FILM REVIEW ANNUAL

1998
Films of 1997

FILM
REVIEW
ANNUAL

1998
Films of 1997

Film Review Publications
JEROME S. OZER, PUBLISHER

Editor: Jerome S. Ozer
Associate Editor: Richard Zlotowitz

ISBN 0-89198-152-7
ISSN 0737-9080

Manufactured in the United States of America

Jerome S. Ozer, Publisher
340 Tenafly Road
Englewood, NJ 07631

TABLE OF CONTENTS

PREFACE

FILM REVIEWS 1

ADDENDUM 1484

AWARDS 1485

INDEX 1495

PREFACE

The FILM REVIEW ANNUAL provides, in a convenient format, a single reference volume covering important reviews—*in their entirety*—of full-length films released in major markets in the United States during the course of the year.

The format of the FILM REVIEW ANNUAL has been kept as clear and simple as possible. Films are reviewed in alphabetical order by title. Following each film title, we provide production information, cast and crew listings, the running time, and the MPAA rating. The reviews for each film are arranged alphabetically by publication. Each review is identified by the name of the publication, the date of the review, the page number, and the name of the reviewer. After the last review of a film, there is an *Also reviewed* section which lists other publications in which the film was reviewed. Because of restrictions in obtaining permission, we were unable to include reviews from certain publications. However, we felt that users of the FILM REVIEW ANNUAL should have help in gaining access to those reviews. Therefore, we included the *Also reviewed* section.

At the end of the FILM REVIEW ANNUAL, we provided full listings of the major film awards, including the nominees as well as the winners.

There are eight Indexes in the FILM REVIEW ANNUAL: Cast, Producers, Directors, Screenwriters, Cinematographers, Editors, Music, and Production Crew.

We have not attempted to force a single editorial style upon the reviews for the sake of achieving consistency. The reader will readily recognize that some reviews were written under deadline pressure and that others were prepared in a more leisurely and reflective style. Some reviews were written to help the moviegoer determine whether or not to see the film. Other reviews assumed the reader had already seen the film and was interested in getting another point of view. We believe this diversity of purposes and styles is one of the major strengths of the FILM REVIEW ANNUAL.

Because of our respect for the integrity of the writers' styles, we made changes from the original only where absolutely necessary. These changes were confined to typographical errors in the original review and errors in the spelling of names. When the reviewer made a reference to another film, we inserted the name of that film. Otherwise the reviews remain as written. British spelling used in English publications has been kept.

We have tried to make the FILM REVIEW ANNUAL pleasurable to read as well as useful for scholars and students of film, communications, social and cultural history, sociology, and also for film enthusiasts. We, the editors, would appreciate your suggestions about how we might make subsequent editions of the FILM REVIEW ANNUAL even more useful.

FILM REVIEWS

AARON'S MAGIC VILLAGE

An Avalanche (a division of Cinepix Film Properties) release of a Benousilio-Volke production in association with Columbia TriStar Home Video. *Producer:* Dora Benousilio and Peter Volke. *Director:* Albert Hanan Kaminski. *Screenplay:* Albert Hanan Kaminski and Jacqueline Galia Renouslio. *Based on the "Stories for Children" by:* Isaac Bashevis Singer. *Music:* Michel Legrand. *Lyrics:* Sheldon Harnick. *Running time:* 80 minutes. *MPAA Rating:* G.

CAST: Fyvush Finkel (Narrator); Tommy Michaels (Aaron); Tovah Feldshuh (Aunt Sarah/ Zlateh the Goat/Matchmaker); Ronn Carroll (Uncle Shlemiel); Harry Goz (Gronam Ox); Ivy Austin (Lantuch).

LOS ANGELES TIMES, 9/19/97, Calendar/p. 18, Jack Mathews

[The following review by Jack Mathews appeared in a slightly different form in **NEWSDAY, 9/19/97, Part II/p. B11.]**

There aren't many animated movies made for so specific an ethnic audience as French filmmaker Albert Hanan Kaminski's "Aaron's Magic Village," and for his stick-to-it-iveness alone, he deserves credit. But even that audience, young Jewish children, may find this a drab piece of business.

"Aaron's Magic Village" is loosely adapted from Isaac Bashevis Singer's "Stories for Children," which also provided the inspiration for Singer's play "Schlemiel the First." It's set in Singer's oft-visited Chelm, a fictional Polish village of fools, where a 10-year-old orphan named Aaron has come with his devoted goat Zlateh to live with Uncle Shlemiel and Aunt Sarah.

Trouble's brewing in Chelm as Aaron arrives. A sorcerer has created the Golem, a monster made of clay and water, and he needs only the secret words contained in the village's Book of Marvels to bring him alive and send him on a rampage. Since Chelm's elders have entrusted the safekeeping of the Book of Marvels to Schlemiel, the original village idiot, the task is a cinch, and the Golem is soon feeling the earth move under his feet.

Only Aaron, being an out-of-towner, has the brains to attempt to retrieve the Book of Marvels from the sorcerer, deactivate the Golem, and save Chelm and the world. And with Zlateh and a brain-addled imp named Lantuch, he sets off for the sorcerer's castle.

The animation is just serviceable, well below the quality of Disney and well above that of Saturday morning TV. But actors Tovah Feldshuh, Fyvush Finkel, Tommy Michaels and Ronn Carroll give uninspired voice performances, and the songs-music by Michel Legrand, lyrics by Sheldon Harnick—are surprisingly flat.

NEW YORK POST, 9/19/97, p. 71, Michael Medved

"Aaron's Magic Village" remains a stubbornly unmagical place, despite a wealth of good intentions and an array of distinguished talent behind the production.

Purportedly adapted from "Stories for Children" by Nobel Prize winner Isaac Bashevis Singer, this animated feature reflects the lost world of Polish Jewry about as convincingly as the cartoon leprechaun on a box of Lucky Charms portrays the riches of traditional Irish folklore.

In fact, this Yiddish-themed shanda seems oddly Irish throughout—with an inexplicable assortment of red-haired characters and uncertain accents, and a boyish protagonist who, with his flowing, carrot-colored locks, pug nose and oversized bowler derby, would look more appropriate on the Auld Sod than riding his goat down the backroads of 19th-century Galicia.

This Little Orphan Aaron (played by the voice of Tommy Michaels from TVs "All My Children") goes to live with his Uncle Shlemiel and Aunt Sarah (the voice of Tovah Feldshuh) in the legendary village of Chelm, notorious in Yiddish folklore as the home of idiots and eccentrics.

To create the requisite "adventure" for contemporary audiences, writer-director Albert Hanan Kaminski concocts an asinine plot about an evil sorcerer who needs to steal a mystical "Book of

Marvels" from the synagogue in Chelm so he can give life to the "golem" he has built—a clay monster he hopes will conquer the world.

The animation is slow, flat and clumsy. Songs, composed by Michel Legrand (of "Yentl" and "Umbrellas of Cherbourg" fame) and lyricist Sheldon Harnick (of "Fiddler on the Roof,") are bland and forgettable.

Filmmaker Kaminski insists that "through the movie, we're telling children and their parents about their true heritage." If so, how can he justify narration (by Fyvush Finkel) that suggests "the Almighty" observed the first Sabbath on Sunday, or images that laughably distort the tradition of Hanukkah candlelighting, in a movie whose dubious flavor suggests hot pastrami—on Wonder bread with Velveeta cheese and mayonnaise.

Also reviewed in:
CHICAGO TRIBUNE, 9/19/97, Friday/p. L, John Petrakis
NEW YORK TIMES, 9/19/97, p. E20, Lawrence Van Gelder
VARIETY, 9/22-28/97, p. 38, Andrew Hindes

ABSOLUTE POWER

A Castle Rock Entertainment release of a Malpaso production. *Executive Producer:* Tim Rooker. *Producer:* Karen Spiegel and Clint Eastwood. *Director:* Clint Eastwood. *Screenplay:* William Goldman. *Based on the novel by:* David Baldacci. *Director of Photography:* Jack N. Green. *Editor:* Joel Cox. *Music:* Lennie Niehaus. *Music Editor:* Donald Harris. *Choreographer:* Shirley Kirkes. *Sound:* Darin Knight and (music) Bobby Fernandez. *Sound Editor:* Alan Robert Murray and Bub Asman. *Casting:* Phyliss Huffman. *Production Designer:* Henry Bumstead. *Art Director:* Jack Taylor. *Set Decorator:* Dick Goddard and Anne D. McCulley. *Special Effects:* Stephen Riley. *Costumes:* Deborah Hopper. *Make-up:* F.X. Perez and Tania McComas. *Stunt Coordinator:* Buddy Van Horn. *Running time:* 121 minutes. *MPAA Rating:* R.

CAST: Clint Eastwood (Luther Whitney); Gene Hackman (President Alan Richmond); Ed Harris (Seth Frank); Laura Linney (Kate Whitney); Scott Glenn (Bill Burton); Dennis Haysbert (Tim Collin); Judy Davis (Gloria Russell); E.G. Marshall (Walter Sullivan); Melora Hardin (Christy Sullivan); Ken Welsh (Sandy Lord); Penny Johnson (Laura Simon); Richard Jenkins (Michael McCarty); Mark Margolis (Red); Elaine Kagan (Valerie); Alison Eastwood (Art Student); Yau-Gene Chan (Waiter); George Orrison (Airport Bartender); Charles McDaniel (Medical Examiner); John Lyle Campbell (Repairman); Kimber Eastwood (White House Tour Guide); Eric Dahlquist, Jr. (Oval Office Agent); Jack Stewart Taylor (Watergate Doorman); Joy Ehrlich (Reporter); Robert Harvey (Cop).

CHRISTIAN SCIENCE MONITOR, 2/21/97, p. 12, David Sterritt

Did you think Hollywood got tired of government-bashing after "Independence Day" blew up the White House and "Mars Attacks!" blasted Capitol Hill to smithereens?

Well, think again. High-tech thrillers may have shifted their sights from bastions of authority to forces of nature like exploding volcanoes and Titanic-sinking icebergs. But lower-tech movies still enjoy tweaking the Washington set, with pictures as different as "Shadow Conspiracy" and "The Beautician and the Beast" taking potshots at politicians and their profession.

Clint Eastwood has never been a fan of official power, as his hugely popular Dirty Harry melodramas showed. These proudly celebrated a lone-wolf cop who didn't mind breaking every rule in the book, or paragraph in the Bill of Rights, if it would bring in the bad guy before the end-credits rolled.

Dirty Harry retired a decade ago, but Eastwood hasn't lost his distaste for what he sees as the hypocrisy and irrelevance of authorities who prefer isolated offices to streetwise reality. His new picture, "Absolute Power," takes on this theme with a vengeance.

Eastwood plays Luther Whitney, a soft-spoken old guy who enjoys working with his hands and admiring beautiful things. By day, this means drawing and sketching as a hobby. By night, it means stealing jewels as a livelihood, sneaking past carefully rigged security systems to indulge his felonious habit.

The story begins with one of these crimes, as Luther ends a long dry spell by breaking into a Washington mansion and scooping up jewels collected by the woman who lives there.

Caught by surprise when she returns for a late-night tryst, Luther scurries into a closet and watches as the woman's lover turns unexpectedly nasty, transforming their rendezvous into a brutal assault, and this part of the movie into a very ugly experience. She tries to fight the pervert off, but two gunmen suddenly appear, killing her on the spot.

Luther has clearly observed an awful crime, but he has also witnessed a political event of seismic proportions. The woman was the wife of an elderly power broker whose influence extends to the highest places. The gunmen were Secret Service agents on active duty. And the sadistic sex partner was none other than the president of the United States.

That's only the first act of this tangled yarn. President Richmond's chief of staff orders a cleanup of the crime and a coverup of the facts. Luther would like to blow the whistle, but his line of work requires anonymity. Meanwhile, a sharp-eyed detective learns the incident had a secret witness, and he puts Luther high on his list of people who might know more than they're telling.

On paper, all this sounds contrived, to say the least. On screen, it's more effective than expected—aside from the scenes of excessive sex and violence, that is—mainly because Eastwood gives one of the most deeply felt performances of his career.

In most of his movies, he has functioned more as a two-dimensional movie star than a three-dimensional actor, relying on the steely face and pent-up persona that have become his trademarks. In recent years he has broken out of this mold to some degree, like using pictures like "White Hunter, Black Heart" and "The Bridges of Madison County" to build well-rounded characterizations.

This trend reaches its high point in "Absolute Power," where his portrayal of a complicated man—skillful but lonely, infamous but isolated, equipped with his own talent for performance and disguise—gives the impression that Eastwood has delved into his own hopes and fears for emotional material to explore.

Always more interesting as a filmmaker than an actor, Eastwood has also directed "Absolute Power" with energy and economy, building smooth suspense episodes and—during scenes with the overeager chief of staff—interludes of mischievous wit.

The movie has major downsides, though. The opening scene of violent sex is more offensive than necessary to make its point. The picture's entertainment value is diminished by its tendency to ramble, as well, and by the implausibility of too many plot twists.

Also troubling are some of the picture's attitudes toward American life and politics. Portraying the president as a sadistic moron is hardly a constructive contribution to present-day dialogues on Washington power. No hint of skepticism is shown regarding the elderly power broker, moreover, although it's unlikely he amassed his money and influence without bending a law in his entire life.

Worst of all is a climactic moment when Luther revenges himself on a man who has injured his daughter in an earlier scene. Luther insists throughout the movie that although he may be a thief, he'd never let anyone be killed. Yet as soon as killing becomes truly tempting for him, he does it as cold-bloodedly as anyone in the picture. Once again, violence prevails in Hollywood.

LOS ANGELES TIMES, 2/14/97, Calendar/p. 1, Kenneth Turan

"Absolute Power's" opening close-up of a painting by El Greco; an impeccable old master, is dead-on appropriate. For the pleasures of this sleek and satisfying entertainment come from the position of its director and star, Clint Eastwood, as the last Old Master in Hollywood, just as reliable in his sphere (at least when he's not co-starring with orangutans) as Rembrandt and Rubens were in theirs.

A twisty tale of coincidence and deceit that might be subtitled "What the Burglar Saw," "Absolute Power" is Eastwood's 40th starring role and 19th film as a director. What he's gained over that stretch of time is an exact knowledge of his own skills, an impeccable sense of what he can and cannot do in front of a camera.

In fact, "Absolute Power," written by veteran William Goldman (from a novel by David Baldacci) and having each of its eight key roles knowingly cast, is a tribute to that increasingly rare commodity, Hollywood professionalism. Yes, this film's plot doesn't make a whole lot of sense, but there is so much pleasure involved in seeing how beautifully old-fashioned movie machinery can be made to work that it seems churlish to object.

As befits Eastwood's increasing age (he'll be 67 in May) and status, "Absolute Power" is hardly "Dirty Harry" territory. It's more of a civilized entertainment, almost a drawing room thriller, unhurried and genteel but enlivened with suspense and surprising bursts of sly, even biting, humor.

And Eastwood's Luther Whitney is not an officer of the law but rather a master cat burglar, a blue-collar version of the tuxedoed brigand Cary Grant played in "To Catch a Thief," able to disarm the most complicated security systems without breaking a sweat. Whitney lives alone in Washington, D.C., with no friends and few acquaintances and spends his days meticulously copying art at the National Gallery.

That same attention to detail pays off when it comes to working nights. "Absolute Power" opens with an extended burglary sequence, shot as calmly and fluidly as the man operates, shadowing Whitney as he breaks into a richly appointed mansion and proceeds to loot a vault room hidden behind a one-way mirror next to master bedroom.

But the building, which is supposed to be empty, suddenly isn't. Into the bedroom comes an inebriated Christy Sullivan (Melora Hardin), the woman of the house, and an even more drunk man we know from a shot of wedding pictures is not her husband. Trapped behind that mirror in the vault room, Whitney sees things he shouldn't, witnesses a shocking series of events that place his life in peril.

A master of disguise and disappearance, Whitney soon finds himself in the radar of a gang of high-profile individuals, including the president of the United States (Gene Hackman), his brittle chief of staff (Judy Davis), a pair of crack Secret Service agents (Scott Glenn and Dennis Haysbert) and one of the wealthiest and most powerful men in the free world (E.G. Marshall).

This crew couldn't be tougher (or more seamlessly acted), and a lesser man would run like hell, which is what Whitney starts to do. But ducking out has rarely been in style for Eastwood's characters, and soon enough Whitney's fury at the hypocrisy of official Washington keeps him hanging around and, in harm's way.

It also puts Whitney into contact with Seth Frank (Ed Harris), a shrewd and sensible detective who is investigating what happened in that fancy bedroom. One of the best scenes in Goldman's screenplay is the verbal fencing the first time these two meet; Whitney's various cracks about being old and in the way are especially well done.

Though Whitney appears to have no family, in fact he does have a grown daughter named Kate ("Primal Fear's" Laura Linney), still resentful about being "the only kid during show-and-tell who got to talk about visiting day." Now a prosecuting attorney, Kate wants desperately to have as little to do with her father as possible, but circumstances inevitably draw her in and make her central to the film's action.

Starting with cinematographer Jack N. Green and including production designer Henry Bumstead, composer Lennie Niehaus and editor Joel Cox, most of "Absolute Power's" key creative personnel have been with Eastwood for years, and the smoothness of their collaboration shows. Adding to the family nature of things, the producer-director has cast two of his daughters, Alison Eastwood (as an art student) and Kimber Eastwood (as a White House guide) in small but visible roles.

What it finally comes down to, however, is the skill and presence of the man who hired them all, an actor who has aged spectacularly well and knows how to make his advancing years work for him on screen. However woebegone the state of current Hollywood may be, without Clint Eastwood's ability to elevate improbable trifles like "Absolute Power," the movie business would be a sadder place still.

NEW YORK, 2/17/97, p. 56, David Denby

I can recommend, in a fragmentary way, Clint Eastwood's latest work as director and star. *Absolute Power* has a terrific opening sequence. Clint, wearing his years with increasing grace, plays a serious career thief, a mild-looking man in glasses and cap who spends much of his time in art museums. With no apparent fuss or fear, the thief enters an enormous Washington, D.C.

mansion, disables the elaborate security system, and penetrates a treasure-filled vault situated behind a two-way mirror. Happily emptying jewelry and cash into his sack, he suddenly realizes, to his horror, that the young mistress of the house has returned with a very powerful and famous man, and further that she plans to have carnal relations with that famous man on the other side of the mirror, only a few feet away. When the sex gets rough, and then violent, and then ends in murder, the thief passes through varying stages of prurient interest, fear, and disgust. The couple have been caught in flagrante. But then, so has he.

Now, what makes this neo-Hitchcock episode successful—apart from a healthy dose of sensationalism and violence—is Eastwood's adherence to the old-fashioned notion that the respective positions of two people or forces threatening one another should be clearly visible to the audience. This may seem elementary or merely academic. If two gunmen are firing at each other, you have to know—don't you?—how great a risk each one is taking when he sticks his head out from behind a boulder. Obvious or not, it's an idea that has been largely ignored in recent years, when most action directors, trying for the pace of TV commercials or MTV, have given up on continuity and clarity and have viciously jammed one explosive shot into the next. So here is Clint Eastwood calmly, methodically laying out a sensational scene, keeping the space clear and distinct, so we can enjoy the thief's fear of exposure, the moral ambiguity of the violator passively watching a greater violation—and then on to the scene's murderous conclusion and its coda detailing the thief's attempted escape. Alas, nothing in the rest of the movie is remotely as good as this long opening sequence. The plot descends into opportunistic gimmickry (William Goldman adapted David Baldacci's novel), with heavy doses of cynicism, sentiment, and sadism. A day later, only the smashingly effective opening sequence remains in one's head.

NEW YORK POST, 2/14/97, p. 43, Michael Medved

Clint Eastwood is such a graceful old pro, as both actor and director, that he can sometimes make even the most mediocre material seem watchable and compelling. "Absolute Power," adapted from the lurid best seller by David Baldacci, indeed boasts scenes of wry humor and expertly calibrated tension, but no amount of style or skill can ultimately transform this contrived melodrama into a hard-edged political thriller.

Eastwood plays a lonely ex-con and master thief who has spent months planning the biggest job of his career. He breaks into the estate of the richest power broker in Washington (E.G. Marshall), and gathers loot from the vault—when he's shocked to see he's not alone.

Marshall's glamorous young wife (Melora Hardin) stumbles into the bedroom, drunk, and while Eastwood watches from behind a one-way mirror, she engages in rough sex with her husband's best friend, the President of the United States (Gene Hackman).

This nasty scene leaves behind an inconvenient female corpse and a wounded President, who is whisked away by two fanatically loyal Secret Service agents (Scott Glenn and Dennis Haysbert) and his chief of staff (Judy Davis), after meticulous efforts to cover up the killing. When they discover that a burglar has been on the scene, they decide to pin the crime on him, but the expert thief has expertly made off with a key bit of evidence.

The rest of the movie is a far-fetched game of cat and mouse, with Eastwood's hunted character dueling the real crooks in the White House. Ed Harris does his usual superb work as an honest, sympathetic police lieutenant assigned to the case, and Laura Linney is affecting as Eastwood's estranged daughter—a rising young prosecutor who's the only one in the world he cares about.

The interaction among these sympathetic characters works far better than the violent confrontations with the cartoonish, shabbily acted villains.

One scene in particular, with Ed Harris questioning Eastwood about the crime, is a marvelously witty chess game full of between-the-lines intensity. The movie needed more of such subtlety and far less of clumsily staged presidential receptions and press conferences which, despite expensive sets, seem thoroughly inauthentic.

That's especially true for the preposterous twist that finishes the story, where Eastwood blurs details and rushes to a jarring conclusion, as if embarrassed by the substance of his script. The director may show the skill of a master thief, but he can't overcome a plot so sloppy it could have been concocted by this story's White House bunglers.

NEWSDAY, 2/14/97, Part II/p. B2, John Anderson

Clint Eastwood's trademark squint-and-grimace is as much a signature gesture as John Wayne's walk. Or Mae West's. But it's seldom haphazard. No, it usually signals a moment of such appalling conduct that even Eastwood's hard-bitten persona—be it Dirty Harry, William Munney, Bronco Billy or Josey Wales—can't quite fathom the decayed state of the human soul.

In "Absolute Power," the look makes its first appearance shortly after master thief Luther Whitney—interrupted while robbing the home of vacationing power broker Walter Sullivan (E.G. Marshall)—begins watching through a one-way mirror as Sullivan's wife, Christy (Melora Hardin), gets it on with the president of the United States (Gene Hackman). The sex will turn rough, then tougher, then murderous and then, after Christy stabs her president, Secret Service agents will burst into the bedroom and blow away the First Bimbo. All of which is worth more than one squint from Clint.

We might want to grimace a bit ourselves at the idea of Eastwood playing so fast and loose with the image of the current White House occupant (imagine Arkansas troopers instead of Secret Service agents, if you will) and apparently pining for Republican presidencies gone by ("There you go again," Luther says at one point, and it sounds like an elegy.) But why does Luther grimace even before the violence starts? Because people are having sex? Because the *president* is having sex? Because Luther is in the ridiculous position of having to watch? Or because a squint, is as good as a wink?

"Absolute Power," on the surface as flat a film as Eastwood has ever directed, is exciting, charming and not to be taken seriously—except perhaps as a commentary on this type of film and this type of career. It's not as if Eastwood the director hasn't toyed with his own screen image. In "Unforgiven," the onetime western star made the supreme anti-western; in "A Perfect World," his best movie, Eastwood deconstructed idea of a Hollywood tradition and used Gary Cooper-manique Kevin Costner to do it. Given "Absolute Power's" perspectives on age, duty, family—and the betrayal of public trust inherent in President Alan Richmond's pathological lust—Eastwood seems to be turning the formulaic plot device of government treachery against itself, in a kind of "Out of the Line of Fire."

But in addition to some leaden lines, the screenplay by William Goldman contains a platterful of cookie-cutter characters—beginning with Luther, who, if he were played by anyone but Eastwood, would be a goof. The burglar as Renaissance man, Luther sketches Old Masters in museums. He eats alone, but by candlelight. One of his cultivated eccentricities (given that he's a thief) is to keep his house key in a flower box just outside his door. He has a bitter daughter he loves (Laura Linney, the latest in Eastwood's catalog of wan blondes). And his decision to take the president down—he has this letter opener, you see, marked with Richmond's blood and Christy's fingerprints—arises from Richmond's exploitation of his mentor during Sullivan's time of grief. "You heartless whore," Luther hisses, in moral indignation.

He was a war hero, of course, although violence has never been part of his M.O. Which is why, while police detective Seth Frank (Ed Harris) knows Luther was capable of the robbery, he questions the Secret Service attempt to pin the killing on him. The agents are quite a pair: as Bill Burton, Scott Glenn is too controlled to be true—unlike his partner, Tim Collin (Dennis Haysbert), whose eyes light up at the thought of Luther's assassination. Judy Davis, a truly great actress, is shoehorned into the cartoonish role of shrewish, calculating chief of staff Gloria Russell. Even Hackman isn't given much to do, other than that strange sex scene.

Which probably saves energy, given Eastwood's ability to diminish his fellow actors—not including Harris, who more than holds his own and, in one game of cat-and-mouse between Seth and Luther, participates in the movie's smartest scene. Which may not be saying much, although "Absolute Power," for all its nasty political innuendo, packs sufficient bang for your buck, along with plenty to think about.

NEWSWEEK, 2/17/97, p. 67, David Ansen

Luther Whitney, the perfectionist cat burglar played by Clint Eastwood in *Absolute Power*, is as meticulous in his craftsmanship as Vermeer, as adept at disguise as Alec Guinness, as elusive as Houdini, as solitary as a monk and, when he wants to be, as crustily charming as ... well, as Clint Eastwood has ever let himself be.

This veteran prince of thieves is pulling off his felonious masterpiece—cleaning out the manor of a rich Washington power broker—when unexpected intruders force him to hide behind a one-way mirror. There he witnesses a young woman and an older man engage in some drunken foreplay that turns rough, then nasty, then ends when two men in suits enter the room and blow the woman away. Unfortunately, Luther knows both participants. She was the wife of the tycoon he was robbing. The adulterous man (Gene Hackman) is the president of the United States. Oops. The men with guns (Scott Glenn and Dennis Haysbert) are Secret Service agents, and the Machiavellian virago who now rushes into the bloody bedroom and starts cooking up the cover-up is Gloria Russell (Judy Davis), the White House chief of staff. What's striking about the queasy, tense scene that Luther witnesses, as they concoct an outrageous story about a burglary attempt gone awry, is that it is also terribly funny.

There has never been a movie quite as deeply cynical about the leader of the free world as "Absolute Power." President Alan Richmond is an unscrupulous swine and will do everything he can to eliminate the one witness, our hero. The widower (E.G. Marshall), led to believe that Luther is his wife's killer, hires his own freelance assassin as well. How will the old thief get out of this one?

In ways that are as preposterous as they are delightful. In screenwriter William Goldman's blithe adaptation of David Baldacci's best seller, Luther's solitary battle with all the president's murderous men plays out not as a paranoid thriller but as a comedy of bad political manners. The tale's cynicism never curdles because we're under no obligation to take anything in this movie seriously, except its skill in entertaining us.

As a director, Eastwood is at his effortless, slyboots best: he deftly cranks up the suspense at the beginning, but by the end he's cruising along so briskly that he can afford to throw away the climactic, violent scenes other directors would belabor—or even leave them out entirely. As a star, he's at his most disarming. Watch him playing cat-and-mouse with Ed Harris's homicide detective: rarely has Eastwood had such playful chemistry with another guy. The whole cast looks to be having a fine old time, particularly Davis, the infernal screwball villainess. What a fun, nutty movie Eastwood and Goldman have conjured up. And what a beguilingly improbable protagonist: Luther Whitney, the first Hollywood superhero to claim he's a member of AARP.

SIGHT AND SOUND, 6/97, p. 44, Tom Tunney

Veteran cat burglar Luther Whitney breaks into the mansion of wealthy political power broker Walter Sullivan. Through a two-way mirror which looks directly into a bedroom, Whitney watches Sullivan's wife Christy enter with US President Alan Richmond. A seduction turns sour when Richmond roughs up Christy, and during the struggle Secret Servicemen Bill Burton and Tim Collin burst in and shoot Christy dead. White House Chief-of-Staff Gloria Russell suggests a cover story of a burglar murdering Christy and the trio set about sanitising the crime scene. However, they leave a bloody letter opener behind which Whitney steals.

Before leaving the country, Whitney attempts to patch things up with his estranged daughter Kate. But after seeing the President publicly offering his condolences to Sullivan on television, Whitney is disgusted and decides to stay. He leaves a note for Russell at the White House. Meanwhile, Detective Seth Frank is convinced Whitney is implicated in the crime, but equally can't believe he's guilty of murder. After quizzing both Whitney and his daughter, Frank persuades Kate to meet her father again. Having tapped their phones, Burton and Collin lie in wait and Collin tries to shoot Whitney as he arrives to meet Kate. Whitney escapes and phones Frank who tells him that the Secret Service are now 'responsible' for his daughter's security. Realising that this is her death warrant, Whitney speeds across town only to arrive as his daughter's car is being bumped over a cliff.

Kate survives but Collin prepares to murder her in her hospital bed with a lethal injection. Whitney surprises him and injects the poison into his neck instead. Whitney gets to Sullivan, tells him the true account of what happened to his wife and proffers the fatal letter opener. Sullivan enters the White House and the story subsequently breaks on television that the President has killed himself with a letter opener. Russell is arrested and Burton is discovered dead by his own hand. Whitney is reunited with his daughter.

The title *Absolute Power* ostensibly refers to the corrupting nature of political office. The film's President Richmond's ready smile is a front both for his own amoral nature and a ruthless political machine for which image is everything and personal integrity counts for nothing. However, this is also pre-eminently a Clint Eastwood star vehicle and, having set up that premise of a President without principles, the narrative quickly becomes a celebration of Eastwood's absolute moral and physical powers. Even his character's name, "Luther Whitney", has an apt Protestant ring to it. He is a cleansing hero who enters into the corrupt church of Big Government, is astonished by what he sees and decides to do something about it.

By this stage in his career, Eastwood the director knows Eastwood the actor so well that there's scarcely a foot of surplus footage expended in the exposition of Whitney's predicament. After the murder and his escape, a different director and star would insist on a lot of hectic running around, anxious facial close ups and fast cutting. Not Eastwood. Instead, there's the deceptively simple scene of him casually walking into his local bar. In its own quiet way it's the most significant moment in the film because it asserts Eastwood's near transcendent sense of calm: his absolute authority. This is a man who isn't afraid, who stoically accepts his new situation and then, using his customary extra-special skills and powers, single-mindedly goes about turning it to his advantage. The rest of the film is thus simply a matter of him asserting this dominance.

Throughout his career, Eastwood's most characteristic expression has been a look of narrow-eyed and tight-lipped contempt, shot in low angle close-up in *Dirty Harry, Pale Rider* and a host of other movies where he plays a ruthless avenger. A mixture of disgust and astonishment at the foibles and failings of lesser mortals, it's the look of a superior (and usually isolated) individual who finds it impossible to recognise any common humanity between himself and the target of his wrath. A martial aristocrat rather than a democrat, Luther Whitney conforms to the established Eastwood type. This time it's Secret Service man Collin who follows in the ignoble tradition of Dirty Harry's Scorpio and many, many others and gets the steely-eyed executioner treatment which inevitably comes with a few choice words (Collin: "Mercy!' Whitney: "I'm clean out!").

However, though it's a pleasure to see Eastwood giving such a proficient workout to his customary screen persona, the economy of its handling here exacts a severe penalty. By limiting the scope of the drama so narrowly to Whitney's battle of wits with the authorities, the film is stripped of any credible political or social context. What works so well within the austere confines of the Western is stretched way beyond its limits within the much more complex context of the modem political thriller. From the first moment Gene Hackman as the President flashes that patented shallow, too-ready smile of his, it's obvious exactly what type of off-the-shelf character he's playing, yet we learn nothing of his presidential policies. But then again, the film's insistent sarcastic message is that the political system in the US is beyond redemption. The only option for a rugged individual like Whitney is to take the law into his own hands.

The Conversation, All the President's Men (which writer William Goldman also scripted) and even *Three Days of the Condor* were all prime 70s exhibitions of paranoia and pessimism about the state of US officialdom. *Absolute Power* plugs into the same cynical zeitgeist, but fails to paint the people working within the system with any subtlety or shading. Instead, the film is keen to tar them all with the same brush.

TIME, 2/24/97, p. 67, Richard Corliss

The film's poster is boldly simple: a close-up of Clint staring both out of and into the darkness, with a visage as stark and stony as if it were a fifth face on Mount Rushmore. The image is fully aware of its iconic import, of the strength and frailty of stardom in late middle age. So is *Absolute Power*, the movie that fleshes out this hunk of granite. Many of its leading actors were born before the Rushmore carvings were completed in 1941. Eastwood, directing himself as a cat burglar on his eighth or ninth life, is 66, as is Gene Hackman, who plays a sexually reckless U.S. President. E.G. Marshall, in the role of the President's adviser, is 86 and counting. The plot is a doomsday version of Bill Clinton's Paula Jones problem, but the theme is impending mortality—settling scores before time's up.

Screenwriter William Goldman, 65, working from the David Balducci novel, asks you to believe that the burglar has hidden behind a two-way mirror in a room where the President is having nasty sex with his adviser's young wife—and that our larcenous hero does nothing to stop her murder. This old-style thriller sometimes creaks in its joints as it adds an amoral aide (Judy Davis), a canny cop (Ed Harris) and a Secret Service agent (Scott Glenn) as weary as the one

Clint played in *In the Line of Fire*. But Eastwood is less interested in political corruption than in filial care; the warming, nicely played relationship of the burglar and his lawyer daughter (Laura Linney) is the source of the film's absolute power. It's a sweet pleasure to see a fatherly smile crack open that Rushmore face.

VILLAGE VOICE, 2/18/97, p. 80, J. Hoberman

Reasonably tense, enjoyably fraught with pretend political implications, and generally possessed of many appealing hooks, *Absolute Power* is a thriller whose title colors everything—particularly the performance of its star-auteur Clint Eastwood.

Eastwood has directed *Absolute Power* from William Goldman's script (as well as producing and composing the musical theme) but he plays something like the unknown artist—introduced to us, gaunt and elegant, as he sketches at the National Gallery in Washington. ("You work with your hands, don't you?" some relative babe asks admiringly.) The movie is fit to suggest the Old Masters, and Eastwood, it turns out, is a master thief. Indeed, by the last reel, he comes to seem an American Fantômas—not only a consummate cat burglar but an escape artist and wizard of disguise.

In the movie's make-or-break half-hour set piece, Eastwood boosts a fabulous Virginia mansion only to find himself trapped in a secret room behind a false boudoir mirror when an illicit couple return unexpectedly and begin to make love. The stereo goes on and immobile Clint gets his own private show. (Squinting unreadably in reaction to the proceedings, Eastwood is the perfect subject for the Kuleshev effect: whatever you think he's supposed to be thinking, he is.) What this primal scene lacks in wacky Lynchian panache, it gains in dramatic interest as the sex escalates from adulterous to rough to violent to ... world-historic.

The secret of who is doing what to whom will be impossible to maintain, but you won't get it from me. Suffice it to say Eastwood witnesses an "invisible" crime that leads, via a convoluted chain of command and the requisite murky action chase, through the corridors of power straight to the White House. "I'm supposed to have all this power, and I can't even help my oldest friend" whines our maximum leader (Gene Hackman) in the first of several scenes that derive their fun from such presidential consternation. Eastwood is set to take his swag and run but, watching (once more) the tawdry spectacle of American telepolitics, the outraged thief decides to stay on and fight the power.

Recapitulating the structure of *Unforgiven*, *Absolute Power* matches outlaw Eastwood against Hackman's villainous sheriff while, as a meditation on things presidential, the movie effectively revises *In the Line of Fire*. Back in 1993, Eastwood played the veteran Secret Service man who failed to take the bullet for JFK and thus bore the burden of America's subsequent history. Now, entering the diminished realm of Clinton II, there is clearly no president worth dying for—at least as far as Clint is concerned. To reinforce the point, *Absolute Power* orchestrates its own crypto-Dealy Plaza stakeout, replete with security agencies at cross-purposes, and designed to eliminate pesky Eastwood—along with plenty of innocent bystanders. (Here, as in the brainless *Shadow Conspiracy,* it's possible to stage a shoot-out in the middle of Washington without fear of police intrusion.)

Absolute Power may be a one-man show, but Eastwood doesn't stint on support. Although the entertainingly Dostoyevskian fencing between the thief and cop Ed Harris comes to little, Judy Davis provides Hackman with the sort of aide—and dancing partner—he deserves. (It's scarcely coincidental that she lives in the Watergate complex, by now as fateful a D.C. address as 1600 Pennsylvania Avenue.) As befits the movie's patriarchal setting, Eastwood's romantic interest is his estranged daughter, a straight-arrow deputy D.A. (Laura Linney). In a scene both maudlin and creepy, she visits his safe house to discover that, unknown to her, he's managed to photograph her whole life. The sense of supernatural Eastwood as his daughter's guardian angel only emphasizes the disturbed parent-child relationship between the president and his plutocrat benefactor (E.G. Marshall). In fact, one could easily schematize *Absolute Power* as a campaign to see which master criminal, Eastwood or Hackman, is the true father of the land.

As the official cover-up unravels, Goldman's script goes a bit kerflooie. *Absolute Power* is too long and more than a little too feel-good. Still, from *Dirty Harry* and *High Plains Drifter* through *Tightrope* and *Unforgiven*, Eastwood has always given his best performances as the bitter avenger in a corrupt town. The crescendo of reassurance with which the star wraps things up can barely dispel his sense of 1600 as a Coney Island spookhouse or the U.S. as the world's greatest banana republic.

Also reviewed in:
NATION, 3/17/97, p. 43, Stuart Klawans
NEW REPUBLIC, 3/17/97, p. 28, Stanley Kauffmann
NEW YORK TIMES, 2/14/97, p. C5, Janet Maslin
VARIETY, 2/10-16/97, p. 62, Todd McCarthy
WASHINGTON POST, 2/14/97, p. B1, Rita Kempley
WASHINGTON POST, 2/14/97, Weekend/p. 68, Desson Howe

ADDICTED TO LOVE

A Warner Bros. release of an Outlaw Production film in association with Miramax Films. *Executive Producer:* Bob Weinstein and Harvey Weinstein. *Producer:* Jeffrey Silver and Bobby Newmyer. *Director:* Griffin Dunne. *Screenplay:* Robert Gordon. *Director of Photography:* Andrew Dunn. *Editor:* Elizabeth King. *Music:* Rachel Portman. *Music Editor:* Dan Lieberstein and Suzana Peric. *Sound:* Ed Novick and (music) Christopher Dibble. *Sound Editor:* Rob Hein. *Casting:* Amanda Mackey Johnson and Cathy Sandrich. *Production Designer:* Robin Standefer. *Art Director:* Stephen Alesch. *Set Decorator:* Alyssa Winter. *Special Effects:* Connie Brink. *Costumes:* Renée Ehrlich Kalfus. *Make-up:* Joe Campayno. *Stunt Coordinator:* Roy Farfel. *Running time:* 97 minutes. *MPAA Rating:* R.

CAST: Meg Ryan (Maggie); Matthew Broderick (Sam); Kelly Preston (Linda Green); Tcheky Karyo (Anton Depeaux); Maureen Stapleton (Nana); Nesbitt Blaisdell (Ed Green); Remak Ramsay (Professor Wells); Lee Wilkof (Carl); Dominick Dunne (Matheson); Susan Forristal (Cecile); Larry Pine (Street Comic); Debbon Ayer (Gwen); Maurizio Benazzo (Euro-Chic Man); Paolo Calamari (French Bartender); Helmar Augustus Cooper (Bus Driver); Tom Forrest (Astronomer); Shoshanna Gleich (School Teacher); Jacqueline Heinze (Bald Girl); Mike Hodge (Linda's Doorman); Daniel Dae Kim (Undergrad Assistant); Bill Kux (Desk Clerk); Steve McAuliff (Business Man); Conrad McLaren (Motorcycle Man); Bill Timoney (Restaurant Patron); Richard Dreyfuss (Astronomer).

LOS ANGELES TIMES, 5/23/97, Calendar/p. 9, Kevin Thomas

"Addicted to Love," a romantic comedy creepier than cute, should be titled "Addicted to Revenge." This is one of those movies that is more disturbing than its makers seem to have intended.

Matthew Broderick's Sam is an astronomer with his head so much in the stars that he doesn't realize that his girlfriend Linda (Kelly Preston), his sweetheart from childhood, is bored to tears in their idyllic rural community. Sam says he can't get away from work just now, but when Linda flies off to Manhattan alone and fires off a Dear John letter, he's heartbroken.

Rushing to Manhattan, he discovers Linda in the throes of a hot romance with a French restauranteur, Anton (Tcheky Karyo). Lovesick and stunned, Sam sets up a camera obscura in a derelict building so that he can spy on Linda and Anton in Anton's chic loft just across the way. He studies the stars and tells himself that the romance is sure to be soon over and that he wants to be close at hand to reclaim his true love.

This isn't the healthiest of situations, obviously, but it swiftly deteriorates with the arrival of Maggie (Meg Ryan), a tough-talking photographer and Anton's former lover, who's out to bug Anton's apartment while plotting revenge.

Maggie carries wounded pride to such extremes that she clearly needs therapy.

In no time at all, she's maneuvered the wimpy Sam into helping her destroy Anton and Linda's romance, wreck his business and cause him bodily harm. (How Sam and Maggie are able to take off from work to devote their entire lives to this sick endeavor remains a mystery.) All the while Maggie and Sam, into mutual denial, are not surprisingly falling in love.

It is exceedingly difficult to find what's funny in the calculated, obsessive, relentless destruction of Anton, especially when he proves to be the most likable and mature of all four of these people. Maybe "Addicted to Love" might work as a pitch-dark comedy, but in the way Robert Gordon has written it and Griffin Dunne directed it, it gives us the impression that we're supposed to take drastic, irrational revenge as a larky laff riot.

Not all the considerable star power of the four principals can make this material appealing, but at least the director's father, journalist extraordinaire Dominick Dunne, as a restaurant critic, and Maureen Stapleton, as Maggie's grandmother, are fun.

NEW STATESMAN, 8/1/97, p. 40, Jonathan Coe

All the way through this bleak and loveless romantic comedy, I kept thinking how inappropriate the title was. *Addicted to Revenge*—or even *Addicted to Hate*—seemed closer to the spirit of a movie entirely concerned with the breakdown of two relationships, and the vicious series of reprisals that follow.

But what the film makers have rather cleverly done, I suppose, is to take the old love-is-a-drug cliché and follow it to its scary conclusion.

The movie's two protagonists are genuine addicts, and they've had their fix taken away from them. Their behaviour, as a result, is like any other junkie's when forced into cold turkey: desperate, single-minded and at times very ugly to watch.

Most of this will come as a surprise to loyal fans of Meg Ryan, who may be expecting something altogether cosier, in the vein of *When Harry Met Sally* or *Sleepless in Seattle*. Her performance in *Addicted to Love* is rather shocking, not least because it feels so strained. Ryan plays a supposedly punkish, supposedly foul-mouthed artist who appears to have abandoned her vocation (at least, we never see her working on any paintings) in order to make life hell for her former boyfriend Tcheky Karyo.

Karyo, a temperamental restauranteur, has recently discovered domestic bliss with Kelly Preston; and *her* former boyfriend Matthew Broderick (an astronomer—though we don't see him looking at many stars) has followed her to New York and found himself a room opposite the happy couple's apartment, whence he spies on them using a camera obscura.

In these circumstances it obviously makes sense for Ryan to move in with Broderick and use her own technical expertise—she turns out to be a whizz with sound equipment—to plant a few microphones so that they can listen to the lovebirds' every move into the bargain. The scene is thereby set for a weirdly twisted romantic version of *Rear Window:* Preston and Karyo's idyllic canoodling acts as a sort of film-within-the-film, projected on to the whitewashed walls of the obsessive Broderick's apartment, while in the foreground our main focus is on his developing relationship with the even more psychotic Ryan.

Of course, the direction this relationship will take is utterly predictable: Ryan and Broderick will come to their senses in the end, realise that they're made for each other, and fall into a clinch.

What isn't quite so predictable, though, is the tone of the film, which is nastier and more brittle than almost anything Hollywood has given us recently in the name of light entertainment.

Partly this has to do with the dialogue, which is unprecedentedly scatological. When Broderick expresses the wistful hope, for example, that Preston might leave her new boyfriend and come back to him, Ryan retorts: "The only way that girl is coming back is if a blast of semen catapults her across the street to you."

And the look of the film is every bit as dark as its tone. Broderick and Ryan do their spying with the lights turned off, hemmed in by shadows and clutter: they seen to inhabit a lair, not a home, and their occasional ventures into the outside world always seem to take them through soot-black, rain-sodden streets. This is not, in short, a feel-good movie.

Nor is it a particularly sane or healthy one. Ryan's monomaniacal desire to sabotage her ex-boyfriend's new affair takes on ever more extreme and sinister forms. By the end of the film she has ruined Karyo's business, broken up his relationship, afflicted him with a skin disease and reduced him to plaster-encased immobility. "Yes," he admits at this point, when they have finally confronted each other, "We are even."

Did I miss something here? Have he and Preston actually done anything wrong, apart from disentangling themselves from failed relationships and trying to find happiness with someone rather more suitable?

Addicted to Love has been extremely popular in America, where only *The Lost World Jurassic Park (TM)* has kept it from the number one spot at the box office. This makes sense, in a way. The Preston and Karyo characters seem guilty of nothing worse than emotional misjudgments, but Ryan and Broderick hold them responsible for ruining their lives, and demand repayment accordingly.

You would expect this warped morality tale to go down well in a country which operates in a culture of blame, never recognising human error except as the prelude to litigation. It will be interesting to see if it strikes the same chord here.

NEW YORK, 6/9/97, p. 78, David Denby

A young man names Robert Gordon wrote the first version of *Addicted to Love* back in 1989, and I can see why the producers who read the script at that time, Robert Newmyer and Jeffrey Silver, wouldn't let the project die—there's something obsessive and strange in the idea that holds one's interest. The movie that eventually got made, directed by the actor Griffin Dunne (it's his first feature), is a contemporary, halfway-perverse screwball comedy—a near-success that promises more for the future. Matthew Broderick has the James Stewart role—a Midwesterner, a mild-mannered astronomer named Sam who adores Linda (Kelly Preston), a beautiful blonde teacher. The two of them have a rather cloying, faithful-dog relationship (they take turns being the dog). In their little town, Sam turns his enormous telescope on Linda every day at noon, and she stops playing with her pupils and waves to him. But Linda is bored. She goes to work in New York for a while but doesn't come back; she leaves Sam for Anton (Tcheky Karyo), a French restauranteur, tough guy, and all-around great lover. Sam pursues her; he sets himself up in an abandoned loft on Wooster Street, right opposite the Frenchman's apartment, and, using a *camera obscure,* spies on the lovers, projecting an image of the goings-on across the street onto his own wall. He's joined in this peculiar vigil by Maggie (Meg Ryan), Anton's abandoned fiancée, who is some sort of downtown art person—a photographer, a motorcyclist who wears black leather and lots of eyeliner. Maggie quickly bugs Anton's apartment, and she and Sam sit there, day after day, watching and listening in masochistic pleasure and misery as their ex-partners eat, talk, and noisily make love.

At first, I admit, I wanted to walk out. Dunne's direction seemed glib, the sequences flatly unbelievable, and Meg Ryan miscast. Maggie initially enters Sam's crumbling loft by bursting through a glass skylight, though knocking on the door would have done just as well; some of the scenes are jumpy and cartoonish. But the picture settles down. A lot of *Addicted to Love* was shot at night, in Soho, and the black, gleaming streets are both beautiful and slightly sinister; the night city of hip people has never looked better. As they watch, Sam and Maggie talk quite a lot, and Meg Ryan, suppressing her girlish smile, tries and almost succeeds in playing a tough, slightly flaky woman who's been badly hurt.

The material goes further into perversity than most Hollywood movies but, alas, not far enough. In the hands of a sophisticated, malicious European director like Buñuel or Chabrol or an independent like Canada's Atom Egoyan, *Addicted to Love* could have been deliciously dirty: The watching couple might have become so turned on by masochism that ... well, your fantasies are sure to be as lurid as mine. *Addicted to Love* doesn't become erotic in that explicit way; instead, it goes Hollywood in screwball style. Sam and Maggie play all sorts of tricks on Anton, driving Linda away, destroying Anton's restaurant and then messing up his looks, until he's reduced to an enraged wreck. We seem to be in the middle of a rather nastily vengeful "comedy of remarriage" in which the original partners—or at least Sam and Linda—will get back together.

Addicted to Love takes an interesting turn: Sam insinuates himself into Anton's restaurant, as a dishwasher, and Anton takes a liking to him and pours out his soul. It turns out that he's something more than an arrogant stud. A buccaneer, a man who arrived in the States with nothing, he takes enormous risks, and if he's egocentric and overbearing, he is also formidable and wily in many ways. The Turkish-born Karyo, a considerable star in France, has some of Gérard Depardieu's big-jawed, ugly-handsome brio. Karyo is abrupt and decisive, with a threat of violence—he's almost overpowering. His Anton is older than Sam, and he knows what he's doing with women, and Sam is suddenly abashed—this guy, he realizes, is a lot more vital than he is. Maybe Anton deserves Linda.

Karyo lifts the movie out of formula, but the filmmakers are stuck for an ending. What to do with Meg Ryan and Matthew Broderick? They don't really go together. He's mild and reasonable, and she's hard and sarcastic (at least on the surface). Yet they have to be made to like each other—that's the way the plot turns—and so the ending is weak. In general, *Addicted to Love* is just strange and interesting enough to make one angry that it's not fresher and more daring. Griffin Dunne appears to have a talent for character observation and a serious interest in sex; he should cut his Hollywood ties altogether, work independently, and take his material as far into intimacy as he wants.

NEW YORK POST, 5/23/97, p. 50, Thelma Adams

Meg Ryan is the cute queen. When she wrinkles her skinny nose, scrunches her laugh lines and pulls one of those gummy, Chicklets-toothed smiles, audiences get that warm, stroke-a-purring-kitty feeling. They want to stand up and pledge allegiance to the all-American girl.

For an actress, this can get tiresome. Rather than go the Julia Roberts route—trying a brogue and sparring with John Malkovich, a partner who drinks fresh-faced actresses for tea—Ryan gives us every possible shade of cute, from "Sleepless in Seattle" to "When a Man Loves a Woman."

The tousle-haired blonde plays a bruised pixie in Griffin Dunne's sassy romantic comedy "Addicted to Love." She might have borrowed her raccoon-y eyeshadow from Jennifer Jason Leigh, but Ryan's downtown and downtrodden photog can make even the most extreme revenge fantasies appealing.

Ryan's Maggie has just been bounced by Anton (Tcheky Karyo). The caddish French restauranteur has a fab SoHo loft filled with photos of himself and a rotating gallery of gal pals. This steamy chef knows the right places to squeeze whipped cream for a sexual feast.

Anton trades Maggie for Linda (Kelly Preston), a rural schoolteacher on sabbatical in Manhattan. Linda's devoted beau, astronomer Sam (Matthew Broderick), follows his childhood sweetheart to the big city. He thinks Anton is only "a passing meteor shower."

Maggie and Sam collide while spying on Anton and Linda. Robert Gordon's script hits some rough spots trying to exploit the darkly comic potential of Maggie and Sam's voyeurism while keeping to the "meet cute" Hollywood formula.

Broderick's star-gazing nebbish makes a sweet foil for Ryan. Preston is suitably perky. Karyo, best known as a fighter, not a lover, in "GoldenEye" and "Bad Boys," is the surprise ingredient. He adds a rough humor that explodes into slapstick and wins the biggest laughs.

Manhattan plays a supporting role. Actor-turned-director Dunne delivers a puckish love poem to the city's gritty romance. The Flatiron Building rearing against a gray sky, SoHo's architectural gingerbread and puddles glowing amid grimy cobblestones appear as appealing as Ryan's dimples.

On the surface, "Addicted to Love" approaches the manic intensity of the Dunne-starrer "After Hours." But, in the end, its heart belongs to "Lassie." This is both its strength and weakness. It's a comedy torn between two coasts.

Ryan's romance isn't addictive, but it does satisfy my love-story jones this week.

NEWSDAY, 5/23/97, Part II/p. B3, John Anderson

For all its defiance of formula, "Addicted to Love" still weighs in as the lopsided stepchild of commerce and art. It's an understandable misconception. Who, after all, wouldn't want Meg Ryan in their movie—even if her role really calls for Amanda Plummer? Matthew Broderick? Get him! Cast him! Never mind that your movie won't be exactly what it wants to be. If this one makes money, heck, you can make another.

That, we're unhappy to say, is film industry logic at its most arcane. The happy note is that Robert Gordon's script and Griffin Dunne's direction make for twisted comedy, about two jilted lovers out to torpedo their exes, who are sharing connubial bliss in a fabulous SoHo apartment. (It's probably rent-controlled, too.) This is classic screwball, with a perverse spin: The bad guys really do seem to love each other. The good guys, well, they're easy not to like.

Not that they ain't been done wrong. Sam (Broderick) was left twisting in the Midwest wind by Linda (Kelly Preston), who attended a teacher's conference in Manhattan and never went back. Maggie (Ryan), dumped by the well-accented, well-endowed raconteur/restauranteur Anton (French film star Tcheky Karyo), sees herself as the discarded means to a green card. When Maggie breaks into an abandoned loft across the street from Linda and Anton's place, she finds Sam already there, obsessively charting the happy couple's romantic habits and living in a black hole of rejection. Maggie and Sam don't like each other, but they team up, intending to drive Anton into bankruptcy, ignominy and, quite possibly, massive infection.

It's not that "Addicted to Love" doesn't go anywhere; it does. It's just that everyone seems to be trying so damn hard to make it move. Ryan, cast dramatically against type as the punkish Maggie, a sour photographer with a streak of distemper, strives for an uncharacteristic coolness toward both the material and the camera. Broderick, whose Sam is as methodical and naive as any Broderick character's ever been, attempts to make contact with his unseen audience. But Sam's and Maggie's shared fanaticism regarding Linda and Anton isn't very involving. Ryan's attempt at caustic humor isn't very convincing. And Dunne leap-frogs us through the early part of the film with some spasmodic storytelling.

He also gives us high-rent lower Manhattan as a nightmare warren of streaming streets and hellish basements, which is somewhat familiar territory for Dunne—he traveled it in his best re- membered acting job, Martin Scorsese's 1985 "After Hours." But Dunne has an obvious awareness of his medium and his own inheritance. The film is—a la Scorsese—supersaturated with eclectic pop (from "Walk Away Renee" to Luscious Jackson to Ry Cooder & Ali Farka Toure) and a definite sense of history and cinema-as-voyeurism.

In the loft where he and Maggie work out their mutual psychosis, Sam constructs a camera obscura, a 17th-Century device through which reflected light can be projected on a surface. It was of great interest to such artists as Johannes Vermeer, who used it to guide the eye of the viewer to what he wanted stressed. Dunne uses it to similar effect, to make terrific pictures, and to imbue his movie with an organic, if all too erratic, intelligence.

SIGHT AND SOUND, 9/97, p. 36, Geoffrey Macnab

Sam, a small-town astronomer, is devastated when his childhood sweetheart Linda leaves him to start a new life in New York City. He sets off after her, determined to woo her back, but discovers that she is already living with another man, a French restauranteur named Anton. Sam moves into a derelict building opposite the apartment shared by Linda and Anton and rigs up a camera obscura to spy on them. He hopes Linda will tire of her new lover. One night while he is spying, a strange woman comes crashing into his building. She is Maggie, Anton's estranged fiancée. Since she wants revenge on Anton, the two pool resources. Maggie and Sam bug Anton's apartment and organise a series of outlandish but ultimately futile pranks to split up the loving couple.

Sam gets a job as a dishwasher at Anton's restaurant and on the night that an important restaurant critic is visiting, lets loose hundreds of cockroaches in the kitchen. Chaos ensues.

The restaurant is closed down. Linda no longer trusts Anton, who has confessed to having a brief affair with a customer. The couple split up. Anton is severely in debt (Maggie has been on a spending spree with his credit cards) and he turns to Sam for sympathy. Sam realises that the Frenchman really does love Linda and begins to feel guilty about ruining his life. Anton's bad luck continues. He comes out in a rash after Maggie hides some strawberries to which he is allergic under his pillows. He ends up in plaster when Sam tries to save him from a reckless motorcyclist.

Sam hooks up with Linda, who is living in a cheap hotel downtown. But even as he spends time with her, he realises that Maggie is the one he loves. He organises a reconciliation between Linda and Anton and goes after Maggie instead. The story ends with two happy couples.

Although it comes disguised as a romantic comedy, *Addicted to Love* is a commendably nasty tale which hinges on voyeurism, eavesdropping and sexual jealousy rather than on the conventional, dewy-eyed idealism of young lovers. Its astronomer protagonist is first seen peering through a telescope at his childhood sweetheart. He is supposedly a clean-living small-town bloke, but even before she abandons him for the big city, it is made apparent that, beneath his regular-guy facade, he is a peeping Tom who prefers staring down his lens at women rather than up at the stars.

Robert Gordon's screenplay, his first produced, borrows motifs and ideas from screwball comedy and classical drama alike. His two spurned lovers show a capacity for plotting which recalls the manipulative wiles of Vicomte de Valmont and the Marquise de Merteuil in *Les Liaisons dangereuses,* but they also often seem as ridiculous as the cuckolds and romantic castoffs in a Molière play. They may be played by two of Hollywood's blandest stars, but they're still grotesques. Their most ingenious ruses for compromising their arch-enemy in the eyes of his girlfriend are to hire an organ grinder's monkey to put lipstick marks on his collar and to pay a gang of children to spray him with expensive scent from water pistols.

Their spying is done in elegant, ironic fashion. The use of the camera obscura, an old-fashioned contraption seldom seen on film since Powell and Pressburger's *A Matter of Life and Death,* shows that you don't need fancy video technology to keep tabs on the neighbours. As usual in comedies touching so explicitly on voyeurism, the audience is made to feel complicit. Sam and Maggie sit back and peep at Anton and Linda on their homemade screen, but we in turn are peeping at them.

Sam, the innocent abroad in the big city who turns out to be capable of behaving just as unscrupulously as any of the local shysters, is quite similar to the central character *Addicted to Love*'s director Griffin Dunne played in Scorsese's *After Hours,* another skewed nighttime New York romance. *Addicted to Love* is certainly darker and more cynical than such recent comparable West Coast romantic comedies as Michael Lehmann's mawkish *The Truth About Cats & Dogs.*

Unfortunately, what should have been edgy, unsettling entertainment is undermined by ludicrous casting. Meg Ryan is presumably trying to escape from playing ditzy, Goldie Hawn-style romantic heroines (*French Kiss, When Harry Met Sally*), but her old persona continues to cling to her. She is no more comfortable here as Maggie the leather-clad femme fatale than she was as an alcoholic in *When a Man Loves a Woman.* Squeaky-clean Matthew Broderick is also strangely cast as the spying Sam. They're far too cleancut, so that neither their malice toward their former lovers nor the squalor in which they are prepared to co-exist while they set about wrecking the lovers' lives seems convincing.

The tension between the stars and their material is palpable. Any romantic comedy with Broderick and Ryan demands an upbeat, happy ending, but Robert Gordon's screenplay spends so long tapping his characters' darker sides that this kind of ending can't help but seem glib and horribly sentimental. Thanks to Sam and Maggie's antics, the woebegone French chef Anton (played with engaging Gallic braggadocio by Tcheky Karyo, the Turkish-born character actor) has endured sufferings which even Job might have buckled under: his fiancée has jettisoned him, his possessions have been impounded by creditors, his business has been closed down by the health authorities, his skin has turned scrofulous, and to cap it all, he is in plaster with broken arms and legs. It goes against the grain to believe that the couple who visited all these misfortunes on him are at heart decent, folksy Americans. For all their final-reel displays of heartfelt affection, you can't help but suspect that it is their mutual capacity for mischief and malice that has brought Sam and Maggie together.

TIME, 6/2/97, p. 74, Richard Schickel

In life, the jilted who stalk and harass their former lovers are usually seen as forlorn creatures, objects of pity, if not downright contempt. In the movies (*Play Misty for Me, Fatal Attraction*), they are more often seen as menaces of a more melodramatic, if not downright terrifying, kind. What no one up to now has ever imagined is that people caught up in this common form of temporary insanity might possibly provide the premise for a romantic comedy.

But that's precisely what director Griffin Dunne and writer Robert Gordon have up and tried in *Addicted to Love,* and a fine—but not entirely uninteresting—mess they have on their hands. It offers us two voyeurs, one male and moony (Matthew Broderick's Sam), the other female and furious (Meg Ryan's Maggie). They meet (about as uncute as any couple in the history of screwball farce) because Linda (Kelly Preston), his former fiancé, has moved into a Lower Manhattan loft with Anton (Tcheky Karyo), her former lover. Sam, an astronomer, has rigged up a camera obscura in a tumbledown tenement across from their love nest, which he uses to snark on them. He charts the many ups and very rare downs of their affair, hoping to predict a big bang in their happy little universe. Maggie, a photographer, bugs the place, adding sound to his pictures, thereby doubling a misery that in this case does not particularly love company.

It's never easy being a spy in the house of love. It is certainly not as funny as Dunne and Gordon must have thought it could be. But the movie does find some grotesque comic traction when Maggie and Sam move from the passive to the active mode, their prime target being poor Anton. They plant evidence indicating that he's having an affair on the side. They ruin the restaurant he runs by bringing in a horde of cockroaches the night the *New York Times* food critic is dining there. They destroy his fallback career as a model by making him break out in blotches from a food allergy. He finally finds himself virtually immobilized in a body cast, quite literally a broken man.

We, in turn, find ourselves in a theater of cruelty, consoling ourselves with incidental pleasures: the anti-comedic darkness of Dunne's lighting and sensibility; the relentless, half-mad meanness of Ryan's performance; the snarling strength Karyo demonstrates in multiple adversity. These people don't give a hoot if they warm our hearts or lift our spirits, and that's not nothing in a time when mainstream movie comedy is all blandness and ingratiation. Too bad we can't reward their bravery with the sound of more than one hand clapping.

VILLAGE VOICE, 6/3/97, p. 74, Amy Taubin

As and old boyfriend told me: "You don't know what it is to be human until you've been dumped by the person you imagine is the love of your life." I won't bother telling you who was first out the door.

In *Addicted to Love*, two jilted lovers find each other while spying on their former sweeties, who've shacked up together. The jilted ones are Sam (Matthew Broderick), an idealistic Midwestern astronomer, and Maggie (Meg Ryan), a hard-boiled Downtown photographer. Their respective exes are Linda (Kelly Preston), a wholesome schoolteacher who likes her sex a little rougher than Sam ever suspected, and Anton (Tcheky Karyo), a French restauranteur who appreciates Linda's latent impulses.

Having tracked Linda down to an eclectically appointed Soho loft where she's living with Anton, Sam installs himself in an abandoned building directly across the street and builds a camera obscura that he trains on Anton and Linda's unadorned floor-to-ceiling windows. Seemingly less invasive than a telescope, the camera obscura projects the image of what's happening across the street onto the crumbling wall of Sam's abode. It's like he's watching a movie of Linda, which, at least cosmetically, is more tasteful than if he were peering at her directly.

But Sam isn't alone with his lens and fantasies. Maggie, who's bugged the loft where she used to live with Anton, becomes his partner in crime. She's the sound recordist and he's the camera-man, and the moments when they curl up on the sofa with Chinese take-out to watch the cinema verité are wittier than anything else in *Addicted to Love*.

Unlike Sam, who just wants to get Linda back, Maggie wants revenge on Anton for rejecting her. A quiet control freak, Sam believes that if he does enough research into Linda and Anton's relationship, he'll be able to figure out how to rescue his love from the lascivious Anton. Maggie just wants to cause Anton as much pain as possible. But because *Addicted to Love* is meant to be a romantic comedy, and a Meg Ryan vehicle to boot, Maggie is never allowed to seem the least bit dangerous. Underneath her *Irma Vep* leather catsuit beats a childishly vulnerable heart. Maggie's idea of revenge is to hide strawberries under Anton's pillow so he'll break out in an itchy rash. Rolling her baby blues or petulantly sucking on her upper lip, Ryan is even more coy and self-involved than usual. There's zero chemistry between her and Broderick.

Addicted to Love is prettily shot and jauntily edited. Directing his first feature, Griffin Dunne keeps things moving almost fast enough to make us forget that the basic premise is as disreputable and as full of pitfalls as the rickety building where Sam and Maggie do there *Rear Window* routine. As an actor and producer, Dunne never shied away from dark material. And in fact, the most arresting moments here seem like nightmare flashbacks to Scorsese's *After Hours*, the high point of Dunne's acting career. They suggest a more subversive tale than the one that made it on to the screen.

Also reviewed in:
NEW YORK TIMES, 5/23/97, p. C14, Stephen Holden
VARIETY, 5/19-25/97, p. 49, Leonard Klady
WASHINGTON POST, 5/23/97, p. B1, Stephen Hunter
WASHINGTON POST, 5/23/97, Weekend/p. 42, Eve Zibart

AFTERGLOW

A Sony Pictures Classics release of a Sand Castle 5/Elysian Dreams coproduction. *Executive Producer:* Ernst Stroh and Willi Baer. *Producer:* Robert Altman. *Director:* Alan Rudolph. *Screenplay:* Alan Rudolph. *Director of Photography:* Toyomichi Kurita. *Editor:* Suzy Elmiger. *Music:* Mark Isham. *Music Editor:* Steve Borne. *Sound:* Claude La Haye and (music) Ben Rogers. *Sound Editor:* Eliza Paley and Paul P. Soucek. *Casting:* Lucie Robitaille. *Production Designer:* François Seguin. *Art Director:* Collin Niemi. *Set Decorator:* Ann Galea. *Costumes:* François Barbeau. *Make-up:* Micheline Trepanier. *Stunt Coordinator:* Dave McKeown. *Running time:* 113 minutes. *MPAA Rating:* R.

CAST: Nick Nolte (Lucky Mann); Julie Christie (Phyllis Mann); Lara Flynn Boyle (Marianne Byron); Jonny Lee Miller (Jeffrey Byron); Jay Underwood (Donald Duncan); Domini Blythe (Helene Pelletier); Yves Corbeil (Bernard Omay); Alan Fawcett (Count Falco/Jack Dana); Genevieve Bissonnette (Cassie); Michele-Barbara Pelletier (Isabel Marino); France Castel (Gloria Marino); Claudia Besso (Monica Bloom); Ellen David (Judy the Waitress); Don Jordan (The Byrons' Concierge); Bill Rowat (Pedro); Cas Anvar (Frederico); David Francis (Falco's Butler); Ivan Smith (Doctor); John Dunn-Hill (Derelict in Park); Warren "Slim" Williams (Chateau Lenore Pianist); Jean-François Sauvageau (Chateau Lenore singer); Bernard Tanguay (Maitre D'); Dave McKeown (Security Guard); Vanya Rose (Hotel Receptionist); Mark Camacho (Ritz-Carlton Bartender); Amy Kadawaki (Chinese Restaurant Hostess); Salvatore Agostino (Restaurant Owner).

LOS ANGELES TIMES, 12/26/97, Calendar/p. 8, Kevin Thomas

"Afterglow" is a wonderful title for so rich and burnished a film. It is dominated by the enduring radiance of Julie Christie while allowing Nick Nolte, Lara Flynn Boyle and Jonny Lee Miller to shine just as brightly. It marks a gratifying resurgence for Christie and an effective departure for writer-director Alan Rudolph from his multi-character movies of recent years. It is also surprisingly demanding for a romantic comedy.

What Rudolph has done is to take a classically simple situation: Nolte's Lucky and Boyle's Marianne have an affair. Then their respective spouses, Christie's Phyllis and Miller's Jeffrey, have their own dalliance unaware of what's going on between Lucky and Marianne.

This plot is the stuff of classic farce, and although Rudolph doesn't stint on the comic elements, he has layered in concerns and insights to create a film of impressive emotional density that much of the time is simultaneously funny and sad.

Rudolph honors the complexity of the characters he has created by pacing his scenes in accordance to what he senses is psychologically valid for them. He is unerring in this, but it takes adjustment on the part of the viewer, who must be prepared for long sequences and abrupt shifts in tone.

Seven minutes short of two hours is in itself a long running time for comedy, but "Afterglow" is richly rewarding in its comment on the curse of selfishness within relationships and the value of forgiveness between people who truly love each other. What gives it its edge is that as it unfolds we begin to fear that Marianne and Jeffrey are doomed to repeat the mistakes of Phyllis and Lucky.

Lucky is a Montreal contractor, a handyman who is especially handy with the women he meets on the job. Meanwhile, Phyllis, as desirable and vibrant as she is, spends far too much time watching a string of tacky horror pictures she starred in in the '70s. In time we learn that Phyllis and Lucky's marriage has been blighted by a terrible loss.

Meanwhile, when Marianne hires Lucky to do some remodeling we discover her marriage is no less dysfunctional. Jeffrey is a formidably successful young businessman who's eager to break out of his career, and when he comes home to his ultrachic apartment he'd like Marianne to be waiting for him with a warm meal and a sympathetic ear instead of attempting to seduce him in her desperate desire to have the child he in fact does not want.

Rudolph has done a terrific job in involving us in this quartet. Phyllis is a woman of self-deprecating wit and irony, of bitter self-knowledge, and Christie brings her alive in what is surely one of her finest roles, laced with great lines.

Who better to play Lucky than Nolte, a rugged kind of guy in whom maturity is sexy. Lucky, however, is more than a practiced philanderer but a man capable of self-reflection, a man with poetry and pain in his soul that he's hard put to express. Marianne is an especially tricky role, for she often comes across as an airhead, but she knows enough to realize that she's got to either make her marriage work or get out of it. Boyle is consistently nimble in handling Marianne's flightiness and longing. What a contrast Marianne is to the tough dame. Boyle played in "Red Rock West." Miller similarly excels in taking us through the despair, self-absorption and bravado of Jeffrey, a man who can say that he's working "the edge of his charm" and, amusingly, mean it. In one of the details that add so much to the film Jeffrey is so complimentary to his secretary (beautifully played by Domini Blythe), a chic woman older than he, that he unwittingly leads her to hope that something could happen between them.

"Afterglow" has the supple style and sophistication that has long been Rudolph's hallmark, and it exudes with elegance from Toyomichi Kurita's perfectly modulated camera work and Mark Isham's mellow score. "Mellow," in fact, is the word that best describes Christie and the movie as well.

NEW YORK POST, 12/26/97, p. 35, Michael Medved

The film "Afterglow" features some of the season's most compelling characterizations and expert performances, but deploys these impressive people in situations so contrived that, except for the film's prevailing air of solemnity and self-importance, it would resemble the silliest of sitcoms.

Jonny Lee Miller ("Trainspotting") plays a callow, uptight yuppie in Montreal whose consuming career as a rising tycoon leaves him little time for his bored, lonely wife, Lara Flynn Boyle.

She yearns for a child, but can't even lure her husband into sex; after he walks out following a painful spat, she throws herself at the rugged, middle-aged handyman (Nick Nolte) she has hired to build a nursery in defiance of her spouse and in order to disrupt the antiseptic, Architectural Digest perfection of their lavish apartment.

Nolte, natch, endures a troubled marriage of his own, fixing the plumbing of a succession of desperate matrons while his wife, a faded B-movie actress played by Julie Christie, sits home watching videos of her mediocre, long-ago work, and mourning her only daughter, who has mysteriously disappeared from their life.

The film falls apart when the yuppie husband coincidentally stumbles across Christie in a bar and illogically begins coming on to her, conveniently unaware that her husband is simultaneously romancing his wife.

Christie ("Darling," "Doctor Zhivago") gets her best role in some 20 years, persuasively presenting a wry, worldly-wise, battle and embittered survivor, just a few clicks shy of hysteria.

Nolte is predictably appealing as the warm-hearted, home-improving Lothario (annoyingly named Lucky Mann), but the film's real revelation is Boyle sweetly sympathetic, totally vulnerable and achingly sexy, erasing memories of all those unworthy roles in movies such as "The Temp" and "Threesome."

Unfortunately, writer-director Alan Rudolph ("Welcome to L.A.," "Mrs. Parker and the Vicious Circle") undermines the fine acting with awkward stabs at slapstick or farce as well as a much-too-neat resolution, all of which run counter to the jazzy, elegiac tone that incongruously prevails here, as it does in all his movies.

No one can deny the fact that he's shaped characters worth caring about, but they ultimately inspire enough compassion that you long to see them in more plausible and satisfying situations.

NEWSDAY, 12/26/97, Part II/p. B2, Jack Mathews

Troubled couple No. 1 are the Manns: an amiable, womanizing Mr. Fixit named Lucky (Nick Nolte) and his depressed, former B-movie star wife, Phyllis (Julie Christie). Troubled Couple No. 2 are the Byrons: emotionally constricted careerist Jeffrey (Jonny Lee Miller) and his frustrated, ovulating trophy wife, Marianne (Lara Flynn Boyle).

Soon, in Alan Rudolph's "Afterglow," events will mix and match these couples in strange and improbable ways, pointing each individual in the vague direction of healing, while commenting generally on the difficulty of relationships in the days of the millennium.

Love him or hate him, Rudolph is a genuine American auteur, and an incorrigible romantic. Outside the occasional gun-for-hire work on studio pictures like "Mortal Thoughts" and "Made in Heaven," the typical Rudolph film occurs in a kind of poetic warp, where events, characters, and emotions are filtered through a personal prism and radiate out in dreamlike waves from the screen.

When everything comes together, as it did with "Choose Me," Rudolph is a brilliant explorer of the puzzling landscape of contemporary relationships. When it all falls apart, as it did with "Love at Large," he makes films that are unwatchably cloying. "Afterglow," while closer to the former than the latter, definitely claims middle ground.

"Afterglow" covers familiar territory, too. In fact, it's the third mate-swapper of the season, following "The Ice Storm" and "One Night Stand." And the Byrons' marriage is about as easy to warm up to as the Trumps'. Jeffrey is a mess of a human being, rude, narcissistic, sexually ambivalent, and incessantly whiny.   And Marianne's presence has all the excitement of a microscope's view of an egg awaiting an invasion of sperm.

The Manns, on the other hand, are a classically divided couple, the George and Martha of Montreal. Something terrible happened eight years earlier, involving a teenage daughter who may or may not be imaginary, and it created a wall of guilt and recrimination between them.

When we meet the Manns, Lucky is a handyman working out of his truck, and encountering enough undernourished housewives to have developed a glossary of tool box metaphors. He lights cigars to mask the scent of women when he gets home, but he doesn't really need to. Phyllis has pre-authorized any transgressions, in lieu of tending to his needs herself. And she stays in a tranquilized state of nostalgia and self-pity, knocking back airline bottles of gin while watching herself in bad late night movies, and reliving the moment she told her husband her darkest secret.

Needless to say, when Marianne decides to remodel a room in her apartment for her hoped-for baby, Lucky is her man. He'll not only build the baby's room, but while her husband is out trying to decide whether he's gay or straight, he'll help her make the baby, too.

So far, so French. And when Jeffrey happens upon Phyllis in the very Ritz-Carlton bar where Lucky and Marianne were last seen necking, "Afterglow" ventures into the territory of bad bedroom farce.

It's rescued from that by two things, the performances of Nolte, whose residual virility and sense of irony. are helping him carve out a late career niche as an irrepressible letch, and Christie, who hasn't lost an ounce of her allure since "Darling." Christie, who won the New York Film Critics Circle best actress award for the part, almost single-handedly gives "Afterglow" its dramatic pulse.

As we cut back and forth between scenes with Phyllis and Jeffrey, on a trip to a country resort, and Lucky and Marianne, back in town, the film lurches along, giddy at one moment, gloomily portentous the next. And the mix makes it hard to stay engaged, or to feel much of a stake in the outcome of the relationships.

Miller, a far distance from the character of Sick Boy in "Trainspotting," has the film's toughest assignment, playing a totally self-absorbed man trying to convince himself he's not homosexual by attempting to launch affairs with older, less threatening women—first his secretary, then Phyllis. Miller does a convincing job, but Jeffrey, is so insufferable, it's hard to share Phyllis' empathy for him.

Despite some marvelous moments and Christie's good efforts, "Afterglow" leaves less than a glow than a bitter aftertaste.

SIGHT AND SOUND, 6/98, p. 38, Geoffrey Macnab

Montreal, the present day. Self-absorbed businessman Jeffrey Byron has been neglecting his young wife, Marianne. She wants to have children, but he refuses even to have sex with her. Marianne hires a handyman named Lucky, an easygoing, charming man. He and Marianne begin an affair. Lucky's relations with his own wife Phyllis are clouded by some incident from the past which neither partner will talk about.

Phyllis spies on Lucky and Marianne in a hotel bar. They leave just before Jeffrey walks in. He chats Phyllis up and invites her to come away with him on a business trip to the country. In the country, over dinner with Jeffrey, a business associate and his mistress, Phyllis reveals that years before, when she was an actress, she had a brief fling with another actor. She became pregnant, but never told Lucky that Cassie wasn't his daughter. When Cassie was 16, the truth came out and Cassie ran away to Montreal. Phyllis and Lucky followed her there, but haven't been able to find her since.

Jeffrey accompanies Phyllis to her hotel room but they are interrupted and he leaves without doing anything. The next day, when they drive back to the city, they bump into Lucky and Marianne in a bar. Lucky and Jeffrey fight and then all decide to meet at Jeffrey's apartment. Lucky and Jeffrey continue to fight. Phyllis leaves without Lucky. Jeffrey and Marianne have sex. Some time later. Marianne is pregnant but separated from Jeffrey. Lucky spots Cassie and chases her. There is an emotional reunion. With Cassie set to come back into their lives, Lucky and Phyllis seem finally reconciled.

At times, *Afterglow* seems like a caricature of an Alan Rudolph film. With its glittering surfaces, playful structure, and four narcissistic protagonists, it contains elements frequently featured in Rudolph's work. From the sleazy, neon lit small town bars of *Choose Me,* via the 20s Paris of *The Moderns,* to the vaguely futuristic cityscapes featured in *Equinox,* Rudolph has always specialised in creating stylised, self-contained worlds. *Afterglow* is shot and ostensibly set in modern day Montreal, but though some of the action unfolds in the streets and parks, this is nothing like real life. He still manages to make the city seem strangely exotic. The very title might describe his approach to lighting: there is never anything harsh or garish about the film. Again and again, the actors are shown in warm, flattering close-ups. As the lazy, seductive saxophone music which is heard over the opening credits suggests, the mood is supposed to be seductive.

Afterglow is also surprisingly theatrical. With its symmetrical staircases stretching down from either side of one vast room, the chic, modernist apartment where Marianne lives with her businessman husband Jeffrey looks like a stage set. The idea of two married couples whose lives overlap might have been borrowed from Noel Coward's *Private Lives* or even Edward Albee's *Who's Afraid of Virginia Woolf?* Like George and Martha in *Virginia Woolf,* Lucky and Phyllis are caustic-tongued, embittered by some unmentionable incident long in the past, and have their own special house rules to make the marriage endurable. Lucky is allowed to sleep around, just as long as he does so discreetly. He is the handyman as satyr. For all his sophistication, Rudolph can't resist the occasional bawdy gag, such as giving us our first view of Lucky with a very phallic-looking spanner sticking out between his legs, his head under a sink and a scantily clad housewife towering over him.

Rudolph's script is wordy, but he is never beholden to the dialogue. Characters are seen in reflection or the camera swoops around them, or there a cutaways to spectacular sunsets over three city. Sometimes, the action is speeded up for comic effect. The sound editing is likewise self-conscious and playful. Marianne seems to control the soundtrack with her remote control and every time she switches channels, she makes us aware of the way in which film makers manipulate mood through music.

As the film progresses, it becomes apparent that *Afterglow* is not simply the comedy of modern manners it first appears. All the characters are unhappy. Marianne's nervousness, her lapses into grating, pidgin French and her coquettishness are symptoms of her deep rooted misery at being trapped in a loveless marriage. Likewise, Jeffrey's overweening arrogance is a cloak for his impotence and immaturity Even Lucky, the easygoing everyman, seems tormented. The hypochondriac and one-time B-movie actress Phyllis is the unhappiest of all, still agonising over the loss of her daughter.

Like his mentor Robert Altman (who produced *Afterglow*), Rudolph allows his cast a freedom one imagines they rarely experience elsewhere. The achievement of his actors here is to flesh out characters who, at first glance, seem mannered and one dimensional. For all her affectations, Lara Flynn Boyle's Marianne is a sympathetic figure while Julie Christie's Phyllis emerges as a full blown tragic heroine. She is able to say a line like, "my soul needs an overhaul", and get away with it. The camera is fascinated by her. In one comic scene, two men hang on her every word as she recounts a rambling, emotional story at the dinner table. ("You're the most fascinating woman I've met in my entire life," Jeffrey tells her. "Yes, I know," she replies.)

The sudden shifts in tone can be disorienting. Scenes in which the characters seem to be deeply unhappy are played in knockabout, comic fashion. The climactic moment in which the two couples meet and realise just who they have been cheating with is played screwball comedy style, complete with a slapstick fight between Lucky and Jeffrey. Rudolph risks losing his audience at several points. If he doesn't care about the characters' problems, why should we? Just when *Afterglow* threatens to end on a banal, anti-climactic note, he throws in a reunion as heartrending as it is unexpected. Rudolph is often accused of dealing in surfaces, but here, at least, there is no questioning his emotional engagement.

TIME, 1/12/98, p. 84, Richard Schickel

Phyliss (Julie Christie) is sad. A former horror-film star, she spends her days watching her old movies on cassette and brooding about her runaway daughter. Her husband Lucky (Nick Nolte) is ... well, lucky—a handyman with plenty of randy women for clients. Marianne (Lara Flynn Boyle) is one of them, feverish with desire for the baby her financier husband Jeffrey (Jonny Lee Miller) is too preoccupied to provide.

The women—one mourning a lost child, the other yearning to have one—offer mirror images of the mothering instinct. The men—a working stiff grabbing furtive pleasure on the fly and an executive taking stupid risks (Jeffrey likes to tiptoe along balustrades high above the street)—reflect, in their class-differentiated ways, the contemporary male's desperate need for adventure. But *Afterglow*'s writer-director, Alan Rudolph, is not entirely certain whether temporarily mixing and rematching these couples is a funny idea or a poignant one.

There's some door-slamming farce in his film and a certain amount of romantic rue as well. Christie has already won prizes for the knowing weariness of her performance, and Flynn Boyle probably deserves some for her ferociously stated frustrations. But their clarity can't quite cut through the thickness of the film's air or compensate for the wooziness it induces.

VILLAGE VOICE, 12/30/97, p. 66, Amy Taubin

As a filmmaker, Alan Rudolph never learned how to finesse the connection between feeling and form. (The 1984 *Choose Me* is an exception.) Still, at a moment when most films are notable only for their absence of heart, no manifestation of messily human emotion should be taken lightly, even when said manifestation makes you feel as if you've spent two hours with a very sloppy kisser.

So it is with *Afterglow*, the latest in Rudolph's long line of quirkily romantic, revoltingly sentimental comedies. *Afterglow* is a four-hander involving two couples, one young and one middle-aged. The young couple is woodenly played by Lara Flynn Boyle and Jonny Lee Miller. The middle-aged couple is played with slightly more panache by Julie Christie and Nick Nolte. The young couple is rich and in crisis. She wants a baby but he can't oblige her with the requisite fuck because he's begun to suspect that he's gay The middle-aged couple is less affluent but also in crisis. He's a womanizing plumber; she's a former B-picture actress. Their estrangement involves a daughter who has run away. The two couples briefly exchange partners, although nothing of note happens during or as a result of the exchange.

Nolte fashions a performance—the only vaguely interesting one in the film—out of a laid-back, over-the-hill jock physicality. Christie, who seems to have checked her irony at the door to the makeup room, uses her character's movie-star past as an excuse to camp it up, albeit not particularly flamboyantly. For her superficial portrayal of an aging beauty who deprives herself of sexual pleasure in order to maintain power, the New York Film Critics Circle gave Christie its 1997 best actress award.

Also reviewed in:
CHICAGO TRIBUNE, 1/16/98, p. B, Michael Wilmington
NEW YORK TIMES, 12/25/97, p. E1, Janet Maslin
NEW YORKER, 1/19/98, p. 84, Daphne Merkin
VARIETY, 5/19-25/97, p. 58, Emanuel Levy
WASHINGTON POST, 1/16/98, Weekend/p. 32, Desson Howe

AIR BUD

A Walt Disney Pictures release in association with Keystone Pictures of a Robert Vince production. *Executive Producer:* Michael Strange and Anne Vince. *Producer:* William Vince and Robert Vince. *Director:* Charles Martin Smith. *Screenplay:* Paul Tamasy and Aaron Mendelsohn. *Based on the character "Air Bud" created by:* Kevin DiCicco. *Director of Photography:* Mike Southon. *Editor:* Alison Grace. *Music:* Brahm Wenger. *Music Editor:* Pat Caird. *Sound:* Bill "Otis" Sheppard and (music) Steve Culp. *Casting:* Abra Edelman and Elisa Goodman. *Production Designer:* Elizabeth Wilcox. *Art Director:* Eric Fraser. *Set Decorator:* David Chiasson. *Set Dresser:* Troy Hansen, Bob Carson, David Segerts, Tamara Susik, and Spencer Louttit. *Costumes:* Jana Stern. *Make-up:* Joann Fowler. *Stunt Coordinator:* Scott Ateah and Bill Stewart. *Running time:* 97 minutes. *MPAA Rating:* PG.

CAST: Michael Jeter (Norm Snively); Kevin Zegers (Josh Framm); Wendy Makkena (Jackie Framm); Bill Cobbs (Arthur Chaney); Eric Christmas (Judge Cranfield); Jay Brazeau (Referee 1); Nicola Cavendish (Principal Pepper); Brendan Fletcher (Larry Willingham); Norman Browning (Buck Willingham); Stephen E. Miller (Coach Barker); Shayn Solberg (Tom Stewart); Chris Turner (Greg); Christine Kennedy (Melissa); Frank C. Turner (Bailiff); Marian Dodd (Reporter); Ursula Martin (Party Mom); Kevin DiCicco (Referee 2); Jessebel Mather and Kati Mather (Andrea Framm).

LOS ANGELES TIMES, 8/1/97, Calendar/p. 14, Kevin Thomas

[The following review by Kevin Thomas appeared in a slightly different form in
NEWSDAY, 8/1/97, Part II/p. B9.]

If ever there was a 12-year-old boy who needed a dog, it would be Josh Framm (Kevin Zegers) in Disney's delightful family comedy "Air Bud." If ever there was a dog in need of a new master, it's a golden retriever Josh names Buddy.

Josh's mother, Jackie (Wendy Makkena), who has recently lost her husband in an accident, has decided to try to start a new life for herself, her son and her toddler daughter in the idyllic Washington town where her grandparents once lived. Devastated by the loss of his father, Josh has a tough time adjusting to a new environment.

He dreams of playing basketball, but before he gets to open his mouth, the gruff coach at his new school instantly designates him the team's water boy. It's when Josh discovers a basketball hoop adjacent to an abandoned rural church that he meets Buddy, who bounces back the ball to him when it rolls into a thicket. It takes a lot of persuasion and patience—not to mention pudding—on the part of Josh to get Buddy to come out of the bushes, let alone trust him.

What we know and Josh doesn't is that the dog is an escapee from a singularly nasty master, the world's worst juggler, a clown (Michael Jeter) who calls himself Happy Slappy the Clown With a Hound and entertains at children's parties. (This is not so different from what Buddy experienced in real life, according to production notes.) Buddy's ability to bounce back balloons and catch tennis balls in his mouth is the only thing that works in Happy's pathetic act. But then Josh discovers Buddy has an astonishing talent.

Adults will know where this fine film is heading from the get-go, but "Air Bud" is admirable for the way in which writers Paul Tamasy and Aaron Mendelsohn have injected a sense of reality amid lots of rousing fantasy calamities involving the bull-in-a-china-shop Buddy. They are honest about the effect of losing a parent, of how alone an adolescent can feel and how in sports being a team player is as important as winning. They suggest that life can be cruelly unjust and require painful sacrifices while affirming that good can triumph over evil with a lot of effort and determination—and with a little luck, too.

Throughout this handsome film, actor-turned-director Charlie Martin Smith manages to shift the tone between pathos and humor seamlessly as he draws ensemble portrayals from his large cast. "Air Bud" has been made with consistent care and intelligence, and its happy ending is well earned.

Zegers, Makkena, Bill Cobbs, as a school engineer with a surprising secret, and Jeter, who can play hilariously hyper characters like no one else, all have the chance to show us the various facets of the people they play so well. Still, it's the amazingly alert and expressive Buddy, in the film's title role, who's the scene-stealer here—and, guess what, he even performs his own stunts.

NEW YORK POST, 8/1/97, p. 43, Michael Medved

Great dog. Great kid. Great gimmick. Pretty good movie. "Air Bud" has all the elements for first-rate family fun, but they never quite come together due to slack direction and a near fatal overdose of slapstick.

No birthday cake is left unsquished, no paint can is left unsplashed, no cooler of Gatorade is left unspilled.

All of this manic mayhem might inspire giggles from very young moviegoers, but it will needlessly embarrass audience members above 13 who might otherwise feel captivated by the movie's incomparably charismatic canine star.

That justly acclaimed celebrity is Buddy the Wonder Dog, a gorgeous golden retriever who has already fetched fame with his uncanny ability to bonk basketballs with his nose and send them accurately arching even through regulation height hoops.

He's previously demonstrated this stunning skill in frequent appearances on David Letterman, at NBA half-time shows, and on various pet food commercials.

The movie deploys a serviceably sentimental plot. Buddy is initially abused by his cruel master, an angry incompetent birthday party clown (Michael Jeter).

Escaping this torment, the hungry stray makes friends with a shy, lonely boy (the excellent and sensitive 12-year-old actor Kevin Zegers), who has just moved to a new home following the death of his test pilot dad.

His hard-working harried mom (lovely Wendy Makkena) relucantly agrees to keep the dog even before she discovers his astonishing athleticism.

Meanwhile, the boy defies the odds and a local bully to make his middle school basketball team, and helps to rehabilitate the haunted handyman (the wonderfully appealing Bill Cobbs), who lives in the basement below the gym and is secretly a one-time star of the NBA.

This new mentor, and their sharp-shooting furry mascot, inspire the kids to the state championship, but injuries in the big game leave them with only four players—until an emergency replacement arrives in the nick of time.

Director Charles Martin Smith (best known for his acting in "American Graffiti," "Never Cry Wolf" and many other movies) draws appealing performances from his entire cast (especially the irresistible Buddy).

But he handles even possibly thrilling chase scenes with infantile stagey excess and undermines a few big moments of potentially honest emotion.

As a result "Air Bud" remains essentially earthbound: no soaring champion of animal entertainment (no, not "Babe," or even "Homeward Bound"). But in a season starved for family fare, its still a spirited (and welcome competitor.

SIGHT AND SOUND, 11/98, p. 40, Joe Harland

The Northwest of the US. Following the death of his father, adolescent Josh Framm moves with his mother Jackie and infant sister Andrea to a new town. Too shy to try out for the school basketball team, he becomes the team's assistant. One evening, he finds a forgotten basketball court and a dog (abandoned by incompetent clown Norm Snively) and names the dog "Buddy".

Josh has a second chance to try out for the team. While he is pondering whether to enter, Buddy steals Josh's ball and scores a basket by hitting the ball with his nose. At the next game

Josh makes the team and on his debut Buddy joins in and shows that he can 'play' too. The school makes him the team mascot. Arthur, the school's janitor who once played for an NBA team, is made coach, and the team reaches the state finals. Meanwhile, Buddy has become a media star. Realising the commercial possibilities, Snively visits the Framms and reclaims his dog. Josh steals Buddy back, and Snively gives chase. They escape, and Josh sets Buddy free. At the final, Josh's team are losing and down a man through injury, but Buddy reappears, joins the team and they win. Snively returns for his dog, and the case goes to court. The judge rules Buddy may choose his owner; he chooses Josh.

Charles Martin Smith's directorial career started with heavy-metal horror film *Trick or Treat*. Here he once again demonstrates an ability to craft an unchallenging but entertaining tale even with the most ludicrous of central premises. *Air Bud* focuses on a fatherless boy's fight for acceptance in a new town with the help of a basketball-playing dog, a plot the film's US tagline sums up neatly as: "he sits, he stays, he shoots, he scores." *Air Bud* never deviates from the narrative rules of dog-and-kid films (from *Rescued by Rover,* 1905, to the recent *Paws):* Josh, like previous screen tots, is drawn out of his reclusive shell by the love a good hound, Mom Jackie comes to accept the new member of the family even after Buddy has trashed the family home, evil clown-villain Snively is routed, and Buddy gets to save the day. In addition, there's a staple sports movie storyline in which losers become winners.

What lifts *Air Bud* is a sense of unforced pathos (particularly concerning Josh's mourning for his dead Dad), a solid sense of its own limits, and the very real abilities of Buddy. Prior to making this, the golden retriever became a minor television celebrity for his hoop-shooting skills (debuted in the "Stupid Pet Tricks" slot on David Letterman's chat show). *Air Bud* goes out of its way to show him shooting (or, more properly, 'nosing') the hoops in single takes, and after the formula assertion that no animals were harmed in the making of the film, another credit line boasts that no visual effects were used either.

The rest of the film may lack visual flair, and the slapstick chases are undoubtedly grating for a mature audience, but one cannot imagine younger viewers complaining about a story told with such effectiveness. Indeed, that Bud's US-football playing follow up, *Air Bud Golden Receiver,* is already in the can testifies to the enduring popularity of such undemanding fare.

Also reviewed in:
NEW YORK TIMES, 8/1/97, p. C14, Stephen Holden
VARIETY, 8/4-10/97, p. 35, Leonard Klady
WASHINGTON POST, 8/1/97, Weekend/p. 30, Stephen Hunter

AIR FORCE ONE

A Columbia Pictures and Beacon Pictures release of a Radiant production. *Executive Producer:* Thomas A. Bliss, Marc Abraham, and David Lester. *Producer:* Wolfgang Petersen, Gail Katz, Armyan Bernstein, and Jon Shestack. *Director:* Wolfgang Petersen. *Screenplay:* Andrew W. Marlowe. *Director of Photography:* Michael Ballhaus. *Editor:* Richard Francis-Bruce. *Music:* Jerry Goldsmith. *Music Editor:* Ken Hall. *Sound:* Keith A. Wester and (music) Bruce Botnick. *Sound Editor:* Wylie Stateman and Peter Michael Sullivan. *Casting:* Janet Hirshenson and Jane Jenkins. *Production Designer:* William Sandell. *Art Director:* Nancy Patton. *Set Designer:* Peter J. Kelly, Karl J. Martin, Martha Johnson, Harry E. Otto, and Lynn Christopher. *Set Decorator:* Ernie Bishop. *Special Effects:* Terry D. Frazee. *Visual Effects:* Richard Edlund. *Costumes:* Erica Edell Phillips. *Make-up:* Kevin Haney. *Stunt Coordinator:* Doug Coleman. *Running time:* 125 minutes. *MPAA Rating:* R.

CAST: Harrison Ford (President James Marshall); Gary Oldman (Ivan Korshunov); Glenn Close (Vice President Kathryn Bennett); Wendy Crewson (Grace Marshall); Liesel Matthews (Alice Marshall); Paul Guilfoyle (Chief of Staff Lloyd Shepherd); Xander Berkeley (Agent Gibbs); William H. Macy (Major Caldwell); Dean Stockwell (Defense Secretary Walter Dean); Tom

Everett (NSA Advisor Jack Doherty); Jurgen Prochnow (General Alexander Radek); Donna Bullock (Press Secretary Melanie Mitchell); Michael Ray Miller (AFO Pilot Colonel Axelrod); Carl Weintraub (AFO Co-Pilot Lt. Col. Ingrahams); Elester Latham (AFO Navigator); Elya Baskin (Andrei Kolchak); Levani (Sergei Lenski); David Vadim (Igor Nevsky); Andrew Divoff (Boris Bazylev); Ilia Volokh (Vladimir Krasin); Chris Howell (Major Perkins); Spencer Garrett (White House Aide Thomas Lee); Bill Smitrovich (General Northwood); Philip Baker Hall (U.S. Attorney General Ward); Albert Owens ("Football" Colonel); Willard Pugh (White House Communications Officer); Michael Monks (Assistant Press Secretary); Alan Woolf (Russian President Petrov); Messiri Freeman (Future Postmaster General); Thomas Crawford (Steward Mike); Fenton Lawless (Steward Joey); Dan Shor (Notre Dame Aide); David Gianopolous (Agent Johnson); Glenn Morshower (Agent Walters); Richard Doyle (A.F.O. Back-up Pilot); Don R. McManus (F-15 Leader Colonel Carlton); Duke Miglin (F-15 "Halo 2" Fighter Pilot); Pavel D. Lychnikoff and Oleg Taktarov (Prison Guards); Brian Libby (Chief Mechanic); Diana Bellamy (Switchboard Operator); Thom Barry (Ramstein S.O.F. Watch Officer); Harry Hutchinson (Ramstein Airbase Controller); Suzanne Michaels (CNN Anchor); Boris Krutonog (MiG Leader); Alex Veadov (MiG Pilot); Allan Kolman (Kazak Soldier); Dan Barringer (USAF Jump Master); Mark Knutson (Russian Jump Master); Jim Harley (Willis); Aleks Shaklin (Government Official); Igor N. Lobotsky (Russian Official); Koko Kiledjian (Russian Speaker); Gordon Michaels, Robert Peters, and Kristian Sorensen (USAF Radio Specialists); Stuart Nixon (USAF Security); Marty Rosen (CIA Director); Lee Faranda (Russian Bad Guy); Mike Hambrick (CNN Reporter); Catherine T. Yang (Foreign TV Reporter); David MacIsaac (MC-130 Pilot); J. Scott Shonka and Paul Sklar (Pararescue Jumpers); David Permenter (Winch Recovery Master); David O'Donnell (Young Airman).

CHRISTIAN SCIENCE MONITOR, 7/25/97, p. 12, David Sterritt

Look to the skies! Airborne entertainments are definitely in style, from the criminal mischief of "Con Air" to the optimistic space ride of "Contact" and the flying-saucer shenanigans of "Men in Black."

Presidents are also fashionable at the movies. True, last year's "Independence Day" treated the chief executive skeptically, and "Absolute Power" and "Mars Attacks!" were even more irreverent. But the presidency rebounds in "Contact," with Bill Clinton joining the action via TV news footage—a circumstance that displeased the White House, which didn't authorize the filmmakers to edit his image into their story.

And in what has become a minitrend, CNN has been playing a starring role on the wide screen. But after the recent premiere of "Contact," in which numerous appearances by CNN personalities drew criticism, the network has temporarily barred its staff from appearing in movies, according to CNN spokesman Steve Haworth.

Those are some of the developments making minor waves at the movies this summer.

For better or worse, "Air Force One" brings them all together. The main setting is the president's plane. On board is the chief executive, no vacillating bureaucrat but a take-charge hero. Down below are millions of anxious Americans—and an army of CNN reporters ready to update them (and us) whenever the plot grows complicated, or too expensive for the movie to actually *show.*

The picture starts with a violent commando operation by American and Russian forces. The target is a dictator in Kazakhstan, now free of Soviet control but still far from democracy. We meet President James Marshall as he defends the raid in a speech—and promises to repeat it if necessary, shoring up world freedom with American strength. Cabinet members may complain, but he values right-minded action over fleeting popularity polls. He's putting the chief back in chief executive.

Flying home with his wife and daughter, Marshall just wants to watch TV and relax. But a terrorist group has different plans—hijacking Air Force One and threatening to kill hostages until the Kazak tyrant is restored to power. Marshall escapes their clutches, but there aren't many places to hide on an airplane, so we know he'll soon be fighting for his life. More to the point, he's not just a statesman but a family man, too. His loved ones are in danger, and he won't rest until they're safe.

It would take a far more intelligent movie than "Air Force One" to credibly explore the issues raised by this hyperactive plot. For starters, are abrupt executive-branch policy changes really such a great idea? And in an emergency, doesn't the president have responsibilities to his country and his world—as well as to his immediate family?

"Air Force One" doesn't even try to deal with such questions thoughtfully, but it has a great time fooling around with them. It even shows occasional glimmerings of imaginative scriptwriting, as when the villain suggests there's no essential difference between what he's doing to the president's entourage and what the United States military did to Iraqis in the Persian Gulf War.

Government buffs will also enjoy the movie's wry dialogue with real-life political leaders. Is the macho secretary of defense really modeled on former Cabinet member Alexander Haig, whose remark about being "in charge" made headlines during a Reagan administration crisis? Is the Vietnam heroism of President Marshall meant as a rebuke to President Clinton for opting out of military service in the '60s? Only the screenwriters know for sure, but moviegoers can while away the boring scenes by pondering these questions on their own.

The marketing campaign for "Air Force One" is based largely on Harrison Ford's star power, which hit new heights when "Patriot Games" and "Clear and Present Danger" struck box-office gold. This campaign could backfire, since the new movie is longer on hoked-up adventure and shorter on believability.

For the film to earn healthy grosses beyond its first couple of weekends, audiences will have to take it as a two-hour goof, more in the spirit of an Indiana Jones adventure than a New World Order fable. Boosting its chance of success is sensational acting by Gary Oldman, as the cold-eyed terrorist who stalks around the plane muttering about Mother Russia, and Glenn Close, as a vice president so vice presidential that her gender isn't mentioned once. Dean Stockwell is also excellent as the secretary of defense.

"Air Force One" was directed by action specialist Wolfgang Petersen, who honed his ability for close-quarters filmmaking in "Das Boot," set on a submarine almost as cramped as the president's plane. Much of the movie looks like it was filmed in a motel, but Petersen shouldn't be blamed. Claustrophobia comes with this territory, and he handles it as well as anyone in the business.

LOS ANGELES TIMES, 7/25/97, Calendar/p. 1, Kenneth Turan

No, Harrison Ford isn't the president, not even a candidate for the job, but given the chance, who wouldn't vote for him in a Beltway minute? A hero with a human face, Ford projects both rectitude and concern while playing engaging pragmatists who do the right thing no matter what. Wouldn't that be a switch on Pennsylvania Avenue?

"Air Force One," directed by Wolfgang Petersen and starring Ford as President James Marshall, is not going to make anybody think twice about that vote. With the actor confidently in his element as a chief executive coping with the hijacking of "the world's most secure aircraft," this is a display of Ford at his best that holds us in a tight bearhug of tension from beginning to end.

Like Petersen's 1993 film, the Clint Eastwood-John Malkovich "In the Line of Fire," "Air Force One" is at once vigorous and old-fashioned, a piece of expertly crafted entertainment that gets the job done with skill and panache. The director and his production team exhibit the same kind of crisp professionalism as the U.S. commando unit that opens the picture by kidnapping Gen. Alexander Radek, the rogue leader of Kazakhstan whose evil policies have, yes, put the entire free world at risk.

In Moscow three weeks later to celebrate that capture with Russian leaders, President Marshall departs from his prepared text to say (what a guy) he doesn't deserve to be congratulated. Having avoided appropriate action in the past, he vows to never again allow political self-interest to deter the U.S. from doing what it should when confronted by terrorists. Aides like his chief of staff (Paul Guilfoyle) later snivel about consulting our allies first, but Marshall shuts them up with a brisk, "It's the right thing to do and you know it."

Back on the plane home, the president is looking forward to relaxing with wife Grace (Wendy Crewson) and their 12-year-old daughter Alice ("The Little Princess" star Liesel Matthews). The only excitement he's anticipating is watching a tape replay of the latest Notre Dame-Michigan football game. Feeling at ease on an aircraft built to survive the pulse of a nuclear attack is an easy habit to get into.

Unfortunately, no one said, "Hey, that's Gary Oldman; he's always up to no good," when Russian TV newsman Ivan Korshunov claimed a seat in the equivalent of coach. In an unexpected blitzkreig, Korshunov and his cohorts manage to take over Air Force One. They notify the White House, specifically all-business Vice President Kathryn Bennett (Glenn Close), that they will execute one of their numerous hostages every half-hour until their hero, that nasty Gen. Radek, is released.

Fortunately for the honor of the profession, Korshunov is not really a TV journalist but a diabolic Russian ultra-nationalist zealot with zero interest in "the infection you call freedom." "Air Force One" pivots (as did "In the Line of Fire") around a battle of wills between its personifications of good and evil, and Oldman is all he should be as a sadistic madman who is not overburdened with respect for human life.

Though he does indulge in a few of his trademark temper tantrums (they must be in his contract), Oldman is mostly under control and does a convincing job of humanizing a man who says, "I would turn my back on God himself for Mother Russia." He knows everybody's weak spots and is not above responding to verbal attacks from the good guys with a savage: "You murdered 100,000 Iraqis to save a nickel on a gallon of gas."

Korshunov's opponent in the cat-and-mouse game that develops on the plane is not, of course, some desk-bound, lethargic politician. This president just happens to be a battle-hardened Vietnam veteran and Medal of Honor winner, and Ford has all the physicality necessary to make Marshall's ability to handle himself in a brawl completely plausible.

What keeps Ford well ahead of the pack as an action hero, however, is his ability to convey not only emotional intensity but also moral qualms, even worry. Placed in situations where his beliefs have a good chance of putting innocent people, including his own family, in terrible danger, President Marshall's convincing looks of anguish add more to this film's effectiveness than its inevitably explosive special effects.

Screenwriter Andrew W. Marlowe, whose first produced script this is, does more than come up with sharp lines for Korshunov. Though there is back and forth with the White House, most of "Air Force One" is a kind of locked-room mystery, where everything of interest has to happen in a confined environment, and Marlowe's script has a knack for coming up with surprising twists and multiple sources of tension.

Getting the most out of that script is the gift of Petersen and his team, including both a world-class cinematographer (Michael Ballhaus) and a crack editor (Richard Francis-Bruce, responsible for "Seven," "The Rock," "Dead Calm" and "Mad Max Beyond Thunderdome").

Together with Jerry Goldsmith's militaristic score and the across-the-board skill of the film's actors, this gang makes "Air Force One" tenser than it has any right to be. Petersen is a master tactician, adept (witness the remarkable "Das Boot") at moving people around tight spaces and finding the best spot for the camera. His skill makes this film the well-oiled but not intelligence-insulting machine Hollywood escapism used to be and rarely is anymore.

It was in "Das Boot" and its story of World War II German submariners that Petersen first showed the gift for tying action to psychology that is much in evidence here. Given that, it's nice to see him casting Jurgen Prochnow, exceptional as that film's U-boat captain, in the wordless but critical part of Gen. Radek. As an affectionate tip of the hat to a marvelous shared past, it's especially welcome and appropriate.

NEW STATESMAN, 9/12/97, p. 41, John Diamond

Even when the Wild West gave up all that tedious wildness, Hollywood didn't give up making cowboy movies. Instead, the new Westerns became historical rather than contemporary; stories which acknowledged that while the modern Montanan rode the trail in a pick-up truck handing out militia recruitment forms, his grand-daddy had spent a lifetime in a big hat, droving cattle.

Hollywood has yet to find a way of working the same trick with modern history. For years, producers *in extremis* concocted homely tales about the Red Menace and how the inherent contradictions of Marxism naturally meant the commies would forget how to shoot straight in the last scene. Then suddenly there were no commies. Well, there are still a few of course, but we'll probably have to wait a while for *Eric Hobsbawm II: This Time It's Dialectical.*

If Hollywood had followed its own cowboy trail, the modern anti-commie shoot-'em-up would be based on events preceding the Fall of the Wall. Events as recent as that, though, don't count as history but as current affairs, and everyone knows that American movie audiences aren't interested in current affairs.

This means that when Hollywood wants to find a commie enemy for the 1990s, it has to invent one. The great thing about invented commies is that they can be anything you want them to be: the baddies in *Air Force One* are variously described by US officials as fascists, communists and something called Russian Ultra-Nationalist Radicals. Required to construct a manifesto for his band of fascisto-communist Russian Ultra-Nationalist Radicals, Gary Oldman juts his wispily bearded chin, shifts his throat into guttural overdrive and announces that his job will be done only "when Mother Russia becomes one state again and when the capitalists are dragged out and shot in the streets."

Oldman is asking us to believe he is Ivan Korshunov, leader of the six Russian nostalgists who hijack Air Force One as it returns from Moscow, where President Harrison Ford has been celebrating the overthrow by a Russo-American force of the fascisto-communist Ultra-National Radical dictator of Kazakhstan.

The hijack makes the Americans angry: "Dammit—nobody does this with the United States," says a general. Others, led by a subdued Dean Stockwell as US Defence Secretary, are equally angry that the president has committed America to polishing off fascisto-communist UNR wherever it may raise its confused head. They think the answer is to let the president, his wife, daughter and sundry staff die aloft rather than capitulate to terrorism. The vice-president, Glenn Close, comes near to tears, but knows there must be another way.

And there is. Harrison Ford, it turns out, wasn't parachuted to earth in the escape pod which is apparently kept for just such contingencies in the bowels of Air Force One. What's more, President Ford, so to speak, is a war hero: "In Vietnam he flew more rescue missions than any man in my command," the general tells a mobbed Oval Office.

Well of course he did. From here on in this is a straightforward action movie, with Ford coming over all Stephen Segalish and displaying those skills which every president since Nixon has clearly needed in office: he shoots straight, punches hard, knows how to fly a plane and how to sabotage one. He is even fiercely loyal to his wife. Indeed, this is the Democratic president Hollywood probably thought it was supporting when it turned up for all those $1,000-a-plate dinners in Washington.

Even though they may all have thought they were making another *Failsafe,* it is only when the film fesses up as a superior action pic that it makes sense. Wolfgang Petersen knows how to handle a movie with a single claustrophobic setting: he directed *Das Boot* after all. As soon as we recognise that all that political nonsense has been attached to the plot with sixinch nails, we can stop worrying about the crassness of the fascisto-communist RUNR theorising every time it surfaces.

This also means we can better appreciate that moment when Ford and Oldman finally meet. As their faces almost touch, you know what the rules are: one must either spit in the other's face, or slap it. Slap or spit, spit or slap? Since Ford doing angry always looks as if he's working up a mouthful of gob, and since this is a superior action movie, we get both.

We also get some excellent special aerobatic effects, a couple of good shoot-outs and a rendering of the "Internationale" (the only song mentioned in the credits), the like of which I haven't heard since the Battle of Red Lion Square.

All of which makes for a moderately diverting couple of hours. Indeed the only depressing thing about *Air Force One* is that it turns out to be the real president's favourite of the year—which is probably a greater reason to distrust him than any detail of his private life.

NEW YORK, 8/4/97, p. 55, David Denby

Wolfgang Petersen's *Air Force One* is exciting, well-made, and utterly preposterous—a 14-year-old boy's fantasy of being president of the United States.

When a group of crazed neo-Soviet nationalists takes over Air Force One, President James Marshall (Harrison Ford) has the chance to parachute to safety in an escape pod. But the prez has just made a bold speech in Moscow insisting that the United States will never negotiate with terrorists; now he has to prove it.

Instead of escaping, he stays aboard and fights back. A commando holing up, in the baggage compartment, he strikes and retreats; he thrashes terrorists with his fists, slams them on the floor, grabs a machine gun, and shoots off dozens of rounds in the pressurized cabin. Whoopee! It's *Independence Day* all over again. Both movies display a pressing desire to hang testosterone-producing spherical objects on the commander in chief. And both have a very literal-minded idea of what balls consist of. In brief, we've come full circle: Ronald Reagan in office struck poses borrowed from the movies he had acted in; now the movies have turned the president back into the law-and-order sheriff Reagan used to play onscreen and given him an Uzi rather than a shotgun to wield. At last the head of the Free World fights like a man. If only the movies had been this tough 55 years ago, Robert Taylor would have pulled down the barbed wire at Auschwitz with his bare hands.

The first-time screenwriter Andrew W. Marlowe, either on his own initiative or under orders, has structured the script so that Harrison Ford has to do pretty much everything by himself. Onboard the plane, the terrorists instantly kill the president's security men and herd the rest of his staff into a conference room. The staff is out of the picture (literally). Meanwhile, in the White House, Vice-President Kathryn Bennett (Glenn Close) talks tough to the hijacking slimebags on the telephone and fends off an overbearing, loutish (and Haig-ish) Secretary of Defense (Dean Stockwell), who wants to take command in the president's absence. We may be amazed to find the filmmakers scoring dumdum feminist points in the midst of this supermacho atmosphere, but I don't think we need fear that the writer, director, or producers will suffer much shame over this, or any other, issue. The way to make a hit is to focus—relentlessly—on the star. Oh, excitement! But what happened to Harrison Ford's good sense? He's always had great natural authority (I'm on record as a fan), but this performance reeks—for the first time—of vanity and megalomania. His mouth set, Ford is grim and righteous and altogether too solemn for such kick-ass fantasy.

Wolfgang Petersen, the director of *In the Line of Fire,* turns the plane into a maze, and as Ford stalks around, the camera takes his point of view, and we get to know every corner of that embattled craft, from cockpit to baggage compartment. Moment by moment, scene by scene, the picture is beautifully choreographed. There's an exciting episode when the lumbering 747, under the command of the hijackers, skids all over an Air Force base and then takes off again just before slamming into a huge military transport. Some of the actors are at the top of their form, especially Gary Oldman as the head of the hijackers, an angry and contemptuous man who frankly hates the new Russian freedoms.

Air Force One certainly holds our attention, and a few of us, easily manipulated, may brush away a tear when some awed soldiers salute their action-hero president with obvious pride. But *Air Force One* is utterly square. Didn't the filmmakers realize it would have been much funnier and more inventive if their hero had been a president actually like the current officeholder—a little soft, unacquainted with guns, given to cajolery, flattery, charm, and guile, and now forced to deal with an implacably violent ideologue? That might have been an original movie. The film that's been made, however effective, traps us in the disgust of a movie culture that doesn't respect our intelligence and gets away with that contempt season after season.

NEW YORK POST, 7/25/97, p. 41, Michael Medved

When people describe the president of the United States as the most powerful man on Earth, they're not usually talking about his muscles.

But then, they haven't met President James Marshall (Harrison Ford), a tough chief executive with astonishing skill at hand-to-hand combat, combining the best qualities of superhero and super statesman.

With anyone else in this central role "Air Force One" might have played like a bad joke, but Harrison Ford manages the perfect mix of dignity, authority, compassion and bone-crushing physical force.

His adventure begins in Moscow with a triumphant speech celebrating joint U.S.-Russian success in capturing a mass-murdering, ultra-nationalist warlord (Jurgen Prochnow), who's been exploiting the chaotic situation in the former Soviet Union.

On the flight back to Washington, however, the president himself is captured when a brilliantly coordinated band of terrorists hijacks his plane and demands release of their imprisoned leader back in Russia.

The dazzling production design and clever concentration on a host of minute details make this far-fetched caper chillingly believable, aided by a truly superb performance from Gary Oldman as the on-board terrorist mastermind. His character is thoroughly evil, but also captivating and comprehensible, never resorting to the rabid-madman hamminess so typical of villains in contemporary action films.

In control of Air Force One, Oldman negotiates with the nervous but capable vice president (Glenn Close) while executing one new hostage each half-hour.

He thinks the president has escaped through his parachute pod, but unbeknownst to the bad guys, the ever-resourceful chief executive is unwilling to abandon his wife and daughter (Wendy Crewson, Liesel Matthews) who remain on the plane, menaced by murderers.

The clever script (by recent film-school grad Andrew W. Marlowe) allows "Air Force One" to emerge as the summer's smartest, slickest action thriller, consistently engrossing for every moment of its running time.

Director Wolfgang Petersen (who previously handled tension in tight spaces in "Das Boot" and presidential protection in "In the Line of Fire") works wonders with miniatures and special effects, flawlessly choreographing an aborted landing at an air base, a high-tech dogfight with supersonic jets, an attempted mid-air rescue and other edge-of-your-seat set pieces.

His only problem involves the character of the president, who relies much too often on fists and guns (he's supposed to be a decorated Vietnam vet) to confront his enemies. The film would have felt more substantive and credible if he'd used leadership skills and cunning more often, and sweaty, face-to-face wrestling matches a bit less.

The movie also goes over the top when the president puts his own survival second to the welfare of others not just once, but a half-dozen times. This isn't merely implausible. In real life it would be irresponsible—though audiences will no doubt feel uplifted by the bipartisan glow surrounding a noble chief who is unequivocally worth hailing.

NEWSDAY, 7/25/97, Part II/p. B3, Jack Mathews

Of all the American presidents seen in major Hollywood movies recently, Harrison Ford's James Marshall in "Air Force One" is the man! The movie doesn't give a clue as to where Marshall stands on such crucial issues as abortion, welfare, Medicare and having unmarried celebrities sleep in the Lincoln bedroom. But here's a guy who can be drinking a beer and watching the Notre Dame-Michigan game one moment, and taking on a mob of skyjacking terrorists the next.

He's a women-and-children-first kind of hero, a decorated Vietnam vet who has the mental toughness to say what he means and mean what he says, and the physical prowess to back it all up. I don't want to say they don't make them like this in real life, but Jim Marshall isn't going to fall off a campaign stage or Greg Norman's front steps.

"Air Force One" is the kind of wholesale fantasy bunkum we expect from summer movies, but there's no denying that this is the role the star was born or at least aged—to play. Ford's acting range doesn't stretch from the left side of this column to the right, but it does include what's called for here, a man old enough to be president (Ford's actually five years older than Clinton), fit enough to hang from a cable suspended behind a 747, and cool enough to say, as he kicks a terrorist into the void, "Get off my plane!"

The story line is as simple as skyjacking thrillers get. On the return flight from Moscow, where President Marshall has given a dramatic speech challenging terrorism, his own plane is commandeered by radicals from an outlaw Russian state. They intend to hold him, the first lady (Wendy Crewson), their teenage daughter (Liesel Matthews), political advisers and members of the White House press corps hostage until their own leader is released from a Russian prison.

In the excitement of the takeover, the president appears to have escaped from a safety capsule out the back end of the plane, but in fact, he's hiding down there with the bad food and the luggage, using his cunning to make contact with Vice President Katie Bennett (Glenn Close) in Washington, and to launch a one-man counteroffensive.

Director Wolfgang Petersen ("In the Line of Fire") doesn't give us much time to dwell on the improbabilities piling up, and unlike his colleagues on "Con Air," "Batman & Robin" and the other summer follies, he uses his action sequences as logical links connecting the takeover of Air Force One to its explosive midair refueling to its wildly successful finale.

There were times during the movie when I wanted to spit the whole thing out like a hairball. There are ridiculous skirmishes in the White House over constitutional authority, and when Ford is on the verge of weeping, we're on the verge of covering our eyes. But there isn't another actor, not one old enough to run for president anyway, who has the screen presence to pull this off.

Nor has there been a better movie villain this summer than Gary Oldman's Ivan Korshunov, a family man whose political fanaticism has turned him into a most cold-blooded killer. As the president roams the bowels of Air Force One, trying to come up with ways of saving the hostages without negotiating with the terrorists, Ivan begins executing them one at a time, until he gets to the first family, and finally tests Marshall's will.

Great detail has gone into the interior design of Air Force One, creating an environment both claustrophobic and realistic, and the stuntwork—especially in the later scenes,when the passengers start disembarking while the plane's 15,000 feet in the air—is sensational.

"Air Force One" isn't enough to save Hollywood's summer of '97 from disgrace, but it does itself proud.

NEWSWEEK, 7/21/97, p. 66, Howard Fineman

The President is a Medal of Honor winner, handy with Uzis and chokeholds, brave beyond measure and so righteous that he vows—in an election year, no less—to dispatch elite American troops wherever and whenever they are needed to save starving children from the clutches of terrorist dictators. To hell with polls. To hell with isolationists in Congress. To hell with ass-covering advisers. Only his adoring wife (they're still madly in love after all these years, all these campaigns) fully understands—and she's with him all the way when he makes the Big Speech. "Never again," he declares, "will I allow our political self-interest to get in the way of what we know to be morally right!"

Here you thought "Men in Black" had all the fantastical creatures this season. Wait until you see the Leader of the Free World in "Air Force One," in which Harrison Ford plays President James Marshall as a blend of Han Solo, Woodrow Wilson and Jackie Chan. Americans are bored by politics, cynical about leaders, too busy in a good economy to care about Washington. But maybe that's because we've seen too many politicians on C-Span talking about the budget. What if we could watch our president blasting terrorists in Sensurround? In this summer of our content, Hollywood is betting on a president as action hero.

It's a good bet. Ford is the Jimmy Stewart of our time—the epitome of decency under pressure—and "Air Force One" is Frank Capra on "Speed." Winging home from Moscow, the First Aircraft is hijacked by bloodthirsty Russian nationalists, led by the hyperventilating Gary Oldman. If their leader isn't released from prison, they say, they'll kill everyone on board—including the First Lady and First Daughter. The president, they think, has fled the plane in an "escape pod." In fact, our buff and resourceful commander in chief is hiding in the cargo hold. He's vowed never to negotiate with terrorists—and yet here they are, with a gun to his daughter's temple! Oh, the dilemmas of leadership!

This one doesn't last long, or require talks with NATO. Methodically, Ford guns down the heavily accented bad guys with Schwarzeneggerian relish, and pushes one fanatic out the cargo bay. "Get off my plane!" says the triumphant president. It's a more inspiring line than, say, "I am not a crook" or "I didn't inhale." Meanwhile, back in Washington, cheers go up from a hearteningly broad cross section of voters huddled at a candlelight vigil in Lafayette Park. There's even joy in the White House press room—certainly the most unrealistic scene.

There's political Zeitgeist news here. At least for now (or until "Primary Colors" arrives), Hollywood seems to have maxed out on portrayals of the White House as a sinkhole of corruption. "Absolute Power" and "Murder at 1600"—two recent flicks with bad-dude presidents—were weaker at the box office than expected. The same trend prevails in reality-based programming. Fred Thompson's made-for-TV hearings about money corruption aren't generating much public interest. For all the investigations swirling around him, Bill Clinton's approval ratings have never been higher.

So there's room for fanciful institutional cheerleading—and perhaps even a hunger for it. God knows the president could use it. But we're all so jaded, we couldn't possibly take such a preachy message straight. It has to be in cartoon form.

Like any well-drawn cartoon, "Air Force One" bows (briefly) to reality. There is no "escape pod" on Air Force One, and the security procedures are tougher than those portrayed in the film, but the mock-up of the aircraft itself is chillingly realistic, down to the straps in the cargo hold, the earth tones in the cabins and the three-zone digital clocks on the walls. President Marshall is vaguely reminiscent of a certain real leader of the free world. He's fiftyish, a television-sports junkie.   He possesses a savvy, outspoken wife, a spunky daughter—and a humorless vice president (Glenn Close in the Al Gore role).

No wonder Clinton loved the script when he heard about it last summer. If you were president, wouldn't you?   It must have been fun to daydream.   Instead of having to reason with Newt Gingrich, for example, you could just give him a karate chop.   Special prosecutor pestering you? Eat lead, counselor!   Indeed, the president liked the project so much he had a minor role in bringing it to the screen.

The "back story" could be a whole other movie—a satire. Last August Clinton was in Jackson Hole, Wyo., for a poll-driven vacation. (Dick Morris, his polltaker, had conducted extensive surveys to decide where the president should go; hiking in the mountain West was the answer.) Clinton learned about the project from Ford during a dinner at the home of James Wolfensohn, president of the World Bank. Ford, already cast as the president, wanted Close for his veep, and she was at the dinner, seated next to Clinton. Ford approached and proposed that she play the part. The real-life president seconded the motion. "I feel like I was present at the creation," Clinton gushed to NEWSWEEK. "I'm probably the only president who got to pick two vice presidents."

Clinton's support was a boon to director Wolfgang Petersen, whose first hit was "Das Boot" and who was eager to recreate its sense of dramatic claustrophobia aboard Air Force One. Clinton took Ford on a tour of Air Force One in Wyoming last summer, and the production designers also toured portions of the plane. The Pentagon cooperated big time, officially sanctioning the use of airfields and a whole arsenal of aircraft.

Those aren't computer-generated F-15s up there on screen. The producers of "Air Force One" are offering aircraft, not uplift. Director Petersen told NEWSWEEK that he was drawn to the project for one main reason: Ford was in it. The film is an over-the-top thriller, too loosely tethered to reality to be a lesson about anything other than the limits of popcorn consumption. In real life—in the real Oval Office—we're not looking for an *übermensch*, anyway. We'll settle for a *mensch*. Someone who might actually want to pass campaign-finance reform, for example. Still, it may say something about the state of America—or Hollywood—that it took a Japanese studio (Sony) and a German-born director (Petersen) to bring to the screen a creature that we Americans can barely imagine: a president as hero.

SIGHT AND SOUND, 10/97, p. 42, Geoffrey Macnab

James Marshall, the President of the United States, is on his way back home from Moscow aboard the presidential jet, *Air Force One*. Six Russians journalists are also aboard, ostensibly to interview the President. On a signal from a sympathetic US Secret Service agent, the Russians hijack the plane. It seems the President himself has escaped in a special emergency pod. Ivan Korshunov, the leader of the terrorists, establishes contact with the White House. He tells Vice President Kathryn Bennett that unless his leader, the extreme nationalist General Radek, is released from a Moscow prison, he will kill the passengers one by one. He makes it clear that he has the President's wife and child in captivity.

Marshall is actually lurking in the hold. Using his mobile phone, he establishes contact with the White House. He tells the Vice President not to negotiate despite the execution of hostages. Meanwhile, he picks off one of the terrorists, sheds the plane's extra fuel, and eventually helps most of the hostages to escape using parachutes. However, Ivan is still holding his wife and daughter. Rather than see either killed, Marshall instructs Moscow to release General Radek. He and Ivan fight it out and eventually Ivan is throttled by parachute cords. Marshall rings Moscow just in time to prevent Radek getting away.

The plane has become damaged and is rapidly losing altitude. Needing to evacuate, Marshall allows his wife and daughter to leave first. He escapes only in the nick of time. *Air Force One* crashes into the sea, killing the renegade Secret Service agent who is still aboard.

Wolfgang Petersen has a knack for making popular, big-budget thrillers which combine spectacle with at least a degree of plausibility and intelligence. *In the Line of Fire* not only elicited a fine performance from Clint Eastwood as the greying Secret Service agent, but also wittily satirised Washington DC, while getting under the skin of its political assassin villain. *Outbreak* was miscast (Dustin Hoffman isn't a natural action hero) but it tapped into the anxiety surrounding the Ebola virus, worked well as a study in small-town hysteria, and boasted some bravura camerawork from Michael Ballhaus.

In theory, *Air Force One* must have seemed like another ideal vehicle for the German director. The film's action is largely confined to the interior of a hi-tech flying fortress but, as he showed in his brilliant U-boat drama *Das Boot*, Petersen relishes stoking up the tension in constricted spaces. He also usually avoids the most obvious stereotypes. Early on here, as first a renegade fascist general is arrested by US and Russian joint forces, and then as President Marshall makes a rousing Abe Lincoln-style speech in Moscow about human rights, it looks as if he is attempting to move beyond old Cold War caricatures of the Russians. But as soon as Gary Oldman comes into view sporting a ridiculous goatee it becomes apparent that the evil empire is still evil as far as Hollywood is concerned.

Action pics aren't under any obligation to be accurate politically. Even so, Andrew W. Marlowe's screenplay seems deeply muddled. The terrorist boss ostensibly comes from Kazakhstan and yet he warbles on tremulously about Mother Russia. As a nationalist, he ought to hate by rights the old Communist regime but a tear still comes to his eyes when he hears his imprisoned comrades singing 'The Internationale'. Oldman plays him as a virtual pantomime figure, a sort of cross between Count Dracula and a KGB agent. President Marshall is an equally implausible creation. Harrison Ford, one of the few contemporary stars with the gravitas of a James Stewart or a Henry Fonda, starts off in solemn, self-righteous fashion, but quickly reverts to an Indiana Jones type when his wife and daughter are put in danger. Just in case his sudden muscular heroics seem incongruous for a man in late middle-age, we're tossed a line of dialogue about his medal-winning exploits in Vietnam.

After Tim Burton's mercilessly iconoclastic *Mars Attacks!* it's well-nigh impossible to take US generals and politicians sitting in the Oval Office seriously. It doesn't help that Glenn Close's one-dimensional Vice President, forced to negotiate with the terrorists, and Dean Stockwell's hawkish Defense Secretary look as if they have strayed out of Burton's movie. They're so stern-faced that they seem comic. Marlowe's screenplay throws in occasional intentionally self-parodic moments, Ford's gung-ho performance and Oldman's rent-a-Russian mugging are certainly tongue-in-cheek, but on the whole, this is played very straight, with little of the knowing humour of, say, *Last Action Hero*. Stripped of its old-fashioned Cold War gloss, it is essentially an airborne *Die Hard*. And like *Die Hard*, it stands or falls by its action sequences.

There is plenty of noisy spectacle. Once again, Ballhaus' cinematography is fluid and arresting. We prowl up and down the corridors of the plane, and explore its every hidden recess. A near crash landing is handled with tremendous, giddy *élan*, as are the refuelling and parachuting sequences. But Ford's advice to the Vice President not to negotiate with the terrorists—"if you give a mouse a cookie, it'll want a glass of milk"—seems to have been given to the film-makers themselves. The inflationary logic of action pics demands that every time they mount a stunt, they must immediately try to trump it. As a result, the effects become ever more exaggerated and all contact is lost with the characters. Dialogue is reduced to a few clunking soundbites of the "nobody does this to America!" variety. Outside the Manichean struggle between the US President and the Russian terrorist, the other actors are largely ignored. Jürgen Prochnow is wasted as General Radek (we see him being kidnapped by the commandos and walking down a long prison corridor, but he isn't even allowed so much as to speak.) William H. Macy, the venal car salesman in *Fargo*, shows a touching, labrador-like loyalty to the President as a patriotic army major, but is likewise underused. Petersen never really explores the relationship between the hostages and their captors. At times, it seems as if he is taking his cue from Jerry Goldsmith's overblown score. He certainly doesn't skimp on spectacle, but the sheer, pommelling bombast of the film-making is ultimately more enervating than exhilarating. Only the most undiscriminating of boy's own action-adventure fans are likely to be satisfied with it.

TIME, 7/28/97, p. 69, Richard Schickel

Well, finally—the president we deserve, a morally square peg in the Oval Office, a man whose primary emotional color is true blue. James Marshall is the kind of guy who stands up boldly to international thuggery as well as to temporizers on his own staff. He has a nice sense of humor, a good marriage and a daughter who mirrors his virtues. He is also, as it turns out, physically brave and uncannily resourceful under life-threatening pressure. And he looks a lot like the reliably doughty Harrison Ford.

This fantasy—that such an exemplary figure could actually get elected in modern America—is actually wilder than the story *Air Force One* is telling. It concerns demented terrorists who somehow insinuate themselves onto the presidential plane and take the Chief Executive and everyone else aboard hostage. Their offer is lives for a life—specifically that of a genocidal tyrant named General Radek, president of a breakaway Russian republic now being held in a Moscow jail.

Since the American President conspired with his Russian counterpart to abduct the general, there is a certain loopy plausibility to the premise. And since their leader, Korshunov, is played by Gary Oldman, an actor who can go from purring self-pity to coldly homicidal rage in about 10 frames of film, these terrorists are truly terrifying—especially when the psychopath in chief has a gun to the head of the First Lady (Wendy Crewson) or the First Child (Liesel Matthews).

Being quite a provincial foreigner, however, he does not reckon with the power of American pragmatism. Having eluded the invaders, the President (who, we are informed, won a Congressional Medal of Honor piloting a rescue chopper in Vietnam) is stalking the surprisingly capacious byways of the plane, armed mainly with native wit and a "Don't tread on me" philosophy. There is good—sometimes witty—suspense in Marshall's single-handed efforts to coordinate a rescue effort by his Washington staff with his own attempts to set his people free using whatever modest tools—a table knife, a cell phone, a fax machine—come to hand.

One wishes, indeed, that the movie—written by Andrew W. Marlowe and directed by Wolfgang Petersen, who knows his way around both tight spaces *(Das Boot)* and the more suspenseful aspects of presidential life *(In the Line of Fire)*—had retained its claustrophobic intimacy to the end. This, however, would have required its makers to forswear a new Hollywood habit of mind, which dictates that no big-time action film can conclude without an orgy of special effects. As *Air Force One* climaxes, a lot of people fly through thin air on thin wires. Too bad. The stalking struggle between reason and unreason that precedes it is much more gripping—and fun.

VILLAGE VOICE, 7/29/97, p. 71, J. Hoberman

The '70s revival is over. The '80s are back. The Reagan Era nostalgia implicit in the current TV ads for those anthologies of half-forgotten hits by Frankie Goes to Hollywood and Duran Duran receives an even more powerful boost with the action heroics of *Air Force One*.

Synthesizing elements of *Rambo* and *Top Gun,* referencing the Conquest of Grenada and the Battle over Sidra, resurrecting the threat of the Evil Empire, Wolfgang Petersen's high-altitude thriller is premised upon the entertaining, utopian notion of an American president tough enough to dangle, like some national phallus, from an airplane at 15,000 feet. The man doesn't break a sweat (let alone suffer a coronary). Even more incredible, he's a president without fear of public opinion polls.

Promoted from the CIA director he played in *Clear and Present Danger,* Harrison Ford is here a first-term chief executive—not to mention a decorated Vietnam War hero (former pilot of the Millennium Falcon), devoted husband, and (just like Michael Douglas in *The American President)* the father of an adoring 12-year-old daughter. What's more, having personally toured a refugee camp outside Moscow, Ford has become a born-again international interventionist—a buff, two-fisted Woodrow Wilson with an attitude, if not quite an agenda.

Basically a cross between an elaborate assassination caper and a crippled-plane disaster flick, *Air Force One* justifies its plot as blowback from a joint U.S.-Russian operation in a neofascist, nuclear-armed Kazakhstan. Andrew Marlowe's high-concept script spends so much time bragging about the Air Force One specs (while telling the audience just how righteous a dude the First Passenger is) that it's actually a relief when Gary Oldman hijacks the flying Oval Office, complete with the presidents wife and daughter. (Only marginally less flamboyant here, but sporting an even worse haircut than in *The Fifth Element*, Oldman plays a crazed Russian Kazakh communazi nationalist-cum-aggrieved veteran of the Afghani War as though he were the lost Karamazov brother.)

"Damn it, nobody does this to the U.S." somebody whines, during a lull in the Kalashnikov concerto, thus establishing the necessary, pre-Reagan mood of narcissistically wounded national pride. (The movie of course finds it grotesque that the Russians are acting on the same principle.) To add to the dilemma, the American vice president is ... Glenn Close, promoted from First Lady in *Mars Attacks!*, raising the humiliating possibility that the U.S. will be stuck with a woman president (a la Jimmy Carter).

Made by a director who staged a three-hour movie in a submarine and mainly impressive as a kindred feat of cramped, one-set engineering, *Air Force One* features much crouching amid the baggage and Coke cartons, as well as a strategically adroit missile attack. The latter is given an additional twist for being monitored via cellular phone by Close and the rest of the War Room gang-including, in another '80s flashback, a hysterical Alexander Haig-style secretary of defense. That's about as clever as *Air Force One* gets—although Petersen does make one weirdly sentimental inside reference by casting *Das Boot*'s old submarine commander (Jurgen Prochnow) in the nonspeaking role of the Kazakh dictator. Verbally, less is more: the longest, most difficult patch of dialogue has to do with sending a fax (generating a suspense ploy which is inexplicably abandoned) while the movie's well-edited trailer flags the only possible tagline: Harrison Ford's heartfelt "Get off my plane!"

The first half of *Air Force One* had the preview screening crowd a-chuckle at its campy, theatrics, leaden banter, and Rambotic derring-do. By the end of the movie, however, something must have kicked in. ("That was *fantastic*!" I heard a man in my row, excitedly bark at his college-age daughter.) Who could resist the bad guys' triumphant singing of the Internationale, not to mention the ecstasy of sending our F-15s to take out their MiGs? For a brief shining moment, amplified by the clarion calls of Jerry Goldsmith's score, *Air Force One* recaptures the full stand up and pray, salute, and cheer mentality of 1984. Born in the U.S.A., America rools, the pride is back—patriarchally speaking, of course. (Just as the president achieves maximum heroism in the role of father, so the agonized Glenn Close can't bring herself to sign a cabinet document and Take the Power.)

Unlike *Contact*, which has apparently irked our real-life maximum leader by appropriating his ectoplasmic image and thus gumping him into the role played to smarmy perfection by Jack Nicholson in *Mars Attacks!*, *Air Force One* enjoyed full White House approval. Indeed, the president bragged to *Newsweek* that he was instrumental in selecting Glenn Close for the role of veep. And, speaking of self-promoting news management, here, as in every other Event movie this summer, CNN has managed to acquire exclusive rights to covering the crisis. Isn't there some sort of antitrust legislation that would give the E! channel a shot at the action?

Also reviewed in:
NEW REPUBLIC, 8/25/97, p. 24, Stanley Kauffmann
NEW YORK TIMES, 7/25/97, p. C1, Janet Maslin
NEW YORKER, 7/28/97, p. 77, Terrence Rafferty
VARIETY, 7/21-27/97, p. 37, Todd McCarthy
WASHINGTON POST, 7/25/97, p. D1, Stephen Hunter
WASHINGTON POST, 7/25/97, Weekend/p. 48, Desson Howe

ALBINO ALLIGATOR

A Miramax Films release in association with Motion Picture Corporation of America of a Brad Krevoy/Steve Stabler production. *Producer:* Brad Krevoy, Steve Stabler, and Brad Jenkel. *Director:* Kevin Spacey. *Screenplay:* Christian Forte. *Director of Photography:* Mark Plummer.

Editor: Jay Cassidy.   *Music:* Michael Brook and Amanda Scheer-Demme.   *Sound:* Mark Weingarten and (music) Bill Jackson.   *Sound Editor:* Per Hallberg.   *Casting:* David Rubin.   *Production Designer:* Nelson Coates.   *Art Director:* Burton Rencher.   *Set Decorator:* Linda Sutton.   *Set Dresser:* Christie Herndon-McGeachy.   *Special Effects:* Lou Carlucci.   *Costumes:* Isis Mussenden.   *Make-up:* Felicity Bowring and Kimberly Greene.   *Stunt Coordinator:* Doug Coleman.   *Running time:* 105 minutes.   *MPAA Rating:* R.

CAST: Matt Dillon (Dova); Faye Dunaway (Janet); Gary Sinise (Milo); William Fichtner (Law); Viggo Mortensen (Guy); John Spencer (Jack); Skeet Ulrich (Danny); Frankie Faison (Marv); Melinda McGraw (Jenny); M. Emmet Walsh (Dino); Joe Mantegna (G.D. Browning); Doug Spinuzza (Agent #1); Spencer Garrett (Agent #2); Enrico Colantoni (Agent #3); Tulsy Ball (ATF Agent); Travis Appel (Another Agent); Brad Koepenick (Browning's Assistant); Jock Worthen (Medic); Willie C. Carpenter, Alexander Smith, and Michael Unger (Reporters); Toni Montgomery (Female Officer); Jeff Hoffman (Jenny's Cameraman).

LOS ANGELES TIMES, 1/17/97, Calendar/p. 4, Jack Mathews

[The following review by Jack Mathews appeared in a slightly different form in
NEWSDAY, 1/17/97, Part II/p. B13.]

On the walls of Dino's Bar, where almost all the action in veteran character actor and freshman director Kevin Spacey's stylishly derivative "Albino Alligator" takes place, there are movie posters featuring tough guys James Cagney and Humphrey Bogart. The Cagney poster is for the 1935 "G Men" and the Bogart, presumably, for the 1948 "Key Largo."

The title on the Bogart poster isn't visible, and with a smaller image of co-star Lauren Bacall on it, the film could just as well be "The Big Sleep" or "To Have and Have Not." But since "Albino Alligator" is all about honoring the spirit of old gangster movies, and "Key Largo," in particular, we'll make the leap.

"Albino's" hotel is Dino's Bar, its Key Largo is modern New Orleans, and the storm keeping everyone inside, mixing the combustible elements of swindlers, sociopaths and frightened hostages, is the swarm of ATF agents—G-men!—who think they have a gunrunner cornered.

Dino's, a basement haunt that's been serving liquor since its speakeasy days, is about to close when three men, one bleeding and being carried over another's shoulder, burst in. We've already met these guys, hoods whose bungled robbery attempt ended in a car crash. Dova (Matt Dillon) is their nervous leader, Milo (Gary Sinise) is his injured brother, and Law (William Fichtner) is the psycho running with them.

Soon, a gun is drawn, and Dino (M. Emmet Walsh), the bar's mush-mouthed proprietor, his feisty barmaid Janet (Faye Dunaway) and three customers—a passive young man (Skeet Ulrich), a defiant older man (John Spencer) and a mysterious French-Canadian (Viggo Mortensen)—are being held hostage.

The screenplay, a first effort by 25-year-old Christian Forte (son of '50s pop star Fabian), offers Spacey an opportunity to blend his experience from both film and theater. The opening chase sequence is exhilaratingly choreographed. When the getaway car slams into another, we watch from an overhead camera, and whoever's body it is we see crashing through the window and landing on the car in front gets our early vote for stunt of the year.

Once the three men have limped inside Dino's, "Albino Alligator" becomes a very tight character drama, with the gang members bickering among themselves over the fate of their hostages. We go outside now and then, to see ATF boss G.D. Browning (Joe Mantegna) joust with TV crews, but the questions carrying the story are simply who will get out alive, and how.

Spacey plays with the story and its characters like a kid with a chemistry set, mixing, ingredients together and waiting for reactions. The most volatile combination is Law, who's itching to go on a rampage, and Milo, who rejects any plan that will kill hostages.

There's another test of wills between Dova, a control freak with no ideas of his own, and Janet, who seems determined to push him.

The title "Albino Alligator" comes from a legend, laboriously recalled by Law, about the habit of alligators to sacrifice weaker members of their own group in order to trap and destroy their rivals. Law offers it as advice in a pool game, but it's so clearly intended to set up the last act that all we can do is guess who will be asked to sacrifice for whom.

"Albino Alligator" doesn't break any new ground for the genre, but it's a nice first piece for Spacey. Inevitably, the interior of Dino's becomes a stage, and the actors are given to theatrical monologues. But the production is so smoothly orchestrated—with fluid camera movements and tightly controlled editing—that we feel as if we're in among the characters rather than looking on from the orchestra seats.

The performances are all solid, but Sinise, the one with the most stage experience, stands out. If Spacey were to have taken a role for himself, Milo's the one best suited for him. He left it in good hands.

NEW YORK POST, 1/17/97, p. 49, Michael Medved

Most of the acclaim for the haunting, intriguing new film "Albino Alligator" will focus on Kevin Spacey, who here makes his skillful directorial debut.

But the real hero of this project is its first-time screenwriter: a 25-year-old Berkeley graduate named Christian Forte, who just happens to be the son of legendary '50s crooner Fabian.

Forte has here written a taut, challenging melodrama that unfolds like an intense, even award-winning stage play—a resemblance that represents both its greatest strength and its primary weakness. The action of the film takes place almost entirely in one claustrophobic location—a basement bar (and former Prohibition-era speakeasy) in New Orleans.

Following a botched robbery and bloody car crash, three small-time hoods (Matt Dillon, Gary Sinise and William Fichtner) invade the premises, taking as hostages its patrons and proprietor (M. Emmet Walsh).

Unbeknown to these humbling desperadoes, they have just disrupted no-nonsense federal agent Joe Mantegna's elaborate stakeout of a major crime figure.

Director Spacey, one of the most accomplished character actors in the business, elicits from his actors superb performances, tracing the relationships between captors and hostages as they're all suddenly surrounded by a huge strike force.

Faye Dunaway gets her best role in years as an aging cocktail waitress who refuses to feel intimidated by the gunmen, and Viggo Mortensen (currently appearing in vastly different roles in "The Portrait of a Lady" and Sly Stallone's "Daylight") plays the most soft-spoken but cunning of the hostages.

William Fichtner (who turned in a similarly showy performance in the little-seen "The Underneath") steals the movie as the most dangerous of the invaders, playing a charismatic, sadistic, psychotic ex-con as effectively as this sort of role can possibly be played. The reliably brilliant Gary Sinise is also riveting as a grievously wounded member of the gang, and the only one of the three with a conscience.

The only weak link in the casting, in fact, is Matt Dillon, playing the leader of the crooks who is torn between the evil influence of Fichtner and the decent, responsible urgings of Sinise, portraying his older brother.

Dillon spends most of the picture suspended between heaven and hell, and between winning or losing forever the sympathies of the audience, but his character comes across as too irresistibly likable, too confoundedly handsome, to give this role the proper balance.

Nevertheless, the script keeps dazzling us with twists and revelations, with each new sequence forcing a thorough reevaluation of what we've seen before.

"Albino Alligator" (the title refers to an arcane bit of bayou lore described by Fichtner) makes demands on both the intelligence and attention of its audience, remaining one of those rare films nuanced enough to deserve a second viewing.

Unfortunately, the smoothly directed interludes showing Mantegna and his men surrounding Dino's Last Chance Bar bear an uncomfortable resemblance to the scenes that screenwriters arbitrarily add to "open up" stage-bound dramas. In fact, the intricate script, with its significant moral questions (how far will you go to survive?) and its showcase roles for an ensemble cast might work even better as the basis for some future theatrical production.

SIGHT AND SOUND, 8/97, p. 36, Stella Bruzzi

A band of robbers, Milo, Dova and Law, set off an alarm during a robbery in New Orleans. While escaping, they kill three Federal agents, and Milo is badly wounded. They seek refuge in a basement bar and take the staff and two guests hostage. The cops and FBI form a barricade around the building. The robbers think this is because of them, but in fact the FBI have been tipped off that an arms dealer named Guy is in the bar. Dino, the bar owner, tries to get his hidden shotgun out from below the bar, but is spotted and murdered by Law.

Milo, who has been unconscious, suddenly wakes up. Guy offers to liaise with the cops, but first the barwoman Janet answers the police's call and conveys the robbers' demands for the removal of all the agents. Milo realises that Dino's bar, once a speakeasy, must have a concealed exit and is shown where the tunnel is. Guy comes up with a plan: they'll tell the police that they're releasing the hostages one by one, but instead they'll 'release' themselves. An image of Guy is shown on the news and it is announced that he is a suspected gun dealer. The cops prepare to raid the bar. Milo wants to turn himself in but Dova, his kid brother, stops him. Milo surreptitiously cuts his wrists and dies. In the confusion and final shoot out, Guy and Law are killed. The cops think Dova is a hero, and Janet chooses not to blow his cover.

Perhaps it is damning Kevin Spacey's directorial debut *Albino Alligator* with faint praise to classify it as sub-David Mamet cinema-theatre. The film's setting echoes the mainly on-set-bound *Glengary Glen Ross* (which featured Spacey as an actor), but it replaces the intense atmosphere of the down-at-heel real estate office with Dino's dingy, lovingly preserved speakeasy. *Albino Alligator* is an engaging film, but one which ultimately fails because it is too predictable. This familiarity is partly due to the Mametisms—the terse one-liners, fractious, complicated relationships and the cold, insular characters—but also the result of its heist movie-heritage. As with so many films of this genre (from *The Asphalt Jungle* to *Reservoir Dogs*) the narrative premise for *Alligator* is the inevitable failure of the perfectly planned robbery.

The problem—which Spacey never quite finds a solution to—is what to do once the gang members are trapped in a confined location with the cops outside waiting to pounce. The only plausible avenue is to focus on the dynamics between the characters, to substitute unexpected personal revelations for action twists and turns. This enforced constriction necessarily places the dramatic emphasis on the actors and the dialogue rather than on pyrotechnics. Here, there is something heavily theatrical about both elements.

Spacey reputedly rehearsed the film almost as if it were a play, working with the actors one-to-one before spending six days on set without the cameras, and *then* filming in sequence to create performance continuity. This approach works, for example, with Gary Sinise, who here gives his most refined and varied screen performance since the film version of Sam Shepard's *True West*. He plays Milo, an intelligent older robber and a welcome respite from the brutish stupidity of his brother Dova and the psychotically inclined Law. When Milo finally stirs from his injury-induced stupor, *Albino Alligator* likewise comes to life, and starts to make psychological sense. For a fleeting moment he offers a crucial glimmer of hope that this shambolic band of robbers might extricate itself from this mess.

But when Sinise resigns himself to the inevitable, so does the film. For the most part, we are made to care little for this bunch of desperadoes as they wait for the inevitable smashing down of the bar door. As the brainless Dova, Matt Dillon (never the most understated of performers) is especially in need of action to get the best from him, as is Faye Dunaway who does sardonic drabness particularly unconvincingly and has only ever been powerful—as she was in Chinatown—when playing a beautiful, and perhaps vacuous, enigma.

Perhaps the actors shouldn't be the only ones blamed. Christian Forte's script is an odd mixture of show-off quips (like Dova's "when push comes to shove, I'll shove"), slapdash character development (we hardly care when a young pool-player in the background turns out to be Janet's son instead of her toyboy) and wayward structuring. Why bring the cops screeching to the scene so soon if they're then to be abandoned to their tepid coffees until the manic dénouement? Apart from some visually arresting sequences, such as the inquisitive close-up tracking shot along the devastated bar following Dino's brain-mashing, *Albino Alligator* is also stylistically conservative. Classic robbery movies, as compensation for their formulaic plot, are often quite extreme in some way—think of the unbearable silence of *Rififi* or the macho posturing in *Reservoir Dogs*. Spacey hasn't found an equivalent; he holds back from excess and is too dependent on such laboured sign-posting as the poster of Bogart that hangs on the bar wall. As a result, this is an unexceptional though watchable film.

VILLAGE VOICE, 1/21/97, p. 70, Amy Taubin

Anyone, who's even had even a fleeting thought about film release patterns knows that January is the pits. Presuming that viewers are sated after an orgy of holiday movie-going, distributors dump their surefire losers into the first available theaters. Thus we have *Albino Alligator*, Kevin Spacey's directorial debut, oozing out of Miramax's storeroom, and *Inside*, Arthur Penn's made-for-cable chamber piece, pushed, inappropriately, onto the big screen by Strand.

In *Albino Alligator*, Matt Dillon, Gary Sinise, and William Fichtner play a trio of low-level burglars who take refuge in a neighborhood bar after they blunder into an FBI stakeout and accidentally run down some agents. Surrounded by the cops, they hold the bar's occupants as hostages while they play for time.

A half-baked mélange of *The Desperate Hours* and all those Tennessee Williams plays that hinge on reptilian metaphors *(Night of the Iguana, The Fugitive Kind)*, *Albino Alligator* is as pretentious as it is bloody, though sadly lacking in brains. Working in close quarters, Spacey soups up the inaction with lots of camera movement and an ominous musical score that, I suppose, is meant to suggest the inner turmoil of the stock characters cluttering the screen.

As an actor, Spacey has made anonymity his identity (no mean feat even when it verges on shtick). As, a director, however, he's no more than the latest, not very stylish member of a filmmaking boys' club that ran out of energy long before he applied. *Albino Alligator* takes itself too seriously to work as genre; on the other hand, its devices are too shopworn to allow for a personal or original point of view.

With the exception of the resourceful Sinise (most alive here when he's quietly bleeding to death) and the charismatic newcomer Skeet Ulrich, the actors (including Faye Dunaway as a high-strung bartender) seem to be laboring under the delusion that *Albino Alligator* will transform their careers. And the larger their talent, the more embarrassing it is to watch them work so hard to no avail. At one point Dillon's character has a heart-to-heart with himself in the mirror. "I should have settled down and gotten married," he mutters. What's evoked is not another possible world but merely the opposite, though no less clichéd, strain of Amerindie. Dear Matt, just because *Albino Alligator* turned into a rout doesn't mean you have to get all warm and fuzzy the next time around.

Also reviewed in:
CHICAGO TRIBUNE, 1/17/97, Friday/p. D, John Petrakis
NEW YORK TIMES, 1/17/97, p. C10, Janet Maslin
VARIETY, 9/9-15/96, p. 119, Lisa Nesselson
WASHINGTON POST, 1/17/97, p. D6, Richard Harrington

ALIEN RESURRECTION

A Twentieth Century Fox release of a Brandywine production. *Producer:* Bill Badalato, Gordon Carroll, David Giler, and Walter Hill. *Director:* Jean-Pierre Jeunet. *Screenplay:* Joss Whedon. *Based on characters created by:* Dan O'Bannon and Ronald Shusett. *Director of Photography:* Darius Khondji. *Editor:* Herve Schneid. *Music:* John Frizzell. *Music Editor:* Abby Treloggen. *Sound:* Richard Bryce Goodman and (music) Dennis Sands. *Sound Editor:* John A. Larsen. *Casting:* Rick Pagano. *Production Designer:* Nigel Phelps. *Art Director:* Stephen Cooper. *Set Designer:* John Chichester, Jann K. Engel, Mick Cukurs, Richard Fernandez, Luis G. Hoyos, Maya Shimoguchi, and Randall Wilkins. *Set Decorator:* John M. Dwyer. *Alien Effects Design:* Alec Gillis and Tom Woodruff, Jr. *Special Effects:* Bruce Devan. *Costumes:* Bob Ringwood. *Make-up:* Barry R. Koper. *Make-up (Sigourney Weaver):* Linda De Vetta. *Make-up (Winona*

Ryder): Naomi Donne. *Stunt Coordinator:* Ernie Orsatti. *Running time:* 105 minutes. *MPAA Rating:* R.

CAST: Sigourney Weaver (Ellen Ripley); Winona Ryder (Annalee Call); Dominique Pinon (Vriess); Ron Perlman (Johner); Gary Dourdan (Christie); Michael Wincott (Elgyn); Kim Flowers (Hillard); Dan Hedaya (General Perez); J.E. Freeman (Dr. Wren); Brad Dourif (Gediman); Raymond Cruz (Distephano); Leland Orser (Purvis); Carolyn Campbell (Anesthesiologist); Marlene Bush (Scientist); David St. James (Surgeon); Rodney Mitchell (Soldier with Glove); Robert Faltisco (Soldier Shot Through Helmet); David Rowe (Frozen Soldier); Steven Gilborn (Voice of "Father"); Nicole Fellows (Young Ripley); Tom Woodruff, Jr. (Lead Alien); Joan LaBarbara and Archie Hahn. (Newborn Vocals).

LOS ANGELES TIMES, 11/26/97, Calendar/p. 1, Kenneth Turan

If you need to read a review to decide if you want to see "Alien Resurrection," you absolutely shouldn't be going.

The fourth film in a series that started with Ridley Scott's widely appreciated 1979 original, the current "Alien" has devolved into something that's strictly for hard-core horror junkies who can't get enough of slime, gore and repulsion.

While progress in some areas of civilization is problematic, one thing that continues to go from strength to strength is the ability of special-effects technicians to up the ante for state-of-the-art revulsion. There's an audience for this kind of stuff, as there was for public executions, and starry-eyed movie executives no doubt stand up and cheer when new levels of disgust are reached and surpassed.

The studio hero this time around is French director Jean-Pierre Jeunet, whose fascination with highly stylized grotesquerie and pretentious dead-end weirdness was last on display in the unfortunate "City of Lost Children."

Working with some of the same actors and technicians from that film, Jeunet has also reteamed with cinematographer Darius Khondji. His visual style, grandly described in the press kit as "signature chiaroscuro lighting and muted colors," in practice means that "Alien Resurrection" looks as if it were shot under the sickly fluorescent lighting of a decrepit hospital emergency ward.

One reason "Alien Resurrection" places so much emphasis on the stomach-turning is that only so much can be done with these films in terms of plot. In fact Ellen Ripley (Sigourney Weaver) neatly summarizes what's to come when she says of the monster, "She'll breed, you'll die, everyone will die."

Yes, Ripley is back, more or less. Dead herself for 200 years, she's been cloned from a drop of her blood (ain't technology grand?), returned to life by screenwriter Joss Whedon with one of those unspeakable aliens growing inside of her.

All this takes place on the Auriga, a renegade space laboratory under the command of Gen. Perez (Dan Hedaya at his most Nixonian). Having missed the previous films, the general's noxious minions are under the illusion that the aliens can be made practical use of. "The potential for this species," one of them smugly says, "goes way beyond urban pacification." You don't say.

Though she's done this three times before, Weaver is actually the best thing in the new "Alien." Playing someone dead seems to have liberated the actress in unexpected ways, and her Ripley, fortified with superhuman strength and skills this time around, has enough confidence and panache to amuse and entertain.

The film's other big name is Winona Ryder, who plays Annalee Call, a crew member on the tramp freighter the Betty that brings food for the aliens. (No, they don't care for Alpo.) Attracted to the role apparently because she's a serious sci-fi fan, Ryder, whose naturalness is her strength, mostly looks lost in the film's overstylized environment.

To the surprise of no one in the audience, the creatures waste little time in finding a way to get loose. This forces the Betty's crew to huff and puff their way from one end of the spaceship to the other a mere step ahead of beasts who drip acidic slime and chomp on everyone in sight. There's even an underwater chase, inspired perhaps by old Esther Williams movies but nowhere near as charming.

Given that Ripley is the world's leading authority on these monsters, it would make sense for people to listen to her, but they rarely do. Ripley also has no effect on the film's forced jokey sensibility, over-the-top acting and loser pickup lines like "If you don't want to play basketball, I know some other indoor sports."

Simple as all this is in outline, the film's plot still contains a number of too-tricky twists that are explained so fast (it is an emergency, after all) that no one but buffs will be able to figure out what is happening. As an example of the mindless pursuit of misguided self-interest, "Alien Resurrection" is not much different from the deluded scientists it so archly mocks.

NEW YORK, 12/1/97, p. 121, David Denby

You would think that a graduate of Stanford and Yale—in fact, *anyone* would get tired of running slime through her fingers, but no, in *Alien Resurrection*, Sigourney Weaver is back in the gunk again as Ripley the indefatigable fighter against the dastardly Other. Weaver, whose career in movies has been rather peculiar, stoops to pick up oozing white stuff. *They* are here: "You will die," she informs the other humans. *Alien Resurrection*, the fourth in a series that began in 1979, is a movie of monstrous deaths, monstrous births. Dead 200 years, Ripley is reconstructed by scientists from her DNA, and when she is full-grown, the alien she was carrying inside her when she died in the last movie (remember?) is also ready for life. Scientists extract the creature, which is what they really want—Ripley, it turns out, was only a "carrier." The men in white coats mutter something about getting "vaccines" from the resurrected alien, but apart from that, we never really know why they bring back an animal that enjoys chewing on the human race. It's as if the filmmakers—writer Joss Whedon, director Jean-Pierre Jeunet—were saying to the audience, "Look, no one has to offer a *reason* for keeping a movie franchise alive, so just go along with it, okay?"

Ripley, not quite human, has some ambivalent moments. Can she kill the alien she carried within her own body? Her features frozen, Weaver gives off a certain sardonic coldness toward the humans—she's disdainful of both the scientists and the scruffy crew of a pirate spaceship (including Winona Ryder) that shows up with additional human "carriers" for the scientists to play with. Sigourney Weaver is an imposing figure (without being an interesting screen actress), and Jeunet gives her some eerie scenes: Ripley the superwoman, facing down the pirate thugs, plays basketball and stops the ball cold with outstretched palm as if her hand were lined with crazy glue.

It would be too easy, and probably wrong, to say that Jean-Pierre Jeunet is just another European director slimed by Hollywood. Jeunet has a screw-loose visual style; he likes everything to be a little off. His 1990 picture *Delicatessen*, which was about a butcher slicing up his neighbors into meat patties, showed a certain talent for "dark" (i.e., disgusting) comedy. I don't, in other words, think that Jeunet is cynical, or working against his instincts. In *Alien Resurrection*, Jeunet and his cinematographer, Darius Khondji, provide some visual excitement early on—steamy corridors in a black spaceship, an exciting underwater sequence. But a franchise becomes a franchise because it delivers certain staple pleasures or shocks, and payoff time in *Alien Resurrection* comes soon enough in the usual form of dripping, fanged, death's-head creatures with iron teeth ripping through bodies. There's all that terrific primal ooze, the pullulating matter and viscous limbs. The movie is fueled by a powerful disgust, but disgust at what? Made-up creatures? Who is the enemy in movies like this one and *Starship Troopers?* Welcome to the movies of the late nineties: rage without purpose, threat without meaning, horror without relief. And why is this summer-season movie coming out now? Is this Twentieth Century Fox's idea of a Thanksgiving present?

NEW YORK POST, 11/26/97, p. 45, Thelma Adams

It strikes me that there are two essentials for a good "Alien" movie: slurpy, skeletal extraterrestrials with permanent P.M.S. and Sigourney Weaver in butch overdrive.

"Alien Resurrection" has both and more. Director Jean-Pierre Jeunet has turned the future into another "City of Lost Children," the French movie he directed with Marc Caro: Its aggressive visual style is flamboyantly Grimm: Hansel and Gretel in techno-hell.

Believe it or not, Ripley (Weaver) has been resurrected (she died in "Alien 3"). Evil scientists aboard a remote, government sponsored station have cloned her and harvested the queen beast she carried in her belly.

Through the miracles of future science, and Joss Whedon's darkly comic screenplay, there's been some DNA leakage: Ripley and the alien have a mysterious bond—and Ripley's got a whole new bag. She's as tense and suspicious as ever and her people skills haven't improved, but her strength has ben supersized.

While Ripley warns General Perez (Dan Hedaya) and Doctor Wren (J.E. Freeman) that they know nothin' about birthin' aliens (She'll breed; you'll die"), her heart seems to belong to that ferocious, purple acid-spitting monster, held at bay behind alien-proof glass.

Meanwhile, smugglers interrupt the science experiments, bringing with them a load of human lunch. Gravel-voiced he-man Michael Wincott leads the band of chunky-boot-wearing rowdies. They include two"Lost Children" stars: Ron Perlman and Dominique Pinon as a nasty giant and a gentle cripple.

Also stepping awkwardly into costume designer Bob Ringwood's unisex jumpsuits is Winona Ryder as Call. While she tries to pass herself off as smuggler, she has "hidden agenda" written all over her pale face. It turns out, she's the warrior waif.

With Call as the cavalry and Ripley's loyalties split, all hell breaks loose when the aliens crack their cage. We return to basics. We're in a haunted house horror movie and the primary question is: who's space food and who's not.

Throughout the elaborate chase, the special effects are suitably nauseating. The goopy aliens with their punching months are more horrifying than ever, despite their familiarity. But their shining moment arrives in a scene of surprising grace. The horrors trap their human prey underwater in a flooded kitchen and swim in pursuit with the alarming fluidity of octopi, fierce and beautiful to behold.

The human effects are a little lighter. As a villain, Hedaya's general is most notable for having the hairiest shoulders in the business. The existential twinges of Ryder's Call seem like a distraction, a "Star Trek: The Next Generation" subplot, rather than an addition.

We're not surprised that Ryder is more gentlewoman than supergirl. The same can't be said for Weaver. Ripley is the character she plays best, the sinewy Amazon whose material tendencies can never be confused with vulnerability. In the end, the movie seems poised for yet another "Alien" installment, as the clone Ripley views Earth for the first time and says: "I'm a stranger here myself." Not for long.

NEWSDAY, 11/26/97, Part II/p. B10, Jack Mathews

Frankenstein's monster, Count Dracula, the Werewolf, Godzilla, Freddy Krueger, Michael Meyers, Jason ... As every horror movie fan and studio executive know, you cannot keep a good monster down. Audiences have to see them die at the end of each story, to enjoy their phantasmagasms, as it were, but they then happily await the monsters' return in the sequel.

This doesn't require a suspension of logic. Monsters are by definition immune from the laws of nature. Many of them are dead to begin with. It's another matter altogether bringing back a dead hero.

Audiences identify with mortal heroes, personalize their danger, walk in their shoes, exalt in their courage. When you kill one of them off, you'd better be ready to say "the end," and mean it. And if you do bring one back, you certainly need a better explanation than the one provided for the reanimation of Sigourney Weaver's Ripley in the monotonously formulaic "Alien Resurrection."

The fourth episode of the series, begun with Ridley Scott's classic 1979 "Alien," has "whoops" written all over it. Twentieth Century Fox and the "Alien" producers allowed Ripley to die a martyr's death at the end of the 1992 "Alien3" figuring that with science-fiction out of vogue, they could only get one more squeeze out of it. But "Independence Day" triggered a quick revival of sci-fi, and the series was returned to active duty.

But what to do about Ripley?

The answer is as easy as A-B-C ... C for cloning, the all-purpose dramatic hook for fantasies of the '90s. It's 200 years after Ripley sacrificed herself in order to kill the alien queen fetus growing inside her. But blood samples left behind give a spectacularly naive generation of scientists—not to mention horror fans—an opportunity to see her again, and see her deliver that baby.

Here's the twist: Ripley 2 of Alien 4 is a hybrid. She has the memories, morals and courage of her human forebear, but she also has some of the strength, and the metal-piercing blood, of the aliens. Just whose side, we are meant to wonder, is she on?

Once Ripley is back, "Alien Resurrection" follows the path of its predecessors. She and a host of disposable others are trapped in a claustrophobic place in space, frantically attempting to both escape the aliens and kill the things—in this case, before they reach Earth and go to work on Alien 5.

Joining Ripley in the endeavor are a team of mercenaries, led by the cool Elgyn (Michael Wincott) and his sear-faced sidekick Johner (Ron Perlman), the alien scientists, whose number includes the martinet general Dan Hedaya, would-be alien trainer Brad Dourif, and the evil Dr. Wren (J.E. Freeman), plus freelance alien hunter Annalee Call (Winona Ryder, who looks as lost as Alice in Wonderland).

French director Jean-Pierre Jeunet has given "Alien Resurrection" that distinctively dark, gridlike look of his last film, "The City of Lost Children," and adds moments of quirky black comedy, which his fans relished in "Delicatessen." The laughs are welcome relief, not so much from the tension created by the chase scenes as from the boredom of them.

How many times, and how many different ways, can you show the same monsters terrifying and dismembering people before it gets tiresome? I must report that there was much delighted gasping over the gore and mayhem at the promotional screening I attended, but call me jaded, if you've seen one skull crushed, you've seen them all.

The only interesting element of this episode is Ripley's personality. Having alien blood gives her a macabre sense of humor, to go with her divided loyalties and her added maternal conflicts. As all actors portraying recurring heroes eventually do, Weaver gets to ham it up and crack jokes about her character's persona.

Her self-parody, plus the human malice given to this batch of aliens, brings the series to the brink of campiness, and that would be OK with me. If there has to be an Alien 5, I'd rather see the creatures singing and dancing on Broadway, or climbing the Empire State Building, than crunching heads.

SIGHT AND SOUND, 12/97, p. 36, Kim Newman

On the military research space habitat *The Auriga*, two hundred years after being impregnated with an alien queen and killing herself to save humanity, Ellen Ripley is cloned by Drs Wren and Gediman. They view her as a "meat by-product" of their project to recreate the extinct alien species. *The Betty*, an outlaw ship captained by Elgyn, arrives at *The Auriga*. General Perez buys from Elgyn a supply of cryogenically frozen people who've been kidnapped en route to a mining colony; they will incubate the alien eggs laid by the queen.

The crew of *The Betty* includes Call, a revolutionary who wants to stymie the project, and pirates Johner, Vriess, Christie and Hillard. Call breaks into Ripley's cell planning to kill her, but discovers that the alien has already been removed. The aliens escape from their secure cages by killing one of their number so that its corrosive entrails eat through the floor. Perez, Elgyn and most of the military and scientific staff of *The Auriga* are swiftly killed. Ripley, Call, Wren, military-officer Distephano and some pirates struggle through flooded areas and fight off aliens while trying to make it to *The Betty* and escape. As the aliens proliferate, Wren reveals that an automatic fail-safe, triggered when the crisis began, is taking *The Auriga* to Earth, where the aliens will run rampant. Ripley discovers seven earlier, unsuccessful alien-human hybrid clones of the original Ripley and destroys them.

Purvis, one of the kidnapped people, has survived. Ripley tells him he is incubating an alien which will kill him. Hillard, Elgyn's lover, is killed. Wren seems to kill Call, but she survives and reveals herself to be a runaway robot, programmed for compassion. Christie sacrifices himself to save his paraplegic friend Vriess. Ripley falls into the clutches of the queen, and Gediman—preserved in a cocoon—explains that the alien has inherited from Ripley the ability to give birth without going through the alien egg-cycle. The queen spawns an alien-human monster, which eats Gediman's head and pursues the crew to *The Betty*.

Wren commandeers *The Betty* but is killed by Purvis, who aims the alien punching through his chest at the scientist's head. Purvis is then destroyed by Johner and Distephano. *The Betty* escapes from *The Auriga*, which burns up on re-entry. But the alien-human attacks Call so Ripley has to use her corrosive blood to open a hole in a window, through which the alien is sucked. Ripley and Call bond as they view the Earth for the first time.

It is clear from the beginning of *Alien Resurrection* that Twentieth Century Fox learned their lesson from *Alien³* and that the resurrection promised by the title refers not simply to Ripley and the alien queen, but to a profitable franchise. Though the services of another visionary director have been retained (after Ridley Scott and James Cameron), it is notable that Jean-Pierre Jeunet is not partnered here with his usual co-director-designer Marc Caro. Jeunet has also been kept well away from the screenplay, entrusted instead to Joss Whedon, who remains best known for his *Buffy the Vampire Slayer* movie and television series. It is, of course, a challenge to make part four of anything fresh and imaginative when straying too far from the series template tends to put off longtime fans without attracting new audiences, as *Alien³*'s director David Fincher discovered. However, it's a shame that this effort—though far more coherent, entertaining and exciting than *Alien³*—should be the first film in the series to be almost anonymous.

There are calculated references to earlier episodes. The computer on *The Auriga* is called Father (in *Alien*, it was Mother)—though the scene establishing this seems to have been snipped. When told of the security procedures which will keep the aliens safely penned, Ripley replies with a paraphrase of the little girl from *Aliens*' line, "that won't matter". Brad Dourif's character, apparently killed off early, turns up later to explain some biology before having his head chewed off, and an inelegant, failed Ripley-clone begs her successor to kill her—two elements drawn from an excised scene from *Alien* involving Tom Skerritt's character.

Whedon also employs such series staples as: the illogical race-against-time (a stupid return-to-Earth safety device is revealed as a pointless non-threat when *The Auriga* burns up on re-entry); the macho face-off as Ripley shows up grunting male slobs (Sigourney Weaver does some one-on-one basketball with a scarred Ron Perlman); and the stubborn belief that twentieth-century culture will still be relevant 500 years from now (there are jokes about *Gilligan's Island* and *Popeye*).

In *Alien Resurrection*'s future, the Company is now out of business, its plot-function in this film replaced by a nefarious but muddled military conspiracy. The androids of the earlier entries make way for a surprise revelation that Call, played by Winona Ryder, is an artificial person one generation on from the earlier models. The term Whedon coins for the new-model Call, an android (gynoid?) built by other androids, is "Anton", which happens to be the name of a race of plastic monsters that lumbered around *Dr. Who* in the early 70s. In fact, *Alien Resurrection*, like *Alien* itself, is something of a mutation of the cramped style of that fondly remembered BBC science-fiction show, with endless running around corridors. There's also a bit of genetic-generic material from disaster movies, with a *Poseidon Adventure*-like swim through a flooded kitchen, while the fanged nasties pick off anyone humourlessly militarist or unsympathetic but leave the obvious survivors, predestined by billing or eccentricity, illogically safe.

There are a few nice character touches, with Ron Perlman and Dominique Pinon grouching and gurning amusingly as the sexless stooges. (Pinon was the star of Jeunet's first film, *Delicatessen*, while both he and Perlman appear in Jeunet's second, The *City of Lost* Children.) The best new invention is the mild-mannered and bespectacled Purvis, who wakes up from cryosleep to find he has been kidnapped, sold, impregnated and doomed but spends the rest of the film kidding himself that he has a chance of survival (and gets to dispose of the chief human villain). The monsters, CGI-augmented this time, drool more than usual—especially during a neat training game with Dourif—and remain fearsome beasties, though the last-reel mutant can't match the escalation of ghastliness provided by the original queen in *Aliens*.

While the *Alien* series has taken a leisurely 18 years to get to number four, during that time there has been of proliferation of novel spin-offs and comic books (including cross-over encounters with *Predator, Superman* and *Batman*), not to mention a line of successful action figures. This is the first film to take back all the merchandising and incorporate it into the plot. Thus, the damp-squib human-alien monster of the finale makes little sense in plot terms, but the continual mutation of the alien species is renumerative excuse for more variant toys.

There are a few fascinating ramifications to the dodgy science. It's suggested that the cloned Ripley has her personality intact because of inherited generational memory and a parallel is made between the unnatural births of Ripley, the queen, Call and the new monster, which give them strengths unattainable by men of woman born. However, none of that material is really explored in the mad scramble to fire off more guns or chew off more heads.

TIME, 12/1/97, p. 84, Richard Schickel

Familiarity also breeds affection. The aliens still have pretty teeth, ooze slime from every pore and maintain their relentlessly hostile attitude toward all things human. But by now—*Alien Resurrection* is their fourth screen appearance—there's something funny about their reliable malevolence. It's sort of like Mr. Magoo's nearsightedness; you await its inevitably disastrous consequences with high comic anticipation.

Naturally, the creatures' old nemesis, Ellen Ripley (Sigourney Weaver), has been—literally—reincarnated, and her wit and toughness were not forgotten in the cloning. Nor did screenwriter Joss Whedon (of TVs *Buffy the Vampire Slayer*) neglect to provide her with a spaceship of fools who refuse to believe her warnings of impending carnage. He has even given Ripley a soul sister (Winona Ryder) to bond with. O.K., she's a robot, but she's got a heart of gold as well as buns of steel.

The director, Jean-Pierre Jeunet, hurries us past all the desperate explanations required by sequels to movies that ended up pretty definitively (the last we saw of Ripley in *Alien 3* she was taking a dunk in molten metal). Since most of these are incomprehensible anyway, especially as they are constantly interrupted by fires, floods and explosions, Jeunet is eager to get on with the really scary stuff. This is not, given the movie's self-satirizing impulse, as terrifying as it once was. But on the whole, the eek-for-yuks trade-off is more than fair—hip without being campy or condescending to one of the better movie franchises.

VILLAGE VOICE, 12/2/97, p. 79, J. Hoberman

In the fall extraterrestrial-combat sweepstakes, *Alien Resurrection* is the yin to *Starship Troopers*'s yang. Where the crypto-fascist Verhoeven flick is an enjoyably simpleminded cartoon, the latest installment of the antiauthoritarian "Alien" saga is a provocatively irrational mess. If *Starship Troopers* is almost campy in its hard-edge gung ho, *Alien Resurrection* is aggressively touchy-feely—the credits plunge you into an immediate ick of seething protoplasm.

Showcasing a strong action heroine, Sigourney Weaver's Lieutenant Ellen Ripley, and steeped in reproductive issues, the first three "Alien" films managed to be simultaneously feminist and gynophobic. So too *Alien Resurrection*, which features a pair of graphic birth scenes—three, if you count the requisite rib-cage explosion of a new-born alien from its unwitting human host (*Starship Troopers* is obsessed with territorial conquest. *Alien Resurrection*, like its predecessors, is a film about interiors.) The movie opens with the cesarean required to extract the alien fetus implanted inside Ripley at the end of *Alien³*, some 200 years before. The final movement is triggered when the fast-maturing alien, a queen no less, gives birth to Ripley's grand-whatzit.

Those who saw *Alien³* may recall that it ended with the impregnated Ripley, hair shorn á la Joan of Arc, diving backwards into a pit of molten lead as she held the alien that had just erupted out of her midsection. The Ripley of *Alien Resurrection* is, as it turns out, a clone just like the movie. (She's even been resurrected for the same reason. As always in the "Alien" cycle, official greed and idiocy reign eternal.) In the process of bringing Ripley back, however, her human DNA has merged with that of the alien within. This accounts for her super strength, leather wardrobe, and general meanness. For much of the movie, Ripley even seems to be an alien symp, gloating over their inevitable victory like the spider-eating Renfield at the approach of Dracula. Once the aliens spawn, however, her human genes win out. She joins the hapless crew in a battle for control of a spaceship that's become a veritable water bed of alien slime.

To explain Ripley's mind-set, screenwriter Joss Whedon and director Jean-Pierre Jeunet contrive a gene-splicing nightmare. The spaceship, where all of the action takes place, contains a secret laboratory full of pickled mutants. Ripley, when she discovers this *Island of Lost Souls* freak show, is moved by pity to torch the place. Her comrades are nonplussed. "What's the big deal, man?" one Neanderthal asks. "Fucking waste of ammo. Must be a chick thing."

Be that as it may, *Alien Resurrection* is not a pretty picture. Occasional cutaways to the ship's exterior suggest a humongous, calcified dog turd floating through the endless sewer of deep space.

(Its destination, per one character, is the "shit hole" Earth.) But despite this and a reported $70 million budget, *Alien Resurrection* has disappointingly little of the baroque set design and droll mise-en-scène of Jeunet's two previous features, *Delicatessen* and *The City of Lost Children*—both codirected with cartoonist Marc Caro.   What *Alien Resurrection* does have is the dubbed-sounding, grade-school dialogue favored by Euro sci-fi, as well as the presence of *Lost Children* stars Ron Perlman and Dominique Pinon (here waging war from a wheelchair).

At least *Alien³* had intimations of mythological grandeur.   Too tepid to be satire, *Resurrection* has reached the point of diminishing returns.   The cloned Ripley ultimately makes a tactical alliance with an equally ambiguous entity played by Winona Ryder.   "No human being is that human," Ripley sneers of her new found friend.   Together, the women (or "women") save the earth—thus leaving the hatch ajar for Fox to concoct an *Alien 5* or perhaps recombine its DNA with *Speed*.

Also reviewed in:
CHICAGO TRIBUNE, 11/26/97, Tempo/p.1, Michael Wilmington
NATION, 12/22/97, p. 35, Stuart Klawans
NEW YORK TIMES, 11/26/97, p. E1, Janet Maslin
NEW YORKER, 12/1/97, p. 102, Anthony Lane
VARIETY, 11/17-23/97, p. 63, Derek Elley
WASHINGTON POST, 11/26/97, p. B1, Stephen Hunter
WASHINGTON POST, 12/28/97, Weekend/p. 60, Desson Howe

ALIVE AND KICKING

A First Look Pictures release of a Channel Four Films presentation of an M.P. production. *Producer:* Martin Pope.   *Director:* Nancy Meckler.   *Screenplay:* Martin Sherman.   *Director of Photography:* Chris Seager.   *Editor:* Rodney Holland.   *Music:* Peter Salem.   *Choreographer:* Liz Ranken.   *Sound:* John Midgley.   *Sound Editor:* Peter Baldock.   *Casting:* Janey Fothergill. *Production Designer:* Cecelia Brereton.   *Art Director:* Philip Robinson.   *Costumes:* Monica Howe.   *Make-up:* Sally Jaye.   *Stunt Coordinator:* Peter Brayham.   *Running time:* 100 minutes. *MPAA Rating:* R.

CAST: Jason Flemyng (Tonio);   Antony Sher (Jack);   Dorothy Tutin (Luna);   Anthony Higgins (Ramon);   Bill Nighy (Tristan);   Philip Voss (Duncan);   Diane Parish (Millie);   Aiden Waters (Vincent);   Natalie Roles (Catherine);   Freddy Douglas (Luke);   Kenneth Tharp (Howard); Michael Keegan-Dolan (Alan);   Ruth Lass (Night Nurse);   Linda Bassett (Doctor);   Hilary Reynolds (Nurse);   Dickon Tolson (Mugger);   David Ashton and Annabel Leventon (Paris Mourners);   David Phelan (Mourner);   Dugald Bruce Lockhart (Man at Club);   Ian Abbey (T-Shirt Man);   John Baxter (Man at Bar);   Jason Cheater (Smoking Man);   Ellen Van Schuylenburch (Dance Teacher);   Mary Cruickshank (Woman at Party);   Allan Corduner (Therapist at Party);   Richard Hope (Karaoke Doctor);   Martin Sherman (Man at Pub);   Sakuntala Ramanee (Hospital Doctor);   Frank Boyce (Man in Park).

LOS ANGELES TIMES, 7/25/97, Calendar/ p. 12, Kevin Thomas

[The following review by Kevin Thomas appeared in a slightly different form in **NEWSDAY, 7/25/97, Part II/p. B9.]**

"Alive and Kicking," one of the strongest films in the recent Outfest '97, takes us into the world of dance—a world that has been decimated by AIDS.   Any reluctance to submit to yet another film on the dread disease is understandable, but "Alive and Kicking" is full of surprises. Its people are sharply, even rigorously, delineated. And it develops into an unexpected love story of uncommon honesty with a great deal of insight about life, art and values.

Written with equal parts perception and compassion by playwright Martin Sherman in his screenwriting debut, "Alive and Kicking" was directed by his London-based fellow American,

Nancy Meckler. She brings to the film the same acute observation of human behavior and attention to detail that characterized her mesmerizing 1995 debut film, "Sister My Sister."

"Alive and Kicking" begins somberly. The members of a London ballet company are visiting one of its dancers, Ramon (Anthony Higgins), who's in the final stages of AIDS. He's the mentor of one of the company's stars, Tonio (Jason Flemyng), who lost his lover to AIDS a year ago. He has AIDS himself but so far has had only one incident of AIDS-related illness. He is determined to complete what will be the company's final season; the company has lost too many dancers to AIDS, and its distinguished choreographer (Dorothy Tutin) is a victim of failing memory.

Talk about depressing! Talk about piling it on! However, Sherman, best known for his play "Bent," and Meckler are daring us to stick with them, instead deciding, "Enough already."

First, they snare us with Tonio, who is tall, pale, auburn-haired and handsome in that aristocratic, hawk-profiled British way. Tonio has the arrogance of a young gay man who knows his sex appeal. He faces up squarely, if understandably bitterly, to his AIDS status, but anyone less than gorgeous should approach him with peril.

One man who does anyway happens to be the one individual nobody recognizes at Ramon's funeral. It turns out he's Jack (Antony Sher), the dead man's AIDS counselor, a man of intense dedication who is all but overwhelmed by his work.

Attracted to Tonio, Jack begins to pursue him with the kind of single-minded passion he brings to his profession. Although many would find Jack attractive, he's a stocky, masculine, not conventionally handsome Bob Hoskins type who falls for below Tonio's standard of male beauty.

But Jack's hunger for love begins to equal Tonio's need for support. What cinches "Alive and - Kicking" is the honesty Tonio and Jack possess in regard to themselves and each other: Were not Tonio facing the prospect of death, he wouldn't have the time of day for Jack, a truth that cuts to the heart of values in gay society with its premium on looks and youth.

But "Alive and Kicking" takes on a larger perspective, celebrating the importance of art. As ephemeral as dance seems to be in comparison with other arts, the film consoles us that, in the face of mortality, art can endure and possesses the power of redemption.

Under Meckler's firm direction, her cast, which includes Diane Parish as Millie, one of the company's star dancers and a staunch friend to the tempestous Tonio, positively crackles. What versatile actors Flemyng and Sher are: in the recent "Hollow Reed," Flemyng played a macho contractor and secret child abuser while Sher is winning praise for his stylish Disraeli in the current "Mrs. Brown." Meckler steers her actors clear of those theatrical mannerisms and vocal inflections with which English actors on the screen can drive you up the wall.

An attempt at lovemaking on the part of Tonio and Millie, a lesbian, slips into self-consciousness. But that's a minor flaw in a fine film that embodies its title. "Alive and Kicking" is just that.

NEW YORK POST, 7/25/97, p. 51, Larry Worth

The script is familiar, the directions a mixed bag and the title—"Alive & Kicking"—sounds like a cliche. So what possible reason is there to check out the umpteenth tale of an HIV-positive guy's love life?

Actually, there are two reasons: Jason Flemyng and Antony Sher.

Sher is an ongoing revelation. Having recently earned plaudits on Broadway in "Stanley," he followed with a superb interpretation of British Prime Minister Benjamin Disraeli in "Mrs. Brown." Now, playing a squat and querulous counselor to AIDS victims, he brings unexpected dimension to what could have been a walking stereotype.

As for Flemyng, he's almost Sher's equal. Last seen as a gay-bashing child abuser in "Hollow Reed," he masters a 180-degree-turn by bringing a dying, self-absorbed ballet star to glorious life.

But Martin Sherman's flawed script not only relates the ballet troupe's travails but plays an Alzheimer's-stricken impresario and her bisexual hubby for laughs. That's a mistake.

So is a climactic twist that calls for an incredibly overwrought dance sequence. It's as if Sherman didn't put enough trust in the film's dynamic duo to let them end on a less grandiouse note.

But Nancy Meckler, whose lesbian-themed "Sister My Sister" clearly showed potential, imbues the dramatics with a heart-rending quality. She never shies away from sarcoma-dotted bodies and provides unexpected levity at various death-bed scenes.

On the other hand, Meckler makes the erotic encounters a bit too graphic, wastes time on dream sequences and squanders locales that range from London to Athens.

But when Sher and Flemyng are front and center, none of that matters. Their combined efforts leave a seemingly moribund genre "Alive & Kicking."

SIGHT AND SOUND, 7/97, p. 35, Vicky Allan

Tonio is a dedicated young ballet dancer diagnosed HTV+. His last boyfriend died because of Aids and his best friend, Ramon, is in hospital suffering from Aids-related illness. All three worked with the Ballet Luna dance company. Despite his doctor's warnings against pushing himself too far, Tonio is determined to dance. When Ramon dies, Tonio and other company members attend the funeral. After the ceremony, the Ballet Luna's director despairs at its declining numbers: the choreographer Luna has Alzheimer's disease and many of the dancers have died because of Aids. His solution is that they should revive a dance originally performed by Ramon, a *pas de deux* for men called 'Indian Summer', with Tonio taking a role.

After a rehearsal, Tonio and other members of the company go out to a club where Tonio meets Jack, an older man who was once Ramon's therapist. When Jack comes on to him, Tonio tells him that he has Aids. Later Jack pursues Tonio, inviting him out to dinner. They end up going to bed together and start to see each other regularly.

While Jack becomes increasingly domestic, Tonio tries to resist the development of a proper 'relationship'. Meanwhile he's rehearsing 'Indian Summer' with the increasingly forgetful Luna. Jack persuades Tonio to go on holiday with him to Greece where they are able to appreciate the culture, scenery and each other. When they return to London, Tonio becomes absorbed in dance rehearsals and a rift forms between them. Jack is increasingly beset by work troubles. Shortly before the day of the performance, Tonio wakes up to find himself paralysed. He is taken to hospital where Luna comes up with a creative solution. 'Indian Summer' will go ahead, but with Tonio performing in his paralysed state, supported by other dancers. It is a triumphant performance, after which Tonio recovers his ability to walk. His relationship with Jack also begins to heal at last.

Alive and Kicking is a film about a dancer with Aids, yet it contains only one extended dance sequence. The camera moves in close on the bodies of the dancers. Using slow-motion, with rhythmically repeated shots that work against the music, this sequence exaggerates the idea of dance as a metaphor for sex, with filmic choreography replacing bodily choreography. It's a scene designed to provoke an ecstatic sympathy with the suffering of the protagonists, but it only serves to remind us how unadventurous and stagy the film has been up until this climactic point. Its innovation comes as an isolated relief.

Too much of British film-making cleaves to theatrical concerns. Here, limited movement and devotion to set pieces are the marks of a film director in thrall to a strong theatrical tradition. That Nancy Meckler comes from a theatre background would be obvious to anyone who has seen either of her feature film *Sister My Sister* or *Alive and Kicking*. Indeed, the former, a tale of two murderous and incestuous sisters, uses its staginess well to effect an appropriately constrained and bizarre quality of claustrophobia. This same theatricality, however, is the fundamental weakness of *Alive and Kicking*.

Jason Flemyng stars as Tonio, the Aids-afflicted dancer. Antony Sher is Jack, Tonio's lover. Physically gorgeous and appropriately camp, Fleming keeps hold of his character's state of emotional denial. He makes Tonio a bright spark who refuses to give in to his illness. It is Sher, though, who is meant to be the sympathetic crux of the film—his Jack feels all the frustrations of dealing with Tonio's Aids—but Sher lacks subtlety in key scenes and his overall performance is too big for the camera. Though sometimes funny, the script, by playwright Martin Sherman (who wrote the acclaimed play *Bent*), is also more often clumsy than cinematic.

Alive and Kicking is exclusively gay in the same way *Sister My Sister* was exclusively female. Nearly all of the characters are homosexual or lesbian, and the one scene in which Tonio decides to get together with his female dance partner, Millie (Diane Parish), ends with sex being rejected in favour of a cuppa. The difficulties the two dancers have in dealing with each other's genitals ("bits keep getting in the way") make a cutting point about heterosexual incomprehension of gay practices. There's also a neat appropriation of the Haagen Dazs adverts when Tonio and Jack fight using chocolate fudge American ice cream. These sexual jokes are the most audience-inclusive moments of *Alive and Kicking*. They work against the decadence and pretensions of the dance world which otherwise tend to be rather off-putting, with such in-jokes as the comment at a funeral, "No one here from the Arts Council, did you notice?" Sherman has to be admired for producing an admirably unsentimental script about dealing with being HIV+. It's a pity it is so bound up in theatrical presentation.

VILLAGE VOICE, 7/29/97, p. 78, Dennis Lim

Like *Box of Moonlight* [see Lim's review], the London-set *Alive & Kicking* wraps a well-worn scenario around a calculatedly mismatched couple—in this case, dancer Tonio (Jason Flemyng) and therapist Jack (Antony Sher), lovers separated by age, disposition, and HIV status. Films about AIDS have often reverted to disease-movie blueprints, which explains why they're cowardly, apolitical, and downright dishonest Scripted by Martin Sherman *(Bent)*, *Alive & Kicking* is no breakthrough, but it is at least reluctant to smooth over emotional awkwardness (though given the spotty writing, you wonder if that's always intentional).

The relationship between the HIV-positive Tonio, a petulant queen who's lost his lover to AIDS, and the pensive, portly, much older Jack feels credible, thanks mostly to Sher, who's as malleable and magnetic as ever. The filmmakers must have anticipated charges of theatricality, what with the teaming of Sher, Sherman, and the experienced West End director Nancy Meckler (whose first film was the claustrophobic *Sister My Sister*). But, if anything, *Alive & Kicking* has a touch of the old BBCs unabashedly drab mise-en-scène.

A dance company turns out to be an unfortunate milieu. There's much stereotypical campery afoot, and one especially dubious-looking routine, which also happens to be the climactic set piece. This culminating dance is a supposedly groundbreaking queer pas de deux, which (for misjudged comic relief) the Alzheimer's-afflicted choreographer can barely remember, and which (for dramatic effect) the semi-paralyzed Tonio is hell-bent on performing. After wading through some laudably real and messy situations, the film finally settles for platitudinous uplift, saying little beyond: Carry on dancing.

Also reviewed in:
CHICAGO TRIBUNE, 9/19/97, Friday/p. J, Achy Obejas
NEW REPUBLIC, 8/4/97, p. 26, Stanley Kauffmann
NEW YORK TIMES, 7/25/97, p. C14, Stephen Holden
VARIETY, 9/9-15/96, p. 121, Derek Elley

ALL OVER ME

A Fine Line Features release of a Medusa Pictures production in association with Slam and Baldini Pictures. *Executive Producer:* Andreas Bühler, Stephen X. Graham, and Nina M. Benton. *Producer:* Dolly Hall. *Director:* Alex Sichel. *Screenplay:* Sylvia Sichel. *Director of Photography:* Joe DeSalvo. *Editor:* Sabine Hoffmann. *Music:* Bill Coleman and Miki Navazio. *Casting:* Lina Todd. *Production Designer:* Amy Silver. *Costumes:* Victoria Farrell. *Running time:* 90 minutes. *MPAA Rating:* R.

CAST: Alison Folland (Claude); Tara Subkoff (Ellen); Cole Hauser (Mark); Wilson Cruz (Jesse); Ann Dowd (Claude's Mom); Leisha Hailey (Lucy); Pat Briggs (Luke); Shawn Hatosy (Gus); Vincent Pastore (Don).

LOS ANGELES TIMES, 4/25/97, Calendar/p. 6, Kevin Thomas

First-time director Alex Sichel and her sister, writer Sylvia Sichel, have said that their beguiling collaboration, "All Over Me," is their attempt to answer the timeless question, "How did we ever survive being teenage girls?" Alex and Sylvia, a playwright in her screenwriting debut, have proceeded with the belief that "every one secretly knows their best friend was their real first love."

Alison Folland's 15-year-old Claudia—called Claude by everybody except her mother (Ann Dowd)—and Tara Subkoff's Ellen live across the street from each other in Manhattan's Hell's Kitchen. Claude is a beautiful redhead, but she feels big and overweight in contrast to Ellen, an exquisite fragile-looking blond; the truth is that Claude is voluptuous without knowmg it while Ellen looks borderline anorexic.

In any event, they're best friends, with Ellen spending much of her time in Claude and her mother's cramped apartment. They have dreams of forming an all-girl rock band. (Patti Smith is a particular idol of Claude's.) Their friendship has so far survived the strains of growing up, but it's about to be put to its most severe test.

Two things happen swiftly. First, Ellen has become caught up in a romance with Mark (Cole Hauser), who's a rugged macho guy. He's possessive of Ellen and a danger to her, and she has turned to taking cocaine to cope with the pressures of the relationship. Second, Luke (Pat Briggs), a very together gay man, has just moved into Claude's building, and he and Claude strike up an acquaintance immediately. In an ugly incident at the pizza parlor where Claude works part time, Luke stands up to Mark's crude homophobia—with drastic consequences.

As this dark, slow-to-be-resolved episode casts a pall over the girls' friendship, Claude is increasingly coming to terms with the fact that her love for Ellen involves sexual attraction and that Ellen seems to be heading for bigger trouble than either of the girls can handle. The entire trajectory of "All Over Me" deals with Claude's self-discovery of her sexual orientation, her priorities and values.

Folland expresses beautifully the vulnerability, pain, confusion—and gathering strength and determination—that Claude experiences in her personal odyssey.

There's a raw slice-of-life quality to "All Over Me" typical of gritty low-budget New York movies, but the Sichels' vision, although admirably clear-eyed, is one of tenderness and compassion. Mark is a hateful guy, but the Sichels allow him to be the one who craves for warmth and affection beyond sex in his relationship with Ellen.

Miki Navazio has composed a vibrant score, and music supervisor Bill Coleman has included songs by the likes of Ani DiFranco, Helium and Cornershop. Alex Sichel is just great with her cast, which includes Wilson Cruz as a wary gay teen and Leisha Hailey (of the Murmurs) as an appealing rock singer with hot-pink hair. If Sichel's pacing is sometimes ragged, it does blend in with the film's shot-from-the-hip low-budget feel.

NEW YORK POST, 4/25/97, p. 49, Larry Worth

With all the hoopla about Ellen DeGeneres' closet-busting antics, audiences may have OD'd on the subject of lesbian love. One can only hope "All Over Me" won't get lost in the shuffle.

As directed by Alex Sichel and written by her sister, Sylvia, it's a jarring, gritty and decidedly unsentimental look at teen angst, unrequited love and the painful process of growing up.

Set in the less-then-scenic environs of Hell's Kitchen, the story centers on 15-year-old Claudia, or, as she's known to her friends, Claude. She's an aspiring rock singer who works at the local pizza parlor and happens to be head-over-heels for her best friend, Ellen.

Though not adverse to flirty kisses with Claude, Ellen's both enthralled and overpowered by a thug-like, gay-bashing boyfriend who satisfies her need to be mistreated. And so it goes, until a local's shocking murder precipitates a crisis destined to alter them all.

But director Sichel wisely puts less emphasis on the crime than the youths' varied reactions, kind of mixing "River's Edge" with "My So-Called Life." The results aren't always pleasant to observe, but they have an undeniably hypnotic effect.

In addition, Sylvia Sichel's sometimes rambling dialogue has a nice, improvisatory feel that taps into punk-flavored adolescents' mindset. Then again, some things never change, humorously exemplified as Claude's distracted mom asks: "Honey, what did I tell you about eating crap all the time?" Claude, in delicious deadpan, responds: "I can't imagine how I forgot."

As the film is less plot-oriented than character-driven, the actors' uniformly fine performances prove essential to its success. In particular, Alison Folland's Claude is a stunning mix of confusion, anger and youthful ardor, perfectly complemented by Tara Subkoff's pouty, destructive Ellen.

Meanwhile, the boys are almost as impressive, starting with Cole Hauser's frighteningly memorable delinquent. He's truly the stuff of nightmares. Pat Briggs and Wilson Cruz also offer standout support as hard-luck members of the gay community.

And that's not even mentioning the moody alternative score. Its harsh tones and incisive lyrics help establish, and maintain, the dark-and-always-getting-darker ambience.

As a result, "All Over Me" not only smells like teen spirit. It has the look, sound, feel and taste.

NEWSDAY, 4/25/97, Part II/p. B13, Jack Mathews

As most of us non-androids know from experience, going through adolescence is hell. But in case you don't remember, the Sichel sisters—director Alex, writer Sylvia—have prepared an anguished 90-minute reminder titled "All Over Me."

Set significantly in Manhattan's Hell's Kitchen, "All Over Me" is the story of best friends Claude (Alison Folland) and Ellen (Tara Subkoff), high school girls of wildly different temperaments and sensibilities whose relationship is about to be tested by their blossoming sex drives.

Ellen, a flashy, impulsively adventuresome blonde, has begun dating Mark (Cole Hauser), a neighborhood thug, while the dowdy, self-conscious Claude is resisting confusing sexual attractions to both Ellen and Lucy (Leisha Hailey), a raspberry-dyed lesbian who plays guitar in a nearby punk bar.

Whatever mutual interests sustained Claude and Ellen's friendship over the years are mostly gone. Ellen now is eager to experiment with sex and drugs, while Claude is occupied by attempts to discover who she is, and neither has any interest in the other's new directions. Yet habit, and Claude's conviction that she's in love with Ellen, keeps them together through increasingly bitter conflicts.

The problems facing the girls' relationship are handled authentically enough, and Folland's reflective performance makes it easy to empathize with Claude. But the self-destructive Ellen is a bit banal, and the major subplot, about the off-screen murder of one of Claude's friends by Mark, is handled with a clumsiness that strips it of all drama.

"All Over Me" is at its best in the moments between Claude and Ellen, when they're alone and trying to share feelings about things that are no longer of mutual concern. There's a real sense of the pain of their inevitable separation, especially from Claude.

The movie would have worked better if we didn't even meet Mark, or Lucy, and if there were no murder.

The Sichel sisters have fallen into a familiar trap of independent filmmakers on wee budgets, attempting to blend European intimacy with Hollywood melodrama, the latter in hopes of finding an audience. The result is a film that is alternately stilted and overwrought. A little like adolescence itself, but that's not a recommendation.

VILLAGE VOICE, 4/29/97, p. 71, Amy Taubin

I turned up the new Sleater-Kinney album and brooded about my crabby reaction to Alex Sichel's *All Over Me,* the latest contribution to the not exactly burgeoning genre of teen-girl coming-of-age films.

All Over Me has a heartbreak cast and an exhilarating soundtrack that runs the postpunk girl-group gamut from Patti Smith to the aforementioned Sleater-Kinney—enough to make some cinematically deprived riot girls and their putatively more mature fellow travelers embrace it wholeheartedly. I, however, could not get past Alex Sichel's anemic, flat-footed direction and sister Sylvia Sichel's awkwardly plotted script. This rule-bound filmmaking betrays its subject—a young girl breaking out, defining her sexuality and desire.

Fifteen-year-old Claude (Alison Folland) is hopelessly, abjectly in love with her best friend Ellen (Tara Subkoff). Claude, who's solidly built and wears her shoulders bunched up like the incredible hulk she imagines herself to be, worships the fragile, blond Ellen, which is exactly what Ellen, teetering on the edge of smack oblivion in her Jodie Foster-in-*Taxi Driver* rickety sandals, doesn't want or need. "You know I'm your dog" whispers Claude, having just saved Ellen from ODing by sticking her fingers down her throat and holding her while she vomits. Ellen pauses just long enough to apply lipstick to her mouth and to Claude's ("That looks weird," she says, her zonked eyes regarding the unfamiliar red slash on Claude's defiantly naked face) before rejoining her Neanderthal boyfriend, the local pusher and gay basher.

The most knowing thing about *All Over Me* is that it makes the breakdown of Claude and Ellen's friendship turn not so much on Claude being gay and Ellen being straight as it does on Claude's desire for love and Ellen's need for abuse. "Claude's my knight in shining armor," says Ellen, but the harder Claude tries to rescue her, the more desperately she runs away.

Exceptionally well-cast, *All Over Me* is best when it gives the actors the time and freedom to play together. Cole Hauser is properly dull-witted and nasty-tempered as Ellen's menacing boyfriend, and Wilson Cruz as Claude's gay high school chum and Pat Briggs as a sightly older gay rocker are just as fine. In a misguided attempt to jack up the action, the rocker is stabbed to death by Ellen's boyfriend—but not before he's had a chance to send Claude to the club where she finds both music to set loose her soul and fresh, true-hearted love with a fuschia-haired guitar player played by tough and spritely Leisha Hailey.

Tara Subkoff makes Ellen's strung-out hysteria so believable it's easy to overlook what a complicated performance she's giving. But crucial as Subkoff is, *All Over Me* is Folland's film; her work takes an otherwise skimpy indie to another level. Folland has a slightly hesitant, husky voice reminiscent of Linda Manz and a wide-boned, soft-featured face made to map mixed emotions. Her mouth curls back as if to mock its own hunger; her gaze is simultaneously guarded and searching. Her Claude is of a piece with the vulnerable teenager she played in Gus Van Sant's *To Die For*—but here she has more room to stretch and grow.

Although not quite enough. About halfway through *All Over Me,* Claude goes home with the lesbian guitar player who's obviously attracted to her. Claude's attracted, too, but the more turned on she gets the more she feels she's betraying her devotion to Ellen. Putting Patti Smit's "Pissing in the River" on the the stereo and muttering about "dangerous music" she begins to dance by her herself. And as she dances, she falls apart. It's the kind of naked expression—of pain, desire, and confusion—that one almost never sees onscreen (Folland is in Gena Rowlands territory here). And what does Sichel do with this amazing gift? Instead of just letting the scene roll, she chops it into pieces, intercutting it with a scene of Ellen trying to get her boyfriend to fuck her on Claude's bed (which, on its own, would have been pretty strong as well). Why would a director make such a pointless juxtaposition, diminishing both her actresses in the process? Because she's afraid of violating Hollywood standards of editing and pace? Because she's scared of emotional display? I have no idea, but the sequence made me want to run for the exit.

Lacking an expressive visual style, *All Over Me* relies on cliché images (the circular pans around Claude's room; the shot of Ellen, dressed in black, glimpsed through the metal bars of the local playground). The film has so little authentic sense of place that its Hell's Kitchen settings could have passed for Toronto. As filmmakers, the Sichel sisters have an eye for casting—and an ear for music—and not much else.

Also reviewed in:
NEW YORK TIMES, 4/25/97, p. C19, Janet Maslin
VARIETY, 7/29-8/4/96, p. 59, Emanuel Levy

AMERICAN WEREWOLF IN PARIS, AN

A Hollywood Pictures release in association with Cometstone Pictures and J&M Entertainment of a Richard Claus production. *Executive Producer:* Anthony Waller. *Producer:* Richard Claus. *Director:* Anthony Waller. *Screenplay:* Tim Burns, Tom Stern, and Anthony Waller. *Based on characters created by:* John Landis. *Director of Photography:* Egon Werdin. *Editor:* Peter R. Adam. *Music:* Wilbert Hirsch. *Sound:* Roberto van Eyden and (music) Frank Reinke. *Sound Editor:* Andreas Musolff. *Casting:* Gail Levin. *Production Designer:* Matthias Kammermeier. *Animation Director:* James Satoru Straus. *Art Director:* Hucky Hornberger. *Set Decorator:* Andrea Schlimper. *Set Dresser:* Manu Demoulling. *Special Effects:* Harald Ruediger. *Visual

Effects: John Grower and Bruce Walters. *Costumes:* Maria Schicker. *Make-up:* Katja Reinert. *Stunt Coordinator:* Stuart St. Paul. *Running time:* 100 minutes. *MPAA Rating:* R.

CAST: Tom Everett Scott (Andy); Julie Delpy (Serafine); Vince Vieluf (Brad); Phil Buckman (Chris); Julie Bowen (Amy); Pierre Cosso (Claude); Thierry Lhermitte (Dr. Pigot); Tom Novembre (Inspector Leduc); Maria Machado (Chief Bonnet); Ben Salem Bouabdallah (Detective Ben Bou); Serge Basso (Officer with Flashlight); Charles Maquignon (Bouncer); Jochen Schneider (First Lycanthrope); Alan McKenna (Second Lycanthrope); Herve Sogne (Third Lycanthrope); Edgar Kohn (Fourth Lycanthrope); Jean-Claude Deret (Professor Martin); Isabelle Costantini (Serafine's Mother); Davis Freeman (Nightclub Visitor); Christian Magnani (Bruno); Chris Bearne (Surgeon); Pierre Bodry (Waiter on Train); Peter Riemens (Waiter in Restaurant); Emile Cappachione (Bodybuilder); Serge Hugel (French Car Driver); John Waller (British Car Driver); Anthony Waller (Metro Driver).

LOS ANGELES TIMES, 12/24/97, Calendar/p. 8, Kevin Thomas

[The following review by Kevin Thomas appeared in a slightly different form in NEWSDAY, 12/24/97, Part II/p. B11.]

"An American Werewolf in Paris" is a painfully anemic variation on John Landis' 1981 winner, "An American Werewolf in London." While the original had both wit and poignancy—and an affectionate and knowing tip-of-the-hat to werewolf movies past—this slapdash, silly new edition is so cut-rate it has Luxembourg and Amsterdam standing in for the City of Light. Only the least discriminating segment of the "Scream 2" audience need bother.

Not even Julie Delpy, exquisite and persuasive as she is, can make the difference. Delpy's Serafine is about to jump off the Eiffel Tower when Tom Everett Scott's nice guy Andy, on a European vacation with his two likable pals, Brad (Vince Vieluf) and Chris (Phil Buckman), steps in to save her. The attraction between Serafine and the tall, boyishly handsome Andy is instant, but Serafine tries to put him off until the inevitable moment she speaks that literally deathless line, "There's something I must tell you ..."

It seems that Serafine and her scientist stepfather (Thierry Lhermitte) have devoted themselves to finding a cure for her, but her surly ex-boyfriend Claude (Pierre Cosso) has injected himself with her blood and in turn infected a group of like-minded right-wing xenophobes so that they can cleanse Paris of what they regard as human scum—by feeding upon them. This plot plays itself out as ludicrously as it sounds, and the overly parochial political angle gets lost amid horror picture clichés.

The well-established Delpy will doubtless survive this debacle, and hopefully so will Scott, Vieluf and Buckman, who are capable, good-looking young actors. "An American Werewolf in Paris" is no fun at all. Not even the special effects are special.

NEW YORK POST, 12/24/97, p. 34, Michael Medved

Until now, you may have thought the worst things about the French were their mad passions for Jerry Lewis and stinky cigarettes. But "An American Werewolf in Paris" provides a new basis for Francophobia. The movie presents an army of exceptionally ugly and vicious werewolves on the prowl in Paris, indulging a special taste for hip, young Americans.

Three such tourists conveniently turn up during college vacation, and one of them (Tom Everett Scott) heroically rescues a beautiful, moody, mysterious French girl (Julie Delpy) from suicide—not knowing she's an unwilling part of the werewolf pack.

As their relationship develops, they bond as good werewolves who battle bad werewolves and befuddled Paris cops (including popular French star Thierry Lhermitte), hoping all the while to find an escape from their moon-driven curse.

Intended as a follow-up to the much-admired 1981 John Landis film "An American Werewolf in London," this project is slicker, sillier and far less scary than the original. We see much more of the hairy, ravenous, awesomely muscled beasts and they are, in repose, impressively imaginative creations—even though their movements remain mechanical, stilted and jerky.

Also jerky is the central character, with Scott displaying none of the edge or intelligence he showed in "That Thing You Do."

Julie Delpy ("Before Sunrise," "Europa Europa") is still one of the most radiant, appealing screen presences on either side of the Atlantic, but she needs some intrepid soul to rescue her from fare such as this.

Director/co-writer Anthony Waller (who previously created the stylish Moscow-based thriller "Mute Witness") provides one knockout sequence on the Eiffel Tower to begin his story, and a similarly socko scene at the Statue of Liberty to end it, but in between he goes for gross-out laughs (including bad condom jokes) rather than psychological chills.

A yellowish, glowing version of "Werewolf Vision" provides an intriguingly altered point of view for his transformed beasts, but to normal eyes this picture (which spends far too much time in underground tunnels) will seem drab and unfocused.

SIGHT AND SOUND, 12/97, p. 37, Kim Newman

In Europe on a "daredevil tour", young American Andy ascends the Eiffel Tower one night with his friends Chris and Brad. Just before Andy makes a bungee jump from the top, a young woman named Sérafine attempts suicide from the same spot. Andy jumps after her and saves her life. Later, Andy tracks Sérafine down and badgers her into going on a date with him, but she warns him to stay away.

Claude, a mysterious friend of Waller offers the three Americans free tickets to a club event. They go to the club. Then Chris returns to Sérafine's house looking for her. When he tells her the others are at the club, she gets him to free her from a cage she's locked inside of. At the club, Claude and his henchmen transform into werewolves, slaughtering the guests. Brad is killed but Sérafine turns up in wolf-form to rescue Andy. Sérafine tells Andy, whom she thinks she has bitten, he is now a werewolf. Andy leaves in disbelief but transforms that night and kills Amy, an American girl on holiday.

The spirits of Brad and Amy explain to Andy that they will walk the earth until the werewolves who killed them are destroyed. Andy can only cure himself by eating the heart of the werewolf who first bit him. Sérafine's late scientist stepfather developed a serum which had the unforeseen effect of enabling werewolves to transform without the moon being full. Claude's gang steal samples of the serum and stage a rave at which they plan to slaughter a crowd of American tourists. Andy and Sérafine intervene, the latter transforming herself to fight the evil werewolves. Accidentally shot by Andy, Sérafine begs Andy to save himself by eating her heart, but it transpires that it was Claude, not she, who first bit Andy. During a fight on the Métro, Andy bests Claude and eats his heart, curing himself. Later, Andy and Sérafine get married while bungee-jumping from the Statue of Liberty.

In 1981, *An American Werewolf in London* and *The Howling* both took advantage of new special-effects technology. Using a canny mixture of horror, sly comedy and genuine emotional content, each revived the apparently played-out werewolf movie sub-genre. It's taken 16 years for a sequel to John Landis' hit to be made, but in the intervening years Joe Dante's *The Howling* has spawned six follow-ups. Anthony Waller (whose debut *Mute Witness* was also about horrors afflicting Americans abroad) reuses some of the new 'rules' of lycanthropy Landis laid down. But some of *An American Werewolf in Paris'* plot points—such as the gang of racist, skinhead lycanthropes, the serum that duplicates the effects of the full moon and the legless werewolf invalid penned in the cellar—would fit more comfortably into the cheapskate, anything-goes tone of *The Marsupials: The Howling Three* or *The Howling VI: The Freaks.*

The usual quandary of sequelmakers is the need to deliver the same material with surprises. Here, the problem is exacerbated by Waller's indecision over how much of Landis' plot and approach to reuse. It's never clearly stated by the script, but it is implied that Sérafine is the daughter of Jenny Agutter's nurse and the hero of *Werewolf in London*. But it's *Werewolf in Paris'* Andy who goes through most of the suffering David Naughton's character experienced the first time round. Waller's movie seems more rip-off than sequel. For example, he ditches the first film's distinctive use of evocative pop songs (all of which had "moon" in the title) in favour of an album's worth of eminently forgettable Eurorock.

The early stages of the film manage Landis' lightness of tone, though the amiable leads have slightly duller material to work with (one sustained gag about condoms excluded). Landis' subtle observations about British hospitality are paralleled by a parade of French stereotypes (pipe-smoking policemen, snooty waiters, abusive club bouncers, unattainable blondes). The plot tours such archetypal locations as the Eiffel Tower, Notre-Dame, Jim Morrison's grave (suspiciously lacking in graffiti), and the sewers made famous by *Les Misérables*. However, the fact that the movie was mostly filmed in Luxembourg prevents it from making its city as much a character as London was in the first film. As in *Mute Witness*, Waller relishes gothic locales. He opens with close-ups of storm-washed gargoyles and a werewolf attack, intercut with a choral concert. But the running-around-tunnels of the rest of the film soon wears thin.

The centrality of Sérafine and Andy eclipses the film's most interesting character, Pierre Cosso's villainous Claude. A potential highlight comes when Claude delivers an ironic speech about how much he loves Americans before slaughtering a batch of them on the Fourth of July. Yet the scene is fumbled completely by cutaways to other business, curbing a rare moment where hilarity and horror genuinely mingle. The second half of the film is so busy that one suspects some tampering to beef it up, because several plot threads get dropped. The ending leaves the ghosts of Amy and Sérafine's mother literally hanging around in limbo. And the key emotional scene, in which Sérafine begs Andy to kill her and eat her heart, is rushed through too swiftly to have the impact it needs.

In retrospect, the miracle of the first film was that it managed to work in sweetness and shivers between the amazing special effects. *Werewolf in Paris* tries for this mixture again, with variable results, but the real arena of competition between the two movies is, of course, in the monsters. Since 1981, there has been a drift away from physical effects towards computer-generated opticals, and this is the first werewolf movie to make extensive use of CGI. These beasts are impressively fearsome, though slightly more simian than lupine. Waller stages one masterly coup as Andy transforms while submerged in a pool and explodes out of the water to shake himself dry. However, like a lot of CGI creatures, the werewolves have little individuality, so it becomes a problem figuring out who exactly has bitten Andy. More problematically, in the battles between good-guy and bad-guy werewolves, it's impossible to know whether our side is winning or not.

VILLAGE VOICE, 12/30/97, p. 72, Gary Dauphin

The only surprising thing about an *American Werewolf in Paris*'s stupid (but occasionally funny) comedy shtick and its lightweight (but intermittently effective) horror moves is that they don't quite suck as badly as you'd think. Not so much a sequel as a cheesier, more nasal copy of John Landis's 1981 original, *Werewolf* chugs into the multiplexes like a kid trying to keep up with an older, meaner sibling: it scores points for effort among potential victims in the audience, but we all know what it really wants is screams.

Werewolf moves its predecessor's basic plotline across the English Channel, plopping three American tourists in Paris so that one of them can get the bad-luck bite and chew on friend and frog alike. Andy (Tom Everett Scott) meets the lycanthropic and suicidal Serafine (Julie Delpy) at the Eiffel Tower (Andy saves her life via a digital bungee jump in *Werewolf*'s best effects sequence). Bitten first just by the love bug, he follows her into a Parisian postpunk werewolf underground and soon gets the real, toothy thing. Andy becomes a howling creature of the damned and predictable mayhem ensues, but whereas the London branch of the franchise drew its considerable energies by slowly backing its hero into a corner, this one is more concerned with looking for a convenient out for Andy, Serafine, and their slightly gag-producing romance.

Director Anthony Waller—who debuted with the fine, low-tech thriller *Mute Witness*—invests *American Werewolf in Paris* with some charm, and Scott's Andy is just right as a pathetic, backpacking sap. But the movie does lack punch, especially on the all-important effects tip. 1997's computer-generated wolfen are nowhere near as horrific as the hairy latex animatronic work F/X-meister Rick Baker created for the original. Digital might work for spaceships, but movie gore is best done the old-fashioned way.

Also reviewed in:
NEW YORK TIMES, 12/27/97, p. E3, Stephen Holden

VARIETY, 11/3-9/97, p. 99, Derek Elley
WASHINGTON POST, 12/25/97, p. C20, Stephen Hunter
WASHINGTON POST, 12/26/97, Weekend/p. 36, Steven Hunter

AMISTAD

A DreamWorks Pictures release in association with HBO Pictures. *Executive Producer:* Walter Parkes and Laurie MacDonald. *Producer:* Steven Spielberg, Debbie Allen, and Colin Wilson. *Director:* Steven Spielberg. *Screenplay:* David Franzoni. *Director of Photography:* Janusz Kaminski. *Editor:* Michael Kahn. *Music:* John Williams. *Music Editor:* Kenneth Wannberg. *Sound:* Ronald Judkins and (music) Shawn Murphy. *Sound Editor:* Charles L. Campbell and Louis L. Edemann. *Casting:* Victoria Thomas. *Production Designer:* Rick Carter. *Art Director:* Chris Burian-Mohr, Jim Teegarden, and Tony Fanning. *Set Designer:* Patty Kalwon, Susan Wexler, Nancy Deren, George Lee, Pamela Klamer, and Easton Michael Smith. *Set Decorator:* Rosemary Brandenburg. *Set Dresser:* Kristin Frances Jones. *Special Effects:* Tom Ryba. *Costumes:* Ruth E. Carter. *Make-up:* Ve Neill. *Make-up (Morgan Freeman):* Mike Hancock. *Stunt Coordinator:* M. James Arnett. *Running time:* 150 minutes. *MPAA Rating:* R.

CAST: Morgan Freeman (Theodore Joadson); Nigel Hawthorne (Martin Van Buren); Anthony Hopkins (John Quincy Adams); Djimon Hounsou (Cinque); Matthew McConaughey (Roger Baldwin); David Paymer (Secretary Forsyth); Pete Postlethwaite (Holabird); Stellan Skarsgård (Tappan); Razaaq Adoti (Yamba); Abu Bakaar Fofanah (Fala); Anna Paquin (Queen Isabella); Tomas Milian (Calderon); Chiwetel Ejiofor (Ensign Covey); Derrick N. Ahsong (Buakei); Geno Silva (Ruiz); John Oritz (Montes); Ralph Brown (Lieutenant Gedney); Darren Burrows (Lieutenant Meade); Allan Rich (Judge Juttson); Paul Guilfoyle (Attorney); Peter Firth (Captain Fitzgerald); Xander Berkeley (Hammond); Jeremy Northam (Judge Coglin); Arliss Howard (John C. Calhoun); Willie Amakye (Folowa); Luc Assogba (Gbatui); Mariah Campbell (Masery); Stephen Conteh (Morlai); Monguehy Fanzy (Fabanna); Jimmy Fotso (Kwong); Adekunle Ilori (Kahei); Sheriff Kargbo (Almamy); Saye Lah (Kessebe); Sylvestre Massaquoi (Santiglie); Samson Odede (Kpona); Chike Okpala (Sorie); Willie Onafesso (Jina); Samuel Pieh (Suuleh); Lansana Sawi (Morlu); Abu Sidique (Tsukama); El Hadj Malik Sow (Golabu); Lamine Thiam (Mahmud); Austin Pendleton (Professor Gibbs); Daniel Von Bargen (Warden Pendelton); Rusty Schwimmer (Mrs. Pendelton); Pedro Armendariz (General Espatero); Frank T. Wells (Crier); Michael Massee (Prison Guard); Roy Cooper (Pickney); Jake Weber (Mr. Wright); Victor Rivers (Captain Ferrar); Joseph Kosseh (Birmaja); Steve Passewe (Cinque's In-Law); Sherly Acosta Williams (Cinque's Wife); Matt Sarles (Young Aide); George Gerdes (Marshal); Jerry Molen (Magistrate); Kevin J. O'Connor (Missionary); Robert Walsh (Guardsman); Sean McGuirk (Courier); Tony Owen (Farmer); William Young (Businessman); Michael Riley (British Officer); Leon Singer (Don Pablo); Castulo Guerra (Spanish Priest); Harry Groener (Tecora Captain); Hawthorne James (Creole Cook); Ingrid Walters (Woman Overboard with Baby); Harry A. Blackmun (Associate Justice Joseph Story); Curtis Shields (Bassie); Charles Udoma (Kessebe); Tony Onafesso (Baa); Clarence Mobley (Kenei); Edward Appiah (Followolo); Paul Mwakutuya (Sessi); Samuel Orekhio (Fawni); Ransford Thomas (Alkali); Issac Mayanja (Sampa); Roosevelt Flenoury (Njaooni); Carlos Spivey (Chike); Andrew W. Josiah (Tamba); Peter Mansaray (Kapr); Brian Macon (Yauai); Denver Dowridge (Kpau); Rory Burton (Vakina); Omo Lara Tosin (Kula); Juliette Darko (Teme); Charlean Isata Bangalie (Margru); M.S. Kaleiwo (Kaleiwo).

CHRISTIAN SCIENCE MONITOR, 12/12/97, p. 12, David Sterritt

Steven Spielberg is most acclaimed for fantasy-adventures like the "Jurassic Park" and "Indiana Jones" movies, which rank among the most profitable pictures ever made.

But three years ago his career took an unexpected turn with "Schindler's List," where he tackled a dark and difficult subject—Nazi genocide—with enough power and insight to establish his long-awaited credentials as a genuinely mature filmmaker.

"Amistad" his first production for the DreamWorks studio and one that has been surrounded by copyright controversy, again tries to dramatize a daunting historical event in compelling mass-audience terms. This time the results are a lot less impressive.

One episode, showing the Holocaust-like suffering of Africans on a slave ship, gains the massive emotional force its subject deserves. Other scenes suffer from Spielberg's habit of squeezing rich material into Hollywood formulas. Many are stilted, simplistic, and woodenly performed.

The tale begins with a violent uprising of captive West Africans against the Spanish slave-traders who are shipping them into bondage. Adrift at sea, they are tricked into navigating toward the American coast, where they are captured and imprisoned for their mutiny.

This raises complicated questions about how US law should treat the refugees. Are they mere possessions? Or full-fledged humans with a right to freedom? Or slaves-in-the-making whose destiny depends on whose control they happen to fall under?

While the group languishes in a Connecticut jail, some freedom-minded Americans—a black abolitionist, a white lawyer—decide to champion their cause. But their hard-won victory is reversed for political reasons, leading to a Supreme Court battle, in which former President John Quincy Adams fights for their liberty. Against him is Martin Van Buren, the current president, who wants to woo Southern voters and placate the Spanish queen.

This is gripping material, hardly needing cinematic gimmicks to boost its power. Spielberg delves into his bag of tricks anyway, chopping the story into heavily edited sequences that leap from shot to shot as frenetically as a hard-sell TV commercial. Some images are stunning to look at, but they rarely stay around long enough to savor. The overall pace leaves little time to think about the story, much less absorb its historical subtleties and learn the lessons they might teach.

David Franzoni's screenplay is also manipulative, turning inherently dramatic speeches and con-versations into ponderous word-fests delivered by gifted actors (Anthony Hopkins, Morgan Free-man) with little conviction.

As if to liven things up, one courtroom debate is interrupted when the main African character breaks into a plaintive chant accompanied by lachrymose music on the soundtrack—for no reason except Spielberg's apparent worry that the legal stuff might get boring, so he'd better kick in some sentimentality for good measure.

Also irksome is the decision to allow just one African character, a man named Cinque, to emerge as a fully rounded individual; the rest are treated as an undifferentiated group. "Schindler's List" was criticized for similar treatment of its Jewish characters.

The white "Amistad" characters don't fare much better. In one plot twist, for instance, a young judge has the courage to make a very unexpected ruling, but this is depicted as an arbitrary surprise, with no hint of the inner struggle—psychological, moral, even spiritual—that must have led up to it.

In its publicity, DreamWorks claims that Spielberg and cinematographer Janusz Kaminski prepared by studying the paintings of Francisco Goya, which were "characterized by their un-romanticized realism." This is a flat-out misrepresentation of "Amistad," which is drenched so stiflingly in romanticized mistiness that "realism" is one of the last words an honest account would choose to describe it.

Despite its many shortcomings, "Amistad" has the energy and earnestness of most Spielberg pictures, and these qualities—along with the clear importance of its subject matter—might turn it into a middling success, if not an outright hit. This makes it all the more regrettable that the filmmakers didn't probe their potentially riveting material more deeply and truly.

LOS ANGELES TIMES, 12/10/97, Calendar/p. 1, Kenneth Turan

While it's tempting but unfair to see him as Dr. Jekyll and Mr. Hyde, Steven Spielberg does have a split in his filmmaking personality. The work of America's most successful director has in recent years alternated between the extremes of noble, serious films like "Schindler's List" and feeble no-brainers like "The Lost World: Jurassic Park" with no time left for anything in between.

Leaving aside the theoretical question of whether this drastic division, the wholesale avoidance of what might be called intelligent entertainment, is a welcome thing in such a capable filmmaker, the well-intentioned "Amistad"—the story of the momentous aftermath of a 1839 shipboard rebellion of 53 African slaves—shows the practical dangers of the split.

For though it's an engrossing piece of work that once again displays the director's impressive mastery of mainstream filmmaking, "Amistad" also shows that Spielberg's system is not working. There's been leakage from the no-brainers to the quality stuff and, in a cinematic version of Gresham's law, bad habits picked up in the mindless movies are driving out better ones. This has kept "Amistad" from being the film it might have been, the film its director intended.

"Amistad" is, of course, laden with virtues. It takes on a difficult and important story and largely tells it well, especially in visual terms. Few directors have Spielberg's fine pictorial sense, his understanding of the narrative power of cinematic storytelling. Many of "Amistad's" most lasting moments, like the raggedy slaver silently passing an elegant party listening to shipboard chamber music, do without any kind of dialogue at all, and the feeling occurs more than once that the silent film era would have suited this director's talents superbly.

The scene that opens "Amistad" shows how it's done. Starting with a tight close-up of an eye alive in darkness, Spielberg, cinematographer Janusz Kaminski and editor Michael Kahn create a compelling montage of the rebellion on board La Amistad off the coast of Cuba that leaves the Africans and their leader, Cinque (Djimon Hounsou), in charge of their destinies. Desperate to sail back to their homeland but tricked by the Spaniards they trusted to navigate the ship, the Africans ended up in American coastal waters. They're captured and taken to New Haven for a trial to determine whether they are to be considered as property or free men.

Though it's shown in flashback, "Amistad's" strongest scene, a depiction of the tortures of the Middle Passage—the journey newly sold slaves made from Africa to the Caribbean—also plays without dialogue. Never have those horrors been treated so graphically in a major Hollywood film, and the influence on Spielberg's style of the "Schindler's List" experience (also shot by Kaminski) is unmistakable.

In the same way, the Africans, who don't learn English until late in the picture, come off much better in the film than Americans of either color. Speaking subtitled Mende, the language of the region (now Sierra Leone) from which they were kidnapped into slavery, they are portrayed, even during their worst, most confused moments, as shrewder, more alive than most of the Americans they come in contact with.

This is especially true for the character of Cinque, the Africans' reluctant leader. Though Benin native Hounsou, who modeled for Herb Ritts before starting an acting career, does not have extensive training or experience, his English dialogue is minimal and his strong presence while speaking Mende projects a remarkable dignity and bearing that is exactly what the part calls for.

There are, however, Americans in "Amistad," and overall they come off as actors playing dress-up but not fooling anyone. This is where the habits of the "Jurassic Park" films, so pathetic in terms of character they should have been embarrassing but apparently weren't, have rubbed off on Spielberg. Rusty with people and unaware of how flat his English dialogue is playing, he's allowed many of his protagonists and situations to come across as unnecessarily broad and buffoonish. The Steven Spielberg who oversaw Robert Shaw and Richard Dreyfuss in "Jaws" has apparently left the building.

"Amistad's" screenplay is credited to David Franzoni (HBO's "Citizen Cohn"), but it is known that Steven Zaillian, an Oscar winner for "Schindler's List," did considerable rewriting (though unrealistic Writers Guild rules did not permit his name on the screen). While any speculation as to who did what is pure guesswork, there are moments, especially in the closing speeches of John Quincy Adams, that Zaillian's welcome touch is felt.

As played by Anthony Hopkins, Adams, son of Founding Father John Adams, himself a former president and currently the grand old man of the Senate, is a treat to behold, easily the best of "Amistad's" English speakers. Though his acting here is the kind of showy impersonation that exists largely on the surface, watching this masterful performer grumbling his way through the role of a cranky old galoot creates a surface that is satisfyingly rich and amusing.

Adams gets involved because abolitionists Theodore Joadson and Lewis Tappan (Morgan Freeman and Stellan Skarsgard, both underutilized) want to turn the trial of the imprisoned Africans into a media event that would publicize the horrors of slavery.

The former president initially turns down the offer to lead the defense because of his age: He's 73 and hasn't argued a case in court for three decades. But, sounding like a creative studio executive, he offers some sage advice: "Find out who they are, find out their story."

If Hopkins is the strongest of the English-speaking actors, Matthew McConaughey is at the weak end. He plays Roger Baldwin, the hustling attorney who does take the case, treating it at first like a simple matter of property and gradually coming to embrace the Africans' humanity. (The real Baldwin was a more impressive and committed attorney who ended up governor of Connecticut.) Presumably hired for his star power, McConaughey is unimpressive in his sparse, Horace Greeley-type beard, and it's hard not to agree with the Africans when they compare him to the dung scrapers they knew back home.

Most of the film involves the process by which the captives, aided by a bilingual translator, find their voices and get their stories told, and how Adams, in part angered by the manipulations of President Martin Van Buren (Nigel Hawthorne), agrees to plead the Africans' case when it goes before a slave-owning Supreme Court.

It's a tribute to Spielberg's ability and serious intentions that "Amistad" is laced with memorable moments, but while they are the best Hollywood has to offer, they are pure Hollywood nevertheless. What saved "Schindler's List" from this self-conscious nobility was the ambiguity of Oskar Schindler's personality and Spielberg's willingness to treat incendiary material coolly. The lesson he seemed to have learned there, that the strongest stories call for the greatest restraint, is one he has at least partially forgotten here.

NEW YORK, 12/15/97, p. 63, David Denby

So much of the violence in movies is fashioned as cynical entertainment that violence intended seriously—violence that acquaints us with the worst people have endured—seems almost indecently demanding. Stunned, we can hardly believe our jaded eyes. Steven Spielberg has made a stiff but powerful film, *Amistad*, about an actual revolt aboard a slave ship in 1839 and the constitutional struggle that followed in its wake. The best thing in the movie is very violent indeed, though it's not the revolt itself, which appears right at the beginning of *Amistad*.

The Africans rise up after they've already been transported to the New World. They've come across the Atlantic (exactly how, we don't know at first). They've been sold in Cuba and transferred to a Spanish ship, the *Amistad*. At night, in a storm, Cinque (Djimon Hounsou), their informal leader, breaks his shackles and liberates the others. The Africans slaughter most of the crew, ordering the two Spanish survivors to take them back to Africa. But the Spaniards trick them and steer the *Amistad* north, and the ship is finally intercepted off the coast of Connecticut by the American Navy. Put on trial for murder and piracy, the Africans are defended by abolitionists, who hire a callow real-estate lawyer, Roger Baldwin (Matthew McConaughey), to try the case. The question arises: Were they born as slaves—on a plantation, say, in the West Indies—or as free men in Africa? If they were born free men, they were exercising their right, as far as a northern court is concerned, to overthrow illegal imprisonment. Silent until then, Cinque finally speaks (through a translator) and recounts the entire tale: The Africans, mostly from the Mende tribe, were kidnapped by rival tribesmen, kept in a slave fortress off the coast of Sierra Leone, and then taken across the ocean in an illegal Portuguese slaver, the *Tecora*.

As Cinque speaks, we see it at last—the voyage, the excruciating transit in the cargo hold known in accounts of the slave trade as "the middle passage." Spielberg stages these scenes with a power that perhaps he alone in film history is capable of. He works in brief flashes of terrifying physical action that burst the frame the way a flood bursts wooden dikes. Herded naked onboard the *Tecora*, the men and women are shackled stomach-down, side by side. Some are whipped, some are fed a revolting lumpy oatmeal, no more than a handful—the doling-out of punishments or rewards seems arbitrary. And the details are unnerving: As the Portuguese crew beats a man to death, a woman, calmly, almost smiling, with a baby in her arms, slips over the side and into the sea. Later, a whole group of men and women, naked and screaming and chained to heavy rocks, are pulled down an incline at the ship's edge and into the water. It seems the Portuguese couldn't feed everyone and decided to dump part of their cargo. As we watch, part of our dismay comes from having seen these men and women in a relative state of tranquillity in a Connecticut courtroom. Now we know that they may suffer all this again if they lose their case.

The high-contrast color cinematography (by Janusz Kaminski, who also did *Schindler's List)* causes the faces to glow in a supernal darkness. Kaminski has gone deep into the tonalities of black and near-black, as in a painting by Ad Reinhardt. We can't always see every comer of the ship's cargo hold, but we're enlisted in the panic of people, born free, who have no way of comprehending what is happening to them. The press notes say that the actors playing the Africans—recruited from West Africa, England, and the United States—wept on the set, and I believe it, for the middle-passage scenes are marked not just by degradation and suffering but by a purely unnecessary cruelty (a spectacle that links *Amistad* to *Schindler's List*). There are, I suppose, less sensational ways of doing this material: A director might have emphasized the maddening duration of the voyage, hopelessness gathering like a disease; or the relations among the African men and women. But Spielberg's way is astonishing, and the shock for us lies both in the images themselves and in the realization that we have never really *seen* this primal American story. By contrast, the comparable passages in *Roots* are no more than genteel.

There are other superb things in *Amistad*—the first meetings of black and white people, for instance. Spielberg, producer Debbie Allen (who initiated the project), and screenwriter David Franzoni have worked hard to create the sheer strangeness of it—the hubbub of voices, the mutual incomprehension (the movie uses subtitles for the Mende dialogue), as well as the sense of violation, the brutal comedy of alien dispositions butting against one another. In Cuba, the shackled black men, about to be sold, recoil in rage as Spaniards lather them with soap in order to clean them up and make them glow. In Connecticut, gazing at the pious abolitionists holding their little Bibles, these same Africans remark that their white benefactors look unhappy and sick—for why are they down on their knees? It is a good joke on the creepier side of abolitionist fervor.

Such scenes are charged by a furious or beatific sense of the elemental forces in life. The rest of the movie, however, is no more than intelligent and morally alert and I say that with both regret and full recognition of how rare these virtues are in our cinema. *Amistad* is an inspirational story that mixes courtroom drama and theatricalized historical instruction. The filmmakers' point of view is that the *Amistad* incident was a central way station between the imperfectly executed Declaration of Independence (which insisted that "all men are created equal") and the inevitable Civil War. Many of the players are conscious of the significance of the moment. The opportunistic, cunning President Martin Van Buren (Nigel Hawthorne), afraid of losing the South in the coming election, wants the Africans returned as property to Queen Isabella of Spain. The abolitionists, both white (Stellan Skarsgard) and black (Morgan Freeman), see the *Amistad* affair as Armageddon in the New World—the trial of Christian faith, of humanity's right to be saved.

Only the real-estate lawyer seems unaware of history marching on, and this lack of consciousness feels right. For him, it's initially a property matter. But as Baldwin learns by degrees that his view is inadequate, Matthew McConaughey fusses and fumbles—he's not an actor but a man using his mouth, beard, and fingers to show us that he's acting—and the stages of Baldwin's enlightenment, ending in a fervent handshake with Cinque, are mostly banal. There are other inspirational moments that some may find exciting—Cinque, having mastered a little English, shouting in the courtroom "Give us free! Give us free!"—but I nearly choked on the lump in my throat. (Opera, I think, should always be performed on an opera stage.) And there's much of the familiar sawing back and forth of courtroom drama, with its lawyers' ploys and speeches and grandstanding moments. I realize that legal procedure is lodged like a canker in the American soul, even in the drama of slavery, but as a movie subject, courtroom drama has worn us out.

McConaughey, draped in thick coats as well as a wispy beard, hides his good looks. Djimon Hounsou flaunts his. A beautiful and powerful man with thick muscles in his back, neck, and arms, Hounsou was born in West Africa but moved to Paris when he was 13. He has appeared in music videos and worked (as a model, I assume) for designer Thierry Mugler. He knows how to present himself to the camera, and in *Amistad* there are moments when Hounsou looks like an idealized model of black pride. He is posed in sullen reserve, or angrily, against fire, or in lightning flashes, his face a sculpted mask. He's monumentalized to an almost intolerable degree as an exemplar of his race (by contrast, Spielberg chose Ben Kingsley to represent the Jews in *Schindler's List*).

Just when *Amistad* is about to perish from nobility, Anthony Hopkins, as John Quincy Adams, saves the day. The sixth president of the United States (from 1825 to 1828), and still at it, in the House of Representatives, at the age of 74, Adams, at first, doesn't want to be bothered by the

Amistad affair. He is almost rude to the abolitionists who come to see him in Washington; he turns his back to them, plucking at little plants in the Capitol gardens. Setting the character, Hopkins is very funny: seemingly preoccupied, almost doddering, extremely vain, with a suggestion that he is offended by the abolitionists' insistent virtue. Those of us who have seen a lot of movies know that JQA is just bored, or possibly faking—that the hero will rise from his slumber. The voice is reedy, flat, New Englandish, with an added Hopkins specialty, that loving, drawn-out caress of the final syllable of a sentence. When the Africans win their Connecticut case, Van Buren appeals to the Supreme Court to have it overturned, and Adams, outraged, pulls himself together and joins the battle. His summation to the Supreme Court is a finely judged, exquisitely modulated piece of American rhetoric. It comes to an unexpected climax with the sudden, vicious ripping of a piece of paper—a symbolic version of the Declaration of Independence. For that is what will happen to that particular document, Adams says, if the Africans are ruled the property of Queen Isabella. And by extension, that is what will happen if slavery is never abolished.

NEW YORK POST, 10/10/97, p. 49, Michael Medved

Steven Spielberg's "Amistad" is actually two films, separate but unequal.

When focusing on its African heroes, the movie proves powerful, lyrical, affecting and effective.

More frequently, however, the picture highlights its white American characters, and these sequences suggest a gaggle of goofy, overacting kids playing dress-up in the attic with grandpa's silly old clothes.

Hokey historical tableaux ultimately smother the undeniably brilliant elements with slack, portentous and miscast melodrama, distorting essential aspects of the dramatic incident that inspired the project.

In 1839, 53 Africans escaped their chains on board the Spanish slave ship Amistad, killed most of the crew and tried forcing the two survivors to sail them back home from the Caribbean.

Eventually captured by the U.S. Navy, the rebellions slaves and their charismatic leader, Cinque, went through a series of complicated legal proceedings as their fate became a *cause celebre* for the anti-slavery movement.

Former President John Quincy Adams ultimately pleaded their case for freedom before the U.S. Supreme Court.

In telling this important tale, Spielberg's greatest asset is Djimon Hounsou, a native of the African nation Benin and a former fashion model who brings leonine grace, muscular self-assurance and spectacular emotional range to the role of the legendary Cinque.

His monumental presence lends visceral force to all his scenes, particularly the harrowing, epic flashbacks of his "middle passage" on a trans-Atlantic slaver.

Unfortunately, the movie Cinque gets inept legal representation in his seemingly endless court battles. As Roger Baldwin, the mutineers' principal attorney, Matthew McConaughey is a flatout disaster. He looks ridiculous in his honeyed curls and granny glasses, wavering among various odd accents, wildly mugging and gesticulating with no focus or purpose.

The always formidable Morgan Freeman is wasted in a pointless (and totally fictional) role as a black abolitionist. As John Quincy Adams, Anthony Hopkins growls a lot and frets interminably over his potted plants (heavy-handedly emphasizing African violets).

His big speech before the nation's highest court is not only utterly falsified, but pathetically pedestrian; perhaps Spielberg knew it, and so left many of Hopkins' key lines largely unintelligible, while underscoring the whole snoozy, dishonest drone with supposedly "inspiring" music by John Williams.

Even the most trivial conversations occur here with heavy breathing and exaggerated intensity, as if Spielberg were deliberately sculpting for Mount Rushmore rather than letting real people talk to one another.

This is particularly true for scenes involving President Martin Van Buren, inexplicably mischaracterized by Nigel Hawthorne as a clueless clown—hardly an appropriate image for the notoriously slick, scheming politician universally known in his era as "The Little Magician." Complaints about such distortions may seem beside the point for a movie that represents an honorable, long-overdue attempt by Hollywood to deal seriously with the shame of slavery.

But when a movie presents itself so self consciously as a "history lesson," an "A for effort" shouldn't be enough to excuse its factual shortcomings and dramatic disappointments.

NEWSDAY, 12/10/97, Part II/p. B3, Jack Mathews

Damned if you do, damned if you don't.

Steven Spielberg may soon be uttering that phrase, as critics, historians, black leaders and others weigh in on "Amistad," his occasionally brilliant, more often tedious, historical drama about an 1839 mutiny aboard a U.S.-bound slave ship, and the landmark trials and Supreme Court case that followed.

Those are crucial events in both African-American history and the abolition movement that preceded the Civil War, and involve everyone from the Spanish slave galley La Amistad to a former and a sitting president of the United States. Spielberg, perhaps the only filmmaker who could bring that overlooked chapter in history to the screen, deserves some credit for having done so.

On the other hand, couldn't he have found a way to tell the story from the mutineers' point of view rather than from that of the white men defending them in court? Which story has the most inherent drama: the plight of free people being kidnaped from their homeland, herded in shackles aboard a slave ship and finally rebelling against their captors, or a star-studded reenactment of the political and legal debates that determined their fate?

Either story would be incomplete without the other, and "Amistad" tells both. But Spielberg and screenwriter David Franzoni have the weight ratio backward. Less than 20 minutes of the film's two-and-a-half-hour, running time is devoted to the Africans' adventure.

The rest of the time, we see them only when they're visited in prison by their defenders—first, Matthew McConaughey's young real estate attorney, then Anthony Hopkins' oracular John Quincy Adams—or when they're sitting in court, perplexed by proceedings they don't understand. They become both defendants and props in a white man's courtroom drama.

The lone exception is Cinque (South African actor Djimon Hounsou), the mutineers' proud leader, who communicates with his lawyers through a translator. Hounsou is a potent force, commanding every inch of the screen while uttering barely a word of English. We'd like to know more about him, what his life was like as a rice farmer in Sierra Leone, how he thought and felt before his kidnaping, and how the experience, which compels him to murder, changes him.

Instead, we get a flashback summary of the kidnaping and subsequent events aboard Amistad, and while that middle passage, prompted by testimony at one of the trials, is extraordinarily powerful, it merely whets the appetite for the kind of movie this might have been.

Whether it was a personal or commercial choice to hold the spotlight on the defenders, the abolitionists and their opponents, the result is that rare Spielberg movie ("The Empire of the Sun" is the other) that doesn't move so much as lurch forward, to the obtrusive interpretation of John Williams' score.

Only in the mutiny sequences does Williams' music work with the images. Elsewhere, it dominates and diminishes them. Hopkins' brilliant 10-minute Supreme Court speech, defending both the mutineers and the Declaration of Independence, is almost muted by the patronizing choir music rising above it.

Before that speech, Hopkins' appearance qualifies as little more than a cameo. The main character through most of the film is Roger Baldwin (McConaughey), an inexperienced but bright and tenacious attorney (think of the hero of any John Grisham novel) who becomes the great white hope for the mutineers and the abolitionists funding the defense.

Spielberg, of course, did a similar thing with "Schindler's List," telling the story of a conscience-stricken Nazi who became the savior of concentration camp Jews. And in both cases, the underlying power comes through the spirit and dignity of the captives.

But there's a big difference between the treatments of these two events. "Schindler's List" drew us into the concentration camps, made us feel through the Jewish characters the terror and indignity of living under a policy of genocide. "Amistad" touches on the fear and anger of the Africans, but only through the eye of the camera and the sympathetic observers.

The one black man among the abolitionists is the fictional Theodore Joadson (Morgan Freeman), a former slave who rallies a business partner (Stellan Skarsgard) to help finance the defense, and then fades into the background, serving as little more than a symbol of the freeman in the North.

A lot of historical detail and characters are shoehorned into Franzoni's episodic script, and you may need a scorecard to keep straight the villains claiming ownership of the West Africans: the southern plantation owners who bought them at a slave market in Cuba, the naval salvagers who found Amistad foundering off Montauk and Spain's pubescent Queen Isabells II (Anna Paquin), who loves her slave trade almost as much as she does her dolls.

There's also a battery of high-ranking pro-slavery government officials, including the Secretary of State Forsyth (a badly cast David Paymer), federal prosecutor Holabird (Pete Postlethwaite) and President Martin Van Buren (Nigel Hawthorne), who is cowed into appealing a lower court's acquittal of the Africans by avid proslavery Sen. John C. Calhoun (Arliss Howard) and public opinion in the South.

There's not much tension in any of this, given the untenable positions of the proslavery forces, and the generally known outcome. The real human drama of the Amistad story rested with the would-be slaves, and that's where Spielberg misses the boat.

NEWSWEEK, 12/8/97, p. 64, David Ansen & Allison Samuels

Born with our eyes on the future, we Americans are notoriously oblivious to history—our own or anyone else's. Unless we are personally involved, our attitude goes, it's nothing to get worked up about. Did anyone, other than a few spoilsport movie critics, take umbrage when the new animated film "Anastasia" claimed that Rasputin's curse caused the Russian Revolution?

History to us is a wallflower. She sits neglected in the corner, drab and demure, uninvited to the dance. What does it take to get us to notice her? A suitor, of course. The most popular boy in the class, say, who suddenly sees her there and proclaims her beautiful. Someone like ... Steven Spielberg.

Having unleashed his prodigious talent upon the Holocaust in "Schindler's List," Spielberg now casts his eyes on an extraordinary event that neither he, nor most of us, was ever taught in school. In 1839, aboard the Spanish slave ship La Amistad, 53 Africans rose in mutiny, slaughtering all but two of their captors. They were imprisoned in New Haven, Conn., for their deed, and their case was ultimately argued before the Supreme Court by former president John Quincy Adams.

But not everybody is happy that Spielberg has asked this girl to dance. This is a piece of history—of African-American history—in which many people do feel personally involved. On the eve of next week's opening of this $35 million production, Spielberg and his studio, DreamWorks SKG, find themselves embroiled in controversy and territorial disputes. There's novelist Barbara Chase-Riboud's $10 million lawsuit claiming that the film steals significant elements of its story from her 1989 novel "Echo of Lions." (In retaliation, DreamWorks now says she ripped off "Black Mutiny," the 1953 history used as a source for "Amistad.") There's the internal dispute over screenwriting credit: David Franzoni was awarded sole credit by the Writers Guild even though Spielberg believed it should have been shared with Steve ("Schindler's List") Zaillian.

Within the black intellectual community, there is heated debate about the appropriateness of a white director's presenting African-American history. Says author Haki Madubuti, owner of the Third World Press publishing house, "We have to be in control of our own stories—just like our destinies. I'm not saying that Spielberg isn't capable of making a decent film about blacks. What I'm saying is that blacks should be given first chance at our own stories." (For a stunning film about slavery by a black director, rent Charles Burnett's 1996 "Nightjohn," originally made for television.)

Harvard sociology professor Orlando Patterson disagrees. "What's important is that it's finally getting made—no matter who made it and as long as it's quality work." Producer Debbie Allen, the choreographer and actress who's been trying to get this story on film since 1982, thinks "Steven was the right person to do this film, and I knew it." Indeed, many black directors—like Spike Lee and John Singleton knew of the story but believed they could never get financing. And as Spielberg points out, "This story is about American history, not just African history."

As the lone African-American at the forefront of the film, Allen assumed the role of guardian of black culture—making sure the tribal dialects and traditions were true to history, seeing that scenes with the African prisoners were restored when it seemed the movie was becoming too much about the white people who fought for their freedom in court. The filming of the Middle Passage sequences, in which the actors playing the slaves had to be shackled, stripped and beaten, was a powerful and agonizing experience that called for special sensitivity. Only black crew members were allowed to put the chains and shackles on the actors. "It took amazing stamina to film those scenes," recalls Djimon Hounsou, the 33-year-old West African actor who plays Cinqué, the leader of the revolt. "It was hard not to cry, and so many of the others did cry, which made us all shed tears. Because you knew this was what my people went through."

These harrowing Middle Passage scenes will not be forgotten by anyone who sees Spielberg's movie: the horrors of the slave trade have rarely been captured in such indelible, painful images. Nor will the film's stunning seabound opening section. "Amistad" begins with Cinqué's breaking his shackles and murdering the crew. Spielberg makes two unconventional choices here: presenting the bloody uprising before he shows us the brutalizing events that led up to it, and having the Africans speak in their native tongues without subtitles. He's deliberately flirting with the stereotype of the Savage, putting us in the position of a white 19th-century American first encountering The Other and not knowing what to make of him. Later Spielberg allows us to see white society through the Africans' eyes—even finding some humor in the vision of dour New England abolitionists singing Christian hymns on the jailhouse steps. Who are these weird people? the prisoners wonder. "They must be entertainers," Cinqué speculates.

The tale is rich in reverberations. The legal battle that ensues over the fate of the mutineers is waged over the issue of property rights, but mighty interests—political and philosophical—are at stake, from those of Queen Isabella of Spain, who insists that the slaves belong to Spain, to those of President Martin Van Buren (Nigel Hawthorne), who, facing an election, fears that a victory for the Africans will lose him the Southern vote. Van Buren cynically overturns the lower court's first decision—won by John Baldwin (Matthew McConaughey), an inexperienced real-estate lawyer—and handpicks a judge who will, he thinks, give him the decision he wants.

Most of this is riveting—but there are moments when you feel you're watching a history pageant or civics lesson. McConaughey, saddled with granny glasses and an unlocatable accent, takes considerable getting used to: he's incorrigibly contemporary. Morgan Freeman is wasted in the underwritten role of a black abolitionist who has little to do but look sorrowful. The ease with which he navigates white New Haven society seems more 1990s than 1840s. This is Spielberg's first venture into an earlier century; understandably uncertain of 19th-century behavior, he sometimes falls back on fussy shtik—like John Quincy Adams's puttering among his plants—that is uncharacteristically stagy.

But if "Amistad" falls short of Spielberg's highest accomplishments, it still has power to burn. In Djimon Hounsou, whose Cinqué cuts a figure of stunning strength and grace, he has discovered an actor of astonishing charisma. (A decade ago Hounsou was homeless on the streets of Paris. His striking looks caught the attention of a photographer; a modeling and acting career followed.) Anthony Hopkins, under mounds of makeup, is deeply moving as the flinty, eloquent John Quincy Adams, coaxed at the age of 74 into arguing for the Africans' freedom in front of a Supreme Court in which six of the nine justices were slave owners. These two actors are the strong, beating heart of the movie. Spielberg will be hailed for nobly resurrecting this important piece of history, and he deserves to be. But he's no fool: he knows a great story when he sees one. And he has always known that in America, and in the movies, the way to reach the conscience is through the gut.

SIGHT AND SOUND, 3/98, p. 36, Philip Strick

Cuba, 1839. After being chained in the hold of the Spanish ship La Amistad, 53 African slaves break free, killing most of the crew. Led by Sengbe Pieh, known as Cinque, they demand to be taken back to Africa, but the helmsman steers north instead, up the US coastline. After two months, the Amistad is stopped by an American naval patrol and the Africans are imprisoned at New Haven to stand trial for murder. The ship's owners, its salvagers, and the Spanish throne make separate claims to 'own' the slaves.

Taking up the Africans' cause, leading abolitionists Joadson and Tappan employ a young attorney, Roger Baldwin.

Struggling to communicate with Cinque, Baldwin finds evidence that the slaves were brought illegally to Havana in the notorious Portuguese slave ship *Tecora*. As the case becomes a national issue, President Van Buren is nervous that an abolitionist victory would prejudice his re-election prospects among the pro slavery southern states, and has a new judge appointed. But Baldwin and Joadson have found an interpreter for Cinque, who describes his abduction in Sierra Leone, his imprisonment in the Lomboko slave fortress, and the *Tecora*'s horror-fraught Atlantic crossing. His story is validated by a British naval officer, and Judge Coglin releases the Africans.

Their celebrations are cut short by news that Van Buren has ordered a retrial in the Supreme Court. In desperation, Baldwin and Joadson appeal to former President John Quincy Adams to argue the Africans' cause. Adams delivers a powerful appeal to the Supreme Court and the Africans are freed. His two-year ordeal at an end, Cinque sets out on the voyage home.

Properly disinclined to unshackle the *Amistad* case from its well documented history, Steven Spielberg entangles himself in a number of complications as a result. Perhaps the most inhibiting is that, as history, the *Amistad* story invites contradictory interpretations: at face value, it centres on a murder trial in which the accused are at last exonerated, while it also represents one of the causes of the Civil War and of the ultimate abolition of slavery. The *Amistad* was indeed a slave ship, yet its cargo, in this instance, according to legal definition (via the Supreme Court ruling of 1841), consisted not of slaves but of "free" men. Whatever the perceptions of the time, the real *Amistad* story is a kind of whodunit, in the sense conveyed by Adams' advice to his petitioners on the Africans' behalf: "Find out, not their names, but *who* they are." To understand why the crew of the *Amistad* were killed requires an understanding of the men who killed them.

It would be logical for this process to begin in Sierra Leone among the Mende tribe from whom slave-leader Cinque is suddenly abducted. However, forced by dramatic necessity to deconstruct the natural order of events, Spielberg follows the classic crime story pattern. Leading off in fine style with the *Amistad* killings, he moves forward into the court proceedings and flashbacks from these into the gradually rediscovered past. This structure, ironically, does little to help us understand Cinque, except at a most basic level: springing from nowhere, strikingly gifted with strength, intelligence, eloquence and simplicity, the archetypal martyr and natural-born leader, he is a non-American struggling for recognition of his entitlement to an American-defined freedom. In the achievement of that recognition, the solution to the whodunit emerges: it is Cinque's accusers and defenders who are the true culprits for having tolerated, condoned and perpetuated (by inaction if not direct profit) the slave trade economy.

While not particularly at ease with these twists of identity, Spielberg grasps the opportunity to craft some immaculate adventures: the shipboard mutiny, the courtroom debate, the presidential banquet, the multi-costumed street scenes, the flame-lit dungeons of prison melodrama. The whole opening section, described from nobody's particular point of view except Spielberg's, observes Cinque's escape as a ferocious awakening. The first close-ups of flesh have a near Jurassic texture, while the extracted nail that leads to freedom demands to be emblematic of an era which, now unpinned, will inevitably fall apart.

Accompanied by crashes of light and thunder, as is usual with Spielberg's crises, these portents herald the protracted death of the ship's captain, transfixed by a single sword-thrust, considered both from above and below with an air of grave collusion between victim and assailant. Without admitting whether the victorious image is his or theirs, Spielberg frames the Africans against the revolving stars, looming superheroes on an epic vqyage. He then reduces the whole venture to farce when they encounter a cyclist at first landfall, and then to inscrutable tragedy as the escaping Cinque is miraculously recovered just when he appears to have drowned, a distracting incident leaving all that follows open to question.

What does follow is something of a parade of distractions. The eccentrics of Spielberg's *Empire of the Sun* are here transmuted not only into the overdressed attorneys and diplomats but also, in gentle but demeaning mockery, to every available figure of authority—from the 11-year-old Queen Isabella to the tight-lipped British officer who supports Cinque's evidence in a state of trembling fury that anyone might doubt his word. Absurd, mannered and performed on the edge of buffoonery, these pantomime figures preside over a society of incalculable priorities. Only by overcoming their amusement at so clownish an environment can the Africans (fresh recruits to Spielberg's regular army of beleaguered innocents, who gradually acquire more elegant clothes for themselves as the arguments over their case grow more complex) hope to regain control over their own fate.

Against this background, Cinque himself, safely underplayed with stoical dignity by Djimon Hounsou, emerges persuasively as a paragon of sanity and wisdom, much matured from the bloodied and rainswept icon we first meet.   With all the best lines, thanks to subtitles and subsequently an interpreter, he embodies two useful precepts: the willingness to take on a fight whether it can be won or not (represented by the lion's-tooth talisman), and communion with one's ancestors.   Briskly adopting both of these, John Quincy Adams, his doddering defender—performed by Anthony Hopkins with a fine array of stops, starts, and piercing stares—shifts the blame for the *Amistad* once again by claiming "who we are is who we *were*", an appeal which works wonders on the ancient Supreme Court judges.

Except for the startlingly clumsy sequence in which the Africans discover for themselves the story of Christ, crashingly intercut with their judge's prayer for guidance, Spielberg puts it all together with great polish, only to fall on his face at the end as the hard facts of history preclude his trademark scenes of reunion and reconciliation.   In a bewildering succession of visual footnotes, he retires the meddling President Van Buren, kills off the Confederacy of Atlanta in 1864 (a two-shot battle scene), destroys the evil Lamboko fortress amid a quick vista of scrambling crowds, and reveals that Cinque returned to a ruined country, his family lost in slavery.   Cruelly marginalised in this way, the story of Cinque's fight for justice is short on consolation: clearly we must hang on as best we can to our lion's teeth, to our ancestors, and above all to our subtitles.

VILLAGE VOICE, 12/16/97, p. 71, J. Hoberman

Tis the season, and after a summer sojourn on Dino-Death Island, Steven Spielberg directs America's attention to one of the nation's original sins.   In making *Amistad* the highest authority—moral and otherwise—in American show business has bestowed eternal name recognition upon a 19th-century Spanish slave-ship, as well as the insurrection and legal case that followed.

College notwithstanding, it took the Symbionese Liberation Army to acquaint me with the story of the *Amistad*—the group's leader named himself Cinque after the African captive who liberated the ship and then secured his freedom in an American court. Anyway, what citizen of a country where the National Air and Space Museum mounts an exhibit called *"Star Wars*: the Magic of Myth" a city whose Museum of Natural History lusted for synergy with *The Lost World,* or a borough wired for a History Channel devoted mainly to old Hollywood movies will dispute *Amistad*'s educational use-value?

The intent is admirable; the execution spotty. Going straight for the jugular, Spielberg opens *Amistad* with a slave revolt shot in mega-close-up. Thunder rolls and the strobe-lit decks run red with blood as the unfettered Cinque (West African model and U.S. video icon Djimon Hounsou) advances out of the storm, machete in hand. The sequence is a daring instance of "unmotivated" vengeance although its nightmare is soon dispelled by the briskly detailed daylight scene in which the Africans are captured by the American navy off the coast of Connecticut.

As always with Spielberg, Otherness is a problem. Bizarrely, *Amistad* only begins to translate the captives' dialogue as they are dragged through New London. The subtitles thereafter come and go as the Africans oscillate between unknowable uncanniness and anthropomorphized hyperhumanity. Their case is founded on a legalism—e.g., to whom do they belong? The competing claims are presented as interesting, the defense lawyer less so—self-absorbed Matthew McConaughey peering over spectacles, scarcely more convincing here than as the president's guru in *Contact.*

Once the Africans dub their lawyer "dung scraper," it's understood that they have begun to learn the white man's mumbo jumbo. As Cinque contributes to his own defense, so one of his colleagues figures out the story of Christ from an illustrated New Testament. It's a religious epiphany—although Jesus has little to do with it. Here, as at the *Close Encounter*'s climax, the movie medium salutes its own capacity for communication. Still, how much off the universal language known as "Spielberg" is really composer John Williams? No less than the African's grasp of scripture, *Amistad*'s emotional high points are rigorously cued. A subliminal Beethoven pastiche wells up as Cinque—demonstrating his command of English for the first time—interrupts the trial to cry, "Give Us Free!" (The over-orchestrated reactions of wonder that greet his declaration are pure Spielberg.)

Amistad's most important sequence is the relatively spare and vivid account of the slavery machine: Africans capture other Africans, selling them to the European slavers who process these chained captives through a concentration-camp fortress, packing them like sardines into a ship's fetid hold, beating a few to death, starving others, drowning more, then finally auctioning the survivors on the block in Havana. The middle passage has not been represented in a Hollywood movie in the 60 years since Tay Garnett's seldom-shown *Slave Ship* which, if memory serves, also included a horrific scene of manacled Africans being thrown overboard.

Djimon Hounsou's Cinque radiates and is able to convey righteousness but, as in *Schlindler's List,* power resides with the white protagonist. In this case, though, the ultimate hero is not a matinee idol but rather a lovably irascible codger, former president John Quincy Adams-wax-museum perfect and played by Anthony Hopkins as a Disney curmudgeon. Considerably less individuated, costar Morgan Freeman has the Ben Kingsley role of an inexplicably wealthy former slave—a fictional abolitionist named Theodore Joadson, who functions as free-floating, conscience-salving sidekick.

Threatened, by Senator John Calhoun, with civil war—or, at least, defeat in the upcoming election—President Martin Van Buren (Nigel Hawthorne) overturns the first Amistad trial, setting the stage for Adams to re-argue the case before the Supreme Court. It matters not whether Cinque and Adams actually bonded over the former president's cultivation of a rare African violet nor if, in the midst of his highly abstract legal brief, Adams really did spin Cinque and crew as American-style freedom fighters. The light behind Adams grows ever more halated and Joadson beams in silent approval as redemption approaches; Cinque thanks his dung scraper with the Black Power handshake, but it is Adams who is the director's mouthpiece.

"In a courtroom, whoever tells the best story wins" Adams earlier told Joadson, proceeding to instruct the dumbstruck Joadson in the dramatic potential of Joadson's own story. It's ironic that novelist Barbara Chase-Riboud's plagiarism suit largely depends on *Amistad*'s alleged appropriation of the Joadson character. Although Morgan Freeman has a unique capacity for giving the illusion of depth to whatever role he takes, his part here is so ephemeral that a DreamWorks lawyer would have no trouble arguing it doesn't exist.

Also reviewed in:
NATION, 1/5/98, p. 34, Stuart Klawans
NEW REPUBLIC, 12/22/97, p. 24, Stanley Kauffmann
NEW YORK TIMES, 12/10/97, p. E1, Janet Maslin
VARIETY, 12/8-14/97, p. 110, Emanuel Levy
WASHINGTON POST, 12/12/97, p. C1, Rita Kempley
WASHINGTON POST, 12/12/97, Weekend/p. 56, Desson Howe

ANACONDA

A Columbia Pictures release of a CL Cinema Line Films Corporation production. *Executive Producer:* Susan Ruskin. *Producer:* Verna Harrah, Leonard Rabinowitz, and Carole Little. *Director:* Luis Llosa. *Screenplay:* Hans Bauer, Jim Cash, and Jack Epps, Jr. *Director of Photography:* Bill Butler. *Editor:* Michael R. Miller. *Music:* Randy Edelman. *Music Editor:* Joanie Diener. *Sound:* Douglas B. Arnold. *Sound Editor:* Rick Franklin. *Casting:* Mindy Marin. *Production Designer:* Kirk M. Petruccelli. *Art Director:* Barry Chusid. *Set Decorator:* Daniel L. May. *Special Effects:* Chuck Gasper. *Animatronic Effects:* Walt Conti. *Visual Effects:* John Nelson. *Costumes:* Kathy Monderine. *Make-up:* James Kail. *Stunt Coordinator:* Webster Whinery. *Running time:* 90 minutes. *MPAA Rating:* PG-13.

CAST: Jennifer Lopez (Terri Flores); Ice Cube (Danny Rich); Jon Voight (Paul Sarone); Eric Stoltz (Dr. Steven Cale); Jonathan Hyde (Warren Westridge); Owen Wilson (Gary Dixon); Kari Wuhrer (Denise Kalberg); Vincent Castellanos (Mateo); Danny Trejo (Poacher).

LOS ANGELES TIMES, 4/11/97, Calendar/p. 4, Kenneth Turan

"When you can't breathe," the ads for "Anaconda" sternly warn, "you can't scream." But nobody said anything about laughing.

Though it's not clear if the humor is intentional or whether its audience will be limited to connoisseurs of movies born to be bad, "Anaconda" is such a classic combination of feckless dramaturgy and rampant excess that giving way to giggles is the only sane response.

It wasn't supposed to end like this. Lots of effort, not to say money, went into turning out impressive 40-foot snakes in both animatronic and computer-generated versions, snakes so nasty they'd swallow both you and a friend without a second thought. There's even a gruesome shot from inside a snake's mouth as it's about to ingest a luckless victim. Let Wes Craven try to top that.

But all this hard work is as nothing against the presence of Jon Voight, who gives an irresistible performance, overripe to the point of bursting, as Paul Sarone, native of Paraguay and snake hunter of mystery. Those with fond memories of Voight as a convict so fierce he had to be welded to his cell in Andrei Konchalovsky's "Runaway Train" can get ready for another round.

Sarone is not initially on the passenger list for the plucky riverboat that chugs its way down the mighty Amazon. In charge is Dr. Steven Cale (Eric Stoltz), an expert in looking effete and finding lost tribes. It's the Shirishama he's after this time out; that's right, "the elusive people of the mist." And he's brought a rather diverse film crew with him to document the experience.

The crew's director is Terri Flores, played by Jennifer Lopez, and, given the success of "Selena," wouldn't she give anything to get this one back? Her cameraman is Danny Rich (Ice Cube), who has to be satisfied with sidekick lines like, "That's it, I'm getting the hell back to L.A."

Her narrator, Warren Westridge (Jonathan Hyde), arrives with Cartier suitcases filled with French wine. Gary the sound mixer is Owen Wilson, an accidental tourist on loan from "Bottle Rocket." And production manager Denise (Kari Wuhrer) is around to model the abbreviated outfits that are just the thing in the steamy jungle.

Just around the, Amazon's first bend, this Ship of Fools comes upon Sarone, stranded on a derelict boat. Snakes are his life, he says, and he's soon the life of the party with tales of his old pal, the anaconda. "It holds you tighter than your true love," he says, courtesy of the Hans Bauer and Jim Cash & Jack Epps Jr. script, "and you get the privilege of hearing your bones break before the power of their embrace causes your veins to explode." Thanks, guys, I needed that.

Possibly having gotten a peek at the rest of the script, Stoltz's Dr. Cale beats a strategic retreat and spends much of the movie breathing uncertainly under a gauze tent. With the doctor gone, no one else on board can handle Sarone, even after it's clear that he will stop at nothing, nothing do you hear, in his mad quest to bring one of those 40-foot anacondas back alive.

Neither, under the uncertain direction of jungle veteran Luis "Fire in the Amazon" Llosa, are any of the other performers capable of standing toe-to-toe in the acting department with the force of nature that is Voight in overdrive.

With a sinister leer always playing over a face like a gnarled tree root, Voight's snarling-scowling performance is one of those leaps into the void that must be seen to be appreciated, kind of like watching "The Wolf Man's" wizened crone Maria Ouspenskaya come back to life as a pumped-up desperado.

The screenwriters have also given Sarone all the good lines. Or at least they seem good in Voight's nominally Paraguayan accent. "Don't make me out a monster, I didn't eat the captain," Sarone plaintively croaks in a moment matched by the scene where he runs his admiring hands through a tangle of young snakes and purrs, "Come on, babies. So young, so lethal."

As they strove to hang onto their sanity in this bizarre mix, the actors in "Anaconda" must have identified with the sentiments of Lopez's film director, who brought down the house in one preview screening when she said, "This film was supposed to be my big break and it turned out to be a big disaster." It's a jungle out there, kids, and don't you forget it.

NEW YORK, 5/5/97, p. 80, David Denby

The characters in the cheesy big-snake movie *Anaconda* are very casually disposed of—so casually that the movie almost seems a joke, like one of the hapless B movies ridiculed in the cable show *Mystery Science Theater 3000*. Here we are on a barge in the Amazon with a documentary-film crew, and every time someone looks at the jungle he or she gets attacked by something. A couple having sex is set upon by a wild boar; an anthropologist hopping into the water gets a poisonous beetle in his mouth. All preparatory, of course, to the appearance of the Big Guy, a 40-foot anaconda, thick as an elephant's leg and flexible as an electrified Slinky. It leaps up into trees and pulls people down and eats more than Bruce the shark in *Jaws*.

The characters have been created as types that will appeal to urban audiences—black and Hispanic heroes, a snooty Brit, and, as a villain, Jon Voight is a boss white man who kills and deceives. *Anaconda* is almost unimaginably bad, but at least it's short—a mere 90 minutes. One suspects the filmmakers threw away a good deal of footage. That the movie has become a hit doesn't make me wish any less fervently that they had thrown all of it away.

NEW YORK POST, 4/11/97, p. 37, Thelma Adams

Squeeze me, baby. I'm a sucker for the man-eating snake spectacular "Anaconda."

Luis Llosa's "Jaws" on the Amazon makes a few detours into what evil lurks in the hearts of men territory, but its most pressing question is: Who'll be the next snake snack?

Which member of the obnoxious documentary film team in search of primal man will be munched first? Will it be know-it-all anthropologist Eric Stoltz? Ambitious director Jennifer Lopez ("Selena")? Street-smart, river-dumb cameraman Ice Cube? Snotty anchorman Warren Westridge?

Where's Agatha Christie with a clue? The mystery scribe must be on the Nile when the crew picks up a hitcher. Fallen priest and snake pro Jon Voight's main goal isn't saving the rain forest. He's got boas on the brain.

If Voight captures a live anaconda, he'll make a million skins. And, for the loopy reasons provided by screenwriters Hans Bauer, Jim Cash and Jack Epps Jr., he needs the help of the egocentric city folks to snare his prey. These man-eaters like take-out—and monkeys are only an appetizer.

Voight, with a slithery Paraguayan accent, is scarier than any 25-foot-long, 3-foot-wide semi-aquatic squeezer. With a nasty fang scar on his cheek and a hungry, snake-head sneer, Voight bites into his role like Marlon Brando falling off Ultra Slim-Fast.

Not only does the "Rosewood" star get the best lines, the full-service predator also constricts the nubile production manager between his thighs while delivering the Last Rites. An extra-added bonus is the pen-knife tracheotomy given to the annoying anthropologist after he swallows a deadly wasp. It's something, as a critic, I've yearned to perform on Stoltz but never had the guts.

Snakes, snakes and more snakes make "Anaconda"—and its sly refusal to see them as a symbol of anything larger—a creepy, crawly guilty pleasure. Sometimes a cigar is just a cigar. From the title to the snake's-eye view of its prey, we know who's the star here.

In his smooth and swift adventure, Llosa ("The Specialist") makes a last-ditch effort to have the audience identify with a dashing Lopez and a smoldering Cube—but it's too little, too late. We're already in thrall to the animatronic anaconda, who refuses to let good taste get in the way of filmmakers who taste good.

NEWSDAY, 4/11/97, Part II/p. B11, John Anderson

Just sit right back and you'll hear a tale, a tale of a fateful trip. It may not be as fateful as the trip to the theater to *see* "Anaconda," but it does have seven stranded castaways, the unfriendly Amazon and a reptile as big as Jon Voight.

Who is played—ba-da-boom—by Jon Voight. As the evil poacher and ne'er-do-well Paul Sarone, he affects an untraceable South American accent and the look of an actor en route to a big meal. As fun as the giant snake is in "Anaconda," Voight is far more interesting, far more evil and a lot funnier.

The latest entry in a genre that has already exploited sharks ("Jaws"), birds ("The Birds"), frogs ("Frogs") and giant mutant brain-eating crabs ("Attack of the Crab Monsters"), "Anaconda" proudly lifts from each, tossing in a twist of "Tremors" and a dash of "Dune." There are too many false alarms, cheap thrills and not-so-special effects to make this anything but a cheap date movie, but if you're in the right mood it may provide a laugh.

Voight's character is found on a derelict boat by the documentary team led by director Terri Flores (Jennifer Lopez) and her scientist adviser, Dr. Steven Cale (Eric Stoltz). Unwisely, they take him on board, where he terrorizes the rest of the crew—Danny (Ice Cube), Warren (Jonathan Hyde), Gary (Owen Wilson) and Denise (Kari Wuhrer)—and manages to turn their filmmaking expedition into a search for the giant ... anaconda.

Did I mention "King Kong"? Paul wants to take the snake alive, which rather provokes the otherwise innocent animal; blowing up a dam full of baby snakes supplies the story's maternal-revenge element (did I mention "Beowulf"?). The computers provide the rather ludicrous shots of the snake itself, coiling cartoonishly out of the water, into the sky, up a waterfall or around whatever victim is going to have the life squeezed out of him. I wouldn't expect "Anaconda" to offer much in the way of zoology or herpetology or anthropology, but it does contain a good deal of aberrant sociology.

In classic movie/TV fashion, "Anaconda's" river-going expedition has been assembled as if it were "Grand Hotel," each actor playing to his/her strength: Lopez gets to strut in damp tank tops; Hyde practices his golf swing; Ice Cube attitudinalizes in Converse All-Stars and shorts. Stoltz, rendered non compos mentis for most of the movie, is the preppy professor. And, like Robinson Crusoe, they're primitive as can be.

SIGHT AND SOUND, 7/97, p. 35, Kim Newman

The Brazilian rain forest. Anthropologist Dr Steven Cale and documentary film-maker Terri Flores set out on an expedition in search of the long-lost Shirishama tribe. Also on the expedition are cameraman Danny Rich, sound recordist Gary Dixon, production manager Denise Kalberg and narrator-presenter Warren Westridge. They travel upriver on a boat captained by local resident Mateo.

En route, the group pick up hunter Paul Sarone, who suggests they take a detour into an area where he can trap a valuable 40-foot anaconda. When they refuse, Sarone slips a deadly wasp into Cale's scuba mask, injuring him and forcing the group to take the detour to get Cale to a hospital. Sarone convinces Gary to help him take over the boat so he can pursue the snake, which later on swiftly kills Mateo and Gary. The others band together and knock Sarone out, but he kills Denise to escape and the snake kills Westridge. After Terri and Danny kill the snake, Sarone is about to kill them but Cale surprises him with an anaesthetic dart and Sarone is pitched overboard.

The boat runs aground at an abandoned factory, where Sarone, who has survived, traps Terri and Danny and ties them up as snake-bait. Another snake kills Sarone, but Terri and Danny manage to kill it. Having defeated the snake, the survivors are welcomed by the Shirishama tribe.

Putting even the ludicrous *Congo* to shame, *Anaconda* is the most ridiculous jungle adventure since James Whale's delirious *Green Hell* of 1939. Obviously conceived as the herpetophobe version of *Jaws*, this stirs into its wok of clichés elements from diverse sources: from *Cannibal Holocaust* (1979) to *Aguirre, Wrath of God* (1972).

The cast is an immaculate cross-section of born losers. There's Jon Voight as the villain Sarone, just back from the career-dead, managing to upstage the 40-foot, plastic-headed and computer-generated monster with his absurd 'Paraguayan' accent. There's Jennifer Lopez and Ice Cube as the heroes glumly trudging through the terror, both of whom ought to get out of typecasting into mainstream commercial movies. Eric Stoltz plays a white-bread-scientific stooge who spends most of the film mutely sick below-deck; Stoltz must feel he's made enough high-integrity, low-paying indie films to deserve fat fees he can win with little effort. Then there's Kari Wuhrer as the secondary babe and victim. Add an English-accented arrogant twit who cops most of the funny lines (Jonathan Hyde) and a few snarling, sinister greasy locals (Vincent Castellanos, Danny Trejo) to prove that there are films still unembarrassed to use ethnic stereotypes, and you have snake-food to go in jumbo portions.

Our merry bunch of sweaty fools brave the usual hazards of such ill-advised ethnological ventures. ("The last time I was in water like this I spent the night picking leeches off my scro-tum," whines one.) But they also have to handle a plot which continually plays variations on characters being constricted and chomped to death. The horror movie tactics are pretty thread-bare: low-angle, water's surface tracking shots towards hapless victims; a sinister totem pole to suggest that the monster is feared as a god in these parts; a monster and a villain who continually come back from the dead. (Sarone even returns after ingestion as the snake sicks up so that, covered in digestive goo, he can have a last sinister wink.) Incidental gruesome bits feature jungle fauna, and a musical score that works overtime to drown out the absurd dialogue.

Director Luis Llosa, who almost managed this level of hilarity with *The Specialist,* clearly didn't set out to make something as entertainingly camp as *Anaconda* rather wonderfully manages to be. However, the touch for suspense displayed in *Sniper* seems to have deserted him. Though Voight snarls his way through the regulation speech about the fearsomeness of his opponent, the snake itself is seen too early and too often to be that frightening. In the end, it turns out to be two monsters, a green one which is easily dispatched and a black one that shows up just for the finale and is a lot harder to kill. Mimicking the snake by constricting Denise to death with a neck-snapping leg-lock, Sarone's perfidy is so deep it goes beyond sheer deviltry (expressed by numberless underlit close-ups of him chuckling nastily) and exists simply as a plot contrivance. One wonders why he bothered to hijack this bunch of amateurs rather than go upriver with his own confederates. As the distributors—who handed out hissing snake-in-the-tin toys and bottles of anaconda serum at the press screening—doubtless realise, *Anaconda* is truly terrible but no means unentertaining.

VILLAGE VOICE, 4/22/97, p. 82, Gary Dauphin

The premise that 40-foot man-eating snakes lurk in the Brazilian rainforest sounds pretty plausible to this reviewer, but then I should say up front that I believe in a lot of odd, lurking things. At first glance, the reptilian pitch behind *Anaconda*—already slithering in theaters—seems good fodder for decent genre hijinks, a nice pre-summer sub-Event flick that promises kooky crytozoology along the lines of *In Search of ... The Loch Ness Monster,* with the digital kicks of a *Jurassic Park* thrown in for good measure. "When you can't breathe, you can't scream" is a pretty neat tag line—best I've heard this year, really—but unfortunately, the truth is that *Anaconda* doesn't quite live up to its poster "When you're yawning, you can't scream" being more this movie's speed.

Anaconda starts out on the edges of the Amazon, with anthropologist Steven Cale (Eric Stoltz) about to lead a documentary team into the heart of darkness on a beat-up river trawler. He's looking for a long-lost Brazilian tribe, the People of the Mists, and he's backed up by a multiculti production team: there's Terri, the Latina director and Stoltz's ex (Jennifer Lopez); Danny, the d.p. from L.A. (Ice Cube); a slacker soundman and his girlfriend (Owen Wilson and Kari Wuhrer); and a crabby Brit narrator (Jonathan Hyde).

The ensemble offers *Anaconda* a chance to rise above the usual horror flick. Normally the people of color, the aged, and the sexually active would be offed up front, but *Anaconda* plays slightly smart with expectations of fated, impending demise. The camera sneaks up on people for a long while before blood spills and bones crunch, the roster of potential victims mixed up enough that, with the exception of Lopez, you're never sure who's about to buy the watery farm.

Their guide into People of the Mists land is Paul Sarone, who Jon Voight plays as some sort of squinting river-dog. Although there is a line about him being a defrocked French priest, he mostly comes off as an unplaceable ham. His accent suggests the Baltics instead of France, and while he's the only one on the boat who seems to know anything about, like, surviving in the rain forest, he's a much more palpably malevolent presence than the big snakes hiding in reserve. When Cale comes down with a poisonous wasp bite (falling into a coma so he can rise at a propitious moment in the last reel), Sarone forces the group to help him hunt the mother of all snakes.

The main problem with *Anaconda* though, is not that its plot is stupid but that the main visual event is unimpressive. The anacondas of the title are part giant foam swingy things and part digital effect, and although they swim nicely, hiss, and wrap themselves around a helpless human in the blink of an eye, the mechanical parts seem like stock footage from the age of puppet monsters. Unable to inspire wonder or incite terror, *Anaconda* is just kind of there, the image believable enough to bore in the way of a bad nature-show close-up. Of course, it could just be that snake phobias aren't particularly high on my list (air crashes and pus-producing infectious disease are scarier these days), but if you're going to charge audiences for monsters, you should at least pay for them in the first place.

Also reviewed in:
NEW YORK TIMES, 4/11/97, p. C5, Stephen Holden
NEW YORKER, 4/21/97, p. 96, Terrence Rafferty

VARIETY, 4/14-20/97, p. 91, Joe Leydon
WASHINGTON POST, 4/11/97, p. B7, Rita Kempley
WASHINGTON POST, 4/11/97, Weekend/p. 42, Desson Howe

ANASTASIA

A Twentieth Century Fox release of a Don Bluth/Gary Goldman production. *Executive Producer:* Maureen Donley. *Producer:* Don Bluth and Gary Goldman. *Director:* Gary Goldman and Don Bluth. *Screenplay:* Susan Gauthier, Bruce Graham, Bob Tzudiker, and Noni White. *Animation Adaptation:* Eric Tuchman. *Editor:* Fiona Trayler. *Music:* David Newman, Stephen Flaherty, and (lyrics) Lynn Ahrens. *Music Editor:* Brent Brooks and Ken Karmen. *Sound:* Robert Renga, Craig Heath, and (music) John Kurlander. *Sound Editor:* Mark Server. *Casting:* Brian Chavanne. *Production Designer:* Mike Peraza. *Conceptual Artist:* Suzanne Lemieux Wilson. *Production Coordinator:* Martha Richter. *Layout Design:* Philip A. Cruden. *Background:* Robyn C. Nason. *Continuity:* Cathy Goldman. *Rough Inbetweens:* Anne Murray-O'Craobhach. *Clean-up Animation:* Eileen Conway Newberry. *Special Effects Animation:* Peter Matheson. *3D Animation:* Thomas M. Miller. *Scene Planning:* Vincent Clarke. *Digital Checking:* Colum Slevin. *Animation Color Styling:* Carmen Oliver. *Special Effects Painting:* Shirley 'Sam' Mapes. *Digital Scanning:* Frank Richards. *Digital Painting:* Liam T. Hannan. *Compositing:* Jeannette Maher. *Running time:* 90 minutes. *MPAA Rating:* G.

VOICES: Meg Ryan (Anastasia); John Cusack (Dimitri); Kelsey Grammer (Vladimir); Christopher Lloyd (Rasputin); Hank Azaria (Bartok); Bernadette Peters (Sophie); Kirsten Dunst (Young Anastasia); Angela Lansbury (Dowager Empress Marie); Liz Callaway (Singing Voice of Anastasia); Lacey Chabert (Singing voice of Young Anastasia); Jim Cummings (Singing Voice of Rasputin); Jonathan Dokuchitz (Singing Voice of Dimitri); Rick Jones (Czar Nicholas/Servant/Revolutionary Soldier/Ticket Agent); Andrea Martin (Phlegmenkoff/Old Woman); Glenn Walker Harris, Jr. (Young Dimitri); Debra Mooney (Actress); Arthur Malet (Traveling Man/Major Domo); Charity James (Anastasia Imposter).

LOS ANGELES TIMES, 11/21/97, Calendar/p. 1, Kenneth Turan

In the topsy-turvy world of feature animation, the best news about "Anastasia" would be bad news anywhere else. Every aspect of what's on the screen, from attractive lovers to campy villains and too cute animal sidekicks, is as familiar as familiar can be, with one exception: The logo on the film reads Fox Animation Studios, not Walt Disney.

The Disney parallels are not surprising, given that the film's producing-directing team, Don Bluth and Gary Goldman, both have extensive Disney experience on such films as "Robin Hood" and "The Rescuers." But Bluth and Goldman have been on their own for nearly 20 years, and this is the first feature they've done that has the potential to attract the same audience as the Disney epics. With DreamWorks' "The Prince of Egypt" due in November 1998, Disney's unprecedented monopoly on high-end animation may be coming to a close.

The first animated film to be shot in CinemaScope since 1959's "Sleeping Beauty" (which Bluth worked on), "Anastasia's" strongest aspect is its epic visual sense, its computer-aided ability to reproduce the vistas of Russia before the revolution and Paris in the 1920s.

One class of viewer "Anastasia" won't be attracting are red diaper babies. Though suggested by the saga of the real-life youngest daughter of Russian Czar Nicholas II, who some claim survived the massacre of her family (though recent DNA evidence says otherwise), "Anastasia's" plot makes a hash of history. It shows czarist Russia as a swell place to live and insists that the revolution took place only because the mad monk Rasputin literally sold his soul to the devil in a fit of pique to make it happen, which is a little like saying a toothache of King George's caused the American Revolution. Sales of Marx's "Das Kapital" are sure to plummet when that news gets out.

Actually, Anastasia's story sounds like unlikely material for an animated feature all the way around. But Bluth and Goldman, aided by a quartet of writers, have managed to put a teen-responsive spin on it. What we get is a lonely girl who wishes she were a princess, an unwanted child eager to find out who she is and desperate for the love only a home and family provide. Surely the Anastasia Barbie is not far behind.

Before all that can happen, "Anastasia" flashes back to 1916 and a grand ball for the 300th anniversary of the Romanov dynasty. There young Anastasia (Kirsten Dunst) shares a tearful tête-d-tête with her grandmother, the Dowager Empress Marie (Angela Lansbury). About to go back to France, the Dowager gives the girl an elaborate music box and a key to wind it that says "Together in Paris."

Those happy plans are interrupted by gloomy party-crasher Rasputin (Christopher Lloyd) and his albino bat sidekick Bartok (Hank Azaria). Looking like Fagin on a bad hair day, Rasputin fumes at no longer being in the royal family's favor and with the devil's assistance soon brings the Romanovs down. If not for plucky kitchen boy Dimitri, Anastasia would not have survived.

Cut to 10 years later. A winsome Anya (Meg Ryan), "a skinny little nobody with no past and no future," is leaving the orphanage where she grew up. She doesn't know a thing about her parents, but a certain key around her neck clues the audience in. After picking up a painfully cute dog named Pookah, Anya heads for St. Petersburg to see what life has to offer. Ah, youth.

Already in St. Pete is a grown-up Dimitri (John Cusack). He and pal Vladimir (Kelsey Grammer) are genial rogues with a plan for instant riches. They'll find a likely girl and teach her to play the part of Anastasia, thus collecting a fat reward from the old Dowager Empress in Paris.

Naturally Anya gets the job, and just as naturally takes such a dislike to Dimitri ("Were you a vulture in another life?" is a typical endearment) that romance is inevitable. Also not surprising is the appearance of a dead but still mobile Rasputin, determined to see his curse on the Romanovs extend to the family's youngest member.

All this is pro forma for feature-length cartoons, and some of the actual animation is on the rickety side. The same goes for the words and music to the eight songs written by Lynn Ahrens and Stephen Flaherty, the team responsible for "Ragtime" on stage. With lyrics like "Heart don't fail me now, courage don't desert me," these tunes are not likely to rock any boats.

"Anastasia's" dialogue, with its insistently modern tone and reliance on phrases like "Can you believe it?" and "What goes around comes around," is also off-putting at times. On the plus side, though, the voicing by a capable group of actors is excellent, with high marks going to Azaria's Bartok the bat, who advises Rasputin "stress is a killer, sir" in an indefinable yet delicious accent.

Though originality is not one of its accomplishments, "Anastasia" is generally pleasant, serviceable and eager to please. And any film that echoes the landscape of "Doctor Zhivago" is hard to dislike for too long.

NEW YORK POST, 11/14/97, p. 45, Michael Medved

At times, the romantic chemistry between the two leads of "Anastasia" becomes compelling and even magical that you must forcibly remind yourself that these are "only" animated figures.

This outrageously ambitious project from veteran producers-directors Don Bluth and Gary Goldman ("An American Tail," "The Land Before Time") takes their art to a dizzying new level, creating the most convincing, complex and endearing human characters in the history of animation.

In the process, the filmmakers uncannily transfer a forbidding old story into an enchanting experience for both children and adults.

The tale begins with 8-year-old Anya living the life of a fairy-tale princess in a gorgeously detailed rendering of Czarist Russia.

Ten years later, long after the Revolution has killed the royal family, a sassy orphan (the voice of Meg Ryan) turns up, and she bears a strinking resemblance to the legendary lost princess Anastasia. Charming con man Dimitri (John Cusack) and fallen aristocrat Vladimir (Kelsey Grammer) together train her to impersonate royalty before taking her to Paris to meet the Dowager Empress (Angela Lansbury), who dreams of reconnecting with her granddaughter.

All of this bears only the flimsiest connection to history, or to previous stage, screen and TV-movie versions of the Anastasia story. In an unnecessary nod to cartoon convention, the movie turns mad monk Rasputin (Christopher Lloyd) into a fiendish villain who defies death with his supernatural powers. But with an albino bat (Hank Azaria) as his deadpan comic sidekick, the bearded baddie combines scary, ridiculous and gross elements in a diabolically amusing manner.

Savvy adults will notice witty references to famous movies about Russia ("Doctor Zhivago") and a Paris populated with cameo appearances by Gertrude Stein, Josephine Baker, Maurice Chevalier and Charles Lindbergh.

Songs by Stephen Flaherty and Lynn Ahrens (the Broadway-bound musical "Ragtime") feature six sturdy, serviceable numbers and one haunting, unforgettable gem ("Once Upon a December"), while computer-generated effects in a spectacular train chase provide thrills to compete with lavish live-action films.

In dramatizing the fall of the Romanoff dynasty, this product of the audacious new Fox Animation Studios will shake the formerly all Disney empire down to its very foundations.

NEWSDAY, 11/14/97, Part II/p. B3, Jack Mathews

This is a big weekend for children's movies. At theaters around the country, Walt Disney Studios' "The Little Mermaid," the 1989 animated musical that heralded the rebirth of the Disney legacy, returns for a 17-day encore. And at the Ziegfeld Theater, Twentieth Century Fox' "Anastasia," also an animated musical, does a one-week warmup for its national release next Friday.

"The Little Mermaid" is a huge entertainment, and there are new millions of kids ready to discover it. But Disney isn't rereleasing it as much for their benefit as to blunt the launch of "Anastasia," a movie that industry observers see as a most serious threat to Disney's domination of the animation market.

Fox is just one of the studios mounting an offensive. Warner Bros. has an animation unit, and so does the new DreamWorks, cofounded by former Disney guru Jeffrey Katzenberg. But Fox is first up with "Anastasia," directed by "An American Tail" animators Don Bluth and Gary Goldman, and it won't fail for lack of quality.

"Anastasia," based on the legend of the lost Russian princess, is state-of-the-art animation, made with a budget estimated at $50 million, and is the first done in Cinemascope widescreen format since the 1959 "Sleeping Beauty." It combines classical, 24-frames-per-second hand-drawn illustrations with computer graphics that adds breathtaking dimension to the illusion of movement. There's a runaway train sequence so taut and fast-paced that you can almost feel the wind against your face.

There also are moments of sublime beauty, with the camera roaming the ornate palatial halls of St. Petersburg and Paris. And great cartoon sequences with a wretched villain and ghostly hobgoblins. And, there is fairy-tale romance, between Anastasia (voice of Meg Ryan) and Dimitri (John Cusack), the former kitchen boy who tries to reunite her with her grandmother, the Dowager Empress Marie (Angela Lansbury).

"Anastasia" follows the general myth of the last Romanov, who was rumored to have escaped the Bolshevik executions that took her parents, Nicholas and Alexandra, and her four siblings. The story, since discredited, was told to dramatic perfection in Anatole Litvak's 1956 "Anastasia," in which Ingrid Bergman gave an Oscar-winning performance as the lost Grand Duchess.

For the animated "Anastasia," Bluth and Goldman and their writers were handed a natural larger-than-life villain in Rasputin (Christopher Lloyd), the seductive faith-healer of Czar Nicholas' court. Here, he is a bearded, black-robed menace who trades his soul for the power to destroy the Romanovs.

During the siege of the Bolsheviks, fueled by Rasputin's new-gained power, a kitchen boy leads 8-year-old Anastasia and the Dowager Empress to safety through a hidden passage. But the girl is separated from her grandmother at the train station, and spends the next 10 years in a paupers orphanage.

Booted out of the home at 18, Anastasia, renamed Anya, sets out for St. Petersburg, following the lead of a playful puppy she takes as a sign from God, and there has a fateful reunion with Dimitri, the kitchen boy. Neither of them recognizes the other. Anya has amnesia, and only remembers she has a family somewhere, while Dimitri and his pot-bellied partner Vladimir (Kelsey Grammer) are scheming to find an Anastasia lookalike to foist off on the Dowager Empress and claim the reward.

Naturally, Anya fits the bill, and soon they are all on their way to Paris where the Empress is in exile.

This sounds complicated for a children's movie, but it plays as a straightforward quest, with Anya, Dimitri, Vladimir and the irrepressible pup Pooka having to overcome that runaway train, Rasputin's curses and a stormy sea.   The film intercuts their adventures with scenes from Rasputin's purgatory, where he and his sidekick, a skeptical, wisecracking albino bat named Bartok (Hank Azaria) plot against them.

The song score by Lynn Ahrens and Stephen Flaherty, who also did the songs for the upcoming Broadway musical "Ragtime," is solid if unspectacular—I can't hum anything after one viewing—and Bartok, the film's primary source of comic relief, is badly underwritten. He just isn't funny.

"Anastasia" wouldn't make anyone forget who's boss of big screen animation, but it certainly proves that Disney is no longer great the only place where great animation is done.

NEWSWEEK, 11/17/97, p. 90, Yahlin Chang

There's something screwy about a movie that makes you lament the fall of the Russian Empire this late in the century. But given the way *Anastasia* revamps history, you almost can't help yourself. The 8-year-old princess revels in royal luxury until the revolution spoils all the fun. "Since the revolution our lives have been so gray!" the Russians sing. Turns out that the revolution's nothing more than a curse upon the Romanovs wrought by evil Rasputin. Ten years later, disgruntled communists are selling off fake royal memorabilia. Anastasia inexplicably turns up at an orphanage with no idea of who she is, but with the help of a con man, Dimitri, she reclaims her imperial heritage. Yes, it's ridiculous (the Bolshevik legacy has certainly been trampled enough). But imperialist nostalgia has become a merchandiser's cash cow—not unlike a successful animated musical.

As Fox's bid for a stake in the animated market, "Anastasia" has clearly borrowed elements of the Disney formula, like toy-friendly comic sidekicks. If you ignore the historical mangling (another Disney influence), there's fun to be had. Hank Azaria is hilariously deadpan as the voice of Rasputin's bat. Meg Ryan lends her trademark feistiness to Anastasia, and John Cusack makes Dimitri eminently likable as a sheepish hustler who redeems himself in love. "Anastasia" relies on proven Broadway conventions: rousing show tunes, big dance numbers, a lilting minor-key ballad. The score's unapologetic cheer is infectious. Kids over 5 will like it, and you'll probably smile yourself (and feel a little silly for it).

SIGHT AND SOUND, 5/98, p. 41, Leslie Felperin

St. Petersburg, 1917. At a grand ball, Princess Anastasia, one of the youngest members of the Romanov royal family, is given a music box by her grandmother, the Dowager Empress Marie, that can only be activated by a special key. The ball is interrupted by the entrance of the sorcerer Rasputin, who puts a curse on the family. Before long, the Russian Revolution commences. Anastasia escapes the palace, but loses her music box which the servant boy Dimitri (who helps her escape) finds and keeps. Missing her train to Paris, a run in with Rasputin leaves Anastasia amnesiac.

Years later, Anastasia, now called Anya, is 18 years old. Dimitri and his partner Vladimir are conmen, searching for a girl to pass off as Anastasia. They select Anya and train her up in courtly ways and Romanov family history as they travel to Paris to present her to the Dowager Empress. Meanwhile, Rasputin has risen from the dead and tries to use magic to kill Anastasia. In Paris, Anya's locket turns out to be the key to the music box: she really is Anastasia. She is reunited with her grandmother. Rasputin's last attempt to kill her is foiled by Dimitri and he and Anastasia declare their love for one another.

Disney's control of the animated feature film genre has been near total in recent years. So at the very least Twentieth Century Fox's *Anastasia* is to be welcomed for auguring the introduction of a new stall into the marketplace, soon to be joined by DreamWorks SKG with their *Prince of Egypt* due later this year.

For inspiration, *Anastasia*'s director Don Bluth (*All Dogs Go to Heaven*) and Co. have opted to adapt freely a more modern, pseudo historical tale, one which started life as a television play, moved to the stage and has since been filmed at least five times. The best known version,

Anatole Litvak's 1956 film, starred Ingrid Bergman as the orphaned princess and heir to the Romanov royal fortune.

Not surprisingly, this latest version places less emphasis on witty repartee and the rituals of court life. Instead, the main engines driving the narrative are magic (the Russian Revolution is provoked by the curse of a disgruntled sorcerer named Rasputin, not by anything silly like mass disgruntlement with imperialist oppression) and musical numbers (fairly bland and unmemorable). Pared down of contextualising history, this *Anastasia* clarifies how much the source material (there were several women who claimed to be Anastasia in real life) works out a common fantasy of many children that they are foundlings, destined to find riches and a better family. But as with the Bergman movie, the pleasure of finding this new family is quickly upstaged by the more mature pleasure of finding a mate.

The seduction of this fantasy is helped along here by finely executed animation. Colours are rich and intense, augmented by computer generated effects which make tiaras and assorted jewellery sparkle invitingly like nebulas. Characters move with fine grace, although the faces are occasionally less consistently drawn. But as a whole, it's a charming film and bodes well for the diversification of the animation industry.

VILLAGE VOICE, 11/25/97, p. 96, Laurie Stone

A Cold War cartoon about the murdered Romanovs would probably have pictured Lenin ushering in an evil empire, but in Fox's animated, post-Cold War version of the Russian Revolution, there is no social vision, only a curse against the czar, invoked by a vindictive Rasputin. In a nod to the good old days of bad Communism, factory workers bleat a wan number about life's grayness since the revolution. But mostly there is Anastasia (Meg Ryan), the czar's youngest daughter, and Dimitri, the kitchen boy who saves her life. The two make their way to Paris to convince the Dowager Empress, Anastasia's grandmother, that she is the real McRomanov. The movie feels rehashed, from the music to the computer-enhanced graphics to the romantic sparring of the leads to the Mrs. Teapot voice of Angela Lansbury's Dowager. Nothing is allowed to excite or disturb. Even the villain is more clownish than scary, and he's paired with a cuddly bat (Hank Azaria).

Revisionism adds one progressive note: while Anastasia acknowledges that every "lonely girl wishes she were a princess," at the end she ditches the royals to stick with her bloke of the folk.

Also reviewed in:
CHICAGO TRIBUNE, 11/21/97, Friday/p. D, Michael Wilmington
NEW YORK TIMES, 11/14/97, p. E22, Stephen Holden
VARIETY, 11/10-16/97, p. 39, Todd McCarthy
WASHINGTON POST, 11/21/97, p. C1, Stephen Hunter
WASHINGTON POST, 11/21/97, Friday/p. 50, Desson Howe

ANGEL BABY

A Cinepix Film Properties release of an Australian Film Finance Corporation presentation of a Stamen/Meridian Films production. *Producer:* Timothy White and Jonathan Shteinman. *Director:* Michael Rymer. *Screenplay:* Michael Rymer. *Director of Photography:* Ellery Ryan. *Editor:* Danny Cooper. *Music:* Chris Gough. *Sound:* John Phillips. *Casting:* Alison Barrett and Greg Apps. *Production Designer:* Chris Kennedy. *Art Director:* Hugh Bateup. *Costumes:* Kerri Mazzocco. *Running time:* 105 minutes. *MPAA Rating:* Not Rated.

CAST: John Lynch (Harry); Jacqueline McKenzie (Kate); Colin Friels (Morris); Deborra-Lee Furness (Louise).

LOS ANGELES TIMES, 1/31/97, Calendar/p.4, Kevin Thomas

Michael Rymer's "Angel Baby" swept the 1995 Australian Film Institute Awards in every major category and won at least five other Down Under prizes.

On the one hand, all this acclaim testifies to Rymer's considerable skill at shamelessly manipulating audience emotions with a sentimental and ultra-romantic treatment of mentally ill lovers, not to mention the potent charisma of his young stars, John Lynch and Jacqueline McKenzie.   On the other hand, such acclaim is not an encouraging sign for the once-groundbreaking Australian cinema.

Dark and lean, looking like a twentysomething Sam Waterston, Lynch's Harry is a sweet-natured guy who lives with caring brother (Colin Friels) and sister-in-law (Deborra-Lee Furness) while regularly attending group therapy and taking drugs that keep at bay the voices that only he hears. He seems to be doing fine when he meets a new group member, Kate (McKenzie).

She's an auburn-haired beauty with porcelain skin who was raped in childhood by her father and whose mental equilibrium is markedly more fragile than Harry's. Kate believes she is watched over by a guardian angel, whom she calls Astral, who communicates with her through Vanna White's equivalent in the Australian version of "Wheel of Fortune." She also believes that anybody who touches her blood has instant power over her.   Both Kate and Harry are slaves to numerology.

The pair swiftly fall passionately in love, and they want everything a normal couple wants, *right now*. Each receives some kind of government stipend, and Harry talks his way into a computer job while Kate does laundry.   They move into an apartment that looks like some sort of government housing structure. Harry's relatives and their therapists are understandably concerned that they're moving too fast, but they seem to be coping—until Kate becomes pregnant.

There's the makings of a good movie here, but Rymer goes for a swooningly romantic Romeo-and-Juliet approach that's sure to turn everyone not caught up in the movie's sugary spell. Rymer tries a love-conquers-all declaration when his story is telling us the reverse: that love, wonderful and welcome as it is, is not enough and that those with mental problems need to be especially careful about being able to deal with powerful emotions and responsibilities.

Rymer piles on the couple's escalating disintegration so extravagantly that you find yourself wondering just how much the government tab will be for picking up the pieces of their lives. So totally self-absorbed are Harry and Kate, and so big a burden do they become on others, that it's a terrific relief when Harry's brother finally loses his temper. If only, alas, Harry and Kate were as real as Harry's relatives.

When Harry and Kate make love, which is frequently, they go in for lots of lighted candles. When you think about it, love by excessive candlelight has become such a cliché that it's got to be a sure sign of a bad movie.

NEW YORK POST, 1/24/97, p. 48, Larry Worth

Cinematic depictions of mental ward inmates can go either way: "One Flew Over the Cuckoo's Nest" and "King of Hearts" won critical and popular success; Dudley Moore's "Crazy People" and Michael Keaton's "Dream Team" became video-store dust collectors.

Then there's the likes of "Angel Baby," which falls squarely between those cracks.

The production's strength is its superb acting. Ireland's John Lynch and Australia's Jacqueline McKenzie both stand out as troubled souls given to bouts of psychosis.

The weakness is a sometimes iffy script, penned by Michael Rymer, the film's director. Too many details don't add up, and a penchant for the mystical—McKenzie receives predictions of the future via TVs "Wheel of Fortune"—never jells within the plot's fragile frame.

The bulk of the story takes shape after the protagonists meet at a Melbourne psychiatric clinic and fall head over heels. That much is fine, as is their decision to share an apartment. But when she gets pregnant and opts off medication to save the baby, things spiral downhill in a hurry.

But while Rymer seems to think he's delivered a "David and Lisa" for the '90s, his sharp changes in tone—from whimsical to bleak to otherworldly—remain at odds with the overall concept.

Rymer's better with small touches, as when the lovers choose an abode based only on the number of lucky digits in the address. Ditto for a quirky scene in which bondage incites panic, not lust.

Speaking of torrid encounters, "Angel Baby" has its share, some almost reminiscent of "9½ Weeks." Each is erotic without being exploitive, starkly shot in sometimes unflattering light.

Lynch, with his gaunt face and darting eyes, and McKenzie, always on the verge of an emotional outburst while sinking into unreality, give such moments a frightening intensity. In addition, Colin Friels, as Lynch's concerned brother, is consistently engaging.

That's why it's disappointing as the inspired moments never coalesce. But "Angel Baby" at least earns points for asking tough questions—and providing no easy answers.

VILLAGE VOICE, 1/28/97, p. 61, Amy Taubin

The Australian film establishment seems partial to films that romanticize psychosis. In 1996, *Shine* racked up all kinds of awards; the year before, it was Michael Rymer's *Angel Baby*. Unlike *Shine*, Rymer's first feature doesn't end on an altogether upbeat note, no doubt the reason it's taken longer to make the journey from Down Under.

Angel Baby stars the brooding John Lynch and the mercurial Jacqueline McKenzie as Harry and Kate, psychotics who meet at an outpatient clinic and fall in love. For them, it's literally *l'amour fou*. After weeks of feverish sex in telephone booths and prettily lit back alleys, they decide to move in together. Harry, the more stable of the two (he had a psychotic break while working for IBM) gets a computer-programming job, and Kate earns some extra change doing their neighbors' laundry. Every evening, they settle down to watch *Wheel of Fortune*. Kate believes that her guardian angel Astral uses the show to transmit coded messages. (McKenzie and Lynch are most compelling when they're mesmerized by the TV screen.) Their domestic bliss is shattered when Kate becomes pregnant and they decide to go off medication to protect the health of the fetus.

Gifted, creative actors, Lynch and McKenzie throw themselves into their characters. If Rymer had trusted them more, *Angel Baby* would have been a more forceful film. Instead he soups up their madness with spinning, out-of-focus camera moves and lots of world-beat drumming. I somehow doubt that psychotics addicted to *Wheel of Fortune* would have aboriginal drum riffs banging around in their heads when they go off the deep end, but film conventions die hard, especially when they're tinged with racism. The music gives away Rymer's clichéd vision of psychotics as the Other—purer, more primitive, more sensitive than we boring, so-called normals. *Angel Baby* condescends to Harry and Kate by putting them on a pedestal. It would be more complicated to show how much like everybody else they truly are.

Also reviewed in:
NEW YORK TIMES, 1/24/97, p. C6, Janet Maslin
VARIETY, 9/4-10/95, p. 76, David Stratton
WASHINGTON POST, 5/2/97, Weekend/p. 43, Stephen Hunter

ANGEL DUST

A Northern Arts Entertainment release of a Twins Japan, Euro Space production. *Executive Producer:* Satoshi Kanno. *Producer:* Taro Maki, Kenzo Horikoshi and Eiji Izumi. *Director:* Sogo Ishii. *Screenplay (Japanese with English subtitles):* Yorozu Ikuta and Sogo Ishii. *Director of Photography:* Norimichi Kasamatsu. *Editor:* Hiroshi Matsuo and Sogo Ishii. *Music:* Hiroyuki Nagashima. *Production Designer:* Tomoyuki Maruo. *Running time:* 116 minutes. *MPAA Rating:* Not Rated.

CAST: Kaho Minami (Setsuko Suma); Takeshi Wakamatsu (Rei Aku); Etsushi Toyokawa (Tomoo); Ryoko Takizawa (Yuki Takei).

NEW YORK POST, 1/24/97, p. 49, Larry Worth

Ambition can be a dangerous thing, as Macbeth so nicely demonstrated.

Granted, director-writer Sogo Ishii wasn't driven to murder, but his out-of-control aspirations for "Angel Dust" prove the kiss of death.

That's a shame, because the premise is among the most terrifying in recent memory. Plain and simple, there's a serial killer on the loose in Tokyo who rides the subway each Monday at 6 p.m., sticking a lethal needle into some lovely in the crowd.

A pretty psychologist is asked to help police crack the case. But the madness hits too close to home when the trail leads to her mentor, a mysterious analyst whose specialty is deprogramming religious cultists.

Let the mind games begin, with the shrink finding her ex-colleague's actions duly suspicious, as well as those of her husband. Suddenly, her own safety is no longer a given.

Thankfully, Ishii never employs cheap just-out-of-the-closet jolts to generate suspense. It's pulled off via effective lighting, tight editing and an ability to convey urban paranoia.

But what starts as a thinking man's thriller degenerates beyond belief in the second hour. Momentum slows to a crawl, dialogue turns to psychobabble and there's an infusion of hothouse erotica.

It gets worse. Ishii introduces outrageous developments that belong in an entirely different movie, then segues to Nietzsche discussions. Any semblance of logic or clarity evaporates in a haze of David Lynch-like nonsense.

One gives the performers credit for persevering regardless. In particular, Kaho Minami makes a compelling heroine, nicely expressing growing alarm as her world implodes. Takeshi Wakamatsu and Etsushi Toyokawa also impress as her properly ambiguous love interests.

Ironically, viewers may root for the monster anyway, assuming mercy kills are the kindest exit for all concerned.

Except Ishii, of course. He needs to stick around and learn the value of leaving well enough alone.

VILLAGE VOICE, 1/28/97, p. 61, Amy Taubin

A less reverent vision of psychosis [The reference is to *Angel Baby*; see Taubin's review.] Sogo Ishii's *Angel Dust* is a visually elegant, deliberately confused serial-killer movie—a mix of *Silence of the Lambs* and Ishii's own *Panic in High School*. Made in 1994, it virtually predicts the Aum cult subway poison-gas killings.

Insanely plotted, *Angel Dust* focuses on a female criminologist (the poised, fabulously well-dressed Kaho Minami) who's brought in to assist a baffled male detective squad investigating a series of murders in the Tokyo subway. The victims, all young women, have been killed at rush hour by lethal injection. The criminologist has learned her unorthodox method of merging her mind with that of the killer from a former lover who specializes in deprogramming religious cultists and who, she suspects, may be involved in the murders. Plunging in and out of sensory deprivation chambers, volcanic caverns, and hivelike subway passages, *Angel Dust* depicts the unconscious as an omnipresent underground, churning out eroticized visions of chaos and annihilation. When one of the leading characters turned out to be a hermaphrodite, I was too tripped out to care.

Also reviewed in:
NEW YORK TIMES, 1/24/97, p. C20, Stephen Holden
VARIETY, 6/20-26/94, p. 44, David Rooney

APOSTLE, THE

An October Films release of a Butchers Runs Films production. *Executive Producer:* Robert Duvall. *Producer:* Rob Carliner. *Director:* Robert Duvall. *Screenplay:* Robert Duvall. *Director of Photography:* Barry Markowitz. *Editor:* Steve Mack. *Music:* David Mansfield. *Music Editor:* Sharon Smith. *Sound:* Steve C. Aaron and (music) Dan Gellert. *Sound Editor:* John Nutt. *Casting:* Renee Rousselot and Ed Johnston. *Production Designer:* Linda Burton. *Art Director:* Irfan Akdag. *Set Decorator:* Lori Johnson. *Set Decorator:* Dea Jensen. *Costumes:* Douglas

Hall. *Make-up:* Allison Gordin and Lily Gart. *Stunt Coordinator:* Ethan Jensen. *Running time:* 148 minutes. *MPAA Rating:* PG-13.

CAST: Robert Duvall (Euliss "Sonny" Dewey, The Apostle E.F.); Farrah Fawcett (Jessie Dewey); Todd Allen (Horace); John Beasley (Brother Blackwell); June Carter Cash (Mrs. Dewey, Sr.); Walton Goggins (Sam); Billy Joe Shaver (Joe); Billy Bob Thornton (Troublemaker); Miranda Richardson (Toosie); Paul Bagget (Tag Team Preacher 3); Lenore Banks (Female Sonny Supporter); Mary Lynette Braxton (Mother Blackwell); Brett Brock (Helper); Christopher Canady and Christian Canady (Sister Johnston's Twins); Elizabeth Chisolm (Singer); William Atlas Cole (Bayou Man); Frank Collins, Jr. (Soloist 4); Carl D. Cook (Civic Auditorium Preacher); Naomi Craig (Scripture Reader); Wayne Dehart (Liquor Store Preacher); Rick Dial (Elmo); Jan Fawcett (Needy Receiver 2); James Ivey Gleason (Young Priest); Chili Graham (Tag Team Preacher 5); Bobby Green (Tag Team Preacher 1); Stuart Greer (Texas State Trooper); John E. Hawkins (Sonny Supporter 1); Hunter Hayes (Child Accordionist); Daniel Hickman (Flashback Preacher); Emery Hopkins (Virgil); Brenda B. Jackson (Faith Healer 2); Jewell Jernigan (Sister Jewell); Charles Johnson (Tag Team Preacher 2); Julie Johnson (Baptism Soloist); Vera Kemp (Faith Healer 1); Joseph Lindsey (Soloist 1); Sharon K. London (Church Woman); Zelma Lloyd (Sister Johnson); Fernie E. McMillan (Doctor); Jimmie J. Meaux (Church Member 2); L. Christian Mixon (Bodyguard); Richard Nance (Church Man 2); Douglas Perry (Louisiana State Trooper); Harold Potier, Sr. (Coroner George); Kevin Rankin (Young Man in Car); Pat Ratiff (Accident Witness); Jay Robicheaux (Sonny, Aged 12); Terence Rosemore (Man Saying 'Amen'); Joyce Jolivet Starks (Sister Delilah); Christina Stojanovich (Jessie Jr.); Nicholas Stojanovich (Bobbie); Ronnie Stutes (Needy Receiver); Ruby Francis Terry (Soloist/Choir Director); Graham Timbes (Church Man 1); James B. Towry (Nosey Neighbor); Renee Victor (Latin Translator); Jesse Waldrop (Sonny Supporter 2); Steve White (Tag Team Preacher 4); Fay Winn (Tag Team Preacher 5); Melete Woods (Soloist 3); Jerry H. Skelton (Organist).

CHRISTIAN SCIENCE MONITOR, 11/14/97, p. 12, David Sterritt

Many moviegoers are pleased to find religion playing an ever-larger role in popular films. The latest examples are an interesting bunch, suggesting that as more pictures explore faith-related issues, their treatments may become more complex, going beyond heartwarming drama to examine conflicts and contradictions in lives touched by religious matters.

The most recent to arrive is *The Apostle*, written and directed by Robert Duvall, a skilled and insightful filmmaker who's best known for his on-screen work in movies by other directors. Already a hit at the recent New York Film Festival, it will have a limited run next month to qualify for the coming Oscar race, then arrive in theaters everywhere early next year.

Duvall plays a Pentecostal preacher named Sonny Dewey, who presides over a thriving evangelical church in Texas with his wife and a young partner. He's clearly a sincere, devoted, and energetic man. But he's burdened with bad qualities including a dangerously nasty temper, which flares out of control when he's hit with the one-two punch of his wife's infidelity and a successful move to oust him from his ministry.

Fleeing the law after a burst of violence, he lands in Louisiana and starts life afresh. Taking on a new name, The Apostle E.F, he plants new roots and gathers a new congregation. Establishing his friendly, racially mixed One Way Road to Heaven Church in a broken-down building on the outskirts of town, he becomes an eccentric but respected figure in the area. Still uncertain is whether his past will catch up with him.

"The Apostle" paints a superbly vivid portrait of Sonny and his companions, thanks partly to Duvall's astonishing performance and his sensitive screenplay. The film is at once a persuasive sociological drama, based on Duvall's sharp-eyed research in churches, and a sympathetic view of a man whose earnest faith has not yet lifted the weight of human weakness from his shoulders.

Critical Care is being promoted as a biting satire on current issues in the health-care industry. This is accurate, but it overlooks a religious dimension that provides some of the movie's most memorable moments.

James Spader plays a young physician being trained at a major hospital. He wants to cure the sicknesses and assuage the sufferings of his sadly afflicted patients.

But the hospital administrators think mainly about two other aspects of their profession: technology and profit. The medical experts are obsessed with high-tech gizmos that allow them to treat illnesses without going near the people diagnosed as having them. The financial experts are infatuated with the checks that roll in from insurance companies—spurring more and more procedures in even the most hopeless cases.

Issues like these are the main concern of "Critical Care," which may jar some viewers with its graphic scenes of illness. Directed by the prolific Sidney Lumet from Steven Schwartz's intelligent screenplay, the film scores many sardonic points against money-driven health care and mechanical approaches to human well-being.

Yet the picture's most touching moments occur in fantasy scenes involving emissaries from the afterlife, who engage earthly characters in dialogues about the true meanings of health, fulfillment, and life itself. Couched in terms of popular entertainment, these scenes don't go deep enough to qualify as genuine religious discernment. But they add a thought-provoking dimension to a film that already has impressive credentials as one of the year's most timely social satires.

A third movie, *Eye of God*, focuses on a woman (Martha Plimpton) who marries an ex-convict, unaware that his new commitment to fundamentalist Christianity hasn't curbed a violent streak in his personality.

Written and directed by newcomer Tim Blake Nelson, the drama makes only superficial use of a biblical subtext drawn from the story of Abraham and Isaac. "Eye of God" recognizes the importance of religion in many American lives, however, and reminds us of the cautionary fact that Scripture can be quoted as easily by guilty characters as by innocent ones.

FILM QUARTERLY, Fall 1998, p. 34, Felicia Feaster

The Apostle is the kind of film that separates the wheat from the chaff: either one responds to its almost documentary-like evocation of the South and its peculiar religious subculture or one dismisses the film out of hand as embarrassingly, unchicly spiritual. It has become customary in the United States to now categorize entire geographies and lifestyles as irrelevant or uncouth—and *The Apostle*'s respectful treatment of the backwater regions of the South and its evangelical religion doubly damn it. One only has to contrast the amusing but dignified treatment of a river baptism in *The Apostle* with John Schlesinger's depiction of the same event in *Midnight Cowboy* as a freakish, inbred travesty to sense the unfashionable, iconoclastic perspective Duvall offers in the film he wrote, produced, directed, and stars in.

Molecularly precise in its rendition of Southerners and the subculture of charismatic ministry, *The Apostle* is something Duvall envisioned 13 years ago ... an homage to what he calls "one of the truly American art forms." *The Apostle* is a response to a Hollywood which has insistently "caricatured the American preacher" and concurrently portrayed Southerners as the kind of people simple enough to dwell in the primordial darkness of religious fervor and plainly displayed emotion. Boasting an absolutely searing performance by Duvall in a sublime impersonation of Texas preacher, *The Apostle* is the culmination of the actor's longstanding interest in the region and an artistic highpoint in his already estimable career.

When Texas preacher Euliss "Sonny" Dewey (Robert Duvall) has his wife (Farrah Fawcett) and congregation wrested away from him by a clean-cut youth minister, he first brains her lover with a baseball bat in front of his children's Vacation Bible School ("I think he may be on the road to glory," Sonny quips with the understated, razor wit of the Southern temperament), and then flees the scene of the crime. In what turns out to be a decidedly spiritual take on the road movie, Sonny lets the Lord determine his course, and winds up in the Louisiana coastal town of Bayou Boutte, where he professes to be reborn, baptizing himself "The Apostle E.F." Resurrecting a humble country church, E.F. draws a devoted, rag-tag assemblage of disciples with his spiritual and earthly charisma. Recalling *Tender Mercies* in its story of a man who leaves his past behind for a new life, *The Apostle* also carries elements of the Western, with its enigmatic outsider who blows into town and changes it irreparably. And just as the motives of Clint Eastwood's "Man with No Name" are carefully concealed, so are E.F.'s intentions never truly clear. The film leaves us to wonder whether he seeks redemption or evasion, whether he is a true visionary or a Gantry-esque huckster.

E.F's most compelling quality is his divided nature. Equal parts manipulative smoothie and bone-deep believer, Duvall suggests the charismatic preacher as sexualized, cock-of-the-walk rock star, utterly beguiling his disciples with his magnetic performance style, wit, and silver tongue. Where *Slingblade* wrapped our identification around a tragic, gentle victim in Gumpian tradition, Robert Duvall's minister is a less immediately loveable, shape-shifting thing. A Lothario one moment, a snake in the grass the next, E.F. succumbs to the lure of violence and whiskey, and applies his charismatic, evangelical charms toward sexual conquest, even wooing a member of his flock (Miranda Richardson). Though a vastly imperfect man, the E.F. portrayed in Duvall's wily performance is a vehicle through which spirituality acts; the preacher's personal flaws are ultimately irrelevant because of the joy and unity he brings to his congregation.

The Apostle's most harrowing scene—and one which exemplifies the jumble of emotions inspired by this complex film—involves a lonely, awkward young man, Sammy (Walton Goggins, in a delicate, wrenching performance reminiscent of Jon Voight's acute vulnerability and degraded innocence in *Midnight Cowboy)*, one of the lowly, ordinary small-town people E.F. inspires. The impact the wayward preacher has had on the community is crystallized in a prolonged sermon delivered by E.F. at the height of his inspiration. When one least expects it, the emotional focus of *The Apostle* shifts to Sammy as he listens to E.F's message. His puppy-dog commitment to E.F.'s cause is heartbreaking, his social clumsiness—enhanced by a sad little pompadour and slightly bucktoothed grin—in touching contrast to E.F's smooth, confident masculinity. While Sonny demonstrates how religion can move an audience through a human agent, Duvall's and Goggins' performances show how acting can seduce a film audience into a secular epiphany.

The Apostle is, for the traditionalism of its subject and milieu, an unusually brave and subversive film. Like Billy Bob Thornton's similar redemption of the South in *Slingblade, The Apostle* shares a concern with the dignity of society's more marginal members, people whom Hollywood and the American public might deem inconsequential. *The Apostle* is an outlaw film for the respect it gives an institution often dismissed by liberals as ignorant and lowbrow, and often approached by conservatives with a bosom-hugging proprietary obnoxiousness. Despite occasional laps into kitsch (seen in an embarrassing musical interlude of a flock of children cleaning E.F.'s Bayou Boutte church), *The Apostle*'s sincerity and attention to the smallest of details rescue it from forays into the overtly melodramatic. Imbued with a penetrating realism, it precisely and often humorously nails its sub-culture, from E.F.'s vanity-plated Lincoln Continental to his good-old-boy, bow-legged shuffle, to the wary deference shown by an older black man—obliged to offer Southern hospitality even in the face of possible danger—when the road-tripping E.F. shows up in his fishing cove incoherent and sweating buckets.

A film about racial community rather than the estrangement thought of as more characteristic of Southern relationships, *The Apostle*'s treatment of race strives—like *Slingblade*'s advocacy for its gay characters—to right decades of misperception about the South's vilification of all difference. Though its thematic connections often feel incomplete, *The Apostle* suggests it was Sonny's seminal boyhood presence at his caretaker's fire-and-brimstone black church which inspired his own flamboyant, sensational preaching. Sonny's associations with Bayou Boutte's African Americans gives him an integrity in *The Apostle* which, even for its feel-good clichés, imbues the film with a gentle optimism about the potential for harmony in the South.

A performance that provocatively distills some of Duvall's former incarnations, E.F. is the culmination of the actor's roles as the gung-ho, explosive alpha male of *Apocalypse Now*, the wayward fathers of *Tender Mercies, The Great Santini*, and *Rambling Rose* and the actor's continued fascination with understated portraits of masculine motivation. *The Apostle* also continues Duvall's longstanding interest in the South as psychological locale, from his film debut in *To Kill Mockingbird* to 1972's *Tomorrow. Tender Mercies, The Great Santini, A Family Thing*, and *Rambling Rose* are all evidence of the South's significance for Duvall, its function as an entry point where masculinity and its performance crumble, revealing fissures in its facade. It's the tenderness at the heart of even the most gruff leathery, hardened men that Duvall's work consistently reveals and that recalls Southern tough-guy Harry Crews' fiction (he was initially commissioned to write *The Apostle*'s screenplay) tempered by the sensitivity of Horton Foote (with whom Duvall has maintained a lengthy professional and personal association), imbuing *The Apostle* with its odd mix of grittiness and grace.

LOS ANGELES TIMES, 12/17/97, Calendar/p. 1, Kenneth Turan

The consummate American actor, Robert Duvall has spent a lifetime crafting roles for other filmmakers. Now, in writing and directing "The Apostle," Duvall has created for himself what could be the defining role of his career.

In a string that began with "To Kill a Mockingbird" and includes 1982's Oscar-winning performance in "Tender Mercies," Duvall has managed to work for 35 years, through all kinds of cinematic weather, without ever setting a foot wrong. Able to disappear inside his characters no matter how often we see him, the actor has an impeccable gift for finding the sparks of authenticity and truth that make his people come alive on screen. Yet, even for him, "The Apostle" is something special.

The story of a life-changing crisis that transforms a Pentecostal preacher, this film has been a personal project of Duvall for more than a decade. It's an excellent fit because the connections between actor and minister—the necessity of belief, the ability to convince, the power of personality and the mastery of the rhythmic cadences of language—are numerous and durable.

Even in a Hollywood that's in general uncomfortable with religion, alternating between the extremes of hagiography and exposé, the committed hellfire and damnation preacher Duvall portrays is a type that gets the shortest shrift. So it is not the least of "The Apostle's" accomplishments that it doesn't condescend to belief. Rather it quietly explores how religion works in people's lives, what it can and cannot do for those who preach and those who practice.

Though we see him as an even younger child mesmerized by a blind black minster, the call officially came to Euliss "Sonny" Dewey (Duvall) at the age of 12. "The Apostle" features the adult Sonny in numerous charismatic preaching situations, eager to compare the virtues of "Jesus' mailing list" to "the devil's hit list" and exulting in the expansive glory of "Holy Ghost power."

Driving past a wreck on a Texas highway, Sonny pulls over and scampers (the man never just walks) toward a seriously injured couple, intent on getting them to "accept the lord Jesus Christ" as their personal savior. When he returns to his car, he proudly tells his beloved mother (country music's June Carter Cash), "Momma, we made news in heaven this morning."

Sonny's relations with his wife, Jessie (a surprising Farrah Fawcett), the mother of his children and his partner in the Temple of the Living God church, are less serene. It's through her, not only in what she says but the fearful way she looks at him, that we learn of the man's darker, womanizing side. When Jessie determines not only to get out of the marriage but to take the church with her, it's a staggering blow.

Wound terribly tight, capable of jealousy and fury as well as religious fervor, Sonny *in extremis* has the frightening quality of Robert Mitchum in "Night of the Hunter." The other side of his positive energy, of his belief that he has a direct line to the Lord, is Sonny's sense that he's a law unto himself, a conviction that leads to a brutal act.

Forced to leave Texas, Sonny erases everything of his past except his deep commitment to religion, rebaptizing himself as "the Apostle E.F." A great self-dramatizer and self-mythologizer, he has conversations with God on his lonely road, assuring the Lord in ringing tones, "wherever thou leadest, I will follow." He ends up in the tiny town of Bayou Boutte in Louisiana, where another kind of preaching life, another opportunity to get right with God, is waiting for him.

Both as a writer and director, Duvall has put himself at the service of this intriguing character, but that hasn't harmed the rest of the film. In fact, unlike the classic star turn that obliterates the competition, the integrity of Duvall's acting brings almost everyone else's work, including the film's nonprofessionals, up a notch. Especially telling is the performance of a gaunt, almost unrecognizable Fawcett, whose portrait of a suffering wife makes us believe.

Duvall's unhurried, naturalistic directing style (a recent Film Comment interview mentioned his admiration for Ken Loach's exceptional "Kes") fosters the best kind of unhurried authenticity. Though a lot happens in it, "The Apostle" is not plot-driven, and despite its subject matter it's the opposite of preachy. Confident of the energy inherent in his character, Duvall has been able to create drama that is no less gripping for being quiet and low-key.

Any discussion of "The Apostle" inevitably comes back to its protagonist, to the way Duvall has created as complete a person as the screen allows, a man who can be discussed as fully as a flesh-and blood acquaintance or even a close friend. It's an effortlessly complex portrayal that relishes the contradictions and complexities of someone capable of both exalted and debased behavior, a shape-shifter it is possible to be fascinated, repelled and compelled by, all at the same time.

In that same thoughtful Film Comment interview, Duvall mentions a sign his old acting teacher Sandy Meisner had over his desk: "There's no right and wrong, only truth or non-truth." By that criteria, or any other you want to name, the Apostle E.F. is screen acting to cherish and remember.

NEW YORK, 1/12/98, p. 47, David Denby

In *The Apostle*, Euliss "Sonny" Dewey (Robert Duvall), a Pentecostal preacher in rural Texas, is driving along the highway with his elderly mother when he comes across a gruesome multi-car accident. For Sonny, it's good times—he gets to work. Pulling over, he hops out of his car, Bible in hand; skips past the highway patrol; and sticks his head into the window of one of the wrecked automobiles. The driver, a teenage boy, is stunned and bloody, and so is the girl sitting next to him. But Sonny tells them that God loves them, that they have to take Jesus into their lives so they can be saved.

"There are angels, *angels* right here in this automobile," he insists, badgering the boy, who stares before him with dead eyes. Duvall keeps his voice low, but Sonny's intrusion is meant to be an outrage: These two sinners need an ambulance. Yet as the boy stirs and begins to weep, Duvall half convinces us that the teenagers may need Jesus too. *The Apostle* (which played a week in December to qualify for the Oscars and is opening again at the end of January) is the best movie ever made about a man of God—which is to say, the most honest and morally the most ambiguous. Sonny is egotistical and manipulative; a con artist, a brawler, a womanizer; a man who falls into bathos as easily as a soldier falls into erotic reverie. Yet he's a kind of genius, too, a gifted, sometimes inspired preacher who rounds up isolated and demoralized people and forges them into a community. Sonny is a warrior against forlornness.

Duvall wrote and directed the picture himself, using some of his own money when no one in Hollywood was much interested in bankrolling him. In truth, his past efforts as a director, *We're Not the Jet Set* and *Angelo, My Love*, would not have sent me reaching for my checkbook, either. Nor can I say that I've always been a fan of his acting. I see what other people admire—the clarifying hardness and power, the edge of mockery, the muscular grip on reality. You certainly can't catch Duvall in false moments. But you also don't catch him relaxing and giving the audience a good time. It's not always easy to look at his mean slit eyes and evil grin, and I think actors who bellow are a pain in the neck, even when they're meant to be playing blowhards. Duvall can be dry and overbearing, almost priggish, as if he thought the mere absence of charm were a virtue in itself.

But in *The Apostle,* he's completely on top of what he's doing. Sonny bellows, but with professional skill, in the rhythmic, incantatory style that he has copied from the black preachers he heard as a boy. He's overbearing, all right—devastating as he zeroes in on whatever person is before him. Duvall makes him fast, very fast, a shrewd and enterprising man, spry as a water bug, who senses what people want and adjusts instantly. This noisy super-salesman for God—the world's greatest shouter, a tent-revival spellbinder—is capable of modulating his voice to a whisper when he needs to get intimate with someone. At times, the performance has an almost effervescent gaiety. Now in his middle sixties, Duvall has never seemed to enjoy himself so much. There's a little hop of anticipation in Sonny's step; he rushes out of his house in the morning, thrilled with himself, thrilled to be doing God's work, chattering and revving himself up—he's scoring a touchdown for the Lord. Sonny pulls depressed people out of their torpor; he makes the quest for Jesus about the most exciting adventure anyone ever heard of. Even when he's at his most outrageously self-serving, he's sure he's doing God's work, and Duvall gives him an edge of bravado and merriment. He's almost daring God not to admire Sonny's effectiveness.

And Duvall has picked up speed as a director, too. Right after the opening, there's a montage of Sonny preaching to different congregations that turns into a kind of musical revue. In one sequence, Sonny rushes back and forth across the stage and then hands the microphone off to different preachers, who, like star tap dancers, surge forward one at a time and do their own supercharged riffs; in another, he's working with a Hispanic woman who's having a glory fit, and he translates her words and moves with her as they march in triumph together through the valley of the shadow of death. Hallelujah! *The Apostle* openly acknowledges that the heat and excitement produced by charismatic showmanship are a major part of Pentecostal evangelism it acknowledges as well how much black speech rhythms dominate the style of the religion. Like Tarantino's *Pulp Fiction* and *Jackie Brown*, it is one of the new movies in which whites and blacks do something together—and race is not much of an issue. White people think Sonny sounds black, and they like his style; black people accept him as a man with a gift. Duvall puts some of the black church women he's met in the South into the picture; they are exalted people with the strangeness of those lost in a dream of God.

At night, on the road, Sonny has a vision: His wife (Farrah Fawcett, who is perfectly good) is sleeping with a handsome young minister. He returns home in a drunken rage, and, with half the town watching, takes a baseball bat to the minister's head. Sonny has to disappear fast—in any case, there's nothing holding him to the town, since his wife has already persuaded his church to throw him out as pastor. After deep-sixing his car, his past, his identity, he hits the road and emerges as a newborn itinerant man of God, a preacher without a congregation. The movie slows down and Duvall opens himself to the softer beauties of the southern landscape—for a while, *The Apostle* becomes a middle-aged *Huckleberry Finn*. Sonny finally settles into a bedraggled but pleasant Louisiana town called Bayou Boutte, where, identifying himself as "E.F., The Apostle," he joins forces with a retired black minister and builds a congregation from the ground up.

This is Sonny's period of grace—the time of his time. Committing an evil act and then escaping from it delivers him into goodness. He's not so much a hypocrite as a man perfectly able to re-create himself without losing a step. The last third of *The Apostle* is not as exciting as the rest, and the movie sags a bit as Duvall romances Miranda Richardson, who plays a genteel southern lady both attracted to and repelled by the dynamic preacher. Still, *The Apostle* gets at something authentic and challenging—the insistent goodness of a man never free of dishonesty or sin. Compared with this movie, films like *Elmer Gantry* that "expose" the evangelist figure as a phony seem shallow and beside the point. For whatever judgment you might make of Sonny, he certainly delivers the goods. And so does Robert Duvall, who has made a movie devoid of both illusion and cynicism. In his own life, Sonny is too much a sinner simply to possess God. He remains an eternal suppliant, a candidate for blessedness, and therefore, despite everything, a hero.

NEW YORK POST, 12/17/97, p. 60, Thelma Adams

"The Godfather" star Robert Duvall finally gets to play Sonny in "The Apostle." Only this time, the character in question isn't the short-fused, oversexed scion of the Corleone clan. Duvall's Euliss (Sonny) Dewey is a short-fused womanizing Pentecostal preacher.

The Texan talks directly to God ("I always called you Jesus; you always called me Sonny."). But the preacher has problems communicating with his cranky wife, Jessie.

Played by Farah Fawcett in her "The Burning Bed" mode, we see the actress as she might have looked after going a few rounds with someone: raccoon-eyed, strung-out but still sinewy and appealing and capable of throwing a mean curve.

When Jessie steals Sonny's church and kids and leaves him for a younger preacher, this son of God breaks a few commandments and takes it on the lam. Dewey reinvents himself as The Apostle and starts anew in a Louisiana backwater called Bayou Boutte.

Sonny travels deep into Flannery O'Connor territory. Along the "Wise Blood" way, Sonny woos an almost unrecognizable, but recognizably brilliant, Miranda Richardson. He also faces the devil in Billy Bob Thornton and strikes up a partnership with black preacher John Beasley. June Carter Cash plays his mama.

Writer, director, producer and star Duvall pairs professional and nonprofessional actors in his character-driven study about an egotistical man who's a saint, a sinner and a true believer.

Heartfelt, funny and raw, "The Apostle" may be short on dramatic tension, but Duvall commands attention with his intense, physical portrayal of a complicated, charismatic American original. Praise the Lord!

NEWSDAY, 12/17/97, Part II/p. B11, Jack Mathews

When Karl Marx called religion the opium of the people, he'd never seen a Sunday service conducted by a Pentecostal preacher like Euliss "Sonny" Dewey, a k a "The Apostle." If he were around now to observe Sonny, Marx might adjust the metaphor and call religion the crystal meth of the masses.

Sonny, played to the rafters and beyond by Robert Duvall, is a shake, rattle and Holy Roller, a Texas zealot who draws faith into his soul with every breath, and exhales nothing but the word. He's been preaching since answering the call at the age of 12, and an hour doesn't pass without his having a talk with God, or with somebody about Him.

And lately, he's had a lot to talk to God about.

Sonny's wife (Farrah Fawcett), with whom he guides a congregation in Texas, has fallen in love with a younger minister and wants a divorce. In addition, she has convinced the church leaders to expel him for her convenience, and he fears that their two children—his "beauties," he calls them—are drifting away from him, as well. The capper: at his son's Little League game, a drunk Sonny snaps and whacks his wife's lover with a baseball bat, leaving him in a coma and turning himself into a fugitive.

What follows is Sonny's efforts, under a new identity, to develop a congregation in a Louisiana bayou town, and find redemption, not just for the crime but for his own infidelities and other presumed abuses of his wife.

"The Apostle" is a different kind of evangelical tale. Duvall, who also wrote, directed, and produced the film, was intent on doing a serious character study, without the condescending tone and demeaning stereotypes that infuse most Hollywood films about southern religion. And though he often overindulges himself with run-on sermons, he's created a, fascinating and—within the narrow world Sonny inhabits—deeply complex man.

Sonny is flawed, but not a fraud. He's ambitious, but incorruptible. And like the Bible he quotes, the hellfire sermons he gives and the demonstrative reaction he gets, there is both inspiration and a sense of violence to the spectacle. Sonny is thoroughly intoxicated by his faith, and intoxicated people often do irrational things.

In the opening moments, Sonny and his mother (June Carter Cash) drive onto the scene of a terrible multi-car crash. Sonny parks, then sneaks past the police to get to one of the involved cars, where he urges the badly injured driver to accept Christ and be joined by angels. The moment is transcendent for Sonny, if not the driver, and he returns to his own car in a state of hyper-exhilaration.

"We made news in heaven this morning, Mama," he says.

Later, in Bayou Boutte, the rural, mostly black Louisiana town where he believes God has led him, Sonny finds enough yearning souls to keep him high for a lifetime. With the help of the Rev. Blackwell (John Beasley), whose heart condition forced him out of the fire and brimstone business, and a community roused by Sonny's thundering radio sermons, he "resurrects" a run-down church, renames it "One Way Road to Heaven," and begins the process of restoring himself.

Meanwhile, he's bearing the burden of bad news relayed from home, where both his mother and his wife's boyfriend lay near death, and dreading the inevitable moment when his past catches up with him.

Duvall filled the church scenes with non-actors recruited from Louisiana parishes, and they lend a wonderful authenticity to their scenes. The professionals all turned in solid performances, particularly Billy Bob Thornton, playing a redneck with a soul in need of saving, and Miranda Richardson, the radio station secretary who is both attracted and repelled by Sonny's intensity.

Still, this is essentially an all-Duvall show. He's in virtually every scene, and besides his writing, directing, and producing chores, he even paid for it. Technically, that makes "The Apostle" a vanity production, but to quote the Bible, "Every man at his best is altogether vanity."

NEWSWEEK, 12/22/97, p. 84, David Ansen

[*The Apostle* was reviewed jointly with *Wag the Dog*; see Ansen's review of that film.]

SIGHT AND SOUND, 6/98, p. 38, Robin Doughtery

Rural Texas. Euliss 'Sonny' Dewey, a Pentecostal preacher, learns that he's been voted out of the church he helped to found. Angry about this indignity and the fact that his wife Jessie is involved with a younger minister, he shows up at his children's baseball game and swats his wife's lover Horace with a bat. Fearing that he's killed the man, Sonny leaves town, ditching his car in a lake. He asks God to make him an apostle, rebaptises himself "the Apostle E.F." and sets off for Louisiana to start a new church.

Sonny has a gift for preaching (flashbacks reveal that he grew up attending services at a black church). In Louisiana, he sets up a new congregation, raising money by working as a short order cook and preaching evangelicalism over the radio. Soon after he opens the One Way Road to Heaven Holiness Temple, Jessie hears him on the radio. Sonny, unaware just how close he is to capture, confesses to the murder to a fellow minister and is overheard by his faithful sidekick Sam. Sonny hints that he may not be around forever. One day, police officers arrive at an evening service. Sonny's animated preaching builds to a crescendo. He leaves the church and walks to the waiting policemen.

Robert Duvall put up $5 million of his own money to produce *The Apostle,* which he also wrote and directed, so it's no surprise that he comes across on screen as the film's mover and shaker. His character Sonny rarely out of sight during the film's 133-minute trek—describes himself as "a genuine Holy Ghost filled preaching machine", an apt description, because here Duvall is a heaven-inspired acting machine. The role won him an Oscar nomination, but it gives moviegoers something far more impressive: a depiction of a minister that draws on all the stereotypical details but ultimately transcends them.

Unlike, say, Burt Lancaster in *Elmer Gantry* (1960) or Steve Martin as a charlatan preacher in the recent *Leap of Faith,* Sonny is not out to exploit his congregation. Although he's a charismatic charmer—a loose-limbed combination of a game show host and a Morris dancer he's not in it for the money at all. Sonny actually believes. He stops his car in mid-intersection to get out to pray, literally asking God for directions. But Sonny's religion has a dark side. He's a man who loves and hates God at the same time. When he finally self destructs, Sonny experiences his downfall as a religious experience. In fact, the film is framed entirely by Sonny's religious perspective, and makes no concessions for any unbelievers in its audience.

As an actor-director, Duvall has a knack for tapping emotions through his visuals, more deft here than in his earlier ventures, the 1975 documentary *We're Not the Jet Set,* and 1983's *Angelo, My Love.* He stirs up the images of rural America in picture book panoramas. In one, Sonny's tomato-red church bus is ferried across a river along a saturated, candy-coloured horizon. In another moment, he gives us children painting the church while energetically sing-chanting the books of the Bible. Duvall also carries out the texture of rural America by casting people we already associate with Southern culture: country music matriarch June Carter Cash plays Sonny's mother and Billy Bob Thornton is a troublemaker whom Sonny converts.

Most importantly, *The Apostle* depicts the startling energy, of Sonny's evangelicalism through an affectionate use of music. The film's score includes such gospel classics as 'Oh How I Love Jesus' as well as Dolly Parton's new song, 'Shine On'. But even these powerful vocal testaments can't drown out Duvall, whose character is never more than a syllable away from invoking Jesus. All those hallelujahs and shouted prayers fill up their own cathedral.

TIME, 1/26/98, p. 69, Richard Corliss

He seems to live in the skin of characters whose skin you might not even want to touch. His trick is to find the surprising private clue: that, say, Adolf Eichmann, whom he played in a TV movie, "loved his kids, doted on them. That gave me a starting point." Or that Stalin (an Emmy-winning HBO turn) could force himself to talk sympathetically to his daughter—"I felt that was as good a work as I've done." So to get inside America's greatest underrated actor, we should look for that secret quirk, that strange but true passion ...

Robert Duvall loves to tango!

Books on the tango decorate the living room coffee table on his 200-acre Virginia farm. Tango records are scattered about. A favorite partner in this dance fever is his dark-haired, thirtyish live-in mate, Luciana Pedraza, who hails from an upper-class Argentine family. The news has to flummox moviegoers who'd have guessed that the only music the 67-year-old actor could move to would be a Sousa march.

A rear admiral's son who grew up on Navy bases around the country, Duvall is best known for playing men with a military bearing about them, a sense of history and tightly coiled power. Think of Stalin and Eichmann, but also Eisenhower (twice), Jesse James, Joseph Pulitzer, Holmes' Dr. Watson. He doesn't just embrace their contradictions; he Heimlichs them to compelling life. The men may be good or bad or (Duvall's favorite) both; he will inhabit them forcefully and without editorializing. His credo of acting is his credo of life: "Don't judge too quickly. Don't patronize. Don't make statements. Don't set people aside. Give them their due."

Since his 1962 debut as Boo Radley, the monster and savior of two Alabama children in *To Kill a Mockingbird*, Duvall has given more than their due to some indelible movie creatures. The names Frank Burns (*MASH*), Tom Hagen (*The Godfather*), Lieut. Colonel Kilgore (*Apocalypse Now*), Bull Meechum (*The Great* Santini), Mac Sledge (*Tender Mercies*) and Gus McCrae (*Lonesome Dove*) summon sharp, overlapping impressions. The odor of anachronism hangs on most of these characters; they are uneasy with and suspicious of the modern world. While everyone else has gone slack and disorderly, they mulishly hew to an old or private code they dare not question. They alone remain *semper fi*.

To this gallery, add two miscreants from films opening this month: *The Gingerbread Man*'s Dixon Doss, a wily Georgia eccentric who is sort of Boo Radley grown old and gone wrong; and, more important, E.F. ("Sonny") Dewey. E.F. is the Texas preacher in *The Apostle*, a complex, cantankerous drama that Duvall wrote, directed, stars in and—after all the studios turned down the $5 million project—paid for. This renegade Pentecostalist has the spiel and showmanship to fill a tent or a temple; when E.F. talks, people listen. "I'm a genu-wine, Holy Ghost, Jesus-filled preachin' machine this mornin'!" He can woo a dying man to the Lord, but he can't heed his own gospel. He menaces his frazzled wife (Farrah Fawcett) and clubs a rival with a baseball bat; when the man falls into a coma, E.F. shows no regret or remorse. He flies away, landing in Louisiana and hoping to build another church. Jesus' retailer needs a new store.

Is E.F. a madman? A hypocrite? A messed-up guy chained to his one gift? In his brave, alert performance, Duvall typically doesn't try to reconcile, or even explain, the discrepancy between E.F.'s life-defying faith and his death-defying sociopathy. He leaves the judging to audiences. His job, which he does better than anyone else in movies, is to watch the world with those icy blue eyes.

"It's the main work he does as an actor," says Billy Bob Thornton, whose *Sling Blade* was partly inspired by Boo Radley, and who plays a pivotal cameo in *The Apostle*. "He observes characters." Screenwriter Horton Foote (*Mockingbird, Tender Mercies*), who recommended that Duvall play Boo Radley, praises his "eye and ear for specifics of character. He has a feel for the Southern idiom, but he brings variations to it. For *Tender Mercies* he tape-recorded people, then studied the accent till he got it right."

Duvall is an ethnographer at heart, pounding the back roads, keeping his eyes open, taking notes. "I don't watch other movies to study acting," he says. "I go to documentaries. And I learn from people. There are things you pick upon mannerism or gesture, one little subtle thing." Before making *Lonesome Dove* he was visiting the Texas home of Slingin' Sammy Baugh, quarterback for the '40s Washington Redskins. "He had a way of pointing"—Duvall cocks a finger and throws his hand in the air—"and a particular way of talking. I put that into the character." Thus did an old football star become a driven cattle driver.

The Apostle required 35 years of watching and waiting. In 1962, during rehearsals for an off-Broadway show in which he was to play a man from Hughes, Ark., Duvall broke up a transcontinental trip to stop in Hughes. "I got off the Trailways bus," he recollects, "and wandered into this little church. There was a lively preacher; the congregation was stomping and moving and feeling the spirit. I said I'd like to play one of these guys one day." When he asked Foote to do the screenplay, the author encouraged the actor to try it himself. In 1984 Duvall began writing. "I pieced it together from stuff that I had found out about this kind of life, just traveling around and absorbing like I do." Sonny is a composite of preachers from rural Texas, Virginia and Tennessee. "I listened to the way they whoop," he says, "then hold the note and cut it with a cadence." If you expect a Jimmy Swaggart-style spellbinder, who coaxes near operatic melodrama from his rich baritone, E.F. will disappoint you. The narrow range of Duvall's voice can convey muscle and danger; the music is lacking." His whoop is a thing of will, not an expression of soulful exuberance. For that, listen to the real preachers Duvall hired for small roles. Black or white, they'll have you lining up to be baptized in the nearest creek or bayou.

On his farm, Duvall is a gentleman farmer who has just finished renovating a barn into a posh party space, with a bar, a pool table and, of course, a dance floor. He can afford it. October Films paid $6 million for U.S. rights to *The Apostle*. He also earns a nice paycheck on gigs like this year's *Deep Impact* (sci-fi with Morgan Freeman) and *A Civil Action* (courtrooms with John Travolta). That leaves something in the bank for his own projects; he and Thornton are planning a Merle Haggard biopic. "The best of it all," he says, "is I'm a late bloomer. I get better as I get older; I learn more and have a lot to draw from. I'm going to try to maybe direct some things and produce some others. But if my film company was suddenly destroyed—which won't happen—I have a good career as a hired hand."

And in the unlikely event that his film career dries up, Duvall could try Broadway. We hear they're auditioning understudies for *Forever Tango*.

VILLAGE VOICE, 12/23/97, p. 84, Amy Taubin

Like Robert De Niro, Robert Duvall is very good at playing characters whose rigid body armor is a defense against their feelings. While most actors are dedicated to getting in touch with their emotions, Duvall is most convincing when he seems most disassociated. Whether he's playing a nutcase like the major in *Apocalypse Now* or an ordinary neurotic like the L.A. detective in *True Confessions*, he doesn't quite compute. It's as if he's desperately trying to rouse something inside him that's missing in action, the something that even atheists like me imagine as a soul.

In *The Apostle*, Duvall plays Sonny Dewey, a Texas Pentecostal preacher who's so busy talking to God, he wouldn't be able to hear Him if He answered. Sonny's like a rooster, rushing around his flock of hens and clucks with his chest stuck out and his ass lagging behind, pumping his elbows like wings, clucking "Thank you, Jesus" at every step. A zealot who admits no opposition in his religious or his personal life, Sonny's turns violent when crossed. His wife (Farrah Fawcett) is sick of his prayers and his physical intimidation. When she tells Sonny that she's leaving him and taking the kids, he responds by applying a baseball bat to the skull of the young minister with whom she is in love. Sonny's in big trouble, but rather than turning himself in, he goes on the lam, and, having asked God for directions, winds up across the state tine in a tiny, mostly black Louisiana bayou town. With the blessings of the town's black minister, who's been sidelined by a bad heart, he rebuilds the local church, puts the word out over the radio, and attracts a full house of worshipers. But no matter how many souls he saves, he still has killed a man, and for that, he's damned to hell.

Written and directed by Duvall, *The Apostle* (which is 20 minutes shorter than when it screened in the New York Film Festival) is basically a character study of a religious fanatic. What's most interesting about the film is Duvall's obvious ambivalence about a guy who is possessed by a fundamentalist notion of God but lacks wisdom, tolerance, compassion, or moral fiber. Unlike the smarmy, sentimental *Sling Blade*, *The Apostle* doesn't try to win us over to its protagonist's side. Sonny does really horrible things: he brutalizes his wife, he kills her lover, he abandons his children, he refuses to go to the bedside of his dying mother (June Carter Cash) lest he be caught by the police, and he tries to seduce one of his parishioners (Miranda Richardson) without letting her know about the heavy baggage he's carrying. This is not a guy you'd want to have around the house. For him, the business of saving souls outweighs personal responsibilities.

Which is not to say he's not suspect in the evangelical department as well. When a local redneck (who else but *Sling Blade*'s own Billy Bob Thornton) threatens to flatten Sonny's "nigger church" with his tractor, it takes only five minutes for Sonny to get him on his knees weeping and waiting and embracing Jesus Christ as his personal savior. But since the guy seems just as delusional after he's found God as he did before, anyone in his/her right mind knows it's as likely as not that he'll be back tomorrow to finish what he was distracted from today.

The scene raises more problems than Duvall wants to deal with. Until Thornton enters the picture, *The Apostle* seems to exist in an ahistorical never-never land where the politics of race, not to mention abortion, don't intrude in the house of the faithful. But Thornton's character is too unimportant to carry the entire burden of the racism that, however unconscious, compromises the film. *The Apostle* plays much too easily into a white racist agenda that wants to keep control of the church in the South. You have to ask yourself why the retired black minister never called up another black minister and asked him or her to take over his congregation, 90 per cent of which is black. Why did he just sit passively at home waiting for the white guy to save his church? You might also wonder why this strangely impotent minister is the only black character in the film to be named in the credits. I know we're all God's children, but it just seems a little bit unfair that when the pews are filled with black bodies, only white people have agency.

Also reviewed in:
CHICAGO TRIBUNE, 1/30/98, Friday/p. A, Michael Wilmington
NEW YORK TIMES, 12/7/97, p. E10, Janet Maslin
NEW YORKER, 2/2/98, p. 82, Daphne Merkin
VARIETY, 9/15-21/97, p. 69, Emanuel Levy
WASHINGTON POST, 1/30/98, p. D1, Stephen Hunter
WASHINGTON POST, 1/30/98, Weekend/p. 48, Desson Howe

AS GOOD AS IT GETS

A TriStar Pictures release of a Gracie Films production. *Executive Producer:* Richard Sakai, Laurence Mark, and Laura Ziskin. *Producer:* Bridget Johnson, Kristi Zea, and James L. Brooks. *Director:* James L. Brooks. *Screenplay:* Mark Andrus and James L. Brooks. *Based on a story by:* Mark Andrus. *Director of Photography:* John Bailey. *Editor:* Richard Marks. *Music:* Hans Zimmer. *Music Editor:* Zigmund Gron. *Sound:* Jeff Wexler and (music) Alan Meyerson. *Sound Editor:* Dennis Drummond. *Casting:* Francine Maisler. *Production Designer:* Bill Brzeski. *Art Director:* Philip Toolin. *Set Decorator:* Clay A. Griffith. *Set Dresser:* John H. Maxwell, Gary Rizzo, Bart C. Hubenthal, Scott G. Jones, Todd Jacques, and John D. Maskovich. *Special Effects:* William B. Doane. *Costumes:* Molly Maginnis. *Make-up:* Michele Burke. *Make-up (Jack Nicholson):* Perry Michael Germain. *Make-up (Cuba Gooding, Jr.):* Stacye Branché. *Stunt Coordinator:* Ken Fritz and Walter Scott. *Running time:* 130 minutes. *MPAA Rating:* PG-13.

CAST: Jack Nicholson (Melvin Udall); Helen Hunt (Carol Connelly); Greg Kinnear (Simon Bishop); Cuba Gooding, Jr. (Frank Sachs); Skeet Ulrich (Vincent); Shirley Knight (Beverly); Yeardley Smith (Jackie); Lupe Ontiveros (Nora); Jill (Verdell); Bibi Osterwald (Neighbor Woman); Ross Bleckner (Carl); Bernadette Balagtas (Caterer); Jaffe Cohen, Laurie Kilpatrick, and Alice Vaughn (Partygoers); Brian Doyle-Murray (Handyman); Kristi Zea (Mother at Table); Annie Maginnis Tippe (Daughter at Table); Shane Black (Cafe 24 Manager); Peter Jacobson (Man at Table); Lisa Edelstein (Woman at Table); Stan Bly (Cafe 24 Customer); Randall Batinkoff (Carol's Date); Jesse James (Spencer Connelly); Jamie Kennedy and Justin Herwick (Street Hustlers); Maya Rudolph (Policewoman); John F. O'Donohue (Detective Ray); David A. Kipper (Hospital Doctor); Mary Elizabeth Still (Nurse Receptionist); Chloe Brooks and Cooper Brooks (Children at Cafe 24); Sharon L. Alexander and Holly Denys (Female Passersby); Lawrence Kasdan (Dr. Green); Alison Rose and Kathryn Morris (Psychiatric Patients); Wood Harris (Cafe 24 Busboy); Linda Gehringer (Publisher); Julie Benz (Receptionist); Harold Ramis (Dr. Bettes); Antonia Jones (Nurse); Kaitlin Hopkins (Woman in Lobby); Jimmy Workman (Sean from the Bakery); Danielle Spencer (Veterinarian); Todd Solondz (Man on Bus); Tom McGowan (Maitre'd); Danielle Brisebois (Singer); Matt Malloy (Men's Store Salesman); Paul Greenberg (Bar Waiter); Kirk Ringberg (Food Waiter); Dave Hawthorne (Bartender).

LOS ANGELES TIMES, 12/23/97, Calendar/p. 1, Kenneth Turan

Before computer-generated images, before blue screens and the optical printer, even before stop-motion animation, there existed the most special effect of all, the power of the written word.

James L. Brooks is royalty in this non-digital domain, and in "As Good as It Gets," his mastery of the nuances of language and emotion has turned the most unlikely material into the best and funniest romantic comedy of the year.

Calling this film's scenario unlikely is being kind. Even for a writer-director like Brooks (a multiple Oscar winner for "Terms of Endearment" and nominee for "Broadcast News") it's difficult to make a story line about a cute dog, a gay artist, an earthy waitress and an author who is certifiably mentally ill sound coherent, let alone appealing. Stars like Jack Nicholson and Helen Hunt help, of course, but can they do enough?

In fact it's a mark of how magically written, directed and acted "As Good as It Gets" is that we end up loving this film despite knowing how haphazard, scattershot and almost indefinable its charm is. Like its troubled characters, convinced to make the best of things despite being perennially on the edge and at least a little bit crazy, "As Good" surmounts its weaknesses to make moving, amusing, quintessentially human connections.

At home with mania and delighted to be pushing against conventional perceptions of the boundaries of humor and romance, Brooks and co-screenwriter Mark Andrus (working from Andrus' original story) have come up with perhaps the choicest dialogue of the entire year. Ranging from killer one-liners (a crack about HMOs invariably beings down the house) to wise and evocative arias about love and relationships, these words bind us to their characters with the force of contract law.

Character is, once again, too mild a word for the personality of Jack Nicholson's Melvin Udall. Having written 62 top-selling romance novels, he may be a productive member of society, but he can stand no one in it and no one can stand him. Homophobic, racist, anti-Semitic and all-around misanthropic, Melvin is a sarcastic, sadistic terror whose idea of a good turn is tossing a neighbor's pesky insect dog down the garbage chute of their Manhattan apartment house.

That dog, given name Verdell, belongs to Simon Bishop (Greg Kinnear), a gay artist who lives on the same floor as Melvin. Like everyone else, Simon is strafed by Melvin's acid tongue: "Do you like to be interrupted," the writer says with a snarl in one of his milder sallies, "when you're dancing around in your little garden?" Fortunately, Simon has an art dealer friend named Frank Sachs (Cuba Gooding Jr.) who is able to keep Melvin more or less in line.

Melvin is more than a true bastard, he's in thrall to an obsessive-compulsive disorder. Unwilling to be touched or to step on cracks in the sidewalk, addicted to bars of Neutrogena soap he throws away after just one use, insistent on bringing wrapped plastic utensils with him on trips to restaurants, Melvin is as much a prisoner of his routines as the Man in the Iron Mask.

The only person Melvin can tolerate turns out to be Carol Connelly (Hunt), a waitress at the neighborhood restaurant where he has his daily breakfast. Still living with her mother (Shirley Knight) in Brooklyn, Carol is both unaffected and unafraid, but her life has its manias as well. She's furiously concerned and over-protective about her 7-year-old son, Spencer (Jesse James), who suffers from pervasive allergies that unhinge his life.

To Melvin, Simon and Carol, three people who barely tolerate one another, crises come calling. An unexpected altercation puts Simon in the hospital, and someone has to be found to take care of Verdell. And Carol, increasingly distraught about her son's health, takes what may be a permanent leave of absence from her job. Both these situations put pressure on Melvin to do the unheard of and reconnect with the human race, and the unexpected repercussions of what he does do are the core of what "As Good as It Gets" is about.

To see Nicholson, who frequently gives the appearance of coasting through his roles, working as hard as he does here is a wonderful thing, Discarding almost all his familiar mannerisms, Nicholson takes more care than usual with this role, maintaining the mastery of bravura humor and timing that leads to big laughs while allowing his character to be honest and vulnerable for the first time in years. As Melvin struggles, ever so tentatively and delicately, with the possibility of being a better person, we are grateful for the synergy between actor and director that allowed it to happen so truthfully.

As all-stops-out as Nicholson is, "As Good as It Gets" wouldn't succeed without its excellent costars, especially Hunt. Best known for her starring role in TV's "Mad About You," she has done excellent work in under-seen films like "The Waterdance" and "Kiss of Death." There's a newly visible maturity and a feisty stability to her characterization of Carol that works beautifully with Nicholson's swooping highs and lows. It's a class act and hopefully it means Hunt's days of A-list stardom are just beginning.

While Gooding reaffirms the positive impression he made in "Jerry Maguire," the fact that Kinnear does everything the part calls for is a surprise after his "Sabrina" debut. Also unexpected is the presence of several other directors like Harold Ramis, Lawrence Kasdan and Todd Solondz in cameo roles. Maybe it's them the closing credits are referring to with the line, "The actors used in this film were in no way mistreated."

Watching these people warily circle one another, trying to decide if the chance to form closer attachments is worth the risk of pain, it's impossible not to be struck again and again by Brooks' nonpareil ability to create humor out of catastrophe. While his obsessive characters invariably worry, as Melvin asks at one point, "What if this is as good as it gets?" it's good to know their creator, maybe even against his better judgment, believes in the existence of something more.

NEW YORK, 12/22-29/97, p. 134, David Denby

In one of those coincidences that seem to strike movies now and then like twin flashes of lightning, *As Good As It Gets*—James L. Brooks's new picture—also features a scene in which the self-confidence of an unhappy young woman (Helen Hunt) is restored by an artist (Greg Kinnear) drawing her in the nude. James L. Brooks has worked a great deal in TV, and his movies are rich in what TV offers at its best—an empathic understanding of what people need to be happy. Hunt plays Carol, a straight-talking single mother obsessed with the care of her severely asthmatic young son. Carol has neglected herself, and she falls into the one thing in the world that she needs least—a relationship with a matchlessly rude writer, Melvin (Jack Nicholson), who suffers from obsessive-compulsive disorders. Among other things, Melvin is incapable of offering a woman a compliment. Ferociously intelligent but mad as a hatter, Melvin needs two bars of Neutrogena to wash his hands and hates to be touched or even spoken to. Retreating behind his bulky forehead, Nicholson can play this role as broadly as he wants and get away with it. He pronounces Melvin's bigoted tirades with delighted, vindictive skill.

Melvin torments his neighbor in Manhattan—a gay artist (Kinnear)—but the movie, as we can tell early on, is a Scrooge story. The question is not when Melvin will melt but how. Brooks avoids commonplace sentiment by cultivating his idiosyncratic sense of character and a series of unstable moods. He lets the scenes play at length, giving each of the actors plenty of time to develop a mood. Helen Hunt, holding the screen at times in silence, has never seemed more powerfully sane. She virtually stares the ridiculous Melvin into becoming a man. *As Good As It Gets* is a superbly written and acted tearjerker—a welcome gift from television.

NEW YORK POST, 12/23/97, p. 47, Thelma Adams

A compulsive curmudgeon. A work-weary single mom. A pampered gay painter. A dog so ugly, he's cute.

If James I. Brooks combined all these elements, threw a couch center stage and teased a stairway off in the background leading toward bedrooms never built, he might have a popular sitcom: "Unmarried ... With Children and Pooch."

Instead, Brooks, working from a witty script he co-wrote with Mark Andrus creates another laugh-until-you-cry, cry-until-you-laugh modern comedy that follows logically from his "Terms of Endearment" and "Broadcast News."

Loneliness is life as a single New Yorker in "As Good as It Gets," a title which, when delivered by Jack Nicholson's misanthrope, sounds more like that pathetic old song, "Is That All There Is?"

Nicholson vents his spleen as Melvin Udall, a romance writer as isolated as "The Omega Man." With his compulsive hand-washing, lock-checking and sidewalk-crack jumping, Melvin couldn't get close enough to a woman to launch a romance.

His only semi-sociable contact in the West Village is with Carol Connelly (Helen Hunt). Shes a waitress with a heart of gold and worry lines creasing her forehead. While Melvin's life is all about Melvin, Carol is lost to the care and cares of her sickly son.

We first see Melvin dropping his neighbor's dog down a trash chute. Needless to say, this angers dog-owner Simon Bishop (Greg Kinnear), but he's too much of a gent to confront Melvin. That's left to Simon's lover, played by Cuba Gooding Jr.

Of course, the dog starts the conflict, the conflict starts a war, the war leads to an uneasy truce and this draws Carol in. Melvin, Simon and Carol end up on a road trip to Baltimore in an unlikely incarnation of Hope, Crosby and Lamour.

The movie would benefit from trimming to achieve a brisker comic pace, but few recent scripts have been so bitingly funny. When a secretary asks Melvin how he writes women so well, he responds: "I think of a man and I take away reason and accountability."

Nicholson plays nasty, but Mel becomes increasingly sympathetic as we realize how little control he has over his behavior, how uneasy he is within his skin. It's a winning performance the actor struggles toward; even stars can't afford to go on cruise control for as long as Jack has.

Hunt long ago proved her cross-over potential. She has the power to make audiences laugh and cry as she reaches toward real women in all their complexity and misplaced anger; never underestimate the uniqueness of the girl next door.

Kinnear steals the movie. He matches emotional range with perfect timing and a wicked Nicholson imitation. Mainstream movies have made so much progress in portraying gay men that Kinnear's Simon can be unapologetic. Since he no longer has to be a role model, like Tom Hanks in "Philadelphia," he can finally be a man. And, for Hollywood, that's about "As Good as It Gets."

NEWSDAY, 12/23/97, Part II/p. B3, Jack Mathews

Imagine that instead of living in Queens, browbeating his wife, daughter and son-in-law from his favorite wing-back chair, Archie Bunker was single, writing romance novels and living in a swank West Village apartment building, taunting the gay artist who lives next door.

What's that? You say you can imagine someone like that *dying* in the West Village but not living there? Ah, just the point. James L. Brooks' "As Good as It Gets" is a situation comedy written for the big screen, and few situations can match Archie Bunker in the West Village.

Add Jack Nicholson as Bunker's slightly upscale soul-mate Melvin Udall, and you're guaranteed as many lung-clearing laughs as you're likely to get this season,

"As Good as It Gets" doesn't quite live up to its title. The movie vacillates between extremes of outrageousness and sentimentality, and the shifts are too jarring for the, sentiment to take hold. But the script, by Brooks and Mark Andrus, contains some of the year's sharpest, chiseled-to-shock lines, and Nicholson hasn't been as endearing since "The Witches of Eastwick. "

Though his "Eastwick" devil and Melvin Udall share a certain overt arrogance, Melvin isn't innately evil. He is an insecure, obsessive-compulsive, socially inept loser who uses his gift for insult as a defense (or is that offense?) mechanism. In real life, this guy would be living in the next cabin over from Ted Kaczynski.

Instead, Melvin hides out in his apartment, banging out bodice-rippers on his typewriter, and going out just long enough to toss his neighbor's dog down the garbage chute, harangue his shrink and indulge his own compulsive breakfast ritual. Every morning, same restaurant, same table, same waitress, same abusive language.

But events are conspiring to threaten Melvin's schedule. First, his neighbor Simon (Greg Kinnear) is mugged so badly by gay-bashing burglars that Melvin is asked to look after the dog, Verdell, while Simon recuperates in the hospital. Then, his regular waitress, Carol (Helen Hunt), quits her job to attend full-time to her asthmatic son.

Melvin, under the threat of bodily harm from Simon's friend Frank (Cuba Gooding Jr.), agrees to take care of Verdell, falling in love with the pooch in the process. And to get Carol back to work, he insists on covering the costs of her son's medical care, and falls in love with her in the process, too. Eventually, Melvin introduces his unlikely friends and they head off on a road trip to Baltimore.

If the events sound contrived, they are. But no matter. The pleasure is all in the writing and in the performances. Melvin's grab-bag of neuroses is catnip to Nicholson, and he's in rare form. One moment, he's doing screeds on homosexuals or immigrants; the next, he's arching that most famous of all archable brows, trying to comprehend what he's doing wrong. It's one of those performances that makes you aware how much fun the actor is having, and you're pleased to go along with him.

At times, Hunt and Kinnear seem to be working in a different movie. As much fun as he is, Melvin is more caricature than a fully dimensional person. He's alternately rude, sensitive, confident and confused, all the things that make a good comic foil, but there's little attempt to explain his behavior.

Carol and Simon are serious, well-defined characters, and the actors are terrific. Hunt brings as much intelligence, humor and compassion to a role as any actress around, and even while you're saying "There is no way this woman ends up with this man, " she makes you believe it's plausible.

Kinnear proves that his acclaimed debut in "Sabrina" was no fluke. He's made a couple of bad choices since then, starring in the back-to-back dreadfuls "Dear God" and "A Smile Like Yours," but as down-on-his-luck Simon, an artist who's lost his looks (to a road map of scars), his apartment, his inclination to draw, and faces the prospect of a final, humiliating rejection by his parents, Kinnear shows the range of a veteran, and charismatic, star.

"As Good as It Gets" is a better movie in its specific moments than as a whole, but for adult Hollywood comedy these days, it's as good as you could expect.

NEWSWEEK, 12/22/97, p. 84, David Ansen

[*As Good As It Gets* was reviewed jointly with *Wag the Dog*; see Ansen's review of that film.]

SIGHT AND SOUND, 3/98, p. 38, Xan Brooks

Manhattan, the present. Melvin Udall is a neurotic romance writer who torments his gay artist neighbour Simon and terrorises the diners and staff at his local restaurant. Only his regular waitress, Carol, has any time for him., But when Simon is hospitalized after being attacked by burglars, Melvin is forced to look after Simon's dog, Verdell, and an emotional thaw begins to set in.

Discovering that Carol is missing work because of her asthmatic son, Melvin arranges for a private doctor to treat the child, giving him proper medical attention for the first time. Later, when Simon is bankrupted by his medical bills, Melvin agrees to drive the man to Baltimore to ask his estranged parents for money. At Melvin's request, Carol accompanies them on the trip, but a budding romance is wrecked when Melvin and Carol argue at a restaurant and she storms back to the hotel. There, Carol agrees to let Simon sketch her in the nude. His interest in art rekindled, Simon decides he does not need his parents' money. The three return to New York where Simon finds his flat has been let out to new tenants. Melvin invites him to move into his spare room. That same night, Melvin visits Carol at her home in Brooklyn. They kiss, and an unlikely romance is set in motion.

Melvin Udall: "a wonderful man" or "an absolute horror of a human-being"? The success or otherwise of James L Brooks' contemporary Good Samaritan fable depends on which side of the line the viewer eventually falls. *As Good As It Gets'* basic set-up follows the same tack attempted by Jane Austen in *Emma*. Invent the most outwardly dislikable character possible and then spend the rest of the story convincing the audience that he/she is actually a sweetheart. Hence Jack Nicholson's writer of quasi-Mills and Boon novels is racist, sexist, homophobic and virulently anti-Semitic. He has a Howard Hughes-style obsession with cleanliness and his interactions with his fellow New Yorkers veer between blatant insult and twitchy emotional autism. His crawl towards lovability is the film's principal journey.

Except that somewhere along the way a strange thing occurs. For the more cuddly this Mr Misanthrope becomes, the more irksome, flawed and dubious Brooks' picture proves to be. In short, *As Good As It Gets* is finally too glib to honour its initial premise. Melvin Udall moves from racist, sexist villain to curmudgeonly philanthropist in an eye-blink, his protracted conversion apparently triggered by nothing more than a liquid look from a little doggy. Brooks (who also co-wrote the script with Mark Andrus) opens with a brave attempt to make a genuinely prickly mainstream comedy and then cops out worryingly. Worse, one suspects that this game was rigged from the start.

Much of this odds-stacking stems from Nicholson's Golden Globe-winning performance. It's not that he's bad in the role—on the contrary he produces what is possibly his most subtle, rounded work in years. It's simply that he brings a bulk of excess baggage (charm, vitality, a certain moral authority) that works against the shabbier aspects of Melvin's character. This is not exactly Nicholson's fault, but springs more from the combination of the rampant public image and directorial mishandling. Brooks has worked with Nicholson before (in both *Broadcast News* and *Terms of Endearment),* so surely he realised the effect would be to sweeten—or at least energise—an otherwise pathetic character. To borrow from the courtroom scene in *A Few Good Men, As Good As It Gets* can't handle Nicholson. He burns too brightly. He bleaches out the plot's darkest, most interesting corners. He bursts out of the persona he is meant to inhabit. And you sense that this is precisely what Brooks wants.

But this strategy brings dangers. One sometimes has the impression that Brooks is coercing the audience into laughing along with Melvin's racist and sexist abuse, inviting us to regard it as mere convention-bucking banter—the sort of stuff we'd all love to say if we weren't so timid, stuffy and middle class. Thus Greg Kinnear's gay neighbour and, to a lesser extent, Cuba Gooding Jr's black art-dealer are essentially relegated to fall-guy positions. Indeed, of the supporting cast, only Helen Hunt breaks loose of the Nicholson orbit to turn her love-interest role into a properly three-dimensional figure: a damaged but resilient soul who offers him "too much reality for a Friday night".

By contrast, *As Good As It Gets* gives us reality-lite: dirty old life in a deodorised, de-fanged format. It says much for the respective skills of those involved, then, that the finished product still boasts a certain low-grade charm. After all, Nicholson is an endlessly watchable performer and Brooks a past master at this brand of sophisticated big-screen soap opera (much of the dialogue is honed to perfection). It's just that, at the day's end, *As Good As It Gets'* much-trumped risk-taking feels tentative and phoney. Melvin Udall starts off as monstrous and redeems himself through expensive gestures and the loan of his spare room to a down-in-the-dumps homosexual. Such behaviour earns him the love of a good woman and the chance of a fresh start in life. But because Brooks never does more than scratch at the psychology of this troublesome man, the final message proves over-cosy and conservative. We all have our crosses, Brooks' film argues, but they're nothing that a cute pooch and a small fortune can't remedy. Ah Jim, if only life were that simple.

VILLAGE VOICE, 12/30/97, p. 66, Laurie Stone

To derive the full benefit of the feel-good prescription *As Good as It Gets,* you have to believe that Carol—the intelligent, quirky, sensuous woman in her thirties that Helen Hunt plays—ought not to aspire higher in a mate than the creakily mannered, pouchy-faced, thick-waisted crank past 50 that Jack Nicholson plays. You have to believe that when a gay man is robbed in his apartment, brutally battered, and left facing a long convalescence, none among his preattack army of gay friends will come to his aid, and that there are no support groups equipped to help. Only the thick-waisted, het crank, who is also rabidly homophobic, racist, and anti-Semitic will save the day. Not even the thick-waisted hets green-lighting Hollywood could buy this fable, though they must believe there's a demographic out there that will.

The individual stamp of director-writer-producer James L. Brooks, co-creator of the innovative *Tracy Ullman Show* and *The Simpsons,* is evident in his own films, *Terms of Endearment* and *Broadcast News,* movies that pretend benevolence toward women while enjoying their frustration and suffering. Brooks celebrates the ability of smart, vivacious women to sacrifice, lose, and do without. There would be no kick in their capitulation if they lacked spunk. Here Hunt plays a waitress with a chronically ill young son and a live-in mom (Shirley Knight). No one can see her fabulousness except an obsessive-compulsive freak named Melvin (Nicholson), a wealthy writer of romances.

Simon (Greg Kinnear), the gay character, is consigned to a female role in the film's scheme. Like Carol, he is very, very nice and for his virtue is wounded and denied sex. This het friendly homo, an artist, can't even be shown to crave sex, so that when a street hustler he means to paint disrobes, thinking he's meeting a trick, Simon primly tells him to get dressed.

The three principals are brought together by an overacting dog. Nicholson overacts more, with bared teeth and spiking eyebrows, clown shtick as fresh, though not as amusing, as a rubber nose and big shoes. Hunt's lack of vanity is sadistically pushed to the edge with frumpy clothes and muddy makeup, and Kinnear escapes his saccharine role only when flashing a satiric impression of Nicholson. Brooks is able to wring some comedy and pathos from scenes, but they don't eclipse the movie's sentimentality or its fantasy that, in watching all the energy of the other characters funneled into humanizing an odious daddy, we will cheer rather than gasp with disbelief.

Also reviewed in:
NEW REPUBLIC, 2/2/98, p. 25, Stanley Kauffmann
NEW YORKER, 1/5/98, p. 76, Daphne Merkin
NEW YORK TIMES, 12/23/97, p. E1, Janet Maslin
VARIETY, 12/15-21/97, p. 58, Todd McCarthy
WASHINGTON POST, 12/23/97, p. D1, Desson Howe

ASSIGNMENT, THE

A Triumph Films release of an Allegro Films production. *Executive Producer:* David Saunders and Joseph Newton Cohen. *Producer:* Tom Berry and Franco Battista. *Director:* Christian Duguay. *Screenplay:* Dan Gordon and Sabi H. Shabtai. *Director of Photography:* David Franco. *Editor:* Yves Langlois. *Music:* Normand Corbeil. *Music Editor:* Michel Gauvin. *Sound:* Claude Hazanavicus and (music) Ian Terry. *Sound Editor:* Michel B. Bordeleau. *Casting:* Mary Margiotta, Karen Margiotta, and Lucie Robitaille. *Production Designer:* Michael Joy. *Art Director:* James Fox. *Set Decorator:* Frances Calder. *Set Dresser:* Manon Girard. *Costumes:* Denis Sperdouklis. *Make-up:* Nicole Lapierre. *Make-up (Special Effects):* Adrien Morot. *Running time:* 122 minutes. *MPAA Rating:* R.

CAST: Aidan Quinn (Annibal Ramirez/Carlos, "The Jackal"); Donald Sutherland (Jack Shaw/Henry Fields); Ben Kingsley (Amos); Claudia Ferri (Maura Ramirez); Céline Bonnier (Carla); Vlasta Vrana (KGB Head Officer); Liliana Komorowska (Agnieska); Von Flores (Koj); Al Waxman (Carl Mickens, CIA); Mitchell David Rothpan (Joey Ramirez); Grégory Hlady (KGB Aide); Gabriel Marian Oseciuc and Frederick Desager (KGB Agents); Kliment Denchev (KGB Technician); Yonathan Gordon (Yoni); Ndiouga Sarr (Nigerian Oil Minister); Manuel Aranguiz (Venezuelan Oil Minister); Leni Parker (OPEC Receptionist); Jacques LaVallée (Du Foltiere, DST); David Francis (Naval Aide); Gouchy Boy and Tim Post (CIA Aides); Daniel Pilon (Admiral Crawford); Richard Jutras (Commander Scowcroft); Hisham Zayed (Libyan Customs Official); Ted Whittal (Norfolk Police Captain); Francis Delvecchio (Injured Paris Boy); Lisa Wegner (Berlin Lover); Lucie Laurier (Paris Lover); Neil Kroetsch (Ramirez' Father); Matthew Dupuis (Young Ramirez); Paul Stewart (Hospital Father); Claude Genest (Baseball Dad); Michael Caloz (Baseball Kid); David Franco (St. Martin Postman).

CHRISTIAN SCIENCE MONITOR, 9/26/97, p. 12, David Sterritt

One of an actor's hardest tasks is to play a character who embodies opposite qualities. Donald Sutherland meets this challenge in "The Assignment," where he portrays a CIA agent who commits appalling wrongs without losing the conviction that his goal—fighting international terrorism—justifies any conceivable means.

The movie follows him as he joins an Israeli operative (Ben Kingsley) to train a young American commando (Aidan Quinn) for clandestine action against a ruthless terrorist—also played by Quinn, since the US agent is selected because of his physical resemblance to the criminal.

A lot of violence (and sadly impersonal sex) spills across the screen during this operation, but in its best scenes the picture uses such elements to make a moral point: that well-meaning individuals who struggle against evil may become as corrupt as the enemies they seek to overcome, unless they guard vigilantly against this.

"The Assignment" would be a deeper film if it developed this theme more fully. As it stands, it's not a substantial movie, but it has the merit of investing its Hollywood star-power in a story that takes notice of compelling real-world issues.

Sutherland is an ideal choice for the CIA character, bringing all the experience he's gathered in more than 90 films since hits like "M*A*S*H" and "Klute" launched his career. His credits range from art-film classics ("Casanova," "1900") to such recent accomplishments as "JFK" and "Six Degrees of Separation," attesting his skill and versatility.

In person, he is also quick-witted and literate, peppering his conversation with lively quotes from authors as different as William Shakespeare and Alexander Pope.

And he's modest. Breezing past his own contributions to "The Assignment," he gives credit for its good attributes to Christian Duguay, the Canadian-bred filmmaker who directed it. "He's committed to building his stories on truth," the actor said in an interview during the recent Toronto International Film Festival, where the picture had its North American premiere shortly before its US opening.

Duguay recognizes "that audiences go to movies with their eyes and ears," Sutherland continued, "but also with their hearts and souls. An actual [movie theater] is different than television, because [moviegoers] lose part of their critical identity; their hearts and souls become a part of the film. And the heart and soul are quicker than the eye and ear... This director sees that, so his pursuit in storytelling is to base it ... on truthfulness."

While a director must seek truth by objective means, using cameras and microphones, Sutherland feels a performer should seek it by subjective means, using words and actions. "I can't think of a film where I didn't believe that's what I was doing," he says. "I might have failed, but that would just be caused by my personal ignorance."

Asked to define the "truth" that movies can convey, Sutherland smiles and resorts to a metaphor. "It's an artichoke," he says. "Pull away a leaf, and there's another one underneath." Groping for a more specific example, he mentions Italian artist Alberto Giacometti, renowned for his sculptures of thin, elongated figures. "If you look at his early work," the actor says with another smile, "his people were fat. Then gradually they got skinny—because he went for the essence, the energy of them."

The basic "truth" of good movies may be hard to define, but Sutherland is aware that it's linked to how they reflect their society's values. "I don't try to bring political things into play," he says about deciding which roles to accept and which to reject. "But there are certain political areas I will not allow myself to be part of promoting. As for ethical and moral considerations—that's what it's all about! That's the only worthwhile thing in this business!"

Not everyone in the business would agree, Sutherland acknowledges. "The general [Hollywood] mind-set is not to respect the heart and soul of an audience," he says. "Moviemakers cheat [truth] all the time ... with the quick cut, the MTV montage ... and they think people don't see it. But even if viewers don't notice it, it alters their perception ... and it alters the movie's effect on them. We are damaged by that ... There's a lot of trash around today ... and it's the moviemakers' fault. All the pursuit is for profit."

In the long run, though, Sutherland thinks the good will defeat the bad, much as the hero of "The Assignment" ultimately helps the world without permanently losing his integrity.

"I don't see a lot of films anymore," says the star, "because I'm a little disenchanted with the process. I'm not entertained by them. But then, truth is the only really entertaining thing.

"I don't think the movie business will ever be a righteous business," he adds, "but there will always be righteous elements in it ... At its best, [film] contains some of the truest things you've ever thought. And with it, we can approach the human condition. You have to presume that on some level, your heart and soul are connected to everybody else's."

LOS ANGELES TIMES, 9/26/97, Calendar/p. 14, John Anderson

[The following review by John Anderson appeared in a slightly different form in
NEWSDAY, 9/26/97, Part II/p. B13, John Anderson

It requires a certain audacity to take a global tragedy in which the smoke has barely cleared—a genocidal war in Bosnia, let's just say—and turn it into a generic thriller. And it's particularly grating when what is essentially a brainless action film tries to promote vague sympathies for living, breathing doers of evil, because the filmmaker has decided that none of the world's problems can be reduced to black and white (while insisting, at the same time, that everything can be a movie).

Consequently, it's a refreshing lack of grace that provides much of the appeal of "The Assignment," director Christian Duguay's intriguing, fast-paced and very straightforward spy chase, which pits a look-alike U.S. Navy officer against Ilich Ramirez Sanchez—a.k.a. Carlos the Jackal, one of the more successful entrepreneurial terrorists of the '70s and '80s.

The Venezuela-born Carlos has been in custody in Paris since 1994, so he's presumably entered the realm of the ineffective and filmable. Played with panache by the often workmanlike Aidan Quinn, Carlos is a malevolent cancer that must be cut out of the world's hide. And Annibal Ramirez (Quinn again), is just the guy who can do it.

Annibal, however, requires a bit of convincing. And training. And appeasement. While vacationing in Israel, he's abducted by Mossad agents, who interrogate him brutally, convinced that he's Carlos—their faces, with the exception of the eyes, are identical. Annibal finally convinces his captors who he is (when he's says, "I am gonna sue you!" they should have known immediately that he was American). But both the Israeli agent Amos (Ben Kingsley) and CIA ghoul Jack Shaw (Donald Sutherland) realize that through Annibal they can finally trap the Jackal.

Kingsley is quite good, but Sutherland's Shaw is one of the movie's better creations. Having allowed Carlos to slip through his fingers just before the bombing of a Paris restaurant, Shaw is on a personal vendetta—and it makes perfect sense, much more so than if he were characterized as some dispassionate government operative. And with Sutherland's demonic glint, Shaw becomes something other than pure human.

For his part, Quinn is convincingly romantic, both as the pursued and as the pursuer. The first part of the film is dominated by Annibal's training—which, given the constraints of a two-hour movie, is rather thorough. Is it totally convincing? No, but it's fun.

The action sequences are well-handled; a car chase through Beirut, for instance, is electric, as are several airport scenes in which Annibal's cover is blown. Although the chase for Carlos, and his basic nature, are never in doubt, Annibal has a bit of a crisis: With his life dependent on his becoming Carlos, he starts to lose his own identity. He's had to learn to think like Carlos, speak like Carlos, even make love like Carlos; during a brief reunion with his wife, Maura (Claudia Ferri) she notices, and things get dicey. Can this marriage be saved? Can the world?

With all of Duguay's artiness—much of it quite effective—"The Assignment" is, in many ways, an old-fashioned film. It's hokum and hooey and insists on a leap of faith that's breathtakingly long and steep. But in the end, like Carlos the Jackal, it delivers.

NEW YORK POST, 9/26/97, p. 49, Bill Hoffmann

Notorious terrorist Carlos the Jackal has always been good fodder for the movies, and his presence on the big screen continues to pay off, this time in "The Assignment."

Aidan Quinn—whose selection of roles has always been hit and miss—scores a big hit here, in a meaty dual role as both the Jackal and a good-guy lookalike trying to set the terrorist up for a fall.

Quinn is American naval officer Annibal Ramirez, a standup guy and family man who's a dead ringer for Carlos.

An American counter-intelligence agent (Donald Sutherland) and his Israeli counterpart (Ben Kingsley) recruit Ramirez to impersonate Carlos.

His assignment: make the real Carlos appear to be a double-dealing traitor so other terrorists will assassinate him.

So Ramirez begins a quick study of Carlos' bloody history, homework which includes trying to pass muster in the sack with the terrorists' various girlfriends. Yes, being a spy is a tough job but somebody's got to do it!

This leads to a series of delicious double-crosses, misunderstandings and mishaps which zip by at a thrill-a-second pace, thanks to the capable direction of Christian Duguay.

Duguay uses a lot of slow-motion effects, usually the signature of a hack filmmaker without a clue. But within the dark and moody context, they work just fine.

The cast is crackerjack. Quinn, Sutherland and Kingsley have played these types of roles so often, they can virtually sleepwalk through them—and yet they're still a lot of fun to watch.

If there's any complaint, it's that this sort of terrorist-counterspy thing has been done so often its old-hat by now.

Thankfully, there are enough twists and turns in Dan Gordon and Sabi Shabtai's script to keep us interested.

SIGHT AND SOUND, 11/98, p. 40, Danny Leigh

Jerusalem, 1986. Carlos "The Jackal" Sanchez is apprehended by Mossad. During his interrogation, it emerges that Mossad has not arrested Carlos, but his unwitting *doppelgänger*, US naval officer Annibal Ramirez.

Later, the CIA's Jack Shaw visits Ramirez at his Virginia home, demanding he masquerade as Carlos to help capture the terrorist. He and Shaw leave for Siberia, where Ramirez is trained by Mossad agent Amos. Shaw tells Ramirez he will be used to convince the KGB that Carlos has betrayed them. Dispatched to Libya, Ramirez impersonates Carlos so successfully the French secret service tries to kill him. Carlos learns of his mimic's activities; Ramirez survives the subsequent attempt on his life, but Amos is shot dead. Returning to Virginia, Ramirez is unable to readjust to his old ways. He travels with Shaw to East Berlin where Carlos is hiding. The KGB observes Shaw and Ramirez together and vows to assassinate Carlos, believing he has defected to the CIA. Carlos escapes, but Shaw assures Ramirez it is only a matter of time before the KGB locates him. Back in Virginia, the CIA stages Ramirez's death to ensure his safety.

Two years after his imprisonment by the French judiciary, Carlos Sanchez is still obscured by rumour and smokescreen. Alternately reviled and made into an icon (and sometimes both at once), "The Jackal" came to personify the axiom—like no one else in recent history, apart from Che Guevara—that one man's terrorist is another's freedom fighter. A film capable of demystifying someone who bedevilled western governments for three decades is surely welcome.

The Assignment is not, however, such a film. Based on events the writers cannot verify—claiming that to do so would compromise those involved—the storyline renders Carlos a decontextualised caricature, seemingly designed only to lend a cheap *frisson* of reality to an otherwise perfunctory spy thriller. Hinging on a preposterous prince-and-the-pauper conceit, an air of shoddy opportunism infects the entire project. Even for the viewer actively searching for redeeming features, there is nothing here to reward the effort.

Visually proceedings veer between made-for-television stodge and inexpert gimmickry. The use of flashbacks whenever the script demands that Ramirez should appear disoriented grows particularly wearing. Equally, the literal direction by Christian Duguay fails to rouse any of his leads from torpid, autopilot manoeuvres.

But what drags *The Assignment* from the merely tawdry to the outright objectionable is its aggressively reactionary polemics. The writers—both connected to the Israeli military—approach politics with a good guy/bad guy logic so crude it verges on the racist, while the only female characters present are the slack-jawed victims of Carlos' insatiable womanising. As a nod to his identity-crisis sub-plot, Duguay apparently kept on set a copy of the Nietzschean aphorism, "Remember, when you look into the abyss, the abyss looks back into you." The same advice may prove useful to anyone contemplating going to see *The Assignment*.

VILLAGE VOICE, 9/30/97, p. 84, Gary Dauphin

Priced out of the terrorist-flick big leagues, *The Assignment*'s low budget makes it look and feel like it's been sitting in a studio vault for a few years. *The Assignment* is a fictionalization of the capture of '70s terrorism superstar Carlos the Jackal, and it uses the old one-actor-playing-two-men ploy: clean-cut Cuban American navy lieutenant (Aidan Quinn) becomes Carlos (also played by Aidan Quinn) in order to set the real terrorist up for KGB assassitiation. Most of the film is given over to sailor-boy's training in Carlos-ness by old intelligence hands Donald Sutherland and Ben Kingsley (both give credible and therefore misplaced turns), an education that centers on learning to memorize the contents of a refrigerator in two seconds flat and remembering to always eat French women out after pimpslapping them. At its best, *Assignment* has a nicely lurid and over-heated B-movie vibe. Canadian director Christian Duguay also directed the sci-fi quickie

Screamers, so the heavily digitized terrorism set pieces are better than you'd expect. Still, this rehash of bits that have been done better elsewhere lives down to its title: work done quickly for money and little else.

Also reviewed in:
CHICAGO TRIBUNE, 9/26/97, Friday/p. N, Monica Eng
NEW YORK TIMES, 9/26/97, p. E20, Stephen Holden
VARIETY, 9/22-28/97, p. 40, Brendan Kelly

AUSTIN POWERS: INTERNATIONAL MAN OF MYSTERY

A New Line Cinema release in association with Capella International/KC Medien of a Moving Pictures/Eric's Boy production. *Executive Producer:* Eric McLeod and Claire Rudnick-Polstein. *Producer:* Suzanne Todd, Demi Moore, Jennifer Todd, and Mike Myers. *Director:* Jay Roach. *Screenplay:* Mike Myers. *Director of Photography:* Peter Deming. *Editor:* Debra Neil-Fisher. *Music:* George S. Clinton. *Music Editor:* Mike Flicker and Lia Vollack. *Choreographer:* Marguerite Derricks. *Sound:* Mark Ulano and (music) John Whynot. *Sound Editor:* Frederick Howard. *Casting:* John Papsidera. *Production Designer:* Cynthia Charette. *Art Director:* Daniel Olexiewicz. *Set Designer:* Martin Roy Mervel. *Set Decorator:* Bob Kensinger. *Set Dresser:* Laura Maffeo, Daniel Brodo, Beth Emerson, Jeannine Fenton, Kirt Johnson, Steve Lauritzen, and Jennifer Weil. *Special Effects:* Rich Ratliff. *Costumes:* Deena Appel. *Make-up:* Patty York. *Make-up (Mike Myers):* John Jackson. *Make-up (Elizabeth Hurley):* Tracy Lee. *Stunt Coordinator:* Bud Davis. *Running time:* 87 minutes. *MPAA Rating:* PG-13.

CAST: Mike Myers (Austin Powers/Dr. Evil); Elizabeth Hurley (Vanessa Kensington); Michael York (Basil Exposition); Mimi Rogers (Mrs. Kensington); Robert Wagner (Number Two); Seth Green (Scott Evil); Carrie Fisher (Therapist); Fabiana Udenio (Alotta Fagina); Mindy Sterling (Frau Farbissina); Paul Dillon (Patty O'Brien); Charles Napier (Commander Gilmour); Will Ferrell (Mustafa); Joann Richter, Anastasia Nicole Sakelaris, and Afifi Alaouie ('60s Models); Monet Mazur (Mod Girl); Mark Bringelson (Andy Warhol); Clint Howard (Radar Operator); Elya Baskin (Borschevsky); Carlton Lee Russell (Gary Coleman); Daniel Weaver (Vanilla Ice); Neil Mullarkey (Quartermaster Clerk); Joe Son (Random Task); Tyde Kierny (Las Vegas Tourist); Larry Thomas (Casino dealer); Burt Bacharach (Himself); Brian George (UN Secretary); Kay Wade (Mrs. Exposition); Steve Monroe (Son); Vince Melocchi (Dad); Patrick Bristow (Virtucon Tour Guide); Jim McMullan (American UN Representative); Robin Gammell (British UN Representative); Ted Kairys (Eastern European Technician); Tom Arnold (Guy on Toilet); Larry Thomas (Casino Croupier).

LOS ANGELES TIMES, 5/2/97, Calendar/p. 10, John Anderson

[The following review by John Anderson appeared in a slightly different form in
NEWSDAY, 5/2/97, Part II/p. B8.]

Poor Mike Myers. Didn't anyone ever tell him you can't spoof camp? In "Austin Powers: International Man of Mystery," he takes on what seem to be ripe topics for parody—the late '60s spy genre and the Swinging London aesthetic—and discovers that the satire's long been exhausted.

Myers, "Saturday, Night Live" alumnus and the auteur-savant behind "Wayne's World," does triple duty in "Austin Powers": one screenplay, two characters. He's Austin, a preening English fashion photographer by day, undercover agent by night, and round-the-clock playboy. And he's Austin's archenemy, the whiny Dr. Evil. The setup? It's 1967, and Dr. Evil eludes the law by having himself cryogenically frozen and shot into space. Austin is frozen, too, so he'll be there when Dr. Evil returns. The gag? Upon thawing, both characters are so out of touch with '90 mores and crime that the result is a comedy of errors.

Errors, yes. Comedy ... we're not so sure. Most of the films and TV series in which Myers roots the Austin character—"The Avengers," "The Man From U.N.C.L.E.," even the James Bond films—were already spoofs. They seldom took themselves seriously and their concessions to period fashions, were as arch as their dialogue. Myers seems to have missed the joke, approaching all this material as if there were somebody or something to knock off a pedestal. There isn't.

And the sorry fact is, the material satirized in "Austin Powers" was a good deal more self-aware—and therefore hipper—than anything Myers has cooked up. It may be asking a lot, but if one is going to send up a genre, or an era, or even a sense of style, isn't one required to be funnier than one's subject matter? Myers' idea of scintillating wit is naming his Italian vamp Alotta Fagina (Fabiana Udenio) or mocking Dr. Evil for his pre-Nixonian appreciation of the dollar—he wants a million not to destroy the world and is practically laughed out of the movie. Along the way, male-anatomy jokes are beaten into the ground with an insistence that's mortifying.

What's more poignant than funny is how the ever-lecherous Austin, with his pinstripes and pyorrhea (English dental jokes abound), is introduced to post-AIDS sexuality. The lesson is delivered by Vanessa (Elizabeth Hurley), the daughter of Austin's now-retired partner, Mrs. Kensington (Mimi Rogers), who often looks at Austin the way audiences will be looking at this movie.

Sixties-ites Michael York and Robert Wagner are included in the cast, but there are no cameos by Diana Rigg as Mrs. Peel or Robert Vaughan as Napoleon Solo. Had there been, it would have been pointless: "Austin Powers" is a movie whose sense of humor is aimed at those far too young to get the big joke, and all but guaranteed to turn off those who do.

NEW YORK POST, 5/2/97, p. 47, Thelma Adams

"Let's make love, you silly little man," temptress Alotta Fagina coos to superspy Austin Powers over a steaming hot tub.

"Austin Powers: International Man of Mystery" is a silly little movie that takes aim at a sure target—secret agent land from Bond to Matt Helm—and never misses.

Written by Mike Myers—who lives in an exhibitionist "Wayne's World" of his own—the former "SNL" funnyman plays a dual role. With a nod to Peter Sellers, a star of the classic British spy spoof "Casino Royale," Myers is both hero and villain, Powers and his nemesis, Dr. Evil.

Directed by Jay Roach, the comedy opens with a hip-swinging. finger-snapping '60s Carnaby Street be-in that's an airkiss to Richard Lester's Beatles' flicks. Powers leads the high-energy production, pelvis pumping and yellow horsy teeth bared. He's a fashion photog by day, a spy for Her Majesty's Secret Service by night.

Fun-hating Dr. Evil is a stiff, scarred skinhead who strokes a hairy pet cat. When the villain botches a hit on Powers, he flees to the future in a cryogenic unit. The cat-chasing agent follows in frozen pursuit.

The duo blast into the '90s with a '60s mindset. Powers' randy, free-love attitude has become sexual harassment overnight, his crushed-velvet suits are waiter wear. Dr. Evil's scheme to blackmail the Royal Family with evidence of Prince Charles' affair is dead in the water.

What's a rat to do after he's thawed along with the Cold War? "Let's just do what we always do. Hijack some nuclear weapons and hold the world ransom," Evil tells his henchmen No. 2 (Robert Wagner with an eyepatch and a dubious face lift) and Frau Farbissina (Mindy Sterling).

Powers grabs his uptight assistant, Vanessa Kensington (Elizabeth Hurley), and goes through the Bond ritual: meet the villain in a social situation, infiltrate his organization, sleep with the enemy, trip over the secret plan, get captured and set up for a grisly death, slip away and save the day, get the girl.

It's a tossup over who's funnier: Myers as Powers, italicizing all the groovy Bondisms with a fake thatch of chest hair, the prince of smarm-charm; or Evil, attending group therapy with his crabby test-tube son and then annihilating the group for being uncooperative.

Carrie Fisher does a wry turn as the therapist who can't distinguish between a father's desire to kill his son and a killer's desire to eliminate a problem; Tom Arnold relieves himself in a toilet cameo.

Also on hand are Michael York, Fabiana Udenio as Fagina and Mimi Rogers as Kensington's mum, a '60s Emma Peel.

Mama Rogers is hotter, and funnier, than Hurley. While the Estee Lauder mannequin sizzles in a micro-mini, her comic talents are equally short. When Powers tells Vanessa, "I'm sorry that bug up your a-- had to die," he must have been putting her on.

Remember when peace, love and revolution were cool? When Brian Jones looked hip in a velvet suit? It's time to defrost. For those who think "Austin Powers" is too silly, I say: "Don't get heavy, baby."

NEWSWEEK, 5/19/97, p. 84, Rick Marin

Behave, all you swingers out there: here comes the groovy star of the '60s-style spy spoof "Austin Powers: International Man of Mystery." You know: Mike Myers, from "Saturday Night Live." Flick called "Wayne's World" ring your bell? Made about a zillion dollars (not counting the sequel). How about "So I Married an Axe Murderer"? OK, so that one only grossed $15.95 (not counting refunds). Well, anyway, Myers is back, with a brand new bag and more silly catch phrases like "Behave!" and "Shagadelic!" A smashing opening weekend at the box office has returned the 33-year-old Canadian to his rightful place as an International Man of Comedy.

Nutty characters like Wayne Campbell, Dieter and Linda ("Coffee Talk") Richman spring like Chia pets from Myers's head.   Powers is a London fashion photographer/secret agent cryogenically frozen in 1967 and defrosted in 1997 to save the world from his bald, Nehru-jacketed nemesis, Dr. Evil (also Myers).   The whole thing's a time-warped homage to James Bond, Matt Helm, Peter Sellers—and Eric Myers, Mike's late father, a serious comedy fan who used to wake his three sons up at night to watch "Monty Python." Picking at a $5 bagel in the restaurant of his New York hotel, Myers says quietly, "Nobody would have loved this movie more than my dad."

A year ago, Myers started channeling Austin, a '60s swinger stuck in the square '90s. "You're a fabulous bird!" he'd ooze to his wife, Robin. "Do you swing? Do I make you horny?" She told him to shut up and write it down.   He cranked out a script in three weeks, while performing around Los Angeles with his retro-mod band, Ming Tea.   Elizabeth Hurley and Robert Wagner signed on to the project, along with director Jay Roach, who let the cast "do their own thing," as Agent Powers might say.   "About 30 to 40 percent is improv," says Myers.   The rest is shagadelic, baby.

SIGHT AND SOUND, 9/97, p. 37, Ben Thompson

Swinging London, 1967. A fashion photographer by day, an international spy by night, Austin Powers is the living embodiment of the Carnaby Street hipster era. He is on the point of capturing his arch-adversary Dr Evil when the master-criminal escapes by having himself cryogenically frozen. Powers does the same, as insurance against the day when Dr Evil might return from the deep freeze.

Austin finds himself defrosted 30 years later by Her Majesty's Government. Dr Evil is back, at the helm of a shadowy multinational corporation called Virtucon, and planning to hold the United Nations to ransom. Joined by Vanessa Kensington—the daughter of his 60s sidekick, now charged with the awkward task of bringing him up to date on the moral and political realities of the 90s—Austin flies to Las Vegas in his private jumbo jet. His mission is to get to the bottom of Dr Evil's mysterious Project Vulcan.

Austin initially struggles to adjust to an age in which sexual promiscuity and sub-standard dental work are no longer socially acceptable, but he adapts and his sexual allure starts working again. Assisted by Vanessa's potent martial-arts skills and an illicit liaison with Dr Evil's accomplice, Alotta Fagina, he infiltrates Virtucon's headquarters. There, he and Vanessa soon find themselves captured and strung up above a tank of angry mutant seabass, but they escape certain death with the aid of some dental floss. Having foiled Dr Evil's attempt to send a nuclear probe to the centre of the earth's core, Austin is free to enjoy the bounty of a 90s-style monogamous relationship with Vanessa—who becomes the new Mrs Powers.

Has Mike Myers, the man who gave us *Wayne's World,* come up with the swinging-London/Britpoptimeslip, easy-listening-revival comedy we've all been waiting for? Well, almost. Right from the lavish opening sequence, where uniformed policemen flick-flack down Carnaby Street in a display of absurdist choreography that tops anything in *Oliver!* and almost anything in *Absolute Beginners*, it's clear tht no expense has been spared in this quest for high-grade pastiche. But Myers (who wrote the screenplay and stars, in impeccable Manichean fashion, as both the film's eponymous spy hero and its Blofeldesque baddie Dr Evil) has clearly applied brain-power as well as hard cash to the 60s/90s interface.

Powers' catchphrases ("Behave!", "Shall we shag now or shall we shag later?") may not be up to much, but he plays the unthinking hedonism of the 60s off against the conventional wisdoms of three decades on to consistently entertaining effect. In the finest tradition of Zucker and Abrahams, this film throws so much comic mud at the wall that some of it has to stick. The humour oscillates from the coarsest toilet gag to the most elegantly crafted Zen one-liner ("How do I tell them that due to the unfreezing there is no inner monologue?"); from precise stylistic allusion—a hilarious multiplying split-screen effect whereby details of ever-increasing absurdity are given their own celluloid paddock—to broad and timeless slapstick.

In another context this might add up to something of a mish-mash, but for a film aiming to be the *Casino Royale* of the Blairite era, the variegated feel is entirely appropriate. The period detail is approached with beguiling energy rather than anal exactitude: both Matthew Sweet's and Susanna Hoffs' songs and the production design of Cynthia Charette are aptly zappy without being drearily museum-like. And the numerous cameos (and this film has more cameos than a Shropshire antiques fair) are gratuitous in the best possible sense. Celebrities making their seven seconds count include: Larry Thomas (*Seinfeld*'s "Soup Nazi") as a croupier, Burt Bacharach as himself, an eyepatch-wearing Robert Wagner as Dr Evil's rebellious henchman, Tom Arnold as an idiot in a public toilet and Michael York as Powers' secret service contact (the superbly named Basil Exposition). Assuming that Patsy Kensit was unavailable, Liz Hurley is ideally cast as the object of Austin's affection. When demonstrating the martial-arts skills which first helped make her name in the underrated *Passenger 57*, she proves a worthy successor to Honor Blackman and Joanna Lumley. Unfortunately the screenplay also requires her to deliver dialogue.

Happily, Myers' presence in the two lead roles is strong enough to sustain the momentum. Even his knowingness—for example Dr Evil's determination to place Vanessa and Austin in "an easily escapable situation involving an over-elaborate death"—has an agreeable measure of innocence about it. And if it doesn't quite match the exalted standards of his first feature outing in Wayne and Garth mode, *Austin Powers* certainly represents a welcome return to form for the Canadian *Saturday Night Live* veteran. In fact, a more appropriate catch-line than the rather underwhelming "Groovy baby" might have been "It's like *So I Married an Axe Murderer* never happened."

VILLAGE VOICE, 5/6/97, p. 94, Brian Parks

A headcheese of *Thunderball, A Hard Day's Night,* and *Laugh-In, Austin Powers* is a hyperextended TV skit with a fab day-glo soundtrack. Mike Myers plays secret agent Austin Powers, a swinging '60s Englishman in crushed velvet who's pulled out of a 30-year cryogenic freeze to fight the sinister Dr. Evil. Not that the plot matters: the movie is really just Myers's chance to mock all things British. He also gets to satirize every mad-genius film ever made—instead of sharks, Dr. Evil tries to kill Austin with a tank of sea bass. Elizabeth Hurley, as Austin's love interest, wins points for good sportsmanship—especially in a scene using a series of well-placed props to conceal her "naughty bits." *Austin Powers* is patchy comedy but a masterwork of set design—the opening Canaby Street musical number is a tremendous send-up of 60s London, down to Austin's British-flag Jaguar. And with his conspicously prosthetic English dental work, Myers works a mild cinematic coup: he's made a movie where you can't stop watching people's teeth.

Also reviewed in:
NEW YORK TIMES, 5/2/97, p. C7, Janet Maslin

VARIETY, 4/28-5/4/97, p. 99, Leonard Klady
WASHINGTON POST, 5/2/97, p. C7, Rita Kempley
WASHINGTON POST, 5/2/97, Weekend/p. 42, John F. Kelly

BANDWAGON

A Cinepix Film Properties release of a Lakeshore Entertainment and Pamlico Pictures production. *Producer:* Alyson Poole and John Schultz. *Director:* John Schultz. *Screenplay:* John Schultz. *Director of Photography:* Shawn Maurer. *Editor:* John Pace. *Music:* Greg Kendall. *Sound:* Knox White. *Production Designer:* Irina Rivera. *Costumes:* Betzy Reisinger. *Running time:* 99 minutes. *MPAA Rating:* Not Rated.

CAST: Kevin Corrigan (Wynn Knapp); Steve Parlavecchio (Eric Elwood); Lee Holmes (Tony Ridge); Matthew Hennessey (Charlie Flagg); Doug MacMillan (Linus Tate); Lisa Keller (Ann); Steph Robinson (Dizz); Doug McCallie (Chester Mealy); Mary Ellen Williams (Helen); Sally Nussbaumer (Mom).

LOS ANGELES TIMES, 9/12/97, Calendar/p. 19, Kevin Thomas

[The following review by Kevin Thomas appeared in a slightly different form in **NEWSDAY, 9/12/97, Part II/p. B8.**]

John Schultz's "Bandwagon" is a sweet-natured and witty comedy about the knockabout adventures of a Raleigh, N.C., garage band. Consistently funny and warm-hearted, it has a broad, generation-crossing appeal rather than aiming only at the very people it depicts.

In his feature debut, Schultz has hit the right unpretentious throwaway tone and intimate scale for his story and, as a result, his picture ought to entertain a lot of people. It is too affectionate to be a satire in the way "This Is Spinal Tap" was, but when it exaggerates situations for laughs, it never loses its sense of proportion.

"Bandwagon" is a little gem in the way "The Full Monty" is and, like the British film, ought to be appreciated for the deft diversion it is and not be oversold.

Charlie Flagg (Matthew Hennessey) is a naive, long-haired motor-mouth forever spouting New Age nonsense. But he is an aspiring drummer and, since he is still living at home, he *does* have a garage. When a local hard-core band called Spittle is signed by the ultimate indie label Rival Records, Charlie becomes determined to start his own band. It takes lots of doing, much of it comical, but eventually he lines up a gifted but almost pathologically shy singer-songwriter, Tony Ridge (Lee Holmes), who has a shock of dark blond hair.

He then lands Spittle's ex-lead guitarist Wynn Knapp (Kevin Corrigan), a very bright guy with glasses who's not sure he "can handle this rock 'n' roll lifestyle." Rounding out the band (which the members decide to call Circus Monkey) is Eric Ellwood (Steve Parlavecchio), a fiery guy prone to trouble.

The band even succeeds in persuading legendary road manager Linus Tate (Doug MacMillan) to come aboard.

(Schultz certainly has a way in coming up with wonderful yet believable names for his people and casting actors with the same quality of authenticity. He presents Tate as a kind of beneficent enigma, although more definition and clarity of his character and role might have been the more effective way to go.)

If the film's buildup is amusing, it gets even funnier when Circus Monkey hits the road in a beat-up van for its very first tour, involving a grueling schedule of one-night stands through several Southern states.

Some years ago Schultz himself had some band experience, and throughout the film there's the sense that every zany thing that happens conceivably could (and probably has). With its abundance of alternative college rock music, "Bandwagon" is a film rich in telling details and sharp observations. Schultz is wonderfully accomplished in his ability to bring out the idiosyncrasies of four young musicians, both in his writing and in his directing of his stars.

Few comedies are entirely successful if they're entirely froth. "Bandwagon" builds steadily to its inevitable moment of truth when Circus Monkey has to decide whether the music it is making is a means to an end—or is an end in itself.

NEW YORK POST, 9/12/97, p. 46, Thelma Adams

"You're a bunch of deviants making noise in Mommy's garage," cries the drummer's sister in "Bandwagon," a spry, rock 'n roll fairy tale in the tradition of "This Is Spinal Tap.

Circus Monkey has its own Fab Four: drama queen Tony (sulky, sweet newcomer Lee Holmes); ticking time bomb without a cause Eric (blue-eyed Steve Parlavecchio, this year's Jason Priestley); stoner and Zen fisherman Wynn (the ubiquitous, creepy, cuddly Kevin Corrigan); and chick-repellent, talkaholic drummer Charlie (Matthew Hennessey).

First-time writer-director John Schultz road-tests his fictional band in North Carolina on the rockin' Raleigh 'n' roll scene. In the land where the rebel yell was perfected, beneath statues dedicated "to our Confederate Dead," alongside bands named "Spittle" and bullies who threaten their victims by setting their own belly hair aflame, Circus Monkey makes a stand: are they pathetic wannabes or a band, mice or men?

As the Yoda of the road, manager Linus Tate (Doug MacMillan) silently guides the band towards enlightenment on the grits 'n' eggs circuit.

In the end, Schultz jumps on a "Bandwagon" that owes more to the optimism of Mickey Rooney and Judy Garland than Spinal Tap cynicism. Once the drummer utters those fatal last words, "I got a real big garage," we know we're on the road to the American dream. Like Mickey and Judy, Circus Monkey pulls off the big show, and are just as appealing, though not half as innocent, in the process.

VILLAGE VOICE, 9/16/97, p. 89, Amy Taubin

Charming but slight (even for a slacker movie), John Schultz's *Bandwagon* goes on the road with Circus Monkey, a fledgling Raleigh, North Carolina garage band, as it tours the beer-drenched, pot-saturated Southern college circuit in a rusted-out van. The ambience is dead-on, the actors seem like the real thing (even though most of the music is dubbed), and the music's pretty good, although there's not enough of it. Ditto the dialogue. What's rare about *Bandwagon* is that it would rather be a tad boring than hyper.

Though Kevin Corrigan, the only name actor, gets top billing, he has little to do but look scruffy and stoned (I wished he'd tried a bit of a Southern accent but what the hey, maybe he's an emigré from the Bronx). Matthew Hennessey is enthusiastic as the drummer and binge talker. Lee Holmes is appropriately charismatic as the creative force behind Circus Monkey, a singer-songwriter so shy he can only perform when he turns his back to the audience. And as the laconic road manager who spots Circus Monkey's talent and encourages them through their trial by fire, Doug MacMillan steals the picture. MacMillan has the look of someone who's done it all before—whatever it might be. In fact he's the lead singer of the indie band The Connells. His performance here suggests that when he gets tired of the music business, he could have a whole new career as a character actor.

Also reviewed in:
CHICAGO TRIBUNE, 9/12/97, Friday/p. K, Monica Eng
NEW YORK TIMES, 9/12/97, p. C13, Janet Maslin
VARIETY, 1/29-2/4/96, p. 62, Joe Leydon

BANG

A Panorama Entertainment release of an Eagle Eye Films/Asylum Films coproduction. *Executive Producer:* Jude Narita and Sean Kelly. *Producer:* Daniel M. Berger and Ladd Vance. *Director:* Ash. *Screenplay:* Ash. *Director of Photography:* Dave Gasperik. *Editor:* Ash and Daniel M. Berger. *Music:* Orlando Aquillen and Jon Deprudhoe. *Sound:* Bill "Underfoot" Foster and Margaret Duke. *Casting:* Ash, Cynthia Cane, and Yasmine. *Production Designer:* Daniel M.

Berger. *Special Effects:* Mike "Fingers" Sullivan. *Costumes:* Dana Woods. *Make-up:* Donna Cicatelli-Lewis. *Make-up Effects:* Fred Nye. *Running time:* 98 minutes. *MPAA Rating:* Not Rated.

CAST: Darling Narita (The Girl); Peter Greene (Adam); Everlast (Pimp); Michael Arturo (Officer Trotter); James Sharpe (Officer Ham); Luis Guizar (Jezuz); Art Cruz (Juan); David Allan Graff (Peter Fawcette, The Producer); Stanley Herman (Mr. Pettibone, Landlord); Michael Newland (Officer Rattler); Donald "Notorious" D (O.G. on Rooftop); Noble James (Seth, Rooftop Dealer); Eric Kilpatrick (Tucker); Wandi Herman (Piwi on Rooftop); David Conner (Ivan); Stephanie Martini (Joy); Jason Pepper (Newscaster/TV Cop); Lucy Lui (Hooker); David Preston (Cook); Paul Saucido (Drive-by Cholo); Thomas Prisco (Addict); Claudia Kareem (Waitress); Daniel M. Berger (Man on Bus); Gloria Gold (Do-me Girl); Pamela Tomasetti (Beverly Hills Housewife); Roberta Rodman (Audition Model with Peter Fawcette); Rowen Kerr (Beverly Hills Golfer); Darren Lane (Businessman); Juanita Salinas (Latina Woman); Kirk "Homehunter" (Homeless Man).

LOS ANGELES TIMES, 12/12/97, Calendar/p. 9, Kevin Thomas

Talk about bad days. A tall, beautiful young Japanese American (Darling Narita) steps out of her L.A. apartment, and her landlord, angrily citing four months unpaid rent, swiftly locks her out, not allowing her to collect any possessions whatsoever.

She has little time to argue, for she's off to audition for an important role in an upcoming film. Arriving early at a producer's home in a cul-de-sac below the Hollywood sign, she strikes up a conversation with a young homeless man (Peter Greene). Moments later she's rushing out of the house, fleeing the producer's casting couch and obviously distraught. The young man is so upset on her behalf he starts overturning trash cans. A cop (Michael Newland) on a motorcycle soon arrives, the homeless guy flees, and the actress is facing the choice between being arrested and jailed for littering the street with garbage, something she did not do but would be hard-put to prove otherwise, or having sex with the officer.

All this is but a prelude to "Bang," a fast and furious film that lives up to its title and then some. Written and directed by a young British filmmaker who calls himself Ash, "Bang" is infinitely worthier and more exciting than most films that cost 100 times its $30,000 budget. Comparisons with "Falling Down" will be inevitable, as we follow the never-named actress on her awesome day through L.A., but the tragicomic "Bang" is lots less contrived, lots more spontaneous and therefore far more disturbing. It's fearlessly venturesome yet manages to be never less than credible.

In a flash the actress has managed to turn the tables on the cop, leaving him only in his briefs and handcuffed to a tree in the wilderness beyond the cul-de-sac. She's suddenly inspired to don his uniform and take off on his motorcycle.

The instant change of status and perspective is dizzying. Here's a woman, who's just experienced eviction, and two ugly incidents of sexual coercion, and now is suddenly empowered by a police uniform and a motorcycle. She heads off aimlessly in the direction of East L.A., exulting in her new role and enjoying her new power, but through the course of the film she will learn brutally how all this is illusion.

In posing as a police officer she is swiftly confronted with the terrible paranoia and danger that lurk just beneath the surface of L.A. in a series of harrowing, even heart-breaking encounters, that bring her face to face with the horrors of drug trafficking, gang warfare and homelessness. Amid a lethal atmosphere of mutual distrust the actress experiences some gestures of kindness—and the awful toll they can exact in some instances for those who express concern for others.

Ash and his wizardly cinematographer Dave Gasperik give "Bang" a tremendous, unflagging sense of immediacy, and Ash works wonders with a large cast. In her film debut Narita carries the film effortlessly in a grueling role. Greene, who starred in another splendid independent film, "Laws of Gravity," is most affecting as the homeless man, as are Luis Guizar and Art Cruz as two brothers, funny and sweet, as they help out the actress when her motorcycle runs out of gas. Noble James is heart-wrenching as a desperate drug dealer, and Newland and David Allen Graff (as the "producer") are rightly despicable, in a darkly comic way.

"Bang" is surely never going to be selected as the film for an LAPD benefit screening, yet it is too honest not to suggest how overwhelming and life-threatening everyday work can be for the police.

NEWSDAY, 11/28/97, Part II/p. B3, John Anderson

Although it has all the earmarks of a Tarantino/Russ Meyer-inspired, exploitation bloodbath shoot-'em-up, "Bang," the debut film by the single-named Ash, turns out to be a thoughtful and provocative exploration of the strange relationship between cop and public in modern-day Los Angeles. Not to say it isn't fun.

But in what might be described as "The Adventures of Alice in LaLa-Land," Ash gives us as much a journey of discovery as a female revenge fantasy, in which the beautiful unnamed Girl (Darling Narita), your standard oppressed citizen, takes a policeman's uniform and gun and experiences life from the other side.

She's certainly primed for trouble and vengeance. In one afternoon, the Asian-American would-be actress is hit on by a sleazy film producer (David Allan Graff), befriended by a hilarious homeless man named Adam (Peter Greene) and sexually assaulted by a police officer (Michael Newland). Understandably irritated, she flips out, grabs the officer's gun and has him handcuff himself to a tree. Then she takes his gun and bike and hits the streets of L.A., leaving Adam to watch over their hostage.

Far-fetched to be sure, but what the Girl finds out is that life isn't pretty from either end. She's afforded surprising respect from average citizens, treated like one of the boys by her "fellow" cops and fed for free at diners. She lets people off who might otherwise be busted. But she also recoils from the real responsibilities that face her at every turn, is unable to cope with most of them and even finds herself doing things—out of anger and resentment—that the police are condemned for doing for the same reasons.

It's a first-rate adventure, and certainly a well-acted film. Newcomer Narita makes the Girl's fury convincing, and keeps her introspective moments from becoming cloying. Peter Greene, a first-rate actor in independent films (his best known role was probably in "Laws of Gravity"), makes Adam both frantic and funny, sometimes frantically funny. And Ash's script holds the whole thing together well, by balancing righteous indignation with the proper amount of objective reality.

SIGHT AND SOUND, 8/97, p. 38, Andy Richards

Los Angeles. A young Japanese-American, known only as "the girl", is on her way to a film audition. She meets Adam, a homeless man, who tries to befriend her. During her audition, the producer Peter Fawcette tries to molest her sexually. Adam sees this and, angered by Fawcette's behaviour, begins overturning trash cans. A motorcycle cop, Officer Rattler, pursues the girl as she flees into a park. Rattler catches her, and offers an exchange of sexual favours for her release. The girl grabs his gun and forces him to strip before handcuffing him to a tree. She puts on Rattler's uniform and drives off on his motorcycle.

Going into a café, the girl is amazed at how well she is treated by the staff and other cops. She goes downtown and distributes money from the cop's wallet to some homeless people. During a confrontation with a drug dealer, the dealer holds a gun to her head, but breaks down in despair. The girl comforts him, but his associates arrive, and knock her to the ground. Meanwhile, Adam taunts Rattler in the park.

The motorcycle runs out of gas, and the girl enlists the help of two Hispanic gang members. A rival gang drives past and guns down one of the Chicanos. Pursuing the killers, the girl confronts them and shoots one in self-defence. She then meets a Japanese-American prostitute, but is viciously beaten by the prostitute's pimp. The girl bathes in the sea. She returns to Fawcette's house, and humiliates him. She goes back to the park and frees Rattler, and returns his uniform and bike. Rattler is about to shoot her in the back, when Adam intervenes and turns the gun on Rattler. He shoots him dead and makes off with the uniform.

Perhaps unsurprisingly, a substantial number of shoestring US-produced independent films enact the empowerment, even if only temporary, of disenfranchised women. It is almost as if the beleaguered, almost invariably male film-makers see themselves mirrored in the struggles of their female protagonists. *Bang*, helmed by the single-named Ash, is the story of a woman who endures prejudice and abuse before turning on her male persecutors. It's in the tradition of Ferrara's *Ms. 45/Angel of Vengeance*, Meir Zarchi's *I Spit on Your Grave* and Todd Morris' (still unreleased in the UK) *A Gun for Jennifer*. Rage at an intolerable status quo underpins all these films. Here, the unnamed girl protagonist tries on the trappings of power (a stolen police uniform and motorcycle) only to discard them in disgust. Her story might be read as a sardonnic comment on the low-budget film-maker's ambivalence towards the mainstream industry. (Indeed, the Hollywood hillside sign is a prominent and ironic landmark throughout the film.)

What distinguishes *Bang* from similarly themed indie-movies is the compassion it extends towards people living in the margins (especially the homeless) and its aggressive contempt for authority. A comic but telling moment in Ridley Scott's *Thelma & Louise* (a studio-financed role model for many indie female-revenge movies) has a Rastafarian cyclist blowing marijuana smoke through an air-hole into the trunk of car in which the protagonists have locked a policeman. In miniature, this scene encapsulates the united front of gender and ethnicity in the face of white male state power. *Bang*—with its Japanese-American heroine (the beautiful but perhaps deliberately unexpressive Darling Narita) driven to extreme measures by a sexist film director and power-abusing cop—attempts a more thorough examination of the same structures of oppression and opposition.

The picaresque journey of "the girl", embarked on almost as a whim, leads her through a series of encounters that reveal how bitterly entrenched these structures are. Unfortunately, the film is hindered by the huge axe it feels compelled to grind with the police, specifically the LAPD. *Bang* opens with the girl watching news footage of a Rodney King-style illegal police beating, her eyes glazed in apathetic withdrawal. Her time in uniform allows her to understand the tension between Los Angelinos and their appointed guardians. Her stolen uniform excites fear and suspicion wherever she goes, and ultimately triggers bloody responses from the hardened criminal elements she encounters. However, such a simplistic treatise on the abuse of power is as disappointing in *Bang* as it was in James William Guercio's *Electra Glide in Blue*.

Stylistically, *Bang* is a curious amalgam of polemics and pert indie mannerisms, encapsulated in the pairing of London-born Ash (director of the intriguingly titled *Sex Police)* and the actor Peter Greene, perhaps best known for his role as Zed in *Pulp Fiction* as well as the small part of Redfoot in *The Usual Suspects*. As the chorus-like Adam, Greene is the vehicle of several Tarantino-style verbal riffs about a malignant tapeworm, a prostitute who steals her client's liver for the black market, and the historical accident which led Raleigh to import tobacco instead of marijuana. Some of the absurdist incidental humour is certainly reminiscent of Hal Hartley, while the slow-motion scene in which the girl avenges the Chicano's murder is textbook Takeshi. Yet this is a film that, unlike many other recent indie releases, doesn't feel oppressively derivative. There is a rough-hewn integrity to the whole, a refreshing absence of smugness coupled with an unusual compassion, particularly in a scene where the girl distributes money to a crowd of down-and-outs. In this context, *Bang*'s occasionally too-earnest social agenda is actually its strongest card, and its improvisational *verité* approach gives several scenes a genuine resonance.

VILLAGE VOICE, 12/2/97, p. 86, Gary Dauphin

A mess of American diasporic set pieces that have been followed out and fused together by L.A.'s solar energy, *Bang* (directed by Brit first-timer Ash) is a neatly superficial little movie, made mostly of air and well-polished, reflective surfaces. Shot on the cheap in the shadow of L.A.'s military-industrial complex, this buzzy, paranoid tendering of one really bad day in the life of an Asian American actress (Darling Narita) starts out with an eviction notice and barely makes it to lunch before she has suffered sexual harassment and then attempted rape. Improbably getting her hands on a cop's gun, bike, and uniform, Narita cruises into LA-LA-land and finds the duskier citizenry quite taken by the spectacle of a pretty woman of color on a hog—at least when they're not asking her to arrest people, or taking potshots at her. Most of *Bang*'s meandering yet engaging incidents have the feel of well-pruned improvisations, as Narita's actress tries to be a decent human being in the getup even as the getup shapes events around her. Although the film suffers at times from the kind of softheaded, multiculti hipness young Brits like Ash seem to favor in their movies and glossy magazines (think Jamiroquai on the cover of *The*

Face), Bang does have a few slickly interesting things to say about police, power, and the strangeness of wearing evil on your skin 9-to-5.

Also reviewed in:
NEW YORK TIMES, 11/28/97, p. E17, Stephen Holden
VARIETY, 4/10-16/95, p. 47, Emanuel Levy

BAPS

A New Line Cinema release of an Island Pictures production. *Executive Producer:* Michael De Luca and Jay Stern. *Producer:* Mark Burg and Loretha Jones. *Director:* Robert Townsend. *Screenplay:* Troy Beyer. *Director of Photography:* Bill Dill. *Editor:* Patrick Kennedy. *Music:* Pilar McCurry and Stanley Clarke. *Choreographer:* Kenny Long. *Sound:* Russell Williams. *Sound Editor:* Richard Hymns and Frank Eulner. *Casting:* Valerie McCaffrey. *Production Designer:* Keith Brian Burns. *Art Director:* Ashley Burnham. *Set Decorator:* Casey Hallenbeck. *Set Dresser:* Monique Landry. *Special Effects:* Larry Fioritto. *Costumes:* Ruth Carter. *Make-up:* LaLette Littlejohn. *Stunt Coordinator:* Bennie E. Moore, Jr. *Running time:* 90 minutes. *MPAA Rating:* PG-13.

CAST: Halle Berry (Nisi); Martin Landau (Mr. Blakemore); Ian Richardson (Manley); Natalie Desselle (Mickey); Troy Beyer (Tracy); Luigi Amodeo (Antonio); Jonathan Fried (Isaac); Pierre (Ali); A.J. Johnson (James); Bernie Mac (Mr. Johnson); Darrel Heath (Terrance); Vince Cooke (Z.Z.); Faison Love (Tiger J); Rudy Ray Moore (Nate); Darrow Igus (Bartender); Debra Wilson (Flight Attendant); Robin Van Sharner (Airline Passenger); Jessica Page (Audition Dancer); Alex Thomas (Music Store Salesman); Eric Poppick (Vincent); Downtown Julie Brown (Herself); Heavy D (Himself); Idalis DeLeon (Herself); Howard Hewitt (Himself); LL Cool J (Himself); Leon (Himself); Dennis Rodman (Himself).

LOS ANGELES TIMES, 3/28/97, Calendar/p. 25, John Anderson

[The following review by John Anderson appeared in a slightly different form in **NEWSDAY, 3/28/97, Part II/p. B2.]**

Two Georgia peaches have invaded Beverly Hills, and they're wearing pumpkin-colored vinyl, stiletto fingernails and earrings the size of ICBMS.

In Robert Townsend's "B.A.P.S.," which in its goofy way is a kind of immigrant fable, cultures and classes collide, then meld in an ultimately enriched social landscape. Hearts soften; the old ways make accommodation for the new.

It's an old story: the American Genesis. But the conflicts here don't arise from religious oppression, politics or shrinking quotas. They're about too much mouth, too much South and too much mousse.

What are B.A.P.S.? Black American Princesses, of course. Halle Berry, proving she can handle trashy as well as classy, is Nisi, a waitress with blond hair, big dreams and a big gold cap on the occasional tooth. With her girlfriend Mickey (the delightful Natalie Desselle), she spends her days slinging greasy meat and burnt toast in the hash house of the dyspeptic Mr. Johnson (the fleeting but funny Bernie Mac). At night, they frequent the Gold Tooth bar, where their own dental apparel sets the detectors a-twitching.

Their land of limited opportunity is Decatur, Ga. where the girls want to open a combination soul-food restaurant and beauty parlor. But when they hear via MTV that rapper Heavy D is launching a search for a video "dream girl," the two head for Los Angeles like a pair of overdressed 747s.

A Ricki Lake appearance? No, but they do crash-land, blowing the audition and all their money. They're also spotted by an emissary of Isaac Blakemore (Jonathan Fried), who recruits them for a seemingly well-intentioned charade: Nisi is to impersonate the granddaughter of Lily, the long-lost love of his filthy rich uncle (Martin Landau) who is dying of cancer. It would make Blakemore's last days so happy, they're told, and the $10,000 Isaac offers doesn't hurt.

What they don't know yet is that Isaac's up to no good, and they're going to be the elder Blakemore's best friends.

The plot is full of mistaken identity, exaggeration. excess and exaggerations of excess. The running gag, of course, is that Nisi and Mickey are walking fashion crisis and they think they're chic.

Their conflict with Blakemore's ultra-proper butler Manley (Ian Richardson), whom Mickey dubs "Alfred," is clearly going to end up a sticky-sweet alliance. Their unemployed boyfriends Ali (Pierre) and James (A.J. Johnson)—are clearly not out of the picture. The picture is clearly on familiar terrain.

Townsend has the benefit of two really winning actresses—Desselle, of "Set It Off," does a pretty good job of stealing the picture—and a willingness to forgo a lot of the nasty humor that might have come easy here. Although there isn't much vulgarity, it is used to great effect.

But Townsend, whose erratic directorial record has included "Hollywood Shuffle," "Meteor Man" and "The Five Heartbeats," suffers from what might be called Penny Marshall Syndrome. A good director of middle-brow comedy, he loses his composure when matters turn serious. The music swells. So do the tears. The buoyancy goes pooooof, and the film goes slack with sentiment.

Townsend is also hampered by a Troy Beyer script that doesn't make a whole lot of sense. Isaac's scheme to steal his uncle's fortune is too half-baked to be believable. Whether old Blakemore is actually dying of cancer is a question too: Given that the imminent death story was part of the initial scam to get the women to the house, we have no reason to think it's true, and Townsend doesn't straighten us out.

And when Blakemore waxes nostalgic over Lily, the story really gets knotty: They were lovers on Blakemore's family estate, presumably when they were young, because his parents broke them up. Yet, he tells Nisi that "everything I have today I owe to her." Yeah, her and the trust fund, I guess.

It's true that airtight storytelling isn't the reason to see "B.A.P.S.—Desselle and Berry are. But the sloppiness of Beyer's script is symptomatic of what keeps the film from being first-rate.

NEW YORK POST, 3/28/97, p. 53, Thelma Adams

Once upon a time, two black waitresses from Georgia flew to Beverly Hills. Before long, they lost their mile-high hair, their 5-inch nails, their gold teeth and their hubcap earrings. Once their clothes weren't shouting, they discovered how big their hearts were.

Robert Townsend's fish-out-of-water comedy "BAPS," a.k.a. Black American Princesses, is as warmhearted as it is boneheaded. Why should it take a manicure and a haircut to get to the roots of Nisi (Halle Berry) and Mickey (Natalie Desselle)?

Of course. Nisi and Mickey can't validate their existence until they save a white man. Enter dying multimillionaire Mr. Blakemore (Martin Landau) and his butler (Ian Richardson). Blakemore's evil nephew (Jonathan Fired) draws the naive women into a scheme to bilk his uncle. They, in turn, revive Blakemore's health through liberal doses of soul food, rap music and close proximity to warm, young flesh.

In Townsend's odd, integrationist comedy, scripted by Troy Beyer, Blakemore's deep, dark secret is that his family separated him from his only love, a black servant named Lily. That's all a bunch of Mandingo, as Townsend tries to sustain the humor by showing silly white people confronting silly black people in a big old mansion spitting distance away from Rodeo Drive.

Sight gags are everything. See thin-lipped Oscar winner Landau wear leopard suits and dance the frug. See legendary Brit Richardson buy rap music. See beauty Berry waggle her hips in skin-tight orange latex.

As talented as Landau and Berry are, neither are natural comedians. Richardson and Desselle make the best of flat material. There is no way to give a bidet joke new life.

That's no reason to flush Townsend yet. The director gets a good rapport going between his stars, and the film's energy runs high even after the jokes flag.

After the hilarious and pointed "The Hollywood Shuffle," the box office nosedive of the sweet-natured "The Five Heartbeats," and the far from meteoric "Meteor Man," the filmmaker has to choose his material more wisely. It's not enough for a comedy to be well-intentioned. It also has to be funny.

SIGHT AND SOUND, 8/97, p. 38, Peter Matthews

Nisi and Mickey work in a greasy spoon in Decatur, Georgia. They are sick of their jobs and of their boyfriends, Ali and James, who can't even afford to buy them drinks. When Nisi hears of a chance to win a part in a video and $10,000 in a dance audition-competition in LA, she decides to try her luck, and the girls go together. Nisi isn't selected, but Mickey meets the handsome Antonio, the chauffeur of the wealthy but dying recluse Don Blakemore. Antonio introduces the women to Blakemore's nephew Isaac.

At the mansion, Isaac offers Nisi a job impersonating the granddaughter of Lily, a former housekeeper on the estate whom Blakemore once loved. Don is charmed by his new companions, who show him a good time. But Nisi and Mickey feel guilty about the deception and begin to miss their boyfriends. Mickey consoles herself by flirting with Antonio, and one day the two playfully attempt to open the family safe. That night, the girls find a masked intruder in the house who turns out to be Antonio. Isaac tries to blame the robbery on Nisi and Mickey, but the butler Manley clears them.

Blakemore's attorney Tracy reveals that Isaac and Antonio have been plotting to gain control of the estate by having the old man declared senile. Isaac has even taken suggestive photographs of Don and the girls to reinforce his claim. Horrified, Nisi and Mickey resolve to leave. But then, Ali and James unexpectedly appear, invited by Manley. The couples are reconciled. Soon after, Blakemore dies peacefully having known all along that Lily never had children. When the will is read, Isaac is disinherited: the main beneficiaries are Nisi, Mickey and Manley. The girls open a combination hair salon and restaurant in Beverly Hills and the boys start up a luxury cab service.

Twenty or so years ago, Sidney Poitier directed and starred in a string of movies (*Uptown Saturday Night, Let's Do It Again, A Piece of the Action*) pitched at a predominantly black audience. It was fairly obvious then that these genial slapstick comedies were intended to provide a counterweight to blaxploitation. Viewers fed up with the brutality and reverse racism of such superstud action pictures as Gordon Parks' *Shaft* (1971) and Larry Cohen's *Black Caesar* (1973) could unwind a little watching Poitier and Bill Cosby mischievously turn the tables on black baddies. That's roughly the tradition to which Robert Townsend's BAPS (the acronym stands for Black American Princesses) belongs. It has the same escapism and the same simple, hopeful message of black people triumphing over the odds, only this time the image which is being implicitly counterpointed is that propagated by such pessimist gangsta pictures as John Singleton's *Boyz N the Hood* or Allen and Albert Hughes' *Menace II Society*.

In one respect at least, *BAPS* marks an advance: the women in the Poitier films tended to be either red-hot mamas or disapproving wives, trying ineffectually to put the kibosh on their husbands' schemes. Townsend and screenwriter Troy Beyer show black sisters doing it for themselves. Nisi and Mickey make a formidable duo with their gold-capped teeth, three-inch-long nails, leopard-spotted plastic ensembles and, above all, hairdos that go beyond beehives into Vorticist architecture. The familiar fish-out-of-water scenario has the girls bowling over the snooty folks in Beverly Hills with sass, soul food and hidden reserves of common sense.

The heroines' class aspirations, together with their square sexual morality (Mickey touchingly confesses that she's still a virgin), indicate where the audience is presumed to be at. If one were to take this pleasantly tacky movie a bit more solemnly than it takes itself, one might say that it caters to a new black variant of the *bourgeoisie*. Two decades on from the community-based *Let's Do It Again, BAPS* endorses a strictly individualist ethos—Nisi and Mickey pull themselves up by their dayglo bootstraps. It's true that they require the help of a benevolent white *deus ex machina* (in the guise of Martin Landau's wealthy Mr Blakemore); but that fact merely sets the seal on a sociological fairy tale in which enterprise and virtue are promptly rewarded and colour barriers scarcely exist.

Giving black viewers what they appear to crave—an upbeat story, appealing characters, humour and a nice moral at the end—is not the worst reason to make movies, especially as *BAPS*, like all Townsend's previous work (*Hollywood Shuffle, The Meteor Man, The Five Heartbeats*), has been made without an ounce of condescension. When Mickey screws up her face in disgust at a Picasso painting, it reflects the film-makers' determination not to pull rank on their audience. The movin'-on-up premise seems to draw on such formulaic American television comedies as *The Jeffersons* and *Fresh Prince of Bel Air*; and Townsend offers further reassurance with a non-threatening style (flat lighting, bright, clear colour and functional camera set-ups) which is the pure essence of sitcom. As the partners-in-fun, Halle Berry and Natalie Desselle aren't in the same league as Cosby and Poitier, let alone Bob Hope and Bing Crosby: they're more like Lucy and Ethel gone to Hollywood, manhandling celebrities (there are crowd-pleasing cameos by Dennis Rodman and LL Cool J among others) or stirring up madcap trouble with a bidet. Their enthusiasm is, however, infectious, and that's true of the entire movie. It's so disarmingly sweet-natured that maybe it doesn't matter that it isn't very good.

VILLAGE VOICE, 4/8/97, p. 90, Jeannine Amber

There's bad and then there's *B.A.P.S.*, the rags-to-riches, ghetto-to-estate, and (by some of backlighting) Negro-to-white story of two girls from the 'hood who find themselves "livin' large and takin' charge" in luxurious Beverly Hills. With over-the-top performances by Halle Berry and effervescent newcomer Natalie Desselle, and cameos from the likes of Dennis Rodman and Heavy D, this could have been a mildly offensive but enjoyable waste of two hours. But director Robert Townsend seems even more lost in this film than his displaced ghetto princesses. Townsend wanders aimlessly, grasping first at straight-up satire (four-foot weaves and gold teeth everywhere), taking a stab at slapstick (the girls turn on a bidet thinking it's a toilet for "number one" and slip and slide around a marble bathroom for a good three minutes), and finally moving on to morality play (the girls refuse a monetary gift from a kindhearted old man, only to have their goodness rewarded with even mo' money!).

Townsend is lost, the audience is bored, only the BAPS are having fun.

Also reviewed in:
NEW YORK TIMES, 3/28/97, p. C21, Janet Maslin
VARIETY, 3/31-4/6/97, p. 86, Emanuel Levy
WASHINGTON POST, 3/29/97, p. C7, Esther Iverem

BATMAN & ROBIN

A Warner Bros. release. *Executive Producer:* Benjamin Melniker and Michael E. Uslan. *Producer:* Peter MacGregor-Scott. *Director:* Joel Schumacher. *Screenplay:* Akiva Goldsman. *Based on Batman characters created by:* Bob Kane. *Director of Photography:* Stephen Goldblatt. *Editor:* Dennis Virkler and Mark Stevens. *Music:* Elliot Goldenthal and Danny Bramson. *Music Editor:* Michael Connnell. *Sound:* Petur Hliddal and (music) Joe Iwataki. *Sound Editor:* Bruce Stambler and John Leveque. *Casting:* Mali Finn. *Production Designer:* Barbara Ling. *Art Director:* Richard Holland and Geoff Hubbard. *Set Designer:* James Bayliss, Richard Berger, Dawn Brown, John P. Bruce, R. Gilbert Clayton, Mick Cukurs, Keith Cunningham, Eric C. Sundahl, Mindi Toback, Stella Furner, Peter J. Kelly, and Nancy Mickelberry. *Set Decorator:* Dorree Cooper. *Special Effects:* Matt Sweeney. *Visual Effects:* John Dykstra. *Costumes:* Ingrid Ferrin and Robert Turturice. *Make-up:* Ve Neill. *Make-up (Mr. Freeze):* Jeff Dawn. *Stunt Coordinator:* Pat E. Johnson and Alex Daniels. *Running time:* 99 minutes. *MPAA Rating:* PG-13.

CAST: Arnold Schwarzenegger (Mr. Freeze/Dr. Victor Fries); George Clooney (Batman/Bruce Wayne); Chris O'Donnell (Robin/Dick Grayson); Uma Thurman (Poison Ivy/Dr. Pamela Isley); Alicia Silverstone (Batgirl/Barbara Wilson); Michael Gough (Alfred Pennyworth); Pat Hingle (Commissioner Gordon); Elle MacPherson (Julie Madison); Jeep Swenson (Bane); John Glover (Doctor Jason Woodrue); Vivica A. Fox (Ms. B. Haven); Vendela K. Thommessen (Nora Fries); Elizabeth Sanders (Gossip Gerty); John Fink (Aztec Museum Guard); Michael Reid

McKay (Antonio Diego); Eric Lloyd (Young Bruce Wayne); Jon Simmons (Young Alfred); Christian Boeving, Stogie Kenyatta, and Andy Lacombe (Snowy Cones Thugs); Joe Sabatino (Frosty); Michael Paul Chan (Observatory Scientist); Kimberly Scott (Observatory Associate); Jay Luchs and Roger Nehls (Observatory Reporters); Anthony E. Cantrall (Observatory Press); Alex Daniels and Peter Navy Tuiasosopo (Observatory Guards); Harry van Gorkum (M.C.); Sandra Taylor and Elizabeth Guber (Debutantes); Patrick Leahy (Himself); Jesse Ventura and Ralph Moeller (Arkham Asylum Guards); Doug Hutchinson (Golum); Tobias Jelinek, Greg Lauren, and Dean Cochran (Motorcycle Gangs); Coolio (Banker); Nicky Katt (Spike); Lucas Berman (Tough Boy Biker); Uzi Gal and Howard Velasco (Cops); Bruce Roberts (Handsome Cop); John Ingle (Doctor).

CHRISTIAN SCIENCE MONITOR, 6/20/97, p. 12, David Sterritt

Batman has traveled a long road since Warner Bros. revived him as a Hollood superhero in 1989. That road doesn't reach a dead end in the new "Batman & Robin," but it gets so crowded and noisy that audiences may not want to take it much farther in seasons to come.

Let's review the history. "Batman" portrayed the Caped Crusader as a moody, mysterious man played by Michael Keaton. "Batman Returns" did the same, adding a megadose of director Tim Burton's quirky cinematic ideas.

"Batman Forever" marked a major turn for the series, replacing Keaton with Val Kilmer—a more conventional actor with a more extroverted manner and trading Burton's surrealism for the action-movie glitz of director Joel Schumacher, whose credits include high-tech fantasies like "The Lost Boys" and "Flatliners."

Which brings us to this year's episode. Once was apparently enough for Kilmer, who hands the Bat-baton to George Clooney this time around. Clooney's admirers will be delighted, but by now the series has invested so much of its capital in outlandish special effects that it hardly matters whose head is under the pointy-eared helmet. "Batman & Robin" is less a movie than a razzle-dazzle video game.

Not that "Batman & Robin" suffers from a shortage of characters amid the chaos. On the side of the good guys, handsome Chris O'Donnell is back as Robin and perky Alicia Silverstone joins the crew as Batgirl. Also returning are old favorites Pat Hingle as Commissioner Gordon and Michael Gough as Alfred the Batbutler, who provides some of the picture's touching moments by showing a vulnerability rarely found in the macho Batcave.

As usual in Batman movies, the villains are more interesting and (let's face it) fun. Arnold Schwarzenegger plays Mr. Freeze, a coldhearted criminal with a clean-shaven skull, a robot-type outfit, and a mean-looking weapon that can ice a whole city in its tracks. Uma Thurman plays Poison Ivy, a demented botanist with a venomous kiss. The gifted John Glover also makes a brief appearance, giving Ms. Ivy her nasty powers and immediately becoming her first victim.

These are talented folks, and it would be nice to see them in one of those old-fashioned pictures that care about story as well as spectacle. Taking the opposite tack, "Batman & Robin" is about as warm as a blast from Mr. Freeze's ice rifle. Akiva Goldsman's screenplay nods toward family values, with some dialogue about loyalty and a limp father-son conflict between the title characters; and Alfred shows a hint of psychological depth when he faces an illness with uncomplaining courage. But such meaningful moments barely have time to get started before another barrage of action blows them off the screen. On a purely technical level, "Batman & Robin" is a well-made specimen of its big-budget breed. The first action sequence packs a particularly strong wallop through sheer speed and inventiveness, even though its anything-goes editing and Krazy Kat physics don't make a bit of sense.

But every blockbuster so far this season has the glaring problem of lasting too long, trying too hard, and blitzing us with more technological derring-do than anyone could need. Suggestion to Warner Bros.: How about a sequel that pays more than lip service to human values, adding some Bat-intelligence and Bat-thoughtfulness to its overloaded utility belt?

LOS ANGELES TIMES, 6/20/97, Calendar/p. 1, Kenneth Turan

The strutting bully that was the Batman franchise is no more. "Batman & Robin," the fourth film in the series, still preens and blusters, but there's no knockout punch.

Lacking most kinds of inspiration and geared to undemanding minds, this project is so overloaded with hardware and stunts, it's a relief to have it over.

A film that boasts 10 Bat weapons specific enough to be mentioned in the press notes (plus four different "Batarangs"), yet considers lines like "Freeze, you're mad" to be acceptable dialogue, "Batman & Robin" lives and dies by the aesthetic of excess, the familiar idea that anything worth doing is worth overdoing. You may admire its surface, but it is far too slick for even a toehold's worth of connection.

While it would take more time than it's worth to list all the wrinkles of the film's Akiva Goldsman plot, "Batman & Robin" has the eerie feeling of having no beginning, no middle and no end. Watching it is like stumbling into the world's longest coming attractions trailer, or a product reel for a special-effects house. Director Joel Schumacher, usually a genie of popular entertainment ("A Time to Kill," "Batman Forever"), has hit the repeat button once too often and found it stuck.

Having exhausted other plot formulations, this latest foray can be seen as the family values "Batman." Almost from the opening frame, Robin (Chris O'Donnell), the whiniest of heroes, acts up like a rebellious teenager, demanding a car and parental trust from the senior Bat (George Clooney this time around).

Then paterfamilias Alfred (Michael Gough) develops a serious ailment, leading to mumbles about mortality, and Alfred's niece Barbara (Alicia Silverstone) shows up and demands parity as Batgirl. It's bad no one thought of casting Dr. Joyce Brothers as an evil therapist giving deadly psychiatric advice.

Instead, "Batman & Robin" makes do with two more conventional villains, both of whom, as it turns out, are perverted and demented idealists, people who were frustrated in their attempts to do good in the world and ended up terrorizing the vulnerable citizens of Gotham.

Freeze (Arnold Schwarzenegger) was once top scientist Dr. Victor Fries, Olympic athlete, Nobel Prize winner and all-around swell guy. But that was before his wife came down with a dread disease and Dr. Fries fell into a cryosolution that mutated his body something fierce. Now he's a walking Popsicle, a one-man Ice Age who wants millions of dollars to do more research or else he'll freeze Gotham till it turns blue.

Freeze's determination to chill everything in sight leads to a burst of verbal creativity, inspiring—if that's the word—lines like "Stay cool," "Talk about your cold shoulder" and "The iceman cometh." A product tie-in with Foster's Freeze is presumably in the works.

Villain No. 2 started out as mousy Dr. Pamela Isley (Uma Thurman), a scientist devoted to giving plants a fighting chance to take back the Earth. A sinister laboratory accident turns her into the vixenish Poison Ivy, a siren with lips so laced with venom that as she puts it, "I'm literally to die for." Using a potion that clouds men's minds, she makes both Batman and Robin yearn for her charms, which, males being what they are, leads to conflicts that threaten to rip the Batpartnership apart.

While "Batman & Robin" is not lacking in events, its crises are invariably bogus; once the movie is over, it's impossible to differentiate one chaotic stunt-and-special-effect-filled episode from another.

Also, despite the impressive names in the cast, the film is indifferently acted, as if the second team were in to give the regulars a breather. Clooney, charming in "One Fine Day," neither hinders nor advances his chances at movie stardom here, which is more than can be said for his cohorts.

If all else fails, and it invariably does, it is possible to admire the scenery in "Batman & Robin." Really. Production designer, Barbara Ling, working with supervising art director Richard Holland and visual effects veteran John Dykstra, has created a massive Gotham City that never fails to intrigue the eye. The film's look is all that money can buy, and, as always with blockbuster wannabes like this, it's a shame that money can't buy even more.

NEW STATESMAN, 6/27/97, p. 42, Jonathan Coe

This week's most high-profile release seems to have little in common with an independent, low-budget classic from the 1960s, except that one day they will appear on the same page in the reference books. Nonetheless, watching the two films almost side-by-side inspired me to very similar reflections. The intelligent, politicised, emotionally charged naturalism of *The Battle of Algiers* made me think: "Cinema was invented for this."

Ten minutes into *Batman and Robin*, I was already muttering: "Cinema was invented for *this*?"

First, the Batfilm. Not much point, as Dr Johnson once said of *Cymbeline* (and as Igor Stravinsky also said of Disney's *Fantasia*), in wasting criticism on unresisting imbecility. It stars the two most desirable people on the planet, George Clooney and Uma Thurman, which I suppose is a point in its favour, and there's a certain amount of pleasure to be derived from watching these gorgeous specimens cavorting around the screen in various tight rubber outfits.

There's a plot, presumably, but I could not make head or tail of it. The film opens and closes with lengthy action sequences in which a lot of people shout at one another, an orchestra thunders in the background and things explode all over the place. In between, it strives for an occasional lightness of touch, but is constantly dragged down by the heavy-handed witlessness of the script and the presence of Arnold Schwarzenegger as "Mr Freeze", the villain. Surely Hollywood should have noticed by now that casting Arnie in any kind of comedy is like adding suet to a soufflé.

The production design is extravagant but standard: vaulting arches, skewed perspectives, lots of shadows and dry ice. One of the recurring exteriors is pretty spectacular: the asylum where Arnie gets banged up (not long enough, for my liking) is a huge, storm-swept, byzantine citadel, like an M C Escher nightmare. Seeing the kind of money and expertise that has been lavished on this, I began to glimpse distant, melancholic prospects of the kinds of fantasies the American cinema could produce (a terrific *Gormenghast,* for example) if it weren't so fixated on its own trashy culture. Worst of all, *Batman and Robin* doesn't even have a sense of its own shallowness, because various attempts are made to extract pathos from the relationship between Batman and his butler, which are truly woeful. Watching this over-inflated, over-designed confection is a preposterous experience: like arriving at Le Manoir aux Quat' Saisons and being served up Whoppers and fries on a silver platter.

On to more serious business. Last week saw the release of another Hollywood excrescence called *The Devil's Own,* in which the psychology of IRA violence is explored by getting Brad Pitt to drink Guiness, look soulful, and say "Aye" every so often. The director of this travesty, Alan J Pakula, must have seen Gillo Pontecorvo's *The Battle of Algiers* at some point, but he either never absorbed or has long since forgotten its lessons.

Pontecorvo's film, first released in 1966 and now appearing in a new print, charts the progress of the National Liberation Front's rebellion against the French occupying forces. Although it doesn't use any historical footage, it achieves a unique textural and emotional authenticity through its rise of bleached black-and-white photography, restless camera, and the casting of mainly amateur performers, including several key personalities from the real campaign (most notably Saadi Yacef, the FLN's former operational head, who plays himself.

The film, funded with Algerian money, was banned in France for many years and has long been a favorite with left-wing audiences (with significant exceptions, such as Jean-Luc Godard, who perversely called it "harmful to the Algerian revolution and a victory for Hollywood"). While there can be no doubt where its political allegiances lie, what has proved most enduring about the film is its rigorous even-handedness and humanity, its refusal to demonise either the revolutionary or the oppressor. Even Colonel Mathieu, the French commander and apologist for torture, is invested with a measure of sympathy by the film's one professional performer, Jean Martin.

The torture scenes remain the most vivid and haunting in the movie, accompanied as they are by fragments of religious music (a blunt but forgivable irony). But the action sequences, too, are far more pulse-quickening than anything in the bombastic *Batman*. Come to that, Pontecorvo handles these scenes, and the ideological conflicts underpinning them, much more adroitly than Neil Jordan managed in the similarly themed *Michael Collins*. If gunfights, chases and explosions are your thing, then *The Battle of Algiers* is probably the most exciting film in town at the moment.

As a bonus it will also make you think and feel: something Hollywood regularly forgets how to do, even with George Clooney, Uma Thurman and all the dollars in the world at its disposal.

NEW YORK, 6/14/97, p. 48, David Denby

Joel Schumacher's *Batman & Robin* is the most ugly-looking, slovenly, incoherent, and redundant big movie I've seen since *Batman Forever,* which was also directed by Joel Schumacher. The dark-toned, elegant beauty of Tim Burton's two earlier *Batman* films—the nightmare city as dream and desire—has now disappeared altogether, replaced by styleless urban-pop grandiosity and a profusion of interiors of unparalleled gaudiness. Does Schumacher aspire to redecorate Donald Trump's homes? I'm sure no one could do it any better. Schumacher has gone past bad taste and ineptitude. As a director he's achieved an eerie kind of boredom in the midst of frenzy, a void of meaning in the middle of violent sequences composed of shots thrown together from nowhere to nowhere without the slightest relation in space. Two years ago, I insisted that the comparable mess in *Batman Forever* was a sign that basic film aesthetics were collapsing, and despite receiving some chastisement on this point from James Wolcott in a recent *Vanity Fair,* I find no reason to revise my opinion. When you have seen Schumacher's two *Batman* movies, you have seen The End.

Arnold Schwarzenegger shows up as Mr. Freeze, menacing Gotham with blasts of chilling air, and Schwarzenegger, bald, purplish, fanatical, and snarling in his peculiar accent, is frightening enough. But Schwarzenegger does the same thing over and over (there are innumerable shots of him holding a gun and covering people in what is meant to be ice but looks like clear plastic), and after a while, he begins to resemble some goony old wrestler freaking out on a late-night cable show. Chris O'Donnell regresses into teenage nowheresville as a combative Robin, envious of Batman and longing for independence, and he's been given an unappealing mate—Alicia Silverstone, who wants to join the same crime-fighting team. Is this really the actress who seemed so promising in *Clueless?* Some way has to be found of photographing Silverstone so it doesn't appear that a pad is stuck under her upper lip. She seems plagued by baby fat, and her threadbare gung ho enthusiasm turns the picture into a cloying TV teen show. George Clooney, wagging his head as he speaks, and then setting and pointing his chin like a hunting dog, makes a sententious Batman. Give this man a role he can play! The movie's only redeeming feature is Uma Thurman as Poison Ivy, who vamps her way amusingly through naughty-girl clichés, puckering her lips into a satirical pout. Showing off her long-waisted figure as she slinks around, Thurman resembles, believe it or not, Nijinsky as the faun.

NEW YORK POST, 6/20/97, p. 39, Michael Medved

"Batman & Robin" is an absurdly lavish, overlong, merciless assault on the senses, It throws so many jarring, jangling elements onto the screen at once that they each deserve a separate review.

GEORGE CLOONEY AS THE CAPED CRUSADER: He looks great in the sleek, even more anatomically detailed Batsuit, but he never suggests the aching aura of haunted-hero torment that his predecessors (Michael Keaton and Val Kilmer) took pains to project.

CHRIS O'DONNELL AS ROBIN: He's a hoot—far funnier, than before, playing "Bird Boy" as an over-the-top, whining, insecure adolescent desperately eager to win his own place in the world.

ARNOLD SCHWARZENEGGER AS MR. FREEZE: With skin and eyes painted an eerily glowing whitish blue and his head shaved to resemble a radioactive cue ball, the nearly unrecognizable action star makes a shockingly successful villain easily the best in the "Batman" series since Jack Nicholson's Joker.

UMA THURMAN AS POISON IVY: She really does kick some ice, as a statuesque, sinuous seductress (half vine, half Venus) who will raise temperatures of all audience males to hothouse levels, making a persuasive push for plant power.

ALICIA SILVERSTONE AS BATGIRL: She's clueless when it comes to her action scenes, and even in her own black Batsuit she's so puffy and pouty that she looks no more formidable than an overly toasted marshmallow.

BATHOS AND THE BUTLER: In a silly, sentimental subplot, Alfred (Michael Gough) is dying of a mysterious disease and Batman will do anything to save him even listen to the old man's countless, gaseous Zen pronouncements.

FIGHT SCENES: There's no excuse for the chaos that sweeps these sequences—with choppy editing that produces confusion and incoherence rather than fast and furious choreography.

SETS, COSTUMES, SPECIAL EFFECTS: Consistently dazzling, bursting with ingenious detail and breath-taking demonstrations of the expanding power of computer graphic imagery.

THE BABE QUOTIENT: Awesome. In addition to Uma and Alicia there's also the ravishing Elle MacPherson as Bruce Wayne's new girlfriend, and even Vivica A. Fox (the stripper in "Independence Day") in a tiny role.

THE OVERALL FUN FACTOR: Sure, there's too much of everything. But the movie does make an honorable effort to give audiences their money's worth. Director Joel Schumacher pointedly reminds us that the original inspirations for "Batman" are called "comic books" not "tragic books," and, even more than he did with "Batman Forever," he takes Gotham away from the gloomy expressionistic excess of Tim Burton territory.
    In many ways, this new installment is closer to the campy spirit of the '60s TV series—despite some needless scenes of torture that make it too much for little kids. All in all, the outrageous, scattershot, operatic madness retains enough adolescent energy to keep customers in line and the aging series alive.

NEWSDAY, 6/20/97, Part II/p. B3, Jack Mathews

One of the characters in "Batman & Robin," the fourth installment of the "Batman" series and the second directed by Joel Schumacher, is a knockoff of Frankenstein's monster, a grunting hulk with veins sprawled across his biceps like spilled spaghetti. His name is Bane, and as this visually stunning but spectacularly boring episode evolves, he becomes the enforcer for Poison Ivy, one of the film's two central villains.
    Ivy, played by Uma Thurman as a cross among Mae West, Jessica Rabbit and the serpent in Eden, can weaken men with her breath and kill them with a kiss. But when things get rough, she turns to Bane. All of which had me wondering throughout the movie when someone—maybe Arnold Schwarzenegger's Mr. Freeze, maybe Alicia Silverstone's newly introduced Batgirl— would catch Ivy alone and say, "Sorry, no Bane, no gain."
    That the phrase is never uttered might be viewed as a sign of restraint, except that screenwriter Akiva Goldsman's actual groaners are worse! Examples:
• From Mr. Freeze, who clumps around in a metallic, internally lighted, body-formed freezer, carrying a cannon that encases his victims in ice: "The Iceman Cometh!"
• From Batman (No. 3: George Clooney), after Chris O'Donnell's Robin requests his own custom-made car: "That's why Superman works alone."
• And from the moist, soft-porn lips of Poison Ivy, on offering to help Mr. Freeze steal diamonds: "I'll help you grab your rocks."
    I haven't been wild about any of the "Batman" movies, but the further the series progresses into self-appreciation and parody—in other words, the closer it gets to the '60s TV show—the more respect I have for Tim Burton's original. Even though Michael Keaton was a shrimp of a Batman, he played the character with the right combination of brooding psychology, as the Dark Knight, and aristocratic air, as Bruce Wayne. The warmer, taller, square-jawed Clooney looks great in both roles, but the script leaves him with little to do, when not crimefighting, but parry bad puns with his annoyingly whiny sidekick.
    In this episode, Batman and Robin, joined by the athletic niece of Wayne Manor's loyal butler Alfred (Michael Gough), have the task of stopping Mr. Freeze from icing the planet so he can have its diamond supply to himself. Meanwhile, another lab accident has turned frumpy horticulturist Dr. Pamela Isley (Thurman) into a half-human, half-ivy, all-environmentalist vamp. She wants to depopulate the earth and liberate the plants. Together, Freeze and Ivy figure they can both get what they want.

Connecting subplots involve Freeze's wife and Alfred, both of whom are suffering from the same progressive neural disease, and both in need of a cure that only Freeze can find.

The set-up's not bad. It's typical comic book adventure, with outrageously overdrawn characters and impossible plotting. But most of the action set pieces—a hockey game in the Gotham Museum, a motorcycle race in the city's ghetto, a rooftop car chase, the showdown in the Gotham Observatory are too silly and frenetically filmed to work even as fantasy. There isn't a moment of suspense, tension or genuine menace, or enough energy in the performances to overcome the flat, mystifying dullness of the story.

Schwarzenegger's character, his face painted an opaque, silvery blue, and his eyes covered by milky contacts, is a marvelous design, but when he isn't wielding the ice gun or spewing wind-chill cliches, he's playing Mr. Freeze with the despair of Mr. Hamlet. And "though it make the unskillful laugh, it cannot but make the judicious grieve."

Thurman, of course, is easy on the eyes, at least after she is transformed from Amanda Plummer lookalike to the slinky Poison Ivy. Some wonderful makeup and costume design went into her sinuous, colorful guises, and though it quickly grows old, she does a wicked Mae West impression.

In contrast, Alicia Silverstone barely registers as British born-and-bred Barbara Wilson, who arrives in Gotham with an inexplicably flawless American accent and joins the Batman troupe.

Of all the summer's $100-million movies, "Batman & Robin" may have the most, literally, to show for it. Frame by frame, it's the most stunning picture out there, and it certainly has the stars. But the series' great weakness has always been its scripts, and with this, Batman is a step closer to being undone by his real nemesis—the Hack.

NEWSWEEK, 6/30/97, p. 77, David Ansen

It may be profitable, but it's sort of sad what's become of the Batman franchise. The series began, under Tim Burton's twisted gaze, with a grave Gothic grandiloquence that appealed to kids and grown-ups alike. Now it's just silly. *Batman & Robin* is a costume party for 9-year-olds—albeit with kinky, S&M-inspired costumes. Noisy, campy, overproduced, it's abdicated all solemnity in pursuit of a boom-kaboom videogame esthetic.

As his sidekicks proliferate, the new Batman (George Clooney) almost seems superfluous to the story, which is turned over to the villains. This time out it's Arnold Schwarzenegger's Mr. Freeze—a giant human popsicle who turns his enemies to ice—and Uma Thurman's Poison Ivy—an eco-freak femme fatale with a deadly venom kiss—who team up to bring Gotham City to its knees. Arnold's silver-skinned Mr. Freeze makes a wonderful objet d'art, but "Revenge is a dish best served cold" is not a line that trips mellifluously off the Big Guy's tongue. Uma is amateurish as the mousy botanist Dr. Pamela Isley, but once she metamorphoses into the vampy Mae West-ian Ms. Ivy, her appeal is self-evident.

As for our heroes, Chris O'Donnell's Robin has become a petulant brat, Alicia Silverstone's Batgirl is a Valley Girl lightweight, and the attempt to wring pathos from Alfred the butler's terminal illness produces not a single genuine emotion. How is Clooney? He's got all the right stuff to be terrific, and nothing to play. Screenwriter Akiva Goldsman has written quips, not characters: in lieu of a part, Clooney just wears a mischievous little smile to go along with his anatomically enhanced rubber suit.

Joel Schumacher still seems miscast as a Bat-action director: he stages the mayhem confusingly and the comedy too broadly. He does, however, have an eye for spectacle: the one aspect of "Batman" that remains seductive is designer Barbara Ling's Gotham City. There's a potent, dangerous allure to these looming cityscapes. If only the drama were commensurate to their wonder.

SIGHT AND SOUND, 8/97, p. 39, Andy Medhurst

Crime-fighting duo Batman and Robin are notified that a new villain, Mr Freeze, is staging a robbery at the Gotham City Museum of Art. They arrive to find Freeze and his henchmen trying to steal a gigantic diamond. Batman is forced to stop pursuing Freeze in order to thaw out the newly frozen Robin. The Boy Wonder is irritated by Batman's paternalistic attitude towards him.

In a research laboratory, horticulturalist Pamela Isley is horrified to learn that her boss, Dr Jason Woodrue, has been secretly creating a destructive man-monster, Bane. Confronted by her, Dr Woodrue attacks Pamela and leaves her for dead, but she re-emerges as Poison Ivy, part-plant part-woman, with a mission to rid the world of polluting humans. In Gotham City, Batman and Robin learn that Freeze was once Dr Victor Fries, a scientist who cryogenically froze his wife after he was unable to save her from an incurable case of the disease McGregor Syndrome. He accidentally fell into her freezing solution and emerged deformed as Mr Freeze, who needs diamonds to maintain his freezing apparatus.

At Wayne Manor, the home of Batman's alter ego Bruce Wayne, Barbara Wilson comes to visit her uncle, Wayne's butler Alfred. To catch Freeze, Bruce holds a charity ball where diamonds will be auctioned, but Poison Ivy and Bane get there first. Ivy uses pheromone dust to hypnotise both Batman and Robin; they fall for her charms and squabble over her. Freeze attacks the ball and is caught and imprisoned, but not before Ivy is smitten by him. Alfred admits he is in fact seriously ill with McGregor Syndrome. Poison Ivy helps Freeze escape, but she switches off his wife's life support and blames Batman. Freeze vows vengeance, planning to freeze first Gotham and then the world. Discovering the secrets of the Batcave, Barbara reinvents herself as Batgirl and saves Batman and Robin from the clutches of Ivy and Bane. Batman, Robin and Batgirl find Freeze at Wayne Observatory and foil his plan. Batman tells Freeze about Ivy's treachery, and that his wife is still alive. Gratefully, Freeze tells Batman how to cure Alfred's McGregor Syndrome. Both Freeze and Ivy are incarcerated. Batman and Robin realise how much they still mean to each other and forge a new crime-fighting unit with Batgirl.

Potentially *Batman & Robin* is a film with something for almost everyone. Saturday night multiplex thrill-seekers can sit back and revel in the well-oiled spectacular destruction. Slumming psychoanalytic theorists can chuckle at Poison Ivy's enveloping fronds and the white stuff that shoots out of Mr Freeze's great big gun. Devotees of S&M can lap up the acres of moulded rubber. Gay men can muse on the fact that George Clooney and Chris O'Donnell are probably the most ravishing male couple ever to share a house in the history of Hollywood. And nerdy film buffs can tick off the inter-textual reference points that fly faster than the dynamic duo's fists. An initial survey might note *Nosferatu* (1922), *Metropolis* (1926), *Rebel Without a Cause* (1955), *Mad Max* (1979), *The Silence of the Lambs* the Power Rangers and—a nice dig at this product's main marketplace rival this summer—*Jurassic Park*. Given such a semiotic cornucopia, the key question has to be: why does *Batman & Robin* nonetheless feel so hollow and hectoring?

The film's slick professionalism is undeniable—the opening battle in the Gotham City Museum of Art is a breathtaking beginning, dispensing with anything as sissy as narrative build-up in order to plunge the audience head-first into a gloriously excessive display of speed, sets, pyrotechnics and expenditure. It leaves you gawping and punch-drunk, but the very scale of its impact creates a structural problem for the film. The only way left to go is down—as if you'd blown your day at the theme park by going on the wildest, scariest ride first. The subsequent action sequences can only offer more of the same, and a law of diminishing returns inevitably takes hold.

Among the performances, the best news is Clooney, who displays exactly the right note of wry disbelief when in costume and manages not to giggle through the risible family melodrama sections back at Wayne Manor. The pointy ears and packed pouch are surely his for as long as he wants them. The wonderful and under-rated Alicia Silverstone is largely wasted, but acquits herself well enough, while the Uma Thurman purrs and pouts in a way that might impress a few teenagers who've never seen Mae West or Jane Russell but is liable to leave the rest of us mightily unimpressed.

As for Arnie, his Mr Freeze can't help but be a step up from *Jingle all the Way,* but he still looks like a star in a tailspin. His classic *Terminator*-era roles were all premised on the fact that he was less (or more) than human, a machine or a monster splendidly isolated from mere mortals. Here, he is a cartoon surrounded by other cartoons; they're all as extreme as he is, and consequently he looks creaky, ponderous and foolish. He delivers the deliberately bad, cold-related puns ("Allow me to break the ice", "Cool party" and so on) with all the panache of a discount warehouse on legs. Perhaps Poison Ivy's henchman, the man-machine character Bane, has been included primarily to mark out the distance Schwarzenegger's image has travelled—years ago *he* would have been playing Bane, but now he gets to banter with the class actors. Unfortunately, he banters abominably, but in the realm of cinema that *Batman & Robin* exemplifies this doesn't seem to matter. It Schwarzenegger's presence that counts—the fact that this is a *Batman* film (established franchise) with added Arnie (new ingredient! improved taste!) is supposed to leave us so stimulated the very idea that we don't notice the   unsatisfying execution.

More positively, *Batman & Robin* is by some distance the closest the film series has come to the once-reviled 60s television show. The perpetually tilted camera during fights and chases recalls the giddy disorientations and Dutch tilts of the small-screen version, to the extent that a psychedelic "Thwok!' or "Bammm!" would come as no surprise and the brooding interiority of the *Dark Knight*/Tim Burton variants is kept a bare minimum. Better still, two of central, recurring male characters finally say "I love you" before kissing. The fact that this exchange involves Bruce Wayne and a sickbed-confined Alfred rather than Bruce and the Boy Wonder is, as any devotee of Bat-queer subtexts will attest, simply displacement. Bruce and Dick are far too busy gazing soulfully into each other's eyes or quarrelling like tetchy long-term lovers to have time to put their deeper feelings into words.

These, though, are slight and incidental pleasures amid the barnstorming callousness of the whole film. *Batman & Robin* feels hollow for the simple reason that all it can ever be a prodigiously overblown joke, and it feels hectoring because of the deafening artillery of artifice it employs to and shroud that fact. "Look how expensive I am," it shrieks, "look at all stars and the dazzle and the trickery, look how much effort I'm putting into entertaining you!" Indeed you are, viewer answered while pining for less bombastic diversions of *Speed* or *Twister* or *Anaconda*, but do you have to be such an attention-seeking little brat about it?

VILLAGE VOICE, 7/1/97, p. 94, Amy Taubin

A permissive dad-type with a benign bedside manner, George Clooney's Batman probably won't doom the franchise. For one thing, he's not onscreen enough to have that potent an effect. Even more than its three predecessors, *Batman & Robin* reserves the star treatment for the villains: Mr. Freeze (Arnold Schwarzenegger) and Poison Ivy (Uma Thurman).

For reasons too complicatcd to explain here, Freeze and Ivy want to take revenge on the inhabitants of Gotham City by bringing on the second Ice Age. "You remember what happened to the dinosaurs?" inquires Freeze. Indeed we do: they were resurrected in *The Lost World,* a cinematic experience so turgid it makes *Batman & Robin* seem frolicsome by comparison.

Less camp than the Val Kilmer-versus-Jim Carrey installment, *Batman & Robin*—with Joel Schumacher again directing gives a Japanese animation style   punch to what is basically still a disco experience. The actors shout one-liners over the techno-ambient din (Elliot Goldenthal's score mixes Wagner riffs with the Smashing Pumpkins) while navigating their way through sets that have the exaggerated perspective of cycloramas. Even in their "anatomically correct" batsuits, though, the heroes—Batman (Clooney), Robin (Chris O'Donnell), and Batgirl (Alicia Silverstone)—seem too square to have gotten past the doormen.

Despite a garage filled with a new generation of Batmobiles and Batbikes, this trio spends much time at home trying on clothes, sorting out familial relationships, logging on to computers, and worrying about the failing health of Alfred (Michael Gough), Batman's butler and surrogate father. Thus Freeze and Ivy have ample opportunity to party and wreak havoc.

Claiming the role once played in the TV series by another ubermensch, Otto Preminger, Arnold is more Kindergarten Cop than Terminator. Beneath his iridescent baby-blue-and-silver subzero-cold armor beats a still warm heart. And if his comic timing is less than perfect, it's not so off the mark that an editor can't clip it more or less into shape. But Arnold's presence, while still monumental, is no longer surprising.

Which puts him at a disadvantage when he's competing for attention with a quick-change artist like Thurman, who metamorphoses before our eyes from a straggly-haired, twitchy chem-lab researcher into a flamboyantly self-possessed femme fatale.   Thurman can wrap a line with innuendo so that the sound is as slithery as her hips. Her Poison Ivy has more in common with outsized male villains like Alan Rickman in *Die Hard* than with Michelle Pfeiffer's kittenish Catwoman. Like Mae West, she sends up gender without relinquishing power or turning herself into a joke.

"Why are all the gorgeous ones such psychopaths?" whines Batman. I agree that Poison Ivy's plants-over-people politics puts her on the fringe of the ecology movement. But preferring to curl up alone in one's own Venus flytrap rather than make nice to a lug in a rubber suit by assuring him that his half-smile, duck-of-the-head routine is going to make him a movie star—that seems perfectly sane to me.

Also reviewed in:
NEW YORK TIMES, 6/20/97, p. C1, Janet Maslin
NEW YORKER, 7/7/97, p. 77, Anthony Lane
VARIETY, 6/16-22/97, p. 34, Todd McCarthy
WASHINGTON POST, 6/20/97, p. C1, Rita Kempley
WASHINGTON POST, 6/20/97, Weekend/p. 37, Desson Howe

BEAN

A Gramercy Pictures release of a PolyGram Filmed Entertainment presentation of a Working Title production in association with Tiger Aspect Films. *Executive Producer:* Richard Curtis. *Producer:* Peter Bennett-Jones, Eric Fellner, and Tim Bevan. *Director:* Mel Smith. *Director of Photography:* Francis Kenny. *Screenplay:* Richard Curtis and Robin Driscoll. *Based on the character devised by:* Rowan Atkinson and Richard Curtis. *Editor:* Christopher Blunden. *Music:* Howard Goodall. *Music Editor:* William Webb and Andre Jacquemin. *Sound:* Robert Anderson Jr. and (music) Gary Thomas. *Sound Editor:* Matt Grimes. *Casting:* Ronnie Yeskel. *Production Designer:* Peter Larkin. *Art Director:* Kevin Constant. *Set Designer:* Theodore Sharps. *Set Decorator:* Bill Gregory. *Set Dresser:* Deana Albers. *Special Effects:* John Hartigan and Chris Walkowiak. *Costumes:* Hope Hanafin. *Make-up:* Melanie J. Romero. *Stunt Coordinator:* Walter Scott. *Running time:* 92 minutes. *MPAA Rating:* PG-13.

CAST: Rowan Atkinson (Mr. Bean); Peter Egan (Lord Walton); John Mills (Chairman); Peter Capaldi (Gareth); June Brown (Delilah); Peter James (Dr. Rosenblum); Clive Corner (Dr. Cutler); Harris Yulin (George Grierson); Rob Brownstein (Dick Journo); Julia Pearlstein (Phyllis Quill); Peter MacNicol (David Langley); Larry Drake (Elmer); Tom McGowan (Walter Merchandise); Sandra Oh (Bernice Schimmel); Pamela Reed (Alison Langley); Tricia Vessey (Jennifer Langley); Andrew Lawrence (Kevin Langley); Alison Goldie (Stewardess Nicely); Dakin Matthews (Passenger Tucker); Scott Charles (Timmy Pewker Jr.); Thomas Mills (Officer Stubbles); Ronnie Yeskel (Mrs. Goodwoman); Richard Gant (Lieutenant Brutus); Chris Ellis (Detective Butler); Priscilla Shanks (Sylvia Grierson); Richard Hicks (Kart Pusherman); Danny Goldring (Security Buck); Johnny Galecki (Stingo Wheelie); Burt Reynolds (General Newton); Gigi Fields (Nurse Desking); Lela Ivey (Nurse Pots); David Doty (Dr. Jacobson); Robert Curtis-Brown (Doctor Frowning); April Grace (Nurse Pans); Perry Anzilotti (Dr. Squeaking); Janni Brenn (Nurse Dyper); Annette Helde (Nurse Gripes).

LOS ANGELES TIMES, 11/7/97, Calendar/p. 12, Jack Mathews

[The following review by Jack Mathews appeared in a slightly different form in **NEWSDAY, 11/7/97, Part II/p. B11.]**

Have you met Mr. Bean?

Quiet fellow, almost mute, very British in his tweedy appearance, but chronically discombobulated in his manner. He's a man who will get his shirt caught in his zipper just before he's to meet a member of the Royal Family, or sneeze up something disgusting during church service and spend the rest of the sermon trying to dispose of it.

If you've met him, through airings of his BBC show on PBS, you haven't forgotten him. And if you haven't, you can do so beginning today at a theater near you. Mr. Bean, a live-action cartoon figure created by British comedian Rowan Atkinson, has graduated to the big screen in the international hit simply titled "Bean."

Atkinson is one of the freshest visual comedians to come along since ... well, we have to go all the way back to Jim Carrey. There are few direct comparisons to the styles of the two men—Carrey pumps his comic wings to the beat of the hummingbird, while Atkinson moves more to the rhythm of the stork. But they both excel in a field of physical comedy that was on the verge of artistic extinction.

Atkinson, whom you may remember as the tongue-tied priest in "Four Weddings and a Funeral," was inspired by Stan Laurel, and the inspiration show's in the predicaments Bean gets himself into. One simple mistake, one rip in a pair of pants, one carelessly tossed match, one mistaken identity, and Laurel was up to his crying eyes in trouble. And so it goes for Mr. Bean.

In the movie, which has earned a whopping $120 million in international ticket sales, Atkinson's accident-prone character is cast as a tenured security guard at a London gallery, where his unique incompetence so distresses management they give him the task of accompanying a famous painting to America, just to be rid of him for a while.

The Los Angeles gallery that has paid $50 million for the painting, "Whistler's Mother," is expecting a top art expert to introduce it at a handing-over ceremony, and the fact that Bean doesn't know beans about art is the lone notion fueling the entire movie. In vaudeville, where Atkinson's brand of pantomime took root in America, this would be called the set-up, from which all comic digressions spring. And that's what "Bean" is, a feature-length series of mostly silent visual sketches, built around its fish-out-of-water theme.

At the elegant new Grierson Gallery in Los Angeles, Bean is at first taken for an eccentric genius, much like Peter Sellers' Chauncey Gardiner in "Being There." His hosts, the supercilious gallery director (Harris Yulin) and the curator (Peter MacNicol) whose home he is invited to stay in, call him "Doctor" Bean and assume profound knowledge behind a face that suggests a child still learning his ABCs.

That the audience knows Bean's limitations and bumbling nature is the essential ingredient of Atkinson's performance. On the TV show, Bean is a sneaking disaster, trying to cover up some embarrassment while compounding it, all at the inconvenience or expense of hapless bystanders.

In the film, written by Atkinson's longtime collaborators Richard Curtis and Robin Driscoll and directed by Mel Smith ("The Tall Guy"), care is taken to develop some of Bean's comic foils. Notably, the flummoxed curator, his no-nonsense wife (Pamela Reed) and their two children, who feel a sort of age-appropriate kinship to their house guest.

While all this adds a hint of realism missing from the TV skits, it also creates a challenge that Atkinson doesn't always overcome and that will almost certainly—you are warned—leave newcomers to Bean's humor wondering what's the big deal. The idea of Bean fitting into this situation, even disastrously, requires more than suspension of disbelief. It requires a full blackout of reasoning.

But for the converted, and for people with a low threshold for visual comedy, "Bean" amounts to a hill of laughs.

NEW YORK, 11/24/97, p. 70, David Denby

At the beginning of *Bean*, Rowan Atkinson, the semi-legendary British comic, rises for the day and shaves his forehead, his nose, and his tongue (mustn't forget *that*). Atkinson has jet-black hair and a Nixonian five-o'clock shadow, and when he cranes his neck, his nostrils flaring, he has the appearance of an aggressively rutting ferret. Atkinson is an all but silent comic. He may emit a variety of subterranean growls and an occasional self-satisfied, sprightly *hmmm*!, but that's about it. Silence, it turns out, is not his poetry, as it was for Chaplin, but his cover: Atkinson is bursting with infantile greed and fatuous self-approval. When he does speak, in a dry, guttural voice, he can barely get the words out. This is a man who gives away as little as possible—a worm inside the bean, a self-protecting man, but, of course, fantastically maladroit, so that even his most careful calculations go astray. The mixture of egotism and ineptitude is what makes Atkinson funny. He's a fussbudget wild man with a repertory of weird, Pinocchio-like facial tics. He startles us with his oddity, his low instincts.

The character of Bean was first developed by Atkinson and writers Richard Curtis and Robin Driscoll for a half-hour show on the BBC, a show that became an enormous success here (on PBS stations) as well as in England. The movie was written by the same pair and directed by Mel Smith, who is English, and I wish I could say I liked it more than I did. Atkinson is a funny man, but despite some bright spots, the picture is mediocre and finally tiresome. Curtis and Driscoll's story is no more than serviceable. Bean is a sleepy, inept guard at the National Gallery in London. When a pretentious California museum buys Whistler's Mother from the gallery, the Brits, eager to get rid of the unspeakable Bean, send him to the Americans as an alleged expert on the painting. Bean—or Dr. Bean, as everyone calls him—never clears up the confusion and of course wreaks havoc on the nervous, hapless Yanks. Women and children may instinctively loathe him, but the ambitious and the phony treat him with elaborate deference, which he systematically abuses.

There are a couple of classic bits, including a sequence in which Bean gets his pants wet in the crotch and, attempting to dry himself, appears to be copulating, in a men's room, with a hot-air blower. But Bean's not saying anything, his temperamental remoteness, is a limitation. What does Bean want? We never know. In between the inspired moments, Atkinson appears to be marking time, and since the picture is poorly acted and badly lit, the time is not well spent. The major trouble, however, is that Bean isn't a rich enough character for a full-length movie. Atkinson has magnificently awful physical equipment, but at the moment, he's a comic without a soul.

NEW YORK POST, 11/7/97, p. 56, Thelma Adams

I didn't expect to fall for "Bean." I'd seen the barf-bag gags, the endless nose blowing, the tissue stuffed in the nostril schtick. Not for me, I thought.

I spent the comedy's first 10 minutes listening to other people laugh. Who were these people, with their snickers and giggles and howls?

I studied Rowan Atkinson, the British comedian who plays "Mr. Bean" on PBS. I inspected his moles, his ghoulish face, his weasel ears, his roll-y brown eyes—the whole bored, bratty schoolboy package in an adult body.

And then it happened: I started to laugh. And I couldn't stop.

When Bean stuffs his skull into a raw, 25-pound turkey and goes banging about with a bird stuck on his head, it's one of the silliest, funniest things I've ever seen. It's ridiculous—and the payoff to come is even better.

This fish-out-of-water scenario, directed by Mel Smith from a script by Richard Curtis and Robin Driscoll, is greater than the sum of the gags. It starts when London's National Gallery of Art can't fire security guard Bean. The board of directors does the next best thing: It ships him off to America.

"Our loss is America's gain," says one gallery official slyly.

Passed off by the National Gallery as an art expert, Bean arrives in L.A. with "Whistler's Mother" in tow. The Grierson Gallery has purchased the American masterpiece from the English with a $50 million donation from Gen. Newton (Burt Reynolds).

Believing Bean is a brilliant art historian, curator David Langley (Peter MacNicol) welcomes the lunatic into his home—and before long, the curator's family life and career are in jeopardy. MacNicol is a formidable foil for Atkinson. Their duet of The Beatles "Yesterday" is silly and poignant.

The movie's most squirm-causing scene finds Bean mistreating "Whistler's Mother." The set piece is funny and embarrassing, reminding me of those excruciating Lucille Ball routines where she's working in the chocolate factory or selling health tonic.

As Bean says in his extemporaneous speech about "Whistler's Mother": "That's marvelous. Well, that's what I think, anyway."

SIGHT AND SOUND, 8/97, p. 41, Philip Kemp

The disaster-prone Mr Bean is employed as an attendant at the National Gallery in London. Since he enjoys the protection of the chairman, the governors are unable to sack him. The Grierson Gallery of Los Angeles has recently bought Whistler's painting of his mother from the Musée d'Orsay in Paris and are bringing it back to the US. They invite the National Gallery to send a top expert to speak at the ceremony. Seizing the chance to get rid of Bean for a while, the governors choose him to be the gallery's representative.

David Langley, the Grierson's young curator, decides to invite Bean to stay with him, despite the misgivings of his wife Alison and children Jennifer and Kevin. After causing chaos on the plane and at Los Angeles airport, Bean is driven home by David, but after brief exposure to the visitor's eccentricities Alison leaves for her mother's, taking the kids. At the gallery, Grierson and his staff are bemused by Bean's erratic behaviour. David is warned that his career depends on Bean coming up to scratch. That night Grierson and his wife arrive at David's for dinner. Bean attempts to microwave a gigantic turkey, which explodes.

The next day, Bean, left alone with Whistler's painting in the museum, accidentally damages it irreparably. He conceals it behind a security screen, but not before the horrified David has seen it. Foreseeing the ruin of his career, David takes Bean off to drown their sorrows. They arrive home drunk to find Alison has returned; she announces her plans to leave David. That night Bean sneaks into the gallery and substitutes a skilfully doctored reproduction for the damaged original. At the ceremony the next day, the painting is acclaimed. Bean makes a platitudinous speech which is warmly applauded by the gallery's benefactor, General Newton.

News comes that Jennifer Langley is in a coma following a traffic accident. David, along with Bean, rushes to the hospital where Bean is mistaken for a doctor. By sheer luck he saves the life of a shot police lieutenant, and brings Jennifer out of her coma. Now an honoured guest, Bean stays on for several days before taking an emotional farewell of David at the airport. Back home, Bean fondly contemplates Whistler's damaged original on the wall of his room.

The record of British television comedians attempting the transfer to cinema is mainly dismal. Tony Hancock, Frankie Howerd and Morecambe and Wise all appeared sadly diminished on the big screen, overstretched at feature length and snarled up by extraneous plotting. Only the *Monty Python's Flying Circus* team made the transition successfully. However, Rowan Atkinson's Mr Bean fares better than most. The plot, if ludicrously implausible, is clear and coherent, and despite the Bean persona being relocated to LA, the comedy has been kept down to a human scale where the Beanish burnout works best. Atkinson and his collaborators have resisted the temptation to pile on the pile-ups or dwarf their hero with gargantuan special effects. Although *Bean* bills itself as 'The Ultimate Disaster Movie', the biggest thing that explodes in this film is a 35-pound turkey.

From this angle, Bean's closest relative among the great screen comics is perhaps Jacques Tati's M Hulot, who was also at his best when he kept the comedy fine-detailed and intimate. In the Hulot tradition, Bean is mostly inept but can on occasion be crafty and even malicious, and—as did Hulot—he does sometimes talk. (The Bean voice is a rotund, strangulated sub-cockney, sounding oddly like a parody of Alfred Hitchcock.) Bean, though, wholly lacks the Frenchman's wistful poetry; his persona is too impervious to be loveable, and he wisely never attempts pathos. The focus of our sympathy in this case is Peter MacNicol's hapless curator, who at one point dissolves into a lachrymose rendition of 'Yesterday' as he sees his entire life disintegrating around him.

The gags are plentiful and mostly good. Bean's comic forte has always lain in bodily functions, and so it does here, although 12-year-olds of all ages may be disappointed at the relative lack of fart and willy jokes. Still, there's a virtuoso nose-blowing episode, with Bean erupting like an entire troupe of rogue elephants, and a commendably gross in-flight sickbag gag. And the escalating destruction of Whistler's masterpiece, iconoclasm in its most literal sense, is sparked off by one of Bean's snot-rich and uncontrollable sneezes.

Bean's ceremonial speech, on the other hand, comes as a cop-out, especially after getting such a comic build-up: a truly resourceful script would have devised a way for him to deliver the whole thing in mime, like Chaplin's David-and-Goliath sermon in *The Pilgrim* (1923). Fellow-comedian Mel Smith, whose directorial debut *The Tall Guy* also featured Atkinson, directs with assured comic timing, never milking the gags to excess. Setting a comic to direct a comic, as Terry Gilliam's reining-in of Robin Williams in *The Fisher King* also showed, can clearly pay dividends.

VILLAGE VOICE, 11/18/97, p. 85, Gary Susman

In *Bean,* an English museum sends the bumbling man-child Mr. Bean (Rowan Atkinson) to Los Angeles in the guise of an art scholar, as something of a joke on us Yanks, who mistake his silence for brilliance. (Call it *Bean There.*) So it is with the movie, in which Atkinson's acclaimed genius for comedy arrives in Hollywood somewhat dumbed down and made more family-values friendly for the International market. Still, Atkinson and his collaborators—director Mel Smith, writers Richard Curtis and Robin Driscoll—know how to build a gag over time, and though Atkinson indulges in silly slapstick, Mr. Bean is funniest when scheming his way out of a dilemma. The comic payoff is inelegant but satisfying.

Also reviewed in:
CHICAGO TRIBUNE, 11/7/97, Friday/p. J, John Petrakis
NEW YORK TIMES, 11/7/97, p. E22, Lawrence Van Gelder
NEW YORKER, 11/24/97, p. 137, Daphne Merkin
VARIETY, 6/30-7/13/97, p. 65, David Stratton
WASHINGTON POST, 11/7/97, Weekend/p. 48, Desson Howe

BEAUMARCHAIS THE SCOUNDREL

A New Yorker Films release of a Telema/studio Canal Plus/France 2 Cinema/France 3 Cinema production in association with Canal Plus and with the participation of Procirep/Invesimage 4/Sofiarp 2. *Executive Producer:* Dominique Brunner. *Producer:* Charles Gassot. *Director:* Edouard Molinaro. *Screenplay (French with English subtitles):* Edouard Molinaro and Jean-Claude Brisville. *Inspired by an unpublished work by:* Sacha Guitry. *Director of Photography:* Michael Epp. *Editor:* Veronique Parnet. *Music:* Jean-Claude Petit. Choreographer: Pierre Darde. *Sound:* Dominique Warnier, Dominique Hennequin and (music) Roland Guillotel. *Sound Editor:* Patrice Grisolet. *Casting:* Catherine Molinaro. *Set Designer:* Jean-Marc Kerdelhue. *Set Decorator:* Marie-Noelle Giraud and Karen Granger. *Costumes:* Sylvie De Segonzac. *Make-up:* Paul Le Marinel. *Running time:* 100 minutes. *MPAA Rating:* Not Rated.

CAST: Fabrice Luchini (Beaumarchiais); Manuel Blanc (Gudin); Sandrine Kiberlain (Marie-Therese); Michel Serrault (Louis XV); Jacques Weber (Duc de Chaulnes); Michel Piccoli (Prince de Conti); Jean-François Balmer (Sartine); Florence Thomassin (Marion Menard); Isabelle Carré (Rosine); Claire Nebout (The Knight of Éon); Jean Yanne (Goezman); Martin Lamotte (Comte De La Blache); Jean-Claude Brialy (The Abbot); Dominique Besnehard (Louis XVI); Axelle Laffont (Mariette Lejay); Murray Head (Lord Rochford); Patrick Bouchitey (Monsieur Lejay); José Garcia (Figaro); François Morel (Peasant at Court); Alain Chabat (Courtier at Versailles); Pierre Gérard (Comte De Provence); Judith Godrèche (Marie-Antoinette); Evelyne Bouix (Madame Vigee-Lebrun); Michel Aumont (Baron De Breteuil); Jean-Marie Besset (Desfontaines); Roland Blanche (Thevenot De Morande); Jeff Nuttall (Benjamin Franklin).

LOS ANGELES TIMES, 10/24/97, Calendar/p. 16, Kevin Thomas

"Beaumarchais, the Scoundrel" is a glorious, giddy account of a tumultuous 11 years—1773 to 1784—in the life of the great French playwright. The author of "The Barber of Seville" and "The Marriage of Figaro" led an incredibly busy life as a political gadfly, taking aim at corruption in the ruling classes, serving as a royal spy, helping underwrite the American Revolution, living by his wits and pursuing beautiful women.

The son of a watchmaker, Beaumarchais devised the movement, still used, with which a watch keeps accurate time, and he married his way to the top of the social ladder. (Twice widowed, he was accused by his enemies of doing away with his wives.) He was also a magistrate and a lord of the hunt.

Not surprisingly, the legend of Beaumarchais attracted actor-writer-director Sacha Guitry, himself a legend, who brought to his plays and films a sly, humanizing touch to the lives of royals and other historic figures. No less surprising, director Edouard Molinaro, famed for "La Cage aux Folles" for many other delightful French comedies, was tantalized by the prospect of filming an unproduced Guitry play on Beaumarchais.

Retaining some 30% of Guitry's dialogue, Molinaro and his co-writer Jean-Claude Brisville devised an inspired script that's like a piece of lacy iron filigree—light and fanciful but sturdy—that sparkles with wit while zapping an oppressive monarchist government. In Molinaro and Brisville's imaginative hands, Beaumarchais emerges as a modern thinker and a prophet of his times, anticipating the American Revolution so soon to come.

Molinaro has said that without Fabrice Luchini he would have never made the film, and unless Guitry had risen from the grave, it is impossible to imagine anyone else in the role of Beaumarchais. That Luchini is slight and unhandsome merely serves to underline the intense magnetism of his wit, intellect and personality. He's such a commanding presence, his sense of timing and movement so acute, that he actually did steal scenes—or close to it—from Gérard Depardieu in "Colonel Chabert." Luchini radiates confidence and authority with the throwaway gallantry so characteristic of Guitry himself. He's a miracle of discipline—and spontaneity.

Bouncing in and out of ladies' beds and various jails for assaults on the *ancien regime,* Beaumarchais takes on the corrupt Court of Lords. He wins his case with the public but winds up stripped of his livelihood, his title and the right to stage his plays.

Coming to his rescue, thanks to the intervention of the Prince de Conti (Michel Piccoli), is the king himself, Louis XV (Michel Serrault), who saves Beaumarchais by pressing him into service as a secret agent. He is dispatched to London to retrieve an attack plan on England from a glamorous spy (Claire Nebout), apparently a transvestite.

It is during this mission that he becomes involved with the fast-approaching American Revolution. Gun-smuggling to the colonies, love affairs and other adventures culminate in his staging of "The Marriage of Figaro," whose premiere has the effect of firing the first shot in the French Revolution.

"Beaumarchais," filmed gorgeously at Versailles and other historic locales, has that flawless period feel, here enhanced by elegant classical music of the era incorporated into a lovely score, that so many European pictures do so well. It is a film of telling nuance and gesture, none more memorable than a moment when a nobleman, encountering Beaumarchais in the Hall of Mirrors, tries to humiliate him by asking him to repair his exquisite and delicate pocket watch. Ever so deftly Beaumarchais manages to let it tumble from his hands and smash to pieces on the parquet.

NEW YORK POST, 10/24/97, p. 47, Larry Worth

Epic costume dramas have long been an endangered species. And epic costume dramas with wit? Those went out with the unicorn.

That's why "Beaumarchais the Scoundrel" is an unqualified delight—a return to the swordplay and adventurous derring-do made famous by Douglas Fairbanks, the sumptuous period films staged by Luchino Visconti and the sharp humor personified by Pierre Augustin Caron de Beaumarchais.

Who? Beaumarchais never quite found his place in history books, but he penned—and was jailed over—"The Barber of Seville" and "The Marriage of Figaro." That was between running arms for the American Revolution, helping to instigate the French Revolution, romancing numerous ladies, mentoring his apprentice, battling 18th-century censors and swapping bon mots with Ben Franklin, Marie Antoinette and Louis XVI.

Director Edouard Molinaro masterfully captures each aspect of the French commoners' hero, though following the sometimes labyrinthine storyline requires rapt attention on the part of the audience.

That shouldn't be a big tumbling block. Whether playing up Beaumarchais' dicey dealings with kings, a transvestite spy in England or any number of lovelies, the material fascinates. Mixed with a tale of shifting loyalties—never mind the merging of sex, intrigue and politics—there's never a dull moment.

That's in addition to Molinaro's ability to capture the sartorial splendor and pageantry of the times, pull off D.W. Griffith-like crowd scenes and make it all look gorgeous. Heck even the requisite carriage-wheels-over-cobblestone shots could pass for postcards.

Having also co-written the script, Molinaro displays versatility in the process. After gaining fame chiefly from comedies such as "La Cage aux Folles" and "A Pain in the A-" he educates and entertains here while recreating—and sometimes resculpting—history.

A first-rate cast is the perfect complement, starting with Fabrice Luchini's charismatic turn in the title role. As with John Malkovich in "Dangerous Liaisons," the appeal has less to do with appearance than manner, which produces a dazzling performance.

Sandrine Kiberlain, recently seen in "A Self-Made Hero" and "Cyrano de Bergerac," is appropriately fetching as Beaumarchais' wife, while newcomer Manuel Blanc stands out as a dashing acolyte. In supporting roles, Gallic veterans Michel Serrault and Michel Piccoli earn special kudos, as does Jeff Nuttall for his hilarious turn as Ben Franklin.

"Life is cruel," the title character often comments. Granted. But thanks to "Beaumarchais," you couldn't prove it by costume-drama fans.

SIGHT AND SOUND, 9/96, p. 35, Ginette Vincendeau

Paris, 1770, towards the end of Louis XV's reign. Pierre-Augustin Caron de Beaumarchais, the playwright, is also an inventor, magistrate and defender of human rights (he's a former friend of Voltaire's). He acquires a new secretary, Gudin, a young man who admires his writing. As magistrate, Beaumarchais rules for a poor man against the powerful Prince de Conti, for which he is provoked into a duel by the Duc de Chaulnes and then arrested. This leads to a trial, where Beaumarchais is accused of using a false aristocratic name (a privilege he has bought) and of living off his two ex-wives' fortunes. He uses the trial to denounce the corruption of parliament and magistrates, especially that of Goezman. The populace supports him enthusiastically, but he is condemned all the same, losing all rights and privileges, including his right to the name Beaumarchais.

A young woman, Marie-Thérèse, declares her love for him. She becomes his wife, replacing his mistress, the actress Marion Menard. At Versailles, the King pardons him in exchange for a spying mission. He is sent to England to meet the transvestite Chevalier d'Eon in order to retrieve a compromising document. In London he also takes up the cause of American independence. The King, unknown to Beaumarchais, dies. Beaumarchais gets the document but is arrested for dealing with the American 'rebels'. Back in Paris, he completes *The Barber of Seville*, which is a flop on its first performance, but, after some editing by Gudin, becomes a triumph. He translates the American Declaration of Independence into French. The new King, Louis XVI asks him to negotiate with the Americans under the cover of trading. He does so, at the price of bankruptcy. Meanwhile, under pressure from his friends, including the Prince de Conti now on his death bed, Beaumarchais agrees to write a sequel to *The Barber of Seville*.

The Marriage of Figaro is passed by censorship despite its revolutionary political allusions. The premiere is a triumph but the King orders the arrest of Beaumarchais at the end of the performance and the play has to be banned. Later on, Beaumarchais is pardoned but he demands as a condition of his release that *The Marriage of Figaro* be performed again. A voice-over informs us that the King agrees, thereby "unwittingly signing one of the birth certificates of the French Revolution".

Within the growing body of historical heritage films, *Beaumarchais* will inevitably be compared with *Cyrano de Bergerac*. Though the period is different—*Beaumarchais* takes place in the late eighteenth century, Cyrano the seventeenth—the films have much in common. Both centre on a dashing, iconoclastic hero, share high production values and large casts, and they put the accent on the theatrical. The first scene of *Beaumarchais*, indeed, is set in a theatre, where Beaumarchais urges the actors to "just say their lines", recalling Depardieu's debunking of the pompous *Comédie Française* acting style at the beginning of *Cyrano*. Equally the Duc de Chaulnes, played by Jacques Weber (who fights with Beaumarchais, but later comes round to his side) evokes the relationship between the Comte de Guiche, played by the same Weber, and Cyrano. But where Cyrano was distinguished by a tight, though sweeping, narrative, *Beaumarchais* has an episodic style reminiscent of Sacha Guitry's 'historical' pageants of the 30s-50s, unsurprisingly since the film is based on a Guitry text. As in Guitry's own films, an impressive roll-call of French stars is on hand for cameo parts: Michel Piccoli (The Prince de Conti), Jean Yanne (Goezman), Michel Serrault (Louis XV), and Jean-Claude Brialy (the Abbot), among others.

One can see why the veteran director Edouard Molinaro (best known for his comedies, especially *La Cage aux folies* I and II) would have gone for Beaumarchais as a subject. In fact, picaresque as the hero's adventures may seem, the real Beaumarchais' life was much more fantastic than that depicted in the film, which leaves out copyright lawsuits, allegations that he murdered his first wife (whose name Beaumarchais took), harp lessons for the King's daughters, and arms dealing in Holland. The decision to simplify was, however, a wise one, and indeed *Beaumarchais*' problem is whether it wants to show its multifaceted hero Beaumarchais as playwright, political activist, philanderer or opportunist. In the end, the film opts for the pleasing myths of eighteenth century France—as the cradle of revolution culture and libertinage—all rolled into one character, played by the gifted Fabrice Luchini.

Luchini emerged as one of Rohmer's key actors in the 80s and later won startling roles in a few other auteurs' films. He rose to mainstream status with his brilliant performance as the lawyer in Yves Angelo's *Le Colonel Chabert* in 1994. *Beaumarchais* gives him the opportunity to develop further his persona of the cunning, effortlessly refined operator and to use his best asset, his melodious voice, in a wealth of well-crafted lines. But talent and craft are not enough. Larger doses of charisma, Depardieu-style, are needed to carry a large ensemble piece such as this, but Luchini's characteristic manner is too nice to be a vehicle for *Beaumarchais'* ferocious drive and opportunism.

Although *Beaumarchais* is inevitably cloaked in the relatively naturalistic garb of 90s costume drama, it is better seen as a Guitry-style romp through famous historical locations (there's Versailles!) and characters (here's Marie-Antoinette!). As in the Guitry pageants which are its points of reference, the performance of history aims to be tongue-in-cheek. Connoisseurs of well-crafted costume dramas will find much pleasure in Beaumarchais (decors and costumes are glorious) and should rush to see it in the cinema.

VILLAGE VOICE, 10/28/97, p. 88, Elliott Stein

Edouard Molinaro's best-known films—*La Cage aux Folles* and *La Cage II*—have been highly commercial comedies, so *Beaumarchais the Scoundrel*, a lavish wide-screen historical pageant, comes as a surprise.

This fictionalized biopic on the life of the great French dramatist is not primarily concerned with him as the author of *The Barber of Seville* and *The Marriage of Figaro*, but with him as the liberal magistrate who favored the lower classes, the founder of the first French union, and a staunch friend of the American colonists. Extremely episodic, it's full of incident, but almost plotless. The sole sequence with any dramatic punch concerns Beaumarchais's trip to London, where he has been sent by Louis XV to recover a copy of France's secret plan to invade England; it has fallen into the hands of the transvestite spy, the Chevalier d'Eon (played by the striking actress Claire Nebout).

The production is richly handsome—it looks like a big-budgeted Gallic opus of the 1950s. Fabrice Luchini gives an intelligent, astringent performance in the title role, but one drawback is that the impeccable Beaumarchais is always right about everything and most of the other characters seem to exist merely to admire him.

Also reviewed in:
NEW REPUBLIC, 11/17/97, p. 26, Stanley Kauffmann
NEW YORK TIMES, 10/24/97, p. E12, Janet Maslin
VARIETY, 4/1-7/96, p. 56, Stephen O'Shea

BEAUTICIAN AND THE BEAST, THE

A Paramount Pictures release of a Koch Company production in association with High School Sweethearts. *Executive Producer:* Roger Birnbaum, Fran Drescher, and Peter Marc Jacobson. *Producer:* Howard W. Koch, Jr. and Todd Graffe. *Director:* Ken Kwapis. *Screenplay:* Todd Graff. *Director of Photography:* Peter Lyons Collister. *Editor:* Jon Poll. *Music:* Cliff Eidelman. *Sound:* Richard Goodman. *Casting:* Jane Jenkins and Janet Hirshenson. *Production Designer:* Rusty Smith. *Art Director:* Steve Cooper. *Set Designer:* John D. Jefferies, Sr. *Set Decorator:* Sara Andrews. *Costumes:* Barbara Tfank. *Running time:* 107 minutes. *MPAA Rating:* PG.

CAST: Fran Drescher (Joy Miller); Timothy Dalton (Boris Pochenko); Ian McNeice (Grushinsky); Patrick Malahide (Kleist); Lisa Jakub (Katrina); Michael Lerner (Jerry Miller); Phyllis Newman (Judy Miller).

LOS ANGELES TIMES, 2/7/97, Calendar/p. 8, John Anderson

[The following review by John Anderson appeared in a slightly different form in
NEWSDAY, 2/7/97, Part II/p. B2]

Fran Drescher's voice should be hooked up to an oscilloscope, because there are things going on there that defy explanation. The piggy-backed harmonics, the simultaneous octaves, the symphonic whine disturbing the peace like a rusty razor, all lead one to suspect that somewhere among her multiple waves of Flushing-accented effusiveness Drescher is producing sounds that only dogs can hear.

Explaining her appeal, on the other hand—either on TV's "The Nanny" or in its spiritual descendant, "The Beautician and the Beast"—is a snap. Drescher's a traditionalist, basically, inasmuch as minority humor and self-abasement are American comedy institutions. Drescher's Lucy-Desi schtick is a combo platter of ethnicity (Queens Jewish), innate absurdity (striking good looks married to a voice like bad radio reception) and the fact that she's everybody's equal, by virtue of being culturally hamstrung.

Of course, Drescher is also no idiot, which is why "The Beautician and the Beast," a lime-and-fuschia-flavored "King and I," is so much more appealing than either its premise or its trailers suggest. As beauty school instructor Joy Miller, Drescher is talky, sexy, inappropriate and smart. And until director Ken Kwapis allows sentimental seriousness to overtake the humor, so is the movie.

Based on the same setup as about a hundred TV sitcoms and dubious films, "The Beautician and the Beast" finds Drescher's colorful Joy in the drab gray former Soviet socialist republic of Slovetzia. It's a mixup, of the classically sitcom variety: Grushinsky (Ian McNeice), emissary of Slovetzia's dictator, Boris Pochenko (Timothy Dalton), has hired Joy as governess to Pochenko's children, thinking she's a science teacher. ("Teach it?" she says later. "I didn't even pass it.") Joy, under the impression Grushinsky needs a beautician, is happy to go along for the ride, especially since the job she really wanted—doing hair for the women who pick Lotto numbers on TV—has gone to someone more chi-chi.

Joy doesn't exactly sing "Getting to Know You," but once in Slovetzia she wins the children over, befriends the locals ("Svetlana! Wait up!"), organizes a union at one of Pochenko's factories, and makes Boris steam. But with steaming, Boris also softens—prompting his malevolent prime minister, Kleist (Patrick Malahide) to speculate whether there isn't room at the top.

There's a romantic subplot about Pochenko's daughter Katrina (Lisa Jakub of "Mrs. Doubtfire") and an anti-government subversive, and of course the growing affection between Boris and Joy. Dalton, not by nature a comedian, is actually quite good as the Stalin-mustachioed Boris, precisely because informality seems to be so hard for both of them. Everyone, however, comes off as stiff next to Drescher, who leaves her dainty high-heel marks all over "The Beautician and the Beast."

"I used to give pedicures to women who wore plastic shoes in summer," she tells Grushinsky. "What's a tougher gig than that?" Well, it's not being Fran Drescher, she of the emery-board voice and tacky charm, who makes all this stuff about class and status seem very easy indeed.

NEW YORK POST, 2/7/97, p. 47, Michael Medved

If "The Nanny" strikes you as the epitome of sophisticated wit and wisdom, then you might actually enjoy "The Beautician and the Beast." Otherwise, this embarrassing bomb offers an experience that is somewhat less pleasant than having your legs waxed.

Fran Drescher plays much the same character she does on television—a cheerfully ditsy blabbermouth from Queens, who here teaches a night-school class on the science of beauty. When a poorly staged fire breaks out in her classroom, she rescues her students and various lab animals, earning a front page picture in The Post.

This exposure attracts the attention of a mysterious foreigner (Ian McNeice). He approaches Drescher on the street and persuades her to travel to his remote Eastern European country, where she will work as a tutor for the four children of the nation's president-for-life.

None of this makes the slightest sense, but the movie only gets worse when she flies to "Slovetzia" and meets her new boss, Boris ("The Beast") Pochenko. Timothy Dalton plays the role with moustache, hair style and uniform obviously meant to evoke Stalin—as if the image of a murderer of millions were an appropriate element for fluffy romantic comedy.

His lame accent, bug-eyed overacting and appalling lack of chemistry with his leading lady represent career worsts for this falling star, who has wandered several galaxies off-course since his days with the Royal Shakespeare Company.

Rather than indulging his "beastly" ways, the script asks Dalton to act charmed by the visiting American, who tells his children of her hero worship for Thurgood Marshall, organizes workers in a state-owned factory to strike, pleads for release of a handsome political prisoner, and urges her boss to "be a mensch."

Didn't anyone behind this film consider the fact that several centuries of Eastern European anti-Semitism might have interfered with the instantaneous acceptance of this whining visitor from Queens?

The movie slavishly steals from "The King and I" for key plot points and whole scenes, but offers none of the charm of the original. Drescher's colorful costumes cunningly play her admirably well-toned figure, while the Czech locations look atmospheric and authentic.

But no amount of superficial polish could make this nonsense watchable. In addition to all its other flaws, the movie is much too long (107 minutes), making it entirely appropriate that the national symbol of fictional Slovetzia should be the boar.

VILLAGE VOICE, 2/18/97, p. 84, Laurie Stone

Against the backdrop of an Eastern Bloc totalitarian regime—so demoralized that its political dissidents are barely of drinking age, there are still peasants laboring in feudal servitude, and factory workers stare blankly at the concept of striking—the Nanny romances her stuffy, dumb lunk. Not Maxwell Sheffield, the uptight producer of Broadway fluff for whom she lusts on her sitcom. No, in *The Beautician and the Beast* Fran Drescher, playing her patented wise primitive (here named Joy Miller), melts the dictator. You know what pushovers those guys are underneath, and how American directness and spiels about democracy are chicken soup for any fascist infection. American democracy and Fran's tush, which twitched and posed with enough fanfare to make Mae West's vamping look modulated, a tush, for all its blatant packaging, that's a tease, baiting the chosen shmendrick for marriage or nothin'.

There are momentary flashes of the street smarts and loopy vulgarity that enliven the TV show. Catering a state affair, Joy has cases of La Choy cocktail egg rolls flown in. Hunting for a midnight snack in the castle kitchen, she assures her studly Stalin, played by Timothy Dalton, "I can find food at Gandhi's house." But the movie is lifeless—even putting aside the politics, which manage to be at once chauvinistic about America and rosy-eyed about fascism. Drescher, who is also one of the movie's executive producers, recycles old shtick that just lies there. Her character's interplay with the children she's charged to teach is generic. Sexual chemistry doesn't ignite with Dalton, whose role is humiliating, as he scowls one moment and then shows he's succumbing to Joy's charms by attempting to control and silence her. The scenes have an odd, s/m edge, though they're unerotic, like the movie as a whole—all fake staginess and no heat.

Also reviewed in:
NEW YORK TIMES, 2/7/97, p. C12, Stephen Holden
VARIETY, 2/10-16/97, p. 63, Emanuel Levy

BENT

A Channel Four Films and Goldwyn Entertainment Company release in association with NDF, Inc., Ask Kodansha Company Ltd., and The Arts Council of England. *Executive Producer:* Sarah Radclyffe and Hisami Kuroiwa. *Producer:* Michael Solinger and Dixie Linder. *Director:* Sean Mathias. *Screenplay (based on his play):* Martin Sherman. *Director of Photography:* Yorgos Arvanitis. *Editor:* Isabel Lorente. *Music:* Philip Glass. *Music Editor:* Isabel Lorente.

Choreographer: Wayne McGregor. *Sound:* Simon Bishop and (music) John Billingsley. *Sound Editor:* Gerard McCann. *Casting:* Andy Pryor. *Production Designer:* Stephen Brimson Lewis. *Art Director:* Andrew Golding. *Special Effects:* John Markwell. Visual Effects: Frédéric Moreau. *Costumes:* Stewart Meachem. *Make-up:* Trefor Proud. *Stunt Coordinator:* Tom Delmar. *Running time:* 104 minutes. *MPAA Rating:* NC-17.

CAST: Mick Jagger (Greta/George); Clive Owen (Max); Brian Webber (Rudy); Nikolaj Waldau (Wolf);   Jude Law (Stormtrooper);   Gresby Nash (Waiter); Suzanne Bertish (Half-Woman, Half-Man); David Meyer (Gestapo Man); Stefan Marling (SS Captain); Richard Laing and Crispian Belfrage (SS Guards); Ian McKellen (Uncle Freddie); Johanna Kirby (Muttering Woman); David Phelan (Fluff in Park); Peter Stark (Guard 1 on Train); Lothaire Bluteau (Horst); Rupert Graves (Officer on Train); Charlie Watts (Guard 2 on Train); Holly Davidson (Girl on Train); Rupert Penry Jones (Guard on Road); Paul Kynman (Corporal); Paul Bettany (Captain); Rachel Weisz (Prostitute); Sadie Frost (Max's Nightclub Friend).

LOS ANGELES TIMES, 11/26/97, Calendar/p. 8, Kevin Thomas

[The following review by Kevin Thomas appeared in a slightly different form in **NEWSDAY, 11/26/97, Part II/p. B10.]**

At the beginning of the powerful, galvanizing "Bent," a spotlight picks up a black-stockinged singer in silhouette, perched on a steel circle as it is lowered into a vast warehouse turned into a nightclub, where a veritable pan-sexual orgy is going on.

As the camera draws closer, the singer—singing a very Marlene Dietrich-like song called "The Streets of Berlin"—looks to be Sandra Bernhard, only a bit older. It turns out to be Mick Jagger, however, playing Greta, the drag queen star and proprietor of the club.

We seem at first glance to be back in the bad old Berlin of "Cabaret," but we're much later in the day than that. Hitler has now come to power and is moving swiftly against gays and lesbians, so swiftly it would seem that many homosexuals—accustomed to the laissez-faire policies of the Weimar Republic—are caught unawares. "Bent," in fact, opens on June 30, 1934, the Night of the Long Knives, when homosexual Nazi commander Ernst Rohm and many others were purged by Heinrich Himmler on Hitler's orders. That very evening the Gestapo raids Greta's club, and eventually caught up in the state police's ever-widening web are Max (Clive Owen), handsome playboy scion of a wealthy family, and his lover Rudy (Brian Webber), a dancer at the club.

With dizzying speed the lovers are heading for Dachau on a freight car, where Rudy meets a truly unspeakable fate, while a fellow prisoner, Horst (Lothaire Bluteau), tells Max what he must do if he is to survive. Once at Dachau, Horst must wear the pink triangle, designating the wearer as homosexual, but Max gets a yellow Star of David, believing that he will be better off thought of as a Jew than a homosexual.

Year in and year out there remains a fairly steady flow of dramas and documentaries dealing with the Holocaust in regard to the fate of Europe's Jews. Only one documentary on gay victims of the Holocaust comes to mind, and therefore "Bent"—a remarkably deft transposition by Martin Sherman of his successful play to the screen—verges on the unique. (Estimates on how many gays and lesbians died in the camps range from a ridiculously low 5,000 all the way up to 600,000.)

Once in Dachau Max manages to have Horst assigned to him in their daily task of moving a pile of rocks from one side of a quarry, an activity with no purpose beyond attempting to drive the two men out of their minds. Having instilled in Max the will to survive, Horst dares to take a further step, encouraging Max to try to feel, although the men dare not touch each other, even avoiding glances at each other. It is in fact a declaration of love on Horst's part, which Max instinctively resists as dangerous.

Love between two men in Dachau, even if not consummated by physical contact, is in fact paradoxical, strengthening each man's will to survive yet rendering him emotionally vulnerable in his concern for the other. Yet the love that develops between Max and Horst gives them dignity, a way in which to give their long days of pointless, exhausting labor meaning. Sherman does not confuse sheer survival with living life to the fullest possible in the most abominable of circumstances.

Directed with unfailing aplomb by Sean Mathias, "Bent" is nevertheless all but unbearable in its bleakness. Thankfully, it has a saving humor, and it is the kind of material that, combined with the shrewd judgment of Mathias' direction, inspires actors to create towering portrayals, calling upon them to reach deeply within themselves, which is clearly what Owen and Bluteau (memorable in the title role of "Jesus of Montreal") have done. Webber is equally fine as the sometimes foolish, ill-fated Rudy. The film moves well, heightened by Philip Glass' pulsating score, more varied than usual for him.

Jagger is amusingly bitchy as the treacherous Greta, who reassumes his real name, George, trading in his gowns for business suits. So is Ian McKellen as Max's uncle, a gay dandy who's prepared to try to help his nephew but not Rudy. (McKellen created the role of Max, which Sherman wrote with him in mind, in the 1979 premiere stage-production of "Bent.") In cameos you can spot Jude Law and Rupert Graves (as Nazis), Sadie Frost (as a nightclubber) and Rachel Weisz (as a prostitute). "Bent" may be hard to take, but it's easy to admire.

NEW YORK POST, 11/26/97, p. 47, Thelma Adams

I'm on the barbed-wire fence about "Bent." On one side, it's a well-acted, impassioned drama about an historical event that has been sidelined in Holocaust cinema: Hitler's vicious persecution of homosexuals beginning with the Night of the Long Knives. On the other, as a movie, "Bent" has trouble breaking out of its dated theatrical trappings.

Sean Mathias, best-known for his recent Broadway production of "Indiscretions," first directed Martin Sherman's "Bent" in London in 1979. Ian McKellen starred in the lead role of Max, a Berlin bon vivant who bids goodbye to his cabaret days and hello to Dachau.

Nearly 20 years later, Mathias makes his film debut with Sherman's adaptation of his play and McKellen in the brief but tasty role of Max's uncle. British actor Clive Owen fills the role of Max, making him a callow charismatic charmer who discovers true love and free will in the camps.

The movie splits between two acts. The first finds Max loving the nightlife at a boite called Greta's. His boyfriend Rudy (Brian Webber) writhes onstage in a hideously post-modern production number. A bewigged Greta (Mick Jagger) decends from above, struggling with one of Philip Glass' catchless tunes, part of a lackluster Glass score.

Despite its tacky S&M rave scenes, Mathias sets the drama sharply in motion. Owen and Webber quickly differentiate their characters and the depth and tricky nature of their love. Jagger campily dons Greta's knickers, but he gains a sininster power as her alter-ego, the strait-laced George who sees the direction of the political tide and sells out those in his path.

Following the Night of the Long Knives, Max and Rudy flee Berlin. A year later, when Max's uncle offers him a single ticket to Amsterdam, he refuses. He'll go only with Rudy.

But after the pair are rounded up and shipped to Dachau in a series of scenes that are as shattering as they are economical, Max sacrifices his lover in order to survive. On the train, he meets Horst (Lothaire Bloteau), a fervent homosexual.

Once Max and Horst arrive at Dachau, the movie settles back into a two-person play set against a chilly, oversized backdrop that recalls a Robert Wilson piece. As Max and Horst move rocks from one corner of the frame to the other, carrying out their assigned tasks, their actions match the repetitive cadence of the Glass score.

While Bluteau ("Jesus of Montreal") and Owen connect strongly, their characters' learning how to make love without touching, to communicate from the heart without looking into each other's eyes, the movie becomes increasingly stagy and self-conscious.

In the end, "Bent" closes in on itself, wrapping itself in barbed wire. The final scenes are static in their symbolism. Max and Horst become detached, less vivid, as Mathias moves them across the set like rocks stuck within the limits of an invisible proscenium.

SIGHT AND SOUND, 3/98, p. 39, Nick Kimberly

Berlin, 1934. At Greta's, a nightclub, Max picks up a beautiful Nazi soldier, much to the chagrin of Rudy, Max's lover. The three men are terrified when soldiers burst into their room. Max and Rudy escape, but see the intruders cut the soldier's throat. They turn to Greta for help, but he reveals that, in the current climate, he has decided to act straight and go by the name of George. Max's Uncle Freddie arranges his nephew's escape to Amsterdam, but Max insists Rudy must accompany him, so Freddie can't oblige. The lovers are eventually tracked down, and sent to a detention camp. On the prison train, Rudy is tortured, and Max is forced to collude. Finally, Rudy is thrown off the train. Another prisoner, Horst, tells Max they're on the way to Dachau. Max tries to make an ally of Horst, who at first resists. In the camp, Max pretends to be a Jew, and wears the Jews' yellow triangle instead of the homosexuals' pink triangle.

Max charms an officer into allowing Horst to join him moving rocks around a huge chamber. Horst resents the gesture, but as the two work together, they develop an affection which becomes sexual. They manage to fulfil their desire for each other without touching. Horst develops a cough which attracts the attention of a Nazi officer, who torments him, and eventually has him shot while Max looks on. Ordered to dispose of the body, Max changes into Horst's uniform, including the pink triangle. In a final gesture of love and despair, he impales himself on the electrified barbed wire surrounding the camp.

In their quest for a racial purity purged of corrupting influences, the Nazis industrialised degradation, torture and murder. To make their prison camps into death factories mass-producing corpses necessitated an element of mob psychology, and that makes Nazism difficult to represent through individual encounters. The larger cruelty can only be glimpsed through smaller acts of brutality, perpetuated, as in *Bent* by types rather than characters. One corrupt camp commandant stands for a whole regime of murder. (It's revealing that one of the most painful fictional accounts of the concentration camps, Art Spiegelman's *Maus,* is a comic featuring cartoon mice: not much realism there.)

Realism's need to personalise gives rise to the set of signals which regularly stand for Nazi inhumanity: here, jackboots, belts tightly cinched round leather great coats, chiselled jawlines, and a cool, clear gaze prefiguring bullying sadism. It's to the credit of *Bent* that it's fully aware how closely that iconography approximates certain homoerotic images. These Nazis are beautiful pin-ups made flesh, yet they wield their power with consummate cruelty We get a real sense of the salivating prurience just beneath the surface of their intolerance of another sexuality.

Martin Sherman' s adaptation of his own 1979 play retains a theatricality, but the movie is in no way constrained by that, repeatedly breaking free to enter a realm of painfully hallucinatory spaces. If director Sean Mathias encloses most of the action in tightly framed verbal encounters, the effect is all the greater when the screen does open up. The seething, tainted sensuality of Greta's club is conventionally contrived, but there's a weird air of carnival, or at least circus about it, only heightened by the sight of Mick Jagger in drag singing from a trapeze. Jagger's presence may be a commercial sop, but his eerie transformation from the dangerous figure of Greta to the utterly safe George produces a neat cameo that Mathias is at pains not to overplay.

The movie's arresting imagery is nowhere more apparent than when protagonist Max is carrying rocks from one pile to another and back. Prisons are usually represented as claustrophobic, but here we feel, in an almost physical way, the sheer belittling pointlessness of Max's solitary labour as the camera finds his tiny figure in the distance, trudging endlessly back and forth in a vast monochrome chamber: a disused furnace, I'd guess, here standing in for who knows what bleak prison facility. In fact, Mathias repeatedly makes telling use of modern industrial wasteland as a visual correlative of the shattered fabric of Nazi Germany.

Perhaps less convincing is the script's suggestion that the Nazis' persecution of gays was even more vicious than their anti-Semitism. In this context, establishing a hierarchy becomes all but meaningless. Perhaps it's a narrative device to allow Max to appear in a less than flattering light: after masquerading as a Jew to avoid the worse treatment, he finally comes out in the most painful way, donning his lover's pink triangle before killing himself.

As Max, Clive Owen has the onanistic insouciance of the sex object, but he's not quite so convincing as a prisoner: a shaven head and sunken cheeks suit him rather too well. Lothaire Bluteau, on the other hand, is remarkable, his features charged with rodent intensity, notably when Horst and Max bring each other to orgasm in the prison yard, neither man touching the other, or indeed, himself. At such moments, Nazi persecution slips gently into the background, to be replaced by an extraordinary love story. It's no disgrace that *Bent* renders that story as movingly as it reminds us of the depths of Nazi hatred.

VILLAGE VOICE, 12/2/97, p. 84, Amy Taubin

Adapted from Martin Sherman's play about the Nazi persecution of homosexuals, Sean Mathias's debut film is baroque, violent, and terribly disturbing—which is as it should be. Opening during the infamous Night of the Long Knives, *Bent* follows Max (Clive Owen), the gay son of a German munitions manufacturer, from the nightclubs of Berlin (where Mick Jagger is the featured drag act) to the stone quarries of Dachau, where Max and the man he tries to befriend (Lothaire Bluteau) carry rocks back and forth from one pile to another.

Rather than trying to naturalize Sherman's theatrical text (you can hear Beckett echoing through it), Mathias designs the film as a series of set pieces filled with flamboyant camera moves and filmed in locations that seem abstract even when they are realistically detailed. The style of the film owes something to Derek Jarman's *Edward II*, but it also marks Mathias, an accomplished theater director, as a filmmaker in his own right.

Also reviewed in:
CHICAGO TRIBUNE, 11/27/97, Tempo/p. 9, Achy Obejas
NEW REPUBLIC, 12/1/97, p. 32, Stanley Kauffmann
NEW YORK TIMES, 11/26/97, p. E5, Stephen Holden
VARIETY, 5/26-6/1/97, p. 66, Emanuel Levy

BEVERLY HILLS NINJA

A TriStar Pictures release of a Motion Picture Corporation of America production in association with Brad Krevoy & Steve Stabler. *Executive Producer:* Jeffrey D. Ivers, John Bertolli and Michael Rotenberg. *Producer:* Brad Krevoy and Steve Stabler. *Director:* Dennis Dugan. *Screenplay:* Mark Feldberg and Mitch Klebanoff. *Director of Photography:* Arthur Albert. *Editor:* Jeff Gourson. *Music:* George S. Clinton. *Music Editor:* Mike Flicker. *Sound:* Jonathan Stein and (music) John Whynot. *Sound Editor:* Robert Shoup. *Casting:* Gary M. Zuckerbrod. *Production Designer:* Ninkey Dalton. *Art Director:* Christa Munro. *Set Designer:* Lori Rowbotham and Phil Toolin. *Set Decorator:* Jan Pascale. *Set Dresser:* F. Alan Burg, Michael J. Miller, Phoebe O'Connor, J. Brent Rice, Cynthia Rebman and Jeff Hay. *Special Effects:* Joseph P. Mercurio. *Costumes:* Mary Claire Hannan. *Make-up:* Angela Moos. *Make-up (Nicollete Sheridan):* Laura Gorman. *Stunt Coordinator:* Rick Barker. *Running time:* 105 minutes. *MPAA Rating:* PG-13.

CAST: Chris Farley (Haru); Nicollete Sheridan (Alison); Robin Shou (Gobei); Nathaniel Parker (Tanley); Soon-Tek Oh (Sensei), Keith Cooke Hirabayashi (Nobu); Chris Rock (Joey); Francois Chau (Izumo); Dale Ishimoto (Old Japanese Man); Da Ming Chan (Head Kobudosai); Burt Bulos (Mr. Ozaru); Curtis Blanck (Billy); Tom Bailey (Billy's Dad); Jason J. Tobin (Busboy); Richard Kline (Driver); Anna Mathias (Female Traveler); Nathan Jung (Fisherman); John Farley and Kevin Farley (Policemen); Gerry Del Sol (Porter); Cynthia Allison and Francesca Cappucci (Reporters); Hideo Kimura (Security Person); Saachiko (Woman); James Laing (Guard); Robbie Thibaut, Jr. (Grandson at Hotel); Michael Cardenas (Patron at Hoop Louie's); Brett Golov and Joe Decker (Club Patrons); Charles Dugan (Man with Shoes); Jason Davis (Young Haru); Alexandra Stabler (Girl on Rodeo Drive); Nicolas Stabler (Boy on Rodeo Drive); Tania L. Pearson, Lisa C. Boltanzer, and Nancy Howard (Dancers); Conrad Goode, Bryan Hays Currie, and Caesar Luisi (Bouncers); Rick Miller (Motorcycle Rider); Eric C. Charmelo (Guy at Plant); Sarah Pierce (Poodle Lady).

LOS ANGELES TIMES, 1/20/97, Calendar/p. 4, Kevin Thomas

A Japanese martial arts clan is taught that a white child will one day appear to become the greatest ninja of them all. Sure enough, at the beginning of the lively, funny "Beverly Hills Ninja," a steamer trunk with a white male baby inside washes up on the beach near the clan's retreat. But the kid grows up to be hefty Chris Farley.

Given the name Haru, he is raised by the clan's loving sansei (Soon-Tek Oh) alongside the master's own son (Robin Shou). But Haru is such a hopeless self-deluding klutz that even his kindly foster father is forced to admit in exasperation that, "He's fat, a fool and an embarrassment to ninja everywhere." (Didn't anybody think of sending Haru off to a sumo wrestling academy?)

While everyone else is off to a competition, Haru is alone at the retreat when a striking blond (Nicollette Sheridan) shows up looking to hire a ninja to tail her boyfriend (Nathaniel Parker) to a meeting at a nearby harbor. She explains she's beginning to suspect that he's up to no good—and not merely two-timing her.

A couple of fast plot developments send Haru off to Beverly Hills to try to locate Sheridan, convinced she's a lady in distress, and right smack in the middle of Parker's complicated international counterfeiting schemes. That Haru one night finds himself performing at a topless joint is typical of his exploit. (Note: the tops stay on—this is a PG-13 picture).

All the elements of "Beverly Hills Ninja" are classic: The overweight jerk everyone has written off as a loser persists to win the day—and the fair lady. The slapstick and the sight gags come thick and fast, as they have throughout a hundred years of screen comedy, yet director Dennis Dugan and writers Mark Feldberg and Mitch Klebanoff keep everything light and bouncy.

"Beverly Hills Ninja" (which wasn't screened for critics) isn't a thigh-slapper, but it's diverting and affectionate—a satisfying and sturdy vehicle for Farley that ought to please his fans, youngsters especially.

Pasadena stands in for Beverly Hills much of the time, as does the more picturesque Chinatown for Little Tokyo. But Dugan and his crew—ingenious production designer Ninkey Dalton and cameraman Arthur Albert in particular—make everything come together. There is in fact, an unpretentious, throwaway, let's get-on-with-it quality about "Beverly Hills Ninja" that is appealing and nowadays rare in Hollywood productions.

While Farley carries the picture easily enough, with deft turns by Sheridan, Soon-Tek Oh and others, he may be a Hardy who needs his Laurel. This is the first picture he's done without his fellow "Saturday Night Live" alumnus David Spade, and it leaves us wishing that hilarious Chris Rock, cast as a sly Beverly Hills hotel bellboy, could have had the chance to emerge as a full-fledged sidekick.

NEW YORK POST, 1/18/97, p. 21, Larry Worth

Does fat necessarily mean funny?

Chris Farley seems to think so, using his girth for the thrust of comic throwaways like "Black Sheep" and "Tommy Boy." Now he's encased his larger-than-life physique in a succession of kimonos to portray a "Beverly Hills Ninja."

The results aren't pretty. But the sight of Farley's massive belly hanging over the get-up's belt is meant to leave viewers rolling in the aisle. Not the case. And by the time he does a striptease, there may be a stampede to the exit.

It all begins when Farley is adopted and reared by a group of ninjas in Japan. (Don't ask.) After demonstrating his bull-in-a-china-shop attempts at martial arts he's assessed by his "big brother" as follows: "He's fat, a fool and an embarrassment to ninjas everywhere."

Sure enough, the "Saturday Night Live" alum leaves a never-ending trail of destruction in his wake. And so it goes until a femme fatale asks for Farley's help. He follows her to Beverly Hills and tries to nab some murderous counterfeiters.

Naturally, big brother is secretly along for the ride, and he salvages Farley's blunders with flying fists to the various heavies. But will Farley ultimately save the day in spite of his avoirdupois? Do ninjas wield nunchakus?

The real problem isn't predictability. It's that Farley provides nothing beyond his size, unlike the kind of talent offered by John Belushi or John Candy. The result is an ongoing irritation.

The supporting cast—Nicollette ("Knots Landing") Sheridan, Chris ("SNL") Rock and Robin ("Mortal Kombat") Shou—supplies the requisite cleavage, cut-ups and chop-socky, respectively. But they're outweighed, in every sense of the word, by Farley's failings.

Hack director Dennis Dugan brings matters from bad to worse, unable to deliver the kick this "Ninja" so desperately needs.

Also reviewed in:
CHICAGO TRIBUNE, 1/20/97, Tempo/p. 1, John Petrakis
NEW YORK TIMES, 1/18/97, p. C20, Stephen Holden
VARIETY, 1/20-26/97, p. 45, Leonard Klady

BLISS

A Triumph Films release of a Stewart Pictures production in association with Pacific Motion Pictures Corporation. *Executive Producer:* Matthew O'Connor. *Producer:* Allyn Stewart. *Director:* Lance Young. *Screenplay:* Lance Young. *Director of Photography:* Mike Molloy. *Editor:* Allan Lee. *Music:* Jan A.P. Kaczmarek. *Music Editor:* Christopher Kennedy. *Choreographer:* Trudi Forrest. *Sound:* Michael McGee and (music) Rafal Paczkowski. *Sound Editor:* Dessie Markovsky. *Casting:* Glenn Daniels. *Production Designer:* John Willett and David Lloyd Fischer. *Art Director:* William Heslup and Eric Norlin. *Set Decorator:* Mary-Lou Storey and Barry Kemp. *Set Dresser:* Macleod Sinclaire and Dermuid Conway. *Special Effects:* Randy Shymkiw. *Costumes:* Jori Woodman. *Make-up:* Rosalina Da Silva. *Stunt Coordinator:* Jim Dunn. *Running time:* 105 minutes. *MPAA Rating:* R.

CAST: Craig Sheffer (Joseph); Sheryl Lee (Maria); Terence Stamp (Baltazar Vincenza); Casey Siemaszko (Tanner); Spalding Gray (Alfred); Leigh Taylor Young (Redhead); Lois Chiles (Eva); Blu Mankuma (Nick); Ken Camroux (Hank); Pamela Perry (Dottie); Eli Gabay (Carlos); Molly Parker (Connie); Hiro Kanagawa (Doctor); Merrilyn Gann (Motel Woman); Gillian Barber (Therapist); Pete Kelamis (Neighbor); Norman Armour (Patient); David Glyn-Jones (Priest); Quincy Welch and Carson Welch (Boys); Serena Bodnar (Girl); Kristin Lehman (Scope/Steps Woman); Akesh Gill (Therapy Woman).

LOS ANGELES TIMES, 6/6/97, Calendar/p. 10, Kevin Thomas

"Bliss" is an earnest yet half baked message movie about how the source of sexual dysfunction in marriage can be caused by a repressed memory of childhood incest. That this is obviously a very serious, tricky subject doesn't excuse writer-director Lance Young from turning out so academic and uneven a film. This is yet another of those blah Canadian movies that provide such a contrast to the venturesome work of two north-of-the-border mavericks, Atom Egoyan and David Cronenberg. (If only either one of them, Egoyan especially, had made this film!)

Maria (Sheryl Lee) and Joseph (Craig Sheffer) seem a perfectly normal, attractive upper-middle-class young couple who six months after their wedding wind up in the office of a marriage counselor (Spalding Gray). Their complaints with each other seem petty, but Joseph goes into a tailspin when Maria finally admits she fakes her orgasms. Then he discovers she's seeing a controversial sex therapist, Baltazar (Terence Stamp), who believes that having sex with his female patients is the only way to cure them.

When Joseph angrily confronts Baltazar, the sexual healer unleashes a torrent of statements as to the delicacy of Maria's mental state. "She's a borderline personality ... in a state of repressed paranoia ... childhood trauma," declares Baltazar to Joseph, who seems far more concerned with breaking through his wife's frigidity than with whatever may be contributing to it. In an incredible twist, Joseph insists successfully that he replace his wife as Baltazar's patient so that he can improve his lovemaking techniques. (You get the impression that Baltazar's key text may be the Kama Sutra.)

Young doesn't give us the scene in which Baltazar tells Maria she can no longer be his patient, but then throughout most of the film, he has her therapists and husband *tell* us about her rather than letting us discover her for ourselves. Essentially, all we know about her is that she seemingly is frigid, vaguely unhappy and determined to rid her house of an invasion of ants.

Young gives us plenty of R-rated scenes of the couple struggling to achieve sexual ecstasy but gets coy once Baltazar and Joseph strip down to their shorts in preparation for the therapist teaching the young husband the secrets of great love-making.

Where the film does strike a valuable chord is to show that once Maria's repressed memories of incest with her father surface, she discovers that she must deal with the guilt over the pleasure she did experience innocently within that incestuous relationship during its duration. It's a shame that such an important point isn't being made in a much better film.

Sheffer, very good at portraying a husband determined to go the distance in the name of true love, and Lee are actually quite effective, and Stamp and Gray are imperturbable in the tradition of movie therapists.

But "Bliss" ultimately leaves you wishing that, more perhaps than even Egoyan or Cronenberg, it had been made by a woman.

NEW YORK POST, 6/6/97, p. 44, Thelma Adams

"Bliss" it isn't! Porn shouldn't be as dull—or as tortured—as Lance Young's yuppie angst-fest about orgasm-challenged young marrieds.

Bland boy Craig Sheffer ("A River Runs Through It") is Joseph, the dullard husband. Sultry Sheryl Lee ("Twin Peaks") is Maria, the repressed wife. As names go, Joseph and Maria are ironically biblical for a sexually dysfunctional couple.

The irony ends there. "Bliss" poses this snorer: Is Maria a borderline personality, or is she just frigid? Only her male therapists know for sure.

Spalding Gray's couples counselor is so recessed as to be hardly worthy of a monologue. We know his Freudian is b.s. because he's never allowed to be anything but. For God's sake, his name is Alfred, like Batman's butler!

Enter violin-playing, interior-decorating, flamboyantly named Baltazar Vincenza. Terence Stamp plays the silver-maned sexual surrogate as if he were Christopher Lee in a Hammer studios horror flick.

How does a contemporary sexual exploration have the guts to come out and call its heroine "frigid," as Vincenza does? Fortunately, Maria's faked orgasms are just a symptom of that current favorite deeper, darker secret—the kiss of incest. Oh, daddy dearest!

Under the G-spot guru's tutelage, Joseph learns sexual healing in a way that would confound Marvin Gaye. He's like an overachiever studying for his LSATS.

Not only does the staid studmuffin get Maria off and over her twisted past, the couple travel to the ninth dimension of orgasmic ecstacy. Who knew?. And with first-timer Young directing from his own script, who cares? In some cases, when a couple get behind closed doors, they should stay there.

NEWSDAY, 6/6/97, Part II/p. B8, John Anderson

People who've died and come back—on the operating table, for instance—often tell of having seen their dearly departed, those who've already passed over to the other side, beckoning them toward a great white light. Those who've seen "Bliss" may feel that they, too, have passed over into another state of being, although instead of waving people on, we're screaming, "NO!! Go back!!" Marrying romantic comedy that isn't romantic or funny with a psychodrama about the repressed memory of childhood sexual abuse, it's a film that imbues one with an unexplainable sense of both loss and empowerment—a feeling that you've joined some sad fraternity for whom nothing can ever be quite as bad, nor ever the same agean.

Written and directed by Lance Young, "Bliss" which stars Craig Sheffer and Sheryl Lee as newlyweds with a sex problem and Terence Stamp as the man who's going to help them—may be Exhibit A as to why mainstream movies have reached the point they have. Young's bio says he has spent most of his career on the business end of film production—he's worked with Steven Spielberg, he's worked at Warner's, and at Paramount—and no doubt has the one thing essential to the auteur of tomorrow: connections! He also makes a pretty good case for the licensing of film directors.

Sheffer's Joseph and Lee's Maria (very New Testament) are wealthy, not too wise and not very happy; she calls him at work a lot, so she's clearly suffering from deep-seated trauma. They go to a therapist Spalding Gray, who gets one of those slow-pan "star" introductions—and during one session, she confesses she's never had an orgasm. Not with her husband, anyway. This causes Joseph great distress, but nothing like the apoplexy he suffers when he finds she's visiting the rogue sex therapist and concert violinist Baltazar (Stamp), who happens to look like Gray's evil twin.

They both bear a resemblance to Maria's father, but there is so much wrong with "Bliss" that merely to tell what happens feels like some sort of validation. The characters are strictly movie creatures; their connection to real life, which the film so much wants to establish through Maria's incest-rooted sexual dysfunction and Joseph's erotic course of study with Baltazar, is laughable. That the film presumes a serious stance on sexual problems and then seizes every opportunity to show its characters naked and coupling isn't much more than bad taste. But Young has the gall to recycle what has now become repressed-memory shtick and further trivialize something that in many cases is a serious issue. And it's really unforgivable.

A lot of movies suffer from a poverty of ideas or dollars. "Bliss" suffers from a poverty of soul. Sheffer gets to stand around looking buff and perplexed; Lee, when she's not hysterical, looks puffy and perky, and Stamp gets to wear a lot of really luxurious shirts and do an impression of what New Age guru Marianne Williamson might sound like if she swallowed "The Kama Sutra." "Bliss" is, in short, better than death. But I'm not sure by how much.

VILLAGE VOICE, 6/10/97, p. 74, Laurie Stone

"I fake my orgasms," confesses Maria (Sheryl Lee) to her shrink (Spalding Gray), while her husband Joseph (Craig Sheffer) squirms on the couch. *Bliss,* a first film by writer-director Lance Young, fakes its orgasms, too, for while the ads suggest a softcore skinfest, the movie remains sleazily, teasingly prim. It's a sex-ed lecture, proclaiming its sensitivity to women while enlisting male experts (one female counselor makes a token appearance) to make its case. The men in this film take on the challenge of becoming sensitive not by being interested in women but by trying to score 10s in the Empathy Olympics.

Even before marriage, Joseph knows Maria is a nut—she cleans compulsively and fervently swats flies—but he means to fix her. He soon finds he needs help, and Maria also reveals that, as a child, her father repeatedly had sex with her. When conventional shrinkage falls, Joseph consults sex guru Baltazar (Terence Stamp), who guides him through tantric techniques, professing he can "heal" Maria. "She needs to be completely reparented," he intones, without a smidgen of irony.

There is no story apart from this tutelage, which is so mirthless it's unintentionally hilarious, Baltazar instructing Joseph on how to breathe by hanging by his ankles and how to locate a woman's "magic spot." (Clue: it's in her vagina.) Encouraged to "love himself," Joseph confesses to having a large, powerful penis, but do we see this member? We do not. Not so much as a bulge ripples the ubiquitous towels sported by bare-chested, puffed-pecs Sheffer, a *joli-laid* in the style of Malcolm MacDowell, who takes shower after shower, though, given Baltazar's injunctions against ejaculation, he seems little in need of washing. Lee, who was the excellent corpse of Laura Palmer on *Twin Peaks,* is barely alive here, either, save for a scene in which she ties up her hubby—not to generate sparks for the audience but so that Joseph, who winces and says "ouch" a lot, can take notes on "women's anger." Baltazar, with his exquisite taste in furniture and music, is a creepy Miss Manners, so absorbed in setting the table, nobody gets to eat.

Also reviewed in:
NEW YORK TIMES, 6/6/97, p. C10, Stephen Holden
VARIETY, 4/28-5/4/97, p. 100, Todd McCarthy

BLOOD & WINE

A Fox Searchlight Pictures release of a Recorded Picture Company presentation of a Jeremy Thomas production. *Executive Producer:* Chris Auty and Bernie Williams. *Producer:* Jeremy Thomas. *Director:* Bob Rafelson. *Screenplay:* Nick Villiers and Alison Cross. *Story:* Nick Villiers and Bob Rafelson. *Director of Photography:* Newton Thomas Sigel. *Editor:* Steven Cohen. *Music:* Michal Lorenc and Peter Afterman. *Sound:* Leslie Shatz and (music) Armin Steiner. *Casting:* Dianne Crittenden. *Production Designer:* Richard Sylbert. *Set Decorator:* William Kemper Wright. *Special Effects:* Rick Jones. *Costumes:* Lindy Hemming. *Make-up:*

Manlio Rocchetti. *Stunt Coordinator:* Bud Davis. *Running time:* 101 minutes. *MPAA Rating:* R.

CAST: Jack Nicholson (Alex Gates); Stephen Dorff (Jason); Jennifer Lopez (Gabrielle); Judy Davis (Suzanne Gates); Michael Caine (Victor Spansky); Harold Perrineau, Jr. (Henry); Robyn Peterson (Dina); Mike Starr (Mike); John Seitz (Frank); Mark Macaulay (Guard); Dan Daily (Todd); Marta Velasco (Gabriella's Cousin); Thom Christopher (1st Jeweler); Mario Ernesto Sanchez (Artie, Fishing Ace); John Hackett (Gas Station Attendant); Hector Montano (Gabriella's Grandfather); Vanessa L. Hernandez (Cuban Little Girl); Carmen Lopez (Head Nurse); Antoni Corone (Caribbean Club Bartender); Jim Torres Towers (Father of Gabriella's Cousin); Alice Montano (Gabriella's Grandmother).

LOS ANGELES TIMES, 2/21/97, Calendar/p. 16, John Anderson

[*The following review by John Anderson appeared in a slightly different form in* **NEWSDAY, 2/21/97, Part II/p. B9.**]

Since their initial, countercultural collaboration—writing The Monkees' movie "Head"—Jack Nicholson and Bob Rafelson have certainly gone down different paths. But their occasional associations have composed a mini-ouevre all its own: "Five Easy Pieces" with its complex characterizations; "The King of Marvin Gardens" with its contrarian casting; "The Postman Always Rings Twice," with its deglamorized take on murder and adultery.

Now, with "Blood & Wine" which Rafelson has declared the last in a trilogy that includes "Five Easy Pieces" and "Marvin Gardens"—they've made another film that works out of stylistic assumptions and defied expectations. A caper-romance-domestic drama-film noir with casual political overtones, "Blood & Wine" is set up the way it ought to be (not that there are any precedents), but how it unfolds, and how its characters unravel, is an always-different story.

Consider, just for starters, Alex Gates (Nicholson), a financially and, of course, morally bankrupt wine dealer who first, appears semi-smirking from behind a morning paper (Rafelson's "star intros" are close to hilarious). He has little to smirk about.

Out of money, out of time, his marriage to wife Suzanne (Judy Davis) is on the rocks, his relationship with stepson Jason (Stephen Dorff) is a prickly mess and he's about to rob a client of a million-dollar diamond necklace. Worse, he's having a conspicuously foolhardy affair with the conspicuously overripe and clearly dangerous Gabrielle (Jennifer Lopez). Nicholson, perhaps for the first time in his career, is playing a character for whom we feel pity.

Rafelson has said that he met newcomer Lopez ("Money Train," "Jack" and the upcoming "Selena") six times before casting her. "The third time, I noticed she had a good body." Right. And Nicholson was cast for his hairline. Let's just say that Lopez, high-heeled and high-maintenance, simmers volcanically while providing the catalyst for the Alex-Jason meltdown and proving that movie bad girls, sometimes, are simply bad.

She's not, however, the most fascinating thing about "Blood & Wine." That prize goes to the venomous relationship between Alex and his larcenous confederate Victor Spansky (Michael Caine), a safecracker with advanced emphysema and a lethally short fuse. Rafelson makes the mistake at several points of cutting back and forth between Jason and Gabrielle, waxing dreamy, and Alex and Victor, malevolently scheming and avoiding each other's horns. In terms of sheer acting, it's simply no contest.

Amid the introspective evil, plans gone awry and the tug-ofwar over the necklace—which takes on the symbolic importance of Steinbeck's "Pearl"—is the marvelous Davis. She is directed to better effect by Rafelson than by Clint Eastwood in "Absolute Power" but is still underutilized. At the same time, she makes a strong impression as the wronged wife—she cold-cocks Alex at one point, in a statement of feminist ferocity and cinematic mischief—while exuding a certain unmotherly attraction for/to Jason.

But "Blood & Wine" is a deeply eroticized movie, almost to the point of distraction: Alex and Gabrielle, Gabrielle and Jason, Gabrielle and her wardrobe; Alex and Suzanne; Jason and his mother—even Alex and Victor. There's a scene in which the two thieves struggle, with Nicholson straddling Caine like a confused bull in a pasture for the fragile and unelastic.

None of this is serious, of course, just Rafelson making merry among the corrupt and unredeemable, whom he endows with a complexity that's probably undeserved, but occasionally very compelling indeed.

NEW YORK, 2/24/97, p. 122, David Denby

The best thing in the doggedly sincere *noir* thriller *Blood & Wine* is the saturnine acting partnership of Jack Nicholson and Michael Caine. A little portly but still formidable, Nicholson is the wine dealer Alex Gates, an apparently prosperous man with a beaming smile and a wardrobe of dark-blue shirts; actually, Alex is broke and desperately eager to end a painful marriage (to Judy Davis) so he can run away with his beautiful young Cubana mistress (Jennifer Lopez). Caine is an English ex-con, Victor Spansky, a safecracker with a vile temper and dyed hair. Wheezing and hacking from emphysema, Victor is on his last bit of leg, but he's a thief, and he needs to steal something, so he joins Alex and together they rip off a diamond necklace from a Miami mansion. These two lazy, egotistical bastards lunge at things and make mistakes. Once they steal the necklace, everything goes wrong, and they begin to despise each other. What's funny is that Nicholson and Caine seem to be outdoing each other in murderous contempt. Like an elderly couple who have been at it for years—joined by spite and lost without each other—Nicholson, glowering, sends vicious remarks in Caine's general direction, and Caine, gasping for breath, turns the remarks around and sticks them into Nicholson's hide. The two men never even make eye contact.

Lust, rage, greed—the usual trio of forties-*noir* emotions—send the plot rushing along, but without any particular distinction. Director Bob Rafelson appears to be paying tribute to such John Huston crime pictures as *The Asphalt Jungle* and *Key Largo*, but Rafelson mucks up the movie (he always does) with earnest, plodding stuff about "relationships." Alex has a stepson (Stephen Dorff), a lost, moody boy loyal to his mother. Meeting Alex's mistress—he doesn't know who she is—awakens the boy's drive and energy; soon, he's struggling with his stepfather over the stolen necklace and then over the woman too. The picture has some emotional density; no one could say it's just another collection of chases and shootouts. But the conflicts are too familiar to us. Gee, a father and his son: Rafelson is going back to the Freudian banalities of *Five Easy Pieces*, which he made, with Nicholson as the son, almost 30 years ago.

Absorbing as it is while you are watching it, *Blood & Wine* doesn't have enough style to resonate in your memory an hour after it's over. It's too straight, almost TV-movieish. Rafelson shot the story (which he devised with Nick Villiers) in Miami, but he makes little use of the city's distinctive light and color, and the conflicts never explode the way they should. As the mistress—a modern equivalent of a forties good-bad girl—Jennifer Lopez (from *Living Color* and the movie *Money Train*) walks around town like a tomato about to burst: Spilling out of her clothes, she's almost comically overripe. But when Lopez sits down and talks to Stephen Dorff, Rafelson directs her well, and she becomes intense and decisive, an actress. And my God, what a great-looking actress! The flesh seems to glow from inside. Dorff looks at her longingly, and we wait, tongues hanging out. Is Dorff going to become a man—even a leading man? Is there going to be a great sex scene between them? Instead, the movie goes all discreet and ambiguous. Who edited this thing—William Bennett? *Blood & Wine* doesn't come across.

NEW YORK POST, 2/21/97, p. 47, Michael Medved

"Blood & Wine" begins clobbering you over the head with its heavy-handed symbolism in its very opening sequence—showing a grubby, sullen, twentysomething punk (Stephen Dorff) waiting all night to land a deadly shark and then butchering the fierce fish at dawn.

The human counterpart to this killer from the depths is Jack Nicholson, so you can rest assured that the beast has teeth. Smilin' Jack plays Dorff's stepfather, an upscale Florida wine merchant (hence the title) whose flashy lifestyle has driven him deep into debt.

To escape this trap and his resentful wife (Judy Davis), he plans to run away with his young Cuban mistress (the alluring but obtuse Jennifer Lopez) after he has stolen a million-dollar necklace from the home where she works as a nanny.

To crack the safe in this closely guarded estate, Nicholson recruits a veteran thief (Michael Caine), a Cockney who simultaneously chain smokes and coughs up blood, hoping to pull off one last haul before his lungs give out.

Unfortunately for the conspirators, a violent confrontation between the wine merchant and his wife disrupts their carefully laid plans, and the rest of the movie involves a vicious struggle between Nicholson and Caine, on the one hand, and Davis and her son (Dorff), on the other.

Along the way, in Oedipal element predictably pops up, with Nicholson's hot-blooded mistress becoming dangerously attracted to his stepson.

Director Bob Rafelson is an old hand at lurid melodrama ("Black Widow" and the Nicholson remake of "The Postman Always Rings Twice"), and he gives this story an eerie glow and decadent stench of a beached eel rotting in the moonlight.

He is betrayed, however, by uneven casting; The battle-scarred veterans (Nicholson, Caine, Davis create vastly compelling characterizations, but the two younger performers (Dorff, Lopez) come across as blank, empty and insubstantial.

Nicolson's amoral but seductive vitality so completely overwhelms Dorff's stone-faced posing that you're forced to root for the bad guy, every step of the way—throwing the entire lunatic structure out of whack.

Rafelson has directed Nicholson four times before, resulting in artful, unforgettable triumphs ("Five Easy Pieces," "The King of Marvin Gardens"), as well as one full-blown disaster—1992's "Man Trouble," a turgid comedy about a dog trainer. "Man Trouble" is so profoundly embarrassing to both men that it's not even mentioned in the press notes.

"Blood & Wine" represents an obvious improvement over this career low point, but its blood still seems thin and the wine is a cheap, flat, undistinguished vintage.

SIGHT AND SOUND, 3/97, p. 41, John Wrathall

With the help of his Cuban girlfriend, Gabriella, and a dying English safecracker, Victor, Miami wine merchant Alex Gates steals a diamond necklace from one of his wealthy clients. While packing for a trip to New York, where he can sell the necklace, Gates is confronted by his wife Suzanne, who finds air tickets for him and Gabriella. They fight, and Suzanne knocks him out with her walking stick. Deciding the marriage is over, she runs away with her shark fisherman son Jason (from a previous marriage), who, unknown to Gates, is also romantically involved with Gabriella. Unwittingly, Suzanne takes the suitcase in which Gates has hidden the necklace.

Hiding out on a houseboat in Key Largo, Jason finds the necklace and takes it to a jeweller, who tells him it's worth $1 million. Following a tip-off from the jeweller, Victor and Gates arrive in Key Largo, but Jason beats up Victor, and escapes with Suzanne. During the ensuing chase, Suzanne crashes her car, killing herself and injuring Jason. Gates tries to retrieve the necklace from their car, but has to flee before the police arrive. When he regains consciousness in hospital, Jason returns to the family home in Miami, where Gabriella has taken up residence. Confronted by Victor, Jason learns that Gates was driving the car which caused the accident. In revenge, Jason tells Victor that he has already given the necklace back to Gates.

Victor goes to Gates' house and attacks him with a golf club, but collapses, short of breath, and is suffocated by Gates. Jason, meanwhile, arranges to run away with Gabriella, but she tips off Gates that the necklace is hidden on a boat Jason has bought with the proceeds of one stone from the necklace. Arriving at the boat, Gabriella and Gates are confronted by Jason, who gives the necklace to Gabriella and allows her to escape. In the ensuing fight, Jason deliberately backs his boat into Gates, breaking his legs. Gabriella, on second thoughts, returns and finds Gates lying helpless on the jetty. She gives the necklace back to him, and he throws it in the sea. Jason sails away into the sunset.

As an actor, Jack Nicholson has now made five films with Bob Rafelson (he also co-scripted Rafelson's first, *Head*), more than with any other director, and Rafelson sees *Blood and Wine* as the final part of a loose trilogy studying a man's problematic relationship to his family. Each of the three films stars Nicholson—as son *(Five Easy Pieces)*, brother *(The King of Marvin Gardens)* and now stepfather. His characters in the three films aren't by any means the same person, but they're all downwardly mobile intellectuals, cultured men (a pianist, a radio raconteur, a wine merchant) who find themselves, through ambition or the want of it, in a seedier world of scams and compromises. (Not, perhaps, unlike Rafelson himself, who was born into an Upper West Side, intellectual Jewish family, dropped out of Dartmouth, and finally drifted into movies through his role in the creation of The Monkees.)

The latest incarnation, Alex Gates, is a perfect role for Nicholson, who is so good at a weary, almost amused sort of rage, looking down contemptuously at the little obstacles which get in his way, as much angry at himself for letting them grind him down. One moment in *Blood and Wine* harks back to Nicholson's character's row with a diner waitress in *Five Easy Pieces:* waiting for his stepson to regain consciousness so he can recover the necklace, Gates goes to the hospital cafeteria with Victor (Michael Caine)—two 60-'ish men of the world, slightly turning up their noses at their tawdry surroundings. "There's no place to sit," complains Caine, confronted by tables covered with other people's dirty plates—whereupon Nicholson simply sweeps the whole lot onto the floor, sits down and eats. He has another great, seething scene later on when, unable quite to believe that he has been reduced to bargaining for the return of Gates casually but lethally accuses Jason of causing his mother's death by getting too ambitious.

Though his last two films, *Mountains of the Moon* and *Man Trouble*, both proved major disappointments, Rafelson's reputation and the prospect of working with Nicholson have combined to attract a formidable cast, not least Judy Davis as the codeine-addicted Suzanne and Michael Caine doing first real acting in a decade as Victor, the emphysema-afflicted safecracker, desperate for a place in the sun before it's too late. ("This is not an ocean-front suite in Marbella," Caine deadpans bitterly to Nicholson in one grotty motel room. "Did you notice that?") But despite these attractions, and a glossy *noir* look from *The Usual Suspects* cinematographer Newton Thomas Sigel, *Blood and Wine* never quite shakes off the feel of a tired television thriller inhabited by unusually interesting characters. It might have been more absorbing to see the Gates family self-destruct without the additional diversion of assault with a golf club, suffocation on a sun lounger and the nifty shark-killing contraption wielded by Jason in his final stand-off with his stepfather. (*Marvin Gardens*, remember, also ended with a murder, but never had to fall back on thriller formulae.) Rafelson is too interested in his characters to worry much about the plot, but the unexpected turns in the narrative—one of his trademarks—seem laboured here when linked to that oldest of Macguffins, the stolen diamond necklace. (Wine, mentioned in the title but seldom afterwards, might have been a more interesting booty for Gates to set his eye on.)

Still, for what it's worth, *Blood and Wine* is Rafelson's best film in a decade—and perhaps a more worthwhile use of Nicholson's time than *Mars Attacks!*

VILLAGE VOICE, 2/25/97, p. 70, Amy Taubin

In Bob Rafelson's *Blood & Wine,* the red stuff is even more free-flowing [The reference is to *Touch*; see Taubin's review.] Jack Nicholson and Michael Caine play sclerotic ex-cons who bungle a million-dollar jewel heist. Judy Davis plays Nicholson's much abused wife and Stephen Dorff his resentful stepson. Despite the neonoir Florida setting, the oedipal conflict (the son hates his stepfather for beating up on his mother, then hates him even more when he discovers they have a girlfriend in common), some adroit car chases, lots of brutality, and four intense performances, *Blood & Wine* is drained of life from start to finish.

Also reviewed in:
NEW YORK TIMES, 2/21/97, p. C15, Stephen Holden
NEW YORKER, 2/17/97, p. 92, Anthony Lane
VARIETY, 9/30-10/6/96, p. 181, David Rooney
WASHINGTON POST, 2/21/97, Weekend/p. 43, Desson Howe

BOOGIE NIGHTS

A New Line Cinema release of a Lawrence Gordon production in association with the Ghoulardi Film Company. *Executive Producer:* Lawrence Gordon. *Producer:* Lloyd Levin, Paul Thomas Anderson, John Lyons, and Joanne Sellar. *Director:* Paul Thomas Anderson. *Screenplay:* Paul Thomas Anderson. *Director of Photography:* Robert Elswit. *Editor:* Dylan Tichenor. *Music:*

Michael Penn. *Music Editor:* Ron Finn. *Choreographer:* Adam Shankman. *Sound:* Stephen Halbert and (music) Casey Stone. *Sound Editor:* Dane A. Davis. *Casting:* Christine Sheaks. *Production Designer:* Bob Ziembicki. *Art Director:* Ted Berner. *Set Decorator:* Sandy Struth. *Set Dresser:* Martin Milligan. *Special Effects:* Lou Carlucci. *Costumes:* Mark Bridges. *Make-up:* Tina K. Roesler. *Make-up (Burt Reynolds):* Brian McManus. *Stunt Coordinator:* Cliff Cudney. *Running time:* 152 minutes. *MPAA Rating:* Not Rated.

CAST: Don Cheadle (Buck Swope); Heather Graham (Rollergirl); Luis Guzman (Maurice TT Rodriguez); Philip Baker Hall (Floyd Gondolli); Philip Seymour Hoffman (Scotty J); Ricky Jay (Kurt Longjohn); William H. Macy (Little Bill); Alfred Molina (Rahad Jackson); Julianne Moore (Amber Waves); Nicole Ari Parker (Becky Barnett); John C. Reilly (Reed Rothchild); Burt Reynolds (Jack Horner); Robert Ridgely (The Colonel); Mark Wahlberg (Eddie Adams/Dirk Diggler); Melora Walters (Jessie St. Vincent); Stanley DeSantis (Jerry); Nina Hartley (Little Bill's Wife); Michael Jace (Jerome); Howard Morris (Mr. Brown); Joanna Gleason (Dirk's Mother); Laurel Hollowman (Sheryl Lynn); Thomas Jane (Todd Parker); Jack Wallace (Rocky); Joe Doe (Amber's Husband); Jonathon Quint (Johnny Doe); Rico Bueno (Hot Traxx Waiter); Samson Barkhordarian (Hot Traxx Chef); Brad Braeden (Big Stud); Lawrence Hudd (Dirk's Father); Michael Stein (Stereo Customer); Patricia Forte (Teacher); Kai Lennox (High School/College Kid); Jason Andrews (Johnny, Limo Driver); Amber Hunter (Colonel's Lady Friend); Greg Lauren (Young Stud); Tom Dorfmeister and Jake Cross (Watchers); Selwyn Emerson Miller (Hot Traxx DJ); Jamielyn Gamboa (Colonel's Hot Traxx Girlfriend); Melissa Spell (Becky's Girlfriend); Raymond Laboriel (Becky's Girlfriend's Friend); Tim "Stuffy" Soronen (Raphael); Alexander D. Slanger and Thomas Lenk (Floyd's Kids, Boys); Lexi Leigh and Laura Gronewald (Floyd's Kids, Girls); Vernon Guichard, II (Mugsy Jack's Bartender); Tony Tedeschi (New Year's Eve Young Stud); Leslie Redden (KC Sunshine); Gregory Daniel (Minister); Michael Penn (Nick the Engineer); Don Amendolia (Bank Worker); Summer and Skye (Jacuzzi Girls); Robert Downey, Sr. (Burt, Studio Manager); Veronica Hart (Judge); Jack Riley (Lawyer); Cannon Roe (Surfer); Mike Gunther, Michael Raye Smith, and Michael Scott Stencil (Surfer Punks); Dustin Courtney (Donut Boy); Allan Graf (Man with Gun); José Chaidez (Puerto Rican Kid); B. Philly Johnson (Rahad's Bodyguard); Joe G.M. Chan (Cosmo, Rahad's Boy); Goliath (Tyrone); Israel Juarbe and Gregory Anthony Rae (Maurice's Brothers) Eric Winzenried (Doctor).

CINEASTE, Vol. XXIII, No. 3, 1998, p. 40, Thomas Doherty

"Lincoln does not have the phallus," wrote the editors of *Cahiers du cinéma* in a scandalous and very French review of John Ford's *Young Mr. Lincoln* back in 1970. "He is the phallus." Dirk Diggler not only has the phallus; he *is* a dickhead.

Smartass lines and smarmy puns are well-nigh irresistible given the length and breadth of the singular off-screen presence and ultimate, end-reel revelation in *Boogie Nights*, twenty-six-year-old director Paul Thomas Anderson's slick homage to the halcyon days of celluloid pornography. Packed with enough subplots and supporting players to fill a season's worth of ER episodes, clothed in enough redeeming social value to escape amputations of overt sleaziness, and whipping out more than enough cinematic prestidigitation to hypnotize the crowd, this Altman-by-way-of-Scorsese-and-Tarantino pop melodrama is a delirious exercise in scopophilia, the peek-a-boo prurience at the core of cinema. A lot may be wrong with this heady mesh of X-rated tastes and G-rated brains, but it is never boring and is always easy to look at.

Set amongst the congenial and nurturing environs always associated with the hard-core sex trade, *Boogie Nights* tracks that awful passage in American culture when the blight of the videotape revolution snuffed out the uncompromising artistry of *Deep Throat, The Devil in Miss Jones*, and *Behind the Green Door.* Though the film chronicles other sad transitions in the zeitgeist from the late 1970s to the mid-1980s—disco-thumping dance tracks to MTV pop, good cocaine highs to bad cocaine highs, sex to violence, platform to sensible shoes—the obvious element left out of the mix is a structured absence bigger than anything that pops out on screen, namely AIDS.

The film is a triumph of style over substance from the opening shot, a long-take, hotshot intro that curves and cranes in to a garishly lit, frenetically agitated disco nightclub. The soon-to-be central characters bob and weave into frame, among them porn producer Jack Horner (Burt Reynolds, in the role he was born to play), porn queen with the heart of gold Amber Waves (Julianne Moore), starstruck nightclub owner Maurice TT Rodriguez (Luis Guzman), sleek California babe Rollergirl (Heather Graham), whose swiveling ass beckons to cap off the traveling shot, and last, but certainly not least, busboy Eddie (Mark Wahlberg), well endowed in an organ that is emphatically not his brain.

A man with an eye for below-the-belt talent, Jack recruits Eddie with the siren call of "adult films, exotic pictures." The posters on Eddie's bedroom wall back home in Torrance, California (supermodels and red Corvettes) signpost his aspirations, and that bulge in his pants highlights his key qualification. If his way to wealth via this "one special thing" isn't quite what Ben Franklin had in mind, his materialism and work ethic are pure American Dream. Since his hellish home life is pure American nightmare (glimpses of his harridan Mom and impotent Dad make Jack's extended porn family seem like the Huxtables), the leap into onscreen sex is less a descent into perdition than a chance at salvation.

During the next big choreographed set piece, more members of the cast and crew float by with Altmanesque precision: Little Bill (William C. Macy), the cinematographer with the extravagantly adulterous wife; Scotty (Philip Seymour Hoffman), the lovelorn tub of lard with a crush on Dirk; the black cowboy and failed entrepreneur Buck Swope (Don Cheadle); the dirty old man who holds the purse strings, The Colonel (Robert Ridgely); and sidekick Reid Rothchild (John C. Reilly), who measures up to Eddie in IQ only. Welcomed into the household, Eddie begins his Horatio Alger trajectory as a self-made man making others. He rechristens himself "Dirk Diggler," the name coming to him as an explosive vision in purple and green neon. At this point, Thomas cuts to a neon sign ("Dirk Diggler"), an explosive vision in people and green.

As a sleek job of skillful filmmaking, *Boogie Nights* is suitably eye-popping. Thomas's camera is fluid and mobile, always active, but not nervous and jumpy in the manner of so many lensers weaned in the age of cable. He prefers moving and craning and sloping to cutting and jerking and zapping. Though the drama is structured as a kind of unregenerate Pilgrim's Progress, the film works best as a demonstration of exuberant set design and florid fashion tapestries. Late 1970s verisimilitude can be really scary. Look at the gaudy evocations of disco nightclubs where geeks hustle by in sub-Travolta threads or the sub-glam parties at Jack's house where hot tubs bubble, coke whores OD, and semibeautiful people struggle to make small talk. Mimesis also abounds in sequences that re-create the visual quality of 1970s porn, complete with cheap film stock, trashy lighting, and bad acting. Like Orson Welles, that other wunderkind who fabricated a spot-on imitation of *The March of Time* for *Citizen Kane*, Thomas lovingly conjures the ambiance of a quite different genre: the raw footage of Amber and Dirk's first consummation; the cheezoid credit sequence to Dirk's porn-film detective series; and Amber's debut behind the camera for a video profile of Dirk.

From opening to end credits, the cutting-edge music of the era sends out a thumping wall of sound that serves as a nonstop, sledgehammer Greek chorus. The lyrical irony is witless but it is meant to be witless, so maybe it's clever: Three Dog Night's "Mama Told Me Not to Come," when Eddie enters Jack's lair; Styx's "Lonely Boy," when Amber's off screen child telephones amidst the uproar looking for his working Mom; and the Beach Boys' "God Only Knows" for the calm after the Big Epiphany. Perhaps having captured the look of the 1970s with such appalling accuracy, Thomas permits himself to cheat on the musical time line with the soundtrack.

No matter: *Boogie Nights* isn't about L.A. in the 1970s any more than *L.A. Confidential* is about L.A. in the 1950s. The film is about the appropriation of a style and the evocation of a mood, the adoption of music, clothes, habits, and the ethos of a different time, an exercise in the creation of a usable cinematic, as opposed to historical, past. No wonder the sudden appearance of two portraits of Ronald Reagan and Jerry Brown in a California state office are so jarring: they are references to an off-camera, not a filmic, reality.

At this juncture of Hollywood history, it is wearisome to bemoan but negligent not to note that even in the porn trade, the women are either mothers or whores and sometimes both: nurturing matriarch/porn queen (Amber) or little girl lost/blow-job artist (Rollergirl). Yet the personal trait that crosses gender lines is stupidity. To a man and woman, the people who populate *Boogie Nights* are truly dumb fucks. Between the ears at least, Dirk, Reid, Buck, Heather, and Amber seem clinically deficient, as if God has only so much largess to parcel out to any one body.

Watching the rushes from his latest achingly bad Dirk Diggler opus on the moviola, porn auteur Jack Horner speaks the lines of an equally clueless Ed Wood: "This is the best work we've ever done. This is the film I want them to remember me by."

Blessed with a higher IQ, director-writer Thomas configures the porn trade as just the next level south on the media food chain, an only slightly less downscale version of Hollywood moviemaking and, by extension, the whoring endemic to all business enterprises. The acceptance speeches and heartfelt thanks at the Adult Film Awards ceremony are every bit as unctuous as the posturing at the Oscars presentation at the Dorothy Chandler Pavilion. In interviews, Thomas has spoken of the forbidden curiosity he felt as a youngster upon hearing that a house on his block was being used to make a porn film. Never repressed, the obsession returns to animate *Boogie Nights,* whose focus is the ethnography of pornography, not its depiction on screen. Having lived his own dream, Thomas is finally backstage, off-camera, directing the action.

For all the vaunted uncompromising courage of Thomas's exploration into the hard-core sex tirade, precious little nudity and no hard-core sex push the envelope of an R-rating. "A" list performers will talk the talk but not walk the walk of hard-core sex, and directors are leery of defiling their characters before a mainstream audience. The lie at the heart of *Boogie Nights* is not just the FX in Dirk's pants, but the limp practice of making a soft-core film about a hard-core industry, of being more linguistically than visually explicit, more talk dirty to me than the devil in Miss Moore. Just as *The People vs. Larry Flynt* refused to think pink, *Boogie Nights* blinks in the face of a money shot.

Suddenly the bucolic 1970s enter a new decade and, like a karmic wheel turning, things fall apart. No, not Reagan: videotape. *Après le déluge,* at a symbolic New Year's Eve party, Jack is confronted with a sinister businessman who declares that videotape is the future of porn, that film is just too damn expensive. Dirk snorts his first lines of cocaine. Bill finally gets seriously annoyed with his wife's exhibitionist infidelities, blows her away, then dispatches himself *Full Metal Jacket*-style. (Needless to say, the party broke up.) The Colonel James is busted for child porn (Jack is appalled). Worst of all, Dirk has trouble getting it up and angrily walks off the set to strike out on his own. (Amusingly, Dirk and Reid's first stopover on the slide down from porn degradation is a yet lower circle of hell: the recording industry.)

Two scenes show the porn crew pathetically trying to cope with normal life. Amber encounters the justice system during a custody hearing for her never-seen child. Her husband (John Doe) argues that a porn set with free-flowing coke might not be a reasonable environment for the kid. Denied custody, of course, Amber sobs in an alley. Buck encounters the hard laws of commercial banking while trying to secure a loan for a stereo shop. Denied the loan, of course, Buck sputters uncomprehendingly. So well equipped for one world, they are woefully ill equipped in another.

In the final act of *Boogie Nights,* parallel editing juxtaposes the ups and downs of the no longer parallel lives. Compromising his artistic integrity, Jack succumbs to the videotape revolution, prospering with a mail-order business and a cable-access TV show. Meanwhile, over in nightmare alley, coke-addled Dirk is forced to hustle ten bucks for a jack-off he can't quite perform. In the back of a limo, Jack cruises the streets for an amateur sex partner to star with Rollergirl on videotape. While Dirk is bashed by homophobes, the Rollergirl's pick-up turns out to be a former high-school tormentor. The jerk crosses the line when he insults Jack's oeuvre. Jack and Rollergirl beat him to a bloody pulp. "Don't you disrespect me!," screams Rollergirl. Imagine: You pick a guy up off the streets for videotape sex and he treats you like a tramp.

The last big set piece is a Tarantino playlet by the numbers. Loud music and bad craziness portend trouble when a seriously demented Alfred Molina refuses to play his role as an easy mark during a planned ripoff that can climax only in gunplay. In the background a Chinese boytoy tosses off firecrackers, the loud retort never failing to make Dirk and Reid jump out of their skin. As Rick Springfield's "Jessie's Girl" blares and Molina performs an unhinged lip synch, Dirk fades back, transported by the wistful tune of teenage envy. He smiles and seems to achieve a moment of peace, and, what is rarer for him, understanding. The violence erupts on cue, but Dirk dodges the crossfire and gets out with his skin intact. When his Red Corvette symbolically runs out of gas, he finds himself back at Jack's door, where comfort and forgiveness await from his surrogate Dad, the great patriarch, the real big dick.

Restored to Dirk-dom, backstage again, looking into a mirror like Jack LaMotta in *Raging Bull* Dirk rehearses his lines and gets pumped for his comeback. Finally, inevitably, he pulls out what has been the off-screen object of so many gazes in all its ruler-length, prosthetic glory. "I am a star!," he declares firmly. But, really, he is just the supporting player.

LOS ANGELES TIMES, 10/17/97, Calendar/p. 1, Kenneth Turan

Welcome to the movies, but not the kind that advertise in family newspapers. Movies without development deals, agents or talky scripts, where crews are small and lighting is haphazard because the director understands "there are shadows in life." Movies where the camera is always focused on "the Mr. Torpedo area, the fun zone." Welcome to the hard-core world of "Boogie Nights."

Written and directed by the formidably precocious 27-year-old Paul Thomas Anderson, "Boogie Nights" is a startling film, but not for the obvious reasons. Yes, its decision to focus on the pornography business in the San Fernando Valley in the 1970s and '80s is nerviness itself, but more impressive is the film's sureness of touch, its ability to be empathetic, nonjudgmental and gently satirical, to understand what is going on beneath the surface of this raunchy "Nashville."-esque universe and to deftly relate it to our own.

If, as John Huston's "The Asphalt Jungle" memorably insisted, "crime is a left-handed form of human endeavor," Anderson has been shrewd enough to see pornography in the same relation to show business in general and Hollywood in particular, to show it attracting the same kinds of dreamers desperate to make something halfway meaningful out of their lives.

But more than working a gleeful twist on traditional star-struck success stories, "Boogie Nights" understands that its characters, engaged though they may be in a quintessentially adult occupation, are in emotional terms no more than children looking for a family, for a home. With its surprising emphasis on the earnestness, the almost innocence of its people, "Boogie Nights" could practically be subtitled "Babes in Pornoland."

While it features extremely adult material, male and female nudity, simulated sex, violence and language strong enough to melt steel, "Boogie Nights'" dispassionate tone keeps it from being exploitative or even erotic. Unlike traditional pornography, its aim is to examine and fascinate, to amuse not arouse, but although its subject matter makes it a likely candidate for NC-17, its R rating makes a kind of sense.

Though the temptation must have been great, "Boogie Nights," expertly acted by a diverse and knowing cast that ranges from, magician Ricky Jay to real-life adult film star Nina Hartley, also manages not to condescend to its characters. The film is bemused and entertained, as we are, by this pack of sexual extremists, and the eye it casts on them is both benevolent and wry. It's not the lower depths we're watching, but a parallel world, where everything is simultaneously different from our own, yet the same.

Masters of this universe, its king and queen, are Jack Homer (Burt Reynolds) and Amber Waves (Julianne Moore). Dressed to impress in a red jumpsuit and gold chains, Jack is a primo director of "exotic films" and Amber, whose real name has vanished into the mists of time, is the very spacey top star who lives with him.

Jack didn't get where he is by being timid; he knows how to ferret out young talent like the teenage Rollergirl (Heather Graham) who never ever takes her skates off. And on this particular 1977 night in a Reseda disco, he's looking over a hunky busboy named Eddie Adams (Mark Wahlberg). "I got a feeling," Jack says, casting a practiced eye on the practically blushing young man, beneath those jeans something wonderful is waiting to get out."

Eddie, it turns out, is more than someone whose anatomy becomes his destiny. A high school dropout abused and belittled by his sour mother (Joanna Gleason), he is, lord help him, a kid who wants to follow his dream. "Everyone is blessed with one special thing in his life," Eddie tells his girlfriend, and the talents of a porno star just might be it for him.

As the boyish Eddie, who in an unexpected leap of imagination decides to rename himself Dirk Diggler, Wahlberg, a.k.a. underwear icon Marky Mark, gets his best film role to date and is indispensable to the success of "Boogie Nights."

Earnestness itself, equal parts ordinary and charismatic, Wahlberg's Dirk is unstoppably naive and completely convincing in his "I Just Wanna Be Me" determination to succeed.

Dirk Diggler is not the only one to have dreams both understandable and preposterous. Jack Horner wishes wistfully for the day when he can make an adult film where the story is as powerful a lure as the sex. And Amber Waves, who sloughed off her son along with her name, doesn't want her porn stardom to interfere with her determination to act like a mother.

Everyone's dreams come together in the most audacious way when Dirk makes his porno debut having sex with Amber under Jack's direction. With its ability to examine unexamined lives and a willingness to understand how the unconventional often mimics the conventional, "Boogie Nights" displays this interlude both for what it is and what its characters badly hope it will become.

Covering seven years with a casual epic flair, writer-director Anderson also follows the fortunes of several more peripheral porno players. These include durable leading man Reed Rothchild (John C. Reilly), country-western-loving African American Buck Swope (Don Cheadle), the money man known only as the Colonel (Robert Ridgely), wistful homosexual Scotty J. (Philip Seymour Hoffman) and the always worried Little Bill (William H. Macy), whose wife (Hartley) has a thing for public sex with other men.

The first part of "Boogie Nights," the introduction to this cockeyed world, is its most successful. Like any rags-to-riches story, it's engaging to watch Dirk Diggler (a character inspired in part by real-life L.A. porn star John Holmes, a.k.a. Johnny Wadd) make a series of James Bondish features that take him, ingenuous as ever, to the top of his profession.

When the '80s hit, a variety of factors, including drugs, cause the adult world and its participants to take a major hit, leading to a "wages of sin" section that is the film's weakest and most predictable. But "Boogie Nights," in yet another unexpected reversal, manages to pull out of this tailspin and right itself before its two hours and 35 minutes is done.

The film's wealth of ensemble performances are a major factor in this. Aside from Wahlberg, especially good are Reynolds, whose veteran been-there presence brings an essential stability to the father figure role, and Moore, that most adventurous of actresses, who provides Amber Waves with a sad and inescapable poignancy.

Perhaps the most exciting thing about "Boogie Nights" is the ease with which writer-director Anderson, whose debut film was the little-seen "Hard Eight," spins out this complex web. A true storyteller, able to easily mix and match moods in a playful and audacious manner, he is a filmmaker definitely worth watching, both now and in the future.

NEW YORK, 10/20/97, p. 54, David Denby

Boogie Nights, an American independent film that some critics are treating as a classic, ends with a shot of Mark Wahlberg lowering his pants and revealing what Mel Brooks would call an enormous *swanstücker*—partly a fake, as it turns out, since Wahlberg (the former model and rap singer who was known as Marky Mark) has been fitted with a prosthetic device. Still, fake or not, the prodigious prong is startling, and we realize that it's meant to sum up the movie and this boy's existence: The possession of that tool transforms a 17-year-old uneducated dropout, Eddie Adams, into the famous porn star Dirk Diggler. It's his distinguishing characteristic but also his limitation—all he is, and all he ever will be. *Boogie Nights,* the second feature made by the 26-year-old writer-director Paul Thomas Anderson *(Hard Eight* arrived earlier this year), is a kind of ragamuffin epic about the San Fernando Valley porn industry. The movie stretches from 1977 to 1984—the disco-and-cocaine period of bellbottom L.A.—and covers the varying fortunes of a small group of porn actors, filmmakers, and hangers-on gathered under the wing of Jack Horner (Burt Reynolds), an avuncular producer who likes to have people hang out at his house. Much of *Boogie Nights* is funny and touching, and even rather sweet. It's a good but not great movie—a movie conceived realistically, without falsifying glamour, but without great insight or excitement either. Anderson has a rather simple idea about these people. They are all screwed up in some way—unloved or brainless or addicted, with an endless capacity for sex but little capacity for life. Orphans in the storm, they gather together in a kind of strange new family with Horner as protector. *Boogie Nights* doesn't inflate its minor subject, but it's not as sharp as it should be, and despite all the sex it never really gets into eroticism as a subject at all.

Jack Horner, a very shrewd fellow, takes one look at Eddie Adams, a busboy in a Valley club, and decides (somehow) that Eddie has got the stuff. He picks up Eddie by using one of his minor actresses, Rollergirl (Heather Graham)—a waitress who never removes her skates in life or on film—as a lure. A strapping blonde, Rollergirl strips down to her skates and jumps on Eddie at Horner's house, while Jack, appraising, watches the show. These goings-on, and all the other sexual events, are treated in a completely matter-of-fact way. The sex just happens. There's no anticipation, no mystery, no violation, no passion, no guilt, no sin, no aftereffects or longing. It's all in fun.

The trouble with all-in-fun, however, is that it's a pornographic, rather than a dramatic, strategy. Anderson hasn't done what he might have, which is to make a movie about the power of eroticism as obsession. After all, this is supposed to be the "real" story of the porn world, not a variation on what the public saw at a triple-X theater. In *Boogie Nights,* the sex genuinely lacks meaning. These performers aren't even self-conscious enough (as Warhol's "superstars" were) to have any attitude about doing something dirty. Sex is simply what they do, and that's all there is to it. End of discussion.

Mark Wahlberg may have something in his pants, but there's no gleam in his eye. Short, pale, with a blank face, he's an inexpressive actor, and he uses his body inexpressively, too. What Wahlberg does best is convey Eddie's desperation. The pain and pleading in his voice when his mother calls him stupid is his sole truly naked moment. His Eddie is just an unassuming kid who longs for acceptance. He wants success and money, but he doesn't desire anyone; he wants other people to desire him. Perhaps that's enough of an idea for an interesting portrait, but narcissism has to be acted, like any other character trait, and Wahlberg doesn't glow like Richard Gere. Since sexuality is the principal dimension to his personality, his blankness leaves very little for us to stay interested in.

In Wahlberg's scenes with Julianne Moore—who plays Amber Waves, a female porn star—Moore does most of the work. Moore, a great actress, has red, red lips and lambent flesh, yet her eyes are anxious; she's a kind of neurotic siren, lewd and always available but frantically unhappy, an erotic icon out of an expressionist painting (touch her, and you will be lost forever). Amber, a druggie, has been separated by a divorce court from her little boy, and she's guilty over it. The way Julianne Moore plays the character, Amber's sadness and vulnerability make her even more desirable. But Dirk doesn't seem to want her, and she needs him more as a kid brother or even as a son than as a lover or co-star. They work together on-camera, but then nothing happens when the camera shuts off. The big scene we are waiting for never arrives. Amazingly, Anderson never plays with the juiciest and funniest possibilities of his subject—the relationship between sex when the camera is rolling and sex when it isn't.

Boogie Nights is made up of many vignettes—parties, drugs and more drugs, teenage girls overdosing, sex as work, work as sex. Anderson is a good observer, with a light, easy touch, and the sun-drenched, fleshy squalor of the scene is often funny. But he hasn't really shaped the screenplay. The vignettes don't comment on one another, as they do in a good Robert Altman movie. One thing happens and then another, over a period of seven years, and the characters stay pretty much the same. As long as they hang out at Horner's house and keep working in his films, they are fine; as soon as they rebel and leave his outfit, going off on their own, they get in trouble. They can't handle the regular world of banks and courts; they can't pull off a robbery without disaster. The sex-and-drugs regimen wears them down; they get diminished. But the forlorn realism of this group portrait isn't enough for us.

Who, for instance, is Jack Horner? In 1977, Jack thinks that "adult" films could become an art form. He has dreams of respectability, and when the moneymen tell him (a few years later) that it's time to switch to videotape, he's outraged: Tape means that pornography will turn into fodder (he's right). Yet earlier in the movie, before the transition to tape, we have *seen* what Jack can do when he has the freedom to invent. He pairs up Dirk Diggler and another performer, Reed Rothchild (John C. Reilly), in a series of James Bond-style action movies, with explicit sex added. Anderson shows us some of these films, and they are made to look pathetic and amateurish. So what do Jack's dreams mean? If he's just fooling himself about "art," then the only thing lost in the switchover to video is the porn workers' illusion that they are part of the film world. There they are, lolling at Jack's swimming pool, boasting like crazy, acting out an unwitting parody of the deluxe movie-star life. But Paul Thomas Anderson doesn't need to "expose" illusions that none of us took seriously in the first place.

Anderson comes close to satire at times, but he wants to be kind to these people, whom he portrays as harmless, even innocent. Drugged-out young girls may die at these poolside parties, but no one means any harm. They all get hurt because they are weak. The movie has its giddy moments (the porn milieu might be an exaggeration of the sexual freedom the rest of the country enjoyed twenty years ago), but in the end *Boogie Nights* is peculiarly depressing. Everyone in it—even the stars, even the kindly Jack Horner—seems like a hanger-on. *Boogie Nights* is gentle, and that's a surprise. But the movie is being overpraised, perhaps because people are astounded that the porn world can be used as a subject at all. Unfortunately, it hasn't been used as a *dramatic* subject. Anderson reports on the industry, perhaps accurately, but he doesn't really satisfy our curiosity about this pleasure-driven but pleasureless, fascinating but wan way of life.

NEW YORK POST, 10/8/97, p. 49, Thelma Adams

"I've gotta feeling that underneath those jeans is something wonderful just waiting to get out," porn director Burt Reynolds tells disco busboy Mark Wahlberg.

It's a line as old as "A Star Is Born"—the Janet Gaynor version—and certainly older than the flashy, trashy '70s, where writer-director Paul Thomas Anderson ("Hard Eight") plots his porn star's rise and fall.

The decade we love to hate—and Hollywood suddenly adores—gains fabulousness in 26-year-old Anderson's hindsight. The details are all there: Shirts are polyester, shoes are platform and sideburns are mutton chops. The pelvic thrust is in. Moralizing is out. Cocaine snorting is called drug use, not abuse.

"Boogie Nights" begins in 1977, the year of "Saturday Night Fever." Eddie Adams, a.k.a Dirk Diggler, (Wahlberg) has as much chance of stayin' alive as John Travolta. But Diggler has one special gift, and it's not dancing.

Under the guidance of smutmeister Jack Horner (Reynolds), Diggler is an instant hit. But stardom is a heavy crown. Ask Gaynor, ask Garland, ask Streisand, ask Travolta.

Horner introduces Diggler to the gang: Amber Waves (Julianne Moore), Little Bill (William H. Macy), Buck Swope (Don Cheadle) and Rollergirl (Heather Graham).

The Horner clan are the family Diggler always wanted but never had: They shower him with unconditional love. They also film sex for money, lots of money. But money can't buy respect.

Reynolds does much to make this alternative family-values pic seem valid. His acting can be described by that great California adjective: mellow. As his wife, Moore gives him strong, quiet support. The redhead brings beauty and pathos to the drug-addicted porn queen who abandoned her own son to become a mother for the sex set.

Wahlberg, formerly Marky Mark, aggressively proves that fairy tales can come true: Even an underwear model can become a star. But the sheer volume of characters cracks the writer/director's concentration. Cheadle and Macy get big violent scenes, but they remain cyphers.

"Boogie Nights" climaxes in a jaw-dropping set piece dominated by Alfred Molina as a jacked-up coke-buyer. But, by this point, the movie has escaped the young filmmaker.

Is Anderson saying that these pornographers are people, too, an X-rated Brady Bunch? Is he saying, as he so aptly demonstrates, that porn leads to violence and perversion? In a very what-you-see-is-what-you-get '70's attitude, he cops out.

Do we respect "Boogie Nights" in the morning? Not entirely, but it's a trip.

NEWSDAY, 10/8/97, Part II/p. B10, Jack Mathews

Everybody is born with a special gift, says Eddie Adams in Paul Thomas Anderson's brilliantly audacious satire "Boogie Nights," and Eddie's gift—at that brief, peculiar moment in popular culture when it's worth its weight in gold—is a sex organ the size of the star of "Anaconda."

The peculiar moment was the late '70s, when porn movies arose from the rubble of the Sexual Revolution to gain a certain middle-class cachet, when porn theaters boasting Triple-X fare moved into suburbia, and when the talents of such folks as Linda Lovelace, Marilyn Chambers and Johnny Wadd were routinely analyzed at cocktail parties.

"Boogie Nights" ducks behind the scenes of the flourishing porn trade, headquartered in Los Angeles' San Fernando Valley, with a story about an ambitious 17-year-old busboy who breaks into the business by way of his special gift, and enjoys the illusion of stardom before his ego and the arrival of the video revolution give him an abrupt introduction to reality.

Despite its sensational subject matter—and more nudity, simulated sex, profanity, drug use and graphic images (including a gander at Eddie's Promethean member) than you'll see in any recent R-rated movie—"Boogie Nights" is anything but an exploitation film. It's a brilliantly candid study of the corrupting power of the American Dream and of the moral deterioration that is a byproduct of social upheaval.

Eddie (Mark Wahlberg) wants two things in life, a career as an actor and a sense of belonging that hasn't been provided at home. He gets both when he's discovered by porn filmmaker Jack Horner (Burt Reynolds). The year is 1977, the same year that David Cronenberg gave porn star Chambers the lead role in his horror film "Rabid." Why wouldn't a teenager with self-confidence, professional encouragement and a special gift think he could make the leap himself.?

Wahlberg, the former model Marky Mark, plays Eddie with a perfect blend of innocence and guile, and Reynolds, who was on the verge of typecasting himself as an aging letch, makes Jack such a richly complex character that he may be contending for some of those year-end acting honors that have always eluded him.

Horner is an essentially decent person and a sincere father figure to his troupe. He's simply caught up in the same self-deception and ungoverned lifestyle that drive them all. For all the sex and drugs and vulnerable misfits around him, Jack sees himself as a serious filmmaker, with ambitions about revolutionizing popular pornography.

"My dream," Jack says, "is to make a film that's true and right and dramatic." Even while fulfilling its obligation to show copious hardcore sex.

Eddie wants the same thing, and he has an idea that leads to a series of Horner hits starring himself—under the marquee name Dirk Diggler—as a street version of James Bond. And, as they say, a star is born. Eddie is honored with X equivalents of the Oscar, he drives a fresh red Corvette, has a house in the Hollywood Hills, and is warmly nurtured in the safety of the Horner empire.

Among Eddie's adopted family, are his frequent co-stars Amber Waves (Julianne Moore). a numb, melancholy dropout who lives with Jack and serves as den mother to the clan, and Roller--girl (Heather Graham). a child-woman with a disabling self-image. Among the guys are actor Buck Swope (Don Cheadle), a black man searching for his identity; gay hanger-on Scotty J (Philip Seymour Hoffman), who has a serious crush on Eddie, and crew boss Little Bill (William H. Macy), an older man being driven to violence by his promiscuous wife and his suppressed shame.

This is life in a fast lane that inevitably leads to the abyss, and the falls here—triggered by jealousy, insecurity and the introduction of a better mousetrap (home video)—are spectacular. The 26-year-old Anderson, working from his own script, sends Eddie and the others to such extremes of humiliation that he actually pauses with a title card at one point to warn us that he's not through yet.

Anderson, with just one film behind him (the stylish "Hard Eight"), shows tremendous command of his subject. "Boogie Nights" is a maturely provocative piece of work, a film that can be seen as an indictment of the sex industry, as an indictment of the overall excesses of the '70s, as an indictment of the cheap cult of celebrity that our thin culture encourages, or all of the above.

In any event, it's an original work, a rare enough event these days, and one of the year's most enjoyable entertainments.

NEWSWEEK, 10/6/97, p. 74, David Ansen

"Everyone's blessed with one special thing," boasts 17-year-old busboy Eddie Adams (Mark Wahlberg) from Torrance, Calif. Eddie; who will rename himself Dirk Diggler and become a shining star in the world of "adult entertainment," is blessed with an exceptionally large penis. It will take him for quite a ride.

Paul Thomas Anderson, the 27-year-old writer and director of "Boogie Nights," which charts Dirk's meteoric rise and fall, has one special thing, too—an enormous talent for making movies. Gloriously alive from its virtuoso opening shot that swerves through a Reseda, Calif., nightclub to its revealing conclusion—in which Dirk's special thing is unveiled in all its absurd, slumbering glory—"Boogie Nights" is one of those breakthrough movies that leaves no doubt you are in the presence of a natural-born filmmaker. Like Spielberg's "Sugarland Express" or Scorsese's "Mean Streets," Anderson's mesmerizing movie announces the arrival of a major career.

Who could have foreseen that an epic about the porn business in the late '70s and early '80s would turn out to be the most invigorating, deeply entertaining American movie so far this year?

The milieu is sleazy, the era is vulgar, the people are dumb ... and for almost 2½ hours, a gifted filmmaker convinces you there's no more fascinating place to be. A stunning provocation, "Boogie Nights" asks us to consider the meaning of the term "family values" from the vantage point of a makeshift band of pornographers living and working in the San Fernando Valley. The father figure in this constellation is porno filmmaker Jack Homer (Burt Reynolds), who discovers Dirk/Eddie in the kitchen of a valley nightclub and realizes he's stumbled upon a "17-year-old piece of gold."

The exhilarating, often hilarious first hour, set in the disco-driven, polyester-clad year of 1977, introduces us to Horner's professional "family," a wonderfully motley crew. There's porno star Amber Waves (Julianne Moore), the unofficial den mother, who takes Dirk under her alternately seductive and maternal wing. There's Rollergirl (Heather Graham), a high-school dropout turned sex star, who will shed any item of clothing except her roller skates. There's the country-music-loving "actor" Buck Swope (Don Cheadle) and Dirk's dim best friend, Reed Rothchild (John C. Reilly), who plays Dirk's screen sidekick in Horner's action-movie porn films. On the other side of the camera is William H. Macy's Little Bill, whose insatiable wife (played by real porn actress Nina Hartley) cuckolds him at every opportunity, and Horner's strictly business cameraman (sleight-of-hand artist Ricky Jay).

Anderson's take on this tacky Californian subculture is at once blusteringly satirical and compassionate. These self-deluded denizens of the fringes of the entertainment world are the pathetic residue of the American lust for celebrity. Anderson mocks Dirk's bad taste in clothes and furniture (the art direction is a marvel of late-'70s kitsch), but his movie never turns sour with condescension—he has a genuine affection for these lost souls. Good anthropologist that he is, he lets us see the workaday normality of the job, and the way these folks create an alternative family to replace those they've fled. Anderson doesn't spare us the lurid, exploitative aspects of this milieu, but his movie never feels like exploitation.

As the '70s turn into the '80s—and video replaces film as the medium for porn movies—Dirk lets his "stardom," not to mention piles of cocaine, go to his head. If the first half of "Boogie Nights" is a kind of parody of the Hollywood rags-to-riches musical (Anderson says he had "Singin' in the Rain" in mind), the second half charts Dirk's crash and burn, as he is banished from Horner's stable and bottoms out on drugs, hustling and his own fractured ego. Though there are moments when Anderson's perfect pitch fails him (the bizarre shoot-out in a doughnut shop belongs in another movie) the fever-grip of his filmmaking holds you in thrall. And at the end of the trip is a bittersweet homecoming far more provocative than the wages-of-sin finale a conventional moralist would have provided.

The big ensemble cast shines from top to bottom. The former Marky Mark (slimmed down for a pre-pumped-up era) may not be a trained actor, but he navigates this tricky role with amazing assurance. Reynolds is the best he's been in decades: he brings a weary dignity to Horner, a man who choreographs sex for a living but seems to have no sex life of his own. Moore, who can turn on a dime from suffering Madonna to lipsmacking porn performer, is heartbreakingly good. There must have been moments when these actors wondered where their director was taking them, and if it was worth the risk. It was: "Boogie Nights" doesn't play it safe, and everyone involved in it comes up smelling like roses.

A few months ago, Paul Thomas Anderson found his second-grade school notebook: "My name is Paul Anderson. I want to be a writer/director/producer/ special effects man. I know how to do everything. I know it all." He was 6 at the time. When he was 17, a high-school kid in Van Nuys, Calif., he got a video camera and made a half-hour movie called "The Dirk Diggler Story," partly inspired by the sad tale of the late legendary porn star John Holmes, partly inspired by his curiosity about what was going on behind the walls of the anonymous warehouses he'd seen growing up in the San Fernando Valley. There was never any doubt he was meant to make movies.

The intense, slightly built Anderson was too impatient to get to work to linger in school. He spent two semesters as an English major at Emerson College, and two days at NYU film school. A short film led to an invitation to the Sundance Lab, where he developed the script for his first feature, "Hard Eight." It was a striking debut (starring Gwyneth Paltrow, Samuel L. Jackson, John C. Reilly and Philip Baker Hall), but few people saw it. Hollywood, however, was not blind to his talent. When he approached New Line with his script about the porn industry, it jumped aboard. A deal was cut: New Line would let Anderson make a 2½ hour movie, but it had to get an R, not an NC-17, rating.

Getting his R took months of back-and-forth negotiations with the MPAA ratings board. The board let him know it loved the movie—indeed, it told him it wanted it to be an NC-17, to restore class to a category it felt had been sullied by "Showgirls." Though the board asked him for numerous trims, to its credit it never had a problem with the dramatically crucial revelation of Dirk's 13-inch member (a prosthetic device, by the way).

When Wahlberg first heard about that scene—before he'd read the script—it reminded him of "all the stuff I wanted to get away from. My past, making a fool of myself." When he first met Anderson, the suspicious former Calvin Klein model asked him: "Is it about the Marky Mark thing?" But it didn't take long for him to realize the director was after bigger game. "It took five minutes of talking," Wahlberg says. "There were so many positives. The screenplay was phenomenal." Wahlberg, who's eager to shed his old reputation as a roughneck street kid, claims that making "Boogie Nights" "helped me in my personal life. All this shit I went through growing up" he saw reflected in Dirk Diggler's struggles to make his mark. "I realized I could be man enough to deal with it and put it behind me. I wasn't playing me, but I still kind of told the truth." Already "Boogie Nights" has changed both Wahlberg's and Anderson's lives. Wahlberg just accepted a part as a boxer opposite Robert De Niro in a movie called "Out on My Feet." Playing a porn star has made him respectable. Anderson is suddenly the hottest new kid on the Hollywood block. He shrugs it off. "At least I know now I can make another movie—at least one," he says. He's underestimating the impression his movie is making. This kid's going to be around for the long haul.

SIGHT AND SOUND, 1/98, p. 36, Linda Ruth Williams

1977. In a San Fernando Valley nightclub, porn director Jack Horner spots talent in 17 year old busboy Eddie Adams. After a row with his mother Eddie leaves home and accepts Jack's offer of work in the hardcore industry. At a party, Eddie meets the members of Jack's entourage: male studs Reed Rothchild and Buck Swope, female stars Amber Waves and Rollergirl, crew member Little Bill, and Jack's financial backer, The Colonel. Eddie changes his name to Dirk Diggler and shoots his first scene with Amber, amazing the crew with the size of his penis and his sexual prowess on set. Dirk becomes a star, and with Reed develops the screen personae of Brock Landers and his sidekick Chest Rockwell, who feature in a series of successful films. Dirk wins awards at the Adult Films Awards Ceremony and becomes rich.

Things begin to go wrong as the 80s dawn. Little Bill shoots his unfaithful wife, her lover and then himself. The Colonel is imprisoned for possession of child porn. Amber makes a documentary about Dirk, whose cocaine addiction is making him increasingly arrogant. Jack employs a new young stud to replace Dirk. Jack's original group begin to pursue careers outside the porn industry. Dirk tries the pop business, but eventually turns to prostitution and drug dealing to fuel his own habit. After failing to rip off a cocaine dealer with Reed and another friend, Dirk returns to Jack, who has been coming to terms with the rise of video. The two reunite to make adult films in this new format.

When is a sex film not a sex film? When it's a film about the sex industry. Paul Thomas Anderson's *Boogie Nights* is one such film, a hilariously engaging and at times bleakly disturbing chronicle of the rise, fall, and rise again life of a hardcore porn stud from the mid 70s to the mid 80s. But while *Boogie Nights* is *about* sex, and about the gloriously cheesy opportunists who gave 70s hardcore its peculiar quality, sexiness is not its foremost pleasure.

Performance, however, *is*. The ensemble cast are flawless, although Mark Wahlberg stands out as the well hung ingénu Eddie, a boy next door who only ever wanted to be Bruce Lee. Changing his name to Dirk Diggler as he gets a grip on the enormity of his god-given talent ("Everyone's blessed with one special thing," he says to his member, in the first of a series of confidence boosting man-to-penis discussions), our hero moves from excessive success to sordid arrogance and despair as decadence takes its toll. Raunch may be his stock in trade, but eager to please enthusiasm is the young Dirk's prime characteristic, which lends itself to a number of supreme comic moments. In response to the crew's failure to catch on film the obligatory 'money shot' (a close up of a penis ejaculating) during Dirk's first scene, the boy only seconds after his last climax helpfully pipes up: "I could do it again if you need a close up". A star is born.

Yet the effect of sex is curious. What Dirk most readily provokes in others is not arousal but sympathetic protectiveness. To say that there are no sex scenes in this film might seem absurd, but indeed there *are* practically no sex scenes if we exclude the scenes performed *on set,* in the films-within-the-film, and the distant and mechanical scenes of Little Bill's wife rutting her various lovers. Otherwise, characters embrace, they cuddle, they support and line up coke for each other. One couple even has a baby. But, except when directed by Jack, none of them apparently fucks. Screen (within a screen) sex is plentiful, self-parodically awful and played for laughs, but the real relationships are as asexual as apple pie.

Despite experiencing simultaneous orgasm with Dirk on set, Julianne Moore's kooky and vague actress Amber Waves who has lost custody of her own child, makes Dirk into a substitute son. As Amber and Rollergirl sink into coked out derangement and let their psychological barriers tumble, they fantasise that Amber is Rollergirl's mother, and decide Rollergirl should go back to school. *Boogie Nights* refuses to ascribe an Oedipal resonance to these feelings. And in this lies its appeal to a mainstream audience: whilst we trip through the episodic structure of beautifully crafted but disparate vignettes, overall coherence is maintained by the arc of immutable 'family' loyalty. Brilliantly played by Burt Reynolds (extending the skin trade sleazeball he developed in *Striptease),* fictional director Jack Horner is many things: a porn auteur, priding himself on the filminess of his films; an endearingly humble professional in his cinematic ambitions (he dreams of making a film which is "true and right and dramatic"), and a Big Daddy to them all. Though at first coming on like wicked, fairy-tale step parents (Jack to Eddie: "I've got a feeling in those jeans there's something wonderful waiting to get out"), Jack and Amber develop into the good carers their entourage always lacked. Thus a kind of surrogate family structure is forged, an anchor of stable unconditional support for the drifters who find a home getting their kit off. (A similar self-created family is to be found in Anderson's first feature, *Hard Eight.)*

But sexual display as a bonding force is only one of *Boogie Nights'* reassuring feelgood elements. Its classic 70s soundtrack is skilfully deployed both as an anthemic celebration and as an oblique, ironic comment on the action. (Melanie's rollerskating referring 'Brand New Key' will never sound the same aqain.) And now that we have all revisited the decade that fashion forgot and are once more happy in flares and platforms, *Boogie Nights'* overflowing wardrobe of fabulously hideous flyaway collars in tangerine and chocolate seems both laughably passé *and* contemporarily hip. Much of the film's humour is at the expense of pathetically obsolete technology (the 8 track cartridge, exemplifying glorious Hi-Fi, is a ready target). Yet the way in which *Boogie Nights* affectionately comments on these objects and sounds also makes the excesses of public sex and mountains of coke look far less alien. The gloss of nostalgia make the unfamiliar seem rather more homely.

So is this pre-Aids past a foreign country? While the consequences of casual, commodified sex are as clearly displayed as the pleasures, *Boogie Nights* refuses to pass judgement since such freedom is now entirely the stuff of fiction. Instead, it just lets its characters slide down their self constructed slippery slopes and shows how hard they land. There are edgily disturbing moments: the scene where Dirk and friends attempt a rip off of Alfred Molina's crazed drug dealer is so tense it's almost impossible to watch.

Later, we see characters swallowing their pride (amongst other things) in a number of painful transition scenes. But energy levels stay high, maintained by the powerful music and the dynamic period design. A post-Aids message about alternative pleasures also shines through in *Boogie Nights'* most exuberant moments. Though sex is ever near and always possible, good times are to be had as much on the dance floor as in the sack—for the tightly choreographed disco scenes are only one of the delights that *Boogie Nights* has to offer.

TIME, 10/6/97, p. 88, Richard Corliss

Eddie Adams couldn't be more common. The 17-year old idles at school and works nights as a dishwasher in a disco. But Eddie, who believes "everyone's blessed with one special thing," is opulently endowed "down there in the Mr. Torpedo area," as an admirer says. At any other time in history, that would win a fellow not much more than respect in the barracks shower. But this is the 1970s, and porno films are big business. Folks looking at Eddie's endowment gasp as if it were the Washington Monument. He is pornography's future: the Holy Groin. Those 13 inches in his pants will make Eddie a big bright shining star. With a star's neon name: Dirk Diggler.

Boogie Nights, written and directed by Paul Thomas Anderson, is itself a size freak; the movie is in love with bigness. It spends 2 hrs. and 32 min. spanning eight years in the lives of a dozen or so denizens of the porn biz. Loosely based on the life of John C. Holmes, porn's biggest male star, *Boogie Nights* has panoramic ambitions: a tapestry-style narrative, labyrinthine tracking shots, explosions of random, firecracker, violence. *Nashville* meets *GoodFellas* meets *Pulp Fiction.* The film doesn't quite get there, but it packs a wad of compelling entertainment on its road to triple-X oblivion.

Jack Horner (Burt Reynolds, relaxed and in charge) is a director with a dream: he wants to make a film that keeps customers in the theater even after they've been sexually satisfied. His lover and star, Amber Waves (a nicely wasted Julianne Moore), is almost as devoted to the son she never sees as she is to her cocaine stash. Rollergirl (Heather Graham, before whose beauty all gentlemen genuflect) performs sex on skates. And Eddie (Mark Walberg, a nice surprise) is just a dim, polite kid, not strong enough for the burden of stardom.

They're the folks next door. They argue over money, worry about their kids, get crazy jealous of their loved ones. They have just this one eccentricity: they don't mind making the most intimate act of their lives a spectator sport. They see no reason to explain this, and neither does this defiantly noncommittal film. At the start for example, Eddie is already exhibiting himself for money. We don't learn why he and Amber and Rollergirl descended into the netherworld of sexual showmanship; they have dwelt in that Valley from the start.

This is no porn-biz exposé. It shows no women lured into fornicating on film; it doesn't finger the Mafia as a crucial investor. When Eddie inevitably splits with Jack, he has nowhere to go; Jack is apparently the only director in pornland. Nor is there much eroticism; indeed, except for the film's final shot, where we get to see Eddie's penis (granted, a nifty prosthetic effect), *Boogie Nights* has little nudity—it's a sex film that stints on the sex. And Holmes, who died of AIDS in 1988, had a life far more bizarre and instructive than Eddie's.

Mention these cavils to Anderson, and he might quote a line from the movie: "That's not an MP. that's a YP—your problem." He made his film, and a pretty good one, about a community of working stiffs; the people fascinate him more than their product. So here's a tip for those attending this handsomely acted, epic-length little film. Ease into the sleaze, stare at the party animals, look but don't touch, and, oh, boogie all night.

VILLAGE VOICE, 10/14/97, p. 85, J. Hoberman

There's a new Tarantino in Tarantino-ville. Paul Thomas Anderson's B movie-ish first feature *Hard Eight* attracted little more than good notices when it opened last January. His second, you may have heard, catapults the 27-year-old, L.A.-born writer-director to the head of the A-list.

Boogie Nights, which plays the New York Film Festival this evening (before opening theatrically Sunday), has been compared to *GoodFellas* and *The Player,* and Anderson's models are a measure of his ambitions. Densely populated and richly metaphoric, *Boogie Nights* can't match *GoodFellas* formal brilliance but it is a scoop—and not just for featuring the former Marky Mark as a prodigiously endowed porn performer who names himself Dirk Diggler. Anderson has beaten out several generations of senior directors to go full frontal (so to speak) on the nation's real dream factory.

Challenging Scorsese and Altman from the get-go, Anderson opens by sending the camera wheeling through the revels of a *Saturday Night Fever*-era San Fernando Valley disco, introducing half the cast, to settle on the future Diggler (Mark Wahlberg) washing dishes backstage. Discovered by the paternal porn director Jack Horner (Burt Reynolds) and his concubine-star Amber Waves (Julianne Moore), Dirk is a sweet, happy dumbo, always eager and ready to fuck. Is his "one special gift" an evolutionary advance? The film's continual references to the star's unrepresentable firehose provide a running gag and a superb punchline.

At once light and studied, drenched in late disco and early power pop, *Boogie Nights* rolls from set piece to set piece. As the downbeat Reno fable *Hard Eight* made clear, Anderson has a nose for stale plush and an eye for the placeless place. The mise-en-scène may be more eloquent than the dialogue, but the cast is uniformly inspired. Moore manages to be at once genuinely maternal and professionally salacious; Heather Graham gives a touching performance as Dirk's female equivalent, a high school dropout given the nom de porn Rollergirl. Not the least of Anderson's coups has been recruiting Reynolds. It's a warm, totally deadpan performance with an a prior authenticity derived from the film's being set (1977-84) at the rancid height of Burt's reign.

For its first half, *Boogie Nights* is a sunny comedy of success—a prancing disco line dance led by Dirk's happy mock-Travolta. Anderson's porntopia has strong echoes of early Hollywood. The sweet smell of success mixes with other bodily fluids. Margaret Mead's Samoa had nothing on the happy simpletons of the sex biz. A cocaine overdose is but a passing cloud in the daylong pool party of innocent sybarites basking in the sunshine of lotusland. But then a prophet of doom (Philip Baker Hall) shows up at Jack's 1979 New Year's Eve bash predicting a revolution about to rock the industry: "Don't get me wrong," he tells the hysterical Jack.   "I like cinema. Specifically, I like to see people fucking on film. But videotape tells the truth."

Thus, the downward spiral begins. Featuring enough coke to give your sinuses a contact burn, *Boogie Nights* seeks to rub the viewer's nose in its characters degradation. What makes it all go bad—is it drugs, video, old age, Reagan? Dirk suffers his first difficulty in getting his dick hard and, freaking out on aggression, throws a memorable star fit: "I'm ready to shoot! Who do I have to fuck?" The bells are tolling but Anderson has scarcely uncorked his final set piece—the Christmas Eve robbery of a Dunkin' Donuts is topped by a late-in-the-film visit to a Beverly Hills degenerate (Alfred Molina) who has french-fried his brain on freebase. Distilling the sum total of the film's delusions, it's as powerful a study in behavioral and staged lunacy as any I've seen since the Dennis Hopper scene in *Apocalypse Now*—an imaginary world observed totally from the outside.

The porn people may be living out collective fantasies but that doesn't preclude their own. Jack dreams of making serious stroke flicks—"This is the film I want them to remember me by," he says, paraphrasing Tim Burton's Ed Wood, after starring Dirk in a blithely idiotic kung-fu fuck film.   Dirk wants to be a pop star—in a comic digression, evoking the history of mass entertainment as well as the actor's own past, he attempts the shift from porn to rock. Amber wants to be a mom. And what is the director's attitude? *Boogie Nights* joins our other current favorite, *Nenette et Boni*, in making exemplary use of the Beach Boys singing "God Only Knows."

Bold in revising the Oedipal scenario, *Boogie Nights* is rather more timid in visualizing other imaginary scenes (racial integration, homoeroticism). But the bottom line: Anderson has made a real movie about the end of movies, a cautionary star vehicle on the subject of stardom, a porn flick with family values, a two-and-a-half-hour picture with scarcely a boring moment.

Treating the rise and fall of an adult entertainment star without flinching from its allegorical potential, Anderson has produced what may be the American movie of the year on what is surely the subject of the age.

Also reviewed in:
CHICAGO TRIBUNE, 10/17/97, Friday/p. A, Michael Wilmington
NATION, 10/10/97, p. 36, Stuart Klawans
NEW REPUBLIC, 11/10/97, p. 32, Stanley Kauffmann
NEW YORK TIMES, 10/8/97, p. E1, Janet Maslin
NEW YORKER, 10/13/97, p. 97, Daphne Merkin
VARIETY, 9/15-21/97, p. 68, Emanuel Levy
WASHINGTON POST, 10/17/97, p. D1, Rita Kempley
WASHINGTON POST, 10/17/97, Weekend/p. 32, Desson Howe

BOOTY CALL

A Columbia Pictures release of a Turman/Morrisey Company production. *Producer:* John Morrissey. *Director:* Jeff Pollack. *Screenplay:* Takashi Bufford and Bootsie. *Director of Photography:* Ron Orieux. *Editor:* Christopher Greenbury. *Music:* Robert Folk. *Music Editor:* Josh Winget. *Sound:* Douglas Ganton. *Sound Editor:* Darren Paskal. *Casting:* Mary Vernieu and Ronnie Yeskel. *Production Designer:* Sandra Kybartas. *Art Director:* Armando Scrignuoli. *Set Decorator:* Hilton Rosemarin and Danielle Fleury. *Special Effects:* Martin Malivoire. *Costumes:* Vicki Graef. *Make-up:* Marilyn Terry. *Stunt Coordinator:* Roy T. Anderson. *Running time:* 98 minutes. *MPAA Rating:* R.

CAST: Jamie Foxx (Bunz); Tommy Davidson (Rushon); Amy Monique Waddell (Arguing Woman); Wiley Moore (Arguing Man); Vivica A. Fox (Lysterine); Tamala Jones (Nikki); Kam Ray Chan (Ug Lee); Ric Young (Mr. Chiu); Ammie Sin (Yoyo); Scott LaRose (Singh); Bernie Mac (Judge Peabody); Olivia Yap (Judge's Woman); Bill MacDonald (Hold Up Man); John Moraitis (Greek Cabbie); Karen Robinson (Admitting Nurse); Donna Preising (Triage Nurse); Johnie Chase (Guard); Amanda Tapping (Dr. Moore); Beatriz Pizano (Pregnant Woman); Bootsie (Old Man); James Mainprize (Another Patient); Pedro Salvin (Male Nurse); Robert Bidaman (Dr. Zevroloski); Julia Paton (Nurse); Valerie Boyle (O.R. Nurse); David Hemblen (Dr. Blade); James Kidnie (Mummified Man).

LOS ANGELES TIMES, 2/26/97, Calendar/p. 10, John Anderson

[The following review by John Anderson appeared in a slightly different form in
NEWSDAY, 2/26/97, Part II/p. B7.]

What is the true meaning of love? What is the true meaning of manhood? What do women really want? Can men, especially when they're bonding like the herd animals they are, ever drop their macho facades and treat their lovers with the sensitivity and respect that they truly deserve?

And, most important, will they be getting any tonight?

These are the burning questions posed by "Booty Call," which wins the prize for least-subtle title of the year, and has a movie to match. Two male friends in hot pursuit of sexual relief run up against two female friends with their own ideas about courtship, class and safe sex. We've seen this kind of thing before, of course. We've just rarely seen it stripped down to its essence with such industrial efficiency.

Playing the four young urbanites on the "double date from hell" are four very talented people trapped in the script from hell. Jamie Foxx ("The Jamie Foxx Show"), who plays the in-your-face, anatomically obsessed Bunz, and Tommy Davidson ("Ace Ventura: When Nature Calls"), who's the far more refined Rushon, are both graduates of "In Living Color" and are gifted co-medians. Likewise, Vivica A. Fox ("Independence Day") and Tamala Jones (TV's "Dangerous Minds"), who play the upwardly mobile Lysterine and the sexually conservative Nikki, are quite capable of holding their own against the rapid-fire repartee of their co-stars.

But as the four wend their way through a night of clichéd mishaps, New York stereotypes and the search for the perfect condom, the relentless humiliation visited upon the couples becomes more than a bit tiresome. And while most of the humor is unprintable, let us just say that Glad Wrap and surgical gloves will probably never again enjoy such innovative product placement.

Basically, Bunz and Rushon are derided for being male; sexual desperation isn't a pretty thing. Lysterine and Nikki are depicted as harpies for insisting on some very basic bedroom precautions that the men should have taken care of beforehand. Stupidity isn't all that funny. Neither are ethnic jokes, which are tossed off casually and somewhat cruelly.

It's not that the movie is never funny. It's just that you don't feel very good when it is.

NEW YORK POST, 2/26/97, p. 40, Thelma Adams

A film clip in which two rhinos do the nasty with a clear view of what makes a male a male and a female rhino a happy mammal is about as classy as "Booty Call" gets.

What's the premise of Jeff Pollack's crass safe-sex comedy? Will Bunz and Rushon get lucky before dawn? You can bet on it. The boys—played by "In Living Color" pals Jamie Foxx and Tommy Davidson—do.

Bunz and Rushon put the moves on Lysterine (Vivica A. Fox) and Nikki (Tamala Jones). "Lysty" claims she doesn't "mess with anyone who does not have class." That doesn't explain why she calls her blind date, Bunz, a "ham-hock eating wildebeaste" one minute and bumps uglies with him the next.

Meanwhile, Nikki and Rushon have the seven-week itch. After nearly two months, they still haven't done the deed. Why don't they do what normal couples do? Go on "Oprah."

The actors approach the homophobic, hormonal material with good humor. The jokes at the expense of Chinese people and gays are excruciating, but there are yuks. A routine at a quickie mart with two Punjabi clerks—one played by the brilliant "Jewel in the Crown" star Art Malik—is raunchy but funny.

Who knew the sexual potential of Glad Wrap? Get Martha Stewart on the horn!

By the comedy's end, the girls are on top, but the screenplay (by Takashi Bufford and Bootsie) has touched bottom too many times. Stay tuned for next month's sequel about nooky in a German sub: "Das Booty Call."

SIGHT AND SOUND, 12/97, p. 39, Richard Falcon

New York. Well-mannered Rushon invites his fast-talking friend Bunz to join him and his girlfriend Nikki on a double date with Nikki's friend Lysterine. During dinner, Bunz and Rushon make a friendly bet on whether Rushon and Nikki will have sex for the first time that night. Nikki invites them all back to her apartment. Eventually, Nikki and Rushon go off to have sex. When Nikki's dog chews up Rushon's last condom, Nikki sends Rushon out to get some more with Bunz. The men return, but with useless lambskin condoms from a Chinese herbalist.

On their second outing, the friends buy latex condoms from a convenience store. When they return, Nikki will not allow Rushon to perform oral sex on her without a dental dam. The men go back to the store and become embroiled in a robbery. Returning with cling film, the men wrap themselves up in it. The women tease them for their ignorance and Bunz leaves, but the other three follow him. During a row, Bunz lets it slip about the bet and Nikki is upset.

When Bunz stops a cab in the street, the frightened taxi driver draws a gun on him and Rushon is hit in the leg by a ricocheting bullet. At the hospital, Rushon is refused admission at first because he doesn't have his insurance card with him. Bunz disguises himself as a doctor to seek help but gets involved in delivering a baby. Later, he and Lysterine finally have sex in one of the wards. Rushon is nearly surgically castrated when a patient swaps clipboards with him. At last, Rushon and Nikki go home and make love and Lysterine and Bunz start exploring S&M together.

Simultaneously a black, urban sex comedy and a 'date movie' built around sensible Rushon and his hip buddy Bunz's quest for prophylactics in New York City, *Booty Call* addresses its niche market with textbook single-mindedness. Viewers who considered *Dumb & Dumber* to be the *ne plus ultra* of no-brow comedy will be amazed to see that film bested by *Booty Call*, which features a scene in which the heroes, both misunderstanding what a 'dental dam' is, wrap themselves in cling film from head to foot.

Booty Call comes on like the repressed of *love jones,* the recent film which featured an all-affluent, young, black cast. Such upwardly mobile aspirations are burlesqued here in the figure of Lysterine (Vivica A. Fox in an enjoyably raunchy performance), a landmine of libido in search of a "classy" partner. What she gets is the "hood rat" Bunz. ("Tarantula-haired fool looks like Predator," she opines.) But he soon finds a way to her heart with his impersonations of such powerful black men as Jesse Jackson and Bill Cosby during foreplay. The film is unembarrassed in its use of stereotyping, exemplified by Bunz's macho boasts about his own virility. Nonetheless, these are soon deflated: when he finally has sex with Lysterine, he climaxes immediately and is mocked by a patient in a full-body cast. As if intended to be a provocation to political correctness, there's also a gay Chinese waiter and two Punjabi convenience store clerks with "Goodness gracious me" accents.

But this caricaturing is prompted by an occasionally surreal comic logic whereby everybody, below the surface, is a "hood rat" like Bunz. When Bunz, at Lysterine's request, pleads with a cigar-smoking triad boss in fluent Cantonese (learnt from kung fu videos) and the subtitle reads "If you don't put out the smoke, we'll get no ass", the gangster relents immediately, a brother under the skin. The camp waiter responds to Lysterine and Bunz's Cantonese insults by slipping into street jive. In a screenplay which would gladden the heart of a lexicographer of sexual synonyms, even the dog's barks are subtitled with street slang. But the biggest joke is as much on the audience itself, lured by the sexist poster which for the British market has the O's of the title encircling a curvaceous pair of female buttocks in tight shorts when the film's only nudity is a shot of Rushon's backside.

Booty Call is a traditional sex comedy at heart, right down to the *Pillow Talk*esque split-screen in which Nikki and Lysterine co-ordinate their demands for safe sex. With its public service homilies ("no glove, no love" being as pithy a slogan for safe sex as health educators could want), its two strong female characters, its lively hip-hop soundtrack and the comic adeptness and charm of all four leads, *Booty Call* emerges—when you've forgiven yourself for chuckling at so many bad-taste gags—as an endearing and unpretentious comedy.

VILLAGE VOICE, 3/11/97, p. 74, Gary Dauphin

In *Booty Call*, Jamie Foxx and Tommy Davidson are two young New Yorkers out on a double date with Tamala Jones and Vivica Fox (who was last seen in *Set It Off* and should have known better). Even though the evening starts out badly, the four end up back at the ladies' Chinatown digs, the only thing standing between them and a matched set of beasts-with-two-backs a thin layer of latex. The fellas trudge back and forth between the bedroom and the bodega in a losing game of prophylactic rock-paper-scissors with their partners (lambskin-latex-Glad Wrap), immigrant sales clerks, and the like foiling them at occasionally funny turns.

Booty Call's main problem is that it seems unsatisfied with just keeping things raw, so besides gut-bucket set pieces like the one involving Jamie Foxx's asshole and a dog's tongue, it's also chock-full of terribly insincere safe-sex homilies and perfunctory calls for the fellas to treat the ladies right. *Booty Call*'s images of black sexuality here aren't *all* awfully familiar racial stereotypes (just 90 per cent are), but really, if you're going to step into a cesspool and roll around, you might as well go whole hog.

Also reviewed in:
NEW YORK TIMES, 2/26/97, p. C16, Stephen Holden
VARIETY, 2/24-3/2/97, p. 75, Leonard Klady

BOX OF MOONLIGHT

A Lakeshore Entertainment and Trimark Pictures release of a Lemon Sky production. *Executive Producer:* Michael Mendelsohn, Tom Rosenberg, Sigurjon Sighvatsson, and Steven Sherman. *Producer:* Marcus Viscidi. *Director:* Tom DiCillo. *Screenplay:* Tom DiCillo. *Director of Photography:* Paul Ryan. *Editor:* Camilla Toniolo. *Music:* Jim Farmer. *Music Editor:* Jim Flatto. *Sound:* Matthew Price. *Sound Editor:* Eliza Paley. *Casting:* Marcia Shulman and Jayne E. Morgan. *Production Designer:* Thérèse DePrez. *Art Director:* Steve Brennan. *Set Decorator:* Nick Evans. *Special Effects:* Mike Weesner. *Costumes:* Ellen Lutter. *Make-up:* Lydia Milars. *Stunt Coordinator:* Dan Barringer. *Running time:* 107 minutes. *MPAA Rating:* R.

CAST: John Turturro (Al Fountain); Sam Rockwell (Buck, the Kid); Catherine Keener (Floatie Dupre); Lisa Blount (Purlene Dupre); Annie Corely (Deb Fountain); Rica Martens (Doris); Ray Aranha (Soapy); Alexander Goodwin (Bobby Fountain); Dermot Mulroney (Wick); Mike Stanley (Doob); Robert Wightman (Dex); James Richardson (Taco); Stephen Dupree (Elwood); Eugene Wolf (Lyle); Reathel Bean (Luvven Coddle); Betty Wills Stephens (Wynelle Coddle); Linda Libby (Curious Waitress); Ernest R. Ogg (Old Motel Clerk); Gary Lowery (Earl Sykes); Bodi Soham (Willard Snarp); Horace E. Smith (Barnett); Stuart Greer (Stinky); John E. Davis (Sheriff); Gene Patterson and Kristin Hoke (Newscasters); Buddy Landel (Uncle Samson); Chaz Warrington (Castroater); Glenn Ruth (Saddam Insane).

LOS ANGELES TIMES, 8/1/97, Calendar/p. 16, John Anderson

[*The following review by John Anderson appeared in a slightly different form in* NEWSDAY, 7/25/97, Part II/p. B8.]

Writer-director Tom DiCillo works in absurdity the way other men work in masonry or actuarial charts.

It was this flair for illogic that made his "Living in Oblivion" such a critical and popular success. When you make a comic, albeit fact-based, story about the making of underfunded independent film, you're in the bizarro land already: Nothing should succeed. That it ever does is a testament to a chaotic universe. And that's something nearly everyone can embrace.

At the same time, DiCillo's deliberate absurdism was what made his first film, "Johnny Suede," so off-putting for so many: Its self-delusional rock-star wannabe, even when played by Brad Pitt, was a hard hero to embrace, given how obtuse he was. And how unlikely it was that he'd ever emerge from his intellectual fog.

Where DiCillo lands with his third feature, "Box of Moonlight," is somewhere between full-blown cognitive anarchy and an atoll of truth. His protagonist, the anal-retentive engineer Al Fountain (John Turturro), is the boss you love to hate, although it's really too easy. Away from home, managing the installation of a rural power generator, he's the type to start his crew on a new job at quarter to 5; he can't tell a joke, or get one.

A humorless prig, he's invited to play poker by co-workers who hope he won't show up. His control-freak urges make his world much less benign, and his wife back home (Annie Corely) basically thinks he's ridiculous (that a woman would marry someone she thinks is ridiculous just makes Al's world more of a disturbing place).

But the thing is, Al knows he's a jerk—he rehearses sounding casual when he's by himself but then can't pull it off. We see what the world doesn't: that Al would like to change. And by putting us inside Al's tidy but unhappy head, DiCillo makes us both sympathetic and complicit.

Al's quasi-liberation from himself—you didn't know this was coming?—arrives via Buck (Sam Rockwell), a Daniel Boone impersonator who lives in half a house trailer, deals in hot lawn ornaments and eats a heaping bowl of Hydrox and milk for breakfast. He's off the grid, he tells Al, and is striving for total self-sufficiency—the kind of solar-powered, Mother Jones-endorsed existence that would be possible only with Al's brand of technical expertise. Buck is as much of an anomaly as Al, but he's a lot happier.

Their mutually enlightening exploits—imagine a comfortable territory somewhere between "Ulysses" and "Dumb & Dumber"—involve a swimming hole, a tomato fight, a bar brawl that doesn't even get inside the bar and an encounter with two sisters (Catherine Keener and Lisa Blount). Constructing a contemporary parable on two contemporary types—the back-to-nature Buck, who hasn't a clue, and the emotionally stifled Al, who can fix a car but has nowhere to go—DiCillo presents us with a two-sided schematic for the modern man.

Adding the flesh and blood are Rockwell, who's hilarious, and Turturro, who gives, Al a posture that says "kick me"—both of whom are quite fine and, as the movie progresses from its disoriented opening scenes, engaging and convincing.

The other jewel in "Box of Moonlight" is Keener, the most criminally underused actress in the business. As Floatie Dupre, a woman with a port wine stain and nasty lack of self-worth, she gives us a character who, like Al, is wrestling with a skewed sense of self. Convinced she's not bright and too busy worrying about it to show that she is, Floatie is the flip side of Al—controlled rather than controlling, a casualty of misguided expectations.

Keener, like DiCillo, makes us believe in someone and something that's elusive, perhaps a little closer to home than we care to loiter but that in the end—and after all the offbeat humor and Al's robot walk—is pretty human. That's unlike much else you're going to see this summer.

NEW YORK POST, 7/25/97, p. 49, Thelma Adams

Tom DiCillo's adventures in filmmaking, so funny in "Living in Oblivion," were much more entertaining than is the magical mystery tour of male midlife crisis in "Box of Moonlight."

John Turturro plays Al Fountain, an uptight electrical engineer who's no fountain of youth. While on a job away from his Chicago home, he discovers his first gray hair. About the same time, he begins to hallucinate. He sees time running backward: water flowing into a pitcher, coffee into the pot, a golden-haired boy cycling in reverse.

When the assignment ends early, Fountain resists returning home to his wife and child for Independence Day. Instead, he returns to a site of youthful happiness and rebellion, only to find that the secluded lake is now a toxic dump.

We should have known when he leased a Taurus at Circle Rent-a-Car on the eve of July Fourth that we were in for a picaresque spiritual journey into the heart of the American male. When Fountain nearly runs into a full-grown man in a Galaxie 500 with a plaster deer in the front seat, the die is cast.

The heavy hand of whimsy descends when the character is known only as The Kid (Sam Rockwell). Is it too much that he's wearing a Davy Crockett costume, complete with coonskin cap? Yes. DiCillo takes the long way 'round to put us in touch with Fountain's inner brat.

As in "Living in Oblivion," writer/director DiCillo, working with casting director Marcia Shulman, has assembled a bright troupe of offbeat actors.

Rockwell is a kinder, gentler Steve Buscemi. Catherine Keener and hubby Dermot Mulroney (both "Oblivion" alums) thread their way through the shallow plot as a failed phone-sex operator and a burnt bully.

As Mrs. Fountain, Annie Corely has little to do but be exasperated, a feeling I shared. Turturro's manic intensity and studied ticks never let us forget it's Turturro the hipster playing a corporate gnat. At the movie's climax, he breaks out in a stiff, funny, funky dance of independence. It's wonderful as an acting set piece, but easy, almost oily, as a resolution to Fountain's spiritual angst.

Despite the comedy's romantic, upbeat title, "Box of Moonlight" spends most of its meanderings in a state of low-level depression. While most scenes take place al fresco, afterward, I felt as if I'd spent two hours cramped in a box.

SIGHT AND SOUND, 5/97, p. 38, Rob White

Al Fountain is supervising a construction job in the American Midwestern town of Drip Rock: he's humourless, pedantic and disliked by his workers. In his hotel room after work, he hallucinates that water is flowing up out of a glass back into a jug. He phones his wife and son, checking on the latter's homework and offering banal fatherly advice. He overhears the workers laughing at him. The next day the job is unexpectedly cancelled. Instead of going home for the Fourth of July holiday, Al hires a car to visit a lake he remembers fondly from childhood. He has more hallucinations of events happening in reverse. When he arrives at the lake, it's contaminated by industrial pollution and patrolled by two elderly Christian fundimentalists. Later, on the road, he stops to help a young drop-out named Kid whose dilapidated car has broken down. He tows the car back to Kid's trailer which is surrounded by ceramic lawn ornaments. Al phones his wife, pretending that the job is still on, and stays the night at Kid's.

Al fixes Kid's car. They warm to each other and after Al's car-keys mysteriously disappear, they embark on various impulsive adventures: stealing fresh tomatoes from a farmer's vine and then eluding the local sheriff, swimming naked in a lake; smashing up the half-built factory which Al had been working on: fighting with local rednecks. Al stays on, despite having acquired some replacement car-keys, and lies again to his family. At the swimming lake, two local women, Floatie and Purlene, turn up. Al sleeps with Floatie in the trailer's ornament-strewn precinct. As Al leaves for home, Kid gives him a box which earlier he had seen Kid 'catch' moonlight in. Back home in Chicago, Al doesn't pester his son about his schoolwork and is affectionate to his wife. He gives her the box of moonlight. Inside are his missing car-keys which Kid had apparently stolen.

One strand of US-independent filmmaking is often excessively preoccupied with society's drop-outs and opt-outs. Off-beat personalities—dreamers, crooks, drifters—trying to escape the banality of everyday life, are often the focus whereas 'ordinary' characters, such as Marge and Norm in Joel and Ethan Coen's *Fargo* are more likely to be parodies. The first two feature films by one-time Jim Jarmusch collaborator Tom DiCillo are certainly in this vein. *Johnny Suede* is too immersed in the eccentricities of its bequiffed protagonist; *Living in Oblivion* embraces a broader range of characters but also revels in the solipsism of lengthy dream-sequences and is set in that paridigm of unreal environments, a film-set. One of the reasons *Box of Moon Light* is so accomplished and satisfying is that it introduces the ordinary—represented here by the emotionally stifled, socially awkward Al Fountain (John Turturro)—into an off-the-rails, left-field world. In this collision, Fountain's character is not undone but changed and broadened by his encounter with an alternative way of living. The film-makers describe *Box of Moon Light* aptly as "a modern fable without a moral".

Al's sense of order is giving way to anxiety about impending middle age, which DiCillo sums up succinctly by having him hallucinate, 'seeing' events happening in reverse. It's at this time of crisis that he meets and is befriended by Kid (Sam Rockwell who has the face and physique of Brad Pitt, only flawed, more goofy), an elfin, slightly disturbed young man. What follows is an engaging series of misadventures and misdemeanors: Al is led away from routine work and family and, in Kid's eccentric, unpredictable company, he rediscovers a youthful spontaneity. In return, Al offers Kid comfort which, though temporary, protects Kid a little from the delirium to which he's often so close. Their relationship is less a meeting of minds than a reciprocal tolerance of difference and idiosyncracy. In this sense, *Box of Moon Light* doesn't have a moral. Instead it suggests that it is unhelpful to generalise about how people experience disillusionment and that there are no formulas which explain how to recover front pain. The experience is different every time, and the recovery (if it comes) is likely to be improvised.

It's an intricate, richly textured film which gestures towards generic conventioiis without being too detained by them. For example, road-movie elements give structure to the first half of the film but they're wittily downplayed by Al's commentary on his trip ("life is a drive down the road"). And though this is an odd-couple buddy picture, the emphasis is less on the comedy of the pairing than on its unexpected, almost erotic intimacy. DiCillo has a fine, intuitive eve for situations and locations which are intriguingly metaphorical without being directly allegorical. Kid's trailer, opened out to the woods and surrounded by garden gnomes and ceramic or wooden animals is a magic garden. It's a space of transformation but also, like a bag-lady's shopping trolley, a totemic scrap yard, an ambiguous shrine for consumerist detritus and kitsch. The fable about the regenerative power of unforeseen friendship is balanced by darker images. The lake which Al visits, drawn by boyhood memories and nostalgia, turns out to be off-limits, polluted by local industry and patrolled by shell-suited Christians (whom we later glimpse on the television being arraigned for murder).

Turturro excels as a man who has valued routine over emotion, whose formality and politeness is a social defence but also a clumsy expression of kindness. But the outstanding performance in the film is Rockwell's as the damaged angel Kid. He's an *idiot savant*, frantically glued to the spectacle of rigged television wrestling-matches, eating chocolate biscuits and milk for breakfast, weeping at the world around him, skinny-dipping, trying to find a way of living "off the grid" with trauma always about to catch him up knowingly able to open life up to Al but facing an uncertain fate himself.

VILLAGE VOICE, 7/29/97, p. 78, Dennis Lim

Not long into *Box of Moonlight*, it becomes apparent that the inner child of the uptight central character will soon be making an appearance. Al Fountain (John Turturro) is an engineer caught in a midlife crisis that appears to have metaphysical side effects (he sees things happening in reverse). On an uncharacteristic whim, he takes a backwoods detour, stumbles upon a goofy, New Age-y individualist known only as The Kid (Sam Rockwell), and loses his inhibitions.

In outline, Tom DiCillo's third feature—following the amiable movie-movie *Living in Oblivion* and the arch retro-hip pose *Johnny Suede*—seems a celebration of regression; Al, in the throes of back-to-nature spiritual rejuvenation, even composes the quasi-Gumpism, "Life is a tomato right off the vine." But this is a film that revels in deception, setting up colossal clichés only to sidestep them by the narrowest of margins. The logic of this method grows increasingly questionable, but when it works, it nudges this id-superego buddy pic into a pleasing disequilibrium.

The subtle acting also undermines the predetermined roles. Turturro uncovers ambiguities in his straight-arrow working stiff, and newcomer Rockwell—playing a straggly-haired flake who hawks stolen garden ornaments, and lives off solar power in a tinsel-strewn trailer—somehow resists full-blown kookiness.

DiCillo's feathery comic touch makes welcome interventions throughout, and each of the few scenes that feature Catherine Keener seems almost to levitate, but *Box of Moonlight* ultimately fails to transcend its familiar premise. Worse, its philosophic side tends toward leaden metaphors (Al returns to a childhood haunt to find it contaminated; his discovery of personal freedom coincides with the Fourth of July weekend). The Kid—who's presented as some kind of latter-day Thoreau—proudly describes himself as "off the grid"; the movie, try as it might, is never quite.

Also reviewed in:
NEW YORK TIMES, 7/25/97, p. C3, Janet Maslin
NEW YORKER, 8/4/97, p. 78, Anthony Lane
VARIETY, 9/9-15/96, p. 116, David Rooney

BOXER, THE

A Universal Pictures release of a Hell's Kitchen production with the assistance of The Irish Film Board. *Producer:* Jim Sheridan. *Director:* Jim Sheridan. *Screenplay:* Jim Sheridan and Terry George. *Director of Photography:* Chris Menges. *Editor:* Gerry Hambling *Music:* Maurice Seezer, Gavin Friday, and Alex Steyermark. *Music Editor:* Maisie Weissman. *Choreographer:* Kathy O' Kennedy. *Sound:* Kieran Horgan. *Sound Editor:* Robert Hein. *Casting:* Nuala Moiselle. *Production Designer:* Brian Morris. *Art Director:* Fiona Daly and Richard Earl. *Special Effects:* Yves De Bono. *Boxing Consultant:* Barry McGuigan. *Costumes:* Joan Bergin. *Make-up:* Maire O'Sullivan. *Stunt Coordinator:* Patrick Condren. *Running time:* 107 minutes. *MPAA Rating:* R.

CAST: Daniel Day-Lewis (Danny Flynn); Daragh Donnelly, Frank Coughlan, and Sean Kearns (Prison Officers); Lorraine Pilkington (Bride); Niall Shanahan (Groom); Father John Wall (Priest); Maria McDermottroe (Betty); Oliver Maguire (Prison Governor); David McBlain (Sean); Emily Watson (Maggie); Sandra Corbally (Cake Decorator); Eleanor Methven (Patsy); Gerard McSorley (Harry); Tess Sheridan (Pianist); Brian Cox (Joe Hamill); David Hayman (Joe Hamill's Aide); Ciaran Fitzgerald (Liam); Josie Doherty (Singer); Joseph Rea (Agnes' Son); Joan Sheehy (Agnes); Peter Sheridan (Peter Mallon); Ken Stott (Ike Weir); Larry Byrne (Old Man in Shelter); Sean Brunett (Boy on Bicycle); James Hayes (Bomb Victim); Joe Gallagher (Car Bomb Driver); Jack Waters (Soldier on Roof); Richie Piggott (Sean's Helper); Padraic O'Neill (Doorman at Gym); Mark Mulholland, John Cowley, and Don Foley (Old Men in Gym); Tim McDonnell (Caretaker of Gym); Kenneth Cranham (Matt Maguire); Philip Sutcliffe (Boxer on Pads); Britta Smith (Mrs. Boots); Gavin Kennedy (Bootsy); Eamon Brown (Referee, 1st Fight); Martin Lynch (Journalist); Gavin Brown (Liam's Opponent); Noel O'Donovan (Timekeeper, 1st fight); Joe Colgan (Danny's Cornerman); Damien Denny (Eddie Carroll); Nye Heron (Eddie's Trainer); Paul Ronan (Eddie's Cornerman); Liam Carney (Mr. Walsh); Veronica Duffy (Mrs. Walsh); Des Braiden (Mr. Orr); Joan Brosnan Walsh (Mrs. Orr); Sean Donaghy (Mickey); Brian Milligan (Ned); Vinny Murphy, Mick Nolan, and Berts Folan (Danny's Supporters); Juliet Cronin (Cardgirl, 1st Fight); Kirsten Sheridan (Girl with Drinks); Mickey Tohill (Billy Patterson); Ian McElhinney (Reggie Bell); Conor Bradford (TV Announcer); Anna Meegan (Woman at 2nd Fight); Al Morris (Referee, 2nd Fight); Ian Thompson (Child at 2nd Fight); Paul Wesley (Danny's Sparring Partner); Michael James Ford (Head Waiter); John Cooke (Toastmaster); Cornelius Carr and Norman Kelly (London Fighters); Gerry Storey (Cornerman); Fred Tiedt (Referee, London Fight); Clayon Stewart (Akim); Jer O'Leary (Timekeeper, London Fight); Jules Kingelesi and Dennis Mika (Akim's Corner); David Heap (Maitre D'); John Hewitt (Ike's Drinking Buddy); Janine McGuinness (Cardgirl, London Fight); Tom Maguire (Policeman at Checkpoint).

CHRISTIAN SCIENCE MONITOR, 1/5/98, p. 10, David Sterritt

The political and religious troubles in Northern Ireland have caused untold suffering for more decades than anyone would like to remember, capturing the world's sympathy but frustrating all efforts to resolve them on a permanent basis. When a solution does arrive, part of the credit will belong to novelists, filmmakers, and other storytellers who have kept attention focused on the region's predicament in a sincere and intelligent way.

No artists stand out with more distinction in this regard than Jim Sheridan and Terry George, who coscripted "The Boxer," cinema's latest exploration of the militant Irish Republican Army and its effects on both private lives and public policies.

Sheridan and George previously wrote "In the Name of the Father," still the most incisive account of how IRA activism can affect the experiences of people entangled with it. George also wrote and directed "Some Mother's Son," based on the wrenching history of an IRA hunger strike. Sheridan's credits include "My Left Foot," an international hit for Daniel Day-Lewis, whose intensive acting gives "The Boxer" some of its most powerful moments.

The title character of "The Boxer" is a prizefighter who's spent the past 14 years in a British prison for IRA-related violence. He stayed true to his code during this long incarceration, refusing to inform on associates still at large. Returning to his old neighborhood when his sentence is over, he expects to be treated with a reasonable amount of dignity and loyalty.

But the political climate is still volatile, and old cronies are suspicious of his new desire to stay as far away from trouble as possible. Adding to the highly charged atmosphere is his renewed romance with a long-ago sweetheart. As the daughter of an IRA officer and wife of a man currently jailed for IRA activity, she has become a walking flash point for rivalry, jealousy, and territoriality among her neighbors.

As fascinating as the story of "The Boxer" frequently is, it never builds the fierce emotional power of "In the Name of the Father" or "Some Mother's Son," which were more successful at infusing their historical topics with unabashedly human feelings.

The screenplay of "The Boxer" spends too much time and energy setting up the basic situations of its plot, then does a spotty job of blending the material's personal and political aspects. The film often seems oddly detached, as if its makers were more interested in the social and cultural ingredients of their tale than in the living, breathing people who populate it.

The performances often rise above these problems. Day-Lewis reclaims his position as one of today's most dependably talented young actors, and Emily Watson follows up impressively on the promise many felt she showed in 1996's "Breaking the Waves," for which she won numerous prizes. British stage and screen veterans Brian Cox, Gerard McSorley, and Ken Stott head the solid supporting cast. Chris Menges, whose work includes Neil Jordan's historical drama "Michael Collins," did the dark-hued cinematography.

LOS ANGELES TIMES, 12/31/97, Calendar/p. 1, Kenneth Turan

Maybe it's because the situation has gone on for decades, maybe it's because internecine warfare is made for drama, but the fierce "troubles" in Northern Ireland have had so many cinematic representations the conflict's motto might well be "No justice, no peace, no end of movies."

As a result, many of the key players in "The Boxer," the latest look at the agonies of Belfast, have been involved in at least one previous film set in the North. Star Daniel Day-Lewis made "In the Name of the Father" with "The Boxer's" director/co-writer Jim Sheridan and co-writer Terry George, and George himself directed "Some Mother's Son," which he and Sheridan also co-wrote.

All this practice means that the level of craft and storytelling in "The Boxer" is lean and effective and, under Sheridan's strong direction, its story of a man trying to pick up the pieces of his life after 14 years' imprisonment for Irish Republican Army activity initially plays like a story that hasn't been told before.

But as "The Boxer" unfolds, its over-familiarity becomes a burden and, though it's a long time coming, the core of the romantic side of its plot also turns out to be old hat. The film's initially close-mouthed characters dissipate our sympathy once they start talking, and the key question becomes whether good acting can redeem borderline banal material.

One thing "The Boxer" doesn't have to apologize for is Day-Lewis' portrayal of 32-year-old Danny Flynn, who spent almost half his life behind bars. More of a chameleon than most leading men, Day-Lewis is believably hard and taciturn as a once-promising athlete who is well aware that he unwittingly tossed the heart of his athletic life away.

Known for throwing himself into his parts, Day-Lewis trained off and on for three years as a fighter, including time spent with Irish world featherweight boxing champion Barry McGuigan. He succeeded in turning himself into a world-class rope jumper and shadow boxer as well as a convincing ring tactician.

The one person most affected by Danny's release is Maggie, played by Emily Watson. She was the boxer's girlfriend before he went inside, and in the interim she has married his best friend and had a son with him. The husband, whom we never see, is also imprisoned, and the code of loyal IRA wives insists that any kind of familiar contact between her and Danny is out of the question.

This inability to communicate works very much to the film's advantage. The brooding and charismatic boxer wastes few words reconnecting with his old coach, Ike Weir (Ken Stott), and determining to reopen the nonsectarian Holy Family Boxing Club they both were affiliated with before his arrest.

Watson, memorable and Oscar-nominated in last year's "Breaking the Waves," is an actress who is Day-Lewis' match in presence, and the scenes of their constrained early communication, marked by no more than the exchange of troubled, longing looks, are especially effective.

Inevitably, these two will at least talk to each other, and when they do, you wish they'd been aware of Dianne Wiest's celebrated "don't speak" advice from "Bullets Over Broadway." They take a walk along the seashore, she tells him, "You used to make me laugh," he pleads, "I gave you up in my head but my body's crying out for you," and her son wonders what's going on. The high drama we'd imagined in our heads before these two became voluble turns out to be more involving than what they actually say.

Both the boxing saga and the romance play out against a background of standard-issue IRA dramatics. Maggie's father is IRA district leader Joe Hamill (Brian Cox), whose weary face shows the strains of constant battles with Harry (Gerard McSorley), the local hothead. Eaten up with bitterness, Harry gets high on constant violence and views the possible coming of peace as a betrayal of everything he's worked for.

In the end, as one unconvincing plot twist follows another, "The Boxer" can't sustain the initial interest it aroused. With Day-Lewis' most effective work done without words, and Watson being constrained by the limits of an underdeveloped character, this film's desire to illuminate the complexities of a terrible situation ends up unfulfilled.

NEW YORK, 1/12/98, p. 48, David Denby

Just as the Irish Troubles seem to have gone on forever, movies about the Irish Troubles have also gone on a bit, and so I may, perhaps, escape censure if I merely salute The Boxer in passing as yet another forceful, honestly made drama about Belfast, fanaticism, explosions, and the blue-gray light of desperate hope. Like In the Name of the Father, this picture was written by Terry George and directed and co-written by Jim Sheridan, and it's about an IRA man, Danny Flynn (Daniel Day-Lewis), who comes out of prison after fourteen years and no longer feels hatred for anyone. Danny wants to get back into the ring, where he was once a promising Irish fighter. He likes the discipline of training, and after so many years of numbing self-suppression, he actually needs to feel the pain of being hit. Day-Lewis brings to the role his usual rapt physical and mental absorption in what he is doing. Silent and wary much of the time, with hawklike eyes and a closed-off face, he bursts out, now and then, in tirades of memorable bitterness. The movie's acts of violence and betrayal may be familiar, but the filmmakers' obvious contempt for people given over to fanaticism is enormously welcome—a call for the most elementary kind of sanity. Even in the smallest roles, the acting is exceptionally strong. As long as such English and Irish powerhouses as Emily Watson, Brian Cox, Gerald McSorley, and Ken Stott are ready to make these movies, they will continue to be made.

NEW YORK POST, 12/31/97, p. 31, Thelma Adams

Imagine they threw a wedding reception and the groom stayed away. It's this striking situation—a prison wedding followed by a Belfast party where the bride arrives stag—that opens Jim Sheridan's gripping drama "The Boxer."

In Sheridan's most morally complex story about "the troubles" in Northern Ireland, the director and his writing partner, Terry George follow "In the Name of the Father" with a love story in which the father of the bride also becomes her jailer.

From the opening scene, Sheridan and George draw a parallel between Irishmen imprisoned in English jails and the women back home, trapped in a society where no acts are private, and Irish Republican Army loyalists monitor the fidelity of prisoners' wives.

Into this highly charged environment, and under the circling helicopters of "peacekeeping" forces during an uneasy truce, Danny (Daniel Day-Lewis) emerges from prison. He has served 14 years for an IRA bombing.

A boxer, Danny's imprisonment has left him emotionally boxed in. He returns home, silent, apolitical, alone. His primary desire? To lead a life of dignity, to fight fairly in the ring where the rules are applied equally to all. In the ring, an opponent's religion or nationality is subordinated to the power of his fists, the stamina of his legs.

As in all of Sheridan's contemporary Irish dramas, an individual's desire for autonomy conflicts with the demands of society at large. Danny's reunion With Maggie (Emily Watson) amplifies this friction.

The two parted as lovers 14 years before. Maggie, then married Danny's best friend, and mothered Liam (Ciaran Fitzgerald). Liam's father is now in prison and she is the model prisoner's wife. Maggie's IRA princess—her father is an IRA honcho—must set an example for the community.

Sheridan & Co. give urgency to Maggie and Danny's struggle toward love in this Rocky O'Balboa underdog story. Watson, who made a splashy debut and received an Oscar nomination for "Breaking the Waves," proves she is England's hottest export.

That's saying a lot in a year when English actresses Helena Bonham Carter, Kate Winslet, Julie Christie and Judi Dench should dominate the Oscars.

Watson, with her pale moon face shy of makeup and flashy mannerisms, brings a gentle strength to her mother in love. The actress' power is in her ability to listen and to make us listen with her, seeing the world anew through her honest blue eyes.

Paired with Oscar winner (for Sheridan's "My Left Foot") Day-Lewis, who cracks the strong, silent stereotype by reinventing himself yet again, Watson makes up one half of the best screen lovers of 1997.

NEWSDAY, 12/31/97, Part II/p. B14, Jack Mathews

With "The Boxer," Irish filmmakers Jim Sheridan and Terry George either complete a trilogy about the impact of war in Northern Ireland, or are drawing out a series on the futility of terrorism as an instrument of political change. Either way, it's an admirable ambition, but as works of dramatic art, let's hope they call it a trilogy and move on.

Sheridan and George have co-written all three scripts, but the first two films, "In the Name of the Father," directed by Sheridan, and "Some Mother's Son," directed by George, were based in varying degrees on factual events. "In the Name of the Father" told the story of wrongly imprisoned Gerry Conlon's long battle to win his release from a British prison. "Some Mother's Son" is about two fictional women whose sons are involved in the 1981 IRA prison hunger strike.

"The Boxer," about a paroled IRA soldier (Daniel Day-Lewis) who returns to his old neighborhood determined to rebuild his life as a non-political person, is a pure fiction. Though its scenes of violence and ravaged neighborhoods have the same jolting authenticity, it reaches for metaphors that overwork the obvious and underwork the audience.

As you might expect, the central metaphor of "The Boxer" is boxing, and the movie is so intent on drawing parallels between the senselessness of the sport and the violence in the streets, you may begin to wonder which is the primary target. One of the pivotal scenes occurs in a supper club arena in London, where Day-Lewis' Danny Flynn and his Ethiopian opponent are pulverizing each other's face, to the bloodlust encouragement of upper class Brits who seem to be parodying Romans at a gladiator outing.

For people who hold the view that boxing is an anachronism in modern society and should be outlawed, the metaphor will doubtless be poignant. To everyone else, the comparison of boxing to the troubles in Northern Ireland should be just plain asinine.

In any event, the ring and street fighting are given equal weight, along with the rekindled romance between Danny Flynn and his teenage sweetheart Maggie (Emily Watson of "Breaking the Waves"). When Danny went to prison 14 years earlier, he was 18 and disillusioned with the IRA. In prison, he didn't talk with other IRA inmates, nor did he write to Maggie, who eventually gave up on him and married his best friend.

When Danny returns, Maggie's husband is in jail, and she's raising a son on her own, while living with her father Joe Hamill (Brian Cox), a weary IRA leader. Despite her apparent interest in him, Danny keeps his distance, knowing that any sign of affection between them will be seen as treasonous by the IRA and put both their lives at risk.

Meanwhile, Danny has plans of rebuilding the local gymnasium where he had trained as a fighter, and starting a nonsectarian youth boxing program. Rescuing his embittered old trainer (Ken Stott) from the bottle, Danny goes to work, with the encouragement of the local police, who donate equipment, and to the severe consternation of diehard IRA warrior Harry (Gerard McSorley), who contributes a car bomb.

Somewhere along the way, "The Boxer" veers into clichéd boxing melodrama. There's the quiet, honest hero struggling for dignity in a savage racket; the girlfriend who stands by her man, despite pressure from the mob; the kids who turn on their idol when he disappoints them.

Day-Lewis has worked himself into incredible shape for the role; his workouts with a jump rope are dazzling. And the makeup team has reshaped the bridge of his nose to show real ring wear. However, the fight scenes themselves and they go on too long for us not to notice—are typically bogus.

Beneath all this boxing overlay is a fascinating story of a couple trying to make sense of their lives, and possibly to justify a life together, in an atmosphere that breeds irrational behavior. In some ways, the dilemma facing Danny and Maggie mirrors that of Marlon Brando's Terry Malloy, another fighter, and Eva Marie Saint's Edie Doyle in "On the Waterfront." They both want to do the right thing, and the obstacles in their path ultimately fuel their passion.

Boxing served as that film's metaphor for violence, too. But "Waterfront" director Elia Kazan knew better than to devote actual time to the ring, and risk the damage that its phony choreography could do to the reality-based story, let alone allow it to be overwhelm the essential human drama. Sheridan and George obviously have the best intentions, but by linking a sport to a grand scale human tragedy, they've overstated the horror of one at the expense of the other.

NEWSWEEK, 1/12/98, p. 61, David Ansen

The Boxer reunites Daniel Day-Lewis, director Jim Sheridan and writer Terry George, the team who brought you the rousing "In the Name of the Father," in another highly charged tale of the Irish Troubles. Where the earlier film effectively worked up an audience's loathing of the English, the villains of the new piece are the hard-core fanatics of the IRA, who will do anything to fan the flames of war.

Danny (Day-Lewis), a former boxer of promise, was once an IRA member himself. Now, out of jail after 14 years, he renounces violence and starts a boxing club that will admit both Protestant and Catholic kids. Strong, silent and haunted, Danny carries inside him a loathing for his IRA past and an unspoken love for his old sweetheart Maggie (Emily Watson). She still loves him, too, but matters are not so simple. She's married to a political prisoner, her son resents Danny's romantic presence in her life and her father (Brian Cox) is an IRA leader trying to negotiate a truce that the more rabid members of his fold would like to undermine. Any impropriety on his daughter's part could be ruinous for his cause.

"The Boxer" is three movies in one: a love story with as many obstacles keeping the lovers apart as "Romeo and Juliet"; a boxing story, complete with an alcoholic trainer who sobers up when Danny Boy, returning to the ring, gives him a will to go on, and a political drama replete with car bombings, assassinations and the by-now-familiar vision of war-ravaged Belfast streets. The fusion of these three formulas results in some explosive drama, but also in a sense of *déjà vu*. There's one too many melodramatic elements in "The Boxer" for its own good. The situation in Northern Ireland is tragic enough in its own right; it hardly needs such a hard sell to tell us what we already know.

What holds the movie together is the fiercely self-contained commitment of Day-Lewis's performance and the palpable chemistry between him and Watson. When two performers of such intensity train their amorous energy upon each other, there's bound to be a laserlike heat. Cox plays Maggie's conciliatory father with brooding, blunt power, and Gerard McSorley is the somewhat too broadly villainous IRA fanatic Harry, eager to exploit Danny and Maggie's relationship for political gain. It's hard to deny "The Boxer's" power; it's equally hard not to notice the strain to achieve it.

SIGHT AND SOUND, 3/98, p. 41, Geoffrey Macnab

Belfast. After 14 years in prison, ex-IRA member and boxing hero Danny Flynn is released. He bumps into Ike, a drunk who used to coach the local boxing team. Danny and Ike decide to reopen the gym which brings Danny into contact with his old sweetheart, Maggie, who works next door. Danny's rejection of terrorism bewilders his old colleagues. He and Maggie still have strong feelings for each other, but while he was behind bars, she married his best friend, also an IRA member, now in prison himself. Maggie risks being ostracised if she starts an affair with another man.

The gym blossoms, attracting young fighters from both sides of the sectarian divide. The IRA declares a ceasefire. This is put in jeopardy when a senior RUC officer is blown up outside the venue during Danny's second comeback fight. In the ensuing riots, Maggie's teenage son Liam, jealous of her relationship with Danny, sets fire to the gym. Danny goes to London to pursue his career as a fighter. Ike is murdered after taunting Harry, an embittered ultra-violent IRA veteran who is opposed to the peace process.

Danny comes back to Belfast and starts seeing Maggie again. She has been warned that her father Joe, a prominent IRA leader, can no longer protect Danny. When she and Danny are driving through the city, they're stopped by a band of IRA thugs led by Harry. The thugs look set to kill Danny, but at the last minute, the assassin levels the gun at Harry instead. The attack was a smokescreen: it was Harry that the IRA leadership wanted dead all along.

Whether they are stories of ferociously driven fighters who lose all sense of moral perspective in their drive to reach the top, or grim tales of losers on their way down, boxing movies tend to focus on individuals. Think of John Garfield in *Body and Soul* (1947), Kirk Douglas in *Champion* (1949), Robert Ryan in *The Set-Up* (1949) or De Niro in *Raging Bull* (1980): in each of these films, bravura performances are delivered by actors prepared to suffer as much as the fighters they portray. On one level, *The Boxer* conforms to this type. It has been well publicised that its star, Daniel Day-Lewis, spent three years preparing for his role as Danny, two of them under the watchful eye of his personal trainer, ex-World Champ Barry McGuigan, who professed himself suitably impressed with Day-Lewis' talent in the ring.

Terry George's screenplay is not embarrassed about invoking old fight- movie clichés. The opening image—a shot of Day-Lewis in the distance, shadow boxing in the prison court-yard—might have been borrowed from Scorsese. Danny is the boxer as loner, a taciturn, introspective figure with a streak of masochism. He welcomes the blows he receives in the ring, he tells his beloved Maggie, because they make him feel pain, and after 14 years behind bars, his emotions are frozen. With his close-cropped hair and awesome self-discipline, he is like a Jesuit priest with gloves. The sub-plot, about an old drunk (played with rambunctious charm by Ken Stott) who does his bit for community relations by reopening the boxing gym, echoes the storyline of Shane Meadows' forthcoming, *TwentyFourSeven* and of countless other sports yarns of years past.

There are the obligatory slow-motion fight sequences with reverberating thwacks on the soundtrack whenever anyone lands a blow. The film-makers go out of their way to present a convincing portrait of the fighters' world. They show the training routines in meticulous detail and chart that strange father/son bond which inevitably blossoms between the wily old coach and his young charge. Even so, the fact that Danny is a boxer is ultimately an irrelevance. It doesn't affect the relationship between the various characters, all of them part of a closely knit community where ordinary values have been distorted by the years of violence.

Chris Menges' brilliant cinematography provides an austere but often lyrical backcloth. His lighting accentuates the desolation of a city under siege. Apart from the blood in the ring, there are precious few primary colours. Skies always seem grey. Using aerial photography of Belfast, as if shot by surveillance helicopters, and the mandatory footage of British soldiers and RUC officers at checkpoints, the street scenes aim for documentary-style realism. Sheridan clearly knows this world from the inside. There is one extraordinary sequence in which Joe, an IRA leader, pays a visit to his daughter Maggie. As curtains are pulled apart, where interior walls used to be there's nothing, and we realise that the entire street is like a warren. Joe and his minders pass from house to house without ever going outdoors. By honing in on the relationship between Danny and Maggie (and the opposition to it), Sheridan and George try to show in microcosm the misunderstandings, lingering bitterness and bigotry which threaten the peace process as a whole. The plotting is a little contrived. Danny and Ike's gym just happens to be in the same building that Maggie works in. Danny's transition from former jailbird into fully fledged professional boxer is remarkably swift. There are constant references to the past—in particular to some murky incident in which Danny was betrayed by fellow IRA recruit Harry—but we never learn quite what happened or why. *The Boxer* suffers from a certain generic confusion—it seems unsure whether it wants to be a sports movie, a romance or a political drama.

Nevertheless, Sheridan directs the set-pieces—the fight sequences, riots and fires—with plenty of gusto while eliciting quietly intense performances from Day-Lewis and Emily Watson as Maggie. George's screenplay may deal in stereotypes, but it also acknowledges the complexity of the political situation. The martyr-like Danny apart, there are no clear-cut heroes or villains. From Brian Cox's battle-weary IRA chief to the belligerent, bloodthirsty Harry, everybody is scarred by the years of conflict. As in *Some Mother's Son* (George's directorial debut, co-written with Sheridan), there is an attempt to foreground women's experiences—to show how the machismo and brutality of the menfolk distorts their lives too. The image of the dead terrorist cradled by his grief-stricken wife may be an obvious one, but it still makes its point.

TIME, 1/12/98, p. 84, Richard Corliss

A critic of mild demeanor (aren't we all?) sat in a screening room, sucking on a Ricola as he watched *The Boxer*, with Daniel Day-Lewis as Danny Flynn, a Belfast prize fighter unjustly jailed on a bombing rap, and Emily Watson as the girl he left behind. The critic dutifully tabulated each blunt plot point, each refried cliché ("I'm not a killer, Maggie, but this place makes me want to kill"). And yet, when Danny's nemesis did something monstrously rotten, the critic was so enraged by the dastardly act that he had to stop himself from spitting his candy at the screen. Extraordinary how potent cheap movies are.

The mass audience has paid scant attention to films about the Irish Troubles, but this one may find friends precisely because it renounces political nuance for emotional bullying and old Hollywood-style blarney. The movie's forebears are '30s Warner Bros. melodramas like *Kid Galahad* (a fighter and his trainer KO the crooks) and *Angels with Dirty Faces* (the Dead End Kids learn who's the real tough guy). *The Boxer* could even be a *Going My Way* without priests—it's that hokey.

Jim Sheridan, the director and co-writer here, who also worked with Day-Lewis on *My Left Foot* and *In the Name of the Father*, may have figured that subtlety has no place in a story about the lunatic fervor of Irish extremist politics. Or maybe he figured his cast could make the gritty fantasy plausible. Day-Lewis very nearly does. His laser stare and world-class rope skipping, his very devotion to the project, elevate the film to check-it-out status and get the crowd cheering for him and his quest. Even in a slim tale like *The Boxer*, Day-Lewis is the serious-actor, movie-star goods.

VILLAGE VOICE, 1/6/98, p. 66, Dennis Lim

As a tale of hopeless love in a hopeless situation, *The Boxer* makes the spectacularly hollow romance of *Titanic* look even more fraudulent. Northern Ireland may not be as picturesque as a sinking ship (some would argue the similarities), but the latest Jim Sheridan-Terry George collaboration is, for its relative understatement, perhaps the year's most visceral love story.

With a typically obsessive three-year training period under his belt, Daniel Day-Lewis stars as Danny Flynn, a Belfast boxer and former IRA member who's spent virtually all his adult life behind bars (his face somewhere between gaunt and chiseled, Day-Lewis definitely looks the part). Released from prison at age 32, Danny promptly returns home, to the scene of old grudges and festering secrets, in the hope of a reconciliation with his teenage sweetheart Maggie (Emily

Watson). The daughter of an IRA big gun, she's now unhappily married to Danny's best friend (since imprisoned), with whom she has a young son.

Sheridan and George's script relies on the actors to inhabit the most awkward gaps; seeing each other for the first time in 14 years, Danny and Maggie are initially able to communicate only in embarrassed glances and silences. "We're not kids anymore," Maggie insists. "But we are" counters Danny—and he's right. At heart, they're two smitten teens, cruelly stopped in their tracks, and starting over is proving all but impossible. The film owes much of its vigor to the two leads. Habitually electrifying, Day-Lewis is an actor who practically charges his surroundings and in Danny, he has his most substantial role in years. As for Watson, few young actresses can match her uncanny instincts.

The wholly convincing central romance notwithstanding, there's a certain depressing familiarity to *The Boxer*—the violence is numbingly predictable, dead-meat characters are instantly identifiable. Sheridan and George were attacked by segments of the British press for *In the Name of the Father* and *Some Mother's Son*, fact-based movies that weren't afraid to take creative liberties, but *The Boxer* should prove uncontroversial even among their harshest critics. A reformed rebel "now fighting within the rules" (as a fight promoter puts it), the title figure embodies the film's political message.

Sheridan and George sketchily outline the split of the IRA into pro-and anti-violence factions, and their film set against the backdrop of a fitful ceasefire, is unequivocal in taking sides—to the extent that Harry (Gerard McSorley), the character who symbolizes the hard line, is an all-out thug, and—boo, hiss—also the main obstacle standing in the way of the lovers' happiness.

Film's inherent reductiveness has rarely been more evident than in the growing subgenre of Northern Ireland political dramas (let's not even consider Hollywood's attempts), but *The Boxer*—a hard look at the personal toll of a culture of violence—succeeds largely by keeping its ambitions on a human scale.

Also reviewed in:
CHICAGO TRIBUNE, 1/9/98, Friday/p. A, Michael Wilmington
NEW REPUBLIC, 2/9/98, p. 27, Stanley Kauffmann
NEW YORK TIMES, 12/31/97, p. E1, Janet Maslin
NEW YORKER, 1/19/98, p. 86, Daphne Merkin
VARIETY, 12/22/97-1/4/98, p. 59, Todd McCarthy
WASHINGTON POST, 1/9/98, Weekend/p. 41, Desson Howe

BOYFRIENDS

A First Run Features release of an Essex Features presentation. *Producer:* Neil Hunter and Tom Hunsinger. *Director:* Neil Hunter and Tom Hunsinger. *Screenplay:* Neil Hunter and Tom Hunsinger. *Director of Photography:* Richard Tisdall. *Editor:* John Trumper. *Sound:* Alan Snelling. *Art Director:* James Dearlove. *Running time:* 82 minutes. *MPAA Rating:* Not Rated.

CAST: James Dreyfus (Paul); Michael Urwin (Matt); David Coffey (Will); Mark Sands (Ben); Andrew Ableson (Owen); Darren Petrucci (Adam); Michael McGrath (James); Russell Higgs (Mark).

NEW YORK POST, 2/14/97, p. 50, Larry Worth

Love is definitely in the air when three couples spend the weekend at an English country estate to discuss, discard and discover "Boyfriends."

As they make up to break up, the fact that all the participants are male doesn't really matter. But the fact that all the participants are cliches matters a lot.

The story opens by introducing Paul and Ben, Matt and Owen, Will and Adam in separate vignettes. But they're all variations on He-Man and Nancy Boy, stereotypes that have been done to death from "The Boys in the Band" to "Love! Valour! Compassion!"

After more than an hour of musical beds, secret confessions and enough soap opera twists to dwarf "Dynasty," the big question emerges. Which pair of lithesome lovers will survive the weekend? Better still, who cares?

As directed and written by Neil Hunter and Tom Hunsinger, the results are consistently predictable. Heck, they even drag out the old "Lets make a movie" routine, giving each participant the chance to sit in front of a video camera and spill his guts.

The overall structure is equally hackneyed. It's either A) endless talk sessions as couples find and lose that loving feeling or B) musical montages of packing, primping and playing Twister. Welcome to the world of deja vu, ad infinitum.

On the plus side, the pairings are never graphic, the filmmakers maintained good production values on a relatively low budget, and the actors—all unknowns with the exception of James ("Absolutely Fabulous") Dreyfus—are at least palatable.

But the real highlight is hearing classic songstress Dinah Washington warble "I Wish I Knew the Name of the Boy in My Dreams" over the end credits. Then again, her unique sense of style shows what was missing in "Boyfriends" all along.

VILLAGE VOICE, 2/25/97, p. 72, Laurie Stone

The shoestring look of *Boyfriends* and its improvised casualness sit cozily, like a lap rug before the fire, as three gay male couples romp during a country weekend. The film, which cost $25,000 and was shot in 18 days, developed from interviews Brit writer-directors Neil Hunter and Tom Hunsinger conducted with 100 actors, sifting through life stories and fantasies to arrive at a spectrum of types. There's the rough-hewn, randy 20-year-old Adam, who squashes a tube of lube while making a morning getaway. There's Will, the older social worker who once counseled him and with whom Adam tricks. Nerdy and romantic Matt wants narcissist Owen to move in with him after three months of dating. And long-suffering Ben identifies with a dying plant abused by his lover of five years, morose, bitchy Paul.

We got shades of Chekhov and *The Return of the Secaucus Seven,* and a pinch of *Boys in the Band,* as Paul digs into sore spots with his video camera. Now dalliances sprout and wither, confessions dart from breasts, and potatoes are peeled with so much sullen woundedness that the skins fly off in oneness with the peeler's vulnerability. Some dialogue clanks and the acting's uneven, but these blemishes go with the turf—friendly pimples on verité complexions. The movie weaves a spell with its simple focus: What do men want? Not success in the world, or money. We don't even learn how most of the characters earn their livings. Men want love, even if they are sometimes wont, in the woods, to drop trou for a wanking with a stranger. Quotidian comfort earns its prominence: good jam at breakfast, someone to name bullshit, pleasure at greetings, the right moment for pig noises.

Also reviewed in:
NEW YORK TIMES, 2/14/97, p. C12, Stephen Holden
VARIETY, 3/25-31/96, p. 69, Derek Elley

BOYS LIFE 2

A Strand Releasing release. *Running time:* 74 minutes. *MPAA Rating:* Not Rated.

MUST BE THE MUSIC: *Producer:* Rafi Stephan. *Director:* Nickolas Perry. *Screenplay:* Nickolas Perry. *Director of Photography:* Steve Adcock. *Editor:* Craig A. Colton. *Sound:* John Roberts. *Casting:* Aaron Griffith. *Running time:* 20 minutes.

CAST: Michael Saucedo (Eric); Justin Urich (Kevin); Travis Sher (Dave); Milo Ventimiglia (Jason).

NUNZIO'S SECOND COUSIN: *Executive Producer:* Camille Taylor.   *Director:* Tom DeCerchio. *Screenplay:* Tom DeCerchio. *Director of Photography:* Steve Poster. *Editor:* Mike Murphy. *Music:* Robert Folk. *Casting:* Ferne Cassel. *Art Director:* James Stewart. *Running time:* 18 minutes.

CAST: Vincent D'Onofrio (Tony Randozza); Miles Perlich (Jimmy);   Eileen Brennan (Mrs. Randozza); Harry Walters, Jr. (Tony's Date).

ALKALI, IOWA: *Producer:* Anne Ruark. *Director:* Mark Christopher. *Screenplay:* Mark Christopher. *Director of Photography:* Jami Silverstein. *Editor:* Gloria Whittemore. *Music:* Julian Harris. *Art Director:* Ed Check. *Running time:* 17 minutes.

CAST: Mary Beth Hurt (June Gudmanson); J.D. Cerna (Jack Gudmanson); Kent Broadhurst (Blondie); Ellen Hamilton-Latzen (Carol); Ed Seamon (Bill Gudmanson); Greg Villepique (Jacko).

TREVOR: *Producer:* Peggy Rajski and Randy Stone. *Director:* Peggy Rajski. *Screenplay:* James Lecesne. *Director of Photography:* Marc Reshovsky. *Editor:* John Tintori. *Music:* Danny Troob. *Art Director:* Leslie McDonand. *Casting:* Avy Kaufman. *Running time:* 19 minutes.

CAST: Brett Barsky (Trevor); Stephen Tobolowsky (Father Joe); Judy Kain (Trevor's Mom); John Lizzi (Trevor's Dad); Jonah Rooney (Pinky); Allen Doraine (Walter).

VILLAGE VOICE, 3/11/97, p. 78, Abby McGanney Nolan

Two years ago, *Boys Life,* an anthology of gay-themed shorts, turned into a surprise hit. Quick on the uptake, the folks at Strand Releasing have assembled four more coming-of-age dramas to rouse moviegoers, memories. Production values have been upped—rather radically—but the first anthology's upbeat outlook has been retained. Satisfaction is in sight for these boys.

Nunzio's Second Cousin stars Vincent D'Onofrio as a gay, loose-cannon cop who invites a homophobe to Sunday dinner. In *Must Be the Music,* four high school kids cruise Los Angeles's nightlife—three are gay and one is along for the ride—but the tale is a little too abbreviated for its own good. From Mark Christopher, the director now at work on a Studio 54 feature, comes *Alkali, Iowa,* a well-filmed farmboy's story of connecting the dots. The highlight is *Trevor,* writer James Lecesne and director Peggy Rajski's portrait of a 13-year-old suburbanite (sweetly played by Brett Barsky) who loves his Diana Ross records and just can't got excited about the girl next door. His parents do their best to ignore Trevor's nicely staged mock-suicides, but he's an irrepressible soul and decides to go ahead with life anyway.

Also reviewed in:
CHICAGO TRIBUNE, 8/15/97, Friday/p. E, John Petrakis
NEW YORK TIMES, 3/7/97, p. C12, Stephen Holden
VARIETY, 3/10-16/97, p. 79, Emanuel Levy

BRASSED OFF

A Miramax Films and Channel Four Films presentation of a Steve Abbott/Prominent Features production. *Producer:* Steve Abbott. *Director:* Mark Herman. *Screenplay:* Mark Herman. *Director of Photography:* Andy Collins. *Editor:* Mike Ellis. *Music:* Trevor Jones. *Brass Band Music:* John Anderson. *Sound:* Peter Lindsay and (music) Simon Rhodes. *Sound Editor:* Dennis McTaggart. *Casting:* Priscilla John and Julia Duff. *Production Designer:* Don Taylor. *Art Director:* Felicity Joll. *Set Decorator:* Brian Read. *Costumes:* Amy Roberts. *Make-up:* Tricia Cameron. *Stunt Coordinator:* Sean McCabe. *Running time:* 107 minutes. *MPAA Rating:* R.

CAST: Pete Postlethwaite (Danny); Tara Fitzgerald (Gloria); Ewan McGregor (Andy); Stephen Tompkinson (Phil); Jim Carter (Harry); Philip Jackson (Jim); Peter Martin (Ernie); Sue Johnston (Vera); Mary Healey (Ida); Lill Roughley (Rita); Melanie Hill (Sandra); Peter Gunn (Simmo); Stephen Moore (McKenzie); Ken Colley (Greasley); Olga Grahame (Mrs. Foggan); Toni Garlacki (Gary); Sky Ingram (Kylie); Luke McGann (Shane); Christopher Tetlow (Craig); Bernard Wrigley (Chapman); Ken Kitson (Heavy 1); Adrian Hood (Heavy 2); Sally Adams (Ward Sister); Tubby Andrews (Bus Driver); Katherine Dow Beyton (Nurse); Adam Fogerty (Miner); Vanessa Knox-Mawer (Mother 2); Sally Ann Matthews (Waitress); Jacqueline Naylor (Mother 1); Bob Rodgers (Halifax Judge); Max Smith (Nightwatchman); Ronnie Stevens (Albert Hall Judge); Peter Wallis (Elderly Man).

LOS ANGELES TIMES, 5/23/97, Calendar/p. 9, John Anderson

[The following review by John Anderson appeared in a slightly different form in
NEWSDAY, 5/23/97, Part II/p. B8.]

The recent near-expurgation of Tories from British political life may take some of the wind out of "Brassed Off," a very earnest David vs. Goliath tale that also pitches art vs. livelihood and Margaret Thatcher vs. the rest of humanity. But not to worry. It's got plenty of wind to spare.

Written and directed by Mark Herman—last seen perpetrating the Bronson Pinchot comedy "Blame It on the Bellboy"—"Brassed Off" takes place in the aptly named town of Grimley, where the Thatcher government is preparing to close the local coal mine. This will effectively render the town obsolete, its people unemployable, its families torn asunder and the local brass band defunct—not necessarily in that order.

To the band's conductor, Danny (Pete Postlethwaite), the Grimley Colliery Band is not just the town's major concern, it's the only concern. Oblivious to the upcoming "redundancy" vote in which the town's miners will decide whether to keep the colliery open or take a government buyout, Danny is intent on taking the band to the national finals at Albert Hall, even as his players—including his son Phil (Stephen Tompkinson)—are busy watching their world collapse.

Postlethwaite is terrifically moving and "Brassed Off" is his movie, even if Andy and Gloria—played by Ewan McGregor ("Trainspotting," "Emma") and Tara Fitzgerald ("Hear My Song," "Sirens," "The Englishman Who Went Up a Hill . . .")—dominate the action as each other's love interest. They are fine, and fine together, despite their mini-crisis. Gloria, unbeknownst to anyone in town, works for the British Coal Board, which poses obvious problems for miner and horn player Andy. But it's Postlethwaite's Danny who represents all the movie's key themes: the self absorption of art, the art of self absorption and the Nero-esque disposition of a British public whose industry is being kicked out from under it.

The difficulty is that "Brassed Off" operates at an emotional pitch that starts at a crescendo and never relents—rendering almost everything equally inconsequential. When local-girl-made-good Gloria adds her fluegelhorn to the colliery band—playing an excerpt from Roderigo's "Concierto de Aranjuez" as if she were conservatory-trained—we have an emotional peak. When the band plays "Danny Boy" outside Danny's hospital room—"black lung" having laid him low—we have another (given that the group can make a 12-by-20 room sound like Carnegie Hall, the question becomes: If not mining, why not a world tour?).

When Andy plays pool to redeem his horn from a local hustler and thus make the trip to the finals, we have one more irresistible catharsis. And at the end, there are so many emotional peaks you might feel like one of Thatcher's miners—manipulated, misled and maneuvered into an emotional corner.

Sloppily dubbed (to avoid moments of troublesome dialect) and, equally sentimental, "Brassed Off" provides a colorful cast of characters, but its tone is never as casual as it should be. The vulgarity is too deliberate, the jokes too forced. This kind of thing has been done well, of course, but not necessarily here.

NEW YORK POST, 5/23/97, p. 50, Thelma Adams

In Steven Spielberg's "The Lost World, Etc.," Pete Postlethwaite plays a supporting role. His great white hunter tracks the ultimate trophy: a T. rex buck.

In Mark Herman's micro-budgeted "Brassed Off," bravely opening today in the dino's shadow, Postlethwaite stars as a member of an endangered species: a Yorkshire coal miner in Maggie Thatcher's England.

While coughing up black bits of lung, Pete draws a paycheck from the "pit" and satisfies his soul by leading the legendary Grimley Colliery Band. He's no radical. The brass band is everything to him. But there's a problem: if the Tories shut the mine, can the band play on?

Herman, who directed and wrote the script, fills the ensemble with a cast of offbeat characters. Toothy Tara Fitzgerald ("Sirens") is a local girl made good.

When she returns home and blows her fluegelhorn, the band will follow her almost anywhere—until they discover she works for management.

Fitzgerald's love interest is hot new thing Ewan McGregor ("Trainspotting"). Playing the youngest union activist, the actor often disappears behind bruised, downcast eyes. Stephen Tompkinson, the band leader's trombonist son, stands out as a good egg who cracks under the strain of supporting a family and the bitter irony of moonlighting as a clown.

Like the band leader he plays, Postlethwaite, the pale actor with the thrusting cheekbones ("The Usual Suspects"), holds the ensemble together. His stubborn, brooding miner earns the band's respect—and ours. His awakening to the larger world outside the brass band repertoire and radicalization—is an emotional achievement.

By turns simplistic and sentimental, Herman undermines the dramatic power of "Brassed Off." His bald Thatcher-bashing seems tired, particularly in light of the recent rise of England's Labor Party. A shot of a clown dangling by a rope from Grimley Colliery is so much clumsier than Postlethwaite's wrenching transition.

"Brassed Off" opens and closes with written definitions, real and tongue-in-cheek. In the opening credits we learn the title is slang for ticked off. At the end, for "conclusion," we are told to draw our own. The problem is that Herman is not brave enough to let us.

SIGHT AND SOUND, 11/96, p. 44, Geoffrey Macnab

A small mining community in North Yorkshire, 1992. As the Tory Government prepares for a fresh round of pit closures, the local colliery band practises for a forthcoming national competition. Several band members, convinced that their pit is doomed, want to quit, but they're held in line by their passionate band leader, Danny. Their spirits soon revive when they're joined by Gloria, the beautiful granddaughter of a former band leader, who has recently returned to her hometown to take up a new job.

Gloria starts an affair with band member Andy, her former childhood sweetheart. Their relationship is interrupted when Andy and his colleagues discover she is researching the viability of their pit for the British Coal Board. The brass band wins the National semifinals. But the musicians' celebrations are cut short by the news that their miners have voted for redundancy. Danny, whose health is precarious from a lifetime in the pits, collapses with pneumoconiosis and is rushed to hospital. His son, Phil, imprisoned during the 1984 miner's strike, is still trying to pay off old debts. Loan sharks have stripped Phil's house bare and his wife and children have left him. He attempts suicide.

The colliery band play what they imagine is their final concert outside the hospital where Danny is recovering. They can't afford to take up their rightful position in the finals, which are to be held in the Albert Hall, London. However, Gloria, who now realises she was hoodwinked by her British Coal bosses, offers to stump up the £3000 needed. The band travel to London and sure enough win the competition. Danny, who has sneaked away from his hospital bed, joins them on stage and makes an emotive speech about how the miners have been betrayed.

Colliery brass bands, like Methodist choirs, temperance leagues and working men's clubs, seem anachronistic—throwbacks to Britain's lost industrial past. A film about them risks lapsing into cosy nostalgia for the working-class culture described so evocatively in Richard Hoggart's *The Uses of Literacy;* an "authentic" culture predicated on home, hearth and workplace, the antithesis of the "ersatz" values represented by consumerism, rock'n'roll, television and Hollywood. Even in 1957, Hoggart was writing as if this culture was in terminal decline. *Brassed Off,* set during the pit closures of 1992, suggests how prolonged its dying throes have been.

On the surface, this seems another British comedy along Ealing lines in which a small community fights back against the big, bad bureaucrats who are destroying its way of life. Early on, as the band members grumble about the kitty, make chauvinistic remarks behind the back of their new woman recruit Gloria (they witlessly dub her "Gloria Stitts") and go on a drunken bus tour of nearby villages, the film strikes a deceptively whimsical note. Writer-director Mark Herman (who made the comedy *Blame It on the Bellboy)* doesn't skimp on the stereotypes. The coal board boss (Stephen Moore) is as oleaginous as any pantomime villain. The miners' wives gossip under hair dryers and henpeck their husbands. Even the love affair between Gloria (Tara Fitzgerald), a Coal Board 'mole', and young band member Andy (Ewan McGregor) seems strictly routine. Rambunctious character performances, notably from Jim Carter, an ageing teddy boy who always spends a small eternity combing his quiff after stints at the coal face, and Philip Jackson, who scowls and hisses venom at 'scabs', are combined with moments of knockabout comedy, and a happy ending. The music itself is surprisingly rousing and emotional, a swirl of flugelhorns, trumpets, cymbals and trombones.

However, beneath the cheerful bluster, a much darker, sadder story is being told. The shadow of the 1984 strike hangs over the film. "10 years ago," one of the band members is told by his wife, "you were so full of fight. Now you just blow your bloody trumpet." There is a sense that the band's struggle to stay in existence is just a coda to a battle which has already been lost. It comes as no surprise when the miners, lured by Coal Board redundancy bribes vote themselves out of a job in the ballot which closes their pits.

It's rare for mainstream British filmmakers to tackle class and politics as directly as Herman does here. His approach isn't subtle in the slightest. Every so often, the narrative is held in suspension as characters deliver some piece of soap box oratory. At one point, part-time clown Phil interrupts a performance for well-off kids at the local church to launch into a bitter tirade against the evil baroness, Thatcher. The fact that he's still wearing his red nose, silly hat and oversize shoes gives the rant a surreal, disconcerting quality, but such didacticism is hardly necessary: simply showing Phil's predicament—he's skint and suicidal, his wife and kids have abandoned him, his father is ill in hospital, loan sharks have ransacked his house—spells out the same message in much more effective fashion. That said, the equally emotional speech coughed out by his ailing band leader father Danny (beautifully, very solemnly, played by Peter Postlethwaite) at the Championship Finals in London works perfectly. just when the film is threatening to turn into a saccharine wish-fulfilment fantasy, Danny's rasping words bring viewers back to the reality of the story. The pit has closed and the band members are all without work. Even the band's future is uncertain. As one character observes, "you can't have a colliery band without a bloody colliery."

It's easy to imagine *Brassed Off* shorn of its star names and done in far bleaker fashion. By the same token, it could also have been made—in defiance of the events it portrays—as an out and out feelgood movie. Instead, Herman steers a middle course. The sheer gravitas of such actors as Pete Postlethwaite, Jim Carter and Philip Jackson ensures that the miner-musicians never seem like comic caricatures. Stephen Tompkinson's mercurial performance, which sees him clowning one minute, lurching close to despair the next, sums up the way the film as a whole oscillates in mood. Still, as a tribute to the defiance of a community under siege, as an indictment of those who betrayed it, as a gritty, melancholic comedy, and most of all as a celebration of the big brass band, *Brassed Off* rings loud and clear.

VILLAGE VOICE, 5/27/97, Film Supplement/p. 22, Amy Taubin

A blast against nearly two decades of Tory rule (and, by implication, the cool 'n' cynical British films it inspired), *Brassed Off* is an old-fashioned leftist political-consciousness-raiser paced by a rousing brass-band score.

The setting is a small town in northern England where a still-viable coal mine is about to be shut down, making several thousand workers redundant. Unlike the dozens of British documentaries made in the '80s about the miners' strike, *Brassed Off* embraces populist entertainment values. Taking the decimation of the British coal-mining industry as a given, it focuses on how workers, deprived of a livelihood that goes back generations, can retain their sense of identity and community.

Danny (Pete Postlethwaite), a retired miner, is the leader of the Grimley marching band. He believes it to be the expression of the Grimley community and history and that it must continue. Pete is secretly dying of black lung disease. It's not until his condition becomes clear to the band members that they rally to his cause and, in so doing, discover a way to make their voices heard.

Ably directed by Mark Herman, who balances uplift and pathos without leaving one feeling overly manipulated, *Brassed Off* is buoyed by a half-dozen performances. In addition to the flinty Postlethwaite, there are Tara Fitzgerald and Ewan McGregor as the young lovers (McGregor, who starred in *Trainspotting* and whose penis is prettily on view in the soon-to-open *The Pillow Book,* is that rare thing, an unabashedly romantic actor). Best of all is Stephen Tompkinson in his feature-film debut as Danny's son, torn between his loyalty to his father and the demands of being a provider for his wife and kids. Danny's only source of income is the clown act he performs at children's parties; he faces tragedy in three-foot-long shoes. Like the film itself, Tompkinson barges clumsily into melodrama and with a fine sense of truth.

Also reviewed in:
NEW REPUBLIC, 6/9/97, p. 30, Stanley Kauffmann
NEW YORK TIMES, 5/23/97, p. C16, Stephen Holden
NEW YORKER, 5/26/97, p. 88, Anthony Lane
VARIETY, 10/28-11/3/96, p. 71, Derek Elley
WASHINGTON POST, 5/30/97, p. B7, Stephen Hunter
WASHINGTON POST, 5/30/97, Weekend/p. 41, Desson Howe

BREAKDOWN

A Paramount Pictures release in association with Dino De Laurentiis and Spelling Films. *Executive Producer:* Jonathan Fernandez and Harry Colomby. *Producer:* Martha De Laurentiis and Dino DeLaurentiis. *Director:* Jonathan Mostow. *Screenplay:* Jonathan Mostow and Sam Montgomery. *Story:* Jonathan Mostow. *Director of Photography:* Doug Milsome. *Editor:* Derek Brechin and Kevin Stitt. *Music:* Basil Poledouris. *Music Editor:* Daryl B. Kell. *Sound:* Felipe Borrero (music) Timothy Boyle. *Sound Editor:* Jon Johnson. *Casting:* Carol Lewis. *Production Designer:* Victoria Paul. *Art Director:* Lee Mayman. *Set Decorator:* Peg Cummings. *Special Effects:* Rick Zarro and Ron Zarro. *Costumes:* Terry Dresbach. *Make-up:* Dennis Liddiard, Jr. *Stunt Coordinator:* Jim Arnett and Pat Romano. *Running time:* 105 minutes. *MPAA Rating:* R.

CAST: Kurt Russell (Jeff Taylor); J.T. Walsh (Red Barr); Kathleen Quinlan (Amy Taylor); M.C. Gainey (Earl); Jack Noseworthy (Billy); Rex Linn (Sherriff Boyd); Ritch Brinkley (Al); Moira Harris (Arleen Barr); Kim Robillard (Deputy Len Carter); Thomas Kopache (Calhoun); Jack McGee (Bartender); Vincent Berry (Deke Barr); Helen Duffy (Flo); Ancel Cook (Barfly); Gene Hartline (Tow Truck Driver); Steven Waddington (Cowboy in Bank); Rick Sanders (Truck Stop Trucker).

LOS ANGELES TIMES, 5/2/97, Calendar/p. 1, Jack Mathews

[The following review by Jack Mathews appeared in a slightly different form in **NEWSDAY, 5/2/97, Part II/p. B2.]**

It's so simple, it ought to be banal. A couple on a cross-country drive from New England to Southern California are stranded with engine trouble on a desolate stretch of highway in the Southwest desert. A passing truck pulls over, and its friendly driver offers them a ride to a nearby diner where they can call for help. The husband stays with the car; the wife goes with the trucker ... and vanishes.

The rest of writer-director Jonathan Mostow's "Breakdown" follows the confused and frantic husband's attempts to find his wife and rescue her from kidnappers. Mostow, with his first feature, has made such a convincing, fast-paced, edge-of-the-seat thriller that you'd swear you'd never seen anything quite like it.

We did see these kinds of movies regularly in the pre-computer, pre-marketing era of Hollywood, when a special effect might be a matte shot or a car stunt instead of a computer-generated volcano, and when the thrills came through our identification with the characters' distress rather than some sense-battering, optical ooh-aah.

Mostow has gone back to that style, with a flair that Hitchcock would have appreciated. In fact, "Breakdown" loosely plays off the wrong-man theme so favored by the suspense master.

Jeff Taylor, played with absolute conviction by Kurt Russell, is an ordinary man forced to muster his wits and courage to fight against forces who think he's someone else. Not literally. J.T. Walsh's Red, a trucker and family man who moonlights as the leader of a gang of desert pirates, knows who his victims are, but he also thinks that because they're driving a new Jeep, they have a lot of money.

The truth is that Jeff and his wife, Amy (Kathleen Quinlan), are down on their financial luck. They've got about $5,000 in the bank, and owe about $25,000 on their car loan and are driving across country to start over in Southern California. But once Jeff gets to know his wife's captors, he realizes she's dead the moment they learn there's no money.

Like Steven Spielberg's great TV movie "Duel," about a traveling salesman being terrorized by a trucker in the desert, "Breakdown" functions as an existential western. The Taylors become victims simply because they're there, vulnerable city slickers in a virtually lawless frontier. The only cop within view of a smoke signal thinks Jeff's crazy, and the locals are either in on the scheme or determined to look the other way.

It's a measure of Mostow's and Russell's success that we identify with every decision Jeff has to make, and though the movie missteps in a couple of places near the end, the payoffs come in the logic and legitimacy of Jeff's choices. You can question his judgment—especially when he lets his wife get on that truck in the first place—but almost everything he does afterward is rational, given the circumstances.

A glaring exception is a sequence where Jeff chases after a big rig turning onto a highway, gets a tenuous grip on its undercarriage and crawls forward to the back of the cab, where he hides for the duration of the trip. He's no longer Joe Average rising to the occasion; he's Indiana Jones on a busman's holiday, and the seconds devoted to this action interrupt the emotional flow of the story.

And it's unnecessary, since Mostow had a better option already set up. Earlier, Jeff gets a look at the sleeping space behind the truck driver's seat; why not have him slip in there when the driver's away and hope he doesn't get caught? It would be both more believable, and more suspenseful. It's what you'd do; sure it is.

But "Breakdown" is less likely to be remembered for the clichés it embraces than the ones it resists. This is a really solid first feature, and the best cardiovascular work out you're likely to have in a sitting position this year.

NEW YORK, 5/26/97, p. 66, David Denby

Breakdown, the road-movie thriller starring Kurt Russell, can't, by its very nature, offer the richness or complexity of a great film. But taken for what it is, the picture is very good—lean and tense, without a superfluous shot, an extravagant performance, or a slip in tone or style anywhere. Russell and Kathleen Quinlan play a Boston yuppie couple crossing the country in a red Jeep Cherokee, a perfectly fashionable and competent car that mysteriously breaks down on the open road. In the middle of nowhere—in Utah or perhaps Arizona, with reddish-brown desert and faceless bluffs all around—Quinlan, trying to get help, climbs into a passing truck. And promptly disappears. Has she been kidnapped? The truckdriver (J.T. Walsh) had seemed friendly enough. Baffled, Russell sets out to find her, without much help. He's a big-city boy, and the emptiness of the landscape mocks him: There are very few people around, the police are ineffective or perhaps treacherous, and under an enormous barren sky the road stretches on forever and goes nowhere.

Breakdown may be a genre movie, but it presents a kind of primal American nightmare—the great wilderness as a glaring, hollow space that offers little reflection of the human presence. Russell is *our* representative; he's accustomed to an urban business civilization in which the rationality of enterprise and organization keeps people accountable—or at least recognizable. But in this wasteland, no one is accountable; people feel little need to make sense or explain themselves. In his polo shirt and slacks, Russell enters a fly-specked "café," and the people hunkering over food stare at him as if he had stepped out of a Martian spaceship. Are they hostile or just indifferent? Has he become paranoid, or is he just a loser? He can't tell, and neither can we. Russell's loss of confidence is both social and metaphysical; the breakdown is complete.

Compare *Breakdown* with the typical big-scale action picture of the nineties *(The Rock, The Fifth Element)*, in which everything is exaggerated or burlesqued and the shots are thrown together from nowhere to nowhere. Making his first feature, the director Jonathan Mostow doesn't overstate anything; he sticks to his business, gets us cleanly and coherently from one place to another, and pulls the line of tension taut. Since Mostow confines us to Russell's point of view, we experience each shock, each puzzling hostile situation, as he does. From the opening shots, we're immersed, emotionally and physically, in the experience onscreen. What a relief! Mostow restores the world to its normal dimensions. The movie is violent but not cartoonish or sadistic. Mostow even stages an original car chase, ending on a high trestle—a chase that comes close to fantasy but doesn't pass over into it.

The bad guys—a grisly ring of kidnappers and extortionists—are led by J.T. Walsh, the bland, puffy, unreachable American who feels no sympathy for his fellow humans. And Mostow gives us a recognizable hero, not a superman but an unremarkable (though physically fit) American male who has to take things in to his own hands. When Kurt Russell does his smoky-voiced super-macho pose, in movies like *Escape From New York,* he becomes synthetic and forgettable. This time, he stays within the bounds of plausibility, and he goes through the various stages of disbelief, rage, and defiance with precision and detail. With Mostow's help, Kurt Russell reinvents the classic American myth: Violence doesn't come easily to a man of his temperament, but when pushed he will fight, and once he gets the taste of it, he becomes rather adept. *Breakdown* doesn't raise many issues; it's as lean as a pole, but it does the old forgotten movie work of convincing us that what it has to show us could actually have happened. The pleasure is made more intense by the simple realization that such a demonstration isn't likely to be repeated soon.

NEW YORK POST, 5/2/97, p. 39, Michael Medved

After its chillingly believable opening sequence, "Breakdown" quickly breaks down—eventually hurtling off the road into a bottomless canyon of hyper-violent cliches, preposterous paranoia and absurdly implausible super-hero stunts.

Worst of all, this slick, sick piece of cinematic exploitation cunningly connives to implicate the viewer in its own sadistic excesses, struggling to elicit cheers for the brutal dispatch of each one of its unspeakably evil bad guys.

The nightmare begins as Boston yuppies Kurt Russell and Kathleen Quinlan drive their shiny new Jeep Grand Cherokee across the continent to a new life in San Diego. After some brief roadside unpleasantness with a pair of snarling rednecks direct from Central Casting (M.C. Gainey, Ritch Brinkley), their car breaks down on a lonely stretch of road in Utah's fabled Monument Valley—where some 400 previous (mostly better) films were shot.

A polite, clean-cut trucker (J.T. Walsh) with an American flag on his baseball cap pulls up his 18-wheeler to help, and offers to take Quinlan to a nearby cafe to call a tow truck while her husband waits with the Jeep.

After she fails to return, Russell manages to repair a loose wire himself and then finds no sign of his wife at the diner. Next, he intercepts Walsh, forcing him off the road—only to find that the trucker denies they've ever met.

An earnest sheriff finds no evidence of the missing woman in the Teamster's rig, leaving Russell desperate and desolate in the desert.

Russell, always a persuasive Everyman, makes his character's situation powerfully compelling, but his solid acting can't hide the stupidity of the plot. His efforts to rescue his wife eventually uncover a ludicrous conspiracy, which he combats with far-fetched derring-do and altogether ridiculous good luck.

The movie tries for the old ordinary-man-pushed-to-extraordinary-heroism formula, but Russell ends up performing feats that even Stallone or Seagal might envy. The only hint that he's still supposed to be a regular guy comes from innumerable grunts and gasps looped onto the soundtrack in post-production.

Director and co-writer Jonathan Mostow (who created the similarly paranoid TV movie "Flight of the Black Angel") handles the big chase scenes with aplomb, but the visceral thrills seem embarrassingly manipulative. Mostow might seek to place his film in the long tradition (from "Easy Rider" through "Deliverance" to "Thelma and Louise") of scare movies purporting to show the vicious cruelty beneath the rustic earthiness of America's rural heartland, but his nasty little thriller lacks the unmistakable passion of its predecessors.

The advertising for "Breakdown" warns: "It could happen to you," but this foolishness could actually happen only in the glib, soulless nihilism of today's Hollywood.

SIGHT AND SOUND, 3/98, p. 42, Kim Newman

Jeff Taylor and his wife Amy, moving from Massachusetts to San Diego, are driving across the desert in their new jeep when they have a minor traffic altercation with Earl, an aggressive cowboy. The jeep breaks down and Red Barr, a trucker, offers the Taylors a lift to the pay-phone at Belle's Diner. Amy goes with Red but Jeff stays with the jeep. Discovering a pulled wire in the jeep's engine, Jeff repairs it. At the diner, the locals claim never to have seen Amy. Jeff drives Red off the road and claims to Sheriff Boyd that Amy has been kidnapped, but the lawman can find no evidence and releases Red. Jeff meets Billy, a local boy, who alleges the police are in on the kidnap scheme and dupes him into pursuing Earl. Billy, Earl and Al, another redneck, are in league with Red, preying on unwary passing motorists for saleable goods and money. Jeff almost escapes, but the gang capture him.

Amy has claimed that Jeff is a wealthy doughnut tycoon, so Red forces him to withdraw a ransom from a bank. Jeff gives Earl the bankroll, $5,000 rather than the $90,000 he expects, and attacks him. Boyd intervenes and is wounded, though he shoots Earl dead. Jeff stows away on Red's truck and is taken back to his homestead, where Amy is a prisoner. Jeff rescues her and escapes from the kidnappers in a stolen pick-up truck. Billy and Al are killed in the chase and Red's truck crashes into Jeff's vehicle on a bridge. The two men struggle and Red falls to the riverbed. Jeff rescues Amy, who, noticing Red is still alive, drops the truck on him.

In the early 70s, movies frequently depicted the American hinterland as a savage place where unwary city slickers were tormented by monstrous rednecks. *Breakdown* is a return to the days of *Macon County Line* (1973), *Race with the Devil* (1975) and *Jackson County Jail* (1976): every roadside stop is full of unhelpful, resentful, ignorant locals. When Jeff tells the proprietor of Belle's Diner that Amy is wearing a Benetton sweater, the sweaty lowbrow has no idea what he means and mishears the brand name as "button-on". Smiling, brutal crooks in cowboy hats live off goods stolen from passing city folks. In its assembly of baddies, the film is exemplary. Red, the folksy mastermind, dotes on his wife and small son even as he treats outsiders as less than human. Billy, apparently mentally handicapped, displays a nasty eloquence when revealing to Jeff that he has fooled him. Earl has a black cowboy hat and *Easy* Rider moustache to go with his courtly air of menace, and Al, the regulation goon, gets in the way and listens to explanations.

It is tempting to see this return to an earlier decade's paranoia as symptomatic of a resurgence of the city-country conflicts that marked the protest era, and a swing away from the more sympathetic depictions of rural folk (see the farmers-in-trouble films *Country* and *Places in the Heart*) of the 80s. After all, even the seminal *Thelma & Louise*, which dwells at length on the threat of the roadside, was crucially about women from the sticks who happened to wake up to the everyday nastiness all around. However, it seems more likely that director-writer Jonathan Mostow (hitherto the direct-to-video toiler of *Beverly Hills Bodysnatchers* and *The Flight of Black Angel*) merely realised a workable suspense pattern had fallen into disuse and could profitably be revived without even a superficial update.

Like *Duel* (1971), *Deliverance* (1972) or even *The Texas Chain Saw Massacre* (1974), *Breakdown* sets up its everyman heroes as city folks from Back East and makes much of their feelings of helplessness at not knowing how extensive Red's gang is. Mostow relishes the lonely roads and the desert's sinister splendours as much as he does the all-action chases and fights. He establishes the menace with enough creepy touches to ground the pay-off set-pieces in something like reality. The film's subtlest stroke is that the misunderstanding works both ways: because they are from Massachusetts and have a snazzy new jeep, Red assumes Jeff and Amy are wealthy, whereas they're in between jobs and about to go into debt.

The moral of the plot (as it often was in the 70s predecessors) may be a warning to redneck villains to stay away from city softies who might not be the easy pickings they seem. Faced with the loss of his wife, Kurt Russell's Jeff Taylor doesn't retreat into the existential dilemma of the hero in George Sluizer's original film of *The Vanishing,* but transforms from an amiable clod into an action hero. He drives daringly into a river to elude pursuit, turns the ransom handover to his advantage, and crawls (in a textbook suspense scene) along the underside of Red's speeding truck to find a safe perch. Finally, he goes *mano a mano* with the always reliably fiendish J.T. Walsh in the creaking hulk of a lorry cab that is hanging precariously off the edge of a bridge.

The callous punchline, as Kathleen Quinlan squashes her tormentor, might not exactly be on a level with the devastating descents into bestiality that afflicted the avengers of Sam Peckinpah's *Straw Dogs* (1971) or Wes Craven's *The Last House on the Left* (1972), but it still draws a slightly disturbing cheer from a satisfied audience.

VILLAGE VOICE, 5/13/97, p. 79, Justine Elias

Large summer movies have helpful messages like *Killer aliens and molten lava—make a mental note to avoid!!!* More modest films, like *Breakdown* and *Underworld,* also have their genteel advice for better living: *Shoot to kill—right away—or you'll be sorry!*

Kurt Russell, in his muscular, ticked-off everyman mode, learns this hard lesson late in the game in *Breakdown,* which begins as a decent paranoid thriller but quickly degenerates into an overheated fantasy of an urbanite's revenge. This type of nightmare journey, done best in *Deliverance* and *Duel,* begins as an ordinary man, traveling through an unfamiliar landscape, becomes unhinged by isolation and an unprovoked assault, only to discover that his true nature is more craven, ruthless, or sadistic than he once believed. And on a certain level he likes it that way.

In *Breakdown,* Russell and Kathleen Quinlan are a childless couple heading west through the Utah desert in their excellent new sports vehicle. But they're not on holiday, they're broke, between jobs, and uncomfortable with each other. In these early scenes, writer-director Jonathan Mostow conveys some of the blunted paranoia and dislocation of movies like *Frantic, The Trigger Effect,* and *Unlawful Entry,* in which an apparently solid marriage is easily fractured by an accident or crime. But when Russell and Quinlan's car breaks down, they take a really stupid risk: he stays behind to guard their possessions while she hitches a ride—alone—with a truck driver, whose told them that his CB radio is broken, but that its only five miles to the nearest telephone. Apparently neither of them sense the irony in trusting the trucker (J.T. Walsh, the scariest ordinary-looking guy in films) enough to refrain from raping and murdering Quinlan, but not quite enough to ask him to drive the five miles and call AAA by himself, if he's so damn helpful. After Russell received a ransom demand for his missing wife, *Breakdown* becomes a disappointingly standard road-rage revenge movie in which an otherwise enraged and violent hero is somehow unable to kill his wife's assailants until after he's tried tying them up, locking them in the barn, and hitting them a little. May I suggest the intermediate step of malicious wounding?

By contrast, the well-dressed thugs of *Underworld,* a tiresome attempt at surreal gangster comedy, err on the side of caution: they like to execute everyone they meet. The exception is Denis Leary, as a mad-at-the-underworld ex-con who punishes his father's apparent killer (Joe Mantogna) by forcing him at gunpoint to listen to a monologue about menswear, showtunes, and the pain of losing a family member. When Mantegna asks dispiritedly, "Should I be jotting any of this shit down?" he really to seems to be saying, "Shoot me."

Also reviewed in:
NEW YORK TIMES, 5/2/97, p. C10, Janet Maslin
VARIETY, 4/28-5/4/97, p. 99, Todd McCarthy
WASHINGTON POST, 5/2/97, p. C1, Stephen Hunter

BRILLIANT LIES

A Castle Hill Productions release of a Bayside Pictures production in association with the Australian Film Finance Corporation. *Producer:* Richard Franklin and Sue Farrelly. *Director:* Richard Franklin. *Screenplay:* Peter Fitzpatrick and Richard Franklin. *Based on the play by:* David Williamson. *Director of Photography:* Geoff Burton. *Editor:* David Pulbrook. *Sound:* Lloyd Carrick. *Casting:* Greg Apps. *Production Designer:* Tracy Watt. *Art Director:* Brian Alexander. *Set Director:* Jill Eden. *Costumes:* Roger Kirk. *Make-up:* Amanda Rowbottom. *Running time:* 93 minutes. *MPAA Rating:* Not Rated.

CAST: Gia Carides (Susy Connor); Anthony La Paglia (Gary Fitzgerald); Zoe Carides (Katy Connor); Ray Barrett (Brian Connor); Michael Veitch (Paul Connor); Catherine Wilkin (Marion Lee); Neil Melville (Vince Williams); Jennifer Jarman Walker (Ruth Miller); Grant Tilly (Steve Lovett); Beverley Dunn (President); Brad Lindsay (Registrar); Barry Friedlander (Mr. Buxton); Iain Murton (Mr. Hall); Tim Elston (Young Brian); Nathalie Gauchi (Young Katy); Emily-Jane Romig (Young Susy); Daniel Holten (Young Paul); Lisa Aldenhoven (Stephanie Fitzgerald); With: Caroline Henricks, Leo Taylor, John Morris, and Louise O'Dwyer.

LOS ANGELES TIMES, 7/25/97, Calendar/p. 10, Bob Heisler

[The following review by Bob Heisler appeared in a slightly different form in **NEWSDAY, 7/11/97, Part II/p. B13.]**

Welcome to Australia, land of the damaged, where claiming victimhood is the goal and there are no rules, just expectations. No heroes here, just schemers—in life, business, love and family.

"Brilliant Lies," the oddly quiet film by Richard Franklin of Australian David Williamson's play about the quest for power, is an anti-summer movie. No special effects, no aliens, no action of any kind, Just talk and more talk.

The production has the modest, made-for-TV feel of a play with a soundtrack. But it takes more than moving the dialogue from a stage to an office or a gym or a golf course to open up a play and make it hold your attention.

At first glance, Williamson and Franklin seem to be a thoughtful, emotional confrontation between employer Gary Fitzgerald (Anthony La Paglia) and his assistant, Susy Connor (Gia Carides), who was fired after an incident that may have been the basest sexual harassment: do this or lose your job. There is hatred far beyond the bounds of modern management manuals. She wants $40,000. Despite the publicity of a trial, he refuses to submit to blackmail and settle.

But early on, the focus shifts from the office to the Connor family, reducing Fitzgerald's activities to a subplot. Susy and her sister Katy (Zoe Carides) seem to be on opposite ends of the sexual spectrum—Susy is a party girl who sees men as her rightful meal ticket, and Katy is a sometime architect and angry lesbian (which in this case means speaking in cliches about male oppressors) who falls for the mediator in her sister's harassment hearing.

The movie seems to be saying their lives are different reactions to the same act. As adolescents, they were groped by their father, a thoroughly awful lout named Brian (Ray Barrett). Brian, true to form, sees himself as the victim in the family—his business fortune now gone, he's alone and in need of heart surgery that could be paid for by Susy's settlement, if she were a good daughter.

La Paglia charges hard and rarely comes up for air. Gia Carides struggles to find a dimension to Susy beyond tart and manipulator. Barrett plays the father with a whine and a whimper.

Not that you would want to know these sad characters any better, but "Brilliant Lies" suffers from not knowing where to put the audience. We're kept at a distance in our theater seats while the conversation continues on the screen.

NEW YORK POST, 7/11/97, p. 40, Michael Medved

On a few key points in their bitter harassment dispute, both contending parties (Gia Carides and Anthony La Paglia) manage to agree.   •

There's no question that she's a drug-indulging party girl who enjoys wearing provocative outfits to her secretarial job at a Sydney insurance company that she held for just seven months before her abrupt dismissal. Nor will anyone deny that he's a crude, hard-driving, demanding boss who's found it difficult to get along with a series of prior female employees.

The essential conflict involves what happened one night at the office when they worked together after hours. She says he grabbed her breasts from behind, mumbled some nonsense about the "twin peaks of womanhood," and exposed himself before she ran from the building. He says that he merely complained about her sloppy work and warned she might be sacked, so she filed the harassment complaint in the hopes of a juicy payoff. Since no one witnessed their fateful interchange, it's simply his word against hers, and both parties seem credible.

This carefully calibrated sense of balance, artfully maintained until the very end of the picture, makes "Brilliant Lies" a brilliant success, far richer and more compelling than one-sided, self-pitying harassment melodramas like "Disclosure" or "Oleanna."

Flashbacks from both points of view, presented in the classic "Rashomon" style, keep the audience guessing, and puzzle the fair-minded conciliation lawyer (Catherine Wilkin) who initially hears the case.

As the story unfolds both characters emerge as fundamentally flawed. Carides wants her lonely lesbian sister (superbly played by her real life sister, Zoe Carides) to lie for her, testifying that she's heard long-standing complaints about the abusive environment in the office. La Paglia pursues a devious scheme to take over the company from his initially supportive associate (Neil Melville). Meanwhile, it turns out that the phrase "twin peaks of womanhood" actually originated with Carides' alcoholic father (Ray Barret) who long ago molested both his daughters.

Obviously, none of these characters is about to win ardent affection or admiration from the audience, but the performances are all so strong and subtle that they are fascinating anyway. La Paglia, best known for playing ethnic New Yorkers, may surprise movie-goers with his effortless Aussie accent—but he came by it honestly, since he was born and raised in Adelaide.

Based on the recent play by Australia's most acclaimed dramatist, David Williamson (known in this country as the screenwriter of "Gallipoli" and "The Year of Living Dangerously"), the film's been directed in crisp and compassionate style by Richard Franklin, whose disappointing American films ("Psycho II," "Link," "FX2") offer little hint of the skill and self-assurance he displays with this complex and challenging material.

VILLAGE VOICE, 7/15/97, p. 68, Amy Taubin

Adapted from David Williamson's play, Australian director Richard Franklin's *Brilliant Lies* is something like early David Mamet but without the misogyny—if such a dissection can be imagined. And, inevitably, it will be compared to Neil LaBute's more complicated *In the Company of Men* (opening next month). Both films make the connection between sexual harassment and a Darwinian corporate culture. But where LaBute foregrounds rogue male egos, Franklin focuses on women's not necessarily admirable responses to the male power structure that keeps them bent out of shape.

Self-styled bad girl Susy Connor (Gia Carides) accuses her boss (Anthony La Paglia) of sexual harassment and demands $40,000 in compensation. Her sister (Zoe Carides) begins to doubt Susy's story when she recognizes a phrase Susy puts in her boss's mouth as something she heard their own father say. It turns out that the sisters were both sexually abused by Dad, who refuses to admit that copping a feel was any big deal and, futhermore, expects Susy to turn over most of the settlement, should she win, to pay for his bypass surgery.

Franklin imposes a rigorous, basically comic structure on material that otherwise might have seemed as clichéd as talk TV. The film is constructed as a series of blackout sketches; each scene reveals the mixture of lie and truth in the scene that preceded it and adds some new ugly detail that will be partially supported and contradicted in the next. The method is compelling from beginning to end, but the aftertaste is gimmicky. Sexual power struggles lose their primal element when they're so elegantly contained.

Also reviewed in:
NEW YORK TIMES, 7/11/97, p. C10, Stephen Holden
VARIETY, 5/13-19/96, p. 68, David Stratton

BROKEN ENGLISH

A Sony Pictures Classics release of a Village Roadshow Pictures Worldwide presentation of a Communicado production in association with The New Zealand Film Commission. *Executive Producer:* Timothy White. *Producer:* Robin Scholes. *Director:* Gregor Nicholas. *Screenplay:* Gregor Nicholas. *Director of Photography:* John Toon. *Editor:* David Coulson. *Music:* Murray Grindlay. *Sound:* Michael Hedges and (music) Graeme Myhre. *Casting:* Fiona Edgar. *Production Designer:* Mike Kane. *Art Director:* Clive Memmott. *Costumes:* Glenis Foster. *Make-up:* Dominie Till. *Running time:* 90 minutes. *MPAA Rating:* NC-17.

CAST: Rade Serbedzija (Ivan); Aleksandra Vujcic (Nina); Julian Arahanga (Eddie); Marton Csokas (Darko); Madeline McNamara (Mira); Elizabeth Mavric (Vanya); Zhao Jing (Clara); Yang Li (Wu); Temuera Morrison (Manu); Michael Langley (Jura); Morena Tutugoro (Sashka); Mona Ross (Auntie Marja); Barbara Cartwright (Jasmin); Patrick Wilson (Dave); Greg Johnson (Doug); Chris Ruka (Reverend Essie); Nui Tuakana (Essie's Wife); Chris Anderton and Dominic Blaazer (Palermo Band); Fred Sy (Chow); Gilbert Goldie (Cab Driver); Emma Lovell (Nina & Eddie's Daughter); Amanda Rees (Nurse).

NEW YORK POST, 5/2/97, p. 46, Larry Worth

It's being advertised as "From the producers of 'Once Were Warriors,'" but those expecting the power and originality of "Warriors" in "Broken English" are due for disappointment.

That's because, for the most part, "Broken English" is yet another "Romeo and Juliet" retread.

Granted, the Capulets aren't squaring off with the Montagues. But Croatian immigrants are reacting pretty similarly to Maori natives in present-day New Zealand.

So, trouble's not far off when the beautiful daughter of a fiercely loyal Croatian family falls head over heels for her handsome Maori co-worker. Her overly protective father soon sets a chain of events in motion that could have earned a screenplay co-credit for Avon's favorite bard.

Subplots about the assimilation process, prejudice's tragic fallout and an Asian-based "Green Card" knockoff don't help. Nor does director Gregor Nicholas' penchant for clunky symbolism about family trees.

But Nicholas isn't without his strengths. Specifically, he uses the Down Under locales to full advantage, incorporates some striking cinematography (including Balkan home movies) and keeps the proceedings moving at a brisk pace.

He also elicited striking performances from two of his cast members. Rade Serbedzija's violence-prone, guilt-ridden papa displays a side of his talents only hinted at in "Before the Rain" and "The Saint." As a frightening amalgam of passion and rage, he's a knockout.

And Julian Arahanga, best known as the stalwart older son in "Once Were Warriors," capably fuses tenderness and steely resolve. His lovestruck twentysomething emerges as a memorable, utterly commanding presence.

Then there's newcomer Aleksandra Vujcic's comely heroine. Her limited acting range is obvious from the outset. Ditto for her ability to raise undulation to an art form.

Speaking of which, Nicholas lets Vujcic and Arahanga engage in a steamy coupling that resulted in the film's NC-17 rating. Seeming somewhat gratuitous to the plot, it appears more of a gimmick to generate publicity.

As such an ardent Shakespeare devotee, Nicholas should have remembered that the play's the thing.

NEWSDAY, 5/2/97, Part II/p. B8, Jack Mathews

The casting director working on Gregor Nicholas' interracial love story "Broken English" spotted Alexandra Vujcic, the young woman who would become the film's costar, in an Auckland, New Zealand, bar. It was a good break for Vujcic, who didn't mind giving up her receptionist job, and an even better break for Nicholas.

Vujcic not only had the dark good looks that Nicholas was looking for, she also shared her character's Croatian background, and brought cultural and experiential detail to the role—not to mention a natural accent—that helped refine the script. The result of the collaboration is a terrific film and a stunning debut by Vujcic, who brings a wrenching honesty to this story of a Croat-New Zealander's attempt to follow her heart without losing her family.

Vujcic plays Nina, the youngest of three children of a New Zealander mother and a Croatian father, a family that has survived the war in the Balkans and moved to Auckland to start a new life. Her father, Ivan (Rade Serbedzija), and her brother, Darko (Marton Csokas), have started their own entry-level immigrant business—selling drugs—while she's waiting tables at a Chinese restaurant.

It's there that Nina meets Eddie (Julian Arahanga), a Maori cook, and their mutual attraction develops into an immediately passionate romance. The problem: Dad is a bullying racist who doesn't want his daughter dating anyone, let alone a Maori, and though she's legally an adult, Nina doesn't have the resources to strike out on her own.

So, she grasps at the one solution presenting itself, and agrees to marry the fiancé of a Chinese co-worker, to make him a New Zealand citizen, and uses the money they pay her to buy a car and set up housekeeping with Eddie. All of which infuriates Nina's father and puts her lover and her family on a violent collision course.

Vujcic, Arahanga and Serbedzija, a major star in former Yugoslavia, give strongly emotional performances in a film that Nicholas has staged with a bluntness that caused embarrassed Hollywood censors to slap an adults-only NC-17 label on it. The official reason accompanying the rating is "explicit sexuality," but it's no more explicit than that in numerous R-rated film. Could it be that the raters are making a racial statement of their own?

In any event, the NC-17's a shame, because this is the kind of movie—dealing honestly with issues facing people every day on this shrinking planet—that thoughtful parents might want their children to see. At least, it ought to be their choice.

SIGHT AND SOUND, 8/97, p. 42, Laura Miller

New Zealand. During a party at the home of Ivan, a Croatian émigré, Ivan's daughter Mira sneaks out of the house for a tryst with another Croat. Ivan and his son Darko destroy the man's car with baseball bats. Ivan's other daughter, Nina, leaves for the Chinese bar and restaurant where she works. There, she strikes up a flirtation with Eddie, the new Maori chef. She explains to him that Jasmin, the owner, profits from finding spouses for immigrants who wish to become legal residents, such as Wu, the boyfriend of the dishwasher Clara. Nina approaches Jasmin and offers to marry Wu for a fee. Eddie and Nina become lovers, but when Nina tries to move in with Eddie her father attempts to make her stay. They argue, he hits her and she leaves. Clara and Wu insist on moving in as well to make the forthcoming marriage seem credible. Nina discovers she's pregnant.

Ivan invites Nina to a feast celebrating the arrival of Ivan's aunt from Croatia. Nina brings Eddie, Wu and Clara. Wu gets drunk and tells Ivan that he will marry Nina and Ivan strikes him. As Nina and her friends leave the party, she fights with Eddie over their cultural differences. The next day, Eddie fails to show up at work, having gone back to his hometown by the sea.

Nina finds him, but Eddie refuses to return with her. Back in the city, Nina almost miscarries and is hospitalised. Infuriated, her father brings her back to his house and imprisons her. Eddie learns that Nina is pregnant and goes to Ivan's house to find her. Ivan and Darko try to attack him but he gets the better of them. Nina leaves with Eddie. Sometime later, Eddie plays with their child in the surf while Nina watches and relates in voice-over that her father still refuses to speak to her.

Despite a star-crossed lovers storyline that's anything but fresh, *Broken English* shows that sheer charisma can make shopworn material absorbing. When you imagine how this film might have turned out recalling how this kind of tale has so often been told by earnest young directors with a burning message—its modest charms seem especially savoury.

Aleksandra Vujcic as Nina and Julian Arahanga as Eddie glow with the radiant sexiness of nascent stardom, their characters all the more compelling for not being too innocent. Nina is no demure Juliet, as her taste for liquor and tight outfits indicates. "I wanted to do what I wanted to do, no matter what," she explains blithely to Eddie as she tells him a story about braving the bombs in Croatia on a lark. Her determination to indulge her emotional impulses whatever the danger ignites most of the lovers' troubles, but it's also the source of her charm. To Vujcic and director Gregor Nicholas' credit, she comes across as brave and often foolishly wilful, but never spoiled.

Arahanga provides Vujcic with an apt match. Hollywood's predominant image of masculinity these days—brooding, sarcastic, bunkered in muscle—seems all the more pathological compared with the unselfconscious virility he exudes. *Broken English* somewhat romanticises the Maoris as open-hearted and earthy (compared with the war-embittered Croats) but Arahanga's warmth and strength make this feel like more than just preachy mythologising. Ironically, he's exactly the man anyone sensible would want his daughter to marry.

But it's the third major player in the cast who takes *Broken English* deeper than most dramas of interracial love. Rade Serbedzija's Ivan is a shaggy, embattled patriarch, a vulgar Lear, whose efforts to control his daughters betray his dread of seeing the family's ethnic identity melt away in this new world. During the feast scene, he and his Croatian buddies glower behind aviator sunglasses in his dusty, cinderblock-enclosed yard, supervising the roasting of a spitted pig and muttering about the jubilant Maori party next door. Sensitive production design plays up the contrast between Ivan's compound and the exhilarating vistas of Eddie's seaside home. The Croatian wives, encrusted with the garish sunglasses and plastic jewellery of immigrant aspiration, are juxtaposed with the Maoris' insouciant beachwear and flower garlands.

Nicholas (who has directed several shorts and the feature *User Friendly*) builds the story's dramatic intensity by focusing on scenes that limn the turbulent bond between father and daughter, a reckless, passionate connection always on the verge of violence. Choices like this make Nicholas' foray into such familiar territory more engaging than its many predecessors, but in the end, it's still well-travelled ground. *Broken English* begs a question: what these talented performers and film-makers might be capable of should they venture further out.

VILLAGE VOICE, 5/6/97, p. 92, Elisabeth Vincentelli

When Nina (Aleksandra Vujcic) falls in love with Eddie *(Once Were Warriors*'s Julian Arahanga), complications ensue—mostly because Nina's dad is a bully with a short fuse. If you already know where this is going, you're 90 minutes ahead of the director. Most of the ingredients in this New Zealand film are familiar: an abusive dad, a silent but sympathetic mom, and star-crossed young young lovers sharing an intense physical passion. (Don't get excited by the NC-17 rating: the love scene that earned it is tame.) There's even a star supposedly in the making. Despite limited acting ability, Vujcic is already being touted as the next bombshell—Salma Hayek, start worrying. The only intriguing element is the ethnic makeup: Nina emigrated from Croatia, while Eddie is Maori. Indeed, the interesting aspect of *Broken English* is its peek at the Croatian immigrant community. And not a pretty peek: an independence-day celebration lets us contemplate the sight of women in tight clothing subordinated to violent, beer-swilling men. I'm waiting for the Croatian Anti-Defamation League to call the producers.

Also reviewed in:
NEW YORK TIMES, 5/2/97, p. C16, Janet Maslin
VARIETY, 9/16-22/96, p. 71, Daniel M. Kimmel
WASHINGTON POST, 6/6/97, Weekend/p. 62, Desson Howe

BROTHER'S KISS, A

A First Look Pictures release of a Rosefunk Pictures Ltd. production. *Executive Producer:* Jim Walton. *Producer:* Bob Potter and E. Bennett Walsh. *Director:* Seth Zvi Rosenfeld. *Screenplay (based on his stage play):* Seth Zvi Rosenfeld. *Director of Photography:* Fortunato Procopio. *Editor:* Donna Stern. *Music:* Frank London. *Sound:* Jan McLaughlin. *Casting:* Francine Maisler and Tracy Marable Moore. *Production Designer:* Roger Fortune. *Art Director:* Rona Taylor. *Set Decorator:* Jim Lillis. *Costumes:* Carolyn Greco. *Running time:* 92 minutes. *MPAA Rating:* R.

CAST: Nick Chinlund (Lex); Michael Raynor (Mick); Cathy Moriarty (Doreen); Rosie Perez (Debbie); Marisa Tomei (Missy); John Leguizamo (Lefty Louie); Justin Pierce (Young Lex); Joshua Danowsky (Young Mick); Michael Rapaport (Stingy); Talent Harris (Vic); Frank Minucci (Uncle Mac); Adrian Pasdar (Doper).

LOS ANGELES TIMES, 7/18/97, Calendar/p. 10, John Anderson

[*The following review by John Anderson appeared in a slightly different form in* **NEWSDAY, 4/25/97, Part II/p. B9.**]

Tracing the concentric circles of modern urban hell, "A Brother's Kiss" offers pain without redemption and despair without a lot of root causes. So, like a lot of the life it portrays, its reason for being comes down to relationships.

And in Lex and Mick, the ill-fated brothers of Seth Zvi Rosenfeld's debut film—adapted and directed from his off-Broadway play of 1989—"A Brother's Kiss" has a near-classic pair of urban types, the kind originated in '30s crime drama and transplanted to late '70s East Harlem.

Here, the extroverted, streetwise Lex (played as a boy by Justin Pierce) plays adolescent father to his little brother, Mick (Joshua Danowsky), while their alcoholic mother, Doreen (Cathy Moriarty), offers herself and the kids' dinner to whatever itinerant male happens to be passing through the apartment. All too obviously, it's a tableau ripe for disaster.

Rosenfeld doesn't portray the family as unloving. Far from it. Doreen is a mess, but she shows flashes of maternity; Mick defends her to Lex, who in turn defends Mick to the point of felonious assault: One night in Central Park, he stabs a cop who is sodomizing Mick and is sent away. Life is irretrievably altered.

That it's Mick (played as an adult by Michael Raynor) who winds up joining the police force while Lex (Nick Chinlund) pursues his hopeless dream of a basketball career isn't an aspect of the story that's probed particularly deeply by Rosenfeld, who has Lex on the fast track to doom and keeps him there.

Always a just-say-no kind of guy (thanks to Mom's voracious thirst), Lex reacts to his dead-end job, his unsettling wife (Rosie Perez) and their child by succumbing to the drugs infecting their Harlem streets.

We've seen variations on this story before, but we may never have seen this particular city before: It's a New York movie that doesn't look like a New York movie because Rosenfeld uses locations that seldom get any screen time. No landmarks, just the picturesque sites of the upper-Upper East Side, where Lex's story arrives at its inevitable cul-de-sac.

Despite a bit of stiffness on the part of Rosenfeld, "A Brother's Kiss" does have two volatile, standout performances. Raynor probably has the less gratifying role as the controlled, internalized Mick, but Chinlund's Lex is a bravura turn, embracing all the fractured pride, humiliation and grief of a man whose dreams were never in his reach, who advertises his own strength but ends up crumbling—like any of the other street kids around him—when his life becomes its own burden. He saves Lex from stereotype, which is as much salvation as we're going to get here.

NEW YORK, 5/12/97, p. 58, David Denby

A Brother's Kiss, made from his own play by Seth Zvi Rosenfeld, is about two white brothers growing up in East Harlem. The older and tougher Nick Chinlund raises his kid brother Michael Raynor but then, when they are both grown up, falls apart and becomes dependent on him. This fervently written little movie about the disintegration of the city is brilliantly acted by a large, streetwise cast, including Cathy Moriarty, Michael Rapaport, John Leguizamo, and Marisa Tomei.

NEW YORK POST, 4/25/97, p. 51, Bill Hoffmann

Seth Zvi Rosenfeld's independent feature "A Brother's Kiss" weighs in as the season's most powerful and passionate drama.

This gripping story of the turbulent lives of two brothers who started out in East Harlem may not be the most original idea on the planet, but Rosenfeld has gathered an incredible cast of pros to portray an eye-popping menagerie of winners, losers, good guys and pond scum.

And along with some beautifully atmospheric location photography by Fortunato Procopio, the results are dazzling.

It's 1979, and boisterous Lex (Chinlund) and his shy kid brother Mick (Raynor) are making the best of life with their alcoholic, peroxide-blonde mom Doreen (Cathy Moriarty), whose bedroom should be fitted with a revolving door.

Lex is incredibly protective of Mick, and the two seem well-adjusted despite their surroundings—until a creepy, late-night visit to Central Park changes everything.

Mick is raped by a renegade cop who's then stabbed by Lex. Sure, it's a case of self-defense, but the word of two ghetto kids is no match for the cops, who haul Lex off to reform school, leaving a traumatized Mick to fend for himself.

Sixteen years later, Mick is a terrified-of-sex, by-the-book cop and Lex is doing odd jobs, having squandered a promising basketball career after impregnating and marrying his girlfriend (Rosie Perez).

Soon it's straight-arrow Mick vs. headed-to-the-gutter Lex, who has gone into the drug-pushing biz when he's not using the stuff himself.

Chinlund and Raynor are great as the about-to-blow brothers, but it's the supporting cast that makes the film so explosive.

As the garish but good-hearted mom, Moriarty does her best work since "Raging Bull"; the always-reliable John Leguizamo shines as a drug kingpin; and Marisa Tomei is hypnotic as Lex's sleazy, stoned-out mistress.

VILLAGE VOICE, 4/29/97, p. 76, Gary Dauphin

I've known plenty of kids like Lex and Mick, the leads in *A Brother's Kiss*, white boys whose parents didn't flee darkening neighborhoods for various reasons and who lived accepted and generally down among black and Latino peers. The Lexes were would-be hardrocks with cheerfully outsize personalities and inner-city troubles: early brushes with the law, early fatherhood, and the like. The Micks were awkward boys who survived long enough to move out, taking with them an appreciation of life at the margins of American society. You've heard both those stories before, but Seth Zvi Rosenfeld's debut (adapted from his 1989 play) turns them into strong family drama.

A Brother's Kiss starts out with a late-night phone call, Lex (Nick Chinlund) calling Mick (Michael Raynor) out to his crack-hotel cot to save him from some unexplained troubles. Rosenfeld flashes back from there to the pair's childhood, a rough-and-tumble street life where "Happy birthday, punk" can sound like a kind pat on the head. Lex grows up into a jangling white amalgam of urban disaster—wants to be a ballplayer but ends up a crackhead—while Mick becomes a cop, his tightly coiled lack of affect the sign of a personality struggling to hold itself together.

The sights and sounds are perfectly early hip-hop, and the surrounding cloud of expert secondary players (Rosie Perez, John Leguizamo, Cathy Moriarty, and Michael Rapaport) sutures the two leads into a dramatic context that's solidly believable. The textured background in turn gives Lex and Mick room to fill their common tragedy with the kind of fierce, startling love that you can only share with a sibling who causes you great pain.

Although *Kiss* is a notable debut for Rosenfeld, there's an unsettling familiarity throughout. There are plenty of Lexes and Micks in the world, but at its core, *Kiss* is essentially hanging old tropes about young black and Latino men on white bodies. It works for this film, but it raises a question about empathy, namely why some folks get it for free, while others have been deemed media clichés.

Also reviewed in:
CHICAGO TRIBUNE, 10/10/97, Friday/p. N, John Petrakis
NEW YORK TIMES, 4/25/97, p. C15, Stephen Holden
VARIETY, 7/28-8/3/97, p. 58, Leonard Klady

BROTHERS IN TROUBLE

A First Run Features release of a Renegade Films production in association with Kinowelt Filmproduktion and Mikado Film. *Executive Producer:* George Faber. *Producer:* Robert Buckler. *Director:* Udayan Prasad. *Screenplay:* Robert Buckler. *Based on the novel "Return Journey" by:* Abdullah Hussein. *Director of Photography:* Alan Almond. *Editor:* Barrie Vince. *Music:* Stephen Warbeck. *Sound:* Roger Slater and (music) Steve Parr. *Casting:* Lucinda Syson. *Production Designer:* Chris Townsend. *Art Director:* Mike Stallion. *Set Decorator:* John Bush. *Special Effects:* John Markwell. *Costumes:* Andrea Galer. *Make-up:* Deborah Taylor. *Running time:* 102 minutes. *MPAA Rating:* Not Rated.

CAST: Om Puri (Hussein Shah); Pavan Malhotra (Amir); Angeline Ball (Mary); Ahsen Bhatti (Irshad); Bhasker (Gholam); Pravesh Kumar (Sakib); Badi Uzzaman (Old Ram); Harmage Singh Kalirai (Sher Baz); Kumall Grewal (Akbar Dal); Omar Salimi (Raja); Pal Aron (Zamara); Shiv Grewal (Shona Mian); Avin Shah (Tara Mian); Lesley Clare O'Neill (Prostitute); Kulvinder Ghir (The Agent); Riz Abbasi (Asif); Freddie Fletcher (Redway); June Broughton (Beryl); William Maxwell (Doctor); Huggy Leaver (Market Porter); Aftab Sachak (Sakib's Uncle); John Lambert (Registar); Tich Saunders (Driver); Judy Monahan (Nurse); Peter Silverleaf (Belgian Docker); Maria Redmond (Nurse); Mellan Mitchell (Café Owner); Shereen Wheeks, Sian Holland, and Luke Johnson (Baby Michael).

NEW YORK POST, 5/14/97, p. 39, Larry Worth

England's Pakistani subculture might seem an unlikely gold mine for one cinematic gem after another, but it has already resulted in "My Beautiful Laundrette," "Sammy and Rosie," "Wild West" and the "Buddha of Suburbia."

"Brothers in Trouble" isn't quite in that league, but it still has plenty to recommend it.

The story begins as a middle-aged Pakistani is shoved into a vegetable crate and shipped to Britain circa 1960. Arrangements have been made for him to settle in an urban home with 20 other illegals and begin work in "the land of opportunity."

As it turns out, employment is in a local mill, where he's assigned to shovel manure. Clearly, the labor serves as a metaphor for his less-than-idyllic existence.

Thankfully, screenwriter Robert Buckler doesn't stop with easy analogies. He paints a bleak, sharply detailed picture of the grueling assimilation process, the goal of which is walking the streets unnoticed. That means not only changing vocal mannerisms but memorizing inanities such as "Look before you leap."

Taking matters one step further, Buckler indicates that the Pakistanis' worst danger isn't from British immigration officers, it's from fighting among themselves. That's particularly true after a pregnant Englishwoman settles in their abode, igniting events that are bound to end tragically.

All that's well and fine, but director Udayan Prasad spends too much time on the mother-and-child domestic squabbles. A first-rate cast helps perpetuate the characters' allure, with Om "Jewel in the Crown" Puri delivering a finely nuanced turn as the household's stalwart leader. Pavan Malhotra also compels as the newcomer, while Angeline "The Commitments" Ball does her best to flesh out the voluptuous lady lodger.

Collectively, the cast compensates when the tale moves in the wrong direction. The result: Like its displaced characters, "Brothers" stands out in spite of itself.

SIGHT AND SOUND, 10/96, p. 37, Philip Kemp

The early 1960s. Amir, an illegal immigrant, arrives in Britain from Pakistan concealed in a vegetable crate and is conveyed to a terraced house in a midlands city. Crammed into the house are 18 other illegals, including Sakid, a young would-be writer, army veteran Gholam, and house leader Hussein Shah. Appalled by the squalid conditions, Amir is warned by Gholam to keep his head down. He is given menial work in the wool-washing sheds of a textiles factory, sends money to his wife and children, and gradually settles into the restricted routine of his life.

To everyone's surprise, Hussein Shah brings home a young white woman, Mary, to live with him. Initially dismayed, the rest of the household—especially Sakid—are won over by her warmth and sense of fun, while she responds to their gentle adoration. But when she proves to be pregnant their fears revive, and only at Ravi's insistence do they summon a midwife to the birth. It's evident that the baby isn't Hussein Shah's.

The humiliated Shah decides Mary will contract a 'paper marriage' with his nephew, Irshad, so that the young man can enter Britain legally. Mary reluctantly agrees. Secure in his legal status, Irshad begins acting recklessly, getting drunk and openly flirting with his 'wife', to his uncle's fury. Sakid, wretchedly besotted with Mary, joins Irshad on his pub-crawls. Tensions rise, culminating in a knife fight in which Irshad fatally stabs Hussein Shah. As Sakib stands over the body in a state of mental collapse, Mary and the other men flee the house—all except Amir who, unable to abandon Sakib, phones the police.

Two years later. Amir, now legally resident with a good job and about to bring his family over, encounters Mary with her son. At first she seems happy, but reveals she is trapped in an abusive relationship. Amir proceeds to the mental home where Sakib has been staying, and where the young man's uncle is due to arrive to take him home to Pakistan. After seeing Sakib off, Amir strolls contentedly through the fields.

The recurrent image of *Brothers in Trouble* is of a group of men crammed into a stairwell, gazing upwards with frightened eyes, listening to events unfolding over which they have no control and which may bring down disaster on their heads. Udayan Prasad's film vividly conveys the sense of helplessness and pervasive fear in which 'illegals' exist. On the rare occasions Amir ventures out into the street he scurries along like a man in a downpour, head bent and hugging the walls, desperate to efface himself, reading hostility and suspicion in every white face he passes.

The paranoid mood is enhanced by Alan Almond's sombre lighting. Most scenes take place at night, and even during the day the cramped little terraced house feels shadowy and oppressive. Mary's arrival literally brings light: she rigs up electric bulbs (which the illegals have never dared use), clapping with childlike glee as the current is switched on and light floods the room. But the shadows soon gather again. In the opening sequence we get Amir's subjective view through the slats of the crate in which he's concealed, and the same narrow slit-vision increasingly recurs as jealousy and suspicion infect the household and people spy on each other through door-cracks. When disaster strikes it's again at night, and the illegals spill forth from the house and scatter off into the darkness, like wild nocturnal creatures panicked from their burrow.

The coda, by contrast, is played out in broad daylight, first in open bustling streets and then on the fringes of the countryside. For the first time we see Amir as he must have been in his home country, outgoing, gregarious and even playful, confident enough to talk back to a bossy nurse who ticks him off. In the final shot, observing "Who would have thought this country could be so beautiful?", he strides jauntily away across the meadows. It's an upbeat ending, but it doesn't let us forget that the one who came through leaves behind him one dead, one mentally broken, and his other housemates scattered who knows where. The pain and damage of the illegals' twilight world is overcome, but not obliterated.

Brothers in Trouble, directed by television documentary and drama director Udayan Prasad (who made the Screen Two dramas *102 Boulevard Haussmann* and *Femme Fatale*) and adapted from a novel by the Urdu writer Abdullah Hussein, ties in with the recent wave of 'post-colonial' writing—often by second-generation children of the original immigrants—that sets out to examine and redefine the immigrant experience. It shares with the work of such writers as Meera Syal, Andrea Levy or Caryl Phillips the knack of giving a white British viewer a chance to see Britain as an alien territory. By the time Prasad's film takes us—along with Amir and Sakid into a local pub, we've grown so used to the claustrophobic commune of the terraced house that it's the pub that appears exotic and dangerous. Not that the white Brits are demonised; at worst, like the woolshed foreman, they're contemptuously tolerant. The smoothly rapacious Pakistani agent, battening on the illegals, is the nearest we get to a villain.

If the film has a fault (besides the title, which sounds like a Boulting Brothers comedy), it lies in the ambiguity of its narrative focus: it's not always clear whether the main story we're following is that of Amir, Hussein Shah or Sakid. But this is perhaps a backhanded way of acknowledging that the ensemble acting is so good, even the secondary characters seem fully-defined enough to carry the storyline. It says a lot for Angeline Ball (*The Commitments*), who plays Mary, that even up against Indian actors of the calibre of Om Puri she holds her own, bringing to her role just the right balance of naive and flirtatious calculation.

VILLAGE VOICE, 5/20/97, p. 71, J.Hoberman

A less virtuoso treatment of similar material, [The reference is to *La Promesse*; see Hoberman's review.] Udayan Prasad's *Brothers in Trouble* is made from the illegal-alien perspective—indeed, the movie opens with its bewildered protagonist, Amir (Pavan Malhotra), arriving in England inside a vegetable crate.

Greasing palms each step of the way with his dwindling supply of dollars, Amir is transported to a clammy Midlands city, installed in a group home with 15 or so other Pakistani illegals, and given a job shoveling sheep shit at one of the local mills. When a foreman appears, Amir instinctively ducks away, inspiring a more experienced compatriot an opportunity to impart the movies basic wisdom: "The bosses love a man with no papers—no papers, no existence, no rights."

Compared to the multiculti madhouse that is chez Igor, the hovel where Amir finds himself is almost genteel. (So too the movie's mise-en-scène. The pace may be hectic, but the lighting in this BBC production is strictly made-for-TV.) The illegals here are generally courteous to each other and even supportive. Those from Karachi may look down on the Bengalis but, all good Muslims, they pray together—as well as attend Sunday-morning shows of Hindi musicals en masse, cheering the wet-sari dance numbers before trotting home to line up for a neighborhood hooker's weekly house call.

Despite its ensemble pyrotechnics, *Brothers in Trouble* lacks narrative tension until the household elder, Hussein (veteran Indian actor Om Puri), takes up with a round-faced, friendly colleen named Mary (Angeline Ball). Consternation: Is the white woman a police informer? Is she a tart? It turns out that Mary is a sister in trouble and, for 20 minutes or so, the movie becomes a bizarre gloss on *Snow White and the Seven Dwarfs,* only to shift focus once more when Hussein insists that Mary—a character more vivid than valid—enter into a paper marriage with his nephew, with predictable results.

Lurching from situation to situation, *Brothers* has the feel of a boiled-down mini-series with movies and music, if little else, cueing a '60s time frame. That the underlying ethos is nostalgic only becomes clear in the unconvincing postscript. Amir, now mysteriously legalized, is awed by the green garden beauty that is England. In retrospect, it becomes apparent that he was always the best groomed, least Muslim, and most respectable of the bunch—less an unreconciled foreigner than a latent Englishman.

Also reviewed in:
NEW YORK TIMES, 5/14/97, p. C16, Stephen Holden
VARIETY, 8/28-9/3/95, p. 68, Derek Elley

BUDDY

A Jim Henson Pictures and Columbia Pictures release of an American Zoetrope production. *Executive Producer:* Francis Ford Coppola, Stephanie Allain, and Brian Henson. *Producer:* Steve Nicolaides and Fred Fuchs. *Director:* Caroline Thompson. *Screenplay:* Caroline Thompson. *Story:* William Joyce and Caroline Thompson. *Based on the book "Animals Are My Hobby":* Gertrude Davies Lintz. *Director of Photography:* Steve Mason. *Editor:* Jonathan Shaw. *Music:* Elmer Bernstein. *Music Editor:* Kathy Durning. *Sound:* Robert Eber and (music) Keith Grant. *Sound Editor:* Rick Franklin. *Casting:* Carrie Frazier. *Production Designer:* David Nichols and Daniel Lomino. *Art Director:* Roland Rosenkranz and Thomas Fichter. *Set Designer:* William

Ryder, Nancy Deren, and Dale Allan Pelton. *Special Effects:* Dennis Petersen. *Costumes:* Colleen Atwood. *Make-up:* Robin L. Neal. *Stunt Coordinator:* Dennis R. Scott. *Running time:* 84 minutes. *MPAA Rating:* PG.

CAST: Rene Russo (Gertrude "Trudy" Lintz); Robbie Coltrane (Dr. Bill Lintz); Alan Cumming (Dick); Irma P. Hall (Emma); Paul Reubens (Professor Spatz); John Aylward (Mr. Bowman); Mimi Kennedy (Mrs. Bowman); Jon Simmons (Theatergoer); Kathleen Klein (Movie Woman); Russell Young (Usher); Frank Collison (Zoo Keeper); Al Weber (Barker); Philip Baker Hall (Minister); Kyle Galyean (Bellowing Man); Dane Cook (Fair Cop); Michael Reid Mackay (Skinny Man); John Ennis and Jeff Hatz (Policemen); Bradley J. Lesley (Ali Baba); Julianna Wheeler (Cornered Woman).

CHRISTIAN SCIENCE MONITOR, 6/6/97, p. 12, David Sterritt

What has exotic animals, interactions with frequently puzzled humans, and lots of special effects?

"The Lost World: Jurassic Park" fits that description, but there's another right answer too—and the second one is a lot friendlier to mayhem-shy moviegoers who'd rather watch animals develop relationships with humans than munch them at snack time.

It's called "Buddy," and while it's not one of the season's best pictures, it provides an oasis for audiences seeking a quieter experience than Steven Spielberg's blockbuster offers.

Based on real events, "Buddy" focuses on Gertrude Lintz, a 1920s socialite with a passion for animals and a bank account big enough to indulge it. Her luxurious home swarms with everything from horses and dogs to rodents, serpents, and fish. Her husband, a successful physician, supports her hobby without quite sharing her enthusiasm. A good-natured assistant helps her cope with unexpected challenges that arise from time to time.

Trudy loves all her pets, but her favorites are four chimpanzees so cute and smart they "almost seem human," to use a familiar phrase. Taking that expression literally, Trudy raises them as if they were children teaching them to eat human foods, play human games, even pretend to say human prayers when they go to bed at night.

It's this aspect of her personality that makes Trudy a potentially interesting movie character—not just a millionairess with a hobby, but a single-minded eccentric whose dedication has crossed the line into obsession. Is her odd treatment of the chimps a legitimate expression of animal-loving good intentions? Or is she preventing them from having the sort of natural, noncivilized life they were born for?

Such questions grow more pressing when Buddy comes along. He's a baby gorilla with serious health problems, and there's no doubt, that Trudy's loving care saves his life and restores his health. She adds him to her domestic menagerie and looks forward to years of household happiness—forgetting that gorillas change their temperaments as they get older, reverting to habits more suited to a jungle than a well-manicured estate.

Which raises still more questions. Will his unusual upbringing enable Buddy to stay in Trudy's special world? Or will the call of the wild make him an unfit member of even this unorthodox household?

"Buddy" would be a better movie if it probed more deeply into issues of animal behavior and human-animal relations, and if it treated Lintz's treatment of her chimps as a moral issue instead of a mere oddity.

Also disappointing is the portrayal of Buddy not by a real gorilla, but by an actor and a remote-control team equipped with a high-tech "animatronic" costume. True, casting a gorilla in the role would have led to intractable training problems not unlike those Lintz faced. But the artificial beast never looks as real as the genuine animals it shares the screen with, and this hinders the movie's overall credibility.

Rene Russo gives a fittingly extravagant performance as Lintz, and Robbie Coltrane is enjoyably offbeat as her long-suffering husband. Alan Cumming and Paul Reubens head the supporting cast. The picture was written and directed by Caroline Thompson, whose earlier screenplays range from "Edward Scissorhands" and "The Nightmare Before Christmas" to "The Addams

Family" and "The Secret Garden," all of which are more adventurous and memorable than her new movie.

"Buddy" has a good heart, but that's not enough to make a successful summer entertainment.

LOS ANGELES TIMES, 6/6/97, Calendar/p. 6, John Anderson

[The following review by John Anderson appeared in a slightly different form in **NEWSDAY, 6/6/97, Part II/p. B9.**]

'Tis the season of special effects, almost all of which will be used to raze buildings and raise blood pressure. Like the cheese they are, they stand alone, with little incorporation into plot or purpose, because they are the plot and the purpose.

And then, just when your biases against movie technology are firmly in place, along comes "Buddy," a sweet fairy tale of a movie from the accomplished screenwriter Caroline Thompson ("Edward Scissorhands," "The Addams Family," "The Secret Garden"), who made such a striking directorial debut with "Black Beauty." Through her liberated visual style and sense of wonder, Thompson is able to bestow pure magic even on a fact-based story; Gertrude Davies Lintz (Rene Russo), whose Brooklyn estate-menagerie is the setting of the film, really did raise dogs and fish and geese and apes.

But Thompson is also ably assisted by the animatronic wonders of Jim Henson Pictures, which makes Buddy (inside of whom is noted gorilla-portrayer Peter Elliott) as convincing as an animal character's ever been—and, coincidentally, rescues technology from the Neanderthals.

"Trudy" Lintz, given a very warm and ethereal performance by Russo, collected animals. Her gorilla-sized husband, Bill (Robbie Coltrane), was a physician and Trudy was an award-winning breeder of Briard dogs. She held to the then-controversial theory (given the Scopes trial) that man and apes were one large family. Her chimps are dressed by Bergdorf-Goodman, they dine at the table and their behavior, with some exceptions, is similar to that of some normal but rambunctious human children.

But it isn't until Buddy—a gorilla foundling—is deposited in her care that Trudy becomes missionary in her zeal, intent on proving that even this more volatile species could join her household. Things go well. and then things go badly. But Thompson makes it all ring true, with very little silly sentiment and a lot of honest emotion.

The sequence that seems askew is the same one that sets Buddy's crisis in motion: the 1933 Chicago World's Fair, to which Trudy is persuaded to bring her apes and put them on display. Given the dignity with which she's treated the animals thus far, it seems uncharacteristic that she'd submit them to such an undignified exhibition. But it all proves immaterial when Buddy gets loose, wanders among the terrified crowds and has to take refuge from police and his own fear until Trudy can rescue him.

What's really intriguing about Buddy's transition from malleable household pet to self-asserting ape is the element of shame he feels: His memory of the fear and loathing he felt at the fair haunts him, makes him brood—to the point that when Trudy interrupts his sullen reverie, he strikes out, compounding his own trauma and the fears of the family.

We're left with the lessons of Trudy's hubris and, of course, the lingering image of a very sensitive, very introspective ape, who's a lot more endearing than most of the humans populating this summer's movies.

NEW YORK POST, 6/6/97, p. 45, Michael Medved

The animatronic baby gorilla featured in early scenes of 'Buddy' may be a stunning, cunning piece of machinery, but it will never convince an audience that it's a living, breathing animal rather than an ingenious prop.

In the same way, it's easy to respect the craft and good intentions behind this intriguing project, and to appreciate all its carefully assembled working parts, but it never comes to life as the classy, classic family movie its makers intended.

Rene Russo plays Gertrude Lintz, a real-life socialite of the 1920s who maintained an exotic menagerie on her Brooklyn estate and wrote an autobiography about her experiences with animals.

She raises four chimpanzees, for instance, as if they were her own children, teaching them table manners and providing tailor-made clothes from Bergdorf-Goodman. Then she tries the same approach with an orphaned, half-dead infant gorilla she rescues from a zoo and calls Buddy.

The beast develops an uncomfortably intimate, yearning attachment to his mistress, which initially she cherishes, but then comes to fear as Buddy matures.

Displayed as a prime attraction in a special pavilion at the 1933 Chicago World's Fair, the animal runs wild and provokes a frightening incident (shades of "King Kong" coincidentally released that same year) and becomes more and more difficult for his adoring owner to handle.

This slender plot unfolds so slowly that the movie feels padded—with lots of 'comic relief' scenes of those lovable chimps doing mischievous things on the Lintz estate—like riding horses, roller skating, or releasing other animals from their cages.

These chimps easily upstage the 'gorilla' who is the movie's main focus, because they're honest-to-goodness animals, while Buddy is just an electronic gorilla doll and then, as he gets bigger, an agile guy in a gorilla suit.

Sure, the computer-controlled facial expressions are fascinating and expressive, but it's still a dubious impersonation. The much-too-immaculate, implausibly elegant period costumes and sets add to the air of unreality, while Russo is so glamorous and wholesome that she never projects the air of wacky obsession her part demands.

Writer-director Caroline Thompson (who previously wrote "Edward Scissorhands" and "The Nightmare Before Christmas," and directed the recent "Black Beauty") again offers a darker, more somber alternative in children's entertainment.

"Buddy" effectively delivers a few scenes of horror and pain that may well prove too much for young moviegoers: My own 8-year-old, Shayna, suffered nightmares from the film and even 24 hours later still wept over scenes showing the adored gorilla turning against his mistress.

Her reaction doesn't make this a bad movie, by any means, but it does raise questions about what audience—if any—the picture is intended to please.

VILLAGE VOICE, 6/10/97, p. 76, Amy Taubin

Buddy isn't Babe, but then, what 800-pound gorilla is?

Adapted from the autobiography of Gertrude "Trudy" Lintz, a pioneer animal activist, *Buddy* focuses on the relationship between Trudy and Buddy, the gorilla she rescued in infancy and raised—along with a quartet of chimps—as a member of the family. An immensely wealthy women, Lintz cared for an impressive variety of animals. But she was most passionate about her primates, who—dressed in made-to-order clothes from Bergdorf's—sat at the table with her and her very patient physician husband.

As directed by Caroline Thompson, *Buddy* tries to be a movie for both children and adults, and probably won't be totally satisfying for either. Kids will adore the chimps, who skate, ride horses, and even do a little fan dancing (Lintz's primates were a main attraction at the 1933 World's Fair). On the other hand, the love story may have them squirming in their seats.

I found the tale of the impossible love between this impulsive, self-assured, generous woman and the ape—who could only find frustration in adulthood where he found bliss in infancy—fantastically compelling. By confronting the myth of *King Kong* (Buddy gazing at Trudy as she combs her waist-length blond hair), Thompson is free to go further in giving Buddy's inchoate longing and Trudy's forbidden desire the gravity they deserve.

The human actors Rene Russo and Robbie Coltrane make eccentricity seem like the healthiest possible adjustment to society. But in the end it's Buddy's movie. The most elaborate animatronic creation of Jim Henson's Creature Shop, Buddy basically involves a collaboration between an actor (Peter Elliott) who's inside the gorilla form and a puppeteer (Mark Wilson) who controls the movements of Buddy's face through a computer system.

Unlike all the man-made gorillas who came before him, Buddy moves his eyes the way real-life gorillas do—independently of his skull. In fact, gorillas have a greater range of eye movement than humans. In a medium where the eyes have the last word, Buddy looks like the better man.

Also reviewed in:
NEW YORK TIMES, 6/6/97, p. C12, Janet Maslin

VARIETY, 6/9-15/97, p. 69, Steven Gaydos
WASHINGTON POST, 6/6/97, p. B7, Stephen Hunter
WASHINGTON POST, 6/6/97, Weekend/p. 62, Desson Howe

BUGIS STREET

A Margin Films release of a Jaytex Prods. (Singapore) production. *Executive Producer:* Godfrey
Yew. *Producer:* Katy Yew. *Director:* Yonfan. *Screenplay (English and Chinese Dialogue):*
Yonfan. *Story:* Katy Yew. *Director of Photography:* Jacky Tang. *Editor:* Kam Ma. *Music:*
Chris Babida. *Sound:* Benny Chu and Brian Schnegmann. *Production Designer:* Ned
McLoughlin. *Art Director:* Ma Man Bing. *Costumes:* Cynthia Lim. *Running time:* 100 minutes.
MPAA Rating: Not Rated.

CAST: Hiep Thi Le (Lian); Michael Lam (Meng); Benedict Goh; Ernest Seah (Lola); Greg-O
(Drago); Maggie Lye (Maggie); Gerald Chan and Godfrey Yew.

LOS ANGELES TIMES, 11/21/97, Calendar/p. 14, Kevin Thomas

Near the beginning of Hong Kong filmmaker Yonfan's endearing "Bugis Street," its naive 16-
year-old heroine Lian ("Heaven and Earth's" Hiep Thi Le), newly arrived from Malacca, takes
a job at a picturesque Singapore Hotel.
Writing to a friend back home, she reports breathlessly that "it's just like "The World of Suzy
Wong."' Almost but not quite, for Lian has not yet discovered that the glitzy glamour girls of the
wonderfully named Sin Sin Hotel on notorious Bugis Street are in fact men, with a far greater
percentage of them transvestites than transsexuals. The time is the '60s.
Like countless drag queens everywhere, the denizens of Bugis Street turn to prostitution in order
to survive while dreaming of true love. Some, like Lola (Ernest), are long-term residents of the
Sin Sin, others rent by the hour, arriving arm-in-arm with their johns, many of them American
and European servicemen on leave from the Vietnam War.
The Sin Sin, run by a plump, kind woman with a pudgy little son, may be a hot-sheet hotel,
but it is well-maintained, with Lian quickly adapting to her job cheerfully as an all-purpose
servant. With its courtyard, lush foliage and charming colonial architecture the hotel might pass
for one in New Orleans; indeed the delicate fretwork of its transoms recall the cast-iron filigree
of French Quarter balconies.
In adapting a story by his producer Katy Yew, Yonfan suggests that such an establishment might
not be such a bad place for a young girl to come of age after all. Lola, who keeps a handsome,
muscular, no-good lover (Michael Lam), and the other working girls can be shrill and flighty, but
by and large they are, underneath the false eyelashes and feathers, tough cookies surviving in a
hostile world despite their vulnerability.
They are kind and loving to Lian, and they have lots to teach her about men and women, life
and love. Lian's special mentor is Drago (Greg-O), back on a visit from Paris to visit his dying
mother. Drago is an ultra-chic, ultra-affected cosmetics salesperson, but beneath all the exaggerated gestures and attire, a devoted son and a worldly mentor to Lian.
Yonfan has an amazing control of tone. He doesn't hesitate to exploit the muscular bodies of
the hunky men who attract the Bugis Street ladies, yet there is an admirable detachment in his
compassion. "Bugis Street" can be very steamy, not to mention outrageously over the top, yet
Yonfan can step back and frame his highly urban, decidedly lurid and sentimental tale with
beautiful, leafy, rain-drenched images.
There's more to "Bugis Street" than mere sensationalism, just as there's more to the real-life
transvestites and transsexuals who populate this film than their makeup and sequins. "Bugis
Street" is alternately funny and gritty and ultimately wise and touching.
Don't go looking for Bugis Street, however, when visiting Singapore, for it has been leveled,
just as New Orleans' long-abandoned Basin Street brothels were nearly 50 years ago. (The film
was shot in a nearby area.) Civic reformers and urban developers everywhere seem to have little
appreciation for the beguiling architecture of palaces of pleasure.

NEW YORK POST, 11/15/97, p. 28, Larry Worth

When Oliver Stone had snakes dropped down Hiep Thi Le's blouse for a torture scene in 1993's disastrous "Heaven and Earth," she probably thought it couldn't get much worse.

But that was before she signed on for "Bugis Street," a laughably unfocused look at one of Singapore's most notorious brothels in its '60s heyday. Hiep Thi Le has the unenviable task of playing a naive 16-year-old who evolves from Milquetoast maid to woman of the world.

Of course, this walk on the wild side is meant to be different from every other coming-of-age tale. Here, the bordello appears to be stocked with pretty ladies, but it actually features—gasp!—transvestites and transsexuals.

OK, that means "Bugis Street" has got a cliche storyline and over-the-top camp. And as veteran writer-director Yonfan ups the ante, the worse it gets.

The real-life locale might have made for an interesting documentary. But in its fictionalized version, "Bugis Street" doesn't merit a visit.

VILLAGE VOICE, 11/18/97, p. 85, Dennis Lim

The first Singaporean feature to earn a U.S. release is, unfortunately, not one of Eric Khoo's stark social critiques, but this insulting and irredeemably sophomoric attempt at titillation. Set In '60s Singapore, Hong Kong director Yonfan's sniggering non-story plants a virginal 16-year-old naif *(Heaven and Earth's* Hiep Thi Le) amid a gaggle of transvestite and transsexual prostitutes, plus one all-male hunk (all nonactors, clearly). Inept both as coming-of-age story and drag fairy tale, the film suffers from a grating woodenness that suggests grotesquely mutated Fassbinder.

Also reviewed in:
NEW YORK TIMES, 11/14/97, p. E33, Lawrence Van Gelder
VARIETY, 10/30-11/5/95, p. 78, Ken Eisner

CAFE SOCIETY

A Raymond De Felitta release in association with The Screening Room. *Executive Producer:* Carl-Jan Colpaert, Frederic Bouin, and Jim Steele. *Producer:* Steve Alexander and Elan Sasson. *Director:* Raymond De Felitta. *Screenplay:* Raymond De Felitta. *Director of Photography:* Michael Myers. *Editor:* Suzy Elmiger. *Casting:* Sheila Jaffe and Georgianne Walken. *Production Designer:* Markus Canter and Stuart Canter. *Set Decorator:* Betsy Alton. *Costumes:* Juliet Polcsa. *Running time:* 110 minutes. *MPAA Rating:* R.

CAST: Peter Gallagher (Jack Kale); Frank Whaley (Mickey Jelke); Lara Flynn Boyle (Patricia Ward); John Spencer (Ray Davioni); Anna Thomson (Erica).

NEW YORK POST, 7/18/97, p. 47, Thelma Adams

Bright lights, big city, dim bulbs.

Throw together trust-funder Mickey Jelke, goldigger Pat Ward and vice cop Jack Kale, and you wouldn't have the wattage to light up the marquee for "The Sweet Smell of Success," the 1957 Manhattan melodrama that newcomer Raymond De Felitta tries to rekindle in "Cafe Society." The story—based on a real, high-profile '50s New York scandal opens with playboy Jelke (Frank Whaley) spying Ward (Lara Flynn Boyle) at El Casbah. It's the, kind of smoky nightspot with zebra-striped walls where patrons sip sidecars.

"A pretty girl is like a melody," Jelke says, but anyone can see Pat's a bad tune—even Kale (Peter Gallagher).

The crusading cop with the matinee idol looks is at the swanky club seeking more than the perfect martini. He's sniffing around 'sweet smell' territory for dirty laundry.

The story's generic Mr. Bigs need scandal to fuel their political careers. They exploit the moral low road while riding on a platform of the moral high road. Besides, the low road makes for better copy—and ludicrous scenes of girdle-clad girlies engaged in alcohol-drenched bacchanals at Jelke's flat.

When Jelke's family cuts him off, he makes Ward an indecent proposal. He'll pimp her until they have enough money to wed. It doesn't take a genius to know it's not time to reserve the Waldorf.

Kale urges Ward to accept the proposal—then arrests Jelke as the crown pimp of Cafe Society. Ward turns over on her round heels and gives state's evidence. While the trio mulls the nature of whoredom, the poor little rich boy walks away with the movie's best self-justification: He's no upper- crust criminal, he's just a "pervert." How '90s of him!

Whaley ("Swimming With Sharks") has a talent for playing smart, weak-willed weasels, normal guys with a crucial screw loose. Here, he never reaches the heights of his pompadour, he's just a little boy playing dress-up.

Gallager ("To Gillian on Her 37th Birthday") has little more to work with than his devilishly dark eyebrows. His character's transition from hooker-happy party boy with a badge to bleeding heart doesn't have a whiff of truth to it.

Boyle lacks the sweet smell of successfully passing herself off as the sophisticated woman of mystery at the center of the Manhattan prostitution scandal that smeared real-life oleo heir Jelke.

The "Twin Peaks" star has the power to make even Demi Moore feel superior as an actress. Ward's saga of rape, abortion, prostitution and suicide comes across with the emotional punch of lather-rinse-repeat.

As Jelke says of his go-along gal pal: "I haven't seen a performance that bad since the talkies."

NEWSDAY, 7/18/97, Part II/p. B9, Jack Mathews

With cigarettes in one hand and highballs in the other, behind mannered glances and improbably quick wits, the stars of Raymond De Felitta's "Cafe Society" quickly turn what the first-time filmmaker assures us is a true story into a dress-up charade that plays more like a deflating New Yorker cartoon, minus the irony.

"Cafe Society" is based on a sex scandal involving New York playboy and oleomargarine heir Mickey Jelke (Frank Whaley), who went to prison in the early '50s for running a call-girl ring out of the nightclubs that were, as he might have put it, his oyster. Much to the political benefit of crusading cops and politicians, the scandal exposed the decadence of high society's spoiled urchins and helped hasten the demise of the New York club scene.

Writer-director De Felitta sorted through that history and apparently fell in love with its setting—the array of Midtown clubs, like the El Morocco, where the swells came to see and be seen, to hustle drinks and invitations to after-hour parties, and to play a cruel game called "Really, now ..., " where they lash each other with sarcasm.

Like "True Confessions," which was loosely based on the murder of a Hollywood starlet in the late '40s, "Cafe Society" is postwar sensationalism done up as film noir. Unlike "True Confessions," which grounded itself in gritty realism, De Felitta's picture is an exercise in artifice, as empty as it is stylish.

In the newsreel footage of club life intercut with the opening dramatic scenes, the natives seem to be lost in liquored revelry; in De Felitta's story, they're mostly drunk with ego, each one harboring a secret agenda for personal gain at another's loss.

Besides Mickey Jelke, "Cafe Society's" circle of friends includes Jack Kale (Peter Gallagher), an undercover cop seeking headlines in a scheme to befriend and betray Jelke; Pat Ward (Lara Flynn Boyle), the beauty who wanders into the El Casbah with dreams of stealing into Mickey's heart and fortune, and Ray Davioni (John Spencer), a press agent who, while dishing the dirt for power and profit, doubles as a pimp.

The story hinges on Mickey's brat-boy instincts, his willingness to trust the most dubious acquaintances, and on Jack's willingness to sacrifice Pat, who has fallen in love with him, to get to Mickey.

De Felitta attempts to heat all this up into romantic melodrama, and he coaxed enough tears and recriminations from his cast to flood a confession booth. But there isn't a moment of genuine emotion, or psychological honesty.

Boyle's good girl/bad girl role is one that would have been played by Lizabeth Scott when she and film noir were young, and Boyle doesn't have the range or sense of mystery to make it work. Whaley is adrift in a blur of pathetic rich-boy clichés, and Gallagher, doing his best to remind us of Robert Mitchum, doesn't do much but pose and sulk.

Really, now.

VILLAGE VOICE, 7/29/97, p. 78, Rebecca Louie

Based on a 1952 prostitution scandal, Raymond De Felitta's debut tries to capture the dog-eat-dog world of crooked law enforcement and New York nightclubs, but *Cafe Society*'s characters are all dressed up with no place to go. Frank Whaley sports stylin' 50s threads as the rich, 23-year-old Mickey Jelke (the playboy who gets caught in a D.A.'s plan to play "moral guardian"), and his lovely girlfriend turned call girl Patricia Ward (Lara Flynn Boyle) could own the Easter parade in her series of extravagant ensembles. Even Peter Gallagher as undercover cop Jack Kale gets into the act with a tuxedo or two, so who cares if their conversations are clichéd and their characters two-dimensional? Their clothes match the set, the soundtrack wails the blues, and they're holding martinis in every other scene.

The actors try hard, every now and then pulling a "real moment" between characters, but *Cafe Society* needs to serve up something a lot stronger than fabulous fashions and noir nuances to got you properly buzzed.

Also reviewed in:
NEW YORK TIMES, 7/18/97, p. C16, Stephen Holden
WASHINGTON POST, 9/26/97, Weekend/p. 50, Stephen Hunter
VARIETY, 6/5-11/95, p. 38, Todd McCarthy

CAMP STORIES

An Artistic License Films release of a Forensic Films production. *Producer:* Robin O'Hara and Scott Macaulay. *Director:* Herb Beigel. *Screenplay:* Herb Beigel. *Director of Photography:* Paul Gibson. *Editor:* Meg Reticker. *Music:* Roy Nathanson. *Production Designer:* Deana Sidney. *Running time:* 99 minutes. *MPAA Rating:* Not Rated.

CAST: Jerry Stiller (Schlomo); Zachary Taylor (Young David); Elliott Gould (Older David); Susan Vanech (Sally); Ted Marcoux (Chaim); Kris Park (Young Paul); Richard Council (Older Paul); Paul Sand (Moishe); Talia Balsam (Chaim's Wife).

LOS ANGELES TIMES, 2/28/97, Calendar/p. 10, Kevin Thomas

Summer camp movies usually spell hilarity and nostalgia, but Herbert Beigel's engaging, semiautobiographical "Camp Stories" is bittersweet to the utmost.

It's set in a fading orthodox Jewish camp in the Poconos in 1958, where 15-year-old David Katz (Zachary Taylor) has been sent much against his will by his parents, who figure their movie-nut son could use some fresh air in a presumably morally uplifting setting. There is some humor and warmth in Beigel's look back, but his film is mainly a record of misery endured during two long, tedious months, relieved by David's first experience of love with a pretty Westport, Conn., shiksa (Susan Vanech) vacationing nearby.

Surprisingly, there are no scenes of religious observance and instruction, and "Camp Stories" suffers somewhat from this lack. What we're left with are some glimpses of desultory sports activities in an overly long tale of ultra-conservative adults constantly hectoring teenagers for the slightest infractions in behavior, while most everybody, adults and kids alike, do an awful lot of nothing much.

Right from the outset, David, who's nice-looking, intelligent and self-possessed, is locked into an edgy situation with one of his cabin mates, the unhappy Paul (Kris Park), who's in his third summer—and whose parents haven't bothered to visit him since his first. Making matters far worse for David is the hotheaded Chaim (Ted Marcoux), caught in a deteriorating marriage and vying with the gentle, ineffectual Moishe (Paul Sand) to take over the camp upon the impending retirement of its pompous leader (Jerry Stiller). A petty, jealous tyrant, Chaim has mistakenly got it in his head that his attractive, fed-up wife (Talia Balsam) is having an affair with David.

Beigel's clear commitment to his people and their stories and some good actors—Taylor, especially—keep us involved, even though the film tends to be repetitious and could benefit from some trimming. "Camp Stories" has a prologue and an epilogue set in the present, which gives it a feeling of evening up old scores. Elliott Gould and Richard Council play the middle-aged David and Paul, respectively.

NEW YORK POST, 4/19/97, p. 28, Michael Medved

The movie "Camp Stories" is a 1960s coming-of-age saga that marks the feature film debut of writer-director Herbert Beigel, a 52-year-old attorney, philanthropist and aspiring actor (he once played a small part in TVs "Law and Order") who audaciously invested his own time and money in the effort.

While aging baby-boomers may instinctively applaud his courage, they can hardly enjoy his film a dramatically dreadful, dismally dishonest mess that gives even well-intentioned amateurism a bad name.

The story centers on 15-year-old David Katz (played by Zachary Taylor of NBC's "I'll Fly Away," looking 10 years too old for the part) who is forced to attend an Orthodox Jewish camp in the Poconos in the summer of 1958.

The founder of this institution (Jerry Stiller) suffers from a terminal illness, leaving two of the senior counselors competing to take his place.

One of them, Moishe (Paul Sand), is a kindly but ineffective bumbler, while the other, Chaim (Ted Marcoux), is a muscular, sadistic disciplinarian.

Chaim's wife (Talia Balsam) is an indolent sexpot, and we know their marriage is in trouble since she can't even pronounce her husband's name.

Another counselor (Ben Shenkman) is supposed to be a gung-ho, uniformed veteran of the Israeli army, but his bizarre accent sounds more Swedish (or sometimes even Cuban) than Hebrew.

Did director Beigel never consider hiring a real Israeli to play this part?

Meanwhile, Beigel has portrayed his frankly autobiographical protagonist as such an impossibly perfect kid that the film feels embarrassing and uncomfortable to watch.

Our hero is brilliant (and a devoted movie buff), handsome, incomparably athletic, considerate, moral, mature, self-reliant and, in a singularly hackneyed bit of plotting, endearing romantic— suavely capturing the heart (and body) of a gorgeous blonde gentile girl (Susan Vanech), who's visiting town with her parents.

If this tacky characterization is one-dimensional, the portrayal of the camp is even worse. Despite its purportedly religious orientation, we never see campers at prayer or study, observing the Sabbath, working at arts and crafts, or even hiking or boating.

The only portrayal of camp life shows the administration struggle to enforce meaningless rules, giving the summer sessions the aura of a sitcom concentration camp and awkwardly recalling an especially weak episode of "Hogan's Heroes."

The whining klezmer music in the background (by Roy Nathanson) incongruously suggests that the melodrama amounts to some profound, heart-wrenching Jewish statement, while even the most trivial details (is Beigel really unaware that Orthodox tradition frowns on mixed dancing?) are abysmally botched.

The acting is never above the level of a bad summer camp pageant, while Elliott Gould (who plays the hero as an adult, looking back on his adolescence) gets the film's best part since he appears on screen for only 90 seconds.

VILLAGE VOICE, 4/22/97, p. 86, David Finkle

Director-screenwriter Rule No. 7: Never have a character spout, "It's like a bad movie," unless you're making a good movie. Herbert Beigel wasn't. Although there's something appealing about the klezmer fright-music underscoring, it's the best that can be said for *Camp Stories*, Beigel's apparently autobiographical first film. Young David Katz is forced to leave his Cincinnati home during the summer of '58 to attend Camp Ararat for Orthodox Jewish boys and girls; he encounters *lanzmen*, a sympathetic shiksa, and life's ambiguities. The learning-when-to-break-the-rules plot may make perfect sense to Beigel but is murky as day-old borscht to everyone else. Among the actors who were undoubtedly scratching their yarmulkes over illogical lines are Zachary Taylor (effective as David against all odds), Jerry Stiller, and the rarely seen Paul Sand. *Feh!*

Also reviewed in:
NEW YORK TIMES, 4/18/97, p. C10, Stephen Holden

CAPITAINE CONAN

A Kino International release of a Les Films Alain Sarde/Little Bear/TF1 Films production with the participation of Canal+ and Studio Images 2. *Producer:* Alain Sarde and Frederic Bourboulon. *Director:* Bertrand Tavernier. *Screenplay (French with English subtitles):* Bertrand Tavernier and Jean Cosmos. *Based on the novel by:* Roger Vercel. *Director of Photography:* Alain Choquart. *Editor:* Luce Grunenwaldt, Laure Blancherie, and Khadicha Bariha-Simsolo. *Music:* Oswald D'Andrea. *Art Director:* Guy-Claude Francois. *Costumes:* Jacqueline Moreau and Agnes Evein. *Running time:* 130 minutes. *MPAA Rating:* Not Rated.

CAST: Philippe Torreton (Conan); Samuel Le Bihan (Norbert); Bernard Le Coq (De Scève); Laurent Schilling (Beuillard); Jean-Yves Roan (Rouzic); Phillipe Helies (Grenais); Tonio Descanvilles (Caboulet); Eric Savin (Corporal Armurier); Olivier Loustau (Hahut); Jean-Marie Juan (Lethore); Catherine Rich (Madeline Erlane); Francois Berleand (Commandant Bouvier); Claude Rich (General Pitard de Lauzier); Andre Falcon (Colonel Voirin); Claude Brosset (Pere Dubreuil); Crina Muresan (Ilyana); Cecile Vassort (Georgette); Francois Levantal (Forgeol); Pierre Val (Jean Erlane); Roger Knobelspiess (Major Cuypene); Frederic Pierrot (Train Officer); Jean-Claude Calon (Officer Greffier Loisy).

LOS ANGELES TIMES, 10/10/97, Calendar/p. 6, Kevin Thomas

Bertrand Tavernier's superb "Capitaine Conan" takes us into the Balkans as World War I ends for a subtle and resonant study of friendship, politics and class differences as the men who helped win the war for France are exploited for covert warfare long past the Armistice.

When World War I ended on Nov. 11, 1918, French troops had been engaged in a bloody struggle with the Bulgarians. They were eager to be demobilized yet were still fighting there intermittently seven months later. They remained because France and its allies were concerned about Bulgaria's territorial ambitions. France's lagging also positioned its men for further combat with the advancing Red Army.

This is just a portion of the complex and conflicting national interests and allegiances at play that made the Balkans such a volatile region then and now.

It is against this background that "Capitaine Conan" unfolds. It was adapted by Tavernier and veteran screenwriter Jean Cosmos from Roger Vercel's 1934 autobiographical novel.

Tavernier is France's master storyteller in the grand tradition. For more than 20 years he has proved that a classic screen narrative that grapples with themes and issues as well as character and destiny remains vital. As a result, he has emerged as one of the world's great contemporary filmmakers, as much at ease with the broad canvas as the intimate sketch. Many of his films are marked by an interplay of shifting scale, none more than "Capitaine Conan."

Tavernier devotes his first half-hour to warfare to convey vividly not only just what a dirty, brutal business it is but also what kind of fearless and cagey men it takes to fight it successfully.

None are better in battle than Capitaine Conan (Philippe Torreton). He is a shrewd working-class man, fully aware that it is men like him—the men who fought hand-to-hand combat—who won the war for France. Once past the Armistice and moved into Bucharest and later Sofia, Capitaine Conan and especially the men he commands find it difficult to remain mobilized while ordered not to fight as France commences engaging in what it euphemistically calls "the theater of external—or expeditionary—operation."

Post-Armistice Bucharest is a glittery, dangerous wide-open town. In an elaborate old palatial structure, the French military is beginning to conduct court martials of some of its bravest soldiers for the most petty infractions; upstairs in the same building is a luxe brothel only officers could afford. In this way, the French ruling classes are reasserting themselves over the very men who saved their nation.

One of the few officers Conan actually respects, Lt. Norbert (Samuel Le Bihan), has been assigned to the tribunal to defend the accused soldiers. Their friendship becomes severely strained when two of Conan's men rob a nightclub, leaving two women dead. But as circumstances shift again, in Sofia, Conan and Norbert once again join forces to try to save the life of a hapless 20-year-old aristocrat who is facing death for a desertion he claimed he did not commit.

Tavernier has provided a rich context of exotic settings and complicated incidents to reveal the many facets of character within Conan and Norbert, men of exceptional strength of character and resolve for whom mutual respect, tested mightily, becomes profound. Torreton bears some resemblance to Tommy Lee Jones, though a smaller, wirier man, and has much of his temperament and forceful presence. Le Bihan, tall and clean-cut, makes of Norbert—who in fact was Vercel's alter ego—an intellectual of quiet courage. Veteran actor Claude Rich epitomizes the absurd obtuseness and arrogance of the French military elite.

As a period piece of exacting and, precise detail and as a triumph of assured filmmaking in every aspect, "Capitaine Conan" is a challenging and enriching experience. It possesses the resonance and subtlety of Jean Renoir's "Grand Illusion."

"Capitaine Conan" is the second of what Tavernier hopes will be a World War I trilogy that began with the memorable "Life and Nothing But" in 1989.

NEW YORK POST, 9/10/97, p. 40, Michael Medved

One of the many indelible images in Bertrand Tavernier's "Capitaine Conan" shows weary French troops in 1918, shivering in the rain, listening to a pathetically pompous general reading them a flowery proclamation of the Armistice.

As their gray-haired commander blathers endlessly about the "immortal glory" they have won, many of the men are unable to avoid breaking ranks to relieve themselves, suffering from "the runs" due to the rotten food they've been eating at the front.

This wry, earthy, view of the everyday realities of war is typical of the film at its most effective, but a slow middle section about adjustments to peacetime assignments is far less compelling; the movie adapts to the changed circumstances just as awkwardly as its characters.

Chief among those rugged personalities is Conan (the formidably fierce Philippe Torreton), a scruffy, irreverent hyper-kinetic officer who leads a celebrated group of unconventional commandos insisting that he's "a warrior, not a soldier."

After the armistice, Conan remains ferociously loyal to his men and contemptuous of his fellow officers when his unit's moved to Bucharest, Romania, but never allowed to return home.

Veteran filmmaker Tavernier ("'Round Midnight," "The Watchmaker") often combines epic elements with intimate intensity, but the huge battles in this film work far better than the private confrontation.

Using nearly 1,000 extras, Tavernier conveys the smell and taste of warfare with startling immediacy and unpredictability, often using a hand-held camera that functions as one of the troops at the front.

French expeditionary forces in the Balkans (they stayed there for more than a year after World War I, ultimately fighting Lenin's Red Army) remain little known in the U.S., but "Conan" (based on Roger Vercel's 1934 autobiographical novel) makes their experience real and riveting.

The complex peacetime tribunals, however, maintain a rambling, fuzzy, docudrama feel, suggesting that Tavernier, like Conan himself, loses energy and focus when removed from the battlefield.

NEWSDAY, 9/12/97, Part II/p.   B11, John Anderson

To compare Bertrand Tavernier's "Capitaine Conan" to "Grand Illusion," "Paths of Glory" or any of the truly great antiwar war films wouldn't be misleading. Or unwarranted. But it would distract somewhat from the fact that Tavernier makes his rapier points while creating a movie more exciting than any shoot-'em-up we've seen this past summer.

Is he trying to have his torte and eat it, too? To a degree. The action sequences in "Capitaine Conan"—which takes place just before and after the 1918 armistice, among men for whom the war may never end—depicts warfare as we seldom see it on screen. Human bodies are fragile, human psyches equally so. War isn't about smart bombs and anonymous, long-range killing, it's about maiming, throat slitting and things going bang in the broad daylight. A soldier's mind shutting down on his way up a strategic hillside. A situation in which terror, rather than bravado or machismo, is the predominant emotion, because these are reasonably intelligent people and they *should* be scared to death.

At the same time, "Capitaine Conan"—which won Cesars (French Oscars) last year for best director and best actor—is also about human nature, its colors and variations and how they're perverted by the unnatural/natural order of war. And how the institutions that demand these wars—governments, churches, industries—are compelled to distance themselves from the fighting once the fighting stops. And, lastly, the way that armies—20th-Century armies at least—tend to feed on themselves when the enemy disappears. Not that there aren't enemies in "Capitaine Conan," but one is occasionally a bit unsure of which uniform they're wearing.

The title character (played by Philippe Torreton, of Tavernier's "L.627") is introduced to us at night, along the trenches of a war that's still officially on. Conan and his band of French irregulars make guerrilla incursions that are designed to demoralize and terrify; "butchery," Conan calls it. When the armistice is announced—during a rain-soaked ceremony in which a quarter of the troops fall out with dysentery—it doesn't mean anyone's going home. It means an undeclared war in the Balkans, whose targets are "Trotskyites, Bolsheviks" or whatever untidy element needs cleaning up before the world can be declared safe for democracy.

This is bad news for most, but good news for Conan. Leader, killer, lover, he is a classic character: the outsider within the established order, whose tactics are considered unacceptable or unsavory, basically because he accomplishes the goals of his superiors without the niceties of gentlemanly pretense or realpolitik. Clint Eastwood has made his career playing types like Conan, and we respond to him because he represents uncluttered truth. Conan has no delusions about war, or about himself. "He's a soldier," he says of De Sceve (Bernard Le Coq), a career infantry officer of noble birth whom Conan admires. "I'm a warrior."

The other man Conan respects, but whose own sense of honor will put them at odds, is Lt. Norbert (Samuel Le Bihan), a scholar who was not born for war but knows his duty. When he's assigned to head a military tribunal—by virtue of his degree in literature—he does what he can to see justice meted out. When Conan's own men are arrested for a brutal nightclub robbery and the murder of two women, Norbert's sense of outrage overwhelms his sense of friendship.

But these soldiers, who've been through so much, and of whom so much has been asked—who can condemn them? That is Conan's question and it's a good one.

Likewise, who can rightfully condemn the pathetic Erlane (Pierre Val), a congenital coward who's going to be hanged? The pleas of his mother (a terrific Catherine Rich) fall on the deaf ears of De Sceve, who feels Erlane has betrayed their class. It's Conan who makes the case against execution; he understands that men like Erlane—and men like him—are born, not made.

Norbert understands it all, but also understands that there must be only one law. Conan understands action. Arrested for assaulting the husband of a woman he was sleeping with, Conan himself is muzzled like a pit bull. But when the fighting resumes, his nature is unleashed in a last-ditch effort to express itself. Because, after war ... what? The ending of "Capitaine Conan" contains its own kind of terror, a terror not of war but of peace. It might just leave you shellshocked.

VILLAGE VOICE, 9/16/97, p. 98, Leslie Camhi

Valor and slaughter drive the men of *Capitaine Conan*, an epic French production set in the trenches of the Great War. Bertrand Tavernier's film is adapted from Roger Vercel's 1934 novel, which follows infantry officers fighting in the Balkans. Captain Conan (Philippe Torreton) leads a special guerrilla unit. "My job isn't soldiering," he says, "it's butchery." His friend Lieutenant Norbert (Samuel Le Bihan), a schoolteacher in civilian life, admires Conan's grit but is puzzled by the moral riddle of the captain's unmitigated masculinity. They both dislike most officers, but admire De Scève (Bernard Le Coq), an aristocrat who chose the infantry over the cushier cavalry.

While their troops muck around in Romania, slitting throats and suffering from pernicious diarrhea, the legendary battles are fought elsewhere. Though exhausted after a ragged victory, they continue to serve in an undeclared war against the Red Army.

Things get complicated when, quartered in Bucharest, Conan's men are suspected in a ruthless nightclub robbery. Norbert is assigned to prosecute them and begins to consider the peacetime consequences of their trained brutality.

In terrifying battle scenes, Tavernier captures the physical confusion of war most convincingly. The Balkan setting is thick with history and recalls the muddled moral conflicts of recent years. Yet, in an age of "smart" bombs, *Capitaine Conan* feels not just historical but old-fashioned, nostalgic for a time when valor was a more important weapon than technology. Still, its a curiously melancholy action picture, an extended meditation on an almost extinct species of men.

Also reviewed in:
CHICAGO TRIBUNE, 1/2/98, p. P, Michael Wilmington
NEW REPUBLIC, 9/22/97, p. 30, Stanley Kauffmann
NEW YORK TIMES, 9/10/97, p. C11, Janet Maslin
VARIETY, 10/7-13/96, p. 90, David Rooney
WASHINGTON POST, 4/3/98, p. F1, Stephen Hunter

CAREER GIRLS

An October Films release of a Channel Four Films presentation of a Thin Man Films production. *Producer:* Simon Channing-Williams. *Director:* Mike Leigh. *Screenplay:* Mike Leigh. *Director of Photography:* Dick Pope. *Editor:* Robin Sales. *Music:* Marianne Jean-Baptiste and Tony Remy. *Sound:* George Richards. *Casting:* Stern and Parriss. *Production Designer:* Eve Stewart. *Art Director:* Helen Scott. *Costumes:* Rhona Russell. *Make-up:* Christine Blundell. *Running time:* 87 minutes. *MPAA Rating:* R.

CAST: Katrin Cartlidge (Hannah); Lynda Steadman (Annie); Kate Byers (Claire); Mark Benton (Ricky); Andy Serkis (Mr. Evans); Joe Tucker (Adrian); Margo Stanley (Ricky's Nan); Michael Healy (Lecturer).

CHRISTIAN SCIENCE MONITOR, 8/8/97, p. 12, David Sterritt

The trouble with making a runaway hit is that people start expecting more of the same.

Mike Leigh labored for years at quirky, bittersweet little films about ordinary people leading ordinary lives. A few, like "High Hopes" and "Life Is Sweet," gained respectful attention but proved limited in their appeal.

He made a breakthrough with the 1993 drama "Naked," winning top awards on the film-festival circuit. Then came last year's "Secrets & Lies," launched with the grand prize at Cannes and saluted by Hollywood with an impressive showing in the Academy Award nominations.

Leigh has clearly been on a roll. Will his new picture, "Career Girls," carry him to still greater heights? Or is it time for his rising roller coaster to take a dip—maybe even a heart-sinking plunge?

"Career Girls" is no disaster, but it's definitely a dip if one measures it by the high standards Leigh has set for himself in the past. Its problems aren't easy to pin down, since the acting and camera work have all the unpredictable twists and offbeat rhythms that Leigh's admirers have grown to love.

Trouble comes less from the story or characters than from the picture's overall tone, which can't decide whether it's rooted in the here-and-now of everyday life or the less tangible atmosphere of deep-down hopes and dreams. In short, the tale doesn't always seem sure where it's going, and for once in his career, Leigh doesn't always appear to have a firm grasp on his project.

The main characters are Hannah and Annie, college chums getting together for the first time since graduation six years ago. Both have come a long way, conquering problems that tormented them during their school days. But they still feel connected by the experiences they went through together.

Overcoming a new set of differences caused by their unequal positions in the professional world, they spend a long weekend in each other's company, hashing over the past and revealing their hopes for the future. Along the way they run into friends and foes from bygone years.

This is a promising movie idea, well suited to Leigh's filmmaking methods. Here as in his previous pictures, he has developed the story and characters in partnership with the cast, writing the screenplay only after much brainstorming and improvising.

No artistic system is foolproof, however, and this time Leigh's time-tested procedures have let him down. The performances are convincing and the London backgrounds have plenty of gritty authenticity. But the action becomes less focused and more meandering, and the characters never grow much richer.

In an apparent effort to save the movie from these problems, Leigh and company try to build psychological interest through an increasingly odd series of coincidences and chance meetings. This is a legitimate tactic—life is certainly full of unexpected surprises—but "Career Girls" relies so heavily on the device that even the characters start wondering what's going on.

You can't help feeling the story has lost its bearings. This impression is supported by Leigh's decision to drench much of the picture in fizzy pop music—like using a spicy sauce to hide the taste of a dish that didn't quite turn out.

The performers do their best under the circumstances, led by Katrin Cartlidge—widely applauded for "Naked" and "Breaking the Waves"—and newcomer Lynda Steadman. Andy Serkis and Joe Tucker are effective as two of the creeps our heroines deal with during their weekend. Mark Benton overdoes it as the most maladjusted of their old friends.

The film's original music was composed by Tony Remy and the multitalented Marianne Jean-Baptiste, an Oscar nominee for her wonderful acting as the adopted daughter in "Secrets & Lies." The flashback scenes are accompanied by far too many pop songs from the Cure.

FILM QUARTERLY, Spring 1998, p. 52, Karen Jaehne

[*Career Girls* was reviewed jointly with *Secrets & Lies;* see Jaehne's review in *Film Review Annual, 1997.*]

LOS ANGELES TIMES, 8/8/97, Calendar/p. 10, Kenneth Turan

"Career Girls" isn't going to cause the fuss that "Secrets & Lies" did, but that's not the point. How often, after all, does a psychologically acute British independent film win the Palme d'Or at Cannes, get nominated for five Oscars and gross $40 million theatrically worldwide?

But for a smaller-scale work, this look at the weekend reunion of two former college roommates puts even into sharper relief what makes writer-director Mike Leigh unique among his contemporaries. It underlines the qualities his more than a dozen films share that makes each linger in the memory, as this one does, long after the efforts of other filmmakers have faded to black.

What Leigh's celebrated work method—the growing of characters from the ground up in close collaboration with actors—creates is an inescapable and compelling sense of reality. No one captures tough human moments better than he does, and no one else's people are so persuasive that it's difficult to get them out of your mind. That's true even when, as here, the people have pain-in-the-neck aspects that keep each other and us at arm's length for a while. "Career Girls" has rewards, but they must be waited for.

Annie (Lynda Steadman, in her film debut) hasn't seen her old roommate Hannah ("Naked's" Katrin Cartlidge) for six years, but she's taking the train into London to spend a weekend with her. Before she arrives, Annie flashes back to what their college days were like, and the film alternates between showing how things were then and experiencing what they're like now as it examines the strength of shared memory and the place of the past in current lives.

Given how much more pulled together and successful both women are now, it's a shock to see what they were like as students at North London Poly. They called themselves "the Bronte sisters" because "we always get the brunt of everything," and consulted a dog-eared copy of "Wuthering Heights" for advice like it was the I Ching, "except you don't have to scratch it."

That questionable pun would be from Hannah, who was all hard edges at school, tactless and aggressive, capable of saying to Annie, a twitchy, grimacing neurotic with a terrible facial rash, "you look like you've done the tango with a cheese grater," a statement that couldn't help but lead to tears.

When Annie and Hannah's pal Ricky (Mark Benton), an overweight basket case whose pants are always just about falling off, is added to the mix, the result is a dubious menagerie that is close to out-and-out grotesqueness. While this emphasizes the awkward side of that time of life and provides a contrast to how the women are now, the feeling that the actors are overdoing it is hard to avoid.

As successful young professionals, Annie and Hannah are much more involving and easier to experience, even if they are awkward with each other at first. There is a kind of wariness and uncertainty between them as they attempt to reestablish a relationship that apparently fell apart under not the happiest of circumstances.

The women end up passing their time in make-believe apartment hunting in some of London's most posh areas, a quest that leads to the film's best line, a retort from Hannah who takes in the view from a dizzying high-rise balcony and snaps: "I suppose on a clear day you can see the class struggle from here."

The people encountered on the apartment search, including an obnoxious, conspicuous consumer (Andy Serkis) and a rental agent with a link to the women's past (Joe Tucker), each gets a segment of the film. Dealing with these men forges a new bond between the old friends and draws them closer to each other, perhaps closer, finally, than they've ever been before.

Though its plot frequently falls back on coincidence, so much so that the characters joke about it, "Career Girls" has the almost magical ability to involve us emotionally with these women even though there are points when we would've sworn that wouldn't be possible.

Secrets get revealed as well as lies, moments of real sadness and sharp humor are experienced, and everyone gets a better understanding of why (aside from a mutual admiration for the Cure, six of whose songs are on the soundtrack) the friendship came into being and why it's likely to last. Against considerable odds, a bond of genuine intimacy is forged on screen, and movies that can accomplish that have come to be Mike Leigh's trademark.

NEW STATESMAN, 9/19/97, p. 40, John Diamond

It is a time before North London Poly was required to masquerade as the University of North London. After a few drinks a stuttering, fat student explains what he's learnt from his psychology course so far. "There's like three different sorts of traits," he tells Hannah and Annie, two flat-sharing Poly girls. Ain't that the truth? Which Mike Leigh film has ever allowed for more than three sorts of trait?

There's the neurotic whose head twitches with the effort of maintaining all that *amour propre*, there's inferiority in the guise of superiority, represented by the nervously jokey loudmouth; and there's the physically-odd-with-a-heart-of-gold represented by the stuttering fat boy.

You know them: they've been played by Brenda Blethyn, Alison Steadman, Timothy Spall and the rest of the gang for years. This time a different group of actors are constrained by the phoney liberty of those improvised scripts. Somehow one knows those improvisations: the actors searching and searching until, deep within themselves, they discover the character they must play, knowing the character is right when it sounds like someone in a Mike Leigh film. All characters in Mike Leigh films sound like characters in Mike Leigh films.

The Mike Leigh character is as recognisable as the Pinter character, except that the latter's taciturnity has some dramatic purpose. Leigh's trait-ridden characters are there, well, because they're there. Art may hold a mirror to life, but in Leigh's world that's all it does. *Career Girls* is rarely more than Leigh saying, "You know what I've noticed about people? I've noticed this, this and this ..."

In fact much of what Leigh has noticed about the lives and mores of the aspirational lower-middle classes is pretty banal and none the less so because of the smug implication that, like some Captain Cook of the modern soul, he is the first to have come across all these traits.

Hannah (a superb Katrin Cartlidge) and Annie (Lynda Steadman—no relation) were at the North London Poly in the Thatcherite 80s—when else?—and now, ten years later, Annie has come back down from her native Wakefield to spend the weekend with her college flatmate. Then, Annie was a flutey-voiced wreck with hennaed knife-and-fork haircut and nervous, scabby skin; now she's merely small and uncomfortable, talking in the language of the high street fortuneteller: "I trust people too much" and "I've never been given the love I deserve."

Student Hannah, tall, pinch-faced, was the hard case, screwing up her eyes and shooting punny little sarcasms out of her tight mouth; now she's the low-level career girl, all Ikea and company car.

Annie and Hannah drive around north London, remembering the old days in a series of interwoven flashbacks. In a series of coincidences they also come across all the characters from their student days—the third flatmate, the gigolo who has them both, the mad stuttering fat boy driven madder by Annie's rejection.

In a film less boastful of its stark realism, the coincidences might have worked. Here they come across as desperate attempts to turn observation into narrative, never mind that Leigh excuses his artifice by having Hannah and Annie comment on it.

But artifice is what Leigh is about. For all the celebrated improvisation and naturalism, artifice is what, all he does. Since his admirers tend to belong to a different class than the one he patronisingly depicts, they're happy to take his word for it. Moreover he tricks the viewer into feeling that to doubt him, to doubt his characters, would be to commit an ideological solecism. To appreciate his work, it follows, is to show one's *bona fides*. But any honest punter can see that, far from naturalistic, his characters and scripts are as mannered as *commedia dell'arte*.

This, in itself, wouldn't matter: there is no dishonour in non-realism, in anti-naturalism; but what is lowering is experiencing the *ars est celare artem* in reverse, as it were. At his best, Leigh produces the odd nod of recognition, even something that, were it less wrung out of one, might approach compassion. At his worst, he produces a kind of emotional dyspepsia. To be depressed by a picture's vision, to be left irritated and angry by it, is no bad thing; to be left with the fuggy grizzle of low-level flu is intolerable.

And that is the trouble with *Career Girls* (and what message lurks, in cowardly fashion, behind the pitying irony of the title?) which manages to be bleak, lightweight and histrionic at the same time. Even Leigh aficionados might balk at such unrelenting toothlessness.

NEW YORK, 8/11/97, p. 53, David Denby

Katrin Cartlidge, who dominates Mike Leigh's new film, *Career Girls*, is tall and thin, with the aspect of a beautiful scarecrow. You may remember her as one of the young women David Thewlis made love to in Leigh's earlier film *Naked*, where she appeared as a sort of twittering yet oddly withdrawn siren. Cartlidge has a ghostly pallor, a pointed witch's nose, and a thatch of flung-about hair, and she's definitely something new in British actresses. She doesn't possess-how shall I put it?—that Royal Shakespeare Company equipoise. She isn't fiercely lucid (Emma Thompson) or beautifully melancholic (Kate Winslet) or passionately sincere (Helena Bonham Carter) or any of the other wonderful things that young British actresses usually are. She's abrupt and helter-skelter; you never know quite what she's going to do. Nervously combative, and then suddenly quiet and recessive, she's a funny and vulnerable actress who seems to discover each emotion as she goes along. Katrin Cartlidge is mysteriously touching, and that's what makes me think she could go far—we are attracted by what's inaccessible or inexplicable in her temperament, which makes us want to see more of her, and we're also held by her odd, convoluted emotional power, which rewards our curiosity.

Darting here and there in *Career Girls*, she is Hannah—or, as she grandly announces herself, drawing out the last syllable in mock-duchess hauteur, Han*naaah*. Whatever her name is, she's a student in London looking for a roommate, and when tiny Annie appears, Hannah both accepts her and makes fun of her. Annie (Lynda Steadman) has the worst case of dermatitis in history (one side of her face has been ravaged), and she speaks in a high voice, suddenly jerking her head down and away from people in shame. She's almost comically pathetic, and Hannah slams right into her—and then apologizes. In temperament and appearance, Hannah and Annie are very different women, but they share a sense of humor as well as a taste for rawness, and a friendship is struck for life (a third roommate gets quickly cast aside).

When the movie opens, Hannah and Annie are 30 and well established professionally yet unsettled in their personal lives. Annie, who has been living up north, takes the train to London, and as she sits in her compartment, and later that night in bed in Hannah's flat, she plays through her mind moments from their lives together as students. Mike Leigh has constructed the movie as a reverie on time and friendship; he shifts back and forth between the drab student past, in which each girl, in a different way, was a mess, and the rather comfortable present (the lighting scheme emphasizes the contrast). Working in the business world, the women have learned to smooth out the rougher edges and hide their discontent. But if we see the ways they have changed, we also see the ways they haven't changed—and can't change. To our relief, the mysteries of personality remain intact. There is something stubborn in each of them that resists "maturity" (i.e., the job market)—call it an essence, and that essence is what their friendship is built on. It may also be what their unhappiness is built on.

As in his last movie, *Secrets & Lies,* Leigh is interested less in dramatic resolution than in portraiture and mood. Yet *Career Girls* is hardly without tension. Cartlidge drives through each scene in a fury. In her student days, her Hannah is a tempest of jokes, quotations, put-downs, little bits of patter and profanity, the Cartlidge tongue moving faster than light. We don't get, or even hear, everything she says—the De Niro and Brando imitations that flash by, the quick mocking voices, the rapid and scathing commentary on everything. But we may be ravished by it nonetheless. Leigh has dramatized something that remains part of the past of many in the audiences time at school when wit and friendship and shared references to movies were the things that mattered most. Thirty years ago, Jean-Luc Godard got some of this onto the screen, but always with elements of Parisian glamour, even chic, that Leigh, the English realist, disdains. There is, for instance, a recurring game in which one person holds up a copy of *Wuthering Heights* and the other asks, in a pleading voice, such questions as "Ms. Brontë, Ms. Brontë, will I have a fuck soon?" and the answer is procured by flipping open the novel and pouncing on the first word that comes into view. The results are oddly bleak—a little punch in the jaw each time. Ms. Brontë has nothing but dark advice to offer.

Mike Leigh gets his rough, spontaneous surface in an unusual way. He doesn't improvise. Instead, he spends months rehearsing with actors who are living as their characters (Leigh gives them the idea, not the specific words). The script that develops out of these sessions is finally set down and shot. The results, to my ears, are much more pointed and affecting than what, say, John Cassavetes achieved twenty years ago using improvisation to develop a written script. Cassavetes's work all too often fell into nagging repetition or wandered off into blind alleys. For every revelation, there was also the embarrassing sight of an actor stranded, desperately trying to fill the dead air, and the movies, for all their moments of power, made a blurry impression. In Leigh's movies, the texture of ambiguities and contradictions, layered in well before shooting, is much more precise. The actors know where they are going; they can fool around with confidence.

As students, Hannah and Annie don't do much of anything; they just talk, cook, and hang out with a few friends, particularly the unfortunate Ricky, who squints when he tries to say something, then touches his closed eye with an alarmingly mobile forefinger, and speaks at last in impassioned fragments. "I'm not an idiot," he says. "I'm an idiot savant. I just haven't found the savant part yet." Leigh's touch with character is idiosyncratic and almost always deeply moving. He digs deeper into people than any other directors now working in movies, and he never touches cliché. Each of his characters is an original.

When the women link up again at 30, they keep running into people from their past, including Ricky as well as a young man with whom they both had affairs and who doesn't recognize them. For all its jokes and its spirit of female solidarity, the movie has an overall melancholy. The past hasn't stopped hurting either of these women. It's part of Leigh's complexity of mind that he makes us see that they've been hurt without reducing the hopes that we have for them in the future.

NEW YORK POST, 8/8/97, p. 53, Michael Medved

Those filthy, angry, immature, egotistical, impossible, pseudo-intellectual strangers—could they possibly be us during bygone college days?

Mike Leigh's latest film, "Career Girls," raises that question as it explores the painful, funny and bittersweet process of escaping the embarrassments of adolescence.

Though crammed with distinctive references to a specific time and place—mid-1980s London, with the music of the Cure blaring in the background—the movie achieves a surprising sense of universality and timelessness.

Like Leigh's other productions, it features remarkably rich characterizations and spectacularly skillful acting. But unlike last year's Oscar-nominated "Secrets & Lies," there's no melodramatic plot twist to help hook a mainstream audience.

In fact, there's no real plot at all, just a sensitive portrayal of a weekend reunion between two old friends from university who haven't seen each other in six years.

Their low-key, chatty time together is punctuated by intense, occasionally overwrought flashbacks emphasizing the way the two women have changed.

Annie (splendid newcomer Lynda Steadman) used to be a shy, twitchy, nervous wreck, with hair dyed orange and "scabby face" cruelly scarred by dermatitis. As a struggling student, she shared a gray, grungy and chronically unkempt flat with a tall, hawk-beaked fellow student, Hannah (the ferociously fine Katrin Cartlidge, best known from director Leigh's "Naked"), a cruel, smart-mouthed, affected, rebellious know-it-all who quickly assumes a complex role as both the new girl's mentor and tormentor.

In the movie's present tense, the two women have mellowed and matured, and they come across as sleek, self-assured, sophisticated urbanites proud of their promising careers. They enjoy elegant meals in pleasant surroundings, but feel horrified by the extremes of "sell-out" materialism they see in Andrew Serkis, an insufferable yuppie who's trying to sell them his trendy condo.

In a series of absurdly implausible coincidences, the two friends also just happen to bump into each of the three people who played the most important roles in their university days. This silly contrivance doesn't distract from the power of the performances—especially by Mark Benton as the sad, stuttering, overweight truth seeker who has found a unique means of keeping faith with his long-ago self.

One of the movie's major strengths is the convincing way it portrays dramatic differences and consistent elements in the past and the present of each of its characters. These details emerge as a triumph of makeup, costume design and, above all, intelligent acting.

The portrayal of the characters' "good old days" is far too honest in its emphasis on grime and self-pity to qualify as conventional "bright college years" nostalgia; the film suggests that the now thirtysomething "Career Girls" may be far less obnoxious than they once were, but they're also, somehow, less alive.

NEWSDAY, 8/8/97, Part II/p. B2 , John Anderson

There's a sense of intermission about Mike Leigh's latest, a sense of work being done for the sake of work—of a project that, like a Shakespearean sonnet or Beethoven arrangement of a Scots folk song, falls somewhat short of "Hamlet" or the Ninth Symphony.

Which is not to say that "Career Girls" isn't a thoroughly enjoyable piece of work—so much so that citing its all-too-obvious flaws feels somewhat curmudgeonly. But allow me to blame Leigh himself. His winning streak—which has been going on for all of the '90s and includes "Life Is Sweet," "Naked" and last year's Oscar-nominated "Secrets & Lies"—has led us to expect a masterpiece a year.

And that is something "Career Girls" is decidely not. Its rather slight story—two young women, roommates during college, are reunited after six years and find each other profoundly changed and profoundly the same—spins together enough coincidence and kismet that the characters themselves are compelled to comment on it.   And when characters don't just break the fourth wall but fairly demolish it, the spell has usually been broken, too.

But the performances.   Let's talk about the performances.   Leigh, as usual, developed this film through improvisations with his cast and the results are characters that are artfully developed, complete and whole—even if we have no idea how Hannah (Katrin Cartlidge and Annie (Lynda Steadman) metamorphosed from the callow creatures they were to the more neatly packaged but insecure people they are.

Traveling by train to visit Hannah, Annie—this is Steadman's first film and she's terific—sees herself in flashback: a nest of nervous tics, with lesions of dermatitis rivering one cheek. (Years later, her skin clear, she still reaches for that cheek during moments of stress.) Hannah ("It's Hann*aaahh*," says with faux-imperiousness) is a caustic piece of work, her spit-fire vulgarity recalling, Johnny, the central character in Leigh's "Naked" (in which Cartlidge co-starred). When Annie meets her friend again, Hannah is well-dressed, well-coiffed and self-assured. But her feral qualities linger.

Mellower, wiser, still not quite sure of themselves or life, they revisit the past, meeting an old flame who slept with both but can't remember either; mocking a supposed ladies' man who wants to sell them an apartment; encountering the tragic Ricky (Mark Benton), an old school chum and apparent mental defective whose appearance is both too unlikely and too predictable not to upset the movie.

But where "Career Girls" succeeds—the title, by the way, is facetious, not a euphemism for prostitution—is in exploring that tender territory where old friends, once so intimate, try to rediscover what they knew in each other.   They stumble around the unfamiliar in search of the past, rekindle memories that might be best forgotten.   In the case of Annie and Hannah, what they find is what they want—but of course, that may be Leigh's point.

SIGHT AND SOUND, 9/97, p. 38, Stella Bruzzi

Annie arrives in London by train to see Hannah Mills, who was her closest friend at college but whom she hasn't seen for six years.   The action cuts between the present and flashbacks of their undergraduate years.   Six years earlier, North London Polytechnic student Annie answers an advert on the flatshare noticeboard and moves in with Hannah and Claire.   Eventually Annie and Hannah move into a flat on their own.   Their times at college are mapped by the relationships they form with Claire, the unstable Ricky Burton (who declares his love for Annie but is spurned) and Adrian Spinks, with whom they both have a brief fling.

The present-day action takes place over a weekend.   The two women are now both in their thirties.   The first evening, Hannah cooks Annie a meal and the two go to sleep.   On Saturday, they pretend to be rich house-hunters and make several appointments to see expensive London properties.   Their first call is to a Docklands apartment, owned by a fast-living city slicker.   They go onto another flat, where the estate agent showing them round turns out to be Adrian.   He vaguely recognises Hannah but not Annie, and tells them he's now married and has a child.   That night, the women go out for a meal.

On Sunday, Annie and Hannah go walking on Hampstead Heath where they see Claire jogging. On the way to the station, they drop by their old student flat.   Ricky, by now severely mentally ill, is sitting on the step of the boarded-up chip shop below it.   After a brief conversation Annie and Hannah leave.   In the car they both start crying.   They have an equally tearful farewell at the station.

Mike Leigh is to fiction film what the best *cinéma vérité* filmmakers are to documentary: an acute observer of nuance who constructs drama out of incidental events we would otherwise not notice at all.   It is the accuracy of the observation that counts, and Leigh's films have the capacity to evoke a cultural moment or a class difference through detail alone.   They revolve around the lives of the very ordinary.   But there is remorseless pathos which is far from simplistic; we are simultaneously distanced from the characters, who are observed through exaggerated comedy, and inexorably sucked into identifying with them via a painful process of self-recognition.

Often at the heart of Leigh's observational method is an object around which an array of emotional and social subtexts evolve that lend it an importance far outstripping its superficial-seeming significance.   In *Abigail's Party* (1977), for example, there was the bottle of Beaujolais that the *nouveau riche* Beverly puts in the fridge, crystallising at once the character's flawed upward mobility and the ugly snobbery of the middle-class audience who instantly recognise her *faux pas*. In *Career Girls* there is a flashback in which Annie cooks a student meal involving coarsely chopped, eye-stinging onions, giving Hannah the opportunity to complain that she can't cry herself. In the midst of this, prominently displayed, is a smudgy plastic bottle of oil. Every student house had a dirty bottle of oil like this in those days, as every student house seemed to have a troubled undergraduate who did a transparently bad job of pretending to be harder than s/he was. The bottle thus becomes a simple sign of the times as well as a metonym for Hannah's inner anguish.

A similar duality is at work in Leigh's predilection for caricature. Hannah and Annie start off (when students) as stereotypes, the former self-critical and defensively abrasive, needing to dominate every situation she's in, the latter nervy, twitchy and cringingly retiring. Both are hysterics whose mannerisms and bodies display their personalities. Thus Annie when younger hides behind a particularly gross dermatological complaint, while Hannah emits a barrage of clumsy puns or oneliners, such as "living in the pasta" or (about her flatmate's skin), "You look like you've danced the tango with a cheese grater." Taking mannerisms to their grotesque extreme becomes an unsuccessful affectation if, as in *High Hopes,* there is little feeling of tenderness between actor and caricature. But in a great Mike Leigh film, such as *Secrets & Lies*, the audience finds itself laughing with disdain and crying with recognition at the same time.

As with *vétité,* however, Leigh's works are deeply schematic despite their observational veneer, and *Career Girls* offers the ultimate meta-commentary on the Leigh method. Like a Richard Rogers building, in which normally internal structures are displayed on the outside, *Career Girls* flaunts its own artifice, deliberately announcing itself as a deeply implausible tale. Not only do Annie and Hannah meet by chance (over a single weekend) the three characters featured prominently in the flashbacks of their undergraduate days, but they discuss (and laugh at) the improbability of these freak encounters. This self-conscious narrative technique is liberating for the audience, who are invited to collude in and enjoy their own gross manipulation. By relying on repetition and coincidence, *Career Girls* helps itself to the raw intensity of a good melodrama, and by the end the audience wait expectantly for the final unbearable moment when the only release is tears.

This emotional purging comes as Annie and Hannah bump into Ricky, Annie's humbling, unstable, sporadically brilliant former suitor. Given the meetings with other characters, we know by a simple process of elimination that this meeting is coming, but this shields us not a jot from the torture of witnessing (along with the two women) Ricky's tumble into half-lucid schizophrenia. As he sits on the step of the old chip shop cradling an oversize blue elephant and explaining to his old friends "I'm not an idiot, I'm like an *idiot savant,* I just haven't found my savant yet," the final flashback begins: Annie and Hannah tracking Ricky down to his seaside home town after being rejected by Annie; he becomes abusive and accuses them of being "nosy parkers". The juxtaposition of these two meetings could be emblematic of the whole film. Like Annie and Hannah, we are left bereft in the knowledge that we feel for Ricky, but are ultimately powerless to help him. *Career Girls* is not an unsatisfying film, but it is a harsh one. Rather than let us feel comforted and replenished by our cathartic experiences, it confronts us with the futility of film's love of emotional identification. We the audience are *idiots savants* too.

TIME, 8/11/97, p. 75, Richard Schickel

Annie (Lynda Steadman) is recessive—a shy, nervous little thing with a tendency, in her younger days, to break out in psychosomatic rashes. Hannah (Katrin Cartlidge) is excessive—a noisy, knowing, angry woman with a tendency, untempered by the passing years, to break out in devastating tirades at anyone who disappoints her.

Roommates in college, they are getting together for a weekend in London after a six-year hiatus in their relationship. Since this takes place under the auspices of writer-director Mike Leigh, you know going in that you are volunteering for a movie in which cramped spaces will be crammed with intensely realistic acting. And that the past, which his characters are almost never able to put safely behind them, will keep nipping, biting, chomping at his *Career Girls*.

Compared with that past, indeed, the girls' careers are nothing much, just jobs that pay them enough to replace their former undergraduate scruffiness with low-budget chic. Otherwise, their work makes them vaguely restless in ways that are scarcely worth discussing. This is not to say that frequent flashbacks to the bad old days—when the pair lived, squabbling and self-obsessed, in a rundown flat above a Chinese takeout restaurant—are finally any more conclusive. Or that the girls' chance encounters with figures out of that past—a slick, careless lover they once shared; a weird, enormous former roommate now lost to schizophrenia (and played with great and tender ferocity by Mark Benton) are particularly illuminating.

Like virtually all Leigh's characters, Annie and Hannah are trapped in the hopelessness of modern life. Or should we make that modern English life? Educated to the point of glibness, but not to the point of wisdom, they know just enough to recognize the constraints of class, gender and material longing, but not enough to break through them, to achieve the freedom of mind and spirit that modernity keeps promising but never quite delivers. This leaves them at once ranting and wistful, delivering those arias of discontent—often funny, sometimes touching, always brutally frank—that are the hallmark of the director's famously improvisational style.

Though our heroines' initial wariness gives way to a tentative reawakening of a friendship less abrasive, possibly more trusting, than it once was, nothing much happens, dramatically speaking, in *Career Girls*. It is less scarring than Leigh's *Naked*, less poignant than *Secrets & Lies*. But still it offers a behavioral truthfulness and a passionate engagement with the despairs of dailiness that put most movies to shame.

VILLAGE VOICE, 8/12/97, p. 67, Amy Taubin

"I suppose on a clear day you can see the class struggle from here quips the snarly, snaggle-toothed, altogether brilliant Hannah (Katrin Cartlidge) as she looks over the Thames from the window of a flat she can't quite afford to buy. Cartlidge's Hannah is the main reason to see Mike Leighs slightly too tidy *Career Girls*. But films that get a handle on female friendship are so rare that I'm happy to cut it some slack.

Six years after they graduated from a London college, former roommates Hannah and Annie (Lynda Steadman) spend a weekend together. Annie, who majored in psych, has a personnel management job ("mostly pushing papers") up north. Hannah, who took a first in literature, works for a high-end stationery company in a management position that offers such perks as use of the company car and a home fax machine.

Dissimilar personalities, Hannah and Annie bonded over their shared sense of social unease and their somewhat dubious prospects for an independent, middle-class lifestyle. In college, Annie's cross was the red, scaly patch of allergic dermatitis covering one side of her jaw that lured her fingers into an ambivalent dance of pointing and caressing. "You look like you've done the tango with a cheese grater," observed the caustic Hannah in a flashback moments after they first met. The remark sent Annie flying into the bathroom in tears, leaving Hannah to bang her forehead in despair at her cruel tongue. The flood of conflicting emotions (and s/m undercurrents) released by this encounter developed over the course of four years into a relationship that was probably as close to love as either of them had known before or has experienced since.

The best thing about *Career Girls* is that it shows how women are complicit with the social order in marginalizing the most rewarding (and potentially disruptive) relationships in their lives until they become virtually nonexistent. Not only is this the first time Hannah and Annie have seen each other since college; it also, despite their tearful protestations to the contrary, may be the last.

For the most part, however, Leigh seems bent on proving a more simplistic thesis. Segueing back and forth between present and past, *Career Girls* reveals that two friends can have vastly different memories of supposedly shared events. To jog this thesis along, Leigh invents an improbable series of coincidences: in the course of 36 hours, Hannah and Annie cross paths with three crucial characters from their college days. Too canny to let such a bald literary device go unmarked, Leigh points it up (not unlike the way Annie can't resist calling attention to her angry skin) with a bit of dialogue about the odds against such coincidences.

The moment is symptomatic of more than a flaw in this one film. Leigh's Achilles heel is his contempt for the very fictional tropes he depends on to keep his films in line. In *Career Girls*, the more crudely Leigh shoves his characters into the past, the more we resent him for keeping them so straitjacketed in the present.

Despite these structural limitations, the actors are all fine, especially the hyperkinetic Cartlidge, who, in her rare moments of stillness, reveals the most intelligent gaze of any actress currently on the screen, and Mark Benton as Ricky, the self-described idiot savant whom Hannah and Annie couldn't save. Ricky's regression is the measure of the career girls' success.

Also reviewed in:
NATION, 8/25-9/1/97, p. 50, Stuart Klawans
NEW REPUBLIC, 8/25/97, p. 24, Stanley Kauffmann
NEW YORK TIMES, 8/8/97, p. C3, Janet Maslin
NEW YORKER, 8/11/97, p. 83, Terrence Rafferty
VARIETY, 6/2-8/97, p. 53, Todd McCarthy
WASHINGTON POST, 8/15/97, p. G1, Stephen Hunter
WASHINGTON POST, 8/15/97, Weekend/p. 32, Eric Brace

CATS DON'T DANCE

A Warner Bros. release of a Turner Feature Animation presentation. *Executive Producer:* David Steinberg, Charles L. Richardson and Sandy Russell Gartin. *Producer:* David Kirschner and Paul Gertz. *Director:* Mark Dindal. *Screenplay:* Roberts Gannaway, Cliff Ruby, Elana Lesser, and Theresa Pettengill. *Music:* Steve Goldstein and Randy Newman. *Art Director:* Brian McEntee. *Music:* Natalie Cole. *Running time:* 80 minutes. *MPAA Rating:* G.

VOICES: Scott Bakula (Danny the Cat); Jasmine Guy (Speaking Voice of Sawyer the Cat); Natalie Cole (Singing Voice of Sawyer the Cat); George Kennedy (Mr. Mammoth); John Rhys-Davies (Woolie the Elephant); Kathy Najimy (Tillie the Hippo); Ashley Peldon (Darla Dimple); Matthew Harried (Pudge the Penguin).

CHRISTIAN SCIENCE MONITOR, 4/15/97, p. 13, David Sterritt

[*Cats Don't Dance* was reviewed jointly with *Paradise Road*; see Sterritt's review of that film.]

LOS ANGELES TIMES, 3/26/97, Calendar/p. 6, Jack Mathews

[*The following review by Jack Mathews appeared in a slightly different form in* **NEWSDAY, 3/26/97, Part II/p. B9.**]

For those of you with toddlers who are crazy about old MGM musicals, love sendups of long-gone Hollywood stars and tycoons and delight in such hip references as King Kong being portrayed as a whiny stagehand, the animated "Cats Don't Dance" may be the cat's pajamas. For those with normal children, good luck.

"Cats Don't Dance," the first film out of Turner Feature Animation, is a startling miscalculation. It has lots of cute animals, some jaunty Randy Newman songs and solid, if uninspired, animation work. But blending parody and nostalgia about an era half a century removed from the lives of the core audience seems a foolish indulgence.

The story, gang-conceived and written, according to the credits, starts out like "A Star Is Born" and ends like "Singin' in the Rain." It's the tale of a Kokomo cat named Danny (voice of Scott Bakula) who arrives in Hollywood on the bus to broken dreams only to discover that animals—no matter how talented—are third-class citizens in the studio system.

The studio where Danny goes to work is Mammoth Pictures, run by cigar-chomping L.B. Mammoth, a caricature of Louis B. Mayer. Mammoth's franchise star is singing and dancing Darla Dimple, a demonic version of Shirley Temple, who was actually Fox's franchise.

When Danny, in the chorus line of a Dimple movie, gets carried away and stretches his one line ("Meow") into a scene-stealing croon, the curly-haired star is roused to a wrath that threatens the career of every bird, mammal and reptile on the lot.

Among the potentially exiled are Woolie (John Rhys-Davies), an elephant who plays a mean rag piano; Tillie (Kathy Najimy), a soprano hippo with a heart as big as her bottom; a cynical old goat; a cowardly tortoise; a pudgy penguin; and the lovely feline Sawyer, a starlet-turned-secretary lured back to the Klieg lights for the love of Danny.

On the other side is Max, Darla's bodyguard, a giant with the body of Frankenstein and the name, face and peevish manner of Erich von Stroheim's butler in "Sunset Boulevard." And seen along the way—on the street, in restaurants, at premieres and on a lot that even looks like old MGM—are such "familiar" faces as Bette Davis, Clark Gable, and Laurel and Hardy.

"Cats Don't Dance" treads this territory with a whimsy that will be over the heads of young kids and too unimaginative for adults.

Newman's songs are theatrical and lively, and Natalie Cole, the singing voice of Sawyer, does a sensational ballad. But despite a credit to the late Gene Kelly for some early choreographic guidance, Danny's animated dancing—as any 5-year-old with an encyclopedic knowledge of old Hollywood will agrees—a far cry from Jerry the Mouse's in "Anchors Aweigh."

NEW YORK POST, 3/26/97, p. 40, Larry Worth

What can you say about a full-length musical cartoon that ends with the credit: "No animals were harmed in the making of this film, but some were erased and redrawn"?

For starters, you can say that the razor-sharp humor of "Cats Don't Dance" remains intact through its final frame. Better still, the production's level of charm, energy and wit make it as much a winner for parents as for children.

Set in the heyday of Hollywood musicals, the action begins when a feline named Danny leaves his Indiana roots to rub whiskers with Tinseltown's fat cats. Determined to become a star, be immediately finds work on a big-budget lensing of Noah's travails, "Little Ark Angel."

Trouble arrives via the show's lead: Darla Dimple, a Shirley Temple wannabe with the soul of Joan Crawford. With the help of her monstrous butler Max (shades of "Sunset Boulevard"), Darla makes Cruella de Vil come off like PETA's pal.

Under Mark Dindal's smooth direction, the colorful results not only entertain but deliver apt messages about believing in one's dreams and fighting all forms of prejudice.

And that's not even mentioning Randy Newman's consistently pleasing score, which incorporates the singing talents of Scott Bakula and Natalie Cole. The voices of Jasmine Guy, Don Knotts, George Kennedy and Kathy Najimy—a standout as a happy hippo—round out the cast of winners.

As he did with Jerry the mouse in "Anchors Aweigh," the late Gene Kelly brilliantly choreographed one and all through there cartoonish paces. The film, dedicated in his memory, thus doubles as a lovely valentine to his talents.

So, is it any wonder "Dance" is the cat's meow?

Also reviewed in:
NEW YORK TIMES, 3/26/97, p. C18, Lawrence Van Gelder
VARIETY, 3/24-30/97, p. 33, Todd McCarthy

CHASING AMY

A Miramax Films release of a View Askew production. *Executive Producer:* John Pierson. *Producer:* Scott Mosier. *Director:* Kevin Smith. *Screenplay:* Kevin Smith. *Director of Photography:* David Klein. *Editor:* Kevin Smith and Scott Mosier. *Music:* David Pirner. *Music Editor:* Brian Mackewich, David Glaser, and Sean McAuliffe. *Sound:* William Kozy. *Sound Editor:* Brian Mackewich. *Casting:* Shana Lory. *Production Designer:* Robert "Ratface" Holtzman. *Art Director:* Jim Williams. *Set Decorator:* Susannah McCarthy. *Costumes:* Christopher Del Coro. *Make-up:* Jane Choi. *Running time:* 105 minutes. *MPAA Rating:* R.

CAST: Ben Affleck (Holden McNeil); Joey Lauren Adams (Alyssa Jones); Jason Lee (Banky Edwards); Dwight Ewell (Hooper); Jason Mewes (Jay); Kevin Smith (Silent Bob); Ethan Suplee (Fan); Scott Mosier (Collector); Casey Affleck (Little Kid); Guinevere Turner (Singer); Carmen Lee (Kim); Brian O'Halloran and Matt Damon (Executives); Alexander Goebbel (Train Kid); Tony Torn (Cashier); Rebecca Waxman (Dalia); Paris Petrick (Tory); Welker White (Jane); Kelli Simpkins (Nica); John Willyung (Cohee Lundin); Tsemach Washington (Young Black Kid); Ernie O'Donnell (Bystander); Kristin Mosier (Waitress); Virginia Smith (Con Woman).

LOS ANGELES TIMES, 4/11/97, Calendar/p. 12, Kevin Thomas

Kevin Smith's "Chasing Amy" is a little movie with big truths, a work of such fierce intelligence and emotional honesty that it blows away the competition when it comes to contemporary romantic comedy.

It could be a career-maker for its three stars, Ben Affleck, Joey Lauren Adams and Jason Lee, and for key supporting player Dwight Ewell. It also marks a strong comeback for Smith, who in the end credits of the film actually apologizes for his second feature, "Mallrats." That film caused widespread disappointment among fans of "Clerks," his knockout no-budget debut film, a semi-autobiographical comedy about a pair of New Jersey convenience store employees.

"Chasing Amy" is an unpretentious, modestly budgeted American movie of potentially wide appeal that dares to show its smarts. It could not be a more welcome experience.

That romantic comedies don't come more serious than this gem doesn't mean it isn't as uproarious as it is shattering. Smith, who cameos as the man whose painful experience gives this film its title, has clearly delved deep within himself and confronted every emotion and insight he discovered. "Chasing Amy" is both raunchy and as all-American as apple pie, but it has mature sophistication—especially in regard to fluidity in sexual orientation—that is usually reserved for foreign films.

Affleck's Holden, tall and goateed, and the full-bearded Banky (Lee) are childhood friends and partners in the creation of a cult-hit comic book, "Bluntman and Chronic." (Holden describes it as "Rosencrantz and Guildenstern meet Vladimir and Estragon.") They work in a nifty office on the charming Victorian main street of Red Bank, N.J. At a comic-book convention in Manhattan's historic Puck Building, they meet Alyssa (Adams), a husky-voiced, sultry comic-book artist.

Alyssa and Holden hit it off from the start, even though she's an upfront lesbian. That doesn't stop them, however, from falling in love, which in turn makes Banky jealous, possibly for reasons he's not prepared to examine.

The things Smith has been able to discover within this situation are altogether amazing: how men can accept one kind of sexual past in a woman but not another; the devastation that disparate levels of sexual experience can bring to a relationship; how crucial candor can be, yet how even the most intelligent and forthright of individuals can smash smack into the heart's all-too-human limitations.

An example of such limitations in empathy is Hooper (Ewell), also a comic-book artist. He is the movie's Eve Arden, quick with the wisecracks. Black as well as gay, he finds himself resenting the trendy acceptability of "lipstick lesbians." (Interestingly, Smith goes for inclusiveness in regard to sexual attractions, contrasting another current New York-based romantic comedy, "The Daytrippers," which uses homosexuality—or bisexuality—merely for shock value.)

Smith alternates between pain and hilarity to a degree that seems groundbreaking for a mainstream movie. But "Chasing Amy," while mainstream, is likely to appeal mainly to the most open-minded moviegoers. Ewell sets the tone for outrageous humor with a speech at the comic-book convention in which he demolishes the "Star Wars" trilogy as racist.

In turn this scene is matched by a diner sequence in which Banky and Alyssa try to top each other with accounts of their sexual exploits. (There's actually not a lot of sex in "Chasing Amy," but the bluntness of its talk about that subject will push the envelope for some moviegoers.)

"Chasing Amy," in which Smith wrote great parts for his actors and then knew how to draw out astonishing, selfless performances from them, concludes his New Jersey trilogy. In being so in touch with himself and with the people he has brought to such intense life, Smith has created a film comedy that has all the hallmarks of a classic.

NEW STATESMAN, 11/14/97, p. 49, John Dugdale

In the credits of *Clerks*, his shoestring, Cannes-fêted first film, the writer-director Kevin Smith thanks such indy-flick forerunners as Spike Lee, Richard Linklater and Jim Jarmusch. God gets the nod instead for his third, *Chasing Amy*, but it's the thoroughly profane figure of David Mamet who seems the real presiding deity.

Like the young Mamet of *Sexual Perversity in Chicago*, Smith knows what he does best is guy-talk—the dirty, idle, sprawling dialogue of the two convenience-store assistants in *Clerks*. But both writers feel compelled to advance to what they ought to produce: purposively constructed stories with a moral, even instructive, even constructive content.

This imperative is also sensed by Holden (Ben Affleck), the cartoonist hero of *Chasing Amy*, who longs to progress to "more personal" work at the expense of the cult strip co-created with Banky (Jason Lee), his belligerently macho partner. Even though TV execs want the New Jersey double-act to transform Bluntman and Chronic into the next big animation series.

Cartoon culture operates as the film's comfortable guy-world, the equivalent of the diner, the sports arena and the "hood" in other cinematic tales of belated growing up. Shared scorn for this subculture supplies the basis for Holden's instant rapport with Alyssa (Joey Adams), a squeaky Manhattan-based illustrator whose resemblance to a miniature Madonna perhaps informs the title's echo of another story of the Big Apple v the 'Burbs, *Desperately Seeking Susan*.

As in Susan Seidelman's film, no one is quite what they seem and the plot of *Chasing Amy* depends on a series of discoveries about Alyssa's sexual preferences. Always imagining that he has finally solved the conundrum she poses, Holden is "weirded out" again and again, only appreciating too late "that in love you have to put the individual ahead of their past actions"—the sampler motto which concludes the solo-written strip called *Chasing Amy* he is drawing in the film's full-circle coda.

Although this moral is imparted as if it were a revelation, only the graphic sexual detail differentiates *Chasing Amy* from a gamut of comedies about men who can't accept women with a Past, the most recent example of which is Patrick Marber's smash-hit play *Closer* at the RNT. To compare Smith with a playwright may seem perverse, but his movies barely qualify as cinema. He plonks his characters down side-by-side in two-shots facing the viewer, just like theatre, and gives them long, unnaturally fluent speeches, just like theatre. Visually negligible, his work lacks any formal playfulness.

All of which makes you wonder why Smith, as projected through Holden, is so preoccupied with creative independence. He has no political agenda, as Spike Lee does; no compulsion to innovate right across the board, in the manner of Quentin Tarantino. What would Hollywood actually stop this outsider from doing?

The answer is confusing. At the end, in *Chasing Amy* the cartoon, Holden has fused independence with maturity and you're supposed to believe they are indissociable: that working solo allows Holden/Smith to create girly strips/films about feelings, to stop the "fart and dick jokes" he despises. But of course Hollywood would like nothing better than an ABCD story leading to the message that love conquers all: if Alyssa's past were wholly hetero, she would be played by Meg Ryan. What Hollywood would excise would be the really filthy stuff the filthy, clerkly stuff at the beginning of the film.

Smith, however, is too canny to erase all the comic guy-talk. And, just as with Mamet, this is what you remember from the coruscating one-scene cameo with Jason Mewes as the white dude speaking flawless, bitch-hating ebonics, to the trademark seminars on cunnilingus. For this director, that's the "personal work", not the humdrum women's magazine homilies. Come back to the convenience store, Kevin Smith, Kevin Smith.

NEW YORK, 4/21/97, p. 52, David Denby

There are a couple of wild erotic monologues and some very funny riffs in Kevin Smith's low-budget *Chasing Amy* which is the story of a love affair between two comic-book artists—Holden (Ben Affleck) and Alyssa (Joey Lauren Adams), who is a lesbian. Holden, it turns out, can deal with the lesbianism but not with certain other erotic events in Alyssa's past. Yet despite its uproarious carnal humor and knowledgeable reporting on the comic-book scene, the movie becomes rather trying: What could have been a good dirty lyric on the evanescence of love turns rather turgid and emotionally overexplicit.

NEW YORK POST, 4/4/97, p. 45, Michael Medved

What happens when the creative team behind the gross-out slacker comedy "Mallrats" suddenly turns its adolescent attentions to an overwrought melodrama about sexual identity and the nature of true love?

If, for some reason, you're intrigued by this odd question, then "Chasing Amy" provides the awkward answer. It's a contrived, consummately clumsy confection that takes itself much too seriously and embarrasses some likable young actors far better suited to whimsical comedy.

Ben Affleck and Jason Lee (both survivors of "Mallrats") play boyhood chums from Red Bank, N.J., who collaborate on a series of hip, popular comic books.

Joey Lauren Adams (another denizen of "Mallrats") is their fellow graphic artist who instantly attracts the handsome, goateed Affleck with her sexy, flirtatious ways.

The only problem is, she's an aggressively promiscuous lesbian with no interest in men. Still, they nonetheless develop a friendship. Mr. Affleck's comic book partner (Lee) opposes this relationship as a threat to his friend's creative genius—though several characters comment that this apparent jealousy may reflect Lee's own unresolved homosexual longings.

Though Adams seems to enjoy her adventurous gay lifestyle and ridicules the notion that she secretly needs a man, the script flatters every fatuous male fantasy by showing her instantaneous "conversion" to straight sexuality after one passionate night with our sulky hero.

Their only remaining problem involves an inevitable confrontation with some dark secrets from her past.

Adams flashes winning smiles and gives her all to this impossible role, but her hysterical intensity only emphasizes the insipidity of the script. Both male leads come across as despicable dorks (and Gen X stereotypes), while the level of romantic charm and insight ("F --- ing isn't always about penetration, Banky!") makes Howard Stern look like Lord Byron.

Even those hoping for glimpses of hot, kinky passion will be disappointed. The movie features raunchy talk about the mechanics of coupling, but not even the briefest (gay or straight) sex scene.

The supposed comic highlight comes when Adams and Lee tediously compare notes on the painful injuries each endured while engaged in sex with women.

Writer-director Kevin Smith previously created the mildly amusing festival favorite "Clerks" before he made "Mallrats," so "Chasing Amy" represents the completion of his "New Jersey Trilogy"—recalling the fragrance and elegance of the Garden State's least-appetizing oil refineries.

Smith also plays an intriguing cameo role as Silent Bob, one of two mysterious stoners who have turned up in all three films. The line at the end of the credits announcing that these two will return in Smith's next film feels, after "Chasing Amy," more like a threat than a promise.

NEWSDAY, 4/4/97, Part II/p. B13, John Anderson

Kevin Smith's "Clerks" was one of the funnier films of recent years, because his dialogue was so ambitiously offensive. In fact, the movie might have been a radio play, given its visual economy and budgetary, shall we say, limits.

In his new film, "Chasing Amy," a romance-cum-therapy session, Smith spends more money and gets a lot more serious not so much that the humor is completely evaporated, but the jokes are secondary to the autopsy he performs on the heterosexual male mind. It's a messy business, full of sloppy swinging and erratic gestures. But the corpus is a singular specimen, whose like is seldom seen on screen.

New Jerseyites Holden (Ben Affleck) and Banky (Jason Lee) draw an underground comic book called Bluntman and Chronic—based on the "Clerks" characters Silent Bob (Smith) and the pot-pushing Jay (Jason Mewes). Told by a fan at a comics convention that his characters are like "Bill and Ted meet ... Cheech and Chong!!!" Holden responds, "I think of them more like Rosencrantz and Guildenstern meet Vladimir and Estragon." You could cut the pretension with a knife.

But generally, Holden and Banky are regular members of the beer-and-whine set who obsess on sex, or lack thereof, and lead limited suburban existences. Enlightenment arrives via Alyssa Jones (Joey Lauren Adams), who lights a fire under Holden and sets Banky's teeth on edge. When she turns out to be a lesbian, Holden is stunned. Banky is elated.

What's going on here? It seems to be Smith's examination of sex, lies, true love and himself. Holden and Alyssa become close friends, discussing in clinical depth the mechanics of hetero-, homo- and idealized love. But for Holden it's not enough: He professes his love for Alyssa (while thunder actually crashes), asking her to renounce the sisterhood and jump into his bed. She becomes enraged at his insensitivity. But she sleeps with him anyway. Which makes Banky crazy.

What's going on here, part two? Banky, we presume, has an uncomfortable attraction for Holden, hates Alyssa for stealing his heart, and sets out to sabotage their affair—which he does by uncovering some unsavory episodes in Alyssa's heterosexual past, with which Holden cannot deal.

Much about "Chasing Amy" simply doesn't work: It assumes that it reaches a level of hilarity it seldom achieves; its characters laugh too hard and too often. The dialogue is anatomically obsessed without a lot of substance; the speeches Adams has to deliver sound like they came off a poster of a sunset, or some inspirational speaker on a PBS fund raiser.

But what's fascinating is the triangulated construct of his characters—Banky the repressed, Holden the explorer and Smith himself, who as Silent Bob delivers the story behind the title and offers Holden some wisdom about love. It's as if the director had done a psychological autopsy on himself. As such, a lot of "Chasing Amy" is forced and unfunny, but a lot of it is like something you've never seen.

NEWSWEEK, 4/7/97, p. 73, David Ansen

A lot of people who fell in love with "Clerks," Kevin Smith's funky convenience-store comedy, were worried, after the dismal "Mallrats," that New Jersey's scruffiest independent filmmaker was a one-hit wonder. You can now banish the thought. With *Chasing Amy*, Smith more than redeems himself: he grows up. He hasn't lost his raunchy, bad-boy humor, and he's back to working on a shoestring. But instead of cool twentysomething irony, Smith startles us with raw emotional honesty.

"Chasing Amy" looks plain, but it takes some big risks. For starters, it's about a straight white dude-comic-book artist Holden (Ben Affleck)—who falls in love with a lesbian comic-book artist named Alyssa Jones (Joey Lauren Adams). Holden's best friend and partner Banky (Jason Lee) is at first concerned, then jealous and horrified when the bright, wild, sexy Alyssa reciprocates. (Undoubtedly some gay women will be appalled, too.)

But "Chasing Amy" is no paean to heterosexuality. Ultimately this funny, surprisingly moving love story is a devastating critique of the hetero male ego, a victim of arrested development. Holden, so cool about Alyssa's flings with women, goes haywire when he's confronted with her promiscuous heterosexual past. Adams will tear your heart out as she fights to bring Holden back to his senses. Who would have expected that Smith could write a female part with such passion and insight? But whether discussing comics, cunnilingus or their deepest feelings, all of Smith's vibrant characters seduce us with their blunt and heartfelt eloquence.

SIGHT AND SOUND, 11/97, p. 36, John Wrathall

At a comic-book convention, Holden and Banky, creators of *Bluntman & Chronic*, meet Alyssa, creator of *Idiosyncratic Routine*. Attracted to Alyssa, Holden is horrified to find out that she has a girlfriend, and claims never to have slept with a man. However, they still become friends.

One night, Holden tells Alyssa he loves her, she reciprocates, and they start sleeping together. Jealous, Banky tries to break up the relationship by telling Holden that a friend of his was once in a threesome with Alyssa and another man. After Holden questions her about this, Alyssa admits it's true. They have a bitter row, and split up.

Moping, Holden bumps into Silent Bob, who tells him he once broke up with a girl, Amy, under similar circumstances. He now realises that the reason they split up was because he was intimidated by her level of experience. He has regretted it ever since. Inspired by Bob's advice, Holden asks Alyssa and Banky to dinner and suggests that the three of them have sex together. Banky reluctantly agrees, but Alyssa refuses. Regretfully, she leaves. At the comic-book convention a year later, Holden is no longer working with Banky. He finds Alyssa and gives her a copy of his new comic book, *Chasing Amy*.

Whether or not Kevin Smith has ever dated a lesbian, there's a definite streak of autobiography in this, his third film. When, in the final scene, Holden presents Alyssa with a copy of his new comic book, *Chasing Amy*, he tells her it's his first "personal" work after his *Bluntman & Chronic* comics. The same goes for Smith: *Chasing Amy* is his first mature work, following *Clerks* and *Mallrats*, both of which featured the screen alter egos of *Bluntman and Chronic*, the obnoxious drug dealer Jay and his sidekick Silent Bob (played by Smith himself).

That's not to say that *Chasing Amy* is a totally new departure for Smith. Jay and Silent Bob are back, as are Smith's magnificently foul-mouthed dialogue (demonstrated, for example, in Alyssa and Banky's duet about injuries incurred during cunnilingus) and his far-fetched riffs on *Star Wars* mythology (such as friend Hooper's interpretation of the attack on the Death Star as a "cracker's" raid on Darth Vader's "'hood"). Though the final credits contain the dedication "To the critics who hated our last flick—all is forgiven", *Chasing Amy* has much in common with its much-reviled predecessor in Smith's self-described New Jersey trilogy. All three of *Chasing Amy*'s leads appeared in *Mallrats*—in different roles, though Jason Lee, as Banky, once again plays the crude, stubborn sidekick to a more romantically inclined hero (here Ben Affleck's Holden).

Like both Smith's previous films, much of *Chasing Amy* depends on the simple formula of two guys talking. But the view of male friendship he puts forward here is much more complex, embracing both a gay subtext and a new awareness, in the film's poignant coda, that friendship doesn't necessarily triumph over adversity. Smith wittily punctures male vanity: in the party scene, Holden glows with self-satisfaction as Alyssa sings him a love song, unaware that she's really serenading her girlfriend. His characters have always been marked by their ability to construct elaborate theories about the mysteries of life and popular culture. But Holden is the first character in whom Smith sees this tendency as a flaw. When Alyssa turns down Holden's offer of a threesome, it's because his "solution" to their problem is just another clever theory, not a real emotional response.

Smith is less adept with his female characters, and he is not helped by Joey Lauren Adams' shrill performance as Alyssa. But he still conveys the complexities of her predicament: falling in love with a lesbian, for a straight man, is just exotic, but for a lesbian to reciprocate entails a comprehensive upheaval of her lifestyle and self-image. (*Clerks* might have seemed the antithesis of political correctness, but here Smith receives an official lesbian endorsement via the cameo appearance of Guinevere Turner, the star and co-writer of *Go Fish.*)

Shot for $250,000, *Chasing Amy* marks a return to the scratchy independent style of *Clerks* after the glossier and less successful *Mallrats*, a film which proved that Smith's lack of visual flair isn't solely down to low budgets. There are a few stylistic flourishes here—like putting the camera above a dart board so that Holden and Alyssa are aiming at us as they play—but by and large *Chasing Amy* confirms that Smith is a far more interesting writer than director. The other disappointment, in such a witty and unexpectedly sensitive account of a love affair, is that there's no real sense of sexual attraction between any of the characters.

TIME, 4/7/97, p. 76, Richard Schickel

[*Chasing Amy* was reviewed jointly with *Inventing the Abbotts*; see Schickel's review of that film.]

VILLAGE VOICE, 4/8/97, p. 79, J. Hoberman

A twisted, twentysomething *Affair to Remember* Kevin Smith's *Chasing Amy* is seriously romantic in a way that would drive the guy protagonists of Smith's first two movies to distraction. Smith names his hero "Holden" and sends him traipsing through the rye to catch a glamorously free-spirited and self-professed lesbian.

You could accuse *Chasing Amy* of being a cartoon, but the movie admits to that freely. Looking like *Mallrats* and sounding like *Clerks*—a film of bright, inert compositions and constant chatter—*Chasing Amy* begins at a crazy New York ComiCon attended by a pair of super star slackers, Holden (Ben Affleck) and Banky (Jason Lee, Shannon Doherty's boyfriend in *Mallrats*).

The artistic team responsible for the cult comic book, *Bluntman and Chronic*, they have ventured in from New Jersey and—tales of the city—wind up on a panel with the beautiful Alyssa (Joey Lauren Adams), a less well-known cartoonist with a more developed sense of sexual bravado.

Adams, a mannered performer with a teasing, moonfaced sneer and Kewpie-doll voice, who appeared to some advantage in the chaotic *Mallrats*, is here charismatic by default. Just as the black militant cartoonist (Dwight Ewell) who mau-maus the convention turns out to be a swishy queen, so her character turns out to have a secret identity: Convinced that she's hot for him, Holden follows Alyssa down to Meow Mix, an East Village den of lipstick lesbianism complete with *Go Fish* and *Watermelon Woman* star Guinevere Turner. His dumbfounded expression when he watches Alyssa lip-lock with another gorgeous chick is almost worth the price of admission. (As the practical Banky points out, where else could guys like them get to see this for free?)

Smith's self-referential New Jersey world has evidently expanded to comment on the independent film scene. Indeed, *Chasing Amy* seems to have been conceived at the 1994 Sundance Film Festival, where both *Clerks* and *Go Fish* had their premieres under the shrewd auspices of producer rep John Pierson. The chaste Rocky Mountain romance between the "clerky boys" and "go-go girls" figures prominently in Pierson's indie memoir, *Spike, Mike, Slackers & Dykes:* "Kevin described Guinevere poignantly: 'Such a pretty girl. It is cool that she's gay because you can play with her, talk smack, and not get crossed wires. Good fences make good neighbors.'"

Pierson notes that the "very curious" Smith discovered far more than he about the go-go girls' sex lives. Thus, the question that dominates *Chasing Amy*'s first half ("How can a girl fuck another girl?") is less crudely hostile than unabashedly clueless. That the movie's comic set piece—a montage in which Banky and Alyssa briefly bond in swapping hyperbolic instances of cunnilingual misadventure—winds up as a brief for better sexual communication is an early clue to the progressive direction of the Smith agenda. Political correctness notwithstanding, youth wants to know. "Since you like chicks, do you just look at yourself naked in the mirror all the time?" Banky asks Alyssa.

Not everyone is going to find *Chasing Amy* endearing—as Smith has anticipated. The uptight Holden and tantalizing Alyssa become friends, even sharing an evening of skeeball on the South Shore. "How was your pseudodate?" jealous Banky whines. Holden is soon accusing his partner of "passive-aggressive gay bashing," and, with their (creative) marriage on the rocks, the smitten cartoonist raises the stakes by declaring his love to Alyssa. The scene, scored to some sort of Swingle Singer drone, is as risky for Smith as for Holden—it's matched by another, lifted from *Go Fish*, in which Alyssa informs her friends that she's dating a man.

Colorful language, explicit description, and a brief bit in which Banky purports to share his stroke book with a seven-year-old notwithstanding, *Chasing Amy* isn't raunchy so much as it is didactic. Although Affleck may be even more stodgily earnest than his part was written, Smith seems to have taken the idea of a straight man literally. By the time the filmmaker appears in his standard cameo as mallrat dope-dealer Silent Bob, *Chasing Amy* has become almost embarrassingly sincere. Smith is clearly trying to work something through—that it turns out to be the venerable dichotomy between the virgin and the whore is less than anticlimactic.

Holden's lugubrious solution to the problem of Banky, Alyssa, and Alyssa's past—"We've all got to have sex together"—suggests an afternoon spent pondering old R. Crumb comix without getting the jokes. Still, it takes guts for Smith to cast his alter ego as something like Mr. Natural's foil. (Actually, *Chasing Amy* is full of Smith surrogates: not only does Affleck resemble the writer-director, Silent Bob is the model for Holden's Bluntman.) "Smith is as personal a filmmaker as ... Stan Brakhage," one of the director's fans assured me heatedly. While Smith's particular form of male psychodrama has less to do with *Scenes From Under Childhood* than the real-life Sunday afternoon alternative radio show where a zonked pair of New Jersey fat boys mix Led Zeppelin with Sinatra while ranting about wrestling and "the queers," there's no denying that *Chasing Amy*, was made from some inner necessity.

Self-absorbed as it may be, *Chasing Amy* isn't smug; however provocatively sexist it seems, the movie still spends most of its time chasing its own tail. The nature of this activity, no less than the place where it winds up, suggests that the filmmaker himself is the work in progress.

Also reviewed in:
NEW REPUBLIC, 5/5/97, p. 24, Stanley Kauffmann
NEW YORK TIMES, 4/4/97, p. C3, Janet Maslin

NEW YORKER, 4/7/97, p. 97, Terrence Rafferty
VARIETY, 2/3-9/97, p. 46, Todd McCarthy

CHEF IN LOVE, A

A Sony Pictures Classics release of a Les Films du Rivage/Studios Adam et Eve/La Sept Cinema/Studio Babelsberg/CMC/Sotra/Innova coproduction. *Executive Producer:* Thomas Baumeister and Telmour Borlouani. *Producer:* Marc Ruscart. *Director:* Nana Djordjadze. *Screenplay (French, Georgian, and Russian with English subtitles):* Irakli Kvirikadze. *Director of Photography:* Guiorgui Beridze. *Editor:* Vessela Martschewski and Guili Grigoriani. *Music:* Goran Bregovic. *Sound:* Claude Bertrand and Francois de Morant. *Production Designer:* Vakhtang Rouroua. *Art Director:* Teimour Chmaladze. *Running time:* 100 minutes. *MPAA Rating:* PG-13.

CAST: Pierre Richard (Pascal Ichac); Micheline Presle (Marcelle Ichac); Nino Kirtadze (Cecilia Abachidze); Teimour Kahmhadze (Zigmund Gogoladze); Jean-Yves Gautier (Anton Gogoladze).

LOS ANGELES TIMES, 4/23/97, Calendar/p. 2, Kenneth Turan

The European release title of "A Chef in Love," a Franco-Georgian co-production, was "The Thousand and One Recipes of a Chef in Love," and that more meandering name is truer to this film's leisurely, haphazard spirit.

Starring French comedy veteran Pierre Richard ("The Tall Blond Man With One Black Shoe"), "Chef" is one of those decorous and decorative films from the Continent that are dear to viewers of a certain age. Not surprisingly, "Chef" was nominated for the best foreign language film Oscar, losing to the more accomplished but philosophically similar "Kolya."

"Chef" starts in Paris, where Georgian Anton Gogoladze (Jean-Yves Gautier) has gone to hang a show of his celebrated fellow countryman, Pirsomani. There he meets a cigar-smoking gastro-nomic photographer named Marcelle (Micheline Presle), who says she's the niece of Pascal Ichac and wants to know what that name means to him.

It turns out that Pascal Ichac, author of a renowned cookbook about Georgian cuisine, was a particular hero of Anton's mother. Even more coincidentally, Marcelle has a manuscript in Georgian that details a personal relationship between Ichac and that very mother. Would the astonished Anton like to read and translate it for her?

With these preliminaries out of the way, "A Chef in Love" spends most of its time in languorous flashbacks to 1920s Georgia. As directed by Nana Djordjadze, "Chef" offers a series of picture-postcard prettified displays of a land apparently filled with colorful local people prone to breaking into spontaneous song and dance at any moment.

To this fairy tale place comes French gourmand Ichac (Richard), an explorer in search of new tastes. On a train he meets the gorgeous red-headed Princess Cecilia Abachidze (Nino Kirtadze) and, despite the difference in their ages, they are soon so much in love that they're crushing grapes together. Yes, it's that kind of a movie.

With a graying beard and hair more unruly than Einstein's, Richard's Pascal Ichac is a character we've seen before, the unrestrained artist so bursting with *joie de vivre* that he makes your teeth hurt. Prone to saying poetic things like, "I want to photograph the silence," Ichac is forever flummoxing the locals with the strength of his life force. "He's crazy," people say, and the inevitable rejoinder is, "he's French."

In love with Georgia as well as with Cecilia, Ichac opens one of the world's great restaurants in Tbilisi, where he wouldn't mind living happily ever after. But after his superb sense of smell saves the life of that country's president (it's a long story), the chef gets more involved in local politics than he ever wanted to be.

Given the film's time frame, politics means the long shadow of the Communist revolution. Soon the crass and slovenly Bolsheviks, whose appreciation of fine food is nil, have overrun Tbilisi. Making things worse, one of their leaders, the dread Zigmund (Teimour Kahmhadze), is infatuated with Cecilia.

Despite its soft heart, "Chef in Love" is inexplicably determined to show the world a different face. The story line of Irakli Kvirikadze's script increasingly strains for relevance and bittersweet poignancy as the Bolshevik stranglehold tightens, but given what's come before, it's difficult to take these ambitions seriously.

Since both Ichac and his modern niece live for food, "A Chef in Love" does not stint on loving pictures of elaborate dishes, though a successor to "Big Night" it's not. The film's philosophy is summed up by Ichac when he presciently states, "Bolshevism will disappear; fine cuisine won't." And neither apparently, will old-fashioned films like this.

NEW YORK POST, 4/25/97, p. 48, Larry Worth

Food-based dramas have suddenly become their own genre, with entries ranging from "Babette's Feast" to "Like Water for Chocolate," "Eat Drink Man Woman" and "Big Night." As the latest addition, "A Chef in Love" never quite equals its predecessors. But the Oscar-nominated production from the republic of Georgia still proves deliciously entertaining.

The story zips back and forth between present-day Paris and 1920s Georgia as a middle-aged art dealer finds a manuscript describing his beautiful Russian mother's relationship with a renowned French chef. As the son flips between letters and documents, the narrative bounces between episodes in the pair's affair.

Viewers know almost from the start that there's no happy ending in sight. Flashbacks show the young boy witnessing his mother's death at the hands of her murderous husband. As for how this lover's triangle came about, the serialized answer is the stuff of epic romance, told against the backdrop of revolution.

Director Nana Djordjadze effortlessly glides between whimsical humor, poignancy and political drama, mixing in healthy doses of local color and fantasy along the way. And, of course, enough time is spent in the kitchen to justify the titular character's passion for food as well as life.

Sadly, writer Irakli Kvirikadze isn't as dexterous, sometimes settling for the obvious and forcing home plot points. But his lapses are easily forgiven amid the lovely sets, costumes and scenery.

In addition, the cast makes each of the principals into appropriately bigger than life creations. Pierre Richard, best remembered as "The Tall Blonde Man With One Black Shoe," uses his standard over-the-top tendencies to fine effect as the tousled haired, ever-eccentric adventurer and epicurean expert.

As the ginger-haired love of his life, newcomer Nino Kirtadze is properly appealing while Teimour Kahmhadze's villainous spouse overcomes the character's black-and-white qualities. Unfortunately, present-day anchors Jean-Yves Gautier and Micheline Presle aren't nearly as charismatic.

OK, so the end result isn't perfect. But "A Chef in Love" still has the basic ingredients for a good time at the movies.

NEWSDAY, 4/25/97, Part II/p. B7, Jack Mathews

What do gourmet dining and rapturous romance have in common with the Russian Revolution? Absolutely nothing, and their incompatibility is just the point of Georgian director Nana Djordjadze's deliciously sentimental "A Chef in Love."

One of this year's five Oscar-nominated foreign-language films, "A Chef in Love" is inspired by the true story of a great French chef who fell in love with the natives on a visit to pre-Soviet Georgia and stuck around to launch a swank restaurant for the privileged class of Tbilisi. When the proletariat put the aristocrats on the run in 1921, the chef's dream turned into a nightmare, and he died of starvation and a broken heart on the roof of his restaurant.

Djordjadze, working with a script by her husband, Irakli Kvirikadze, uses that story as the spine of a much richer tale of romance and political crisis, set on the impact point of the old and new orders of Eastern Europe. Like "Eat Drink Man Woman," about a Taipei chef's strained relationships with his westernized daughters, and the recent "Big Night," about immigrant brothers going broke serving northern Italian cuisine in pizza-happy New Jersey, "A Chef in Love" uses fine food as a metaphor for radical cultural change.

It never ceases to work. Good taste and a good appetite inevitably produce sympathetic characters, and you won't find many more sympathetic on the screen this year than Pierre Richard's Pascal Ichac. Told in flashback from contemporary Paris, where the son of Ichac's lover is reading through his dusty memoirs, "A Chef in Love" follows Pascal on an adventuresome scouting trip to Georgia.

Already famous at home, Pascal ventures into the Caucasus to sample regional foods and the country's spectacular wines, and before long, he's fallen in love, with everything the country has to offer, including the beautiful Princess Cecilia (Nino Kirtadze), whom he meets on a train.

Though Pascal is more than twice Cecilia's age, his senses and his appetite for life blur the difference, and the couple are soon living a life of mad bliss—especially after Pascal sniffs out a bomb under the Georgian president's ballet seat and is rewarded with his own restaurant—until the Cossacks and the Revolution arrive. Soon, Pascal is living in an attic, and Cecilia, to save his life, is married to a zealous army officer.

There is the whiff of Hollywood melodrama to much of this. The flashback structure resembles, and is about as distracting as, that in "The Bridges of Madison County." But the Georgian part of the story is really marvelous—sad, romantic, tragic and illuminating all at the same time.

VILLAGE VOICE, 4/29/97, p. 78, Francine Russo

Forget Lutèce. Forget Daniel. I want to dine at the New Eldorado, the sumptuous palace de cuisine in Tbilisi. Alas, this grand café wafts its intoxicating aromas only in the French-Georgian collaboration *A Chef in Love*, set in the decadent 1920s. But you can gorge yourself on the scrumptious cinematography; not just table after table of steaming delicacies but riotous shots of fleshly delights that rival the great food-as-sex scenes on film.

The chef is Pascal, singer, gigolo, and gourmet. The aging French scoundrel falls in love with a gorgeous young Georgian princess, and saves the Georgian president from an assassin. He opens a dazzling restaurant, then refuses to abandon it even as barbaric revolutionary soldiers invade.

As Pascal, Pierre Richard gives a bravura performance, from triumph to mad defiance—King Lear with a twinkle. Nino Kirtadze—all bones and fire—sizzles as Cecilia. Open-hearted, full of humor, Nana Djordjadzer's film puts a fairy-tale gloss on Pascal's character. His destructive selfishness is idealized, and the film's dark side—filmed as surreal and fantastical—is underplayed.

Still, the film's images are startling: black-robed pipers prancing through a deserted grassy valley, Cecilia in her wedding dress, dancing drenched in flour. And then there's all that hot sex. Don't be fooled by its PC-13 rating—it's amazing what you can do with sheets.

Also reviewed in:
NEW YORK TIMES, 4/25/97, p. C3, Stephen Holden
VARIETY, 6/3-9/96, p. 52, Deborah Young
WASHINGTON POST, 5/16/97, Weekend/p. 46, Desson Howe

CHILDHOOD'S END

A Plainview Pictures release of a Plainview/Open City production. *Producer:* Jason Kliot and Joana Vicente. *Director:* Jeff Lipsky. *Screenplay:* Jeff Lipsky. *Director of Photography:* Victoria Ford. *Editor:* Sabine Hoffman. *Sound:* Tom Varga. *Casting:* Diana Jaher. *Production Designer:* Wing Lee. *Art Director:* Mark Helmuth. *Costumes:* Angela Wendt. *Running time:* 113 minutes. *MPAA Rating:* Not Rated.

CAST: Cameron Foord (Evelyn); Heather Gottlieb (Rebecca); Sam Trammell (Greg); Colleen Werthmann (Denise); Bridget White (Chloe); Reiko Aylesworth (Laurie); Philip Coccioletti (Harvey); Ellen Tobie (Miranda); Maureen Silliman (Mrs. Meyer).

NEW YORK POST, 4/4/97, p. 49, Larry Worth

Imagine a universe where everyone talks in lyrical metaphors, is completely in touch with feelings and analyzes everyone else with therapeutic ease.

A bad "Twilight Zone" episode? Not quite. Welcome to the world of "Childhood's End," an exercise in self-indulgence that may induce primal screams.

Set in Minneapolis of '93, the psychobabble fest is geared to three recent high school grads and their lovingly dysfunctional families. In a sad-sack version of "Knots Landing," one and all play musical beds, but without glitz or intrigue.

In fact, first-time writer-director Jeff Lipsky goes out of his way to de-glamorize the characters' day-to-day activities, lensing their goings-on in a purposely unpolished manner.

That includes some unexpectedly graphic bedroom encounters, where passion is surpassed by posing. Specifically, he showcases a host of not-so-perfect bodies in decidedly unflattering positions.

Par for the course is when a lumpy Mrs. Robinson-wannabe engages in pillow talk while popping her young lover's blackheads. So much for romance.

Actually, that might be the point. But "real-life" honesty needn't seem so strained and phony, as Britain's Mike Leigh recently demonstrated in "Secrets & Lies."

Matters only get worse as the supposedly daring subject matter moves to lesbianism, masturbation and incest. With unerring consistency, each is overdone to the point of parody,

And there's simply no excuse for Lipsky's ever-indulgent dialogue and refusal to edit. Must he allow every conversation to run for more than 10 minutes? Clocking in at a nearly interminable two hours, quantity has been badly confusing with quality.

Meanwhile, the ensemble cast is composed principally of big-screen newcomers, most of whom come off like an amateur actors' workshop. Only Heather Gottlieb's gawky outcast and Bridget White's aspiring model convey some level of credibility.

That's why, despite its endless I'm-OK-you're-OK philosophizing, little's OK about "Childhood's End."

NEWSDAY, 1/23/97, Part II/p. B8, Jack Mathews

Jeff Lipsky had 20 years' experience distributing difficult independent films in the United States before deciding to try his hand at directing, and the result of that effort "Childhood's End"—may be his most difficult distributing challenge yet. It's certainly one of his least watchable pictures.

"Childhood's End," partly filmed in Lipsky's home town of Plainview (standing in for suburban Minneapolis), is a ragged soap opera about a clutch of graduating high school students entering adulthood in an assortment of unconventional relationships. Greg (Sam Trammel), a gifted photographer about to become the art director of a magazine, begins an affair with the mother (Cameron Foord) of his lesbian friend Denise (Colleen Werthmann), who is about to hit on the pathologically shy Rebecca (Heather Gottlieb), who has a secret crush on Greg.

Meanwhile, Greg's older sister, Chloe (Bridget White), an aspiring model, is putting together her portfolio, which will include a series of stunning nude photos that we get to see being shot by ... Greg!

You can detect the influence of European filmmakers on Lipsky by the casualness of the nudity, and the nonchalant dialogue on such delicate topics as oral sex and whether lovers should squeeze each other's blockheads. His camera is the proverbial fly on the wall, watching Greg and Evelyn being totally at ease with their sexuality, and unblinking as Denise initiates the virginal Rebecca.

Lipsky seems to have confused candor with content. The relationship between Denise and Rebecca has a sweet awkwardness about it, but every second spent with Greg and Evelyn is a second without a point.

That Greg would think himself suitable for an older woman, and that she'd be in the mood for an all-day lover, aren't such stretches. But this is not a strictly sexual relationship. Greg and Evelyn, who have an emotional wind-chill factor of about 50 below, strain friendships and family ties to be together, for reasons impossible to fathom from their vacuous conversations.

There isn't much about "Childhood's End" to validate the wisdom of Lipsky's career shift. His script is badly paced, its dialogue is wooden and the actors seem to be flailing around inside the shells of their characters. Even his camera direction is clunky.

After working for New Yorker Films, Skouras Pictures and the Samuel Goldwyn Co., where he helped distribute such films as "My Dinner With Andre," "My Life as a Dog" and "Sid and Nancy," Lipsky cofounded October Films, one of the premium boutique distributors in-America. October currently has two films—"Secrets & Lies" and "Breaking the Waves"—contending for Oscar nominations.

We need every savvy distributor with good taste we can get, and we wish Lipsky a speedy return.

VILLAGE VOICE, 4/8/97, p. 85, Laurie Stone

Don't be put off by the dumb director Jeff Lipsky's first film, an odd, intentionally unpolished comedy of manners that listens in on all the damaged inner children careening through America's malls. The movie zeroes in on a gaggle of Minneapolis teens on the brink of adulthood and their parents—their mothers, actually, the fathers figuring as stubbly shadows on the landscape who seem as hounded and hormonal as their offspring. The moms, variously sex-gorging, isolated and fog-bound, are merely observed. The give monologue to, the camera or each other. No one knows how to have a conversation; rather, they take turns spilling, the confessional mode—which makes no reference to the world or politics, only to feelings—their perfected form. The movie is like a collection of performance art's greatest hits.

Its charm is its matter-of-factness and disinhibition, both in the camera work and dialogue. David Lynch gasps at suburbia's underbelly, finding creeps wearing gas masks. Lipsky's vision is less seismic, something closer maybe to *Blue Velveeta*. His surveillance equipment picks up people who gleefully squeeze blackheads and masturbate in front of each other, a brother and sister who exchange incest-tinged kisses without so much as provoking a raised eyebrow from mom—she's passed through denial into a post-*Oprah* shrug. The movie centers on a boy who has been universally adored and yet remains aloof and two girls who are unrecognized in their families but come together in good fit connection. We shuttle between their lives, catching big and little moments, seeing that self-understanding is the central drama in these lives. That and the collision of skin. The film's physical nakedness is unairbrushed and in its way poignant, revealing a dimpled, mottled map of the times.

Also reviewed in:
NEW YORK TIMES, 4/4/97, p. C25, Stephen Holden
VARIETY, 9/23-29/96, p. 132, Emanuel Levy

CHILDREN OF THE REVOLUTION

A Miramax Films release in association with the Australian Film Finance Corporation of a Rev Kids production. *Producer:* Tristram Miall. *Director:* Peter Duncan. *Screenplay:* Peter Duncan. *Director of Photography:* Martin McGrath. *Editor:* Simon Martin. *Music:* Nigel Westlake. *Sound:* Gethin Creagh. *Sound Editor:* Andrew Plain. *Production Designer:* Roger Ford. *Costumes:* Terry Ryan. *Running time:* 101 minutes. *MPAA Rating:* R.

CAST: Judy Davis (Joan Fraser); Sam Neill (Nine); F. Murray Abraham (Stalin); Richard Roxburgh (Joe); Rachel Griffiths (Anna); Geoffrey Rush (Welch); Russell Kiefel (Barry); John Gaden (Dr. Wilf Wilke); Ben McIvor (Young Joe); Marshall Napier (Brendan Shaw); Ken Radley (Bernard Shaw); Fiona Press (Mavis); Alex Menglet (Yuri); Rowan Woods (Colin Slansky); Harold Hopkins (Police Commissioner); Heather Mitchell (Mrs. Savage); Paul Livingston (Beria); Stephen Abbott (Malenkov); Dennis Watkins (Khrushchev); Ron Haddrick (Allan Miles); Barry Langrishe (Ted); Robbie McGregor (Minister); Roy Billing (Police Sergeant).

LOS ANGELES TIMES, 5/1/97, Calendar/p. 14, Kenneth Turan

Imagine, just imagine, that Joseph Stalin had a love child. Could the boy settle down and become a regular Joe, or would his life prove that heredity is destiny? And what kind of a woman would have a mad romantic fling with Stalin in the first place?

"Children of the Revolution," the feature debut of Australian writer-director Peter Duncan, answers those questions and several others you might not have thought of. A gloss on the disillusion that came with the embracing of communist ideals that is part playful farce, part dark satire, this unclassifiable film, both comic and strange, always holds your attention even when it doesn't seem to know where it's going.

Providing "Revolution's" driving force is the whirlwind Judy Davis, who brings her trademark intensity and sense of humor to full boil here. Few actresses can get as comically riled up as Davis, and this fire-in-the-eyes part is made to order for her abilities.

Davis plays Joan Fraser, introduced as the Red terror of 1951 Sydney, a firebrand Communist who can't wait for the bloody proletarian revolution, the bloodier the better. "Overthrowing the government is not a hobby," she informs hangdog suitor Welch (Geoffrey Rush, much calmer than he was in "Shine"), and when he mentions the possibility of arrest she snaps, "Anyone who's anyone has been in prison."

Convinced that "what's going on in Russia has to be better than what's happening here," Joan's idea of a hobby is spending her spare evenings writing long, passionate letters to the world's top Communist, the man she reverentially calls "Comrade Uncle Joe."

Those letters do not go unnoticed. First they elicit a visit from a mysterious government agent known only as Nine (Sam Neill at his most unctuous). And they capture the fancy of Comrade Stalin's devoted male secretaries, eager to divert a boss who is grouchy from trying to give up smoking. Soon Stalin is dancing on air and inviting Joan Fraser to be his guest at Moscow's 1952 Communist Party congress.

Expertly played by F. Murray Abraham, Stalin is a comic opera villain who would be at home in producer Max Bialystock's "Springtime for Hitler." Toadied to by the trio of Beria, Malenkov and Khrushchev he calls "the three stooges," Stalin is willing to do anything, even break into a chorus of "I get no kick from champagne," to impress our Joan.

Things don't necessarily go as planned behind the Kremlin's closed doors, however. Complications with Stalin as well as the surprising appearance of agent Nine lead to Joan arriving back home a bit dazed and pregnant enough to agree to a marriage of convenience to the compliant Welch.

Much of "Children of the Revolution" focuses on the life of Joan's son Joe (Richard Roxburgh), who spends so much time behind bars during his formative years due to arrests at demonstrations his mother has dragged him to that he inevitably falls in love with a handcuff-wielding member of the local constabulary (Rachel Griffiths).

That handcuff routine is typical of "Revolution's" subversive and unpredictable nature. Writer-director Duncan has a gift for twisty, outrageous plot details; while another film would have just given the adult Joe a mustache, he invents an unbelievably elaborate rationale for its appearance.

Constructed around a series of mock documentary interviews, "Children of the Revolution" has no intention of sticking to a single dramatic tone, and that can be a problem. Sometimes funny, sometimes unsettling, sometimes just off the wall, "Revolution" is much too various to settle for being simply a comedy. While ambition is usually a good thing in a filmmaker, Duncan's sometimes gets out of hand.

Still maybe Joseph Stalin put it best. "Never underestimate Australians, Yuri," he says to a loyal assistant. "They are not as silly as they sound."

NEW YORK, 5/26/97, p. 77, David Denby

Children of the Revolution is moderately entertaining to watch, but it's bloody hell to review: The movie has been made with more love than inspiration, and no one enjoys putting down a labor of love. *Children of the Revolution* is a comedy about a fanatic—Joan Fraser (Judy Davis), an Australian Communist who believes every cliché of party ideology and who loves Josef Stalin, to whom she writes ardent letters. Joan gets called to Moscow by the great man and at the end of a drunken evening winds up in bed with him. In an excess of ardor, she kills him and has to be spirited out of the country, pregnant. Joan raises her little boy—named Joe, of course—and marries the dull, devoted Australian (Geoffrey Rush) who hangs around the party for her sake. Communism has been discredited and reviled everywhere, but Joan doesn't know it; she still carries a red flag to party rallies. Little Joe becomes a young man, and the only thing he enjoys about revolutionary activity is being arrested; the handcuffs, wielded by a pretty policewoman (Rachel Griffiths), turn him on. The movie is a comedy of twisted genes: Joe likes prisons, the place to which his father sent so many people, and he has a Stalinist drive for power and control. To his mother's horror, he joins "the fascists" and takes over the police union.

Children of the Revolution was written and directed by Peter Duncan (it's his first feature), and I wish I could say the movie hangs together. Joan is an utterly serious—even tragic—figure, but the movie keeps falling into feeble whimsy on all sides of her. Stalin, as tendered by F. Murray Abraham, is just a vain fool (the Kremlin scenes are pretty clownish all around), and the bondage eroticism never seems more than a conceit. The mix of seriousness and absurdism is hard to get a handle on, and not because anything wild or daring is going on. The movie is slow, and from time to time I fell into a stupor, depressed by the drab sets, the dead camera, the needlessly deliberate pacing of ordinary expository scenes. Some of the mock potted Australian history (newsreels, interviews, etc.) is fun, but in the end, we have little to respond to but Judy Davis's rage. Her Joan is a passionately sincere woman who notices nothing, a mixture of idealism, indignation, and stupidity. She continues to fight for the cause year after year, and though there's a trace of nobility as well as foolishness in her fury, the movie undercuts her, surrounding her with ciphers. Judy Davis furrows her brow and works like a demon. But the movie Duncan has created isn't worthy of its star.

NEW YORK POST, 5/2/97, p. 47, Thelma Adams

"Never underestimate Australians. They're not as silly as they sound," says Josef Stalin in Peter Duncan's refreshing intellectual comedy about coming of age as a Red diaper baby Down Under.

Duncan's grandfather, a Communist true believer, inspired the first-time feature film director and screenwriter to make "Children of the Revolution." Like Duncan's grandpa, Joan (Judy Davis) has a blind faith in a workers' revolution.

It's 1949. By day, Joan tries to rally her groggy gang of socialists at the local pub. She spurns Welch (Geoffrey Rush), a regular guy who'd rather be wed—to Joan—than Red. At night, Joan pens passionate letters to Stalin.

Those letters bring her to the attention of Nine (Sam Neill), an Australian-Russian double agent. They also catch the eye of Stalin (F. Murray Abraham). He invites Joan to the Kremlin.

Joan refuses Welch's marriage proposal and accepts Stalin's invite. "Anyone who's anyone in revolutionary politics has gone to Russia," she tells Welch.

Stalin charms Joan. In a showstopper, the dictator serenades Joan with American pop, backed up by his "Three Stooges," Beria, Malenkov and Khrushchev.

The night is young. Stalin is old. He dies in bed. A guilt-stricken Joan turns to Nine for comfort. She returns home, subdued and pregnant. Joan marries Welch and gives birth to a son, Joe.

Joan raises Joe to be a revolutionary. As a schoolboy, he knows zip about Churchill but all there is to know about Stalin. All, that is, except for the purges and genocide. Mom won't let anything obscure her utopian visions—including the facts.

Joan leads Joe (Richard Roxburgh) on a guided tour of radical causes. Grown up, Joe is dutiful, but he's more turned on by the uniformed police than by the peaceniks. When he meets mounted policewoman Anna (Rachel Griffiths), Joe starts getting arrested just so she'll cuff him.

It turns out Joe has a congenital case of creeping fascism. After a stint in jail as a conscientious objector, he's politically reborn as a defender of jailers. His ambitions escalate and, in 1989, he nearly topples the Australian government backed by the forces of law and order. Mama wanted a revolution, just not this one.

Strongly supported by Neill, Abraham, Rush and Griffiths, Davis and Roxburgh create a sharp, passionate, evolving portrait of a mother and son bound by a love colored by ideology. Because of this, Duncan achieves an emotional, as well as a comic, payoff to "Children of the Revolution."

As the saying goes: If you want a revolution, you have to break some eggs. The problem is, you never, know how the omelette is going to taste.

NEWSDAY, 5/1/97, Part II/p. B7, Jack Mathews

She has spent most of her life praying at the altar of Soviet communism, and worshiping from afar its leader, Joseph Stalin. At a young age, she even taught herself Russian so she could write mash notes to the Kremlin, and though her native Australia wouldn't seem to be red meat for the revolution, that is her dream.

Meet Joan Fraser, the rebel groupie of writer-director Peter Duncan's delightfully absurd political fable "Children of the Revolution," the epic tale of how Australia is brought to the brink of chaos in the mid-'90s because she goes to Moscow in the early '50s, and returns carrying Stalin's son.

That's right. During her one night in the Kremlin, she ends up in bed with Uncle Joe, and though the exercise is fatal to him, his genes are passed along, and as the boy grows to manhood Down Under, he becomes more than a chip off the old block—he's the spitting, rabble-rousing image.

This is a wonderfully nutty idea, but what makes it go the distance as a feature film is the earnest, dead-pan performance of Judy Davis. You'd think Joan Fraser was a character in "Reds" rather than some loony comedy, and wrongheaded as Fraser is, Davis makes her as essential to the fun as a pole at a May Day celebration. (Speaking of which ... Miramax Films, never one to miss a marketing opportunity, is releasing "Children of the Revolution" on a Thursday because May 1 is a holiday associated with the labor movement that fed the revolution. So if you live in Moscow, get to the theater early.)

Duncan, directing his first feature, structures "Children" as a dramatic news feature, opening it with interviews suggesting a political crisis in Australia brought about by the dangerously radical politician Joe Welch (Richard Roxburgh), Joan's fortysomething son.

The movie then flashes back to the postwar period, where Joan, almost single-handedly, is keeping the Australian Communist Party alive.

Joan's been writing letters to Stalin for years, but it's not until she leads a successful campaign against a referendum to ban the party that the Soviet leader takes notice, and invites her to Moscow. Her visit with Stalin (F. Murray Abraham, in a rare, broad comedy role) is a hoot. He may be a cold-blooded dictator, but he has a warm feeling about Joan and begins to seduce her with his rendition of "I Get a Kick Out of You." She sleeps with him anyway.

Back home, Joan marries her blinded-by-love suitor, Zachary ("Shine's" Geoffrey Rush), not able to tell him for certain whether her baby is the son of Stalin or David Hoyle (Sam Neill), the double-agent who keeps hovering over her life. But time, given the power of little Joe's double ration of revolutionary genes, will tell.

Roxburgh has fun taking Joe through the stages of political metamorphosis, from ordinary kid to activist to messianic radical. And Rachel Griffiths, the rising Australian star best known in this country as Toni Collette's ill-fated friend in "Muriel's Wedding," is terrific as Joe's lover and his eventually wary wife.

It took a lot of nerve for first-time director Duncan to make a comedy about Stalin and communism. Not because they're political hot potatoes, but because they're so passé. Happy May Day.

VILLAGE VOICE, 5/6/97, p. 79, J. Hoberman

Glib, jolly, and not overly concerned with anyone's lost innocence, the Australia-Miramax Cold War comedy *Children of the Revolution* explores another page of the post-modern scenario.

Like *Irma Vep*, this is a star vehicle about stardom. The most hardcore fanatic in the Australian Communist Party, Judy Davis's Joan Fraser is introduced circa 1951 launching into a heartfelt rant, disrupting the rhetoric of an anti-Soviet newsreel. It's a great comic turn. The actress's intensity—her all-over emotional vibrato—keeps her character from ever seeming a half-wit despite the traps contrived by writer-director Peter Duncan. The impassioned letters written by this starstruck, would-be red Saint Joan to the Great Stalin not only make the Russian censors weep but secure her an invitation to visit the Kremlin. Joan returns, pregnant with Stalin's child, to marry a timidly admiring fellow-traveler played by Oscar laureate Geoffrey Rush. (Only scarcely less outlandish, Duncan managed to get Davis, Rush, and Sam Neill, as a government double—or perhaps triple-agent, for his first film.)

Children of the Revolution intermittently pretends to be a pseudo-documentary but seems most at home in the realm of campy farce. Stalin (F. Murray Abraham) calls the Russian people his "pussycats" and refers to henchmen Beria, Malenkov, and Khrushchev as "The Three Stooges." The sub-Mel Brooks scene—where he get them to sing backup while he belts "I Get a Kick Out of You" is blithely tasteless but perhaps not quite tasteless enough. This Gumpish Cold War gloss eventually assumes the cutie-pie in-your-face quality of Australian comedies like *Strictly Ballroom* and *Muriel's Wedding*. Despite Duncan's thesis that Communism runs in families, like hemophilia or the Hapsburg jaw, *Children of the Revolution* loses momentum when the emphasis shifts from crazy Joan to her crazy son Joe (Richard Roxburgh) and his fixation with a leather-clad policewoman (Rachel Griffiths).

No way to fault Davis. She ages beautifully into a crotchety old crank watching Gorbachev on television and ranting about McSocialism. In an alternate universe, the subject of her rage might well be McMovies.

Also reviewed in:
NEW YORK TIMES, 5/1/97, p. C18, Janet Maslin
NEW YORKER, 5/12/97, p. 104, Anthony Lane
VARIETY, 8/5-11/96, p. 49, David Stratton
WASHINGTON POST, 5/9/97, p. D1, Stephen Hunter
WASHINGTON POST, 5/9/97, Weekend/p. 57, Jane Horwitz

CHRONICLE OF A DISAPPEARANCE

An International Film Circuit release of a Dhat Productions, Norma Productions in association with the Fund of the Promotion of Israeli Quality Film, European Union Media Project and CNC and Independent Television Service. *Executive Producer:* Assaf Amir. *Producer:* Elia Suleiman. *Director:* Elia Suleiman. *Screenplay (Arabic, Hebrew, French and Russian with English subtitles):* Elia Suleiman. *Director of Photography:* Marc Andre Batigne. *Editor:* Anna Ruiz. *Music:* Alla, Abed Azrie, Leonard Cohen, and Natacha Atlas. *Sound:* Jean-Paul Mugel. *Art Director:* Samir Srouji and Hans ter Elst. *Running time:* 88 minutes. *MPAA Rating:* Not Rated.

CAST: Elia Suleiman (E.S.); Ula Tabari (Adan); Nazira Suleiman (Mother); Fuad Suleiman (Father); Jamal Dehar (Owner of the Holyland Shop).

LOS ANGELES TIMES, 10/31/97, Calendar/p. 10, Kevin Thomas

"Chronicle of a Disappearance's" title refers to the lack of a story to tell on the part of filmmaker Elia Suleiman, a Palestinian returning to his native land after a 12-year absence. He seems to have arrived at a moment of calm in Palestinian-Israeli relations, and as it turns out, this suits his purpose perfectly in what is a demanding, beautiful and understated experimental film of unexpected impact.

Suleiman has described his film as "a journey in search of what it means to be Palestinian." Neither documentary nor fiction but partaking of both, "Chronicle" is best described as a journal expressing the filmmaker's emotions and state of mind as he observes daily life about him. What he creates is a Palestinian's sense of marginalization as well as pride in a series of vignettes, some dryly amusing, others expressing powerful emotions.

For example, Suleiman expresses great affection when he shows his father, seen through a window, enjoying the camaraderie of friends and besting them at arm wrestling. This is a film rich in references and nuances, and the exceptionally detailed synopsis provided reviewers reveals that far more extensive subtitles or perhaps narration in English added to the soundtrack really is needed to convey the full experience of the film available only to Arab-speakers.

Suleiman divides his film into two parts, "Nazareth Personal Diary" and "Jerusalem Political Diary," but the transition between the two is gradual, a kind of looking into one's self giving way to a looking outward. Warm observations of his relatives alternate with views of a listless, aimless existence, epitomized by the dull routines of the proprietor (Jamal Dehar) of a souvenir shop, the Holyland. One moment he's seen filling bottles of holy water—from his own tap—another trying to keep a cheap camel statuette from falling over. Suleiman often sits out front of the store with the proprietor.

A triumph of succinct images and adroit structure, "Chronicle" gains focus and intensity, especially when it moves on to Jerusalem, where he witnesses an attractive Arab woman (Ula Tabari) experience repeated rejection when over the phone she tries to rent an apartment in Jewish West Jerusalem.

After an especially comic sequence, Suleiman falls heir to an Israeli policeman's walkie-talkie, which allows him to evoke with alternating humor and fear an overwhelming sense of paranoia that a Palestinian can feel in regard to Israelis—and vice versa. (At one point what looks to be a terrorist's hand grenade turns out to be a cigarette lighter.) The sense of absurdity over the entire Israeli-Palestinian predicament grows as "Chronicle" unfolds, and it ends with an image of profound alienation.

NEW YORK POST, 5/30/97, p. 52, Larry Worth

People are shown taking a snooze in the first and last scenes of "Chronicle of a Disappearance." In between, viewers may do the same.

Included as part of this year's New Directors/New Films series, Elia Suleiman's look at Palestinians in present-day Israel isn't really a drama, nor a documentary, nor a travelogue. Rather, its a series of largely unrelated scenes in which actors try to convey a specific time, place and state of mind.

Sadly, the results aren't nearly as intriguing as the concept. In fact, it occasionally seems a parody of cinema verite.

Divided into two main section about Nazareth and Jerusalem, the narrative is then broken down into mini-segments. With most of them titled "The Day After," it becomes obvious that almost nothing changes in the subjects' mundane existences. And while that may be the point, the results are downright soporific.

For instance, there's scene after scene of two owners of a souvenir shop sitting outside the store, staring into space. A penny for their on-screen thoughts would rack up millions. But so what? Ditto for a later sequence when one of them uprights a plastic camel that falls over, six—count 'em six—times.

Things pick up slightly in the more politically based second half. Even then, Suleiman indulges his unique storytelling manner, exemplified by a tableau of the director sitting down for a smoke and beer.

But within such time-wasting, interesting moments sneak in, as when a female apartment-seeker confronts anti-Arab sentiments. Equally arresting is when a Nazareth resident comments on the pollution-induced scum making it possible for anyone to walk across the water that Jesus did.

Ironically, such highlights confirm the rest of the production's lackings. And while photography of ancient Israel and a lively soundtrack are duly evocative, they can't compensate for the overwhelming sense of ennui.

The bottom line: "Chronicle" has much to say, but communicates precious little.

VILLAGE VOICE, 6/3/97, p. 65, J. Hoberman

The lost world in Elia Suleiman's *Chronicle of a Disappearance* that of an "invisible" national identity. After a dozen years of self-imposed exile in New York, a thirtysomething, Israeli-born, Arab filmmaker returns to Nazareth, the sleepy hometown he shares with Jesus Christ, to make this elegant, serenely ironic movie—the one Israeli avant-documentarian Amos Gitai has always longed to make.

Conceived in the aftermath of the Oslo accords, Suleiman's accomplished first feature—shown in March as part of "New Directors/New Films"—is effortlessly prismatic. Part documentary, part psychodrama, part structuralist investigation, and part absurd comedy, *Chronicle of a Disappearance* is unified by a methodological emphasis on presence that paradoxically emphasizes the filmmaker's own sense of dislocation. Few movies give a more vivid sense of Israeli geography; none, in my experience, have limned it more ruefully from a Palestinian perspective. Deliberate and deadpan, *Chronicle of a Disappearance* is largely composed of discrete bits of business. Suleiman begins the first half, "Personal Diary," by contemplating the weathered landscape of his father's face. He then segues into the doings in and around the Holy Land souvenir stand, where the proprietor begins his day by filling little vials of holy water from the tap, Japanese tour buses disgorge their pilgrims, and close-ups of the postcards in the outside rack provide a model for the film's own style.

As spare and formalist as it is, *Chronicle of a Disappearance* has been compared to Jim Jarmusch's *Stranger Than Paradise* and Suleiman to Jacques Tati. Suleiman's sophisticated orchestration of the ordinary also has a generic resemblance to James Benning's ruminations on the look of the upper Midwest and to Chantal Akerman travelogues *News From Home* and *D'Est*. The difference is that Suleiman uses actors (often family members playing themselves) and that where Akerman was abroad in New York or Eastern Europe, Suleiman has gone home—equally a tourist.

Midway through he becomes even more so—even while providing the overt "Palestinian" content his subject would seem to warrant. Suleiman's "Political Diary" begins with the laconic statement: "I moved to Jerusalem to be closer to the airport." Here, the filmmaker abandons a fixed-camera perspective to figure in the action as a suitably expressionless, largely mute, observer of increasingly bizarre events. Having found and brought home a police walkie-talkie dropped on the ground by a gang of Uzi-toting Keystone cops, E.S (as he credits himself) monitors the cryptic transmissions of the Zionist entity. (So do his parents, last seen asleep in their living-room easy chairs as Israeli TV signs off with "Hatikva").

One is reminded of the title of the Turgenev novel, *Diary of a Superfluous Man*. Brought to lecture before a Palestinian audience, E.S. is prevented from uttering even a single word by a faulty microphone, an inept, darting technician, and ultimately the disinterest of the audience. A more political form of absurdity is embodied by the dilemma of the statuesque Adan, who is unable to rent an apartment in east Jerusalem because she is a single woman or in the city's western sector because she is an Arab. Is Adan a performance artist or a member of a terrorist cell? "To be or not to be ... Palestinian," is how one intertitle poses the dilemma.

Also reviewed in:
NATION, 6/16/97, p. 35, Stuart Klawans
NEW REPUBLIC, 6/30/97, p. 26, Stanley Kauffmann
NEW YORK TIMES, 5/30/97, p. C18, Janet Maslin
VARIETY, 9/23-29/96, p. 131, Deborah Young

CITY OF INDUSTRY

An Orion Pictures and Largo Entertainment release of an Evzen Kolar production. *Executive Producer:* Barr Potter. *Producer:* Evzen Kolar and Ken Solarz. *Director:* John Irvin. *Screenplay:* Ken Solarz. *Director of Photography:* Thomas Burstyn. *Editor:* Mark Conte. *Music:* Stephen Endelman. *Music Editor:* Joe Milner. *Sound:* Walter Hoylman and (music): Gary Chester. *Sound Editor:* Anthony J. Miceli. *Casting:* Dory Zuckerman and Cathy Henderson. *Production Designer:* Michael Novotny. *Special Effects:* Joe Lombardi. *Costumes:* Eduardo Castro. *Make-up:* Janeen Schreyer. *Stunt Coordinator:* Ernie Orsatti. *Running time:* 97 minutes. *MPAA Rating:* R.

CAST: Harvey Keitel (Roy Egan); Stephen Dorff (Skip Kovich); Famke Janssen (Rachel Montana); Timothy Hutton (Lee Egan); Wade Dominguez (Jorge Montana); Michael Jai White (Odell Williams); Reno Wilson (Keshaun Brown); Lucy Alexis Liu (Cathy Rose); Dana Barron (Gena); Tamara Clatterbuck (Sunny); Brian Brophy (Backus); François Chau (Uncle Luke); Flex (A Roc); Brian Shen (Pai-gow Dealer); Ai Wan (Gwen); Cyrus Farmer (Steady); Eli Ruiz (Henry Montana); Vien Hong (Gingerhead); Michael Trac (Shrimp Boy); Evzen Nolar

(Droutzkoy);   Jonathan Schmock (Jewelry Manager);   Raymound Ma (Paradise Hotel Clerk); Georg D. Rice (Royal Sentry Security Guard);   Brian Habicht (Phone Company Employee); Arthur Louis Fuller (Bouncer);   Sarah Sullivan (Nurse);   Jane Crawley (Waitress);   Antonio Molina (Mailman);   Philip Tan (Jimmie);   Stuart Quan (Onion Head);   Anthony James DeJesus (Jorge Jr.);   John Koyama (Two Gun);   Steven Ho (Gang Member);   Brian Imada (Sweet Plum); Leo Lee (Redman);   William Leong (Jesse);   Andrew Markell (Kangol);   Eddie Yansick, Eddie Mathews, and Tim Rigby (Bodyguards);   Fred Lerner (Security Guard);   Elliott Gould (Gangster).

LOS ANGELES TIMES, 3/14/97, Calendar p. 6, Kenneth Turan

Everything about "City of Industry" is reminiscent of something else, but that doesn't have to be bad. Bringing professionalism and style to familiar genre material, this is a modest, efficient little thriller whose strength is not where it's going but how it gets there.

Yet another of those modern film noirs where evil bakes in the amoral California sun, "City of Industry" owes a considerable debt one of its most celebrated predecessors, the John Boorman-directed "Point Blank," taken from a novel by Donald Westlake writing as Richard Stark.

That 1967 film featured Lee Marvin as an unstoppable golem of crime, a berserk avenger who only wants what's owed him. All kinds of people think they can handle Marvin's Parker, but they don't know what they're getting into.

As written by Ken Solarz (whose credits include TV's "Miami Vice" and "Crime Story") and directed by John Irvin, "City of Industry" passes Marvin's mantle to Harvey Keitel, who dominates this film with a powerful presence and a look of inexorable determination.

Before Keitel's Roy Egan makes an appearance, there are other members of an L.A. criminal team to meet, starting with his brother Lee Egan (convincingly played against type by a bearded, bristling Timothy Hutton), a hoodlum who steals cars as casually and as often as he changes shirts.

Hutton's main confederate is Jorge Montana (Wade Dominguez), (convicted on a weapon's charge and about to be sentenced. Jorge is a family man with two small children and a wife (Famke Janssen, "GoldenEye's" Xenia Onatopp) who is, yes, tired of a husband who makes his living outside the law.

Apparently unaware of the movie odds against hard guys determined to take down one last big score, Egan and Montana plan a job in Palm Springs big enough to attract the attention of Lee's brother, Roy. The target is the West Coast distribution center for a Russian diamond cartel, where a robbery will have the added fillip of giving the Russkies "a crash course in free enterprise."

Every crime team needs a wheel man and this crew has Skip Kovich (Stephen Dorff, very different as Candy Darling in "I Shot Andy Warhol"). A flashy, amoral hot-head—and that's on his calmer days—Skip is oversupplied with attitude and is clearly a person who never met a risk he didn't like.

As in all movie robberies, it doesn't matter how good the planning is or how quick and brutal the gang is on the job, the frailty of human nature is guaranteed to mess things up. Which is the signal for Roy Egan to become a veritable god of vengeance.

Operating on the savage theory that "I'm my own police," Egan proves to be undeterred by normal human emotions and as difficult to kill as the Whitewater controversy. Except for a scene of out-of-control emotion, possibly thrown in for old time's sake, Keitel's acting is as refreshingly spare and pared down as Al Pacino's is in "Donnie Brasco." If this turns out to be a trend, no one will be upset.

Veteran director Irvin, who has made everything from "The Dogs of War" to "Widow's Peak" in a 30-plus year career, has gotten involved in this story. "City of Industry" has a nice feeling of craft and tightly wound concision about it. And its attempt to showcase unusual L.A. locations, including a cheap motel tour of the city, is worthwhile even if some of the locales are as venerable as the abandoned oil refinery in Santa Fe Springs that was the location for James Cagney's last stand in "White Heat."

"City of Industry" has its share of weak areas, including plot points that won't stand up to heavy analysis and a tendency to dip heavily into on-screen violence. But even if breaking new territory isn't one of it's strengths, this film gives fans of grown up Dead End Kids exactly what they bargained for.

NEW YORK POST, 3/14/97, p. 51, Thelma Adams

"I'm my own police," says Roy, the grizzled avenging angel in John Irvin's "City of Industry." About Fulsom Prison, his brother, Lee, says: "That's me and Roy's alma mater."

Ouch! If Roy (Harvey Keitel) and Lee (Timothy Hutton) bit that dialogue any harder, it would bite back. The brothers talk tough, but they aren't smart enough to know the No. 1 lesson of armed robbery:

Never go into business with a guy named Skip.

Skip (Stephen Dorff) is a screaming, one-man disaster area from the first slangy words that fall from his curled lips in an armchair-hard script by Ken Solarz (of TV's "Crime Story" and "Miami Vice," both of which are better credits). With the exception of Dorff's Candy Darling in "I Shot Andy Warhol" and his turn as the fifth Beatle in Ian Softley's overrated "Backbeat," the young actor has become a sign of a movie in trouble (masochists should rent "S.F.W.").

Roy, Lee, Skip and Jorge (Wade Dominguez) join forces for a big diamond score in Palm Springs. Jorge's wife,, Rachel (Famke Janssen), sits around the house in frumpy shorts, an accessory after the plot; maybe Janssen's bored and angry because she got to kill guys with her bare thighs as Xenia Onatopp in "GoldenEye."

The boys score, but Skip does what comes naturally to a little, flame-haired guy on an elephant's dose of amphetamines: He double-crosses his partners. This leads to Roy having tantrums (luckily, he tosses the furniture but not the Budweiser) in tatty hotel rooms on the seedy side of the Big Orange. Then Roy gets really ugly—but not as ugly as the L.A. blight Irvin presents with an earnestness previously reserved for Jacques Cousteau's exploration of the undersea world.

Why Keitel would want to take another dip in "Reservoir Dogs" territory with Irvin's neo-noir is more of a mystery than this less-than-thriller offers. Another enigma: How does Irvin, an experienced director of movies as various as "Widows' Peak" and the Schwarzenegger vehicle "Raw Deal," achieve that first- time-filmmaker look?

NEWSDAY, 3/14/97, Part II/p. B9, John Anderson

It probably doesn't qualify as a trend, but the makers of "civilized" pictures ("chick flicks" being far too outré a description) seem to be feeling their oats.

First, Mike Newell ("Four Weddings and a Funeral," "Enchanted April") comes up with the bracing-yet-human "Donnie Brasco." Then John Irvin, best known for "Widows Peak" and "A Month by the Lake," turns out "City of Industry," which is all nerve-racking violence and deglamorized dishonesty.

Down, boys. OK maybe it's not a trend. Maybe it's just a rite of manhood. In any event, Irvin's very entertaining movie is a crime thriller as might be prescribed by William Bennett—it's about received values, professional ethics, the struggling small business of crime. As Bob Dylan once sang, "To live outside the law, you must be honest." Irvin's film is about what happens when you're not.

Set in and around a seedy Los Angeles and among conscientious losers, "City" finds the overly confident Lee (Timothy Hutton) putting together a heist of Russian diamonds from a Palm Springs dealer. Already on board is Jorge (Wade Dominguez), who's lost his appeal of a prison term on another case, but wants to get in on the action. En route to town, making pit stops for guns and with the heavy metal on full blast, is Skip (Stephen Dorff), who seems as untrustworthy as he is volatile. And, getting off a bus from somewhere, is Lee's brother Roy, played by Mr. Earthy Integrity himself, Harvey Keitel.

Keitel doesn't so much star in as preside over the film. If John Wayne had a walk that defined screen machismo for the studio era, Keitel moves with the motions of postmodern, post-nuclear solitude. He's existential energy and simmering rage, weathered and unbeaten.

As Roy, he's also a pro. He takes one look at Skip and sees trouble; he's not so sure of Lee either, who's dangerously overconfident and willing to put his trust in Skip.

Strictly '90s hoods, the four view crime as an occupation, and go about it with vicious efficiency. But it's not their only concern in life. Jorge's worried about his long-suffering wife, Rachel (Famke Janssen), and their kids; Roy and Lee discuss whether their mother should go into a home. Only Skip is without roots or responsibilities, and since he's a sociopath anyway, this makes him a time bomb. And he goes off almost immediately.

Roy, who declares at one point "I am my own police," may be self-sufficient, but he exists within, and respects, the limits of a defined universe. Skip does not. The most profound thing about "City of Industry" is the way it serves as a metaphor for a disintegrating society (Bennett again?). Roy may be a thief, but he's got integrity. Skip's self-aggrandizing attitude is very '80s, and knows no moral boundaries. Their battle, which involves a cross-section of ethnic mobsters and a hint of romance between Roy and Rachel, is epic, violent and hinges on the very things that keep society from flying completely apart. Does it have a happy ending? That may depend on your politics.

SIGHT AND SOUND, 8/97, p. 44, Rob White

Lee Egan has planned a robbery in Palm Springs with brother Roy, driver Skip, and friend Jorge. Skip buys guns from a black gang. The robbery is accomplished quickly. Skip kills Lee and Jorge to keep the money for himself. But Roy escapes. Roy drives to LA and breaks into Lee's apartment to tell his wife what's happened. She tells him about the Wildlife Lounge where Lee and Jorge used to meet. Roy beats up the barman there until he reveals the name of Skip's lawyer. Roy confronts the lawyer and gets phone numbers for Skip. At a strip bar, Roy tracks down one of Skip's girlfriends. Skip puts out a contract to have Roy killed.

Roy goes to visit Rachel, Jorge's wife. Asian gangsters jump Roy at his motel. He kills them, but is injured. Rachel nurses him and agrees to help him track Skip in return for $100,000. She takes him to the sweatshop base of Skip's fence, Luke. Roy beats up Luke and takes the money he's laundered for Skip. Luke phones Skip at a disused refinery to tell him what's happened and where Roy is (Luke knows because Roy had dropped his room key). A shoot-out at the motel ends in the death of Skip's men. Two black gang members take Skip's girlfriend hostage. Skip kills them and her.

Skip calls Roy at Rachel's house. Roy drives to the refinery. Despite being shot, he kills Skip's henchmen and batters Skip to death. Rachel drives him to a hospital but he disappears while she runs to find help, leaving her the money. She and her kids move to the coast where a letter arrives for her containing a medallion she had given Roy.

City of Industry is a contemporary crime thriller based around fairly conventional situations: theft, betrayal, retribution. It begins with a quickly and coolly executed heist carried out by a gang comprised of Lee Egan, his brother Roy, Jorge Montana and Skip Kovich. But when Skip turns on his partners, Roy manages to get away and sets about avenging his brother's death in the most implacable fashion, with the help of Jorge's wife Rachel. However, the film is anything but ordinary in the elaboration of its plot. Stripped down to the very barest narrative bones, it opts for an almost clinical minimalism in order to reimagine the thriller genre.

The action covers a couple of days, but it feels as if one coherent unit of time is being observed, as if the duration of the action isn't much different from the duration of the film. This effect can be attributed to *City of Industry*'s remarkable formal discipline. No scene is longer than a few minutes and each seems to be about as long as every other. The effect is of an absolutely controlled, insistent, almost percussive rhythm which, as the film progresses, lends it the quality of abstraction. This rhythm seems more important than any opportunity for prolonged spectacle or suspense, staginess or burnout. The film doesn't try to elicit excitement, outrage, surprise, identification (although these reactions aren't excluded). It's worth pointing out that there are no cops in *City of Industry*: "I'm my own police," Roy says, underlining the fact that the film seeks neither to juxtapose Roy's sense of justice with what's socially permissible, nor to present any variation on the cop/criminal double which would otherwise be standard. In *City of Industry*, betrayal isn't important for its social or psychological dimensions—it's simply the minimum condition of the plot—and retribution is no more or less than closure, an ending to narrative. In its detached way, the film seems to be trying to get at the quintessence of revenge movies, free of all superfluity.

To complement the economy of the narrative, Harvey Keitel performs with a compelling mixture of feral edginess and emotional containment—as if he were still in *The Piano*. He's taking a revenger-role more readily associated with Schwarzenegger or Van Damme, but playing it with art-film techniques. A lifetime of pain and disillusionment is stored up behind his eyes and coiled in the controlled violence of his actions. But all this overspills only once. In a motel room just after Lee's murder, he sits playing patience. Suddenly he loses control, hurling the cards and the table across the room as if buckled by his loss. It's all over in a flash—but for a moment trauma has punctured the narrative in a quite unexpected way. Roy's moment of temporary disarray rhymes with another moment when Rachel, having just been told the details of Roy's betrayal, stumbles in her garden and almost collapses. She doesn't acknowledge this instant of breakdown. Because so much is left implicit here, the scene is immeasurably more arresting and affecting than if it had been teased out and glossed. Narrative precision and formal organisation lend *City of Industry* rigour and structure; moments like these lend it pathos and complexity. The blend is masterful.

The city of the title is, of course, Los Angeles and the film-makers are clearly interested in the violence, ethnic diversity and cultural fragmentation which virtually define LA. There are traces of moral panic in the film's array of racially distinct gangs (traces, that is, of a view of LA which laments the city's cultural diversity). But what is much more prominent is a kind of quizzical distance which, rather than trying to construct a unified aesthetic of the city, views it in fragmented, disparate ways. So we have a brief sequence of black-and-white shots of bridges and flyovers, snatches of slow motion and a whole array of interiors: a strip club washed in blue light (shades of Michael Mann here, with whom writer Ken Solarz collaborated on *Crime Story* and *Miami Vice*); a sweatshop lit the colour of parchment; various seedy, impersonal motel rooms.

This is a composite picture, as heterogeneous as its subject, made up of shards of other pictures. The effect is academic rather than polemical or involved, not least because *City of Industry* relates itself to film history. Several scenes take place in the precinct of an abandoned refinery (where a chimney spurts fire). On the one hand, the classic 1949 *White Heat* in which James Cagney's character meets his death while standing on the tower of a refinery is recalled here, and on the other, *Blade Runner*. The setting invokes classicism and post-modernism, the American city as crucible of social history and as dizzying premonition of the future.

VILLAGE VOICE, 3/18/97, p. 76, Laurie Stone

John Irvin's no-fat direction has nearly comic economy. *City of Industry* is noir pulp with nothing but pulp. Harvey Keitel, whose face has weathered to a moon surface and whose nose is spreading into a Karl Malden warp, is tired con Roy, whose younger brother, played by a skanky Timothy Hutton, ropes him into a Palm Springs jewel heist. The rat pack—when these guys do a car, you can kiss your Club goodbye—includes a pretty Latino played by Wade Dominguez and wheelman Skip (Stephen Dorff), named as if he were a sunny lad from a 50s sitcom instead of a jittery psycho with hair bobbed by nail scissors. Everyone wears stylish sunglasses, including the armies of black and Chinese thugs who throng the movie and who, given no distinct characters, are treated like warrior ants. But Skip's craziness leaks out beyond his Guess jeans-addict chic look, in his taste for headbanger rock and his rough way with the babes.

The movie is mostly a silly, repetitive cat-and-mouse chase waged between Roy and Skip, but it hits an authentic note in its view of machismo. In this world, women are peripheral and at risk. Men have all the aggression and, terrified of other feelings, consist of nothing but aggression. Mourning his murdered brother, Roy can do nothing but smash his hotel room. Men here burn to break bones and to bloody faces, preferably with their fists, though a rifle butt will do. What distinguishes scuzzy but true brutes from irredeemable scum is whether they are driven by anything but greed and whether they use women's bodies as a battlefield to prove their masculinity. The movie spares us insight into Skip's barbarisms, and Keitel is too intelligent to turn his martyred tough guy into a hero—the way an actor like John Wayne would have. Keitel gives us space not to care about him as he seeks vengeance on pure malice.

Also reviewed in:
NEW YORK TIMES, 3/14/97, p. C19, Stephen Holden
NEW YORKER, 3/24/97, p. 84, Terrence Rafferty
VARIETY, 3/3-9/97, p. 67, Emanuel Levy

COLD AROUND THE HEART

A Twentieth Century Fox release of an Illusion Entertainment Group/Baumgarten-Prophet Entertainment production. *Executive Producer:* Richard Rutowski. *Producer:* Dan Halstead, Craig Baumgarten, and Adam J. Merims. *Director:* John Ridley. *Screenplay:* John Ridley. *Director of Photography:* Malik Hassan Sayeed. *Editor:* Eric L. Beason. *Music:* Gerry Gershman and Mason Daring. *Casting:* Mary Vernieu and Ronnie Yeskel. *Production Designer:* Kara Lindstrom. *Running time:* 96 minutes. *MPAA Rating:* R.

CAST: David Caruso (Ned); Kelly Lynch (Jude); Stacey Dash (Bec); Chris Noth (T); John Spencer (Uncle Mike); Pruitt Taylor Vince (Cokebottles); Richard Kind (Habbish).

LOS ANGELES TIMES, 12/5/97, Calendar/p. 8, Kevin Thomas

"Cold Around the Heart" is lowdown, outrageous trashy fun, a nifty neo-noir/pursuit picture charged with a torrid love affair straight out of "Duel in the Sun."

We've seen what writer-director John Ridley serves up many times before, but he makes its familiarity a sit-back-and-relax pleasure while bringing to his picture a sharp-edged freshness and dimension. Such are the joys of genre done with panache that amusingly threaten to go right over the top.

Advertised as simply "Cold Heart" but still reading "Cold Around the Heart" on the screen and bearing a 1996 copyright, the movie opens strongly and never lets up.

A couple (David Caruso, Kelly Lynch) are zooming down a desert highway with a police car gaining on them when suddenly their passenger-side door flings open, leaving Caruso's Ned Tash sprawled on the highway, hauled off to a small city hospital for treatment of minor injuries and facing charges of armed robbery of a jewelry store that left three people dead.

Ned escapes with comparative ease, determined to track down Lynch's Jude, who did the actual shooting, and made off with $250,000 in jewels. Consumed with revenge, he is obsessed with killing her, but as a pretty hitchhiker (Stacey Dash) tells him, he must love Jude very much to be so determined to waste her.

While Ned and Dash's Bec, running away from a sexually abusive father, commence developing a wary mutual trust and respect, Jude, laying low, enlists the aid of a seemingly thick-headed guy she picks up in a bar (Chris Noth, in a sly portrayal) to protect her when Ned catches up to her with an inevitability that occurs more often in the movies than in real life. (Ridley clearly knows his movie owes more to other movies than to actuality and accordingly proceeds with a light touch.)

However, we're by now in such a thicket of double-crosses it's hard to know whom to believe; trusting anyone is out of the question.

Ridley is really shrewd: In Ned and Jude he creates characters with a recklessness combined with sexual magnetism that are just what a satisfying escapist fantasy needs. He then makes them sufficiently self-deluding so that we don't have to care too much what happens to them.

Lynch's adamantine blond, who is certainly "cold around the heart," and Caruso's scrappy red-head are a terrific-looking couple and their mutual attraction is palpable. Dash is most appealing as a young woman who learns an awful lot awfully fast in such dangerously mercurial company. John Spencer is memorable as an old pal of Ned's who gives him shelter but is not so benignly avuncular as he at first seems; it is he who aptly labels Jude and Ned as "the low-rent Bonnie and Clyde."

Whether production designer Kara Lindstrom found actual untouched locales or dressed them to be the epitome of wonderfully tacky low-class taste that has always been a mainstay of roadside Americana, she has contributed crucially to "Cold Around the Heart's" atmospheric appeal.

"Cold Around the Heart," which has a zingy Mason Daring score, may not be nearly as witty or inspired as "Red Rock West" or "The Last Seduction"—the maker of those films, John Dahl, by the way gets a thank you in the end credits, but it's good enough to have rated a week at the Nuart or the Sunset 5 with their sophisticated audiences. Meanwhile, Caruso, who has famously left and returned to TV after a shot at the big screen, should nonetheless hang in there for further movie breaks.

NEW YORK POST, 11/7/97, p. 56, Larry Worth

Midway through the disastrous "Cold Around the Heart," David Caruso tells his buddy, "Don't ever call me stupid again."

That's a hard order since he's gone from one cinematic fiasco to another after jumping ship from TVs "NYPD Blue."

This time around, Caruso's a jewel thief bent on tracking down his double-crossing lover (Kelly Lynch, doing a poor imitation of Ellen Barkin).

Directed and written by John Ridley, it's a slight variation on Oliver Stone's "U-Turn" (which Ridley scripted), minus the black humor. The only memorable moment is when Lynch deadpans to her new amour, "You've got a way of making dumb look good."

The same can't be said for "Cold Around the Heart."

Also reviewed in:
NEW YORK TIMES, 11/7/97, p. E14, Lawrence Van Gelder
VARIETY, 11/17-23/97, p. 64, Robert Sklar

COMMANDMENTS

A Gramercy Pictures release of a Northern Lights Entertainment production. *Executive Producer:* Ivan Reitman. *Producer:* Michael Chinich, Joe Medjuck, and Daniel Goldberg. *Director:* Daniel Taplitz. *Screenplay:* Daniel Taplitz. *Director of Photography:* Slawomir Idziak. *Editor:* Michael Jablow. *Music:* Joseph Vitarelli. *Music Editor:* Allan K. Rosen and Patty Von Arx. *Sound:* Alan Byer and (music) Daniel Wallin. *Sound Editor:* Patrick Dodd. *Casting:* Lynn Kressel. *Production Designer:* Robin Standefer. *Art Director:* Stephen Alesch. *Set Decorator:* Kate Yatsko. *Set Dresser:* Larry Amanuel, Harvey Goldberg, Henry Kaplan, and Douglas Fecht. *Special Effects:* Connie Brink. *Visual Effects:* Joseph Grossberg. *Costumes:* John Dunn. *Make-up:* Allen Weisinger. *Stunt Coordinator:* George Aguilar. *Running time:* 87 minutes. *MPAA Rating:* R.

CAST: Aidan Quinn (Seth Warner); Shirl Bernheim (Sylvia); Courteney Cox (Rachel Luce); Peter Jacobson and Patrick Garner (Bankers); Marcia Debonis (Receptionist); Anthony LaPaglia (Harry Luce); Pamela Gray (Melissa Murphy); Lisa Louise Langford (Paramedic); Chris McGinn (Nurse); Louis Zorich (Rudy Warner); Scott Sowers (Detective Mahoney); Pat McNamara (Police Chief Warren); Jack Gilpin (Gordon Bloom); Amy Sedaris (Scholar); Stephen Pearlman (Rabbi); Frank Girardeau (Bartender); Tom Aldredge (Mr. Mann); Alice Drummond (Mrs. Mann); Stephen Singer (Mr. Neer); John Tormey (Desk Sergeant); Michael Badalucco (Detective); Stu "Large" Riley (Inmate); Tom Riis Farrell (Marine Biologist).

LOS ANGELES TIMES, 5/2/97, Calendar/p. 14, John Anderson

[The following review by John Anderson appeared in a slightly different form in
NEWSDAY, 9/2/97, Part II/p. B7.]

What a lot of stories need, at their center, is a really rotten subordinate character to capture our hearts and minds. "Othello" has Iago, for instance. In "Paradise Lost," Satan manages to steal most of the scenes. In "Commandments"—a promising debut by writer-director Daniel Taplitz—it's Anthony LaPaglia.

LaPaglia's Harry Luce—journalist, adulterer and all-around ne'er-do-well—isn't the centerpiece of the story. But he lurks about its perimeter, providing the link to sordid humanity that keeps "Commandments" at least remotely in touch with our planet.

Harry's brother-in-law, Seth Warner (Aidan Quinn), has the real problems. He's lost his pregnant wife to the sea, his house to a freak tornado, his job to the caprices of bureaucrats. He asks why, and lightning strikes him. It even maims his dog. So he decides to break each of the Ten Commandments, just to see if he can get a rise out of God.

Taplitz is on audacious ground—does thunder make him nervous? Through Seth, he's asking those questions that have plagued agnostics since time began: If there's an all-powerful, all-merciful God, then why is there suffering in the world? Taplitz obviously can't answer his own question and his ending is a complete cop-out. But at the same time, this isn't your normal comedy material. And, like Satan, it keeps you interested.

Having moved in with Harry, Harry's wife Rachel (Courteney Cox) and Harry's guitar collection, Seth starts out violating the easier commandments—he worships at a Buddhist temple, carves a graven image of an Indian death goddess, blasphemes in a library, dishonors his father at his synagogue (Seth's late mother was Christian, so he's a pan-denominational sinner). He doesn't observe the Sabbath. He covets Rachel and it's mutual. Adultery isn't going to be a problem.

His task gets stickier when he gets to "Thou Shalt Not Kill," which I always thought was the Fifth Commandment but here is the Sixth (it all depends on how you read Exodus, presumably). Harry—a newspaper reporter who sleeps with his sources, lies with bravado, collects guitars he can't play and is investigating the police chief (Pat McNamara)—gets some well-deserved comeuppance via Seth's Old Testament wrath, including the aforementioned wife-coveting.

Quinn is fine as Seth, although his character's rather radical plan of action is never entirely put across; explaining what he wants to do is something the film has to get over with so it can proceed to the actual sinning. Cox is lovely, but a bit inaccessible. LaPaglia, though, is refreshingly vile and ultimately humanized.

What's most troublesome about "Commandments" as a film, though, is the way it swings so casually from urban fantasy to urban realism without marrying the two in a really convincing way. It's OK that Seth isn't given any counseling or Prozac as long as the rest of the film's tone falls into line. But a lot of scenes—to say nothing of the theology—seem illogical or contrived. Taplitz, for all the promise he shows, does seem sincere about his questions, but he has remember: Thou Shalt Not Commit Unresolved Differences With the Almighty to Film Without Fear of Retribution.

NEW YORK POST, 5/2/97, p. 54, Larry Worth

It's a question that's been asked since the days of Job: Why do bad things happen to good people, and what kind of god allows it?

Any film that even tries tackling that subject in the '90s earns credit for sheer audacity. But in writer-director Daniel Taplitz's "Commandments," the query proves more interesting than the answers.

Aidan Quinn stars as Seth, a modern-day Job who endures his wife's death, being fired, having his Brooklyn house destroyed by tornado and his faithful dog's loss of a leg. Taking a stand on the edge of a rooftop and demanding an explanation from the Almighty, he's then hit by lightning.

Seth provides the followup thunder by vowing to break each of the 10 Commandments, convinced his actions will force an explanation from on high. Temporarily lodged with his fetching sister-in-law (Courteney Cox) and her philandering husband (Anthony LaPaglia), Seth has no problem "coveting thy neighbor's wife."

Taplitz initially uses that premise to fine effect. The surreal quality that infuses the goings-on—heightened by interesting lighting and cinematic gimmickry—provides a sharp mix of humor and quirkiness.

But Taplitz can't maintain the high-wire balancing act, ultimately slipping into a too-cute tone that bottoms out with an absurd, laughably symbolic finale. Adding a "who's sane amidst all this insanity" theme only worsens matters, invoking the likes of treacly chestnuts such as "King of Hearts."

To his credit, Aidan Quinn maintains an edgy charm as the walking pariah. He delivers a level of conviction and compassion that makes his rantings impossible to dismiss.

As the woman who tempts Seth (and supplies the other half of a tastefully erotic encounter), Courteney Cox is consistently effective. She's properly appealing while subtley registering hurt, confusion and the vagaries of love.

And as the third side of the fractured triangle, Anthony LaPaglia provides his standard slow boil, which proves as effective as it is familiar. One keeps hoping he'll move on to a new schtick.

The bottom line is that "Commandments" leaves viewers in cinematic purgatory: inspired by a divine premise and disappointed by a divine premise and disappointed by the hellacious follow-through.

VILLAGE VOICE, 5/6/97, p. 86, Jennifer Vandever

Commandments is one of those movies where you can hear the pitch in the background: "Imagine Job hooks up with one of the cast members of *Friends* and decides that life isn't so bad after all!" Aidan Quinn plays Seth Warner, a decent young doctor who in one fell swoop loses job, home, and family and decides he's the object of a cruel divine conspiracy. Deciding to give God what for, Seth resolves to break all of the Ten Commandments. In fairly short order he moves in with his dead wife's sister Rachel (Courtney Cox) and her philandering husband, Harry (Anthony LaPaglia), and starts sinning with a vengeance. He dispenses with the boring, false-idols-type commandments rather quickly, concentrating instead on the buildup to the big hubba-hubba of # 7 (guess who?) and the requisite redemptive fifth act.

But with the exception of *Adam's Rib*, the Old Testament makes rather poor fodder for romantic comedy. In spite of the filmmaker's earnest attempt to fashion a darkly comic fable about Big Themes, the story never resolves its conflicting tones of tragedy and comedy. The film relies on a kind of glib mysticism that seems to indicate a screenwriter who's watched those Joseph Campbell tapes too many times.

Also reviewed in:
NEW YORK TIMES, 5/2/97, p. C36, Lawrence Van Gelder
VARIETY, 1/27-2/2/97, p. 82, Leonard Klady
WASHINGTON POST, 5/2/97, Weekend/p. 42, Rita Kempley

CON AIR

A Touchstone Pictures release of a Jerry Bruckheimer production. *Executive Producer:* Chad Oman, Jonathan Hensleigh, Peter Bogart, Jim Kouf, and Lynn Bigelow. *Producer:* Jerry Bruckheimer. *Director:* Simon West. *Screenplay:* Scott Rosenberg. *Director of Photography:* David Tattersall. *Editor:* Chris Lebenzon, Steve Mirkovich, and Glen Scantlebury. *Music:* Mark Mancina and Trevor Rabin. *Music Editor:* Will Kaplan, Zigmund M. Gron, and Bob Badami. *Sound:* Arthur Rochester and (music) Steve Kempster. *Sound Editor:* George Watters, II. *Casting:* Victoria Thomas, Jeanne McCarthy, and Matthew Barry. *Production Designer:* Carl Griffin. *Art Director:* Chas Butcher. *Set Designer:* Barbara Mesney. *Set Decorator:* Debra Echard. *Special Effects:* Chuck Stewart. *Visual Effects:* David Goldberg. *Costumes:* Bobbie Read. *Make-up:* Kris Evans. *Special Make-up Effects:* Thomas R. Burman, Bari Dreiband-Burman, Allen Barlow, Patrick Gerrety, Peter Moraiti, Frank Diettinger, and Becky Ochoa. *Stunt Coordinator:* Kenny Bates and Steve Picerni. *Running time:* 115 minutes. *MPAA Rating:* R.

CAST: Nicolas Cage (Cameron Poe); John Cusack (Vince Larkin); John Malkovich (Cyrus "The Virus" Grissom); Steve Buscemi (Garland Greene); Nick Chinlund (Billy Bedlam); Rachel Ticotin (Sally Bishop); Colm Meaney (Duncan Malloy); M.C. Gainey (Swamp Thing); Ving Rhames (Diamond Dog); Brendan Kelly (Conrad); Mykelti Williamson (Baby-O); Danny Trejo (Johnny 23); Renoly (Sally Can't Dance); Jesse Borrego (Francisco Cindino); Dave Chappelle (Pinball); Carl N. Ciarfalio (Con #1); Jerry Mongo Brownlee (Ajaz); Steve Eastin (Falzon); Jose Zuniga (Sims); Ned Bellamy (Chopper Pilot); John Marshall Jones (Gator); John Roselius (Devers); Fredric Lane (Pilot); Martin McSorley (Co-Pilot); Dylan Haggerty (Starkey); Matt Barry (Chambers); Monica Potter (Tricia Poe); Landry Allbright (Casey Poe); Dan Bell (Fuel Jockey); Robert Stephenson (Ted the Pilot); Scott Ditty (Bus Guard); Tommy Bush (Sheriff); Lauren Pratt (Debbie, 6 years old); Steve Hulin (Ronnie); Don Charles McGovern (Smoke);

Angela Featherstone (Ginny); Doug Hutchison (Donald); Jeris Poindexter (Watts); David Ramsey (Londell); Conrad Goode (Viking); Emilio Rivera (Carlos); Jeff Olson (Uncle Bob); Dawn Bluford (Female Baggage Handler); Charlie Paddock (Transportation Officer #1); Randee Barnes (Stickman); Don Davis (Man in Car); Barbara Sharma (Woman in Car); Brian Hayes Currie (Cop in Vegas); Ashley Smock (Huey Pilot); Charles Lynn Frost (DEA Agent); Joey Miyashima (Tech Guy); Scott Burkholder (Air Traffic Controller); Kevin Cooney (Judge); Gerard L'Heureux (Guard Renfro); Pete Antico (Guard Garner); John Robotham (Guard Ryan); George Randall (Old Con on Plane); James Bozian, Harley Zumbrum, and Doug Dearth (Cons); David Roberson (Supervisor); Alexandra Balahoutis (Waitress); Dick "Skip" Evans (Airplane Pilot); Sheldon Worthington (Co-pilot); Robert Taft and Robert White (Soldiers); Chris Ellis (BOP Official Grant); John Campbell (BOP Bus Driver); Brian Willems and Bill Cusack (Paramedics).

LOS ANGELES TIMES, 6/6/97, Calendar/p. 1, Kenneth Turan

"Con Air" is a big, loud, noisy movie made with almost scientific precision for people who like big, loud, noisy movies. Numbing but not boring, it's finally more dispiriting than exhilarating, like a wild night of debauchery that leaves only a fearsome hangover for a souvenir.

Producer Jerry Bruckheimer, having made "Top Gun," "Bad Boys," "The Rock" and similar fare with his late partner Don Simpson, knows the drill for this kind of picture. Pump up the volume, add on the crashes, blasts and explosions, increase the body count and sit back and count the money.

New to Jerry's world are Simon West, a British commercial director making his feature debut, and screenwriter Scott Rosenberg, best known for "Things to Do in Denver When You're Dead." Their contributions, combined with a capable group of actors, improve on business as usual, but the change isn't enough to make this trip necessary for the uninitiated.

The story of how "every creep and freak in the known universe" combine to take over a U.S. Marshals Service prison airplane, "Con Air" starts with a glimpse of its hero, human killing machine Cameron Poe (Nicolas Cage), at a high point in his life.

A newly minted Army Ranger, Poe has barely had time to receive a welcome home kiss from his pregnant wife in Mobile, Ala., before he gets involved in a barroom altercation and ends up drawing a seven- to 10-year sentence for justifiable homicide.

Passing the hours studying origami and staying fit, Poe also finds time to write mushy letters to his wife and the daughter he's never met, notes that Cage reads in an Alabama accent so thick it makes George Wallace sound like David Niven. It's the signature of a borderline parody performance that warns "Anaconda's" Jon Voight he'd best look to his laurels.

Paroled after eight years, Poe is just an airplane ride away from his family. But the plane he calls "my sweet bird of freedom" is in reality' an airborne snake pit, taking a group of criminal monsters to a new superprison designed to "warehouse the worst of the worst."

The demented leader of this particular pack is Cyrus "The Virus" Grissom, "poster child for the criminally insane," neatly played by a gleeful John Malkovich. Among his henchpersons are Nathan "Diamond Dog" Jones (Ving Rhames), a murderous black separatist; the aptly named Billy Bedlam (Nick Chinlund); and serial rapist John "Johnny 23" Baca (Danny Trejo).

Much to the chagrin of the good guys on the ground, ranging from the shrewd Vince Larkin (John Cusack) to Duncan Malloy (Colm Meaney), hot-headed enough to have "AZZ KIKR" on his license plate, these menaces to society commandeer the plane and make a try for freedom.

Plot contrivances being what they are, Cameron Poe has a chance to walk away from this messy cargo. But, as chivalrous as his accent, he stays on board to protect best friend Baby-O (Mykelti Williamson) and a female guard (Rachel Ticotin) Johnny 23 has in his sights. "I can't trade a friend's life for my own," he says, a grand sentiment for sure.

Director West is adept at keeping things moving and writer Rosenberg does provide some good lines, like Cyrus' sincere "love your work" aside to Hannibal Lectorish mass murderer Garland Greene (Steve Buscemi).

But with a noise level so high the dialogue has to be screamed and more silly moments than sane ones, "Con Air" is an animated comic book put together to pound an audience into submission, not entertain it. It gets the job done, but a pretty picture it is not.

NEW YORK, 6/16/97, p. 51, David Denby

Anyone going to American movies this season can easily visit a whorehouse one evening and a Quaker meeting hall the next. The vagaries of the summer schedule have thrown together the following combination of new movies: *Con Air*, one of the big-budget summer blockbusters, a low, cynical, violently entertaining spectacle; and *Ulee's Gold*, which is about a saintly Florida beekeeper, a movie made in an austerely disciplined style that manages to hide a considerable degree of self-satisfaction beneath its dignified surface.   The split between these two movies—between the big-budget studio marketing vehicle and the independently made little moral drama—couldn't be more extreme. At the same time, that contrast defines the twin poles of our dissatisfaction. Both of these movies, in their wildly different ways, are fairly good, but neither is good enough, and taken together they do little to discourage the notion that making first-rate movies in this country has become impossible. The structure of the American cinema will not allow it: The middle ground in budgets, and the great middle ground in popular art between mere commerce and mere high-mindedness—the area in which Hollywood excelled for decades—has now been ruled out of existence.

Con Air sets up its absurd premise very quickly (before the credits sequence is over). Nicolas Cage is Poe, an ex-U.S. Ranger who returns to his wife after duty, gets into a barroom brawl, and kills some nameless thug in self-defense. A morally innocent man, he's nevertheless shipped off to federal prison for eight years, where he does nothing but exercise religiously in his cell and think about the little daughter he's never seen. When he gets paroled, just in time for her birthday (he holds a stuffed bunny as a present), he hitches a ride home on a U.S. Marshals prison plane, a plane that is flying the worst criminals in the country to a new maximum-security facility.   Rapists, mass murderers, drug dealers—gee, everything but serial jaywalkers—all together on one plane, and each with his specialized form of craziness. Up in the air, Grissom (John Malkovich), the most intelligent of the convicts, leads a rebellion and takes over the plane, brutalizing the guards and setting off a pursuit led by a U.S. marshal (John Cusack). Should the plane be shot down? Poe has an opportunity to get off, but he refuses; he won't leave behind a diabetic convict and a female prison guard. We're informed that he wants a chance to serve his country once again, but one glance at Nicolas Cage—who looks crazed-tells us he's as close to murder as any of the professional killers. He's dying to take on the animals.

A collection of out-of-control killers running amok may sound a good deal like last summer's movie produced by Jerry Bruckheimer, *The Rock,* but the real spiritual father of his *Con Air* is *The Dirty Dozen*, the nihilistic bone-crusher from 1967, in which a bunch of psychos are given a chance to redeem themselves in a World War II suicide mission. The gimmick in both cases is to let the killers run wild, each doing his thing, and to cast the hippest possible actors, so the audience can have the guilty pleasure of enjoying the criminals for their weird specialties (and then of seeing them killed off, which releases the audience from guilt).

Malkovich, bald, with an ugly goatee, does his hyper-literate satanic routine, exuding conscious enjoyment of evil as he strings out long, archly intelligent sentences.   Malkovich is now so deep into irony he couldn't order dinner straight.   Ving Rhames, as some sort of black-revolutionary murderer, caresses each word in his rich, appraising manner as if he were running diamonds through his hands. An elaborately masked, cuffed, trussed, and bound super-killer turns out to be the familiar, cranky Steve Buscemi, offering brilliant sophistries in defense of murder. Dave Chappelle, the stand-up comic front *The Nutty Professor*, races happily through the high-tension dialogue created for him by screenwriter Scott Rosenberg, whose profane, wise-ass script turns every situation into a bristling confrontation. In scene after scene, one guy wins, another loses. Rosenberg's style of dramaturgy is not creative, exactly, but it's not boring, either, and it frees the actors to try out their pet aggressive moves, and to chew each other up.   Low and violent as it is, *Con Air* has some life to it. The movie is very nasty fun.

As always in these quasi-fascist entertainments, anarchic violence, after running loose for a while, has to be restrained by righteous violence (for instance, Lee Marvin's authoritarian officer in *The Dirty Dozen).* Nicolas Cage has gone from the Everyman reluctant hero in *The Rock* to a superman style that can only be called neo-Clint. His Poe is primed to explode, and when he does, lean yet bursting out of his undershirt, with ropy trapezium muscles leading up to his neck, he becomes a spectacularly violent man—a superhero who speaks, like Clint, in sardonic little sentences. Cage, a great, daring actor, underplays, holding the screen with sheer concentration; for all his gallantry as Poe, he's faintly inhuman (and will probably become a huge box-office star because of that inhuman quality). Fortunately, there's someone else in the movie for us to look at—John Cusack, who represents rational intelligence and who plays the marshal as a decent fellow out of his depth in all this violence but game for it nevertheless.

The director, Simon West, a Brit maker of commercials, has just enough technique, in his feature-film debut, for what he has to do here—that is, he's good at moving men and machinery around, and he's good at brutal action. *Con Air* may be nonsense, but it has some new settings—the prison plane and then an ancient Nevada airstrip with lots of abandoned aircraft from World War II—and that matters a lot in these enormous action movies. Jaded by spectacle, we don't want to see the same old explosions and car crashes over and over. When West hits the airstrip, he turns the movie into part demolition derby, part war film. The final scene, however—a crash landing in the middle of Las Vegas—is nuttily pointless even by summer-season standards.

Con Air is a cartoon that combines extreme violence and extreme sentiment, a classic American duo. Through all the carnage, Poe supposedly wants only to save his diabetic buddy; save the woman guard, who is chained up and menaced by a rapist; and get back to his wife and daughter. He drags that bunny right through the movie and finally presents it to his flaxen-haired little girl. That's the Jerry Bruckheimer touch—a bit of "heart" that allegedly makes the hero appealing to the audience. My guess is that a good part of the audience will ridicule the cynicism of "heart" for the outrageous cornball crap that it is. *Con Air* has about as much heart as an F-16. It does fly, though, a lot higher and faster than anyone would have expected.

NEW YORK POST, 6/6/97, p. 37, Michael Medved

"Con Air" tries so hard to qualify as the noisiest, silliest, most excessive and explosive midsummer buster on the block that it ends up undermining its own considerable cleverness and charm.

That's a shame, because the childish explosions ultimately overwhelm the polished (if unoriginal) writing and the solid acting that constitute the movie's most substantial assets.

If you've seen one of the "Die Hard" films, or any of their nearly two dozen big-budget imitators ("Speed," "Cliffhanger," "Under Siege," "Passenger 57"). then you already know the basic plot of this one: "Con Air" is "Die Hard" on a prison plane.

This time it's Nicolas Cage (with impressively new musculature) who gets to play the soft-spoken, reluctant-but-deadly hero: a decorated Army Ranger from Alabama who's wrongly imprisoned for defending his wife (Monica Potter) in a barroom brawl.

After serving his time, he's ready to return home and to connect with the adorable 8-year-old daughter he's never met, but he hitches a ride on a prison transport plane carrying some of the nation's most vicious and notorious criminals.

John Malkovich plays "Cyrus the Virus" Grissom, the mass murderer and evil mastermind (a staple of this format), who ingeniously schemes to hijack the plane, assisted by a colorful band of capable actors (Ving Rhames, Steve Buscemi, M.C. Gainey) enjoying their chance to play vicious psychopaths.

Intrepid U.S. Marshal John Cusack soon realizes that Cage represents his only ally on the captured plane and his only chance to rescue the hostages (including prison guard Rachel Ticotin).

To protect his new-found friend, Cusack must dissuade a hotheaded D.E.A. agent (Colm Meaney) from simply blowing the plane out of the sky.

All of the performances are superior, and these vivid characters keep the movie richly entertaining for most of its running time.

Cage (despite a pathetic attempt at a Southern accent) makes his character both comprehensible and sympathetic.

The fight-and-flight scenes are also expertly edited, with director Simon West (a British specialist in commercials and music videos here making his feature film debut) deploying an infectious sense of humor to break up the action and tension.

It's only in the movie's final 15 minutes that this tongue-in-cheek approach totally takes over, ruining any real thrills and turning the story into a grotesque cartoon.

In the end, the plot line (literally) crashes and burns; the ludicrous fireballs, laughable chase scenes, sadistic mutilations and wanton demolition of countless miniatures of the Las Vegas strip, represent a sadly anti-climactic climax and needlessly insult the audience.

Producer Jerry Bruckheimer ("The Rock," "Bad Boys," "Top Gun") clearly believes in giving moviegoers their money's worth, but when it comes to over-the-top destruction and severed or punctured limbs, he ought to know by now that less can definitely be more.

NEWSDAY, 6/6/97, Part II/p. B3, Jack Mathews

The CD-ROM press kit that the Walt Disney Co. produced for its summer action spectacle "Con Air" is a thing of beauty. With full-color graphics and a soundtrack that will pin you to the back of your seat, you can absorb every marketing detail, from the furiously fast-paced trailer, to sound-bite interviews with the cast and crew, to still photos promising an orgy of fireballs, death and destruction.

And it's honest work. The movie, about a transport plane skyjacked by its lethal cargo of felons, delivers all of the above. People are punched, shot, stabbed, burned and decapitated. Bodies are dropped from planes onto the tops of cars passing below. The plane crash-lands not once, but twice, the second time down the neon corridor of the Las Vegas strip.

But what the CD-ROM, played on a small PC monitor, cannot begin to suggest is the enormity of the sense-numbing insult that "Con Air" actually hurls at its audience. It's a big, loud, smug, empty, obnoxious cartoon that is shoved through your eyes and ears like gruel down the throat of a Strasbourg goose. The audience I saw it with couldn't get enough.

Which makes me wonder, what have we geese come to expect from popcorn adventure? We've been on an escalating scale of sensory excess for so long, we must have surpassed the high-end threshold by now. Can we actually hear those 20 or 30 extra decibels, or process mayhem that rains down from the screen like meteor showers?

And what has become of Nicolas Cage? He wins an Oscar for "Leaving Las Vegas," at last receiving recognition for 15 years of brilliant dramatic work, and he's now stealing roles from Steven Seagal?

In "Con Air," directed by British newcomer Simon West for venerable action producer Jerry Bruckheimer, Cage plays Cameron Poe, a Gulf War veteran and paroled killer whose flight to freedom—and into the arms of his wife and their 8-year-old daughter—is interrupted by his fellow convicts' plan to skyjack their way to Mexico.

Among the new crew are sadistic leader Cyrus Grissom (John Malkovich, who has turned smarminess into performance art), insane black militant Diamond Dog (Ving Rhames) and Garland Greene (Steve Buscemi), a deceptively mild-mannered psychopath whom guards, in a clear steal from "Silence of the Lambs," accord the respect reserved for Hannibal Lector.

Poe is given a chance to get off the plane in California, but to help his diabetic cellmate Baby-O (Mykelti Williamson) and tough-cookie guard Sally Bishop (Rachel Ticotin), he decides to stay on board and, in his own words, "save the day."

Meanwhile, there's a jurisdictional battle royal between U.S. Marshal Vince Larkin (John Cusack), who realizes Poe is an ally in the sky, and hothead Drug Enforcement Agency employee Duncan Malloy (an insufferably overacting Colm Meaney), who wants to knock the plane down with a missile.

Though screenwriter Scott Rosenberg was reportedly inspired by an article about actual air transports of dangerous felons, nothing in his script has a jot of credibility. That includes the opening scene showing how nice-guy Poe ends up in prison by delivering a death blow to one of three thugs who are out to knife him and rape his wife. This wouldn't even be a close call on Court TV; give the man a book contract and leave him alone.

Most action films are heightened reality, but "Con Air" is heightened shtick, with dialogue and scenes so cutely crafted, you can almost see Rosenberg clucking to himself as he taps it all out on his word processor. There is the occasional good line, the best cheerfully delivered by Buscemi, but not one that seems spontaneous.

Ultimately, Rosenberg's script is film-school fantasy writing, a procession of reworked genre clichés that under the guise of showing us a good time, shows us instead what fools we be.

NEWSWEEK, 6/9/97, p. 74, David Ansen

"Welcome to Con Air," purrs the bald brilliant psychopath Cyrus (The Virus) Grissom (John Malkovich), having just skyjacked a prison transport plane carrying a gaggle of the most twisted felons in the land. Also on board is the one man crazy and heroic enough to foil the escape: the just-paroled Cameron Poe (Nicolas Cage), heading home to deliver a stuffed bunny rabbit to the 8-year-old daughter he's never met.

Welcome to Con Air, another pumped-up, amphetamine-paced action movie from the producer of "The Rock," Jerry Bruckheimer. In the production notes, Bruckheimer comments on screenwriter Scott Rosenberg's project. "It was certainly great writing, but I instantly surmised that the script needed more heart. It had to be more character driven, which is a common theme throughout all my films, no matter what the action content might be."

Maybe I missed something (the thunderous noise level makes it hard to catch all the character-driven subtleties of the script), but it did seem to be the "action content" that was grabbing the crowd. Dozens of seat-shaking explosions, a crash landing on the Vegas strip, attempted rapes, one bloody impalement and a motorcycle-and-firetruck chase are among the highlights, while the characterizations are all outlined in cartoon strokes. Steve Buscemi, shackled like Hannibal Lecter, is the comically depraved serial killer ("I like your work," says Malkovich to Buscemi). Ving Rhames is a militant murderer with a reputation for "killing more men than cancer." While these bad dudes are bumping off U. S. marshals by the dozen, good guy Cage is improbably fixated on finding a syringe to save his pal (Mykelti Williamson) from a diabetic attack.

The saving grace of "Con Air" is its sense of its own absurdity. Rosenberg and director Simon West seem to know just how preposterous their story is: the "heartfelt" moments between Cage and his family are as over the top as the macho *grand guignol* of a planeload of raving psychopaths. "This film is a story about redemption," says Bruckheimer, and let's hope he's pulling our legs. If you can't take "Con Air" as a big, noisy joke, why would you want to take it at all?

SIGHT AND SOUND, 7/97, p. 37, John Wrathall

Paroled after serving eight years of a manslaughter sentence, ex-Army Ranger Cameron Poe is heading home on the "Jailbird", a convict transport plane operated by the US Marshals Service. Other passengers include Poe's diabetic cellmate Baby-O and master criminal Cyrus "The Virus" Grissom, who unpicks his handcuffs using a pin he has smuggled on board embedded in his flesh, and then hijacks the plane with his accomplices. In the struggle, the syringe Baby-O needs to administer his insulin is broken.

At the first scheduled stop, Carson City, Grissom drops off the crew, gagged and disguised as prisoners, and picks up six more convicts, including Francisco Cindino, an heir to a Colombian drug dynasty, and a pilot. Given the chance to get off, Poe stays on the plane to look after Baby-O, who will die if he doesn't get insulin in two hours. Meanwhile, US Marshal Vince Larkin has got wind of the plan after finding blueprints of the plane in Grissom's cell. But he arrives too late to stop the jailbird from taking off again.

During the flight, Grissom lets slip to Poe that they will be landing at the remote Lerner Field in Nevada, where Cindino's gang will be waiting to fly them out of the country. Poe writes their destination on the tee-shirt of a corpse which he throws out of the plane. Larkin gets the message, but his colleagues are all off chasing a scenic tours plane on which one of Grissom's accomplices has planted the Jailbird's transponder.

Larkin arrives alone at Lerner Field, in time to see the Jailbird crash land. Double-crossing Grissom, Cindino tries to escape with his gang, but Larkin stops their plane from taking off, and Grissom kills them. Before the Jailbird can take off, more police arrive, and are ambushed by Grissom. In the ensuing battle, Poe finds a syringe and races back to the plane to save Baby-O—which means he is still on board when it takes off again.

The police give chase in helicopters, and are about to shoot the Jailbird down when Poe forces the pilot to crash land in Las Vegas. Grissom escapes on a fire engine, but Poe and Larkin give chase on motorbikes. Grissom is killed in a collision with an armoured car. Poe is reunited with his wife and daughter.

The death of Jerry Bruckheimer's producing partner Don Simpson has apparently done nothing to soften the loud, flashy style of film-making for which they became famous in the 80s. Like its immediate predecessors in the Simpson and Bruckheimer action-film canon, *Crimson Tide* and

The Rock, Con Air takes a stock action formula—in this case the convict-in-transit hijack movie, a lacklustre genre exemplified in recent years by the likes of *Passenger 57* and *Turbulence*—and pumps it full of stars and steroids until the whole thing verges on parody.

Though it throws together a Black Power terrorist, a white supremacist, a serial rapist, a Colombian cocaine baron, asserted mass murderers and even a transvestite for good measure, *Con Air* never exploits the internecine mayhem you might expect from such a gathering of villains. When John Cusack's college boy US Marshal drops a quote from Dostoyevsky, "The degree of civilisation in a society can be judged by observing its prisoners," it's a tease: no one's really expecting its to take *Con Air* as any sort of meditation on the state of US prisons or society. Though Ving Rhames' militant Diamond Dog hints at one point that he has his own agenda, he and the other convicts settle down meekly into the role of Grissom's henchmen. This is particularly disappointing in the case of Steve Buscemi's Garland Greene who, after a magnificently overblown entrance in full Hannibal Lecter regalia, has very little to do except smile his creepy smile. Like everything else in *Con Air*, he's simply a pretext for some great gags: "Love your work," quips John Malkovich's Grissom as he peers through the serial killer's armour of restraints and masks.

Another Bruckheimer hallmark is the choice of a new director from the world of advertising (see also Tony Scott on *Top Gun*, Adrian Lyne on *Flashdance*, Michael Bay on *Bad Boys)* who can be counted on to supply the necessary sheen without perhaps bringing too much in the way of personal vision. On *Con Air,* Simon West does an admirable job getting all the explosions in the right places. Rather more distinctive is the work of screenwriter Scott Rosenberg, who supplies acid dialogue (to the question "Have you lost your mind?" Malkovich's Grissom snaps: "According to my last psych test, yes") and some delightfully absurdist throwaway touches, such as Buscemi serenading a Barbie doll with "He's Got The Whole World In His Hands" and the jailbird slicing the neck off the Hard Rock Cafe's giant neon guitar as it plummets towards Las Vegas.

In a way, writing a good script for a Jerry Bruckheimer film is a wasted effort: the plot doesn't have to make sense (and there's an unnecessary muddle here about exactly how many guns there are on the plane) and much of the dialogue is drowned out under the relentless music and sound effects. What a Rosenberg script can do, as his previous efforts *Things to Do in Denver When You're Dead* and *Beautiful Girls* proved, is attract an outstanding ensemble cast, and therein lies *Con Air*'s greatest strength. Malkovich, after languishing in too many lugubrious art movies, seizes the chance to camp it up as the irredeemable Grissom. The film's slightly lunatic tone also suits Nicolas Cage's acting style, which depends as ever on projecting an exaggerated seriousness in the midst of chaos—a mood perfectly encapsulated by the line Cage deadpans when, amid mounting carnage, he looks out at the sports car which has somehow become tied to the Jailbird and is being dragged through the air in its wake: "On any other day, that might seem strange."

VILLAGE VOICE, 6/17/97, p. 70, Gary Dauphin

The action-figure plastic spine of a plot that holds up *Con Air*'s manly protoplasm coincidentally enough involves a prison break, but there the similarities to *Dust of Life* end. First-time director Simon West cut his teeth doing Budweiser commercials, making this essentially a two-hour expansion of the yahoo, frat-boy sensibility that made beer, frogs, and Bob Marley such a winning combination.

Con Air starts out with recently paroled ex-army ranger Nic Cage boarding a prison transport flight for the trip home to wife and daughter. When the plane is promptly hijacked by a purported Who's Who of celebrity cons, Cage gets to do his thing in the air while a bright, bleeding heart of a U.S. marshal (John Cusack) runs around on the ground speculating about whether or not they have "a guy up there." Between that and a few nice stunts, *Con Air* is serviceable summer crud, but its basic problem is that there are a few *too* many guys up there. From the gleaming metal cage of the title's propeller plane to the nicknames used by baddies John Malkovich, Ving Rhames, Steve Buscemi, et al. (Cyrus the Virus is my favorite), *Con Air* suggests nothing so much as the pro-wrestling superfight, where an awful lot of wrestlers pile into an enclosed ring and slam each other against a fence over and over again. Fun stuff, but unfortunately for *Con Air,* there's no controversy about whether or not its blood is real, making it not only crap media, but crap-crap media.

Also reviewed in:
CHICAGO TRIBUNE, 6/6/97, Friday/p. A, Michael Wilmington
NEW YORK TIMES, 6/6/97, p. C5, Janet Maslin
NEW YORKER, 6/9/97, p. 107, Anthony Lane
VARIETY, 6/2-8/97, p. 53, Todd McCarthy
WASHINGTON POST, 6/6/97, p. B1, Rita Kempley
WASHINGTON POST, 6/6/97, Weekend/p. 62, Desson Howe

CONSPIRACY THEORY

A Warner Bros. release of a Silver Pictures production in association with Shuler Donner/Donner productions. *Executive Producer:* Jim Van Wyck. *Producer:* Joel Silver and Richard Donner. *Director:* Richard Donner. *Screenplay:* Brian Helgeland. *Director of Photography:* John Schwartzman. *Editor:* Frank J. Urioste and Kevin Stitt. *Music:* Carter Burwell. *Music Editor:* Adam Smalley. *Sound:* Tim Cooney and (music) Michael Farrow. *Sound Editor:* Mark Mangini and George Simpson. *Casting:* Marion Dougherty. *Production Designer:* Paul Sylbert. *Art Director:* Gregory William Bolton. *Set Designer:* Lauren Cory, Joseph G. Pacelli, Jr., and Thomas Betts. *Set Decorator:* Casey Hallenbeck. *Special Effects:* Mike Meinardus. *Costumes:* Ha Nguyen. *Make-up:* Lee Harman. *Make-up Special Effects:* Kevin Yagher. *Stunt Coordinator:* Conrad Palmisano. *Running time:* 135 minutes. *MPAA Rating:* R.

CAST: Mel Gibson (Jerry Fletcher); Julia Roberts (Alice Sutton); Patrick Stewart (Dr. Jonas); Cylk Cozart (Agent Lowry); Stephen Kahan (Wilson); Terry Alexander (Flip); Alex McArthur (Cynic); Rod McLachlan, Michael Potts, and Jim Sterling (Justice Guards); Rich Hebert (Public Works Man); Brian J. Williams (Clarke); G.A. Aguilar (Piper); Cece Neber Labao (Finch's Secretary); Saxon Trainor (Alice's Secretary); Claudia Stedelin (Wilson's Secretary); Leonard Jackson (Old Man in Bookstore); Donal Gibson (Doctor, Roosevelt Hospital); Joanna Sanchez (Nurse, Roosevelt Hospital); Michael Shamus Wiles and Mik Scriba (Cops, Roosevelt Hospital); Patrick Wild (Intern in Jerry's Room); Mushond Lee, Kevin Kindlin, and Troy Garity (Interns); J. Mills Goodloe (Jonas' Aide); Michael Kurtz (Well Dressed Man); Pete Koch (Fire Captain); Kevin Jackson, Nick Kusenko, and Karl Makinen (CIA Agents); Darren Peel (Geronimo Cleet); Marian Collier (Geronimo Cook); John Harms (Agent Murphy); Christine Toy Johnson (Bookstore Clerk); David Koch, Danny Smith, and Juan Riojas (Techs); Paul Tuerpé and Dean Winters (Cleets); Jose Ramon Rosario and Louis Cantarini (Angry Vendors); Sean Patrick Thomas and Peter Jacobson (Surveillance Operators); Edita Brychta (Finch's Receptionist); Sage Allen (Grouchy Nurse); Thomas McCarthy (Helicopter Spotter); K.T. Vogt (Woman in Mental Hospital); Joshua Fardon (Hospital Guard); Joan Lunden (TV Announcer); Charles McDaniel (Bureaucrat); Matte Osian and David Hamilton Simonds (Operatives); Rick Hoffman (Night Security, Federal Building); Edward J. Rosen (Old Man in Diner); Bert Remsen (Alice's Father); Lincoln Simonds (Cop by Laundry Chute); Bill Henderson (Hospital Security); Jay Fiondella (Patient); James Louis Oliver (Man in Justice Department); Kerry Palmisano, Victory Grace Palmisano, and Kate Bayley (Nurses' Aides); Irene Hillary (Justice Department Receptionist); Stephen Liska (Hospital Orderly); Don Stanley (Justice Department Guard); Lorna R. Millen (Charge Nurse); John Schwartzman (Sniper); Raymond King and Jared Crawford (Bucket Drummers); Jeremy A. Graham and Chad Santiago (Rappers); Christo Morse (Taxi Patron); H. Clay Dear and Daniel Nugent (Traffic Cops); Andrew Lauren, Tom Schanley, and Kenneth Tigar (Lawyers); Maureen Lauder (Lady with Dog); Judy Woodbury (Woman Lawyer).

LOS ANGELES TIMES, 8/8/97, Calendar/p. 1, Kenneth Turan

Even a blind hog, or so they say, finds a truffle now and then. So could it be that Jerry Fletcher, conspiracy theorist extraordinaire, has actually stumbled on the truth?

Fletcher is a New York City cabdriver who unnerves his passengers and everyone else in earshot with the crackpot ideas that go into his newsletter, circulation all of five. He believes that fluoride weakens your will, that the Grateful Dead tour so much because they're in the British Secret Service, that the Vietnam War was fought over a bet Howard Hughes lost to Aristotle Onassis.

It all sounds farfetched, but some very powerful people take Jerry Fletcher seriously enough to want to kill him. The problem is, he can't figure out over what. Only Alice Sutton, the plucky Justice Department lawyer he's developed an awkward crush on, even half believes him, and it's not clear what these two can do against the bogeymen of the world.

That in brief, is the outline of "Conspiracy Theory," written by Brian Helgeland, and as premises go it is a promising one. It might even have made a good film, but it hasn't. In the hands of stars in denial about their stardom and a director who can't be bothered to take things seriously, it has come out implausible and unsatisfying, a comic thriller that is not especially funny or thrilling.

The stars are Mel Gibson and Julia Roberts, and while you might think being those two on screen sounds pleasant enough, Gibson and Roberts beg to disagree. They use this film as a kind of joint plot to avoid the kinds of parts that made their careers, a hooky-playing opportunity to escape from what they're good at. Go figure.

Gibson, best known for being handsome and heroic, is frankly unconvincing as the mentally defective, just about drooling conspiracy theorist who continually mutters to himself and secures his refrigerator with a combination lock.

Eager though he is for a chance to play offbeat, to hide his classic features behind a coating of oatmeal (don't ask), Gibson can't camouflage the fact that he is miscast, that the part needs more of a traditional character actor to be effective. But a character actor wouldn't make a box-office-secure romantic pair with Roberts, so plausibility soon went out the window.

As for Roberts, her determination to play as many dour and troubled characters as possible is becoming the stuff of show business legend. As attorney Sutton, she gets to be upset about the recent mysterious death of her father as well as the constant attention of the crazed Fletcher, and even manages a scene where she breaks down in agony with her hands covered in blood.

While Roberts, like Gibson, has the perfect right to choose whatever parts she pleases (and she chose exceptionally well in "My Best Friend's Wedding"), the truth is that in roles like this, where the actress rations her smile as parsimoniously as Ebenezer Scrooge, she is simply not as convincing or involving a performer as roles where it's in the nature of her character to laugh freely. No one ever said life was fair, even for actors.

The evil force in this morality play is Dr. Jonas, a psychiatrist with the highest governmental connections, sharply played by Patrick Stewart, last seen in "Star Trek: First Contact." When Jonas comes looking for Fletcher, the plot kicks into its anemic version of high gear, bringing the present and the past together in a way that ought to be more involving than it is.

Riding herd on all of this is veteran director Richard Donner, glimpsed in an unbilled cameo as Fletcher's first worried taxi passenger. With theatrical credits that go back more than, 30 years and major hits like the "Lethal Weapon" series behind him, Donner is confident enough of mass appeal to allow his films—and this one is no exception—to slip into a genial contentment with the obvious.

So it's Donner we have to thank for indulging Gibson's mugging when he should have been reining it in. And because the director tends to look on everything as some kind of a gag, the film's exposition is listless and the tentative feelings between Fletcher and Sutton are unconvincing. A double star vehicle where neither party is eager to step up and be the star, "Conspiracy Theory" is a mystery that isn't worth the effort to solve.

NEW YORK, 8/25/97, p. 148, David Denby

In the first half of *Conspiracy Theory*, Mel Gibson, playing a thoroughly fortified paranoid—he keeps his tapioca and his coffee beans sealed with a combination lock—races through nut-brain fantasies with a stumbling panache. Gibson, who can be truculent and boring in standard heroic roles (*Braveheart* and *Ransom*), is at his loose-limbed and loose-tongued best, starting and stopping sentences, adding sane little quips to impossibly mad rants—and all without losing the beat. His New York taxi driver is physically hyperactive yet flummoxed. (At one point he barrels down a staircase strapped in a wheelchair.) The guy's head has been messed with, yet he still has the memory of sanity, so he mixes real events with dreams, horrifying memories with sheer fantasy.

As long as writer Brian Helgeland and director Richard Donner are teasing us, the movie is hip and entertaining—it plays with the dreams of nutters and cranks while granting them a little piece of truth. But when the film becomes soulful, romantic, and violent, we could be watching a great many other thrillers. Conventionality takes over, which is too bad. For the first time, Richard Donner, director of the numskull *Lethal Weapon* series with Gibson, comes close to breaking into the clear and becoming a true film creator. Maybe next time.

NEW YORK POST, 8/8/97, p. 45, Michael Medved

Even paranoids have enemies.

Jerry Fletcher (Mel Gibson) is just such a paranoid: an unequivocally deranged New York cabbie who rants to his unsuspecting fares about hovering black helicopters, poisoned drinking water and CIA schemes to use the space shuttle to provoke deadly earthquakes.

He lives in a rat's-nest SoHo apartment crammed with rusting file cabinets and piles of old newspapers—that is equipped with innumerable locks (even on the food in his refrigerator) and early-warning devices designed to protect him from the invasion that he expects "they" will launch against him any day.

In this environment, he publishes a crude newsletter dense with tiny type and dire warnings and prepares for frequent meetings with a bemused young Justice Department attorney (Julia Roberts) he once rescued from a mugger and around whom he's built a romantic obsession.

Roberts feels sorry for this seedy, stuttering lunatic whose wild dreads connect with her own doubts about the official explanation of the mysterious murder of her father, a federal judge.

Gibson delivers a complex, risky, multi-layered performance, making Jerry simultaneously appalling and endearing, pathetic and prophetic. Unfortunately, this intriguing characterization and director Richard Donner's sleek, ominous, spellbinding visual imagery (deliberately meant to evoke the far superior "Taxi Driver") are ultimately undermined by the lurid plot (scripted by "Assassins" co-writer Brian Helgeland) when Jerry's tormented terrors become nightmarishly real.

Patrick Stewart is potently menacing as a sadistic CIA psychiatrist who kidnaps and ruthlessly tortures the poor guy, asking questions that the victim's addled intellect can't even comprehend, until Jerry escapes and the movie's big chase begins.

Gibson's sudden transformation into a super-capable (and even calculating) action hero is completely unconvincing, as is the preposterous on-the-run romance that develops with Roberts.

The underlying revelations are both anti-climactic and internally inconsistent, meant to persuade only those audience members who still believe that Elvis is alive and that the American intelligence establishment is both all-powerful and all evil.

In the "Lethal Weapon" movies (also directed by Donner), Gibson successfully combined killer competence with an edge of insanity, but those movies sensibly maintained a breezy, self-mocking, comic attitude to put the impressive action scenes in proper perspective.

Here, some of the chases and confrontations are also spectacularly staged, but they are gratuitously grim and gory; director and star end up treating paranoid delusions with glum intensity and misplaced seriousness, not only exploiting but encouraging the most far-fetched fears and demented delusions of the audience.

The messages are both aesthetically unsatisfying and socially irresponsible, producing a movie that is not only disappointing, but also potentially dangerous.

NEWSDAY, 8/8/97, Part II/p. B3, Jack Mathews

"I don't know what I know, but I know that it's big."

So says Mel Gibson's paranoid New York taxi driver Jerry Fletcher at some frenzied point early in "Conspiracy Theory." We might add that whatever this thing is, it is also murky, stupendously implausible, alternately campy and overwrought, and somehow, crazily, satisfying.

Gibson has never given a performance like this one. Take him at his wildest in the "Lethal Weapon" movies and multiply him by Robin Williams. He is at times so unnervingly manic and animated, he threatens to spin off the screen. He's "Taxi Driver's" Travis Bickle on a caffeine high, a blur of tics and jitters, and the words pour out of him at speeds approaching Mach 1. Was it just me, or was the entire audience on the brink of screaming back at the screen "Mel ... SHUT UP!!!!"?

At other times, Gibson's poster boy for schizophrenia is droll, melancholy, enraptured, euphoric, pensive, playful, heroic, and as helpless as a child. It is a virtuoso star turn, making silk of a sow's script, and so dominant that you only occasionally notice that the girl of Jerry's fevered dreams is none other than Julia Roberts.

"Conspiracy Theory," directed by the "Lethal Weapon" series' Richard Donner and written by Brian Helgeland ("Assassins"), is a stew of comically twisted ingredients from "Taxi Driver," "The Manchurian Candidate" and "Marathon Man." Gibson's Jerry Fletcher is a man with a past he can't remember, a romantic obsession he can't explain, and a posse of G-men on his tail who literally want to pick his brain.

When we meet him during the opening credits, Jerry seems a harmlessly motormouthed cabbie, regaling each of his bored fares with bizarre conspiracy theories. ("Jerry Garcia is dead. That's what they want you to think.") As we follow him to his booby-trapped New York walk-up, where he has locks on everything from his front door to his coffee canister, he's a checklist of paranoia. And when he's professing his love to a woman he's watching through his binoculars, there's the brief sense of real danger.

That woman is Alice Sutton (Roberts), who turns out to be the U.S. attorney Jerry is counting on to alert the White House to various assassination plots he's uncovered. Any chance for story plausibility is lost the moment he bursts into the federal building, a raw nerve flailing against the marble walls, and is rescued by her from the security guards. No, no. He'd be whisked off to Bellevue in a New York minute.

But Alice sees something safely earnest and likable in Jerry, and when he returns later with blood pouring out of a belly wound, mumbling about having been kidnaped and tortured, she's down for the adventure. She patches him up, listens to him, even goes with him to his apartment!

So, go along ye Mel Gibson fans, and abandon all reason. What follows, as Jerry and Alice try to evade hordes of murky federal agents and solve the mysteries of his mind and her father's murder (could they be related?), gets progressively more outrageous and entertaining.

With almost anyone else playing Jerry, we might be talking about the worst movie of the year. The character, not to mention the baroque plot and Jerry's budding romance with Alice, is that absurd. But Gibson, turning the most mundane scenes into comic relief, creates enough of a genial illusion for us to care how Jerry makes out.

Roberts, keeping her double-jointed smile in check, makes an effective straight man for Gibson, while Patrick Stewart walks through his role as Dr. Jonas, a clear knockoff of Laurence Olivier's sadistic interrogator in "Marathon Man."

"Conspiracy Theory," with its stars and its array of elaborate stunts, is an expensive operation, but unlike the directors of other high-ticket summer fare, Donner never lets the focus veer far from his stars. He not only avoids many of the cliches of the season, he has his characters pause to make fun of them.

Romantic comedy, action parody, tongue-in-cheek thriller ... Whatever this thing is, it's a welcome breeze in one of Hollywood's most arid summers.

SIGHT AND SOUND, 9/97, p. 39, John Wrathall

Jerry Fletcher, a Manhattan cab driver who publishes a newsletter called *Conspiracy Theory* is obsessed with Justice Department lawyer Alice Sutton, whom he pesters with tip-offs about conspiracies. Spotting mysterious government agents on the street one day, Jerry follows them to the criminal courts building where the CIA has an office. As he leaves, he is kindnapped. Under torture, Jerry bites the nose of his interrogator, Dr Jonas, and escapes from what turns out to be an abandoned mental hospital. When Jerry tries to tell Alice about his ordeal, he is arrested, taken to hospital and sedated. Before he loses consciousness, he asks Alice to switch his chart with another patient's. The next morning the other patient is dead. Called in to identify the body, Alice notices that the CIA doctor—Jonas—has a bandaged nose. Jerry escapes from hospital, finds Alice and gives her a list of *Conspiracy Theory*'s five subscribers. When agents attack

Jerry's flat, Jerry and Alice escape, but not before Alice notices a picture of herself on Jerry's wall. Realising he has been stalking her, she tells him to get lost.

Tracking down the five subscribers to *Conspiracy Theory,* Alice finds they have all recently died, except for one. Visiting him at the criminal courts building, she discovers it is Jonas, who reveals that he once worked on now-terminated CIA mind-control experiments. The technology has been stolen, he tells her, and Jerry, one of his former guinea pigs, is the assassin who murdered her father, a judge. He convinces her to help catch Jerry.

Alice goes to a rendezvous with Jerry, who takes her to the scene of her father's death. His memory jogged, he remembers that he was helping the judge blow the whistle on Jonas' programme, but failed to prevent his murder. Jonas arrives and captures Jerry, but Alice escapes. She tracks Jerry down to the mental hospital. As they try to escape, Jonas shoots Jerry and is shot by Alice. She visits Jerry's grave, then goes riding. Watching her from a car is Jerry. As long as Jerry is presumed dead, an agent explains, she will be safe.

The opening credits of *Conspiracy Theory* are an obvious pastiche of *Taxi Driver,* with neon signs reflected in the windows of a yellow New York cab as it cruises slowly through puddles. Like Travis Bickle, Jerry Fletcher is obsessed with a beautiful career woman, whom he pesters relentlessly, although she is clearly out of his league. And Jerry, if anything, has even worse psychological problems than Travis: flashing lights trigger hallucinations and he talks like David Helfgott.

One has to admire Mel Gibson for his willingness, unlike his peers on the Hollywood "A" list, to play disturbed, pain-racked characters on a regular basis. At times he conveys a vivid sense of Jerry Fletcher's suffering, not just when he is being tortured but also, more poignantly, when he tries to declare his love for Alice, and has to resort to the lyrics of Sting's 'Every Little Thing She Does Is Magic'. But unfortunately these moments of twitchy commitment are undermined by Gibson's equal insistence on coming across as a loveable, wacky guy, and Richard Donner, directing Gibson for the fifth time, only eggs him on.

Brian Helgeland's script has a dark, cynical strain of humour, best expressed by Jerry's conspiracy theories (Oliver Stone was "employed to spread disinformation for George Bush") and Dr Jonas' passing hints about CIA history (his mind-control programme was wrapped up after John Hinckley shot Reagan). Donner has the makings here of a first-class, paranoid-conspiracy thriller and thanks to cinematographer John Schwartzman, he has the appropriate look too, not least in the hallucinatory interrogation sequence, which draws visually on *Jacob's Ladder* and *Natural Born Killers.* But, in the tradition of his *Lethal Weapon* films, he also want to play it for laughs: there's a daft running joke about an FBI agent who doe not lose consciousness when he's hit over the head, and a wildly inappropriate sing-a-long at the end, only moments after a traumatic scene of Jerry apparently bleeding to death. Every such comic interlude stops the mounting suspense and paranoia cold, with the result that the plot has to resort to yet another chase. There are no fewer than nine sequences in which Jerry and/or Alice have to escape from Jonas and his agents. While the first genuinely terrifying, with Jerry careening downstairs strapped to a wheel chair, later ones (depending on a baddie conveniently popping into the line of fire just when a sniper has Alice in his sights, or Alice hearing the captured Jerry singing down a ventilator shaft in the hospital) are evidence that ideas are running very thin indeed. What these repetitive chases do achieve, however, is to drag the running time out to 135 minutes.

TIME, 8/18/97, p. 62, Richard Schickel

We meet Jerry Fletcher (Mel Gibson) in mid-rant, and our first impression is of a typical New York City cabbie of the old, or native-born, variety, full of mis- and dis-information delivered in a rush that permits no quibbling interruption. Assassination plots both current and historical, a unique slant on the militia movement, even (heaven help us!) inside dope on the Vatican's plans for world domination—the man's a full-service paranoid.

Then, having frightened his last fare witless—he drives as wildly as he talks—Jerry pulls up in front of an apartment house, trains his binoculars on a window behind which a woman, obviously above his station and equally obviously a love object, is exercising, and we get really nervous. For we seem to be entering Travis Bickle country, an essentially inimitable place that one wants to visit only once in a lifetime.

But no, this is just the writer, Brian Helgeland, and the director, Richard Donner, having their little misleading joke. For we soon see that underneath the crazy bluster, there is a certain woozy sweetness about Jerry, something suggesting that he is in occasional touch with rationality. Alice (Julia Roberts), the Justice Department attorney he's spying on, notices it too. She's uncommonly patient on the several occasions when he bursts out of the shadows and intrudes on her otherwise orderly life, babbling—well, yes—*Conspiracy Theory*.

It turns out, of course, that there is nothing theoretical about the conspiracy that primarily obsesses Jerry. We learn that decades earlier it seized and victimized him (among many others) in a government-supported attempt to create our very own Manchurian candidates; that this program has been directed undetected all these years by the visibly wicked Dr. Jonas (Patrick Stewart), one of those shrinks who in life would lose their license but whose malpractices are never questioned in the movies; and that it is the purity of Jerry's love for Alice that is bringing him back to his senses, in intermittent but ever increasing flashes.

Finally, we don't believe a word of this. (A black helicopter hovering unremarked over a crowded Union Square? I don't think so.) But Gibson blurs the line between lunacy and lucidity very funnily, Roberts is a woman who could drive any man sane, and some of the film's offhand observations about the life-styles of the poor and nutty are goofily persuasive (Jerry padlocks his refrigerator and keeps its contents in combination-locked canisters). Caught up in the movie's intricacies, we go along with it, momentarily distant kin to those people who cling desperately to some convoluted explanation for a national tragedy. Conspiracy theory may be reason's most rickety scaffold, but it is more comforting than its alternative, which is chaos theory. Wouldn't want to see a movie about that, would you?

VILLAGE VOICE, 8/19/97, p. 81, Amy Taubin

Like slightly drunken reveries, the late, great Hitchcock films make light of logic while illuminating primal fears and desires. (Let's face it, in a flesh-and-blood world, Jimmy Stewart never would've survived the opening sequence of *Vertigo*.) Richard Donner's *Conspiracy Theory* is a bit like Hitchcock's *The Man Who Knew Too Much* scrambled with Terry Gilliam's *Brazil,* John Frankenheimer's *The Manchurian Candidate,* and a couple of screwball comedies of which I seem to have forgotten the names (must be all that lead in the water). A movie that offers Mel Gibson suffering the embarrassments of middle-aged memory loss and conspiratorial mind-warp and that also made me wake up singing "I Love You, BA-A-BY" for a week should not be faulted, as I overheard several churlish guys doing after a preview screening, for playing fast and loose with plausibility.

The most pleasurable studio movie in a dismal season, *Conspiracy Theory* is a loopy romantic thriller that melds the rescue fantasy crucial to romance since the age of chivalry with an up-to-the-minute conspiracy paranoia (a prominent feature of which is an us-against-them mentality that also comes to the fore—what a coincidence—when people fall in love.)

Gibson plays Jerry Fletcher, a deranged New York cabbie who's obsessed with conspiracies because he has fractured memories of having been a victim of some maverick C.I.A. experiment himself. Julia Roberts plays Alice, a Justice Department lawyer who hasn't the heart to close her door to the raving Jerry because, despite his obsessions and his inability to speak in complete sentences, he hasn't lost what can only be described as an essential Mel-ness. (It makes more sense that Alice is drawn to the sweetly crazed Jerry than that Cybill Shepherd agrees to go to the movies with Robert De Niro in *Taxi Driver,* to make an obvious comparison.) Jerry and Alice also share a bit of back story, part of which they're consciously aware of, part of which is buried in that area of the unconscious reserved for oedipal traumas, and none of which I'm going to reveal here.

Roberts is more endearing than in any film since *Pretty Woman*. Gibson is as convincingly schizoid, recklessly hyper, and just plain moving as he's ever seen. Richard Donner's kinetic and witty direction gives you a map to Jerry's fried brain without going so far as to put you inside his head—which would have been unbearable. And how can any New Yorker resist a movie that lands a fleet of black helicopters in Union Square to abduct the hero, who's been traced to Barnes & Noble, where he's indulging his compulsion to buy up all available copies of *The Catcher in the Rye?* Had *Conspiracy Theory* come out three months later, it also might have solved the mystery of Andrew Cunanan.

Also reviewed in:
NATION, 9/8-15/97, p. 35, Stuart Klawans
NEW YORK TIMES, 8/8/97, p. C1, Janet Maslin
NEW YORKER, 8/18/97, p. 78, Anthony Lane
VARIETY, 8/4-10/97, p. 34, Todd McCarthy
WASHINGTON POST, 8/8/97, p. D1, Stephen Hunter
WASHINGTON POST, 8/8/97, Weekend/p. 32, Rita Kempley

CONSPIRATORS OF PLEASURE

A Zeitgeist Films release of an Athanor/Delfilm/Koninck International production. *Producer:* Jaromir Kallista and Jan Svankmajer. *Director:* Jan Svankmajer. *Screenplay:* Jan Svankmajer. *Director of Photography:* Miloslav Spala. *Editor:* Marie Zemanova. *Sound:* Ivo Spajl and Francois Musy. *Animation:* Bedrich Glaser and Martin Kublak. *Puppet Designer:* Eva Svankmajer. *Set Designer:* Karel Vanasek. *Costumes:* Ruzena Blahova. *Make-up:* Petr Kokes. *Make-up:* Eva Vosahlikova. *Running time:* 83 minutes. *MPAA Rating:* Not Rated.

WITH: Petr Meissel (Mr. Peony); Anna Wetlinska (Mrs. Beltinska); Gabriela Wilhelmova (Mrs. Loubalova); Jiri Labus (Mr. Kula); Barbora Hrzanova (Mrs. Malkova); Pavel Novy (Mr. Beltinsky); Frantisek Polata; Eva Vidinska; Ervin Tomenendal; Josef Chodora; Marie Zemanova; Jan Daniel; Martin Kublak; Eva Vosahlikova; Martin Radimecky; Jiri Pesek; Miroslav Vranka; Karel Firt; Milan Brasna; Jesef Vilim; Karel Fifer; Jiri Liska; Renata Chlustinova; Zdenek Baborovsky; Pope John Paul II; Milan Uhde.

LOS ANGELES TIMES, 9/19/97, Calendar/p. 17, Kevin Thomas

"Conspirators of Pleasure" is an apt, elegant title for the great Czech surrealist Jan Svankmajer's latest work, a brilliant fable of sexual longing and gratification at its most furtive and kinkiest.

Yet another of Svankmajer's inspired blends of live-action and animation, it uses compulsive-obsessive sexual behavior as a metaphor for a society long repressed by religion and oppressed by politics.

Svankmajer belongs to a rich Eastern European tradition in animation and experimental cinema that views the universe as a absurd mechanism that remorselessly grinds down the individual often to the sound of a tinkling music box, itself an intricate, self-contained device. Until its bravura final sequences, "Conspirators of Pleasure" is entirely live-action but its people are so driven by lust that they might well be puppets; it's not for nothing that Svankmajer belonged to the famous Lanterna Magika puppet theater when he entered films.

There is pitch-dark humor here, but it's matched by an acute sense of pathos.

As if it were clockwork, the film is set in motion by a diffident young man, Mr. Pivonka (Petr Meissel), purchasing a Playboy from a vendor (Jiri Labus) who is tinkering with some sort of electronic device. The magazine centerfold sets off in Pivonka the most elaborate and macabre sexual fantasies.

Meanwhile, a post woman, Mrs. Malková (Barbora Hrzanová), presents him with a letter containing the message, "On Sunday." Pivonka then asks his blowzy landlady, Mrs. Loubalová (Gabriela Wilhelmová), to kill a chicken for him.

Mrs. Malkova makes a delivery to the home of an attractive newscaster (Anna Wetlinska), who happens to be the object of the news vendor's passion and whose husband, a police commissioner (Pavel Novy), proves to be just as impassioned fetishist as everyone else in the film.

Not one word is spoken throughout the film, but Svankmajer typically makes portentous use of everyday sounds.

Even though Svankmajer acknowledges his obvious debt to Sigmund Freud, Luis Buñuel, Max Ernst, the Marquis de Sade and Leopold von Sacher-Masoch, you really have to wonder how he came up with so much kinky stuff:

How much was research, how much was imagination?

It seems safe to say that most of those who see this picture will have their minds boggled. Yet the kinkiness is never just for its own sake but to give way to a chilling large view of individuals in profound isolation, deprived of the highly tactile sensuality Svankmajer evokes with a lush, bold outrageousness. Sex and religion intermingle in the bizarre rituals these individuals construct for themselves, frequently involving reworking the most mundane items. (Tear apart a couple of umbrellas and you've got a great pair of bat wings.)

Some of these people's fantasies seem harmless enough, but Pivonka and Malková reveal a darkly destructive aspect to their fantasies of each other. It's part of Svankmajer's assured artistry that you can't tell for sure that these six people connect with one another except on some psychic level, if at all. It may all just be coincidence that they are interlinked in the unique universe Svankmajer inevitably projects with such dazzling force and originality.

NEW YORK POST, 8/20/97, p. 42 , Larry Worth

Any director whose end credits list the Marquis de Sade, Luis Bunuel, Max Ernst and Sigmund Freud as inspirations is either (a) admirably open to all schools of thought or (b) a very sick pup.

Judging from "Conspirators of Pleasure," Jan Svankmajer is both.

His look at obsessive, fetish-like behavior of six individuals whose lives criss-cross in a small town is wildly imaginative, amusing and fresh—and undeniably gross, sick and twisted.

The unique narrative jumps from one oddball character to the next, starting with one man's painstaking creation of a papiermache rooster head. The camera then hovers over a woman who fashions tiny balls of dough from loaf after loaf of bread, as well as a guy who's creating a kinky moving sculpture and a lady who dreams of having carp suck her toes.

As the individuals concoct their outrageous schemes, there's no clue whatsoever to the method in their madness—or how the various elements all mesh. Therein lies the fun.

And the main drawback? The anticipation far outweighs the anticlimactic payoffs. In fact, two denouements which involve pixilation are just plain stupid.

Worse, the Czech director gets redundant with all his phallic symbols and sexual innuendoes, sometimes repeating the exact same image over and over. A soundtrack full of amplified slurps, sucking noises and heavy-duty squishes grows tiresome, too, though accomplishing the goal of making viewers squirm on cue.

But there's a positive for every negative. As in earlier efforts such as "Alice" and "Faust," Svankmajer injects witty social commentary into his surreal journey. Here, the director's takes on pornography, voyeurism, misogyny and male-bashing are welcome complements to the wild goings-on, proving as eerie and disturbing as they are hilarious.

The cast, meanwhile, is perfectly suited to their bizarre tasks, performed with no dialogue whatsoever. Among the leading players, Peter Meissel and Gabriela Wilhelmova stand out as battling neighbors whose love-hate antics lead to the deliciously warped ending.

Viewers may have a similar love-hate reaction to "Conspirators". But, at the very least, they'll never think of carp in the same way again.

NEWSDAY, 8/20/97, Part II/p. B9, John Anderson

The conspirators of "Conspirators of Pleasure" never conspire, but then again their pleasure is hardly rapturous either. The latest by the celebrated Czech filmmaker Jan Svankmajer—who credits Freud, de Sade, Luis Bunuel and the artist Max Ernst as inspirations for this film—follows a group of middle-class Pragueites in their ritualistic preparations for highly arcane erotic exercises. Unspeakable practices and unnatural acts, the stuff that surrealist dreams are made of.

Virtually wordless and drily funny, "Conspirators of Pleasure" moves Svankmajer further from the fabulist animation that made his reputation (including his best known short, 1982's "Dimensions of Dialogue"). But his devilish humor is given full due here, as the modern world's oxymoronic, many-headed hysteria fueled by puritanism, neuroticism and sensualism gets lanced like a boil.

Svankmajer is insistent on one image informing the other—a baby picture and a piece of pornography, for instance, with the sexual conflicts between procreation and lust floating about like metaphorical spores. There is also the ever-present suggestion of pleasure being not just what separates but isolates his various characters, with the near-misses of human contact setting a constantly ironic tone: The love doll of our main character, Mr. Peony (Peter Meissel) resembles his neighbor, Mrs. Loubalova (Gabriela Wilhelmova), and hers resembles him (the dolls are brought to life, and their abusers' fantasies into reality, in Svankmajer's single, outlandish Claymation sequence). Mrs. Beltinska (Anna Wetlinska) is a newscaster neglected by her fur-fetishist husband (Pavel Novy) but worshiped by the news vendor Kula (Jiri Labus), who constructs a many-armed masturbation machine in her honor.

Mr. Peony creates a huge rooster's head out of papier-mâché, which itself is made out of pages from girlie magazines; a set of wings constructed from two umbrellas completes the outfit, a chifforobe provides his sanctuary. Mr. Beltinsky, the police commissioner, is attracted to women by the size of their fur stoles, from which he takes surreptitious trimmings to be used in gothic, rubber-fingered sculptures. The postmistress, Mrs. Malkova (Barbara Hrzanova), scoops out the soft innards from loaves of rye bread, which she rolls into balls and sucks up her nostrils.

Svankmajer isn't ridiculing his characters, although they are ridiculous, but he is critiquing their desperation, and the fact that they must hide from the world when they do what they do. It's a world, after all, that made them what they are in the first place—and a world that goes about its often horrible business shamelessly and openly while these poor souls must hide their heads. If surrealism means locating the incongruous within the absurd, then Svankmajer is being true to his art. And his inspirations.

SIGHT AND SOUND, 2/97, p. 39, Leslie Felperin

In Prague, Mr Pivoine, an unmarried man, buys some pornography from his local newsagent, Mr Kula, and returns home. A postwoman, Mrs Malkova, gives him a letter which reads "On Sunday" in cut-out letters. In secret, she then rolls pieces of bread into little balls and carries them in her satchel. Pivoine asks his neighbour, Mrs Loubalova, to slaughter a chicken for him. Using the leftover feathers and papier-mâché made from the porn, he constructs a chicken head and fabricates wings made from umbrellas. Meanwhile, police captain Beltinsky buys rolling pins and pan lids from the same shop that sells Pivoine's umbrellas. Using these items plus stolen pieces of fur and sharp things, Beltinksy constructs unusual objects in his workshop. His wife, a newsreader named Beltinska, feels neglected and buys some live carp. She is unaware that Kula is in love with her image and has constructed a machine rigged to stroke and masturbate him when she is on television. Pivoine and Loubalova construct life-size effigies of each other.

On Sunday, Pivoine drives to the country with his effigy while Loubalova takes her effigy to an abandoned crypt containing a closet, a chair with candles and a basin of water. Loubalova emerges from the closet and whips her straw effigy, which (being animated) reacts. Pivoine dresses in his chicken outfit and struts around his similarly animated effigy, eventually crushing it with a boulder while Loubalova drowns hers in the basin. At home, Malkova shoves an unfeasible number of bread balls in her nose and ears and takes a nap. While Beltinska strokes her carp and feeds them the bread balls Malkova later delivers, Beltinsky strips naked in his work shop and rolls and rubs his objects over his body. When Beltinska reads the news, Kula turns on his machine and climaxes at the same time that she does, stimulated by the carp sucking her toes under her desk.

On his way home, Pivoine is fascinated by Beltinska's image in a television shop window and stops to buy electronic equipment magazines at Kula's shop. Kula is now covering rolling pins with feathers; Malkova looks longingly at a carp in a fishmonger's windows. Pivoine discovers that Loubalova has been killed in her flat by a boulder that has seemingly dropped through her roof: Beltinsky is investigating. Entering his own flat, Pivoine sees the chair with candles and the basin of water awaiting him. His closet door slowly opens.

If western animators have tended to emphasise the procreative nature of their work, boosting their ability to give life to objects and drawings, the Czech surrealist film-maker and animator Jan Svankmajer continually reminds us of the technique's deadly flipside, its fascination with destruction and its power to take back the "life" it gives. Steeped in Prague's alchemical traditions, his magic is a black one, from the murderous puppets of *The Last Trick* (1964) to the sorcery of his *Faust* (1994). Although *Conspirators of Pleasure* only features small bursts of 3-D animation, one level of the film continues to comment on animation's sadism. For example, the neighbours Pivoine and Loubalova lovingly craft effigies of each other which are brought to life by a strange voodoo of lust. The camera lingers especially on Poivine's drawer of modelling clay, a substance familiar in its texture from many of the director's earlier films (*Dimensions of Dialogue*, 1982; *Darkness Light Darkness*, 1989; *The Death of Stalinism in Bohemia*, 1990). The neighbours then crush, whip and drown their creations, acts which mysteriously lead to their counterparts' deaths. The use of live actors adds a menacing realism to these rituals which would never be possible in the all-cartoon world films of the similarly sadistic Tex Avery.

However, it would be reductive to insist that this is the only theme the film explores. Western critics probably find it easier to latch onto the self-reflexivity of Svankmajer's work at the expense of exploring his more political and polemical ideas. In his writings about and interviews for the film, the director has emphasised the centrality of issues of freedom and rebellion. Citing the influence of Freud and De Sade, Svankmajer seems to see the film as an illustration of their ideas about perversity's social importance, of the power of the pleasure principle to rub, *frottage*-like, against the restrictions of the reality principle.

No doubt that sounds rather clinical, if also perhaps somewhat fustily redolent of 60s avant-garde idealism. But in illustrating these ideas, the director has a light touch. While Kula, the newsagent who is fixated on the newsreader, Beltinska, prepares his pleasure-machine, the television set shows footage of wars abroad. Beltinsky, the abrasion buff, turns out to be a policeman, a repressive state apparachik, who in the end is called in to investigate Loubalova's murder.

Yet for all these characters, the larger structures of power and social order mean less than the tenuous community forged by the sly glances and knowing smiles they share amongst themselves. Thus there is a real political dimension to the 'conspiracy' of their pleasures.

Against this ideological ballast, *Conspirators of Pleasure* is still a pleasure to watch. Deeper issues aside, the film can also be read as a black sex comedy, a merry *La Ronde* of self-loving romantics. The cast (none of whom speak apart from Beltinska the newsreader, played by real life Czech newsreader Anna Wetlinska) bring a necessary warmth to the proceedings, an unglamourised humanity with their cuddly, lumpy bodies and soft features. With his characteristically impeccable timing, Svankmajer manages the pace just right: the slow start, with its slightly quizzical banality, crescendoes gradually towards an orgy of surrealist moments, hilarious but icily undercut by the entrance of death at the end.

VILLAGE VOICE, 8/26/97, p. 78, Dennis Lim

Having punctured the Romantic myth of Faust and purged the Victoriana from *Alice in Wonderland*, Jan Svankmajer turns to less literary, but no less subversive, pursuits. *Conspirators of Pleasure*, the Czech animator-surrealist's mostly live-action third feature, is a witty, almost entirely wordless rondo of ritualized autoeroticism. Conceived nearly three decades ago, but blocked by the Communist censors (Svankmajer was, in fact, banned from filmmaking for seven years), the film chronicles the ornate sexual escapades of six Prague residents.

As much as the director's boldly updated *Faust*, *Conspirators* is rooted in the tradition of Surrealist art as social criticism; the titular conspiracy is against the reality principle (Freud and De Sade are thanked in the end credits). The main character, a nervy, weasely fellow played by Peter Meissel, conducts an elaborate ceremony involving the slaughter of a rooster (plucked, then cooked in its own blood), the construction of a bat-wing cape (shredded umbrellas) and a giant rooster's head (*Hustler*-centerfold papier-maché, adorned with feathers), and eventually, the fanciful brutalization of a life-size effigy. All of which, apparently, constitutes but one half of a symmetric, sadomasochistic covenant that binds the character to his corpulent neighbor (Gabriela Wilhelmová).

The other "conspirators" are a postmistress who gets off on clogging her ears and nostrils with bread balls (and who has a somewhat, well, doughy complexion); a police inspector with a brush-and-feather fetish (and a knack for DIY); his newscaster wife (played by real-life Czech TV anchor Anna Wetlinska), who's discovered a novel use for live carp; and a shifty shopkeeper, engaged in an onanistic, *Videodrome*-style relationship with the newscaster's pixilated likeness. All six characters are linked—directly, tangentially, or downright absurdly; the postmistress, for instance, delivers her used bread balls to the newscaster, who feeds them to her fish (the immaculate serendipity would probably have pleased Kieslowski).

Faultlessly paced and edited (with mood music from the Brothers Quay), the film is essentially an awesomely fastidious foreplay session, climaxing in six rhapsodic, hypertactile orgies. Svankmajer manages a couple of post-coital flourishes, too: an inspired gag suggesting transmigrating fetishes and one final masterstroke that carries the movie's rigorous dream logic over into a macabre coda.

While *Conspirators* contains only fitful explosions of animation (deployed most conspicuously when gleeful dismemberment is called for), the human characters' mystic, obsessive rites are every bit as involved and alchemical as Svankmajer's wizardly brand of animation. The director has previously treated puppets and real-life actors interchangeably, but *Conspirators of Pleasure* evinces an unexpected grasp of human perversity. In the end, it's the film's fleshly dimension that makes it at once funny, compassionate, and disconcerting.

Also reviewed in:
NEW YORK TIMES, 8/20/97, p. C11, Stephen Holden
VARIETY, 10/14-20/96, p. 64, David Rooney

CONTACT

A Warner Bros. release of a South Side Amusement Company production. *Executive Producer:* Joan Bradshaw and Lynda Obst. *Producer:* Robert Zemeckis and Steve Starkey. *Director:* Robert Zemeckis. *Screenplay:* James V. Hart and Michael Goldenberg. *Based on the novel by:* Carl Sagan. *Director of Photography:* Don Burgess. *Editor:* Arthur Schmidt. *Music:* Alan Silvestri. *Music Editor:* Ken Karman. *Sound:* Randy Thom, William B. Kaplan and (music) Dennis Sands. *Sound Editor:* Phil Benson. *Casting:* Victoria Burrows. *Production Designer:* Ed Verreaux. *Art Director:* Lawrence A. Hubbs and Bruce Crone. *Set Designer:* James Claytor, Josh Lusby, Kristen Pratt, Evelyn Barbier, Easton M. Smith, Dean Wolcott, and Mariko Braswell. *Set Decorator:* Michael J. Taylor. *Visual Effects:* Ken Ralston. *Special Effects:* Allen Hall. *Computer Graphics Designer:* Steve Sexton and Simon Knights. *Costumes:* Joanna Johnston. *Make-up:* Hallie D'Amore. *Stunt Coordinator:* Bud Davis. *Running time:* 142 minutes. *MPAA Rating:* PG.

CAST: Jodie Foster (Eleanor "Ellie" Anne Arroway); Matthew McConaughey (Palmer Joss); Tom Skerritt (Dr. David Drumlin); Angela Bassett (Rachel Constantine); John Hurt (S.R. Hadden); David Morse (Theodore "Ted" Arroway); Rob Lowe (Richard Rank); William Fichtner (Kent); James Woods (Michael Kitz); Geoffrey Blake (Fisher); Jena Malone (Young Ellie); SaMi Chester (Vernon); Timothy McNeil (Davio); Laura Elena Surillo (Cantina Woman); Henry Strozier (Minister); Michael Chaban (Hadden Suit); Maximilian Martini (Willie); Larry King (Himself); Thomas Garner (Ian Broderick); Conroy Chino (KOB-TV Reporter); Dan Gifford (Jeremy Roth); Vance Valencia (Senator Valencia); Donna J. Kelley, Leon Harris, and Claire Shipman (Themselves); Behrooz Afrakhan (Middle Eastern Anchor); Saemi Nakamura (Japanese Anchor); Maria Celeste Arras (Latina Anchor); Tabitha Soren and Geraldo Rivera (Themselves); Ian Whitcomb (British Anchor); Jay Leno, Natalie Allen, Robert D. Novak, Geraldine A. Ferraro, and Ann Druyan (Themselves); Jake Busey (Joseph); Kathleen Kennedy (Herself); Michael Albala (Decryption Hacker); Ned Netterville (Decryption Expert); Leo Lee (Major Domo); William Jordan (Chairman of Joint Chiefs); David St. James (Joint Chief); Jill Dougherty (Herself); Haynes Brooke (Drumlin Aide); John Holliman, Bobbie Battista, Dee Dee Myers, Bryant Gumbel, and Linden Soles (Themselves); Steven Ford (Major Russell); Alex Zemeckis (Major Russell's Son); Janie Peterson (Major Russell's Daughter); Phillip Bergeron (French Committee Member); Jennifer Balgobin (Doctor Patel); Anthony Fife Hamilton (British Committee Member); Rebecca T. Beucler (NASA Public Relations); Marc Macaulay (NASA Technician); Pamela Wilsey (Voice of NASA); Tucker Smallwood (Mission

Director);   Jeff Johnson (Mechanical);   Yuji Okumoto (Electrical);   Gerry Griffin (Dynamics);   Brian Alston (Communications);   Rob Elk (Pad Leader);   Mark Thomason (Security);   José Rey (Controller 8);   Todd Patrick Breaugh (New VLA Technician);   Alex Veadov (Russian Cosmonaut);   Alice Kushida (Scientist);   Robin Gammell (Project Official);   Richardson Morse (Mission Doctor);   Seiji Okamura (Japanese Ensign);   Bernard Shaw (Himself);   Mak Takano and Tom Tanaka (Japanese Techs);   Catherine Dao (Life Support);   Kristoffer Ryan Winters (Dynamics 2);   Valorie Armstrong (Woman Senator);   Jim Hild and Bill Thomas (Reporters);   Diego Montoya (Schoolboy).

CHRISTIAN SCIENCE MONITOR, 7/11/97, p. 12, David Sterritt

Pathfinder is beaming snapshots from Mars, repairs are under way on the Mir space station, and the American military is again trying to squelch pesky stories about aliens at an Air Force base. Science is booming in real life, so is it surprising that science fiction is booming at the box office?

It's been that way all season, from the campy heroics of "The Fifth Element" to the faux pale-ontology of "The Lost World: Jurassic Park." Even the heroes of "Batman & Robin" are equipped with as many high-tech doodads as a "Star Wars" spaceship.

This reflects widespread interest in science-related enterprises—and if the media are as influential as many observers believe, such fascination with on-screen technology could encourage more political and financial support for actual science projects.

The ticket-selling champ of the current SF crop is "Men in Black," a comic look at spacepersons in our midst. But the most substantial entry is "Contact," directed by fantasy specialist Robert Zemeckis and based on a novel by Carl Sagan, whose "Cosmos" television show did for astronomy in the '80s what Zemeckis would like to do today. The film's mixture of scientific and religious elements is unusual and sometimes compelling, although its ideas are ultimately less venturesome than one might wish.

Jodie Foster plays Eleanor Arroway, an astronomer with a vision. Since childhood she's dreamed of probing distant galaxies with earthbound instruments, and as an adult she's traded academic prestige for a career of scanning the skies with telescopes. Her goal is to pick up a message from outer space, thus proving a lesson her father taught her: If there's nobody in the universe except us humans, that would be an awful waste of space.

Her wish comes true when a radio telescope picks up a purposeful signal from Vega, a star 26 light-years away. After much puzzling, pondering, and decoding, she and her colleagues piece together its meaning. Passed along to the government, this leads to construction of an unearthly machine designed to propel one individual into the reaches of space, toward a destiny only Vegans could foretell.

Other characters include Tom Skerritt as Eleanor's rival, James Woods as a national-security adviser who hones skepticism into a fine art, and John Hurt as a business magnate whose wit and wisdom keep the project going.

Most interesting is Matthew McConaughey as a young theologian who's made his reputation by reminding the world that scientific knowledge is no substitute for spiritual awareness. He becomes Eleanor's lover and confidant, engaging her—and the audience—in an ongoing discussion about the limitations of logic and the primacy of religion as a source of true insights and values.

As entertainment, "Contact" is a slow-going drama that would have more impact if it trimmed away unneeded characters and dropped some gimmicky video episodes. But special effects are superbly rendered in two major sequences, both involving the space-travel machine.

Foster brings commendable passion to her role, ably supported by Hurt and William Fichtner as a blind astronomer with a great ear for interstellar transmissions. By contrast, McConaughey seems less interested in his dialogue than in flashing his increasingly famous smile.

As philosophy, "Contact" is more thoughtful than most Hollywood pictures, but not as bold or innovative as it could have been. For all the screenplay's talk about religious values, its ultimate message favors humanism over metaphysics, suggesting that faith must reside in the heart rather than the mind, and that people (of whatever planet or galaxy) have "only each other" to preserve them from utter loneliness in the universe.

Zemeckis's last picture, the hugely successful "Forrest Gump," was criticized by some family-friendly viewers for conveying the idea that intelligence and education are luxuries rather than necessities. Traditionally minded spectators may scold "Contact" for a similar tendency to substitute feel-good imaginings for earnest, practical thought about important issues.

Disguised as a comic-book knockoff in the dubious "Judge Dredd" and "Barb Wire" tradition, "Men in Black" brings a needed dose of hilarity to the SF scene by telling us something we've always suspected: Those people we meet who look, sound, and act like aliens really are aliens! Their aim is to infiltrate Earth by hiding in human bodies. Their problem is that the disguise doesn't work very well.

Who'll save us from this menace? The fabled Men in Black, ever on the lookout for creatures who don't follow the rules of intergalactic etiquette. The tools of their trade are high-energy blasters, cars faster than the Batmobile, and a handy gizmo that erases the confusing memories caused by close encounters of the third kind. Their main field of action is Manhattan.

"Men in Black" gets its comic momentum from three sources. One is the razor-sharp acting of Tommy Lee Jones, as a veteran MIB who can spot a space invader in the most motley crowd of New Yorkers, and Will Smith, as a new agent whose on-the-job training goes less smoothly than expected. Vincent D'Onofrio is superb as an alien whose human form is barely under control—his performance recalls Steve Martin in "All of Me"—and Rip Torn is his usual persuasive self as the MIB boss.

The film's second powerhouse is Ed Solomon's witty screenplay, full of zingy one-liners and outrageous story developments. The third and most important is Barry Sonnenfeld's ever-surprising directing style, alternating scenes of broadly physical slapstick with unexpectedly subtle gags relying on split-second timing.

The film's only major downside is a weakness for jokes aimed at people who seem "weird" or "different," echoed in the regrettable ad campaign, portraying Earth as a "gated community" staving off outsiders with every weapon they can find. A comedy this funny doesn't need xenophobic overtones to up its hilarity quotient.

LOS ANGELES TIMES, 7/11/97, Calendar/p. 1, Kenneth Turan

Whatever's Out There has always fascinated people Down Here, especially movie people. But these days, instead of watching the skies (as those 1950s films encouraged everyone to do), people are listening to them. "Contact" tells us what one woman heard and how the world reacted.

Starring Jodie Foster in an exceptional performance as the radio astronomer who listened, and directed by Robert Zemeckis in his first outing since "Forrest Gump," "Contact" is superior popular filmmaking, both polished and effective. But despite its success and its serious intentions, it's finally a movie where the storytelling makes more of an impact than the story.

Balanced between wanting to deal with the philosophical and scientific issues that concerned Carl Sagan, who wrote the original 1985 novel, and making sure to satisfy the cravings of a mass audience, "Contact" manages to have it both ways most but not all of the. time. Not as profound as it would like to be, with a decidedly soft central message, it is nevertheless thoughtful and intelligent for the Hollywood summer entertainment it basically is.

Expertly directed by Zemeckis, who makes this kind of prestige studio production look easier than it is, "Contact" never loses touch with its "who are we and why are we here" sense of wonder about the universe that is its greatest strength. While it has a strongly sentimental side and wanders into conventional territory more often than it realizes, "Contact" manages an almost gyroscopic ability to right itself whenever absolutely necessary.

Much of this is due to Foster, whose skill and presence seem to increase with each picture and who dominates "Contact" in the best possible sense. Her portrayal of astronomer Ellie Arroway, a character she knows intimately, demonstrates why no one is more persuasive at conveying intelligence and single-minded passion to the point of confrontational anger. Foster is "Contact's" lodestar, and when she is on screen, the film can't help but be engrossing.

Arroway is first encountered in a prologue as an 8-year-old shortwave radio buff with a gentle father (David Morse) and an eagerness (well-conveyed by young actress Jena Malone) to hear from far-away places. Dad also ignites her interest in extraterrestrials with a folksy "if it is just us, seems like an awful waste of space" homily the film likes enough to use three times.

As an adult astronomer who has come to trust her work more than people, Arroway has turned into someone accurately characterized as "brilliant, driven, a major pain in the ass ... obsessed with a field that's considered professional suicide." That would be her affiliation with SETI, the Search for Extraterrestrial Intelligence, a group of scientists who listen doggedly for a signal from the skies.

Arroway's superior, National Science Foundation head David Drumlin (Tom Skerritt), is markedly unsympathetic, typically greeting her with a dismissive, "Still waiting for E.T. to call?" A further run-in with Drumlin leads Arroway to reclusive billionaire S.R. Hadden (an assured John Hurt), who lives on an airplane and knows exactly what he wants to do with all his money.

Arroway also connects with a different kind of man, Palmer Joss, played by heartthrob *du jour* Matthew McConaughey. A kind of self-defrocked priest, "a man of the cloth without the cloth" who "couldn't live with the whole celibacy thing," Joss is a writer who feels the modem passion for technology and science is corroding the world's moral values.

Though the science vs. religion, does-God-exist discussions he has with Arroway are some of "Contact's" most interesting, Joss has a tendency to come off as a ruggedly handsome signboard for the film's ideas. Also, the James V. Hart and Michael Goldenberg script upgrades Joss to much more of a conventional love interest than he was in Sagan's book. It's a transition that has its bumpy aspects as Joss, a construct more than a fully fleshed-out character, pops in and out of events in a not-always-convincing way.

Clocking in at 2½ hours, "Contact" is most alive during its central section, when Arroway, sitting next to a photogenic group of dish-shaped radio telescopes near Socorro, N.M., and hoping as per usual for a sign from the cosmos, hears what is unmistakably a signal from the beyond.

The source turns out to be Vega, a spot 26 light-years away, and how Arroway and her colleagues take the numerous steps necessary to decipher that message, what it says, and how Arroway fights to retain a part in its implications, are conveyed in a rush of images and sequences that are so invigorating it's possible to be swept away and overlook how skillfully it's all been put together.

For this, much credit has to go to director Zemeckis, cinematographer Don Burgess and editor Arthur Schmidt. The wizardly storytelling style they employ is seamless and involving, with all manner of elegant camera moves. Even bravura sequences like tracking Foster as she runs from her car through the lab to check on the signal (a scene that according to American Cinematographer was shot in two separate locations months apart) are so intrinsic to the narrative they never seem showy or excessive.

"Contact" has difficulty maintaining this momentum through its extended final segment. Partly it's that the initial section, the quest, makes the best use of the strengths of Foster's characterization, of Arroway's almost painful eagerness to make intergalactic contact. Also—and this goes to the heart of what "Contact" is lacking—the idea of the search turns out to be more involving than the knowledge that ends up being found.

Not helping is the tendency of the plot (despite appearances by James Woods as the president's national security advisor and Angela Bassett as a White House power) to get increasingly contrived and unsatisfying as the story unfolds. Even more than usually involving visual effects (supervised by Ken Ralston) can't fill that gap.

Still, when you think of how little to chew on summer films usually give us, "Contact" has to shine by comparison.

NEW YORK, 7/21/97, p. 47, David Denby

Robert Zemeckis's metaphysical sci-fi movie, *Contact*, from a novel by the late Carl Sagan, explicitly asks the big-bowwow questions: Are we alone in the universe? Does scientific reasoning threaten religious faith? The movie deals in wonders and miracles; it may be the biggest miracle of all that Zemeckis and his screenwriters (James V. Hart and Michael Goldenberg) were able to provide answers to these riddles that aren't completely ludicrous or banal.

Contact is a half-good movie: Part of it is a large-scale noisy production, overpadded and self-important, with tumultuous public scenes—White House press briefings and cabinet meetings and masses of people gathering and demonstrating. But at the heart of *Contact* there are patches of rapt silence and a lonely young woman, Dr. Ellie Arroway (Jodie Foster), an orphan, madly intense, asexual, an astronomer with spiritual longings, or at least hungers. Ellie has been obsessed since girlhood with hearing messages from outer space. There she sits in the New Mexico desert, a modern anchorite, listening through headphones to whatever is picked up by an array of powerful radio telescopes. Finally, she hears something—a steady metallic pulse that sounds rather like an Abrams tank grunting on a cold day. It is clearly a message from a major brain. When Ellie makes the discovery public, the White House becomes alarmed, the media go into a frenzy, and religious groups sense blasphemy or the end of the world. The government sets about building a space vehicle, designed according to specifications provided by the aliens. Someone's got to go out there and meet them. Or perhaps I should say *Them.*

Jodie Foster plays a driven personality all too successfully. Only 34, Foster already looks like one of those Lauren Bacall ladies on Madison Avenue who have had three nip-and-tucks—the skin is pulled tightly over her face (by sheer will power I assume), and she gives off a glint of humor, but no more than a glint. We know, of course, what Foster is up to. She wants to suggest how an obsessed woman—and a woman intellectual at that—would make herself half-crazy from isolation and ambition. The material, following Sagan's bent, has been given a feminist tilt: The big-shot White House science adviser (Tom Skerritt) who is Ellie's former mentor keeps taking the credit for her discoveries and pushing her out of the way, and Ellie has to suffer and fight. We are constantly asked to worry about Ellie's career moves and whether she's getting proper credit for her genius, all of which seems a little odd if not trivial in a movie offering to solve the eternal questions of the universe. Foster is effective but not much fun to watch; her performance is almost grindingly sincere, and often on the tremulous side.

Ellie's been given a lover, a defrocked clergyman named Palmer Joss who shows up every once in a while to argue with her about God. In the person of Matthew McConaughey, he looks like a moist-eyed sex hustler that people are unaccountably taking seriously (Palmer even sits in on White House cabinet meetings). Someone has to turn this man into an actor.

As he did with *Forrest Gump,* Robert Zemeckis puts everything into the movie: the pageant and frenzy of national media life, the president and his advisers, a megalomaniacal billionaire in the Howard Hughes mold (John Hurt), religious figures of various sorts, and so on. Zemeckis keeps trying to make the national myth, and though I'm glad he's got an intellectual rather than a simpleton at the center of his film this time, I wish he would rein himself in and tell a story more simply and coherently. There's too much going on in *Contact,* and not all of it is of the highest quality (the scenes with the billionaire are downright trashy). I often felt, as I have at other big-budget movies this season, that the director was throwing in redundant scenes and hordes of extras merely because he had the money to do so and imagined that audiences would feel cheated if the movies weren't filled with clutter. The monster budget may have destroyed what is left of Hollywood's sense of form.

The movie is best in its moments of Spielbergian awe—for instance, when Jodie Foster sits among the radio telescopes in the New Mexico dusk and her eyes, closed in sleep, electrifyingly pop open at the first sounds of life. At the end of the movie, when Ellie journeys (perhaps) into a new dimension, Zemeckis gives us a *son et lumière* show that tops Stanley Kubrick's famous trip at the end of *2001: A Space Odyssey.* Arriving at a distant galaxy, Ellie reaches out and touches the atmosphere on a beautiful beach as if it were a veil of translucent plastic. Does she really go someplace, or does she only imagine contact with extraterrestrials out of an unappeasable human desire for company? In its finest moments, *Contact* merges spectacle, science, and a genuine religious impulse.

NEW YORK POST, 7/11/97, p. 35, Michael Medved

Grandly ambitious, painfully earnest and profoundly disappointing, "Contact" may not be the worst film of the year, but it could count as the most frustrating.

The appalling waste of talent begins with producer-director Robert Zemeckis, who displays neither the whimsy and tenderness of "Forrest Gump" nor the pacing and humor of his "Back to the Future" trilogy.

Instead, he has adapted Carl Sagan's 1985 best-seller as a lumbering, self-important saga as joyless and cold as its main character: a supposedly brilliant astronomer played with an edge of hysteria by Jodie Foster.

Because she is a lonely orphan girl, this fanatical protagonist risks her promising career to sweep distant space for evidence of intelligent life, while her only human contact is a brief, heavy-breathing, Harlequin Romance-style affair with a pompous, goofy, New Age guru played by the confused (and embarrassed) Matthew McConaughey.

The film's very title indicates that it's only a matter of time before Foster gets her message from the great beyond, so the entire first third of the movie feels plodding and predictable.

But at least it's more believable than what follows.

Unseen aliens command earthlings to construct a gigantic machine, without ever explaining how it works or what it does, and the leaders of the planet cheerfully comply.

To make this plot point more credible, President Clinton turns up some half-dozen times in a singularly distracting cameo, provoking audience titters each time he appears.

Meanwhile, James Woods and Angela Bassett play bickering members of his White House staff, Tom Skerritt is an ambitious federal science chief and John Hurt is an eccentric, ailing billionaire who funds Foster's research.

Promoted as a "thinking person's" alien adventure, "Contact" is actually no less preposterous than "Independence Day" or any little-green-men Hollywood fantasy.

Why, for instance, do the governments of the world jointly invest $330 billion on a huge interstellar travel machine which, inexplicably, contains a seat for only a single crew member? And which intrepid space cadet do you think demands the right to journey to new worlds as the official representative of the human race? (Hint: It's not Al Gore.)

Such comic-book material is accompanied by pseudo-intellectual dialogue, including two (count 'em!) discussions of the medieval philosophical concept known as "Occam's razor." The dialogue also includes such scintillating profundities as "I always believed that the world is what we make of it" and "In all our searching, the only thing we found that makes the emptiness bearable is each other."

The movie's emptiness is made no more bearable by its ugly, unmistakable grudge against organized religion—with, as the most obvious bad guys, a band of drooling evangelical terrorists (led by deranged preacher Jake Busey), an a Ralph Reed-style political smoothie named Richard Rank played by Rob Lowe!). Fosters most heroic moment involves her refusal to declare a belief in God, even though such candor threatens her career.

At least the film's climax offers an explosion of genuinely dazzling special effects (vaguely recalling "2001: A Space Odyssey) that provide a suddenly spellbinding 10 minutes—but even this artistry is quickly trashed by a singularly gutless "Maybe-it-was-all-a-beautiful-dream"ending.

For those who spent good money to see this mess, "Contact" feels less like a lovely dream and more like a manipulative nightmare.

NEWSDAY, 7/11/97, Part II/p. B3, Jack Mathews

A little intellectual provocation in a movie counts for a lot in this summer of brain-dead action films, so for the scope and integrity of its subject matter alone, we welcome Robert Zemeckis' "Contact" into the parched wasteland of the multiplex.

Adapted from the late Carl Sagan's Promethean 1985 novel, exploring man's place in the cosmos, "Contact" takes on issues no smaller than the question of God's existence, the meaning of life, and the arrogance of both science and religion. It puts us in our place all right, as confused microcosmic specks in a universe so vast, we don't know the billionth of it.

The movie is awash in ideas that are overwhelming for their implications, and the story, about an obsessed astronomer who picks up and decodes a radio signal beamed from 400 million miles away, evolves from the most convincing science. Yet, for all of its empirical and philosophical weightiness, "Contact" is still a summer movie, with a space agency budget and executive lives on the line, and Zemeckis hasn't forgot it.

The result is a film whose brainy intentions are often dulled with chintzy melodrama. Zemeckis enchanted the world three summers back with "Forrest Gump," but here on the other end of the IQ scale he doesn't have the same faith in his audience and throws out clichés, like so many life preservers, to keep viewers comfortable.

The screenplay focuses on Sagan's central heroine, Dr. Ellie Arroway (Jodie Foster), a brilliant astronomer dedicated from early childhood to putting an ear to space. Ellie's patience and determination pay off, and she ends up in White House meetings discussing her findings and a course of action.

In the stacks of digital data from space are blueprints for a machine that will presumably transport its occupant—only room for one!—to the source's location in the galaxy of Vega. Even at the speed of light, a round trip would take 50 years of Earth time. Naturally, Ellie wants to go. So does her ex-boss, ambitious presidential science adviser David Drumlin (Tom Skerritt) and so might S.R. Hadden (John Hurt), the eccentric billionaire electronics mogul who's been bankrolling Ellie's project.

This is hot stuff, and despite miles of techno-jargon and the total absence of conventional action, the film builds up tremendous pressures. Will Ellie go? Will the machine fly? Who might she find out there? And how will all this cosmos fraternizing set with the Religious Right, represented by the Ralph Reed-inspired Richard Rank (Rob Lowe), by the nutcase religious fringe, represented by the evil-eyed, Bible-thumping blond (Jake Busey), and the thoughtful religious scholars, represented by Ellie's unlikely lover Palmer Joss (Matthew McConaughey).

Religious groups already threatening protests of "Contact" are right in saying their views aren't getting a respectful hearing. Except for Palmer Joss, the religious reps are a nutty bunch, and he is such a complete pre-fab romantic figure, even his vow of toleration for secular humanism sounds like a come-on.

Ellie and Palmer meet in a Puerto Rican jungle, where they're following the beat of different drums in the heavens, and overcome the great divide of their viewpoints to prove the scientific maxim that "opposites attract." In comparison to their romance, everything else—the outerspace signals, the government's willingness to crash the national budget to build the transport, S.R. Hadden's willingness to spend the same fortune for a Japanese-made backup—seems perfectly plausible.

Foster, her presence as intense and commanding as we've ever seen it, makes Ellie such an unstoppable force, she seems to be going against her nature in the coyly staged scenes with McConaughey. And Hunk of the Moment that he may be elsewhere, McConaughey is very ordinary in her company. In fact, with the exception of Hurt, no one rises to the occasion, least of all a self-parodying James Woods.

Zemeckis, using the same illusory tricks that delighted us in "Forrest Gump," overdid it with the Bill Clinton clips. The president appears so often, he may qualify for residuals. And instead of calling Central Casting to fill the electronic journalist roles, Zemeckis called CNN. Among the moonlighters are Larry King, Bernard Shaw and "Crossfire" hosts Geraldine Ferraro and Robert Novak. Doesn't Ted Turner pay these people a living wage?

For all its flaws, "Contact" is, by several lights years, the smartest film in the summer market. Technically, the movie is packed with enough scientific detail for it to become a teaching aid. It's just too bad Zemeckis didn't take the same care in creating authentic relationships. In the end, "Contact" could have used a little less astronomy, and a little more chemistry.

NEWSWEEK, 7/21/97, p. 68, David Ansen

In *Contact*, playing astronomer Ellie Arroway, Jodie Foster looks haunted, driven. Behind the fierce intelligence of her eyes, you can see the hurt child who grew up motherless, and then lost her father when she was 9. Her drawn face hints at a lifetime spent hopefully, fruitlessly gazing at the stars, awaiting a signal. Ellie's conviction that we are not alone in the universe arises from a deep need. As Robert Zemeckis's movie makes clear, the contact she seeks from the heavens—and ultimately finds—is a recompense for the deep solitude she holds in her heart.

Foster brings a passionate conviction to this ambitious, 2½-hour adaptation of Carl Sagan's science-fiction best seller, which labors mightily to merge the personal and the cosmic in a resonant metaphor. Filled with lofty debates about the conflict between science and religion, more interested in stirring awe than whipping up action, "Contact" is being positioned as the "thinking man's" summer movie, an heir to "2001 " and "Close Encounters of the Third Kind." At its most seductive moments—the rousing sequence when Ellie and her team first pick up a signal from the star Vega at their New Mexico listening site, and the shocking visual image they decode on their monitors—we're drawn inside Ellie's passion, sharing her sense of wonder at the infinite possibilities Out There.

But Zemeckis's beautifully shot movie is frustratingly uneven. When it's good, it's very good. And when it's not, it can be as silly and self-important as a bad '50s sci-fi movie. Screenwriters Michael Goldenberg and James V. Hart have written a terrific part for Foster, as a bruised. headstrong scientist battling a skeptical establishment, but their inspiration runs aground with the other characters.

The pressure to pump up a love story has resulted in Palmer Joss (Matthew McConaughey), a lapsed seminarian whose character is as improbable as his name. The Reverend Joss first appears, in hippieish garb in Puerto Rico, where the novice Dr. Arroway is conducting her search for extraterrestrial intelligence. They share a night of love, which the emotionally skittish Ellie refuses to pursue. Some years later, when the signal from Vega has put her at the center of a national controversy, the now resplendently coiffed Joss, a bestselling New Age theologian, reappears as a most unlikely consultant to the president, just about every scene with the philosophical reverend is a clinker, and he keeps popping up in implausible places to continue his debate with Ellie about the existence of God. It's a role that could make any actor look bad, and McConaughey, too young and too pretty for it, cuts a ludicrous figure.

As the sinister national-security adviser who is, of course, paranoid about the extraterrestrial's intents, James Woods brings his patented rancid malevolence, overstated but amusing. John Hurt turns up as a powerful, mysterious industrialist who funds Ellie's project before the government hones in on the act. Tom Skerritt is Ellie's spotlight-stealing scientific boss, and rather too old for the astronaut role he's asked to play. Even Bill Clinton gets shoehorned into the act: Zemeckis, using his "Forrest Gump" tricks, inserts actual Clinton press conferences into the story's context, a distracting device that doesn't quite feel kosher. Shouldn't the president have a say in whether he wants to be a bit player in a summer movie?

There are a few glimmers of the satirical Zemeckis of old, as the Vegan contact brings out every crackpot demonstrator from fundamentalist zealots to Elvis worshipers, but most of the time the director is in a reverent mode. It must be said that the great insight revealed at the end of Ellie's fantastic voyage isn't much more than a fortune-cookie platitude. The story finds a way to resolve its science-vs.-faith theme by having it both ways, with a little spiritual frosting atop its secular-humanist cake.

But if "Contact" is disappointingly soft in the head, it can also enthrall. Zemeckis is such a potent imagemaker that he is capable, for long stretches at a time, of sweeping you up in his vision. His intricate, virtuoso camera moves and elegant compositions often rise to the celestial occasion. At the heart of this unwieldy but intriguing entertainment is a primal sense of cosmic curiosity that all but the most cynical will find hard to resist. We've all gazed up at the stars and asked ourselves big, dumb questions about the meaning of it all. "Contact" can be forgiven its big, dumb answers.

SIGHT AND SOUND, 10/97, p. 44, Philip Strick

Orphaned at the age of nine, Ellie Arroway grows up obsessed with the possibility of communication with distant planets. She joins the SETI (Search for Extraterrestrial Intelligence) project and uses the giant radio telescope in Puerto Rico to scan the stars for a coherent message. When presidential Science Adviser David Drumlin withdraws funds, Ellie secures support from the billionaire recluse S.R. Hadden and transfers her unit to Socorro, New Mexico, where an array of telescopes is tuned in to space. Just when her time has almost run out, an unmistakable signal is received.

Originating from the dwarf star of Vega, the message first consists of prime numbers but soon becomes more complex. Ellie is interrogated by top-level government officials, including Drumlin and National Security Adviser Michael Kitz. Integrated with other images is a mass of digital data. Summoned by Hadden, Ellie is guided by him into decoding what turns out to be the blueprint for a vast construction and some kind of spaceship. Drumlin is chosen over Ellie to 'fly' in the ship to the Vegans. However, during the first testing of the machine, it is blown apart by a deranged evangelist and Drumlin is killed. Ellie grows close to ex-priest Palmer Joss, now a presidential adviser. Hadden tells Ellie the Japanese have secretly put together a second ship: she will be the passenger. Locked into the machine with a miniature videocamera, Ellie hurtles through tunnels of light and space.

She lands 18 hours later on a tropical beach where she is welcomed by her father. He is in fact an alien, taking shape from her memories. His main message is that Earth's participation in extraterrestrial activity must be gradual. Whisked back to the launch site, Ellie finds that only seconds have passed and the mission is declared a failure. She tries to convey the splendour of her experience but her videocamera shows only static and she is publicly humiliated by Kitz, who accuses her of helping Hadden to perpetuate a monstrous hoax. Ellie retreats to Socorro, where she lectures children and watches each night as the stars come out. It transpires that her camera recorded 18 hours of static.

It began life in 1981 as a film treatment and was then converted into a blockbuster novel after much comment and input, from, among others, the passionate science-fiction guru Theodore Sturgeon. Translated back to the screen in time to participate in the current meteor swarm of 'alien' movies, the late Carl Sagan's *Contact* reaches us in a kind of decaying orbit, bearing the impacted scars of multiple amendment and afterthought. Although co-produced by Sagan and his wife, Ann Druyan (cowriter of the original treatment) it is no longer a didactic affirmation of the two astronomers' predictions about life on other worlds. Instead, thanks to considerable extrapolation from hints and details in the novel, it has become a Robert Zemeckis film. That means—recalling the eccentricities of the *Back to the Future* trilogy, *Death Becomes Her* and *Forrest Gump*—it's become a tale of delusion and disorientation told with a startling technical expertise.

Unconstrained by normal inhibitions and well suited to Jodie Foster's intense and haunted performance, the Ellie Arroway of the film is subconsciously hunting for irrefutable proof that her dead parents continue to exist in some other plane or on some other planet in accordance with religious promise (despite her stated rationalism). In the book, Ellie's mother remains alive, although on the wane; in the film she is disposed of from the start, leaving the way clear for Ellie's more acute concern, the resurrection of her father. The film painstakingly surrounds Ellie with father-figures, personifying such paternal qualities as authority (Ted), accusation (Kitz), manipulation (Hadden), unreliability (Drumlin), support (Kent), near-omniscience (the alien), and unlimited affection (Joss).

Of these, she finally settles for Palmer Joss, promoted for the screen from his written role as theosophical irritant on the margin of Ellie's cause. While remaining an unlikely intrusion, he becomes a handy bit of love-interest in that his physical charms and his doctrinal arrogance render him both irresistible and repugnant to Ellie at the same time, a contradiction that mirrors her own insecurity. At the end, in uneasy compromise, they accept a cautious faith in each other and, more importantly since Ellie is alone with the stars when we last see her, faith in whatever the heavens may choose to reveal. Repossessed of her lost parent through Joss, Ellie now awaits communication from a new century. Sagan set out three main questions in his book (are there aliens, how should we deal with them, and what will they tell us about God?) and provided three respectable answers (unquestionably, carefully, and nothing we can't work out for ourselves). His most vital assertion, reassuringly bolstered by mathematical logic but otherwise leaving us to our own faiths and devices, is that "in the fabric of space and in the nature of matter, as in a great work of art, there is, written small, the artist's signature". Sagan's Ellie, carrying a symbolic palm frond and accompanied by four co-witnesses on the trip to Vega to substantiate her story, has no doubt about what she has seen. Zemeckis, on the other hand, seemingly unpersuaded and eager not to offend, stays firmly within the limits of his Ellie-as-troubled-orphan reading: Ellie on film has visions, dreams, memories and hopes, but no signed proof of anything. Worse still, she seems likely to have been duped by the wildly powerful S.R. Hadden, centre-staged from his peripheral usefulness in the novel to become, as joyously performed by John Hurt, a resonant combination of the Dalai Lama and the dead, deranged leader of the Heaven's Gate cult. While presumably he would have been unable to influence Ellie's fantasy about Vega, a sparkling tropical beach derived from the rather spare painting of Florida she did as a child, he is Ellie's guide to an understanding of the 'alien' text and to the stand-by space-pod awaiting her when the first is sabotaged. He could even perhaps have prompted the sabotage itself in order to get Ellie's adversary, the odious Drumlin, out of her way in what Hadden terms "the game of the millennium'.

Since this interpretation, more Philip K. Dick than Sagan, leaves his aliens exceedingly thin on the ground by contrast with the massed hordes of *Independence Day, Mars Attacks!* and *Men in Black*, Zemeckis generates all kinds of alternative visual excitements. His intergalactic opening is so spectacular, in fact, that his first Earthbound scenes take a while to settle down. The camera has to be dragged in from the garden to concentrate on the indoor exchanges between Ellie and her father. When, later, the father collapses, all 'normal' viewpoints are discarded: all we see of his body is scattered popcorn, while Ellie's rush to the medicine cupboard becomes a slow-motion panic filmed through a mirror. Rather predictably, the arrival of the first alien signal prompts a frantic scramble of hand-held camerawork, but Ellie's rollercoaster ride through the wormholes is as satisfying a lightshow as anything since: *2001: A Space Odyssey.*

Although a major step away from the goofy slapstick of his previous films, *Contact* retains plenty of Zemeckis humour, as well as the trademark 'documentary' shots, here Bill Clinton among the film's cast and the cheerful use of irreverently meaningful names such as Kent Clark. There are moments, too, of appealing delicacy: the pan across a row of radio telescopes to embrace the curve of Ellie's straw hat, the sight of a compass in free fall with all sense of direction lost, or the simple evocative close-up of a handful of grains of earth. If the whole exercise, falling back to Earth, is something of an anticlimax in concluding that aliens probably know more than we do—but not much—while true believers will claim that God put Hadden up to it, Zemeckis and his team have at least subjected Sagan's elaborate thesis to an enthralling realignment.

TIME, 7/21/97, p. 69, Richard Schickel

The movie *Contact* is something like one of those mysterious asteroids that get the astronomers all worked up: a large body of gaseous matter surrounding a relatively small core of solid substance.

You would not, however, characterize it as "hurtling" through space to that theater near you. It proceeds very slowly through many banal deliberations about cosmic enigmas to a comfortably reassuring conclusion in which scientific humanism and vaguely uplifting religiosity are squashily reconciled.

This is not, frankly, a place at which one is rooting for Jodie Foster's Ellie Arroway to end up. Foster has always been an actress who gives intelligence a good name, and she's very attractive here as a stubbornly obsessive scientist, convinced there are brainy beings out there in deep space trying to get in touch with us, then triumphantly picking up their mysterious signals from the void.

The movie, adapted from Carl Sagan's novel, is good—up to a point—on the inevitable hubbub that follows. Leading it are a national security adviser (James Woods) going nastily paranoid about space invasion; a presidential science adviser (Tom Skerritt) trying to shunt Ellie out of the loop as the government builds the shuttle (plans kindly provided by the aliens) needed to penetrate our newly defined outer limits; and—oh yes, oh help—Palmer Joss.

He is sort of a New Age Billy Graham who has wormed his way into the high councils of state as spiritual consultant to the President. He is played with a nice shiftiness—you really wouldn't want to trust this guy with a church-collection plate—by Matthew McConaughey. Yet director Robert Zemeckis lets him carry the movie's message. That is to say, Joss, not Ellie—bless her sternly rational soul—happens to be right; there is, just as he has so tiresomely predicted, a metaphysical dimension to deep space.

It turns out to look like a Club Med and to offer reunions with the dear departed, but without any sectarian representation of a deity. This turns cerebral Ellie into numinous jelly, but it is an alarming comedown from the director who played so entrancingly with time travel in the *Back to the Future* movies and gave us the delightful alternative reality of *Who Framed Roger Rabbit.* The success of *Forrest Gump* has made him Hollywood's philosopher-king, free to spend a fortune doing for the simple pieties what he recently did for simplemindedness: make them look like a nice easy road to spiritual fulfillment. Zemeckis and his colleagues have been all over the press congratulating themselves on throwing an intellectually challenging movie into the summer maelstrom. What this tells us about them—and if *Contact* is a hit, the rest of us—is too depressing to contemplate.

VILLAGE VOICE, 7/22/97, p. 65, J. Hoberman

Hyped as the summer's only serious $90 million movie, *Contact* is an example of hardcore Spielbergism delivered—sans the Spielberg pizzazz—by the master's most grimly successful disciple.

In *Who Framed Roger Rabbit?*, Robert Zemeckis may have given us the '80s' supreme metaphor for how we live now; *Contact,* by comparison, is a multiple regression. Adapted from the Reagan-era bestseller written by the late public-TV-astro-popularizer Carl Sagan, this account of the most benign interplanetary interaction since the heyday of *E.T.* falls somewhere between the golden anniversary of the Roswell Event and NASA's own summer blockbuster, Pathfinder on Mars. Mainly, however, it's a search for the lost daddy—a spectacle at once laughable and glum.

The orphan of Bedford Falls, astro-genius Ellie Arroway (Jodie Foster), has developed her precocious interest in ham radio into an obsessive search for life in the cosmos, most pithily (if pitifully) summarized by the flashback to her prepubescent post-funeral shortwave plea: "Dad—are you there?" Never less than earnest, even when enjoying a postcoital struggle with resident hunk Matthew McConaughey, Foster battles the bureaucratic blob blocking her "journey to the heart of the universe," but seems most at home in the role of a grade-school teacher. She's a gracious fount of wisdom who ends the movie posed as Rodin's thinker.

Is the star wondering why *Contact* is a movie where fathers proliferate faster than the pods in *Invasion of the Body Snatchers?* Ellie's extraterrestrial efforts are thwarted by her rogue mentor David Drumlin (Tom Skerritt), an enemy of "pure research" who opportunistically reverses himself the nano-second his former student's obsession bears fruit. Supposedly more positive male authority is provided by Palmer Joss (perpetually smirking McConaughey), a freelance spiritual advisor who claims no particular back channel to the Supreme Being but pops in and out of the plot, amazing Ellie with his uncanny ability to paraphrase her long-dead dad. Video transmissions of our presidential pop (Bill Clinton) further hover over the proceedings, as does a trillionaire benefactor (John Hurt). The hilarious embodiment of mobile, transnational capital, Hurt's character beams personal missives into Foster's computer, jesting with her in somewhat the same creepy way as Anthony Hopkins did in *Silence of the Lambs.*

No less than any other summer blockbuster, the universe here thrives upon synchronicity and synergy: the plug is about to be pulled on Ellie's project and Palmer is making his debut on *Larry King Live* as the president's personal New Age guru (Michael Lerner, eat your heart out) when the Master Programmer in the sky contrives to dispatch a mega static blast from the vicinity of the Vega star cluster. Enter the petulant government functionaries—played with bracing villainy by James Woods and Angela Bassett—plus every talking head in the CNN stable.

Contact leaves the unmistakable impression that CNN has acquired exclusive rights to what is repeatedly billed as the most important event in human history. What Time Warner has wrought, so Time Warner's CNN must report! (Or, as Richard Corliss wrote in *Time* itself on the occasion of the Heaven's Gate mass suicide: "Here's our scoop. The real conspiracy is the mind-clouding cocktail of pop culture and hard news.") Whatever other forms of communication it celebrates, *Contact* offers Hollywood's most intense mix ever of newsreaders and celebs—dwarfing the dogged promotion of *Independence Day*'s Murdoch serfs.

So much for corporate logic. *Contact*'s more enjoyable irrationalities include an astronaut contest between our heroine and a character too old to stay up for Jay Leno, let alone take a rocket to Vega. This willing suspension of disbelief is reinforced by holy man Palmer's pragmatic suspension of personal ethics—although this may be social satire, as the movie makes him Bill Clinton's spiritual adviser. Indeed, while all *Contact*'s performances seem a bit constricted, the most blatantly constructed belongs to our starstruck Fearless Leader. I always thought that Clinton was the secret subject of Zemeckis's *Forrest Gump; Contact* proves it. News footage of the president is edited into some scenes and glimpsed into at least one shot, focusing like a laser his concentrated sincerity and all-purpose cliché babble on the problem of deep messages from deep space. "Let's deal with this on the facts."

Facts, as Ronald Reagan famously said, are stupid things. Despite Ellie's persecution during government hearings for being an agnostic, *Contact* is most affecting for embodying the pathos (or pathology) of faith. Although the movie attempts to inoculate itself against charges of religious pandering with a clumsy reference to Heaven's Gate, its most naturalistic scenes naturally feature the full panoply of American true believers—old hippies, pseudo Indians, neo-Nazi skinheads, Jesus freaks, Elvis imitators—massing with hucksters in the desert. The movie's alleged critique of fundamentalism notwithstanding, it shamelessly promotes an infantile yearning as profound (if not as convincingly dramatized) as that of *Close Encounters.*

Contact is not quite celebrating itself when it evokes "the most expensive single project in all of human history," although it does advocate privatized space research as well as raise the specter of copyright news. Still, specialists may prize the movie as the incoherent convergence of many agendas. Zemeckis's special effects-driven sense of world history as a series of highly malleable media events meets Foster's alienated, didactic streak; Time Warner's self-promotion blends with that of the White House. Something here for everyone. (Who, I wonder, is responsible for locating our media-driven culture in Nazi Germany?)

As *Contact* leisurely wends its way toward cosmic closure, the requisite references to *Close Encounters* (and the bizarre ones to *Silence of the Lambs)* give way to a klutzy mix of *2001* and *Mr. Smith Goes to Washington.* How do things turn out? Suffice to say: Tinkerbell Lives!

Various reviewers of the Village Voice felt so strongly about Contact that they wrote individual reviews in addition to J. Hoberman's review. The reviews appeared on 8/19/97, p. 86 under the headline "Ranting About the Summer's most Obnoxious Movie."

Dull, windy, and rife with logic chasms at least as vertiginous as the wormhole Jodie Foster bobsleds down in the film's climax, Robert Zemeckis's film agonizes tirelessly over the cramps religious faith gives society and science. But the deck is stacked. The notion that the Clinton White House would ever allow Christian Coalitioners to attend cabinet meetings or that it would keep a studly young evangelist on call is a gas—as if God would ever overrule greed and self-interest on Capitol Hill. This goatwash is all justified, according to the film, by the fact that "95 per cent" of us believe in God (by my almanac, atheists, Buddhists, Confucians, and the nonreligious comprise nearly a quarter of the world population). Despite it all, Zemeckis & Co. still try to appear fair—Matthew McConnaughey's beatific "reverend" even pleads for a "middle ground" between blind faith and hard science, which, as author Carl Sagan knew, is like asking for a compromise between Oz and Oshkosh. How many real churchgoers would claim to have informed opinions about extraterrestrial interfacing, anyway? It's not quite the same as knowing what you don't like about *Ellen.* —MICHAEL ATKINSON

No filmmaker has done more for the self-esteem of the IQ-deprived than Robert Zemeckis: *Forrest Gump* allowed idiots to feel good about being stupid; *Contact*, no less penuriously, allows them to feel smart. Mulling solemnly over cosmos-sized, jargon-smattered questions, it's apparently tailored for the thinking moviegoer (not to mention the gullible critic). It left me patronized, offended, bored out of my mind, and marveling at the irony of a fanatical, universe-wide search for intelligent life that itself contains none. The film positively reeks of Zemeckis's monomania, his questionable appetite for spectacle, his dunderheaded belief that verisimilitude equals import (hence moonlighting CNN journalists and a gumped president). As directed by a compulsive reductionist, *Contact* conjoins Ellie "Science" Arroway and Palmer "Religion" Joss. The movie's ideological tussle is rigged; poor, foolish, agnostic orphan Ellie doesn't stand a chance. When no one believes her story about whizzing through space straight into Daddy's arms, she's cured of her heathenish ways, finally appreciating the power and incommunicability of faith. According to its admirers, *Contact* is serious, sincere, and cause for celebration in a summer awash in thoughtless F/X. If this is your kind of spiritual balm, then fine, but don't try telling me that this film has anything to do with thought. —DENNIS LIM

For a movie whose central intellectual metaphor involves, you know, listening, *Contact* sure has an awful lot of stupid talk in it. Prespun as an "intelligent," big-idea alternative to the summer movie crapfest, to me *Contact* boiled down to an endless-seeming string of yammer scenes whose whiny undercurrents were more the stuff of your average episode of *Sally* than *Cosmos.* From the familiar cadences of "My daddy's dead!" to the odd watercooler extravagances of "They took my grant money!" and "They won't send me to Vega because I slept with the hot guy on the international selection panel!" *Contact* is so much the product of the recent television-talk era that it's dramatic and (purportedly) transformative payoff scene isn't the patently ripped-off wormhole sequence (from *2001* to *Brainstorm,* you've seen it before) but the Congressional Hearing—historically the site of some important talk to be sure but at its purest *Ricki Lake* for wonks. Most alarming though is that a film concerned ostensibly with the Most Important Event in Human History hasn't a single word in its emotional or intellectual vocabulary that isn't lifted directly from the New Age feel-goodism of everything from *The Celestine Prophecy* to the *Oprah-* and PBS-endorsed blatherings of Deepak Chopra. Stripping itself of its associations with the late Carl Sagan (who was no friend of the New Age himself) with every pseudo-meaningful look,

Contact replaces Sagan's love of the big questions with a thin soup of ridiculously vague dithering about "belief" and "happiness' so masturbatory and self-obsessed that a civilization-transforming event is just another metaphor for "personal fulfillment." —GARY DAUPHIN

Is it a nasal mist or a movie? A nasal mist *and* a movie! I forgot all about the film five minutes after it was over, but my general impression was: Jodie is too butch for Matt. Matt's cute and he's a lot of fun, but I just don't buy him as, you know, another throbbing hetero Hollywood boner. I'd prefer to see Matt in a light romantic comedy with Leonardo DiCaprio and Tom Cruise, something like *Matt Sandwich*.—GARY INDIANA

Also reviewed in:
NEW YORK TIMES, 7/11/97, p. C3, Stephen Holden
NEW YORKER, 7/21/97, p. 81, Anthony Lane
VARIETY, 7/14-20/97, p. 43, Todd McCarthy
WASHINGTON POST, 7/11/97, p. B1, Rita Kempley
WASHINGTON POST, 7/11/97, Weekend/p. 37, Desson Howe

CONTEMPT

A Rome-Paris Films (Paris), Films Concordia (Paris), Compagnia Cinematografica Champion (Rome) production. *Producer:* Georges de Beauregard and Carlo Ponti. *Director:* Jean-Luc Godard. *Screenplay (French, English, Italian and German with English subtitles):* Jean-Luc Godard. *Based on the novel "Il disprezzo":* Alberto Moravia. *Director of Photography:* Raoul Coutard. *Editor:* Agnès Guillemot. *Music:* Georges Delerue and (Italian) Piero Piccioni. *Sound:* William Sivel. *Costumes:* Tanine Autre. *Make-up:* Odette Berroyer. *Running time:* 101 minutes. *MPAA Rating:* Not Rated.

CAST: Brigitte Bardot (Camille Javel); Jack Palance (Jerry Prokosch); Michel Piccoli (Paul Javel); Giorgia Moll (Francesca Vanini); Fritz Lang (Himself); Jean-Luc Godard (Assistant Director); Linda Véras (Siren); Raoul Coutrad (Cameraman).

CHRISTIAN SCIENCE MONITOR, 7/9/97, p. 14, David Sterritt

"Contempt" begins with a shot of Godard's camera gazing at us from the screen. Then it shifts to the dramatic story of a writer trying to adapt "The Odyssey" for a Hollywood producer who's more impressed with his own power than the glories of ancient Greece.

Also involved in the tale is a great filmmaker whom the writer—like Godard himself—admires. But the writer's attention wanders when his wife loses respect for him, convinced he's allowing the producer to flirt with her. The movie reaches its climax during a sun-drenched visit to a Mediterranean island, stunningly filmed in a setting that combines modern architecture with the timeless beauty of exquisite landscapes and seascapes.

At once intelligent, deeply emotional, and original, "Contempt" deserves its reputation as a brilliantly absorbing work. Godard's enthusiasts will be thrilled with the newly made wide-screen prints being shown in its current revival, and newcomers can now make the acquaintance of a movie long unavailable in its original form.

LOS ANGELES TIMES, 7/4/97, Calendar/p. 8, Kenneth Turan

It's one thing for a film to retain every bit of its worth after more than 30 years, but more impressive is the ability to be increasingly relevant and moving with the passage of time. Such is the case with Jean-Luc Godard's 1963 "Contempt."

Perhaps how thin the cinematic gruel has become over the past decades is what makes us appreciate the thematic strengths of this work. And there's also the cool beauty of Raoul Coutard's wide-screen cinematography, unmistakable in the new print struck for this two-week revival at the Nuart in West Los Angeles.

Or maybe it's the impression made by the film's unlikely polyglot cast, which includes a gorgeous Brigitte Bardot at the height of her stardom, Michel Piccoli at the beginning of his, Jack Palance at his most magnetic and the great Fritz Lang playing himself near the end of a long directing career.

Most important, however, is the unexpected and potent connection between director and material. For perhaps the only time in his career, Godard, the gifted *provocateur* of the French New Wave who could take film apart and put it together any way he pleased, made a picture based on conventional material, a novel by the Italian Alberto Moravia.

What resulted is, along with "Breathless," as memorable a film as Godard ever made, a kind of "where love has gone" meditation on the crumbling of two kinds of passion, one romantic, the other cinematic.

"Contempt" was partially financed by American mogul Joseph E. Levine, and one of the intriguing ways this film folds back on itself is that Godard is said to have modeled Palance's crass American producer Jerry Prokosch on Levine himself.

More than that, it was Levine and producer Carlo Ponti's horror at the lack of nude shots of sex symbol Bardot in the film's rough cut that led to "Contempt's" celebrated opening, where an unclothed Camille (Bardot) lounges on the bed with husband Paul (Piccoli) as he tells her he loves her "totally, tenderly, tragically." What the producers didn't bargain for was that Godard shot the sequence with the distancing device of alternating red and blue filters, giving the producers what he wanted in the guise of giving in.

Paul is a novelist-turned-screenwriter whom Prokosch wants to hire to add some sex scenes to an adaptation of Homer's "Odyssey" that Lang is directing. Will Lang be willing to work with him, Paul wonders. "He will direct whatever is written," Prokosch says, and he means it.

Perhaps because he is the film's unapologetic dark force, Palance's Prokosch completely holds our attention. His portrait of the producer as a pompous, predatory ignoramus always quoting from a tiny book of maxims (an interesting counterpoint to Rod Steiger's monster executive in Palance's earlier "The Big Knife") is stunning. Whether he's tossing film cans around a screening room or saying, "Whenever I hear the word 'culture,' I bring out my checkbook," he epitomizes the industry's worst tendencies, both then and now.

For it is one of this film's sad tasks to recognize that the sophisticated art of movie-making (epitomized by the cultured, multi-lingual Lang) is crumbling like the decrepit studio Prokosch has set up shop in. Though Godard's own work contributed in a very different way to the death of classical filmmaking, "Contempt" always reflects the director's sense of loss.

What gives this film its special poignancy, however, is its exploration of romantic loss, of a relationship that starts to unravel not just when Camille meets Prokosch in his red sports car but when Paul starts to work for the producer. For Camille alone can sense, almost instinctively, what a threat the man is to anything that aspires to lasting value. Paul either doesn't notice, or pretends not to, until it is too late.

All this comes to a head in a half-hour scene between husband and wife in their new, partially furnished apartment. It's a devastating sequence as we see, for no apparent reason yet for any number of intangible ones, a relationship disintegrate in front of our eyes. In its vision of small disputes getting painfully but inevitably out of hand, it's as emotionally telling as anything in Godard's body of work.

There is, in this focus on personal and artistic relationships gone sour, a sense of quiet tragedy hovering over "Contempt," a mood heightened by Georges Delerue's lush and moody score. Melancholy and sensual, "Contempt" is the one Godard film it's impossible to mistake for any other, and the director, perhaps sensing this, puckishly cast himself as Lang's officious assistant director. It's a nod to greatness that, 30-plus years later, the film itself returns in kind.

NEW YORK POST, 6/27/97, p. 42, Thelma Adams

Jean-Luc Godard's 1963 "Contempt" is less a brilliant, but misplaced, masterwork than a reminder of what used to draw American audiences to foreign cinema: naked women; Yankee bashing; the canonization of the male, European auteur, and a level of critical discourse most useful for impressing chicks at the coffeehouse after the show.

Adapted by Godard from Alberto Moravia's novel "A Ghost at Noon," the movie, currently in re-release, immediately tops the printed page by laying out Brigitte Bardot in all her nubile nakedness. Godard presents her with tousled hair on tousled sheets, but she is as much flesh on a silver platter as Peter Greenaway's corpses.

The typist-turned-housewife(Bardot) asks her screenwriter hubby (Michel Piccoli), over-dressed in rumpled white T-shirt and boxers, if he loves various parts of her anatomy. What's not to like? The creases on her firm, tan bum are as crisp as Connecticut khakis.

When Camille finally turns her gaze from the mirror to Paul, her homely hubby, it's no wonder she's stung by contempt. Piccoli's ugliness is more than mug deep. His character is as weak as his jaw; his commitment to art as much a pose as his tiny fedora.

Godard soon tests Paul's mettle. Hollywood producer Jerry (Jack Palance) asks Paul to rewrite scenes in his current production of "The Odyssey"—for a price. The wavering playwright is caught between the maniacal capitalist and the film-within-the-film's famed German director, Fritz Lang (playing himself), between the exploiter and the *artiste*.

In Godard's in-joke on international filmmaking, the game becomes money or art—with the girl as the prize. The marital sparring between Bardot and Piccoli is excruciating: John Cassavetes without the booze. The only thing interesting about this couple is her beauty and Godard's obsession with it. For the director, art is as hard as a library chair; female flesh offers a rare respite.

Godard's contempt for the producer's brand of checkbook filmmaking fuels the French film-maker's dogmatic attacks on easy targets. He goes so far as to have Lang liken Jerry's tactics to Nazism, equating dirty American movie money with Adolf Hitler's guns—Irving Thalberg as architect of the Holocaust.

Palance plays the manic producer as if he'd just walked off Mount Rushmore. His Yankee is larger than life, arrogant, predatory, confident. He says of his movie-in-the-making: "I like gods ... I know exactly how they feel."

That Palance, the son of Russian immigrants, can carry such hogwash underscores a perform-ance that belies Godard's chic anti-Americanism. The actor might not be able to articulate what he's doing, but his star power is as striking as the Capri backdrops.

Lang plays himself with an Old World courtliness that's beyond "Contempt." His haute, and well-earned, superiority echoes the irony of Erich von Stroheim in Billy Wilder's "Sunset Boule-vard." Like Palance, he finesses such Philosophy 101 whoppers as: Did God create man or man create his gods?

Godard can impress some by quoting Bazin: "Cinema substitutes a world that satisfies our desires." Cool!

While "Contempt" is more accessible than much of Godard's later work, and presents Palance and Lang in teasing, tasty roles, it doesn't satisfy my desires. It certainly doesn't leave me "Breathless."

NEWSDAY, 6/27/97, Part II/p. B8, John Anderson

Given this summer of exasperating, sneer-producing movies, what better moment for "Contempt"? Restored, refreshed and still raring to offend the cinema status quo, Jean-Luc Godard's 1963 masterpiece of discontent delivers a backhanded slap at Hollywood's view of the world, the Americanization of world cinema, the prostitution of European culture and the global triumph of style over substance. In 1963, it was a nouveau nightmare. Today? It's a documentary!

However and whenever one views/viewed it, "Contempt" remains a lament—for both cinema and love, Godard's two great themes, and for the sad fact that people always have their reasons (as Godard progenitor Jean Renoir might have put it). As blistering as it is about the all-too-human business end of art and the emphasis on technology over content (Godard's use of Cinemascope in this, his first big-budget movie, is hilarious), it's also a primer in Godardian film philosophy. Casting charter Sex-Kitten-Hall-of-Fame member Brigitte Bardot in a Godard movie is an attempt at esthetic paradox regardless of how one views Bardot's acting. (Which can't, in this context, be held to traditional standards). It also gives Godard the opportunity to make "BB" jokes.

"Contempt's" central characters are French writer Paul Javel (Michel Piccoli), his drop-dead-gorgeous wife, Camille (Bardot), and the American producer who wants to seduce them both (him figuratively, her literally), Hollywood über-boor Jerry Prokosch (Jack Palance). Jerry wants Paul to rewrite his production of "The Odyssey," which is being directed by the legendary German filmmaker Fritz Lang (played by ... Fritz Lang, Godard's icon/confederate). Lang is interested in filling the film with meditative shots of Greek sculpture; Jerry wants it filled with naked mermaids. He'd also like Paul to consider the plot possibility that Penelope was unfaithful while Odysseus was away. And to get out of the way while he tries to bed Camille.

Palance, despite apparent friction with Godard, plays Jerry with just enough irony to let us know that he knows that we know what's going on. Reportedly modeled after Joseph E. Levine (who with Carlo Ponti produced "Contempt"), Jerry is the ugliest of Americans. "I found this book of Roman paintings that I thought would help with 'The Odyssey,'" he says, revealing a respect for mythology equal only to Disney's. He carries a book of pithy axioms, which he delivers with great bravado. He can't speak French (occasionally, Godard allows Jerry and Paul to converse in different languages, despite the presence of the translator played by Giorgia Moll). More insulting to Jerry, however, is that this supposedly archetypal American can't drive: He constantly grinds out the gears on his Alfa Romeo, driving with too much gas and not enough brains (and subtley foreshadowing of the film's conclusion). Jerry's just too much, too often.

With its Homeric echoes and "Sunset Boulevard"-esque casting, "Contempt" is almost too ripe with metaphor to be contained, even in Cinemascope. From the narrated credits, which bestow a faux-gravity on the first frames of the picture, to the extended, marriage-dissolving sequence shot in Paul and Camille's underfurnished apartment—in which the camera moves in what can only be viewed as defiance of its widescreen format—"Contempt" is a comedy, wrapped in a tragedy.

After an introductory quote from critic Andre Bazin—"Cinema replaces the world with one that conforms to our own desires"—we get not surprisingly, a naked Bardot, face down on a bed, talking with Piccoli. It's a scene that was ordered up by Levine and Ponti after they saw Godard's cut and decided the film needed more BB. But Godard, shooting his actress through blue, white and red filters (for *liberté, egalité, fraternité?*) has her ask her husband, "Do you like my legs? ... Do you like my breasts?..." Cataloging herself while splayed across a wide screen, she's actually talking to the producers. And what we're actually watching is warfare, played out on film and fought with the modern weapons of words, images and money.

NEWSWEEK, 7/28/97, p. 69, David Ansen

The reissue of this 1963 Jean-Luc Godard film has proved to be the surprise hit on what used to be called the arthouse circuit. And it will remind you why art and movies were once discussed in the same breath. Brigitte Bardot, Michel Piccoli and Jack Palance star in a movie about (among other things) the making of a movie based on "The Odyssey," the dissolution of a marriage, the clash of classicism and modernism, Hollywood and Europe, the death of love and the beauty of B.B.'s butt. A British critic has called it "the greatest work of art produced in postwar Europe." Nonsense. It's not even Godard's best (I vote for "Pierrot le Fou"). It's merely wonderful: challenging, gorgeous, moving, bitterly funny and graced with a Georges Delerue score ravishing in its melancholy.

SIGHT AND SOUND, 9/96, p. 55, Colin MacCabe

Le Mépris opens in Rome's Cinecitta, made empty by the economic crisis of Italian (and European) cinema. An American producer, Jeremy Prokosch is trying to engage a young playwright, Paul Javel, to rewrite the scenario of the film of *The Odyssey* which Prokosch is currently shooting with the great German director Fritz Lang. Prokosch's *Odyssey* is no sword and sandal epic: he wants a modern psychological love story in which Penelope and Odysseus are estranged. Meanwhile, Fritz Lang is attempting to catch on film the classical art of Greece.

As the three male protagonists watch the rushes together with the translator, Francesca Vanini, it becomes clear that Prokosch has no time for Lang's untroubled classical serenity and that he is certain of his ability to buy Paul's talents. After the projection, Paul is met by his young and devoted wife Camille. Prokosch is immediately struck by Camille and offers her a ride in his Alfa Romeo. Camille is reluctant to accept this offer but Paul insists, saying that he will take a taxi. When he arrives late at the villa, Camille is furious with him but Paul is keen for her to honour Prokosch. He also makes a perfunctory pass at Francesca.

The action now moves to Paul and Camille's apartment, symbol both of their coupledom and the economic need which makes Prokosch's offer so attractive. For 30 minutes Paul talks with increasing desperation to Camille. Paul wishes to retrieve the situation which has been ruined by his complacent attitude towards Prokosch. At the same time he wishes to persuade Camille to accept Prokosch's offer to join him and the rest of the crew at Capri. The more he talks, however, the more the situation worsens. Finally Camille is goaded into admitting that she feels contempt for him.

The action moves to Capri. Paul and Lang discuss *The Odyssey* once more. Paul is now half persuaded of Prokosch's interpretation as he tries to read the problems of his own marriage into the relationship between Penelope and Odysseus. However, Lang remains unmoved in his commitment to a classical vision. Camille is now heading for Prokosch. Even Paul's refusal of Prokosch's offer and his determination to return to his first love, the theatre, fails to impress her. Camille tells Paul that she no longer loves him, that he is not a man. She leaves a note saying that she is leaving for Rome. On the way, the red Alfa Romeo crashes, killing both Camille and Prokosch. On Capri, Paul bids farewell to Lang who is about to make a shot of Odysseus regarding his homeland after his ten years' wandering. This shot, noisily prepared by Lang's assistant (played by Godard himself), closes the film.

In many ways *Le Mépris* is Jean-Luc Godard's most orthodox movie, with a best selling novel, a star cast, the largest budget he ever worked with, and a relatively developed narrative. But the film is also as cinematically adventurous as any other by Godard. The colours are primary: yellows, reds and blues which emphasise the stark contrast offered by the scenario. The central scene of the movie is a 30 minute dialogue of Beckettian impoverishment between the writer, Paul (Michel Piccoli) and his wife, Camille (Brigitte Bardot). And the film bears what is, and was even by 1963, Godard's trademark: all human relations are modelled onto the history and structure of film production.

Historically, *Le Mépris* bears witness to the swift disillusionment that the young *Cahiers du cinéma* critics-turned directors felt for Hollywood cinema. No sooner had they discovered the joys of Hawks and Ford, and the Monogram and Republic studios' films than the whole economic basis of the golden age of studio production collapsed. Hollywood shifted from being a Utopia six thousand miles away to a competitor muscling in on European cinema and a failed patron who would no longer employ the Rays, Fullers and Langs whom the Cahiers critics so adored.

Prokosch is a figure of unredeemed banality—his visions are predictable and clichéd, his relation to others a mixture of brute power and crude manipulation. But there is something about his vitality which makes him attractive and besides which Paul is doomed. Crucially this struggle between writer and producer becomes a struggle about the future of cinema.

What in Alberto Moravia's original novel had been a simple opposition between commerce and art is internationalised by Godard so that American producer confronts French writer. And Moravia's German director Rheingold is turned into Fritz Lang, who stands for a classical cinema suddenly rendered as distant as Homer.

Le Mépris thus consciously opposes a European classicism to an American modernity, as tellingly embodied by the apartment full of consumer durables as it is by Jerry Prokosch's boorishness. Nowhere is this boorishness so evident as in Prokosch's inability to speak any language other than his own. While the great Lang moves effortlessly from French to English to German with a passing nod at Italian, Prokosch depends on his translator for all communication. Where Fritz Lang quotes Hölderlin, Prokosch mouths inanities about poetry. The linguistic complexity of the film, which also involves making the translator into a significant character, gives *Le Mépris* some claim to be one of the few examples of a genuinely European film.

It would be quite wrong, however, to assume that *Le Mépris* simply rehearses a tired opposition between American money and European culture. The cinema renders all such oppositions dubious and as central to *Le Mépris* as Homer's *Odyssey* is the image of a woman. Never was Bardot better served by a director. The nudity demanded by the producers is rendered part of an experimental documentary about modern life. Her face is used for a series of portraits of heart-stopping beauty which punctuate the film. Bardot's beauty is the element which proves resistant to the comfortable male perspective of Fritz Lang and Paul Javel. For them B.B. is Bertolt Brecht and the complaint against the necessity to sell one's artistic talents to the highest bidder;

for the film B.B. is Brigitte Bardot and the extraordinary power of cinema to render physical beauty.

It is this power which now seems definitively placed in the hands of Americans who none the less are unaware of its true significance and whose representative, Jeremy, drives uncaringly towards the most modern of deaths: the car accident. As Godard has grown older, his pessimism has become more and more insistent. What *Le Mépris* reminds us is that this pessimism is constitutive to all his work and was there from the beginning: cinema is always an art which has already been betrayed. But then it becomes clear why Godard's note is so frequently elegiac. It is at the moment of death that the beauty of life is seized. As European cinema dies, victim to a global entertainment business which has also destroyed the secret artists of the studio system, Godard constructs a film which moves from Hölderlin to Bardot, which mixes modernity and classicism, which draws on four languages and which is constantly of a breathtaking visual beauty. This is the greatest work of art produced in postwar Europe.

VILLAGE VOICE, 7/1/97, p. 89, J. Hoberman

Jean-Luc Godard and the corporate entity formerly known as "Walt Disney" have done more than anyone else to chart the parameters of the post-cinema universe. It's natural, then, that when contemplating the origins of Western civilization, they would peer into the pre-Judeo-Christian mist of ancient Greece and see the pagan religion of ... movies.

Contempt, Godard's 1963 stab at a "commercial" feature, self-reflexively imagines *The Odyssey* as a similarly failed attempt to challenge the gods and make a film; *Hercules,* Disney's latest blockbuster, is no less self-referential in taking Greek mythology as a metaphor for marketing a star. *Contempt*—which after 30 years withdrawn from circulation, returns to the Ithaca of art-house distribution—is a mournful ode to Hollywood hegemony. *Hercules* opening at 'plexes throughout the universe on the same day, is nearly as damning in demonstrating that hegemony.

Equally allegorical, both movies feature caricatured Hollywood types as their villains. But while *Contempt* recalls a time when the now quaint term *sellout* was some sort of epithet, *Hercules* cheerfully obliterates the memory that said time ever existed.

As spectacles of antiquity, *Contempt,* and *Hercules* are idiosyncratic versions of the grandiose and tawdry sword-and-sandal genre the French call the *peplum* (a term derived from the Greek word for the flowing dress worn so fetchingly by Hercules's animated inamorata). Enjoying a golden age from the late '40s through the early 60s, the *peplum* was, in effect, Europe's last indigenous form of mass-audience movie. Indeed, both of *Contempt*'s producers were *peplum* meisters—Carlo Ponti produced the Kirk Douglas *Ulysses* and Joseph E. Levine made his fortune by importing the Steve Reeves *Hercules* to America.

Many *peplums* were international co-productions, filmed in Rome with French or British money and American actors. So, too, *Contempt*—an international co-pro, adapted (with surprising fidelity) from Alberto Moravia's bestseller, shot (at Cinecittá) in TechniColor and CinemaScope, and starring Jack Palance and Brigitte Bardot. Godard had become briefly bankable when the aging sex kitten let it be known she wanted this movie-crazed hipster to direct her next picture.

At once a movie of outrageous formalism (bold colors, abstract chunks of sound) and documentary verisimilitude (cast speaking an undubbed mixture of French, English, Italian, and German), *Contempt* is the story of a French writer (Michel Piccoli) who takes a job from an American producer (Palance) and, as a result, loses his wife (Bardot). The plot is distilled to anecdote in the sun-smacked Mediterranean light and further fractured by the struggling melancholy of Georges Delerue's musical theme, not to mention the inserts of Bardot skinny-dipping demanded by Godard's producers. At one point the movie is interrupted by the message that "Joe Levine is calling from New York." *Contempt* begins with a charged quote from Godard's mentor André Bazin—"Cinema replaces the world with one that conforms to our desires"—followed by a close-up of Brigitte Bardot's world-famous *derrière.*

Moravia's novel was translated as *A Ghost at Noon,* and Godard's movie has the quality of a daylight haunting; an empty studio is populated by a collection of movie apparitions. The tawny nexus of desire (and token of male exchange), Bardot is never other than a platonic image of herself—although she sometimes wears the wig that Godard's then muse Anna Karina wore in

Vivre sa vie. Piccoli, whose stingy-brim fedora, rolled up shirt sleeves, and loosened tie suggest a refugee from the set of *Some Came Running* (Godard wanted Sinatra), has been hired to rewrite the *peplum* Odyssey being shot by a philosophically world-weary Fritz Lang (who "actually plays himself," *The New York Times* noted with surprise).

Given to big pronouncements quoted from a tiny book of wisdom, producer Palance enters the deserted Cinecittà lot in a mood of fatuous melancholy: "Only yesterday there were kings here." Beloved by *Cahiers* for his portrayal of a star in revolt in *The Big Knife,* Palance plays the producer as if reprising his Attila the Hun in the Hollywood *peplum, Sign of the Pagan.* (His big, brutally energetic and self-important child is said to be modeled after Joe Levine, although the type may be immortal—it's no stretch to imagine him producing *Con Air* or running Miramax.)

Thanks to Lang's ill-starred production, the Olympians preside over the modern story. "I like gods, I know exactly how they feel," Palance declares in the midst of trashing the master's rushes. (A famous quotation from Louis Lumière is inscribed beneath the projection-room screen: "The cinema is an invention without a future.") Afterward, Palance coaxes an unwilling Bardot to ride in the red Alfa Romeo that serves as the story's deus ex machina. Later, back home and betoga'd in towels, Bardot and Piccoli pace and squabble through a half-furnished apartment—enacting the disintegration of their marriage in the stunning, half-hour tour de force that provides the movie with its centerpiece.

Godard called *Contempt* the "story of castaways of the western world, survivors of the shipwreck of modernity." Thirty-odd years later, it seems like an elegy for European art cinema, at once tragic and serene. If *Contempt* is a myth about the baleful effect of the movie god on the lives of two mortals, it is also the story of Godard's victory over a similar seduction. Lashed to the mast of irascible genius, he heard the song of the sirens and lived to tell the tale.

Also reviewed in:
CHICAGO TRIBUNE, 9/5/97, Friday/p. A, Michael Wilmington
NATION, 7/14/97, p. 36, Stuart Klawans
NEW YORK TIMES, 12/19/64, p. 25, Bosley Crowther
NEW YORKER, 7/7/98, p. 78, Anthony Lane
WASHINGTON POST, 7/25/97, p. D6, Stephen Hunter
WASHINGTON POST, 7/25/97, Weekend/p. 49, Desson Howe

COP LAND

A Miramax Films release of a Woods Entertainment production. *Executive Producer:* Bob Weinstein, Harvey Weinstein, and Meryl Poster. *Producer:* Cary Woods and Cathy Konrad. *Director:* James Mangold. *Screenplay:* James Mangold. *Director of Photography:* Eric Edwards. *Editor:* Craig McKay. *Music:* Howard Shore. *Music Editor:* David Cabonara. *Sound:* Allan Byer and (music) John Kurlander. *Sound Editor:* Phil Stockton. *Casting:* Todd M. Thaler. *Production Designer:* Lester Cohen. *Art Director:* Wing Lee. *Set Decorator:* Karin Wiesel. *Set Dresser:* David Gagnon, Mike Leather, Alan Muzeni, and Jeff Rollins. *Special Effects:* Wilfred Caban. *Costumes:* Ellen Lutter. *Make-up:* Lori Hicks. *Make-up (Sylveste Stallone):* Scott Eddo. *Make-up (Ray Liotta):* Judy Lovell. *Make-up (Robert De Niro):* Ilona Herman. *Stunt Coordinator:* Jery Hewitt. *Running time:* 105 minutes. *MPAA Rating:* R.

CAST: Sylvester Stallone (Freddy Heflin); Harvey Keitel (Ray Donlan); Ray Liotta (Gary Figgis); Robert De Niro (Moe Tilden); Peter Berg (Joey Randone); Janeane Garofalo (Deputy Cindy Betts); Robert Patrick (Jack Rucker); Michael Rapaport (Murray Babitch); Annabella Sciorra (Liz Randone); Noah Emmerich (Deputy Bill Geisler); Cathy Moriarty (Rose Donlan); John Spencer (Leo Crasky); Frank Vincent (PDA President Lassaro); Malik Yoba (Detective Carson); Arthur J. Nascarella (Frank Lagonda); Edie Falco (Berta); Victor L. Williams (Russell); Paul Calderon (Hector, Medic); John Doman (Lassaro's Aide); Deborah Harry

(Delores); Vincent Laresca (Medic #2); Oliver Solomon (Black Man); Terri Towns (Black Woman); David Butler (Thin Cop); Brad Beyer (Young Cop); Charles Dumas (TV Cyril Johns); John Johnson (News Anchor); Frank Pellegrino (Mayor); Robert John Burke (Officer B); John Ventimiglia (Officer V); Terry Serpico (Tony, Wincing Cop); Method Man (Shondel); Sean Cullen (Other Cop); Paul Herman (Game Operator); Mel Gorham (Monica); Graciela Lecube (Spanish Woman); Chris Conte (Gordon); Anthony Citro (Young Freddy); Alexandra Adi (Young Liz); Mark Cassella (Fireman); Timothy Stickney (Window Yeller); William Kalaidjian (Police Chaplain); Sean Runnette (IA Detective #1); Michael Gaston (IA Detective #2 (Rubin)); Ben Ellerin (Little Kid with Gordon); David Diaz (Funeral Reporter); Tracy O. Emory (Video Camera Operator, News Segment); Robert Castle (Chaplain at Joey's Funeral); Bruce Altman (Counselor Burt Kandel); Carly Fordham (Liz's Daughter); Tony Giorgio (Ceremonial Officer); Kevin O'Sullivan (Head Pall Bearer/Flag Holder); Louis D'Alto (Exiting Cop); Sylvia Khan (Deli Lady); Ronn Munro (Chief of Police); John Henry (Officer in Alleyway); Richard Lisi (Officer in Alleyway "Charlie"); Hans Moody (Sergeant in Alleyway); Garry Pastore (Core Cop "Johnny B"); Tony Sirico (Toy Torillo); Peter Wise (Plaza Cop #1); P.J. Brown (Plaza Cop #2); Manuel Corrado (Plaza Cop #3); Jeffrey Kaufman (Plaza Cop #4); Europe Harmon (Plaza Cop #5); Rene Ojeda (Plaza Cop #6).

CHRISTIAN SCIENCE MONITOR , 8/15/97 p. 12, David Sterritt

Miramax Films is promoting "Cop Land" as a breakthrough movie, and in some ways it is. It's a breakthrough for writer-director James Mangold, who earned deserved respect for his small-scale drama "Heavy" a year ago and now emerges as a major talent in the mass-market melodrama field.

And it's a breakthrough for independent film in general, since it's almost unprecedented for so much top-of-the-line star power—Sylvester Stallone, Robert De Niro, Harvey Keitel, Ray Liotta—to appear in a single picture with such a modest budget and low-key style.

Not that "Cop Land" tells a gentle story. The setting is a New Jersey town across the river from Manhattan, populated largely by New York cops who've moved to the suburbs so their kids can grow up away from big-city chaos and confusion.

Stallone plays the local sheriff, a lonely man whose career was stalled years earlier by an injury. He spends his time flagging down speeders, remembering the past especially his one moment of glory, the heroic rescue that left him with damaged health—and envying the "real cops" who live all around him.

His illusions about them are shaken when an internal-affairs investigator comes to town, probing a scandal that may involve several of the officers he sees every day. Gradually he realizes that their loyalty and solidarity are masks for conspiracy and corruption; slowly he sees that his friendships and duties are on a collision course.

Tales about dishonest lawmen and codes of silence are familiar stuff, but Mangold makes "Cop Land" fresh by caring more about the characters—especially the sheriff, a strikingly real and sympathetic figure—than the increasingly nasty skulduggery around them.

The dialogue is crisp and realistic. Liotta does his sharpest work since "GoodFellas," and there are moments when De Niro and Keitel almost recapture the electricity of their indelible "Taxi Driver" portrayals. It's a special pleasure to see Stallone doing solid work in a solid movie for a change. Has he grown out of his action-movie phase at last?

"Cop Land" would be even stronger if it built to a more meaningful climax—its final shootout is a letdown after such an absorbing story—and if Mangold had avoided a few trite devices, like an almost-love-affair between two characters and the year's umpteenth scene in a topless-dancing joint.

Back on the positive side, some of the movie's most awful violence is suggested rather than shown, and the screenplay makes intelligent points about the good and bad aspects of suburban communities. Of particular interest is its recognition that people drenched in "family values" rhetoric sometimes use this as a deluded justification for selfish and even destructive behavior toward those outside the domestic circle.

In all, "Cop Land" is easily the year's best-acted movie, and one of the smartest, too.

LOS ANGELES TIMES, 8/15/97, Calendar/p. 14, Kenneth Turan

"Stallone Acts!" may not resonate the way "Garbo Talks!" did once upon a time, but it's the main attraction of "Cop Land," an independently produced police drama whose entire budget is close to Sly's usual salary for the brawny epics that are his specialty.

Determined to return to his "Rocky/Lords of Flatbush" roots and a less exclusively physical style of acting, Stallone not only took a considerable pay cut here, he also gained so much weight (a reported 39 pounds) for the part that a shot of him looking especially paunchy had to be cut after it pulled preview audiences right out of the picture.

Written and directed by James Mangold, who debuted with the Sundance hit "Heavy," "Cop Land" also takes the precaution of surrounding Stallone with Harvey Keitel, Ray Liotta, Robert De Niro, Peter Berg and Michael Rapaport, a coterie of actors who have been down this particular road before.

The result is familiar territory, one of those hard-case movies where the guys talk tough and the women are long-suffering. Like Stallone's much-anticipated performance, "Cop Land" is involving in individual moments but not compelling as a whole. Always watchable, it ends up promising more than it can deliver, an independent film that can't camouflage its too-schematic Hollywood soul.

Cop Land is not a state of mind, it's a place, a town called Garrison, N.J., that's just over the George Washington Bridge from Manhattan. It's an enclave inhabited almost exclusively by New York cops and their families, guys who took advantage of a loophole to flee the city's criminal element and get a little fresh air in the bargain.

Not just anyone can be the law in a town full of lawmen; the job apparently calls for an ineffectual dupe washed up before his time, someone for whom pride and ambition are just a memory. Ray Donlan (Keitel), the man to see in Cop Land, knows he's found the perfect candidate in Sheriff Freddy Heflin (Stallone).

An NYPD wannabe whose bad ear, damaged in an underwater rescue years before, has kept him off the force, Heflin is a wistful lost soul with a big gut and a sad sack attitude, the kind of guy who spends his days returning lost stuffed animals to their owners and his nights dozing off to Springsteen melodies.

Most of the cops in Garrison barely notice the sheriff, and some, like Joey Randone (Berg), who married Liz (Annabella Sciorra), the woman whom Heflin rescued and still loves, hold him in contempt. Only the troubled Gary Figgis (Liotta), prone to sticking darts up people's noses when he gets upset, tolerates the big lug and thinks he's worth treating decently.

Heflin's lethargic existence gets shaken up after an incident on the George Washington Bridge. Murray "Superboy" Babitch (Rapaport), a cop who is Ray Donlan's nephew, gets into an altercation so serious that the young man has to be made to disappear. No one's supposed to know where Superboy is, but a quirk of fate reveals that information to the sheriff.

Complicating things even more is the appearance in Garrison of Moe Tilden (De Niro), a determined investigator from the NYPD's Internal Affairs section. He's suspicious of Babitch's disappearance and focuses on the sheriff as the weak link in the wall of silence. "I see a man waiting for something to do," Tilden tells Heflin, but the sheriff, a Sampson with his hair still shorn, turns him down. For now.

When as public an actor as Sylvester Stallone takes a new career turn, it's tempting to talk about it in extremes, to flatly say he shouldn't have bothered or to instruct Daniel Day-Lewis to look to his laurels. In this case, however, neither position is accurate.

Well-cast and looking especially woebegone with a bandage on his nose for most of the picture, Stallone gives a solid, capable performance as the flabby sheriff, but it's rather on the one-note side and lacks the charisma of his best roles. He has no trouble holding his own with his co-stars, but seems a bit rusty, and he doesn't bring as much to the table as he might.

As to those other actors, they've done this kind of work so often it's to Mangold's credit that things don't become completely routine. As a director, he shows his people to their best advantage and is especially good at heightening individual moments, like the scene in which De Niro's Tilden says he's visiting all-police Garrison because "I heard it was a way of life," and Keitel's Donlan snaps back, "What are we, the Amish now?"

But if the film's many sharp scenes make a fine attractions reel, they do not come together in a satisfying way. "Cop Land's" script has so many contrivances, coincidences, dark secrets and last-minute changes of heart that its plot starts to resemble the standard Hollywood nonsense its star is nominally trying to flee. While Stallone's return to simpler fare is successful enough to have been worth doing and worth repeating, it would be wishful thinking to call it or the film it inhabits unqualified successes.

FILM QUARTERLY, Summer 1998, p. 28, James Morrison

In his past roles, Sylvester Stallone's hang-dog countenance, sleepy with mournful aggression, has concealed explosive, righteous rage. In James Mangold's *Cop Land*, it reveals entrenched and stubborn melancholy. Despite a climactic shoot-out with cool overtones of *Taxi Driver*, the explosion never really comes. Stallone's face—its droopy, baleful gaze, downturned lips, nascent jowls—bears the imprint of this movie's distinctive sensibility as surely as Pruitt Taylor Vince's pasty, moist-eyed face did that of Mangold's previous film, *Heavy* and Stallone's performance as Freddy Heflin, the small-town sheriff who wanted to be a big-city cop, is the film's unlikely set-piece, to be admired, like so much in the film itself, for everything it does *not* do.

On the strength of *Heavy* and his new film, Mangold appears to be striving to forge an authentically ascetic style within the decidedly inhospitable climate of contemporary Hollywood. His decision to follow the anomalously quiet *Heavy* with a police-procedural that appears at least superficially to be in the up-to-the-minute blockbuster mode feels a bit like an exercise, an experiment in spiritual temptation-and-resistance, and the news here is that Mangold has *not* sold out, as so many young filmmakers do after a first independent hit. Once the conventions of the genre have been set in place, Mangold goes on to work against every one of them in a manner that might feel systematic if that impulse too had not been rejected as too worldly. In fact, although the film carefully chronicles the textures of its characters' lives, it does so almost entirely in their moments of repose. The inertia of the film's action sequences feels calculated, the sign of the movie's tone of detached curiosity—sometimes tender, sometimes doleful. Although the movie carries the force of subdued conviction, it's difficult at first to locate that conviction, because the film has little interest in exploring the usual subjects or provoking the ordinary audience responses typical of the police-procedural genre. It's a cop movie steeped in stillness.

The film's dramatic situation is rooted in a casually audacious fiction. A tightly knit group of cops migrates from New York City to a burg across the river: Garrison, New Jersey—"population 1280," a road sign informs us in an offhanded and uncharacteristically sly nod to the title of a Jim Thompson thriller about a criminal sheriff, filmed by Bertrand Tavernier *as Coup de Torchon,* a film which in its dour, quiet style is an important forerunner of *Cop Land.* In Garrison, the cops stake out territory to live apart from the depredations of the city while continuing collectively to manipulate networks of corruption from a safe distance, running drugs for the mob. A title informs us at the end of the film, if we weren't aware of it already, of the fictive status of this central conceit. In fact, New York police officers are required to live within the city limits. This is no small point, for it reveals the insularity of the film's vision of the contemporary American sociocultural landscape.

A pivotal plot event is an instance of racial violence at the beginning of the film. An unseasoned, hot-headed cop known as Superboy shoots two black men in a highway skirmish, then feigns suicide with the aid of his cronies to escape investigation, fleeing back to Garrison. But the movie's interest in the causes or effects of racial violence is so limited that a few scenes that would be crucial in a more conventional piece are rendered almost completely opaque in this film. For example, we get a glimpse of a black spokesperson decrying the media emphasis on the cop's suicide over the deaths of these "black children," and the comically inappropriate designation of the murdered punks is presented in feyly broad, sourly satirical terms. The moment seems here less indicative, however, of the paradoxically hysterical intellectual complacency of DePalma's film than it does of a sort of committed indifference to the sociology of current realities in Mangold's film. The film is not oblivious of racial politics, but its account of the genesis of corruption does not reside in the standard versions of urban anomie. The vision of the city in *Cop Land* is largely free of the fulminating, Scorsesean moral horror or the virulent Schraderesque disgust one finds in a film like *Taxi Driver,* in part because Mangold is interested in the image of the metropolis only insofar as it sets into relief the meditation on private consciousness and small-town torpor that are the film's true concerns. In *Cop Land,* New York isn't a circle-of-hell or a pervasive state-of-being, the oppressive projection of a dankly morbid consciousness, but just a place you look at from across the river; and if the city is thus deprived of the internal aspect it is routinely granted in such films, it is also thereby denied the geeky mythic grandeur or the lame-brained romance so typical of lesser manifestations of the genre—*Night Falls on Manhattan*, say, or the remake of *Kiss of Death.*

A quality of obliquity in the narrative's construction defuses any real sense of urgency in the film's cop-movie theatrics. (The one later scene involving careening police cars and frenzied officers running in all directions feels totally obligatory and, by that point in the film, decidedly out of place.) During an early scene of exposition, Heflin glances out the precinct window and sees a mother drive away with her kid's toy, a stuffed green turtle, on the roof of her van. This collateral set-up pays off later, but it functions at the time as a mark of the eccentricity of the movie's construction, its abiding concern with sidewise detail. Again and again Mangold displaces the drama of a given scene with such seemingly peripheral observation, or neutralizes volatility by angling a scene through the perspective of a calm or marginal observer—usually the doggedly passive Heflin. The distancing effect of such strategies enables a double focus on the cop-movie material, potentially satisfying the viewer who wants that but also allowing the gradual emergence of the movie's real subjects in the margins.

With like obliquity, Mangold's previous film told the story of an overweight restaurant owner (Pruitt Taylor Vince) in love with a beautiful waitress (Liv Tyler). Recognizing the hopelessness of this desire, he doesn't even try to articulate it to anyone, and as a result his inner life grows so remote even to himself that when his mother dies he doesn't tell anyone about that either. It's a film with a deep reserve of feeling for the unspoken and a hushed, evanescent atmosphere of delicacy—you watch it breathlessly, the way you'd watch a lovely, tiny bird that might take flight at the slightest movement. It's filled with Ozu-like cutaway-shots to transfixing sky-scapes or inserted nonnarrative tableaux with a formalized, still-life quality, and the fragility of the film's texture derives from the balance between such techniques and a methodical observation of the operations of diurnal ritual in characters' lives.

As *Heavy* demonstrated, Mangold's keenest feelings as a director appear to be for the textures and the rhythms of small-town life, and the conceit of *Cop Land* allows Mangold to play those textures and rhythms against the more conventional materials of the police-procedural action-adventure film. In its treatment of these themes, the earlier movie concerns the relation between states of transfixedness and states of fixation. The promise of spiritual escape in *Heavy* is predicated on an arrested emotional condition—and the film is interested in both the promise and the condition—that makes escape finally impossible. The movie's main characters are constantly discovered in day-dreamy postures of concentration—mooning at the sky, or looking at photos of one another—which are nearly indistinguishable from their moments of distraction, as they gape at TV screens or swap banal small talk. In the middle of the night, they park at an airport and watch planes take off, and in an inspired lyric gesture, Mangold refuses to show the planes (except in the film's first and last shots, where we see distant planes in vacant skies with no clear observer), showing in these moments only the reflections of their lights on the car windows or playing on the awe-stricken, upturned faces, stunned with pleasure, of the watchers whose hopeless aerial aspirations are stoked by the dazzlement of what they see and we do not. Through such poetic counterpoint, the scenes manage simultaneously to convey wonder and lack. The restaurant owner fantasizes saving the waitress from drowning, and the fantasy soon takes on the aura of a familiar hallucination. With its pensive gravity, the movie carefully shows how what is obsessive shades over into what is quotidian.

Cop Land has a different feeling, but it's surprisingly not as different as one might expect, and it shares a number of concerns with the earlier film while presenting them in a more literalized, plot-bound form. The movie deals with secret maneuvers and covert operations, but unlike more standard cop movies, it provides next to no exposition for the viewer, letting the secrets emerge by implication rather than explication. Even when all the characters are in on something—the plot to hide Superboy, the assorted entanglements and adulteries of the cops and their wives—the viewer is often left out, left to fit the pieces together through accumulation. The film's closest connection to *Heavy* is through Stallone's character, Heflin. Prevented from being a New York cop by deafness in one ear sustained in his youth during the heroic rescue of a drowning woman, Heflin lumbers through the daily routines of small-town sheriff-hood with a blank, amiable obliviousness, stopping repeatedly to gaze across the river at the city with the same kind of distracted concentration with which the characters in *Heavy* inhabit their lives. Constantly shadowed by the looming cityscape, the town of Garrison becomes an archetypal image of unfulfilled aspiration. Simply by bringing them together, *Cop Land* exposes the dual (and competing) myths of small-town America as at once the stronghold of clean living and pure values and the repository of crushed hopes and abandoned dreams, the haven of those who couldn't cut it in the big time.

The emotional textures of delusion, self-aggrandizement, and failed aspiration are the film's real interest, and just about every star performance in the film surprises us by revealing some new aspect of these textures. Having assembled such a constellation—Stallone, Robert DeNiro, Harvey Keitel, Ray Liotta—Mangold arranges the stars into a genuine ensemble instead of an aggregate of disconnected star turns. He doesn't do this by asking them to play against type. In some ways, indeed, the performances of the most familiar actors here play like mildly restrained pastiches of their previous roles. Keitel brings to his part the self-important, slightly philistine leisure-suited smoothness of his recent gangster roles with a submerged self-hatred which has associations that go back to his performance in *Fingers* (1978). Ray Liotta, meanwhile, incorporates his trademark coiled, desperate anger with an impatient humaneness. DeNiro as an Internal Affairs officer draws on something of the righteous moral solemnity that has cropped up in some of his recent performances, like the one in *Sleepers,* but he gives it a spin with residual echoes of, say, his Rupert Pupkin from *The King of Comedy*, sporting a 70s haircut, polyester blazers, and a shaggy mustache, and giving a sing-songy derision to some of his intonations, as when he tells Stallone, "You bleeeew it!"

It may be simply our familiarity with these actors in Scorsese movies that enables them to gel here, but the self-referential quality of the acting allows the incorporation of others into the ensemble so that even Stallone, who is in some ways cast against type, appears to be not so much departing radically from his usual persona as he is returning to some of the attitudes of his mid-1970s film performances. There is a kind of consistency in this ensemble that comes in part from the mosaic quality of the movie's structure, setting lots of subplots in motion but not granting real primacy or giving sustained attention to any subplot at any one time. In larger part, though, this consistency comes from the decision to make Stallone the mutable center of the ensemble. The result is that, because we see the other performances continually as they play off Stallone's less expressive performance, their performances are toned down by Stallone's function as a foil, and all the actors seem to be doing the same thing, geared toward the same end.

Stallone's performance can't exactly be called restrained, though its rhetoric is that of understatement, because you don't really feel there's anything that would be coming through if it were not being held back. It's a little like watching some of Marilyn Monroe's performances, especially the later ones, in *Some Like It Hot* or *The Misfits*, where Monroe's palpable effort to remember what she had been told to do in front of the camera translated into an ineffable, clumsily ethereal vulnerability. Stallone is capable of achieving nuances in the role: the way his voice breaks in a scene with Annabella Sciorra playing the woman he has saved, for instance, or the paltry bravado he musters when he tells a group of schoolkids to move along "before I kick your ass." But the poignance of the performance clearly comes less from the performance itself than from the way the director uses it; some of the effects Mangold gets this way could almost be called Bressonian, and the irrevocably alienated quality of the final siege links it as surely to *L'Argent* as to *Taxi Driver*.

When Heflin realizes Superboy is still alive and decides to bring him in, the movie might have turned up the emotional thermostat, taken an urgent turn toward the thematics of redemption, as in Scorsese. But Mangold uses Stallone's performance to insure that the film remains focused instead on the lassitude of inevitable failure. Stallone walks through the final shootout like the Terminator, and the showdown itself is robotic and without volition, like something out of Fritz Lang. Despite the film's overriding concern with interiority, it has little concern with the dynamics of epiphanic insight, and its end brings no redemption. The explanatory aftermath provided by DeNiro's voice-over is notably perfunctory, and the last sequence shows Heflin still gazing across the river with what can by this time no longer be called yearning. Stallone's performance is a remarkable found object, beautifully used: it is not only *about* absence but, in crucial ways, it *enacts* that condition, illustrates it, making the film's meditation on oblivion all the more piercing. The blankness of Stallone's final look, itself evanescent, not lingered over, feels emotionally wrenching only in memory, after the film is over. It is then that you realize the film has been about not the sadness of unfulfilled desire, but about the sorrow of desire that persists after its origin is lost, when it no longer matters whether the object of desire—the ubiquitous city across the river, or the woman the empty-faced man might once have loved—vanishes or remains.

NEW YORK, 8/25/97, p. 147, David Denby

Many of our movies, pitched for the overseas audience, have been simplified to death, their dialogue pared down, their local detail drained away. *Cop Land*, a New York-area movie written and directed by the young filmmaker James Mangold and starring Sylvester Stallone, Harvey Keitel, Robert De Niro, and Ray Liotta, suffers from an unusual fault. *Cop Land* is actually too complicated. There's too much going on in it, too much "back story"—the secondary plotting and bits of detail and personal history that give a movie texture. The cops in question, all from the same New York City precinct, have grown disgusted with the violence and mess of the city. Led by Harvey Keitel's baleful Ray Donlan—a tough little mother with an annihilating tongue—they consider themselves victims, the good soldiers who get no respect. (One of the things that's blurry about the movie: It seems to be set in the present, yet the attitudes come out of the seventies.) At night, the men cross the George Washington Bridge to Jersey, where they live with their families in a tiny paradise "Garrison" (a fictional name), a town at the edge of the Hudson that has splendid views of the Upper West Side and offers shelter and quiet.

A young cop who is part of this group, Babitch (Michael Rapaport), gets into trouble on the bridge, killing two black teenagers after a misunderstanding; his older police friends instantly arrange his disappearance, pretending that he's jumped into the Hudson, then hiding him in Garrison. The cops are so brazen that they allow Babitch to expose himself to the gaze of Garrison's sheriff, Freddy Heflin (Sylvester Stallone)—Freddy the nice guy who doesn't know the score, the local hero who lost part of his hearing saving a girl from drowning and can't get on the New York force. Freddy is not going to turn Babitch in; he's too passive, too dumb.

All of this, and more, is presented in jagged fragments—highly suggestive scenes cut off in the middle. By degrees, Mangold lets us know that the New York cops have entered into cozy relations with the mob, who repay the police by making life easy in Garrison. Mangold has something serious in mind—the way cops whose jobs are tough, and who run into trouble with parts of the community, think of themselves as victims and seize on their difficulties to justify corruption. But Mangold buries the issue in a welter of past events alluded to but not dramatized, and what's actually before us—such as a scene in which the cops try to kill Babitch when he threatens to spill the beans—is so ineptly managed, we can't tell what's going on. Mangold scatters his attention; he wants to do everything, and he doesn't seem to know what's important in his picture and what isn't.

Characters jump forward as if they are about to take over the movie, only to recede immediately into the buzzing but useless background. Robert De Niro, for instance, shows up as a former cop buddy of Keitel's who has gone over to Internal Affairs and now investigates police corruption. Mangold has spoken of seeing, as a boy, Keitel's and De Niro's names on a theater marquee for *Taxi Driver* and of his longing to bring them together again. Early in the movie, De Niro and Keitel face each other with bristling mock politeness. Nodding and smirking, they get a rhythm going together, and the audience sighs in appreciation. But the scene quickly ends, and there's no payoff to the tensions built up. De Niro tries to goad Stallone's Freddy into pursuing the bad guys, and he then retires into a corner of the movie.

Janeane Garofalo, of all people, is part of Freddy's police force in Garrison, and after playing a tiny role in the story, she grandly announces that she's leaving town. What's going on here? There are two tormented young men wandering around the Garrison bush and coming out of the night—not just Rapaport's Babitch, whose behavior we never understand, but also a cop played by Ray Liotta, who is part of Keitel's group but feels betrayed and shut out. Liotta, always an intense actor, makes the most of his scenes, but he can't fight his way into the center of the movie. That place, I'm afraid, is left to Stallone, who has gallantly added pounds of flab to play Freddy. The role is Stallone's attempt, after a long debauch in terrible action movies, to give a quiet, realistic performance, and it would be nice to say that it succeeds, but Stallone doesn't have the focus to suggest the stirrings of intelligence and revolt in a somnolent man. His face as well as his body is flaccid. He hardly seems a star at all. The performance goes nowhere for a long time and then lurches forward into rage. Freddy redeems himself—the most movieish, least interesting thing in *Cop Land*. All of a sudden, Mangold abandons his idiosyncratic setting and theme and turns his hero into the lone sheriff in an old Western. The picture comes to a climax in a slow-mo shootout that is one of the saddest admissions of defeat in years.

NEW YORK POST, 8/15/97, p. 35, Michael Medved

In "Cop Land," Sylvester Stallone's physical transformation signifies his serious acting intentions as the erstwhile superhero gets back on the "Rocky" road as a lovable underdog.

Extra poundage provides a comfortable paunch for this "heavy" role (from the acclaimed writer-director of last year's "Heavy"), and Sly's old athletic swagger has given way to a slow, bear-like roll. His wounded character is supposed to be deaf in one ear, and his sad, puppy-dog eyes go moist at the slightest provocation.

Stallone handles this collection of quirks with conviction and intensity, reminding the world what a fine character actor he can be. Unfortunately, the movie built around this admirable performance is an overwrought, melodramatic dud.

The plot centers on the faked suicide of decorated New York cop Michael Rapaport after an embarrassing shooting incident; his uncle (Harvey Keitel) is an influential veteran officer who wants to avoid a damaging investigation.

Keitel is protecting a vast web of corruption and deceit involving virtually all his fellow residents of a New Jersey town known as "Cop Land"—a gritty, suburban refuge for hard-working officers, just across the river from the big, bad city. Ray Liotta plays an embittered former member of Keitel's "inner circle" and Peter Berg is a handsome hothead involved in a messy affair with Keitel's slatternly wife, Cathy Moriarty, while abusing his own woman, Annabella Sciorra.

Robert De Niro, with a chip on his shoulder and a bad toupee on his head, plays an obnoxious Internal Affairs officer who's determined to expose all the crooked creeps of Cop Land.

The key to his investigation is Stallone, the slow-witted, big-hearted sheriff of the police-infested village. He admires all the New York officers in his town, and might have joined them on the force except for his bad ear which he injured while rescuing Sciorra from a car crash years before.

Like many young filmmakers, 33-year-old James Mangold bases his work on old movies instead of observed reality, but at least he's got the good sense to imitate Martin Scorsese directly rather than worshiping at the altar of Quentin Tarantino.

In fact, Mangold is such a shameless wannabe that he fills four crucial roles with, actors indelibly associated with Scorsese: De Niro, Keitel, Moriarty and Liotta.

These gifted veterans could handle such hackneyed parts while sound asleep, and "Cop Land" displays none of the moral or emotional complexity of "Mean Streets"—or, for that matter, of "High Noon," which it also ham-handedly evokes. Here, Keitel and his cronies are one-dimensionally wicked, with no hint of charismatic qualities—such as fierce loyalty to brother cops or devotion to wife and kids—that might have made them watchable villains.

Mangold mangles a considerable opportunity in his odd determination to turn New York's Finest into New York's Foulest. In contrast to vastly superior films about cop corruption (like Sidney Lumet's recent, unjustly ignored "Night Falls on Manhattan"), his single-minded hostility leads to a host of implausible, unauthentic details and ultimately self-destructs in an orgy of show-offy indulgence.

NEWSDAY, 8/15/97, Part II/p. B3, Jack Mathews

In James Mangold's urban western "Cop Land," Sylvester Stallone plays a pathetic, heavy-drinking, hard-of-hearing sheriff compelled by his conscience to rise up against his New Jersey town's enclave of rogue New York City cops. For the part, Stallone quit working out and ate pancakes until his waist size reached 39 inches.

This was no small sacrifice for the hourglass ego whose body once reigned as the god of international action films. And Stallone has gamely acknowledged he did all this, plus working for scale, plus risking personal embarrassment in the stellar company of costars Robert De Niro, Harvey Keitel and Ray Liotta, in order to give his waning career a dramatic kick in the pants.

In effect, Stallone cast himself as Hollywood's Rocky Balboa, a pug actor climbing into the ring with New York's De Niro, whom he refers to as "America's greatest living actor," figuring that anything short of his own knockout would be a moral victory.

On that score, Stallone succeeds. He's perfectly fine as Sheriff Freddy Heflin, and is still on his feet at the end. At the same time, we are so aware of the restraint he's showing that his performance begins to feel like a stunt. Look what Sly's doing! And that restraint becomes more apparent as we begin to realize that "Cop Land," in the end, doesn't really add up to much.

Mangold, whose one previous film, "Heavy," was a sensitive, plodding character study of a socially withdrawn pizza chef, shows a coolly deft hand at the kind of street theatrics we expect from Martin Scorsese films. And he fashioned some terrifically showy scenes for De Niro, as the internal affairs investigator prodding Sheriff Freddy, Keitel, the baddest of the bad cops living in Garrison, and Liotta, the tormented, coke-sniffing cop who eventually becomes Freddy's ally.

The impressively large cast also includes Annabella Sciorra, as a cop's abused wife and Freddy's fever dream; Cathy Moriarty, as the town vamp; Janeane Garafalo, as Freddy's brooding deputy, and Michael Rapaport, the impetuous young cop whose killing of two unarmed black youths starts a chain reaction that spans the George Washington Bridge.

Mangold's script is inspired by the loathing that many New York cops project for the people they're supposed to protect, and by their dejection at being taken more for villains than heroes in those communities. They're outcasts, so they become outlaws, moving to the frontier—or at least the other side of the Hudson—to create their own utopian outpost.

Garrison is a crime-free paradise for the cops and their families, crime-free because they grant themselves open immunity from the law, while discouraging outsiders from dropping in. Freddy, whose lifelong dream of joining the NYPD ended when he lost half his hearing during a river rescue, is a toothless rent-a-cop for the townfolk he envies. His job entails ticketing the occasional out-of-town speeder, mediating family disputes and turning his deaf ear to criminal plotting.

That last challenge gets harder and harder with De Niro's Moe Tilden pushing him to behave like a real cop, and with Freddy's realization that his idol, Keitel's Ray Donlan, has had his own friends killed to protect Garrison's sovereignty, and is about to do it again.

On the surface, "Cop Land" has no glaring deficiencies. It's nicely shot, by Eric Edwards, Mangold's dialogue is sharp, and his direction sure-handed, and the performances—especially from the Scorsese troupe—are all solid. But in fusing two genres—the urban cop drama to the western—and filling the pivotal role with a slumming action star, Mangold has created a nice charade and not much more.

NEWSWEEK, 8/25/97, p. 73, Jack Kroll

[*Cop Land* was reviewed jointly with *G.I. Jane*; see Kroll's review of that film.]

SIGHT AND SOUND, 12/97, p. 41, Geoffrey Macnab

Police officer Murray Babitch is on his way home to Garrison, New Jersey, after a night out in New York. Two joyriders almost force him off the road as he crosses the George Washington Bridge and aim what appears to be a gun at him. He reacts by firing his own gun at them and accidentally drives into their car, killing them both. The cops swarm to the scene of the accident. Senior policeman Ray Donlan, Babitch's uncle, quickly realises that the joyriders were in fact pointing a steering wheel lock, not a gun, at Babitch. Donlan and his colleagues plant a gun in the car.

Claiming that Babitch committed suicide by jumping off the bridge, they spirit him back to Garrison where many of New York's cops live.

Freddy Heflin, Garrison's local sheriff, always dreamed of working for the NYPD. But after losing the hearing in one ear while rescuing a girl from drowning, he had to accept that he would never make the force. None of Garrison's cops has any respect for Freddy's authority. His only ally is undercover cop Gary Figgis, a loner who knows how corrupt Garrison really is. Freddy is secretly in love with Liz Randone, the girl he saved from drowning years ago, who's now married to a cop. Internal Affairs officer Moe Tilden suspects a cover-up in the Babitch case and investigates, but Freddy refuses to cooperate. Donlan decides he no longer needs the hiding Babitch alive, so he and his associates try to drown him, but Babitch escapes. Freddy takes a stand against Donlan and the corrupt cops and brings in Babitch. Figgis leaves town with the money from an insurance scam, but is drawn back by his loyalty to Freddy. In a shootout, Freddy and Figgis kill Donlan and his henchmen. Freddy delivers Babitch to Moe Tilden's New York office.

Writer-director James Mangold's script for *CopLand* (his second feature after *Heavy*) may be a contemporary police thriller, but many of its ideas and motifs are drawn from the Western. Its protagonist, a small-town sheriff looking for redemption, is reminiscent of Gary Cooper in *High Noon* and of countless other flawed Western heroes who only prove their mettle in the final reel. This time, he's neither an alcoholic nor a coward. It's his deafness which hampers him.

There is an element of cruelty about the casting. Sylvester Stallone, effective in punch-drunk boxer and muscular action-hero parts but hardly one of the great Method actors of his generation, is put up against Robert De Niro and Harvey Keitel. He's a lumbering, awkward presence who shuffles in and out of frame like somebody auditioning for the part of Lenny in a remake of *Of Mice and Men*. At times, the role seems to be mocking him, reminding him that just as Sheriff Freddy Heflin isn't fit to join the NYPD elite, as an actor Stallone himself is not up to the standards of his co-stars.

Stallone's acting is fascinating. One is reminded of Lev Kuleshov's famous experiment (in which he induced audiences to read grief, hunger and joy by intercutting the same image of an actor with shots of different objects) because Stallone seems to have only one expression, a sort of goofy leer. But Freddy is supposed to be gauche and ill-at-ease. In a perverse way, Stallone's performance is imperfectly judged.

Mangold's debt to Scorsese is apparent throughout the film. He starts with a voice-over by De Niro (shades of *Taxi Driver*) and tries to capture the same wisecracking, bar-room banter and male camaraderie that Scorsese specialises in. There are plenty of scenes of the off-duty police officers chewing the fat in the local bar. Ray Liotta's hyper-charged, paranoid Figgis could almost be a continuation of his character in *GoodFellas*. The only real difference here is that the corrupt organisation he turns against isn't the Mafia—it's the cops themselves.

Sometimes, Mangold matches Scorsese's dynamism—there is one brilliantly handled scene which ends with Liotta about to slit apart a colleague's nostrils with the sharp end of a dart. But even this seems a little derivative. It is presumably intended as a nod in the direction of *Chinatown*, while his character's name and the corrupt-cop plot also gesture towards Mike Figgis' *Internal Affairs*. Throughout, Mangold treads a fine line between witty, knowing intertextuality and clumsy pastiche.

However, neither Keitel nor De Niro is on his best form here. As if to announce that he's in character-actor mode and that we shouldn't expect a major performance, De Niro (playing an Internal Affairs officer) sports a bad haircut and silly moustache. Keitel's corrupt cop Donlan may have an Iago-like ability to dissemble, but is too clear-cut a villain: he lacks the sense of introspection and moral ambiguity that made Keitel so memorable in, say, *Bad Lieutenant*.

Mangold's central conceit is ingenious. On one side of the river lies big, bad New York City. On the other is the sleepy little town of Garrison, NJ. As the film unfolds, we gradually learn how the former has contaminated the latter. But the film seems weighed down by its surfeit of heavyweight character actors and stars. As well as De Niro, Keitel and the others, *CopLand* also features, *inter alia*, Janeane Garofalo in a cameo as a prim, naive policewoman and Annabella Sciorra as the woman Stallone saved from drowning all those years ago. (She's a betrayed wife and now it's up to him to save her again.) With so many characters to deal with, Mangold inevitably loses focus.

Ultimately, *CopLand* is a surprisingly underwhelming experience. What might have worked as a low-budget indie film seems stifled by its own production values. (This is the kind of conventional, bloated cop drama you'd expect from a big studio, but not from Miramax.) But even if the film lacks urgency and narrative tempo, the set-pieces (car crashes, shootouts and so on) are effectively handled. Mangold offers an enjoyable enough rehash of old genre clichés, and it's impossible not to be intrigued by Stallone's cumbersome but strangely effective performance.

VILLAGE VOICE, 8/19/97, p. 81, Amy Taubin

I chortled when I heard that Sylvester Stallone was going to star in *Cop Land*, the second film by James Mangold, whose *Heavy* was among the most untalented debuts to benefit from indiscriminate indie hype. If Stallone was looking for a boy genius to do for his skidding career what Tarantino did for Travolta's, he chose unwisely. Even more bizarre is that a Scorsese-nurtured crew of actors who should have known better—Robert De Niro, Harvey Keitel, and Ray Liotta—also signed on. To a man, they give dreadful performances.

Stallone plays Freddy Heflin, the sheriff of a small New Jersey town that is home to a bunch of New York City cops who do many more awful things than flout the rule about not living out of state. Once *Cop Land* gets rolling there are enough incidents of boys in blue offing one another to keep the tabloids busy for months.

Freddy, who was left partially deaf as a result of an adolescent act of heroism, still dreams of jolting the NYPD despite the police corruption he's forced to witness up close and personal. And no one is more corrupt than his mentor (Harvey Keitel), the ruler of "Cop Land."

In the interest of verisimilitude (and following the example of De Niro's preparation for *Raging Bull*), Stallone put on about 40 pounds, the extra weight accentuating his already saggy hound-dog eyes, jowls, and belly. Liotta and De Niro seem to have been indulging in a bit of competitive overeating as well. (One could speculate how much the Tribeca Grill tab added to *Cop Land*'s budget, which reportedly ballooned to $35 million during production.)

A more skilled director than Mangold might have found a tactful way to tell Stallone that it's redundant for him to expend so much energy acting like a doofus since he already *is* a doofus. (Stallone is a more resourceful performer than he appears to be here.) And a more skilled director also might have suggested that the supporting players keep their tempers in check, since no amount of yelling was going to fill the holes in the script. (The actors with the smallest parts—Annabella Sciorra, Cathy Moriarty, and the always vibrant Michael Rapaport—do the best work.)

Unlike *Conspiracy Theory*, [see Taubin's review] *Cop Land* aspires to a realist genre (the police exposé) that requires an airtight narrative. But, in both writing and directing, Mangold lurches between ambiguous subjective sequences that leave the audience confused about what actually happened and clunky blocks of dialogue that fail to explain what we need to know. Cinematographer Eric Edwards insures that the image is always pretty to look at, though his expert use of natural light can't compensate for the staginess of the blocking. Howard Shore's faux-symphonic score, on the other hand, is probably, what Mangold wanted; it's exactly what he deserves.

(Both *Conspiracy Theory* and *Cop Land* feature actors with bandages or scabby wounds covering the bridges of their noses á la Jack Nicholson in *Chinatown*, a mode of scarification that could become the fashion trend of next year's Academy Awards.)

VILLAGE VOICE, 9/9/97, p. 88, Gary Susman

Why does Sylvester Stallone seem so authentic in *Cop Land*? If you read the film's New York City as Indie Land, the home of Miramax (*Cop Land*'s distributor), It's clear that Sly is playing himself in an allegory of his own bid for actorly credibility, trying prove himself in an independent film milieu that turns out to be as cynical and corrupt as the world he would escape from.

Stallone plays a lawman who established himself as a hero years ago yet remains a figure of ridicule. The out-of-shape flatfoot gazes at the skyline of New York, wishing he could be like the tough guys who are respected and feared there. Sly takes a chance and goes toe to toe with Harvey (Keitel) and Bob (De Niro), hoping to earn the respect of the Manhattan establishment. Yet he discovers that the coercion, greed, and fondness for violence to which he'd turned a deaf ear in his own fiefdom also characterize the players in the city, who hide behind badges of honor and integrity. In the end, despite his dogged heroics, Sly's still not welcome on the force in New York. Now, however, he'd rather not work there anyway.

Also reviewed in:
NEW YORK TIMES, 8/15/97, p. C3, Janet Maslin
NEW YORKER, 8/18/97, p. 77, Anthony Lane

VARIETY, 8/11-17/97, p. 56, Todd McCarthy
WASHINGTON POST, 8/15/97, p. G1, Rita Kempley
WASHINGTON POST, 8/15/97, Weekend/p. 32, Stephen Hunter

COSI

A Miramax Films release in association with The Australian Film Finance Corporation of a Smiley Films production in association with Meridian Films. *Executive Producer:* Phaedon Vass. *Producer:* Richard Brennan and Timothy White. *Director:* Mark Joffe. *Screenplay (based on his stage play):* Louis Nowra. *Director of Photography:* Ellery Ryan. *Editor:* Nicholas Beuman. *Sound:* John Schiffelbein. *Casting:* Alison Barret. *Production Designer:* Chris Kennedy. *Art Director:* Hugh Bareup. *Costumes:* Tess Schofield. *Running time:* 100 minutes. *MPAA Rating:* R.

CAST: Ben Mendelsohn (Lewis); Toni Collette (Julie); Barry Otto (Roy); Pamela Rabe (Ruth); Jacki Weaver (Cherry); Colin Hay (Zac); David Wenham (Doug); Paul Chubb (Henry); Colin Friels (Errol); Rachel Griffiths (Lucy); Aden Young (Nick).

LOS ANGELES TIMES, 4/11/97, Calendar/p. 6, Jack Mathews

[The following review by Jack Mathews appeared in a slightly different form in
NEWSDAY, 4/11/97, Part II/p. B13.]

They can't sing, they don't speak Italian, and most of them are heavily medicated. Nevertheless, with the help of their young theater director and against the orders of the administration, the patients at a mental institution in Sydney, Australia, are determined to mount an in-asylum production of Mozart's comic opera "Cost Fan Tutte."

Something like this actually happened to playwright Louis Nowra in the early years of his career, providing the inspiration two decades later for "Cosi," a highly successful Australian stage production and Mark Joffe's current film of the same name.

Politically incorrect as it may be to build a comedy around the antics of the mentally ill, "Cosi" is a warmly human and often uproarious ensemble piece, a sort of "Everyone Flew Over the Cuckoo's Nest" that will be offensive only to those with a purist's ear for Mozart.

Heading the superb Australian cast is Ben Mendelsohn, reprising his stage role of Lewis, the young man hired to keep patients amused with a theater production. Lewis' plans for a simple variety show are quickly scuttled by the irrepressible Roy (Barry Otto), an opera aficionado who cows him into taking on "Cost Fan Tutte" instead.

After a series of riotous auditions, Lewis' cast is filled out by the delusional Roy, the recovering heroin junkie Julie ("Muriel's Wedding's" Toni Collette), aging nympho Cherry (Jacki Weaver), anxious musician Zac (Colin Hay), active pyromaniac Doug (David Wenham), and the emotionally tense introverts Henry (Paul Chubb) and Ruth (Pamela Rabe).

Nowra's script follows a predictable arc, as the rehearsals and the patients' behavior become more and more frantic, before the coldly uncaring administrators provide the catalyst that brings everyone—and the show!—together in a life-affirming finale. But the incidents and the relationships developed along the way give it a wily balance of farce and sentiment.

The theme of tested fidelity in "Cost Fan Tutte" is played out in a pair of weakly developed romantic subplots—one, Lewis' mutual infatuation with Julie and the other an attempt by his best friend (Aden Young) to seduce Lewis' frustrated live-in lover, Lucy (Rachel Griffiths). Fortunately, neither of these is given enough time to detract from the great pleasures, and laughs, as Lewis and his eccentric cast prepare for opening night at the asylum.

NEW YORK POST, 4/11/97, p. 44, Michael Medved

"Cosi" is altogether too cozy in its treatment of an Australian mental institution and its patients, sentimentalizing these people in the hackneyed Hollywood fashion.

Solid acting by the gifted cast can't redeem a silly structure or make up for an overblown and anticlimactic finale.

Ben Mendelsohn ("The Year My Voice Broke") plays Lewis, an amiable but aimless slacker who falls into a job as drama coach at a psychiatric hospital.

He wants to stage a simple variety show, but one of the patients, a talkative, manic-depressive intellectual (superbly played by Barry Otto), bullies and badgers Lewis to dare instead a lavish production of Mozart's opera "Cosi Fan tutte."

Eventually won over, the drama coach and the hospital's head nurse (Colin Friels) go forward with this irrationally ambitious undertaking.

Of course, they encounter huge obstacles along the way, especially after one of the stars of his in-house production, a sex-crazed pyromaniac nicely played by David Wenham, burns down the hospital playhouse where they've been rehearsing.

Lewis loses his job, but the cutesy psychos inevitably lure him back onto hospital grounds to work with them in secret in an abandoned barn.

There's also a conspicuously clumsy life-imitates-art subplot involving the rocky relationship between Lewis and his sexy live-in girlfriend (Rachel Griffiths).

Just as Mozart's opera focuses on a bet about whether two superficially devoted ladies can be induced to cheat, Lewis makes a wager with his best friend (Aden Young), a pretentiously intense actor and director, insisting on his sweetheart's faithfulness.

Meanwhile, Lewis himself is distracted by the most talented member of his own operatic troupe (Toni Collette, star of "Muriel's Wedding"), a recovering drug addict who plainly adores him.

Brief glimpses of absurdly overwrought productions by the hero's ambitious actor-pal seem richly amusing precisely because such inane excesses are believable. That quality of credibility is utterly absent, however, in the operatic extravaganza for which the entire picture has served as preparation.

Director Mark Joffe ("The Efficiency Expert"), adapting a successful Australian stage play, tries to make this long-awaited show within a show seem simultaneously magical and mad, but in the process equips the performers with wildly whimsical costumes that make no sense within the story line.

Moreover, those moviegoers unfamiliar with more traditional stagings of the real "Cosi" will get no hint of the opera's spiritual richness or infectious wit.

The movie fails to generate much nostalgia or affection since the patients and the production that are intended as the focus of those emotions never seem in any way authentic.

VILLAGE VOICE, 4/15/97, p. 76, Laurie Stone

You don't have to be a big studio throwing around money to make a lousy movie. You can be a little guy, distributed by Miramax, and come up with the Australian-made clinker that is *Cosi*. Its sentimentality about theater is matched by its sentimentality about crazy people. Slacker Lewis (Ben Mendelsohn) lands a job directing plays in a looney bin. He's never finished anything, so this is a chance to prove himself, and one of the inmates wants to stage *Cosi Fan Tutte*, although no one can sing except the pretty drug addict-depressive Julie (Toni Collette). The rest of the inmates are psychos and veggies left over from *Marat/Sade* and *David and Lisa*. Back home, Lewis's leggy, law student girlfriend (Rachel Griffiths) scoffs at *Cosi*'s "misogyny," the opera presenting the moral that women are by nature fickle.

The punitive lighting makes pimply complexions look like geographical relief maps. And for no reason, Lewis finds in *Cosi* an exemplum for romance and begins doubting his girlfriends honor, at the same time flirting with Julie. Every line of dialogue is as calculated for cuteness as the blizzard of reaction shots—calling upon the actors to pop eyes, flap wattles, or stare glumly. A cat-incinerating psycho wafts some libido, but, alas, he's locked up through most of the flick.

Also reviewed in:
NEW REPUBLIC, 3/3/97, p. 30, Stanley Kauffmann
NEW YORK TIMES, 4/11/97, p. C16, Stephen Holden
VARIETY, 3/25-31/96, p. 67, David Stratton

COUCH IN NEW YORK, A

A Northern Arts Entertainment release of a Les Films Balenciaga/France 2 Cinema/M6 Films (Paris) Paradise Films, RTBF-Television Belge (Brussels)/Babelsberg Film Produktion (Berlin) production, with participation of Canal Plus, Film Board Berlin Brandenberg. *Executive Producer:* Robin O'Hara. *Producer:* Regine Konckier and Jean-Luc Ormieres. *Director:* Chantal Akerman. *Screenplay (French and English with English subtitles):* Chantal Akerman and Jean-Louis Benoit. *Director of Photography:* Dietrich Lohmann. *Editor:* Claire Atherton. *Music:* Paolo Conte and Sonia Atherton. *Sound:* Pierre Mertens and Gerard Lamps. *Production Designer:* Christian Marti. *Art Director:* Patricia Woodbridge. *Costumes:* Stephane Rollot. *Running time:* 105 minutes. *MPAA Rating:* R.

CAST: William Hurt (Henry Harriston); Juliette Binoche (Beatrice Saulnier); Paul Guilfoyle (Dennis); Stephanie Buttle (Anne); Richard Jenkins (Campton); Kent Broadhurst (Tim); Henry Bean (Stein); Barbara Garrick (Lisbeth); Bernard Breuse (Jerome).

VILLAGE VOICE, 11/18/97, p. 82, J. Hoberman

An uptight New York shrink (William Hurt in the Cary Grant role) swaps apartments, sight unseen, with a hang-loose Paris gamine (relaxed and charming Juliette Binoche). He starts fielding her lovers, she starts treating his patents, and ... actually *A Couch in New York*, Chantal Akerman's English-language screwball comedy, is not nearly the disaster advance word might indicate.

A soupçon of Tashlin-esque gadget humor notwithstanding, Akerman's jokes are more droll than uproarious or, put another way, less funny than formalist. In the Akerman oeuvre, *A Couch in New York* is closest to her last, not so frivolous romantic escapade, *Night and Day*. As an example of Franco-American counterintuitive artistry, *A Couch in New York* makes an interesting comparison to Woody Allen's *Everyone Says I Love You*. (There's even a magical Central Park.) Given a bit of time, a clever and sympathetic viewer could tease out the psychoanalytic subtext.

Also reviewed in:
NEW YORK TIMES, 11/19/97, p. E3, Janet Maslin
VARIETY, 2/12-18/96, p. 81, David Rooney

CRASH

A Robert Lantos and Jeremy Thomas presentation in association with Fine Line Features of an Alliance Communications production. *Executive Producer:* Jeremy Thomas and Robert Lantos. *Producer:* David Cronenberg. *Director:* David Cronenberg. *Screenplay:* David Cronenberg. *Based on the novel by:* J.G. Ballard. *Director of Photography:* Peter Suschitzky. *Editor:* Ronald Sanders. *Music:* Howard Shore. *Music Editor:* Suzana Peric. *Sound:* David Lee and (music) Gary Gray. *Sound Editor:* Andy Malcolm. *Casting:* Deirdre Bowen. *Production Designer:* Carol Spier. *Art Director:* Tamara Deverell. *Set Decorator:* Elinor Rose Galbraith. *Special Effects:* Michael Kavanagh. *Costumes:* Denise Cronenberg. *Running time:* 98 minutes. *MPAA Rating:* NC-17.

CAST: James Spader (James Ballard); Holly Hunter (Dr. Helen Remington); Elias Koteas (Vaughan); Deborah Kara Unger (Catherine Ballard); Rosanna Arquette (Gabrielle); Peter MacNeil (Colin Seagrave); Yolande Julian (Airport Hooker); Cheryl Swarts (Vera Seagrave); Judah Katz (Salesman); Nicky Guadagni (Tattooist); Ronn Sarosiak (Assistant Director); Boyd Banks (Grip); Markus Parilo (Man in Hanger); Alice Poon (Camera Girl); John Stoneham, Jr.; (Brett Trask).

FILMS IN REVIEW, 1-2/97, p. 70, Julien Lapointe

David Cronenberg's *Crash* is as single-minded and as blatantly provocative as its title suggests. The film, a success at Cannes and in Canada, has been deemed the director's masterpiece. In a sense it is, but its alleged greatness is so self-conscious one feels turned off—though I'll admit even that might be an intended effect. What makes *Crash* at once both annoying and competing is that it remains dramatically obscure, yet also exquisitely eccentric. There wasn't a moment when I wasn't hoping for this macabre film to end, but I didn't dare walk out. Cronenberg, with all his skill, uses 'art' to grab hold of our sensibilities and coaxes us into sitting through his morbid fantasies to the very end.

The main characters are James (James Spader) and Catherine Ballard (Deborah Unger). They spend their time practicing sodomy with each other and anyone else they meet. They also share their adulterous adventures in a monotonous, detached manner. These people are so empty that sex is the only emotional sensation they can relate to, and their indulgence in it serves only as an escape from the reckless boredom of their lives. But then James meets the enigmatic Vaughan (Elias Koteas, a regular of Egoyan's films), a psychopath who stages car wrecks and is sexually aroused by the sight of bloodied corpses and scarred flesh. Vaughan gets the enervated James and Catherine hooked into his dirty (and dangerous) games. The main dramatic conceit is that this depraved sexuality doesn't corrupt the young couple; it fulfills them, bringing excitement to their lives. James and Catherine eventually make love while fantasizing over Vaughan's accident-wounded body and their mutual fascination for this pervert allows them to connect emotionally. It fills their void.

Cronenberg doesn't structure his plot or seek dramatic clarity, and he isn't concerned with plausibility either. He presents the action in a matter-of-fact manner and, staging much of it within closed areas—with claustrophobically dark, dull colours—he creates a repellent austerity. The occasional lapses of humour act as an oasis within this very dry film, and although its and tone is not without intensity, one can't help but wonder how much better it would have been if pushed into the realm of black comedy. But Cronenberg takes himself so seriously that he undermines any dramatic flourishes *Crash* could reveal. He makes the picture dull and then expects us to be moved by his drab aesthetics.

It isn't that he doesn't care for his characters, it's that he doesn't care for what he *thinks* of them. He hollows them out with his simple-minded narrative—they're just one-dimensional sexually driven beasts and that's all that really seems to interest him. The various performers (the cast also includes Holly Hunter and Roseanna Arquette) have emotionality wearied features that suggest psychological complexities Cronenberg never explores.

In the end, we're left more perplexed than awed. The final shot has James and Catherine coming out of a car wreck and engaging in passionate sex. Ah, the honorably deranged Vaughan has brought out the beasts in these two lovers and thus saved their marriage. I wish this were intended as some sort of a sick joke, but I'm afraid it isn't. *Crash* is about the redemptive amorality of sexual perversion. Take it or leave it.

LOS ANGELES TIMES, 3/21/97, Calendar/p. 10, Kenneth Turan

A few years ago a handwritten sign was spotted outside a theater in one of Manhattan's more dismal neighborhoods. "Now!" it proclaimed, "The First Bondage Film With a Believable Story Line!" History does not tell us whether the picture lived up to that promise, but if it did it would be a leg up on the mind-numbing "Crash."

The latest film by Canadian director David Cronenberg, "Crash" is not exactly about bondage; an ice-cold, sadomasochistic linkage of sex and pain is more its game. And the result is so far from being involving or compelling, so intentionally disconnected from any kind of recognizable emotion, that by comparison David Lynch's removed "Lost Highway" plays like "Lassie Come Home."

"Crash" is the same film that won a Special Jury Prize at Cannes last year "for originality, daring and audacity." But it was an award that so split the panel that, in an unprecedented moment, President Francis Ford Coppola announced from the podium that some jury members demanded a public statement that they had abstained.

Make no mistake, Cronenberg, a veteran filmmaker ("Rabid," "The Brood," "Videodrome," "Dead Ringers") who has always been intrigued by what's out of conventional bounds, has made exactly the film he, his devoted cast and expert cinematographer Peter Suschitzky intended. How much interest it will arouse outside that small circle is less secure.

Based on a 1973 cult novel by science-fiction writer J.G. Ballard (whose equally cold but quite different "Empire of the Sun" attracted Steven Spielberg's attention), "Crash" is set in an undefined time frame, half present, half future. Its protagonists are a semi-detached couple, James Ballard (James Spader) and his wife, Catherine (Canadian actress Deborah Kara Unger).

"Crash" doesn't have a plot per se, it simply follows the fortunes of this non-monogamous pair after James gets hurt in a major automobile accident that kills a man and seriously injures his wife, Dr. Helen Remington (Holly Hunter).

In some inexplicable way that's presented as a given, that crash serves as a powerful aphrodisiac for both Ballard and Remington, who begin to compulsively share distant sex in cars while talking about the mechanics of accidents.

Soon the couple is in communication with Vaughan (Elias Koteas, recently in Atom Egoyan's "Exotica"), part cult leader, part mad scientist, part performance artist. A scar-covered veteran of numerous collisions whose ideas include staging a re-creation of the crash that killed James Dean, Vaughan includes among his accident-freak followers a seriously injured young woman named Gabrielle (Rosanna Arquette) who doesn't let the braces and full-body harness she wears stand in the way of pleasure.

Though these people engage in frequent sex, it is impossible to over-emphasize how cold, non-erotic, almost intentionally asexual these acts are. Vaughan may consider crashes "liberating events" and his followers may get so turned on by accidents they treat footage of crash test dummies as if it were pornography, but the filmmaking here is so glacially paced (the final script, was only 62 pages for a 100-minute film) and enervating that boredom is the most frequent result.

Director Cronenberg, whose passion for automobiles will extend to his projected next film, a Grand Prix drama called "Red Cars," devoted an exceptional amount of time to "Crash's" crashes. According to the press notes, "more than 200 picture vehicles and over 60 stunt drivers were employed [and] 25 automobiles were demolished or pre-wrecked for crash aftermaths."

This concern for clashing metal notwithstanding, frank indifference is the most likely reaction to "Crash," its proudly worn NC-17 rating notwithstanding. In that connection, it's amusing to note that great pains are being taken to label this film as "controversial." Remember "Showgirls," remember "Striptease" and remember that for a canny marketing department "controversial" is the last refuge of the tedious. Kicks may be getting harder to find, but "Crash" is not a great place to look for new ones.

NEW STATESMAN, 6/6/97, p. 38, Jonathan Coe

In the week in which David Cronenberg's *Crash* finally goes on release although not in most of London's West End, thanks to Westminster Council—here are the critical comments to ponder. "A piece of nauseating muck." A film with "all the morals of an alley cat and all the sweetness of the sewer". A film which would "pervert the minds of the British people". A film which deserved "a 'D' certificate—for disgusting". "The most sickening display of brutality, perversion, sex and sadism ever to be shown on the screen ... it is an extraordinary oversight on the part of the British Board of Film Censors that this monstrosity has been passed for public showing."

No, they're not referring to *Crash*, as it happens. Think back 49 years instead, to 1948 and the release of *No Orchids for Miss Blandish,* that silly, insipid British attempt to imitate the American gangster movie. Now almost forgotten—except for the occasional, untrumpeted screening on television—this film caused the most astonishing uproar at the time, provoking even reputable critics (that last quotation is from the *Monthly Film Bulletin*) to spasms of self-righteous apoplexy which have recently found a chilling echo in the outrage generated by Cronenberg's film.

"Beyond the bounds of depravity" was the headline dreamt up by an *Evening Standard* sub-editor to accompany Alexander Walker's first thoughts on the matter, while the real architect of the anti-*Crash* campaign has been Christopher Tookey of the *Daily Mail* who has bizarrely claimed, among other things, that this rather bland and cerebral film about consensual sex promulgates "the morality of the satyr, the nymphomaniac, the rapist, the paedophile, the danger to society."

Crash is a film about a group of fetishists who get sexual kicks out of car crashes. There is no rape in the film, and no paedophilia (or even any children). So what prompted Tookey to misdescribe it so wilfully? Why did he go on to write a further full-page article urging *Mail* readers to boycott products made by Sony, the parent company of the film's distributors Columbia TriStar? And why has the *Daily Mail* subsequently homed in on the marital status not just of TriStar's managing director ("single and childless"), but of 14 examiners employed by the British Board of Film Classification ("the secret censors who refused to put a ban on *Crash*) in a tacky double-page exposé that even listed the values of their homes?

Clearly by this stage we have moved some way beyond the realm of film criticism, even beyond the boundaries of campaigning journalism, and into the world of witch-hunts and attempted character assassination. To remind ourselves of how downright peculiar the *Mail*'s campaign has been (the word "fetishistic" springs to mind in this context, too), it's necessary to emphasise—as other writers have done—what an extremely unremarkable film Cronenberg has made in *Crash*.

We're back in *No Orchids for Miss Blandish* territory. In 1948 the BBFC was simply perplexed by the furore unleashed by that wretched film. "We don't know what the excitement is about. As far as we are concerned it is a normal gangster film, no more brutal than many made in Hollywood."

That's certainly how everybody would see it now and, by the same token, *Crash* is a normal Cronenberg film: hugely less brutal than the average Schwarzenegger or Abel Ferrara movie, and containing no more sex than the films Westminster Council benignly allows to play at the Astral Cinema in Brewer Street every night.

The comparison with porn films isn't entirely inappropriate, because *Crash* deploys much of the logic and vocabulary of pornographic cinema. This isn't so much a matter of the sex scenes, which follow each other in relentless succession, but more its brazen narrative assumptions. Just as every dolly bird encountered by the hero in a porn film will oddly—but invariably—be gagging for it, so every character James Spader meets in *Crash* just happens to share his particular predilection, and can't wait to submit to a serious rogering in the back of the nearest Buick or Mustang.

Far from being erotic (which was clearly not Cronenberg's intention), this gives the film a dream-like, affectless tone, drawing the audience into a world that has been comprehensively drained of plausible human feeling.

It also, I'm afraid, makes the movie numbingly boring. These are dull people with dulled emotions and dull obsessions, and the film registers this dullness with scrupulous fidelity. While it would certainly take a colossal numbskull—or perhaps a *Daily Mail* writer—to think the film was in any way endorsing (let alone "promulgating") these characters' behaviour, it's also a cause for regret that Cronenberg has so rigorously denied himself the vocabulary that would enable him to make a critique of it. Fans of James Spader, Holly Hunter and Rosanna Arquette will find these capable performers sleeping their way through parts that could just as easily have been played by crash-test dummies. And yes, of course that's part of the point, just as the suffocating lack of humour is part of the point. (There's only one good joke about sex and technology in the film—when Spader tweaks Deborah Unger's nipple as they make love in a car, and the electric windows slide up and down.) But none of this can disguise the fact that there's a deep failure of artistic energy somewhere at the heart of *Crash*. The studied inconsequentiality of the dialogue, the actors' expressionless intonation, the aloofness from satire—all these things create an impression, finally, of immense self-satisfaction; of enormous pride taken in the audacity and significance of a central conceit (technology equals lack of emotion) which is, in fact, the very last word in banality.

On one hand, then, we have a clamorous and incomprehending mob howling for censorship, and on the other we have a film so smugly convinced of its own daring that it feels no obligation to entertain or inform us. A depressing situation, you'll agree; but not a totally unfamiliar one. History, especially film history, is littered with examples of censorship battles being fought over films which, under normal circumstances, would scarcely be worth speaking up for.

One thinks of Ken Russell's lurid *The Devils* and Sam Peckinpah's sweaty, posturing *Straw Dogs*, of *Visions of Ecstasy*, a slight piece of homoerotic soft porn which fell foul of the blasphemy laws when a shrug of indifference would have been the more appropriate response; of *The Night Porter* and *The Wild One*, *A Clockwork Orange* and *120 Days of Sodom* ...

The point about these films is that they are all at the very least flawed, and in some cases are among the weakest works of their illustrious directors. It's enough to make you think that there might be something in the very nature of transgressive cinema that condemns it to artistic failure: a fatal tendency on the filmmakers' part, perhaps, to assume the act of transgression itself justifies the whole enterprise, so that there's no real need to attend to the more routine satisfactions (coherence, variety, intelligibility) which an audience would normally demand. Even the most daring work, in other words, can bore very quickly if daring is all that it has to offer. Daring is not enough to keep us glued to the screen for two hours, as *Crash* all too glumly testifies.

But in the end, for all its faults, there's no doubt that we have to speak up for *Crash* against the cultural vandals of the press and Westminster Council. The discovery that it is essentially no good may be disappointing, but it doesn't detract at all from Cronenberg's right to make such a film and to have it exhibited. It's to be hoped that once members of the public are able to see the film for themselves, the tide of media hysteria will begin to recede.

Otherwise we could be in for some rocky times. In a pernicious extension of the Neighbourhood Watch culture, the moralists at Westminster Council (led by an antique dealer in his late sixties who rejoices in the name of John Bull) have not only banned *Crash* from the borough's West End screens, but have now invited concerned citizens to draw their attention to any other releases that might be considered offensive. Since, in a rather pathetic bid for political correctness, they have attacked *Crash* for its "sexual humiliation of women" (although no women are sexually humiliated in the film), this could pose problems for the new David Lynch movie *Lost Highway*, which contains an intensely and disturbingly erotic scene in which Patricia Arquette is made to strip at gunpoint in front of a bunch of gangsters.

So, will Lynch make it past the Westminster worthies? I'd urge Tom Clarke, Labour's new minister for films, to look into this matter with some urgency. It's all very well handing out Lottery money to the British film industry, but as a centre for exhibition London could soon become a global laughing stock if the work of some of the world's best directors can't get shown here, simply because of a handful of philistine, authoritarian bureaucrats whose last visit to the cinema was to see *Bedknobs and Broomsticks*.

We may be about to enter the most repressed and heavily censored era in British cinema history. It would be ironic, to say the least, if this happened under new Labour rather than the Conservatives.

NEW YORK, 3/31/97, p. 81, David Denby

"Why do they have to bury the bodies so quickly?" whispers Catherine (Deborah Kara Unger), a stunning blonde with flattened cheekbones. Catherine always whispers when a normal speaking voice would get the job done. "They should let them sit around for days," she breathes. The hushed, monotonal characters in *Crash*—a highbrow pornographic movie directed by David Cronenberg—are neither ghouls nor necrophiliacs, though they certainly get off on death. In some nameless gray city, the pleasure-seekers prowl the freeways, banging their cars into one another, exciting themselves with near-death experiences. In order to prolong the ecstasy, they then make love in the wreckage. *Crash*, a rapt erotic-trance movie, is conducted in whispers and shot in the sleekest car-metal colors—silver, gray, and black. The sky never betrays a patch of blue, and there's no red anywhere, except for the sexy blood on the mangled bodies. The movie is based on J.G. Ballard's cult novel from 1973, but the entire picture seems to be taking place in David Cronenberg's head: car crashes as orgasm, the slicing of bodies as ecstasy. I can't be the first to say this, but I'm not strong enough to resist: The movie gives new meaning to the term *autoeroticism.*

The two Davids, Lynch and Cronenberg, always weird, have turned into out-and-out mannerists. Their latest movies, however, are quite different from each other. David Lynch's *Lost Highway* is dreamy, hallucinatory, and anti-realistic but all within the familiar structure of a fatalistic *noir* movie from the forties. Cronenberg, by contrast, is a literalist from scene to scene but methodically mad (like the Marquis de Sade) in his overall intention. Both directors let erotomania do the work of dramatic construction. We're in the hands of two obsessional directors, and their movies are certainly not boring. But they're not art either. *Lost Highway* holds together visually but makes no discernible sense; *Crash* is an exhaustive exploration of a single nut-brain fetish—car crashes as eros and death combined. It's a great movie for intellectual analysis written in French (what a shame Michel Foucault had to die before he could take it on).

The press notes describe the movie as "a cautionary tale of how we might adapt to the environment that we have ourselves created, sterile and isolated from nature." This is absolute nonsense: The movie is an eager embrace of that environment. *Crash* doesn't look like any work of pornography you've ever seen, but I don't know what else to call it. The characters have no jobs or lives to speak of; erotic reality, erotic time, is the only dimension they inhabit. In the opening scene, Deborah Kara Unger slowly leans forward, stimulating a nipple into erection against a cold, cold surface (an airplane fuselage, I believe) while getting worked on from behind and below by some man we don't yet know. Later, in bed, Catherine narrates the events to her husband, James Ballard (James Spader), a producer of television commercials who entertains her with *his* day spent dallying on the set. The two of them use the narrated sexual acts to stimulate their own lovemaking. (The character name *Ballard,* which also appears in the novel, is intended, I suppose, as an act of candor implicating the author in the goings-on. Sex, you might say, is a form of narrative, and the writer is always a seducer and fantasist, and so on.)

On the road, Ballard inadvertently crashes into a doctor, Helen Remington (Holly Hunter), whose husband dies in the crash. Dr. Remington, however, is turned on, and sitting in the wrecked car, defiantly exposes a breast. (Holly Hunter does this with her usual precision and snap, like the bravest girl in acting class.) The two crash victims then meet in the hospital, and thereafter things turn increasingly automotive, what with the couple fornicating awkwardly in the mangled cars and then attending a kind of public performance, a crash derby in which the man who made love to Catherine—Vaughan, his name is—restages the crash death of James Dean, complete with the same kinds of cars and an actual collision.

Everyone politely applauds the demonstration. That gentle patter of applause for an atrocity would seem to suggest a sneaking sense of humor, even a dash of self-satire. Cronenberg, after all, made *The Fly* and *Dead Ringers,* two obsessional yet witty explorations of surgery and violation. In the past, he's been able to combine fixation and humor, freakishness and jokes. But *erotic* fixation and humor do not mix—not if you want to keep an audience aroused, that is—and Cronenberg has made his choice. Solemnity seals the mood: Whisper, whisper, don't break the trance. The movie turns ritualistic. The scarred Vaughan, played by a very creepy Elias Koteas, serves as guru to a circle of crash addicts. Vaughan is purely sexual, purely death-haunted—the ultimate fetishist. At home, his mangled little group, sitting in their braces and leather body sheaths (Rosanna Arquette is barely held together: she has scars like fissures), repeatedly watch slow-motion footage of test-dummy crashes, and they all get hot together.

Vaughan gets Ballard hooked, and since Ballard wants Catherine to be happy—there's some romantic Tristan-and-Isolde-ish feeling in their linked death wish—the two of them take part in the wild rides around town. The sex grows more and more baroque and voyeuristic. There is a sequence in a car wash, with a couple making love while brushes and hoses spray the car—the closest thing in the movie to a cliché. And there are many, many more crashes and much licking of scars. How do you end a dirty novel or movie? For artists as well as junkmeisters, the problem is notorious. In porn, acts are repeated and repeated, and varied and then repeated again, with no end in sight, and the only artistically satisfying way to conclude is with the death of the love object. Cronenberg's movie is just mad for death, and its last line (which will become deservedly famous) sets us up for the extinction of its two main characters. He has taken pornography to its logical conclusion. For some this may amount to a radicalism of spirit; it also marks Cronenberg's departure from life.

Peter Suschitzky is the cinematographer, and I don't know how he did some of the highway collisions (they don't look fake). This is an extremely controlled piece of filmmaking, without an ugly or discordant shot anywhere. Formally, *Crash* is a triumph. But it's too remote and specialized to be of more than passing interest, and its techno-fetishism is familiar to anyone who has sampled avant-garde fiction over the past 30 years. One wants to give Cronenberg credit for his madness, but there's a banal problem standing in the way: The men and women who make TV commercials have sensed the connection between automobiles and eroticism for decades. *Crash* has the conceptual brilliance of a great ad campaign, the silver-gray gleam of high-tech graphics. Whether you're selling automobiles or automobile-death-fetishism, there may not be all that much of a difference. Either way, there's that sexy chill of flesh meeting metal.

Cronenberg's chic eroticism focuses everything on desire and rules out the rest of human experience. Sometimes the women undress slowly, raptly, thoughtfully; sometimes both men and women pull off their clothes and go to it. The movie is certainly arousing. But this is a limited recommendation. The very concentration that makes *Crash* successful as pornography limits it as art. *Crash* may not be funny, but it's almost always ludicrous.

NEW YORK POST, 3/21/97, p. 49, Thelma Adams

David Cronenberg has always driven against the flow. With "Crash," he cruises the erotic intersection where sex and cars collide.

James Spader—the badboy Robert Redford—plays James Ballard. The name's significant. Cronenberg jump-starts J.G. Ballard's existential sci-fi thriller following his adaptation of William Burroughs "Naked Lunch."

"Crash" is kinky from the get-go. TV ad-man Ballard "produces a segment" with an assistant on a set surrounded by machinery. Meanwhile, his wife, Catherine (Deborah Kara Unger), rubs against a plane while having sex with an anonymous man. Fate intervenes and it's coitus interruptus for hubby and wife.

The Ballards reunite and talk dirty as they talk over the day's events. Their coupling produces more friction than heat.

That's the beginning of a cautionary tale that's sexually explicit but less shocking than expected. The sophisticated Ballards are, emotionally stunted. To compensate, they take unnecessary risks.

While reading and driving, Ballard bumps into Dr. Helen Remington (Holly Hunter, raising more than Arizona). Her husband takes a header into Ballard's front seat and a kinky relationship is born. Before long, the widow Remington and Ballard are tossing their canes and steaming up the windows of Ballard's sedan.

Remington draws Ballard into an intense world of car-crash survivors who have developed an appetite for sex and death and refuse to diet. The group's guru, is, the scarred Vaughan (Elias "Exotica" Koteas). Gabrielle (Rosanna Arquette) is a maimed sex kitten who sports prosthetic gear like S & M chic.

In addition to re-creating famous car wrecks (James Dean's, Jayne Mansfield's), Vaughan drives like a madman and closely admires the scars of both sexes. He pontificates about crashes, "... a liberation, of sexual energy that mediates the sexuality of those who have died with an intensity impossible in any other form." Don't mistake this for Cronenberg's meaning; the director expects us to see through Vaughan.

Catherine's simple refrain, repeated by Ballard at the movie's end, is more to the point: "Maybe the next one, maybe the next one." How far will the couple go to reach orgasm? How far will we travel with them?

Not since "Last Tango in Paris" has a movie pushed so many erotic buttons, but Cronenberg doesn't butter up the audience. The far-fetched erotica in "Crash," which was vilified but also rewarded with a special jury prize at Cannes, is more distancing than arousing.

This is where it crosses the line from genre pic to art. Cronenberg plays chicken with the audience's imaginations. By luring us into the theater with the promise of a tale more lurid than any we've seen outside the New York Underground Film Fest, the director climbs out on a limb to prove how far out we are in our quest for thrills—and what an emotional dead end that is.

NEWSDAY, 3/21/97, Part II/p. B9, John Anderson

As they used to say in the car ads, this is not your father's Oldsmobile.

"Crash," David Cronenberg's audacious, erotic and strangely profound movie about sex, death and car crashes, cruises the intersection of flesh and technology with a dreamy, jaundiced eye. It's blackly funny, but morbidly serious; alluring, but obvious—its initial image is a naked breast being pressed against the hard, glazed shell of a private jet, so we have a good sense of where we're heading. The main questions are about route and horsepower.

Based on the cult novel by J.G. Ballard, whose work also includes "Empire of the Sun" (the basis of the Spielberg film), "Crash" is about people who've gone beyond the pedestrian fascination with vehicular disasters into a subculture of fetishized smashups, leg braces, scar tissue and death wishes. The highway wreck is erotica, fender benders are foreplay; celebrity fatalities—James Dean, Jayne Mansfield—are sublime.

You have to give Cronenberg credit for nerve, among other things. And Ballard, too. The main character here is named James Ballard (James Spader), a TV producer who's introduced to full-metal arousal after he causes the crash that kills the husband of Dr. Helen Remington (Holly Hunter). Both James and Helen are hospitalized, but their initial impact has had an eroticizing effect: When they run into each other again (no pun intended), they have a full-frontal collision of the libidinous kind.

Ballard and his wife, Catherine (played by the seemingly custom-ordered Deborah Kara Unger), have a marriage in which each thrives on the knowledge of the other's adultery. They're prime candidates for the loose association of crash fans led by Vaughan (Elias Koteas), a "scientist" obsessed by the "reshaping of the human body by technology." Accompanied by the multi-braced Gabrielle (Rosanna Arquette), he stages theatrical re-enactments of famous wrecks, drives the same model Lincoln in which JFK was shot and subjects Catherine to a brutalizing sexual ravaging, while James drives the car.

But like the protagonists in a Bunuel film, the Ballards are very bourgeois thrill-seekers. They might be aroused by the screech of metal and the smell of transmission fluid, but they visibly wither when their sports car is dented. "They bury the dead so quickly," Catherine sighs. "They should leave them lying around for months." Unger gives Catherine an ethereal air; her eyes effect a look of blindness. But we see her clearly enough: Her faux vampirism is all middle-class boredom and erotic adventurism.

So "Crash" actually is a conservative film in its way, because Cronenberg is taking to its extreme conclusion a cultural esthetic that promotes body-piercing, moshing, thrash metal and the "heroin chic" of Calvin Klein. His characters are in hot pursuit of the repellent, attracted by the unattractive *because* it's unattractive. When Ballard and Vaughan have sex—as do Gabrielle and Helen it's because they're *not* gay. They've programmed themselves to find pleasure in what doesn't come naturally. It's an anti-esthetic, really, which is ultimately soul-killing. And that's how Cronenberg portrays it.

So consider the man who's been burdened with a "king of weird" reputation—for such films as "Naked Lunch," "The Fly," "Scanners" and "Dead Ringers"—as the moral arbiter of our times. Ted Turner has dubbed this film "sick." But Cronenberg really only wants what's best for his characters.

NEWSWEEK, 3/24/97, p. 79, Jack Kroll

Since death is the ultimate experience, it was inevitable that death would be the ultimate movie trend. And of course it would be hooked up to sex; after all, orgasm has been called "the little death." The trend may have arrived. David Lynch's "Lost Highway" was the first of the necro-*noir* movies. But David Cronenberg's *Crash* blows it away in terms of impact and controversy. Greeted at the Cannes Film Festival last May by a storm of cheers and boos, the film won a Special Jury Prize "for originality, daring and audacity." Those words could also apply to two other upcoming films, *Sick*, a powerful and unsettling documentary about a sadomasochistic performance artist, and *Kissed*, a movie about the ultimate taboo of necrophilia, which was a prize winner at the Toronto festival. "Crash" is rated NC-17, the others are unrated, which in these cases means not exploitative junk, but films for grownups—and not for all of them.

Cronenberg, a Canadian, has been the thinking fiend's horror director with films like "Scanners," "The Fly" and "Dead Ringers." In "Crash" (based on J.G. Ballard's 1973 novel), he's made the hydrogen bomb of shock movies. Its opening scene shows Catherine Ballard (Deborah Unger) rubbing her bare breast against an airplane's fuselage. That's sex. Catherine's husband, James (James Spader), is in a terrible car crash that kills the husband of Dr. Helen Remington (Holly Hunter). That's death. James and Helen, recovering from their injuries, have carnal congress in a car. That's sex/death. They get involved with Vaughan (Elias Koteas), a "scientist" who stages re-enactments of "celebrity car crashes" (James Dean, Jayne Mansfield) for a chit of crash obsessives, including Gabrielle (Rosanna Arquette), who wears leg braces and a slutskirt.

"Crash" has no plot to speak of. It's a cinematic tone poem of collisions and coitus. James, Catherine, Helen, Vaughan and Gabrielle engage in every possible pairing, hetero and homo.

It's the apotheosis of auto eroticism. And, being the work of Cronenberg, it's deadly serious. Cronenberg has a millennial vision of a transformed sexuality that bears the paradoxical possibilities of death and love. He's a master of seductive visuals and editing. He can be both compelling and pretentious. For all the blood and bodies, the film is cold, and the hushed solemnity of its dialogue verges on self-parody, despite what can only be called a courageous cast.

"Crash" will disturb many viewers, not so much with its sexual explicitness but with its linkage of sexual gratification with the near-death experience of car crashes. Ted Turner, whose Fine Line Features is releasing "Crash" in the United States, at first balked at the movie but later relented. The film, which cost $9 million, has made $18 million outside the United States and was chosen best picture of 1996 by the French cinephile bible Cahiers du Cinéma. Bernardo Bertolucci calls it "a religious masterpiece." But Cronenberg's agent told him, "Do not do this movie. It will end your career."

Cronenberg deserves the Cannes prize for audacity (even though he wasn't audacious enough to break the line on male frontal nudity). He says he's grateful to Holly Hunter, who went after Cronenberg just as she went after Jane Campion for the erotically charged "The Piano" (which won her an Oscar). Some Cannes jurors worried about copycat crashes. This film has been seen by 5 million people, and the traffic statistics have remained constant," says Cronenberg. As for a breakout of sex in cars, he says, "I'd like to take credit for that, but I can't. There was a whole generation spawned in the back seats of Fords."

"Sick" and "Kissed" are more shocking than "Crash" but quieter. "Sick" tells the story of Bob Flanagan, a performance artist who suffered from cystic fibrosis and died last year at the age of 43.   Director Kirby Dick fashions an unblinking biography of "supermasochist" Flanagan. Audiences will not be unblinking the scenes of self-mutilation are for strong eyes and stomachs only. These scenes are relieved by others in which Flanagan does hilarious riffs on the world of S&M. One scene outshocks one of the most famous scenes in movies, the slitting of an eyeball in Luis Buñuel's surrealist classic, "Chien Andalou." But "Sick" is real, a compassionate account of perversion as a tragicomic kind of salvation.

"Kissed," a first feature by Canadian Lynne Stopkewich, does the impossible, treating necrophilia with delicacy and tenderness. Molly Parker, as a woman who becomes an embalmer because she's fascinated by death, turns another perversion into a twisted gesture toward transcendence. Stopkewch calls her film "a first-date movie for the millennium." Not as wild a date as Cronenberg's: the couple that crashes together bashes together.

SIGHT AND SOUND, 6/97, p. Leslie Dick

Television commercial producer James Ballard and his wife Catherine live in Toronto, Canada, and have an open marriage, although they still have sex together. One night, James' car accidentally collides with another vehicle. The driver of the other car is killed, but his wife, Dr Helen Reminton, and James survive with injuries. At the hospital, James meets a scarred man named Vaughan coming out of Helen's room.

After being released from hospital, James becomes fascinated with cars and finds himself sexually excited by road accidents. He meets a similarly aroused Helen at the police pound and offers her a lift. At an airport parking lot, they have sex in the car. Helen invites James to a recreation of James Dean's fatal collision staged by Vaughan. Through Vaughan, James meets Vaughan's strange entourage: Colin (a stuntman), his wife Vera, and their disabled friend Gabrielle.

After a menacing car chase during which Vaughan almost forces Catherine off the road, James introduces Catherine to Vaughan. While the married couple make love, Catherine fantasises aloud about Vaughan. The three of them encounter a freeway crash which was caused by Colin recreating Jayne Mansfield's fatal accident. Later, Vaughan has bruise-inducing sex with Catherine in his car while James drives them through a car wash. In another car, James penetrates a wound in Gabrielle's leg with his penis to their mutual satisfaction. Later, Vaughan and he have sex, after which Vaughan threatens to run him down with his car. Vaughan once more chases Catherine, but suddenly Vaughan hurtles off the freeway into a bus and is killed. Afterwards, James buys the wrecked hulk of Vaughan's car and uses it to help Catherine experience the pleasure of her own accident.

Leaving aside for a moment the howling outrage elicited in Britain by *Crash*, it is striking to note that some Ballard fans condemn the film for the opposite reasons: not violent enough, not extreme enough, not transgressive enough. A no-win scenario, in which a film is denounced as both shocking and dull. However, I would propose that this film is indeed both shocking and dull: any obsession that one doesn't share is undeniably dull, while often shocking. This film turns its medical gaze on an obsession, and it does not seduce us into partaking in the obsession, nor does it invite us to identify with the obsessed. Indeed it refuses to provide us with those narrative trappings like motivation or personality which would allow us to identify in any conventional sense. Not a pornographic text, *Crash* is rather a text on pornography, a cool, detached look at sexual obsession itself.

People who are into cars are also disappointed—the crash sequences are shot with the same detachment as the sex scenes, they feel strangely unreal, artificial, despite (or because of) the obsessive attention to detail. Again, it's a clinical look, Cronenberg's speciality. In *Crash*, Vaughan's (Elias Koteas) car has mythic dimensions, a black Lincoln Continental the same as the one Kennedy was shot in, thereby proposing JFK's assassination as another kind of crash, but James Ballard (James Spader) drives a generic sedan, an American car, while Catherine (Deborah Kara Unger) drives a Mazda Miata, a sexy, diminutive sports car. Still, Cronenberg eschews the conventional formulas; neither television car ad nor Hollywood crash sequence, the cars in *Crash* have a conceptual presence that outweighs their styling. They are representations of technology, imbued with the promise of sex and death, not consumer desirables.

The opening of *Crash*, in a light aircraft hangar, sets the terms for sexuality as an encounter of bodies and technology. Catherine, in high heels and straight skirt, a homage to Helmut Newton, presses her magnificent breast up against a plane, before being fucked from behind by some anonymous man. I was irritated by the lingerie-advert-style satin bras that keep appearing until I understood the technologic parallel: the gleam on the protuberant satin like the shine on the bulging wing of a car or nose of a jet. The topic of *Crash* is the intersection of (sexual) bodies, (automobile) technology, and (catastrophic) medicine, with the cars standing in for modern society, becoming sheer representations of the death drive, and it seems Freud's idea that people are driven towards death and destruction as much as towards survival and reproduction is still wildly transgressive.

For J.G. Ballard, the novel *Crash* was a dystopian satire, a counter-blast to consumer-safety advocate Ralph Nader. Ballard saw cars as the totem of American culture: aggressive, wasteful, violent, sexual, with a functional dimension. Naderism was an attempt to draw a veil over this reality, to pretend that seat-belts and crumple-zones and baby seats would make safe this killing machine, domesticate it. But to Ballard, this was a lie, like the lie that the home itself is a safe place.

The sexual obsession in this movie is idea-driven, and while it presents an unutterably bleak and dark view, it also allows for a vein of wit that occasionally moves forward into outright comedy. Obsession is on some level absurd, and when Vaughan breathes heavily over James' wounds, or Helen Remington (Holly Hunter) fumbles for the remote, at the mercy of an urgent need to see the end of the crash test video she's hooked on, it is a great comic moment. Cronenberg presents Vaughan's cronies as a typical subcultural scene, rolling spliffs on an old sofa in front of the box, while Vaughan plans the next great performance art crash, very Survival Research Lab, very punk. Gabrielle (Rosanna Arquette) is an avatar of punk style, encased in black leather orthopaedic corset, braces, trusses and supports, the back of her thigh revealing (through black net stockings) a fissure, a cleft, the trace of some unspeakable wound. When James gets around to fucking it, it is both shocking and very amusing, because we can't forget the taboos around disability, this ultimate site of the forbidden.

The weakness of the film is in the characterisation of Vaughan, who is the heart of darkness, the black hole towards which all the others are ineluctably drawn. His sexual dynamic is too physical, I think, yet despite this the film does convey the poignancy of this strange relationship, as James and Vaughan first use Catherine as their sexual link, and then finally fuck each other. The car wash scene, with James at the wheel while Vaughan and Catherine do it in the back, is very beautiful, the suds like a psychedelic light show framing James' expressionless face, the clunky convertible roof automatically extending itself as Vaughan descends on Catherine's body.

Crash is a brilliant, brave film non-narrative, anti-realist, cool as a cucumber, it sticks to its conceptual guns, refusing to situate the audience comfortably, calmly bringing forward a celebration of sex and death, as if for our consideration. It is this very calm—the stylisation, the use of tableau, the subtle intensity of Howard Shore's score, the emptiness of the characters—that makes the film so disturbing, witty and dispassionate, as it studies an obsession that is itself shocking, and necessarily, as obsession must be, a little dull.

TIME, 3/24/97, p. 88, Richard Corliss

At last May's Cannes Film Festival it won a hotly disputed prize for "originality, daring and audacity." In November it nabbed five Genies (Canada's Oscar equivalent), including one for director David Cronenberg. It also earned a chilling blast of invective from Ted Turner, boss of bosses of the film's U.S. distributor, Fine Line Features (and vice chairman of Time Warner, parent of TIME). Now *Crash*—from J.G. Ballard's notorious 1973 novel, and with an NC-17 warning sticker affixed—finally opens in the country that invented car culture.

Its premise is custom-made to shock: five people take their pleasure by making love in the twisted wrecks of cars. Not simple thrill seekers, these folks have turned their kink into a cult, elevated making out in the backseat to sado-masochistic levels, converted rubbernecking into a black art. They preach "the reshaping of the human body by modern technology." Their grail is James Dean's Porsche Spyder 550; their relics are photos of Jayne Mansfield's fatal collision. Kinda creepy, huh?

Fade in on a luscious blond, sleek as a vintage Corvette, who presses her breast against a car hood while an anonymous man caresses her skin as if it were rich Corinthian leather. The scene is from a film being shot by director James Ballard (James Spader), and the star is Ballard's wife Catherine (Deborah Kara Unger).

But this is just fun and games. The real show begins when Ballard's car jumps a barrier and head-ons another car; the driver is killed, but his wife, a doctor (Holly Hunter), survives. Ballard meets her at the hospital, and in a trice they are having urgent sex in an airport garage. The doctor tells of her other sexcapades in cars: "They felt like traffic accidents." She loves making love to men with scars; to her, each wound is an orifice, and auto eroticism is an aphrodisiac. It is more—a sacrament—to Vaughan (Elias Koteas), whose obsession with celebrity crashes has made him a priest of the car cult. He seeks immortality in heavy-metal scrapes with death.

Cars and sex do have things in common: acceleration, aggression, contact, combustion. Cinema, eternal celebrant of the stupid-funny car crash, is the ideal medium to anatomize America's fetishizing of the automobile. And Cronenberg is the very guy for the job. His first commercial film, *Fast Company* , was about stock-car racing; his brilliant remake of *The Fly* was a parable of love, decay and death, of man misguidedly using machinery to transform himself.

An intellectual and a sensualist, Cronenberg graces *Crash* with philosophical musings, acres of pretty flesh and even more penis talk than on some 8 o'clock sitcoms. For all that, Crash doesn't work. Sexual without being sexy, the film moves smoothly but slowly, like a Caddy on a revolving showroom platform. Dialogue scenes are conducted in a reverent whisper; only the brakes screech, just after a climax or before a death. Even the carnographic love play—in which each character has predictably weird sex with most of the others—is too studied. The fine actors disport themselves solemnly, like giant hood ornaments of lust.

Maybe a little careering delirium would have helped. It may seem perverse to demand that an outrageous film go still further, faster, wilder. But if it had, *Crash* wouldn't be the honorable chore it finally is—less a joyride than an endless traffic jam.

VILLAGE VOICE, 3/25/97, p. 75, J. Hoberman

Booed at Cannes and banned in London, dissed (so they say) by Francis Coppola and disowned (temporarily) by distributor Ted Turner, David Cronenberg's *Crash* arrives here laden with baggage. Will this metaphoric meditation on sex, death, and automobile crack-ups achieve sufficient visibility to be denounced by Bill Clinton or Mothers Against Drunk Driving? Suffice to say, that, while not for every taste, the most controversial Canadian movie of all time is also the wittiest, most poetic, and best-crafted commercial feature to open so far this year.

Does *Crash* deserve the scarlet NC-17? Perhaps prospective viewers should submit to a mandatory IQ test or first apply themselves to J.G. Ballard's cult novel. (The 1973 *New York*

Times review began *"Crash* is, hands down, the most repulsive book I've yet to come across." Erotic, *and* anti-erotic, *Crash* the movie begins boldly enough with a vacantly lissome blonde (Deborah Kara Unger) dreamily unbuttoning her jumpsuit to press a bare nipple against the enamelized surface of an airplane fuselage before allowing a total stranger to take her from behind. The tone is so solemn audiences might be tempted to laugh—were this not the first of three increasingly peculiar sex scenes.

Sex, largely in cars, is pretty much a *Crash* constant, but Cronenberg, who wrote as well as directed, actually distills a narrative out of Ballard's laconic phantasmagoria. The film's protagonists are a jaded married couple—morose swingers with a taste for risky liasons and a need to regale the other with an account of their extramarital exploits. Or perhaps it's just that James (James Spader, an actor who exudes spoiled hedonism) is trying to attract the attention of his hilariously self-absorbed Catherine (Unger). At once dazed and hyperalert, she is forever looking sidelong off-camera. No sooner does her husband initiate a caress than her eyes slide away like marbles on a table.

James's accidental encounter with Dr. Helen Remington (Holly Hunter, earnest but miscast)—namely a head-on collision that kills her husband—brings the couple in contact with a sexual subculture of car-crash enthusiasts. Alienated isn't even the word for these thrill seekers, who are led by the charismatic Vaughan. (Elias Koteas brings to this hospital-ghoul the insinuating, obsessive quality of his work with Atom Egoyan.) Catherine and James have their hottest sex fantasizing about rough-trade Vaughan ... and his wheels. ("I'll bet he's fucked lots of women in that big car," Catherine sighs. "I'll bet it smells of semen." "It does," her husband assures her.)

In the novel, Vaughan is obsessed with crashing his 1963 black Lincoln convertible (the JFK death car) into Elizabeth Taylor's limousine. In the movie, he restages famous crack-ups "The Fatal Crash of James Dean"—on a deserted nighttime road. His announced project is to use modern technology to "reshape the human body"—a process Cronenberg has himself explored quite memorably in *Videodrome* and *Dead Ringers*. The cult's mascot Gabrielle (a splendid Rosanna Arquette) is, in fact, a sort of cyborg—the Dr. Strangelove of sex, wrapping a leather miniskirt around customized braces that manage to suggest a prosthetic limb, a hockey goalie's shinguard, and some unnamed s/m device.

Cronenberg's hypnotic affect does not preclude an extremely dry humor. Just as Ballard's entire novel might be described as a gloss on the phrase "autoeroticism," so the movie's funniest jokes—if that's the correct term—are purely visual. Most are puns in which automobiles mimic the human sexual response or vice versa—a closeup of an automatic car window slowly rising, the running-gag equation of tail-gating and rear-entry sex. In one memorable scene, the cult sits around getting off on videotapes of Swedish test crashes, as if to clinch the identification between Volvos and vulvas.

Its tone perfectly sustained throughout, *Crash* manages the tricky feat of feeling like sci-fi while looking like Now. Most of the movie is set in the generic nowhere of Toronto's bland highrise-cum-industrial outskirts—an antiseptic location rendered all the more dreamlike by the characters' activities (as well as the lush drone of Howard Shore's atonal score). Having survived their accident to land in an otherwise empty airport hospital, both James and Helen conclude, pace *Invasion of the Body Snatchers,* that something is different: the world is filled with ever more traffic.

A highway cloverleaf may seem creepily organic but, scarcely a gross-out, *Crash* is too stylized for splatter and too astutely edited to be porn. And, despite several choreographed instances of highway bumper cars, it's hardly an action film. "This is a work of art," Vaughan exclaims as he raptly photographs the vast multivehicle pile-up that Cronenberg has devised. So, too, are the movie's fastidiously created scars, suggestively oblique montage, seductively, fetishized surfaces, and deadpan fantastic medical devices. The impact is largely cerebral, with every shot designed to wring pathos from trauma.

In short, *Crash* is one brilliantly worked out film. Although following some of Ballard's baroquely detailed sexual scenarios, Cronenberg has his own agenda. The lyrical tour de force, in which James uses the rearview mirror to watch Vaughan and Catherine screwing in the backseat as the sex machine they're riding in passes through the sudsy deluge of an automatic car wash, is matched only by the mad passion with which he rips Gabrielle's mesh stockings to fuck the new orifice that some automobile or surgeon has cut in her leg. Sex is also a technology.

Uncompromising in its melancholia, *Crash* establishes a profound sense of seeking comfort in the crevices of a lacerating, metallic world. In the context of this brilliant science fiction, our species is imagined as vulnerable bits of oozing, sucking, coupling, retracting, yearning protoplasm. Does the thought disturb you? Shown on a double bill with *Speed* or *Star Wars* (or *The English Patient* for that matter), *Crash* would emerge as an infinitely more honest and moral movie.

Also reviewed in:
NATION, 4/14/97, p. 36, Stuart Klawans
NEW REPUBLIC, 4/21/97, p. 26, Stanley Kauffmann
NEW YORK TIMES, 3/21/97, p. C3, Janet Maslin
NEW YORKER, 3/31/97, p. 106, Anthony Lane
VARIETY, 5/20-26/96, p. 30, Todd McCarthy
WASHINGTON POST, 3/21/97, Weekend/p. 48, Desson Howe

CREMASTER 5

Producer: Barbara Gladstone and Matthew Barney. *Director:* Matthew Barney. *Screenplay:* Matthew Barney. *Director of Photography:* Peter Strietmann. *Music:* Jonathan Bepler. Sound: Jeno Banyai. *Set Designer:* Robert Wogan. *Running time:* 54 minutes. *MPAA Rating:* Not Rated.

CAST: Ursula Andress (Queen of Chain); Matthew Barney (Diva/Giant/Magician); Joanne Rha and Susan Rha (Queen's Ushers).

VILLAGE VOICE, 10/28/97, p. 79, Amy Taubin

Matthew Barney has been tinkering with video for as long as he has been making sculpture. Barney fans will recall the videos of the artist as gymnast, navigating dangerous-looking trapeze-like structures, and the ridiculous sci-fi pieces shown on tiny, suspended monitors in his first Whitney Biennial installation.

The tapes in the *Cremaster* series are of a slightly different order. Transferred to 35mm and running slightly under an hour apiece, they are intended for viewing in theatrical situations. *Cremaster 4* and *Cremaster 1,* the first and second films in the series, played at the Film Forum about a year ago. *Cremaster 5,* the third and most recent *(Cremaster 2* and *3* have yet to be made), is a giant leap forward. At long last, it seems to have dawned on Barney that editing is a major component of cinematic expression.

While not lacking provocative images, *Cremaster 4* and *Cremaster 1* employed only the most primitive parallel editing, clunkily cutting back and forth between, say, the yellow "pace car" and the blue "pace car" as they zoomed around the Isle of Wight, or between a giant football field filled with Busby Berkeley-style chorus girls and the minuscule interior of the cabin of a Goodyear blimp, where a bevy of female flight attendants hovered over a dish of grapes. *Cremaster 5* is also structured around two locations, both atmospheric relics of 19th-century Budapest—an elaborate red-and-gold opera-house interior and a similarly baroque pale-green tiled pool in a disused bathhouse. But here the movement from one to another is as sinuous as the movement within the individual sequences.

Although *Cremaster 5* has a text, it's no more a narrative than the earlier pieces. A skeletal opera with a libretto written by Barney in Hungarian (oh, why not?), it involves four characters: the Queen of Chain (a haggard but regal Ursula Andress) and what one might think of as her three suitors—the Diva, the Magician, and the Giant—all played (I use the word loosely) by Barney.

A hybrid of film and performance art, *Cremaster 5* owes something to Werner Schroeter and even more to Robert Wilson (I'd add Jack Smith, except that Smith would have been revolted by Barney's seamlessly fabricated, spare-no-expense aesthetic). Barney's visual imagination, however, is as original as the allegorical system that underlies his entire oeuvre. Where else would you find a flock of fragile white Jacobin pigeons fluttering at the ends of long ribbons attached to the groin of a half-naked man (the Giant)? The groin, in case you didn't know, is where the cremaster is located; it's the muscle that, contracting or expanding according to temperature, causes the testicles to move closer to or further from the torso. Part of the pleasure of Barney's work is hermeneutical but even more is purely aesthetic. It's possible to be baffled by *Cremaster 5* and still be ravished by its beauty.

Also reviewed in:
NEW YORK TIMES, 10/22/97, p. E5, Stephen Holden
VARIETY, 3/30-4/5/98, p. 43, Derek Elley

CRITICAL CARE

A Live Entertainment release in association with Village Roadshow-ASQA Film Partnership of a Live Film and Mediaworks production. *Executive Producer:* Don Carmody. *Producer:* Steven S. Schwartz and Sidney Lumet. *Director:* Sidney Lumet. *Screenplay:* Steven S. Schwartz. *Based on the novel by:* Richard Dooling. *Director of Photography:* David Watkin. *Editor:* Tom Swartwout. *Music:* Michael Convertino. *Sound:* Bruce Carwardine. *Casting:* Avy Kaufman. *Production Designer:* Philip Rosenberg. *Art Director:* Dennis Davenport. *Set Designer:* Gord White. *Set Decorator:* Carolyn Cartwright and Enrico Campana. *Costumes:* Dona Granata. *Running time:* 107 minutes. *MPAA Rating:* R.

CAST: James Spader (Dr. Werner Ernst); Kyra Sedgwick (Felicia Potter); Helen Mirren (Stella); Margo Martindale (Connie Potter); Jeffrey Wright (Bed Two); Wallace Shawn (Furnaceman); Anne Bancroft (Nun); Albert Brooks (Dr. Butz); Philip Bosco (Dr. Hofstader); Edward Herrmann (Robert Payne); Colm Feore (Wilson); James Lally (Poindexter); Al Waxman (Sheldon Hatchett); Harvey Atkin (Judge Fatale).

CHRISTIAN SCIENCE MONITOR, 11/14/97, p. 12, David Sterritt

[*Critical Care* was reviewed jointly with *The Apostle*; see Sterritt's review of that film.]

LOS ANGELES TIMES, 10/31/97, Calendar/p. 20, Jack Mathews

[*The following review by Jack Mathews appeared in a slightly different form in* **NEWSDAY, 10/31/97, Part II/p. B6.**]

It says more about the intellectual vitality of Hollywood and the passive mood of the country than it does about 73-year-old Sidney Lumet that his excoriating satire of television, the 1976 "Network," is followed two decades later by as tepid a parody of the U.S. health system as "Critical Care."

"Network," like many studio films of the '70s, was punishing in its irreverence, isolating its targets—ratings-obsessed TV executives, amoral careerists, megalomaniacal anchors, opportunistic activists and everything else about the medium, that made screenwriter Paddy Chayefsky madder than hell—and attacking them with the precision of smart bombs. It was a cynical, zero tolerance assault on an industry being driven by greed toward social irresponsibility, and one so dead-on in its vision that it's come to be regarded as a work of prescient social criticism.

By contrast, "Critical Care," set in an intensive care unit where patients exist on life support, is a bowl of hospital oatmeal. It's a mushy combination of doctor jokes, clumsy fantasies and over-earnest moralizing about issues so obvious that people in the health care industry may be its best audience. The film has its own set of worthy targets—bottom-line hospital administrators, dispassionate lawyers and insurance companies, egocentric doctors and misguided relatives of dying patients—but no one is seriously hurt.

The script, a first effort by television producer Steven Schwartz, cracks these issues by spending a few days with Dr. Werner (James Spader), a bright second-year resident in the heroic care unit of a spotless, state-of-the-art urban hospital. He looks after patients for whom all hope is lost, but who—providing they are fully insured—are kept alive anyway. These are not merely people in a persistent state of vegetation, they're cash cows.

Dr. Ernst is looking forward to doing his final year of residency in the hospital's high-tech wing, where the future of medicine is being configured with holograms and research grants. But after he goes to bed with the daughter of one of his patients, and gives illicit advice about pulling the plug on Dad, he is caught in a career-threatening legal web.

Seems that Felicia Potter (Kyra Sedgwick) and her Bible-hugging half-sister Connie (Margo Martindale) are fighting over a potential $10-million inheritance. If their father dies in the next three weeks, all the money goes to Felicia. If he lingers beyond that, the prize goes to Connie. Felicia, with videotaped evidence, is blackmailing the doctor, giving him the options of pulling the plug himself, helping her convince the court it should be done legally or having his ethical lapse, among other things, exposed.

Spader and Sedgwick seem to be acting in different movies when they're in the same scenes. Ernst cracks the occasional joke but Spader otherwise plays him with dead and deadening seriousness. Meanwhile, Felicia is played with such high vamp voltage by Sedgwick that she's barely more than a blur of giggles, lipstick, legs and bright pastel leather.

The bulk of the film's laughs are provided by a heavily made-up Albert Brooks, playing the hospital's alcoholic, absent-minded administrator. And Helen Mirren brings honest humanity to to her role of an intensive care nurse tempted to honor the wishes of a patient begging for death. At the other extreme is Wallace Shawn, repulsively unfunny as Satan's emissary in a series of ill-conceived fantasy sequences.

It's understandable, on some level, how the ideas behind "Critical Care" drew Lumet's interest. In the 40 years since his first film, "12 Angry Men," no American director has tried harder to stay on the course of a social dramatist, or succeeded more often. But the heyday of Hollywood social drama has passed, and the pickings among finance-able, issue-oriented scripts are slim.

"Network" was a major studio movie, with full resources, a large, rich cast, a script by a mature, productively cynical veteran, and a wide audience eager for pointed entertainment. "Critical Care" has none of those advantages. Schwartz's script may have stood out for its subject matter, and for that, the younger Lumet might have given it an E for effort. But it's hard to imagine him making it.

NEW YORK POST, 10/31/97, p. 50, Michael Medved

In contrast to the heroic hunks who staff TV's "ER," the medical weasels in Sidney Lumet's "Critical Care" never lose sight of their selfish, shallow priorities: inflated insurance billings, lawsuit avoidance, hospital profits, prestigious fellowships, meaningless technical advances and seduction of vulnerable bimbos.

In this glistening, high-tech hospital setting of cold chrome and blue-glycerin mattresses, James Spader plays a hotshot second-year resident assigned to the Intensive Care Unit.

His mostly comatose patients ("I have lettuce in my refrigerator with a better chance of becoming conscious than this guy!") place few demands on him, leaving him free to explore the aphrodisiac powers of his new title, "Dr."

One target of his lust is a bubble-brained, bleached-blonde model (Kyra Sedgwick,) who yearns to disconnect her elderly father from life support, but must overcome the objections of her frumpy half-sister (Margo Martindale), a demented Bible-thumper.

Spader flirts shamelessly with Sedgwick, and they soon tumble into bed together, where she secretly videotapes him admitting that her father has no chance of escaping his "vegetative" state.

This tape then turns up in a lawsuit to force the hospital to pull the plug—since her father must die within three weeks or she won't inherit his $10 million estate.

Meanwhile, the hospital's senile, alcoholic chairman emeritus of critical care (an unrecognizably aged—and very funny Albert Brooks) also concentrates exclusively on money, as does its bullying chief attorney (Edward Hermann).

Only a cynical, cancer-surviving nurse (Helen Mirren) shows compassion for the patients.

The wised-up screenplay focuses more on distorting elements of greed in modern medicine than timeless, intractable questions of the right to die.

Director Lumet plays too many surrealistic games with heavenly blue backgrounds vs. hellish reds, introducing an other-worldly nun (Anne Bancroft) and a diabolical "furnaceman" (Wallace Shawn).

The combination of comical insanity and sobering issues in a hospital at the edge of collapse inevitably recalls 1971's memorable Arthur Hiller-Paddy Chaveysky collaboration "The Hospital," but this edgy effort lacks its predecsor's warm-hearted emotion, providing no characters worthy of respect or affection.

Nevertheless, the uncompromising intelligence, style and polished performances of "Critical Care" produce strong vital signs that stand out in a season of mostly comatose and brain-dead new releases.

VILLAGE VOICE, 11/4/97, p. 79, J. Hoberman

The comprehensive health care plan Bill Clinton promised us may have flatlined back in the fall of 1994, but Americans were scarcely left uncovered. That same season brought the weirdly comforting, phenomenally popular TV show *E.R.*—"At last, a health program that works" in *Newsweek*'s classic cover line.

E.R. is a fantasy in which all can share—the actual health care system is a reality we get to experience as individuals, without necessarily living to tell the tale. This paradox, not unlike the heavenly scenarios put forth by organized religion, helps muddle Sidney Lumet's *Critical Care*—a well-meaning muckraker, burdened with the additional problem of how to out-*E.R.* the TV juggernaut.

Scarcely up to the level of Paddy Chayefski's 1971 *Hospital,* a madcap metaphor for the Great Society's collapse, the Lumet screed is a movie with precious few vital signs. It's set in an antiseptic intensive-care ward that's hushed by the presence of medical priesthood and backlit to suggest some sort of sci-fi heaven. Can satire be soothing? The pace is beyond deliberate, its slowness accentuated by a sober absence of music, save for the failed levity of the credit song, "Dem Bones," and an occasional Mozart spasm.

The dirty secret of the film's underpopulated IC unit, and by extension American medicine, is that terminal cases are being kept alive to drain their health insurance into the hospital coffers. "I have lettuce in my refrigerator with a better chance of becoming conscious than this guy," ambitious young resident Dr. Ernst (James Spader) riffs with the wise veteran intensive-care nurse (Helen Mirren). Another patient, young enough to inspire pathos and sufficiently alert to beg his caretakers for death, has the additional horror of hallucinating a demonic Wallace Shawn perched at his bedside. (As if this visionary interpolation was not lame enough, Lumet throws in another with the gracious Anne Bancroft haunting the hospital corridors as a mystical blue nun.)

James Spader has made his career playing yuppie scapegoats, and such satisfaction as *Critical Care* offers is largely predicated upon the dubious pleasure of watching him squirm. After the randy Dr. Ernst is purposefully seduced by the lettuce man's floozy daughter (Kyra Sedgwick in a funny, one-note performance), Lumet segues from bedside melodrama to his preferred legal wrangle. Unaccountably heroic after his ethical system collapses, Dr. Ernst tries to go it alone—speaking up for himself and the rights of all patients. (Their rights to do what is never made clear.)

The futuristic notion of a patient as a file of digitized symptoms notwithstanding, *Critical Care* trots out its managed-care critique most elaborately in the several Socratic dialogues Dr. Ernst has with his supposed mentor, the cigar-chomping, bourbon-swilling chief resident Dr. Butz (Albert Brooks, made up to resemble a 65-year-old country lawyer). Broad as it is, Brooks' drunken Cliff Arquette routine brightens up the movie, which is scarcely subtle enough to resist his cynical curmudgeon totally committed to the idea of medicine as a business.

The barbaric steps taken to maintain the dying will scarcely surprise those who have had a loved one attached to a ventilator. They may, however, derive a certain bleak vindication from Dr. Butz's disclosure that he carries no health insurance—it is, as he explains to Dr. Ernst, a more effective way to safeguard against extreme measures than a living will.

Also reviewed in:
CHICAGO TRIBUNE, 10/31/97, Friday/p. E, Michael Wilmington
NEW REPUBLIC, 12/1/97, p. 33, Stanley Kauffmann
NEW YORK TIMES, 10/31/97, p. E20, Stephen Holden
VARIETY, 10/13-19/97, p. 84, Todd McCarthy
WASHINGTON POST, 11/14/97, p. D7, Rita Kempley
WASHINGTON POST, 11/14/97, Weekend/p. 52, Desson Howe

CYCLO

A CFP Distribution release of a Les Productions Lazennec film in coproduction with Lumière, La Sept Cinema, and La SFP Cinema in association with Salon Films Ltd. and Gai Phong Film Studio. *Producer:* Christophe Rossignon. *Director:* Tran Anh Hung. *Screenplay (Vietnamese with English subtitles):* Tran Anh Hung. *Director of Photography:* Benoit Delhomme. *Editor:* Nicole Dedieu and Claude Ronzeau. *Music:* Ton That Tiet. *Sound:* Dominique Dalmasso. *Sound Editor:* Marie-France Ghilbert. *Casting:* Nicolas Cambois. *Art Director:* Daniel Zalay. *Set Designer:* Benoit Barouh. *Costumes:* Henriette Raz. *Make-up:* Valerie Tranier. *Running time:* 120 minutes. *MPAA Rating:* Not Rated.

CAST: Le Van Loc (The Cyclo); Tony Leung-Chiu Wai (Poet); Tran Nu Yen Khe (Sister); Nguyen Nhu Quynh (Madam); Nguyen Hoang Phuc (Tooth); Ngo Vu Quang Hai (Knife); Nguyen Tuyet Ngan (Happy Woman); Doan Viet Ha (Sad Woman); Bjuhoang Huy (Crazy Son); Vo Vinh Phuc (Cyclo's Friend); Le Dinh Huy (Grandfather); Pham Ngoc Lieu (Little Sister); Le Tuan Anh (Handcuff Man); Le Cong Tuan Anh (Drunken Dancer); Nguyen Van Day (Lullaby Man); Bui Thi Mingh Duc (Poet's Mother); Trinh Thinh (Foot Fetishist); Nguyen Dinh Tho (Poet's Father); Nguyen Viet Thang (Cocaine Policeman); Thanh Lam (Singer); Gia Khoan (Government Official); Huang Kiem (Man at TAK-47); Mao Can (Urine Fetishist); Chu Hung (Money Thief); Tran Manh Cuong (Cabaret Man); Tran Quoc Hung (Gorilla); Vo The Vy (Dancer No. 2); Truong Thanh Nghi (Victim of the Lullaby); Pham Hai Truong (Nguyen Thi Hoa Servant); Tran Loc (Fire Man); Tran Minh Tuan and Pham Duy Huong (Old Men); Nguyen Van Tung (Petrol Seller); Le Thai Ngoc Hoan (Child of the Fountain); Ba Phan Chalatoan (Napping Client).

LOS ANGELES TIMES, 8/1/96, Calendar/p. 2, Kevin Thomas

With his Oscar-nominated "The Scent of Green Papaya," writer-director Tran Anh Hung took us into a French-Indochinese world of ritual and tradition so enclosed that he was able to shoot it on a sound stage in France, using several interiors that provided only glimpses of narrow streets outside.

He made us feel the fragility of this world, so soon to crumble, but with his dazzling new film "Cyclo" he plunges us, in jolting contrast, into the hectic heart of downtown of today's Ho Chi Minh City, picking out in the crowded streets a slight, wiry 18-year-old man (Le Van Loc), whom we will know only as the Cyclo (pronounced CEE-clo). He's one of countless men earning a grueling living pedaling a bicycle-taxi known as *cyclos*.

Only a year before, his father, a *cyclo* before him, was killed in a traffic accident, and he has vowed to make a better life for his family: his beautiful older sister (Tran Nu Yên Khé, the exquisite star of "The Scent of Green Papaya"), who delivers pails of water to a vast outdoor market; his younger sister, who shines shoes there; and his 70-ish grandfather, who repairs *cyclo* tires. They live in a tiny apartment behind a beauty salon that at least looks out onto a lovely, foliage-lined stream.

The world of this gentle family, however, proves to be just as fragile as the one depicted in "Green Papaya." When the Cyclo's pedicab is stolen, he is swiftly sucked into a nightmarish underworld in order to pay his steely boss, (Nguyen Nhu Quynh), for its loss. She is in her mid-30s and has a retarded son whom she constantly pets and croons to as if he were a large dog.

The Sister's lover, the Poet (Tony Leung-Chiu Wai, a major Hong Kong star and a marvel at playing passive characters), is a sober, handsome man of much ambiguity and cynicism who supports himself pimping and who is driven to degrade the Sister by prostituting her as well.

The question becomes whether the Cyclo and the Sister will be able to pull themselves back from the path of certain destruction involving connections between individuals of which both are unaware.

At first the shock of rawness, the outright savagery of "Cyclo," is so blinding that it's hard to believe that it was made by the same man who made "Green Papaya." But the two films are really companion pictures, taking us into a Vietnam on the brink of destruction and again two decades after the conclusion of the Vietnam War.

In both instances Hung reveals himself to be a supreme sensualist, marveling in the beauty of a woman's ivory complexion, the flowing and splashing of water and, here, even the metallic glow and flow of spilled paint. Once again, Hung is working with his master cinematographer, Benoit Delhomme, and his equally expressive composer, Ton That Tiet, to create images and moods that border on the surreal.

In his previous picture, Hung showed us a civility about to be swept away, and here he goes further to play innocence against corruption, beauty against cruelty, tenderness against brutality, luxury against poverty to drive home the terrible legacy of the war and a Third World nation ripe for economic exploitation by superpowers.

There are images of self immolation, of fistfuls of American dollars and even a glimpse of a chopper, a war trophy displayed on a tiny plot in the middle of a busy street, suddenly tipped over during a street skirmish. But Hung is not being merely antiAmerican or anti-French, for that matter; instead he is looking deeply to the eternal relationship between good and evil and contemplating how this paradox has played out so drastically over the decades in Southeast Asia.

With its finely shaded portrayals, "Cyclo," which took the Golden Lion at Venice last year, is another superb picture from Hung, a world-class filmmaker if ever there was one.

NEW YORK POST, 2/12/97, p. 38, Thelma Adams

"Cyclo" is profoundly mysterious. Like "The Scent of Green Papaya," Tran Anh Hung's latest, more wrenching drama about a pedal cab driver in the former Saigon, opens at a glacial pace. Using a pointillistic approach, Hung layers dot on dot of color to reveal the complex texture of ordinary life.

In a radical break from the hothouse debut that made Hung's reputation and won the Camera D'Or at Cannes in 1993, "Cyclo," shot on location in Vietnam, escalates to a fever pitch that rivals the hum of Ho Chi Minh City, a ceaseless, exhausting hustle for money and satisfaction in a corrupt post-war economy.

In 1995, "Cyclo" won top honors at the Venice Film Festival before making its American debut at the New York Film Festival. It is about a common man who comes of age in an uncommon situation. The nameless cabby at the story's center is a cyclo; the appellation refers equally to driver and vehicle. Played with a silent grace and pathos by Le Van Loc, the cyclo emerges in the details, recently orphaned, cycling in his late father's footsteps, supporting his two sisters and grandfather.

Thin from overwork, threatened with impotence—the cabby's disease—and beatings at the hands of roving gangs protecting their turf, the cyclo is one dot in the whoosh of traffic. His life is a circular pattern of long hours of labor, brief respites of food and sleep. Or is it?

When thugs steal the cabby's cyclo, the event threatens his family's fragile economy. The situation is complicated by the suggestion that it was not rival gangs who stole the bike, but men in the employ of the cyclo's boss, an alcoholic godmother with a retarded son and her own circular tale of woe.

In order to repay his debt for the lost cab, the cyclo is drawn into a murky underground. A short career as an arsonist puts him on the road to becoming a paid assassin. He falls under the thrall of a nattily dressed poet pimp, played with a smoky charisma by Hong Kong superstar Tony Leung-Chiu Wai ("Chungking Express").

Like the cyclo, Leung's character also mourns a lost father. The poet rose from the slums by vice, his father, still living, rejects his corrupt son and his blood money. Deadened by the pain of loss and the horrible acts he performs as a gang member, the poet gains satisfaction by turning innocents into prostitutes.

When the poet initiates the cyclo's virginal sister ("Papaya"'s incandescent Tran Nu Yen Khe) into the trade, he closes the drama's circle and writes the final stanza on his dark spiritual journey. After a brief moment of rubber-necking, the traffic in Ho Chi Minh City surges on.

At times baffling, often stirring, filled with fits of wonder and rage, unabashedly poetic, "Cyclo" is a masterpiece by a young director in absolute control of his craft who is able to explore the mysteries of life without presuming he holds the key.

NEWSDAY, 2/12/97, Part II/p. B7, John Anderson

There is a poem by Ezra Pound titled "In a Station of the Metro" that reads, in its entirety,
The apparition of these faces in the crowd;
Petals on a wet, black bough.
In its enigmatic fashion, Tran Anh Hung's haunting "Cyclo" is like Pound's poem made plastic. It certainly shares many of the same qualities: a haiku-like economy, a sense of fleeting encounter and fleeting beauty. It is stationary, and yet it moves; in its impressionistic imagery it is elusive, yet never goes away.

"Cyclo" is also a masterpiece. Set in a current time, among an underclass, the film concerns the plight of an unnamed cyclo (Le Van Loc), who drives his bicycle taxi through the seething streets of Ho Chi Minh City. His grandfather fixes flats; his tiny younger sister shines shoes; his older sister, the statuesque, Mona Lisa-like Tran Nu Yen Khe (of Tran's "Scent of Green Papaya"), is a water-bearer who is swiftly coming under the sway of The Poet (Tony Leung-Chiu Wai), a homicidal pimp, drug dealer and thug, whose linen suit and dangling cigarette would make him ludicrous—if he weren't so dangerous.

The family is divided by generation, and by generational ethics: When a bathroom scale arrives in the mail by accident, Cyclo wants his grandfather (Le Dinh Huy) to use it to make money; it'll be easier than pumping flats, he says. But the grandfather wants to wait, resisting even the vaguely illicit gesture, clinging to a nostalgic morality.

"Cyclo" is a chronicle of corruption foretold: When the cyclo's pedal cab is hijacked, his boss (Nguyen Nhu Quynh) demands full payment. Cyclo is compelled to begin a life of crime, sabotaging rice stockpiles, tossing Molotov cocktails, joining forces with the same Poet who's turning his sister into a specialty hooker (her clientele is largely fixated on feet).

There are images of startling effrontery, and startling violence: The tiny bugs that crawl across his face after a fleeing Cyclo has emerged from a muck-filled river, an execution by Mr. Lullaby (Nguyen Van Day), who opens a crimson fountain in an enemy's throat, with the doomed man's face distorted by plastic wrap. The Poet has a chronic nosebleed (caused by nerves or cocaine) and he tends to drip in places that create beautiful pictures.

The camera of Tran Anh Hung is an organic presence; it finds, in interior spaces, a kind of sanctuary, a quiet counterpoint to the raucous, congested streets of the city. It responds to imminent trouble by averting its gaze, rising from the street to the trees, from a building to the sky. It's an intelligent entity within the film: When Mr. Lullaby is about to dispatch his victim, and he does so within a kind of garage, the camera hurries outdoors, at least momentarily, preferring the riot of the street for the insanity inside.

The effect is to give the audience a tangible connection to the film, something Tran accomplishes with motion the same way he did with stillness in his Oscar-nominated "The Scent of Green Papaya." That film, created entirely on indoor sets representing a pre'60s Vietnam, serves as a prelude to "Cyclo," a cinematic prod to faulty national memories and post-war complacence.

The point has been made by some critics—ever since "Cyclo" debuted here at the 1995 New York Film Festival—that there may be no political or moral conscience to it. I think that's wrong. The family unit we begin with remains intact throughout the film, but the father has always been missing; he was killed in a cyclo accident sometime earlier, and his presence hangs over the son. But so does the patriarchy of the United States, whose money is the only currency we see and whose legacy is viewed at least through, the eyes Tran Anh Hung, as one of abandonment and its consequent dysfunction.

SIGHT AND SOUND, 4/96, p. 42, Tony Rayns

Present-day Saigon. The cyclo, 18-year-old driver of a *cyclo-pousse* pedicab, lives with his grandfather and two sisters; his mother died in childbirth and his father (also a cyclo) died in a road accident. His employer, the Boss Lady, allows him to keep 5,000 *dong* of his daily earnings; she has a retarded son of about his age. One day the cyclo's vehicle is stolen and he is beaten up by the thieves when he attempts to give chase. Reporting the theft to the Boss Lady, he is told to follow her mysterious employee the Poet and his two heavies, Knife and Tooth. They lead him to a bare room with faulty wiring and tell him to stay out of sight and await orders.

They soon begin training him in crime. He takes part in an operation to spoil rice in a warehouse (they punish him for detouring to rescue a drowning man during a getaway.) He lobs a Molotov cocktail into the garage of a rival cyclo garage. He is taken to see the gang's executioner Mr Lullaby, who sings to his helpless victims while slitting their throats. Meanwhile the Poet recruits the cyclo's elder sister to work alongside the two prostitutes (one sad, one jolly) he already controls. But he cherishes her innocence: clients are forbidden to deflower her, and the Poet takes her to meet his parents.

The next phase of the cyclo's education is to courier heroin (sewn into sides of pork) across the city. He is almost caught in a police check, an incident which makes him dream of the accident in which his father died. The Poet offers sado-masochistic sex with the elder sister to a businessman, who gets carried away and rapes her; the Poet personally executes him. The cyclo asks the Boss Lady if he can clear his debt to her some other way. He sees one of the men who stole his pedicab (also her employee) and manages to hit him in the face without being seen or caught.

As Tet (the New Year festival) approaches, the cyclo is readied for his first murder: he is provided with a gun and with pills to boost his courage. But instead of carrying out the hit he takes all the pills and becomes delirious, wrecking his room and daubing it and himself with blue paint. The Boss Lady's son is startled by a firecracker placed between his legs by kids; he falls in the path of a passing truck and is killed. The Poet has already retreated to his apartment; he knocks back whisky and an hallucinogen, sets fire to the place and dies in the conflagration.

Next morning the elder sister, grieving for the Poet, has her pocket picked while praying amid crowds at a temple, but is then invited to eat with a family of street-dwellers. Tooth and Knife find the cyclo out cold on the floor of his room; they tell him he was lucky not to be sent to Mr Lullaby, and discharge him from their service. The Boss Lady cradles the cyclo as if he were her son.

Some time later, the cyclo drives his grandfather and two sisters through the streets of the rapidly changing city in a new pedicab.

Cyclo offers a vivid and intensely physical picture of street-level life in present-day Vietnam, but it could not have been made by anyone in Vietnam's domestic film industry. Neither could it have been made by any of the French directors who have lately used Vietnamese locations for nostalgic evocations of the colonial past. Tran Anh Hung rediscovered his native country while failing to negotiate permission to shoot his first feature *The Scent of Green Papaya* in Saigon, and *Cyclo* clearly reflects not only his profound fascination but also the outsider's detachment which tempered his feelings of involvement and engagement. Everything in the film, from the composition and colour of individual shots to the near-surrealist use of fish, insect and lizard imagery, springs from Tran's particular identity as a foreign-educated Vietnamese.

The film begins as an archetypal "third world" movie, with scenes establishing the sights and especially the sounds of Saigon's bustling streets and sketching the daily routines of the cyclo and his family: the grandfather mending punctures at the roadside, the elder sister delivering water to market stalls, the younger sister shining shoes and the cyclo himself carrying a wide variety of passengers about the city. The point at which social realism shades into stylised morality play is impossible to determine, because the shift is as gradual as the intensification of the imagery. Is it the startling scene in which the cyclo (who has been led through a seemingly derelict, flooded building) enters a throbbing underground disco, where he is told to help carry out a young man who has overdosed on something? Or is it the moment when we first glimpse the Poet, wanly lighting the first of countless cigarettes as he loiters outside the Boss Lady's window, his downcast expression unreadable? Or is it even earlier, when the cyclo first finds himself facing the Boss Lady's retarded son, the boy who will turn out to be his spiritual twin and whose death will eventually, in some unfathomable way, replace his own?

Tran's achievement here is to make the film's metaphorical register explicit and engrossing without losing touch with the underlying level of accurate sociological observation. He makes this work largely through the way he proposes parallels between characters and correspondences, between images and incidents. The clearest parallel throughout the film is that between the cyclo and the Boss Lady's son, one motherless, the other nurtured by an 'evil' mother; both are associated with fish—with the silent need expressed so eloquently by a fish's jaw movements—and both at different times daub themselves with paint. But the image of the Boss Lady cradling her fully-grown son is also paralleled by the image of the executioner Mr Lullaby quasi-parentally cradling his victim at the point of murder: two images of distorted 'parenting' which counterpoint the film's many sidelong glances at more orthodox parent-child relations in everyday life. All of the film's parallels and correspondences cut more than one way, and they are never schematic.

At heart, though, Cyclo is about father-son relations, seen both in the traditional Asian way (the continuation of a family line, the perpetuation of a moral ethos) and in a post-Freudian way (a symbolic crisis in patriarchal values). Over the very first shot of the cyclo working on the streets of Saigon we hear his late father's voice, reminding him that three generations of the family have worked as cyclos and expressing the hope that he will be able to pass on some better inheritance to his own children. There is a strong suggestion that the cyclo later finds the strength to resist falling into total corruption by feeling that he is coming to inhabit the sinews, veins and skin of his father's body. (Here, as throughout the film, the risk of declining into French-style intellectual pretentiousness is kept at bay by the sheer physicality of the detail.)

The Poet, on the other hand, has been disowned by his father, who physically beats him and refuses to allow any of his 'dirty money' into the house. But the Poet also becomes a kind of surrogate father to the cyclo and his elder sister, testing both of them by exposing them to all kinds of evil and secretly (judging by Tony Leung's indelible, introspective performance and by the two Vietnamese poems that he speaks in voice-over) willing them to resist. In these terms, the Poet's psychedelic suicide represents the implosion of patriarchy which has failed both itself and its dependents.

In that the entire film is in some sense a cypher for Vietnam today, Tran is making an unfashionably moralistic point about the country's rush to embrace capitalism and its mercenary values. That he sustains his vision with such credibility and force is a measure of his skill in marshalling his resources and of the extraordinary range of his imagination. There is not one false note in any of the performances, many of them by untrained or inexperienced actors, and the choice of locations and production design are unfailingly expressive. Cyclo does several things that no other film from the 'developing world' has yet dared to do: it attacks the fetish of 'social realism' while showing sexual fetishes for what they are and celebrating the enduring strength of 'innocence' without trading on sentimental pieties. And it is also one of the cinema's most visceral and deeply-felt descents into hell. It is, in short an astounding film.

VILLAGE VOICE, 2/18/97, p. 80, J. Hoberman

The corrupt brutes of Eastwood's D.C. would scarcely seem out of place running the rampantly criminal contemporary Saigon that affords the backdrop for Tran Anh Hung's Cyclo. [The reference is to Absolute Power; see Hoberman's review of that film.]

Paris-based and cinematically Frenchified, Tran first attracted international attention for The Scent of Green Papaya (1993), a delicately hyper-real evocation of the director's lost homeland, which reconstructed a 1950s upperclass Saigon milieu on a European soundstage. Cyclo, included in the 1995 New York Film Festival and opening at Film Forum, was shot in the actual Vietnam but—combining bloody action and languorous chic—this high-powered, low-life melodrama is a no-less-stylized movie.

Cyclo's skinny, impassive hero—an 18-year-old pedicab driver or cyclo (himself the son of a cyclo)—ekes out a living in the midst of Saigon's unending traffic until his pedicab is stolen. In order to repay the "boss lady," from whom he leases his vehicle, he becomes an apprentice criminal in her underworld gang. Vividly detailing the rickshaw life, Cyclo has a definite neorealist component, but it's a lot closer to *Taxi Driver* than to *The Bicycle Thief*. Tran shoots the street from every possible angle. Immersed in traffic, his nameless characters are like the tropical denizens of an urban aquarium—a point made visceral by the slo-mo shot in which the cyclo plunges his mud-flecked face into a goldfish tank.

There's no mistaking Tran for anything other than an aesthete. (Albeit more florid in its effects, his sensuous mix of mega close-ups and modernist documentary montage suggests the recent work of Claire Denis, another displaced French colonial.) Dream overwhelms reality. Carrying dope in sides of pork, the cyclo is stopped by cops, caught in a riot, and wakes from a nightmare. The movie is populated by fantastic characters—singing executioner Mr. Lullabye, Boss Lady's autistic son, and a pimp known as the Poet (HK star Tony Leung) who captivates the cyclo's innocent sister. Played by *Green Papaya's* Tran Nu Yen Khe, this timorous creature—whose goofy Buddha smile suggests abashment at her own beauty—is fetishized within and without the narrative. The Poet, subject to mysterious bleeding from his nose, keeps the sister's virginity intact while having her perform all manner of acts for a variety of kinky clients. As elegant as it is sordid, *Cyclo* is eliptical, distanced, and barely interested in social reality. (There is no evidence of communism beyond a fleeting reference to some neighborhood committee or the glimpse of a schoolgirl's red scarf. Even the whores are paid in U.S. dollars.) *Cyclo* has its share of operatic carnage, but its oddly tranquil climax of death and conflagration, amid the celebration of the Buddhist new year, suggests that the title of this outsize and disturbing vision refers not simply to the world of pedicabs but to some karmic cycle of the universe.

VILLAGE VOICE, 2/18/97, p. 75, Laura Winters

"For me, filmmaking is a way to show the poignant spectacle of unresolved lives," said Tran Anh Hung, speaking quietly in French. The 34-year-old Paris-based director left Vietnam with his family at the age of four, returning for the first time in 1991. What he saw inspired his portrait of Vietnam in *Cyclo*: "A country caught in the middle of transformation," he recalls, "heading towards modernity after almost 20 years of American embargo. There was a huge energy, but an equally huge exhaustion."

Hung filmed *Cyclo* entirely on location in Ho Chi Minh City in 1994, using a hidden camera for many of the street scenes. He searched three months for a boy to play the pedicab driver, and finally found his actor on a street in Danang.

The depiction of random violence in *Cyclo* carries a moral weight "The violence in classic American films is dangerous, because it's justified," Hung says. "In the end, the bad guy always dies. Then you have the violence of Tarantino, which is playful, almost jubilant. But I think that for violence to be seen as a moral thing it needs to come about in a gratuitous way. In *Cyclo* not only do thieves steal the boy's bike, but they come back just to beat him up. Their violence doesn't serve any purpose. So when it happens, you experience its full horror."

As one of the few Vietnamese filmmakers working today, Hung feels his responsibility keenly. "Sadly, there is no real movement of Vietnamese cinema," he says. As for Westerners' notions of Vietnam, "I don't care for the mode of Asian cinema in the West. It carries an exotic image of Asia's past that has no importance today. Let's just say that my film is the first to speak of today's Vietnam. But it will take many films to create a mosaic where one can see Vietnam at close range."

Also reviewed in:
CHICAGO TRIBUNE, 11/1/96, Friday/p. F, Michael Wilmington
NEW YORK TIMES, 2/12/97, p. C18, Janet Maslin
VARIETY, 9/11-17/96, p. 108, David Rooney
WASHINGTON POST, 9/13/96, p. F6, Hal Hinson

DANGEROUS GROUND

A New Line Cinema release of a Gillian Gorfil/Darrell Roodt production; an Ice Cube/Pat Charbonnet production. *Executive Producer:* Ice Cube and Pat Charbonnet. *Producer:* Gillian

Gorfil and Darrell Roodt. *Director:* Darrell James Roodt. *Screenplay:* Greg Latter and Darrell Roodt. *Director of Photography:* Paul Gilpin. *Editor:* David Heitner. *Music:* Stanley Clarke. *Music Editor:* Steve Hope and Lee Scott. *Sound:* Nicky De Beer. *Casting:* Marina Van Tonder. *Production Designer:* Dimitri Repanis. *Art Director:* Emelia Roux. *Set Dresser:* Ninon De Klerk. *Costumes:* Ruy Filipe. *Make-up:* Gabi Molnar. *Stunt Coordinator:* Roly Jansen, Isaac Mavimbela, and Andy Anderson. *Running time:* 92 minutes. *MPAA Rating:* R.

CAST: Thokozani Nkosi (Young Vusi); Ron Smerczac (Interrogation Policeman); Wilson Dunster (Heavy Policeman); Ice Cube (Vusi); Sechaba Morojele (Ernest); Peter Kubheka (Igqira); Roslyn Morapedi (Vusi's Mother); Elizabeth Hurley (Karen); Mabel Mafuya (Woman); Fana Mokoena, Maimela Motubatse, and Nkululeko Mabandla (Youths); Robert Whitehead (Sandton Hotel Receptionist); Gresham Phetjaulima (Bellboy); Toni Caprari (Bar Owner); Temsie Times (Black Hooker); Prophets of Da City (Band in Nightclub); Helge Janssen (Crack Dealer); Anthony Bishop and Ross Preller (White Thugs); Greg Latter (Sam); Eric "Waku" Miyeni (Steven); Ving Rhames (Muki); Candy Jack Lee (Chinese Girl); Robin Smith (Iron Guard); Gys De Villiers (Detective Sergeant); Veronica Mitchell (Muki's Wife).

LOS ANGELES TIMES, 2/12/97, Calendar/p. 6, John Anderson

[The following review by John Anderson appeared in a slightly different form in **NEWSDAY, 2/12/97, Part II/p. B2.]**

OK, let's get this straight. The sometime rapper, sometime actor Ice Cube is cast as a onetime member of the South African resistance who left his homeland for Los Angeles at age, let's say, 12. Returning on the occasion of his father's funeral, he addresses his relatives—all of whom speak in high-toned English—in a diction straight off the streets of South Central L.A.

Assimilation is one thing, but what Ice Cube's character Vusi has accomplished is a tour de force of linguistics and cultural accommodation.

This is not noted in order to make fun of someone's speech patterns, just to mark the glaring unlikelihood that someone who left one country for another at such an advanced age would have also left his native accent, or his native character for that matter, so far behind. At the same time, this is hardly the most incredible aspect of "Dangerous Ground," which transplants a rather standard drama from the 'hood to post-apartheid South Africa. The lesson: with freedom comes responsibility.

So does movie-making, but as long as we're asking for miracles, why not try for an explanation for why Elizabeth Hurley, playing the exotic dancer Karen—who's also the girlfriend of Vusi's crack-addict brother Steven (Eric Miyeni)—makes her first appearance bursting through a door in a T-shirt and leather bikini briefs, with a beautiful tousle of hair and her Estee Lauder undisturbed? There must be an empowerment lesson here someplace, but I was distracted.

Together, Vusi and Karen search for Steven, who owes a big pile of drug money to Muki (Ving Rhames) but can't get off the pipe. Vusi, who represents moral vigor and strength—a refreshing change for the way Americans abroad, even immigrant Americans, are usually portrayed—raises the cash, which doesn't prevent a full-scale blood bath intended to drive home the ideas that liberty costs and that all Africans are brothers.

This is a vanity production for Ice Cube—a really convincing actor even when he's growling, but who's in distinct danger of becoming one-dimensional. He gets to strut his stuff while Hurley struts hers, and together with Sechaba Morojele (who plays Vusi's other brother, Ernest), they compose a kind of nouvelle Mod Squad, dedicated to the good fight in a South Africa going American. It's a posturing film that's boring in its indignation, and marks a real come-down for director Darrell Roodt, who made the heartbreaking "Cry, the Beloved Country," which concerned the same geography, but a world view several light-years away.

NEW YORK POST, 2/12/97, p. 38, Thelma Adams

Prim Estee Lauder mannequin Elizabeth Hurley enters "Dangerous Ground" in a hot pink T-shirt and black thong bikini. Hugh Grant's galpal is all pale thighs and bedroom eyes that promise a roll in dirty sheets. Does the name Divine Brown ring a bell?

Not since Cindy Crawford began and ended her acting career in "Fair Game" has so much attitude been attached to so little talent. Rarely has hair and makeup worked so hard.

Like the Demi Moore character in "Striptease," Hurley's crack-addled stripper claims, "I like dancing." Like Moore, there's no glimmer in the model's icy blues to show she's enjoying a rump bump with a metal pole.

Ice Cube is equally miscast in Darrell Roodt's unintentionally funny guided tour through the new South Africa. The chunky rapper's California grad student never cracks a book, but he has an uncanny ability to crack heads. Did Mr. Cube's Vusi minor in weapons training?

A former teen-aged firebrand, Vusi fled South Africa at gunpoint. A dozen years later, he returns to bury his father. In the puffed-up narration, Vusi claims he "left as an African and came back an American."

Like Roodt's "Cry, the Beloved Country," this new film is an outsider's quest for understanding and reconciliation. Here, Roodt and co-writer Greg Latter have gone pop. The movie rocks with furious pumped-up visuals that shift from black and white to color, dispensing political wisdom along with easily digestible visual nuggets.

After burying the old man in the pastoral Transkei, Vusi heads for Soweto and Johannesburg to find his younger brother, a wayward crackhead. Vusi collides with his brother's girl (Hurley) and a Nigerian drug jackal, Muki (Ving Rhames). Along the way, black thugs jack Vusi's rented Beemer, skinheads diss his girl and he nearly caps a neo-Nazi in broad daylight.

In a few short days, Vusi goes from tourist to avenging angel. One minute, he's studying African lit 101, the next he's majoring in AK47. One minute "Dangerous Ground" is a philosophical quest for the soul of democratic South Africa, the next it's a slumming shoot 'em up straight outta Jo-burg Vice.

Roodt's laudable ambition is to get under the skin of an uncharted country, to show that the end of apartheid was also the beginning of social disarray, that with democracy also came drug dealers and an uneasy coexistence among the races. When Roodt takes the high road, Vusi's liable to apologize: "We've been oppressed by the white man for so long, all we know is oppression."

It's no wonder that the guilty pleasures lie on the low road: Rhames, that most gentle of giants ("Pulp Fiction"), sucking, sucking on a white chicken foot; or Hurley, up for anything, even when that means applying a lamp cord to a villain's lap.

SIGHT AND SOUND, 6/97, p. 49, Chris Darke

After 12 years living in exile in the US, Vusi, a young black man, returns to visit his family in post-apartheid South Africa to mourn the death of his father. His younger brother Steven is missing, so Vusi goes looking for him in Johannesburg. Before embarking, Vusi is car-jacked by a group of hostile black youths. He discovers that Steven's flat is empty but meets Karin, Steven's white drug-addicted girlfriend, who offers to help.

After a nightclub encounter with some racist skinheads, Vusi visits a drug dealer where he spots Steven who, failing to recognise Vusi, flees. Vusi gives chase but loses him. Vusi meets Muki, a Nigerian drug lord to whom Steven owes money. Muki threatens to kill Steven and his entire family if the debt is not paid. Vusi and Karen finally track Steven down. Vusi takes Steven, who's coming down from a hit, to visit Muki where he pays off his brother's debt. Muki shoots Steven dead in front of Vusi and Karin. Out for vengeance, Vusi and his middle brother Ernest unearth an arms cache and go back to Muki's hotel and kill him with the help of Karin. Vusi decides to settle in South Africa and invites his girlfriend to join him. Karin accepts Vusi's invitation to join him with his family where she can kick her drug habit.

One of the most depressing consequences of liberation facing any country newly emerging from under the yoke of oppression is the prospect of American-backed pulp movies being shot on location to add a little local colour to their tired generic shenanigans. Occasionally such films declare themselves to be studies of "the current political climate and social malaise effecting the nation." Then maximum cynicism is in order.

Dangerous Ground is just such a film. Taken lightly, it's a routine gangster movie relocated to Johannesburg in which Ice Cube acts with his furious cedilla-like eyebrows and Liz Hurley wears a number of short skirts but avoids appearing grungy despite the fact that her character is a crack addict. Taken seriously, however, (and with a film as preposterous as this that's asking a lot) *Dangerous Ground* is fairly offensive. It offers itself on several occasions as a movie with a political agenda: "You can't fall into the same trap that the black Americans did in the 70s. They got free, then they got high," Cube lectures at one point. "Drugs have taken over where apartheid left off." But the film wastes no time in showing its true colours, jettisoning the high-minded sermons and giving in to a run-of-the-mill gamut of brawls, car chases and shoot-outs, culminating in a De Palma-style *Scarface*-like bloodbath. As with so many thrillers about righteous anger, the political simply gets boiled down to vigilante justice.

Director Darrell Roodt, who made the Alan Paton adaptation *Cry the Beloved Country*, has stated that the film "was made to be accessible to the MTV generation." Judging from *Dangerous Ground*, he can't be thinking that this generation demands much in the way of depth, characterisation or plausibility. Roodt indulges in all the tricks in the MTV book, layering almost every scene with music, regardless of the atmospheric demands of particular moments and reducing the secondary characters to such paper-thin walk-ons as a fey slob of a drug dealer, a lizard of a strip-club owner and a corrupt high-ranking cop. However, producers of forthcoming James Bond films should take note: should they require a seriously hyperbolic Bond villain then Ving Rhames' magisterially camp turn as Muki the Nigerian drug baron is highly recommended.

Roodt handles the action with necessary competence but little tension and favours a *National Geographic* aesthetic for his shots of the Transkei landscape. He seems completely at a loss when it comes to generating anything of interest in the scenes between Cube and Hurley. Their dialogue is risible and there's little sense even of basic dramatic dynamics in the scenes and absolutely no chemistry between the two. But then Hurley's character is so underwritten that her Khalashnikov-toting intervention at the film's finale is hilarious. Having been shot in South Africa doesn't save *Dangerous Ground* from being a third-rate gangster film, it just gives it a specious frisson of self-serving 'relevance'.

VILLAGE VOICE, 2/25/97, p. 70, Gary Dauphin

The archetypal myth of African Americans recrossing the Atlantic to do the prodigal son thing in the Motherland gets a rather awful update in *Dangerous Ground*. Action-identity fluff from Darrell Roodt (the director of *Sarafina!* and *Cry, the Beloved Country*), *Ground* is part *Shaft in Africa*, part *Boyz 'n the Hood,* and although that's a curious enough pedigree, this film is much, much less than the sum of its parts. Putting African American notions about Africa and homeland onscreen demands care and subtlety, but unfortunately *Ground* is the kind of film whose most extended metaphor involves smearing actor Ving Rhames's face with cocaine and then equating him visually with a big old albino bull. I suppose that's not astoundingly egregious as images of black folks go, but it's also not anything particularly new or interesting.

Ground's actual star isn't the mandingo-cum-drug kingpin played by Rhames, but Ice Cube. Shaft to South Africa's, well, Africa, Cube is what you'd call a bit of an international other here, a South African who returns home after a 12-year exile in the Bay Area. While in America Vusi's not only lost his accent and "African heritage" (he refuses to ceremonially slaughter one of the aforementioned bulls), but he's also lost actual touch with his family. One sibling has become a bitter crank who pines for his days with the ANC planting mines in Boer driveways, while youngest brother Stephen (Eric Miyeni looking like Larry Fishburne playing Ike Turner) has disappeared into Johannesburg's drug underworld. Vusi goes looking for Stephen as a favor to his mother, and thus begins *Ground*'s homage to *Boyz*'s tale of guns, gangs (the aforementioned Rhames), and family vengeance. He'll find, lose, and avenge his brother in short order, director Roodt doling out action sequences and earnest monologues with all the élan of a straight-to-video hack.

Although its plot arc follows *Boyz* quite closely, *Ground*'s textural details are straight out of *Shaft*'s lurid blaxploitation universe. For example, although Vusi is ostensibly a graduate student in African literature, he's also Ice Cube the gangsta, so when it comes time to peel a cap in some nig—I mean *African*'s—ass, he's well up to the task, taking to his brother's old ANC AK-47 like a fish to water. Then there is Elizabeth Hurley, who plays the missing Stephen's girlfriend with a loopy gusto. A white girl with a fetish for black boys, Hurley is also a saucily fun-loving crackhead, her vices providing Cube and *Ground* with two strangely codependent soapboxes: one problack love, the other anticrack. Hurley earns her keep with the black folks through a combination of miniskirted perkiness and good deeds, but it is clear throughout that *Ground* figures both miscegenation and crack cocaine are "problems" the new South Africa is going to have to overcome (or something). Drawing on his experiences in the New World, Vusi does beg his South African brethren to avoid the fate of Black America, which "got free, then got high," but on the white girl problem his feelings are closer to Superfly's than John Shaft's.

Also reviewed in:
NEW YORK TIMES, 2/12/97, p. C10, Stephen Holden
VARIETY, 2/17-23/97, p. 70, Joe Leydon

DANTE'S PEAK

A Universal Pictures release of a Pacific Western production. *Executive Producer:* Ilona Herzberg. *Producer:* Gale Anne Hurd and Joseph M. Singer. *Director:* Roger Donaldson. *Screenplay:* Leslie Bohem. *Director of Photography:* Andrzej Bartkowiak. *Editor:* Howard Smith, Conrad Buff, and Tina Hirsch. *Music:* John Frizzell. *Music Editor:* Abby Treloggen and Jim Weidman. *Sound:* Dave MacMillan and (music) Dennis Sands. Sound Editor: Richard L. Anderson and George Simpson. *Casting:* Mike Fenton and Allison Cowitt. *Production Designer:* Dennis Washington. *Art Director:* Tom Targownik Taylor and Francis J. Pezza. *Set Designer:* Louisa Bonnie, Mary Finn, and David M. Haber. *Set Decorator:* Marvin March. *Set Dresser:* Rich Chirco, Richard Wright, Kevin Chambers, and Greg Lynch. *Visual Effects:* Patrick McClung. *Special Effects:* Roy Arbogast. *Costumes:* Isis Mussenden. *Make-up:* Richard Snell. *Stunt Coordinator:* R.A. Rondell. *Running time:* 112 minutes. *MPAA Rating:* PG-13.

CAST: Pierce Brosnan (Harry Dalton); Linda Hamilton (Rachel Wando); Jamie Renée Smith (Lauren Wando); Jeremy Foley (Graham Wando); Elizabeth Hoffman (Ruth); Charles Hallahan (Paul Dreyfus); Grant Heslov (Greg); Kirk Trutner (Terry Furlong); Arabella Field (Nancy); Tzi Ma (Stan); Brian Reddy (Les Worrell); Lee Garlington (Dr. Jane Fox); Bill Bolender (Sheriff Turner); Carol Androsky (Mary Kelly); Peter Jason (Norman Gates); Jeffrey L. Ward (Jack Collins); Tim Haldeman (Elliot Blair); Walker Brandt (Marianne); Hansford Rowe (Warren Cluster); Susie Spear (Karen Narlington); David Lipper (Hot Springs Man); Heather Stephens (Hot Springs Woman); Ingo Neuhaus (National Guardsman); Patty Raya Macmillan (News Stringer); R.J. Burns (Man at Helicopter); Tammy L. Smith (Town Meeting Woman); Christopher Murray (Pilot); Justin Williams (Paramedic); Donna Deshon and Tom Magnuson (Road Block Newspersons); Marilyn Leubner (Babysitter).

CHRISTIAN SCIENCE MONITOR, 2/7/97, p. 12, David Sterritt

Whirling tornadoes and hostile aliens made "Twister" and "Independence Day" two of last year's most, popular pictures, and now "Dante's Peak" is erupting in theaters everywhere.

Disasters are the order of the day, with "Volcano" and "Titanic" on tap when the warm-weather season arrives. TV networks are also contributing to the calamity craze, placing items like "Asteroid" and "Pandora's Clock" on their agendas. And don't forget the Broadway stage, where "Titanic" will sink to a musical beat starting next month.

Is it a trend? Most critics say no, since only a few major titles are involved, and they're spread over too much time to build truly trendlike tremors.

The current scene is a pale shadow of the 1970s, when Hollywood racked up monumental grosses with epics like "The Poseidon Adventure" and "The Towering Inferno."

True, the '70s disaster wave played itself out before long, but Hollywood has never been famous for learning from the past. The new cycle will end quickly if earnings don't stay high, since "event pictures" bursting with special effects are expensive to produce. Look for plenty more, though, if audiences cotton to the current screen catastrophes.

Early signs are making producers happy. Mountains of "Dante's Peak" publicity have American moviegoers panting to see it, and overseas audiences won't be far behind. The entertainment paper Variety reports that Universal recently unveiled its $100 million epic for exhibitors in Singapore, garnering a prediction that the movie will do "Twister"-type business, i.e., a non-US gross of some $270 million.

Kaboom!

"Dante's Peak" has so much in common with "Twister" that there's every reason to believe the optimistic forecasts. Once again there's a man and a woman, a bucolic American setting, and a disgruntled Mother Nature at the heart of the story. And once again the dramatic ingredients are just a flimsy framework for high-tech effects meant to blow our collective socks off at carefully calculated intervals.

This time the background is a Pacific Northwest community that's just won second place in a contest for most livable American town. Obviously this is one trophy the villagers shouldn't get too attached to, and sure enough, something peculiar is going on at the local volcano. The ground starts trembling, tap water turns a funny color, and a couple of skinny-dippers get boiled in their swimming hole.

A handsome volcanologist shows up, muttering about acid levels and seismic activity. The townspeople resist his bad news, since the prospect of volcanic death would put a hefty dent in the tourist trade. The aptly named Dante's Peak cares nothing for such concerns, of course, and proceeds to blow its top. Everyone flees in a panic, leaving the handsome volcanologist to escort the lovely mayor, her adorable kids, and their feisty old grandma to safety.

Sound familiar? Of course it does, since every moviegoer over 12 has seen all this before in many films. If a lava flow of money does start pouring into Universal's coffers today, it will be yet another testament to the power of entertainment formulas perfected by Steven Spielberg, whose "Jaws" revitalized screen adventure back in 1975.

"Dante's Peak" begins with a sneak preview of volcanic horror—an eruption in Colombia that kills the volcanologist's wife—just like the scary-shark uproar that gets "Jaws" going. Even the soundtrack music is a dead ringer for the pulsing theme (dum-da-dum-da) that boosted Spielberg's suspense.

The mountain town is divided between money-driven ostriches (an eruption would ruin property values!) and right-thinking realists (she's gonna blow whether we like it or not!) exactly like the beach-front citizens of "Jaws," who also debated the dollar value of facing facts and fleeing for their lives.

And for a movie set in the Northern Cascades, there's a surprising number of water-centered scenes. "Jaws" lives again!

It's likely that the makers of "Dante's Peak" are fully aware of these resemblances, and far from being embarrassed, they're probably congratulating themselves for pulling off their Spielbergian stunt so successfully.

So instead of chiding them for lack of originality, it might be more worthwhile to ask whether they recognize the moral liabilities built into the disaster genre as a whole, which raises the uncomfortable question of how nourishing it is for the human spirit to wallow in meticulously produced views of death, disorder, and destruction.

Some specimens—Alfred Hitchcock's classic "The Birds" is a good example—show how physical dangers can draw out inner resources in ordinary people; others, like the recent Sylvester Stallone flop "Daylight," induce us to cheer for a handful of photogenic heroes while ignoring the suffering and extinction of everyone else.

"Dante's Peak" is cleverly constructed, attractively acted by Pierce Brosnan and Linda Hamilton, and impeccably filmed by director Roger Donaldson and cinematographer Andrzej Bartkowiak, who gives some of the most frightening moments a sheen that can only be called beautiful.

But all this lies on the surface. Deeper down, the movie falls into the category of unfeeling thrillers that care less for the welfare of the characters than for the jump-in-your-seat value of the next shocking surprise.

LOS ANGELES TIMES, 2/7/97, Calendar/p. 1, Kenneth Turan

Disaster movies have become Hollywood's version of the seven plagues, a series of natural catastrophes inflicted by the lords of studio misrule on defenseless audiences who can do no more than hope to survive and then survey the damage.

After wind ("Twister"), water ("Daylight") and alien invasion ("Independence Day"), the latest plague to make the rounds is volcanic eruption. "God's big show" has rarely been dealt with since "The Last Days of Pompeii" and "Krakatoa, East of Java," which was most notable for not understanding that Krakatoa is in fact west of Java.

"Dante's Peak" is customary for the genre, with convincing special effects sharing screen time with standard-issue characters and situations. Despite being directed by Roger Donaldson, apparently a geologist *manque*, and with three PhDs listed as "volcanology advisors," this is still the kind of movie where someone's darn dog runs off at the worst possible moment.

One of the things "Dante's Peak" does demonstrate is that the volcanic act itself, accompanied as it is by massive clouds of the most impenetrable black smoke, is not ideal disaster movie material. And I that's not even mentioning the avalanche of snowy ash that makes the appearance of Sgt. Preston of the Yukon seem imminent.

When it comes to the flow of superheated lava, which ought to be the movie's signature element, "Dante's Peak." is curiously coy. Though computer-generated lava is certainly a factor, at one point impressively setting a cabin and surrounding forest on fire, its screen time is limited, more like a cameo appearance than the starring role it deserves.

"Dante's Peak" treats its volcanic eruption as if it were a mass murderer stalking a small town. Ominous music makes the knowledge that something terrible is going to happen unavoidable, but the potential victims in Leslie ("Daylight") Bohem's predictable script are blithely oblivious to the danger they're facing. Except for Harry Dalton (Pierce Brosnan), a steely-eyed volcanologist who's let a bad experience he had when a mountain blew up under him in Latin America turn him into a tireless workaholic "better about volcanoes than people" who neither smiles nor takes vacations.

Harry has been dispatched by the U.S. Geological Survey to the bucolic Pacific Northwest town of Dante's Peak to check out some suspicious readings. It turns out to be a swell spot, celebrated by Money Magazine, "beautiful, safe, a wonderful place to raise a family," according to mayor-single mom Rachel Wando (Linda Hamilton), a town so attractive that powerful Blair Industries is about to invest $18 million in hundreds of new jobs.

Not so fast, says Harry. Even though the odds are 10,000-to-1 against it, he feels the dormant volcano that gives the town its name is a ticking time bomb. Harry's timid boss Paul Dreyfus (Charles Hallahan) says he's out of line, the mayor's cranky mother-in-law (Elizabeth Hoffman) agrees, but Harry, apparently the only person in the film who got an advance copy of the script, keeps insisting that Dante's Peak is going to blow.

When, after an hour of clearing its throat, the inevitable finally happens, "Dante's Peak" becomes not so much a volcano movie as a smorgasbord of selections from other disaster spectaculars. Buildings collapse, rivers go wild, freeway ramps and bridges buckle, crowds panic, and the mayor's cute kids conveniently head right into harm's way. Where's a little extra lava when you need it most?

NEW YORK, 2/17/97, p. 55, David Denby

We know that big snow-capped mountain is going to blow. Out there in the Pacific Northwest, in the idyllic, clear-aired town of Dante's Peak, which is situated at the base of a dormant volcano, Linda Hamilton, of *Terminator* fame, is the mayor, and Pierce Brosnan shows up, a handsome but troubled volcanologist (can that really be what they are called?). It seems there are some mysterious rumblings down below. Brosnan is the only one who takes the threat seriously, but we know the doubters are foolish; after all, there's no movie if the damn thing *doesn't* blow. All through the picture—*Dante's Peak* is the initial offering of the volcano season, which is starting early this year—we can see the plot devices falling into place. There's the stubborn grandma who won't come down from her mountain and has to be rescued by little children, and the cute little dog that disappears just as the lava is beginning to flow. (Myself, I would have let the dog and maybe grandma get toasted, but we won't go into that.) We've seen disaster movies before, and we've certainly seen *Jaws*, some of whose plot elements have been recycled here. *Dante's Peak* is movieish, corny, imitative, and absurdly plotted (by screenwriter Leslie Bohem). Still, the stupid thing gets the job done.

After some mini-quakes and a couple of lovers roasted while frolicking in the hot springs, and so on, the mountain erupts, with nuclear force, and the scenes of panic and devastation in the small town are scary enough. Buildings explode, and a disgusting gray ash falls everywhere. Fiery rocks fly through the air, conking mini-vans and trucks on the head. (God appears to be throwing billiard balls down on his children.) Director Roger Donaldson, or perhaps second-unit director Geoff Murphy, stages a fine scene in which a raging river sweeps away a bridge and a man trapped on the bridge has a passing moment of recognition in which he accepts his fate. Here and there, the movie hits a note of genuine awe.

But why, I wonder, can't we get past the peculiar moral economy of Hollywood disaster movies in which characters who are stubborn and Refuse to Take the Dangers Seriously are always the ones who suffer death? I thought the point was that a natural disaster like an earthquake or volcanic eruption eliminates anything and anyone in its path, guilty, innocent, or merely neutral. On the one hand, Hollywood is telling us that nature is awesome, irresistible, devastating, etc.; on the others it's telling us that we still live in a morally coherent world in which a greedy capitalist gets tried for his poor fault.

Pierce Brosnan somehow survives such lines as "I'm better at figuring out volcanoes than people or politics." Brosnan has always seemed a preposterously handsome man searching for a personality, but in recent years, as he's passed 40, he's developed some sense of how to engage the camera. He has more weight than usual, more substance, even a touch of reserve and melancholy. Pierce Brosnan has grown into his perfect features. For the first time, he seems a genuine movie star.

NEW YORK POST, 2/7/97, p. 37, Michael Medved

"Dante's Peak" erupts with such unexpected force that moviegoers may feel nearly as stunned as the fictional Pacific Northwest town that's blown away in the course of the film.

No, this is not just "Twister" with lava; director Roger Donaldson ("Smash Palace," "No Way Out") instead confounds skeptics by showing as much care for his characters as for his spectacular effects, thereby shaping the most skillful, satisfying disaster movie Hollywood has yet made.

In a suitably eerie prologue in South America, an intrepid researcher (Pierce Brosnan, in unusually sympathetic form) escapes from an exploding volcano but loses his fiancee in the process.

Four years later, still haunted by the experience, strange seismic measurements draw him to a picturesque Cascades Mountain village, proud of the majestic, snow-packed "Dante's Peak" towering over the town.

The mayor, a cafe owner and single mom played with earthy intensity by Linda Hamilton, knows that jittery reports from the visiting volcanologist might jeopardize her hard-won plans for economic development.

Nevertheless, a friendship develops as Hamilton and Brosnan display chemistry nearly as combustible as the worrying rumbles and sulfurous emissions from the mountaintop.

Tension builds gradually, stressing the idyllic beauty of the pre-eruption village, rather, than instantly clobbering the audience with non-stop special effects. As a result, when the otherwordly dazzlements begin assaulting the senses (and characters we care about) halfway through the movie, the impact is truly awesome.

Some of the imagery, relying in part on superbly detailed computer graphics, is unforgettable: floods from melted glaciers sweeping away forests, dams and bridges; gas clouds exploding with the force of a million atom bombs (as with previous real-life eruptions), a formerly tranquil mountain lake suddenly turned to a deadly sea of acid, battered trucks driving across cooling lava fields as tires explode into flame.

Unlike other movies of this type, there's no tongue-in-cheek winking or nudging to break the tension, even though Donaldson does surrender to one of the most obnoxious conventions of disaster movies: it's understandable why you need threatened kids and old ladies, but was it really necessary to throw in the lost dog?

All complaints are finally overwhelmed by the movie's thrills, with superior acting and flawless pacing as bonuses you'd hardly expect in this sort of fare. In any event, "Dante's Peak" is easily powerful enough to insure that you'll never again look at lava lamps the same way.

NEWSDAY, 2/7/97, Part II/p. B2, Jack Mathews

When the volcano in Roger Donaldson's "Dante's Peak" finally blows, it's not just lava and rocks and ash that come spewing out. It's an eruption of action-adventure history, 100 years worth of cliché build-up—the plaque of hacks!—projectile-vomited off the screen.

It all comes raining down in a fury. A quiet hero fighting jaded officials. A stubborn old woman who won't come down from the mountain. Kids who won't stay where they're told. A family dog that runs off, and has to be whisked from the humid breath of a lava flow. Romance developing amidst the rubble. Scientists who won't run from anything, even Mother Nature with the heaves.

"Dante's Peak," like Mt. St. Helens, takes time blowing its top, but when that happens, the movie becomes a blur of hairbreadth escapes. It's like the TV commercial where a four-wheel drive vehicle races down a mountain, narrowly missing an elk, spilled logs and falling boulders before carving a new trail through the canyon and bringing its driver safely home.

In "Dante's Peak," the wonder vehicle is an even sturdier Chevy Suburban truck, and anybody living in the shadow of the apocalypse should have one.

With six weeks of winter remaining, we welcome the year's first pure summer movie, and the first of the year's two volcano disaster pictures. This one stars Pierce Brosnan as volcanologist Harry Dalton, who leads a crew of technicians to the small Pacific Northwest town of Dante's Peak to check the pulse of its slumbering volcano.

For Dante's Peak's mayor, cafe owner and single mom, Rachel Wando (Linda Hamilton), the last thing she needs is the last thing anybody needs—a natural disaster. Her community is just pulling out of a depression, and looking forward to an infusion of jobs and cash from a company she lured to locate there.

But when the sulfur-scorched bodies of a young couple are found in a hot spring spa, Harry quickly attributes their deaths to a volcanic acid burp and urges Rachel to put the town on alert. The mood of Dante's Peak is suddenly as tense as that of coastal Amity in Steven Spielberg's "Jaws."

Donaldson, with an "original" script by Leslie Bohem ("Daylight"), keeps the unlikely "Jaws" parallel going further than you could imagine. He turns the volcano into a monster, a huge, lurking killer ready to consume anything in its path. And like the Great White, it actually seems capable of malice.

It is not, however, capable of turning back, and once it has stopped teasing and threatening the town with seismic rumbles, and begins to barf in earnest, "Dante's Peak" is a runaway Suburban ride—down the mountain, across rivers, through ash storms—with a tidal wave of lava lapping at its wheels.

Donaldson is a veteran studio director with a better record at character-driven thrillers ("No Way Out") than special-effects spectacles ("Species"). Bohem's thin script doesn't give him much to work with in the way of characters, but Brosnan, moonlighting from his new job as James Bond, and Hamilton, the heroine of the "Terminator" movies, make an engaging pair.

While an effort is made to give Harry and Rachel some psychological weight—Harry's fiancée is killed in another volcanic eruption at the start of movie, and we learn that Rachel and her two kids have been abandoned by her husband—there isn't much more to the couple in "Dante's Peak" than those in last summer's zero IQ "Twister."

However, the images—mixing live-action with miniatures and computer-generated lava flows - are often sensational.

For disaster buffs, the year's second volcano movie—the Mick Jackson-directed "Volcano" is due to erupt in theaters this fall.

NEWSWEEK, 2/17/97, p.66, David Ansen

The disaster movie is back, though I'm not sure anybody was asking for it. Why the sudden torrent of twisters, volcanoes and alien invasions? We could give you a sociopolitical tap dance about the post-cold-war Zeitgeist, and how we're projecting our fears of communism back onto Mother Nature, but it would be hard to keep a straight face. No, Hollywood is cranking out this stuff because it needs to put its new high-tech toys to work. When you can create piping-hot streams of lava entirely inside a computer, and digitalize rolling black clouds of smoke and ash, why not make *Dante's Peak*, the first of 1997's two volcano lavapaloozas?

The special effects are definitely the best thing about this curiously bland disasterthon: three cheers for the collapsing freeway, the broken dam, the cool miniatures of collapsing buildings and the swirling volcanic ash (but no cheers for our first glimpse of the peak itself, as phony as a velvet painting). Unfortunately, attached to this fine display of technology are a story and something resembling characters, and we have to wade through a full hour of said "story" before the darn mountain blows.

Pierce Brosnan is the volcanologist with a Tragic Wound. (His fiancée, who also loved volcanoes, was killed by one: we know because it's the first scene in the movie.) Now he sees in Dante's Peak, Wash., all the signs of another looming disaster, but of course no one will heed his warnings, because it might scare off big business coming to town. Supplying the generic love interest is Linda Hamilton as a single mom and the model city's mayor.

Leslie Bohem's script is almost self-parody, but director Roger Donaldson keeps a straight face throughout, even when the obligatory family dog is rescued from the encroaching lava and Granny gets her legs parboiled in an acid lake. It's a sign of how badly awry the human dimension of this movie has gone that Granny's death, played for pathos, evokes only relief. If only those computers could generate virtual emotion.

SIGHT AND SOUND, 4/97, p. 38, Philip Strick

Volcanologist Harry Dalton, studying an eruption in Colombia, makes a belated getaway. His fiancée Marianne is killed in the truckseat beside him. Four years later, Paul Dreyfus, Harry's boss at the Vancouver Observatory's seismology unit, asks Harry to investigate some minor tremors around the town of Dante's Peak. Harry arrives to find the town celebrating its annual Founders' Day; the mayor, Rachel Wando, announces a deal that will boost the region's prosperity. Harry accepts Rachel's guided tour of the region, meeting her children Lauren and Graham, and their Grandmother Ruth. While visiting the hot springs in the woods, they discover two corpses. Harry notifies his boss, but when Dreyfus and his team arrive to conduct tests, Dreyfus says there is no need to warn the townsfolk.

Harry and Dreyfus study the peak. One of the crew, Terry, is injured in a rock-slide, but there is no evidence of seismic activity. Dreyfus decides they might as well leave. Enjoying a farewell evening with Rachel, Harry discovers the town's water-supply is polluted with sulphur. He warns Dreyfus, and the reinstated monitoring equipment suddenly indicates trouble. Rachel announces a town meeting and advises Ruth to leave her home, but she refuses to budge. The townsfolk scatter in panic as the first tremors occur; following a series of explosions, rocks and volcanic ash begin to pelt down on the escaping people.

Frantic to rescue Graham and Lauren, Rachel and Harry find that the children have driven off to collect Ruth; they catch up with them as her house is invaded by a flood of molten lava and the five make their escape by boat across a lake of acid. Ruth jumps overboard to help them reach the shore before the boat sinks; fatally burned, she dies the next day. Meanwhile, Dreyfus and his team make their getaway across the town's main access bridge as flood waters surge over it. The bridge is shattered and Dreyfus is swept away in the torrent. With Rachel and the children, Harry drives into the ruined town just as the Peak explodes with climactic force. They shelter in the disintegrating tunnels of a disused mine where Harry manages to switch on a signalling device that eventually brings a rescue team.

Hollywood's portents of disaster, currently the flavour of the millennium, seem to be confirming a global interest in extinction. While echoing the unstable 70s era of *Earthquake, Jaws* and *The Poseidon Adventure*, the present fears concentrate on vengeful onslaughts from the heavens, a scathing downpour of asteroids, aliens and dispossessed angels. Popular demand, if cinema is any accurate reflection, is apparently for a bombardment that will reduce us, like the dinosaurs, to our properly primordial condition. Such celebrations of vulnerability form a litany of fireballs, tidal waves, tornadoes, hurricanes, and laser-blasts from malignant visitors. And, as illustrated by *Dante's Peak*, subtlety becomes superfluous as soon as the mountain starts to rumble: the rest of the show is simply a series of struggles for survival.

Although lightly sprinkled with aphorisms—sex, for instance, is peculiarly linked to riding a bicycle (once mastered, never forgotten)—Leslie Bohem's script for *Dante's Peak* paraphrases his scenario for *Daylight* with characterisation and plot similarly paper-thin and well-perforated. Scaling down the perky Stallone of *Daylight* to an unassuming Brosnan charmer the film offers no parallels between its hero and a smouldering volcano, consigning him instead to the thankless role of rock-watcher. Mysteriously, despite his unsubstantiated but much-touted skills, he seems to operate mainly on intuition, able to forecast in an urbane Cassandra-ish way that a major catastrophe will follow a minor rock-slide. Equally improbable is Linda Hamilton's craggy but conveniently available town mayor who distractedly drenches visitors at her log-cabin café and conveys the powerful impression that her civic eminence could only have been won in a rigged tombola.

To watch Roger Donaldson's cast attempting to flesh out these cursory sketches is to experience a lesson in sheer bravado, rather as with previous yarns *The Getaway* or *Species*, in which his players adopted trancelike states in evident desperation. Mostly required to utter one-liners, they fill their screen time with bits of business like kicking furniture and drinking coffee while the director pauses before his next emergency. In fact, the only pause that really works in *Dante's Peak* is the Grandmother's death-scene, where the dialogue is largely confined to sobs and the setting is a ghastly billow of volcanic ash. Otherwise, the film alternates its escalating programme of traps and last-moment escapes with an exasperating collection of puzzles, such as why the discovery of two corpses fails to act as an early warning signal or why the seismic-detection equipment is stubbornly dormant until too late.

The justification for its piecemeal structure is in the unarguable magnificence of its visuals, which blatantly re-stage the cinema's latest hits—the exploding buildings from *Independence Day*, the flying projectiles from *Twister*, the underground burrowing (and even the dog-rescue) from *Daylight*. Since eruptions appear to incorporate not only lava-flows and flaming rocks but also an epileptic frenzy of lighting bolts, acid lakes and shockwaves comparable to nuclear blasts there is plenty to bother us. The sight of a packed motorway writhing into fragments or of an entire town bursting into instant ruin is spectacularly disconcerting. Removing the ground from under the feet, Andrzej Bartkowiak's camera wanders on an indecisive trajectory, as unsettling in its revolves and asides as all the lively instability it reveals. And again taking its cue from the multiple pile-ups of other movies about urban breakdown, much of the suspense of *Dante's Peak* takes place behind the wheel, whether escaping from a river-bed or from the incendiary centre of lava-flow, so that surviving becomes a matter of acceleration, tyre pressures and roof-strength, defining an extended MOT for the disaster-prone motorist. While the film's other messages may be less than persuasive, *Dante's Peak* at least makes a strong case for keeping the family saloon both well tanked-up and watertight.

TIME, 2/17/97, p. 80, Richard Schickel

The obsessed scientist whose instincts for catastrophe are more finely tuned than any predictive instrument; his bureaucratic superiors whose waffling makes a bad situation worse; businessmen determined to stifle talk about threats to life, limb and, above all, property for fear of the impact on their interests; a woman, scared but spunky and available for romance when she is not dodging falling objects; and, if possible, an adorable dog to be lost in whatever chaos the movie is trafficking in, then found and daringly rescued to the cheers of an audience that has stoically watched hundreds of anonymous human extras perish.

Disaster movies are our millennial No plays, totally stylized, totally predictable, but comforting in their familiarity. Whether the threat to domestic tranquillity is a ferocious shark, invading spacemen or a rogue volcano (as in *Dante's Peak),* it reassures us that nice people, if they are smart, brave and quick on their feet, will somehow survive.

Writer Leslie Bohem and director Roger Donaldson brush briskly through the standard scientific and romantic blather. They know that in movies like this, complexity is the province of the special-effects people. It's the same with the actors. Cool Pierce Brosnan and warm Linda Hamilton understand that their job is mainly to provide human scale for the lava flows and firestorms, the lake that turns to acid (the better to eat their boat) and the blizzard of volcanic ash that eventually buries a small town. We want to feel for them. But not too much. We want our doomsdays to be thrilling. But not scarily final. Or fatal to anyone's pooch.

VILLAGE VOICE, 2/18/97, p. 80, Amy Taubin

In an era of low expectations, predictable is not the worst thing a natural disaster movie can be. Based on the model that's been in force from *Jaws* to *Twister*, *Dante's Peak* serves up some attractive Northwest mountain scenery, some campy dialogue ("A man who stares at a rock must have a lot on his mind"), one or two engrossing action sequences (involving sturdy automotive vehicles and fast moving molten lava), lots of fiery special effects, and a dog trained in the art of jumping into a car just in the nick of time.

Newly certified as the second most desirable place to live in the U.S. with a population under 20,000, the town of Dante's Peak is nestled in the Washington Cascades on the slopes of a dormant volcano that's giving signs of becoming the next Mount Saint Helens. For starters, a couple of nubile backpackers are incinerated while frolicking in a hot spring.

Enter Harry Dalton (Pierce Brosnan), a volcanologist who trusts his instincts rather than the readings on his high-tech monitors. Harry wants Dante's Peak's miniskirted mayor (Linda Hamilton) to put the town on alert, but his boss thinks Harry's just an alarmist. The boss wants more evidence before he scares off the tourists. Why blight a burgeoning economy if nothing bad is going to happen?

A skilled action director, Roger Donaldson keeps things moving nicely from the first seismic shocks, exploding buildings, and highway collapses, all the way through "God's big show" (although I can't believe that God doesn't have a more advanced special effects studio than whatever generated that smokey Baked Alaska of a mountain). *Dante's Peak* doesn't convince one of the dangers of the great Northwest so much as it reassures Hollywood folk that, compared to the possibility of volcanic eruptions, an 8.5 on the Richter scale is a piece of cake.

Also reviewed in:
NEW YORK TIMES, 2/7/97, p. C10, Janet Maslin
VARIETY, 2/10-16/97, p. 62, Todd McCarthy
WASHINGTON POST, 2/7/97, p. D1, Rita Kempley
WASHINGTON POST, 2/14/97, Weekend/p. 43, Eric Brace

DAYTRIPPERS, THE

A Cinepix Film Properties release of a Fiasco Photoplays & Trick Films production. *Executive Producer:* Lawrence S. Kamerman, David Heyman, and Campbell Scott. *Producer:* Nancy Tenebaum and Steven Soderbergh. *Director:* Greg Mottola. *Screenplay:* Greg Mottola. *Director of Photography:* John Inwood. *Editor:* Anne McCabe. *Music:* Richard Martinez. *Sound:* David Powers. *Sound Editor:* Steve Hamilton. *Casting:* Sheila Jaffe and Georgianne Walken. *Production Designer:* Bonnie J. Brinkley. *Costumes:* Barbara Presar. *Make-up:* Kim E. Behrens and Tracy A. Sassano. *Running time:* 87 minutes. *MPAA Rating:* Not Rated.

CAST: Hope Davis (Eliza D'Amico); Pat McNamara (Jim Malone); Anne Meara (Rita Malone); Parker Posey (Jo Malone); Liev Schreiber (Carl Petrovich); Campbell Scott (Edward "Eddie" Mazzler); Stanley Tucci (Louis D'Amico); Andy Brown (Ronnie); Marc Grapey (Aaron); Marcia Gay Harden (Libby); Marcia Haufrecht (Molly); Paul Herman (Leon); Carol Locatell (Doris); Douglas McGrath (Chap); Amy Stiller (Amy Corinne Fairbright-Lebow); Stephanie Venditto (Cassandra); Jill Rowe (Monica); Peter Askin (Nick Woodman); Adam Davidson (Libby's Ex-boyfriend); Tracey Barry (Monica's Friend); Ford Evanson (Sandy).

LOS ANGELES TIMES, 3/21/97, Calendar/p. 2, John Anderson

[*The following review by John Anderson appeared in a slightly different form in* NEWSDAY, 3/5/97, Part II/p. B3.]

All those might-be-apocryphal tales of modern life—about alligators in toilets and homicidal maniacs on the upstairs telephone—are popular because they're true, at least in what they say about our deep-seated fears. What those fears say, of course, can be even scarier than the stories themselves.

Which isn't to say that Greg Mottola's "The Daytrippers" is a horror movie—unless the idea of finding a love note to your husband on your bedroom floor and then spending the day scouring Manhattan for him with your parents, sister and sister's boyfriend is your idea of horror. But it does resolve in a way that's as Freudian as the aforementioned alligator, with a similar kind of bite.

Smartly nuanced and darkly comedic, "The Daytrippers" takes place on the day after Thanksgiving—as anticlimactic as any on the calendar and one ripe with potential indigestion. Such is the fate of Eliza (Hope Davis), a woman happily in love with her publishing agent husband, Louis (Stanley Tucci), living with him somewhere in the cozy confines of Huntington, L.I. (there's a cameo by the Walt Whitman Mall), and who starts the day by finding that note.

First problem: She takes the letter—complete with 17th century love poetry and expressions of undying romance—to her mother, Rita (Anne Meara), who is, as they say, difficult. Second problem: Rita unilaterally orders a full-family assault on Manhattan to find Louis and straighten everything out. Then the real fun begins.

Mottola's Malone family is a fully realized creation, as familiar as your own phone number. Rita picks on her husband, Jim (Pat McNamara), out of habit; he ignores her, out of habit. Eliza's sister Jo (a nicely restrained Parker Posey), home from college with her boyfriend, Carl (Liev Schreiber), ignores both of them. Carl, whose erudition would be forgettable except for the company he's keeping, regales everyone with the plot of his novel, about a messianic figure with the head of a German short-haired pointer. Each is a hermetically sealed universe, bumping off the others with very little cross-pollination.

Eliza's the exception. While the others treat their expedition like some Agatha Christie-inspired cruise across uncharted waters (the East River), the sweetly distressed Eliza is faced with real questions—about Louis, about their life together. That her family is so oblivious to her pain is part of Mottola's wry commentary on the general self-absorption of the modern individual. But strictly in terms of this movie, it's the stuff of very subtle comedy.

Here and there, the film shows its seams. There are Cassevetian close-ups and an assumption about the profundity of the offbeat. But at the same time there's this double helix of dissatisfaction and new possibilities running through "The Daytrippers," mutating the dynamics of the characters, finding fault lines in their geography.

The city itself, an exotic locale for Rita and Jim, has an aphrodisiac effect on the younger set: Jo flirts with Eddie (Campbell Scott), one of Louis' authors; Eliza warms up to Ronnie (Andy Brown), whose apartment they invade when Rita has a fainting spell. Jim has a moment of manhood. And the always precise and balanced Tucci, of whom we see much too little here, has one moment as Louis that is so haunted and fearful that he, might be looking at the abyss. Or, perhaps, his in-laws.

NEW STATESMAN, 7/24/98, p. 43, Gerald Kaufman

[*The Daytrippers* was reviewed jointly with *The Gingerbread Man*; see Kaufman's review of that film.]

NEW YORK, 4/21/97, p. 52, David Denby

The Daytrippers is a shaggy-dog story that turns into a bittersweet comedy about mismatched couples and loneliness. A suburban woman (Hope Davis) happily married to a New York publishing executive (Stanley Tucci) discovers a mysterious love letter in her husband's things. Is he having an affair? With her dissatisfied parents, her bickering sister, and her sister's boyfriend improbably in tow, she searches through Manhattan for her husband, who seems to be spending the day with his lover.

As these loquacious people travel about, they have one odd adventure after another, picking up and discarding various strangers in the city, and by the end of the day, as long-held irritations come to the surface, it has become clear that both the young wife and her sister have been forced into unsuccessful relationships by their pile-driving mother. The writer-director, Greg Mottola, shares with David O. Russell, the director of *Flirting With Disaster,* a satiric, picaresque style—

loosely inclusive, chatty, naggingly funny. Mottola depends on vignettes that push just slightly past realism. It takes us a while to realize what the film is about—that the mother and her two daughters are the center of it. At first we're inundated with talk, some of it very funny and good, including a weird kind of running commentary provided by the boyfriend, who recites the plot of his goofy sci-fi novel.

Mottola also shares with Russell a penchant for working very close to embarrassment. Both directors put people we like on the screen and then force them to make fools of themselves. Here it's Anne Meara as the mother who gets pushed into an almost Shelley Winters-style hysteria. Monstrous but lovable, Meara's crazy mom favors men for her daughters who share her emotionalism; she sets herself up for betrayal and then can't believe it when it happens. In its small way, this New York independent movie is very penetrating. See it for the actors, including Campbell Scott as a cruising novelist, Parker Posey, as the sister, and, as Parker's boyfriend, Liev Schreiber, playing a painfully self-conscious prig who discovers, as he talks his way into trouble, an abyss opening at his feet.

NEW YORK POST, 3/5/97, p. 37, Michael Medved

Our closest relatives may be weird, tacky and relentlessly annoying, but at times of crisis it's still comforting to count on their support.

"The Daytrippers" uncannily captures this sense of warmth and reassurance, while sketching the hilarious follies and foibles of each of its flawed, ultimately endearing family members.

The central figure in this splendid film is a sensitive school teacher (Hope Davis) in suburban Long Island who seems to enjoy a passionate, perfect marriage with her witty book-editor husband (Stanley Tucci).

On the day after Thanksgiving dinner, however, she discovers what appears to be a love note addressed to him and then drives to Irish-American parents' blue-collar home to discuss her suspicions.

Her domineering, opinionated and incurably talkative mother (Ann Meara) suggests a family field trip to Manhattan to confront the possibly straying husband at the publishing house where he works.

Feeling numb and stunned, the worried wife joins her mother and her silent, long-suffering dad (Pat McNamara) for the long ride in their battered station wagon, along with her rebellious kid sister (Parker Posey) who's home from college with her fatuous boyfriend (Liev Schreiber).

One of the movie's most amusing elements is this earnest lout's insistent, appallingly detailed descriptions of the novel he plans to write: "It's an allegory about spiritual survival in the contemporary world ... It's about a man who's born with the head of a dog."

Liev Schreiber does a superb job making us care about this pathetic yutz, and, in fact, all the movie's performances are world-class.

Best of all is Hope Davis in the lead role: She's an acclaimed stage actress who has previously played bit parts in forgettable films like "Flatliners" and "Mr. Wrong" but here shows unmistakable potential for first-rank stardom.

There's a pristine, transparent quality to her loveliness, conveying her character's ordeal with heart-breaking dignity. Campbell Scott also makes a sensitive impression in a small but crucial part as one of her editor-husband's rising novelists.

And speaking of rising talents, 32-year-old writer-director Greg Mottola makes one of the most accomplished, original debuts since Steven Soderbergh stunned the movie world with "sex, lies, and videotape"—an apt comparison, since Soderbergh is credited as one of the producers on "The Daytrippers."

This movie delivers more than its share of surprises and revelations, and even though none of these plot points seem especially earth-shattering, it's hard to imagine any film of 1997 presenting a richer, more captivating family of characters.

SIGHT AND SOUND, 8/98, p. 36, Liese Spencer

Long Island, New York. Eliza D'Amico finds a love letter to her husband Louis from someone called Sandy. She shows the letter to her parents Rita and Jim Malone, her sister Jo, and Jo's boyfriend Carl. Hoping to confront Louis, Eliza and the family cram into the family car and drive to Louis' Manhattan publishing company. Rita and Eliza are told he has the day off, but will be attending a book party later. Going through Louis' desk, Rita discovers a photograph of him with a woman. Pressing redial on his phone, Rita hears an answering machine say, "Hi, you've reached Sandy and Monica."

Spotting a restaurant in the photograph, the family track it to SoHo. Parked outside, they see Louis take a cab with the woman from the photo. Rita, chasing on foot, faints, and the family end up in a young passer-by's apartment, where they meet his father. Leaving the others in the car, Jo and Carl go into the book party to find Louis, while Eliza meets two sisters squabbling over their dead mother's possessions. Louis isn't at the party, but Jo flirts with an author named Eddie. Jo and Carl leave the party, but Jo goes back and kisses Eddie. Outside, Jo finds he has given her his number; she calls him from a phonebox. Carl overhears and they argue. Still searching for Louis, the family drive to Sandy's apartment, where there's a party going on. Eliza goes in and sees Louis kissing another man—Sandy. She runs away, chased by Louis who tells her his affair with Sandy has been going on for a year. They argue. Eliza walks into the night, followed by Jo.

Produced by Nancy Tenenbaum and Steven Soderbergh (executive producer and director respectively of *sex, lies and videotape),* this assured debut from writer/director Greg Mottola is a bit like 'sex, lies and the family slide show'. A wry road movie, instead of allowing its protagonists to escape family ties in a sexy soft top, *The Daytrippers* squashes them into a station wagon and gives them a tour of the emotional cul de sacs that characterise their adult relationships. The film opens with happily married couple Eliza and Louis D'Amico returning from a family Thanksgiving to make love in their Long Island home. However, when Louis leaves for work the next morning, Eliza finds a cryptic love poem to him on the bedroom floor. Domestic bliss is blown apart and the stage set for a jaunt into nuclear-family meltdown.

Summoning the universal childhood memory of fractious family outings, Mottola squeezes Eliza, her parents Rita and Jim, sister Jo and Jo's boyfriend Carl into one cramped car, then sends them on a decidedly adult adventure: to find and confront Louis. But despite the authentically queasy air of expectation the clan drum up for their quest, this show of family solidarity soon curdles into claustrophobia. As the station wagon leaves behind suburban malls for skyscrapers, Mottola's cramped, car-bound compositions act as a visual metaphor for the confines of familial relationships. Often jamming his characters into a single frame, the director subtly skeins invisible lines of tension into their small talk and strategic silences. When Carl (a superbly smug Liev Schreiber) sees some ugly buildings and pronounces, "Architecture is dead," for instance, Jo rolls her eyes, Rita glows with an uncomprehending maternal pride, and Eliza merely continues to gaze pensively out of the window.

On reaching New York City, a series of chance encounters with other families—a son harbouring his alimony-outlaw father, two sisters squabbling over their dead mother's out-of-date medicine—serves to underline humorously Mottola's theory of relativity: "there is no such thing as a 'functional' family." Whether it's the pretentious Carl hopelessly championing a return to feudalism, or the bathetic thrill of "the world's shortest car chase", Mottola demonstrates a wickedly funny eye for human frailty without succumbing to cynicism or misanthropy. Thanks to naturalistic performances and deft writing, such scenes can feel almost desultory, but Mottola handles his episodic narrative with ease, coaxing great ensemble performances from his cast (of whom Anne Meara deserves a special mention as the infuriating Rita) before shifting up a gear for the whiplash denouement.

For much of *The Daytrippers* the tone is lightly satirical, but Mottola almost imperceptibly darkens the mood. Swapping to a handheld camera, he follows his characters as they erupt from the confines of the car and spill out on to the pavement. Shouting at each other on empty street corners, they are suddenly lonely, isolated figures, back-lit by the window displays of closed shops, their words drowned by the roar of city traffic. The casual cruise into alienation is complete when a lone Eliza gatecrashes a party to discover the truth about Louis. Running into the night, she briefly climbs into the car, only to disappear into the human traffic of Manhattan's streets with her sister Jo. It's a surprisingly sombre ending but, on reflection, proves more hopeful than a thousand family reunions, illustrating as it does the sisters' ability to reinvent themselves beyond their stalled relationships, and resume—on the hoof—the road movie's traditional search for self-fulfillment.

VILLAGE VOICE, 3/11/97, p. 78, Amy Taubin

Anyone traumatized by excursions in the family car—stuffed into the back seat with restless sibs while, up front, Mom and Dad bicker about driving skills, the route, the radiator, the radio, the amount of gas left in the tank, and whether Dad nodded off during that last red light—will be sympathetic to *The Daytrippers,* Greg Mottola's likeable, neatly produced first feature. *The Daytrippers* is very good at capturing the outrageous invasion of privacy otherwise known as family life, despite the fact that it's impossible to believe that the actors we see on the screen are related by either blood or marriage.

When Eliza (Hope Davis) finds a note written to her husband Louis (Stanley Tucci) that any idiot would realize was proof of his infidelity, she goes running to her parents to find out what they think. Her mom Rita (Anne Meara), the most aggressive, self-centered screen mom since Shelley Winters's "noxious baba" in *Lolita,* opts for immediate confrontation. So Mom, Dad (Pat McNamara), younger sister Jo (Parker Posey), her boyfriend (Liev Schreiber), and the quietly distraught Eliza pile into the car and head for New York, where Louis works in a classy publishing house. Finding him inexplicably absent from his office, Mom rifles through his desk, chattering within ear-shot of his colleagues about the possible identity of his paramour. Then, following the clues she's uncovered, they try to track him down at various literary parties and picturesque Soho locations.

An inevitable question for low-budget filmmakers is whether to use the best available actors or to choose less-compelling actors who might be more appropriate for the parts. One of the main problems in *The Daytrippers* is that Hope Davis, an unusually resourceful and luminous actress, is never believable as Eliza. Davis's Eliza is maybe a little too passive for her own good, but she lacks the neurotic masochism that would cause her to just hang around while her mother humiliates her and messes up her life. Similarly, Parker Posey's kid sister never seems as if she's grown up in a blue-collar Long Island household with brown kitchen appliances and ochre-and-puce-patterned wallpaper.

The discrepancies between the actors and the characters make the plot of *The Daytrippers* seem more contrived than it might have. Similarly, the conventionally correct production values dilute the sense of place (the difference between Manhattan and the 'burbs) that's crucial to the film's meaning. Like too many recent indies, *The Daytrippers* has a bridge-line look (as DKNY is to Donna Karan, *The Daytrippers* is to *Father of the Bride 2).* As for the surprise twist at the end, I saw it coming all too soon.

Also reviewed in:
NATION, 3/31/97, p. 36, Stuart Klawans
NEW REPUBLIC, 3/10/97, p. 30, Stanley Kauffmann
NEW YORK TIMES, 3/5/97, p. C17, Janet Maslin
NEW YORKER, 3/24/97, p. 85, Terrence Rafferty
VARIETY, 3/18-24/96, p. 48, Emanuel Levy
WASHINGTON POST, 3/28/97, Weekend/p. 51, Desson Howe

DECONSTRUCTING HARRY

A Fine Line Features release of a Sweetland Films presentation of a Jean Doumanian production. *Executive Producer:* J.E. Beaucaire. *Producer:* Jean Doumanian. *Director:* Woody Allen. *Screenplay:* Woody Allen. *Director of Photography:* Carlo DiPalma. *Editor:* Susan E. Morse. *Sound:* Les Lazarowitz. *Sound Editor:* Bob Hein. *Casting:* Juliet Taylor. *Production Designer:* Santo Loquasto. *Art Director:* Tom Warren. *Set Decorator:* Elaine O'Donnell and Susan Kaufman. *Special Effects:* John Otteson. *Costumes:* Suzy Benzinger. *Make-up:* Rosemarie Zurlo and Margot Boccia. *Running time:* 93 minutes. *MPAA Rating:* R.

CAST: Caroline Aaron (Doris); Woody Allen (Harry Block); Kirstie Alley (Joan); Bob Balaban (Richard); Richard Benjamin (Ken); Eric Bogosian (Burt); Billy Crystal (Larry); Judy Davis (Lucy); Hazelle Goodman (Cookie); Mariel Hemingway (Beth Kramer); Amy Irving (Jane); Julie Kavner (Grace); Eric Lloyd (Hilly); Julia Louis-Dreyfus (Leslie); Tobey Maguire (Harvey Stern); Demi Moore (Helen); Elisabeth Shue (Fay); Stanley Tucci (Paul Epstein); Robin Williams (Mel); Hy Anzell (Max); Scotty Bloch (Ms. Paley); Philip Bosco (Professor Clark); Robert Harper (Harry's Doctor); Shifra Lerer (Dolly); Gene Saks (Harry's Father); Annette Arnold (Rosalee); Stephanie Roth (Janet); Dan Frazer (Janet's Dad); Joel Leffert (Norman); Lynn Cohen (Janet's Mom); Joe Buck (Yankee Announcer); Jane Hoffman (Grandma); Frederick Rolf (Harvey's Doctor); Elisabeth Anne Cord (Rosalee's Sister); Lortensia Hayes (Jennifer); Alicia Meer and Victoria Hale (Women in Shoe Store); Irving Metzman (Shoe Salesman); Sunny Chae (Lily Chang); Ralph Pope (Death); Tony Darrow (Camera Operator); Jonathan LaPaglia (1st Assistant Cameraperson); Jeff Mazzola (2nd Assistant Cameraperson); Timothy Jerome (Director); Pete Castellotti (Crew Member); Judy Bauerlein (Actress); Joseph Reidy (1st Assistant Director); Phyllis Burdoe (Script Supervisor); Barbara Hollander (Mel's Daughter); Adam Rose (Mel's Son); David S. Howard (Mel's Doctor); Amanda Barudin (Beth Kramer's Daughter); Juliet Gelfman-Randazzo (Baby Hilly); Floyd Resnick (Israeli Patient); Brian McConnachie (Doctor Reese); Peter Jacobson (Goldberg); Tracey Lynne Miller (Goldberg's Girlfriend); Jennifer Garner (Woman in Elevator); Irwin Charone (Bar Mitzvah Host); John Doumanian, Alexa Aronson, and Kenneth Edelson (Bar Mitzvah Guests); Viiola Harris (Elsie); Si Picker (Wolf Fishbein); Howard Spiegel (Mr. Farber); Eugene Troobnick (Professor Wiggins); Ray Aranha (Professor Aranha); Paul Giamatti (Professor Abbot); Marvin Chatinover (Professor Cole); Daniel Wolf (Professor Wolf); Waltrudis Buck (Dean of Adair University); Arden Myrin (Mary, a Student); Daisy Prince (Elevator Voice); Peter McRobbie (Damned Man); Dan Moran (Devil); Ray Garvey (Policeman on Campus); Linda Perri (Policewoman on Campus); Tony Sirico (Policeman at Jail).

LOS ANGELES TIMES, 12/12/97, Calendar/p. 1, Kenneth Turan

People are going to be furious at Woody Allen's latest film and it's not difficult to see why. Writer Harry Block, played by Allen himself, is petty, spiteful and vindictive and his self-absorbed, misogynistic antics are painful to experience.

But "Deconstructing Harry" is also bracingly funny from a dramatic and psychological point of view, it is compelling viewing. A bravura act of self-revelation, its vivid portrait of one man's fears, fantasies and neuroses uses a mixture of reality, imagination and comedy to create one of the writer-director's most involving films.

What makes "Harry" especially fascinating is the way it counterpoints recent Allen films like "Mighty Aphrodite" and "Everyone Says I Love You." There, too, he played an unlikely Lothario who always manages off-putting romantic scenes with young and attractive actresses. But while those films have been unhappy masquerades, trying without success to pass off their smarmy aspects as light entertainment, Allen here drops the mask.

So though Harry Block's actions are familiar, no attempt is made to paint them as charming. Allen, in fact, originally wanted to title his film "The Worst Man in the World," and the jazz standard "Twisted," with lyrics like "My analyst told me I was out of my head," runs over the opening credits. Spiritually bankrupt and sexually obsessed, Harry is uncompromisingly presented as an unsavory scoundrel, albeit one with a sense of humor. Told that his life is all about nihilism, sarcasm and orgasm, Harry shoots back, "In France, I could run on that ticket and win."

Less a *mea culpa*, than an *ecce homo*, "Harry" feels, despite pro forma disclaimers to the contrary, like the most nakedly autobiographical of Allen's recent works, complete with the usual references to baseball, Chinese food, therapy and Manhattan's Upper West Side. In this, his 28th theatrical feature, the director has come closest to the lacerating and defiant self-revelation of one of his idols, Ingmar Bergman, though it goes without saying that Allen's soul is both funnier and considerably more Jewish than Scandinavian.

Twenty-eight is a lot of features, and while some have a tossed-off, who-cares feeling about them, "Harry" is the opposite. Its intricate and carefully worked out structure would be beyond a less experienced director, and Allen, collaborating once again with cinematographer Carlo

DiPalma and editor Susan E. Morse, has worked more substance into his 95 minutes than many of this season's behemoths have managed at twice that length.

"Harry's" opening sequences give an indication of Allen's method. Lucy (Judy Davis) is shown furiously exiting a Manhattan cab on a rainy night not one but some half a dozen times, the repetition emphasizing the extent of her rage. Then comes a vacation home scene where a writer named Ken (Richard Benjamin) is seen having farcical sex with his sister-in-law Leslie (Julia Louis-Dreyfus).

Next it's back to Lucy, who has come to Harry's house with the intent of murdering him because his last novel caused the breakup of Lucy's marriage and created a rift between Lucy and her sister Jane (Amy Irving), Harry's third wife. The farcical sex scene we've just seen turns out to be a dramatization of Harry's novel, and Lucy is the real-life sister-in-law who's had to face the effects of Harry's callous use of personal experience in his fiction. "You take everyone's suffering and turn it into gold," Lucy hisses at him as only Judy Davis can. "I want to kill the black magician."

Lucy may be hysterical, but she is dead-on correct. Harry has always heedlessly exploited the people closest to him for his work and been indifferent about the consequences. And among this film's cleverer aspects are dramatizations of Harry's earlier fiction, including a deft Kafkaesque story about an actor named Mel (Robin Williams) who discovers that he's literally gone out of focus. Harry even meets one of his fictional doppelgangers outside the Red Apple Rest, a venerable New Jersey roadside restaurant, and has a conversation with the double about the kind of person he's become.

"Deconstructing Harry" also exposes us to the contorted personal side of a blocked writer who drinks too much, swallows pills to counteract depression, is ambivalent (at best) about being Jewish and complains to his latest analyst about the way his compulsive sexual fantasies have wreaked havoc with his life. "Did Raoul Wallenberg," he muses, "want to bang every cocktail waitress in Europe?"

After being simultaneously involved with wife Jane and sister Lucy, Harry left, both of them to carry on with the (what else but) younger and more attractive Fay (Elisabeth Shue). And the writer's selfish attempts to manipulate her life for his own short-term benefit is one of the film's major strands.

In the midst of all this, Harry learns he's to get an award from Adair, the college that expelled him once upon a time. Not surprisingly given his repellent personality, no one wants to go with him to the presentation, and the group he ends up with—including his young son, old friend Richard (Bob Balaban) and a hooker named Cookie (Hazelle Goodman)—leads to absurdist scenarios that are comical and devastating.

Allen has helped make the film's problematic scenario involving by assembling his usual command performance cast and utilizing them in unexpected ways. Who else would have Eric Bogosian as a religious zealot or even think of casting Demi Moore as an Orthodox wife fervently reciting blessings in Hebrew? And Allen's sense of humor, with its irresistible zest for the dark side ("To evil," a toast runs, "it keeps things humming") is as sharp as ever.

But what feels like "Deconstructing Harry's" almost compulsive honesty is its strongest lure. When Harry says, "I'm no good at life but I write well," it's a fitting coda to a scathing look at one man's disastrous experiences with marriage, adultery and the literary life. Self flagellating and fearless, "Deconstructing Harry" does a lot of things but holding back because of what an audience might find objectionable is not one of them.

NEW YORK, 12/22-29/97, p. 134, David Denby

There are some excruciatingly funny moments in Woody Allen's *Deconstructing Harry*. I don't think, for instance, that I will soon forget Demi Moore as a grim, super-Jewish wife, saying her prayers, eyes lowered, before performing oral sex on her husband. But scandalously entertaining as parts of it are, the picture still left me in the foulest of foul moods. *Deconstructing Harry* is all promising bits that add up to very little. Ostensibly, it's about a selfish writer, Harry Block (Woody Allen), who travels to his alma mater in order to accept an honorary degree. Harry is at an impasse in both his creative and his personal life, and as he tries to get someone to accompany him on his trip, various women show up and tear into him—he has cheated on them, he has used their experiences with him in his novels and stories, he's a shit, a twerp, a betrayer, and so on.

Woody Allen stages the fictional version of various marital events, drawn from Harry's books, and then he shows us the people that the fictions are based on—often very different from the originals. The movie is meant to be a Philip Roth-like comic demonstration of the existentially ambiguous relations between art and life, and much of it is very free in form. At times, Harry is reminded of something and simply begins telling us a funny little story, which we also see. *Deconstructing Harry* should give us the delight of something that feels made up as it goes along, but the movie, despite many bright flashes, is blurry, redundant, and exasperating, without the beautiful lucidity of, say, Buñuel's *Discreet Charm of the Bourgeoisie,* which also enfolded stories within stories. There are so many similar women hurling accusations in *Deconstructing Harry* that after a while we don't care what level of fiction or reality the movie is in.

I leave to the literal-minded the task of working out the relation between *Deconstructing Harry* and Woody Allen's tangled life. It's not an interesting question, and what the movie says about such issues should discourage people from pursuing that connection (it won't, though). Since Harry is self-serving, dishonest, and weak, the literal-minded may also be induced to see the picture as Woody Allen's mea culpa. But "mea gloria" might be a more proper description. Harry may be an utter dog, but he attracts and disappoints one beautiful young woman after another—and what could be a greater ego blast than that kind of "self-criticism"? What Allen doesn't show us is why everyone is so wild about Harry. This churlish writer doesn't do anything except fend off other's people's attacks. Woody Allen has wound up making a fetish of himself, and it's beginning to be embarrassing. Yes, we accept that he has built, over the years, a comic persona onscreen, and we hardly expect that figure to look like Alec Baldwin. Still, it's getting a little creepy to watch a short, pale 61-year-old man kissing (in one movie) Elisabeth Shue, Judy Davis, Hazelle Goodman, Amy Irving, Kirstie Alley, etc., etc. I have nothing against egocentricity, but in *Deconstructing Harry,* Woody Allen doesn't seem to realize that he's left the impression that women are drawn to Harry only because his creator is a famous movie director.

NEW YORK POST, 12/12/97, p. 57, Michael Medved

Why should a bespectacled, middle-aged guy feel sorry for himself if he (or his fictional alter egos) enjoys passionate sex with an endless array of gorgeous women, including Elisabeth Shue, Amy Irving, Kirstie Alley, Judy Davis, Demi Moore, Julia Louis-Dreyfus and many others?

Woody Allen manages to answer that question in "Deconstructing Harry," a brilliant, bleak, bitter and very funny movie that leaves a sulfurous aftertaste as one of the most depressing comedies of recent years.

Woody plays Harry Block, an acclaimed comic novelist and world-class womanizer who in many ways resembles Philip Roth. Like one of Roth's recent novels, the movie focuses on the complex connection between experience and fiction, offering flashbacks of Harry's many loves, but also showing the way he transmutes his experiences into his writing.

Different actors play fictional characters inspired by the real people in his life: For instance, Alley is earthy and angry as Harry's psychologist second wife; Moore plays the fabricated psychlologist/wife in the dramatization of one of his stories.

Davis draws some of the film's biggest laughs as the foul-mouthed, explosive mistress whose unsuspecting sister (Amy Irving) is Harry's third wife; Louis-Dreyfus is the imaginary sister-in-law who performs quick, furtive oral sex on Harry's (and Philip Roth's) alter ego, Richard Benjamin.

While skillfully juxtaposing flashbacks from "reality" with images from "fiction," Allen also salutes his old idol Ingmar Bergman by structuring the movie like "Wild Strawberries." Most of the action occurs during a single day when Harry drives upstate to the leafy campus that expelled him as a student nearly 40 years ago, but where the administration now plans an "Honoring Day" in recognition of his literary achievements.

His initial inability to find anyone to share the occasion (he pays a brassy black hooker, played by Hazelle Goodman, $500 to ride along with him) emphasizes the anti-hero's desperation, especially since his latest love (the radiant Shue) has left him in order to marry his glib old friend, Larry (Billy Crystal).

This fast-moving film fairly bursts with inventive elements, including a Kafkaesque (and Rothian) tale about a movie actor (Robin Williams) who goes suddenly, inexplicably, incurably out of focus, and a visit to the lowest level of a lurid, glowing-red, devil-infested hell.

Allen also projects a ferociously angry, surprisingly obsessive hostility to Jewish religiosity, particularly to those (like several characters in the film) who discovered faith as adults.

Woody displays reckless cinematic courage in betting his entire picture on such a manipulative and despicable character, with no traces of the tender romanticism or stubborn moral concerns displayed by his more familiar, lovably neurotic schlemiel. At the end of the film we know Harry extraordinarily well, but it remains all but impossible to like him.

NEWSDAY, 12/12/97, Part II/p. B3, Jack Mathews

If Woody Allen's 1980 "Stardust Memories" expressed contempt for his fans, as so many offended critics concluded, "Deconstructing Harry" seems intent on taking it all back. This brilliantly inventive, often vulgar, deeply self-critical work, about a writer who can only function through his art, plays like self-addressed hate mail.

The film is not autobiographical, but like the novel within the movie, it's enough of a *roman à clef* to make everything but names and neuroses clear. And though he's as bitter as he is apologetic, we end up hearing the confession of a man who seems to be acknowledging his narcissism and pleading to be loved, if not for himself, then for his art. Its message is the exact reverse of "Stardust Memories."

I love "Stardust Memories," precisely for its revealing honesty. No question, it was an insult to his over-indulgent fans. He was saying, in effect, that people couldn't love him as much as they said because it wasn't love he was getting from them, but some kind of iconographic reflex. That was *his* problem.

There's a scene in "Deconstructing Harry" where Allen's Harry Block meets a beautiful young fan (Elisabeth Shue) in an elevator, and rather than being offended by her interest, he begins to seduce her. When she tells him she fell in love with him before they met, he builds a wall between them by saying she's in love with his work, and that the man and the work aren't the same.

But, of course, they are, when the work is as direct an extension of the creator as Harry Block's, and Woody Allen's. Seventeen years, an enormous scandal and a media full-court press after "Stardust Memories," Allen seems finally to realize the love he gets for his work is genuine, and, for a guy lacking the graces of the society judging him, maybe it should be enough.

"Deconstructing Harry" is beautifully constructed. Like "Stardust Memories," its narrative hook is an out-of-town honorarium. Harry is to receive an award at an upstate school from which he was once expelled (for giving the dean's wife an enema, among other things). But with few friends left after his book, he ends up making the trip with a $200-a-night hooker (Hazelle Goodman), a deathly ill acquaintance (Bob Balaban) and a young son (Eric Lloyd) he kidnaps from his mother.

The movie opens, however, with an hilarious scene from that scandalous novel. Where Harry's alter ego (Richard Benjamin) and his wife's sister (Julia Louis-Dreyfus) are caught mid-tryst by her dotty grandmother during a family picnic. In the next scene, the real sister (Judy Davis) storms into Block's apartment, threatening to shoot him for revealing the dirty details of their sex life.

The parallel stories continue throughout the film, with different surrogates playing Block. In one anecdote, Stanley Tucci plays a neurotic patient who marries his shrink, played by Demi Moore. For a while, she's the perfect mate, because she knows all his kinks and quirks and puts up with them. But after having a baby, she becomes a "born-again Jew," and runs off with another patient who's more spiritual.

In fact, Harry had married his analyst, Joan (Kirstie Alley, giving the film's most winning performance), but she hadn't left him for a better Jew; she left him because he had an affair with one of her patients. When she confronts him, he defends his actions by saying that since she works at home, her patients are the only strangers he meets.

Gradually, the profile of Harry that emerges is the exaggerated profile of Allen—minus child-abuse allegations—that emerged through the Mia dustup and the Soon-Yi affair. Harry is a womanizing, misogynistic, vulgar, hard-drinking, pill-popping, God-hating, whoring, condescending, antisocial monster. And even if Allen intended all of this as a dark sendup of his media-tainted image, even if he still sees himself as a victim of character assassination, the portrait resonates with underlying truth.

One of the film's funniest digressions is Harry's story about an elderly woman who discovers after 31 years of marriage that before they met, her husband had killed and eaten his wife, his mistress and two other people. If that's the kind of myth-making rumor to which Allen has been subjected, hey, the old man doesn't deny it.

The recurring theme of "Deconstructing Harry," underscored by an actor (Robin Williams) who suddenly becomes out of focus, is that "our lives consist of how we choose to distort it," and that you can't expect the world to adjust to the distortion you've become.

That sounds like insight to me.

"Deconstructing Harry" is often uncomfortably rank, particularly in a hell fantasy where the devil (Billy Crystal) and Harry compare notes on the joy of abusing women. But disturbing as it may be, it's an almost unprecedented piece of self-analysis, and it is, in its best moments, as laugh-out-loud funny as anything Allen has ever done.

NEWSWEEK, 12/22/97, p. 84, David Ansen

[*Deconstructing Harry* was reviewed jointly with *Wag the Dog*; see Ansen's review of that film.]

SIGHT AND SOUND, 5/98, p. 42, Melanie McGrath

At a country-house picnic, Leslie has illicit sex with Ken, her sister's husband. In New York, Lucy threatens to shoot her ex-lover Harry, a writer, to avenge his literary cannibalisation of their affair (the Leslie and Ken story we have just seen) in his latest novel. Eventually, Lucy calms down and Harry recalls his story about a young married writer named Harvey who borrows a friend's apartment for a tryst with a prostitute, only to discover Death arriving for the occupant. Later, Harry's psychiatrist reminds him of another story in which an actor, Mel, becomes out of focus to everyone who looks at him, a cipher for Harry's expectation that the world adjust to the distortion he has become.

Harry has been asked to an honouring ceremony at his old school. He asks his ex-wife Joan to allow him to take their son, Hilly. Joan refuses. She, too, is angry at her portrayal in Harry's novel, in which a psychiatrist, Helen, seduces her patient Paul then transmogrifies into a shrewish religious obsessive after the birth of their baby. Anxious not to go alone, Harry asks his friend Richard and his ex-lover Fay to accompany him but neither can. Harry is shocked to hear that Fay is getting married to Harry's old friend Larry.

Harry has a prostitute named Cookie over to his apartment and asks her to beat him. After sex, Harry remembers first meeting Fay when he was on his way to meet Lucy, the sister of his third wife Jane. Cookie agrees to accompany Harry to the ceremony. The next day, Cookie and Harry are about to leave when Richard unexpectedly turns up. The three of them drive off together. Harry drives by Hilly's school and kidnaps his son. En route he runs into his autobiographical character Ken, who illuminates Harry's relationship with Lucy, Jane and Fay.

Still en route, Harry's party drop in on Harry's half-sister Doris, who is angered by Harry's fictional portrayal of her as a religious obsessive. Harry meets his character Helen, an amalgam of Doris and Joan. Meanwhile, Richard has died in the car. The party arrive at Harry's college where Harry is arrested for snatching Hilly. In jail, Harry confesses to Richard's ghost that he's a failure at life. Newlyweds Fay and Larry arrive to bail Harry out. In a dream version of the honouring ceremony, Harry meets the characters from his stories who remind him that without him they would not exist. Back in his apartment, Harry begins a story about a character only able to live fully and successfully through his art.

Deconstructing Harry marks a return to Woody Allen's autobiographical cinema of complaint. It possesses neither the sweetly clumsy tone of *Mighty Aphrodite* nor the charming amateurism of *Everyone Says I Love You*, but shares with both those films (and with his early comic fiction) an obsessive interest in formalism. From the title sequence with its repeated shot of Lucy emerging from a cab, there's little doubt that you are in a filmic exploration of psychological fragmentation. Cutting between scenes from fiction-writer Harry's present life and flashbacks and sequences from his stories, the film becomes a kaleidoscopic picaresque tale, even swapping cast in the middle of a sequence to emphasise its protagonist's failure to distinguish between his inner and outer lives and the business of his fiction. In *Deconstructing Harry*, Allen has made an efficient and impressive frame on which to hang his thematic obsessions.

Yet *Harry*'s terrain—featuring a bewildered, lust-laden, self-reflexive male protagonist bent on his own dissolution is a disappointment after the refreshing divergence of direction *Everyone Says I Love You* seemed to promise. True, there are some strikingly good one-liners and verbal turns (attempting to reassure his ailing friend Richard about his medical condition, Harry remarks: "Science is okay. Between air-conditioning and the Pope, I'll take air-conditioning"). Robin Williams' out-of-focus actor Mel is a brilliantly witty sortie, but Allen needs new pastures. However bewitching, Allen's one-liner wit feels like an add-on that makes one long for the character-centred slapstick of his early work.

Harry's women make up a typical Allen list of frigid shrews, exotic tarts with hearts and compliant saints, all distant promises or realised disappointments. So far, so familiar. More troubling is Allen's seeming willingness to drain the colour from and subdue such compelling and charismatic actresses as Elisabeth Shue, Judy Davis (who shines nonetheless) and Mariel Hemingway in order to glamorise his hero's overblown psyche. Dressed down and filmed flatly, these women are all rendered the banal objects of Harry's resentment, nothing more than so much material to be recycled into art. It is not so much that Harry/Allen hates women, but that he cannot be a man, let alone an artist, without consuming them.

Only a cast as good as the one Allen has assembled could make much of the patchwork of schematic ciphers *Harry* serves up as characters. Allen's technique of sending each actor only his or her pages and allowing no rehearsals before principal photography can bring freshness to a rich script, but in Harry it produces a skittish cobweb of performances linked only to and by the central protagonist himself. Allen the director has a way of corralling his performers back to the centre of the action where they can be safely defused by the frantic mannerisms of Allen the actor, whose presence on screen always, ironically, comprises the still hub of the action. Since Allen the actor is only convincing as Allen the man the film inevitably turns in on itself. Why does Allen continue to cast himself? Even the overweening Tarantino has not been so vain as to continue ploughing what is so obviously arid terrain.

At its best, *Harry* is an architectural journey around the memory palace of an ageing man, a twisted homage to Ingmar Bergman's *Wild Strawberries* (1957), though without Bergman's emotional generosity or moral decency. As the deconstruction of a psyche, Harry serves only to translate the lexicon of self-deprecation into the language of self-aggrandisement. In the end, the best that can be said for *Deconstructing Harry* is that it is the very funny retreat of an artist who, finding himself defeated by his picture, makes a dazzling job of tarting up its frame.

TIME, 12/22/97, p. 83, Richard Schickel

The grim reaper knocking at the door, the failures of psychiatry, reality and fantasy getting all mixed up in people's minds, vengeful former spouses—certain images and ideas do tend to keep turning up in Woody Allen's movies. And that says nothing about his recurring sexual tropes—older men lusting after much younger women or, still more disastrously, after their sisters-in-law. Lately, sex with an agreeable prostitute as a way of staying out of deeper trouble seems to have become his new fixation.

Deconstructing Harry, in which Allen plays a novelist with the unfortunate habit of drawing a little too obviously on the facts of his life for his fiction, is a compendium of the writer-director's well-known obsessions—an anthology of angst, if you will. It has a great if often underutilized cast and some bold comic conceits: an actor who literally loses his focus, appearing as a blur on-screen and in the eyes of his loved ones, lovers caught en flagrante by an elderly blind woman who thinks that what they're really doing is stirring a pitcher of martinis.

But on the whole, the movie feels regressive and dispassionate, especially when you compare it with the sustained inventiveness of *Bullets over Broadway* or the serene surrealism of *Everyone Says I Love You*. Worse, Allen's character is shrill, sour and even somewhat irrelevant in ways it was not when Allen's neuroses were still touched by romantic hope and when the sexual revolution had not yet entered its present grimly Stalinoid phase.

VILLAGE VOICE, 12/16/97, p. 71, J. Hoberman

It used to be possible to oppose Spielberg and Woody Allen as Mr. Mass and Mr. Class. Now the dialectic has changed. If the former has, post-*Schindler*, become Steven the Good ("I'm breaking my neck looking up at that guy," Jeffrey Katzenberg told the *New Yorker)*, the latter, post-Mia, has aged into Woody the Bad.

Compulsively morbid and tawdry, *Deconstructing Harry* offers further proof that the Woodman will not go gentle into that good night. The saga of a rumpled, foulmouthed, pill-popping, skirt-chasing, blocked novelist (guess who?), *Deconstructing Harry—* which might alternatively have been titled *Justifying Woody*—mixes daydream-and-reality conceits swiped from musty art-house flicks like *8½* and *Wild Strawberries* with the dirty-old-man crankiness of Philip Roth's *Sabbath's Theater*. There are two hookers of color (Hazelle Goodman and Sunny Chae), and the word *fuck* is used so often it could bring a maidenly blush to Joe Pesci's cheek. The star gets to lock lips with his ingenue du jour Elisabeth Shue while providing just enough jump cuts and one-liners to keep things lively for the rest of us not to mention a particularly brutal bit of bar mitzvah mise-en-scène and an excellent running sight gag.

The supporting cast is typically extensive. Caroline Aaron and Kirstie Alley share honors for worst harridan. In a further turn of the dialectic, Julia Louis-Dreyfus (playing one of Harry's fictional characters) suffers the greatest onscreen humiliation, while Judy Davis (Louis-Dreyfus's "real life" model, referred to by Harry as "a world-class *meshuggeneh* cunt,) proves once again that she's equal to anything.

Also reviewed in:
NATION, 1/5/98, p. 36, Stuart Klawans
NEW REPUBLIC, 1/19/98, p. 24, Stanley Kauffmann
NEW YORK TIMES, 12/12/97, p. E1, Janet Maslin
VARIETY, 9/1-7/97, p. 74, David Stratton
WASHINGTON POST, 12/25/97, p. C19, Rita Kempley
WASHINGTON POST, 12/26/97, Weekend/p. 35, Rita Kempley

DEEP CRIMSON

A New Yorker Films release of a Ivania Films/IMCINE/MK2 Productions/Wanda Films with Fondo de Fomento a la Calidad Cinematografica, Gobierno del Estado de Sonora, Television Española, Les Productions Traversière with the collaboration of Canal+ and with the support of FONCA. *Executive Producer:* Tita Lombardo. *Producer:* Miguel Necoechea and Pablo Barbachano. *Director:* Arturo Ripstein. *Screenplay (Spanish with English subtitles):* Paz Alicia Garciadiego. *Director of Photography:* Guillermo Granillo. *Editor:* Rafael Castanedo. *Music:* David Mansfield. *Choreographer:* Jorge Bartolucci. *Sound:* Gabriel Romo, Carlos Faruolo, Antonio Betancourt, and (music) Dan Gellert. *Casting:* Leticia Córdoba. *Art Director:* Monica Chirinos, Patricia Nava, Marisa Pecanins, and Macarena Folache. *Set Decorator:* Antonio Muño-Hierro. *Costumes:* Mónica Neumaier. *Make-up:* Carlos Sánchez. *Running time:* 109 minutes. *MPAA Rating:* Not Rated.

CAST: Daniel Giménez Cacho (Nicolás Estrella); Regina Orozco (Coral Fabre); Marisa Paredes (Irene Gallardo); Verónica Merchant (Rebeca Sanpedro); Julieta Egurrola (Juanita Norton); Patricia Reyes Spindola (Mrs. Ruelas); Rosa Furman (Mrs. Silberman); René Pereyra (Iduarte, Policeman); Alvaro Carcaño (Home Run Motel Clerk); Alejandra Montoya (Ifi); Esteban Soberanes (Barman); Sherlyn González (Teresa Fabre); Fernando Soler P. (Don Dimas); Gastón Melo (Ticket Seller); Alexandra Vicencio (Imelda); Bianca Florido (Mercedes Sanpedro); Paco Mauri (Post Office Clerk); Giovanni Florido (Carlitos Fabre); Juán de la Loza (Car Salesman); Oscar Castañeda (Doroteo).

LOS ANGELES TIMES, 10/31/97, Calendar/p. 22, Kenneth Turan

In the hands of virtuoso Mexican director Arturo Ripstein, "Deep Crimson" is the color of melodrama, passion and death. A strange and deeply twisted romance, "Deep Crimson" never strays from its uncompromising vision of the dark power of a destructive couple madly, deeply and perhaps truly in love.

Though his work is not often seen in this country, Ripstein is probably Mexico's preeminent filmmaker, a man who has directed 24 films since his career began in 1965. Ripstein makes use of his accumulated skill, to control this deliberately paced film as it holds a twisted and pitiless mirror to conventional notions of romantic love.

Set in northern Mexico in 1949, "Deep Crimson" is based on the same true-life source material that inspired Leonard Kastle's memorable 1970 "The Honeymoon Killers," starring Tony LoBianco and Shirley Stoller as a grotesque couple who preyed on lonely, desperate and gullible women.

That description certainly fits Coral Fabre (Regina Orozco), a woman of considerable size who lives in cluttered poverty with her two children. A morgue worker and part-time nurse, Coral is aware the stench of formaldehyde and death clings to her, but that doesn't stop her from devouring romance magazines and developing a fixation on suave movie star Charles Boyer.

Always on the verge of a nervous breakdown, a mother who alternately mistreats and then sobs over her children, Coral impulsively answers an ad in a lonely hearts column, figuring, "What can I lose?" If she only knew.

The ad was placed by Nicolas Estrella (Daniel Gimenez Cacho). He runs a lonely hearts scam, using his would-you-believe Charles Boyer looks and charm to swindle money from unwary victims. He himself, meanwhile, is insecure enough to practically foam at the mouth if he's discovered without his hairpiece. He meets Coral, gets physically attacked by her in the intensity of her passion, and, somewhat unnerved, decides never to see her again.

Nicolas reckons without, however, the unyielding madness of Coral's love. She uproots herself to follow him, vowing to rid herself of her children and even her life if he doesn't submit to her ardor. She discovers the nature of his chicanery and swears to help him, proposing traveling as his sister and helping him decide which women to victimize. Astonished and even flattered at the frenzy of her emotions, Nicolks agrees.

So begins a squalid spree of seduction of women (including one played by Pedro Almodóvar stalwart Marisa Paredes) who are as delusional about love as their victimizers. And because Coral's jealousy knows no bounds, these women are often murdered, clumsily, horrifically, almost as an afterthought.

Yet once the murders are committed, Coral and Nicolas view them as a kind of consecration of their love, a strengthening of the bond between them "Providence brought us together," he tells her, "or maybe the devil."

Working from an expert script by Paz Alicia Garciadiego, director Ripstein conjures up an unblinkingly grotesque vision of love in a state of hysteria. From the carefully chosen muted colors to cinematographer Guillermo Granillo's elegant compositions, to the ironic counterpoint provided by composer David Mansfield's neo-romantic score, everything combines to create a disturbing scenario we view in both horror and fascination. "You must learn to watch your heart," Nicolas says at one point, but no one in "Deep Crimson" has bothered to listen.

NEWSDAY, 10/8/97, Part II/p. B13, Jack Mathews

Every country seems to have its own shocking true story of killer couples on the road, and each one is source material for that venerable class of movies called "mad love."

In the United States, we have the '50s killing spree of Charles Starkweather and Caril Ann Fugate, the inspiration for both Terrence Malick's 1973 "Badlands" and the TV two-parter "Murder in the Heartland." In Mexico, they have Raymond Fernandez and Martha Beck, whose string of murders in 1949 Sonora were dramatized first in Leonard Kastle's 1970 "The Honeymoon Killers" and now in Arturo Ripstein's deeply troubling "Deep Crimson."

The new film is troubling both for its content and Ripstein's approach. For the bulk of the picture, its style is cleverly sophisticated black comedy, so seductively offbeat and whimsical that we are lulled into a kind of false security, able to laugh at foul deeds because they don't seem quite real.

Then, with little warning, the tone shifts to starkly jolting realism, and this cartoonish couple is transformed into the self-absorbed monsters that Fernandez and Beck no doubt were. The effect on the audience is one of punishment. We're made to feel like accomplices in their last crimes because we aren't sufficiently alarmed by the earlier ones.

The Fernandez/Beck spree in 1949 was dubbed the "Lonely Hearts Murders" because of the couple's MO of contacting, robbing and killing widows found through the personal ads in newspapers. In "Deep Crimson," the couple's names are Nicolas (Daniel Gimenez Cacho) and Coral (Regina Orozco), who meet under the same circumstances.

Nicolas is the handsome, toupeed cad with a Spanish accent who responds to the obese and desperately lonely nurse Carol's ad. Fighting off his physical repulsion, Nicolas sleeps with Carol, then robs her and makes off with her money. The next day, she shows up at his door with her young children in tow, convinced that they are destined for each other.

When Nicolas rejects her, gently assuring her he can't support her kids, she abandons the children at an orphanage, and her display of commitment wins Nicolas over. Soon, they're reading the personal ads, planning to go out as brother and sister and sucker widows out of their savings.

But Carol goes plumb nuts with jealousy, and kills every woman who seems to be stealing affection from Nicolas. Initially frightened by her intensity, Nicolas becomes perversely pleased by it, considering it a sign of divined passion. Alone, they may be self-loathing losers, but together, they have strength and purpose—each other!

"Deep Crimson" is a superbly made movie, and the performances of Orozco and Gimenez Cacho are dead-on. But it is perverse in its own way that Ripstein makes these sad creatures vaguely sympathetic, mostly through the humor in their low self-images, then asks the audience to pay for their crimes.

In real life, Fernandez and Beck were executed in prison. Here, they meet a more romantically tragic end, in a pool of mud and blood along a Mexican road. And we're right in it with them.

NEWSWEEK, 10/20/97, p. 70, David Ansen

In real life they were known as the Lonely Hearts Killers. They were called "The Honeymoon Killers" in Leonard Kastle's 1970 cult movie. Now the tale of the couple who murdered lonely widows has been stunningly remade as "Deep Crimson" by Arturo Ripstein, Mexico's finest living director. An obese nurse whose breath reeks of the morgue (Regina Orozco) falls for a gigolo (Daniel Giménez Cacho) who reminds her of Charles Boyer. Abandoning her children to be with him, she poses as his sister as the two, answering lonely-hearts ads, cross the Mexican countryside in the 1940s fleecing and slaughtering their victims. Ripstein and his wife, writer Paz Alicia Garciadiego, lure us in with black comedy, inviting us to feel pity for the grotesque nurse and the vain gigolo, only to horrify us when the movie wades into the deep end of evil. A former assistant to Luis Buñuel, Ripstein shares with him a coolly unsentimental vision flecked with perverse wit. This monstrous love story serves up film noir at its most darkly authentic: it plays for keeps.

SIGHT AND SOUND, 9/97, p. 40, Paul Julian Smith

Mexico, 1949. Coral, an overweight nurse and single mother, answers a lonelyhearts advert in the local paper. The "Spanish gentleman" who has placed the advert proves to be Nicolás, an aging but charming Mexican conman in a wig. After the desperate Coral forces him to make love to her, Nicolás steals money from her purse and absconds. Coral tracks him down and arrives on Nicolás' doorstep with her children. She discovers that he has murdered his wife. Abandoning Coral's children at an orphanage, the couple set off across rural Mexico, with Coral posing as Nicolás' sister.

When Coral sees Nicolás dancing with the aging widow Juanita Norton, she poisons Juanita's drink. The couple next pose as missionaries for the benefit of a devout Spanish widow, Irene Gallardo. Mrs Gallardo sets off with the couple, 'marrying' Nicolás in an improvised ceremony in a graveyard on the wedding night, however, the jealous Coral cannot allow the marriage to be consummated. Coral kills Mrs Gallardo and the body is secretly buried on the plain. The couple's final victim is Rebeca Sanpedro, a young and beautiful widow. When Rebeca is made pregnant by Nicolás, Coral performs an abortion on her, after tricking her into taking anti-coagulants. Grievously ill, Rebeca is finished off by Nicolas; Coral also kills Rebeca's young daughter, who is a witness to her mother's murder. Apparently tiring of their criminal career, Nicolás calls the local police and confesses. The couple are shot in the back by the police and die together, face down in a puddle.

The first shot of *Profundo carmesi/Deep Crimson*, which is typical of this film, shows sluttish Coral (the disturbingly impassive Regina Orozco) reading a cheap novella in a bedroom cluttered with star photos, clothes, and cosmetics. Her face is fragmented by a cracked mirror. This combination of the grotesque with the romantic is a technique characteristic of Arturo Ripstein, who is Mexico's most accomplished director. One of his earlier successes (*El ligar sin limites*, 1977) told a similar tale of tragic *amour fou* through the equally disquieting figure of a drag queen in a brothel. And if Ripstein claims to take his title from Thomas De Quincey, the style and set-ting of *Deep Crimson* are more reminiscent of the kitsch world found in the novels of the Argentinian Manuel Puig *(Kiss of the Spider Woman)*, This sensibility extends to the soundtrack, which features not flagrantly sentimental Mexican rancheras, but instead melancholic Argentinian tangos.

Ripstein has written that his film, based on the real-life story of the "lonely hearts killers" (whose story inspired *The Honeymoon Killers* of 1969, directed by Leonard Kastle to whom *Deep Crimson* is dedicated), explores the extremity of an absolute passion which dignifies even such "mean" and "narrow-minded" characters as his central couple. The subtle performances here certainly hint at depths you wouldn't expect from the initial serial-killers-on-the-run premise. Because the principals consistently underplay their grotesque roles, the murders appear as inevitable and even comprehensible effects of an externally bizarre but internally logical relationship. The gallery of supporting cameos is equally assured. If Marisa Paredes, most familiar to audiences outside Spain for her three features with Almodóvar, has been cast to satisfy co-producers Spanish state television (TVE), the theme of the Spanish presence in post-War Mexico is also central to the film's plot: it is Nicolás' rare ability to mimic the Peninsular lisp which renders him impossibly seductive to Mexican widows. But while Spaniards are praised as romantic caballeros, they are also dismissed as poor immigrants, even as gypsies. Erotic fantasies of nationality thus fuse with curious gender reversals: forever fussing over his appearance, the lady's man Nicolas attracts timid widows through his very femininity; conversely, it is the curvaceous Coral who initiates all action, whether amorous or murderous. Sacrificing her own hair to make a new wig for her lover, she will also batter a victim's body with a length of piping while Nicolas crouches whimpering in a cupboard.

Typically, however, the violence is as underplayed as the psychological melodrama. The camera pans slowly over the floor to the pipe, but the act itself is only shown reflected in a mirror on the wall. Elsewhere the camera keeps its distance: scuttling behind a low wall as the doomed Rebeca plays happily with her child and the treacherous Nicolás; slowly tracking the three characters (murderous couple and future victim) as the widow Norton drinks and flirts in the tawdry Café Intimo. In such sequences and from the bleached expanses of the meseta to the claustrophobic interiors of parlours and bedrooms thick with religious and romantic icons, both exteriors and interiors are shot with an atmospheric intensity which transcends the 'period' label that might be applied to the film. Although Ripstein favours long takes in which his actors are given room to explore their spatial relation to one another, his mobile camera and clever cutting hold the viewer's attention until the end. So if the conclusion seems somewhat cursory (with no motivation given for the characters' sudden decision to call a halt to their murders), *Deep Crimson* remains a highly accomplished and surprisingly commercial film. It's also one which successfully maintains a nasty taste in the audience's mouth even as it celebrates the fatal passion which turns all-too ordinary people into monsters.

TIME, 10/20/97, p. 105, Richard Corliss

[*Deep Crimson* was reviewed jointly with *A Self Made Hero*; see Corliss' review of that film.]

VILLAGE VOICE, 10/14/97, p. 85, J. Hoberman

Emerging from the depths of the human heart and loins (not to mention the NYFF), Arturo Ripstein's *Deep Crimson* is a dark tango transposing the true story of the Lonely Hearts Killers —inspiration for the cult classic *The Honeymoon Killers*—to 1940s Mexico. A fading gigolo and the obese nurse who adores him ruthlessly prey upon a succession of vulnerable widows.

Built like an R. Crumb ingenue or an old DeSoto, the nurse Coralita (Regina Orozco) is a fantastic creature—indolent, slovenly, inept, and selfish, yearning for love and reeking of the morgue. Orozco is an opera singer and her presence underscores Ripstein's mock melodramatic style; as the love of her life, the madly profiling Daniel Gimenez Cacho is no less knowingly stylized. The movie's bravura performances are matched by superb production design. The tones are warm, the forms round, the light sculpted. Ripstein's trademark tawdry mise-en-scène is never more evident than in the sequence where a decorous doña (Spanish actress Marisa Paredes), half-crazed with lust, offers herself amid the baseball decor of the Motel Home Run, or the reverse dolly from a couple making love inside a derelict Chevy, rocking on its flat tires in a rubblestrewn dirt yard.

Mexico's maestro of the feel-bad, Ripstein thrives on dysfunctional families and sexual degradation. (He'd have been the perfect director for this summer's audacious but inept *Star Maps*.) But *Deep Crimson* is something rarer than an alienated saga of mad love or an accomplished black comedy—this is a convincing movie about evil, with vanity and greed the deadliest of sins. (*Kiss or Kill*, the NYFF's other murderous-couple saga, is vacuous fluff by comparison.) At once svelte and savage, *Deep Crimson* inspires a certain awe. It pities its monsters and dares us to feel for them.

Also reviewed in:
CHICAGO TRIBUNE, 1/16/98, Tempo/p. 5, Michael Wilmington
NATION, 10/27/97, p. 34, Stuart Klawans
NEW YORK TIMES, 10/7/97, p. B8, Stephen Holden
VARIETY, 9/9-15/96, p. 118, Leonardo Garcia Tsao

DEF JAM'S HOW TO BE A PLAYER

A Gramercy Pictures release of a PolyGram Filmed Entertainment presentation of an Island Pictures production in association with Outlaw Productions. *Executive Producer:* Robert Newmyer, Jeffrey Silver, and Stan Lathan. *Producer:* Mark Burg, Todd Baker, Russell Simmons, and Preston Holmes. *Director:* Lionel C. Martin. *Screenplay:* Mark Brown and Demetria Johnson. *Story:* Mark Brown. *Director of Photography:* Ross Berryman. *Editor:* William Young. *Music:* Darren Floyd. *Sound:* Mathew Markey. *Sound Editor:* Sam Gemette. *Casting:* Jaki Brown-Karman and Robyn M. Mitchell. *Production Designer:* Bruce Curtis. *Set Decorator:* Claire Kaufman. *Set Dresser:* Bill Butler. *Costumes:* Mimi Melgaard. *Make-up:* Vonda K. Morris. *Stunt Coordinator:* Eddie Watkins. *Running time:* 94 minutes. *MPAA Rating:* R.

CAST: Bill Bellamy (Drayton Jackson); Natalie Desselle (Jenny Jackson); Lark Voorhies (Lisa); Mari Morrow (Katrina); Pierre (David); Jermaine "Big Hugg" Hopkins (Kilo); A.J. Johnson (Spootie); Max Julien (Uncle Fred); Beverly Johnson (Robin); Gilbert Gottfried (Tony the Doorman); Bernie Mac (Buster); Stacii Jae Johnson (Sherri); Elise Neal (Nadine); J. Anthony Brown (Uncle Snook); Amber Smith (Amber); Devika Parikh (Barbara); Bebe Drake (Mama Jackson); Gillian Iliana Waters (Shante); Tara Davis (Cute Party Girl); Marta Boyett (C.C.); Jazmin Lewis (Pookie); Licia Shearer (Nikki); Jerod Mixon (Kid #1); Jamal Mixon (Kid #2); D.D. Rainbow (Jealous Girl); Natashia Williams (Pink Bikini Girl); Edith Grant (Peaches); Jesse Collins (D.J.); Melissa Cross (Sales Girl); Claude "Pete" Bryant (Chess Player).

LOS ANGELES TIMES, 8/8/97, Calendar/p. 6, Kevin Thomas

[The following review by Kevin Thomas appeared in a slightly different form in
NEWSDAY, 8/8/97, Part II/p. B8.]

"Def Jam's How to a Player" is a rambling, shambling, good-natured comedy that tries to have fun with unbridled male sexual prowess while making sure its hero gets an obligatory comeuppance at the very last moment. However, by then we have every reason to be confident that Bill Bellamy's fast-talking sexual superman Dray Jackson will manage to handle his trusting steady girlfriend, Lisa (Lark Voorhies), when she at last catches him with another woman.

While adults won't bother taking this picture seriously—in the unlikely event they happen to see it—you have to wonder about its impact on young males. What writers Mark Brown and Demetria Johnson are essentially saying is that it's in the nature of men to score with as many women as possible, and the trick is merely for them not to get caught doing it by their girlfriends.

They're further saying that, even if the man is a liar, if he's handsome enough and slick enough, most women will ultimately forgive him. They don't have much to say about women's sexual prowess but, again at the last possible moment, they do suggest a gorgeous woman can temporarily bring down an overconfident playboy. You have to be grateful that "Def Jam's How to Be a Player" at least makes it clear that Dray uses condoms.

The entire film—which is saturated in raunchy language, some of it truly tasteless—takes place during a holiday, with Dray having one rendezvous after another with his many beautiful lovers while his nerdy pals wait in his vintage Thunderbird convertible. There's a stopover at his mother's house for a barbecue, where there's a cameo with Max Julien, cast as Dray's brother and role model. (Julien was a definitive player in the blaxploitation pictures of the '70s.) The film culminates at a Malibu party.

Meanwhile, Dray's disapproving sister (Natalie Desselle) and her classmate in anthropology (Mari Morrow) are focusing on Dray's lifestyle as a possible class project. A number of actors display personality and presence, but Lionel C. Martin's direction is uneven to the point of seeming nonexistent.

NEW YORK POST, 8/6/97, p. 37, Michael Medved

"Def Jam's How to Be a Player" is crude, witless, smug, exploitative, immature ... and so shamelessly politically incorrect in its Neanderthal, misogynistic outlook that many moviegoers will instinctively embrace its adolescent arrogance.

The producers and stars (who've previously worked together on HBO's hip, popular "Def Comedy Jam") show no shame in pandering to the most irresponsible male fantasy of them all: portraying a suave hero who effortlessly enjoys sensational sex with six different big-breasted glamour girls in a single day.

Bill Bellamy, previously best known as a stand-up comic and MTV host, plays the lucky guy—a slickster with a stylish apartment, a closet full of expensive athletic shoes, a cherry-red '63 Thunderbird, and some unspecified job at a record company to which he devotes no time or energy at all.

Bellamy displays a boyish smile, but never comes close to generating the sort of on-screen electricity that might explain why gorgeous women all find him irrestible.

This playboy (or "player," in current urban terminology) hides his adventures from his classy, steady girl (Lark Voorhies) at the same time he drives around LA with a trio of frustrated wannabes (Pierre, Jermaine "Big Hugg" Hopkins, A.J. Johnson), dispensing wisdom in between stops for sex at the homes of an array of adoring airheads.

The lothario's chubby sister (Natalie Desselle) feels outraged at his behavior, and teams with yet another seductive sweetie (Mari Morrow, the most arresting screen presence in the film) to invite all the various "flavor" in his life to the same Malibu beach party in hopes of embarrassing him into a reformation.

From Mozart's "Don Giovanni" to Eddie Murphy's "Boomerang," the theme of a seducer getting his well-deserved comeuppance has been a staple of Western culture, but "How to Be a Player" isn't Mozart, or even Murphy, and it's considerably less cultured than spoiled yoghurt.

The main character's principal conquests have been achieved before the story begins, so we don't even get the modest thrill of watching him demonstrate his technique.

Instead, the, movie tries for its biggest laughs with fat jokes and a slapstick routine about breaking wind in someone's face.

The women are, however, uniformly stunning, and their outfits are colorful and provocative.

Director Lionel C. Martin, a music video specialist making his feature film debut, never achieves the energy or style you'd expect in this material.

The, dialogue ("I can never have too many girls, my brother!") is flat and clumsy, and the movie earns no image awards for its portrayal of African-American manhood, but you can't get too snooty when the subject is booty.

SIGHT AND SOUND, 1/98, p. 37, Andrew O'Hehir

Drayton, a playboy, wakes from a dream in which his girlfriend Lisa catches him with another woman.   Lisa arrives to cook him breakfast, and Dray allays her suspicions about his philandering. Dray's sister Jenny shows up and Lisa leaves for work. Jenny chastises Dray, but when Jenny's friend Katrina appears, he invites her to a pool party in Malibu that evening.

Dray departs with his friends Kilo and Spootie, leaving Jenny and Katrina in his apartment, where they gather material for an anthropological study of him. Dray, Kilo, and Spootie must first retrieve their friend David, who has been caught cheating by his girlfriend, Nadine. Then Dray has trysts with three more women.   Meanwhile, Jenny and Katrina devise a plan to invite all Dray's lovers to the Malibu party, hoping to force him to repent. After a barbecue at Dray's mother's house, everyone reconvenes at the pool party, where Dray cultivates several new conquests before six of his current and former lovers begin arriving. Dray successfully disperses the women and evades an angry cuckolded husband. Jenny and Katrina appear foiled. As David and Nadine reunite, Dray goes home in triumph to await Lisa's return. But Katrina gets there first and seduces Dray. When Lisa arrives, the dream from the opening scene has become reality and the ultimate player has been "busted".

A quickie sex farce evidently concocted to cash in on the popularity of music-video host Bill Bellamy, *Def Jam's How to Be a Player* isn't quite as awful as it could be.   There's nothing wrong with the basic idea of transposing the oft-retold legend of Don Juan, the original 'player', into an urban African American setting, complete with earthy street dialogue.   This adaptation may have just enough raunchy humour to accompany its parade of pulchritude, its luxurious fantasy of the LA lifestyle, while its soundtrack featuring numerous well-known rap and R&B artists shines. But it lacks the distinctive wit and originality necessary to subvert the moralising of its source material.

Undeniably handsome, with a sly naughty-little boy smile, Bellamy's suave televisual demeanour does not, however, translate to the big screen.   He mugs his way through one formulaic episode after another, uncertain how to position himself for the camera and unable even to pretend to listen to other actors. (As any real player will tell you, listening is central to the game of seduction.) Bellamy seems more comfortable addressing the camera directly.   Poor craft would be bad enough but Bellamy isn't even convincingly sexy and the sex scenes are too anodyne to come off as Rabelaisian excess.   Only the final coupling between Dray and Katrina has any erotic heat, and even then it's in the magenta-mood tradition of late-night pay-television pornography.

Director Lionel C. Martin seems more at home with purely visual, painstakingly constructed sequences than with action and dialogue.   A scene in which images of Dray's various women dressing for the evening are sequentially superimposed over a clock face, its hands slowly rotating, is the film's most intriguing sequence.   In contrast, most dialogue-driven scenes seem built half-heartedly around their lewd laugh lines, unimaginatively filmed and choppily edited. Much of the humour is mean-spirited—amid the ribald talk of "bitches" and "hoes", we are asked to laugh at fat children, asthmatics, and unattractive women. Most of the acting is so lamentable that character players—including Natalie Desselle as Dray's aggrieved sister Jenny and Max Julien as Dray's Uncle Fred, clad in vintage 70s blaxploitation attire—shine in minor parts. These idiosyncratic glimmers of promise provide the barest outline of what *How to Be a Player* might have been.

Also reviewed in:
NEW YORK TIMES, 8/7/97, p. C16, Lawrence Van Gelder
VARIETY, 8/11-17/97, p. 58, Todd McCarthy

DELI, THE

A Golden Monkey Pictures release in association with Caminer-Gallagher Productions. *Executive Producer:* John Dorrian. *Producer:* Sylvia Caminer. *Director:* John Gallagher. *Screenplay:* John Dorrian and John Gallagher. *Director of Photography:* Robert Lechterman. *Editor:* Sue Blainey. *Music:* Ernie Mannix and Janice Ginsberg. *Sound:* Melanie Johnson. *Casting:* Judy Henderson and Alycia Aumuller. *Production Designer:* Lisa Frantz. *Costumes:* Melissa Toth. *Running time:* 90 minutes. *MPAA Rating:* Not Rated.

CAST: Mike Starr (Johnny); Matt Keeslar (Andy); Judith Malina (Mrs. Amico); Brian Vincent (Pinky); Ice T (Phil the Meat Man); Michael Imperioli (Matty); David Johansen (Cabbie); Heather Matarazzo (Sabrina); Debi Mazar (Teresa); Jerry Stiller (Petey Cheesecake); Frank Vincent (Tommy Tomatoes); Burt Young (J.C.). *WITH:* Michael Badalucco; Heavy D; Iman; William McNamara; Gretchen Mol; Chris Noth; Tony Sirico; Shirley Stoler.

NEW YORK POST, 11/7/97, p. 56, Larry Worth

John Gallagher's talents as a writer-director are pretty much nil, as demonstrated in his hopelessly amateurish comedy, "The Deli." But he must be one of the world's best snake oil salesmen.

How else to explain extended cameos from Heather Matarazzo, Debi Mazar, Ice T, Jerry Stiller, Iman, David Johansen, Heavy D and a half-dozen others as "neighborhood eccentrics,"' never mind landing tunes from David Bowie, Marvin Gaye and the Posies?

It certainly couldn't have been the nearly laughless script. Trying to rip off both "Smoke" and Damon Runyon, the plot concerns a beefy deli owner (Mike Starr) who robs Peter to pay Paul as his gambling debts get worse by the minute, not unlike the production itself.

Though the main players—relative unknowns Starr, Matt Keeslar and Judith Malina—give their all, "The Deli" will have viewers gagging from rancid baloney.

VILLAGE VOICE, 11/11/97, p. 86, Porochista Khakpour

Next time you walk into a New York deli, look around and try to absorb the ambience. Chances are any rumination will yield more in the way of good cinema than the 98 minutes of John Gallagher's culinary calamity. In terms of cinematic sustenance, *The Deli* delivers much of yesterday's cheese sandwiched within an undigestible storyline.

The Deli's plot is one long runaround involving the deep-in-debt gambling gastronome Johnny Amico (Mike Starr) and his brother Andy (Matt Keeslar), who is smitten with the catering-client's daughter.

Aspiring for a *Smoke*-esque improvisatory feel, Gallagher and coscreenwriter John Dorrian settle for rambling monologues and runaway dialogue. The movie is similarly stocked with New York perennials—including Debi Mazar, Heather Matarazzo, Heavy D, Ice T, and Chris Noth— but no one in the cast goes further than championing his or her assigned New York caricature. Worst of all is the endless barrage of embarrassing slapstick, courtesy mostly of Pinky, Brian Vincent's Curley-meets-Carrey cretin. Rarely has a movie provided so little to chew on.

Also reviewed in:
NEW YORK TIMES, 11/7/97, p. E16, Janet Maslin
VARIETY, 6/2-8/97, p. 59, Joe Leydon

DELINQUENT

A Rice Arts Management release of a Big Bad Productions film. *Producer:* Peter Hall. *Director:* Peter Hall. *Screenplay:* Peter Hall. *Director of Photography:* Todd Crockett. *Editor:* Thom Zimny. *Music:* Gang of Four. *Sound:* Juan Rodriguez. *Casting:* Maureen Fremont. *Art Director:* M.E. Guamaccia and Annette Mohr. *Running time:* 84 minutes. *MPAA Rating:* Not Rated.

CAST: Desmond Devenish (Tim); Shawn Batten (Tracy DeLors); Jeff Paul (Ben); Marisa Townshend (Mrs. Richman); Ian Eaton (Eddie).

LOS ANGELES TIMES, 9/12/97, Calendar/p. 15, Kevin Thomas

[*The following review by Kevin Thomas appeared in a slightly different form in* **NEWSDAY, 9/12/97, Part II/p. B8.**]

"Delinquent" is one of those great little near-no-budget movies that every now and then seem to come out of nowhere to give hope for a truly independent American cinema. It marks a stunning feature debut for writer-director Peter Hall, who never makes a false move as he builds suspense right from the start.

"Delinquent" is a somewhat misleading title in that the word is so automatically modified by "juvenile." But if anyone in this picture is a delinquent, it's the parent, Jeff Paul's Ben is an ignorant, racist, mean-tempered, hard-drinking single father much hated by his only son, 15-year-old Tim (Desmond Devenish), who blames him for driving his mother to her recent suicide. After hitting the skids, Ben has managed to land a job as a cop in an upstate New York village near the town where he and his family once lived.

The brutal, raging Ben demands respect from Tim but succeeds only in instilling in his son an escalating fear mixed dangerously with defiance. For all his intelligence, Tim is too young and too blinded by emotion to be able to see over the wall of anger between them to realize that his father is grief-stricken over his wife's death. Ben believes his new job has given him a second chance.

Outraged that Tim, heretofore an outstanding student, is on the verge of flunking out of school, Ben sees his new career potentially jeopardized by any wayward behavior on the part of his son. Thus, the cramped trailer this father and son share seems like a tinderbox: You become filled with dread as you become sure something awful is going to happen between them.

Having established an atmosphere of increasing tension so deftly, Hall expands upon it as, after a typically volatile father-son argument, Tim runs off and ends up breaking into a lovely old house in a beautiful rural setting.

As we grow increasingly concerned with Tim, who is a likable youth of sensitivity and imagination in the throes of burgeoning sexual maturity, Hall then switches to Tracy (Shawn Batten). The daughter of the family that owns the house Tim breaks into, Tracy is a pretty young teenager with whom Tim has become infatuated once he's discovered a home video of her. As it turns out, Tracy is in the midst of a major personal crisis.

As in a Claude Lelouch movie, you begin to wonder whether these two young people, attractive and intellectually sophisticated, will ever meet and, if so, what the consequences will be. Hall is breathtakingly astute at involving us in these young people's destinies and in never letting up as his film becomes increasingly taut.

"Delinquent," which boasts an effectively nerve-jangling score by Gang of Four, its first for a film, is a highly accomplished work in which its cast is never less than compelling. This is one suspense picture that gives way to a larger contemplation of the interplay of fate and emotion.

NEW YORK POST, 9/12/97, p. 50, Larry Worth

As tales of troubled youth go, "Delinquent" will never be mistaken for "Rebel Without a Cause." Then again, writer-director Peter Hall earns credit for putting his own spin on James Dean's spiritual successors.

In his debut behind the camera, Hall at least tries to redefine age-old themes—sometimes capably sometimes not.

With subjects running the gamut from abusive dads and teen pregnancy to voyeurism and attempted murder, Hall might have done better to keep his ambitions—no matter how admirable—in check.

He gets the most mileage from the 15-year-old hero, Tim. Sharing a cramped trailer with his booze-swilling father, Tim is slapped around once too often. Running off to a deserted summer house, he finds videos of one of its inhabitants, a pretty adolescent named Tracy.

As it turns out, Tracy has as many troubles as Tim. Specifically, she's pregnant with her English teacher's child. But it isn't until Tim and Tracy's paths cross that the makings for tragedy are set in motion.

Unfortunately, Hall's blending of their storylines is far from seamless. The problem is exacerbated via long stretches with little dialogue, making the goings-on take far too long to kick in.

But when they do, Hall switches into overdrive. His hand-held camera-work becomes properly jarring, setting the tone for a non-Hollywood ending that's downright inspired.

Meanwhile, the acting ranges from alluring to excruciating. In the latter category, Jeff Paul is a virtual cartoon as Tim's violent father, while associate producer Marisa Townsend is utterly laughable as Tim's former teacher. Hopefully, she'll keep her talents off-camera in the future.

The good news is that Desmond Devenish is a real find as Tim, conveying emotions only hinted at in the script. Shawn Batten also holds her own as the duly confused Tracy.

It's chiefly due to their efforts, coupled with Hall's obvious potential, that "Delinquent" has something to offer bad boys and cineastes alike.

VILLAGE VOICE, 9/16/97, p. 98, Gary Susman

The protagonist of *Delinquent* is not your standard streetwise, swaggering, sexy teen reprobate. Rather, he's a small-town, mixed-up, abused introvert whose potential for violent crime exists primarily within his own mind. The title's suggestion of a lurid teensploitation flick seems intentionally ironic. Indeed, everything about *Delinquent* challenges preconceptions, not just about genre, but also about adolescent behavior and psychology.

Set in an upstate New York hamlet called Cold Mills, *Delinquent* tells the story of Tim (the spot-on Desmond Devenish), a 15-year-old boy whose soul is up for grabs. Tim's life has been upside down since his mother killed herself a year ago, leaving Tim to discover the corpse. His father, Ben (a cartoonish Jeff Paul), lost his job and house and moved himself and Tim into a trailer in a strange new town, where he now works as a cop.

Seeking refuge from his father's alcohol-fueled temper, Tim sneaks into an unoccupied house. His imagination stirs as he explores the personal effects of Tracy (Shawn Batten), a boarding-school girl his age whose family keeps the place as a summer home. Differences in sex and class aside, Tracy appears to be going through a similar process of painful self-discovery, as evidenced by a videotape implying an affair with one of her teachers.

It's the feminine sphere—the artifacts that Tracy has left behind and the concern of a former English teacher who once saw promise in Tim—that offers him some small hope of redemption. While juvenile-delinquent movies from *Rebel Without a Cause* to *Boys 'N the Hood* blame teen-age sociopathy on absent or insufficiently masculine fathers, *Delinquent* indicts hyper-masculinity. Away from his mother or the English teacher, Tim's only role models are his jock friend Eddie and his authoritarian, abusive dad who, when he sees Tim reading Tracy's copy of Virginia Woolf's *A Room of One's Own,* rips it to shreds.

Tim, Tracy, and Ben eventually do cross paths, but the way their climactic confrontation plays out defies expectations yet seems devastatingly apt. Writer-director-producer Peter Hall, who apparently fashioned the film from incidents in his own troubled childhood upstate, presents a debut feature that, while self-assured and sure-handed, is as raw, restless, contemplative, and haunting as its antihero.

Also reviewed in:
CHICAGO TRIBUNE, 1/23/98, p. I, Michael Wilmington

NEW YORK TIMES, 9/12/97, p. C18, Lawrence Van Gelder
VARIETY, 1/16-22/95, p. 96, Todd McCarthy

DELTA, THE

A Strand Releasing release of a Charlie Guidance production. *Producer:* Margot Bridger. *Director:* Ira Sachs. *Screenplay:* Ira Sachs. *Director of Photography:* Benjamin P. Speth. *Editor:* Alfonso Gonçalves. *Music:* Michael Rohatyn and Adam Feibelman. *Sound:* Iddo Patt. *Sound Editor:* Tom Efinger and Damian Volpe. *Production Designer:* Bernhard Blythe. *Art Director:* Yin Ling Wong. *Costumes:* Stevan Lazich. *Make-up:* Linda Wood. *Running time:* 85 minutes. *MPAA Rating:* Not Rated.

CAST: Larry Reynolds (Man in Park); Shayne Gray (Lincoln Bloom); Thang Chan (Minh Nguyen, "John"); Angelique Owens (Donut Shop Clerk); Leigh Walden (Cece Bloom); Gene Crain (Sam Bloom); Charles Ingram (Gary Bloom); Ron Gephart (Ken Bloom); Kim Newman (Denise Bloom); Polly Edelstein (Debbie Bloom); Vanita Thomas (Bernice); Rachel Zan Huss (Monica); Randall Reinke (Danny); Melissa Dunn (Tina Clifton); Erin Grills (Jacquie Clifton); Kate Davis (Gloria Clifton); Alluring Strange (Club Band); Mark Hyman (Club Bouncer); Michael Locke (Michael, Kid on Bike); Robert Hathaway (2nd Kid on Bike); Lamar Sorrento (Ted); Richard Daggett (Pick-up Driver); Anthony Isbell (Jerry, Man in Hotel); J.R. Crumpton (Joe); Patricia A. Gill (Joe's Wife); Moses J. Peace (Policeman); Nhan Van Dang (Minh's Roommate); Bay Thi Ho (Old Vietnamese Woman); Hoang N. Pham (Minh's Friend); Mai Ballard (Pool Hall Owner); Colonious Davis (Ricky Little).

LOS ANGELES TIMES, 8/15/97, Calendar/p. 4, Kevin Thomas

Ira Sachs' tender, wrenching "The Delta" takes us not into the charming old Memphis of the Peabody Hotel and other genteel landmarks, or such tourist attractions as Beale Street and Graceland. Instead it takes us to the city's more impersonal side streets and suburbs, some of the same seedy, territory covered by, Jim Jarmusch's "Mystery Train."

"The Delta" begins in the dark of night, on a highway in a park area where gay men cruise one another. A young man with a motorbike approaches another in his car. They have sex and go their separate ways, not to cross paths for another 35 minutes of this succinct, flawless and intimate 85 minute film. Sachs deftly uses these intervening minutes to establish the distinct and rarely intersecting worlds of these two young men.

Shayne Gray's Lincoln Bloom is a twentyish youth, handsome in a wholesome boy-next-door way, who still lives at home with his affluent businessman father. On the surface, the pleasant, well-behaved Lincoln fits in perfectly with family and his contemporaries, who tend to hang out a lot in a totally ordinary way. His girlfriend (Rachel Zan Huss) is a demure blond beauty, and they're a sweet, attractive couple. But underneath his ultra-conventional surface, Lincoln is drawn sexually to men. He hasn't yet discovered whether he is gay or bisexual.

The other young man (Thang Chan) looks to be the same age as Lincoln but is actually a decade older. He calls himself either Minh or John, depending on the circumstances. Born of a Vietnamese mother and an African American father never known to him, Minh has been in the U.S. for three years. (Chan himself was settled in Seattle in 1993 by the U.S government as part of a program to bring the children of American soldiers to the U.S.)

When Minh and Lincoln run into each other a second time in an adult entertainment arcade, Minh zeros in on Lincoln immediately. Minh is direct, passionate and openly gay; you believe him when he tells the bowled-over Lincoln that he fell in love with him the first time they met. The young men eventually head for Lincoln's father's boat, and a romantic idyll downriver in Mississippi.

But the question is this: How can they possibly develop their relationship in small-city Southern society? Minh has been marginalized to the max, fitting in neither the black nor Vietnamese émigré communities of Memphis, and facing much discrimination in his native land because of the color of his skin. He is a nervy, edgy man desperate for love and acceptance.

Meanwhile, Lincoln is completely conventional, apart from his uncertain sexual orientation. That he could have a gay Vietnamese-African American lover would surely be inconceivable to his family and friends. Will he ever find it within himself to pursue such a relationship in such an environment, or have the courage, let alone the desire, to take off with Minh?

In making his feature debut, Sachs returned to his native Memphis, where he spent six months reabsorbing the atmosphere. There, he discovered both Chan, a Seattle fishing cannery worker vacationing in Memphis, and Gray, an Arkansas rock drummer in the city for one night only. Neither of them had ever acted before.

Sachs' ability to draw deeply affecting, completely open and unself-conscious performances from Chan and Gray and other nonprofessionals as well is most impressive and highly effective. Working with masterly New York cinematographer Benjamin P. Speth. Sachs has created in "The Delta" an achingly poignant portrait of alienation and longing so evocative that it is poetic in its impact.

NEW YORK POST, 8/15/97, p. 42, Thelma Adams

"The Delta" puts a new twist on the idea of cruising the Mississippi. Ira Sachs' groping, awkward drama opens with a privileged Jewish teen and an Afro-Vietnamese drifter meeting and mating on the back streets of Memphis.

Sachs, who also wrote his debut feature, creates a boy-meets-boy, boy-dumps-boy, boy-exacts-revenge story that would make for an alternative country hit, something about wet kisses across the tracks down by the river, the weeping river.

Lurching between Lincoln Bloom (Shayne Gray) and Minh Nguyen (Thang Chan), Sachs is reaching for something more, something beyond the grasp of his filmmaking skills. The lighting is ineffective, the sound garbled, the dialogue clunky. The structure is a leaky vessel, hobbled by missed opportunities and sudden shifts in direction.

Gray is a dimpled newcomer with a Costner charm and a 50-50 chance of showing his best side to the camera. Chan, his thick accent intensified by poor miking, is hard to understand. His physical charms are left to the imagination.

In the few scenes in Vietnamese with subtitles, Chan gives the movie rhythm it desperately needs. The anger beneath his glib surface hints at the shocking climax the movie must reach despite itself.

Sachs has a novelist's insight into rich material, without the skills to mine it. He has been summoned back to Memphis after his college years at Yale to find the hidden city: the crossroads between drug-addled teens, and a gay netherworld, the shadowy corners where prosperous white boys soul-kiss the dark men they avoid during daylight hours.

He shuns the city's landmarks for the strip malls, dive bars, video arcades and cheesy modern flats that could be anywhere.

The writer/director comes close to breaking new ground when he shows Lincoln slipping between his passive trophy girlfriend (Rachel Zan Huss) and Minh. He sets up juicy potential conflicts, then drops them, resolving differences with jarring violent acts that are dramatically unsupportable.

"The Delta" has made the festival rounds: Sundance, Los Angeles Outfest, the San Francisco Gay and Lesbian Film Festival. It should make its splash where gay rage is all the rage, technique be damned. But it's not ready for a theatrical release. It's no Memphis Belle, even in drag. "The Delta" is Sachs' "Slackers," his "The Doom Generation" but he's not yet a Richard Linklater or a Gregg Araki.

NEWSDAY, 8/15/97, Part II/p. B8, John Anderson

Five minutes into Ira Sachs' feverishly inert little drama "The Delta," the two principals lock lips (I'm being discreet) and spend the rest of the movie pushing us away. OK so they want to be alone. I'm more than willing to oblige them.

The title is evocative enough, of course—blues, Robert Johnson and poison whiskey coming immediately to mind—but "The Delta" is more like a fluvial deposit of filmmaking silt. The documentary-style setups, the overlapping live sound, the dispassionate perspectives, none of it has any essential purpose in telling this story which is vaguely about culture clash and coming out.

It all feels borrowed and rather pointless, as does its riff-with-a-half-twist on Huck Finn-as-homoerotic-hero. Leslie Fiedler, call your lawyer.

Lincoln (Shayne Gray)—and, yes, his name is Lincoln—is the scion of a well-to-do Memphis family who has a quasi-girlfriend but spends his evenings cruising the city's gay strip. (He's repressed, obviously, as well as confused, but we're supposed to think he's special nonetheless.)

One evening, John (Thang Chan), the Amerasian offspring of a black soldier and Vietnamese woman, gets into Lincoln's car and we're off on a proto-American joy ride to the land of milk, honey, sexual guilt and a throwaway murder.

Having Lincoln and John take to the Mississippi—using Lincoln's father's cabin cruiser for their metaphorical raft—is clever, but that's about it. There's little resonance in the story, less in the dialogue, especially when Sachs is putting together his patchwork portrait of Lincoln's aimless teenage coterie.

Quite often, what the characters say, especially Lincoln, has us squirming with its dead-on banality (such lines as "If you want me to," "Do you want me to?" and "I want you to" occur with such regularity you begin to think it *is* a documentary). But all this effort, and discomfort, is for very little gain. In the end, "The Delta" feels like a movie made by a director whose budget was burning a hole in his pocket.

VILLAGE VOICE, 8/19/97, p. 90, Dennis Lim

A willfully scraggly study of sexual repression, The Delta—like Larry Clark's *Kids*—wants to be read as ethnography. Its dispassionate gaze fixed mainly on a white, upper-middle-class Memphis teen, Ira Sachs's first feature tunnels deep into the city's homosexual, youth, and immigrant subcultures. The director himself gay, white, and Memphis-raised—records the psychosexual tumult of his protagonist, Lincoln (Shayne Gray), a fresh-faced high schooler juggling a girlfriend and an active nightlife on the local gay cruising circuit.

The film opens with Lincoln picking up a twentysomething man and giving him a blowjob in the front seat of the family station wagon (like the few other sexual episodes in the film, it's a decidedly ungainly affair). The older guy, Minh (Thang Chan), is half black, half Vietnamese, the son of an American G.I.

Sachs turns what seem like budgetary constraints into pseudorealist tactics: the cast consists of non-actors (it shows); the soundtrack is smothered in unfiltered background noise; and the film is barely lit, struggling at times to emerge from a thick murk. The camera hangs back, often inert, observing provocatively long and uneven scenes.

But a self-conscious tripartite structure underlies the painstakingly engineered casualness: the first section follows Lincoln, the third Minh, and the pivotal middle sequence depicts an overnight encounter between the two. Every inch a Deep South drama, The Delta is never less than hypercognizant of race and class; Lincoln and Minh—the latter plainly in thrall to the former—come across as an erotically shackled master and servant. Sachs, unable to resist the queer Huck-and-Jim scenario staring him in the face, sends the pair floating down the Mississippi.

Though it will probably be billed as a doomed romance, The Delta has very little to do with love. Gruelingly pessimistic, it plays like the inverse of a coming-out movie. And yet, its denunciation of the closet could not be more emphatic. Sachs's subject is self-loathing—and the tragic, pathetic lie to which it can reduce a life. In one memorably discomforting scene, Lincoln, attempting to woo his girlfriend, regurgitates Minh's half-flirtatious, half-imploring declarations from the night before.

For Sachs, repression is a profoundly destructive evil, and the movie's finale goes out of its way to prove this thesis. But unlike, say, Chantal Akerman's *Jeanne Dielman,* in which a culminating act of violence shifts an ultraminimalist narrative into full-scale tragedy, The Delta's final jolt of brutality (an oedipal impulse, we're led to conclude) feels cheaply sensational. For all its strenuous aspirations to authenticity, the film ends up with its emotional honesty compromised.

Also reviewed in:
NEW YORK TIMES, 8/15/97, p. C14, Stephen Holden
VARIETY, 12/16-22/96, p. 83, Emanuel Levy

DESIGNATED MOURNER, THE

A First Look Pictures release of a BBC Films presentation of a Greenpoint Film production. *Executive Producer:* Mark Shivas and Simon Curtis. *Producer:* Donna Grey and David Hare. *Director:* David Hare. *Screenplay (based on his play):* Wallace Shawn. *Director of Photography:* Oliver Stapleton. *Editor:* George Akers. *Music:* Richard Hartley. *Sound:* Clive Winter. *Production Designer:* Bob Crowley. *Art Director:* John Ralph. *Running time:* 95 minutes. *MPAA Rating:* R.

CAST: Mike Nichols (Jack); Miranda Richardson (Judy); David de Keyser (Howard).

LOS ANGELES TIMES, 6/6/97, Calendar/p. 14, Kevin Thomas

"The Designated Mourner" is as demanding a movie-going experience as you're ever likely to have. Director David Hare, one of Britain's most celebrated playwrights, has brought Wallace Shawn's play, a London sensation last year, to the screen with the utmost rigor and simplicity.

Mike Nichols, Miranda Richardson and David de Keyser, in recreating their stage roles, are seated, a table in front of them, with a gold-leafed wall behind them. Without any exposition whatsoever they talk for 94 minutes, which means we are left to make sense of Shawn's torrent of words the best we can.

Even exerting the utmost concentration, you may have trouble figuring out what's going on. It seems that Jack (Nichols), in the title role, married Judy (Richardson), the daughter of de Keyser's Howard, a literary lion, a poet and thinker imperiled by an ever more oppressive regime. Although shrewd, Jack could never quite measure up to the rarefied and humane intellectual circles of his father-in-law and wife, which the government is eager to crush as a source of dissent.

Therefore, Jack finds it not so difficult to slide into the dispassionate "low-brow" mode now advocated by the government. Ultimately, it's left to him to lament the loss of a world he at once envied and disdained because he felt excluded from it.

The country in which all this is happening is never revealed, even though the universal is best perceived in the particular rather than the vague. Even so Shawn's passionate anti-totalitarian stance is clear enough, as is his ability to enjoy the simple pleasures of life—the latter a characteristic he displayed in "My Dinner With Andre," an equally talky but considerably more accessible film.

Shawn seems to be attempting to illuminate the human condition free of conventional dramaturgy and in this he succeeds, although to wearying effect, at least on the screen. He seems to be suggesting that traditional storytelling is unnecessary and even distracting in eliciting the entire range of human emotions—love, envy, despair, boredom, fear, etc. In Nichols (in his first major screen role), Richardson and de Keyser, he's got actors who are able to express this wide range brilliantly.

Yet Hare's approach, which has his three actors directly addressing the camera most of the time, only rarely talking to one another, presents acute challenges to attention spans. The case is invariably made for such talkathons that the camera peers right into the souls of the characters the actors are playing. However, under the weight of an avalanche of words, you may find yourself drifting and thereby become caught up in appraising the superb technique of the actors—how expressive they are, what wonderful voices they all have, what they can do with a pause, a gesture, a movement of their bodies.

Acutely visual directors from D.W. Griffith to Michelangelo Antonioni and beyond have bared many a soul but have also expressed many of the same emotions and similar concerns with memorably enduring images; this Hare does not do. It is entirely understandable and admirable that Hare et al would want to film "The Designated Mourner." This simply means hard work for the viewer, for there is nothing like the steady gaze of a long-held camera to drain meaning from a verbal barrage.

NEW YORK POST, 5/2/97, p. 54, Bill Hoffmann

We know Mike Nichols can direct. And with "Designated Mourner," now we know he can act. And my question is: What took him so long? Nichols is the front and dramatic center of this three-character play-turned-movie penned by actor Wallace Shawn.

He's also the compass that keeps this absorbing but sometimes confusing story on track.

Nichols is Jack, a self-confessed "lowbrow" whose marriage to Judy (Miranda Richardson), daughter of a renowned poet, Howard (David de Keyser), puts him smack in the middle of the intellectual elite.

As the film begins, Howard has just died and Jack appoints himself as a "designated mourner"—to eulogize the end of an intellectual era.

With New York City's elite always complaining about the Big Apple's cultural decline, it seems like "The Designated Mourner" should be set in New York.

Instead, Shawn places his characters in an unnamed country with an oppressive government that stomps on all sources of dissent—particularly writers.

As Nichols, Richardson and de Keyser (in spirit) talk about their city's once great past and its grim future, the play becomes a funeral for the slow death of American culture.

In Shawn's eyes, yesterday's literary geniuses are becoming today's dust.

With its mythical setting, Shawn's play, directed for the screen by David Hare, sometimes delves into the Orwellian and veers toward obscurity.

But Nichols and Richardson are such strong and engaging actors that you can't take your eyes off them.

Nichols was always a natural on stage—totally relaxed and genuinely likable in the standup act he did with his ex-wife, Elaine May.

Let's hope with his new success, well be seeing more of Nichols in front of the camera.

NEWSDAY, 5/2/97, Part II/p. B3, John Anderson

Think of popular movies as being on two distinct, quasi-evolutionary paths one ending with an inarticulate grunt and a hand grenade, the other in pure verbiage.

It's an apt consideration, given "The Designated Mourner," which is not just as talky a movie as you'll ever see, but contains among its various themes the growing disparity between the lumpen and the intellectual. Adapted from the successful play by occasional actor Wallace Shawn ("Clueless"), and directed by another playwright, David Hare, "The Designated Mourner" in its roundabout manner is an elegy for art, culture and memory.

Continuing its daisy chain of playwrights, actors and directors, the film also includes a rather terrific performance by Mike Nichols, who at one point in his career was a performer (Nichols and May), went on to direct a few films of his own ("The Graduate," "Who's Afraid of Virginia Woolf," "The Birdcage," etc., etc.) and makes his on-screen performing debut as Jack, whose alternately self-indulgent and self-recriminating observations supply the basis of Shawn's psychological meditation.

Set in an unknown country in an unknown time, "The Designated Mourner" contains three characters, all addressing the audience directly, almost never interacting with each other, and speaking as if the others weren't there. I didn't see the original, which Hare first staged at London's National Theater last year (with Nichols' much-praised performance), but the capacity of the camera to get in the faces of the characters adds a degree of intimacy impossible on the stage—and which is frequently uncomfortable here.

What is revealed by Jack, a failed student of literature; his wife, Judy (Miranda Richardson), and, in a much more limited way, Judy's father (David de Keyser), a celebrated essayist, poet and enemy of the regime, progresses from Jack's rather Prufrockian anxieties to something profoundly Orwellian. To reveal too much would be to betray Hare, whose careful translation of the play depends on the gradual surrender of detail, the dissolving of facades and the catharsis of begrudging emotional release.

Shawn's is an ingeniously written piece. His characters circle their subject matter warily, ignore it, avoid it, digress and dance around their histories with an agility that reveals socially ordered lives and iron reserve. Their bon mots are courtesy of "so and so" and "such and such," but they could well be quoting themselves and are perfectly capable of doing so.

Richardson is her usual possessed and transporting self, imbuing Judy with both heartache and armor. But Nichols gets the attention, not just because he has the larger part and because he's a revelation. Jack is a fully realized character; his self-appointment as the dying society's "designated mourner"—a reference to the practice among certain cultures of appointing someone to officially grieve—is the saddest of acts, because he's never appreciated literature or art or anything "highbrow." He surrenders to baseness, breathes in the anesthesia of ignorance, and is just an observer of how, with the evaporation of his memory, all vestiges of culture will die.

Shawn's is a funny, witty play that's now a horror movie. Nichols is his Frankenstein, and his monster.

VILLAGE VOICE, 5/6/97, p. 94, Leslie Camhi

If all the readers of poetry slowly disappeared, extinguished by the forces of order and attrition, would we really miss them? Or would we simply enjoy the pleasant if vacant aimlessness of a world where the knotty complications of art and morality had finally been eliminated? *The Designated Mourner*, playwright Wallace Shawn's unnervingly lyrical and harshly elegiac requiem for humanistic values and culture, is set in an unknown country sometime in the future. This screen version borrows its director (David Hare) and cast of three from the play's London production.

Years ago, Jack (Mike Nichols), a "former student of English literature," married Judy (Miranda Richardson), the cultivated daughter of Howard (David de Keyser), a writer and leading dissident intellectual under an increasingly repressive (if nondescript) regime. Howard calls Jack a man so lazy "his favorite foods ... were soup, risotto, mashed potatoes, and ice cream." Jack describes his father-in-law as remarkable for both his great culture and his limitless capacity for contempt. Howard, he says, could suffer with equal ostentation over both gross social injustices and the closing of his favorite espresso bar or the razing of his favorite grove of trees.

But that was long ago, when things were different, Jack informs us. He is the "designated mourner," there to bear witness to the orchestrated extinction of that strange tribe, the cultural elite, the lovers of art and poetry. It's a tribe he married into, with a son-in-law's envy of their ease and scorn for their rituals; he alone could see how narrowly circumscribed their world had become. To survive, he had to abandon them and betray their ideals; he learned to make friends with the TV screens and pornographic magazines, and to content himself with firework displays at night. Yet he knows that with their passing something oddly worthy and beyond his understanding was lost.

The three characters, Jack, Howard, and Judy, sit around a table, talking to the camera and occasionally addressing each other. Howard and Judy exist largely at the service of Jack's memory. Together with director David Hare, Shawn (whose screen credits include the *raconteur* classic, *My Dinner With Andre*) has once again tried to fashion a film wholly from words and the flitting theater of facial expressions. Does it work? Not entirely, though Mike Nichols's breath-taking performance as Jack goes a long way toward carrying this picture. His timing is flawless, his speech peppered with strange pauses through which we grasp the full weight of his irony, derision, and sheer incredulity at the peculiarity of the human phenomena that surround him. As Howard, David de Keyser manages to convey the cerebral haughtiness that often passes for a superior moral conscience. Only Miranda Richardson seems woefully miscast, entirely too smooth, hard, and perfect to play a weather-beaten female intellectual. But the real star of this film is Shawn's language, as indirect as human interaction, and as incisive as art.

Also reviewed in:
CHICAGO TRIBUNE, 11/7/97, Friday/p. M, John Petrakis
NEW REPUBLIC, 3/24/97, p. 28, Stanley Kauffmann
NEW YORK TIMES, 5/2/97, p. C7, Stephen Holden
NEW YORKER, 5/19/97, p. 97, Terrence Rafferty
VARIETY, 3/10-16/97, p. 81, Derek Elley

DEVIL'S ADVOCATE, THE

A Warner Bros. release in association with Regency Enterprises of a Kopelson Entertainment production. *Executive Producer:* Taylor Hackford, Michael Tadross, Erwin Stoff, Barry Bernardi, and Steve White. *Producer:* Arnon Milchan, Arnold Kopelson, and Anne Kopelson. *Director:* Taylor Hackford. *Screenplay:* Jonathan Lemkin and Tony Gilrory. *Based on the novel by:* Andrew Neiderman. *Director of Photography:* Andrzej Bartkowiak. *Editor:* Mark Warner. *Music:* James Newton Howard. *Music Editor:* Jim Weidman. *Sound:* Tod A. Maitland and (music) Shawn Murphy. *Casting:* Nancy Klopper and Mary Colquhoun. *Production Designer:* Bruno Rubeo. *Art Director:* Dennis Bradford. *Set Decorator:* Roberta Holinko. *Special Effects:* Rick Baker. *Costumes:* Indianna Makovsky. *Make-up:* Luigi Rocchetti. *Stunt Coordinator:* Gary Davis and Frank Ferrara. *Running time:* 130 minutes. *MPAA Rating:* R.

CAST: Keanu Reeves (Kevin Lomax); Al Pacino (John Milton); Charlize Theron (Mary Ann Lomax); Jeffrey Jones (Eddie Barzoon); Judith Ivey (Mrs. Lomax); Craig T. Nelson (Alexander Cullen); Connie Nielson (Christabella); Tamara Tunie (Jackie Heath); Ruben Santiago-Hudson (Leamon Heath); Debra Monk (Pam Garrety); Vyto Ruginis (Weaver); Laura Harrington (Melissa Black); Pamela Gray (Diana Barzoon); George Wyner (Meisel); Christopher Bauter (Gettys); Connie Embesi (Mrs. Gettys); Jonathan Cavallary (Getty's Son); Heather Matarazzo (Barbara); Murphy Guyer (Barbara's Father); Leo Burmester (Florida Prosecutor); Bill Moor (Florida Judge); Neal Jones (Florida Reporter); Eddie Aldridge (Florida Bailiff); Mark Deakins (Florida Lawyer #1); Rony Clanton (Junkie); George Gore II (Boy); Alan Manson (Judge Sklar); Brian Poteat (Pie Face); Daniel Oreskes (Metro, D.A.); Kim Chan (Chinese Man); Caprice Benedetti (Manage a Trois woman); Don King (Himself); Ray Garvey and Rocco Musacchia (Fight Fans); Susan Kellermann (Joyce Rensaleer); James Saito (Takaori Osumi); Harsh Nayyar (Pavathi Resh); M.B. Ghaffari (Bashir Toabal); Nicki Chochrane (Multi-lingual Party Guest); Fenja Klaus (Female #1); Gino Lucci (Limo Driver); Novella Nelson (Botanica Woman); Vincent Laresca and Benny Nieves (Big Guys); Franci Leary (Babs Coleman); Gloria L. Henry (Tiffany); Jorge Navarro (Spanish Restaurant Manager); Jose Fernandes Torres (Flamenco Guitarist); Antonio Vargas Cortes (Flamenco Singer); Elena Camenuz Andujar (Flamenco Dancer); Monica Keena (Allesandra); Linda Atkinson (Therapist); William Hill (Feeney); Juan Hernandez (Paparazzi); Mel Wei (Gizelle); E. Katherine Kerr (Woman Judge); Liza Harris, Bill Boggs, and Bo Rucker (Reporters); Michael Lombard (Judge Poe); Marc Manfro and J. Nester (Bailiffs); John Rothman (Broygo); George Sperdakos (Technician); Hollis Granville and Edward Seamon (Old Men); Patrick Joseph Byrnes and Gregory Lichtenson (Joggers); Socorro Santiago (Nurse); Marcia DeBonis (Nurse 2); Marie Stuart Vassallo (Marie the Patient); Tom Riis Farrell (Priest); Harold Suratt (Orderly 1); Cadillac Moon (Band).

CHRISTIAN SCIENCE MONITOR, 10/20/97, p. 15, David Sterritt

If a Hollywood producer wanted to retell the "Faust" legend in a contemporary setting, it's easy to guess the main character would be a lawyer. Not an old-fashioned attorney endowed with fair-minded logic and seat-of-the-pants wisdom, but a late-century shyster burdened with stereotypical traits like unbridled ambition, hired-gun ethics, and a conviction that triumph in the courtroom is the only thing that counts.

And so we have Keanu Reeves in "The Devil's Advocate," playing a talented young Southerner who wins every case he tries—first as a prosecutor, then as a defense attorney who's not overly concerned whether his clients are guilty or not. Wooed by a wealthy Northeast firm, he moves to New York despite warnings from his deeply religious mother, who tells him Manhattan is a latter-day Babylon crawling with sin and temptation.

Ensconced with his beautiful wife in a posh apartment, he rises rapidly in his profession, earning mountains of money and generous praise from the firm's mysterious boss. It seems too good to be true, and of course it is. The firm appears more immoral every day, the demands on his time and energy are crushingly hard, and his wife misses the attention he used to lavish on her.

And what's behind the nightmarish visions that start tormenting the couple as they sink ever deeper into their strange new life?

Without revealing too many of the movie's secrets, it's fair to say that the insidious firm and its supernatural boss turn out to be literally infernal, using the modern-day legal system to manipulate society and lure weak-willed opportunists to perdition.

In the end, "The Devil's Advocate" carries a lesson about the wiliness of temptation and the need for personal responsibility that's as strait-laced as a medieval morality play. But be warned that the filmmakers drape their story in more lascivious sex and shocking violence than a traditional "Faust" rendition. This is the year's most vivid example of what a filmmaker once called the Cecil B. DeMille sin-and-scripture syndrome, following Hollywood's age-old practice of deploring evil while plastering it all over the screen.

The picture was directed by Taylor Hackford, a versatile filmmaker whose credits range from the melodrama of "An Officer and a Gentleman" to the documentary of "Chuck Berry Hail! Hail! Rock 'n' Roll." He keeps the overlong action flowing rapidly, helped by Andrzej Bartkowiak's spooky camera work and Mark Warner's energetic editing.

The only technical disappointments come from the special-effects department. It tries to make the villains look like living gargoyles in some scenes, but the images lapse into clichés that were already stale when "I Married a Monster From Outer Space" trotted them out in the 1950s.

Reeves gives his most persuasive performance to date as the misguided lawyer, and Al Pacino is devilishly devious as his wicked boss, who flashes hypnotic glances and always travels by subway so he'll be close to home. The strong supporting cast includes Charlize Theron, Judith Ivey, Jeffrey Jones as an ill-fated accomplice, and Craig T. Nelson as the firm's most scoundrelly client.

LOS ANGELES TIMES, 10/17/97, Calendar/p. 10, Kenneth Turan

If Satan were the senior partner in a major Manhattan law firm, would anybody notice? What difference would it make in standards and practices? And if the Prince of Darkness is so powerful, why is he bothering to run a law office in the first place?

"The Devil's Advocate," starring a determined Keanu Reeves as an ambitious young lawyer and Al Pacino as you-know-who, is a potboiler with something on its mind which is not always a good thing. Directed in bold, energetic strokes by Taylor Hackford, "Devil" is fine disreputable fun at first, a stylish and matchable hoot. But then its tone changes, the plot goes gimmicky and bombastic speeches about the nature of good and evil clutter the airwaves and confuse the issue.

"Devil's Advocate" shies away from initially saying who John Milton (Pacino) of Milton, Chadwich, Waters is, but anyone who's read the title and seen the trailer will guess in a New York minute, and that knowledge makes things much more fun. In fact the only person in the entire film who's in the dark so to speak, is young Florida attorney Kevin Lomax (Reeves).

First glimpsed in a Gainsborough courtroom, Lomax is that rare individual who, first as a prosecutor and now as a defense attorney, has never lost a case. And, faced with a shaky teenage victim (Heather Matarrazo of "Welcome to the Dollhouse") in a molestation case, he knows exactly what needs to be done.

These formidable courtroom skills come to the attention of that New York firm, which offers to bring Lomax and his fetching wife, Mary Ann (an appealing Charlize Theron), to Manhattan. Off they go despite the qualms of his God-fearing mother (Judith Ivey), who is fond of quoting Ecclesiastes to the effect that "fallen, fallen is Babylon, it has become a dwelling place of demons." Little does she know ...

Watching this young couple fall under the away of the kind of swank life only a major league New York firm can provide is part of the fun of "Devil". Much of that pleasure comes from Pacino's relish in playing the showy role of malevolent malefactor, riding the subway for pleasure, hobnobbing with pals like Don King and Sen. Alfonse D'Amato and sweet-talking Mary Ann with lines like "A woman's shoulders are the front lines of her mystique." Who knew the devil read Harlequin novels in his spare time?

Gradually, however, things get things get dicier. Lomax's workaholic tendencies take over his life, and he finds himself attracted to Christabella (Connie Nielson), one of the firm's more attractive partners. There's little time for poor Mary Ann in all this, and she starts to have a nervous breakdown that worsens when Lomax begins the defense of Andrew Cullen (Craig T.

Nelson), a Donald Trumpish developer (the Donald's Fifth Avenue penthouse makes a cameo appearance) accused of a messy triple murder.

As written by Jonathan Lemkin and Tony Gilroy from a novel by Andrew Neiderman, "The Devil's Advocate" also has some amusing subtexts, like the idea that all attorneys are Satan's pawns and the perverse notion that it's not idle hands but the determination to work endless hours that makes the devil happy.

But at a certain point in the exposition, a pair of unwelcome tendencies assert control of "The Devil's Advocate," and things begin to spiral out of control. One is the increasingly common need to add needless complications to the plot, which run the length to an unnecessary 2 hours and 23 minutes, and the other is the willingness to confuse the film with a freshman seminar on moral philosophy.

What that means is that Pacino, who's been under control for most of the movie, explodes into a series of bloated speeches that are declaimed like leftovers from the benighted "Looking for Richard." Although it's nice for a film to be ambitious, there is such a thing as overreaching. As the devil himself puts it (and who should know better), "Vanity, that's my favorite sin."

NEW YORK, 10/27/97, p. 80, David Denby

The Devil's Advocate is the kind of preposterously entertaining movie that people discuss more intensely than they do saner and better works. Steaming and redolent, with the wordiest script since the late Paddy Chayefsky sheathed his quill, it's about Satan, New York, fornication, and the practice of law (in ascending order of evil). It is, I suppose, very much in the line of *Rosemary's Baby* and *The Exorcist*, though less maliciously artful than the first and more fun than the second. Al Pacino stars as John Milton, the loquacious head of an international law firm in New York that has a spectacular view of the bridges over the East River. Milton recruits a hotshot lawyer from small-town Florida who has never lost a case—Kevin Lomax (Keanu Reeves), who arrives in the dazzling big city with his beautiful wife, Mary Ann (Charlize Theron), and receives the best of everything. Pacino does the grandstanding; he has the big florid speeches about the power of evil and the inhumanity of God (guess which part he plays). But Reeves holds the movie together. He's lean and square-jawed, forceful in his lawyer suits. His performance says, "No more fooling around: I want to be a movie star." He's so serious a young man that he makes succumbing to temptation sexier than a more relaxed actor ever could.

I know one reason *The Devil's Advocate* will be popular around the country, and so do you: The movie conveys the idea that anyone who wants success in New York must be ready to sell his soul (which must be a consoling view if you live in Fresno). Taylor Hackford, the director, working with a script by Jonathan Lemkin and Tony Gilroy (from Andrew Neiderman's schlock-gothic novel), has a very square idea of evil. Kevin Lomax is corrupted by vanity and by his desire to win his cases at all costs. The rewards are an apartment on Fifth Avenue, gorgeous women who disrobe with gratifying regularity, and invitations to parties at which Al D'Amato is received not as a disgrace but as a celebrity.

Square or not, Hackford, the director of *The Idolmaker, An Officer and a Gentleman,* and *Everybody's All-American,* has always been a good storyteller, and passages of this movie are very satisfying. Hackford and special-effects whiz Rick Baker don't get freaky right away (for a long time, the movie holds to a realistic framework). Kevin takes on the case of a big-deal real-estate developer (Craig T. Nelson) who may have killed his wife, but as he becomes absorbed in the case he neglects Mary Ann, who gets set upon by Satan and his minions. The wife of another lawyer bares her breasts and makes gargoyle faces at Mary Ann; she has disgusting visions, Satan sleeps with her, and she loses her sanity. All this may be gothic nonsense, but the lush, bow-lipped Charlize Theron gives a full-scale dramatic performance, and she's very touching. In a genuinely erotic scene, Keanu Reeves makes love to her and to Connie Nielson at the same time (that is, one woman becomes another, and then back again—ah, the magic of the movies). Parts of the movie are disturbingly sensual, and the scenes of deluxe New York life, conventional as they are, might easily impress a small-town boy as the height of sophistication. At the end, however, when Pacino takes over and delivers his Devil's sermon at the top of his lungs, and Keanu shouts back at him, we go beyond entertaining gothic kitsch into some never-never land of movie awfulness. Hellfires burn, bodies writhe, and the movie goes up in flames. But *The Devil's Advocate* is fun for a while.

NEW YORK POST, 10/17/97, p. 41, Thelma Adams

A New Yorker has to love a devil who rides the subway.

Al Pacino is old red eyes, and the joke is that Lucifer is a lawyer in "The Devils Advocate." Taylor Hackford's slick, campy son of "Rosemary's Baby" is a sinfully guilty pleasure.

Pacino has never seemed to enjoy a role more than that of the infernal John Milton, senior partner of Milton, Chadwick, Waters.

Pacino's Milton is a sexy charmer. He has piercing brown eyes under a vault of eyebrows, a towering marble forehead like Lugosi's Dracula—and heel lifts.

The devil can see into men's hearts, up women's skirts and be in two places at once. And, of course, in Jonathan Lemkin and Tony Gilroy's sharp, Faustian script, he gets the best lines.

On his way to summoning the anti-Christ, Milton sets out to sink the soul of one vain Florida lawyer with a talent for picking juries and getting sweaty child abusers acquitted.

Enter Kevin Lomax (Keanu Reeves), the kind of cocky S.O.B. with slicked-back hair and a widow's peak who can actually have a victory party after breaking an honest, abused teen witness (well-played by Heather ["Welcome to the Dollhouse"] Matarazzo).

Reeves' accent is pure Gator Bowl. We no more believe he's a hot-shot attorney than we buy Nicole Kidman's nuclear genius in "The Peacemaker." But the actor's vanity is believable—and it's through Lomax's self-love that the devil plots the young sharpie's fall.

Lomax should know that Milton's big-city-job offer is too good to be true—but his egotism clouds his vision. He wants to be a player. His Bible-thumping mama (Judith Ivey) warns him about Manhattan ("a dwelling place of demons"). But his bodacious wife (Charlize Theron) can't resist the Classic Eight with Central Park views that Milton offers.

Disturbingly erotic, spiked with gyno-horror that would make David Cronenberg squirm, "The Devil's Advocate" is a knowing, urbane, character-driven thriller which never loses touch with its characters.

While the script cops out in its several endings and gives Pacino his inevitable howling valedictory, "Advocate" shrewdly examines the character issue: what is a man made of, what tempts him, and where does he draw the line before he looks in the mirror and views the devil himself?

NEWSWEEK, 10/27/97, p. 70, Jack Kroll

Some movies are so silly that they cross over into some mystical land of superkitsch, where they take on a kind of crazy grandeur. They don't come any kitschier than *The Devil's Advocate* which has McDeep things to tell us about Good and Evil, love and lust, free will and fate. Screenwriters Jonathan Lemkin and Tony Gilroy have taken a god-awful little novel by Andrew Neiderman and pumped it up into this Macy's Parade balloon of a film about a young lawyer, Kevin Lomax (Keanu Reeves), who's plucked from the Florida courts by a big-time New York law firm, headed by John Milton (Al Pacino). Lomax has never lost a case; he's mastered all the tactics needed to successfully defend repulsive types like teachers who sexually abuse their young female pupils. He doesn't like these creeps, but he loves riding their constitutional rights to his own superstardom.

Milton recruits Lomax, seducing him with money, a lavish apartment and a corporate setting that looks like the digs of a Renaissance doge, complete with hot and hotter running bimbos. Lomax manfully tries to resist the bimbos, but he can't resist Milton, whose vast office contains a huge, blazing fireplace, who speaks all languages, who travels only on the subway (underground, get it?). Well, long before poor Lomax has gotten it, everyone in the audience knows that Milton is the Devil. Even his name is a devilish gag. Don't these Southern boys take English lit? John Milton wrote "Paradise Lost," the epic of warfare between God and Satan. Meanwhile, Lomax's wife, Mary Ann (Charlize Theron), is getting sicker and sicker as she senses the encroaching evil.

James Newton Howard's score clangs and bangs, smiting you with ponderous sonic clues to the satanic situation, and Andrzej Bartkowiak's cinematography turns New York into a hell that's erupted into a high-rise parody of heaven. In the climactic face-off, Lomax and Milton engage in a verbal duel that itself is a parody of "Paradise Lost." Written with brio and staged rousingly by director Taylor Hackford, this confrontation is good, kitschy fun. Milton proclaims that lawyers are the new Antichrist army who defend human evil, "winning acquittal after acquittal until the stench rises" to overwhelm virtue. The film ends with a double switcheroo, a cop-out that cops out again. But how can you hate a movie that casts litigators as the new legions of Lucifer?

Pacino hasn't had such fun since he exposed the devilish doings among New York cops in "Serpico." But the new news is Charlize Theron, a 22-year-old South African-born actress who made a knockout debut as a hit woman in the noirish "2 Days in the Valley." As sexy as Stone, as beautiful as Pfeiffer, Theron has a spontaneity and pure screen presence that says "star" with every breath she takes. I mean, Keanu Reeves is a star, right? There's his name, *above* Pacino's name in the credits! He must have one of those Luciferian lawyers.

SIGHT AND SOUND, 1/98, p. 38, John Wrathall

Florida-based defence lawyer Kevin Lomax is defending a guilty sex offender, Gettys. Lomax goes to the bathroom to wrestle with his conscience, then returns to the courtroom and wins the case. When Lomax is headhunted by a powerful New York law firm run by John Milton, his mother warns him not to go. Undeterred, he comes to Manhattan with his wife Mary Ann. Lomax is attracted to one of his colleagues, Christabella. Both Lomax and Mary Ann start to have hallucinations. One of the firm's biggest clients, Alexander Cullen, is accused of multiple homicide. Milton gives Lomax the case. Increasingly preoccupied, he has little time for Mary Ann, who grows lonely and depressed, but he refuses Milton's offer to leave the case. Lomax gets Cullen off even though he's probably guilty. Mary Ann unfeasibly claims that Milton raped and mutilated her. Lomax has her committed to a psychiatric hospital where she kills herself. His mother reveals that Milton is his father. Lomax confronts Milton, who is the Devil incarnate. He wants Lomax to take over the family business with his half-sister Christabella, who will bear his child, the Antichrist. Lomax shoots himself.

Suddenly Lomax finds himself back where he started in the Florida courthouse bathroom. He announces that he is unable to defend Gettys. On the way out of the courthouse, he is approached by a reporter who applauds his ethical stance and promises to write a profile that will make him a star. When Lomax agrees and leaves, the reporter turns into Milton.

A young couple moves into a Central Park apartment block inhabited by devil worshippers. While the husband, eager to get ahead, socialises with them and prospers, his lonely wife cracks up after a radical change of hairstyle, and starts believing she has had sex with the Devil. Roman Polanski's achievement in *Rosemary's Baby* (1968) was to invest this storyline with a level of psychological realism. Three decades later, Taylor Hackford plays it strictly as pantomime. Even less progressively, he chooses to focus on the husband, who is literally, the Devil's advocate. As for the wife, despite the best efforts of Charlize Theron as Mary Ann, she is left picking out colours for the apartment walls and dreaming that the Devil has stolen her ovaries—a very distasteful sequence, and the closest this preposterous film comes to a real scare. Then, when she's no longer necessary to the plot, she abruptly slits her throat. So much for girl power.

The maker of *An Officer and a Gentleman* and the Chuck Berry documentary *Hail! Hail! Rock n'Roll*, Hackford discovered horror and interesting women late with his 1995 Stephen King adaptation *Dolores Claiborne*. But *The Devil's Advocate* shows that he has forgotten about them already, despite reuniting him with that film's scriptwriter, Tony Gilroy (one of two credited writers here). Hackford doesn't really believe in horror; apart from a couple of time-lapse shots of the New York skyline, and endless ominous rumbles on the soundtrack, the film is brightly lit and bizarrely jaunty. The script toys with biblical allusions, most memorably in the scene when Milton takes Lomax to the top of the mountain/skyscraper to tempt him. (Keanu Reeves has already played Buddha, so why not Christ?) But Christianity is represented here by a Southern church full of gospel singers and Lomax's bible-bashing mother who denounces New York as Babylon, a dwelling-place of demons; in short, it's just as much a caricature as Satanism. There's no sense that good is really good, or evil really evil.

Of course, the only reason to even consider seeing this film is to watch Al Pacino as the Devil. As if in atonement for, the subtlety he displayed in *Donnie Brasco,* Pacino lets loose with his full range of mannerisms—the inappropriate laugh, the snakelike tongue hovering between his lips—and even gets to mime along to Frank Sinatra.   Plastered with Grecian 2000 until he resembles Robert Maxwell, tottering around on stacked heels (the 90s answer to cloven hooves), he's a flamboyant figure, but hardly a sinister one.   We see him getting a blowjob in a restaurant, and boiling a font with the tip of his finger.   But crucially, when it comes to Milton doing something really horrific—such as raping Mary Ann and slashing her body—Hackford chickens out and just shows us the aftermath.   That's taking sympathy for the Devil a bit too far.

VILLAGE VOICE, 10/28/97, p. 79, Amy Taubin

Just as baroque, though much more vulgar and nearly three times as long, [The reference is to *Cremaster 5;* see Taubin's review.]   *The Devil's Advocate* stars Keanu Reeves as Kevin Lomax, a hot-shot Florida defense attorney recruited by a high-priced New York law firm headed by John Milton (Al Pacino), who, as anyone who's seen the TV trailer knows, is Satan himself. Aspiring to the mix of quotidian and supernatural that made *Rosemary's Baby* so memorable, *The Devil's Advocate* falls way short, thanks to Taylor Hackford's plodding direction and a glut of ostentatious, clichéd special effects.

Lawyers may get a kick out of the notion that theirs is the devil's chosen profession. New York bashers will enjoy Hackford's hideous depiction of the city, which, despite numerous apartments and offices overlooking Central Park (one gold-encrusted horror is, in fact, where Donald Trump hangs his hat), lacks any sense of cosmopolitanism.

The only fun in *The Devil's Advocate* comes from watching Pacino and Reeves. Newly slim, agile, and irresistibly earnest, Reeves is almost believable as the courtroom star whose ambition gets the better of his moral convictions. Barely an actor but very much a star, he manages to hold his own against Pacino, who's both of those in spades and also gets the best lines. "God likes to watch ... he's a tight-assed sadist, an absentee landlord," raves the devil, invoking an obsession with real estate that's as close to a genuine New York mentality as this ersatz film ever gets.

Also reviewed in:
CHICAGO TRIBUNE, 10/17/97, Friday/p. A, Michael Wilmington
NEW YORK TIMES, 10/17/97, p. E12, Janet Maslin
VARIETY, 10/13-19/97, p. 77, Todd McCarthy
WASHINGTON POST, 10/17/97, p. D1, Stephen Hunter
WASHINGTON POST, 10/17/97, p. 33, Desson Howe

DEVIL'S OWN, THE

A Columbia Pictures release of a Lawrence Gordon presentation. *Executive Producer:* Lloyd Levin.   *Producer:* Lawrence Gordon and Robert F. Colesberry.   *Director:* Alan J. Pakula. *Screenplay:* David Aaron Cohen, Vincent Patrick, and Kevin Jarre. *Based on a story by:* Kevin Jarre.   *Director of Photography:* Gordon Willis.   *Editor:* Tom Rolf and Dennis Virkler.   *Music:* James Horner. *Music Editor:* Todd Kasow and Jim Henrikson. *Sound:* James Sabat and (music) Shawn Murphy. *Sound Editor:* Ron Bochar. *Casting:* Alixe Gordin. *Production Designer:* Jane Musky. *Art Director:* Robert Guerra. *Set Decorator:* Leslie Bloom. *Set Dresser:* Jim Archer. *Make-up:* Michael Laudati.   *Stunt Coordinator:* Doug Coleman.   *Running time:* 115 minutes. *MPAA Rating:* R.

CAST: Harrison Ford (Tom O'Meara); Brad Pitt (Frankie McGuire/Rory Devaney); Margaret Colin (Sheila O'Meara); Ruben Blades (Edwin Diaz); Treat Williams (Billy Burke); George Hearn (Peter Fitzsimmons); Mitchell Ryan (Chief Jim Kelly); Natascha McElhone (Megan Doherty);   Paul Ronan (Sean Phelan);   Simon Jones (Harry Sloan);   Julia Stiles (Bridget

O'Meara); Ashley Carin (Morgan O'Meara); Kelly Singer (Annie O'Meara); David O'Hara (Martin MacDuff); David Wilmot (Dessie); Anthony Brophy (Gerard); Shane Dunne (Young Frankie); Martin Dunne (Frankie's Father); Gabrielle Reidy (Frankie's Mother); Samantha Conroy (Frankie's Sister); Baxter Haris (Customs Agent); Hassan Johnson (Teenager); Scott Nicholson (Rookie Cop); Jonathan Earl Peck (Jerry); Sixto Ramos (Hispanic Man); Mya Michaels (Hispanic woman); Jessica Marie Kavanagh (Hispanic Girl); Brendan Kelly (Teddy); Kevin Nagle (Thug); Greg Salata (Tony); Joseph Dandry (Joey the Bartender); Jack McKillop (Jack Fitzsimmons); Mac Orange (The Maid); Malachy McCourt (Bishop); Marian Tomas Griffin (Cousin Eileen); Peggy Shay (Aunt Birdie); Danielle McGovern (Brooke); Ciaran O'Reilly (Father Canlon); Rob McElhenny (Kevin); Donald J. Meade, Patrick Reynolds, and Peter Rufli (Irish Musicians); Debbon Ayer (Tour Guide); Mario Polit (Young Dominican); Chance Kelly (Masked Burglar); Greg Stebner (Uniformed Cop); William Paulson (Detective); Bill Hoag (Trucker); Victor Slezak (Evan Stanley, FBI); Damien Leake (Art Fisher, FBI).

LOS ANGELES TIMES, 3/26/97, Calendar/p. 1, Kenneth Turan

With two of the world's biggest stars in tow, the creators of "The Devil's Own" can be forgiven for figuring that nothing else really mattered. If you've got Harrison Ford and Brad Pitt, do you really need a coherent script? Unfortunately for everyone concerned, the answer is yes.

Even without reading news reports about the back-and-forth between the two leads and director Alan Pakula about what constituted a film-able screenplay, no one seeing "The Devil's Own" can miss the fact that its IRA-gunman-meets-N.Y.C.-cop story line feels random, haphazard, even patched together.

While Kevin Jarre's original work conceivably had its strengths, the current document, credited to David Aaron Cohen & Vincent Patrick and Jarre, is considerably less than compelling in its final created-by-committee incarnation.

Paradoxically, while the two stars might have been better served if they'd kept out of the script-doctoring business, neither of them can be faulted for their work on screen. In fact the jolts of star power that Ford and Pitt provide make "The Devil's Own" watchable even when it shouldn't be.

The difficulty is that in their apparent rush to see that neither performer got short-changed, the filmmakers ended up creating a pair of equal but separate scenarios. Ford has his own half-movie, thank you very much, and Pitt has his, and though they collide at times, they mostly glide by each other like supertankers in the night.

Pitt's Frankie McGuire is on stage first, introduced as an 8-year-old living such an idyllic life with his family on the coast of Ireland you know it can't last. Tragedy strikes almost immediately, and the film flashes forward to Belfast in 1992 and a grown-up and bearded McGuire as an IRA stalwart so deadly and deceptive he's "never seen the inside of a cell."

What looks like half the British army tries to change that, but McGuire is too much for them and soon he's arriving at Newark Airport with a clean shave, a fake passport and a new identity as Irish immigrant Rory Devaney.

McGuire's American contact, a sympathetic judge, places him as a boarder with salt-of-the-earth New York City cop Tom O'Meara, played by Ford, who thinks the young man is spending his days working construction. Instead, McGuire is refitting a derelict ship and trying to fill it with enough Stinger missiles to change the balance of power back home.

Though McGuire and O'Meara spend a bit of time together doing standard movie bonding at bar-room pool tables and the like, they're mostly involved in their own affairs. Pitt does very well as the charismatic McGuire, steely in an acceptable Belfast accent as he negotiates for the missiles with slippery bar owner Billy Burke (Treat Williams) yet soft enough for romance with Colleen Megan Doherty ("Surviving Picasso's" Natascha McElhone).

Ford is equally good and always an object of audience affection as an ordinary cop with a sweetheart for a wife (Margaret Colin) and three young daughters. On the force for 23 years, O'Meara may not be as quick on his feet as he used to be, but he retains a sympathy for the less fortunate and his belief in doing what's right.

So far, so OK, but in what feels like an attempt to give Ford more screen time, an extraneous subplot about a moral crisis that arises between O'Meara and his partner Edwin Diaz (Ruben Blades) is awkwardly grafted onto the proceedings.

More troublesome is that, as noted, "The Devil's Own" never coheres into an involving drama even when O'Meara, not the sharpest knife in the drawer, finally discovers the true identity of the hunk in his basement. The qualities that are most wanted—urgency, authenticity, a sense of lives at stake—are absent under Pakula's uninvolving direction, with the script's increasingly clunky improbabilities not helping much either.

Though their scenes together do have a cross-generational summit conference quality, for the most part Ford and Pitt manage to share the screen nicely, giving "The Devil's Own" a wistful what-might-have-been quality.   But maybe that was inevitable. As Devaney tells O'Meara—"Don't look for happy endings, Tom. It's not an American story, it's an Irish one."

NEW YORK, 4/7/97, p. 57, David Denby

Pound for pound, Harrison Ford has the highest specific gravity of any American actor since James Stewart (alive but inactive). Other actors may occasionally resemble grown-ups, but in the eighties and nineties a gift for seriousness—by now, I have begun to think of it as a gift, like the ability to play the piano—is pretty rare. Nick Nolte has it in some of his roles, and Harvey Keitel, and Steven Hill in the TV series *Law & Order,* and a few others; when such men tell you something, you believe them. But generally, our culture is too derisive and self-conscious to support much weight on the screen. Anyone who tries too openly to buck the skittish tone can come across as a stiff—a minor player, an Edward Herrmann. Not that Harrison Ford lacks humor. When he was young, he was rakish and witty (I always assumed his performance as Han Solo was conscious parody). But he really blossomed in middle age as a sober-sided, responsible man thrown into extraordinary circumstances—the gravely challenged realistic action hero of *Witness, Patriot Games, The Fugitive, Clear and Present Danger.* He has no magic powers; nor does he hang by cables like Tom Cruise in *Mission: Impossible.* He keeps his feet on the ground. He is credible, determined, unspectacular, a mensch rooted to the center of the earth in a pop-cult world.

In *The Devil's Own,* Ford brings strength and sureness to what would have been an iron mask of a role for anyone else—an honest New York cop. His Tom O'Meara doesn't commit violence easily; he's the kind of cop who chases a runaway suspect for blocks. He wants to bring the guys to the station house in one piece; he has a sense of justice. But into his home comes a young man who kills without remorse. Brad Pitt is the IRA assassin and terrorist Frankie McGuire, who saw his father killed when he, Frankie, was only 8, and who believes in nothing but the endless struggle against British rule of Northern Ireland. Frankie has been sent to the U.S. to buy the Stinger missiles that will bring down British helicopters. Pretending to be an ordinary construction worker, he enters Tom's home and falls in with his happy family and community life. The boy without a father finds a man who has two daughters.

Many writers, some not credited, worked on the screenplay, and there has been talk in the press of dissension on the set. But for all its alleged troubles, *The Devil's Own* has turned out to be a pretty solid piece of work—Alan J. Pakula's best piece of direction in a long time. An opening gun battle between the IRA and the British in Belfast has the extreme violence and acrid bitterness of longtime enemies engaged in a familiar ritual. The scenes of routine police work in New York—a different kind of war, smaller and less violent but also between familiar enemies—are done with respect for truth and human fallibility. And Pakula doesn't embarrass us in the surrogate-father-son scenes between Ford and Pitt. He stays close to the actors but refuses to milk the emotions. Harrison Ford is crusty but warm-spirited—an ideal father. Pitt, clean-shaven, masters the Belfast accent; he gives an easygoing, glamorous performance—Steve McQueen would have been proud of him. But Pitt is not enough of an actor to give Frankie the other things the role needs, shades of menace and danger. When Pitt tries to be tough, he just comes off as flippant, an angel-face posing as a tough guy.

The central idea is clear enough: Each man comes from a different moral universe. Apart from some junky scenes with a crooked arms dealer, the movie doesn't glamorize violence. The Irish are warriors who say they can't afford the luxury of justice, but the movie suggests that they are wrong—trapped in an endless cycle of killing without meaning. It's their destiny because they make it their destiny. What Harrison Ford's cop does—prevent violence—is harder and braver than what a terrorist does. That may be a square idea, but the filmmakers have cast the one American movie star who can put it across without making a fool of himself.

NEW YORK POST, 3/26/97, p. 39, Michael Medved

"The Devil's Own" is an eloquent, affecting apology for murderous terrorism.

Brad Pitt plays the cutest, cuddliest, cold-blooded killer you've ever met—an IRA thug whose brooding, rebel-with-a-cause demeanor is supposed to suggest that he somehow feels conscience-stricken about the bodies that pile up around him.

The movie opens with this character at age 8, watching his father being killed at the family's dinner table by a masked gunman. This shocking scene, repeatedly mentioned through the movie, is meant to render all future excesses not only justified, but inevitable.

Fleeing Belfast after a bloody and implausible escape from a British ambush, Pitt flies to New York for another desperate mission: He's supposed to purchase Stinger missiles on the black market, and then sail them across the Atlantic in a little fishing boat so they can wreak havoc back home.

He's assisted by a smug Manhattan judge (George Hearn) who's a secret IRA sympathizer and finds Pitt a place to live in the Staten Island home of an Irish-American police sergeant (Harrison Ford).

Neither Ford nor his adoring wife (Margaret Colin) nor their three lovable daughters knows anything about their visitor.

Director Alan J. Pakula ("All the President's Men," "Sophie's Choice") is at his best in describing this wonderfully warm, blue-collar family and the quiet, inviting neighborhood in which they live.

To make sure we never lose sympathy for Pitt's character (who, after all, is secretly using and endangering these fine people), Pakula draws his chief antagonists (Simon Jones as an evil English agent, Treat Williams as the brutal mobster who sells him the Stingers) as savage caricatures.

Ford's character, on the other hand, is almost impossibly perfect—an honest, compassionate cop with such an unshakable moral center that only Ford himself among all contemporary stars could play the part with conviction.

Inevitably there's a climactic, father-and-son-style conflict between this upright officer who abhors violence and the Irish trigger man who is immersed in it, but Pakula cops out by suggesting that both men are appropriate products of their respective cultures.

Pitt's performance, despite a less-than-perfect Belfast brogue and a marked tendency to deliver his most important lines in a pleading whisper, is spell-binding in its intensity, and the rest of the fine cast is similarly impressive.

No amount of acting excellence, however, can cover the movie's devilish attempt to rationalize and, ultimately, to glamorize the most deadly sort of political violence.

NEWSDAY, 3/26/97, Part II/p. B2, Jack Mathews

On more than one occasion in Alan J. Pakula's "The Devil's Own," Brad Pitt's IRA leader Frankie McGuire reminds Harrison Ford's Irish-American cop Tom O'Meara that "it's not an American story, it's an Irish story."

True, the ongoing battle to which McGuire refers—between Northern Ireland's Catholic minority and the British government—is one with no imminent Hollywood ending. But the movie itself suffers no such ambivalence. "The Devil's Own," which is two-thirds of a terrific movie, has a classically American ending, one that opts for staged melodrama over its own developed objectives.

"The Devil's Own" is a textbook example of how today's Hollywood undermines its best ideas and filmmakers, and its timing helps explain why the major studios are mostly sitting out the Oscars these days. They cannot help themselves from insisting on tidy endings aimed at pleasing the least attentive members of the audience, even if it betrays the film and insults everyone else.

The script, credited to more people than we have space for here, adopts the violent political strife in Northern Ireland as a backdrop for a story about two men who share an ethnic heritage but live in different worlds. Frankie McGuire is a Belfast Catholic who has been devoted to the IRA cause since his father was shot to death by a masked assassin at the family dinner table when he was a kid. Tom O'Meara is the highly principled New York cop who takes in McGuire as a temporary boarder.

Tom, his wife (Margaret Colin) and their three daughters form immediate bonds with their friendly guest, knowing nothing of his past—which includes the killing of 13 British soldiers and

11 cops—or of his plan to ship missiles to Ireland. And the bonds are genuine for McGuire, too, especially with Tom, with whom he develops an almost father-son connection.

In Pakula's heyday—during the '70s, when he did "Klute," "The Parallax View" and "All the President's Men" there were few directors who could match his ability to develop tension through characters. And throughout the first hour of "The Devil's Own," he's operating at that level. He opens the film with bluntly violent sequences in Belfast, but once the story settles in New York, its focus stays mostly on the relationship between Tom and Frankie, and Ford and Pitt play off each other superbly.

Pitt, managing a consistent and credible Belfast accent, brings tremendous sympathy to a character dedicated to killing. He doesn't force the boyish charm, but it comes through, in scenes that play as melancholy glimpses into the life he may have led. Frankie loves and envies the O'Mearas, and Pitt makes us feel his struggle of conscience.

Ford's role is the more conventional, and the story takes a decided downturn into Hollywood melodrama in a fabricated subplot about Tom's break with his longtime partner (Ruben Blades), after the partner panics in a foot chase and shoots an unarmed burglar in the back. Tom's conflict between loyalty to a friend and keeping faith with his oath plays as an obvious dress rehearsal for coming events with Frankie.

The earnest performances of Ford and Pitt are finally overshadowed by the clichés of the genre. There's a forced romantic subplot with Frankie and an Irish loyalist (Natascha McElhone), and not one but two cardboard-cutout villains—a thug Irish-American arms runner (Treat Williams) and a sadistic British intelligence officer (Simon Jones).

And then there's that ending, like a knock-off from a bad western, that betrays whatever goodwill had been earned before.

SIGHT AND SOUND, 6/97, p. 50, Philip Kemp

Northern Ireland, 1972. Eight-year-old Frankie McGuire watches in horror as his fisherman father is gunned down for being a Republican sympathiser. 1992. Frankie is now a senior member of the IRA. He decides to leave for New York to buy Stinger missiles. Travelling under the name of 'Rory Devaney', Frankie is met by judge Peter Fitzsimmons, a secret supporter of the Republican cause, who has arranged for him to lodge with Tom O'Meara, a sergeant in the NYPD. Tom, married with three daughters, welcomes 'Rory' to his Staten Island home, believing him a simple refugee from the troubles. Frankie meets up with his IRA colleague Sean Phelan; together they plan to transport the missiles across the Atlantic on a fishing boat. Club-owner Billy Burke will supply the weapons. The money, raised by Fitzsimmons, is delivered to Frankie by Megan Doherty another friend from Belfast.

The bond between Tom and Frankie grows stronger. The missile purchase is delayed, and Burke takes this badly. Tom, who has never killed in the line of duty, is devastated when his partner Eddie Diaz shoots an unarmed fugitive. He tells his wife he wants to quit the force. They find three masked intruders in the house. Frankie helps Tom fight them off, but realising the thugs were sent by Burke, goes to confront him. Burke shows him a beaten Sean and demands payment.

Tom finds the cash in Frankie's room. Frankie returns and confesses his true mission. Tom and Eddie arrest him, but Frankie shoots Eddie dead, escapes with the money and delivers it to Burke, who has already killed Sean. The booby-trapped bag kills Burke and his henchmen. Refusing to help the FBI or the British Secret Service, Tom sets out to track down Frankie. In a shootout on the fishing boat, both men are wounded, Frankie fatally, and he dies in Tom's arms.

The last time Harrison Ford tangled with the IRA was in Phillip Noyce's inane Tom Clancy adaptation, *Patriot Games*. That had Richard Harris popping up to explain that the bad guys involved must be an extremist splinter faction, since the IRA proper would never be so irresponsible as to put innocent lives at risk. *The Devil's Own*, though not short of Hollywood narrative clichés, never descends to anything so crass. Indeed for a big-budget studio product, Pakula's film makes a laudable attempt to take on board the complexities of the situation in Northern Ireland. Though it ultimately fails, it's still Hollywood's best shot to date at a famously intractable subject.

"Don't look for happy endings," terrorist Frankie (Brad Pitt) tells Tom (Ford). "It's not an American story—it's an Irish one." Well, yes and no. The ending of *The Devil's Own* may not be a happy one, but it's right in line with traditional Hollywood morality: the terrorist, no matter how well-motivated, must die, and the good cop, no matter how sympathetic he feels, must be the one to kill him. *The Devil's Own* has been damned in some quarters as "an apology for terrorism". This, of course, is the routine response to any film that fails to depict all IRA members as having three heads and devouring babies.

Still, *The Devil's Own* could be said to be sympathetic to the Republican cause since theirs is the only side to be given a hearing. The Loyalists never feature except (presumably) as the hooded gunmen who murder Frankie's Dad in the pre-credit sequence. The British are seen only as soldiers, or as Simon Jones' arrogant Secret Service man, and it's on them that Frankie unequivocally lands the blame: "You're dealing with a government that's failed everyone—on both sides." That's the nearest we get to political analysis. As ever, when forced with political conflict Hollywood instinctively narrows it down to a clash between individuals. So although Tom admits that, if he'd been through what Frankie has, he'd have done the same, in the end his rationale comes close to Bogart's stark creed as he sends Mary Astor down in *The Maltese Falcon* (1941): "When a man's partner's killed, he's supposed to do something about it."

If, prior to this showdown, the relationship between Frankie and Tom is a touch over-schematic—one finding the father he lost, the other the son he never had—it's at least played out on a fairly unportentous level. ("Good to have somebody round here that pees standing up," observes Tom.) Pitt's performance rather touchingly suggests a young man briefly experiencing something of the carefree youth he never had time for earlier. (He also makes a fair stab at a Belfast accent.) But what *The Devil's Own* really lacks is any sense of encroaching menace.

Pakula was once the great master of paranoia: *Klute* (1971), *The Parallax View* (1974), *All the President's Men* (1976), even the confused and confusing *Rollover* (1981) contained scenes in which the feeling of nameless terror lurking in the shadows created a quivering tension. *The Devil's Own* should have provided the perfect vehicle for just such another exercise, what with Frankie lodging in the cellar and the dark forces of the Troubles moving in on Tom's quiet Staten Island home. But all we get are a few bursts of violent action, efficiently staged but never generating much atmosphere.

Perhaps the mere fact of setting a film about Northern Ireland in the US inevitably carries with it its own distancing effect. The most effective treatments of the current troubles—such as Neil Jordan's *Angel*, Ken Loach's *Hidden Agenda* and Jim Sheridan's *In the Name of the Father*—have conveyed the effect of a conflict that's corrupted an entire society; rather than showing the same poison affecting America, Pakula's film finally reduces the whole matter to a little local difficulty. Like those wartime Hollywood movies that tried to make sense of the Nazis by likening them to Chicago gangsters, *The Devils Own* leaves the impression that there's nothing going on in the Six Counties that couldn't be dealt with by a few old-fashioned, straight-arrow New York City cops.

TIME, 3/31/97, p. 78, Richard Schickel

The budget—not all of which, frankly, is visible on the screen, reached a reported $90 million. The two stars did not get along during the shoot, and one of them has publicly dissed the movie prior to its release. Sounds like they're dressing up *The Devil's Own* for a fall, doesn't it?

Maybe yes, maybe no. But before either the studio or the audience takes a write-off on this one, we should recall that those two stars, Harrison Ford and Brad Pitt, are known for their ability to open a picture. More important, we should take into account the fact that this is really quite a good movie a character-driven (as opposed to whammy-driven) suspense drama—dark, fatalistic and, within its melodramatically stretched terms, emotionally plausible.

Pitt's Frankie McGuire is an assassin for an unnamed group of Northern Irish terrorists sent to America to evade the British secret service, whose noose is beginning to tighten around him. He carries a vast sum of money and instructions to purchase a shipment of Stinger missiles capable of rebalancing the power in Belfast. Given an assumed name and occupation, he enters the country, and the home of Ford's Tom O'Meara, as an ordinary immigrant needing a sponsor. Since Tom is a New York City cop of unquestionable honesty, Frankie's cover is perfect.

As it turns out, a little too perfect. For Tom, though a devoted husband and a father to two daughters, likes having another man around the house—someone with whom he can share a pint of beer, a game of pool, a few confidences. For obvious reasons, Frankie has to be a little guarded in the last department. On the other hand, he became a terrorist because as a young boy he witnessed his father being gunned down by Unionist terrorists, and gruff-tough-sentimental-principled Tom fills an obvious need for him.

The script (by David Aaron Cohen, Vincent Patrick and Kevin Jarre) is good about not making too much of this relationship, subtly foreshadowing the betrayal that must end it but allowing these figures room to draw normal human breath. It diverts us by showing each man dealing with a dangerous professional problem. In Tom's case it is a hot-headed, trigger-happy yet likable partner (well played by Ruben Blades) who tests his loyalty and affection. In Frankie's, it is an arms dealer (Treat Williams, slithering from smooth menace to surprisingly vicious sadism) who tests his nerve—and to a degree his commitment to his cause. Frankie can't help contrasting the dank underworld he is obliged to work in with the cozy warmth of the O'Mearas' house.

It may be that Pitt and the script cheat a little with his character, not investing him with quite the fanatical glitter a political gunman ought to exhibit. But you have to balance that against the reality of Ford's work—no one half-suppresses, half-reveals strong feelings better than he does—and director Alan J. Pakula's analogous strengths. Pakula (*Klute, Presumed Innocent*) develops his story patiently, without letting its tensions unravel. At a moment when everyone is saying the studios have lost the knack for making solid, broadly appealing entertainments, *The Devil's Own* suggests the skill may be only mislaid. Of course, it helps when you hire grownups to do the job.

VILLAGE VOICE, 4/1/97, p. 72, Michael Atkinson

The most surprising thing about Alan J. Pakula's blustering, Hollywood-does-the-Troubles melodrama *The Devil's Own* is that it's not a whole lot of fookin' shite. Playing with its hand of cards in full view, the movie still manages its action crisply. The screenplay quietly locates a few sneak attacks amid the cliché bog (the corned beef controversy is subtle and telling), and most of all, Harrison Ford steadies the boat with the same formidable gravity that's made him the most inconspicuous and least objectionable movie star of the '90s. He looks real, for one thing (hard to say that about golden costar Brad Pitt, whose brogue is as flat as fortnight-old draught Guinness). Ford has acquired with the years such a naturally stabilizing, graceful presence that every gesture or focused gaze has a beneficent, Dad-like aura. He's patriarchy you can trust.

Ford digs in here as cop and father-o'-three Tom O'Meara, who innocently accepts undercover IRA gunman Frankie McGuire (Pitt) into his Brooklyn home and family. Big mistake, as it happens, since the young whelp is arranging to buy missiles to ship back home, and the deal has the O'Meara household crossing paths with both Treat Williams's blithe crime lord and British Intelligence. The tale's doglegs bristle with only middling contrivance, the emotional crises are believable, and the vagaries of North Irish politics are shunted aside in favor of an it's-all-a-bloody-shame slough of despond. ("Don't look for happy endings, Tom," Pitt burbles not once but twice. "It's not an American story. It's an Irish one.") *The Irish Story* was, we should recall, in the interests of perspective, the working title for Ron Howard's shamrock rash *Far and Away*. Warm-blooded, earnest, and resisting, barely, the natural tendency to pistol-whip us with glib moralisms, *The Devil's Own* may not be an Irish story, but it's not quite Hollywood as usual.

Also reviewed in:
NEW REPUBLIC, 4/21/97, p. 28, Stanley Kauffmann
NEW YORK TIMES, 3/26/97, p. C11, Janet Maslin
NEW YORKER, 4/7/97, p. 97, Terrence Rafferty
VARIETY, 3/24-30/97, p. 33, Todd McCarthy
WASHINGTON POST, 3/26/97, p. D1, Rita Kempley
WASHINGTON POST, 3/28/97, Weekend/p. 51, Desson Howe

DIARY OF A SEDUCER

A Leisure Time Features release of a Gemini Films production with the participation of the National Center of Cinematography and Canal Plus. *Executive Producer:* Paulo Branco.

Producer: Philippe Saal. *Director:* Daniele Dubroux. *Screenplay (French with English subtitles):* Daniele Dubroux. *Based on an essay by:* Soren Kierkegaard. *Director of Photography:* Laurent Machuel. *Editor:* Jean-Francois Naudon. *Music:* Jean-Marie Senia. *Sound:* Henri Malkoff and Gerard Rousseau. *Production Designer:* Patrick Durand. *Costumes:* Anne Schotte. *Running time:* 95 minutes. *MPAA Rating:* Not Rated.

WITH: Chiara Mastroianni (Claire Conti); Melvil Poupaud (Gregoire Moreau); Hubert Saint Macary (Hubert Marcus); Serge Merlin; Mathieu Amalric (Sebastien); Daniele Dubroux (Anne); Jean-Pierre Leaud (Hugo); Micheline Presle (Diane Dremond).

LOS ANGELES TIMES, 7/25/97, Calendar/p. 6, Kevin Thomas

Don't be taken in by the title of the glum French film "Diary of a Seducer." There's no ooh-la-la here but instead a solemn treatise on the psychology of love and desire inspired by existentialist philosopher Soren Kierkegaard's essay of the same name. It's writer-director Daniele Dubroux's notion that the essay actually does possess darkly magical powers for anyone who reads it.

The idea that the written word could have such impact in this electronic age is rather touching, but there's no magic in Dubroux's direction, which has no pace or rhythm. Plot developments kick in—about an hour into the picture—that might make you sit up and take notice, but it's awfully late in the game.

By the time the film is over, it's possible to see that Dubroux the writer has been on to something that could have worked, but that it's beyond the abilities of Dubroux the director to make it come alive on the screen.

(The film has been described as a comedy, but humor seems in short supply.)

This 1995 production marks the first starring role for Chiara Mastroianni, the lovely and talented daughter of the late Marcello Mastroianni and Catherine Deneuve. She plays Claire, a Paris university student who is not too interested in her major, which is psychology.

Claire lives with her mother (played by Dubroux), a hospital staff doctor on the night shift.

Somehow an unhandsome and pushy acquaintance (Mathieu Amalric) of Claire's has managed to get the mother and daughter to let him sleep on their couch. Nothing if not a pragmatist, he zeros in on the older woman when it becomes clear that he's not going to be able to seduce her daughter. (This substantial subplot seems extraneous.)

Along comes Gregoire (Melvil Poupaud), whose copy of Kierkegaard's essay on the aesthetics of seduction Claire borrows and reads without realizing its supposed dangers. A handsome, pale and thin philosophy student who takes Kierkegaard seriously, Gregoire makes no move toward Claire.

This, of course, makes Gregoire all the more attractive to her, with his classic romantic hero looks and moody personality. Gregoire lives with his glamorous but deranged grandmother (Micheline Presle) in a big dark old apartment in a rundown building. Claire is swiftly obsessed with Gregoire.

Dubroux's idea seems to be to show how all kinds of people can be seduced by their concept of love and the art of its pursuit rather than by love itself She puts it across so heavy-handedly that her film too much of the time is a chore rather than a pleasure to watch, and her actors aren't as able to make as strong an impression as they should.

Leave it to Presle, still beautiful and dynamic after nearly 60 years before the camera, to shine brighter than anyone else.

NEW YORK POST, 5/2/97, p. 54, Bill Hoffmann

If you've ever been to Paris, then you know that it is the world's most magical city—particularly for romance. In "Diary of a Seducer," Paris' powerful charms are even more dangerous, thanks to a magical book that bewitches everybody who comes in contact with it.

Claire (Chiara Mastroianni) finds that out when she discovers a lost copy of Kierkegaard's classic novel "Diary of a Seducer"—about a boy's step-by-step plan to bed an innocent young woman—and returns it to its rightful owner, Gregory (Melvil Poupard).

The book has magical powers to turn hearts to mush, and Claire falls hard for Gregory.

This leads to a bizarre meeting with Gregory's reclusive grandma, Diane (Micheline Presle), the shocking discovery of a frozen corpse and a weird dinner party at the home of a trigger-happy college professor (Jean-Pierre Leaud, the French New Wave star who first charmed us in Truffaut's "The 400 Blows" 38 years ago).

It's an unusual and mostly successful combination of melodrama, comedy and mysticism. And it's all very, very French.

NEWSDAY, 6/13/97, Part II/p. B13, John Anderson

How to define "French," as in film? You could describe the air of insouciance, the casual intelligence, the ennui-ridden sense of distance, which so laughably masks a burning hunger for reckless passion. Or, just show 'em "Diary of a Seducer."

As French as a movie can get, Daniele Dubroux's dark comedy of manners and sex is more clever than stirring, but it does have a winning actress in Chiara Mastroianni, who is charmingly bemused while all those around her are slightly daft.

They include the student Sebastien (Mathieu Amalric), a shameless liar and would-be Lothario who, being without a home, is taken in by Claire (Mastroianni) and her mother, Anne (Dubroux). He sets his sights on Claire as an object of desire, will tell any lie to win her—this includes his supposed sexual "confusion," which seems like a clever ruse—and will settle for Mom if he can't get the girl.

Mom isn't exactly averse to the possibilities (that the director plays the one self-possessed character in the film isn't exactly a coincidence). But Claire is far more interested in Gregoire (Melvil Poupaud), a dark, Byronic philosophy major who gets her reading Kierkegaard's "Diary of a Seducer," a book that acts on the film's characters like an aphrodisiac. Or a time bomb. But for all his romantic posturing, Gregoire is not a man of action, either. In "Diary of a Reducer," there is far more diary than seduction (Sebastien's journal entries supply comic counterpoint to Kierkegaard's) and anything that actually *happens* here does so because of a woman.

This includes the body in the freezer at the house shared by Gregoire and his zany grandmother (Micheline Presle), a corpse that can only be seen as further evidence of male entropy. Dubroux goes a bit wide of the mark, perhaps, in erecting her absurdist universe, but she has an elusive target: The modernist tendency toward overanalyzing a situation—even love—to the point of paralysis. It's no wonder she opens the film with an amnesiac, wandering the streets of Paris looking for his past.

"Diary of a Seducer" tries a bit hard at times to be as coolly mad as it wants to be, but sometimes it doesn't have to try at all: Jean-Pierre Leaud, maturing poster boy of the French new wave, does a wonderful bit as Gregoire's thoroughly unhinged professor. He contrasts smartly with Mastroianni, who, with a roll of her eyes or that sympathetic smile, can set the whole crazy world back on its axis while the rest of the movie is pushing it off.

VILLAGE VOICE, 5/6/97, p. 86, Amy Taubin

Call it a Lacanian screwball. Daniele Dubroux's *Diary of a Seducer* makes Paris seem as alluring and mysterious as it did in all those early-'60s New Wave films. Dubroux's fourth feature (the earlier ones were never released in the U.S.) owes something to Rivette and Ruiz, but it's less indulgent than the former and less heavy-handed than the latter. Best of all, it manages to be delirious and sensible all at once.

The perversely named Claire Conti (Chiara Mastroianni) is the heroine of a narrative as elliptical and circuitous as a recurrent dream. Claire, a psychology student at the Sorbonne, finds a copy of Kierkegaard's *Diary of a Seducer.* The book, which acts as a kind of love potion, has caused havoc in the life of its owner, Gregoire (Melvil Poupard), an intense and fragilely glamorous philosophy student. A woman he barely knows becomes so obsessed with him that she commits suicide; the corpse of her former boyfriend reposes in his refrigerator. The charmingly passive Gregoire doesn't have a clue what to do about any of this. But Claire, who, of course, falls in love with him at first sight, has the practicality that he lacks.

Claire and Gregoire are hardly the film's oddest couple. Claire's mother (played by Dubroux herself), a doctor who prefers night duty because she doesn't like to sleep alone, has an affair with Claire's classmate Sebastien (Mathieu Amalric), who's keeping a diary of his own attempts at seduction. Gregoire's professor (Jean-Pierre Leaud) nurses a passion for Gregoire's extravagantly eccentric and reclusive grandmother (Micheline Presle). And Claire's psychoanalyst (Hubert Saint Macary), a specialist in "breakups," develops an uncontrollable counter-transference after Claire lends him the Kierkegaard book. "I can't help you" he informs a desperate patient. "Beware of everyone: Freudians, Jungians, Kleinians, Lacanians. ... There is no answer to existence." The send-up of psychoanalysis notwithstanding, *Diary of a Seducer* is an ode to the surrealist version of the unconscious—as the anarchic source of desire and aggression, eroticism and wit. This is an exhilaratingly heady film, as smart as it is romantic, its lyricism bent by irony. Dubroux's direction has a fine-tuned nervous energy, and she's immensely assisted by all the actors, by Laurent Machuel's elegant cinematography, and particularly by Jean-Marie Senia's score, which sounds like something Stravinsky might have written for the Ballet Russe. A buoyant film about the fatality of love, *Diary of a Seducer* turns gallows humor loose on romantic angst; one leaves the theater feeling lighter than air.

Also reviewed in:
CHICAGO TRIBUNE, 10/31/97, Friday/p. N, John Petrakis
NEW YORK TIMES, 5/2/97, p. C32, Stephen Holden
VARIETY, 12/11-17/95, p. 87, Greg Evans
WASHINGTON POST, 9/5/97, Weekend/p. 41, Desson Howe

DIFFERENT FOR GIRLS

A First Look Pictures release of a BBC Films presentation in association with CiBy Sales Limited and Maurice Marciano/Great Guns of an X Pictures production. *Executive Producer:* George Faber and Laura Gregory. *Producer:* John Chapman. *Director:* Richard Spence. *Screenplay:* Tony Marchant. *Director of Photography:* Sean Van Hales. *Editor:* David Gamble. *Music:* Stephen Warbeck and Charles Negus-Fancey. *Sound:* Mark Holding. *Casting:* Andy Pryor. *Production Designer:* Grenville Homer. *Art Director:* Melanie Allen. *Special Effects:* Stuart Brisdon. *Costumes:* Susannah Buxton. *Make-up:* Fae Hammond. *Stunt Coordinator:* Jim Dowdall and Chris Webb. *Running time:* 101 minutes. *MPAA Rating:* R.

CAST: Steven Mackintosh (Kim Foyle); Rupert Graves (Paul Prentice); Miriam Margolyes (Pamela); Saskia Reeves (Jean); Charlotte Coleman (Alison); Neil Dudgeon (Neil); Nisha K. Nayar (Angela); Lia Williams (Defense Solicitor); Ian Dury (Recovery Agent); Robert Pugh (DS Cole); Philip Davis (Taxi Driver); Rick Warden (PC Ken); Kevin Allen (PC Alan); Gerard Horan (Sergeant Harry); Edward Tudor-Pole (Prosecuting Solicitor); Adrian Rawlins (Mike Rendell); Peter-Hugo Daly (Barry Stapleton); Shand (Biker Jim); Llewella Gideon (Receptionist); Charles De'Ath (Young Man at Gig); Robert Demeger (Magistrate); Malcolm Shields (Soldier); Graham Fellows (Dispatch Manager); Ruth Sheen (Nosey Neighbor); Christie Jennings (Waitress); Stephen Walker (Karl Foyle); Blake Ritson (Young Prentice); James D. White (Finer); Colin Ridgewell (Shrimp); Jamie Leyser (Matthew Payne).

LOS ANGELES TIMES, 9/12/97, Calendar/p. 6, Kenneth Turan

[The following review by Kenneth Turan appeared in a slightly different form in
NEWSDAY, 9/12/97, Part II/p. B8.]

Even in this sexually brazen age, romantic comedies involving transsexuals are not the usual thing. Filmmakers, not surprisingly, aren't rushing to create genial romps about people who've turned to surgery to change their sex because, explains a dictionary, they have "the physical characteristics of one sex but a strong and persistent desire to belong to the other." Which is why the British "Different for Girls" is different for sure.

The story of a relationship between a prim writer of poetry for greeting cards and a brawny, leather-wearing motorcycle messenger, "Different for Girls" is one of those films for which a lot has to be forgiven.

Its plot, direction and writing have the slapdash quality of mid-range British TV dramas, for which the film's creators have done considerable work. But there's an exceptional performance, a memorable character at the center of things that makes that forgiveness worth the effort.

"Different for Girls" begins with a prologue at a British public school where a teenage boy named Karl is tormented and beaten in the shower for thinking he's a girl. He has only one defender, a solid, fearless lad named Paul Prentice.

Flash-forward 15 or 16 years. Karl, after surgery and hormone treatment, is now a woman named Kim, leading a quiet life working for busybody Miriam Margolyes at Bon Mot Greeting Cards. Prentice is a beer-swilling biker with a perky girlfriend, "not pension plan material," who has gone through a collection of odd jobs without ever quite managing to get himself sorted out.

A cute meet is the ticket for these two, facilitated by a crash of Prentice's motorcycle into the taxi Kim's in. Though Prentice knows it "sounds like a line from 'Top Gun,'" he's convinced he's seen Kim before, and soon enough he figures it out. Sort of.

Faced with a world of sexual choices he never knew anyone had, Prentice is initially dazed and confused, unable to figure out what Kim's sexual orientation is. Gay seems an obvious choice, which infuriates Kim: "I'm not a [expletive] drag queen," she snaps.

Rupert Graves, who plays Prentice, is better known to American audiences through roles in films like "The Madness of King George" and "A Room With a View" than Steven Mackintosh, the actor who plays Kim. Though he makes Prentice too much the bull in the china shop at times, Graves selflessly provides the necessary dramatic foil for Mackintosh's altogether remarkable work.

As Kim, who never doubts her choice but nevertheless feels sometimes trapped in a world she herself helped make, Mackintosh gives a performance of dazzling tact and delicacy that is as difficult to describe as it must have been to accomplish. Mackintosh couldn't be more exactly nuanced as a woman who once was a man, someone who is understandably horrified at being mistaken for a drag queen.

The initial sections of "Different for Girls," with Prentice and Kim tentatively renewing their friendship, trying to decide if it's worth their time to surmount the inevitable awkwardness, are the film's most satisfying. She learns to ride a motorcycle, he reads a book on transsexuals and mollifies his suspicious girlfriend (Nisha K. Nayar), and they both try to navigate their way through a relationship that lacks ordinary guidelines.

A plot does have to kick in eventually, and as written by Tony Marchant and directed by Richard Spence, what there is is not particularly inspired. It involves an unfortunate arrest, a sadistic policeman, the tabloid press, Kim's supercilious sister (Saskia Reeves), her drill sergeant husband (Neil Dudgeon) and considerable amounts of sentimental boilerplate that isn't up to the subtlety and sensitivity of the film's best moments.

But those best moments, when they occur, are worth the trouble. Watching Kim and Prentice dancing—half alone, half with each other—to a record they both remember from school is to see something quite special, to feel nourished by an image and a relationship that is both out of the ordinary and as everyday as falling in love.

NEW STATESMAN, 4/10/98, p. 44, Chris Peachment

Lindsay Anderson used to say that writing about British cinema was the critic's equivalent of doing National Service. He's dead now, but a stint in the paras still looks like a cinch compared with having to analyse the sheer range of films the Brits are cranking up nowadays. *Different for Girls,* directed by Richard Spence and starring Rupert Graves, is about a transsexual. In a thin week for movies you could do worse than try it out—the film, that is, not the operation.

Graves is that rare thing: an English actor who knows how to perform for film. Unlike so many theatre-trained actors, he has discovered the knack of restraining himself for the camera and communicating by thought more than action. He seems to keep himself away from the starrier side of the business, which may explain why he hasn't yet received his due recognition. Here, he's at the lower end of the social scale, playing a motorcycle courier who is broke and constantly trying to fend off the repo men. He's loud and he's mouthy, a role streets away from the well-mannered types you may remember from films such as *A Room With a View*.

One day his bike crashes into a taxi carrying the dusty blonde Kim Foyle. He knows her vaguely from somewhere, but for the life of him can't place her face. As it happens, they were best friends at school, when Kim went under the name of Karl. She's had the operation. Graves' neediness leads on to predictable scenes of distaste, followed by curiosity and later something like commitment.

There's a dust-up with the police, who make the usual comments about transsexuals before beating up Graves. When he sues for assault, the crunch comes down to whether Kim will adopt her usual position of staying out of harm's way or stand up for her man in court.

It's really not much more than the boy-meets-girl routine, but jiffed up no end by the twist that this girl used to be a boy. Inevitably this leads to all sorts of speculations, at least on the part of this heterosexual, transsexually ignorant viewer. Why is it that transsexuals are such bad dressers? If I had a woman inside me bursting to get out, the first thing I'd do would be to take her down to Versace and let her choose a slinky black number that would emphasise my 42-inch chest while concealing my footballer's knees. Kim looks as though she shops from a 20-year-old mail order catalogue and dresses by the light from the fridge.

Steven Mackintosh, as Kim, does do a Full Monty. This is brave by any standards, since he can't disguise the fact that he still has a man's body with bits added to the upper half and subtracted from the lower. Still, a small Oscar should be awarded to the make-up people: you cannot see the joins.

When they do finally twang the bed springs, Rupert's cry of joy is: "It fits!" This may leave something to be desired in the gallantry department, but it does answer the nasty question lurking in the basement of my mind.

The movie more or less stops there. If only it had gone on to explore just what it means to be a man committing the act of darkness with a woman who was once a man. The mere thought of it gives me the jitters in a way I can't quite explain, and if a movie gives you the jitters it's usually doing something right.

NEW YORK POST, 9/12/97, p. 46, Michael Medved

Accidentally crossing paths with a school chum for the first time in 20 years, a leather-jacketed, working-class Londoner played by Rupert Graves can't help notice how much his old friend has changed.

In fact, that sensitive, abused boy he once befriended and protected has taken on an entirely new identity ... as a woman.

Given the enormous popularity of transvestite comedies ranging from "Mrs. Doubtfire" to "To Wong Foo ...," it was only a matter of time before movies crossed this final frontier and focused on the most radical masquerade of them all: dramatizing the life and loves of a transsexual.

An accomplished British actor named Steven Mackintosh plays the key part with such subtlety and vulnerability that even those who find the subject matter inherently distasteful will feel sympathetic to his character.

Mackintosh (who in real life is unequivocally male; married, with children) plays Kim, whose uptight, understated life since her operation is the very opposite of drag queen flamboyance.

She believes that the best way to win acceptance as a woman is to avoid being noticed at all, and so she works diligently at her job in a greeting card company, occupies a pink-and-white, antiseptic flat, and enjoys no social life whatever ... until she reconnects with her earthy old friend from school.

For his part, that comrade now works for a motorbike delivery service and stubbornly holds onto the remains of his rebellious adolescent identity from the punk era of the 1970s.

Though previously best known for upper-crust roles, Graves is explosively appealing as a loudmouthed lout who renews a friendship with the fastidious Kim in part because he's curious about some of the lurid details of transsexual transformation—details with which this film is entirely too generous.

The inevitable nude scene, in "The Crying Game" tradition, shows Mr. Mackintosh alarmingly transformed, with movie magic convincingly adding and subtracting key equipment.

The audience also gets totally gratuitous flashes of Mr. Graves' private parts—show-offy displays that upstage the underlying story of friendship and, yes, love.

The film's central relationship is supposed to be powerful enough to overcome superficial obstacles, so why this cinematic focus on flesh?

Transsexual Kim may never seem as seductive or feminine as Jaye Davidson of "The Crying Game," but she is far more human—making the leering emphasis on mechanics and plumbing even more difficult to justify.

SIGHT AND SOUND, 4/98, p. 37, Andy Medhurst

Motorcycle courier Paul Prentice is involved in a minor accident with a London taxi. The taxi's passenger turns out to be Kim Foyle, formerly Karl, once a friend of Paul's when they were at boys at school together. Intrigued, Paul asks Kim to meet him for a drink, but the occasion turns sour when Paul makes insensitive remarks about Kim's change of identity. The next day, he turns up at her office with flowers and an apology. They visit a club and go back to Paul's flat, where they almost kiss. Deceiving his girlfriend Angela in order to keep meeting Kim, Paul goes to Kim's flat for a romantic dinner, but feels confused.

Despite Kim's attempts to keep him quiet, he makes a drunken, noisy commotion in the street, scandalises the neighbours and is arrested. One of the arresting policemen viciously beats Paul up, then fabricates a charge against him. Kim's evidence could save Paul, but the police rely on her fear of publicity and jail to prevent her from going to court. Kim flees to stay with her sister Jean, whose marriage is on the rocks. Paul's attempt to persuade Kim to testify seem to have failed, but on the day of the trial she appears and he is merely fined. Outside the court, a sleazy tabloid journalist offers the couple money for their unusual story, threatening that it will be revealed whether or not they consent. Back at Kim's flat, she and Paul finally make love. Their story is splashed all over the paper, but they have the money and are too in love to care.

Smart, moving, witty and brave, this transsexual *My Beautiful Laundrette* is one of the best British films of the decade. Some will dismiss its small-scale, no-frills look and its character-based talkativeness as televisual, but in an era when "cinematic" means the hectoring, amoral bombast of *Titanic* that's no bad thing. Besides, the CVs of its writer (Tony Marchant), director (Richard Spence) and producer (John Chapman) include some of the most important small-screen series in recent British television—*Holding On, Making Out* and *Common as Muck*. Those are all texts distinguished by their ability to interweave social comment with involving drama, a tradition *Different for Girls* upholds splendidly. It isn't flawless—some of its peripheral participants and subplots are only hazily sketched in—but it takes risks (offering not just a transsexual heroine but telling attacks on police ethics and military machismo), breaks new ground and tickles the heart and mind in equal measure.

Given its storyline, much depends on the actor playing Kim. Getting her wrong would have tipped the film into ungainly farce or clod-hopping propaganda, but happily Steven MacKintosh (whose previous best work was the Billy Idol-ish punk singer in the BBC serialisation of *The Buddha of Suburbia*) delivers a superb performance. His Kim is a brilliant study in wary poise, pinpointing exactly the right blend of courageous single-mindedness and anxious conformity. Kim' s shifting feelings around Paul—happy memories, fears of being 'outed', growing attraction, oscillating degrees of delight, mistrust, exasperation and desire—form the emotional core of the film, and MacKintosh never puts a foot wrong. He also, in Kim's climactic disrobing scene, gets to take part in a striptease far more radical than the evasive and over-praised kit-off finale of *The Full Monty*. That film fought shy of full-frontal display, thus ultimately celebrating the masculinity it earlier threatened to critique. But *Different for Girls* goes all the way, revealing Kim to Paul and to us in all her post-operative glory. It could have been a finale of damaging bathos, but thanks to subdued lighting, MacKintosh's chutzpah and heaven knows how much Sellotape, it becomes a moment of tender, triumphant revelation.

As Paul, Rupert Graves buries his dubious Merchant Ivory past and emerges as a convincingly laddish romantic—imagine, if it were possible, a puppyish Keith Allen. Stuck in a dead-end job and a dingy flat, he postpones growing up by still playing the records he loved as a teenager (the film boasts a tremendous late 70s soundtrack) and getting into scrapes that hardly suit a man of his age. "It's about time you came through puberty," his girlfriend Angela tells him, the irony being that it won't be her who finally hauls him into adulthood but the far more complex and perplexing figure of Kim.   His bafflement around the latter, as he tries to reconcile their developing love with a less-than-sophisticated grasp of sexuality and gender, is handled very neatly "I am straight, you know,' he tells Kim with rattled assertiveness.   "So am I," she truthfully yet confusingly replies.

Here and there, Graves is made to stand too clumsily for the straight-man-in the audience the film wants to educate, but these are momentary blips of didacticism.   More interesting are the brief flashbacks to schooldays, where Paul was Karl/Kim's protector against homophobic bullying: these hint at a bond between them that predates and prefigures their new romance and add a welcome twist of ambiguity to the proceedings.   Similarly, the film doesn't shy away from the prurient interest most of us have, on meeting transsexuals, in the anatomical small print of surgery, hormones and eventual plumbing.   The scene where Kim gently explains the details to an increasingly entranced Paul is deliciously reminiscent of that point in *Brief Encounter* (1945) when Alec and Laura fall in love over a recited catalogue of respiratory ailments—though Paul's startled/delighted cry of "I've got a hard on" would no doubt have sent Celia Johnson scuttling headlong out of the waiting room and under the next express.

Different for Girls is a genuine original, simultaneously a warm and affecting love story and a breakthrough in sexual representation.   Most impressively of all, it fuses those two strengths, offering passion and politics in equal measures, and it even avoids the dreariness of naturalism by giving its nonconformist heroes a 100 per cent, rose-coloured happy ending.   Rarely has 'normality' been made to look so drab, cramped and compromised, which in my book makes this a film to be treasured.

VILLAGE VOICE, 9/16/97, p. 100, Michael Musto

Boy meets boy.   Boy loses penis.   Boy gets girl.

That's pretty much the premise of *Different for Girls,* but, rather than squeeze rip-roaring comedy out of it, the ultra-sincere film mostly goes for an understated drama about preconceptions in relationships.   The film—a first-time feature by Brit TV director Richard Spence—goes one-up on *The Crying Game* by hinging on the thesis, "Not only weren't you always a girl, babe, but when you were a boy, you were my best friend at school!" That's promisingly daft—though the result tries so hard not to be sensational, it verges on a textbook recitation that's even downright *tasteful* at times.

The London-set film has macho messenger Paul Prentice (Rupert Graves) running into Kim Foyle (Steven Mackintosh), a delicate transsexual who writes verse for a greeting card company. In a matter of seconds, Paul realizes Kim is actually his old buddy Karl, and their personality clash takes on a more fascinating subtext when they notice a certain sexual tension that wasn't necessarily there under the old gender assignation (though Paul *was* always Karl's protector).   The two gradually adapt to each other's excesses and even start to seem like a workable pairing of chromosomes.   Kim learns to ride motorcycles and dance to rock.   Paul develops an ability to apologize via floral bouquets.   And they make love, but not until Paul asks Kim for a free viewing of her new topography.

Even when they do finally connect, a lot of what follows sounds like it came out of a transsexual primer (the press kit assures us that a male-to-female consultant named Adele Anderson was asked for pointers).   There's tons of clinical talk, as we learn that estrogen makes your nipples darker and you can alter your voice by moving it from your chest to your head. "There was a growth coming out of me," Kim explains to Paul.   "The way you deal with growths—you get rid of them."   One senses one has wandered into a daytime talk show, but at least it becomes a good one when Kim adds, "You're obviously quite attached to yours."

The flick is better when it catches the lovers being specifically fallibly human—not walking billboards for male- and femaleness who are there to tell us everything we always wanted to know about sex changes.   Fortunately, there are enough such moments, and ample sweetness in the approach and the performances, to ultimately, offset the threat of blandness and make *Different for Girls* more than the same old thing.

Also reviewed in:
CHICAGO TRIBUNE, 10/10/97, Friday/p. B, Michael Wilmington

NEW YORK TIMES, 9/12/97, p. C8, Stephen Holden
VARIETY, 2/5-11/96, p. 63, Joe Leydon

DISAPPEARANCE OF GARCIA LORCA, THE

A Triumph Films release of a Miramar Films-Esparza/Katz coproduction. *Producer:* Marcos Zurinaga and Enrique Cerezo. *Director:* Marcos Zurinaga. *Screenplay:* Marcos Zurinaga, Juan Antonio Ramos, and Neil Cohen. *Based on the books "The Assassination of Federico Garcia Lorca" and "Federico Garcia Lorca: A Life" by:* Ian Gibson. *Director of Photography:* Juan Ruiz Anchia. *Editor:* Carole Kravetz. *Production Designer:* Gil Parrondo. *Art Director:* Eduardo Hidalgo and Antonio Paton. *Costumes:* Leon Revuleta. *Running time:* 114 minutes. *MPAA Rating:* R.

CAST: Esai Morales (Ricardo Fernandez); Edward James Olmos (Lozano); Andy Garcia (Federico Garcia Lorca); Gonzalo Penche (Jorge Aguirre); Marcela Walerstein (Maria Eugenia); Jeroen Krabbé (Colonel Aguire); Giancarlo Giannini (Taxi Driver); Miguel Ferrer (Enforcer).

LOS ANGELES TIMES, 9/12/97, Calendar/p. 16, Kevin Thomas

[The following review by Kevin Thomas appeared in a slightly different form in **NEWSDAY, 9/12/97, Part II/p. B13.]**

"The Disappearance of Garcia Lorca" is one of those films that is so artificial that it would be impossible to believe in it even if it were based wholly on facts instead of largely on fiction. It's a ponderous period piece that tries halfheartedly to be a thriller while going for a glowing romantic look and mood that's death to any form of suspense.

Overly complicated and further loaded down with trite characterizations and dialogue plus a leaden pace, it's a hopelessly lifeless film despite yeoman efforts of Esai Morales, Andy Garcia, Edward James Olmos and others.

Director Marcos Zurinaga and his co-writers imagine a solution to the identity of who pulled the trigger of the weapon that killed the great Spanish playwright and poet Federico Garcia Lorca, who was executed by fascist rebels in Granada at the outbreak of the Spanish Civil War in 1936.

The one thing you can say for the film's tediously complicated flashback-within-flashback structure is that it does allow Garcia to keep popping up often enough to give us a persuasive portrayal of Lorca as a dashing, witty, self-aware and courageous man—and to wish that he were in fact the center of the film.

The key character is instead Morales' dull Ricardo Fernandez, a Granada native who as a teenager fled with his family to Puerto Rico with the ascent of Francisco Franco. Now it's 1954, and Fernandez, a journalist struggling with writing a book about Garcia Lorca, his boyhood hero, decides he must return to Granada to try to solve his murder if he is ever to finish his project.

Breathtakingly naive at every turn, the doggedly sincere Ricardo stays with a family friend, a Franco colonel (Jeroen Krabbé) who displays a Third Reich medal in his study. Ricardo proceeds as if he were researching Cervantes instead of a martyr of the Spanish Civil War at a time when Franco had 21 years to go in his iron rule.

Olmos has some edge as a seeming Garcia Lorca enemy who may in fact have been a friend; Miguel Ferrer is a key bad guy; and Giancarlo Giannini is a taxi driver conveniently concerned with Ricardo's welfare. Morales is game but Ricardo's blandness—and dispiriting lack of smarts—prove taxing.

"The Disappearance of Garcia Lorca" means above all to evoke the tormented legacy of the Franco years, but many Spanish films have done this far better than this lackluster international coproduction shot in English.

NEW YORK POST, 9/12/97, p. 46, Thelma Adams

Director Marcos Zurinaga's "The Disappearance of Garcia Lorca" is a drama of missed opportunities. A compelling mystery ripped from the history books, a stellar cast and more local color than a flamenco troupe's wardrobe can't rescue this original film about the famed Andalusian poet's death.

Andy Garcia—largely in flashbacks—plays Lorca: handsome, lively, brave in spirit and physically weak. Lorca's life is a poem shouted until he is hoarse and silenced.

But this Lorca is a hero, not a human. On the screen, his homosexuality is as shrouded in mystery as are the details of his 1936 assassination by Franco's minions during the Spanish Civil War.

In the quiet moments, Garcia delivers what the director can't coax—or impose by the showy, dramatic lighting that frames the "Blood Wedding" writer as if he were a portrait in the National Gallery. He projects a sense of depth and soul, playfulness and warmth.

Zurinaga surrounds Garcia with strong character actors: Edward James Olmos as a fascist publisher, Miguel Ferrer as a cloudy enforcer, Jeroen Krabbe as a charming Franconista. The fabulous Giancarlo Giannini is along for the ride as an enigmatic cabby.

Esai Morales ("La Bamba") is not an actor who conveys much with silence. He plays the movie's lead, Ricardo, a 31-year-old journalist who returns to his native Granada in 1954, to ask: "Who shot Garcia Lorca?" Morales is as phony as the freshly pressed ascot Ricardo pulls out of his suitcase each day.

"Disappearance" makes a good companion piece to Mary Harron's "I Shot Andy Warhol." Harron took a historical footnote—the story of Valerie Solanas, the woman who achieved her 15 minutes of fame by shooting Warhol—to understand the power the artist held over his contemporaries and re-examine his place in history.

Zurinaga's decision to focus on a fictional journey fails where Harron succeeded. He puts distance between us and a fascinating era, teasing us with a delicious mystery that gains in power as the movie reaches its conclusion, but never clarifying the power Lorca had over his native country and the symbolic death that nation died with his murder in 1936.

VILLAGE VOICE, 9/16/97, p. 100, Ed Morales

Federico Garcia Lorca is one of the literary world's great martyrs. The most important Spanish poet and playwright of his time, he was murdered by a regime intolerant of difference. *The Disappearance of Garcia Lorco* is based on a real-life investigation of the poet's shadowy death at the hands of Franco's fascist followers.

The film follows a young reporter, Ricardo Fernandez (Esai Morales), who returns to Spain to unearth the gory details about his childhood idol's demise. Zurinaga, who debuted with the leaden but elegantly shot *La Gran Fiesta,* captures the hot colors of Andalusia and Garcia Lorca's deep roots in that culture. But oddly, his homosexuality is only obliquely referred to.

Morales's moody calm makes the Fernandez character compelling, but Andy Garcia, playing the poet with the awkward pose of a Mafia hit man, is horrendously miscast. Zurinaga muddles the plot twists, but the film still delivers a haunting message about the Spanish Civil War and the silence that surrounded its brutal excesses.

Also reviewed in:
NEW YORK TIMES, 9/12/97, p. C5, Stephen Holden
VARIETY, 3/10-16/97, p. 80, Jonathan Holland

DONNIE BRASCO

A TriStar Pictures release of a Mandalay Entertainment presentation of a Baltimore Pictures/Mark Johnson production. *Executive Producer:* Patrick McCormick and Alan Greenspan. *Producer:* Mark Johnson, Barry Levinson, Gail Mutrux and Louis DiGiaimo. *Director:* Mike Newell. *Screenplay:* Paul Attanasio. *Based on the book by:* Joseph D. Pistone and Richard Woodley. *Director of Photography:* Peter Sova. *Editor:* Jon Gregory. *Music:* Patrick Doyle. *Music*

Editor: Robin Clarke and Roy Prendergast. *Sound:* Tod A. Maitland and (music) Paul Hulme. *Sound Editor:* Ian Fuller. *Casting:* Louis DiGiaimo. *Production Designer:* Donald Graham Burt. *Art Director:* Jefferson Sage. *Set Decorator:* Leslie Pope. *Set Dresser:* Claudette Didul, Dennis Zack, Steve Swanson, Deborah Dreyer, Deborah Moses, and Frank DeCurtis. *Special Effects:* Ronald Ottesen, Jr. *Costumes:* Aude Bronson-Howard and David Robinson. *Make-up:* Margot Boccia. *Stunt Coordinator:* George Aguilar. *Running time:* 121 minutes. *MPAA Rating:* R.

CAST: Al Pacino (Lefty Ruggiero); Johnny Depp (Donnie Brasco); Michael Madsen (Sonny Black); Bruno Kirby (Nicky); James Russo (Paulie); Anne Heche (Maggie); Zeljko Ivanek (Tim Curley); Gerry Becker (Dean Blandford); Robert Miano (Sonny Red); Brian Tarantina (Bruno); Rocco Sisto (Richie Gazzo); Zach Grenier (Dr. Berger); Walt MacPherson (Sheriff); Ronnie Farer (Annette); Terry Serpico (Strip Club Owner); Gretchen Mol (Sonny's Girlfriend); Tony Lip (Philly Lucky); George Angelica (Big Trin); Val Avery (Trafficante); Madison Arnold (Jilly); Delanie Fitzpatrick, Katie Sagona, and Sara Gold (Daughters); Larry Romano (Tommy); Tim Blake Nelson and Paul Giamatti (FBI Technicians); James Michael McCauley (FBI Agent); Jim Bulleit (U.S. Attorney); Andrew Parks (Hollman); Keenan Shimizu (Japanese Maitre D'); Rocco Musacchia and Joe Francis (Trafficante's Men); Sal Jenco (Mare Chiaro Bartender); Billy Capucilli and Laura Cahill (Communion Party Couple); John Horton (FBI Director); Dan Brennan (FBI Photographer); Lajuan Carter, Sandy Barber, and Joyce Stovall (Singers).

CHRISTIAN SCIENCE MONITOR, 2/28/97, p. 12, David Sterritt

Like artists in other fields, filmmakers don't like being locked away in narrow pigeonholes. This may be why director Mike Newell has taken such an unexpected turn in his latest movie.

Audiences have cheered him as a gentle storyteller, with pictures like "Four Weddings and a Funeral" and "Enchanted April" among his crowd-pleasers.

But with the new "Donnie Brasco," he invades the territory of darker talents like Martin Scorsese and Francis Ford Coppola, spinning the tale of an undercover FBI agent (Johnny Depp) and a fading criminal (Al Pacino) whose trust and friendship the cop has sworn to betray. It's a fact-based story, taken from real events, and a violent one, to the point of real horror at times.

Donnie Brasco is the assumed name of special agent Joe Pistone, a young Fed who manages to infiltrate the mob that dominates New York's hyperactive crime scene. His assignment begins when he worms his way into the confidence of Lefty Ruggiero, an aging assassin who's connected in one way or another with every gangster in town.

Lefty is interesting to the Feds not for any clout of his own; despite his age and experience, he's still a small-time operator with little to show for his years of criminality. What makes him valuable is that he knows—quite literally—where all the local skeletons are buried. He accepts so-called Donnie as a protégé, vouching for his loyalty and introducing him to the Brooklyn contingent of a powerful Mafia family.

The plot's most dramatic twists arise from two developments neither of them could have predicted. For one, Donnie soon bypasses Lefty in the mob's complex hierarchy, rising to a higher level despite his desperate efforts to stay near his mentor in the mediocre middle.

For another, their branch of the mob explodes into war within itself, bringing nerve-jangling instability to every aspect of the power structure. Your best friend today might be the one who "whacks" you tomorrow.

Finally, as if all this weren't enough to contend with, Joe's wife and young daughters lose patience with the unexplained absences and complicated excuses that his profession inflicts on them. Even the pathetic Lefty has a more satisfying home life in some respects, and domestic pressures begin to trouble Joe as acutely as the life-threatening risks of his undercover career.

The main ingredient making "Donnie Brasco" a reasonably smart and involving gangster yarn is the pair of performances at its heart. The poignancy of Pacino's acting comes partly from the nature of his role, and partly from the way this contrasts to his most famous earlier work. He became a top-flight star by taking iron-willed control of a Mafia family in "The Godfather Part

II" more than 20 years ago, so there's a special irony in his sad-eyed portrayal of a crook who never made the grade and is now losing the tiny bit of status he did manage to accumulate.

Depp is less resonant but equally convincing as the increasingly troubled Joe, reconfirming his reputation as a hugely versatile actor who can swing from the comedy of an "Ed Wood" to the tragedy of a "Dead Man" and the fantasy of an "Edward Scissorhands" without losing an ounce of credibility.

The strong supporting cast includes Michael Madsen as a mid-level mob boss, Anne Heche as Joe's frustrated spouse, and Bruno Kirby as a clone of the wormy little crooks played so effortlessly by Joe Pesci in one Scorsese picture after another.

The echo of Pesci in Kirby's performance raises the question of whether "Donnie Brasco" would have been a better picture if a mob-movie specialist like Scorsese—or Coppola, whose "Godfather" films still dominate the genre—had taken the reins of Paul Attanasio's screenplay.

The answer is almost certainly yes. Newell's talent for eliciting good performances is at its best in projects where charm and elegance are major selling point, which explains why audiences have embraced the delights of "Enchanted April" and "Four Weddings and a Funeral" more enthusiastically than the more brooding qualities of "The Good Father" and "Dance With a Stranger," which he also directed.

The gritty realities of "Donnie Brasco" aren't geared to his strong points, leading to awkward scenes (e.g., a maudlin moment with Joe's oldest child) and mishandled details (e.g., the way Lefty's social clumsiness comes and goes). Scorsese's sense of style (see "GoodFellas" for a classic example) or Coppola's sense of nuance (see the first two "Godfather" epics) would surely have served the story better. As it stands, "Donnie Brasco" is a competent picture with a true-life story that might have been more powerful still.

CINEASTE, Vol. XXIII, No. 1, p. 42, Thomas Doherty

In *Hollywood on Trial* (1976), the documentary about those who 'named names' and those who didn't during the HUAC hearings, actor Zero Mostel recalls the famous scene from John Ford's *The Informer* (1935), when the British Black and Tan uses his riding crop to push thirty figurative pieces of silver across the table to the traitor Gypo Nolan, refusing to sully his own hands with the transaction. To bond with men, break bread with them, and then betray them is a primal kind of crime, a violation of unspoken codes of conduct from the playground to prison. Even the undercover man on the side of the law, the police agent who risks his life to gain the confidence of the bad guys and bring them down, seems soiled by his actions, the infiltrator being an eyelash away from the informer, the most despised of creatures.

Told from the perspective of real-life FBI agent Joe Pistone (Johnny Depp), who under the name of Donnie Brasco burrowed into the ranks of the New York Mafia, *Donnie Brasco* is a sleek, brooding gangster noir. As directed by Mike Newell *(Four Weddings and a Funeral)* and written by Paul Attanasio *(Quiz Show)* from the book *Donnie Brasco: My Undercover Life in the Mob* by Pistone and Richard Woodley, the film delves less into the violence of the mob and the suspense of imminent exposure than the moral torment of the infiltrator. In the course of a prolonged identity transformation, Joe becomes implicated in the lives and enamored of the men in his cross hairs. The clear-cut divide between cops and robbers is undercut not by a glib equivalence between government agents and deviant types but the compromises the one group must make to penetrate and destroy the other. Bleeding into his work, FBI agent Joe Pistone becomes whom he pretends to be, the underworld underling Donnie Brasco.

The film opens with a slick montage of video stills and 35mm contact sheets, a sequence of grainy, black-and-white, and neon soaked images that look like still lifes but are actually surveillance tapes and hidden camerawork, a bit of visual trickery forewarning of the duplicities to come. Donnie's mentor in crime is rank-and-file hoodlum Lefty Ruggiero (Al Pacino). "I'm just a spoke on a wheel," he says, a factotum with no illusions. Yet he is a wise guru to the eager acolyte with the secret agenda. "A wiseguy never pays for a drink," instructs this veteran of "twenty-six fucking hits." Lefty lays down the dress code—no mustache, no jeans ("This ain't a fucking rodeo") and teaches Donnie the military-like ranking of "connected guy" to "made guy." It is a world of huge Lincolns and Cadillacs, real waterbeds on wheels, driven by guys in leather jackets waving huge pinky rings. When the boys are out on the town, *Donnie Brasco* evokes with frightful fidelity, the fashion risks of the mid-Seventies, notably the polyester disco-wear of that other Brooklyn Italian film, *Saturday Night Fever* (1977).

In the ballet of hunter and game, or the courtship of spider and fly, Donnie waits for Lefty to make the first move and come to him. "I got him—I got my hooks in the guy," he boasts to his FBI handler, before Lefty becomes more than a fish to reel in. The Darwinian nature of the relationship is transmitted via the heavy-handed symbolism of the *National Geographic* documen-taries Lefty watches on TV, where hyenas attack cheetahs and the law of the jungle reigns all around. Justifiably paranoid about his job security, when he is 'sent for' by an ominous associate, Lefty warns Donnie that the fatal hit, when it comes, will come from a friend, someone close. The irony is ladled on thick—Lefty is trusting and generous, Donnie secretive and reserved. Lefty puts himself on the line for Donnie; Donnie tapes their conversations and gathers evidence.

From *White Heat* (1949) to television's *Wise Guy,* the infiltrator has linked himself to the leader of the pack. Here he doesn't attach himself to the charismatic top dog but to the junk-yard mongrel. Newell underscores Lefty's subordinate status when headman Sonny Red (Robert Miano) disses him and Lefty, eats the insult, or when Lefty breaks up a parking meter for the coins, showing just how nickel and dime he really is. Grunts and foot soldiers, beefy guys on more familiar terms with pasta makers than Nautilus equipment, Lefty and his fellow mobsters have little of the stylish elan of the Roman centurions of Scorsese or Coppola. Only the quietly sinister Sonny Black (Michael Madsen) has his eyes on the main chance while the hapless jester Nicky (Bruno Kirby) can barely manage to pull off drug deals in Florida.

Animating the byplay between Donnie and Lefty at the textual level is the face-off at the level of acting between Johnny Depp and Al Pacino. A type-A actor, Pacino turns down his natural electricity and screen volume to register as a lowly subaltern. Lately, in *Scent of a Woman* (1992), *City Hall* (1996), and *Heat* (1995), Pacino's performances have been so bombastic and over the top, just plain LOUD—that his diminution from cock of the walk to a desexualized schlump devoid of status is a stunning transformation. Stars know how to turn on the charisma, which is why they're stars. It is harder to turn the voltage off. Pacino assumes a slumping gait and modulates his vocal range. With his sad, droopy eyes and ill-fitting hats, he seems a born second-rater. To a highlight reel already packed with memorable hoods—the coldblooded Michael Corleone, the explosive Tony Montoya, the stalwart Carlito—he can add the small-time, stand-up guy Lefty Ruggiero.

For his part, Johnny Depp graduated from pretty-boy teen idol to A-list actor with his blithe portrayal of the unsinkably chipper Z-movie *auteur* in *Ed Wood* (1994). His is the controlling intelligence, the gaze that directs the vision of *Donnie Brasco.* While Pacino talks and shrugs, Depp is all reactive interiors, communicating with his eyes, alert, wary, and fearful. Only once does Donnie break character, to wink at himself (not Lefty), during a shopping excursion for just the right Hallmark greeting card to help grease the palms of a senior mobster.

Newell's understated style suits this low-key mob milieu. *Donnie Brasco* is a character study, not a sweeping portrait of a criminal organization or a bright showcase for directorial razzle-dazzle. The film boasts no lovingly choreographed ballet of violence, no dreamy montages of slow-mo gunplay and bloodletting, paced action-adventure style, like the rhythm track of a dance mix. When it comes, the violence is blunt, businesslike, and abrupt. Thus, a sudden deadly ambush is followed by a ghastly disposal operation where the boys hack up the designated corpus delicti, plus a surprise last-minute addition.

A smart and engrossing gangster picture is no mean task when tracking over such well-trodden territory (especially, one is tempted to add chauvinistically, for an Englishman whose previous credits include the gauzy pantheism of *Enchanted April* [1991] and *Into the West* [1993]). The release of *Donnie Brasco* coincided with the twenty-fifth anniversary rerelease of *The Godfather* (1972), a timely reminder not only of the enduring influence of the Coppola-Puzo masterpiece but also of how rich the gangster genre has been since its third great awakening. *(Little Caesar* [1930] kicked off the first; *White Heat,* the second). The mobbed-up work of Coppola, Scorsese, and even DePalma, has bequeathed an indelible cast of characters, quotable lines, and exemplary montages, a pantheon of wiseguys and goodfellas making unrefusable offers and bashing each other with baseball bats. Neatly bridging the Watergate crisis of 1972-1974, *The Godfather* epic set the pattern for the more serious enterprises of the genre, the executive actions of the mob being a handy metaphor for the ruthlessness of capitalism and the dirty business of money-mad, success-driven America.

Yet the subversive impulses of the genre were mainly diversionary. The family affections, the boy-boy bonding, and the strict adherence to the rules of the crime game dripped nostalgia for the old country—that is, not Sicily in the 1890s but America before the 1960s. Like the original gangster films, born in the nadir of the Great Depression as a twisted version of the American Dream, the mobbed-up gangster films affirm the classic American values of individual enterprise, upward mobility, and regeneration through violence. On balance, it is a deeply conservative genre. Ethnic verisimilitude alone can't account for all the Catholicism, the persistent religious imagery and the adherence to ceremony, wafting across the screen like incense. As in the *Star Wars* trilogy, that other great Seventies recycling of a matinee genre, the young rebels eagerly perform ritual obeisance and supinely accede to the codes of their fathers in dress, language, and beliefs.

Not least, the sons of *The Godfather* hark back to the stern laws of primogeniture. The female principle is absent or subordinate in the mob milieu, the last of the exclusive all-male clubs. As Donnie Brasco, Joe has no relations with women at all; as Joe, he literally phones in his role as husband and father. Newell's *mise-en-scène* and the set design imply that Joe's flight from the domestic sphere is motivated by more than FBI duty. His home is cluttered and claustrophobic, a space owned by a wife and three daughters. Cool and in control at work, he is tense and rattled at home, where only hassle and guilt await him (he neglects his loving wife, he misses his daughter's first communion). Bolting from the high-estrogen atmosphere, Joe soars as Donnie Brasco. No wonder that, like Joe, the spectator may want to fast-forward through the domestic complications between Joe and his very long-suffering wife (except perhaps for a priceless scene in a marriage counselor's office where Joe is urged not to "play out the old pathology" by a touchy-feelic shrink).

Newell's suspense strategy is classic enough and still surefire: lock the spectator into Joe's undercover perspective and set off ticking time bombs. A tape recorder concealed in Donnie's boot sets in motion an ugly mugging when he refuses to remove his incriminating footwear in a Japanese restaurant. Rather than blow his cover, he incites his pals into brutally beating the Japanese-American restaurateur. It is the most unnerving scene in the film—not just because of the racist assault on a total innocent but also because of its tragic necessity.

But the real action is in watching Pacino and Depp color in the emotional shadings between Lefty and Donnie. The older man seeks a surrogate son, a blood kinsman to whom he can pass on his hard-won lessons, a need Joe cagily exploits when he says he is an orphan. In any number of man-to-man talks—in the privacy of a car, in Lefty's low-rent apartment, or, most movingly, when a repentant Donnie comes to the hospital to sit with Lefty while his biological son lies in a coma from a drug overdose—the pair play father and son. As Lefty assumes paternity, Donnie comes more and more to dread his scripted role in the oedipal drama.

Being a third-wave gangster film, *Donnie Brasco* challenges the easy moral complacency of its predecessors. In *Little Caesar*, Rico Bandello was bad to the bone; in *White Heat*, Cody Jarret was a certifiable nut case. The Mafiosi keep you guessing. They are men with home lives, friends, and convivial personalities who happen to be in a business of appalling violence and stone cruelty. The schizophrenia is epitomized in the scene from Scorsese's *GoodFellas* (1990) where the boys drop by for some of Mom's home cooking (and a carving knife) while their still-living victim writhes outside in the car trunk. When Sonny Black and the gang travel to Florida to stake out some new prospects, they behave like frat boys on spring break—taking in the sights, picking up babes, burying each other in sand. This is not black humor but moral complexity and psychic disorientation: how can such likable goombahs be such vicious beasts?

Internalizing the mob's value system (as the shrink would say), Donnie certainly comes to feel more at ease with mobsters than the FBI (which saddles him with a dangerously incompetent undercover partner) or his wife (who breaks his concentration). With Lefty as his vulgar cultural informant and example, Donnie fully assimilates the local folkways. When Sonny Black recruits him away from Lefty, he feels he has betrayed his first mentor—not as an FBI agent but as a mob protégé. Context is everything. Thus a moment of quiet reflection finds Joe with his FBI comrades, listening to the wiretaps and trying to explain to the flat-footed feds the layered meanings of "fuhgeddaboutit," the all-purpose interjection whose meaning shifts from denial to agreement, depending on intonation and stress.

In the last reel, Joe is brought in from the cold and Lefty remains behind to take the heat. The returns for Joe Pistone's service as Donnie Brasco are paltry—a perfunctory awards ceremony where the mayor mispronounces his surname and hands him a $1500 check and a medal. Meanwhile, Lefty gets the dreaded but not unexpected phone call. 'Sent for' for the last time, he removes his rings and watch, kisses his crucifix, and marches to his fate. Lefty abides by the rules he taught Donnie and forgives his prodigal son. "Tell Donnie, if it had to be anybody, I'm glad it was him," he whispers to his girlfriend before walking out the door.

A jump cut to the sound of gunshots finds Donnie, rather Joe, on an FBI firing range blasting a target, the hunter bagging his game. *Donnie Brasco* ends where it began, with a close-up on the eyes, the window on the soul, which reveal that Joseph Pistone will not soon forget about it.

LOS ANGELES TIMES, 2/28/97, Calendar/p. 1, Kenneth Turan

How much Mafia can you take? Are you entranced by the Talmudic distinctions between a wise guy, a made guy and a connected guy? Do you relish hearing cold-eyed thugs mumbling, "I don't mean no disrespect"? "Donnie Brasco" is waiting for you.

For those without a Mafia habit, things are more problematical. "Donnie Brasco" is an ambitious film with an effective and modulated performance by Al Pacino that should make "forget about it" (pronounced *"fhuggedaboudit,"* more or less) a national catch-phrase, but its aims are often unrealized and undercut.

This is not only because Mafia pictures are overly familiar, a glut on the market. "Donnie Brasco's" look at the stresses of undercover work has also been done earlier and to better effect in a pair of Sidney Lumet films, "Prince of the City," which starred Treat Williams, and "Serpico," headlined by Pacino himself.

Those films involved infiltrating the police, not the mob. And they didn't have "Donnie Brasco's" focus on showing what happens when genuine friendships are formed between the spider and the fly. But problems in both structure and casting leave these themes hanging, and even the fresh eye of eclectic British director Mike Newell ("Dance With a Stranger," "Four Weddings and a Funeral") can't make this film feel other than second-hand.

Based on a true story of FBI penetration of the mob in the 1970s, "Donnie Brasco" was written by Paul Attanasio before he did the much-applauded script for "Quiz Show." Its intention is to delineate character, to put a more human face on the lower end of the Mafia food chain.

As Lefty Ruggiero, "Left" to his intimates, Pacino carefully creates the role of a good mob soldier with 26 hits under his belt, "a spoke in the wheel" who does the dirty work and never complains.

Trading on his deep eyes and shopworn dignity, Pacino shrewdly underplays Lefty, leaving us with an affecting portrait of an old warrior weary in the service of the dons and hungry for some human contact and appreciation. After the showy work of "Heat" and the outright hamminess of "Looking for Richard," it's a welcome change.

A chance encounter in Little Italy introduces Lefty to Donnie Brasco, a.k.a. "Don the Jeweler" (Johnny Depp). The aging veteran takes a shine to the new fence on the block, treating him like a son (his own is an addict) and teaching him the myriad rules of wise guy behavior, things like carrying your money in a roll, not a wallet.

More important, Lefty vouches for Donnie, giving confederates his personal assurance that the kid is OK. With his support, Lefty says, "even Jesus Christ couldn't touch you." Which is good news for Donnie, who in real life is FBI man Joseph Pistone, an agent consumed with getting inside the mob so he can help destroy it.

"Donnie Brasco's" main concern turns out to be the conflicts Pistone faces in his double life, the strains that enter his relationship with his family and, as the two get closer, with Lefty as well.

Neither of these areas comes off as planned, but Pistone's inability to connect with his wife, Maggie (Anne Heche), and their small daughters is the film's least successful section. And part of the reason is a simple question of structure.

The film introduces us to Pistone when, undercover for two years, he's already turned into a mob type. We never get to see him as a regular guy, never know what he was like before his undercover job started eating him alive, and the change in him that so upsets his family is weaker for having to be taken on faith.

Despite the presence of a fine young actress like Heche, the scenes with the agent's family are the weakest parts of "Donnie Brasco." It's almost like the filmmakers, as in love with the chance to make believe they're tough guys as Pistone is, can't wait to revel in that repetitively macho world of made men talking tough and whacking each other.

Handled better is what happens between Donnie and Lefty. Though the agent boasts to his superiors, "I got my hooks in this guy," in fact the relationship, like those hooks, cuts both ways. As a line from the wildlife documentaries Lefty watches in his spare time puts it, "hunter and hunted, predator and prey, the endless cycle of nature."

Hampering this part of "Donnie Brasco," however, is Depp's performance. The actor's most characteristic work, from "Edward Scissorhands" and "Benny & Joon" through "Ed Wood" and "Dead Man," called on Depp to be a cipher whose emotions are difficult to read. That bland, opaque quality is a disadvantage here; whatever else this star is capable of, making audiences feel his pain is not at the top of the list.

With only Lefty to empathize with, "Donnie Brasco" is more one-sided than anticipated. Though the outline of what the film has tried to do is visible, so little feels at stake emotionally that anyone intending to care about these characters would be well advised, for want of a better phrase, to simply *fhuggedaboudit*.

NEW YORK, 3/17/97, p. 55, David Denby

"What am I gonna do with a truckload of razor blades?" wails one of the minor thugs in *Donnie Brasco*, the serious and touching new film about the Mafia directed by Mike Newell. Set in the late seventies and early eighties, and based on a true story, *Donnie Brasco* catches the mob at a period of confusion and relative decline. In Brooklyn, a crew of "soldiers" (made men, but nowhere near the top) hang out in the back of their dark little social club and play cards and struggle to meet the weekly "vig"—the $50,000 owed regularly to higher-ups for granting the boys control of the territory. These men are not crime lords but thieves and murderers imprisoned by myths that have long since worn out. When one of the great chiefs goes by, the men's jaws drop; they are as awestruck as real soldiers might have been by, say, the appearance of Douglas MacArthur. God walks the earth—with a cigar, no less. But God, it turns out, regards the believers as mere fodder. The men are part of a machine, held in place by medieval codes of loyalty that are both absolute and incomprehensible. Betrayal seems an inevitable part of "loyalty." You are loyal up to the moment at which you murder the friend you've been working with for years.

Donnie Brasco isn't a satire, nor is it nostalgic for the great old days of the mob (nostalgia made Martin Scorsese's last mob movie, *Casino,* seem a little off). *Donnie Brasco* is a bloody gangster film about corrupt and stupid men, but it has the honesty to avoid inflating its subject. The ace screenwriter Paul Attanasio (*Quiz Show, Disclosure)* examines all the fascinating ambiguities of "loyalty," and he's acute on minor details of protocol and linguistic etiquette, such as the difference, when introducing a new man to mob elders, between the phrases "This is a friend of mine" and "This is a friend of ours." An insider patiently explains to outsiders the five separate meanings of "Fuhgedaboudit!" Such niceties are paramount in closed societies, though in this particular society blood threats linger around the words. And Attanasio has built a wonderful emblematic figure—a new movie icon of failure—out of the mobster Lefty Ruggiero (Al Pacino).

Lefty is a longtime hit man, but his authority is now dwindling; he's been repeatedly passed over, and he grumbles like a corporate hotshot who got a corner office when young but somehow never made vice-president. Everyone has heard his complaints, and no one cares. When Lefty meets an outsider, the svelte young jewel thief Donnie Brasco (Johnny Depp), who listens to him and seems to admire him, he warms to Donnie immediately. Lefty desperately needs a protégé, and Donnie seems to have all the right instincts. Lefty sets about getting the young man accepted into the mob. What he doesn't realize is that Donnie is an FBI agent.

Donnie Brasco is based on the adventures of the real-life FBI mole Joe Pistone, and the material is not altogether fresh. We've seen these mole stories before, and we're familiar with their tensions and conflicts. The picture isn't an event or a work of art; it's just a very solid and entertaining movie. It sticks to its business, it's well-acted, the milieu seems true—so true that it's funny—and the details are closely observed and startling. Donnie, wearing a tape recorder in his boot, refuses to take off his shoes at a tradition-bound Japanese restaurant and stands by while his mob friends beat up a persistent maitre d' who wants the shoes removed. What's horrifying about the moment is its ambiguity: Johnny Depp, with a few glances, manages to suggest that Donnie, a cop, enjoys his power in the mob, even the power to get an innocent waiter beaten up.

At the heart of the movie is the relationship between two characters, and two actors. Pacino wears an awful little hat—a small-timer's porkpie—and he looks exhausted, with sunken but glittering eyes and a hoarse voice. His Lefty blusters a lot, but he's a frightened man. He may kill people (on orders), but he knows that the day will come when he will be whacked himself. "When you're called for, you go," he explains to Donnie, as if that were all there is to say. Pacino's performance is a beautiful piece of work—moving, in part, because it is offered utterly without irony or condescension. Lefty may be a murdering fool, but Pacino knows that even a fool longs for dignity and tries to justify himself. At some level, Lefty senses that everyone in the mob is finally out for himself, but he's stuck—he's got to believe in the myths because he's got nowhere to go (turning informer like Joe Valachi or Henry Hill is not possible for him). If he can get Donnie to believe with him, then he will feel he isn't a failure. Pacino makes Lefty a pathetic but almost lovable man—a murderer who refuses to be cynical. The performance is perhaps the most melancholy of his career, the most convincingly fatalistic.

Johnny Depp's handsome, Kabuki-mask face has held our interest in weird or preposterous roles in *Edward Scissorhands, Benny & Joon,* and *Don Juan DeMarco.* In this film, he says good-bye to his gentle-flower act, which is a relief. This actor can move: As Donnie, he's very graceful, with a knifelike speed in violent moments. We can believe that the mob might take him for a tough, ambitious young hood—he has the wariness and the self-confidence that creates an aura. And Depp's emotional reticence works for the role. We can't tell after a while whether Donnie wants to nail these hoods or become one of them. He's in very deep, caught in the stupid but mesmerizing tangle of betrayal and violence. The rubouts, the beatings, the eroticized power—it tops anything his family, even his sexy wife (Anne Heche), can offer him. Donnie doesn't want to live without that danger and excitement, and he turns his family feelings to Lefty, who needs him.

Who is Mike Newell? It's a pleasant mystery. The talented British director has given us the ice-cold, blue-shadowed erotophobia of *Dance With a Stranger,* the anguished realism of *The Good Father,* the stumbling, ramshackle cheerfulness of *Four Weddings and a Funeral*: all good films, but each in a different style. Newell may be a master without a style—for critics and filmgoers, an anti-auteurist's auteur. In *Donnie Brasco,* Newell doesn't take many risks with the camera. There are no wild flights, no outbreaks of Scorsesean poetry. But his movie is coherent and emotionally satisfying—a good, realistic gangster film, just when everyone thought the genre was exhausted.

NEW YORK POST, 2/28/97, p. 35, Thelma Adams

Every time I get fed up with Al Pacino, he pulls me back in. In the sharp, slangy gangster flick "Donnie Brasco," Pacino plays a Bonanno underling with a shattering, soft-spoken grace.

Gone are the whisper-now, shriek-later excesses of "Heat." Stooped, broken, sweating, trapped in '70s leisure suits, Pacino's Lefty Ruggiero is an old soldier on his final march.

Passed over for a promotion, facing the disappointments of his junkie son, Lefty drags his feet along the Willy Loman, "Death of a Salesman" trail. "Even a dog gets a warm spot on the sidewalk," says the aging hitman.

Johnny Depp artfully plays a role that's the lead in title only. His portrait of a disco-era G-man, Joe Pistone, a.k.a. Donnie Brasco, shows the mature, quiet self-confidence that has elevated Depp above his peers.

Working undercover, Pistone gains Lefty's confidence. Before long, Ruggiero is vouching for Brasco and putting his own neck in a noose to do so. "This is my own family," the mobster says of the Cosa Nostra, "even more than my own family."

Pistone underestimates the power of this bond. A principled G-man, he's unaware of how alien and sterile the FBI environment is—or how fragile family ties are. Pistone gravitates to the mob: the camaraderie, the ethnicity, the sense of Old World order. Like a frog tossed into cold water that is gradually heated to a boil, Pistone doesn't realize he's in hot water until it's too late.

Brasco assists in escalating crimes, peering over murder's abyss. By the time his own life and sanity are endangered, his loyalties are divided. What's worse, Brasco knows that his retreat would result in the execution of the man who has become like a father to him.

Michael Madsen, Bruno Kirby and James Russo lead the strong supporting cast as members of Lefty's crew. As Mrs. Pistone, a Botticelli beauty with a Jersey lilt, Anne Heche breaks hearts without melodrama. She struggles to be a lifeline to her husband, but refuses to drown along with him.

Based on Pistone's real-life account, Paul ("Quiz Show") Attanasio's script is ripe with mobisms ripped straight from FBI surveillance tapes. Whether the mobsters are discussing the relative merits of Lincolns and Cadillacs or explaining that it's bad form for an enforcer to say the name of the guy he's just whacked, the dialogue rocks.

Who knew that director Mike Newell, of "Four Weddings and a Funeral" fame, could also stage a mob hit? If there's a problem with "Donnie Brasco," it's the pacing. Every time Newell gets the mob story kicking he yanks us into a scene of domestic drama—and doesn't quite know how to regain the suspense.

This is a small lapse in a movie that showcases Pacino at his very best. When Lefty responds to his druggie son's coma with a smothered sob—a mere peep—the underplayed emotion clinches the film's true killer moment.

NEWSDAY, 2/28/97, Part II/p. B3, John Anderson

In his actor's confessional, "Looking for Richard," Al Pacino's passion for playing Shakespeare's hunchback seemed just slightly redundant: Hadn't he already played Richard III, as Michael Corleone? And wasn't he part Faust in "Carlito's Way," part Caliban in "Scarface," part Coriolanus in "Serpico"? Isn't his ability to elevate the lowest of lives to the level of literature the reason he's Al Pacino?

Yes, and it's how he gets away with playing one more mobster, one more time. In "Donnie Brasco" he reprises his New York hood as a middle-class wretch and draws from an aptly modest inspiration: Willy Loman. "Even a dog gets a warm piece of the sidewalk, " rues Lefty Ruggiero, who's worked for "our thing" for 30 years and whose little American Dream, criminal though it is, is never coming true. He's a mug. Somewhere he knows it.

But when Donnie Brasco (Johnny Depp) appears, Lefty sees new vistas, fresh possibilities and, most of all, a protégé. Together they'll work the angles, dodge the cops, play political footsie with the dangerous and upwardly mobile Sonny Black (Michael Madsen). And what will give added poignancy to Lefty's needy state is that Donnie's an undercover agent for the FBI.

Pacino's a bagman of acting technique. He creates a moment outside the mob's social club—when Lefty watches the entrance of the local don with a mix of worship, failed ambition and mute awe—that is simply heartbreaking. And as Lefty schools Donnie in the finer points of '70s Brooklyn mobdom, one can see Pacino and Depp involved in a similar line of succession.

Not that Depp needs much help. He's among the best actors of his generation, and consistently picks challenging, offbeat films in which to ply his craft. He may even have the tougher role here, playing someone who's acting. He makes Donnie's metamorphosis from college-educated fed to quasi-vicious wiseguy an almost imperceptible process.

At the same time, though much of what "Donnie Brasco" has to say is valid, it's also a bit old hat: that the infiltrator and the infiltrated share the same moral rung, that heroes go unappreciated, that one organization may be no better than the other. The FBI here is less concerned with Donnie's safety than the fact he wears a mustache and uses mob-cultivated profanity. "I'm a Mormon," barks his supervisor. "Clean it up, mister!!" This stuff is hilarious—as is Donnie's explanation of the etymology of "fuggedaboudit." It's also profoundly sad.

Director Mike Newell, of the oh-so-pleasant "Four Weddings and a Funeral," "Into the West" and "Enchanted April," seemed an unlikely choice to direct a mob movie. He still does. Much of the attempt to evoke a '70s gangland esthetic hits one over the head (the bottle of Sambuca, the tacky clothes, the elephantine Cadillac, etc.). And on several points we're, left hanging entirely. Lefty accepts Donnie as a confidant far too easily. Donnie's marriage to Maggie (Anne Heche) goes from troubled to incendiary and is a complete cipher. Granted, we meet Donnie two years into his masquerade, and Maggie's left virtually alone with the kids for years at a clip. But we get no clue as to what their relationship once was, nor what expectations Maggie had—given that she's married, theoretically, to the mob.

That organized crime Italian-style retains its romance is partly due to the benevolent Catholicism hanging over it (the ethos of modern gangs being far less appealing), but mostly to do with the movies. "Donnie Brasco" doesn't glamorize crime; there's little glamor here at all. What it's about, despite the occasional burst of violence, is humanity, something that is embodied in its two lead performances.

NEWSWEEK, 3/3/97, p. 69, David Ansen

You're telling yourself: I need another wiseguy movie like I need to pay more taxes. Al Pacino as a two-bit mafioso? Is the pope Catholic? Johnny Depp as some goombah named Donnie Brasco? Fuggedaboudit ...

There are plenty of reasons to be skeptical about "Donnie Brasco," but give this movie 20 minutes and you'll change your tune. The story, based on true events, is so good, and the characters so rich, that the familiarity of the turf becomes irrelevant. Screenwriter Paul Attanasio ("Quiz Show") and jack-of-all-genres director Mike Newell ("Four Weddings and a Funeral," "Dance With a Stranger") don't seem worried that hundreds before them have marched down these mean Italian-American streets; after all, we haven't been there with Lefty Ruggiero—the small-time hit man Pacino plays—or with Depp's Donnie Brasco. Donnie is actually FBI undercover agent Joe Pistone, a man who is so successful insinuating himself inside the mob that he doesn't know how to get back out again-or whether he wants to. Pistone is a great actor and an agile seducer: playing his role as "Donnie the jewel man," he makes Lefty feel like he's found a son and a bright new future. The love and trust Lefty feels for his protégé isn't playacting, and Pistone is pulled in by it. He's a man torn by too many families and too many loyalties—to the Feds, to the mobsters, and to his wife (Anne Heche) and children, who never know where he is or what he's really doing. As with most whose lives are a performance, his sense of his own identity is a slippery thing.

What's compelling about the way Newell and Attanasio tell this story—with a riveting mixture of comedy, dread, warmth and brutality—is that the audience isn't sure which side to take. Depp's character is in a classic tragic bind, and family values have rarely been so ambiguous. There's a brilliantly tense scene at a Japanese restaurant, where the maitre d' orders Donnie and his Mafia colleagues to take off their shoes. We know if Donnie does he'll be killed, because that's where his tape recorder is hidden. Donnie improvises adroitly, playing on his comrades' xenophobia to turn them against the Japanese host. We're relieved—and then we're horrified when the mafiosi, pumped up with "family" loyalty, viciously stomp the maitre d'. For Donnie, the price of saving his own skin keeps getting higher.

This is Depp's coming-of-age role, and he's terrific. Pacino, who's shown more flash than substance recently, reminds us how great he can be when he loses himself inside a character. The bond between these two makes Newell's film sing. It's a wiseguy movie, but it's also a doomed love story—funnny, sad and bitter on the tongue.

SIGHT AND SOUND, 5/97, p. 40, John Wrathall

New York, 1978. FBI agent Joe Pistone, working under cover as jeweller "Donnie Brasco", wins the trust of Lefty Ruggiero by spotting a fake diamond a debtor has tried to palm off on him. In return Lefty takes Joe under his wing, introducing him to his local Mafia crew, which includes Sonny Black and Nicky. The murder of a high-ranking boss leads to the promotion of Sonny Black over Lefty's head. Joe gets more involved with the crew's operations. Visiting a Japanese restaurant with the crew, he is asked to remove his boots, one of which contains his tape recorder. To cover himself, he picks a fight with the waiter, and joins in when the crew beat the waiter up.

Joe's FBI controllers ask him to vouch for another agent, Richie Gazzo, who is under cover in Florida running a bar, King's Court. At Joe's suggestion, the crew flies to Florida to take over Richie's bar. In order to placate the local boss Santos Trafficante, Lefty takes him out on a yacht, which Joe arranges through FBI contacts. The night of its grand reopening, King's Court is busted and the crew arrested. Lefty suspects there must be a "rat". In fact, the bust was arranged by Trafficante as a favour to Sonny Black's rival Sonny Red, who plots to kill the crew when they return to New York. On the plane back, Joe sees a photo of the yacht in a *Newsweek* article about FBI stings. Back in New York, Sonny Black's crew ambush Sonny Red's crew, and Lefty kills Nicky, assuming he was the "rat". Joe has to help chop up the bodies. Sonny Black becomes the local boss.

The FBI decides to pull Joe out. But Joe knows that if he blows his cover, Lefty will be killed for having vouched for him. Meanwhile, Lefty entrusts Joe with his first contract killing. On the way to the hit, Lefty shows Joe the *Newsweek* cutting, but Joe convinces him he is not an informer. When Joe and Lefty arrive at the hit, they are arrested by the FBI. With Joe safe, the FBI tells Sonny Black that "Donnie" was one of their agents. Lefty gets a call late one night and leaves his valuables in a drawer before going out to certain death. The FBI rewards Joe with a medal and a cheque for $500.

Paul Attanasio wrote the script for *Donnie Brasco* (from Joe Pistone's memoir *Donnie Brasco: My Undercover Life in the Mafia*) in 1989, but the arrival of *GoodFellas* the following year delayed its progress to the screen. The subject matter—middle-level New York Mafiosi falling out during the 70s—is certainly similar, but producers Mark Johnson and Barry Levinson (for whose Baltimore Pictures Attanasio went on to write *Quiz Show*, *Disclosure* and the television series *Homicide Life on the Street*) have shrewdly opted for a director fresh to this sort of material, in the shape of *Four Wedding's and a Funeral*'s Mike Newell. While the choice of someone like Newell ensures a very different style of film from *GoodFellas*, it also makes sense in terms of the narrative: here we learn about the Mafia not from a Little Italy insider (like *GoodFellas'* Henry Hill, or Scorsese himself) but from an outsider, 'Donnie Brasco', the undercover FBI agent. (The sense that we are seeing the film through Joe's eyes is established by the close-ups which bookend the film.)

Some of the film's early scenes have an almost anthropological quality, as Lefty explains to "Donnie" (and us) the mysteries of Mafia rituals and turns of phrase (the difference, for instance, between describing someone as "a friend of mine" and "a friend of ours", or later, as the by now thoroughly initiated Joe explains to two FBI colleagues, the five different meanings of "Forgetaboutit"). The sense that we are observing a strange tribe through a telephoto lens is reinforced by the use of freeze frames, as unseen agents snap surveillance photos of Lefty and his cohorts, and wittily echoed by the David Attenborough wildlife documentaries which Lefty continually watches at home. We also learn about the tribe's social structure: the Mafia operates on an almost feudal system, a pyramid in which everyone is somebody's "man", and must pay tribute to his immediate superior. 'Donnie' constantly has to 'lend' Lefty money he will never see again, while, further up the ladder, Sonny Black has to produce $50,000 a month for his overlord. The FBI, meanwhile, isn't much different: there's a neat joke early on when Joe's Mafia and FBI superiors both tell him to shave off his moustache, as it's against regulations; and the film ends with Joe becoming the FBI's equivalent of a "made man"—the reward Lefty has been promising him all along.

With the exception of a couple of Scorsese-esque montage sequences outlining, respectively, the crew's violent routine in New York and their moneymaking at the King's Court bar, Newell plays it very straight. His director of photography Peter Sova (another Levinson veteran) has given the film a refreshingly drab look—shallow focus and a palette of browns—which seems both more authentically 70s than, say, *Casino* or *Carlito's Way*, and a great deal more honest. We don't sympathise with Lefty because he's cool but because he's human. Despite 26 hits to his name, Lefty is conspicuously uncool, a laughing-stock among his colleagues; it's his desire to impress and befriend the manifestly more cool 'Donnie' that is his undoing.

Far more restrained than of late, and never sinking to being comic or loveable, Pacino brings enormous dignity to the role of Lefty, the self-confessed "spoke in the wheel" who outlives his usefulness—Newell's likening of the film to *Death of a Salesman* isn't far off the mark. Equally astutely cast is Johnny Depp, whose customarily blank, unknowable demeanour is perfect for Joe, a man who has had to erase his own personality in order to survive. There's a very uncomfortable scene in which Joe listens impassively to the tape recording of the attack on the Japanese waiter in which he participated. Is he relieved at his narrow escape from exposure, horrified at what he has become, or has he stepped so far outside himself that it's simply another piece of evidence? Depp's face lets us decide for ourselves.

VILLAGE VOICE, 3/4/97, p. 65, J. Hoberman

Movie stars with "muscle" is how the hero of Martin Scorsese's *GoodFellas* described his *Cosa Nostra* cohorts. Right—and when movie gangsters age, they become raging Method actors. Al Pacino may play mafioso mentor to *Donnie Brasco*'s title character, but there's scarcely a memorable scene in Mike Newell's engrossing mob-informant melodrama that isn't defined by Pacino's voluptuously sagging features—or that doesn't have his toothmarks all over the set.

Donnie Brasco is based on the sensational true story of FBI agent Joseph Pistone, who invented the "Brasco" identity and, between 1976 and 1982, infiltrated the Bonanno crime family so successfully that he was on the verge of full induction (not to mention Murder One) when the Bureau brought him in from the cold. But, as deadpan Johnny Depp goes undercover himself playing Brasco, the movie belongs to Pacino, who uncorks a characterization to place alongside his chilly Michael Corleone and coked-up "take a look at the bad guy" Scarface.

Sporting a massively lacquered pompadour topped by a porkpie hat, dressing in a red velour jogging suit and peering through aviator bifocals to cook Christmas-day coq au vin, taking a mallet to a sawed-off parking meter in the midst of a mobster coffee klatch, Pacino plays hit man Lefty Ruggiero as a maniacally kvetching, chain-smoking, lovable goombah—never mind that he's responsible for 26 whacks. Unlike the dread Joe Pesci, Pacino can nuance his hysteria. We feel his pain when, fearing he's been cast aside, he hoarsely whines that "even a dog gets a warm piece of the sidewalk."

More than a Pacino-thon, *Donnie Brasco* is filled with snappy tough-guy stuff. Michael Madsen and Bruno Kirby are thugs to remember and screenwriter Paul Attanasio has written a showy set piece for Depp on the semiotics of the term *fuhgeddaboudit*. Set mainly in Little Italy and South Florida during the late '70s, the movie parlays its disco mileage for an enjoyably cheesy period feel. If the premise and milieu unavoidably suggest *GoodFellas* (the success of which, according to one of the movie's producers, delayed Attanasio's script for half a dozen years), the movie never feels superfluous. Unlike last fall's sodden *Sleepers, Donnie Brasco* has something on its mind.

Steeped in the minutiae of the *Cosa Nostra* code, not to mention that of the FBI (which only recognized organized crime's existence after J. Edgar Hoover's death), the movie depicts a war of rival bureaucracies, themselves rife with intra-agency intrigue. Like Attanasio's script for *Quiz Show, Donnie Brasco* is founded on an active moral confusion. The scene in which the FBI man protects his identity by inciting his mob pals to trash a Japanese restaurant approaches Scorsese in its disturbing quality—not to mention in its rabble-rousing. The informer comes closest to being caught when he borrows, from the FBI Abscam sting operation, a yacht on which to entertain the venerable Florida don Santos Trafficante. Newell edits the sequence to suggest multiple betrayals—bereft Lefty wanders morosely around the ship, while back in Queens, Brasco's daughter receives her First Communion.

Unlike murderous Lefty, the hero Brasco is definitely not lovable—squabbling with his wife in the course of an infrequent home visit, then furtively banging her on the carpeted stairs of their semidetached Queens house. The none too subtle point is that, playing Donnie Brasco, agent Pistone becomes a regular little mob monster. Indeed, the duplicitous lawman is ultimately more like a gangster than the gangsters themselves. While Attanasio's script runs this tiff into the ground, staging the Pistones' session with an idiot marriage counselor, the fact is Mrs. Pistone has good reason to be jealous. The title of *Donnie Brasco* could just as easily have been *Waiting for Lefty*.

Also reviewed in:
NATION, 3/31/97, p. 35, Stuart Klawans
NEW REPUBLIC, 3/31/97, p. 26, Stanley Kauffmann
NEW YORK TIMES, 2/28/97, p. C4, Janet Maslin
NEW YORKER, 3/17/97, p. 121, Anthony Lane
VARIETY, 2/24-3/2/97, p. 75, Todd McCarthy
WASHINGTON POST, 2/28/97, p. C1, Rita Kempley
WASHINGTON POST, 2/28/97, Weekend/p. 42, Desson Howe

DOUBLE TEAM

A Columbia Pictures release of a Mandalay Entertainment presentation of a Moshe Diamant production and a One Story Pictures production. *Executive Producer:* Don Jakoby and David Rodgers. *Producer:* Moshe Diamant. *Director:* Tsui Hark. *Screenplay:* Don Jakoby and Paul Mones. *Based on a story by:* Don Jakoby. *Director of Photography:* Peter Pau. *Editor:* Bill Pankow. *Music:* Gary Chang. *Music Editor:* Richard Whitfield. *Sound:* Daniel Brisseau and (music) Armin Steiner and Brian Reeves. *Sound Editor:* Sandy Gendler. *Casting:* Penny Perry and Illana Diamant. *Production Designer:* Marek Dobrowolski. *Art Director:* Damien Lanfranchi. *Set Designer:* Christian Calviera. *Special Effects:* Bruno Van Zeebroeck. *Costumes:* Magali Guidasci. *Make-up:* Zoltan. *Special Action Choreographer:* Samo Hung. *Stunt Coordinator:* Charles Picerni. *Running time:* 90 minutes. *MPAA Rating:* R.

CAST: Jean-Claude Van Damme (Quinn); Dennis Rodman (Yaz); Mickey Rourke (Stavros); Paul Freeman (Goldsmythe); Natacha Lindinger (Kath); Valeria Cavalli (Dr. Maria Trifioli); Jay Benedict (Brandon); Joelle Devaux-Vullion (Stavros' Girlfriend); Bruno Bilotta (Kofi); Mario Opinato (James); Grant Russell (Carney); William Dunn (Roger); Asher Tzarfati (Moishe); Rob Diem (Dieter Staal); Ken Samuels (Stevenson); Sandy Welch (Delta Two); Jessica Forde (Delta Three); Malick Bowens (Delta Four); Dominic Gould (Delta Five); Frederick Renard (Delta Six); Dufaut Cyrille (Bravo One); Eric Gauchy (Bravo Two); Patrick Gauderlier (Bravo Three); Orso Maria Guerrini (Colony Resident); Alexander Koumpaan (Russian Man); Hans Meyer (British Man); Jesse Joe Walsh (Jaseck); Peter Nelson (American CIA Agent); Paolo Calissano (Rome CIA Agent); Pascal Lopez and Dominique Fouassier (Stavros' Men); Paolo Paoloni (Old Monk); Jean-Pierre Stewart (Yamir); Ted Russof (Brother Ramulu); Umberto Raho (Brother Regulo); Adam Kaci (Cyrus); Xin Xin Xiong (Stavros' Man, Hotel); Pascaline Girardot (Domestic); Nathalie Grac (Mermaid); M. Benabiles (Pilot); M. Szolnic (Co-Pilot); Sigal Diamant (Giada); Angelo Ragusa (Stavros Goon); Gabriella D'Olive (Nurse); Nick Brett (Hospital Guard).

LOS ANGELES TIMES, 4/4/97, Calendar/p. 16, Kevin Thomas

[The following review by Kevin Thomas appeared in a slightly different form in
NEWSDAY, 4/4/97, Part II/p. B9.]

"Double Team" offers a triple-threat trio in Jean-Claude Van Damme, Dennis Rodman and Mickey Rourke plus director Tsui Hark, the hallowed Hong Kong maestro of mayhem, that jump-starts the action-thriller genre, which could use some fresh juice. This is one slam-banger that looks to connect with action fans at home as well as abroad.

Much is familiar—there seems to be an explosion a minute, for example—but writers Don Jakoby and Paul Mones prove ingenious in maneuvering Van Damme through a secret-agents-can-never-retire plot, and Hark, in his American debut, brings to it a most welcome light touch.

Best of all, there's plenty of humor along the way, which plays to the strengths of both Rodman, who scores big in his first major screen role, and Hark, expert at combining comedy with endlessly inventive go-for-broke Hong Kong-style action. Gorgeously photographed European locales, principally Rome, are another asset. From Hong Kong, Hark brought another legend, Samo Hung, to serve as special action choreographer, and cinematographer Peter Pau who shot Hark's hilarious "The Chinese Feast."

Van Damme thinks he's retired as America's top counter-terrorist to his luxurious South of France villa with his pregnant wife, but we know better. He's yanked back into service to go after super bad guy Rourke and is taking aim at him when Rourke's little son rushes into his father's arms. Van Damme hesitates before shooting, then realizes to his horror that he's killed the child rather than the father.

A couple of plot twists later, Van Damme teams up with Rodman, playing a CIA operative/Antwerp arms dealer every bit as flamboyant as the basketball star is in his own life. "Who does your hair," Van Damme asks, "Siegfried or Roy?"

That Van Damme and Rourke are both family men, despite their ruthless trades, lends emotional intensity to the action, while Rodman provides the humor, as well as impressive backup for

Van Damme. Rodman is more partner than sidekick, and he and Van Damme form a dynamic duo.

"Double Team" is one of Van Damme's best, and he's the linchpin when all's said and done. Also in his best work in some time, Rourke is a nasty, brooding villain further enraged by the loss of his son. And Rodman is a natural for the movies. He's got a star's wit, personality and presence, and clearly his role has been tailor-made for him. (Amusingly, for much of the picture Rodman wears a well-cut suit, a tie and a fedora-classic attire that makes him look great.)

All three stars are in shape to the max, with Rourke having beefed himself up considerably. "Double Team" marks Van Damme's third teaming with an ace Hong Kong director—Hark was preceded by John Woo ("Hard Target") and Ringo Lam ("Maximum Risk")—and it is arguably the most effective.

NEW YORK POST, 4/4/97, p. 44, Michael Medved

No, it's not true that all performances in "Double Team" are painfully inept.

A 500-pound Bengal tiger named Tiaga turns up near the end of the movie (commanding nearly as much screen time as Dennis Rodman) and plays a commanding and convincing role in the action.

As for the human actors (including Rodman), they're all stiffs, delivering performances that run the gamut from merely embarrassing to outrageously awful.

Of course, Jean-Claude Van Damme's diehard fans don't particularly care about nuanced, naturalistic acting, but they do expect coherent action scenes, which "Double- Team" pointedly fails to provide.

The flashy, frenetic editing and camera work (supervised by Hong Kong cult director Tsui Hark in his bleak U.S. debut) is so choppy and sloppy that you can't follow whose foot is crashing into whose face.

In the end, that confusion hardly matters since the story line itself is so muddled it defies intelligible description. Van Damme plays a secret agent who, as the film opens, undertakes one last mission to rescue plutonium from Croatia, crashing a big yellow truck through platoons of pursuers and a speeding train.

Next, he's in the midst of yet another last mission, apprehending terrorist mastermind Mickey Rourke from an Antwerp carnival. Rourke escapes a bloody shootout, but the wounded Van Damme wakes up a prisoner in a CIA compound called "the Colony."

Here, they keep a collection of snarling, over-acting secret agents from various countries who are "too valuable to kill, too dangerous to let go."

Van Damme escapes anyway (by graphically slicing off his own thumb print) and sets out to rescue his pregnant wife (Natacha Lindinger) from the vengeful Rourke.

Along the way, our hero hooks up with an eccentric weapons dealer (Rodman) whose hair comically changes color from scene to scene and who can't stop making unfunny quips about basketball.

In his few scenes, Rodman offers an oddly likable screen presence, but his mincing mannerisms, phoned-in delivery and clumsily choreographed fights all suggest that he shouldn't give up his NBA career any time soon.

In a few of Van Damme's recent films (especially the nifty hockey rink thriller "Sudden Death"), the Muscles from Brussels began to show evidence of latent acting ability, but here he takes several giant, grunting steps backward. Director Hark handles him like a kid throwing around a poker-faced, plastic GI Joe to see just how much punishment it can take.

And how much punishment can the audience take? The movie lasts 90 minutes, but before the climactic appearance of that terrific tiger you'll probably be reviewing grocery lists (or basketball scores) in your mind.

SIGHT AND SOUND, 5/98, p. 44, David Tse

Special agent Jack Quinn is brought out of retirement to hunt down terrorist Stavros. The mission fails when Quinn hesitates to shoot Stavros in front of his family, causing Stavros' escape and the death of Quinn's backup team. Quinn finds himself incarcerated on The Colony, a luxurious prison island for former agents. On learning Stavros is holding his pregnant wife hostage, Quinn performs a daring underwater escape.

In Antwerp, Quinn enlists the help of flamboyant arms dealer Yaz. The duo survive a trap set by Stavros. Assisted by a band of computer-wizard 'cybermonks', the duo outsmart Stavros in a Rome hotel and save Quinn's wife. Quinn and Stavros duel in the Roman Colosseum for Quinn's newborn son. Stavros is dispatched, and the heroes depart.

Directing a Jean-Claude Van Damme movie has become an initiation rite for Hong Kong film-makers trying to break into Hollywood: after John Woo and Ringo Lam, here comes Tsui Hark bringing zest to Van Damme's latest screen adventure. Tsui has already had a phenomenal career. A pioneer of the special-effects fantasy film that is by now a stable game of Hong Kong cinema, he is also the head of the trend-setting Film Workshop, whose alumni include Woo and Ching Siu-Tung (*A Chinese Ghost Story*). Regrettably, Tsui is to moviemaking what Brian Eno is to pop music: they are better as producers than solo artists. In his own rough-hewn films, Tsui often exhibits a wilful disregard for continuity that alienates all but the most tolerant viewers.

American backers notwithstanding *Double Team* bears the hallmarks of a Film Workshop production, including a colourful palette, breakneck pace and plentiful stunts. Tsui is prodigious with visual ideas virtually every shot of this movie has been digitally doctored or contains a visual punchline. In an early gunfight scene, there are deft trick shots such as selective motion blurs (with only the hunted man in focus among indistinct crowds) and superimposed after-images (we are running so fast that a 'ghost image' of the past overlaps on to the present). When Van Damme is trapped on a mysterious prison island *à la The Prisoner*, the inmates all wear blank wristwatches.

The problem is that the movie has been filmed and edited like a trailer: it's all payoffs without build-ups. A Film Workshop production frequently works because it is largely studio-bound, thus providing some kind of visual unity to the film. Here, the manic visual inventions never gel into a coherent narrative. A possible explanation is that the story is not fantastical enough for Tsui; he feels compelled to turn a routine actioner into a constantly arresting post-modern collage: part existential spy yarn, part sci-fi high jinks, with a dash of medieval iconography thrown in. The final scene at the deserted Roman Colosseum is a homage to Bruce Lee's classic duel in *Enter the Dragon* (1973). But Lee's film announced the arrival of an international star, while *Double Team* gives the erroneous impression that Tsui would make a great music-video director. And as for Van Damme himself, he is out-acted by basketball sensation and sometime actor Dennis Rodman. Van Damme's relative longevity testifies to a continuing audience demand for a kickboxing action man who can't emote, but we deserve better movie heroes than this.

VILLAGE VOICE, 4/15/97, p. 74, Gary Dauphin

Dennis Rodman probably has a thing or two to say about shifting identity and incomprehensible exchanges, but that'll have to wait for his next starring role. Currently Rodman costars in *Double Team,* the new Jean-Claude Van Damme flick, and the most surprising thing about his acting debut is that he's not that bad. Sure, he plays a CIA operative/arms dealer who assists rogue agent Van Damme in his quest to take down a master terrorist (Mickey Rourke, who is as cut as the proverbial brick shithouse here), and yes, his dialogue is a god-awful string of basketball clichés ("Airball!" "Nothing but net!" "The best offense is ..." and the like). Director Tsui Hark and fight coordinator Samo Hung (both Hong Kong action luminaries making Hollywood debuts) understand, though, that no turn of plot is too predictable or ridiculous if accompanied by kewl fight sequences that make the leads look like stone kung fu killers. Under Hark and Hung's expert eyes, both Rodman and Rourke become surprisingly credible fighters, while Van Damme looks like the Larry Bird of martial arts (i.e., best white guy playing in someone else's sport). As acting basketball players go, Rodman isn't quite as blandly polished as Michael Jordan, but he is leaps and bounds better than Shaquille O'Neal. To make the other obvious comparison, *Double Team* is no *Game of Death,* because Van Damme and Rodman are no Lee and Abdul-Jabar. But really: anything that keeps Dennis out of the WWF is fine and good in my book.

Also reviewed in:
NEW YORK TIMES, 4/4/97, p. C7, Janet Maslin

VARIETY, 4/7-13/97, p. 43, Emanuel Levy
WASHINGTON POST, 4/4/97, Weekend/p. 44, Desson Howe

DREAM WITH THE FISHES

A Sony Pictures Classics release of a 3 Ring Circus Films presentation. *Executive Producer:* John Sideropoulos and Charles Hsiao. *Producer:* Johnny Wow and Mitchell Stein. *Director:* Finn Taylor. *Screenplay:* Finn Taylor. *Story:* Finn Taylor and Jeffrey Brown. *Director of Photography:* Barry Stone. *Editor:* Rick Le Compte. *Music:* Tito Larriva. *Music Editor:* Joe Binni, Raymond Lee, and Charles Raggio. *Sound:* Michael Emery. *Sound Editor:* Josh Rosen. *Casting:* Joseph Middleton. *Production Designer:* Justin McCartney. *Art Director:* Christopher Frank. *Set Decorator:* Katherine Purchas. *Set Dresser:* Andrew Kemler, Karl T. Hirsch, and Melinda Sugino. *Costumes:* Amy Brownson. *Make-up:* David Clark. *Stunt Coordinator:* Mickey Breitenstein. *Running time:* 96 minutes. *MPAA Rating:* R.

CAST: David Arquette (Terry); Brad Hunt (Nick); Cathy Moriarty (Aunt Elise); Kathryn Erbe (Liz); Patrick McGaw (Don); J.E. Freeman (Joe, Nick's Father); Timi Prulhiere (Michelle); Anita Barone (Mary); Allyce Beasley (Sophia); Peter Gregory (Pharmacist); Richmond Arquette (Sheriff); George Maguire (Funeral Director); Kristina Robbins (Terry's Bowling "Date"); Katherine Copenhaver (Nick's Bowling "Date"); Gary Brickman (Drug Dealer); Nina Peschcke-Koedt (Psychic); Orril Fluharty (Priest); Michael Halton (Liquor Store Clerk); Mike Por (Donut Shop Clerk); Chris Pay (Emergency Room Doctor); Felix Justice (Nick's Doctor #1); James Carraway (Nick's Doctor #2); Michael Vaughn (Bank Security Guard); Beth Daly (Librarian); Banda El Rincon (Band in Bar); Michael Hsiao (Restaurant Pianist); Alec Ingalls (Bartender); Jack A. Roe (Angry Taxi Passenger); Xris (Convenience Store Clerk); Greg Love, Ken Cunningham, and Mike Price (Cops at Funeral/Pharmacy); Roldan Abasolo (Aquarium Security Guard); Sophia Stefanek (Mary's Daughter); Mark Hager (Garbage Man).

LOS ANGELES TIMES, 6/20/97, Calendar/p. 8, Jack Mathews

[*The following review by Jack Mathews appeared in a slightly different form in* NEWSDAY, 6/20/97, Part II/p. B9.]

If its story were summarized in an ad line, Finn Taylor's "Dream With the Fishes" would sound like a lot of buddy movies we've seen—tales of unlikely companions whose relationship is built on the tottering foundation of suspicion, anger and desperation, ultimately held together by a shared humanity.

But this first feature by writer Finn Taylor ("Pontiac Moon") is hardly derivative or predictable. Its characters, both pathetic losers in the beginning, develop their own charisma, and the fragile nature of their relationship creates a second, equally strong bond with the audience.

"Dream With the Fishes" is about a healthy man who wants to die and a dying man who wants to live. David Arquette is Terry, a voyeur so socially disconnected that he has created an entire life through the end of his binoculars. But even he knows it's a desperate, impossible existence and, emboldened by whiskey, he plans to end it all with a leap from the Oakland Bay Bridge.

There, not to stop him but to ask for his watch, is Nick (Brad Hunt), a man we have already learned this about: He lives with his girlfriend across the way from Terry and has unknowingly been one of the stars of Terry's nightly voyeurism, and he was planning to rob that liquor store when Terry came in to buy his courage.

What we soon learn is that Nick is dying from some fast-moving disease, probably a brain tumor, and that he needs money for the expensive painkillers that keep him going. Before their first strange evening together ends, Nick has made Terry an offer: If Terry will finance Nick's final days and a few of his fantasies, Nick will pick an opportune moment to fulfill Terry's death wish.

Terry agrees, partly because even this morbid arrangement gives him a connection to another person, but he treats Nick with the wariness of someone who's just walked out of a screening of

Alfred Hitchcock's "Strangers on a Train." Is this guy nuts? Will he deliver on his promise? And does Terry really want him to? Taylor keeps these questions dangling until near the end, keeping both Terry and the audience off balance. And he does it with raw-nerve honesty. These characters do begin to steady each other and lend moral support but never in the overtly manipulative ways we're accustomed to with mainstream films.

Their relationship grows not in leaps and bounds, but with one tenuous step at a time, and often with quick steps backward. Even scenes created for humor have emotional consequences. They spend one evening together in a bowling alley, which Nick has rented with Terry's money, for a few lines of nude bowling with a pair of hookers. But the sporty event ends badly because Terry is terrified of the socialization involved.

Eventually, Nick and Terry drive to Nick's hometown, where he has some unfinished business with an old girlfriend and an abusive father. But with his dependency on painkillers growing and his behavior becoming more erratic, Nick needs the kind of friend Terry has never been. With time running out, we'll see how far they've come.

The performances here are superb. Arquette plays a pitifully lost soul with enough contradictory impulses to make him simultaneously off-putting and irresistible. Terry's a man clinging to reality by his fingertips, forced out of his own despair to connect with another human being, and Arquette pulls off the transformation with amazing subtlety.

Hunt has the more conventional role, gregarious roustabout, but it's one for which natural appeal is essential, and he has it. There's also strong work by Kathryn Erbe, as Nick's caring lover, and Cathy Moriarty, as his salty Aunt Elise.

This may be a small film in a summer of towering adventures, but so far, it's shown more humanity than the lot of them.

NEW YORK POST, 6/20/97, p. 44, Michael Medved

"Dream With the Fishes" is an abysmal, bickering buddy movie about the madcap adventures of two generation Xers on complementary death trips.

David Arquette is a healthy but nervous type who tries repeatedly to kill himself, while Brad Hunt is a lifelong Bohemian dying of leukemia.

This is not the sort of setup that offers a rollicking good time at the movies, and this project is every bit as bad as its pathetic premise suggests.

Oddly enough, this misguided movie muddle actually opens with a touch of energy and originality. In a San Francisco liquor store, unwashed, long-haired, pistol-packing Hunt watches Arquette, who's wearing an expensive suit and wire rims, buy a huge bottle of rot-gut booze to dull his pain.

He follows the stranger out onto a bridge and interrupts him just before he jumps to his death. He asks for the would-be suicide's expensive watch since he presumably won't be needing it, then persuades him to come over to his apartment to end it all in more painless fashion with an overdose of available sleeping pills.

Their relationship develops from there and the movie goes straight downhill. As Arquette discovers that his new pal is a doomed man who wants to avoid the hospital during his last weeks of life, he quickly forgets his own troubles (his adored wife has perished in a car crash) to concentrate on helping his friend make the most of his remaining moments.

In one scene they, live out the dying man's fantasy of nude bowling with two fun-loving prostitutes. Later, they travel to a small Northern Californian town to re-connect with Hunt's hyper-macho unforgiving father (J.E. Freeman) and his charmingly eccentric aunt (Cathy Moriarty), a lusty, one-time exotic dancer.

Hunt's grieving girlfriend (Kathryn Erbe) impulsively gives herself to the uptight Arquette as some sort of life-affirming gesture while the man she really loves slips deeper into his disease.

Arquette lacks the kinetic screen presence of his big sisters, Rosanna and Patricia, playing his impossible part like an obtuse neurotic whose suicidal tendencies seem neither convincing nor comprehensible.

Hunt brings more star quality to his role, but his robust, athletic good looks (and muscular, frequently bared torso) seem incongruous for a character who's supposed to be expiring from a terminal disease.

Meanwhile, the critical ailment for the picture itself is the immature, self-important indulgence of debuting director Finn Taylor.

SIGHT AND SOUND, 7/98, p. 40, Xan Brooks

San Francisco. Terry, a depressed voyeur, wants to kill himself. Meanwhile, his free-spirited neighbour Nick is dying of a terminal illness. The two reach an agreement: if Terry will bankroll Nick's few surviving weeks, Nick will return the favour by killing him. Nick abandons his girlfriend Liz and sets out on the road with Terry. En route, the pair drop acid and hold up a local drugstore to get Nick's medication.

Upon reaching Nick's rural hometown, they stay with his Aunt Elise, a former stripper, and hook up with Nick's old schoolfriend Don, while Nick makes peace with his violent father Joe. Nick offers to fulfil his side of the bargain, but Terry is now enjoying life and rejects the offer. The pair are tracked down by Liz, but Nick's health is deteriorating and he is admitted to hospital after collapsing during a bank heist. In the hospital, he and Liz are married. Later, Terry sneaks into his room and assists with Nick's suicide. Returning home, Terry burns his stash of illicitly taken photos and prepares to rejoin the land of the living.

Dream with the Fishes is clearly dreaming of the 70s. Even the title is a twist on the "he sleeps with the fishes" line from *The Godfather* (1972). Finn Taylor, making his debut as a writer-director, and cinematographer Barry Stone have engineered a photographic process that consciously apes the redundant film stock employed by such revered cinematographers as John A. Alonzo (on *Chinatown* 1974), Gordon Willis (on *The Godfather)* and Laszlo Kovacs (*Five Easy Pieces* 1970). Thus *Dream with the Fishes* fairly wallows in evocative high-contrast colour, bottomless pools of shadow giving way to glaring expanses of light. The plot also recycles the concerns of that bygone era. Such movies as *The Last Detail* (1973), *Midnight Cowboy* (1969) and *Five Easy Pieces* were fixated on the role of the American man in a post-feminist climate and the survival of the pioneering spirit in a constricting modern world. Taylor's film follows suit, with its blaze-of-glory last excursion of ailing Nick and suicidal Terry. Its underlying mantra is the one espoused by Neil Young on that classic 70s album *Rust Never Sleeps:* "It's better to burn out than to fade away." Or, as Nick puts it: "If you're gonna go, go with a fucking bang."

As a homage to the pictures that influenced him, Taylor's film looks seamless. As an original film in its own right, it feels synthetic. *Dream with the Fishes'* screenplay is too elementary, leaning heavily on that old chestnut, the terminal illness, for its emotional effect. Its odd couple characters are archetypes (the repressed modern man, the wild liberating angel); its line of symbolism crude and heavy-handed. Taylor is so focused on men and male values that his female characters are left wafer-thin, mere facilitators for the macho experience. Cathy Moriarty's Aunt Elise is an aging good-time floozy, Liz the feisty, good-hearted girlfriend. Nick's mum merely smiles wanly from behind the screen-door of the family home, and barely gets to say a word.

Undigested in parts and never wholly successful, *Dream with the Fishes* nonetheless takes flight during its middle act, Abruptly liberated from its schematic set-up, the film flourishes for a brief, giddy spell before the redemption-by-numbers finale clips its wings again. Here, Taylor's script grows more assured, his direction turns supple and effortless, the lead performers click together, and there comes a crop of vibrant cameos (Peter Gregory as the menaced pharmacist; Gary Brickman as a cocksure, wheelchair-bound dope dealer). For about 30 or 40 minutes, one catches a glimpse of what could have been—the seductive, honest, earthy picaresque tale Taylor was striving to fashion. But on the whole *Dream with the Fishes* is overrun by hand-me-down plot devices and style. The result is an expert but suspect line in cinematic pastiche, messy, modern-day masculinity smoothed over with an airbrush. In the end, it simply fades away.

VILLAGE VOICE, 6/24/97, p. 82, Amy Taubin

A more puerile expression of male camaraderie [The reference is to *Frank & Ollie*], animates Finn Taylor's *Dream With the Fishes*, which has built its ad campaign around a nude bowling scene that occupies about 30 seconds of screen time. Creative in the mode of Miu-Miu polyester shirts combined with recycled bell-bottoms, Taylor's first feature has a vaguely '70s look (flat, high-contrasty, with supersaturated colors) and suggests the influence of many movies in which guys come together in weird circumstances (Wim Wenders' great *The American Friend* and Robert Altman's overrated *California Split* among them).

While attempting to commit suicide, Terry (David Arquette) encounters Nick (Brad Hunt), a junkie dying of a rare blood disease. Nick promises to kill Terry before he kicks the bucket himself if Terry helps him live out some last-minute fantasies (the aforementioned nude bowling among them). The two hit the Northern California highways and byways, quickly run afoul of the law, and take refuge in Nick's hometown, where the dying man becomes reconciled with his past and Terry realizes that life is too great a gift to be thrown away. If this sounds hackneyed, it is, but Taylor adds enough whimsical curlicues to the narrative to distract you from the obvious (that is, if you have a taste for whimsy).

Arquette, who cut such an edgy figure in the otherwise awful *Johns*, is less impressive here. (He seems like a paler Jeremy Davies.) Most of the other actors, including Cathy Moriarty as Nick's stripper aunt, downplay the outlandish aspects of their situations and come off as mildly appealing. Which also is the best that can be said about *Dream With the Fishes*. Oh yeah, and the scene where the cop inadvertently drops acid is very funny.

Also reviewed in:
NEW YORK TIMES, 6/20/97, p. C21, Janet Maslin
VARIETY, 1/27-2/2/97, p. 76, Dennis Harvey

DRUNKS

A Northern Arts Entertainment release of a Seagoat Films and Kardana Films presentation of a Shooting Gallery production. *Executive Producer:* Larry Meistrich, John Hart, and Tom Caruso. *Producer:* Peter Cohn. *Director:* Peter Cohn. *Screenplay (based on his play "Blackout"):* Gary Lennon. *Director of Photography:* Peter Hawkins. *Editor:* Hughes Winborne. *Music:* Joe Delta. *Sound:* Andrew Morad. *Casting:* Lina Todd. *Production Designer:* Michael Shaw. *Art Director:* Daniel Goldfield. *Costumes:* Kim Druce. *Running time:* 88 minutes. *MPAA Rating:* R.

CAST: Richard Lewis (Jim); Faye Dunaway (Becky); Dianne Wiest (Rachel); Parker Posey (Debbie); Amanda Plummer (Shelley); Howard Rollins (Joseph); Lisa Gay Hamilton (Brenda); Spalding Gray (Louis); Laurie Taylor-Williams (Francine); Geroge Martin (Marty); Anna Thomson (Tanya).

LOS ANGELES TIMES, 5/30/97, Calendar/p. 8, Kevin Thomas

Adapted by Gary Lennon from his play "Blackout," "Drunks" is said to be the first film to take us inside an Alcoholics Anonymous meeting from start to finish. Allowing for a certain theatricality, "Drunks" is totally persuasive in its account of recovering alcoholics helping one another in a painful and often desperate struggle for sobriety.

Although it ends on a note of hope, "Drunks" is hard to take—especially for those of us who've had to deal with alcoholics for a large chunk of our lives. Yet there is no doubt that this is a worthy endeavor that could just possibly impact upon people's lives.

Although "Drunks" is an ensemble endeavor sprinkled with distinguished names, comedian Richard Lewis, in his first leading dramatic role, is undeniably its star and a commanding one at that.

Lewis' Jim is a man whose sobriety is coming unraveled in the face of the sudden death of his wife some months before. He finds the pressure too much to bear when asked to speak at an AA meeting, held in the basement of a Times Square area church, and flees to go on a binge.

Jim serves as a solid dramatic device, allowing director Peter Cohn to cut away from the meeting from time to time to follow the man as he plunges into a despair. But this character is no mere device, for Jim comes to represent the individual who must finally confront the truth that he must be honest with himself and with others on other issues—that admitting to alcoholism while lying about something crucial in your life is not the way to staying sober.

What horror stories the AA members have to tell.   None, however, would surprise any alcoholic or any of us who've attended Alanon meetings for friends and relatives of alcoholics. Here's Faye Dunaway's elegant Becky, deeply afraid that she may return to the bottle if she should lose custody of her son; Dianne Wiest's doctor, long sober, but who's become concerned that she's become a workaholic to avoid doing the real work of becoming a truly recovered alcoholic; the late Howard Rollins as a father consumed with grief and guilt over his responsibility in injuring his small son in a drunk driving accident; and Spalding Gray's Louis, who tries to convince us and himself that he's stumbled on the meeting purely by accident, saying he was coming to the church for choir practice.   Other troubled people are played by Parker Posey, Amanda Plummer and many others.

You can only hope "Drunks," which has already played on cable, reaches people with its belief that you can take charge of your life no matter how hard the struggle to do so may be.

NEW YORK POST, 3/14/97, p. 50, Michael Medved

"Drunks" is an audacious experiment in minimalist cinema that fails courageously and conclusively.

Adapted from the play "Blackout" by first-time director Peter Cohn, the movie presents the discussion at an Alcoholics Anonymous meeting one cold winter's night in the basement of a Times Square church.

Some dozen characters take turns speaking to the camera and delivering confessions of their destructive drinking.

The late Howard Rollins Jr. is especially effective as a guilty father who pointlessly injured his 5-year-old son. Dianne Wiest plays a prominent physician whose boozy blackouts threatened her high-pressure career. Faye Dunaway is masterful as a divorcee whose superficial elegance hides her shattered life.

These characters listen patiently to each of the stories, but they never interact meaningfully with one another, so the picture lacks all dramatic momentum.

The only hint of a plot centers on Richard Lewis, playing a shaken slickster who's asked to kick off the meeting by describing the recent death of his wife. Lewis grabs hold of this part with admirable intensity, but his normal comic persona remains firmly enough in place so that you're never sure whether we're supposed to assume he's telling the truth.

Neither the script nor his performance makes clear why the character storms out of the church and onto the snowy streets, plunging into a binge of booze and heroin.

For the rest of the picture, scenes of his hellish descent alternate with the earnest presentations by the others who have stayed with the continuing meeting.

Among these is Spalding Gray in the movie's best performance as a confused, well-spoken fellow who has arrived in church on the wrong night for choir practice, stumbles onto the AA meeting by accident, and then offers his own revealing and poetic monologue about why he doesn't think he qualifies as an alcoholic.

Though the producers claim that each of the players improvised their lines, Gray's performance is the only one that seems spontaneous.

Too many other narratives seem as if they're being read from words on a page, with frequent "ers" and "uhs " inserted in a vain stab at realism.

The truth about America's millions of recovering alcoholics, gaining control of their lives "by the grace of God, one day at a time" offers one of the most important and potentially compelling stories of our time, but in its desperate attempt at honesty and understatement, this grim, monochromatic film never manages to transcend its own restrictive and claustrophobic format.

VILLAGE VOICE, 3/18/97, p. 80, Leslie Camhi

In a Times Square church basement, Jim (Richard Lewis) testily perks the coffee for an AA meeting. Two years ago, he stopped drinking and using; now he's dealing with his wife's death. Assorted characters file in: Rachel (Dianne Wiest), a dope-addicted doctor; Becky (Faye Dunaway), a drunk divorcée; Debbie (Parker Posey), a wild child and NFL fanatic; Francine (Laurie Taylor-Williams), a shopaholic and "social imbiber"; Joseph (Howard Rollins Jr.), an ex-con and former drunk driver; Louis (Spalding Cray), who stumbles in for choir practice and is drawn to their stories. Jim speaks because he's asked to, then storms out on a bender from which he may never return.

Drunks's star-studded cast offers stellar performances, but fame sometimes gets in the way of the film's everyman aspirations. The script is clever and edgy, though at times it betrays its theatrical origins. Still, steering clear of both sermonizing and mindless celebration, *Drunks* offers a series of funny, moving, and sobering reflections on our consuming needs for things, people, and most of all, stories.

Also reviewed in:
NEW REPUBLIC, 4/14/97, p. 28, Stanley Kauffmann
NEW YORK TIMES, 3/14/97, p. C20, Stephen Holden
VARIETY, 9/11-17/95, p. 106, Daniel Kimmel

DUST OF LIFE

A Swift release of a Swift production in association with 3B Productions/Hamster Productions/La Sept Films/IVP/TeleMunchen/Paradise Film/Salon Films. *Executive Producer:* Charles Wang. *Producer:* Jean Bréhat. *Director:* Rachid Bouchareb. *Screenplay (French and Vietnamese with English subtitles):* Bernard Gesbert and Rachid Bouchareb. *Based on the novel "Fanta Hill" by:* Duyen Anh. *Director of Photography:* Youcef Sahraoui. *Editor:* Hélène Ducret. *Music:* Safy Boutella. *Running time:* 87 minutes. *MPAA Rating:* Not Rated.

CAST: Daniel Guyant (Son); Gilles Chitlaphone (Bob); Léon Outtrabady (Shrimp); Jéhan Pagès (Little Hai); Siu Lin Ham (Greaser); Eric Nguyen (One-two); Yann Roussel (Steel Muscles); William Low (Commander).

NEW YORK POST, 6/11/97, p. 42, Bill Hoffmann

If you lived through the Vietnam War era and aren't a veteran, most of your memories probably focus on what was happening here: the escalating draft, the raucous protests, the backroom politics.

There have been plenty of movies made about our perceptions of the Vietnam War and its aftermath, and how they affected the United States. But the Vietnamese side has gotten the short shrift.

Thankfully, "Dust of Life," will help change that.

A French-Algerian production made in 1994, "Dust of Life" focuses on the often brutal government "re-education" of tens of thousands of "half breed" kids—born of Vietnamese mothers and American soldier dads.

These young outcasts lived in a social twilight zone—abandoned by their parents and shunned by their prejudiced countrymen.

Branded the "dust of life," these kids were rounded up off the streets where they worked as pickpockets and beggars and taken to a jungle boot camp to be cleansed of Western (i.e., American) ideology.

Director Rachid Bouchareb focuses on 13-year-old Son (Daniel Guyant) who, along with other boys, quickly begins dreaming of getting out.

The kids are like cows in a slaughterhouse, except they can think; and the only way to survive is to flee—at any price. Some will survive, many will perish.

Please don't let the downbeat nature of the subject scare away. The movie—based on Duyen Ahn's autobiography "Fanta Hill"—serves as both stirring history and gripping cinema.

The film has the added bonus of being filmed in wide-screen. Of course, lots of mainstream Hollywood flicks come in wide-screen. but not many recent entries have used the large frame as well as "Dust of Life," in which each shot is so well constructed, not a bit of space is wasted.

VILLAGE VOICE, 6/17/97, p. 70, Gary Dauphin

At the fall of Saigon in 1975, there were some 40,000 Amerasian children, born of American GIs and Vietnamese women, in Vietnam; they were derisively called the 'dust of life.' Algerian director Rachid Bouchareb, whose extremely fine 1991 film *Cheb* was a trek through the landscape of French-Algerian hyphenation, uses the fate of one of them as a jumping-off point for his latest film, *Dust of Live.*

Dust is based on a true story that begins with 13-year-old Son Nguyen (Daniel Guyant) trying to get into the collapsing U.S. Embassy compound in Saigon. Son is denied entry despite having an American father and soon ends up thrown into a truck and shipped to the countryside with a group of other "orphans." The more savvy Bob (a sadly handsome Gilles Chitlaphone) befriends Son, protecting him from the other kids when they arrive at a remote reeducation camp, where work and violence are the main lessons and the unseen "tiger cage" awaits anyone who dares attempt an escape.

Son also meets the tiny but surprisingly tough Little Hai (Jehan Pages), and the two discover they're both closet Christians, kneeling down in a stream for forbidden Hail Marys. The cross soon becomes one of Son's talismans, as does the pen. The only child in the camp who can write, he soon starts recording the names of dead children, obsessively writing his way through the drudgery and unpredictability of incarceration.

From the very beginning, *Dust* has the feel of tragedy (Bouchareb has a talent for elegiac imagery). The boys eventually plan a painfully naive escape that brings them to the tiger cage and the limits of their endurance. In the process Son eagerly undergoes a transformation that's almost as frightening, going from crying mama's boy to a budding leader with a martyr's glow in his eyes. There's something wrenching about hearing a 13-year-old say, "Christ doesn't smile upon his cross" but coming from Son and *Dust of Life* it's perfectly (and horribly) believable.

Also reviewed in:
CHICAGO TRIBUNE, 11/7/97, Friday/p. O, John Petrakis
NEW YORK TIMES, 6/11/97, p. C15, Stephen Holden
VARIETY, 9/5-11/94, p. 56, Ken Eisner

EAST SIDE STORY

A Kino International release of an ANDA Films/WDR/DocStar/Canal+ production. *Producer:* Andrew Horn. *Director:* Dana Ranga. *Screenplay (English, German, Russian and Romanian with English subtitles):* Dana Ranga and Andrew Horn. *Director of Photography:* Mark Daniels. *Editor:* Guido Krajewski. *Sound:* Heino Herrenbruck and Martin Ehlers. *Costumes:* Suse Brown. *Make-up:* Volker Langwagen and Jo Braun. *Running time:* 78 minutes. *MPAA Rating:* Not Rated.

CAST: Andrea Schmidt, Brit Kruger, and Barbara Harnisch (Communist Party Girls). *INTERVIEWS WITH:* Karin Schröder, Brigitte Ulbrich, Helmut Hanke, Hans-Joachim Wallstein, Maya Turovskaya, Chris Doerk and Frank Schöbel.

LOS ANGELES TIMES, 8/29/97, Calendar/p. 2, Kenneth Turan

You've never seen anything like "East Side Story," but then again neither has anyone else. At least not on this side of the former Iron Curtain. Smart and sassy, this smashingly entertaining documentary introduces the West to the world of socialist musicals, a genre so unlikely even its creators were often chagrined at what they'd accomplished.

Imagine, if you can, hearty machinists bursting into a chorus of "in the hot blast of the coal oven, the coal press begins to stomp." Or ecstatically happy peasants taking part in a stupendous wheat harvest choreographed to the rhythms of massive machinery. Or a glamorous swineherd singing, "Hey, piggies, time to eat, come to your trough and have a little meal." It's all here, and more.

But "East Side Story" is not just a "That's Entertainment!" compiled from communism's most eye-popping production numbers. As put together by Dana Ranga and Andrew Horn (she directed, he produced, they co-wrote), the film examines how these unlikely epics came to life in the face of serious obstacles. And it does so with irresistible style, typified by a puckish thank-you to Karl Marx, "without whom none of this would have been necessary."

"A socialist musical film has to be a crazy idea," says the movie's sly voice-over, partly because "fun and music in a world of ambiguity and suspicion" is an unlikely scenario. Also, the seriousness of socialism, its humorless determination to raise the political consciousness of the working class, led party functionaries to dismiss mere entertainment as unworthy of the great cause.

Yet some 40 socialist musicals with catchy titles like "Tractor Drivers" and "Cossacks of the Kuban River" were made behind the Iron Curtain, mostly in the USSR and East Germany but with stubborn outcroppings in Bulgaria, Poland, Romania and Czechoslovakia. "East Side Story" uses a generous selection of clips and pithy interviews with experts, participants and ordinary fans to show how the impossible came to be.

It all started with Russian Gregory Alexandrov and his unlikely patrons in high places. Alexandrov was the great Sergei Eisenstein's assistant director, but after the two of them returned from a 1931 trip to Hollywood, Alexandrov went out on his own and made the first Soviet musical, the merry, syncopated "The Jolly Fellows."

Naturally, the film was promptly baned, but Alexandrov took it to writer Maxim Gorky, who liked it so much he personally showed it to Joseph Stalin himself. Against considerable odds, Stalin was wowed, allegedly commenting that "anyone who made a movie as funny as this has to be a brave man."

With backing that potent, Alexandrov and his actress wife, Lyubov Orlova (who was so popular she regularly got fan letters signed by thousands), were able to make several musicals, including the celebrated "Volga Volga" about local talent determined to make it big in Moscow. That film was Stalin's favorite. He watched it more than 100 times and even gave a copy to wartime ally Franklin D. Roosevelt, whose own reaction is not recorded.

Both Alexandrov and the other key Soviet musical director, Ivan Pyriev, created dreams, but they were specifically Communist ones, where optimistic workers were always smiling and fulfilling quotas was a joy not a duty. But when Stalin died, the heart went out of the USSR musical, and it fell to the German Democratic Republic to pick up the slack.

But not right away. The East German film bureaucrats preferred to turn out turgid tales like "Ernest Thalmann, Class Leader" that idealized the heroic albeit boring struggle against capitalism. But in the days before the Berlin Wall, what East German audiences preferred was to cross over and spend their money on the potent fantasies that Hollywood produced. Entertainment, it turned out, had a powerful imperative of its own.

So, reports actress Karin Schroder, known in her heyday as "the Doris Day of the East," the GDR power structure, having determined that "we have attractive people, we have sex, we have all that here," decided to go into the musical business themselves and pocket the profits.

Their first product, 1958's "My Wife Wants to Sing," starring a former Miss Bavaria and the actor who'd played Ernest Thalmann, boasted the daring theme that communism supported women who wanted to work. It was an immediate hit even in the Soviet Union, where it earned 11 million rubles in just four weeks.

Eventually East Germany got bold enough to attempt brassy teen musicals with names like "Hot Summer" and "No Cheating Darling," but the lack of governmental support and recognition—not to mention that the shoots used so much electricity they threatened the power supply of entire cities—led inevitably to their extinction.

Even in their heyday, what with lack of experienced personnel and official pronouncements condemning them as "the most flagrant offspring of the capitalist pleasure industry," creating these musicals was never easy. In fact one of the most charming of the East German films, "Midnight Review," focused on the difficulties and featured a lyric complaining:

"It's enough to make you tear your hair out!
It's easier to wait 10 years for a car.
It's simpler to go ice-skating in the desert
Than to make a socialist musical!"

Viewed today, the clips featured here are both musically engaging and endearing in their earnestness, a view of an intriguing parallel universe influenced by Hollywood but doing things not quite the same way. "Who knows," "East Side Story" asks with a tinge of regret, "how things would have turned out if socialism could just have been more fun?" How indeed.

NEW STATESMAN, 10/16/98, p. 41, Gerald Kaufman

Although Sergei Eisenstein was regarded as a progenitor of socialist realism on film, the movies he particularly liked were Hollywood musicals. The creator of *The Battleship Potemkin* was addicted to masterworks such as *Star-Spangled Rhythm*, and was a devoted fan of Judy Garland.

It may be speculated that Eisenstein had to look westward for his musical kicks because of the paucity of Soviet song-and-dance movies; and it is true that in 40 years only 40 musicals were made on the eastern side of the Iron Curtain. But the chance provided by *East Side Story*, a compilation documentary, to view extracts from a couple of dozen of these musicals offers a more depressing judgement. Although many of these films were lively, energetic, colourful and good-natured, almost all of them seem to have been dreadful, whether they subscribed to socialist dogma or did their best to escape it.

Some of them were so silly as to be endearing; for example, a plump lady in a pinafore—presumably on a collective farm—singing a serenade to pigs. Some of them were so dire as to be fascinating, most prominently *Midnight Review*, a musical about making a musical featuring an ingredient never before believed to have existed: East German humour.

It is not that the performers were without talent. The tradition of ballet in the Soviet Union meant that there was no shortage of accomplished dancers. Although some of the singers were overly winsome, such stars as the East German Karin Schroder ("the Doris Day of the East") had bags of personality. The problem was the material they were given to work with.

Efforts were made to pillage or plaglarise Hollywood musicals. *East Side Story* shows one film clip of a dancer whose routine was clearly stolen from the "Embraceable You" sequence in *An American in Paris*. A session with rollerskates harks back to Gene Kelly gliding along in *It's Always Fair Weather*. Silhouettes of musical instruments derive from several MGM musicals. There is a homage to the dream sequence in *Singin' in the Rain*, as well as a dance number which indicates that its choreographer might have caught a furtive glimpse of *West Side Story*. Too many of the dance arrangements, however, owe more to *Come Dancing* than to Kelly or Astaire. Most of the songs (though one East German film's soundtrack does contain intriguing echoes of Kurt Weill) would gain nul points in the Eurovision Song Contest.

The Romanian director Dana Ranga does, however, earn high marks for her diligence in unearthing these unlikely treasures. Moreover, at least a couple of the extracts made me wish I could see the whole movie. A Czech film called *Women on the Rails* contains sequences imaginatively tailored for the travelling camera. A Russian movie, *Cossacks of the Kuban River*, includes a production number based on harvesting methods which, like the barn-raising episode in *Seven Brides for Seven Brothers*, turns physical labour into inventive choreography.

Ranga links the excerpts from the musicals with talking-head reminiscence from former stars (such as Chris Dork, East Germany's Elvis) and analysis from film scholars. Of these, my favourite is a severe lady called Maia Turovskaia who, apart from delighting with her frequent references to "Gollywood" (the Russian alphabet being bereft of a letter "h"), utters an important truth not only about eastern-bloc musicals but about all popular entertainment: "Sometimes people need untruths so as to survive."

SIGHT AND SOUND, 10/98, p. 42, Julian Graffy

This examination of the Socialist musical begins with extracts form East European, predominantly East German, musicals of the 50s and 60s, intercut with interviews with people who worked at the East German DEFA studios. A former functionary of the East German State Committee for Entertainment recalls combing the works of Lenin for ideological justification for their endeavours. The beginnings of the genre in the Soviet Stalinist musicals of the 30s and 40s are explored, and extracts from the films of Grigorii Aleksandrov and Ivan Pyriev are interpreted by the Russian film historian Maia Turovskaia.

With the end of Stalinism, the Soviet film musical went into decline just as the new East German state began to experiment with the genre. Footage from such East German musicals as Hans Heinrich's *My Wife Wants to Sing* (1958), Gottfried Kolditz's *Midnight Revue* (1962) and *The Lovable White Mouse* (1964), as well as the 'teen' musicals *Hot Summer* (1968) and *No Cheating, Darling* (1973) is shown. Reminiscences of the participants accompany those of audience members. But *No Cheating, Darling* marked the end of the genre, preceding by about a decade the demise of the system that spawned it.

Director Dana Ranga describes the Socialist musical as a genre that ought not to have existed and her own film as a personal journey to discover why it did. The first part of *East Side Story* is a dazzling kaleidoscope of scenes from such genre masterpieces as the Romanian *I Don't Want to Marry* (1960) in which, in a sub-Busby Berkeley routine, girls discard their work overalls for pretty dresses; or the Czech *The Wayward Wife* (1965), where the heroine is seduced by a roller skating gigolo. Actually, however, the territory of the Socialist musical is not quite as uncharted and mysterious as Ranga seems to think, and it is a relief when Ranga turns to historian Maia Turovskaia and her analysis of the genre in the Stalin period.

The musical comedy in Russia dates from the early 30s, its birth precipitated both by the visit of Grigorii Aleksandrov (its first major practitioner) to Hollywood with Eisenstein, but also, most importantly, by the coming of sound to Soviet cinema. Sound was seized upon by Party and cinema bureaucrats as an effective means of increasing and channelling the ideological thrust of Soviet films, including musicals. Thus the ideological content of Aleksandrov's films increased as the decade passed.

If Aleksandrov's films involved the journey of the heroine to artistic or ideological success in Moscow, the work of the other great practitioner of the genre, Ivan Pyriev, hymned life on the periphery, on the collective farm. Ranga's coup here is to include a sequence from the original version of Pyriev's *Tractor Drivers* (1939) in which the eponymous heroes bring in the harvest while singing their loyalty to Stalin, a sequence removed after the leader's death. She also shows the bizarre opening of Pyriev's *The Swineherd and the Shepherd* in which (in 1941!) the heroine sings her piglets a song of plenty ("Eat, eat, and then I'll give you more!").

Turovskaia has many wise things to say about these works, surmising that both directors were wilier than they seemed. She knows (having done pioneering work on film reception in the Stalinist period) that these films delivered both propaganda and entertainment, and not always in the way the Party may have intended. The films of both directors stressed the role of women. This was not just because both Aleksandrov and Pyriev were married to their stars, Liubov Orlova and Marina Ladynina respectively, and needed vehicles for them, but also because the transformation of the role of women in society was Socialism's proudest boast. In fact, as Turovskaia and the film extracts show, Socialism and the musical were made for each other since both promised a fairy-tale transformation in which obstacles and barriers would melt away.

In Russia, the musical almost died with the post-Stalinist Thaw, which brought earnest demands for truthfulness, whereas the most famous of the post-war musicals, Pyriev's *Cossacks of the Kuban River* (1949), was seen as the paradigm of the "varnishing of reality". Besides, the musical stars (especially Orlova and Ladynina) were now middle-aged and the Thaw was obsessed with youth. It is ironic that at this stage the East Germans attempted to resuscitate the genre, since, as Ranga observes, the three key points of reference the musicals made by the Nazis, Hollywood and Soviet Stalinism—were all ideologically suspect (though one assumes that a keen eye was trained upon West German experiments in the genre).

The third, East German section of *East Side Story* shows the musical absorbing new social influences: for example, the liberation of women in *My Wife Wants to Sing,* in which the wife of a department-store manager leaves her kitchen for the stage, and, a decade later, the self-assertion of local youth. Perhaps the most interesting of the East German works of the time is *Midnight Revue,* a film about making a musical which explicitly addresses the ideological and financial problems that beset the DEFA workers. This last part of the film also includes works from other countries, notably the bizarre Czech film *Woman on the Rails* (1965), in which female construction workers are given facials in a beauty parlour and warned not to lose their femininity. Through all of the examples she chooses, Ranga provides an eloquent social and political history, for the problems and the fates of the musicals are microcosmic of the problems and fates of 'socialism' in these countries.

Above all, her achievement is to unearth and display an extraordinary richness of visual material, from the delirious primary colours of the dance numbers in *Midnight Revue* to the self-conscious uppitiness of youth in *Hot Summer*. Watching them provokes a range of reactions, from nostalgia for their innocence and naivety to cringing at their datedness and absurdity. Like the recent past in general, they are both dismayingly familiar and frighteningly remote. In this sense, Ranga's archaeological researches are highly evocative, and she gleans a number of perceptive comments from her interviewees, not least from Turovskaia, who describes how her own attitude to the films has changed from, at the time, finding them appallingly lacking in "truth to life" to her present realisation that their comforting lies were lies that people everywhere turn to in mass culture "so as to survive".

TIME, 7/14/97, p. 81, Richard Corliss

There's one simple explanation for the triumph of capitalism over Soviet communism: we had Astaire and Marilyn; all they had were boy-loves-tractor pictures. As the battle of the ideologies was fought on movie screens around the world, the edifying drabness of Soviet-bloc films couldn't compete with America's glamorous, sexy, lilting pop culture. As Dana Ranga, director of the terrific documentary *East Side Story*, puts it, "A specter was haunting communism: the specter of Hollywood."

Now and then, Communist filmmakers tried entertaining the masses with what the official press derisively called "the most flagrant offspring of the capitalist pleasure industry": musical comedies. *East Side Story* is the history of that glorious, doomed attempt to create an all-singing, all-dancing genre within the unsmiling dictates of socialist realism.

Some Commusicals did fit the stolid stereotype—Mikhail and Judit shouting, "Let's harvest the beet crop right here!" but many have an enduring buoyancy. Grigori Alexandrov's pioneering *The Jolly Fellows* (1934) percolates with jaunty jazz, Cubist compositions and a Dietrichish blond in a party hat. The amazing *Midnight Revenue* (G.D.R., 1962) is a comically cynical parable about the difficulty of making a musical when your producer is not Arthur Freed but a pack of philistine bureaucrats. We can't approve your film, the apparatchiks sing; it's "too hot!"

This plot was no joke. Many Commusicals were censored for having a decadent Westernized tone. As an officious official bellows to a young dancer in *Carnival Night* (U.S.S.R., 1957), "We want to raise the consciousness of our workers. But what do you expect to raise with naked legs?" Only about 40 Soviet-bloc musicals were made in 40 years, from *The Jolly Fellows* to the glossy, ginchy *No Cheating, Darling* (G.D.R., 1973). Yet these films brought vigorous fun to an audience starved for it. Their makers deserved to be named Heroes of the Soviet People.

Like Hitler, who insisted on a steady stream of musicals from the German studios, Stalin was a big fan of the genre; he saw Alexandrov's *Volga, Volga* (1938) 100 times. And busy as he was in 1933, supervising the forced starvation of 7 million Ukrainians, Stalin took time out to see *The Jolly Fellows*. It was his enthusiasm that overruled the censors' original ban.

The only Soviet specialists in musicals were Alexandrov and Ivan Pyriev, the man who made the tractor movies. Pyriev's peasants in *Tractor Drivers* (1939) sing, "With shellfire thundering and gleaming steel,/ The machines will race ahead to lead the march." In Alexandrov's factory fantasy *The Bright Path* (1940), workers sing, "Whether you work a machine or break through rocks/ A wonderful dream reveals itself and calls you forward." Naive, yes, but ferociously pertinent for the Russian audience—propaganda in its noblest form.

The Russian musical died with Stalin, but the '50s and '60s saw a little bloom in Soviet-bloc musicals that were much more in step with Hollywood films. In three 1965 movies you'll see a dapper gent figure-skating around a woman in her bedroom (the Czech-East German *The Wayward Wife)*, a DayGlo-bright production number in a spa (*Woman on the Rails*, Czechoslovakia), a Bulgarian Connie Francis in full taunt (*The Antique Coin*). But the syncopated clock was ticking; Commusicals fizzled out, as Hollywood song shows did, in the early '70s.

Beautifully assembled by Ranga and producer Andrew Horn, *East Side Story* reveals the need for fantasy in any social system. Now the "wonderful dream" of Soviet socialism is dead; and these films, reviled in their time, still live. Thirty or 60 years later, in their passionate innocence, they sing to us.

VILLAGE VOICE, 7/1/97, p. 96, Elliott Stein

A young woman serenades an audience of piglets—showgirls with bouffant '60s hairdos busily spin atop a giant turntable; on a city street, a dozen chorus boys hoof up a storm, attired in Day-Glo outfits color-coordinated with their gleaming new convertibles. Hollywood kitsch? Tinseltown camp? Think again. The flashy chorus-boy scene, pure fantasy, was shot on a Prague street at a time of the dreariest Stalinism. These are but three of the 22 production numbers from inspirational Marxist musical movie extravaganzas, made during the Communist era in the Soviet Union and Eastern bloc countries, excerpted in Dana Ranga's entertaining *East Side Story*. Most of these films were never exported to the West and will be novelties even for the most zealous cineastes.

Ranga's fascinating doc begins with a barrage of heady clips from half a dozen '50s and '60s musicals from Romania, Czechoslovakia, Poland, and East Germany, alternating with interviews with actors and technicians from these state-run film industries. Its next segment, presented by Russian film historian Maya Turorskaya, takes us back to the outset of Eastern tuners, when Soviet musical comedy was founded by *Jolly Fellows* (1934), a landmark movie directed by Sergei Eisenstein's assistant, Grigori Alexandrov. Wild, lyric, goofy, influenced by Hollywood, but full of a comic invention all its own, it made a star of soprano Lyubov Orlova, the director's wife. She later belted her way through his *Volga Volga* (1938) and *The Bright Path* (1940). Volga was produced during one of the most terrible periods of Soviet history. While the film's crowds of peasant extras were chanting "Our happiness is blossoming like wheat!" millions were being murdered.

In *Path,* a socialist version *of Cinderella,* Orlova is an illiterate servant girl who becomes a leader in the textile industry. Like many other Soviet musicals of the period, it perpetuated the myth that a simple farm girl or worker could become a sports champion, film star, or prime mover. It was one of Stalin's favorite pictures; he gave it its title and is said to have seen it dozens of times. (Three of Alexandrov's musicals were recently released here on video—see review by J. Hoberman, April 1, 1997.)

Although not as well known as Alexandrov, Ivan Pyriev was a prolific director of musicals, which he alternated with screen adaptations of Dostoyevsky novels. Judging from the four excerpts of his work on view, all starring warbler Marina Laynina, his films were brightly melodic, handsomely produced, and polished—ideal escapist fare for the Soviet citizenry during particularly hard times.

When Uncle Joe died, the Soviet musical quickly petered out, whereas in East Germany, the DEFA studio, eager to compete with light-entertainment films from the West, went into high gear and continued to turn out tuners for another two decades. They often featured fantasy song-and-dance routines rigged out with tempting luxury consumer goods. These Hollywood-parroting musicals are not without a klutzy charm. There were cloned Busby Berkeley geometric numbers, Rockette-type high-stepping sequences, and Funicello-esque beach-party teenage-romp romances. Best of all, there was the radiant Karin Schroder, "the Doris Day of the East," who presents a clip from her biggest hit, *The Lovable White Mouse* (1964).

Diverting and novel as it is, *East Side Story* has been unevenly assembled. A sort of Greek chorus of "Communist party girls" who comment on the clips is a silly conceit that doesn't fit in with the rest of the picture. Image quality is thin; what we're looking at is apparently a video transfer. My most serious beef is that not once are any of the interview subjects—veterans who worked on the films—ever asked a tough question. How about: "How did you feel working at a studio like DEFA where the story editors were known to be informants of the state police?"

Also reviewed in:
CHICAGO TRIBUNE, 1/9/98, Friday/p. K, John Petrakis
NEW YORK TIMES, 6/25/97, p. C13, Janet Maslin
VARIETY, 2/24-3/2/97, p. 90, Todd McCarthy
WASHINGTON POST, 12/5/97, Weekend/p. 57, Desson Howe

EDGE, THE

A Twentieth Century Fox release of an Art Linson production. *Executive Producer:* Lloyd Phillips. *Producer:* Art Linson. *Director:* Lee Tamahori. *Screenplay:* David Mamet. *Director of Photography:* Donald M. McAlpine. *Editor:* Neil Travis. *Music:* Jerry Goldsmith. *Music Editor:* Kenny Hall. *Sound:* Eric J. Batut and (music) Bruce Botnick. *Sound Editor:* Jay Wilkinson. *Casting:* Donna Isaacson. *Production Designer:* Wolf Kroeger. *Art Director:* Rick Roberts. *Set Decorator:* Janice Blackie-Goodine. *Set Dresser:* Bruce Shibley. *Special Effects:* Mike Vezina. *Costumes:* Julie Weiss. *Make-up:* Christine Beveridge. *Make-up (Alec Baldwin):* Carl Fullerton. *Stunt Coordinator:* Betty Thomas. *Running time:* 120 minutes. *MPAA Rating:* R.

CAST: Anthony Hopkins (Charles Morse); Alec Baldwin (Robert Green); Elle Macpherson (Mickey Morse); Harold Perrineau (Stephen); L.Q. Jones (Styles); Kathleen Wilhoite (Ginny); David Lindstedt (James); Mark Kiely (Mechanic); Eli Gabay (Jet Pilot); Larry Musser (Amphibian Pilot); Brian Arnold, Kelsa Kinsly, and Bob Boyd (Reporters); Gordon Tootoosis (Jack Hawk).

LOS ANGELES TIMES, 9/26/97, Calendar/p. 4, Kenneth Turan

Few movie spectacles are more satisfying than great performers playing deadly rivals, than natural-born antagonists going at it fang and claw, so to speak. "The Edge" has such a rivalry going, but it's not quite what you might expect.

For though the movie is set up as conflict between Anthony Hopkins remote billionaire and Alec Baldwin's flashy fashion photographer, the battle that gives "The Edge" its power and excitement is the one between Hopkins and Bart the Bear, two consummate professionals who hold nothing back.

They don't give Oscars for best supporting bear, and Bart is probably not on the American Film Institute's short list for a life-achievement award. But his performance here, the capstone of an illustrious career, is a milestone in ursine acting. Here's hoping the guy didn't have to work for scale.

Given that "The Edge" was written by David Mamet and directed by Lee Tamahori ("Once Were Warriors," "Mulholland Falls"), no one will be expecting a remake of "Lady Windermere's Fan." But that doesn't mean that "The Edge" isn't something of a surprise.

For though Mamet's recurrent themes of rivalry and betrayal, extreme behavior and men put to the test are present, the confrontations here are more physical than verbal. What Mamet and Tamahori have come up with is a pleasantly old-fashioned man-against-nature epic that could have been written by Jack London or appeared in one of those 1950s magazines with names like Saga and Argosy. "Men at their most primeval," the cover line would likely have read, "stripped bare by the wilderness and the demons in their souls."

"The Edge" also fits neatly into the adventure-disaster, genre that is the trend of the moment, with books on killer storms off New England and big trouble on Mt. Everest high on national bestseller lists. While the film has a tendency to tilt toward the too insistently macho, Hopkins' well-grounded performance and Bart's bear-like ability straighten things out.

For his part, Mamet has come up with an effective premise of men with every reason to despise each other needing to cooperate to survive. The point of contention between them is, not surprisingly, a beautiful woman named Mickey (Elle Macpherson, naturally), the wife of one man and the favorite model of the other.

Charles Morse (Hopkins) is the husband, and if there is such a thing as the average billionaire, it's not him. Gifted with an appetite for arcane knowledge and the ability to recall it at will, he seems to know everything, even why a rabbit is calmly smoking a pipe though threatened by a predator on a piece of native Alaskan art. "The rabbit is unafraid," says Morse, "because he knows he's smarter."

Morse is in Alaska, specifically in a ramshackle lodge run by an old trail rat named Styles (Sam Peckinpah veteran L.Q. Jones), to accompany his wife on a fashion shoot run by Robert Green (Baldwin). Spending his time reading a book called "Lost in the Wild" given to him by his secretary, Morse is ill at ease, partly because that's his natural state and partly because he suspects his wife and Green are having an affair.

Almost on a whim, Green, his assistant Stephen (Harold Perrineau, the blazing Mercutio in Baz Luhrmann's "Romeo & Juliet") and Morse get into a rickety plane to search for a photogenic old hunter. The ride isn't what they expect, and soon enough they're on the ground, forced to try to walk out of the wild together if they are to stay alive.

It's at this point the rivalry between the two men is supposed to take center stage (and the film would've benefited if it had) but Baldwin's Bob Green is more of an idea for a character than a real person. A slick emotional blowhard, he creates as little interest lost in the wilderness as he did anywhere else.

Hopkins, by contrast, uses his great gift for being convincing to subtly but unmistakably change on screen as he comes to embody the masculine credo "what one man can do *another* can do." Morse's face gets more alive, his physical demeanor peps up, he blooms in the wilderness like a cold weather version of a cactus flower. It's a transformation all the more remarkable for appearing in a film so dependent on physical not psychological dynamics.

In no time at all a formidable antagonist enters the survivors' lives, a large and vicious Kodiak bear who has gotten used to feasting on humans, a habit, apparently, as tough to break as cigarettes. He trails the group as relentlessly as Natty Bumpo, and the men come to understand they may run from the beast but there is nowhere they can hide.

As photographed by veteran Donald McAlpine, edited by "Dances With Wolves" Neil Travis and directed by Tamahori (who has said, "I wanted to instill in the audience the same terror experienced by these characters"), the scenes of bear attacks are the strongest in the film, always believable and clearly energizing to Hopkins.

As for Bart, at this stage in his career, after starring in "The Bear" and "Legends of the Fall," he could have rested on his laurels, or whatever it is bears rest on. But under the training of Doug and Lynn Seus, Bart goes all out and pilfers the picture.

Compared to these bestial heroics, the rivalry between the film's two fallible men can't help but be less involving. Yet "The Edge's" fusion of Mametspeak with a true life adventure remains brawny entertainment, even if it is difficult to take as seriously as the filmmakers intend. But when Bart is on his game, nobody is going to notice anything else.

NEW YORK, 10/6/97, p. 66, David Denby

In *The Edge*, a very rich man (Anthony Hopkins), his beautiful wife, a model (Elle Macpherson), and a young fashion photographer (Alec Baldwin) who covets the beautiful model travel to Alaska for a photo shoot. After certain preliminaries, the two men get stranded in the wilderness without weapons or food, and the movie proper gets under way. Who survives and who doesn't? Who's the stronger, and why? Will the young man kill the older in order to take his woman, or will they work together for common survival? Or will they both succumb to despair and get eaten by a giant Kodiak bear (Bart the Bear)? These questions are chased up and down mountains, through piney forests, across yawning chasms, and alongside ponds, lakes, and glinting streams.

The Edge was concocted by David Mamet, but Mamet, deep in his crewcut-and-cigar mode of macho philosophizing, has done little more than tone up a *Men's Journal* fantasy of hanging tough. A certain banality comes built into the survivalist competition. The older man is an intellectual, an entrepreneur, a rugged individualist, the young man a cynic and moral weakling—he embodies the corruption and shallowness of the media. There's no doubt who's the more honorable person, but in the freezing wastes, does virtue lead to survival? The issue is fought without the slightest reference to the woman, who, we are left thinking, is not only treacherous but stupid. (She will, apparently, accept either one as the winner.)

Director Lee Tamahori makes the most of the Canadian Rockies, which double for Alaska's terrain; and Tamahori puts his two stars through a great deal of wet and cold and general misery. As a physical adventure, *The Edge* is often pictorially thrilling, and it remains to be said that the bear is just great. Huge and fierce, with a spectacularly ugly nose and mouth, it paws the ground, swipes at the air, and in general gets the director, writer, and actors out of trouble whenever the movie begins to expire in the forest. I didn't, myself, care which of the two men got Elle Macpherson. Perhaps the bear should have her. He certainly works the hardest.

NEW YORK POST, 9/26/97, p. 48, Michael Medved

For years, Sylvester Stallone has been talking about his dream of playing Edgar Allan Poe on screen—an ambition only slightly more bizarre than the notion of Sir Anthony Hopkins taking on the heroic lead role in a muscular, hyper-macho action picture about man-eating bears and other horrors of the Alaskan wilderness.

Sly must continue to wait for his chance to play the doomed Bard of Baltimore ("Yo! Raven!"), but Hopkins surely makes the most of his chance to defy audience expectations in the uneven but exhilarating "The Edge."

He plays a bookish millionaire with a super-model wife (played by Elle Macpherson in a piece of startling casting). Accompanied by hip, hot-shot photographer Alec Baldwin, his dreadlocked assistant (Harold Perrineau), and other hangers-on, they travel to a rustic lodge in the Alaskan back country for a combination fashion shoot and vacation.

While Macpherson stays behind at the inn, the men set off on a seaplane excursion, giving Hopkins the chance to confront Baldwin with suspicions about the younger man's involvement with his glamorous wife.

In the midst of this dramatic encounter, their small craft suddenly goes down, bouncing off a mountainside and plunging into a lake in perhaps the most horrifying, staggeringly well-staged plane crash ever filmed.

Hopkins, Baldwin and Perrineau all survive and must work together in order to stay alive in the wilds and attract the attention of rescuers.

The chief threat to survival is a 1,400-pound "man-killer" bear who has already developed a notorious taste for human flesh.

As played by veteran thespian Bart the Bear ("The Bear," "Grizzly Adams" on TV), with the aid of an indistinguishable animatronic stand-in, this formidable creature energizes the chilling, gory and utterly riveting man-and-beast confrontations.

Unfortunately, the man-to-man interactions are considerably less intriguing, largely because Baldwin's slippery, cynical character never quite comes into focus.

While Hopkins persuasively portrays the transition from reserved, pampered plutocrat to manly, resourceful leader, Baldwin's attitude suggests confusion rather than the ironic ambiguity that screenwriter David Mamet (yes, that David Mamet) intended.

New Zealand director Lee Tamahori (best known for his stunning debut, "Once Were Warriors") makes the most of breathtaking locations and gripping set pieces (dangling from a log over a raging waterfall, etc.), but he lets the contrived, overly tidy resolution fall flat.

Tamahori's adrenaline-pumping intensity assures that the film is always bear-able, but it does lose force and ferocity when its chief characters no longer face their formidable, furry foe.

NEWSDAY, 9/26/97, Part II/p. B11, Jack Mathews

The most indelible image on the movie screen this year appears about two-thirds of the way into Lee Tamahori's "The Edge." It is a scene where Anthony Hopkins' Charles Morse, stranded in the Alaskan wilderness, is patiently fishing with a makeshift dropline when he hears a noise behind him.

He turns his head to the left, and sees nothing, then turns to the right. As he does, the screen is suddenly filled with a Kodiak bear standing a few yards away. The Kodiak, largest of all land carnivores, is immense—9 feet tall on his hind legs, and nearly a ton in weight—and having seen him in action earlier, we know by the protruding pout on his lower lip that he means business.

In the year of the villain, amidst all the psychopaths, sociopaths, aliens, giant insects, dinosaurs, devils and demons, none is more frightening than this creature. He's played by veteran character bear Bart ("Legends of the Fall"), an animal actor who's described by co-star Alec Baldwin as a "tame old movie bear who should send the film editor a fruit basket every day for making him look so scary."

Whoever deserves credit for Bart's performance, it's a scene-stealer, and welcome relief in a film that, for all its outdoor spectacle, is an otherwise tight and occasionally tedious two-man stage play. "The Edge" was written by playwright David Mamet, and it is, for Mamet, a typical struggle between conflicting egos.

The stage is cleared for Morse and for Baldwin's fashion photographer Robert Green soon after they arrive in Alaska with Morse's trophy wife and Green's favorite model Mickey (Elle Macpherson). The two men, along with a photo assistant (Harold Perrineau) and a pilot (Larry Musser), head out the next day for a remote lake, searching for a Native American that Green wants to use in a photo spread. But the plane crashes, killing the pilot, and stranding the other three, one of whom quickly becomes bear bait.

Now it's just Morse and Green, an odd couple in Jack London country. Morse is an insecure tycoon, book-smart, filthy rich, and convinced that his wife and Green have invited him along on the trip to do away with him. But once the two men are alone against nature, they become edgy co-dependents.

At least, Green is dependent on Morse. The rich man's font of knowledge, particularly about survival, is extraordinary, and as he draws one successful technique after another from his photographic memory, he becomes the stronger man—physically, mentally, and emotionally. Whatever Green's plans are, they're moot, at least until they return to civilization.

Hopkins and Baldwin are operating on reverse arcs. Morse is a character developing power as he goes, while Green is growing increasingly weak. Morse is obviously the more interesting character, and with any other set of actors, he would dominate our attention. But with Hopkins in the role, giving Morse a steady balance of intellect and control, Baldwin nearly fades into the snow-clad landscape.

There are excesses in the film. The older, and admittedly sedentary Morse is given a physical stamina that violates the laws of biology and Gold's Gym. He runs for miles without becoming short-winded, and when he finally stands his ground against the stalking bear, you know the animal is in trouble. Nonetheless, Hopkins invests Morse with so much character detail, you overlook the hyperbole in his actions.

Ultimately, film is the art of illusion, and Tamahori ("Once Were Warriors") has whipped up some gems, chiefly the crash of the plane, and the multiple encounters with the bear. Somewhere in the film's credits is mention of a human bear double, suggesting that we are occasionally being scared out of our skins by a man in a bear suit.

It doesn't matter. The illusions are perfectly realistic, and Bart the bear—man or beast—is worth his weight in serial killers.

SIGHT AND SOUND, 2/98, p. 41, Geoffrey Macnab

Charles Morse, a billionaire, accompanies his beautiful young wife, fashion model Mickey, to Alaska where she is due to take part in a fashion shoot. They stay in a remote cabin with photographer Robert Green and his crew. Robert invites Charles to join him on a short plane trip across the lakes in search of an old Native American hunter, but he's not at home. They take off again, but their plane crashes after low-flying geese smash the windscreen. The pilot dies. The three survivors—Charles, Robert, and Robert's assistant Stephen—are stranded. Realising that they have little chance of being found in the wilderness, they resolve to walk back to civilisation. Stephen is mauled and eventually killed by a man-eating bear which then begins to track Robert and Charles.

Charles hatches a plan to kill the bear. Miraculously, they succeed. Many days later, Robert and Charles find a cabin on the edge of the woods. Charles finds a receipt for a watch that reveals that Robert was having an affair with his wife. Robert threatens to kill Charles, but before he is able to do so, falls into a bear-pit, injuring his leg horribly. Charles rescues him and, finding a canoe, takes him downriver. A helicopter appears, and Charles attracts its attention, but by now Robert is dead. Charles arrives back at the cabin. He pushes through the huge awaiting pack of journalists and presents his wife with Robert's watch. She realises he knows about her affair.

David Mamet is an urban writer *par excellence*. His characters, whether swindlers, con artists, estate agents, or university professors, tend to be savvy and sardonic. They speak in that clipped vernacular which is his trademark. His classic play *Glengarry Glen Ross* may sound like a Highland epic, but it's about selling real estate. Even his most recent film, *The Spanish Prisoner*, is set in the duplicitous, big-city business world. He is just about the last writer you would expect to turn out an action-adventure about two men adrift in the great American wilderness.

The Edge, directed by Lee Tamahori *(Once Were Warriors, Mulholland Falls)* from Mamet's script, isn't quite as radical a departure for Mamet as it first seems. On one level, the rugged, *National Geographic*-style mountains, lakes, forests and big blue skies (all marvelously shot by Donald M. McAlpine) are merely window dressing. What matters more are the dynamics of the relationship between Charles, a billionaire with a beautiful wife 20 years younger than himself, and Robert, a cocksure fashion photographer. One man covets the other's wife and wealth, perhaps even wants to kill him, but in the wilderness, both are dependent on each other for survival. You can almost hear Mamet chuckling as he deposits Charles and Robert in the middle of nowhere and takes away every crutch that civilisation offers them.

Tamahori goes out of his way to make the characters' plight credible. Charles and Robert are resourceful and intelligent, but they are not action-heroes. They improvise compasses, build fires, even—somewhat improbably—design themselves bear-skin outfits. Their survival is a matter of common sense. In addition, *The Edge* boasts awesome effects, notably in the scene in which their little plane plummets down into a frozen lake after its windscreen is smashed by geese. The man-eating bear, which comes sniffing after Charles, Robert and their hapless colleague Stephen, is not one of those latex-and-fur creations that pop up in low budget horror movies, but a huge, terrifying predator.

On one level, this is a typical boys' own adventure and obeys the generic rules. The moment we see Charles reading an old book called *Lost in the Wild,* we know that the title will prove prophetic. Before he loses the book, he learns one key axiom: people who perish in the wilderness really "die of shame", so full of regret about their blunder, they despair instead of thinking ahead. Sustaining interest in a story about two men adrift in Alaska poses Tamahori a considerable formal challenge. As they clamber up the next icy mountain or repel yet another bear attack, the repetition threatens to become numbing.

But the real strength of the film lies less in its formulaic plotting than in its attention to character. The attritional relationship between Hopkins and Baldwin rekindles memories of Roger Donaldson's underrated *The Bounty*, in which Hopkins' Captain Bligh was pitted against Mel Gibson's Fletcher Christian. Again, there is a very obvious Oedipal subtext and the conflict between the characters is underlined by the casting—the British actor takes on the American star. Hopkins is bookish and withdrawn; Baldwin arrogant and loud.

Charles' isolation is understandable: everybody wants something from the billionaire. Even the rugged, seemingly honest cabin owner Styles can't resist turning a friendly conversation into a pitch for money.

Mamet plays with the conventions of the buddy movie. On one level, this is yet another tale about city slickers who rediscover their masculinity by traipsing round the wilds. There is plenty of male bonding. (If you've killed a bear together, sat by the same fire and suffered the same privations, you're friends for life.) But the usual clichés are turned on their head. There is an edge between the characters, a hint of barely suppressed enmity about their relationship. They're like rugged, National Park counterparts to Vladimir and Estragon—two clowns condemned to each others' company.

Mamet shrouds the key moments of the film in ambiguity. In the early scenes, when Charles is watching helplessly from the sidelines as the younger man flirts with his wife, we realise that for all his wealth and power, he is an emasculated figure. "You're an angel ... everything except the wings," his wife tells him, but as events later prove, this is a very barbed compliment. When the fashion photographer confronts him with a gun, it is never quite apparent whether he intends to pull the trigger. Even the seemingly conventional ending is laced with irony. On the surface, Charles has learned the usual life-affirming lessons about loyalty, friendship and human endurance. But when he comes back to civilisation, he knows more than ever that he can't trust anybody.

TIME, 9/29/97, p. 100, Richard Corliss

Charles (Anthony Hopkins) is rich beyond the dreams of greed—his dreams, anyway. Other people may have other ideas. Take Robert (Alec Baldwin), a fashion photographer who seems way too chummy with Charles' supermodel wife (Elle Macpherson). On a photo shoot in the Great White North, the two men—Robert with strength and youth, Charles with loads of book learning—fly off in a small plane to an even remoter location. "So," Charles asks Robert, "how are you planning to kill me off?" Seconds later, the plane crashes.

The Edge, from a screenplay by David Mamet ... Oh, excuse us while we ask, "Huh?" The *Übermensch* of Urban Menace with a wilderness script? Mr. American Buffalo out where the, well, elk roam? Yes, and this is genuine Mametiana: a two-character piece with threats crowding in from the elements (vast space, cold weather, an angry bear) and from a man's bitter, murky soul. It doesn't have much of the Mamet dialogue tang; that is on dazzling display in his forthcoming thriller, *The Spanish Prisoner.* Still, *The Edge,* directed by Lee Tamahori, offers enough of what a melodrama demands: two strong characters in mutual creative distrust.

In a small role Macpherson is a mere cartoon character (her name in the film: Mickey Morse). But Bart the grizzly, who starred in 1989's *The Bear,* deserves a Best Supporting Animal award for his ferocious work. Baldwin is persuasive in his familiar persona, the cagey sleazebag. And as the polymath plutocrat, Hopkins manages to make erudition sexy; a library intelligence and a steely intellect make him Baldmin's ideal adversary. *The Edge* merits a modest cheer as an action film that celebrates not brute force but survival of the smartest.

VILLAGE VOICE, 9/30/97, p. 84, Gary Dauphin

For his third picture, New Zealander Lee Tamahori *(Once Were Warriors)* teams up with David Mamet for an Alaskan man-versus-everything epic. *The Edge* is a coldly beautiful and resolutely low-tech action film that dumps three men in the stark, frozen wildness and asks them to contend not only with the usual inner and outer obstacles (the elements, a man-hungry Kodiak bear, and themselves), but with weirdly abstract, patently Mametesque guy stuff. As if snow and animals weren't enough, *The Edge* has paranoia about cheating wives, intimations and accusations of gayness, and more importantly, all kinds of shame that you might be the wrong man at the wrong time.

Our trio consists of a bookish billionaire (Anthony Hopkins), a cynical fashion photographer (Alec Baldwin), and a black guy (Harold Perrineau, playing walking bear bait). They've come to Alaska to shoot the billionaire's model-wife (Elle Macpherson) against glacial backdrops, and they're trapped far from the lodge after the photo leads them on an ill-advised search for an "authentic" Native American extra. Hopkins's distracted rich man suspects that Baldwin's smarmy lensman is not only fucking his wife but actually wants him dead, but Hopkins becomes the party's would-be-savior anyway. Besides being a captain of industry, he's a voracious reader of frontier lore. They're barely out of their plane's wreckage before he's built a compass out of a leaf and a paper clip.

The Edge has already been linked to *Deliverance,* but it has more in common with *Scream.* Hopkins is up to the task of survival because, much like kids who know you need to watch horror films to combat knife-wielding maniacs, he's indulged in the appropriate fictions and therefore knows the rules. Mamet's dialogue (which benefits enormously from Tamahori's hyper-macho handling) attributes Hopkins's durability to a lack of imagination, but that's a tease, as *The Edge* is really about testing different kinds of imagination. It's pretty easy to pick the survivor among men with their heads in books, men snorting coke off models' hips, and black men, but credit Tamahori and Mamet for making something so predictable and schematic work as well as it does.

Also reviewed in:
CHICAGO TRIBUNE, 9/26/97, Friday/p. A, Michael Wilmington
NEW REPUBLIC, 10/27/97, p. 26, Stanley Kauffmann
NEW YORK TIMES, 9/26/97, p. E10, Janet Maslin
VARIETY, 9/8-14/97, p. 75, Todd McCarthy
WASHINGTON POST, 9/26/97, p. C7, Rita Kempley
WASHINGTON POST, 9/26/97, Weekend/p. 49, Desson Howe

8 HEADS IN A DUFFEL BAG

An Orion Pictures release in association with Rank Film Distributors of a Brad Krevoy & Steve Stabler production. *Executive Producer:* Jeffrey D. Ivers. *Producer:* Brad Krevoy, Steve Stabler, and John Bertolli. *Director:* Tom Schulman. *Screenplay:* Tom Schulman. *Director of Photography:* Adam Holender. *Editor:* David Holden. *Music:* Andrew Gross. *Music Editor:* Lee Scott. *Sound:* Ed White and (music) John Kurlander. *Sound Editor:* Mike Wilhoit. *Casting:* Janet Hirshenson. *Production Designer:* Paul Peters. *Art Director:* Tomas P. Wilkins. *Set Designer:* Scott Herbertson and Cleone Balsam. *Set Decorator:* Amy Wells. *Set Dresser:* Josh Ian Elliott. *Special Effects:* Lou Carlucci. *Costumes:* Sanja Milkovic Hays. *Make-up:* June Brickman. *Make-up (Special Effects):* Greg Cannom. *Stunt Coordinator:* Rawn Hutchinson. *Running time:* 90 minutes. *MPAA Rating:* R.

CAST: Joe Pesci (Tommy Spinelli); Andy Comeau (Charlie); Kristy Swanson (Laurie Bennett); Todd Louiso (Steve); George Hamilton (Dick Bennett); Dyan Cannon (Annette Bennett); David Spade (Ernie); Anthony Mangano (Rico); Joe Basile (Benny); Ernestine Mercer (Fern); Frank Roman (Paco); Howard George (Big Sep); Tom Platz (Hugo); Endre Hules (Marty); Calvin Levels (Jamal); John Zurlo (Little Joey); Roger Cobra (Frank); Jeff Sanders (Isaiah); Ric Sarabia (Benito); Tony Montero (So-So Stu); Michael Groh (Bad Frank); Wendy Clifford (Woman with Baby); Matthew Fonda (Organ Carrier); Michael Nickles (Juan the Bandito); Suzanne Krull (Woman at Phone); Miguel Perez (Customs Inspector); John Webber (Airline Ticket Agent); Eduardo Ricard (Hotel Doctor); Sally Colon (Maid #1); Irene Olga Lopez (Maid #2); Charles Martiniz (Airport Security Guard); Glenn Taranto (Mr. Escobedo); Bart Braverman (Rental Dealer); Philip Suriano (Gangster); Ellis E. Williams (Newark Porter); Horacio LeDon (Airport Customs Inspector); Joe Xavier Rodriguez (La Purisima Police Officer); Darius Anderson (Mexican Man).

LOS ANGELES TIMES, 4/18/97, Calendar/p. 2, Kevin Thomas

Tom Schulman's "Eight Heads in a Duffel Bag" is consistently inventive without being consistently funny and comes up with about half as many laughs as it works so hard to get. While there are a number of funny moments, "Eight Heads" suggests just how difficult it can be to create and sustain an all-out farce.

In his directorial debut, writer Schulman brings to the film a curiously varied background: an Oscar-winning script for "Dead Poets Society" and the screenplays for "What About Bob?," "Honey, I Shrunk the Kids" and "Medicine Man." What's more, he has at his disposal a large and effective cast. But his experience and a lot of talent in front of the camera don't add up to a thigh-slapper.

Having virtually repeated his "GoodFellas" role in "Casino," Joe Pesci seems to be parodying the not-too-smart, hot-tempered and ruthless gangster that he maybe should be giving a rest. In any event, he's Tommy Spinelli, who must fly from the East Coast to San Diego with a duffel bag full of eight heads as proof to "the big guy" that he fulfilled his contract as a hit man.

Naturally, his black bag gets mixed up with that of Andy Comeau's nice guy Charlie, who's to meet his girlfriend Laurie (Kristy Swanson) and her parents (George Hamilton and Dyan Cannon) and head for a vacation at a posh Baja resort. Poor Charlie; not only does he wind up with eight dead heads south of the border but also with, the news that Laurie wants to break off with him. (This, of course, sets him up to rise to the occasion and emerge a hero.)

In his film debut, Comeau comes across likably, and Hamilton, as a stuffed shirt, and Cannon, as a brand-new teetotaler, know all the right moves and are a pure pleasure.

Threatening to steal the picture, however, are David Spade and Todd Louiso as Charlie's hapless fraternity brothers, tracked down by Tommy, who's prepared to kill them if they fail to figure out where Charlie has gone in Mexico. Spade is very funny as a guy who can't resist a retort even in the most negative circumstances, and Louiso may be even funnier as a young man who can't relinquish his concern for ethics even in the most absurd predicaments.

Keith Vanderlaan of Cannom Creations devised some admirably realistic heads, and Schulman was resourceful in his use of Southern California locales to stand in for Mexico. It was probably just as well "Eight Heads" wasn't filmed in Mexico because Schulman indulges, although good-naturedly, in some Latino stereotypes that will not amuse everyone.

NEW STATESMAN, 11/28/97, p. 45, John Diamond

Just think of the number of reasonable scripts the Hollywood studios must turn down each year in order to make films as infuriatingly bad as this, and weep. Yes, I know: each week brings any number of bad films, films made by producers who understand that x million people will always stump up y million dollars to see Dolph Lundgren lose his shirt, but that is a sort of honest badness. *Eight Heads in a Duffle Bag,* on the other hand, is trying so hard to be a good film, and probably thinks it is, that it counts as dishonest badness and thus worthy of your tears. Or mine, anyway.

I imagine *EHIADB* must have looked a killer when stuffed into its original one-page synopsis (although the title *is* the one page synopsis, give or take) and before it became apparent that the director was no more up to the job than the writer. In fact these malefactors are one and the same: Tom Schulman, who wrote *Dead Poets Society* but has never been allowed to direct before.

His story concerns a Mafia man (Joe Pesci) charged with taking to his boss on the west coast the proof of eight rivals getting whacked. The duffle bag full of heads is—guess what—identical to the duffle bag full of clothes owned by the schlemiel of a medical student (Andy Comeau, doing an American Hugh Grant for all he's worth) who is off to be introduced to his girlfriend's parents in Mexico. Comeau is seated on the plane next to the Mafia man. Got it? OK, you have five minutes to go away and come back with the rest of the synopsis.

Two minutes! That *was* quick. Did you get the bit in about the run-in with the Mexican police? About the *I Love Lucy* set-ups between putative in-laws? The car chase with the mobsters? Well, of course you did.

And at the end, have you written that this is a comedy in the vein of *It's a Mad Mad Mad Mad World*? No, of course you haven't, because you know that that film was put together by somebody who understood the mechanics of farce, not to say the mechanics of a movie camera, while this one has been put together by a man who thinks that a change of scene is what you have when the previous one has run out of puff. Schulman, by the way, compares his work to *It's a Mad Mad Mad Mad World*? If only films could sue for libel.

The deal with any farce is that large chunks of plot have little more than an entirely mechanical function—to get the maid into the wardrobe, the boyfriend under the bed and, if you insist, the duffle bag into the wrong storage bin on the aeroplane. A good *farceur* will mask the mechanics with diverting dialogue, but there are long periods in this film where *everything* serves that same uncamouflaged mechanical function, where you sit there waiting for each element to be dragged on—the dog, the Mexican waiter, the dypso wife—so that they can all just get on with whatever they've come on for and we can move on to the next tortuous set-up.

And I mean tortuous. Throughout the film you can see, as though they were painted on the screen, the points where Schulman said to himself the like of "Heck! We need some way of losing a head and then finding it again but not being able to fit it in the bag. I know! How about suddenly and for no apparent reason the medical student has to take a present back to the US which happens to be precisely the same size as.. . "

Worse is the soppy obeisance to Hollywood morality. In order for the denouement, such as it is, to work, the Pesci character mustn't be a murderer himself, merely a courier of the results of other people's murders. You have no idea how long it can take to draw such a fine moral line on screen. Or, come to that, why the same morality requires Pesci to get spare heads from the already dead at a cryogenic research lab rather than plucking fresh heads himself—even though he seems quite willing to shoot an extra couple of innocent parties.

Worst of all, Schulman has never learnt the single most important rule which every constructor of a tight plot understands, which is that you're only allowed one impossible plot twist or coincidence to go unremarked. In *EHIADB* we have to believe that Charlie's first response on discovering he has somebody else's bag and that it's full of heads is not to go to the police. OK, I'll buy that. But I won't accept that, as character after character makes the same discovery, they all have the same response.

Is there a single redeeming feature? Well, perhaps just the one: in an age where every film is an epic, *EHIADB* lasts for just 95 minutes. And remember, moviegoers, that means that if you want to leave angrily halfway through, you need to be out after 47½ minutes exactly.

NEW YORK POST, 4/18/97, p. 45, Michael Medved

Eight heads are not necessarily better than one—especially when the one head that's missing is the organizing vision of a capable comedy director. Screenwriter Tom Schulman ("Dead Poets Society," "What About Bob?") provides a potentially amusing script but stumbles badly in handling his own material in his directorial debut.

Stumbles is the right word here, because it's the inept slapstick in "8 Heads in a Duffel Bag" that ultimately decapitates the picture.

Schulman's endlessly repeated scenes of various characters screaming or fainting when they see severed human heads are embarrassing rather than funny, and fall to the floor with their own exaggerated thud.

In this context, the cast deserves credit for its energy and professionalism—especially Joe Pesci in an effectively (and uncharacteristicly) understated role as a veteran hit man.

He draws the assignment of transporting eight heads of murdered mobsters from New Jersey to California to prove that his associates have successfully fulfilled the terms of a contract.

On the flight west, however, the duffel bag containing this precious cargo gets switched with the luggage of a mild mannered medical student (likable newcomer Andy Comeau) who's spending spring break with his girlfriend (Kristy Swanson) and her parents.

Those parents (George Hamilton and Dyan Cannon) take the kids to a resort hotel in Mexico where Comeau discovers the grisly contents of the bag he has unwittingly picked up.

The frenetic and tedious schtick that follows involves insultingly stereotypical Mexican bellmen, bandits, maids, police officers and even a snapping little dog.

Dyan Cannon, still looking improbably fresh and sexy, struggles with a thankless role as a recovering alcoholic and pill popper whose encounter with the gory heads drives her back—wouldn't you know it—to her supposedly comic addictions.

The movie picks up a bit when Pesci finally follows his bag to Mexico after kidnapping two of Comeau's fellow med students (Todd Louiso and the amusingly droll David Spade).

For a while the confusions, complications and chase scenes begin to echo the cross-cutting, character-driven chaos of "It's a Mad, Mad, Mad, Mad World"—one of Schulman's obvious inspirations for the film.

There's even a fanciful dream sequence where the eight heads—grotesque in the childish traditions of Halloween rather than convincingly gruesome—croon "Mr. Hit Man" to the tune of "Mr. Sand Man."

These touches, however, arrive too late to save the project—especially after all those lame puns, including even the archaic use of "head shrinker" as slang for psychiatrist.

In several scenes, Schulman even tries to get laughs by dressing his Everyman protagonist (Comeau) in the same vomit-splattered shirt. No wonder the whole movie begins to smell stale.

NEWSDAY, 4/18/97, Part II/p. B2, John Anderson

So here's da deal. The unsavory Tommy Spinelli (Joe Pesci) has to drag a duffel bag full of heads from New York to California, from one mobster to another, so the first one can verify to the second that he fulfilled the contract on the eight guys whose beans are in the bag.

On the plane to San Diego, while acting like a moke, Tommy runs into this nice guy, Charlie (Andy Comeau), who has a similar looking bag. Ba-da-bing, ba-da-boom. The bags get switched.

Tommy, as they say, is not happy. Charlie's holiday in Mexico is not, as they say, going to go well. Gimme, as they say, a break.

"8 Heads in a Duffel Bag" is the kind of movie that makes you say "wha?" A very long, very predictable, occasionally disgusting and not so funny situation comedy (although the heads themselves do a very nice riff on "Mr. Sandman"), it is about hiding the heads, people screaming over the heads, the heads getting lost, the heads getting ripe. The plot getting riper.

The live heads are all very familiar. Kristy Swanson, of the original, immortal "Buffy the Vampire Slayer," is Laurie Bennett, whose stuffed-shirt father (George Hamilton) and not-quite-recovering alcoholic mother (Dyan Cannon) aren't at all pleased with Charlie's inclusion on their Mexican vacation. Chris Farley's habitual sidekick, David Spade, is Ernie, one of Charlie's fellow medical students, who's back home being tortured by Tommy for information on Charlie's whereabouts. Todd Louiso ("Jerry Maguire") is the other pal, Steve, who eventually loses his mind over the entire head situation. We sympathize.

Comeau is cloyingly wholesome, and Pesci, for whom this film was apparently written, seems intent on reprising his "Goodfellas" role, minus the charm. And what Pesci does for Italians, the rest of the movie does for Mexico and Mexicans. The hotel staffers are fawning idiots, the car dealers are thieves, the thieves are would-be rapists. Asked by Laurie to turn the heads over to the authorities in this "Third World country," Charlie declines ("they have no laws here"). More scandalously, when Laurie suggests he ship the heads back to Tommy, Charlie claims there's no Fed Ex service in Mexico. Which of course there is (a nice woman at the 800 number confirmed this).

A large amount of film time is spent with Tommy trying to substitute look-alike heads for the ones he's lost, in the cryogenics lab at Ernie and Steve's med school, and then again in the morgue, providing the kind of scene pregnant with teenage male humor. But if he's already taken the frozen heads, why does he need more? And if he has these heads, why does he then have to chase Charlie down to Mexico, to get the original eight heads back? Is he trying to cast an all-head version of "A Chorus Line"? First-time director Tom Schulman should have remembered what Kipling said about keeping your head when all about you are losing theirs.

SIGHT AND SOUND, 12/97, p. 42, Xan Brooks

Newark, New Jersey. Mobster Tommy Spinelli meets with men Rico and Benny to collect a cargo of eight severed heads to deliver to his boss, Big Sep, on the West Coast. But en route, Tommy's luggage becomes mixed up with bags belonging to Charlie, a young medical student on his way to a Mexican holiday with his girlfriend Laurie where he hopes to impress her parents Dick and Annette.

Determined to locate his luggage, Tommy visits Charlie's college and tortures his nerdy roommates Ernie and Steve. Tommy steals some replacement heads from a college lab. Meanwhile, Charlie and Laurie discover the heads and struggle desperately to conceal them from Dick, Annette and the Mexican authorities. Two are discovered in Dick's travel-bag and he is arrested. Tommy (with Ernie and Steve in tow) arrives in Mexico to pursue Charlie. But now he too is being chased by Rico and Benny, whom Big Sep suspects of not completing the hits.

Charlie and Tommy join forces. Tommy plants the new heads in Rico and Benny's luggage and the pair are arrested at the airport. In the ensuing chaos, Tommy makes his escape back to California with the real heads safely back in his duffel bag. Some time later, Charlie and Laurie are married.

In *A Biographical Dictionary of Film*, the critic David Thomson compares Joe Pesci to 40s star Walter Brennan, observing that each has two ways of acting: "with teeth or without". For the record, then, *8 Heads in a Duffel Bag* is one of the defanged performances.

The Pesci career is a strange and schizophrenic thing. Unlike other stars, he has forged his reputation as a support player, creating memorably chilling portraits of low-lifes, psychos and hoodlums in such films as *JFK*, *GoodFellas* and *Casino*. Yet shift Pesci to the top of the bill and his high-voltage malevolence usually becomes a comic *schtick*, a neutered parody of his screen image in the more high-profile films. (*The Public Eye* in which he played a photographer loosely based on the historical figure of Weegee is the exception.) *My Cousin Vinny*, *The Super* and now *8 Heads in a Duffel Bag* all play Pesci's trademark mania for laughs. When the famous "are you talking to me?" routine from *Taxi Driver* is pastiched in *8 Heads*, it inadvertently underscores the gulf between Pesci's Scorsese work and his comic lead parts.

In this frantic comedy debut from director Tom Schulman, Pesci's familiarity becomes comforting, his frustrated rage endearing. Mob-employee Tommy's delivery of the heads is, we are told, his last job before retirement. For all his colourful threats he makes it through the film without killing anyone. (Even someone he shoves from a speeding jeep shows up alive and well in the end-credit sequence.) This makes *8 Heads* an engaging if thematically garbled hodgepodge. It's partly a bright, poppy diversion which takes aim at a roster of cartoony stereotypes (nerdy students, aspirational parents, crotchety old women). However its depiction of Mexico, spilling over with dodgy food and leering banditos, is worryingly xenophobic. Charlie explains away his girlfriend's shrieking reaction to the dismembered heads by telling hotel staff she's just eaten a Mexican pepper, and conceals his discovery from the authorities because "you don't just call the police in a third-world country. They have no laws here. They'll turn me into a taco." From Welles' *Touch of Evil* (1958) onwards, Mexico has traditionally represented the badlands of the US' collective imagination. Here, however, the portrait is glibly drawn and borders on racism.

On the plus side, there's something pleasingly dark and absurd about Schulman's film. The severed heads become a multiple McGuffin within the narrative, wreaking havoc wherever they pop up. But then Schulman lets the absurdity get just a little too out of hand, making the movie's most ambitious sequence also one of its weakest, in which Tommy is haunted by the eight, suddenly animated heads breaking into a barber-shop rendition of "Mr Headman" (to the tune of "Mr. Sandman"). Arriving out of nowhere, it's a scene that tips the balance too far, exposing an over-excited immaturity in Schulman's style that is his and the film's own undoing.

What we're left with, then, is a sporadically engaging comedy, a slipstream of Christmas cracker-style jokes ("what a headcase!"), and a day-glo pastiche of the gangster-movie terrain sustained by nimble-footed performances. David Spade and Todd Louiso contribute neat comic turns as the hapless college kids, while George Hamilton proves marvellously toxic as Laurie's rich and reptilian dad. However, everyone plays second fiddle to the bustling, bristling, permanently manic Pesci, who buzzes through the narrative like a baleful mosquito. Admittedly, Pesci in this mode doesn't sting, or bite, or even swear much, but there's still some residual energy about the man which makes him always worth watching. Even in these reduced circumstances he looms above the rest of Schulman's film, "the sleaze-bag-you-love-to-hate" as Thomson describes him.

VILLAGE VOICE, 4/22/97, p. 82, Gary Dauphin

Eight Heads in a Duffel Bag is almost as anachronistic as *Gamera*, a comedy like they don't make anymore, or at least added proof of why they don't make them. The retro vibe that creeps through *Eight Heads* might have to do with the presence of George Hamilton and Dyan Cannon, or maybe the studied, early Tom Hanks look of newcomer and star Andy Comeau. In any case this film isn't exactly an argument for a return to light slapstick.

The eight heads of the title belong to a recently rubbed-out mob family, the duffel bag the tool of the trade of bagman Tommy Spinelli (Joe Pesci). Tommy has "gots to gets da heads to San Diego in three days" but accidently switches bags with hapless college student Charlie (Comeau), who is on his way to Mexico to meet his girlfriend's folks (Cannon and Hamilton) for the first time. The comic implications of this little switcheroo are pretty obvious from the get-go, but that doesn't mean first-time writer-director Tom Schuman had to play them that way. Charlie's future mother-in-law discovers the heads and falls off the wagon. His father-in-law gets caught with two of the heads and ends up tortured by the Mexican police, confessing to murder back home, Charlie's college roommates (David Spade and Todd Louiso) are themselves being tortured by Tommy in the films funniest bits, being slapped with wet towels and noogied in a near-perfect frat-boy parody.

Pesci is as good at playing the likable but murderous nut as you'd expect, but even his ease can't hide the fact that *Eight Heads* is a phoned-in, haphazard trifle, unsure of whether its main instinct is meanness or schmaltz. In the end meanness wins out. Besides everything else *Eight Heads* is also one of the more offensive collections of stereotypes about "Mexico—the Great Banana Republic to the South" that I've seen in some time. Since bad movies are made all the time, the question isn't what everyone was thinking during production, but who exactly they figured would be laughing.

Also reviewed in:
NEW YORK TIMES, 4/18/97, p. C10, Janet Maslin
VARIETY, 4/21-27/97, p. 59, Leonard Klady

EIGHTH DAY, THE

A Gramercy Pictures release of a Pan-Européenne Production/Homemade Films/T.F.1. Films Production/RTL-TVI Working Title/D.A. Films Made with the support of Eurimages with the participation of Centre National de la Cinématographie produced with the help of Centre du Cinéma et de l'Audiovisuel de la Communauté Française de Belgique with the patication of Canal+. *Executive Producer:* Eric Rommeluere and Dominique Josset. *Producer:* Philippe Godeau. *Director:* Jaco Van Dormael. *Screenplay (French with English subtitles):* Jaco Van Dormael. *Director of Photography:* Walther Vanden. *Editor:* Susana Rossberg. *Music:* Pierre Van Dormael. *Sound:* Dominique Warnier and Franciois Groult. *Sound Editor:* Philippe Bourgueil. *Art Director:* Hubert Pouille. *Set Decorator:* André Fonsny. *Costumes:* Yan Tax. *Make-up:* Kaatje Van Damme and Cédric Gérard. *Running time:* 114 minutes. *MPAA Rating:* Not Rated.

CAST: Daniel Auteuil (Harry); Pascal Duquenne (Georges); Miou-Miou (Julie); Isabelle Sadoyan (Georges' Mother); Henri Garcin (Company Director); Michele Maes (Nathalie); Laszlo Harmati (Luis Mariano); Helene Roussel (Julie's Mother); Fabienne Loriaux (George's Sister); Didier De Neck (George's Brother-In-Law); Alice Van Dormael (Alice); Juliet Van Dormael (Juliette); Marie-Pierre Meinzel (Saleswoman); Sabrina Leurquin (Waitress); Kim Chi N'Guyen (Mongol Baby); Stéphane Keyser ('Dentofresh' Guy); Roland Depauw (TV Chef); Séréna Ruspoli (Wife); Joe de Backer (Husband); Nathalie Poniot (Spanish Woman); Dieudonné Kabongo, Lotfi Yahia Jedidi, and Patrick Harcq (Dustmen); André Simon (Tramp); Monique Fluzin (Nathalie's Mother); Jean Bollery (Nathalie's Father); Jean-Henri Compère (Teacher); Dominic Gould (Harry's Colleague); Josse de Pauw (Policeman); Alexandre von Sivers (Doctor); Jean Luc Piraux (Pedestrian); Christian Hecq (Shoe Shop Manager); Ebrahim Salem (Hindu); Rémy Julienne (Truck Driver); Pierre Godeau (Georges' Nephew); Marie Godeau (Georges' Niece); Erik de Staercke (Waitress); Pauline Zerla (Little Girl); Olivier Gourmet (Father); Hélène Roussel (Julie's Mother); Laurette Vankeerberghen (Cleaner); Tam Yo (Japanese Pianist); Didier Ferney and Marc Schreiper (Showroom Salesmen); Yves Degen (Showroom Manager); Georges Siatidis (Showroom Security Guard); Raymond Lescot ("Big Vegetable"); Sophie de Kerkhove (Dancing Girl); Bernard Eylenbosch (Dancing Man); Yasmine Van Hevel (Showgirl); Gérard Hernandez, Patricia Houyoux, and Jacqueline Ghaye (Voices).

LOS ANGELES TIMES, 3/7/97, Calendar/p. 16, Kevin Thomas

"The Eighth Day" is a daring film even for so venturesome a filmmaker as Belgium's Jaco van Dormael, whose 1991 ... "Toto le Héros" was such a brilliantly original exploration of fate and identity. What's daring is not so much its teaming of major French star Daniel Auteuil and Pascal Duquenne, who in real life has Down's syndrome, but how close it comes to being like a Hollywood buddy movie only to pull back for a stunning pull-the-rug-out-from-under-you climax.

Duquenne's uninhibited, irrepressible Georges, longing for his mother who so loved him, escapes a rural institution and crosses paths with Auteuil's Harry, a genius at teaching salesmanship but such a disaster at marriage that his estranged wife (Miou-Miou) has forbidden him to see his young daughters after he misses connecting with them at a train station. When Harry gives Georges a lift on a country road, he's as starved for love and affection as Georges is.

Van Dormael finds much humor in Georges' antics, often understandably infuriating to uptight Harry, but ever so gradually, without our noticing it, the tone of "The Eighth Day" becomes more serious as the friendship between Harry and Georges deepens. In form, the film may sound conventional, sentimental even, but it evolves into something quite extraordinary and also unsettling, far more so than either "Rain Man" or "Forrest Gump."

The more the film progresses the more Georges affects Harry and the more they seem fundamentally alike in their longings. By the same token, we become increasingly persuaded that Van Dormael is not merely manipulating our emotions—an easy enough feat in regard to Georges—but has a larger purpose in mind.

There's always the possibility that, despite his wife's adamant stand, Harry will win his family back. But how will Georges ever be able to know the love and independence he so craves? Georges is so sweet-natured and affectionate he can't fail to touch you, but you have to ask yourself if you would be prepared to care for him. How many people are there out there who would really be ready to nurture him as his mother did?

It's not so much that Georges is different as that he's such a big responsibility. Yet if no one does step forward, how can he feel he has any place in society? As before, Van Dormael poses hard questions. Yet as admirable and engrossing as this film is, it is not quite on the level of "Toto le Héros," principally because of an epilogue that softens its climax and redundantly illustrates how Georges has transformed Harry's life. Van Dormael also inspires the kind of performances that receive Oscars. Auteuil has long been established in the French cinema as an actor of seemingly limitless range, depth and passion, qualities that characterize his portrayal of Harry. Yet Duquenne, who has appeared on stage for more than a decade and was in "Toto le Héros," is every bit as accomplished as a man with a spirit that soars but who is tethered by cruel realities that he is only too aware of.

"The Eighth Day" is the kind of picture you'd hate to miss but would probably find too harrowing to sit through a second time.

NEW YORK POST, 3/7/97, p. 46, Thelma Adams

Georges and Harry are no Jules and Jim. With "The Eighth Day," director Jaco Van Dormael single-handedly proves that French-language cinema can be as saccharine and sentimental as any Hollywood big-budget heart-tugger.

John Travolta would be the perfect Harry. Instead, brilliant, broody Daniel Auteuil plays the upwardly mobile salesman who his lost his smile. When Harry looks in the mirror, his reflection is as vacant is a vampire's. Harry's wife (the cryptic Miou-Miou) has taken their two daughters and left the workaholic for the worst reason imaginable: no reason at all.

One day, driving from his beach house to his townhouse in a rainstorm (why is it always raining?), Harry lets go of the wheel. He almost hits Georges (Pascal Duquenne). The self-described "Mongol" has escaped from the institution where he lives with a community of Down's syndrome adults. With suitcase in hand, Georges is just embarking on the road Harry is so eager to leave.

Like "Rain Man," "Forrest Gump," "Being There" and "Sling Blade," it's the childlike other, the abnormal one, who guides the normal adult back to his inner child and a healthy relationship with the real world. Arrrgghh! If there's one kind of movie that tortures me the most, this is it. I find idiot savants more irritating than hookers with golden hearts.

Belgian Van Dormael, working from his own script, tells his story with a heaping spoonful of visual whimsy wedged between misty moments. When he is happy, Georges has recurring visions of colorful crooner Luis Mariano in Mexican drag; while Harry sleeps, a singing mouse and a pair of dancing trousers entertain Georges until his mother visits him from heaven to remind her son that he is "the kindest person in the world."

Georges and Harry hug trees, listen to grass hum, follow the flight of a ladybug and walk not so miraculously on water. Auteuil ("Les Voleur") and Duquenne (who also starred in Van Dormael's "Toto the Hero") chew the material like ants demolish sugar: in baffling amounts well over their body weight.

The two jointly won the best actor award a year ago at Cannes. It's the kind of soft-hearted gesture we've come to expect from the Oscar folks; now, the French can't blame Americans for all cinematic bad taste.

NEWSDAY, 3/7/97, Part II/p. B13, John Anderson

Harry (Daniel Auteuil) is in a rut. We can tell by the way his nattering radio chirps *bonjour* each morning, the way his boring toast pops up, the way his bourgeois automobile pulls out into anxious a.m. traffic. While teaching sales techniques to corporate Brussels, he stresses one thing above all else: You must maintain control. In the meantime, he's losing his.

It's understandable. His wife (Miou-Miou) has left him for reasons unknown even to her and is living on the coast with their daughters. They won't speak to him either, but it doesn't help that he's forgotten them at the rail station, where they've had to take a return train home. He smashes the office espresso machine, so inanimate objects are already in danger. He's a man living close to the edge.

Into his life walks, or wanders, Georges (Pascal Duquenne), a young man with Down's syndrome who's skipped his institution, attaches himself to Harry and restores sanity to his life. Thus, the Gumpification of cinema proceeds like a sling blade, inexplicably and unabated.

In his 1991 black comedy "Toto the Hero," Belgian writer-director Jaco Van Dormael employed startling imagery and a freedom of movement that gave his story of a bitter old man a sense of buoyant magic. In "The Eighth Day," the magical realism continues—at times, we see things through Georges' eyes, and we really *see things*—but the sentimentality inherent in Van Dormael's treatment of Georges is like an unstoppable *blancmange,* engulfing everything in its path.

Duquenne, who shared the best actor prize at Cannes last year with co-star Auteuil, really has Down's syndrome and he can be a source of impressive on-screen power.

His Georges is a volatile fellow, as capable of spontaneous kindness as he is of pawing the errant woman, writhing on the floor in frustration or emitting a frightening animal growl (which seems to indicate displeasure). But it's how he's seen by his director—as a source of therapeutic innocence, but also as something of a pet—that occasionally leaves one staring at the screen. in dumbfounded amazement.

Together, Harry and Georges engage in several capers: disrupting a corporate convention, liberating the clients of Georges' facility, winning back the love of Harry's daughters and maybe even his wife. The denouement is something you'd never see in an American movie. At the same time, the lessons learned are lessons we've learned before and are just as suspect here as there. The suffocated Harry is liberated by Georges, whose handicap comes with the door prize of unfettered frankness and an open heart. But the exaltation of the simple-minded is too easy a way to pathos, and even if he were trying to be cruel, it seems unlikely that Van Dormael could have been any more dismissive.

SIGHT AND SOUND, 11/96, p. 48, Chris Darke

Georges, a young man with Down's Syndrome, runs away from a residential home followed by the institution's dog. The dog is run down by Harry, a harassed sales guru, separated from his wife and children. Harry gives Georges a lift. After trying vainly to entrust Georges to the police, Harry lets him stay at his house for the night. The next morning, Georges has collapsed after an eating binge. The doctor diagnoses an allergic reaction to chocolate. Harry drives Georges to an address in Holland, which he claims is his Mother's house. Harry learns that Georges' mother died two years before, but he gets the address of Georges' sister. When Georges gets him in a fight with a lorry driver, Harry leaves him alone at a crossroads, but when it starts to rain, he returns.

George's sister refuses to take him in but gives Harry the address of the home. Harry decides to take George back. At a restaurant on the way, Georges is smitten by a waitress and tries to charm her but she backs off, frightened when she see his eyes. Harry phones his wife Julie to tell her that he wants to deliver an early birthday present to his daughter. She refuses to let him because he forgot to pick the two girls up from the railway station the last time she sent them to see him. Harry drives Georges to the seaside. Georges wanders off into the heavy fog and almost falls into the sea but is saved by the sound of Harry's carhorn. The next morning Harry leaves Georges in the car and goes to see his wife. Outside the house, Georges meets Harry's two daughters and accompanies them into the house where he has to restrain their father. Harry takes Georges back to the home.

Nathalie, Georges' girlfriend, leaves the home to return to her family. On an outing to an art gallery, Georges and his friends steal a car from a car showroom and break into a sales conference in which Harry is participating. They steal fireworks, pick up Nathalie and break into a fairground. Harry lets off the fireworks on the beach facing Julie's house. Georges and Nathalie make love in a caravan. The police arrive and Nathalie's parents take their daughter away. Georges, in anguish, runs away, pursued by Harry. They go to a disco where Georges tries to dance with several women who reject him. Harry and Georges fall asleep on a bench. When Harry awakes Georges has gone, taking Harry's wallet with him but leaving the photographs of his daughters. Harry is reconciled with his family. Georges goes onto the roof of the building where Harry works, eats a box of chocolates and throws himself to his death.

Jaco Van Dormael's *Toto the Hero* was an extraordinary first film, with a visual flair and a command of its switchback narrative structure that promised great things from its director. *The Eighth Day* comes as something of a shock in comparison. Where *Toto* was a hard stare at the ambiguous memories of childhood, *The Eighth Day* is a misty-eyed attempt to locate the 'the child within'. The film's premise is familiar from *Rain Man, Forrest Gump*, even from *Being There:* an uptight regular guy undergoes a life-changing encounter with a man suffering some kind of disability. But whereas in these other examples, disability is performed—Hoffman with his method autism, Hanks and Sellars as remedial holy fools—in *The Eighth Day* it's the performer himself who is disadvantaged. Pascal Duquenne, who plays Georges the young man with Down's Syndrome, has the condition himself. This gives his performance the appearance of an unmediated intensity. The successful pairing of Duquenne with Daniel Auteuil—whose screen persona is rapidly becoming that of a man permanently wall-eyed with shock and rigid with repression—saw the duo share the Best Actor award at Cannes this year.

While the authenticity of its casting might help *The Eighth Day* overcome some of the similarities it shares with American counterparts, the film also ups the ante in its treatment of the story's emotion. It doesn't so much tug at your heartstrings as riffle out sentimental arpeggios on them. *The Eighth Day* searches for a cinematic language to express excessive emotion. There's a basic melodramatic structure of sundered relationships—Harry with his wife and kids, Georges with Nathalie—embroidered with sequences of hyperbolic stylistic excess that are also often remarkably cinematic. The opening sequence is a tour de force, in which the two characters—Georges on the ground Harry in the sterile enclosure of airliner's business class—are linked by the flight of a ladybird. But such pyrotechnics soon become wearing, particularly when the ersatz Latin crooner Luis Mariano (played by Lazlo Harmati) keeps appearing as the embodiment of Georges' interior life. These moments are naive in their unrestrained emotion but artful in their execution. Imagine Douglas Sirk directing a Pierre and Gilles designed fantasy sequence and you'll have an approximation of the stylistic terrain.

Dormael's commitment to the emotional honesty and immediacy of Georges dictates the film's style. But the pay-off, which has Georges dying so that Harry may live an emotionally richer life, seems dishonest and cruel. Particularly when Georges' suicidal leap is followed by an appallingly misjudged *Singing Detective*-style burst of ensemble singing. Like so many of its moments of stylistic excess, it's a telling one, an indication that, in the absence of the narrative origami that distinguished *Toto*, Dormael seems to be chaffing at the bit of linear narrative, that what he really wants to do is sawdust and tinsel spectacle or old-fashioned musical show-stopping routines. These moments only serve to add glitter to a predictable story underwritten by the highly conventional 'othering' reflex familiar from the film's Hollywood precursors where the disabled character is always an idiot savant, a repository of humanising influences to be absorbed by the repressed sidekick. It's as if *The Eighth Day* cannot make up its mind whether it is a film of childlike emotions for adults or a film of adult emotions for children.

VILLAGE VOICE, 3/11/97, p. 80, Joanne Gallo

Among the mentally challenged characters in current films like *Shine, Breaking the Waves,* and *Sling Blade,* Georges of *The Eighth Day* is the real party animal. As played by Pascal Duquenne, this randy young man with Down's syndrome flirts madly with every other pretty girl he sees. He also burps loudly, curses at truck drivers, and gulps down beer—that is, after he runs away from his group home and collides with Harry (Daniel Auteuil), the successful salesman with an unsuccessful personal life. Georges attaches himself to Harry, coerces him into a road trip, and along the way teaches him to stop and smell the flowers —or more literally, hug a tree.

Jaco Van Dormael's follow-up to his Camera d'Or-winning debut *Toto the Hero, The Eighth Day* is a less restrained film culminating in a wacky climax. Like a merry band of frat boys, Georges and a posse from the institution wreak havoc on the outside world through a series of exuberantly wild acts that resolve Harry's problems with the wife and kids and get Georges some action as well.

Although the concept is predictable—a French-Belgian *Rain Man* lite, if you will—*The Eighth Day* possesses its own quirky charm. Much of this lies in the film's imaginative visuals, such as Georges's vision of mariachi singer Luis Mariano singing atop Harry's Mercedes in motion. At Cannes last year, Auteuil and Duquenne walked off with a shared Best Actor award, and though their performances are solid they're not particularly nuanced. Still, the unselfconsciously emotional relationship between the two men is sweet. And I'd much rather watch Daniel Auteuil than Tom Cruise any day.

Also reviewed in:
NEW YORK TIMES, 3/7/97, p. C23, Janet Maslin
NEW YORKER, 3/17/97, p. 123, Anthony Lane
VARIETY, 5/20-26/96, p. 37, David Rooney

END OF SUMMER

A JGM Enterprises release of a Showtime production. *Executive Producer:* Ted Swanson and Karen Goodwin. *Producer:* Linda Yellen. *Director:* Linda Yellen. *Screenplay:* Jonathan Platnick and Linda Yellen. *Director of Photography:* David Bridges. *Editor:* Jan Northrop. *Music:* Patrick Seymour. *Production Designer:* Bob Ziembicki. *Costumes:* Martha Mann. *Running time:* 95 minutes. *MPAA Rating:* Not Rated.

CAST: Jacqueline Bisset (Christine); Peter Weller (Theo); Julian Sands (Basil); Amy Locane (Alice); Elizabeth Shepherd (Madame Vera).

LOS ANGELES TIMES, 7/4/97, Calendar/p. 4, Kevin Thomas

In the period piece "End of Summer," Jacqueline Bisset is radiant as a rich, aristocratic turn-of-the-century spinster who unexpectedly has a second chance at love. The hourglass silhouette, the long skirts, the leg o' mutton sleeves of the gowns of the era are highly becoming on Bisset in this 1995 Showtime production now receiving theatrical release. Bisset is "End of Summer's" key strength in a focused, reflective portrayal of a Victorian woman whose passion is imprisoned in false pride and the puritanical mores of her time and station in life.

Unfortunately, "End of Summer" is not on Bisset's level as producer-director and co-writer Linda Yellen wavers between Henry James and Harlequin romance. The writing, acting and directing are wildly uneven, with the result that the film's various anachronisms in production design and script are more distracting than they would be in a sturdier production. "End of Summer" cries out for the meticulously detailed and subtle Merchant Ivory touch, as it does for a co-star more along the lines of Tom Selleck than Peter Weller, an accomplished and versatile actor but miscast here as a dashing romantic leading man.

Bisset's Christine is spending the summer at a Saratoga Springs resort, where she is stunned to encounter Weller's Theo. The two were once students together, and a spark had ignited between them. But before it could catch fire, Theo was deeply hurt by another woman, a "shameless flirt." Once poor, Theo has made a fortune out west and has returned a rich—and unattached—man. In their sedate, proper fashion, things look promising for Christine and Theo when a reckless young woman (Amy Locane), daughter of Christine's close friends, turns up and sets her cap for Theo. Lots more complications ensue.

Inadequate writing and direction do Locane no favors and do even worse to Julian Sands as a singularly dense and deplorable clergyman. Yet the character of Madame Vera, a society adventuress of a certain age, is strikingly well-written and beautifully acted by Elizabeth Shepherd. If "End of Summer" can be said to have made one point well, it is the vulnerable position women held in 19th century society. But it's a comment that's already been made in numerous better pictures in recent years.

NEW YORK POST, 6/13/97, p. 48, Michael Medved

One of the most puzzling movie developments of recent years has been the sudden surge of cinematic interest in the late 19th century novels of Edith Wharton and Henry James.

So far, the films resulting from this odd trend (including "Ethan Frome," "The Age of Innocence" and "The Portrait of a Lady") haven't exactly generated a tidal wave of public interest, so it's hard to understand why anyone would attempt a pallid, ersatz imitation of these literary classics like "End of Summer."

This flimsy film makes little effort at either psychological complexity or historical authenticity, and echoes the real works of Wharton or James to the same extent that bodice-ripper romances resemble Shakespeare.

If it weren't for an unusually able cast providing solid performances, "End of Summer" would have resulted in an End of Patience for most moviegoers.

Jacqueline Bisset is radiant and sympathetic as a millionaire's daughter in 1897 New York, just coming to terms with her spinsterhood. She makes a habit of spending her summers at scenic Saratoga, and when she arrives this year she is stunned to encounter a rugged but wealthy Westerner (Peter Weller) who had romanced, then rejected, her some 20 years before.

Miraculously, he is still single and their old connection is instantly rekindled, but Bisset must soon face uncomfortable competition from a flirtatious teen-ager (Amy Locane) she is supposed to chaperone.

Meanwhile, an ambitious and altogether unscrupulous clergyman (Julian Sands) tries to enlist Bisset's help in persuading her ailing father to leave him most of his wealth in order to build a huge cathedral that will become a wonder of the age.

Part of the problem with the plot is the insipidly steamy way it handles sex, as if turn-of-the-century Saratoga represented some Adirondack answer to "Melrose Place—which is the TV show, by the way, on which Locane appeared.

It's not that people never had illicit sex in 1897, but they would certainly have behaved more discreetly and felt more guilt-ridden than some of the inexplicably free spirits in this silly film.

Producer/director/writer Linda Yellen has worked on several acclaimed TV movies ("Prisoner Without a Name, Cell Without a Number," "Playing for Time") and she certainly has a way with actors—helping to project subtle but powerful chemistry between Bisset and Weller, for instance.

The plot, remains so preposterous, however, that other than providing an excuse for splendid costumes, gleaming carriages and elegant locations, it's hard to imagine her purpose in pursuing this peculiar project. A treacly, banal musical score (by Patrick Seymour) creates problems of its own, hyperventilating with an overwrought climax that makes the movie's abrupt and awkward conclusion especially difficult to endure.

NEWSDAY, 6/14/97, Part II/p. B7, John Anderson

Precious, libidinous and crashingly inconsequential, "End of Summer" features a group of what might be Edith Wharton refugees acting like they're on "Melrose Place." It's not as refreshing as it sounds.

A Showtime production directed by the multiple Emmy-winning Linda Yellen, "End of Summer" stars Jacqueline Bissett as Christine, a love-wounded heiress who makes pottery and who is surrounded by a collection of characters worthy of a road company of Merchant-Ivory productions: The sophisticated frontiersman (Peter Weller), the long lost love of Christine's life; the ineloquent, lecherous preacher (who's annoying, but played perfectly by Julian Sands); the unsettling blonde (Amy Locane) who's too beautiful and callow for her own good, and the unscrupulous Madame (and we do mean madame) Vera, played by Elizabeth Shepherd.

Hampered by rococo dialogue and gingerbread gestures, "End of Summer" is shoehorned into its historical period, without any sense of naturalness; the characters all sound the way you think *they* think late-19th-Century dilettantes would sound, except that when you hear it there's no music. The film is clean, bright, ornate and soulless.

Weller's character, Theo Elliott, represents the American ethics of nature and ingenuity; Basil the preacher, Vera and Locane's Alice are all cast in a moral anemia that's lingeringly European and decadent.

But don't take this too seriously. In "End of Summer," both the sex and the party scenes go on far too long, which is usually a sign that the director is running out of things to say, and thinks we'd be shallow enough to settle for gaiety of the public or private varieties. Hah!

Weller does look appropriately consumptive, but his lines are leaden. Locane seems to be imitating Sharon Stone in "Casino." Bisset? The best of the bunch, she manages to maintain a discreet distance from the sordid goings-on—which may keep her unsullied, but doesn't do much for the movie.

VILLAGE VOICE, 6/17/97, p. 70, Laurie Stone

When casting a repressed American spinster in turn-of-the-century New York, of course you think of smoldering Brit Jacqueline Bisset. Bisset looks like she wants to scream throughout Linda Yellen's yawn of a romance, *The End of Summer,* originally made for Showtime in 1995. Everything about the movie has a K-Mart feel—low-end Wharton and *Masterpiece Theater.* Bisset plays Christine, who summers in Saratoga, turning out clay pots her philistine father scorns as inferior to mass-produced ones. Old-flame Theo (Peter Weller) shows up and begins to woo her, until young bombshell, Alice (Amy Locane) snags him. Ambitious, social-climbing minister Basil (Julian Sands) is also aboard, smarming randily. Locane is ludicrously out of context with her modern sex-kitten manner. Bisset acts her part entirely with her culturally stiffened upper lip. Even Sands's ass looks fake in the suspiciously choppy editing of a sex scene meant to evoke *A Room With a View*—but not exactly.

Also reviewed in:
NEW YORK TIMES, 6/13/97, p. C22, Stephen Holden

END OF VIOLENCE, THE

An MGM Distribution Company release of a CiBy 2000 presentation of a CiBy Pictures/Road Movies/Kintop Pictures coproduction. *Executive Producer:* Jean François Fonlupt and Ulrich Felsberg. *Producer:* Deepak Nayar, Wim Wenders, and Nicolas Klein. *Director:* Wim Wenders. *Screenplay:* Nicolas Klein. *Story:* Nicolas Klein and Wim Wenders. *Director of Photography:* Pascal Rabaud. *Editor:* Peter Przygodda. *Music:* Ry Cooder and Sharon Boyle. *Sound:* Jim Stuebe. *Casting:* Heidi Levitt and Monika Mikkelsen. *Production Designer:* Patricia Norris. *Set Decorator:* Leslie Morales. *Special Effects:* Gary P. D'Amico. *Costumes:* Patricia Norris. *Make-up:* Katharina Hirsch. *Stunt Coordinator:* Chris Howell. *Running time:* 122 minutes. *MPAA Rating:* R.

CAST: Bill Pullman (Michael 'Mike' Max); Andie MacDowell (Paige Stockard); Gabriel Byrne (Ray Bering); Loren Dean ('Doc' Block); Traci Lind (Cat); Daniel Benzali (Brice Phelps); K. Todd Freeman (Six); John Diehl (Lowell Lewis); Pruitt Taylor-Vince (Frank Cray); Peter Horton (Brian); Udo Kier (Zoltan Tibor); Enrique Castillo (Ramon Gomez); Nicole Parker (Ade); Rosalind Chao (Claire); Marisol Padilla Sanchez (Mathilda); Marshall Bell (Call); Frederic Forrest (MacDermot); Sam Fuller (Louis Bering); Chris Douridas (Technician); Soledad St. Hilaire (Anita); Sal Lopez (Tito); Ulises Cuadra (Jose); Aymara De Llano (Florinda); Henry Silva (Juan-Emilio); Ulysses Cuadra (Jesus); Andy Alvarez (Philipo); Karen Ross (Fluffball); Reg Rogers (Jack); Sam Phillips (Singer); Michael Massee (Guy in Bar); O-Lan Jones (Barmaid); Black Encyclopedia (Rapper 1); Me'Shell Ndegeocello (Malike); Victoria Duffy (Female Cop).

LOS ANGELES TIMES, 9/12/97, Calendar/p. 8, Kevin Thomas

[*The following review by Kevin Thomas appeared in a slightly different form in*
NEWSDAY, 9/12/97, Part II/p. B7.]

By the time Wim Wenders' audacious and seductive "The End of Violence" is over, its title has changed meaning, signifying not the elimination of violence but its cumulative effect. As complex as it is beautiful, it has echoes of "1984" and "The Conversation" and offers a shrewdly observed panorama of contemporary L.A. in general and Hollywood in particular.

"The End of Violence" has a large and distinctive cast; low-key yet stunning cinematography by Pascal Rabaud; a lovely, languorous Ry Cooder score, one of the year's best; and the soundtrack boasts a clutch of wonderful newly commissioned work by such artists as Tom Waits, Los Lobos, a duet by U2 and Sinéad O'Connor, and a duet by Michael Stipe and Vic Chesnutt.

"The End of Violence" may be an impressive and even satisfying achievement for Wenders aficionados, but it is also extraordinarily demanding for a major studio release. In its complicated plot, it is a thriller. But it is first and foremost a moody, contemplative European-style art film by a master of the New German Cinema movement who has always been fascinated by American pop culture.

Best known today for his surreal "Wings of Desire" and its sequel, "Faraway, So Close!," Wenders has already made two memorable American films, "Hammett" and "Paris, Texas."

In "The End of Violence," a brusque, hard-driving Hollywood producer, Michael Max (Bill Pullman), has a film currently shooting and a beautiful wife (Andie MacDowell) he seriously neglects. His loyal, conscientious secretary (Rosalind Chao) tells him that he has received a hefty tome via e-mail on a new surveillance system, but he has no time to look at it. It apparently has been sent to him by a NASA-trained FBI surveillance expert, Ray Bering (Gabriel Byrne), he met briefly at an electronics convention.

Meanwhile, Ray is holed up in the Griffith Planetarium setting up this breakthrough surveillance system that allows for constant observation of L.A.'s city streets. (It involves hidden cameras installed all over L.A. streets at what must be an astronomical cost.) Ray's boss (Daniel Benzali) intends it to speed up crime response 200%. He remarks, "It could mean the end of violence as we know it."

Because Ray is beginning to have misgivings about the surveillance system in its Big-Brother-is-watching-you implications, he reached out, it would seem, to Mike in the belief that someone outside the FBI should know about it. Mike is subsequently amused that, as a ruthless Hollywood type, he would be entrusted with such vital information.

The crux of Wenders and writer Nicolas Klein's plot, which requires at times leaps of faith, is that there is a mind-boggling aspect of the surveillance system that Ray does not know about—that is, until, by the long arm of coincidence, the system saves the life of Mike, who is in danger of losing it at the hands of a pair of buffoonish crooks (Pruitt Taylor-Vince, John Diehl) intent on stealing his Mercedes. Remembering his secretary's memo on the e-mailed surveillance material, Mike winds up laying low and is given shelter and work by some gardeners (Enrique Castillo, Sal Lopez and Ulises Cuadra) led by a kindly patriarch (Henry Silva).

That all this just sets the film in motion suggests how intricate "The End of Violence" is. While in hiding, Pullman has a chance to think about his life and character, to realize what an SOB he has become and to discover that change within individuals is the only way society can be transformed, as idealistic as that seems. Wenders and Klein come up with amusing commentary on the workings of Hollywood, and there is a consideration of how so many peoples' lives are affected by violence in all its forms, including movies.

As "The End of Violence" unfolds in all its implications and permutations, it involves us with an extraordinary number and range of individuals, all of them engagingly played, although MacDowell seems out of her element as a woman who evolves into the hard, self-absorbed type of individual her missing husband had become.

Among those making vivid impressions are Traci Lind as a stuntwoman with acting ambitions; Loren Dean as a shrewd, ambitious young cop attracted to Lind; K. Todd Freeman as an opportunistic film composer; KCRW-FM's Chris Douridas as Ray's assistant; Marisol Padilla Sanchez as a new planetarium cleaning woman; Frederic Forrest (who played the title role of "Hammett") as a veteran cop; Nicole Parker as a challenging poet; and most especially director Sam Fuller as Ray's frail but feisty father. Singer Sam Phillips pops up briefly, and you can try to spot singer Meshell Ndegéocello.

Although "The End of Violence" is probably too complicated for its own good, it is clearly the work of a major visionary artist in whom it is always possible to recognize truths about the lives we live—a filmmaker who for once doesn't exploit violence as he protests it. It would be terrific to see it on a double bill with Robert Altman's "Short Cuts" or Michelangelo Antonioni's "Zabriskie Point."

NEW YORK POST, 9/12/97, p. 47, Michael Medved

In his latest project, the moody, wistful German filmmaker Wim Wenders ("Paris, Texas," "Wings of Desire") comments on America's "culture of violence" by creating an assortment of oddly connected characters, each of whom illustrates some aspect of the subject.

● Bill Pullman plays a powerful, desperately driven Hollywood producer, noted for artistic and wildly successful extravaganzas of gore.

● Andie MacDowell is his bored, beautiful wife who suffers the "violence" of a husband who ignores her.

● Trace Lind is a tough, ambitious stuntwoman who is injured in one of Pullman's films.

● The promising leading man Loren Dean is a police inspector who falls in love with her while investigating the producer's mysterious disappearance (and possible murder).

● Gabriel Byrne is a brilliant but hermetic surveillance expert with photographic clues to that mystery, as he develops a network of hidden cameras to record street crime for a super-secret government agency (represented by the ominous,Daniel Benzali).

● Marisol Padilla Sanchez portrays Byrne's housekeeper (and eventually his lover), who has survived massacres and mutilation in her native El Salvador.

As if these disparate plot elements weren't enough, "The End of Violence" also indulges self-conscious, irrelevant references to the paintings of Edward Hopper, films by Antonioni and Rafelson and numerous other literary, cinematic and painterly predecessors.

Frankly, the result is a slow-moving, meandering mess—but at least it's a consistently interesting mess, thanks to its compelling characterizations and haunted, shimmering visions of L.A. by debuting cinematographer Pascal Rabaud.

Director Wenders portrays the City of Angels with the same ironic detachment with which his glum, sympathetic angels viewed Berlin in "Wings of Desire " capturing Southern California with surprisingly fresh (though unmistakably alien) eyes:

Pullman is convincing in the central role as a ruthless moviemaker, but he strains when asked to depict his character's redemption as a humble, anonymous, adopted member of a family of sweaty, honest, hard-working and (excessively) admirable Mexican gardeners.

Ultimately, the paranoid conspiracy that's supposed to connect the dots of the movie's scattered elements seems a cheap device unworthy of its more intriguing ambitions.

The film feels far longer than its two-hour running time, and long before the gloppy, strange ingredients finally begin to gel, "The End of Violence" already will have reached "The End of Patience" with many moviegoers.

SIGHT AND SOUND, 1/98, p. 40, Nick Roddick

Cat, a stuntwoman working on an action movie, *The Seeds of Violence,* is slightly injured in an explosion. The film's producer, Mike Max, whose career has been built on high-concept action movies, receives an e-mail from his wife Paige, who says she is leaving him. Mike visits Cat in hospital and gives her an acting role in the film. While calling Paige, Mike is abducted by two men. They take him to a piece of wasteground underneath a freeway interchange.

Meanwhile, in the Griffith Park Observatory, former NASA scientist Ray Bering is completing a computer surveillance system linked to cameras all over the LA area. On one of them, he sees Mike with the two men. Later, Mike is discovered unconscious by gardener Ramon Gomez and his crew. The cops arrive and find the dead bodies of the two abductors. Investigating police detective 'Doc' Block visits the set of the film and is very taken with Cat. Mike recovers at Ramon's house, where he gradually becomes part of the family.

Paige takes over Mike's business. Mike accesses his e-mail and discovers that a huge file, apparently containing classified information, has been sent to him. Ray's boss, Brice Phelps, introduces him to his new cleaner, Salvadorean refugee Mathilda. Mike begins to realise that his abduction has to do with the secret file, which was sent to him by someone he met at a computer fair. Doc is taken off the case, but visits the film set again to see Cat. Mike spies on the shooting of Cat's big scene, and sees Paige shut down the picture. Mike warns Cat of the danger, passing her details of the man who sent him the mysterious information. Establishing contact with Paige, he agrees to her separation terms.

Ray begins to become aware that he is also being watched. Doc tracks down Cat, who is hiding out in South Central, and gets the number of the man who had sent Mike the file, who turns out to be Ray. Doc and Ray meet in Griffith Park, but the latter is shot by an unseen assailant before he can tell Doc anything. Later, Mathilda meets up with Phelps (who appears to have hired her to spy on Ray) on Santa Monica Pier while, some distance away, her daughter chats to Mike, who is staring out over the ocean.

Set in modern Los Angeles and weaving together film-industry people, computer experts, Latin American immigrants and cops, *The End of Violence* is not Wim Wenders' most straightforwardly narrative movie. Nor, however, is it his most discursive. The story concerns a film producer, Mike Max (Bill Pullman), a maker of violent films, who is abducted and ends up hiding out amongst Mexican gardeners. Max's abduction is seen on a long-range surveillance camera by Ray (Gabriel Byrne), who works for a shadowy figure named Brice Phelps (Daniel Benzali). The cop (Loren Dean) who investigates Mike's abduction is a fan of his films, and eventually all three plot strands start to overlap in surprising ways.

On one level, it is a whodunit for the paranoia generation, to which the answer can be found in the single word: Them. As in *The Parallax View* and *The Conversation* (both 1974), "they" did it. The films anti-hero Max says in one of his growling voiceovers: "Paranoia is our number one export. Everybody needs an enemy." And indeed, in this, everybody seems to have one. "They" could be the hidden forces who dynamite the lives of Max and his alter-ego Ray; or the death squads who have traumatised Phelps' employee Mathilda (Marisol Padilla Sanchez) in San Salvador, or the father evoked in a poem about child abuse in one of the film's truly disturbing scenes.

But this is not to imply that this is primarily a film with a message. As with almost all the director's films, *The End of Violence* is about what happens when a familiar world be to unravel (taking with it, conventions, all sense of cause and effect). And it is about the process of film-making, in the way in which any self-respecting modernist text is about its own articulation. Wenders has asserted in many interviews that it is a film about violence without being a violent film. Yet *The End of Violence* is not really concerned with the ethics of making violent films. We see next to nothing of *The Seeds of Violence,* the film which Zoltan Tibor, played by Udo Kier (the personification of evil in so many European films), is directing for Mike beyond the opening stunt and a few glimpses of stuntwoman Cat's scene in a bar (the latter so obviously a reconstruction of Edward Hopper's painting *Nighthawks* that it is hard to see the scene behind the homage). Nor does Mike's final renunciation of his *métier* in the film's closing helicopter shot tell us much about the modern-day Hollywood referred to in the press notes. "We all think it is perfectly normal to drive down Sunset Boulevard and see one billboard after another of all our favourite stars raising guns that are more and more threatening," Wenders notes there. But *The End of Violence* has more to do with his own personal journey.

However, violence permeates both the film's world (the career of Max and all those who depend on him is fuelled by it) and its language. "Shoot!" growls Sam Fuller in his final cameo as Ray's father, even if all he means is "Tell me about it!" or perhaps "Film it!", for the process of film-making—of framing and movement and the decoding of images—is central to the whole film. It also accounts for some of the exquisite pleasures which *The End of Violence* has to offer, most of them thanks to the limpidly beautiful colour palette of director of photography Pascal Rabaud. Not since Vilmos Zsigmond shot Robert Altman's *The Long Goodbye* has the peculiar beauty of Los Angeles, its adjacent ocean and hills, been so stunningly captured on celluloid.

In fact, for all the star power and big words that float around in the dialogue, *The End of Violence* is an essentially simple film, speedily prepared. Wenders and screenwriter Nicolas Klein admit to knocking the script together in six weeks because they were fed up with waiting for pieces of their sci-fi epic *The Billion Dollar Hotel* to fall into place. It was also quickly made (a six-week shoot) and, by Wenders' own admission, rather too hastily assembled for its world premiere in Cannes in May, 1997. Since then, five minutes have been removed.

The 122-minute version has certainly solved some of the rhythmic problems, but it has not nor could it have addressed the films two main weak points: the misjudged comedy scene as the two kidnappers bicker over who is to shoot Mike (from which I fancy at least a minute has gone since

I first saw the film), and the generally underwritten character of Paige, performed with something akin to discomfort by Andie MacDowell. But then, characters who are functions of an idea rather than ordinary people have always been one of the director's predilections. The only member of the New German Cinema movement still to be more or less continually active, Wenders has rarely progressed beyond the sense of alienation faced by the central character in his first commercial feature film, *The Goalkeeper's Fear of the Penalty* (1971), who leaves a job (in which as he bitterly observes, they only really notice you when you fail) in order to set out on an odyssey of self-discovery.

Wenders' characters have been making those odysseys ever since, most unforgettably in *Kings of the Road (1976)*, most emotionally in *Paris, Texas*. And Mike Max, jarred out of his routine in mid-phone call, is no exception, effectively reinventing himself as a Mexican gardener. Thus, he becomes one of California's invisible men (Wenders has some fun in a couple of scenes where the mainstream Angelenos who are seeking him look straight through him), in order to put his life back together.

But there is a new element at work in *The End of Violence*. It is the first film Wenders has made since his collaboration with Antonioni on *Beyond the Clouds,* and the new film has about it something of Antonioni's sense of spatial relationships between people and objects—a plastic equivalent of the characters' alienation—which marked *L'avventura* and *La notte*. The result is an intriguing and extremely matchable movie, which functions both as a kind of spaced-out detective story and as a modernist *conte philosophique* in which the intertwining of the characters' destinies is never quite neat enough to suggest a pattern, nor loose enough to imply free will.

VILLAGE VOICE, 9/16/97, p. 94, Laurie Stone

With a tight script by Nicolas Klein and with cinematographer Pascal Rabaud framing bold, beautifully colored tableaux, Wim Wenders's comic meditation *The End of Violence* injects the screen with so many ideas it's a marvel the plot can contain them. Not every puzzle proves solvable. Was Mike Max (Bill Pullman), the movie producer hijacked by two thugs, the one to blow off their heads, or did someone else do the deed? Mike claims he didn't fire. And Ray (Gabriel Byrne), the NASA-trained surveillance jockey working on a secret FBI project, captures only blurry footage of the scene, at which one of his video cameras was installed. The movie ripples out from these men who are isolated from other people and wedded in different ways to screens: the moviemaker so famous for violence-licking flicks that even his hit men and the cop-shrink assigned to investigate his disappearance are cultish fans; and the techie wizard, credulous enough to believe that studding L.A. with concealed cameras will so speed police response that violence will be obviated.

Speaking in voiceover, Pullman's Mike remembers early paranoia, a childhood conviction he would be blindsided by a stalking enemy. The movie richly plays with this notion, showing how paranoia is the ultimate form of narcissism—the need to see the self as the obsessive focus of others and the inability to bear that most collisions, whether producing ruinous or fortunate consequences, are random. Though hardly anyone likes Mike, Ray meets him by chance, takes a fancy to him, and then places his life in peril by sending him an e-mail detailing the FBI project. On the other hand, one of the killers hired to whack Mike hesitates to pull the trigger because, he confesses to his fuming partner, "I like him."

Which doesn't mean Wenders is naive about foul schemes. They are as rife as chance occurrences: from the FBI plot, to the subverting machinations of Mike's lawyer (a delightfully wormy Peter Horton), to the boinking by Mike's music director, gangsta rapper Six (K. Todd Freeman), of Mike's wife (passivity-incarnate Andie MacDowell), to the string-pulling of Ray's boss (a sharkish Daniel Benzali), who preys with equal relish on emotional cripples like Ray and survivors of Latin American torture like the indebted maid-spy (Marisol Padilla Sanchez) he hires to keep tabs on Ray. Each character struggles to distinguish love from aggression, and Wenders wittily shows how nearly impossible this is.

The movie remains buoyantly absurd, a style enhanced by leads Pullman, MacDowell, and Byrne, whose collective woodenness works here, required as they are to play bundles of sociological elements more than people. Wenders's satire admits the allure of his targets. He basks in his fascination/repulsion with L.A., a world that willy-nilly mixes spiritual rebirth, studio deals, and performance art, while so worshipping financial status that Mike, who takes refuge with Mexican gardeners, doesn't have to disguise himself because no one really looks at him. Pushing the envelope of how much can be squeezed into one movie, Wenders, riffing on voyeurism and framed scenes, homages Antonioni's *Blow-Up* and Hopper's *Nighthawks,* and in the dialogue of his menagerie of minor characters, the deadpan, reference-spiked speech David Lynch used to droll effect in *Twin Peaks.* While purging his screen of violent images, Wenders pleasurably ponders all kinds of murder.

Also reviewed in:
NEW YORK TIMES, 9/12/97, p. C5, Stephen Holden
VARIETY, 5/19-25/97, p. 51, Todd McCarthy

EVENT HORIZON

A Paramount Pictures and Lawrence Gordon release of a Golar production in association with Impact Pictures. *Executive Producer:* Nick Gillot. *Producer:* Lawrence Gordon, Lloyd Levin, and Jeremy Bolt. *Director:* Paul Anderson. *Screenplay:* Philip Eisner. *Director of Photography:* Adrian Biddle. *Editor:* Martin Hunter. *Music:* Michael Kamen. *Music Editor:* Graham Sutton, Chris Brooks, and Alex Gibson. *Sound:* Chris Munro and (music) Steve McLaughlin. *Casting:* Deborah Aquila and Jane Shannon-Smith. *Production Designer:* Joseph Bennett. *Art Director:* Malcolm Middleton. *Set Decorator:* Crispian Sallis. *Special Effects:* Neil Corbould, Clive Beard, Trevor Wood, Paul Corbould, and David Williams. *Visual Effects:* Richard Yuricich. *Mechanical Effects:* David Nunez. *Costumes:* John Mollo. *Make-up:* Pauline Heys. *Stunt Coordinator:* Marc Boyle. *Running time:* 97 minutes. *MPAA Rating:* R.

CAST: Lawrence Fishburne (Captain Miller); Sam Neill (Dr. William Weir); Kathleen Quinlan (Emergency Technician Peters); Joely Richardson (Navigator Starck); Richard T. Jones (Emergency Technician Cooper); Jack Noseworthy (Engineer Justin); Jason Isaacs (Doctor D.J.); Sean Pertwee (Pilot Smith); Peter Marinker (Kilpack); Holley Chant (Claire Weir); Barclay Wright (Denny); Noah Huntley (Burning Man); Robert Jezek (Rescue Technician).

LOS ANGELES TIMES, 8/15/97, Calendar/p. 16, Kenneth Turan

In the area of science-fiction horror, state-of-the-art technology gives and takes away. It makes possible wonders no one could have imagined and creates terrors so excessive it's dreadful to look at the screen. "Event Horizon" has a knack for both, and that's something of a shame.

For watching the dark doings that result when spaceship Event Horizon returns from a mysterious trip "beyond the boundaries of known scientific reality" leads to the odd wish it had been made in a different time. Yes, you'd sacrifice the special effects and the excellent model work, one of the film's prime assets, but you'd also sidestep the current hip fascination with creating repulsion, sickening and revolting an audience. Maybe that's not strictly a trendy desire, but it's not previously been joined with the kind of killer technology that makes it so graphically possible.

There are, as it turns out, several things to appeal to an adult audience about "Event Horizon." With stars like Laurence Fishburne, Sam Neill, Kathleen Quinlan and Joely Richardson, it's especially well-cast for what is basically a piece of pulp fiction. And Philip Eisner's script holds our interest, partly via a plot twist that fans of "Forbidden Planet" will find familiar.

Director Paul Anderson, whose—last film was "Mortal Kombat," well knows how to build suspense and increase tension. But counter-balancing all of that is "Event Horizon's" position as a sci-fi splatter film, intent on drenching the screen in blood and gore whenever possible. Though the script provides an excuse for the charnel house ambience, that doesn't make it any more pleasant to watch.

"Event Horizon" opens in the year 2047 with some startling news: The spaceship of the same name, having disappeared without a trace seven years before in the midst of a mission to explore the boundaries of our solar system, has suddenly come back into radio contact on the outskirts of Neptune.

Sent to find out where the ship has been and what happened to its crew is the Lewis & Clark, a seven-person American search-and-rescue ship run by the laconic, no-nonsense Capt. Miller (Fishburne), whose idea of a big speech is: "You know the rules, people: Someone drops the ball, we get the call."

Also on the Lewis & Clark is Dr. William Weir (Neill), the troubled scientist who designed the Event Horizon. He explains that the lost ship was able to in effect fold space, creating what he calls "a dimensional gateway" that enabled it to evade the laws of physics and fly faster than the speed of light.

The Event Horizon, it's soon determined, is a ghost ship with its crew—who have left behind a strange and terrifying captain's log—all dead and gone. It's also an extremely spooky place that causes all kinds of aberrant instrument readings. So no one is too happy when disastrous circumstances force Dr. Weir and the Lewis & Clark crew to temporarily abandon their ship and set up on the derelict vessel.

Though explaining exactly what's happening and why is not always this film's strength, it becomes clear, that the Event Horizon is playing frightening mind games with everyone on board. Dr. Weir seems to understand more than he's willing to let on, and those who remember the strange powers of "the monsters from the id" in "Forbidden Planet" will know some of the places this film is headed to sell this kind of B-movie material, an A-cast is always helpful, and, starting with the always-convincing Fishburne, "Event Horizon" has one. Why fine performers want to be reduced to saying lines like "optimum approach angle is 14 degrees" is unclear (unless it's a desire to have a "Star Trek" knockoff experience) but the film is better off for their presence.

It's also helpful that several of the actors, the director and key production personnel are British. It gives "Event Horizon" a bit of a different feel, as does the arresting production design by newcomer Joseph Bennett. Expertly photographed by Adrian Biddle, who shot James Cameron's "Aliens," Bennett's brooding, at times almost medieval sets are as convincing as they are different.

Director Anderson gets points for skillfully choreographing all of this, but he loses them for a consistent desire to brutalize the audience. Even before scenes with gouged-out eyes, "Event Horizon" uses over-amplified sound and a shock style of editing to unmercifully pulverize viewers.

This technique can't help but be effective up to a point, but the number of people who equate being efficiently tortured with being well entertained is, one hopes, a finite one. Otherwise the prognosis for film and society is about as grim as the doings on that sinister ghost ship.

NEW YORK POST, 8/15/97, p. 43, Michael Medved

"Event Horizon" may not scare you to death (as it clearly intends to do), but it almost certainly will gross you out.

About the time that a big pane of glass bursts on a stricken spaceship, undamming a cascading torrent of foamy blood that threatens to drown major characters (and to give new meaning to the word "bloodbath"), you might as well give up on finishing that tub of popcorn.

If nothing else, this ambitious, often original special-effects extravaganza emphasizes the crucial difference between movies that are profoundly frightening and those that are merely sickening.

First-time screenwriter Philip Eisner cunningly combines your basic lost-in-space, sci-fi adventure with your basic demonic-possession, haunted-house gore fest.

The horrors begin in 2047 when a search-and-rescue spacecraft commanded by Laurence Fishburne heads toward the planet Neptune. The mission is to salvage the Event Horizon, an experimental ship that disappeared seven years earlier while attempting to be the first space vehicle to travel faster than the speed of light.

Accompanying the rescue crew (Joely Richardson, Kathleen Quinlan, Jack Noseworthy, Richard T. Jones) is the designer of the lost craft, Dr. Weir as in Dr. Weir(d)—capably played by Sam Neill.

He seems intrigued rather than appalled when they board the long-missing ship and discover that all members of its original crew died grisly, mysterious deaths.

"When she crossed over, she was just a ship," he admiringly declares. "But when she came back, she was alive! Isn't she beautiful?"

Most of the sets and miniatures are indeed beautiful, displaying a flair, inventiveness and eye for telling detail that other space adventures (such as the durable "Star Trek' series) can only envy.

The acting is also strong, with each member of the crew crisply and competently characterized, and a solid ensemble sensibility linking the entire cast.

Why, then, does "Event Horizon" feel so unsatisfying by the time it has finished battering our senses? In part, because the skillfully layered tension of the first half simply dissolves in outrageous excesses of carnage that can't cover up for the lack of adequate answers to intriguing questions.

Like so many other big studio releases in this dismal cinema summer, the demand for some supposedly shattering, thrill-ride climax of explosions and fireballs and hairbreadth escapes simply obliterates all sense of proportion or integrity.

The final revelation that "the devil made me do it" feels here merely like an excuse. Promising young British director Paul Anderson previously created "Mortal Kombat," and it's unfortunate that he ultimately turns this far-more-challenging material into just another bloody, demonic video game.

NEWSDAY, 8/16/97, Part II/p. B5, John Anderson

Its forebears are numerous and unsettling, but the film evoked most strongly by "Event Horizon"—an "Alien"-esque sci-fi nightmare bedecked with arcane theology, pure math and pure evil—is a 1963 movie about New England eccentrics and a haunted house. "The Haunting," starring Julie Harris and Claire Bloom and based on a Shirley Jackson story, concerned customized horror: Regardless of the nature of the unseen evil dwelling at Hill House, it knew the innermost fears of the people within it. We're talking about niche-market nightmares for the clairvoyant, and a frightening movie.

So, for the most part, is "Event Horizon," which stars Sam Neill as a mathematician-spaceship designer who takes Laurence Fishburne's reluctant crew out toward Neptune to find the Event Horizon—a ship that disappeared once it passed behind the planet, and whose fate is the stuff of apocalypse and perdition. What they find is horrendous; what they experience is hellacious. And the evil that inhabits, or possesses, the lost ship knows each of them personally.

Unfortunately for both them and us, it all goes on too long and at a pace that needs to accelerate constantly to maintain its momentum. It eventually careens into a black hole of its own creation, even while producing a healthy number of chills. Director Paul Anderson ("Mortal Kombat") uses sound to disorienting effect—see "Event Horizon" in a theater with the best system, because you'll literally levitate at certain moments. But he goes to the well once too often. After a while these otherworldy clangs and bangs get as overdone as the bloodshed and dismemberments.

But when it is good, it is very good. Neill's Dr. William Weir gets stranger and stranger, Fishburne's Capt. Miller is all business and brio, but Richard T. Jones really stands out as Cooper, the crew member who provides just the right amount of comedy relief in times of evisceration and Weir's pontifications on curved space and bent time. That the voices they all hear on the tapes of the slaughtered Event Horizon are in Latin lends the film a certain theological gravity, even if it's as bogus as Weir's math lessons, but you do get the inkling that time and history might recur in sweeping, circular motions. And movies, too.

SIGHT AND SOUND, 10/97, p. 46, Mark Kermode

2040. The experimental deep-space ship *Event Horizon* disappears beyond Neptune. Seven years later, the search-and-rescue vessel *Lewis and Clark* is despatched to Neptune under the command of Captain Miller, with *Event Horizon* designer Dr William Weir on board. En route, Weir explains that the *Event Horizon* disappeared when engaging its faster-than-light gravity drive that generates black holes which allow it to travel through wormholes in space. The ship has recently resurfaced, issuing a single harrowing distress signal to which the *Lewis and Clark* is responding.

Orbiting Neptune, the *Lewis and Clark* docks with the *Event Horizon*. The older ship shows no sign of life despite extraordinary bioscope readings. Distorted video images in the ship's log suggest that the crew perished in hellish torment. Soon, the *Lewis and Clark*'s crew are themselves beset by nightmarish visions: Dr Weir is confronted by his dead wife; Peters, a technician, by her son whom she's left behind on Earth; Miller by the burning soldier he once left to die. After being sucked into the gravity drive (an event which damages the *Lewis and Clark*), a haunted engineer named Justin jettisons himself unprotected into space and suffers extensive injuries before being rescued.

Lewis and Clark navigator Starck concludes that the *Event Horizon* is generating the hallucinations as a self-defence system. Meanwhile, ship's doctor D.J. translates the recorded Latin phrase gurgled by the *Event Horizon*'s captain as "Save yourself from Hell". As oxygen levels on the ship decrease, the crew's hallucinations worsen. Beset by visions, Peters plunges to her death and D.J. is discovered ritually disembowelled. Miller's attempts to abandon ship are thwarted by Weir who plants a bomb which destroys the *Lewis and Clark*, killing its pilot Smith and sending a technician named Cooper spinning into space. Weir gouges his own eyes out, is possessed by the ship and proclaims Hell the *Event Horizon*'s ultimate destination. Miller triggers a self-destruct system in the tubular body of the *Event Horizon:* both he and Weir and the rest of the ship are sucked into the gravity drive's black hole. Starck, Cooper and Justin, secure in the head of the ship, are blown free. Some time later, the hibernating crew are rescued but hallucinations still haunt them.

Director Paul Anderson (*Shopping, Mortal Kombat*) has likened his lavish sci-fi/horror epic to "*The Exorcist* in space", a description actually first used by the publicists of Ridley Scott's groundbreaking *Alien*, to which *Event Horizon* owes an obvious debt. Other generic touchstones range from *The Haunting* and *The Shining*, to *Lifeforce* and even (bizarrely) *Hellraiser IV: Bloodline*, while the plot concerning a 'living' inert structure which taps characters' subconscious minds invokes *Solaris*. But to dismiss this as merely a hotchpotch of borrowed motifs is to do *Event Horizon* a grave injustice. Despite the wooden delivery of some frankly ropey dialogue, Anderson's eye-pleasing fantasy achieves numerous moments of creepy terror and generates an atmosphere of delicious unease sadly lacking in most mainstream fantasy films.

The star of the show is undoubtedly the ship itself, beautifully photographed by *Aliens* cameraman Adrian Biddle, to which Anderson and production designer Joseph Bennett have brought a glorious combination of hi-tech futurism and medieval gothic. Modelled upon the Notre-Dame cathedral, the *Event Horizon* becomes the perfect location for a tale of deep-space demonism, suggesting a craggy haunted castle cast adrift on the very edge of space, beyond the reach of man or God.

Mining this rich thematic seam, Philip Eisner's script maintains an edgy balance between the sacred and the scientific, with Jason Isaacs relishing the chance to deliver the best lines as he realises too late the true significance of the late Captain's Latin gasps. Terror, too, lurks in the horribly fleeting video images of hellish torment which taunt both the crew of the *Lewis and Clark* and the audience of *Event Horizon*. Scenes of tongue-lolling torture appear and disappear so abruptly (and to such cacophonous accompaniment) during the climactic sequence showing Hell at the end that we are left unsure as to what we have actually seen, and how much we merely imagined. Here, the editing is nothing less than masterful. Elsewhere, however, the movie seems crippled by a too-rigid reining-in of the material. Indeed, the brutal and often illogical pacing of the less spectacular scenes seems to suggest that the finished movie has actually been unsuccessfully pared down from an earlier, more languid cut—certainly you are left with the feeling that there should be more here than eventually meets the eye. Whether or not Anderson will at some point unveil a wealth of unseen footage for a special-edition video or laser disc (now the fashion in this genre) remains to be seen. For the fans, at least, such a prospect would be enticing.

VILLAGE VOICE, 8/26/97, p. 78, Gary Dauphin

You don't have to be a genre connoisseur or video-store clerk to identify the many predigested parts of *Event Horizon*, derivative in the desperately workmanlike way that results from a lot of professionals simultaneously running out of ideas while on deadline.

Event Horizon is the name of an experimental starship that resembles a Klingon bird of prey—which, in the way of experimental starships, disappears without a trace on its maiden voyage. Seven years later, it reappears just outside of Neptune, so a search-and-rescue team is dispatched to the dimly lit hulk, basically in order to stand around asking dumb questions of its designer (Sam Neill, just along for the ride in a number of ways) while getting increasingly creeped out until the compartments start explosively decompressing. The rescue team is a reasonably functional crew-ensemble fronted by a gruff leader (Laurence Fishburne, looking pissed at the gig's inherent lack of star power), but the poor plotting and Paul Anderson's lazy direction give them little to do except make like drugged visitors to a science fiction-flick museum: here we have the *Nostromo* crew quarters from *Alien,* there the HAL brain rooms from *2001* and *2010,* there you'll find entire sections from Disney's *The Black Hole.*

Horizon flirts with hard sci-fi (the ship uses man-made black holes to bend space) but winds up mainly trying to impress fans of the *Hellraiser* cycle (if you bend space, creatures with extravagantly scarred skin will tie you up with barbed wire and probe your orifices with drills). Much less fun than the sum of its ill-fitting parts, *Event Horizon* turns the theater into a working model of the astrophysics concept hijacked for the title: a region of space where gravity slows light to a crawl.

Also reviewed in:
NEW YORK TIMES, 8/15/97, p. C16, Stephen Holden
VARIETY, 8/18-24/97, p. 30, Joe Leydon
WASHINGTON POST, 8/15/97, p. G6, Stephen Hunter

EVE'S BAYOU

A Trimark Pictures release of a Chubbco/Addis-Wechsler production. *Executive Producer:* Mark Amin, Eli Selden, Nick Wechsler, and Julie Silverman Yorn. *Producer:* Caldecot Chubb and Samuel L. Jackson. *Director:* Kasi Lemmons. *Screenplay:* Kasi Lemmons. *Director of Photography:* Amy Vincent. *Editor:* Terilyn A. Shropshire. *Music:* Terence Blanchard. *Music Editor:* Lori Slomka. *Choreographer:* Mariama. *Sound:* Benjamin A. Patrick. *Sound Editor:* Jay Nierenberg. *Casting:* Jacki Brown-Karman and Robyn M. Mitchell. *Production Designer:* Jeff Howard. *Art Director:* Adele Plauche. *Set Decorator:* Joanne Schmidt. *Special Effects:* Christopher R. Brady. *Costumes:* Karyn Wagner. *Make-up:* Marietta Carter-Narcisse. *Stunt Coordinator:* Marvin Walters. *Running time:* 109 minutes. *MPAA Rating:* R.

CAST: Samuel L. Jackson (Louis Batiste); Lynn Whitfield (Roz Batiste); Debbi Morgan (Mozelle Batiste Delacroix); Vondie Curtis Hall (Julian Grayraven); Branford Marsalis (Harry Delacroix); Lisa Nicole Carson (Matty Mereaux); Roger Guenveur Smith (Lenny Mereaux); Ethel Ayler (Gran Mere); Meagan Good (Cisely Batiste); Jurnee Smollett (Eve Batiste); Diahann Carroll (Elzora); Jake Smollett (Poe Batiste); Afonda Colbert (Henrietta); Lola Dalferes (Lynette); Marcus Lyle Brown (Hosea); Alverta Perkins Dunigan (Paige); Ron Flagge (Vendor); Sharon K. London (Hilary); Carol Sutton (Madame Renard); Victoria Rowell (Stevie Hobbs); Oneal A. Isaac (Bus Driver); Julian Dalcour (Bartender); Leonard Thomas (Maynard); Allen Toussaint (Proprietor); Billie Neal (Ghost of Original Eve); Tamara Tunie (Narrator).

LOS ANGELES TIMES, 11/7/97, Calendar/p. 16, Kevin Thomas

There has never been a film quite like Kasi Lemmons' shimmering "Eve's Bayou." There have been plenty of mood pieces about white Southerners, usually decadent types, and there have been films about hardships of oppressed blacks. But "Eve's Bayou" is virtually unique as a fable about an old Louisiana Creole family living in an antique-filled manor house that's every bit as elegant as a white aristocrat's plantation.

The Batistes are clearly more prosperous than the people of Julie Dash's more stylized "Daughters of the Dust," the film it most closely resembles. As a memory piece of acute psychological insight it is as evocative of time and place as a work by Truman Capote or Tennessee Williams. "Eve's Bayou" is an inspired achievement, with superb cinematography by Amy Vincent, absolutely crucial to the film's success. The same can be said for Terence Blanchard's lovely, languorous score and the impeccable production design by Jeff Howard and costume design by Karyn Wagner. There are no false notes in this fine, venturesome film, one of the year's best.

We witness not a single instance of racial discrimination or bigotry but instead share in a mystical experience of what it means to be a black woman—proud, beautiful, vulnerable yet resilient. You can't improve upon the film's description offered by its distributor, Trimark: "The true topography of 'Eve's Bayou' is a locale somewhere between the material and spiritual worlds, where truth and its perception can change shape, depending on the light of day."

Geographically speaking, the film takes place in a small backwater Louisiana community in the '50s. It unfolds from the point of view of a 10-year-old girl; it is her voice as a woman looking back over the decades that serves as the film's narration. She tells us that the community's name, Eve's Bayou, comes from the name of a slave woman whose medicines saved the life of a white planter, Jean-Louis Batiste, who set her free and gave her land. Our narrator, named Eve in honor of her ancestor, informs us wryly that the original Eve in turn presented Batiste with 16 children.

The present-day head of the family is Dr. Louis Batiste (Samuel L. Jackson), who lives in that gracious old home with his beautiful, glamorous wife Roz (Lynn Whitfield), their 14-year-old daughter Cisely (Meagan Good), Eve (Jurnee Smollett) and 9-year-old son Poe (Jake Smollett) and the proud and proper Gran' Mère (Ethel Ayler). We meet the Batistes during a gala party in their home. Everyone seems to be beaming with happiness but already we have evidence that this impression is misleading, as Louis dances vigorously with a woman who flaunts her lush body outrageously.

Dr. Batiste is a world-class charmer who sincerely loves his wife and family but is a constant philanderer who seems oblivious to the pain he causes his wife—and the daughters who, as worshipful as they are of him, are on the verge of comprehending his infidelity and its impact on their mother and themselves.

In a very real sense "Eve's Bayou" is a gallery of portraits of women. The most vivid is Debbi Morgan as Mozelle, Louis' gorgeous, fiery sister, a self-described "psychic counselor" who can see into the futures of many but was never able to foretell the deaths of her three husbands, something that understandably haunts her.

In contrast to Mozelle is the ferocious local voodoo woman Elzora (Diahann Carroll) whose fortunetelling so scares the already unhappy Roz that she becomes terrified to leave her three children out of her sight. Together, Moze and Elzora represent, the range of superstition, the mix of Catholicism and Yoruba that persists into modern times.

Carefully observing though not fully understanding all that's going on around her, Eve is coming of age. The key relationship of the film is that between the childless Mozelle and Eve, the child she is determined to protect while strengthening her to deal with whatever life holds for her.

Lemmons not only sees all these people in the round but also understands that human relations can be a "Rashomon"—that truth can seemingly vary depending on the point of view. This shifting view of reality, coupled with the spiritual longings of Lemmons' people, give "Eve's Bayou" a distinctive richness. Lemmons' command of cinematic style, her appreciation of the chimerical aspects of life and her ability to inspire actors to give remarkably faceted portrayals mark "Eve's Bayou" a first film of exceptional promise.

NEW YORK POST, 11/7/97, p. 56, Michael Medved

From its instantly gripping opening lines of narration ("The summer I killed my father, I was 10 years old ..."), "Eve's Bayou" never loses its uncanny power to startle—and to satisfy its audience.

First-time director (and veteran actress) Kasi Lemmons captures shimmering images that project a kaleidoscope mastery of shifting, intricate moods, but it is her stunningly self-assured screenplay that represents an even more significant achievement.

Writing so rich in character, incident and atmosphere misleadingly suggests an adaptation of some classic but previously unknown Southern memory novel, but this is, after all, an audacious movie original.

Samuel L. Jackson plays a popular small-town doctor in Louisiana of the 1950s who admires his elegant but tightly wound wife (Lynn Whitfield) and three children but can't stop himself from taking advantage of lusty loose women in his village.

His beautiful sister (Debbi Morgan) suffers romantic torments of her own; after the deaths of three consecutive husbands, this psychic healer feels convinced she operates under an inescapable curse.

The family saga unfolds through the eyes of the middle child, Eve (played with remarkable range by 10-year-old Jurnee Smollett), who feels jealous of her all-conquering adolescent sister (Meagan Good) and sadistically contemptuous of her sensitive younger brother (Jake Smollett).

Thanks to the consistently superior performances, each of these relationships comes across with unexpected clarity and dynamism, with especially moving moments showing the passionate love-hate connection between sisters.

Much of this material resonates with the bittersweet, nostalgic intensity of "To Kill a Mockingbird," though the fatal-flawed philanderer who heads this household is a far cry from the heroic father figure in that book and movie.

Jackson (who also coproduced the movie) manages to make the proud papa so undeniably charming that it's easy to understand why his kids worship him as they do, even though they know his faults.

Among the movie's few faults, the only one that counts is the awkward overlay of mystical elements, represented in part by resentful voodoo priestess Diahann Carroll; director Lemmons only distracts from her electric and unpredictable human relationships with these half-hearted invocations of the supernatural.

Far more impressive magic involves the sulfur risk-taking of this audacious and imaginative adventure, which placed an aristocratic black family in a setting (and time period) instantly associated with Tennessee Williams, and created a motion picture experience that is simultaneously fresh and unforgettable.

SIGHT AND SOUND, 8/98, p. 38, Linda Ruth Williams

1962. The prosperous Batiste family hold a party in their Louisiana home. Jealous of her sister Cisely's close relationship with their father, local doctor Louis Batiste, ten-year-old Eve escapes to the carriage house. She is disturbed by the spectacle of her father having sex with neighbour Matty Mereaux. Eve then dreams that her Uncle Harry is killed, and soon afterwards he dies.

She becomes close to his widow Mozelle, a psychic whose powers Eve shares. Eve's mother Roz, disturbed by Louis' infidelities, has her fortune told and, believing that her children are in danger, confines them to the house. After Roz and Louis argue, Cisely withdraws into herself and is sent to a psychiatrist. She tells Eve that Louis molested her one night when she tried to comfort him. Eve vows to kill their father and consults a voodoo practitioner to that end. Louis is murdered soon after by Matty's husband, but Eve finds a letter from her father to Mozelle saying that Cisely had been the sexual initiator in their encounter and that he had rebuffed her. When Eve confronts Cisely, she admits that she does not know who was to blame.

Despite its heady Southern-gothic mix of infidelity, voodoo and murder, Eve's Bayou is not one of Tennessee Williams' hothouse flowers. Its ancestors are the women's film and the coming-of-age story, and actress-turned-director Kasi Lemmons presents distorted memory and a child's-eye view of the adult world with a dispassionate care. The wealthy, black bourgeois Batiste family is elegantly sketched, their story played out in a series of gorgeous Southern-style Ideal Homes (circa 1962) interiors which frame, and indeed cool, the heated shenanigans of the grown-up players. But more than this it is ten-year-old Eve's perspective which keeps the adults' passions at arm's length. Beautifully played—and sometimes skillfully underplayed—by Jurnee Smollett (who was ten when she took on the role), her view gives the film a detachment partly born of childish misrecognition.

This directness of view gives Eve's Bayou a focus which enables it to carry off a number of complex thematic feats. With Eve as its subjective centre, the film shifts between past, present and future in a manner which is illuminating rather than confusing, making it a generational saga that opens the question of how the past haunts the future. Eve anchors person to property: *Eve's Bayou* (rather like the House of Usher) is both the place she inhabits (after which she was named) and the world she constructs. This, incidentally, is the only moment when the film overtly stakes its racial political claim: "The town we lived in was named after a slave," Eve tells us, and a female slave at that. A female slave who gave not only the town, but Eve herself, a name—Eve being her affluent descendant.

The sympathy we feel for Eve also enables us to accept the film's most difficult issue: its suggestion that incest might not be a locus for blame or simple responsibility, but the result of a melting pot of unresolved desires emanating from both parent and child. That Eve finally eschews blame means that the film itself can also do something rather more complex than turn its flawed characters into heroes or villains. In particular, Samuel L. Jackson's seductive but family-loving philanderer manages to be deeply likable, in a performance played beautifully against type.

The theme of passing on and seeing through the past is carried through in the film's double pun on the word sight. As the opening and then the closing voice over (by the adult Eve) tells us, "Memory is a selection of images ... Like others before me I have the gift of sight. But the truth changes colour depending on the light." This 'sight' is the second sight of Mozelle and Eve, itself an instance of the past passed on. It is also the opening for a number of visual plays on the notion that memory has no single truth, position or perspective. Like photographic film itself, memory here changes colour depending on the light. Key epiphanic moments—Louis' initial infidelity; flash-photo shots of family members; the kiss between Louis and his eldest daughter—are frozen, slowed or bleached into grainy black and white to underline their ambiguous significance out of time. Less successful, because less cinematic, is the contrived and stagy device of 'projecting' memories in mirrors. But this is an uncharacteristic off-note, since the precise cinematography and performances evoke in a very cinematic way the question of how memory is rewritten through its reworking through time.

Clairvoyance—literally 'clear visior' may be Mozelle's gift to Eve, but the hidden past and unlived future the women see is anything but clear in its significance, and the picture keeps shifting. Here *Eve's Bayou* seems to suggest that the camera (or clairvoyant) which reads and replays another's memories neither lies nor tells the truth: it's not what you see that's important, but how desire filters the way you see it.

While Eve is the film's fulcrum, *Eve's Bayou* demonstrates that no single perspective can possibly account for the complex truths of family life, compromised by secrets and desire. So in the way that it both withholds and rewrites the truths of its own past, *Eve's Bayou* does more than gear up narrative suspense when it shows you what it *won't* tell as well as what it *will*. With Cisely's final revelation that Oedipal desire can work in both directions, and that who does what to whom is rarely clearly delineated, the film puts on hold the possibility of accessing the truth plain and simple, demonstrating that the family saga might be the best place to reassess how we understand the deceptions and revelations of memory.

TIME, 10/13/97, p. 88, Richard Corliss

Once is a fluke, twice a hope, three times a trend. So, with the pretty box-office numbers for *Soul Food* following the $70 million that *Waiting to Exhale* earned in early '96, and with the highly touted *Eve's Bayou* opening in two weeks, maybe Hollywood will stop being surprised every time the black middle class goes to see itself on screen.

Quality is another, nearly irrelevant matter; no film has to be well made to be well liked. Indeed, one reason for the popularity of *Soul Food* is that it pushes emotional buttons with all the subtlety of a poke in the baby-back ribs. It could be a distillation of some unaired black soap opera, so predictable, are the plot contrivances—adultery, pregnancy, illness, missing money—and so cartoonishly are the characters drawn. Mother Joe (Irma P. Hall) is warm, loving, doomed. One daughter, Maxine (Vivica A. Fox), is heart-smart and, since she's a mother, a font of family wisdom. Another, Teri (Vanessa L. Williams), a successful lawyer who has subsidized most of the family's extravagances, is, of course, the villain of the piece. Poor Williams: her pretty mouth is forever prissed in disapproval at her more sympathetic sibs.

At the movie's center is a wise child: Ahmad, 10, brings the warring family together. As Ahmad, Brandon Hammond is superb: his serious eyes are alert, his bearing natural. He points the film up the road it should have taken. Didn't, though. The dialogue plays like song cues without the songs, and the rest of a talented cast is wasted. *Soul Food* aims to be a banquet of feelings, but mostly it serves up tripe.

An attractive, adulterous man; a woman trying to preserve her family; a child who sees and remembers too much. The same elements presented so coarsely in *Soul Food* come piercingly alive in *Eve's Bayou*. From the opening voice-over—"The summer I killed my father, I was 10 years old"—the film weaves a spell of magnolia and menace. This 10-year-old is Eve (Jurnee Smollett), second daughter of Dr. Louis Batiste (Samuel L. Jackson). Louis pushes charm as much as pills, and the local ladies swoon at his touch. "To a certain type of woman," he notes, "I am a hero. I need to be a hero." Eve and her sister Cisely (Meagan Good), 14, need him to be one too, and when he proves a sinner, they are devastated. His crime may have been that he didn't dance with Eve or that he danced too close to Cisely. But since Aunt Mozelle (Debbi Morgan) tells fortunes, and lives out bad ones, Eve is a voodoo priestess once removed. Her curse on her daddy could be fatal.

In rural Louisiana in the '60s, and in the humid swamps of the Southern Gothic imagination, tenderness and terror are first cousins destined to marry. With scary assurance, novice writer-director Kasi Lemmons invades Faulkner-McCullers territory and makes it her own. There are a few visual and character clichés, and we wish that, just once in movies, a fortune teller's dire prophecy would not automatically come true. But the folks here believe in its power, and they compel the viewer to abandon skepticism, to hide with Eve in the Batiste closet, where skeletons whisper vengeance.

Jackson wears Louis' shroud suavely; he can seduce everyone except Eve. But this is a woman's film, and a showcase for superb actresses. Morgan does especially fine work as a sorceress whose gift runs away with her. The poise and passion in *Eve's Bayou* leave one grateful, exhausted and nourished. For the restless spirit, here is true soul food.

VILLAGE VOICE, 11/11/97, p. 82, Amy Taubin

In Kasi Lemmons's *Eve's Bayou*, Samuel L. Jackson plays the dad of every little girl's wildest dreams. When we first see Dr. Louis Batiste, he's dirty dancing with a friend's wife while the other women in his life (his two daughters, wife, mother, and sister) watch with mixed emotions, each in her own way trying to deny that she's seeing what she's seeing. "You must be very proud of your son—he's the best black doctor in Louisiana," says one partygoer to Dr. Batiste's mother, as the object of desire displays his lasciviousness like a charm.

Eve's Bayou is a rare film in that it's about female desire, and, in particular, the desire of a 10-year-old girl to secure the affections of her father, whose sexuality both binds and disrupts family life. Couched as a memory piece, it seems to lay its cards on the table right at the beginning. As the camera floats across the dark waters of the bayou country, we hear the voice of the grown-up Eve announcing, "I was 10 the summer I killed my father."

The death of the father, thus, has an inevitability that offsets the ambiguity of the feelings and events that precipitate it. That growing up is about learning to live with dreadful ambiguity is precisely Lemmons's point. Eve will never know for certain whether her father committed the terrible act that made her want him dead, or whether she caused his death through magic or through her precocious understanding of the explosive power of sexual jealousy.

This is ambitious stuff, and it's no wonder that a first-time director doesn't have it entirely under control. Or maybe the problem is that Lemmons wants to exert too much control, tying inchoate desires, contradictory motives, and elusive memories into an overly conventional package so as not to alienate a potential mass audience. In any event, the expressivity of the filmmaking doesn't quite measure up to the ideas and feelings that inspired *Eve's Bayou*.

That said, this is still a wonderfully talented and intelligent film. Lemmons mixes the mysterious and the mundane in her depiction of a wealthy, creolized black culture that's never been shown in depth on the screen. And her obvious empathy with the actors (Lemmons was a performer before she became a director) encourages them to give performances that are as complicated as the characters they embody.

In a white Hollywood terrified of black male sexuality (think of how Don Cheadle is de-balled in *Boogie Nights),* Jackson has been straitjacketed in roles that displace his libido into violence or humor. Here, he's as startlingly carnal a presence as the young Brando was in *Streetcar.* Not content to be merely charismatic, he shows how Dr. Batiste's irresistible joie de vivre is inseparable from his guilt and self-hatred.

As Eve, Jurnee Smollett—who can do a 180-degree emotional shift within a single shot—is equally compelling. Lemmons allows her to be as broad and awkward in the expression of feeling as children often are in life and almost never are on screen. It's a remarkably unsentimental performance.

In the supporting roles, Meagan Good (as Eve's 14-year-old sister whose heart belongs, even more perilously, to Daddy) and Debbi Morgan (as Mozelle Batiste Delacroix, Dr. Batiste's sister, who either has the gift of sight or is a little nuts, or maybe both) are particularly fine. In a film that proposes female bonding as a counterbalance to the power of heterosexual desire, it's satisfying that the largely female cast has a rapport that's as complicated as it is understated.

Also reviewed in:
CHICAGO TRIBUNE, 11/7/97, Friday/p. H, John Petrakis
NEW YORK TIMES, 11/7/97, p. E14, Stephen Holden
VARIETY, 9/8-14/97, p. 80, Emanuel Levy
WASHINGTON POST, 11/7/97, p. G1, Stephen Hunter
WASHINGTON POST, 11/7/97, Weekend/p. 48, Desson Howe

EXCESS BAGGAGE

A Columbia Pictures release of a First Kiss production. *Producer:* Bill Borden and Carolyn Kessler. *Director:* Marco Brambilla. *Screenplay:* Max D. Adams, Dick Clement, and Ian La Frenais. *Story:* Max D. Adams. *Director of Photography:* Jean Yves Escoffier. *Editor:* Stephen Rivkin. *Music:* John Lurie. *Music Editor:* Lia Vollack. *Sound:* Eric J. Batut and (music) Pat Dilletti. *Sound Editor:* Patrick Dodd. *Casting:* Mike Fenton and Allison Cowitt. *Production Designer:* Missy Stewart. *Art Director:* Richard Hudolin. *Set Decorator:* Elizabeth Wilcox. *Special Effects:* William H. Orr. *Costumes:* Beatrix Aruna Pasztor. *Make-up:* Victoria Down. *Stunt Coordinator:* Betty Thomas. *Running time:* 105 minutes. *MPAA Rating:* PG-13.

CAST: Alicia Silverstone (Emily Hope); Benicio Del Toro (Vincent Roche); Christopher Walken ("Uncle" Ray Perkins); Jack Thompson (Alexander Hope); Harry Connick, Jr. (Greg Kistler); Nicolas Turturro (Stick); Michael Bowen (Gus); Robert Wisden (Detective Sims); Leland Orser (Detective Barnaby); Sally Kirkland (Louise); Hiro Kanagawa (Jon); Brendan Beiser (Man on Pay Phone); Demetri Goritsas (Surveillance Van Cop); Jorge Vargas (Mini Mart Clerk); Danielle Saklofsky (Monique); Stacy Grant (Car Showroom Receptionist); Callum Rennie (Motel Manager); Carrie Cain Sparko (Waitress at Diner); Nicole Parker (Waitress at Knotty Pines); Bill Croft, C. Ernst Harth and Adrien Derval (Truckers); Claire Riley (Dream Reporter); Dean Wray (Barge Mate); Fulvio Cecere (Sharp Shooter); David Longworth (RV Gas Pumper).

LOS ANGELES TIMES, 8/29/97, Calendar/p. 14, Jack Mathews

[The following review by Jack Mathews appeared in a slightly different form in **NEWSDAY, 8/29/97, Part II/p. B3.]**

It seems like just 10 minutes ago that Alicia Silverstone was being discovered in a throwaway thriller about a deranged adolescent girl who develops a lethal "Crush" on Cary Elwes, and maybe five minutes ago that she was "Clueless." Now, she's a full-fledged star of the '90s, with the power to produce her own major studio movies, even if they only amount to "Excess Baggage."

What a cool thing to be a teenager with a multimillion-dollar budget, to be able to pluck a fun role out of a stack of scripts, cast a hunk like Benicio Del Toro as her romantic co-star, hire her own director and then fight with him over creative differences! Hats off to erstwhile Columbia chief Mark Canton, who got to Silverstone first, got to her before her wisdom teeth were even in, and gave her First Kiss Productions the go.

For the rest of us, the news isn't so good. "Excess Baggage," a scruffy romantic comedy about a despairing rich girl who hatches a kidnapping scheme to test her father's love, is an aimless waste, a star vehicle without a compass. It wants very much to be both funny and poignant, but is more often just noisy and pointless.

Silverstone did pick a role ready-made for her. Emily Hope could be the girl from "The Crush," after her release from the mental hospital: better, but not quite cured. Still a manipulative brat. Her wealthy father (Jack Thompson) is too busy with his shady international dealings, to give her the attention she needs, so she creates increasingly elaborate pranks to distract him.

This last one is a pip. She's holding herself hostage and demanding a $1-million ransom, while her father, the FBI and her mysterious Uncle Ray (Christopher Walken) try to find her. But her plan goes awry when a professional auto thief named Vincent (Del Toro) steals her green BMW from the pickup spot, unaware that Emily, self-bound and gagged, is in the trunk.

Once Vincent and Emily formally meet, they evolve from hostile enemies to reluctant companions to ... well, let's just say the arc of their relationship generally follows that between crusty Clark Gable and petulant heiress Claudette Colbert in "It Happened One Night." They're on the road together in the Pacific Northwest, Vincent not wanting to go down for kidnapping as well as grand theft auto, and Emily determined not to go home.

Though John Lurie's soundtrack music breaks its strings trying to convince us scenes are funnier than they, the resources devoted to "Excess Baggage" do cover many of its weaknesses. The cinematography of Jean Yves Escoffier is terrific, as is the scenery in British Columbia. And for what they're given to do, Del Toro, Thompson, Walken and Nicolas Turturro, a Joe Pesci impressionist who plays one of Vincent's dangerously unhappy clients, give solid performances.

Walken, whose name suggests how he now gets through most of his roles, plays former CIA assassin Uncle Ray as a deliberate, confident fellow with a smile that hints of both whimsy and sadism. Nobody plays this character better than Walken, and "Excess Baggage" should have taken better advantage of him.

From published accounts, it seems that Silverstone played her scenes to suit herself, rather than take direction from Marco Brambilla ("Demolition Man"), and to her credit, she stays within her demonstrated range. If she's the star everyone is telling her she is, "Excess Baggage" will do OK.

If not, we can hope that both she and spendthrift studio executives will take a lesson from it, and give experience a chance.

NEW YORK POST, 8/29/97, p. 56, Michael Medved

Car thief Benicio Del Toro feels proud of the handsome, late-model BMW he manages to steal from a parking garage. Back at his warehouse headquarters, however, he opens the trunk and discovers "Excess Baggage" in the person of a bound-and-gagged Alicia Silverstone.

The result of this encounter is an uneven but occasionally intriguing romantic comedy that takes Hollywood's obsession with high concept "Cute meets cutthroat" to absurd new extremes.

Silverstone plays a sulky heiress who staged her own kidnapping in a desperate bid to win attention from her widower father (Australian star Jack Thompson), a shady international entrepreneur.

When Del Toro steals her car, he disrupts her elaborate plans and they must overcome their instinctive hostility to work together in dodging dangers from bumbling cops and his vicious, impatient criminal colleagues (Nicolas Turturro, Michael Bowen, Harry Connick Jr.). They also face the determined pursuit of her unstoppable 'Uncle' Ray (Christopher Walken), a suave but deadly former-CIA-operative who now handles impossible jobs for her tycoon father.

Ever since Clark Gable and Claudette Colbert hit the road together in "It Happened One Night," poor little rich girls have been encountering penniless, cynical rogues (with secretly soft hearts) in big-screen romances. "Excess Baggage" audaciously varies this ancient theme by treating both of its principals as pathetic, shallow, lonely, low-life losers, consuming—in between Ms.

Silverstone's countless cigarettes—prodigious quantities of Jack Daniels, vodka, gin, rum and wine (never mind that her character is a pointedly underage 18).

Silverstone slips into this deglamorized role with surprising assurance and ease while Del Toro, despite a mumbling tendency to imitate Christian Slater imitating Jack Nicholson, lends slimy, sad humanity to his peculiar part.

Unfortunately, the overwritten and meandering plot, full of illogical twists and double-crosses, is both less realistic and less interesting than the characters. Scenes shift jerkily among various picturesque but unfocused locations, with Vancouver standing in for Seattle.

Director Marco Brambilla, whose one previous film (the futuristic Stallone/Snipes bloodbath "Demolition Man") featured almost nothing beyond mindless action, here seems so eager to show he's capable of substantive work that the various chase and fight scenes display a lackadaisical, perfunctory quality.

In the end, you can almost sympathize with the characters' self-pity and boredom since the insipid story line leaves these vividly creepy but compelling people trapped in the trunk of a shiny but tinny stolen vehicle.

SIGHT AND SOUND, 11/97, p. 37, Nina Caplan

Poor little rich girl Emily Hope is so desperate for her father Alexander Hope to switch attention from managing his millions to her that she stages her own kidnapping. Unfortunately, while she awaits deliverance from the boot of her BMW, car thief Vincent Roche steals it. He takes the car back to his stolen-car-filled garage and discovers her in the boot. Vincent drives Emily out of town, and dumps her in the countryside far from a phone. On the way back, he sees on the news that his garage has burnt down (due to a lit match accidentally left by Emily) and that she is a millionaire's daughter. He goes back to rescue her and leaves her at a motel.

Vincent's partner Greg is in trouble with mobsters Stick and Gus who were to collect the stolen, now burnt, cars. They want the $200,000 they paid in advance, which Vincent has, and set off to look for him. Meanwhile, Mr Hope's head of security Ray finds Vincent and forces him to take him to Emily. Although he realises Emily faked the kidnapping, Ray plans to get Vincent arrested for it to avoid the scandal, but Emily helps Vincent escape.

The couple spend a passionate night together, but are surprised by Stick and Gus in the morning. They kidnap Emily, then demand that Vincent give them the original $200,000 and extort $1 million from Mr Hope. However, Hope refuses to pay. Vincent and Ray go to rescue Emily themselves although she breaks free herself. Later, when the longed-for emotional reunion with her father is not forthcoming, Emily leaves to be with Vincent.

Most good comedies have an inherently funny situation at their core. In Marco Brambilla's *Excess Baggage*, parental neglect is the premise for a romantic comedy of mismatched characters who fall in love. But this is an odd variation of the formula that doesn't really work because it lacks an underlying sense of stability. In Howard Hawks' comedies, for example, a surreal disorder is always counterpointed against a domestic calm which frames the action. Here, however, we are presented with an already loveless environment which has clearly damaged Emily emotionally.

With one exception, everyone in this film is running after money. Even Emily, who claims in the initial voice-over that her fake kidnap is not financially motivated, is chasing her father, a monolithic figure whose power and complete absence of emotion make him a living symbol of wealth. While Stick and Gus are the perennial uncomplicated wrongdoers chasing the big loot, Vincent is the disadvantaged criminal with morals but no other way out of the poverty trap. Benicio Del Toro turns in a fine performance as the muttering hoodlum with a heart, but the role is clichéd and insubstantial.

One ray of wintry sunshine is Christopher Walken as Hope's hitman Uncle Ray, who attempts to protect Emily because of his love for her and loyalty to her father. But his motivation, the only one that doesn't spring from greed, never seems convincing. This is typical of a film which never quite rings true: it is a capitalist fable where money can't buy love; a story of a princess who doesn't need rescuing; a crime flick with no thrills. The one authentic touch is the fine noir-ish cinematography. Reflecting Emily and Vincent's feelings for them, the dark, sleek cars are lovingly photographed: lights slide across their windows as they move between rain-swept highways and brightly lit petrol stations.

The film is littered with excess baggage, both physical and emotional. Despite attempts to make Emily seem vulnerable (such as a dream sequence in which she imagines a rapturous reunion with Daddy), Silverstone, who heads the film's production company, seems too much in control. Brambilla directed *Demolition Man*, and *Excess Baggage* suggests that his vision of the present is as bleak as his revisions of the future. Lust is read as love, attention as affection and all objects are replaceable. When trying to extract ransom money from an indifferent Mr Hope, Vincent is astonished to realise he cares more about Emily than her father. It's an unsettling note in a comedy. Vincent states at one point that he has always known the potential of failure. As a film for the grab-it-and-run 90s, *Excess Baggage* should have been more convinced of its own ability to succeed.

VILLAGE VOICE, 9/2/97, p. 78, Dennis Lim

"All I ever wanted was a father who loved me," sighs Alicia Silverstone in the first minute of her producing debut, *Excess Baggage*. It's soon apparent that the film's principal ingredients are Silverstone, handcuffs, duct tape, and the Electra complex, and that director Marco Brambilla has no idea how to stitch them together with any coherence. Silverstone plays Emily Hope, a petulant heiress (like *Clueless*'s Cher, only not funny) who stages her own kidnapping in a last-ditch bid to get Daddy's attention. All goes to plan, until a car thief (Benicio Del Toro) intervenes, and Emily (in the fashion of an Almodovar heroine) falls for her captor.

The witless script never calls upon Silverstone's impeccable comic timing, simply surrounding her with a succession of older men, all of whom want to either harm or protect her. Del Toro, whose demeanor here suggests a simian Brad Pitt, is an intermittently fascinating presence, but the film is otherwise teeming with rotten performances; Christopher Walken as Emily's crazy uncle Ray deserves special condemnation.

Also reviewed in:
CHICAGO TRIBUNE, 8/29/97, Friday/p. A, Michael Wilmington
NEW YORK TIMES, 8/29/97, p. C10, Stephen Holden
VARIETY, 9/1-7/97, p. 75, Timothy M. Gray

EYE OF GOD

A Castle Hill Productions & Minnow Pictures release. *Producer:* Wendy Ettinger and Michael Nelson. *Director:* Tim Blake Nelson. *Screenplay:* Tim Blake Nelson. *Director of Photography:* Russell Lee Fine. *Editor:* Kate Sanford. *Music:* David Van Tieghem. *Sound:* Mack Melson. *Sound Editor:* Mary Ellen Porto. *Casting:* Avy Kaufman. *Production Designer:* Patrick Geary. *Art Director:* Richard "Tudor" Williams. *Set Dresser:* Barry Greene. *Costumes:* Jill O'Hanneson. *Make-up:* Salina Jayne. *Prosthetic Make-up:* David Atherton. *Running time:* 84 minutes. *MPAA Rating:* Not Rated.

CAST: Mary Kay Place (Claire Spencer); Nick Stahl (Tom Spencer); Chris Freihofer (Les Hector); Woody Watson (Glen Briggs); Martha Plimpton (Ainsley Dupree); Margo Martindale (Dorothy); Kevin Anderson (Jack Stillings); Wally Welch (R.J. Prichard); Larry Flynn (Jim Nutter); Richard Jenkins (Willard Sprague); Maggie Moore (Janice); Vernon Grote (Fast Food Customer); Gary Ragland (Lee); Hal Holbrook (Sheriff Rogers); Caroline Wickwire (Mrs. Rogers); Toby Metcalf (Officer #1); Darryl Cox (Officer #2); Karen Carney (Mrs. Sprague); Robert Peters (Del); Lisa Benavides (Nurse); Gail Peister (Female Doctor).

CHRISTIAN SCIENCE MONITOR, 11/14/97, p. 12, David Sterritt

[*Eye of God* was reviewed jointly with *The Apostle*; see Sterritt's review of that film.]

LOS ANGELES TIMES, 10/31/97, Calendar/p. 20, John Anderson

[The following review by John Anderson appeared in a slightly different form in **NEWSDAY, 10/17/97, Part II/p. B7.**]

Does God smile on Oklahoma, where the wind comes sweeping down the plain? Let's examine the evidence: Mickey Mantle, Will Rogers and J.J. Cale; 168 dead in a terrorist bombing; and the banning of "The Tin Drum." The question seems open to debate.

Debuting writer-director Tim Blake Nelson seems convinced that the place suffers from deity deprivation, judging by "Eye of God," a dark little tale that borrows the Genesis story of Abraham and Isaac as its opening conceit but really deserves something out of Revelations. Murder. Madness. Fundamentalist hysteria. And a strain of apocalyptic malevolence running throughout that occasionally blossoms into real tension.

On the other hand, there's so much flashing (back and forth, forth and back) that the movie should be wearing a raincoat. Time here is a very, very flexible thing, so much so that just keeping track of when and where you are is enough to keep you from noticing how slim the story is. We encounter young Tom Spencer (Nick Stahl) as a happy kid watching TV, then in a post-traumatic catatonia, then as a vaguely unhappy kid, very quickly and without enough immediate detail to establish what's happening when. It's not an ineffective technique; when Atom Egoyan does it in the upcoming "Sweet Hereafter," it works both dramatically and logically. It just doesn't quite work here.

The other characters are caught up in same space-time discontinuum: Ainsley Dupree (Martha Plimpton), for instance, who's waiting at the local lunch counter for Jack Stillings (Kevin Anderson), her just-released-from-prison pen pal. Plimpton is marvelously unsure of herself as Ainsley; Anderson is not quite believable (which would be good, if it weren't the fault of the script) as the born-again ex-con come to sweep her off her feet. Their whirlwind romance ends in a marriage that becomes increasingly oppressive for Ainsley and seems headed for disaster. Except the disaster's already happened. Or has it?

The acting is uniformly fine, and Nelson exhibits terrific control over the sequence that closes the film. Getting there, however, involves transversing a too-belabored and confusing series of plot pieces, stacked in a rather mad manner. Without the narrative trickery, on the other hand, the story is exposed as a fairly predictable bit of business.

NEW YORK POST, 10/17/97, p. 48, Thelma Adams

Martha Plimpton plays wispy blondes brushed with tragedy. With her slim, long-distance-runner's body, the "Parenthood" star can appear to be blown sideways by life—but she's anchored, rangy, a survivor. She plays plucky, stubborn young women who like to break the rules.

In Tim Blake Nelson's American grotesque "Eye of God," the doe-eyed Plimpton is Ainsley Dupree. The Oklahoma short-order cook breaks all the rules.

1: The Menendez rule: Never initiate an epistolary romance with a convict.

2: The Marv Albert rule: Never marry the lunk before you have all the facts.

3: The Gwyneth Paltrow rule: Don't date a guy who's prettier than you.

Kevin Anderson, as convict Jack Stillings, is such a guy. He's one of those soft-talking, God-fearing, curl-tumbling-over-his-forehead psychopaths who just breathe plot twists. (On TV, he's making ambivalence cute again as the preacher star of "Nothing Sacred.")

On the day Stillings leaves jail, he meets up with pen pal Plimpton at a diner. The coffee has hardly cooled before they're married and he's maniacal.

Sheriff Rogers (Hal Holbrook) gets pulled into their domestic mess when the lawman encounters Tom (Nick Stahl), a blue-eyed, blood-drenched boy who's seen too much.

As the local sheriff says, "Sooner or later, a cop has to deal with God." In narrative voice-over, the world-weary lawman lays down the central theme.

Sheriff Rogers recounts the tale of Abraham. Called on by God to slay his own son Isaac, Abe obeys unconditionally. The story reflects the mystery of God's will and the need for the individual to have faith, to submit.

Director Nelson, adapting his own stageplay, attempts an interesting twist. The drama is meant to be Isaac's story, the vision of the innocent, the groping toward faith of those who are apparently out of range of God's voice.

But it's the pulpy story of Ainsley and her prison pen pal that swallows the movie. "Eye of God" opens with a portentous clarity that promises something more than a corpse dredged up from an Oklahoma lake. Sooner or later, a filmmaker has to deal with God, but it's easier if he throws in a nude body and a glass eye.

VILLAGE VOICE, 10/21/97, p. 94, Gary Dauphin

First-time writer-director Tim Blake Nelson's *Eye of God* is a real magic trick of a movie, a simple and depressingly familiar small-town story that looms larger than you'd expect thanks to fine, detailed performances and sleight-of-hand plotting. On one level *Eye* is just the downbeat tale of Jack (Kevin Anderson) and Ainsley (Martha Plimpton)—two not-quite-kids from the heartland who'd be the perfect stuff of a darker, more violent John Cougar Mellencamp song—but it's also an ambitiously nonlinear film where incidents are rearranged in time like cards being showily shuffled. It's a stacked deck, of course, but even if you don't buy *Eye*'s numerous nominations about fate there's still something awfully impressive about how deftly it deals out bad hands to the people onscreen.

Eye's primal scene is a nighttime trip to the banks of a weed-clotted watering hole where the mazelike flashbacks begin and end. In the opening moments, a local teen (Nick Stahl) is found there—blank, bloody and so traumatized he's unable to speak. It's where the hapless and rangily pretty Ainsley takes ex-con and Jesus freak Jack a-courtin' soon after he's paroled and where Ainsley will run once he turns controlling and violent. The aging local sheriff (Hal Holbrook, doing a fine job of seeming fatigued) goes to the pond as well, but late in the game, long after it's obvious that something predictably nasty has happened between Ainsley, Jack, and the mute boy. Mirroring *Eye*'s own priorities, he isn't trying to find out what occurred there so much as he's desperately looking for just one person to save.

The first few scenes and flashbacks make it clear that Ainsley come to grief, but the curious thing about *Eye of God* isn't the how or why of her fate but the wonder it evokes regarding her ability to live with some kind of hope as her world begins to contract. Director Nelson flirts consistently with disaster by bleeding *Eye of God* so thoroughly of suspense or even order, but the gambit works because of a graceful, low-key shooting style that sticks closely throughout to the details of everyday life. It also works because of Plimpton. Her Ainsley is a real marvel, the kind of lonely young woman who hangs out at lunch counters hoping to just sit a spell and talk, and she's so likable and genuine that even when she makes patently foolish decisions, they don't seem stupid but brave in a flinty, fragile way. *Eye of God* obviously believes (and with some self-importance) in the unavoidabilty of fate, but Plimpton's Ainsley is about the possibility of faith, and there are ways in which that's just as powerful.

Also reviewed in:
CHICAGO TRIBUNE, 1/30/98, p. J, Michael Wilmington
NEW YORK TIMES, 10/17/97, p. E12, Stephen Holden
VARIETY, 1/27-2/2/97, p. 77, Joe Leydon
WASHINGTON POST, 11/14/97, Weekend/p. 50, Stephen Hunter

FACE/OFF

A Paramount Pictures release of a Douglas/Reuther production, WCG Entertainment, David Permut production. *Executive Producer:* Michael Douglas, Steven Reuther, and Jonathan D. Krane. *Producer:* David Permut, Barrie M. Osborne, Terence Chang, and Christopher Godsick. *Director:* John Woo. *Screenplay:* Mike Werb and Michael Colleary. *Director of Photography:* Oliver Wood. *Editor:* Christian Wagner and Steven Kemper. *Music:* John Powell. *Music Editor:* Sally Boldt. *Sound:* David Ronne and (music) Alan Meyerson. *Sound Editor:* Mark P. Stoeckinger. *Casting:* Mindy Marin. *Production Designer:* Neil Spisak. *Art Director:* Steve

Arnold. *Set Designer:* Steven Schwartz, Gerald Sullivan, Barbara Ann Spencer, and Suzan Wexler. *Set Decorator:* Garrett Lewis. *Special Effects:* Lawrence J. Cavanaugh and R. Bruce Steinheimer. *Visual Effects:* Boyd Shermis and Richard Hollander. *Costumes:* Ellen Mirojnick. *Make-up:* David Atherton. *Make-up (Special Effects):* Kevin Yagher. *Stunt Coordinator:* Brian Smrz. *Running time:* 150 minutes. *MPAA Rating:* R.

CAST: John Travolta (Sean Archer); Nicolas Cage (Castor Troy); Joan Allen (Eve Archer); Alessandro Nivola (Pollux Troy); Gina Gershon (Sasha Hassler); Dominique Swain (Jamie Archer); Nick Cassavetes (Dietrich Hassler); Harve Presnell (Victor Lazarro); Colm Feore (Dr. Malcolm Walsh); John Carroll Lynch (Walton, Prison Guard); C.C.H. Pounder (Hollis Miller); Robert Wisdom (Tito Biondi); Margaret Cho (Wanda); Jamie Denton (Buzz); Matt Ross (Loomis); Chris Bauer (Dubov); Myles Jeffrey (Michael Archer); David Mccurley (Adam Hassler); Thomas Jane (Burke Hicks); Tommy J. Flanagan (Leo); Dana Smith (Lars); Romy Walthall (Kimberly); Paul Hipp (Fitch); Kirk Baltz (Aldo); Lauren Sinclair (Agent Winters); Ben Reed (Pilot); Lisa Boyle (Cindee); Linda Hoffman (Livia); Danny Masterson (Karl); Michael Rocha (Priest); Megan Paul (Hospital Girl); Mike Werb (Hospital Dad); Tom Reynolds (LAPD Cop); Steve Hytner (Interrogating Agent); Carmen Thomas (Valerie, Reporter); John Bloom (Prison Medical Technician); Walter Scott (Port Police Commander); Brooke Leslie (ER Nurse); Cam Brainard (Dispatcher); David Warshofsky (Bomb Leader); John Neidlinger and Norm Compton (Bomb Technicians); Gregg Shawzin (Lock Down Guard); Clifford Einstein (Restorative Surgeon); Marco Kyris (Recreation Guard); Tom Fridley (Prison Guard); Andrew Wallace (Altar Boy); Jacinto Rodriguez (Prisoner); Chic Daniel (FBI Squad Leader); Laurence Walsh (Walsh Clinical Nurse).

LOS ANGELES TIMES, 6/27/97, Calendar/p. 1, Kenneth Turan

John Woo is known for a cinema of violent delirium so breathtaking it plays like visual poetry; and "Face/Off," though his third film in Hollywood, is the first to expose mainstream audiences to the master at his most anarchically persuasive.

But as those who've seen the director's cult favorite Hong Kong movies like "A Better Tomorrow," "The Killer" and "Hard Boiled" can testify, Woo is also known for the sincerely sentimental underpinnings of his work. Bonding between men links all his films, which classically feature an emotional connection between the hero and the villain that's the strongest one on screen.

Which is why, though it was written by the team of Mike Werb & Michael Colleary before either one had seen the Hong Kong films, "Face/Off" is a kind of ultimate John Woo movie. Its tale of identity-switching takes the director's usual themes to their logical extreme, resulting in a delicious inside-out double-reverse movie that's as outrageous and over the top as anyone could want.

For "Face/Off"'s title refers not only to the inevitable confrontation between good and bad but to a literal switching of physical identities as well. It's a film that demands that its stars play two roles, one nestled inside the other like interlocking toy dolls, a task that's been handled so persuasively by John Travolta and Nicolas Cage that they've inspired Woo to do his best work in years.

The director, who didn't seem to be quite hitting his stride with his first two American films, "Hard Target" and "Broken Arrow," here offers a demonstration of action as it should be done. In its best moments, "Face/Off" practically mainlines fury, leaving audiences no time to think or even breathe.

With an offbeat sense of humor, an eye for small visual touches and a weakness for white doves added to an intuitive grasp of the mechanics of large-scale pyrotechnics, Woo ensures that no one's eyes will be leaving the screen when he's spinning his apocalyptic web.

After a brief prologue set six years ago that establishes the reason for the enmity between Sean Archer (Travolta) and Castor Troy (Cage), "Face/Off" moves up to the present, with Archer as the driven, humorless leader of the usual supersecret government anti-terrorist team.

Archer's main target is, no surprise, Castor Troy and his sniveling sociopath brother Pollux (Alessandro Nivola). Castor is no bargain either, establishing himself early on as a showy and bombastic homicidal maniac, a terrorist-for-hire whose huge gold-dipped handguns decorated with custom-made dragon grips are the least flashy thing about him.

Castor and Pollux get defanged in "Face/Off's" initial action sequence, coming out on the short end of a tussle with Archer, an unhappy man who has let his relationships with wife Eve (Joan Allen) and pouty teenage daughter Jamie (Dominique Swain) deteriorate in his manic quest to nail his nemesis. "It's over," he tells Eve after the battle, but we know better.

It turns out that no one but Castor, who's in one of those movie comas, and Pollux, who's in prison, know exactly where the pair have planted a poison gas bomb that will decimate Los Angeles in just a few days. The only way to save the city is for Archer to assume Castor's identity and worm the info out of the imprisoned Pollux.

We're not talking a fake driver's license here. Thanks to an experimental surgical procedure involving something called a "morphogenetic template," Archer, in a sequence that owes a lot to Georges Franju's indelible "Eyes Without a Face," manages to disappear behind Castor's face and inside his body type. Everyone assures him it's reversible but it's still awfully creepy.

Creepier still is what happens when, for no apparent reason, Castor wakes up and, because it's the only one not spoken for, ends up grabbing Archer's face and body. So both men: each looking like his own worst enemy, try to complete the jobs they started when they looked like themselves.

"Face/Off's" script is not strong on dialogue or conventional plausibility, but its themes are sound, and one of its more intriguing ones is how flummoxed Archer and Castor are by having to live the lives of their hated opponents. Imprisonment and dissipation in no way agree with Archer, and Castor, despite sharing a bed with Archer's wife and leering at his daughter, finds married life is more complex and onerous than he anticipated.

Cage and Travolta are equally successful with their double-barreled roles, and in fact both do better playing the self-loathing that comes with being a frustrated personality in an unwanted body. Travolta, when in the grip of Castor's persona, even gets to make some disparaging comments about his own chin. It's that kind of movie.

It's safe to say that Joan Allen, not usually found in films of this sort, will not get a third Oscar nomination for her work as Archer's sorely tried wife, but it's precisely her skill at making her character both grounded and believable that is essential in giving "Face/Off" what reality it has.

Not surprisingly, it's John Woo, able to provide a nautical sequence that shames "Speed 2" plus carnage choreographed to Olivia Newton-John singing "Somewhere Over the Rainbow," who is the real star of "Face/Off." It's difficult to describe the jolt his films deliver when he's on, and he is on with a vengeance here.

NEW YORK, 7/14/97, p. 47, David Denby

In *Face/Off*, the surprisingly daring and extremely odd John Woo action thriller, John Travolta is an agonized FBI agent and family man, and Nicolas Cage is the terrorist and assassin Travolta is obsessed with catching. The Travolta character, whose name is Sean Archer, is a scrupulous and caring fellow, but he's cut off from life—consumed (as they say) by rage—and Travolta plays him as a miserable obsessive, with a rigid body and a constant grimace of pain. Some years earlier, Cage's Castor Troy tried to eliminate Archer with a high-powered rifle and wound up killing Archer's little boy; Archer has been paralyzed by thoughts of vengeance ever since. The Castor Troy he hates is not only a killer but a jaunty nihilist with a brazenly disruptive sense of humor. Arming a bomb that could release biological agents into the air of Los Angeles—a "biblical plague," in terrorist-speak—Castor dances and swings his arms in mock reverence, a celebrant of his own dastardly transgressions. Cage does what can only be called heterosexual camping—he's flamboyant, ironic, mocking. Sean Archer and Castor Troy are temperamental as well as moral opposites, about as far apart as two men could be. Or so we think.

From the beginning, the cinema has reveled in spooky transformations, in transactions, sometimes solemn, sometimes mischievous, between essence and persona. Is the actor acting "himself," or is he the mimic of another person? Usually the questions are asked, the riddles posed, in artistically serious movies, but Woo and the screenwriters Mike Werb and Michael Colleary (who first conceived this movie back in 1990) are making a violent commercial thriller. The aesthetic risk-taking in *Face/Off* has a special excitement precisely because it arrives so unexpectedly amid the shootouts and falling bodies.

Early in *Face/Off,* the virtuous Archer captures Castor Troy and his genius-lunatic brother Pollux (Alessandro Nivola), who designed the biological bomb, which is still ticking. But where is the bomb? Archer doesn't know; Castor, injured in the arrest, lies in a coma and can't tell him. Only the imprisoned Pollux knows, so Archer, in order to get close to Pollux, agrees to take part in a bizarre medical procedure. Lasers remove his face (eyes, nose, chin, everything) and Castor's face too. Archer then gets the killer's face sewn on, and after some liposuctional work is done on his body (there are amused references to Travotta's love handles), he looks exactly like Castor Troy. Archer enters the prison to cosy up to brother Pollux. Troy, meanwhile, awakens from his coma and takes Archer's face, which has been floating like a mask in a saline solution. Have you understood the situation? The actor John Travolta is now playing Castor Troy but in his own face and body; and Cage is playing Sean Archer but in *his* face and body.

Realism is not at issue here. John Woo is a balletmaster action director, the veteran of countless Hong Kong productions featuring people floating through the air in slow-motion. In Hong Kong movies, a villain is really villainous, a snarler, and everything is exaggerated, cartoonish: the standard of characterization is brevity and vividness, not actuality, and nothing has any weight. Woo is part magician, part schlock-movie maker, a director who loves violence and guns. His last American production, *Broken Arrow* (1996), also with John Travolta, was literally weightless: the film was conducted mainly in the air, with people flying, dangling, falling, jumping, hoisting.

There's plenty of high jinks in *Face/Off*. A helicopter harasses a plane that is trying to take off, shooting, at it, mashing the tail fins, until the plane plows into a hangar. Inside the hanger. Woo stages the first of many shootouts. Bodies whirl, tumble, fall through glass windows; gunmen shoot while flying through the air, which may be a new Woo signature. In all of this mayhem, there's death but no pain—the heroes keep jumping up to shoot again. In later scenes, police in black jackets, fodder with little function except to die, get mowed down by the dozen. The new aesthetic of weightless action is producing a new morality of weightless death—that is, death that has only a formal meaning as a compositional element in Woo's air ballet. Woo is saying this violence is not life, not real, but there's still, for us, an element of uneasiness in his manic aestheticism. When will death *ever* matter to this director?

On several occasions, Woo shows us a bullet hurtling straight toward us and at one point in the hangar sequence, Cage, his body itself turned into a projectile, is shot like a bullet into a wind tunnel. Woo's natural bent is to turn bodies into flying objects. That's why the movie is so odd: because some of it is rather touching, even anguished, as when Castor Troy, now in the body of Sean Archer, makes love to his wife (Joan Allen), and she's puzzled by his new attentions; or when Sean Archer, now in the body of Castor Troy, lies abandoned in prison, the authorities convinced he's a terrorist.

Every time Sean Archer looks in the mirror, he sees the face of the man who shot his son. Woo, where is thy rue? A director raised in a humanist tradition would realize that violent air ballet and tender character observation don't really go together, but Woo pushes the extremes as far as he can; the movie is exciting, unstable, flimsy, and profound at the same time, a gimmick that hurts.

What most people are likely to remember is the two stars playing each other. Travolta, taking over Cage's body language, is liberated into swinishness. He smiles, intrudes on everyone's privacy; he's suddenly a free-and-easy egotist, dancing his way into rooms, insinuating, vicious. He freaks out Dominique Swain (the Lolita-to-be, if the movie is ever released), who plays Archer's rebellious teen daughter. Brazenly coming on to the girl, he suddenly gets tough with her—monster that he is, he sees that she's going wrong, and acts like her father.

Cage, by contrast, taking Archer's anguish into himself, is now frozen, stricken, his eyes suffused with pain. Goodness locks him up. But in another way, he's liberated. Archer no longer needs to commit only righteous violence, the violence certified by the state. He has the appearance of a cruel and anarchic man: he can do what he wants. The gimmick becomes unsettling when the two personalities merge. A man, we realize, may have no essence at all; the suppressed side of him will be released the minute he can get away with it. We are not a single unchanging personality. We are evil and goodness, cynicism and faith. So is John Woo, who is ready perhaps, to return to earth. Hong Kong's airy days are gone. Gravity awaits.

NEW YORK POST, 6/27/97, p. 35, Michael Medved

"Face/Off" doubles everything—providing double identities for its intrepid hero, double identities for its ruthless villain, double roles for both its superstar leads and double meanings for its clever title.

"Face/Off" here not only refers to a deadly confrontation between two implacable foes, but also signifies the process of surgically removing a human face and then attaching it to a different body.

This ghastly (and implausible) procedure is at the heart of the story about a determined FBI agent (John Travolta) ready to do whatever it takes to apprehend a psychopathic terrorist-mastermind for hire (Nicolas Cage).

In the movie's horrifying prologue, Cage kills Travolta's 5-year-old son, but the G-man gets his revenge during a thrillingly staged airport chase scene in which he puts his adversary in a coma.

The only problem is that Cage has already planted a devastating biological weapon in an undisclosed location, and so to go undercover and disarm the bomb, Travolta takes on Cage's identity—literally stripping the face from his body in a top-secret experimental procedure.

The only problem is that Cage soon arises from his comatose state and is less than pleased to find his head a bloody, faceless pulp. He borrows Travolta's face (from its convenient nearby storage in saline solution), then assumes his rival's job at the FBI and even moves into his home, cruelly menacing his wife and daughter (Joan Allen and Dominique Swain).

Meanwhile, the real hero—who now resembles the world's most notorious terrorist, with the only officials who knew about his deception murdered by his enemy—must reclaim his own identity and defend his family.

This preposterous plot requires a huge suspension of disbelief, but Travolta and Cage are both so good that they make you want to go along with the sci-fi silliness.

For the record, Cage is somewhat more effective as the long-suffering good guy (because of his vulnerable, everyman quality) and Travolta is a bit better as the dangerous creep (because he doesn't play it with quite the broad hamminess that Cage brought to that part of his role).

Each star revels in the actor's dream of playing absolute evil and indestructible goodness in the same movie, and other performers (including Gina Gershon as the terrorist's lovelorn girlfriend) also acquit themselves honorably.

Director John Woo became a legend in Hong Kong for his stylish action films, but as with his previous American effort, "Broken Arrow," the most impressive element here is the vivid characterizations.

In fact, the furious gun battles and breathless chase scenes all display a tendency to go on too long (and to shatter too much glass), distracting from the intriguing interplay of the personalities on screen.

"Face/Off" is not for the faint of heart, but despite its sadistic excesses, it won't cause Woo (or his capable cast) to lose face.

NEWSDAY, 6/27/97, Part II/p. B3, John Anderson

There's a point somewhere around the midsection of "Face/Off" in which FBI agent Sean Archer, wearing the face of psycho-terrorist Castor Troy, has to explain to his wife (Joan Allen) just what's been going on.   And while the reader should, by all rights, be totally confused already, his rap goes something like this:

"Honey ... [deep breath] I managed to put Castor Troy, the killer of our son, on life support. But he and his brother had already planted a bomb that would have leveled a square mile of Los Angeles. So in order to get the location from his brother, they transplanted Castor's face onto mine and they also gave me his voice, which is why I don't even sound like me. But then Castor came out of the coma [Archer starts to lose it, because he knows how loopy he sounds], he took my face, my life, killed everyone who had any knowledge of my covert assignment and is about to take over the FBI.

"Oh, and by the way, the guy you've been sleeping with for the last week ... "

It takes a lot of nerve to film a story like this; it takes pure gall to summarize it more than halfway through the picture. But it takes a kind of impudent, flamboyant abandon to make it all work as well as "Face/Off" does.

This is not first-rate Woo, but let's do a little summarizing ourselves: Woo has been virtually deified by fans of his Hong Kong action films, and his Hollywood output—"Hard Target," and "Broken Arrow" with John Travolta has indicated a distinctly upward trajectory. He's also shown that combining action with intelligence—despite all the evidence supplied by "Speed 2," "Con Air" and "Batman & Robin" isn't an unnatural act.

The high-velocity action-of "Face/Off" may be its calling card, but the story also gives us a big old psychological rubber toy to chew on: How would someone feel if he looked in the mirror and saw the one person he hated more than any other? Castor Troy (Nicolas Cage) once tried to assassinate Archer (Travolta) and killed his son instead. So the "face switch" is something more than another assignment.

What should have been "Face/Off's" triumph is actually a failing: the alter-ego acting of Cage and Travolta. Cage is a wildly libertine Castor, hip-shaking his way through murder and mayhem, feeling up a choir girl while impersonating a priest; Woo does a marvelous slo-mo bit where Castor's coattails, whipped by the wind as he gets out of a car, is given a kind of vampire snap by the soundtrack. And Travolta, when he becomes Castor, at least tries to tart himself up to fit the man within (although Cage still gets the "Ain't it cool?" line lifted from "Broken Arrow"). Cage doesn't do much to impersonate Travolta's stolid Archer, though. He must have left his enthusiasm on the "Con Air" shuttle.

But Woo is the real star of the film. However intense his action becomes, you always have a sense of where you are in space: Watch the first 10 minutes of "Batman & Robin" to see how bad it can get when you don't. He pays little tributes to himself—Cage's twin pistols, for instance, trademark of Hong Kong star Chow-Yun Fat. And he creates moments of pathos and insight, even if he does fall victim to some Hollywood overkill: The last 10 minutes of "Face/Off," with its gratuitous boat chase and maudlin coda, are ridiculous. But Woo's playing the game. And besides, these little problems are hardly enough to keep "Face/Off" from being the smartest pure action film of the summer.

NEWSWEEK, 6/30/97, p. 78, David Ansen

Imagine the shock: every time you look in the mirror you see your own worst enemy, the man who murdered your son. This is the outlandish predicament that faces FBI antiterrorist agent Sean Archer (John Travolta), who has surgically replaced his own face with that of the man he hates the most—the evil genius Castor Troy (Nicolas Cage). Castor has planted a bomb somewhere in Los Angeles. Now he's in a coma, and the only person who knows the bomb's location is his unhinged brother Pollux (Alessandro Nivola), who happens to be locked up in a high-tech prison. So Archer borrows Castor's identity to save L.A., but one major glitch arises in his plan. The wily and now faceless Troy arises from his coma, hijacks Sean's mug (and voice) and is running around town impersonating the FBI agent—not to mention fulfilling his marital duties. Meanwhile, good guy Sean—looking like bad guy Castor—is stuck in prison, where of course no one believes his farfetched story of who he really is.

Does this sound nuts, or what? Well, if only more action movies were this marvelously loopy, we'd all be having as much fun as we're pretending to have at "Speed 2," "Con Air" and "The Lost World." "Face/Off" is a summer movie extraordinaire: violent, imaginative, crazily funny and, even more surprising, oddly moving. Hollywood has finally wised up and let Hong Kong auteur John Woo strut his stuff in all its undiluted, over-the-top glory. Closer in spirit to his delirious Hong Kong thriller "The Killer" than to the homogenized "Broken Arrow," "Face/Off" is grandly operatic pulp.

The writing team of Mike Werb and Michael Colleary have taken this cartoon-metaphysical premise—what if Good and Evil exchanged bodies in a fight to the death—and wrung some whoppingly clever complications from it. The movie really strikes gold in the casting of Travolta and Cage, who are obviously having a ball playing off each other's performances. Their delight is contagious. Each actor, in effect, gets to play a one-man duet: Travolta plays Cage playing Travolta while Cage plays Travolta playing Cage. It's a brilliant collaboration of two of the most daring, physically intuitive, soulful performers on screen, each getting to enact both stalwart hero and flamboyant villain in one body. Playing off their baroque style, Joan Allen, as Travolta's wife, more than holds her own: her unadorned emotional honesty anchors the movie in something like reality. Their teenage daughter is played, with fine spirit, by Dominique Swain, star of Adrian Lyne's forthcoming "Lolita."

Woo, a master of poetical carnage, mixes kitsch, sadism, sentiment and comedy with choreographic precision. Who else would stage an elaborately bloody shootout to "Somewhere Over the Rainbow," or set a bullet-ridden confrontation in a beachside chapel midst a flock of flying doves? What separates his sense of humor from the cartoon mayhem of many other summer action flicks, however, is its lack of cynicism. The absurdity of this parable's premise doesn't stop Woo from taking it seriously. And with Cage and Travolta embodying the extremities of human nature, damned if we don't too.

SIGHT AND SOUND, 11/97, p. 38, Robin Dougherty

FBI agent Sean Archer captures slick terrorist Castor Troy, who killed Archer's son six years earlier. Castor and his computer-nerd kid brother Pollux have just planted a bomb, scheduled to go off in six days somewhere in LA. Pollux is imprisoned, but Castor remains comatose. To find out where the bomb is, the FBI arrange for surgeons to cut Archer's face off his head and save it. They remove Castor Troy's face and attach it to Archer's head. Archer is to assume Castor's identity (Archer's voice and body shape will also be altered), go into the prison holding Pollux and get him to reveal the location of the bomb.

Inside the prison, Archer instigates a fight and meets up with Pollux. Meanwhile, Castor comes out of his coma and has his henchmen force the FBI surgeon to attach Archer's face to him. As Archer, he arranges Pollux's release and tells Castor that he's torched the FBI surgery and everyone who knew about the identity switch. He assumes Archer's identity at home. The real Archer escapes from prison with another felon.

After 'heroically' defusing the bomb, Castor convinces the government to put him in charge of antiterrorism activities. He goes home and makes love to Archer's wife Eve and shows Archer's daughter Jamie how to defend herself with a switchblade. Soon, he gets a call from Archer, who has returned to LA and put the FBI on alert. Archer goes to Castor's waterfront hangout, where he greets Castor's henchmen and, to prevent them from becoming suspicious, ingests some drugs. He passes out and when he comes too, Castor's girlfriend Sasha is seducing him. She tells him that her son Adam is his. He apologises for his hurtful behaviour in the past.

An FBI SWAT team storms the building and a huge gun battle ensues between the two factions. Castor shows up and, after most of the SWAT team and terrorists are killed, Archer and Castor confront each other in a hall-of-mirrors shootout. Both escape and Archer finds his wife. A doctor, she becomes convinced of his true identity when she types a sample of his blood. Archer's boss tells Castor to put a stop to his activities, but Castor kills the boss and makes it appear a heart attack. At the boss' funeral, the two men confront each other. Sasha shows up and gets killed in the gunplay. Archer's daughter also arrives and realising who her real father is, stabs Castor with her switchblade. Eve phones the FBI and explains what's transpired. At the docks, Archer and Castor engage in a speedboat chase until both boats crash into a pier. Finally, the real Archer harpoons his nemesis. The FBI arrive and tell Archer that they've got a surgeon on the way. Back in his original body, Archer returns home and reunites with his wife and daughter. He introduces them to Adam, who needs a place to live.

In John Woo's most fully realised English-language film to date, two characters literally become their own worst enemies. The movie propels itself on this role-switching gimmick and on Woo's trademark excess. It's a star vehicle, a tenderly executed acting exercise, and a bone-crunching, hilarity-inducing example of what fans hoped would happen when the Hong Kong director's cartoon pyrotechnics collided with Hollywood production values and matching budgets.

A sci-fi film wrapped around a Shakespearean romantic comedy of assumed identities and exchanged lovers, *Face/Off* turns Woo into the ultimate crowd-pleaser, which, in this case, is not a bad thing. In sci-fi, medical experiments gone wrong lead to violence. In romantic comedy, mistaken identities resolve with domestic stasis. Here, we get both, and the result is as suspenseful as it is liberating. Can a person right his *doppelgänger*'s wrongs? It appears so. The script requires that its stars John Travolta and Nicolas Cage take over each other's roles, which they do, gleefully sending up each other's mannerisms. More importantly, the ensuing confusion leads to transformation and redemption for each man: as Archer, Castor makes the FBI drone care about his life. As, Castor, Archer makes amends for the terrorist's actions.

Like Woo's Hong Kong work—as well as his two earlier English-language films *Hard Target* and *Broken Arrow*—*Face/Off* is punctuated with gravity-teasing acrobatics, comic mayhem, and mind-boggling sentimentality, which somehow manage not to cancel each other out. Cheeky scenes occasionally mock the outré nonsensicalness of it all ("It's like looking in a mirror, only not," says Travolta at one point). In one scene, a gun battle seethes around a little boy whose stereo headset is playing 'Over the Rainbow' while the grown-ups around him shoot it out in slow motion. In another, an actor announces the movie's theme—"good versus evil"—after parodying the posture of Christ on the Cross.

The secret of Woo's appeal is that he takes all the familiar clichés and throws them back at us. Not only does he use, without an ounce of compunction, the hackneyed plot device of a lawman out for revenge against a villain who killed his son, but he stages this murder, in a breathtaking sepia-and-slow-motion style, on a merry-go-round, complete with sad calliope music. Trite, yes, but so over-the-top trite it makes a statement.

Woo seems determined to prove that any plot event can be turned into a flaming inferno, as in the overextended finale in which every piece of wood in an LA harbour, drenched or not, seems transmuted into a stick of self-combusting dynamite. With his dark, Deco-futuristic sets and set-pieces, Woo quotes from such sci-fi classics as *Metropolis* (1926) and lesser-known works like *Seconds* (a 1966 film in which men bored with their lives elect to have a face-swap) as well as, with its hall-of-mirrors shootout, such noir dramas as *Lady from Shanghai* (1948). Woo drops in these allusions not just to show off but because he knows we also love the spot-the-influence game. Indeed, *Face/Off* is, at heart, a high-budget B-movie with great B-movie moments. One of the finest is when Archer, residing in Troy's body and confined to an Orwellian hellhole of a prison, learns that Troy has escaped and is impersonating him. Our hope for his salvation sinks even lower than his below-floor-level prison cell.

Face/Off's screenplay, originally written for Sylvester Stallone and Arnold Schwarzenegger, leaves plenty of room for hamming it up. But it also contains the magic that works the spell that unravels a world in which one man inhabits another's body. It helps that Cage and Travolta seem like separate ends of a large blob of taffy—a tug on one end affects the other. What's amazing is that on such a big canvas, both Travolta and Cage set down their small moments with delicate strokes. "I'm Castor Troy," yelps Archer as he tentatively tries out his new identity. Then louder: "I'm Castor Troy." We watch him go through a baptism of fire and come out laughing all the way.

TIME, 6/30/97, p. 65, Richard Corliss

[*Face/Off* was reviewed jointly with *The Lost World: Jurassic Park*; see Corliss' review of that film.]

VILLAGE VOICE, 7/8/97, p. 69, J. Hoberman

Opening with the murder of the five-year-old child who might well have concocted its central gimmick, *Face/Off* is a nightmare of crazed blood lust and exuberantly one-dimensional characterizations. John Travolta plays an angry, revenge-obsessed FBI man; his nemesis, Nicolas Cage, is a flamboyantly lunatic terrorist. Thanks to reconstructive surgery a third of the way through, these two indestructible action figures trade faces—and hence personalities.

A movie whose action pyrotechnics are matched only by its motivational flip-flops, *Face/Off* is further distinguished by its casual sadism—"Relax, he's a turnip," a nurse tells the good Travolta, stubbing out her cigarette on the bad Cage's arm—and its bizarre religiosity. "Oh God, what are you asking me to do?" the Job-like Travolta asks heaven before allowing a plastic surgeon to slice off his face (which is conveniently left floating in a laboratory jar) and graft on Cage's. If the operation has the poetic quality of Georges Franju's mad-doctor horror-classic *Eyes Without a Face,* the dialogue is just a horror. "What about my voice?" "I've implanted a microchip in your larynx."

The joke of having to go through life looking like Nicolas Cage is compounded by the Cage character's complaint at being transformed into Travolta: "This hair, this nose, this ridiculous chin." Within the agency, the new, bad Travolta is understood as an improvement. "Sir," an assistant inquires, "did you just have a surgical procedure—was the stick successfully removed from your ass?" The movie's most perverse aspect ties audience sympathy into a pretzel by allowing the bad Travolta to pay attention to the good Travolta's neglected wife (Joan Allen) and troubled teenage daughter.

So much for psychology. In addition to Travolta doing Cage and vice versa, the films set pieces include a spectacular instance of cop-car airplane-runway tag, a prison shoot-out in ricochet heaven, a mad grenade attack on a druggy pleasure dome with the unmistakable Woo touch of having a five year-old kid with a headset listening to "Somewhere Over the Rainbow" amid bloody slo-mo carnage, a church funeral that escalates into a Mexican stand-off worthy of Sergio Leone, and the climactic, exhausting, on-the-water chase of launched flaming speedboats.

Men in Black is cute pulp; *Face/Off* has a cold, Langian fatalism exaggerated by the absurd conviction of its *Robot Monster* logic. With its choral requiems and gleaming skyscrapers, compulsive doubling and outrageous mayhem, this is the first of Woo's Hollywood movies to suggest the nuttiness of his best Hong Kong films. The writers had to wait years for the right man to direct this script. As for family values, suffice to say that in the beatific finale, the good Travolta's daughter has removed the ring from her nose.

Also reviewed in:
NEW YORK TIMES, 6/27/97, p. C1, Janet Maslin
NEW YORKER, 7/14/97, p. 84, Terrence Rafferty
VARIETY, 6/23-29/97, p. 93, Todd McCarthy
WASHINGTON POST, 6/27/97, p. D1, Stephen Hunter
WASHINGTON POST, 6/27/97, Weekend/p. 43, Desson Howe

FAIRY TALE—A TRUE STORY

A Paramount Pictures release of an Icon Productions/Wendy Finerman production. *Executive Producer:* Paul Tucker. *Producer:* Wendy Finerman and Bruce Davey. *Director:* Charles Sturridge. *Screenplay:* Ernie Contreras. *Story:* Albert Ash, Tom McLoughlin, and Ernie Contreras. *Director of Photography:* Michael Coulter. *Editor:* Peter Coulson. *Music:* Zbigniew Preisner. *Sound:* John Midgley and (music) Rafal Paczkowski. *Sound Editor:* Sarah Morton and Peter Bond. *Casting:* Mary Selway and Sarah Trevis. *Production Designer:* Michael Howells. *Art Director:* Sam Riley. *Set Decorator:* Totty Whately. *Special Effects:* Dave Beavis. *Costumes:* Shirley Russell. *Make-up:* Peter King. *Stunt Coordinator:* Jim Dowdall. *Running time:* 97 minutes. *MPAA Rating:* PG.

CAST: Florence Hoath (Elsie Wright); Elizabeth Earl (Frances Griffiths); Paul McGann (Arthur Wright); Phoebe Nicholls (Polly Wright); Bill Nighy (Edward Gardner); Bob Peck (Harry Briggs); Harvey Keitel (Harry Houdini); Peter O'Toole (Sir Arthur Conan Doyle); Anton Lesser (Wounded Corporal); Tim McInnerny (John Ferret); Jason Salkey (James Collins); Lara Morgan (Jean Doyle); Adam Franks (Adrian Doyle); Guy Witcher (Denis Doyle); Joseph May (Houdini's Assistant); John Bradley (Portly Gentleman); Anna Chancellor (Peter Pan); Leonard Kavanagh (Stage Manager); Lynn Farleigh (Mrs. Thornton); Sarah Marsden (Lucy); Tara Marie (Judith); Alannah McGahan (Margie); Peter Mullan (Sergeant Farmer); Jim Wiggins (Albert, the Postman); David Calder (Harold Snelling); Anthony Calf (Geoffrey Hodson); John Grillo (Mr. West); Benjamin Whitrow (Mr. Binley); Dick Brannick (News Vendor); Barbara Hicks (City Woman); Christopher Godwin (City Businessman); Andrew Cryer (First Soldier); Paul Poppelwell (Second Soldier); David Norman (O'Neill); Matilda Sturridge (Dorothy); Charlotte Champness (Alice); Anna Ramsey (Charlotte); Peter Wight (Newspaper Editor); Willie Ross (Old Print Worker); Ina Claugh (Lady Calling to Fairies); Carol Noakes (Station Photographer); Stephen Chapman (Boy in Hospital); Bill Stewart (Chess MC); Don Henderson (Sydney Chalker); Stewart Howson (Red-faced Man); James Danaher (Joseph Wright); Martin Gent (Pushy Photographer); Anthony Collin (Older Photographer); Tom Georgeson (First Reporter); Angus Barnett (Second Reporter); THE FAIRIES: Sue Barton (Lutey); Ali Bastian (Lull); Anna Brecon (Elabigathe); Sean Buckley (Mr. Bandylegs); Lindsey Butcher (Tib);

Norma Cohen (Nanny Button Cap); Matt Costain (Prince Malekin); Philip Fowler (Fenoderee); Katie Gibbon (Pinket); Sophy Griffiths (Sib); Sara Li Gustafsson (Loireag); Tara Kemp (Gull); William Lawrance (Tom Cockle); Caleb Lloyd (Lob); Marianne Melhus (Florella); Genevieve Monastesse (Morgana); Simon Penman (Peerifool); Briony Plant (Yarthkins); Anna-Louise Plowman (Shellycoat); Jane Read-Wilson (Asrai); Isabel Rocamora (Queen Mab); Thomas Sturridge (Hob); Mark Tate (Habetrot); Hayley Tibbins (Patch); Mel Gibson (France's Father).

LOS ANGELES TIMES, 10/24/97, Calendar/p. 10, Kevin Thomas

"Fairy Tale—A True Story" is an enchanting, gorgeous-looking movie recalling "The Little Princess" and "The Secret Garden" that, like them, involves a spunky little heroine on her own coping in a new environment. It is even set in the same early 20th century era as the two earlier pictures.

It's 1917 and World War I is raging. In the audience at London's Duke of York Theater is 10-year-old Frances Griffiths (Elizabeth Earl), riveted by the sight of Peter Pan flying across the stage. For a brief moment Frances is transported from her grief over her parents. Her mother is dead, and her father has been declared missing in action—she is old enough to know what that most likely means.

Frances has just arrived from Africa, where her father served in the military, to come to live with her Aunt Polly Wright (Phoebe Nicholls), Polly's husband Arthur (Paul McGann) and their 12-year-old daughter Elsie (Florence Hoath).

The elegant Wrights live in a handsome, spacious manor house in West Yorkshire. Nearby there is the most beautiful brook you could ever see. The Wrights welcome Frances with open arms and understanding hearts, for they have just lost their own son. Even in such sad circumstances, Frances could not possibly have fared better. But there is more—much more—quickly at hand.

This occurs when Elsie shares with Frances her great, incredible secret: that there really are fairies inhabiting that babbling brook. Sure enough, the fairies soon make themselves visible to the overjoyed Frances as tiny humans dressed in elegant medieval attire and fitted with hummingbird-like wings.

But, as this is the 20th century, the girls do something very modern: Using Arthur's new Midg camera, they take pictures of the fairies—and, as word gets out, they find themselves at the center of what today has become an all-too-familiar media circus.

As the debate rages over whether the pictures are real or fake, Sir Arthur Conan Doyle (Peter O'Toole) and Harry Houdini (Harvey Keitel), who is currently performing in London, become involved and befriend the Wrights and the little girls as well. Both Conan Doyle and Houdini, who were old friends, had long been interested in spiritualism and the possibilities of the supernatural. Whereas Houdini had become a skeptic, a crusader in exposing fake mediums, Conan Doyle had become a believer over the decades, especially with the recent loss of his son in the war. He is convinced, in fact, that through a medium was able to communicate with the son.

As this substantial outline suggests, "A Fairy Tale—A True Story" has all the ingredients for an exceptional entertainment, and Ernie Contreras' script and Charles Sturridge's direction make the most of all of them. At heart it's a story of a need for faith and hope in a terrible time—Britain had suffered horrendous war losses by 1917.

The presence of such legendary and respected figures as the greatest magician of them all and the creator of the greatest detective of them all—Sherlock Holmes—gives the film added depth and dimension. O'Toole is an elegant and humane Conan Doyle, and Keitel is flat-out perfect for Houdini, intellectually and physically. The rest of the cast, including young Earl and Hoath, are up to O'Toole's and Keitel's level.

"A Fairy Tale" is an example of impeccable craftsmanship, with a flawless sense of period in its production design and costumes. (World War I is a tricky era to reproduce, a subdued transitional Beaux Arts-ish period between elaborate Victorian styles and the radical Art Deco designs and flapper styles to come.) Zbigniew Preisner's sweeping score appropriately soars, and Michael Coulter's camera work complements Sturridge's carefully nuanced direction.

And as for the all-important fairies, they are absolutely convincing.

NEW YORK POST, 10/24/97, p. 46, Michael Medved

If you don't believe in fairies, then "Fairy Tale"—A True Story" might just change your mind. Surely, some form of supernatural enchantment represents the best explanation for the magical skill behind every detail of this superb film—easily one of the most satisfying and surprising releases of 1997.

The subject is a famous series of 1917 photographs casually snapped by two English cousins, aged 10 and 12, and played here by the effortlessly adorable Elizabeth Earl and Florence Hoath.

The pictures seemed to show a number of tiny fairies with fluttering wings, surrounding the children as they played along a lush, idyllic country stream near their Yorkshire home.

When the mother (Phoebe Nicholls) of one of the girls showed the photos to a visiting spiritualist (Bill Nighy), he quickly brought the astonishing images to London where Sir Arthur Conan Doyle (Peter O'Toole), world-renowned creator of Sherlock Holmes, became a tireless champion of their authenticity.

At the same time, Doyle's friend Harry Houdini (the perfectly cast Harvey Keitel) knew enough about misleading special effects to maintain a consistently skeptical attitude, even as the seemingly innocent country girls and their earth-shaking photographs passed rigorous scientific tests.

The movie compresses events that actually stretched over six years into a few months during the darkest days of World War I—a switch which makes dramatic sense even if it seriously alters the story.

Director Charles Sturridge ("A Handful of Dust," "Gulliver's Travels" for TV) also abandons any claim of objectivity on the still controversial Cottingley photographs by creating captivating movie images of scores of gorgeously costumed fairies interacting with the two girls.

These breathtakingly beautiful, bewitching and wistful scenes help to make this movie not only a delight for sophisticated adults, but also one of the finest films of recent years for children who will respond to its charms on a more visceral, enthusiastic level.

The heart-tugging conclusion, involving the sudden, startling appearance of one of Hollywood's biggest stars in an uncredited role, will send everyone home happy, still glowing from the Oscar-quality camera work (by Michael Coulter of "Sense and Sensibility") and lush, dazzling musical score (by Zbigniew Preisner).

Regardless of your opinions on brownies, pixies and sprites, "Fairy Tale" should serve to shore up waning faith in the all-conquering magic of movies.

SIGHT AND SOUND, 3/98, p. 45, Rob White

1917. In London, Harry Houdini performs his escape routines and is congratulated by Sir Arthur Conan Doyle.

Frances Griffiths arrives in Yorkshire from Africa to stay with her uncle Arthur Wright, his wife Polly and their daughter Elsie. The Wrights' son Joseph, a prolific painter of fairies, has died recently of pneumonia. Frances and Elsie begin to see fairies in the woods. Polly visits theosophist meetings; the talk of spiritual forces assuages her grief for her dead son. Frances and Elsie take photographs of the fairies, Arthur is shocked to see them appear when he develops the film, and Polly delivers the pictures to theosophist Mr Gardner. A photographic expert authenticates them.

Gardner informs Conan Doyle, who visits the Wrights, accompanied by Houdini. The photographs are reported in the *Strand* magazine and crowds descend on the Yorkshire woods. A reporter, John Ferret, harasses the girls. The fairies take flight. While the Wrights are in London, Ferret breaks into the Wrights' house where he finds cut-outs of fairies. He flees in terror when confronted with the ghost of Joseph. Fairies steal into the girls' bedroom after they return home. Elsie is entranced, but Frances doesn't notice, as at the moment of the fairies' arrival her father, who had been believed lost in action in France, arrives at the house.

In 1917, two young girls, Elsie Wright and her cousin Frances Griffiths, took a number of photographs which seemed to show the girls in the company of fairies several inches high. These photographs were publicised by Sir Arthur Conan Doyle and became celebrated around a world. It is remarkable that this story should have so fired recent cinematic imaginations, inspiring both *Fairytale: A True Story* about the girls and last year's more adult-centred *Photographing Fairies*.

Fairytale is directed by Charles Sturridge, who made *Brideshead Revisited* for television, and has specialised since in literary adaptations, including an engaging version of Evelyn Waugh's *A Handful of Dust*. Here, Sturridge collaborates with *Forrest Gump*'s producer Wendy Finerman on a confection that combines the worst of British literary nostalgia with Hollywood moral simplifications: *Gump* meets *Peter Pan*. In *Fairytale,* we are urged if not to credit the photographs' authenticity, then at least to savour their innocently offered solace to a war-torn world. We are urged, that is, to delight in artifice rather than in evidence.

Providing at least some depth to the film is the first-rate supporting cast, but this talent is squandered. Peter O'Toole is lively enough in the limited role of Conan Doyle, but Harvey Keitel is very subdued—perhaps because he is playing Houdini, a militant sceptic when it came to spiritualist claims, and this is not a film much fuelled by skepticism. The one villain, the newspaper hack John Ferret who identifies the girls, never threatens any real malignancy, and ends up white with terror at the sight of Elsie's brother's ghost. It is probably too much to have expected *Fairytale to* attend to the psychological connections between trauma (World War One, childhood death) and a belief in supernatural beings. But one can be forgiven for having expected a bit more variety in characterisation—if not Roald Dahl, then at least Walt Disney: any maker of distinguished children's fiction would never have passed up, as *Fairytale's* makers have, the opportunity to give voices to a band of fairies.

Film has made strong connections between childhood and the supernatural, from *The Exorcist* to *E. T. Fairytale* is much closer to the latter, depicting childhood, especially in its intersection with the occult realm, as a privileged state of instinctive moral correctness. In one scene, for example, Frances sits in a train opposite a horribly disfigured soldier. She reacts to him without a blush, a blink or a stare, accepting him for what he is. This same all-accepting attitude gives her access to the fairy world. And just as there is an idealisation of childhood on offer here, so is there a quasi-Victorian notion of the conventional family, which finds its culmination in the appearance of Frances' father returning from war at the film's end.

Fairytale's cloying message—that if you believe in something enough it may as well be true—postulates gullibility as a credible moral position. This is problematic enough in itself, but there is the added complication that it is precisely gullibility that is, a willingness to treat digitally engineered images as real—which so much mainstream filmmaking relies upon summoning up in its audience. In a way, the aesthetic opportunities offered by new visual technologies carry a politics of characterisation in their wake: Forrest Gump is not only a model citizen unquestioning, docile—but also a model filmgoer. And likewise there could hardly be more ideal spectators of a certain kind of contemporary product than children who might once have been fascinated by fairies. These ideal spectators are made the protagonists within films like *Gump* or *Fairytale*, and in these protagonists we are confronted with what Hollywood would have us, as consumers, be.

The two girls' ingenious fakery was an amateurish precursor of today's digital technology. Now, their photographs do not look very convincing. They probably once did when people instinctively believed that what could be photographed was necessarily real. But, as the historian Tom Gunning has shown, early photographs—and particularly spirit photography—were often felt to be uncanny, frightening pictures of a reality that could not be seen by the eye. It is interesting to speculate that digital technology is taking us not forward, but back—to a time just before the cinema, when photographs could not be trusted. If this is so, it is encouraging to think that a film such as *Fairytale* fails because it overestimates an audience's capacity to be deceived either by visual tricks or by highly oversimplified ideas about the moral dimension of gullibility.

VILLAGE VOICE, 10/28/97, p. 84, Leslie Camhi

In London, in 1917, the zeitgeist is distinctly melancholy. Women in droopy hats and shapeless brown dresses, men in uniform missing half their faces, crowd the quays and throng the rainy streets. Ten-year-old Frances Griffiths (Elizabeth Earl), whose mother is dead and whose father is missing in action, travels by train to stay with her aunt's family, in a caretaker's house on a large estate in Yorkshire.

Her grief-stricken aunt (Phoebe Nicholls) dabbles in theosophy; she hopes to make contact with the young son she lost to pneumonia. Her kind but skeptical uncle (Paul McGann) is busy electrifying the local mill for the profit of his landlord. Frances and her 13-year-old cousin, Elsie

(Florence Hoath), take refuge from the household's persistent gloom near the woodland stream at the back of their garden, where the girls seem to commune with fairies.

Fairytale—A True Story is based upon a historic hoax and the uproar it occasioned, when photographs that the two girls claimed to have taken of their sprightly friends were shown to Sir Arthur Conan Doyle, the creator of Sherlock Holmes. The eminent Peter O'Toole plays the eminent Doyle, a man of reason undone by grief; after the wartime loss of his son, Doyle became an ardent spiritualist, and took the photographs for definitive proof of the life of spirits. Harvey Keitel brings his considerable charisma to bear on the role of Doyle's friend, the masterful Harry Houdini, who, on the subject of spectral emanations, remained curious but unconvinced. Yet in an England ravaged by the twin losses of war and industrialization, the published photographs of the Cottingley fairies provoked a form of mass psychosis, providing a comforting interlude of nature and fantasy.

Director Charles Sturridge and his crew of designers have artfully recreated the drab look of wartime London and the compelling artifice of its theatrical spectacles. More forceful still is his depiction of the emotional climate that caused soldiers to see spirits hovering over the front lines, and the bereaved to imagine conversing with their deceased loved ones. I wish he'd given a similarly turn-of-the-century feel to the fairies, but alas, these insect-like creatures sporting pointy ears and woodland costumes are too Disney-esque to be truly moving. Harvey Kietel's sweet-natured performance suffers from his Brooklyn accent, and the script from occasional anachronisms. ("Cover your ass!" he warns the gullible Doyle.) But the two little girls are magically innocent and knowing.

The film comes down rather wholeheartedly on the side of the fairies' existence. And though no one wants to identify with the cynical journalist who keeps sniping away at the girls' reputation, I couldn't help wondering if the meaning of their story wasn't rather the saving grace of fantasy in a world that's all too real.

Also reviewed in:
CHICAGO TRIBUNE, 10/24/97, Friday/p. D, John Petrakis
NEW YORK TIMES, 10/24/97, p. E12, Stephen Holden
WASHINGTON POST, 10/24/97, p. D7, Stephen Hunter
WASHINGTON POST, 10/24/97, Weekend/p. 55, Jane Horwitz

FALL

A Capella International and Five Minutes Before the Miracle release. *Executive Producer:* Tom Gamble. *Producer:* Eric Schaeffer. *Producer:* Terrence Michael. *Director:* Eric Schaeffer. *Screenplay:* Eric Schaeffer. *Director of Photography:* Joe De Salvo. *Editor:* Thom Zinney. *Music:* Amanda Kravat. *Casting:* Sheila Jaffe and Georgianne Walken. *Production Designer:* Michael Shaw. *Set Decorator:* Kara Cressman. *Costumes:* Kim Marie Druce. *Running time:* 94 minutes. *MPAA Rating:* Not Rated.

CAST: Eric Schaeffer (Michael Shiver); Amanda DeCadenet (Sarah Easton); Rudolph Martin (Philippe); Francie Swift (Robin); Lisa Vidal (Sally).

LOS ANGELES TIMES, 6/27/97, Calendar/p. 8, Kevin Thomas

"Fall" is an act of bravado on the part of actor-writer-director Eric Schaeffer that is never less than involving, despite some silly asides. It is convincing as a scorchingly intense love affair and, as such, it is considerably more intelligent than, for example, "9½ Weeks."

Schaeffer, who first came to attention with his films "My Life's in Turnaround" and "If Lucy Fell," stars himself as Michael Shiver, a New York cab driver and writer who considers himself a cabby first. When fabled model Sarah Easton (the aptly cast Amanda DeCadenet, a former model and British talk-show presenter turned actress) gets into Michael's cab, he is swiftly transfixed. Never mind that Sarah is married to a handsome European aristocrat (Rudolph Martin), who conveniently will be abroad for the next two months.

Michael is implacable and totally confident in his pursuit of Sarah. Schaeffer doesn't give us much time to ponder the deathless question of whether two people from such different worlds can a romance. And, actually, Michael and Sarah as lovers is no stretch. Michael is not handsome and is shorter than Sarah, but he has an interesting George C. Scott-Roy Scheider nose and is in good shape. He has a deep, resonant voice, recites love poems and has a down-to-earth blue-collar masculinity. As such, he represents a refreshing contrast to the glittery world in which Sarah travels and, try as she might, she can't resist him.

Michael and Sarah come across as adults who are trying to keep their eyes wide open about their relationship, but the chemistry between them is truly torrid. Since Schaeffer and DeCadenet get this couple just right, it's too bad Schaeffer doesn't stick to that.

But instead he has Michael pretentiously admit that 10 years ago fresh out of school he wrote a bestseller but lost his ambition amid all the hullabaloo it brought him. (As if Thomas Pynchon feels he has to go on book tours and talk shows!)

Then there's this problem of Michael having as best buddies two beautiful women, one of them about to be ordained as an Episcopal priest and who has a penchant for outré performance art. They hang on his every word about the progress of his romance. This makes Michael and, in turn, Schaeffer himself come across as men of overweening ego and self-regard.

Even so, Michael does emerge as a man willing to risk everything for love, and in "Fall," it's the man rather than the woman who's the true romantic.

VILLAGE VOICE, 7/1/97, p. 96, Hillary Posner

In Eric Schaeffer's first feature, *My Life's in Turnaround,* a character reads aloud the reviews of her friends' play. "Why, why do these untalented children persist in spewing their uninteresting, unenlightened, clichéd, trite complexities on the public?" one critic has written. "They bored me to tears." My compliments to Schaeffer; he pretty much anticipated the reviews of *Fall.*

This *Penthouse Forum*-style mate-fantasy features Schaeffer as a taxi driver who hits on women in his cab. His chosen prey is married supermodel Sarah Easton (Amanda De Cadenet), who falls for him far too easily to be believed—he lures her to his apartment for tea, then gives her an orgasm in about 10 seconds merely by talking dirty to her. What follows is Schaeffer's embarrassing rendition of Mickey Rourke in *9½ Weeks,* minus any sex appeal or chemistry with De Cadenet.

There are a few compelling moments, like the scene in which the lovers gorge on three different kinds of takeout or when he flies to Paris, only to learn that Sarah is back in supermodel mode and will have none of him. And Schaeffer scores points for his use of male nudity (himself). But the film never delves deep enough beneath its characters' dull exteriors to seem anything more than one self-indulgent writer-director-actor-producer's ego trip.

Also reviewed in:
NEW YORK TIMES, 6/20/97, p. C28, Lawrence Van Gelder
VARIETY, 6/30-7/13/97, p. 66, Steven Gaydos

FAMILY NAME

An Opelika Pictures release of an Opelika Pictures production. *Executive Producer:* Nicholas Gottlieb. *Producer:* Selina Lewis. *Director:* Macky Alston. *Screenplay:* Macky Alston and Kay Gayner. *Director of Photography:* Eliot Rockett. *Editor:* Sandra Marie Christie and Christopher White. *Music:* Camara Kambon. *Running time:* 89 minutes. *MPAA Rating:* Not Rated.

LOS ANGELES TIMES, 10/10/97, Calendar/p. 14, Kevin Thomas

When Macky Alston was a child living in Durham, N.C., his father, a Presbyterian minister and civil rights activist, placed him in an all-black public school, where he was amazed to discover that he shared with many of his classmates the same surname. Death threats on account of his father's activities later drove the family from Durham when Macky was 8 to relocate in Princeton, N.J., where his father still preaches and lives.

But the memory of his shared-name classmates provided the inspiration for Alston, now 32 and living in New York, to embark upon a project that has resulted in his deeply moving "Family Name."

Alston is descended from 18th century slave-owning North Carolina aristocrats—you get the impression that every other plantation in the state belonged to an Alston. It is common knowledge that slaves took their masters' surnames and that many a plantation owner exercised his *droit du seigneur* with female slaves.

On a return visit to North Carolina several years ago, Alston was struck by the fact that two large Alston family reunions, one black and one white, took place within a few miles of each other, and yet none of the members of each gathering were aware of the other reunion. Macky Alston, with his multiethnic crew, was the only Alston to attend both events. Alston believes that because much of his own life involved a secrecy—he is gay, and he only came out to his parents at age 19—he was driven to delve into other kinds of family secrets, to pore over actual documentation of his ancestors' ownership of slaves and to discover blood relations between the black and white Alstons. The first task was relatively easy, the second, far harder.

As a filmmaker and as a family historian, Alston learns as he goes along, which imparts his film with a beguiling sincerity. Not surprisingly, Alston finds both white and black Alstons reluctant to talk about a painful past. Eventually, he makes connections, first with Fred Alston Jr., a noted symphony orchestra bassoonist, whose ancestors turn out to have been owned by Macky's. Macky then learns of Charles Alston, an esteemed painter of the Harlem Renaissance who died in 1977 but left behind much archival material. What strikes Alston is how light-complexioned Charles Alston and his family were; Charles' sister in fact admits that in the course of her life she had been able to pass for white.

"Family Name" becomes suspenseful as Alston grows closer to proving that Charles Alston's father Primus, a prominent turn-of-the-century African American minister in Charlotte, was the son of Macky's great-great-great-uncle, a slave owner. By the time "Family Name" is over, Alston has filled the screen with Alstons of every shade, creating a powerful image of the unity of the human family.

"Family Name" has an ending you could never anticipate at the outset—the first-ever gathering of Alstons, black and white.

NEW YORK POST, 9/3/97, p. 40, Bill Hoffmann

To put it simply, "Family Name" is a remarkable documentary.

Filmmaker Macky Alston attacks his intriguing subject with the energy of an Olympic runner—and emerges with a movie so engrossing and alive with history, it sets new standards for all future projects of its type.

As a white boy growing up in Durham, N.C., Alston noticed there were dozens of families sharing his last name. But oddly, all of them were black except for him.

Twenty-five years later, Alston, 31, decided to find out why and took his camera along to oversee the investigation. An amazing journey of discovery—and self-discovery—followed.

The filmmaker learns that his ancestors were once well-to-do plantation owners with hundreds of slaves who routinely give their children the master's last name, as was the custom then.

At this point, Alston would have easily taken the easy way out by photographing the library archives and interviewing a few historians. But he didn't.

Instead, the moviemaking dynamo began a trek from Alabama to New York, traveling to family reunions, housing projects, churches, graveyards and even the original Alston plantations.

There, he interviews the descendants of those slaves, picking their brains for details passed down from generation to generation, as well as bravely introducing himself as the great-great-great-grandson of the man who once owned their families.

There are dozens of great stories told here—some are hysterically funny, others tenderly poignant and still others heartbreakingly tragic.

Since master-slave sex was rampant in the days of slavery, Alston is eventually forced to face the inevitable: that he is a distant blood relative to some of his subjects.

In particular, Alston discovers the work of a painter named Charles "Spinky" Alston, whose striking style emerged during the Harlem Renaissance.

While Spinky died in 1977, he left a rich archive of photos and taped interviews which Alston extensively taps to discover that he and the artist may be related.

The filmmaker's hard work and insightful storytelling make for a riveting 89 minutes that beautifully blend elements of history, mystery, myth and melodrama. It's drop-dead great filmmaking.

VILLAGE VOICE, 9/9/97, p. 86, Amy Taubin

Macky Alston's *Family Name* is a fascinating film—as much for what it represses or disavows as for what it makes explicit. Like most good documentaries, it raises the possibility of a dozen other films that could be made by taking different routes through the same terrain. It opens more cans of worms than it knows how to deal with. And it might make you want to dig for what's not on the screen, exactly as the filmmaker digs for what's unacknowledged in the family history that is his subject.

The nagging sense of there being another film buried beneath this one explodes when, at the very last moment of *Family Name*, Alston discloses a bit of information that makes us see the film in a different light. Which is not to say he's been devious, but only that no one is ever entirely cognizant of his or her motives—especially when the sticky issue of origins is involved.

Alston is the descendant of North Carolina plantation owners. When he was a child, his family moved from its hometown because his father, a Methodist minister and civil rights activist, had received death threats. He was sent to a progressive school in Durham where there were many other Alstons, all of them black. Later he discovers the answer to this mystery: as property, slaves were labeled with their owner's name.

Twenty years later Alston finds himself wanting to know more about the relationship between the black Alstons and the white Alstons. How does this shared history of slavery affect their lives today? He goes back to his hometown with a small camera crew. He interviews black Alstons and white Alstons (all of whom look as if they can't get away fast enough once the word *slavery* is mentioned). As a gay man, Alston knows about open secrets, but that doesn't necessarily make him less of a blunderbuss when probing what other people prefer to leave unspoken.

When he discovers that one of his ancestors was one of the largest slave owners in North Carolina, he searches for a contemporary who might be a descendant of a slave his family had owned or even one who might be connected to him by blood (owners having capitalized on their property by impregnating their slaves).

A relentless researcher, Alston looks for leads in birth and death records, in wills and property deeds, in graveyards and family albums. He tracks down wonderful archival material about Spinky Alston, a painter of the Harlem Renaissance. He finds Fred Alston, a classical bassoonist and one of the first black musicians with a permanent seat in a symphony orchestra.

This is the liveliest section of the film, but it's also the place where you might start wondering whether there isn't a touch of paternalism in Alston's investigations. What does it mean for a white filmmaker to go around asking black people if they are not, so to speak, all his father's children—especially when the father is the devil incarnate?

But I think there's something more complicated going on that Alston doesn't own up to. "I want to find a black Alston who's connected to me through slavery—who might be my cousin," says Alston. Fine, but then why does he only investigate the paternity of black Alstons (not to mention that his fetishistic relationship to the family name keeps his maternal lineage out of the picture)? Why does he never turn his investigations on himself? Why does he never ask whether he himself might be other than pure white? I suspect that's the question that inspired the film—although Alston may not have been consciously aware of it.

If ever there were a film that proved Freud's theory of the family romance and its repression (the childhood belief, usually denied in adult life, that one may not be the child of one's parents), this is it. The evidence is the text that appears at the very end of *Family Name:* "In the course of his research, Macky Alston discovered that his great, great grandfather was illegitimate. Macky Alston is not an Alston after all" It's a better hook for a sequel than Hollywood ever imagined.

Also reviewed in:
NEW YORK TIMES, 9/3/97, p. C11, Stephen Holden
VARIETY, 2/17-23/97, p. 70, Godfrey Cheshire

FARMER AND CHASE

An Arrow Releasing Inc. presentation in association with Red Sky Films of a Kalmbach/Seitzman production. *Executive Producer:* Douglas Humphreys and Ted Schacter. *Producer:* Scott Kalmbach. *Director:* Michael Seitzman. *Screenplay:* Michael Seitzman. *Director of Photography:* Michael Maley. *Editor:* Doug Werby. *Music:* Tony Saunders. *Casting:* Joan Marechal. *Production Designer:* Doug Freeman. *Running time:* 97 minutes. *MPAA Rating:* Not Rated.

CAST: Ben Gazzara (Farmer); Todd Field (Chase); Steven Anthony Jones (Ollie); Lara Flynn Boyle (Hillary).

NEW YORK POST, 2/7/97, p. 53, Larry Worth

Ben Gazzara fans will leave "Farmer & Chase" with two questions: Who is Gazzara's agent and why hasn't he been fired?

Gazzara hasn't had a role worthy of his vast abilities since John Cassavetes' death in 1989. Having been reduced to glowering at Charlie Sheen in last month's "Shadow Conspiracy," he's now glowering at Charlie Sheen lookalike Todd Field in "Farmer & Chase."

Granted, it's the difference between a supporting and lead role, but they're equally embarrassing. Here, Gazzara plays Farmer to Field's Chase, a father-and-son bank robbery team plotting a "last big heist" before Farmer retires his ski mask.

Tension's already in the air between the bickering duo, heightened when goofy shoplifter Lara Flynn Boyle steals Chase's affections. You know things have reached a nadir when Farmer smells Chase's hand after a big date.

That's in addition to dialogue that never convinces—"Should I pick up some candy?' Chase asks Farmer before holding up a convenience store—and attempts to rip off everything from "Dog Day Afternoon" to "Bonnie and Clyde."

The real blame goes to Michael Seitzman, who wrote and directed this umpteenth try at jumping on Quentin Tarantino's bandwagon. He erroneously believes that focusing on characters' quirky traits usually within life-and-death situations—constitutes entertainment.

Worse, Seitzman incorporates slow-motion sequences, furious cross-cuts, whimsical dissolves and heavy-handed music into the mix, making for an endlessly drawn-out, hopelessly heavy-handed effort.

Aside from Gazzara's presence, the sole element of note is Flynn Boyle. Sadly, her charms are drowned out by the character's non-stop, utterly annoying gum-snapping.

Meanwhile, Todd Field comes across as the gawkiest, least talented performer to clutter the screen since Tori Spelling.

Field proves persuasive only when telling his partners in crime: "Something's not right here." It's the ultimate in understatement.

NEWSDAY, 2/7/97, Part II/p. B10, Bruce Forer

Whenever characters are chain-smoking, you're either watching a French film or a Quentin Tarantino creation. This debut film of writer-director-producer Michael Seitzman is neither, although it seems to be trying hard to resemble the latter.

Add some handguns, a gush of profanity, a formula plot, a respected veteran character actor (Ben Gazzara) and a seductive former "Twin Peaks" star (Lara Flynn Boyle), and the young film-maker is well on his way to a studio contract. "Farmer and Chase" makes more sense as an audition for the big time than as an independent movie with heart.

Chase (Todd Field) is a kid torn between going to community college or following in his dad's footsteps as a low-rent thief. The rub: Farmer (Ben Gazzara) is an extremely disapproving father who proclaims that Chase is too soft and doesn't have what it takes for a life of crime. "I got something more important than college," he says proudly. "I got _____."

When he isn't castigating his son for supposed humanistic impulses, he is making awkward speeches to the camera. There is, in fact, little dialogue in this movie; the characters tend to deliver endless monologues, uninterrupted by others. When does that happen? Only in movies like this one. According to Seitzman, Gazzara hates to rehearse: It inhibits raw energy or emotion—and it shows. "Raw" is the right word.

After Farmer's longtime partner gets killed in a botched job in Chicago, he reluctantly agrees to work with his son, who is now romancing his "Bonnie," Hillary (Lara Flynn Boyle). At first, she's an impediment, but she ultimately wants to relieve the boredom of her suburban life in Northern California more than she fears the consequences of crime. So the three rob a bank. That ends badly for them, but it is inside the bank that the director forgets for a fleeting moment about excessive "style" and a glimpse of drama comes through. Just for a moment, we really do believe we are watching a father and a son going nowhere. It almost redeems the film.

Also reviewed in:
NEW YORK TIMES, 2/7/97, p. C23, Lawrence Van Gelder
VARIETY, 10/16-22/95, p. 97, Dennis Harvey

FAST, CHEAP & OUT OF CONTROL

A Sony Pictures Classics release of a Fourth Floor Productions presentation in association with American Playhouse. *Executive Producer:* Lindsay Law. *Producer:* Errol Morris. *Director:* Errol Morris. *Director of Photography:* Robert Richardson. *Editor:* Shondra Merrill and Karen Schmeer. *Music:* Caleb Sampson. *Sound:* Steve Benes and Fred Burnham. *Sound Editor:* Magdaline Volaitis. *Production Designer:* Ted Bafaloukos. *Set Decorator:* Scott Doonan. *Make-up:* Jeri La Shay. *Running time:* 80 minutes. *MPAA Rating:* Not Rated.

CAST: Dave Hoover (Wild Animal Trainer); George Mendonca (Topiary Gardner); Ray Mendez (Mole-Rat Specialist); Rodney Brooks (Robot Scientist).

FILM QUARTERLY, Spring 1999, p. 43, Karen Jaehne

Sisyphus meets Einstein in *Fast, Cheap & Out of Control*, Errol Morris's contribution to the current debate on evolution and human consciousness. It is overtly a documentary about people who tame or master nature, bending lions or boxwood to their wills, reaching up to map the surface of Mars or tunnelling into the earth to discover the hairless mole-rat. Morris's barrage of images gradually sorts itself out into four human lives, united but also isolated from the rest of mankind by their strange obsessions. Morris discovers spiritual lessons embedded in organic and inanimate matter, brought into focus by the men's explanations of what they do. The film is arguably an elegy for a humanistic vision of Man Invincible, perhaps because it was finished after the death of Morris's parents (to whom it is dedicated).

In his previous work, Morris excelled at the interview, and here again, he uses it is the organizing principle. He introduces four men who are as eccentric or focused as anybody from his previous films (pet cemetery-keepers, the Dallas police). It's safe to say that obsession itself is what attracts Morris. His thinking about the role of obsession in the modern world is conveyed more by anecdote and incident than by argument. In obsessions, human beings evince strange— even weird or humorous—traits that set them apart from the motley crowd. What this augurs for human evolution is a very popular matter of scientific and pop-scientific speculation, of course, and in *Fast, Cheap ...* Morris ruminates on human direction, given the tendencies displayed in his four case studies.

Dave Hoover is a lion tamer whose experience has taught him that "an animal has a one-track mind ... You put the chair up, and ... he has four points of interest ... He can't comprehend these four points. ... His mind now is completely distracted from his original thought: Eat the man in the white pants." Dave and his lions are the first in a series of recurring images of master/subject relationships, including the mammoth, lumbering elephants in chains and shapely female acrobats performing at the behest of the ringmaster.

Ray Mendez studies hairless mole-rats and builds habitats for colonies of this mammal, which exhibits, he opines, the behavior of social insects. "People come and look," he says, "... to find themselves in another social animal." Mendez has an infectious enthusiasm for what he calls the "exploring and finding of animals that have absolutely nothing to do with any control that we ... would have; that feeling that you are in the presence of life ... irrelevant of yourself ... see if you can get the moment where the animal is actually looking at you, and you feel there is contact: I know you are. You know I am."

Although Mendez's rodents prompt an awareness of a commonality between man and mole-rat, artificial-intelligence expert Rodney Brooks seems to feel eclipsed by the robots that are his obsession. "We're not even at cockroach stage with a.i. robots," he claims, standing in a room swarming with small, cheap models of insect-robots. Morris helps Brooks' argument along by inserting clips of Pathfinder on another planet to indicate enormous progress from the ludicrous, rogue robot smashing up an office in old movie footage that recalls the robot's origins in popular culture.

Brooks has an unblinking faith in his chosen life form: "understanding life," is gained "by building something life-like ... Some researchers view building these robots as the next step in evolution ... a step beyond mere human bodies, which decay after 70 years ... building something that can reproduce at a much faster rate and carry on through the life of the universe." Because Morris punctuates much of Brooks' interview with playful images of robots, it is difficult to take Brooks' extreme views seriously. Indeed, Brooks floats the notion that human intelligence will carry on as the intelligence invested in developing robots. If we subscribe to this, we can project ourselves into a new age of exploration, when multitudes of insect-robots are launched under the banner of "fast, cheap and out of control."

In sharp contrast, we see the devotion of George Mendonça, the topiary gardener on the estate Green Animals in Providence, Rhode Island, for some 70 years. His domain may be doomed to decay, and is depicted at the end in hazy landscapes reminiscent of the Twilight of the Gods, yet Mendonça modestly presents himself as hired help—he even tells us how he fell in love with the kitchen maid and how the two of them served Green Animals and their mistress, whom we only sense in shots of an empty salon in the mansion. The union of man and plant is most striking when George shows us how he erected a scarecrow man and gave him a wife in a pricey hat. George strikes no heroic poses; he is more like Noah or Adam in the Garden. His animals are herbaceous, but no less unruly than Dave's lions. "It's just cut and wait, cut and wait," he sighs, "You're fighting the elements, getting them to do what you want." George's boxwood beasts cannot reproduce, and it is clear to George that, after him, nobody else will take over their tender care.

Morris puts together the images to depict animal, vegetable, mineral, celluloid, and even woman (acrobats) as subject to human control. The anecdotes, struggles, and small triumphs of the four men are intercut with footage of circus, cartoons, old sci-fi films, and Saturday morning Clyde Beatty serials, thus tracking the evolution of popular entertainment. As circuses gave way to Saturday serials, so serials became B-movies, etc., right down to prime time footage of Pathfinder. Likewise, the documentary we are watching has gone beyond the watch-and-wait methods of Wiseman, Les Blank, and documentarians who quietly roll miles of footage to be edited later for verisimilitude. Morris's variant teaches us to be alert to variety and replication of the many basic elements in the worlds and worldviews presented to us first-hand.

For instance, the images that accompany mole-rat expert Ray Mendez's explanation of coordinated efforts in a mole-rat colony are of a chain of ants moving breadcrumbs, intercut with the torso of a female circus acrobat, her muscles delineated and flexed, her costume's beaded fringe swinging in a sensual rhythm. Her muscles are developed to a point of physical prowess that is as incomprehensible to the average person as the coordination and social perfection of a colony of insects, which may fumble the bread from moment to moment, but achieves its goal with uncanny determination. Reinforcing this theme of balance underlying the appearance of disorder comes another explanation, this time from Rodney Brooks, that insect-robots are not built for stability, but rather for instability, which is a more common challenge when negotiating a terrain, terrestrial or celestial.

The blow-up of the video images of the chain of ants creates a visual effect of almost neon-like vibration, which echoes the fringe of the acrobat; the push-and-pull effort of the ants finds a corollary in news footage of Pathfinder striking out across extra-terrestrial surfaces, bringing us back to the film's basic concern. Exactly what, if anything, is fast, cheap, or out of control? If the film's title itself is ironic—and I suspect it is—it harks back to a serious scientific proposal for space exploration once made by our champion of technology, Rodney Brooks. To wit, replacing huge robots makes exploration formidably expensive; therefore, using 100 small disposable robots simplifies the process, because the robots can be programmed to map, then die. "If it does find what it's looking for," says Brooks of an efficient exploration robot, "its life is over. It stops where it is ... and you get this automatic map." As an explorer, that certainly sets it apart from Cortez "high on a peak in Darien," as Keats envisioned the conquistador.

Although Keats used the wrong explorer, his aim was like that of Morris, who uses the romance of these old Saturday serials to recall our innocence. The affable lion tamer, Hoover, lingers in our memory, even if he says he is but a pale imitation of the greatest lion tamer of them all, Clyde Beatty. We see Beatty's exploits: swinging from ropes onto citadels, saving maidens, liberating missionary orphans, and being colonially stalwart, in scenes from *Darkest Africa,* his own serial, which captured the imagination of young Hoover and made him literally run away with Beatty's circus. Hoover's dedication to lion-taming even had the sanction of his priest, who told his distressed mother that the world also needs lion tamers. Amen.

Why do we trust the folks Morris has lined up? In *The Thin Blue Line,* the whole point was the credibility of each witness: Could we trust what they said? Their inconsistency is what eventually enabled its subject, Randall Adams, to go free. If trusting the interviewees is the crux of *Fast, Cheap & Out of Control,* then we have to weigh the humanists, Hoover and Mendonça, whose jobs seem to be fading out, against the triumphs in technology that make Brooks and Mendez so proud of their models, as if existence as we know it could persist or be carried on in robot or mole-rat form. Is this evolution or merely the result of fast and cheap, as in our no-deposit/no-return culture?

Quibbling with Morris's subjects may not be productive in a film where Morris wants us to believe them—so much so that in order to bring his interviews closer to confession, he invented the Interrotron (two jerry-rigged TelePrompTers, modified so that Morris and his subjects are talking to each other's images on video because both cameras have a half-silvered mirror in front that functions as a monitor. The interview or A-camera runs Morris's image directly in front of the lens. The B-camera, which is on Morris, carries an image of the interview subject being fed in from the A-camera, so that by looking at each other, they stare directly into the cameras' lenses). "There is something very important ... about someone looking you straight in the eye," says Morris, "certainly in human communication and in communication in general. If you ask me, it is the difference between the first person and the third person." As a result, these four first-person narratives are juxtaposed in such a way as to constantly weigh the value of human life over other kinds of life—insect, beast, celluloid, or silicon.

In Fast, Cheap ... Morris is definitely doing more than showing us how four men's lives have been shaped by the parts of the world that they themselves shape. The narration in the interviews is, according to Morris's comments in the production notes, more than "information about the world, [it] actually gives us information about the speaker; he reveals both his world and the radical disjunction between his world and the world at large. Looking at that disjunction is the enterprise of all my movies." As if that ambition were not grand enough, another masterful purpose is built into Morris's fast-paced cutting and high-relief expressionism. Behind the illusion of "chaos" (an apparently inexorable trend in late 20th-century intellectual history), Morris finds pattern; or rather, embedded in the visual verve of *Fast, Cheap* ... is a debate on the value of human progress, which in turn calls for a kind of interrogation of our assumptions about the progress of film technique itself.

Besides found footage from the archives, Morris works with cinematographer Robert Richardson (who gave us the splashy vulgarity of *Natural Born Killers* and *Casino*) to achieve film styles that differ according to the desired level of discourse with the audience. *Fast, Cheap & Out of Control* interweaves stylized, high-resolution sequences with the neon-vibrancy of video transfers to film, then contrasts this with the archaic style of old sci-fi or photo-montage sequences of shredded American iconography. This all dashes across your field of vision in a display that hints at erudition and subtle purpose, yet remains steadfastly faux-pop. It also gallops along like television, where the average length of a shot is 3.5 seconds, and where the assumption is that the viewers' synapses connect the dots with ease. We are also trusted to sort out another interweaving: sound from one source laid over visuals from another.

Should there be any doubt about the design Morris weaves with the threads of interviews—namely, that human existence is threatened by the existence of freaky life-forms—the footage from *Darkest Africa* provides the symbol of insect-winged warriors swooping down to seize our hero after he has liberated missionaries and damsels in distress. The hierarchy from this relic of pop culture plays out in the hierarchy of interviewees (robot/lion-tamer/gardener/mole-rat) to come full circle. Insect-robots cruise around an M.I.T. lab and are proposed as the apotheosis of intellectual evolution, possibly even human evolution. But can Brooks be trusted, when he has so little regard for his own species?

Brooks says of his flock of robots: "A professor from Germany asked me how you tell the robot what to do, and my only answer was, I don't tell the robot what to do ... I switch it on, and it does what is in its nature." Similarly, Errol Morris has tuned into four diverse lives, and despite the manipulation inherent in editing a film, certain elements in those lives—viewed through the kaleidoscope of Morris's own interests—have led him inexorably to a fin-de-siècle fear of the fragility of life. In the final sequence, we witness the lion tamer retiring and passing his baton to a kinder, gentler tamer who sticks her head in the lion's mouth. Then footage from *Darkest Africa* shows the lost city collapsing, a volcano spewing, and our hero Beatty scrambling for his life, before we return to the brave new world of a robot on lunar terrain, as the circus elephants depart. We see a storm looming over Green Animals, and George the gardener with his shears in his hand holding an umbrella against the raging elements. This bleak conclusion reminds us of the evanescence of human existences: not much survives. Creativity is our only consolation.

In an age and medium that relentlessly insists on celebrity, Morris celebrates ideas. He uses relatively unknown people as his dramatis personae, focusing on their knowledge, labor, and dedication as a microcosm of human progress. The major idea of this film revolves around consciousness, beginning at the level of the mole-rat and arriving at the point where artificial intelligence carries forth human intelligence until human knowledge and being persist as pure ideas. Implicit in this concept is the death of homo sapiens, or as Rodney Brooks dubs it, "carbon-based life," as if to replace carbon with silicon is nothing more than a new and improved version of life.

Death, however, is the dilemma; emphasized by the way Morris encapsulates the film with a visual death knell culled from a macabre "bit" at the circus. In the beginning as well as in the final sequence of the film, a clown races across the screen with a skeleton tied to his back, creating the impression, that it's chasing him. Filmed in grainy black and white this corny vaudeville act sets a droll tone and suggest that death is just a circus act away—unless, somehow, the wizards of artificial intelligence can rescue the entire human comedy. Spliced into these death-chases are the elephants, lumbering off in heavy contrast as the music fades. To be sure, the off-key midway music that lends much of the film a jaunty recherché quality owes as much to the techno-artifice of Philip Glass's studio as to Federico Fellini's famous organ-grinding themes. There is no aspect of *Fast, Cheap, & Out of Control* that Errol Morris has not subjected to the traditional versus modernist tug-of-war.

Will a time come when the modifier "artificial" no longer makes a meaningful distinction? Will we assume the life of robots is subject to certain laws of evolution and also attribute to them a high culture/low culture dichotomy, i.e., HAL versus R2D2? Of course, it's not just the robots that terrorize us. Fast, cheap and outta control is just what everyone most fears about modern times, from Charlie Chaplin at the assembly line to video porn in *Boogie Nights*. And in watching the many layers of life that Errol Morris has assembled, we are very much like Ray Mendez watching his mole-rats: "This is not a form of scientific observation. It's a form of self-knowledge."

LOS ANGELES TIMES, 10/3/97, Calendar/p. 19, Kenneth Turan

At a certain point in "Fast, Cheap & Out of Control," Errol Morris' strange but wonderful new documentary, wild-animal trainer Dave Hoover explains why a brandished chair is an effective foil for a lion. The four legs present four points of interest, and that confuses a beast who had been completely focused on "eating the guy in the white suit."

A one-of-a-kind extravaganza by the most original talent now working in documentary film, the four-pronged "Fast, Cheap" has a similar potential to disorient audiences. Director Morris, whose previous films include "Gates of Heaven," "The Thin Blue Line" and "A Brief History of Time," is intent as always on pushing the envelope of nonfiction filmmaking, on cutting the form as much slack as he can while still remaining in complete control.

What that means here is linking four stories that have only the most tenuous thematic connections by means of fluid juxtapositions of image and sound. "Fast, Cheap" is an intoxicating collage put together (by Morris, Oscar-winning cinematographer Robert Richardson, composer Caleb Sampson and editors Shondra Merrill and Karen Schmeer) using nothing more than instinct and sensibility. It's nervy filmmaking, like facing lions in a cage, that is as powerful as a dream to experience.

Links could of course be found between the four men profiled in "Fast, Cheap." They all tell what the director himself has called "deeply weird animal stories," they're all restless intelligences searching for knowledge while trying to control the natural world. But even as these links are acknowledged, they seem beside the point. The truth, as Morris said when "Fast, Cheap" debuted at Sundance, is that this is "the ultimate low-concept film," a quartet of stories linked only by the directors' fascination with each of its characters.

Dave Hoover is, as noted, an animal trainer specializing in the big cats, as did his mentor and idol, the legendary Clyde Beatty. Now semi-retired, he's a genial raconteur, spinning tales of life inside the ring and letting us know why you never, ever want to wear an expansion band wristwatch when lions are around.

Much more intense, though his animals are considerably smaller, is Ray Mendez, an authority on African mole-rats. These strange little beasts, with monster teeth capable of gnawing through concrete, have the distinction of being the only mammals who live in the same kind of complex society insects do. A photographer who designed a mole-rat habitat at the Philadelphia zoo, Mendez wears a butterfly-shaped bow tie and is positively gleeful about his favorite species.

Just as excited, though his specialty is not flesh and blood, is Rodney Brooks, one of MIT's top robot scientists, who builds machines that are unnervingly life-like. The same goes for the wild beasts sculpted with garden shears by George Mendonca, a topiary artist who's worked at a Rhode Island estate called Green Animals for more than 20 years, turning privet and boxwood into giraffes and bears.

Using the Interrotron, a machine of Morris' invention that enables interview subjects to look directly at the audience, these four tell tales of ordinary madness, offering tasty tricks of the trade and revealing how and why they do what they do. But that is only the first level of what "Fast, Cheap" has to offer.

Added on next is footage by Richardson, who has shot almost all of Oliver Stone's films (his Oscar was for "JFK") and who has done an exceptional job infusing an air of strangeness and beauty to pictures of situations like that topiary garden and the three-ring action of the current Beatty circus.

Equally important is a hypnotic, driving score by Sampson (a founder of the Alloy Orchestra, admired for its silent film compositions) and a wide and impressive variety of other kinds of footage, everything from circus home movies to clips from Beatty-starring serials like "King of Jungleland."

While there is minimal cohesion between the lives of the certified eccentrics the film investigates, all these varieties of film and sound are layered tightly together in the most artful way. Circus footage, for instance, will be on the screen while someone is talking about robots, and shots of robots will be intercut with kangaroos and ostriches. Even without conventional links, the whole thing hangs together beautifully. Don't question this film's structure, just let its images and connections wash over you. We're all at the circus here, and Morris is an unconventional ringmaster whose sense of wonder never flags.

NEW YORK POST, 10/3/97, p. 54, Larry Worth

Finding something extraordinary in the ordinary has become the norm when Errol Morris steps behind the camera. And it's a gift now shown to superb effect in the boldly original "Fast, Cheap & Out of Control."

Basically, Morris profiles the lives of four distinctive gentlemen: an animal trainer who grew up idolizing Clyde Beatty; a topiary sculptor at Rhode Island's Green Gardens; an expert on the habits of Africa's hairless mole rats; and an MIT scientist whose robots resemble insects.

An eclectic group of oddballs, to be sure. But while some directors might make fun of these eccentrics, Morris chooses to celebrate them.

Interweaving shots of the four at work and play, Morris starts spinning parallels between their far-ranging interests. Pretty soon, one guy's narrative seamlessly overlaps into footage of another, as disparate themes and philosophies meld into a deliciously enticing pattern.

Using his trademark skewed camera angles, slo-mo and speeded-up photography, a ton of vintage movie clips and an entrancing score, Morris fashions an utterly enchanting production. If anything, the down-side comes from darting among such fascinating subjects, any one of whom merits his own documentary.

The real-life Edward Scissorhands proves especially spellbinding, as when he tells how it took 15 years to shape a bush into a bear, or when he details what happened when his shrub giraffe was decapitated.

In offering such minutiae, each speaker conveys a passion and devotion to his craft that's not only admirable, but unexpectedly poignant.

Long before its conclusion, "Fast, Cheap & Out of Control" has not only entertained but educated, though one learns a little more than necessary about the mole rats excretory habits. All things considered, it's a small price to pay.

NEWSDAY, 9/30/97, Part II/p. B9, John Anderson

Filmmaker Errol Morris, who's been labeled eccentric more often than Marv Albert's been called kinky, has explored pet cemeteries ("Gates of Heaven"), lionized a wheelchair-bound cosmologist defining the universe ("A Brief History of Time") and gotten an innocent man off death row ("The Thin Blue Line"). With each film, he has not just redefined the documentary, he's reordered the way we look at film.

But what exactly is the unifying essence of "Fast, Cheap and Out of Control"? Is there one? The plot thickens ...

In this purposefully strange, eerie and vaguely melancholy movie, Morris profiles—although "profile" doesn't quite cut it—four very different men with very strange vocations. Dave Hooper is a lion tamer and an acolyte of Clyde Beatty, whom we see in outtakes from some very campy '40s serials. George Mendonca is a topiary gardener who's spent his adult life maintaining a green menagerie in Rutherford, R.I. Ray Mendez works with "naked mole rats," a mammalian species that behave like insects. And Rodney Brooks is a scientist at MIT who has developed crawling robots that operate autonomously of human control.

Animals are certainly a constant here, as is the attempt by all these very obsessive, very precise practitioners of four very odd arts to impose control over the uncontrollable—a control that can be lost, in the case of the garden, with a change in the weather, or, in the lion's cage, by the momentary dropping of one's guard.

But the more compelling theme in "Fast, Cheap and Out of Control" is the way the viewer wants to ascribe human characteristics to other creatures, be they animal, vegetable or computer. It's what Brooks alludes to at one point when he mentions the "Bambi syndrome." We watch the community of mole rats and presume they're like people, something Mendez assures us they're not. The lions that Hoover "tames"—although he admits that every day is square one—don't think like us, and he tells us how. The manner in which Mendonca makes his shrubbery conform to the barest resemblance of animal shapes illustrates how willing we are to see what we want—and how insistent we are in finding thematic unity where it doesn't necessarily exist.

And that's why "Fast, Cheap" is so unsettling and disarming. Morris, mixing film styles and perspectives, is disabusing us of our expectations about what documentary should be, how themes can—or should—be explored and, perhaps, how resistant we are to change. Along the way we get to meet four very interesting men operating on the edges, with the uncredited member of their quintet being Errol Morris himself.

NEWSWEEK, 10/20/97, p. 67, David Ansen

Errol Morris likes to describe his newest movie, *Fast, Cheap and Out of Control*, as "the ultimate low-concept movie—a film that utterly resists the possibility of a one-line summary." Trying to define any Errol Morris movie is a slippery business. This obsessive, cerebral, cosmically ironic filmmaker makes one-of-a-kind movies that are often filed under the category "documentary," a rubric that doesn't begin to grapple with their singularity.

His best-known film, "The Thin Blue Line," an investigation into a Texas crime that resulted in the release of a man wrongly convicted of murder, is the easiest to buttonhole; but even there Morris mixed real interviews with simulated reenactments, blurring the line between fact and fiction. Morris's interviews, in which his subjects speak straight into the camera, have a spookily formal quality that's all his own. This style was evident in his amazing first feature, "Gates of Heaven." Ostensibly about pet cemeteries, its true subject was American speech: we got to know the inner lives of the family that ran the cemetery by how they revealed themselves, and their dreams, through language. In his brilliantly bizarre "Vernon, Florida," the talkers are a gaggle of Southern eccentrics; in "A Brief History of Time," the subject is the physicist Stephen Hawking, who, unable to talk because of his disease, types words that are translated into speech by a computer.

A great listener, this former philosophy student is stalking big game. Concerned with epistemological issues—how do we know what we know?—his brainy, haunting films deliberately fudge the line between actuality and fantasy because Morris himself sees the world as an unstable mixture of the two. The 49-year-old filmmaker is haunted by a question. "How much of the world is our dream of the world, and how much is it itself?" That's why he hates to be called a documentary filmmaker. "My gripe isn't with *cinéma vérité*. It's the metaphysical claim—the idea that style guarantees truthfulness—which I find repellent." Morris's nonfiction films don't pretend to be "capturing" reality: they're probing and poking at it, like a doctor looking for a surface aberration that will reveal an inner secret.

In the mysterious and beautiful "Fast, Cheap and Out of Control," Morris interviews four seemingly disparate men—a topiary gardener whose Sisyphean labors (15 years to create a bear!) could be erased by a single storm; a scientist who studies mole rats as an act of self-investigation; a lion tamer who idolizes Clyde Beatty, and a robot scientist who envisions a future in which carbon-based life is replaced by silicon-based forms of life. Each of these obsessive men is fascinating in his own right, but it's the juxtapositions and connections that Morris creates—mixing his interviews with circus footage, a cheesy old Clyde Beatty jungle movie, the mole rats at work, lion-taming acts—into a collage of animal, human and mechanical images that sets off intellectual fireworks in your head.

Made after the death of his mother and stepfather, it has an elegiac undercurrent that's new in Morris's work—a sense of mortality and loss that anchors its heady playfulness in real feeling. "I had a poem by William Butler Yeats in mind when I made it," Morris says. "The lines in 'Lapis Lazuli': 'All things fall and are built again/ And those that build them again are gay.' It's the idea of the hopelessness of it all, but a surviving nobility notwithstanding."

Morris, who lives in Cambridge, Mass., with his wife and son, made one ill-fated journey into purely narrative cinema: an adaptation of the Tony Hillerman novel "The Dark Wind" for Robert Redford's company. It went straight to video. But he'd like to return to fiction films. One of his long-cherished projects, "The Trial of King Boots," is a true story about a sheep dog in Michigan that was put on trial for murder. He also has hopes of developing a series of bizarre, half-hour, fact-based episodes for TV that will employ his invention, the Interrotron. That is his name for the camera he devised that allows his subjects to look directly into the lens while seeing Morris's face as he interviews them. "Fast, Cheap" was shot this way, and he refers to it as "the first true first-person movie." It's Morris's way of saying, "I am a camera." But he is a camera like no other: what he sees are the things no one else would dream of looking for.

TIME, 10/27/97, p. 111, Richard Corliss

Life is so short, and work so long, that it's a balm to love what you do.

To take pleasure and meaning from work not only gets you through the day-after-day, year-after-year, but it defines your place on this planet as much as anything short of your kids. Yet movies remain fixed on growing-pains farce and lurid fantasy. A distant civilization, judging earthlings from their popular films, would think we are the creatures who cop feels and catch serial killers. They'd never guess we spend something like half our waking hours at work.

Errol Morris' delightful nonfiction film, *Fast, Cheap & Out of Control*, is a testimony to the rest of our lives. A one-line summary of the film: it's about four guys who love their jobs. Five if you count Morris, who has built a unique career on his quirky metadocumentaries (*Gates of Heaven, The Thin Blue Line, A Brief History of Time*). He is just the filmmaker to find four kindred spirits, united only in their fascination with pursuits that have something to do with animals. They might be anyone with the genial obsession to get to the office a half-hour early. Dave Hoover wanted to be a lion tamer ever since he was a kid and saw Clyde Beatty's cheesy jungle movies. George Mendonca went to Rhode Island after the hurricane of '38 and stayed to become a topiary gardener. Ray Mendez, a photographer, had a high school fascination with insects; 20 years later, he learned that there were mammals—naked mole rats—living in colonies like insects, took photos of them, brought them home.

Rodney Brooks is an M.I.T. scientist who loved to build things; now he makes robots whose movements are not programmed but follow the machine's "nature."

The names of these men are shown only briefly at the start. For the rest of the film they are identified by their eccentric clothing (Ray's plaid shirt and butterfly bow tie) or coiffure (Dave's gravity-defying orange comb-over). And they are defined by their jobs; we think of them simply as "the lion tamer" or "the mole-rat guy," and watch their eyes spark as they speak of the work that lights their lives.

To have a vocation means to have patience. "It took me 15 years to build a bear," says George of one of his arboreal sculptures. "I won't live long enough to build another bear like that one." Like carpenters and shoemakers, George represents a dying breed of quiet artisanship. And Dave represents the veteran worker who, having devoted himself to perfection on the job, must eventually give way, training his young, flashier replacement.

Morris beautifully orchestrates the four stories (helped by Caleb Sampson's music, which gaily purloins motifs from Nino Rota and Philip Glass). The film blends interview and location footage with clips from old movies and Super 8, black and white and color. As the styles merge, so do the stories. The real lions, the leaf elephants, the robot insects and the insectoid rodents overlap, abut, merge in a gorgeous fugue of hard work and abiding love. This is a funny, thrilling tribute to people's urge to find play and profundity in the work they do.

VILLAGE VOICE, 10/7/97, p. 73, J. Hoberman

I'll take Big Themes under the Big Top. In *Fast, Cheap & Out of Control*, Errol Morris presents The Meaning of Life—or at least his own version of the old TV show *Animal Kingdom*. In this self-described "ridiculous elegy for the end of the millenniums" our favorite docu-epistemologist intercuts interviews with a topiary gardener, an MIT robot scientist, a melancholy lion tamer, and a guy with an inexplicable jones for the ugly, hairless, nearly cold-blooded slug that is the South African naked mole rat.

The circus is Morris's ruling metaphor for his densely edited meta-meditation on the Fate of the Earth (interspersed are clips from juvenile 1930s serials starring animal trainer Clyde Beatty). Deploying all manner of extreme camera tilts, switching from pixillation to slo-mo and back, yoking together a wide variety of film stocks, *Fast, Cheap & Out of Control* is more garishly expressionistic than previous Morris efforts—it was largely shot by Oliver Stone's favorite cinematographer, Robert Richardson with a found Fellini quality accentuated by Caleb Sampson's faux Nino Rota score.

Still, tawdry title notwithstanding, this is a subtle sideshow: plants are cut to resemble animals and animals imagined to think like humans; machines are designed to believe like insects even as insects provide the social model for certain revolutionarily bizarre animals. Indeed, *Fast, Cheap* is itself an unusual life form—telling all four tales more or less simultaneously. The structural precedent is D.W. Griffith's 1916 *Intolerance*, which similarly conjoined a quartet of stories into one overarching narrative, cutting back and forth between the fall of Babylon, the massacre of the Huguenots, a contemporary tale of miscarried justice, and the Passion of Jesus Christ. Scarcely less cosmic, albeit not so grandiose, Morris expands upon the Griffith worldview to conjure up a vision of pre- and posthuman history.

A movie that finds the evanescence of life in the nocturnal spectacle of a floodlit topiary garden in the rain and records someone describing their sublime moment of eye contact with a mole rat, *Fast, Cheap* programatically blurs the boundaries between life and machines, animal and vegetable, human and ... whatever. The study of mole rats is explained as a means of "self-knowledge", rather than "scientific exploration," while lion tamer Dave Hoover theorizes that his animals are confounded by the four legs of a chair brandished in their face because they can only focus on one thing at a time.

If the wild-animal tamer and the topiary gardener attempt to mold divine creation to human ends, the robots and mole rats are more mystically understood by their enthusiasts to embody a blind, superhuman life force. "I switch the robot on and it does what is in its nature," Professor Rodney Brooks tells Morris. The movie's suggestively lurid title comes from Brooks's proposal that, rather than one, 100 tacky little robot explorers be sent on an expedition to Mars.

Parallels proliferate. The Clyde Beatty serial is set in a mole rat-friendly labyrinth of underground tunnels; a crude robot attack in a '50s sci-fi film is instinctively fended off with a chair unsuccessfully, of course. The insects that provide the model for robot sensors and the mole rats with their ideal social organization feast upon the shrub menagerie: "It's a constant battle all the time," the topiarist states. The circus blends with the chaos of the storm threatening the glamorously photographed topiary garden. Brooks suggests that carbon-based life will be replaced by silicon-based life; an earthquake rocks the Clyde Beatty underground. Will the mole rats inherit the earth? The gardener swears he'll keep his shrub-cut animals (as long as he's alive, that is).

What we have are two optimists and two pessimists—or rather, two futurists and two men who face a disappearing past. To which philosophy does the filmmaker subscribe? In a reverse zoom, Morris ends his movie by dedicating it to his own late parents.

Also reviewed in:
CHICAGO TRIBUNE, 11/14/97, Friday/p. C, Mark Caro
NATION, 10/27/97, p. 34, Stuart Klawans
NEW YORK TIMES, 9/30/97, p. E5, Janet Maslin
VARIETY, 1/27-2/2/97, p. 79, Todd McCarthy
WASHINGTON POST, 11/7/97, Stephen Hunter

FATHERS' DAY

A Warner Bros. release of a Silver Pictures production in association with Northern Lights Entertainment. *Executive Producer:* Joe Medjuck, Daniel Goldberg, and Francis Veber. *Producer:* Joel Silver and Ivan Reitman. *Director:* Ivan Reitman. *Screenplay:* Lowell Ganz and Babaloo Mandel. *Based on the film "Les Compères"by:* Francis Veber. *Director of Photography:* Stephen H. Burum. *Editor:* Sheldon Kahn and Wendy Greene Bricmont. *Music:* James Newton Howard. *Music Editor:* Jim Weidman. *Sound:* Gene S. Cantamessa, Clark King and (music) Shawn Murphy. *Sound Editor:* Howell Gibbens. *Casting:* Bonnie Timmermann and Michael Chinich. *Production Designer:* Thomas Sanders. *Art Director:* Daniel T. Dorrance. *Set Decorator:* Lauri Gaffin. *Special Effects:* David M. Blitstein. *Costumes:* Rita Ryack. *Make-up:* Peter Montagna. *Stunt Coordinator:* Joel Kramer. *Running time:* 99 minutes. *MPAA Rating:* PG-13.

CAST: Robin Williams (Dale Putley); Billy Crystal (Jack Lawrence); Julia Louis-Dreyfus (Carrie Lawrence); Nastassja Kinski (Collette Andrews); Charlie Hofheimer (Scott Andrews); Bruce Greenwood (Bob Andrews); Dennis Burkley (Calvin); Haylie Johnson (Nikki); Charles Rocket (Russ Trainor); Patti D'Arbanville (Shirley Trainor); Jared Harris (Lee); Louis Lombardi (Matt); Alan Berger (Rex); Tom Verica (Peter); Jennifer Crystal (Rose); David Ripley and Ryan "Rhino" Michaels (Roadies); Jason Reitman (Wrong Kid in Alley); William

Hall (Hotel Clerk); Ricky Harris (Bellhop); Paul Herman (Mr. Barmore); Christopher Jaymes (Gas Station Guy); Catherine Reitman (Victoria); Claudette Wells (Ms. Tweesbury); Susan Traylor (Flight Attendant); Dana Gould (Room Service Waiter); Meagen Fay (Megan); Mary Gillis (Slot Machine Lady); Mindy Seeger (Nurse); Jennifer Echols (Ball Park Vendor); Marc Glimcher (Cashier); Geoffrey Infeld (Mime); Harry E. Northup (Cop, Reno Jail); Tamara Zook (Francene, Waitress); Frank Medrano (Mechanic); Elston Ridgle (Security Guard); Kim Shattuck, Ronnie Barnett and Roy McDonald (The Muffs); Caroline Reitman (Lost Girl); Lee Weaver (Airline Passenger); Jose (Esau) Pena (Boat Painter); Andrew Zotoff (Doorman); Kay Ford (Woman in Lobby); Jasmine Rose (Nose-ring Girl); Mel Gibson (Punk with "Prince Albert").

LOS ANGELES TIMES, 5/9/97, Calendar/p. 1, Kenneth Turan

Inoffensive, predictable, obvious, "Fathers' Day" is all the I things a major studio comedy wants and needs to be. If you noticed that funny is not on the list, go to the head of the class.

Because humor, real humor, involves an element of daring, and, even worse, of risk. With Robin Williams and Billy Crystal as its stars, "Fathers' Day" sounds funnier than it is, which is exactly the point. For a Hollywood comedy, it's more bankable to be safe, more important to give the illusion of humor than to attempt the real thing and flirt with the possibility of disaster.

Don't misunderstand. "Fathers' Day" is not the runt of the litter; it has moments that amuse and if you're trapped with it on an intercontinental airplane, it won't be painful to watch. But this example of what happens when commercial calculation rules the day is, so nakedly a machine-made product you can see the gears meshing at every turn.

Like a board of directors picked from heads of Fortune 500 companies, "Fathers' Day's" creative choices all point toward the sleek and unadventurous usual suspects, such as casting Julia Louis-Dreyfus with an eye no doubt toward her "Seinfeld" success. Director Ivan Reitman is a past master ("Junior," "Kindergarten Cop") of this kind of bland corporate comedy, and the writing team of Lowell Ganz & Babaloo Mandel ("Forget Paris") are not far behind.

All these people have been funny at one time or another, but if this film is any evidence, at this point in their careers they're largely doing it by the numbers. This is comedy at its most lumbering, so slow you can practically snooze between the jokes.

Even the film's pretested subject matter of two men who both think they have the same boy for a son speaks to a lack of originality. "Fathers' Day" is based on a successful French comedy, "Les Comperes," written by Francis Veber, himself a middle-of-the-road mainstay with "The Tall Blonde Man With One Black Shoe" and "La Cage aux Folles" to his credit.

"Fathers' Day's" initial dilemma is the disappearance of 17-year-old Scott Andrews (Charlie Hofheimer). His mother, Collette (boomer icon Nastassja Kinski, another bankable choice), thinks he's run off with a girlfriend, but since dad Bob (Bruce Greenwood) is not taking action, she moves into gear. She contacts two of her old lovers, tells each that he's the boy's father and asks for help finding him.

Dad designate No. 1, attorney Jack Lawrence (Crystal) is dubious about the project, asking for a blood test and telling Collette, "I don't find people, I sue them." But despite fears about how his new third wife (Louis-Dreyfus) will take the news, he's soon involved in the search for Scott.

Dad designate No. 2 is Dale Putley (Williams), a reformed mime, failed performance artist and avant-garde poet who is prone to getting emotional. With little to live for (Collette's phone call interrupts a suicide attempt), Putley embraces the idea that he's a dad with considerable relish.

Once they discover what Collette has done to hook them in, the pair weakly bicker about who will likely be the real dad before agreeing to join forces to find Scott. He, it turns out, has run off in search of Sugar Ray, a band with a Grateful Dead-type mobile following. Soon on the road as well is husband Bob, who decides late is better than never in the searching-for-Scott department.

Like one of those supertankers that needs a lot of warning to make a simple turn, everything that happens in "Fathers' Day" is telegraphed well in advance. Also, those who think vomiting, attacks of scalding coffee and portable toilets overturning with people in them is what humor is all about will not be disappointed here.

With Crystal's character depicted as someone who head-butts people to get out of trouble and Williams' pigeon-holed as a walking compendium of outlandish neuroses, neither actor is used to maximum benefit, though Williams does exhibit a few welcome glimmers of madness. One of the film's biggest laughs belongs to neither man, but rather to Mel Gibson making an uncredited cameo appearance as someone with so many rings in his body he looks like a human loose-leaf binder.

As has become the trend in recent years, "Fathers' Day" also dilutes whatever humor it allows in by overwhelming it with waves of sentiment, in this case scenes about the pain of having a father who doesn't listen and the importance of acknowledging parents as people.

This gets so out of hand that when one character says, "Can I give you a little bit of advice here?," it's tempting to yell, "Try to be funny, for heaven's sake." But, prepackaged and pre-sold to a large degree, films like "Fathers' Day" are taking away way too much money to listen.

NEW YORK, 5/26/97, p. 66, David Denby

When the next generation looks back in boredom on American movies in the nineties, they will point to the prematurely arthritic *Fathers' Day* as a typical example of ennui. The movie is no more than trivially bad—it's the kind of thing one watches, half asleep, on a flight to the coast—but it speaks volumes about timidity and sloth. Here are two of the most original talents in the country, Robin Williams and Billy Crystal, joined together in another remake of a French farce. Apart from *The Birdcage,* (a remake of *La Cage aux Folles)*, I can't think of a single one of these French comedies that has worked as an American film. What do the French have to teach us about comedy? The only reason for the remakes is the studios' sheer terror of doing something—anything—that hasn't been done successfully before in one form or another.

The plot seems to have been preserved in a jar. Nastassja Kinski's 16-year-old son runs away, so she enlists the help of two former boyfriends, Billy (a Los Angeles lawyer-prig) and Robin (a Berkeley loser), convincing each that he might be the boy's father. The two men meet and instantly loathe each other, but they join forces, and they almost become friends. Oh, such wonderful adventures they have! They enter rock clubs with as much discomfort as if they had wandered into an inferno. Then there is the great sequence in which Billy Crystal's wife hears, on the telephone, that the boy is in the shower, and concludes that Billy is having a homosexual adventure. That one must have cracked them up in Lyons.

The jokes are beyond square; they're almost cubic. Isn't it a little early for comics who are this young to be warming up for a lack Lemmon-Walter Matthau picture?

Billy Crystal has a few moments: He does a Jack Benny slow burn as a corporate tough guy. He also butts people with his head when he's angry, an aggressive propensity that's never explained (some sort of Marseilles thing?). Robin Williams plays a zhlub—a failed writer, a no-talent sentimentalist. But who wants to see Robin Williams as a zhlub? He's too creative to play anyone so uncreative: Director Ivan Reitman is pouring champagne into a cola can. Williams has a weakness for hairy-leprechaun darlingness that I've often deplored. *Let it out, Robin! You don't really love us all that much. And you should never put us in the position of feeling sorry for you.* And the script doesn't do what we expect and what would have been satisfying—allow him to break triumphantly from shlump-hood. He has one funny moment—one—when he does pidgin German as a Euro-rock promoter. *Fathers' Day* is fundamentally lazy. If Jim Carrey leaves these guys in the dust, they deserve the dry taste in their mouths.

NEW YORK POST, 5/9/97, p. 51, Bill Hoffmann

"Fathers' Day" ranks as one of the biggest disappointments of the year.

It's a by-the-numbers comedy that runs out of gas a third of the way through and has a lame ending that delivers no payoff.

But most distressing about this Ivan Reitman-directed mess is seeing two comic heavyweights such as Robin Williams and Billy Crystal limping their way through 99 minutes of half-baked material.

The cutting-edge, razor-sharp wit that made them two of America's funniest entertainers is gone, their once-great comic timing is off, and they seem very, very tired.

This is a going-through-the-motions movie for the pair—strictly a case of grind it out fast and collect the paychecks.

Crystal plays Jack Lawrence, a married, hotshot L.A. lawyer whose life, is turned upside down when Collette Andrews (Nastassja Kinski), an old college flame, reappears to reveal that she has a 16-year-old-son by him.

A day later, Collette contacts another old boyfriend, Dale Putley (Robin Williams), a suicidal English teacher, and tells him that *he's* the dad.

What gives? Her son, Scott (Charlie Hofheimer), has run off with his bratty teen girlfriend and Collette wants her old loves to track him down.

The trail leads them through a number of largely unfunny encounters in Sacramento, San Francisco and Reno—including a pointless twist in which drug-dealing thugs join in the chase, adding an unnecessary nastiness to the proceedings.

Who turns out to be the real father? I won't say, but, believe me, the answer to the movie's big question is a total rip-off. It's also sad to see the talented Julia Louis-Dreyfus (Elaine on "Seinfeld") wasted in a thankless role as Crystal's wife.

With this inferior remake of the much-funnier 1984 French hit "Les Comperes," Reitman must believe fans will swallow Williams and Crystal in *anything*. I hope he'll be proved wrong when the box-office receipts are totaled.

A lot of Jim Carrey's fans didn't think much of "The Cable Guy" (a wildly edgy movie I thought was brilliant), but at least it showed that he's willing to experiment.

In "Fathers' Day," the only thing Williams and Crystal push is stale Hollywood product. And for that, they should be ashamed.

NEWSDAY, 5/9/97, Part II/p. B2, John Anderson

Whether the sum equals the parts isn't even a question you have to ask about "Fathers' Day," unless you still believe Robin Williams and Billy Crystal are the funniest men on the planet. Remember when they were the comics with ... *edge?* Think of them now as the farm team Lemmon and Matthau, who in, oh, say, 20 years, will be making "Grumpy Old Comedians."

Which doesn't make "Fathers' Day"—the latest in a long line of French remakes—an atrocity. On the contrary, it can be quite funny; Crystal and Williams do the old married couple shtick so well they should open a joint bank account. But what works in the film has little to do with the fact they've been teamed together. They work better, in fact, when they work alone.

Opening with a montage of cozy home video, family-album-style shots and a song that sounds like the Beatles-soundalike Badfinger—and is actually Beatle-soundalike Paul McCartney—"Fathers' Day" strives for pathos before it's even out of the box. And between director Ivan Reitman's longing for sentiment and the Babaloo Mandell-Lowell Ganz script (these guys should just open a recycling center and get it over with), the film conspires to nullify that which is both Williams' and Crystal's strong suits—spontaneity with a streak of anarchy. The brightest moments, you have the very immediate suspicion, are all ad-libbed.

Rather than provide a springboard for the talents of its stars, the story is a speedbump: Colette (Nastassja Kinski) is looking for her son Scott (Charlie Hofheimer), who has disappeared after a fight with his dad, Bob (Bruce Greenwood). She looks up an old boyfriend, Jack Lawrence (Crystal), a shark-like Los Angeles attorney, tells him he's the boy's father and hopes he'll be compelled to join the search. When Jack doesn't bite, she goes to Dale Putney (Williams), a neurotic-compulsive writer and another old flame, and tells him the same story. Dale, who was at the time contemplating suicide ("It's the only thing that keeps me going.") buys the whole yarn.

Jack, however, has second thoughts and the two counterfeit fathers cross paths, join forces, and track down Scott—who himself is following a rock band to Reno. This provides all sorts of opportunities for high jinks, situation comedy and making the point that neither Williams nor Crystal is as young as he used to be. Scenes in a skinhead club provide opportunities for vomit jokes; hot coffee in a lap proves the requisite groin gag; a recurrent subplot about Bob trying to find Scott and getting stuck in an overturned Portosan provides the necessary scatological humor and allows us not to think badly of Bob while keeping him out of the main story.

You get a little pathos, a little violence, a snide view of teenagers, a mean drug dealer (Jared Harris) from whom Scott must be rescued by his "fathers," and a wasted performance by the wonderful Julia Louis-Dreyfus.

Of course, you have to also ask: Why would Colette approach two virtual strangers to help her find her son? Answers to questions like this exist in the Hollywood plot void, swirling endlessly through the vapors of studio story meetings. You have to ignore the inanity of it all and wait for Williams and Crystal to deliver the jokes, which aren't as plentiful as they might have been, but are as good as they get, when they get there.

SIGHT AND SOUND, 10/97, p. 48, Xan Brooks

Successful Los Angeles-based lawyer Jack Lawrence receives a surprise visit from his ex-girlfriend whom he has not seen in 17 years. Over lunch, Collette shocks him with the news that he is the real father of her 16-year-old son Scott, whom she and her husband Bob have raised together. Scott has absconded with his girlfriend Nikki and Collette wants Jack him to find him. The next day, Collette phones failed suicidal writer Dale Putley—an ex-boyfriend from around the same time—to tell him that *he* is Scott's father. Dale and Jack each duly embark on a hunt for the missing boy. However, their quest soon brings them into contact, and they realise they have been duped. They call Collette and she tells them that she doesn't know exactly who Scott's father is. It is either Jack, Dale or Bob.

Jack and Dale find Scott—drunk and abandoned by Nikki—at a concert by the rock band Sugar Ray and take him to a hotel where they discover $5,000 in his shirt pocket. In the morning, Scott escapes and the two men continue their chase to Reno, the next leg of the Sugar Ray tour. Meanwhile, Bob sets off to look for Scott himself but is waylaid by an accident at a roadside outhouse. In Reno, Scott tells them that the money was stolen from two drug dealers, Lee and Matt, who are now chasing him. Jack and Dale fight them off and return Scott to his family. Collette privately confesses that Scott is Bob's son but to spare his rescuers' feelings, Scott takes Dale and Jack aside separately to inform each in turn that he is the real father.

Father's Day sticks like a limpet to the *Three Men and a Baby* formula of overhauling a much-loved (but little-seen) French comedy for Stateside consumption. In this instance it's Francis Veber's odd-couple caper *Les Compères* (1983). It emerges from the Hollywood mill plucked, scrubbed and ready-made for the bantering skills of stars Robin Williams and Billy Crystal. Add Tinseltown insider Ivan Reitman (*Ghostbusters, Twins*) as director and one of the producers and we have a textbook essay in formula film-making. All that's missing is a heart or soul.

Had *Father's Day* been more slickly paced or exuberantly played one might have been able to ignore this absence, but it seems to affect all that surrounds it. *Father's Day* struggles on almost every level. Neither heartwarming nor very funny, it is marked by an indulgent, hands-off style of direction that's at odds with its material; farce requires more control to spoonfeed the audience its entertainment.

Presumably Reitman reasoned that all he needed to do was set up the cameras and tick off the scenes. After all, Hollywood lore has always held that Williams works best when he's off the leash (his turns in *Good Morning Vietnam* and Disney's *Aladdin* both resulted from inspired improvisations). But in *Father's Day* the ruse backfires. In the role of Dale Putley, the weepy wannabe writer, Williams merely lolls on his laurels. He shows a faint flicker of interest when running through a rendition of his self-penned musical 'Hello Doctor, it's Still Swollen', but it's fleeting. Even an extended sequence which has Dale alone in his apartment adopting and discarding various parental personas (the hippy parent, the streetsmart rapper, the suave aristo) falls flat. Only occasionally does he pull off a good line. when crystal's Jack explains how he uses force to get information, Dale exclaims "How Joe Pesci of you! How are you going to get this one to talk? Run her tits through a vice?"

Crystal fares better as Jack, the chalk to Dale's cheese, in a deceptively tricky role. On the one hand, he's the grey, faintly dislikeable foil to the more colourful Dale. On the other, he's the film's proper hero (because it is his journey from sterile careerist to budding father that the movie traces). Underplaying, Crystal manages a certain naturalness and seems at least to be taking the part seriously. He even manages to make a contrived sob story about his childhood dog getting put down on his birthday faintly touching.

Away from these two roles, *Father's Day* offers the leanest of pickings to its cast. Charlie Hofheimer is adequate but under-used in a stock part as the runaway teen, while the talented Jared Harris (who played Warhol in *I Shot Andy Warhol*) sparkles ever so briefly as a twitchy drug dealer before getting beaten up in the climactic fight scene.

But it's the women who are most shortchanged by Reitman's film. Julia Louis-Dreyfus—so good in television's *Seinfeld*—finds herself cast here as the archetypal nagging shrew in a support slot as Jack's current wife. Still more agonising is the sight of Nastassja Kinski assigned only a scant smattering of lines in her pivotal role of Collette, mother of Scott and former lover to both Jack and Dale. Women don't figure much in the *Father's Day* equation. In the handling of Scott's fickle girlfriend Nikki, there's almost a subtle misogyny. Maternity is a given but never explored, just as Collette's telling Jack and Dale they are both the father of Scott is a plot engine with no plausible explanation.

Had the makers been more daring we might have had a different ending in which Jack and Dale set up home together, with Scott snugly ensconced in the guest room. One almost expects something like this to happen based on the associations brought to the film by Williams' recent appearance in *The Birdcage*. Judging by the homoerotic jokes that abound in the film's mid-section (in which a bemused bellhop assumes a *menage-à-trois* upon seeing the two men in the shower with a drunken Scott), this conclusion would have sat quite neatly at the end of *Father's Day*. Chances are it would have for a more interesting movie, too.

VILLAGE VOICE, 5/20/97, p. 78, Laurie Stone

In his movies, Billy Crystal wants to be adorable. But in *Fathers' Day*, playing high-powered lawyer Jack Lawrence, for once he isn't begging to be loved, and he's funny in a new, restrained way. He lets his intelligence find the ironies, and his performance goes a distance in keeping the movie amusingly afloat. Nastassja Kinski—looking like a generic Hollywood blonde (!)—tells her two old boyfriends, played by Crystal and Robin Williams, that each is the real father of her 16-year-old runaway son, Scott (Charlie Hofheimer), in hopes they will search for the boy. Her husband, Bob, the boy's actual father—played by Bruce Greenwood as a WASP who holds in his emotions as tightly as his buff buns—wants Scott to return on his own. The reason mom can't search is that she's blonde and needs guys to do that for her.

The movie tells a story about a shiksa who turns to schmaltzy, caring Jews when Mr. Hardbody goes limp in the feeling department, though it doesn't mean to flare Jewish self-congratulation, only to rub the WASP's tapered nose in his folly. It does in a series of hilariously low toilet sketches, starting when Bob is accidentally tipped over a roadside embankment while inside a foul-smelling 'porta-potty.' Mostly, *Fathers' Day* is an amiable road flick, Crystal odd-coupling it with Williams, who plays his patented outpatient character, a manic-depressive named Dale; when we meet him he quips, "For years the thought of suicide was the only thing that kept me going." The movie's sense of chronology is, shall we say, loose: Crystal and Williams are way too old to have been college flames of Kinski's character. The film wastes Julia Louis-Dreyfus and generally treats females as the chicory garnish you look at but don't eat. Still, it's easy to overlook these lapses during several out-and-out howlers: Greenwood being hosed down after his parta-potty adventure, and Crystal, having tracked Scott to a headbanger concert, disentangling his cuff link from a young girl's nose ring.

Also reviewed in:
NEW YORK TIMES, 5/9/97, p. C3, Janet Maslin
NEW YORKER, 5/19/97, p. 96, Terrence Rafferty
VARIETY, 5/5/-11/97, p. 67, Todd McCarthy
WASHINGTON POST, 5/9/97, p. D7, Stephen Hunter
WASHINGTON POST, 5/9/97, Weekend/p. 56, Desson Howe

FEMALE PERVERSIONS

An October Films release of a Trans Atlantic Entertainment and Mindy Affrime production. *Executive Producer:* Zalman King, Gina Resnick and Rena Ronson. *Producer:* Mindy Affrime. *Director:* Susan Streitfeld. *Screenplay:* Susan Streitfeld and Julie Hebert. *Based on "Female Perversions: The Temptations of Emma Bovary"* by: Louise J. Kaplan. *Director of Photography:*

Teresa Medina. *Editor:* Curtis Clayton and Leo Trombetta. *Music:* Debbie Wiseman. *Music Editor:* Mark Jan Wlodarkiewicz. *Choreographer:* Kim Blank. *Sound:* Ed White and (music) Dick Lewzy. *Casting:* Christine Sheaks. *Production Designer:* Missy Stewart. *Set Designer:* Don Merkt, Leslie Thomas, and Patricia Owen. *Set Decorator:* Karen Manthey. *Special Effects:* J. Ignacio Alvarez. *Costumes:* Angela Billows. *Make-up:* Suzanne Diaz. *Stunt Coordinator:* J. Ignacio Alvarez. *Running time:* 119 minutes. *MPAA Rating:* R.

CAST: Tilda Swinton (Eve Stephens); Amy Madigan (Madelyn Stephens); Karen Sillas (Renee); Laila Robins (Emma); Clancy Brown (John Diehl); Frances Fisher (Annunciata); Pauline Porizkova (Langley); Dale Shuger (Ed); Lisa Jane Persky (Margot); John Diehl (Jane Rock); John Cassini (Gas Station Attendant); Sandy Martin (Trudy, License to Flirt); Marcia Cross (Eve's Mother); Shawnee Smith (Make-up Salesgirl); Nina Wise (Lingerie Saleswoman); Judy Jean Berns (Boutique Saleswoman); J. Patrick McCormick (Wallace); Abdul Salam el Razzac (Homeless Man); Elizabeth Cava (Female Jail Guard); Scotch Ellis Loring (Joey, Cab Driver); Rick Zieff (Office Boy); Don Gettinger (Eve's Father); Marra Racz (Earthwoman); Ruben Knight (Judge); Russ Gething (Courthouse Guard); Bailee Bileschi (Young Eve); Kim Blank (Mother in Boutique); Robert Rider (Old Man in Boutique); Eva Rodriguez (Latina Cleaning Woman); Bea Marcus (Old Lady on Bus Bench); Jim James (Detective); Evangelina Rodriguez (Latina Corn Seller); Kirstie Tyrone (Young Madelyn); Wade Durbin (King); Azalea Davila (Queen).

LOS ANGELES TIMES, 4/25/97, Calendar/p. 10, Kevin Thomas

"Female Perversions" sounds like a porno title, but it is in fact a deadly serious exploration of how society—indeed, the entire weight of culture and history—shapes and can distort a woman's sense of her own sexuality, consciously and unconsciously, and therefore her identity as well. It suggests how this in turn affects her whole life—her self-esteem, how she sees herself and how she conducts herself at every turn of her existence.

Directed by Susan Streitfeld and adapted by her and Julie Hebert from a book of case histories by Dr. Louise J. Kaplan, "Female Perversions" is nothing if not ambitious. Even if it works better as a provocative psychological treatise than as art, it does come alive and does provide major roles for Tilda Swinton and Amy Madigan, formidable actresses who are more than up to the challenge.

And it stands as a powerful argument that as the end of the 20th century approaches, women still need to liberate themselves in regard to their psyches and how such liberation remains crucial to self-confidence and self-fulfillment in all aspects of their lives.

An ever-venturesome Scottish actress in her American film debut, Swinton plays a stunningly beautiful Los Angeles public prosecutor up for a governor-appointed judgeship. Her Eve has a ruggedly handsome and successful lover (Clancy Brown), a nifty loft, a fabulous wardrobe (designed by Bela Freud, a descendant of Sigmund!)—and a cool demeanor that hides gnawing insecurities.

Just as Eve's anticipating the all-crucial interview with the governor, she has to cope with the arrest for shoplifting of her sister (Madigan), a UCLA graduate student in feminist studies up for her doctoral exams. The sisters' mother died when they were young, and their father, described as a "brilliant banker," remains remote. Both women could use therapy—it seems there may be repressed family secrets as well. They need to learn to help each other.

As a first-time director, Streitfeld has taken on too much. There's a whole slew of images supposedly welling up in Eve's dreams and imagination that vacillate between the too literal and the too obscure. There are too many other characters in the film, serving all-too-obviously as illustrations of various types of female hang-ups. Streitfeld has trouble differentiating between taking herself and her film seriously, a problem that of course chronically afflicts critics as well as filmmakers.

The film's strength lies not in glimpses of bondage rituals and a repeated shot of Eve's family's swimming pool, which just happens to have been designed in the shape of a cross and in which she feels she's drowning. It's in Eve's worrying about a loose thread dangling from the hem of her skirt during that all-important gubernatorial interview; in a moment of one-upmanship between Eve and her public prosecutor successor (Paulina Porizkova) when they discover they use the same new lipstick; and in Eve's hot fling with a lesbian psychiatrist (Karen Sillas) in a state of such self absorption she never considers her impact on the lesbian's emotions.

It is unfortunate that Streitfeld did not trust the power of what she has to say to reveal itself in such detailing and skip the surreal stuff entirely.

Too didactic in tone, "Female Perversions" has its share of foolish, over-the-top moments, but it is also brave, illuminating and honest. There are worse sins than pretentiousness.

NEW YORK POST, 4/25/97, p. 51, Thelma Adams

"Female Perversions": The title titillates and sounds like a chapter in a Psych 1 text. Susan Streitfeld's provocative, pretentious, pornographic drama is an uneasy mix of academics and arousal.

"Perversions" revolves around Eve (Tilda Swinton). The lawyer on the verge of a judgeship reads like a clinical case study tarted up for a women's magazine: a Type "A" in revealing Rodeo Drive togs, she's tough on the outside, crying on the inside. Her life's empty, but success permits unlimited shopping.

The attorney swings between two ideal lovers: John (Clancy Brown) and Renee (Karen Sillas). He's an earthquake expert with Fabio looks. She's a busty blonde shrink who gives it up on the first date, but longs for commitment.

Fueling Eve's predatory sexuality is a desperate little girl longing for daddy's love. In case we don't get the connection, Streitfeld pastes signs on walls and bus stops to guide the unenlightened. "Perverse scenarios are about desperate need," reads one.

Eve's pivotal memory is a snippet of domestic porn: Mama seduces academic papa by tracing a circle around her erect nipple with a fountain pen; papa rejects Mama, pushing her to the ground; guilt-stricken daughter comforts the cold father rather than the love-starved mother.

While Eve lets off steam shopping and having sex, her sister, Madelyn (Amy Madigan), shoplifts. This hobby reunites lawyer and criminal when the Ph.D. candidate gets arrested the week before defending her thesis on Mexican matriarchy. Maddy tells Eve that kleptomania gives her an orgasm when nothing else will. Daddy Dearest twisted both sisters, it seems.

The moon-faced Swinton ("Orlando") imperiously marches through the material, creating an L.A lawyer as far from Susan Dey as possible. Eve makes no sense, but Swinton fills up the hollow bits with conviction and intensity.

Equally compelling but incompatible, the earthy Madigan plays her scenes in a realistic vein at odds with Swinton, who appears to be fleeing a Derek Jarman film. Sillas adds a heft and heart to her sexy shrink that isn't on the page. Frances Fisher arrives for a striptease and a discourse on giving men what they want; pubescent Dale Shuger mutilates herself in anticipation of womanhood.

Streitfeld's feminist sloganeering is instantly forgettable; not so the sex. It's no surprise that soft-core pornster Zalman King ("Wild Orchid") executive produced "Perversions." Eve and Renee's hammock frolic ranks among the top 10 lesbian lovemaking scenes ever. And in an era of sitcom outings and it-couple Anne Heche and Ellen DeGeneres, what's so perverse about that?

NEWSDAY, 4/25/97, Part II/p. B9, John Anderson

Hot-shot attorney Eve Stephens (Tilda Swinton) is delivering a lethal courtroom summation, reducing the opposition to ash, and all eyes are on her—her hips, her lips, her legs, her cleavage. Her words? Like ether, they evaporate in the fevered atmosphere of a collective male gaze.

Eve is high-caliber. A legal assassin. She's about to be nominated for a judgeship. What did she actually *say* in court? I have no idea, which is just one of the little epiphanies of "Female Perversions," a title guaranteed to elicit conclusions without proof of purchase, but a film of extraordinary intelligence, wit and erotic heat.

Inspired by the book by Freudian theorist Louise J. Kaplan, it opens with a Kaplan quote it really doesn't need: We know quickly enough that the "perversion" in question is "normal"—in that female self-definition is dictated by male standards and even the most successful woman is plagued by racking doubts and fears. Within the deliberately arch, subtly flamboyant settings of director Susan Streitfeld, Eve looks for validation from men, even as she's unaware how deeply she's programmed, how much her sense of self depends on clothes and cosmetics. A walking

Vogue ad, she lives in fear that her "flaws" will be found out. Her career has been a series of lucky breaks. She's put one over on the world. And the more she accomplishes, the more severe her self-recriminations and loathing.

Is she an anomaly? Hardly. Her circumstances may be singular; her basic plight seems universal. Her sister, Maddy (Amy Madigan), a doctoral candidate (anthropology, I think), reacts to her own sense of suffocation by shoplifting things she doesn't even want. Maddy's housemate, Emma (Laila Robins), is emotionally enslaved by her boyfriend. Annunciata (Frances Fisher), a stripper, is the essence of sexual cynicism. And Emma's daughter Ed (Dale Shuger) is dealing with oncoming puberty with self-mutilation and dread.

When Maddy's arrested, Eve has to venture out of her safe urban center—which includes a relationship with John (Clancy Brown) that seems strictly sexual and a sexual relationship with a doctor, Renee (Karen Sillas), that might be more. She finds a world in which women, defensively perhaps, prey on one another emotionally.

Director Streitfeld doesn't succeed at everything she tries. The recurring visual hallucinations about ropes and bondage are stylized to the point they seem borrowed from Peter Greenaway, or maybe even Derek Jarman, and are overheated in the way the Swinton-starring "Orlando" was. The chemical peel given Eve's psyche is caustic but occasionally misapplied: When she screams at her secretary, Margot (Lisa Jane Persky), "I'm going to be a judge!!!" and they both dissolve in girlish shrieks, I'm not quite clear what Streitfeld is saying, or whether she knows, either.

But Eve is played brilliantly by Swinton and the rest of the cast is first rate, too. It would mean nothing to say "Female Perversions" is the season's smartest film because the season has been mentally deficient. But it offers what smart movies do: a fresh introduction to the all-too-recognizable.

SIGHT AND SOUND, 5/97, p. 43, Claire Monk

About to be interviewed by the State Governor as a prelude to her likely appointment as a judge, successful Los Angeles attorney Eve Stephens looks set to break into the echelons of power. But Eve thinks of herself as a fraud—a belief expressed in masochistic fantasies. Though in an sexual relationship with man, she starts an affair with Renee, a psychiatrist, but Renee quickly identifies her as neurotic and treats her with caution.

Eve's older sister Madelyn has just completed a PhD on a Mexican matriarchal community, and is a compulsive shoplifter. When she is caught and arrested, Eve drives out to the small desert town where she lives and tries unsuccessfully to bail her out. Eve spends the weekend in Madelyn's room, and meets Madelyn's landlady Emma, Emma's sullen teenage daughter Ed, and Ed's flamboyant aunt Annunciata. Later, a released Madelyn reacts furiously to a moral lecture from Eve. The two part on bad terms and Eve returns to the city.

On the night before Eve's judicial interview, Madelyn—defending her thesis in LA the next day—arrives uninvited to stay over, and departs early, stealing Eve's interview suit. At the interview, Eve is thrown off-balance when the Governor asks about her nonexistent marriage plans. Going to pieces, she drives out of town to confront Madelyn. Their fight forces Eve to confront herself, and a reconciliation follows. Watching a family home movie, Eve realises that one of her recurring dream/fantasy images dates from childhood, when she saw her father spurning a seduction attempt by her mother and rushed to placate not her, but him. A cathartic dream leaves her traumatised, but she is soothed by Madelyn. As Eve leaves, news arrives that the Governor is proposing her as a judge; seeing Ed in distress on a mountain near the road, she comforts her.

As a concept, *Female Perversions* couldn't get much weirder if you dreamt it. It's a fictional feature based on a Freudian feminist study of female behaviour and sexuality (Louise J. Kaplan's *Female Perversions)*, directed by the former agent of Danny Glover and part-executive-produced by, Zalman King (screenwriter of *Nine½ Weeks*). Stranger still, it relocates Tilda Swinton—the most uncompromisingly anti-mainstream of major British film stars—to LA, kits her out in tiny Bella Freud suits and impossible heels and requires her to get steamy with Karen Sillas (from Hal Hartley's *Simple Men* and *Flirt*) in a hammock.

In practice, Susan Streitfeld's first feature is one of the most disturbing, intriguing feminist films in years. Its hard-edged visual gloss and cool focus on unsisterly sisters make a welcome antidote to the safe sentimentality of most recent Hollywood women's films whose political lexicon never seems to progress beyond 'B' for bonding. The film's opening epigraph—taken from Kaplan's book—suggests that for a woman to express her full sexual, emotional and intellectual capacities "would entail who knows what risks", but that the alternative—the ongoing performance required to conform with 'normal' femininity—is itself a "perversion". Thus the "female perversions" of the title refer not only to Eve's (neurotic and erotic) fantasies of being sexualised and belittled by men (particularly, her father) but also to the social performance she enacts in the struggle to reconcile her fragile status and power with 'acceptable' femininity.

If this set-up sounds tough-going, Streitfeld makes its cinematic realisation unsettlingly recognisable and often cynically funny. The spheres of shopping and shoplifting, beauty and fashion provide rich opportunities for satire, and are lampooned here, for example, when Eve parades in her teddy across a high-fashion emporium. Throughout the film, seemingly realistic scenes slide into perverse scenarios to illustrate Eve's troubled unconscious rather than objective reality. As she argues powerfully to an all-male court panel, the camera takes on the leering character of a male voyeur, and whispered obscenities suggest Eve's insecurities; but when her sister Madelyn sees her interviewed about the case on television, Eve appears authoritative and powerful, suggesting a corrective to Eve's loathing of herself.

In presenting Eve's oppressions as self-inflicted, Streitfeld risks confirming the opinions of misogynistic viewers. Yet this risk—embodied above all in Swinton's enjoyably unsympathetic performance as Eve—is also what makes *Female Perversions* effective. The film does indeed suggest that the compulsive performance of femininity functions as a powerful instrument of self-oppression. Though Madelyn's kleptomania marks her as a 'deviant' woman, she appears more normal than Eve or her ridiculously feminine landlady Emma, a single parent with a penchant for pink stretch lace and an irrational faith in marriage.

Above all, this is a film in which clothes and cosmetics are of more than passing significance. Whether neurotically pacing her apartment in heels and a flesh-coloured teddy or plagued by a permanent loose thread on her skirt, Swinton's Eve is in constant conflict with her executive femme drag. Her obsessive reapplication of lipstick at inappropriate moments becomes an eloquent recurrent emblem. In one hilarious scene, she is too busy fixing her lips to notice that Langley, the assured young female lawyer being groomed as her successor, is standing next to her. Professional rivalry is displaced into lipstick oneup(wo)manship: 'I think we have the same lipstick,' says Langley. 'No, I don't think so—this is a new Fall colour,' snipes Eve.

But there's a more startling moment: as an elderly woman sits down on a street bench to fix her lipstick, Eve parks nearby and—blind to the woman's presence—eerily mirrors her gestures as she applies lipstick herself. The bench itself carries a text: "In a perversion there is no freedom—only conformity to gender stereotypes." It's an image worthy of the artist Barbara Kruger (whose work appears in the film), posing provocative questions about gender and post-feminist competitiveness. Significantly, Eve's lover Renee, the one female character in the film who seems at home with herself, wears no lipstick; and when one of the Mexican matriarchs who are the subject of Madelyn's thesis appears to Eve in a dream she is naked.

VILLAGE VOICE, 4/29/97, p. 82, Leslie Camhi

Voyeurism, fetishism, exhibitionism, necrophilia—why do men have all the fun? Until recently, psychoanalytic definitions of perversion tended to focus on men's sexual proclivities. A few years ago, though, in a book called *Female Perversions*, psychoanalyst Louise Kaplan argued that "normal" women's desperate fixation on the accoutrements of femininity—lipstick, lingerie, and the like—bordered on pathological obsession.

First-time director Susan Streitfeld was casting about for a story when she came across Kaplan's book. Theoretical treatises don't usually lend themselves to film. (Can you imagine *Das Kapital*, the film?) But Streitfeld molded characters from the range of symptoms Kaplan described, and *Female Perversions* became a movie.

The brilliant Tilda Swinton (Sally Potter's Orlando) plays Eve Stephens, a high-profile L.A. prosecutor in line for a court appointment. Eve is as sleek and mannered as the Dialogica furniture that fills her apartment. We first meet Eve as she's having energetic sex with her hunk of a seismologist boyfriend (John Diehl). Cut to a courthouse where, hours later, in tight ivory suit, she's giving her summation in a case of white-collar corruption. Eve is a piece of work.

Her calculated gestures clothe her commanding intellect with an archly feminine allure, and even the judge fingers his gavel as he listens to her.

Yet, though perfect, Eve is also a perfect disaster. Shopaholic and bulimic, she's addicted to lipstick, codependent on her dry cleaner, manipulative, and deeply superstitious. In nightmares and while having sex, her unconscious fantasies of domination and submission spin wildly out of control. All along she feels she's faking her fragile mastery of power.

Eve's sister Madelyn (Amy Madigan)—dumpy, kleptomaniacal, butch—lives far outside L.A. in the desert, where she's writing her dissertation on "a small Mexican town where the women have all the power." They both cope with a gnawing sense of lack; Eve shops and Madelyn shoplifts, in vain efforts to appropriate the love and worth that their philosopher dad has denied them.

On the eve of Eve's interview for the judgeship, Madelyn is arrested, and Eve drives out to the desert to help her. There she meets Madelyn's landlady, Emma (Laila Robbins), a masochist forever at her boyfriend's mercy, and Emma's daughter "Ed" (Dale Shuger), a tomboy in mournful revolt against her mother's girlish simpering. They're soon joined by Ed's Aunt Annunciata (Frances Fisher), a stripper with a muscular back and a way with men. Amid this hothouse collection of feminine styles, Eve is in for some revelations.

Film and femininity share an obsession with the image, and *Female Perversions* is a pleasure to watch. Its dialogue is snappy and its looks are smart, though the film suffers from some alarmingly literal dream sequences that are almost Jungian in their campiness. There's a sly quality to Streitfeld's filmmaking, as if we're all in on some great Freudian joke; her camera focuses on tiny details like an annoyingly able shrink. The many scenes of cutting—film sliced, flesh carved by little feminine fingers—were heavy-handed in their evocation of castration anxiety, though they certainly had me squirming. Clinical pronouncements appear embroidered on Eve's pillowcases. Is she imagining them? In fact, *Female Perversions* is so suggestive in part because it walks an uncertain line between fantasy and reality. Kudos go to Streitfeld for mucking around in the murky realm of the unconscious, where we're all working from someone else's script.

Also reviewed in:
NEW YORK TIMES, 4/25/97, p. C8, Stephen Holden
VARIETY, 1/29-2/4/96, p. 65, Emanuel Levy
WASHINGTON POST, 5/16/97, Weekend/p. 45, Desson Howe

FETISHES

A Cinema Village Features release of a Lafayette Film production. *Executive Producer:* Sheila Nevins. *Producer:* Nick Broomfield and Michelle D'Acosta. *Director:* Nick Broomfield. *Director of Photography:* Christophe Lanzenberg. *Editor:* Betty Burkhart and Nick Broomfield. *Music:* Jamie Muhoberac. *Sound:* Dick Farner. *Running time:* 90 minutes. *MPAA Rating:* Not Rated.

WITH: Mistress Natasha and Mistress Raven.

VILLAGE VOICE, 5/13/97, p. 86, Amy Taubin

A cooler though no less hokey brand of British humor pervades *Fetishes*, a Nick Broomfield documentary made for HBO's "America Undercover" series. [The reference is to *Twin Town*; see Taubin's review.] This theatrical version includes several scenes of nipple piercing and penis torture that HBO deemed unfit for even their midnight slot.

Broomfield spent two months at Pandora's Box, which he describes in laconic voiceover as "a legal fetish and S&M house of domination, the most cheerful of all the places we visited, and easily the most lavish and expensive." Broomfield hangs with the mistresses at work, treats them and their clients to some light interviewing, and occasionally follows them home for a quickie consensual invasion of privacy. Mistress Raven, the proprietor of Pandora's Box (which occupies the top floor of an office building in the Flatiron district), must be pleased with Broomfield's creative work because she's been offering working press a promotional tour of the premises in conjunction with the film's release.

And in fact, *Fetishes* is quite funny—although anyone expecting either erotic thrills or serious investigative journalism is going to be sorely disappointed. Broomfield sets himself up as an unreliable narrator right from the start, commenting over sonic "archival" footage from a '40s spanking flick that "S&M was something I'd heard of over the years, but didn't really know much about." This from the maker of the brilliant *Heidi Fleiss: Hollywood Madame*. Not to mention that Broomfield hails from a country where tabloids routinely feature prominent members of parliament who've been less than discreet about their rubber bondage and erotic strangulation habits. Isn't sadomasochism known as "the English vice"?

Given that S&M is stagey by definition, does it matter that some of the scenes Broomfield records are deliberately staged for the camera? It just adds a neat layer of irony. As does the fact that Broomfield expends no more energy on the film than the mistresses do on their clients. Its a day's work for a days pay, and it's clear that everyone involved—including some of the clients—would rather be elsewhere.

Still, *Fetishes* has its hilarious moments: Broomfield trying to figure out where to put the mike in an interview with a client who has his head in a toilet bowl; the receptionist, who has a thick Franco-Russian accent that makes what she says almost incomprehensible, questioning a Jewish client with a Nazi fantasy about the level of verbal abuse he prefers ("Is Jew boy enough, or do you prefer something more intense, like you rotten fucking Jew?" she inquires benevolently).

If it's the the mainstreaming of S&M that Broomfield's after, then he succeeds pretty well. I just can't buy his insistence that Mistress Raven was once among the most famed dominatrices on the East Coast. Anyone who's seen *Chelsea Girls* knows she's no competition for Mary Woronov.

Also reviewed in:
NEW YORK TIMES, 5/9/97, p. C18, Stephen Holden
VARIETY, 7/1-14/96, p. 36, David Stratton

FIERCE CREATURES

A Universal Pictures release of a Fish Productions/Jersey Films production. *Executive Producer:* Steve Abbott. *Producer:* Michael Shamberg and John Cleese. *Director:* Robert Young and Fred Schepisi. *Screenplay:* John Cleese and Iain Johnstone. *"The Fierce Animal Policy" based on an idea by:* Terry Jones and Michael Palin. *Director of Photography:* Adrian Biddle. *Editor:* Robert Gibson. *Music:* Jerry Goldsmith. *Music Editor:* Ken Hall. *Sound:* Chris Munro. *Sound Editor:* Colin Miller. *Casting:* Priscilla John. *Production Designer:* Roger Murray-Leach. *Art Director:* David Allday and Kevin Phipps. *Set Decorator:* Brian Read and Stephenie McMillan. *Costumes:* Hazel Pethig. *Make-up:* Paul Engelen. *Stunt Coordinator:* Simon Crane and Greg Powell. *Running time:* 93 minutes. *MPAA Rating:* PG-13.

CAST: John Cleese (Rollo Lee); Jamie Lee Curtis (Willa Weston); Kevin Kline (Vince McCain/Rod McCain); Michael Palin (Bugsy Malone); Ronnie Corbett (Reggie Sealions); Carey Lowell (Cub Felines); Robert Lindsay (Sydney Small Mammals); Bille Brown (Neville Coltrane); Derek Griffiths (Gerry Ungulates); Cynthia Cleese (Pip Small Mammals); Richard Ridings (Hugh Primates); Maria Aitken (Di Admin); Michael Percival (Ant Keeper); Fred Evans (Flamingo Keeper); Lisa Hogan (Sealion Keeper); Choy-Ling Man (Parrot Keeper); Tim Potter (Vulture Keeper); Jenny Galloway (Aquarium Keeper); Kim Vithana (Tiger Keeper); Sean Francis (Buffalo Keeper); Julie Saunders (Rodent Keeper); Susie Blake (Woman in Red Dress); Pat Keen (Woman's Mother); Denis Lill (Woman's Husband); Gareth Hunt (Inspector Masefield); Ron Donachie (Sergeant Scott); Paul Haigh (Sergeant Irving); Leon Herbert and Stewart Wright (Octopus Security Guards); Kerry Shale (Frightened Executive); Mac McDonald (TV Producer); Amanda Walker (Zoo Secretary); Terence Conoley (Man in Straw Hat); Tom Georgeson, John Bardon, and Anthony Pedley (Sealion Spectators); Kevin Moore (Hotel

Manager); Leslie Lowe and Iain Mitchell (Assistant Hotel Managers); Valerie Edmond (Hotel Maid); Nick Bartlett (Policeman); Ricco Ross and Kate Harper (TV Journalists); Nicholas Hutchison (TV Reporter).

LOS ANGELES TIMES, 1/24/97, Calendar/p. 6, Jack Mathews

[The following review by Jack Mathews appeared in a slightly different form in NEWSDAY, 1/24/97, Part II/p. B2.]

If it's not a sequel, or a remake, what is "Fierce Creatures," the long-awaited reunion film of the cast from "A Fish Called Wanda"?

Kevin Kline, who won an Oscar for his performance in "Wanda," is quoted in the production notes as calling "Fierce Creatures," "an equal." He must have said that before the movie was finished, before preview audiences held their noses and it was sent back for more work.

"Fierce Creatures," release was delayed by about a year while a new director, Fred Schepisi in for Robert Young, reassembled the cast and shot new footage. Finally, here it is, by no means the equal to "Wanda," but a charming mess with moments of hilarity.

The script, written by John Cleese and British critic Iain Johnstone, shares nothing with "Wanda," other than their vague pets-in-jeopardy themes, and is a far less clever concoction. But the inspiration is present in each of the characters.

Cleese again plays a kind of bumbling authority figure, a London zoo manager shocked at the attention paid him by Jamie Lee Curtis' seductive American. Michael Palin, no longer a stammerer, is a motor-mouthed zookeeper with a deep attachment to his pet tarantula. And Kline, the son of Murdoch-mocking media baron Rod McCain (also played by Kline) is the crazed egotist who doesn't know when he's not wanted.

Vince McCain is a vacuous, simple-minded character with little of the irresistible looniness of his ("Don't call me stupid!") Otto in "Wanda," and Kline mostly flails around doing shrill physical shtick. He's much better as the old man, a flatulent Australian empire builder whose buy-pillage-sell philosophy sets events in motion at his newly acquired Marwood Zoo.

The task facing Cleese's Rollo Lee is to get zoo profits up by 20%, even if it means killing passive animals to make room for the fierce creatures the public really wants to see. Naturally, the zoo staff isn't up to executing their furry friends, and mutiny is in the air when Vince and Willa Weston (Curtis) arrive, as emissaries of Octopus Inc., to take charge.

Willa's plan is to develop the zoo as a model for a chain of theme parks. Vince wants to merchandise the animals by selling sponsorships to their cages (among the sponsors he corrals are Pizza Hut, Panasonic and Saddam Hussein) and pocket the income.

The problems uncovered in the preview screenings of "Fierce Creatures" are apparent in the film's rambling, anecdotal story line. As in his Monty Python days, Cleese comes up with great bits, but there's not much forward momentum here.

In fact, the presumably new ending, with Rod McCain showing up at the zoo for a darkly comic showdown with his son, seems only distantly related to the events preceding it.

Stranger yet, the ending works, as its own extended sketch. It is better developed and more controlled, and in ways that can't be explained by good editing. The performances actually feel different, especially Kline's. It's as if he's finally gotten a handle on Vince and reigned him in just enough to make him sympathetic.

To whomever pulled it together, nice work. "Fierce Creatures" won't make anyone forget "A Fish Called Wanda"—or remember it, for that matter—but it gets the year off to a good laugh.

NEW YORK POST, 1/24/97, p. 43, Michael Medved

Something fishy is going on at Marwood Zoo—because that's where the stars (and much of the production team) from "A Fish Called Wanda" have reassembled for another irresistible assault on good taste and sanity.

The result, "Fierce Creatures," isn't intended as a sequel to the 1988 smash hit, since the actors each play strikingly different characters. But as an oddball ensemble they still project peerless comic chemistry and generate the sort of magnificently manic energy that makes this new movie even funnier—and fiercer—than the original.

Once again, Kevin Kline (who won a supporting Oscar for "Wanda") leads the way with a triumphal, hilarious, tour-de-farce performance.

He plays Rod McCain (also known as "Rod Almighty"), a boorish, billionaire Australian tycoon (with no known resemblance to any actual Australian tycoons you may have read about) whose Octopus Industries are gobbling up enterprises all over the world. Kline also plays McCain's unloved and feckless son, who is less concerned about corporate profits than he is with the bottom line of a curvaceous new executive in the conglomerate (Jamie Lee Curtis).

Together, they're assigned to milk more money from a quaint, picturesque zoo in England that McCain has just purchased, and where they're supposed to work with blustery by-the-book company man John Cleese in making the necessary changes.

The concept Cleese wants to put into practice is a zoo filled entirely with fierce, deadly creatures—since violence and danger promise boffo box office.

Some of the movie's funniest scenes show the distraught zookeepers attempting to persuade Cleese that their cutest, cuddliest beasts (like lemurs, meerkats, anteaters, coatis and sea lions) are actually ferocious man-eaters, so that these adorable animals won't be cruelly dispatched to make room for deadlier game.

Michael Palin plays the leader of the keepers, a pompous know-it-all who can't stop talking—in contrast to the tongue-tied stammerer he played in "Wanda."

All the performances are topnotch—with Kline, in particular, working miracles of acting subtlety in a sequence where one of his two characters imperfectly attempts to impersonate the other.

The innumerable sight gags demand close attention from the audience (such as "celebrity sponsorships" for animal exhibits from beloved figures ranging from Bruce Springsteen to Saddam Hussein) and the madcap climax, seems so ingenious and appropriate that it's hard to believe it came as a second thought—reshot (with a second director, the formidable Fred Schepisi) nearly a year after the rest of the film.

It's true that some of the sexual double-entendre becomes a bit tiresome, and there perhaps a few too many leering, drooling views of the (admittedly spectacular) breasts and legs of Ms. Curtis, but it's all so well-constructed that it's hard to complain.

The movie may be rude, crude, vulgar, immature and insufferable silly, but these "Fierce Creatures" are also ferociously funny.

SIGHT AND SOUND, 3/97, p. 46, Leslie Felperin

England, the present. Marwood Zoo has just been bought by ruthless Australian media baron Rod McCain, who rules that all his acquisitions must show a 20 per cent return on investment or he will shut them down. McCain employee Rollo Lee, a former policeman, is assigned to run Marwood. Drawing on his experience at a Hong Kong television station, Rollo decides that fierce creatures (such as lions, tigers and gorillas) are the most popular attractions and that all cuddly or inoffensive animals must be disposed of. The zookeepers are horrified. He pretends to kill five especially cute animals to show his mettle, but in fact keeps them all at his flat.

Meanwhile, ambitious McCain executive Willa Weston asks to be assigned to Marwood. McCain's corrupt son Vince, lusting after Willa, requests a transfer there too. Upon arrival, Willa and Vince demote Rollo, and Vince installs intrusive advertising hoardings all over the zoo and sets up bogus celebrity sponsorships of the animal pens. Willa, growing fond of the animals and turning away from the McCains' materialistic policies, mistakenly assumes that Rollo is a sex-crazed girl-magnet and finds herself growing attracted to him, and he to her.

Rod McCain flies to England with plans to sell the zoo off to a property developer. Willa and Rollo find this out and that Vince has been skimming off the profits from the advertisers and sponsors. After they confront him, he tries to escape with the money but gets into an argument with his father on the way out of the zoo. By accident, Bugsy Malone the insect-keeper shoots Rod McCain dead. All the zoo staff help Vince to disguise himself as his father in order to sign a new will leaving all Rod's money to Vince. They then fake Rod's 'suicide'. Vince inherits the fortune, and Willa and Rollo stay to care for the zoo together, the fierce animal policy now abandoned.

A Fish Called Wanda, directed by Ealing comedy veteran Charles Crichton and written by Crichton and its star John Cleese, was the most financially successful British comedy of all time until *Four Weddings and a Funeral*. Faring remarkably well in the US despite its slightly xenophobic attitude towards Americans, the cruelty-tinged fun of *Fish*, with its biting one-liners, made a worthy successor to the Ealing tradition of black burnout. Closest to the British funnybone was *Fish*'s running gag of animal cruelty, involving the crushing of a poodle by a falling safe and the eating of Michael Palin's character's precious tropical fish.

Despite its title, *Fierce Creatures*, the "sort-of-sequel" to *Fish* which stars the same core cast, is a more toothless affair. It focuses on a beleaguered zoo where a new director at first insists that only 'fierce animals' will be featured because customers prefer to see violence or its potential. This central premise derails the film from the start. It might have been used as an indication of Rollo's ineptitude that he suggests the policy in the first place, but surely someone at the zoo would have the sense to point out its lack of business acumen. Instead, all are merely horrified at its cruelty. At a time when the BBC's *Animal Hospital* and shows such as *Badger Watch* get high ratings, it beggars belief that anyone could be so naive as to think the public only likes animals if they're vicious. After all, the film itself is being sold as much on the cuteness of its supporting cast of lemurs, Patagonian maras and baby ostriches and the like, as it is on the appeal of its human cast.

No animal is seen to be harmed during the film, on or off screen, which is a pity since it was the spectre of death that gave *Fish* its edge. An ending of this film in which Kline's character Vince, the greedy son of the zoo's owner, is killed off had to be abandoned after negative test screenings in the US. This is why two directors, Robert Young (of *Splitting Heirs* and the television series *G.B.H.*) and Fred Schepisi (*Roxanne* and *Six Degrees of Separation*) were needed—Schepisi shot the new ending because Young was "unavailable".

Neither as funny nor as cruel as its predecessor, *Fierce Creatures* still has charm and satirical bite. Its main targets are corporate greed and the 90s cult of the soulless leisure industry for which zoos are interchangeable with golf courses and television stations. Starting with a tortoise 'sponsored' by Bruce Springsteen, Vince brings in more sponsorship and advertising until the zoo is crammed with vulgar hoardings and demeaning product placements (a tiger wears a jacket reading "Absolut Fierce".) The irony is that the advertisers get to send up themselves up and still get their names into the film. Given that Cleese refused to write a fourth series of *Fawlty Towers* to order; it is odd that, even as this film lampoons money-lust, it should so accommodate it.

Ultimately, it is the reconstituted cast which *Fish*-fans will want to see again. All are on good form here even if the script flags in places. Cleese presents yet another of his bumptious bureaucrats, a Basil Fawlty-esque pompous git trying to maintain dignity even when his office is transferred to an unused animal cage. He wins the girl in the end—Jamie Lee Curtis as a smouldering siren with a talent for slapstick. As in *Fish*, Kevin Kline shows off his gift for mimicry (he plays both American Vince and his Australian father Rod, and in a *tour de force* Vince playing Rod). His superb comic timing is properly employed, and he again gets the best lines (explaining why a puppy was an unwanted present when he was a little boy, he says, "I guess I didn't need anything fetched").

Palin is nicely irritating as the kind of nasel-voiced little man he specialised in during his and Cleese's *Monty Python* years. A nice spin on his *Fish*-character's stutter has him unstoppably loquacious here. Robert Lindsay (overacting just a trifle) and Ronnie Corbett (cute as the sea mammal-keeper) fill out lesser roles. It's a finely interlocking ensemble, reminiscent of the troupe of players who meshed so beautifully in Ealing's heyday (Alec Guinness, Alastair Sim, Joan Greenwood), but ultimately *Fierce Creatures*, for all its gentle venom, fails to measure up to such classic British satires as *The Man in the White Suit*, *Whisky Galore!* and Crichton's own *The Lavender Hill Mob*.

TIME, 1/27/97, p. 68, Richard Schickel

Fierce Creatures is not a sequel in the usual sense of the word. But it does reassemble the key zanies of *A Fish Called Wanda*: Kevin Kline, all ego and libido and stupid schemes; John Cleese, all British pomp, phlegm and cluelessness; Jamie Lee Curtis, still innocent of the effect her form encased in a tight dress can have on impressionable males; Michael Palin, just plain innocent, but with his former stammer replaced now by another verbal disability-logorrhea.

This time they are the mismanagers of a commercial zoo that has been acquired by a Murdochian media buccaneer (Kline plays him too, complete with Down Under accent). They are charged with getting its profit margin up to his brutal rate (20%). Their plan is to dispense with all the zoo's sweet little fuzzballs and stock the place exclusively with man-eaters. If violence sells on TV and in the movies, why shouldn't it do the same for them?

As comic premises go, this is not exactly a world-beater. But soon enough, the keepers—gentle souls all—are funnily up in arms defending their pets. A wandering tarantula motivates a genteel striptease, and the mean mogul gets his comeuppance. The script, by Cleese and Iain Johnstone, lacks *Wanda*'s mean and giddy inventiveness, and the directors, Robert Young and Fred Schepisi, don't wind their material very tightly. Still, this good-natured movie is very much in the spirit of those ancient comedies from Ealing Film Studios in which nice, silly people defend some enclave of old-fashioned sanity against the forces of brute modernism. And that's a tradition worth reviving.

VILLAGE VOICE, 1/28/97, p. 70, Howard Feinstein

Fierce Creatures recasts the leads from 1988's *A Fish Called Wanda* (the second-highest grossing British film of all time). Like the great British music-hall parodies that inspired them, the films *Privates on Parade* and *The Wrong Box* successfully combined dryness and vulgarity, but this force about a nasty international media conglomerate called Octopus—whose greed threatens rare animals in a British zoo—eschews the former entirely and renders the latter inert. Endless close-ups of cute'n'cuddly critters can't vivify this dud: it feels like it's been directed by a taxidermist.

Two taxidermists. Schepisi *(Six Degrees of Separation)* was reportedly brought in to clean up the mess wrought by Young, whose Eric Idle vehicle *Splitting Heirs* (1994) should have been the swan song for Pythonite features. (The zoo story is left over from a pre-Python Michael Palin-Terry Jones idea.) John Cleese scripted *Fierce Creatures,* along with British film critic Iain Johnstone.

If you couldn't stomach Kevin Kline in *Wanda,* you'll lose your bouillabaisse at his relentless mugging in a dual role here. (I guess his Supporting Actor Oscar gave him double clout.) He plays Octopus's Kiwi-born, Murdoch-like magnate Rod McCain (based in Turner's Atlanta, get it?), as well as McCain's despised American-born scion, Vince. Eager to please Dad, Vince and ambitious now employee Willa Eston (Jamie Lee Curtis, who spends most of her time thrusting her tits and responding to juvenile sexual innuendo and puns like "I like him breast of all") take over the quaint menagerie that's been temporarily run by eccentric Rollo Lee (Cleese, really forcing it) as a spectacle of "fierce animals" geared to a bored public.

Willa's conversion by a cute gorilla ("I made contact!") pushes her toward Rollo, a closet animal lover, and away from the company line. Vince accelerates the species hype by bringing in illicit celebrity endorsements (Bruce Springsteen, Saddam Hussein) and corporate sponsors like Guinness, Pizza Hut, and British Airways. (Does this count as product placement?) Plot thickens, or thins, rather, when Vince's efforts fail to impress Daddy, who has bigger fish to fry. Fish. Get it?

Also reviewed in:
CHICAGO TRIBUNE, 1/24/97, Friday/p. J, Mark Caro
NEW YORK TIMES, 1/24/97, p. C5, Janet Maslin
NEW YORKER, 2/3/97, p. 85, Anthony Lane
VARIETY, 1/20-26/97, p. 44, Leonard Klady
WASHINGTON POST, 1/24/97, Weekend/p. 30, Desson Howe

FIFTH ELEMENT, THE

A Columbia Pictures release of a Gaumont production. *Producer:* Patrice Ledoux. *Director:* Luc Besson. *Screenplay:* Luc Besson and Robert Mark Kamen. *Story:* Luc Besson. *Director of Photography:* Thierry Arbogast. *Editor:* Sylvie Landra. *Music:* Eric Serra. *Sound:* Mark Mangini. *Casting:* Lucinda Syson. *Production Designer:* Dan Weil. *Art Director:* Jim Morahan and Kevin Phipps. *Set Designer:* Jean "Moebius" Giraud, Jean-Claude Mézières, Sylvain

Despretz, Patrice Garcia, Sean Hargreaves, Kamel Tazit, Hélène Giraud, Jacques Rey, Michel Gibrat, Humbert Chabuel, and Pierre-Alain Chartier. *Set Decorator:* Maggie Gray and Anna Pinnock. *Special Effects:* Nick Allder and Neil Corbould. *Visual Effects:* Mark Stetson. *Costumes:* Jean-Paul Gaultier. *Make-up:* Lois Burwell. *Make-up (Bruce Willis):* Amanda Knight. *Stunt Coordinator:* Marc Boyle. *Running time:* 105 minutes. *MPAA Rating:* PG-13.

CAST: Bruce Willis (Korben Dallas); Gary Oldman (Zorg); Ian Holm (Cornelius); Milla Jovovich (Leeloo); Chris Tucker (Ruby Rhod); Luke Perry (Billy); Brion James (General Munro); Tommy "Tiny" Lister, Jr. (President Lindberg); Lee Evans (Fog); Charlie Creed Miles (David); Tricky (Right Arm); John Neville (General Staedert); John Bluthal (Professor Pacoli); Mathieu Kassovitz (Mugger); Christopher Fairbank (Mactilburgh); Kim Chan (Thai); Richard Leaf (Neighbor); Julie T. Wallace (Major Iceborg); Al Matthews (General Tudor); Maiwenn Le Besco (Diva); John Bennett (Priest); Ivan Heng (Left Arm); Sonita Henry (President's Aide); Tim McMullan (Scientist's Aide); Hon Ping Tang (Munro's Captain); George Khan (Head Scientist); John Hughes (Head of Military); Roberto Bryce (Omar); Said Talidi (Aziz); Bill Reimbold (Mactilburgh's Assistant); Colin Brooks (Staedert's Captain); Anthony Chinn (Mactilburgh's Technician); Sam Douglas (Chief NY Cop); Derek Ezenagu (NY Cop); Indra Ove, Nicole Merry, and Stacey McKenzie (VIP Stewardesses); Sophia Goth (Check In Attendant); Martin McDougall (Warship Captain); Peter Dunwell (Diva's Manager); Paul Priestley and Jason Salkey (Cops); Stewart Harvey Wilson, Dave Fishley, Carlton Chance (Ruby Rhod Assistants); Gin Clarke (Diva's Assistant); Vladimir McCrary (Human Aknot); Clifton Lloyd Bryan (Mangalore Aknot); Aron Paramor (Mangalore Akanit); Alan Ruscoe (Mangalore Kino); Clifton Lloyd Bryan (Airport Guard); Christopher Adamson (Airport Cop); Eve Salvail (Tawdry Girl); Kaleem Janjua (Shuttle Pilot); Tyrone Tyrell (Shuttle Co-pilot); Kevin Brewerton (Shuttle Mechanic); Kevin Molloy and Vince Pellegrino (Ground Crew); Ian Beckett (Baby Ray); Sonny Caldinez (Emperor Kodar Japhet); Zeta Graff (Princess Achen); Eddie Ellwood (Roy Von Bacon); Laura De Palma and Yui (Fhloston Hostesses); Michael Culkin (Hefty Man); Lenny McLean (Police Chief); Robert Oates (Phloston Commander); John Sharian (Fhloston Captain); Fred Williams (Hotel Manager); Sibyl Buck (Zorg's Secretary); Scott Woods and Leon Dekker (Lab Guards); David Garvey, Stanley Kowalski, and Omar Hibbert Williams (Staedert's Technicians); Robert Clapperton (Robot Barman); Robert Alexander (Warship Technician); Mia Frye (TV Stewardess); Leo Williams and Keith Martin (Power Operators); Marie Guillard, Renee Montemayor, Stina Richardson (Burger Assistants).

LOS ANGELES TIMES, 5/9/97, Calendar/p. 1, Kevin Thomas

There's no doubt about it, when it comes to saving the world, Bruce Willis is your man. He does it with smarts and style, humor and courage. He's rugged and tough, yet remains vulnerable and tender. And whatever they paid him to appear in "The Fifth Element," it was worth it.

Willis holds together French filmmaker Luc Besson's elaborate, even campy sci-fi extravaganza, which is nearly as hard to follow as last year's "Mission: Impossible." But it is also a lot warmer, more fun and boasts some of the most sophisticated, witty production and costume design you could ever hope to see. As with the Tom Cruise-Brian De Palma blockbuster, just go along with "The Fifth Element" because all becomes clear enough at the finish.

"The Fifth Element" refers to the Greek belief that four elements—earth, air, fire and water—gathered together to create the fifth one—life itself. What if, Besson speculates, there could be a negative form of life in a parallel dimension? And what if every 5,000 years there opened a window of opportunity between the dimensions enabling the forces of darkness to extinguish all light and life in our universe?

After a prologue set in an Egyptian tomb in 1914 done in the style of a silent movie epic—in the manner of early Cecil B. DeMille or Michael Curtiz and featuring aliens that look like gold-plated armadillos—"The Fifth Element" moves 300 years ahead in time when the President of the Federation (Tommy "Tiny" Lister Jr.) is confronted with the appearance in the sky of a fiery dark planet. The priest Cornelius (Ian Holm), who knows of the parallel dimension legend, advises him not to fire at this malevolent-looking mass, but the president orders bombs away. This scheme backfires when the mass increases in size the more it's fired upon.

What an amazing world Besson and his legions of craftsmen have created for us to behold—and in such imminent danger of destruction! Production designer Dan Weil has envisioned New York as a kind of city-state that seems to pay homage to Fritz Lang's "Metropolis" in which all manner of vehicles move through the air in deep, deep canyons created by immensely tall skyscrapers in the Beaux Arts style. (It would seem here that Art Nouveau is in but Art Deco is out.)

The population now includes the immense, canine-like Mangalores, who happen to be mercenaries of this film's Ming the Merciless: Gary Oldman's Zorg, "agent of all that is evil," which means he's the contact man for that dark planet, natch. Then within a huge glass cylinder materializes none other than the Supreme Being herself, Leeloo (Milla Jovovich), who for the world looks like a Jean-Paul Gaultier model, a blond with an overlay of a near-phosphorescent red dye on her locks for a neo-punk look. (You check your credits and, guess what, Gaultier *is* the film's costume designer.)

One tricky plot development after another brings together the lissome Leeloo, Willis' Korben Dallas—a retired major in an elite military force and now a cabby living in South Brooklyn—and Cornelius in an attempt to defeat the forces of evil.

Adventures take Leeloo and Korben, who of course fall in love, to a vast cruise ship with interiors that would make Donald Trump's Taj Mahal casino seem understated. They encounter a super-frenetic TV disc jockey/interviewer diva called Ruby Rhod (Chris Tucker), who, in turn, makes RuPaul—or for that matter Dennis Rodman—seem as calm and sedate as Whistler's mother.

The look and feel of "The Fifth Element" is clearly more important to Besson, than, the narrative—oh, for a soupçon of old-fashioned clarity!—and it recalls "Blade Runner" with a touch of Gallic "Barbarella" insouciance thrown in for good measure. (Pastiche is clearly Besson's passion here.)

In some sequences there is that grunge look that harks back beyond "Star Wars" to John Carpenter's "Dark Star" (1974), which may be the most influential least-known movie of the past couple of decades. These days, it all but goes without saying that the special effects, indeed all technical and creative aspects of the film, are stupendous.

The cast is a delight, but it's Willis who is the film's true "fifth element," giving it life, depth and humanity.

NEW YORK, 5/19/97, p. 63, David Denby

The *Fifth Element* a frantically boisterous science-fiction spectacle, is about the end of the world. (Has there ever been a science-fiction movie that wasn't about the end of the world?) The movie is also about absolute evil and absolute good, a diva who sings Donizetti, a screechy-priss disk jockey who broadcasts from outer space, a gun that shoots arrows, creatures with faces like dogs, and other creatures with faces like ants. It's about everything and nothing. The *Fifth Element* is the dream project of the noisily ungifted French director Luc Besson *(La Femme Nikita, The Professional)*, a man trying awfully hard to make American "event" movies, Besson imagines that the way to make them is to put every goddamn thing in the world into them. The movie has enormous sets—an airport, a hotel lobby, an opera house—filled with costumed idiots running around and posing. In the end, the sets are blown up, the people scattered and sent screaming. Besson works with a kind of fitful volatility that I find almost sinister. What do these people rushing around the sets imagine they're doing? How can filmmakers devote a year, even two years of their lives to such overwrought, crumbling nonsense? I suppose it's absurd to ask such questions. If the movie is a hit, I will have my answer.

The *Fifth Element* is set (mostly) in the twenty-third century, and one of its few successful elements is an animated version of a future Manhattan, with traffic whizzing through the air at many different levels and fast-food stands suspended from the sides of buildings way up high, maybe a mile from the ground. Bruce Willis is master of this high-flown chaos; he does his hairy-ape prole-Everyman thing, and he's very good at it—relaxed, modest, with that familiar smirk that says, "I'm ready for anything." Willis eases us through the whirling gibberish, which seems to bounce off his benevolent puss. Without his familiar face and sanity, *The Fifth Element* would be completely unwatchable. Willis plays some sort of defrocked special agent reduced to driving a cab, and into his lap falls a beautiful female creature who has been reconstructed from

DNA. She, of course, is the force of absolute good, and in the person of model Milla Jovovich she has a long-waisted figure and ripe kissy lips. The lips seem to be Jovovich's principal instrument as an actress; she parts them in an attitude of perpetual anticipation. At the same time, great actors stand around projecting bits of business into a void—Ian Holm, fussing and giggling as a benevolent priest, and Gary Oldman, straight hair flapping to the side like Hitler's, vamping the camera in ecstasies of nastiness.

The world is saved, or lost, or something—does it matter? Except for Bruce Willis, *The Fifth Element* is a carnival of geeks, and though a few moments are funny, you may feel an immense weariness, as if lead weights had been attached to your eyelids. The mass of elaborately built and gaudily destroyed sets is a perfect emblem of the emptiness of big movies now. Besson has a taste for pointless grandiosity combined with a habit of goosing every element into farce. It's possible, of course, that he could throw a hell of a Halloween party, but I don't see much evidence that he can make a good movie.

NEW YORK POST, 5/9/97, p. 43, Michael Medved

"The Fifth Element" unmistakably recalls, "Stargate," with its kitchen-sink combination of occult/Egyptian elements, splashy sci-fi special effects and save-the-world heroics, but this new film displays a more refreshing sense of humor and a far more imaginative visual sensibility.

In fact, French writer-director Luc Besson ("La Femme Nikita," "The Professional") has created the most fascinating futuristic fantasy since "Blade Runner," substantially aided by visual-effects supervisor Mark Stetson, who previously worked on that landmark film.

The year is 2259, and cosmic anti-life forces that come together every 5,000 years now gather into a black, expanding planet that threatens to destroy all forms of existence.

Hulking metallic aliens with strange, tiny heads make their way toward Earth to assist humanity, but they're intercepted and destroyed by the forces of Zorg (the hilariously effective Gary Oldman), a lisping industrialist with a Southern-boy accent, who has allied himself with the forces of death.

Earth's only hope is the "supreme being" the aliens had with them in the athletic, semi-nude form of former supermodel Milla Jovovich. This sexy savior somehow escapes destruction and crashes through the ceiling of an air taxi driven by New York cabbie (and former ace fighter pilot) Bruce Willis.

As mystical priest Ian Holm explains, she's the Fifth Element of prophecy, who must now combine with the ancient stones representing the other four elements (earth, wind, fire and water) to defeat the forces of destruction.

Despite attacks by cruel, Robocopish police officers and the bulldog-faced alien warriors employed by Zorg, Willis must help his new-found friend recover the stones.

This jokey, jazzy plot provides an abundance of fast-moving fun, with splendid effects designed to serve a well-structured story rather than a clumsy story constructed as an excuse for spectacular effects.

The costumes by high fashion's bad boy, Jean-Paul Gaultier, are dazzling, though Jovovich's stringy, gaudy, fire-engine-red hair is a pointless distraction.

Willis makes a likable urban Everyman, but Chris Tucker, as a swishy, jive-talking intergalactic radio host, becomes intrusively annoying as unneeded comic relief.

Besson's fascination with huge explosions and ferocious, futuristic guns also misfires, but he does provide a blue, tubular, 9-foot-tall diva who belts out Donizetti in a scene that instantly becomes one of the movies' most memorable operatic performances.

A politically correct conclusion forces a hard-bitten male to say "I love you" as the price of saving the universe, and if the emotions "The Fifth Element" inspires aren't quite true love, it's still easy to appreciate a project that never runs out of energy or ideas.

NEWSDAY, 5/9/97, Part II/p. B2, John Anderson

Given the way it roams free of any logic or context, "The Fifth Element" was the perfect opener for this week's 50th Cannes Film Festival, representing as it does the state of its particular art. A manic, martial sci-fi extravaganza, an asteroid shower of high-tech distractions, the film abdicates whatever lingering obligation there is on the part of popular film to tell a coherent story, choosing instead to celebrate the victory of the tangential over the substantial. Call it, if you'd like, the dark side.

Starring Bruce Willis and directed by the once-promising French filmmaker Luc Besson ("La Femme Nikita"), "The Fifth Element" may actually be a milestone in moviemaking, given how blithely it relies on the accessories of film narrative rather than the fabric. Explosions, wisecracks, anachronistic gags and a seemingly complex background story—which is all but ignored—make it amusing enough, as long as you abandon any desire for a plotline.

Which is frighteningly easy. The prelude, taking place in 1914 Egypt in a tomb where western archeologists (including a truly anemic Luke Perry) are discovering the gruesome secret of the universe and being visited by malevolent aliens in orthopedic combat boots, provides the kind of quick-drying mythology that has become the stock in trade for this kind of faux-historic horror film. But unlike "The Exorcist," to cite just one example, there's no Jungian connection being tapped here, no haunted sense that what we're learning about the past has anything primal about it, or any link to our present.

No, we blow right by the present to the 23rd Century, South Brooklyn and Bruce Willis, who as cab driver Korben Dallas is about to face another tour of duty on the streets—or rather the midair traffic patterns—of New York City. It looks as if it's gonna be one o' doze days. And is, as soon as a mysterious, jabbering redhead, being pursued by government agents, crashes through his cab roof and persuades Korben on a very hormonal level to help her escape.

Who is she? What is she? Out of a scarred, old artifact—it looks like the armor-clad piece of a space alien, but don't hold me to it—scientists have regenerated the lithesome, gibberish-spouting Leeloo (Milla Jovovich), who according to a weird cleric named Cornelius (Ian Holm) is speaking the original language of the universe. It is she, you see, who must salvage humankind from the evil designs of Zorg (the profoundly strange Gary Oldman) and complete the movie's framing device by getting them all back to Egypt, an ancient ritual and the marriage of the Earth's other ancient elements (earth, water, air, fire). She, obviously, is the "fifth."

And this, just as obviously, is all hooey. What "The Fifth Element" is really about is Willis smirking, bad guys exploding and the lampooning of society from a vantage point of two centuries. Oh yes, and the kind of seamless movement of words and camera that presupposes an audience attention span of about 13 seconds.

The filmmakers have expressed pride in attempting to create a world based on what current conditions might eventually dictate—the vertical construction of Manhattan, for instance, or the high-security cubbyholes in which people live.

What's far more fascinating is what *hasn't* changed. Racial and ethnic differences—even regional accents—are pronounced. The president, Tommy (Tiny) Lister Jr., sounds like a heavy on "NYPD Blue." There's modesty about nudity, no computers in sight (pneumatic tubes apparently make a comeback in the year 2214) and fashions—created for the film by Jean-Paul Gaultier don't look so different from what you see on "Style With Elsa Klensch." "Ellen's" progress aside, the campiness of a screaming, mincing faux-gay radio personality named Ruby Rhod (Chris Tucker) still packs a media punch. Jovovich is adorable. Willis is as annoyingly postmodern as ever. South Brooklyn survives, as does McDonald's. Will you? Will film? "The Fifth Element" may in fact be The Last Straw.

SIGHT AND SOUND, 7/97, p. 39, John Wrathall

Egypt, 1914. Fearing the coming war, the Mondoshawan, an alien race, revisit a temple they established in antiquity to take back four mystic stones, representing the four elements, and a casket containing the fifth element which is the Supreme Being.

The twenty-third century. An evil force appears in the universe, and Cornelius, a priest of an order founded by the Mondoshawan, warns that it can only be defeated by a weapon made from the five elements. A Mondoshawan ship approaches Earth but is destroyed by Mangalore warriors, aliens in the employ of Zorg, an ally of the evil force. A remnant salvaged from the Mondoshawan ship is regenerated into a female humanoid, Leeloo, who escapes from a government laboratory and falls in with New York taxi driver Korben Dallas, who takes her to Cornelius. The priest tells Korben to leave. Cornelius realises that Leeloo is the fifth element and must be reunited with the four element stones, which the Mondoshawan have entrusted to an alien opera diva on the resort planet of Fhloston.

Korben, a former space soldier, is conscripted by General Munro to go to Fhloston and get the stones, which are also being sought by Zorg and a band of Mangalore. Munro rigs a contest so that Korben wins two tickets to Fhloston and winds up travelling with Leeloo, who is gradually learning to understand humanity. On Fhloston, the stones turn out to be inside the diva. After a battle in which Zorg and the Mangalore are wiped out, Korben, Cornelius and Leeloo return to the temple in Egypt, where the stones are arranged to transform Leeloo. The evil force nears Earth. At the last moment, Leeloo—who has learned about humanity's history of war—has to be convinced that the world is worth saving by Korben, who admits his love for her. The evil force is nullified, and Korben and Leeloo become lovers.

Luc Besson began working on the story of *The Fifth Element* when he was 16 years old, when he might just conceivably have taken some of it seriously. But from the first sight of John Bennett's stuck-on chin beard and tremulous face-pulling as the priest in the 1914 prologue, it is evident that this project has been transformed from an intense exercise in philosophical science fiction adventure (note that when Besson was 16, *Star Wars* had just come out) into something more like a French farce of the future. Various factions dash about an overpopulated universe colliding coincidentally with each other, so that the chaotic second half even stirs distant memories of such 60s larks as *Casino Royale* or *Modesty Blaise*. The most subtle joke comes when, on Fhloston, the alien diva performs in an auditorium which is, we are told, a perfect recreation of the Royal Opera House, prompting an audience aware of Euro-funding to muse cynically that a fortune has just been saved on big sets. The pay-off is that parts of the opera house are then comprehensively trashed in a big shoot-out, suggesting that it is a James Bond film-sized set after all.

After 20 years in development, the script seems to encompass elements from all five of Besson's earlier fiction films. Leeloo, the inhuman waif with incredible skills and a mixture of naivety and ruthlessness, follows similar figures in all Besson's films, combining especially Jean-Marc Barr in *The Big Blue* and Anne Parillaud in *Nikita*. The more grounded, grouchy, mock-cynical Korben (who has to catch up on the millennia-old plot) evokes the secondary figures played by Jean Réno in *The Big Blue* and Natalie Portman in *Léon*, but aspects of his life (his cat stands in for Léon's hapless plant) suggest that he too has the stuff of Besson's ironic adventurer heroes. As always with Besson, there is a tension between likeable absurdism and faintly embarrassing Big Thinks, and the miracle is that character does survive amid the kinetic, visual razzle-dazzle.

Bruce Willis is quite charming, but feels a little too much like a Jean Réno stand-in, but former model Milla Jovovich, previously an adornment to clinkers like *Return to the Blue Lagoon* and *Kuffs*, makes an appealing impression as the wild child Leeloo, with a Raggedy Ann hairdo and bikini bandages, developing manipulative skills long before she masters English.

In its unashamed poaching of bits and pieces from all over the place to dress up its tour of the future, there is quite a bit of the teenage comic-book fan to the picture. It is, however, hard to tell the intentional borrowings from the coincidental parallels. There is a certain cachet in elaborating on an episode from Gerald Potterton's *Heavy Metal* movie (as opposed to the *Heavy Metal* comic it is based on) in Korben's routine as a New York air cabbie in a Metropolis-like urban hell. This also applies to the incorporation of visual ideas from *bande dessinée* artists like Moebius and Jean-Claude Mézières and costume designer Jean-Paul Gaultier. But seeming to evoke the Alien Egyptology of *Stargate*, the ancient evil Shadows of *Babylon 5*, the punchline (dignitaries intent on congratulating the world-saving heroes find them making love) from *Moonraker* and even the floating palace of *The Return of the Jedi* is to tap into a seam of mainstream naff that is hard to rationalise as homage, parody or subversion.

The anything-goes looney-tunes attitude—Gary Oldman, with Bugs Bunny teeth, appears to be doing some sort of Mel Blanc southern accent—also encourages even such models of acting restraint as Ian Holm to overdo the bumbling. The worst offender is Chris Tucker, in the role of a twenty-third-century radio star like something out of a lost Almodóvar *House Party* sequel, who stretches out a one-scene satirical bit into an excruciating running joke that seriously mars the second half of the film. What tips the balance in Besson's favour is that he can pause for astonishment, as when the blue-tentacled opera singer belts out a bit of *Lucia di Lammermoor*, as well as speed up for action when the aria shifts into disco overdrive and a musical number is intercut with several brilliantly staged and edited shoot-outs. Some set-pieces trump recent attempts at the genre: here, the gene-engineered babe of *Species* and the three-dimensional car chase of *Judge Dredd* are done right at last, simply because charm and emotion have been added to special effects and stuntwork.

Given that large-scale science fiction adventures have become formulaic in the last 20 years, and are liable to do so all over again in the wake of the *Star Wars* reissue, Besson's comic irreverence is welcome as it downplays the over-familiar Big Alien Threat to the Universe plot engine in favour of inspired comic goofiness. If it weren't for footnote jokes like the trickle of sweaty hair dye that tracks down Oldman's forehead as he takes a phone call from the most evil being in the universe, or the flying Chinese food junk that calls at Bruce Willis' literal hole-in-the-wall apartment, it would be hard to accept the dumb-bell plot coincidences. One example is Leeloo fortuitously falling in with the cab driver who is also independently the space hero who will be charged with sharing her mission. The just-plain-crazed emotional climax when a being genetically engineered as a perfect warrior is horror-struck by the whole idea of war is a daft final irony.

VILLAGE VOICE, 5/20/97, p. 71, J. Hoberman

The fate of the universe may be at stake, but for all its outré violence, French genre-king Luc Besson's long-gestating sci-fi epic is at least as comic as it is cosmic—an outlandish showcase for 23rd-century Gaultier clothes. Space-shuttle stewies come packaged in baby blue bondage-fitted Naugahyde; the big action scene keeps cutting back to an aqua-latex opera diva with a tentacled perm. The numerous throwaway gags include the notion that the cigarettes of the future have inverted the current tobacco-to-filter ratio. It's hard to get those Euroepicenes to take the majesty of *Star Wars* seriously.

The major Lucas influence here is the *Star Wars* cantina. Closer in its whimsically garish clutter to Terry Gilliam or the team of Caro and Jeunet, *The Fifth Element* entertains a premise that's borderline cheesy. A retired military something or other, Bruce Willis is drawn from his "South Brooklyn" lair into the millennial struggle when, rattling on about her mission in what sounds like pidgin Hungarian, a winsome creature with bright orange hair (Milla Jovovich) crashes through the roof of his flying taxicab. (New York City has evidently built up into the ozone layer so that the traffic floats like confetti in the skyscraper canyons.)

Battling a horde of nouveau Clay People and a bucktoothed, Hitler-coiffed, Texas-twanged Gary Oldman (even more wired here than in Besson's *The Professional*, Willis is continually upstaged, not only by the set design but also by stand-up comedian Chris Tucker's interpretation of a space-age Oprah Winfrey as a sort of manic Morse Code-spouting amalgam of Dennis Rodman and Diana Ross. Then, as now, doomsday is visualized as an endless presentation of the Grammys.

Also reviewed in:
NATION, 6/2/97, p. 34, Stuart Klawans
NEW YORK TIMES, 5/9/97, p. C3, Janet Maslin
VARIETY, 5/12-18/97, p. 63, Todd McCarthy
WASHINGTON POST, 5/9/97, p. D1, Rita Kempley
WASHINGTON POST, 5/9/97, Weekend/p. 56, Desson Howe

FIRE

A Zeitgeist Films release of a Trial by Fire Films production. *Executive Producer:* Suresh Bhalla and David Hamilton. *Producer:* Bobby Bedi and Deepa Mehta. *Director:* Deepa Mehta. *Screenplay:* Deepa Mehta. *Director of Photography:* Giles Nuttgens. *Editor:* Barry Farrell. *Music:* A.R. Rahman. *Sound:* Konrad Skreta. *Production Designer:* Aradhana Seth. *Art Director:* Sunil Chhabra. *Costumes:* Neelam Mansingh Chowdhury and Anju Rekhi. *Make-up:* Lizbeth Williamson. *Stunt Coordinator:* Amin Ghani. *Running time:* 108 minutes. *MPAA Rating:* Not Rated.

CAST: Shabana Azmi (Radha); Nandita Das (Sita); Kulbushan Kharbanda (Ashok); Jaaved Jaaferi (Jatin); Ranjit Chowdhry (Mundu); Kushal Rekhi (Biji); Karishma Jhalani (Young Radha); Ramanjeet Kaur (Young Radha's Mother); Dilip Mehta (Young Radha's Father); Vinay Pathak (Guide at Taj Mahal); Alice Poon (Julie); Ram Gopal Bajaj (Swamiji); Ravinder Happy (Oily Man in Video Shop); Devyani Mehta Saltzman (Girl in Video Shop); Sunil Chhabra (Milkman on Bicycle); Avijit Dutt (Julie's Father); Shasea Bahadur (Julie's Brother); Meher Chand (Goddess Sita); Bahadur Chand (God Ram); Kabir Chowdhury (Boy in Video Shop).

LOS ANGELES TIMES, 8/27/97, Calendar/p. 5, Kevin Thomas

Deepa Mehta's graceful and daring "Fire" begins with a deceptively tranquil image of some women and a little girl sitting in the midst of a field of flowers. A voice-over tells us that these people have never seen the sea and long to see it, concluding with the remark of a wise old woman, "Sometimes you just have to see without looking."

It's an image that's repeated as a memory of a beautiful but sad woman as she looks out at New Delhi from an apartment above her husband's shop, a fast-food restaurant and video rental store on a bustling thoroughfare. She doesn't know it, but she's about to start seeing "without looking"—as she was advised to do when she was that little girl.

The woman, Radha Kapur (Shabana Azmi), is resigned to her fate. She is unable to bear children, but she is too kind, wise and just plain weary to hold it against her husband, Ashok (Kulbushan Kharbanda), that—in response to the disgrace of her barrenness—he has become celibate in the thrall of a swami who preaches that "desire is the root of all evil." Radha spends her days divided between working in the shop and caring for her aged mother-in-law, who was felled by a major stroke that has left her mute and unable to walk but still alert.

Sharing the tasteful but small apartment is Ashok's younger brother and business partner Jatin (Jaaved Jaaferi) and his bride Sita (Nandita Das). The handsome Jatin is in the midst of a passionate affair with a Chinese Canadian woman (Alice Pon) too independent to marry into a traditional Hindi family but has succumbed to pressure from his brother and mother to wed Sita.

Thus it is a far from happy family into which the trusting but intelligent Sita has married. Scarcely radical or revolutionary, Sita is in fact a perfectly conventional young woman. She's capable of respecting tradition yet lives in the modern world. Consequently, when she and Radha bond in the face of mutual respect—and misery—it is Sita who is young enough, sufficiently unhappy enough and open-minded enough to act upon the growing sexual attraction between her sister-in-law and herself.

In the context of the Kapur family and their narrow world, what Sita has done is shocking and an invitation to calamity, just as the film itself was, when it was screened at the International Film Festival of India, where a man threatened to shoot Mehta for having made it.

At last report, "Fire" remains banned in India. That's a shame because, beyond depicting in the Indian cinema the unthinkable—a lesbian relationship—it reveals a tug between past and present beliefs and values that must affect the lives of millions, especially women, entrapped in an oppressive patriarchal society.

As India's longtime preeminent screen actress, Shabana Azmi was understandably apprehensive about agreeing to play Radha, and surely it was no small act of courage on her part to accept the role. In her understated yet inimitably expressive manner, the exquisite Azmi blends right into the flawless ensemble of actors Mehta has assembled.

Heightening the drama through out is A.R. Rahman's shimmering score. For American audiences "Fire" has an additional plus: It is in "Hinglish"—English seasoned with occasional Hindi expressions.

NEW YORK POST, 8/22/97, p. 42, Thelma Adams

When two frustrated wives bond, their passions catch "Fire." Deepa Mehta's lush, layered, English-language romance heated up audiences at last year's New York Film Festival.

Let's meet the Kapurs. They're just a typical New Delhi family—the Cleavers of contemporary India.

Eldest brother Ashok has taken a vow of celibacy. His infertile wife, Radha, suffers in guilty silence. For 13 years she has helped hubby test his faith by lying next to him, untouched. She's cranky but devoted.

Brother Jatin is a handsome video dealer. He idolizes Jackie Chan and Bruce Lee. Pressured by family nagging for an heir, he makes an arranged match with the beautiful virgin Sita. But the pompous hipster's heart belongs to his Chinese mistress. Unlike Radha, Sita's not one for silent suffering. She's too fiery to stay devoted for long.

Mundu, the family servant, is at the low end of the food chain. He has a bad habit of watching dirty videos in front of Biji, the bedridden matriarch made mute by a stroke. She can ring her bell all night long, but she can't control the desires unbound in her extended family.

Writer-director Mehta ("Camilla") gives a face, heart and soul to each member of the Kapur clan while showing the budding sexual relationship between Radha and Sita as one sensual step away from tradition and toward self-realization. She also embroiders her tale with ritual, religious fables and formative memories that enrich the modern drama.

Indian movie star Shabana Azmi, as the older wife, and Nandita Das, as Sita, delicately show the progression from companions trapped in a traditional society that appears to offer few choices to lovers who must make their way in a land where, as Sita tells Radha, "There is no word in our language to describe what we are to each other."

NEWSDAY, 8/22/97, Part II/p. B8, John Anderson

A menage á trois of Indian esthetics, American mores and feminist aggravation, Deepa Mehta's "Fire" concerns two love-starved, culturally oppressed women who find each other as they lose their chains. You can see it all coming; amid the lush sensuality of Mehta's English-language love story, there are few surprises, except perhaps for the two characters involved.

But Mehta—whose previous films include "Sam and Me" and "Camilla"—isn't out to shock anyone. Not her American audiences anyway. (A male moviegoer in India, on the other hand, apparently threatened to shoot her.) She's using the lesbian story not to titillate but to pry the lid off Indian family life, and off India itself. And so it's a much gentler mission Mehta's on than one of provocation. Which is why the movie works as well as it does.

There is, generally, a distinctly different sensibility at work in Indian films than American, in terms of color, motion and allegory; characters, regardless of their humanity, can't seem to help but become symbolic. It's true of Radha (the celebrated actress Shabana Azmi) and Sita (Nandita Das), sisters-in-law drawn together by need. They're not just representative victims of oppressive Indian manhood, but of colonization—and the colonization of the colonized by the colonized. Their sex is almost chaste, although their impulses are heated.

There's a lot of anger in Mehta and she parcels it out fairly deftly, although the men in the movie are, to a man, lice. Radha's husband Ashok (Kulbushan Kharbanda) is seeking spiritual enlightenment through celibacy; he tests himself with Radha, but for 15 years they haven't had sex. Ashok's younger brother, Jatin (Jaaved Jaaferi), has just married Sita but continues his longtime affair with a Chinese girlfriend—who wouldn't marry him because of his family.

Jatin also sells porn tapes in his video store, unbeknownst to almost everyone but Mundu (Ranjit Chowdhry), the household servant, who engages in onanistic activity while watching the tapes in the same room with the family's paralyzed and mute granny (Kushal Rekhi), who bangs her one good hand in wild disapproval.

So you can't say Mehta doesn't have a sense of humor, although this is one unhappy metaphorical family, in a world that prefers that unhappiness not be expressed, much less remedied, and where bad behavior is not to be acknowledged. Of course, in this Mehta has found the common ground of two cultures. And she does a pretty good job of bridging them.

SIGHT AND SOUND, 1/99, p. 46, Rachel Malik

Contemporary New Delhi. Young and newly married Sita comes to live with the family of her husband Jatin. The family run a busy take-away restaurant and video shop and Sita is soon busy helping with the business and taking care of her husband's elderly, invalid mother Biji. Sita is frustrated with Jatin who makes no effort at friendship or affection. She develops a close friendship with her sister-in-law Radha. Jatin spends most of his time with his mistress Julie while Radha's husband Ashok spends his evenings at religious meetings. Soon the two women become increasingly close and fall in love.

For a period, their relationship thrives undetected but they are discovered by Mundu, a servant. Radha discovers him watching pornography in the living room while the mute Biji looks on in horror. Mundu is humiliated and tells Radha he knows about her and Sita. Ashok insists Mundu should have a second chance but Mundu, determined on revenge, tells Ashok, who then discovers the two women making love. The two women confirm their plan to leave. Sita packs and goes but Radha is determined to speak to her husband first. In an angry encounter, Radha's sari catches fire and the room goes up in flames. As Sita waits, Radha appears in her burnt clothes, seemingly unscathed, and the two women are reunited.

Ever since Princess Diana was photographed visiting the Taj Mahal alone, the building has become an ironic international signifier of romantic love. In Deepa Mehta's *Fire*, Sita, one of the film's heroines, makes a honeymoon visit there with her sullen husband. The tour guide's extolling of this ultimate expression of love and the couple's obvious unease are the first markers of the film's distrust of romance. Sita does find love—although it will be with her sister-in-law Radha rather than her husband.

"There is no word in our language for what we are," Sita says of Hindi, and this very silence is an opportunity. A patriarchy which so rigorously genders the division of work and leisure and presumes masculinity as the beginning and end of sexuality by that very fact also creates possibilities for friendship and love between women. While the film charts the difficulties of extended family living, the household regimen also allows moments of privacy. When Radha's husband calls to her, she can linger a moment with Sita, knowing that he will wait (although surprised) for her to attend him. The two women erotically reinscribe an array of modern and traditional codes of the sub-continental feminine: Sita oils Radha's hair, Radha presents Sita with bangles, they sing karaoke versions of popular love songs, Sita in drag, in front of their mother-in-law Biji.

But here 'a secret love' is neither desirable nor possible: not desirable because their relationship leads them to challenge common-sense duty and obedience; not possible because entrenched inequality fights back, a process personified by the actions of Biji and the resentful servant Mundu. Voyeuristic Mundu knows words to describe Sita and Radha—from the pornography he consumes in front of the traumatised Biji. It is he who tells Radha's husband that his wife and sister-in-law are lesbians, an act of bitterness which is also, however paradoxically, the act of a 'faithful' servant. And Biji knows too. Silenced by a stroke and abused by Mundu, she still maintains some authority: her bell must always be answered. Her knowledge of their relationship, in part the result of her forced education, also seems to issue from the keen powers of observation that arise out of women's oppression.

An intertextual play of references offers another means of understanding and possibly overcoming this patriarchal status quo. Hindu parables are enacted within the narrative of the film in a variety of idioms: morality play, soap opera, Bollywood. The testing of a mythical Sita by her husband the god Rama is the most repeated parable; and while Radha emerges from her trial by fire unscathed—the mark of her virtue—she is still condemned to exile. These narratives of female obedience and the realism of the film are sharply contrasted in a sequence which is repeated and expanded as the film progresses. We are shown a lyrical field of yellow flowers, the setting for another seemingly fantastical story that centres on the possibility of envisaging the sea. Simultaneously a memory, a fantasy and a vision of a possible future, this space is contructed by a different logic. Radha's literal trial by fire binds this symbolic narrative of freedom to the film's resolution. One of the most powerful achievements of *Fire* is to represent a form of desire which is not an escape, but a political challenge.

VILLAGE VOICE, 8/26/97, p. 80, Leslie Camhi

The passions that ignite us sometimes start as *coups de foudre,* but often they build more slowly, with smoldering combustion. Deepa Mehta's *Fire* finds erotic heat in the prosaic recesses of a middle-class New Delhi household, and between women whose sexual lives appear to be over.

Fire opens with a young Indian couple on their honeymoon at the Taj Mahal, but that monument to conjugal love is an ironic counterpoint for the story that follows. Radha (Shabana Azmi) has been a dutiful Indian wife for some 15 years, though her husband Ashok (Kulbushan Kharbanda) took a vow of celibacy over a decade ago. He won't touch her, but spends his evenings massaging the feet of a shoddy swami. They live in a faceless high-rise with Ashok's mutely imperious, elderly mother, Biji (Kushal Rekhi), his callow younger brother, Jatin (Jaaved Jaaferi), and Mundu (Ranjit Chowdhry), their clownish servant. Jatin loves Julie (Alice Poon), a Chinese hairdresser and would-be actress; bowing to tradition, he marries Sita (Nandita Das), a young Indian woman, but spends most nights away from home.

Between working for the family's takeout video-rental business, caring for Biji, and hanging out the laundry, Radha and Sita are drawn to each other, through a shared love and ambivalence for the rituals that bind them, and from which they ultimately unbind each other.

Fire is lusciously photographed, with several fine performances; the beautiful Shabana Azmi, in particular, makes Radha's journey from self-forgetfulness to erotic awareness entirely convincing. Sometimes the "Hinglish" dialogue seems melodramatic or forced, especially in scenes between Jatin and Julie, whose fake American accent is strangely grating.

But Mehta manages to capture a New India, where sacred scenes from the life of Ram are performed in kitschy street theater next to video stores renting contraband porn. She's attuned to the minute shifts of women's inner experience, and to the varieties of masculine inattention and indifference. *Fire*'s seeming quiet is unsettling and deeply subversive.

Also reviewed in:
CHICAGO TRIBUNE, 9/19/97, Friday/p. F, Michael Wilmington
NEW YORK TIMES, 8/22/97, p. C22, Lawrence Van Gelder
VARIETY, 9/16-22/96, p. 69, Brendan Kelly

FIRE DOWN BELOW

A Warner Bros. release of a Seagal/Nasso production. *Executive Producer:* William S. Gilmore and Jeb Stuart. *Producer:* Julius Nasso and Steven Seagal. *Director:* Felix Enriquez Alcala. *Screenplay:* Jeb Stuart and Philip Morton. *Story:* Jeb Stuart. *Director of Photography:* Tom Houghton. *Editor:* Robert A. Ferretti. *Music:* Nick Glennie-Smith. *Sound:* Charles Wilborn. *Casting:* Shari Rhodes and Joseph Middleton. *Production Designer:* Joe Alves. *Art Director:* Mark Mansbridge and Bill Hiney. *Costumes:* Rosanna Norton. *Stunt Coordinator:* Bobby Brown. *Running time:* 99 minutes. *MPAA Rating:* R.

CAST: Steven Seagal (Jack Taggart); Marg Helgenberger (Sarah Kellogg); Harry Dean Stanton (Cotton); Stephen Lang (Earl Kellogg); Kris Kristofferson (Orin Hanner); Levon Helm (Reverend Goodall); Ed Bruce (Sheriff Lloyd); Brad Hunt (Orin Hanner Jr.); Mark Collie (Hatch); Alex Harvey (Sims); Richard Masur (Pratt); Randy Travis (Ken Adams).

LOS ANGELES TIMES, 9/8/97, Calendar/p. 6, Gene Seymour

You see this guy, right? And he looks like he's the lineal descendant of a ferocious jungle cat. But, what the hey, you and your six or seven buddies take him on. In seconds, you and your buddies are lying on the ground in pieces, and he's still standing.

With me, so far? OK, here's my problem: Knowing what this cat is capable of, *why do you and your six buddies insist on taking him on again? And again? And AGAIN?*

Understand, now, that this is a relatively minor point to deal with in "Fire Down Below." But it sufficiently represents the many improbabilities you have to live with in a Steven Seagal film.

Begin with the fact that our brooding, broad-shouldered hero has taken his avenging angel persona and dressed it in eco-populist trapping. The Environmental Protection Agency—honest!—is deploying this one-man battalion to investigate the illegal dumping of toxic waste in a Kentucky coal mine. Several people have gotten sick. A pondful of fish has died—as has a handful of Feds who have mysteriously died trying to get the goods on this corporate atrocity.

Seagal's character poses as a humble carpenter going from house to house near the dump site, asking questions and generally annoying so-called peace officers and local thugs, all of whom are in the employ of the slimy billionaire who's depositing poison into the Earth.

Kris Kristofferson is the baddie and he's just one of many classic country-rock stars scattered throughout the scenery. Levon Helm's the town preacher, and I guess that really is Randy Travis as a fast-drawing Fed who is not what he seems. There are also fine actors including Stephen Lang, Harry Dean Stanton and the shamefully underemployed Marg Helgenberger.

And Seagal is ... well, Seagal. Which is to say he is, by turns, torpid, charming and scary, sometimes all at once. His one big dramatic moment comes in a sermon at the church, where he's exhorting the townspeople to stand up for themselves against wealthy elites. That he does so wearing a leather coat that, as one of the characters says, probably costs a year's salary of an underpaid miner says as much about Seagal's moxie as his capability in hand-to-hand combat.

Also reviewed in:
CHICAGO TRIBUNE, 9/8/97, Tempo/p. 2, John Petrakis
NEW YORK TIMES, 9/6/97, p. 18, Lawrence Van Gelder
VARIETY, 9/8-14/97, p. 76, Leonard Klady
WASHINGTON POST, 9/6/97, p. D1, Stephen Hunter

FLAMENCO

A New Yorker Films release of a Juan Lebron Producciones production. *Executive Producer:* Jose Lopez Rodero. *Producer:* Juan Lebron. *Director:* Carlos Saura. *Screenplay:* Carlos Saura. *Director of Photography:* Vittorio Storaro. *Editor:* Pablo del Amo. *Music:* Isidro Munoz. *Sound:* Chris Munro, Jesus Bola, and Andrew Glen. *Production Designer:* Jose Lopez and Carlos Regido. *Art Director:* Rafael Palmero. *Costumes:* Rafael Palmero. *Running time:* 100 minutes. *MPAA Rating:* Not Rated.

WITH: Paco de Lucia; Manolo Sanlucar; Enrique Morente; Joaquin Cortes; Jose Menese; Lole y Manuel; Mario Maya; Jose Merce; Matilde Coral; Carmen Linares; Merche Esmeralda; Chocolate; Manuela Carrasco; Farruco; Fernanda de Utrera; La Paquera de Jerez; Mananita; Ketama; Agujeta; Moneo; Paco Toronjo; Maria Pages; Aurora Vargas; Remedios Amaya; Juana la del Revuelo; La Macanita; Chano Lobato; Rancapino; Potito; Duquende; Relen Maya; El Grilo.

LOS ANGELES TIMES, 8/22/97, Calendar/p. 20, Kenneth Turan

To see "Flamenco" is to be swept up in a performance dream, to experience a vibrant musical tradition as filtered through Spain's top director and one of the world's preeminent cinematographers. If you're not an aficionado when you go, you might be persuaded to become one by the time you leave.

Veteran director Carlos Saura, with more than 30 films to his credit, has dealt expertly with performance before in, among others, "Carmen" and "Blood Wedding." In "Flamenco," he has employed an estimated 300 performers—singers, dancers, guitar players, chanters and rhythmic clappers—to take stock of an ageless tradition at this particular time and place.

Flamenco, a brief crawl at the film's beginning tells us, is a half-a-millennium-old fusion art, a creation of elements of Gypsy, Arabic, Jewish, African and other music that came into its own in Andalucia around 1850. Though the film uses subtitles to identify styles of flamenco like *bulerias, guajiras* and *alegrias*, no attempt is made to define or describe the characteristics of each.

Similarly, though the press notes let on that such flamenco luminaries as Paco de Lucia, Manolo Sanlucar and dancer Joaquín Cortés appear in the film, unless you know these folks by sight you won't figure out who they are. (Cortés, recognizable from Pedro Almodovar's "The Flower of My Secret" and dancing a fierce bare-chested *farruca*, is the one exception.)

But though viewers may occasionally entertain the perverse wish that Ed Sullivan was around to say, "Let's hear it for Paco de Lucía, what a performer," most of the time not knowing who's who is an acceptable price for the pleasure of feeling we've stumbled onto the flamenco show of a lifetime. Though obviously carefully planned, "Flamenco" creates the illusion of unfolding spontaneously, a found event not a planned extravaganza. Information can be gotten later; for now, we're happy to let the music flow.

None of this would work well without the expressive work of director of photography Vittorio Storaro. A three-time Oscar winner for cinematography ("Apocalypse Now," "Reds," "The Last Emperor"), Storaro makes even standard shots come off as elegant and involving. A key player in the film's visual invention, its use of single-color backgrounds and the way it blends light, dark and shadow, Storaro demonstrates that you can be a genius even photographing an empty stage.

Both director and cinematographer must share a fascination with faces, because everyone who appears on camera in "Flamenco" has a keenly expressive one. Or it could be that involvement with this intense, passionate music makes deep character lines inevitable.

Several different styles of flamenco dance are on display, executed by some of the youngest and oldest performers in the film, the physical energy of the former contrasting with the sense of dignity of the latter. It's quite a combination.

It is the unmistakable sound of flamenco singing, however, that is the most haunting of this film's experiences. With voices that verge on shouts of pain and songs that seem to leave the singers continually on the edge of tears, this is a sound that intoxicates.

"Flamenco" also demonstrates how exciting it can be to perform in an art form that venerates tradition while valuing personal expression. The words on the film's Spanish CD package say it succinctly; "Ritmo, Pasion, Fuerza y ... arte, much arte." Rhythm, passion, strength and art, much art.

NEW YORK POST, 4/25/97, p. 52, Thelma Adams

Famed Spanish director Carlos ("Carmen") Saura exercises his passion for flamenco in a stripped-down, sensual song-and-dance marathon. "Flamenco" showcases the flowering of a vital, evolving art that fuses gypsy melodies, Andalusian rhythms, Hindu songs, Gregorian chants, Jewish laments and Persian tunes, among others.

Set in an abandoned train station in Seville and structured like an all night rave that begins in the afternoon and continues until the shoe leather wears thin at dawn, 'Flamenco' features the best singers and dancers of the flamenco renaissance. The cast mixes the internationally famous—Paco de Lucia, Manolo Sanlucar, Lole y Manuel—as well aspiring artists and huge families of performers never before seen outside of their native Spain.

Photographed by famed cinematographer Vittorio ("The Conformist") Storaro, "Flamenco" wastes no time on talking heads. Subtitles are few and far between, disclosing a song title or type. The music speaks from the heart and for itself.

Among the documentary's highlights is a duet between an old grandpa and a youth: One dancer has the benefits of confidence and technique, his footing assured beneath his round belly; the other has the agility and newfound pride of a boy reveling in a God-given talent.

Another high point is Joaquin Cortes' bare-chested, stylized stomp called *farruca*. His movements are school-trained, dramatic, assertive, sexual. A moment after he stops he exhales a "phew" of exertion and relief. The 27-year-old gypsy dancer is only a human after all; we see behind the scrim.

Another emotional peak is the performance of legendary guitarist de Lucia. He has influenced exceptional musicians outside the flamenco circuit, from John McLaughlin to Al Di Meola. Considered the foremost flamenco guitarist, de Lucia lives up to his reputation in a series of tangos.

Seated on a simple wooden chair set on a low platform, he leads two brothers and a group of musicians in soul-filling riffs. De Lucia remains the image of cool until he breaks into a final, thin smile of joy.

This joy in "Flamenco" is so contagious it's a wonder the chairs don't start dancing on their wooden legs.

NEWSDAY, 4/25/97, Part II/p. B7, Jack Mathews

Carlos Saura's passion for Spain's native folk music has resulted in several memorable films, notably the dance trilogy "Blood Wedding," "Carmen" and "El Amor Brujo." But this performance movie may be the capper. Filmed entirely (and brilliantly, by Vittorio Storaro) in an empty train station in Seville, "Flamenco" brings together Spain's greatest singers, dancers and musicians for what appears to be the ultimate flamenco jam. This is not the tabletop clop-'n'-castanets show put on for tourists in Madrid bars, but the pure thing, a mixture of grace, power, sensuality, passion and storytelling. With no introductions preceding them, "Flamenco" moves smoothly through a series of numbers—from dance, song and guitar solos to a celebratory finale with more than 300 performers—and covers most variants of an art form that has evolved over centuries of cultural mixing in southern Spain. The songs, sung in a wailing cant clearly more Arabic than Spanish, are strange and grating to these uninformed ears, but the dances, choreographed against craftily lighted, minimalist backdrops, are sensational.

VILLAGE VOICE, 4/29/97, p. 76, Laurie Stone

With percussive feet ruling in the ingenious, juiced shows *Stomp*, *Noise/Funk*, and *Top Dogs*, this might be the season for *Flamenco*, too. But while the stage evenings homage tap traditions, they also rewire and extend them. Carlos Saura's performance film *Flamenco* is an archive and a snore. You feel the solemnity and deadness almost from the start. The setting is a dance studio, the cast 300 of Spain's most renowned singers, guitarists, and dancers, who parade their routines in an unbroken procession. Notes flashed onscreen and included in the press packet explain that flamenco developed over 500 years, combining the religious chants of Spanish Jews who migrated to Flanders (hence Flamenco) and the customs of gypsies, Muslims, and Christian dissenters from the Spanish Inquisition. The resulting folk art is communal and mostly sexually segregated. In the movie, it comes across largely unerotic; only one number involves a man and woman dancing together, and even here they don't touch.

Saura (*Carmen, Blood Wedding*), working with famed cinematographer Vittorio Storaro, stresses pure tradition, and to infuse the sets with a drama they lack often uses chiaroscuro, shooting figures in semi-darkness and in silhouette. It's a frustrating technique, making it difficult to see the dancers. The rhythmic combinations, songs, and guitar licks are divided into categories that vary, the way blues and gospel forms do, but the overall effect remains repetitive. Most of the songs, whether lamentations or jubilations, are wailed. Few of the dancers have flair, though all are committed. What emerges is a sense that the participants—spanning a great range of ages and physical abilities—are engaged in something authentic and moving to them. It's refreshing to see the gnarled and elderly appreciated, but after a while it's like being trapped at an endless family gathering, where all the aunts and uncles get a chance to perform.

Also reviewed in:
NEW YORK TIMES, 4/25/97, p. C4, Stephen Holden
VARIETY, 9/18-24/95, p. 99, Deborah Young
WASHINGTON POST, 7/18/97, Weekend/p. 42, Desson Howe

FLIPPING

A Dove Entertainment release of a Mon Frere Motion Picture production. *Executive Producer:* Michael Woods. *Producer:* Gene Mitchell and David Amos. *Director:* Gene Mitchell. *Screenplay:* Gene Mitchell. *Director of Photography:* Phil Parmet. *Editor:* Kevin Krasny. *Sound:* Benjamin Patrick. *Casting:* Pat Melton and Paul G. Bens. *Production Designer:* Diane Hughes. *Costumes:* Nadine Reimer. *Running time:* 112 minutes. *MPAA Rating:* R.

CAST: David Amos (Michael Moore); David Proval (Billy White); Gene Mitchell (Shot); Shant Benjamin (Hooker); Barry Primus (Joey); Paul Klar (Dennis); Tony Burton (Chuckie); Mike Starr (C.J.); Keith David (Leo Richards).

LOS ANGELES TIMES, 2/21/97, Calendar/p. 15, Kevin Thomas

[The following review by Kevin Thomas appeared in a slightly different form in NEWSDAY, 3/7/97, Part II/p. B15.]

"Flipping" flops. Gangster pictures don't come any phonier than this misfired attempt to set down a bunch of sub-Scorsese goodfellas, none of whom seems to have ever spent a moment west of New Jersey, on the side streets of Hollywood. Writer-director Gene Mitchell's first feature plays like an actor's workshop exercise—"Flipping" did in fact begin in a workshop—that had no business being filmed for public consumption.

It's dismaying to see as many proven actors come across so overly theatrical and therefore unconvincing. The key exception is the veteran Barry Primus, who clearly realizes the distinction between playing under a proscenium and for the camera.

One thing makes sense: Nobody but a bunch of dummies would work for as violent, cheap and mercurial a leader as Keith David's Leo. (Get this: Leo is also a wannabe cabaret singer.) The entire film is composed of double-crosses upon double-crosses, to the extent that by the time that a long-winded 102 minutes have passed, everyone has killed off everyone else.   There's absolutely no reason to be concerned with these crooks: They're stupid, brutal and unfunny. They're not drawn from life but from the countless underworld movies that preceded them.

The one fresh idea that Mitchell has is to have a gay undercover cop (David Proval) fall in love with the most ambitious member of the gang (David Amos), but this relationship not only rings false but remains peripheral until the film's ending. In the credit-where-credit-is-due department, let it be noted that Phil Parmet's fluid, highly atmospheric camera work is better than "Flipping" deserves.

NEW YORK POST, 3/7/97, p. 46, Thelma Adams

"I have the right to my degeneracy," detective Billy White in Gene Mitchell's crime of a crime drama, "Flipping." It's the most memorable line in the most forgettable movie of 1997.

Stretched thinner than a hunger striker, writer, director and coproducer Mitchell also plays Shot, a trigger-happy thug. Given a movie this bad, Mitchell should be Shot.

The actor/auteur has stumbled behind the wave of two independent cinema trends: the neo-noir gorefest with hard-boiled dialogue, and the tortured, explicit drama of homosexual angst that ends in violence.

If there is a theme animating "Flipping"—cop-lingo for turning a criminal into an informant—it's ugliness for its own sake. Mitchell ("Surf Nazis Must Die") substitutes wanton violence for drama while assembling a group of actors so unappealing they make Peter Lorre look like Miss Venezuela.

Det. White (David Proval) thinks he has "flipped" gangster Michael Moore (David Amos). White wants Moore to finger his crew and its kingpin, Leo (Keith David). Moore has another agenda. The cop's jones for the criminal—a salivating wolf who suffers from insomnia—complicates the plan.

Moore could be a Jim Thompson protagonist: amoral, violent, charming, capable of anything and essentially unknowable. But Mitchell is nowhere near as daring as Thompson who has become the Mark Twain of the pulp fiction revival. Making Moore sexually ambiguous is less imaginative than trendy.

"Flipping's" pockmarked, red-eyed weasel of a cop may have a right to his degeneracy, but we have a right to reject it. I get paid to go to movies like this so that you can avoid them. As Leo tells Shot, "If you think you're hot sh--, think again."

VILLAGE VOICE, 3/11/97, p. 78, Frank Ruscitti

This homage to all things Scorsese comes complete with a wedding, several murders, and loads of blood. The only thing missing are the cannolis. *Flipping* recounts the tale of how some low-level Hollywood wiseguys planning to double-cross a local crime boss ultimately get theirs. Okay, okay, we know you've seen this one before; what's striking, however, is how well it all comes off. An excellent cast brings a new vitality to roles we're quite familiar with, giving Joe Pesci and his boys a run for their money as the most regular-guy killers around. Keith David almost steals the film as the local ruthless kingpin.

The subplot, involving a love affair one of the mobsters and an undercover cop, makes no sense and nearly ruins the picture. Once the novelty of two men soul-kissing on the big screen wears off, you're left with a nervous Ron Silver-having-a-bad-hair look-alike in love with a square-jawed Van Damme type and a believability quotient of zero.

Also reviewed in:
NEW YORK TIMES, 3/7/97, p. C7, Lawrence Van Gelder
VARIETY, 1/22-28/96, p. 100, Emanuel Levy

FLUBBER

A Walt Disney Pictures release of a Great Oaks production. *Executive Producer:* David Nicksay. *Producer:* John Hughes and Ricardo Mestres. *Director:* Les Mayfield. Screenplay: John Hughes and Bill Walsh. *Based on a story by:* Samuel W. Taylor. *Director of Photography:* Dean Cundey. *Editor:* Harvey Rostenstock. *Music:* Danny Elfman. *Music Editor:* Ellen Segal. *Sound:* Agamemnon Andrianos and (music) Shawn Murphy and Robert Fernandez. *Sound Editor:* Scott Martin Gershin and Wylie Stateman. *Casting:* Nancy Foy. *Production Designer:* Andrew McAlpine. *Art Director:* James E. Tocci. *Set Designer:* Erin Kemp. *Set Decorator:* Daniel May. *Set Dresser:* Emilio R. Aramendia. *Special Effects:* Stan Parks. *Costumes:* April Ferry. *Make-up:* Cheri Minns. *Stunt Coordinator:* Freddie Hice. *Running time:* 93 minutes. *MPAA Rating:* PG.

CAST: Robin Williams (Professor Phillip Brainard); Marcia Gay Harden (Sara Jean Reynolds); Christopher McDonald (Wilson Croft); Raymond Barry (Chester Hoenicker); Clancy Brown (Smith); Ted Levine (Wesson); Wil Wheaton (Bennett Hoenicker); Edie McClurg (Martha George); Jodi Benson (Voice of Weebo); Leslie Stefanson (Sylvia); Malcolm Brownson (Father); Benjamin Brock (Window Boy); Dakin Matthews (Minister); Zack Zeigler (Teenage Boy); Samuel Lloyd (Willy Barker); Scott Michael Campbell (Dale Jepner); Bob Sarlatte (Rutland Coach); Bob Greene (Referee); Tom Barlow (Medfield Basketball Player); Scott Martin Gershin (Voice of Flubber); Julie Morrison (Voice of Weebette).

LOS ANGELES TIMES, 11/6/97, Calendar/p. 6, John Anderson

[The following review by John Anderson appeared in a slightly different form in NEWSDAY, 11/26/97, Part II/p. B3.]

With all the resilience, elasticity and recoil of Robin Williams' career, "Flubber" bounces into theaters today to begin the holiday marketing march.

In remaking 1961's "The Absent Minded Professor," which starred Fred MacMurray as the creator of flying rubber, producer-screenwriter John Hughes and Co. have chosen to change the title to something far more commercially viable than "Disorganized, Middle-Aged Science Teacher." And they've made a few other changes, too. Professor Phillip Brainard (Williams), a kind of Wallace sans Gromit, has been given an airborne computer pal named Weebo (voice of Jodi Benson). Flubber itself has been given an actual personality, somewhere between primordial ooze and Chris Farley. And MacMurray's old jalopy has been replaced by a 1963 T-Bird, which is very nice and able to fly.

Otherwise, this is your basic audience-friendly comedy with a crisis—the imminent closing of Medfield College. And a couple of thugs—Smith and Wesson (Clancy Brown and Ted Levine). And their boss—the college-foreclosing Chester Hoenicker (Raymond J. Barry). There are two love triangles: One among Phillip, Weebo and Sara (Marcia Gay Harden), whom the addle-pated Phillip has left at the altar three times. (What she's doing with him in the first place? Oh, never mind.) And one among Phillip, Sara and Wilson Croft (Christopher McDonald), who wants to steal Phillip's invention and his fiancee and who gets her to wager herself on the results of the big basketball game.

Harden and McDonald are good. Ted Levine is very good (he was the killer in "Silence of the Lambs" and the police chief in "Mad City"). But amid all the Professor Irwin Corey-inspired double-talk about what makes Flubber Flubber, the bigger mystery is what Williams contributes to all this. He's a likable enough personality, but Flubber itself is an uncomfortable reminder of what he used to be—antic, unpredictable and vaguely dangerous. Although there were hints of his dormant comedy talents in "Fathers' Day," in which he got to play the off-kilter half of a comedy team, what he's required to do here is act, often in the most maudlin situations. What this usually amounts to is Williams tightening his upper lip, jutting out his lower and enunciating very carefully, thus indicating emotional distress.

And there's a bit too much emotional distress in "Flubber" and not quite enough of the energetic slapstick that takes place at the big basketball game, which Phillip fixes with Flubber (yes, kids, he's cheating!) or the abuse that Smith and Wesson take via the bowling ball and golf ball that begin bouncing at the beginning of the film and return to Earth periodically with hilarious timing and accuracy. Director Les Mayfield ("Miracle on 34th Street") has his moments, of course, but what ultimately was needed in the case of "Flubber" was a movie with more bounce and less talk.

NEW YORK POST, 11/26/97, p. 47, Michael Medved

In the feckless "Flubber," Robin Williams plays a professor so appallingly absent-minded that he has totally forgotten the key elements of the source material that inspired the movie—charm, warmth and whimsy.

In painful contrast to Disney's delightful 1961 Fred MacMurray film "The Absent Minded Professor," this inept remake comes across as a crude, cruel, tedious slapstick extravaganza, insulting the intelligence of even those sadistic 9-year-olds who seem to comprise its intended audience.

Williams plays Professor Phillip Brainard, so obsessed with his experiments he misses his own wedding three times.

Marcia Gay Harden looks stunned and uncomfortable as his long-suffering fiancee and president of the college, trying to save her struggling institution from bankruptcy.

Raymond Barry is the unsavory tycoon scheming to close the campus, and Clancy Brown and Ted Levine play "Smith and Wesson", his two cartoonish, bumbling goons—since every John Hughes film since "Home Alone" must, by binding statute, feature two cartoonish, bumbling goons.

The non-fun begins when the professor discovers "flubber" (or flying rubber), a gravity defying green goo (that inexplicably giggles and dances), using it to win a school basketball game or to power his antique Thunderbird for air travel.

Even the showy special effects look lame, considerably more forced and distracting than the easygoing magic of the 1961 original, and the biggest special effect of all—Robin Williams—never kicks in for a moment.

Obviously eager to play a clumsy, cuddly genius, he comes across as oddly muffled, giving no hint of his trademark manic energy or improvisatory, stream-of-consciousness comedy. This eccentric chemist displays no chemistry whatever with his purported love interest, but tearfully, embarrassingly overacts when his cute, seductive computer (an idiotic addition for this update) gets smashed by the bad guys.

Les Mayfield (who previously crafted the radiant remake of "Miracle on 34th Street") draws the dubious director's credit, but of course it's cowriter/co-producer John Hughes who'll get most of the blame.

The dark, demented, kiddie-gothic atmosphere, however, incongruously echoes the work of Tim Burton rather than Hughes—though with none of Burton's quirky imagination or originality.

For family audiences, "Flubber" represents the season's most acute disappointment and will be remembered as a feeble flub for all concerned.

SIGHT AND SOUND, 3/98, P. 47, Darren Arnold

Philip Brainard, an absent-minded professor at debt-ridden Medfield College, is due to marry his colleague Sara Reynolds. On their wedding day, Philip becomes engrossed in an experiment which produces a gelatinous high-energy green substance which he names Flubber. Flubber's bounciness causes some mischief in the neighbourhood, and Philip misses his wedding. At the church, Sara is sweet-talked by Wilson, Philip's old rival. Meanwhile, wealthy Chester Hoenicker is enraged by his son Bennett's poor performance in Brainard's class. He sends his two henchmen, Smith and Wesson, to find blackmail material to use against Philip, and they see him working with Flubber.

While flying in his car with Flubber's aid, Philip overhears Wilson persuade Sara to go away with him for the weekend if his college's team wins the big basketball game against Medfield. Philip attaches pieces of Flubber to the shoes of the Medfield players, ensuring them a surprise victory. Weebo, Philip's faithful flying robot, goes to Sara's house and plays her a recording of Philip saying how much he loves Sara. Mollified, Sara meets Philip and asks him to consider using Flubber to develop air travel. The two henchmen break into the laboratory, destroying Weebo and stealing Flubber, but Sara and Philip manage to steal it back. Philip sells the formula for a vast sum of money, thus saving the college, and finally marries Sara.

Since *Flubber*'s story centres on the success of a scientific formula, it's ironic that it should also neatly illustrate a formulaic movie gone awry. A lazy screenplay (written by John Hughes and Bill Walsh) must shoulder most of the blame, along with Les Mayfield's pedestrian direction and Robin Williams, putting in another cloying turn as the absent-minded inventor of the title's material. Given the success of the recent Eddie Murphy-starring remake of *The Nutty Professor,* it was inevitable that someone would remake the similarly titled 1960 Fred MacMurray vehicle *The Absent Minded Professor.* However, *Flubber,* having changed both the focus and the title of its source material, seems very unsure of what it actually wants to be: the marketing refers to *Flubber* as a remake, yet *The Absent Minded Professor* is not directly mentioned in the credits. So it comes as no surprise that the film's actual content is remarkably lop-sided. In the original, Fred MacMurray's professor used the substance he'd created to help him fly his car, a project which was of paramount interest to both scientist and movie (as befitted the automobile- and space-travel-obsessed early 60s). In this version, Williams' Brainard seems rather underwhelmed by his flying 60s car (shown in a few near-throwaway scenes), and instead continually marvels at the green gunge itself. Moreover, the professor's robot sidekick Weebo is infinitely more endearing and impressive than Flubber, as both a character and an invention. After all, Weebo has an advanced artificial intelligence, can perform numerous household tasks, and can fly to boot. Indeed, the film's one real moment of poignancy comes with Weebo's demise. Flubber is anodyne to a fault, and it's quite some way into the picture before we see it become anything remotely resembling a character. Admittedly, when this happens, it's a brilliantly executed vignette as Flubber subdivides and recreates a selection of Busby Berkeley's finest moments.

Although Danny Elfman's suitably rousing score and Dean Cundey's cinematography are two of *Flubber*'s strongest points, there is really precious little else to recommend this film. The combination of the routine central performance and the Disney/Hughes staple of two evil henchmen who are there to disrupt the main character's idyll reminds us how often, and how much better, we've seen *Flubber*-y films done before (including, in their different ways, *The Nutty Professor* and the original *Home Alone*). One would have thought that the recent cloying and unimaginative *Miracle on 34th Street* would have been more than enough to discourage Mayfield from tackling any other remakes.

VILLAGE VOICE, 12/2/97, p. 79, Dennis Lim

Dragging 1961's *The Absent-Minded Professor* into an age of rampant cross-promotional possibilities, Disney has called this inevitable remake *Flubber,* deftly shifting the focus from the forgetful academic of the original title to his eminently marketable creation: a hyper-kinetic, flamboyantly elastic substance—what Jim Carrey would be if he were a fluorescent green, gravity-defying blob.

Though flying rubber—to give flubber its full name—apparently has revolutionary potential in the energy industry, its chief function here is to galvanize a musty save-the-school plot. Robin Williams, in the fuddy-duddyish Fred MacMurray role, is less flubbery than usual—which is just as well, since the green stuff is itself quite a scene-stealer. Flubber '90s style isn't merely F/X-enhanced, but aggressively anthropomorphized, reinvented as a cuddly, face-pulling star with a knack for large-scale musical numbers. The substance has its vulgar side, too. After Williams wins back his girlfriend (Marcia Gay Harden), the unctuous rival (Christopher McDonald) gets to ingest and excrete flubber by way of comcuppance.

In a creepy contemporizing touch, Williams's jealous personal assistant, Weebo, is a breathy-voiced, flying saucer-shaped robot that interposes semi-ironic commentary throughout on a flip-up screen (and flying goo is supposed to be the radical invention?). The movie's nominal director is Les Mayfield, but the rancid undercurrent can be traced to cowriter John Hughes, indulging in the cruel humor that stunk up his *Home Alone* films. *Flubber*'s goons have a very high threshold for pain, and a running gag involves scaring a little boy out of his wits. The "kids are cruel" argument may be true, but it doesn't quite justify being cruel to kids.

Also reviewed in:
CHICAGO TRIBUNE, 11/26/97, Tempo/p. 1, Rick Kogan
NEW YORK TIMES, 11/26/97, p. E8, Janet Maslin
VARIETY, 11/24-30/97, p. 63, Joe Leydon
WASHINGTON POST, 11/26/97, p. B1, Stephen Hunter
WASHINGTON POST, 11/28/97, Weekend/p. 60, John F. Kelly

FOLLOW ME HOME

A New Millennia Films release. *Producer:* Alan Renshaw, Irene Romero, Peter Bratt, and Benjamin Bratt. *Director:* Peter Bratt. *Screenplay:* Peter Bratt. *Director of Photography:* Garett Griffin. *Editor:* Robert Grahamjones. *Music:* Cyril Neville Speech and Roy Finch. *Production Designer:* Katerina Keith. *Running time:* 104 minutes. *MPAA Rating:* Not Rated.

CAST: Alfre Woodard (Evey); Jesse Borrego (Tudee); Benjamin Bratt (Abel); Calvin Levels (Kaz); Steve Reevis (Freddy).

NEW YORK POST, 2/28/97, p. 44, Larry Worth

Ever heard the one about a group of troubled souls taking a physical and spiritual journey across America?

OK, been there, done that. But how about if the troubled souls are a mix of African-American, Native American and Hispanic American graffiti artists, all headed to the White House to do their thing on one of its walls?

Welcome to "Follow Me Home." Yes, it's "Easy Rider" meets the Rainbow Coalition, with the bickering sightseers agreeing only on the fact that "white people need a good kick in the motherf-----g a--."

They get to prove the point when running smack into a Yankee convention of Civil War-outfitted Crackers in the Midwest. Conveniently, that gives even the itinerant group's bad boy—a drug-imbibing, gun-toting, multi-tattooed misogynist—a chance to show his heroic side.

The rest of the film is just as manipulative, whether ripping off "Five Easy Pieces" with an incredibly labored restaurant scene or insulting filmgoers of all colors with its sophomoric, condescending tone and simplistic dialogue.

Speaking of dialogue, the script may set a record for repeated use of the word "bro," never mind howlingly cliched one-liners meant to sum up America's troubled race relations: "Am I a black dude?" one character rhetorically asks. "Why can't I just be a dude?"

As if all that's not heavy-handed enough to sink the project, first-time writer/director Peter Bratt inserts symbol-laden black-and-white dream sequences, poetry readings and slo-mo ventures into the surreal. "This is art," one of the, principals shouts, but viewers may need more convincing

Then there's the one-note acting. But its hard to fault Benjamin Bratt (virtually unrecognizable from his persona on TVs "Law and Order"), Jesse Borrego, Calvin Levels and Steve Reevis for failing to enliven walking stereotypes. Alfre Woodard's also along for the ride, but doesn't fare much better. What were they thinking?

Equally puzzling is why Salma "Fools Rush In" Hayek shows up and then disappears after a pointless cameo. Maybe she was just savvy enough to sum up the situation and cut her losses.

The others should have followed suit.

VILLAGE VOICE, 3/4/97, p. 72, Valerie Burgher

Two parts road flick and one part Rainbow Coalition rallying cry, *Follow Me Home* is an impressive cinematic step toward an Americanism of color.   Tudee, a West Coast Latino, convinces his working-class artist cronies—his wild-child cousin, a soft-spoken Native American, and an unsmiling Afro-spiritualist—to embark on a pilgrimage. They load up their van and prepare to take their talents to D.C., where they will adorn La Casa Blanca with murals representing "our colors' " En route through Nebraskan wheat fields the men encounter Evey (Alfre Woodard) and piss off a number of Civil War reenactment buffs who resent the brown boho presence riding roughshod over their fair state.

As always, Woodard brings a unique classiness to the role of the strong-willed mother. Few actresses could explain the difference between a woman and a 'ho with such conviction and lack of pretense.   Likewise, Benjamin Bratt transforms himself into Tudee's cousin Abel, a hyped-up *boricua* going on gangsta. Teeth yellowed from crack smoke, jeans riding low, and supplied with an ample lexicon of *hey, bro* and *shee-at,* Abel alternately slices through some of the more highfalutin' multiculturalist verbiage and drives much of the plot.

The brilliant desert colors and a mystical sensibility allow Tudee to float in and out of black-and-white dream states in which he battles a personification of The Man. But the potential p.c. clichés are deftly averted by screen-writer-director Peter Bratt's inventive flourishes: a gun-toting short-order cook who eloquently reminds the rowdy bunch that good manners are universal; a reconstructed Yankee who's been dumped for a Chinese meditation leader; children's rhymes that work magic. *Follow Me Home* occasionally preaches, but does so with an admirable message and distinctive style.

Also reviewed in:
NEW YORK TIMES, 2/28/97, p. C14, Stephen Holden
VARIETY, 3/18-24/96, p. 52, Derek Elley

FOOLS RUSH IN

A Columbia Pictures release. *Executive Producer:* Michael McDonnell. *Producer:* Doug Draizin. *Director:* Andy Tennant. *Screenplay:* Katherine Reback. *Story:* Joan Taylor and Katherine Reback. *Director of Photography:* Robbie Greenberg. *Editor:* Roger Bondelli. *Music:* Alan Silvestri. *Music Editor:* Andrew Silver. *Sound:* Peter J. Devlin. *Sound Editor:* John Morris. *Casting:* Juel Bestrop. *Production Designer:* Edward Pisoni. *Art Director:* David Crank. *Set Designer:* Evelyne Barbier. *Set Decorator:* Leslie Morales. *Special Effects:* Dennis Dion. *Costumes:* Kimberly A. Tillman. *Make-up:* Robin Siegel. *Stunt Coordinator:* Bob Jauregui. *Running time:* 105 minutes. *MPAA Rating:* PG-13.

CAST: Matthew Perry (Alex Whitman); Salma Hayek (Isabel Fuentes); Jon Tenney (Jeff); Carlos Gomez (Chuy); Tomas Milian (Tomas Fuentes); Siobhan Fallon (Lanie); John Bennett Perry (Richard Whitman); Stanley DeSantis (Judd Marshall); Suzanne Snyder (Cathy Stewart); Anne Betancourt (Amalia Fuentes); Jill Clayburgh (Nan Whitman); Angelina Calderon Torres (Great Grandma); Debby Shively (Donna); Mark Adair Rios (Juan Fuentes); Annie Combs (Dr. Lisa Barnes); Shelley Morrison (Aunt Carmen); Maria Cellario (Aunt Yolanda); Irene Hernandez (Aunt Rosa); Josh Cruze (Antonio Fuentes); Angela Lanza (Petra); Randy Sutton and Christopher Michael (Policemen at Dam); Angel Valdez (Carlos); Cesar Santana (Enrique); Garret Davis (Osha Rep); Chris O'Neill (Priest); John Tripp (Man in Lobby); Andrew Hill Newman (Assorted Cheeses); Chris Bauer (Phil); Douglas Weston (Hank); Rupert Baca (Porter); Jan Austell (Bruce Stewart); Cydney Arther (Diane Stewart); Leslie Silva (Process Server); Maryann Plunkett (Heliport Mother); Juel Mendel (Receptionist); Eddie Powers (Elvis); Salvafor Saldaña (Mariachi Singer).

LOS ANGELES TIMES, 2/14/97, Calendar/p. 6, Kevin Thomas

[The following review by Kevin Thomas appeared in a slightly different form in NEWSDAY, 2/14/97, Part II/p. B13.]

"Fools Rush In" is the kind of love story that Hollywood does better than anywhere else when it puts its mind to it. It has magic, glamour and romance yet never forgets that it's taking place in a recognizably real world. It also represents a major breakthrough for its stars, Matthew Perry (of TV's "Friends") and radiantly beautiful Salma Hayek. It's the perfect Valentine's Day release.

Perry plays a Manhattan go-getter sent to Las Vegas to oversee the construction and launching of the latest link in an international chain of nightclubs. Shortly after arriving in Vegas, Perry's Alex Whitman meets Hayek's Isabel Fuentes as they're waiting in a line for the restroom in a small, bustling Mexican restaurant. Isabel, an aspiring photographer, turns her considerable charm on the boyish Alex to let her go in ahead of him. Director Andy Tennant swiftly cuts to Isabel waking up in Alex's bed in his tract house.

Subsequently, Alex and his partner-pal (Jon Tenney) get their club project underway, and Isabel, who left Alex without so much as her last name or a phone number, is out of Alex's life until she appears three months later with the news that she is pregnant and he is the father of the child she is carrying. Alex launches on a "woman's right to choose" speech when she cuts him off, saying she, intends to keep the child, expects nothing from him whatsoever but feels that it is the only honorable thing to inform that he will be a father.

Screenwriter Katherine Reback, who wrote the film's original story with Joan Taylor, director Tennant and their gifted and charismatic stars take it from there with tremendous skill and charm. "Fools Rush In," which dares to take the time needed to set up its story properly, accrues substance and edge with the interplay of the cultures represented by Alex's WASP background and Isabel's proud Mexican American heritage. Distant from his own parents, Alex is told by Isabel that for her, "family is not something you put up with on a national holiday." Even so, she does feel that her relatives need to meet him at least once. You can be sure one thing leads to another.

Reback's script has real substance and perception, with Alex and Isabel emerging as individuals of depth and dimension, and their story is told with humor, passion and wit. "Fools Rush In," a film as good-looking and engaging as its stars, invites us to consider how well many people really know each other when they get married—and how crucial trust and candor are at any stage of any relationship.

NEW YORK POST, 2/14/97, p. 51, Michael Medved

Romantic comedies usually portray the process of lovers trying to get together, but "Fools Rush In" focuses on the more fascinating struggle of a newly married couple trying to stay together.

The result is an ideal date movie for the weekend after Valentine's Day; like other seasonal confections, it may not be particularly nourishing, but it's hard to resist such sentimental sweetness.

Matthew Perry (of TVs "Friends") plays a hard-driving yuppie from Manhattan who's assigned by his company to supervise construction of a new nightclub in Las Vegas. One Friday night in a Mexican restaurant he meets the lustrously beautiful, outspokenly emotional Salma Hayek (who made eye-catching appearances in "Desperado" and "From Dusk Till Dawn"), and they end up sharing a fleeting night of passion.

She then disappears from his life for three months, until turning up to announce that she's pregnant. Impulsively, they marry at an all-night wedding chapel (where a beaming Elvis impersonator gives away the bride), but must soon cope with rage from her loving, deeply religious, Mexican-American family, complete with four muscular, disapproving older brothers.

Meanwhile, his WASPy suburban Connecticut parents (Jill Clayburgh and Perry's real-life father, John Bennett Perry) assume that their boy's new bride is actually the cleaning lady when they first meet her.

Additional problems arise when Perry's career demands that he return to New York, despite his new wife's passionate desire to raise their child in Nevada, close to her family and the desert she loves.

Casting and chemistry are everything with this sort of fluff, and "Fools Rush In" hits the jackpot on both counts. Perry makes an appealing (and occasionally hilarious) leading man, with an everyman quality that effortlessly blends charm and vulnerability.

Hayek, meanwhile, is both a dazzling screen presence and a surprisingly nuanced actress who generates so much warmth (and heat) that whenever she's off screen you fairly ache for her return.

Director Andy Tennant (who previously handled the adorable kiddie comedy "It Takes Two") is hardly a master of subtlety or understatement, and he pushes the ethnic stereotypes further than absolutely necessary, but his big, splashy style feels warm-hearted and sincere.

The movie also offers a few good lines ("You are everything I never knew I always wanted") and a luscious musical score (by Alan Silvestri). All in all, you'd be a fool not to rush in to a picture so cunningly designed to place a smile on your face.

SIGHT AND SOUND, 10/97, p. 50, Peter Matthews

Whitman is an executive for a Manhattan-based company that designs and constructs night clubs. He is assigned a job in Las Vegas, where he meets Isabel Fuentes, a Mexican-American photographer who believes in destiny. The two have a one-night stand, but in the morning Isabel flits. Three months later, Isabel suddenly shows up and tells Alex that she's pregnant. Isabel plans to raise the baby alone, but she asks Alex to meet her family just once. Alex is moved by the Fuentes' close-knit spirit. Realising he loves Isabel, Alex proposes to her and the two are wed that night. The couple live happily until Alex states his intention of returning to New York after the club he has been working on opens. Isabel wants to stay near her relatives, and they argue about this until they agree to go east only after the baby is born.

Alex's parents Richard and Nan visit unexpectedly. The two sets of in-laws arrange to meet, but an argument between the two families only helps to emphasise the cultural chasm between the newlyweds. Alex's boss orders him back east to start up another club. When Isabel hears about his imminent departure, she storms off. Soon after, she claims to have lost the baby. Alex returns to New York and is shortly served with divorce papers. Cathy Stewart, an old friend who's always fancied Alex, asks him to join her on a sailing excursion. However, prompted by a series of mystical signs, Alex rushes off in search of Isabel. Alex finds her at the Hoover Dam, where he discovers that she is about to have the baby. Isabel has a girl, and the new parents are reunited just when their divorce is made final. They remarry, with their families in attendance, at the Grand Canyon.

If the *sine qua non* of romantic comedy is chemistry between the leads, then *Fools Rush In* only narrowly squeaks by. Playing the usual pair of kooky ill-matched lovers, Matthew Perry and Salma Hayek don't exactly light up the sky with mutually generated electricity. You don't especially believe that Hayek's character—the sensual Isabel—would discern her destiny in the form of a corporate dweeb like Perry's Alex. Granted, the screwball heroine's role is often to arrive from left field and liberate the hidebound hero's slumbering potential (a process certified by Alex's line "you are everything I never knew I always wanted"). But still, the two of them rarely suggest that precise complementarity of opposites which the genre sees as the perfect symbiotic union.

All the same, Perry and Hayek's pleasantness together is already enough to place the film a cut above such piteous dreck as *Forget Paris,* where Billy Crystal and Debra Winger seemed to gaze at each other with active loathing. However, sometimes a worse movie can be a 'better' one through the exemplary quality of its cruddiness. Nonetheless, *Fools Rush In* keeps so doggedly to a mean of pedestrian competence and unobjectionable mildness that it remains deeply uninteresting. You can't accuse the director Andy Tennant (director of the recent *It Takes Two*) of high style, but neither is he guilty of particular crassness. Indeed, his only visible trait is a penchant for those pop-scored montage sequences that gaily skip over the protagonists' lives and conflicts and save the film-maker the effort of dramatising them.

Fools Rush In creates the same anodyne impression. While it's refreshing that Las Vegas, where most of the story occurs, isn't depicted as the usual existential hellhole, at times it seems shot to resemble an infomercial from the Nevada tourist board. The panoramic views of Hoover Dam and the Grand Canyon do succeed in fostering an abstract kind of romanticism, but Tennant could have used cardboard sets and back projection for all that these locales feel organically connected to the characters' experience. The source of the problem lies in Katherine Reback's sketchy script, which floats Alex and Isabel in a sort of limbo where they are neither entertaining ciphers nor sharply observed human beings. The picture's premise is that this impulsive couple conduct their courtship backwards: they marry first and then date, only realising later the cultural differences between them.

It's not a bad gimmick, and it might have been carried out profitably in either of two ways. Reback could have gone for full-blown ethnic caricature, with Isabel's hot tamale sexiness and Catholicism rubbing provocatively against Alex's tight-assed WASP propriety. Equally, she could have honed it down to an everyday texture of small frictions. There are intimations of this latter approach in a few tentative, blobby scenes where the duo thrash out their feelings and grope towards a fragile truce. But as if she feared alienating the audience with too much interiority, Reback makes a half-hearted feint at the burlesque option as well. Thus the movie can find no better way of illustrating Alex's disaffection from nature than to stick his behind with cactus prickles after a hunting expedition goes horribly wrong. However, this cartoon register also results in one of the best moments (only seconds long) when Alex's upper-crust parents' faces express synchronised panic when first introduced to Isabel and then instantly recover with expressions of glazed social politeness.

The big quandary of the story is whether our twosome will continue to take it easy in Vegas or join the rat race in New York. It's perhaps symptomatic that while this issue is prodded and probed through nearly the entire running time, the film-makers leave it hanging like a loose tooth at the end. Instead, one gets fobbed off with the idea that babies are universal sticking plasters, rather than the start of a whole new round of frictions. But the only real suspense in the film is whether Matthew Perry (Chandler in the sitcom *Friends*) can hack it as a leading man. He's acceptable, even if his mannerisms—the bunched-up eyebrows, hangdog mouth and twitchy body movements—feed off his befuddled small-screen persona. The trouble with a snappy, lightweight television performer like Perry is that he tends to cut a movie down to his size.

VILLAGE VOICE, 2/18/97, p. 84, Justine Elias

Wake up, young lovers! Do you find a good scare preferable to treacly romantic comedies? The fearsomely inept romance *Fools Rush In* is the last word in cinematic terror. Bad omen number one: the tide's lifted from an old song. Number two: it stars a bewildered sitcom refugee, Matthew Perry of *Friends*. And number three: it's an autobiographical vanity project by two zany producers who are now divorced. Perry plays a workaholic New Yorker who's sent to Las Vegas to oversee the opening of a theme restaurant. There he meets his match in Salma Hayek, cast once again as a quirky Mexican American spitfire. (Her character's described in press notes as "fiery"—¡Ay, caliente! Perry is, of course, an uptight WASP—¡Not especially caliente!) They have sex, get pregnant, marry, and then fall in love. As is typical in comedies of this type, both have cynical throaty-voiced confidants who advise them to bail out of the rocky relationship. Former *Saturday Night Live* performer Siobhan Fallon takes the Janeane Garofalo role, and Jon Tenney is a likable sharpster. Both of these able supporting actors try mightily not to upstage the stars; they fail. Director Andy Tennant is fond of Chamber of Commerce-style montages that explain, for the 20th time, where the story is taking place. I haven't seen this much stock footage since *Godzilla's Revenge*.

Also reviewed in:
NEW YORK TIMES, 2/14/97, p. C14, Janet Maslin
VARIETY, 2/17-23/97, p. 69, Todd McCarthy
WASHINGTON POST, 2/14/97, p. B7, Rita Kempley
WASHINGTON POST, 2/14/97, Weekend/p. 68, Desson Howe

FOR EVER MOZART

A New Yorker Films release of a Vega Film/Aventura Films/Périphéria/ECM production. *Executive Producer:* Jean-Luc Godard. *Producer:* Ruth Waldburger and Alain Sarde. *Director:*

Jean-Luc Godard. *Screenplay (French with English subtitles):* Jean-Luc Godard. *Director of Photography:* Christophe Pollack. *Editor:* Michael Ripps and James Mitchell. *Music:* David Darling, Ketil Bjornstad, Ben Harper, and Györgi Kurtag. *Sound:* François Musy and Olivier Burgaud. *Production Designer:* Ivan Niclass. *Costumes:* Marina Zuliani. *Running time:* 84 minutes. *MPAA Rating:* Not Rated.

CAST: Vicky Messica (Vicky Vitalis, the Director); Madeleine Assas (Camille, the Director's Daughter); Frédéric Pierrot (Jerome, Camille's Lover); Ghalya Lacroix (Camille and Vicky's Arab Maid); Bérangére Allaux (The Actress in "The Fatal Boléro").

CHRISTIAN SCIENCE MONITOR, 7/9/97, p. 14, David Sterritt

Cinema superstar Jean-Luc Godard is making a comeback. This is important news, because it means his stimulating brand of filming will be accessible to a much wider audience than it has had in recent years.

It's even more important if it signals a change in American moviegoing, which would benefit from more openness to works that challenge the sensationalism and commercialism of many Hollywood products.

Whatever the deeper meanings of the development, Godard's films are definitely finding increased visibility on American screens. His newest movie, "For Ever Mozart," is his first picture in several years to have a regular US release, courtesy of New Yorker Films.

At the same time, filmmaker Martin Scorsese and Strand Releasing are presenting a revival of "Contempt," Godard's 1963 masterpiece starring Michel Piccoli as a French screenwriter, Brigitte Bardot as his discontented wife, Jack Palance as a high-powered producer, and legendary director Fritz Lang as himself.

Godard launched France's powerful New Wave movement with his energetic "Breathless" almost 40 years ago, and to this day he inspires high praise. A fellow filmmaker has called him "the one ... who never disappoints me," and a noted critic has hailed "Contempt" as not just a fine movie but "the greatest work of art produced in postwar Europe."

American moviegoers are less receptive to European pictures than they were in the 1960s, however, when Godard's visits to the United States were major events for countless admirers. Compounding this difficulty is the challenging nature of Godard's work, which calls on audiences to shed Hollywood-style viewing habits. While ordinary movies encourage us to be passive consumers, he craves an audience that's alert, engaged, and critical.

"For Ever Mozart" demands just such an attitude, and its success in US theaters may indicate whether the Godard revival will gather more momentum. The main character is a filmmaker whose new picture goes astray when he can't find the proper cast. He goes to work on a theatrical production in Sarajevo instead, but this runs aground as the Bosnian war hurtles toward the city. Godard sees the horrors of war as a symbol for modern greediness and materialism. What he cries out for in their place is a rebirth of art, which can heal society by guiding it toward higher, more refined values.

With its references to wartime savagery and vulgarity in the entertainment world, "For Ever Mozart" is itself less refined than some moviegoers might wish. But its messages are uplifting and its cinematic beauty is breathtaking. It's also very funny—as when it begins its Mozartean voyage with a passage from one of Beethoven's most beloved pieces!

LOS ANGELES TIMES, 9/26/97, Calendar/p. 21, Kevin Thomas

What a smart move the Nuart has made in presenting each night a different major Jean-Luc Godard film as a second feature to his latest, "For Ever Mozart," which opens a one-week run today. That's because "For Ever Mozart"—pared down and elliptical to the utmost—is the most impenetrable picture in his current cycle of work.

Those who find it difficult to get a purchase on this picture might well welcome another chance to see such Godard classics as "Breathless" (the second feature tonight) or even less familiar films such as "Tout Va Bien" (Tuesday's second feature).

Visually, "For Ever Mozart" is typically ravishing, and it has Godard's usual barrage of aphorisms, declarations and pronouncements as well as inspired use of music. Invariably, Godard lets us make connections for ourselves, but here that task is more daunting than usual. The one—

and overriding—connection that is clear enough is that Godard is contrasting warfare—specifically the war in Bosnia—and filmmaking. He discovers them both to be cruel, calamitous and often darkly comical enterprises, fraught with peril from the outset.

The film opens, probably in Switzerland, with a veteran film director, Vicky Vitalis (Vicky Messica), finding it impossible to cast his newest project. It is a war film inspired by Spanish novelist Juan Goytisolo's observation that "the history of the 1990s in Europe is a rehearsal, with slight symphonic variations, of the cowardice and chaos of the 1930s."

Vitalis then agrees to help his daughter Camille (Madeleine Assas) and her lover (Frédéric Pierrot) in their attempt to stage Alfred de Musset's comedy "One Must Not Play at Love" to cheer up the citizens of Sarajevo.

The well-intentioned but naive and innocently condescending members of this enterprise, including Camille and Vicky's Arab maid Dzamilla (Ghalya Lacroix) get caught up in the crossfire of the war in Bosnia with tragic results.

Vitalis, however, had already departed and revives his project, his politically critical "The Fatal Boléro," which allows Godard to satirize the ignominy of trying to make serious movies in the era of the American mega-blockbusters. While Vitalis is clearly Godard's alter ego, he physically more closely resembles Fritz Lang as he appeared in Godard's "Contempt."

(Intriguingly, the difficulty Vitalis has in getting his "Boléro" actress to utter a single word of dialogue is identical to a struggle Lang had with Marilyn Monroe while making "Clash by Night"; only the word is different.)

What makes "For Ever Mozart" worth grappling with, beyond the incontestable stature of its relentlessly uncompromising maker, are Godard's doubts is to whether film truly possesses the redemptive power of art when it comes to dealing with the horrors of war. (Significantly, Godard's publicly expressed his wish that Steven Spielberg had not made "Schindler's List.")

"Knowledge of the possibility of representation consoles us for being enslaved to life. Knowledge of life consoles us for the fact that representation [i.e., cinema] is but shadow," Godard says. When it comes to redemption, Godard, at the end of this densest of films, leaves that to the music of Mozart.

NEW YORK POST, 7/4/97, p. 32, Thelma Adams

My favorite Jean-Luc is the Enterprise's bald captain, not the pedantic French auteur. In "For Ever Mozart," Godard continues his tradition of serious filmmaking spiced with naked ladies. Even Milos Forman, in his "Amadeus," understood that geniuses, like Mozart, aren't serious 24 hours a day.

Godard's cinematic symphony in four movements finds the Director chasing down familiar themes and sulky young women. At the beginning, the Director (note rumpled raincoat, battered fedora, tobacco-stained fingers) is raising money for a new film, the cheerfully titled "The Fatal Bolero."

In the second movement, the Director pursues, then abandons, Albert Camus' unemployed granddaughter. The restless actress (Madeleine Assas) goes to Sarajevo to perform Musset under fire. (Think American college students making the pilgrimage to Nicaragua in the '80s.) She and her fellow travelers are captured, tortured and worse—but not before Godard shoots the women in their undies.

The war scenes are amateurish, despite references to American director John Ford. The locals are comic extras in their own tragedy, the Bilkos of Bosnia. Godard is more comfortable with the fetishes of death. Note the pale flesh, the sensual turn of the foot, in the hastily dug, open grave.

In the second half of "For Ever Mozart," the Director continues his insurgent battle for art against commerce. If you've seen Godard's 1963 model, "Contempt," now at the Film Forum, you'll recognize that this dead horse is as beaten and bloodied as a Bosnian militiaman.

The Director's film-within-the-film dramatizes scenes of Camus' granddaughter, recycling earlier dialogue for those who need a review of Lesson One. To play the philosophizing actress, he employs a woman plucked naked from a corpse heap. He dresses her in an extravagant red costume that looks fabulous against the seaside location.

Throughout, Godard drops quotes on cinema and representation that he was citing over 30 years ago. Without crediting Bazin, as in "Contempt," a character states: "Cinema replaces our gaze with a world in harmony with our hearts." When Godard mentions Musset, Goya, Corneille, Racine, it's high-brow namedropping, the cinematic equivalent of boldface.

In the final movement, "For Ever Mozart" drags its survivors to a concert hall, where a young pianist performs Mozart. Godard's symphony ends with the Director crumpled at the top of a stairway in the symphony hall, virtually at the feet of genius, of Mozart. It's a redemptive moment that can hardly be taken as seriously as Godard takes himself.

TIME, 4/4/97, p. 67, Richard Corliss

Two nude corpses lie on a beach. Then someone quickly covers their bodies: the man's with a tuxedo, the woman's with a formal red dress.

It seems a restoration of dignity after death, but it is only the rough bustle of filmmaking: the corpses are actors, and they must get dressed for the next shot.

This scene, from Jean-Luc Godard's poignant, invigorating *For Ever Mozart*, lasts only a few seconds—yet it serves as a surreal image, a joke and a requiem. After 40 years, Godard can still astonish and amuse in the cinematic shorthand he virtually created. Now two of his films, both about moviemaking, are on view: the 1995 *For Ever Mozart* and *Contempt*, his 1963 meditation on sex, lies and celluloid, newly restored after long being out of theatrical circulation. So it's time to praise Godard for what he was and still is.

His early films—*Breathless, My Life to Live, A Married Woman, Masculine-Feminine*—were acerbic love stories set in Left Bank cafés, sketches of men and women rubbing each other raw, arguing, smoking, drinking, anecdoting their lives away. The scenarios, rambling and aphoristic, could have been scrawled on napkins; their emotions were spiked with absinthe. Films poured out of Godard, two or three a year, and each was an incendiary device—an event for his admirers, an affront to the cinematic status quo. Andrew Sarris called him "the analytical conscience of the modern cinema." Because of Godard, it seemed, movies would never be the same.

Thirty years later, movies are samer than ever—more conservative, more in the thrall of spectacle and sensation. And Godard ... is he still around? In fact, he made 15 films in the '80s, nine more in the '90s. A man in *Mozart* says, "There's no such thing as grownups." Godard, who'll be 67 this year, still has the intellectual energy—the need to know and show everything—of a precocious child.

Contempt is hardly Godard's best or most evocative work, but it exposes his feelings for the seductive lie of movies: that "cinema replaces our gaze with a world in harmony with our desires" (the same line is quoted in *For Ever Mozart*). A French playwright (Michel Piccoli) is hired for a rewrite job by an American producer (Jack Palance) who has eyes for the writer's sexy wife (Brigitte Bardot). With its polyglot cast and mixed-doubles leering, *Contempt* gets the Babel and Babylon of filmmaking down perfectly.

The film's own behind-the-scenes story is also instructive. When producer Carlo Ponti saw the finished film, he was upset at the absence of Bardot nudity. Godard then shot the famous opening scene, of Bardot asking Piccoli if he likes her eyes, breasts, ass—a catalog that commercializes her body, just as Ponti demanded—and Piccoli replying that he loves her "totally, tenderly, tragically."

Godard has always been a canny guerrilla. He knows that film is an expensive art, that someone must subsidize his midnight raids on the prevailing culture. So he subverts the typical narrative by using all the handsome old tools. *Contempt* has movie stars, guns, car crashes, wide screen, beautiful color, the cliffs of Capri, the most rapturous music (by Georges Delerue), its violins sawing and soaring like Philip Glass in ecstasy). And, always, pretty women. A Ziegfeld of the Left Bank, Godard reinvented Jean Seberg and discovered Anna Karina, Juliet Berto, Maruschka Detmers, Myriem Roussel, Juliette Binoche, Julie Delpy—glories of Gallic cinema. In *Contempt* he saves Bardot from cheesecake notoriety. She's smart, sensitive, brutal, doomed.

"War is easy," says a woman in *Mozart*. "It's sticking a piece of metal in a piece of flesh." Moviemaking, though, is hard. Here a crew is in Sarajevo to film an adaptation of Alfred de Musset. The Bosnian war, its carnage everywhere evident, is reflected in the rancor of the filmmakers. An actress must try, hundreds of times, to say the word *oui* correctly; the accountant refuses to sign any more checks. At the end of the war, and the end of the century, are we near the end of our rope? One man thinks so. "When I look at the sky," he says, "I only see what has disappeared." This could be Godard, musing on an art form near exhaustion. Yet he gives the lie to this cynicism in scene after scene of dark beauty. Could he be not the Picasso of cinema but its Mozart?

Toward the end of *For Ever Mozart*, a kid standing in line for the movie we have just seen hears the plot and says, "Let's go see *Terminator 4*." But Godard's films are worth seeing for his encyclopedic with the glamour of his imagery, the doggedness of a man who won't give up on modernism. His crabby films are, in truth, breathlessly romantic—because he keeps searching for first principles in the pettiest human affairs. Godard gazes at the intimate and finds the infinite.

VILLAGE VOICE, 7/8/97, p. 74, Amy Taubin

In the '60s, Jean-Luc Godard made films about art, sexual obsession, and death, though not necessarily in that order. Now in his sixties, Godard makes films about art and death, with sex barely in the picture. "What? No boobs?" whines an outraged filmgoer, standing in line for *Fatal Bolero*, the film within Godard's 1996 *For Ever Mozart*. "Your fucking film is full of corpses? Let's go to *Terminator 4* instead."

Godard's two great films of the '90s—*Germany Year 90 Nine Zero* and *JLG By JLG*—dealt with the death of communism and cinema *(Germany)* and the death of cinema and the director's personal intimations of morality *(JLG)*. After only one viewing, I'm not sure that *For Ever Mozart* is quite in the same league with those two films; I have no doubt, however, that it's the most straight-forward and profound of the films Godard has made about war, beginning with *Les Carabiniers* and including all the work he did under the banner of the Dziga Vertov collective. In other words, it's pretty damn important, and pretty damn moving to boot—which makes its exclusion from the 1996 New York Film Festival pretty damn inexplicable.

Proceeding perhaps from the homily that on the battlefield, the explosion you hear is never the one that kills you, *For Ever Mozart* is a film in which image and sound are disjoined from the start. As the title *For Ever Mozart* bounces onto the screen, we hear a fragment of Beethoven's "Emperor" concerto (written by an Austrian composer to celebrate the victory of a French general who had delusions of unifying all of Europe under his rule). Immediately after that we see a group of men and women chasing after one another and we hear one of the men calling "Sabine, Sabine" suggesting that before we eventually find our way to Mozart, we will have to go through some contemporary version of the rape of the Sabine women. With Godard, the end is always present in the beginning.

A movie director (whose face and voice resemble Godard's but whose world-weary demeanor is closer to Fritz Lang's in *Contempt)*, is preparing a film about war based on the Spanish novelist Juan Goytisolo's claim that "the history of the 1990s in Europe is a rehearsal, with slight symphonic variations, of the cowardice and chaos of the 1930s" The director's daughter, her male cousin, and the family's Arab maid are simultaneously getting ready to go to Sarajevo to put on a theatrical production of Musset's *One Mustn't Play at Love*.

Wandering in the Bosnian countryside, the actors are captured, raped, forced to dig their own graves, and killed in the crossfire when their captors are ambushed by another guerrilla group. "War is simple. It's sticking a piece of metal in flesh" says one of the characters in the film within the film, but this battle scene—as formally precise as it's emotionally devastating—is anything but simple.

Singularly unaffected by the death of his daughter, the director, who's shooting his war epic, refuses to film the battle scenes his gangster producer demands. (He must know we've seen enough of them already.) Instead, he gets stuck doing endless retakes of a single page of dialogue when his leading actress is unable to say the word "yes" to his satisfaction.

"I told you you should have turned the page" says the director's assistant when the opening-day audience rejects the film, leaving the director's career in ruins. Those who haven't rushed off to see *T4* wind up at a concert where one young man is drafted to be the page turner for the piano soloist who is performing a Mozart concerto. Outside the director sits on the stairs, half listening as he smokes a cigarette.

In confronting the failure of art to change the course of history and the moral obligation of the artist to nevertheless bear witness to her/his time, *For Ever Mozart* treads on ground so familiar it can only be played as farce. What's extraordinary about the film is the elegance, grace, and gallows humor with which it deals with issues of form, beauty, classicism—and with why Godard, who in my book is the greatest filmmaker of all time, cannot be Mozart. In the age of unreason, a beautiful image (there's not a single frame in this film that's less than ravishingly beautiful) does not lead logically and inevitably to another. Instead, they collide, fragment, and fly apart. Seductive as they are, page turners belong to the past.

Also reviewed in:
NEW YORK TIMES, 7/7/97, p. C14, Stephen Holden
NEW YORKER, 7/14/97, p. 85, Terrence Rafferty
VARIETY, 9/16-22/96, p. 70, David Stratton

FOR RICHER OR POORER

A Universal Pictures and The Bubble Factory release of a Sheinberg production in association with Yorktown Productions. *Executive Producer:* Richard Baker, Rick Messina, and Gayle Fraser Baigelman. *Producer:* Sid Sheinberg, Bill Sheinberg, and Jon Sheinberg. *Director:* Bryan Spicer. *Screenplay:* Jana Howington and Steve Lukanic. *Director of Photography:* Buzz Feitshans IV. *Editor:* Russell Denove. *Music:* Randy Edelman. *Music Editor:* Joanie Diener and J.J. George. *Choreographer:* Jeanie Love. *Sound:* Jim Sabat and (music) Elton Ahi. *Sound Editor:* Richard LeGrand, Jr. *Casting:* Victoria Burrows. *Production Designer:* Stephen Hendrickson. *Art Director:* Bob Shaw. *Set Decorator:* Beth Kushnick. *Set Dresser:* Elizabeth Weber. *Special Effects:* Joey DiGaetano. *Costumes:* Abigail Murray. *Make-up:* Bernadette Mazur. *Stunt Coordinator:* Walt Scott and Gary Hymes. *Running time:* 122 minutes. *MPAA Rating:* PG-13.

CAST: Tim Allen (Brad Sexton); Kirstie Alley (Caroline Sexton); Jay O. Sanders (Samuel Yoder); Michael Lerner (Phil Kleinman); Wayne Knight (Bob Lachman); Larry Miller (Derek Lester); Miguel A. Nunez, Jr. (Frank Hall); Megan Cavanagh (Levinia Yoder); John Pyper-Ferguson (Henner Lapp); Carrie Preston (Rebecca Yoder); Ethan Phillips (Jerry); John Caponera (Dave); Katie Moore (Anna Yoder); Bobby Steggert (Samuel, Jr.); Michael Angarano (Sammy); Rosemary Knower (Grandma Yoder); David Harscheid (Grandpa Yoder); Hunter Stover and Scout Stover (Baby Yoder); June Claman (Judge Northcutt); Marla Maples (Cynthia); Holly Rudkin (Mary); Crystal Bock (Penny); Monica Deeter (Hanna Yoder); Richard Pelzman (Jonathan Yoder); Madeline Mager (Sarah); Terrence Currier (Elder Joseph); Hal Henderson (Elder Thomas); Michael Howell (Bailiff); Johanna Cox (Emma Yoder); Stefan Aleksander (Jacob Yoder); Holly Atkinson (Teller); Emily Chamberlain (Evelyn); Anthony Azizi (Taxi Driver); David Maples (IRS agent); Markus Flanagan (George); Wes Johnson (Tourist Man); Rick Foucheux (Tom); Drenda Spohnholtz (Waitress); Marla Sucharetza (Stacy).

LOS ANGELES TIMES, 12/12/97, Calendar/p. 18, Kevin Thomas

The chemistry between Tim Allen and Kirstie Alley is so good it's too bad that "For Richer or Poorer" isn't as much fun as they are.

They're cast as a Donald and Ivana Trump-like couple who've soured on each other after 10 years of marriage. They put on a good show for their 10th wedding anniversary, which also serves as a promotion for Allen's latest real estate venture, a thunderingly tasteless Holy Land theme park.

Never fear, the park is not to be, for their accountant (Wayne Knight) has robbed them blind, and they're soon fleeing arrest for tax fraud in a stolen Manhattan taxi, which veers off the road into a pond in the heart of Pennsylvania's Amish country. There, they manage to pass themselves off to a kindly Amish family, headed by Jay O. Sanders and Megan Cavanagh, as relatives visiting from Missouri. You can pretty much take it from there: Hard work and clean living have their salutary effect on the couple's values and regard for each other.

Jana Howington and Steve Lukanic have written well-developed parts for the stars who shine under Bryan Spicer's direction, and they treat Amish customs with affectionate respect. The film's biggest problem is that at nearly two hours it's simply too long for a romantic comedy and that too often its humor is broader than the side of an Amish barn, which undercuts the film's more credible intimate moments. The writers get off some zinging lines, but the film's scale and garish tone are too artificial to encourage suspension of disbelief. Indeed, the spoiled nouveau riche couple are so transparently phony in their Amish gear that we have to leave open the possibility that their Amish hosts aren't fooled for a second.

Still, it is a pleasure to see such pros as Allen and Alley, seasoned by the discipline of TV sitcom, play off each other so well. Michael Lerner lends credibility as the kind of take-charge attorney we all wish we could afford if we got into trouble, and Marla Maples and the Plaza Hotel are on hand just in case we don't make the satiric Trump connection. Allen and Alley, who make an attractive and believable couple, never miss a beat. Unfortunately, that's not the case with "For Richer or Poorer."

NEW YORK POST, 12/12/97, p. 56, Larry Worth

Early on in "For Richer or Poorer," Tim Allen rests against the posterior of Wall Street's raging bull statue and declares: "This is bulls--t."

Truer words were never spoken.

This oh-so-lame comedy's plot teams Allen with Kirstie Alley, another TV star, whose abilities are better show-cased on the small screen. Here, they play Mr. and Mrs. Nouveau Riche Yuppie Scum, who flee their Manhattan penthouse after making the IRS' most-wanted list.

Minutes later, the battling Bickersons show up in Intercourse (yuk, yuk), Pa. So, in the heart of Amish country, the materialistic city slickers don Mennonite attire and try to blend in with their God-fearing neighbors.

Those who howl at the thought of farmer Allen plowing a field in zigzag patterns, milkmaid Alley getting squirted by an errant udder or the twosome engaging in a high-speed car chase that lands them in a mud pond are in for a treat. All others should head for the hills.

That includes the Amish, who—a la last year's "Kingpin"—are treated in a stupid, downright offensive manner. A moratorium on "Children of the Corn" jokes would be a start. Then again, those who paid the price of admission aren't treated any better.

Quality control isn't a priority for director Bryan Spicer, as demonstrated with his ham-fisted efforts on "Mighty Morphin Power Rangers: The Movie" and "McHale's Navy." This time around, his idea of a hoot is exemplified by a Jerusalem theme park featuring Bedouin breakfasts. 'Nuff said?

OK, so the film's lacking in humor and originality. But can't it at least be brief? Apparently not. At 122 minutes, it's 10 minutes longer than the drama to which it so often alludes, Peter Weir's "Witness."

Whatever funny moments result—and they're few and far between—basically come from stars Allen and Alley. But once they stop yelling at each other, the pair try to be credible as their characters rediscover their kinder, gentler selves. It's a valiant struggle.

In supporting roles, the versatile Jay O. Sanders is sadly wasted as the Mennonite clan leader—complete with glue-on beard—while Marla Maples was clearly hired to deliver her line: "I'm just glad someone's happily married, even if it's not moi." A real talent, that Marla.

And things only go downhill from there, as "For Richer or Poorer" forsakes better for worse.

NEWSDAY, 12/12/97, Part II/p. B9, John Anderson

There is a type of film, rare though it may be, that provides a blissful immersion in another world, while at the same time it elevates our minds and—yes—our very lives to a better, finer, more graceful state of being ... a film that transcends the mundane, the insensitive, the crass, the pedestrian ... a film that fulfills the oft-broken promise of cinema, that touches our souls, that may even make us better people.

And then there is that kind of film which, from its opening moments, makes you want to tear your own head from your shoulders.

"For Richer or Poorer," ladies and gentlemen, is that movie.

Starring Tim Allen and Kirstie Alley, two performers whose careers should be the subject of an "X-Files" episode, this Bryan ("McHale's Navy") Spicer-directed comedy contains the kind of contradictions of which, perhaps, only a big-budget studio movie is capable. While everything about it screams money, it wants to tell us that money isn't everything. While it gets a lot of mileage snickering at a simple, sectarian lifestyle, in this case the Amish, it also wants to assure the audience that said lifestyle is superior to theirs. And despite the fact that the best comedies have always been 90 minutes or less, it insists on prolonging both our mutual agony and a tired old plot for more than two hours. "For Richer or Poorer" does get better however marginally—as it goes along, although at no time do you have any doubt where it's going. Brad Sexton (Allen), an ostentatious entrepreneurial gas bag, uses his 10th anniversary party to pitch his latest project—Holyland, a theme park "inspired by God himself." Such behavior does nothing for his image, or his marriage to the shrewish Caroline (Alley), who promptly asks for a divorce.

Ah, but divine intervention arrives via the IRS, which wants to nail Brad and Caroline for tax fraud, even though their violations are all the work of Brad's sweaty accountant Bob (Wayne Knight), who promptly takes it on the lam—as do Brad and Caroline, who find themselves among the Mennonites.

Further exploration of the plot would be pointless, since you already know what happens. Any exploration of the insultingly obvious illogic of the story would be futile, because "For Richer or Poorer" already has everything that makes for a big-screen success, which is smallscreen stars.

But it simply isn't funny. Allen, the "Home Improvement" star and Alley, of "Cheers" and now "Veronica's Closet," are tiresome and shrill at the outset of the film; when they make peace, it's worse. The jokes are older than an Amish couture (something Caroline, in one of the movie's more tasteless episodes, sets out to tart up). And even though the lampooning of the IRS and its agents—via Larry Miller's mercenary Derek Lester—may gratify a lot of people, it doesn't atone for the other endless minutes of unrelenting shtick.

SIGHT AND SOUND, 11/98, p. 49, Edward Lawrenson

New York City. Caroline Sexton demands a divorce from her husband Brad after they return home from their wedding-anniversary party. The following day, Brad, the unwitting victim of tax fraud by his accountant Bob Lachman, escapes from gun-touting IRS agent Derek Lester in a stolen taxi, inadvertently picking up Caroline along the way.

Brad crashes near an Amish settlement named Intercourse, and at the village store overhears that a local family, the Yoders, are expecting the arrival of their married cousins from Missouri. Brad and Caroline turn up at the Yoders' door, dressed as Amish and passing themselves off as the cousins. Over the next few weeks, Brad helps out on the farm, Caroline in the home. Slowly they grow fond of their hosts and fall in love again. At the wedding of the Yoders' daughter Rebecca and Henner, a local youth, Lester appears and exposes Brad and Caroline as impostors. At their trial, Brad's lawyer Phil Kleinman arrives with Bob, who confesses to tax fraud. Brad and Caroline are acquitted.

Early on in *For Richer or Poorer*, a snippet from *It Happened One Night* (1934) is glimpsed on a television set. What director Bryan Spicer *(Mighty Morphin Power Rangers: The Movie, McHale's Navy)* was thinking about in including such a clip is anyone's guess, but one thing is clear: apart from the comic couple-on-the-run plot structure, this achingly unfunny film is about as far as anyone could get from Frank Capra's classic. Expecting us to laugh at the very mention of the word "Intercourse" (the name of the Sextons' adopted Amish village), or the sight of Kirstie Alley slipping in pig shit, the comic world of *For Richer or Poorer* seems as wilfully out of synch with the sensibilities of today's audience as the Amish settlement is to the uncomprehending Sextons. Offering a relentless onslaught of weak *double entendres* and shameless mugging, *For Richer or Poorer* is closest in tone to the very worst of the *Carry On* series—the ones even the most revisionist of cultural critics now prefer to forget.

Worse still, *For Richer or Poorer* lacks *Carry On*'s trademark irreverence for all things serious which at least excused the bad jokes. Once the Sextons knuckle down with the Amish, a lazy sentimentality takes hold. As a crass, Donald Trump style tycoon, Brad Sexton might have been a vehicle for some fun among the simple, trusting Amish, but Tim Allen struggles unconvincingly in the part. It's only when he lends a hand around the farm that he hits his stride. Fixing up carts, struggling manfully to plough a field, Allen effectively reprises his role as Tim Taylor, the

DIY enthusiast he played in the US sitcom *Home Improvement*. The Amish of this film—neighbourly types who take pride in their property and pleasure in the simple, small things of life—present less an alternative to mainstream America (as they did in Peter Weir's *Witness*) than an embodiment of the suburban values which made *Home Improvement* such wholesome (and dull) viewing.

Glimpses of the wicked knockabout *For Richer or Poorer* could have been are provided by the ever reliable Alley's reaction to her changed circumstances. At one point, she disgustedly sums up the Amish who have kindly taken her in: "They're like Children of the Corn." This, one of the film's few funny lines, also has a mawkish truth to it: over the course of events, Alley's conversion from shopaholic to homemaker and loving wife suggests it's not the Amish she's been living with but the good folk of Stepford.

VILLAGE VOICE, 12/23/97, p. 79, Gary Dauphin

That Amish people make funny backdrops (funny ha-ha and funny peculiar) is a Hollywood truism, the dark hats and drawn carriages instantly promising comedy á la *Kingpin* or riffs on cultural difference á la *For Richer or Poorer* is a definite comedy-yuck-type movie, as it takes a glitzy, predivorce New York couple on the run from the IRS (tube boobs Tim Allen and Kirstie Alley) and plops them down in Amish country. It's the start of harvest season, all the better to reap the obvious fish-out-of water hilarity and a side yield of sensitive, interpersonal discovery. On the yuck end, real estate mogul Tim plows a field by fast-walking the horse (yuck yuck) while society maven Kirstie puts on a fashion show to introduce the local ladies-who-scrub to colors like "aubergine" (yuck). On the really yucky but purportedly sensitive end it seems that living in a religiously enforced time warp cleans Kirstie and Tim's relationship palates (like a bracing orthodox sorbet, perhaps), thereby allowing them to, you know, savor the sweetness of true love.

None of this is particularly egregious as big-screen vehicles for sitcom stars go, and these leads do come up with some chemistry, albeit a creepy kind (Tim and Kirstie approach the comic reinvigoration of marriage like two people who've just discovered that wonderful erection-producing pill). Still, *For Richer or Poorer* is a direly predictable, only intermittently funny movie. Given Tim Allen's Middle American megastardom and perhaps Kirstie Alley's eyebrows, it'll make millions. But *Kingpin* (or even Weird Al's rapping Amish) it ain't.

Also reviewed in:
NEW YORK TIMES, 12/12/97, p. E16, Lawrence Van Gelder
VARIETY, 12/8-14/97, p. 111, Leonard Klady
WASHINGTON POST, 12/12/97, p. C6, Stephen Hunter

FOR ROSEANNA

A Fine Line Features release. *Executive Producer:* Ruth Vitale, Mark Ordesky, Jonathan Weisgal, and Miles Donnelly. *Producer:* Paul Trijbits, Alison Owen, and Dario Poloni. *Director:* Paul Weiland. *Screenplay:* Saul Turteltaub. *Director of Photography:* Henry Braham. *Editor:* Martin Walsh. *Music:* Trevor Jones. *Casting:* Nina Gold. *Production Designer:* Rod McLean. *Costumes:* Annie Hardinge. *Running time:* 99 minutes. *MPAA Rating:* PG-13.

CAST: Jean Reno (Marcello); Mercedes Ruehl (Roseanna); Polly Walker (Cecilia); Mark Frankel (Antonio); Giuseppe Cederna (Father Bramilla); Renato Scarpa (Dr. Benvenuto); Luigi Diberti (Capestro); Roberto Della Casa (Rossi); Trevor Peacock (Iaccoponi); Fay Ripley (Francesca); George Rossi (Sgt. Baggio); Romano Ghini (Umberto).

LOS ANGELES TIME, 7/2/97, Calendar/p. 10, John Anderson

[The following review by John Anderson appeared in a slightly different form in NEWSDAY, 6/18/97, Part II/p. B2.]

Its lead actors are about as Italian as steak and kidney pie—in Bearnaise sauce, with a side of slaw. But "For Roseanna" has its charms, which do not include that cloying title but do include a cast that makes what might have been a trifle into a whimsical, bitter-sweet romance.

And by romance, we don't necessarily mean straining bustiers and perspiring peasants (although British actress Polly Walker is dutifully distracting). Striving for an "Il Postino"-like rusticity and native charm, "For Roseanna" is about people and the character thereof. And its three stars—Walker, French demi-idol Jean Reno and American virtuoso Mercedes Ruehl—make those characters buyable if not totally believable; insane, but certainly endearing.

The film also does what any ethnicized soap opera is supposed to: make itself universal. That it happens to take place in an insular, less-than-postcard-perfect Italian village allows the kind of internecine sniping and enforced intimacy that occur in small, tight communities. But it might as easily have taken place in Lindenhurst as Tuscany.

Or in Travento, which is where the discombobulated Marcello (Reno) is busy keeping everyone alive. He's very concerned about the local birth of twins (Is everyone healthy?). He yells at hunters shooting too close to town. He cuts off customers in his restaurant when they order more wine ("You have a long drive home."). He even does rounds at the local hospital, ensuring that the terminally ill remain plugged in.

His concern is somewhat egocentric: His beloved wife, Roseanna (Ruehl), terminally ill with a weakened heart, wants just one thing: to be buried beside their daughter in one of the parish's few remaining plots. The wealthy lawyer Capestro (Luigi Diberti), for reasons all his own, has refused to sell any adjoining land to the church.

By keeping the rest of the village safe, Marcello hopes there'll be a place for Roseanna, thus putting him in the unenviable position of having to pray for the quick death of the person he loves the most.

With unquestionably saintly and just as maddening generosity, Roseanna wants Marcello to remarry when she's gone—and to marry her beautiful sister Cecilia (Walker). And, as if Marcello doesn't have enough to worry about, into this mix of melancholy and anarchy, writer Saul Turteltaub inserts a Mafia subplot.

Insanity, you say? Not really. The Marcello-Roseanna-Cecilia imbroglio would be tough sledding for 90 minutes, and something has to give. It does, via the squat, angry figure of Fredo Iaccoponi (Trevor Peacock), a kidnapper who, after a 20-year sentence, is expecting to be greeted by his banker Rossi (Roberto Delta Casa) and the millions of lira in ransom money with which Rossi was entrusted. The banker, however, has spent most of the money on his voluptuous, voracious mistress Francesca (Fay Ripley), and things are not going to go well.

There are many more twists to this bowl of pasta, which might easily have been an ungodly mess; Paul Weiland, who's done a lot of British TV (including Rowan Atkinson's Mr. Bean), has directed just one previous feature, the eminently dismissible "City Slickers II." But Reno is as watchable a character as there is on screen; Ruehl is a national treasure. With Walker, they give fluff a spine and serve up sentiment.

NEW YORK POST, 6/18/97, p. 38, Thelma Adams

A mime crosses a crowded Italian graveyard on a tightrope. He nearly loses his footing as he drops roses on a series of wooden caskets. Fall in, I plead, fall in!

Rarely has it been so clear in the opening shot that the movie reeks as in the first, brief moments of Paul Weiland's "For Roseanna."

An entire family of aerialists have tumbled to their deaths. This fact enrages Marcello (Jean Reno). He might not like mimes any more than I do, but that's not why he's angry.

Marcello's ailing wife, Roseanna (Mercedes Ruehl), has a dying wish: She wants to be buried in the tiny Travento cemetery. The Roman performers have filled five spots in the local boneyard. Only three plots remain. (And that's three plots too many for Saul Turteltaub's one-joke script.)

Marcello goes to ridiculous, but hardly comic, extremes to make death take a holiday in scenic Travento. Meanwhile, Roseanna's sister Cecilia (Polly Walker) flirts with the local landowner's nephew. His uncle can grant Roseanna's dying wish by deeding adjacent land to the church. Why doesn't he? The secret's long-buried, but obvious.

Only Ruehl, her face dusted with powder, survives with grace. Her monolog at her young daughter's grave has a heart and soul absent in the rest of "For Roseanna."

VILLAGE VOICE, 6/24/97, p. 84, Jennifer Vandever

Italian trattoria owner Marcello works tirelessly to keep his fellow villagers alive. It seems the village cemetery is down to its last three plots and his dying wife Roseanna's last wish is to be buried there. Unlike American cemeteries, Italian ones don't take reservations. This would be a rather leaden comic premise to keep airborne were it not for the comic talents of French actor Jean Reno as Marcello. And luckily, Roseanna (played with sexy nobility by Mercedes Ruehl) suffers from an unspecified illness whose only symptom is heightened wistfulness. But as the body count begins to climb, the cast can't keep the proceedings from becoming mired in morbidity. With subplots involving a bitter old rich guy, his hunky nephew, a slutty Roman mistress, and a Mafia hit man come back from the slammer, the film starts to feel like a wacky Italian version of *Knots Landing*. Though admittedly it's a version with more charm and a much better locale.

Also reviewed in:
NEW YORK TIMES, 6/18/97, p. C14, Janet Maslin

FOREIGN LAND

A Riofilme and Videofilmes release. *Producer:* Flavio R. Tambellini. *Director:* Walter Salles and Daniela Thomas. *Screenplay (Portuguese with English subtitles):* Walter Salles, Daniela Thomas, and Marcos Bernstein. *Director of Photography:* Walter Carvalho. *Editor:* Walter Salles and Felipe Lacerda. *Music:* Jose Miguel Wisnik. *Sound:* Geraldo Ribeiro. *Art Director:* Daniela Thomas. *Costumes:* Cristina Camargo. *Running time:* 100 minutes. *MPAA Rating:* Not Rated.

CAST: Fernanda Torres (Alex); Fernando Alves Pinto (Paco); Luis Melo (Igor); Alexandre Borges (Miguel); Laura Cardoso (Manuela); Joao Lagarto (Pedro); Tchecky Karyo (Kraft).

NEW YORK POST, 10/24/97, p. 46, Thelma Adams

Lisbon is called the white city. In "Foreign Land," the Portuguese capital comes alive in black and white.

"Lisbon is the ideal place to lose someone or get lost," according to a character in Walter Salles and Daniela Thomas' thriller with a mourning heart. All roads that lead to the port city end in chaos, displacement and incurable homesickness.

"Foreign Land" shifts to Brazil, the former Portuguese colony. It's 1990 and the Latin American nation is faring no better than its mother country. Brazilian President Fernando Collor freezes all savings accounts.

A Spanish-born seamstress watches the news on TV. With the speed of a toothpaste commercial, her life savings disappear along with her dreams of returning to her Basque homeland. When she dies from shock, her only son, Paco (Fernando Alves Pinto), joins a generation of displaced Brazilians.

An antiques dealer named Igor (Luis Melo) gives Paco the chance to fulfill his mother's destiny and visit her birthplace. All Paco has to do is deliver a suitcase to Lisbon. Schemes go awry and Paco gets snared in an intrigue beyond his ken (signaled by the arrival of Tcheky Karyo in a cameo as a black marketeer).

Paco's underground adventures lead him to Alex (Fernanda Torres), a Brazilian waitress with Sonia Braga hair and a six-shooter. Their fates are sealed in noir and white.

Beset by homesickness, outraged by local prejudice, strapped financially, Alex toys with returning to Sao Paulo. It's one of the more conventional moves in this beautifully shot tale of foreigners in a foreign land, that Paco and Alex briefly find a home in each other's arms.

Rhythmic and soulful, "Foreign Land" is a thriller in plot only. Its crosses and double crosses, diamonds tucked in violin cases and smoking guns are an alluring pretext to explore a generation of Brazilian slackers and a fallen empire twisting in the global wind.

VILLAGE VOICE, 11/28/97, p. 79, Amy Taubin

A taut, angst-ridden thriller about young Brazilians recruited to ferry stolen jewels from Sao Paulo to Lisbon, *Foreign Land* is the kind of movie that dozens of American Indie directors have tried and failed to make.

Set mostly in "the White City," where huge numbers of immigrants from Latin America and Africa struggle for a foothold in Europe, *Foreign Land* makes palpable the terrors of being without a home, a family, a passport, a future. Alex, daughter of the Brazilian middle classes, and Paco, son of an immigrant seamstress, are both part of a desperate generation that fled Brazil in the early '90s as a result of the insane monetary policies of the Collor government. Attempting to extricate themselves from a Lisbon underworld of crooks and smugglers, they fall in love.

An extremely intelligent, heartfelt film that's directed with great sophistication by Walter Salles and Daniela Thomas, *Foreign Land* is reminiscent of early Wim Wenders crossed with Cinema Novo. Shot in richly textured black-and-white, filled with off-kilter compositions and vertiginous camera moves, the film evokes the sense of being isolated in a teeming city. The editing is jagged and tense but allows time for character nuance.   The largely unknown cast perform with understated conviction.   Last but not least, the fado-inflected score provides a dark, sinuous undercurrent without being all intrusive. Put together with old-fashioned cinematic values, *Foreign Land* is a thoroughly modern movie.

Despite racking up a slew of prizes (including a big one at Sundance), *Foreign Land* is still without an American distributor. It plays at the Anthology for a week. Aside from *Happy Together*, it's the only current film worth going out of your way to see.

Also reviewed in:
CHICAGO TRIBUNE, 3/13/98, p. I, Michael Wilmington
NEW YORK TIMES, 10/24/97, p. E18, Lawrence Van Gelder
VARIETY, 10/2-8/95, p. 42, David Rooney

FORGOTTEN SILVER

A First Run Features release of a WingNut Films Production. *Executive Producer:* Jamie Selkirk and Peter Jackson.   *Producer:* Sue Rogers.   *Director:* Peter Jackson and Costa Botes. *Screenplay:* Peter Jackson and Costa Botes. *Director of Photography:* Alan Bollinger and Gerry Vasbenter. *Editor:* Eric De Beus and Mike Horton. *Music:* Dave Donaldson, Steve Roche, and Janet Roddick. *Sound:* Ken Saville. *Production Designer:* John Girdlestone. *Running time:* 53 minutes. *MPAA Rating:* Not Rated.

NARRATOR: Jeffrey Thomas.

LOS ANGELES, 1/16/98, Calendar/p. 6, Kenneth Turan

Imagine the surprise of New Zealand director Peter Jackson when a casual remark led him to a cache of ancient nitrate stored in a shed at the bottom of a neighbor's garden. Found there were "the most extraordinary collection of films, films I never heard of. Imagine if a film like 'Citizen Kane' suddenly came out of the blue."

Imagine also the surprise of the viewers of "Forgotten Silver" as they come to realize that the man who directed those lost silent films, New Zealander Colin McKenzie, never really existed.

For what Jackson (whose impudent sense of humor was on display in "Heavenly Creatures" and "The Frighteners") and co-director Costa Botes have created is a classic mockumentary, a charming tongue-in-cheek jest that is both cleverly conceived and exceptionally well executed.

Owing a great deal to the spirit of Woody Allen's "Zelig" as well as "This Is Spinal Tap," "Forgotten Silver" combines interviews with real people like actor Sam Neill, film critic Leonard Maltin and Miramax Chairman Harvey Weinstein with elaborately faked silent film footage and still photographs that really look as if they were created between the turn of the century and the 1920s.

If you are going to create an imaginary director, you might as well make him a master, and "Silver" is rife with deeply felt encomiums to McKenzie as one of the greatest filmmakers who ever lived, delivered with magnificent straight faces by all concerned.

Born and raised in rural Timaroo, young Colin had a passion for mechanical invention, and is given overdue credit here for creating the world's first tracking shot—even though the bicycle he mounted his home-made camera on promptly crashed.

This penchant for disaster was a sad constant in McKenzie's career. Having come up with an egg-based film emulsion, his need for more and more film led to the following provocative headline in the local newspaper: "2,000 Dozen Eggs Stolen."

Another gleeful theme of "Forgotten Silver" is how important pint-sized New Zealand would be if the true history of the 20th century could be written. For instance, a piece of splendidly splotchy film taken by McKenzie reveals that it was N.Z. farmer Richard Pierce, not the Wright Brothers, who should be credited with the world's first manned flight.

Further triumphs and setbacks followed, like the first use of sound in a feature (1908's "Warrior Season"), marred by the fact that all the dialogue was in Chinese—leading New Zealand audiences, Maltin somberly informs us, to "just walk out in droves."

"Forgotten Silver" is mostly concerned with McKenzie's masterpiece, the four-hour "Salome," the only biblical epic to be jointly financed by a crude slapstick clown, a gang of mobsters and Joseph Stalin. Dragging 15,000 extras and the woman you love to a huge biblical city constructed in the center of the jungle couldn't have been easy, and Jackson and Botes have considerable fun with "Salome's" shaggy-dog travails.

It can't be overemphasized how carefully "Forgotten Silver's" sham edifice is constructed, and with what a sharp sense of humor. Seeing Weinstein say that if McKenzie were alive today, he'd prefer the newly truncated version of "Salome" to his original is a scene for the ages.

NEW YORK POST, 10/3/97, p. 48, Larry Worth

Colin McKenzie may never be mentioned in the same breath with Paul Bunyan or Pecos Bill. But directors Peter "Heavenly Creatures" Jackson and Costa Botes' tall tale is one for the record books.

Welcome to "Forgotten Silver," a hilariously solemn mockumentary about the one-and-only Colin McKenzie, a New Zealand-born genius whose cinematic accomplishments pre-dated those of Thomas Edison and D.W. Griffith.

Mixing "just discovered archival footage" of McKenzie and interviews with actor Sam Neill, film historian Leonard Maltin and Miramax honcho Harvey Weinstein, the film is a joyful sendup of the filmmaking biz and one man's Sisyphean struggle to succeed.

Paired at the Quad Cinema with "Signing Off,"a wonderfully witty 15-minute gem about an aged deejay's last work day, the 53-minute "Forgotten Silver" confirms that short and sweet needn't leave viewers shortchanged.

VILLAGE VOICE, 10/7/97, p. 80, Michael Atkinson

Like the film history mock docs before it, Peter Jackson and Costa Botes's *Forgotten Silver* is predicated on the addictive notion of a secret movie history—indeed, though barely a century old, cinema seems preternaturally fascinated with what it might not know about itself. (See Theodore Roszack's novel *Flicker* for the ultimate expression of moviehead arcanum.) Kind of like a Peter Delpeut movie with a bellyful of cheap New Zealand lager, *Silver* tells the story (through faux archival footage) of Colin McKenzie, a completely forgotten NZ film pioneer who seems to have done everything first. McKenzie made stock out of flax and egg whites, was the first to invent a color process and sound, and even shot the first man in flight, six months before the Wrights. His tumultuous career disappeared with his unfinished epic *Salome*, whose lost-city set is discovered in the overgrown western jungles. A modest made-for-NZTV satire on the excavation-restoration craze, *Forgotten Silver* is rarely funny—Jackson and Botes instead push their ruse as far as they can while still keeping a straight face. Their point, however, is strange and clear: that a complete grasp of film history, brief though it is, shall always elude us.

Also reviewed in:
CHICAGO TRIBUNE, 1/2/98, p. M, Michael Wilmington
NEW REPUBLIC, 11/3/97, p. 29, Stanley Kauffmann
NEW YORK TIMES, 10/3/97, p. E22, Lawrence Van Gelder
VARIETY, 5/27-6/2/96, p. 69, David Stratton

4 LITTLE GIRLS

An HBO release of a 40 Acres and a Mule Filmworks production. *Executive Producer:* Sheila Nevins. *Producer:* Spike Lee and Sam Pollard. *Director:* Spike Lee. *Director of Photography:* Ellen Curas. *Editor:* Sam Pollard. *Music:* Terence Blanchard. *Sound:* J.T. Takagi. *Running time:* 102 minutes. *MPAA Rating:* Not Rated.

LOS ANGELES TIMES, 10/24/97, Calendar/p. 2, Kenneth Turan

From "Do the Right Thing" to "Get on the Bus," director Spike Lee has made some of the most hard-edged and unsettling American films on racism and its effects. Yet none has been as moving as this, his first feature-length-documentary, simply titled "4 Little Girls."

Lee's first short feature, "Joe's Bed-Stuy Barbershop: We Cut Heads," was a documentary, and the desire to bear witness to history has often been a factor in what he's done, from the stately Denzel Washington-starring "Malcolm X" biography through possible projects on baseball stars Jackie Robinson and Curt Flood.

The best of documentaries—and "4 Little Girls" is one of them—often have a piercing, heart-rending quality that insists we look with fresh eyes at material we think we know. Made for HBO, which will broadcast it during Black History Month early next year, Lee's film tells a story of such power that even those who think it sounds familiar will find themselves completely involved.

On one level "4 Little Girls" details the Sept. 15, 1963, bombing of Birmingham, Ala.'s 16th Street Baptist Church that claimed four young victims who were attending Sunday school in the building's basement. "At that moment," TV anchor Walter Cronkite says, "America understood the real nature of the hate that was preventing integration, particularly in the South, but also throughout America. This was the awakening."

One of the film's aims, which it realizes, is to make these four girls, ages 11 through 14, into real people whose absence we feel as much as the parents, relatives, friends and neighbors who are interviewed about their loss. It is especially shocking, somehow, to see the girls' childhood friends, not frozen in time like the victims, but now adults in their 40s still haunted by what went on.

But "4 Little Girls" goes further. With the ability to smoothly interweave the personal and the political, it serves as a window into the entire civil rights movement, a look at a society that needed to change and at the people who saw to it that change took place.

Though known as "The Magic City" for its rapid industrialization, Birmingham also was, journalist Howell Raines explains, a place with a long history of labor violence involving dynamite as well as enough institutional racism for Dr. Martin Luther King to call it "the most thoroughly segregated city in the country."

Paralleling its stories of those girls growing up, Lee uses people like historian Taylor Branch, author of the landmark "Parting the Waters," and civil rights veterans like the Rev. Wyatt T. Walker and Andrew Young to describe how the movement came to the city and what kind of reception people like public safety commissioner Eugene "Bull" Connor, "the walking *id* of Birmingham," prepared for them. It also can't resist current footage of former Alabama Gov. George Wallace, physically wasted and apparently troubled by his segregationist past.

Mostly, however, "4 Little Girls" is blessedly straightforward and restrained, confident enough of the heart-breaking nature of its story to relate it with a dispassion that is always effective. Lee and his collaborators have also prepared with thoroughness, interviewing nearly 50 people on camera, utilizing more than 20 archive sources and striking just the right opening note with Joan Baez's searing version of Richard Farina's "Birmingham Sunday" on the soundtrack.

Those interviews, all conducted by Lee himself, are the core of the film. The girls' families especially seem to find a kind of empathetic solace in the director's presence that allows them to unburden themselves, to tell their painful stories with honesty and dignity.

In contrast to some of Birmingham's white leaders, who talk of the early '60s as a bucolic time, the city's African Americans remember the debilitating pain of segregation. Christopher McNair, for instance, tells of taking his daughter, Denise, later one of the bombing victims, to a department store and trying to explain to her why she couldn't get a sandwich at the segregated lunch counter.

"It was as if the whole world of betrayal had fallen on her," he says slowly, adding that telling her the facts of racism was as difficult a moment as seeing her in death after the bombing. More than the twisty tale of how the church bomber was finally brought to justice, more than the way the violence of the incident galvanized the civil rights movement, moments like this father's terrible sadness have an indelible impact.

Scenes like that are also a powerful argument for seeing "4 Little Girls" during its current theatrical engagement. While all credit has to go to HBO for its continued support of excellent documentaries, only on a big screen does the cathartic effect of a film like this play out to maximum effect.

NEWSDAY, 7/9/97, Part II/p. B2, Jack Mathews

Most of Spike Lee's movies, and all of his good ones, have more than a little documentary fire burning in their bellies. Stoking "Do the Right Thing," "Malcolm X," and "Clockers," to name three of Lee's best pictures, and even "School Daze," "Mo Better Blues," and "Crooklyn," his three worst, is a highly flammable mix of intellectual outrage and personal bitterness, the last of which has often diluted his skills as a storyteller.

But with the superb "Get on the Bus," and his latest film, the documentary "4 Little Girls," there is evidence of a more mature and vastly more effective Spike Lee, a filmmaker finally able to temper his anger so the audience can react to its own.

And there is plenty of reason for universal anger in "4 Little Girls," which recalls the lives of the black victims of the Ku Klux Klan bombing of a church in 1963 Birmingham, Ala. The horror of that event drove home to the rest of America the tyranny of segregation and Southern racism, and helped launch the civil rights movement.

"4 Little Girls" was funded by HBO, where it will presumably air after its theatrical run. Combining interviews, newsreel footage and still photos, along with controlled measures of his own outrage, Lee sets out in "4 Little Girls" to bring the victims back, to let us get to know them as distinct individuals, rather than as faceless martyrs, and to drive home the losses still felt by their friends and families 34 years later.

Their names (and ages) are Addie Mae Collins (14), Carol Denise McNair (11) Cynthia Wesley (14), and Carole Rosamond Robertson (14), and they are the stars of the movie, recalled over and over in still photos, home movies, on cemetery markers, and, at one wrenchingly dramatic moment, in ghastly morgue photos. We hear from their parents and siblings about their ordinary lives and varied personalities, and about their final hours.

Years after the bombing, a former Klansman was convicted of the crime. It was an act, like most acts of terrorism, that had the opposite effect of that intended—it didn't disabuse southern blacks of the desire for freedom. Instead, it encouraged a full-out fight, and it created broad support across the country.

Though we see this man smirking and joshing with guards and lawyers, Lee barely acknowledges him, as if saying his presence would be a further insult to his victims. He's not even mentioned in the press kit. Besides, his was not a lone act. He represented a large constituency of mad-dog racists and, by extension, a white America that bred him.

A younger Lee might have made that last connection the focus of his piece, forcing the white members of the audience to identify with the demon and share his shame.

Instead, Lee takes the constructive approach of humanizing the victims, giving them back their voices and showing how they inspired positive change.

Lee filmed his interviews in such extreme close-up, they're almost overwhelming on the big screen. Not to mention being spectacularly unflattering to his often elderly subjects—among them a stroke-debilitated George Wallace, the "segregation forever" Alabama governor whose relatives were trying to get his scenes excised from the film.

Given the mischief Wallace caused three decades ago, including him here, pathetically showing off his black assistant to prove his color-blindness, hardly qualifies as cruel and unusual punishment.

VILLAGE VOICE, 7/15/97, p. 65, J. Hoberman

No tragedy that befell the nonviolent Civil Rights movement was more searing than the Sunday, September 15, 1963, bombing of Binningham's 16th Street Baptist Church—an act of white supremacist terror (scarcely two weeks after Martin Luther King's world-historic Washington speech) that resulted in the death of four black children: Addie Mae Collins, Denise McNair, Carol Robertson, and Cynthia Wesley.

No evil more evident; no martyrs more innocent. It is the victims who are the subject of Spike Lee's first documentary, *4 Little Girls*. Made for HBO, *4 Little Girls* is a tender film that begins with the incongruously lilting Joan Baez song "Birmingham Sunday" and includes extensive interviews (seemingly conducted by the filmmaker himself) with the girls' parents, siblings, school friends, and neighbors. These recollections are interspersed first with an evocative mix of snapshots, later with news photos and newsreels of the demonstrations that rocked Birmingham, as well as the world, in the spring of 1963.

Birmingham was the movement's first urban battleground. *4 Little Girls* invokes the local traditions of labor violence, lynchings, Ku Klux Klan display, and raw intimidation. The neighborhood to which middle-class blacks began to move in the mid '50s was called Dynamite Hill—the city itself referred to as Bombingham. King, who was physically assaulted there by an American Nazi in late 1962, called the Alabama steel town "the most thoroughly segregated city in the United States."

In early 1963, as the Southern Christian Leadership Conference prepared to shift its attention to Birmingham, *The Saturday Evening Post* proclaimed it "A City in Fear." The events of April and May epitomized the struggle. Police commissioner Bull Connor (a candidate for mayor, shown patrolling the streets in his personal tank) used police dogs and fire hoses to attack the peaceful demonstrators—many of them school children—who were attempting to integrate the city's downtown stores. King was jailed. Terrorists simultaneously bombed the home of his younger brother and the motel room where he himself was thought to be staying—the latter event serving as pretext for an invasion by club-swinging National Guardsmen.

Alabama's new governor, George Wallace, became a national figure that spring—"a dynamic expression of the derangement of white people," in the words of one interviewee. In a scene recreated for *Forrest Gump*, Wallace barred the door at the University of Alabama. (Lee allows the sick old Wallace a cameo, babbling about his best friend being a black man.) The events in Alabama forced President Kennedy, after nearly two and a half years in office, to take a clear public stand against segregation. The same night that JFK made his televised address, NAACP leader Medgar Evers was assassinated in Mississippi. The spring of 1963 initiated America's nine-year run of domestic violence which ended, more or less, with Wallace's own shooting. At the time, it seemed as though the Birmingham police riots, the Evers murder, and the church bombing had lit the fuse for the Kennedy assassination seven weeks later.

That was a different America, and Lee's motives may not be simply political in encouraging those interviewed to describe how segregation felt—rather than what integration meant. *4 Little Girls* was made for TV, and, like TV, it's focused on emotion and immersed in the personal. Lee counts down to the bomb blast, building a terrible tension by crosscutting between the various witnesses and survivors. (One woman remembers her first reaction as being "Russia had sent a Sputnik bomb.") As with *Get on the Bus,* the event is privileged over its context, the human over the historical. Thus, a now elderly woman's prophetic dream is more significant than the information that the September 1963 school term began in Birmingham with two bombs demolishing the home of a prominent black attorney. Nor is there any mention of the postbombing riot in which two black youths were shot dead by Bull Connor's police.

King, who called upon Kennedy to put Birmingham under martial law, warned of "the worst racial holocaust this nation has ever seen." In one of the last interviews, Lee asks one bereaved mother about her feelings of hatred and anger. (Her unfashionable refusal to elaborate seems to surprise him.) The filmmaker's own, typically guarded anger is most clearly expressed in the footnotes citing the current wave of church burnings and the conviction 14 years after the bombing of a single, smiling perpetrator, Robert "Dynamite Bob" Chambliss.

Also reviewed in:
CHICAGO TRIBUNE, 10/24/97, Friday/p. A, Michael Wilmington
NATION, 7/28-8/4/97, p. 35, Stuart Klawans
NEW YORK TIMES, 7/9/97, p. C11, Janet Maslin
VARIETY, 7/21-27/97, p. 38, Todd McCarthy
WASHINGTON POST, 9/19/97, p. C1, Stephen Hunter
WASHINGTON POST, 9/19/97, Weekend/p. 51, Desson Howe

FOUR MILLION HOUSEGUESTS

An ABC/Kane Productions International and Imax Corporation release. *Executive Producer:* Andrew Gellis, Dennis B. Kane, and Jonathan Barker. *Producer:* Sandy Dundas, Barbara Kerr, and Lorne Orleans. *Director:* Paul Cox. *Screenplay:* Paul Cox, Barbara Kerr, John Larkin, and Margot Wiburd. *Director of Photography:* Vic Sarin. *Editor:* Barbara Kerr. *Music:* Richard Robbins. *Running time:* 40 minutes. *MPAA Rating:* Not Rated.

WITH: Charlotte Sullivan; C. David Johnson; Gosia Dobrowolska; James Garner (Narrator).

NEW YORK POST, 5/9/97, p. 50, Larry Worth

IMAX movies have never been known for their strong plots. And the latest, "Four Million Houseguests," doesn't exactly break new ground.

But having Australia's award-winning director Paul Cox at the helm certainly helps. His strong sense for entrancing visuals and storytelling—even when the script is relatively thin—brings a much-needed flair and sense of style.

The narrative begins as an inquisitive teen arrives at her grandfather's country cottage, assuming she's to endure a boring two weeks with her relatives. But Gramps is off on his own vacation and has left a treasure map of clues through which she'll discover his "four million houseguests."

Those houseguests range from particles of dust to spiders to bacteria, all of which take on a whole new look when magnified 100 times via the magical patriarch's microscopes and futuristic gizmos.

But Cox services the production best by incorporating the 3-D effects into the script. Here, objects don't arbitrarily "jump" into viewers' laps and standard scenery takes on equal import.

Accordingly, establishing shots of the rustic hideaway and its tranquil setting are as breathtaking as floating soap bubbles, a pop-up book's pages or the thrusts of a wonderfully unique cuckoo clock.

In addition, magnified examinations of the "houseguests" will fascinate kids and adults alike. Ditto for time-lapse photography of decomposing fruit that proves jaw-droppingly impressive.

Complemented by James Garner's reassuring narration, the acting from Charlotte Sullivan as the adventurous adolescent and C. David Johnson and Gosia Dobrowolska as the harried parents is perfectly serviceable. Granted, the end product isn't going to change history, IMAX's or otherwise. But "Houseguests" nicely demonstrates that a talent like Cox's can bring new dimension to the genre.

VILLAGE VOICE, 5/13/97, p. 90, Abby McGanney Nolan

The latest 3-D extravaganza from IMAX puts a little magic into two weeks at a summer house. Elly (Charlotte Sullivan) is an 11-year-old who's been given mysteries to solve by her absent grandfather. He's equipped his exquisitely rustic lakefront house with clues and keys and discoveries for her to make about the natural world.   What she finds under the microscope—insects, mold and other tiny household items—is blown up magnificently on the IMAX.

Australian director Paul Cox, a regular on the film circuit opens with a gorgeous shot of a lakefront—you want to reach out and grab the greenery—and maintains a pleasingly gentle tone throughout. Sullivan does well as a sweet, sullen preteen, and the film offers a reassuring tour of the microscopic world. Luckily, it doesn't show the tiny organisms that may well be residing on the 3-D headsets.

Also reviewed in:
NATION, 6/2/97, p. 36, Stuart Klawans
NEW YORK TIMES, 5/9/97, p. C14, Stephen Holden
VARIETY, 5/12-18/97, p. 64, Ray Richmond

FRANK AND OLLIE

A Buena Vista Pictures release of a Theodore Thomas Productions production. *Producer:* Kuniko Okubo and Theodore Thomas. *Director:* Theodore Thomas. *Screenplay:* Theodore Thomas. *Director of Photography:* Erik Daarstad. *Editor:* Kathryn Camp. *Music:* John Reynolds. *Running time:* 89 minutes. *MPAA Rating:* PG.

WITH: Frank Thomas; Ollie Johnston; Sylvia Roemer; John Canemaker; John Culhane; Glen Keane; Andy Gaskill.

LOS ANGELES TIMES, 10/20/95, Calendar/p. 6, Kenneth Turan

Think of Frank Thomas and Ollie Johnston as the eighth and ninth of Snow White's amiable dwarfs. Or, from a darker point of view, as the miscreants who killed Bambi's mother. But whatever your perspective. to encounter them in the sprightly documentary "Frank and Ollie" is to understand what the phrase "charmed lives" means.

The closest of friends since they met as art students at Stanford in 1931, Frank and Ollie more or less stumbled into animation when it paid $17 a week, only to discover both had such a gift for the process that their work changed its essential nature.

As the most prominent of the "Nine Old Men," Walt Disney's shock troop of key animators, Frank and Ollie had a hand in creating some of the most well-known images on the planet. And now happily retired with dozens of films and books to their credit, they have the pleasure of appearing in this charming documentary written and directed by Frank's son Theodore Thomas.

Since feature-length animation dates back only to 1937s "Snow White and the Seven Dwarfs," Frank and Ollie were literally present at the form's creation, giving this film an importance as irreplaceable oral history.

But the greatest pleasure of "Frank and Ollie" is the opportunity it offers to simply spend time with these amiable codgers, possibly the world's eldest kids, who laugh easily and refuse to take themselves awfully seriously, despite their considerable accomplishments.

Working separately but often on the same project, what Frank and Ollie did was pioneer and refine the concept of character or personality animation. Contributing heavily to films like "Pinocchio," "Peter Pan" "The Jungle Book," "Bambi" and "Lady and the Tramp", these animators got inside what they drew; that a bunch of sketches could seem as real as flesh. One of this film's special treats is seeing both of them act out the characters they created and marveling at how close their pencils came to what their minds imagined.

With all their closeness (their families still live next door to each other in La Canada Flintridge and their first children were born less than a week apart), it can be difficult to tell Frank from

Ollie except by their hobbies. Frank, the more analytical at the drawing board is shown playing ragtime piano (he helped found the Firehouse Five+2) while Ollie, an intuitive artist whose pencil "kissed the paper," is a serious model train enthusiast.

Given the genesis of this project, no one should expect "Frank and Ollie" to be a tough look at Walt Disney and the sometimes controversial way he ran his operation. Rather it is a loving tribute to two gifted and delightful men whose way of looking at the world first put the magic in the Magic Kingdom.

NEW YORK POST, 6/21/97, p. 21, Larry Worth

They made "Snow White and the Seven Dwarfs," "Pinocchio,""Fantasia' and so many more. But Frank Thomas and Ollie Johnston seemed destined to be known as the men who killed Bambi's mom.

Now, the striking documentary "Frank & Ollie" also identifies them as two of cinema's most talented animators—never mind a couple of the sweetest guys to ever hit Hollywood.

Granted, there may be a slight prejudice at work here. The film was written and directed by Frank's son, Theodore. But the film's sentimental, homey touch feels appropriate, given its slice-of-life subject matter.

Thomas and Johnston are actually two of Disney's Nine Old Men, the think tank whose cartoon creations became the stuff of legend and made their creators renowned in their industry.

As well as offering a compelling look at the twosome—lifelong best friends and neighbors as well as colleagues—the production delivers enchanting insight into the overall animation process.

Viewers get to watch how Johnston and Thomas would act out the parts of their four-legged characters before committing them to paper, then trade ideas on how to make the likes of Lady and her Tramp into poignant representations of human emotions.

The process was truly one of collaboration, to the point that Thomas and Johnston could, and still can, finish each other's sentences.

Collectively, the results fascinate, although they're broken up by annoying title cards such as "How Ollie Works," followed by "How Frank Works." In addition, a few of the at-home scenes with the boys' spouses feel a bit forced. Did the camera just happen to catch them struggling over that crossword puzzle?

But those are minor quibbles. particularly given the generous amount of clips from "Alice in Wonderland," "The Jungle Book," "Sword in the Stone" and all the old gems. One keeps wishing the hit parade would never stop.

Accordingly, it's a real tribute to both Frank and Ollie that, when the focus switches from Bambi and pals back to the titular duo, they come off as equally engaging.

VILLAGE VOICE, 6/24/97, p. 82, Amy Taubin

While they may not have been solely responsible for the death of Bambi's mother, Frank Thomas and Ollie Johnston, by taking personality animation to a level even Walt Disney hadn't imagined, made us believe that a young deer could experience bereavement and joy just like a human child. Collaborators and best friends since they first met in the Stanford University art department in 1931, they worked on 23 features, had four books published, and were still going strong in 1995 when Franks son Theodore Thomas premiered his bewitching documentary, *Frank & Ollie*, at Sundance.

The best antidote to the lumbering *The Lost World, Frank & Ollie* explores the mysteries of animation and friendship in ways that children and adults should appreciate. What better granddads than these two octogenarians, who not only have instant access to clips from *Snow White, Bambi, Pinocchio,* and *The Lady and the Tramp* but also can demonstrate how they brought a pathos worthy of Chaplin to cartoon animals. For aspiring animators, *Frank & Ollie* is a terrific primer.

Fascinated by the animated shorts they saw in Los Angeles movie theaters, Thomas and Johnston went to work for Disney in the mid '30s and stayed for over 40 years. Though their working methods differed (Thomas is more analytic, Johnston more intuitive), they both specialized in conveying the emotional life of their hand-drawn characters. Thomas says that he and Ollie are romantics "in that we draw the connections between ourselves and animals and plants—the whole thing. If you're going into an imaginary field like animation, you'd better be equipped with that."

Shot in Thomas and Johnston's adjacent Los Angeles houses (they married and had their first children almost simultaneously and have lived next door to each other for their entire adult lives), *Frank & Ollie* isn't quite as lively as its two subjects. Thomas *fils* tries a little too hard to keep a professional distance, but he also shies away from the thorny issues of Disney animation in its "golden age" and after. At Sundance, during a postscreening discussion, Thomas and Johnston remarked on how the fast pace of contemporary animation made their particular passion—the expression of complex emotions—impossible. Disney might not have been pleased had such a critique made its way onto celluloid, but since they've not released *Frank & Ollie* either theatrically or on video, what does it matter? And how come they can't recognize a love letter when they see one?

Also reviewed in:
CHICAGO TRIBUNE, 5/3/96, Friday/p. L, Michael Wilmington
NEW YORK TIMES, 6/20/97, p. C30, Stephen Holden
VARIETY, 1/23-29/95, p. 73, Leonard Klady
WASHINGTON POST, 5/10/96, p. D7, Rita Kempley

FREE WILLY 3: THE RESCUE

A Warner Bros. release in association with Regency Enterprises of a Shuler Donner/Donner production. *Executive Producer:* Lauren Shuler Donner, Richard Donner, and Arnon Milchan. *Producer:* Jennie Lew Tugend. *Director:* Sam Pillsbury. *Screenplay:* John Mattson. *Based on characters created by:* Keith A. Walker. *Director of Photography:* Tobias Schliessler. *Wildlife Photography:* Bob Talbot. *Underwater Photography:* Pete Romano. *Editor:* Margie Goodspeed. *Music:* Cliff Eidelman. *Music Editor:* Darrell Hall. *Sound:* Rick Patton and (music) Bruce Botnick. *Sound Editor:* Isaac "Scud" Strozberg, Sean Kelly, Sophie Hotte, Kevin Townshend, and Real Gauvreau. *Casting:* Judy Taylor and Lynne Carrow. *Production Designer:* Brent Thomas. *Art Director:* Douglasann Menchions. *Set Decorator:* Louise Roper. *Special Effects:* Tony Lazarowich. *Whale Effects:* Walt Conti. *Costumes:* Maya Mani. *Make-up:* Taylor Roberts and Gina Hole. *Stunt Coordinator:* Mike Nomad. *Running time:* 90 minutes. *MPAA Rating:* PG.

CAST: Jason James Richter (Jesse); August Schellenberg (Randolph Johnson); Annie Corley (Drew); Vincent Berry (Max Wesley); Patrick Kilpatrick (John Wesley); Tasha Slimms (Mary); Peter Lacroix (1st Mate Sanderson); Stephen E. Miller (Dineen); Ian Tracey (Kron); Matthew Walker (Captain Drake); Roger R. Cross (1st Mate Stevens); Rick Burgess (Smiley); Roman Danylo (Pizza Kid).

LOS ANGELES TIMES, 8/8/97, Calendar/p. 8, Kevin Thomas

It's time to set Willy, the orca whale, free once and for all. "Free Willy 3: The Rescue" is sparked by its two young stars, Jason James Richter and newcomer Vincent Berry. But it is otherwise dull and tedious, which so often is the case with films shot in Canada.

Richter, who has starred in all three films, returns as Jesse, now 17. He has gotten a job for the summer tracking whales aboard a research vessel with his mentor Randolph (August Schellenberg, also reprising). The beautiful setting is the Northwest Pacific coast, where there has been a disturbing decline in the orca population.

Meanwhile, 10-year-old Max (Berry) is going to sea for the first time with his father, John (Patrick Kilpatrick), captain of a salmon fishing boat. John's key source of come is from the illegal slaughter of whales for sale to countries where whale meat is considered a delicacy. So who should turn up in Botany Bay but Willy and his new mate?

In his film debut, Berry is most impressive as a youngster torn between his love for his father and horror at his discovery of the illegal whaling. Richter is likewise effective as a youth on the edge of adulthood, struggling to be taken seriously by his elders and trying to persuade Max to help him save Willy, et al. Among the key adult characters, only John has dimension and an edge, a man enraged that the way in which his forebears supported themselves for generations is now against the law.

Unfortunately, everyone else is blah. Sam Pillsbury's direction is so earnest he allows for no humor along the way and little suspense. But then writer John Mattson's script is not exactly inspired.

The film's climactic sequence, while predictable, is unintentionally unsettling.   While preservation of the orca whales and obeying the law are of paramount importance, "Free Willy 3" actually suggests that seriously endangering John's life is less important than saving the life of a whale—indeed, John, entrapped in rope netting, would surely have drowned had not Willy himself miraculously saved him.

Would little Max really rather see his father die than Willy? You're left to wonder. What's more, you're also left wondering how John can support his family without resorting to illegal whaling.

NEW YORK POST, 8/8/97, p. 52, Michael Medved

Parents will have mixed emotions, about a kiddie morality play featuring a father whose lifelong vocation has been totally destroyed by his son's betrayal, confessing to that self-righteous 10-year-old: "You were right. I was wrong."

To which the smug twerp responds by patting his pathetic pa on the shoulder and telling him: "That's all right, Dad. You just made a mistake."

"Free Willy 3: The Rescue" makes its own mistake in transforming a merely dull and vacuous "family film" into an actively obnoxious one by hammering home its "kids [and whales] know best" theme with such heavy-handed intensity.

The story shows maturing teen-ager Jesse (played yet again by the appealing young actor Jason James Richter) getting a summer job on a whale-tracking research vessel off the rugged coast of the Pacific Northwest, where he's reteamed with his wise, warm-hearted Native American mentor, Randolph (August Schellenberg).

They set out to reconnect with Willy, the altogether admirable Orca they jointly freed from a theme park two movies ago, learning that the big guy and his whale wife, Nicky, face deadly danger.

Scowling Patrick Kilpatrick plays a fishing boat captain and third-generation whaler who refuses to give up the family business to respect international conventions protecting the marine mammals.

His cute, tousle-haired boy (Vincent Berry) sails along with him for the first time, but is outraged by his father's bloody trade.

Directed by little-known New Zealander Sam Pillsbury, this new "Willy" displays a nice feel for its picturesque locations and the entirely robotic whales (considerably improved since machines altogether replaced real whales in the second film in the series) are more versatile and convincing than ever.

Along with obligatory scenes of Jesse riding Willy's back, however, this new film promotes some decidedly radical messages. The script unequivocally justifies the idea of kids breaking and entering, stealing (and wrecking) boats, disregarding all notions of private property and even putting a parent's life and livelihood in dire jeopardy, as long as the goal is saving whales.

At least Patrick Kilpatrick brings some unexpected sympathy to the glowering role of the grim whaler, trapped by his family's past, but even his well-aimed harpoons can't prevent the movie from dragging its flippers in the water: "Free Willy 3" feels so much longer than its 90 minute running time that by the end most moviegoers will feel personally ready for "The Rescue."

"Maybe Willy's smarter than we are. Or more human," Jesse declares. Apparently, Warner Bros. believes the public yearns to revere some higher, wiser form of life. "Contact" therefore exalted unseen, all-knowing aliens and, even more prepostetously (and pathetically, "FW3" worships animatronic mechanical whales.

NEWSDAY, 8/8/97, Part II/p. B9, John Anderson

About 50 discriminating moviegoers average age, oh, about 7—filed into a Tuesday screening of the latest "Free Willy" installment. The smell of bologna lay heavy in the air. "They're not fish!!!" they all sang out, when some bad guy misidentified the killer whales (which, as all us good guys know, are mammals). When Willy made his first appearance, a buzz of recognition coursed through the room. The crowd was primed, loaded and ready for action.

Kids don't know much about the law of diminishing returns, but they know what they like. And they didn't seem to like "Free Willy 3: The Rescue," which pits a rather underutilized Willy against poachers and had the kids talking, running to the bathroom and twisting themselves into the kind of pretzels that only bored 7-year-old bodies can achieve.

Of course, children will talk and squirm and contort, but there wasn't much that got their attention here besides a bar fight between loathesome whale killers and angelic environmentalists, and that didn't seem like such a good thing (the fight, of course, not the characterizations). There was a lot of terrific photography—sun sparkling on water, boats making wakes, Pacific Northwest vistas and those photogenic whales. But we, and they, know what's going to happen: Willy's going to be endangered and Jesse—played for the third time by young Jason James Richter—is going to get him out of it.

Some things do change, of course: Richter is older, heading for a kind of Fred Savage adolescence, while Jesse has gotten a job on a research ship, working for the prickly Drew (Annie Corley) beside his old mentor Randolph (August Schellenberg). The hook: There's been a decline in the orca population and they don't know why.

As the 7-year-olds might say—I know! I know! It's Max's dad! Max (Vincent Berry), who has a passing resemblance to Larry Fine, is eager to accompany his father John (Patrick Kilpatrick) on a fishing expedition, until he finds out that it's whales Dad is after. And they're not even Japanese! Max finds himself in the middle of what you night call a crisis of conscience.

Max and Jesse hook up, there are moments of expense—I mean suspense—and there is some absolutely fascinating footage of the birth of a baby killer whale (Willy and the missus having, well, you know). But there's a heckuva lot of treading water before we get to the payoff. Personally, I'm going to go have a bologna sandwich.

SIGHT AND SOUND, 10/97, p. 51, Andy Richards

The Pacific Northwest. Jesse, who has had a long friendship with an orca (or killer whale) named Willy, is now 17 years old and is starting a summer job on an oceanic research vessel, the *Noah*, with his mentor Randolph Johnson and Drew, a research scientist. They want to investigate the cause of a mysterious decline in the local orca population. By broadcasting sonic waves from the boat, Jesse summons Willy. Drew is impressed.

Ten-year-old Max Wesley goes out on his first fishing trip with his father John on the boat *Botany Bay*. The crew pursue some orcas and begin slaughtering them, and Max's excitement turns to revulsion. He falls overboard, but is rescued by Willy. Max becomes disillusioned with his father when he learns that John is illegally harvesting whale meat for blackmarkets abroad.

Willy, wounded by John's harpoon, returns to Jesse who removes it. The research crew realise that John and his crew are hunting Willy and his family, but they cannot convince the authorities without proof. Willy now has a mate, who is pregnant. Jesse sneaks onto the *Botany Bay*, but is discovered by Max and his father and told to leave. Wanting to let the whales escape, Max deliberately acts incompetently on his next fishing trip, and the whales get away. Jesse befriends Max, but realises that he cannot ask him to betray his father.

The *Noah*'s crew pursue the *Botany Bay*, hoping to save Willy's family. They ram into John's boat, and he falls overboard. Willy saves John. The authorities now close in on the poachers. John repents, and is reconciled with Max. Willy's mate gives birth. Jesse decides to name the baby Max.

Surprisingly, this latest instalment of the *Free Willy* saga is a rather better film than its predecessors, although it hardly departs radically from the series' established formula. Once again, a dysfunctional family bonds through assisting a family of whales. (It's a formula which also underpins the series' growing ranks of imitators, such as the seal-starring *Andre* and polar-bear movie *Alaska*.) Nonetheless, *Free Willy 3 The Rescue* serves up a more complex set of issues than you might expect.

This time around, Jesse is peripheral to the main action, which centres on the dilemma faced by Max Wesley. Max's newly discovered respect for the sanctity of Willy and his family makes it increasingly hard for him to support his father's fishing activities. John Wesley makes for an intriguing anti-hero, rather more so than the corporate villains from the earlier films. John is a hunter from a long line of hunters, intent on preserving a tradition through his young son. When challenged by Max, he asserts that "you have a right to be what you are, and to make a living", whilst conceding that it is hard to see procuring "sushi for the Japanese" as God's work.

The issue is well balanced, and our sympathies are curiously divided. Indeed, at times the film almost seems to want to establish Jesse and his whale-loving colleagues Randolph and Drew as self-righteous liberal meddlers, disrupting the workings of a traditional, blue-collar economy. When John and his crew are described by Randolph as "monsters", it is hard to concur (this is at least partly due to Patrick Kilpatrick's restrained, dignified playing). John is at worst delusional; his code of blood and iron, deriving from an earlier phase of American civilisation, has no place in the eco-aware 90s. The film's resolution of this crisis of masculinity through John's repentance is, however, disappointingly contrived. When John plunges into the sea and, like *Moby Dick*'s Ahab and *Jaws'* Quint before him, comes face to face with his nemesis, it's rather disappointing that Willy rescues rather than devours him. But in this kind of film, characters invariably gain self-respect through the acceptance of responsibility, and *Free Willy 3* could hardly be expected to rock that particular ideological boat.

The theme of fatherhood is mirrored in Willy's development: the film's coda shows his mate giving birth. The waters stain with blood, mirroring the film's opening scene in which a whale is killed in a shower of harpoons. Such touches do credit to New Zealand-based director Sam Pillsbury (*The Scarecrow, Zandalee)*, whose darker palette pays dividends, dispelling memories of the bland and charmless *Free Willy 2* and restoring confidence in what is one of the better family franchises.

Also reviewed in:
NEW YORK TIMES, 8/8/97, p. C8, Anita Gates
VARIETY, 8/11-17/97, p. 57, Leonard Klady

FULL MONTY, THE

A Fox Searchlight Pictures release of a Redwave Films production. *Producer:* Uberto Pasolini. *Director:* Peter Cattaneo. *Screenplay:* Simon Beaufoy. *Director of Photography:* John de Borman. *Editor:* Nick Moore and Dave Freeman. *Music:* Anne Dudley. *Music Editor:* Graham Lawrence. *Choreographer:* Suzanne Grand. *Sound:* Alastair Crocker and (music) Chris Dibble and Steve Price. *Sound Editor:* Ian Wilson. *Casting:* Susie Figgis. *Production Designer:* Max Gottlieb. *Art Director:* Chris Roope. *Special Effects:* Ian Rowley. *Costumes:* Jill Taylor. *Make-up:* Chris Blundell. *Stunt Coordinator:* Terry Forrestal. *Running time:* 90 minutes. *MPAA Rating:* R.

CAST: Robert Carlyle (Gaz); Tom Wilkinson (Gerald); Mark Addy (Dave); Lesley Sharp (Jean); Emily Woof (Mandy); Steve Huison (Lomper); Paul Barber (Horse); Hugo Speer (Guy); Deirdre Costello (Linda); Bruce Jones (Reg); William Snape (Nathan); Paul Butterworth (Barry); Dave Hill (Alan); Andrew Livingstone (Terry); Vinny Dhillon (Sharon); Kate Layden (Bee); Joanna Swain (Sheryl); Diane Lane (Louise); Kate Rutter (Dole Clerk); June Broughton (Lomper's Mum); Glenn Cunningham (Police Inspector); Chris Brailsford (Duty Sergeant); Steve Garti (Policeman); Malcolm Pitt (Job Club Manager); Dennis Blanch (Director); Daryl Fishwick (Social Worker); David Lonsdale (Repossession Man); Muriel Hunt (Horse's Mum); Fiona Watts (Beryl); Theresa Maduemezia and Fiona Nelson (Horse's Sisters); British Steel Stocksbridge Band (Brass Band).

LOS ANGELES TIMES, 8/13/97, Calendar/p. 5, Kevin Thomas

At the beginning of the bittersweet British comedy "The Full Monty," we're treated to a promotional film touting Sheffield, England, as the "City on the Move" and boasting that the city's mills produce the finest steel in the world. But that was 25 years ago, and today factories are either more mechanized or stand abandoned, just as they are in America's Rust Belt.

When a couple of Sheffield's long-out-of-work guys notice that a night spot is packing in the local lasses with a Chippendale-style revue, they reflexively react with scorn—at least until they start calculating the take. The unthinkable gradually becomes thinkable: Why not work up a male strippers act themselves and make some money?

Why not, indeed? Right away, the difference between Gaz (Robert Carlyle) and his pals and the buffed-out young guys who are *de rigueur* for Chips performances is an instant source of humor and discomfort for Gaz and company—and probably for most of the men in the audience who are either out of shape or not so young, or both. Writer Simon Beaufoy understands this, fortunately, and he and director Peter Cattaneo balance broad humor with much affection.

Like the recent "Brassed Off" and countless other British films, "The Full Monty" deals with people coping with unemployment and the toll it exacts on self-esteem, especially in blue-collar men who've always prided themselves as reliable breadwinners. Gaz is especially desperate for money, for he is in danger of losing partial custody of his beloved small son (William Snape).

The idea of taking off their clothes in public of course strikes Gaz's friends as humiliating, but as the men gradually bond, they begin to be less self-conscious. We in turn realize how easy it is to be filled with loathing for our own bodies should they fail to measure up to the physical perfection so relentlessly promoted in the media. While too sharp-featured to be considered handsome, Gaz has a trim build and is not a bad dancer. His best friend Dave (Mark Addy), however, is a bear-like guy. Although he's a rugged man who actually carries his bulk well, he is uncomfortable about his body. He only reluctantly allows Gaz to persuade him to participate.

Others they line up for their act are their former foreman, Gerald (Tom Wilkinson), a skilled ballroom dancer who will also serve as choreographer, and Horse (Paul Barber), who can do the Bump, the Stump and the Funky Chicken despite a "dodgy" hip. Gerald and Horse are well into middle age but are in good shape.

Rounding out the act are Guy (Hugo Speer), the one man who actually looks like a Chippendale alumnus but who is a klutzy dancer, and Lomper (Steve Huison), a pale, scrawny red-haired young man.

As their "Hot Metal" revue commences rehearsals—to the sounds of Donna Summer, Hot Chocolate, Gary Glitter, Sister Sledge, Tom Jones and the like—the men realize that if they're going to draw a full house for what they intend to be a one-time-only venture, they must do "the full monty"—i.e., take it *all* off (we see them from the back).

If you don't go expecting the depth and subtlety of a Mike Leigh working-class film, "The Full Monty" can be heart-warming fun with more serious undertones than you might have expected.

NEW YORK POST, 8/13/97, p. 39, Michael Medved

If you tear away a male's dignity as a breadwinner, a husband, a father and a productive citizen, how can he possibly affirm his manhood?

The engaging new British comedy "The Full Monty" suggests that there's always the most essential, irreducible indication of masculinity—even if it's merely displayed in a demeaning Chippendale's-style nude-dancing revue.

This odd notion of manhood literally stripped down to its bare essentials works well here only because the men in question emerge as such sympathetic and compelling characters.

Robert Carlyle (who made such a strong impression as a psychotic junkie in "Trainspotting") is funny, edgy and painfully vulnerable as a divorced father and out-of-work steelworker who's desperately eager to retain the respect of his precocious 9-year-old (the splendidly spunky William Snape).

Carlyle's best friend (Mark Addy) is overweight and impotent with his earthy and uncomplaining wife (Lesley Sharp) who singlehandedly supports the family since her husband lost his job.

The marvelous Tom Wilkinson (who at times nearly walks away with the movie) is their fussy former supervisor, clinging to a charade of middle-class respectability, putting on his tie and pretending to go to work each day so his wife won't know he's unemployed.

These lovable losers enlist three other victims of the fading steel industry in gritty Sheffield in a desperate scheme to earn quick cash and long-term redemption.

Noting that a one-night performance by the Chippendale's dancers provoked an enthusiastic response from local women, the six unemployed, out-of-shape blokes plan to one-up these well-muscled visitors by offering curious customers "the full monty" providing the total exposure, with no protective G-strings, that professional dancers avoid.

The movie itself pointedly avoids such full-frontal display (thereby preserving its R rating, rather than NC-17), but English TV director Peter Cattaneo handles his debut feature so skillfully that even without such scenes the audience feels well informed about the individual equipment of the main characters.

Nonetheless, there's a surprising sense of innocence to this material as the boys clumsily choreograph the immortal music of Donna Summer, Sister Sledge and Tom Jones—so much so that it feels strangely appropriate for Carlyle's young son to take part in their preparations.

Unlike the musical miners of the somewhat similarly themed "Brassed Off," there's no political edge to this naive, eccentric response to economic adversity.

Some of the scenes are hysterically funny, and the development of the friendships (and in one instance something more) among the principals is warm-hearted and persuasive.

The film does feel a bit padded as it winds through the inevitable twists and obstacles on its way to the big performance, but ultimately these characters triumph precisely because they're so well-endowed—with humanity.

NEWSDAY, 8/13/97, Part II/p. B9, John Anderson

From this end of the pond, it seems as if British film since Margaret Thatcher has been nothing more than a constant, bilious commentary on her policies of economic jungle law. But what's just as noteworthy is how few American films have dealt even remotely as well with the same subjects. Downsizing, social Darwinism, a heinous redistribution of wealth, the exaltation of capital, the demeaning of work. None of it gets any attention on the big screen here, where there is—just for instance—far less concern about 185,000 Teamsters than about prompt deliveries from the Underpants of the Month Club.

And speaking of underpants: Take 'em off, and what you have is the full monty, the titillating title of Peter Cattaneo's very broad and occasionally very pointed comedy about how low people will go when they're pushed. Disguised as a farcical comedy about a group of laid-off-steel-workers-turned-male-strippers, "The Full Monty" has a subtext of pain that could only be palatable if people were being made to look ridiculous.

And, God knows, they are. Gaz, played by Robert Carlyle, the psycho beer drinker of "Trainspotting," is among the Sheffield unemployable. He takes his son on excursions to steal scrap metal; his ex-wife is suing for back maintenance and full custody. When he and his pal Dave (Mark Addy) sneak into a Chippendale's show and see how much money is being made, they resolve to take it all off. And rake it all in.

That the idea is purely preposterous—Gaz is skinny, Dave is fat, the others they recruit are a bit less than buff—is what gives "The Full Monty" both its goofy humor and its gravity. With a script full of Stooge-isms, Cattaneo has constructed a comedy that operates, very literally, on two levels: One is the baggy-pants, no-pants slapstick of relatively unattractive men strutting their stuff; the other is about their willingness to humiliate themselves to an excruciating extent because they need to feed their families, pay their rent and rebut the official government position that they're obsolete.

What's a relief is that "The Full Monty," with a few scenes excepted, doesn't subject us to too much agony, as Gaz and Co.—his old boss Gerald (Tom Wilkinson), the near-suicide Lomper (Steve Huison), the over-the-hill hoofer Horse (Paul Barber)—try to pull off a male version of "Flashdance" (disco is back, by the way). Gaz' son Nathan (William Snape) has to leave the room when his father starts doing the Gypsy Rose Lee, but that's understandable, and Nathan eventually comes around, even after the whole kickline is arrested for indecent exposure and he's questioned by social services.

The choreography of the "The Full Monty" follows a fairly recognizable pattern: Underdogs beat the odds, make good and exit, stage right, with a big emotional finale. Like "Brassed Off," another recent British version of "Rocky", "The Full Monty" plays a bit fast and loose with our emotions. The difference—without being too cute about it—is a little more naked anguish. And Tom Jones singing "You Can Leave Your Hat On."

NEWSWEEK, 9/1/97, p. 67, David Ansen

In a drab governmental office in Yorkshire, rows of unemployed men stand dolefully in line when suddenly a radio begins to play Donna Summer's "Hot Stuff." Almost imperceptibly one of the men begins to roll his shoulder to the beat, then another. A third traces dance steps with his feet, while a fourth, a fifth and a sixth suddenly succumb to the siren call of disco, momentarily transforming a bureaucratic hellhole with Wednesday Afternoon Fever.

The six men, whom we have come to know well by this midway point in *The Full Monty*, are a motley gaggle of out-of-shape, out-of-work steelworkers. Desperate for money and inspired by a visit to Sheffield by a Chippendales troupe of dancers, they have concocted the lunatic notion of putting on their own strip show, which they have been clumsily rehearsing in an abandoned warehouse. Studying tapes of "Flashdance" for inspiration (though highly critical of Jennifer Beals's welding) and battling their macho sense of shame as they stuff their variously scrawny, overweight and middle-aged bodies into G-strings, these beleaguered troupers are a wonderfully particularized group of Everymen, learning to survive in a world where all the rules have changed. In that enchantingly funny moment when they lose themselves to Donna's shake-your-booty rhythm, the audience knows that redemption is in sight. Get down tonight!

Something is afoot in the Zeitgeist when the two most crowd-pleasing imports of the season—this delightful British comedy and the sweet, more wistful "Shall We Dance?" from Japan—employ a dance floor to drag their reluctant, hidebound heroes into a new, more flexible concept of masculinity. In musicals, dancers are a strutting, extroverted breed, but for the solemn, officebound husband in Masayuki Suo's film and the put-upon working-class mates in Peter Cattaneo's movie, strutting your stuff in public is a fear-inducing, taboo-breaking leap into the unknown. What does it say that American audiences are responding so warmly to these fantasies, grounded in the embarrassment of male display? They strike a chord most Hollywood movies have neglected: our films are filled with Nautilusized young stars playing characters with egos as impregnable as their bodies.

The jobless men in "The Full Monty" (the title is Brit slang for "showing all") have nothing to fall back on and have egos easily bruised. The jaunty ringleader, Gaz (Robert Carlyle), is a divorced dad who'll lose visiting rights to his son if he can't come up with some cash. The pudgy Dave (Mark Addy) has become impotent. Lomper (Steve Huison) is shy and suicidal. The haughty Gerald (Tom Wilkinson), their ex-foreman, can't even tell his wife he's lost his job. Horse (Paul Barber) is considering penile enlargement to live up to his name, while Guy (Hugo Speer), the youngest, fittest and most exhibitionistic, has only his size to recommend him. Cattaneo, writer Simon Beaufoy and their terrific cast turn these guys into a most endearing dirty half dozen. "The Full Monty" finds both pathos and laughs in its farfetched conceit, avoiding the pitfalls of sappiness and shtik. Odds are good you'll exit grinning.

SIGHT AND SOUND, 9/97, p. 43, Nina Caplan

Gaz and Dave are young, unemployed steelwelders in Sheffield. Gaz needs money to retain joint custody of his son Nathan; Dave's loss of self-respect is making him fat and impotent. When the male stripping group The Chippendales visit the city, Gaz, Dave and a reluctant Nathan gatecrash. The sight of the strippers, cheered on by hysterical women, and the amount of money they make, impress Gaz.

Gaz and Dave foil fellow-steelworker Lomper's attempt to gas himself. The three men decide to persuade their former foreman, Gerald, an expert ballroom dancer who has not told his wife that he has been unemployed for six months, to help them form a strip act. Persuasion involves ruining Gerald's job interview by distracting him with a puppet-show battle using garden gnomes outside the window behind the interviewers' heads. Gerald agrees to coach the act.

Reinforcements include an old black man named Mr Horse and Guy, a pretty and well-hung young man who can run up walls like Donald O'Connor in *Singin' in the Rain*. The group realise they have only one chance of drawing a lucrative crowd: to go "the full monty" and completely undress. But anxieties soon set in. Gerald is afraid of a "stiffy" onstage; Dave, worried he may never get it up again, backs out of the act. The dress rehearsal goes ahead, but a policeman stops by to investigate and Gaz, Gerald and Mr Horse are arrested for indecent exposure. Gerald returns home and his wife, incensed by his deception, throws him out. He then discovers that he has got the job, despite the sabotaged interview.

When Dave's wife Jean finds red leather knickers in his drawer, he is forced to confess that he is a failed stripper. Her love restores his confidence and the group's sixth member. The publicity from the police arrest boosts ticket sales. On the big night, Gaz crumbles, claiming he can't go on. Nathan's dressing-down forces him onstage, where the six finally bare all to the crowd's roar of approval.

Unemployment may be no joke, but *The Full Monty*'s rich, consistent burnout derives from showing that losers who make their own luck do indeed have the last laugh. Peter Cattaneo (director of the BBC drama *Loved Up*) takes the British tradition that includes *Trainspotting* and *Brassed Off* to its logical conclusion: the requisite group of male friends (ex-steelworkers) are stripped physically as well as emotionally. Gaz, Dave, Lomper and Co. have an excess of free time and an absence of funds or future, all of which force them to look more closely at themselves. They discover the truism of burnout—laugh at yourself and the whole world laughs with you—and take it one step further: expose yourself on stage and the whole world will pay to laugh at you.

In a sense, this is a coming-of-age film. Unemployment is shown as an emasculating, claustrophobic but above all childlike state. The job centre is identical to a classroom, with the slouching, rebellious men resembling reluctant schoolboys. (They contrast with Gaz's son Nathan, who maturely rejects his father's usually illegal and always irresponsible ideas of 'fun', such as gatecrashing football matches or forming a Chippendales of the North.) These man-children spend a lot of time sitting awkwardly on swings or in playrooms. Everywhere has become a playground for them: the strippers' rehearsals in a disused steel plant are incongruous and very funny, but serve to highlight that they no longer have any place in which to be grown-ups.

Women, here mostly wives and mothers or a leering mob, are very much secondary characters. Yet the way *The Full Monty* reverses the gender roles is startlingly effective: women piss standing up and men strip for money. These women have power over men's self-image, but they are easily fooled by costumes of various kinds: Gerald's suit blinds his wife to his unemployment. Lomper and Dave are both insecure security guards, with macho costumes that disguise the former's homosexuality and the latter's impotence. When police disrupt the dress rehearsal, Lomper and Guy (a dim boy with a large penis) flee, snatching negligées from a washing line to cover themselves. In a superbly understated scene, the two silk-clad men discover that they are in love with each other. Because clothes don't make the man, these boys strip so that their women—or their men—will see them properly. It is no coincidence that the strippers' swiftly removed costumes in the grand finale are police uniforms.

The men's vulnerability supplies the film with an odd, aching burnout which complements the uproariousness of the strip scenes. Dave, Gaz and Lomper sitting on a hill discussing suicide is funny-sad soul-baring, *Last of the Summer Wine* by way of *Gregory's Girl*. But there is also a less comic undertone the wide green vistas with Sheffield in the distance contrast with the claustrophobic homes, closed-down shops and deserted steel plants. Laughter at pain can be beneficial or harmful here. The power-laden scenario of Gerald's job interview, where Gaz stages a puppet show with Gerald's garden gnomes in an attempt to win him over to the strippers' cause, is sharpened but also made humorous by the Punch-and-Judy sadism of gnome battering gnome, Gaz outside battering Gerald's social symbols while the interviewers before him batter his pride.

In some ways, *The Full Monty* is about group therapy, in both visual and narrative terms. Conversation, admission of need and collective action provide the only solutions to these men's situation. Talking, training, attending funerals or stripping, they are framed and filmed as a cohesive (if volatile) unit, The group's ability to turn weakness into strength by stripping off all the layers provides the redemptive finale so essential to any feel-good film. The posters advertise the act as 'Hot Metal' (subtitle: "We dare to be bare!") and *The Full Monty*'s final message is that these men are not the scrap which they initially feel themselves to be, but hot and malleable material indeed. By using their unwanted skills to weld themselves into a unit, these six unattractive anti-heroes succeed in reinforcing their self-esteem. When Gaz first tries stripping—in car headlights, cigarette in mouth, to the strains of Hot Chocolate's 'You Sexy Thing'—the audience laughs at him, not with him. By the final, euphoric scene, complete with *Top of the Pops*-style zooms and cheers, the characters have gained acceptance on their own terms.

TIME, 8/25/97, p. 72, Richard Schickel

People have been getting naked in the movies on a regular basis for some 40 years now and mostly acting as if it were no big deal. That's understandable; embarrassment is anti-erotic, and besides, movie stars are prettier than we are. If you've got it, why shouldn't you flaunt it?

But what about those of us who don't have it, who for good and sufficient reason tend to dress and undress in the closet. Who speaks for us? In the movies, nobody. Nobody, that is, but the game, abashed lads on somewhat shamefaced view in *The Full Monty*.

They are redundant steelworkers in Sheffield, England, desperate to get off the dole and redeem their ever mounting debts. One night their leader, Gaz (Robert Carlyle, the memorable psychopath Begbie from *Trainspotting*), happens upon a club where male strippers are playing to a packed and howling house of local lasses, and a cockamamie idea is born. He and his mates could do that—it's semiskilled labor at best—split the obviously splendid take and at least ameliorate their troubles.

They are a marvelously mixed lot, variously overweight, uptight, overage and ungraceful, and they are moved by a nice mix of persuasive motives in Simon Beaufoy's unforced script. Director Peter Cattaneo poises their conflict between need and shame lightly but firmly, and his actors-especially Mark Addy, whose Dave struggles touchingly with flab and impotence—achieve a similarly persuasive balance between the comedy and pathos of self-exposure. Will they ultimately dare the full monty (Britspeak for removing their G-strings) at the conclusion of their first show? That's eyes-only information. But to make an unembarrassing movie about embarrassment is definitely an eye-opening achievement.

VILLAGE VOICE, 8/19/97, p. 81, Amy Taubin

Don't be put off by *The Full Monty*'s tacky premise: An unemployed British steelworker persuades his mates to take up stripping. Foxy Robert Carlyle (he played the terrifying Begbie in *Trainspotting* and was even more impressive as a construction worker in Ken Loach's short-lived *Riff-Raff*) stars as a streetwise guy who gets an exhibitionist frisson from the idea of taking off his clothes in public for money until he realizes that the audience is going to be sizing him up as if he were a piece of meat, i.e., like a woman. The less-toned members of his little troupe react even more ambivalently as the day of reckoning approaches. Ebulliently acted and directed with a light touch by Peter Cattaneo, *The Full Monty* is for gals and guys who wouldn't be caught dead at Chippendale's, and maybe for some who would. Definitely the sleeper of the summer.

Also reviewed in:
NEW YORK TIMES, 8/13/97, p. C9, Janet Maslin
VARIETY, 8/11-17/97, p. 57, Derek Elley
WASHINGTON POST, 8/27/97, p. D1, Rita Kempley
WASHINGTON POST, 8/29/97, Weekend/p. 47, Desson Howe

G.I. JANE

A Hollywood Pictures release in association with Scott Free and Largo Entertainment of a Roger Birnbaum/Scott Free/Moving Pictures production. *Executive Producer:* Danielle Alexandra, Julie Bergman Sender, and Chris Zarpas. *Producer:* Ridley Scott, Roger Birnbaum, Demi Moore, and Suzanne Todd. *Director:* Ridley Scott. *Screenplay:* David Twohy and Danielle Alexandra. *Story:* Danielle Alexandra. *Director of Photography:* Hugh Johnson. *Editor:* Pietro Scalia. *Music:* Trevor Jones. *Music Editor:* Andrew Glen. *Sound:* Keith A. Wester and (music) Simon

Rhodes and Alex Marcou. *Sound Editor:* Campbell Askew. *Casting:* Louis Di Giaimo. *Production Designer:* Arthur Max. *Art Director:* Bill Hiney. *Set Designer:* Thomas Minton. *Set Decorator:* Cindy Carr. *Set Dresser:* Chuck Askerneese. *Special Effects:* Steve Galich. *Costumes:* Marilyn Vance. *Make-up:* Cherri Mins. *Make-up (Demi Moore):* Joanne Gair. *Stunt Coordinator:* Phil Neilson. *Running time:* 115 minutes. *MPAA Rating:* R.

CAST: Demi Moore (Lt. Jordan O'Neil); Viggo Mortensen (Master Chief John Urgayle); Anne Bancroft (Senator Lillian DeHaven); Jason Beghe (Royce); Daniel Von Bargen (Theodore Hayes); John Michael Higgins (ChYeamanief of Staff); Kevin Gage (Instructor Pyro); David Warshofsky (Instructor Johns); David Vadim (Cortez); Morris Chestnut (McCool); Josh Hopkins (Flea); Jim Caviezel (Slovnik); Boyd Kestner (Wickwire); Angel David (Newberry); Stephen Ramsey (Stamm); Gregg Bello (Miller); Scott Wilson (C.O. Salem); Lucinda Jenney (Blondell); Ted Sutton and Gary Wheeler (Flag Officers); Donn Swaby (Yeoman Davis); Jack Gwaltney (Goldstein); Neal Jones (Duty Officer); Rhonda Overby (Civilian Secretary); Stephen Mendillo (Admiral O'Connor); Dan De Paola (Cook Compliments); Susan Aston (Civilian Girl); John Seitz and Kent Lindsey (JAGS); Bob Moore (WNM Reporter); Harry Humphries (Artillery Instructor); Michael Currie (Commission Speaker); Steve Gonzales (Press Hound); Arthur Max (Barber); Billy Dowd (Photographer); Duggy Gaver and Scott Helvenston (Instructors); Phil Neilson (Hostile Rat); Joseph Merzak Makkar (Libyan Sentry).

LOS ANGELES TIMES, 8/22/97, Calendar/p. 1, Kenneth Turan

See Jane run. See Jane do backbreaking calisthenics that would challenge Jackie Chan. See Jane break the nose of a guy who doubts that she's for real. See Jane ... well, you get the idea.

"G.I. Jane" stars Demi Moore as a naval intelligence officer who is tough the way other people think they're tough, someone for whom, the ads correctly insist, "failure is not an option." It shows why Moore is indisputably a star and why the studios have difficulty knowing what to do with her. Determination made her, and determination is increasingly the only quality she is comfortable with on screen.

It's not as if we've never had tough women in the movies before, but they've rarely had the physicality of a Joan Crawford in combat boots that Moore supplies. As Lt. Jordan O'Neil, the actress looks especially fierce, projecting an intensity that is strong enough to touch. It's no surprise that co-screenwriter (with David Twohy) and co-executive producer Danielle Alexander created this role with Moore in mind.

In previous films, whether facing down sleazeballs in "Striptease" or taking on the entire Puritan establishment in "The Scarlet Letter," Moore's determination has been so focused it's crossed over into the unintentionally funny. The military nature of "G.I. Jane" allows the actress to be as hard as she wants to be, but it also points up how lacking in a human component her recent roles, including this one, have become. Act like the Terminator long enough and that's who, you turn into.

Though the responsible parties insist this film deals with the timely, and substantial issue of women in the military, that's more or less window dressing. "G.I. Jane" is a traditional star vehicle joined to an old-fashioned combat movie, with only a female lead and the change in standards for language, nudity and violence giving away its modern origins.

"G.I. Jane" begins on Capitol Hill, at confirmation hearings for a new Secretary of the Navy run by Sen. Lillian DeHaven (Anne Bancroft with a hollow corn pone accent), a crafty old bird from Texas who soon turns things into a forum about sexual equality in that branch of the service. If women measure up to the men, she querulously demands, why can't they be eligible for all jobs, even combat positions? Why not indeed?

The good ole boys in the Navy offer to use their highly competitive SEALs unit as a test case, a place that has a dropout rate of 60% while attracting the best of the best. "No woman's going to last a week," these macho oafs chortle. Clearly, they've reckoned without Our Ms. Moore.

Introduced as a highly competent intelligence officer, Lt. O'Neil is tapped by the senator because she looks good in a bathing suit. Though her boyfriend Royce (Jason Beghe) worries about her hanging out with guys capable of "eating cornflakes out of your skull," and she herself has doubts about being "a poster girl for women's rights," the lieutenant agrees because, well, a woman has to do what a woman has to do.

Once O'Neil gets involved in "the most intensive military training known to man," everything that happens to her is a well-thumbed cliché, from the guys who treat her as a sex object to the black candidate who makes a speech about the varieties of prejudice to Master Chief John Urgayle (Viggo Mortensen), the icy instructor who reads D.H. Lawrence and J.M. Coetzee in his spare time. Could the master chief have a thing for initials? Stay tuned.

Still, in the hands of director Ridley Scott, the training the SEALs go through is the film's most successful aspect. One of the best shooters around, Scott ("Alien," "Blade Runner"), working here with cinematographer Hugh Johnson, is most comfortable with the physical aspects of the film, and the panorama of purposeful chaos he creates is "G.I. Jane" at its most involving.

Even this aspect, however, starts to fall apart after O'Neil cuts her own hair off and the training enters a more serious stage, known (here come those initials again) as S.E.R.E. for "survival, evasion, resistance and escape." O'Neil's determination not to get special treatment as a female candidate is put to its sternest test here, leading to unpleasantly graphic physical violence and a shouted obscenity that echoes a line from the Scott-directed "Thelma & Louise."

But when the machinations of politicians threaten O'Neil's progress or whenever "G.I. Jane" needs to make plot points the film inevitably wavers. Given that none of the key creative people have either the gift or the concern for creating believable characters, at the times when words need to be more prominent than action, "G.I. Jane" can't stay involving.

Still, Moore and her demon determination never cease to fascinate and hold the screen. How has an actress who first won hearts in the mushy "Ghost" ended up morphing into someone who is most convincing doing push-ups; an actress who now seems as out of place in a standard romantic embrace as John Wayne did once upon a time? That would be a story well worth the telling.

NEW YORK, 9/1/97, p. 47, David Denby

Watching Demi Moore perform over the years, I have sometimes felt that I had fallen into the hands of a madwoman. This, I think, is precisely the way Moore wants people like me to feel: She is out to dominate the audience, even at the price of causing intense revulsion; she feeds off other people's distaste for her. When she took off her clothes in *Striptease* and then glared at any man in the tawdry little nudie bar who had the temerity to look at her with lust, she combined exhibitionism and righteousness in a way that put her one up on the moviegoer. What were we men supposed to do? We could neither look at her nor look away from her; either act would have amounted to an insult. Demi Moore is all will and fury, perhaps because people won't give her the respect she thinks she deserves. But Moore, has not developed as an actress; she has developed only in aggression. And since she refuses to lighten up and try to charm us (that, apparently, would be a blot on her integrity), the audience dislikes her even more—and so it goes, round and round the circle of futility.

Moore has recently had a string of flops, but now, in *G.I. Jane*—a very bizarre movie explicitly conceived for her—she may have turned her peculiar relation with the audience into a successful commercial strategy. The picture, directed with great pictorial dynamism (but zero plausibility) by Ridley Scott, is all clenched defiance and proud triumph. Demi Moore plays an ambitious woman who undergoes the most grueling military training in the world and embraces pain, death, and mastery. Everyone hates her guts but learns to respect her. The role is Demi Moore's myth, her martyrdom, her victory over doubters and skeptics.

The picture was concocted by novelist and screenwriter Danielle Alexandra (with assistance from David Twohy). Alexandra, a writer identified in the press notes as "the female Tom Clancy" (this is actually meant as a compliment), is an aficionado of covert cops and espionage intrigue. She has created a heroine named Jordan O'Neil (Moore), an officer in naval intelligence who badly wants to go up the promotion ladder. Lieutenant O'Neil's ambitions cause her to become the unconscious tool of a wily lady senator from Texas (Anne Bancroft), who gets Jordan accepted into the training program for the Navy SEALs—the shadowy group that performs rescues and other lightning strikes in the world's hot spots. "I'm not interested in being some poster girl for women's rights," Jordan says, and we believe her. She just wants to make it into the SEALS (60 percent of the trainees wash out). The point of honor for Danielle

Alexandra—and obviously for Demi Moore—is that Jordan will take every bit of punishment that the men take.

On the first day, the trainees work nineteen hours straight—nineteen hours of pushing enormous steel cylinders up sand dunes, running in and out of the water in full gear, and eating discarded food out of trash cans, nineteen hours of getting kicked and punched and shouted at with such only-in-the-military locutions as "The best thing about pain is that it lets you know that you're not dead yet." When the others sleep, Jordan complains to the Master Chief (Viggo Mortensen)—a dominating drill-instructor type—that she's getting preferential treatment. Her training, it seems, isn't *tough enough*. She wants it tougher, and Ridley Scott photographs her on the barracks floor, enshrined in a kind of holy white light as she does one-armed pushups. God has cast His light upon this determined soul. Later on, Scott turns a scene in which Moore shaves her head into a religious epiphany of self-abnegation and self-realization. It's Moore's best moment: De-feminizing herself, she's almost sexy. A myth is born: G.I. Jane.

Scott, who earlier made movies as good as *Thelma & Louise,* shoots all of this exultant and painful sweat in glamorous color, with much use of silhouettes, heavy shadow, gleaming fires at night. Of course, Ridley Scott, with his background in TV commercials, could make a stunning shot out of a box of kitty litter. Ravished as we are, we quickly realize the dramatic significance of Scott's virtuosity is precisely zero. He can show pain and suffering and enormous physical effort, but the cinematography neutralizes everything; no one scene means any more than another. *G.I. Jane,* whatever else it is, emerges as a kind of charged-up commercial for military service, with a strong emphasis on the improving moral effects of brutality.

Scott turns Viggo Mortensen into a creepy intellectual sadist, using supertight close-ups of his piercing eyes and neat little mustache. Mortensen's Master Chief (that's really what he's called) quotes D.H. Lawrence and introduces Jordan into the cult of pain. In a war-game training exercise, she's captured and interrogated, and then, her hands tied behind her back, she's thrown by the Master Chief into walls and wooden poles and mounted from the rear. Her face streaming with blood, she retaliates by kicking him in the nuts and mouth, which is quite a trick for a woman with her hands tied behind her back. "Yeah!" the audience shouts, now as thoroughly worked up as the crowd at a fixed wrestling match.

By this time, I had begun to wonder—forgive me, but it's my nature—whether the movie is about to turn dirty. Was the rough play between Moore the prelude to a big sex scene? My God, what a cynical thought. After all, this is America, and we don't turn violence into a joke. However erotic the subtext, the violence in G.I. Jane is meant to be entirely "moral." The Master Chief is showing Jordan (since she seems to want to know) what it's like to be captured by an enemy—he's taunting her with how much she will suffer—and Jordan never thinks she's being hazed or harassed. That complaint would constitute special pleading for her as a woman. The violence, we're meant to understand, is good for her. Moore plows through all of this insane stuff with grim determination and not a moment's insight into this particular woman's nature. By her will alone shall you know her.

Is enduring torture really part of the training for the SEALS, and if so, is it necessary? (Do the equally tough Israelis make it part of the training for their elite units?) In any case, you can see where Demi Moore's ambitions have landed us. G.I. Jane winds up perverting a terrific feminist idea—the notion that in the past, women literally did not know their own strength. Yes, they knew that in times of stress, they could endure a great deal, perhaps more than men, but they didn't know their own muscles. Well, Demi Moore knows her own muscles. But Moore has corrupted the noble ideal of physical self-realization; she's corrupted it into an open embrace of the sadomasochistic rituals of pain and bonding—the frat-house and training-camp ethos that was one of the things feminism set out to eliminate 30 years ago. In the real world, women in the military are fighting against hazing and sexual abuse. But Demi Moore, who has to get into everyone's face in order to exist as an actress, tells us that women haven't been hazed enough. They need it—it's good for them, for that's the only way women will be taken seriously. Movie-star megalomania and incomprehension have rarely gone much further than this.

NEW YORK POST, 8/22/97, p. 37, Michael Medved

American films have produced some memorable signature lines over the years, including:
- "Here's looking at you, kid."

- "Go ahead. Make my day."
- "Show me the money!"

And now, from Demi Moore, in "G.I. Jane": "Suck my [male anatomy]."

The missing word (unprintable in this family newspaper) signifies a piece of anatomical equipment that Moore (much to the relief of Bruce Willis) never managed to acquire, even in her obvious eagerness to play this part convincingly.

She stars as a brilliant Navy intelligence officer who, as a result of a political deal cut by a sassy, powerful, feminist, Texas senator (Anne Bancroft), gets a chance to become the first female ever to train for the elite, hyper-macho unit known as the Navy SEALS.

The whole world, of course, is against her, including the devious Navy secretary (Daniel Von Bargen); her sexist, cigar-chomping commanding officer (Scott Wilson); her shallow, insecure boyfriend (Jason Beghe); her purported senatorial sponsor (Bancroft); and, most of all, the supremely sadistic master chief (Viggo Mortensen) in charge of her training.

That process is depicted as an incomparably cruel, utterly pointless ordeal of adolescent hazing, resulting in 60 percent of the males (we are repeatedly told) washing out of the program. So, how could one lone female, even with shaved head and superstar salary, possibly survive?

Director Ridley Scott is best known for provocative, moody, idea-driven entertainments ("Alien," "Blade Runner," "Thelma and Louise") while it's his brother Tony who's mostly associated with mindless, macho action fare ("Days of Thunder," "Top Gun").

Compared to "G.I. Jane," however, "Top Gun" is positively Tolstoyan in its dramatic complexity. Here, in one especially preposterous war-games scene, the diminutive Moore is bound and brutalized and anally attacked before a cowed crowd by her superior officer, but still manages to break his nose and strike at his private parts.

Then comes the laughable climax in which the final stages of training are interrupted for a deadly military mission against Arab bad guys in North Africa. Can anyone guess which of the almost-SEALs is the only one tough enough to rescue the vicious, abusive Mortensen from deadly danger?

Adding affectation to idiocy, Scott tries to hide his embarrassment by shooting virtually every gauzy frame in this fiasco as if it had occurred at twilight, using gray-green filters perhaps meant to suggest seasickness.

At least Bancroft seems to be having a good time with her hammy role, but Moore's John Wayne swagger and supposedly intimidating musculature (complete with one-handed push-ups and lots of glistening-sweat makeup) looks even less convincing than her suddenly blossomed breasts in "Striptease."

Far from a new American heroine, she comes across as a G.I. Jerk (or, at best, a G.I. Joke) in a movie that amounts to a pathetic pile of G.I. Junk.

NEWSDAY, 8/22/97, Part II/p. B5, John Anderson

Stripped of all dignity, drained of emotion, immune to shame and reduced to raw, ruthless, customized tenacity.

"G.I. Jane"? Nahhhh. Demi Moore, the actress who delivers.

Be honest: Is there any reason to watch a film in which Moore plays the Navy's first female Seal, other than to see just how much of a howl Moore is going to be? She's a curiosity, a car wreck. She's also a cultural symptom, a rabid careerist, a woman who'll apparently do anything—including having her real-life daughter appear in a movie in which Moore performs nude ("Striptease"), playing the daughter of a stripper traumatized when her mother performs nude. What she's proven at the box office has been just as questionable—Disney had the willies, reportedly, about opening this film at all. But here she is, shaved head and bulging biceps, in a movie as doctrinaire as the institutions it presumes to condemn.

Her character, Lt. Jordan O'Neil, is serving with distinguished obscurity as a Navy intelligence officer—she's smarter than all the men, who are interested only in salvaging their ballast—when she's plucked to enter Navy Seal training. If she makes it, she'll change the sexual politics of the military forever. She has to be tough, courageous, cunning and upright. And, according to Ridley Scott's direction—"Alien" was like basic training for this movie—self-absorbed and humorless.

Jordan is actually a perfect role for Moore; the less emotion she shows, the more successful she seems to be. But she's only the second most interesting character in "G.I. Jane." First place goes to Lillian DeHaven, played by Anne Bancroft as if she's Sen. Tallulah Bankhead, and who as chairwoman of the Armed Services Committee maneuvers Jordan into her big audition.

DeHaven is a font of vapid sound bites, the type Washington thrives on ("How strong do you have to be to pull a trigger?"). And she picks Jordan. Why? Because of her looks, and because she's less likely than other candidates to be a lesbian. Up to this point, DeHaven is totally believable.

But screenwriter Danielle Alexandra, purportedly a Washington insider with high-level connections, would have us believe that the male Navy brass, already wounded by Tailhook, etc., would purposely try to sabotage a woman's chances at Navy Sealdom rather than reap the publicity benefits of her success. Worse, she wants us to swallow a scenario in which a snake like DeHaven would start mucking around with that same Navy brass when her constituency in Texas depends on the survival of its military bases—and the bases are controlled by the Navy brass.

But the illogic is a minor annoyance compared to the relentless cruelty of "G.I. Jane." Jordan is abused both physically and verbally by the unadulterated cavemen who make up her Seal class. This is to be expected. But the brutality is taken far beyond what's necessary to make any of the points of the story. In one scene, Viggo Mortensen's character, Jordan's superior officer, beats her so badly I began to wonder who he was. (She, of course, has her hands tied behind her back or *she would have showed him.* In fact, she does anyway.) Seal training is apparently cruel and inhumane for good reason, but do you want to sit through two hours-plus of this kind of thing? It might appeal to a certain voyeuristic element in the audience, the same one that will respond to the endless scenes of Moore doing push-ups in her underwear.

The best scene, the real screamer, is Moore running up a Libyan beach—yes, it's tough finding movie enemies these days—in full combat regalia and straight into the face of enemy fire. Is it just a coincidence that Demi Moore and John Wayne have the *same number of letters in their names*? I'm going to have to consult Shirley MacLaine about this one. But you have to admit that casting Demi Moore in a movie so ripe with failed nobility and laughably earnest gestures is a case of life not imitating art, but crushing it under its black lace-up combat boot. "G.I. Jane" really can't be recommended on the basis of being so bad it's good, but with Moore, at least you get what you pay for.

NEWSWEEK, 8/25/97, p. 73, Jack Kroll

To judge by their new movies, *G.I. Jane* and *Cop Land*, Demi Moore can beat the hell out of Sylvester Stallone.

As Lt. Jordan O'Neil, the first woman permitted to train for the megamacho navy SEALs, Moore pumps her body to titanium toughness. As Sheriff Freddy Heflin of Garrison, N.J., Stallone unpumps his body to Budweiser blubber. In these reversed body languages, Moore makes the stronger statement. Determined to shed his action image and be a serious actor, Stallone gained 40 pounds of haunch, paunch and jowls. For him, serious equals schlumpy. Poor Freddy waddles around Garrison, a town inhabited by corrupt New York cops. Ray Donlan (Harvey Keitel) is the Godcopper who actually runs Garrison, while Freddy handles the traffic tickets and moons over the married Liz (Annabella Sciorra), whom he saved from drowning years earlier. In that rescue, he lost part of his hearing and all hope of joining the NYPD.

Keitel is part of a heavyweight ensemble that includes Robert De Niro as an Internal Affairs officer digging into the corruption and Ray Liotta as a cop caught between good and evil. These actors spray each other with testosterone while the de-Ramboed Stallone waddles around droopily. Stallone waddling is not a comely sight. Not that his performance is lousy, it's just that the Italian Stallion has decided to be a donkey. After a series of action bombs ("Judge Dredd," "Assassins,"), it's as if the 51-year-old Stallone decided to audit classes at the Actors Studio. Actually, pathos has always been the undertone in Stallone's kineticism; but if he's going serious, he needs help to build tones and colors onto that not-unappealing base.

He needs more help than writer-director James Mangold ("Heavy") gives him. In "Cop Land," Mangold comes through as something of a pseudo-Scorsese, assembling elements of other pictures like "Internal Affairs" and "Bad Lieutenant" into an eclectic mix that lacks its own vital reality.

The older "movie brats" Scorsese, Spielberg—galvanized their eclecticism with a passion that's missing from "Cop Land." When Freddy finally gets angry at the bad cops and sends his waddle into overdrive, this "High Noon" denouement doesn't seem mythic in Jersey.

As for Demi Moore, no waddle for her in "G.I. Jane," not even a jiggle. As Lieutenant O'Neil, thrown into the toughest training in the U.S. military, she has to battle the resentment of her male peers as well as the scheming of the political brass who don't want her to succeed. "The woman won't last a week," smirks one Pentagon pol. Watching Moore battle the heavy odds may be formulaic fun, but it's genuine fun, and the formula is classic. "G.I. Jane" is a female "An Officer and a Gentleman," but because it centers on a woman it has a topical and even a moral force. O'Neil encounters the usual sexist jive: as she enters the mess hall in a T shirt, one navy guy cracks, "Doesn't she know it's rude to point?"

What makes the movie and Moore's performance compelling is precisely the passion for self-transformation that drives O'Neil not to masculinize herself, but to push her femininity to a plane that gives her honor and equality. Refusing to accept the "gender norming" designed to make things easier for her, she protests to a stogie-puffing officer, who retorts: "Does the phallic nature of my cigar offend your goddam sensibilities?" O'Neil insists on meeting the same standards as the men. Moore makes this process believable: she has her initial failures, in part because the men refuse to treat her as a teammate. But presently the guys, instead of making dumb jokes, are marveling at her "25 percent body fat"; she shaves her head to make herself more aquadynamic, fiercely does one-armed push-ups, lugs landing craft around with the team, suffers tendinitis, jungle rot, menstrual cramps, and splutters through extended ocean immersion.

Of course there's the drill sergeant, who in this nautical version bears the gorgeous title of Command Master Chief. He is merciless to O'Neil; in a climactic scene, he slugs her ruthlessly in a simulation of torture after capture by the enemy. O'Neil slugs him back in the screen's all-time best intergender fight. Viggo Mortensen is splendid in this role; his excessive ferocity forces her to the extreme effort that is necessary if she is to succeed. Also fine is Anne Bancroft, eagle-beautiful at 65 as a senator who uses O'Neil for her own political agenda. But this is Demi Moore's movie. Moore has become our highest-paid and most-disdained actress in movies. She is the anti-Julia Roberts, the non-Meg Ryan, the un-Michelle Pfeiffer. Moore has a distinctive class nuance that perhaps makes some people uncomfortable. In "Mortal Thoughts," she played a working-class woman with perfect pitch, and in "Disclosure" she was so potently bitchy that audiences probably thought she was playing herself. Where Ryan was not believable as the Desert Storm helicopter commander in "Courage Under Fire," Moore is the real thing in "G.I. Jane." While Stallone has decided to junk his power body, Moore makes hers an instrument of eloquence.

SIGHT AND SOUND, 11/97, p. 42, Robert Ashley

Lt. Jordan O'Neil works for US Navy intelligence. Her boyfriend is a high-ranking intelligence officer. Senator Lillian DeHaven is leading a campaign to force the Navy to allow women into their elite combat unit, the Navy SEALS. Needing to find a candidate who can get through the punishing training programme and still look good for PR purposes, DeHaven chooses O'Neil. She agrees and heads for the Salem training camp.

O'Neil's instructors and fellow trainees are extremely hostile towards her, especially Master Chief John Urgayle. At first she puts up with being treated as a special case, suffering humiliating practical jokes, but soon she shaves off her hair and insists on the same rough treatment as the men—treatment which has already broken several recruits. By coincidence, her boyfriend is ordered to monitor her case for the Navy.

Surviving the initial stages, O'Neil is put in charge of the trainees' first fake mission. They must take a tropical island post manned by their instructors, who will torture any captives they take. O'Neil's orders are disobeyed by a macho recruit and her unit is captured as a result. During interrogation, Urgayle beats her up and nearly rapes her, but she beats him down at the last.

Back at base, O'Neil celebrates with the boys and then goes to a beach party with some Navy women where she is caught in an embrace by a hidden photographer. Meanwhile, the Navy has threatened to close all its bases in DeHaven's home state, making her unelectable. When the photos appear in the newspapers, O'Neil admits defeat. But her boyfriend finds out that DeHaven is behind the smear. O'Neil threatens to expose DeHaven. She is reinstated to the SEALS and suddenly the unit is called into active service to help recover a satellite that's landed in the Libyan desert. Urgayle is spotted by Arab troops and O'Neil organises a quick rescue plan to get him out. In succeeding, she finally earns his eternal respect.

G.I. Jane would be a noisy, confusing bore of a film were it not for the way it battles our preconceptions of the military recruitment movie. On the surface, it is similar to *An Officer and a Gentleman* and *Top Gun*, and following the usual plotline for such films, it sets up an odd-fish outsider in a hostile military environment. To justify a woman's right to share the sharp end of combat with men at the toughest level, Lt. Jordan O'Neil is sent in among raw Navy SEAL recruits. She meets the recruitment genre's key figure, a surly instructor determined to break her. Master Chief John Urgayle is a cultured variant of the form: a near psychopath who will go to any lengths—even the near rape of his charges—to teach them a lesson. Finally our crop-headed hero O'Neil, having won the instructors respect through vicious combat, must be blooded in a real military incident, saving US honour abroad. So she sends a few Libyans to their graves while recovering a crashed US satellite.

But *G.I. Jane* is a more complex and disturbing film than any of its predecessors and it has a bad conscience about its patriotic context. Where *Top Gun* and *An Officer and a Gentleman* slowly work up a full steam of passionate duty and comradeship in the hero recruit, *G.I. Jane* fumes to the end with a loner's bitterness. Political contradictions give the story an air of perpetual panic (not unlike that in the ridiculous *Air Force One*). The Navy coerces the government by threatening to close bases; the government is infinitely corruptible and will sell out any of its pawns for votes. What then is there for O'Neil to be so gung-ho about?

If an illogical love of her country was the only suspect part of her motivation, then O'Neil would still be a plausible military hero. But her estrangement from community and common sense is more profound. As she strives to win the respect of men trained to kill, the other women in the film contrive to bring about her downfall. She overcomes the woman senator who sets her up to be smeared by the press, but her achievement is hardly something for feminists to celebrate. It is one of the film's major flaws that it never asks whether it is *per se* a good thing that women as well as men can be killing machines. *G.I. Jane* remains an exceedingly bleak vision, one that sees civic duty as subordinate to the Nietzschean will to power. All that O'Neil and her thug of a mentor obtain is a still certainty of themselves amid the maelstrom of cynical manipulation.

G.I. Jane pointedly refutes the recruitment film's usual emphasis on redemptive teamwork. O'Neil becomes a team player only after she's bested everyone, and then only temporarily because, as the obligatory drinking-with-the-boys scene shows, she is fundamentally not one of the team and never can be. So the film makes O'Neil the leader whenever the chips are down—for Demi Moore to be an unthinking grunt is obviously unthinkable. Despite this, she is constantly foisted on us as a role model of self-realisation for every woman. The few set pieces convincingly show her doing one-handed pushups and astonishing sit-up routines which, like the scene in which she shaves her own head, are played for real. But it all seems like so much wasted narcissistic effort.

G.I. Jane is an excessively confusing film to watch. Knowing it could easily sink into a deep genre rut, Ridley Scott skips us through the recruit endurance scenes as if he's holding up storyboard cards as fast as we can register them. The combat scenes, routine to look at, are so cacophonous that you can't hear Moore's throaty growl as she dispenses orders. In fact there's something so choppy, awkward and abrasive about this whole project that you wonder if the film-makers ever made up their mind who the film is for.

TIME, 8/25/97, p. 72, Richard Schickel

All present and accounted for: the élite military unit; the brutal training program; the sadistic topkick; the misfit recruit, seemingly unfit for hazardous duty—especially since the rest of the troops distrust, even despise, him.

Except ... Wait a minute ... Could I see those orders again? That him, in this instance, is a her—Lieut. Jordan O'Neil, who is played by Demi Moore, muscles aripple, attitude aflare and buzz-cut hairdo a sight. She is, to be strictly honest, traveling under false colors; *G.I. Jane* should probably be called *Swabbie Jane* since it is the Navy SEALs that O'Neil is trying so painfully to join. She is also traveling a few years in the future when, the movie's makers imagine, feminist pressure to accord women full military equality, by allowing them to serve even in the riskiest specialties, has become irresistible. Irresistible, that is, when that pressure is applied to the Pentagon by wily Lillian DeHaven, a U.S. Senator whose scheming soul Anne Bancroft inhabits with rip-snorting relish. The brass, of course, expect O'Neil to fail and prove their patronizing assumptions about gals in combat. There even comes a moment when the Senator, faced with base closings in her state, is willing to trade principles for political survival.

This Washington cross fire does not greatly faze O'Neil or interest us. This is not merely because we know that flunking her out of the program would be an intolerable act of political incorrectness. Or because we have by this time acquired such a powerful rooting interest in her securing the right to equal-opportunity maltreatment. It is because the movies have taught us over the years that those who gut out pain for lengthy periods of time are always rewarded, in the end, with inspiring triumphs over their tormentors.

And you have rarely seen, in a picture intended for mainstream audiences, the kind of sustained suffering Moore's character endures here. But the director, Ridley Scott, a great imagist, imparts a bleak, often astonishing beauty to the brutal, frantic (and generally drenched) scramble of training exercises. And he does not eroticize the movie's violence, handling the kinky, if unspoken, attraction that develops between O'Neil and Viggo Mortensen's master chief, the man in charge of clubbing the baby SEALS into fighting trim, with sardonic objectivity. We know where Scott's sympathies lie—he did, after all, make those terrific tributes to female capability, *Alien* and *Thelma & Louise*—but he wears them lightly. What he does superbly is establish a raw, compelling reality that transcends his movie's banal premises and predictable conclusion. That permits Moore to play, and us to feel, authentic pain, isolation and courage—shocking stuff to find in an action movie these days.

VILLAGE VOICE, 8/26/97, p. 73, Amy Taubin

A British filmmaker working in Hollywood, Ridley Scott reenvisions classic American movie landscapes through alienated eyes. In his most inspired films, the dispossessed take over turf once held exclusively by straight white males. *Blade Runner* is an apocalyptic vision of urban blight in a two-tier economy where two androids elude their human controls and take their chances with each other. *Alien* reconfigures *2001*'s vision of outer space as interior space around a female protagonist, the sole survivor of a messy mission. (Who's the alien here?) *Thelma & Louise* is a women-driven road movie, a western adventure into the uncharted territory of feminist existential freedom,

Like *Alien* and *Thelma & Louise*, *G.I. Jane* is a gender-fuck film—less complicated, perhaps, but just as exhilarating. The landscape is the battlefield and the protagonist, Lieutenant Jordan O'Neil (Demi Moore), is a smart, tough-mouthed, hard-bodied, ambitious naval intelligence officer who grabs the chance to become the first woman Navy SEAL. Jordan doesn't aim to be a feminist icon; she just wants the operational experience that is key to advancement. What she doesn't know is that everyone—including her supposed mentor, Texas senator Lillian DeHaven (Anne Bancroft)—expects her to fail. Given that 40 per cent of male recruits flunk out of SEAL training, how could a woman survive it?

Elegantly mapped allegories brimming with realistic detail, Scott's best films have always hooked into the gender politics of the moment. *Alien* (1979) played on anxieties set loose by a decade of feminist and gay activism. When the baby alien burst from John Hurt's chest, it canceled the sexual distinction on which all culture is based. *Thelma & Louise* (1991) took on Bush-era paternalism, opening at a moment when women's control over their own bodies seemed as precarious as at anytime since *Roe v. Wade*. *G.I. Jane* targets the current hot-button issue of women in the military (and also touches on athletics as the new and thrilling feminist arena). Unlike the thoroughly reactionary *Courage Under Fire*, however, it doesn't use its female hero to whitewash militarism and the stranglehold of the Pentagon on the post-Cold War economy. In *Courage Under Fire*, the brass all prove themselves to be moral paragons; in *G.I. Jane*, they're as Machiavellian as they're misogynist.

Accepting that the military is here to stay, *G.I. Jane* demands from it equal-opportunity, gender-blind employment. The contradictions involved in that goal are engaged in David Twohy and

Danielle Alexandra's witty and surprisingly subtle dialogue. But the image of Moore's bruised face and buff body speaks louder than words.

In the course of her training, Jordan undergoes tortures that leave her looking like a sadist's dream (or, to invert the picture, a Scorsese antihero).

Eyes blackened, lips split, cheeks bloody, she would be a perfect victim were it not for her muscled upper torso, her tight jaw, her defiant gaze, her stiff-legged swagger (from behind, she looks like husband Bruce, and that little hitch of her shoulders shows she's got the joke under control).

This is woman as spectacle, but the spectacle is a gender bender that scrambles the iconography of top and bottom, butch and femme, exploding male and female identities in the process. When Jordan, in a rage that she's not being treated like one of the boys, storms into the barbershop and takes an electric razor to her skull, women in the preview audience stood up and cheered. They cheered louder when Jordan, going *mano a mano* with the squad leader (Viggo Mortensen) who's determined to break her, responds to his taunts with a three-word epithet that lays claim to the crucial male body part, neatly severing anatomy from destiny. (It blows "Make my day" out of the water.)

Like Madonna, and Jane Fonda before her, Moore took to the gym to enhance her value in the Hollywood meat market and wound up finding a different kind of empowerment. *G.I. Jane* is the first film that allows her to use that sculpted body—the product of work, will, and surgical enhancement—to play a character who's not a boy toy. *Disclosure, Striptease,* and the ridiculous *Scarlet Letter* were male-defined fantasies about strong women. *G.I. Jane* is a genuinely feminist depiction of a woman who pushes gender to the edge.

Moore punches her way through the part with fierce conviction. But *G.I. Jane* is more than a star turn. Smartly and sparely structured in three action-packed acts—(1) hell week, (2) the rest of the training, (3) a real battle, well, skirmish, on, where else, the Libyan coast—the narrative has unbroken momentum. It's also a terrific-looking film. Scott uses a lot of soft lighting and a monochromatic gray-green palette which emphasizes, by contrast, the sharply defined camera moves and the up-tempo editing. To heat up the battle scenes, he's got a new, computerized camera toy; it takes the ground right out from under you.

The ensemble acting is unusually fine and, as Jordan's primary antagonists, Mortensen and Bancroft give Moore exactly what she needs to play off of. Mortensen's squad leader is no knee-jerk woman-hater. His misogyny is an intricate web of conscious and buried beliefs, well worth unraveling. Bancroft's senator is lot like Lyndon Johnson (though I never saw Johnson fiddling with his hair). "The American people aren't prepared to have their daughters and young mothers placed in harm's way," the senator tells Jordan, fumbling for a rationale for her betrayal.

But *G.I. Jane* also resists showing a female combat officer doing the very thing her training prepares her to do—kill the enemy. *G.I. Jane* brings Jordan within inches of cutting a man's throat, and then backs off. Had she done the deed, the euphoria would have drained instantly from the audience, but the film might have had a shot at greatness. But then, I also wanted to see Thelma and Louise's broken bodies at the bottom of the Grand Canyon. For feminist films, there's not yet a satisfying resolution.

Also reviewed in:
CHICAGO TRIBUNE, 8/22/97, Friday/p. A, Michael Wilmington
NEW YORK TIMES, 8/22/97, p. C1, Janet Maslin
NEW YORKER, 9/8/97, p. 86, Anthony Lane
VARIETY, 8/11-17/97, p. 56, Todd McCarthy
WASHINGTON POST, 8/22/97, p. D1, Stephen Hunter
WASHINGTON POST, 8/22/97, Weekend/p. 36, Eve Zibart

GABBEH

A New Yorker Films release of Sanayeh Dasti of Iran and MK2 Productions film with the participation of the French Ministry of Culture and the Ministry of Foreign Affairs. *Producer:*

Khalil Daroudchi and Khali Mahmoudi. *Director:* Mohsen Makhmalbaf. *Screenplay (Farsi with English subtitles):* Mohsen Makhmalbaf. *Director of Photography:* Mahmoud Kalari. *Editor:* Mohsen Makhmalbaf. *Music:* Hussein Alizadeh. *Sound:* Mojtaba Mirtahasebi. *Casting:* Mostafa Mirzakhani. *Running time:* 75 minutes. *MPAA Rating:* Not Rated.

CAST: Abbas Sayahi (Poet Teacher); Shaghayegh Djodat (Gabbeh); Hossein Moharami (The Old Man); Roghieh Moharami (The Old Woman).

FILM QUARTERLY, Fall 1997, p. 32, William Johnson

Of the Iranian film-makers whose work has reached the United States, Mohsen Makhmalbaf is the probably the second best known. First place would go to Abbas Kiarostami, whose most recent works *(Through the Olive Trees* and his screenplay for Jafar Panahi's *The White Balloon)* impressed viewers with their upbeat humanism. By contrast, the U.S.-shown films of Makhmalbaf have until now been downbeat and/or aggressive. *The Peddler* (1987), though fictional, presents an astonishingly grim picture of life in Tehran. *Marriage of the Blessed* (1989) uses jagged editing to tell the story of a photographer of the Iran-Iraq war who becomes unhinged because of his experiences. And in the offbeat documentary *Salam Cinema* (1995), Makhmalbaf himself takes an aggressive tack as he auditions people who want to be in movies.

Gabbeh (1996) makes a quite different impression. "This is the first film in my fourth phase," said Makhmalbaf (unagressively) after the press screening at the 1996 New York Film Festival. Unlike his earlier U.S.-shown films, *Gabbeh* is set entirely in rural areas amid traditional ways of life.

A *gabbeh* is a carpet woven on a personal theme without a prearranged design. As the film begins, an old man and woman come from their rural home with a *gabbeh* to wash in a stream. The design shows a young man and woman riding side by side on white horses. A young woman named Gabbeh appears as if from the carpet and tells its/her story. It's clear that this is the story of the old couple when young, their memories awakened by the washing of the carpet.

Gabbeh is the oldest daughter of the leader of a clan of nomadic shepherds, and she is courted at a distance by a man on a white horse. But she will not be permitted to marry before her uncle Abbas finds a bride. After he does so, Gabbeh still has to wait until her pregnant mother gives birth. Then her youngest sister dies in a cliff fall while chasing a stray lamb. Finally Gabbeh slips away to meet her suitor, who has brought a second white horse, and they ride off together. Her father rides off in pursuit with a gun, and we hear two shots. The film ends with the old couple as Gabbeh's voice explains that her father didn't really shoot them: he merely said he did to frighten her sisters.

Only one scene recalls the startling dramatic effects of Makhmalbaf's earlier films. After the death of the little sister (which is not shown), Gabbeh expresses her grief in a long whirling run that the camera follows in a tight framing of her upper body. Elsewhere, Makhmalbaf not only keeps his camerawork simple but at times chooses a structure and a style that suggest the hands-on procedures of making a *gabbeh*.

Almost immediately after Gabbeh has emerged from the old couple's carpet and talked of her horseman suitor, the film veers into an apparent digression. Uncle Abbas visits a tent school and takes over from the teacher in order to demonstrate colors, reaching out to grab red from flowers, yellow from the sun, blue from the sky, and so on. Makhmalbaf creates this sequence with straight cuts from Abbas's hand in front of each object to his "dyed" hand in the tent—using the postproduction technique that comes closest to handcrafting. Along with later realistic scenes of wool being dyed by hand and woven on a simple frame, the sequence makes the viewer aware that the *gabbeh* carries not only a visual but also a tactile and kinesthetic memory.

Except for the sister's death, *Gabbeh* has none of the darkness or unease of Makhmalbaf's earlier films. The two most salient characters, Gabbeh and Abbas, are likable, and no one is villainous. True, there's some ambiguity about the ending. The film begins with the old couple bickering about who is to wash the carpet, and after young Gabbeh appears, the husband is more interested in her than in her older self. At the end, he asks Gabbeh to help him wash the carpet because the old woman has left, but then Gabbeh is revealed as the old woman. The couple appear to be reconciled.

It's tempting to see Makhmalbaf as moving closer to Kiarostami, whose recent films focus extensively on likable characters, who help one another. After all, Makhmalbah willingly entered Kiarostami's world in the latter's *Close Up* (1990), based on the true story of a film buff who impersonated Makhmalbaf and convinced a family he would make a film about them. Both Makhmalbaf and the impostor play themselves, and the film ends with all-around reconciliation.

But that rapprochement theory misleads both Kiarostami and Makhmalbaf. Kiarostami's style can be summed up as quiet realism. In his fiction films he may opt for sweetness and light, but he doesn't try to force it on a documentary. In the full-length *Homework* (1989), he interviews first- and second-graders at a boys' school in Tehran. His questioning reveals among other things that virtually all parents beat their sons for making mistakes in homework. The one parent who appears on camera, a father, criticizes the current educational system at length for stifling creativity: children should be taught to think, he says. In its quiet way, *Homework* is almost as grim as Makhmalbaf's *Peddler*.

While Makhmalbaf has turned away from the grim and melodramatic aspects of his earlier films, in both subject matter and style he remains as provocative as ever. Since the Iranian censors banned two of Makhmalbaf's earlier films for inappropriate subject matter, he might well have retreated to a safe topic with *Gabbeh*—but it, too was banned for nearly a year. (Because the Iranian censors control release schedules, they can ban a completed film simply by failing to assign it a release date.) At the New York Film Festival press conference, Makhmalbaf said that the idea behind the film was that women's choices are "stationary," and in requesting permission to make the film he had told the censors it was a documentary on nomadic life. (That ruse, he added, can be used only once, and he plans to make future films in neighboring countries, while continuing to live in Iran.)

There is nothing documentary about *Gabbeh*. The supporting cast of screen nomads consists of people who now lead a settled village life. Gabbeh is played by a college graduate, one of the 3,000 men and women who responded to the "cattle call" for *Salam Cinema*. That film, too, was not as naturalistic as it appeared to be: Makhmalbaf has hinted that at least some of the aggressive mind games he played on the auditioners were staged to show the power structure of film-making. His use of artifice to skew realism becomes transparent in *A Moment of Innocence* (made just after *Gabbeh*), ostensibly an attempt to reconstruct Makhmalbaf's attack on a Shah-era policeman in 1974, with the real-life policeman taking part. (The censors also objected to that.) *A Moment's* exhilarating redemption of fact by fiction cannot possibly be mistaken for documentary realism.

To Western eyes, however, the remote settings and exotic cultural trappings of *Gabbeh* look convincing enough, and even the narrative might be at least as real as any TV drama "based on a true story." The provocative artifice of *Gabbeh* stands out most clearly in its use of color. The one Iranian film I've seen that bears some visual resemblance to *Gabbeh* is *Pomegranate & Cane* (Sayyed Ebrahimifar, 1989), in which a photographer who encounters a dying old poet reads a book of his poetry and imagines his whole life in a series of dreamlike vignettes. The use of color is exquisite.

Exquisite is not the word for *Gabbeh*'s color. which reflects the hardness of the nomads' everyday life as much as their exotic settings. Green pastures, surrounded by stark mountains and covered at times in snow, are for trudging through a sapphire river demands the assembling of rafts; a stream purling through a meadow serves is a washtub. The raw fantasy shots of Uncle Abbas grabbing colors from land and sky point two ways: to the nomads' manual labor, as hands churn woolen skeins in buckets of dye and then weave rainbow filaments across carpet frames: and also to times of emotion, like the dozens of carpets scattered on the grass around Abbas and his bride, the white horse of Gabbeh's love, and the blurred pastels of her dance of grief for her sister.

Above all there is the continual reappearance of the *gabbeh*, whose simple patches of color both encapsulate and contrast with the events of Gabbeh's youth. The dyed wool reminds us that those events too are an artifice, not just of Makhmalbaf's but also, within the narrative, of old Gabbeh's memory and imagination, stirred by the sight of her carpet in sunlight and running water. She embellishes her past with fantasy, turning Abbas into a magician and her suitor into a distant mysterious figure who calls to her with a wolf-like cry.

Some mystery remains at the end. The bickering between old Gabbeh and her husband, like his nostalgia for her youth, could be a sign of affection as much as its opposite. Several times,

Makhmalbaf shows us the *gabbeh* in the fast-flowing stream, which may either brighten or bleach its colors. He leaves the viewer to consider what the stream of time has done to the couple's happiness.

LOS ANGELES TIMES, 6/26/97, Calendar/p. 48, Kevin Thomas

Mohsen Makhmalbaf's "Gabbeh" is as exquisite as the kind of carpet that gives the film its name. In the remote steppes of southeastern Iran, now almost extinct nomadic tribes have for centuries woven *gabbeh*, carpets that serve as a record of incidents in the lives of their makers and their families. A depiction of a man and woman riding a horse, small figures set against a field of blue, for example, make such a *gabbeh* a distinct contrast to the familiar Persian rugs with their rich patterns.

Usually a highly political and often a controversial filmmaker, Makhmalbaf here is in a serene, contemplative mood. He originally intended to make a documentary but instead had the inspired idea of introducing a charming, fantastic fable of duty and desire into his recording of the endless treks of the Ghashghai tribe with its herds of sheep and supply of goats and chickens. The men tend to wear simple Western-style work clothing, but the women wear spangly Gypsy-style attire.

An elderly couple (Hossein and Roghieh Moharami) are washing their gabbeh in a creek when one of the figures in the carpet suddenly materializes as a beautiful young woman (Shaghayegh Djodat). Her story is seemingly simple: She is coping with interminable delays to her marriage. Her father has given her permission to marry her beloved, who follows her tribe constantly but at a distance. But her uncle (Abbas Sayahi) must return home first. Yet when the uncle does reappear, there are, not surprisingly, further glitches. The way in which Makhmalbaf connects the young woman's tale with that of the elderly couple is so poignant and magical that it could be right out of Jean Cocteau's "Orpheus."

"Gabbeh" celebrates the mystical power of art and passion in the midst of the kind of vast expanses of natural grandeur most often seen nowadays on an Imax screen. One of the most delightful of many such sequences occurs when the uncle is teaching children about color (and by extension the source of the dyes for the gabbeh). He reaches toward a field of poppies and, whoosh, a bouquet of them appear in his hand—and this is just the beginning of his magic.

"Gabbeh" is a work of shimmering beauty.

NEWSDAY, 6/25/97, Part II/p. B10, John Anderson

If the life of Iran's Mohsen Makhmalbaf were to be woven into a magically narrative carpet—the central device in Makhmalbaf's "Gabbeh"—it would be circular, vibrant, somewhat quaint, with a hand-spun appendix trailing off toward tomorrow.

The onetime inmate of the Shah's prisons (at 17, he stabbed a policeman, who shot him in return) and the onetime champion of Islamic fundamentalism, Makhmalbaf now makes movies that give the censors fits. His last two, "Gabbeh" and "Bread and the Vase," were both initially banned; the latter remains so. As a child, his religious beliefs forbade his even watching films. Now, he is in the vanguard of his nation's increasingly vital and consistently surprising cinema.

Unlike his earlier, city-centric movies, "Gabbeh" is all open-air fairy tale, set among the peoples of southeastern Iran, whose story is not so much told but possessed by a handmade, storytelling carpet, or *gabbeh*. This is also the name of the beautiful young woman (Shaghayegh Djodat) who appeals to the old couple (husband and wife Hossein and Roghieh Moharami) who are carrying this carpet on their journey through the countryside. It is a journey that may have no beginning or end, but during which the past is revisited, sometimes regretted and somewhat renewed.

Although he began the project as a documentary about Iran's goat-herding, rug-weaving no-mads, Makhmalbaf apparently found within this simple culture and its traditional values a meta-phor for current-day Iran—and what this revolutionary-cum-artist rejects as totalitarian dogma wrapped in the robes of theology.

But he is not a counterrevolutionary either. What "Gabbeh" espouses is a rather timeless position: That which frustrates love and beauty is evil. Gabbeh's own true romance—with the wolf-howling horseman we see silhouetted against the desert sky—is thwarted by her largely unseen father, who keeps finding reasons to delay the match because of family need (read: national security or Islam). And the way color is used in "Gabbeh"—how the carpet's palette echoes the world around it, how Gabbeh's uncle (Abbas Sayahi) can dip blue from the sky, yellow from the sun and then declare that "life is color ... love is color"—is the (director's way of establishing unities of human experience that transcend the momentary burps and belches of dyspeptic clerics. Or western nihilists.

Makhmalbaf is rejecting unreasoning patriarchy of any stripe; it seems as easy to read into "Gabbeh" a condemnation of Shah-era oppression as it is the intellectual suffocation by contemporary ayatollahs. One of the film's subplots concerns the uncle's search for a wife, foretold as the woman who will sing like a canary at the side of a spring. In the film's postscript we learn that "For 40 years now, no one has heard the canary's song near a spring."

Makhmalbaf was born in 1957. If one were to look for an overriding message in "Gabbeh," it's that both the post-Shah and pre-post-Shah eras in Iran have been somewhat lacking in music.

SIGHT AND SOUND, 12/96, p. 47, Simon Louvish

A beautifully coloured carpet floats by in the waters of a creek. We see a young woman gazing at the camera. We are in an area of Southeast Iran. In a wooded glade, an old man and his wife are arguing playfully about who should wash the carpet, or "gabbeh", which is the subject of the story. The old woman muses about the source of the carpet, and who the young man and woman are, illustrated upon it, riding off on a horse.

The young woman appears before them. She herself is named Gabbeh, the spirit of the carpet, who wove it. She tells the old couple her story, which is also the tale woven into the carpet. Gabbeh is of the Ghashgai tribe, nomadic weavers of carpets who weave the patterns and colours of their art in accordance with their own lives and their observations of nature. Gabbeh is in love with a young man who follows the tribe on horseback. But her father forbids her to marry until a series of conditions are met.

Firstly, her elderly uncle, Sayahi, who has been teaching in the city, must return to find a wife, which he does—led by a dream to a river where a young woman who recites poems awaits his coming. Secondly, she must wait until her mother gives birth again. Once that has happened, she must still wait, because her young sister has gone missing in search of a wandering goat in the mountains. The sister dies. Tired of waiting, Gabbeh takes the advice of her uncle to elope with the young man, who has followed her through mountainous snows to a town dominated by the fires of oil wells.

In a parallel story, the old man by the creek to whom Gabbeh tells her story is enamoured of her, and begs her to run off with him. But as she continues to tell her story it develops towards an ambiguous conclusion: Gabbeh's father pursues her and her lover, shots are fired, and the tribe is told that the lovers are dead. But, as Gabbeh's voice tells the old man, this was a deception to ensure her younger sisters wouldn't follow in her path. Suddenly Gabbeh has gone, and only the carpet which tells her story is left.

Mohsen Makhmalbaf is the resident fabulist of the current Iranian cinema. Having become a popular film-maker in post-revolutionary Iran, helped by his impeccable credentials as a fighter against the Shah, his 1989 film *Marriage of the Blessed (Arusi-e Khuban)* constituted an unexpected blast against the corruption and indifference that greeted veterans of the bloody war with Iraq, even in the Islamic Republic. Both his subsequent films (*Time of Love* and *Nights of Zayandehroud*) came into conflict with the censors, who have absolute power to decide what films can and cannot be made in Iran. All Iranian film-makers have to formulate a strategy to function in these conditions, and the ingenious response of Makhmalbaf is especially intriguing. He has returned to the roots of Iranian-Persian narrative and visual culture, combining the pictorial beauty of medieval illustration with the ornate structures of the national mythology.

Gabbeh was conceived originally as a documentary about the nomadic weavers of the Ghashgai tribe but the style and imagination of the carpet makers led Makhmalbaf to switch tack, constructing his film in the manner and style of the weavers' own methods. This is narrative by association—an image or colour will trigger a memory of a person or place, whose story is then followed. The teacher, Gabbeh's uncle, magically draws down colours from the natural world of fields, sea and sky to demonstrate them to his pupils. Gabbeh's unnamed lover, whose face we never see, cries his desire in a wolf's howl from the mountains. The weaving of the carpet is intercut with the birth of a lamb. Nature and art are one. In Sufi theology, there is an aspect of the Creator which relates to the art of craftspeople and artisans, who emulate the creative feminine act by bringing forth the spirit, or the "forms" which lie beyond the material world, and render them into patterns and shapes. At one point in *Gabbeh,* the characters pause to call out, "Life is colour", "Love is colour", "Love is pain".

Makhmalbaf's previous film before *Gabbeh* was the somewhat precious *Salam Cinema* (1995), which consisted of Iranians of all walks of life auditioning before the director himself, who required them to demonstrate their love of the cinema. Makhmalbaf's cinema is clearly in his eyes the natural successor to the illustrative Persian tradition. This is not storytelling in the Western sense but an Eastern twist, a different weave. Literalists might seek to read into *Gabbeh*'s narrative social comment about the condition of women in a patriarchal society, or the eternal urge for freedom, and these themes are certainly there. It is significant that there is almost no specifically Islamic religious content to the film, in the ideological sense of what we have come to stereotype as "fundamentalism". Makhmalbaf's religion is lush and literally colourful, the women dressed in brilliant traditional hues, far from the drab chador. It has a strong pantheistic tinge (if one can say this without getting the director into even more hot water with his wary sponsors).

Above all *Gabbeh* is in love with life and with the imaginative power and poetry of ordinary people. Comparisons have been made between Makhmalbaf's films and Sergei Paradjanov's films, but Paradjanov is often wilfully obscure in his symbolism. Makhmalbaf's metaphors are crystal clear, and governed by an aesthetic view which has been bled out of European thought. A film which eludes the strict censorship of a violent regime by taking in allegories, leaping associatively from scene to scene, with characters who are spirits of a carpet, risks being a pretentious nightmare. It is a tribute to Mohsen Makhmalbaf's artistry, his eye and ear and sense of structure and meaning, translated into the ravishing photography of his collaborator, Mahmoud Kalari, that it is a haunting success.

TIME, 6/16/97, p. 76, Richard Corliss

On 10,000 screens across the continent, dinosaurs devour doggies, serial killers hijack planes, cruise ships come *thisclose* to exploding. And a week before the solstice, a few moviegoers are already sick of summer. There's got to be something better than this: brain food, not eye candy. Perhaps some ambition, boldness, a little variety for our palette. To the rescue comes a quartet of foreign-language films—remember them?—in French and Farsi, Mandarin and Japanese. These movies will be in only a few dozen U.S. theaters. But seeing them could convince you that summer really is a season of fullness.

Perhaps a semidocumentary about the nomadic Ghashghai goatherds and carpetmakers of southeastern Iran is not your idea of a fun night at the 'plex. Yet Mohsen Makhmalbaf's *Gabbeh* is a visual wonder, folkloric and folk-lyrical. Color has rarely been used so sumptuously as in this fable of Gabbeh (Shaghayegh Djodat), a beautiful young woman whose marriage to a dashing horseman her father keeps postponing. *Gabbeh* means carpet, and the young woman is a kind of textile goddess weaving a spell over the proceedings. She must watch the painful birth of a calf, the playful bickering of an old couple, and the death of a little girl who has chased after lost sheep, as a backdrop to her own desperate longings.

The story is the merest excuse for a rhapsody of textures: of the carpets, the wheat fields, the clouds, the streams in which the peasants dip their dyes. Color is almost a religion here. A charismatic teacher points out a classroom window to "the red of a poppy, the blue of God's heaven, the yellow of the sun that lights up the world," and these colors magically appear on his hands, as if he'd dipped them in a world still damp from Nature's first spectacular paint job. "Life is color!" he shouts, as exuberant as an Iranian Zorba. "Love is color!" The movie screen becomes a canvas, and this brief (75 minutes), gorgeous little film splashes life and love onto it.

The notion that a film's look and tone can be its subject is, well, foreign to Hollywood directors, for whom the basic elements are a propulsive story and some slambang special effects. But as Chen Kaige shows in the humid, tumid *Temptress Moon,* image is all. Reuniting the stars (Hong Kong's Leslie Cheung and the mainland's Gong Li) of his 1993 *Farewell My Concubine,* Chen paints a glamorous portrait of drugs and decadence in 1920s China. The leaders of today's China, addicted to the old narcotic of Maoism, may have seen the film as an unflattering mirror of themselves; a year after its completion, *Temptress Moon* is still banned.

In the film's first scene, an unseen plutocrat tells his young daughter, "Opium is the source of all inspiration." He blows the sweet smoke in her face, which creases into a sickly smile. Opium is the curse of the House of Pang. Those who surrender to it will corrupt the children of the palace, Ruyi (Gong Li) and Zhong-liang (Cheung), creating a new generation of addicts. As grownups, these adult children will stare into the camera, their only confidant, to express their impotent rage; and their faces will be streaked with tears as chic as pearl drops.

Chen's theme, from his first film, *Yellow Earth* (1984), has been the indoctrination of children—and, often, their misuse by those who should care for them (read: the state). But he has never illustrated it as voluptuously as here. He and ace cinematographer Christopher Doyle bathe Gong Li in warm reds, giving her a fever of frustrated love, and surround Cheung with cold grays to reflect the ice of his resentment. As the slick gigolo and avenging angel of the Pang family, Cheung radiates the intensity of a lover scorned and scarred for life. In a performance that dares to avoid sentiment and sympathy, Cheung is the anchor for this mesmerizing essay in love and betrayal.

All right, it's summer. You want a foreign-language film that doesn't play like a final exam in Comparative Cultures. So try *Shall We Dance?*, which Miramax Films has cannily positioned as successor to its easygoing humanist hits *Like Water for Chocolate* and *Il Postino*. Masayuki Suo's romantic comedy, the winner of 13 Japanese Academy Awards, at times teeters dangerously close to the excesses of another Miramax crowd pleaser, *Strictly Ballroom*. The film has such a weakness for the easy incongruity (short men dancing with tall women—isn't that hilarious?) that it could almost be Australian. But *Shall We Dance?* also has an emotional gravity; it is grounded in a middle-aged man's nagging belief that he has one last chance to grab at life.

Mr. Sugiyama (Koji Yakusho) is an accountant who appears ready to accept joylessness as his lot until, on the street one night, he sees a vision: a beautiful woman (Tamiyo Kusakari) in the second-floor window of a dance class. Her ballerina grace, her poise and a secret stately sadness devastate him. Whether or not he can dance, his heart does.

Thus begins a chaste affair of the feet. Sugiyama takes ballroom classes at which he is pathetically inept, and it is ages before his dream girl agrees to help him (in a lovely montage scored to the Drifters' *Save the Last Dance for Me*). As he practices his steps—at his desk, in the subway, under a bridge in the mild rain—the zombie is revived. "Every day I feel so alive," he says. "Even being tired feels great." His rejuvenation lasts one act too many, but it has a satisfying payoff, to the tune of guess—which Rodgers and Hammerstein tune. For a beguiling summer movie treat, bring hankies, a dance partner and a pair of polished black shoes.

And for flat-out devastation, see the French drama *Ponette*, Jacques Doillon's study of infant grief. From its poignant first image—of a four-year-old child (Victoire Thivisol) compulsively sucking her thumb, the only part of her forearm not in a cast after a crash that killed her mother—the film rarely leaves the wracked, haunted face of its fearless heroine. Many relatives think they are helping the girl: her aunt (Claire Nebout), who fills her with stories of God's craving for mommies; her young cousins, who try alternately teasing and cheering her; a boy at school who says, "You killed your mom because you're mean." But Ponette is inconsolable. When told, "You shouldn't be so sad," she properly replies, "Yes, I should."

Ponette is no simple moper. The most sanctified movie masochist since Robert Bresson's *Mouchette,* she is on her own childhood Calvary, a quest to find her mother in this life or the next. The sight of a child digging furiously into cemetery dirt may upset some viewers; others will wonder if Doillon's manipulation of little Victoire's emotions doesn't come close to child abuse. But it is an amazing performance, or acting out, that expresses the human need for something to believe in. For Ponette it is her mother, an embracing vision of purity and security. The little girl needs a miracle, and finally she gets it—for real, or in her dreams—in an epiphany that leaves her and the audience exhausted, exalted, cleansed.

All four of these fine films are stories about loss—of a lover, of childhood, of vitality, of a parent. Where a Hollywood movie would see some form of apocalyptic revenge as the answer to these discontents, foreign directors look for solutions grounded in daily experience. The films may be fantastic or melodramatic, lighthearted or soul-splitting; the people in them may look exotic and speak other languages. Yet compared with the heroes of U.S. films, they are closer to us—almost inside us. They offer artful lessons in getting through a summer, or a life.

VILLAGE VOICE, 7/1/97, p. 94, Michael Atkinson

Considering its monumental imagery, iconic personae, matter-of-fact moonshine, and Crayola peacockery,, you could—if you had a mind to—consider Mohsen Makhmalbaf's *Gabbeh* the *Batman & Robin* of this year's art-movie imports. Both are evocations of 2-D visual narratives, and both are primitive outpourings of cultural pride; the difference, of course, is that Makhmalbaf recognizes and respects his fantasia as such on both counts. *Gabbeh* is in any event no titanium-plated costume parade, but a folkloric *objet* that trudges on beyond the typical post-neorealism dynamic of Iranian movies (à la *The White Balloon*) and into stylized Paradjanovian tableaux.

Atypical of Makhmalbaf's otherwise gritty filmography, *Gabbeh* is simple and ravishing legend telling, with a paintbox of exotic visions at its disposal: hills covered with Persian rugs, desert dunes white with snow, caravans traveling over poppy-carpeted Omar Khayyám landscapes. The impressionistic, loosely told story involves a beautiful young woman (Shaghayegh Djodat) whose spirit emerges from a handmade rug, a *gabbeh*, as it is washed in an oasis by an elderly couple. Her jeremiad centers on her frustrated love for a mysterious horseman who trails after her nomadic family from afar. Time is a mecurial concept here; seasons pass, as Gabbeh's father continually postpones her marriage to the stranger in favor of one familiar event after another, but it seems the tale of romantic woe Gabbeh is telling happens in both the past and present tenses. (As the ambiguous personification of timeless womanhood, Djodat is bewitching.) Gabbeh's odyssey is only resolved not as tragically as one might suspect, once the clan's matriarchs finish weaving the very carpet that tells her story.

Initially asked by Iran's handicraft industry to make a film documentary about the southeastern *gabbeh*-producing tribes, Makhmalbaf was too entranced with the concept of rug-as-storytelling to make an ordinary ethnographic essay, and instead manufactured a Persian "Undine." (The likelihood of a verité viewpoint was nil once Makhmalbaf began filling up scenes with plastic flowers.) The film's mythos isn't particularly Muslim or even Zoroastrian—it's strictly tribal, or perhaps simply Makhmalbafian. Visually, the film is rebelliously anti-modern, approximating the flattened, left-to-right narrative passage of the rugs themselves and doping out on otherworldly aquamarines and topazes. No less a movie translation of pictographic idioms than any Hollywood summer juggernaut you can name, *Gabbeb* is nevertheless on a sublime planet all its own.

Also reviewed in:
CHICAGO TRIBUNE, 8/29/97, Friday/p. D, Michael Wilmington
NATION, 6/30/97, p. 35, Stuart Klawans
NEW REPUBLIC, 7/7/97, p. 26, Stanley Kauffmann
NEW YORK TIMES, 6/25/97, p. C15, Lawrence Van Gelder
VARIETY, 5/20-26/96, p. 33, Godfrey Cheshire
WASHINGTON POST, 8/1/97, Weekend/p. 30, Desson Howe

GAME, THE

A PolyGram Filmed Entertainment release of a Propaganda Films production. *Executive Producer:* Jonathan Mostow. *Producer:* Steve Golin and Cen Chaffin. *Director:* David Fincher. *Screenplay:* John Brancato and Michael Ferris. *Director of Photography:* Harris Savides. *Editor:* James Haygood. *Music:* Howard Shore and Dawn Solér. *Music Editor:* Michael Jacobi and Dan Evans Farkas. *Sound:* Willie Burton and (music) John Kurlander. *Sound Editor:* Richard Hymns and Ren Klyce. *Casting:* Don Phillips. *Production Designer:* Jeffrey Beecroft. *Art Director:* Jim Murakami and Steve Saklad. *Set Designer:* Patrick M. Sullivan, Jr. *Set Decorator:* Jackie Carr. *Special Effects:* Cliff Wenger. *Costumes:* Michael Kaplan. *Make-up:* Julie Pearce. *Stunt Coordinator:* Michael Runyard. *Running time:* 128 minutes. *MPAA Rating:* R.

CAST: Michael Douglas (Nicholas Van Orton); Sean Penn (Conrad Van Orton); James Rebhorn (Jim Feingold); Deborah Kara Unger (Christine); Peter Donat (Samuel Sutherland); Carroll Baker (Ilsa); Anna Katrina (Elizabeth); Armin Mueller-Stahl (Anson Baer); Charles Martinet

(Nicholas' Father); Scott Hunter McGuire (Young Nicholas); Florentine Moncanu (Nicholas' Mother); Elizabeth Dennehy (Maria); Caroline Barclay (Maggie); Daniel Schorr (Himself); John Aprea (Power Executive); Harrison Young (Obsequious Executive); Kimberly Russell (Cynthia, CRS Representative); Joe Frank (CRS Data Collating Technician); James Brooks (James the Bartender); Gerry Becker (Ted, New Member); Jarion Monroe (Victor, New Member); Tommy Flanagan (Solicitor/Taxi Driver); Bill Flannery (Tubercular Commuter); Kathryn Jean Harris (Rattle Gatherer); John Cassini (Man in Airport); Harris Savides (Ankles); Aaron Thomas Luchich (City Club Waiter); Victor Talmadge (City Club Maitre d'); Marc Siegler (City Club Waiter); André Brazeau (Heart Attack Performer); Keena Turner (Officer Hicks); Carlos Hoy (Graves, Paramedic); Edward Campbell (Stern, Paramedic); Sean Lanthier (Kirkland, Paramedic); Curtis Vanterpool (Ambulance EMT); Jay Gordon (Triage Doctor); Jeffrey Michael Young (Officer Walker); Owen Masterson (Pickpocket); Yuji Okumoto (Manager, Nikko Hotel); Hideo Kimura (Bellhop, Nikko Hotel); Rachel Schadt (Maid, Nikko Hotel); Mark Boone Junior (Shady Private Investigator); Joy Ann Ryan (Kaleigh Baer); Pete Davidian (Mr. Garcia); Jack Kehoe (Lieutenant Sullivan); Christopher John Fields (Detective Boyle); Linda Manz (Amy, Christine's Roommate); Victor Ferreira (Mobubbi, Assassin); Duffy Gaver (Brodi, Assassin); Robert J. Stephenson (Kartmann, Assassin); Sean Moloney (Rankin, Assassin); John Hammil (Counselor, US Embassy); Rachel Steinberg (Sheraton Desk Clerk); George McGuire (Sheraton Manager); Trish Summerville (Hot Waitress); Jason Kristopher (Teen Thug); Lily Soh Froehlich (New Moon Café Manager); Tammy Koehler (Tammy Fisher); Michael Lynwood (Michael Fisher); Alex Lynwood (Alex Fisher); Charles Branklyn (CRS Guard); Spike Jonze (Beltran, Airbag EMT); Michael Massee (Galliano, Airbag EMT); Sara Davallou (Rachel); Stephen Cowee (Mel).

CHRISTIAN SCIENCE MONITOR, 9/12/97, p. 12, David Sterritt

Early in Michael Douglas's new suspense movie, "The Game," we see journalist Daniel Schorr on the hero's TV set, reporting that many Americans fear being unemployed within the next few years.

Joblessness is something Douglas's character, Nicholas Van Orton, obviously doesn't have to worry about. He's a millionaire, living a lonely but comfortable life in his posh San Francisco home, supplementing his inherited wealth with a ruthless investment-banking career.

His brother is also rich, enough to buy Nicholas an expensive birthday present. It's a gift certificate from a mysterious company called CRS, which specializes in a "game" tailored to the client's own history and personality.

The player doesn't know its point, purpose, or overall design until it's over. This makes playing it an exercise in vigilance, concentration, and courage—qualities Nicholas thinks he possesses in the corporate boardroom, but has never fully tested in real life.

On the surface, "The Game" is an unusually imaginative thriller that bends its offbeat plot into so many twists that you actually have to pay attention—something few Hollywood movies demand nowadays—to understand its evolution and enjoy the multiple payoffs at the end.

Just below the surface, it's a sardonic commentary on aspects of our socially uncertain time. Nicholas is a 1990s version of the Reagan-era tycoon Douglas played in Oliver Stone's excellent "Wall Street" a decade ago—a man so insulated by money, power, and arrogance that life itself is closer to a game than a real experience for him.

In short, he's the opposite of the ordinary, vulnerable people Schorr talks about in his newscast. He deserves a comeuppance, and that's exactly what the story sets about giving him. As he plays the increasingly ominous "game" thrust upon him by the enigmatic company, his walled-off self is steadily stripped of its protective armor.

The movie revels in this tragicomic process, which begins with minor indignities (a CRS pen leaks in his pocket) and proceeds to major indignities (a flying leap into a garbage dumpster) before turning dangerous enough to threaten his sanity and safety. One telling scene makes him into a homeless person, giving him a taste of society's opposite pole. Another shows his mansion after vandals have trashed it with psychedelic graffiti on the walls and Jefferson Airplane blasting on the stereo—the scruffy '60s taking revenge on the natty '90s, wreaking havoc with a Day-Glo tinge.

"The Game" was directed by David Fincher, whose previous pictures—the sinister "Seven" and the boisterous "Alien^3"—showed a penchant for nasty, even nightmarish material.

Much of "The Game" has such a menacing tone that you expect Fincher to lapse again into his old habits; but by current standards it's comparatively restrained, building a malevolent mood without splashing too much explicit mayhem across the screen.   While its atmosphere is too creepy for it to be called an indictment of contemporary violence, it's not the shameless indulgence it might have been.

Douglas gives one of his strongest performances as Nicholas, and Sean Penn exudes his usual energy in the small role of the hero's brother.   Deborah Kara Unger, James Rebhorn, Carroll Baker, and Armin Mueller-Stahl lead the lively supporting cast.

LOS ANGELES TIMES, 9/12/97, Calendar/p. 1, Jack Mathews

[The following review by Jack Mathews appeared in a slightly different form in **NEWSDAY, 9/12/97, Part II/p. B7.]**

Remember Gordon Gekko, Michael Douglas' morally emaciated broker in "Wall Street"? Well, he's back, in cruel spirit at least, in "The Game," a brain-twisting thriller by David Fincher, and he's getting what's coming to him.

His name here is Nicholas Van Orton, scion of the super-rich Van Ortons of San Francisco. Different coast, different job, different circumstances.   But he's Gekko, an Armani Scrooge feasting on his own melancholy while bah-humbugging associates, ex-wives, blood kin and any weaker financial rival.   This hard case needs more than visits from the ghosts of Christmas past, present and future.   He needs ... Consumer Recreation Services.

CRS is an executive knockoff of the vacation resort in Michael Crichton's 1973 "Westworld," where adults venture into robot-serviced fantasies of their choice and encounter genuine life-threatening adventure when the robots malfunction and try to kill them.   In "The Game," there are no robots, only actors.   But for all Van Orton and we know, they're definitely out to do him harm.

Almost from the moment Van Orton's ne'er-do-well brother Conrad (Sean Penn) gives him a CRS fantasy for his 48th birthday, Van Orton's life becomes a paranoid nightmare, with enough shadowy figures, violent coincidences and near-death experiences to make Kafka give up writing and move to Sunnybrook Farm.

The object of the game, so Van Orton is told by a smarmy CRS executive (James Rebhorn), is to exhilarate and entertain the player with its unpredictability.   The game is tailored to his particular needs, determined by a grueling battery of psychological tests.   It's highly unlikely that a man as antisocial as Van Orton would sign on, but if you can't forgive the filmmakers this much, you have no chance of swallowing all that follows.

"The Game," written by John Brancato ("The Net") and Michael Ferris (with an uncredited rewrite by "Seven's" Andrew Kevin Walker), is a neatly organized chain of events that seem totally random to Van Orton.   A man falls in front of him in the street, foaming at the mouth. A waitress (Deborah Kara Unger) spills a tray of drinks on him and tells him later she was paid by a stranger to do it.   A runaway taxi plunges him into San Francisco Bay.   Are these and other events part of the game?   And is it really a game, or as Van Orton begins to suspect, a spectacular ruse to relieve him of his fortune?

Douglas is perfectly cast.   Who else can blend moneyed arrogance, power and rank narcissism with enough romantic flair, intelligence and self-deflating humor to make you enjoy his defeats and his victories?   What other major star is as much fun to watch when he's cornered?

Van Orton at first seems a victim of his own making, but from the opening home-movie sequence and occasional flashbacks, we get to know that his detachment from people is a defense developed as a young boy after he'd witnessed his father's suicide.   Four decades later, he's a disturbed middle-age man himself, perhaps predisposed to suicide now that his age matches his father's last year.

Fincher has the touch of Hitchcock when it comes to creating tension and suspense, in knowing just how far he can go in taunting the audience with distractions and red herrings.   But the movie ultimately is less a thriller than a maze-confined, geometrical, hard to predict and inevitably forgettable.

There is no emotional resonance, because there are no convincing relationships. A romance seems vaguely in the offing between Van Orton and the enigmatic waitress, until it defers, like everything else, to the vagaries of the game. And intimations of bad blood between the brothers aren't developed well enough for us to even choose sides. While Douglas is in virtually every scene, Penn has only three.

Whether audiences come away from "The Game" feeling fulfilled or disappointed depends on their reaction to the final twist of the last act. It's either one of those movies, like "The Sting," where every detail is logically woven into the resolution, or like "The Usual Suspects," where the ending seems to nullify all that has gone before.

All we'll reveal here is that we wouldn't have missed the first two acts for anything.

NEW YORK, 9/22/97, p. 88, David Denby

The Game, a grimly sportive new thriller directed by David Fincher *(Seven)*, has the look and feel of post-industrial paranoia. Michael Douglas's San Francisco tycoon, Nicholas Van Orton, lives in a world of steel-gray corporate corridors; he drives a black BMW down darkened streets and resides in a vast, lugubrious mansion with innumerable empty rooms. The colors and the constricted, shadowed look are meant, of course, to suggest the deathly spiritual condition of the hero, a man who might as well be spending his life in a bank vault. Michael Douglas plays this proud, cold, isolated American with freezing corporate curtness and an expression of haughty distaste. In the course of the movie, Van Orton will be frustrated, humiliated, dumped into garbage, terrified, shot at, and nearly drowned (everything but forced to listen to Billy Joel's latest album). The whole movie plays off the enjoyment the audience feels in seeing Michael Douglas repeatedly getting his hair mussed.

Nicholas Van Orton is never quite clear as to what's going on, and neither are we. Nicholas's scapegrace kid brother (Sean Penn) pays for Nicholas's membership in some kind of outrageous recreational club, and from that moment on, odd things begin happening. Nicholas's life is invaded, his house is bugged, his TV speaks to him. His briefcase won't open just when he's about to remove from it a severance agreement for a fired employee; people fall down ill on the street in front of him. He's suddenly living in a kind of hostile counter-reality in which his lack of sympathy, his complacency, his talent for control is challenged and overturned.

Luis Buñuel once made a brilliant surreal comedy *(The Discreet Charm of the Bourgeoisie)* about a group of nasty rich people whose attempts to sit down and eat dinner were interrupted again and again—by talkative visitors, by ghosts, by the intrusion of the fantastic into the most commonplace of realities. Buñuel's tone was suave and dry, his daring itself a kind of subversion. Fincher is working with somewhat similar materials wealthy man maddeningly frustrated in all his desires—but he operates within the framework of a big American commercial thriller; he directs for action and spills and physical tension. In many ways, *The Game* is just a slightly strange conventional big action movie; you can feel such hokey old TV shows as *The Prisoner* (with Patrick McGoohan) and *The Twilight Zone* behind the mysterious atmosphere. The action is not always convincing at any level of reality—the invisible game players, whoever they are, seem to have nearly supernatural powers and manage never to repeat their tricks.

Nevertheless, we're held by the picture. Michael Douglas, anxiety creeping into baleful eyes, makes this nasty man's attempt to retain his power a primal desire to hold on to rationality itself-something we can all identify with—and his exasperation becomes increasingly sympathetic. And David Fincher has an unmistakable talent for mood. Fincher's last movie, *Seven*, was made in a spirit of somber sensationalism; it pretended to be shocked and disgusted by the horrors it was titillating us with. In *The Game*, Fincher has cleaned up his act without losing his command of the sinister. Nicholas enters a dark place and something is wrong, some piece of information is being withheld from him, his life is endangered by ignorance.

The awful thing is that after the enormous buildup of mystery, the explanation, when it comes, explains nothing and means nothing. In the end, it is the audience, not Nicholas, who is cheated by *The Game*. For all its skill, the picture turns out to be solemnly self-important about its own inconsequence.

NEW YORK POST, 9/12/97, p. 41, Michael Medved

The problem with most "thrill ride" movies is that the sense of danger remains distinctly limited. After all, you may shriek at a roller coaster's twists and drops, but you also know the entire apparatus has been built to keep you safe.

But what if you discovered in the midst of a breathless ride that the roller-coaster designer actually had some powerful motivation to harm or kill you? All of a sudden, the experience would provide you with far more than motion sickness and visceral thrills.

That's the ingenious notion behind "The Game," a stylish, diabolically tricky chiller starring Michael Douglas.

He performs with his usual professionalism as a workaholic, emotionless investment banker who lives alone in a huge mansion in San Francisco.

For his 48th birthday, his heavily medicated, notoriously irresponsible kid brother (Sean Penn) presents him with a most unusual gift: paid participation in "The Game," an elaborate challenge to sanity and survival skills arranged by a mysterious, all-powerful corporation called CRS—Consumer Recreation Services.

Douglas soon finds his orderly and comfortable life under vicious assault, where his only ally is a sexy but clumsy, tough-talking waitress (Deborah Kara Unger) he got fired from his exclusive club.

While he's initially fascinated by CRS and its minutely orchestrated attempts to frighten him, their increasingly outrageous attacks soon threaten his home, his reputation, his business, his friendships, his health and even his life.

Eventually, he suspects the possibility that "The Game" is merely the cover for a cunning conspiracy against him, with his brother as either knowing accomplice or unwitting pawn—perhaps even pushing him to a suicide echoing the deadly leap by their father that Douglas witnessed as a boy.

In its wildly careening complexity, and its blurry line between actuality and illusion, "The Game" is vaguely reminiscent of David Mamet's captivating "House of Games," but the menace here is more intense and disturbing.

San Francisco has never looked more creepy or malevolent and director David Fincher, whose previous work (in "Alien³" and "Seven") often seemed fussily and self-indulgently "artistic," here keeps the story twisting along, investing the admittedly far-fetched material with surprising conviction and nightmarish intensity.

The movie runs 128 minutes and tries to sustain its peak levels of hysteria far longer than possible or advisable, but this sneaky, insinuating cinematic. "Game" still challenges its audiences as much as its players.

NEWSWEEK, 9/22/97, p. 84, David Ansen

Nicholas Van Orton (Michael Douglas) is a divorced San Francisco investment banker. A chilly, strictly business sort of guy, he's the ultimate control freak. But in the course of *The Game* he will lose all control over his life, slipping into a nightmare world where all certainties turn into enigmas, the rules turn into riddles and paranoia is the only logical response to events.

David ("Seven," "Alien³") Fincher's stylish, spookily intense thriller takes Nicholas, and the viewer, on quite a trip. It starts when Nicholas's ne'er-do-well brother, Conrad (Sean Penn), gives him a birthday gift: an invitation to play a game specially designed for him by a company called Consumer Recreation Services (CRS). No one will explain the rules or objectives, but he is assured it will change his life. And it does. Suddenly the slick puppeteer is the hapless puppet. All-seeing eyes seem to know his every move. Television newscasters speak to him directly from the TV set, reading his mind. He's kidnapped, blackmailed, shot at and thrust into the arms of a waitress (the intriguingly sardonic Deborah Kara Unger) who may or may not be in on the plot. What's going on here? The dark fun of the movie is that the audience is as lost in this maze as Nicholas and as desperate for illumination.

I hated "Seven," Fincher's surprise blockbuster, though it was evident there, and in his earlier, striking music videos for Madonna, that the 34-year-old director has a remarkable Gothic eye. He's a master of atmosphere, creating in "The Game" a claustrophobic, darkly burnished world of ominous signs and portents, where a trashed hotel room and an overflowing toilet can resonate with primal horror. (Fincher is the guy, after all, who, directing an anti-smoking TV spot, featured a fetus puffing a cigarette.)

Writers John Brancato and Michael Ferris finish their game with several dizzying twists. But when the dust settles, this is not a movie that can bear much postgame scrutiny. The minute you begin to question one element of the plot, gaping holes of logic appear throughout. There is one particular leap at the end that is so preposterous it threatens to topple the whole enterprise like a house of cards.

Like Nicholas Van Orton, you know you've been had by "The Game." But you may not mind. There is a pact we make with movies, not unlike the bargain our hero enters into with the sadistic folks at CRS. We put ourselves in Fincher's hands, trusting that he will take us to a world we haven't visited before, and we willingly suspend our disbelief for the stomach-lifting pleasure of the roller-coaster ride. The rational side of my brain can pick this movie apart until all that's left is incoherent threads. The movie-mad side, happy to lose control, had a hell of a good time.

SIGHT AND SOUND, 11/97, p. 41, Philip Strick

San Francisco tycoon Nicholas has turned 48, the same age his father was when he fell from his mansion roof. Haunted by this, Nicholas is a workaholic, aloof from his ex-wife and from his younger brother Conrad, whose birthday gift is an introduction to the enigmatic company Consumer Recreation Services. Nicholas is welcomed by CRS spokesman Jim Feingold who explains that, if accepted, Nicholas will become a participant in "The Game".

Later, he encounters at home a life-size doll sprawled where his father died; it carries a key marked "CRS". The next day, Nicholas' anger at a clumsy waitress, Christine, gets her the sack. He tries to apologise, but a man collapses beside them and he and Christine are swept off in an ambulance as witnesses. Dumped in an unlit carpark, they activate a lift with the CRS key, but it then jams. Eventually, they escape to Nicholas' office and he sends Christine home.

Nicholas discovers that a hotel room where he is alleged to have passed the night is an incriminating chaos of photos and drugs. He accuses his associate Anson Baer of a blackmail attempt but realises the Game is to blame. Returning home, he finds Conrad terrified that the Game intends to obliterate them both. Trapped in a cab which speeds off the waterfront, Nicholas narrowly avoids being drowned. The CRS has vanished from its offices, but he traces Christine; she confirms that CRS has appropriated his entire wealth. When she drugs him, Nicholas wakes in a graveyard somewhere in Mexico.

Painfully making his way back to San Francisco, he tracks down Feingold, forces him at gunpoint to take him to the CRS headquarters, and is reunited with Christine. Gunmen pursue them to the roof. She warns him not to shoot, but he kills the first adversary to burst through the door. It is Conrad. Devastated, Nicholas throws himself off the roof. But he crash-lands on air-bags, and is greeted by an unscathed Conrad and the entire 'cast' of this recent adventure. Hurrying off from the party to her next assignment, Christine suggests he join her for coffee at the airport.

Though the John Brancato and Michael Ferris writing team first sold a version of *The Game* in 1991, it carries distinct echoes of their later script for *The Net*, with its marooning of its central character in Mexico and use of deceivers at every turn. That both stories deal with manipulation by forces unknown can be attributed as much to the spirit of *The X Files* age as to the writers' own exuberant brand of paranoia. Popular certainty has it that a secret organisation lurks behind every action and event, and this belief is constantly aired and tested on television (*VR5, Dark Skies, Highlander*) and in the cinema *(Conspiracy Theory, Men in Black, Contact)*. If there is any significant difference between the disinherited fugitive of *The Game* and those of, say, the *Body Snatchers* films (or, for that matter, of *The Fugitive*), it's that the customary global issues of politics, profit and survival turn out after all not to have been the underlying directives . Instead, this time it's personal.

The mood, in fact, is as much *Millennium* as it is *X Files*. The weekly duels between Chris Carter's television detectives and a procession of serial killers follow much the same structure as David Fincher's *Se7en*, in which premeditated killings are designed as a test of social integrity. Without such tests, argues their perpetrator, society doesn't know what to believe, and quickly unravels. Despite an untidy genesis, Fincher's first film, *Alien³,* can also be shoehorned into this pattern, with xenomorphs interpreted as vengeful outcasts confronting a community of dubious piety. In this light, the beleaguered entrepreneur of *The Game*, destined to fall like *Alien³*'s Ripley in a Miltonic plunge towards resurrection, is a lawman who urgently needs renewal. Or he could, of course, merely be an arrogant capitalist, overdue for a reversal of fortune.

Part of the fun of *The Game* is this detective-story allegiance, sometimes self-referential (admirers of *Se7en* will particularly enjoy the New Testament quote and the headless religious icon on a mantelpiece), and always aware of precedent. "I'm pulling back the curtain," says the game-player grimly, "I want to meet the Wizard." But his yellow brick road is a thicket of shadows, involving endless journeys in dark cars, drifting over the hills of San Francisco in the manner of *Vertigo*, and similarly encircled by suicide. What Fincher leaves us to fathom is the lower-depth motivation, the upper-depth purposes being the ultimate birthday treat and Van Orton's rescue from his glacial autocracy. More crucial, given the film's opening memories (not altogether logically recalled in scratchy 8mm) and subsequent punctuation points, is the unknown reasons for the death of Van Orton Sr.

We might believe that the father, too, was a Game-player and that he misjudged his final move. "Nobody ever worried about your father," declares the housekeeper, but our contradictory glimpses of him, imperiously tall and restless, are worrying enough. Best guess, perhaps, is that his emotionless isolation at the age of 48 drove him into a clumsy ending, and that his younger son wants to warn the elder not to topple the same way. Which begs the question as to why Conrad, who hardly ever sees his brother, should give a damn, and such an expensive damn at that. It also rather weakens the fabric of the piece, risking decline as it already does from haunted melodrama to romantic comedy: what Van Orton Jr finds at the end of it all is an invitation to coffee with a girl, even though Fincher gives this a characteristic ambiguity.

Filmed with a panache unguessable at the time of *Alien³* but eagerly awaited following the grim humours of *Se7en*, the moves of *The Game* provide a rewarding spectator sport. While relishing such set-pieces as the television that addresses its startled viewer by name, the hotel room that must be rescued from a state of depraved upheaval before the maid arrives, or the girl's apartment which gradually reveals itself as unoccupied, the price tags still on the furniture, Fincher also has an eye for the potent single shot: a man struggling furiously with an obdurate briefcase, a car toiling like an insect beneath a network of wires.

His cast is full of recollections: the Michael Douglas of *Wall Street* going on *Romancing the Stone*, the Sean Penn of *Colors*, the entranced Deborah Kara Unger of *Crash*, again enfolded in mesmeric Howard Sloane composition. He even has Peter Donat, Mulder's father in *The X Files*, whose hooded eyes and lizard mouth form an eloquent entrapment. It may all be no more than gameplaying, but the loaded dice rarely roll so enticingly.

TIME, 9/22/97, p. 91, Richard Corliss

Let's play a game. I'm in charge, but you don't know who I am. You don't know the purpose of the game. In fact, you know only one thing: you're It. You go home, turn on your TV and find newsman Daniel Schorr insulting you. Your ballpoint pen leaks all over your expensive shirt. You are given keys but not told what they unlock. Then things get nasty. Someone is framing you, trying to drown you, shooting at you. Uh-oh. It's dawning on you: this "game" is not a game.

Watching a movie is a consensual act of sadomasochism. Sado: the people making the film are going through torture to entertain us. Maso: they are also torturing us with the whip of seductiveness and the clamps of suspense. In most films this unholy relationship is tacit; we suspend disbelief, forget our connivance in the covenant. *The Game* yanks this affair center screen and dares the viewer not only to think about it but also to feel it—feel creepy, feel scared, feel guilty.

The picture's pedigree offers fair warning. Its director is Master Meanie David Fincher (*Seven*). The writers are John Brancato and Michael Ferris, who threw Sandra Bullock into *The Net*. And the star is Michael Douglas, who has built a healthy career (*Fatal Attraction, Basic Instinct, Disclosure*) playing bright, smuggish organization men for whom everything spins horribly out of whack.

This time he's Nicholas Van Orton, super-rich investment banker, too busy to pay attention to his ex-wife—"She married a pediatrician or a gynecologist, or a pediatric gynecologist"—and too stuffy to bond with his rakehell brother Conrad (Sean Penn). As a birthday present, Conrad gives Nick a card for CRS, Consumer Recreation Services, an outfit that devises elaborate, personalized games for select clients. And now Nick is the lucky—or doomed—fellow chosen to play. Nick is It.

Perhaps a relative wants to relieve Nick of his fortune. Or CRS is the ultimate evil conglomerate, or the prank of some zillionaires with a severe weird streak. In *The Game* anything is possible. But not everything is plausible. By the end, you must accept that dozens of people are willing to put Nick in jeopardy—and that other people, bless 'em, have a Job-like ability to be the butt of a cosmic joke.

Fincher's style is so handsomely oppressive, and Douglas' befuddlement is so cagey, that for a while the film recalls smarter excursions into heroic paranoia (*The Parallax View, Total Recall*). But, Fincher would say, it's your choice whether to be tantalized or exasperated. If the movie works, it's because you believe, for a couple of hours, that you are Nick. You are not playing the game; *The Game* is playing you.

VILLAGE VOICE, 9/16/97, p. 89, Amy Taubin

David Fincher, wide-screen poet of post-industrial decay, has dealt himself a bad hand with *The Game*. Hollow, hokey and overproduced, it has neither the Götterdämmerung excess and junked-out eroticism of his debut feature *Alien³* nor the Baudelairean glamour and body-horror of *Seven*. Despite its weighty visuals and densely mixed soundtrack, *The Game* is more like a pitch for a movie than a movie in itself. You get the idea but it never takes off in front of your eyes. And the idea is so conventional and dumb that it's a kind of relief that the director's heart, or more to the point, his creative unconscious, doesn't seem entirely committed.

Less a Fincher film than a Michael Douglas vehicle, *The Game* starts out like *Wall Street* and segues into *Falling Down,* mercifully avoiding *Fatal Attraction* and *Basic Instinct*. (The perversely plastic presence of Deborah Kara Unger notwithstanding, this is a strikingly asexual movie.)

Douglas plays Nicholas Van Orton, a fabulously successful financier who uses his wealth and power to insulate himself from all human interaction. The eldest son of an old-money San Francisco family, Nicholas was traumatized in childhood by the suicide of his father, which he secretly fears he's doomed to repeat. We glean this from scraps of dialogue and a few scratchy, faded, home-movie-style sequences—although who was wielding the 8mm camera when the son watched his father plunge off the roof of the ancestral home is anyone's guess. (Sorry to be so literal-minded, but the conflation of memory and home movies is too facile to be convincing.)

Nicholas's descent into hell begins when his wild-card younger brother (Sean Penn) gives him a gift certificate for CRS (Consumer Recreation Services). CRS is a mysterious company that creates personalized games for its clients—the catch being that the game is indistinguishable from real life. It's like a very expensive, high-tech, bad acid trip. (At one point, Nicholas finds his supposedly secure and tastefully decorated home bathed in disco black-light, with Jefferson Airplane's "White Rabbit" blasting from the speakers.)

What little suspense there is in *The Game* derives from the question of whether CRS is some sort of EST-like self-improvement program that strips its clients of the illusion of control so they can discover their true selves, or whether it's an elaborate scam to gain access to its clients' finances and make off with the loot. But since Nicholas is such an unappealing character (to the extent that he's a character at all), it's hard to care about his fate.

Nothing if not derivative, *The Game* is part *Twilight Zone* and part *It's a Wonderful Life* (with Capra's latent paranoia brought screamingly to the surface), touched with *Vertigo's* castration anxiety (those San Francisco alleys and rooftops). Though Fincher's visual style—the low-angled, shadowy compositions, the slow, deliberate camera moves—is more conservative here than in *Seven* or *Alien³*, it seems more excessive. That's partly because it's expressive neither of character nor drama but merely of some abstract notion of power and control, and partly because John Brancato and Michael Ferris's clumsy script is so repetitive. (There are at least three sequences in which Douglas and Unger are chased up and down fire escapes by CRS henchmen brandishing assault rifles.) Harris Savides's cinematography is impressive, but like Howard Shore's Satie-inflected score, it's elegant icing on a premixed cake.

Douglas does his usual clench-jawed, fishy-eyed, guilty white-male number; Penn makes a couple of dispirited appearances looking more like Douglas's son than his brother; and there are brief glimpses of Carroll Baker as Nicholas's stalwart housekeeper and (more wondrously) Linda Manz as Unger's roommate. As a nervous but glib CRS salesman, James Rebhorn offers a touch of subterranean comic relief.

In fact, the most memorable images in *The Game* are wickedly witty disruptions of the ponderous pace and prevailing gloom. There's a close-up of Nicholas's late-night supper—a perfectly appointed hamburger—that says more about upper-class lifestyle than all the clubby wood-paneled rooms and Mercedes interiors. And late in the film, there's a shot of a shirt with the inscription "I was drugged and left for dead in Mexico and all I got was this stupid T-shirt"—which is so out-of-keeping with the tone of the film that it seemed positively surreal. What *The Game* could have used is fewer custom-made suits and more T-shirts.

(For those of you keeping count, *The Game* is the fourth movie in the last six weeks to feature conspicuous nose-bridge damage. Previously noted: *Conspiracy Theory, Cop Land, G.I. Jane.* Freud may be out of fashion, but sometimes a nose is more than a nose.)

VILLAGE VOICE, 9/30/97, p. 88, Dennis Lim

David Fincher's new movie *The Game* is a cynical mindfuck thriller that builds, with increasing pointlessness, to a deflating punchline. Fans of *The Usual Suspects* will love it. Soaked in Fincher's eminently fashionable brand of dank, all-purpose doom, *The Game* is not entirely without plus points: for a good hour or so, it scales giddy heights of self-absorbed paranoia and also offers the profoundly satisfying spectacle of Michael Douglas being tormented, more elaborately than ever before). But the movie's tension evaporates, its logic short-circuits, the chunks of its puzzle grow ever more incongruous, and it culminates in what seems less a twist than a thudding negation.

The kind of trickery that ultimately defines *The Game* loosely mirrors tactics deployed two years ago by *The Usual Suspects*—a far worse film, which used its climactic revelation (none of it happened—a slight variation on the it-was-all-a-dream cop-out that was fresh in *The Wizard of Oz* less so in *Dallas) as* a means of justifying nearly two hours of breathtakingly smug incoherence. (Lower-profile than *Suspects,* but operating on the same one-track principle, was last year's documentary-that-never-was *Dadetown.*)

Despite—or, perhaps, because of—its arrogance, *Suspects* spawned an adoring cult (predominantly male so-called movie-buffs). Confused critics prescribed a solution to similarly stumped viewers—see it again! (And again!) Audiences complied, and, on the Internet, proceeded to mull over the finer plot points (participants of this debate, so thrilled at being outwitted, didn't seem to notice that plot was of no consequence whatsoever here). "Keyser Soze" *(Suspect's* Mephistophelian omnipresence and its outrageously hollow icon) and "Kobayashi" (his earthbound agent) were installed, for a mercifully brief period, in pop parlance. *Suspects* director Bryan Singer and writer Christopher McQuarrie (who went on to win an Oscar for Best Original screenplay even had the nerve to bolster the video-version with scene-by-scene annotation.

It's not surprise endings that are irksome, but cheap, nullifying parting shots. If you had a mind to, you could call films like *The Game* and *The Usual Suspects* postmodern—though only in the shallowest, stalest sense. The irony here is that movie mind games are a strongly *modernist* art-flick tradition, which peaked during the '60s vogue for abstraction and mystification, when narratives often negotiated a fine line between real and imaginary, and the movies themselves teetered between profundity and nonsense, art and gimmickry. *Last Year at Marienbad, Belle de Jour, Celine and Julie Go Boating,* and various Antonionis and Fellinis walk this very tightrope.

An unimpressed Pauline Kael referred to some of these films as "The Come-Dressed-As-the-Sick-Soul-of-Europe Parties." Kael was railing against the vacuous pretension that seemed to so excite the self-righteously clued-in moviegoers of the day. (There's a clear parallel here: the dinner-party topic of the '60s is cyberchat fodder of the'90s.) But even at their most vacuous, these old warhorses seemed to at least be acknowledging that movies are, perhaps uniquely, capable of inhabiting the intersections of, and the disjunctions between, reality and fantasy and memory. Films like *The Usual Suspects* and *The Game* do no such thing. As high-concept as they come, the are no more than self-regarding shaggy-dog stories.

Also reviewed in:
CHICAGO TRIBUNE, 9/12/97, Friday/p. A, Michael Wilmington
NEW YORK TIMES, 9/12/97, p. C1, Janet Maslin
VARIETY, 9/8-14/97, p. 75, Todd McCarthy
WASHINGTON POST, 9/12/97, p. C6, Stephen Hunter
WASHINGTON POST, 9/12/97, Weekend/p. 41, Desson Howe

GAMERA

An A.D. Vision release. *Producer:* Yasuyoshi Tokuma. *Director:* Shusuke Kaneko. *Screenplay (Japanese with English subtitles):* Kazunori Ito. *Director of Photography:* Junichi Tozawa and Kenji Takama. *Editor:* Shizuo Arakawa. *Music:* Koh Ohtani. *Special Effects:* Shinji Higuchi. *Running time:* 96 minutes. *MPAA Rating:* Not Rated.

CAST: Tsuyoshi Ihara (Yoshinara Yonemori); Akira Onodera (Naoya Kusanagi); Ayoko Fujitani (Asagi Kusanagi); Shinobu Nakayama (Matumi Nagamine).

NEW YORK POST, 4/16/97, p. 40, Thelma Adams

Wanted: giant turtle; with fangs; able to fly; taste for man-eating pterodactyls; commuting distance to Tokyo; good with kids.

Any one-shelled wonder other than "Gamera: The Guardian of the Universe" need not apply. In the pantheon of Japanese movie monsters, the good-natured, if misunderstood, Gamera is Apollo to godzilla's Zeus.

From 1965 to 1971, the turbo-charged, 200-foot turtle fought giant lizards, huge birds, an outer-space squid with mind control and assorted other bloated uglies with super powers and mean spirits.

In 1981, the beast who's so big he's easily mistaken for a floating atoll fought them all in "Supermonster Gamera."

Is it soup time for the avenging turtle with a soft spot for the human race? Never. For the next two weeks, Film Forum will serve up Japan's most recent, high-tech (look, Ma! no strings) Gamera adventure.

Under Shusuke Kaneko's assured direction, from Kazunori Ito's script, Gamera bites into his old foes, the Gyaos. The Japanese military tries to contain the man-eating winged lizards in the Fukuoka (say that a few times quickly) Astrodome, but only Gamera can exterminate the pesky pterodactyls.

The army's lame, and so are the flat-footed human subplots. The government recruits a dewy ornithologist (Shinobu Nakayama) into action after she discovers her mentors death by digging elbow deep into Gyao dung and retrieving the guy's glasses and pen.

Meanwhile, a dashing naval officer (Tsuyoshi Ihara) discovers the floating atoll that turns out to be Gamera. After he gives a souvenir of the event to his boss's pre-teen daughter, she becomes a Gamera priestess with a psychic link to the gentle giant.

The plot unravels with the somber seriousness of wartime military propaganda films. The strength of "Gamera" is its stern refusal to wink at the audience. This isn't kitsch, it's a super clash where humans are just so many ants at the picnic. The highlights are the most excellent pitched battles between the fire-spewing turtle and the churlish lizard-birds. Gamera to Gyaos: You guys are prehistory!

VILLAGE VOICE, 4/22/97, p. 82, Gary Dauphin

The problem of electronic image processing and realism isn't one that comes up very much in *Gamera: The Guardian of the Universe,* which is as it should be. The 1995 return of Japan's favorite giant turtle is crisp looking, slightly gorier than I remember, and appropriately millennial (the lost city of Atlantis is a major theme). Even better, a guy flopping around in a turtle suit still looks like a guy flopping around in a turtle suit. (Some things are better left alone.)

The Gamera series started in 1965, with the nuclear unlocking of a very large, very violent, and very pissed-off turtle from an Arctic iceberg. The creature quickly turned into a good-guy character in much the way pro wrestlers are periodically converted, Gamera teaming up with small children with names like Tibby, cute Japanese tykes whom he would wink at, save from other monsters, let ride in his shell, et cetera. There is no shell ride this time around but the overall theme remains the same: when an ancient, winged demon named Gyaos is suddenly spotted on a remote Pacific island, Gamera rises from slumber, breathing fire and saving the world, stepping all over Tokyo in order to rescue it.

The unconscious anxiety that propelled even the most cartoonish King Kong versus Godzilla outing was always Japan's national atomic nightmare. Here it's been displaced by an ecological unease about nuclear power plants, contemporary to be sure but suggesting that even in Japan the atom bomb can recede in memory, given enough time. The more telling cultural fascination in *Gamera* is with the impotence of the modern-day Japanese military. The Defense Forces have always been outmatched by the Monsters, but here the stone-faced generals go so far as to request permission from the Diet to "return fire" on Gyaos and an initially misunderstood Gamera. It's a passing procedural nicety to be sure, but anyone searching for pop-culture cues about Japanese cultural attitudes will find plenty beyond a love of foam rubber in *Gamera.*

Also reviewed in:
CHICAGO TRIBUNE, 8/29/97, Friday/p. J, John Petrakis
NEW YORK TIMES, 4/16/97, p. C16, Janet Maslin
VARIETY, 9/4-10/95, p. 77, Todd McCarthy

GANG RELATED

A Metro-Goldwyn-Mayer release of an Orion Pictures presentation of a Brad Krevoy & Steve Stabler production. *Executive Producer:* Lynn Bigelow-Kouf. *Producer:* Brad Krevoy, Steve Stabler, and John Bertolli. *Director:* Jim Kouf. *Screenplay:* Jim Kouf. *Director of Photography:* Brian J. Reynolds. *Editor:* Todd Ramsay. *Music:* Mickey Hart. *Music Editor:* Gary Todd and Howard Cohen. *Sound:* David B. Chornow and (music) Tom Flye. *Sound Editor:* Gary Gerlich. *Casting:* Carol Lewis. *Production Designer:* Charles Breen. *Set Decorator:* Stephanie Ziemer. *Set Dresser:* Bruce Fuselier, Christopher Kennedy, Scott Belshe, Jared Scardina, and Regina Lee Hervé. *Special Effects:* John Hartigan. *Costumes:* Shari Feldman. *Make-up:* Whitney L. James. *Make-up (Dennis Quaid):* Craig Reardon. *Stunt Coordinator:* James M. Halty and Steve Kelso. *Running time:* 111 minutes. *MPAA Rating:* R.

CAST: James Belushi (Divinci); Tupac Shakur (Rodriguez); Lela Rochon (Cynthia); Dennis Quaid (William); James Earl Jones (Arthur Baylor); David Paymer (Elliot Goff); Wendy Crewson (Helen Eden); Gary Cole (Richard Simms); T.C. Carson (Manny Ladrew); Brad Greenquist (Richard Stein); James Handy (Captain Henderson); Kool Moe Dee (Lionel Hudd); Victor Love (Hooper); Robert LaSardo (Sarkasian); Perry Anzilotti (Vic); Gregory Scott Cummins (Clyde); Tiny Lister, Jr. (Cutless Supreme); Thomas Mills (Patrolman Mahoney); Rick LaFond (Desk Officer); Anthony C. Hall (James); Catero Colbert (Cortez); Steve Wilcox (Dave); Alexander Folk (Reverend); Paul Gold (Lineup Suspect); Douglas Bennett (Guard); David Weisenberg (Doctor); Will Jeffries (Dunner Attorney); Jason Bagby (Young Man); Chris Hendrie (Judge Weinberg); Bob Apisa (Dunner Bailiff); Terrance Ellis (Gun Seller); Todd

Patrick Breaugh (Steven J. Allen);   Yuri Ogawa (Jury Foreperson);   Joseph Hieu (Asian Man);
Deborah Rennard (Caroline Divinci);   Edward Edwards (Sgt. Gardner);   Fred Ornstein (Officer);
Taylor Anderson (McCall's Butler);   Tom Ormeny (Nathan McCall);   Tony Perez (Judge Howard
W. Pine);   Ron Cummins (Baliff);   Elizabeth Maynard (Newscaster);   Charlene Simpson
(Manny's Secretary); Jimmie F. Skaggs (Duncan); Leonard O. Turner (Guard at Cynthia's Jail);
Andrea C. Robinson, Dafidd McCracken, and Nellie Sciutto (Reporters);   Donald Craig
(Sunclair);   Lisa Dinkins (Nurse);   Teddy Lane, Jr. (Guard at County);   Reginald W. Miller,
George Christy, and Jesse J. Donnelly (Detectives);   Peter Navy Tulasosopo (Bob the Bouncer);
Myles Derussy III (Officer).

LOS ANGELES TIMES, 10/8/97, Calendar/p. 4, Kenneth Turan

"Implausible" is a mild word for the shenanigans "Gang Related" expects us to swallow.
Writer-director Jim Kouf has loaded a lifetime's worth of ploys and contrivances, feints and jabs,
into this unpleasant, interminable, more-than-usually pointless film.

Kouf's script, about a pair of scum-of-the-Earth cops who panic when their amoral scam starts
to fall apart, must have read better than it plays. A more-than-respectable cast, from stars James
Belushi and the late Tupac Shakur through supporting players Lela Rochon, James Earl Jones and
Dennis Quaid, have signed on, but it matters not.

For a combination of credulity-straining coincidence, characters it's difficult to care about and
the violence and foul tempers that we've come to both expect and dread in similar urban dramas
means "Gang Related" is not going to make anyone's day. The more Kouf and his actors try to
make this abrasive muddle believable, the less they succeed.

The particularly violent and cynical con game police partners Divinci (Belushi) and Rodriguez
(Shakur) are running has been going on for some time when "Gang Related" opens, and it does
have a certain brutal simplicity.

Pretending to be drug dealers, the guys sell a bag of good stuff to known dealers, pocket the
money and almost immediately murder their helpless victim.   They write the homicide off as
"gang related," deftly recover the bag of drugs, wash the blood off and start the whole cycle all
over again.

Aside from convincing themselves that they're performing a public service by ridding the streets
of evil, the partners need the money.   Rodriguez has a nasty gambling habit, and Divinci, who
uses his exotic dancer girlfriend Cynthia (Rochon) as bait in the scam, dreams of retiring to
Hawaii, source of the multicolored shirts he favors.

Not a bad scheme, or plot device, but then things start to go sour. One of the murdered marks
turns out to be an undercover operative for the Drug Enforcement Agency, and Divinci and
Rodriguez have to deal with federal agents thirsting for revenge while figuring out whom to frame
for a crime they themselves committed.

Their selection, born of desperation and sheer script idiocy, is a battered, filthy, just about
comatose street person (a grunged-up Quaid) who literally can't remember his own name. A
person too out of it to stay awake is hardly likely to make a convincing murder suspect, but
Kouf's script plunges ahead nevertheless.

That's because "Gang Related" has yet another farfetched scenario involving Mr. Comatose that
it wants to fuse with what's gone before. The result is a bad luck story with way more twists and
turns than it's worth the time and trouble to negotiate.

Not helping is the surliness and unlikability of just about everyone in the film.   "Gang Related"
has much pointless violence, vile language, bad tempers and people happy for the chance to call
one another "pus head." It's especially sad that rap star Shakur, who had a considerable amount
of promise as an actor, would end up having a film like this be his last.

Writer-director Kouf has an eclectic résumé, including writing credits on "Stakeout" and
"Operation Dumbo Drop." His work here results in a disjointed film whose attempts at intrigue
end up no more than irritating.

If "Gang Related's" press kit is any judge, Kouf and his wife, executive producer Lynn
Bigelow-Kouf, are especially pleased with their life on a ranch in Montana, a locale noticeably
lacking in the kinds of lowlifes this film presents. It's too bad they can't resist the impulse to
inflict these kinds of steazeballs on the rest of us.

NEW YORK POST, 10/8/97, p. 49, Larry Worth

It's just about a year since Tupac Shakur's death, and the late rapper is still being showcased as an actor of unexpected depth and range. That being said, he's the only reason to check out "Gang Related."

Shakur plays a savvy police detective who's up to his eyeballs in debt. That's what motivates his participation in corrupt partner James Belushi's scamming of drug dealers, who are quickly killed by Belushi once the transactions go down. Fellow boys in blue assume the deaths to be "gang related."

All's well for the deadly duo until one mark turns out to be an undercover DEA agent. Suddenly, the heat's on to find a fall guy for the murder. Belushi's girlfriend, who's also in on the scheme, leads them to a homeless derelict hanging around her apartment. But as luck would have it, the bum has a few surprises of his own.

That's more than you can say for the script, penned by Jim Kouf, cowriter of the dismal "Operation Dumbo Drop." Enough said? Unfortunately not, since he also plays director to ill effect.

In his efforts to evoke classic crime-dramas filled with double-crosses and ironic twists, Kouf lays a giant egg. The results come close to parodying the genre.

Not helping is James Belushi's over-the-top, hideously cartoon-like depiction of sleaze with a badge. For all his subtlety, he might as well be sporting horns and a tail.

And as a down-and-out stripper who's his main squeeze, Lela "Waiting to Exhale" Rochon is way too stiff and one-dimensional. Supporting turns from James Earl Jones, David Paymer, Wendy Crewson and Gary Cole are only marginally better.

But the biggest raspberry is earned by Dennis Quaid, meant to be unrecognizable as the street person set up to take the blame. He looks straight out of makeup with his perfect smudge marks, glued-on beard and wigged-out ponytail. Quaid's way too talented for such slumming.

Then there's Shakur, who delivers all his lines with a credibility and dead-on style that soars above the rest of this nonsense. The fact that "Gang Related" is dedicated to his memory proves far more ironic than anything in the script.

NEWSDAY, 10/10/97, Part II/p. 83, Gene Seymour

They made movies like "Gang Related" a lot more often in the late 1940s than they do now. If you're an aficionado of true *noir*, you know the program: The protagonist is a bad cop, often played by Robert Ryan or Dan Duryea, who routinely does bad things and then one night does a *really* bad thing and pays gruesome dues in the end.

Nowadays, moviegoers want their *noir* lightened with more redemption. Even "L.A. Confidential" is far more romantic than its seductively dark contours suggest. "Gang Related" has no heroic escape hatch. It comes on like a generic cop-buddy movie that goes haywire at the start and winds up being a taut, astringent parable about justice. And about who is (or isn't) a human being in the eyes of the law.

The advance buzz about "Gang Related" has swarmed around the late Tupac Shakur, who was shot to death not long after the film was completed. Shakur plays Rodriguez, one of two detectives who have been setting up fake drug deals in which they keep the money and kill the dealer in "drive-by" fashion. Rodriguez's partner, Divinci (James Belushi), uses his stripper-girlfriend Cynthia (Lela Rochon) as bait for the dirty deals, whose violent outcomes are always written off as "gang-related."

Rodriguez has gambling debts to pay and Divinci can almost smell early retirement on a beach in Maui. What's the harm anyway? ("Drug dealers are animals," the slovenly Divinci says while scratching himself.) Then it turns out that their latest victim (Kool Moe Dee) is an undercover DEA agent whose furious boss (Gary Cole) seeks quick and effective action from the two detectives in charge of the resulting investigation. Guess which two?

You get a mild case of the grins and grimaces watching these hapless bozos contrive a cover-up. Their usual suspects all have alibis for the Night In Question. (One was in jail, another was shot and so on.)

With pressure building, Divinci finds a confused derelict (Dennis Quaid) sprawled in an alley near Cynthia's building and convinces everyone, even the bum, that the shooter's been nailed.

That anyone would, for a moment, buy the idea of a Smith & Wesson ending up in a vagrant's hands is hard to swallow as a plot point. Still, the flimsy scenario holds until a famous attorney (James Earl Jones) discloses the derelict's true identity. Now Divinci and Rodriguez really have to scramble. Or, maybe, punt.

As with the scruffy, low-budget *noir* flicks of two generations ago, "Gang Related's" off-the-rack, ready-for-video veneer is charming camouflage for its acerbic theme. The plot twists are well-paced and the acting is solid throughout.

It's regrettable that another beautiful African-American woman is compelled to play a stripper, but Rochon's resolute command of her character's divided emotions is one of the movie's pleasantest surprises.

Shakur's role isn't as broadly defined as Belushi's. But he displays enough verve and wit here to make you regret all the more that his fine promise was blown to bits in Las Vegas.

SIGHT AND SOUND, 8/98, p. 41, Danny Leigh

In a nameless US city detectives Divinci and Rodriguez meet drug dealer Lionel Hudd in a motel room. Hudd is later shot dead, his drugs and money stolen. The killers are Divinci and Rodriguez, hoping to finance early retirement and settle gambling debts respectively.

Assigned to the apparently 'gang related' case, Divinci and Rodriguez learn Hudd was working undercover for the Drug Enforcement Agency. Panicked, they frame an alcoholic vagrant, Joe, appropriating a gun intended as evidence against Clyde, a murderer they themselves arrested. Clyde walks free. The pair convince Joe he shot Hudd while drunk, while Divinci's girlfriend Cynthia agrees to testify as an eyewitness. Attorney Arthur Baylor realises Joe is William McCall, a wealthy client missing for seven years. In court Baylor defends Joe/William. The trial collapses when Cynthia admits perjury. After discovering Rodriguez informed on him, Divinci flees. A loan shark executes Rodriguez. Four months later the fugitive Divinci attacks Cynthia then hires a driver to transport him to safety. The chauffeur is Clyde, who shoots and kills Divinci.

Days after completing *Gang Related* the 25-year-old actor/rapper Tupac Shakur was killed in a Las Vegas drive-by shooting. Shakur had established himself as a considerable screen presence in Vondie Curtis-Hall's *Gridlock'd* and the morbid irony of his death is hard to escape while watching his final performance.

At first glance, despite the grim thematic congruence, this hardly appears an ideal epitaph. Dialogue rarely rises above the functional, the narrative trajectory often creaks under its own contrivances, and the lack of visual distinction betrays director Jim Kouf's background as the journeyman behind such fodder as Disney's *Operation Dumbo Drop*. Yet by inverting the threadbare premise of a crime-fighting odd couple, ostensible flaws assume a radically different complexion. Rather than a hackneyed crime thriller, *Gang Related* emerges as a consummately subversive recasting of the *Lethal Weapon* prototype as a pitiless morality play. The basic elements remain inviolate: street weary cops—one black, one white—with messy private lives and a maverick *modus operandi* wisecracking their way around irascible police chiefs and criminal caricatures. Except here there are no good guys, and justice, however poetic, is served by chance.

Nowhere is this acid twist made clearer than in Divinci and Rodriguez's bumbling attempts to find a patsy for their crime. Before happening upon the hapless Joe, they question a series of local thugs, each with an iron-clad alibi, as the police department grows restive under pressure from the DA. The scenario is tired, even anachronistic, but revitalised by a darkly comic cynicism: there is no killer to be found, simply someone to be framed.

Divinci and Rodriguez cannot even dissemble their crime as vigilantism. Despite paying the idea periodic lip service, their self-justifying talk of "taking out the garbage" is soulless and routine; they're only in it for the money. Though both *Bad Lieutenant* and *CopLand* share this feral-lawmen leitmotiv, *Gang Related* is ultimately more sardonic and less bombastic than either. While Abel Ferrara deals in Catholic absolution and James Mangold allows a heroic archetype to save the day, the corrosively amoral Divinci and Rodriguez are checked only by their own ineptitude.

Assisted by his lead actors' restrained self-possession, Kouf's anonymous direction creates a self-consciously generic locale, where happy endings and resolutions come, if they come at all, wholly arbitrarily. As a mordant comment on the buddy movie, it's enthralling; sadly, it also makes a perfect coda to the death of Tupac Shakur.

VILLAGE VOICE, 10/14/97, p. 94, Gary Dauphin

If the still-evolving line about the late rapper Tupac Shakur is that he was better than most people knew, then *Gang Related* is an appropriate if not satisfying coda to his acting career. Tupac's last film is a scattered and unpleasant bit of would-be urban grit about two homicide detectives (Tupac and Jim Belushi) who set up phony drug deals in order to kill the buyers and pocket their money, and there's not a thing to recommend it except for Tupac himself. Belushi's barely watchable, and as Belushi's stripper girlfriend Lela Rochon has little to do except shake and be watched in the worst possible way. While Tupac doesn't exactly shine in the role of a crooked cop trying to protect a scrap of conscience, he does show the flashes of humor, intelligence, and, most importantly, effort that are otherwise missing here. What doesn't save *Gang Related*, but it does suggest the better movie this could have been as well as the better movies Tupac could have made if there'd been anyone offscreen to save him.

Also reviewed in:
CHICAGO TRIBUNE, 10/8/97, Tempo/p. 1, Michael Wilmington
NEW YORK TIMES, 10/8/97, p. E3, Lawrence Van Gelder
VARIETY, 10/6-12/97, p. 54, Todd McCarthy
WASHINGTON POST, 10/8/97, p. D1, Stephen Hunter

GATTACA

A Columbia Pictures release of a Jersey Films production. *Producer:* Danny DeVito, Michael Shamberg, and Stacey Sher. *Director:* Andrew Niccol. *Screenplay:* Andrew Niccol. *Director of Photography:* Slawomir Idziak. *Editor:* Lisa Zeno Churgin. *Music:* Michael Nyman. *Music Editor:* Bunny Andrews. *Choreographer:* Maurice Schwartzmann. *Sound:* Stephan Von Hase-Mihalik. *Sound Editor:* Richard King. *Casting:* Francine Maisler. *Production Designer:* Jan Roelfs. *Art Director:* Sarah Knowles. *Set Designer:* Stephen T. Alesch and Randall Wickins. *Set Decorator:* Nancy Nye. *Special Effects:* Gary D'Amico. *Costumes:* Colleen Atwood. *Make-up:* Ve Neill. *Stunt Coordinator:* Mike Cassidy and Norman Howell. *Running time:* 112 minutes. *MPAA Rating:* PG-13.

CAST: Ethan Hawke (Vincent/Jerome); Uma Thurman (Irene); Gore Vidal (Director Josef); Xander Berkeley (Lamar); Jayne Brook (Marie); Elias Koteas (Antonio); Maya Rudolph (Delivery Nurse); Una Damon (Head Nurse); Elizabeth Dennehy (Pre-School Teacher); Blair Underwood (Geneticist); Mason Gamble (Younger Vincent); Vincent Nielson (Younger Anton); Chad Christ (Young Vincent); William Lee Scott (Young Anton); Clarence Graham (Personnel Officer); Ernest Borgnine (Caesar); Tony Shalhoub (German); Jude Law (Jerome/Eugene); Alan Arkin (Detective Hugo); Carlton Benbry (Gattaca Hoover); Grace Sullivan (Sequencing Customer); Ken Marino (Sequencing Technician); Cynthia Martells (Cavendish); Loren Dean (Anton); Gabrielle Reece (Gattaca Trainer); Ryan Dorin (Twelve Fingered Pianist); Dean Norris (Cop on the Beat); Russell Milton (Gattaca Detective); George Marshall Ruge (Beaten Detective); Steve Bessen (Blood Test Detective); Lindsey Lee Ginter (Mission Commander).

LOS ANGELES TIMES, 10/24/97, Calendar/p. 6, Jack Mathews

[The following review by Jack Mathews appeared in a slightly different form in NEWSDAY, 10/24/97, Part II/p. B6.]

In the brave new world of writer-director Andrew Niccol's "Gattaca," genetics is God. People are designed in petri dishes, not conceived in passion. Their gene pools are swept and filtered to remove any potential of mental or physical imperfection, and they arrive in the world naked as ever but genetically dressed for success.

Not so the movie. Niccol's script, which has the earnest simplicity of a freshman philosophy paper, is merely naked exploitation, a sci-fi snow job that projects a contemporary ethical question—would a perfect human be human?—into a solemn future where the worst-case scenario unfolds as conventional Hollywood melodrama.

According to an early title card, "Gattaca's" future is just up the road, a stone's throw from a cloned sheep, where the vast bulk of the population is genetically pure beyond anything ever envisioned by Hitler. Potluck babies like Vincent (Ethan Hawke), who was conceived the old-fashioned way, in a tangle of desire in the back seat of a Buick, make up the new underclass.

Ethnic differences may be a thing of the past, but science has yet to isolate the gene that causes the superiority complex, and the naturals—a.k.a., "faith babies," "in-valids" and "de-gene-er-ates"—provide handy negative stereotypes. Some of them are born diseased, or disabled, or predisposed to who knows what kind of behavior.

Vincent, who has poor vision, a terminal heart defect and a meek physique, is thus the black sheep of his family. He's an embarrassment, despite his romantic genesis, and a true weakling in the company of his young brother, Anton, whose carefully presorted genes make him taller, stronger, smarter and infinitely more employable. Sibling rivalry exists here, but it's no contest.

At least, not until Vincent proves the film's ad slogan, that there is no gene for the spirit, and summons the strength to beat the smug Anton so thoroughly in an endurance swimming contest that he has to save Mr. Perfect from Mr. Deep. The event calls for a rematch in the film's ludicrous finale.

In the meantime, Vincent will assume the identity of a petri person named Jerome, an Olympic athlete (Jude Law) paralyzed in a car accident, and set out to achieve his greatest goal—to travel in space before his heart poops out.

Along the way, he'll fall in love with a designer baby (Uma Thurman, as emotionally uninvolved as ever), who has her own cross to bear, and become the target of a murder investigation that threatens to expose him before his spaceship sails.

Good science fiction develops from premises and situations that, no matter how fantastic, seem a logical extension of where we are, politically as well as scientifically.

Aldous Huxley's "Brave New World" projected from the advancing science of 1932 a future 600 years forward where mankind is genetically bred in a cheerless utopia. The novel was commenting more on totalitarianism than science-run-amok. The same can be said of George Orwell's "1984," written 17 years later, on the rising tide of Cold War paranoia.

"Gattaca" has less political undercurrent than an episode of "3rd Rock From the Sun." Niccol's world, too close to ours by centuries, is a one-trick pony. Because the genetic engineering of flawless people now seems conceivable, he envisions a result that could only occur if we drop everything else. No drug, surgical or transplant options for Vincent's heart? No solution to his astigmatism, other than glasses or tell-tale contacts?

This is an unimaginative, claustrophobic future, set mostly in the sleek corridors of Gattaca, the space exploration company where Vincent transforms himself from janitor to astronaut. The film's one effective conceit is that employees are routinely and instantly identity-screened with urine, blood, saliva, skin cell and hair follicle tests, compelling Vincent to carry Jerome's prepackaged specimens under his clothing.

The loss of a single personal eyelash, however, puts wise Detective Hugo (Alan Arkin) and his overbearing boss (Loren Dean) on Vincent's genetic trail, and with the clock ticking toward launch time, he must summon the superior traits of his betters to squeak through.

"Gattaca" might have worked as a "Sleeper"-like comedy, where such happy inventions as the orgasm machine at least give the future a fair shake. We have to have something to look forward to. Instead, Niccol has fashioned a deadening cautionary tale; it's far too serious to be taken seriously.

NEW YORK, 11/10/97, p. 61, David Denby

Gattaca, the first feature by the writer-director Andrew Niccol, is about a genetic tyranny of the future in which society is rigidly divided into humans perfectly engineered and those known as faith babies—people with the ordinary mix of strengths and physical susceptibilities. Ethan Hawke, clean-shaven and very fit, is one of the latter, who nevertheless penetrates to the inner sanctum of the perfect ones. Always on the verge of being discovered, he meets a kind of mate in the elongated and smirking Uma Thurman, who, like him, has an ailing heart. *Gattaca* is not pop science fiction in the *Star Wars* mold but a serious and intelligent movie, with an inexpensive but handsome design, good music by Michael Nyman, and perceptive observations of such all-too-human elements as friendship and rivalries between brothers.

NEW YORK POST, 10/24/97, p. 39, Michael Medved

The sleek, fascinating, future world of "Gattaca" turns discrimination and oppression into sciences.

Genetic engineering enables privileged parents to create flawless "designer" babies in the laboratory, but those unfortunate children conceived the old-fashioned way will be evaluated within moments of delivery.

Such DNA analysis reveals the newborn's entire future, including adult IQ and life expectancy, with those who display even minor chromosomal shortcomings receiving the dreaded "in-valid" designation and toiling forever in demeaning jobs.

Ethan Hawke plays one such invalid (he's likely to suffer an early heart attack) who refuses to accept his fate and longs for the bright prospects that his genetically engineered, petri-dish-conceived brother (Loren Dean) enjoys.

In particular, Hawke dreams of service as an elite navigator in a Saturn expedition planned by the all-powerful Gattaca Corp., but to advance his ambitions he must obtain the genetic identity of one of his privileged peers.

An underground DNA broker (Tony Shalhoub) puts him in touch with a superior specimen (Jude Law). His privileged identity has become useless to him because of a paralyzing accident, so he agrees to sell his genetic material to the pretender.

The film's intricate story line describes every detail of their deception, in which Hawke borrows bags of urine, sachets of blood and even hair and eyelash samples from his wheelchair-bound better.

Unfortunately, two developments at Gattaca threaten his painstakingly plotted imposture. First, the murder, of a corporate official sends suspicious detectives (led by Alan Arkin) swarming over the facility. And second, our hero begins to feel a mutual attraction for one of his co-workers (Uma Thurman).

New Zealand-born commercial director Andrew Niccol makes a startlingly self-assured debut as both writer and director in a movie that simultaneously stirs emotions and stimulates the mind.

The cast (solid rather than spectacular) displays the cold, haughty airs of Vogue models, while corresponding costumes and sets show a gleaming, timeless, soulless, "modernistic" surface that is at once futuristic and old fashioned (and which utilizes the exterior of a famous Frank Lloyd Wright building).

Some hair-breadth escapes may seem far-fetched and fortuitous, straining credibility even within this fanciful universe, but the story provides enough substance that its own genetic code—a carefully thought-out script and design—can be read as smart and superior.

SIGHT AND SOUND, 3/98, p. 48, Jonathan Romney

"The not-too-distant future." DNA engineering makes it possible for people to be born with high intelligence and near-perfect physiques, with their genes predicting their future; naturally born people are stigmatised as 'In-Valids'. Vincent Freeman, myopic and at risk of dying of a heart condition after 32 years of age, feels inferior to his 'Valid' younger brother Anton, until he saves Anton's life in a swimming contest.

As a member of the underclass, Vincent can only become a cleaner at the Gattaca Corporation, a centre for the genetic elite. Vincent dreams of joining Gattaca's space mission to Titan. A broker arranges for him to swap identities with Jerome, a swimming star made paraplegic in an accident. Using Jerome's blood and urine in tests, Vincent rises through Gattaca's ranks, becomes romantically involved with his co-worker Irene, and is chosen for the Titan mission.

When Vincent's mission director is found murdered, an investigation is led by Detective Hugo and a senior policeman. A hair found at the crime scene puts the police on Vincent's trail. They raid Vincent's apartment, but Jerome successfully covers for him. The real killer is revealed to be Gattaca Director Josef. However, the senior policeman, in fact Vincent's brother Anton, continues to pursue Vincent. They challenge each other to a second swimming contest; this time, Anton saves Vincent. Vincent is reunited with Irene, who accepts his genetic imperfection. On the day of the space flight, a technician reveals that he's always known Vincent was an In-Valid, but he lets him off anyway. Jerome commits suicide as Vincent heads for the stars.

Andrew Niccol's DNA dystopia story is well timed, not only because it taps into current anxieties that genetic engineering may lead towards a new prescriptive eugenics. For comparable fears surround the future of cinema itself in which, already, 'flawed' imagery is routinely corrected with digitals, and ideas out of step with mainstream criteria risk being relegated to oblivion, condemned as 'In-Valid'.

Gattaca hardly represents a corrective to this tendency, at least in visual terms. Instead, it pushes its cultivation of surface elegance to a parodic extreme. Its most striking images are shot through a range of blue, yellow and green filters, as though the camera would pass out any imperfections in this fictional world. Yet this hyper-cosmetic style makes *Gattaca*'s look, if not its substance, stand out from the usual run of Hollywood futurology. Its visual style, at times echoing Truffaut's *Fahrenheit 451* (1966), is above all European: the glacial photography is by Slawomir Idziak, known for his work with Zanussi and Kieślowski, and the chilled-chrome monument of the Gattaca centre is by Dutch designer Jan Roelfs, who was so instrumental in creating the look of Greenaway's films. The heroic swells of the score are by Michael Nyman, here operating closer to *The Piano* than to his Greenaway mode.

New Zealand-born director/writer Niccol made his name working on commercials in Britain, and *Gattaca,* it must be said, rather brings to mind those mid-80s vodka-ads featuring futuristic lounge lizards in an Orwellian London. Although the film's brittle chic central to its argument, there is nevertheless something counterproductive about it. Niccol can't quite anchor his too-seamless cool world to any recognisable present reality.

But present reality is, or should be, very much at stake in this future society. The opening intertitle placing the action in 'The not-too-distant future' is a giveaway—in dystopian science fiction, these words invariably signal that we are dealing not with fantasy but with a hypothetical extrapolation of our own present. *Gattaca* simply follows to its extreme our society's obsession with human perfectibility. In the DNA-engineered society that has created Gattaca (the name is derived from the initials 'G', 'T', 'C' and 'A", which represent the four key components in DNA), the most valued human qualities are completeness and quantifiability—its citizens must live up to their genetically predetermined potential, without exceeding it.

This entails a problem endemic to dystopian fiction, especially of the sort concerned with *Metropolis*-style social hierarchy: we are so often asked to take an interest in a monotone, predictable world inhabited by monotone, predictable characters. What ought to enliven *Gattaca* is Vincent's determination to break the mould, to demonstrate (as the *films* tagline puts it) that "there is no gene for the human spirit." Yet, however radical the methods for achieving it are, Vincent's dream of space travel is entirely conventional. *Gattaca* is really a generic story of single-minded social climbing, a sci-fi version of the boardroom-politics yuppie *Bildungsroman* movie of the 80s.

What's also missing is any kind of back story. Future fiction is often drastically hamstrung by spelling out such imagined histories, and yet here we have to take it on trust that *Gattaca'* s world arises naturally out of its premise. Nothing quite explains how a social fetish for the genetically packaged self could blossom into a fully fledged ideological totalitarianism; so the world of *Gattaca* ends up looking too much like pure speculative metaphor. Besides, these streamlined future people could surely have retained some hedonism or at least humour. It's hard to sustain an interest in a world so blandly stylish, in which the only remaining pleasures seem to be well-tailored suits, lounge jazz and sleek monumentalist architecture. But Niccol also denies us any transgressively appealing outside world, of the sort that has been a structurally essential part of dystopia fiction since Zamyatin's 1920-21 novel *We*.

Instead, *Gattaca* is bolstered by an elaborate, often impressive series of riffs on identity and disguise. This works both on the level of smart one-liners—"My real resumé was in my cells"—and of visual details, like the opening montage of business with fake fingerprints, borrowed blood and urine. The play with 'authentic' genetic identity and its possible signs is nothing if not thoroughgoing—when Vincent's real identity is discovered, he is given away by his penis, which he holds with the wrong hand. This chimes with the suggestion of Vincent's old-world phallic potency, a theme that has its bathetic climax on the battleground of machismo, in his swimming showdown with his brother.

Gattaca's most consistently intriguing stylistic aspect is its visual reworking of familiar imagery into an anachronistic world based largely on 50s America, much as *Brazil* reworked the British 30s. Alan Arkin's plebeian cop is a *Dragnet*-style gumshoe complete with fedora, although the brim looks somehow just *not quite right*. Even Vincent's dream of interplanetary freedom is straight out of 50s pulp sci-fi, rocket science as the last word in exotic modernity. The film's most evocative shot has Vincent in a roomful of retro furniture, poring over a dusty old copy of *Space Navigation*.

Finally, however, the film alienates by trying to have it both ways—tut-tutting at *Gattaca*'s body fascism while asking us to feel for leads as pedigree-bred and crisp-frozen as Uma Thurman and Ethan Hawke, who hardly reveals any heretical passions beneath Vincent's zipped-up surface. Meanwhile, the authentically battered likes of Alan Arkin, Gore Vidal and an under-used Ernest Borgnine get short shrift. You begin to suspect that production decisions were made to strictly eugenic criteria.

TIME, 10/27/97, p. 116, Richard Schickel

In the very near future the world is divided into the genetic haves and have-nots. The former are designed in labs prior to conception; with a twist on this DNA strand, a tug on that one, they come out smart, handsome and spared even such minor inconveniences as lefthandedness. The have-nots, products of their parents' taking a romantic free fall into the gene pool, are condemned to hard labor in support of their superiors. They are also burdened with flightier emotions.

Literally so, in the case of an "invalid" (nice pun there) named Vincent (Ethan Hawke), who since childhood has dreamed of being an astronaut. As we discover him at the beginning of *Gattaca*, he's on the brink of achieving this goal—he has formed an alliance with a valid (Jude Law) who has been invalidated by an accident. For a fee, the valid supplies Vincent with the stuff he needs—including blood and urine—to satisfy the endless identity checks at the space agency where he works.

This is not a bad premise for a cautionary science-fiction tale. And anyone who has cheated on an expense account can identify with a character like Hawke's, working a much bigger scam on a bureaucracy quiveringly alert to genetic impostors. A lost eyelash, a bit of exfoliated skin left on his keyboard could undo him—especially when the cops, led by a very querulous Alan Arkin, suddenly descend on his facility and, as they investigate a murder, start subjecting everyone's detritus to genetic spot checks.

Writer-director Andrew Niccol, a New Zealander up out of commercials and making his debut in features, is less successful with the big things than he is with these little ones. His vision of a heavily sanitized and overrational future is perhaps inevitably more chilly than chilling. And since emotion has been bred out of most of the people he's concerned with, the movie's relationships—notably a romance between Vincent and a co-worker played by Uma Thurman—tend to be distant and not very involving.

Still, one has to admire a lot of his refusals. Niccol doesn't turn his film into a big chase or gunfight. He has serious matters on his mind and attends to them soberly, with the humanistic intensity—naively instructional yet rather touchingly earnest—that marked the sci-fi of the 1950s, when it was widely discovered that the future might not be all it was cracked up to be.

VILLAGE VOICE, 10/28/97, p. 84, J. Hoberman

In the future, as we should know from watching old science-fiction movies on television, the landscaped industrial park has become the new urban paradigm and anyone who is anyone will be if not an actual robot, then a cold and emotionless intellectual zombie.

So it is in Andrew Niccol's curiously retro *Gattaca,* an acronym for the elements of DNA. A form of social science fiction rooted in *Brave New World,* the young New Zealander's somberly soporific debut feature is minimal in effects as well as affect—positing an antiseptic future America where all the best babies have been genetically programmed—thus eliminating the "glorious creative chaos of diversity" extolled in the studio press notes. As a voiceover takes pains to explain, once upon a time there were two brothers, one natural and the other DNA designed. The natural—or "In-Valid" brother (Ethan Hawke) harbors the impossible dream of becoming an astronaut, an honor that is reserved for the elite. He consequently must engage in an elaborate campaign of subterfuge, involving everything from secret bodybuilding to assuming the superior identity of a prime genetic specimen (Jude Law, British don't you know).

Given the atmosphere of total surveillance in which a single hair is a dead giveaway, not to mention the official Nazi ideology of genetic superiority, *Gattaca* makes most sense as a Jew-passing-for-Aryan story set in the Third Reich. Niccol prefers to play it as an Ayn Rand-ish scenario extolling free will over determinism and raising the individual above the collective. It's serious stuff. Law's belligerently supercilious turn notwithstanding, the closest the movie offers to a smile is Hawke's crooked smirk of deception—like who could ever believe his genetic inferiority? Although there is, of course, no popular culture (when the Hawke and his coworker Uma Thurman go out on a date, it's to listen to Schumann), suffice to say that, whatever else has been programmed out of our genes, the future still believes in *Rocky.*

Also reviewed in:
CHICAGO TRIBUNE, 10/24/97, Friday/p. A, Michael Wilmington
NEW REPUBLIC, 11/17/97, p. 26, Stanley Kauffmann
NEW YORK TIMES, 10/24/97, p. E18, Janet Maslin
VARIETY, 9/15-21/97, p. 70, Emanuel Levy
WASHINGTON POST, 10/24/97, p. D1, Rita Kempley
WASHINGTON POST, 10/24/97, Weekend/p. 54, Desson Howe

GENTLEMEN DON'T EAT POETS

A Live Entertainment release of a Xingu Films production. *Executive Producer:* Stephen Evans. *Producer:* Trudie Styler. *Director:* John-Paul Davidson. *Screenplay (based on his novel "The Grotesque"):* Patrick McGrath. *Director of Photography:* Andrew Dunn. *Editor:* Tariq Anwar. *Music:* Anne Dudley. *Choreographer:* Carol Fletcher and Sue Leften. *Sound:* Graham Ross. *Sound Editor:* Christopher Ackland. *Casting:* Joyce Nettles. *Production Designer:* Jan Roelfs. *Set Decorator:* Michael Seirton. *Special Effects:* Stuart Brisdon. *Costumes:* Colleen Atwood. *Make-up:* Peter Owen. *Running time:* 98 minutes. *MPAA Rating:* R.

CAST: Alan Bates (Sir Hugo Coal); Theresa Russell (Lady Harriet Coal); Trudie Styler (Doris Fledge); Sting (Fledge); Jim Carter (George); Anna Massey (Mrs. Giblet); Lena Headey (Cleo Coal); Maria Aitken (Lavinia Freebody); James Fleet (Inspector Limp); Steven Mackinstosh (Sidney Giblet); John Mills (Sir Edward Cleghorn); Chris Barnes (John Lecky); Timothy Kightley (Harbottle); Richard Durden (Sykes-Herring); Nick Lucas (Hubert Cleggie); Annette Badland (Connie Babblehump); David Henry (Freddy Hough); Bob Goody (Father Pim); Edward Jewesbury (Sir Edward Tome); David Killick (Sir Humphrey Stoker); Geoffrey Freshwater (Jury Foreman); Jeffry Wickham (Justice Congreve); Michael Cronin (Dr. Walter Dendrite); Eleanor Church (Nurse).

LOS ANGELES TIMES, 3/14/97, Calendar/p. 12, Jack Mathews

[The following review by Jack Mathews appeared in a slightly different form in NEWSDAY, 3/7/97, Part II/p. B7.]

Is it the quality of the photography or the mood that makes first-time director John-Paul Davidson's "Gentlemen Don't Eat Poets" seem so murky? Either way, it makes this dreary black comedy more work than fun.

"Gentlemen," adapted by Patrick McGrath from his novel, "The Grotesque," is in the British tradition of the gothic, evil-servant thriller, served up with a dash of aristocratic bitters and a couple of dark twists. But it is not nearly clever enough to sustain even its relatively brief one-hour, 38-minute running time.

Reminiscent of both Joseph Losey's "The Servant" and Harold Prince's "Something for Everyone," "Gentlemen" tells of events at a crumbling estate in 1949 England after the arrival of a servant couple with a mysterious past. The estate is occupied by the Coal family, Sir Hugo (Alan Bates), a financially drained aristocrat preoccupied with the dinosaurs he reassembles in his barn; his American wife, Harriet (Theresa Russell), whose sexual needs have gone unattended for 10 years, and their grown daughter, Cleo (Lena Headey), who's about to become engaged to the effete would-be poet Sidney (Steven Mackintosh).

Into their lives come Fledge (Sting), a butler with snaky eyes, a smug disposition and high ambitions—and his wife, Doris (Trudie Styler, Sting's real-life mate and the film's producer), who manages to whip up sensational meals despite her daylong drinking bouts. While Doris quaffs her way through the Coals' wine cellar, her husband is busy sabotaging what weakened connections still hold the family together.

To that end, Fledge seduces Harriet and Sidney, flaunting both affairs before Sir Hugo's bemused eyes. Hugo is happy to have Harriet reclaim her glow and, as a man of science, he's thrilled to be shown a reason for driving the useless poet out of his daughter's life.

But when Sidney disappears, with foul play suspected by the clumsy local constable, the question arises: Who would be most apt to do Sidney harm? Sir Hugo, Fledge or the suspicious pig farmers (Jim Carter, Chris Barnes) lurking about? And why is the Coals' ham suddenly tasting so gamy?

Beyond its athletic lovemaking, "Gentlemen Don't Eat Poets" plays like a cheap homage to "Alfred Hitchcock Presents." It telegraphs its punch lines well advance and has exhausted its wit by the final anticlimatic note.

What the film does have is a wonderful, full-throated performance by Bates, an actor we don't see often enough these days. Bates has a great time lurching around in his larger-than-life character. Sir Hugo is half-bombast and half mad, a man determined to add his own luster to his storied family history, even if it is with some cockeyed theory about dinosaurs having been birds.

Sting does well enough with the one-note Fledge, and Headey adds moments of common grace as Cleo. But there aren't enough of those moments of grace, not to mention humor or originality, to make "Gentlemen Don't Eat Poets" any kind of a feast.

NEW YORK POST, 3/7/97, p. 46, Michael Medved

"Gentlemen Don't Eat Poets" features characters with names such as "Inspector Limp," "Connie Babblehump," "Lavinia Freebody" and poor "Sidney Giblet," who may—or may not—have been unwittingly consumed in an episode of genteel cannibalism.

Such droll details suggest a witty, scandalous drawing-room romp, but this badly botched British import offers few laughs and less originality, while indulgently dwelling on its own darkest, most deviant elements.

In the end, the movie lives up to the title "The Grotesque," which originally was attached to the 1988 Patrick McGrath novel that inspired it.

The story unfolds in the years following World War II in the shabby, eccentrically appointed estate of Sir Hugo Coal (Alan Bates), an aging adventurer obsessed with assembling the skeleton of a previously unknown dinosaur.

His mad passion for this project leads him to ignore his bored American wife (Theresa Russell) and their sensitive daughter (Lena Headey), who is secretly infatuated with aspiring poet Sidney Giblet (Steven Mackintosh).

The arrival of a smug, conniving butler (Sting) and his alcoholic wife (played by Sting's real-life wife and this film's producer, Trudie Styler) introduces new problems into this dysfunctional household.

The bisexual butler quickly commences a torrid affair with the restless lady of the house, while simultaneously seducing the effete young poet.

Sir Hugo implacably opposes the engagement of this confused suitor to his vulnerable daughter, and arouses guilty suspicions when the poet disappears from the premises one dark night.

As the mystery deepens, the police also interrogate the pig farmer and hog butcher (Jim Carter), who is Sir Hugo's best friend.

All members of the cast perform with the elegant expertise we've come to expect in English ensemble pieces, but the parts they play remain cartoons rather than characterizations.

Bizarre plot twists involving butchery, hanging and a cruelly paralyzing stroke take attention from potentially intriguing relationships—as does the distracting focus on a poisonous pet toad and confusing symbolism involving crows.

Sting is especially good at projecting malice, menace and near-hypnotic power but, like the other performers, he deserves stronger material.

Veteran documentary director John-Paul Davidson falters in his feature-film debut, making far too much of the heavy-handed connection between Sir Hugo's dinosaur obsession and his own status as representative of the nearly extinct aristocracy.

With its tired theme of power passing from master class to servant class, "Gentlemen Don't Eat Poets" begins to feel like one giant, ungainly, dusty and musty fossil.

SIGHT AND SOUND, 8/96, p. 50, Chris Darke

England after World War Two. A new butler, Fledge, arrives with his wife at Crook House, the country home of Sir Hugo Coal and his American wife, Harriet. Hedge ingratiates himself with Lady Harriet, while Sir Hugo tries to seduce Hedge's alcoholic wife. Sir Hugo's daughter, Cleo, announces that her boyfriend, Sidney Giblet, is to visit. Sidney, an aspiring poet, announces that he and Cleo wish to marry. That night, Sir Hugo dreams of having sex with Fledge's wife, who then turns into Fledge himself.

Fledge and Lady Harriet have sex, watched unawares by Sidney. When Sidney visits Fledge in his den to tell him what he knows, Fledge grabs him by the throat and kisses him. The next day, Sidney has disappeared. A local policeman, Inspector Limp, comes to investigate. Cleo discovers Sidney's lighter in Fledge's den.

Sydney's mother, Mrs Giblet, arrives with her companion Miss Freebody. That night Cleo dreams of Sidney with his throat cut and wakes up screaming. She tells her father that Sidney said Fledge's name in the dream. Sidney's body is discovered, butchered and gnawed by pigs. Suspicion falls on George Lecky, the gamekeeper. George tells Sir Hugo that his brother, John, disturbed someone burying a sack. John brought the sack back, dismembered the body, and fed it to the pigs. The police arrest George. Mrs Giblet confronts Cleo with her suspicion that it was Sir Hugo who killed her son.

Cleo is watching as her mother and Fledge have sex. Rifling through Fledge's belongings, she uncovers press clippings about the suspicious death of Hedge's former employer. George goes on trial. Sir Hugo confronts Fledge, is knocked down and reduced to the state of a vegetable by a stroke. George is found guilty of Sidney's murder. Mrs Giblet accuses Sir Hugo: his daughter accuses Fledge but George is hanged. Cleo spikes Fledge's pipe with poison. She watches as Fledge and her mother dance together waiting for him to pick up his poisoned pipe from the mantelpiece. Sir Hugo dies dreaming of his dead friend George. The pipe has been taken from the mantelpiece.

The Grotesque lays claims to be part of a neglected sub-genre of British satire that hinges on the savage caricaturing of class. Another name for this sub-genre might be 'Rotten Gothic', its roots traceable in Mervyn Peake's *Gormenghast* trilogy and such past cinematic examples as Vivian Stanshall's slice of English absurdism *Sir Henry at Rawlinson's End*. Adapted by Patrick McGrath from his novel, and directed by television documentary producer and director, John-Paul Davidson, *The Grotesque* has the requisite elements: a crumbling stately pile, Crook House, and an eccentric aristo incumbent Sir Hugo Coal. Representing the encroachment of the lower orders are Sir Hugo's American wife Harriet—who carries the arriviste connotation of 'new money'—and Fledge, the butler with ambitions to move upstairs, via Her Ladyship's chamber.

Half ramshackle manor, half menagerie, Crook House teems with animal imagery: Fledge's arrival is shadowed by a cloudburst of ravens and Sir Hugo describes the new butler as "cunning as a fox". The presence of nature 'red in tooth and claw' is clearly meant to extend the class war going on inside the stately home, to lampoon the notion of aristocracy as a 'natural order' of things. Sir Hugo's interest in palaeontology underlines the fact that he is a dinosaur in social terms and that the more predatory Fledge is in the ascendant. When we see Sir Hugo snoozing beneath a book brazenly entitled *Extinct Animals*, it's not so much an example of over-extended symbolism as a lack of imagination. Redundant images also underline the dialogue: Sir Hugo, after his stroke, is described as being 'a vegetable' just as we see a plate of cabbage being dollied up to the old curmudgeon.

The performances are equally unimaginative. Alan Bates' Sir Hugo appears to want to reclaim the term "crusty" from the anarcho-veggie contingent of youth. But his portrayal falls well short of Trevor Howard's brilliant, self-parodying crustiness in *Sir Henry at Rawlinson's End*. Sir Hugo's death generates little pathos and not much is done with his relationship to his loyal game-keeper, George Lecky, of whom he says, "We shared as much as men can share," and whose conviction and execution comes and goes like the narrative contrivance it is. Sting, as the ambiguous interloper, Fledge, reprises his *Brimstone and Treacle* turn. When lit in the right way, he exudes a gimlet-eyed menace, but he never approaches the seething class hatred and cold Machiavellian stealth that might have made Fledge a butler to rival Dirk Bogarde's in *The Servant*. At one point, a dinner guest at Crook House complains about having to battle with "gamey ham". It's a sentiment with which anyone watching the gurning on display here will sympathies.

VILLAGE VOICE, 3/11/97, p. 74, Brian Parks

Sir Hugo has a problem with the butler. And it's not that he's played by Sting. No, his problem is that the new valet is starting to wear gentleman's clothes and acting like lord of the manor. Which he may soon be.

A rogue paleontologist with a theory that dinosaurs were actually birds, Sir Hugo (Alan Bates) lives on a crumbling estate with his bored wife (Theresa Russell) and lovely daughter (Lena Headey). His marriage, though, has gone as cold as the bones he studies. So when the calculating new butler arrives, the servant's omnisexual exploits quickly throw the house into chaos—a situation not helped by a grisly murder involving a ham.

Gentlemen Don't Eat Poets is an amusing plate of English gothic served up with some nicely restrained camp. Based on Patrick McGrath's novel *The Grotesque*, the film is both successful creepshow and self-conscious romp (characters boast names like "Connie Babblehump" and "Dr. Dendrite"). And its obvious pleasure in the stew of sex, death, and food makes it a tasty bit of Greenaway lo-cal.

Also reviewed in:
NEW YORK TIMES, 3/7/97, p. C7, Janet Maslin
VARIETY, 9/25-10/1/95, p. 95, Joe Leydon

GEORGE OF THE JUNGLE

A Walt Disney Pictures release of a Mandeville Films, Avnet/Kerner production. *Executive Producer:* C. Tad Devlin. *Producer:* David Hoberman. *Director:* Sam Weisman. *Screenplay:* Dana Olsen and Audrey Wells. *Story:* Dana Olsen. *Based upon characters developed by:* Jay Ward. *Director of Photography:* Thomas Ackerman. *Editor:* Stuart Pappé and Roger Bondelli. *Music:* Marc Shaiman. *Music Editor:* Scott Stambler. *Choreographer:* Adam Shankman. *Sound:* David Kelson and (music) Dennis Sands and Robert Fernandez. *Sound Editor:* Tim Chau and Todd Toon. *Casting:* Amanda Mackey Johnson and Cathy Sandrich. *Production Designer:* Stephen Marsh. *Art Director:* David Haber and Mark Zuelzke. *Set Decorator:* Kathryn Peters. *Set Dresser:* David Elton. *Visual Effects:* Tim Landry. *Costumes:* Lisa Jensen. *Make-up:* Ben Nye, Jr. *Stunt Coordinator:* Phil Adams. *Running time:* 92 minutes. *MPAA Rating:* PG.

CAST: Brendan Fraser (George); Leslie Mann (Ursula Stanhope); Thomas Haden Church (Lyle Van de Groot); Richard Roundtree (Kwame); Greg Cruttwell (Max); Abraham Benrubi (Thor); Holland Taylor (Beatrice Stanhope); Kelly Miller (Betsy); John Bennett Perry (Arthur Stanhope); John Cleese (Voice of an Ape named "Ape"); Michael Chinyamurindi (N'Dugu); Abdoulaye N'Gom (Kip); Lydell Cheshier (Bateke); Keith Scott (The Narrator); Spencer Garrett and Jon Pennell (Male Guests at Party); Lauren Bowles, Afton Smith, and Samantha Harris (Ursula's Friends); Rodney Johnson (Jailer); Peter F. Giddings (TV Weatherman); Terilyn Joe (TV Anchor); Michel Camus (Cameraman); Valerie Perri (TV Reporter); Willie L. Brown, Jr. (Himself); Carrie Zanoline (Perfume Lady); Garrett Griffin (Fireboat Captain); Harve Cook and Aristide Sumatra (Bongo Drummers at Dance Studio); Noah John Cardoza and Benjamin John Cardoza (George Jr.).

LOS ANGELES TIMES, 7/16/97, Calendar/p. 5, Kenneth Turan

[The following review by Kenneth Turan appeared in a slightly different form in **NEWSDAY, 7/16/97, Part II/p. B2.]**

"Watch out for that tree!" people are always screaming at George of the Jungle, and not without reason. Plucky but maladroit, this Tarzan knockoff is liable to bang into almost anything but, like those old Timex watches, he takes a licking and keeps on ticking.

Created by Jay Ward, who also came up with Crusader Rabbit plus the dream team of Rocky squirrel and Bullwinkle moose, George was an animated staple of late 1960s television. Now he's been brought back as a live-action kind of guy, and if you're looking for something silly, you've got nothing to worry about.

This version of "George of the Jungle," directed by Sam Weisman and starring Brendan ("Encino Man") Fraser as the vine-swinging stalwart, tries to recapture the wised-up cleverness of the original but only partly succeeds. Sporadically playful, it ends up wearing as thin as any film geared to a preteen sense of humor is bound to do.

What that means is that audiences who might be charmed by the film's self-mocking attitude have to endure a long string of jokes about flatulence and people getting hammered in the crotch. When George's predilection for slamming into things gets factored in, that's an awful lot of low-level slapstick to put up with from anybody who is not Jim Carrey.

"George" appropriately opens with a cartoon prologue, newly created in the Ward style, locating the country of Bujumbura in the heart of Africa (as opposed to the liver and the colon) and describing the accident that left baby George stranded in the jungle and raised by tolerant apes.

Unseen but all-important is the narrator (Keith Scott), whose mellifluous voice delivers knowing asides referring to things like "the big and expensive waterfall set." It also moves us "46 vines away" from George's territory to introduce the "terrifying intruder" who turns out to be madcap heiress Ursula Stanhope (Leslie Mann) on an adventure-seeking safari in Africa.

Soon enough Ursula is joined by her arrogant snob of a fiancé, Lyle Van de Groot (Thomas Haden Church of TV's "Ned & Stacey"). He's accompanied by a pair of poachers thinly disguised as guides, one of whom, sharp-eyed Max, fans of Mike Leigh's "Naked" will recognize as the landlord from hell.

Those poachers are ever so interested in jungle legends of a gigantic White Ape, 7 feet tall with the strength of many. Lyle pooh-poohs the White Ape notion ("sounds like a drink"), but soon enough Ursula is gone, and it just might be that the big galoot has made off with her.

That galoot, of course, would be George, who, not surprisingly, given all the knocks on the head he's taken, is not the sharpest coconut in the jungle. Though the character is meant to be an innocent, Frasier's playing is closer to feeble-minded and befuddled, which puts a crimp in his audience appeal.

Naturally Ursula ends up in George's split-level treehouse, hanging out with the big guy and his menagerie. That includes Tookie-Tookie, a nosy bird; Shep, the elephant who (courtesy of computer-generated imagery) frolics like a dog; and Ape (voiced by John Cleese), an English-speaking simian who is more cultured than his vine-ripened pal could ever be.

One of the film's series of animatronic apes, including a swinging band (all masterminded by the Jim Henson Creature Shop), Ape is the most successful of the film's nonhuman characters. More comfortable painting a still life than grunting through the jungle, Ape is also dismissive by nature. When his human friend talks of passing on tricks of the jungle trade, Ape sniffs, "George's Secrets: There's the shortest book ever written."

This kind of off-handed humor appears often enough to keep "George of the Jungle" genial, but even by the standards of the genre, there is not a banana's worth of plot in the Dana Olsen and Audrey Wells script to offer narrative nourishment.

George does make a detour to Ursula's hometown of San Francisco, but only to get a great swinging-from-the-Bay Bridge stunt (performed by Joey Preston) into the picture. The film's main focus is on George's courtship of Ursula, whom he initially views as "a funny-looking fella," which is about the level of sophistication of the rest of the romance.

"George's" other preoccupation is product placement, with clothes by Armani and shoes by Nike getting prominent display. The film remains mildly amusing, but this kind of stuff ends up canceling out the humor and the innocence.

Given that "King of Jungle only here to help" is George's constant refrain, he could have started by bailing out his own film.

NEW YORK POST, 7/16/971 p. 45, Michael Medved

Sure, "George of the Jungle" is infectious and frenetic fun, but it just might threaten the physical well-being of your children. After watching the movie, my 4-year-old son, Danny, begged me to install jungle vines in our home.

"But Danny," I replied, "Don't you remember that each time George goes swinging through the jungle, he crashes right into some giant tree?"

"That's okay," the budding critic solemnly nodded. "I know he never gets killed."

He knows because the resonant, all-knowing voice of the film's narrator (Keith Scott) assured him at one tense moment early in the film: "Don't worry. Nobody dies in this movie. They just get really big booboos."

This running commentary on the action ("Meanwhile, at a very big and very expensive waterfall set ...") helps recapture the antic, wise-acre spirit of the original "George of the Jungle" animated TV series, created in 1967 by the incomparable Jay ("Rocky & Bullwinkle") Ward.

That good-natured Tarzan spoof featured a fearless, musclebound doofus in a loincloth, portrayed here by Brendan Fraser with a lithe athleticism and vulnerable edge all his own.

As with his previous role in "Encino Man," Fraser does a nice job of suggesting that his character is sweet, innocent and primitive, rather than outright-dimwitted.

In fact, George shows his intelligence by falling for Ursula (the appropriately gushy and dewy-eyed Leslie Mann), a San Francisco heiress who's gone on jungle safari to escape from her snooty, devious fiance (Thomas Haden Church).

She's naturally impressed by George's noble savage savoir-faire, and by his rapport with animal companions, including a bespectacled, chess-playing gorilla (with the bemused Alfred-the-butler voice of John Cleese) and an elephant, Shep, who thinks he's a faithful dog.

This panting, playful pachyderm, combining footage of a real elephant with computer generated images, fetches logs hurled in his direction or rolls over and plays dead; he's an especially bewitching cinematic creation that alone justifies the price of admission.

The movie flags only during the inevitable interlude when Ursula brings George back to her world of San Francisco to meet her disapproving parents, and, despite one spectacular stunt on the Bay Bridge, we go through predictable pratfalls (as in dozens of movies from "Crocodile Dundee" to "Jungle to Jungle") of nature boy in the cruel big city.

Fortunately for both the characters and the audience, the action ultimately returns to George's leafy home, where we get a climactic, sensational chase scene and a truly inspired sight gag for the film's conclusion.

Director Sam Weisman previously created two likable but limited films ("Bye Bye Love" and "D2: The Mighty Ducks"), that gave little chance for originality or visual dazzlement, yet here his wit and inventiveness are not only entertaining, they're exhilarating. But watch out for that tree!

SIGHT AND SOUND, 1/98, p. 43, Leslie Felperin

An airplane crashes in the middle of an African jungle. Infant-survivor George is taken away by gorillas and raised as one of their own. Twenty-five years later, beautiful heiress Ursula Stanhope sets off with an expedition party into that same jungle to find the legendary "white ape" (George). Ursula's snobby fiancé Lyle tags along. Ursula and Lyle are confronted by a lion; Lyle is knocked unconscious, but Ursula is saved by George and whisked away on a trapeze of vines to his hut, where he lives with Ape, a talking gorilla, Shep, a canine-like elephant, and Tookie, a toucan. Lyle and the others search for Ursula.

George and Ursula begin to fall in love. After he is injured by a poacher's bullet meant for Ape, Ursula brings George back to San Francisco with her. Her parents are disgusted by George's uncouth ways, but when George saves a workman from falling off a bridge, he becomes a hero. Back in the jungle, Lyle and the poachers have captured Ape—Lyle plans to make Ape a showbusiness attraction back in the US. Tookie flies to San Francisco to tell George what has happened and George returns to the jungle to save Ape. George is reunited with Ursula and the two stay on in the jungle, while Ape pursues his singing career abroad.

British viewers are probably less familiar than North American ones with the original cartoon series *George of the Jungle,* a satire of the Tarzan films whose hapless hero was forever colliding with trees as he swung on vines through the rainforest. It was the last gaudy blossom of a series (1967-70) put forth by Jay Ward Productions, the creators of such legendary characters as Bullwinkle and Rocky, Dudley Do-Right, and Crusader Rabbit (whose own show, conceived by Ward and Alex Anderson, was the first animated series made exclusively for television). Crudely drawn and simply animated, Ward's cartoons managed to outshine rival companies by virtue of their extraordinarily amusing scripts, full of intrusive narrators and tongue-in-cheek wit. *The Simpsons, Ren and Stimpy,* and *Beavis and Butt-head* all owe far more to the spirit of Ward's work than they do to Hanna-Barbera's.

George of the Jungle the film makes a more than noble effort to recapture some of the original's charm and parodic sense of humour, which means that most of the best lines belong to the narrator, voiced with due seriousness by Keith Scott. As in the original series, a running gag involves him describing events seconds before they happen, only to react in frustration when the characters don't act the way they should. For example, he describes how, on seeing an impressive vista, the expedition party "reacted with awe", only for the party to sigh with a collective "ahh!" as if they had just seen a bunny rabbit. Another throwaway gag links scenes with "Meanwhile, back at the big and expensive jungle set ..."

Indeed, with flashy CGI effects that create an elephant that thinks he's a dog and a top-notch stunt involving our hero swinging from the Golden Gate Bridge, this is a fairly big and expensive movie, an extra, not so-funny irony considering that the original series was modest and cheap. The cartoon's cult following was built partly on an admiration for its audacity in smuggling something so subversive into the Saturday morning and after-school television schedules. (*George* mark one had a proto-queer quality, founded on George's inability to comprehend what a woman was, and that his mate Ursula was one.) Produced by Disney, *George* mark two repackages and restrains that subversiveness and sells it back to us bit by bit, from the film itself to the inevitable tie-in meal deals at fast food restaurants. Thus, another irony is that while the two *Brady Bunch* films managed to make something far darker and more caustic out of their source material, *George of the Jungle* fashions a more anodyne and family-friendly product from its.

Nonetheless, as updated, reheated nostalgia films go, *George of the Jungle* is fairly fresh. Director Sam Weisman *(Bye Bye Love, D2 The Mighty Ducks)* keeps things bouncing along and knows that the mixed-aged audience he's aiming for wants a seamless mix of jokes, pratfalls, and effects, with a romance for the girls (and boys) inclined to swoon over the toothsome figure of Brendan Fraser. It's a very likeable film, but one can't help thinking that if Jay Ward were alive and involved in its making, he would have pinched up the cheekiness, thrown in a sarcastic remark about Michael Eisner and at least a swat at *Hercules.*

Also reviewed in:
NEW YORK TIMES, 7/16/97, p. C18, Lawrence Van Gelder
VARIETY, 7/14-20/97, p. 43, Leonard Klady

WASHINGTON POST, 7/16/97, p. D1, Rita Kempley
WASHINGTON POST, 7/18/97, Weekend/p. 41, Desson Howe

GOING ALL THE WAY

A Gramercy Pictures release of a PolyGram Filmed Entertainment presentation of a Tom Gorai/Lakeshore Entertainment production. *Executive Producer:* Tom Rosenberg, Ted Tannebaum, and Michael Mendelsohn. *Producer:* Tom Gorai and Sigurjon Sighvatsson. *Director:* Mark Pellington. *Screenplay (based on his novel):* Dan Wakefield. *Director of Photography:* Bobby Bukowski. *Editor:* Leo Trombetta. *Music:* Tomandandy. *Music Editor:* Tom Paul. *Sound:* Tom Paul. *Casting:* Ellen Chenoweth. *Production Designer:* Thérèse Dèprez. *Art Director:* Keven Lock. *Set Decorator:* Nick Evans. *Set Dresser:* Todd Ian Cole and Brian Scott Buteau. *Special Effects:* Gary Linn Rittenhouse. *Costumes:* Arianne Phillips. *Make-up:* Raqueli Dahan. *Stunt Coordinator:* Johnny Cann. *Running time:* 110 minutes. *MPAA Rating:* R.

CAST: Jeremy Davies (Sonny Burns); Ben Affleck (Gunner Casselman); Amy Locane (Buddy Porter); Rose McGowan (Gale Ann Thayer); Rachel Weisz (Marty Pilcher); John Lordan (Elwood Burns); Bob Swan (Luke); Jill Clayburgh (Alma Burns); Lesley Ann Warren (Nina Casselman); Richard Gaeckle (Conductor/Ticket Taker); Teri Beitel (Beautiful Young Girl); Everett Greene (Waiter); Jerry Panatieri (Religious Man); Jeff Buelterman (Blow Mahoney); Nick Offerman (Wilks); Pat Daley (Meadowlark Resident #1); Charlie Webb (Meadowlark Resident #2); Wendy Carter (Deedee); Dave Webster (Crooner); Ted Steeg (Minister); Adrienne Reiswerg (Farmer's Wife); David Aikens (Farmer #1); Dan Wakefield (Farmer #2); John Craig (Doctor).

LOS ANGELES TIMES, 12/19/97, Calendar/ p. 9, John Anderson

[*The following review by John Anderson appeared in a slightly different form in* NEWSDAY, 12/19/97, Part II/p. B7.]

Consider the Woody Allen-Bill Gates trajectory of American manhood over the last 30 years, and there's only one conclusion: Nerds rule! Al Gore is vice president. Ben Stein has his own TV show. And Jeremy Davies, who appeared in "Spanking the Monkey", and is now starring in "Going All the Way," has timed his career to the height of the geek revolution.

Davies will take the misfit portrayal to even further extremes in the upcoming "Locusts," and is walking on the thin ice of stereotype. That said, he's nearly perfect in this adaptation of Dan Wakefield's popular novel, a tale of what else?—rites of passage, coming of age and sexual education under Eisenhower.

Based on a 1970 novel set in the '50s, and directed by '80s and '90s MTV auteur Mark Pellington (Pearl Jam, U2, Public Enemy), "Going All the Way" shows a pan-generational sympathy for the plight of males in need. Could it have been set during any other period? Probably not: Its subtext about women, marriage and men-as-prey wouldn't really wash outside of the Cleaver Years.

At the same time, the film's erotic landscape seems more like the '60s; for all the reputed sexual repression that made Elvis Presley possible, the terrain of "Going All the Way" is pretty freewheeling.

And Sonny Burns (Davies) would like to get in on the action. Returning home to Indiana after the Korean War (he served in Kansas City), Sonny meets an old hometown acquaintance, Gunner Casselman (Ben Affleck of "Chasing Amy"). Gunner has also been discharged, and it's Gunner, the former sports star, who strikes up with Sonny, the former high school photographer. It's an odd match, but there's something solid about Sonny to which Gunner responds; for all of Gunner's pretentious talk about Japan and art and the ways of Zen, something in the war has changed him, something never articulated but always present.

This unspoken, Hemingway-esque war ghost lends gravity to the friendship between the two young men, each of whom has his own female trouble. Sonny's mother, Alma (played with a combination salve and acid by Jill Clayburgh) is a smothering manipulative holy roller who wants Sonny to marry Buddy (Amy Locane), his faithful, uninspiring girlfriend. Gunner's mother, whom he calls Nina (Lesley Ann Warren), refers to herself in the third person and reveals a vicious anti-Semitic streak—and probable Oedipal impulse—when (Gunner takes up with the savvy Jewish art student Marty Pilcher (Rachel Weisz). Sonny's most agonizing moments come with Gale Ann Thayer (retro-bombshell Rose McGowan), a pitiless siren who leaves him in an emotional ditch.

So much male bonding, male pain. And so many women with men's names. Like the crankcase on a '57 Chevy, the Wakefield-Pellington perspective on gender relations is a black and viscous thing, full of unpleasant possibilities. Pellington bestows on the film a distracting if occasionally effective, amount of video technique, and Wakefield's story is rich and often truthful.

On the other hand, neither seems have learned the lessons of their movie: That "going all the way" doesn't really refer to sex. And that when men resist their basic nature is when they finally become adults.

NEW YORK POST, 9/19/97, p. 52, Thelma Adams

Male coming of age doesn't get any fresher when set in Indianapolis after the Korean War. The cars were bigger, the girdles sturdier and there wasn't any Internet, but anatomy was basically the same.

Mark Pellington's "Going All the Way" exchanges the summer of '54 for the "Summer of '42." Based on Dan Wakefield's adaptation of his novel, this energetic period piece goes all the way through male desire, overbearing mothers, masturbation, religious rejection, provincialism, drunken hazes, performance anxiety, a suicide attempt and a life-changing car crash.

Since soldiers Sonny Burns (Jeremy Davies) and Gunner Casselman (Ben Affleck) are no longer virgins when they return to Indiana from their military postings, going all the way comes to mean getting out of Dodge: leaving their mothers and high school girlfriends and heading for New York.

Davies ("Spanking the Monkey") and Affleck ("Chasing Amy") are well cast as the high school nerd and big man on campus who bond on the train home, but their story is as old as a catcher in the rye, the wheat, the oats, whatever ...

When Sonny mentions Holden Caulfield it's just too obvious how overtilled this fictional soil is.

Jill Clayburgh and Lesley Ann Warren are boxed into nagging maternal stereotypes: one's an overprotective Bible-thumper, the other an overprotective lush and anti-Semite. Rachel Weisz and Amy Locane, in particular, make the best of their supporting roles.

SIGHT AND SOUND, 8/98, p. 44, Claire Monk

1954. On a train home to Indianapolis, two young GIs—confident Gunner Casselman, returning from the Korean war, and shy, repressed Sonny Burns, back from the army—recognise each other from high school and become unlikely friends. Sonny, smothered by his religious mother Alma, envies Gunner's liberal home life and sexual experience. Sonny tries to dump his girlfriend Buddy. Gunner pursues Marty, a sophisticated Jewish art student soon to move to New York. His ardour wins out, but Gunner's anti-Semitic mother Nina opposes the relationship.

To steer Sonny away from Gunner's influence Alma finds him a born-again Christian mentor. Marty sets up Sonny with her sexually experienced college friend Gale but he drinks to excess and fails to perform. Later he slashes his wrist but is saved by Gunner, who drives him into the country by night. A storm strikes and they crash. Badly injured, Sonny comes round in hospital to learn that Gunner was unhurt and has gone to New York with Marty. Sonny returns to his parents' care. One day they instruct him to take Buddy out. To his relief, Buddy is engaged to someone else. Sonny travels one-way to New York.

Going All the Way may have left UK screens by the time you read this review. This would be a shame, because despite the *Grease*-like trinity of kitsch, saccharine and raunch its title suggests, this acute and funny coming-of-age film has a lot to recommend it. Its pleasures owe much to

Dan Wakefield's script, adapted from his own highly regarded 1970 novel, and to the fine central performances, most crucially from Jeremy Davies as the shy, hormonally tormented Sonny, returning from service as a GI to a suffocating 50s family home where adulthood as well as sexuality is vehemently denied. Most impressively, *Going* comes close to doing for the 50s what *The Ice Storm* did for the 70s, playing with the decade's sexual, social and design tropes with an eloquence that transcends cliché. Debut feature director Mark Pellington and his production designer Thérèse Deprez distil the film's themes into its visuals with dexterity. The details of Sonny's grim bedroom, from the sports-print wallpaper to the childish bunk bed, tell us almost all we need to know about his familial oppression.

Unusually, rather than treating sexual repression as a generic 50s trait, *Going* portrays it as a site of generational conflict and dissent, and lucidly roots it in the wider bigotries of the McCarthy era. Sonny's mother may murmur "God save your eternal soul" when she finds his porn mags, but the film's younger generation reject such morality. Gunner and Sonny dream of sex without strings, and the young women they make out with are uninhibited. The most mould-breaking figure is Gunner's mother Nina: wealthy, unattached and attractive, she seems unexpectedly liberated. The opposed mores of the two boys' families are given gorgeous expression in the interior design: gingham frills for the Burns, mid-century modern furniture and abstract art for Nina. But Nina's taste coexists with snobbery and anti-Semitism, making Gunner as eager to escape as Sonny. The contrasting characters of Sonny and Gunner are amusingly signalled through physical type: Ben Affleck's blank handsomeness provides a foil for the short, nervy Jeremy Davies. Oddly, the substance of their friendship is *Going*'s most elusive element, but the film's sharpness as social commentary more than compensates.

VILLAGE VOICE, 9/23/97, p. 90, Amy Taubin

"Painting leads to pussy," says Gunner Casselman (Ben Affleck) to his friend Sonny Burns (Jeremy Davies) as they are distracted in their contemplation of a modernist masterpiece in Indianapolis's Museum of art by the sight of a real live woman. Like *My Sex Life,* Mark Pellington's *Going All the Way* is a film about masculinity during the critical transition from adolescence to adulthood. That thematic aside, the two films have remarkably little in common.

At best, *Going All the Way* is a not-bad American indie. Predictably plotted and suffering from the prevalent Amerindie fetishization of art direction as a substitute for eloquent camerawork and editing, it nevertheless takes life from its two leading actors. Davies and Affleck play Korean War veterans who are having a hard time returning to the confines of mid-'50s, midwestern suburbia. As the shy Sonny, who stubbornly refuses the life his parents have laid out for him, Davies skitters around the clichéd dialogue and comes up with some surprisingly moving moments. Affleck has much the better role. His Gunner is a former high school jock whose brief contact with Japanese culture has opened him to new worlds within and without. Adapting the '50s lingo of David Reisman, he ingenuously describes himself as an outer-directed guy who's trying to be more inner-directed. Affleck, who's like a less neurotic version of the young Warren Beatty, has a physical ease and generosity that's extremely seductive. If *Going All the Way* is remembered at all, it will be as a stepping stone in his brilliant career.

Also reviewed in:
CHICAGO TRIBUNE, 10/10/97, Friday/p. O, John Petrakis
NEW REPUBLIC, 10/6/97, p. 28, Stanley Kauffmann
NEW YORK TIMES, 9/19/97, p. E14, Stephen Holden
VARIETY, 2/3-9/97, p. 45, Todd McCarthy
WASHINGTON POST, 10/10/97, p. D6, Stephen Hunter

GONE FISHIN'

A Hollywood Pictures release in association with Caravan Pictures of a Roger Birnbaum production. *Executive Producer:* Jill Mazursky Cody. *Producer:* Roger Birnbaum and Julie Bergman Sender. *Director:* Christopher Cain. *Screenplay:* Jill Mazursky Cody and Jeffrey Abrams. *Director of Photography:* Dean Semler. *Editor:* Jack Hofstra. *Music:* Randy Edelman. *Music Editor:* John LaSalandra. *Sound:* Tim Cooney and (music) Elton Ahi. *Sound Editor:* Mark P. Stoeckinger. *Casting:* Rick Montgomery and Dan Parada. *Production Designer:* Lawrence Miller. *Art Director:* Michael Rizzo and Phil Dagort. *Set Designer:* Barbara Mesney, Andrew Neskoromny, Greg Papalia, and Mark Poll. *Set Decorator:* Cloudia. *Special Effects:* Jeff Jarvis. *Visual Effects:* Erik Henry. *Costumes:* Lizzy Gardiner. *Make-up:* John M. Elliott, Jr. *Make-up (Joe Pesci):* James Sarzotti. *Make-up (Danny Glover):* Diane Hammond. *Stunt Coordinator:* Shane Dixon. *Running time:* 94 minutes. *MPAA Rating:* PG.

CAST: Joe Pesci (Joe Waters); Danny Glover (Gus Green); Rosanna Arquette (Rita); Lynn Whitfield (Angie); Willie Nelson (Billy "Catch" Pooler); Nick Brimble (Dekker Massey); Gary Grubbs (Phil Beasly); Carol Kane (Donna Waters); Edythe Davis (Cookie Green); Jenna Bari (Gina Waters); Samantha Brown (Tracy Green); Jeff DiLucca (Mack Waters); Jamil Akim O'Quinn (Gregory Green); Frank Nasso (Young Joe); Raynor Scheine (Glenn); Robyn Hackett (Nicky); James R. Greene (Bubba); Steve Wise (JP); Claudia Haro (Julie); Jonathan Avildsen (Parking Valet); Bob Noble (Manager); Jeff Prettyman (Maitre D'); Judy Clayton (Deana Bernini); Antoni Corone (Front Desk Clerk); Dana Adamstein (Reporter #1); Valerie J. Boey (Reporter #2); Joseph Scalora (Officer); Tommy DeVito (Construction Foreman); Leonard Termo (Vending Worker #1); Alfred Nittoli (Vending Worker #2); Gary Morgan (Bergman); Lisa Hewlett Keen (Dining Room Guest); Dave Corey (Actor); Baynor Foy Crane (Actress); Mark Futch (Seaplane Pilot); Al Guthery (Helicopter Pilot); John Griffen (Blind Driver).

LOS ANGELES TIMES, 6/2/97, Calendar/p. 3, Gene Seymour

[The following review by Gene Seymour appeared in a slightly different form in NEWSDAY, 6/2/97, Part II/p. B7.]

You have to wonder what in the name of Curly Howard possessed acting powerhouses Joe Pesci and Danny Glover to play a pair of minus numbers from Jersey in "Gone Fishin'," a mirthless, graceless slapstick comedy with little to recommend it except some Florida scenery—which, come to think of it, isn't all that scenic.

The only possible explanation for this movie's existence—and this is a stretch and a half—is that somebody, somewhere, liked the chemistry between Pesci and Glover in two consecutive "Lethal Weapon" movies enough to think they could commit entertaining mayhem anywhere.

But somebody, somewhere, should have figured out that playing dumb requires a tricky balance of abandonment and timing in order to make an audience laugh. And despite their considerable, well-deserved credentials, neither Pesci nor Glover is as good at doofus shtick as, say, Jim Carrey or Jeff Daniels in "Dumb and Dumber."

Then again, it may be that Glover is just too dignified to be believed as the kind of guy who shatters everything he touches. Pesci fares better, especially in a fancy restaurant scene when he's slurping red wine. But you wish the story gave him a chance to explode as only he can.

Ah, yes. The story. Pesci and Glover are longtime chums who win a fishing vacation in Florida. Pesci's wife, the shamefully underused Carol Kane, foresees trouble. Sure enough, they haven't been in the Sunshine State for a minute before their car is swiped by a sinister con man who is himself the target of a search by two women (Rosanna Arquette, Lynn Whitfield). Why are they looking for him? Why are they even in this movie? To give Pesci and Glover someone to ogle?

The listless succession of scenes in which boats crash (stuntwoman Janet Wilder was killed last year doing one such stunt), furniture breaks and rooms explode gives fresh meaning to the expression "senseless violence." Willie Nelson's literally incandescent cameo as the boys' fishing hero gives flickering hope that something unusual might happen. But he drifts away with the wreckage. Hope they paid you well, cowboy.

NEW YORK POST, 5/31/97, p. 21, Larry Worth

About midway through "Gone Fishin'," Joe Pesci says to Danny Glover: "You know what? This is going nowhere."

Truer words were never spoken.

But that doesn't stop director Christopher Cain from throwing in everything but the kitchen sink in a bid to animate this moribund mess.

Specifically, he has Pesci and Glover on a runaway boat in a crowded marina, threatened by a murderer, dodging explosions, navigating swamps with a treasure map, being struck by lightning, cursed with sleepwalking and chased by crocodiles.

Worse, that's all meant to garner laughs, since Pesci's and Glover's characters have the collective IQ of a slug. In reality, those on-screen crocodiles will be the only ones smiling.

Director Cain's best quality is that he seems to mean well. In a bid to provide suitable entertainment for the family, the yuks are never mean-spirited. Stupid, yes. But never mean-spirited.

Meanwhile, Pesci and Glover, the duo that ignited endless comedic sparks in two of the "Lethal Weapon" films, display virtually no chemistry here.

Granted, it's nice to hear Pesci recite something besides his standard obscenity-laden dialogue. But he never convinces as a sad-sack family man. Worse, this comes on the heel of his disastrous contribution to "Eight Heads in a Duffel Bag."

Pesci's career isn't the only one requiring rethinking, evidenced by Glover's lame attempts at physical humor. For that matter, how does one explain Rosanna Arquette, Lynn Whitfield, Willie Nelson and Carol Kane embarrassing themselves with paint-by-number supporting roles? Were they that desperate for a paycheck?

Hopefully, their next efforts won't leave fans with such a sinking feeling.

Also reviewed in:
NEW YORK TIMES, 5/31/97, p. 20, Lawrence Van Gelder
VARIETY, 6/2-8/97, p. 60, Joe Leydon

GOOD BURGER

A Paramount pictures release in association with Nickelodeon Movies of a Tollin/Robbins production. *Executive Producer:* Julia Pistor. *Producer:* Mike Tollin and Brian Robbins. *Director:* Brian Robbins. *Screenplay:* Dan Schneider, Kevin Kopelow, and Heath Seifert. *Based on characters created by:* Dan Schneider, Kevin Kopelow, and Heith Seifert. *Director of Photography:* Mac Ahlberg. *Editor:* Anita Brandt-Burgoyne. *Music:* Stewart Copeland. *Music Editor:* Michael Dittrick. *Choreographer:* Dave Scott. *Sound:* Veda Campbell. *Sound Editor:* John Benson. *Casting:* Jaki Brown-Kaman and Robyn M. Mitchell. *Production Designer:* Steven Jordan. *Art Director:* Robert J. Bacon. *Set Designer:* Charlie Vassar. *Set Decorator:* Cloudia. *Special Effects:* John R. Peyser. *Costumes:* Natasha Landau. *Make-up:* Emily E. Katz. *Stunt Coordinator:* Al Jones. *Running time:* 93 minutes. *MPAA Rating:* PG.

CAST: Kenan Thompson (Dexter Reed); Kel Mitchell (Ed); Abe Vigoda (Otis); Sinbad (Mr. Wheat); Shar Jackson (Monique); Dan Schneider (Mr. Bailey); Jan Schwieterman (Kurt Bozwell); Ron Lester (Spatch); Josh Server (Fizz); Ginny Schreiber (Deedee); Linda Cardellini (Heather); Shaquille O'Neil (Himself); George Clinton (Dancing Crazy); Richard Hale (Huge Scary Man); Robert Wuhl (Angry Customer); Corrie Harris (Corey); Lori Beth Denberg (Connie Muldoon); Marques Houston (Jake); Matthew Gallant (News Reporter); Teresa Ganzel (Woman Customer); Brian Peck (Upset Customer); Hamilton Von Watts (Troy); J. August Richards (Griffen); Kevin Kopelow (Sad Clown); Floyd Levine (Ice Cream Man); Brett Jones

(Driving Attendant);   Brad Wilson (Scared Customer);   Melissa Spell (Frightened Customer);
Andres Aybar (Mondo Worker);   Eve Sigall and Jo Farkas (Elderly Ladies);   Paul Parducci and
Kim Delgado (Police Officers);   Wendy Worthington (Demented Hills Nurse);   Chet Nichols and
Carl A. McGee (Guards);   David Shackelford and Rob Elk (Attendants).

LOS ANGELES TIMES, 7/25/97, Calendar/p. 14, Gene Seymour

[The following review by Gene Seymour appeared in a slightly different form in
NEWSDAY, 7/25/97, Part II/p. B9.]

In this epoch of children's pop entertainment, where action figures still monopolize the landscape, it's reassuring to know that kids can still be captivated by the simple spectacle of two
goofy guys dropping things, walking into walls, making yet Another Fine Mess.

It's far too soon to bestow upon Kenan (Thompson) and Kel (Mitchell) the iconic dimensions
owned by Laurel and Hardy, Abbott and Costello, Martin and Lewis, Kramden and Norton ...
or, for that matter, Wayne and Garth.

But it's also mildly amazing that in the three years that they've been doing their odd-couple
shtick on the Nickelodeon network, Kenan and Kel have become cult figures among post-toddlers
and preteens who make room in their crowded schedules to watch them on Saturday nights.

"Good Burger," K&K's inevitable first movie, will satisfy their audience's appetite for basic,
messy silliness while leaving many grown-ups mildly bemused by the fuzzy obviousness of its
humor, the gawky pacing of its sight gags and the second-handedness of its slapstick—almost all
of which is redeemed by the eager but never cloying charm of its two stars.

The movie gives full rein to one of Kel's recurring TV personas: Ed, the dread-locked idiot
savant who's always ready to take your order at Good Burger, a humble little joint that, as the
movie begins, is in danger of being ground into oblivion by Mondo Burger, a glitzy competitor
run by a smarmy little martinet named Kurt (Jan Schwieterman).

Among the Good Burger coworkers joining Ed in foiling Mondo's evil machinations are Dexter
(Kenan), a high school student who's not above exploiting Ed for his own schemes; Monique
(Shar Jackson from "Moesha"), a comely counter girl; and Otis (Abe Vigoda), who wakes up
from perpetual stupor long enough to help the good guys throw icky stuff at the bad guys.

Sinbad heroically sheds his dignity to play Kenan's hopelessly stuck-in-the-'70s teacher, while
the great George Clinton drops by to help out in an impromptu performance of (what else?) "Do
Fries Go With That Shake?"

It's nowhere near a masterpiece. But then, few thought "Buck Privates" was a masterpiece
when it came out in 1941. Yet it guaranteed Abbott and Costello's marquee value for at least the
next decade-and-a-half. By this standard, "Good Burger" may be just good enough (i.e. not too
embarrassing) to pass mustard—um—muster.

NEW YORK POST, 7/25/97, p. 49, Larry Worth

Those who habitually tune into the Nickelodeon channel apparently know and love teenaged
heroes "Kenan and Kel." As such, the TV characters' first cinematic offering, "Good Burger,"
has a ready-made audience.

But for non-devotees, "Good Burger" can't even pass as cinematic junk food; there's too much
that sticks in the craw.

Especially unpalatable is Kenan Thompson, the smart-mouthed, alleged brains of the operation.
He's kind of a full-grown version of Gary ("Diffrent Strokes") Coleman, who previously reigned
as TVs most irritating presence.

Then there's Kel Mitchell whose corn-rowed pageboy lets him pass for Janet Jackson on a bad
hair day. He's actually the equivalent of a dumb blonde; someone tells him to "watch your
butt," he spends the next five minutes turning in circles.

The simplistic story could have been fun, dealing with the titular Good Burger restaurant—
staffed by dim-witted Kel and wise-cracking Kenan—and a fight against neighboring Mondo
Burger and its fascist employees.

But as directed by newcomer Brian Robbins, the good vs. evil story quickly loses its way.
Although the vehicle is presumably geared to youngsters, a number of unsettling areas surfaces.

For starters, there's a smarmy onslaught of sexual innuendoes, as when Kel asks Kenan to check out his "special place," or when a sex kitten tries to seduce Kel into surrendering his "secret sauce."

Even worse, the action later switches to an insane asylum, where the troubled inmates become fodder for cheap laughs. A scene in which they break into an MTV-style dance is particularly demeaning.

And that's not even mentioning a scene of Kel in frilly ladies' underwear, or half-baked storylines about Kenan's deadbeat dad and the dangers of illegal food additives. Did the writers really think this stuff was suitable as kiddie fare?

As for the star attractions, Kenan and Kel muster zero appeal on screen, no matter how much charm they've generated on TV. Aside from Kenan's ability to roll his eyeballs and Kel's penchant for working "dude" into every sentence, their assets are hard to discern.

Even sadder are pathetic supporting turns from Abe Vigoda, Sinbad and Shar Jackson, along with and inexplicable cameo from Shaquille O'Neal. Were they that desperate for exposure to the Nickelodeon crowd?

A ton of shameless Coca-Cola and Rold Gold plugs, an inappropriate soundtrack geared to sell CDs and special effects that are considerably less than special leave viewers even less to savor.

That's why—for all but Kenan and Kel diehards—"Good Burger' goes down badly, then leaves a nasty aftertaste.

SIGHT AND SOUND, 3/98, p. 49, Andy Richards

Ed works at Good Burger, an old-style fast-food retailer whose business is threatened by corporate controlled Mondo Burger across the street. High-school pupil Dexter Reed accidentally collides with a car and is forced to work at Mondo Burger to pay for the damage. But Dexter is soon sacked by his tyrannical boss Kurt and Ed gets him a job at Good Burger. Dexter tries some of Ed's delicious homemade sauce, and gets Ed to sign a contract entitling Dexter to 80 per cent of Ed's profits from patenting the sauce. Due to the sauce, business thrives. Staff worker Monique agrees to go out with Dexter but when she learns about the contract, she berates him. Kurt sends over a sexy cohort to coax the secret recipe from Ed, but he resists.

Ed and Dexter, suspicious at the size of the Mondo Burgers, infiltrate their kitchens. Discovered by Kurt, they are imprisoned in Demented Hills asylum. Kurt and his men poison the special sauce at Good Burger. Otis, a loyal and elderly worker, catches them at it and is also dispatched to the asylum. Ed, Dexter and Otis manage to escape and race back to Good Burger, where they prevent any customers tasting the poisoned sauce. Ed and Dexter discover that the Mondo Burgers are produced using illegal food additives. Ed causes the burgers to explode, destroying the restaurant. Kurt is arrested, and Ed is feted as a hero. Dexter tears up his contract for Ed's sauce.

Good Burger feels like a mediocre television comedy sketch stretched beyond breaking point to feature length which, it transpires, is exactly what it is. Young stars Kenan Thompson and Kel Mitchell achieved fame in Nickelodeon's sketch comedy series *All That* (in which the burger sketch made a regular appearance), before collaborating on their own show *Kenan & Kel*. Director Brian Robbins, who holds a co-creator and executive producer credit on both shows, attempts a bright, feel-good charm, saturating his flat visuals with day-glo colouring. But this film, in the tradition of other television-sketch spin-offs (such as *Wayne's World*), succeeds only in delivering sporadic flashes of wit amid the weak, forced gags and lazy one-dimensional characterisations. Certainly, it is hard to see the film finding an audience in this country, and equally hard not to feel that, with its tedious banter and clumsy exposition, it hardly merits one anyway.

Admittedly, Mitchell and Thompson generate a certain chemistry, and their dominant skills—for physical and verbal comedy respectively—complement each other well. However, Mitchell's almost unfeasibly deep voice very quickly starts to grate, and his Ed character is too limited to sustain a feature film. It is dispiriting to encounter yet another film whose narrative is sustained by the antics of an *idiot savant* whose stupidity is supposed to be endearing. Thompson, while at least capable of lucid speech, merely huffs, puffs and rolls his eyes.

It seems curious that the film's narrative can nostalgically celebrate the simple virtues of a hamburger joint where staff members are obliged chirpily to intone, "Welcome to Good Burger, home of the Good Burger. May I take your order please?" (the original sketches' catchphrase) and where bureaucratic inefficiency is endemic. To British eyes, accustomed to a landscape colonised by US-style fast-food outlets, there may not seem much of a quantifiable difference between Burgers Mondo and Good, thereby rendering this disposable piece of cinema even more irrelevant.

Also reviewed in:
NEW YORK TIMES, 7/25/97, p. C10, Anita Gates
VARIETY, 7/28-8/3/97, p. 57, Leonard Klady
WASHINGTON POST, 7/25/97, Weekend/p. 49, Stephen Hunter

GOOD LUCK

An East West Film Partners release. *Executive Producer:* Bob Comfort. *Producer:* Richard Hahn and Shirley Honickman Hahn. *Director:* Richard LaBrie. *Screenplay:* Bob Comfort. *Director of Photography:* Maximo Munzi. *Editor:* Neal Grieve. *Music:* Tim Truman. *Sound:* Brett Grant-Grierson. *Casting:* Rik Pagano. *Production Designer:* Jane Ann Stewart. *Set Decorator:* Ellen Zuckerman. *Running time:* 95 minutes. *MPAA Rating:* R.

CAST: Gregory Hines (Bernard Lemley); Vincent D'Onofrio (Tony Olezniak); Max Gail (Farmer John); James Earl Jones (James Bing); Joe Theismann (Himself); Roy Chunk Firestone (Himself); Robert O'Reilly (Bartender); Maria O'Brien (Peggy).

LOS ANGELES TIMES, 3/7/97, Calendar/p. 10, John Anderson

[*The following review by John Anderson appeared in a slightly different form in* NEWSDAY, 3/7/97, Part II/p. B13.]

A black guy, a white guy—one maimed in a car crash, one blinded playing NFL football; one prodding the other to get off his self-pity and into a white-water race so they can prove they're stilt men. Is this the stuff of nauseatingly upbeat melodrama or what?

You have to give director Robert LaBrie credit for biting off such a large chunk of standard-issue tar pit like this and then spitting out "Good Luck"—which is just what you'd tell him. Certain audiences, and they're not necessarily right, of course, would emit a low moan of discomfort at the mere mention of the plot synopsis. Buddy movies, triumph-over-adversity movies, moral-triumph movies, they're all wrapped up here like a rapidly ripening fish.

But it's not so simple. From the outset, LaBrie establishes a certain goofy freedom that keeps the film from imploding, and it actually surprises you—not always, but often enough. And Vincent D'Onofrio and Gregory Hines, never known for restraint, are precisely what they should be.

Tony "Olee" Olezniak, for instance, played by D'Onofrio, is a nationally recognized tight end for the Seattle Seahawks, the type of player police like to escort to games when he's late and speeding. When a vicious tackle leaves him blind because of a spinal injury, his life takes the predictable downward trajectory. When he learns his tell-all book about life with a washed-up, impotent football star, he throws the TV and everything else out the window (it's D'Onofrio, the frequent Orson Welles look-alike, doing the tantrum scene from "Citizen Kane"). He ends up in jail. His life in the toilet, Olee chooses not to bail himself out.

Injured in an auto accident eight years earlier, Bernard Lemley (Hines) sees Olee's story and, remembering that he'd tutored the ballplayer years before, goes to the jail. He has this dream of entering the rigorous Gold City Regatta, a raft race on Oregon's Rogue River, and wants Olee's strength to fight the white water. They meet, they butt heads, they bond.

Clearly, the whole premise is absurd, and at this point you're wondering if they'll run into Meryl Streep while bobbing along the Rogue. But there's a loose, irreverent quality about the fact-based "Good Luck," an ability to do an end-run around the plot conventions, that gives the film a fresher than expected feel. There are also little bits of tossed-off comedy (I heard something about "Murder in the Cathedral" starring Pia Zadora) that keep the whole thing from becoming as maudlin as it could easily have been. And Hines and D'Onofrio work really well together and separately.

Hines makes Lemley a cross between Stephen Hawking and Steve Urkel. D'Onofrio, who possesses the ability to swing from sour to soulful in a heartbeat, turns Olee's bombast into a plea for help. The heart of the film isn't the race, of course, it's the interaction of the antagonist-pals—a game of chicken on a railroad tracks. a game of blackjack in a roadside casino, sex talk, childhood trauma, hopes, dreams and some unlikely feats by a blind man. Also, a little too much slo-mo in the climactic moments. But the remarkable thing is how well Hines and D'Onofrio make you forget their characters' disabilities, which is rather the point of the whole thing.

NEW YORK POST, 3/7/97, p. 51, Michael Medved

How's this for tawdry, tear-jerking high concept?

A famous pro football star (Vincent D'Onofrio) goes blind after a freak NFL accident. Wallowing in self-pity after a destructive rage puts him in a Seattle jail cell, he's approached by a paraplegic dental technician (Gregory Hines) with a daring plan to enable both men to recover their manhood.

Hines wants to enter a celebrated whitewater rafting race on Oregon's Rogue River, showing the world that they can overcome their disabilities.

A blind, blue-collar white guy and a crippled black guy risking their lives in one of the most demanding, dangerous sports in the world? Would any savvy moviegoer care to bet against such audacious underdogs?

While the clumsily titled "Good Luck" sounds like some wretched TV movie, it's actually much worse than that—treating us to all sorts of gratuitous information about D'Onofrio's impaired sexual performance and his troubled bowel movements.

There's also the inevitably brassy-but-kind-hearted tramp (Maria O'Brien) who helps our sad, sightless star rebuild his bedroom confidence, and an assortment of sloppy sketches intended to represent what the press notes describe as "hilarious encounters with the colorful denizens of rural America."

One of these "colorful denizens" is a mellow pot grower and former college quarterback (Max Gail of "Barney Miller") who helps the boys challenge the rules of the rafting race that prohibit disabled entrants.

Considering that the whole interminable picture is supposed to lead up to this thrilling whitewater adventure, the actual scenes of rapids-running are pathetically brief and unconvincing.

While it's true that screenwriter Bob ("Dogfight") Comfort comes up with a surprisingly smart and unexpectedly affecting ending, the final five minutes can't save this putrid picture any more than the fine acting by both stars.

VILLAGE VOICE, 3/11/97, p. 74, Jason Vincz

A particularly sensitive young man once said, "I'd never yell 'good luck!' at anybody. It sounds terrible when you think about it." And there is something terribly uncomfortable about parts of *Good Luck,* a film that's not above sending its disabled protagonists tumbling down a ramp, and playing it for laughs.

Still, as a person who suffers sympathetic embarrassment at every affliction from phlegmy coughs to bedhead, it's liberating to watch a film treat blindness and lameness with such insouciant tactlessness. People do stumble and fall, some more than others, and if psychological atavism forces onlookers to sentimentalize the causes—and cringe, or cluck, or laugh—that's their problem. The stumblers have more important things to talk about.

Good Luck's more important thing is a raft race, typifying the films unromantic, untortured, normal-guy view of physical incapacity. Tony Olezniak (Vincent D'Onofrio) is a depressed ex-football star whose career ended with a blinding spinal injury, and Bernard Lemley (Gregory Hines) is the paraplegic dental technician who convinces the star to reclaim his life by challenging him to enter the race.

Reveling in cute improbabilities, *Good Luck* barely even tries to convey any anguish, and while that approach may seem phonily, calculatedly uplifting (like much of this very Hollywood entertainment), the films unifying theme—that disability needed be tragic—finds its best expression in the two guys' resilient jokiness.

Also reviewed in:
NEW YORK TIMES, 3/7/97, p. C, Lawrence Van Gelded
VARIETY, 12/2-8/96, p. 67, Emanuel Levy

GOOD WILL HUNTING

A Miramax Films release of a Lawrence Bender production. *Executive Producer:* Su Armstrong, Bob Weinstein, Harvey Weinstein, and Jonathan Gordon. *Producer:* Lawrence Bender. *Director:* Gus Van Sant. *Screenplay:* Matt Damon and Ben Affleck. *Director of Photography:* Jean-Yves Escoffier. *Editor:* Pietro Scalia. *Music:* Danny Elfman. *Music Editor:* Kenneth Karman. *Sound:* Owen Langevin and (music) Dennis Sands. *Sound Editor:* Kelley Baker. *Casting:* Billy Hopkins, Suzanne Smith, and Kerry Barden. *Production Designer:* Melissa Stewart. *Art Director:* James McAteer. *Set Designer:* Adam Scher. *Set Decorator:* Jaro Dick. *Set Dresser:* David Charles. *Special Effects:* Brian Ricci. *Costumes:* Beatrix Aruna Pasztor. *Make-up:* Leslie Sebert. *Stunt Coordinator:* Jery Hewitt. *Running time:* 125 minutes. *MPAA Rating:* R.

CAST: Matt Damon (Will Hunting); Robin Williams (Sean McGuire); Ben Affleck (Chuckie); Stellan Skarsgard (Lambeau); John Mighton (Tom); Rachel Majowski (Krystyn); Colleen McCauley (Cathy); Casey Affleck (Morgan); Cole Hauser (Billy); Matt Mercier (Barbershop Quartet #1); Ralph St. George (Barbershop Quartet #2); Bob Lynds (Barbershop Quartet #3); Dan Washington (Barbershop Quartet #4); Alison Folland, Derrick Bridgeman, and Vic Sahay (M.I.T. Students); Shannon Egleson (Girl on Street); Rob Lyons (Carmine Scarpaglia); Steven Kozlowski (Carmine Friend #1); Minnie Driver (Skylar); Jennifer Deathe (Lydia); Scott Williams Winters (Clark); Philip Williams (Head Custodian); Patrick O'Donnell (Assistant Custodian); Kevin Rushton (Courtroom Guard); Jimmy Flynn (Judge Malone); Joe Cannons (Prosecutor); Ann Matacunas (Court Officer); George Plimpton (Psychologist); Francesco Clemente (Hypnotist); Jessica Morton and Barna Moricz (Bunker Hill College Students); Libby Geller (Toy Store Cashier); Chas Lawther (M.I.T. Professor); Richard Fitzpatrick (Timmy); Patrick O'Donnell (Marty); Frank Nakashima (Executive #1); Chris Britton (Executive #2); David Eisner (Executive #3); Bruce Hunter (NSA Agent); Robert Talvano (2nd NSA Agent); James Allodi (Security Guard).

LOS ANGELES TIMES, 12/5/97, Calendar/p. 1, Kenneth Turan

By this time everyone who cares knows about the fairy tale beginnings of "Good Will Hunting." Actors and boyhood friends Matt Damon and Ben Affleck, disgruntled with the material they were seeing, wrote a film for themselves to star in, a film that would let them shine.

A good deal of this "Hey, kids, let's put on a show" charm is still visible in "Good Will Hunting's" story of how a blue-collar math genius with a chip on his shoulder comes to terms with civilization. Having lived with this material for years, both actors (who went on to burgeoning careers, Damon starring in "John Grisham's The Rainmaker" and Affleck in "Chasing Amy") are strong and believable and generate considerable appeal. Would that were enough.

But what Damon and Affleck considered one of their script's commercial strengths, a character they'd written specifically to attract a major star, turns out to be a flaw. And the process of turning "Good Will Hunting" into a $15-million to $20-million film, co-starring Robin Williams and directed by Gus Van Sant, magnified that flaw as only the movie business can.

The result is an uneasy hybrid of old and new Hollywood, where the engaging and independent spirit the actors provide coexists shakily with the kind of traditional sticky sentimentality that characterized films like "Dead Poets Society," "Awakenings" and "Mr. Holland's Opus."

"Good Will Hunting's" premise, however, is a clever and delicious one. It starts when a professor named Lambeau ("Breaking the Waves"' Stellan Skarsgard), the star of MIT's math department, posts an especially difficult problem on the blackboard outside his class. Mysteriously, the answer appears, but no one confesses to having put it there.

What the audience knows that Lambeau doesn't is that the problem solver is Will Hunting (Damon), a part-time MIT janitor and full-time roughneck who grew up poor and scrappy as an orphan in South Boston, a working-class neighborhood known as Southie.

Will may live a life, of beer, brawls and belches with best friend Chuckie (Affleck) and their buddies, but under the surface he is one of the great math geniuses the world has known. Plus, he's got a photographic memory that enabled him to memorize the sum of human knowledge for, as he puts it, "$1.50 in late charges."

Since being an unrecognized genius is probably a common fantasy, this is a pleasant and shrewd scenario, and it works especially well in a scene where Will simultaneously deflates an arrogant Harvard guy (yes, there are some) and makes a favorable impression on Skylar (Minnie Driver), a feisty pre-med student who likes his style. Damon is so effective and charming in this tailor-made role he compels us to be on Will's side even when he's at his most bratty.

Never too busy to get into a brawl, Will hits the wrong person and ends up facing serious prison time. But Lambeau, who has figured out who solved his problem, offers to get Will released if the lad promises to get therapy to curb his antisocial tendencies.

Will agrees, but since messing with people's minds is one of his hobbies, your average therapist is unable to deal with him. But then Lambeau remembers his old college roommate Sean McGuire (Williams). Not only is he a therapist, but he's unconventional, a fellow Southie, and someone who also had difficulty fulfilling his potential. What a coincidence!

If this appears a bit contrived, it's just the beginning. While the idea of therapist able to rescue Will from himself is perhaps inevitable, the part as written is pat. As much improvisers as writers of their own roles, Affleck and Damon lack the craft to give McGuire speeches that aren't so fake-sensitive it's amazing Will doesn't laugh the healer out of the room. And giving the therapist a problem that maybe Will can help him work out plays as by the numbers as it sounds.

Though it's unexpected given the nature of his stand-up work, Williams has played a conventionally understanding if eccentric mentor so often that his presence in a film like this has become a tip-off that it's going to be unremittingly middle of the road. The practice has made Williams better at the part, but his is still the most stodgy and unconvincing aspect of an otherwise lively film.

If Williams seems intent on turning his career into a big-screen version of "Father Knows Best," eccentric director Gus Van Sant is apparently determined to become the next Frank Capra. While it's nice to see Van Sant challenging himself (no one in their right mind wants to see "Even Cowgirls Get the Blues: The Reunion"), it would be nice if some of the edge he brought to the mainstream "To Die For" found its way to the screen here.

With a resolution as tidy as the patterns we see a single scull's oars make on the Charles River, what Van Sant has directed conforms to Hollywood's patterns in every way that counts. While the charismatic performances of Damon and Affleck make "Good Will Hunting" a difficult entertainment to resist, doing just that is not as hard as the film would like to think.

NEW YORK, 12/8/97, p. 62, David Denby

Early in the morning, in *Good Will Hunting*, Chuckie (Ben Affleck) raps on the door at the ratty house of his friend Will Hunting (Matt Damon) and silently hands him a cup of coffee. The two men—20 years old and lifers in the Irish working-class neighborhood of South Boston—head off to their jobs in construction or maintenance. At night, Chuckie and Will drink with a couple of friends at a neighborhood pub, and the four of them, a white-boy gang—Southies—drive around in an old car, cruising the neighborhood, egging one another on to brilliant flights of profanity. They get into brawls, and Will, at least, has been arrested again and again. The movie was written by Affleck and Damon, who grew up together in Cambridge. The two actors seem to walk together in mutual rhythm; they share such an easy, slangy rapport onscreen that they can slip sideways into conversation, speaking in fragments—a helter-skelter grace that Gus Van Sant, the director, reinforces with speed and spontaneity, with rapidly changing moods, half-told jokes, rage that boils up out of nowhere and rapidly drops away. The pleasures these two men share bond them together; adolescent recklessness bonds them, too. Thirty years could slip away without a beat. They have only one immensely troubling problem. Will Hunting is a genius.

No education to speak of, but a photographic memory, an easy way with excruciatingly difficult problems in advanced mathematics, a detailed knowledge of history picked up from library books—there's something mysterious (and not always believable) about Will's divine gray matter, but we go along with the movie's premise, because Affleck and Damon work it for a new kind of ironic realism.   At least Will wasn't bounced on the noggin by God like Travolta in *Phenomenon*.   What if an extraordinary mind was put into the body of an orphaned, abused Southie, a boy contemptuous of career and status, a boy with a violent streak—even a bit of a thug? Mopping up at M.I.T., Will casually solves problems left on the blackboards, problems intended to stump the best mathematical minds in America. The formidable Professor Lambeau (Stellan Skarsgard), recognizing Will's uncanny talent, takes the boy under his wing, keeping him out of jail by agreeing to get him into therapy. Will lands in the office of Lambeau's old friend and rival Sean McGuire (Robin Williams), a bit of a screw-up himself, a damaged man, grief-stricken and defensive, but perhaps the one shrink in Boston who can understand Will. The boy doesn't want to be "saved." He wants to be left alone.

Matt Damon's Will has a careless mop of hair, funny ears, a big-toothed smile. He's halfway between beauty and ugliness, and there's something disturbing about him, stirrings of consciousness and pain beneath the working-class boy's cocky façade. Will is vain about his intellectual powers, and even more vain about his ability to throw away his "potential" like a used condom. He's above striving for what other people want. Three people turn themselves inside out trying to help him: Lambeau, Sean McGuire, and the beautiful and funny Harvard senior (Minnie Driver) he negligently attracts during a trip to a Cambridge bar. He repels them all; he even has a mean streak—he attacks the weak spot of anyone who tries to break through his bravado.

Good Will Hunting (the title, of course, is a pun) starts out brilliantly. Affleck, Damon, and Van Sant don't condescend to the Southies, but they don't sentimentalize them, either. There's enormous vitality to their lives, but they are trapped, partly by Boston's class divisions, partly by apathy and fear (i.e., "pride"). Will clings to a romantic working-class leftism; he convinces himself that success is corrupting. At its best, this movie lays open the conflicts within smart people, the conflicts that make them cranky, ornery human beings. Not only does Will fight with his shrink, but Sean and Lambeau, their relationship unresolved, go at each other like mid-dleweights.   This movie has wit and temperament to burn—there isn't a dead scene in it anywhere. Gus Van Sant may no longer be as original a hipster-artist as he was in the days of *Drugstore Cowboy* and *My Own Private Idaho*, but he has gained in coherence and accountability. In the end, however, he's betrayed by the script, which takes a disastrous turn toward conventionality. Shrink and patient fall into each other's arms, just as Judd Hirsch and Timothy Hutton did in *Ordinary* People. "Feelings" take over; Robin Williams, sharp up to that point, turns cuddly, and the air goes out of the movie. What I will always remember is an edge of temper. *Good Will Hunting* persuades us that genius is of incalculable worth but utter hell to live with.

NEW YORK POST, 12/5/97, p. 49, Thelma Adams

Part coming-of-age saga, part town-and-gown drama, part love story, part "Forest Gump" fairy tale, Gus Van Sant's "Good Will Hunting" is totally disarming.

Matt Damon stars as Will Hunting, a moniker that accounts for the cutesy and initially confusing title. Hunting is a charismatic and conflicted character: a math genius with no formal education, a South Boston orphan bolstered by a ring of blue-collar pals, a charmer with the ability to escape his limited options and the inner demons to keep him shackled to low-paying nowhere jobs.

The young man works as a janitor at prestigious MIT when he's not hanging out with his Southie gang, putting away pints and leading with his fists.

Just when he comes to the attention of a prize-winning MIT professor (Stellan Skarsgard), police arrest Hunting for assault.

Professor Lambeau promises to take Hunting under his wing and introduce him to a good therapist in exchange for his parole. After a number of misfires (and an over-the-top cameo from

George Plimpton, who utters the line: "No more shenanigans, no more tomfoolery, no more ballyhoo" before exiting, stage left), enter Sean McGuire (Robin Williams).

This South Boston shrink and professor gradually draws Hunting out while healing himself in the process.

Like his name, Hunting is on a search—a search for adulthood, for his status as a man, for his place in the world. It's up to the four people who mean the most to him—the ambitious Lambeau, the empathetic McGuire, best friend Chuckie (Ben Affleck) and dream pre-med student Skylar (Minnie Driver)—to help Hunting realize the good in himself.

Damon, who co-wrote the multi-layered script with co-star Affleck, is as disarming as the movie. He has the big star smile of the next Brad Pitt on the body of a high school wrestling champ. But as "John Grisham's The Rainmaker" made clear, he has power and intelligence as an actor. He's a listener, an underplayer, and has a sharp emotional edge beneath his good looks.

Affleck ("Chasing Amy") gives strong support as Hunting's best friend, a role he also plays in real life. Williams is shtickless, funny where he should be and emotionally true. Skarsgard ("Breaking the Waves") is engrossing as a brilliant man driven by equal parts and arrogance and insecurity, afraid of being unmasked at any moment.

Driver is everything she should be as the dream girl of Affleck and Damon's imagination; she also carries a raw power in the emotional scenes where she tries repeatedly to break down Hunting's walls while baring herself in the process.

With "Good Will Hunting," director Van Sant delivers his most natural least flamboyant work to date. This may be a disappointment to some die-hard fans. Smooth but not slick, "Hunting" lacks the archness of "To Die For," the edge of "Drugstore Cowboy" or the frantic fantasy of "Even Cowgirls Get the Blues."

Working with his accomplished design team—costumer Beatrix Pasztor and designer Melissa Stewart—and cinematographer Jean-Yves Escoffier, Van Sant offers a soulful contemporary fable with the flavor of Boston and a universal heart.

NEWSDAY, 12/5/97, Part II/p. B2, Jack Mathews

Posted on a chalkboard outside a world-renowned math professor's classroom at MIT is a problem so difficult that the first student to solve it before the end of the term is promised an honored seat at the prof's dinner table. But what if the genius who provides the answer, virtually overnight, turns out not to be a student at all; rather, he's a young janitor with a photographic memory, a rap sheet and a bad attitude?

The second equation is the premise of Gus Van Sant's "Good Will Hunting," a psychological study of a blue collar savant named Will Hunting (Matt Damon) and his relationships with the four people trying to solve *him*.

Those helpful souls are: the MIT professor (Stellan Skarsgard), who's humbled by Will's genius and determined not to allow the next Einstein to escape his mentorship; psychiatrist Sean McGuire (Robin Williams), a grieving widower with whom Will begins a tortured battle of wills; Skylar (Minnie Driver), the rich Harvard girlfriend pushing Will to open up emotionally; and boyhood pal and adult beer buddy Chuckie (Ben Affleck), who wants Will to use his head and escape their dead-end existence in South Boston.

Will Hunting is a great character, a rebel without a cause for the '90s. He's a brooding, complex, psychologically scarred outsider who hides his gentle nature behind a tough guy veneer and keeps his ego in a shell of stress-tested defense mechanisms. But he doesn't hide his brilliant mind, and that creates a mystique that's irresistible to people both in the film and in the audience.

Damon created Will Hunting himself, in a short story he wrote while a student at Harvard, and with his longtime friend and fellow actor Affleck, developed the character and story into a full-length script. It's Grade A Hollywood material, meaning that it is derivative enough for easy marketing, and Damon is now poised to repeat the Cinderella tale of Sylvester Stallone, who refused to sell "Rocky" without having himself cast in the title role.

Damon has been on the rise, earning good notices with his supporting role as a troubled soldier in "Courage Under Fire" and the lead role of a novice attorney in the recently released "John Grisham's The Rainmaker." But it is Will Hunting who will make him a major star.

In fact, you may have to go back to Jack Nicholson's Bobby Dupea, the pianist-cum-oil rigger in "Five Easy Pieces," for a similarly blessed marriage of star to role, and Damon's performance is no less magnetic. He has a commanding presence on screen, mixing boyish good looks with a voice fermented in oak, and he has the ability to seem simultaneously dangerous and sympathetic.

Will is damaged goods, an orphan and perpetually abused foster child, who's ready to take his anger out on the world with either his fists or his tongue. In one of the film's best scenes, Will confronts a condescending Harvard student in a Cambridge bar, and humiliates him with an onslaught of knowledge.

"Good Will Hunting" means to please, and in doing so, it doesn't leave audiences much to think about afterward. The script is a schematic piece of work, essentially four minidramas that are tied up so neatly at the end, they betray the psychological messiness that makes them interesting in the first place.

The most compelling of the four relationships is that of Will and McGuire, the fifth psychiatrist Will is taken to after being bailed out of jail by the MIT professor, and the only one willing to work with him beyond one session. Will, you see, is so smart, he immediately assesses the vulnerabilities of the shrinks and attacks them, in order to protect himself.

McGuire's weakness is his obsessive grieving over the death of his wife, and Will's exploitation of that quickly changes the patient-client dynamic to something better described as mano a mano. Williams has never been better in a dramatic role, and despite the predictable outcome of the psychological struggle, his scenes with Damon have undeniable power.

The performances are all solid, and Van Sant ("To Die For"), on his second director-for-hire assignment, has guided it with a fluid, transparent style, allowing the relationships to run their course at a seemingly natural pace. But in the end, "Good Will "Hunting" is less a great movie than a great opportunity. For Matt Damon, it's "A Star Is Born."

SIGHT AND SOUND, 3/98, p. 50, Liese Spencer

Will Hunting works as a janitor at MIT, and spends his spare time drinking with his friends. One night, he scrawls the answer to a maths challenge on a blackboard anonymously. Following a violent brawl, Will is sentenced to a jail term. Luckily, Professor Lambeau has identified him as the genius who solved his problem, and gets the judge to suspend Will's sentence if he studies with him and receives counselling.

Out drinking in a bar, Will's friend Chuckie chats up medical student Skylar, but is put down by an arrogant student. Will bests the student intellectually, before getting Skylar's phone number. They go on a date but Will doesn't call her back. The following week, he asks her out again, and they begin a relationship. After a series of failed therapy sessions, Will agrees to meet with therapist Sean McGuire. During a series of angry and emotional skirmishes, Will discovers that McGuire's unhappiness began after the death of his wife, while McGuire forces Will to talk about the abuse inflicted on him by his foster father. When Will resists Lambeau's attempt to get him a job, the professor challenges McGuire. The men argue over Will's fate. Will argues with Skylar, who leaves to study in California. Chuckie encourages Will to take a job that uses his brain. Will does, but leaves shortly after to seek Skylar.

As Will's car disappears over the horizon at the end of *Good Will Hunting*, it's hard not to fantasise an alternative, less conventional ending, in which the boy genius is heading off not to be reunited with his girlfriend but on his way to a chess championship. Such a triumph of intellect over emotion could never be allowed, of course. But it's a measure of how convincingly Gus Van Sant handles his subject that, for a while at least, you almost believe it could.

A rites-of-passage story of how a 20-year-old orphan comes to terms with childhood abuse and his exceptional mathematical gift, *Good Will Hunting* is the most mainstream movie Van Sant has directed to date. Its character-driven drama could have been sentimental were it not for its caustic and often very funny script by star Matt Damon and co-star Ben Affleck. The screenwriters have produced an engaging blue-collar superhero, with a brain to match his brawn. Will may sound at times as though he's swallowed an encyclopedia, but he's no nerd.

Playing out the disempowered-teen dream of winning all the fist fights and having all the answers, Damon and Affleck's screenplay offers wish-fulfilment to relish. In one scene, Will crushes a supercilious Harvard student with choice cuttings from his photographic memory, winning the amused admiration of the woman his rival is trying to impress. While the Harvard boy's drubbing is enjoyable enough, a subsequent scene, in which Will embarrasses him in front of his friends by showing him that he got her phone number as well, adds a delightfully dishonourable authenticity.

Full of adolescent swagger, new face Matt Damon proves himself a charismatic and compelling actor in a role which calls for rapid changes, between violent rage, insouciance, clowning and injured vulnerability. Ben Affleck and Minnie Driver are able foils, while the shifty-looking Stellan Skarsgard is well cast in the role of the vicariously ambitious Professor Lambeau who tutors Will. But the real laurels among the supporting cast must go to a remarkably restrained Robin Williams. Free of his usual attention-grabbing tics and mannerisms, the stillness of Williams' performance lends it a real depth and dignity. And even if the odd one-liner sounds like his invention (leaving his psychology class, he promises to tell them next week, "why Freud took enough cocaine to kill a small horse"), they slot so well into the smart, wisecracking script they don't jar.

Like Van Sant's previous *Drugstore Cowboy* and *My Own Private Idaho*, *Good Will Hunting* focuses on an outsider. But while those films captured the vibrancy life on the streets with an often stylised sensibility, Van Sant here adopts a more straightforward visual approach to sketch the different enclaves of his class divided characters. The groves of academia are bland and featureless, while Boston's rowdy bars and sidewalks are shot with a raw naturalism in tune with the unvarnished vigour of their inhabitants. There's an energy here which can erupt into salty humour or violence at any time. Eschewing poetics for much more discreet observation, Van Sant contents himself with the odd slow-motion fight or grainy cut-away to a television, and visualises Will's thoughts as a kind of kaleidoscopic prism.

Just as Van Sant's presence is subtle in the visuals, it pervades and pleasingly inflects the screenplay's sometimes over-schematic struggle between emotion and intellect, self-realisation and loyalty to one's roots. Van Sant subversively hints that homoerotic feelings might be mixed up in the battle of wills between girlfriend, best friend, emotional and academic mentor. Everyone wants a piece of Will, and none more so than the possessive, infatuated Lambeau. The womanising professor may flirt with girls, but his real relationship has, up until now, been with his male research assistant Tom. When Will usurps that role, Van Sant enriches the ostensible relationships at play with an economical shot of Tom, watching with wry resignation as his tutor throws an arm around the beautiful boy.

Indeed, as Van Sant moves between Will's laddish bonding with his mates and his relationships with his male mentors, he suggests that Skylar may be the real outsider. Nonetheless, the movie moves inexorably in its second half towards a neat resolution. Conflicts are tied up, relationships resolved, and emotion triumphs over intellect in line with the wisdom of popular therapy. And since Hollywood and most of the audience believe so strongly in romantic love, that's the belief Will must live by.

TIME, 12/1/97, p. 80, Richard Schickel

[*Good Will Hunting* was reviewed jointly with *The Rainmaker*; see Schickel's review of that film.]

VILLAGE VOICE, 12/9/97, p. 69, Amy Taubin

Long on charm, short on logic, *Good Will Hunting* is a movie to love in spite of your better judgment.

There are a couple of ways to read the title. Will Hunting (Matt Damon), a math genius from South Boston, is the lead character, and, as his psychotherapist (Robin Williams) is wont to say, he's a *good* kid. Know also that you could hunt through a bunch of multiplexes this holiday season without finding another movie that engenders as poignant a feeling of good will toward man (and the occasional woman) as this one.

Now that cynicism is pro forma for the young and hip, it's downright risky to make a coming-of-age movie that's flagrantly sentimental (granted that cynicism and sentimentality are two sides of one coin). The difference, however, between the sentimentality of *Good Will Hunting* and that of, say, *Phenomenon* (another movie about unlikely genius) is that the people involved in making *Good Will Hunting* depict the world as they wish it were, while the people involved in *Phenomenon* depict a world they think audiences will lap up. It's the difference between a sentimentality that reflects heartfelt idealism and a sentimentality that's Hollywood's most mendacious formula for box-office success.

Set in Boston, where the hostility between the resident working-class population and the transient cultural and technocratic elite of Harvard and M.I.T is knotted into the fabric of daily life, *Good Will Hunting* is a fairy-tale-like story about a townie whose exceptional talent for mathematics would be his ticket out of Southie—if only he didn't feel so damn guilty about taking advantage of it. An orphan who was bounced from one abusive foster home to another, Will Hunting has settled into a life of immediate though limited gratification. He enjoys hanging with his friends, playing ball, getting drunk, beating up the Italian kids he's hated since kindergarten. He also gets a perverse kick out of his job as a janitor at M.I.T. From this lowly position, he can look down on privilege, reveling in the secret knowledge that he's smarter than everyone else on campus.

One day, his all-American competitiveness having gotten the better of his desire for invisibility, he's caught by a celebrated professor of higher mathematics (Stellan Skarsgard) scrawling the answer to a problem that was supposed to have kept graduate students busy for another year. The professor makes Will an offer he'd refuse if the alternative weren't so dire. He can avoid doing jail time for assault if he agrees to become the professor's student and go into psychotherapy. Enter Robin Williams as Sean McGuire, a therapist whose unresolved conflicts mirror Will's own.

Although much can be learned about the collective unconscious by putting fairy tales on the couch, it's more problematic to subject a fairy-tale *character* to psychoanaylsis. The reality principle begins to intrude and before you know it you're wondering if Will lacks the obsessive traits that would make him race through every mathematics text he could lay his hands on, let alone invent theories to up-end them. And exactly when, in his active boy's life, could he have fit in trips to the library?

Narratively speaking, *Good Will Hunting* falls apart after the shrink comes into the picture. And the more frayed the story gets, the more the filmmakers feel obliged to tie up the loose ends into one big happy ending. So you get awful stuff like Will having a cathartic cry during one session and being sent out into the world to "follow his heart" in the next.

Still, there are amazing scenes scattered through the film from beginning to end. There's a playground fight that's like revved-up Cocteau, the dreamy eroticized slo-mos of boys going at one another breaking open into real-time bone crunching and bloodletting. There's an understated moment early in Will's therapy where he is forced to confront the fact that he hasn't a clue about what he really wants to do with himself. And there's a barroom scene in which Minnie Driver as the Harvard pre-med student who has captured Will's imagination (and vice versa) slaps a brogue on top of her upper-class English accent and tells a hilariously filthy Irish joke, much to the delight of Will's friends. Will says nothing but we know he has to be wondering if she knows how condescending she's being. The most complicated interaction in the film, it's dropped much too soon, but still, it gives you an inkling of irreconcilable differences that no one wants to face.

Written by Damon and Ben Affleck (who plays the relatively thankless role of Will's best friend), *Good Will Hunting,* for all its narrative holes, is right on the mark about the guilt and insecurity that's inflicted on Irish-American working-class kids. It's also one of the rare movies in which the dialogue is as smart as the characters are meant to be. (The speech in which Will makes hash out of a couple of National Security Agency headhunters is a classic.) Having written himself a part that's a foolproof star-maker, Damon wisely got someone with a little distance to direct, thus avoiding the narcissistic trap Ed Burns lurched into with *She's the One.*

Working as a director-for-hire, Gus Van Sant mixes high spirits with lyricism while soft-pedaling the aching sense of loss and abandonment that colors his best films, *Mala Noche* and *My Own Private Idaho.* It's wise not to compare *Good Will Hunting* or *Idaho,* or for that matter Damon to River Phoenix. This film and its star are about simpler pleasures. Van Sant's camera gazes perhaps too adoringly at Damon's beautiful, slightly clownish face, with its toothy, mocking grin, and his hunky, slightly bowlegged body (if this sounds like boy porn, the film, at moments, is right on the edge). But he also taps into Damon's volatile emotional range, into the violence that underlies his antic humor.

The other actors do very nicely, too (Williams has never been less obnoxious, even though the need to give him a character arc commensurate with his star status weighs on the film at the end).

Driver is an inspired choice for the love interest. Although the part, conceptually, is no more than that, she not only holds her own in a boys-only world, she blows its insularity wide open. The film is luminously and exactingly photographed by Leos Carax's long-time cinematographer, Jean-Yves Escoffier, who also shot Harmony Korine's *Gummo*. As a coming-of-age flick, *Good Will Hunting* is *Gummo*'s better-socialized twin.

Also reviewed in:
NEW YORK TIMES, 12/5/97, p. E10, Janet Maslin
VARIETY, 12/1-7/97, p. 73, Emanuel Levy
WASHINGTON POST, 12/25/97, p. C1, Desson Howe
WASHINGTON POST, 12/26/97, Weekend/p.35, Desson Howe

GRAVESEND

A Manga Entertainment release of a Brooklyn Woods Productions film. *Executive Producer:* Daniel Edelman, Toni Ross, and Mark Ross. *Producer:* Salvatore Stabile. *Director:* Salvatore Stabile. *Screenplay:* Savatore Stabile. *Director of Photography:* Joseph Dell'Olio. *Editor:* Miranda Devin. *Music:* Bill Laswell. *Sound:* Phillip Apperle, Molly Harris, Noah Cross, Patrick Dundass, and Ali Futoran. *Sound Editor:* Donny Black, Jason Candler, Ray Kapicki. *Casting:* Harriet Bass. *Running time:* 85 minutes. *MPAA Rating:* R.

CAST: Thomas Brandise (Mikey); Tom Malloy (Chicken); Michael Parducci (Ray); Tony Tucci (Zane); Sean Quinn (Mark); Carmel Altomare (Zane's Mother); Teresa Spinelli (Zane's Grandmother); Glen Sparer (Tow Truck Driver); Macky Aquillino (Jo Jo the Junkie); Yoni Berkovits (Junkie); David Auerbach (Tony); Miranda Devin (Mary); Dora Irizzary (Mary's Mother); Ray Picirillo (Mary's New Boyfriend); Maurice Carr (Terence); Jinn S. Kim (Korean Clerk); Fritz Zernike (Annoying Customer); Gil Machucha (Mexican Store Owner); Greg Bello (Cop); Mike Kaves (Dispatcher Voice); Megan Gray (Disc Jockey Voice); Armando J. Cerabino (Mikey's Father); Kira Burke (Father's Girlfriend); Anne Rollins (Mikey's Sister).

LOS ANGELES TIMES, 9/19/97, Calendar/p. 12, Kevin Thomas

When Salvatore Stabile, an NYU film school dropout, began making his galvanizing "Gravesend" at the age of 19—he's now 22—it was as if he jumped off the highest diving board he could find. He pulls us into the dark undertow that ensnares four young men from the Brooklyn neighborhood of the film's staggeringly apt title, an Italian American enclave located right across from Coney Island.

Stabile has said he improvised the entire film with his actors, drawing upon his characters from a novel he wrote at 15. He narrates his story off screen, saying that "thank God" he wasn't along with his purportedly fictional pals on a certain night. They are Tony Tucci's mustached and goateed Zane, who has a hair-trigger temper; Michael Parducci's Ray; Tom Malloy's Chicken; and Thomas Brandise's Mikey, the sensitive hanger-on of the group and its scapegoat. Mikey's also the smartest of the four and the only one capable of anything resembling reflection.

The guys are hanging out, getting high and loud in the basement den in a row house owned by Ray's older brother, who comes downstairs to clear them out because he has to get up for work at 6:30 the next morning. Zane and the brother immediately clash, and Zane pulls a gun that of course is not supposed to have any bullets in it. Not that Zane particularly cares one way or another. The brother winds up dead, and the four friends suddenly have a corpse on their hands.

Stabile is a natural storyteller with a camera, and he shows the sureness of his instincts with a fast black-and-white montage revealing that the dead man is no great loss. Stabile's too smart to imply that this justifies shooting the guy, accidentally or otherwise, but it's a shrewd way of mollifying us, buying just enough time to catch us up in the adventure the young men have embarked upon. At this point, Stabile starts injecting humor into the proceedings. It's so unexpected, so dark-beyond-dark, that astoundingly you may find yourself actually moved to laugh out loud.

The guys hit upon the neighborhood's local fixer and drug dealer, JoJo (Macky Aquilino), to help them dispose of the body, which the tubby middle-aged man agrees to in return for $500 plus one of the victim's thumbs(!). How to come up with the cash?

As Stabile is generating the most outrageous humor out of the quartet's predicament, he's also acquainting us with the four young men, all of whom are scarred by terrible family lives and are clearly not going anywhere in life. Stabile doesn't start out asking us to like them but instead lets us see a brutal, indifferent world through their eyes. He's such an instinctive, assured artist that he involves us with their fates, and we find ourselves caring about what happens to them in spite of ourselves.

Gradually, "Gravesend" grows darker and darker as we realize that these four really only have one another to rely upon—and even that allegiance is provisional. The rage that so easily surfaces in them—Zane in particular—reflects the virtual absence of love throughout their lives, "Gravesend" plays like the back story to many of those seemingly inexplicable street catastrophes that open the evening news day in and day out.

The film has such panache it's no wonder it has proved to be a calling card for Stabile, who already has a two-picture deal with Steven Spielberg. Surely, "Gravesend" can only enhance the careers of its talented actors as well as Stable's formidably resourceful cameraman, Joseph Dell'Olio, and terrific edgy composer, Bill Laswell.

Savagely comic nihilism coupled with genuine sentiment and a no-holds-barred style is sure to command attention. But now that Stabile has illuminated the lives of losers—a familiar story—perhaps he'll be tempted to tell us about how a guy like him ended up a winner.

NEW YORK POST, 9/5/97, p. 58, Thelma Adams

F*#&! S*#!! Rooster*#?!: In Salvatore Stabile's "Graves-end," that's the way we talk in Brooklyn. It makes it easy for film school dropouts like Stabile to write dialogue.

As for action, debut director/writer/producer Stabile reaches right out and grabs you by the lapels, shakes you, stuns you with a sloppy right hook and then tosses you on the sidewalk school of physical communication.

The professional wunderkind's vision of his old stomping ground—a Brooklyn neighborhood nowhere near as deadly as its name—makes the violent, pagan world of "Kull the Conqueror" look like it's just a subdivision away from "Leave It to Beaver."

Narrated by a character named Sal Stabile (how post-modern), the drama follows one tragic night in the life of four obnoxious Brooklyn buddies: the pathological Zane (Tony Tucci), the doper Chicken (Tom Malloy), the weakling Mikey (Thomas Brandise) and the man in the moral middle, Ray (Michael Parducci).

After Zane pulls out a gun, the plot follows a path as stupid as the gang. Zane shoots Ray's brother. These guys are too dumb to call 911. Mikey suggests they call 411 to get the number. Instead, they spend Saturday night trying to dispose of the corpse—and adding to their collection.

There are brief moments of promise, blurry black-and-white flashbacks to a Christmas confrontation between Ray and his brother, a stinging war of words between Zane and his spoon-wielding Italian mama. The performances are rough-hewn and natural.

But, by Sunday morning, the boys have all shown the grim, threadbare cloth they're cut from. Since it's a Brooklyn film, all roads lead to Coney Island. In the final scene, silent comes the dawn to the Wonder Wheel, a symbol of faded dreams, lost hopes, youth cut short, yadda, yadda, yadda.

"Gravesend" crosses "Mean Streets" with "Clerks" and gets jerks. Despite the stupidity around him that Stabile vigorously records, the Brooklyn auteur is as sharp as he is tacky.

Not only has Stabile created a hornets' nest of buzz for "Gravesend" in the two years since a rough cut screened at the Hamptons Film Festival, he closed the deal and got results. Oliver Stone "presents" the drama; Steven Spielberg has signed the young genius for a two-pic deal.

Salvator (Sal) Stabile: remember that name. If only to avoid buying tickets for "Gravesend."

NEWSDAY, 9/5/97, Part II/p. B3, Jack Mathews

You've heard this story before. A young filmmaker comes out of nowhere with a movie financed on credit cards or pop bottle refunds and sends shivers up the spines of festival mavens and critics, who hear the words "genius" and "prodigy" and "not since Orson Welles" escaping their lips before they've had time to think about it.

In the case of Sal Stabile's "Gravesend," which had its world premiere in rough cut form at the 1995 Hamptons International Film Festival, the huzzahs came literally before anyone had time to think about it.

Then Hamptons director Darryl Macdonald told critics and reporters at a private screening of "Gravesend" that it was the first time in his career that he'd shown an unfinished film, and said from the moment he saw it, "I knew this was the work of a genius, raw talent."

We'll see. "Gravesend," which finally makes it commercial debut, is remarkable mostly for its minuscule budget, reportedly $5,000, and its native energy. Stabile, who grew up in Brooklyn's Gravesend neighborhood, was 20 when he made the picture, with just two years of film school training behind him, and he certainly has early command of his vision.

Shot mostly with a hand-held camera, and edited in ways that give it a jittery, frenetic pace, "Gravesend" is a dark comedy about four aimless Gravesend youths whose normal Saturday night routine of TV watching, badgering each other, and fighting on street corners is interrupted by an accidental shooting.

Zane (Tony Tucci), the neighborhood loco, kills the older brother of his friend Ray (Michael Parducci), claiming he didn't know the gun was loaded, and then talks the others into disposing of the body rather than calling the cops.

This happens in the first 10 minutes of the movie. The rest of the way, we follow Zane, Ray, insecure Mikey (Thomas Brandise), and mentally disturbed Chicken (Tom Malloy) as they drive around Gravesend, with corpses piling up in their trunk and their panic rising, trying to beat the dawn.

Stabile is obviously hyperbolizing his own street life observations in Gravesend, and he attempts to expand the well-traveled genre. With impressionistic black-and-white flashbacks, he gives us glimpses into the past lives of the four boys, suggesting not only how they got to this point, but how they may behave as the night wears on.

The question is, do you want to go along? Do you want to spend the night with four screaming, pushing, fighting, taunting kids who, in real life, you'd drive 10 miles out of your way to avoid? In the end, Stabile doesn't so much add insight into the timeless cycle of teen violence as confirm our stereotypes. Zane is a bad seed, and the others are peer-pressured chumps. What's new?

"Gravesend," blown up from 16-mm. to 35, is a smart calling card for Stabile, but if he goes on to have the career predicted by Darryl Macdonald, he'll remember the movie for what it did for him rather than what it did for audiences.

SIGHT AND SOUND, 6/98, p. 45, Mark Sinker

Four friends—Zane, Ray, Mikey and Chicken—are in the basement belonging to Ray's brother Mark in Gravesend, Brooklyn. Zane accidentally shoots and kills Mark with a gun he thinks isn't loaded. Ray wants to go to the police, but the others agree with Zane that they should get Jo Jo the junkie to dispose of the body. Constantly quarreling, they put it in the trunk of Mikey's father's Buick and go search for Jo Jo.

Jo Jo wants $500 to bury the body, but the friends have no money. They try to sell some dope but get ripped off. Zane's ex-girlfriend Mary won't lend them any, so they try unsuccessfully to hold up a store. Chicken robs another store, but only gets potato chips. Mikey borrows money from his father, catching him with a prostitute. He gets Zane's gun and kills both his father and the girl. Jo Jo agrees to bury Mark and burn the other bodies. They're to return early next morning. They sleep on the Coney Island seafront, waking to find Mikey gone. Ray tries to go to the police, and Zane shoots him. Chicken then shoots Zane, and sets fire to car and bodies.

Generally when a movie deals in the folkways and subcultures of the film maker's own undercelebrated community—Gravesend is the name of a much overlooked part of Brooklyn—it will pick at least something special, compelling if not appealing, to pull outsiders in, such as a charismatic central character. First-time director Salvatore Stabile gives us Tony Tucci as Zane, the cause of a violent death and thus this film's dynamo, in whose chaotic, manipulative wake the other three main characters swirl. He's slim, not unhandsome, not uncharming, certainly the most stylish and memorable of the four—and yet he's also a volatile blank, a sinkhole of energy.

Scenes alternate between panicky tussling about what to do and ones of the four sitting quiet in a cruising Buick, emphasising the lack at the core of this all-male teen mini-gang. They are unable to be even momentarily honest with one another in such a crisis. Even the uninflected voice over narration (by the 22-year-old Italian-American director himself, ostensibly the fifth member) seems constantly to veer between sentimental self-delusion about the "code" of the Gravesend street and a cool distancing, congratulating himself for being absent this fateful Saturday night (as if to say, "whatever faults brought my buddies to this pass, I don't share them"), and for having a perspective his erstwhile friends hadn't.

In fact, with no one who *was* there now around to recount what actually happened, the whole movie is a betrayal couched as a loyal salute, a dramatic recreation by extrapolation from the worst of the narrator's memories of his friends, with brilliantly sly emphasis on their stupidity, their credulity, their confusion, their shocked fright, clad in the remnants of a faked bravado. However fictional the tale he's telling may be, it's hard not to feel that Stabile has portrayed the world he's saying made him with virtuoso contempt, at the same time as he's feeding off its furious drives and filtering its many voices. The performances—all from unknowns are as remarkable as those in, say, *Nil by Mouth* (there are several characters, mostly women, that you want to see more of). The camerawork and construction are seamlessly fluid and cunningly artless, especially the endless flashes forward and back.

Gravesend is impressive even when it's imitative (particularly of Scorsese and Tarantino). And yet all the immense energy of conception and execution seems to circle back to the blocked hopelessness of the central characters. There's something deeply enervating about the director's insistence on foregrounding people who hadn't the wherewithal he's clearly been able to barter into the creative skills. Where Harmony Korine's superficially similar *Gummo* is daring to the point of lunacy, and humane even in its least deluded moments, this film is a self-celebratory cheat, albeit the cheat and the swank of a serious new talent.

VILLAGE VOICE, 9/9/97, p. 88, J. Hoberman

Because the universe loves a good coincidence, *The Keeper* isn't this week's only self-produced, backstory-rich urban-horror flick by a first-time Brooklyn filmmaker. [See Hoberman's review.] Also open Friday: Salvatore Stabile's *Gravesend*.

The discovery of the celeb-stocked Hamptons International Film Festival, where it was shown as a work-in-progress in October 1995, *Gravesend* arrives endorsed by the likes of Steven Spielberg and Oliver Stone, as well as heralded by a *New Yorker* profile which—less persuaded than these Hollywood heavies by Stabile's street-kid persona—wisely chose to focus on the neophyte writer-director's promotion of his movie, rather than the movie itself. Far more convincing than *Gravesend*'s first-person account of murder and anomie in the teenage lower-depths—a rondo of mindless volatility and rote scuffling in tight hallways—is its simulation of a hand-to-mouth feature willed into existence by a 21-year-old NYU dropout clever enough to have made a close study of Martin Scorsese's *Mean Streets* and Matty Rich's early career moves.

A group of kids hanging out one Saturday night shoot the brother of one of their number by mistake. Too dumbfounded to call 911, they drive off—cursing and squabbling—into the night to see a fat fixer in a tam-o'-shanter. With everyone acting like they're acting in a movie, this 85-minute slice of life among the mentally challenged was surely more fun to make than it is to watch. *Gravesend*'s interminable ride-around, remarkable mainly for a record use of the expletive *fuck*, is being spun as black comedy. Whatever its intent, *Gravesend*'s wittiest moment trumps the tired notion of Louis Armstrong's "What a Wonderful World" wafting out of the car radio by having one of the resident dopes observe that "this guy has a horrible voice."

If the climactic bloodbath feels anticlimactic, it may be because virtually every previous scene escalates into a shouting match—the raw realness perhaps that persuaded Oliver Stone, as with the egregious *Zebrahead* of several years back, to give his imprimatur—twice the size of Stabile's on the press book. Following the fashion established by Kevin Smith, Stabile ends the final credits by thanking everyone—his friends for their support and, with a Nietzchean bellicosity, his foes for steeling his resolve.

The person to whom Stabile should really express gratitude is cinematographer (and Gravesend resident) Joseph Dell'Olio, who shot the film on spec in handheld 16mm without a lighting assistant and seems responsible for its most authentic and professional aspects. An ex-cop who put himself through NYU film school, Dell'Olio might even be the movie's real story.

Also reviewed in:
CHICAGO TRIBUNE, 9/26/97, Friday/p. Q, John Petrakis
NEW YORK TIMES, 9/5/97, p. C5, Stephen Holden
NEW YORKER, 9/15/97, p. 94, Daphne Merkin
VARIETY, 6/10-16/96, p. 42, Ken Eisner

GRAY'S ANATOMY

A Northern Arts Entertainment release of an Independent Film Channel production in association with BBC Films. *Executive Producer:* Jonathan Sehring, Caroline Kaplan, and Kathleen Russo. *Producer:* John Hardy. *Director:* Steven Soderbergh. *Screenplay:* Spalding Gray. *Based on the monologue by:* Spalding Gray and Renée Shafransky. *Director of Photography:* Elliot Davis. *Editor:* Susan Littenberg. *Music:* Cliff Martinez. *Sound:* Paul Ledford. *Production Designer:* Adele Plauche. *Set Decorator:* Cynthia Wigginton. *Running time:* 80 minutes. *MPAA Rating:* Not Rated.

WITH: Spalding Gray.

LOS ANGELES TIMES, 5/9/97, Calendar/p. 12, John Anderson

A Spalding Gray film means equal parts humor and dread, digressions and absurdity, meditation and mania, personal confession and Yankee reserve. Add a desk, a mike and a glass of water, and you've got the basic formula.

But there's at least as much different as there is the same about "Gray's Anatomy," the third filmed version of a Gray monologue (after the Jonathan Demme-directed "Swimming to Cambodia" and Nick Broomfield's "Monster in a Box"), and the most cinematic of the group.

This time, Steven Soderbergh takes Gray (who appeared in his little appreciated gem "King of the Hill") places, he's never been onscreen. Motion, color and brazen stylizing enhance what is at times a genuinely hysterical work on rationalized terror.

Sprung from Gray's experience with an eye ailment—"macula pucker" is the diagnosis, a term we come to know and love—Soderbergh chooses to open not with Gray but with a series of first-person accounts of other people's eye problems. One concerns a fishhook, another, oven cleaner; one man who had steel in his eye tells how he had to finish the brake job on his truck before he could drive himself to the hospital. These are occasionally gruesome stories, but they're told so casually that they're funny.

And they set us up perfectly for Gray. What he does, through his measured, literate and wryly knowing persona, is convince you he's a rational man. His response to his disorder, of course, is to flee reason for the arms of New Age humbug, an American Indian sweat lodge ceremony (where he becomes so unnerved he forgets to "give up" his pain) and a Filipino "psychic surgeon" who sounds like a cross between Jackie Chan, Elvis Presley and the Amazing Kreskin.

Although a continuous, seamless piece, "Gray's Anatomy" has certain individual episodes that shine. The sweat lodge. The Philippines trip. A guilt-ridden bit on Gray's Christian Science upbringing. And an experience as a day laborer for some Brooklyn Hasidim. Certain he was going blind in one eye, it reassured him that there was work he could do if his other eye went, too.

Never mind that Gray talks for a living, and presumably could, and would, continue to do so whether he could see or not. But imagine, the anxiety. Soderbergh would have to film in 3-D.

NEW YORK POST, 3/19/97, p. 37, Bill Hoffmann

"Gray's Anatomy" is enthralling entertainment and brainy food for thought that is not to be missed.

If you're already a fan of Spalding Gray, you'll no doubt be racing over to Film Forum for a fresh new dose of wild, whimsical philosophy from America's master of the monologue.

If you've never seen this gregarious, gray-haired gabber in action—get ready for a cinematic revelation. How can one man blabbering on for 80 minutes be that great? Trust me, he is.

In fact, in his newest talkfest, Gray goes a hold step beyond his previous efforts, "Swimming to Cambodia," "Monster in a Box" and an HBO special.

This time, Gray takes us to the blackest period of his life, one you'll relate to in spades: the fear your health is shot and you're one step from the boneyard.

Gray's nightmare began when he awoke to find himself nearly blind in one eye—a terrifying condition that led him on a strange globe-trotting odyssey to find the cause and cure.

Director Steve Soderbergh ("sex, lies & videotape") precedes Gray's weird adventures with the real testimonials of people who almost lost their sight.

It's chilling to hear one woman tell how she reached for eye drops and mistakenly poured super-glue into her eye. One man cheerfully tells how he accidentally drove a nail through his eye, while another relates how he was pierced by a carelessly cast fish hook.

My first reaction to these icky tales was: Stop horsing around and bring on Spalding! But Soderbergh knows what he's doing—and uses terror tales to remind us of how fragile our lives really are. How one second we can be on top of the world and the next, just seconds from the morgue slab.

Gray's journey from doctor to doctor is a twisted digest on just how screwed up the world of health care can get as he tells of bouncing from one high-priced Manhattan specialist to the next.

Getting no satisfaction, the panicky Gray tries a Far East healer, then a wacky nutritionist and ends up flying West for an ancient "Indian sweat box" ceremony in the nude.

When those methods fail, Gray flips out and flies to the Philippines to see the "Elvis Presley of psychic surgery," a doctor who greets him in white, Palm Beach-style leisure shoes and a bloody butcher's apron!

How it all turns out won't be revealed here, but suffice to say that after hearing Gray's jaw-dropping recollections, you'll never again laugh at those cheesy "skin peel" ads in the subway and you'll count good health as the Lord's greatest blessing.

Director Soderbergh mixes Gray's stories with striking visuals and camerawork. Some works, some falls flat. The bottom line is that Gray is the show and no amount of visual hanky panky matters.

A line once screamed at the great Groucho Marx in "Animal Crackers" is very appropriate here: "Hooray for Captain Spalding!"

VILLAGE VOICE, 3/25/97, p. 75, J. Hoberman

Based on Spalding Gray's 1993 monologue concerning his attempts to avoid surgery for a rare ocular disease, *Gray's Anatomy* is also concerned with reshaping the human body through technology, or fear of same. Accidents will happen: director Steven Soderbergh immediately goes for the visceral, prefacing the piece with a bit of a 1950s educational film ("Think how many things you know because your eyes tell you") and using a chorus of interviewees describing their own humorously gruesome eye injuries to annotate Gray's performance.

Typically, Gray believes that he developed a macula pucker on his left retina because of professional self-absorption: "All that I, I, I!" Brought up as a Christian Scientist, he is drawn to alternative therapies that range from submitting to an Indian sweat lodge and a regime of nutritional ophthamology to flying to Manila to meet the Elvis Presley of psychic surgery. The monologue is increasingly manic and extremely funny. Perhaps in response to the material, the movie is hysterically visual. Switching Gray's backdrop, cutting from indoors to outdoors and back, lighting the monologuist in silhouette, placing the camera beneath a glass table, Soderbergh's mise-en-scene ranges from the busy to the overwrought.

Not surprisingly, the most potent visual reference (and pithiest film allusion) is verbal. Gray describes a videotape of his inevitable surgery as *The Andalusian Dog* magnified 100 times. And nothing is more piercing than Gray's own cri de coeur: "I don't want medicine. I want magic and miracles."

Also reviewed in:
NEW YORK TIMES, 3/20/97, P. C19, Janet Maslin
VARIETY, 9/16-22/96, p. 68, Todd McCarthy
WASHINGTON POST, 5/30/97, p. B1, Stephen Hunter
WASHINGTON POST, 5/30/97, Weekend/p. 41, Desson Howe

GRIDLOCK'D

A Gramercy Pictures release of a PolyGram Filmed Entertainment presentation of an Interscope Communcatins production. *Executive Producer:* Ted Field, Russell Simmons, and Scott Kroopf. *Producer:* Damian Jones, Paul Webster, and Erica Huggins. *Director:* Vondie Curtis Hall. *Screenplay:* Vondie Curtis Hall. *Director of Photography:* Bill Pope. *Editor:* Christopher Koefoed. *Music:* Stewart Copeland. *Music Editor:* Michael Dittrick. *Sound:* Craig Woods and (music) Jeff Seitz and Steve Krause. *Sound Editor:* Steven D. Williams. *Casting:* Robi Reed-Humes. *Production Designer:* Dan Bishop. *Art Director:* Scott Plauche. *Set Decorator:* Kristen Toscano Messina. *Set Dresser:* David Elton, Win Craft, and Nashon Petrushkin. *Costumes:* Marie France. *Make-up:* Vonda K. Morris. *Stunt Coordinator:* Julius Leflore. *Running time:* 90 minutes. *MPAA Rating:* R.

CAST: Tim Roth (Stretch); Tupac Shakur (Spoon); Thandie Newton (Cookie); Charles Fleischer (Mr. Woodson); Howard Hesseman (Blind Man); James Pickens, Jr. (Supervisor); John Sayles (Cop #1); Eric Payne (Cop #2); Tom Towles (D-Reper's Henchman); Tom Wright (Koolaid); James Shanta (Patrolman #1); Jim O'Malley (Patrolman #2); George Poulos (Chuck); Debbie Zaricor (Clerk); Mik Scriba (Officer #1); Lucy Alexis Liu (Cee-Cee); Richmond Arquette (Resident Doctor); Billie Neal (Medicaid Woman #1); Debra Wilson (Medicaid Woman #2); Rusty Schwimmer (Nurse); Elizabeth Anne Dickinson (Admissions Person); Joey Dente (Vendor); Darryl Jones (Panhandler); Jasen Govine (Medicaid Security Guard); Tim Truby (Man with Directions); Venessia Valentino (Woman in ER); Ron Cummins (Man in ER); Bradley Jordan Spencer (Paramedic #1); Rory J. Shoaf (Paramedic #2); Tracy Vilar (Screaming Woman); Roslyn McKinney (Female Clerk); Roderick Garr (Welfare Security Guard); William Long, Jr. (Right Wing TV Show Host); Mark Ericson (Bill the Anchor Man); Tonia Rowe (Woman on TV); Lynn Blades (Alexia Cruz); Kasi Lemmons and Henry Hunter Hall (Madonna and Child); Vondie Curtis-Hall (D-Reper).

LOS ANGELES TIMES, 11/29/97, Calendar/p. 1, Jack Mathews

[*The following review by John Anderson appeared in a slightly different form in* **NEWSDAY, 1/29/97, Part II/p. B5.**]

It's the same whenever you're watching a movie featuring an actor who has died between his performance and the film's release. Feelings of dread or sadness hang over each of his scenes. your mind does a double-read of dialogue that is now darkly ironic, and you have to consciously push out the post-production news to stay with the story.

"Lately, I've been feeling that my luck's running out," says the late rap star Tupac Shakur's Spoon, early in the black comedy "Gridlock'd."

It's his drug addiction that has Spoon down, but as we look at this handsome, vibrant young actor, it's impossible not to leap ahead to that intersection in Las Vegas where, last fall, Shakur's luck finally did run out, in a hail of bullets that left him fatally wounded.

We'll never know whether the violence-prone Shakur could have beaten back the demons that had him in constant scrapes with the law, but underscores the waste of his talent. Cast against type as the gentler of two musician junkies trying to burrow through the bureaucracy to enter a rehab clinic in Detroit, Shakur has the relaxed screen presence of a young Wesley Snipes and plays perfectly off the delirious Tim Roth.

Written and directed by actor Vondie Curtis Hall ("Passion Fish"), "Gridlock'd" follows Spoon and Roth's Stretch through a chaotic day of bureaucratic runarounds and street chases. The New Year's Eve overdose of Cookie (Thandie Newton), the singer in their jazz/performance art trio, has prompted a resolution from Spoon to enter rehab. His pal Stretch, for whom anything new is a potential high, decides to sign on with him.

But getting past the clerks and the paperwork stacked up between them and detox is more than the strung-out junkies can bear, and they spend as much of their time trying to stay high and out of trouble as they do trying to find help.

Curtis Hall, in his directing debut, has created an effective mix of comedy, drama and action. Though things descend into slapstick at times, the basic premise—that government red tape does as much to foil rehabilitation as facilitate it—adds a nice satiric edge, and Roth and Shakur have terrific chemistry.

Roth, who seems to get every social misfit role that Gary Oldman doesn't, has never been as spring-loaded wacky as he is here. Stretch is a white guy who thinks he's a brother, and gets himself and Spoon into trouble trying to use the N-word as an affectation and challenges killers to act on their impulses. It's a funny, dark, almost spooky performance.

Newton, seen mostly in flashbacks, is also very good as Cookie, a fledgling Billie Holiday both on stage and in her drug haze. But it's Shakur, who has one more movie ("Gang Related") coming before the book is closed on his film career, who attracts most of our attention. With his tattooed and bullet-scarred torso on display in several scenes, he's like his own catalog of bad times and a promo for the trouble ahead.

His fans will have more reason to mourn now than ever.

NEW YORK POST, 1/29/97, p. 39, Michael Medved

In making movies about drug addiction, filmmakers face an abundance of risks.

On the one hand, if they make their junkie characters too witty, stylish and hip, they will end up glamorizing a tragic habit.

If, on the other hand, the addict heroes are too dirty, dumb and self-destructive, the weary audience will feel that spending two hours in their company is some sort of penance or punishment.

In the case of "Gridlock'd," it's safe to say that no one will accuse its two detestable and dim-witted protagonists (Tim Roth and Tupac Shakur) of an excess of charm or charisma.

Unfortunately, the most intriguing figure in the film (played by the radiantly sexy Thandie Newton) goes into a coma in the movie's first five minutes and spends nearly the entire picture in that sad state.

Newton's New Year's Eve overdose forces her two partners (Roth and Shakur) to reevaluate their pathetic lives.

The movie concentrates on their wearying efforts to secure Medicaid funding so that they can get rehabilitation. Bouncing from one crowded office to another, they encounter no end of rude clerks and angry social workers.

Shakur (who was shot to death at age 25 last September) demonstrated a natural, riveting screen presence in "Juice" and "Poetic Justice," and does so again here.

Tim Roth draws the more broadly comic role, and his performance is an extravaganza of twitches and grimaces.

The editing and camera work suggest real promise for first-time director Vondie Curtis Hall but, with "Gridlock'd," both his talents and his audience seem trapped in a dead end.

SIGHT AND SOUND, 6/97, p. 52, Kim Newman

New York City, New Year's Eve. Stretch and Spoon, both heroin addicts, celebrate at home after a successful gig for their improvisational jazz/poetry trio. Cookie, the third member of the group, tries heroin for the first time and goes into a coma. Having taken Cookie to a hospital, Stretch and Spoon irritate the admissions bureaucrat when they express their frustration at being asked to fill out forms and provide details of the medical insurance Cookie doesn't have. Spoon decides that he will kick his habit, prompting the less-determined Stretch to share his New Year's resolution. They rip off money from crime figure D-Reper and visit their dealer to buy their 'last' heroin. At a detox clinic, they learn they have to be on Medicaid—state medical insurance—to qualify.

Returning to their dealer, they find he has been murdered by D-Reper and scavenge the drugs. Stretch shoots up so he can cope with more queues and forms as they go from government office to office, trying to get into a detox program. D-Reper pursues them, hoping to get the dealer's stash, and the police—who have put them at the site of the murders—are also on their trail. They realise the only way they can get into a program is if they are admitted to hospital as casualties—Stretch has been shot by D-Reper and Spoon insists his friend stab him. D-Reper is caught by the police and charged with the dealer's murder. Stretch and Spoon turn up at the hospital but are thwarted by the admissions person they earlier annoyed and told to fill in forms and wait. Cookie comes out of her coma and leaves a message on the pair's answering machine, suggesting they get off heroin.

It was claimed, not least by the comedians themselves, that Cheech and Chong's marijuana-based comedy routines were essentially stoned updates of the traditional 'drunk acts' that were staples of vaudeville, silent cinema and the booze-fuelled humour of W.C. Fields or Dean Martin. The comic potential of heroin, touched on in *Trainspotting* is a fair trickier prospect, and *Gridlock'd* never quite gets round to making fun of the death-tinged junkie lifestyle. Instead it wrings sick humour from its feckless heroes' forlorn attempts to get the monkeys off their backs, trying to escape from a habit they don't really enjoy any more: "We just take this stuff to stop us feeling sick."

However, Stretch (Tim Roth) and Spoon (Tupac Shakur) seem so defined by their identities as junkies that their day-long attempt to kick looks as temporary as the jobs Laurel and Hardy used to take up and then abandon in time for the next film. If it weren't for the subsequent death of rap-music star Tupac Shakur, you could imagine these characters recurring like Abbott and Costello in a series of comedies, always complaining about the drugs they can't say no to. As 90s comedy teams go, Stretch and Spoon are more in the spirit of *Dumb & Dumber* than Beavis and Butt-head. Oddly estranged from their gritty urban roots, they're sweet-natured holy fools rather than horrifying exemplars of dead-end American nihilism.

As in *Trainspotting, Gridlock'd*'s comic approach is initially disorienting. The milieu—grotty studio apartments, garbage-strewn streets, chaotic hospital admissions rooms, faded government offices—is familiar from 'serious' films about urban losers (from 1971's *Panic in Needle Park* to *The Saint of Fort Washington*, leading us to expect a far more serious, downbeat and familiar essay. It comes as something of a shock when you realise how close it is to a classical Hollywood comedy-team vehicle with recurring supporting characters popping up at each location and malign circumstance contriving to frustrate the heroes. Veteran character actors take on cameo roles as deadbeats and bureaucrats, with Howard Hesseman as a blind Vietnam veteran who terrorises a social security office with his vicious dog and Elizabeth Peña (acting here under the name Elizabeth Anne Dickinson) making the unhelpful hospital admissions person a Margaret Hamilton-esque comedy villain.

The film's modest success is also attributable to the adept playing of its two leads, both of whom have to overcome their own images. An actor of Roth's intensity and a rapper of Shakur's legend might be expected to come on angrier and grungier, but they play off each other with the mix of affection and exasperation that characterises the great comic teams. Roth even mimics a few of Stan Laurel's mooncalf mannerisms while Shakur plays the straight-man surprisingly well with a strange flux of optimism and resignation. In a grim and audacious moment, Spoon admits that he is HIV-positive, which qualities him for the instant medical aid they've been trying to get, but which he hadn't thought to mention earlier.

As with all great clowns, the enemy is not really their own weakness for drugs but the world itself, represented by the endless waiting rooms, queues (even when there's no queue, the pair have to wind through a roped-off maze to get to a counter), forms, plexiglass-caged bureaucrats, snarling gangsters and suspicious cops. *Gridlock'd*'s debutante writer-director Vondie Curtis-Hall, best known as a stern actor, plays the comically cool D-Reper, and works much harder with his actors than with his straggley storyline. To go along with the film, you must take on trust contrivances such as the trio's ability to sustain a musical career (real addicts don't hang on long to cash-convertable musical instruments), or that all the government offices shown would be open on New Year's Day.

TIME, 2/3/97, p. 66, Richard Corliss

Perplexing chasm separated the two Tupac Shakurs. As rap's Public Gangsta No. 1, he spumed venom on CD, reeked menace onstage, wore his tattoos like a war hero's medals, did time for violent crimes and, at 25, got gunned down in Las Vegas last September. As a budding film star, though, he pinwheeled charm and emotional purity. Shakur, who had acted professionally since he was 12, wasn't quite Sidney Poitier, but in a decent range of roles (in *Juice, Poetic Justice, Above the Rim*) he showed power and promise.

In *Gridlock'd*, an ambitious first film as writer-director by actor Vondie Curtis Hall, Shakur plays Spoon, a musician who resolves to say aloha to heroin after his singer girlfriend Cookie (radiant Thandie Newton) nearly dies from a drug overdose. The plot has Spoon and his nutsy pal Stretch (wild man Tim Roth) fleeing a Detroit drug lord (Curtis Hall) who's peeved that the lads stole his stash. But the real story is of the runaround Spoon and Stretch get from social-service employees who can't be bothered to help addicts get into rehab programs. This is an action comedy about two guys waiting in line for nothing to happen: Samuel Beckett rewritten for Simpson-Bruckheimer.

Alkies and druggies of old movies *(The Lost Weekend, Days of Wine Roses, The Man with the Golden Arm)* didn't need government rehab to shake the monkey off their backs. Part of the joke here is that Spoon and Stretch, who are less performance artists than petty criminals, suffer from welfare-state dependency. And in Michigan, this is the wrong state to depend on. Public servants are ignorant or lazy or just plain crazy. But Spoon and Stretch aren't your ideal victims. Their signature act of social aggression is to smoke cigarettes in government offices. Their way of bonding is for one to give the other a gut wound with a penknife. They're the Jerky Boys, playing mortal pranks on themselves.

The film's villains are from Central Casting, the cops from Keystone. But that's not what matters. Taking a page from the Martin Scorsese handbook, Curtis Hall smartly heightens moments with epic visual declarations (slo-mo, negative images, gigantic closeups). The speeches are arias, the shots operatic, complex.

The performances are also big; nearly everyone in this Act-O-Rama gets a screaming scene. The tone is set by Roth, the Brit of choice for those directors who think Gary Oldman just doesn't push it far enough. It's cartoon work, really (imagine Henery Hawk trying to be the Tasmanian Devil), but fun to watch. And Shakur, as the sensible guy, plays nicely off Roth. He is both Stretch's keeper and the film's conscience. "When gettin' high becomes a job," he muses, "what's the point?"

Shakur also serves as his own elegist. "All the things we talked about," he says of Cookie when he thinks she might be dead, "things she wanted to do—then she ups and dies. I don't wanna go out like that." Later he speaks one of the most introspective lines in the Afro-action canon: "Somehow I don't think this was my parents' dream for me." With Shakur's death, Hollywood lost part of its own dream to become a robust rainbow cinema. *Gridlock'd* gives a taste of what the movies are going to miss.

VILLAGE VOICE, 2/4/97, p. 70, Amy Taubin

Gridlock'd Vondie Curtis Hall's first feature, is brimming with gallows humor and plain old joie de vivre. Its exuberance is contagious; I would've happily sat through it twice.

Set in Curtis Hall's native Detroit, *Gridlock'd* is part social satire, part screwball comedy, and part buddy movie. The buddies are a pair of junkies played by Tim Roth and Tupac Shakur, an odd-coupling so inspired that I can't imagine the movie without them. This is Tupac's second-to-last acting role (in case you've been on Mars, he was shot to death last fall at age 25), and the fine grain of sadness underlying the film's antic humor is weighted by our knowledge of his real-life fate, "Lately, I've been feeling like my luck's run out," he says, and we gasp because, suddenly, its not just the character talking. Because the movie tries so hard not to be exploitative, something more complicated than sentimentalized necrophilia is going on here. We have a glimpse of the gifts of prophecy and memory that all films potentially offer.

Stretch (Roth) and Spoon (Shakur) are best friends and members of an edgy jazz trio that's been derailed by drugs. When their singer (the fragile Thandie Newton) ODs and winds up in the hospital, Spoon decides it's time for them to kick. (Faced with a damsel in distress, our boys try to rescue each other.) *Gridlock'd* follows their frenetic daylong attempt to enter the heaven of rehab.

Much to their amazement, the social service system doesn't welcome even such motivated junkies with open arms. Instead they're told to take a number, fill out the forms, and wait. Wait all day so that they can wait six weeks, and then six more weeks. It's crazy, because waiting is the very thing junkies can't do. If they were capable of delaying gratification they probably wouldn't be junkies in the first place. Frustrated by one institutional double bind after another, Stretch and Spoon take time out for a last fix. That's when they get into serious trouble. Their dealer's been shot dead, and suddenly they're being pursued by the cops, who believe they're the murderers, and by the murderers, who know they've stolen the stash.

Curtis Hall proves his talent by keeping the film precariously balanced between everyday weirdness and pointed burlesque. The scene in which Stretch and Spoon shoot up with the dealer lying dead in a pool of blood less than 15 feet away could have been played for cheap laughs. Instead, Curtis Hall gives it an offhand logic by sticking to his characters' point of view. And from the point of view of a junkie, even a still-warm corpse fades into the woodwork when he's having a fix.

Unlike most of the new breed of actors turned directors, Curtis Hall has a rare sense of how to make film space come alive. *Gridlock'd* is built around Roth and Shakur's performances, but there's nothing stagy in the way they're presented. When Stretch drops a one-line bombshell that transforms Spoon's (and our) relationship to him, he blurts it out from behind the closed door of a toilet stall. Separating word and image adds to the expressiveness of the scene without taking anything away from Roth or the character he embodies. It's a tiny moment, but it suggests a real filmmaker at work.

The film's classy producers have surrounded Curtis Hall with some major talent: cinematographer Bill Pope (*Darkman* and *Clueless*) and production designer Dan Bishop are responsible for the film's muted hyperrealist look and editor Christopher Koefoed (*Menace II Society*) for its skittery, breakneck pace. The crucial element, however, is the chemistry between Roth and Shakur—the sense of trust and freedom that they bring to all their scenes together.

The bandy-legged Roth, with his strutting torso and scrunched-up face, is so alive it hurts me to say he's been better elsewhere (there's a trace too much Ratso Rizzo in Stretch). Shakur, however, takes the opportunity to play a thoughtful character on the verge of conquering self-destructive impulses and runs with it. We know immediately why these two characters are so entwined: Stretch is so crazy that he makes Spoon feel sane and Spoon's sanity keeps Stretch from losing it completely. *Gridlock'd* rests on the friendship between a black man and a white man. Roth and Shakur show us the intricacies of the relationship and let us know that it's for life.

Also received in:
NEW YORK TIMES, 1/29/97, p. C12, Janet Maslin
VARIETY, 1/20-26/97, p. 45, Todd McCarthy
WASHINGTON POST, 1/29/97, p. D1, Richard Harrington
WASHINGTON POST, 1/31/97, Weekend/p. 44, Desson Howe

GRIND

A Castle Hill Productions and Kodiak Productions, L.L.C. release. *Executive Producer:* Tom Staub. *Producer:* Laura Lau. *Director:* Chris Kentis. *Screenplay:* Laura Lau. *Director of Photography:* Stephen Kazmierski. *Music:* Brian Kelly. *Sound:* William Cozy and (music) Scott Anthony. *Sound Editor:* Dan Sable. *Casting:* Laura Lau, Melissa Powell, and Cassandra Han. *Production Designer:* Therese Deprez. *Art Director:* Michael Krantz. *Costumes:* Katherine Jane Bryant. *Make-up:* Nicky Jasney-Ledermann. *Running time:* 96 minutes. *MPAA Rating:* Not Rated.

CAST: Billy Crudup (Eddie); Adrienne Shelley (Janey); Paul Schulze (Terry); Frank Vincent (Nick); Saul Stein (Jack); Amanda Peet (Patty); Steven Beach (Jimmy); Jason Andrews (Joey);

Arthur Nascarella (John); Nick Sandow (Lenny); Tim Williams (Scott); Angela Pupello (Pam); Lydia Radzull (Liz); Tim Devlin (Scully); Joe Pallister (J.J.).

LOS ANGELES TIMES, 5/9/97, Calendar/p. 11, Kevin Thomas

Chris Kentis' "Grind" will surely be noted as the first film of Billy Crudup's already promising career. With any luck, it will also launch Kentis, here in his feature debut, and give boosts to the ongoing careers of Paul Schulze, who made his mark in "Laws of Gravity," and Adrienne Shelley, who first came to attention in Hal Hartley's "Trust" and "The Unbelievable Truth."

In the meantime, it should be hastily made clear that "Grind" is a fine and involving accomplishment in its own right, not just for what it promises for its writer-director and his young actors. Kentis takes us into a blue-collar New Jersey family without a trace of condescension or stereotyping to bring alive a group of people you can care about.

Crudup's Eddie shows up at his brother Terry's home after serving an 18-month sentence after getting in a drunken car race in which the other participants wound up dead. A loving brother, Terry (Schulze), takes in Eddie and promptly gets him a job at a treadmill factory where Terry and the two brothers' father (Frank Vincent), who's about to retire, work.

Terry even loans Eddie money to buy a car so he can resume his beloved car racing. (OK, that the factory makes treadmills may be a bit too symbolic, like the sign telling us that Terry lives on a dead-end street—but it's no big deal in either instance.)

Eddie doesn't mind at all when he's switched to the night shift because he figures it will give him more time to work on his car. It also, however, throws him together with his lonely sister-in-law, Janey (Shelley).

Kentis gets lots going here. Eddie has a reckless streak but he's also more imaginative than his relatives. Racing has given him a sense of freedom that makes it impossible for him to consider a permanent job on an assembly line. Janey and Terry haven't gotten their lives together either, although they're into denial.

Having a baby has made Janey realize that maybe she's settled down too early and finds that her life seems boring and lonely. If the men are ground down at work, Janey is drifting because clearly nothing in her experience has given her the inner resources to create a fulfilling life for herself along with being a housewife and mother.

A traditionalist, Terry never considers that encouraging, let alone approving, Janey to get more education to enable her to get a decent job might be a better course for both her and for their marriage than his participating in a car theft/insurance scam to bring in more income so that they can better make ends meet.

In any event, Eddie has a sexy sensitivity, which along with his immaturity, is going to make it different for Janey to resist him after one spontaneous, even innocent kiss on his part. Clearly, all three of these likable, fundamentally decent and intelligent people are going to have to do lots of growing up, not just Eddie, and we can only hope that they make it.

"Grind" is a fine, intimate film of considerable insight and much compassion.

NEW YORK POST, 4/11/97, p. 44, Bill Hoffmann

The independent film world certainly gave Hollywood a run for its money last year, as the recent Oscar ceremonies showed.

Was it a fluke? The answer is a very welcome "no," as proven by the compelling new psychodrama "Grind."

Filmed on a shoestring budget, this gritty little gem from first-time director Chris Kentis loaded with so many emotional twists and turns that it will have you breathlessly trying to keep pace.

In her most challenging role to date, Hal Hartley alumna Adrienne Shelley plays the newly married Janey, who's gradually but uneasily settling into the role of a suburban housewife with her boozing, factory worker hubby, Terry (Paul Schulze), and their 6-month-old baby.

For Janey, life in and about blue-collar Clifton, N.J., is as boring as it gets—until Terry's kid brother, Eddie (Billy Crudup), drops in one morning, fresh from an 18-month stint in the pen.

There's no question that Eddie is trouble, but he's got an edgy energy and smoldering sex appeal that his brother will never know.

And with the antsy Eddie hanging about the house all day with the bored Janey and a sleeping baby as reliable ol' Terry does the 9-to-5 grind, the inevitable happens.

With sharp albeit spare dialogue and a fine cast, director Kentis slowly and methodically turns up the heat under a sexually charged pressure cooker. Crudup ("Sleepers," "Inventing the Abbotts"), who is bound for stardom, simmers as the lusty loser of a brother who seems to spoil everything he touches. And Schulze, so good in "Laws of Gravity," is fabulous as a by-the-book factory worker who dabbles in the stolen car biz for extra cash.

Also notable is the wonderful dramatic performance of Adrienne Shelley, who is finally breaking out of her tiring rep as a Hartley staple.

Helping bring things to the dramatic boiling point is the wonderful location shooting, which makes suburban living seem like residing in hell.

Devoid of culture and with a downbeat landscape of cookie-cutter housing, the folks here don't have much to do but spend weekends at a raceway park and play pool at the local gin mill.

This movie will make you thank God you live in New York City, warts and all.

NEWSDAY, 4/11/97, Part II/p. B11, John Anderson

Sunday! Sunday! Fuel-injected funny cars! Sunday! Sunday! Nitro-burning dragsters! Sunday! Sunday! Ex-cons, small-time thuggery, intrafamilial sex, sibling rivalry! Sunday! *SUNDAY!*

Okay, it's Friday. But "Grind" has all of the above, in various doses and potencies and, more important, a true sense of the blue-collar soul of semisuburban New Jersey. Set in Clifton—the home of Rupert Pupkin—it's a small tale about small people, whose plotline is about as well land-scaped as the Newark sequence of the New Jersey Turnpike. But at the same time, this debut feature by director Chris Kentis employs enough irregular rhythms, potent moments and visual mobility to generate interest in the director, if not always the film.

And the cast is first-rate, a pit crew of independent-film veterans who lend solid support to their soon-to-be-superstar leading man, Billy Crudup. Currently on view in "Inventing the Abbotts" and starring in the upcoming "Pre" (he was also in "Sleepers"), Crudup may well have been the reason this intimate little film finally got released; shooting was completed in 1995. Whatever the reason, it's good to see it. And Crudup.

Eddie, the drag racer and ex-con who returns to Clifton for a stab at real life, is the kind of character who usually runs right into a wall of cliches and attitude. But Crudup manages to add dimension to what might have been a Brad Pitt-by-way-of-Brando knockoff, fleshing out the hunk. Eddie's exchanges with his obnoxious, car-heisting brother Terry (Paul Schulze), his desperate affair with Terry's wife, Janey (Adrienne Shelley), and his estrangement from his father, Nick (Frank Vincent), all ring true. Even the glimpse we're given of his expired relationship with the gum-popping Patty (a very-big-haired Amanda Peet) is genuine love-as-lingering-death.

Eddie moves in with Terry and Janey and their baby, starts work in the treadmill (nice touch) factory where Nick and Terry work, and tries to avoid the car-boosting scam run by Jack (the always scary Saul Stein). But his heart is in racing, and racing takes money and one thing leads to another and Eddie with more looks than intelligence, and more hormones than wisdom—watches things start to go up in flames.

There is, of course, the scandalous suggestion in "Grind" that a working-class existence and a few cut-rate dreams inevitably lead to crime. Also, the perhaps more reasonable assertion that Eddie's problems are rooted in a class system that discriminates, and a justice system based on wealth. His crime was a street race in which his Mustang beat a Porsche. "They lived. I didn't," Eddie says, with all the fatalistic resignation of the perpetual antihero.

But such are the conventions of cinema. Kentis does a good job of avoiding most conventions. He just gets tripped up at the wire.

VILLAGE VOICE, 4/15/97, p. 72, Laurie Stone

First-time writer-director Chris Kentis captures blue-collar entrapment with a visual economy that matches his characters' few-words minimalism. He nails the gerbil routines of assembly-line Joes and baby-bottle Jills, the stubbly-faced, leftover-cake-for-breakfast vérité of their tract-house mornings. The scene could be the '50s or '90s, not intentionally retro but a timeless groove. Janey (Adrienne Shelley) isn't sure how in a year she went from a summertime romance with factory worker Terry (Paul Schulze) to counting out her days with coffee spoons and their infant's diapers. Into this ménage slips Terry's brother Eddie (Billy Crudup), fresh out of jail for a speeding incident that, though not his fault, resulted in a death. Eddie's passion is souping up and driving drag cars. It means independence and glamour, but he takes a job at the factory where his brother is installed and where his father—humiliation rising off him like a tang—waits retirement.

Eddie is so drop-dead gorgeous—his cheekbones like shelves you could arrange bric-a-brac on—you wonder why he doesn't get a gig modeling Guess? jeans. Actually Kentis uses Eddie's beauty. It's part of his vulnerability and what separates him from the other males who've been coarsened by the world's disregard for them. In this enclave, there is little romance or pride apart from youth's body, before it is damaged and used up. As Janey, Shelley is a fugitive from a John Mellencamp ballad, a passive creature with her intelligence kept under wraps. Suffocating in inarticulable longings, Janey falls in love with Eddie, who is tender, and he responds to her kindness because it's not freighted with deals. Their kisses are like mouth-to-mouth resuscitation, awakening each other from sleep. Their affair makes trouble, but it also allows them to see the machinery, understand they are meant to be cogs. Love inspires them to honor themselves and mourn their class: "Everything in this room was made by somebody," Eddie observes sadly. "The fringe on that ugly lampshade was somebody's life."

Also reviewed in:
NEW YORK TIMES, 4/11/97, p. C10, Stephen Holden
VARIETY, 4/22-28/96, p. 92, Leonard Klady

GRIZZLY MOUNTAIN

A Mega Communications, Inc. release in association with Napor Kids and Legacy Releasing of a Parkinson/Konstant/Furla production. *Executive Producer:* Eric Parkinson, Nicholas Konstant, and George Furla. *Producer:* Anthony Dalesandro and Peter White. *Director:* Jeremy Haft. *Screenplay:* Jeremy Haft and Peter White. *Based on a story by:* Eric Parkinson. *Director of Photography:* Andy Parke. *Editor:* Richard Westover and Anthony Dalesandro. *Music:* Jon McCallum. *Sound:* Victory Pictures. *Production Designer:* Joe Schilling. *Art Director:* Christine Schulman. *Set Designer:* Patrick Danz. *Costumes:* Diane Hansen. *Running time:* 96 minutes. *MPAA Rating:* G.

CAST: Dan Haggerty (Jeremiah); Dylan Haggerty (Dylan); Nicole Lund (Nicole); Kim Morgan Greene (Betty); Perry Stephens (Boss Man Burt); Robert Patteri (Roscoe); Andrew Craig (Bailey); Robert Budaska (Jones); E.E. Bell (Mayor); Marton Kove (Marshal Jackson); Don Borza (Bill Marks); Marguerite Hickey (Karen Marks).

LOS ANGELES TIMES, 10/31/97, Calendar/p. 22, Kevin Thomas

"Grizzly Mountain" marks the return of Dan Haggerty, star of the popular "Grizzly Adams" TV series and subsequent movies. While it's nice to have the burly, amiable portrayer of mountain men back after a near-fatal motorcycle accident, it's too bad "Grizzly Mountain" is such an amateurish effort.

Actually, its premise has possibilities for a family entertainment. A surveyor (Don Borza) for the state of Oregon takes his family along when he starts mapping out a condo development in a beautiful forest a two-hour drive from Portland.

His two older children (Dylan Haggerty, Nicole Lund) go off to do a little exploring on their own, entering a cave that transports them back to 1870. With their walkie-talkies and other 1990s toys, they end up helping Haggerty's Jeremiah and a local Indian tribe fend off some rapacious developers. When the children are reunited at last with their family, their father gets the conservationist message.

Sadly, Haggerty is surrounded by more mediocre acting than he is gorgeous wilderness scenery. Jeremy Haft hasn't a clue as to how to direct actors, and he and his cowriters send their politically correct messages with a heavy hand. The bad guy (Perry Stephens) has three knucklehead sidekicks whose antics make the Three Stooges masters of subtlety in comparison, and they make the movie all but unwatchable. You can't in good conscience recommend "Grizzly Mountain" to anyone over the age of 5.

NEW YORK POST, 10/31/97, p. 50, Michael Medved

"Grizzly Mountain" cheerfully skips along the dividing line between childlike and childish, innocent and amateurish.

While betraying its low-budget origins with splotches of sloppiness and silliness, its fresh, out-doorsy atmosphere and lovable leading man provide rollicking family fun that will particularly please the youngest members of the audience.

The story begins in the present day, when a Portland, Ore., family heads to the mountains for a weekend camping trip.

The two oldest kids (Nicole Lund and Dylan Haggerty) go exploring and wander into a cave where flashes of purple-and-yellow animation, along with a suddenly shaky camera, signal that they've just gone through a mysterious time warp.

When they emerge it's 1870 and they meet a genial, beefy, full-bearded mountain man, Jeremiah (Dan Haggerty, TV's "Grizzly Adams"), who seems oddly unfazed by these young visitors from the future.

He introduces them to his animal companions (a fun-loving bear and well-trained golden eagle) and soon involves them in a local dispute: Jeremiah has joined with a friendly Indian tribe in resisting schemes by greedy frontier developers to destroy the pristine paradise of Grizzly Mountain.

Three bumbling bad guys work for the eager exploiters and provide embarrassingly bad comic relief, while the visiting kids use nifty 1990s toys they've carried in their backpacks to prevent dynamite charges from blowing up the forest.

This puerile plot unfolds with such easygoing geniality that the well-deserved "G" rating might appropriately stand for "goodnatured."

Some 19 years after his TV show went off the air (and a decade after a near-fatal motorcycle accident nearly ended his career), Dan Haggerty still projects a reassuring combination of cuddly compassion and rugged, big-daddy virility; the fact that two of his own kids play key roles in this film only adds to the wholesome aura of these proceedings.

If the rest of the cast lacks Haggerty's effortless charisma, it hardly matters to enchanted small fry, who will pay more attention to friendly forest creatures and goofy slapstick than to subtle displays of acting expertise.

Also reviewed in:
CHICAGO TRIBUNE, 10/31/97, Friday/p. O, John Petrakis
NEW YORK TIMES, 10/31/97, p. E24, Lawrence Van Gelder
VARIETY, 11/3-9/97, p. 100, Lael Lowenstein

GROSSE POINTE BLANK

A Hollywood Pictures release in association with Caravan Pictures and New Crime Productions of a Roger Birnbaum & Roth/Arnold production. *Executive Producer:* Jonathan Glickman and Lata Ryan. *Producer:* Susan Arnold, Donna Arkoff Roth, and Roger Birnbaum. *Director:* George Armitage. *Screenplay:* Tom Jankiewicz, D.V. DeVincentis, Steve Pink, and John Cusack. *Director of Photography:* Jamie Anderson. *Editor:* Brian Berdan. *Music:* Joe Strummer and Kathy Nelson. *Music Editor:* Angie Rubin. *Sound:* Arthur Rochester. *Sound Editor:* David Hankins. *Casting:* Junie Lowry Johnson and Ron Surma. *Production Designer:* Stephen Altman. *Art Director:* Scott Meehan. *Set Decorator:* Chris Spellman. *Set Dresser:* Matthew Altman.

Special Effects: Ron Trost. *Costumes:* Eugenie Bafaloukos. *Make-up:* Cindy Jane Williams. *Prosthetic Make-up Effects:* Todd Masterson. *Stunt Coordinator:* Buddy Joe Hooker. *Running time:* 106 minutes. *MPAA Rating:* R.

CAST: John Cusack (Martin Q. Blank); Minnie Driver (Debi Newberry); Alan Arkin (Dr. Oatman); Dan Aykroyd (Grocer); Joan Cusack (Marcella); Hank Azaria (Lardner); K. Todd Freeman (McCullers); Mitchell Ryan (Mr. Newberry); Jeremy Piven (Paul Spericki); Michael Cudlitz (Bob Destepello); Benny Urquidez (Felix); Duffy Taylor (Ultimart Carl); Audrey Kissel (Arlene); Carlos Jacott (Ken); Brian Powell (Husky Man); Ann Cusack (Amy); D.V. DeVincentis (Dan Koretzky); Barbara Harris (Mary Blank); Wendy Thorlakson (Melanie the Waitress); Belita Moreno (Mrs. Kinetta); Pat O'Neill (Nathaniel); Jenna Elfman (Tanya); Steve Pink (Terry Rostand); K.K. Dodds (Tracy); Bill Cusack (Waiter); Traci Dority (Jenny Slater); Doug Dearth (Eckhart); Colby French (Bartender); Brent Armitage (Cosmo); Jackie Rubin (Marie); Sarah DeVincentis (Dr. Oatman's Patient); Eva Rodriguez (Nurse); David Barrett (Bicycle Messenger).

LOS ANGELES TIMES, 4/11/97, Calendar/p. 1, Kenneth Turan

It's live ammunition that's coming at you in "Grosse Pointe Blank." A wild at heart, anarchic comedy that believes in living dangerously, it follows is hit man to his high school reunion and survives to tell the tale.

John Cusack, vividly watchable as always, does more than star as morose assassin Martin Q. Blank; he has organized a kind of Cusack conglomerate of relatives and friends to bring this darkly playful project to fruition.

It starts with sister Joan Cusack as Martin's eccentric assistant Marcella, prone to calling him "sir," as in, "Sir, I'm starting to worry about your safety." Two other siblings, Ann Cusack and Bill Cusack, have small parts, and a friend from high school in Evanston, Ill., Jeremy Piven of TV's "Ellen," has a key co-starring role as, yes, an old high school friend.

Two other Evanston buddies, D.V. DeVincentis and Steve Pink, also have bit parts and joined with Cusack as co-writers of the script, along with original story writer Tom Jankiewicz, who managed a screen credit despite the lack of an obvious Evanston connection.

Nimbly making his presence felt amid all these homeboys is director George Armitage, who is developing one of the tastiest if slowest simmering of movie careers. Armitage turned out a quartet of uncomplicated exploitation films with names like "Private Duty Nurses" and "Vigilante Force" in the 1970s and then didn't direct again until 1990's "Miami Blues," a roguish black comedy starring Alec Baldwin, Jennifer Jason Leigh and Fred Ward that was one of the year's most distinctive films.

That same feeling for darkly ironic farce animates this film, and it's a pleasure to see Armitage connecting with sympathetic material once again. "Grosse Pointe" has its share of Hollywood twists and doesn't always make a whole lot of sense, but seeing a vehicle this outlandish is reward enough by itself.

Having been an assassin for a decade, Martin Blank is ripe for a crisis of confidence. His hits are not going as smoothly as they used to, and his archrival Grocer (Dan Aykroyd) is trying to form a kind of hit-person's union that would include everyone from murderous dwarfs to those notorious "mad stabbers from the Philippines."

Blank is worried enough to have gotten into therapy with the celebrated Dr. Oatman (played, in a possible nod to the classic "The In-Laws," by Alan Arkin), author of "Kill Who? A Warrior's Dilemma." But Oatman is too terrified of his client to be much help. "Don't kill someone for a few days," he offers. "See what it feels like."

Adding complications, the mercurial Marcella pressures Martin to attend his 10th reunion at tony Grosse Pointe High because she finds it "amusing that you came from somewhere." The man himself is dubious about the kind of impression he'd make ("What can I say—that I killed the president of Paraguay with a fork?") but when an assignment in nearby Detroit brings him to the area anyway, Martin decides to go.

Of course, he has another reason for attending. Having stood up his high school sweetheart Debi Newberry (the always effective Minnie Driver) on prom night and then disappeared without a trace, Martin has dreamed about his lost love every night for 10 years. Maybe reconnecting with Debi will help him figure out what his life is supposed to be all about.

Once he arrives in Grosse Point, however, Martin finds that few things about the town he left behind are as he expected. And the presence of rival hit men and cynical federal agents, all angling for an opportunity to end his life, help make this a weekend to remember.

In both incident and character, "Grosse Point Blank" manages to be consistently surprising, down to minor characters like a quirky rent-a-cop (played by co-screenwriter Pink) who feels overly protective about the houses he guards. And one of the film's clever running jokes is how unimpressed everyone is when Martin breaks down and reveals what he does for a living. "Good for you," says Debi's father dryly. "It's a growth industry."

Clever enough to make jokes about Greco-Roman wrestling and make them funny, "Grosse Pointe Blank's" greatest success is the way it maintains its comic attitude. Working with a smart script and actors who get the joke, director Armitage pulls off a number of wacky action set pieces. Even if you think you've heard actors say, "I love you, we can make this relationship work," in every conceivable situation, this film has a few surprises in store.

NEW YORK, 4/28/97, p. 102, David Denby

In the immensely enjoyable *Grosse Pointe Blank*, John Cusack plays a criminal—a professional assassin who goes home to his ten-year high-school reunion and picks up where he left off with Minnie Driver, the girl he abandoned on prom night. Driver, a local radio personality who doesn't yet know her old boyfriend's profession, is more than amenable, and the reunited couple are getting along very well, moving from the school dance floor to the nurse's office, when suddenly Driver stops him. "There's something missing here," she says. "What—too fast?" he says anxiously. "Something missing," she says, thinking it over and then she whams him one across the face. Cusack looks stunned but smiles in acknowledgment of her point. The two then resume kissing.

That's the movie in a nutshell. It slaps us hard with the unexpected, waits an instant for us to catch up, and then begins tricking us all over again. *Grosse Point Blank* is as funny as *Get Shorty* and as hip as *Pulp Fiction,* though not as sleek and high-powered as the first or as ostentatiously ironic as the second. It has a modest satiric style all its own. George Armitage, who made *Miami Blues,* directed, and his tempo is fast, fast, faster—sometimes so fast you want to see the movie again to be sure you really heard the outrageous things you think you heard. But *Grosse Pointe Blank* is a real charmer—a dark comedy that is too romantic and affectionate to be called black.

The premise is no more than a joke, but it's a good joke. In the opening scene, Cusack stands at a hotel window, busy shooting someone (another hit man, on a bicycle), while at the same time his secretary (played by his sister Joan Cusack) reads him a letter over the telephone. The comic point is that John Cusack's character—Martin Blank is his name—conducts himself as though he had a completely normal job. His secretary, a demanding, over-explicit woman, gives him careful advice and worries over him just the way Humphrey Bogart's secretary worried over her boss in *The Maltese Falcon.* Martin has pushy clients, he has supply problems (that late shipment of 9-mm. shells), and he has rivals who want to dominate him. The market for hit men has apparently been flooded with ex-Stasi thugs and tiny, knife-wielding Filipino ladies posing as hotel maids. Things are tough all over, but Blank's problems are different: His morale is low, and he may be losing his touch, too. He botches a couple of jobs; his heart is no longer in it. Depressed, and worried that he has chosen the wrong line of work, Martin goes to a shrink, the great Dr. Oatman, who is very frightened of his earnestly troubled patient. Alan Arkin, holding his bald dome in anguish, has his funniest bit in years. "Try not killing anyone," the doctor says.

That John Cusack was likable became clear as early as *The Sure Thing* and *Say Anything*, that he was a terrific film actor became obvious in *The Grifters.* Now it's evident as well that he knows how to be a movie star. Cusack optioned a screenplay by Tom Jankiewicz, then worked with a couple of writing pals from his Chicago theater crowd—D.V. DeVincentis and Steve Pink—to reshape it into a vehicle for himself. The role has a quality almost ... Cusackian. Dressed in black, Cusack has filled out—he looks more substantial than before, and he comes across as suave and self-confident but in a light, unemphatic way. With his long, pale face and small mouth, Cusack can look like a degenerate or a choir boy, and his smoky voice has surprising registers. He's very adroit with tiny, rapid shifts of mood, from mild mockery to sweet literalness and then back again. He's easy to take and unassuming, and you feel generous toward him; you want him to succeed.

His Martin Blank is an improvisatory personality and an honest man. He dissembles, but he won't lie to himself. He dresses in black, but he's not the usual macho loner. (No actor with a trace of awareness can do the hired killer straight anymore.) Cusack makes him a modern, self-conscious guy, a hustler, an operator, even a yuppie slightly embarrassed by how much he once enjoyed killing people. *Grosse Pointe Blank* is the sport of a satirical age, a joke not on murder but on what people once took seriously in the movies. Martin Blank may be getting tired of killing—he even longs for "the redemption thing"—but he still has the moves. Cusack hits his stride in his first scene with Dan Aykroyd, a fellow assassin. The two approach each other warily—sidewise, with their hands inside their coat pockets, ready to draw on each other, and they banter in hostile jive nonsense, the jargon of the professional-killer trade. Aykroyd goes a mile a minute in his machine-gun style, and Cusack impressively matches him. The movie never comes down from that giddy moment.

In this spoof, killing is everyone's profession. Assassins are hired like business consultants, and government hit men are always lurking around, waiting to knock off the freelancers. In the end, they all plug away at one another and fall down in a heap. In *Grosse Pointe Blank,* violent death becomes ridiculous, not because death is ridiculous but because the way movies usually treat it has no meaning. Martin and some obscurely motivated French thug shoot it out in a convenience store, the blasted Fritos and Cokes flying every which way, and the bullets never touch either man. The violent scenes are way over the top. Aykroyd holds his guns right out in front of him, blazing away as nonchalantly as a kid with a cap pistol. The filmmakers are teasing us for the way we respond to violent thrillers. Directors know that we would *like* to care about death—they are willing to indulge the pretense. But they also know we don't really care, that we just want the thrill. Laughing at this movie is a strike against hypocrisy.

Arriving home, Martin meets old friends who are extremely angry at him for disappearing ten years earlier without a word. When they ask him what he does, he always tells them the truth. They sell real estate or cars; he's a professional killer. But they assume he's putting them on, and without hesitating more than an instant, they come back at him with wisecracks. The filmmakers twist the usual awkward comedy of high-school reunions into half-sinister farce. Nobody believes Martin because everyone lives in a David Letterman world of put-ons and gags. Reality has been showbizzed; everyone has his shtick. Even Martin's old history teacher, a sardonic woman about half his size, riffs on his black clothes. Some of the friends who stayed behind—including Jeremy Piven (from the TV series *Ellen)* as a real-estate salesman—are made almost hysterical by their envy of Blank. His name is emblematic; they project their fantasies onto him. The joke goes sky-high when assassins come after Martin in the school.

The one thing done (mostly) straight is the renewed love affair between Minnie Driver and Cusack. Driver, who is British, was a little stiff in *Big Night;* here, she's loose and funny, an adorable good girl with a mop of curled hair, a bright smile, and a way of running from place to place—her arms moving like pistons—that is a shot of pure joy. Her Debi can't believe her luck: The one man she clicked with has come back to her. The two of them move ahead fast, like a couple in a thirties screwball comedy. Her rage when she finds out he's not kidding about killing is a beautifully graded shift from disbelief to pain to shocked exasperation. The ending of the movie is a little too easy and unambiguous—an escape into standard romantic comedy that seems weak after what we've seen—but the picture has entertained us so much, we can forgive it almost anything.

NEW YORK POST, 4/11/97, p. 45, Michael Medved

Anyone courageous enough to attend a high school class reunion will instinctively attempt to put the proudest possible face on all career achievements.

Marvin Q. Blank (John Cusack), part of the Grosse Pointe High class of 1986, is no exception: While reconnecting with his classmates in Detroit's most posh and privileged suburb, he matter-of-factly informs them that he's achieved success as a professional assassin.

They of course, assume this is one more example of his dry sense of humor, but it turns out he's telling the truth.

In fact, he's combining his nostalgic trip home with a profitable contract killing in the area.

He also means to reconnect with the high school sweetheart (Minnie Driver) he left behind 10 years ago, and who has no idea of the bizarre, bloody direction his life has taken since the night he disappeared and stood her up at the prom.

This set-up for "Grosse Pointe Blank" yields a few irresistibly amusing moments, but for the most part the filmmakers (director George ["Miami Blues"] Armitage and four credited writers, including Cusack himself) can't figure out what to do with their promising premise.

Beyond a few furious, fancifully staged gun battles, very little happens leaving Cusack and Driver too much screen time to gaze longingly at one another while exchanging zingers about their painful pasts.

Yes, Cusack's in top form, making even his icy-veined killer seem ironic and likable, while Driver, so profoundly appealing in "Circle of Friends" and "Big Night," reinforces her status as one of today's most lovable leading ladies.

Her part, however, is so poorly written that the character never emerges as much more than a convenient plot device: She broadcasts a confessional daily radio show from a storefront in downtown Grosse Pointe, and we're asked to assume that no other man has arrived to fill the empty space in her life in the decade since Cusack ditched her.

Other characters are also colorful caricatures—including Joan Cusack (John's real-life sister) as his wacky, unflappable secretary; Alan Arkin as his exasperated psychiatrist; and Dan Aykroyd as a bullying rival trying to organize a professional killers union—but since they're intended primarily as comic distractions, their absurd excesses are more or less appropriate.

And speaking of excess, the movie tries to create the illusion of energy with an annoyingly intrusive soundtrack featuring songs by Motorhead, the Cure and many other groups intended to make the project seem hip by association.

"Grosse Pointe Blank" may generate some noisy explosions, and a few random shots may actually strike the target, but in the end, the whole project seems to be shooting blanks.

NEWSDAY, 4/11/97, Part II/p. B2, Jack Mathews

Ever wonder what became of those classmates whose names appear on the "Lost Sheep" list attached to your high school reunion invitations? Where the heck have they been? Organizing Democratic fund raisers in Beijing? Waiting for space ships in California? Doing Dennis Rodman's hair? Is it something we said?

There's rich material on those lists for anyone with a lively imagination, and the gang of writers who contributed to "Grosse Pointe Blank" had theirs fully engaged. Their lost sheep, John Cusack's Martin Q. Blank, is indeed alive, and thriving in a dark occupational loop way outside the mainstream. He's a globe-hopping, government-trained, stubbornly independent commercial assassin.

Now, 10 years after vanishing from the posh Detroit suburb of Grosse Pointe where he grew up, he's returning to combine business with curiosity. As luck would have it, he has to be in the Motor City for a killing on the same weekend as his first high school reunion, and—at the urging of his sentimental secretary (Joan Cusack)—decides to look in on the lives he left behind. Maybe he can even rekindle a romance with the childhood sweetheart he left all dressed up with no place to go on prom night.

"Grosse Pointe Blank" is exactly the lark it sounds, and it's great fun. John Cusack reportedly nursed the project along from story to completion, earning a co-screenwriting credit, and it was worth the effort. The black humor perfectly suits his deadpan style, and director George Armitage, whose 1990 "Miami Blues" anticipated "Pulp Fiction," knows how to blend genres while turning them on their heads.

"Miami Blues" was panned by many critics for being too violent, though their real problem seemed to be with its mixing of graphic violence and comedy. It was a discomfiting blend, to be sure, just as "Pulp Fiction" would later be, but for those who went with it, Armitage delivered a riotously guilty pleasure.

"Grosse Pointe" is much too silly to create any guilt, and its characters are far brighter and more upscale than those in "Miami Blues." But its humor builds from the same types of violent situations. Marty is a cold-blooded killer with a warm heart and a vulnerable ego. He's a generous employer, a meticulous craftsman, and he spends as much time on his psychiatrist's couch as he does plotting his next killing.

There are some hilarious bits between Marty and Alan Arkin's Dr. Oatman, who refuses to accept Marty as a patient even though he never misses an appointment, and between Marty and the Grocer (Dan Aykroyd), a rival assassin who's trying to organize a hit men's union.

But the central relationship is the rejuvenated romance between Marty and his high school girlfriend, Debi (Minnie Driver), a local radio deejay still carrying a torch and a broken heart. Driver, in her biggest screen role since charming audiences in the Irish coming-of-age story "Circle of Friends," brings a lot of fun to a character who seems to have been invented as little more than a date for the reunion.

That reunion, of course, is the film's major set piece, laced with quirky moments between Marty and his classmates, most of them brutal caricatures of suburban yuppies, and capped by a death struggle with another killer who shows up with a contract on him.

Don't look for any hidden messages here, or any messages at all. "Grosse Pointe," like "Miami Blues," like "Pulp Fiction," is a total goof, and though I've never been to one, I'm sure it's more fun than a high school reunion.

NEWSWEEK, 4/21/97, p. 67, David Ansen

I don't think what a person does for a living really reflects who he is," argues the dissatisfied Martin Q. Blank (John Cusack) to his shrink Dr. Oatman (Alan Arkin). Though millions of people, no doubt, feel exactly the way Martin does, few of them are professional hit men. Martin is, which helps explain why his shrink is scared to death of him and also why Martin's quest for inner peace will be a rocky one.

Just consider—as the fresh, darkly funny *Grosse Pointe Blank* asks us to—how awkward it might be for an assassin to navigate his 10th high-school reunion. What kind of small talk will suffice? "I killed the president of Paraguay with a fork. How have you been?" When Martin shows up in Grosse Pointe, he has more than etiquette problems on his hands. He's supposed to rub someone out in nearby Detroit; his biggest rival (Dan Aykroyd) hurt that Martin refuses to join his hit men's union, wants him dead, and the Feds are on his tail. On top of all this, Martin is hoping to rekindle a romance with his high-school flame Debi (Minnie Driver), whom he stood up 10 years earlier at their senior prom, and who is much too decent to be happy about his career choice.

A premise this preposterous must be carried off with unflappable comic conviction, and Cusack is just the right man for the job. His comic timing hasn't been this precise since "Say Anything," and he's become downright debonair as a romantic partner, making sweet chemistry with Driver. Under director George Armitage who hasn't made a movie since the terrific "Miami Blues" in 1990—everyone from the stars to the supporting players Joan Cusack, Michael Cudlitz, Jeremy Piven) seems turned on by the project. A spontaneous, improvisatory glee lights up the best scenes. As a satire, "Grosse Pointe Blank" doesn't completely add up—the parts are greater than the whole—but it's very much alive and kicking.

SIGHT AND SOUND, 8/97, p. 45, John Wrathall

Bored hired killer Martin Black's latest job goes wrong after the intervention of his rival, Grocer, who is trying to start a hitmen's guild to regulate the trade. To keep his employer happy, Martin has to do an unscheduled assassination of a Federal witness in Detroit, which happens to coincide with his high-school reunion in the nearby suburb of Grosse Pointe.

Returning to Grosse Pointe, Martin finds that his family home has been demolished to make way for a convenience store. He tracks down his old girlfriend, Debi, whom he hasn't seen since he stood her up at the prom ten years earlier. Now a DJ at the local radio station, she has mixed feelings about his reappearance, and embarrasses him by having a phone-in on her show about whether she should get back together with him.

Returning to the convenience store, Martin is attacked by a rival assassin, Felix. Martin is also being trailed by Lardner and McCullers, two government agents whom Grocer has tipped off about the hit: they plan to catch him in the act and kill him. Despite the danger, Martin decides to take Debi to the reunion, where they finally declare their love. But before they can leave together, Martin is attacked by Felix, whom he kills with a ballpoint pen. When Martin admits what he does for a living, Debi runs away in horror.

Alone again, Martin opens the envelope containing the details of his next target, who turns out to be Mr Newberry, Debi's father. He catches up with Newberry just as Grocer is about to shoot him. They escape to the family home, where Martin protects Newberry and Debi in a bloody shoot-out in which Grocer, Lardner and McCullers die. Martin asks Debi to marry him, and Newberry gives them his blessing. Martin and Debi drive out of Grosse Pointe together.

John Cusack is one of the generation of American actors who came to prominence in the teen movies of the mid-80s (in his case, notably, *Sixteen Candles*, *The Sure Thing* and *Say Anything*). Part of the delight of this satire about a hitman returning to his ten-year high-school reunion, lies in the way it plays with memories of those films. The soundtrack of 80s hits played at the reunion and by Debi on the local radio station during her special '80s weekend" (shades of *Reservoir Dogs*) is deployed to wonderfully absurdist effect. At one point during the reunion, Martin sneaks away alone to look at his old school locker. His nostalgic reverie is interrupted by the arrival of Felix, the Basque terrorist-turned-hitman, whom Martin bloodily dispatches with the complimentary ballpoint pen just pressed on him by a former classmate (who now sells insurance). It's a moment of pure black comedy, irresistibly heightened by the song which suddenly echoes up from the dance floor, Nena's inane, pacifist Euro hit '99 Luftballons'.

Tom Jankiewicz's original script has been extensively rewritten by Cusack in collaboration with two old associates (D. V. DeVincentis and Steve Pink, with whom the actor founded Chicago's New Crime Theater). The emphasis is less on the story itself (though it's perfectly coherent) than on engineering a succession of sketch-like encounters which highlight the incongruity of Martin's very ordinary worries, his slick, businesslike demeanour and his lethal profession.

The banal day-to-day concerns of the hitman have long been a source of wry diversion in American thrillers (the tradition stretches back from *Pulp Fiction* to Don Siegel's *The Lineup* and *The Killers*). But here director George Armitage (whose last film, the wonderful *Miami Blues*, explored a similarly black vein), pushes the formula into outright comedy. A particular joy is Martin's session with his psychotherapist Dr Oatman (a very droll Alan Arkin). Not wanting to be "withholding" in therapy, Martin has told Oatman what he does for a living, with the result that the doctor is terrified of him. But Oatman's suggestion that his client's problems may have something to do with killing so many people is rebuffed by Martin, who protests that he doesn't want to just talk about work.

In Martin Blank, Cusack, who also receives a credit as co-producer, has fashioned a perfect role for his slightly uneasy talent: on the one hand, he's boyish enough to be just ten years out of high school, but on the other, as in *The Grifters*, he's pinched and shifty enough to make a plausible killer. Minnie Driver, little more than part of the furniture in such blockbusters as *Sleepers* and *GoldenEye*, also comes into her own as Debi, supplying enough spark and warmth to make the romantic ending a believable development rather than just a neat contrivance.

But for all its lightness of touch and upbeat 80s hits, *Grosse Pointe Blank* leaves a very bitter aftertaste. As Martin bumps into his old classmates—an insurance salesman, an estate agent, a car dealer, and a trigger-happy security guard—we realise that the class of '86, the generation so full of idealism and promise in the films of John Hughes *et al.* have all turned into killers.

TIME, 4/28/97, p. 73, Richard Schickel

The concept couldn't be higher—that is to say, simpler: a professional assassin goes to his high school reunion. Ha-ha. Can't you just see the double takes when Martin Q. Blank (John Cusack) tells all those suburban housewives and real estate salesmen what he's been doing since graduation?

But *Grosse Pointe Blank*, its title punning nicely on a famously grim movie about a hit man, is not a one-joke comedy. Nor is it, despite its Disney auspices, cozy family fun. In its soft-spoken way, it is fierce, shaggy and deeply weirded out.

For Martin is a haunted man. What's put him on the couch of Alan Arkin's understandably nervous psychiatrist is lack of job satisfaction—killing the President of Paraguay with a fork just isn't the kick it might once have been—and the fact that he still pines for his high school sweetheart, whom he stood up without explanation on their long-ago prom night. Since she is played by the divine Minnie Driver—now working as a disk jockey but still smitten, it turns out, and still warily available—his feelings are understandable.

But Martin is also a hunted man, mostly by Dan Aykroyd's Grocer, a goofily rational rival determined either to bring him into a hired killers' union that he is intent on forming or, failing that, to off the competition. Curiously enough, Grocer and his henchmen blend quite easily into the suburban scene. Grosse Pointe may have grander homes and less snow than, say, Fargo, but spiritually they are sister cities—places where everyone tries to maintain an air of chipper blandness in the face of postmodernism's disorder.

People there pop pills to raise their depressed spirits. They cover their paranoia with clenched-jaw politesse. They don't quite understand Martin's dismay when he discovers that his boyhood home has been replaced by a convenience store—where the clerk gets so lost in a noisy video game that he fails to notice a real-life gun battle breaking out in his aisles. Therein lies this movie's fundamental irony: anarchy may bloom from Martin's gun barrel, but unlike his old pals, he is not in denial about it. He is still trying to nurture the shoots of old-fashioned squareness that remain rooted in his soul.

Cusack is one comically cool dude, and the movie, which he and some of his high school pals helped write, is directed with sly sobriety by George Armitage. For once, a big studio has apparently let some smart people run free, and the result is as fresh, funny and acute as any Sundance winner. See, guys, you can do it; you just have to loosen the reins a little.

VILLAGE VOICE, 4/22/97, p. 77, Michael Atkinson

Agreed, there was little reason to hope that a Disney-released, Gen-X blabbermouth comedy about the redemption of a baby-faced hitman wouldn't lay flat on your plate like sour ham, but *Grosse Pointe Blank* cooks, in a full pot and at high boil, fully justifying the faith we dubiously kept in director George Armitage during the years since the reckless and cruel *Miami Blues*. Still, much of the credit must go to star producer John Cusack who also happens to be this intensely clever movie's largest speed bump—however much he may be a master at dry line deliveries, who can buy this guy as a slick 28-year-old hired assassin? Casually burping up more sarcastic dialogue, throwaway laugh lines, idiosyncratic story gags and hilarious fringe perfs than any other '90s studio movie, *Grosse Pointe Blank* moves (and talks) so fast your doubts are swallowed whole in the first 10 minutes.

The story does read preciously: Cusack is Martin Blank, a smooth gunman who hesitantly returns to Grosse Pointe, Michigan, for his 10-year high school reunion, and therein falls in again with his old girlfriend (Minnie Driver). Cusack & Co. wrote the shit out of this caper, but Armitage's touch is downright Hawksian. He even makes Dan Aykroyd (as a rival mercenary) look good for the first time since the doing-Tom Snyder days; Alan Arkin and Jeremy Piven are so concisely hilarious they even steal scenes they're not in. Negotiating queasily between domestic pratfall and pragmatic gunplay ("I know I can make this relationship work," Cusack blurts sincerely, spattered with blood), Armitage's screwball drollery may be an unmarketable nightmare for Disney, but it's the kind of movie Hollywood would regularly produce in an ideal world.

Also reviewed in:
NEW REPUBLIC, 5/12/97, p. 26, Stanley Kauffmann
NEW YORK TIMES, 4/11/97, p. C8, Janet Maslin
NEW YORKER, 4/21/97, p. 97, Terrence Rafferty
VARIETY, 3/31-4/6/97, p. 85, Leonard Klady
WASHINGTON POST, 4/11/97, Weekend/p. 42, Desson Howe

GUANTANAMERA

A Cinepix Film Properties release of an Icaic/Tornasol Films/Alta Films/Prime Films/Road Movies coproduction. *Executive Producer:* Camilo Vives. *Producer:* Gerardo Herrero. *Director:* Tomás Gutiérrez Alea and Juan Carlos Tabío. *Screenplay (Spanish with English subtitles):* Eliseo Alberto Diego, Tomás Gutiérrez Alea, and Juan Carlos Tabio. *Director of Photography:* Hans Burmann. *Editor:* Carmen Frias. *Music:* José Nieto. *Sound:* Raul Garcia. *Production Designer:* Frank Cabrera. *Art Director:* Onelia Larraide. *Running time:* 101 minutes. *MPAA Rating:* Not Rated.

CAST: Carlos Cruz (Adolfo); Mirtha Ibarra (Georgina); Raúl Eguren (Candido); Jorge Perugorria (Mariano); Suset Pérez Malberti (Iku); Pedro Fernandez (Ramon); Luis Alberto Garcia (Tony); Conchita Brando (Aunt Yoyita).

LOS ANGELES TIMES, 8/1/97, Calendar/p. 12, Kevin Thomas

"Guantanamera!" is a screen valedictory most filmmakers would envy, a funny and poignant comedy unfolding on a trouble-plagued journey from Guantanamo to Havana. The film is a heartfelt expression of a love of life and a brave acceptance not only of the inevitability but the necessity of death.

With his health failing, Cuba's leading director, the late Tomás Gutiérrez Alea, collaborated with Juan Carlos Tabío, an esteemed writer and director in his own right, on two final films, this one and "Strawberry and Chocolate."

Both show a Cuba beset by poverty and hardship, an economic system breaking down before our eyes. Yet at the same time, both films celebrate the Cuban people in their warmth, humor and resilience and both abound with a love of Cuba.

Gutiérrez Alea, who died last year after a long battle with lung cancer, first made his mark in world cinema with his 1968 masterpiece, "Memories of Underdevelopment." It was a penetrating study of a handsome upper-middle-class man, not unlike Gutiérrez Alea himself, who makes a last-minute decision not to flee with his family to Miami when Castro takes power and instead stays to see what the Communist future holds for him.

An early idealistic Castro supporter and a founding member of Cuba's respected Cinematographic Art and Industry Institute, Gutiérrez Alea expressed in his films his attempts to embrace Marxism and his increasing disenchantment with its consequences.

"Guantanamera!," accompanied by the famous song on the soundtrack, involves a journey, one of the most ancient metaphors for the passage of life that, on-screen, has yielded such classic movies as John Ford's "Stagecoach" and Ingmar Bergman's "Wild Strawberries."

In "Guantanamera!," Carlos Cruz plays Adólfo, a government bureaucrat who has lost his standing. He sees a chance to regain it with a cumbersome gas-saving, cost-cutting scheme that would require that a hearse be stopped at every town along the way to a burial destination to have its casket transferred into a local hearse (thus no given city would use more than its gas ration). When someone close to Adódlfo dies, he finds himself at the mercy of the time-consuming system he has devised.

So many stops allow for much to happen, most significantly the continual crossing of paths of Adólfo's wife, Gina (Mirtha Ibarra), and one of her former students, Mariano (Jorge Perugorria).

A respected and outspoken economics professor, Gina has given up her career in sheer frustration over the state of Cuba and her sense of powerlessness to do anything about it and has resigned herself, more or less, to be a dutiful, traditional Latina wife.

Mariano, who was smitten by his elegant professor and even once sent her a love letter (she was flattered but didn't respond), is stunned to see her again.

A truck driver, Mariano regularly travels between Guantanamo and Havana with his partner, Ramon (Pedro Ferndández), and is used to having casual sex along the way. But the handsome, husky Mariano is confronted with the emptiness of his life when he encounters Gina for the first time in several years.

A woman in her 40s, Gina is beautiful but worn; seeing Ramon again has made her look and feel young again. A family friend, Cándido (Raúl Eguren), traveling with Adólfo and Gina, warns her that he let his own life become "smaller and smaller." Gina sees a way out with Mariano, but will she take it?

Meanwhile, Adólfo becomes increasingly exasperated with the constant transferring of the casket from hearse to hearse.

Gutiérrez Alea and Tabío recall Jean Renoir in their ability to embrace people in their love of nature and with all their flaws. Crucial to "Guantanamera!'s", impact is that the filmmakers are able to view Adólfo, despite his insensitivity and self-absorption, with compassion.

They're able to see him as a man who has struggled to play by the rules, even if those rules are unjust and ineffective, and as one who is struggling to avoid being crushed by them. Thus, Cruz is able to make the not very sympathetic Adólfo quite human.

Ibarra, Gutiérrez Alea's wife of 22 years and his frequent leading lady, and Perugorría make Gina and Mariano as irresistible as the characters they played so unforgettably in "Strawberry and Chocolate." Perugorría created in the earlier film one of the most memorable gay characters in world cinema, a man who might be effeminate and at times flamboyant but is of staunch character and principles. Here, Perugorría plays a rugged guy whose macho looks and behavior mask considerable sensitivity.

Ibarra played Perugorría's next-door neighbor, an endearing former prostitute of much vulnerability. In "Guantanamera!," Ibarra is portraying a woman of dignity and superior intelligence forced to admit that her life is drying up on her.

We've met many Ginas and Marianos in films before this, but the direction, the writing and the acting combine to make them seem extraordinary here. What's more, the rest of the cast and their roles are up to the standards of the film's stars.

Funny, rueful, infinitely moving, "Guantanamera!" does not take its leave without a lovely touch of magic realism. And Gutiérrez Alea has taken leave of us with a film that has a quality of abundance—of wit, affection and wisdom—that so often seems to have all but vanished from the screen.

NEW YORK POST, 7/25/97, p. 48, Thelma Adams

A stubborn bureaucrat. A lonely wife. A randy truck driver. A broken-hearted musician. A beautiful corpse. All are traveling from "Guantanamera" to Havana.

"Guantanamera" is the bittersweet social comedy from Juan Carlos Tabio and the late Tomas Gutierrez Alea. During their previous collaboration, "Strawberry and Chocolate," Gutierrez Alea learned he had cancer. "Guantanamera" is his swan song, the culmination of a half-century of filmmaking that included the unforgettable "Memories of Underdevelopment."

"Guantanamera" treats one of Gutierrez Alea's central themes: the indomitable Cuban spirit, bent but not broken by Castro's dystopia. It is a film as lovely, graceful and down-to-earth as its star, Mirtha Ibarra, Gutierrez Alea's widow.

Ibarra played the suicidal neighbor in "Strawberry and Chocolate." Here, she's Georgina, the wife of the bureaucrat Adolfo (Carlos Cruz). Their marriage is the island's political situation writ small: his tyrannical small-mindedness crushes her spirit.

A former economics professor, Georgina dutifully accepts a union in which passion, if it ever existed, is dead. She's abandoned her personal dreams and ambitions. Georgina embodies a common theme: the individual versus the collective. As in "Strawberry and Chocolate," which treated the Cuban government's repression of homosexuals, the individual wins a small triumph without dismantling the collective.

Events get kicked into gear when Georgina's aunt (Conchita Brando), a famous singer, returns to Guantanamera after 50 years. Almost immediately, she dies in the arms of her long-lost love, Candido (Raul Eguren).

When Georgina and Candido try to accompany the corpse to Havana for burial, they become tangled in Adolfo's plot to resurrect his failing political career. He's engineered a nutty money-saving scheme for transporting bodies across country lines: a Pony Express with hearses and cadavers.

The death and funeral cortege give Gutierrez Alea and Tabio, working from a script they wrote with Eliseo Alberto Diego, a running start on a road movie. Along the way, we get a guided tour of Cuba's interior. The villages are in ruins. The radio DJ reports productivity gains, but food is scarce. Dollars are the currency of choice. Cuba is a Third World country, a ruined beauty.

The black comedy is tempered by optimism. A woman gives birth. A studly trucker rescues Georgina from her loveless marriage. The bureaucrat is humbled and ignored. Death and birth are a snake joined head to tail; the individual spirit thrives whatever the political climate.

With his final, beautiful film, Gutierrez Alea, supported by his family of artists, was a man at death's door who opened the window of his heart to life. His legacy is the clearest answer to Adolfo's question: "If everybody starts doing what they feel like, where will it end?"

VILLAGE VOICE, 7/29/97, p. 71, Laurie Stone

The Cuba of *Guantanamera*, Tomás Gutiérrez Alea's final, genial film, is a dusty bone gnawed by toothless bureaucrats. There are no lawyers, guns, or money—nor food at the cafés, nor public transportation. Clustered at roadsides, people fling themselves onto passing trucks. Beneath the dried-up riverbed of the revolution flows a black market of ingenuity. Garlic and bananas suddenly appear, sold for dollars not pesos, and the savvy know about tavernas that serve roast pork. This unorganized, serendipitous culture is a libidinous current pulsing through the unstrung society. And sex itself—private experience with its lick of rebellion—gets people though the frustrating, lazy afternoon of their existence.

A sweet patience rises off Alea's compatriots, a people fettered but not fooled. The little moments in which they're revealed, seemingly in the background, deliver the movie's power, as well as Alea's means of contrasting careful observation with the plans hatched by blinkered apparatchiks. One of them, Adolfo (Carlos Cruz), still reveres party politics; he's also a prig and a bully. And he's the piñata that will be unstuffed as his tamped-down wife Georgina (Mirtha Ibarra) makes a break for love with Mariano (Jorge Perugorria), a former college student of hers. A comical road movie, *Guantanamera* shows love blossoming as Mariano, now a trucker, tries to evade women along his route, and Georgiana commandeered into her husband's grandiose plans to bury a corpse, is clued to life's brevity by the nearness of death. The movie is like an asthmatic jalopy that takes a while to got cranked but hums once it's rolling.

Also reviewed in:
CHICAGO TRIBUNE, 11/28/97, Friday/p. A, Achy Obejas
NATION, 8/25-9/1/97, p. 48, Stuart Klawans
NEW REPUBLIC, 7/28/97, p. 26, Stanley Kauffmann
NEW YORK TIMES, 7/25/97, p. C12, Stephen Holden
VARIETY, 9/18-24/95, p. 100, David Stratton
WASHINGTON POST, 8/8/97, Weekend/p. 33, Jane Horwitz

GUMMO

A Fine Line Features release of an Independent Pictures production of a Harmony Korine Film. *Producer:* Cary Woods. *Director:* Harmony Korine. *Screenplay:* Harmony Korine. *Director of Photography:* Jean-Yves Escoffier. *Editor:* Christopher Tellefsen. *Music:* Randall Poster. *Sound:* Brian Miksis. *Sound Editor:* Melissa Zaroff. *Casting:* Nicole Hennessey. *Art Director:* Amy Beth Silver. *Pyrotechnics:* Mike Weisner. *Costumes:* Chloe Sevigny. *Make-up:* Mia Thoen. *Animal Coordinator:* Ernie Karpeles. *Running time:* 95 minutes. *MPAA Rating:* R.

CAST: Jacob Sewell (Bunny Boy); Nick Sutton (Tummler); Lara Tosh (Girl in Car); Jacob Reynolds (Solomon); Darby Dougherty (Darby); Chloe Sevigny (Dot); Carisa Bara (Helen); Jason Guzak and Casey Guzak (Skinheads); Wendall Carr (Hantz); James Lawhorn and James Glass (Cowboys); Ellen M. Smith (Ellen); Charles Matthew Coatney (Eddie); Harmony Korine (Boy on Couch); Bryant L. Crenshaw (Midget); Daniel Martin (Jarrod); Nathan Rutherford (Karl); Max Perlich (Cole); Bernadette Resha (Cassiday); Linda Manz (Solomon's Mother); Donna Brewster (Albino Woman); James David Glass (Tummler's Father); Mark Gonzales (Chair Wrestler); Berniece N. Duvall (Grandmother); Kristi Faye Randolph (Deaf Woman); William Dickinson (Deaf Man); Bill Evans (Bald Guy); Jeffrey Baker (Terry); James Baker (Phelipo); Rose Shephard (Woman in Bed).

FILM QUARTERLY, Winter 1998-9, p. 42, Felicia Feaster

Breathtaking and creepy, Harmony Korine's *Gummo* is one of the few truly risk-taking independent films of recent years. The debut film from the 23-year-old Korine, *Gummo* offers the kind of nasty truthfulness more often seen in the esoteric, documentarian work of British photographer Richard Billingham's images of his alcoholic, ruined family members, Jim Goldberg's journalistic portraits of homeless teens captured in a photography exhibit and book, *Raised By Wolves,* or the devastating child-murder documentary *Paradise Lost.* Korine's population of the film with friends from his own Nashville upbringing lends a further verité element which grounds *Gummo* in a personal documentary tradition in keeping with the autobiographical photography of his benefactor Larry Clark, Billingham, Nan Goldin and their progenitor, Diane Arbus.

Gummo opens with distorted video footage of a stretch of Hell known as Xenia, Ohio devastated as if by demonic or angelic intervention by a vengeful tornado, a catatonic child's voice narrating the destruction like some fairy tale waif. By the film's end, one can appreciate—even invite—the twisted worldview that could support both Satan worship and the religious belief in the righteousness of a tornado wiping this sorry place off the face of the Earth.

Gummo's is a world depopulated of grown-ups. Their very absence is attested to in the blank generation they have spawned. Hanging out on concrete slab front porches, shooting cats full of BBs, sniffing glue, sustaining themselves with meals of corndogs and milkshakes, *Gummo*'s monstrous, tragic children play in the shade of their diseased family trees. Having fun, getting high, wasting time, their rage and desperation to express or get affection comes out warped into sadism or self-abuse, their pleasures greedily horded with animalistic intensity.

Korine made his breakthrough into film by writing photographer Larry Clark's *Kids,* but Korine is already years ahead of his guru. An intuitive, self-taught filmmaker, Korine bucks the current tradition of Scorsese and Tarantino-indoctrinated film grads who recycle ad infinitum the road films and caper violence of an addled modern imagination. Instead, Korine uniquely envisions the ugliness and pain of a subculture of abandoned kids; skinheads, deviants, perverts, sluts, victims all, with sickening accuracy and a sympathetic delicacy *Kids* never achieved. *Gummo*'s children are free agents. A condition once romanticized in the verdant, unencumbered child's paradise of *Huckleberry Finn*, in *Gummo* such freedom has lapsed into all unromantic parental abandonment of children to Satanic cults and junkyards and sexual abuse.

Korine shows how every perversion in *Gummo,* like the older boy (Max Perlich) who pimps his retarded sister to best pals Solomon (Jacob Reynolds) and Tummler (Nick Sutton), is relativized by environment. With no standards to measure sociopathy next to where adults are drunkards, rapists, pornographers, jailbirds, mad—these kids become, by process of elimination, the prophets and heroes. In *Gummo*'s wire-crossed circuitry of powerlines, child molesters, cancer and retardation, Korine weaves a nightmare fairy tale of a poisoned world eating up its inhabitants from the guts out. The trampy teenage sisters Dot (Chloe Sevigny) and Helen (Carisa Bara), who shave their eyebrows and strip their hair of color, suggest little girl sexuality defined by exposure to porn and incest, and sexual imaginations steeped in artifice, pain and fetishism. The boys and even grown men of *Gummo* operate within the same twisted notion of gender roles. Masculinity in *Gummo* is unnaturally brutal, whether seen in the gladiatorial men fighting a kitchen dinette set in one of the film's most disturbing and amusing moments, or in the angry, vicious homoerotic love expressed between two wrestling skinhead brothers.

Every aspect of *Gummo* feels polluted, from the boy who dresses in nothing but shorts and pink rabbit ears (Jacob Sewell) to the budding serial killers—yet another caricature of masculine aggression—who play-torture Bunny Boy. Everything is permissible, Korine shrugs, the most grotesque psychological damage worn as silly costume. And the most disturbing element of *Gummo* may be the impression it gives, that Korine didn't have to coax such brutal vignettes from his "actors"—that what he's done in this spellbinding film is capture the reality of his white trash roots in a new form. Korine has capped the mason-jar lid on these raging, helpless moths so we can watch their struggles behind the clouded glass. Using found footage, a verité style mixed with unnervingly distorted imagery, Korine employs technique as Francis Bacon's paint evoked tissue and blood, as yet another indication of his thematic sickness. Blurring out characters' faces or fluttering hysterically around them like a swarming insect, Korine slices the world up, making its people into monsters so that the only truth can seem fleeting and dreamlike: Did it happen, or did we just dream it after a huffing binge? Typical of *Gummo's* fog of chemically and genetically distorted minds, is a vignette of a sad-eyed little girl playing in the mud, as her voice-over narration recounts her molestation at the hands of her stepfather. *Gummo* is a toxic swamp of such lacerating truth and the erratic behavior, tics, sadism, rage that distorts it into a dreamy, fuzzy unreality. This impression of a nightmare wrapped in the trappings of a children's fairy tale powerfully conveys Korine's view—that as much as its children beat against the glass, they are unable to escape, trapped within the viciousness and horrors their parents have visited upon them.

Korine's technique is a skin-crawling and electric assault on the eyes and brain, which disorients as much as the vignette-based, non-linear format of *Gummo,* alighting on one character, only to jump to another, and shattering filmic time and space in a disorienting way. The largely negative response to *Gummo,* trickled down from *The New York Times* reviewer Janet Maslin's definitively repulsed reaction, suggests an objection to style equally balanced by objections to *Gummo's* disturbing subject matter. Maslin's effusive, hysterical pronouncement of Clark's *Kids* "a wakeup call to the world," typifies how its more traditional narrative approach, adult perspective and the faux-moralizing of Clark's AIDS warning is more palpable to audiences. Korine refuses to sift out such moral lessons from *Gummo's* chaos.

As Gus Van Sant noted of the film's unusual vantage, *Gummo* is "made by a young person speaking through a sophisticated and refined cinematic dialogue of modern cultural influences." What's more, Korine's failure to latch this story onto one character's consistent viewpoint alienates and fractures our response to the film, a unique strategy for conveying the disorienting, centerless amorality of the world he documents. To center a film on one protagonist is to buy into a classical Hollywood schemata invested in America's self-identity; of heroism, of objectives ultimately rewarded, of authority, which it is Korine's goal to shatter. These children grow up in a world with no such heroes, no parents, no authority, and to yoke a film to such a concept would therefore be disingenuous.

In an *Interview* magazine discussion with the filmmaker, Werner Herzog likens *Gummo* to a science fiction film; "a scary vision of the future: a loss of soul, a loss of spirituality." *Gummo* offers a poisoned glimpse of the Apocalypse, of a world where a decayed moral center allows incest, violence, self-abuse and neglect to flourish. The essence of this psychological deterioration is reflected in the clutter of these characters' homes and their yards where objects are horded into piles of filthy debris, and children are thrown away. The small instances of tenderness between Solomon and his alcoholic mother (Linda Manz) thus occur in a claustrophobic house whose clutter squashes such frail expressions of love. By the same token, a scene of a little boy lifting a picture from his living room wall to uncover a colony of roaches and the insect bites which pock his legs somehow speak more profoundly for the familial cesspool which is illustrated more clearly in his zoned-out mother sniffing glue on their couch.

Korine's casting decisions in *Gummo* capitalize on this atmosphere of disorder, his characters gleaned from the authentic flotsam of a diseased consumer culture. Paint sniffer Nick Sutton captured Korine's imagination on an episode of the Sally Jesse Raphael show titled with the tabloid screech "My Child Died From Sniffing Paint," and found his titular star Jacob Reynolds in a Dunkin Donuts commercial.

Where *Gummo* stumbles is in its literalization of Xenia's freakishness: a black midget, a deaf couple arguing in sign language, a horny albino girl, who become overly symbolic signposts leading to Korine's assertion that this viciously constricted, impoverished town has made its occupants in vitro victims of its moral contamination, pickled in the sins of their parents. In a world where degradation is commonplace, Korine suggests such evil is tangible, like some poison leached into the soil to deform the locales, or literalized as a vengeful tornado which erases sin with a mythic fury.

LOS ANGELES TIMES, 10/17/97, Calendar/p. 6, John Anderson

[The following review by John Anderson appeared in a slightly different form in **NEWSDAY, 10/17/97, Part II/p. B13.]**

Snapshots: A rough tryst in an old wrecked car. A dead cat who "looks like my mom." Young girls practicing to be strippers. A bare-chested kid wearing pink rabbit ears. A dog impaled on a rooftop antenna.

This is the tourist brochure to the tornado-ravaged world of Harmony Korine's Xenia, Ohio, a town as bereft of hope as Dante's ninth circle and a soulless cancer ward of glue-sniffing, drunkenness, child abuse and animal torture. A place where all these exposures of full-frontal ugliness will somehow coalesce into ... something unified and enlightening? We hope, we wait. To no avail.

Korine, the 23-year-old onetime wunderkind who wrote the screenplay to Larry Clark's "Kids," has been given his own movie to direct. That in itself may be disturbing, but what he has produced is as unsettling and irritating a work as we're likely to see this year.

The reasons aren't all on the screen; many more of them have to do with how and why movies get made, why no one smells disaster until a film gets finished, and how we've gotten to the point where so much depends upon the marketing of smug decadence and spiritual bankruptcy. And "Kids" was a primer compared with "Gummo."

Clark's film, which was largely a voyeuristic indulgence on the part of its director, portrayed a New York City stratum of hedonistic, vacant and sexually predatory teenagers, a sort of diseased "Peanuts" where no adults existed and no overriding conscience ruled. However vaguely implied, there was still a hint of, or wish for, soul.

"Gummo" is a series of exercises in gross-out humor and outright depravity, all of which are nothing but what they say they are: postcards from hell. Korine isn't editorializing. This isn't agitprop cinema. It's button-pushing, pure and simple, made on the cynical assumption that the only way to get our attention is to make a mess.

And so, it's merely childish. "Look at me!" Korine says. And that's it. Just "Look at me!" We look, and to keep our attention, he pushes his two main characters—Solomon (Jacob Reynolds), whose face looks as if it's being reflected in a doorknob, and Tummler (Nick Sutton), whose haircut alone qualifies him as a charter member of White Trash Nation—a little further into the abyss. Of course, in a film where everything is stripped of meaning, the abyss is, too.

There are moments in "Gummo" that are pure hilarity and others that are frighteningly real. Linda Manz, featured 20 years ago in Terrence Malick's "Days of Heaven," plays Solomon's mom and does a tap-dancing tribute to her late husband that's too odd not to be infectious. A scene in which a bunch of shirtless local drunks break up a kitchen is so angry and unstable you almost hope it's documentary, because questions of how and why it was staged become a bit too troubling.

The film is being positioned commercially as a movie for teenagers—and knowing how well pointlessness plays these days, they may respond. If nothing else, "Gummo" does challenge perceptions and presumptions: Is the perspective of youth in this country really so devoid of significance, and their existence so septic? These are good questions, although "Gummo" provides neither answer nor solution, or even thematic cohesion.

When Tod Browning made "Freaks" back in 1932, the point was that community exists even among the most Godforsaken of creatures. With "Gummo," divinity isn't even part of the equation.

NEW YORK, 11/3/97, p. 52, David Denby

In *Gummo*, the shock avant-garde feature directed by young Harmony Korine, a group of people (generically, white trash) stand around in a messy suburban split-level house and watch a grown man destroy a kitchen chair. He smashes it, bangs it, butts and elbows it. He just destroys the damn chair. But why does he do this? We have no idea. We have seen some of these people before, the men with lank hair and tattoos, the women frizzed, wearing sweaters and jeans; we have seen them drinking beer and arm-wrestling, but they don't figure prominently in the movie, which, in any case, has no plot and only a few recurring characters. Nor is there anything earlier in the movie that would lead us to believe that the destruction of the chair has a particular social meaning—that the scene is an attack on, say, consumerism, or on sitcoms set in perfect kitchens, or on Martha Stewart, or on anything else. The man smashing a chair is simply a man smashing a chair.

What's going on here? I think it's obvious that Harmony Korine, the screenwriter of *Kids*, recently profiled in these pages as a snarling little show-off ["Dis Harmony," by Richard Regen, October 20], knows what he is doing. That is, Korine, who is 23, knows perfectly well that the kind of people *Gummo* is about will never see it. He knows as well that the only possible audience for it—the educated urban bourgeoisie and their hip, art-loving children—cannot be shocked, in movies, by eroticism, violence, or death. That is what they always see in movies, and for Korine, that stuff is mere commercial cliché, phony and dead. The only thing this audience can be shocked by is disorder. *Gummo* has been fueled by an aesthetic of ugliness and by youthful contempt that is meant to needle an audience expecting its art to be beautiful or "powerful"—or just to make sense. *Gummo* is hell to sit through; it's boring and redundant, a series of mock outrages, some of which want so badly to be revolting (two kids shooting a catatonic old woman in the foot) that one can only laugh at the thoroughness of the effort.

So why write about *Gummo*? After all, Harmony Korine has no more than a glimmer of talent. *Gummo* is worth writing about because it's an instructive artifact of the late twentieth century—an example of extreme disgust with the media that expresses itself in the media. (Where else could it express itself? Korine longs to be noticed.) Korine wants to blow up the MTV-advertising world of perfect, chic imagery and fluent salesmanship. He wants to cleanse, to burn, to destroy. If only he knew how to do it! There may be some trace here of Diane Arbus's photographs of freaks and giants, but in its bleak nihilism, *Gummo* is inadvertently closer to those "reality TV" programs in which a cop bursts into a trailer and arrests someone while a baby sits bawling on the floor surrounded by junk. It is beyond redemption.

A prologue of sorts acquaints us with a tornado in Xenia, Ohio, in 1970, and presumably what follows is a portrait of a tornado-shocked community. But this prologue, it turns out, is just an excuse for Korine to show off the kind of rubbly world he's comfortable in. Indeed, anyone taking *Gummo* as a serious essay on social breakdown should be sent to a home for retired liberals. *Gummo*, it turns out, was shot not in Ohio but in Korine's hometown, outside Nashville. With the help of a famous cinematographer (Jean Yves Escoffier) and a few professional actors (Linda Manz and Max Perlich), he persuaded a lot of his childhood friends and neighbors to do ridiculous things and to trash themselves.

The movie is composed of rough and discontinuous vignettes—dejected little home movies, or fake cinéma-vérité scenes of poverty and squalor. Women with thick calves sit around on porches bad-mouthing their neighbors; little boys wander about and attack one another; girls do odd things to their nipples and slowly lick their lips for the camera—the movie has some of the pimply teen carnality of *Kids*. It is all dank, affectless, bedraggled, and photographed without pity or outrage. Nor does Korine spare himself. He turns up as a messy little drunk making homosexual advances to an embarrassed old friend, an encephalitic black dwarf. The levels of exploitation in that scene are too sick to contemplate.

The only semblance of purposeful activity is the efforts of two skanky teens, Tummler (Nick Sutton) and his diminutive sidekick, Solomon (Jacob Reynolds), to kill as many cats as they can. They drown them and shoot them, then sell them to a butcher for money to buy glue to sniff. America, your cats are dying! Korine wants to frighten us with brat nihilism. In this context, the most startling thing in the movie is an interview with an elderly woman in a parking lot who says she had a cat once, and it died, and she misses it—an oddly humane touch. Most of the rest—the fatties, the dwarf, the prostitute sitting in bed and servicing the little teens—is just carnival theater. Harmony Korine is too arrogant to understand that it's much harder to tell a story coherently than it is to string together a series of meaningless "cruel" vignettes. But that's a mistake that can be put down to youth. What can't be forgiven is the habit of aestheticizing the poverty and troubles of helpless people.

Yet Harmony Korine must be granted half a victory: He won the Critics' Prize at the recent Venice Film Festival, and he won another kind of critic's prize in New York when Janet Maslin, in the *Times*, called *Gummo* "the worst movie of the year." That, of course, is an enormous distinction, one that a 23-year-old can dine out on for months. Korine may not have much talent for filmmaking, but he knows how to play his elders. In *The New Yorker*, Kurt Andersen, trying to put spin on spin after interviewing Korine, compared the filmmaker to Arthur Rimbaud (then withdrew the comparison) and teased the idea that *Gummo* was a revolutionary work of art and that anyone who didn't like it was an aging hypocritical yuppie. Korine spun the spinning Andersen as if he were an empty top.

NEW YORK POST, 10/17/97, p. 48, V. A. Musetto

"Gummo" plays like a red-neck "Kids." which is no surprise, since it's written and directed by Harmony Korine, the 23-year-old skateboarder who helped pen the controversial "Kids" for Larry Clark.

Opening today at the Angelika, "Gummo" is no less provocative.

Using 35mm and grainy video, as well as a cast of mostly nonprofessionals (Chloe Sevigny of "Kids" is one of the exceptions), the plotless "Gummo" portrays life in backwards Xenia, Ohio.

It's the kind of burg where "fun" means killing cats and selling them to a meat supplier for a buck a pound ("Wanna be paid by the cat or the pound?" the butcher asks first), pulling the respirator plug on a comatose old lady, offering your Down's syndrome sister for prostitution, or just plain sniffing glue.

Most wonderful moment: a deaf couple arguing in sign language at a bowling alley.

Most disgusting: a kid eating spaghetti in a bathtub full of vile, filthy water. It could turn you off to baths and/or Italian food for life.

Both perversely funny and disturbingly sad, Korine's directorial debut is welcome at a time when too many filmmakers go out of their way to make bland, cookie-cutter movies designed to offend absolutely nobody.

In the usual hyperbole of movie ads, "Gummo" is touted as "the most original film of the decade!" That it definitely isn't (the work of sadly unknown Canadian helmer Guy Maddin comes immediately to mind).

But like a kid acting up for attention, the wise-ass Korine wants desperately to be in your face—to offend and provoke. And he does a damn good job getting his way. If for no other reason, Korine deserves our thanks and "Gummo" deserves to be seen.

SIGHT AND SOUND, 4/98, p. 38, Gavin Smith

Two youths, Tummler and Solomon, ride their bicycles around the town of Xena, Ohio, searching for stray cats to kill and then sell to a local supermarket owner. Teenage girls Dot and Helen use electrical tape to enhance their nipple size. Tummler and Solomon sniff glue in the woods. Dot and Helen watch their friend Eddie practise tennis and he tells them about his Attention Deficit Disorder. A boy talks to a midget on a couch; another wanders around town wearing a rabbit-ear hat.

Tummler and Solomon pay a visit to their competition in the cat-hunting trade and then go to a prostitute. Solomon's mother chances on him working out in the basement and shows him her tap-dance moves. Tummler writes in his diary and then later visits friends who amuse themselves by arm-wrestling and destroying a chair. Tummler and Solomon break into a friend's house, discover photos of him wearing women's clothes and switch off his comatose grand-mother's respirator. Dot and Helen search for their lost cat and are nearly molested by a man who claims to know where the cat is. Solomon bathes and his mother serves him spaghetti and a candy bar on a tray in the bath. We last see Tummler and Solomon standing in the rain shooting their 'BB' guns at a dead cat.

On the face of it, Gummo's director Harmony Korine, the precocious co-screenwriter of photographer of Clark's kids, has transposed the How It Is aesthetic and lurid, teenage-wasteland ethnography of Clark's remarkable New York-based film to white-trash Middle America. In the process, however, he has discarded the narrative and stylistic overdetermination of kids in favour of a hallucinatory, displaced tone. Gummo has a sketchy, unstructured episodic drift, and relaxes even further than kids any sense of a larger social order to which his juvenile milieu is answerable.

In the film's prologue, protagonist Solomon recalls a tornado that recently devastated the town, and which serves as the film's historical ground zero. This catastrophe in a sense dictates not only the film's traumatised and jumbled form but more importantly its moral ruptures, and the otherwise inexplicable absence of all but a few adults and all forms of social authority: "It killed the people left and right ... a lot of people's fathers died ... I saw a girl fly through the sky and I looked up her skirt. School was smashed ..." With all authority and social restraint swept away by an act of God, Korine's kids live in a world where all transgression seems permitted and unchallenged.

The narrative, such as it is, follows the wandering misadventures of a teenager, Tummler, and his pre-pubescent sidekick Solomon (nominally hunting and killing stray cats for money), intermittently shifting focus to tag along with a secondary duo of teenage girls, and more peripherally, the wanderings of an even more aimless skateboarder wearing a pink rabbit-ear hat. This scripted material is interpolated with improvised scenes. These function as crude but often compelling anthropological showcases for Korine's 'found' subjects—people enlisted on location to perform as 'themselves'. The film's fragmented collage effect is completed by the incorporation of artfully crude home-video footage that presents Korine's nonactors in an even more informal register. Some of the video footage is teasingly accompanied by Solomon's intoning, whispered voice-over, unmistakably imitative of Sadie Benning's PixelVision video journals. But Korine refrains from resolving the video footage into a fictive subjectivity—an indication of the director's shrewd flair for the purposeful incoherence that characterises the film's formal derangement and which he has described as "mistake-ist".

Korine's predilection for improbable associations and the coexistence of incompatible opposites suggests a strategy of paradox, contradiction and studied perversity. Hence the film's ostensibly poignant closing rendition of 'Jesus Loves Me' by two women is immediately followed by a black metal song with satanic associations. The soundtrack of contemporary heavy-metal songs is pointedly at odds with numerous on-screen T-shirts featuring passé early 80s metal groups. In one of the film's more memorable scenes, Solomon pauses while taking a bath to eat spaghetti and a fudge bar simultaneously. On several occasions, characters reveal unmotivated and unlikely talents for public performance: in a complete break of character, Tummler delivers a Jimmy Durante vaudeville routine for the amusement of a man who rents out his wife's sexual services. Solomon's mother performs an impromptu tap dance. And at a convivial redneck get-together featuring an arm-wrestling contest, one character performs a kitchen chair-wrestling routine for an appreciative group of onlookers until one of the rednecks intervenes and pulverises the chair. All three instances partly reflect Korine's transparently too-cool-for school gambit of investing his characters with the fashionably unfashionable trappings of underground or obsolete pop culture, the more surely to establish their marginality—and the authority of his subculture connoisseurship. (The film's title, a reference to Gummo Marx, one of the lesser-known Marx brothers, also invokes vaudeville.)

But Tummler's and Solomon' s mother's routines are also manifestations of the film's wider impulse to cancel or problematise distinctions between character and performer. Hence the familiar neo-realist strategy of using mostly non-actors playing versions of themselves. But for all the film's documents mannerisms and aspirations to the *sui generis* realism of Werner Herzog, its uniformly affectless cast are unapologetically selected for their bizarre appearance or physical deficiencies (an albino woman, a black midget, a deaf couple) and manoeuvred into situations which seem chiefly rigged to yield the maximum sensationalism or grotesqueness. It is this which has left Korine open to entirely understandable but unprovable accusations of exploitation on a par with that of tabloid television talk shows. While Korine insists his film is a celebration of the dispossessed, fashioned to honour the dignity of his performers, others may just as readily see an affront to the predicaments of the powerless and unfortunate.

Besides, such humanist compassion scarcely seems compatible with the film's matter-of-fact nihilism. It is hard to discern the dignity revealed by an apparently retarded girl's cheerleader routine and incoherent anecdote. And Korine's own inconsequential cameo, a drunken monologue of supposed self-exposure culminating with him pouring a drink over his own head and attempting to kiss the midget sitting beside him, seems a half-hearted contrivance to disarm potential criticism by substantiating his identification with his performers and demonstrating a willingness to look just as foolish. Even the film's most spectacular or poignant incidents, such as the chair-wrestling episode, teeter on the brink of travesty, and indeed, this is part of the film's considerable aesthetic value.

If on one level *Gummo* represents a high watermark of 90s White Trash Chic, on another its resurrection and flagrant deforming of the neo-realist impulse harbours a longing to invent a Cinema of Abjection. In this project, Korine is far from alone. It may be that he derives his inspiration from the early 90s 'abject art' trend extolled by such artists as Mike Kelley. (Closer to home, young British artist Richard Billingham's *Ray's a Laugh* photo series has much in common with *Gummo*.) Korine shares his strategy of recruiting performers from the socially disenfranchised with Canadian videomaker Donigan Cumming, whose troubling and cryptic *A*

Prayer for Nettie and *Cut the Parrot* feature a non-actor repertory company of the moribund, the sick and the grotesque. The best instances of this nascent Cinema of Abjection to date are Russian film-maker Kira Muratova's *The Asthenic Syndrome* (1990) and Hungarian Bela Tarr's extraordinary eight hour *Satantango* (1994); its worst would be Russian film-maker Artur Aristakisian's *Palms (Ladoni)* (1994), which mobilises Christian mysticism to sanctify the homeless beggars and cripples of Moldavia. Lacking the philosophical resources or clear, detached vision of these films, however, *Gummo* is ultimately stranded between a fearless, uncompromised commitment to its material and a refusal to interpret otherness/outsideness on the one hand and a naive, idealising search for authenticity in abjection and a self defeating Fuck You Cinema attitude on the other.

VILLAGE VOICE, 10/21/97, p. 96, Amy Taubin

Gummo is the first feature directed by Harmony Korine, the fabulously talented 23-year-old who wrote the screenplay for Clark's *Kids*. When *Gummo* is good, it illuminates what it's like to grow up in a sub-cultural scrap heap as nothing else quite has before. When it's bad, it makes me want to do to Korine what his two adolescent protagonists do to the cats they sell to the local butcher for a dollar a pound: shoot him, toss him in a vat of filthy water, string him up and beat him to a pulp, et cetera, et cetera.

Set in the rust-belt suburb of Xenia, Ohio, *Gummo* opens with a vertiginous jumble of images that summon up the tornado that decimated the town some time in the not-so-distant past. On the soundtrack, a disembodied voice describes the ghastly event. "A lot of people's fathers were killed ... my neighbor was killed. They never found his head. I always thought that was funny." Just in case you missed that this violent natural catastrophe is *Gummo*'s myth of origin, Korine also mixes in a child's singsong invocation of that place from which we all come: "My mother has a pussy ... a li'l tiny PUSSY ..."

Like *Kids*, *Gummo* follows the perambulations of a pair of asocial teenage boys, Solomon and Tummler. The resemblance stops there. Where *Kids*'s spare, arrow-straight plot line is motored by its antihero's permanent hard-on, *Gummo*'s course is more meandering. So meandering, in fact, that it results in a film that's less a narrative than a collection of portraits, vaudeville routines, and shaggy-dog stories. What's most remarkable about *Gummo* is its uncompromising depiction of the random sequencing and fractured time lines of teenage daily life. There are no driving desires, and hardly any acknowledgment of causality—just a low-level curiosity and a taste for scavenging for bad jokes, cheap drugs, and nasty sex.

In fact, the only governing principle in *Gummo* is pastiche. Korine mixes low-grade video with 35mm, ethnographic investigations with outlandishly stagey skits, professional actors with kids off the block. The film doesn't lack for memorable sequences: a skinny, fragile-faced boy clad only in bicycle shorts and long pink rabbit ears shivering on a highway overpass; a trio of dazzling bottle blonds (the stunningly composed Chloe Sevigny among them) achieving instant breast augmentation by applying electrical tape to their nipples.

But too often Korine's penchant for giant whoppers and surrealist gimmicks short-circuits what's original and moving in his work. Jacob Reynolds, who plays Solomon, has one of the most strangely proportioned faces in the history of cinema. It's a face that calls all definitions of beauty into question. Why mock his looks by shooting him through an anamorphic lens? And what's a black dwarf flaunting an "Israel" T-shirt doing at a party of white-trash ex-cons? Moreover, the filmmaker's squeamishness about "mommy's pussy" results in some truly grotesque images of women.

Korine tries to ward off potential charges of exploitation by including himself in his film, acting as freakish as anyone else. It doesn't wash. Korine isn't a freak. He isn't stuck in the rubbish heaps of Xenia, Ohio. He's a young filmmaker of considerable power and authority. And the only thing that could stop him from maturing as an artist is his reluctance to examine his relationship with the others he puts on the screen.

Its wise-ass shriek notwithstanding, *Gummo* takes more risks with form and content than any American indie film in years. Think of it as the avant-garde *Boogie Nights*, born out of a similar love for subcultural detritus, but refusing to conform to industry standards. Gummo was, after all, the Marx brother who bowed out when the others went legit.

Also reviewed in:
CHICAGO TRIBUNE, 3/6/98, p. G, Mark Caro
NEW YORK TIMES, 10/17/97, p. E12, Janet Maslin
VARIETY, 9/8-14/97, p. 80, Emanuel Levy

HABIT

A Glass Eye Pix release in association with Passport Cinemas. *Producer:* Dayton Taylor. *Director:* Larry Fessenden. *Screenplay:* Larry Fessenden. *Director of Photography:* Frank DeMarco. *Editor:* Larry Fessenden. *Music:* Geoffrey Kidde. *Sound:* Bill Chesley. *Art Director:* John Arlotto. *Costumes:* Loren Bevans. *Running time:* 112 minutes. *MPAA Rating:* Not Rated.

CAST: Larry Fessenden (Sam); Meredith Snaider (Anna); Aron Beall (Nick); Patricia Coleman (Rae); Heather Woodbury (Liza); Jesse Hartman (Lenny).

LOS ANGELES TIMES, 10/29/97, Calendar/p. 2, Kenneth Turan

If an attractive member of the opposite sex with "kind of a timeless quality" came on to you at a hip New York party, would you wonder if this was one of the undead or just be pleasantly surprised? If the best sex of your life resulted, how much would it matter if you started feeling weaker and began noticing what look suspiciously like bite marks on your body? Would you assume the worst or just think your tired mind was playing odd little tricks on you?

Larry Fessenden's impressive "Habit" takes a great deal of pleasure in ambiguously playing around with the vampire tradition. It allows viewers to experience these dilemmas in the same way the protagonist does, gradually but surely imprisoning us and him in an obsessive situation from which escape may not be possible or even desired.

An adroit arty/spooky example of what's come to be known as no-budget filmmaking (projects under $200,000), "Habit" helped win Fessenden—who wrote and edited the film along with starring and directing—last year's Someone to Watch Award from Swatch and the Independent Feature Project.

Though his work has rarely surfaced in theaters, Fessenden has been making films for more than a decade, and his experience shows in how confidently he and cinematographer Frank DeMarco create an air of haunted and unsettling menace out of the rather pedestrian streets of Lower Manhattan.

Sam (Fessenden) is a heavy-drinking restaurant manager, a guy known among his friends for getting wasted early and often. A shambling and feckless wastrel who's never bothered to replace a front tooth lost in a mugging, Sam thinks he's hipness personified, but in fact he's just another lonely boy in the big city, more of a psychological soft touch than he can imagine.

Having just lost his father and opted for a trial separation from his artist girlfriend Liza (Heather Woodbury), Sam is at greater loose ends than usual when Anna (Meredith Snaider) seems to materialize in front of him at a Halloween party. There's an immediate connection between them, but Sam is too drunk to effectively capitalize on it, and as hard as he tries once he sobers up, he can't find her.

Then, just when he's given up hope, Anna finds him at a Little Italy street fair, holding out two Ferris wheel tickets and offering "the ride of your life." They have an intense sexual encounter that very night, and when Sam wakes up alone in Battery Park the next morning, there is a prominent wound on his lower lip.

The pattern of that voraciously physical first encounter becomes the norm for this relationship. Appearing unexpectedly, Anna teases Sam into having sex in unlikely public places, even in a hospital morgue, while steadfastly refusing to reveal anything about herself "The less you know about me, the longer you'll be interested," she tells him. "Men like to fall in love, not stay in love."

While his friends ineffectually worry about how strung out he's looking and how physically wrecked he's become, Sam, completely intoxicated with Anna, doesn't care to hear it. The question "Habit" asks is not so much can he escape Anna's influence, but does he even want to.

Though many of the performances in "Habit" mark time at best, Snaider makes a powerful impression in her film debut as the direct, soft-spoken, preternaturally composed Anna. Her assured, attractive characterization is the critical element in the film's success, and she manages to be so genuinely otherworldly you start to wonder if she only worked after dark.

Part of the spooky fun of "Habit" is noticing how Fessenden has discreetly sprinkled traditional vampire film paraphernalia throughout his story. We catch glimpses of a derelict ship and a pack of wolves, a Van Helsing-type character makes a brief appearance, and Anna is troubled by the smell of garlic.

Some of these elements pay off in expected ways, some do not, but all fit with a satisfying smoothness into a '90s urban environment. Imagining you're seeing the undead all around once you leave the theater is a hazard of watching "Habit." You might even be right.

NEW YORK POST, 11/14/97, p. 50, Larry Worth

So what's the connection between indie filmmakers and vampire movies? More important, why are all the end results so anemic?

In the wake of ill-fated, low-budget productions like Abel Ferrara's "The Addiction" and Michael Almereyda's "Nadja" comes the even more dismal "Habit," a virtual one-man show from Larry Fessenden—who directed, wrote, edited and stars as the alcoholic hero.

The problem is that Fessenden's vision far exceeds his talents: Direction is sluggish, his writing labored, editing disjointed and acting amateurish. Need one, say more?

NEWSDAY, 11/14/97, Part II/p. B13, John Anderson

If it had been made in Hollywood for $25 million, pundits would be touting the urbanely macabre "Habit" as the Wellesian tour de force of the '90s. Given that it was made in New York for a little less than $200,000, in little more than a month, we'll just have to call it amazing.

Erotically charged and infused with dread, "Habit" is set in New York's version of Transylvania (the East Village), where Sam (Larry Fessenden), a part-time bar manager and full-time alcoholic, is on the express train to oblivion. His father has recently died anal it pains him; his romance with Liza (Heather Woodbury) has deteriorated. Although she loves him, she's leaving Sam anyway.

These relationships aren't particularly clear-cut; neither is Sam's battle with himself—not at first, anyway. Over the course of the film, history asserts itself, but Fessenden refuses to dump his characters' stories in our laps. He lets them leech out, the way they would naturally. He startles us with visual asides, odd angles and eerie visages—his intermittent cutaways to a ship in New York harbor evoke the vampires' journey in "Dracula"; the sound of a ferris wheel in Little Italy, whose joint-creaking clangor sounds like cracking bone, augments the Manhattan Gothic texture that "Habit" creates.

It's at a Halloween party thrown by his friends Nick (Aaron Beall) and Rae (Patricia Coleman) that Sam, drunk and vaguely destructive, meets Anna (Meredith Snaider). Sly and physically suggestive, she makes an unqualified sexual overture and they hit the streets, where she promptly disappears. But she'll be. back, with increasing frequency. And appetite.

In linking Sam and Anna's furious sexual coupling with Anna's need to tap Sam's corpuscles, Fessenden is following a bloody tradition, running from Bram Stoker to Federico Garcia Lorca to Tod Browning to Francis Ford Coppola, that draws out of the vampire legend not just its metaphorical content but its vein of profoundly predatory sexuality. But Sam is also draining off his own life through alcohol. And never does it strike him that a drink-sodden bar manager with fewer teeth than possibilities might not have a lot to offer a woman as sophisticated as Anna. Unless it was a high platelet count.

Ego is always one part of the vampire story; how else would one justify living forever? Force of personality is another; in any relationship, the legend implies, one partner feeds while the other drains. It's a very modern myth that suggests drugs and AIDS and has been explored in recent years by Abel Ferrara in "The Addiction" and Michael Almareyda in "Nadja." Fessenden's version, in which the monster intrudes upon a thoroughly convincing contemporary world, is the most convincing of all.

And this makes "Habit," which Fessenden wrote, directed and edited, a scary film. "Habit" was selected Best Film at the '96 Long Island Film Festival. Good choice, because filmmaking, clearly, in is his blood.

VILLAGE VOICE, 11/18/97, p. 85, Amy Taubin

Even if you've had it with vampires, you might be unmoored by *Habit*, a Dostoyevskian East Village romance between an alcoholic restaurant manager with a penchant for slicing up his arms at parties and a mysterious woman who may or may not be drinking his blood.

Written by, directed by, and starring Larry Fessenden (winner of the 1997 Independent Feature Project's "Someone To Watch" award), Habit is a quintessentially New York film—as paranoid a portrait of the city as *Rosemary's Baby* or *Taxi Driver*. Not particularly scary while you're sitting there, it packs its power punch after it's over, altering your perception of familiar streets and seemingly ordinary people, alerting you to the vampire within and without.

It's Halloween, and Sam (Fessenden) is on the street chatting up an intense woman he's just met at a party. Sam is compelling, though a bit too burnt out to be attractive. A runty Jack Nicholson look-alike with stringy hair and tired skin, he's wearing a papier-mâché Pinocchio nose and a white ostrich plume pinned rakishly to the back of his head. The defiantly phallic effect is midway between comic and creepy (one could say the same thing about the film as a whole). As Sam sways drunkenly, the handheld camera is forced to make tiny adjustments to keep him in the frame. The movements are small enough to pass unnoticed, but there's no doubt that they have a cumulative kinetic effect. It's this camera strategy, as much the narrative, that leaves you feeling at the end of *Habit* as if the rug has been pulled out from under you. Which is to say that Fessenden is a real filmmaker, not just a guy with a personal story to tell about alcoholism, abandonment, castration anxiety, and other such nifty things.

Having recently lost his father and broken up with his girlfriend, and with his drinking habit out of control, Sam is in bad shape. Vulnerable and adrift, he plunges into an affair with Anna (Meredith Snaider), the mystery woman whose sexual aggression balances his extreme passivity. But soon he begins to feel as if she's draining the life out of him. "I think you've been having very unsafe sex" answers a practical-minded friend when Sam wonders whether Anna's biting habit, not to mention her abstinence from food and drink might be evidence of vampirism. But whether Anna's powers are supernatural or merely projections of Sam's alcohol-damaged psyche, the effect is the same. Sam is desperate to escape from Anna, even if they both have to die in the process.

Shot and edited with great sophistication, *Habit* (which cost a mere $190,000) has a caught-on-the-fly, oversaturated look that's perfectly suited to its unkempt, hobo milieu. Fessenden (who was the best thing in Kelly Reichardt's *River of Grass)* is at least as talented an actor as he is a filmmaker. His Sam is a mix of gallows humor and raw emotion, driven by guilt and a perverse exhibitionism, the goal of which is to look as repellent as possible. Whatever you make of *Habit*, a film that begs for interpretation, it's anything but a vanity production.

Also reviewed in:
NEW YORK TIMES, 11/14/97, p. E33, Lawrence Van Gelder
VARIETY, 4/29-5/5/96, p. 135, Joe Leydon

HAMSUN

A First Run Features release. *Executive Producer:* Lars Kolvig. *Producer:* Erik Crone. *Director:* Jan Troell. *Screenplay (Swedish, Danish, Norwegian, and German with English subtitles):* Per Olov Enquist. *Based on the book "Processen mod Hamsun":* Thorkild Hansen. *Director of Photography:* Jan Troell. *Editor:* Ghita Beckendorff and Jan Troell. *Music:* Arvo Pärt, Johann Strauss, and Richard Wagner. *Running time:* 160 minutes. *MPAA Rating:* Not Rated.

CAST: Max von Sydow (Knut Hamsun); Ghita Norby (Marie Hamsun); Anette Hoff (Ellinor Hamsun); Asa Soderling (Cecilia Hamsun); Gard B. Eidsvold (Arild Hamsun); Eindride Eidsvold (Tore Hamsun); Ernst Jacobi (Adolf Hitler); Erik Hivju (Psychiatrist).

LOS ANGELES TIMES, 11/21/97, Calendar/p. 16, Kevin Thomas

A little girl approaches a tall, distinguished-looking old man, throws a book at him and, saying her mother told her to, asks, "Why did you become a traitor?" In his remarkably compelling 160-minute "Hamsun," veteran Swedish writer-director Jan Troell succeeds stunningly in making us understand how Norwegian novelist and poet Knut Hamsun, winner of the 1920 Nobel Prize for literature, came to be one of the few major European artists to support Hitler.

As Hamsun, Max von Sydow crowns a long, distinguished and richly varied career with arguably his greatest portrayal of a literary lion in winter, a great, tragically naive writer coming to terms with his failures as a man and as a patriot as he copes with encroaching age.

The epic scale comes naturally to Troell, long one of Sweden's finest filmmakers and best known for "The Emigrants" and its sequel, "The New Land." The saga of Hamsun, whom the king of Norway proclaimed was his country's very soul, demands such scope, even though Hamsun is already 76 when we meet him in 1935. It is a darkening period for Hamsun, suffering from a loss of self-respect over his long-term writer's block, as well as for all of Europe.

Marie (formidable Ghita Norby, grande dame of Norway's actresses), his 22-years-younger wife of nearly 30 years, lashes out at him in her despair for having made her give up her career as an actress, for banishing their four children from his presence as soon as they disturbed the peace he demanded as a writer and, above all, for failing to live up to the ideals he proclaimed in his work.

Their marriage has deteriorated to the point that Hamsun leaves his immense country manor house to go off to live in an inn in Oslo for a year. What brings the Hamsuns to the point of a wary truce is their common admiration for Adolf Hitler.

The impassioned speeches of Norwegian Nazi leader Vikun Quisling stressing idealism, family solidarity and respect and opportunity for women enthrall Marie, whose several books for children have been popular in Germany.

(During World War II even youngsters knew "quisling" as an expression meaning "traitor.") Hamsun loathes the imperialism of the British and buys into Hitler's promise that Norway will have a more prominent role to play in the new world order.

Marie swiftly becomes an all-out Nazi convert and her facility in German, a language her increasingly deaf husband does not speak, causes her to speak for him, often in terms more strongly than he actually believes or states. No wonder Hamsun's longtime publisher remarks in dismay to a colleague in regard to his client, "To think that the Germans have such a magic flute at their disposal."

It's only when the German Army of Occupation starts turning Norway "into a blood bath." to borrow the description Hamsun uses in a humiliating visit to Hitler to plead to the Führer to stop destroying Norway, that Hamsun begins to grasp the specter of Nazi evil. With the end of World War II Hamsun commences the final, most dramatic chapter of his life.

When you consider the countless movies that sail by without a thought in mind it is amazing what "Hamsun" accomplishes.

It is above all a cautionary tale about the artist isolating himself from the world and from his family at great peril. It is a love story at its most tempestuous and agonized. It is a World War II picture told from an unusual and provocative perspective, and as such, a splendid period piece. It is a haunting portrait of valiant old age.

As formal in style as von Sydow's Hamsun is, it is work of profound psychological insight, grasping firmly the conflicting motives and emotions of the human heart. "Hamsun" is easily one of the year's finest films.

NEW YORK POST, 8/6/97, p. 37, Thelma Adams

Max von Sydow, Knut Hamsun; Swedish actor, Norwegian novelist. They're two great tastes that go great together in "Hamsun"—but they make a heavy meal.

Hamsun lived from 1859 to 1952, long enough to receive a Nobel Prize for his 1917 novel "Growth of the Soil" and to become a "magic flute" for the cause of national socialism as Hitler swept Europe.

While the staunchly anti-British author—near deaf and past 80—remained in his study, penning support for Hitler and a free Norway, his wife traveled Germany, delivering public readings of Hamsun's novels.

Jan Troell ("The Emigrants"), working from Per Olov Enquist's screenplay, tries to explain the author's motives for supporting the losing team in the crucial conflict of the 20th century, while also dissecting the Hamsun family saga.

According to "Hamsun," Marie, an actress 20 years her husband's junior, found her greatest role as Hamsun's wife. As Hamsun's ability to function in public withered with his hearing, she became his mouthpiece.

When the movie opens, in the 1930s, the couple's marriage is unraveling. The unfulfilled Marie (Ghita Norby) blames the self-obsessed *artiste* for her lost dreams; their four grown children suffer to varying degrees from his neglect.

Marie finds an outlet for her pent-up acting ambitions and feminist yearnings in the Nazi cause. Danish star Norby ("The Kingdom") brings warmth and vulnerability to a Lady MacHamsun part. Norby's Marie must bear a heavy load for a movie that is as much an apologia for the great man as the author was an apologist for Hitler.

The film's shortcomings are few, but critical. "Hamsun," which spans the final decades of the author's life and straddles World War II, never gains the piercing emotional resonance of Ingmar Bergman (who Troell consciously imitates) as it vibrates from fact-based historical drama to intimate family saga. Its multiple climaxes flatten into melodrama and it takes nearly as long to die as the author himself.

For all that, von Sydow delivers a towering performance. He is among the world's greatest living actors. His artist, Nazi sympathizer, father, husband, patriot and traitor is unforgettable—even for those who don't know Knut from Newt.

NEWSDAY, 8/6/97, Part II/p. B5, John Anderson

Behind every misguided Norwegian Nobel Prize-winning Nazi sympathizer is an unhappy woman, yoked to an insensitive husband and a culture that doesn't appreciate her. Such is the case in "Hamsun," the story of Knut Hamsun the author/icon whose support of the Nazi occupation of his country has made his name synonymous with betrayal—and his wife, Marie, whose motives may have been far more base but are much more understandable.

How much one knows about either Norway's plight during World War II, or Knut Hamsun himself—who ranks second only to Quisling (he makes an appearance here, too) among Scandinavian scoundrels—will color one's perception of the film; except for allowing his esteem to be co-opted by fascist invaders, Hamsun seems to have done very little for the German cause. But this isn't a war story. It's an examination of deeply complex characters. And with seductively understated and ultimately transporting performances, Max von Sydow and Ghita Norby make those characters very real. And disturbing.

Directed by Jan Troell—whose "The Emigrants" of 1972 is one of only five foreign films ever nominated for a Best Picture Oscar—"Hamsun" opens in 1935, and with a marriage as volatile as Europe itself. Knut, who won his Nobel in 1920 and hasn't written much since, is an increasingly deaf, ever-irascible egoist whose bad temper and self-absorption have left his family in emotional ruins. Marie, whose career as an actress and children's book writer was derailed early on by Knut, seethes over missed opportunities, the adulation of her husband and the resentments of her children (including the alcoholic Ellinor, smartly played by Anette Hoff). Their verbal battles are massive, the venom potent.

It is words, ironically, that betray Knut Hamsun. Although he is perceived by his countrymen as "the soul of Norway"—a writer—whose pioneering modernist works ("Hunger," "The Growth of the Soil") gave Norwegian literature global stature—his hatred of the British (for their "arrogance") and his theories of ethnic unities push him toward Hitler's camp. But when he tries to backpedal, his intentions are often distorted—either by the manipulating Nazis, or by his wife, who, when it suits her purposes, mistranslates her husband's speeches. Hamsun, for all his Teutonic empathy, has never bothered to learn German.

And so Knut, the literary artist, is rendered mute. During a misbegotten meeting with Hitler (Ernst Jacobi) he can't communicate; a speech before Berlin journalists, in which he pleads for Norway, is translated into a "kill the Brits" tirade. Within this Norwegian-Danish-Swedish-German coproduction is something pronouncedly Greek. Shot by Troell himself, "Hamsun" has a rich look. The story follows its subject through his postwar disgrace, confinement in a mental hospital (where Troell draws not-too-subtle parallels between the totalitarianism of psychiatry and the fascism of the Germans) and his trial, which Norway didn't want but Hamsun demanded. It's a quixotic mission, his search for redemption, one that never quite comes off. But "Hamsun" accomplishes something meaningful, making us face the uncomfortable humanity in the most discomfiting of humans.

VILLAGE VOICE, 8/12/97, p. 67, Elliott Stein

No fluffy summer movie this. Swedish director Jon Troell's solemn, nearly three-hour biopic focuses on the last two decades of the life of the controversial Norwegian author Knut Humsun. Its time frame extends from the mid 1930s, when the Nobel laureate's fascination with Hitler was becoming an obsession, to his trial for treason after World War II. He had not only sided with the Nazis, but when Norway was invaded, had urged his countrymen to lay down their arms and welcome the occupying German forces.

Hamsun is a rambling affair, remarkable only for Max von Sydow's authoritative, finely controlled performance in the title role. Winning even a modicum of sympathy for such a customer is no easy task. Von Sydow is up to it. He lights up the screen, particularly in two memorable vignettes of isolation and pain: the old man fussing with his appearance, essaying a show of sartorial dignity on the way to his trial, and in the film's key scene, realizing for the first time the full horrendousness of what he has condoned when he's shown footage of the death camps.

A disproportionate amount of the movie is taken up by the stormy relationship of Hamsun and his wife, Marie (the veteran Danish actress Ghita Norby). By demonizing Marie, presenting her as a harping Hitler groupie, Troell appears to let Hamsun off the hook a tad easily, blurring the question of why one of Norway's greatest figures turned traitor.

Hamsun's work—its extraordinary lyric pantheism—has been especially admired, by other writers. His disciples include as diverse a lot as Henry Miller, Thomas Mann, Arthur Schnitzler, and Isaac Bashevis Singer. Troell's film conveys next to nothing about the originality of that significant oeuvre.

Also reviewed in:
NEW REPUBLIC, 5/19/97, p. 26, Stanley Kauffmann
NEW YORK TIMES, 8/6/97, p. C15, Stephen Holden
VARIETY, 4/22-28/96, p. 90, Gunnar Rehlin

HAPPY TOGETHER

A Kino International release of a Jet Tone Productions and Block 2 Pictures Inc. production in association with Prenom H. Co., Ltd. and Seowoo Film Co., Ltd. *Executive Producer:* Chan Ye-Cheng. *Producer:* Wong Kar-Wei. *Director:* Wong Kar-Wai. *Screenplay (Cantonese, Mandarin and Spanish with English subtitles):* Wong Kar-Wai. *Director of Photography:* Christopher Doyle. *Editor:* William Chang Suk-Ping and Wong Ming-Lam. *Music:* Danny Chung. *Sound:* Leung Chi-tat and Tu Duu-chih. *Production Designer:* William Chang Suk-Ping. *Running time:* 93 minutes. *MPAA Rating:* Not Rated.

CAST: Tony Leung Chiu-Wai (Lai Yiu-Fai); Leslie Cheung (Ho Po-Wing);   Chang Chen (Chang).

LOS ANGELES TIMES, 10/31/97, Calendar/p. 9, Kevin Thomas

The title of Wong Kar-Wai's wrenching, jagged "Happy Together," taken from the popular song, is decidedly ironic. Shot alternately in high-contrast black and white and rich color, it has a harsh charcoal-sketch look in either mode as it charts the coming apart of a gay love affair.

Photographed by Wong's usual collaborator, the award-winning Christopher Doyle, "Happy Together" is as fragmented in style as the relationship it depicts with relentless emotional honesty. The result is a take-no-prisoners movie from one of Hong Kong's most idiosyncratic, shoot-from-the-hip filmmakers that's the very antithesis of sentimental gay love stories. Don't say you weren't warned.

It opens with a helicopter shot of Iguazu Falls, along Argentina's border with Brazil, but Lai Yiu-Fai (Tony Leung Chiu-Wai-so designated to avoid confusion with the other, taller Tony Leung) and Ho Po-Wing (Leslie Cheung) never make it there together.

They've been in Buenos Aires for a time, seeking new experiences and hoping that flight from Hong Kong will revitalize their relationship. But it's clearly crumbling long before they're hit with car trouble on the highway to the falls, which according to legend is a place in which to dump your emotional problems.

Lai is the stable one. He's willing to take a series of menial jobs—doorman at a tango bar, dishwasher at a Chinese restaurant, slaughterhouse worker—but luxury-loving Ho takes to the streets as a hustler, undermining their affair. The lovers have already split up bitterly when Ho turns up badly beaten.

Lai takes him to his tiny room, the acme of picturesque squalor, and lovingly nurses Ho back to health. But Ho is too much the playboy, too much the wastrel, for the steady, loving Lai to accept. As Lai digs in, dealing with his loneliness and survival in Buenos Aires, Ho commences a familiar downward spiral.

But it's Wong's inspired touch to allow us to see Lai in a different light when he perversely, selfishly—pointlessly—refuses to give Ho his passport, even though he ultimately wants to return home to Hong Kong just as badly as Ho does. Ho may be foolish, even worthless, but for all his otherwise admirable character traits, Lai is finally small-minded and lacking in imagination in this petty, dangerous gesture. The exile experience in "Happy Together" heightens the sense of alienation and isolation felt by both Lai and Ho.

Tony Leung Chiu-Wai and Leslie Cheung are Hong Kong superstars of remarkable range and versatility. Wong has placed the utmost demands upon them, and they in turn make this harrowing, disintegrating relationship seem absolutely authentic. Chang Chen plays a likable, friendly young restaurant co-worker who Lai comes to realize is straight—much to his disappointment.

Wong, who took the best director prize at Cannes this year for "Happy Together," doesn't push it, but the tango certainly does serve as the perfect metaphor for Lai and Ho's relationship, with their good looks, fiery mutual attraction and constant struggle for dominance. Surely, countless young gay male couples will recognize themselves in Lai and Ho.

TIME, 10/27/97, p. 111, Richard Corliss

As the major (virtually the only) maker of art films in rampantly commercial Hong Kong, Wong Kar-wai is a goad and a threat to his competitors. He releases a movie—say, the 1990 *Days of Being Wild*—and they release a parody, *Days of Being Dumb*. He uses a pensive voice-over narration in *Chungking Express*; soon every Hong Kong film hero is talking to himself. He wins the Best Director prize at this May's Cannes festival for *Happy Together*, and within three months there's a movie *(Those Were the Days)* about a prizewinning director sent back to the '60s as punishment for never having made a popular picture.

It's tough being the object of all this scornful veneration—so tough that Wong left town, went to the opposite side of the world and made a movie about gay men stranded in Argentina. Yet *Happy Together* is also a twist on a familiar Hong Kong genre: the Heroic Bloodshed films of John Woo. Instead of making war, Ho (Leslie Cheung) and Lai (Tony Leung Chiu-wai) make love as war. They arouse and annoy each other, fall out of love and back in. When the two aren't arguing, they are folding into each other for shelter from the storm within. The film is full of pathetic hugs and sweet cuddles; the lovers share cigarettes, tango dances, sponge baths and one fabulous kiss in the kitchen. They make each other miserable, yet they are also groping toward the unlikely ideal of being happy together.

With its Kodachrome oranges and petrochemical sunsets, *Happy Together* looks as if it had been printed on ancient nitrate stock about to catch fire, like the loins of its heroes. Wong's U.S. career could do the same when audiences discover this this sexy, spiky love story.

VILLAGE VOICE, 10/21/97, p. 85, J. Hoberman

The old Hong Kong is no more, but, after a half-dozen years as a legend of the Chinatown/midnight/festival circuit, hyperromatitic HK action aesthete Wong Kar-Wai is edging toward mainstream consciousness. His last two features—the garish and melancholy *Fallen Angels* and its relatively subdued follow-up *Happy Together*—were featured in the 1997 New York Film Festival and both are scheduled for commercial release.

Happy Together is both a bravura love story and an attitudinous buddy film. Acerbic, moody, and provocatively slight, it's a movie of apparent non sequiturs and privileged moments. Daring himself to miss the Crown Colony's last days, Wong went on location to Argentina and, together with his longtime cinematographer Chris Doyle, reimagined Buenos Aires as something like the Chinese equivalent of 1920s expatriate Paris—with outermost Patagonia standing in for the edge of the world.

Set mainly in a nocturnal city of vague specifics and visceral details, *Happy Together* posits a love affair between two major Hong Kong stars, Tony Leung and Leslie Cheung, both reborn from Wong's *Ashes of Time*. There's no particular explanation for how the guys wound up stranded in Buenos Aires; suffice to say they're a long way from home. Where Leung (last seen here as the poet-pimp in *Cyclo)* is serious, introverted, and responsible, baby-faced Cheung (most recently Gong Li's gigolo nemesis in *Temptress Moon)* plays his spontaneously heedless opposite.

Wong needs only one or two setups to get sex out of the way—catching the stars' lovemaking as it is reflected in the dirty mirror of a seedy hotel room—before settling down for a voluptuous immersion in the couple's emotional detritus. A shocker by HK standards, *Happy Together* makes explicit the homoerotic content of the male-bonding bloodbaths that have characterized the post-John Woo Hong Kong action film. (On the other hand, in Cannes, where *Happy Together* won Wong a prize for best direction, the movie was given the politically suggestive subtitle *A Story About a Reunion.)*

After their breakup (for no real reason) en route to the fabulous Iguazu Falls—the film's equivalent of the Holy Grail—Leung finds work in Buenos Aires steering tourists to a tango bar while Cheung drifts into hustling. They patch things up (unhappy together) while Cheung recovers from some trick-inflicted injuries and Leung washes dishes in a Chinese restaurant. Leung is initially unwilling to start over but his attempt to hold Cheung backfires. The two split once more, for a prolonged period of loneliness—complete with a frenetic cruising sequence shot vérité-style from a moving car. Working nights in an abattoir, Leung haunts public toilets and porn theaters as the urban nocturne yields a quick flash of the Hong Kong skyline, filmed upside down on the other side of the globe.

A long, jagged still life, replete with landscape and documentary inserts, *Happy Together* swoons in and out of scorched color. The movie was shot, as Wong tends to work, off the cuff. Albeit less densely edited than *Fallen Angels, Happy Together* has the narrative fragmentation of early Godard. (The lengthy scene in which Leung cares for Cheung in his impossibly narrow digs all but quotes the epic room service that took up perhaps a quarter of *Breathless.)* just as Wong's new wave sword flick *Ashes of Time* was more extravagantly mournful than violent, so *Happy Together* saves most of its passion for regret. As the solitary Leung finally contemplates Iguazu Falls, the same mist that sprays his face clouds Cheung's eyes back in Buenos Aires.

Wong's romanticism has always drawn sustenance from rock 'n' roll. While offering ample Astor Piazzolla (and even some Frank Zappa), *Happy Together* sets its last pixilated cityscape to the eponymous Turtles anthem; it's less a distended rock video than the feature-length prolegomenon to a pop song. If this is the most cosmopolitan of Wong's films, it is also the most provincial. The movie goes around the world to find the perfect look-back vantage point.

In the end, homesick Leung arrives in Taiwan just in time to catch the televised news of Deng Xiaoping's death. Loss mixes with relief. It's the cosmonauts return. Leung boards a driverless train on the notorious new Taipei subway. China rules ... in more ways than one.

Also reviewed in:
NEW YORK TIMES, 10/10/97, p. E10, Stephen Holden
VARIETY, 5/19-25/97, p. 50, Derek Elley

HARD EIGHT

A Rysher Entertainment release of a Green Parrot production in association with Trinity. *Executive Producer:* Keith Samples, Hans Brockmann, and Francois Duplat. *Producer:* Robert Jones and John Lyons. *Director:* Paul Thomas Anderson. *Screenplay:* Paul Thomas Anderson. *Director of Photography:* Robert Elswit. *Editor:* Barbara Tulliver. *Music:* Michael Penn and Jon Brion. *Sound:* Mark Deren and (music) Lois Foraker. *Sound Editor:* Jeffrey R. Paine. *Casting:* Christine Sheaks. *Production Designer:* Nancy Deren. *Art Director:* Michael Krantz. *Set Decorator:* David A. Koneff. *Set Dresser:* Martin Milligan and Lloyd Brown. *Special Effects:* Lou Carlucci. *Costumes:* Mark Bridges. *Make-up:* Lydia Milars and Alyson Murphy. *Stunt Coordinator:* Cliff Cudney. *Running time:* 101 minutes. *MPAA Rating:* R.

CAST: Philip Baker Hall (Sydney); John C. Reilly (John); Gwyneth Paltrow (Clementine); Samuel L. Jackson (Jimmy); F. William Parker (Hostage); Phillip Seymour Hoffman (Young Craps Player); Nathanael Cooper (Restroom Attendant); Wynn White (Waitress); Robert Ridgely (Keno Bar Manager); Kathleen Campbell (Keno Girl); Michael J. Rowe (Pitt Boss); Peter D'Allessandro (Bartender); Steve Blane (Stickman); Xaleese (Cocktail Waitress); Melora Walters (Jimmy's Girl); Jean Langer (Cashier); Andy Breen (Groom); Renee Breen (Bride); Jane W. Brimmer (Aladdin Cashier); Mark Finizza (Desk Clerk); Richard Gross (Floorman); Cliff Keeley (Aladdin Change Booth Attendant); Carrie McVey (El Dorado Cashier); Pastor Truman Robbins (Pastor); Ernie Anderson, Wendy Weidman, and Jason "Jake" Cross (Pants on Fire People).

LOS ANGELES TIMES, 2/28/97, Calendar/p. 2, John Anderson

[The following review by John Anderson appeared in a slightly different form in **NEWSDAY, 2/28/97, Part II/p. B9.]**

For some actors, the perfect role comes early, makes them stars, occasionally makes them headaches. For others—Philip Baker Hall, for instance—it arrives after years of being a well-known face unconnected to a name, an actor on the edges of the spotlight and perhaps waiting for and ripening into his ideal character.

For Hall, the role is Sydney, an aging, gentlemanly gambler with the heart of—is it really gold?—who's the main fascination of Paul Thomas Anderson's "Hard Eight."

The title, we noncrapshooters learn, refers obliquely to an eight rolled with a four on each of the dice. Courteous, chivalrous, neatly if not well-dressed, Sydney may be a sucker for betting the hard eight but he's also a survivor, an intelligent professional who dwells on the edge of legitimacy, surrounded by what basically is the scum of the earth. Gambling, we gather, is the flaw that keeps him from being a great man—and keeps him a tragic masterpiece. Anderson, making modern film noir á la John Dahl ("The Last Seduction"), gives us a mystery, then wraps him in an enigma.

Why would the obviously crafty and cultured Sydney virtually adopt the destitute and uninspiring John (John C. Reilly) off the front steps of a Nevada dinner, teach him the tricks of his trade, steer him toward a romance with full-time casino waitress/part-time hooker Clementine

(Gwyneth Paltrow, in her best role yet) and try to protect him from the clearly malevolent Jimmy (Samuel L. Jackson)? We hunger to know.

And at the same time we don't. Anderson, who makes as impressive a directing debut as has been seen in some time, creates a perfectly modulated mystery that doesn't even feel like one. It's a character play, and Hall, Reilly and Paltrow are so convincingly damaged they take on the properties of fine china. A wrong move, and we're all goners. That Anderson gets himself, and us, out of this predicament with only the slightest shattering of sensibility is a sign of enormous talent.

With some terrific hand-held camera work by Robert Elswit, Anderson also finds unexplored territory in the over-filmed milieu of Nevada's casino-land. It's sympathetic cinematography: Sydney views Reno as his workplace, not an amusement park. Through such eyes, all that tawdry splendor becomes not just garish but trite.

It's far too early to be talking about the year's best this and the year's best that, but if "Hard Eight" is forgotten when the awards start flying around at the end of '97, it'll be a shame. As well as a mystery.

NEW YORK POST, 2/28/97, p. 44, Michael Medved

"Hard Eight" focuses on the odd, intense relationship between a stone-faced, sleekly groomed, tightly controlled professional gambler named Sydney (Philip Baker Hall) and a blubbering goofball (John C. Reilly) young enough to be his son.

They meet one morning when the unwashed, shivering kid crouches at the door of a Reno, Nev., coffee shop, desperate to find enough money to pay for his mother's funeral.

Sydney takes pity on him, providing cigarettes and coffee and helping him get the cash he needs by playing games of chance at the casinos.

The story then shifts to two years later, with the once hopeless kid looking prosperous and confident, striding between hotels and gaming tables while slavishly following the guidance of his grim but indulgent mentor and father figure.

Unfortunately, he also strikes up a friendship with a loud-mouthed hustler and part-time security guard (Samuel L. Jackson) whose risky braggadocio undermines Sydney's a stabilizing influence.

Their connection is also complicated by a pathetically dim-witted but sexy cocktail waitress and part-time hooker (played with no condescension by Gwyneth Paltrow) who convinces no one with her favorite refrain: "I'm not stupid!"

Eventually she ends up in a seedy motel room with the overconfident kid and the brutalized body of a half-conscious john, engaged in a badly botched ransom attempt. Naturally, they turn to the seemingly all-powerful Sydney to deal with the situation and get them out of their mess.

"Let's listen to Syd!" his pusillanimous protege wails. "Syd knows. He knows!"

The most impressive achievement of "Hard Eight" is that it somehow convinces us that Syd, indeed, knows—though we're never quite sure about the nature of that knowledge.

Veteran character actor Philip Baker Hall delivers a superbly authoritative performance that wordlessly conveys world-weary wisdom and existential depth, setting up the dark secret that almost allows this strange plot to come together and make sense.

The presence of hot, distinguished actors such as Paltrow and Jackson reflects the undeniable talent of writer-director Paul Thomas Anderson, who developed this debut film project through the auspices of the prestigious Sundance Institute.

His moody, artfully composed images, inventive camera work and uncanny eye for detail are all extraordinary, promising formidable future achievements.

This film, however, not unlike many another debut, seems to be rooted not so much in reality as it is in other movies—particularly classic film noir, seasoned with a splash of Quentin Tarantino's wacky and sadistic irony.

On his first roll of the directorial dice, young Anderson may not break the bank, but he still beats the odds by coming out substantially ahead.

SIGHT AND SOUND, 1/98, p. 44, Richard Falcon

John has just lost all his money in Las Vegas. He is approached by Sydney, an older well dressed stranger, who offers him a ride to Reno, $50 and a lesson in turning the money into a deluxe room for the night through a complex but legal scam. The scam succeeds. Two years later, John is Sydney's protégé and the pair of them live off gambling in Nevada casinos. One night, Sydney meets Clementine, a cocktail waitress. John arrives and introduces Sydney to Jimmy, who claims to have heard of Sydney's once betting on "the hard eight" (both dice coming up four) in a crap game.

Sydney realises Clementine is moonlighting as a hooker and puts her up for the night in John's room at their suite. The next evening, Sydney plays the hard eight at a crap table and loses $2,000. In the early hours, a panicked John summons him to a seedy motel: John has married Clementine and straight after the wedding, she turned a trick. The client refused to pay, so John and Clementine are holding him hostage. Sydney tells John and Clementine to leave for Niagara Falls immediately and gives them money. After their departure, Jimmy tells Sydney that he knows the reason for the older man's altruism towards John: in Atlantic City, Sydney murdered John's father. Jimmy threatens to tell John unless Sydney gives Jimmy $6,000. Jimmy goes off to the crap tables and has a streak of luck playing high stakes on the hard eight with Sydney's money. When Jimmy returns home with a hooker, Sydney shoots him dead and takes the remaining winnings. As Sydney sits alone in the diner where he met John, John and Clementine continue their drive to Niagara.

In the game of craps, a hard eight is a dice combination of two fours rather than a five and a three or any another combination to make eight. In film-making, as much as at Reno crap tables, there are clearly harder and easier combinations to play. In writer-director Paul Thomas Anderson's debut feature, made two years ago and held up because its US distributor went bankrupt, the choices lay evidently somewhere between the 'soft eight', lower-risk strategy of plot driven, low-budget *noir* and the higher yielding 'hard eight' of a character study turning on questions of dignity, quiet desperation, hope and loneliness.

In its gripping opening 20 minutes, *Hard Eight* employs a rigorous austerity. Everything is excluded from the mysterious exchange between grifter Sydney and grifter-in-the-making John but coffee cups, cigarettes and the lined face and measured voice of Philip Baker Hall as Sydney (reminiscent of Edward G. Robinson in *The Cincinnatti Kid* of 1965). Even the pair's subsequent drive across the desert maintains the opening's mesmerising tone of claustrophobia. Refusing transitions, it concentrates on intimate two-shots and close-ups of Sydney as he succeeds in gaining John's confidence. So much is going on in these close-ups, that even with the appearance of Samuel L Jackson, we resist lending any obvious iconographic significance to Sydney's dark suit and white shirt: it would be trite to see only the superficial resemblance to Tarantino's gangsters, and to miss the more evocative correspondence between Sydney and the benign angel of *It's a Wonderful Life* (1947). Indeed, right up to the concluding song that starts "Alone at Christmas ...", we receive hints that something more may be at stake beyond the isolation and desperation of the diners, seedy motels and anonymous casino courtesy rooms which circumscribe the characters' world.

So focused is the movie on its intriguing minimalism that we start to expect from it the hardboiled poetic existentialism of a Mamet play, or even the metaphysical conundrums of *The Music of Chance*. However, after a fascinatingly plausible demonstration of how to turn $50 in slot tokens into a courtesy room for the night, we return from a two year ellipsis to a more prosaic world of US indie neo-*noir*. *Hard Eight* nevertheless almost succeeds in turning our disappointment into a virtue. For example, holding John and Sydney in an agonisingly prolonged two-shot in the doorway of a motel room, the movie seems reluctant to release us into the chaotic tableau of bloody handcuffed trick on the bed and Clementine crouched despairingly in the corner which will kick start the plot mechanics.

But Anderson still has two strong cards to play in Jackson and Gwyneth Paltrow. The first is all scene-stealing malevolence, creaking menacingly in a leather jacket, while the latter offers an affecting sketch of amorality and childish chaotic thinking. Both evince the kind of defective self-esteem which Sydney aims to correct in the hapless John. In a riveting scene between Jackson and Hall, built like a lot of *Hard Eight* around play with a cigarette (don't see this if you're trying to quit), Jackson holds our attention so completely that we can almost forgive his character for spelling out the slightly pat revelation which explains Sydney's 'altruism'. *Hard Eight*'s lurch into contrivance at this point prepares us for the too-neat dramatic irony whereby Sydney finally achieves his big payout on the hard eight. It's a flaw similar to an earlier flashback illustrating why John never uses matches, a rare lapse into film school referentiality and mannerism.

If the neatness and formal rhymes of the plotting thwart our grander hopes as spectators for *Hard Eight* the movie nevertheless remains an affecting and resonant experience. This resonance is oxygenated by its ambiguous little details: Sydney hiding his bloodstained cuff, an edit between Sydney's silver-grey Plymouth and John's similar car which momentarily relieves Sydney's isolation by placing Clementine in his passenger seat. When, earlier, Clementine asks Sydney whether his intention was to "fuck" her, Sydney replies, offended: "Never ask a question like that unless you already know the answer". In *Hard Eight* Anderson and his brilliant quartet of performers prove that they know a great many questions. This evocative, memorable movie would perhaps have been even better if it had left one or two more of the answers to us.

VILLAGE VOICE, 3/4/97, p. 65, J. Hoberman

Hard Eight, writer-director Paul Thomas Anderson's assured, Sundance-incubated debut, is another May-December gangster romance.

Here, an aging Reno sharpie named Sydney (superbly played by unsung vet Philip Baker Hall) takes a dim-bulb drifter (John C. Reilly) under his dapper wing. The kid is hardly a double agent; the guilty secret belongs to his mentor, who is as cool a customer as Pacino's wiseguy was hot.

Experience personified, voice honed to a mellow rasp by a million cigarettes and an ocean of Johnny Walker, Sydney shows his protégé how to dress, act, and establish himself as a pseudo-high roller through the artful recirculation of casino chips. He even plays Cupid when the kid falls for a goofy, angel-faced waitress (canny Gwyneth Paltrow) who augments her tips by turning tricks on the side.

As fastidious (and unbelievable) as enigmatic Sydney, *Hard Eight* has a precise narrative structure and a clean, vérité look. As a director, Anderson tends toward the analytical, favoring close-ups while feasting on the garish colors and stale plushness of Reno's posh neon night—as a writer, he plays his cards less cautiously, withholding key info until well after the movie unexpectedly plunges into a Cassavetes morass of untrammeled id. *Hard Eight* takes another mad lurch, thanks to the routinely electrifying Samuel L. Jackson as a slaphappy hustler, before resolving itself with a symmetry that bodes well for Anderson's own future projects.

Also reviewed in:
NEW YORK TIMES, 2/28/97, p. C7, Stephen Holden

HEAD ABOVE WATER

A Fine Line Features and InterMedia Films release of a Tig Productions/Majestic Films production. *Executive Producer:* Guy East and Tristan Whalley. *Producer:* John M. Jacobsen. *Producer:* Jim Wilson. *Director:* Jim Wilson. *Screenplay:* Theresa Marie. *Based on a screenplay by:* Geir Eriksen and Eirik Ildahl. *Director of Photography:* Richard Bowen. *Editor:* Michael R. Miller. *Music:* Christopher Young. *Music Editor:* Thomas Milano. *Sound:* Richard Bryce Goodman and (music) Robert Fernandez. *Sound Editor:* Robert Fitzgerald. *Casting:* Elisabeth Leustig. *Production Designer:* Jeffrey Beecroft. *Art Director:* Joseph P. Lucky. *Set Decorator:* Susan De Havenon. *Costumes:* Colleen Atwood. *Special Effects:* Eric Rylander. *Make-up:* Bernadette Mazur. *Stunt Coordinator:* George Aguilar. *Running time:* 92 minutes. *MPAA Rating:* PG-13.

CAST: Harvey Keitel (George); Cameron Diaz (Nathalie); Craig Sheffer (Lance); Billy Zane (Kent); Shay Duffin (Policeman).

LOS ANGELES TIMES, 6/25/97, Calendar/p. 4, Jack Mathews

[The following review by Jack Mathews appeared in a slightly different form in NEWSDAY, 6/25/97, Part II/p. B9.]

On a sparsely populated island off the coast of Maine, three people—two men and a woman—are playing a game of cat and mouse. Or, more accurately, a game of life and death.
. George (Harvey Keitel) is a middle-aged judge, Nathalie (Cameron Diaz) is his young wife, and Lance (Craig Sheffer) is her childhood friend, an artist who doubles as the island's caretaker. He lives next door.

For a brief time in Jim Wilson's "Head Above Water," there is a third man, Kent (Billy Zane), Nathalie's ex-lover. But he dies early in the film, leaving behind a naked body that sends George into a jealous rage and leaves us wondering which is the most dangerous character—the corpse, the judge, his wife or their neighbor?

If this black comedy sounds familiar, you may have caught it on HBO, where it aired earlier in the year. It's not unusual these days for a particularly engrossing cable film to take a theatrical second breath, but "Head Above Water" is not a particularly engrossing movie. Its island setting is gorgeous, better served for sure on the big screen. But the story is as slight as an episode of "Tales From the Crypt," another HBO presentation.

These kind of keep-the-audience-guessing whodunits depend on the dialogue and the actors' chemistry, and "Head Above Water" fails both tests. Keitel is badly miscast as the comically jealous husband; Sheffer, the brooding, older son in Robert Redford's "A River Runs Through It," doesn't begin to convey the mystery implied by Lance; and Diaz, while clearly talented at light comedy, is stuck in the middle, sputtering in confusion over which is the better man.

By the time "Head Above Water" reaches its "Perils of Pauline" ending, it's a question of interest only to Nathalie. If you have to spend time with a corpse at the beach, this is better than "Weekend at Bernie's." But it's a near thing.

NEW YORK POST, 6/25/97, p. 41, Michael Medved

"Head Above Water" is a slick mayhem-and-mutilation comedy with two fundamental problems: It's hard to like any of its four characters or to believe the horrifying happenings that befall them.

Harvey Keitel plays an uptight, seemingly upright middle-aged judge who has just married the much younger Cameron Diaz—a gorgeous alcoholic and pill-popper who happened to pass through his courtroom and now wants to straighten out her life.

The newlyweds vacation at her parents' summer home on a scenic Maine island, where the only other inhabitant is the beautiful bride's boyhood friend (and longtime admirer), a lonely sculptor played by rugged Craig Sheffer.

While Keitel is away with Sheffer for an overnight fishing trip, Diaz is surprised by an unexpected visit from her former lover—a charismatic, fast-talking scoundrel played by Billy Zane in the movie's most energetic performance.

He makes a determined effort to seduce her (and the audience never learns if he succeeds), but the next morning she finds him in another part of the house, nude and dead. With her husband returning home any moment, she hides the corpse under the floorboards and tries to dispose of the dead man's clothes.

The Maine seascape is beautiful to behold, as is the glamorous Diaz—who is forced to spend most of the movie bound and gagged and gasping for help. At the "Perils of Pauline"-style climax, she is seated atop a steep ramp overlooking the ocean, with hands bound behind her back and feet embedded in a tub of concrete.

Scenes like this one are supposed to count as dark comedy; unfortunately, director Jim Wilson never lets you forget it.

Unlike Alfred Hitchcock or even Quenton Tarantino, who play their macabre material fairly straight, Wilson constantly nudges us in the ribs to remind us that these shenanigans are supposed to be hilarious—and such smug, self-conscious jabs seem far more annoying than good-natured.

SIGHT AND SOUND, 9/97, p. 44, Mark Kermode

George, a judge, holidays on an island off Maine with his wife Nathalie. Her friend Lance is the only other inhabitant. While George is out on a fishing trip with Lance, Nathalie's former flame Kent arrives, insisting his impending visit had been announced by a postcard. Kent drinks George's vodka, flirts with Nathalie, then dies while naked.

Fearful of George's reaction, Nathalie consigns Kent's clothes and stolen rowboat to the sea and hides Kent in the cellar, where George unknowingly breaks the corpse's neck. George assumes that Kent died by drinking the methanol he keeps in the vodka bottle. Worried about explaining a naked corpse to the authorities, he resolves to lose the body at sea, but then Lance shows up. When Lance finds the clothes and rowboat, Nathalie gives the suit to a drunken George to clothe the corpse. But George has now chainsawed Kent's body to pieces and cemented him into the gazebo steps. Assuming that George hid the postcard and planned the killing, Nathalie flees in Lance's boat but is caught by George and locked in the cellar.

When Lance questions George about a loose gun cartridge in his boat, George replies that Nathalie had become suicidal. So when Nathalie flees, Lance turns her back over to her husband, although he does agree to humour her by digging up the gazebo steps. While Lance digs, Nathalie discovers proof of George's innocence, but she arrives at the gazebo too late to stop George shooting at Lance, who retaliates by knocking George unconscious. Nathalie now suspects lovelorn Lance, who declares his love for her, but he is shot by George who then cements Nathalie into a bowl of concrete. George accidentally swigs from the bottle which contains the methanol, and collapses. Nathalie attempts to free herself with a chainsaw, but ends up decapitating the gazebo, which fatally skewers George, and sends Nathalie tumbling into the sea. When a passing policeman attempts to rescue her, he is pulled from his boat, which smashes onto the rocks. As Nathalie recounts her story to the cop, he discovers a bottle of vodka...

An unacknowledged remake of a quirky 1993 Norwegian black comedy directed by Nils Gaup (*Pathfinder*) entitled *Hodet over vannet*, this lumpen stodge has none of the speed, wit or sparkle necessary to power its comic engine. While farce must evoke a manic melange in which characters are driven to extremes by misunderstandings, *Head Above Water* proceeds at the kind of workaday pace which constantly invites the audience to ask why these people don't just stop behaving so stupidly. Events do not pile one atop the other, but are instead foisted with great effort into a burgeoning mountain of calamity more likely to annoy than amuse.

Throughout, apparently throwaway gags are signalled with enough visual honking and blowing of sirens to awaken even Billy Zane from his untimely grave. When Lance foils George's corpse-disposal plans by hurling a crucial make-weight over board, he declares (with unknowing irony) "Your problems are over." So too is the joke, but still we cut back to a reaction shot of Harvey Keitel's George and Cameron Diaz's Nathalie mugging desperately to a script direction which must surely have read "They look at each other in desperation!"

Elsewhere, the discovery of the deceased Kent's suit provokes inevitable horror from Nathalie, but Lance still has to tell her "You look like you've seen a ghost." Meanwhile, the usually talented Christopher Young's musical score goes 'tooty tooty toot' in a manner which suggests a level of wacky hilarity sadly absent from the screen. All of which is a shame, because any movie in which Harvey Keitel chainsaws a body to pieces because he's too drunk to do anything else should occasionally be fun. Instead, the audience (like the cast) is left sadly at sea by the onscreen antics, heads below water, not waving but drowning.

VILLAGE VOICE, 7/8/97, p. 74, Lauren P. Fritz

Bronzed pill popper Nathalie (Cameron Diaz) finally got it right. After years of bad men, she met George (Harvey Keitel) at one of her court hearings (he was the judge), and at the start of the film their happy, I'm-in-love faces beam as they take their first vacation. Two more men then enter the scene: Lance (Craig Sheffer), Natalie's childhood friend who is now the caretaker of the island, and a soon-to-be-dead ex-boyfriend (Billy Zane). It seems that all—even the seemingly benign-to-the-point-of-stupid Lance—have something to hide, and *Head Above Water* soon spins into a who-did-what-to-whom semithriller that leaves the audience confused but somehow entertained. Keitel and Sheffer sleepwalk through their roles until the frenzied last 40 minutes, while Diaz escapes from being tied up at least three times. Director Jim Wilson signals the scary parts with music, topping that off with grotesque moments that shift the film to a sickly comic story. *Head Above Water* is billed as a "black comedy" but should probably be called a "savage tan comedy," thanks to Cameron Diaz.

Also reviewed in:
NEW YORK TIMES, 6/25/97, p. C15, Stephen Holden
VARIETY, 11/11-17/96, p. 58, Derek Elley

HERCULES

A Walt Disney Pictures release. *Producer:* Alice Dewey, John Musker, and Ron Clements. *Director:* John Musker and Ron Clements. *Animation Screenplay:* Ron Clements, John Musker, Irene Mecchi, Donald McEnery and Bob Shaw. *Story:* Barry Johnson. *Editor:* Tim Finan. *Music:* Alan Menken and (lyrics) David Zippel. *Music Editor:* Earl Ghaffari and Kathleen Fogarty-Bennett. *Sound:* Gary Rydstrom and (music) John Richards and Frank Wolf. *Sound Editor:* Tim Holland. *Casting:* Ruth Lambert. *ANIMATION: Adult Hercules:* Andreas Deja. *Baby & Young Hercules:* Randy R. Haycock. *Phil:* Eric Goldberg. *Hades:* Nik Ranieri. *Meg:* Ken Duncan. *Pegasus:* Ellen Woodbury. *Zeus & Hera:* Anthony DeRosa. *The Muses:* Michael Show. *Pain & Panic:* Marc Eoche Duval. *Titans & Cyclops:* Dominique Monfery. *Amphitryon & Alcmene:* Richard Bazley. *The Fates/Thebans:* Nancy Beiman. *Hydra:* Oscar Urretabizkaia. *Art Director:* Andy Gaskill. *Production Designer:* Gerald Scarfe. *Visual Effects:* Mauro Maressa. *Running time:* 87 minutes. *MPAA Rating:* G.

VOICES: Barbara Barrie (Alcmene); Roger Bart (Young Hercules, Singing); Mary Kay Bergman (Earthquake Lady); Corey Burton (Burnt Man); Jim Cummings (Nessus); Keith David (Apollo); Danny DeVito (Phil); Tate Donovan (Adult Hercules); Paddi Edwards (Fate); Susan Egan (Meg); Samantha Eggar (Hera); Cheryl Freemen (Muse); Kathleen Freeman (Heavyset Woman); Matt Frewer (Panic); Bobcat Goldthwait (Pain); Bug Hall and Kellen Hathaway (Little Boys); Charlton Heston (Narrator); Hal Holbrook (Amphitryon); Joshua Keaton (Young Hercules, Speaking); Wayne Knight (Demetrius); LaChanze (Muse); Aaron Michael Metchik (Ithicles); Patrick Pinney (Cyclops); Amanda Plummer (Fate); Roz Ryan (Muse); Paul Shaffer (Hermes); Carole Shelley (Fate); Vaneese Thomas (Muse); Rip Torn (Zeus); Lillias White (Lead Muse); James Woods (Hades).

CHRISTIAN SCIENCE MONITOR, 6/27/97, p. 12, David Sterritt

A lot is riding on "Hercules," the new feature-length cartoon from Walt Disney Productions.

True, this powerful studio still has a solid lock on the sizable market for family-friendly entertainment in the warm-weather season. And its animation division still has the best name-recognition in the business. Parents fondly recall masterpieces like "Dumbo" and "Pinocchio," while kids treasure more recent memories of "Aladdin" and "The Little Mermaid."

Still, not all the fantasy-merchants in Disneydom have been earning smiles lately. Their last two pictures, "Pocahontas" and "The Hunchback of Notre Dame," made piles of money—but smaller piles than unqualified hits like "The Lion King" and "Beauty and the Beast" pulled in.

Were these movies weakened by inappropriate stories, or were the characters unappealing, or was the cartooning too tame for eyes accustomed to action pictures with high-tech special effects? Or has the old Disney magic simply waned with the passing years?

Different observers have different theories, but all agree a top-grossing smash would renew the studio's luster while assuring fans that the Disney name can still be depended upon. Hence the high stakes for "Hercules," Disney's 35th animated feature.

The tale begins when Hercules is born to Zeus and Hera, who welcome their baby with a special gift: little Pegasus, a winged horse destined to grow large and strong enough for a brawny Greek god to be proud of. Little do the proud parents know, however, that Hades—the evil god of the underworld—is plotting to take over their domain.

The three Fates tell Hades he'll succeed if Hercules doesn't take up arms against him. So the villain kidnaps our hero and—after failing to destroy him—leaves him stranded in the mortal world, ignorant of his Olympian origins and uncertain why he doesn't fit in with ordinary folks. He eventually learns the truth and triumphs over Hades, of course, but not before fighting some dangerous battles and falling in love with a woman almost as imperiled as he is.

Does this add up to an animation milestone, or just a pop-culture rehash of a story that's survived for millennia without Hollywood's help?

Sad to say, the second answer hits closer to the mark. Straining to be classical and contemporary at once, Disney has steeped the timeless characters in its own well-worn formulas—ancient Greeks or not, they look and sound exactly like mass-market cartoon figures—while twisting the complexity of an age-old myth into the three-act structure of a standardized screenplay.

And the songs don't help. Sung by a quintet called (inevitably) the Muses, they aim for the toe-tapping uplift of high-energy gospel but land near second-class Motown, a genre composer Alan Menken clearly hasn't mastered. While some pop fans may go for them, many will find them one of the movie's major downsides.

Fortunately, there are some upsides as well. The cartooning is fast and clever, especially in the underworld scenes, and some of the voice-performances are fine. James Woods is an excellent Hades, both sinister and hilarious. Danny DeVito is good as our hero's mentor Philoctetes, and it's fun to hear cultivated talents take on smaller roles like Rip Torn's thundery Zeus, Hal Holbrook's lovable Amphitryon, and Amanda Plummer's wizened Fate sister. Bobcat Goldthwait and Matt Frewer are especially lively as Hades' bumbling assistants.

Back on the downside, parents should be careful about "Hercules" if they're thinking about taking young children. While the smallest hint of smarminess is usually enough to earn a PG for a picture, the rating authorities will pass surprisingly large amounts of violence into the G category if the movie is based on a myth or some other source with bedtime-story credentials.

With its underworld god, River of Death, multiheaded monster, and so on, "Hercules" has more scary material than any G-rated picture since the non-Disney adaptation of "Pinocchio" last year. Older kids will handle it fine, but the littlest viewers should sit this one out.

LOS ANGELES TIMES, 6/25/97, Calendar/p. 1, Kenneth Turan

Hollywood being the kind of place it is, people out there are waiting for the powerhouse that is Disney animation to get its comeuppance. The good news about "Hercules," at least for the rest of us, is that they're going to have to wait awhile longer.

Light on its feet and continually amusing, this free-spirited show-biz version of Greek mythology ranks with the best of modern Disney animation. Cleverly constructed to appeal to boys and girls, children and adults, it also has in "City of Angels" Tony-winning lyricist David Zippel, the first person since the late Howard Ashman who's been able to write the kind of snappy musical patter these features thrive on.

The guiding spirits here, the writing, directing and producing team of John Musker & Ron Clements, worked with Ashman and "Hercules" composer Alan Menken on "Aladdin," and this film combines much the same wisecracking aura with a dollop of romantic poignancy.

It's been done with subject matter—the Greek hero who was the strongest man on the planet while coping with a rather painful personal history—that is unlikely. But Musker & Clements (working with co-writers stand-up comics Bob Shaw & Donald McEnery and have done a brisk and successful cut-and-paste job on the original material, nervily mixing and matching elements from all over classical mythology. In comes the flying horse Pegasus to be the big guy's pal, out goes Hercules' destructive fits of madness, not to mention the time he cut the noses and ears off an unlucky group of messengers.

Kudos is also in order for how deftly the project's "A Funny Thing Happened on the Way to the Forum" comic tone has been combined with traditional Disney life lessons for little folks. Who would have guessed that Hercules was the kid who didn't fit in, the adolescent who needed to prove himself to his father and, finally, the young adult who has to discover that heroism is something measured only by strength of heart. It kind of chokes you up, it really does.

"Hercules" isn't slow in unveiling its comic tone. Narrator Charlton Heston gets to read no more than a handful of somber words before he's cut off with a sassy, "Will you listen to him? He's making this story sound like some Greek tragedy. Lighten up, dude."

Those words come from the Muses, cut down from the original nine to a manageable five (Lillias White, Cheryl Freeman, LaChanze, Roz Ryan, Vaneese Thomas) and transformed into a Greek chorus that is part Motown girl group and part gospel choir. Their trio of the Gospel Truth numbers introduce characters, provide back story and jump-start the film into an up-tempo gear it never abandons.

Though no one can duplicate what Robin Williams did for "Aladdin," the irresistible James Woods as Hades, the cynical, fast-talking king of the underworld, comes surprisingly close. Introduced at a party Zeus and Hera, king and queen of the gods, are giving for baby son Hercules, he enters with a Don Rickles wisecrack ("I haven't been this choked up since I got a chunk of moussaka caught in my throat") and never pauses for breath.

Hades, you should know, is not a happy god. He has a plan to replace Zeus and get the hell out of the underworld, but the Fates, who know all about the future and tell a bit ("Indoor plumbing—it's going to be big"), inform him that he won't succeed unless he's able to neutralize Hercules.

Working with comic sidekicks Pain (Bobcat Goldthwait) and Panic (Matt Frewer), Hades manages to turn Hercules human, but he still retains his godlike strength.

Here grows up to be a gawky teenager, teased as Jerkules for his clumsiness, but his life takes a better turn when he discovers that Zeus is his father and that proving himself a hero on Earth can make him a god once again.

Philoctetes, Phil for short, is a pudgy satyr who knows all about heroes. He's trained the best of them, from Achilles on down, but having "been around the block before with blockheads like you," he considers himself retired.

Naturally, Hercules changes his mind, and as played by Danny DeVito, Phil is the film's energy source when Hades isn't around. The kind of guy who calls everyone "kid" and tells people to keep their togas on, Phil has a Borscht Belt vocabulary and a determination to make Hercules the greatest there ever was.

On the way to Thebes, the Big Olive, "a big tough town, a good place to start building a rep," Hercules runs into Megara (Susan Egan), a.k.a. Meg, a different kind of Disney heroine, the kind of been-around, good-bad girl who could have been voiced by Barbara Stanwyck. She arouses Phil's suspicion and incites Pegasus to jealousy, but the look in Hercules' eyes tells us she'll be sticking around.

Given the kind of guy he is, it's inevitable that Hercules (Tate Donovan) battles lots of strange monsters. The most impressive (and the film's only nod to Hercules' storied 12 labors) is the protean Hydra, a beast that grows new heads whenever one is cut off. A technological marvel, the Hydra is the film's most impressive computer-generated character, and no wonder. The press notes say a team of 15 artists and technicians worked on the five-minute sequence for two years.

When our hero becomes "the greatest thing since they put the pocket in pita," a process detailed in the rousing "Zero to Hero," the film delights in satirizing Disney's well-known penchant for merchandising, including omnipresent Air-Herc sandals and the hot-selling "30-minute workout scroll, 'Buns of Bronze.'"

But, like any protagonist, Hercules has to discover that "being famous isn't the same thing as being a true hero," and the process of doing so involves him more intimately with Meg in a way that sentimentalists will find satisfying.

Though they're not big star names, without the excellent, feeling work of Donovan as the adult Hercules and Egan as Meg, "Hercules" would have considerably less impact. The animation, with an assist from British illustrator Gerald Scarfe, has just enough of a different look to it to make things interesting. What remains the same is the ability of Disney feature-length cartoons to entertain like crazy. It's hard to believe that lines that move can move us so much, but they do.

NEW YORK, 7/7/97, p. 54, David Denby

The animated Hercules takes off right at the beginning, when the muses painted on some shapely Greek vase come to life and metamorphose into five gospel singers with interesting hair.

They narrate the story, in high-powered, hip-jamming song (written as usual by Alan Menken), and the movie enters a plane of gratifying silliness. As far as the Greek myths are concerned, *Hercules* is pretty much a hash, an amalgam of Ovid and everything else, not to mention all of contemporary media culture (this Hercules becomes a T-shirt). But who cares? Hercules, after all, is not a tragic hero like Oedipus or Prometheus. His story is almost pop fiction to begin with; even in ancient Greece, the myths surrounding Heracles (as he was known) were pumped by stories about other heroes.

The cleaning of the Augean stables is gone, as are many other less redolent feats. In this version, Hercules is born to Zeus and Hera. A powerhouse even in swaddling clothes, he grows up to be the most awkward teenager of all—a dopey blond bimbo, as brutal and innocent as Wagner's Siegfried. Hades (spoken by James Woods), lord of the underworld, tries to rob him of his godhead, for Hercules is the only one who can stop Hades from overthrowing the resident deities on Mount Olympus. Woods, the best thing in the movie, plays Hades as a chiseling con man, a Hollywood agent desperate for a deal and therefore both propitiatory and bullying. Hades uses the ripe Megara to trap the young champion, and Susan Egan does a slightly hyped version of a good-bad girl, tough, sexy, and self-sufficient, like Stanwyck or Bacall.

The team of John Musker and Ron Clements, which was also responsible for *Aladdin,* does best with the evil characters. Zeus (spoken by Rip Torn) is all hearty bluster and swelling beard and chest, but Hades, flaming at the top (literally, a hothead), is wickedly entertaining, and such monsters as Hydra and the Titans billow up and loom over us in classic Disney style. Greek myth and Greek art are a fertile source of the instant heroic: Decorative figures on plates and pots come to life, friezes unfreeze and dance. The whole movie dances.

NEW YORK POST, 6/13/97, p. 43, Michael Medved

"Hercules" is funny, frisky and refreshing—especially for those families who have felt frustrated by the somber, self-important tone of Disney's last two animated offerings, "The Hunchback of Notre Dame" and "Pocahontas."

This zippy, zingy new musical extravaganza never strains to achieve masterpiece status; it's proud to be sassy rather than classy, offering irreverent and inventive entertainment for the widest possible audience.

Serious students of mythology may be the only dissenters, since these splashy adventures of "Herc" the Hunk bear very little resemblance to the disturbing trials of the Heracles of Greek legend.

Here, we get to know the future super-hero as a shy, klutzy teenager, derided by popular kids as "Jerkules."

At the Temple of Zeus, a statue of the big guy springs to life, informing the outcast of his Olympian origins, reuniting him with a flying horse, and urging him to contact a grubby, grouchy satyr named Philoctetes (brought to amusing life through the face and form of Danny DeVito) to prepare him for his career as a hero.

After an intensive training regimen, the newly muscular Herc (voiced by Tate Donovan) and Phil journey to Thebes ("the Big Olive"), where he becomes an overnight sensation (with his own line of celebrity sandals and drinking urns) after slaying a slew of menacing monsters.

The only threat to his newfound fame is that Hades, Lord of the Underworld (marvelously portrayed with the diabolically cynical voice of James Woods) wants to get rid of "Wonder Boy" to rebel against Zeus (voice of Rip Torn) and the other Olympians.

To this purpose, he employs the saucy, seductive Megara, who's sent to discover Herc's weak spot but ends up falling for the big lug in spite of herself. As superbly sung and spoken by Susan Egan (of Broadway's "Beauty and the Beast"), this Meg is an especially splendid creation—displaying a cynical but vulnerable Barbara Stanwyck sexiness without the voluptuous Barbie-doll excesses of Pocahontas or Princess Jasmine from "Aladdin."

Production and character design by renowned British satirist Gerald Scarfe provide a sharp, spiky edge that suggests that this is one "animated feature" pleased to accept the designation "cartoon."

The multi-headed Hydra is an awe-inspiring demonstration of the power of computer graphics imagery, but most people who return to see the movie a second or third time will do so to pick up missing bits of witty, rapid-fire dialogue (the half-goat DeVito character complains of a "fur wedgy") rather than to thrill again to breathtaking images.

It may seem tasteless to use gospel music to sing of pagan gods and titans (including an introductory number called "The Gospel Truth"), but the score (by Disney veteran Alan Menken, again) is reasonably tuneful and infectious, if never outright inspired.

All in all, this "Hercules," as both character and film project, may not qualify as a lofty Olympian, but he's still a thoroughly likable guy.

SIGHT AND SOUND, 10/97, p. 52, Leslie Felperin

Ancient Greece. On Mount Olympus, the gods celebrate the birth of Hercules, son of mighty Zeus and beautiful Hera. Zeus fashions a winged horse named Pegasus to be Hercules' playmate. However, bitter Hades, ruler of the underworld, is plotting to release the Titans (ancient beings who were once vanquished by Zeus) and take over the world. The Fates predict that Hercules will stop him, so Hades despatches his henchmen Pain and Panic to kidnap Hercules, make him mortal and then kill him. The two demons botch the job and Hercules survives, retaining a drop of immortality. He is found by a childless couple and raised as their own.

Prodigiously strong, Hercules grows up to be a handsome man but is clumsy with his strength. After learning about his origins, Hercules is told by Zeus that to become a god again he must prove himself to be a true hero. Reunited with Pegasus, Hercules seeks out the satyr Phil, a trainer of heroes. After a prolonged training period, Phil sends Hercules to Thebes, a city plagued by a monster. In Thebes, Hercules kills the monster, a many-headed hydra. He begins a career of heroic deeds—killing the Nemean lion, slaying sea monsters and so on—and becomes famous.

Hercules falls in love with the bewitching Megara ("Meg"), but she is secretly in thrall to Hades with whom she once traded her soul for the life of a former lover. Hades threatens to kill Meg unless Hercules gives up his power for 24 hours. Hercules agrees, and Hades sets free the Titans who besiege Olympus. Meg is killed in the mêlée, but Hercules manages to survive the ordeal of saving her soul from the underworld because of his remaining drop of immortality. Restored to godhood, he defeats Hades at last. The Titans are also defeated, and Zeus offers Hercules a place on Mount Olympus. Hercules refuses, choosing to become mortal again and stay with Meg.

With their robustly one-dimensional heroes, symbolic narratives and amazing feats, the myths and legends of Ancient Greece (and the pagan world in general) have often been described as the oral comic books and cartoons for the Golden Age. This being the case, it's odd that animation has neglected for so long this mythic storehouse of stories and tales, leaving it to such live-action film-makers as Ray Harryhausen and the makers of the recent sword-and-sandals television series *Hercules* to bring these stories to the screen. Perhaps the Greek myths, with their high incidence of animal slaying and virgin ravishing, were thought a bit too spicy for children. Disney's only other significant attempt to blend Greek mythology with animation is the anodyne Beethoven's *Pastoral* section of *Fantasia* (1940) which, with its proto-My-Little-Pony centaurs and bikini-garlanded nymphs, was one of the low points of that film.

After the success of Disney's accomplished (albeit most contentious) recent feature *Aladdin*, the way must have seemed clearer to depict a character who lives in a pagan world and has to slaughter animals on a regular basis, even if they are horrible monsters (in one case, a lion which bears an uncanny resemblance to the evil Scar in *The Lion King*). Nonetheless, classicists will be disgruntled to see how far the film strays from its source material, just as historians picked a few bones with *Pocahontas* and Hugo-fans with *The Hunchback of Notre Dame*. *Hercules'* scriptwriters have been selective about which elements of the story's many variants they chose to use. Thus, the infant Hercules slaughters snakes from his basket as he does in many ancient versions of the story, but the so-called thirteenth labour of Hercules (there's often just 12 cited) in which he must sleep with 49 women in one night has been left out, strangely enough.

On its own terms, *Hercules* is a delight: zippily paced, wittily written, and beautifully animated. Directors John Musker and Ron Clements, who co-directed *The Little Mermaid* and *Aladdin*, have a knack for fashioning Disney films that appeal to both children and adults simultaneously. Children will like *Hercules'* knockabout slapstick, its scary monsters (especially the seemingly unkillable Hydra) and likable he-man hero. Grown-ups will titter at the film's sly in-jokes, including the self-reflexive dig at the cult of merchandising ("I'm an action figure!" says Hercules) and Hades' droll lines, such as "It's a small underworld after all". James Woods' demonic voice—characterisation of Hades (drawn to look like the actor and at one point sporting his trademark Havana cigar) is a hoot, as is the hero's stupidity.

What really sets Hercules apart, though, is the coherence of its overall design. This is something of a trademark of Musker and Clements, but its linear energy owes an enormous amount to the work of the British cartoonist Gerald Scarfe, who was hired to do some key character sketches and stayed on to work as production designer for the whole film. His contribution has given the film a lovely comic solidity. Details, such as little spirals on Hercules' elbows, nipples and knees which rhyme with the swirls in the Ionic columns' capitals, knit the film together elegantly.

If the film has a serious flaw, it's the same one that has plagued most of the recent Disney films: atrocious ballad songwriting. Stuck in a syrupy paradigm, Alan Menken and David Zippel's songs, such as Hercules' lament that no one loves him and the main love song, 'I Won't Say (I'm in Love)', are colourless ditties, fashioned for an audience that isn't expected to want more from them. Far better are the Muses' chorus-like expository numbers, done as brassy gospel-style showstoppers that create an interesting bouncy distancing effect. There is nothing Grecian about them, but then again, this is a Disney film.

TIME, 6/23/97, p. 76, Richard Corliss

The Disney full-animated feature is the most profitable franchise in movies, maybe in the entire entertainment industry. The pressure to keep producing the tiniest variations on a winning formula must be severe. So it was brave for the Disney artists to try tiptoeing away from what worked. *Pocahontas* had soaring melodies to match its do-gooding intentions; *The Hunchback of Notre Dame* came within two deaths and three cute gargoyles of being the first grownup singing-cartoon romantic tragedy. But these two movies also had an almost toxic serioso content. At times they got so solemn they could have been Broadway musicals in the fashionable I'm-miserable-I'm-a-monster-I'm-a-Times-Square-whore-my-ship-is-sinking mode. Songs for suicides.

Hey, guys, welcome back. *Hercules* is a happy reminder that the genre was once called musical *comedy.* Directors John Musker and Ron Clements (*The Little Mermaid, Aladdin*) could have gone for a decorous retelling of Greek mythology, but a funny thing happened on the way to decorum. They decided to give the musical form what it has sorely lacked: pinwheeling, knockabout fun.

Don't look for this plot in Bulfinch. It's a shaggy-gods story with the requisite Disney theme of adolescent self-discovery: a cub becomes a lion; a mermaid becomes a maid; a geek kid becomes a Greek god. Hercules (voiced by Tate Donovan) is your basic mythic hybrid-half man, half deity—recast as a clumsy teen. Superman-strong and Bambi-naive, Herc is an ideal foil for wily Meg (a subtle siren, wonderfully voiced by Susan Egan). She plays Barbara Stanwyck to his Eddie Bracken, while a gruff satyr (Danny DeVito) acts as Herc's mentor and parries the anti-Olympus scheming of Hades (James Woods).

Woods portrays the Lord of the Underworld as a sour, conniving Hollywood agent. He works every meeting, with gods, mortals or demons, as if it's a bored crowd in a Vegas lounge ("So is this an audience or a mosaic?" he asks after a gag bombs). Even his compliments have the bite of insults: "You look like the Fate worse than death," he purrs to one of three haggish wraiths. And when he blows his smoldering top, it's like Krakatau in orgasm. In character, design and performance, Hades has it all.

This is a bright movie, in both senses of the word. The visual style, inspired by the pointy illustrations of Gerald Scarfe (who served as production designer), challenges the eye: blink, and you'll miss the sign in the sky indicating that Marilyn Monroe isn't just a star, she's a whole constellation. The script by Musker, Clements, Bob Shaw, Donald McEnery and Irene Mecchi is rife with Oedipus riffs, Achilles spiels, Zeus zingers and roman-numeral jokes—"Somebody call IX-I-I." The Greeks had a word for it: shtick.

Composer Alan Menken, on vacation after the operatic *Hunchback* score, hasn't delved this deeply into pop pastiche since his 1982 off-Broadway hit, *Little Shop of Horrors.* The quintet of Muses, like *Little Shop's* black-thrush trio, tells the story, doing justice to the jaunty R.-and-B.

inflections ("and then along came Zeus") of David Zippel's serviceable lyrics. The ballad *Go the Distance*, as pummeled by Michael Bolton, is the tune you'll hear coming from every radio, music store and elevator this summer.

The eighth or ninth version of anything (except Beethoven's symphonies) is likely to seem less fresh than the first, and for all its bustle *Hercules* hasn't quite the wit to make one forget *Aladdin*. But one shouldn't look a gift horse in the mouth, especially if it's Pegasus. Sixty years after *Snow White*, *Hercules* proves that Walt's art form is still sassy and snazzy.

VILLAGE VOICE, 7/1/97, p. 89, J. Hoberman

Back in Lotusland, *Hercules* consecrates the triumphant merger of Broadway brass and animated pizzazz. The movie's infectious vulgarity (not to mention its gold-fuchsia-turquoise color scheme) trumps anything *Contempt*'s producer might have imagined. With Hermes envisioned as *Late Show* bandleader Paul Shaffer and the Muses an r&b gospel chorus out of *Bubblin' Brown Sugar*, Mount Olympus is a delightfully celeb-stocked Vegas lounge while, tie-ins be damned, the Underworld is compared to McDonald's—five billion souls served so far.

The favorite character of Italian *peplums*, Hercules here sports a Kirk Douglas chin cleft and a credo cribbed from a box of Wheaties: "I'm on my way—I can go the distance." Hunkules, as the Muses dub him, is coached to the superstardom that will be celebrated in Michael Bolton's strident finale by the bouncy, bulbous-nosed satyr—voice supplied by Danny De Vito—and vamped by a slinky vixen named Meg (short for Megara), modeled on screwball wise-girls like Jean Arthur or Barbara Stanwyck.

Executed from designs by Gerald Scarfe by the team responsible for *Aladdin*, *Hercules* is a genuinely funny and inventive animated cartoon. It's also confident enough to encompass its own critique. After killing a computer-generated Hydra, Hercules's success includes the Hercules Store, Hercul-Ade, Air-Herc, et al. "I'm the most famous hero in all Greece—I'm an action figure," he cries at the climax of a scene that seems less satire than social realism. (The morning of the pagan celebration consecrating midtown Manhattan to Disney's latest creation, I received a mailorder catalogue selling limited-edition Hercules coins, lithographs, watch-and-figurine chotchkes, and musical snow globes, as well as more plebeian swimsuits, bike shorts, T-shirts, and toys.)

"How cute—a couple of rodents looking for a theme park," Meg riffs on seeing Hades's little helpers in cartoon-character disguise. Hades himself (modeled on and given voice by James Woods) is a sarcastic showbiz hustler with a flame of blue hair and a motor-mouthed shpritz filled with Yiddish-isms. An unmistakable Hollywood agent, plotting a "hostile takeover" of Olympus, this devil suggests Michael Eisner's paranoid fantasy of Michael Ovitz's palace revolt.

Also reviewed in:
NEW YORK TIMES, 6/13/97, p. C1, Janet Maslin
NEW YORKER, 7/7/97, p. 78, Anthony Lane
VARIETY, 6/23-29/97, p. 94, Leonard Klady
WASHINGTON POST, 6/27/97, p. D1, Rita Kempley
WASHINGTON POST, 6/27/97, Weekend/p. 44, Desson Howe

HOLLOW REED

A Cinepix Film Properties release of a Scala/Senator Film/Channel Four Films presentation of a Scala production. *Executive Producer:* Nik Powell and Stephen Woolley. *Producer:* Elizabeth Karlsen. *Director:* Angela Pope. *Screenplay:* Paula Milne. *Story:* Neville Bolt. *Director of Photography:* Remi Adefarasin. *Editor:* Sue Wyatt. *Music:* Anne Dudley. *Sound:* John Pritchard. *Casting:* Susie Figgis. *Production Designer:* Stuart Walker. Art Director: Diane Dancklefsen and Charmian Adams. *Costumes:* Pam Downe. *Running time:* 106 minutes. *MPAA Rating:* Not Rated.

CAST: Martin Donovan (Martyn Wyatt); Joely Richardson (Hannah Wyatt); Ian Hart (Tom Dixon); Jason Flemyng (Frank Donally); Sam Bould (Oliver Wyatt); Edward Hardwicke (Judge); Douglas Hodge (Hannah's Lawyer); Annette Badland (Martyn's Lawyer).

LOS ANGELES TIMES, 5/2/97, Calendar/p. 21, Kevin Thomas

"Hollow Reed" is one of those intelligent, understated traditional-style films in which fairly early on you think you know where it's headed. Even so, you can be caught up in this taut, excellent British picture because it has such an acute grasp of the twists and turns of human psychology and emotions and becomes loaded with a deeply involving, increasingly harrowing suspense.

In his British film debut, Martin Donovan plays an English physician, Martyn Wyatt, in a sizable unidentified city in England. He has settled into a solid relationship with another man, Tom (Ian Hart), in a small apartment, but has only limited access to his 9-year-old son Oliver (Sam Bould). Oliver lives with his mother, Hannah (Joely Richardson), and her lover Frank (Jason Flemyng), an architect who recently moved into their spacious, airy home.

The film opens with the boy—a bad cut, along his right eyebrow—streaking through the night to the home of his father, who does not have the right to keep his son overnight. According to the boy, he was attacked by another child, but when Martyn finds this not to be true and when Oliver later ends up with a broken hand, the father becomes suspicious. Martyn's lawyer tells him he must on all accounts keep his cool—but he can't.

Marked by insight and compassion for Martyn and the vulnerability of his status as a gay parent, "Hollow Reed" quite possibly gains special dimension because it was both written and directed by women—Paula Milne and Angela Pope, respectively.

One evidence of this is that, unlikable as Hannah becomes, she also is understandable, which is absolutely crucial if the film is to work. Here's a woman of pleasant if unexceptional looks and equally unexceptional intellect. Her self-confidence has been undermined by the failure of her marriage, and she's carried away by her hot new romance. She's enraged and embittered at her ex-husband, one of those men who repress their homosexuality only to marry disastrously.

While one by one the adults around him behave recklessly—and worse—Oliver struggles to survive, keeping his own counsel for good reason. (One nifty touch: Oliver, profoundly wary of the world, has rigged a little cart, like a toy, that he pulls around the halls at the top of his home's open staircase. He has attached a rearview mirror to it for surveillance; he also frequently peeks through Venetian blinds.)

If Milne has written roles of exceptional depth and dimension for the actors, Pope in turn has directed them to maximum impact. Bould is impeccable in what had to have been a very difficult role for him. Richardson wisely doesn't ask us to try to like Hannah, and Hart (memorable as John Lennon in "Backbeat") and Flemyng are similarly first-rate.

Donovan is a marvel of versatility; in a comparatively short time, he's come a long way from the quirky world of Hal Hartley films to his prize-winning portrayal of the sensitive suitor Nicole Kidman should have gone for in "The Portrait of a Lady," to this limning of a gay man facing the very real prospect of losing both his son and lover.

NEW YORK POST, 4/18/97, p. 44, Larry Worth

Abused children. Gay parents. Courtroom truth-twisting. Cinematically speaking, they've been recycled to point of tedium.

But if a pretty compelling reason is required to sit through the last variation, "Hollow Reed" has three: stand-out acting, an unusually intelligent script and tension-filled direction.

It starts with the image of a little boy with a badly bloodied face running through the woods. Showing up on his divorced dad's doorstep, he claims school chums beat him up.

Subsequent injuries force the father to suspect that his ex-wife's live-in boyfriend is hitting the child. But getting custody is a sticky issue since dad is living with a male lover.

What follows is exceptionally compelling since the main players—mother, father and their significant others—prove flawed, vulnerable individuals. Instead of settling for a gay "Kramer vs. Kramer" knockoff, director Angela Pope moves the production to a more challenging plane, devoid of easy answers.

In addition, Pope never sensationalizes the material.

Scenes of child abuse and sexual encounters merely set a tone, artfully complementing Paula Milne's stunningly honest dialogue.

Then there's the cast which is just about flawless. Martin ("Portrait of a Lady") Donovan is in especially fine form. Aside from adopting a convincing British accent (to accommodate the Bath, England, setting), he superbly communicates an anguished father's concerns and frustration.

Almost as good are Joely ("101 Dalmatians") Richardson's lonely, blinders-wearing mom, Ian ("Backbeat") Hart's sentient gay lover and Jason ("Rob Roy") Flemyng as a Jekyll/Hyde who's as monstrous as he is appealing.

But that's not to forget Sam Bould as the terrified center of attention. He could write the book on avoiding precious child shots.

The result will never be called the feel-good movie of the year. But "Hollow Reed" is proof-positive that talent can put new life in the most tired of subjects.

NEWSDAY, 4/18/97, Part II/p. B13, John Anderson

Before surrendering to the movie-of-the-week proclivities that have been lurking about its hedge-rows, "Hollow Reed" is an enormously subtle film, a movie that seethes in its understatement and acts like a hand grenade in the war over gay parenthood.

Set in England, but thematically transatlantic, it poses the question: Is a child better off with his mother and her abusive boyfriend? Or with his gay father and his lover? It seems like a no-brainer, but then the movie doesn't really *ask* the question either. This is a story with a definite agenda. But as is usually true with propaganda, the end can justify the means.

As British director Angela Pope showed in her first feature, "Captives," she has an eye and ear for the fringes of English society—although the elements of "Hollow Reed" are a few rungs farther up the ladder. Martyn Wyatt (Martin Donovan) is a mild, thoughtful doctor, with a live-in lover named Tom (Ian Hart) and a son named Ollie (Sam Bould). The child's mother, Hannah (Joely Richardson), works nights and leaves Ollie home with her boyfriend, Frank (Jason Flemyng). And Ollie has been having a lot of "accidents."

When he shows up bloodied at Martyn's house, he lies that some boys roughed him up. But he doesn't have to say much. Pope sets up her characters' interconnections and festering resentments with enormous economy, substituting deft visual storytelling for wordage. What dialogue there is sounds like outtakes from the notes of a failed social worker:

"Kids lie, don't they?"

"You don't know what it's like trying to get love from a child who won't give it to you."

"My father used to slap me. It made me respect him."

"It'll never happen again."

It's no secret what's going on. The crux of the story is what happens to Ollie (given a precise and moving performance by young Sam Bould) once his father starts fighting for him. Donovan and Hart prove themselves among the most adept actors around, Richardson is deliciously despicable as the mother in denial, but Flemyng gives a really remarkable performance, one that's almost unthinkable in any similar American production.

Maybe the fact that Frank is involved with a woman who was married to a homosexual is gnawing at his manhood. Maybe the fact that Ollie is the son of a homosexual increases the friction. But there's also the glint of pleasure in Frank's face each time he prepares to strike Ollie. It's as dislikable a role as is apt to come along in Flemyng's career, and it's remarkable how he keeps the character unsympathetic without consigning him to pure evil.

"I must learn to control the excesses of my nature," Ollie recites at Frank's commands, and these are words that could serve as the movie's mantra. In its reserved English manner, "Hollow Reed" is as indignant a tale about child abuse as we're likely to see.

VILLAGE VOICE, 4/22/97, p. 77, Amy Taubin

Most actors know a little something about psychology. It's a rare actor who understands how people are defined by the contingencies of history. The young British actor Ian Hart brings that understanding to every role he plays. That's what made his performances as the Communist freedom fighter in Ken Loach's Spanish Civil War film *Land and Freedom* and as the young John

Lennon in both Christopher Munch's *The Hours and Times* and Iain Softley's *Backbeat* so complicated. Add in his concentrated energy, inventiveness, chameleon-like powers, and his uncanny ability to let you know what's going on inside his character's head without a word or a discernible gesture, and you have one stunning actor, someone who pulls your eyes whenever he's onscreen.

You can get a fair idea of the range of Hart's talent from his radically different roles in two British films opening here within a week of each other. In Angela Pope's *Hollow Reed,* he's the ardent gay lover of a divorced doctor who's fighting for custody of his young son; in Thaddeus O'Sullivan's *Nothing Personal,* he's a paramilitary psycho killer at war with the IRA. Skillfully constructed, character-driven social dramas, both films are distinguished by unusually fine ensemble acting, but Hart's performances are a cut above.

Based on a true story, *Hollow Reed* is a slightly didactic suspense film about child abuse played against a landscape of homophobia. Martin Donovan plays Martyn Wyatt, a doctor who divorces his wife Hannah (Joely Richardson) when he falls in love with Tom Dixon (Hart), a gay bookstore owner. When Martyn discovers that his son (Sam Bould) is being physically abused by Hannah's new lover, he sues for custody. Desperate to protect his child, Martyn is torn between going back in the closet or trying to convince the court that his son is better off living with his openly gay father than with a mother who refuses to recognize that her properly heterosexual but psychopathic boyfriend has been beating the kid to a pulp every time he's left alone with him.

Straightforwardly directed (although a little too heavy-handed with mood music), *Hollow Reed* keeps the focus on the actors. Richardson is unsparing and unsentimental as the intelligent, professional woman whose sexual involvement warps her judgment. Her Hannah is all the more frightening for not being a monster (although the film is too bent on stacking the deck against her). As the child who keeps silent about his abuse out of terror and because he doesn't want to interfere with his mother's happiness, Bould is properly fragile and completely convincing. And Donovan has finally escaped the mannerisms of his Hal Hartley period. He has a solidity and passion here that he's never shown before.

As for Hart, he seems to have metamorphosed into a Greek god. The characters he played in previous films, however extraordinary, would never get checked out on the street. But here, his features look finely chiseled, the lines of neck, shoulders, and torso perfectly proportioned and aligned. He's a babe, and an unmistakably gay babe to boot. (Hart and Donovan have a love scene that's all the hotter for being brief.) But what's interesting is that, for all his beauty, there's no narcissism in the performance. Hart's transformed himself specifically to show how little investment this character has in his own beauty. No one-night stand, Tom's the guy who's around for the long haul; he's good-humored, loyal, emotionally generous, and far too honest to lie about his sexuality even for his lover's sake. For Tom, being openly gay is a moral choice, one that at the end of the 20th century is still subversive.

Also reviewed in:
CHICAGO TRIBUNE, 9/24/97, Tempo/p. 4, John Petrakis
NEW REPUBLIC, 5/5/97, p. 24, Stanley Kauffmann
NEW YORK TIMES, 4/18/97, p. C4, Stephen Holden
VARIETY, 2/5-11/96, p. 62, Leonard Klady
WASHINGTON POST, 6/6/97, Weekend/p. 63, Stephen Hunter

HOME ALONE 3

A Twentieth Century Fox release of a John Hughes production. *Executive Producer:* Ricardo Mestres. *Producer:* John Hughes and Hilton Green. *Director:* Raja Gosnell. *Screenplay:* John Hughes. *Director of Photography:* Julio Macat. *Editor:* Bruce Green, Malcolm Campbell, and David Rennie.. *Music:* Nick Glennie-Smith. *Music Editor:* Laura Perlman. *Sound:* Jose Antonio

Garcia and (music) Malcolm Luker. *Sound Editor:* Mike Wilhoit. *Casting:* Billy Hopkins, Suzanne Smith, Kerry Barden, and Jennifer McNamara. *Production Designer:* Henry Bumstead. *Art Director:* Jack G. Taylor, Jr. *Set Designer:* Cate Bangs, Kevin Cross, David W. Krummel, Leslie Thomas, and Jim Wallis. *Set Decorator:* Richard Goddard. *Set Dresser:* Joe Bristol, Heidi Hublou, Tim McGee, Jon Nicholson, and John R. Ziganto. *Special Effects:* Ron Bolanowski. *Costumes:* Jodie Tillen. *Make-up:* Linda Boykin-Williams. *Stunt Coordinator:* R.A. Rondell and Freddie Hice. *Running time:* 97 minutes. *MPAA Rating:* PG.

CAST: Alex D. Linz (Alex); Olek Krupa (Beaupre); Rya Kihlstedt (Alice); Lenny Von Dohlen (Jernigan); David Thornton (Unger); Haviland Morris (Karen); Kevin Kilner (Jack); Marian Seldes (Mrs. Hess); Seth Smith (Stan); Scarlett Johansson (Molly); Christopher Curry (Agent Stuckey); Baxter Harris (Police Captain); James Saito (Chinese Mob Boss); Kevin Gudahl (Techie); Richard Hamilton (Cab Driver); Freeman Coffey (Recruiting Officer); Krista Lally (Dispatcher); Neil Flynn (Police Officer #1); Tony Mockus, Jr. (Police Officer #2); Pat Healy (Agent Rogers); James L. Chisem (Police Officer #3); Darwin L. Harris (Photographer); Adrianne Duncan (Flight Attendant); Sharon Sachs (Annoying Woman); Joseph L. Caballero (Security Guard); Larry C. Tankson (Cart Driver); Jennifer Daley (Police Photographer #2); Darren T. Knaus (Voice of Parrot).

LOS ANGELES TIMES, 12/12/97, Calendar/p. 22, David Kronke

[The following review by David Kronke appeared in a slightly different form in **NEWSDAY, 12/12/97, Part II/p. B8.]**

"Home Alone 3" follows in the, er, proud tradition of "The Sting 2" and "Jaws 3-D," movies that have nothing to do with the original film that inspired them, except a flaccid adherence to the formula that made the first a success.

If you have a name brand product, need you bother to clutter the equation with name-brand stars? Macaulay Culkin has evolved from the once-adorable moppet of the first two flicks to a teenager who could afford his own wing of the new Getty museum. Likewise, the producers figured out that virtually anyone with a SAG card can feverishly mug and indulge in pratfalls, so what's the point in ponying up for pricey talent like Joe Pesci and Daniel Stern, Culkin's erstwhile antagonists?

The principal constant in this series' current outing is John Hughes, the inexplicably successful master of teeth-rattling, mean-spirited slapstick of the sort that he brings not only to his own increasingly banal material ("Career Opportunities," "Baby's Day Out"), but also to crass updating of beloved classics ("101 Dalmatians," "Miracle on 34th Street," "Flubber"). He's so busy these days, he probably saves time by reducing his pitch meetings to a single, succinct sentence—"Impossibly cute kid/animals/wad of goo sadistically rout bad guys, resulting in wacky mayhem until an insanely maudlin conclusion."

Hughes' scenario this time around is characteristically bland. An invaluable Air Force computer chip is stolen—one bad guy intones dramatically, and expositorily, "Whoever possesses this chip could dominate the entire region.' (Evidently, someone did research finding that children are more impressed by the word "region" than, say, "planet.")

So, of course, said chip improbably winds up in the hands of our hero, Alex (Alex D. Linz, Michelle Pfeiffer's son in "One Fine Day"), who is suddenly stricken by a rare strain of chickenpox that induces neither fatigue nor discomfort and takes care not to mottle telegenic faces. Which means Alex, and Alex alone, is around to detect this crack group of international villains descending upon his neighborhood. In their quest to recapture their prize, these elite ne'er-do-wells search one whole house a day (apparently, it's not that vital to locate the microchip).

And even though Alex gets in endless trouble for perceived prank calls to the police—the bad guys, of course, elude Chicago's finest, if not an 8-year-old—his mom still sees fit to leave him at home with no protection against the Big Bad World, or vice versa.

Unfortunately, this takes way too long to set up. Hughes handed the directing chores to Raja Gosnell, a veteran film editor who astonishingly allows the first two-thirds of the film to sag badly.

The slapstick finale is vintage Hughes-crude (two guys get their genitalia smashed; one is showered with fecal waste), unnecessarily rough (two guys endure Dolby-ized electroshock; a woman absorbs two violent cracks to her delicately sculpted face; one guy takes spray-paint in his eyes) and simultaneously overly elaborate and drearily predictable. Kids will laugh as much as adults groan.

If Hughes isn't pummeling his characters senseless, his wit is benign to the point of nonexistent: His idea of a huge laugh is sending Dad off to work in a suit coat, shirt and tie—and boxer shorts. He also creates a smart-aleck parrot who serves as a sort of pre-pubescent Greek Chorus, cracking witless one-liners that might amuse 8-year-olds. No danger of your sides splitting here.

NEW YORK POST, 12/12/97, p. 56, Michael Medved

"Home Alone 3" qualifies as one of the season's more pleasant surprises by confounding the low expectations surrounding its release.

After all, this movie represents an unnecessary extension (with a no-name cast) of a series that already seemed sadly exhausted with "Home Alone 2."

To replace Macaulay Culkin, now a moody teenager, writer-producer John Hughes installed 8-year-old Alex D. Linz as his puerile protagonist, suggesting no plot connection at all between the characters in the previous films and those in this purported sequel.

That hardly matters, since it turns out this new kid (who appeared in McDonald's commercials and "One Fine Day" with Michelle Pfeiffer) is terrific—wholesome, smart, natural, charming and cuddly without becoming cloying.

His character comes down with chicken pox while dad (Kevin Kilner) is away on a business trip. Despite the fact that mom (Haviland Morris) wants to stay home to care for him, she goes to her office for a business emergency, leaving the sick boy conveniently home alone.

Due to a chance switch of parcels in an airport, the child winds up with a remote controlled car with a top secret Air Force computer chip hidden inside it. A group of international criminals will stop at nothing to get it and to sell it to terrorists.

The suave bad guys (led by Polish actor Olek Krupa, and the undeniably glamorous Rya Kihlstedt) assume they'll make short work of the kid, knowing nothing of his elaborate booby traps and sadistic home defense strategies.

In contrast to the two bumbling burglars of the first two "Home Alones" (and in Hughes' unfortunate, "Flubber"), the four villains here seem more appropriately fierce and formidable—deploying high-tech wizardy and wearing black turtlenecks in the style of the "Man From U.N.C.L.E." TV show.

Raja Gosnell, the veteran film editor, makes a solid directorial debut, though this new film lacks the sweet, seasonal sentimentality of its predecessors. In fact, the action is oddly set in January, and John Williams' magical, Christmas music from the first two films has been replaced by a serviceable, nondescript score by Nick Glennie-Smith.

Moviegoers won't be dazzled or inspired by the crude-comedy yuks of this predictable project, but they won't feel cheated either.

SIGHT AND SOUND, 1/98, p. 44, Jamie Graham

Hong Kong. Four thieves acquire a $10 million top-secret computer chip. To smuggle it, they hide the chip inside a toy remote control car. But at the airport, the thieves make off accidentally with the wrong package, while the real one is picked up by Chicago-bound Mrs Hess. She gives the car to her neighbour, Alex Pruitt, a child who lives opposite. The thieves track the car to Mrs Hess' street and covertly begin searching each house.

Alex develops chicken-pox and, during his illness, witnesses the thieves breaking into two houses across the street. The police don't believe him so he videos a third break-in with a camcorder taped to the remote-control car. The thieves catch the car and retrieve the videotape, but Alex manages to regain the toy. Suspicious, he opens it and finds the chip, which he reports to a US-Army recruiting office. The thieves' North Korean boss gives them 24 hours to salvage the chip or they will be "nullified". They attempt to break into the Pruitts' house, but Alex foils them with various homemade defence measures. Having been contacted by the recruiting office, the police and FBI arrive and apprehend the four burglars. Alex's father returns from business and gives Alex another remote-control car. Arrested, all four thieves have come down with Alex's chicken-pox.

Whatever your feelings about Macaulay Culkin, a *Home Alone* film without him and his trademark screams is like a *Die Hard* movie minus Bruce Willis and his vest. The essence of the *Home Alone* series is the confrontation between a seemingly vulnerable child and the intruders he bests with DIY tortures. But the film-makers have made the decision to ditch Kevin (Culkin) altogether, probably because he has now reached an age where being left home alone is no longer an issue.   With Culkin gone, the opportunity for a complete springclean presented itself. However, instead of seizing the occasion, writer/producer John Hughes and director Raja Gosnell (who edited the first two *Home Alone*'s) have delivered a mish-mash of the old and the new.

The opening sequence, set in Hong Kong and introducing the computer chip Macguffin, promises much in the way of innovation. In place of Joe Pesci and Daniel Stern we have a crack team of international thieves; the crowbars, woolly hats and petty crimes are gone (as, regrettably, are the laughs), while hi tech gadgets, designer suits and multi million pound heists are in. You won't catch these villains poking their heads through cat-flaps.

Modernity is further achieved by the bold decision to discard John Williams' Christmas-flavoured music for a more dynamic score. Nick Glennie-Smith is best known for his work in Bruckheimer and Simpson's explosive event films *(Con Air, The Rock, Crimson Tide)*. Here, his urgent industrial music sits comfortably with this more action-orientated third instalment. The scene in which Alex (played by Alex D Linz, Culkin's replacement) records the burglary of a neighbour's house with a camcorder strapped to a remote-control car is of particular note: music, editing and fluent camerawork are deftly synched together to create a fast-moving set-piece unlike anything in the first two films.

It is a disappointment, then, that the promising opening and technical assurance are mired by a plot that slowly segues into all-too-familiar territory.   A string of coincidences places the computer chip in Alex's home, and once again the villains embark on a climactic siege of the protagonist's house (albeit with electronic keypads). It is no surprise that they are thwarted by a torrent of cartoon violence. The film-makers would no doubt argue that this adherence to an established formula ensures the series' overall coherence; it's unfortunate, however, that such slapstick brutality acts as the constant thread in a children's franchise, which reaches new heights of cruelty when a lawnmower's rotating blades descend on an upturned face.

Also reviewed in:
NEW YORK TIMES, 12/12/97, p. E16, Stephen Holden
VARIETY, 12/8-14/97, p. 112, Joe Leydon
WASHINGTON POST, 12/12/97, Weekend/p. 56, Desson Howe

HOODLUM

A United Artists Pictures release of a Frank Mancuso, Jr. production. *Executive Producer:* Bill Duke, Laurence Fishburne, and Helen Sugland. *Producer:* Frank Mancuso, Jr. *Director:* Bill Duke. *Screenplay:* Chris Brancato. *Director of Photography:* Frank Tidy. *Editor:* Harry Keramidas. *Music:* Elmer Bernstein. *Music Editor:* Kathy Durning and Patricia Carlin. *Choreographer:* Otis Sallid. *Sound:* Curt Frisk and (muisc) Keith Grant. *Sound Editor:* Gregory M. Gerlich. *Casting:* Amanda Mackey Johnson and Cathy Sandrich. *Production Designer:* Charles Bennett. *Art Director:* Gary Baugh. *Set Decorator:* Maria Nay. *Set Designer:* Patrick Raney, Chris Phillips, Kerry Sanders, Timothy Mann, and Cydney Harris. *Set Dresser:* Cyril Mathys Jr., Scott Troha, and Juan Vela, Jr. *Special Effects:* Guy Clayton. *Costumes:* Richard Bruno. *Make-up:* Stacye Branche. *Make-up (Andy Garcia):* K.G. Ramsey. *Make-up (Vanessa L. Williams):* Kate Best *Special Effects Make-up:* Bill "Splat" Johnson. *Stunt Coordinator:* Greg Elam. *Running time:* 130 minutes. *MPAA Rating:* R.

CAST: Laurence Fishburne (Ellsworth "Bumpy" Johnson); Tim Roth (Dutch Schultz); Vanessa L. Williams (Francine Hughes); Andy Garcia (Lucky Luciano); Cicely Tyson (Stephanie St. Clair); Chi McBride (Illinois Gordon); Clarence Williams, III (Bub Hewlett); Richard Bradford

(Captain Foley); William Atherton (Thomas Dewey); Loretta Devine (Pigfoot Mary); Queen Latifah (Sulie); Mike Starr (Albert Salke); Beau Starr (Jules Salke); Paul Benjamin (Whispers); Joe Guzaldo (Bo Weinberg); Ed O'Ross (Lulu Rosenkrantz); J.W. Smith (Calvin); Eddie "Bo" Smith, Jr. (Tee-Nincy); John Toles-Bey (Vallie); David Darlow (Johnny "Figures" DiPalmero); Steve Pickering (Lucky's Henchman);   Ellis Foster (Undertaker);   Bill Henderson (Mr. Redmond);   Juan A. Ramirez (Enrique "Henry" Miro);   Kevin Morrow (Waldo);   Tony Fitzpatrick (Dutch's Driver); Robert Cornelius (Hobo); Tab Baker (Willie Brunder); Joe Van Slyke (Warden); Daniel Bryant (Hep-Cat Man); Don James (Piano Man); Sulanya "Sue" Conway (Miss Philmore); Paul Eckstein (Dutch's Thug); Christian Payton (Jimmy); Jackie Taylor (Mrs. Andrews); Dick Gjonola (Owney Madden); David Nisbet (Man in Cotton Club); Nancy Nickel (Woman in Cotton Club); Ted Love and Kenya Cagle (Runners); Jim Saltouros (Lieutenant); Marc Vann (Dutch's Liquor Henchman); Cheridah Best (Prostitute); Colin Bradley Sylvester (Chee Chee); Iris Lieberman (Female Prison Guard); Leonard Roberts (Tyrone); John Watson, Sr. (Manager of Pool Hall); Lisa Boltauzer (Dancer); Michael McCary (Osgood); Eric Kilpatrick (Security Guard); Demetrice O'Neal (Singer); Tony Powell (Rent Party Singer); Kevin Morrow (Church Conductor); Louis Price and Vernon Oliver Price (Church Singers); Laurnea Wilkerson (Cotton Club Singer); Tony Rich (Duke Ellington); Kim Adams (Show Girl); David A. Jansen (Doorman); Fred Nelson (Sideline Musician).

LOS ANGELES TIMES, 8/27/97, Calendar/p. 8, Kenneth Turan

Laurence Fishburne is one actor who has charisma to burn, but even his incendiary performance can't ignite "Hoodlum," a would-be gangster epic that generates less heat than a nickel cigar.

Fishburne does his best, and as Ellsworth "Bumpy" Johnson, the numbers king of 1930s Harlem, that best is considerable. With the thinnest possible mustache and a glare that could melt steel, Fishburne's Bumpy is fierce, magnetic, irresistible, the kind of handsome, nerveless desperado every crime drama needs. But even this actor, whose Ike Turner in "What's Love Got to Do With It" still burns in the memory, can only do so much.

There's nothing wrong with "Hoodlum's" designs on being a Harlem-based "Godfather," but the film has turned out more ambitious and physically impressive than dramatically accomplished. While the scenes that are supposed to create audience involvement are easy to spot, they don't play as intended, and the result is a plodding epic that tends to the lethargic and lackadaisical.

Director Bill Duke has done a considerably better job than Eddie Murphy did with the same period in "Harlem Nights," but "Hoodlum" lacks the kind of energy and interest that marked Duke's fine directing debut, "A Rage in Harlem," or his later "Deep Cover," which also starred Fishburne.

But while "A Rage in Harlem" had a juicy novel by Chester Himes as source material, "Hoodlum" has to make do with a problematic first produced screenplay by Chris Brancato. He's loaded his work with self-conscious period slang like the mysterious "You better not frog up on me," but it still feels inauthentic and incapable of getting even slightly below the surface.

Better writing would have helped most of Fishburne's costars, but it might not have had much effect on Tim Roth's portrayal of rival gangster Dutch Schultz.

Roth, who could people an entire episode of "The Untouchables" with all the crooks and lowlifes he's created, plays the Dutchman as a scrappy but genial psychopath who kills without blinking. It's the kind of self-conscious performance that encourages remarks like "interesting acting choice" instead of sweeping you away the way Fishburne's work does.

Fishburne's Johnson, who became Dutch Schultz's ultimate nemesis, is introduced (on the day he's getting out of Sing-Sing prison) as a kind of one-man Harlem Renaissance who writes poetry, plays chess and thinks deeply about the books he's read.

Returning to Harlem and hooking up with his cousin, Illinois Gordon (Chi McBride), Johnson is disturbed at the way Schultz's thuggish minions are treating old pal Stephanie St. Clair (Cicely Tyson), the regal monarch of Harlem numbers known as Madame Queen. He offers to help and is soon thrown by circumstances into a position running the entire operation.

Big a job as that is, it leaves Johnson time to romance the attractive Francine Hughes (Vanessa Williams), a do-right member of Marcus Garvey's United Negro Improvement Assn. who does not usually hang with lowlifes. But it's not every thug who understands racial empowerment and can talk about the numbers racket as "the only home-grown business we got in Harlem," and soon Francine's moral objections prove as disposable as yesterday's policy slips.

Williams does all she's asked to do in this largely window-dressing role, which is more than some of the rest of the cast can manage. Many, including Andy Garcia as mob boss Lucky Luciano, are infected by the film's lack of tension and can't bring their usual sharpness to bear.

Much of the film is taken up with the battle between the Dutchman and Bumpy for control of Harlem's numbers, which may be the only thing in "Hoodlum" that actually happened. The film ends with a lengthy disclaimer reminding viewers that "the events, places and most of the characters ... are purely fictional," which will be good news to admirers of squeaky-clean special prosecutor and future Republican presidential candidate Thomas Dewey (William Atherton), here depicted as practically drowning in bribes.

"Hoodlum's" main points vis-a-vis Johnson, that he was passionate about African American dignity and solidarity but at some point risked losing his soul because of his bloody war with Schultz, is not convincingly made. The movie may turn on Bumpy for a time, but audiences will remain unconvinced. He's the only thing on screen that's alive, and no one will want to question his choices, no matter where they lead.

NEW YORK POST, 8/27/97, p. 43, Michael Medved

The bloody struggle over control of the numbers racket in Harlem of the 1930's hardly qualifies as a crucial battleground in the struggle for African-American dignity and equal rights.

Nevertheless, that intra-mural gangster grudge-match receives the full Robin Hood(lum) treatment in this surprisingly rousing formula flick that uses spectacular star power to overcome its own lack of subtlety, originality or historical accuracy.

Laurence Fishburne portrays the heretofore little-known Ellsworth (Bumpy) Johnson, an uptown enforcer originally associated with an exotic crime queenpin, played by Cicely Tyson.

As the movie embellishes the story, Bumpy protects her enterprises when she goes to prison and fights the efforts of the murderous, explosive Dutch Schultz (Tim Roth) to extend his empire into Harlem.

In the process, Johnson defies the all-powerful mob boss Lucky Luciano (Andy Garcia) and emerges as a much-admired neighborhood folk hero.

"Hoodlum" focuses too much on its protagonist's predictably tortured relationships with two altogether fictional characters: an idealistic, aristocratic love interest (Vanessa Williams) and an earthy, overweight cousin (Chi McBride) who becomes his most faithful (and inevitably abused) lieutenant.

The movie also senselessly smears three-time New York governor and crime-busting prosecutor Thomas E. Dewey, portrayed here by William Atherton, as a greedy, corrupt, bribe-hungry toady to the mob.

Of course, few moviegoers know or care enough about the real Tom Dewey—or about Bumpy Johnson, Dutch Schultz, or Lucky Luciano for that matter—to complain about details of characterization, especially when the performances are as splashy and satisfying as they are here.

Roth is particularly effective (and horrifyingly funny) as a hair-trigger psychotic who is far less complex—and far more riveting—than the Dustin Hoffman version of Dutch Schultz in 1991's "Billy Bathgate."

Garcia is lucky as Luciano, effortlessly exerting cobra-like hypnotic power and suggesting the raw menace behind an exaggeratedly elegant exterior.

Fishburne is also perfectly cast, projecting an impressive combination of heroics and savagery, but remaining too indestructibly sympathetic when the plot takes pains to prove (yawn!) that even admirable battles against evil unavoidably lead to their own evil excess.

Like other Depression Era shoot-'em-ups, "Hoodlum" indulges in plenty of antique cars, snappy costumes, New Deal references, and ritualistic invocations of Duke Ellington and the glamorous Cotton Club.

But director Bill Duke ("A Rage in Harlem," "Deep Cover") never lets settings upstage his larger-than-life characters.

Showing steady improvement in handling actors, and in the energy and elegance of his images, Duke never crushes his puny plot with weighty messages about the nature of racism, capitalism, or cosmic justice.

The garish and decidedly old-fashioned melodrama may feel operatic, but at least it never tries to be "Twilight of the Gods."

NEWSDAY, 8/27/97, Part II/p. B2, John Anderson

Far less a gangster movie than a movie about gangster movies, Bill Duke's "Hoodlum" revisits some familiar turf. The war for the '30s Harlem rackets fought by the psychopathic Dutch Shultz and his uptown nemesis Bumpy Johnson—and controlled by the Sicilian puppetmaster Lucky Luciano.

It's a great story, as we've already seen—in E.L. Doctorow's novel, "Billy Bathgate," for instance, as well as Francis Ford Coppola's film "The Cotton Club," obviously, with varying degrees of success.

Somewhere in the middle of novelistic gravity and Hollywood pomposity lands Duke's movie, which presents Bumpy—a poetry-writing, chess-playing ex-con portrayed by Laurence Fishburne—as a Prohibition Robin Hood. Tim Roth is the homicidal, foul-mouthed Schultz, who's muscling in on the numbers game of "Queen" Stephanie St. Clair (Cicely Tyson), leaving a trail of blood and body parts along Lenox Avenue. Andy Garcia, one eye drooping, is Luciano, who just wants everyone to play nice and the black people to stay uptown.

That Duke wants to make a hero of Bumpy Johnson (here, he's a virtual auxiliary member of the Harlem Renaissance) or depict the numbers racket as a form of black enterprise, certainly are areas for debate. But the reasons "Hoodlum" fails to work as a film have more to do with the rococo script by Chris Brancato—whose attempts to recreate the era through constant period references are ham-handed at best—and because Duke is just as subtle in his choice of camera movements, backgrounds and the way he directs his actors.

The overbroad characterizations and the set design (think of a slightly less garish "Dick Tracy") don't seem to meld with Duke's apparent wish to make a film that works in one genre (the western) while simultaneously parodying another (the Warners Prohibition-era gangster flick). Bumpy's spiritual redemption in the midst of all this comes very close to satire.

All of the actors are good; none performs up to his or her potential. Fishburne has too tough a time juggling nobility, ruthlessness and romantic appeal; his affair with the upstanding, Christianly Francine Hughes (Vanessa Williams) goes nowhere, although she does get to blow away some bad guys. Garcia is mostly mugging, and Roth, who can do sociopathic scum while standing on his head, is a bit cartoonish, partly because every other word out of his mouth is _____. Maybe there should be a promotional contest, with the winner correctly counting how many times he says it.

Duke is much better choreographing action sequences than he is constructing moral parables. The shootouts are fairly electric, the various forms of mayhem abrupt and startling. "Hoodlum" would have been much better, though, had he expended less effort making a tortured demigod out of Bumpy and simply let him be a man.

VILLAGE VOICE, 9/2/97, p. 73, Amy Taubin

As florid in tone as *The Godfather,* as pictorially vivid as *The Cotton Club, Hoodlum*—Bill Duke's biopic of the black gangster Bumpy Johnson (Laurence Fishburne)—is filmmaking on a grand scale. Though the influence is undeniable, the film also has a style of its own. The slow and swooping camera moves, saturated colors, lush Ellington-inflected score, performances give an old-fashioned theatrical twist to a Depression-era fable with painful relevance to our own time.

Hoodlum focuses on Johnson's war with Dutch Schultz (Tim Roth) for control over the numbers racket in Harlem. The first white gangster to realize that poor black people putting pennies on the numbers added up to a million-dollar business, Schultz tried to muscle in on the turf of Stephanie St. Clair (Cicely Tyson), Harlem's queen of policy and Bumpy's mentor. For Bumpy, it was worth taking up arms to keep the numbers a black-owned and operated business with the profits circulating back into the Harlem economy. As the bodies pile up, Bumpy's nearest and dearest either are killed or abandon him. Only after he wins the war, does he have the luxury of wondering if he's lost his soul.

"The two most successful creations of American movies are the gangster and the Westerner: men with guns," writes Robert Warshow in his stunning 1954 essay "The Westerner." Warshow argues that the point of the western is not violent itself but rather "a certain image of man, a style, which expresses itself most clearly in violence. Watch a child with his toy guns and you will see: what most interests him is not (as we so much fear) the fantasy of hurting others, but to work out how a man might look when he shoots or is shot. A hero is one who looks like a hero"

There's a moment early in *Hoodlum* when Bumpy, fresh out of prison, is gifted with a gun. As Bumpy tests out his weapon, the camera isolates him on the right side of the frame, using slo-mo to magnify his movements as he draws and aims. Gun in hand, he becomes superhuman—he has control of time itself.

As fetishistic as anything in the oeuvres of Scorsese or Eastwood, the sequence has an extra layer of complexity because it's a black man taking control of his turf with firepower. Bumby's no 17-year-old homeboy destined not to come of age. Neither is he a psychopath, nor a member of a separate kingdom (like the Corleones). The Bumpy of *Hoodlum* is cool, intelligent, and brutally pragmatic. He calculates the risk of going to war with an occupying army; he wins and lives to tell the tale. He is the outlaw hero, a seductive fusion of tradition and transgression, fiction and fact.

As a fantasy of empowerment, *Hoodlum* is often thrilling. But the film despite it's stylized surface, also plays on its real-life basis. And though the filmmakers make a last-minute attempt to skew the film toward a cautionary tale, Bumpy is more role model than not. He has no choice but to pick up the gun. Only after he's proved himself a warrior can he make the treaty that brings peace to the streets. Fishburne doesn't soft-pedal Bumpy's brutality. The contradiction is that he's closest to being a tragic hero when the bodies pile up and the friends flee in disgust. It's lonely at the top.

So the thought occurs: with 25 per cent of young black men currently incarcerated, or having been so at some point in their lives, is it the moment to glorify gangsterism even for righteous ends? I suspect from *Hoodlum*'s off-the-wall finale that the question troubled Duke as well.

Roth matches Fishburne's energy, but his Schultz—the proto-skinhead, defiantly prole and maddened with race hatred—is a bit too broadly drawn. As Downtown boss Lucky Luciano, Andy Garcia nearly steals the picture. Garcia knows the devil is in the details—the drooping eyelid that makes his expressions impossible to read, the contemptuous twitch of his shoulders when he makes a fool of an adversary. When he goes one-on-one with Fishburne or Roth, he takes control of the rhythm of the scene. By stretching a pause, or speeding up a phrase, he forces them to pay attention to him. Bumpy Johnson may have been the Robin Hood of Harlem, but it would be sentimental to forget that Luciano held the strings.

Also reviewed in:
NEW YORK TIMES, 8/27/97, p. C16, Stephen Holden
VARIETY, 9/1-7/97, p. 75, Leonard Klady
WASHINGTON POST, 8/27/97, p. D1, Stephen Hunter

HOTEL de LOVE

A Live Entertainment release of a Village Roadshow Pictures and Pratt Films production. *Executive Producer:* Peter Heller, Graham Burke, Alex Waislitz, Greg Coote, and Heloise Waislitz. *Producer:* Michael Lake and David Parker. *Director:* Craig Rosenberg. *Screenplay:* Craig Rosenberg. *Director of Photography:* Stephen Windon. *Editor:* Bill Murphy. *Music:* Brett Rosenberg. *Sound:* Gary Wilkins, Steve Burgess and (music) Ross Cockle. *Sound Editor:* Glenn Newnham. *Casting:* Maura Fay and Lou Mitchell. *Production Designer:* Simon Dobbin. *Art Director:* Brian Dusting. *Set Decorator:* Marian Murray and Marita Mussett. *Special Effects:* Laurie Davidson. *Costumes:* Bruce Finlayson. *Make-up:* Kirsten Veysey. *Stunt Coordinator:* Chris Peters. *Running time:* 95 minutes. *MPAA Rating:* R.

CAST: Aden Young (Rick Dunne); Saffron Burrows (Melissa Morrison); Simon Bossell (Stephen Dunne); Pippa Grandison (Alison Leigh); Ray Barrett (Jack Dunne); Julia Blake (Edith Dunne); Peter O'Brien (Norman); Belinda McLory (Janet); Caleb Cluff (Bruce);

Cassandra Magrath (Suzy); Andrew Bibby (Matt); Alan Hopgood (Ronnie); Raelee Hill (Emma Andrews); Margaret Hoctor (Bridesmaid); Bayard Templin (Melissa's Father); Robert Lowe (Priest); Leo Faust (Brett); Alan Stone (Minister); Sally Lightfoot (Maid); Barbara Burder (Mrs. Fielding); Robert Tuttleby (Mr. Fielding); Craig Gillespie (Young Man); Madonna Munasinha (Eleanor, Young Woman); Michelle Twigden (Young Girl, Nail Biter); Cameron Nugent (Young Man She Kisses); Paul Crossley (Handsome Guy); Bettina Petrone (Handsome Guy's Girlfriend); Stephanie Turner and Andrew Russell (Lovers); John Forsythe (Newspaper Man); Danny Stone (Singer, Wedding Band); Simon Patterson (Guitar, Wedding Band); Peter Melberg (Bass, Wedding Band); Richard Montgomery (Keyboards, Wedding Band); Russell Smith (Drummer, Wedding Band); Ben Hall (Barman); John Baird (Cart Driver).

LOS ANGELES TIMES, 2/7/97, Calendar/p. 10, Kevin Thomas

[The following review by Kevin Thomas appeared in a slightly different form in **NEWSDAY, 2/7/97, Part II/p. B10.]**

It's hard to imagine Craig Rosenberg's "Hotel de Love" appealing to anyone who isn't hung up on romance novels, but if you're into unrequited love, this may be for you. The twist in this exceedingly minor Australian romantic comedy is that this time it's the men instead of the women who are pining away for love.

Simon Bossell's Stephen tells us how he and his fraternal twin, Rick (Aden Young), fell hard for a visiting beauty, Melissa (Saffron Burrows). Although only Rick has been intimate with her, both brothers are still obsessed with her a full decade later. Neither has been able to fall truly in love with anyone else.

In that time, Stephen has become a workaholic stockbroker while the increasingly cynical Rick has become the manager of a garish honeymoon hotel. (Its interiors seem to have been inspired by San Luis Obispo's famous Madonna Inn.) Wouldn't you know, Melissa and her fiancé (Peter O'Brien) turn up one day, which says little for their taste in resorts. Also popping up for a visit are Stephen and the twins' parents, whose marriage has gone stale over the decades.

The young stars are attractive and capable, but "Hotel de Love" is as synthetic as an old "Love Boat" episode.

NEW YORK POST, 2/7/97, p. 48, Thelma Adams

"Don't analyze me. I'm too shallow," says Rick, a womanizing fraternal twin with kiss-me lips and lyin' eyes. The caution applies to "Hotel de Love." Australian Craig Rosenberg's romantic comedy is slighter than a one-night stand.

The summer after high school, Rick (Aden Young) and his birdy brother, Stephen (Simon Bossell), fall for dreamgirl Melissa (Saffron Burrows), Rick scores; Stephen moons; Melissa enters college without her virginity.

Ten years pass. Ditched at the altar by another woman, a cynical Rick manages the Hotel de Love, a tacky wedding mill featuring theme-based love nests.

Incurable romantic Stephen, still fantasizing about the girl he never had, visits the hotel with his parents, Jack (Ray Barrett) and Edith (Julia Blake). The bickering pair have returned to the site of their honeymoon to renew their vows—if they don't kill each other first.

Having contrived to reunite his characters in Act II, Rosenberg inserts Melissa into the scene like a Barbie in a portable pink plastic playhouse. Now a philosophy don, she brings along her adorable but sexually so-so steady, Norman (Peter O'Brien).

While the movie's opening wasn't fresh, Rosenberg managed to throw a halo of youthful energy around the same old cliches. By the time all the players have checked into the Hotel de Love and the director rolls up his sleeves to tickle out the meaning of love, the fizz is out of the cheap champagne.

Playing the twin faces of male desire, Young and Bossell are appealing, if uneven. Burrows, who made a strong impression in "Circle of Friends," walks the Andie MacDowell beat. She's a riveting, self-possessed love object, but her range is untested.

A woman in the review audience critiqued Burrows' facial moles in the post-preview elevator wrap-up. Don't blame the statuesque model-turned-actress for being beautiful; blame the director for leaving so much dead time between jokes in this land-locked "Love Boat."

SIGHT AND SOUND, 8/98, p. 45, Kim Newman

Australia. Stephen Dunne spends his free time in an airport, wondering about romance. He tells the story of an obsessive love that began for him as a teenager at a party where he was struck by Melissa. But Melissa loses her virginity to Rick, his less sensitive twin. Ten years later, Rick—cynical about women after breaking up with his girlfriend Alison—is the manager of Hotel de Love, a tacky romantic theme resort. Stephen arrives there with the brothers' parents, Jack and Edith, who intend to rededicate their marriage vows after 32 years of misery. Melissa also turns up, with her boyfriend Norman.

Norman and Melissa get engaged, but have doubts, especially when Melissa tells Norman about Rick's sudden declaration of love for her. Stephen finally gets up the nerve to tell Melissa he loves her too, but falls for Alison, who turns out also to have been at the party where the brothers met Melissa. When Edith discovers that Jack has been sending her anonymous romantic notes, they settle their quarrels. Melissa marries Norman, but she instantly asks for a divorce and a year later marries Rick. Alison leaves for Barcelona, and Stephen obsessively meets every plane which might be bringing her back. Finally, she returns to him.

What chance *Hotel de Love* might have had as a romantic comedy is undone by fatal overplaying which leads most of the cast (especially Simon Bossell) to challenge characters from *Fawlty Towers,* so that even reasonably smart lines are punctuated with tics and bug eyed stares. This tone most disastrously spreads to a score that clumsily signals whether scenes are meant to be funny or touching, a necessary strategy given that the writing and playing aren't up to either tickled ribs or warmed hearts.

As the title suggests, the centrepiece of the film is its setting, a resort motel that boasts a three-foot waterfall ('Niagara Smalls'), a lounge pianist everyone seeks advice from, and rooms kitted out in a variety of romantic themes: a sports arena with cheering crowds around the bed, a garden of Eden with fake foliage and a dayglo apple, and a subterranean grotto. The decor works a few laughs, but it has been invented for the film, which makes the whole a mere cartoon rather than anything touching or grotesque.

The relationship between the long-married couple who are so committed to verbal arguments that the husband can only woo his wife with typewritten anonymous poetry is potentially the most moving. But the revelation that Jack Dunne is his wife's secret admirer is so obvious that their renewal of vows is thrown away in a climax that strives not to rip off *The Graduate* (1967) while reprising the same basic situation. The twist that prolongs the agony is that Melissa changes her mind after she has gone through with the marriage rather than before, but it's hard to care which way Saffron Burrows will decide, since her two suitors—supposedly insensitive softie Rick and bookish, lukewarm Norman—are differentiated mostly by the amount of screen time they get. Aden Young's smug playing of Rick almost forces you to sympathise with fall guy (and part-time impotent) Norman.

Only Pippa Grandison as a palmist is appealing enough to get by the forced eccentricities writer-director Craig Rosenberg lumbers his characters with. Her nicest moment comes when she looks into Rick's hand and predicts that he will be chucked, prompting him in mid-sneer to realise that she has broken up with him. Like its heroes, *Hotel de Love* wants to get away with being romantic and cynical at the same time, winning hearts with laughter while all the time being aware of the tackiness that goes along with true love. The problem is that its cynicism isn't funny enough to bite—the supposedly comic confrontations between Rick and Melissa are especially laboured—and its romance is predicated on an audience caring about unconvincing characters who witter on about their feelings and are so wrapped up in themselves you wonder why the extras hit them.

Also reviewed in:
NEW YORK TIMES, 2/7/97, p. C14, Stephen Holden
VARIETY, 9/23-29/96, p. 127, Ken Eisner

HOTEL MANOR INN, THE

A Manor Films release. *Producer:* Wayne Chesler. *Director:* Wayne Chesler. *Screenplay:* Wayne Chesler. *Director of Photography:* Michael McCurry. *Editor:* Wayne Chesler. *Music:* Alan Schwartz. *Sound:* Derek Felska and Roy B. Yokelson. *Production Designer:* Pilar Turner. *Costumes:* Marianne Powell-Parker. *Running time:* 92 minutes. *MPAA Rating:* Not Rated.

CAST: John Randolph (Gus); Sam Trammell (Nolan); Jennifer Corby (Kathy); Fred Norris (Pete); Lawrence Vincent (Ed); Burke Moses (Brian Armor).

NEW YORK POST, 3/28/97, p. 52, Thelma Adams

If it's any consolation to Hollywood in this era of the "independents," for every movie like "The English Patient," there are at least 50 like "Hotel Manor Inn."

Brooklyn auteur Wayne Chesler has made one of those sincere, inept black comedies that only a mother could laugh at. It was for movies like this that channel surfing was born.

Chesler's shining achievement is the casting of John Randolph ("Prizzi's Honor") as the cheery manager of a Massachusetts barrier-island inn. Gus (Randolph) goes to extreme lengths to protect his dream of reviving the old Victorian to its General Douglas MacArthur-slept-here glory. Sometimes, a man just wants an inn of his own.

Of course, there are obstacles to free enterprise. A dime-store Norma Desmond with a confessional streak and a poisoning in her past; a drunken idiot who just shouts "Make me a corpse!"; the shrewish heir to the property; her talkie Aussie mate; and a kidnapper in a kangaroo suit all threaten Gus' plans for "The Shining" by the sea.

The biggest threat to Gus' dreams is a cheesy tab TV show called "The Smoking Gun." Fronted by Brian Armor (overplayed by Broadway actor Burke Moses), the show is an easy target for obvious jokes.

By mistake, "The Smoking Gun" assigns an intern to Gus' island hideaway. Distracted by his hormones, Nolan (nerdy Rob Lowe look-alike Sam Trammell) is so busy rubbing against island girl Kathy (appealing Jennifer Corby) that he ignores the burgeoning body count.

Meanwhile, in the corners of the frame, Gus dumps corpses with the same industriousness as he tends his inn. During these scenes, the movie's so bad that it's almost funny. Almost.

Howard Stern sidekick Fred Norris grins from the sidelines as a local bartender. Watching him stranded on this island of lost laughs is a reminder of how funny his near silent act was in "Private Parts."

Also reviewed in:
NEW YORK TIMES, 3/28/97, p. C21, Stephen Holden
VARIETY, 8/12-18/96, p. 35, Lisa Nesselson

HOUSE OF YES, THE

A Miramax Films release of a Spelling Films presentation of a Bandeira Entertainment production. *Executive Producer:* Robert Berger. *Producer:* Beau Flynn and Stefan Simchowitz. *Director:* Mark Waters. *Screenplay:* Mark Waters. *Adapted from the play by:* Wendy MacLeod. *Director of Photography:* Mike Spiller. *Editor:* Pamela Martin. *Music:* Jeff Rona. *Casting:* Mary Vernieu. *Production Designer:* Patrick Sherman. *Costumes:* Edi Giguere. *Running time:* 87 minutes. *MPAA Rating:* R.

CAST: Parker Posey (Jackie-O); Josh Hamilton (Marty); Tori Spelling (Lesly); Freddie Prinze, Jr. (Anthony); Genevieve Bujold (Mrs. Pascal); Rachael Leigh Cook (Young Jackie-O).

LOS ANGELES TIMES, 10/10/97, Calendar/p. 10, John Anderson

[The following review by John Anderson appeared in a slightly different form in **NEWSDAY, 10/10/97, Part II/p. B11.]**

"Excuse me," Mrs. Pascal (Genevieve Bujold) tells her assembled children as they await Thanksgiving dinner at the family home in Washington, D.C. "I'm going to go baste the turkey and hide the kitchen knives."

Things are getting a little dicey at Chez Pascal, the setting of Mark Waters' "The House of Yes." More-than-unstable daughter Jackie-O (Parker Posey) is back in her pink Chanel suit and pillbox hat, still lusts after her twin brother, Marty (Josh Hamilton), and is scheming to get Marty's fiancé Lesly (a surprisingly capable Tori Spelling) out of the house, perhaps feet first. Brother Anthony (Freddie Prinze Jr.) is maneuvering Lesly into bed, while Jackie and Marty perform their erotic reenactment of the Kennedy assassination downstairs in the living room. Mom, looking like a funereal raisin, is in deep denial. Imagine "You Can't Take It With You" as envisioned by Chas. Addams (or Charles Busch).

To say that there's been a paucity of good writing in movies lately would be stating the painfully obvious, but it must be said. But having said it, and having seen "House of Yes," one realizes that good writing is not everything. In addition to its terrifically bratty performance by the epically bratty Posey, "House of Yes" contains some of the smarter (and smarter-assed) writing of the year. Kaufman and Hart could get laughs caricaturing the American family (everyone, after all, has their eccentric relative) and Addams was really doing the same thing with Gomez and Morticia. But unless incest between twins has gained a popularity I'm unaware of, the situation in the Pascal home is too unorthodox to make any common connections.

That said, "House of Yes" has some very funny moments (Posey's delivery being well-suited to the Waters-MacLeod material) and almost inadvertently lampoons our national Kennedy fascination. Dad, it seems, left Mom on the night of Nov. 22, 1963 (the film takes place exactly 20 years later), and this convergence of events is blamed for the family's deep-rooted dementia—if not its central fixation ("When Jackie was born, her hand was holding Marty's penis," Mrs. Pascal says solemnly).

All this is absurdist in its nature, but the film also wants to provide us with comedy of the high, low, black and baggy-pants variety as in this exchange between Jackie-O and the ditsy Lesly:

"Would you like a glass of Liebfraumilch?"

"No, I'll just have a glass of wine."

"It is wine."

"Oh. I don't speak French."

All of which is fine, but the lack of stylistic focus makes us less than willing to engage the wackier aspects of the Pascal chronicles. "I can't believe you guys," says the exasperated Lesly. No, and for all the snappy gags, that's our problem, too.

NEW YORK, 10/20/97, p. 80, David Denby

If you believe Wendy MacLeod, her play *The House of Yes*—which has been made into an entertaining little movie—is about "amorality" and "the insularity I see in the upper classes, people who have cut themselves off from the rest of the world and are living by the rules they have invented." MacLeod's solemn explanations have a scolding, moralistic tone. But her play offers something very different from moralism. *The House of Yes* is actually about a witty group of monsters who enjoy playing tricks on one another. I suppose one could deduce from the material some Marxist lesson about the irresponsibility of the American upper classes, but not without hypocrisy, since the money, the liberties, the big house, and the absence of work that MacLeod apparently disapproves of are precisely the elements that make her play entertaining—and that allow it to exist as a stage and film piece in the first place.

In the eighties, young Marty Pascal (Josh Hamilton) returns home to his mother's house in Washington, D.C., with his innocent fiancée (Tori Spelling) in tow. It's a Tennessee Williams house, a big bad house with a Secret. Marty's dad died—was shot, perhaps—the same day that JFK was shot, and Marty's sister, who calls herself Jackie-O (Parker Posey), has become obsessed with both deaths and lives in a mad dream world in which she is Jackie, always Jackie, with a pink dress and a pillbox hat and dark hair in a bouffant turned up at the cheek. Her mother (Genevieve Bujold) makes malicious and ironic jokes, sometimes at her own expense, and then disappears into the recesses of the house; her younger brother (Freddie Prinze Jr.) is some sort of school dropout who puts the moves on Marty's fiancée as quickly as he can. There's something weird and sexual going on between Marty and Jackie-O, which isn't very hard to figure out, and there's a gun that is part of a repeated ritual and that goes off the way guns in plays are supposed to go off (at the end).

None of this can be taken seriously as psychological drama, much less as an indictment of wealth and privilege—it's all too glib and flamboyant, and too obviously stage-bound. The characters put each other on and make brittle, insinuating remarks, echoing each other mockingly in the Albee manner. The movie is fun precisely because the director, Mark Waters (it's his first film), embraces the gamesmanship, the posing and teasing theatricality. The nifty opening sequences home movie of a teenage Jackie-O showing off the mansion, footage that gets intercut with the real Jackie showing off the White House—sets the tone of sinister farce, and the actors are skillful enough to keep the macabre flights aloft.

Parker Posey, looking tense as an electric wire in her Jackie rig, narrows her eyes into slits and speaks such lines as "I spend most of my days with my head in the toilet ... throwing up pills" with as much eccentric force as a young Kate Hepburn. At first glance, Josh Hamilton does indeed look like a conventionally handsome rich boy. But when he and Parker get their brother-sister attraction going, some sort of gleam comes into Hamilton's eyes, and he is lost and naughty at the same time. Director Waters knows what he is doing. He may have adapted a play, but he has a firm grasp of film grammar. The moving camera is impressively dreamlike; the point-of-view shots are used strategically, as they would have been in a forties Hollywood movie. *The House of Yes* is a hothouse plant and only of limited interest, but it's the kind of small demonstration piece that could open up a variety of careers. If Mark Waters can get out of that big house, he could become a famous movie director.

NEW YORK POST, 10/10/97, p. 48, Thelma Adams

What's prohibited any more? What's taboo? It's gotten to the point where incestuous twins re-creating the Kennedy assassination as foreplay—the central image of "The House of Yes"—seems like the stuff of a People magazine profile.

Like the title of Mark Waters' black comedy, we're living in a house of yes, where nothing is taboo, everything's allowable. Sorry, Nancy Reagan, we can't just say no any longer.

Based on Wendy MacLeod's stageplay, Waters' adaptation never quite cracks out of the premium. On a dark and stormy night, we enter a drawing room in a memory-haunted D.C. mansion where rich people in evening clothes use dialogue to cut and paste their hearts.

Parker Posey plays Jackie-O, an acid-tongued twin whose passion for her brother Marty (Josh Hamilton) led her to madness or is it the other way around? Mama Pascal (Genevieve Bujold) is a chip off Morticia Addams, while younger bro Anthony (Freddie Prinze Jr.) isn't as naive as he seems.

When Marty returns home for Thanksgiving with his fiancee Lesly (Tori Spelling), a doughnut shop cashier who, he says, "smells of powdered sugar," the stage is set for a nuclear family meltdown.

Bujold and Posey are a mother-and-daughter tag team of melodrama queens who make every one else suffer for their love. Bujold ("Coma") shows a flair for brittle comedy, delivering such lines as "I'm going to go baste the turkey and hide the kitchen knives" like well-aimed silver ice picks.

In the poison-in-pearls role, the perfectly cast Posey ("The Daytrippers") is affected and affecting, laugh-out-loud funny and sexually provocative.

Spelling ("Beverly Hills 90210") is a perfect foil. In high, lacy collars, her Lesly's no competition for Jackie-O—even though the poor, normal girl doesn't recognize the enemy. "I don't think you're insane," she tells Jackie, "I think you're just spoiled."

The piercing dialogue and pitch-perfect performances compensate for a stagy story that's hermetic and often emotionally dry. But, in a season of movies with chilly family Thanksgivings ("The Ice Storm," "The Myth of Fingerprints"), the Pascals certainly host the most hellish.

VILLAGE VOICE, 10/14/97, p. 85, Abby McGanney Nolan

In *The House of Yes*, Parker Posey is pretty in a pink pillbox hat, a Jackie 0. obsessive with a fixation on her twin brother Martin (Josh Hamilton). Stuck overnight in the sprawling family home with an eccentric mother (Genevieve Bujold), a dullard younger brother (Freddie Prinze Jr.), and Martin's absurdly clueless fiancée (Tori Spelling), the pair deal with such demons as a dead father, incest, and quirkily precious dialogue.

Like *The Ice Storm*, Waters's directorial debut involves a major weather occurrence on a Thanksgiving of the past. Here it's 1983—the 20th anniversary, we're reminded, of JFK's assassination—and the pounding rain outside unsubtly accentuates the trouble started when Martin brings his fiancée home to meet his family. Posey's character, always referred to as Jackie O., is ravingly jealous from the start (Mom offhandedly recalls her first inkling that these twins might be closer than normal—"Jackie was holding Marty's penis when they were born.") Posey clearly revels in her glamorous, fresh-from-the-mental-hospital loon, but Hamilton is less than convincing as the ambivalent brother. At least he's not costumed as distractingly as Tori Spelling's Lesly, a Donut King waitress who favors Laura Ashley-style getups.

The film opens with old footage of Jackie Kennedy giving her tour of the White House. Along with a campy reenactment of the Dealey Plaza shooting, the historical reference leads heavy-handedly to a conflation of dad's death with JFK's death and then on to more death. The film never succeeds in creating a sense of claustrophobia, but it is creepy.

Also reviewed in:
CHICAGO TRIBUNE, 10/17/97, Friday/p. L, John Petrakis
NEW YORK TIMES, 10/10/97, p. E10, Stephen Holden
VARIETY, 1/27-2/2/97, p. 73, Dennis Harvey

HOW I SPENT MY SUMMER VACATION

A Cinema Guild release of an Alan James Gay production for Castleway Entertainment. *Producer:* Alan James Gay. *Director:* John Fisher. *Screenplay:* John Fisher. *Director of Photography:* Charles Mills. *Editor:* Alan James Gay and Norman Todd. *Music:* Johnny Barrow. *Sound:* Palmer "Whit" Norris. *Casting:* Shay Bentley-Griffin. *Art Director:* Tim Dempsey. *Costumes:* D'Carol Randle and Wayne Van Nuygen. *Running time:* 75 minutes. *MPAA Rating:* Not Rated.

CAST: RonReaco Lee (Perry); Deanna Davis (Stephanie); E. Roger Mitchell (Joseph); Mike Ngaujah (D'Angelo); Jade Janise Dixon (Tammy); Darren Law (Nolan); Maude Bond (Monica); T'Erika Jenks (Kim).

NEW YORK POST, 11/19/97, p. 46, Larry Worth

It sounds like the topic for a 500-word essay to be penned by a bunch of grade-schoolers.

Instead, "How I Spent My Summer Vacation" concerns college students who fall in and out of love. So how come it reflects a grade-schoolers level of sophistication?

Written and directed by first-time filmmaker John Fisher, the low-budget production is harmless but numbingly familiar in its examination of an attractive young couple caught in makeup-to-breakup pattern.

The tale's recycled quality is obvious from the lame startup: Cross-cutting between Perry and Stephanie's memories of their first date,. Needless to say—with apologies to Maurice Chevalier and Hermione Gingold, never mind and Lerner and Loewe—they don't remember it well.

So it's no surprise when Stephanie calls it quits once again. Before long, Perry is seeing a new lady and Stephanie has found another man. But as their paths keep crossing, each mulls reconciliation.

In the meantime, the pair's friends serve as something of a Greek chorus, not only making predictions on the lovebirds' future but offering anecdotes from their own troubled romances. Unfortunately, none of it adds up to much, with viewers having virtually no stake in the outcome.

After all, this is hardly an amour to rival that seen in "Annie Hall" or "She's Gotta Have It," despite Fisher's tips of the hat to both Woody Allen and Spike Lee.

That isn't to say the film is without merits. It's got a sweetness and simplicity that shines past the script's lack of originality. And some snippets of dialogue certainly ring true.

Further, RonReaco Lee and Deanna Davis are undeniably appealing, though their chemistry makes for sparks rather than a blaze. And in supporting roles, E. Roger Mitchell, Mike Ngaujah, Darren Law and Jade Janise Dixon do their best to enliven a slew of tired situations.

But "How I spent My Summer Vacation" still boils down to an elongated he says/she says exercise—one where all's been said to many times before.

NEWSDAY, 11/19/97, Part II/p. B11, Gene Seymour

Early in "How I Spent My Summer Vacation," Stephanie (Deanna Davis), a vivacious coed, finds herself grasping for something nice to say about Perry (RonReaco Lee), another student from whom she's just broken free of a roller-coaster relationship. "Charming" is the first word that registers. Upon reflection, it seems to be the only word she can think of.

A similar conundrum occurs when trying to come up with the saving graces of John Fisher's debut feature. Despite the presence of cinematographer Charles Mills ("Boyz N the Hood" "Days of Thunder"), the film lacks visual flow and graceful pacing. Sometimes, you swear you can hear the camera rolling in the background. Like Stephanie, you try hard to think of a superlative for the film and "charming" is once again the first word that comes to mind.

But what's also apparent is that while Perry, and Fisher's film, have lots of charm, Fisher's film is a *whole* lot smarter than its hapless male protagonist, whose skill at navigating love's perilous waters is as considerable as his ability on the basketball court: not much happening in either venue.

And there's something to be said, at the outset, about a feature film that dares to show a young brother who not only can't play hoops, but is so deluded about his ability that he thinks letting his girlfriends watch him play constitutes a substantial date.

Fisher, a 23-year-old Howard University film school grad, may not have well-developed technical chops, but his eyes and ears are wide open to what his peers talk about when they talk about love. Not since Spike Lee's "She's Gotta Have It" has a black male filmmaker shown such knowing empathy for his sisters. And it's hard to think of any black filmmaker willing to give his central character enough dimension to come across as both well-intentioned and a jerk.

When the decline of Perry and Stephanie's relationship is recounted through flashbacks, it's clear that the former's annoying fastidiousness (even the way she pours milk on cereal starts an argument) and the latter's unreasonably high expectations show them to be a match made not in heaven, but the Other Place.

Yet, in Perry's case, he can't bring himself to believe it's over when it's over. And his fumbling efforts to compensate—from driving his roomies Joseph (E. Roger Mitchell) and D'Angelo (Mike Ngaujah as a slacker in dreadlocks) crazy with his grief, to stumbling his way toward other women—are recognizable enough to make anyone (white, black, young, old) cringe.

VILLAGE VOICE, 11/25/97, p. 100, Gary Dauphin

Black love done kinder, gentler, New South-style, *How I Spent My Summer Vacation* is a neat little film, a wry comedy that doesn't linger much in the head but that does find a place in the mental Rolodex under noteworthy debuts. Twenty-three-year-old Howard grad John Fisher may be from Georgia, but he tells the tale of the on-again, off-again relationship of two black college students like an up-and-coming New York neurotic, setting his actors down before the camera for full-frontal kvetching about their love lives. The end result doesn't have quite the energy or gloss of *She's Gotta Have It* or *love jones*, but it does charm in a quietly understated way.

Stephanie and Perry (relative newcomers Deanna Davis and RonReaco Lee) are the couple having *Vacation's* central summer of nonlove. Two sophomores living in the snug confines of undergraduate Atlanta (black-college ground zero), they're riding on different emotional trains, both of them seeing the same scenery but coming away with he-said, she-said spins. After yet another goodbye (it's a passing idea of his, but she takes it seriously), Perry's season of relationship hell begins. The likable but confused young man cycles through a gamut of post-breakup states—joy, denial rebound, stalking—as his two roommates (comic quick sketches who should have been named Afrocentric Brother and Pre-professional Brother) offer him a nice mix of tepid support and bad advice.

There is a definite thinness to *How I Spent My Summer Vacation*—the characters are only as complicated as their onscreen chatter, and the film is confined to a handful of cramped, dormlike locations—but things still work, thanks to Fisher's ear for how certain young black men talk to one another. *Vacation* gives Perry and company so much room to blunder through obsessions—the proper way to pour milk on cereal, the dreaded bad dick report—that you realize the real love here isn't between the boy and the girl but among the boys. *Vacation*'s young writer-director casts a rosy glance back at an age he's just barely outgrown. It's not exactly very deep, but then 18-to-21 isn't always as heavy as older folks like to remember.

Also reviewed in:
NEW YORK TIMES, 11/19/97, p. E5, Stephen Holden
VARIETY, 11/17-23/97, p. 64, Godfrey Cheshire

HUGO POOL

A BMG Independents release of a Nomadic Pictures presentation in association with Northern Arb Entertainment of a Downey/Ligeti production. *Executive Producer:* Douglas Berquist, Mike Frislev, and Chad Oakes. *Producer:* Barbara Ligeti. *Director:* Robert Downey, Sr. *Screenplay:* Robert Downey and Laura Downey. *Director of Photography:* Joseph Montgomery. *Editor:* Joe D'Augustine. *Music:* Danilo Perez. *Production Designer:* Lauren Gabor. *Costumes:* Jocelyn F. Wright. *Running time:* 93 minutes. *MPAA Rating:* R.

CAST: Patrick Dempsey (Floyd Gaylen); Robert Downey, Jr. (Franz Mazur); Richard Lewis (Chic Chicalini); Malcolm McDowell (Henry Dugay); Alyssa Milano (Hugo Dugay); Cathy Moriarty (Minerva Dugay); Sean Penn (Leprechaun).

LOS ANGELES TIMES, 12/12/97, Calendar/ p.12, Jack Mathews

[*The following review by Jack Mathews appeared in a slightly different form in*
NEWSDAY, 12/12/97, Part II/p. B9.]

We hate to hit a man when he's down, but what a week for Robert Downey Jr.! On Monday, a judge orders him to jail for six months for violating probation on past drug offenses, and today, "Hugo Pool" opens, putting on public display one of the worst performances he or any major star has recorded on film.

It would be better for all concerned if the movie were being shown only in Downey's cell. Being forced to watch himself playing Franz Mazur, a punch-drunk, homicidal, tongue-tied Dutch film director, in this woebegone farce would be tough love indeed.

Mazur is one of the many oddball customers being serviced by Hugo Dugay (Alyssa Milano, from TV's "Who's the Boss?"), a self-employed Los Angeles pool cleaner, who awakes one day in the midst of a drought to a backlog of 44 jobs. To get them all done, she enlists her drug- and alcohol-addicted father, Henry (Malcolm McDowell), who devotes most of his sober moments to spouting verse that rhymes with "ring-dang-do," and her mother, Minerva (Cathy Moriarty), an addicted gambler who's trying to earn enough money to pay off her bookie ("Gong Show" emcee Chuck Barris) without having to sleep with him.

Early on, Henry is sent to the Colorado River to steal enough water to fill a mobster's pool, while Mom tags along with Hugo, serving no discernible purpose. Along their separate ways, Henry picks up a companion (Sean Penn), whose blue shoes Henry takes for the Holy Grail, and Hugo and Minerva pick up a client named Floyd (Patrick Dempsey), a mute, keenly spirited man in a wheelchair who is in the final stages of amyotrophic lateral sclerosis, or Lou Gehrig's disease.

At this point, at least halfway through the movie, "Hugo Pool" becomes what it's really intended to be, an ode to unconditional love. Hugo, a young woman with no prior romantic illusions, falls in love with the sensitive Floyd and begins to shed the lunatics around her to focus on him.

The director, Robert Downey Sr. ("Putney Swope" and not much else), co-wrote the script with his wife, Laura Downey, who died of ALS at the age of 36 and whose "beautiful absurdist sense of nonsense," he says, inspired the spirit of the film.

Downey's sentiment is admirable, but "Hugo Pool" doesn't transcend the intimacy of the memory he's honoring. If Floyd were the central character of the story, being amused by the absurdist nonsense, we might at least appreciate the humor vicariously. As it is, the audience seems limited to the director's inner circle.

That circle includes Robert Downey Jr., who has been appearing in his father's films since he was 5, and maybe his manic, presumably improvised performance here is the sort, of thing that rocked the Downey household. But given the actor's off-camera adventures, it's hard not to regard it as the work of someone who's not thinking straight.

NEW YORK POST, 12/12/97, p. 57, Thelma Adams

The title character in "Hugo Pool" is a tattooed, diabetic, Beverly Hills pool cleaner played with pluck and sincerity by TV cookie Alyssa Milano.

Robert Downey Sr. (best known for the 1969 counterculture comedy "Putney Swope") co-wrote the heartfelt but inane comedy with his wife, Laura. She died at 36 of Lou Gehrig's disease.

Their heroine encounters a variety of suddenly whimsical characters as she dumps chlorine in no fewer than 44 pools. Chic Chicalini (comic Richard Lewis) threatens poor Hugo with death if she doesn't fill his pool with water before he lams it to the Betty Ford Clinic.

Courtly, wheelchair-bound Floyd Gaylen (Patrick Dempsey) catches a Hugo's eye though he doesn't have a pool to swim in.

Throughout the day, family dysfunction dogs Hugo. The lithe young woman functions as the adult in her relationship with her drug-addled dad (Malcolm McDowell) and her gambler mom (Cathy Moriarty).

McDowell is no lucky man to be cast as Downey Sr.'s irresponsible alter ego. He coyly refers to heroin as "ring dang do" and in one painful scene has a heart-to-heart with a hand puppet—it's so Shari Lewis meets "The Basketball Diaries."

Moriarty comes across simply, as if she's playing Gena Rowlands in her "Gloria" days.

The biggest victim of the family sweepstakes is Robert Downey Jr. He earns the worst-supporting-actor nod for his excessive portrayal of a Dutch film director.

Sean Penn also can't resist these family affairs. After starting in Nick Cassavetes' "She's So Lovely," he steps into bright blue leather shoes to play a Downey leprechaun. As the puckish drifter tells Hugo's pop: "If words could speak, I'd still have nothing to say." Heavy!

VILLAGE VOICE, 12/16/97, p. 78, Elizabeth Weitzman

Because Robert Downey is the director of the biting cult classic *Putney Swope* and because he has amassed such an impressive cast list, it's tempting to believe *Hugo Pool* is actually a satire of such movies as *Hugo Pool*. Instead it turns out to be more akin to the faux indie film inside Tom DiCillo's *Living in Oblivion*. There are no dwarfs here, but there is a blue-suede-shoed leprechaun (underplayed by a slumming Sean Penn); a drug addict who utters such lines as "'I'm off the snow, no more blow, and vodka had to go. There's only one thing left I do and that's the ring dang do" (Malcolm McDowell, irritatingly channeling James Cagney and Jimmy Durante); an abrasive, gravel-voiced gamblaholic (Cathy Moriarty, irritatingly channeling Cathy Moriarty); a Betty Ford-bound gangster named Chic Chicalini (an absurdly miscast Richard Lewis); a quadriplegic victim of Lou Gehrig's disease (Patrick Dempsey, showing up the others without saying a line); and Dutch, a cave-chested alcoholic filmmaker (funny Robert Downey Jr., whose talents cannot be destroyed no matter what horrors he puts them through). Tying all these people together is the lovely Hugo Dugay (Alyssa Milano), an overworked pool cleaner whose busy day is hampered by all but the wheelchair-bound Floyd, with whom she falls in love. It's too bad that Milano, whose natural performance appears to have been cut and posted from another (better) movie, can't turn around without the camera lewdly ogling her.

Downey's young wife, who cowrote the script, died in 1994 of Lou Gehrig's disease, and he clearly had some sort of mission with this film. But before the first lap is completed, the movie has already begun sinking under the weight of its very determined whimsy. By the end, you feel like you're drowning right along with it.

Also reviewed in:
CHICAGO TRIBUNE, 1/9/98, p. H, Michael Wilmington
NEW YORK TIMES, 12/12/97, p. E26, Stephen Holden
VARIETY, 2/10-16/97, p. 66, Emanuel Levy

I KNOW WHAT YOU DID LAST SUMMER

A Columbia Pictures release of a Mandalay Entertainment presentation of a Neal H. Moritz production. *Executive Producer:* William S. Beasley. *Producer:* Neal H. Moritz, Erik Feig, and Stokely Chaffin. *Director:* Jim Gillespie. *Screenplay:* Kevin Williamson. *Based on the novel by:* Lois Duncan. *Director of Photography:* Denis Crossan. *Editor:* Steve Mirkovich. *Music:* John Debney and Alex Steyermark. *Music Editor:* Tom Carlson. *Sound:* Carl Rudisill and (music) John Richards. *Sound Editor:* Michael Hilkene and C.T. Welch. *Casting:* Mary Vernieu. *Production Designer:* Gary Wissner. *Art Director:* John J. Rutchland, III. *Set Designer:* Andrew Menzies and Alan Hook. *Set Decorator:* James Edward Ferrell, Jr. *Set Dresser:* Scott A. Lawson. *Special Effects:* John D. Milinac. *Costumes:* Catherine Adair. *Make-up:* Bonita DeHaven. *Stunt Coordinator:* Freddie Hice. *Running time:* 100 minutes. *MPAA Rating:* R.

CAST: Jennifer Love Hewitt (Julie James); Sarah Michelle Gellar (Helen Shivers); Ryan Phillippe (Barry Cox); Freddie Prinze, Jr. (Ray Bronson); Muse Watson (Benjamin Willis/Fisherman); Bridgette Wilson (Elsa Shivers); Anne Heche (Melissa Egan); Johnny Galecki (Max); Stuart Greer (Officer); J. Don Ferguson (MC); Deborah Hobart (Mrs. James); Mary McMillan (Mrs. Cox); Rasool J'Han (Deb); Dan Albright (Sheriff); Lynda Clark (Pageant Official); Shea Broom (Contestant #1); John Bennes (Old Man); Jennifer Bland (Contestant #2); William Neely (Hank); Jonathan Quint (David Egan); Richard Dale Miller, Mary Neva Huff, and David Lee Hartman (Band Members).

LOS ANGELES TIMES, 10/17/97, Calendar/p. 16, Kevin Thomas

"I Know What You Did Last Summer" isn't the virtuoso work that "Scream," also written by Kevin Williamson, was. Nor is it as nonstop frightening. But it is fun, energetic and fairly scary.

Its four young stars have exceptional poise and promise, and their presence contributes strongly to the film's enjoyment, as does the film's setting, a charming old, North Carolina coastal community.

It's the Fourth of July, and the four have recently graduated from high school. Helen (Sarah Michelle Gellar), a lovely blond, has been named the queen of a local Independence Day beauty contest and plans to go to New York to become an actress. Her best friend Julie (Jennifer Love Hewitt), a stunning brunette, is off to college, as is Helen's rich jock boyfriend Barry (Ryan Phillippe). Only Ray (Freddie Prinze Jr.), a fisherman who is Julie's boyfriend, is staying behind.

After a romantic idyll at the beach, the two couples get into Barry's father's expensive car with Ray insisting on driving because Barry has had too much to drink. Ray is driving safely on a deserted highway when suddenly there's a loud thwack! In an instant the lives of the four young people are shattered by having struck a man who for some reason was standing in the darkness in the middle of the road.

Julie, the most intelligent and mature of the four, insists on contacting the police immediately about the accident, but for a variety of reasons—well-elucidated by Williams—she is outvoted.

Jump a year ahead, and Julie faces returning home at the end of her first year at college with extreme dread. Guilt has taken its toll. She looks terrible, has nearly flunked out, and upon arriving home, is greeted by an unsigned note: "I KNOW WHAT YOU DID LAST SUMMER." The reign of terror has begun, reuniting the four to try to combat an unknown, implacable, intermittently glimpsed enemy, a looming figure in a dark slicker and a hat that obscures his face. He carries a fisherman's curved knife.

There are a sprinkling of incidents in which we're never sure whether they're real or imagined, and the film's denouement—which of course allows for a sequel—is awfully complicated. You may even find yourself trying to sort it out after the lights go up. But director Jim Gillespie, a Scot in his American film debut, has a terrific sense of pace and allows his talented cast, which includes Anne Heche as a lonely farm woman, to shine brightly.

NEW YORK POST, 10/17/97, p. 49, Michael Medved

Like some shadowy, vengeful, unkillable psycho, the dumbest conventions of past slasher movies come crawling out of their primordial ooze to claw and tear at this once-promising project.

It's a particularly painful process to watch since the first half of "I Know What You Did Last Summer" features slick, sometimes stylish direction (by Scottish BBC veteran Jim Gillespie) and a savvy screenplay (by Kevin Williamson, of "Scream" fame) that seem to promise much more.

The story begins on the Fourth of July in a picturesque seaside village in North Carolina and focuses on four attractive kids who've just graduated from high school together.

While partying on a moonlit beach, local football star Ryan Phillippe consumes far too much alcohol. On the way home, his fancy car strikes a shadowy figure on the road.

The stranger's lifeless form presents a huge problem: When authorities see the liquor-soaked vehicle, the teenagers all surely face arrest and the ruination of their grand plans, which include a scholarship to a prestigious college, a promising acting career in New York, athletic glory, writing fame and so forth.

To protect their dreams, Phillippe and his three friends (Jennifer Love Hewitt of "Party of Five," Sarah Michelle Gellar of "Buffy, the Vampire Slayer" and Freddie Prinze Jr.) toss the corpse off a pier into the ocean, destroying all evidence of their deadly nightmare.

The friends keep their guilty secret during the year that follows, but when they reunite the next summer, they start receiving menacing notes and subtle warnings suggesting that someone is on to them.

The well-developed psychological tension quickly degenerates into a cliche-riddled gore fest, complete with bystanders ruthlessly ripped open; sexually tinged pursuits in showers, bedrooms and locker rooms; screeching, hysterical music on the soundtrack; and a faceless, mysterious, implacable avenger who rivals Jason's hockey mask and Freddy Krueger's steel claws with a fisherman's slicker and rubber hat and a huge, bloody hook.

The acting is generally adequate, with the sleek, sexy women (Hewitt and Gellar) showing more promise than the decidedly hunkish men. There's even an oddball bit part by Anne Heche as a lonely killbilly butcher.

While the exhausted slasher format stubbornly refuses to die, this above-average genre offering demonstrates that even in reasonably competent hands, it also refuses to live.

SIGHT AND SOUND, 1/98, p. 45, Kim Newman

The fishing community of Southport, North Carolina. On the night of the Fourth of July, Helen Shivers wins the Miss Croaker beauty contest. She celebrates by going out with her boyfriend Barry Cox, best friend Julie James and Julie's boyfriend Ray Bronson. Because Barry is drunk, Ray drives the group home in Barry's car, but they run over someone on the coast road. Fearing for their futures if they go to the police, the teenagers decide to dump the body. At the last moment, the victim turns out to be still alive but Barry still tosses him in the sea. All promise to keep this secret.

A year later, Julie receives an anonymous letter reading: "I know what you did last summer." Barry's first suspect is Max, who has a crush on Julie, and so Barry threatens him. Before long, a mysterious figure dressed as a fisherman kills Max and injures Barry. Julie and Helen visit Melissa, the sister of David Egan whose body was found soon after the accident. The girls get a lead on a possible friend of David's who might be the avenger. The fisherman cuts off Helen's hair the night before she has to ride as the outgoing queen in the Fourth of July parade. He then disrupts the celebrations by murdering Barry, a police officer, Helen's sister Elsa and Helen herself.

Julie realises the body they dumped was not David's but Benjamin Willis', the father of a girl who was killed in an accident he blames David for. When they hit him, he had just murdered David. For a moment, Julie suspects Ray is the real killer and flees to a boat owned by Willis, who actually survived the accident. Willis menaces Julie, but Ray saves her and Willis is lost overboard. A year later, Julie and Ray have come through their trouble, but Willis has survived and attacks Julie.

The success of Wes Craven's *Scream*, soon to yield the inevitable *Scream 2*, has clearly given a jump-start to the played out slasher genre. This adaptation of Lois Duncan's well-regarded young-adult suspense novel, scripted by Kevin Williamson—the writer of *Scream*—flirts occasionally with the self-awareness of the Craven movie. Helen and Julie cite Angela Lansbury in *Murder, She Wrote* and Jodie Foster in *The Silence of the Lambs* as they venture out to an isolated farmstead in search of clues, and they take the names "Angela" and "Jodie" while posing as stranded motorists and ineptly questioning a woman about her dead brother. However, Williamson is more careless this time round. Here, he displays without irony hackneyed devices such as a corpse which is found in Julie's car boot but then disappears without trace when she brings her friends back. The smart soundbites of *Scream*-style kidspeak tend to be outweighed by clunky lines ("I'll call the cops on your college quarterback ass") and thumping cliches ("Oh my God, this isn't happening!").

Scream's intricate homage cum-deconstruction approach excused its wholesale pillaging of tropes from other horror movies. Here, the effect is a lot like arrant filching: the shadowy killer in a fisherman's oilskins has been done in the fishing-themed slasher movie *Blood Hook* (aka *The Mutilator*). The small town celebration backdrop recalls *My Bloody Valentine* and *The Prowler* (aka *Rosemary's Killer*). And the cynically callous finale is a less clever twist on the similar punchline of *He Knows You're Alone*. Any other writer might be able to claim unfamiliarity with such 80s sub-*Friday the 13th* sludge, but one of the things demonstrated by the *Scream* screenplay is that Williamson has seen an awful lot of slasher movies and has a pretty good recall for detail.

The major disappointment of *I Know What You Did Last Summer* is that the first reel is rather good. Its quartet of kids have genuinely complex relationships, and their potential big futures are sketched economically, suggesting how imperilled they might be. Ray's status as the upwardly mobile son of a fisherman is contrasted with Max, the loser doomed to a life cutting bait. Helen's beauty queen confidence is subtly contrasted with her embittered, abusive elder sister Elsa (the glamorous Bridgette Wilson, cleverly cast as dowdy). She clearly went the same route and ended up running their father's general stores. Even the odious rich jock Barry (whose fault it all seems to be) and the goody goody lawyer-wannabe Julie are given just enough depth to make their predicament intriguing.

The film starts to drift during the crucial road accident scene which skews the action to exonerate prematurely the four kids. The central section of the film is bogged down by detective work which trots out a great deal of confusing plot information. At least this allows for an evocative cameo by a luminous Anne Heche that shows up the pretty teenage leads. But the shared guilt of the quartet and the *Shallow Grave* style moral choices they make are eventually revealed to be a false premise.

Furthermore, the elaborate probing of motive and backstory is scuppered when the slasher is revealed as an indiscriminate lunatic, the incarnation of the hook-handed madman of urban legend, who ups the body count by gutting enough of the supporting cast to fill the trailer with gory moments.

VILLAGE VOICE, 10/28/97, p. 88, Joshua Cicerone

In the tradition of those carnage-and-cleavage frightfests from the old drive-in cinema, screenwriter Kevin Williamson (*Scream*) continues his revival of the teen-horror flick. Like Williamson's previous hit, which treated the horror film as self-fulfilling prophecy, *I Know What You Did Last Summer* posits the frightening notion of folklore-come-true. Four friends from a small North Carolina town celebrate their last summer before college, drinking around a bonfire and recounting local tales of a hook-fisted madman. The group's terror begins on the way home, when their car hits a man on a dark coastal road. Rather than risk promising futures, they dump their victim into the ocean and swear each other to secrecy. A year later the friends are reunited and discover that somebody knows their secret: a stalker determined to bring the teens to their own bloody endings—with, of course, a huge hook.

Rising above their sexualized stereotypes, Jennifer Love Hewitt (the smart one), Sarah Michelle Gellar (the beauty queen), Ryan Phillippe (the spoiled jock), and Freddie Prinze Jr. (the nice guy) are surprisingly persuasive as the friends whose bonds slowly deteriorate, overcome by mounting suspicion. Hewitt is especially impressive as Julie, the film's moral core and heroine. Still, neither her bravery nor her brains seem to command the unwavering attention the filmmakers give to her breasts.

Under the direction of Scottish filmmaker Jim Gillespie, *I Know What You Did* had the preview audience gasping with every sudden camera movement. While its paranoid mood is somewhat reminiscent of *Cape Fear*—right down to the alone-with-the-stalker-on-a-boatending—the movie works because it is genuinely with the Williamson-penned *Scream 2* on the way this winter, it would appear that teen-terror is back to remind us of all the fun and fear of being in the dark.

Also reviewed in:
CHICAGO TRIBUNE, 10/17/97, Tempo/p. 6, John Petrakis
NEW YORK TIMES, 10/17/97, p. E14, Lawrence Van Gelder
VARIETY, 10/13-19/97, p. 78, Leonard Klady
WASHINGTON POST, 10/17/97, Weekend/p. 33, Richard Harrington

I LOVE YOU, I LOVE YOU NOT

An Avalanche Releasing release. *Executive Producer:* Cameron McCracken, Bob Weinstein, and Harvey Weinstein. *Producer:* Joe Caracciolo, Jr., John Fiedler, and Mark Tarlov. *Director:* Billy Hopkins. *Screenplay (based on her play):* Wendy Kesselman. *Director of Photography:* Maryse Alberti. *Editor:* Paul Karasick and Jim Clark. *Music:* Mark Berger. *Production Designer:* Bill Barclay and Gudrun Roscher. *Running time:* 89 minutes. *MPAA Rating:* Not Rated.

CAST: Claire Danes (Daisy); Jeanne Moreau (Nana); Jude Law (Ethan); Carrie Slaza (Jane); James Van Der Beck (Tony); Kris Park (Seth); Lauren Fox (Alison); Emily Burkes-Nossiter (Jessica); Robert Sean Leonard (Angel of Death).

LOS ANGELES TIMES, 10/31/97, Calendar/p. 16, Kevin Thomas

Billy Hopkins' charming but also piercing "I Love You, I Love You Not," gracefully adapted by Wendy Kesselman from her play, opens with a gracious older woman, a Holocaust survivor, giving an illustrated lecture on concentration camp horrors to students at a posh Manhattan prep school.

The response of the pupils ranges from the pertinent to the shockingly rude and ignorant. So when the guest lecturer asks the young people if anyone of them knows a person with a concentration camp tattoo on his or her arm, Daisy (Claire Danes) does not raise, her hand, much to the consternation of her best friend (Carrie Slaza), one of the school's few African American students.

The friend knows that Daisy's beloved grandmother (Jeanne Moreau, no less), an Auschwitz survivor, has such a tattoo. Daisy, however, like most teenagers, has a desperate need to feet she belongs and wants in no way to be perceived as different. What's more, she's in the throngs of a first-time passion for the school's most outstanding male student, Ethan (Jude Law). Daisy, in fact, pronounces him "perfect": an A-plus student, captain of the lacrosse team, student body president, who's also rich, tall, handsome, well-traveled and sophisticated. What's more, Daisy is pretty and intelligent enough for him to start noticing her.

The cruel irony is that Daisy's instincts are on the money. When she and Ethan, who spend lots of time together in the most beautiful stretches of Central Park, are falling in love and she commences to trust him, she tells him about the grandmother she so much adores. Soon a photo of a starving concentration camp survivor turns up taped to the inside of the door of Daisy's locker, with the question scrawled on the survivor's emaciated arm: "What's your number?"

While it's doubtful that this act of hate was the work of Ethan, it is impossible to believe it could have happened without him having told others that Daisy is Jewish. Pretty soon Ethan is pronouncing Daisy herself perfect, but it's not a compliment: She reads too much, she's too obviously bright, she's—well—different.

The crux of the film may be Daisy's ill-fated first love, but its heart is Daisy's relationship with her grandmother, who lives in a gracious Hudson Valley house surrounded by a beautiful garden. Moreau's Nana is all flowing golden hair and smocks and muumuus; since making this film Moreau has slimmed down dramatically and cut her hair for a more youthful look. But here Moreau is a virtual earth mother, nurturing, wise and playful.

Her Nana is often momentarily overcome by Holocaust memories but has too much spirit, too much love of life, to let them defeat her. It will have to be her loving strength and wisdom that Daisy needs to draw upon if she is willing or able to achieve self-acceptance.

There are moments when the film tends toward, the precious—grandmother and granddaughter do an awful lot of gamboling around that garden—but that's forgivable in the light of the shining portrayals of Moreau and Danes and the deft way in which the film depicts the stubborn, insidious persistence of anti-Semitism. "I Love You, I Love You Not" makes its point implicitly: The people you want to be accepted by usually turn out to be not worth your effort.

NEW YORK POST, 10/31/97, p. 50, Thelma Adams

Call a movie "I Love You, I Love You Not," name the lead Daisy, and you don't need to be a botanist to know that she'll be pulled apart before the movie's end.

Claire Danes is the flower in question in Billy Hopkins' heartfelt Holocaust drama, adapted by Wendy Kesselman from her stage play.

Daisy is torn between two worlds: her tony Upper East Side prep school and the Holocaust legacy she endures as the only grandchild of a survivor.

Like all teens, Daisy's also torn by hormones. But, because she's a big fan of "Anna Karenina," she's more dramatic than the average blossom.

Kesselman embodies the split between past and present in two symbolic characters. Nana, generously played by Jeanne Moreau, is the kind of intuitive, supportive, insightful grandmother we all wish we had (and some of us, luckily, do).

The stunningly handsome Jude Law's Ethan is ubernormal, an Aryan dream, the prep school senior class president, the captain of the lacrosse team, Mr. Popularity.

The drama's emotional weight falls on the heart of Kesselman's original one-act: the relationship between grandmother and granddaughter.

Their bond is touching, intimate, fresh. Nana and Daisy share books, dreams, stories and the ability to express raw emotion with each other when the outside world rewards glosses and denial.

The Daisy-Ethan scenario shifts the movie to weaker ground, poor-little-rich-girl territory.

Danes, who appeared in "I Love You" before she tackled Juliet in "William Shakespeare's Romeo and Juliet," shifts between appealing and cloying. The movie comes dangerously close to "My So-Called Holocaust."

Moreau rises above the material, its blunt comparisons.

The French star ("Jules et Jim") soars not in the set pieces about Nana's tragic past, the speeches meant for drama coaches and auditions, but in the moments where she presses against the drama with a gentle, mocking humor.

When Nana settles Daisy in her lap, the lanky teen disappears in her maternal caresses. Nana cradles the child she has comforted since birth and embraces the woman to come.

The past is present, sadness opens the door to bliss. Moreau finds the emotional truth of "I Love You, I Love You Not" even when the director misplaces it.

VILLAGE VOICE, 11/4/97, p. 84, Laurie Stone

Billy Hopkins's debut feature, *I Love You, I Love You Not*, adopted by Wendy Kesselman from her play, uses the Holocaust to heighten the ordinary growing pains of high schooler Daisy (Claire Danes). It's a blunder, the film winds up equating the Holocaust with an individual's emotional damage. It confuses history with neurosis. Resting on the facts that her Nana (Jeanne

Moreau) survived Auschwitz and Daisy's classmates are mostly rich WASPS, the film contrives an Anne Frank facade for her though there is nothing remotely Anne Frank-like about her circumstances. Frank had Nazis at her door. Daisy falls in love with a shallow guy who dumps her for being too intense.

The filmmakers, on the other hand, go to the absurd length of turning Daisy's classmates into anti-Semites, passing up the more credible exploration of Daisys guilt feelings about sex and her identification with those punished by the Holocaust. Too bad Daisy and Nana don't sort out these matters. Moreau and Danes glow in their scenes together, their two kinds of beauty cutting through the schmaltzy music and jumbled plot.

Also reviewed in:
NEW YORK TIMES, 10/31/97, p. E12, Janet Maslin
VARIETY, 11/10-16/97, p. 41, Lael Loewenstein

ICE STORM, THE

A Fox Searchlight Pictures release of a Good Machine production. *Producer:* Ted Hope, James Schamus, and Ang Lee. *Director:* Ang Lee. *Screenplay:* James Schamus. *Based on the novel by:* Rick Moody. *Director of Photography:* Frederick Elmes. *Editor:* Tim Squyres. *Music:* Mychael Danna. *Music Editor:* Pat Mullins. *Sound:* Drew Kunin and (music) Brad Haehnel. *Sound Editor:* Philip Stockton. *Casting:* Avy Kaufman. *Production Designer:* Mark Friedberg. *Art Director:* Bob Shaw. *Set Decorator:* Stephanie Carroll. *Special Effects:* John Ottesen. *Costumes:* Carol Oditz. *Make-up:* Michael Bigger and James Sarzotti. *Stunt Coordinator:* G.A. Aguilar and Douglas Crosby. *Running time:* 112 minutes. *MPAA Rating:* R.

CAST: Kevin Kline (Ben Hood); Joan Allen (Elena Hood); Henry Czerny (George Clair); Adam Hann-Byrd (Sandy Carver); David Krumholtz (Francis Davenport); Tobey Maguire (Paul Hood); Christina Ricci (Wendy Hood); Jamey Sheridan (Jim Carver); Elijah Wood (Mikey Carver); Sigourney Weaver (Janey Carver); Kate Burton (Dorothy Franklin); William Cain (Ted Shackley); Michael Cumpsty (Philip Edwards); Mala Danziger (Mrs. Gadd); Michael Egerman (Pharmacist); Christine Farrell (Marie Earle); Glenn Fitzgerald (Neil Conrad); Tom Flagg (Train Conductor); Jonathan Freeman (Ted Franklin); Barbara Garrick (Weather Reporter); Dennis Gazomiros (Stephen Earle); John Benjamin Hickey (Mark Boland); Katie Holmes (Libbets Casey); Allison Janney (Dot Halford); Byron Jennings (Pierce Sawyer); Colette Kilroy (Sari Steele); Ivan Kronenfeld (Jack Moellering); Daniel McDonald (Weatherman); Miles Marek (Mr. Gadd); Donna Mitchell (Maria Conrad); Barbara Neal (Helen Wentworth); Nancy Opel (Claudia White); Larry Pine (Dave Gorman); Marcell Rosenblatt (Mikey's Teacher); Wendy Scott (Pharmacy Attendant); Evelyn Solann (Woman in Pharmacy); Jessica Stone (Marge); Sarah Thompson (Beth); Scott Wentworth (Paul's Teacher); Rob Westenberg (Rob Halford).

CINEASTE, Vol. XXIII, No. 2, 1997, p. 41, Robert Sklar

Ang Lee, director of *The Ice Storm*—whom one would not necessarily regard as a stylist—has conceded that his previous films *(Pushing Hands* [1992], *The Wedding Banquet* [1993], *Eat Drink Man Woman* [1994], and *Sense and Sensibility* [1995]) lacked a style, in order to make the point that *The Ice Storm* has one. At his New York Film Festival press conference, Lee noted that the film draws on a photorealist esthetic, adopting an observational approach to the setting. He acknowledged his film's affinity to Susan and Alan Raymond's 1973 documentary *An American Family*, which chronicles the dysfunction and disintegration of a family called the Louds. *The Ice Storm* is set in the same year *An American Family* aired on public television.

It's an intriguing idea to imagine a fiction film taking the form of fly-on-the-wall direct cinema. It makes you wonder what a fly sees. More like morsels of food on the kitchen countertop than moments of human emotion and social interaction. Whatever the Raymonds may have said about their method, when they picked the Louds they had subjects who were primed to act out melodramatic transformations. The flies-on-the-wall had to scamper to keep from getting swatted.

The paradox of *The Ice Storm* is that the filmmakers imagined that by taking a fly-on-the-wall approach they too were required to keep their distance. It's odd to think of them adopting a stance of 'objectivity' toward characters who are completely figments of their imagination. Maybe this tactic would have worked if they had created fictional families as flamboyant and dysfunctional as the Louds appeared, but the film's folks might as well have been called the Quiets. The Louds, to be sure, were Californians, while *The Ice Storm's* families live in prim and proper Connecticut.

Not distance but coldness is the operative word for the filmmakers' viewpoint toward their characters. Director Lee and producer-screenwriter James Schamus, adapting Rick Moody's novel, have conjured a hell on earth from the low end of the thermometer. The torments suffered by the film's Connecticut exurbanites come from lives frozen over long before nature's big freeze occurs on Thanksgiving weekend 1973. People are as brittle as the powerlines and tree branches that snap and break when the temperature drops.

The Ice Storm opens (as we will retrospectively realize) in the midst of the storm that forms the film's temporal climax: In a framing scene, teenager Paul Hood (Tobey Maguire) is riding a late commuter train from Manhattan to New Canaan. He's reading a *Fantastic Four* comic book, and when the power fails and the dark train grinds to a halt, he muses, through voice-over, on how the cartoon quartet resembles a family. "A family, " he says, "is like your own personal antimatter."

You don't need a physicist to tell which way the wind is blowing. Negation and annihilation are this simile's themes for family life, and the film's two families, the Hoods and the Carvers, just happen to qualify numerically and otherwise as fantastic foursomes.

The Hoods, in addition to Paul, are father Ben (Kevin Kline), mother Elena (Joan Allen), and daughter Wendy (Christina Ricci). The Carvers are mother Janey (Sigourney Weaver), sons Mikey (Elijah Wood) and Sandy (Adam Hann-Byrd), and father Jim (Jamey Sheridan). I reverse patriarchal order in the Carvers' case because Jim's business trips are apparently seamless with his presence. "I'm back," he tells his sons on returning. "You were gone?," one replies.

Ben Hood has been having an affair with Janey Carver. Talk about cold! From what we see of it, this ranks with the iciest infidelities in movie history. On the fateful dark and stormy night, Elena Hood has what might be called a sexual encounter with Jim Carver in a parked car (they're left-overs from a spouse-swapping "key party") and Wendy Hood spends a naked night in bed with Sandy Carver.

But don't get the idea that *The Ice Storm* is about the 'sexual revolution.' Sex in this film is more like a grotesque form of humanity's failure to communicate. Perhaps the most harrowing instance comes when Wendy and the older Carver boy, Mikey, start fooling around in the Carver's finished basement rec-room. Wendy finds a discarded rubber Halloween mask of Richard Nixon and puts it on, paradoxically licensing her sexual boldness by masquerading as one of the most wooden and unerotic of all presidential persons (also, of course, by transgendering her identity).

Nixon is, inevitably, the film's ruling metaphor for interpreting its historical setting. The Watergate scandal, with it denouement in an unprecedented presidential resignation less than a year in the future, pulls together the nation's malfunctioning and disintegrating public and private spheres—political criminality, impending defeat in Vietnam, the war between the generations, the implosion of traditional marriages and families (to mention only those disorders that are substantially noted).

Nixon—who is seen on television making one of his fatuous, guilt-ridden, ineffective self-defenses—also functions in another way as the film's primary symbol. He's the failed Fifties father figure. He's the Man in the Grey Flannel Suit, the Organization Man, all those Fifties conformist strivers rolled into one, who persevered and won it all, and now can't hold on to it. Kevin Kline's Ben Hood is the film's junior-grade Nixon. He's climbed the postwar materialist's ladder to a Wall Street job and a cube-shaped house in the Connecticut woods. He's more affable and less earnest than the president, but no less fatuous, guilt-ridden, and ineffective. Now his life, too, is unraveling. (Ben also has, in a way, Nixon's wife—Joan Allen, who portrayed Mrs. Nixon in Oliver Stone's film, plays Mrs. Hood here.)

Schamus's screenplay, a prizewinner at Cannes, leaves out much of the anxiety and sense of failure that Ben suffers in Moody's novel. The book makes more prominent Ben's professional panic, his awareness that he is out of his depth at work; if in the past he might have been able to make a career out of geniality and a good golf game, that time is over. The movie doesn't give us any inkling of the economic crisis that accompanied Watergate and the pullout from Vietnam back in 1973-soaring oil prices, Wall Street down the tube, people shooting each other on long lines at the fuel pump. The Hood and Carver families each seem to be getting by quite nicely on one income, but you wonder for how long (to be sure, you also wonder how long they're going to remain families).

Even though a failing patriarchy is *The Ice Storm*'s overriding issue, the fathers are not exactly engines of the film's dramatic drive. Ben is an energetic presence, but fundamentally he's clueless. Jim Carver, rarely heard from, seems to know what's going on and also that he can't do anything about it. Lee and Schamus are more interested in what happens to wives and children in the void left behind when the traditional father no longer rules.

Homemaker is not exactly the descriptive term for Elena Hood or Janey Carver. Joan Allen as Elena gives another Pat Nixonian performance—preserving her dignity amid constant humiliation, while occasionally breaking out with startling, pathetic bursts of feeling or will, as when she bicycles into the village and shoplifts a trifle from the pharmacy (unknowingly echoing her daughter's earlier actions). Sigourney Weaver creates an enigmatic Janey, sharp-witted, decisive, yet so deeply cynical and disappointed by her life that it's as if she's sleepwalking through it.

The childrens' basic problem is finding the route to maturity while knowing that their parents got sidetracked along the way. Wendy, the one member of the two families who takes an interest in Nixon's downfall, uses her connection to the public world as a bridge toward a private identity. Paul, away at boarding school, develops an acute awareness—he's the film's occasional voice-over narrator—as an outsider even to his own self. Sandy, with his homemade buzzbombs and panicky toy soldier, borrows strength from military struggle that doesn't have to be victorious. Mikey, curious about nature, suffers an annihilation that is not metaphorical.

It sounds compelling in the telling. Yet the film's documentary impulse quashes its human drama. When a ripple of recognition passes through the audience—partly amused, partly appalled—at the sight of the Carvers' water bed, it's the most notable instance of objects in the film taking on more emotional valence than people. Production designer Mark Friedberg, costume designer Carol Oditz, and cinematographer Frederick Elmes have re-created a 1973 world that is cluttered with period things and styles, yet also feels harrowingly empty.

Perhaps that's one of the filmmaker's points, that possessions in this social milieu possessed people: things filled the cupboard while souls starved. The effect is like an old photograph, in which we see evidence of past lives even though the people are no longer living. But film can shape a fiction that makes the past appear to live again, not, as in *The Ice Storm*, hold it at arm's length and say, this frozen image is as close as we can get.

LOS ANGELES TIMES, 10/17/97, Calendar/p. 8, Kenneth Turan

More aptly named than it's prepared to acknowledge, "The Ice Storm's" glacial saga of New England WASPs behaving badly is as frigid as its name. Burdened with a story of some of the world's least interesting people going through a holiday crisis, director Ang Lee and screenwriter James Schamus get as close as any creative team could to making matters involving, but the task is finally too much for these.

The Taiwanese-born Lee, whose last film was "Sense, and Sensibility" finds the milieu of repressed New Canaan, Conn., during 1973's Thanksgiving weekend as fascinating as the remote interior of Papua, New Guinea, and though he, production designer Mark Friedberg, costume designer Carol Oditz and set decorator Stephanie Carroll carefully mimic the period, they can't succeed in making it our concern.

Partly this is because the affluent suburban milieu of martinis and drained swimming pools filled with autumn leaves is overly familiar from the work of novelists John Updike and John Cheever as well as numerous movies about the country club set. More to the point, this stodgy, hermetic world is not one of enormous intrinsic interest, and it's difficult to watch "The Ice Storm" without thinking of Martin Mull's satiric blues lyric, "I felt so low down deep inside, I threw, my drink across the lawn."

Based on a novel by Rick Moody, "The Ice Storm" is filled, in case anyone should miss the point, with images of frost ranging from the natural event of its title to ice cubes in a tray. The first frozen thing we see is a commuter train headed back to Connecticut from Manhattan and containing 16-year-old prep schooler Paul Hood (Tobey Maguire). Waiting for him at the New Canaan station are his parents and his younger sister, each of whom has numerous reasons for looking, as they do, like cast members from the original "Night of the Living Dead."

Father Ben Hood (Kevin Kline) is having an inept and unsatisfactory affair with neighbor Janey Carver (Sigourney Weaver), a predatory suburban virago whose husband, Jim (Jamey Sheridan), is often out of town. And though mother Elena Hood (Joan Allen) does no more than suspect this truth, she's still edginess itself and, like almost everyone else in the film, apparently has forgotten how to smile.

Given that she's 14 years old, it's not surprising that sister Wendy Hood (Christina Ricci of the "Addams Family" films) is loaded with unhapppiness and attitude, unable to decide whether to devote herself to the Watergate crisis or the sexual fantasies of the Carver's two sons, spacey Mikey (Elijah Wood) or explosion-loving Sandy (Adam Hann-Byrd).

Paul has some things he needs to deal with as well, like his crush on wealthy schoolmate Libbets Casey (Katie Holmes). But, as with the rest of the family, the fact that his difficulties are presented with care is no guarantee that we will care about them.

Aside from its final storm, "The Ice Storm's" turning point is that relic of suburbia past, a wife-swapping key party, where the men put their car keys in a bowl and the women go home with (gasp!) the man whose keys they select. The film treats this tedious event as reverentially as Margaret Mead did the coming-of-age rituals of Samoa, even though the tribe in question is so off-putting the anthropologist would likely have fallen asleep or fled in terror.

It's unfortunate that as capable a team as director Lee and screenwriter-producer Schamus (who also collaborated on "Eat Drink Man Woman" and "The Wedding Banquet") should have become fascinated with such unpromising material. And in all fairness, "The Ice Storm" does manage to have some affecting moments, and Lee handles the film's teenage actors with a sure touch.

But the setting has mandated a terribly constrained style of performance for all concerned, encouraging the actors to tiptoe through their words as rigidly as highly choreographed marionettes on the end of a string. Typically hamstrung is Kline, so delightful in farce, who comes off fatuous and close to boring here. Only the blessedly reliable Allen manages to make something real and human out of her character. Otherwise, when one of her co-stars says, "This has been kind of a discouraging evening," it's difficult not to nod in agreement.

NEW YORK, 10/6/97, p. 64, David Denby

In *The Ice Storm*, a late-autumn rain hardens into blue icicles, country roads turn slick and glassy, and the normally protected reaches of New Canaan, Connecticut, are violated by a sinister dry snapping noise—the sound of power lines failing in a shower of sparks. *The Ice Storm* uses the altered physical world as metaphor, and with punishing force, too. Director Ang Lee and his talented cinematographer, Frederick Elmes, have coordinated every shape and color to produce a sense of natural life going into deep freeze. In flashbacks, they show us scenes of autumnal forlornness—a teenage boy, probably high on pot, simply not noticing a football passed in his direction; two teens meeting for a panicked kiss in a drained swimming pool filled with dead leaves. Where are we, at the bottom circle of Dante's *Inferno*, where tears turn to ice? No, only in the land of rich, suburban Wasps, where everything, apparently, is a little weird. (An unhappy teenage girl walks the woods like Little Red Riding Hood seeking the wolf.) As you may have gathered, *The Ice Storm*, which producer-screenwriter James Schamus adapted from the Rick Moody novel, is not sentimental and therapeutic, like *Ordinary People*. It presents its characters with a certain sardonic distaste, holding and controlling them in a framework of austere design. Judgment sits heavily in the film's metaphors. But what have these people done wrong? The movie, though highly skilled and never less than fascinating, leaves one rather baffled. *The Ice Storm* is a case of too much art, too much judgment, and not enough life.

The movie is set in the early seventies. Nixon, seen on TV, sweats and lies, and two families are falling apart. The husband and father (Kevin Kline) in one of these families, the Hoods, is having a tepid affair with Janey Carver, the wife and mother (Sigourney Weaver) in the other; at the same time, Ben Hood's 14-year-old daughter, Wendy (Christina Ricci), who likes to expose herself, is fooling around under the covers and in bathrooms with Janey's two sons (Elijah Wood and Adam Hann-Byrd). The parents on both sides haven't a clue as to what the kids are up to; they talk to them with stiff formality, and the kids, imitating the parents' foolish acts and ignoring their words, just shrug them off. In all, the relations among both the younger and older members of the two families form a portrait of hapless misery.

No one quite says, or even knows, what he is feeling. Janey's younger son blows up his model airplanes and takes a bullwhip to the flowering plants. If the parents are lost, the kids are turning spooky and morbid. The moods as well as the rains are frozen.

Rick Moody's book, published in 1994, was written in a very different vein. The novel *The Ice Storm* is a kind of lewd suburban rhapsody, juicy, detailed, anatomical, adorned with product names and the slop and profusion of American affluence—disorderly houses full of things (including the boys' and girls' naked things). Both the novel and the film are recounted by Paul Hood, Ben's 16-year-old son. Paul's bemused face and hapless attempts to bed a prep-school girl are, in the performance by Tobey Maguire, about the movie's liveliest elements. Maguire delivers the narration Schamus has constructed for Paul, which is mysterious and brooding, and very different from Moody's tone of racy mischief.

For a while, we hope *The Ice Storm* will be funny. Schamus and Lee try to satirize the rich suburbanites who embraced the post-sixties sex-and-drug scene without really having the temperament for it. The Hoods, the Carvers, and their friends would be swingers if only they knew how (a waterbed does nothing for them but jiggle their nighttime reading). The women wear their hair long—Sigourney Weaver, in a dress that unzips down the front, wears hers like Jane Fonda, only she's a Jane Fonda who has gone sour, a pleasureless bitch with a tongue that reduces everything to ashes. At a wife-swapping party, the men in their car-salesman rust-and-gold colors look puppyish or glum; they feel less like studs than like embarrassed householders. Both husbands and wives exchange partners without wildness or even much excitement, as if the act were a mere social ritual expected of them, the way beer drinking is expected of frat boys. The scene is acutely observed and unutterably depressing.

Passivity and square incomprehension make a very limited screen subject. In movies (as opposed to literature), the only way to play this kind of material, perhaps, is Paul Mazursky's way, in such films as *Bob & Carol & Ted & Alice* and *Down and Out in Beverly Hills*—as exuberant and affectionate comedy. But *The Ice Storm*, perceptive as it is, feels pained and embarrassed. These people are just pathetic; they behave badly, and they don't even get any fun out of it. But who are the prigs—the characters or the filmmakers?

The actors are a talented group, but they look haltered. As a fortyish dad who can't reach his children and who bores his mistress, Kevin Kline is touching—weightless, as always, but with a forced good cheer that just barely covers Ben's consciousness that he's striking out. One wants to embrace his Ben Hood, but one loses patience with the character, just as one loses patience with Ben's wife, Elena (a masklike Joan Allen), who knows that Ben is straying and expresses her anger in bouts of shoplifting. Why doesn't any of them do something? Or at least say something? *The Ice Storm* has an overarticulated design, but it's an inarticulate movie. What do these people want? Who are they? Their passivity and cluelessness aren't adequately explained. The director may have made them lifeless in order to feel sorry for them and judge them. On wife-swapping night, Elena and Janey's husband (Jamey Sheridan) have a squalid encounter in the front seat of a car, and they are both ashamed, but the quick grope clears the air of constraint. At least it's an act.

The movie's only voice is its ironclad style—the winter colors, especially colorless colors (water, leafless trees, rain-soaked windows, white-on-white houses), and the sadistically precise editing, which has the unnerving effect of cutting off a scene just as someone is about to gain insight into something. The compositions, which look edged, overdefined, and emotionally neutral, like photo-realist paintings, can be breathtaking in their chilled beauty. Talent certainly isn't what's missing here. Ang Lee's touch is very delicate, and the movie's perfection of bleakness offers a refined pleasure (of a sort). But the material doesn't quite *play*. If, at one end of the spectrum, *The Ice Storm* is like Mazursky without the laughs, at the other it's like Bergman without the anguished brilliance.

Ang Lee has relinquished the warming generosity, the rages and satisfactions of family love that made his earlier movies (*The Wedding Banquet, Eat Drink Man Woman, Sense and Sensibility*) so hopeful a flowering of humanist filmmaking. In this movie, he aims for the poignant and iconic moment—the visual signature of despair, the empty soul in the too thoroughly designed glass suburban house. In the end, his control and his use of the natural world are artistically formidable but humanly appalling. A kind of biblical punishment—violent changes in nature and the death of a firstborn son—falls on these banal suburban sinners, and the punishment doesn't fit the crime. Even the Old Testament God was not so perverse as to strike people down for failing to communicate.

NEW YORK POST, 9/26/97, p. 59, Thelma Adams

Like James Schamus, the Cannes-award-winning screenwriter of "The Ice Storm," I came of age in the '70s. It was the decade the sexual revolution trickled down to the suburbs, the Autumn after the Summer of Love.

At the time, the '50s were the distant past, the Dark Ages of sexual repression. Now, in the '90s, my '70s are the same 20 years and a generation ago. It's a little jarring to see director Ang Lee treat my decade as if it were another period piece, like "Sense and Sensibility."

"The Ice Storm" is set in 1973 in New Canaan, Conn. It's based on Rick Moody's wrenching novel of family loss and redemption. When Lee's drama opens at the New York Film Festival tonight and arrives tomorrow at area theaters, it's deja vu all over again.

The sharply cast movie gives a dark twist to the 1969 group-grope Classic "Bob and Carol and Ted and Alice." Here, two couples come close to discovering that two's company, four's a happening.

Next-door neighbors Janey Carver (a predatory Sigourney Weaver, fab in shag haircut) and Elena Hood (Joan Allen, so Tricia Nixon as yet another tortured spouse) are trying to get in touch with themselves.

Meanwhile, Janey has gotten in touch with Elena's husband. Kevin Kline's Ben is a straight arrow who wants to swing but can't get the rhythm. When Ben gripes about work after a roll on the waterbed, Janey tells him: "You're boring me. I have a husband. I don't feel the need for another one."

Janey's husband (affectingly underplayed by Jamey Sheridan) is clueless, off inventing the "peanuts" that buffer breakables in transit. Meanwhile, their kids orbit, communicating to each other more directly than their parents do.

Schoolboy Paul Hood (Tobey Maguire) narrates the story. His younger sister (Christina Ricci, stealing the movie from the adults) plays sex games with both Carver boys (Elijah Wood and Adam Hann-Byrd).

The movie climaxes with a storm and a "key party"—a bash where couples leave the car keys at the door on entry and the wives change partners by picking different keys on exit. Together, these events lend a new meaning to slippery when wet.

As the roads ice over, the couples get drunker and the latchkey kids run amok, Lee and Schamus create incredible tension. In this deadly game of sexual musical chairs, we become fearful for these families who unwittingly risk all in their folly.

In a Puritanical turn made in hindsight, someone has to pay. The Hoods and Carvers have lost track of themselves and their children; they are frozen and sex cannot thaw them. Ultimately, it's the bond between fathers and daughters, mothers and sons, that shoots out like an electrical current from a cable downed by a freak ice storm.

Lee captures this connection in intense images: Janey waking up to the sound of her husband's mournful sobs, aware of tragedy even before she knows its source; Ben carrying his teen daughter in his arms, her legs squeezing his trunk, her arms circling his neck—a show of physical intimacy that cuts through the brittle chatter. The bond can be bent, but even death cannot break it.

NEWSDAY, 9/26/97, Part II/p. B7, Jack Mathews

Rick Moody's 1994 bestseller "The Ice Storm," about a dysfunctional upscale family in 1973 suburban Connecticut, is so specifically American, its film adaptation would seem to demand a director with a strong background in domestic drama. Instead, it got Taiwan-born Ang Lee, whose only made-in-the-U.S.A. movie, "The Wedding Banquet," contained so much Chinese dialogue, it was nominated for an Oscar as best foreign-language film.

But the selection now looks to be a stroke of genius. The 43-year-old director avoided the clichés that have sunk more than a few ambitious movies about the early '70s to a degree that might have been impossible for someone raised in the culture.

Moody was a teenager in 1973, and two decades later, strained that experience through a prism of time. And though 16-year-old Paul Hood is the narrator of his novel, the author was able to step back to view the events from the adults' points of view, as well. Lee has taken that further, creating such an even balance that both parents and their grown children from the period will find pieces of themselves somewhere in the emotional clutter of the story.

On the surface, "The Ice Storm" seems just another Thanksgiving holiday with a dysfunctional family. But it is too busy probing the individual identification crises, and their threat to the family unit, to spend much time at the dinner table. The Hoods are a family being subverted by the instability of society at large. They're a dysfunctional family in a dysfunctional culture.

It's the period of Watergate, student riots, free love and freer drugs, all chipping away at the foundation of what we now call family values. Adults were tempted by a lifestyle forbidden them a mere decade or so earlier, and adolescents were being thrown into the current with unprecedented peer and cultural pressure.

When we peek in on them, the Hoods are inching toward calamity. Ben Hood (Kevin Kline) is pathologically self-absorbed, searching for ego gratification in a dead-end affair with an equally self-obsessed—and far more cold-hearted—neighbor (Sigourney Weaver). Elena Hood (Joan Allen) is wary of her husband's growing detachment, and of her own loss of passion. Paul (Tobey Maguire) is testosterone-charged at a time when everybody seems to be having sex but him. And 14-year-old Wendy (Christina Ricci) is in that awkward zone between childhood and adolescence, made all the more treacherous by the tenor of the time.

The story takes place mostly on a day that will end with a brutal ice storm, which is both the dramatic catalyst and the movie's overriding metaphor. Lee frames it as a flashback, opening in the dawn after the storm, with Paul's train from Grand Central to New Canaan creaking back to speed after being stalled all night on the frozen tracks.

In the end, we see him get off the train and meet his family, three people whose lives have been permanently changed by the events of the previous day.

The movie intercuts scenes of each family member's experiences. Ben's deflating relationship with Janey Carver (Weaver). Wendy's tenuous sexual contact with the Carver boys, the outgoing Mikey (Elijah Wood) and his emotionally troubled younger brother Sandy (Adam Hann-Byrd). Elena Hood's open rebellion. And Paul's own adventures with his roommate and the girl they go to visit in Manhattan.

The film's centerpiece is a party that the feuding Ben and Elena attend, only to learn when they get there that it's a swap meet. The men throw their car keys into a fish bowl, and after an evening of drink, the women blindly grab a key and go home with whomever it belongs to.

Swap parties have been parodied to death in movies, but Lee's tack is painfully realistic. These are suburbanites caught in a scary fantasy, and the looks on most of the faces aren't the sort you see when someone's about to break a piñata.

There are scenes of people slipping on the icy carpet left by the storm, and you feel that instability in the characters throughout the movie. Kline, as far removed from his character in "In & Out" as possible, makes Ben Hood a study in confusion and self-destruction. He's desperate to be part of a social wave he doesn't understand, and in showing his dawning revelations, brought on by error and tragedy, Kline gives a heart-wrenching performance.

All of the performances are exceptional, but special mention is deserved for Allen, whose character absorbs most of the emotional blows and survives, almost heroically, and for Ricci, as gifted a young actress as there is on the scene today. And kudos to everyone involved in creating the look of "The Ice Storm." I haven't felt this cold since "Dr. Zhivago."

SIGHT AND SOUND, 2/98, p. 42, Lizzie Francke

New Canaan, Connecticut. November 1973. The Hood family prepare for Thanksgiving. There is a slight chill between Ben Hood and his wife Elena, but they still go through the yearly ritual with their teenage children Paul (who is travelling up from a New York prep school) and Wendy.

Ben is having an affair with his neighbour Janey Carver. Wendy is experimenting sexually with the eldest Carver boy Mikey, while his younger brother Sandy pines for her.

Over at the Carvers for a tryst with Janey, Ben discovers Wendy with Mikey making out and escorts his daughter home. Despite storm warnings, Paul visits a potential girlfriend, Libbets, in New York City only to find his schoolfriend Francis there. Hoping to spoil Francis' chances, Paul gives him sleeping pills, but Libbets insists on taking them as well and both of them pass out. Paul catches the last train, but it's delayed by the ice storm.

Elena has guessed by now that Ben is having an affair. Together they attend a neighbour's annual party only to find that it's a wife swapping event. Though somewhat disconcerted, they stay on. Ben gets very drunk. As each wife fishes out a set of car keys to select the night's partner, Ben makes a fool of himself when Janey is escorted out by a friend's son. Elena is paired off with Janey's husband Jim and they have disappointing sex in the car. Meanwhile, Wendy goes over to the Carvers and ends up in bed with Sandy. Mikey has set out into the night to experience the storm, only to be electrocuted by a storm-damaged pylon. Later, Ben makes his way home and discovers Mikey's body. He brings him back to the Carvers. The following morning, the Hoods meet Paul at the station and watching him in the car mirror, Ben bursts into tears.

With its spare, circular story line, the ability to crystallise so much of what it is about in its visuals, and an exceptional cast delivering the most precise of spoken lines, *The Ice Storm* is cinema at its most immaculate. Everything from Mark Friedberg's wonderfully researched production design though to Frederick Elmes' crisp cinematography and Mychael Danna's wintry wind-instrument based score is perfectly conceived. Undoubtedly, it confirms its director Ang Lee *(Sense and Sensibility)* and his regular producer/ screenwriter James Schamus as a world class film-making team.

Based on Rick Moody's novel written in 1994, it is also one of the most intelligently observed appraisals of the 70s and, more precisely, of the watershed year of 1973. The reference points are brilliantly assembled—toe socks, and the television show *Divorce Court* and Philip Roth's *When She Was Good* are ever so briefly glimpsed—and used not as decorative retro accessories but as means of commenting on the dislocation of the moment and the confusion of those trying to live through it. Importantly, obvious historical referents are threaded through but don't dominate the film. Nixon and Watergate are as much part of the texture as crocheted tank-tops. (Though a hilarious scene showing the sexually precocious 14-year-old Wendy wearing a Nixon mask while she and Mikey attempt sex makes a somewhat oblique but wry comment on the political shenanigans of the era.

On the other hand, key 1973 phenomena are wisely left implicit. For example, acerbic Janey Carver's calculated view of sex surely signals that she h mastered the "zipless fuck" of Erica Jong's imagination. Indeed, *The Ice Storm* is bourgeois lives that are cluttered up with goodies and ideas to be tried on for size. The more conservative Hoods, whose home is a discordant mix of two-or-so decades' furnishings, are straining to swing with the rest of them, an effort signalled equally by the buying of new chinawear and Elena's purchase of proto-New Age philosophies. In contrast the Carvers, with their cool Philip Johnson- style glass house that ostensibly signals openness about their lives, have severed themselves from a past predicated on picket-fenced ideals.

Architecture is essential to the film and director Lee has a rare skill: the ability to communicate via the spatial relationship between the characters and the things around them. A brief scene depicts Ben at work in the city, a bored man in a board meeting, sitting as stiffly as the skyscrapers glimpsed in the window behind him. His sense of discomfort with power and himself is neatly secured in this wordless moment. (By way of contrast, Janey's voracious appetite for domination is economically conveyed when she toys with her son's cowboy whip out in their back garden, a delicious moment which Sigourney Weaver makes her own.)

Perhaps the most symbolic and dangerously gaping space of them all in the film is Mikey's haunting ground, the swimming pool empty of water and collecting dry leaves. Like some waiting mass grave, it implies the deep dead-end of affluence while firmly rooting the film in John Cheever country (Frank and Eleanor Perry's adaptation of *The Swimmer* of 1968 would make an interesting double bill with *The Ice Storm,* as would the 1970 Perry movie, *Diary of a Mad Housewife).* The empty pool also augurs the tragedy to come, *The Ice Storm's coup de grâce* that finally underscores the fragility of relationships and life itself.

TIME, 9/29/97, p. 98, Richard Corliss

Forget the dictates of retrochic: the typical '70s family was not the Brady Bunch. It might have been closer to the Hoods and the Carvers, neighboring clans in New Canaan, Conn., who make up one big unhappy family in *The Ice Storm*. Ben Hood (Kevin Kline) is having a fruitless tryst with Janey Carver (Sigourney Weaver), while Ben's wife Elena (Joan Allen) screams silently, so as not to wake the kids, and Janey's husband Jim (Jamey Sheridan) has so little impact on his brood that when he calls out a cheery, "I'm back," his son Mikey (Elijah Wood) replies, "You were gone?"

Playtime for the kids, on this Thanksgiving weekend of 1973, means sexual one-upmanship. Precocious Wendy Hood (Christina Ricci) insists on wearing a Nixon mask during foreplay with Mikey Carver and goads his shy younger brother Sandy (Adam Hann-Byrd) into a game of mutual exhibitionism. Wendy's brother Paul (Tobey Maguire) goes to a Manhattan party where, once again, a pretty girl treats him as just a friend. For the adults the big social event is a Key Party. The men drop their car keys into a bowl, the women blindly pick them out, and new sexual partnerships are formed—a surer route to public embarrassment than to private ecstasy. The omens are clear: the founderings of all these nice people will lead to trouble. A child must be sacrificed; men must sob at their loss. *The Ice Storm*, says Ang Lee, director of this daring epic in miniature, is "a disaster movie. Except the disaster hits home."

The '70s, in Rick Moody's 1994 novel, is a time of profound unease—when '60s free love got to the suburbs, and the folks there knew they had to try it but didn't know how to enjoy it. Promiscuity became one more burden of middle-class life. And the climactic ice storm is nature's way of saying, Don't try this at home. "At first it comes down like water, really soft," says Lee, 42. "Suddenly it freezes and wraps everything. It adds weight to the objects, eventually causing them to shatter. It's a crystal world."

A world with elaborate, often suffocating behavioral codes that its inhabitants try desperately to obey—this is the milieu of all five of the Taiwanese director's films, from his Mandarin-language "Father Knows Best trilogy" (*Pushing Hands, The Wedding Banquet, Eat Drink Man Woman*) to *Sense and Sensibility* and *The Ice Storm*. His characters' failure to achieve an artificial ideal makes the films both comedies of manners and bourgeois tragedies. Especially this one, thanks to a superb script by Lee's frequent collaborator James Schamus. When Janey joins Elena in her kitchen to help with the dishes, the hostess whispers a steely, "Don't touch them!" It is Elena's amusingly fierce marking of her turf, it is also a socially acceptable way for her to bark at her husband's mistress and uncork her hatred of her life.

"This movie is about uncomfortableness," Lee says. "Whatever you do is somehow wrong." So the actors could not feel self-assured about their performance. It's not about performing; it's about people being observed in an uncomfortable situation." The viewer should feel the same way. A squirming sympathy is the only proper reaction to the clumsiness of the parents' attempts to connect with their kids, like Ben's solemn advice to his son on masturbation ("Don't do it in the shower"). Yet the film's lesson is that, God help us and them, we are our parents. The kids and their folks share all kinds of little sins, from shoplifting to casual sex to peeking in a neighbor's medicine cabinet. Home, the film says, is a school where we mostly learn bad habits.

When the local hippie minister makes a mildly suggestive remark to Elena, she says, "I'm going to try hard not to understand the implications of that." That is the cardinal rule here: Don't ask, don't dwell. One of the chilliest moments in *The Ice Storm* comes in an edgy scene where Ben tells Elena, "I guess we're just on the verge of saying something—saying something to each other." Saying something harsh and truthful would be a breaking of the code, of the lies that sustain their marriage and keep it arid.

Lee's exquisitely watchful face may suggest a softness of temperament. Don't be fooled: he knows what he wants. "I like to communicate in a civilized way, if my English can accommodate it," says Lee, who came to the U.S. for college in 1978 and has lived here ever since. "Sometimes my English is a little brutal. But that's all right. I get understood."

The grace of an Ang Lee film is in his avoidance of the gaucheries his characters cannot escape. He calls this "a costume drama," but doesn't push the period. "I haven't seen the '70s treated realistically. Most films mock the '70s. But it's both period and very fresh in our memory. That ambiguity fascinated me."

And of course Lee will not pass draconian judgments on his sweet, sad characters. "My Oriental upbringing made me bring sympathy to them," he says. "it also gave me the fear of nature, fear and respect for something bigger than life, something unknown that you can't control." He could mean not just the ice storm in his delicately devastating film, but the wayward impulses that rage in every human heart.

Also reviewed in:
CHICAGO TRIBUNE, 10/17/97, Friday/p. C, Michael Wilmington
NATION, 10/27/97, p. 34, Stuart Klawans
NEW REPUBLIC, 10/13/97, p. 30, Stanley Kauffmann
NEW YORK TIMES, 9/26/97, p. E1, Janet Maslin
NEW YORKER, 9/29/97, p. 86, Daphne Merkin
VARIETY, 5/19-25/97, p. 49, Todd McCarthy
WASHINGTON POST, 10/17/97, p. D6, Rita Kempley
WASHINGTON POST, 10/17/97, Weekend/p. 32, Desson Howe

IMAX NUTCRACKER, THE

An Imax Corporation release of a Sands Films production. *Executive Producer:* Andrew Gellis. *Producer:* Oliver Stockman and Lorne Orleans. *Director:* Christine Edzard. *Screenplay:* Christine Edzard. *Based on the story "The Nutcracker and the Mouse King" by:* E.T.A Hoffmann. *Director of Photography:* Noel Archambault. *Music:* V.I. Tchaikovsky. *Production Designer:* Annabel Hands, Neale Brown, and John McMillan. *Art Director:* Annabel Hands, Neale Brown, and John McMillan. *Costumes:* Claudie Gastine, Sabine Dutilh, and Sadie Frederick. *Running time:* 40 minutes. *MPAA Rating:* Not Rated.

CAST: Miriam Margolyes (Sugar Plum); Heathcote Williams (Drosselmeier); Lotte Johnson (Clara); Benjamin Hall (Nutcracker Prince); Harriet Thorpe (Mother); Patrick Pearson (Father); Daniel Wylie (Frederick); Tamara Rojo (The Sugar Fairy).

LOS ANGELES TIMES, 11/26/97, Calendar/p. 12, Jan Herman

To all those sincere, affectionate community productions of "The Nutcracker," we may now add a sincere, affectionate screen version, "The IMAX Nutcracker." Clearly intended as a fuzzy-warm Christmas evergreen for children, it makes tasteful use of 3-D cinematography and avoids any startling special effects, dark themes or, for that matter, a ballet company.

Although E.T.A. Hoffmann's early 19th century fairy tale "The Nutcracker and the Mouse King" is most familiar nowadays as a story ballet, this brief outing of less than 40 minutes sticks to a more ordinary, not to say pedestrian, mode of storytelling. The movie offers a lovingly told narrative—accompanied somewhat haphazardly by the lush music of Tchaikovsky's "Nutcracker Suite"—about 8-year-old Clara's visit to Uncle Drosselmeier's house with her brother and her parents one snowy winter day in London and the fantastic events that befall her on the way home.

Drosselmeier, played by a monocled Heathcote Williams with the slightly ferocious stare of someone mildly possessed, is no ordinary boring uncle. He's a gadget collector who has filled his well-appointed home with antique marvels: dolls and puppets, music boxes, toy soldiers, marionettes and, the *pièce de resistance* of his collection, a miniature castle made of spun sugar that must be kept under glass to protect it from mice. Of course, Drosselmeier also has a wonderful Christmas present for Clara: a very dignified Nutcracker carved out of wood to look like a Hussar in a flamboyant red-white-and-blue officer's uniform.

Despite its brevity, the movie manages to go slack midway through the story, following the imaginary battle between the Nutcracker's troops and the Mouse King's. And it loses its narrative drive altogether during Clara's dreamscape voyage to the Sugar Palace with her handsome escort, the Nutcracker, who has been magically transformed into a young prince. But young viewers probably won't notice. Clara's stagy boat ride on billowing clouds of dry ice is not likely to discourage their fantasies any more than it does hers.

The action picks up again nicely at the palace, where she and the prince are greeted by Sugar Plum and a circus troupe of tumblers, stilt-walkers, clowns and, at last, the Sugar Fairy, a slim ballerina doing an exquisite series of piqué turns. When all is said, moreover, "The IMAX Nutcracker" evokes a poetic mood that requires only a short attention span, making it ideal as an intimate introduction for young children to a wholesome Christmas tradition.

NEW YORK POST, 11/26/97, p. 45, Larry Worth

It sounded like an inspired idea: lensing E.T.A. Hoffmann's classic "The Nutcracker and the Mouse King" tale in the wonders of 3-D IMAX.

But what could have become a cinematic holiday tradition is the equivalent of coal in one's stocking. Under Christine Edzard's inept direction, the fantasy universe in which Clara and her Nutcracker Prince battle a six-headed mouse before sailing to his sugar palace looks cheesy and unconvincing.

The clumsily staged action appears to have been choreographed by Gomer Pyle. Meanwhile, the updated story—which has Clara falling through thin ice after visiting Uncle Drosselmeier—leads to a ludicrous "There's no place like home" finale.

And although veteran actress Miriam Margolyes tries hard to convince as Sugar Plum (now rewritten as the prince's full-bodied pastry chef), she can't mask the monotonous drone of Lotte Johnson's stilted Clara or the rote actions of Benjamin Hall's Nutcracker.

Thankfully, the sounds of Tchaikovsky's glorious score prove somewhat distracting, along with the IMAX 3-D's special effects. Even then, Edzard missed a great opportunity by skipping over the family Christmas tree's magical growth scene.

Like the rest of "The IMAX Nutcracker," the evergreen remains stunted, unadorned and unappealing.

NEWSDAY, 11/26/97, Part II/p. B12, Gene Seymour

It may be a tad grinchy to demand that this "IMAX Nutcracker" present anything comparable to what you'll find across the street and down the block from where it's playing. But let's say this at the outset: If you really want a "Nutcracker" with the kind of heart-in-the-throat thrills that an IMAX show customarily provides, you're a lot better off getting in line for tickets to the venerable New York City Ballet production at Lincoln Center.

The IMAX version, by contrast, is a shiny little contraption with all kinds of bright, whirring activity jammed in its tight corners. The Tchaikovsky music can be heard throughout in the background of this version of the Hoffman tale, set in contemporary, snow-covered London. There is a little girl named Clara (Lotte Johnson), here saddled with a pair of whiny parents and a bratty brother (Daniel Wylie).

And there is Drosselmeier (playwright Heathcote Williams), depicted as your standard-issue eccentric surrounded by bright, whirring antique toys. Clara, of course, is enchanted by a nutcracker, which bratty brother soon tosses onto a pond of thin ice. She scrambles and slides after it and just as she reaches the thing, she dreams herself and the nutcracker into a warm, glowing room.

You know what happens next. Maybe you don't. Anyway these giant mice—which, magnified, look like a stampede of winter hats—attack all these toys which have either grown as big as Clara or have stayed small as Clara has shrunk. Whatever.

The battle, like much else in the film, is a confounding welter of furry bodies and plastic faces. All you want to do when watching this is move your elbows back and forth to get these detracting creatures out of your way.

Eventually, the nutcracker reveals himself to be a handsome prince (Benjamin Hall) and there's a dance by one fairy (Tamara Rojo) and some business involving someone named Sugar Plum (Miriam Margolyes).

If I'm making this sound both dense and perfunctory, that's exactly what this movie feels like. It's not a bad way to spend part of a crowded shopping day, but it'll melt away in your memory bank like the spun sugar that made Drosselmeier's house.

VILLAGE VOICE, 12/2/97, p. 86, Francine Russo

If this *Nutcracker* were not an IMAX, no one would bother. Ballet is a tiny element, Tchaikovsky's gorgeous score is subordinate, and the story line—simple as it is—slightly confusing. But the 3-D spectacle is its own breathtaking reason for being. Stroll along a wintry London street hearing the snow crunch under your boots, stare upwards at snow-dusted spruces, and gaze close-up at intricately pointed and carved toys and costumes. See sad-eyed monkeys strum mandolins while trapeze artists in tulle somersault practically into your lap.

Writer-designer-director Christine Edzard has whipped up an imaginative feast for the senses on the order of grand opera, with every spectator sitting in the first row. Never mind that the young actors speak their lines woodenly or that the battle scene between the toys and the mice looks like a crowd jostling each other in a movie line. The acrobats, puppets, and dancers put on a spirited show, and there are delightful cameos by Heathcote Williams and Miriam Margolyes. Here's 40 minutes of Victoriana and Christmas plum cake via one high-tech headset.

Also reviewed in:
CHICAGO TRIBUNE, 11/26/97, Tempo/p. 10, Michael Wilmington
NEW YORK TIMES, 11/26/97, p. E5, Stephen Holden
VARIETY, 12/1-7/97, p. 73, Lael Loewenstein

IN THE COMPANY OF MEN

A Sony Pictures Classics release of a Stephen Pevner/Atlantis Entertainment production in association with Fair and Square Productions. *Executive Producer:* Toby Gaff, Mark Hart, and Matt Malloy. *Producer:* Mark Archer and Stephen Pevner. *Director:* Neil LaBute. *Screenplay:* Neil LaBute. *Director of Photography:* Tony Hettinger. *Editor:* Joel Plotch. *Music:* Ken Williams and Karel Roessingn. *Sound:* Guy Camara and (music) Tony Moskal. *Make-up:* Joe Moyer. *Running time:* 93 minutes. *MPAA Rating:* R.

CAST: Aaron Eckhart (Chad); Stacy Edwards (Christine); Matt Malloy (Howard); Michael Martin (Co-Worker 1); Mark Rector (John); Chris Hayes (Co-worker 2); Jason Dixie (Intern); Emily Cline (Suzanne); Roxanne Butler (Flight Attendant); Chan Aye (Courtesy Van Driver); Nisa Janek (Waitress); Bob Werling (Bartender); Brandy Runyan (Temp Secretary); Tony O'Dell and Adam Simcoe (Painters); Michael C. Barnhouse and Laura L. Bartels (Dinner Crowd); Peter Springer (Jeweler); Sarah Springer (Jewelry Patron); Sara Valentine (Coffee House Waitress); Paul E. Wilson, Jr. (Garage Passer-by); Ken Petruska and Mike Thena (Elevator Men); Fred Coffee (Bank Mangager).

CINEASTE, Vol XXIII, 1997, No. 2, p. 40, Paul Arthur

If Neil LaBute were playing poker, someone would want to shoot him. His debut film, *In the Company of Men*, announces itself as a cutthroat round of stud poker involving two seasoned players and a mark. As the cards are laid it becomes apparent that the dealer is holding a pat hand. Even worse, just before the final bets, the rules change to include wild cards. What begins as a high-stakes game of sexual chance is on closer inspection little more than a (phallic) shell game whose slick gestures hide an elusive thematic pea.

Opening at the tail end of summer's commercial sludgefest, *Company* was almost universally hailed as a tough, darkly-etched social satire on empty suits behaving badly for fun and profit. According to the director, the story is a simple case of "boys meet girl, boys crush girl, boys giggle." Allowing for a certain amount of poetic license—only one boy giggles; the girl does not seem crushed—LaBute's encapsulation sounds like a screwball comedy gone sour, a post-feminist battle of the sexes in which the side with all the weapons gets skewered.

What transpires is at once more ambitious and less clearly motivated. Two former college buddies perched on the same generic corporate ladder are sent for six weeks to a branch office in a nameless heartland city in order to oversee some vague data installation and training program.

Chad (Aaron Eckhart) and Howard (Matt Malloy) are a typical odd couple: the former is brash, deadly handsome, and verbally adept; the latter is a diminutive nerd replete with glasses, receding hairline, and a bad case of the mumbles. What binds them psychologically are deep-seated grievances against women, what they view as the power to manipulate and humiliate them in romantic relationships. They agree that things are getting out of balance and that there's going to be hell to pay down the line.

Although they decry the absurdity of not being able to tell lewd jokes at work, the gender competition they imagine is primarily sexual, not economic; strangely, the only women evident in the corporate structure are typists. During a long night of drinking and venting en route to their new assignment, Chad coerces Howard into a scheme in which they will target and mutually seduce a woman from the local office, someone so physically disadvantaged and undesirable that she doubts the possibility of romance. Then they will dump her and laugh about it, Chad explains, "until we are very old men."

They settle on Christine (Stacy Edwards), a clerical temp who is deaf, lives with her mother, and speaks with a halting nasal drone. The object in this game of payback is to maintain perfect control, a constant theme as well as emblem of the film's visual design. As Fate or narrative convention would have it, Howard, and possibly Chad, become emotionally involved, forcing them into same-sex competition and eventual betrayal. By the end, Howard is completely undone, a physical wreck who has been demoted to customer relations and reduced to pitiful groveling in front of an unresponsive Christine.

In what the film passes off as biting irony, it is learned that Chad's account of his mistreatment by a lover is all a hoax. The suggestion is that, despite an overarching viciousness and anger directed at the social order in general, Chad's ulterior motive in concocting the seduction scheme has been status envy, the subversion of Howard's superior position in the corporate hierarchy. In other words, the manipulation of sexual power has served as a cloak for intrafraternal warfare: boys hit on girl, boys fuck each other up, boys exchange job descriptions.

Unfortunately for the narrative logic, the rivalry over who will bed Christine is itself a hoax. Howard is presented as needy, cuddly, and awkwardly sincere, a mixture of Woody and Dilbert. Chad is a tad chilly yet, given that both he and Christine look as though they have stepped off the pages of *Vogue,* there is scarcely a moment's doubt as to which guy will get the nod; indeed, the only mystery is why Christine is not the object of *more* romantic attention. For a while at least, *Company* sticks to its guns, maintaining a strict perspectival focus on the men (although always slightly favoring Chad as mediator of knowledge). In the body of the film, scenes shift between the two men alone and their various romantic encounters with Christine. She is given no independent life and her feelings about her sudden popularity remain a cipher. There is an admirable rigor involved in the decision to cordon off the victim's subjectivity.

It then becomes all the more shocking, and inexcusable, when the rules of engagement are broken. In the second of two climactic scenes, Chad admits to Christine that Howard's revelation of the pact between the suitors is true. After Chad departs, the camera lingers on a two-minute overhead closeup of Christine's silent agony, the most blatantly mawkish and invasive shot in the entire movie (Oh, did I mention that one-eyed jacks are wild?). The same formal misprision is repeated, and amplified) in the final scene as, weeks later, Howard comes barging into a cavernous bank where Christine is now temping. As he entreats her to give him another chance, his voice is abruptly deleted from the soundtrack, making us privy not only to Christine's optical but also her auditory perspective.

These calculated lapses in the film's stylistic program would perhaps feel less damaging were it not for the insistent emphasis on hard-edged, almost clinical disengagement from contact with the characters' inner lives, a method LaBute refers to as minimalism. The majority of scenes unfold in long-take, fixed-camera, frontal compositions—many from unnaturally high or low angles—which display the two predators like insects in a museum exhibit. The physical environment they inhabit parallels the impersonal, functionless work they presumably perform: not quite colorless but antiseptic surfaces, a series of compartmentalized spaces in which the exercise of gratuitous insult is muffled by an aura of synthetic uniformity (a design stunningly realized by cinematographer Tony Hettinger). The effect is reminiscent of Kubrick's visions of male technocracy, a comparison heightened by two scenes of male intimacy staged in the executive bathroom—think of *The Shining* or *Full Metal Jacket.*

Further, a dynamic tension between aggression and compartmentalization is established by a clipped cadence of six discrete sequences or chapters corresponding to the progression of weeks, bracketed by a prologue and epilogue. Paradoxically, the degree of distance and control inscribed in the image eventually registers as a mirror for the consciousness of control-freak Chad. In this sense, not only is *Company*'s narrative economy weighted towards Chad's willful deceptions, its visual patterning corresponds to Chad's buffed, meticulous demeanor.

Since Howard never has a fighting chance, and Chad is virtually Jack the Ripper in Brooks Brothers garb, it is hard to understand what critics found so controversial, incendiary, or instructive about *Company*'s discourse on misogyny. Rather than being implicated in the attitudes or behaviors of the schematic seducers, the male viewer can shrug off any stigma of identification by simply dismissing the characters as either patently pathetic or borderline psychopathic. If there is a need to articulate the relationship between masculine self-definition and the wielding of sexual power within the workplace, that goal is surely not achieved by creating characters so exaggerated that any possible defense of their actions becomes moot.

Company does contain one truly incendiary scene, but like much else in the film it turns out to be a red herring. In a private conference, Chad interrogates an African-American intern about a minor infraction, dangling the possibility of corporate advancement if he has the balls. When the intern responds affirmatively, Chad demands to see if they are literally big enough, and after some hesitation—and assurance from Chad that he is no homo—the poor guy obliges. Are we to conclude that Chad's sexism is integrally linked with racism? That his competition with Howard is actually grounded in inchoate homoerotic attraction? The film pursues neither question; instead, they are merely tantalizing diversions, like the grand flourish of a card sharp as he slides one off the bottom of the deck.

A frequent connection has been made between LaBute's film and the work of David Mamet, an insight that seems dead-on, if not in the way it was intended. At both his best and his worst, Mamet is a practitioner of what might be called the slippery allegory, in which individual characters are invested with abstract social or psychological or moral attributes. In traditional—as opposed to postmodern—literary allegories such as Bunyan's *The Pilgrim's Progress,* a character who stands for, say, Christian virtue will encounter a series of figures and situations that will test and ultimately define the ideal nature of the abstract concept. In Mamet's plays and films, there is often the veneer of a hidden parable, some ethical lesson to be derived which remains just hazy enough to allow for conflicting interpretations. The dehumanizing, degrading but also possibly redemptive rituals of persuasion enacted in *Glengarry Glen Ross* (1992) is a useful example. When the social issue at stake is defined too narrowly or clumsily, and the deck of allegorical traits is stacked from the beginning, as in the egregious fakery of *Oleanna's* (1994) gender struggle, the house of cardboard figures collapses under its own weight.

Something similar occurs in *Company*. It is never clear whether the trope of corporate competition as directed by Chad is a displacement for or a generative model of male heterosexual rage. Are these two behavioral trajectories being equated, paralleled, or situated in a causal chain (i.e., the frustrations of mindless, alienated labor produce sexual predation; or alternatively, the inability to find romantic completion leads to cutthroat business tactics)? The deaf typist whose limited powers of speech prohibit dissimulation, the nameless computer application of a nameless corporation located in a nameless city, all conspire to place the drama of *In the Company of Men* in a suprarealistic realm. Chad and Howard are not to be taken literally, as real people, but as exemplars of... what? The film can never quite decide; there is something up its sleeve and the suspicion is that it is nothing more, or less, than the long arm of patriarchy.

LOS ANGELES TIMES, 8/1/97, Calendar/p. 6, Kenneth Turan

Writer-director Neil LaBute's "In the Company of Men" is a one-trick pony, a movie that has a gift only for making audiences squirm. Something of an accomplishment, no doubt, in this blasé age, but not satisfying enough to base an entire film on.

It's not that the pair of corporate executives who seethe with resentment toward women and hatch a cynical, sadistic plan to wreck revenge on a vulnerable member of the opposite sex don't have a basis in reality. But, while men acting monstrously can cause considerable havoc both on and off screen, the spectacle is not dramatically involving in and of itself.

Bad behavior doesn't have to be soft-pedaled to capture our interest, but it does need to be illuminated and dissected, not merely presented. While no film character has been a more vicious misogynist than David Thewlis' blistering, abrasive Johnny, the protagonist of Mike Leigh's "Naked," that film enabled us to experience his character in completely unexpected ways.

There is hardly anything surprising, by contrast, about the way "In the Company of Men" unfolds, and the only thing that changes in our attitude toward its males is a steady increase in the level of revulsion they inspire.

Chad (Aaron Eckhart) and Howard (Matt Malloy) are two white-collar executives, employees of a nameless corporation headed for a six-week assignment in an anonymous town. Howard is the senior of the pair, but he is a mousy, timid soul with none of the confidence of the brash and preening Chad, an arrogant type given to expressions such as "As a race, men like us are doomed" and "Life is for the taking, is it not?"

One thing these two do have in common is problems with women. When Howard reveals he's been dumped by his girlfriend, Chad says his has left him as well. Working himself up to a fine rage, Chad decides it's payback time for all the pain of relationships. "Let's hurt somebody," he says to Howard, and he reveals a plan.

The idea is to find a woman, "vulnerable as hell, a wallflower type who felt romance was lost to her forever." Both Chad and Howard would simultaneously hit on her, making her believe she was the love of their lives, and then coldly tell her the truth before leaving town. "She'll be reaching for the sleeping pills within a week," Chad gloats, "and you and me, we'll laugh about this until we're very old men."

Howard reluctantly agrees, and Chad almost immediately spots Christine (Stacy Edwards,), his idea of the ideal victim. Deaf since the age of 8, Christine is a typist who keeps to herself and speaks with difficulty. "She has a voice like a dolphin. It's like having a chat with Flipper," Chad exults adding with typical mean glee "She's one of the kindest people I've ever had spray spit in my face."

Broken up into segments, one for each of the weeks Chad and Howard are out of town, "In the Company of Men" details what happens when these men put their scheme into operation, plus the difficulties that simultaneously begin to crop up on the business side of their lives.

It's not a pleasant picture for any number of reasons, mainly because Chad is so off-putting a character. A bully and a liar, a master game player and manipulator who we watch casually crushing a young co-worker (Jason Dixie), Chad's practiced humiliation stance has none of the fascination of memorable double-dealers like Robert Mitchum's Love/Hate preacher in "Night of the Hunter." We simply want to be free of his presence as quickly as possible.

Ironically, given that it prides itself on its toughness, "In the Company of Men" would be more painful (and more honest) if it were as nervy as it pretends. For the film pulls its punches by casting Edwards, a quite attractive actress whose vocal problems (learned for the film) are not that troublesome. The kind of victim Chad says he's after would be much more woebegone, but that kind of truth is out of this film's range of possibility.

Well-received at Sundance, "In the Company of Men" has a share of virtues. It's convincingly acted, and writer-director LaBute has a gift for a certain kind of comic-scabrous dialogue as well as a sure idea of what he wants to accomplish. Yet as shrewdly put together as this film is, it's hard to shake the feeling that what we're watching is a well-made psychological snuff film. If that's your preference, you know where to find it.

NEW YORK, 8/18/97, p. 50, David Denby

At the beginning of *In the Company of Men*, the camera follows two young corporate guys waiting for their connecting flight somewhere in the Midwest.

Dragging their sorry butts from airport lounge to bar, they suffer the kind of soul-destroying boredom that might lead even Winston Churchill to the brink of self-pity, and for a moment, we feel sympathy for them.

The two men, Chad (Aaron Eckhart), tall and handsome with a cleft chin and a wide, eager smile, and the diminutive Howard (Matt Malloy), who has a receding hairline and a small, mean mouth, are flying to a six-week assignment in a branch office of their company. It's a lousy assignment, and they complain sourly about work and about the women back home—girl-friends—who have done them dirt.

Or at least Chad complains. Howard, who is Chad's dim echo and patsy, doesn't so much speak as murmur in assent. A terrific pair: Chad the snake, Howard the worm. In the airport, Chad proposes, and Howard agrees, that they should claim some revenge. During their six weeks in purgatory, they will take turns attracting a defenseless woman ("a corn-fed bitch") and then dumping her. It's payback time.

Though the men are not presented as stupid or crazy, they think the same way that psychopaths and the dimmest of frat boys think: Screw everyone in sight and therefore become more powerful men. We are not intended to wonder how their hurting some stranger could possibly punish another person or a business organization a thousand miles away. We are meant instead to be both shocked and amused by the men's viciousness and to find it entirely characteristic of the corporate world. That is, their "revenge" is significant precisely because it's senseless; they've been bred to perform in a certain way, and now "motiveless malignity" (Coleridge's phrase for Iago's behavior) is the result. *In the Company of Men,* which was written and directed by the 34-year-old playwright Neil LaBute (it's his first film), is a didactic fable of how the dog-eat-dog ethos turns working stiffs into predators, shiv artists, and weaklings. Can the movie be taken seriously? It has certainly received extraordinary reviews. Some people seem dazzled by its vicious tone, which they take for accusing truth; they really think some bold protest, some act of revolt, has been staged against American insensitivity. Yet *In the Company of Men* is a repellent experience—a schematic, coldly cynical work that pretends to expose coldness and cynicism. It's the season's conversation piece, no doubt, but far from a work of art.

LaBute is from the David Mamet, or "never apologize, never explain," school of dramaturgy. In imitation of such Mamet works as *Glengarry Glen Ross* and *Oleanna,* LaBute writes terse, flat-toned dialogue charged with spasms of hatred and dismay. Two people sit side by side or across a table facing each other, the camera never moving as one or the other rants on and on in a self-serving fit. The sequences last forever, and the brutally reductive language, unanswered, unchecked, glowers meanly in the sterile atmosphere. LaBute is going for quintessence, not realism: He doesn't tell us what city we're in, or what the company's name is, or what product or service it offers. The office is decorated in faceless corporate modern, and the men, whose business talk is devoted to process (organizing, programming, taxing, presenting), wear identical white shirts. They aren't robots, exactly, but every one of them (not just the two principals) is nasty, craven, and low. Is *Company* funny? No, it's too tight and angry for satire. LaBute is zeroing in for the kill. Between the different sections of the story, he fills the soundtrack with thudding drums and a screech of tenor sax—a howl of violence and absurdity that jumps out at us like a grinning mask. We're in the presence of Chaos itself. Nothing sullies the purity of the indictment.

What LaBute actually offers is an aesthete's paranoid view of corporate life. The movie has the pared-down abstractness—the absence of ordinary messy life—one used to find in a tendentious Off Broadway play, and we respond with assent or anger to its argument (that corporate work produces monsters) because there's little else to respond to. There's not much life here, and in the absence of life, it's easy to hurl extreme indictments.

The two men get down to work and take turns flirting with the perfect victim—a secretary, Christine (Stacy Edwards), who is a lovely person, with a beautiful figure and dark hair and eyes. Christine has a way about her, an aura of dignity and gentleness. She is also stone-deaf, and Chad makes fun of her slightly hooty voice while tenderly seducing her; Howard, meanwhile, actually falls in love but remains too frightened and duplicitous to retrieve the situation from disaster. LaBute bores in like a jackhammer: For these men, sexist gamesmanship is not only a pleasure in itself but the natural result of the atmosphere of extreme competitiveness. Christine isn't even a trophy for Chad; she's a mere instrument. His real victim is someone else.

The game with Christine does have a certain sinister fascination—sadism always does—and I would guess, from the length of the shots, and from the way the scenes just sit there, that LaBute means to confront us with our own sneaky enjoyment of what's going on. "C'mon," he's saying, at least to the men. "Admit that there's a little bit of Chad in every one of you." Well, critics are no better human beings than anyone else, so I can do little more than hope to escape the charge of hypocrisy if I say I genuinely did not enjoy *In the Company of Men*—that I felt slightly sordid watching the men play stupid tricks on a deaf woman and that my indignation, once aroused, was turned not against Chad and Howard, who are merely figments of their creator's imagination, but against LaBute for putting me in the position of watching these two pint-size devils. In the same way, the scene in which Chad humiliates an African-American subordinate by making him expose his genitals is so weird that one's indignation collapses into simple disbelief. In a movie, with the clear possibility of life breaking in, one inevitably wonders how Chad can avoid being discovered, denounced, or opposed. When the black man submits to his own humiliation without protest, some of us just feel disgust at the filmmaker. Our retort to LaBute becomes "That's *your* made-up outrage on the screen. Don't point your finger at us."

In other words, LaBute creates a closed world of Machiavellian manipulation and pathetic victimization by making his Satan invincible and the victims hapless. He's dropped out most of the richness and complexity of life and mounted an inadequate fiction: Chad's victories are too easily gained. Aaron Eckhart has a laughing charm, and he uses his college-stud handsomeness to reassure people; he gives a convincing performance in an unconvincing framework. But Matt Malloy, as crawling-on-his-belly Howard, is really too sad to bear watching. Perhaps a comic like Bill Murray could have played Howard without masochism. But Howard's miseries have been realistically conceived, and we have to suffer through every stage of his disintegration. We wind up taking the punishment for what he does.

Mamet's characters in *Glengarry Glen Ross* are older than these guys, and they've had some dreams, taken some hits; they're human enough to know desperation. LaBute has approximated Mamet's nihilistic world without Mamet's redemptive pity or the driving rhythms and vituperative glories of his speech. Mamet makes poetry out of the broken discourse of American futility and greed, but the language in *In the Company of Men* is truly refuse. LaBute has no ear. The movie is clever but preposterously bitter and hollow—a nasty stunt. The great reviews it has received suggest that our cinema is now so bland, so devoid of adult content, that a tiny weed of spite strikes our critics as the very flowers of evil.

NEW YORK POST, 8/1/97, p. 42, Michael Medved

"In the Company of Men" dares to emphasize the darker side of men behaving badly—focusing on brutality rather than boorishness, and highlighting treatment of women that is calculatingly cruel rather than merely crude.

Some observers will welcome the manipulative malice of these characters ("Let's hurt somebody!") as a courageous confrontation with eternal and terrifying truths about masculinity, while others will dismiss it as politically correct posturing and trendy male-bashing.

There is, however, no denying the film's disturbing dramatic power, as young playwright and first-time film director Neil LaBute draws extraordinary performances from three little known actors.

The glib, charming Chad (Aaron Eckhart) and the shy, bespectacled Howard (Matt Malloy) toil away as unappreciated junior executives in a nameless company that has dispatched them to complete a six-week project in some provincial city.

Waiting for a late-night plane, they lick their wounds and share horror stories about rejection by their respective girlfriends.

To avenge themselves on the female of the species, they agree to find some vulnerable, lonely woman in the town they're visiting and jointly pursue her.

Then they'll drop her abruptly and, as Chad proudly predicts, "She'll be reaching for the sleeping pills within a week, and you and me, we'll laugh about this until we're very old men."

They settle on Christine (Stacy Edwards), a lovely deaf woman working in the typing pool, as the target of their scheme.

With her beautiful and transparently expressive face, painfully awkward speech (flawlessly rendered by the actress, who is not hearing-impaired), and fearlessly direct expression of her emotions, this unforgettable character connects powerfully with the audience—and, ultimately, with her tormentors.

As the six weeks progress, nothing in their hateful game turns out exactly as they had intended.

The director's minimalist vision of anonymous, nondescript offices, airports, restrooms, motels and restaurants appropriately oozes loneliness and yearning, and only in one unfortunate scene (in which Chad insists that an abused African-American intern display his genitalia) does the film descend into caricature.

For nearly all of its running time, the men in this movie offer company that is disturbing—but worth keeping.

NEWSDAY, 8/1/97, Part II/p. B11, Jack Mathews

While introducing "In the Company of Men" to a Cannes Film Festival audience earlier this year, first-time American filmmaker Neil LaBute said that of those who'd already seen the picture, most men considered it a big lie and most women thought it was a documentary. I think people who see it as either one need counseling.

"In the Company of Men," the story of a pair of narcissistic white-collar Neanderthals who seek out a vulnerable woman to date and destroy, is a sexploitation film, without sex, sensuality or a trace of sensitivity. It is a jagged wedge being driven into the gender gap, a corrosively vile parable of men behaving badly, and of women behaving like lambs to slaughter. And it is so devoid of moral judgment that it calls into question LaBute's motivation for even making it.

Is the filmmaker touting misogyny? Not likely. Is he so cynical about men's nature that he's doing a mea culpa for us all? Possibly. Or is he merely a crafty opportunist, fashioning an alarmist film that is as certain to rouse its audience as someone screaming "Fire!" in the theater? I think that's it.

"In the Company of Men" is a straight shot of misanthropy, and you walk away from it feeling as if you'd witnessed a rape that you'd done nothing to stop. In reminding us of film's enduring power to move us, if only to recoil at the reflection of the beast within, I suppose LaBute has achieved something special.

But did this picture win a trophy at Sundance because it is strong storytelling, or because it provokes strong reactions? Has film sunk to the level where the ability to agitate is itself artistry, and where provocation alone equals excellence?

"In the Company of Men" opens with an odious conversation between Chad (Aaron Eckhart) and Howard (Matt Malloy), would-be corporate ladder-climbers who, motivated by past rejections—at both work and play—conspire to punish a random woman for their specific pains.

"Let's hurt somebody," says the tall, handsome Chad, to the stumpy, insecure Howard. Wouldn't it be swell, Chad giggles, to cut a weak heifer from the herd, bolster her with attention, fill her heart with false affection, then break it and watch her bleed?

"She'll be reaching for the sleeping pills within a week," Chad says, "and you and me, we'll laugh about this until we're very old men."

Their chosen victim is Christine (Stacy Edwards), an office temp who is pretty, intelligent, sweet-natured ... and deaf, her disability being a sure sign to the boys, and apparently LaBute, that she must also be lonely and desperate.

As the calculated "love" triangle begins taking shape, LaBute's second agenda emerges. Chad, it seems, is just as anxious to hurt Howard, who's a weak romantic rival but a serious threat in the company. This would have been a far stronger subplot if their victim had also been a potential rival. Two birds with one wicked stone.

Instead, LaBute isolates Chad's all-encompassing meanness as the story's central concern, and there is nothing in that for us. Eckhart, in his screen debut, is superbly evil—of all the summer's sociopaths, there's not been one quite like Chad—but there's no reward for putting up with him. Though we don't need an ironic, table-turning ending to validate our outrage, LaBute denies us any moral outlook at all.

The upshot is that men are compelled to watch this movie from the dock, as defendants charged with genetic culpability in crimes against women. And women can only identify with it as silent, emotionally scarred witnesses to the evil that men do.

In the ritual of male-female relationships, there is some truth in both roles. But the roles are reversed often enough to discredit the film's stark generalizations. LaBute, who's already working on another, supposedly even more severe tale from the gender war, has avoided the gray shades of life for in-your-face sensationalism. He's made a horror movie designed to shock, and nothing else.

NEWSWEEK, 8/4/97, p. 71, Jeff Giles

This past winter Neil LaBute had Sundance raving—not to mention ranting. The director's first film, *In the Company of Men*, is the story of two thirtysomething Yuppies who break a deaf woman's heart for kicks. One executive at the festival told LaBute that "Company" made him sick. Another was quoted as saying, "My wife would never forgive me if I picked up that movie." LaBute's actors didn't get off lightly, either. Aaron Eckhart, who plays a chiseled misogynist named Chad, was accosted at a party. "A woman literally came up to him and said, 'I hate you'." says LaBute, 32. "Aaron was like, 'You mean you hate Chad.' And she was like, 'No, I hate *you*.'" LaBute snagged the Filmmaker's Trophy for Best Dramatic Feature. But what on earth had he won?

"Company" is a brutal black comedy. It asks real questions and takes real chances, which is no doubt why it spooked Hollywood. Chad and his neurotic colleague Howard (Matt Malloy) fly into an unnamed city to work on an unnamed project for their unnamed company. Both have recently been dumped, so Chad persuades Howard to play a game: they'll both woo a lonely deaf typist (Stacy Edwards), watch her blossom under the attention and then drop her cold. "You know, to restore a little dignity to our lives," says Chad.

Howard is predictable: you figure he won't have the stomach for this scam, and he doesn't. But Chad is a startling creation. His frat-boy charm degenerates into misanthropy—and still there are times when you wonder if he's actually falling in love. "Company," clearly influenced by David Mamet, absolutely nails the tussle of male egos and the lewd poetry of thirtysomething banter. LaBute's script relies solely on the power of words—but then words are all you can afford when you're shooting a $25,000 movie near home in Fort Wayne, Ind.

LaBute, a playwright and former drama teacher, wrote "Company" as a study of banal, everyday evil. At Sundance, some audience members figured the movie was autobiographical and the director himself was a misogynist. "You want to say, 'Can we stop being silly and go get something to eat?' The movie is *fiction*. Do these people run screaming out of 'Richard III'?"

LaBute left the festival without a U.S. distributor. Harvey Weinstein of Miramax was quoted online saying he didn't think women would be wild about the movie. "I was really depressed when that came out," says LaBute. "I thought, 'If you don't like it, that's cool, but don't crush us under your boot heel'." Six weeks after Sundance, Sony Classics finally signed on. As it happens, women, in screenings and in reviews, have mostly embraced LaBute's movie as an exposé of sexism and a brave bit of truth-telling. It's men who should be worried.

SIGHT AND SOUND, 2/98, p. 44, Peter Matthews

Chad and Howard, friends since college, work together for a large nameless corporation in a nameless city. Sent for six weeks to a branch office to complete an important project, the two commiserate over their lots. Both have been recently dumped by their girlfriends, so Chad proposes a twisted payback scheme against women. He and Howard will choose a wallflower type, someone not accustomed to romance, and both men will date her in turn. At the end of the six weeks, they will ditch her simultaneously. They select a beautiful, deaf woman named Christine, who works in the typing pool.

Chad soon gets her into bed, but makes cruel jokes about her disability in private. He also begins undermining Howard with their co-workers. Howard starts to feel genuinely attracted to Christine. One day, he asks her out for lunch, but she claims to be snowed under. Later, he encounters Chad and Christine together and expresses annoyance at her lie. Christine is shocked to discover that the two men know each other. Having safely packed Chad off to the home office to make a presentation, Howard goes away for the Fourth of July holiday weekend with Christine. He tells her that he needs her, but she confesses that she loves Chad. Angry, Howard informs Christine of the plot. Thunderstruck, she confronts Chad who owns up and laughs in her face. Chad's corporate sabotage finally bears fruit: Howard is downgraded, while Chad receives a promotion.

Sometime later, Howard visits Chad and admits that he really loved Christine. Chad reveals that he's still with the girlfriend who supposedly dumped him; they never broke up at all, and Howard realises that Christine wasn't the only dupe. Howard flies out to see Christine and finds her working in a bank. He screams at her desperately, but she refuses to read his lips.

The movie medium is well suited to a kind of informal anthropology: it can show the concrete particulars of a way of life in a way necessarily stylised theatre never can. That may be why the vaguely corporate setting of writer director Neil LaBute's debut feature *In the Company of Men* is so disconcerting. Far from fleshing out his fictional world with details, LaBute strips the film's office environment down to its barest components. You can't pinpoint where the story occurs or when and it's anybody's guess what business the middle management team of Chad (Aaron Eckhart) and Howard (Matt Malloy) get up to when they're not plotting to pay women back on behalf of their sex. The office space itself is carved up into identically gloomy cubbyholes where the same few items (terminals, telephones) recur like totems of anonymity.

Almost no attempt is made to create the usual illusion of a reality beyond the film frame. Indeed, LaBute draws explicit limits to his created world, providing glimpses of a gaping void (a construction site) just beyond the periphery of the action. The shuttered, synthetic atmosphere plainly derives from *film noir*. However, it's no surprise to learn that the director has also written plays. *In the Company of Men*'s nefarious twists are mostly conducted through the medium of talk. LaBute favours long takes where the characters vent their spleen. The effect isn't uncinematic exactly, but it's close enough to dramaturgy to suggest one probable antecedent: David Mamet. His plays carry a similar charge of bravura nastiness and feel just as remote from life.

It's pretty clear how we're meant to interpret the lack of specific context: the movie is basically saying *plus ça change*. Despite 30-odd years of feminism, the boys are still at it, comparing their dicks and treating women with contempt. (Here, specifically, deaf secretary Christine, played by Stacy Edwards.) That nameless hive filled with corporate drones turns out to be an image of patriarchy in all its pristine ugliness. Chad's honeyed smile conceals a killer sting, and what you make of the film as cultural diagnosis largely depends on what you make of Chad. The character is permitted to spew some of the rankest misogynist abuse ever heard in film. The raw aggression of his language would seem to express a primal anger, long bottled up and finally daring to speak its name. On one level, Chad is the post-feminist bogeyman, mad as hell and eager to get his own back. Shy, deaf Christine is the easy mark he chooses to seduce and then crush. But LaBute's wheels-within-wheels script eventually works round to the idea that partner-in-crime Howard is the real pigeon. In short, business as usual: women are only ciphers of exchange, denied a voice (here, almost literally) in the power games played by men.

As if two ironic *coups de grâce* weren't sufficient, LaBute finds a third. It isn't treacherous Chad who's the *bona fide* misogynist, it's Howard the schmuck. Where sovereignty seeking Chad hates everybody impartially, Howard shows human weakness (and capacity for redemption) falling in love with his dupe, until she rebuffs him, when he lashes out even more cruelly than Mephistophelean Chad. Chad's motives seem almost supernaturally based, because by daylight the movie's whole premise is flawed. Such an ultra narcissist would never be seen dating a deaf girl—not in *that* office, with *those* colleagues.

You have to swallow even harder to accept the film's showstopper the sequence where Chad forces a young black intern to exhibit the "balls" needed for a cut-throat corporate career. While there's certainly an undercurrent of homosexuality to this virtually all-male movie, it's a bit much to suppose that Chad would deliberately open himself up allegation. The scene is ostensibly there to prove that in terms of dispensing humiliation, Chad runs a very broad church. Primarily there to titillate, risqué touches like these—racial or erotic innuendo—can make a movie seem hot and controversial; in this regard, Chad is a publicist's dream. In old Hollywood, the likes of Cecil B. DeMille excited the mass audience by depicting vice while salving its conscience with a show of sanctimony. It seems to me that LaBute is pulling the same stunt—except for a modern liberal audience. When Chad delivers a line like "I don't trust anything that bleeds for a week and doesn't die," you can cheerfully get your rocks off at his saying the unsayable, yet you can still feel virtuous for attending a radical, alternative and deeply disturbing feminist movie.

TIME, 8/18/97, p. 60, Richard Corliss

Chad, a nice-looking fellow with the soul of Satan, sits next to Christine, the deaf secretary he has bogusly courted for the sole pleasure of dumping her. As she registers the enormity of his betrayal, Chad stares at her and says, "So how does it feel?" This moment in Neil LaBute's *In the Company of Men* packs such a sick smack that at a showing at the Samuel Goldwyn Pavilion in West Los Angeles last week, a woman gasped and shook her head in disgust; another, supplying a retort for Christine, said, "I feel like cutting your cojones off."

In the Company of Men is cool, shiny, handsomely made and, in its compelling-repelling way, mordantly funny—imagine an atrocity tale told with Noël Coward insouciance. But the most interesting part of the film comes after it's over. That's when the real knives come out. At the Sundance Film Festival, where this pitch-black comedy was an award winner, LaBute was widely rebuked by the sensitivity patrol. After a Manhattan screening, a male publicist was punched. Well, he was a guy. Probably deserved it.

Aaron Eckhart, the 29-year-old actor who plays Chad, has yet to be slapped by any female moviegoers (it's early; be patient). But he says, "I've had women come really close. The right hand is back, and they go, 'I just want to slap you.' And I go, 'All right.' They don't, and then they laugh. But I'm sure if I demonstrated any Chadness while they were in midswing, they'd go all the way."

For LaBute, 34, a playwright making his debut as screen auteur, the flush of anger is a career-making dream. "I'm more than happy that people are polarized," he says. "I'd much rather have somebody hate my movie than be indifferent about it." He would get his wish if he listened to TIME film critic Richard Schickel: "Other pictures that have broken out on the basis of sociological buzz, like *Thelma & Louise*, had appealing characters confronting interesting issues in suspenseful or comic fashion. But here all we are dealing with is sociopathic behavior that has no real-world resonance. The movie's sheer grimness militates against anyone other than a masochist volunteering to pay money to see it."

There must be a lot of masochists in New York City and L.A.: the film (which cost a preposterously meager $25,000, and which Sony Pictures Classics bought for less than $50,000) earned $196,157 its first week on just eight screens. And if tickets could be sold for discussion groups after the show, it would have made even more. "Women love the movie," says Tom Bernard, co-president of Sony Classics. "It shows men behaving badly, and women feel like a fly on the wall watching the things men do." Stacy Edwards, the Juliette Binoche look-alike who beautifully embodies Christine, says, "I've had men come up to me and say it was really uncomfortable for them. It profoundly moved them; they had tears in their eyes." This is the first hate story that could become a big date movie.

Chad and Howard (Matt Malloy) are two thirtyish corporate types on a six-week assignment in a new city. Howard has been dumped by the fiancé he adored. Chad, who tells Howard he too has been abandoned, proposes an elaborate scheme of gender revenge. They will choose a vulnerable woman, begin dating demurely, get her to fall in love. And then drop her. "Let's do it," Chad says. "Let's hurt somebody."

Their designated victim is Christine, winsome and delicate, her eyes signaling sweet intensity and a ladylike itch for passionate release. In her presence Chad is darling; he has the shy-guy, sensitive-man patter down pat. He convinces Christine, and perhaps the audience, that he is falling for her. To Howard, though, he says he despises Christine (he even makes fun of the way she reads lips) and her entire sex. "Women—nice ones or the most frigid of the race; it doesn't matter in the end—inside, they're all the same. Meat and gristle and hatred, just simmering. And I for one have had it with their s___."

Says LaBute, a Mormon married to a family therapist: "I was drawn to the idea of a lover's triangle and to the theme of betrayal, which I find a very intimate, devastating thing. The template was Restoration comedy; I love that kind of gamesmanship, the verbal wit." Chad's surname is Piercewell, its rapier malice nicely echoing Congrevean namesmanship. "I saw a parallel from the 1690s in the 1990s in the tendency not to fight with fists but instead to tear and devastate with words." That's Chad's forte. With just a flick of a phrase, he can devastate his boss, an intern or the woman who's come to love him.

Few will be rooting for Chad, but he does have a way about him: the purring amorality, the artist's attention to detail, the born salesman's blinding self-assurance. He is, in short, a perfect Chad—a winner at any cost. Howard is perfect only as Chad's opposite and victim. All the women he loves dump him. But who wouldn't? His devotion is a pillow that doesn't comfort but smothers; he's forever tripping over his big dopey heart. His clumsy pursuit of Christine will have the decent guys in the audience replaying their dankest romantic humiliations. Says LaBute: "I despise the things about him that are most like me." Chad is the super-Nazi, Howard the "good German."

Chad is also a prototype and a throwback: the streamlined 1997 model of caveman. He's not a sexist so much as he's an inhumanist, for he is contemptuous of other guys as well. "Working in the company of men," he says of his colleagues, "they still want their mommies to wipe their bottoms every time they go potty." By taking the title from this harangue, LaBute clarifies his intentions. The true arena of this extreme game is business, not sex, and the person Chad wants to screw, so to speak, is not the secretary but his old friend and current boss. Christine is just a means to Howard's end.

"You got the balls for this?" Chad asks a young black intern whom he orders to pull down his pants in the film's most humiliating scene. "You need the big brass ones for the task ... That's what business is all about: who's sporting the nastiest sac of venom, and who's willing to use it." Ultimately there are two kinds of men: predator and prey. A few millenniums of civilization have refined man's hunter instinct; we now see a subtle but lethal damage that man can inflict on the competition. Male or female, for business or pleasure—doesn't really matter.

LaBute says there is a moral: "Be careful about whom you pretend to be, because that is often the person you turn into." But the movie is careful not to give Chad his comeuppance, and the audience must fish for any lessons the story offers. Men are welcome to X-ray their hearts for a hint of Howard or an edge of Chad. Women can take a peek at—and, if they wish, confirm their suspicions of that dangerous and perplexing house pest, the modern middle-class male. The camera lingers in elegantly immobile, anthropological medium shot—a distance that respects the danger of the creature it is photographing. Chad prowls and roars and claws for us in his cage, separated not by bars but by our final appreciation that this is, after all, fiction. It's all right, the mother says to her panicked child at the end of a bedtime fairy tale; it was just a story. And still the child cries deep into the night.

"The tendency today," says LaBute, "is for movies to rush over you with everything but thought. A wave of stimuli rather than the most important thing, which is something to take home in your head." In the Company of Men is the toxic antidote to such disposable entertainment. Love it or loathe it, the picture sticks to you like guilt sweat after adulterous sex. It leaves a little spoor trail. Food for thought? No, a banquet for debate and denial.

VILLAGE VOICE, 8/5/97, p. 67, J. Hoberman

A direct attack on machismo, In the Company of Men is itself sufficiently macho to walk a tightrope through the fog of gender paranoia without the benefit of a safety net. Neil LaBute's first feature—shot entirely in Fort Wayne, Indiana—is a remarkable stunt, at once a ruthlessly demonstrated thesis and a comedy so edgy that you feel implicated if you laugh.

Opening in the male heart of darkness (an airport men's room), Company initiates a quick litany of masculine complaint. Two executives in their early thirties—the nerdy, needy Howard (Hal Hartley veteran Matt Malloy) and the more tigerishly confident Chad (Aaron Eckhart), old college buddies and current coworkers—are discussing their uniform frustration with rejection, both in their relationships with women and in their capacity to advance their careers. Indeed, the two have just been shuttled off by company headquarters to implement a six-week program at a branch in some unnamed city. It is not, one gathers, a prize assignment.

En route to Palookaville, Chad (whose rage is exacerbated for having hapless Howie as his nominal superior) proposes a sadistic scenario that should keep them amused while providing balm for wounds they've suffered in the gender wars. The pair will select a vulnerable local woman and, after overwhelming this gratefully bewildered wallflower with unexpected attention, simultaneously dump her. "She'll be reaching for the sleeping pills within a week," Chad laughs. Even better, he and Howard will be forever bonded: "We would always have this thing." Seduced, himself, by the force of his colleague's personality, Howard agrees.

Once installed in their featureless workplace, Chad zeroes in on Christine (Stacy Edwards), an attractive, hearing-impaired newcomer to the office typing pool. The choice of a handicapped woman is a brilliant bit of nastiness, as is the implication that Chad is genuinely turned on by her deafness and imperfect mastery of speech—In the Company of Men should make it difficult to ever feel the same way about the innocent sweetness with which Charlie Chaplin falls for the blind flower girl in City Lights. With courtship reduced to strategy, the situation becomes all the more fraught once the fast-talking Chad and slow-thinking Howard begin to deceive each other in the competition for Christine's affections.

Conceptualized three years ago, at the widely publicized heyday of the Angry White Male, In the Company of Men is an entertaining gloss on the Michael Douglas oeuvre of privileged self-pity—to which, as an unsubtle sort of counterpoint, LaBute works in a specifically racial component by having each of the guys relate, from a position of authority, to a black coworker. The movie is borderline allegorical, making much of the business ethos whereby each man is a potential rival and all women are objectified tokens of exchange. The action is neatly parsed and interspersed with frantic sound interludes that suggest the savage beast that beats beneath the imitation Armani suit. The recurring phrase, "It's no big deal," only serves to reinforce the duplicitous nature of the power relations.

Gender psychology is also neatly schematized. The scenario suggests that there are two kinds of men—the passive aggressive sulky nebbish who "falls in love" and the blithely predatory sociopath who needs to score. The woman, meanwhile is (in line with feminist film theory of the 1970s) excluded from the realm of linguistic authority. Christine's powers of enunciation are displaced onto her eloquent gaze, at first deeply interested in the men who pursue her and then increasingly stricken as their intentions become ever more dubious. (Edwards's tremendously appealing performance only serves to compound audience discomfit.)

Modeled, per its author-director, on Restoration comedy, *In the Company of Men* is exceedingly well-written, with a rigorously worked-out structure that's all the more disturbing for its clarity. (LaBute's detached precision and latent misanthropy have led more than one reviewer to hail him as a young Kubrick.) The movie's didacticism is justified by a willingness to push a concept past the polite limits. If the characters sometimes suggest mice wandering through a maze of corporate cubicles—that's part of the joke.

As its triangle implodes, *In the Company of Men* builds to a series of lacerating, one-on-one confrontations predicated on Christine's pitiful honesty in the face of her suitors' apparently unlimited capacity for inflicting emotional pain. There are those who believe the film's ending goes too far, but then, once the mindfuck vengeance machine is set in motion, it would hardly seem fair to spare the viewer's feelings. That the film's violence is exclusively psychological only compounds the mood of anticatharsis.

A few technical glitches aside, *In the Company of Men* is a fully achieved chamber work. Moreover, based as it is on the dialectic of sincerity and manipulation, it's a movie of admirable integrity. See it at your peril. This has got to be the most incendiary dating flick in the decade since *Fatal Attraction* and I mean that as a compliment.

Also reviewed in:
NEW REPUBLIC, 9/1/97, p. 24, Stanley Kauffmann
NEW YORK TIMES, 8/1/97, p. C32, Janet Maslin
VARIETY, 1/27-2/2/97, p. 73, Emanuel Levy
WASHINGTON POST, 8/22/97, p. D1, Stephen Hunter
WASHINGTON POST, 8/22/97, Weekend/p. 36, Desson Howe

IN LOVE AND WAR

A New Line Cinema release of a New Line production in association with Dimitri Villard Productions. *Executive Producer:* Sara Risher. *Producer:* Dimitri Villard and Richard Attenborough. *Director:* Richard Attenborough. *Screenplay:* Allan Scott, Clancy Sigal, and Anna Hamilton Phelan. *Story:* Allan Scott and Dimitri Villard. *Based on the book by:* Henry S. Villard and James Nagel. *Director of Photography:* Roger Pratt. *Editor:* Lesley Walker. *Music:* George Fenton. *Music Editor:* Kevin Lane. *Sound:* Simon Kaye, Jonathan Bates, Gerry Humphreys, and (music) Dean Humphreys and Tim Cavagin. *Casting:* Jeremy Zimmerman, René Haynes, and Clare Walker. *Production Designer:* Stuart Craig. *Art Director:* Neil Lamont. *Set Decorator:* Stephenie McMillan. *Special Effects:* Richard Conway. *Costumes:* Penny Rose. *Make-up:* Daniel Parker. *Stunt Coordinator:* Eddie Stacey. *Running time:* 115 minutes. *MPAA Rating:* PG-13.

CAST: Sandra Bullock (Agnes Von Kurowsky); Chris O'Donnell (Ernest Hemingway); Mackenzie Astin (Henry Villard); Emilio Bonucci (Domenico Caracciolo); Ingrid Lacey (Elsie "Mac" MacDonald); Margot Steinberg (Mabel "Rosie" Rose); Tara Hugo (Katherine "Gumshoe" De Long); Colin Stinton (Tom Burnside); Rocco Quarzell (Roberto Zardini); Ian Kelly (Jimmy McBride); Vincenzo Nicoli (Enrico Biscaglia); Alan Bennett and Terence Sach

(Porters); Carlo Croccolo (Town Mayor); Gigi Vivan (Italian Child); Giuseppe Bonato (Grandfather); Allegra Di Carpegna (Loretta Cavanaugh); Diane Witter (Adele Brown); Mindy Lee Raskin (Charlotte Anne Miller); Tracy Hostmyer (Ruth Harper); Kaethe Cherney (Veta Markley); Lauren Booth (Anna Scanlon); Rebecca Craig (Elena Crouch); Frances Riddelle (Katherine Smith); Wendi Peters (Emily Rahn); Laura Nardi (Teresa); Maria Petrucci (Sonia); Valeria Fabbri (Anna Maria); Quinto Rolman (Italian Man); Raph Taylor (Francesco); George Rossi (Triage Medic); Todd Curran (Skip Talbot); Matthew Sharp (Joseph Larkin); Nick Brooks (Louis Burton); Tom Goodman-Hill (Houston Kenyon); Doreen Mantle (Emilia); Tim McDonell (Adjutant); Vincenzo Ricotta (Italian Officer); Reno Porcaro (Italian Photographer); Bruno Majean (Alberto Zardini); Joseph Long (Italian Doctor); Bruce Lidington (American Surgeon); Colin Fox (Dr. Hemingway); Kay Hawtrey (Grace Hemingway); Roseline Garland (Carol Hemingway); Evan Smirnow (Leicester Hemingway); Avery Saltzman (Oak Leaves Reporter); Rodger Barton (Sun Times Reporter); Richard Blackburn (Tribune Reporter); Gil Filar and Noah Reid (Boys); Richard Fitzpatrick (Mailman); Philippe Leroy (Count Sergio Caracciolo); Laura Martelli (Isabella Caracciolo); Cyril Taylor (Maitre d'); Milan Rosandic (Waiter).

LOS ANGELES TIMES, 12/18/96, Calendar/p. 1, Kenneth Turan

[*The following review by Kenneth Turan appeared in a slightly different form in* **NEWSDAY, 1/24/97, Part II/p. B3.**]

As depicted in Richard Attenborough's "In Love and War," young Ernest Hemingway is anything but earnest. Cocky, conceited and self-absorbed, the novelist-to-be is played by Chris O'Donnell as the last person you'd expect to find in love with anyone but himself.

And in truth there is so little convincing passion in this tepid story set in northern Italy during the closing days of World War I that "In Love and Snore" might be a more appropriate title. Glossy, genteel, conventional through and through, "In Love" likely never would have made it this far if Hemingway wasn't one protagonist and Agnes Von Kurowsky, the model for the heroine of his "A Farewell to Arms," wasn't the other.

It's Aggie (brightly played by Sandra Bullock) we meet first, a 26-year-old American Red Cross nurse who looks so pristine that a small Italian boy thinks she's an angel from heaven. Devoted to her work, she is indifferent to the admiring glances she attracts from older locals, though other nurses are not above noticing that "these Italian gents sure are gallant."

Some miles away, brash 18-year-old Red Cross volunteer Ernie Hemingway (he lied about his age to get in) is bored with his assignment manning a coffeepot. So he bicycles to the front lines to hand out cigarettes to Italian soldiers and ends up getting shot in the leg, the first American casualty in that country.

Naturally Ernie is taken to Aggie's hospital, where she notices that gangrene is starting to set in. No slouch in the medical department, Aggie applies a new irrigation technique to the wound and even changes the mind of the suave Italian doctor (Emilio Bonucci) who wants to amputate as a precautionary measure.

No sooner does Ernie regain consciousness than he starts to put his teenage hustler moves on Aggie. Other men are interested in her as well, including Ernie's pal Henry Villard (nicely played by Mackenzie Astin) and the good doctor, who turns out to be an aristocrat with a *palazzo* in Venice with a heck of a view of the Grand Canal.

But for reasons that three separate screenwriters (Allan Scott, Clancy Sigat and Anna Hamilton Phelan) have been unable to make either clear or convincing, Aggie has eyes only for Ernie. Never mind that he's a fatuous jerk too irrepressibly juvenile for words, never mind that Aggie accurately says, "You are such a child, when are you going to grow up?"—the movie treats him like the catch of the decade.

Part of the problem is that there is little on-screen chemistry between the two leads. O'Donnell's character is so busy being stuck on himself that any emotion he directs toward anyone else seems just a reflection of that self-love. And Bullock, who looks completely at home in period dress, never seems much more than bemused by the person she and everyone calls "Kid." Plus the supposed eight-year difference in their ages, of which a great deal is made, is not visible at all to the camera.

Adding to this difficulty is the script's determination to spend much of its time showing the buildup to this romance and its sour aftermath. The actual love affair itself is treated so briefly and cursorily it is hard to take it as seriously as we're expected to.

The main source for this story is "Hemingway in Love and War: The Lost Diary of Agnes Von Kurowsky" co-authored by the real-life Henry Villard, a book that apparently takes the view that this relationship ran into problems because Agnes didn't have the courage to keep her commitments to a too-much younger man.

What we see on screen is some thing very different, not a grand amour that floundered but an inconsequential liaison that was obviously never meant to be. Instead of blaming Aggie for her lack of nerve, we feel like congratulating her for a narrow escape from a life with Mr. Attitude. Not even Richard Attenborough of "Gandhi," maybe especially not Richard Attenborough of "Gandhi," can make a moving love story out of such unpromising material.

NEW YORK POST, 1/24/97, p. 49, Michael Medved

If you think of Sandra Bullock as the chirpy, girl-next-door heroine of comedy or action film, then "In Love and War" will force you to think again.

This wildly popular actress here delivers a performance of remarkable weight, depth and intelligence, playing a courageous woman painfully torn between common sense and emotion.

Her richly appealing, thoroughly nuanced characterization would make this an absorbing World War I love story even if its principals had been fictional or unknown characters.

But the fact that these two people are Ernest Hemingway and Agnes Von Kurowsky, his first great love, provides this unusually challenging film with additional rewards—and difficulties.

Chris O'Donnell plays the 18-year-old Hemingway, arriving in Europe in 1918 as a volunteer ambulance driver assigned to the Italian front.

Bullock plays Von Kurowsky, a plucky Pennsylvania girl of German extraction (hence the misleadingly Teutonic name) who serves as a nurse at a Red Cross hospital and cares for Hemingway after he is grievously wounded in the trenches while trying to rescue a stricken Italian soldier.

The movie nicely captures the bittersweet, sometimes tragic atmosphere of a military hospital, focusing on the future novelist and his angel of mercy but a full range of other patients, doctors (especially a chivalrous Italian nobleman played by Emilio Bonucci) and nurses.

Particularly important among this supporting cast is a recent Harvard grad named Harry Villard (Mackenzie Astin), whose own recollections of his friend Hemingway, along with Von Kurowsky's secret letters and diaries, became the basis for the 1989 book that inspired this movie.

Director Richard Attenborough has made a specialty of sprawling epics about heroes of the 20th century—including "Ghandi," "Young Winston," Stephen Biko in "Cry Freedom" and C.S. Lewis in "Shadowlands."

Here, he makes the daring and intriguing decision to treat his historic titan (Hemingway) as a supporting player, while focusing on the inner turmoil of the little-known Von Kurowsky, who's desperately worried over the fact that she's eight years older than her teen-age lover.

The problem is that Attenborough (and Chris O'Donnell) go much too far in making young "Ernie" a fresh-faced, corn-fed, gee-whiz, aw-shucks, ardent and ordinary Midwestern rube— giving the brilliant, self-confident Von Kurowsky no reason to fall so hard for him other than his obvious good looks.

Given his tormented family background and his already consuming ambitions, it seems certain that the real Hemingway, even at age 18, would have displayed more shadows and substance than the shallow, callow youth depicted here.

Nevertheless, the leisurely, lyrical pace of the picture proves seductive, the authentic Italian scenery is spectacular and the two stars produce convincing chemistry in one of the more poetic, impassioned and believable love scenes of recent years.

If Chris O'Donnell, a reliably charismatic and sensitive leading man, may seem sadly miscast in a pivotal role, it's still possible to put aside the movie's literary trappings and appreciate it as a tale of two unknown Americans finding love and loss amid the unspeakable butchery of World War I.

SIGHT AND SOUND, 3/97, p. 50, Philip Kemp

Northern Italy, 1918. Italian forces, hard pressed by a massive Austrian advance, are retreating with huge losses. Agnes von Kurowsky, a 26-year-old American Red Cross nurse, arrives to tend the Italian wounded. Soon afterwards Ernest Hemingway, an ambitious 18-year-old reporter from Kansas, also reaches Italy, having conned his way into the Red Cross. Against orders, he makes his way to the front and starts interviewing Italian soldiers in the trenches. A shell-blast kills most of them, but leaves Ernest unharmed. He tries to carry a mortally-wounded survivor, Roberto, to safety but is shot in the leg.

Ernest is taken to the hospital where Agnes works. The surgeon, Domenico Caracciolo, diagnoses gangrene and plans to amputate, but Agnes persuades him to let her try a newly-developed technique of bathing the wound with acid. Though agonising, the treatment works and Ernest's leg is saved. Dr Caracciolo, impressed by Agnes' determination, invites her out, but she and Ernest are increasingly drawn to each other—to the jealousy of Ernest's friend Harry Villard, hospitalised with jaundice. Another American patient is Red Cross aide Jimmy McBride, badly burnt by a phosphorus shell.

With Ernest now walking on crutches, Agnes takes him and Harry on a picnic. Needled by Harry, Ernest claims to have slept with Agnes. She slaps his face. Soon afterwards Jimmy kills himself, having left unfinished a letter to his parents she was dictating to Agnes. Ernest dictates another to her, after which they kiss for the first time. Agnes, along with Dr Caracciolo, is sent to the front, and Ernest is ordered to return to the US. He seeks her out and they spend the night together in the only available accommodation: the local brothel.

Caracciolo invites Agnes to his aristocratic parents' palazzo in Venice. Home in Kansas, Ernest is fêted as a hero, but worried he has heard nothing from Agnes. She pays a second visit to Venice; during dinner the Armistice is declared. Caracciolo shows her round the disused factory he plans to turn into a great hospital, and proposes. Torn between the two men, Agnes finally accepts Caracciolo and writes to Ernest to tell him. On receiving the letter he goes crazy with rage and grief. Eight months later, Agnes meets Harry for lunch in New York. Unable to forget Ernest, she has broken her engagement. Harry tells her Ernest is holed up in a lake cabin, fishing and writing. She goes there and tells him she loves him but, proud and angry, he rejects her and she leaves. End titles add that Agnes later married and lived to a ripe old age. Ernest Hemingway became a great writer, married four times and shot himself at 62.

"It's when we feel pain that we're most alive." The line comes, not from *In Love and War*, but from Richard Attenborough's previous film *Shadowlands*, and his latest work amplifies and develops very much the same themes. In fact the two films, taken together, dovetail perfectly, each illuminating and complementing the other. Both are about a writer faced with a traumatic love affair which brings him both joy and suffering. In the case of C.S. Lewis it comes late in life, at a time when he's ceased to expect it, and for all the agony it causes him he survives as a warmer, deeper, far more human person, connected to life in a way he never was before. To Hemingway it comes too early before he's able to handle it, and makes him cut off a whole area of himself from the risk of intimacy, souring his emotional life and his response to women forever. "The hurt boy," Agnes' voice-over muses at the end of the film, "became an angry man", as we see the bitter, disappointed features of the ageing writer. Love and suffering, these two films imply, may well be beneficial if they come when we're ready for them; but coming at the wrong time they can destroy us.

The youthful Hemingway certainly courts suffering—though not the sort he finally gets—rushing impetuously off to the front to grab his "last chance to see action". It's to Chris O'Donnell's credit that he never tries to make the young pup particularly likeable. Indeed he's so wholly convincing as the brash, bumptious young lover (if less so as the embryo novelist) it seems as if Agnes might have been a damn sight better off with the charmingly courteous Dr Caracciolo (or even with Mackenzie Astin's shy Henry Villard). But in acting terms this is Bullock's film. The unforced, natural appeal that's always been her strength has matured, in *In Love and War*, into a warm, troubled tenderness that makes her indecision in no way coquettish. It stems from a misguided desire to be fair to both her lovers, which being impossible, injures them both.

"Why love if loving hurts so much?" asks Lewis in *Shadowlands*. "The pain then is part of the happiness now," responds Debra Winger's Joy Gresham, "that's the deal." But that's exactly the deal that Hemingway rejects, demanding all the good and none of the bad. All-or-nothing, in fact, is his credo: "If I'm going to end up less than all of me," he tells Agnes when amputation is considered, "I'd rather be dead." And dead, emotionally at least, is just how he ends up.

Attenborough is never a director to be hurried, and *In Love and War* unfolds at a steady, even pace that sometimes feels at odds with its story of impetuous young love. George Fenton's over-lush score further weights it down. But the battle scenes, the more horrible for being played out in glorious hill-scenery rather than the mud-hell of the trenches, have a brutal immediacy that reminds us Attenborough cut his directorial teeth on *Oh! What a Lovely War*. Hemingway, like Lewis, "enjoys a good fight"; but fighting is often what men do because it's so much easier than loving. Lewis learns that; Hemingway never did.

It may seem odd, even perverse, to treat Attenborough as some kind of auteur; for years the films he's directed have been condescendingly dismissed as "stolid", "worthy" or at best "work-manlike", products of the old-fashioned mainstream school of British film-making: Lean without the flair. But these two latest films suggest that he may be a more interesting director than has been allowed; more interesting, perhaps, than he's hitherto allowed himself to be.

TIME, 2/3/97, p. 66, Richard Schickel

In Italy in 1918, in a relatively quiet comer of World War I, a 19-year-old American ambulance driver is wounded. In the hospital he falls in love with a pretty nurse. They have a brief affair, which she ends rather abruptly with a Dear John letter.

A fairly standard-issue wartime liaison, in short, of no consequence to anyone but its participants—except that it really happened to Ernest Hemingway. And he transformed it (and the rest of his Italian experiences) into some of his most memorable and poignant fiction. Drawing in part on a recently discovered diary of his inamorata, Agnes Von Kurowsky, Richard Attenborough and a squad of writers attempt to penetrate to the truth of the tale in *In Love and War*. They get lost in that no-man's-land where so many biopics come to grief: trying to stay in touch with historical fact, yet eager to convert an intimate romance into something more sweeping and epic.

They are not much helped by Chris O'Donnell as the writer manqué. There is no danger in him. You don't for a minute believe that his "kid" (as Agnes, who was seven years older, called him) is going to grow up to be our macho-crazed Papa. On the other hand, Sandra Bullock is just lovely as Agnes. Their difference in ages bothered her, but you also get a sense of a woman tasting freedom for the first time, wanting to keep all her options for adventure, romantic and otherwise, open—and sensing, more clearly than he did, that her lover needed to do the same. There's a truthfulness, an allure, in her ambivalences that comes close to saving a film careless with facts but dutiful to movie clichés.

VILLAGE VOICE, 2/4/97, p. 70, Laurie Stone

This movie depicts a wartime romance between 18-year-old Ernest Hemingway and the 26-year-old nurse Agnes Von Kurowsky. In the press kit is this caveat: "All of Ernest Hemingway's on-screen dialogue and literary creations are fictional." Say what you want about Papa's chest thumping and clenched-jaw spareness, he could never have produced sentences as insipid as those placed in his mouth here, and he would *plotz* to see the casting of Chris O'Donnell in his role. O'Donnell is Mr. Anyface, undisturbed by emotion or experience. To portray Agnes, an emotionally masked woman, Sandra Bullock delivers most of her lines in a whispery monotone, with eyes cast down. It is the bland leading the bland. Perhaps this film could inaugurate a parlor game of far-fetched casting choices, say Ozzie and Harriet as Antony and Cleopatra.

But no actors could juice the anemic script, credited to Allan Scott, Clancy Sigal, and Anna Hamilton Phelan. Imagine the midnight oil burnt in composing such exchanges as "I couldn't leave without seeing you again" or "I came to tell you I love you, and I will love you forever." Agnes saves Ernest's wounded leg from amputation by bathing it, so he is naturally grateful, but nothing these characters say to one another reveals them as particular or remotely suggests what we are told: that this relationship permanently marked both lives. It comes off as a simple sexual awakening, a fling that director Richard Attenborough tries to enlarge by piping in George Fenton's sappy, heroic music. Everything in the film feels generic: the battlefield combat, the hospital-ward banter, the courting of Agnes by other men. The movie insults its sources and audience. It's not as if something pointed and ambitious has been attempted. Dumbness was the goal.

Also reviewed in:
CHICAGO TRIBUNE, 1/24/97, Friday/p. C, Michael Wilmington
NEW YORK TIMES, 1/24/97, p. C5, Stephen Holden
NEW YORKER, 2/3/97, p. 84, Anthony Lane
VARIETY, 12/23/96-1/5/97, p. 41, Todd McCarthy
WASHINGTON POST, 1/24/97, p. G1, Rita Kempley
WASHINGTON POST, 1/24/97, Weekend/p. 30, Desson Howe

IN & OUT

A Paramount Pictures release in association with Spelling Films of a Scott Rudin production. *Executive Producer:* Adam Schroeder. *Producer:* Scott Rudin. *Director:* Frank Oz. *Screenplay:* Paul Rudnick. *Director of Photography:* Rob Hahn. *Editor:* Dan Hanley. *Music:* Marc Shaiman. *Music Editor:* Nic Ratner. *Choreographer:* Jerry Mitchell. *Sound:* Danny Michael and (music) Dennis Sands. *Sound Editor:* Dan Sable. *Casting:* Margery Simkin. *Production Designer:* Ken Adam. *Art Director:* Charles V. Beal. *Set Decorator:* Leslie A. Pope. *Special Effects:* Albert Griswold. *Costumes:* Ann Roth. *Make-up:* Bernadette Mazur. *Stunt Coordinator:* Jery Hewitt. *Running time:* 105 minutes. *MPAA Rating:* PG-13.

CAST: Kevin Kline (Howard Brackett); Joan Cusack (Emily Montgomery); Matt Dillon (Cameron Drake); Debbie Reynolds (Bernice Brackett); Wilford Brimley (Frank Brackett); Bob Newart (Tom Halliwell); Tom Selleck (Peter Malloy); Gregory Jbara (Walter Brackett); Shalom Harlow (Sonya); Shawn Hatosy (Jack); Zak Orth (Mike); Lauren Ambrose (Vicky); Alexandra Holden (Meredith); Lewis J. Stadlen (Ed Kenrow); Deborah Rush (Ava Blazer); J. Smith-Cameron (Trinia Paxton); Kate McGregor-Stewart (Aunt Becky); Debra Monk (Mrs. Lester); Ernie Sabella (Aldo Hooper); John Cunningham (Voice on "Be a Man" Tape); Gus Rogerson (Danny); Dan Hedaya (Military Attorney); Joseph Mayer (Father Tim); William Parry (Fred Mooney); William Duell (Emmett Wilson); Richard Woods (Reverend Morgan); Kevin Chamberlin (Carl Mickley); Wally Dunn (Cousin Lenny); Larry Clarke (Cousin Ernie); June Squibb (Cousin Gretchen); Alice Drummond (Aunt Susan); Mary Diveny (Cousin Ellen); Anne Russell (Aunt Marge); Patrick Garner (Stan Forrest); Joanna Wolff (Jennifer the Flower Girl); Jane Hoffman (Mrs Baxter); Becky Ann Baker (Darlene); William P. Hoag (Bartender); Danny Canton (Cameraman); Selma Blair (Cousin Linda); Patricia Guinan (Bill's Mom); Nesbitt Blaisdell (Bill's Dad); Jo-Jo Lowe (Awards Event Model); Lisa Emery and Gary Dewitt Marshall (Classroom Reporters); Peter Barmonde (Wedding Photographer); Glenn Close (Herself, Oscar Presenter); Whoopi Goldberg (Herself, Oscar Presenter); Jay Leno (Himself, Chat Show Host).

LOS ANGELES TIMES, 9/19/97, Calendar/p. 19, Kenneth Turan

It's Hollywood's Night of Nights, but no one's picking Cameron Drake for the best actor Oscar. With competition like Paul Newman in "Coot," Clint Eastwood in "Codger," Michael Douglas in "Primary Urges" and Steven Seagal in "Snowball in Hell," how could they?

But Drake's performance in "To Serve and Protect" as a gay soldier betrayed by a copy of "Beaches" discovered in his locker proves the surprise winner. After thanking "my agent and my new agent," Drake remembers Howard Brackett, his old high school English teacher back in Greenleaf, Ind. An inspiration, he says. "And he's gay." Which is big news to everyone back in Greenleaf, especially Howard Brackett and the woman he plans to marry in three days time.

Thought up by producer Scott Rudin after Tom Hanks' public thanking of a gay teacher when he won best actor for "Philadelphia," "In & Out" is a comedy of the moment with laughs that last far into the night. Its coolly funny exploration of what that chance remark does to Brackett's life benefits from a deft collaboration between talents who've not always been as successful on screen as they are here.

Screenwriter Paul Rudnick's previous credits ("Jeffrey," "Addams Family Values") haven't been as consistently funny as the uncredited work he did on films like "First Wives Club" and his stint as fearless Premiere magazine film critic Libby Gelman-Waxner.

With "In & Out," however, he's written sharply satirical lines, taking on not just Oscar night but the O.J. Simpson trial, the Barbra Streisand phenomenon, supermodel bulimia and considerably more. His dialogue is more than funny, it has that rarest of comedic attributes, unpredictability.

Similarly director Frank Oz, after starting with TV's Muppets, has had an erratic feature career, with some of his best work, like "The Indian in the Cupboard," being the least appreciated. But his ability to create a warm and genial atmosphere while respecting the bite of Rudnick's lines keeps "In & Out" balanced between entertainment and relevance.

And while Kevin Kline, who stars as the dazed and confused Brackett, has certainly had successes, he's rarely had a film role that made such fine use of his remarkable gift for the physical side of farce. With moves that Jim Carrey might envy, Kline is just so as the teacher who has his world turned inside out and then outside in by a former student's chance remark.

Brackett is introduced just before Oscar night as one of the best-liked men in Greenleaf, "a great big small town." After a three-year engagement, his forthcoming wedding to former fatty Emily Montgomery (Joan Cusack), who lost 75 pounds in anticipation of the event, delights parents Bernice and Frank (Debbie Reynolds and Wilford Brimley) and causes the basketball team he coaches to break out the champagne.

Then Cameron Drake (Matt Dillon doing a shrewd Brad Pitt imitation) speaks up on Oscar night and Greenleaf goes into shock and searches for explanations. Maybe, one of Brackett's students theorizes, Drake thought, "Smart, well-dressed, kind of prissy and really clean"—Brackett must be gay. Or maybe the actor was swayed by the teacher's loyalty to "Funny Lady" and willingness to get into a fistfight over the merits of "Yentl."

The reporters who make up the national media blitz that invades Greenleaf aren't interested in these niceties, they just want to corner Brackett for a hot sound bite. Peter Malloy (a relaxed Tom Selleck) seems no different, headlining his weeklong series "A Teacher in Trouble, a Town Under Siege, a Journey to the Heartland." But Malloy has a secret agenda that more than unnerves the groom-to be.

One of the pleasures of "In & Out" is its embracing of character comedy. Not only do Dillon, Selleck, Brimley, Reynolds and Bob Newhart (as Greenleaf's weaselly principal) do expert supporting work, many of the smaller parts, like Shalom Harlow as too-thin supermodel Sonya, are precisely cast as well. And as Brackett's loyal fiancée, Cusack has the first role in a long time that she can really throw herself into.

Though the film does itself a perhaps inevitable disservice with its ersatz "Mr. Holland's Opus" ending, overall "In & Out" benefits from the things it has to say about stereotyping and what happens when people are unable to acknowledge who they are. Thoughtful without seeming to be, making jokes that aren't dumb and dumber, "In & Out" takes itself just seriously enough to be a success.

NEW YORK, 9/22/97, p. 54, David Denby

Paul Rudnick, who wrote the comedy *In & Out*, is an affectionate, easygoing satirist who happens to compose some of the funniest one-liners in show business today. As if it weren't enough to be a novelist, playwright, screenwriter, and Nice Jewish Boy, Rudnick is even a film critic of sorts. In *Premiere,* he holds forth in the person of "Libby Gelman-Waxner," a princess with major shopping ambitions and reliably middlebrow tastes. As Libby, Paul Rudnick revels in the lurid badness of big Hollywood movies while relishing the various attractions of the male movie stars. No gay writer ever found a safer, funnier haven. In all, Rudnick cuddles his material, his audience, and himself. He loves moms, he loves Hollywood and American shopping-mall banality. He luxuriates in the anti-p.c. realization that stereotypes are always true—Jews really are Jewish, and gays gay. In *In & Out*, Rudnick and director Frank Oz create a fantasy Hollywood gay movie. It's called *To Serve and Protect* (we see a little of it), and it's an earnest tearjerker in which Matt Dillon plays an all-American war hero drummed out of the

Army for loving the camp Bette Midler-Barbara Hershey epic, *Beaches*. It's characteristic of Rudnick's affection for the kitschier regions of show business that he creates a parody of a movie that doesn't exist. The excruciating *To Serve and Protect* could serve as an example of wish fulfillment. If only Libby could review it.

At the Oscars, accepting the award for his stirring performance, Matt Dillon casually "outs" his high-school English teacher—Mr. Brackett, who still wears bow ties and perfectly pressed mall clothes while teaching *Romeo and Juliet* to somnolent teens. A bachelor, perhaps 40, Howard Brackett (Kevin Kline) is about to be married, after a long, long courtship, to another teacher (Joan Cusack). When the citizens of Greenleaf, Indiana, glued to their sets, hear about his alleged homosexuality, they freeze (literally: No one moves). Brackett denies being gay, but a pack of reporters descends on the sleepy Indiana burg, led by a persistent tabloid-TV personality (Tom Selleck) who really is gay. In the idyllic Indiana countryside, the two men run into each other, and Selleck grabs Kline and kisses him on the mouth for what seems like an eternity. Bazoingas! The teacher is knocked silly, like Buster Keaton clobbered by a brick. So is he or isn't he?

"Should homosexuals be allowed to touch fresh produce?" asks one of the TV reporters hounding Howard Brackett. For Paul Rudnick, homophobia is not so much vicious as preposterous, a compound of dotty misinformation and primal fear. Rudnick has fun with the high-school-locker-room louts who air their solemnly bizarre theories about gay sex. He's not angry at his Indiana hicks. On the contrary, he rather loves them, perhaps because they are so readily shocked by homosexuality. In this regard, *In & Out* feels dated, almost as if Indiana were stuck in the fifties, trapped in a blinkered, pre-media state.

Apart from Brackett, who is smart but unconscious, none of the locals has more than half a brain. The trouble with believing so thoroughly in stereotypes is that it may be impossible to create a character who isn't one. Rudnick dissolves character into performance: Life is all about presenting yourself in one way or another. Howard Brackett has no self, the filmmakers turn him this way and that, using him opportunistically for laughs, and the character never makes much sense. Yet Kevin Kline triumphs over an incoherent idea. His lightweight, I can-do-anything style, which has held him back as a movie star, works for this cipher. He makes Brackett ever so slightly prissy; then, when he's out to prove that Brackett is straight, he mugs and struts like a lumberjack. In his best moment, he breaks into a paroxysm of disco dancing, the movements just bursting out of him in uncontrollable spasms. It's as good a metaphor for orgasm as we are ever likely to see in movies, and it may make Kevin Kline a movie star at last.

Tom Selleck has finally found his way in movies, too. His TV reporter is a second-rate journalist but an honest man, and Selleck, relieved, perhaps, not to be playing an action hero, revels in good-natured candor. Joan Cusack, in an enormous, billowing wedding dress, has one of those abandoned-at-the-altar scenes that could be nothing but a cliché, but she drives the moment so wildly and operatically over the top that she triumphs, too. The laughs arrive in volleys, though many of them are cheaply earned. Rudnick's surface-is-all dramaturgy links his work to classic farce; it also links his work, at its most facile, to television, and far too often *In & Out* feels like a slightly giddy sitcom, with overbright lighting and huggable moments for every character.

Rudnick and Oz and producer Scott Rudin have made this sexual-identity comedy as American as Indiana corn. Their desire for acceptance of gays is inseparable from their desire for the acceptance of their picture as a commercial comedy. The emotional ending to *In & Out*, which turns into a gay rally, may be as melodramatic and silly as anything in the putative *To Serve and Protect*. Still, there's that kiss between Selleck and Kline. People looking for boldness will seize on that kiss. The rest of us will have to live with it in every Oscar-night collage of Hollywood's most romantic moments.

NEW YORK POST, 9/19/97, p. 53, Michael Medved

Near the beginning of the hilarious comedy "In & Out," Glenn Close turns up to present one of the nominees for best actor at a fictional Academy Awards show. She shows clips from a smug, sentimental, cinematic sermon about the struggles of gays in the military ("they defend their country, but they're not free to date!") that is unfortunately typical of the solemn, self-important tone of most previous big studio "gay-themed" movies.

What makes "In & Out" so enjoyable is that not only avoids, but satirizes, such poker-faced preachiness. When an airheaded Brad Pitt-style actor (Wickedly well-played by Matt Dillon) wins that Oscar for his performance as a persecuted homosexual, he makes an acceptance speech thanking his agent ("and my new agent"), then acknowledging an inspirational high school teacher back home in Indiana, defiantly (and thoughtlessly) telling the world that "he's gay."

Unfortunately, this popular basketball coach and member of the English faculty (the superb, irresistibly likable Kevin Kline) has never acknowledged to himself or anyone else anything about his underlying sexual orientation.

After all, he's supposed to be married just a few days after the Oscars to an adoring fellow teacher (Joan Cusack) who's waited three years for these nuptials and lost 75 pounds for the occasion.

His all-American parents (Wilford Brimley, Debbie Reynolds) don't want the scandalous Oscar announcement to interfere with the big wedding celebration, but a media horde suddenly descends on their town, led by smirking TV reporter Tom Selleck (in a juicy role that may get supporting-actor Oscar attention of its own.)

Paul Rudnick's screenplay may be faulted by some for "trivializing" gay identify (defining it largely as love of Shakespeare, skill at using a napkin, an uncontrollable urge to dance to disco music, and an unreasoning passion for Bette Midler's "Beaches" or Streisand's anything), but it probably delivers more unstoppable laughter than any script this year.

Comedy specialist Frank Oz ("Little Shop of Horrors." "Dirty Rotten Scoundrels") treats his fictional Indiana town with real affection, filling it with decent folks eager to make the most of their lives, rather than stereotypical gay-bashers.

One maudlin, manipulative crowd scene may go too far (substituting "I'm gay!" for "I am Spartacus!"), but what ultimately distinguishes "In & Out" isn't its "gayness," but its all-embracing, warm-hearted humanity.

NEWSDAY, 9/19/97, Part II/p. B7, Jack Mathews

The title of Frank Oz' "In & Out" serves a double meaning. From the poster, you might think it's the first part of a sentence that ends "... of the closet." But in a movie where double entendres dance like fireflies in a cave, it more likely comes from a hilariously clumsy theory about homo-sexuality expressed by a high school senior to his pals, on the occasion of the televised "outing" of their English teacher.

The theory has to do with putting things in the wrong places, but its purpose, like so much of Paul Rudnick's marvelously whimsical script, is to show the confusion among heterosexuals.

And that, for anyone looking for a breakthrough mainstream gay film, is about as serious as the politics get. "In & Out" is merely an old-fashioned screwball comedy with a gay theme.

"In & Out" was inspired by Tom Hanks' acceptance speech at the 1994 Oscars, where he was honored as best actor for his performance as an attorney with AIDS in "Philadelphia." Hanks took the occasion to acknowledge the humanity of a gay drama teacher who'd inspired him in college, a gesture that had producer Scott Rudin wondering, "What if that teacher were still in the closet?"

Hanks' teacher was, in fact, out of the closet. But the "what if" premise was delivered up as a hanging curve-ball to Rudnick, a playwright, humorist, and screenwriter, who turned it into something that critics of an earlier era could have mildly described as ... gay!

"In & Out" is the tale of Midwest high school English teacher Howard Brackett (Kevin Kline), who, days before he's to be married, is outed on global TV by an Oscar-winning former student during the Academy Awards. The stunning revelation, news that shocks no one more than Brackett, turns the poor man's life upside-down.

The next day, Brackett and all of tiny Greenleaf, Ind., (a cameo by Northport), are besieged by the national media. He's compelled to issue denials to everyone from his fiancée (Joan Cu-sack) to his parents (Wilford Brimley and Debbie Reynolds) to his current crop of students. And he's being threatened with dismissal by the school's inanely homophobic principal (Bob Newhart).

But as the wedding day approaches, the question haunting Brackett begins to shift away from why his former student would declare him gay on live TV to how he knew. Brackett is apparently a middle-aged virgin, with no sexual experience, and no overt doubts. Yes, he knows every scene of every Barbra Streisand movie, he gushes poetry and rides a bike to school. But until the Oscars, no one had thought to put the signs of the stereotype together.

"In & Out" isn't a mainstream gay film, but a film written by a gay man for a mainstream audience. It's the multiplex equivalent of safe sex. The movie's lone homosexual contact, an impromptu kiss planted firmly on Brackett's lips by Tom Selleck's gay TV reporter Peter Malloy, is a hilariously protracted bit of physical comedy, seen mostly from a distance.

Rudnick, as anyone who reads his pseudonymous column in Premiere magazine knows, is a pop-culture pack rat, and he's got hip references leaping out of every scene. My favorite: Besides Brackett's former student Cameron Drake (Matt Dillon), the best actor nominees at that Oscar show include Steven Seagal, for "A Snowball in Hell," referring to the actor's chances of that ever happening.

There isn't a missed note by anyone in the cast. Selleck has a high time playing a down-on-his-ratings TV star out to reset his career with an up-close-and-personal exposé on Brackett. The extraordinary Cusack finally gets a showcase role, and is a howl as the luckless Emily, a fellow Greenleaf High teacher who had torture-dieted herself into wedding-playing condition, only to find herself without a partner. And Kline, probably the most engaging light film comedian we have, is perfect as a man keeping his sexuality a secret, even to himself, right up to the moment when it's his turn to say, "I do," and he can't.

"In & Out" is nicely directed by Oz, but the clear creative engine behind it is Rudnick. This may not be a breakthrough movie, even if it's a hit. Its gay characters are too likable, too in on the joke to tap into—let alone change anyone's prejudices. But it won't hurt, either. Rudnick has too much fun exploding stereotypes to promote any.

SIGHT AND SOUND, 2/98, P. 43, Andy Medhurst

Greenleaf, Indiana, high-school teachers Howard Brackett and Emily Montgomery are about to marry. A few days before the wedding, a former student of theirs, Cameron Drake, wins an Oscar for playing a gay role and makes an acceptance speech which simultaneously thanks Howard and outs him as homosexual. Greenleaf is invaded by a media circus asking intrusive questions, but Howard staunchly protests his heterosexuality. Nonetheless, his parents, students and Emily all take some convincing owing to Howard's neatness, love of poetry and devotion to Barbra Streisand.

Television reporter Peter Malloy decides to make Howard the focus of a sequence of programmes, interviewing the townspeople and refusing to let the story die. Howard receives a veiled threat from the school principal that he would be sacked if he really was gay. Malloy reveals his own homosexuality to Howard, refuses to believe the latter's denials and kisses him. Howard seeks solace in a self-help tape on masculinity, but finds himself unable to comply with its strictures. At the altar, he stuns everyone by saying "I'm gay" instead of "I do". The principal fires him, his parents try to come to terms with the news, and Emily heads off to a bar to get drunk. There she meets Cameron, en route to his home town to show Howard some moral support, and they become close. At the high school's graduation ceremony, news of Howard's sacking shocks everyone. Cameron arrives to speak up for Howard and the whole town rallies to his support.

Inspired by the legendarily self-indulgent speech Tom Hanks made when receiving his Academy Award for *Philadelphia*, *In & Out* subscribes to the same well-intentioned liberalism of that earlier film, but operates as a mildly didactic comedy of manners rather than a browbeating weepie. Its considerable success in the US is heartening given its gently gay-friendly message, though its ability to tickle mainstream audiences inevitably means that it will seem tame and safe to most queer viewers. It left me with decidedly mixed feelings—part of me wants to applaud a multiplex hit which stresses the benefits of coming out, challenges anti-gay prejudice and lands some welcome slaps against boorish masculinity. But part of me couldn't help feeling short-changed at noticing how evasively the film backs away from doing any more.

Early on in the film, it's often unclear where the humour is directed, leaving some scenes rather queasy. When Howard's students grill him about his sexuality (thus taking their place in a tradition of gay-baiting classroom interrogations that reaches back to *Taxi zum Klo* and *Nighthawks*), it's difficult to be sure whether we're being asked to laugh at their naiveté or his discomfort. Howard's bachelor party is a similarly problematic scene, where his lumpenly hetero friends (who've become converts to Streisand-worship thanks to Howard's enthusiasm for her) fall into bitter wrangling about the respective merits of *Yentl* and *A Star Is Born*. On one level, this is a gag about their ignorance of La Babs' place in gay male culture, yet on another it mocks and baits those queens who take such things seriously. All the same, it's a deliciously funny moment.

The second half of the film is more assured, its targets clearer. Kline's performance, which threatens at times to veer into the Robin Williams zone of shameless posing, settles and matures once Howard has come out. He's ably supported by Tom Selleck who deftly conveys the ease and charm of a man comfortable with who he is. (Selleck's casting is one of the film's more mischievous gambits since he was one of the first targets of the early 90s outing campaigns which also took aim at Jodie Foster) The main casualty of the deepening relationship between Kline and Selleck is Joan Cusack, whose thankless role as Emily reaffirms an unofficial rule of liberal films about male homosexuality—the securing of gay men's self-esteem requires women to be made marginal and ridiculous. The treatment of Emily here is horridly misogynistic: her weight problems and self-loathing are played for easy laughs, she takes the blame for Howard's bid at sham-straightness, and Cusack's unfortunately one-dimensional performance conspires with the film's ideological drift to turn Emily into a total pain. She does, however, get the film's best line when, betrayed at the wedding, she yells at Howard, "Fuck Barbra Streisand and fuck you".

As with many feelgood US films, the ending of *In & Out* seeks to bury its narrative loose ends with a conclusion of vague, communal merry-making. After the affirmations of the graduation day scene, where citizen after citizen defends Howard by standing up to declare with a loyal lie "I'm gay" (a neat and rather touching nod to the "I'm Spartacus" climax of the Kirk Douglas epic), we're returned to the church in which the earlier non-wedding took place. Briefly, the film teases us with the genuinely radical possibility that Howard and Peter are about to marry, before ducking out in favour of a more politically manageable ceremony: Howard's parents re-taking their wedding vows. The film ends with the whole of Greenleaf frugging away to the strains of the Village People, although this still leaves three vital questions unanswered. What kind of life can the now out-and-proud Howard expect in a normative small town like this? Have he and Peter really become an item? And, most intriguing of all, what took place between Howard and Cameron Drake to make Drake so certain about his teacher's sexuality?

None of those riddles can be solved, since their likely answers would make the film less comfortable for heterosexual audiences. As it stands, they can flatter themselves that they, like the denizens of Greenleaf, are live and-let-live liberals, not nasty old bigots like the school principal. After all, in the ideological map of films like this it's permissible to vilify homophobic individuals, but not to attack homophobia as a systematic form of oppression. Going that far would be to reveal the stifling repressiveness of places like Greenleaf, of every community that daily and unthinkingly reaps the benefits of heterosexual privilege—but that's hardly on the cards while Hollywood's profit motive needs to keep all the Greenleafs sweet.

VILLAGE VOICE, 9/23/97, p. 94, Laurie Stone

For *In & Out*, screenwriter Paul Rudnick creates a topsy-turvy world in which a weasely scandalmonger champions self-knowledge, Hollywood's untouchables are fair game for dunking, and the usually serious subject of gay outing is the material of farce. Unlike the majority of TV and movie comedies, where offensiveness is shaved like potentially irritating stubble, Rudnick trounces consensus good manners—the kind that deem sissy gays verboten—and he accomplishes this feat without soft-pedaling fagphobia or stomping the socially weak. He targets pomposity, vanity, anxiety about appearances, and fear of otherness. Frank Oz, a guiding force in creating the Muppets, turns Rudnick's script into a gay fairy tale (no pun intended), the characters coming across as human versions of fuzzy puppets.

It takes a little while for the tone to click into place. We start out in ultra-white-bread Greefleaf, Indiana, and it's unclear if we're meant to gag on the blandness or cuddle up to it, as we watch high school teacher Howard (Kevin Kline) prepare to marry fellow teacher Emily (Joan Cusack), his newly slimmed, longtime fiancée. But the camp banners are soon flying when the scene shifts to Hollywood and Rudnick spoofs Oscar reverence by channeling his alter ego, snarky movie critic Libby Gelman-Waxner. Howards former student Cameron (Matt Dillon in a blond-streaked Brad Pitt do) wins an award for playing a very dumb gay soldier (conflating

Tom Hanks's parts in *Philadelphia* and *Forrest Gump*). The victory is a shoo-in, given that the competition, announced with delirious solemnity by Glenn Close, includes Paul Newman in *Coot*, Clint Eastwood in *Geezer,* and Steven Seagal in *When Hell Freezes Over.*

Riffing off Hanks's Oscar speech for *Philadelphia,* in which he honored a gay teacher, Rudnick has Cameron thank Howard—and add that Howard is gay. Watching the telecast, Howard turns to stone, then tosses the remote control out the window, as if it were a conduit for queerness. Kline is such an intelligent comedian, he leaks the hysteria of the closet case Howard is, while acting like a straight man who's inconvenienced but not disgusted by the "mistake." The fablelike quality created by Oz—lending all the characters a cleverly chosen one-dimensionality—allows us to believe that a middle-aged man could still be trying to straighten himself out. And in a predictable but very amusing set piece, Howard listens to a self-help tape for macho building, every fiber in him straining not to boogie—for "real men don't dance"—when "Disco Inferno" is blasted out as a test.

As the out gay, non-swish entertainment reporter who stalks Howard and plants a juicy smacker on his lips, Tom Selleck is charmingly low-key. And Cusack is perfect as a crazed bride as chagrined by her own naïveté for enduring a chaste, three-year engagement as she is enraged at Howard for his charade. Best are the Rudnick zingers, which chase the movie's sometimes treacly attempts to translate gays to straights. A garish, powder blue tux is dubbed "The Torme." Howard's mother (Debbie Reynolds) vows she would love him even if he were gay—or, as his father (Wilford Brimley) adds, "climbed a clock tower and started shooting" Cameron's super-model girlfriend (Shalom Harlow), balking at a pending trip to Indiana, complains, "I promised Isaac I'd do his show. I have to shower and vomit." And trying to present a manly front at his bachelor party, Howard, feigning weariness with Barbra Streisand, is egged into a brawl when one of the celebrants declares of *Yentl,* "She was too old for the part"."

Also reviewed in:
CHICAGO TRIBUNE, 9/19/97, Friday/p. A, Mark Caro
NEW REPUBLIC, 10/20/97, p. 27, Stanley Kauffmann
NEW YORK TIMES, 9/19/97, p. E12, Janet Maslin
VARIETY, 9/15-21/97, p. 68, Todd McCarthy
WASHINGTON POST, 9/19/97, p. E1, Rita Kempley
WASHINGTON POST, 9/19/97, Weekend/p. 50, Desson Howe

INNOCENT SLEEP, THE

A Castle Hill Productions release of a Timedial Films presentation. *Executive Producer:* Rod Michell. *Producer:* Scott Michell and Matthew Vaughn. *Director:* Scott Michell. *Screenplay:* Ray Villis. *Director of Photography:* Alan Dunlop. *Editor:* Derek Trigg. *Music:* Mark Ayres. *Sound:* Geoff Neate, Geoff Smythe, and (music) Mike Ross-Trevor. *Sound Editor:* Ted Mason. *Production Designer:* Eve Mavrakis. *Art Director:* Bowesy. *Special Effects:* John Fontana. *Costumes:* Stephanie Collie. *Make-up:* Catherine Scoble and Clare Le Vesconte. *Stunt Coordinator:* Rod Woodruff. *Running time:* 96 minutes. *MPAA Rating:* R.

CAST: Oliver Cotton (Lusano); Tony Bluto (Thorn); Paul Brightwell (Pelham); Michael Gambon (Matheson); Rupert Graves (Alan Terry); Campbell Morrison (Mac); Graham Crowden (George); Franco Nero (Cavani); Hilary Crowson (Sheila Terry); Kieran Smith (Newspaper Vendor); Sean Gilder (Police Constable); Brian Lipson (Police Sergeant); Dermot Kerrigan (Willie); Dermot Keanby (Driver); Alex Richardson and Chris Chering (Thugs); Annabella Sciorra (Billie Hayman); Chris Jury (News Photographer); Laura Berkeley (Glamorous Blonde); Hugh Walters (Lewis); John Hannah (James); Crispin Redman (Simon, C.I.D.); Katy Carr (Alice); Chris Armstrong (Dave, C.I.D.); Lehla Eldridge (Morgue Attendant); Struan Rodger (Peter Samson); Stephen Yardley (Drago); Ken Ratcliffe (Stephens); Carmen De Venere (Cavani's Aide); Paul Gregory (Newsreader); Robert James (Hopkin);

Susan Gilmore (News Program Presenter);   Peter Cartwright (Gerald Phillips);   Julian Rivett (Bike Courier);   Patrick Dugan (Landlord);   Peter Howell (Sir Frank);   Ben De Saumserez (Assassin).

LOS ANGELES TIMES, 6/27/97, Calendar/p. 14, John Anderson

[The following review by John Anderson appeared in a slightly different form in **NEWSDAY, 6/27/97, Part II/p. B8.]**

Intrepid reporters, noble homeless, outlaw masons and tutti Mafiosi are the ingredients in "The Innocent Sleep," an English thriller that won't inspire much raising of hair, tingling of spines or biting of nails.   But it does have an intelligent cast and none of them wear capes.

Imagine a fair to middlin' "Prime Suspect" episode—except that in lieu of the severe but sensitive Det. Inspector Jane Tennyson we get the severe but sensitive crime reporter Billie Hayman (Annabella Sciorra).   Her all-but-indecipherable connections to the homeless community of London provides the tip to the biggest story of the year: that the body of an Italian industrialist found hanged from a Thames River bridge wasn't a suicide at all.   And the ripples are international.

The tip comes from Alan Terry, an out-of-luck, out-of-work, out-of-wife drinker who witnesses the crime, in one of the movie's tenser scenes.   He's given a very substantial performance by Rupert Graves ("The Madness of King George," "A Room With a View"), one of the more talented of England's current bumper crop of gifted actors.   Used to less effectiveness is the about-to-be-legendary Michael Gambon ("Mystery!'s" Maigret, recently seen on Broadway in "Skylight"), who imbues his homicidal rogue detective with an unhealthy level of venom.   But why should an actor of Gambon's stature be playing a role meant for Brian Dennehy?

Why, for that matter, is Billie an American?   There's no explanation (none that I remember anyway).   There's certainly nothing wrong with her being American, even if British work rules might make it unlikely.   But without some explanation, we're left to assume that she's American simply because they wanted Sciorra in the movie.   And that puts an unfair burden on an actress who isn't all that endearing to begin with.

Director Scott Michell acquits himself admirably; this is his first feature, and it moves along smoothly, professionally, rhythmically.   OK, so we hear opera every time the good guys, or the police, venture into the beggars' community (an aria sung by Lesley Garrett of the English National Opera and specially composed for this film).   Directors have done a lot worse.   And done it this summer.

"Innocent Sleep"—a title lifted, for no particularly urgent reason, from "Macbeth"—is based on the Roberto Calvi Affair of 1982, in which a presumed suicide, was found swinging under a Thames bridge.   The subsequent investigation revealed a conspiracy that "touched the Vatican and the Italian government of the day," according to the film's press notes.   The filmmakers, having all this to work with, have also implicated Scotland Yard, maligned the working press and tied the whole thing neatly together via a character modeled after Rupert Murdoch.   If the purpose of this kind of conspiracy thriller is to increase our paranoia, "Innocent Sleep" fails, simply because it tries too hard.

NEW YORK POST, 6/27/97, p. 42, Larry Worth

The title for "The Innocent Sleep" comes from a line in Shakespeare's "Macbeth." But a line from "A Midsummer's Night's Dream" sums it up better: "Lord , what fools these mortals be."

How else to explain why script writers Ray Villis and Derek Trigg would take such a well-worn plot and give it an umpteenth going over?

Yes, it's the old chestnut about a man who witnesses a murder and becomes the killers' next quarry. Piling cliche upon cliche, Villis and Trigg quickly make cops the culprits and throw in a governmental conspiracy theme. The rest is similarly by-the-numbers.

So far, so bad. But that's where a first-rate cast comes in handy. Indeed, Rupert Graves, Annabella Sciorra, Michael Gambon and Franco Nero combine forces to—believe it or not—turn the hackneyed suspenser into a moderately entertaining production.

Graves, best known from Merchant-Ivory productions, is particularly convincing as the down-on-his-luck hero, a former yuppy who's been forced to find quarters among London's homeless. He delivers a nicely modulated mix of wide-eyed desperation, distrust and growing horror.

Sciorra provides fine support as a tough-talking journalist who becomes Graves' chief ally. And, as ever, Gambon is deliciously over-the-top as the officious officer working under nasty Nero's orders.

First-time director Scott Michell also does what he can. He makes good use of Tower Bridge locales and conveys a sinister feel via grainy cinematography.

Of course, no amount of smart acting or brisk direction can mask the conclusion's lack of logic. That would take an act of God. As is, the fact that Graves and company make this drivel palatable is miracle enough.

SIGHT AND SOUND, 2/96, p. 44, Geoffrey Macnab

Alan Terry, a young down-and-out, is spending the night in a disused warehouse near Tower Bridge when he hears a scuffle below him. He looks to see what is happening, and quickly realises he is witnessing a murder. The assassins come after him, but he manages to hide. The next day, he tries to report the incident to the police, but is shocked to find that one of the killers is a policeman. He flees from the station. Kindly old drunk George, a former journalist fallen on hard times, believes his story and sets up a meeting with reporter, Billie Hayman. Alan eventually convinces her and she decides to write an exposé on the case for *The London Evening Herald*. It turns out that the murder victim was an Italian businessman. He was assassinated on the order of a wealthy colleague, whom he had betrayed.

The policeman, Matheson, is in the pay of the Italians. He wants Alan dead, and scours London looking for him. Alan is hiding out in Hayman's flat, but when he realises that she values her career more than his life, he decides to take his chances on his own. The policeman narrowly misses catching him on several occasions. But in the search for Alan, he starts a fire at the cardboard city where Alan had been living. George is caught in the flames and receives fatal burns. Alan mistakenly believes that the policeman's real name is DCI Stephens. When he rings the station to tell another officer about the crime, Matheson intercepts the call and sets a trap for him. The two are to meet at the scene of the murder. Hayman is desperate to reach Alan before Matheson does. She speeds to Tower Bridge, but it seems too late. Matheson already has Alan cornered, and is on the verge of killing him. Just before he has the chance, he himself is shot. The Italians ordered his assassination. Despite the Italian connection, the story dies with Matheson. People in high places have told Hayman's editor not to pursue it further.

Pea-soup fogs and policemen with whistles are all that are missing from *The Innocent Sleep*, a brisk little London thriller which gingerly trots through every available genre cliché and, in the process, rekindles memories of the scores of similarly formulaic Edgar Wallace crime dramas the British film industry used to chum out in the 1930s and 1940s. Characterisation is on the stereotypical side: Annabella Sciorra's sassy, chain-smoking crime reporter, Franco Nero's sinister but sartorial Italian businessman and Michael Gambon's leering detective villain are caricatures, as are all the various down-and-outs, drunkards, and heavies who flit in and out of the story. The innocent-man-witnesses-murder storyline is a very old chestnut. There's plenty of overblown, operatic music to lend a portentous feel to events, and the abrupt ending, which cuts off a complex narrative in its prime, is a masterpiece of evasive plotting.

This may be hackneyed material, but at least the film-makers mobilise the old tropes with some élan. They make inventive use of London locations and throw in enough stock characters, MacGuffins (buttons lost in the mud, red herrings about Italian Masonic lodges) chases and explosions to maintain interest, however improbable the storyline becomes. First-time director Scott Michell allows himself occasional Hitchcockian touches—the deliberate way, for instance, he builds up to the moment when Gambon lights his cigar and then tosses the match onto the ground to set off a huge fire. There's also one expressionistic flourish: the down-and-out hero falls asleep in the bath and suffers a lurid nightmare in which Gambon tries to drown him.

Even the casting is in the spirit of the old-fashioned B quickie. Franco Nero follows in the footsteps of such stars as Cesar Romero and Herbert Lom as the exotic foreigner while Sciorra is following a well-trodden path from Hollywood to Britain, a journey undertaken by many once-prominent stars whose careers are in temporary or terminal decline. It seems improbable that she was attracted by the quality of the script. Whatever the case, she attacks her role with commendable verve, barking out her lines and making sure she's never seen without a cigarette hanging out of her mouth. The fact that the storyline doesn't provide her with any romantic interest, save for some corny banter with fellow hack, John Hannah, suggests her role may originally have been written with a man in mind. Perhaps Rupert Graves, more accustomed to appearing in Merchant/Ivory movies than playing down-and-outs, is a little too fresh-featured as Alan Terry, the film's homeless hero, but the same certainly can't be said of Michael Gambon, who sneers his way through the film as corrupt cop, Matheson. (There are clear echoes here of his role in *The Singing Detective*.)

The Innocent Sleep is an oddly apt title. There's something ingenuous and a little somnambulatory about the film's lumbering use of generic conventions. This is a very British thriller, with none of the swagger of Danny Cannon's *The Young Americans*. In truth, it's not a very good one. But, like the old Edgar Wallace movies it emulates, it's always entertaining, in its own creaky, atmospheric way.

VILLAGE VOICE, 7/1/97, p. 94, Laurie Stone

It must have sounded surefire at the story meeting: a conspiracy thriller based on the 1982 murder of Italian banker Roberto Calvi, found hanging from a Thames bridge. The crime's tentacles encircled the Italian government and the Vatican; the film adds corruption in the British police force and a battle of wits between established power and Thatcher-wrought no-hopers camping in London's cardboard city. Shades of Graham Greene, Hitchcock, and Jim Cartwright. Talent got on board: hunky/stubbly Rupert Graves as innocent dosser Alan, who witnesses the homicide and becomes a hunted rabbit; Michael Gambon as a world-weary thug who snuffs out life as easily as a match; and Annabella Sciorra as a tough-cookie reporter. The trouble is, first-time director Scott Michell forgot to care about the story or characters. His by-the-numbers noir is so corny it isn't even lurid. Pulp clichés pass for dialogue and scenery chewing for acting, all to the accompaniment of Mark Ayres's ludicrously tumescent score—each shake of Gambon's jowls seems accented by a clash of cymbals.

Also reviewed in:
NEW YORK TIMES, 6/27/97, p. C12, Stephen Holden
VARIETY, 6/26-7/9/95, p. 84, David Stratton

INSIDE

A Showtime release in association with Hallmark Entertainment of an Elkins Entertainment and Logo Entertainment production. *Executive Producer:* Louis Gossett, Jr. *Producer:* Hilly Elkins. *Director:* Arthur Penn. *Screenplay:* Bima Stagg. *Director of Photography:* Jan Weincke. *Editor:* Suzanne Pillsbury. *Music:* Robert Levin. *Production Designer:* David Barkham. *Costumes:* Leigh Bishop. *Running time:* 94 minutes. *MPAA Rating:* R.

CAST: Eric Stoltz (Marty Strydom); Nigel Hawthorne (Colonel Kruger); Louis Gossett, Jr. (Questioner); Ian Roberts (Guard Moolman); Ross Preller (Guard Potgieter).

LOS ANGELES TIMES, 1/31/97, Calendar/p. 2, Kevin Thomas

"Inside" is as impressive as it is almost too painful to watch in its depiction of the evils of apartheid carried to the extreme. Although set in that racist system's final years in South Africa, it is a timeless depiction of the horrors that can confront any individual who becomes at the total mercy of a monstrous regime. It also makes palpable the fear that can consume people in regard to those different from themselves.

Arrested for treason but without being charged, Marty Strydom (Eric Stoltz) is thrown into a prison run by a Col. Kruger (Nigel Hawthorne). Initially proud and defiant, Marty is systematically beaten so badly that—and given the prominence of his family in South Africa—Kruger determines to drive him to suicide by whatever means at his disposal. A trial for Strydom would only bring further international protests of the South African government and exposure of the hideous treatment accorded its political prisoners.

Just at the point—about half an hour into the picture—when Kruger and his guards' treatment of Strydom is becoming truly unbearable, "Inside" switches to the present, with a black official, known only as the Questioner (Louis Gossett Jr.), interrogating Kruger in regard to Strydom.

As a chamber drama, "Inside" could scarcely have been more adroitly filmed than by director Arthur Penn, working with cinematographer Jan Weincke and production designer David Barkham, resourceful craftsman both. The prison cell door's large peephole becomes the film's dominant, oddly obscene image, through which Marty can communicate with other prisoners—but also receives blasts of a Mace-like spray. Scenes inside cells and Kruger's office are punctuated with shots of the long prison corridors, their darkness pierced by pools of light from occasional ceiling fixtures. Similarly, Penn uses sound to vary and heighten Strydom's terrible predicament. "Inside's" terse 94 minutes is expertly paced.

The director of "Bonnie and Clyde," "The Miracle Worker," "Mickey One," "Little Big Man" and "Night Moves," plus a raft of Broadway successes, Penn has now added another important picture to this list. In doing so, he has inspired in his cast electrifying portrayals. Gossett gives us a man of controlled rage while Stoltz sustains a thoroughly harrowing portrait of a man facing as best he can the most horrible of fates.

Yet it is, not surprisingly, Hawthorne's Kruger who haunts you. It's not too much to say that Kruger is among the most loathesome, despicable men ever depicted in the movies, the very epitome of absolute power corrupting absolutely. Kruger is also the very embodiment of Hannah Arendt's famous "banality of evil"—a man possessed of a small, closed mind but an infinite capacity for cunning. His hatred of blacks is fueled by a limitless paranoid fear that, once in power, they will surely treat the white man the way the white man has treated them.

NEW YORK POST, 1/10/97, p. 48, Bill Hoffmann

Arthur Penn's chilling tale of apartheid in South Africa will shock and jolt you from the opening scenes.

It's 1988 and the P.W. Botha government is at a fever pitch in its violent battle to maintain segregation and white domination.

As the credits roll, horrifying scenes—taken from actual news footage—show an inhumane police force beating, torturing and killing in the name of racism.

It's a grim but appropriate scene setter for the riveting drama to follow.

A psychotic police commander (Nigel Hawthorne) has arrested a young white radical (Eric Stoltz) for alleged "subversive" pro-black acts.

Whether Stoltz is guilty isn't immediately apparent, but Hawthorne is determined to make him confess through horrifying sessions of physical and psychological torture.

Between excruciating beatings, the prisoner is told that his parents have abandoned him and that his girlfriend is in jail and being raped by guards.

The only thing that keeps Stoltz from going off the deep end are the continual pleas from a black prisoner in a nearby cell (Lou Gossett Jr.) to hang in and be strong.

Penn doesn't shy away from the brutality one iota, but what makes it all bearable are the terrific performances by the three principals. Nigel Hawthorne, so great in "The Madness of King George," delivers an Olivier-caliber performance deserving of an Oscar nomination.

His calm, deliberate delivery is filled with a simmering insanity that is positively chilling. It's acting bravado.

Stoltz also comes through with flying colors with a passionate portrayal of an idealist who refuses to bow to corruption, even if it will save his life.

In a neat plot twist, Hawthorne is eventually imprisoned as apartheid ends and Gossett becomes his interrogator. It's particularly nice to see Gossett, an excellent actor who's appeared in too many turkeys over the years, back in action in a meaty role.

Film fans will also be heartened to see Arthur Penn back in the saddle, his directing talents in full gear. I thought that after the abysmal "Dead of Winter" and "Penn and Teller Get Killed" that

Penn had given up the directing ghost. But the man who gave us the American classics "Bonnie and Clyde" and "Little Big Man" still has it—and that's exciting news.

As South Africa moves on to new and exciting social and economic development under the Mandela regime, "Inside" reminds us that it was only yesterday that the country was a living, breathing nightmare.

NEWSDAY, 1/10/97, Part II/p.   B13, Jan Stuart

Much of Arthur Penn's aptly titled "Inside" is glimpsed through a prison-door peephole. This calculated, limiting view is intended to capture the tightness and isolation that informs the daily life of an incarcerated South African freedom fighter played by Eric Stoltz. And it does. Well before the final frame, you will be yearning for a glass of water and an IMAX movie.

A ticket to "Inside" will not buy you grand vistas or subtleties. Stoltz plays a 30-year-old university professor in 1988 whose inclinations toward political martyrdom are telegraphed by his name Marty Strydom. The great-grandson of a South African freedom activist and the son of a prominent conservative lawyer, Marty has been arrested for his anti-apartheid involvement. In prison, he is tortured and beaten by the secret police, who spray spit, Mace and the blood of his fellow prisoners at him through the peephole. The brutality is visceral and scalding.

None of the physical violence works on him quite as potently, however, as the psychological beating he takes from his inquisitor, Col. Kruger (Nigel Hawthorne, affecting an insincere grin that taps into our most primal aggressive impulses). The venomous Kruger twists the truth into a noose to get Marty to admit to his weapons-smuggling activities, and the effort pays off. "Inside" tracks his breakdown, alternating between Kruger's needling interviews, cellbound conversations with Marty's fellow prisoners and an investigation years later in which the colonel's sadistic behavior is unraveled by a Truth Commission interrogator (Louis Gossett Jr.) with his own ax to grind.

For all of the peephole glimpses and birds-eye shots of Marty's tiny cell, the claustrophobia that we experience owes as much to Bima Stagg's hermetically airtight script. "Inside" feels too mapped out and worked-through, more intent on dramatic sleight of hand than character texture. Stagg manages a few surprises, but the inside he never quite reaches is the interior workings of Kruger's head. He's always just another fascist pig: It gets your blood boiling, but it's not very illuminating.

Penn's direction is taut and no-nonsense, helped by some resourceful cellblock camera shots by Jan Weincke that reach for the poetic. All three lead actors are to be admired for their thoroughgoing commitment to their roles, but you can't help but feel they would be better off on a stage. As it happens, there was a time when the theater would be the natural home for a talkfest like "Inside," but that notion of drama has gone the way of apartheid. The most enduring contemporary theater is generally more cinematic than anything in this earnest but overwritten film.

VILLAGE VOICE, 1/21/97, p. 70, Amy Taubin

Arthur Penn takes on the past 10 years of South African history in a film that is both well-meaning and well-made, but which mostly makes one aware of the inadequacy of conventional film fiction. Eric Stoltz plays an intellectual accused in 1988 of conspiring to overthrow the apartheid regime. Nigel Hawthorne plays the army officer who tortures him to death. Nearly a decade later, the colonel is himself the object of an investigation and his interrogator is a former revolutionary (Louis Gossett Jr.) who witnessed the torture from his own prison cell. Segueing back and forth in time, the film makes an emotionally compelling case for the "The Truth Commission"—South Africa's version of the Nuremberg Trials—but leaves one hungry for something more factual and analytical.

Also reviewed in:
NEW YORK TIMES, 1/10/97, p. C18, Caryn James
VARIETY, 4/29-5/5/96, p. 133, Dennis Harvey

INTIMATE RELATIONS

A Fox Searchlight Pictures release of a Handmade Films presentation of a Boxer Films and Paragon Entertainment Corporation production. *Executive Producer:* Gareth Jones. *Producer:* Angela Hart, Lisa Hope, and Jon Slan. *Director:* Philip Goodhew. *Screenplay:* Philip Goodhew. *Director of Photography:* Andres Garreton. *Editor:* Pia Di Ciaula. *Music:* Lawrence Sharagge. *Sound:* Keith Tunney. *Casting:* Susan Forrest and Maximillian Boxer. *Production Designer:* Caroline Greville-Morris. *Art Director:* Annie Gregson and Moving Jim. *Set Decorator:* David Rosen. *Costumes:* John Hibbs. *Make-up:* Victoria Wright. *Running time:* 102 minutes. *MPAA Rating:* R.

CAST: Julie Walters (Marjorie Beasley); Rupert Graves (Harold Guppy); Matthew Walker (Stanley Beasley); Laura Sadler (Joyce Beasley); Holly Aird (Deirdre); Les Dennis (Maurice); Elizabeth McKechnie (Iris); James Aidan (George); Michael Bertenshaw (Mr. Pugh); Judy Clifton (Mrs. Fox-Davies); Christopher Cook (Deirdre's Baby); Candace Hallinan (Pauline); Charles Hart (Hotel Receptionist); George Hart (Car Vendor); Amanda Holden (Pamela); Nicholas Hoult (Bobby); Annie Keller (Jean); Elsie Kelly (Enid); Max (Princess); Gary Meredith (Mr. Jarvis); Sarah-Jane McKechnie (Mrs. Latimer); Lucy Rivers (Valerie); Sonya Sadler (Mrs. Clitherow); Leanne Summers (Girl at Swimming Pool).

LOS ANGELES TIMES, 9/19/97, Calendar/p. 16, Kevin Thomas

In "Intimate Relations," when Julie Walters' Marjorie Beasley—a relentlessly proper housewife in small-town England in the 1950s—asserts that she "would rather be dead than brazen," don't believe her. Beneath her dowdy wardrobe and unbecoming too-tight curls is a woman so consumed with sexual frustration she swiftly seduces her startled new young lodger, Harold (Rupert Graves).

Alas, Marjorie's 13-year-old daughter Joyce (Laura Sadler) is onto the affair right from the start.

Writer-director Philip Goodhew, inspired by an actual incident, goes for dark humor in a predicament that for all the outrageousness of its unraveling is not all that funny. The harder he tries to make Marjorie and Harold's affair symbolic of 1950s repression and hypocrisy, the more their story seems to lack much point.

After all, lurid events with dire consequences lurking behind middle-class propriety has been a staple of true-life British crimes since the Victorian era, if not earlier. In any event, Goodhew needed to have brought more style and point of view to the telling of a story that rapidly becomes increasingly deranged and predictably grisly yet resolutely lacks passion and poignancy.

Beasley's machinist husband, Stanley (Matthew Walker), who lost a leg in World War II, seems a nice guy, though drowning his wife's rejection of him in drink.

But Marjorie insists to Harold that in the boudoir he's "beastly." An innocent quickly in over his head, Harold has a troubled background presented with a needless vagueness that proves distracting.

In any event, the conflict between Marjorie's craving for respectability and craving for sex has clearly unhinged her. Harold hasn't a chance, and Joyce, who fancies Harold for herself, is in a position to blackmail both him and her mother. It's a wonder that this situation takes a couple of years to explode.

Although Goodhew didn't find a satisfactory style for "Intimate Relations," he certainly has inspired some compelling portrayals from his actors across the board. Marjorie is a monster but, thanks to Walters, she emerges as believably human, and Harold remains essentially sympathetic in Graves' portrayal of him.

Ironically, the actual story of the real-life "Harold," who is now in his 70s, is infinitely more sinister and bizarre.

NEW YORK POST, 9/19/97, p. 52, Thelma Adams

Chalk up another high-gloss period flick about female sexual hysteria leading to serial mayhem. Philip Goodhew's "Intimate Relations"—a.k.a. sex—is not quite the black comedy it's billed as, or that the chirpy Rosemary Clooney tune "Come On-A My House" announces at the onset.

Within the fussily papered walls of '50s provincial England, under the stern stare of Queen Elizabeth's portrait, Marjorie Beasley (Julie Walters) is playing at the perfect mum. (Perhaps the young queen's face would have been even sterner if she had known the bent her own domestic life would take.)

Marjorie's husband, Stanley (Matthew Walker), is a shriveled, one-legged war vet.   In Goodhew's fact-based script, this leads to no end of best-foot-forward jokes.

Daughter Joyce (Laura Sadler) has a Lolita complex (another flavor of risky female lust).   The 13-year-old schoolgirl has a taste for grisly anecdotes and tastier lodgers. Enter Harold Guppy (the ubiquitous Rupert Graves).   He looks nothing like Montgomery Clift, although this suggestion sends Joyce into hysterical giggles. Back from the merchant marines, Harold's a pale, beaten, motherless lad with a history of "temper."

"Call me 'mum," Mrs. Beasley tells her new boarder.   But Marjorie's brand of mothering includes rutting in a double bed, with Joyce only a pillow away and Stanley down the hall. Harold just can't say no. Marjorie can't get enough.

What's a mother to do when her husband's touch disgusts her and, to steal a phrase from Steven Seagal, there's a "fire down below"?, What's a pubescent daughter to do when Mummy dearest brings home flesh candy and won't share?

Taken together, the Beasley women are as cuddly as "Heavenly Creatures." Flash forward to the Beasleys', with nothing but a bloody ax and a mourning Stanley.

Walters tries—and fails—to breathe sympathetic angst into her waxwork monster in apron and pin curls. Sorry, Joyce, but Graves, as sulky as he is, is no Clift, a smoldering sexual object divided against himself.

Harold's thwarted desire to recreate the family he never had with the Beasleys seems just the thinnest excuse for a sex-and-sicko story that needn't be retold, but which Goodhew presents as if it were the hottest of National Enquirer scoops.

"Intimate Relations" lets the genie of women's sexual desire out of the bottle—and then offers a damn good argument for bottling it up.

NEWSDAY, 9/19/97, Part II/p. B10, John Anderson

Based on a true story—but fascinating just the same—"Intimate Relations" pulls off the Hitchcockian trick of mining malevolence out of the mundane. But the latent evil doesn't just rest in teacups or rocking chairs. It infects the entire war-reeling, middle-class world of suburban England.

It's 1954, and such stalwart women as Marjorie Beasley (Julie Walters) are keeping hearth and home together, despite shortages and angst. Fourteen-year-old Joyce (Laura Sadler)—"My late blessing!"—is her joy; her husband, Stanley (Matthew Walker), a hero of the war, lives on his memories. But memories don't pay out, except at the pub. So Marjorie decides to take in a lodger. And, she chooses Harold Guppy (Rupert Graves).

Harold is a British Navy vet, the good-looking product of various institutions beginning at age 10, when his mother sent him off for "behavioral problems"—Harold actually has a metabolic malfunction that he keeps in check with candy. Marjorie first looks at Harold like he's Jack Henry Abbott. Then she starts to see him as Montgomery Clift. And from here, the plot is thickened liberally with unspeakable practices and unnatural acts.

It's a kind of counter-feminist construct: Not only has Harold been abandoned by his mother, but her legacy to him is his violent blood-sugar disorder. He's been rejected by his sister-in-law Iris (Elizabeth McKechnie). And he's being metaphorically consumed by his sexually insatiable landlady.   Harold—whom we must view as innocent by reason of body chemistry and sociology—is a child who's been thrown to the wolves.

"Intimate Relations"—which during the shooting was apparently referred to as "Disgusting Familiarities" by the cast and crew—seethes with latent madness under its apron and candy. As Harold tries unsuccessfully to escape Marjorie's tentacles, we see that he cannot resist, and in fact cannot live without, an imposed existence. And we see, as Joyce tries to seduce him too, and Stanley finally gets a clue, the film spiraling uncontrollably toward something dreadful.

Although it's funny—Walters is peerless as an arsenic-dispensing Martha Stewart—"Intimate Relations" is also about being inarticulate. No one can talk about sex, no one can talk about work, and no one can talk about the war. If any one ever did, it would probably open up a floodgate of therapeutic emotion. But they all remain mute. And the atmosphere remains perfectly lethal.

SIGHT AND SOUND, 7/97, p. 42, Claire Monk

1954. Harold Guppy, a young sailor estranged from his family since he was sent away to reform school as a child, drifts to a small English town hoping to renew ties with his brother Maurice. Rebuffed by Maurice's wife Iris, he finds lodgings with middle-aged Marjorie Beasley, the wife of Stanley, a World War I veteran and amputee, and the mother of 12-year-old Joyce.

The Beasleys seem normal, although Marjorie shares a bedroom with Joyce and consigns Stanley to the boxroom, having denied him sex for ten years on alleged medical grounds. Marjorie welcomes Harold, giving him the largest bedroom and insisting that he calls her "Mum". Joyce too takes a fancy to him. But after Joyce's thirteenth birthday party, Marjorie manipulates her way into Harold's bed. Joyce overhears them and insists on joining them, threatening to tell Stanley if they refuse. Marjorie lets her stay, and the pair persuade themselves that Joyce is asleep during their sexual encounter, although she is not.

The situation continues. Though enjoying sex with Marjorie, Harold starts to feel worn down and soon Joyce blackmails him into spending the night with her in a hotel. Harold angrily complies, but cruelly manipulates Joyce's fantasies in a vain attempt to make her leave him alone. To escape, he joins the Army and ignores Marjorie's letters. Hearing that he is engaged, she threatens that if he doesn't come 'home' Joyce will report his hotel 'assault' to the police. Harold returns, but Marjorie's pledge that he will now be her 'son' and not her lover proves false. Trapped and abused, he becomes increasingly angry and violent, and Joyce redoubles her threats.

After a fight with Harold, Stanley leaves, but Marjorie insists he must be brought back to preserve appearances. Harold loses his temper, and Marjorie throws him out, but she is soon stalking him again. Cracking up, he touches up a girl at a swimming bath and returns to Marjorie. But on a picnic, he threatens to report her to the police. Marjorie starts touching him but Joyce attacks her with an axe. Marjorie tries to stab Harold, but he stabs her to death. Joyce tries to kill him and he kills her too. His subsequent suicide attempt fails and a caption tells us that Harold was imprisoned for life.

Writer-director Philip Goodhew's darkly impressive debut feature takes its story from a forgotten mid-50s murder case and the newspaper cuttings about it (with all the names changed). *Intimate Relations* therefore differs significantly from other recent British films which have treated the 50s as synonymous with real-life murder (from *The Young Poisoner's Handbook* to *"Let Him Have It"* to *Dance with a Stranger*) in that its subject-case has no lasting notoriety. Instead it is a film in which the relationship of fiction to fact is flagged from the outset as unstable and problematic.

The film's factual roots nevertheless impose certain structural choices. *Intimate Relations* has a bloody denouement which few fiction screenwriters could have dreamed up. Real life has also supplied Goodhew with characters that would have delighted Joe Orton: arch-conservative housewife Marjorie, her innocent but sexually curious underage daughter Joyce, and their lodger Harold, who, blackmailed into serving as Marjorie's sex-slave and worn down by the sexual demands of both women, eventually murders them. One can see why Julie Walters leapt at the role of Marjorie, rich in ironies and one-liners, but markedly less sympathetic than her usual personae.

Goodhew's treatment of his material fits the bizarre quality of these real-life ingredients and finds them ripe for satire. The film's disturbing comic power and escalating surrealism are intensified his systematic exploitation of instabilities of narrative, psychology and behaviour: so much so that repeat viewings reveal new uncertainties. The slow-burning insinuation that Joyce was fathered by one of Marjorie's wartime lodgers is an obvious example.

This audience-teasing is fitting, for *Intimate Relations* is a film about the construction of social and sexual fictions; a vicious tragicomedy about characters—and a society—committed to maintaining deceptive appearances and blanking out the resulting damage. "The truth?" Marjorie screams at Harold, "The truth frightens everybody to death!" The film's comic moments are peppered with the language of this denial. When Marjorie compliments Harold on his 'distinguished' pajamas, she means she wants to tear them off. When she encourages Harold to call her "Mum", she is priming him for sexual subordination—a situation prefigured early on when Harold points out that her dog, a macho-looking boxer named Princess, is actually a boy. "Yes," she replies, "but he doesn't know that." It is such linguistic dishonesties which later permit Harold to deny to Stanley that he has been having "intimate relations" with Marjorie: it could be argued that he's not lying, just rejecting a coy euphemism.

The true object of this satire isn't hard to fathom. For all its deft historical references (Grace Kelly, Ruth Ellis and the Cold War) and reconstruction of the age of chintz, *Intimate Relations* serves as a razor-sharp condemnation not of the historical 50s but of the mythic 50s so mistily invoked by John Major in his calls for a return to "decency" and "family values". Like Major, Marjorie pays lip-service to decency and morals, most notably when her part-time dry-cleaning job requires her to bring "a woman's touch" to sacking a pregnant teenage colleague—a plot detail juxtaposed with 13-year-old Joyce's attempt to get Harold into bed.

If Joyce's naive—and unrequited—sexual pursuit of her mother's lover can be read as a surreal inversion of the *Lolita* story, it nevertheless skirts close to taboo. Here, Goodhew is fortunate in his choice of actors. As Joyce, 14-year-old Laura Sadler is not at all coquettish in portraying early-teen sexual directness and stubbornness. The unshown details of her spiralling disturbance—interference with her best friend and incessant masturbation—acknowledge the active sexuality of teenage girls. Yet when Harold confronts Joyce in a hotel bed and voices her fantasies about him at a length which could be misconstrued as verbal foreplay—only to throw them back in her face—she reacts as a scared child.

It's an extraordinary scene, a risk which only works because of the audacity and control of Rupert Graves as Harold. Graves (voted Best Actor at the Montreal Film Festival for the film) is outstanding in a deeply ambiguous characterisation. Harold's desire for mothering makes him a complicit participant rather than an innocent victim of Marjorie's seduction/abuse, and as the film descends into horror, his violence towards Joyce becomes as much of a betrayal of her as her mother's evasions. Conversely, while it is difficult not to respond to Marjorie as an ogre, Walters works hard to make us understand that she too is a victim of the repressive politics her character represents.

As Harold becomes increasingly unable to tolerate all that Marjorie stands for, his sexual language becomes more explicit, as if he's stepped out of the 50s setting to denounce hypocrisy and repression from the present. If this aspect of the film is calculated to enrage the Marjories of today, one hopes it will also shake up the critics who seem incapable of writing about Graves without tying him down to two films he made for James Ivory ten years ago. After all, as the lyrics of *Intimate Relations'* closing song—*This Old House*—suggest, we wouldn't really want to live in the past.

VILLAGE VOICE, 9/23/97, p. 90, Gary Susman

Based on a real-life crime that shocked England in the 1950s, *Intimate Relations* stars Rupert Graves as Harold Guppy (the names have been changed to protect the guilty), a drifter with a history of mental illness, who finds lodging with Marjorie Beasley, a frumpy, middle-aged housewife who burns with hidden passions (Julie Walters, of course).

Married to a much older man who lost a leg in World War I, Marjorie quickly sets about seducing Harold. Once Marjorie's sexually curious 14-year-old daughter catches wind of their affair, Harold is trapped in a web of blackmail. He tries to extricate himself from the manipulative mother and daughter, with ultimately violent results. At first writer-director Philip Goodhew satirizes English repression and self-delusion, playing the situation as a black farce and allowing Marjorie to justify her hypocrisy with lines like "It's not a lie. It's a deception." His tone shifts, however, to the tediously didactic, hammering home the point that this tragedy might have been avoided if the English could speak frankly about sex. Moreover, Goodhew goes far too easy on Harold (in real life, a recidivist violent offender), dismissing his short temper as the effect of occasionally low blood sugar. Therein lies Goodhew's most novel contribution to social-problem cinema: the not-enough-Twinkies defense.

Also reviewed In:
CHICAGO TRIBUNE, 9/26/97, Friday/p. O, Mark Caro
NEW YORK TIMES, 9/19/97, p. E22, Janet Maslin
NEW YORKER, 9/15/97, p. 93, Daphne Merkin
VARIETY, 6/17-23/96, p. 53, Ken Eisner

INVENTING THE ABBOTTS

A Fox 2000 Pictures release of an Imagine Entertainment production. *Executive Producer:* Karen Kehela and Jack Cummins. *Producer:* Ron Howard, Brian Grazer, and Janet Meyers. *Director:* Pat O'Connor. *Screenplay:* Ken Hixon. *Based on the story by:* Sue Miller. *Director of Photography:* Kenneth MacMillan. *Editor:* Ray Lovejoy. *Music:* Michael Kamen. *Music Editor:* Graham Sutton, Michael Connell, and Steve Lotwis. *Sound:* John Patrick Pritchett and (music) Stephen McLaughlin. *Sound Editor:* Don Sharpe. *Production Designer:* Gary Frutkoff. *Art Director:* William V. Ryder. *Set Designer:* Louisa S. Bonnie and Steve Cooper. *Set Decorator:* Kathryn Peters. *Set Dresser:* Karin McGaughey, Kinney K. Booker, Terry Doherty, Douglas McKay, Peter Lakoff, and Jim Jackson. *Special Effects:* Jim Fredburg. *Costumes:* Aggie Guerard Rodgers. *Make-up:* Julie Hewett. *Stunt Coordinator:* Shane Dixon and John Moio. *Running time:* 100 minutes. *MPAA Rating:* R.

CAST: Joaquin Phoenix (Doug Holt); Billy Crudup (Jacey Holt); Will Patton (Lloyd Abbott); Kathy Baker (Helen Holt); Jennifer Connelly (Eleanor Abbott); Michael Sutton (Steve); Liv Tyler (Pamela Abbott); Joanna Going (Alice Abbott); Barbara Williams (Joan Abbott); Alessandro Nivola (Peter Vanlaningham); Nicole M. Vassallo (Giggling Girl #1); Amanda Sherman (Giggling Girl #2); Shawn Hatosy (Victor); Garrett M. Brown (Webb Crosby); Julie Benz (Co-ed); Zoe McLellan (Sandy); David Frazier (Ted); Margaret Ash (Store Clerk); Clive Rosengren (Principal); Susan Barnes (Mrs. Porter); Andrea Post (Waitress); Jack Cummins (Funeral Director); David Heckendorn (Pre-Record Singer).

CHRISTIAN SCIENCE MONITOR, 4/15/97, p. 13, David Sterritt

[*Inventing the Abbotts* was reviewed jointly with *Paradise Road*; see Sterritt's review of that film.]

LOS ANGELES TIMES, 4/4/97, Calendar/p. 2, Jack Mathews

[*The following review by Jack Mathews appeared in a slightly different form in* NEWSDAY, 4/4/97, Part II/p. B9.]

In his 1995 "Circle of Friends," Irish director Pat O'Connor told the funny, sad, sensitive story of a trio of teenage girls coming of age in 1950s Ireland. It seemed to capture the confusion of the characters and the period just right—the awkward mix of romantic longing and hesitation, of eagerness and fear, of passion and guilt.

O'Connor travels the same road in "Inventing the Abbotts," but this road is in small-town America, and he lost his bearings somewhere on the transatlantic hop. He seems daunted by the American locale, or at least daunted by the detail of the period as relayed in such Hollywood melodramas as "Rebel Without a Cause" and "Peyton Place."

Those films weren't history lessons, they were allegories, one about the growing postwar generation gap, the other about the loosening moral codes in middle-class America. "Inventing the Abbotts" is pointless soap opera, anecdotal and superficial, mixing sibling rivalry, class conflict and tragic romantic entanglements in a style that mimics fictional life in the '50s more than it illuminates what went on.

Adapted by Ken Hixon ("Grandview, U.S.A from Sue Miller's short story, "Inventing the Abbotts" is the story of the families Holt and Abbott, the poor and the rich of Haley, Ill., 1957-60. The Holts are the widow schoolteacher Helen (Kathy Baker) and her sons Jacey (Billy Crudup) and Doug (Joaquin Phoenix). The Abbotts are office-equipment magnate Lloyd (Will Patton), his resigned wife, Joan (Barbara Williams), and their three daughters, Alice (Joanna Going), Eleanor (Jennifer Connelly) and Pamela (Liv Tyler).

In the beginning of his nearly nonstop voice-over narration, Doug Holt tells us that his older brother is obsessed with the Abbotts, and as the story unfolds, we learn why. Many years earlier, the family traded a patent for a suspension file drawer to Lloyd Abbott for a 1937 Dodge, which the boys' dad then drove to his death on an ice-covered lake on a dare-devil bet. Lloyd, meanwhile, got filthy rich on the Holts' patent, and—if the town's most enduring rumor is true—had a long affair with his widow.

All of which has left Jacey determined to destroy Lloyd, by infiltrating the family through his daughters. First, he has an affair with middle-sister Eleanor, who has already slept with half the senior class of Haley High. Then with the oldest, insecure Alice, after she separates from her husband. And finally, with virginal Pamela.

Each of these triumphs creates its own melodrama, particularly the one over Pamela, who happens to be the girl of Doug's dreams. Doug's relationship with Pamela, from friendship to gawky romance to undying love, is the most promising in the story, but when Jacey's predatory pattern reaches her, it threatens to destroy his own family.

And there you go, as the world turns ...

"Inventing the Abbotts" has none of the humor or interludes of exhilaration in "Circle of Friends." The Holt boys and the Abbott girls are despairing enough to lower the morale at the Heartbreak Hotel. Eleanor, played with unselfconscious raunchiness by Connelly, seems to be having a good time until we realize she's only sleeping around to punish her overbearing father.

Given the one-note nature of their characters, the attractive young cast makes this more tolerable than it might be, and Baker has some fine moments as the resilient Helen Holt. But anyone looking for enlightenment about the '50s, or just a little entertainment, would have better luck at the video store.

NEW YORK, 4/21/97, p. 51, David Denby

Once in a while you meet an appealing man in his late twenties or early thirties who is charming but mysteriously cut off and hidden in some way. Among other things, the lovely new Pat O'Connor movie, *Inventing the Abbotts* shows you the early life of one such cipher. Jacey Holt (Billy Crudup) is a good-looking teenager in the Elvis-permeated late fifties—the time when good-looking American teenagers first realized the world belonged to them. But Jacey carries a sense of grievance that he only half understands. In small-town Illinois, he lives on the wrong side of the tracks: His father is dead, his mother is a teacher, and he has to work in a garage to make money. Jacey becomes obsessed with three wealthy sisters, the Abbott girls, all tall and beautiful, and he sleeps with first one and then another, causing havoc with each affair. He's not in love with any of them; he doesn't even see the girls clearly. He has "invented" them in his head, as something to conquer. *Inventing the Abbotts,* based on a short story by Sue Miller (Ken Hixon did the adaptation), has a theme out of Theodore Dreiser. It's one of the rare American movies that portray the sex drive of a young man as something integrally related to class and social ambition. Jacey is literally consumed by his antagonisms.

We see Jacey through the eyes of his younger and gentler brother, Doug (Joaquin Phoenix), who initially admires Jacey's skills with women and then comes to pity his brother. The two actors go well together. Crudup has straight black hair, dark eyes, and a strong jaw: he's tight and aggressive. Joaquin Phoenix is less conventionally handsome—more retiring and a little hangdog, with a scarred lip but hungry eyes. In the second half of the movie, his Doug slides very slowly into a relationship with the youngest Abbott daughter, Pamela, played by the strapping Liv Tyler, who is awkwardly beautiful. With her mouth primly closed—Pam doesn't want to be taken as a "fast" girl like her older sister Eleanor (Jennifer Connelly)—Tyler does a convincing impersonation of a swan hiding as an ugly duckling. Tyler has a big upper lip, and when she kisses Phoenix, the two of them, with their funny lips, look happily mated.

The charm of the movie, as you may have gathered, lies in its attention to all the hesitations, longings, and emotional transgressions of fifties teen life—a time when sex was still a danger, even a kind of crime, and class mattered a great deal yet still could be transcended by love.

Inventing the Abbotts is slow and a little square; it doesn't have anything of the emotional rawness or tumult of *Rebel Without a Cause* or *East of Eden* or *Splendor in the Grass* the most famous movies about teens actually made in the fifties (or just after), by Nicholas Ray and Elia Kazan. The Irish director Pat O'Connor *(Cal, Circle of Friends)* lacks fire (a fight between Crudup and Phoenix is pretty much a joke), And O'Connor is so eager to maintain an intimate scale that he misses some obvious occasions for glamour and excitement—refusing to photograph the three sisters together, for instance, so we could savor and compare them as the two brothers do. The action is surrounded by voice-over narration delivered by the mature Doug looking back from some safe and wise vantage point—an inherently moralistic device, since he's the "good" brother and our response to Jacey is controlled first by Doug's jealousy and then by his contempt (it might have worked better to alternate Doug and Jacey looking back). It's one thing to be led toward virtue, another to be coerced into it.

Still, this is an intelligent and absorbing romantic drama, beautifully mounted, emotionally saturated. I relaxed into it, grateful to have my tempo slowed down. And it's a strong movie—not soft or nostalgic but respectful of fifties America as a societyv more clearly structured than our own. I enjoyed all the richly colored observation of social life at parties, on porches, and in cars in the time of America's fabled "troubled" adolescents, when the new consumer confidence was beginning to dissolve the wartime austerities. The movie captures the strain, the uncertainty of a country shifting its values.

The past still mattered then: Much of the story falls out of events that took place between the kids' parents a generation earlier. As the boys' mother, Kathy Baker brings a sense of humor to a limited role. She talks straight to her teenage sons, as if they were independent men whose ornery quirks had to be respected. Things haven't gone easily for her character, and Baker is stoic about it; she can't remake her life or help her hyper-ambitious son, who is determined to screw his way into the upper middle class. And Billy Crudup, cool but intense, is a possible star presence. He gives a wary, intriguing performance: The older Jacey gets, the more remote Crudup seems, the less comprehensible to himself. Jacey winds up hurting a lot of people and he doesn't know why. As Doug comes out of his shell, Jacey retires into one—for life, we think.

NEW YORK POST, 4/4/97, p. 45, Thelma Adams

"Inventing the Abbotts" has the geometry of conventional female family fiction. Based on a Sue Miller story, the characters are laid out like the intersection of Main Street and Elm in a generic Midwestern town.

Up the hill are the three rich, beautiful Abbott sisters: the good one, the bad one and the forgotten one (Joanna Going, Jennifer Connelly and Liv Tyler). Across the tracks are the two darkly handsome Holt brothers with blue-collar pasts and college cardigan futures. They're split between the angry, sexy one (Billy Crudup) and the sulky, sensitive narrator (Joaquin Phoenix).

It's the twilight of the '50s in Middle America and the quintet are obsessed wiih each other. Over three crucial coming of-age years and the revelation of one deep, dark family secret that links the Abbotts and the Holts—and a fair amount of cross-pollination for an era when young women still wore girdles—we laugh, we cry, we fall in love with one another again.

As Doug Holt (Phoenix) telegraphs the audience, if the Abbotts hadn't existed, his older brother Jacey (Crudup) would have invented them. It's a corny thing to say about people who were made up to begin with, but at least it explains the title.

For everything that is passe and predictable about this period weepie with its picture-perfect automobiles and overlit soda shops, Pat O'Connor throws himself—and the audience—into the movie as if it had never been done before. The alchemy that made the Irishman's "Circle of Friends" a hit, will surely make "Inventing the Abbotts" the season's date movie.

Crudup lends a method moodiness to his Midwestern seducer with a sympathetic psychological profile. By the bittersweet ending, screenwriter Ken Hixon double knots Jacey's motivations—a deep neediness caused by his father's early death and mother's subsequent grief.

To watch Crudup button and unbutton his gas jockey work shirts is to smell gasoline and Old Spice and feel flushed. (Ironically, it's Billy's older brother, Tommy, soon to join the Rosie O'Donnell show, who's the looker in the family.)

Phoenix is equally good. His touch is gentler than the material. The actor leavens his "social agony" with joy, rolling out a cookie-cutter role in fresh directions.

As the Abbotts' Plain Jane, Tyler gives the performance flacks have been promising in her last three films—and she has yet to deliver. She's vulnerable, gawky, expressive and intelligent. I enjoyed watching her reach deeper into herself and out to the other actors, giving them more than a mannequin to play against.

As working single Mama Holt, down-to-earth Kathy Baker makes the apron an artifact as patriotic as the American flag. She drags women back to '50s values with dignity. When she coughs over the stove, we know it isn't the cold she claims to have—but, bless O'Connor and a first-rate cast, we still have hope.

SIGHT AND SOUND, 11/97, p. 43, Liese Spencer

Haley, Illinois. 1957. Living with their widowed mother Helen, the working-class brothers Doug and Jacey Holt lust after Alice, Eleanor and Pamela, the three daughters of the wealthy Abbott family. Angry at rumours that his mother had an affair after his father's death with the Abbotts' father Lloyd and that she might have sold him a valuable patent, Jacey feels bitter resentment towards the Abbotts' wealth and envy of their lifestyle. After Alice's shotgun wedding to a young man of her social class, Jacey begins a passionate affair with the wild Eleanor before leaving for Penn College. Doug, meanwhile, begins chastely dating Pamela.

Returning from college, Jacey resumes his affair with Eleanor. After taunting her father over the liaison, Eleanor disappears one day (we learn her father has had her committed to a mental hospital). At Pamela's birthday party, Doug, after punching a rival, becomes a social pariah, but he and Pamela resume their romance after graduation. Meanwhile, Jacey pursues the separated and vulnerable Alice, who succumbs. Challenging his mother one day about the rumours of her affair with Lloyd, Doug learns that she actually rejected Lloyd's advances, but was publicly accused by his wife Joan, and found herself ostracised.

Three years later, Doug bumps into Pamela, who is at a neighbouring college. They tentatively begin seeing each other again, but Doug is heartbroken when he discovers that Jacey has had a one night stand with Pamela to revenge himself on Lloyd. When their mother dies, the brothers' rift is healed. On the way home, Doug bumps into Eleanor, now an air hostess. Doug tells Jacey that their mother never had an affair with Lloyd and shows him proof that his father, rather than his mother, sold Lloyd the patent. After visiting Lloyd to verify the story, Doug traces Pamela and the pair later marry.

Like other coming-of-age dramas set in the 50s (such as *Stand by Me*), *Inventing the Abbotts* has a narrative voice-over which lends a retrospective poignancy to its small-town soap opera. While it signals that we are visiting the memories of Doug Holt, the now grown-up teenage protagonist, it's also a device which immediately taps into a collective memory of a decade that's been repackaged repeatedly in the cinema, from *Grease* to *Peggy Sue Got Married*. What distinguishes Pat O'Connor's movie from earlier 50s-set films is the authentic way it inhabits the era, refusing to score easy laughs from old-fashioned mores, and eschewing caricatured nostalgia for a trenchant study of the American class system.

Through the wide eyes of Doug (whose vulnerable sensitivity is made palpable by Joaquin Phoenix's fragility) the film shows how the apparently perfect Abbott family, ostensibly living out a 50s suburban idyll of parties, picnics and big cars, acts as an aspirational lynchpin for his hometown of Haley. What is satisfying about this movie is its slow unravelling of this impossible ideal. At the start of the film, the Abbotts' carefree social success is marked by the eternal raising of their garden marquee to celebrate some new rite of passage for the three Abbott daughters. But when Doug gets trapped in the household after a clandestine sofa date with Pamela, he becomes an unwilling spy into the family's private discord.

While the facade has been punctured for Doug, director Pat O'Connor (*Circle of Friends*) skilfully demonstrates the way the family's wealth and status ensure that "the Abbotts" continue to exist as a powerful social construct which overshadows and influences the lives of all the protagonists. For older brother Jacey, they are a symbol of unattainable sex and wealth, and his desire for their lifestyle is displaced into the seduction of each Abbott daughter.

The repressive norm represented by the Abbott family is best realised in the powerlessness of the Abbott women against the absolute rule of patriarch Lloyd. The film starts with the pregnant eldest daughter Alice forced into what Pamela describes as "an arranged marriage", and throughout the movie female dissent is diagnosed as sickness. Lloyd ends an argument with his wife by telling her to "take one of [her] pills" and sends the sexually active Eleanor to "a nuthouse". More positive is the model of Helen Holt, played with economical pathos by Kathy Baker. As a single mother supporting herself, she appears initially to live a dignified existence beyond the confines of such social strictures, until she is slowly revealed as a lonely pariah, her life destroyed by punitive gossip.

Despite occasionally over-emphatic interpretation from the voice-over, O'Connor's subtle direction generally manages to downplay the melodrama of such revelations, with understated performances complementing Ken Hixon's spare dialogue. This easy naturalism is satisfyingly evident in the relationship between the chalk-and-cheese Holt brothers. Still soft around the edges, Phoenix's Doug is full of questions and puppyish good humour, while rebel Jacey is well portrayed by Billy Crudup as a teenager already emotionally ossified into the adult rules he despises.

In its story of five adolescents growing up in the decade that "invented" teenagers, the film certainly suggests a familiar parallel between the end of childhood and a vanished 50s America on the cusp of a national loss of innocence. But while the movie has all the trappings of period detail, they are less window dressing than unobtrusive visual comment. From the awful fairy-tale princess dresses that imprison Liv Tyler's Pamela (one memorable party frock an awful bile green explosion of starched net), to her earnest exposition of slang "Jacey's 'trig' [cool]. You know, like a pipe smoker," each detail is made to count. Best of all are the Holt boys' ping-pong matches, which act as an acceptable form of unspoken bonding between the warring brothers.

Languidly paced, *Inventing the Abbotts'* luminous photography captures the crisp orderliness of the decade's dress and manners. Interior scenes switching between the grand neo-classical Abbott household and the bare, impoverished Holt home are rhythmically illuminated by shots of the perennially sunny small town. Edited in this way, the film creates a real sense of place and social boundaries, with teenage transgressions talking place outside, away from claustrophobic domestic constraints. While anatomising the specific social hierarchies of the time, the film does not consign them to a quaint "period" past but incorporates them into a wider portrait of the way in which social power and prejudice are continually created and maintained by a collective fiction which exists beyond individuals or even facts. "Inventing the Abbotts was something everyone in Haley did," says Doug at the end of the movie, underlining the myth-making complicity of the whole town. Pat O'Connor doesn't simply deconstruct the mythologised 50s, then, but shows how even in the 50s, that dream world didn't exist anywhere except in a communal imagination.

After the bland *Circle of Friends*, O'Connor's latest work offers a deeper and more satisfyingly ambiguous character drama. Commenting on her unease with the role of "an Abbott" Pamela suggests to Doug that if she could choose between money and her father she'd like to be poor but, "life is not a cafeteria," a nice spin on the "life is like a box of chocolates" homily touted by the ersatz history of *Forrest Gump*. Still, the final, upbeat message of the film is that while the adults have got trapped in that old model, teenagers Pamela and Doug can escape it through true love, and if the rebellious Eleanor does not enjoy this kind of star-crossed lover romance, she at least survives institutionalisation, reappearing late on as that symbol of 60s freedom—the air hostess.

TIME, 4/7/97, p. 76, Richard Schickel

Testosterone is the young man's curse and the moviemaker's blessing. It imparts to the male teenager that preoccupying randiness that drives him to adventures and alliances he's going to regret someday—at best with wry embarrassment, at worst with a sense of loss verging on the tragic. Yet those rioting hormones also power tales of the young and restless that can sell profitably to the young and restless—in other words, date movies for the under-25s.

There are essentially two ways of handling this hot stuff. Gingerly—oh, all right, "sensitively"—as writer Ken Hixon and director Pat O'Connor do in *Inventing the Abbotts*. And raunchily—oh, all right, dirty-mouthed and in your face—as writer-director Kevin Smith does in *Chasing Amy*. On the whole, Smith's is the better way—funnier, smarter and a lot more truthful about the whole experience of being led around by your ... er, base instincts.

In fairness, O'Connor and Hixon have to deal with more distractions than Smith does. Their film, based on the Sue Miller short story, is a period piece, set in 1957, when, especially in small, middle-American towns—they inform us, with a rather touching air of discovery—lots of people were repressed and also more class-conscious than they should have been. Jacey Holt

(Billy Crudup) is unafflicted by the former condition, but the latter has him distinctly under the weather. He lives poor with his much nicer younger brother Doug (Joaquin Phoenix) and his widowed mother (Kathy Baker) and fixates on the wealthy Abbotts. He's convinced that Lloyd (Will Patton), the paterfamilias, got rich by stealing an invention from Jacey's late father and then had a ruinous affair with his mom. In repayment, Jacey will therefore seduce Eleanor (Jennifer Connelly), the least stable of the three Abbott daughters. And then her older sister Alice (Joanna Going), and finally her younger one (Liv Tyler), who happens to be his brother's beloved. The kid is to middle-class propriety what Genghis Khan once was to the trembling civilizations of Asia.

Yet the movie seems unaware of the depths of Jacey's sexual vengefulness. It's played as romantic rebellion, something he'll outgrow. Meantime ain't he cute, girls, all broody and snotty—just the thing to give your parents plenty of sleepless nights. What *Inventing the Abbotts* is aware of are all those lock-up-your-daughters movies of the 1950s, to which for some dotty reason it is eager to prove its superiority of understanding. But the goofy hysteria of something like *A Summer Place* was infinitely more entertaining and emotionally authentic than the distant smugness of this failed clone.

Kevin Smith, by contrast, owes nothing to nobody. As he proved with a few bucks and some black-and-white film stock in *Clerks*, he's an original, a deadpan, dead-on observer of the whole GenX mess. In *Chasing Amy*, he has moved up slightly—color film, more than one setting, scenes with actual extras in them. But he's still a guy making two-shots of people talking about their troubles, working them through on the basis of faulty information and silly suppositions.

Case in point: Holden McNeil (Ben Affleck). He draws underground comic books with his boyhood pal Banky (Jason Lee). Then he meets Alyssa (Joey Lauren Adams), also a comix artist, and falls into obsession. The problem is, she's a lesbian. Well, nobody's perfect. And, indeed, she's not perfectly gay, for eventually she succumbs to Holden's passion. This makes him feel terrific—the super-stud who has conquered the unconquerable. Except that Banky—who has some homoerotic issues of his own to sort out—discovers otherwise. Alyssa has had male lovers in the past. This devastates Holden and wrecks both relationships.

It's a sad and fiercely told story. Smith and his actors catch the stunned manner of a culture that thinks post-modernism is a synonym for postemotionalism. They're always trying to be coolly affectless about hotly affecting issues, hoping blunt, acceptant talk about sexual congress will disarm the subtle pains it always implies. This is a newer, more interesting form of innocence than the '50s kind, and when their true feelings burst through, their breakdowns and breakups are really scary. Like *Inventing the Abbotts*, this movie knows that the questing phallus is the main source of youthful romantic angst. But *Chasing Amy* doesn't try to shift the blame for its heedlessness to its times or the social structure. It doesn't believe there's magic in true love, either. That makes it a true movie rarity: a brutally honest romance. If you loved *Sleepless in Seattle,* you'll just hate it.

VILLAGE VOICE, 4/8/97, p. 79, Amy Taubin

Merely a nubile object of desire in *Stealing Beauty,* Liv Tyler turns up fat (by moviestar standards), sassy, and thoroughly her own person in *Inventing the Abbotts,* a hopelessly overblown and underdeveloped adaptation of a Sue Miller short story. Tyler and her costar Joaquin Phoenix are the only reasons to see the picture, which is set in the Midwest during the Eisenhower era and concerns the adolescent entanglements of two brothers (Phoenix and Billy Crudup) raised by a schoolteacher mom (Kathy Baker) with the three daughters (Tyler, Jennifer Connelly, and Joanna Going) of the wealthiest man in town (Will Patton).

At various moments reminiscent of *Splendor in the Grass, East of Eden,* and *The Great Gatsby, Inventing the Abbotts* is a mélange of production-design epiphanies—a red convertible streaking through waving wheat fields, a powder-blue sedan parked outside a clapboard house, a boy in a plaid cotton shirt reaching into a basement deep freeze—in desperate need of what the pros call a narrative arc. I suspect that director Pat O'Connor could tell you what the film's supposed to be about, but most of the time it's not up on the screen.

Though Crudup is surprisingly pallid as the resentful older brother, Connelly scores as the wildest of the three sisters. Phoenix proves that his haunting performance as a stupefied teen in

To Die For only tapped into a small corner of his talent. Here he's solid enough in body and spirit that his eccentricities seem a sign of mental health. He and Tyler trade quips, glances, and caresses with remarkable spontaneity. "You don't look so plain anymore," he says to Tyler, who at that moment is wearing, inexplicably, the most ill-fitting black wig ever seen in a major motion picture.

Also reviewed in:
NEW REPUBLIC, 4/28/97, p. 30, Stanley Kauffmann
NEW YORK TIMES, 4/4/97, p. C3, Janet Maslin
WASHINGTON POST, 4/4/97, Weekend/p. 44, Desson Howe

IRMA VEP

A Zeitgeist Films release of a Dacia Films production with the participation of Canal Plus. *Executive Producer:* Françoise Guglielmi. *Producer:* Georges Benayoun. *Director:* Olivier Assayas. *Screenplay (French and English with English subtitles):* Olivier Assayas. *Director of Photography:* Eric Gautier. *Editor:* Luc Barnier and Tina Baz. *Music:* Eric Michon. *Sound:* Philippe Richard, Amaury de Nexon, and (music) William Flageoller. *Sound Editor:* Marie-Christine Ratel and Marie-Christine Ruh. *Casting:* Pierre Amzallag. *Art Director:* François-Renaud Labarthe. *Special Effects:* Olivier Zenenski and Grégoire Delage. *Costumes:* Françoise Clavel. *Costumes (Irma Vep):* Jessica Doyle. *Make-up:* Nancy Tong and Isabelle Nyssen. *Stunt Coordinator:* Michel Julienne. *Running time:* 96 minutes. *MPAA Rating:* Not Rated.

CAST: Maggie Cheung (Maggie); Jean-Pierre Léaud (René Vidal); Nathalie Richard (Zoé); Antoine Basler (Journalist Who Loves John Woo); Nathalie Boutefeu (Laure); Alex Descas (Desormeaux); Dominique Faysse (Maïté); Arsinée Khanjian (American); Bernard Missile (Markus); Olivier Torres (Ferninand Moreno); Bulle Ogier (Mireille); Lou Castel (José Murano); Jacques Fieschi (Roland); Estelle Larrivaz (Switchboard Operator); Balthazar Clémenti (Robert, Assistant); Lara Cowez (Script Supervisor); Dominique Cuny (Grip); Jessica Doyle (Jessica, Roland's Friend); Sandra Faure (Sex Shop Salesperson); Catherine Ferny (Policewoman); Maryel Ferraud (Make-up Woman); Filip Forgeau (Camera Operator); Nicolas Giraudin (Unit Manager); Valérie Guy (Valérie, in Mireille's Apartment); Laurent Jacquet (Electrician); Philippe Landoulsi (Inspector); Smail Mekki (Kermor, Unit Manager); Maurice Najman (Maurice, Roland's Friend); Leslie Rain (Stuntperson); Yann Richard (Kevin); Jérôme Simonin (Property Man); Alexandra Yonnet (Lili, Markus's Friend); Pierre Amzallag (Emergency Doctor); Françoise Clavel (René's wife); Françoise Guglielmi (Producer); Odile Horion (Zoe's Assistant); Françoise-Renaud Labarthe (TV Cameraman); Alain Martin (Boy at "Cafe des Oiseaux"); Guy Patrick Sainderichin (TV Dignitary); Willy Martin (Bellboy).

LOS ANGELES TIMES, 5/16/97, Calendar/p. 12, Kevin Thomas

Olivier Assayas' amusing "Irma Vep" is an homage to radiant and versatile Hong Kong star Maggie Cheung—and a blast at contemporary French filmmaking. Assayas displays an intimate, informal style and a sharp sense of proportion that allows him to have some fun, score some points and then wrap it all up before overstaying his welcome. "Irma Vep" is as effortless as a shrug and boasts a film buff's dream cast.

Jean-Pierre Léaud, all but unintelligible in English (which doesn't much matter, as it turns out), plays a washed-up, burnt-out New Wave director who has a not-bad idea: to star Cheung in a film based on Louis Feuillade's 1915 serial "Les Vampires." Cheung would play Feuillade's super-villainess Irma Vep (an anagram for Vampire).

Cheung has the figure for a black latex bodysuit and head mask—Irma's standard gear—in which only her expressive eyes and mouth are visible, and is an action star as well as splendid actress. But from the moment Cheung, who is in effect playing herself, arrives in Paris, nothing goes right.

The rushes that Léaud's René Vidal manages to shoot before experiencing a major nervous breakdown look pretty good, but there's no sense that Vidal is ever really in control of his set, and it swiftly becomes doubtful that he'll ever return to it. Already lots of nasty stuff is happening. Nathalie Richard's Zoé, the production's conscientious, hyper wardrobe mistress, is a lesbian instantly smitten with the gorgeous Cheung—and almost as quickly humiliated when a film executive's harebrained wife (Bulle Ogier) takes it upon herself to inform Cheung of Zoé's attraction to her.

Already treated like dirt by the company"s humorless female assistant director, a gossip and rumormonger of world-class maliciousness, poor Zoé now confronts the widespread assumption that she and Cheung have already commenced an affair. The truth is that Zoé is hesitant even to make the slightest pass at the star, who she assumes is straight.

The new "Les Vampires" is swiftly swamped in backbiting, turf-defending and an awesome obliviousness to Cheung, who's self-possessed, professional and uncomplaining. In a deliciously suspenseful sequence that is quintessential Feuillade, Cheung is not above discovering for herself whether she's up to playing Irma.

A couple of other characters deserve mentioning: Antoine Basler's obnoxious journalist who, while interviewing Cheung, sounds off on the French cinema, past and present, for not being more commercial and eagerly trashes one of the greatest national cinemas in history.

Then there's Lou Castel, a '60s survivor as worn-looking as Léaud's director, as the director lined up to replace him. In a grand dismissive gesture that can only be described as racist, he proclaims he would not have a Chinese playing Irma Vep, who he proclaims is "the Paris underworld! Arletty!"—as if Irma were Marie Antoinette or Sarah Bernhardt. (Actually, Cheung has a certain resemblance to Musidora, the original Vep.) As tumult takes over, Assayas pulls back to create a lovely surreal coda in homage to Cheung.

Zoé keeps saying that she sees no point in remaking Feuillade films, but it has been done several times, never so poignantly as with Georges Franju's 1964 "Judex."

NEW YORK, 5/5/97, p. 79, David Denby

Irma Vep, the new film by the extraordinarily talented French director Olivier Assayas, was shot in four weeks, and it has the intensity, the restless power, the desperation and sheer exhilaration of a single continuous burst of energy. Like Truffaut's *Day for Night* (1973), this is a movie about the making of a movie. *Day for Night* is charming and rather soft: The film we see being made in Nice—a trivial romantic melodrama called *Meet Pamela*—suffers all sorts of problems on the set, but by the time the film wraps, the troubles have been resolved and the crew disperses, peaceful and content. Truffaut wound up celebrating the purposeful chaos of filmmaking, the commonplace pleasures of illusion. *Irma Vep*, I suppose, is a sardonic commentary on Truffaut's good humor. This time the movie within the movie—a misconceived project—stumbles, and then collapses with hilarious and almost frightening force. The chaos is not purposeful but sinister: Ineptitude, madness, and sheer malice take over. What we don't realize at first is that we are watching not a single doomed project but the general dissolution of French film culture.

Jean-Pierre Léaud, who starred in Truffaut's *The Four Hundred Blows* when he was a boy and then appeared in many other New Wave films, plays the (fictional) director René Vidal, a fading genius who has been asked by French TV to undertake a hopeless project—a remake of the French silent classic *Les Vampires*. Directed by the legendary Louis Feuillade, *Les Vampires* is about a gang of cat burglars led by the music-hall performer Irma Vep (an anagram of *vampire).* At night, the thieves scamper about the rooftops of Paris in form-fitting black hoods with slitted eyes, stealing jewelry from the decadent rich. The action is entirely fantastic, but Feuillade worked in a simple and realistic style—a mix of qualities that gives the serials an air of vagrant poetry that appealed to the Surrealists and to comic-book artists (Catwoman is an obvious descendant).

René Vidal, whose hyperintellectual meanderings suggest a second-string Jean-Luc Godard, wants to recapture Feuillade's simplicity and poetry. He casts as Irma Vep not a French actress but the star of Hong Kong quickie action movies Maggie Cheung (a real Hong Kong star), who he thinks has the grace to play the role. A sensible professional actress and good sport, Maggie is willing to do whatever is asked of her, but the poor girl gets thrown into a bog of Parisian vanity and incoherence. René cannot explain what he wants; trying for Feuillade's magical plainness, he produces only weird, dead footage, "an image of an image."

The black hooded costume—now made of latex and purchased in a sex shop—possesses a meaning it did not necessarily have in 1915. Zoé (Nathalie Richard), a lesbian costume designer, gets turned on by Maggie in what now appears to be a bondage rig. Zoé is not a bad person, but she's a born loser—a child could see this—and she becomes a kind of whipping girl, the receptacle for everyone's misery in a production spinning out of control. The mop-haired Nathalie Richard gives Zoé a recognizable desperation—her defiance, her needs provoke aggression in everyone. People feel they are almost doing her a favor by attacking her. A cigarette ever dangling from her mouth, Nathalie Richard is the comic soul of the movie, much more than Léaud, who looks awful and is grimly eccentric (and all too convincing) as the addled René.

Olivier Assayas, who both wrote and directed, keeps the personal and professional disasters moving at an extraordinary pace, and the movie becomes a kind of comedy of catastrophe. Assayas is a whiz with the moving camera: People pass in and out of the frame, and we hear fragments of conversation, only to pick up other conversations as the camera moves around or circles back to people seen earlier in the shot. (Some of these virtuoso shots rival the best of Robert Altman's work.) In all, I don't see how any French person could see this movie without wincing: Assayas seems to be getting at widely shared character flaws—egotism and vanity as well as intellectual pretension substituting for creativity. From the evidence of *Irma Vep*, making a movie in France these days is like going to a very bad party.

The French have a great culture, a great history, but they are in a state of futility. A filmmaking industry that was both artistically innovative and financially resourceful now lies in ruins, destroyed by vanity, inconsequence, and the philistine exuberance of American entertainment, which both enrages the French and leaves them sick with envy: They can't make our movies, and increasingly they can't make their own. René Vidal is so stricken when he sees the early rushes of his Feuillade imitation that he his a nervous breakdown, retreating into insanity.

It is left to his star, Maggie Cheung, to keep things going. In a mysterious scene, Maggie actually becomes a cat burglar at her hotel, entering the room of a woman who lies naked on a bed talking to her lover on the phone. Suddenly Maggie is running across rooftops with jewelry, glistening in the rain, looking evil in her weird costume. For a moment, the movie—Assayas's movie—turns wildly beautiful and savage in Feuillade's style. When we return to the workaday world of squabbling actor and technicians, we feel the decline from magic to realism. In the end, Assayas both deconstructs illusion and creates it all over again. *Irma Vep* may be a bitter lament over a dead art form, but movie itself is an extraordinary sign of life—for the French, one hopes, a collective cleansing of the soul.

NEW YORK POST, 4/30/97, p. 40, Thelma Adams

"Irma Rep" portrays French cinema on the verge of a nervous breakdown—or, at least, a hissy fit.

In Olivier Assayas' black comedy, director Rene Vidal (Francois Truffaut's cinematic alter-ego, Jean-Pierre Leaud) is closer to meltdown than Tommy Lee Jones in "Volcano."

Played by Leaud with a weary, whispered tyranny, the burnt-out French director is remaking Feuillade's classic silent serial "Les Vampires." It's like wanting to remake "Birth of a Nation"—a cinematic unholy grail.

It doesn't inspire confidence that the blasphemous Vidal has cast Hong Kong action star Maggie ("Heroic Trio") Cheung as the French icon Irma Vep (an anagram for "vampire"). Vep is not a bloodsucker, but an amoral queen of thieves who leaps from gig to gig, lover to lover, in a black catsuit.

Casting Cheung seems to purists like smearing tofu on a baguette. But from the moment the Asian superstar arrives on the set, playing herself, she commands the center of the film within a film and "Irma Vep."

On the verge of international stardom, Cheung is a consummate professional, a subtle actress with a deceptive surface simplicity.

Those around Cheung project their desires on her agile figure as if it were a rice-paper screen. As the wardrobe woman Zoe (Natalie Richard) says: "You want to play with her. She's like a plastic toy."

But Cheung's more than an action figure. At night she roams the halls of her hotel, sleepless, uneasy, wearing her latex catsuit, slinking into strangers' rooms, stealing their privacy as well as their jewels. Cheung comes to animate the mystery that is Vep—feminine, unknowable, sensual, decisive, a jump ahead.

"Irma Vep" was a darling of the 1996 New York Film Festival. With a mock casualness, it sharply addresses the convergence of Asian, American and French cinema, with a nod to the Canadian fringe (Atom Egoyan's wife, Arsinee Khanjian, has a nude cameo).

"Vep" skewers and celebrates the chaos that is French filmmaking. It also acts as an equal-opportunity basher, tweaking "Batman" and American excess, John Woo and the exaltation of violence, and French navel-gazing.

As Vidal collapses emotionally and spiritually, we discover that his casting of Maggie was indeed the perfect choice. French cinema is dead. Long live French cinema!

SIGHT AND SOUND, 3/97, p. 51, Chris Darke

Paris, the present. Actress Maggie Cheung arrives three days late at a film company's offices. Director René Vidal wants her to play Irma Vep in a television remake of the French silent serial film *Les Vampires*. Maggie tries on her black latex costume and meets Zoé, the costumier. During the first day's shooting, Zoé argues with the production assistant, Maité. After seeing the dailies, Vidal walks out in disgust. Zoé takes Maggie to a friend's apartment for a meal. Zoé confides in Mireille, her older friend, that she finds Maggie attractive and believes the attraction is mutual. To Zoé's chagrin, Mireille tells Maggie, who is amused and a little shocked.

Back at her hotel, Maggie finds that Vidal has been calling her. She goes to Vidal's apartment. The police are there: he has attacked his wife and is under sedation. He tells Maggie that he despairs of their film. She prowls the corridors of her hotel in her Irma Vep costume, creeps into a woman's room and steals a piece of jewellery. Escaping onto the roof, she drops the jewel over the edge. When she is late on-set the next morning, Maité blames Zoé. Laure, another actress, tells Zoé that Maité told her Zoé had just slept with Maggie. Zoé is furious. Laure mentions that another director, José Murano, called her. Vidal does not appear and the day's shooting is cancelled.

Laure meets José Murano. He tells her Vidal has had a breakdown and that he's been asked to step in. Murano wants to replace Maggie and offers Laure the role of Irma Vep. Later, Maggie and Zoé drive to a nightclub and Maggie recounts her meeting with Vidal. She leaves for the US the next day. Murano watches the footage that Vidal has shot and edited.

Shot in four weeks on a minuscule budget and written by director Olivier Assayas for the Hong Kong action star Maggie Cheung, *Irma Vep* explodes like a firework over its thematic terrain: a mourning for cinema's 'innocent' past. In a film about the making of a television film, Cheung plays herself. She is cast by a burnt-out, middle-aged French auteur René Vidal (Jean-Pierre Léaud) to play Irma Vep, the famous black-clad Parisian criminal, in a remake of the 1915 French silent serial *Les Vampires* (directed by Louis Feuillade). Vidal's *idée fixe* is of Musidora, the original Irma Vep, as an icon of cinema grace and of Feuillade as cinema's brilliant primitive. But he knows that his attempt to revive their purity is little more than a futile seance. Assayas seems to share Vidal's obsessions, yet he seeds this film with telling glimpses of images that suggest that such 'innocence' is still possible. A video screening of the 1968 militant film *Classe de lutte* stands for political purity and Vidal's own terminal film-poem is its poetic equivalent. Although petty rivalries and myopic arrogance characterise the depictions of film people here, Cheung herself is grace incarnate, deliberately demystifying her star persona. When Vidal describes her, in her Hong Kong action persona, as being "like an acrobat," she tells him, "It's all done by stunt men." Yet she displays a touching faith in Vidal, whose intuition about her (which is also Asssayas') proves correct: in her black latex catsuit, she does make an iconic and slinky Irma. Assayas succeeds where the fictional Vidal fails because he can use Vidal as a surrogate conscience to shoulder the weight of film history for him. Where Vidal is creatively exhausted by his fidelity to the past, Assayas can be an urgent force. *Irma Vep* doesn't work out its mourning for cinema with the romantic nostalgia of Godard's *Le Mépris* or *Passion,* it's more like the Mexican Day of the Dead: remembrance as an act of celebration. The theme of cinema history as a dead weight on modern directors is crystallised by the film's ending, when the replacement director, José Murano, watches Vidal's edited footage: a viciously experimental squall of film. Shots of Maggie-as-Irma are bleached-out, out-of-focus, scratched and defaced; the obsessive attention paid to every frame reflects Vidal's state of mind. He's like a child who colours in every letter of a favourite book before trashing it. He can't possess Maggie—Irma is inviolably distant anyway—so he vengefully imposes himself like a spurned lover on his flimsy celluloid material.

Assayas isn't just using the stylistic tropes of experimental cinema for expressionistic atmosphere here. Compared to the similarly distressed opening credits of *Se7en*, there's a greater coherence to René's black-and-white film-poem. A torrent of scratches pours from Maggie's eyes. Her gaze becomes a visual fusillade echoing down from Feuillade's day. On the one hand, the sequence expresses the impossibility of rejuvenating silent cinema's 'innocence'—a theme alluded to when Vidal damns the idea of the television remake of *Les Vampires* as "blasphemy". On the other hand it's about the mystery of cinema's attraction (the television film is entitled *Les yeux qui fascinent*). Cheung says: "Desire. It's what we make films with." But it's also what makes us *watch* films. This circuit of desire unites those who cast lifelike shadows on a wall with an audience that re-animates them in their heads.

Another circuit of desire is played out and projected on and off the film set. Zoé (Nathalie Richard), the bisexual costumier, develops a crush on Maggie; Maité, (Dominique Faysse) the production assistant, attempts to poison Maggie's attitude to Zoé; Mireille vicariously exploits Zoé's attraction to Maggie and Vidal himself harbours barely suppressed desires for his lead. When Maggie prowls the hotel corridors in her Irma Vep outfit and steals jewellery from a room, she's not only losing herself in a character she'll never perform, she's also enacting the play of desire that the film so effortlessly works through.

Formerly a critic on *Cahiers du cinéma*, Assayas has made five films before *Irma Vep*. His last, *L'eau froide* (1994) was a particularly impressive example of intimate portraiture. But *Irma Vep* is an experiment that has paid real dividends. Assayas must now be seen as one of the most exciting European filmmakers currently at work.

VILLAGE VOICE, 5/6/97, p. 79, J. Hoberman

The agony and the ecstasy of making a movie isn't the freshest croissant in the *café* but Olivier Assayas's *Irma Vep* sure makes it seem so. This latest feature by the 42-year-old festival-god was shot, in Super 16, like an on-set doctumentary—at once self-deprecating and megalomaniacal, it's a jagged, speedy rap fueled by cigarettes, coffee, and insomnia.

A wry and witty piece of work, *Irma Vep* puts business first, holds the art for last, and keeps stardom at center screen. Hong Kong action diva Maggie Cheung descends, straight from a 12-hour flight, into a churning maelstrom of production-assistant hysteria. Cheung, known as Maggie and essentially playing herself, has arrived in Paris to take the title role of the black-clad cat burglar *Irma Vep* in a remake of Louis Feuillade's 1915 serial, *Les Vampires*. The original cult film, a baroquely paranoid tale of criminal conspiracy, is to be updated, with some trepidation, by René Vidal, a burnt-out new wave *auteur* (Jean-Pierre Léaud).

For a French cineaste, *Les Vampires* is a cultural childhood lost—representing both an impossible innocence and a virtually forgotten commercial dominance—and *Irma Vep* has the atmosphere of a cheerful haunted house. René whispers cryptic phrases—he's his own oracle—while Léaud's mere presence effectively populates the movie with spectral performances for Godard and Truffaut, especially in the latter's movie-making movie *Day for Night*. (When, at the end of the proverbial day, a gone-to-seed Lou Castel appears as another washed-up '60s director, it allows Assayas a poltergeist reference to R. W Fassbinder's nastier production paean, *Beware of a Holy Whore*.)

René is acutely aware that it is impossible to recreate Feuillade's unselfconscious poetry (as if to demonstrate this, *Irma Vep*'s least successful sequence has Maggie getting into character—slinking around her hotel and stealing a necklace) but, unburdened by such history, his star radiates sweetness and grace. Maggie is enthusiastic, hardworking, modest, and—never less than professional—somewhat baffled by the backbiting antics of her French colleagues. At the same time, as poured into her latex bondage suit, she's the universal fetish object of desire. "You want to touch her, play with her— she's like a plastic toy," the production's hyperfrazzled AC/DC costumier Zoë (Nathalie Richard) confides. This longing is compounded by interpolated scenes of the Feuillade original (Irma's abduction and unmasking), as well as the presence of Maggie's body double also in black latex.

Trapped in the phantom zone, temperamental René storms imperiously out from a screening of his dailies leaving his colleagues in consternation and Maggie abandoned, forced to catch a ride to a crew party on the back of Zoë's moped. Anyone who has seen Assayas's sensational *Cold Water* knows that this director can choreograph a bacchanal. But in the theory-crazed world of *Irma Vep*, the revelers can't stop talking about movies—or even looking at them. Someone has commandeered the VCR to show the post May '68 faux Godard agitprop *Classe de lutte,* an even stranger fossil than *Les Vampires*—as well as another movie about movies. The image of a flickering Steenbeck image is underscored by the militant slogan: "Cinema is not magic: it is a technique and a science."

A different sort of cine-romantic, Assayas may beg to differ with that Marxist formulation although, as Maggie is gracious enough to demystify her own stardom, so *Irma Vep* exudes a restrained cinephilia that repeatedly questions itself. While waiting for René to return, Maggie is interviewed by an obnoxious French film buff who drones on (in English) in praise of John Woo ("*Bullet in the Head*—I think it's a great, great film") and Arnold Schwarzenegger, dismissing French cinema as snobbish, passé, and "nombrilistic" (a wonderful Franglaise coinage for "navel-gazing").

The self-parody is layered—in his days with *Cahiers du Cinéma,* Assayas edited the special issues "Made in U.S.A.' and "Made in Hong Kong"and even dialectical. Just as *Irma Vep* switches off between French and English (the latter serving as lingua franca), so the scene in which temperamental René admires a mad bit of HK swordplay in Maggie's vehicle *The Heroic Trio* also serves to play "natural" Maggie off his mannered postures. Richly hybrid, *Irma Vep* opposes decadent French auteurism with insouciant Hong Kong pop, pits Gallic play against Hollywood materialism, and juxtaposes the urge to recycle the movie past with the desire to represent the moment.

The idea of remakes extends even to the soundtrack, which includes Luna's hipster cover of the gloriously absurd Brigitte Bardot-Serge Gainsbourg duet "Bonnie and Clyde" while, as if in counterpoint, the action is interspersed with a number of gratuitous "pure" film interludes—a conversation shot on a crowded metro, a few minutes of Zoë dancing in a strobe light. (A sharp-featured, stringy-haired bundle of rangy energy, Nathalie Richard may be the nerviest presence in new French movies.) *Irma Vep* is lighter than earlier Assayas but it ends marvelously with a taste of René's vision an act of aggression that, combining kinesis and mystery, achieves a primitive essence of cinema.

I wouldn't want to jinx the miraculous revival of a low-budget, free-wheeling, film-smart French cinema but—*zut alors!*—if it's not already here. *Irma Vep* isn't only about making movies—it demonstrates that making real ones is still actually possible.

Also reviewed in:
NATION, 5/19/97, p. 35, Stuart Klawans
NEW YORK TIMES, 4/30/97, p. C16, Janet Maslin
VARIETY, 5/20-26/96, p. 35, David Rooney
WASHINGTON POST, 6/13/97, Weekend/p. 42, Desson Howe

JACKAL, THE

A Universal Pictures and Mutual Film Company release of an Alphaville production. *Executive Producer:* Terence Clegg, Hal Leiberman, Gary Levinsohn, and Mark Gordon. *Producer:* James Jacks, Sean Daniel, Michael Caton-Jones, and Kevin Jarre. *Director:* Michael Caton-Jones. *Screenplay and story:* Chuck Pfarrer. *Based on the film screenplay "The Day of The Jackal" by:*

Kenneth Ross. *Director of Photography:* Karl Walter Lindenlaub. *Editor:* Jim Clark. *Music:* Carter Burwell. *Music Editor:* Angie Rubin. *Sound:* David John and (music) Michael Farrow. *Sound Editor:* Richard King. *Casting:* Ellen Chenoweth. *Production Designer:* Michael White. *Art Director:* Ricky Eyres and John Fenner. *Set Decorator:* Kate Sullivan. *Set Dresser:* Bruce Seymour. *Special Effects:* Yves De Bono. *Visual Effects:* Tricia Owen. *Costumes:* Albert Wolsky. *Make-up:* Peter Robb-King. *Make-up (Bruce Willis):* Gerald Quist. *Make-up (Richard Gere):* Felicity Bowring. *Running time:* 123 minutes. *MPAA Rating:* R.

CAST: Bruce Willis (The Jackal); Richard Gere (Declan Mulqueen); Sidney Poitier (Carter Preston); Diane Venora (Valentina Koslova); Mathilda May (Isabella); J.K. Simmons (Witherspoon); Richard Lineback (McMurphy); John Cunningham (Donald Brown); Jack Black (Lamont); Tess Harper (The First Lady); Leslie Phillips (Woolburton); Stephen Spinella (Douglas); Sophie Okonedo (Jamaican Girl); David Hayman (Terek Murad); Steve Bassett (George Decker); Yuri Stepanov (Politovsky); Walt MacPherson (Dennehey); Ravil Isyanov (Ghazzi Murad); Maggie Castle (13 Year Old Girl); Karen Kirschenbauer (Speaker); Terrence Currier (Surgeon General); Daniel Dae Kim (Akashi); Michael Caton-Jones (Man in Video); Laura Viederman (Woman in Video); Peter Sullivan (Vasilov); Richard Cubison (General Belinko); Jim Grimshaw (Green Beret Colonel); Greg Miller (Paramedic); Bob Kingdom (Ambassador Koldin); Murphy Guyer (NSC Rep.); Philip Le Maistre (Bored Teenage Clerk); Serge Houde (Beaufres); James McCauley (CIA Rep. #1); Terry Loughlin (Davis); Victor Sobchak (Doctor); Serge Christiaenssens (Immigration Officer); Boris Boscovic (Interrogator); Ewan Bailey (Prison Guard); Danette Alberico and Debra Gano (Women with Champagne); John Bland (Dave); Pamela Poitier (Law Clerk); Jonathan Aris (Alexander Radzinski); Eddie "Bo" Smith, Jr. (Washington Cop); Larry King (Himself); Daniel Ziskie (CIA Rep. #2); Gayle Jessup (Reporter); Bill Collins (Medic); David Gene Gibbs (Pilot); James M. Helkey (Co-Pilot).

LOS ANGELES TIMES, 11/14/97, Calendar/p. 12, Kenneth Turan

Intended as a meat-and-potatoes espionage thriller, "The Jackal" has come off the stove as an overcooked stew of random ingredients. Sporadically effective, it appears not to have particularly excited the people who made it, and that lackadaisical quality is a drawback.

Inspired by the rough outline of the 1973 film "The Day of the Jackal," which focused on a plot to do away with French leader Charles de Gaulle, "The Jackal" probably sounded good enough to fill out the dance card of stars like Bruce Willis and Richard Gere and director Michael Caton-Jones. But if any of them saw this as much more than their next paycheck, it's not evident on screen.

Willis, who plays the title role of a ruthless assassin so secretive no one is sure he even exists, does get to hop in and out of numerous disguises. Val Kilmer did the same thing in "The Saint," and "The Jackal" makes you wonder if the two actors had a side bet going as to who could change identities the most, the loser agreeing to appear in the next "Batman" extravaganza.

Caton-Jones had an equally unhappy task, the cobbling together of numerous disparate elements. These include linking up-to-the-minute violence and a hip soundtrack with the boilerplate of Chuck Pfarrer's standard script about agents and counter-agents chasing each other from Moscow to Washington with stops in Helsinki, London and Montreal thrown in.

The back-story of "The Jackal" is that the Russian Mafia has gotten so powerful that FBI Deputy Director Carter Preston (Sidney Poitier) is helping local intelligence officer Valentina Koslova (Diane Venora) keep the hoodlums in line.

While Preston's main job appears to be supplying platitudes like "It's never easy taking a life," his presence irks Mafia big cheese Terek Murad (David Hayman). Terek plants axes in peoples' heads the way Johnny Appleseed planted trees, and emphasizes his ruthlessness by commenting: "I took no joy in that."

Mafia business must be good in Russia because Terek doesn't blink at the $70-million price tag when he hires the Jackal for a high-level American assassination. "I want to strike fear into the marrow of their bones," he says, sounding like a radical cancer specialist. The Jackal merely nods.

Because Willis, perhaps thinking he's in a remake of "I Walked With a Zombie," often confuses iciness with somnolence, it's hard to tell if the assassin is nodding in agreement or because he's about to fall asleep. At any rate, he takes the job, and it isn't long before the Americans know something is up.

The FBI's search for an anti-Jackal operative takes them to an imprisoned IRA stalwart named Declan Mulqueen, played by Gere with a twinkle in his eye and a lilt in his voice. Mulqueen may be behind bars, but when he tells the FBI that his word is his bond, we know he's one of the good guys. And he bears the Jackal just the kind of dark and secret grudge that screenwriters like to throw in when they're desperate for motivation.

As his credits demonstrate, director Caton-Jones (whose projects include "Scandal," "Rob Roy," "Memphis Belle" and the underappreciated "This Boy's Life") enjoys varying the kinds of films he does. But his lack of flair for the thriller genre shows in the fluctuating excitement levels—now high, now nonexistent—surrounding the Jackal as he goes about his deadly business and the FBI and company as they try to stop him.

Also up and down is the acting of the on-screen ensemble. While the two leads mainly go through the motions, Venora as always brings something unexpected to the role of the Russian intelligence major who believes "the good guys don't hide."

Perhaps the biggest surprise of "The Jackal" is that the actor who provides the glue for the production and whose conviction comes closest to making these proceedings creditable is Sidney Poitier. Though he no longer works steadily and is venerable enough to have won the AFI's Life Achievement Award and be serving as ambassador to Japan from the Bahamas, Poitier has invested himself in these proceedings like no one else. There is a moment near the end of the film, as his character rushes with heedless, eye-widening intensity to save a life, when you can see what "The Jackal" might have become if everybody else cared that much.

NEW YORK, 11/24/97, p. 70, David Denby

In *The Jackal*, Bruce Willis is a killer for hire, and Richard Gere an Irish terrorist with a good heart who tries to stop him from shooting someone very, very important. A master of disguises, Willis wears a variety of bizarre outfits and mustaches, and in one sequence, eager to pick up a gay man in a bar, he dons a blondined wig that makes him look rather cute. These sudden shifts in apparel—Willis might be a guest on an old TV variety show—are about the only amusement in a pedestrian thriller that does everything by rote.

NEW YORK POST, 11/14/97, p. 51, Michael Medved

The jackal is a wily beast, but he feeds on decaying, previously slaughtered flesh. In a similar vein, the new movie "The Jackal" makes a hash of material that's been regurgitated twice before but tries to spice it up with star power and melodramatic excesses.

Both Frederick Forsyth's best seller and the spellbinding 1973 Fred Zinneman film "The Day of the Jackal" re-create a diabolically detailed plot by a master killer (played by Edward Fox) to assassinate Charles de Gaulle.

This time Bruce Willis plays the Jackal, and he's been promised $70 million by the Russian mafia to dispatch an unspecified but prominent target in Washington, D.C.

The always formidable Sidney Poitier plays the FBI's deputy director who joins forces with an intrepid, ruggedly competent and scar-faced Russian intelligence officer (the intense and affecting Diane Venora) to foil the nefarious plot.

Their determination to defeat the evil genius leads them to temporarily release from prison an admirable IRA "idealist" (Richard Gere, complete with wistful and distracting Irish brogue) who's worked with the Jackal in the past and knows how he operates.

Willis provides one of his strongest performances to date as the hyper-competent killer with icy nerves and quiet charisma, and the ingenious disguises he employs to rapidly shift identities will generate their share of audience gasps and chuckles.

Unfortunately, flamboyantly implausible touches (like the Jackal's counter-productively cruel killings on the way to his one big hit) make the plot seem silly rather than chilling, and portray the chief villain as a sadistic psycho rather than a steely nerved professional.

Gere's character, at the other extreme, is simply to good to be true—an even more adorable IRA terrorist than Brad Pitt in "The Devil's Own," who emerges directly from prison to inexplicably risk his life protecting innocent strangers.

Previously associated with character-driven fare such as "Scandal," "Memphis Belle" and "This Boy's Life," Scottish director Michael Caton-Jones handles big-action scenes with too much ponderous slow-motion manipulation and no notable invention or pizazz.

By the time Gere's former girlfriend (French actress Mathilda May) plaintively declares, "I thought this was all behind us! When is this ever going to end?" she could be speaking for the weary audience.

NEWSDAY, 11/14/97, Part II/p. B6, Jack Mathews

It takes courage to include a line like "Is this ever going to end?" at the 90-minute mark of a two-hour movie as mired in clichés as Michael Caton-Jones' "The Jackal." And for that, and for its sporadic bursts of ingenuity, it can't be considered the worst action movie of the year.

But it's in the top 10.

It's hard to believe a film inspired by something as riveting as Fred Zinnemann's 1973 "The Day of the Jackal," itself adapted from Frederick Forsyth's best novel, could be so mundane. At least, not until you consider (a) how many espionage thrillers have been made in the intervening quarter-century, (b) how many of those counted on the heightened paranoia and political insecurities of Cold War audiences for their emotional tension and (c) how consuming Hollywood's obsession with high-tech gadgetry and explosive set pieces has become.

"The Jackal" is a fairly uncomplicated story about a mercenary assassin (Bruce Willis) plotting the killing of a major American political figure at the behest of the Russian Mafia, and the efforts to stop him by the FBI and a temporarily paroled Irish terrorist (Richard Gere) with an old score against him.   One villain, one target, one hero, and a war's worth of incidental death and destruction.

Forsyth's original story was about a plot by French radicals to assassinate Charles de Gaulle, with the future of France hanging in the balance. All their hired Jackal needed, besides his array of disguises and false identities, was a custom-made lightweight rifle, with a silencer, a scope, and a trim carrying case. All these decades later, he's got something the size of a Civil War cannon that fires like a machine gun from the back of a minivan, and which he aims from afar with the use of a hidden camera and a notebook computer. Progress.

And there's no silencer on this banger. It's built to rock and roll, for a Dolby boomer generation that likes to be shaken and not stirred. The Jackal's new gun is so big, so noisy and so destructive that the film's second-biggest action scene occurs when he takes it to the country to try it out. And pity the sidekick who is asked to portray a moving target.

Willis plays the Jackal with the customary iciness of a Hollywood assassin, and his buff frame suits the heavy lifting his character is asked to do. But the film would have been better served if the stars had switched roles. Gere has more experience playing sociopaths and is better at it, and the same can be said of Willis and contrived heroes. As it is, Willis is not particularly scary, and Gere, while managing a fair Irish accent, is not particularly convincing.

The Jackal's disguises are laughably obvious. Willis alternates various colored toupees, adds a mustache now and then, and creates a pot belly for one of his ruses, but only people who've been staring at the sun would fail to recognize him.

The film's greatest weakness, however, comes from reframing "The Day of the Jackal" as a Russian-American conflict. The Stalin-monster archetype is no less a cliché when cast as the head of the post-Cold War Moscow underworld, and his hiring of the Jackal to avenge what he believes was an FBI killing of his brother is hardly the motivational stuff of great espionage fiction.

Incidentally, the conditions of employment set by the Jackal—a $70 million fee, total creative control, and anonymity if anything goes wrong sounds like the deal Willis made with TriStar Pictures for "Hudson Hawk." The results are pretty much the same, too.

There is, in the midst of this baloney, a very good performance by Diane Venora, playing the tough Russian intelligence officer working with the FBI's deputy director (Sidney Poitier) and Gere's Declan Mulqueen.   Battle-scarred but unbowed, Venora's Valentina represents the emerging conscience of free Russia, and the actress makes her come alive in ways the rest of the movie never does.

NEWSWEEK, 11/24/97, p. 73, David Ansen

Bruce Willis tries on a lot of wigs playing the chameleon-like assassin known as the Jackal. Richard Gere tries on an Irish accent as the imprisoned terrorist cajoled by the FBI into helping it track down this nefarious killer before the Jackal bumps off a government bigwig. (Gere, you see, is the only one who knows what makes the guy tick. Heard that one before?) Though both stars have had better days, it's not their fault that this loose remake of 1973's "The Day of the Jackal" is so unpardonably dull. Credit that to a script by Chuck Pfarrer that is at best generic and at worst nonsensical. Sidney Poitier as an FBI director and Diane Venora as a tough Russian cop do their best to liven things up, but the usually reliable director Michael Caton-Jones ("Scandal," "This Boy's Life") hasn't a clue how to freshen up such stale material. If you bite your fingernails, it will only be from boredom.

SIGHT AND SOUND, 2/98, p. 45, David Tse

Russian Mafia lieutenant Vasilov is killed during a police arrest engineered by FBI agent Preston and Russian intelligence officer Valentina Koslova. In revenge, the Mafia hire a contract killer named the Jackal to assassinate the head of the FBI. This information is leaked to Preston and Koslova.

Preston arranges for the temporary release of IRA terrorist Declan Mulqueen who has a score to settle with the Jackal. Adopting numerous disguises, the Jackal travels to Washington, London and Montreal, where he buys a machine gun, fake passports, a yacht and a van that can be camouflaged. He also commissions a remote-controlled gun mount from a mechanic, who is killed in the firing test. The Jackal re-enters the US by taking part in a Chicago regatta race.

Mulqueen and the Jackal identify each other at the pier, and a shootout ensues. The Jackal attacks Mulqueen's ex-lover Isabella at her house; her protector Koslova is killed as a result. Mulqueen guesses correctly that the Jackal's true target is the First Lady, due to appear in the opening ceremony of New Hope Children's Hospital. Preston and Mulqueen push the First Lady out of the firing line and spot the van that conceals the machine gun. Mulqueen tracks the Jackal to the subway, where finally he is shot by Isabella. Preston turns a blind eye to Mulqueen's departure.

The fascinating thing about Fred Zinneman's 1973 suspense classic *The Day of The Jackal* is that it offers absolutely no psychology or motivation to explain its characters. Filmed in stark docudrama style, it tells the story of a solitary contract killer hired by the extremist faction OAS to assassinate President de Gaulle in the summer of 1963 (whose actions inspired the naming of the notorious terrorist "Carlos the Jackal", aka Ilich Ramirez Sanchez, who was recently convicted in France). As played by Edward Fox, the assassin is well-groomed, debonair and immensely resourceful. Since none of his political or social history is revealed (or any other characters'), we gradually build up for ourselves an impression of the Jackal's personality by observing his actions.

So, when word leaked out of this remake with Bruce Willis and Richard Gere, reasonable fears were raised that the film-makers would ruin it by inventing clichéd backstories to 'explain' the characters, or casting Willis instead of Gere as the Jackal (how much better it would have been if the roles were reversed). Sadly, these fears are confirmed. The film-makers have stated in the press notes that they "purposely tried to create characters that people could really be invested in." This means turning once mysterious characters into one-dimensional ones, giving some preposterous thriller names like Declan Mulqueen and Valentina Koslova.

To update the plot, *The Jackal* is unimaginatively set in a vaguely present-day Washington with fictional characters. It eschews the opportunity to mix in some recent historical events, one of the strengths of the original book and film. Despite material that could offer opportunities for great Hitchcockian set pieces, *The Jackal* is instead a flat and cliché-ridden thriller. One says 'flat' in both the emotional and visual senses of the word. The photography is pedestrian, and most of the shots look shallow because of the excessive use of perspective-flattening telephoto lenses.

Whereas Zinneman's film provides an absorbing record of how an individual manages to outsmart instruments of state control (the police, the customs, the military), *The Jackal* follows a conventional hero-versus villain format. Sidney Poitier is lured out of graceful semi-retirement to play the Morgan Freeman role of wise elder black man. Since this is no longer a docudrama but an action movie, the international travels and numerous disguises of Willis' Jackal (copied from the original film) have far less urgency or story necessity. (In a moment of rare wit, the disguise he adopts during the actual assassination resembles Claude Lebel, the detective hero of the original film.)

And where's the challenge in killing someone, as he tries, using a remote controlled machine gun? Without a personal stake, Willis' apparently masterful hitman is just a guy with a button to push. The film-makers probably sensed this, and attempt to raise the emotional stakes (or, in the US, sympathy from anti-Hillary Clinton viewers) by revealing the real target to be the First Lady instead of the head of the FBI.

Director Michael Caton-Jones is no stranger to adaptations, producing sentimental but proficient results with the true story based *Scandal* and the literary *This Boy's Life,* before he finally struck box-office gold with the grimy cartoon of medieval heroics *Rob Roy* set in his Scottish homeland. But *The Jackal* is such a banal and redundant blockbuster, one senses there was no reason to make it, other than the desire to cash in on the stars' names. One might conjecture that their fees ate up the bulk of the budget, leaving the rest of the film a lacklustre thing. The heart of the problem is that the film-makers don't seem to want to thrill, surprise or delight us and don't appear even to understand what's great about their source material.

VILLAGE VOICE, 11/25/97, p. 96, Amy Taubin

The line, and where you draw it, is hardly an issue in *The Jackal* a campy thriller (based on Fred Zinnemann's 1973 *The Day of the Jackal)* that takes exploitation for granted. Bruce Willis plays the Jackal, a sadistic political assassin hired by the head of the Russian mafia to execute an American government honcho. Worried about being overmatched by the Jackal, the FBI guy in charge of the case (Sidney Poitier) asks assistance from an IRA operative (Richard Gere) who's doing a life sentence in a U.S. prison.

The FBI and Gere track Willis, who changes identities with increasing frequency as he travels toward D.C. Though no Alec Guinness, Willis clearly relishes the comic and sinister possibilities afforded by his many wigs and body paddings. Less sanctimonious than in *Red Corner,* Gere plays the straight man with aplomb. Director Michael Caton-Jones underscores Willis's and Gere's star power in two sequences composed of nothing but enormous closeups. (Willis shows unusual restraint by facing down Gere's contemptuously curled lip without a hint of his habitual smirk.)

Caton-Jones knows how to jack up tension in the stalking scenes. Willis has a high-tech gun which he uses to turn minor characters into bloody meat long before he trains its sights on those we're meant to care about. But it's Gere who nails the gun fetishism that's *The Jackal*'s raison d'être. Given an assault weapon to defend himself, Gere pulls it to him like a long-lost love. "It's been a long time since I had a gun in my hands," he murmurs. As if we didn't know.

The only thing to do with dialogue this ludicrous is to throw it away. Willis and Gere do just that. But, Caton-Jones too often demands the other actors to do the opposite. The result is a bunch of unintended laughs, though none of them big enough to destroy the movie. And in fact, I might have enjoyed *The Jackal*—fetishism and all—had it not been for its knuckle-headed gay bashing.

Wanting access to a vehicle with security clearance tags, the Jackal goes to a gay bar where he locks lips with a government closet case who, anticipating a hot date, happily gives him the keys to his house (garage attached). How come it's only gay men who are so vulnerable? Next time, Jackal, be an equal-opportunity assassin. Offer Super Bowl tickets—it's another way to get your foot in the door.

Also reviewed in:
CHICAGO TRIBUNE, 11/14/97, Friday/p. A, Michael Wilmington
NEW YORK TIMES, 11/14/97, p. E19, Stephen Holden
VARIETY, 11/10-16/97, p. 39, Todd McCarthy
WASHINGTON POST, 11/14/97, p. D1, Stephen Hunter
WASHINGTON POST, 11/14/97, Weekend/p. 50, Desson Howe

JACKIE BROWN

A Miramax Films release of A Band Apart production. *Executive Producer:* Richard N. Gladstein, Elmore Leonard, Bob Weinstein, and Harvey Weinstein. *Producer:* Lawrence Bender. *Director:* Quentin Tarantino. *Screenplay:* Quentin Tarantino. *Based on the book "Rum Punch"* by: Elmore Leonard. *Director of Photography:* Guillermo Navarro. *Editor:* Sally Menke. *Music:* Ann Karlin and John Katovsic. *Music Editor:* Tom Kramer. *Sound:* Mark Ulano. *Sound Editor:* Stephen Hunter Flick. *Casting:* Jaki Brown. *Production Designer:* David Wasco. *Art Director:* Daniel Bradford. *Set Designer:* Mariko Braswell. *Set Decorator:* Sandy Reynolds-Wasco. *Set Dresser:* Mark Hutman, Stoney Emshwiller, Sally Reed Protiva, Dena J. Allen, and Dave Coronella. *Special Effects:* T. "Brooklyn" Bellissimo. *Costumes:* Mary Claire Hannan. *Make-up:* Ermahn Ospina. *Make-up (Samuel L. Jackson):* Marietta Carter-Narcisse. *Make-up (Robert De Niro):* Ilona Herman. *Make-up (Michael Keaton):* Bob Mills. *Stunt Coordinator:* Steve Davison and Kiante Elam. *Running time:* 154 minutes. *MPAA Rating:* R.

CAST: Pam Grier (Jackie Brown); Samuel L. Jackson (Ordell Robbie); Robert Forster (Max Cherry); Bridget Fonda (Melanie); Michael Keaton (Ray Nicolette); Robert De Niro (Louis Gara); Michael Bowen (Mark Dargus); Chris Tucker (Beaumont Livingston); Lisa Gay Hamilton (Sheronda); Tommy "Tiny" Lister, Jr. (Winston); Hattie Winston (Simone); Denise Crosby (Public Defender); Sid Haig (Judge); Aimee Graham (Amy, Billingsley Sales Girl); Ellis E. Williams (Cockatoo Bartender); Tangie Ambrose (Billingsley Sales Girl #2); T'Keyah Crystal Keymah (Raynelle, Ordell's Junkie Friend); Venessia Valentino (Cabo Flight Attendant); Diana Uribe (Anita Lopez); Renee Kelly (Cocktail Waitress); Elizabeth McInerny (Bartender at Sam's); Colleen Mayne (Girl at Security Gate); Laura Lovelace (Steakhouse Waitress); Candice Briese and Gary Mann (The Deputies).

CHRISTIAN SCIENCE MONITOR, 1/5/98, p. 10, David Sterritt

With his first two features, Quentin Tarantino became Hollywood's most flamboyant young filmmaker, blending intricate storytelling with enough violence and vulgarity to strain the limits of the R rating.

Traditionalists blanched, but "Reservoir Dogs" made him a rising star and "Pulp Fiction" became an international superhit, earning Oscar nominations along the way. Tarantino was launched, with a vengeance.

His next move surprised friends and detractors alike: He took three years off, cooking up his next project at a leisurely pace and filling his extra time with acting jobs and minor directing stints.

Had he run out of ideas after only two movies? Or was he cleverly raising his market value by building a suspenseful interlude into his career? Or was he just plain tired, and successful enough to take a vacation whenever he felt like it?

Whatever the reasons for his hiatus, Tarantino has returned with a typically loud splash. His new picture, "Jackie Brown," resembles his earlier movies with its raunchy language, throwaway mayhem, and playful way of bending time and space onto unpredictable new shapes.

Yet it's also different in significant respects. For one, it's not an original story but a faithful adaptation of a popular novel, "Rum Punch" by Elmore Leonard, who shares Tarantino's zest for seedy characters in sleazy situations. For another, it tells a single story from beginning to end, with only occasional detours into high-stepping cinema (split screens, instant replays) for its own sake.

Most unexpected of all, it's designed more to explore the vicissitudes of human nature than to shock its audience or show off the latest plot-scrambling techniques. It's hardly a gentle or subtle tale, but it sends a message that's as welcome as it is overdue: Hollywood's boy wonder is growing up.

The bright side of "Jackie Brown" begins with its casting. In a superb stroke, Tarantino has chosen Pam Grier to play the heroine, a 40-something flight attendant whose life is complicated by three men—an old boyfriend with a murderous streak, a burned-out bail bondsman looking for new experiences, and an ambitious cop who'll put her in jail if she doesn't help him collar the crook he's chasing.

Grier was a leading star of the "blaxploitation" craze in the early 1970s, sassing and shooting her way through low-budget melodramas with inner-city settings and African-American characters. Glowingly filmed by Guillermo Navarro's camera, she emerges today as a mature and savvy actress whose checkered career is paying lofty dividends at last.

Equally impressive is the amazing Samuel L. Jackson as Jackie's dangerous boyfriend, offsetting a mean personality with an ultracool style and the snazziest clothes of the season. The key role of the bail-bond broker is sensitively filled by Robert Forster, another half-forgotten face of the '70s revivified by Tarantino's time-machine casting.

Lending able support are Bridget Fonda as a dope-addled bimbo, Michael Keaton as the bright-eyed government agent, and Robert De Niro reaching against-all-odds brilliance as a character so depressingly dumb he's hardly in the movie at all.

Like any Tarantino picture to date, "Jackie Brown" contains enough offensive material to anger a wide variety of moviegoers. While the violence is restrained by "Pulp Fiction" standards, its very casualness makes some of it appear all the more shocking. Its sex is mercifully brief but outrageously raw. The language is grotesquely foul, and nonstop racial epithets will infuriate people who don't share Tarantino's idea that constant repetition may defuse the words' malignant power in contemporary culture.

"Jackie Brown" will also disappoint Tarantino fans who hoped for something even more bizarre and incendiary than his previous pictures. But this is the movie's best quality. Although the boy wonder still has much maturing to do, he's finally on his way to thoughtful use of his prodigious filmmaking talent.

LOS ANGELES TIMES, 12/24/97, Calendar/p. 2, Kenneth Turan

Unlikely as it sounds, "Jackie Brown" is Quentin Tarantino's idea of a nice film. Not that it's everyone's idea of nice: This hotbed of industrial-strength profanity isn't headed for the Disney Channel any time soon. But motivating the writer-director here is not his usual impulse toward outrageousness but what has to be called a sweet desire to pay tribute to two key influences in his creative life, writer Elmore Leonard and star Pam Grier.

This is Tarantino's first film since "Pulp Fiction" won the Palme d'Or at Cannes 3½ years ago, a long enough time for numerous imitators to have clogged cinemas worldwide with rip-offs of his cascading blood and brain matter style.

However, those expecting Tarantino to pick up where he left off will be disappointed in "Jackie Brown." Instead of rearranging audience's sensibilities, he's taken the typically twisty plot of Leonard's "Rum Punch" and run it through his personal Mixmaster. The result is a raunchy doodle, a leisurely and easygoing diversion that goes down easy enough but is far from compelling.

A fan of Leonard for years, Tarantino also realized that by changing the race of "Rum Punch's" female protagonist he could also turn this film into a tribute to Grier. For those with short memories, she's the no-nonsense star of over-the-top 1970s blaxploitation films like "Coffy," "Foxy Brown" and "Sheba Baby" the director is an unabashed fan of.

This decision gives "Jackie Brown" a poignant feeling at times, especially in a closing close-up of Grier's face—that is in an unnerving way reminiscent of the celebrated shot of Garbo at the end of "Queen Christina." But tribute is a hard act for someone with Tarantino's sensibility to master, and "Jackie Brown" casts doubt on whether he's the right director to make "nice" an involving quality.

For one thing, at 2 hours and 40 minutes, "Jackie Brown" plainly takes longer than it should to unfold. Along with that too-leisurely pace, goes a lack of immediacy, a sense that this is the kind of thing that Tarantino not only might have done in his sleep but in fact has.

Helping keep people awake is Tarantino's trademark wall-to-wall profanity, which can be spell-binding but this time around is so dependent on casual usage of the N-word that fellow writer-director Spike Lee was moved to complain publicly about it.

Most of the hard talk comes from Samuel L. Jackson as Ordell Robbie, introduced in an apartment in Hermosa Beach showing a video called "Chicks 'n' Guns" to the very different Louis Gara and Melanie Ralston.

Melanie (Bridget Fonda) is Ordell's girlfriend, a kittenish surf bunny whose ambition doesn't seem to extend past getting high and watching TV. Louis (Robert De Niro) is an old pal of Ordell's who's just gotten out of prison and is looking for a situation.

Ordell himself is a gun dealer, proud of his merchandise ("the AK-47, when you absolutely positively got to kill every [expletive] in the room") but ruthless and menacing to his employees when he needs to be.

One of those workers is Jackie Brown (Grier), a stewardess with a fly-by-night airline that shuttles between L.A. and Mexico. The government, in the person of Alcohol, Tobacco and Firearms agent Ray Nicolette (Michael Keaton), puts pressure on her to turn Ordell in. But Jackie, aided by been-around bail bondsman Max Cherry (Robert Forster) would rather play both sides against each other and get a crack at liberating Ordell's half-million-dollar stash.

Though it's Jackson who provides whatever energy "Jackie Brown" can manage, it is a treat to see Grier, who has the intimidating physicality of a sexy linebacker, be "too cool for school" and face down any troubles the script throws her way.

While Leonard's original novel was set in the Miami area, Tarantino moved it to L.A., which means lines about Roscoe's Chicken & Waffles and key scenes are set in the Del Amo Fashion Center. Tarantino feels at home in the South Bay, maybe too much so. He's relaxed so much he hasn't given this film more than attitude, and even attitude can wear thin after a while.

NEW YORK, 1/5/98, p. 52, David Denby

Jackie Brown, Quentin Tarantino's first full-length film since the revolutionary *Pulp Fiction*, turns out to be not revolutionary or even evolutionary but enormously ... methodical. Working from an Elmore Leonard novel, Tarantino has created a gangster fiction that is never larger than life and sometimes smaller. The movie doesn't so much dramatize the characters as tail them. They come; they go; they meet and talk; they talk again; and finally someone gets shot. Yet *Jackie Brown*, despite its termitelike pace and thoroughness, is not dull; Tarantino is an entertainer, and he's written some scandalously funny lines for Samuel L. Jackson, who plays one Ordell Robbie, an egotistical L.A. gun seller. Ordell wears a full ponytail and a little wispy goatee in Chinese-sage style. In the world of taciturn thugs, this hipster-dandy is a brilliant talker; he's also a mean and dangerous man. Ordell keeps a number of people in his employ, including a libidinous white surfer girl (Bridget Fonda) who sits around getting stoned; a mangy ex-con (Robert De Niro); and a stewardess, Jackie Brown (Pam Grier), who carries cash for Ordell back and forth between Los Angeles and Mexico. Jackie is a tough black woman in her forties; she knows the ropes. The movie is about her attempt to break free of Ordell and fleece him of his money.

Tarantino shows off the lowlife egomania, the endless cadging, cheating, doublecrossing. *Jackie Brown* is often funny (in a squalid way), but it's generally unexciting, and it lacks the shocks and aesthetic daring of *Pulp Fiction*. People expecting something ambitious from Tarantino-people who see him as some kind of savior—will be amazed and disappointed by *Jackie Brown,* which feels like a conscious regression. The picture is actually an elongated and ambitious B-movie—a dogged homage to the kind of atmospheric minor crime picture that Tarantino, having grown up in a video store, enjoys more than he does prestige movies. In *Jackie Brown*, Tarantino has tried to make the most serious and detailed B movie ever. That attempt has caught him in certain contradictions. He has built the movie around Pam Grier, the strapping, bodice-spilling star of such early-seventies black exploitation movies as *Coffy* and *Foxy Brown*. Tarantino has often expressed his admiration for Grier, and in *Jackie Brown* she does seem a terrifically smart and likable woman. Yet she's a limited performer, and she can't really bloom in the realistic, matter-of-fact framework that Tarantino has constructed for her. Revived and made the center of a movie, she holds on to her dignity as if it were a life raft, and the performance doesn't go anywhere.

Grier has only a scene or two with the volatile, profane Samuel L. Jackson, who jostles her and would have drawn her out if they had butted heads more often. Most of the time, Tarantino pairs her with another B-movie actor, the somber, stone-faced Robert Forster, who was in *Medium Cool* in 1969 and has worked in obscure movies ever since. Forster plays a tough, experienced bail-bondsman, Max Cherry, who does business for Ordell. In his late fifties, Max is too set in his ways to make a pass at Jackie, but he admires her and possibly even loves her. He's like a wall, this Max, smart but quiet and self-contained, and when Forster acts with Grier—the scenes are mostly long conversations—we realize what Tarantino is getting at. These two actors, sitting across a table in some dim bar, don't open anything up; they're not particularly expressive. But they're not cheap or flashy either; their strength lies in a kind of impervious power, and it's possible that their very lack of range and flexibility seems a form of integrity for Tarantino. He lets Samuel L. Jackson run free, but he treats De Niro and Fonda like B-movie actors, too—each of them plays a type, with only limited consciousness, clinging to a little bit of psychological turf. Perhaps Tarantino is saying that this is what people in the crime world are really like—sly, mean, and limited. They make mistakes, and they die with barely a flicker of awareness of what's happening to them.

At one point, Jackie, trying to steal Ordell's money, is telling one story to Ordell, another to Max, and still another to a federal agent (Michael Keaton) who's trying to destroy Ordell. The plot is enormously complicated, and Tarantino wants us to see what's at stake for each person at each moment. *Jackie Brown* never speeds up; it never explodes. At the climax, in fact, it slows down: Tarantino shows us the same sequence of events three times consecutively, each time from the point of view of a different character. But he does it only to keep things clear. After the formal bravura of *Pulp Fiction,* it's as if he were saying, "Look, no tricks; everything is exactly as it seems." So it may turn out that Quentin Tarantino is not, after all, the American Godard, not a mall-rat pop genius eager to transform pulp into formally demanding art. He really likes pulp for its stiff, repetitive, bullheaded qualities. He likes it so much, he's made his own sober version of it.

NEW YORK POST, 12/24/97, p. 33, Thelma Adams

Quentin Tarantino's "Jackie Brown" is as flat as its star, Pam Grier, is curvy. The worshipful Tarantino puts Grier on a pedestal, but he doesn't give her what she really needs: a script that matches her talent. It was ever so. Even in her greatest hit, the 1973 "Coffy," the blaxploitation diva was a statuesque head and shoulders above the material.

In Tarantino's punchless adaptation of Elmore Leonard's "Rum Punch," Grier plays Jackie Brown. A stewardess for a second-tier Mexican airline, Brown supplements her income by smuggling cash into the country for an arms dealer (Samuel L. Jackson).

When Brown gets caught by the feds (led by Michael Keaton dog-paddling through an underdefined role), she must make a choice: roll on Jackson or lose her livelihood. She pursues a third, winner-take-all option: feed the arms dealer to the law, take the money and run.

Jackson, in a caper film that's dreadfully overlong but impeccably cast, is as slick and scary as he's ever been. With a fright wig that's alternately braided and Bozo'd, a skinny braid drooling from his chin, he's one intimidating thug. We soon discover his actions speak even louder than the nonstop words Tarantino puts in his mouth.

There are moments when "Jackie Brown" comes alive. A great scene finds edgy ex-con Robert De Niro bickering with Jackson's girlfriend, pot-smoking surfer chick Bridget Fonda. In the middle of an elaborate money switch, he can't remember where he parked their van in a mall lot—and she won't cut him any slack.

Another signature bit finds Jackson riffing on the virtues of various weapons while watching a video of "chicks who love guns." When he starts talking about the street popularity of arms displayed in Hong Kong action movies, it's pure Tarantino.

Some strong scenes find Grier making a leisurely seduction of Robert Forster's impassive bail bondsman while enlisting his aid in her attempt to fleece Jackson and escape the law. There's a peaceful, easy feeling to their rapport that's fresh, lacking the usual expensive lingerie and big-eyes obviousness of contemporary thrillers.

But these isolated scenes never gain the momentum of "Pulp Fiction" or "Reservoir Dogs." And what really shines through, and separates Tarantino from his idols John Woo and Ringo Lam, is the lack of a strong moral center and world view, a reason for being, besides the contact high. With "Jackie Brown," Tarantino creates a hall of mirrors that only has the power to reflect other films, the fragmented images of videos past.

NEWSDAY, 12/24/97, Part II/p. B7, Jack Mathews

Someone who can count faster than I said that Samuel L. Jackson's character in the new Quentin Tarantino film "Jackie Brown" uses the N-word 38 times. I would have guessed much higher. The word goes off in his mouth like a firecracker with every sentence, and his Ordell Robbie is a nonstop talker.

His Robbie character's use of the N-word wouldn't be quite as offensive, or at least as obtrusive, if the movie were as clever, funny, involving or fast-paced as "Pulp Fiction," the 1994 sensation that made Tarantino the hottest flavor in pop culture. Instead, it is a flat, mannered work that takes one of Elmore Leonard's lesser novels and draws it out as if it were Chekhov.

"Jackie Brown," adapted from Leonard's "Rum Punch" and relocated from Florida to southern California, is a simple tale of triple-cross, about a middle-age stewardess (Pam Grier) who, after being caught smuggling money from Mexican buyers to L.A. arms dealer Ordell Robbie, plots to beat both Robbie and the police out of Robbie's remaining half-million-dollar Mexican stash.

Generally faithful to the novel, "Jackie Brown" is told in a linear style, with its major characters and its story line introduced in some crisp opening sequences. First, we see Jackie Brown striding through Los Angeles International Airport, where she's about to be pinched by L.A. cops Michael Keaton and Michael Bowen. Then, we meet the sociopathic Robbie, his perpetually stoned girlfriend Melanie (Bridget Fonda), and his recently paroled friend Louis (Robert De Niro). And, not least, there is Max Cherry (Robert Forster), the bail bondsman Robbie sees about springing Jackie Brown from jail.

The advance word on "Jackie Brown" had Tarantino attempting something completely different from "Pulp Fiction." But while there is less blood-splattering mayhem—only four people are killed—and more time is spent with fewer characters, the most noticeable difference is that the Tarantino flourishes that made "Pulp Fiction" so startlingly fresh have already grown rancidly stale.

"Jackie Brown" has a couple of scenes of shock violence, the sudden death moments that had "Pulp Fiction" audiences gasping and laughing at the same time, but the surprise element is just not there.

Some of the performances are interesting, particularly that of Forster, the one-time TV star ("Banyon") rescued by Tarantino from the motivational speech circuit. Forster gets the best assignment. Max Cherry is a cool character, a man who's seen it all and who knows the criminal justice system like the back of his hand, and yet he is incapable of deviousness or deceit.

Cherry is that rarest of all fictional creatures, an honest bail bondsman. Even when Cherry's infatuation with Jackie Brown draws him into her scheme, he does his job with utter truthfulness, and Forster's calm, unruffled manner makes him one of the year's most likably offbeat heroes.

Elsewhere, Tarantino's effort to create amiably odd-ball characters doesn't quite work. Grier, a frequent star of blaxploitation films of the '70s and '80s, is a strikingly handsome woman at 48, and she has a couple of big scenes, including one with Jackson where her use of the N-word is genuinely funny. But her appearance seems largely to be stunt casting, done both as homage to the black action genre and an attempt to make "Jackie Brown" a cross-over film (the character was white in the novel), and Grier doesn't have the dramatic range the role implies.

Even De Niro seems a little lost in the charade. He's so emotionally reigned in as Louis Gara, he seems more sedated than dimwitted. When Louis finally explodes, in an abruptly lethal, signature Tarantino temper tantrum, it comes off as very forced comic relief.

However, there is no greater misfire in "Jackie Brown" than Ordell Robbie. It's hard to separate this character from the philosophical hit man Jackson played in "Pulp Fiction. " Both men do what they have to do, which often involves cold-blooded murder, but there is no underlying charm, no mitigating wit to Robbie. It's not that Tarantino and Jackson don't attempt to make Robbie a perversely magnetic figure. They simply fail to, and the harsh, repetitious use of the N-word amplifies that failure.

To some extent, Tarantino is a victim of his own success. With "Pulp Fiction" and his earlier "Reservoir Dogs," he had more or less reinvented film noir, taking pulp crime drama and playing it out as convulsive black comedy, and his style has inspired more cheap imitations than Tiffany lamps.

It may be unfair to expect Tarantino to outdo himself with every film, but if he's going to stick with the genre, if he's going to keep making lamps, that's the only way he'll distinguish his work from the knockoffs.

NEWSWEEK, 12/22/97, p. 84, David Ansen

[*Jackie Brown* was reviewed jointly with *Wag the Dog*; see Ansen's review of that film.]

SIGHT AND SOUND, 4/98, p. 39, Stella Bruzzi

Ordell Robbie, a gunrunner, goes to Max Cherry's bail bond office to post the $10,000 bail for a henchman, Beaumont, facing time in jail for arms possession. Ordell then kills Beaumont after he's released. Jackie Brown, who smuggles money for Ordell to supplement her stewardess' income, is stopped by cops at LA airport. They find $50,000 and a stash of cocaine in her bag. Ordell bails Jackie out of jail. She realises, after Beaumont's death, that Ordell will kill her too so she strikes a deal: in exchange for $100,000 if she's convicted, she won't give him over to the police. However, Jackie also makes a deal with the cops, saying she'll help them convict Ordell. She tells Ordell of her visit to the cops, but assures him she's thought up a scam to double-cross them when they come after the money.

Jackie tempts Max to come in with her on a $500,000 deal. Having delivered $50,000 of smuggled cash, Jackie wins the cops' trust. But with a second delivery, Jackie pulls a scam: in a shopping mall changing room, she swaps bags with Ordell's henchwoman Melanie, but hands over a dummy bag containing only some of the $500,000. Louis, an ex-con friend of Ordell's who has accompanied Melanie, shoots Melanie when she irritates him. Ordell realises Jackie has taken the money and shoots Louis. Max, now on Jackie's side, gives Ordell his $10,000 bail bond back and tells him he has the rest of the money in his safe. When Ordell arrives at Max's office, the cops shoot him. Jackie gets away with the bulk of the money. She offers some to Max before leaving for Spain, but he declines.

Jackie Brown, Quentin Tarantino's adaptation of Elmore Leonard's novel *Rum Punch* has been on the cards ever since Tarantino and his producer Lawrence Bender optioned the book just after making *Reservoir Dogs*. It feels like a project that's been knocking around for a while, one that's been mulled over, reassessed, changed and finally made. There's something confidently easy-going about it; it's immensely hard to dislike *Jackie Brown*. However, it is not a particularly good film, it's too long and draws out what is essentially a caper movie way beyond its narrative capability. It does, though, make for an interesting auteur piece, eschewing as it does the trademark frenziedness of both *Reservoir Dogs* and *Pulp Fiction*.

As if to signal this difference, *Jackie Brown* opens with an ostentatiously lazy, prolonged profile shot (which lasts for the duration of the opening credits) of Pam Grier as stewardess Jackie Brown progressing in stately fashion along an airport conveyor belt. Because nothing much else is going on here, we are lured into becoming obsessively attentive to details, such as Jackie's garish company badge, the cheap blue of her jacket contrasting with the rich browns of her hair and skin, the elegant curve in her nose and her ambiguous eyes, both vulnerable and self contained. Whereas previously in Tarantino's films, such expansiveness would have been the exception (Mr Blonde's languid torture of the cop in *Reservoir Dogs,* or John Travolta's heroin-fuelled cruise through town in *Pulp Fiction*), in *Jackie Brown* it establishes the defining mood. It's as if the whole film is viewed through the haze emanating from Ordell's girlfriend Melanie's impressive array of dope pipes. At one point, the already monosyllabic Louis, having smoked perhaps a bit too much grass, is rendered catatonic. He's upright, on the telephone but hardly able to move a muscle. The film is content to grind to a halt with him.

This intriguing, anti-dynamic approach to narration has its drawbacks in what is essentially a 90s homage to the black action movies of the early 70s. The clearest blaxploitation echoes are in the casting of Grier (star of *Coffy,* 1973, and *Foxy Brown,* 1974) and Samuel L Jackson as Ordell, who with his pimp-look outfits and fast talking is a pastiche of Richard Roundtree in *Shaft* (1971) and the mass of street-smart heroes who followed. Ordell is the antidote to Jackie Brown. While she, a none-too-bothered siren, soaks up and deflects energy, he provokes or perpetrates all the film's action and violence. It is almost an auteurist necessity that he blows out both

Beaumont's and Louis' brains at point-blank range. His protracted word firing sprees function as reminders of the genre *Jackie Brown* purports to inhabit.

The uneasy discrepancy between generic framework and tone is exacerbated when it comes to Jackie Brown's double-crossing money-swapping ventures. Her final successful attempt at conning Ordell out of his money and the police out of getting hold of it should provide the fast paced denouement to a twisty plot. Instead, Tarantino elects to film the same changing-room bag-swapping sequence of events from three different subjective angles, thus repeating but also dissipating the tension. Each time new details emerge, such as Louis' half-recognition of Max the bail bondsman, but the three versions are essentially very similar. Again, the most memorable features of this triptych are the insignificant details such as the fetishistic sight of Melanie's bronzed, sandalled feet pacing around under the changing-room door. Claude Chabrol once wrote of the difference between big-theme and little-theme movies, arguing that just because its story is placed within a more grandiose setting, the biblical epic isn't necessarily about more important things than a film about a domestic argument. Tarantino seems to have learnt a similar love of low key nuance, but he still can't quite relinquish action and bombastic stylisation.

Jackie Brown is an intriguing failure. Whereas both *Reservoir Dogs* and *Pulp Fiction* were brashly single-minded films, Tarantino's latest meanders constantly off-course, its narrative and mood rarely compatible. Symptomatic of this is the end: as Max lures Ordell into the police trap, the action movie is resolved with a typically excessive vertical shot of Ordell lying on the floor. The actual end of the film, however, is all about a love of faces and character, concluding with a beautiful, caressing close-up of a chaste farewell kiss between Max and Jackie and then a calm, static shot of Jackie leaving which mirrors her arrival. *Jackie Brown* is an anomaly: an action film that takes us nowhere in particular.

TIME, 12/22/97, p. 80, Richard Corliss

The wait is over. It's 3½ years since *Pulp Fiction* exploded at the Cannes Film Festival, and now everyone can stop wondering what Quentin Tarantino will do next. The answer, in *Jackie Brown*: more of the same, and less.

The film is an elaborate, fitfully funny Tarantoon about chatty folks with big guns. Working reverently from Elmore Leonard's novel *Rum Punch* the writer-director tosses half a dozen wary people into the pit of their avarice and lets us guess who will survive. Pam Grier's title character is a flight attendant running money from Mexico to California for her drug boss Ordell (Samuel L. Jackson), who is variously inconvenienced by his lazily taunting girlfriend (Bridget Fonda), his low-IQ henchman (Robert De Niro), an eager fed (Michael Keaton) and an aging bail bondsman (Robert Forster), whose creased face is a road map of disappointment in the venality of humankind.

There's little moral rooting interest here; the fun comes from expert actors spitting out the lurid rhythms of punk patter. You want affability fragging into menace? Tarantino can write it for you. Jackson and Fonda, especially, can deliver it with a swell sting.

But at 2½ hours, it all plays like the rough assembly of a 90-min. caper film—an anecdote told at epic length. Grier, foxy lady of '70s blaxploitation, is given little chance to radiate; you never even glimpse her magnificent shoulders. As for Tarantino, he is playing peekaboo with his sizable talent. *Jackie Brown* marks time, lots of it, between *Pulp Fiction* and his next great project. The wait goes on.

VILLAGE VOICE, 12/30/97, p. 61, J. Hoberman

One may wonder what inspired Martin Scorsese to make *Kundun*. There is no such mystery to Quentin Tarantino's *Jackie Brown*. Both men belong to the Church of Cinema, but the icon Tarantino worships here is warrior woman Pam Grier. This love letter to the most bodacious action star in Hollywood history reconfigures Elmore Leonard's *Rum Punch* into a brilliantly cast homage to the blaxploitation flicks of Tarantino's childhood.

More a presence than an actress, Grier is as formidable as ever—although, 20-odd years after *Foxy Brown*, her kung fu is largely verbal. Tarantino gives her a stellar introduction, as she glides along on an airport people mover, and a comeback role as a $16,000-per-year stewardess on the L.A.-Baja flight, nailed by the authorities after smuggling currency through customs. The accomplice of a psychotic gun dealer (Samuel L. Jackson sporting a ponytail and symmetrical, braided goatee), Grier plays a complicated double game. Indeed, this is a movie in which everyone is running a scam except the world-weary bail bond agent who helps the heroine out (Robert Forster, another successfully rehabilitated '70s performer).

Actors dearly adore working with Tarantino. The supporting cast includes Bridget Fonda's stoned surfer, as well as Robert De Niro and Michael Keaton in character roles—the former as a grizzled ex-con who joins forces with Jackson, the latter as a virulently vacant, gum-chewing cop. The freshness of their performances is somewhat mitigated by Tarantino's indulgence for shtick—his own included. Just as every performer gets a bit too much space, so do the director's prize conceits. An initially apt use of the Delfonics is run into the ground; ditto the video infomercial Jackson uses to push his product.

Mellow compared to Tarantino's first two features, *Jackie Brown* retains the author's trademark aggression: One killing is staged in long shot, à la Takeshi Kitano, but the rest are presented as laff lines; Jackson, who at one point engages in shameless minstrel-show competition with the equally motormouthed Chris Tucker, is the spigot for a raging torrent of racially offensive dialogue. (One would have to go back 60 years to the Oscar Micheaux jaw-dropper *God's Stepchildren* to find so loquacious an antirace man.)

Can we blame this on the director's youth? On his aesthetic tunnel vision? *Jackie Brown* is still very much a film enthusiast's film. Many of Tarantino's best ideas are casually tossed off—the tribute to *Across 110th Street*, the interpolation of the Meters' "Cissy Strut," the use of obscure LA. neighborhoods and malls, the orientation of the key caper in an intricate *Rashomon* double flashback.

An uncorseted two and a half hours, *Jackie Brown* is so fond of its actors and so far superior to anything else on the crime beat—Francis Coppola's bizarrely overpraised adaptation of *The Rainmaker* in particular—that it deserves at least two cheers. So *chapeaus bas* and doo-rags off? This guy really should make movies more often.

Also reviewed in:
NEW REPUBLIC, 1/26/98, p. 24, Stanley Kauffmann
NEW YORK TIMES, 12/24/97, E5, Janet Maslin
NEW YORKER, 1/12/98, p. 83, Anthony Lane
VARIETY, 12/22/97-1/4/98, p. 57, Todd McCarthy
WASHINGTON POST, 12/25/97, p. C1, Stephen Hunter
WASHINGTON POST, 12/26/97, Weekend/p. 34, Stephen Hunter

JACKIE CHAN'S FIRST STRIKE

A New Line Cinema release of a Raymond Chow/Golden Harvest production. *Executive Producer:* Leonard Ho. *Producer:* Barbie Tung. *Director:* Stanley Tong. *Screenplay:* Stanley Tong, Nick Tramontane, Greg Mellott, and Elliot Tong. *Director of Photography:* Jingle Ma. *Editor:* Peter Cheung and Chi Wai Yau. *Music:* J. Peter Robinson. *Music Editor:* Brent Brooks. *Sound:* Gary Wilkins, Gretchen Thornburn and (music) Frank Fleming and Brian Harman. *Sound Editor:* Paul Clay. *Production Designer:* Oliver Wong. *Art Director:* Benfi Sum and Sarah Stollman. *Special Effects:* Jeff Little, Albert Payne, and Peter Stubbs. *Costumes:* Juanita Cheng and Wendy Law. *Make-up:* Connie Lai, Man Yun Ling, and Jose Perez. *Stunt Coordinator:* Stanley Tong. *Running time:* 110 minutes. *MPAA Rating:* PG-13.

CAST: Jackie Chan (Jackie); Jackson Lou (Tsui); Chen Chun Wu (Annie); Bill Tung (Uncle Bill); Jouri Petrov (Colonel Gregor Yegorov); Grishajeva Nonna (Natasha); John Eaves (Mark); Terry Woo (Uncle Seven); Kristoff Kaczmarek (Commander Korda); Brenton Heeren and Steve Jones (Snipers); Symantha Liu (Channel 7 Reporter); Gary Wilkinson (News Anchorman); Low Houi Kang (H.K. Policeman); Esmond Ren and Jim Hsin (C.I.A. Members); Igro Guleen (USS Agent); N. Leshcinkov (General Gudanov); Rusean Scriprik (Strike Force Leader); Alexander Ustichenko (Major Majenko).

LOS ANGELES TIMES, 1/10/97, Calendar/p. 2, Kevin Thomas

"Jackie Chan's First Strike," yet another amusing action comedy-adventure from the martial arts superstar, is actually No. 4 in Chan's popular "Police Story" series, which finds Chan playing a Hong Kong policeman, Jackie, inevitably thrust into one hair-raising, cliffhanging predicament after another. "First Strike" is a diverting follow-up to "Rumble in the Bronx," which was also directed by Stanley Tong and which also had wide distribution in an English-language version.

"Relax, have fun," says Jackie's commanding officer, "Uncle Bill" (Bill Tung, veteran co-median and perennial Chan sidekick), allowing the CIA to dispatch Chan on a plane to the Ukraine, where he is to observe closely a beautiful young Russian. Upon the plane's arrival in an unnamed city, he dutifully turns over to his CIA contact his notes listing the times the woman went to the restroom. He's off to a good night's sleep and a return flight to Hong Kong the next day.

Of course, he never gets any rest, because the Russian woman is involved in a plot involving a stolen Ukrainian nuclear warhead. In no time, Jackie finds himself snowboarding over Ukrainian mountains and posing as a stilt-walking priest in an elaborate Chinatown funeral procession in Brisbane, Australia, where he winds up fighting for his life in a shark tank. These are just a couple of the flashier moments in Chan's nonstop derring-do as he pursues a rogue CIA agent (Jackson Lou).

The plot is terrifically complicated, which is typical for the genre. That the film has been dubbed into laughably primitive English makes it all the harder to follow, but this is ultimately no big obstacle to its enjoyment. (This dubbing could pose a problem in Chan's more serious films, however.) As always, Chan displays a balletic grace in his elaborate martial arts stunts, performed with the knockabout humor of a born clown. Interestingly, one of the film's most delightful moments is one of the simplest. It occurs when Chan nonchalantly eases himself down a brick wall, bracing his legs against a convenient palm tree. Intricate, awesome stunts are a Chan trademark, but it's his unpretentious, boyish charm that ensures Jackie Chan's position as one of the giants of the international cinema.

NEW YORK POST, 1/10/97, p. 48, Larry Worth

What's with a title like "Jackie Chan's First Strike"?

Has a documentary crew captured the Asian superstar's debut at a bowl-o-rama? Or is it an attempt to avoid confusion with maybe "Jean Claude's First Strike"?

Thankfully, it's just overkill on the producers' part. More importantly, Chan never lets such redundancy affect his universally acclaimed stunts.

They're as fresh and invigorating as ever, served up amid a steady stream of fiery explosions, a hail of bullets, and hands flying from every corner of the screen.

In addition, "Strike" has Chan all over the map, hightailing it from Hong Kong to the Ukraine to Down Under to you name it. Viewers need a triptych to keep up.

But plot never counts for much in a Jackie Chan vehicle. Here, Chan—referenced in the script only as Jackie, no surname—is a cop caught between Hong Kong's boys in blue, the KGB, CIA and Russian Mafia as he tries to collar an arms dealer who smuggled a nuclear warhead from Moscow. Still following?

Not to worry. The good guys are virtually indistinguishable from the bad, particularly as they all make Chan do the high jump sooner or later.

Then again, that's what audiences eagerly await. It's like watching a dumb Busby Berkeley extravaganza, where the spurts of dialogue are endured to get to magically choreographed musical numbers. And sure enough, Chan's fancy footwork is as stunningly realized as the best of Busby.

Here, Chan does his thing with collapsible ladders, stilts, snowmobiles, never mind great white sharks. At one point, he even gives James Bond a run for his derring-do while dropping from one cliff after another on one ski, or engaging in underwater battle a la "Thunderball." All that's missing is a James Barry score.

Through it all, Chan maintains his humbling sense of humor, always proving lovably fallible—especially when rescuing the damsel in distress. Ultimately, he's a presence that's both godlike and human, an irresistible combination.

Sure, one can't help imagining Chan in a quality production—minus the badly dubbed dialogue, continuity snafus and idiosyncrasies of writer/director Stanley Tong. But the pair's meteoric track record indicates that Tong is the ying to Chan's yang.

So—unless talking about one of Chan's priceless limbs—if it ain't broke, why fix it?

NEWSDAY, 1/10/97, Part II/p. B2, John Anderson

Although the title "hardest-working man in show business" has been in James Brown's possession for a long time, the title may really belong to Jackie Chan. The gifted comic actor and Hong Kong martial-arts star, who never uses a stunt double, has broken most of the bones in his body, still has an unclosed hole in his skull (a memento from a stunt on a Yugoslav film set) and isn't a kid anymore. You can tell.

At the same time, "Jackie Chan's First Strike" (Why first? No idea) is the kind of pure entertainment Hollywood hardly makes anymore, an engaging, exciting and amusing romp through several continents, with some amazing fight choreography that may not surpass Chan's best work but certainly equals a lot of it.

The latest in his "Police Story" series, which included last year's re-release "Supercop," "First Strike" finds Chan as Jackie, a Hong Kong police detective being used by the CIA and Russians to retrieve a nuclear warhead. As often happens, Chan's character is carried along by an accelerating series of uncontrollable events, leaving him bemused and frantic, as fight scenes, locales and whatever's lying around is used to comic effect. Chan's films have consistently used found objects around which to build their martial-arts ballets—the major-appliance battle in "Rumble in the Bronx" was a good example—and "First Strike" contains at least one first-rate fight sequence, choreographed by director and fight coordinator Stanley Tong.

The scene: Having been framed for the murder of Chinese mobster Uncle Seven (Terry Woo), Jackie seeks out his daughter, Annie (Chen Chun Wu), to explain his innocence and is waylaid by her friends. The ensuing melee is in a catering hall and employs broomsticks, tables and an aluminum ladder, around and through which Chan travels while fending off his lethal opponents. As has become standard for a Jackie movie, outtakes from the action scenes are shown during the closing credits and indicate just how painful so much of this stuff can he.

The plot isn't much. Jackie is used and misused by a variety of people—Chinese mobsters, Russian mobsters in a variety of settings—Ukraine, Russia, Australia—while chasing and being chased. It's Chan's on-screen appeal. He's often been compared to Chaplin and Keaton as a physical comic. And the individual action sequences make the films special: a snowboard-snowmobile shootout across a frozen Ukrainian mountainside; Chan hanging off a soon-to-be detonated helicopter (hanging off helicopters is another Chan speciality); a lethal pursuit that involves a Chinese funeral and an Australian shopping mall and finds Chan kick-boxing on stilts. And, of course, the climactic car chase, with Jackie piloting a sports car onto a pleasure boat.

So much of the actual circumstances within Chan's movies are the same that it's remarkable how they manage to keep one's interest, but they do. It's a tribute to Chan's perfectionism, and that of Tong, and the enormous energy they expend making the shortest moments on film so fluid and comic. At least the outtakes serve to make Chan seem mortal: At one point, he's stopped in his tracks by a bloody nose. Bloody nose? Jackie Chan? Who thought he bled? Who thought he'd have any left? Or that the hardest-working man in show business is also a tortured artist?

SIGHT AND SOUND, 10/97, p. 49, David Tse

Policeman Jackie Chan's latest assignment is to tail an arms dealer to the Ukraine, a simple task that quickly turns into a death-defying chase at a skiing resort. Rescued from a frozen lake by Russian intelligence officer Colonel Gregor Yegorov, Chan is recruited to track down a missing arms dealer named Tsui who has in fact broken off an illegal nuclear-arms deal with Yegorov). Chan travels to Brisbane, Australia, and befriends Annie, Tsui's sister. An inquiry with Tsui's father, the local Triad boss Uncle Seven, proves fruitless. Chan is outsmarted and briefly captured by Tsui, who reveals Yegorov's true mercenary motive. Seven is murdered by Yegorov. The police suspect Chan is the killer, so Chan goes on the run. He storms Seven's club and eventually Chan's name is cleared.

A final free-for-all takes place in Chinatown in Brisbane, continuing onto the oceanarium where Annie works, with the various parties trying to obtain the all-important uranium core amidst sharks and bursting water tanks.   Eventually Yegorov and Tsui are captured, and Chan is honoured by the Russians.

To test how good a particular Jackie Chan movie is, look at its closing credits, which invariably feature footage of the astonishing stunts Chan has performed earlier, showing us what injuries he avoided or endured for its sake.   *First Strike*'s end credits are exciting but not quite as disturbingly demonstrative of Chan's masochistic streak as were, say, those from the first *Police Story*, which showed Chan nearly electrocuting himself.

Chan is an endearing anachronism, a kamikaze stuntman-superstar in the age of blue-screen effects.   An indefatigable vaudevillian, his mastery of acrobatic sight gags makes him less a successor to Bruce Lee's kung fu fighting mantle than a descendant of the great silent film clowns. In his breakthrough epic *Project A*, Chan dangled himself from a giant clock face (a la Harold Lloyd in 1923's *Safety Last*).   His best film to date, *Miracles/Oiji*, was a disguised remake of Capra's screwball comedy *Lady for a Day* (1933), as if that film had starred Buster Keaton.

This is why the hackneyed James Bond-like international espionage of *First Strike* is not the best backdrop for Chan to shine against: his everyman screen persona is the antithesis of Lee's—and for that matter Bond's—invincible heroics. (Chan has explained that "when Lee hits, he is a superman; after I hit, ouch, I grimace and hold my hand in pain.") *First Strike* is actually the fourth instalment in Chan's *Police Story* series, but since Stanley Tong took the director's megaphone over from Chan himself in the third episode *Supercop*, the mood is a far cry from the gritty policier drama of the first two movies.

Tong is a movie success story, a former stuntman turned coveted action director who was brought in to quicken Chan's notorious perfectionism.   What Tong practises with Chan in *Supercop, Rumble in the Bronx* and *First Strike* is a half-tourist, half-guerrilla kind of filmmaking, where Chan and his crew improvise set pieces according to local environments.   It's an easygoing approach, doubtlessly encouraged by Chan's near-fatal accident, which caused a concussion in the over-zealous *Armour of God* (1986).   Tong makes two mistakes here: he can't resist showing off the exotic locations, often to the detriment of narrative coherence; and the action sequences don't grow out of the story organically.   It makes you miss the way that in Chan's self-directed films, the fight scenes are woven into the fabric of the narrative in a similar way dance sequences are in Stanley Donen-Gene Kelly musicals.

Chan doesn't really get to move until half an hour into the movie, but when he does the screen really lights up.   *First Strike*'s derring-dos here include Chan skiing off a cliff and grabbing a helicopter in mid-air and fighting underwater in the company of some very real sharks.

But the best moments are the simple human ones, such as when Chan scales a building exterior with casual and impossible agility, or deftly holds off scores of villains with commonplace objects like a ladder or an umbrella (a classic Chan device).   At moments like these Chan displays the physical grace, relaxed humour, and breathless invention that would do Harold Lloyd and Keaton proud.

First Strike doesn't stand up to the joyous exhilaration of *Miracles* or the scorching intensity of *Police Story II*.   One can't help wondering why haven't those classics been re-released rather than this lackadaisical lark?   This film's success in US theatres, however, is not difficult to understand. Chan's immense desire to give pleasure to his audience is infectious, and we find ourselves forgiving the maladroit storytelling and the visual plainness.   There are scenes of unintentional hilarity due to the shoddy dubbing, but my guess is that Chan wouldn't mind our laughter at all. The best thing about Chan the performer is that he is utterly ego-free, someone who thinks nothing of donning a silly snow hat or walking on a pair of stilts while doing stunning acrobatics. The amount of unpretentious goodwill towards the audience is so overwhelming, we gladly return the affection.

VILLAGE VOICE, 1/21/97, p. 70, Nathaniel Wice

The pleasures of Jackie Chan draw into sharper relief as his movies evolve into their own action-export genre. *First Strike* the third Chan movie to be released here in dubbed form with an American soundtrack—was originally produced in Hong Kong by Golden Harvest and released in Asia some 10 months ago for Chinese New Year '96, but it's so panoramic and heavy with

Benetton-style internationalism that it qualifies as some new cinematic art form distinct even from Chan's own HK moviemaking.

The globe-trotting spy plot takes Chan, reprising his role as a humble HK cop, to the Ukraine and Australia to fight the post-Soviet spread of nuclear weapons. New Line's abridgment forsakes continuity, but smartly focuses attention on Chan's fluid magic as he slips down a brick wall, runs across a swimming pool, or lands a second-story kick on stilts (!). These are the moments of audible wonder in the audience. The larger-budget scenery is nice but the biggest thrills come in a fight sequence that was probably filmed in an HK soundstage: Chan twirls an A-frame ladder around his body like a majorette's baton.

Movies usually depend on a suspension of disbelief in order to work. The heroism of a Tom Cruise in *Mission Impossible* or Geena Davis in *The Long Kiss Goodnight* to pick up two examples of HK-inflected Hollywood, is diminished when we remember that it's only a movie. But Jackie Chan works in reverse, the illusion of the roles only serves to illuminate the hero who plays them. That's why an Australian policeman who's never met Chan's character in the movie can still refer to him as Jackie (and the U.S. distributor has added Jackie Chan's name to the film title). In this context, Chan's longtime American champions must cheer his overdue crossover success, even if it means wincing through the indignity of dubbing, camp laughter, or, concurrent with the film's release, a Mountain Dew "extreme" ad.

Moviegoers who still don't know Chan will be surprised by his humility, humor, and most of all, the unmitigated physicality he communicates (often obscured in the celebration of risky stunts he is getting too old to do). Even though there's the low rumble of a 007 theme in the soundtrack, when Chan exclaims at one point, "I feel just like James Bond," it's a wry reminder that Pierce Brosnan would never end an action sequence curled up in a fetal position, teeth chattering, on the ice of a frozen lake.

Also reviewed in:
CHICAGO TRIBUNE, 1/10/97, Friday/p. J, Mark Caro
NEW YORK TIMES, 1/10/97, p. C3, Stephen Holden
VARIETY, 5/6-12/96, p. 86, Leonard Klady

JEW, THE

A First Run Features release of an Animatografo production in collaboration with Tato Filmes, Metrofilmes, and A & B Producaos. *Executive Producer:* Antonio da Cunha Tolles. *Producer:* Jom Tob Azulay, Antonio Vazda Silva, and Claudio Kahns. *Director:* Jom Tob Azulay. *Screenplay (Portuguese with English subtitles):* Millor Fernandes, Geraldo Carneira, and Gilvan Pereira. *Director of Photography:* Eduardo Serra. *Editor:* Jose Manuel Lopes and Pedro Ribeiro. *Music:* Ruy Luis Pereira. *Art Director:* Adrian Cooper. *Sound:* Carlos Alberto Lopes. *Marionettes:* Jose Carlos Barnes and Jose Neto. *Costumes:* Maria Gonzaga. *Running time:* 85 minutes. *MPAA Rating:* Not Rated.

CAST: Felipe Pinheiro (António José da Silva); Dina Sfat (Lourença Coutinho); Mário Viegas (King Joao V); Jose Lewgoy; Fernanda Torres (Brites, da Silva's Cousin); José Neto; Ruy de Carvalho; Cristina Ache; Edwin Luisi (Alexandre); Rogerio Paulo; Curado Riberia; Fabio Jonqueiro.

NEW YORK POST, 1/8/97, p. 36, Larry Worth

Salem of 1692 wasn't unlike Lisbon of 1715: Denouncing one's neighbor was the favorite sport. But the Portuguese were less concerned with witches than Jews.

Specifically, countless Jews who had been forced into Christianity were put on trial for maintaining Judaic traditions. Among the most prominent: playwright Antonio Jose da Silva, Portugal's answer to Moliere.

His story, encapsulated in "The Jew," should give viewers a healthy dose of high drama, a horrific history lesson and an emotional workout. But unlike Nicholas Hytner (who just brought

Arthur Miller's "The Crucible" to brilliant cinematic life), director Jom Tob Azulay doesn't know the first thing about storytelling.

What he does know about is establishing time and place: His recreation of the Inquisition's terrors, as well as infinite palace intrigues surrounding the reign of King Joao V, are lovingly realized via superb sets, costumes, photography and lighting.

Unfortunately, establishing characters gets lost in the shuffle. Or, if the characters actually had been established, they fell victim to butcher-knife editing.

The script virtually jumps between crucial moments in the literary genius' life, as when somehow segueing from a quiet moment in da Silva's household to his grueling torture scenes on the rack.

Although none of the actors makes much of an impression, it's hard to blame the individuals. As the titular martyr, Felipe Pinheiro screams competently on cue, but rarely gets to state da Silva's beliefs before the scene arbitrarily changes. Efforts from Mario Viegas (as the scheming king) and Fernanda Torres' turn as da Silva's pretty, ill-fated cousin are equally wasted.

For whatever reason, more time actually goes to puppet-based depictions of da Silva's satiric works. As the ultimate irony, they're the production's least wooden aspect.

VILLAGE VOICE, 1/14/97, p. 63, J. Hoberman

The Jew, a Brazilian-Portuguese coproduction based on the life of the 18th-century playwright António José da Silva and his death at the hands of the Inquisition, is as uncomfortably blunt as its title. It's the only film I know (save Mel Brooks's *History of the World*) that concerns the forced conversion of Iberian Jewry, as well as the anxiety of those Jews who either practiced their beliefs in secret or else adapted, with varying degrees of success, to Catholicism.

Directed by Jom Tob Azulay for deft period reconstruction and near-maximum understatement, *The Jew* opens in 1715 with a group of Lisbon children staging a puppet show that dramatizes the miraculous tears flowing from a statue of Our Lady. One puppet is skeptical. "*Death to the marrano!*" the children shout. Their aunt stops the show and anxiously scolds them because ... they themselves are *marranos* (concealed Jews).

Although the action jumps ahead a decade, the early scene provides Antonio with all the psychological baggage the movie deems necessary—a mix of shame, subterfuge, and theatrically confused identity. Is he really a Jew? Antonio's cousin Brites, a multi-cultural militant *avant la lettre*, gives him a Mogen David amulet. Nevertheless, after confessing on the rack to the "sin" of Judaism, he seems to be successfully passing *converso*—feted by Portugese aristocrats as a successful writer of comedies.

The Jew is interspersed with numerous performances (including repeated versions of a *Don Quixote* puppet show), as if to make the point that Antonio is always playing a role—even using a puppet to court another cousin, who will become his wife. Modestly opulent, the movie makes judicious use of La Tour lighting and museum settings to signify a world of Iberian splendor. It's also somewhat less than translucent in its exposition. Is Antonio to be punished for his writings? The exuberant Brites is reported to the authorities by a nervous lover, her arrest perhaps serving as means to frame her cousin.

Like *The Crucible*, *The Jew* is set in a period of denunciations and heresies—albeit on a far more grandiose scale. The torture scenes are explicit without being exploitative—although, to see this movie is to viscerally understand the ingrained Jewish aversion to the splendors of the Catholic Church. Instructed to incriminate her family, Brites remains feisty enough to argue with the priest. Nevertheless, Antonio is brought before the Inquisition—along with his wife (whose own mother had been previously burned at the stake). There is no real evidence, and, like a pair of agents for Stalin's NKVD, two priests discuss the problems in constructing their respective cases. ("God will inspire you with proof," their superior advises.)

Even as Antonio languishes in the Inquisition dungeon, his irreverent puppet shows continue to be produced in Lisbon taverns. "It's by the Jew," someone remarks significantly after one particularly anti-authoritarian burlesque. The movie's point, of course, is that a far greater show is being staged by the Church's cynical grand inquisitor, with the acquiescence of Portugal's powerless king. The message of that imperial production is that—*marrano* or *converso*—a Jew is still a Jew.

Also reviewed in:
NEW YORK TIMES, 1/8/97, p. C12, Stephen Holden
VARIETY, 8/12-18/96, p. 35, Dennis Harvey

JOHN GRISHAM'S THE RAINMAKER

A Paramount Pictures release of a Constellation Films presentation of a Douglas/Reuther production in association with American Zoetrope. *Producer:* Michael Douglas, Steven Reuther, and Fred Fuchs. *Director:* Francis Ford Coppola. *Screenplay:* Francis Ford Coppola and Michael Herr. *Based on the novel by:* John Grisham. *Director of Photography:* John Toll. *Editor:* Barry Malkin and Melissa Kent. *Music:* Elmer Bernstein. *Music Editor:* Kathy Durning. *Sound:* Nelson Stoll and (music) Dan Wallin. *Sound Editor:* Michael Kirchberger. *Casting:* Linda Phillips-Palo. *Production Designer:* Howard Cummings. *Art Director:* Robert Shaw. *Set Designer:* Scott Murphy. *Set Decorator:* Barbara Munch. *Costumes:* Aggie Guerard Rodgers. *Make-up:* Lois Burwell. *Stunt Coordinator:* Jack Gill. *Running time:* 137 minutes. *MPAA Rating:* PG-13.

CAST: Matt Damon (Rudy Baylor); Claire Danes (Kelly Riker); Jon Voight (Leo F. Drummond); Mary Kay Place (Dot Black); Mickey Rourke (Bruiser Stone); Danny DeVito (Deck Schifflet); Dean Stockwell (Judge Harvey Hale); Teresa Wright (Clarice Birdsong, "Miss Birdie"); Virginia Madsen (Jackie Lemanczyk); Andrew Shue (Cliff Riker); Red West (Buddy Black); Johnny Whitworth (Donny Ray Black); Wayne Emmons (Prince Thomas); Adrian Roberts (Butch); Roy Scheider (Wilfred Keeley); Randy Travis (Billy Porter); Michael Girardin (Everett Lufkin); Randall King (Jack Underhall); Justin Ashforth (F. Franklin Donaldson); Michael Keys Hall (B. Bobby Shaw); James Cunningham (J. Michael Floquet); Frank Clem (Mr. Van Landel); Alan Woolf (Kermit Aldy); Sonny Shroyer (Delbert Birdsong); Pamela Tice Chapman (Vera Birdsong); Trula Marcus (Jewelery Saleswoman); Tony Dingman (Bruiser's Driver); Daniel O'Callaghan (Carl); Tim Kagy and John Yancey (Homicide Detectives); Verda Davenport (Jailer); Chris Gray (Jury Foreman); Johnetta Shearer (Courtroom Clerk); Tammy Wendel (Court Reporter); Nate Bynum (Mr. McKenzie); James W. Redmond (CNN Reporter); John Gray (Hospital Volunteer); Sherry Sanford (Nurse); Billy Ray Reynolds and Mary Lester (Murder Scene Bystanders); Deborah Frazier (St. Peter's Receptionist); Vernon Newman (Great Benefit Salesman); Lynn Carthane (Newscaster); Rodney Peck (Rehab Center Desk Clerk); Bill Lunn (Himself); Terrance Stewart (Boy with Broken Arm); Bridget Brunner (Bruiser's Receptionist); Mike Cody (Tinley Britt Lawyer); Donald Folden (Legal Commentator); Eloise Dukes (Clerk); Katherine Morrow (Deposition Court Reporter); Alex Harvey (Bar Exam Proctor); Melissa Hurst (Waitress at Bar); Anasa Briggs-Graves and Ronnie Dee Blaire (Bailiffs); Danny Glover (Judge Tyrone Kipler).

CHRISTIAN SCIENCE MONITOR, 11/21/97, p. 15, David Sterritt

Hollywood movies have always been eager to capitalize on legal proceedings, which is hardly surprising, given the built-in drama that trials often have. Two new pictures, both inspired by popular books, take us into Southern-style courtrooms.

But that's all they have in common. *The Rainmaker,* adapted by Francis Ford Coppola from John Grisham's bestseller, zeroes in on a Tennessee lawsuit fought by a novice attorney against a corporate enemy. *Midnight in the Garden of Good and Evil,* directed by Clint Eastwood from John Berendt's nonfiction novel, uses a murder trial for dramatic impact while devoting its main energy to portraits of eccentric characters in the colorful city of Savannah, Ga.

The hero of "The Rainmaker" is Rudy Baylor, a recent law-school grad who takes the only job he can find: ambulance-chasing for the benefit of a low-grade shyster who's more interested in profits than professionalism. Rudy hates this sleazy corner of the legal scene, yet he rather likes his new assistant, a venturesome hustler whose only claim to fame is having flunked the bar exam six times. This is hardly distinguished company. Rudy surmounts his lowly status, though, by taking on a handful of cases he truly believes in.

Grisham's novel is long and loquacious enough to follow Rudy through every twist and turn of his new career. Coppola's movie is more condensed, even with a running time of 2¼ hours, and some of the plot's surprises are sprung abruptly enough to seem arbitrary or even gimmicky. Also disappointing is the film's failure to develop any of the female characters in much depth. Some women have significant scenes, but they're mostly portrayed as victims with few inner resources to fall back on.

"The Rainmaker" provides pleasures as well as problems, though. The acting is generally smart, and Coppola has directed the movie with his usual keen attention to atmosphere, texture, and detail. While it's not in the league of "The Conversation" or "Apocalypse Now" or the first two "Godfather" pictures, it's a sturdy achievement that spins a persuasive story while taking unobtrusive note of some troubling contradictions—can money buy justice? Do criminals deserve a good defense? Do underdogs always win?—that are integral to the American judicial system.

"Midnight in the Garden of Good and Evil" begins when a New York journalist named John Kelso arrives in Savannah, Ga., to cover a social event for a magazine. Just when he thinks his little task is completed, one of his new friends—an antiques dealer widely known in the community is arrested for killing a wild-living young employee during a ferocious argument. Staying in town to write about the trial, John makes the acquaintance of various offbeat folks, including a stagestruck transvestite and a woman who weaves voodoo spells in the dead of night.

Berendt's book is as much a Georgia travelogue as a murder-trial narrative, and Eastwood steeps the movie version in moody Southern charm. He also soft pedals the tale's most sensationalistic aspects, although the picture earns its R rating with rough language and much material focusing on gay sexuality.

Eastwood's biggest miscalculation is to shorten the book's engrossing series of trials, thus diminishing its insights into the all-too-human factors (including bigotry) that can sway a courtroom's search for truth.

The picture's most impressive asset is Kevin Spacey's superbly crafted performance as the accused man. Also noteworthy is the soundtrack music, a sweet-sounding potpourri that was surely assembled by Eastwood himself, a jazz connoisseur who numbers the excellent "Bird" among his directorial credits.

LOS ANGELES TIMES, 11/21/97, Calendar/p. 2, Jack Mathews

[The following review by Jack Mathews appeared in a slightly different form in NEWSDAY, 11/21/97, Part II/p. B3.]

Francis Ford Coppola writing and directing an adaptation of a John Grisham novel sounds like the creative mismatch of the decade. What's next, Maya Angelou reciting "Humpty Dumpty"? Wynton Marsalis doing an arrangement for "Three Blind Mice"?

Of course, when you think of it, Angelou and Marsalis would no doubt elevate our appreciation of those simple verses, and that's exactly what Coppola does with "John Grisham's The Rainmaker."

Though he's adapting the same story Grisham always tells, that of an ethical, talented and inexperienced attorney taking on and outwitting powerful and corrupt legal opponents, Coppola has infused "The Rainmaker" with enough humor, character, honest emotion and storytelling style to make it one of the year's most entertaining movies. And the filmmaker manages all this without doing radical surgery on the spine of the novel.

"The Rainmaker" follows recent law school grad Rudy Baylor (Matt Damon) as he struggles to get his career off the ground in lawyer-infested Memphis with a pair of jobs that fell into his lap. One is handling the will of an elderly woman who wants to leave her imaginary fortune to a televangelist; the other is a lawsuit against an insurance company whose denial of a legitimate medical claim is costing a young man his life.

Coppola overcomes some of the episodic nature of the book by quickly doing away with the weak subplot about Miss Birdie's will. She's still around, played with delightful spiritedness by 79-year-old Teresa Wright, as Rudy's landlady, but the comic relief comes from her personality, not her predicament.

A second subplot, about Rudy's relationship with a young woman he attempts to rescue from her abusive husband, remains overplayed melodrama. But Claire Danes' strength as Kelly Riker, and the sincere chemistry between her and Damon, offset the cliché.

The main business of the plot is that insurance case, and it's a pip. A poor family-overworked mom Dot Black (Mary Kay Place), brain-damaged dad Buddy Black (Red West) and their dying son Donny Ray (John Whitworth)are suing Great Benefit, a billion-dollar company that has denied their claim for Donny's bone-marrow transplant, calling it an uncovered experimental procedure.

It's a strong case for someone facing his first bar exam, and Rudy reluctantly turns it over to Bruiser Stone (Mickey Rourke), the disreputable lawyer for whom he works briefly. When Bruiser disappears, after some pursuit by the feds, Rudy finds himself alone in the courtroom, arguing against a battery of high-priced corporate lawyers.

In the voice-over narration, written by Michael Herr, who provided the. same service on Coppola's "Apocalypse Now," Rudy muses that his opponents probably have more than 100 years of experience between them, while his staff—the ambulance-chasing paralegal Deck Shifflet (Danny DeVito)—has failed the bar exam six times.

These are odds Grisham likes. And so, apparently, does Coppola, who takes the opportunity to give corporate America and its legal bodyguards a scorching hotfoot. Great Benefit's dream team, led by the slick Leo Drummond (Jon Voight), is an immoral bunch, ready to defend its sleazy client with all means—legal and illegal—at its disposal. The team's bugging of Rudy's office and the countermeasures taken by Rudy and Deck lead to some hilarious consequences.

Humorless lawyers who think Hollywood has gone far enough in trashing their profession may not enjoy the additional beating they take here, and they will be right in saying that Coppola overstates the wretchedness of our legal system. But for the rest of us, it's great fun.

Coppola's casting is flawless. Damon, a talented young actor on the brink of stardom, gives Rudy just the right blend of innocence, determination and wariness. He makes a preposterous situation as plausible as it can be. DeVito is a riot as Deck Shifflet, a hardworking opportunist who can't pass a person in the hallway without producing a business card.

Voight is having a nice second career playing villains, and he's terrific as Drummond, a condescending Goliath being plumped for the courtroom kill by his unlikely opponent. Even Rourke, as the ironic shyster who keeps live sharks in his office, is fun to watch.

Other familiar faces belong to Dean Stockwell, playing the derelict judge who encourages Rudy to settle out of court for small change; Danny Glover, the pro-plaintiff judge who eventually tries the case; Roy Scheider, the skulking head of Great Benefit; and Virginia Madsen, as a fired claims agent who knows all the insurance company's dirty secrets.

It's hard to say Francis Ford Coppola's "John Grisham's The Rainmaker," but it's a pleasure to watch.

NEW YORK, 12/8/97, p. 63, David Denby

Matt Damon shows up again, [the reference is to *Good Will Hunting*] as Rudy Baylor, the young, just-out-of-law-school hero of *The Rainmaker*. Rudy is an earnest southern boy, gallant by instinct, with a streak of natural piety. Yet Rudy is also a lawyer, and therefore it's his business to consort with crooks and sellouts, and in general to work within a corrupt system that favors the wealthy and the powerful. *The Rainmaker,* adapted and directed by Francis Ford Coppola, is the most heartfelt of the six John Grisham movies—the one that bores most deeply and intimately into lawyering as a calling, a condition of spirit as well as a career. Is it worthwhile being a lawyer at all? Are the compromises too great? Michael Herr's written narration, spoken by Damon, is surprisingly touching, and the actor gives the straightest of straight performances. His lawyer is not some slick mover who eventually finds his conscience, like Tom Cruise in *The Firm;* he's idealistic from the beginning, and also devoid of self-righteousness (in fact, he has a wily streak that grows more and more pronounced as the movie goes on). It's possible to root for this young knight without feeling like a fool.

The Rainmaker is essentially a David-and-Goliath tale. In Memphis, Rudy and his scapegrace helper, Deck (Danny DeVito)—a true lover of the law who never passed the bar—take on a huge insurance company, a crooked outfit that won't pay the claims made by a family with a boy dying of leukemia. A big, nasty insurance company! It's not exactly a moving target, and unfortunately the picture falls into caricature now and then. The company's CEO is a desiccated moron (Roy Scheider), its chief lawyer (Jon Voight) a beautifully coiffed, contemptuous swine who gives himself away at every turn.

Coppola needs a success, and he plays up these populist elements, yet there's something else in his direction, something of the old textured quality. The atmosphere of low-rent lawyering is lovingly dowdy, and Coppola displays his familiar appreciation for the energy of morally compromised people. Rudy's first employer is a cuff-linked gangster-shyster played by a bearded Mickey Rourke with his early modesty and precision—Rourke, hoarse, in the gaudiest of gaudy shirts, makes a gorgeous slimeball. Even DeVito is restrained as the true believer who may not enter the church. Despite its moral simplicities, the movie is highly watchable. It's richly cast from top to bottom (Mary Kay Place, Teresa Wright, and Virginia Madsen show up in small roles), and Damon holds it together. We can even believe that this young Galahad takes care of a battered young housewife (Claire Danes) without having any initial sexual interest in her. Purity is one of the hardest things to bring off with conviction. Damon brings it off.

NEW YORK POST, 11/21/97, p. 47, Michael Medved

John Grisham's novel "The Rainmaker" tells a simple and, in fact, simplistic David and Goliath story: An idealistic law school graduate in Memphis facing his first trial takes on a mighty, utterly corrupt insurance company that's been preying on decent but downtrodden working people.

In the movie version of the book, director-screenwriter Francis Ford Coppola invests this flimsy story structure with surprising depth and intensity, thanks to an abundance of eloquent images and compelling characters.

Of course, Coppola worked similar magic on his signature "Godfather" films—enriching pallid pop fiction with unexpected color and resonance.

Once again, expert casting proves crucial to his success. Matt Damon plays the most persuasive Grisham movie hero to date because, unlike his glamorous predecessors (such as Tom Cruise in "The Firm" or Matthew McConaughey in "A Rage To Kill"), he seems ordinary and unpolished enough to make a plausible underdog—particularly with Coppola's intimate focus on the challenges of his daily life.

Danny DeVito portrays the youthful crusader's cynical Sancho Panza, a "paralawyer" who has repeatedly failed the bar but introduces the newcomer to the joys of ambulance chasing.

All other roles benefit from comparably vivid work, with Mickey Rourke as the deliciously shady legal operator who initially sponsors our hero, Mary Kay Place and Johnny Whitwork as pathetic victims of corporate greed, Danny Glover as a wry, sympathetic courtroom judge, Virginia Madsen as a sassy, mysteriously missing witness and, most notably, the superb Jon Voight as the oily, super-sophisticated, charming, conniving, corporate shyster who seems to outmaneuver his rough-hewn, rookie rival at every turn.

The movie's most significant weakness involves a groan-inducing subplot in which Claire Danes arouses the protagonist's protective instincts as the horrifically battered bride of a sadistic psycho (Andrew Shue). She and Damon project tender chemistry together, but still can't carry a clumsy romance to a satisfying conclusion.

NEWSWEEK, 11/24/97, p. 73, David Ansen

A wonderfully quirky cast under Francis Ford Coppola's direction makes this one of the more enjoyable Grisham movies. The formula is pure David and Goliath: an idealistic young lawyer (Matt Damon) and his ambulance-chasing partner (Danny DeVito) do battle with a corrupt insurance company and its team of expensive lawyers. In a romantic subplot, our hero falls for a battered wife (Claire Danes). The outcome of both stories may be predictable, but the writing (Coppola did the adaptation) is sharp and funny, low-rent Memphis is pungently evoked and the scoundrels are irresistibly hissable. Among the best of a gravel-voiced lot are Mickey Rourke as a flamboyantly shady lawyer, Dean Stockwell as a local judge and Jon Voight as a sleek corporate attorney. The good guys are fun, as well: the naive but shrewd Damon; DeVito at his slob-pit-bull best; a droll Danny Glover as the presiding judge, and Mary Kay Place as the dirt-poor woman who instigates the lawsuit. It's good to have Coppola back in form; he's not taking any big risks here, but he serves up this crowd-pleaser with old-pro panache.

SIGHT AND SOUND, 4/98, p. 50, Philip Kemp

Memphis. Rudy Baylor an idealistic young law student, finds himself obliged to work for Bruiser Stone, a crooked lawyer. Stone assigns Rudy sleazy paralegal Deck Schifflet as his assistant. Rudy has two cases: Clarice Birdsong ("Miss Birdie"), an eccentric old lady constantly revising her will to exclude her grasping family, and Donny Ray Black, a young man stricken with leukaemia whose insurance company, Great Benefit, refuses to pay on the health-insurance policy taken out by his mother, Dot. Rudy meets a young woman, Kelly Riker, hospitalised after her husband Cliff has savagely beaten her. He urges her to divorce Cliff, but fearfully she refuses.

Rudy moves into the apartment behind Clarice's house. With Stone facing indictment for fraud, Rudy and Deck set up on their own. Having passed his bar exam, Rudy represents Dot in court against Great Benefit, coming up against a team of slick lawyers headed by the formidable Leo F. Drummond. The assignment of liberal-minded judge Tyrone Kipler to the case tilts the balance back in Rudy's favour. Donny Ray, gravely ill, gives his deposition at home, but Drummond and Great Benefit block Rudy's access to a key witness, former claims assessor Jackie Lemanczyk. Donny Ray dies.

Kelly, brutalised again, agrees to file for divorce. At her house, she and Rudy are attacked by Cliff. Rudy overcomes him and beats him almost to death. Kelly makes Rudy leave, then finishes Cliff off and takes all the blame. In court, Rudy, with Deck's help, produces Jackie Lemanczyk. Her testimony damns Great Benefit, but is disallowed on a technicality. Deck, via a call to Bruiser, finds a way round this. Rudy demolishes Great Benefit's chief executive, and the jury awards Dot Black $50 million in damages. But the company files for bankruptcy; she will get nothing. Reunited with Kelly, who has been released without charge on a self-defence plea, the disillusioned Rudy considers teaching instead of practising law.

To say that *The Rainmaker* finds Francis Ford Coppola back on form would be an overstatement. We're sadly far from the glories of *The Conversation* (1974) or the first two *Godfather* films. Still, it's a vast improvement over the unspeakable *Jack* from two years ago, as well as being one of the less stodgy adaptations of a John Grisham novel. True, at over two hours it overstretches its slight material, and all the doomy Coppola style—claustrophobic shadows, portentous low-angle camerawork—weighs heavily on what's essentially little more than two or three episodes of a better-than-average television courtroom drama. Nor are the three strands of plot (or rather two-and-a-half, since the Miss Birdie story fades out midway through) ever knitted properly together. But the film's visual solemnity is undercut by a healthy streak of cynicism, and at times a rare thing for Coppola—it's even funny.

The most diverting moments come less from situation or dialogue than from interplay of character. The script is serviceable, but less stylish than might be expected from a film that lists "Poet in Residence" among its credits. But Coppola has always been a fine director of actors, and in *The Rainmaker* he encourages his cast to get their teeth into some rich nutrients. At times, in fact, the film threatens to disintegrate into a string of cameos, with especially ripe turns coming from Dean Stockwell's venal, terminally bronchial judge, and Mickey Rourke as a lawyer so hyped on his own lack of scruple he keeps a tank of baby sharks in his office. Claire Danes, though, unleashes a stark intensity as the battered wife, rescuing the role from being sidelined, while as the hotshot defence counsel Jon Voight gives his best performance in years, superficially complacent but with hints of self-doubt quivering his florid jowls. And whenever the film courts sentimentality there's always Danny DeVito as the gleefully opportunistic Deck Schifflet, sidling away from Donny Ray's lump-in-throat deposition scene to check out a black kid with an arm in plaster as a possible client, or exulting when Donny Ray dies: "Now it's a wrongful death suit: gazillions!"

Schifflet serves as the most prominent outcrop of the film's saving grace—its underlying mood of cynicism about the legal system and US institutions. In its bare outlines, the plot follows that of a thousand courtroom movies: the starry eyed young lawyer's initial success, his unearthing of a surprise witness, the unexpected setback, the final triumph of justice. Less predictable, and dramatically far more potent, is the dying fall that follows the verdict. The insurance company goes bankrupt, robbing Donny Ray's mother yet again without hope of redress, and the brash youngster realises that his triumph is the first step of his possible transformation into his despised opponent, the fat-cat lawyer retained by crooked corporations. He fears becoming "just another lawyer joke". This shadow side is reflected in the film's visual texture, at once lush and edgy, an index of moral ambivalence.

These two edged resolutions have always drawn Coppola's strongest emotional responses. Think of Harry Caul's horrified realisation in *The Conversation* that all his conscientious sleuthing has pointed the exact wrong way; of Willard having slaughtered Kurtz in *Apocalypse Now,* as dead inside as the man he just killed; of Michael Corleone's empty gaze after the final bloodletting of *Godfather II.* *The Rainmaker* falls far short of those masterpieces, no question, but it shares something of their sense of a morally precarious world, where success entails far more dangers than failure.

TIME, 12/1/97, p. 80, Richard Schickel

For the moment, which may extend to Academy Awards night, Matt Damon has cornered the always busy market in youthful, affronted innocence. And you have to admit he's pretty good at it. In *The Rainmaker,* playing Rudy Baylor, a young, undertrained lawyer trying his first case, he shows a nice sneaky knuckler, tracing an erratic path toward the strike zone. In *Good Will Hunting,* he pitches a sharp curve ball as a brilliant autodidact, confused by his own genius, alternately angry and vulnerable. Yet whether Damon has a high hard one, a true star's blowback fastball, is not a question these movies permit him to answer.

But *The Rainmaker,* cleverly adapted by Francis Ford Coppola from a John Grisham novel, is honest, commercial fun, and *Good Will Hunting,* which is written by Damon and his co-star (and old buddy) Ben Affleck, is finally dishonest, but in ways that will delude the impressionable into thinking it's saying something important.

Meantime, however, a couple of cheers for Coppola, who satisfies at least one ruling critical principle: any movie that offers successful employment to Mickey Rourke and Teresa Wright cannot be all bad. He's the only shyster in town who's willing to take a chance on young Rudy; she's his landlady who is nowhere near as ditsy as she looks. And like the rest of a constantly bestartling supporting cast, led by Jon Voight and Danny DeVito as deliciously disparate masters of legal sleaze, they're terrific. Another good rule is not to take Grisham novels as seriously as the writer does when you bring them to the screen, and Coppola fulfills that imperative too. This one is about a big insurance company trying to cheat a poor family out of medical payments that might save a boy's life. Justice in this matter is eventually served, but with comic klutziness and realistic ambiguity.

For a while, it's possible to hope that *Good Will Hunting* may partake of the same exuberant spirit. Damon's title character, Will Hunting (isn't that cute?), is a janitor at M.I.T., solving impossible equations a professor leaves on a blackboard. After hours, though, he joins his lowlife South Boston cronies for stupid boozing and brawling. Class issues, rarely raised in American movies, seem about to be interestingly engaged. But no, Will's inability to find love and embrace his upscale destiny is the product of childhood abuse, the memory of which he must recover. This brings on Robin Williams as—what else?—the humanist shrink, himself a troubled soul, but, like Will, redeemable (they are both baseball lovers). Hearts sinking, we are obliged to endure much pseudo-serious gabble as we head toward another painfully predictable triumph of the human spirit. There must be some better way of hunting our—and Oscar's goodwill.

VILLAGE VOICE, 11/25/97, p. 96, Amy Taubin

Last week it was Dustin Hoffman as a journalist in *Mad City,* this week it's Matt Damon as a lawyer in *The Rainmaker,* both fretting about "crossing the line." With no one except hormonally driven teens and right-wing nutjobs excited about sex anymore, the workplace is Hollywood's current libidinal frontier. Crossing the line is the professional equivalent of falling into the arms of the whore of Babylon. Real men thrill to the opportunity but do not succumb.

Adapted from yet another John Grisham courtroom opus by director Francis Ford Coppola, who knows the box office potential of a potboiler when he reads one *(The Godfather* had its origins in the deathless prose of Mario Puzo), *The Rainmaker* is a David and Goliath story that pits an idealistic, penniless young lawyer against a lying, cheating, billion dollar health insurance company.

Fresh out of law school, Rudy Baylor (Damon) is hired to do ambulance chasing by Memphis sharpie attorney Bruiser Stone (Mickey Rourke). When FBI scrutiny forces Bruiser to skip town, Rudy sets up a storefront office in partnership with Bruiser's enterprising "para-lawyer," Deck Schifflet (Danny DeVito). Rudy's most promising client is Dot Black (Mary Kay Place), whose son Donny Ray (Johnny Whitworth) is dying of leukemia. Donny has been denied coverage for a bone marrow transplant by Great Benefits, a routinely scummy health insurance operation that's made a fortune by selling policies to poor people and then refusing to pay their claims.

Great Benefits expects that Dot, like most of its naive clients, will simply give up and go away. Dot, however, is a fighter, and Rudy encourages her to go to trial. But even with a judge (Danny Glover) who's absurdly on their side, it's a greener-than-grass attorney against a gang of $1000-an-hour lawyers headed by the corrupt dolt Leo Drummond (Jon Voight).

Basically a courtroom drama in which the verdict is never in doubt, *The Rainmaker* tries to pump up suspense with a subplot involving Claire Danes as an abused wife who becomes the object of Rudy's extracurricular rescue fantasy. But because the romance is without heat, it's hard to think of Danes's character as anything but a distraction from the sexier demands of the courtroom.

Following Grisham's lead, Coppola paints his characters all black or all white, which makes *The Rainmaker* duller and less believable than it need be. The exception is Bruiser. With gray hair crimped so stiffly you can smell the curling iron, Rourke makes sleaze irresistible. Too bad he exits early for the Caribbean.

Given that the writer and the director of the film are one and the same, it's peculiar that they seem so at odds. Coppola's script is sentimental and vulgar. His direction is restrained and rather elegant. The combination should please no one.

The most interesting directorial choice Coppola makes is to shoot most of *The Rainmaker* from noticeably low angles. The effect is not that the characters are monumentalized, but rather that you become aware of the various ceilings (in homes, in courtrooms, in hospitals) that keep the little guy down. John Toll's burnished cinematography and Elmer Bernstein's score give an old-fashioned studio feel to what might otherwise have been a movie of the week.

Though Danes is wasted in a thankless role, the supporting actors are fine, particularly Virginia Madsen, as an alcoholic claims officer who pulls the plug on Great Benefits, and Red West (one of Elvis Presley's acting sidemen), as the father of the leukemic Donny Ray. DeVito does his usual sparkplug routine and Voight works his face like silly putty (he's truly unbearable).

Poised but bland, Damon carries the film without making much of an impression. You'd never suspect seeing him here that he's the boychick of the year. (It's not Coppola but Gus Van Sant's turning him loose in *Good Will Hunting* that will make him a star.) Nothing in Damon's true blue performance prepares us for his climactic speech about getting out of lawyering before he finds himself crossing the line. But buried in most Hollywood movies is an allegory of their own making. What line did Coppola cross that he hadn't crossed before when he chose to make this Grisham bestseller his own? Remember *Jack*?

Also reviewed in:
CHICAGO TRIBUNE, 11/21/97, Friday/p. A, Michael Wilmington
NATION, 12/22/97, p. 35, Stuart Klawans
NEW REPUBLIC, 12/15/97, p. 29, Stanley Kauffmann
NEW YORK TIMES, 11/21/97, p. E18, Janet Maslin
VARIETY, 11/17-23/97, p. 63, Todd McCarthy
WASHINGTON POST, 11/21/97, p. C1, Rita Kempley
WASHINGTON POST, 11/21/97, Weekend/p. 50, Desson Howe

johns

A First Look Pictures release in association with Bandeira Entertainment of a Flynn/Simchowitz production. *Executive Producer:* P. Holt Gardiner. *Producer:* Beau Flynn and Stefan Simchowitz. *Director:* Scott Silver. *Screenplay:* Scott Silver. *Director of Photography:* Tom Richmond. *Editor:* Dorian Harris. *Music:* Charles Brown and Danny Caron. *Music Editor:*

Gary Wasserman. *Sound:* Larry Scharf and (music) Samuel Lehmer. *Sound Editor:* Andrew DeCristofaro. *Casting:* Mary Vernieu. *Production Designer:* Amy Beth Silver. *Art Director:* William P. Paine. *Set Decorator:* Jennifer Gentile. *Costumes:* Sara Jane Slotnick. *Make-up:* Kenneth Michael. *Stunt Coordinator:* Rick Avery. *Running time:* 96 minutes. *MPAA Rating:* R.

CAST: David Arquette (John); Lukas Haas (Donner); Wilson Cruz (Mikey); Keith David (Homeless John); Christopher Gartin (Eli); Elliott Gould (Manny Gould); Terrence Dashon Howard (Jimmy the Warlock); Richard Timothy Jones (Mr. Popper); Nicky Katt (Mix); Richard Kind (Paul Truman); Kurtis Kunzler (Hustler at Payphone); John C. McGinley (Danny Cohen); Louis Mustillo (John Wayne, "Rex"); Harper Roisman (Old Man); Josh Schaefer (David); Alanna Ubach (Nikki); Arliss Howard (John Cardoza); Tony Epper (Santa Claus); Sydney Lassick (Al); Ruth Silver (Tourist Mom); N'Bush Wright (X-Mas Junkie); Nina Siemaszko (Tiffany the Prostitute); Craig Bierko (Christmas Preacher on Radio).

LOS ANGELES TIMES, 1/31/97, Calendar/p. 6, Kevin Thomas

[The following review by Kevin Thomas appeared in a slightly different form in NEWSDAY, 1/31/97, Part II/p. B15.]

There's a sentimental streak a mile wide in Scott Silver's "johns," but it's nonetheless engaging and poignant because David Arquette and Lukas Haas bring such vulnerability and likability to the Santa Monica Boulevard hustlers that Silver has written with such care and compassion. A tragicomic tale, "johns" is a minor film, but it fulfills its aspirations.

In interviewing actual hustlers, Silver came away impressed by their survival instincts and disturbed by their belief in the impossibility of friendship. The film opens with Arquette's John waking up in a park, without his lucky sneakers, which have his life savings hidden in them. These were the shoes that were "going to take me places." John is a hustler archetype: a nice-enough-looking, outgoing, none-too-bright young man with self-deluding dreams of becoming an actor. We don't know how long he's been hitting the streets, but he's definitely beginning to look worn and seedy.

In contrast, Haas' fresh, boyish Donner has been hustling only seven weeks, learning the ropes from John and falling in love with him in the process. The film, which unfolds over Christmas, involves John's struggle to scrape up enough money to pay off a $300 debt to the menacing Jimmy the Warlock (Terrence Dashon Howard), Donner's struggle to get John to accept his friendship and also to earn enough money to get them on a bus to Branson, Mo., where a cousin can provide them work and shelter as lifeguards at a resort. Both John and Donner, in different ways, are innocents, Donner surprisingly and dangerously so. As the film shifts into a countdown mode, it begins to fill you with the fear that these two, as they pursue various johns, aren't going to make it out of town after all.

Although "johns" grows ever more ominous, there are a number of funny moments along the way. Elliott Gould is very amusing as a prissy, romantic family man who is one of John's regulars, and so is Harper Roisman as an elderly man who picks up Donner and proves to be one tough, blunt-talking old guy. Even more deceptive is Arliss Howard's shy, stuttering customer, who takes John to a motel.

There's a graceful flow and an aptly noirish look to "johns," thanks to versatile cinematographer Tom Richmond, but you wish that Silver had not allowed his cast to become at times so unnecessarily mannered. Also, too much is too obvious or too pointedly symbolic e.g., the Branson resort is called Camelot, it is set over Christmas, etc. The film boasts a great Charles Brown-Danny Caron score, but some of its songs underline the action too heavily.

Still and all, these are familiar, far-from-fatal flaws typical of a first feature. On the whole, "johns" augurs well for the directing future of Silver, a 1993 American Film Institute graduate.

NEW YORK POST, 1/31/97, p. 42, Thelma Adams

Is it any fresher when the hooker with the golden heart is a boy? Not really, but Scott Silver manages a few new twists in his accomplished debut "johns."

Cruising among Hollywood's hustlers, the writer-director shows he can slum and spin a cliche at the same time. Sure, Silver's anecdotes—plucked from the paid confessions of bona fide street boys—are more graphic than when Shirley MacLaine played a prostitute. She didn't pitch ripe grapefruits at a man's hairy butt to satisfy him—and get beaten up when she laughed at the ridiculousness of the trick.

Lukas Haas' rookie hustler, Donner, fits within the pantheon of bruised good-time girls working the other side of Tinseltown's streets. He views the world through eyes of wonder—when he's not training baby seal beat-me looks on the camera.

Haas has matured since he made "Witness" in 1985. As he approaches adulthood, his signature is the gawky, intelligent man-boy stalled in adolescence. He wears his feelings on his pale skin the way others sport tattoos. A sensitive actor, Haas' gentleness brings out the fire in his co-stars.

Donner's best friend, and unrequited lover, is the streetwise John (David Arquette). Donner cares too much; John protests he doesn't care at all. Yes, it's a buddy movie that moves its homosexual undertones to overtones.

In one long, tragi-comic day, John loses his lucky sneakers, his cash stash, commits a robbery, and gets stabbed and beaten repeatedly. It's both Christmas Eve and the eve of his 21st birthday. His mission? To score the cash to spend the night at a plush Beverly Hills hotel.

Arquette ("Scream") is the movie's live wire, the antsy, edgy, dangerous life force that both invites and delivers danger. When this low-rent Paul Newman removes his shirt, it becomes easy to ignore his yellow teeth and filthy feet. Arquette, in a memorable low-budget performance, takes the anonymity out of the name John. This is a lost boy with soul; the fact that he never mentions or explains his past is explanation enough.

Elliott Gould and Arliss Howard play clients with varying success. Gould heard "johns" was a comedy and plays his married husband role too broadly; Howard gives warmth to an implausible conclusion. As Homeless John, Keith David strikes a Paul Robeson pose; he can't overcome the fact that he's playing a symbol rather than a character.

Among the movie's funnier episodes is a car ride pairing Donner and a horny, spotty senior. While it goes a long way to deglamorize hustling, the scene ends the only way Silver knows how: with escalating violence.

Caught between a laugh and a beating, the audience stops sympathizing with this gutter-chic Beavis and Butt-head. By the forced redemptive ending, Silver has run out of tricks.

SIGHT AND SOUND, 6/97, p. 54, Rob White

John, a male prostitute, wakes up in Los Angeles on Christmas Eve morning just in time to see someone running off with the sneakers in which he keeps his money. This means he'll now need to earn enough once again to fulfil his dream of spending Christmas Day (his birthday) at the Park Plaza hotel. Later, two other hustlers warn John that Jimmy the Warlock—a dealer he owes money to—is looking for him. John finds his friend Donner who tells him how he was beaten up by a date. A family draws up to John and Donner while they're on the street and pay to have their photo taken with Donner. John meets his girlfriend Nikki while Donner looks on sadly.

On a date, John is stabbed and Donner tends the wound. They go to the Plaza where John leaves a $100 downpayment on the room. Donner phones his cousin who offers him and John jobs as lifeguards at a theme park, but John refuses to go. John steals a string of pearls which he pawns. Jimmy and a crony beat John up and take his money, demanding the rest of the debt by midnight. Donner is beaten by an elderly date. John finds Donner, apologises to him, and decides to go to the theme park with him. He retrieves his $100 from the hotel. Donner goes to Jimmy and pays off the remainder of the debt. On the way to the bus station, John decides to meet one last date. In a hotel room, he's murdered after sex. Donner is distraught when he finds John's body. It was he who stole the sneakers, in order to make sure Jimmy was paid off. Donner takes the bus alone.

Recalling *My Own Private Idaho*, *Johns* is a story of unconsummated love between two gay hustlers, but unlike its predecessor it's a graceless film which seems ill at case with its subject-matter. It does feature touching and compelling performances from Lukas Hass (playing Donner) and David Arquette (as John). However, little attention is paid to either the social circumstances of prostitution or the psychology of this central relationship. Instead, novice writer-director Scott Silver presents characters whose compulsions are less emotional or sexual than materialistic. The height of John's ambitions is to spend his birthday in Los Angeles' Park Plaza hotel. At one point, John goes into the hotel, eyes wide, and the normally uninquisitive camera spins and careers around the lobby as if enraptured by the palatial surroundings. All that's needed at this point is for Richard Gere to turn up and take John shopping for the film to turn into a gay *Pretty Woman*.

Towards the beginning, John and Donner are stopped in the street by an out-of-town family in a car. The father asks John to photograph them all with Donner, as if any hick visitors in LA would want to get a snap of a real-life rent boy. It's hard not to read this scene as an inadvertent parody of *Johns*, the fictional correlative of the fantasy of selling a gay-themed movie to Middle America. It's worth bearing in mind that Silver, depressed at not being an overnight success in Hollywood, apparently behaved in a rather similar way to his fictional tourists: he cruised in search not of sex but hustlers' stories which, at $20 a time, could form the basis for his big break.

Though the distributors would have audiences liken *Johns* to *Midnight Cowboy* (1969), it may be more useful to compare it to Bruce LaBruce's *Hustler White*, which has a remarkably similar setting and structure. In that accomplished feature, LaBruce ironises the narrational point-of-view by aligning it with that of a louche writer (played by himself) imperiously researching streetlife. This made the film interestingly camp and self-referential. There's no question in *Hustler White*, as there is with *Johns*, of worrying that the point-of-view might be touristic and prurient. While LaBruce's characters are at home with deviance—with porn, for instance, or sadomasochism— Silver's are scrubbed *ingénus* (John constantly changes his clothes), and conventional. And there's no trace in *Hustler White* of the portentousness which characterises the concluding tragedy of *Johns*. Tragedy in LaBruce's film, such as the death of one hustler's amputee lover, is tucked away amidst edgy satire. LaBruce celebrates sexual and social nonconformity; Silver prefers a superficial, easily intelligible idea of 'the norm'.

This explains the title, which refers both to the slang name for a prostitute's dates and to the fact that John keeps meeting people with the same name as his. The film's overall attempt to appeal to a mainstream audience reaches a peak of triteness with this conceit. Worse still, that universalisation has a funny way of turning into a kind of denunciation. The physical contact between John and Donner is minimal. What intimacy there is takes place between John and his girlfriend Nikki or—repeatedly and violently—between the hustlers and their dates and dealers. John's and Donner's faces are progressively more battered as the film goes on. The result is that sex becomes displaced by violence. The problem is not that violence doesn't have a part in a movie about prostitution; it's that there's virtually nothing in *Johns* to counter the violent apogee—the post-coital murderousness which finally kills John. This is exploitative filmmaking, but it's arguably also reactionary and subtly prurient regardless of its director's intentions.

VILLAGE VOICE, 2/4/97, p. 70, Amy Taubin

Of course, acting alone does not make a film. In *johns*, the talented David Arquette and Lucas Haas are hung to dry by fledgling director-writer Scott Silver. Judging from certain desperate editing effects (like dropping the ambient sound out of a mundane shot of a kid walking down the street and replacing it with high-toned ecclesiastical music), Silver realized too late that a couple of "true" stories about young male L.A. hustlers and their creepy johns don't necessarily add up to a feature film.

Arquette plays an experienced hustler on the run from a drug dealer he's ripped off. Haas plays the gay runaway who's in love with him. *johns* recalls any number of indie films, but primarily *My Own Private Idaho*. Each time Haas or Arquette checked out passing cars for potential clients, I could have sworn they were really looking for Gus Van Sant.

Also reviewed in:
NEW YORK TIMES, 1/31/97, p. C12, Stephen Holden
VARIETY, 1/29-2/4/96, p. 63, Godfrey Cheshire

JUNGLE 2 JUNGLE

A Walt Disney Pictures and TFI International release. *Executive Producer:* Richard Baker, Rick Messina, and Brad Krevoy. *Producer:* Brian Kelly. *Director:* John Pasquin. *Screenplay:* Bruce A. Evans and Raynold Gideon. *Based on "Un Indien dans la ville" by:* Hervé Palud, Thierry Lhermitte, Igor Aptekman, and Philippe Bruneau de la Salle. *Director of Photography:* Tony Pierce-Roberts. *Editor:* Michael A. Stevenson. *Music:* Michael Convertino. *Music Editor:* Ken Wannberg and Michael Ryan. *Choreographer:* Sarah Rudner. *Sound:* Allan Byer and (music) Dennis Sands and David Marquette. *Sound Editor:* Bruce Stubblefield. *Casting:* Renée Rousselot. *Production Designer:* Stuart Wurtzel. *Art Director:* Timothy Galvin. *Set Decorator:* Beth Rubino. *Special Effects:* Steve Kirshoff and Russell Berg. *Costumes:* Carol Ramsey. *Make-up:* Bernadette Mazur. *Stunt Coordinator:* Danny Aiello, III. *Running time:* 105 minutes. *MPAA Rating:* PG.

CAST: Tim Allen (Michael Cromwell); Sam Huntington (Mimi-Siku); JoBeth Williams (Dr. Patricia Cromwell); Lolita Davidovich (Charlotte); Martin Short (Richard Kempster); Valerie Mahaffey (Jan Kempster); LeeLee Sobieski (Karen Kempster); Frankie Galasso (Andrew Kempster); Luis Avalos (Abe); Bob Dishy (George Langston); Rondi Reed (Sarah); Oni Faida Lampley (Madeleine); Dominic Keating (Ian); Carole Shelley (Fiona); Michael Mastro (Gino); Joan Copeland (Mrs. Prelot); Jack McGee (Mr. Uhley); David Ogden Stiers (Alexei Jovanovic); Nicholas J. Giangiulio (Jovanovic Thugs); Christie Toy (Stewardess); Jack O'Connell (Homeless Person); Jake Cooper (Bejamin); Ken Larsen (Ride Operator); Lowell Sanders (Broker); Adam LeFevre (Morrison); John Tormey (Deli Clerk); Diana Roberts ("Hello You" Girl); Derek Smith (Louis); Tanya Memme (Trader's Assistant); R.M. Haley (Hot Dog Vendor); Glen Trotiner (Dart Booth Attendant); Eva Vernonika (Jovanovic's Mother); Georgina Kess (Fish Market Employee); Maureen Beitler (Nurse); SHTHD Right-Turn Clyde (Matitka); Brian M. Reilly (Fingerless Hand); John Pasquin (Bearded Man in Times Square).

LOS ANGELES TIMES, 3/7/97, Calendar/p. 8, Kevin Thomas

More often than not, Hollywood studios buy up foreign films for remakes only to throw out the very elements that made them so attractive in the first place. Disney, however, has been too smart to do that. It picked up "Un Indien dans la Ville," one of France's biggest box-office hits ever, dubbed it as painstakingly as possible and released it last year as "Little Indian, Big City." Now Disney is opening its charming and funny remake, "Jungle 2 Jungle," which fits Tim Allen like a glove while retaining everything that made the original such a delight.

Allen plays Michael Cromwell, a workaholic Wall Street commodities trader who makes a rush trip to the Amazonian jungle to complete his divorce from his long-estranged wife (a wryly amused JoBeth Williams), who left him after he installed a fifth phone line into their apartment, making her feel more a receptionist than a wife. What he could never anticipate was that he would be returning home with their 13-year-old son, Mimi-Siku (Sam Huntington), whom he never knew he had. The son speaks English but has been raised by his mother, a doctor, as an Amazonian native.

A most reluctant father, Michael hits Manhattan accompanied by a barefoot son in a loincloth, carrying a blow gun, a bow and arrow—and in a small wicker basket, his very large pet spider, Myteka. If Michael's vapid fashion designer fiance (Lolita Davidovich, lovely and rightly laughable) is somewhat less than thrilled at the unexpected prospect of becoming a stepmother to so unusual a teenager, she is flat-out aghast at Myteka.

Where the original French writers and their American adapters have been especially clever is in coming up with a lot of farcical plot and sight gags to provide hilarity and adventure to undercut the predictability of the inevitable flowering of a father-son relationship. Michael has unintentionally left his pal and partner Richard (Martin Short, a frantic comic joy) in the lurch over a business deal while off to the Amazon, and that has driven Richard to go to a dangerous Russian mobster (deliciously played by David Ogden Stiers).

Then there's Mimi-Siku's tumultuous weekend visit with Richard's family, which includes Mimi in all innocence roasting Richard's cherished aquarium fish, worth thousands of dollars. Much of the film's humor derives from Mimi's "wild child" behavior, which at once aggravates his self-absorbed father yet also has the effect of gradually liberating him. With so much going on, "Jungle 2 Jungle" creates plenty of opportunities for those serious moments that every traditional comedy must have if it is to work.

All these observations are indicative of what a terrific job of direction John Pasquin, who directed Allen so effectively in "The Santa Clause," has done with richly varied material and a well-nigh perfect cast. Huntington is wonderful at conveying Mimi's combination of naiveté and intelligence, and Allen is a marvel. His amazing expressiveness and his physical grace recall the great silent clowns and bring to the film an extra level of visual and emotional impact. Beautifully designed and well-crafted, "Jungle 2 Jungle" is arguably the equal of the French original and perhaps even better, thanks to Tim Allen.

NEW YORK POST, 3/7/97, p. 47, Michael Medved

Those snooty souls who insist on the natural superiority of French taste and culture must somehow explain several annoying anomalies.

First, there's that puzzling respect they lavish on Jerry Lewis, and then there's the matter of all those insufferably stinky cigarettes.

And finally, how can one account for the appalling popularity of the rancid 1994 kiddie comedy "Un Indien Dans La Ville"?

The Disney company already tried releasing a badly-dubbed English language version of this French folly (under the title "Little Indian, Big City") and now they're back with a slavish remake ("Jungle 2 Jungle") that inexplicably preserves all the obnoxious elements of the original.

Tim Allen plays a workaholic, yuppie commodities trader who travels to the remote Amazon rain forest to get his estranged wife (JoBeth Williams) to sign divorce documents.

She's the longtime doctor to a primitive Indian tribe, who announces that since arriving in the jungle 13 years ago she's born Allen a son he's never met and lovingly raised him among the natives.

This child (played by bland, blond Sam Huntington) is known as Mimi-Siku, or Cat Pee in his native language, and he returns with his new-found father (who he calls Baboon) for a visit to New York.

The fish-out-of-water hi-jinks then include climbing to the crown of the Statue of Liberty, shooting pigeons with bow and arrow, eating rare tropical fish from an aquarium, urinating on house plants, scarfing cat food from a bowl on the floor, and terrifying everyone with his giant spider—especially affrighting his father's airhead, fashion designer fiancee (Lolita Davidovich).

In an especially irritating subplot, Mimi-Siku also finds time to fall passionately in love with the 12-year-old daughter (LeeLee Sobieski) of his father's frantic business partner (Martin Short), who's involved in a needlessly ugly and violent confrontation with the Russian mafia (led by a menacing David Ogden Stiers).

Director John Pasquin ("The Santa Clause") and cinematographer Tony Pierce-Roberts shoot the whole picture as an incongruously radiant valentine to Manhattan—so that it's all the more difficult to accept the preference for rain forest life ultimately displayed by all the major characters.

Tim Allen works hard at his part, but you know he's in trouble when his most amusing scene involves abuse of a fluffy doll that's supposed to represent an unconscious cat.

In the final analysis, not even the most charming and energetic star could possibly kick this dead fur ball into life.

NEWSDAY, 3/7/97, Part II/p. B7, John Anderson

Dilemmas in Disneyland! What do you do when a movie you own contains the corporately acceptable messages of tolerance, open-mindedness and fatherly understanding, but whose humor is based on the fact that people are animals (the reverse, as it happens, of the usual Disney formula)? What to do, what to do ...

The first thing you don't do is remake a movie that didn't need to be made in the first place. "Little Indian, Big City"—which Disney released here just about a year ago—was broad, vulgar and obvious. "Jungle 2 Jungle" is a virtual clone, except less charming.

The problem? It isn't all Tim Allen's fault—although the "Home Improvement" star should, at this lofty stage of his career, be able to demand scripts that don't make him seem like a cranky, humorless old man. As Michael, the highly stressed commodities trader who discovers he has a 13-year-old son named Mimi-Siku (Sam Huntington) living in the Amazon jungle, Allen delivers all the combustion and confusion required.

It would be tough to call him likable, though. Obligated to bring Mimi to New York, he has to appease his ill-tempered fashion designer girlfriend (the always charming Lolita Davidovich, who's beginning to look like Shawn Colvin), keep his trading partner, Richard (Martin Short), from getting them killed by a Russian mobster (David Ogden Stiers), and train Mimi-Siku to be a more cosmopolitan practitioner of the blowgun and bow. Allen does it all with the charm of a Portuguese man-of-war.

"Jungle 2 Jungle" departs from its predecessor by omitting virtually all references to lust (the original jungle boy's libido was a big part of the first film's humor). Huntington is too androgynous-looking to inspire much heat anyway, but let's face it: Pubescent sex, like representations of Satan or smoking, is strictly verboten in the current climate. To compensate, the filmmakers direct their wit in more proper directions, such as excretory functions and flatulence.

Or ethnic-flavored jokes: Allen's "nightmare on bodega street" line when he's on a Venezuelan pay phone. The crude way in which Russians are portrayed (OK, they're gangsters, but why Russians? Because Italians would complain?). The patronizing manner in which the members of Mimi-Siku's tribe are treated, and the tired, obligatory and largely inaccurate joke about how New York City cabdrivers don't speak English. Forget political correctness. This stuff is *boring*. Trite. Lazy. To say nothing of contemptuous.

The kids at the screening I attended liked the pratfalls and slapstick, which are abundant, and involve things they've probably never seen—like someone charging at a door, the door opening at the last minute and the person running through the room, out a window and onto a picnic table. This stuff is funny if you haven't seen it 40 or 50 times. When it comes to "Jungle 2 Jungle," twice is already too much.

SIGHT AND SOUND, 6/97, p. 54, Vicky Allan

Michael is a New York commodities trader, about to marry fashion designer Charlotte. First, he must finalise his divorce from his wife Patricia, who's been living in the Amazon jungle for 13 years. Before leaving, he secures a high-risk coffee deal and entrusts his business partner Richard to sell when he gives him permission.

When Michael arrives in the Amazon, he makes the shock discovery that he has a son, Mimi-Siku. During Michael's visit, Mimi-Siku goes through his rites of passage to manhood, and is given the task of going to the Statue of Liberty and bringing back its fire. Reluctantly, Michael agrees to take him to New York. There, Michael finds that his instructions to sell the coffee while its price was high were not confirmed; the price of coffee has now nose-dived. Also, Charlotte is not entirely pleased with Mimi's habits.

Mimi-Siku goes out to the Statue of Liberty and discovers that the fire is not real. Meanwhile, Richard has set up a deal for the coffee with the Russian mafia. Michael ducks out of the deal, but Richard sells the coffee shares for $1 million, on the promise that coffee will not drop below 75 cents. Michael decides to leave Mimi with Richard's family, including his attractive 12-year-old daughter Karen, while he patches things up with Charlotte. The price of coffee does drop below 75 cents and Richard anxiously buys the coffee shares back from the Russians. His blood pressure soars when he returns home to find Mimi has barbecued his prize fish, then wakes up the next morning to see Mimi in a hammock with his daughter. Worse still, the price of coffee rises, and the Russians, who think Richard duped them, arrive at his home, but Mimi saves him. Despite being a hero, Mimi, who is unhappy, returns to his village, complete with Statue of Liberty cigarette lighter. Soon after, his father, Richard, Karen and family join him there.

"You're an adolescent" concludes Tim Allen's 13-year-old son Mimi-Siku, when dad defines the difference between manhood and adolescence as one of responsibilities not capabilities. From his stand-up routines to his DIY obsessive role in *Home Improvement*, how to be a man today, or rather, how to reconcile traditional macho values with the demands of modern society, has been a recurring theme in Tim Allen's comedy. In his second turn as a movie-lead (his first was in another John Pasquin-directed movie, *The Santa Clause*) he's faced with a similar dilemma again, this time through a bizarre paternity revelation.   This predictable, but reliable Disney comedy joins the tired ranks of other films examining the father-son relationship (*Liar Liar* for example).   Cute adolescent in a loin cloth persuades selfish father to liberate himself from the 'me' society and take on familial 'we' responsibilities in an escapist idyll.   While the film begins with Mimi-Siku (played in innocent deadpan style by Sam Huntington) undergoing his ceremony of passage to manhood, it's really his father's rites of passage that the film is concerned with. Tim Allen's acting style and appearance lend themselves well to the reluctant paternal role.   The man behind the voice of Buzz Lightyear in *Toy Story*, he's more a verbal than a physical comic—though he does get good mileage from his galumphing, big-bellied body.

Jungle 2 Jungle combines the fatherhood film with a revamp of the *Crocodile Dundee* formula. Hence the comedy stems from Tim Allen's city idiot gagging it up in the Amazon, and Huntington's innocent naïf causing chaos in the urban jungle.   With gags like Mimi-Siku barbecuing his host's prize ornamental fish, and tossing aside a tasteless frozen battered cod portion, the majority of the laughs are based on what one character describes as "an intercultural misunderstanding".

Adding to a long tradition of 'primitivism', the film romanticises the appeal of nature.   Right from the opening shots, which cut from Huntington, the son, surrounded by the dramatic peace of the Amazon, to Tim Allen, the father, frantically ducking and diving in the chaos of the city stock exchange, it's clear which location's going to win out.   Working on the principle that you should give the audience what it wants (or at least expects), *Jungle 2 Jungle* is comfortably predictable: it gives the expected payoff to the gags, plays out its slapstick with controlled reliability and ends on a corny but camp cliché.   Allen's return to the jungle is so inevitable that it's hardly giving anything away to mention it.   This conversion to jungle-living is the one way of solving the modern male dilemma: go back to nature and live the Good Life.

Also reviewed in:
VARIETY, 3/10-16/97, p. 79, Leonard Klady
WASHINGTON POST, 3/7/97, p. B7, Rita Kempley

KAMA SUTRA: A TALE OF LOVE

A Trimark Pictures release of an NDF International Ltd./Pony Canyon Inc./Pandora Films presentation in association with Channel Four Films of a Mirabai Films production. *Executive Producer:* Michiyo Yoshzaki.   *Producer:* Lydia Dean Pilcher and Mira Nair.   *Director:* Mira Nair.   *Screenplay:* Helena Kriel and Mira Nair.   *Based in part on the short story "Hand-Me-Downs" by:* Wanda Tabassum. *Director of Photography:* Declan Quinn.   *Editor:* Kristina Boden. *Music:* Mychael Danna. *Choreographer:* Debi Basu and Maya Krishna Rao. *Sound:* Drew Kunin and (music) G. Brad Haehnel.   *Sound Editor:* Stuart Levy.   *Casting:* Susie Figgis, Uma Da Cunha, Dinaz Stafford, and Tula Goenka.   *Production Designer:* Mark Friedberg.   *Art Director:* Nita Desai.   *Set Decorator:* Stephanie Carroll.   *Special Effects:* Arun Patil.   *Costumes:* Eduardo Castro.   *Make-up:* Pat Hay.   *Stunt Coordinator:* Moses Fernandez.   *Running time:* 100 minutes. *MPAA Rating:* Not Rated.

CAST: Naveen Andrews (Raj Singh);   Sarita Choudhury (Tara);   Ramon Tikaram (Jai Kumar); Rekha (Rasa Devi);   Indira Varma (Maya);   Pearl Padamsee (Maham Anga);   Arundhati Rao (Annabi);   Khalid Tyabji (Biki);   Harish Patel (Doctor Mani);   Ranjit Chowdhry (Babu);   Siddarth Anand Kumar (Prem);   Avijit Dutt (Vazir);   Surabhi Bhansali (Young Maya);   Garima Dhup (Young Tara);   Kusum Haidar (Dilki);   Achla Sachdev (Rupa);   Arjun Sajnani (Bashir);   Anjum Rajabali (Madho Singh);   Debi Basu (Dance Teacher);   Rahul Vohra (Royal Messenger);   Manize Boga (Aunt Laila);   Prabeen Singh (Praveen);   Sinia Jain (Begum Para);   Urvashi Nair (Rich Friend);   Bhaumathi Rao (Old Woman);   Vasudeo Bhatt (Astrologer);   Moneeka Misra Tanvir (Madame);   Daphnée Breytenbach and Celesteann Cruz (Swimmers);   Nizami Chattarpur (Deaf Old Man);   Yasmine Stafford (Purnima);   Sunil Chhabra (Smart Aleck);   Himanshu Malik (Young Merchant);   Shubha Mudgal (Singer).

LOS ANGELES TIMES, 2/28/97, Calendar/p. 12, Kevin Thomas

With "Kama Sutra: A Tale of Love," director Mira Nair has incorporated the teachings of the famous 4th century text on the art of love into a heady, tragic tale of the entangled lives of two women and two men in 16th century India.

Nair, maker of the landmark "Salaam Bombay!" and the engaging "Mississippi Masala," has this time over-reached with a story as silly as it is sensual.

Originally, "Kama Sutra," which faces formidable censorship problems on its home ground in India, was more explicit. It was toned down by Trimark Pictures and Nair to emphasize the sensual rather than purely erotic and is being released without an MPAA rating.

Nair and co-writer Helena Kriel have taken themselves far too seriously and have laid a feminist sensibility much too heavily on material that has inherently camp elements—exotic locales, a dastardly villain, improbably gorgeous stars who cannot but bring to mind fond memories of Maria Montez and Turhan Bey and their '40s escapist movies. (Trying to evade campiness is to invite it unintentionally, alas.)

A more effective approach might have been satire, sending up the harem genre as a way of making a feminist comment of the status of women in particular and political tyranny in general. Nair, in short, might better have played her film's various elements and concerns against one another, as directors as different as Jonathan Demme and R.W. Fassbinder have done so successfully, instead of trying to blend them into an awkward, contradictory whole. Not helping matters is that none of Nair's people is intrinsically interesting enough to sustain the traditionally slow pacing and length of Indian films. (Note: "Kama Sutra" is an English-language production.)

In any event, when the beautiful Princess Tara (Sarita Choudhury) slights her even more beautiful servant Maya (Indira Varma), Maya in revenge offers herself to Tara's bridegroom, the king Raj Singh (Naveen Andrews). He's a young and handsome despot who rapes his bride on their wedding night and is already dissolute from the temptations of the harem and the opium pipe.

Maya ends up cast out of the palace, to begin an odyssey that finds her falling in love with the well-muscled royal sculptor Jai Kumar (Ramon Tikaram) and learning the secrets of the Kama Sutra from his friend, a priestess of love (the striking Rekha, a woman of commanding presence). But they are to be lovers as star-crossed as the miserable Tara and the rapidly decaying Raj, who is endangering the security of his kingdom with his epic debauchery.

With its spectacular authentic locales, lavish costumes, lush score and beautiful stars, "Kama Sutra" is visually sumptuous beyond description. Certainly, its notions of love-making are liberating and wise, as are its celebration of sensuality in all aspects of life. But as a movie "Kama Sutra" is, to paraphrase the Doors, not likely to light your fire.

NEW STATESMAN, 6/20/97, p. 42, Jonathan Coe

Mira Nair's new film makes a pointed comparison with last, week's Indian release, *The Square Circle*. Both films purport to challenge national orthodoxies about sexuality, but *Kama Sutra* is by far the more radical and subversive of the two.

The Square Circle starts off as a skewed road movie about transvestites but then slides, through a series of abject concessions to Bollywood conventions (rape scenes, punishment of sexual adventurism), into an extreme form of conservatsm. But *Kama Sutra*, besides being a more technically accomplished and matchable piece of work, offers its female viewers a genuinely empowering treatment of sexual role-playing and self-discovery. Perhaps the most telling commentary on these films is the fact that, while *The Square Circle* has been a big popular hit in India, *Kama Sutra*,—a less violent and prurient film—has been banned by the authorities and still awaits a commercial release.

The movie takes its title, of course, from the famous *Kama Sutra* of Vatsayana, but there are surprises in store for people who know it only as a handbook of sexual positions. That may be the most widely translated section, but there are 34 other chapters dealing with social customs and morality, and these have proved equally inspiring for Nair (whose previous films include *Salaam Bombay* and *Mississippi Masala*) and her co-screenwriter Helena Kriel.

Their story, set in the 16th century, centres upon the friendship and rivalry between two women: a princess called Tara (Sarita Choudhury) and her servant Maya (Indira Varma).

Resentful of the social inequality between them, and tired of having to make do with Tara's hand-me-down clothes, Maya takes her revenge by seducing Tara's husband-to-be, the prince Raj Singh, the night before their wedding. Her treachery is discovered and she is cast out from the palace as a whore, being left to wander through the Indian countryside (stunningly photographed by Declan Quinn) until she comes across a sculptor called Jai, who sets about commemorating her beauty in stone.

Although her relationship with Jai soon comes to grief, his statue indirectly provides her route back to the royal circle: Raj Singh catches a glimpse of it and insists on installing Maya in the palace as his chief courtesan. A ferocious power struggle ensues, with Maya and Tara competing for the (sexual) favours of the prince, while Jai and Raj Singh battle for Maya's heart. Enemy forces are massing outside the palace walls, but the prince is too voluptuously mired in his addictions to sex and opium to take any notice. Finally, the centre cannot hold and gory chaos ensues. But Maya walks serenely through it all and we last see her strolling off into the sunset, older and wiser, reflecting on her new-found assurance and declaring: "My heart is as open as the sky."

As you'd expect it's Indira Varma, a royal Academy of Dramatic Arts graduate making her feature film debut, who has to carry most of the movie, and she copes admirably with both the physical and emotional demands of her role. Given that most Indian film-goers are allowed to see sex on the screen only when it is contextualised by violence (hence the rape scenes in *The Square Circle),* the emotional range of the lovemaking in *Kama Sutra* is salutary: we have playful sex, angry sex, gloomy sex, passionate sex, vengeful sex and acrobatic sex, to name just a few.

It helps, needless to say, that all four of the main participants are exceptionally good to look at: not least Naveen Andrews (most recently seen as the Indian sapper Kip in *The English Patient),* whose hooded eyes and mischievous half-smile—as if permanently amused by his own hedonism—bring a touch of the young Oliver Reed to his portrayal of the dissolute Raj Singh.

In its conflation of western film techniques with eastern eroticism, *Kama Sutra* will probably appeal to the same people who flocked to Peter Greenaway's *The Pillow Book* last year. Nair's film is not as clever or as rigorously organised, but it offers a far richer and more emotionally rounded experience. The word "seductive" can be overused when writing about the cinema, but there were points in *Kama Sutra* when the pervading atmosphere of lush sensuality—sustained in part by Mark Friedberg's opulent sets and by an astonishingly vibrant musical score composed by Mychael Danna—did make me feel that I was being seduced, expertly and assiduously.

After the relative disappointment of the *The Perez Family* this is a blazing return to form by Mira Nair: certainly her most accessible film, and quite possibly her best to date.

NEW YORK POST, 2/28/97, p. 45, Michael Medved

Mira Nair's "Kama Sutra: A Tale of Love" is a triumphantly sensual film, not just in its frank approach toward passionate sexuality, but in its seductive celebration of the colors, clothes, feasts, music, architecture, landscape and sculpture of 16th-century India.

The lush textures of the film—saturated with ocher, burgundy, violet and an abundance of burnished, bronze skin—are so gorgeous that they effectively conceal the undernourished nature of the plot and characters.

Indira Varma, a ravishing actress trained at the Royal Academy of Dramatic Arts, makes a splashy movie debut as Maya, a serving girl raised alongside a haughty princess (Sarita Choudhury of director Nair's "Mississippi Masala").

Regularly humiliated and abused by her royal companion, Maya exacts her revenge on the eve of the wedding between her mistress and a powerful young king (Naveen Andrews, the Sikh bomb-disposal expert in "The English Patient").

Catching the eye of the swaggering groom, Maya allows him to deflower her the night before his wedding. When he enters the bridal chamber with the princess, it is Maya's name that he murmurs.

Banished from the palace, she wanders the countryside; falls in love with an ardent court sculptor (Ramon Tikaram); receives instruction in the 4th-century guide to love, the Kama Sutra; once more attracts the attention of the opium-addicted, increasingly debauched young king; emerges as the favored courtesan in his decadent, pleasure-loving court; and alternately enrages and assists her one-time mistress, now an embittered, abandoned queen in a doomed kingdom besieged by Muslim invaders.

This story line unfolds with an aura of fairy-tale inevitability, in which characters act according to the whims of fate (or the filmmaker), but without making their decisions or emotions coherent and comprehensible. Ramon Tikaram may be handsome and muscular as the brooding sculptor, but his dull, one-dimensional performance makes the key romantic obsession in this melodrama seem willful and arbitrary.

All the other actors acquit themselves honorably, as have the performers in each of Mira Nair's previous films: "Salaam Bombay!" "Mississippi Masala" and the underappreciated "The Perez Family."

This time, she focuses on visual splendor rather than dramatic subtlety; at one point, radiant star Varma appears in an elaborate outfit made up entirely of plastic pearls woven together in alluring strands.

Nuance and substance stand little chance in the face of such superficial dazzlement, and Nair's occasional gestures toward mystic philosophy and sexual politics provide less convincing and appropriate decoration than all the billowing fabrics and sleek, glistening bodies.

NEWSDAY, 2/28/97, Part II/p. B9, John Anderson

Filmmaker Mira Nair, who had a terrific debut with "Salaam Bombay!" and explored the darker side of assimilation in "Mississippi Masala," now casts her eyes to feudal India, a place and time when the senses were heightened and the land fairly churned with unbridled passion before colonialism stripped it of its rampant sensuality the way a randy sea captain might strip an innocent young native ... Uuuh, sorry. Let's just say, before western civilization put a damper on things.

Like the classic Fourth-Century work from which it draws its title, "Kama [love] Sutra [lessons]" is big on variety. Sometimes it seems like an overly ambitious porn film without the payoff. Sometimes it seems like the "Bhagavad Gita" as edited by Helen Gurley Brown. Sometimes, it's a soap opera, with beautiful bodies doing beautiful things and friendships going bad. Sometimes it's a trip to the transcendental '60s. ("Shame: That is an ancient word ..." "A servant is a master in disguise ..." "The art of love is much more than the act itself ...")

Overall, it's a sisterly tale: Maya (Indira Varma), a serving girl, and Tara (Sarita Choudhury), a princess, have grown up together and studied together the ways of the Kama Sutra. In a pique, Maya has put her lessons to good use, seducing Tara's husband-to-be, the debauched Raj Singh, who's also the king (Naveen Andrews, of "The English Patient"). He becomes obsessed with her, especially after Tara turns out to be less than welcoming of his amorous advances. Maya, in turn, hooks up with a hunky sculptor, Jai Kumar (Ramon Tikaram). Things do not go well, although a brief fling between the two women certainly takes matters in a new direction.

For all its color, splendor and general voluptuousness, "Kama Sutra" suffers from ludicrous theatricality and the imposition of '90s values on another time—the coup de grace for any period piece. Indira Varma makes a decent screen debut and certainly possesses the screen when she's on it. But if the culture Nair evokes is so enlightened about sex, why are her characters undone by 19th-Century mores? Her logic gets tied in more knots than her characters.

SIGHT AND SOUND, 7/97, p. 43, Melanie McGrath

India, the sixteenth century. Maya is a servant in the court of the decadent young king Raj Singh. Tara, her childhood companion, is Singh's betrothed. As women, Tara's and Maya's destinies are set: they will marry and become the property of their husbands, but Maya longs to be independent and create her own destiny. The marriage of Tara and Singh is marred by Singh's obvious attraction to Maya. Seeing Maya as her sexual rival, Tara rejects her old friend, who retaliates by seducing Singh before his marriage to Tara is consummated. Ejected from the court for her betrayal of Tara, Maya meets Jai, the court sculptor, who finds her shelter at the house of Rasa Devi, a teacher of the kama sutra, the art of love-making. Maya learns well and captures the heart of Jai, who models an erotic sculpture on her. Singh stumbles on the sculpture during a hunting trip, immediately recognises Maya and determines to find her again.

The love between Maya and Jai becomes soured by Jai's obsession with his work. To help herself forget her lover, Maya becomes Singh's chief courtesan and is interred in the king's harem. The debauched Singh, aroused by Maya but unable to win her love, retreats into a world of opium and sex, ignoring the pleas of his advisers to attend to matters of state. When Singh commissions Jai to carve a statue of his favourite, Maya and Jai resume their affair. Just as they decide to elope together, Singh finds the couple *in flagrante* and sentences Jai to death. Queen Tara, meanwhile, frustrated and humbled by Maya's sexual conquest of the king, slices her wrists and is saved only by the timely arrival of Maya. The two women are united in their contempt for Singh. Jai is executed. Singh's rival storms the palace with his troops and Maya finds herself wandering the countryside, released finally from the pain of desire.

Kama Sutra A: Tale of Love is a slow and oozing sort of film. It deals in bodies and their sex liquids but it also drifts along for nearly two hours quite unhindered by any real change of pace or swell of tide. This is not to say the narrative is boring exactly. There are a couple of quite mesmerising dance sequences, some stirring sex and a nasty fight or two. For the most part though, *Kama Sutra* is, as a story, rather unengaging.

'*Kama sutra*', we are told, means 'love lessons' and we certainly get plenty of coitus, filmed with the sort of celebratory openness rare in contemporary film and positively extinct in Hollywood. Only the most committed killjoy could complain about the sex scenes between Maya and her sculptor lover: they are pleasingly choreographed and performed, erotic without any hint of prurience and mercifully lacking the dreary fumbling that passes for passion in more mainstream films' couplings. This is a real achievement and marks *Kama Sutra* as a film of genuine sexual poetry. If *Kama Sutra* were nothing but an exploration of sensual love, it would go down like honey. It's those 'lessons' that make it hard to swallow.

An awfully didactic piece of work, it wouldn't be so bad if director Mira Nair's message about the joys of uninhibited sex had been thought through. Instead, it's a maze of contradictions. The film explicitly advocates freedom of sexual expression, but the *Kama Sutra* of the title is a book of manners from fourth-century India prescribing quite rigid sexual formulae, a precursor of *The Rules* (the recent dating guide for women by Ellen Fein . Nair does not seem to have noticed this inconsistency. At *kama sutra* school, Nair's girls dutifully learn to distinguish their *yonis* from others' *lingams*, and having mastered a dizzying array of acrobatic poses, cheerily submit to a lifetime of sexual slavery working as court concubines.

There are some startlingly old-fashioned tropes, from Maya's Princess Di-style simpering to the general assumption that classy girls don't, or if they do, they don't enjoy it much. And even though the film departs from familiar narratives of sexual transgression—exacting its punishment on Jai, not Maya—*Kama Sutra* is still knee-deep in Mills and Boon romanticism, that swooning play of surrender and dominance in which pleasure and power are indissolubly linked. When Maya complains that her love for Jai enslaves her to him, her lover hotly replies that "a servant is a master in disguise".

Nair's previous work—*The Perez Family, Salaam Bombay!* and *Mississippi Masala*—gave us so many playful, spirited characters that it's all the more disappointing to find the protagonists in *Kama Sutra* no more complex than the symbols they represent, making Singh 'Decadence', Maya 'Impetuousness', Jai 'Hubris' and Tara 'Imperiousness'. The film's schematic treatment of character, coupled with its historical setting, lends *Kama Sutra* an allegorical feel, as though somewhere inside its realist skin there is a magic realist movie struggling to get out. The dialogue doesn't help, roughly hewn as it is from a block of clichés ("Take me I'm yours," says Maya to her lover) ornamented with the odd aphorism ("Love is a call to ripening," according to *kama sutra* teacher Rasa Devi, played by Bollywood star Rekha).

You feel this film is struggling to be an epic romance. It has both the scale and trappings: grand locations filmed like paintings, rivers of extras, fabulous outfits, a sweeping score and smooth, formal camerawork. But neither the confidence of the art direction nor the atmospheric score can quite carry *Kama Sutra* off. Historical sweep and sensuality prove to be no insurance against a lousy script. For a movie given over to sensuality, *Kama Sutra* is a surprisingly disembodied piece of work.

VILLAGE VOICE, 3/4/97, p. 72, Amy Taubin

An even more inept movie about women and power, [The reference is to *Smilla's Sense of Snow*; see Taubin's review.] Mira Nair's *Kama Sutra: a Tale of Love* makes sex seem so tedious that, had I seen it at an impressionable age, I would have been celibate for life. Set in 16th-century India, *Kama Sutra* follows the transformation of a young servant girl named Maya (Nair never resists the obvious) into a great courtesan. Or something like that.

Jealous of Princess Tara, once her childhood friend and now her mistress, Maya impulsively seduces Tara's husband Raj Singh on the eve of their wedding. As punishment, she's banished from the court. Wandering off, though not very far, she's discovered by the court sculptor, who makes her his muse and his girlfriend but then rejects her because he's afraid of commitment. Those great male artists, they're all alike.

When the Raj sees the statues of Maya, he realizes that he's still obsessed with her and forces her to return to him. Then the artist sees Maya fucking the Raj and realizes that he's still obsessed too. Then Princess Tara gets jealous all over again, even though there's nothing she likes less than having sex with her husband. The resulting quadrangle can only end in disaster. The Raj condemns the artist to be crushed to death by an elephant (a method of execution that makes lethal injection seem civilized). Having thus experienced love and loss, Maya understands that nothing is permanent and journeys on to a higher plain. Or something like that.

This is an exceptionally stupid film. It is also stunningly unerotic. I'm sure it will make its way to the midnight slot on Cinemax very soon.

Also reviewed in:
NEW REPUBLIC, 3/10/97, p. 30, Stanley Kauffmann
NEW YORK TIMES, 2/8/97, p. C19, Janet Maslin
VARIETY, 10/21-27/96, p. 86, Todd McCarthy
WASHINGTON POST, 3/7/97, Weekend/p. 32, Desson Howe

KEEPER, THE

A Kino International release of a Rada Films proudction. *Executive Prouder:* Juan Amalbert and Forrest Murray. *Producer:* Joe Brewster and Jordi Torrent. *Director:* Joe Brewster. *Screenplay:* Joe Brewster. *Director of Photography:* Igor Sunara. *Editor:* Tom McArdle. *Music:* John Petersen. *Production Designer:* Flavia Galuppo. *Art Director:* Tom Jarmusch. *Running time:* 90 minutes. *MPAA Rating:* Not Rated.

CAST: Giancarlo Esposito (Paul Lamont); Regina Taylor (Angela Lamont); Isaach De Bankole (Jean Baptiste); Ron Brice (Clarence Ross); O.L. Duke (Ron Baker); Alvaleta Guess (Officer Jones); Sam E. Wright (Officer Santana); Shiek Mahmud-Bey (Majhid); Victor Colicchio (Officer Corvino); Arthur French (Jimmy Johnson); Jude Ciccolella (Captain Walker); Liza Colon (Officer Melendez); Cory Glover (Martin); Sixto Ramos (Wilson); Curtis McClarin (Joseph); Laurence Mason (Jordi); Dan Moran (Tony); Michael Kirby (Michael); Mitchell Marchand (Horton); Kenshaka Ali (Officer Williams); Gordon Joseph Weiss (Police Officer Guido); Oni F. Lampley (Mrs. Grant); Novella Nelson (Mrs. Lamont, Mother); Emile St. Lot (Mr. Lamont, Father); Aaron Griffin (Young Paul); Diego Lopez (Jose); Jewdyer Osborne (Officer Smith); Lionel Bernard and Constance Bernard (Haitian Musicians); Rocco Iacovone (Hospital Doctor).

LOS ANGELES TIMES, 1/16/98, Calendar/p. 8, John Anderson

[*The following review by John Anderson appeared in a slightly different form in* **NEWSDAY, 9/6/97, Part II/p. B7.**]

That actors of color are so infrequently cast as anything but hustlers and wastrels adds an extra dimension of intrigue to "The Keeper," a fable-like character drama that's the first feature by psychiatrist-cum-filmmaker Joe Brewster and that doesn't need any extra dimensions to be taut and intelligent, thanks very much.

Setting his film in and around jail—the Kings County House of Detention—allows Brewster to thumb his nose at conventional typecasting at the same time it provides the proper cage for his conflicted characters.

Chief among them is Paul Lamont (Giancarlo Esposito), a corrections officer whose place in the gothic universe of the short-term prisoner is as unsettled as his own sense of identity. Half-Haitian—and toting a lot of "issues" about his Caribbean heritage—he is strangely affected by a Haitian inmate, the biblically named Jean Baptiste (Isaach De Bankole of "Night on Earth"), who has been falsely accused of rape.

Paul eventually bails Jean out, and Jean eventually shows up at Paul's home, where his wife, Angela (Regina Taylor of "Fly Away Home"), is at first incensed, and then enchanted, by having Jean in her home.

Brewster doesn't just sidestep stereotypes, he gives us characters with malleable and multifaceted personalities; people are, after all, really different depending on whom they're with.

Angela, for instance, whose daily struggle with her school students and her husband's inner demons has drained her joy, blooms around the spiritually healthy Jean Batiste. Paul has to work each day beside a reverse racist like Clarence Ross (the all-too-rarely seen Ron Brice) and is not immune to the dehumanizing effects of jail house life, despite his intellect. Nor is he immune to jealousy, which erupts when he suspects Jean and Angela of having an affair, evicts Jean and lets those demons overtake him.

Paul is occupied, after all, in the business of pain, some of it personal, some of it institutional. The prison exterminator, Jimmy (Arthur French), explains to Paul that one day he realized how much of his life depended upon the rats and cockroaches he's supposed to kill. So he spares a few; it keeps the population steady, he tells Paul who sees as we do a metaphor for criminal justice in general.

While there's a visual stiffness to "The Keeper," which hasn't quite lost a certain stagy quality transition from script to screen, it's an extremely well-acted movie. And its provocative ideas are explored in a way that's both Kafkaesque and therapeutic.

NEW YORK POST, 9/5/97, p. 58, Michael Medved

"I'm tired of this melodrama!" screams the long-suffering wife of the tormented main character, and long before "The Keeper" lurches toward its odd conclusion, most members of the ex-asperated audience will emphatically agree with her.

This ambitious, original, well-acted film feels frustratingly unfocused and incomplete, eventually collapsing under the weight of its own loose ends, mystical pretensions and pointlessly portentous atmosphere.

The always intriguing Giancarlo Esposito plays an idealistic corrections officer at the Brooklyn House of Detention married to a similarly dedicated school teacher (Regina Taylor).

Their relationship suffers due to the devastating demands of his job and she can't understand why he insists on risking their savings to bail out one of his prisoners.

The proud, dignified Haitian immigrant he liberates may have been wrongly accused of rape, but soon after his release, this mysterious stranger (played by the riveting Isaach De Bankole of the Ivory Coast) turns up at their doorstep and asks for a temporary place to stay. Esposito implausibly agrees, in part because feels lingering guilt about his embarrassed rejection of his own late father's "foreign" Haitian background.

The house guest proceeds to teach the middle-class couple about spicy Caribbean food, music, dance and religion—making enigmatic references to the power of the voodoo deities.

No charms, however, can protect his prison guard host from the deadly poison of jealousy once he begins to suspect his bored and ignored wife of infidelity.

First-time writer-director Joe Brewster once worked as a psychiatrist at the Brooklyn House of Detention and his cinematic presentation of the everyday dreariness of this facility seems eerily authentic—more cold than cruel, more mind-numbing than nightmarish.

"The Keeper" is especially effective at rendering the defensive camaraderie of the nearly all-black guards, and their desperate need to emphasize their differences from the similarly all-black prisoners.

The performances are consistently intense and accomplished, but scenes of climactic violence have been staged with amateurish clumsiness. Brewster's wobbly time sequence and confused continuity add needless layers of confusion while flashbacks and dream sequences are more indulgent than revealing.

The depiction of a wrongly accused Haitian immigrant in Brooklyn may add an air of topical relevance, but for all its moody subtext of sacrifice and otherwordly power, "The Keeper" fails to weave a magic spell powerful enough to draw its disparate elements together.

VILLAGE VOICE, 9/9/97, p. 88, J. Hoberman

There's no trailer like the evening news—timing is the showbiz name for zeitgeist. Thus, *The Keeper*, writer-producer-director Joe Brewster's long-germinating, independent first feature—a movie whose production and distribution vicissitudes were reported in no less than three *Voice* columns over the last 15 months—opens only weeks after an alternative version of its cops-and-Haitians story emerges as the city's most compelling narrative.

The figure of Abner Louima doesn't exist per se in *The Keeper*, but it's impossible not to find his presence dispersed throughout the movie's already nightmarish psychosocial stew of rape, racism, psychosexual angst, police violence, and victimized immigrants. To make *The Keeper*, the 44-year-old Brewster drew on his own experiences as a psychiatrist at the Brooklyn House of Detention. If the movie speaks to Louima's condition, it is because at any given moment, the world is filled with forces waiting to realize themselves as tabloid drama.

Given Brewster's interests, it is hardly surprising that *The Keeper* would be less an action film than a study in character disintegration—including the psychic cost of internalizing the social order and policing the underclass. Troubled by the antipathy exhibited by his (mainly black) colleagues toward their (almost entirely black) charges, Paul, an ambitious and deeply middle-class corrections officer, played by Giancarlo Esposito, bails out Jean-Baptiste (Ivorian actor Isaach De Bankolé), a Haitian prisoner who has been accused, perhaps unfairly, of sexual assault.

No good deed goes unpunished. By bringing the regal Jean-Baptiste home to an already troubled marriage, Paul precipitates all manner of latent violence, psychological and otherwise. As a New York City school teacher, Paul's equally middle-class wife Angela (Regina Taylor) is another sort of professional "keeper" whose real job, as suggested by the remarkably alienated party that the couple throw, may be keeping herself under control. Paul's psychological profile is additionally complicated in that his awkwardly ambivalent feelings of solidarity with Jean are based in unresolved feelings about his own Haitian immigrant father. When Jean-Baptiste shows up at the door, he's the living return of the repressed, Paul's guilt given material form. As the initially hostile Angela warms to their houseguest, the tightly wound Paul grows increasingly paranoid—particulary once Jean-Baptiste brings his benefactors to the Haitian club of voudon frenzy that functions as the movie's site of unconscious desire.

Such exoticism notwithstanding, *The Keeper* is particularly strong on everyday workplace jive—the jargon of the prison law library where Paul works, the bureaucratic rules, the class tension among the cops, the continual riding of a Muslim prisoner, the nutty exterminator who keeps rats and roaches as pets.

The powerful scene in which a coven of guards exact vigilante justice on one prisoner (while bonding themselves in a sort of blood ritual) no longer seems quite as unrealistically melodramatic as it did to some reviewers which *The Keeper* was shown at Sundance in 1996.

Unusual in putting an ineffectual, repressed character at its center, *The Keeper* suffers down the stretch for pulling away from the now pathologically jealous Paul's psychic anguish. (Esposito's measured performance evaporates here.) Call it the breakdown of pedantry. As Brewster sacrifices narrative flow for visual authority, so *The Keeper*'s studied lighting and self-consciously "serious" look parallels Paul's uptight personality. Paradoxically, this weightiness ends up working to the movie's advantage once Paul's world comes apart and flips upside down.

Also reviewed in:
CHICAGO TRIBUNE, 1/16/98, p. J, John Petrakis
NEW YORK TIMES, 9/5/97, p. C12, Janet Maslin
VARIETY, 1/29-2/4/96, p. 64, Emanuel Levy

KICKED IN THE HEAD

An October Films release of a De Fina/Cappa production. *Executive Producer:* Martin Scorsese. *Producer:* Barbara De Fina. *Director:* Matthew Harrison. *Screenplay:* Kevin Corrigan and Matthew Harrison. *Director of Photography:* John Thomas and Howard Krupa. *Editor:* Michael Berenbaum. *Music:* Stephen Endelman and Alex Steyermark. *Sound:* Jan McLaughlin. *Casting:* Sheila Jaffe and Georgianne Walken. *Production Designer:* Kevin Thompson. *Set Decorator:* Ford Wheeler. *Special Effects:* Drew Jiritano. *Costumes:* Nina Canter. *Make-up:* Tracy Warbin. *Stunt Coordinator:* Douglas Crosby. *Running time:* 97 minutes. *MPAA Rating:* R.

CAST: Kevin Corrigan (Redmond); Linda Fiorentino (Megan); Michael Rapaport (Stretch); James Woods (Uncle Sam); Burt Young (Jack); Lili Taylor (Happy); Olek Krupa (Borko); Elliot Cuker (Sheldon); David Deblinger (Escalator Man); Alan Davidson (Subway Gunman); Bianca Bakija (Pearl); Sol Frieder (Elderly Man); Matthew Harrison (Luau Man); Gary Perez (Dean); John Ventimiglia (Man at Party); Royale Watkins (Chicky); Lawton Paseka (Pilot); George Odom (Door Person); Nicole Baptiste (Cop).

LOS ANGELES TIMES, 9/26/97, Calendar/p. 25, John Anderson

[*The following review by John Anderson appeared in a slightly different form in* [NEWSDAY, 9/26/97, Part II/p. B11.]

For a filmmaker to use the Hindenburg as a recurring motif, he might as well call his movie "Kicked in the Head." It's like saying, "Go ahead. Hit me."

If you insist.

"Kicked in the Head" is director-writer Matthew Harrison's follow-up to his Sundance-honored "Rhythm Thief," which not only looked great but managed to combine comedy, existential criminals and a tongue-in-cheek approach to the regrettable conventions of Lower East Side/low budget filmmaking.

If Harrison wanted to move in a new direction with "Kicked in the Head," he pulled it off, in a loony-the-loop: He's made the very type of movie to which "Rhythm Thief" was a positive reaction.

Kevin Corrigan, a fixture in independent New York films who shares screenplay credit for this and currently stars in "Bandwagon," plays Redmond, a jobless, apartment-less would-be author.

His Uncle Sam (an antic James Woods) cons him into doing a drug pickup; his buddy Stretch (Michael Rapaport) is a beverage distributor engaged in a "beer war" against violent rivals. According to a fortune cookie, his "attendant godling has lost her way," which means his guardian angel has left for the coast, which leaves him feeling particularly unhinged: He meets a flight attendant named Megan (Linda Fiorentino) and decides that aviation is next to godliness.

With an increased budget (and an executive producer named Martin Scorsese), Harrison can, and does, indulge himself in gunfights and car explosions; what's funny is that he uses them as parodies in which no one gets hurt and everyone runs from the car before it goes off.

But the laughs are pretty scarce in "Kicked in the Head," which is less a coherent narrative than a series of bits—each featuring Corrigan and one of the well-known co-stars, such as Fiorentino, Burt Young or Woods, none of whom seem to have met. The script is lacking, and although there are some funny lines, Harrison lets them get away by errors in pacing.

It's a likable cast, but with the exception of Lili Taylor—as Redmond's faithful girlfriend, Happy—no one seems particularly engaged; Corrigan, for one, often seems primed to burst out in laughter. They all seem to be having a good time romping about Lower Manhattan. But they should have thought to bring us along.

NEW YORK POST, 9/26/97, p. 48, Thelma Adams

Ouch! I just got "Kicked in the Head."

My sensibilities were attacked by Matthew Harrison's visually spry, spiritually bankrupt downtown-and-out coming-of-age story.

Harrison, whose acclaimed "Rhythm Thief" was more accomplished, an angry young man's "Stranger Than Paradise," has coauthored this harsh comedy with star Kevin Corrigan.

Corrigan plays Redmond, a pop-eyed, talentless poet. Evicted from his apartment, stalked by his girlfriend (Lili Taylor), hoodwinked by his Uncle Sam (James Woods), Redmond crashes with a pal.

Life with Stretch (Michael Rapaport, in another obnoxious, hysterical non-performance) includes booze, drugs, guns and an ugly roundtable discussion about women that also lamely riffs on "Planet of the Apes."

Redmond wants peace, but can't pay the tab. The painfully poetic twentysomething is on "a spiritual quest, a voyage of self-discovery." We know this, in part, because Harrison keeps cutting to scenes of the Hindenberg in flames. Was this found footage on sale?

Martin Scorsese, of all people, executive-produced this twaddle. His imprimatur might account for the stellar supporting cast, including Woods and Linda Fiorentino.

Fiorentino ("The Last Seduction") brings a besotted beauty to the standard-issue stew (er, flight attendant) who must fly as Redmond's guardian angel. For Harrison and Corrigan, love is holding a guy's head over the toilet bowl while he barfs—and giving him a wet kiss afterward. Sweet, huh?

Woods is the biggest kick in "Kicked." He clearly enjoys inhabiting Sam, a two-bit criminal incapable of wising up. When Sam steals a car, there's a dog in it. He tosses the pup on the sidewalk, only to receive a stream of abusive calls on the car phone from the dog's mistress.

Uncle Sam would make a great character in a comedy that was going somewhere besides an epiphany about a dirty navel. Sam's dead-on when he tells Redmond, "Discover yourself later."

VILLAGE VOICE, 9/30/97, p. 86, Dennis Lim

A bustling New York indie with local color to spare, Matthew Harrison's *Kicked in the Head* charts four predictably eventful days in the life of the predictably hapless Redmond (Kevin Corrigan), a newly evicted, out-of-work, Lower East Side soul searcher. Haunted by images of the 1937 *Hindenburg* disaster (so that crashing and burning can serve as the movie's controlling metaphor), Redmond is a *Planet of the Apes* expert who writes horrible poetry and takes fortune cookies seriously; he is, in short, the kind of person you hope exists only in American independent movies.

Failing in his mission to deliver a brick of cocaine on behalf of his small-time scamster uncle (James Woods), Redmond finds himself hurtling through a succession of broadly drawn traumas: he unwittingly antagonizes a company of cartoon hoodlums; moves in with slobby beer-distributor pal Stretch (Michael Rapaport); and falls for a classy flight attendant (Linda Fiorentino) he sees on the B train.

Kicked in the Head suffers from casting: Fiorentino is on call as an unflappable femme fatale; Lili Taylor, as Redmond's groveling ex-girlfriend Happy, puts an embarrassingly dopey twist on her Miss Maladroit number; Rapaport plays yet another vaguely Neanderthal loose cannon, Woods another motormouthed weasel. Corrigan, the affable Amerindie perennial (who cowrote the screenplay), is seen here with much less hair and slightly less charm than usual.

Though clearly more successful with wry absurdities, Harrison (who directed the grittier, cheaper *Rhythm Thief*) opts time and again for strained wackiness (the chief thug growls, "I like precise, with a P, like in *phenomenon*"), and the abundance of tightly framed medium close-ups only makes all this off-the-wall business appear needlessly in-your-face. The detour-littered but pretty much twist-free plot is even more exasperating in hindsight, i.e., when the movie fails to end up anywhere more illuminating than in the realm of straight-guy fantasy.

Also reviewed in:
CHICAGO TRIBUNE, 9/26/97, Friday/p. F, Michael Wilmington
NEW YORK TIMES, 9/26/97, p. E10, Janet Maslin
VARIETY, 5/26-6/1/97, p. 70, Todd McCarthy

KISS THE GIRLS

A Paramount Pictures release in association with Rysher Entertainment of a David Brown/Joe Wizan production. *Executive Producer:* C.O. Erickson. *Producer:* David Brown and Joe Wizan. *Director:* Gary Fleder. *Screenplay:* David Klass. *Based on the novel by:* James Patterson. *Director of Photography:* Aaron Schneider. *Editor:* William Steinkamp and Harvey Rosenstock. *Music:* Mark Isham. *Music Editor:* Tom Carlson and Richard Bernstein. *Sound:* Lee Orloff and (music) Stephen Krause. *Sound Editor:* David Bartlett. *Casting:* Deborah Aquila and Jane Shannon Smith. *Production Designer:* Nelson Coates. *Art Director:* Joseph Hodges. *Set Decorator:* Linda Lee Sutton. *Special Effects:* John Peyser. *Costumes:* Abigail Murray. *Make-up:* Ben Nye, Jr., and Jeff Hamilton. *Stunt Coordinator:* Chuck Picerni, Jr. *Running time:* 117 minutes. *MPAA Rating:* R.

CAST: Morgan Freeman (Alex Cross); Ashley Judd (Kate McTiernan); Cary Elwes (Nick Ruskin); Tony Goldwyn (Will Rudolph); Jay O. Sanders (Kyle Craig); Alex MacArthur (Davey Sikes); Bill Nunn (Sampson); Brian Cox (Chief Hatfield); Richard T. Jones (Seth Samuel); Roma Maffia (Dr. Ruocco); Jeremy Piven (Henry Castillo); Gina Ravera (Naomi Cross); William Converse-Roberts (Dr. Wick Sachs); Helen Martin (Nana Cross); Tatyana M. Ali (Janell Cross); Mena A. Suvari (Coty Pierce); Heidi Schanz (Megan Murphy); Rick Warner (Sergeant Willard); Billy Blanks (Instructor); Dianna Miranda (Jennifer); Mary Major and Melinda Renna (TV Reporters); Loanne Bishop (Kate's Nurse); Tim Ahern (LAPD Sergeant); W. Earl Brown (Locksmith); Brian Brophy (Swim Team Manager); Michael J. Cutt (FBI Agent Hospital); Tricia Vessey (Woman at Nepenthe Bar); John Cothran, Jr., (FBI Agent at Lair); Robert Peters (Agent on Robe); Jill Callaham (Female Reporter in Durham); Nancy Yee (Chinese Grandmother); Christina Ma (Chinese Mother); David Cowgill (Chief Resident); Weston Blakesley (Bellman); Joe Inscoe (Large Cop); Deborah Strang (Dianne Wainford); Robert Overmyer (Competitive Swimmer); Bolse Holmes (Basketball Player).

LOS ANGELES TIMES, 12/13/97, Calendar/p. 12, Jack Mathews

Longtime Hollywood producer David Brown says in the production notes for "Kiss the Girls" that he had been so frightened by John Patterson's source novel that he had to close the blinds in his house while reading it. That's a strange reaction to a story in which the only victims are beautiful young women. Maybe he was afraid someone would break in and steal his wife Helen Gurley Brown's collection of Cosmo covers.

In any event, "Kiss the Girls" is a genuine page-turner of a movie thriller, and if Brown needn't worry about his safety, it will certainly inspire some blinds-closing and double-checking of door locks for a lot of female viewers.

Directed by talented newcomer Gary Fleder ("Things to Do in Denver When You're Dead"), "Kiss the Girls" is a psychopath-on-the-loose movie in the urgent, heavy-breathing mode of "The Silence of the Lambs." Young, pretty, bright women are disappearing in both California and North Carolina, their bodies occasionally turning up in the woods, where they have been raped, bound to trees, had their hair shorn and been left to die.

One of the missing victims in North Carolina is the niece of a brilliant nationally known police detective and forensic psychologist named Alex Cross (Morgan Freeman), who takes leave of his job in Washington to put his own expertise on the case. After striking a fragile agreement with the local authorities, Cross begins finding clues where no one else had thought to look.

Like "The Silence of the Lambs," "Kiss the Girls" is a genre film done as a match of super-intelligence. Cross is up against a sick but agile mind—maybe more than one—and must trust his own deductive reasoning skills against the perverse gamesmanship of his prey. Of course, those skills have never been tested in a case that's personal, and his emotions become his greatest obstacle.

Freeman, who brings intelligence and physical assurance to every role he plays, is perfectly cast as the conflicted psychologist, and he's ably supported by co-star Ashley Judd, playing Kate McTiernan, a young surgeon who escapes her captor and joins forces with Cross to rescue the other victims.

Fleder has directed three-quarters of a terrific movie and one-quarter of pure Hollywood baloney. After carefully building up the suspense and tension through Cross and McTiernan's search, spiked with nail-biting encounters on both coasts, Fleder lets it trail off in anti-climax and banal violence. I didn't read the novel, but the movie creates no profile of the eventual villain. You don't look back and say, "Oh, yeah," because there was no groundwork laid.

All we really know is that the kidnapper collects women he thinks he's in love with and kills them when they disappoint him. With some other ending, that wouldn't be a bad thing, because the pleasure of the movie comes out of the psychology of Cross and McTiernan and their interdependent relationship.

Fleder has Jonathan Demme's knack for insinuating a sense of actual danger in situations that should overtax the imagination. Even McTiernan's physical stamina, her ability to fight her way free from a powerful man, is developed in ways that makes it completely believable when it occurs.

The overdone ending is the norm in Hollywood these days. Whether it's audience research, bad writing or simply not knowing when to say when, it has turned a lot of potentially good movies into very ordinary ones, and "Kiss the Girls" is the latest victim.

NEW YORK, 11/3/97, p. 53, David Denby

It's business as usual in the disgraceful *Kiss the Girls*, the kind of thriller that pretends to sympathize with women who are being mauled and dominated by men but actually exploits the sadism for everything it can get out of it. The movie was the top-grossing picture in the country for two weeks in a row. Is it any wonder that kids like Harmony Korine are running amok?

NEW YORK POST, 10/3/97, p. 55, Michael Medved

"Kiss the Girls" conjures up a criminal wacko who is so diabolical and bizarre that he makes Hannibal "the Cannibal" Lecter look like the boy next door.

Based on James Patterson's gruesome and riveting best seller, the movie delivers an abundance of creepy atmosphere and some well-staged chase scenes, but its grotesque excesses leave believability behind and begin to play like self-parody.

Morgan Freeman plays a brilliant forensic psychologist who works for the Washington, D.C., police department but journeys to North Carolina when his adored niece (Gina Ravera) disappears from her college dorm.

It turns out she's one of nine exceptionally talented and attractive young women who have vanished, claimed by a demented mastermind who identifies himself to police only as "Casanova."

Neither local authorities (Brian Cox, Cary Elwes) nor frantic FBI officials (including Jay O. Sanders) want Freeman to get involved, but his desperate desire to rescue his niece draws him deeply into the case.

He's soon working closely with Ashley Judd, playing a doctor in training (and expert kick-boxer) with a similarly personal stake in capturing the kooky kidnapper; she's the only one who has escaped his clutches, and she can provide crucial clues to the investigation.

Judd does a fine job in her breakthrough role, projecting strength, determination and ferocious intensity that inevitably will remind viewers of Jodie Foster's Oscar-winning role in "The Silence of the Lambs."

Freeman plays the same sort of world-weary, compassionate and intellectual cop he portrayed so effectively in "Seven." the problem with the picture is the kidnapper-killer, whose face we only glimpse in the film's final seconds; depictions of the ludicrously elaborate dungeon deep in the woods where he holds and torments his beauteous victims are not only far-fetched, they're laughable.

The screenplay also throws out so many red herrings that the whole project begins to smell fishy. Young director Gary Fleder (who previously directed the hopelessly mannered, outrageously indulgent "Things to Do in Denver When You're Dead") this time keeps his story moving along with taut and moody eye-catching locations, but he can't escape that torchlit, clammy, contrived dungeon that seems to hold the entire project prisoner.

SIGHT AND SOUND, 3/98, p. 51, John Wrathall

When his niece disappears in North Carolina, forensic psychologist Alex Cross goes to Washington DC to search for her, but the local police, including Detective Nick Ruskin, do not appreciate his interference. Seven other young women are missing and two have been found dead. The killer leaves taunting notes signed "Casanova', and slips a postcard under the door of Cross' hotel room.

Dr Kate McTiernan is abducted by the masked Casanova and kept in his underground lair in the woods, where she hears the voices of the other missing women. She escapes, despite having been injected with an amnesia-inducing drug, which Cross identifies as Systol. Cross finds out that a Los Angeles plastic surgeon called Will Rudolph has bought large supplies of Systol, although he doesn't need it for his work. Cross flies to California and stakes out Rudolph. When Rudolph abducts a woman, Cross is able to save her, but Rudolph escapes. Examining his lair, Cross concludes that he is not Casanova, but must be in touch with him. Cross returns to North Carolina with McTiernan to search the woods where she was found.

Rudolph arrives at Casanova's lair, but Casanova shoots at him. Cross hears the shot and enters the lair, rescuing the captive women and killing Rudolph, but Casanova gets away. McTiernan returns home under police guard. Ruskin relieves the policemen on duty outside and tries to rape her. McTiernan handcuffs him to the cooker, but Ruskin manages to pull it away from the gas supply pipe and threatens to blow them both up with his cigarette lighter. Realising that Casanova's handwriting on the postcard is the same as Ruskin's, Cross races over to McTiernan's house where he kills Ruskin and saves her.

The serial-killer genre, as exemplified by the Thomas Harris adaptations *Manhunter* and *The Silence of the Lambs*, has a different set of rules from the traditional whodunit. Crucially, in those films and lesser examples such as *Copycat*, the identity of the killer is revealed to the audience half way through; he is not someone the investigator knows already, and the suspense lies in whether the latter can use his or her skills to identify and catch this stranger before he kills again.

The influence of *The Silence of the Lambs* is very much in evidence in *Kiss the Girls*. The teaming of veteran investigator and driven, haunted young woman—here Morgan Freeman and Ashley Judd—echoes that of the Scott Glenn and Jodie Foster characters, not least in the absence of romantic entanglement. The look of the film—the Southern forests, the Gothic underground cells—is also reminiscent of Demme's film, while also harking back to the world of fairy tale (notably 'Bluebeard'). The casting of Brian Cox in a brief and very unrewarding role as the reactionary local chief of police could also be seen as a nod to Michael Mann's *Manhunter*, in which the Scottish actor unforgettably played the first incarnation of Hannibal Lecter.

But unfortunately, *Kiss the Girls* also wants to be an old-fashioned whodunit. Two doctors and one policeman are introduced as possible culprits before the final revelation of Casanova's identity (see the synopsis above if you want to know who). But though this shock may surprise us for a moment, it fatally undermines what has gone before. In the first place, while the expertise of Freeman's Dr Cross has been on display throughout, he actually identifies Casanova by recognising his handwriting, something a child could have done, and probably about an hour earlier too. What's most challenging about stories of men who habitually do terrible things to young women—from *M* (1931) to *Peeping Tom* (1960) to *The Collector* (1965)—is usually the insight they provide into the motives and habits of these monsters. *Kiss the Girls,* however, presents us with a man who has hitherto seemed perfectly normal, then expects us to believe he has been leading a double life as Casanova, with only a perfunctory last-minute speech to explain his motives.

Efficiently but heartlessly directed by Gary Fleder *(Things to Do in Denver When You're Dead), Kiss the Girls* dwells gloatingly on the sufferings of women in jeopardy. The sequences in which Judd's Dr McTiernan is stalked round her home, then later sexually assaulted, are calculated to instil terror in any woman who lives alone. Somehow the decision not to show Casanova, dictated by the plot, forces us to share his point of view: we observe the women's agony, without being encouraged to understand why it's being inflicted.

The only notable feature of Casanova's *modus operandi,* rather conveniently for the film-makers, is his preference for pretty and in some way "exceptional" women—which is all the more titillating for a male audience. As a result, the film leaves a very unpleasant taste, without even the consolation that this unpleasantness is in the service of a convincing story. Putting a black psychologist and a kickboxing woman doctor on the killer's trail may have been intended as a compensatory gesture of political correctness, but it's a half-hearted one at best, especially since for all their skills, it's only through a pure stroke of luck that they manage to catch the white male killer.

VILLAGE VOICE, 10/14/97, p. 90, Dennis Lim

Ashley Judd, who plays Clay's patient girlfriend in *The Locusts* [see Lim's review] has a juicier role in *Kiss the Girls;* the film is, however, appallingly threadbare, recycling *Seven* and *The Silence of the Lambs* in a wrongheaded stab at reviving serial-killer chic. Judd plays Kate McTiernan, an iron-willed, kick-boxing medical intern, who teams up with smooth-talking forensic psychologist Alex Cross (Morgan Freeman) to sniff out a "serial collector."

Casanova, as the movie's unimaginative villain calls himself, abducts beautiful young women and stores them in a harem-cellar deep in the North Carolina woods, killing them when they break his rules. The maniac has something of a talent fetish, so only overachievers like Kate and Naomi, Alex's violin-virtuoso niece, meet his standards. Director Gary Fleder delivers shocks on cue, but he needn't have bothered; in the end, it's the stench of exploitation that lingers, overpowering everything.

Also reviewed in:
CHICAGO TRIBUNE, 10/3/97, Friday/p. C, John Petrakis
NEW YORK TIMES, 10/3/97, p. E14, Stephen Holden
NEW YORKER, 10/13/97, p. 98, Daphne Merkin
VARIETY, 9/15-21/97, p. 69, Todd McCarthy
WASHINGTON POST, 10/3/97, p. B1, Rita Kempley
WASHINGTON POST, 10/3/97, Weekend/p. 46, Desson Howe

KISS OR KILL

An October Films release of a Bill Bennett production in association with the Australian Film Finance Corporation. *Executive Producer:* Mikael Borglund and Gary Hamilton. *Producer:* Bill Bennett and Jennifer Bennett. *Director:* Bill Bennett. *Screenplay:* Bill Bennett. *Director of Photography:* Malcolm McCulloch. *Editor:* Henry Dangar. *Sound:* Wayne Pashley. *Casting:* Jennifer Bennett. *Production Designer:* Andrew Plumer. *Costumes:* Ruth de la Lande. *Make-up:* Jennifer Lamphee. *Stunt Coordinator:* Johnny Hallyday. *Running time:* 95 minutes. *MPAA Rating:* R.

CAST: Frances O'Connor (Nikki); Matt Day (Al); Chris Haywood (Hummer); Barry Otto (Adler Jones); Andrew S. Gilbert (Crean); Barry Langrishe (Zipper Doyle); Max Cullen (Stan); Tiffany Peters (Young Nikki); Julie Sobotta (Nikki's Mother); Syd Brisbane (Nikki's Father); Geoff Revell (Paul Nathan); Eliza Lovell (Felicity); Jordan Weldon-Iley (Young boy); Carmel Johnson (Sarah, Hotel Regency Maid); Liz Windsor (Medical Examiner); Paul Rees (Assistant Medical Examiner); Audine Leith (Jules in the Gym); Michael Hill (Jacko); Tracy Bennett and Darren Bennett (Wrong Couple); Beth Dew (Wrong Motel Owner); Rosalind Aylemore (Stan's Cleaning Lady); Marjorie Koch and Ted Koch (Jetty Couple); Dennis Williams (Truck Driver); Stacey Perry ('Surf and Turf' Waitress); Ulli Birve (Waitress in Toilet); Chris Burke ('Sorry' Truckie); Matthew Bartsch (Uniform Cop); John Clarke (Possum Harry); Jennifer Cluff (Bel Jones); Bruce Ross (Roo Shooter); Mary McLaughlin (Publican); Jean Smith (Shop Owner); Don Chapman (Lindsay Klein, Lawyer); Vicki Burfitt (Esperence Hotel Maid); Tony Lynch (Roadblock Cop); Janet Brewer and Peter Carman (Ambulance Personnel).

LOS ANGELES TIMES, 11/14/97, Calendar/p. 16, Jack Mathews

[The following review by Jack Mathews appeared in a slightly different form in **NEWSDAY, 11/14/97, Part II/p. B6.]**

Imagine Terrence Malick's "Badlands" done as black comedy, with the rural atmosphere of "Psycho" and dialogue rubbed against flint, and you are in the general vicinity of writer-director Bill Bennett's deliciously twisted "Kiss or Kill."

The specific vicinity is the vast wasteland between Adelaide and Perth in southwest Australia, where Bennett takes us along on an eventful ride with Al Fletcher and Nikki Davis (Matt Day and Frances O'Connor, both of "Love and Other Catastrophes"), a young .couple deeply in love and even more deeply in trouble. Al and Nikki are small-time cons. She picks up businessmen in hotel bars and goes with them to their rooms, where she drugs them and lets Al in to rob them. But their latest job has gone wrong. Nikki accidentally gave the man a lethal, overdose, and all they've come away with are a few bucks and a briefcase containing a videotape.

The tape, they soon realize, is worth something. It reveals famous rugby star Zipper Doyle (Barry Langrishe) as a pedophile, meaning they may have killed a blackmailer. But before they figure out what to do with the tape, they hit the road for Perth, with a pair of homicide detectives and the frantic Zipper Doyle on their trail. And their pursuers are the least of their troubles.

Between the setup and conclusion of Bennett's story, a lot of miles are covered, a few grisly murders occur, a genuine mystery unfolds, suspicions between Al and Nikki grow, and an amazing amount of character development is realized. It's a measure of the director's sure-handedness, his star's performances and the captivating power of undying love that we can take off with such unappealing characters and come to care for their well-being.

Bennett, an award-winning Australian television reporter, has some experience with road movies. He made himself known to the international film community with his debut film, "Backlash," and then caught Hollywood's eye with his 1994 "Spider & Rose," about the relationship between a cranky ambulance driver and the old lady he has to take on a long journey home.

The upshot was a studio offer to direct "Two If by Sea," another road movie, starring Denis Leary and Sandra Bullock as lovers on the run. It was a bad movie and a worse experience, and Bennett went home to Australia, vowing to stick to films he writes, directs and controls.

"Kiss or Kill" is the work of a free and ambitious spirit. It's a film noir thriller, a love story, a psychological drama, a whodunit and even a bit of a western. And somehow, amid the "Twilight Zone" eccentrics we meet along the road, Al and Nikki hold both our empathy and our fascination.

People are dying around Al and Nikki—in their sleep with their throats slit—and with no one else around, they begin to suspect each other. Al begins to wonder what Nikki does while sleepwalking, and as the body count grows, she wonders how far he will go to commit petty theft.

Bennett has written himself into a corner from which he just barely escapes. He's asking the audience not just to sympathize with the couple, but to put themselves in their place. It succeeds because of the amount of character detail worked into the story. Without sentimentalizing their pull, Bennett gives us enough background to understand how Al and Nikki got to be who they are, and why they need each other so much.

Day and O'Connor have strong chemistry, and so, in a more comic vein do Chris Haywood and Andrew Gilbert, playing the bantering cops tracking them. One of the film's highlights is an improvised scene where one of the cops is interrogating the other about why he doesn't eat bacon.

Other standouts in the cast are Barry Otto as an old man who stows away in Al and Nikki's car, then invites them into his desert shack for a kangaroo dinner, and Max Cullen, as a nutty motel owner who whips them up an ill-fated fondue dinner with a blowtorch.

NEW YORK POST, 11/14/97, p. 51, Thelma Adams

Like its title, "Kiss or Kill" balances between intimacy and violence.

The opening scene of Bill Bennett's quirky thriller sets up this tension, jerking between hearth and horror. A mother and her young daughter happily putter in the kitchen. Someone knocks at the door. What follows is a brutal act that plays like a kick in the solar plexus.

With her mother's death, Nikki's childhood ends. The event also sends two currents rippling through the movie: an amoral criminality and a hungry desire to recreate the family's kitchen-table intimacy.

It's no wonder that when Nikki grows up, the troubled beauty plays Bonnie to Al's Clyde. Frances O'Connor and Matt Day (previously teamed in "Love and Other Catastrophes") play lovers who met at reform school. When one of their cons goes sour, Nikki and Al lam it across Australia.

Jolly cops and a pedophiliac football hero (fittingly named Zipper Doyle) follow in hot pursuit. As the corpses pile up along the road, the fugitives learn a few lessons about love and larceny. As Nikki concludes, "Only kill pedophiles."

Bennett (a successful Australian who made an ill-fated Hollywood pit stop with the Sandra Bullock clunker "Two If By Sea") keeps the thriller plot twisting. He jacks up the pace, keeping the cuts jumping along with the audience.

As adept as he is at thrills, Bennett excels in defining his characters and their inner conflicts. He marvels at the way Nikki and Al, a rumpled James Dean with a flash temper and a daddy complex, try to remain true to each other—even as each suspects the other has made the leap from larceny to serial murder.

Sharply played by O'Connor and Day, Nikki and Al ultimately drop Bonnie and Clyde for Ginger and Fred. Amid shabby motels, abandoned nuclear test sights and truck stops, Bennett allows a shopworn romanticism to conquer cynicism. In the end, Nikki and Al hobble into the sunset and kiss the carnage goodbye—or do they?

SIGHT AND SOUND, 7/98, p. 44, Philip Kemp

Nikki seduces businessmen in hotels and then drugs them so that she and her lover Al can rob them. In Adelaide, their latest victim Paul Nathan dies. In his briefcase, they find a video of football star Zipper Doyle taking a young boy to bed. The pair drive west across the Nullarbor Plain, heading for Perth. Doyle arrives to meet Nathan, realises the tape has been stolen and follows Nikki and Al.

Police detectives Hummer and Crean investigate Nathan's death and also start trailing the young couple. At a remote motel, the owner Stan serves Nikki and Al fondue for dinner. Nikki accidentally burns herself, reviving memories of a childhood trauma. That night, Al sees Nikki sleepwalking. After they leave, Stan is found murdered and robbed. Nikki and Al steal a four-wheel drive and dump their car. Hearing about Stan's killing on television, they each accuse the other. Hummer and Crean hire a tracker, Possum Harry. Nikki and Al find a man named Adler hiding in their car. Adler invites them to stay with him and his wife Bel in their isolated shack. The next morning, Adler and Bel are dead, their throats cut. Convinced Nikki killed them, Al ties her up and drives to a deserted hut, but she frees herself and later almost sets fire to him while sleepwalking.

Aided by Possum Harry, the detectives track the couple down and arrest them. Nikki admits to the killings, but Harry deduces that Adler killed Stan (who was having an affair with Bel), then slit Bel's throat and his own. Hummer and Crean watch Doyle's paedophile tape. A lawyer arrives, apparently from Al's father, demanding Nikki and Al's release. The detectives let them go, hoping they'll act as bait for Doyle. The lawyer takes the pair to Doyle, who kidnaps them at gunpoint and speeds off. The car crashes at a roadblock and Doyle is killed. Nikki and Al get off with a suspended sentence and set up home together. But Nikki is still sleepwalking.

Midway through *Kiss or Kill* two police detectives, Hummer and Crean, are sitting in a diner. Crean refuses bacon on the grounds that he's Jewish. Hummer is taken aback: "I didn't know you were Jewish." Crean elaborates: his parents, who worked for Mossad, died in a plane crash; he has a sister and a brother; he's married and his son has cerebral palsy. Hummer is abashed and apologises—he never knew. "You never asked," retorts Crean. Then he grins, tips back his head and swallows the bacon in a gulp.

It's a neat little scene, played with shrewd timing by Chris Haywood and Andrew S. Gilbert. But it also serves as a comic play on the underlying theme of this new film by Bill Bennett (who directed the flop *Stolen Hearts*): none of us really knows anybody, not even those closest to us. "It looks flat, like a pizza," says Stan the motel-owner about the bleak Nullarbor Plain stretching all around, "but underneath there's all these caves." The hidden reaches of the human mind are clearly what he's really talking about. *Kiss or Kill* takes the classic road-movie scenario, the attractive young criminal couple on the run, and cunningly subverts it, as Nikki and Al come to fear that their chief danger lies less in their pursuers than in each other.

Uncertainty, the sense that nothing and no one can be relied on, quivers through the film. Nikki's response ("I don't hate men—I just don't trust them," she says in voice-over) is to turn perfidious herself, only to find that duplicity is catching. "I don't know who you are," she laments after her lover Al explodes violently at one point, while Al becomes increasingly spooked by her sleepwalking. The film's coda seems like a gag but isn't. Snug in domestic bliss and waking to find Nikki absent, Al discovers her in the kitchen hacking savagely at a piece of meat. She swings round brandishing the knife—then laughs and hugs him. Neither laugh nor hug is the least bit reassuring.

Bennett heightens this sense of unease by the look and texture of the film. There are constant flickering jump-cuts, not between shots but within otherwise static set-ups, causing people to jerk fractionally as though the camera had blinked. The landscape, an immensity with no place to hide, is shot in stark high contrast, accentuating its brooding presence, at once ominous and indifferent. As the fugitive couple Frances O'Connor and Matt Day give edgy, volatile performances. And if *Kiss or Kill* isn't the first road movie to dispense with non-dietetic music, it's certainly the first for years, proving that for sustaining tension, skilfully handled ambient sound can beat a pounding soundtrack hands down.

VILLAGE VOICE, 11/18/97, p. 85, Elizabeth Weitzman

Heard this one before? A pair of crazy young lovers on the lam ... wait, I haven't finished ... go on a cross-country killing spree, piling up corpses ... patience, please ... while the comically inept feds stay just two paces behind their every move. Still here? You must either be very kindhearted or a hopeless fan of a genre that's been, well, pretty much beaten to death by now.

Even Australian director Bill Bennett seems to realize that despite the blistered outback backdrop, he's mostly working with yesterday's news, for he's added a stylistic device guaranteed to keep you on the edge of your seat: jump-cutting! Regrettably, this pointless contrivance, which I guess is supposed to render you as nervously twitchy as the protagonists, may instead turn you fidgety in irritation.

But Bennett does have a more compelling ace up his sleeve: the immensely talented Frances O'Connor, who was also the best thing about last spring's collegiate kvetchfest *Love and Other Catastrophes*. She proved her comedic gifts back then, and now as the emotionally, scarred, needy, and manipulative Nikki, she turns a character we've seen—and been annoyed by countless times before into something satisfyingly unsettling. As the couple's increasingly erratic behavior leads them to warily eye even one another, O'Connor's artful performance leaves us far more agitated than any editing tricks. Fellow down under up-and-comer Matt Day (also a *Catastrophes* alumnus) easily holds his own as Nikki's boyfriend Al, so while he at first appears to be a ducktailed Jason Priestly manqué with a nifty accent, his characterization is no more trustworthy than O'Connor's—and in this familiar setting, that's the highest of complements.

Also reviewed in:
CHICAGO TRIBUNE, 11/21/97, Friday/p. B, Michael Wilmington
NATION, 12/8/97, p. 36, Stuart Klawans
NEW REPUBLIC, 12/29/97, p. 29, Stanley Kauffmann
NEW YORK TIMES, 10/2/97, p. E5, Stephen Holden
VARIETY, 6/30-7/13/97, p. 66, David Stratton

KISS ME, GUIDO

A Paramount Pictures release in association with Kardana/Swinsky Films and Capitol Films of a Redeemable Features production. *Executive Producer:* Jane Barclay, Tom Carouso, Sharon Harel, and Christopher Lawford. *Producer:* Ira Deutchman and Christine Vachon. *Director:* Tony Vitale. *Screenplay:* Tony Vitale. *Director of Photography:* Claudia Raschke. *Editor:* Alexander Hall. *Music:* Randall Poster. *Sound:* William Kozy. *Sound Editor:* Juan Martinez and Thomas O'Shea. *Casting:* Pat DiStefano. *Production Designer:* Jeffrey Rathaus. *Set Decorator:* Wanda Wysong. *Costumes:* Victoria Farrell. *Make-up:* Joanne Ottaviano. *Stunt Coordinator:* Manny Siverio and Norman Douglass. *Running time:* 91 minutes. *MPAA Rating:* R.

CAST: Nick Scotti (Frankie); Anthony Barrile (Warren); Anthony DeSando (Pino); Molly Price (Meryl); Craig Chester (Terry); David Deblinger ("#"); Christopher Lawford (Dakota); Domenick Lombardozzi (Joey Chips); Jennifer Esposito (Debbie); Antonia Rey (Josephina Zito); John Tormey (Patsy Zito); Irma St. Paule (Grandma); Anthony Vitale and Frankie Dellarosa (Pizza Guys); Rebecca Waxman (Wiggy); Tony Ray Rossi (Vinny the Fish); Dwight Ewell (Usher); Marcia Firesten (Real Estate Broker); Bryan Batt (Tino); Craig Archibald (Robbie); Guinevere Turner (Indignant Lesbian); Damien Achilles and Bruce Smolanoff (Tough Guys); Goumba Johnny and Hollywood Hamilton (WKTU-DJ Voices).

LOS ANGELES TIMES, 7/18/97, Calendar/p. 16, Kevin Thomas

[*The following review by Kevin Thomas appeared in a slightly different form in* NEWSDAY, 7/18/97, Part II/p. B9.]

If Tony Vitale's "Kiss Me, Guido" isn't quite the laff riot its trailer suggests, it nonetheless abounds in good-hearted humor, adding up to a perfectly pleasant summer diversion.

What's significant is that Vitale successfully discards political correctness and instead embraces both Italian American and gay stereotypes with so much affection you can laugh out loud at them. At the same time he takes care to suggest how a gay man might actually be a regular guy.

What makes the movie work, however, is its star Nick Scotti, up from the ranks of fashion modeling and acting in the soaps. Scotti is flat-out terrific.

As Frankie, a Bronx pizza parlor worker, he somehow manages to convince us that this young man is absolutely unaware of his good looks. He is then able to make us believe that Frankie is so naive that he thinks that a "GWM" designation in a Village Voice want ad means "Guy With Money." Vitale has amusingly supplied Frankie with strong motivation for wanting to leave home in Belmont, the Little Italy of the Bronx, and answer a roommate ad for an apartment to share in the West Village.

The ad has been placed by Warren (Anthony Barrile), an actor-choreographer who's a whopping five months behind on his rent and faces eviction. Frankie reels from the shock of discovering that "GWM" means Gay White Male, but Vitale is clever enough to think up circumstances dire enough for Frankie and Warren to attempt to make sharing the apartment work, which neither wants to do. That Frankie dreams of being an actor himself helps. (He can do a pretty good Robert De Niro "Raging Bull" impersonation but admits his hero is Sylvester Stallone.)

"Kiss Me, Guido" is often silly, but Vitale makes silliness fun because he doesn't pretend it's otherwise and because he's good at thinking up plot twists. "Kiss Me, Guido" is highly theatrical—indeed, at one point Vitale tried to get it staged as a play—but it flows like the movie it is.

Although Frankie and Warren are the film's focal point, there are plenty of colorful, expertly played supporting characters. Anthony DeSando is Pino, Frankie's irrepressible satyr of a brother—it's this character's seduction of women that, along with blunt language, accounts in large part for the film's R rating.

Craig Chester is Warren's wisecracking best friend—it's the Eve Arden role; Christopher Lawford is Warren's tweedy ex-lover and roommate, an aspiring playwright; and Molly Price is Warren's mercurial landlady. Rounding out the key players are David Deblinger as Lawford's ultra-pretentious colleague and Domenick Lombardozzi as Frankie's sweet-natured co-worker back at the pizza parlor.

Amid a raft of vivid presences, Warren, well-played by Barrile, is at times in danger of seeming colorless. Yet it is key to Vitale's point that friendship, after all, can exist between an ordinary gay man and an ordinary straight man. Although neither as exuberant nor remotely as innocent as Frankie, Warren is as much a normal, everyday man as Frankie is. They could just end up pals.

NEW YORK POST, 7/18/97, p. 46, Thelma Adams

Are second-hand jokes hazardous to your health? Tony Vitale's "Kiss Me Guido" is harmless, but, ask the Surgeon General, humor this tired could use a laugh track.

In Vitale's first time out, the home-grown writer director goes for the classic oil-and-water sitcom situation. Think "My Favorite Martian," with a homosexual twist.

Actor Warren (the dimpled Anthony Barrile) needs a roommate. His cadish boyfriend- (Christopher Lawford, with father Peter's smile and little of his charm) has moved out without covering the rent.

Warren's pal Terry (Craig Chester) puts an ad in the paper seeking a roommate, a GWM—a gay white male. Bronx pizza boy and aspiring actor Frankie (Nick Scotti) thinks Warren is looking for a guy with money. Ah, the cross-culture comedy is endless—or at least it seems that way.

Frankie moves in with Warren and the stage is set. Pretty soon the pair are sharing the sitcom sofa, arguing about whether to watch "The Sound of Music" or the ballgame, whether to brunch out or egg in.

Before you can finish a chorus of "Edelweiss," you know Warren and Frankie will bond. All differences will melt away because it's a small world, after all.

For those out of the loop, the Guido of the title is slang for a macho Italiano. In that spirit, the supporting characters are screaming stereotypes. Frankie's big-haired former fiancee sleeps with his brother Pino, an Italian stallion in love with his Caddie. Their mother never speaks when she can shriek; ditto Warren's Jewish landlady.

Vitale has given opportunities to a number of appealing actors, including Scotti, Barrile, Chester and Anthony DeSando as Pino. Couldn't he have also given them better lines and stronger direction?

SIGHT AND SOUND, 12/97, p. 44, Andy Medhurst

New York. Aspiring actor Frankie works in a Bronx pizza parlour but feels increasingly constricted by his insular family and community. One night, he comes home to find his girlfriend Debbie and his brother Pino making love in the kitchen. This makes him determined to move on. Seeing a flat-share advertised in a magazine, he calls and makes an appointment, thinking that the renter's stipulation that only a 'GWM' need apply means 'Guy With Money'. In fact, it means 'Gay White Male', and the other tenant in the flat is gay actor Warren.

Frankie views the flat, still not realising Warren is gay, but is immediately caught up in a recriminatory argument between Warren and his devious ex-lover Dakota. Once Frankie is aware of Warren's sexuality he says he can't stay. But having stormed out of the family home he has nowhere else to go, so he decides to stay just one night. The two men's suspicions of each other gradually lessen and a tentative friendship slowly develops.

Meanwhile, Warren engineers a romance between his landlady Meryl and Pino, hoping this will deflect her constant demands for overdue rent. Dakota offers Warren the lead role in a new off-Broadway play he has written to try and win him back, but Warren is injured when he and Frankie fight off queer-bashers and Frankie takes the role instead, helped by Warren's coaching. On the opening night, he is a great success, despite the embarrassments caused by his entire family turning up to see him play a gay role. At the first night party, Warren finally sees through Dakota's schemes and he and Frankie, now firm friends, agree to continue sharing the apartment.

No film that boasts a character called "Indignant Lesbian" or features Carol Jiani's 'Hit & Run Lover' (the greatest Hi-NRG record ever made) on its soundtrack can be all bad—but *Kiss Me, Guido* comes close. Its central concept—a straight man and a gay man share a flat, have differences, then make up—feels like a discarded pilot for a liberal 80s sitcom akin to *Kate and Allie*. Its narrative is dispiritingly predictable and its politics veer from the unduly schmaltzy to the downright offensive. If one looks hard for positive aspects, one could mention that there are some nicely judged performances and a well-crafted sense of place and space. The latter might be attributable to the fact that first-time director-writer Tony Vitale once worked as a location manager, but on what can we blame *Kiss Me, Guido*'s glaring flaws?

Most damagingly, the central figure of Frankie lacks credibility, since there cannot feasibly be a man on Earth, especially among North Americans with theatrical ambitions, so totally ignorant about homosexuality. Nick Scotti does what he can with the role, but his main purpose in the film is not to convince us but to set us drooling, and for those with tastes in that direction his dumb-hunk porn-star looks will surely suffice. Underlying the camera's love affair with him, however, is a long-standing, suspect reasoning (which dates back to E. M. Forster and later Quentin Crisp) that straight men, because they are 'real' men, are more attractive. This is a philosophy which can only leave queer men feeling in equal parts self-loathing and unrequitable lust. According to the unbreakable rule of texts that operate within this framework, the gay man doing the lusting cannot be an object of desire himself.

So the gay character of Warren, although smart and charming, has to be shorter, plumper and slightly fem. The urban gay male viewer at whom the film is mostly aimed is consequently invited to identify with the supporting player, reliable but never magical—Edward Everett Horton but never Fred Astaire. For all its supposedly hip 90s trappings, then, *Kiss Me, Guido* plays some of the oldest representational cards in the deck.

There's worse: the crass gullibility of Frankie's fellow Italians (the most unreconstructed lot since Spike Lee's in *Do the Right Thing*) surpasses even Frankie's improbable denseness. This doesn't, however, leave the film open to charges of racism—Italian New Yorker Vitale, presumably, knows the milieu he's handling—but manifests a more subtle and insidious form of prejudice. All is revealed in the film's title, which rests on a piece of American slang. A 'Guido' is, basically, a stupid Italian—macho, sexist, muscled, worshipping Sylvester Stallone, and, crucially, working class. (Imagine, as a provocative parallel, a British comedy about a West Indian called 'Watch It Winston'). "You're such a 'Guido'," Warren tells Frankie, laying bare the real reason he can't imagine their shared domesticity succeeding, and thereby reconnecting us to the Forsterian queer/non-queer dynamic outlined above.

A key inflection in that sensibility was that the straight, desirable man should also be common as muck, while the queer was drenched in middle-class culture. *Kiss Me, Guido* tries to avoid this cliché in its laboured art-bashing parody of the absurdly pretentious play that Frankie reluctantly performs in, but the fact remains that part of Warren's mission is his determination to purge Frankie of his working-class roots and tastes.

Civilising the natives, after all, usually means imposing the conqueror's culture on to the conquered. "No more videos with 'Ninja' in the title" Warren warns Frankie, as they finally prepare to shack up.

The only other point to note about *Kiss Me, Guido* is the timing of its production and release, taking place after years in which Vitale failed to sell the idea. The film emerges firstly in the wake of *The Birdcage*, which proved you could sell fag-centred farce to the multiplex market, and secondly in the era when *Friends* is the definitive US sitcom. For Frankie and Warren, read Joey and Chandler: dishy-but-dim Italian actor and his WASPish roommate. Unfortunately, farces need speed and panache, while *Kiss Me, Guido* remains sluggish and stolid, and *Friends* thrives on sharp wit and real warmth, whereas all Vitale can muster is damp squibs and reheated lasagne.

VILLAGE VOICE, 7/22/97, p. 72, Elisabeth Vincentelli

Let's give writer-director Tony Vitale the benefit of the doubt and assume he used stereotypes instead of characters for his debut, *Kiss Me, Guido,* in order to make us question our own assumptions. Does it mean we have to gloss over the witlessness of the dialolgue, the inanity of the situations, or, for that matter, the entire premise of the movie?

When pizza maker—aspiring actor Frankie Zito (Nick Scotti) decides to move from da Bronx to Manhattan, he ends up sharing an apartment with openly gay Warren (Anthony Barrile). The two boys will eventually realize that a mutual passion for acting and disco music cancel out any smaller differences, but not before Frankie, for whom "fag" is a casual insult, gets an education in Downtown customs. When Warren watches *The Sound of* Music on TV, for instance, Frankie mistakes Julie Andrews for Julia Roberts: "I liked her in *Pretty Woman,*" he offers. After being corrected by the incredulous Warren, Frankie defensively replies, "I liked that movie—it was realistic." Clearly *Kiss Me, Guido* dispenses entirely with witty repartee.

Suspension of disbelief is a customary necessity in summer movies. So we will buy the fact that Frankie thinks the term "GWM" in a classified ad stands for "Guy With Money." But since we are also to believe that Frankie hopes to find an apartment in Little Italy for $200 a month, we can conclude that Vitale has forsaken any last shred of realism in favor of science fiction. Unfortunately he didn't go whole hog: production values are low and there's no flair for the extravagant. Indeed, why stop at one cartoonishly man-hungry straight woman, Warren's landlady Meryl (Molly Price), when there could have been 30 of them in coordinated outfits, catfighting over sales at Loehmann's?

Also reviewed in:
NEW YORK TIMES, 7/18/97, p. C5, Janet Maslin
VARIETY, 1/27-2/2/97, p. 76, Dennis Harvey
WASHINGTON POST, 8/8/97, Weekend/p. 32, Michael O'Sullivan

KISSED

A Goldwyn Entertainment Company release of a Metromedia Entertainment Group presentation of a Boneyard Film Company film produced in association with British Columbia Film. *Executive Producer:* John Pozer. *Producer:* Dean English and Lynne Stopkewich. *Director:* Lynne Stopkewich. *Screenplay:* Angus Fraser and Lynne Stopkewich. *Based on the story by:* Barbara Gowdy. *Director of Photography:* Gregory Middleton. *Editor:* John Pozer, Peter Roeck, and Lynne Stopkewich. *Music:* Don MacDonald. *Sound:* David Ballard. *Sound Editor:* Susan Taylor. *Casting:* Wendy O'Brien Livingstone. *Production Designer:* Eric McNab. *Art Director:* Darryl Dennis Deegan. *Set Decorator:* Laura Morrison. *Special Effects:* Kevin House. *Costumes:* Barb Nixon. *Make-up:* Adina. *Stunt Coordinator:* Jim Dunn and Kevin Stubbs. *Running time:* 78 minutes. *MPAA Rating:* Not Rated.

CAST: Molly Parker (Sandra Larson); Peter Outerbridge (Matt); Jay Brazeau (Mr Wallis); Natasha Morley (Young Sandra Larson); Jessie Winter Mudie (Carol); James Timmons (Jan); Joe Maffei (Biology Teacher); Robert Thurston (Detective); Annabel Kershaw (Mother Larson); Tim Dixon (Father Larson); Amber Warnat (Lisa Brown); Bill Finck (Minister); Janet Craig (Mourner); Edward Davey (Embalming Prof).

LOS ANGELES TIMES, 4/18/97, Calendar/p. 6, Kevin Thomas

Lynne Stopkewich's audacious "Kissed" is as hilarious as it is seemingly serious, a darkly outrageous comedy. It's probably not quite like anything you've ever seen before, although its evocation of weirdness amid a prosaic small-town setting may make you think of David Lynch's "Blue Velvet." But in contrast to Lynch's lush colors, Stopkewich goes for a drab, dun look, a depiction of tastelessness in clothes or interiors that suggests how powerful the pull of the metaphysical can be amid such dullness.

A bizarre yet romantic fable, it tells of an adolescent girl, Sandra (Natasha Morley), who is fascinated with death and given to ritual burials of dead sparrows and chipmunks in the woods near her home. In the midst of one such ceremony, Sandra has her first experience with menstruation, and as a result the sex-and-death equation is firmly cemented in her psyche.

Can it be a surprise that several years later, as a young woman, Sandra (now played by Molly Parker) is drawn to take a mortuary job, becoming a zealous student of embalming and encountering a lonely pre-med student, Matt (Peter Outerbridge)?

Matt falls in love with Sandra. But can he compete with the corpses of the best-looking, most in-shape among the dead males at the funeral parlor? Sandra is sufficiently comfortable with the pleasant-looking Matt to confess that she is in fact a voracious necrophile. Matt is, in turn, sufficiently enamored of Sandra—and sufficiently open-minded to try to take this rather remarkable piece of information in stride.

He wonders what will probably have crossed your mind and asks her if the necrophiba is a power trip for her. She says no, that "it's about crossing over," and explains that it's a kind of mystical experience in which she is able to feel the full impact of the individuality of every male corpse she has sex with.

Now that's a reach, but the amazing thing is Stopkewich makes you believe Sandra may be on the level and not entirely crazy while letting you laugh at the absurdity of the idea. Traditionally, necrophiles tend to be men rather than women, so Sandra's activities take on a feminist tinge.

"Kissed" is the kind of endeavor that demands total control, especially of tone and discretion in regard to dealing with such kinky sex. So much as a single misstep could spell disaster, but Stopkewich never slips up and gets right-up-to-the-edge portrayals from Parker and Outerbridge.

At a certain point, "Kissed" develops a quality of inevitability, and by the time it's over you may be reminded of Nagisa Oshima's notorious "In the Realm of the Senses."

NEW YORK POST, 4/18/97, p. 44, Larry Worth

To Sandra, love means smelling like formaldehyde and having blood under her fingernails. That's because Sandra's a necrophiliac—and the blissfully deluded heroine of "Kissed." Her tale is guaranteed to shock, disturb and upset, mostly because first-time filmmaker Lynne Stopkewich isn't trying to generate cheap jolts. Rather, she tackles Sandra's lifelong obsession with death in a startlingly serious manner.

Stopkewich increases tension by denying audiences the chance to laugh or scream—viewers' standard releases when subject matter calls for squirming. Those reactions prove virtually impossible as one gets sucked into an increasingly warped universe.

As the storyline opens, young, pig-tailed Sandra looks and acts like, Wednesday Addams, creating elaborate funerals for broken-winged sparrows and the like. But even Wednesday never rubbed their feathered corpses across her body or tenderly caressed their beaks.

It's no surprise when Sandra grows up and pursues her dream job: an embalmer at the local funeral parlor. And that's just the beginning for what turns into an all-consuming, tragic passion.

So, is this sick-pup time? No question. But unlike David Cronenberg's purposely emotionless characters in the equally controversial "Crash," Sandra proves consistently sympathetic and all-too-human.

For that, newcomer Molly Parker deserves applause. Her uninhibited presentation of a skewed sensibility is conveyed with a grace that defies all logic. She taps into Sandra's purity and unique vision, translating them with the subtlest of gestures.

Peter Outerbridge dovetails beautifully as Sandra's heart-breakingly sincere lover. Also noteworthy are Jay Brazeau's initially stoic funeral director and Natasha Morley as the young Sandra.

But it's the project's poetic look and artistic feel that make all the difference, along with Stopkewich's penchant for facing incomprehensible topics head-on.

As for scenes' graphic nature, be forewarned. Some tableaus require a strong stomach, particularly embalming sequences in which viewers may learn more than they ever wanted to know.

It's safe to say funeral directors won't be the only ones to take umbrage. But fans and detractors alike must acknowledge Stopkewich's accomplishments: She's not only tackled a tough taboo, but embraced it with unexpected dignity.

NEWSDAY, 4/18/97, Part II/p. B11, John Anderson

Connections between sex and death may be grave, but they're certainly nothing new. In the English poetry of the 17th Century, "dying" could mean sexual climax; the French phrase *le petit mort* defines orgasm as "little death." Taking it a few steps further, being "annihilated" can be a good thing; being "dead in bed" is bad.

On-screen necrophilia, however, is something of a rarity, and that may be the point of "Kissed," a Canadian import and the first feature film by director-writer Lynne Stopkewich. Is sex with the dead a pressing social issue crying out for attention? Is it a ripe metaphor for the state of contemporary sexuality, culture or the Senate? Is it a subject that might get a fledgling director a lot of attention?

I'd rule out A, but B and C seem to be distinct possibilities. In chronicling the morbid curiosity of the child Sandra Larson (Natasha Morley) and the necrophiliac compulsions of her older self (played by Molly Parker), Stopkewich creates a setting and atmosphere not unlike that of many low-budget, young-adult comedies, films dealing with modern individuals resisting the status quo in search of their true selves and destinies. And happiness. In Sandra's case, happiness happens to mean getting it on with a corpse.

And not any particular corpse. Not only is Sandra turned on by rigor mortis, she's promiscuous about it. But let's not quibble. Anyone inclined to be offended by all this has already jumped out the window.

"I've always been fascinated by death," says Sandra, in an opening flashback that begins with ambulances and police and takes us to her young self holding highly ritualized funerals for small dead animals. Stopkewich is convincing enough in her portrayal of a child's embrace of what she finds both compelling and appalling; Sandra's embrace of the unknown, her need for physical contact with the sad animal corpses she buries so tenderly, is not so hard to understand. Death is the big delicious mystery, even for an 11-year-old.

But this chronicle of a fetish foretold loses us when Sandra gets older, goes to college, finds a job in a funeral home run by Mr. Wallis (Jay Brazeau) and decides to become an embalmer. This gives her access to the bodies, of course, and allows her to indulge herself, and the white effect that follows each crescendo of passion is our visual link to Sandra the child—the same obliterating brightness followed each of her childhood episodes. That this visual connection doesn't occur when Sandra goes to bed with her fellow student, Matt (Peter Outerbridge), is Stopkewich's way of telling us that there's a near-organic connection between Sandra and death that's simply her fate—and might be ours, if only we would open ourselves up to it.

No thanks. Stopkewich shows some talent, and Molly Parker (although she bears an unsettling facial and vocal resemblance to Mackenzie Phillips) is a very likeable actress. But the movie's case isn't made. We don't understand Sandra's obsession any more at the end than we did before. Matt's desperate attempts to make a connection with Sandra—being alive, of course, he's at a disadvantage—make little sense at all.

With all the advances in cloning, in-vitro fertilization and battery-operated appliances, there have been a lot of jokes lately about men being obsolete. Some of them are funny. "Kissed," however, is merely tiring.

NEWSWEEK, 3/24/97, p. 79, Jack Kroll

[*Kissed* was reviewed jointly with *Crash*; see Kroll's review of that film.]

SIGHT AND SOUND, 1/98, p. 47, Charlotte O'Sullivan

As a child, Sandra Larson finds death irresistible. She enjoys burying animals at night and rubbing their corpses over her skin, trailing their blood. She tries to induct a friend into her ceremonies, but instead scares her off.

Now a young woman, Sandra takes a job at the local funeral home where she is taken under the wing of Mr Wallis, the proprietor. She is attracted to the young male bodies and begins making love to them. Jan the cleaner tells her Mr Wallis abuses the little boy corpses.

At college, Sandra meets Matt, a young medical student, taking "time out" from his studies. She shares her secret with him and they begin sleeping with each other. However, Sandra is unsatisfied and continues to make night visits to the funeral home while Matt becomes increasingly jealous. Sandra won't let him watch and she won't explain her actions, so his attempts to satisfy her become increasingly desperate. She wants to call the relationship off but suddenly he's the one not returning the calls. She goes to his room and finds him standing naked, on a stool, with a rope round his neck. He wants her to push away the stool. When she won't, he kicks it himself and dies. The ambulance arrives and Sandra, wrapped in a blanket, watches him leave. Life goes on, but she has found true love—after this, all corpses will remind her of him.

The plot of *Kissed* (based on a short story by Canadian writer Barbara Gowdy) couldn't be simpler: necrophiliac girl meets boy, boy dies. And, just as the embalmer Mr Wallis drains blood from his bodies, Canadian director Lynne Stopkewich uses the camera to drain tension from her debut film. We get slow fade-outs and dissolves. Sometimes, while our narrator Sandra muses New Age-style on her hobby, we grind to an absolute halt. Newcomer Molly Parker suits the role perfectly: skeletal-thin, she has skin like a freckled egg and lips so pursed they seem stitched together.

Pretty soon, this relentlessly wan style becomes a problem. Even the necrophilia itself starts to get mundane. At every sexual climax, Stopkewich cuts to cold white light. Like a cameraman's flashbulb, it captures and freezes the moment. But what's in this girl's past? (Even the po-faced *Female Perversions* had flashbacks. And when, one wonders, is she going to be found out?

Meanwhile, Sandra's relationship with besotted boyfriend Matt barely makes sense. He seems too reasonable and glamorous (a dead ringer for the young Peter O'Toole) to fall so heavily.

But then Matt kills himself, and suddenly this corpse of a film comes electrifyingly to life. "You don't love me," Matt tells Sandra, "but you will." And he's right. Sandra's newly-aroused self and resulting euphoria ("his star was the brightest I'd ever seen") sends a shock through the system. We feel two things at once: repulsion (having been lulled by Sandra's controlled voice, we realise the extent of her insanity), but also intense pleasure (Matt, more vulnerable than we thought, has got what he wanted and Sandra has found love—the terrible isolation has been pierced).

How can such a cold film create such heat? Because, without our realising it, Stopkewich has created a world truer to life than art, a world in which desire has no plot. Mr Wallis (as played by the exquisitely restrained Jay Brazeau) demonstrates this perfectly. Initially a low-comedy figure, he is an abuser but also the one adult in authority, an efficient, even paternal figure, full of mordant unintentional wit. Like a character in *Crash*, Wallis is a respectable addict who has tracked down his drug of choice and is feasting off it slowly. He is obsessed by destruction, but not self-destruction.

Hitchcock might not have liked this film, but he would have understood its aims. That you can't keep a good perversion down is the lesson taught by movies like *Marnie*. At some point, the perverted will be dragged into the light of day, filling the psychiatrist's office and/or the blackmailer's pocket. In *Kissed,* there is no light of day. It's not that Mr Wallis and Sandra are "normal", it's that there is no "norm". With shame and blame removed from Stopkewich's piece, other, far stranger, feelings become possible for the viewer.

Kissed is hardly an advert for necrophilia. The *amour fou* of *Breaking the Waves* ended with ringing bells, a metaphorical thumbs up from God. There's nothing in *Kissed* to indicate Matt's done the right thing. Even so, some will no doubt be outraged by the existential calm. Is Sandra's a victimless crime? "The dead can feel it" says Jan the cleaner sadly and Sandra nods in fierce, excited agreement. It's a neatly made point: both necrophiliac and anti-necrophiliac have an investment in believing the dead *do* care. Would we feel differently if the sexes were reversed? Certainly, there's a thrill in seeing the woman on top (Snow White bestowing the kiss on a motionless prince) that wouldn't work the other way round. A male director might be accused of exploitation if he showed female bodies being violated, or a woman offering her life for a lover. But that's not Stopkewich's problem. Hers is a wonderfully disturbing film. And what does it matter that it can only be "enjoyed" in hindsight? *Kissed* may not be scrotum-tightening but, as far as the brain and heart are concerned, it turns the screw.

VILLAGE VOICE, 4/15/97, p. 67, J. Hoberman

Kissed, a minor sensation at the last Toronto Film Festival, features one sexual practice that *Pink Flamingos* forgot—namely necrophilia. Corpse fucking was the subject of much off-screen humor in *Clerks* but, as directed by Lynne Stopkewich from a short story by Barbara Gowdy, this Canadian production is a far more serious affair.

A movie of solemn voiceovers and fragmenting closeups, *Kissed* begins with its heroine's admission that she's "always been fascinated by death." Despite the first-person narration however, the movie is less psychological than anthropological and (unlike *Crash*, for example) more defensive about than fascinated by its particular erotic subcultures. The child Sandra invents her own dead-bird rituals, burying various small animals in the woods. In high school, she can't bear to look at a frog dissection but has no qualms about licking a dead rodent. The New Age yodeling that accompanies this epiphany is a taste of what's to come.

Having grown into a provocatively prim young woman (Molly Parker), Sandra gets her dream job at a local funeral parlor. The movie turns rapturous the first time she kisses a (handsome, young, male) corpse—the screen exploding in white light. Sandra subsequently learns the art of embalming, cuddling cadavers while listening to soft folk music. Surprisingly easy to watch, *Kissed*'s kinkiest aspect is the heroine's affair with an understanding medical student (Peter Outerbridge). After their first tryst, she runs from his bed back to work to mount a handy corpse. Later, she frustrates his desire for some sort of morgue ménage à trois even while stoking his jealousy by extolling the experience: "It's like looking into the sun without going blind."

Kissed touches only glancingly on the suggestion that any mortician might be a closet necrophiliac—or any corpse might be less than perfect. Indeed, the movie is so decorously delicate, so self-consciously poetic, and so sanctimoniously tasteful that it would surely strike John Waters as a comedy.

Also reviewed in:
NEW YORK TIMES, 4/18/97, p. C18, Stephen Holden
VARIETY, 9/16-22/96, p. 69, Brendan Kelly
WASHINGTON POST, 4/25/97, p. G1, Rita Kempley
WASHINGTON POST, 4/25/97, Weekend/p. 49, Richard Harrington

KNOWLEDGE OF HEALING, THE

An In Pictures release of a T&C Film Ag production in association with Schweizer Fernsehen DRS/Kulturfonds Swissimage/Teleclub. *Executive Producer:* Paul Riniker. *Producer:* Marcel Hoehn. *Director:* Franz Reichle. *Screenplay (Tibetan, Russian, Buryat, English, Swiss dialect, and German with English subtitles):* Franz Reichle. *Director of Photography:* Pio Corradi. *Editor:* Myriam Flury and Franz Reichle. *Sound:* Dieter Meyer. *Sound Editor:* Jörg von Allmen. *Running time:* 90 minutes. *MPAA Rating:* Not Rated.

CAST: H.H. Tenzin Gyatso (XIV Dalai Lama of Tibet); Tenzin Choedrak (Senior Personal Physician to His Holiness the Dalai Lama); Chimit-Dorzhi Dugarov (Tibetan Physician, Ulan-Ude); Karl Lutz (Pharmaceutical Entrepreneur, Zollikon); Alfred Hässig (MD, Immunology, Bern); Herbert Schwabl (PhD, Biophysics, Zolikon); Herbert Kilma (PhD, Biophysics, Vienna); Dashinima D. Ayusheyev (MD, Urology, Ulan-Ude); Isaac Ginsburg (PhD, Micorbiology, Bacteriology, Jerusalem); Israel Vlodavsky (PhD, Tumor Biology, Jerusalem); Lobsang Dolker (Patient, Hermitess, Dharmsala); Tenzin Choedon (Patient, Shugsep Nunnery, Dharmsala); Nikita B. Maglayev (Patient, Novo-Nikolayevsk, Irkutsk); Viktoria Tsyrengarmayeva (Patient, Narsatui); Dolgor B. Linkhovoin (Patient, Ulan-Ude); Fritz Sterki (Patient, Thun).

NEW YORK POST, 11/5/97, p. 48, Larry Worth

It's not a particularly catchy title. Indeed, "The Knowledge of Healing" sounds like something better suited to the Discovery Channel than to the big screen.

Actually, it *is* better suited to TV, as well as too long and repetitive. But within the clumsy framework, "Knowledge," proves to be eye-opening and thought-provoking.

Coming shortly after "Seven Years in Tibet" piqued moviegoers' curiosity about Tibetan culture, viewers get an all-encompassing look in the Dalai Lama's medicine cabinet.

Specifically, the film focuses on two practitioners of Tibetan remedies, then analyzes their findings through Western scientists' eyes. Yet, director Franz Reichle fails to turn the footage into compelling cinema.

Ultimately, "Knowledge" is like those Tibetan herbs that defy rational explanation. They're not a perfect science, but the end basically justifies the means.

SIGHT AND SOUND, 12/98, p. 48, Melanie McGrath

A torch illuminates an ancient Tibetan table of herbs or *thangka*. In Dharmsala, northern India, Tibetan medical practitioner Tenzin Choedrak unrolls his *thangka* and explains the fundamental text of Tibetan medicine, the eleventh-century *Gyushi or* "knowledge of healing". A nun is prescribed herbs for injuries sustained during anti-Chinese protests. Choedrak ministers to the Dalai Lama. In Buryatia, Mongolia, an old man is treated for inoperable cancer. A young woman paralysed in a car accident is offered massage. An old woman shares her remembrances of Tibetan medical healers, many of whom were killed by the Chinese during the Cultural Revolution.

Dr Lutz, a Swiss doctor and advocate of Tibetan medicine, explains that a Russian named Badmajew first brought the Tibetan tradition to the west in the 40s. In Jerusalem, scientists make the case for Tibetan medicine. At the Vienna Nuclear Institute physicists conclude that Tibetan healers are able to alter light emissions given off by their patients. Back in India, the Dalai Lama calls for western and Tibetan medicine to be practised in parallel. Some months later, in Buryatia, the young accident victim is making progress and the old man's cancer is now considered operable. Meanwhile, in Dharmsala the nun is more cheerful but no better. Choedrak tells her progress will be slow but she must feel proud of her protest against the Chinese. Choedrak rolls up his *thangka* and the film fades out.

This quiet, old-fashioned documentary fits into the worthy but somewhat trudging tradition of 70s anthropological film-making. If self-serving direction, scripted scenes and plumped-up phoney characters define the contemporary docusoap, *The Knowledge of Healing* is the anti-docusoap, and for that alone it is welcome. The absence of spelled out narrative links, voice-overs or the kind of set-up devices we have become used to seeing in non-fiction filmmaking lends this documentary a simple *vérité* appeal. In affirmation of Buddhist tradition, the action floats, free of the tyranny of preconceived intent. And unlike many of its anthropological antecedents *The Knowledge of Healing* never descends to condescension to either the subject or the viewer.

Perhaps the noble-savage chic with which all things Tibetan are currently regarded in the west, plus the appearance of the Dalai Lama, contributed to this film finding a theatrical distributor. It is, nonetheless, wholly unsuited to the large screen. Maybe it is asking too much of a film about eastern medicine that it conform at least in some part to the accepted grammar of the contemporary non-fiction film. Still, we are western viewers and we live by western values, one of which demands that a roughly 90-minute documentary taking in more exotic locations than a James Bond film give out something greater than a talking-head-and-landscape sandwich. The evidence about the healing properties of light emissions is genuinely new, but most of what *The Knowledge of Healing* has to tell is now familiar from the rhetoric of new-age therapeutics.

Little here delights the eye. The film's one stylistic trick—the use of torches to illuminate the Tibetan texts—appears oddly antiquarian. Otherwise, *The Knowledge of Healing* is flatly, almost dourly directed. Long uncut sequences are piled one upon another without the intervention of music or a change in tone. The camera is too literal and the direction too clumping for the film to feel anything but didactic. And the editor surely must have fallen into a state of catatonia during one Israeli interviewee's prolix exposition, there being no other possible rational explanation for not cutting.

VILLAGE VOICE, 11/11/97, p. 82, Amy Taubin

If *Eve's Bayou* [see Taubin's review] locates the gift of second sight somewhere between Freud's concept of the unconscious and the culture of voodoo, Franz Reichle's *The Knowledge of Healing* documents another non-Western, nonestablishment method of caring for body and soul. That it's one of the least elaborate films in a deluge of last-ditch attempts to record Tibetan culture on the brink of annihilation doesn't make it any less effective.

A 2000-year-old system of healing that relies heavily on the medicinal use of plants, herbs, and minerals, Tibetan medicine is a scientific practice that has successfully treated cancer and coronary diseases, sometimes when Western medicine has failed. Reichle interviews the Dalai Lama and his physician, as well as an impressive array of doctors, biochemists, and biophysicists in Europe and Israel who take Tibetan medicine extremely seriously. He also follows several cases where Tibetan doctors were able to heal people with chronic illnesses after Western doctors had given up on them. One patient is a female Tibetan monk suffering from paralyzing headaches as a result of being beaten and tortured in a Chinese prison. Wiping away his tears, the elderly doctor explains that she should not be ashamed of her pain: "Just remember that you suffered torture not on a personal level, but for the whole of Tibet. Put your mind at rest. The truth will come out in the end."

Also reviewed in:
NEW YORK TIMES, 11/5/97, p. E4, Stephen Holden
VARIETY, 12/8-14/97, p. 113, Ken Eisner

KULL THE CONQUEROR

A Universal Pictures release. *Executive Producer:* Beverlee Dean, Jeff Franklin, and Steve Waterman. *Producer:* Raffaella De Laurentiis. *Director:* John Nicolella. *Screenplay:* Charles Edward Pogue. *Based on the worlds and the characters created by:* Robert E. Howard. *Director of Photography:* Rodney Charters. *Editor:* Dallas Puett. *Music:* Joel Goldsmith. *Music Editor:* Darrell Hall. *Sound:* Reinhard Stergar and (music) Michael Ross. *Sound Editor:* Glenn T. Morgan. *Casting:* Jeffery Passero and Elizabeth Hayden-Passero. *Production Designer:* Benjamin Fernandez. *Art Director:* Pier-Luigi Basile. *Set Decorator:* Giorgio Desidri. *Special Effects:* Kit West. *Visual Effects:* Richard Malzahn. *Costumes:* Thomas Casterline and Sibylle Ulsamer. *Make-up:* Giuseppe Desiato, Lorella De Rossi, Eloisa De Laurentiis, and Eva Vyplelova. *Special Make-up Effects:* Giannetto De Rossi. *Stunt Coordinator:* Paul Weston. *Running time:* 90 minutes. *MPAA Rating:* PG-13.

CAST: Kevin Sorbo (Kull); Tia Carrere (Akivasha); Thomas Ian Griffith (Taligaro); Litefoot (Ascalante); Roy Brocksmith (Tu); Harvey Fierstein (Juba); Karina Lombard (Zareta); Edward Tudor-Pole (Enaros); Douglas Henshall (Ducalon); Joe Shaw (Dalgar); Sven Ole Thorsen (King Borna); Terry O'Neill (Ship Captain); Pat Roach (Zuleki); John Hallam (Mandara); Peter Petruna and Boris Bacik (Slaves); Paul Kynman and Paul Weston (Dragon Legion Guards).

LOS ANGELES TIMES, 8/29/97, Calendar/p. 12, Kevin Thomas

[The following review by Kevin Thomas appeared in a slightly different form in
NEWSDAY, 8/29/97, Part II/p. B8.]

"Kull the Conqueror" is a deliciously silly, ancient times fantasy-adventure that works because its makers know exactly what they're doing and how to do it. Tone is key in any picture but absolutely crucial when reviving an old genre.

Director John Nicolella and writer Charles Edward Pogue, drawing from the writings of Robert E. Howard, who also created "Conan the Barbarian," never condescend to their material or their audience but instead approach their tale with affection and just enough saving tongue-in-cheekery to make it work as a zesty and amusing contemporary entertainment. As a result, "Kull" is fun and fast-moving, avoiding the pitfalls of kitsch and camp.

TV's Hercules, Kevin Sorbo, moves to the big screen with the greatest of ease in the title role. He slays the tyrannical King Borna (Sven Ole Thorsen), but with his dying breath the monarch surveys his court, and decides that his slayer is more worthy of wearing his crown than anyone else.

Kull's ascension to the throne naturally does not sit well with Borna's commander Taligaro (Thomas Ian Griffith) and his followers. The next thing we know, a 3,000-year-old sorceress, Akivasha (Tia Carrere), is being raised from the dead to bring down Kull. But she doesn't reckon with the spiritual power of the proud slave girl Zareta (Karina Lombard) combined with Kull's true grit.

So much for plot. "Kull the Conqueror" proceeds with unstinting panache amid picturesque Slovakian locales and handsome sets. Derring-do and the supernatural are also presented with consistent style and imagination, and Joel Goldsmith's robust score goes heavy metal at all the right moments.

Sorbo displays a welcome dry humor. He can even say a line like, "When I get hold of that bitch demon, I'll tear her heart out," without breaking up. His supporting cast, which includes Harvey Fierstein as an ebullient con man, play it straight without taking themselves too seriously.

"Kull the Conqueror" has a remarkably light, buoyant touch for its genre. As a Universal production, it is reminiscent of the studio's escapist fare of past eras. You can't help envisioning Burt Lancaster as Kull, Maria Montez as Akivasha and Yvonne De Carlo as Zareta.

NEW YORK POST, 8/29/97, p. 49, Michael Medved

"Kull the Conqueror" can teach attentive moviegoers all sorts of valuable lessons—highlighting, for instance, the dangers in trusting any woman who lies about her age.

The blushing bride (Tia Carrere) of the newly crowned King Kull (Kevin Sorbo) tells him she's just an innocent lass of 19, but it turns out she's actually a sorceress who's going on 3,000.

As you might expect, the royal wedding night involves its uncomfortable moments, as Carrere (who looks absolutely ravishing in her campy, slinky Frederick's-of-Babylon outfits) uses her new position to try to enslave the entire kingdom to the tyranny of her Evil Fire.

Kull barely escapes with his life and must journey to the ends of the earth (accompanied by saintly, sexy slave girl Karina Lombard) to acquire the mystical gifts that will allow them to return home and free his subjects from the forces of darkness and deviltry.

This is absurdly silly stuff, of course, but "Kull" conquers by celebrating that silliness. After all, its pectorally privileged protagonist proclaims platitudes like, "My blood is as red as any man's!" and one of the powerful opponents he encounters on his heroic quest is a devious slave merchant in a rhinestone headdress played by ... Harvey Fierstein!

At times, especially when crowds of poker-faced, bearded extras listlessly shake their arms and shout "Long live the king!," this outrageous epic begins to feel like a hip Monty Python takeoff of "Conan the Barbarian"—a resemblance that is no accident, since producer Raffaella De Laurentiis previously committed "Conan," and "Kull" is based on the deathless works of Robert E. Howard, the same pulp-meister who gave the world the barbarian big guy.

Kevin Sorbo, star of TV's inexplicably popular "Hercules: The Legendary Journeys," is not just a Schwarzenegger stand-in; unlike Arnold in his early roles, he seems to be in on the joke, delivering some sly smiles and hinting at some residual smarts, instead of projecting mere muscular stolidity.

Though Sorbo seems occasionally flat-footed in the fast and furious (and well-edited) fight scenes, and the script never explains why his shoulder-length hair is always wet, he displays both the awesome, swaggering body and the raw charisma to become a major big-screen success.

His presence, combined with some spiffy special effects (mostly involving Carrere's devilish dual-identity), make "Kull" a sword-and-sorcery extravaganza that is definitely a cut above—if not downright magical.

Also reviewed in:
CHICAGO TRIBUNE, Friday/p. C, John Petrakis
NEW YORK TIMES, 8/29/97, p. C12, Lawrence Van Gelder
VARIETY, 8/25-31/97, p. 73, Leonard Klady

KUNDUN

A Touchstone Pictures release of a Cappa/De Fina production. *Executive Producer:* Laura Fattori. *Producer:* Barbara De Fina. *Director:* Martin Scorsese. *Screenplay:* Melissa Mathison. *Director of Photography:* Roger Deakins. *Editor:* Thelma Schoonmaker. *Music:* Philip Glass. *Music Editor:* Suzana Peric. *Sound:* Clive Winter and (music) Martin Czembor. *Sound Editor:* Philip Stockton. *Casting:* Ellen Lewis. *Production Designer:* Dante Ferretti. *Art Director:* Alan R. Tomkins. *Set Decorator:* Francesca Lo Schiavo. *Costumes:* Dante Ferretti. *Make-up:* Fabrizio Sforza. *Running time:* 128 minutes. *MPAA Rating:* PG-13.

CAST: Tenzin Thuthob Tsarong (Dalai Lama, Adult); Gyurme Tethong (Dalai Lama, Age 12); Tulku Jamyang Kunga Tenzin (Dalai Lama, Age 5); Tenzin Yeshi Paichang (Dalai Lama, Age 2); Tencho Gyalpo (Mother); Tenzin Topjar (Lobsang, 5-10); Tsewang Migyur Khangsar (Father); Tenzin Lodoe (Takster); Tsering Lhamo (Tsering Dolma); Geshi Yeshi Gyatso (Lama of Sera); Lobsang Gyatso (The Messenger); Sonam Phuntsok (Reting Rinpoche); Gyatso Lukhang (Lord Chamberlain); Lobsang Samten (Master of the Kitchen); Tsewang Jigme Tsarong (Taktra Rinpoche); Tenzin Trinley (Ling Rinpoche); Ngawang Dorjee (Kashag/Nobleman #1); Phintso Thonden (Kashag/Nobleman #2); Chewang Tsering Ngokhang (Layman #1); Jamyang Tenzin (Norbu Thundrup); Tashi Dhondup (Lobsang, Adult); Jampa Lungtok (Nechung Oracle); Karma Wangchuck (Deformed Face Bodyguard); Ben Wang (General Chang Chin-Wu); Kim Chan (Second Chinese General); Henry Yuk (General Tan); Ngawang Kaldan (Prime Minister Lobsang Tashi); Jurme Wangda (Prime Minister Lukhangwa); Robert Lin (Chairman Mao); Selden Kunga (Tibetan Doctor); John Wong (Chinese Comrade); Gawa Youngdung (Old Woman); Tenzin Rampa (Tenzin Chonegyl, age 12); Vyas Ananthakrishnan (Indian Soldier).

CHRISTIAN SCIENCE MONITOR, 12/31/97, p. 15, David Sterritt

Other movies had higher budgets or flashier stories, but "Kundun" might be the riskiest and most audacious picture of the past year.

Focusing on a subject steeped in history and religion, filmmaker Martin Scorsese has steered away from Hollywood-type elements that might distract attention from the seriousness of his theme. There are no movie-star faces—most roles are played by Tibetan actors—and the story covers a 22-year span instead of condensing events into an artificially dramatic structure.

Also missing is the psychological emphasis used by most movies to fix attention on the main character's personality. Melissa Mathison's screenplay cares more about sweeping ideas—faith, nonviolence, the intersection of politics and religion—than the personalized drama found in pictures like the recent "Seven Years in Tibet," which explored similar territory in a far more conventional way.

In sum, Scorsese has dared to direct a high-profile art picture that leaves the incendiary images of his "Mean Streets" and "GoodFellas" for a thoughtful look at historical, biographical, even spiritual issues. The result isn't likely to be a high-grade hit in today's star-saturated movie atmosphere. But seen on its own terms, it's an inspiring epic that deserves a wide audience.

The story begins in 1937, when Tibetan monks identify a two-year-old boy as the latest incarnation of the Dalai Lama, the country's spiritual and secular leader.

Noting the irony of his birthplace, near the Chinese border at a time of growing political tension with China, they bring him to Tibet's capital and start the long process of educating him for his future responsibilities. He's an eager pupil, showing keen interest in the modern world outside the boundaries of his highly traditionalized nation.

China invades Tibet in 1950, when the 15-year-old leader considers himself too unseasoned to take charge of an active resistance. In the last scenes he's a young man in his mid-20s, profoundly shaken by China's brutality and faced with awesomely hard decisions. Should he organize a more forceful response to the occupation, compromising his nonviolent principles and risking his life in the process? Or should he flee his country to struggle in exile, preserving his leadership but depriving the people of his comforting presence?

If this riveting material seems less than compelling at times, it's partly because the film's finely detailed authenticity doesn't always support storytelling intimacy. There are also moments when Scorsese appears uncertain how to handle a scene—most of his career has centered on New York, not the Himalayas—and the film's sacred dimension may have intimidated him a bit, as happened in his earlier religious epic, "The Last Temptation of Christ."

This said, "Kundun" is ultimately a stirring tale, filmed by cinematographer Roger Deakins with striking luminosity. Other key contributors are editor Thelma Schoonmaker, one of Scorsese's most gifted collaborators, and Dante Ferretti, who designed the production, shot mainly on Moroccan locations.

Mathison, whose previous screenplays include "E.T. The Extra-Terrestrial" and "The Black Stallion," wrote the movie with assistance from the actual Dalai Lama.

LOS ANGELES TIMES, 12/24/97, Calendar/p. 6, Kenneth Turan

"Kundun" is a stunningly beautiful object offered in tribute to a holy man, a gorgeous film that is nevertheless burdened by the defects of its virtues. Careful and respectful, it is everything a movie about the Dalai Lama should be except dramatically involving.

Directed by Martin Scorsese, this lovely piece of old-fashioned movie-making recounts the story of the early years of the Tibetan religious leader now in exile in India. And, as an end credit relates, it was "produced with the cooperation and contribution of His Holiness the Dalai Lama."

While obviously no one is suggesting that this revered winner of the Nobel Peace Prize has a hidden dark side the film shied away from exploring, "Kundun" has an inherent drawback because it is an authorized biography.

The difficulty is one of tone. Pure goodness is by definition a tricky subject to film, and being reverential and even worshipful toward "his Holiness," as the filmmakers call him, can stand in the way of drama. More than that, if you are already emotionally invested in a story, as screenwriter Melissa Mathison (whose interest in Tibet is long-standing) and director Scorsese are, it can blind you to the fact that the emotions you feel so strongly are not being consistently transmitted on screen.

"Kundun" does have its strong dramatic sections. Both the early parts of the film, starting in 1937, when a monk on a quest recognizes a 2-year-old boy as the reincarnation of the previous Dalai Lama, and the closing sections, when the then-25-year-old spiritual leader finds himself forced to go into exile in India, are involving. But the extensive middle sections would be completely inert if it weren't for the lush and atmospheric way the story is told.

With Dante Ferretti serving as both production and costume designer and shot by expert cinematographer Roger Deakins ("Fargo," "The Secret Garden"), "Kundun" is a visual cornucopia, filled with pristine, spectacular images that encompass scenery (Morocco doubled for Tibet) and costumes as well as breathtaking shots of sand mandalas that were photographed by Phil Marco.

Equally potent in terms of creating an exotic atmosphere tangible enough to touch is the distinctive Philip Glass score, which mixes his usual hypnotic rhythms with sounds that could only come from Tibet.

The strongest section of "Kundun" is the initial one, detailing the real-life fairy tale story of the holy men from far-off Lhasa who stop to rest at an isolated Tibetan farmhouse and discover to their delight that the playful, self-possessed 2year-old who lives there shows unmistakable signs of being the reincarnation of the 13th Dalai Lama, familiarly known as "kundun" (presence).

Scorsese has given several reasons, including an intense interest in the spiritual, for agreeing to direct Mathison's script, but it may not be farfetched to suggest another one. Perhaps he remembered back to the time when he was a small boy in New York's culturally distant Little Italy, a small boy who similarly felt he was destined for great things in the larger world. Whatever the reasons, Scorsese's empathy for the boy Dalai Lama is evident, and these sections have the slow-motion magic only consummate filmmaking provides.

Once the chosen one gets to the Tibetan capital city of Lhasa and the young boy's spiritual education begins, despite the best efforts of screenwriter Mathison ("E.T.," "The Indian in the Cupboard"), "Kundun" slowly loses our interest. Part of the difficulty is that using four actors for the boy's different ages makes it difficult to identify with him. Also, having to depend on inexperienced children with varying commands of English to tell a story of holiness and belief is especially problematical.

Paradoxically, the entrance of a flesh-and-blood enemy, the invading Communist Chinese, an event that should have added much-needed conflict, does not have that effect. Maybe because the evil is so blatant, both "Kundun" and the earlier and sillier "Seven Years in Tibet" have had trouble making Tibet's plight as moving as it ought to be. And "Kundun's" decision to turn Chairman Mao (Robert Lin) into an oddly fey and borderline campy maximum leader does not help the situation.

Still, "Kundun's" depiction of the Dalai Lama's final journey out of Tibet, complete with apocalyptic visions of disaster, turns out to be serious and moving. But, ironically for a film that helped poison Hollywood's relationship with China, "Kundun" will have its greatest impact not on newcomers to Tibet's tragedy but on those who are already true believers.

NEW STATESMAN, 4/3/98, p. 64, Jonathan Freedland

We're used to Scorsese heroes pacing up and down, feverishly scratching their cheeks and asking, "Are you talking to me?" or, more menacingly, "D'you think I'm funny? Funny how?" before plugging 70 rounds of lead into the unlucky bum who got in their way. So it's a bit of a shock to find Martin Scorsese choosing as his latest protagonist a pacifist do-nothing like the Dalai Lama. Not much of a role for De Niro or Pesci there.

More shocking still that Disney should fund a film about a Tibetan leader whose trademark philosophy is stillness and contemplation. One can imagine the boardroom discussion. "Where are the merchandising opportunities? What kid's gonna buy a toy based on the Dalai Lama? What are we gonna call it: Inaction Man?" A Buddhist movie sounds unlikely to the point of oxymoron, like a Trappist talk show.

And Scorsese does not make life any easier for himself. *Kundun* is not a Tibetan *Cry Freedom*, a thrills-and-spills, tears-and-cheers biopic of one brave man's struggle against evil oppression. Instead the film works hard to match form and content. Since the Dalai Lama acts rarely and speaks seldom—and only then in short, calm sentences—so the film, too, never raises its voice. The pace is meditative, the focus on detail. Scorsese told the *Guardian* that his film is "anti-drama, where the drama is dealing in the spiritual level. It permeates everything—the teacup, the cleaning of the teacup is what its about."

He's not kidding. *Kundun* lingers for non-Hollywood aeons on miniature actions: the cleaning of a wooden bowl, the preparation of a ritual. When characters speak in English, it comes as a jolt: you were expecting subtitles. It looks like a foreign film.

This can induce frustration in the non-cineaste moviegoer. As the threat to tiny Tibet looms from China, the *Mean Streets* or *GoodFellas* fan is waiting for the hero to get angry, slam his fist on the table and summon his advisers for a council of war. We want to see him vow to take no more punches and to exact his revenge. That's what we're used to.

But *Kundun* like the Dalai Lama, will not give us our fix of violence or retribution. The Buddhist chieftain remains impassive, even as he hears word of the latest violation of Tibetan rights by the tyrants in Beijing. Somehow the audience finds itself identifying with the sequence of middle-aged aides to the boy prince, who constantly enter the royal chamber to announce new dangers and to demand a decision, only to be met with expressions of patience and inner faith. *Do* something, we cry from the stalls.

Yet slowly you see the strength in apparent weakness and the drama in "anti-drama". For when these placid waters ripple even slightly, it sounds like a crash of mighty waves. With so little conventional action, the smallest gesture suddenly exerts an enormous impact. A Chinese general dares pour tea for himself in the presence of the Dalai Lama: a mark of disrespect as ruthless as a mafioso beating, and just as painful to watch.

When the Tibetan leader attends a summit with Chairman Mao, offering his hand to the man who has ordered the slaughter of his people, our own flesh crawls at the prospect. Robert Lin's portrayal of—and remarkable resemblance to—Mao is one of *Kundun*'s several gems (along with the performances of the two- and five-year-old Tibetan boys who play the young Dalai Lama). After an apparently courteous meeting, Mao leans over and whispers in the Lama's ear: "Your people are poisoned and inferior." That single line is as lethal as any expletive-packed fusillade from De Niro.

It's tempting to see some parallel between Scorsese and his subject—in *Kundun*, as in *The Age of Innocence,* the director signals that he, too, now believes in the power of restraint. There is one golden opportunity for a shoot-'em-up, but Scorsese admirably refuses to indulge himself. As the Chinese start to massacre Tibetan villagers, reports reach the Dalai Lama of grotesque atrocities. All we see, however, is the briefest flash of a young child forced to aim a pistol at his parents. Again, that fleeting image is more harrowing than any of the lingering gunfights favoured by Hollywood present or Scorsese past.

Visually the film is a treat. The heat and sweat of the ritual which transforms an entranced elder into an oracle, the lavish costumes, the spectacular simulation of the Himalayan landscape (filmed in Morocco); it all makes magnificent cinema. Powerful, too, is the recurring motif of the Buddhist sand painting, a wide and intricately laid mosaic of coloured grains which might take days to produce, only to be blown away in a second. Life may hang by a thread, but even a grain of sand should be handled with reverence.

That's not a common message from Hollywood, and Scorsese is to be congratulated for getting it through. He's proved that not every movie out of LA has to be titanic.

NEW YORK, 1/5/98, p. 51, David Denby

Martin Scorsese sets a mood of innocence and calm right at the beginning of *Kundun.*

In Tibet, in 1937, after the thirteenth Dalai Lama has died, a holy man is looking for a little boy who will grow into the next living spirit of Buddha. He finds such a boy in a small mountain village; the child's parents think their 2½-year-old son is special—his birth was attended by mysterious happenings, and he definitely has a way about him, both self-possessed and gentle. The mood is rapt, tranquil; Scorsese conveys the charm of intelligent people who live by a sense of wonder. As the holy man poses a series of questions, there's a suggestion that the child may be faking—that the eager monk has planted the idea of specialness in the boy's head, and that he's living up to the role. But it's just a suggestion, quickly dispelled, and it becomes clear before long that this boy, as he grows into a teenager, has a spiritual calling. Kundun, the monks call him—he is Tenzin Gyatso (Tenzin Thuthob Tsarong), the fourteenth Dalai Lama, the leader of the Tibetan people. The movie was shot in Morocco and cast with Tibetans living in exile—not trained actors but people apparently so disciplined that they can express what they are feeling through the simplest and most modest of means.

Unlike the fatuous, conventional *Seven Years in Tibet,* this movie has been made with love. It has an assured beauty and an exquisite formality that honor the subject. Roger Deakins's camera moves easily across the mountains and through the sets designed to reproduce a famous temple in Lhasa. And yet, lovely as it is, *Kundun* is of very little dramatic interest—it's an extremely beautiful, boring movie. The boy grows into a gracious and modest young man, a man not always sure that he's up to the role of leader; but still, he has no great spiritual crisis, no awful time of testing, and everyone in Lhasa gathers around and tutors and protects him. It may seem odd to Westerners that Tibetans recognize this teenager as Buddha's representative and, at the same time, instruct and correct him as if he were an ordinary young man, but it's part of the meaning of the film. Spiritual grace is something given, something inherent; the boy matures into the near-divinity that was there inside him from the beginning. The raw edges and tumult of Scorsese's *Last Temptation of Christ*—the striving and torment of a Jesus who was always in doubt—are nowhere in sight. Approaching an alien tradition, Scorsese is entirely respectful, and the respectfulness dulls out the movie.

There are recurring images of great contemplative beauty—the mountain peaks, the sand sculpture with colored grains being dropped to form a picture. Philip Glass's music, with its repeated, chantlike figures, complements the stunning but placid images. But what, I wonder, can any director do with the subject of Buddhism and the Chinese invasion of Tibet? This nonviolent, religious country gets assaulted by a totalitarian dictatorship eager to extirpate religion. A slimy, patronizing Chairman Mao tells the Dalai Lama that "religion is poison" and proceeds to destroy a good part of Tibet's heritage and culture. Except in a few of the Dalai Lama's dreams, Scorsese won't show the torment and death brought on by the Chinese. "They have taken away our silence," one of the monks observes, in reproof of the insistent Communist people's-chorus music suddenly blaring everywhere in Tibet. It is the most aggressive remark made by any of the Tibetans.

Not many of us are likely to respond the way we are clearly meant to respond—with deep satisfaction that the Tibetans maintained their dignity and emerged as the spiritual victors in their struggle with the Chinese. The elements of hope in this movie look rather wistful, even wan. As Orwell said, nonviolence worked for Gandhi because the British had a conscience to appeal to; it wouldn't have worked against the Nazis or the Japanese in World War II—and it didn't work against the Chinese Communists in Tibet. I can't escape the feeling that Buddhism is an impossible subject for the movies. After all, great movie characters are men of overbearing will—Charles Foster Kane, or Vito and Michael Corleone, or Scorsese's Jake La Motta—not characters who *renounce* will.

NEW YORK POST, 12/24/97, p. 35, Michael Medved

In "Kundun," minimalist music appropriately accompanies a minimalist movie; just as renowned composer Philip Glass stresses mood over melody, director Martin Scorsese here emphasizes hypnotic atmosphere, otherwordly images and hazy spirituality over conventional notions of plot or character.

The film begins in 1937 with recognition of a 2-year-old Tibetan farm boy as the reincarnation of the recently deceased 13th Dalai Lama and the new leader of his nation.

Transported to the capital by monastic authorities, the child receives intensive spiritual education as the film struggles gamely (but vainly) to summarize some 1,200 years of Tibetan wisdom in about an hour of screen time.

We already know that this kid's supposed to be an old soul, selected for an extraordinary destiny, so there's little suspense in these long scenes of the boy-Lama growing up.

After the Chinese invasion of 1950, the story threatens to take a more dramatic turn, but Scorsese never manages to make political crosscurrents comprehensible.

The young Dalai Lama meets with Mao (played by Robert Lin in a lifeless, waxworks impersonation) and despite his determination to remain with his people, he eventually heads for exile in India in 1959 (with the film seriously downplaying the full-scale revolt that wracked his country at the time).

Though the movie boasts of recounting "the true story of one of our era's most compelling and inspiring figures," it concludes before its holy hero even begins his real life's work: rallying international support for Tibetan culture and independence.

The cast, comprised entirely of exiled Tibetans with no acting experience, performs splendidly under Scorsese's guidance; the four young people (the oldest is 18) who play the hero at different stages of his development uncannily succeed in combining humanity and divinity in their composite portrayal.

Scorsese also benefits from extraordinarily detailed and loving re-creations of Tibetan monasteries and palaces (filmed in Morocco, of all places!), rich in exotic color and authentic flavor.

Developed over seven years as an act of devotion by writer and co-producer Melissa Mathison, this earnest effort to portray the "reincarnate Buddha of Compassion" can hardly be judged by the standards of ordinary entertainment, but on its own terms it works as a subtly cinematic meditation.

NEWSDAY, 12/24/97, Part II/p. B6, John Anderson

Martin Scorsese's Dalai Lama is "a modern man ... just like he was the last time." Predictably, there's a lot of urgent modernism swirling about him. Will Tibetans ever break their Chinese yoke? Will Michael Eisner get his Sino-Disney theme park? Where's Brad Pitt in all this?

By the end of "Kundun," a spectacularly beautiful biography that is less about story than it is about conscience and belief, none of the more temporal issues really seem to matter. At the same time, permanence, too, has been swept away. Like the mandala, or Buddhist sand painting, that recurs throughout "Kundun," the film itself attempts to become a picture of a spirit, tries to capture the architecture of religious aspiration. Like the mandala, which is often destroyed as soon as it's made, Scorsese's movie strives to be like a prayer at the same time it bows to the fleeting existence of the filmic image.

Whether he was making a film about Jesus or Jake LaMotta, Scorsese has always been a filmmaker inspired or stricken by his own sprituality. But "Kundun" is something else, an attempt not to get a person into a film but to emulate the virtues and vision of its subject. From the time Tenzin Gyatso (the Dalai Lama's real name) is a self-assertive 2-year-old—pushing his father out of his chair at the dinner table, for instance—until he has reluctantly fled his homeland in an attempt to keep body and soul together, Scorsese is mirroring the man's experience as well as his story. The camera technique, the symbolism, the pacing, the breadth of vision all seem to develop along with its subject's. And as trite as this may sound, it combines for a work of singular emotion and humanity.

One can seldom escape the sense of impending doom posed by Mao Zhedong, who enters Tibet in 1950 claiming it is part of China. Dramatically speaking the late dictator is the motor of the movie. As played by Robert Lin, Mao is an unctuous, almost effete dictator whose contempt for religion looks ridiculous in light of the Dalai Lama's, or Kundun's, quiet wisdom—convincingly conveyed by Tenzin Thuthob Tsarong, one of four Tibetan actors who play Kundun at various ages.

There are moments in "Kundun"—filmed in Morocco, from a script by Melissa Mathison ("E.T.")—that are ripe with quiet wonder, or great power. When his father (Tsewang Migyur Khangsar) dies and is given a traditional funeral, his body is hacked to pieces and fed to the vultures; simultaneously, a letter from Mao is heard in voiceover. While the combination may sound heavy-handed it works like few scenes in few movies.

There will be those who say not enough can happen in a story that is basically about spirituality to keep our interest, but Scorsese defies such expectations, both through extraordinary filmmaking and personal investment. You watch the child (Tenzin Yeshi Paichang), who has been picked after years of searching by a team of monks as the reincarnated Dalai Lama, selecting from a group of objects the ones that belonged to his former self, and you imagine a young Scorsese picking out Ford, Hawks and Hitchcock, asserting his own destiny through choice as well as birthright. Not that the director would be so proud as to think this himself, but we can all find a bit of ourselves in "Kundun," and something to embrace.

NEWSWEEK, 12/22/97, p. 84, David Ansen

[*Kundun* was reviewed jointly with *Wag the Dog*; see Ansen's review of that film.]

SIGHT AND SOUND, 4/98, p. 41, Andrew O'Hehir

Tibet, 1937. A roaming monk assigned to find the successor of the thirteenth Dalai Lama happens upon a rural family living near the Chinese border. He becomes convinced that the family's two-year-old boy is 'Kundun', the human reincarnation of the Buddha of Compassion, and thus the next Dalai Lama. He is moved to Lhasa, the capital, to be instructed in the rituals and responsibilities of his future role as religious and secular leader of the Tibetan nation. As he grows and awaits his full investiture on his eighteenth birthday, he becomes increasingly concerned about Tibet's tenuous political situation. After Mao Zedong's Communists take power in Beijing, China's long-standing claim to sovereignty over Tibet is revived, only to be rejected by the Dalai Lama and his ministers. Ultimately, the Chinese army invades Tibet. Now invested, the Dalai Lama travels to a remote monastery for his own protection.

Once the Chinese take control of Tibet, Communist leaders seek the Dalai Lama's cooperation in 'liberating' and modernising the country. He decides to return to his Lhasa palace and use his influence to build a constructive relationship between Buddhism and socialism. When he meets Chairman Mao in Beijing, the Chinese leader is respectful but makes ominous pronouncements on Tibet's future. When the Dalai Lama returns home, he sees the situation rapidly deteriorate: many Tibetans rebel against the occupation, and the Chinese respond with brutal repression. In a series of visions, the Dalai Lama foresees the pillage of his country and the massacre of many monks. Faced with evidence that the Chinese plan to bomb Lhasa and imprison or kill him, he escapes from the palace in disguise and travels over the mountains into exile in India.

From its very conception, *Kundun* had the potential to be a vainglorious disaster, or at least a dull exercise in liberal-chic. The consummate American film director of our era, Martin Scorsese's natural habitat is the tawdry dreams of hustlers, but here he is making a biographical epic about the Dalai Lama, the very embodiment of eastern serenity. Lacking a recognisable star and unloved by its corporate parent Disney—but filmed on four continents at tremendous expense—it's a movie that only someone of Scorsese's stature and ambition could have made. Perhaps Scorsese should face impossible odds and boardroom opposition more often, since the product of his perseverance is nothing short of astonishing. *Kundun* is more than a grand spectacle full of breathtakingly beautiful images (magnificent, but expected). It's a movie that uses its visual and aural palette to build something almost indescribable, revelatory and profoundly moving.

Kundun stems from a deeper and more personal source than a didactic urge to educate Westerners about the tragedy of Tibet. This is a difficult film to categorise, and superficially seems completely at odds with Scorsese's body of work, even *The Last Temptation of Christ*. But the director has made sporadic attempts over the last decade to escape from the wise guys. (He may not have been completely at ease with *The Age of Innocence*, for example, but it's a much better and sexier movie than is generally recognised.) Scorsese's most memorable work—often scenes or sequences rather than whole movies—has always had a symphonic, collaborative aspect, transcending conventional notions of plot and character to create kinetic narrative from the onrushing flow of cinematography, production design and music. (He would have made great silent films—or for that matter great music videos.)

With the stark, improbable beauty of its setting, its marvellously haunting score by Philip Glass and Roger Deakins' remarkable photography, *Kundun* is the apotheosis of this tendency. In it, Scorsese has gathered up everything he has learned about movies and pushed forward into a more mature and subtler kind of film-making than he has ever tried before. There's little point in arguing about whether *Kundun* is his 'best' movie, but for my money it comes dazzlingly close to the mysterious synthesis of landscape, ritual and spirituality that film can only approach once in a great while—in the best work, say, of Dovzhenko, Tarkovsky or Kurosawa.

Despite its storybook beauty and almost mythic grandeur, *Kundun* is certainly not destined to be Scorsese's most popular work. It begins slowly in the peasant household of the Dalai Lama-to-be before abruptly shifting focus to the often baffling pomp and pageantry of the monastic palace in Lhasa, and offers us no pop-psychological insight into its central character. While there was no realistic alternative to having the cast of Tibetan non-actors (headed by the composed performance of Tenzin Thuthob Tsarong as the adult Dalai Lama) speaking in variously accented grades of English, it's not a completely comfortable solution. But whether you like it or not, this film's uncompromising nature is one index of its unique achievement.

To their everlasting credit, Scorsese and screenwriter Melissa Mathison resist preachy explication of Buddhist theology or Tibetan politics. Instead, they use the childish curiosity of the Dalai Lama as the audience's point of access to his miraculously transformed world. After the boy is discovered and moves to Lhasa, the film explodes into a panoply of bright colours and mysterious darknesses. The child Dalai Lama doesn't comprehend the ancient complex of rituals that surrounds him—he explores the palace with all the inquisitive wonder of a plucky children's-book hero, unable to sit still for meditation, fascinated by the rats who clamber on the altar (the Buddha of Compassion, whose mandate is 'to love all living things', can make no exceptions for vermin), examining the portraits of his legendary forebears.

Although we hear fragments of Buddhist catechism and tenuous reports of the mounting Chinese threat, *Kundun* advances its ideas through its many unforgettable images: the Dalai Lama among the teeming wildlife on his summer palace's grounds; the movies, newsreels and maps that introduce him to the world outside Tibet (also archly suggesting the importance the western media would ultimately play in his life); the faceless legions of the People's Liberation Army who appear in a scene that suggests both Fritz Lang and Chen Kaige. We probably learn more about Tibetan Buddhism through a wrenching scene in which monks matter-of-factly tear apart the body of the Dalai Lama's father and feed it to vultures than we would from dozens of earnest disquisitions.

Indeed, the primary representatives of the Word in *Kundun* are the Chinese Communists, who plaster the Dalai Lama's childhood home with propaganda slogans and shatter the calm of Lhasa with loudspeakers. When the Dalai Lama meets Mao in Beijing (on an amazing mid-period Commie-chic set), the author of *The Little Red Book,* in Robert Lin's portrayal, is a menacing, mercurial intellectual, one day explaining that his mother was a Buddhist and the next telling his visitor, "Your people are poisoned and inferior." While some leftward critics have complained that *Kundun* stacks the deck unfairly in its confrontation between Communist materialism and Buddhist spirituality, in fact Mathison's script takes pains to humanise its Chinese characters, and makes it clear that the Dalai Lama had hoped to reform the more autocratic elements of Tibetan tradition.

Kundun does indeed take place entirely within the Tibetan belief system; the legitimacy of the Dalai Lama's reincarnation is treated as a matter of course. But the movie's real concerns—as is usual with Scorsese seem to be the nature and meaning of artistic experience, not religion or politics. *Kundun*'s central visual and conceptual metaphor is the Buddhist sand painting, a colourful and elaborate mandala that monks labour over for hours or days before sweeping it away in an instant. When we first see one being made, the operative symbolism seems trite and obvious: art, like life, is ephemeral, and we vain humans must learn humility. But when we finally see the painting swept away, during the masterful and heartbreaking extended montage that concludes the film after the escaping Dalai Lama has witnessed the imminent destruction of his nation in a series of visions, the metaphor has become ironically and tragically inverted. It is the artifice, in fact, that endures; the movie we are watching will preserve for posterity both an artwork that has been destroyed and an ancient society that has largely been obliterated.

TIME, 12/22/97, p. 81, Richard Corliss

The Bible plays like wild melodrama: a father commanded to sacrifice his child, an ark in a deluge, God's son betrayed and murdered and reborn. Ideal material for Martin Scorsese, as he proved in *The Last Temptation of Christ*, his mean-streets-of-Jerusalem story of a tormented Jesus. By contrast, Buddhist texts are static and serene, antidramatic. And the 14th Dalai Lama of Tibet is the ultimate good fellow, not a goodfella. So what can Scorsese find to make his own in *Kundun*? That turns out to be the wrong question. The director has come to this biography of "the Buddha of compassion, the wish-fulfilling jewel" as a pilgrim. He is in Tibet (actually Morocco) to explore, bend, learn, find new ways of seeing and showing the light. That makes *Kundun* his simplest and most experimental film.

Melissa Mathison's script dares to tell an Asian tale with no Westerners, not even Brad Pitt. At two, Tenzin Gyatso is found in a remote village and proclaimed Buddha's incarnation. Schooled and coddled, he grows to manhood. He confronts Mao and his acquisitive legates, and he finally flees to India.

So far, so sonorous—perhaps soporific. But aided by Roger Deakins' pristine camera work and the euphoric drone of Philip Glass's score, Scorsese devises a poem of textures and silences. Visions, nightmares and history blend in a tapestry as subtle as the Tibetans' gorgeous mandalas of sand. For some, *Kundun* will be a slog. For the open mind and eye, though, this is rapture in pictures.

VILLAGE VOICE, 12/30/97, p. 61, J. Hoberman

More a costume curiosity but less than an exotic masterpiece, Martin Scorsese's *Kundun* is an ahistorical historical epic, an action movie about nonaction. It has intimations of eternity, but it vibrates in place.

Henry Kissinger, the moral philosopher hired by Disney, Scorsese's studio, to explain this celebration of Buddhist Tibet and the Dalai Lama to the Chinese (who occupied Tibet in 1911 and annexed it in 1950), might dismiss *Kundun* as a bit of colorful anticommunist propaganda. The director, however, has dedicated it to his late mother, and *Kundun*, which takes its title from the Dalai Lama's honorific, begs for autobiographical reading. The Dalai Lama's childhood might easily be transposed from backwater Tibet to cold-water Elizabeth Street—the willfull toddler, sickly yet divinely inspired, tyrannizing his humble household or experiencing the revelation of his first motion picture. When civil war breaks out, the slightly older Kundun's surprised exclamation seems pure Scorsese: "The monks have guns?!"

Not for nothing does *Kundun* open on Christmas Day. Filled with inexplicable rituals, often shot from a child's point of view, this is the pageant of an alternative theology, as splendid as a midnight mass and strange as the Hebrew desert religion Scorsese presented in *The Last Temptation of Christ*. Among other things, this is also one of the most beautifully crafted movies in recent memory. The seamless integration of the disparate locations (Morocco, Idaho, British Columbia), the candlelit scenes, and impeccable matte work suggest an imaginary *National Geographic* report on the land of *Lost Horizon*. The red and gold color schemes have the quality of an illuminated manuscript. One long shot—in which Kundun and his monks are spotted in halolike hats—suggests a quattrocento image of a Jesus and his disciples by the Dead Sea.

Cast almost entirely with exiled Tibetan nonactors, *Kundun* is a kind of passion play, albeit not exactly a neorealist one. (In a sense, it's another one of Scorsese's Rossellini-Minnelli syntheses.) The movie may be low-key but—characterized by the nervous virtuosity of dramatic mega-close-ups, abrupt dollies, unexpected overhead angles, and interpolated slow motion—it's hardly austere. Scorsese cuts from foggy mountain crags to the infinitesimal details of a sand mandala; although the persistent, if relatively understated, Philip Glass score promotes a certain detachment, *Kundun* seems at once overwrought and underwritten. The cosmic drama is too often telegraphed as cosmic.

Kundun is a lot less goofy than *Little Buddha,* a million times more nuanced than *Seven Years in Tibet,* and most compelling when Scorsese directs against the grain. The Chinese invasion is given an ethereal quality, as though a host of fallen angels had descended upon Shangri-la. Kundun's trip to Beijing is a small masterpiece of disorientation—rows of children singing socialist realist anthems, Mao addressing a crowd before his own giant image, the flashbulbs of modern demonism everywhere.

Incongruously dressed in ornate hippie embroidery, Kundun briefly imagines there might be a Buddhist socialism. He might as well be talking to Michael Eisner. Treating the Lama like a child, the epicenely condescending Mao (performance artist Robert Lin) tells him that "religion is poison" Typically, the camera is fascinated by the Communist leaders shiny black shoes.

Kundun is sometimes spectacular and somewhat hypnotic—if not perhaps in the way intended. Emotionally, the movie only kicks in during its final half hour with the drama of Kundun's loss. Just as you imagine a universe shatter, the cannonball crashes through the monastery wall. It's a shock and it's real.

Also reviewed in:
CHICAGO TRIBUNE, 1/16/98, Friday/p. A, Michael Wilmington
NEW YORK TIMES, 12/24/97, p. E1, Stephen Holden
VARIETY, 12/15-21/97, p. 57, Emanuel Levy
WASHINGTON POST, 1/16/98, Weekend/p. 32, Desson Howe

L. A. CONFIDENTIAL

A Warner Bros. release of a Regency Enterprises presentation of an Arnon Milchan/David L. Wolper production. *Executive Producer:* Dan Kolsrud and David L. Wolper. *Producer:* Arnon Milchan, Curtis Hanson, and Michael Nathanson. *Director:* Curtis Hanson. *Screenplay:* Brian Helgeland and Curtis Hanson. *Based on the novel by:* James Ellroy. *Director of Photography:* Dante Spinotti. *Editor:* Peter Honess. *Music:* Jerry Goldsmith. *Music Editor:* Kenneth Hall and Paul Rabjohns. *Sound:* Kirk Francis and (music) Bruce Botnick. *Sound Editor:* John Leveque. *Casting:* Mali Finn. *Production Designer:* Jeannine Oppewall. *Art Director:* Bill Arnold. *Set Designer:* Louisa Bonnie, Julia Levine, and Mark Poll. *Set Decorator:* Jay R. Hart. *Set Dresser:* Troy Alan Peters. *Special Effects:* Eric Rylander and Richard Stutsman. *Costumes:* Ruth Myers. *Make-up:* John M. Elliott, Jr. *Make-up (Kim Basinger):* Francesca Tolot. *Stunt Coordinator:* Jeff Imada. *Running time:* 136 minutes. *MPAA Rating:* R.

CAST: Kevin Spacey (Jack Vincennes); Russell Crowe (Bud White); Guy Pearce (Ed Exley); James Cromwell (Dudley Smith); Kim Basinger (Lynn Bracken); Danny DeVito (Sid Hudgens); David Strathairn (Pierce Patchett); Ron Rifkin (D.A. Ellis Loew); Matt McCoy ("Badge of Honor" Star Brett Chase); Paul Guilfoyle (Mickey Cohen); Paolo Seganti (Johnny Stompanato); Elisabeth Granli and Sandra Taylor (Mickey Cohen's Mambo Partners); Steve Rankin (Officer Arresting Mickey Cohen); Graham Beckel (Dick Stensland); Allan Graf (Wife Beater); Precious Chong (Wife); Symba Smith (Jack's Dancing Partner); Bob Clendenin (Reporter at Hollywood Station); Lennie Loftin (Photographer at Hollywood Station); Will Zahrn (Liquor Store Owner); Amber Smith (Susan Lefferts); Darrell Sandeen (Buzz Meeks); Michael Warwick (Sid's Assistant); Simon Baker Denny (Matt Reynolds); Shawnee Free Jones (Tammy Jordan); Matthew Allen Bretz (Officer Escorting Mexicans); Thomas Rosales, Jr. (First Mexican); John Mahon (Police Chief); Tomas Arana (Breuning); Michael McCleery (Carlisle); George Yager (Gangster at Victory Motel); Jack Conley (Vice Captain); Ginger Slaughter (Secretary in Vice); Jack Knight (Detective at Detective Bureau); John H. Evans (Patrolman at Nite Owl Cafe); Gene Wolande (Forensic Chief); Brian Bossetta (Forensic Officer); Michael Chieffo (Coroner); Gwenda Deacon (Mrs. Lefferts); Mike Kennedy (Bud's Rejected Partner); Ingo Neuhaus (Jack's Rejected Partner); Robert Harrison (Pierce Patchett's Bodyguard); Jim Metzler (City Councilman); Robert Barry Fleming (Boxer); Jeremiah Birkett (Ray Collins); Salim Grant (Louis Fontaine); Karreem Washington (Ty Jones); Noel Evangelisti (Stenographer); Marisol

Padilla Sanchez (Inez Soto, Rape Victim); Jeff Sanders (Sylvester Fitch); Steve Lambert (Roland Navarette); Jordan Marder (Officer at Detective Bureau); Gregory White (Mayor); April Breneman and Lisa Worthy (Look-Alike Dancers); Beverly Sharpe (Witness on "Badge of Honor"); Colin Mitchell (Reporter at Hospital); John Slade (Photographer at Hospital); Brenda Bakke (Lana Turner); Kevin Maloney (Frolic Room Bartender); Patrice Walters and Rebecca Jane Klinger (Police File Clerks); Irene Roseen (D.A. Ellis Loew's Secretary); Scott Eberlein (West Hollywood Sheriff's Deputy); David St. James (Detective at Hush-Hush Office); Bodie Newcomb (Officer at Hush-Hush Office).

CINEASTE, Vol. XXIII, No. 3, 1998, p. 41, Paul Arthur

Given our current movie culture, it is easy to forget that *'film noir'* used to mean something more than a vaguely malevolent atmosphere, a criminal misadventure, and a lethal woman. Today even one of those elements is enough to summon the epithet *'noir.'* The term has become a crutch, a cheat, an unearned password to a territory at once broader and more complex than any formulaic rehash of sexual duplicity. Fortunately, Curtis Hanson's *L.A. Confidential,* adapted from James Ellroy's massive *policier,* is dead serious about its historical backdrop, its relation to the generic lineage of *noir* storytelling but also to the social-political climate in which the series flourished and expired. Instead of feeding off the usual suspects, *L.A. Confidential* circles back to the early Fifties to revisit two intertwined but often overlooked branches of the *noir* family tree: the rogue cop saga and the exposé of municipal corruption. Although it engages in the requisite glut of senseless mayhem, there is for a change an insistence on self-recognition, on the grim reciprocity between personal and institutional practices of violence. Equally important, and in keeping with the most accomplished neo-noirs—*Chinatown* (1974), *True Confessions* (1981), and *The Two Jakes* (1992)—Los Angeles is presented as not just a setting but a state of mind, an urban mythology stamped with the false promise of endless opportunity and filtered by the projections of Hollywood's dream factory.

The year is 1953 and the rhythms of postwar prosperity are mingled with a backbeat of organized crime and racial injustice, to say nothing of Cold War anxieties. The recent Kefauver congressional hearings have made a national fetish out of crooked cops and their ties to urban hoodlums. The Supreme Court decision on school desegregation, along with the first glimmers of the civil-rights struggle, are just around the corner. If the city shown in *L.A. Confidential* is a combat zone, these festering social issues form the boundaries within which the personal dramas and practical alliances among a group of detectives are played out. The central characters are introduced in separate sequences offering three alternative versions of how cops make their way through a morass of graft, department infighting, occupational sadism, and media scrutiny. Bud White (Russell Crowe) relies on muscle and a vigilante's code of retaliation, especially against wife-beaters. Ed Exley (Guy Pearce) is a righteous but ambitious straight arrow, refusing petty kickbacks but willing to seize an angle, including informing on his buddies, if it offers advancement within the system. "Celebrity crime-stopper" Jack Vincennes (Kevin Spacey), who says he has forgotten why he became a cop, boasts the sweetest deal: "technical advisor" on a *Drag*net-like TV show; and paid tipster and partner in mischief to the editor of a sleazy gossip rag. It is this consummate insider, Sid Hudgens (Danny DeVito), his fingers knuckle deep in every organ of power, who delivers the film's opening benediction. "You'd think that the place was the Garden of Eden," he tells us, but "They're just selling an image," a scam fabricated for suckers. Thus the trope of illusion/reality, planted at the beginning like a cynical piece of evidence, hangs over much of the following action.

Wedding generic obligation with marketing necessity, there is a mistress of illusion, high-priced hooker Lynn Bracken (Kim Basinger), who has been dolled up to resemble actress Veronica Lake (in his 1967 memoir, *Hollywood,* Garson Kanin reports that there was indeed a local brothel where whores imitated movie stars). She turns out to be the good-bad girl of White's dreams. Although her role in the investigation story is marginal, she is deployed as a nearly transparent conduit for the love-hate bond between White and Exley. Vincennes is given no heterosexual object of desire. Even worse, he manifests a questionable sympathy for a would-be actor *qua* male prostitute for which he is, in essence, condemned to death at the hands of the film's master conspirator, police captain Dudley Smith (masterfully played by James Cromwell).

This crew is ballasted by a host of colorful minor figures and ensconced in an intricately digressive case of mass murder whose resolution is filled with hairpin turns, excruciating betrayals, and an impressive body count. Suffice it to say that the path to justice is, among other more familiar markers of criminal activity, littered with the brutalization—and off-handed killing—of black suspects, the rescue of a Chicana rape victim, and other 'provocative' episodes which could have been cribbed from the audiotapes of another moonlighting technical advisor, Detective Mark Fuhrman. To be sure, although the source novel was written pre-Rodney King and O.J., L.A. Confidential gets plenty of sneaky mileage out of the LAPD's recent notorious public image.

Where Ellroy decorates his numerous paranoid subplots and flashbacks with numbing processual detail—sort of like Thomas Pynchon writ small, or vulgar—screenwriters Hanson and Brian Helgeland more or less cut to the chase, the grudging coalition of three differently-flawed but ultimately noble warriors in a search for Truth and, not incidentally, personal redemption. That the summary effect of this often predigested business works as well as it does is largely attributable to two features: a surfeit of smartly sensual visual style (principally, Dante Spinotti's cinematography, Jeannine Oppewall's production design, and Ruth Myer's costumes) and a tripartite division of character—not Good, Bad, and Ugly (although one feels a touch of Leone's male triangles) but Brains, Brawn, and Cool—that manages to generate subtle shifts, fusions, and a gradual deepening of psychological traits. White and Exley are linked by similarly traumatic past events, the unpunished murders of parents; the slightly older Vincennes has his own psychosexual secrets. Thus, even without the intervention of explanatory flashbacks, these cops are clearly involved in the expiation of longstanding feelings of guilt and inadequacy.

There is, however, a hitch. Unlike more authentically noir characters such as Jake Gittes, their befuddlement is only circumstantial and they are never fully immersed in a recurring cycle of death or abnegation. Their identities undergo substantial change but are not stripped bare; they never face the existential crisis of, say, Double Indemnity's Walter Neff, who declares, "I couldn't hear my own footsteps. It was the walk of a dead man." The physical and mental resources of these cops are not utterly depleted or hopeless in the throes of criminal conspiracy, nor are they completely ostracized from the social regime they are sworn to protect and defend." They are powerful, engaging characters but their police file reads noir-lite, not D.O.A.

Although the comparison may be unfair, the transformation of the rogue detective in The Big Heat (based on a best-selling urban exposé and released in 1953) displaces a comfortably bourgeois optimism with a robotic ruthlessness, the mask worn by many noir characters as they sound the depths of a self-induced liminal underworld. No one in L.A. Confidential quite makes this risky, usually irreversible, journey. White, Exley, and Vincennes may commit stupid or reprehensible acts, yet they maintain a decisive separation from the ultimate Evil, which is violence at the service of venality and the exercise of power for its own sake. In this regard, since they are never alone or lacking a sense of higher purpose, their deadly ordeal resembles the plight of Hawksian professionalism more than it does noir's psychosocial devastation—one reason why Hawks, almost alone among notable postwar action directors, never made a convincing film noir (yes, that includes The Big Sleep).

L.A. Confidential's most satisfying conjuncture with the postwar crime cycle is its canny, and significantly un-nostalgic, evocation of place and decor. Vernacular settings such as a liquor store or the empty interior of the Nite Owl cafe, site of the mass murder, provide a wealth of clues to the fabric of daily routine, not just for cops and robbers but for a wider swath of Fifties' urban dwellers. During Exley's entrance into the crime scene, grimy objects and architectural details scanned by the camera—order pad, sizzling grill, ashtrays—register as pieces of a lived-in world rather than, as is too often the case, collectible trinkets straight from the studio antique shop. The same is true for the blunt outlines of men's suits and the unenviable cuts of their hair; Russell Crowe, in particular, is a study in Nixonian awkwardness of face, clothing, and gesture. According to interviews with the director and cinematographer, visual touchstones for the production included the Fifties' directorial styles of Minnelli, Aldrich, and Kubrick, the iconic attitudes of Sterling Hayden, Dean Martin, and Chet Baker.

In terms of noir esthetics, 1953 is not 1945 or even 1948: the figure of the femme fatale has all but vanished; first-person narration has faded into memory— the private eye is dormant, awaiting its last [sic] hurrah in Kiss Me Deadly; in fact, the bulk of noir investigators are no longer private citizens but public employees, namely local or federal law enforcement officers. In general, protagonists are worrying less about displaced oedipal attachments and more about stolen government microfilm. It is the era of 'public' *film noir*, a period often ignored in the critical literature and rarely invoked in the current onslaught of *noir* subjects. The previous year saw the release of Phil Karlson's *Kansas City Confidential*, the first in a series of B-productions with the names of cities and the word "Confidential" (or "Story") in their titles, whose plots center on the exposure of corrupt agencies of government and law. Working hand-in-glove with popular journalism rather than hard-boiled fiction, films such as Karlson's *The Phoenix City Story* (1955) map a semidocumentary veneer over established narrative patterns of the fall into criminal alienation.

Rogue cop narratives reached their apogee in 1954 with the showcasing of *Pushover, Rogue Cop, Shield for Murder,* and *Private Hell 36,* a trend capped by the great terminus of *noir* itself, *Touch of Evil* (1958). In other words, as atomic-spy trials were intensifying (the Rosenbergs were executed in that same fateful year of 1953), the Blacklist and anticommunistic hysteria was reaching full throttle *(High Noon* and Arthur Miller's *The Crucible* are two contemporaneous treatments), *film noir* is awash in cops crossing over into criminal activity. Even avowedly patriotic testaments to the crime-fighting prowess of federal authorities, such as *The Naked Street* 1955, are suspect in their fascination with undercover agents miming a criminal code. Granted that the transgressions of crooked cops are duly punished, and the stability of the system reaffirmed, this is hardly material in tune with a foreign policy in which America was cast as the Policeman of the World. Nor is it the stuff of Ike's placid vision of social "togetherness."

L.A. Confidential taps into some of the surly, confused mood of Fifties' *noir* but, not surprisingly, updates its thematic or metaphorical subtexts to encompass more contemporary cultural obsessions. Like *True Confessions* or the dreary *Mulholland Falls* (1996), *Confidential* attempts to draw parallels between government, law enforcement, and organized crime as three interlocking, mutually reinforcing but vaguely competitive, forms of free enterprise. Each has a mirroring hierarchy, concealed sexual perversions, a set of common goals and brutal 'business' tactics, and a shared interest in victimizing the city's underclass. The narrative function of this linkage is fairly obvious, presenting a moral opposition between forces of entrenched civic power and previously complicit, but newly enlightened, individualist avengers.

The film also serves up one further player in the corruption sweepstakes, the nexus media/Hollywood, as represented by the trashy editor Hudgens, the television cop show, and the smooth boss of the movie-star prostitution ring. This porno-mogul, in effect a surrogate Hollywood producer, has a business card engraved with the motto 'Whatever You Desire,' a phrase that might fittingly be installed just beneath the MGM lion. *L.A. Confidential* suggests that law enforcement, tabloid journalism, and Hollywood are rackets creating pubic images built on sensationalism; in slightly different ways, they are all flesh industries. Moreover, as the dialog and action make perfectly clear, they each require male 'heroes' to secure their image and hence their economic viability.

It is not simply that these institutions are deceptive, not what they seem on the surface, but that they enact carefully constructed scenarios for both private and public consumption. This turns the film's anecdotal roster of crafty impersonations, shakedowns, fake busts, fake interrogations, and good cop/bad cop routines into related forms of theater. To take one example, when Hudgens and Vincennes stage-manage the pot bust of a budding screen star, the bottomline results have little to do with justice; they will increase magazine sales, add a nice collar to Vincennes's' record and, possibly, even benefit the framed actor (as a similar bust arguably benefited Robert Mitchum).

In distinction to greed-motivated operations of power, however, which in this context are evil by definition, the self-conscious adoption of artifice or playacting becomes a double-edged sword, a weapon wielded as readily in the redress of corrupt practices in their expansion. Exley, White, and the deceased Vincennes are in the end judged as socially redemptive performers while the organizations, and the Organization Men, to which they were initially indebted, are condemned. What is required of dedicated crusaders is a combination of passionate impulse and the ability to recite scripted lines; good actors are also actors for the common good. Despite the unmistakably conservative values embedded in this line of critique, and a lack of overall thematic coherence in their presentation, by current standards it is an ambitious agenda for a commercial action movie. As *L.A. Confidential* implies, to demand more makes you either a crusader or a sucker.

LOS ANGELES TIMES, 9/19/97, Calendar/p. 1, Kenneth Turan

Fascinated by the spectacle of fallible men and fallen women trapped in a corrupt and heartless world that's too cold to care, filmmakers in every generation have never stopped reinventing film noir. From 1940s classics like "Out of the Past" (1947) through the likes of "Kiss Me Deadly" (1955), "Point Blank" (1967), "Chinatown" (1974) and "Body Heat" (1981), each decade has taken its own kind of brooding look at what goes down at the dark end of the street.

"L.A. Confidential," with an exceptional ensemble cast directed by Curtis Hanson from James Ellroy's densely plotted novel, looks to be the definitive noir for this particular time and place. A dark, dangerous and intoxicating tale of big trouble in paradise, smartly done with the blackest possible humor and names like Kevin Spacey, Kim Basinger and Danny DeVito, it's conspicuously contemporary both in its attitudes and its willingness to bend the rules of the game absolutely as far as they will go.

Ostentatiously cynical, hyper-violent, dripping with attitude, "L.A. Confidential" holds nothing sacred. Its intricate plot is so nihilistic and cold around the heart, its nominal heroes so amoral, so willing to sell out anyone and everyone, that the film is as initially unnerving as it is finally irresistible. A cocktail of diverse elements first shaken and then stirred, it takes pride in confounding expectations and leaving us as surprised as its characters by twisting turns of events.

From top to bottom, "L.A. Confidential" enjoys playing around with these notions of appearance and reality. It presents a fearfully corrupt police force the world thinks is a model of decorum, characters who believe in "doing what they have to do for justice" no matter how savage and even murderous their acts may seem, all operating in a city that likes to pretend it's paradise on Earth when it's really seething with pervasive corruption. Welcome to sunny Los Angeles in the year 1953.

This theme begins with the opening sequence, cheery promotional films of the Southland counterpointed by a wised-up and sarcastic narration. "Life is good in Los Angeles," sneers Sid Hudgens (DeVito). "At least that's what they tell you."

Hudgens ought to know. As the energetic editor of Hush-Hush, as in "off the record, on the qt and very hush-hush," always on the lookout for "prime sinuendo," he specializes in running scandalmonger stories like "Ingenue Dykes in Hollywood." Hudgens' monologue not only sets the tone for "L.A. Confidential," it also provides crucial background information: With the removal of major mobster Mickey Cohen, the L.A. crime scene is rudderless and up for grabs and 25 pounds of pure heroin have just gone missing.

Next on the scene, introduced one by one on Christmas Eve, are the three LAPD cops who are the film's protagonists. That night turns out to be crucial for each, involving them in incidents that have implications that gradually play out in bloody and unexpected ways.

Officer Bud White (Russell Crowe, the Australian star of "Romper Stomper") is first up, a relentless and unsmiling one-man wrecking crew with an inflectionless voice and an eagerness to turn psychotic when protecting women in jeopardy.

On Christmas Eve, White meets the beautiful but troubled Lynn Bracken (Basinger), a vision in a black hooded cape with white trim, who immediately lets him know he's got cop "practically stamped on his forehead." With chitchat like that, we know they'll be meeting again.

Sgt. Jack Vincennes (Spacey), a.k.a. "Hollywood Jack" and "the Big V," is a show-biz cop with the cushy job of technical advisor for the mock-"Dragnet" TV series "Badge of Honor." A smoothly corrupt operator who smiles easily but not openly, Vincennes does not disappoint the superior who tells him, "I doubt you've ever drawn a stupid breath in your life. Don't start now."

Vincennes spends his Christmas Eve in one of his frequent collaborations with Hudgens, busting two young contract players for drugs in exchange for a cash payoff and prominent mention in Hush-Hush's next cover story, "The Movie Premiere Pot Bust." Oh, the price of fame.

Ed Exley (Australian Guy Pearce), the son of a martyred cop and about to be made lieutenant, seems the likeliest good guy as a believer in helping people and an enemy of corrupt policing. But the aftermath of a police riot he gets caught in on Christmas Eve shows him to be smug and priggish with an eye for human weakness, a cold-hearted and manipulative careerist who doesn't care what he has to do to get ahead.

None of these men is an obvious hero, and each has enough willingness to transgress conventional morality to have made him a villain in other times and other films. If they're knights, and they certainly don't seem to be, their armor is at best seriously tarnished. When one of them is told, "Don't start trying to do the right thing, you haven't had the practice," it's advice they could all take to heart.

With all this as backdrop," 'L.A. Confidential" kicks into gear with a case big enough to involve the entire police department: the coffee shop shooting deaths of six people, including a policeman, that the press dubs "The Nite Owl Massacre."

Heading the investigation is Capt. Dudley Smith ("Babe's" James Cromwell), an unflappable veteran with a lilting way of calling everyone "boyo." Eventually involved as well are crafty Dist. Atty. Ellis Loew (Ron Rifkin) and Pierce Patchett (David Strathairn), a mysterious Mr. Big that Hudgens characterizes with typical brio as "a powerful behind-the-scenes strange-o."

Diverse as they sound, all these strands and characters eventually come together as smoothly as the finish on the film's vintage automobiles. Ellroy's nearly 500-page novel has so much plot, in fact, that the author thought it was his least likely book to be filmed. But co-screenwriters Brian Helgeland and Hanson have expertly extracted the essence of the proceedings and boiled them down to a concentrated screen story where appearances are deceptive and nobody gives any information away.

Director Hanson has already demonstrated a command of narrative drive in previous work like 'The River Wild" and "The Hand That Rocks the Cradle," and "L.A. Confidential's" clean, relentless storytelling sense, its ability to draw us in while always playing fair with plot details, is its quintessential asset.

Following right behind is strong ensemble acting. Spacey is the essence of corrupt charm, and Basinger provides the film's emotional center as the world-weary femme who's been around more blocks than the Thomas Guide. "L.A. Confidential's" nerviest and most successful decision was using the unknown faces of Crowe and Pearce as two of its key L.A. cops. Anyone who remembers Pearce as the youngest and most flamboyant drag queen in "The Adventures of Priscilla, Queen of the Desert" will be impressed at the transformation.

In its locations, its look and its period soundtrack, "L.A. Confidential's" passion for authenticity has paid off. L.A. native Hanson and cinematographer Dante Spinotti opted to shoot in venerable spots like the Formosa Cafe and Hollywood's Frolic Room, and production designer Jeannine Oppewall, set decorator Jay R. Hart and costume designer Ruth Myers have made sure everything else looks right.

The only potential audience drawback "L.A. Confidential" has is its reliance on unsettling bursts of violence, both bloody shootings and intense physical beatings that give the picture a palpable air of menace. Overriding that, finally, is the film's complete command of its material. "L.A. Confidential" believes in itself because its creators got drawn into its wild story, and what an adventure that turns out to be.

NEW YORK, 9/29/97, p. 50, David Denby

L.A. Confidential is not only the best American movie of the year (thus far) but, in some ways, the only American movie of the year. Much of the picture is so powerfully entertaining that it seems a strange artifact from another age—a time when story, characters, and milieu worked together on the screen as devastating fiction and in the moviegoer's mind as memory and desire. *L.A. Confidential,* based on James Ellroy's 1990 novel, is about corruption and honor in the L.A.P.D., and it's set in 1953, in the period immediately after the imprisonment of the local Mafia boss Mickey Cohen. All of a sudden, power in the crime world is up for grabs; some of the greedier cops are trying to lay hands on it. When a group of people is massacred at the Nite Owl Cafe, the crime is initially blamed on three young black men. But the apparent solution to the murders unravels, and a larger pattern of evil behind the massacre, like a spreading stain, reaches out to cover widely separated elements of Los Angeles society. This is the classically fallen L.A. of Raymond Chandler and Ross MacDonald and of such film masterpieces as *The Big Sleep* and *Chinatown*—the beautiful bad place. Violent, ravenously erotic, deeply cynical but also possessed of a touching faith in the future, a belief in innocence and pleasure. The end of the movie wears a crooked grin: Things are set right again, but not in the standard Hollywood way. Corruption, we realize, may be endemic to power, even to benevolent power.

The material arrives with a corrosive edge supplied by Ellroy and preserved by director Curtis Hanson and screenwriter Brian Helgeland. A merry little crumbbum named Sid Hudgens (Danny

DeVito) provides a sarcastic welcome-to-L.A. narration at the beginning: The city is growing rapidly, Sid tells us, and though the police may be preserving the image of a sunshine paradise, he knows "the truth." The publisher of a tabloid scandal sheet, Sid is a true creator of sleaze journalism; he alerts the police to trivial forms of vice (i.e., sex and pot in a motel room) and then photographs for his magazine a celebrity cop, Jack Vincennes (Kevin Spacey), making the bust.

Sid and Jack work their dirty game for mutual profit and fame; one of the movie's bitter jokes is that life is far dirtier than either of them will ever understand. Apart from its central narrative, *L.A. Confidential* is obsessed with such things as the porno and prostitution rings at the edge of the movie business, the violent racism of the Los Angeles cops, the habitual use of intimidation as a method of police inquiry. The hints and allusions become echoes, producing a pervasive anxiety, a sense of something horribly wrong that can't be fixed.

In the past, in such movies as *The Bedroom Window* and *The Hand That Rocks the Cradle,* Curtis Hanson has shown some skill at building tension but nothing like the sensuality and power he demonstrates here. A bullheaded cop, Bud White (Russell Crowe), who's on a real Galahad trip—he can't stand seeing women hurt—approaches a black Cadillac with a beautiful woman and a wealthy Beverly Hills dandy in the back, and the fifties glamour of the moment arrives with so evocative an aura of danger (the woman's face is bandaged) that we simply slide back 45 years without any sense of entering the past. The period details are there, but what matters are the emotions, the story, the pull of death and despair. Violence and desire bring the period close to us. By the end, the *noir* attitudes—the general fatalism—seem not merely a set of stylistic conventions but a more serious attitude toward evil than anything we have now.

The bandaged woman, it turns out, is a call girl whose appearance has been altered to make her look like a movie star. Wealthy clients pay to sleep with Lana Turner and Rita Hayworth look-alikes. That could be a metaphor for what we all want out of the movies—the erotic power of falsehood. *L. A. Confidential* is even sardonic about its own tropes: One of the cops runs into the real Lana Turner and takes her for a whore. That's a good, raw joke, and the movie has many almost as good.

The violent Bud is one of two heroes, neither of them unblemished. In a masterstroke, Curtis Hanson and producer Arnon Milchan have cast Australian unknowns as these men. As played by Russell Crowe, Bud is a man of abnormal rage who pounds people with his fists on command; he's a follower, a tool of the seemingly benevolent but actually vicious chief of detectives, Dudley Smith (James Cromwell). Bud barely knows himself, and Russell Crowe's features, which seem soft and unformed—puffy, like the face of a pre-moral child—slowly come into focus for us as the movie goes along. Guy Pearce, who plays Ed Exley, a straight-arrow cop, all ambition and calculation, is exactly the opposite: His face is overdefined, his jawline too clean, his mouth too tense (he has Katharine Hepburn's mouth, somehow). The slender Pearce doesn't look like a cop, which is probably why he was cast. His Exley is a young man on the make who uses rectitude as a way of getting ahead, and the other cops despise him. Arrogant and repressed, Exley is the natural enemy of Bud White, but they both slowly change, and it's thrilling for us to discover the gradual alteration in the faces of these new actors. Russell Crowe comes up from brutalism, and Guy Pearce down from moralism, and they meet in the middle and join forces (to our relief).

The movie suggests a deep fallibility in even the best men, a bottomless deceit in the worst, and a wide range of honor and venality in everyone in between. Kevin Spacey makes a major creation out of the suave, nattily dressed son-of-a-bitch Jack Vincennes, a preening cop who serves as adviser to a hit TV series about the L.A.P.D. It takes us a while to realize quite how intelligent Vincennes is (his brain is working even after he's taken a bullet). Jack recovers his soul; so does the Veronica Lake look-alike played by Kim Basinger, an actress who, in the past, has never quite known who she is and discovers herself here as an imitation. Basinger, soft and saddened, is very touching as a guilty hooker, a good-bad girl worthy of the high forties. The movie is filled with wonderful actors—David Strathairn, in a pencil-line moustache, displaying surprising wit as a sleek smoothie living high off the prostitutes; Simon Baker Denny as an eager-to-please young actor-stud too beautifully dumb to stay out of trouble.

There's one cheap scene in which Pearce and Crowe terrorize someone by hanging him out of a window, and, at the end of the movie, the corpses perhaps pile up a little too rapidly. The vicious concentrics that radiate out from Mickey Cohen's death become numerous beyond counting, yet the filmmakers pull everything together in the end. The world, it turns out, is not beyond redemption. Loyalty is possible, even love. This violent story truly earns its quiet, ambiguous final note of exhausted calm.

NEW STATESMAN, 10/31/97, p. 37, John Diamond

Everyone's in showbiz nowadays. The television screens are busy with celebrity doctors, celebrity shrinks, celebrity journalists, celebrity coppers. It wasn't always thus, of course. Back in 1953 the only celebrity policemen were those who—literally—trod the Hollywood beat.

In the mainly fictional *LA Confidential* for instance, the dishonourable sergeant Jack Vincennes (Kevin Spacey) is technical adviser to *Badge of Honor,* a television cop show which is *Dragnet* in all but name. His access to the celeb circuit allows him to make celeb arrests for 1950s-style celeb crimes—dope smoking, gay sex and take a kickback from the sleazy editor of a sleazy celeb magazine (Danny DeVito), who gets to photograph the collars.

Representing the older, thuggish strain of police work is the crew-cut Bud White (Russell Crowe), brought in to flex his muscles when the Irish captain of police wants a hoodlum to scamper back whence he came. And standing straight for the newer, forward-looking brand of policing is the bespectacled, book-reading and incorruptible Ed Exley (Guy Pearce) who manages, at the start of the film, to antagonise everyone in the department by giving evidence against the old guard to a grand jury.

Between the three of them we have a story of institutional rites of passage (police department sees error of oafish ways, spruces itself up for life in the modern world), neatly, carried in the pocket of a piece of *film noir* which only just manages to avoid pastiche.

In fact to say there are just the two films here is to undersell Brian Helgeland and director Curtis Hanson's version of the James Ellroy novel, for there is a point halfway through when the mood of the film changes so completely that for a moment I couldn't remember which film I'd been watching for the first hour or so.

That first hour is spent in full retro-wallow, the screen full of big old Buicks and Oldsmobiles so unnaturally shiny as to suggest the museum curator was waiting, purse-lipped, on the set to get his exhibits back. The backing track is all Sinatra and Crosby and you know that even though you can't see the individual beer bottle labels in the liquor store scene, big money has been spent getting every one of them just so.

The plot is purposefully convoluted, as if somebody had one eye on the bits of Chandler that Chandler said he didn't understand, and the other on *Chinatown.* But essentially it concerns—deep breath—the connection between a high class brothel staffed by film-star lookalikes and run by a millionaire pimp with a heart of gold, the shooting of half a dozen customers of a diner (which number includes a detective sacked after the press got a picture of a group of Mexicans being beaten up and a hooker from above-mentioned brothel), the escape of the black teenagers arrested for the murder, a heroin heist, DeVito's magazine, an ex-directory nightclub and—well, you see what I mean about convoluted.

And then, as the disparate threads are drawn together in an engagingly unlikely way, the second film starts. The Sinatra is replaced by heavy-on-the-bass mood music, unrecognisable as such in 1953, the camera stops lingering on the clever props, the rain starts falling and the rest of the plot, leading up to the inevitable shoot-out, is played out in the shadows.

As the claustrophobia starts the film suddenly isn't so convoluted after all. Or rather one realises that it never really was. Somebody worked out that with a film like this, convolution is part of the shtick but that there are fewer filmgoers around who take pleasure in not quite understanding the whole plot than there were when *Chinatown* was made in 1974. And so although the story is chock-full of elements, we are so carefully guided through them that we can boast at the end about how clever we've been to have understood it all.

Perhaps it's ungenerous to criticise any script for being comprehensible, but I'd have been happy to work harder and guess the denouement a little later. All of which to say that if *LA Confidential* isn't the wonderfully complicated and entertaining film the Americans have been hailing, it is at least undemandingly entertaining almost to the very end. Three minutes from the credit roll Hanson manages to make the final scene look like something substituted at the last moment at the behest of a couple of tryout audiences. It is in fact precisely the ending Ellroy wrote for his book.

LA Confidential isn't really a film about the nature of policing or about America's awkward years in the 1950s or about any of the other profundities which one imagines the producers thought they'd worked into the film. It's about working out who Mr Big is. To the extent that this is what films used to be about, it contains a purer nostalgia that it ever intended.

NEW YORK POST, 9/19/97, p. 45, Michael Medved

Just how good is "L.A. Confidential"?

Suffice it to say that it's the first film in some 20 years that can honestly stand comparison to Roman Polanski's neo-noir masterpiece "Chinatown."

Like its famous predecessor, this new film offers a nostalgic, fascinating tour of L.A.'s past, in this case focusing on the booming 1950s instead of the 1930s of "Chinatown." Both films emphasize moral rot and outrageous conspiracies beneath the sunny California surfaces. And both films create dangerous but irresistible romances, and an assortment of unforgettably vivid characters—though "Confidential" may provide an even richer array of well-written parts and dazzling performances.

Kevin Spacey plays a suave celebrity cop, famous as technical adviser for a popular TV series in the tradition of "Dragnet." On the side, this public hero earns a few illegal bucks by helping the editor of a sleazy gossip magazine (Danny DeVito) set up police busts of Hollywood luminaries.

This sleaziness horrifies an ambitious, by-the-book officer (Guy Pearce) who is hated by his colleagues for attempts to halt their various cruelties and corruptions.

One of the vulnerable officers is a rugged loner—played, magnificently, by Russell Crowe—who viciously attacks anyone who gives even a hint of abusing women.

This tough-but-tender cop inevitably falls for a wounded beauty, played by Kim Basinger—part of a call-girl ring in which each of the women pretends to be a glamorous star of the day.

James Cromwell (of "Babe" fame) is the worldly-wise Irish police captain determined, at all costs, to maintain public confidence in the department.

The film cleverly compacts the dense, complex plot of the James Ellroy novel that inspired it, while cinematographer Dante Spinotti ("Last of the Mohicans") does a brilliant job with images that are simultaneously seductive and dangerous, gleaming and shadowy.

Director Curtis Hanson has done good work before ("The River Wild" and the underappreciated "The Bedroom Window"), but now he wins new recognition as a major stylist.

The climactic confrontation may strain credibility and common sense, but by that time the characters have already captured you so completely that you can't help rooting for them—and their movie—to pull through.

NEWSDAY, 9/19/97, Part II/p. B3, Jack Mathews

James Ellroy is to many people the densest, toughest and smartest crime writer of our time, and what may be his densest, toughest and smartest novel is now a movie bearing the same distinction. Curtis Hanson's "L.A. Confidential" is a richly detailed, intensely played cop drama that is as much a social commentary on post-"Chinatown" Los Angeles as it is a pure, butt-kicking entertainment.

"L.A. Confidential" is set in the early 1950s, at a time when Hollywood's glamor still reigned, despite the steady encroachment on its audience by television. It was a period when corruptibility and the impulse for violence were rewarded skills of police recruits, and when veteran cops often "traded up" from the beat to the mob. It's about a time when the LAPD was shifting from a frontier mentality to one modeled on the military, and when the seeds of racism that would fuel riots 15 and 40 years later were being sown.

Ellroy's novel, efficiently simplified and streamlined by Hanson and co-writer Brian Helgeland, straddles that changeover in a story about two cops—one all muscle and good intentions, the other all brains and big ambitions—who are thrown into conflict by a murder case that stretches from an all-night diner where six bodies are found, to City Hall, where some of the skeletons are buried.

Hanson, trying to avoid the distraction of star casting, tapped Australian actors Russell Crowe ("The Quick and the Dead") and Guy Pearce ("Priscilla: Queen of the Desert") to play the old and new-breed cops, respectively, while filling out the rich array of supporting roles with Kevin Spacey, Kim Basinger, James Cromwell, David Strathairn, Danny DeVito and Ron Rifkin.

With the exception of Pearce, who seems a touch too squeaky clean for his character, the cast is a study in perfection. Basinger is at her sultriest as Lynn Bracken, a high-priced call girl with a Veronica Lake hairdo, who becomes a pawn in the fight between detectives White (Crowe) and Exley (Pearce). Cromwell is the Irish police captain with a brutal streak to match his brogue. Strathairn is a suave racketeer with "big connections." And Rifkin is the compromised DA with an appetite for graft and young actors.

Best of all are Spacey,, striking an impossible balance of smarminess and charm as Jack Vincennes, a sharp-dressing detective who moonlights as technical adviser for a TV show called "Badge of Honor" (it's "Dragnet"), and DeVito, a hilariously oily Sid Hudgens, the reporter, photographer and publisher for Hush Hush magazine (it's Confidential).

Hanson, who toiled in low-budget horror films until breaking out with "The Hand That Rocks the Cradle," works this complex material with the sure-handedness of a magician. Every scene is a link to all the others, and though you can be confused by the sheer number of interrelationships, you look back from the end at a trail that follows a perfectly logical progression.

The "Chinatown" allusion is fair. Just as "Chinatown" used real estate scams of '30s Los Angeles to enrich its film noir story, "L.A. Confidential" uses police corruption and mob influence of the '50s as the basis for pulp crime drama.

Mobster Mickey Cohen (Paul Guilfoyle), whose imprisonment opens the L.A. underworld to would-be successors, and his henchman Johnny Stompanato (Paolo Seganti), were familiar figures to both cops and stars in a time when there was some mutual attraction. Stampanato was the live-in lover stabbed to death by Lana Turner's daughter in 1958, and he and Turner (Brenda Bakke) show up together, in better times, for a very funny scene in L.A.'s landmark Formosa Cafe.

"L.A. Confidential," with its authentically detailed production design and Dante Spinotti's elegantly moody cinematography, also has the romantic gloss of "Chinatown." Los Angeles is a place where the real and the imagined have historically overlapped, and when filmmakers work that margin well, they create their own magic.

Better get to the bookstore. If "L.A. Confidential" is a hit, there'll be more Ellroy to come. He has 10 more novels under option.

NEWSWEEK, 9/22/97, p. 83, David Ansen

For a sunny town, Los Angeles has sure inspired a lot of dark movies. From "Double Indemnity" to "Kiss Me Deadly" to "Chinatown," L.A. has been the capital city of film noir. Time will tell if *L.A. Confidential* has the staying power to warrant inclusion on this august list. It has the right ingredients: a dense and satisfying plot that gives off the pungent odor of corruption, a rich cast of deeply flawed characters whose actions resist snap judgments and a nostalgia-free re-creation of the city in 1953 that lets us see the line that connects the LAPD of the era of Mickey Cohen and Johnny Stompanato to the LAPD of Daryl Gates and Rodney King.

Director Curtis Hanson and his cowriter, Brian Helgeland, have taken a massively complex novel by James Ellroy and boiled it down to a no-flab screenplay that still eludes easy synopsis. A mass murder in a downtown café sets off an investigation that will spiral off in many directions, ultimately encompassing a prostitution ring that features girls surgically altered to resemble movie stars, drug-running mobsters, celebrity gutter journalism, police corruption, political blackmail, the racial biases of the LAPD and even a good, sexy love story.

At the heart of the tale are three cops with radically conflicting agendas who find themselves pursuing the same dangerous truth. Bud White (Russell Crowe) is the most volatile. Used by the chief of police (James Cromwell) for his muscle, he has no compunction about planting evidence if he thinks his guy is guilty. Bud has a thing about rescuing women in peril, and call girl Lynn Bracken (Kim Basinger) definitely arouses his chivalry, as well as his lust. Squeaky-clean Ed Exley (Guy Pearce) is his opposite; brainy and political and wildly ambitious, he's a perfect poster boy for the department's new image. Publicity-hungry Jack Vincennes (Kevin Spacey) is all preening vanity: he's the adviser on a "Dragnet"-like TV show, and he feeds his appetite for the spotlight by working alongside tabloid dirtmonger Sid Hudgens (Danny DeVito), setting up celebrity busts that will increase his fame.

One of the unexpected pleasures of "L.A. Confidential" is that your sympathies (or antipathies) for these guys keep changing. The brutal guy has more brain—and the smart guy more guts—than is first apparent. These are juicy roles, and the three stars do them full justice. (If you can't quite place Pearce, it's because the last time you saw him he was in drag in "Priscilla, Queen of the Desert.") Basinger brings a touching, bruised sultriness to her good-bad-girl role.

Hanson has always been a good craftsman, making solid entertainment out of formulaic material ("The Hand That Rocks the Cradle," "The River Wild"). But here he gets to sink his teeth into meatier stuff, and he raises the level of his game. "L.A. Confidential" asks the audience to raise its level a bit, too—you actually have to pay attention to follow the double-crossing intricacies of the plot. The reward for your work is dark and dirty fun.

SIGHT AND SOUND, 11/97, p. 45, John Wrathall

Los Angeles, the early 30s. Police Captain Dudley Smith tells his ambitious, incorruptible protégé, Sergeant Ed Exley, that he will never make detective unless he's willing to kill men he knows are guilty instead of risking their getting off in court. That same night, officers Bud White, Jack Vincennes and Dick Stensland beat up a gang of Mexicans in police custody. Exley, who tries to prevent the attack, testifies against them, incurring their hatred. White and Vincennes are transferred and Stensland sacked. Exley makes detective.

Stensland and five other bystanders are murdered during a bloody armed robbery at the Nite Owl Café. Exley successfully pins the massacre on three black junkies who have abducted and raped a Mexican woman, Inez Soto. When they escape, he tracks them down and kills them in self-defence during the ensuing shootout. He is decorated with the Medal of Valor. Meanwhile, White investigates another victim of the Nite Owl massacre, Susan Lefferts, and discovers she worked for mysterious millionaire Pierce Patchett, one of whose sidelines is supplying prostitutes who look like movie stars. After spying on another of Patchett's girls, Lynn Bracken, White starts an affair with her.

Exley begins to doubt the guilt of the Nite Owl killers when Soto admits she made up the evidence that implicated them. After agreeing to help Exley find Stensland's real killers, Vincennes reveals his suspicions to Smith, who shoots him dead. Suspicious of White, Exley visits Bracken, and ends up having sex with her. When Smith arranges for White to "accidentally" see photos of Exley with Bracken, White attacks Exley. But Exley convinces White that Smith is their common enemy; Smith is trying to take over the LA underworld with Patchett while gang boss Mickey Cohen is in prison.

Exley and White are called to a motel where they are ambushed by police. Smith shoots White, and is about to finish off Exley when the injured White stabs him. Knowing he can never prove that Smith was the real killer who committed the Nite Owl massacre (as a cover for killing Stensland over a heroin deal), Exley shoots him in the back. In the ensuing cover-up, Smith is depicted as a hero killed in the course of his duties, and Exley receives a second Medal of Valor. White leaves for Arizona with Bracken.

Attempts to compress a 500-page bestseller into a two-hour film often result in hopelessly overcrowded plots peopled with schematic characters. One need only consider the string of recent films adapted from the novels of John Grisham. Doing justice to James Ellroy's *L.A. Confidential* might seem an even more daunting task. For a start, the book is merely one part (the third) in Ellroy's mammoth LA quartet, which traces the secret history of Los Angeles from the 40s to the 60s, with recurring characters and themes throughout. Besides, 500 pages of Ellroy are like a thousand of anyone else's: he writes in a fevered shorthand, cramming information onto the page.

So writer-director Curtis Hanson's achievement with *L.A. Confidential* is all the more triumphant. With his co-screenwriter Brian Helgeland (who wrote *Conspiracy Theory*), Hanson hasn't so much condensed Ellroy's novel as filleted it, lifting out characters, incidents and chunks of juicy dialogue and rearranging them into a more streamlined plot. (One hesitates to say a simplified one because the synopsis above only hints at the narrative complexity of the film.)

One inspired decision is to eliminate Preston Exley, the cop-turned-property-developer who in the novel dominates his son Ed and the city as a whole. This allows Dudley Smith to loom more powerfully as Ed Exley's father figure, *éminence grise* and, ultimately, nemesis. In fact, Smith's opening speech to Exley, in which he tests his willingness to plant evidence, rig crime scenes, beat confessions out of suspects and shoot criminals in the back, belongs to Preston Exley in the novel. Also, in the book it is Preston who is destroyed by Ed's investigations, while Smith lives on, guilty but undeterred. If anything, Helgeland and Hanson's devastating ending, in which Exley can only beat Smith by stooping to Smith's cold-blooded, law-bending methods, improves on Ellroy's.

What Hanson has preserved from the novel is the use of three contrasting protagonists: the repressed Exley, the sleazy Vincennes and the explosive White. The way their investigations intertwine, their methods differ and their relationships develop towards the final, grudging collaboration gives the film a richness far beyond the basic thrills of the police investigation. Thanks to Ellroy, *L.A. Confidential* is also peopled with unusually vivid supporting characters, not least the muck-raking gossip columnist Sid Hudgens, whose role is elevated here from colourful (and short-lived) bit player to occasional narrator, spouting Ellroy's magnificent Walter Winchell-inspired tabloid speak.

A thriller specialist, Hanson's previous work has been marked by an old-fashioned, unflashy emphasis on character and tight plots. Here he manages to capture Ellroy's uniquely raw and brutal tone, but (thanks to Dante Spinotti's luxurious Panavision photography and Jerry Goldsmith's *Chinatown*esque score) within a much smoother and more elegant framework than the book provided.

Hanson's real flair, however, is for casting. In the past, he has credibly reinvented Rob Lowe as an evil genius (in the underrated *Bad Influence)*, Rebecca De Mornay as a psycho nanny *(The Hand that Rocks the Cradle*) and Meryl Streep as an action heroine (*The River Wild*). Surely no one else in Hollywood would have chosen two Antipodeans, Russell Crowe and *The Adventures of Priscilla, Queen of the Desert*'s Guy Pearce, to play White and Exley, but they are both frighteningly driven, while James Cromwell, the kindly farmer from *Babe*, is equally perfect as the avuncular but lethal Smith. More conventionally cast, but clearly relishing their roles, Kevin Spacey and Danny DeVito provide some very cynical light relief as the cop and the columnist who collaborate on busting celebrities.

In fact, despite its bleak catalogue of murder, rape and betrayal, and without ever making light of them, *L.A. Confidential* manages to be a very witty film, thanks to Ellroy's gallows burnout (at one point, a wry pathologist describes one organ as the "stomach of the week") and Hanson and Helgeland's inspired interpolations, not least the moment where Exley mistakes the 'real' Lana Turner, on the arm of Mickey Cohen's lieutenant Johnny Stompanato (also a historical figure), for one of Patchett's movie-star lookalike whores.

TIME, 9/15/97, p. 100, Richard Schickel

Try to imagine this: a mainstream American movie, rife with violent and often murderous behavior, yet so densely plotted, so richly peopled, that you can't summarize it in a sentence. Or a paragraph. Or several of them. Imagine, as well, a film set in the exotic past—Los Angeles in the noirish '50s—that tends to make the mass audience skittish. And imagine too a cast of terrific actors that lacks the reassuring presence of a megastar who can, as they say, open a picture.

Now try to imagine the pitch meeting for this project. Or the nervous marketing meetings that follow. Better still, imagine yourself at the earliest possible showing of *L.A. Confidential*, watching alchemist-director Curtis Hanson (who shares screenwriting credit with Brian Helgeland) turn pulpmeister James Ellroy's brutal, bustling novel into something like cinematic gold.

To cut to the heart of its intricacy, the film basically follows the misfortunes of three Los Angeles cops as they trace the links among the murder of a corrupt colleague, a pioneer of sleazoid celebrity journalism (Danny DeVito, who brings huge comic relish to the role), a shadowy social climber (David Straithairn), who is enamored of underworld glamour, a call girl (an entrancing Kim Basinger) working for a service whose employees are obliged to imitate movie stars (she's the Veronica Lake look-alike), and, eventually, major players in the Los Angeles law-enforcement hierarchy.

Whew! This is Raymond Chandler's penchant for complex high-low conspiracies writ large. And we haven't even mentioned the police riot, the body decomposing in the basement or the hanging of the D.A. out his office window by his heels in order to elicit information. Nor have we considered the natures of the three lead detectives, who, once they start working in atonal concert, sort of add up to one Philip Marlowe.

This trio includes Jack Vincennes (Kevin Spacey, never more engagingly slippery), who is the technical adviser to a *Dragnet*-like TV show and is becoming a celebrity in his own right; Bud White (Australian actor Russell Crowe), who's a sweet, plodding sort of guy unless someone visits violence on women, which turns him into a raging brute; and Ed Exley (Guy Pearce, another Aussie), the departmental priss and spoilsport, thoroughly despised by everyone, as moral centers of amoral enterprises should be—until they turn out to have been right all along.

If you have to spend time in a labyrinth, these are the kind of guys to do it with—tough, canny realists who can follow a tangled thread to daylight. Well, hmmm, daylight. There's not much of that in *L.A. Confidential*. It's a movie of shadows and half lights, the best approximation of the old black-and-white noir look anyone has yet managed on color stock. But it's no idle exercise in style. The film's look suggests how deep the tradition of police corruption runs. And that, paradoxically, makes it as outrageous (and outraging) as tomorrow's headlines will surely be.

VILLAGE VOICE, 9/23/97, p. 85, J. Hoberman

Curtis Hanson's *L.A. Confidential* is a big, intricate noir that manages to corral much of wild man James Ellroy's 500-page, take-no-prisoners fever dream of bloody mayhem and police corruption—and to sanitize even more. Enjoyably hard, fast, and detailed, the movie doesn't have much depth, but it's actively superficial and the surface tension keeps it from spilling over the top.

Set, in 1953, mixing fact with fiction, and predicated upon the connection between gangland warfare, urban development, intra-LAPD intrigue, and the so-called Nite Owl massacre, where a rogue cop was slaughtered along with a half dozen other patrons of a downtown greasy spoon, *L.A. Confidential*'s narrative is sufficiently complex to demand a reasonably alert viewer. There's no end to the setups and bad guys. Even the sympathetic characters are hopelessly bent pretzels of moral compromise.

Kevin Spacey's powerful absence of personality has never been more effective than here, as the ultracool celebrity narc Jack Vincennes, who has parlayed his role in Robert Mitchum's pot bust (he's fake, it's real) to public identification with the (made-up) *Badge of Honor* TV show—itself a force in L.A. politics—as well as, less overtly, an adviser to the *Confidential*-style scandal rag *Hush Hush*, terror of Lotusland. The movie's two other principal cops—Russell Crowe's blank Galahad, Bud White, and Guy Pearce's ambitious do-gooder, Ed Exley—seem by comparison to be deliberately smaller-than-life. Bud is dumb and soulful, Ed is a ferrety RFK type. Brains and brawn ultimately unite in the fight against an absolute evil that the attentive spectator will have no difficulty identifying.

With the *Hush Hush* editor (Danny De Vito) serving as occasional narrator, *L.A. Confidential* plunges into the joy of simulation—invoking actual gangsters Mickey Cohen and Johnny Stompanato, as well as a racket involving a gaggle of classy hookers who have been "cut" to resemble stars—the hyperrealism accentuated by having the cartoonishly generic and terminally unconvincing Kim Basinger as a supposed Veronica Lake look-alike. The movie's best single joke has Ed mistake the "real" Lana Turner for her call-girl doppelgänger. In the end, he learns that there is no justice in L.A. only media coverage. "The press is going to have a field day with this," someone remarks after the big *Dawn of the Dead*-like gorefest in which the LAPD effectively wipes itself out. That's an apt forecast of *L.A. Confidential*'s generally glowing reviews—although there's a different sort of cynicism at work in the movie's bizarrely muddled happy ending.

Taking police thuggery as a given, Hanson's *L.A. Confidential* seems haunted by the specter of the last LA. riot. An entire precinct participates in a Christmas Eve pogrom against a group of Chicano suspects; three black punks are blatantly framed for the Nite Owl bloodbath. And yet, for all the scenes of swaggering Caucasians beating on their "inferiors," the race angle is curiously underdeveloped—eventhough the early 1950s were the heyday of L.A.'s fanatically white-supremacist police chief William Parker, a character in Ellroy's novel, prudently eliminated in the movie.

Ambivalently praising Ellroy's project to recast L.A. history in the tabloid terms of "sex crimes, satanic conspiracies, and political scandals," Mike Davis has suggested that the writer's self-consciously totalizing and sensational neonoir re-created the atmosphere of Ronald Reagan's America—"a supersaturation of corruption that fails any longer to outrage or even interest." I don't think that's entirely fair to Ellroy, who, after all, denies his readers any semblance of the feel-good denial that was part of the Reagan package. But, nihilistic as he is, the novelist gazes into an abyss from which Hanson and his cowriter, Brian (*Conspiracy Theory*) Helgeland, have no choice but to recoil.

This is a conservative noir—not just for its traditional filmmaking values. With its big canvas, mythologized locations, lone golden-hearted whore and multiple shoot-outs, *L.A. Confidential* has the feel of an epic western (even if Crowe and Pearce aren't exactly Bob Mitchum and John Wayne). But on its own genre terms, *L.A. Confidential* is less the *Chinatown* redux some have wishfully termed it than the anti-*Blade Runner*. The movie is not simply, cop copacetic—its terminally cop-o-centric worldview is suffused with nostalgia for the pre-multicultural L.A.

Also reviewed in:
CHICAGO TRIBUNE, 9/19/97, Friday/p. A, Michael Wilmington
NEW YORK TIMES, 9/19/97, p. E1, Janet Maslin
NEW YORKER, 9/22/97, p. 141, Anthony Lane
VARIETY, 5/19-25/97, p. 48, Todd McCarthy
WASHINGTON POST, 9/19/97, p. C1, Stephen Hunter
WASHINGTON POST, 9/19/97, Weekend/p. 50, Desson Howe

LA PROMESSE

A New Yorker Films release of a Les Films du Fleuve, RTBF, Touza Productions, Samsa Film, and ERTT production with assistance from the French Community of Belgium, the Belgian National Lottery, Canal Plus, ACCT, and Eurimages du Conseil de l'Europe. *Producer:* Luc Dardenne and Hassen Daldoul. *Director:* Jean-Pierre Dardenne and Luc Dardenne. *Screenplay (French with English subtitles):* Jean-Pierre Dardenne. *Director of Photography:* Alain Marcoen and Benoit Dervaux. *Editor:* Marie-Hélène Dozo. *Music:* Jean-Marie Billy and Denis M'Punga. *Sound:* Jean-Pierre Duret. *Set Designer:* Igor Gabriel. *Running time:* 93 minutes. *MPAA Rating:* Not Rated.

CAST: Jérémie Renier (Igor); Olivier Gourmet (Roger); Assita Ouedraogo (Assita); Rasmané Ouedraogo (Hamidu).

LOS ANGELES TIMES, 5/30/97, Calendar/p. 14, Kenneth Turan

Morality is a given, in the movies; everyone, even the worst of creatures, knows if they're bad or good. In "La Promesse," an exceptional film from Belgium, all of that is reversed as a sense of right and wrong struggles to emerge in a young man who never knew there was a difference. The conflicts involved are intense and absorbing, proving that compelling moral dilemmas make for the most dramatic cinema.

An exciting discovery at both last year's Directors' Fortnight at Cannes and the New York Film Festival, "La Promesse" makes being politically relevant and philosophically thoughtful so simple and involving that the story seems to be telling itself. Written and directed by Luc and Jean-Pierre Dardenne, a pair of filmmaking brothers, it is made with such unobtrusive sureness that it's able to exert great power without forcing anything.

Though relatively new to features, the Dardenne brothers have 20 years of documentary work in Belgium behind them, and their use of hand-held cameras and probing close-ups gives "La Promesse" the urgency and immediacy of total authenticity. Toss in unknown but persuasive actors and characters whose reality is unmistakable and you get an idea why this film is as bracing as it is.

"La Promesse" is set on the outskirts of the Belgian city of Liege and centers on a 15-year-old apprentice auto mechanic named Igor (Jeremie Renier). An opportunistic sneak thief and smooth liar, Igor is like a small animal with dirty blond hair, casually amoral because in his world the opposite has never been presented as an option.

Igor's universe is completely controlled by his father, Roger (Belgian stage actor Olivier Gourmet), A pudgy, bearded and petty despot, Roger has a lie or a threat or a beating for every occasion. Hot-tempered, violent, a master of casual betrayals, Roger puts together scams without end, but he also cares for his son and values their almost symbiotic relationship.

Roger's business is dealing in illegal immigrants—Turks, Ghanaians, Romanians and Koreans—who sneak into Belgium looking for a better life. Roger hides them in a clandestine rooming house, charging them exorbitant fees for false identity papers while collaborating with the police when a raid is needed to satisfy the local politicians.

In all of this, Igor, made in his father's image and hardened by sharing his lifestyle, is a willing second-in-command. Part man, part boy, he spends the spare moment when he's not conniving with the old man putting together a go-kart with his young friends.

Igor's life begins to change when Assita (Assita Ouedraogo) and her small child arrive from Burkina Faso to join husband and father Hamidu (Rasmane Ouedraogo) in Roger's boarding house. Assita's individuality intrigues Igor, and then a jolt of fate shoves their lives closer. Hamidou has an accident working illegally, Roger refuses to take him to the hospital, and he dies after making Igor agree to take care of his wife and child, the promise of the title.

It's difficult to do justice to how subtly the film develops from here, how unflinching it depends on documentary-style realism and expressive faces to make its points. Though the question of romance never arises, Igor becomes increasingly protective of Assita, which puts him in conflict with his father, the only person who's ever cared about him. It, a predicament that is as difficult a it is compelling.

"La Promesse's" actors have differing levels of experience, with Jeremie Renier, an impressive natural, having the least and Assita Ouedraogo (whose first trip to Europe was to make this film) having appeared in three films of fellow countryman Idrissa Ouedraogo. But they all work so seamlessly here we feel we're eavesdropping on a moral rebellion that is being played out for the highest possible stakes.

Among the many things it does right, "La Promesse" refuses to even consider glib solutions. This film understands that moral choices are a painful, troublesome business, that decisions to do the right thing are not simple to take and hardly make things easier. Nothing in life takes more courage, and no kind of filmmaking offers greater reward.

NEW YORK, 5/19/97, p. 63, David Denby

If you're sick to death of extravagant put-ons like *The Fifth Element,* you may respond (as I did) to *La Promesse,* a story told straight, and with great intensity. In this extraordinary Belgian film, two brothers with a background in documentary filmmaking—Luc and Jean-Pierre Dardenne—dig so deeply into a specific scene that one sees its very bones and arteries. Roger (Olivier Gourmet), an unemployed factory worker living near Liege, runs a scam operation in illegal foreign workers. His chief assistant and disciple is his 15-year-old son, Igor (Jérémie Renier), whom he desperately loves and furiously dominates. Rushing about madly, the two men bring Turks, Romanians, Croats, and Africans into the country and charge them rent to live in abandoned housing; they rip them off and exploit them any way they can, and then, when things get too hot, turn some of the workers over to the police. Roger, an overweight man of about 40, less-than-ordinary-looking, has a kind of demonic energy. Among other things, he has robbed his son of his childhood; the boy is already an accomplished thief and liar. Both men display immense resourcefulness in perpetrating squalid little frauds and deals; their hands are never free of cash.

When an African worker falls and injures himself badly (he may be dying), Igor wants to take him to the hospital, but Roger, fearing that the police will close down his operation, forces the kid to help him bury the still-living man in cement. At first, Igor conceals the gruesome death from the African's wife, a proud and beautiful woman carrying a little baby in a sash. At the same time, he tries to help her escape the awful fate his father has devised for her, but she doesn't want help—she's off in her own world of magic and ritual, seeking answers from the entrails of chickens in the middle of this gray-souled Belgian industrial wasteland. The movie chronicles the beginnings of moral feelings in a boy whose instincts are almost always larcenous—a transformation that forces a break with the father who loves him.

The Dardenne brothers use a handheld camera, and much of the film has a hustling, caught-on-the-run quality; we see little acts of desperation and pleasure as people exchange money or rush down obscure corridors. And because the picture is so brazen and energetic, it is never depressing. The scene has a malign fascination; this endless scrambling, we realize, is the heart of an underground economy. The same thing happens in every dark corner of New York or Los Angeles.

For all the roughness, we see what we need to see, with one major exception. Assita Ouedraogo, a teacher from Burkina Faso who plays the wife, is obviously loath to face the camera. She ducks her head, backs into scenes—the pride extends to a refusal to act or even to be seen. Ouedraogo is a discomforting presence; she makes us feel we are trying to steal something from her. The movie has been shaped as a moral fable about the awakening of conscience, but here, right in the middle of it, is an actress who will not quite yield herself to fiction. Does it matter? It doesn't: By resisting the benevolent intentions of two Western filmmakers obviously outraged on her behalf, Ouedraogo reinforces the movie's theme of exploitation and cultural isolation. The Dardenne brothers must be doing something right.

NEW YORK POST, 5/16/97, p. 42, Bill Hoffmann

If you thought David Helfgott's dad was a mean-spirtited S.O.B. in "Shine," you ain't seen nothing yet.

In "La Promesse," actor Olivier Gourmet plays the sleaziest, nastiest, most vile and immoral parent in movie history.

Calling him the Dad from hell would be positively unkind to the devil.

Gourmet's kinetic performance as this soulless human will have you cringing—while, at the same time, you won't be able to take your eyes off the screen.

But Roger, a Belgian con man, is just one component of a film nearly flawless in its uncensored telling of lives so rotten, it'll make you think long and hard about the nature of the human race.

"La Promesse," filmed in stunning *cinema-verite* style, is a coming-of-age story of a different sort.

Igor (Jeremie Renier) is a lanky teen who knows the score, thanks to his father, Roger, who warehouses illegal immigrants in a foul-smelling tenement and uses them as slave labor.

Roger is repulsive—a man who exploits everything and uses threats, violence and psychological fear on anybody who stands in his way—including his son.

Igor collects the whoppin rents his dad charges the illegals, and he does it with a shrewd skill that tells you he'll grow to be just as monstrous as his dad.

But, maybe not ...

When a black worker is critically injured on a job, Roger has his son bury him in cement rather than take him to the hospital, so the cops won't catch on.

Keeping the dead man's wife (Assita Ouedraogo) in the dark about what happened, Igor promises he'll take care of her if her mate never returns.

From that moment on, you know push will come to shove between father and son. And when it does, watch out!

The Dardenne brothers have made a powerful, must-see film from a horrifying subject. But, as we learned with "Trainspotting," even the most lurid of subjects can make fascinating cinema.

Well, "La Promesse" is Belgium's answer to "Trainspotting."

NEWSDAY, 5/16/97, Part II/p. B9, John Anderson

Tattoed, beer-drinking, chain-smoking Igor (Jeremie Renier) is the heart and soul of the remarkable "La Promesse," and may be the last hope of civilization. For that matter, he may be the ultimate vindication of humankind. Raised and tutored by his Fagin-like father, Roger (Olivier Gourmet), the teenager is an adept thief and an accomplished liar. But his moral conscience will erupt like some spontaneous Big Bang, defying logic, expectation and behavioral science. And while this isn't exactly "Song of Bernadette" it's a miracle nonetheless.

Nothing in "La Promesse" quite feels like a miracle, though. In their spare, unobtrusive, faux-documentary style, brothers Luc and Jean-Pierre Dardenne—who say they found their inspiration in "The Brothers Karamazov"—have devised a fluid and edgily mobile film about a boy's moral awakening that is thoroughly engrossing, totally convincing, almost archetypal.

Roger, a brutish symptom of a post-industrial continent, takes shameless—and felonious —advantage of the dregs of the earth, including refugee Romanians and Africans, whom he smuggles into his midsize Belgian city (via economy-sized cars). He bilks them, he works them, he occasionally offers a few up for sacrifice: When the mayor feels the heat over the influx of illegals, Roger throws the cops a few Croats.

Igor, lab assistant to his Frankenstein father (who's busy making a monster son, as well as a new Europe), parrots his gestures and policies and never protests when his father drags him away from his apprenticeship at a local garage, a job for which he has real talent. Occasionally, Roger gives Igor gifts.

"Thanks, Dad."

"My name's Roger."

What does this mean? That they're not related? There's no mention of a mother, although Igor could use one. Father and son certainly don't resemble each other. There's the possibility that the Dardennes are purposely pitching hardcore genetics theorists against the environmental camp, with a sideswipe at religion: If the two are not related by blood, perhaps Igor is free from Roger's original sin? Either way, as rich in detail as "La Promesse" is—unlike so many movies, you really have to *watch* this one—it's equally rich with intrigue about motivations, emotions and cultural differences.

Nowhere is this more pronounced than in Igor's relationship with Assita (Assita Ouedraogo), who arrives from Burkina Faso with baby on board. Igor watches the woman—with her talismans and spirit medicine—with fascination. But his awe has as much to do with her maternity as her hoodoo. He's never had it, never seen it. And he wants it. And when Assita's husband dies after a building accident—because Roger refuses to blow his cover by taking the man to a hospital—it sets up a three-way confrontation of biblical proportions.

Gourmet is appropriately disgusting as the beery Roger, but young Jeremie Renier is a wonder, able to marry a street-punk sensibility to naked need. His father beats him when Igor gives Assita money to pay her now-missing husband's gambling debts; Roger wants her to go away, by whatever means necessary. This is disturbing, but not as disturbing as Roger's attempts to make up with Igor, dad and son hugging and having a talk about sex, just as if there weren't a dead man hidden in the back yard.

The Dardennes clearly were striving for hyper-realism and unfettered naturalism. Toward that end they have the marvelous hand-held camera work of cinematographers Alain Marcoen and Benoit Dervaux, always agile and revealing without being obtrusive. And a fresh, unpresuming cast—Ouedraogo, for instance, is a schoolteacher in her native Burkina Faso. In "La Promesse," however, she's a primal, sculpted force of motherhood and faith, a means of salvation for Igor and an indictment for most of the rest of the world. After all, you'll be asking yourself later, just what *is* the "promise" of the title?

NEWSWEEK, 6/30/97, p. 79, David Ansen

There's not an ounce of flab or a false move in the breathtaking Belgian film *La Promesse*. Written and directed by the brothers Luc and Jean-Pierre Dardenne, whose background as documentary filmmakers can be felt in the tale's gritty verisimilitude, it's the story of a teenager's hard-won moral awakening. Fifteen-year-old Igor (Jérémie Renier) has little chance to be a kid. He's too busy learning the ropes of his father's shady business: exploiting illegal immigrants who've sneaked into Belgium from Eastern Europe and Africa. Falsifying passports, hiding the workers from inspectors, tricking them into working for slave wages, Igor is well on his way to emulating his scuzzy father (Olivier Gourmet), a monster whose love for his son is nonetheless palpable. Then a dying African worker, fallen from a scaffold, extracts a promise from Igor to take care of his wife and child. To keep his pledge, Igor must betray his father and look at the world with new eyes. Urgently, without sentimentality, "La Promesse" shows us the birth of a conscience, and its cost. This fleet, powerful movie may prove to be a classic.

VILLAGE VOICE, 5/20/97, p. 71, J. Hoberman

From *The Jazz Singer* through *The Godfather* and beyond, the Hollywood immigrant story has been a paean to economic upward mobility. The equivalent European films, more typically, are tales of exploitation and loss. (And they wonder why the world loves American movies.) Far from advertising the lands in which they were produced, the Belgian feature *La Promesse* and the British *Brothers in Trouble* make the sort of appeal to civic responsibility that vanished from our own national radar screen around the time Jimmy Carter went down in flames.

La Promesse, a critical hit at the last New York Film Festival, is also a terrific little movie. Written and directed, with maximum vérité-style kapow, by the brothers Jean-Pierre and Luc Dardenne, it distills an array of moral problems into one supercharged metaphor for patriotism and the fatherland: somewhere in the dank, economically depressed suburbs of industrial Belgium, a quick-thinking—if unformed—urchin and his harried slob of a father are warehousing illegal immigrants and using them for cheap construction work.

The towheaded Igor (neophyte actor Jérémie Renier), small for his 15 years, is a dutiful son and practiced dissembler who has internalized the values embodied by his father Roger—indelibly portrayed by stage actor Olivier Gourmet as an unshaven, tubby lout in incongruously thick horn-rimmed glasses. Whether lying his way to the front of a queue or setting up troublemakers for a government bust (and then forgetting he did so), Roger is shamelessly self-serving. So, in his way, is Igor, who—merged with Roger—is continually called away from his job at the garage to run his father's errands. Symbiotic as they are, the pair even have a father-son barroom routine. (Renier and Gourmet work as a team despite the total absence of physical resemblance because they are so well matched allegorically—the son is small and middle-aged looking, the father overbearing and infantile.)

While Igor retains a boyish enthusiasm for racing go-carts with his neighborhood pals, it is a half-articulated sexual curiosity that creates the first fissures in his loyalty to dad. When the African woman Assita, wife of the worker Hamidou, arrives from Burkina Faso with her baby, Igor is fascinated—spying on the family's room, inventing excuses to learn about their special purification rituals, ogling the tribal fetish that presides over their household. The luckless Hamidou falls from a scaffolding in a pre-inspection panic and, before losing consciousness, makes Igor promise to take care of his family. (An incidental horror: it is unclear whether Hamidou is actually dead when Roger disposes of the body by burying him in the construction site under building debris and poured concrete.)

Having spent 20 years making political documentaries, the Dardenne brothers tunnel into their material with scarcely a backward glance. *La Promesse* is an artfully convincing slice of life. The landscape is casualty devastated; the visual mode is handheld and hectic. The bravura long takes and whizzing camera maneuvers are complemented by the sense of onrushing traffic and harsh street noise. The camera rarely stays still, while most of the cuts are on movement: a scene opens with Roger fully crazed and bludgeoning Igor for giving Assita the wood-burning stove he'd planned to swap for the sexual favors of another immigrant woman.

In fact, Roger is plotting to send Assita back to Africa—or at least get her out of town. Operating by the laws of her own particular universe, however, the unwitting widow reads a chickens entrails to discover that Hamidou is near. (The scene is rhymed by one of a fruitless trip to a police station establishing that Hamdou can't be missing since he doesn't legally exist.) just as the current immigrant infusion has served to rekindle a neorealist impulse in European cinema, so the Dardenne brothers use Roger's sordid scam as the catalyst for Igor's moral awakening. The boy, who is introduced opportunistically pocketing an elderly woman's wallet, ultimately throws his lot in with the victimized and completely unforgiving Assita.

While the actors playing Igor and Roger hurtle through their roles, Assita is portrayed as stiff, unyielding, and irreducibly foreign: Everything about the actress Assita Ouedraoago's body language suggests that she has found herself on some ghastly tundra. Ultimately, she becomes a living reproach. (In this sense, *La Promesse* refers back to the first neo-neorealist film to directly address the First World-Third World divide, Ousmene Sembene's *Black Girl.)* Belgians lie to her, piss on her (literally, as well as figuratively), obliterate her husband, ride their motorbikes over her meager possessions.

When, having impulsively foiled his father's first plan to send Assita packing, Igor attempts to express a measure of ambivalent solidarity, the woman just glares at him. (Soon she will accuse the lad of infecting her baby.) It's one of *La Promesse*'s great virtues that—in charting the course of Igor's own conflict—the more global situation that is Assita's resists easy resolution.

Also reviewed in:
CHICAGO TRIBUNE, 8/22/97, Friday/p. J, Michael Wilmington
NEW REPUBLIC, 5/26/97, p. 30, Stanley Kauffmann
NEW YORK TIMES, 5/16/97, p. C16, Stephen Holden
VARIETY, 5/27-6/2/96, p.75, Derek Elley
WASHINGTON POST, 6/27/97, p. D6, Stephen Hunter
WASHINGTON POST, 6/27/97, Weekend/p. 44, Desson Howe

LAST TIME I COMMITTED SUICIDE, THE

A Kushner-Locke Company, Roxie Releasing and Tapestry Films release of a Bates Entertainment production. *Executive Producer:* Peter Locke, Donald Kushner, Lawrence Mortorff, Peter Abrams, Robert L. Levy, and J.P. Guerin. *Producer:* Edward Bates and Louise Rosner. *Director:* Stephen Kay. *Screenplay:* Stephen Kay. *Based upon a letter by:* Neal Cassady. *Director of Photography:* Bobby Bukowski. *Editor:* Dorian Harris. *Music:* Tyler Bates. *Music Editor:* Bill Black. *Sound:* Mark Weingarten, Roger Stevenson and (music) Robert Carranza. *Sound Editor:* Leonard Marcel. *Casting:* Laurel Smith. *Production Designer:* Amy Ancona. *Art Director:* Rachel Kamerman. *Set Decorator:* Melissa Levander. *Costumes:* Denise Wingate. *Make-up:* Suzanne Diaz. *Running time:* 95 minutes. *MPAA Rating:* R.

CAST: Thomas Jane (Neal Cassady); Keanu Reeves (Harry); Adrien Brody (Ben); John Doe (Lewis); Claire Forlani (Joan); Jim Haynie (Jerry); Marg Helgenberger (Lizzy); Lucinda Jenney (Rosie Trickle); Gretchen Mol (Mary "Cherry" Greenway); Pat McNamara (Father Harlan Fletcher); Kate Williamson (Nurse Waring); Christine Rose (Mrs. Greenway); Meadow Sisto (Sarah); Amy Smart (Jeananne); Alexandra Holden (Vicky); Clark Gregg and Joe Charbanic (Cops); Edward Bates (Player 1); Ted Henning and Josh Randall (Guards); Tom Bower (Police Captain).

LOS ANGELES TIMES, 6/20/97, Calendar/p. 12, Kevin Thomas

There's such a wonderful look and feet to Stephen Kay's "The Last Time I Committed Suicide" that it's a shame it doesn't truly come alive until its climactic sequence. In a singularly audacious and encouraging feature debut, Kay has written his script from the so-called "Great Sex Letter" that Beat icon Neal Cassady wrote to Jack Kerouac, who would immortalize him as Dean Moriarty in "On the Road."

Kay goes for the intense quality of Cassady and Kerouac's writing that is echoed in the film's great bebopping jazz score. The trouble is that Kay doesn't define Cassady sufficiently to allow us to see him as the stuff of legend. Thomas Jane plays him as a likable guy with a reckless streak, but someone who is not all that distinctive. (In short, we wouldn't have much reason to be watching this young man if his name weren't Neal Cassady.) Kay also has a tendency to have Cassady and his poolroom pal Harry (Keanu Reeves) sound a little too literary early in the film.

Still, Kay captures some quicksilver quality of authenticity of place and time, and just when you're sure about to give up on the picture ever coming to life fully, Reeves kicks "Last Time" into a raw, passionate existence. He sets up Jane for Cassady's stunning moment of self-knowledge that will determine the restless, craving-experience course for the rest of his short life. Cassady died in Mexico in 1968 after being found in a coma, having fallen asleep after some partying—by a railroad track during a cold, rainy night. He had just turned 42.

The film is set in his native Denver the late fall and Christmas season of 1945, when Cassady was 19 and working the graveyard shift at Goodyear Tire. Kay tells us nothing about his background, presenting him as a handsome, sexy and increasingly free spirit involved in a romance with an emotionally unstable young woman (Clare Forlani, who played Jean-Michel Basquiat's girlfriend in "Basquiat"). Boy, is Cassady the wrong guy for her!

A flashback shows Neal having a fling with an eager 16-year-old (Alexandra Holden), which will have profoundly crucial consequences. Cassady, already experimenting with expressing himself through writing, is seriously intending to settle down with Forlani's seemingly recovered Joan and trying to land a day job as a taxi driver.

All of Cassady's plans unravel during a prolonged encounter with Harry, an alcoholic who, in a long sequence brilliantly sustained by Reeves, forces Cassady to recognize the "wild demon" within himself, one who at heart doesn't want to be confined by life behind any proverbial "white picket fence." Jane has presence but is not able to break through as Cassady until those climactic moments, and even then he is overshadowed by Reeves' powerful, driving star performance.

"The Last Time I Committed Suicide," already shown on cable a few months ago, is unlikely to have much of a theatrical run. But it is more persuasive than the 1980 "Heart Beat" portrait of Cassady and his relationships, and it does leave you wanting to see what Kay—and Jane, too—will do next. It also leaves you with a feeling of real respect for Reeves for showing up in this modestly budgeted film instead of "Speed 2."

NEW YORK POST, 6/20/97, p. 44, Michael Medved

The library heroes of the postwar Beat Generation wrote novels too sprawling, formless and impressionistic to lend themselves readily to big-screen adaptation, and the rare attempts at movie versions of cult books of the period ("Naked Lunch," "Last Exit to Brooklyn") have proven, for the most part, disappointing.

"The Last Time I Committed Suicide," therefore, employs an audacious new strategy: Instead of dramatizing a full-scale novel, the movie merely adapts a single letter by Beat icon Neal Cassady.

The letter in question, addressed to Jack Kerouac and presented in a brief black-and-white prelude showing Cassady smoking and then sitting down at a typewriter, details a troubled love affair in 1947.

The 21-year-old protagonist (newcomer Thomas Jane) gets involved with a glamorous lost soul named Joan (Claire Forlani), who inexplicably slits her wrists one rainy night in his Denver bathroom.

He spends the few days at her hospital bedside, hoping she'll recover but then giving up on her and finding companionship with a hard-drinking, cynical pool-hall buddy (Keanu Reeves) with highfalutin literary pretensions.

Near Christmastime, the wounded Joan suddenly reappears and reclaims Neal's attention, and he feels himself powerfully drawn to the life of white-picket-fence domestic bliss that this vulnerable, needy spirit incongruously offers him.

At the most inconvenient possible moment, however, he is distracted by a sexy 16-year-old schoolgirl sweetie known as Cherry Mary (Gretchen Mol), who begs to see him one last time.

We also meet assorted friends from Neal's moody, skid-row world, including the iconic, bespectacled, gay-leaning Ben (the excellent Adrien Brody) and a grieving old man (Tom Bower) who worked alongside our hero on the graveyard shift at the Goodyear plant.

All the performances are solid and spicy, with Reeves surprisingly strong in his scene-stealing turn that casts him boldly against type.

In virtually all of his previous work, Reeves played characters who are likable, even heroic, but not very bright; here, he is riveting as a seedy, dangerous figure of corrisive, manipulative, seductive intelligence.

Thomas Jane (in his first starring role) is considerably less intriguing as Cassady, but he does convey some of the restless energy, that odd combination of gee-whiz cowboy innocence with self-destructive decadence, that so captivated Kerouac, Allen Ginsberg and other Beat legends (Cassady became the model for Dean Moriarty in "On the Road").

Jane certainly does better as Neal than the straining, embarrassed Nick Nolte did (in 1980's dismal "Heart Beat"), but for all his subtlety and skill as an actor, he lacks the elemental, animal, on-screen electricity that might have explained why all the other characters circle Cassady like faithful planets orbiting the sun.

Debuting writer-director Stephen Kay handled this odd, slight project with the jazzy editing and off-kilter, atmospheric camerawork that it needed.

His visions of wintry 1940s Denver convey the appropriately bleak aura of yearning and loneliness, while the musical score (by Tyler Bates), heavily flavored with be-bop, is a major asset.

Some of the dialogue tilts toward pseudo-intellectual grandeur: "You're special, man. You're the big cat, destined to wander forever, spreading your sunshine on those of us more or less," or, "The time is now. And now is all that counts."

These adolescent pretensions seem jarring in a contemporary film, but they're true to the spirit of the source material, helping "The Last Time I Committed Suicide" despite its awkward, ill-chosen title) oome as close as any previous film to capturing the elusive, bittersweet Beat mystique.

SIGHT AND SOUND, 6/98, p. 48, Claire Monk

The early 50s. Neal Cassady types a letter to his friend Jack Kerouac recounting the film's events. Neal's girlfriend Joan attempts suicide, but he finds visiting her in hospital too depressing and stops going. He hangs out in bars with his older friend Harry, where they play pool and pick up teenage girls.

One night, a woman named Lizzy picks Neal up at a bar and takes him home. He finds that Joan is living there with Lizzy, and her husband Lew. Reunited, Neal and Joan start planning their future together. Lew offers to set Neal up with a job. Neal suddenly decides that he needs a suit for the job interviews, and abandons Joan to find the suit he shares with three friends. He is waylaid by Harry, who seeks a favour. A few years earlier, Neal had an affair with a 16 year old Catholic girl. 'Cherry' Mary, until her mother intervened. Fancying Cherry himself, Harry persuades Neal to lure her to a meeting. Neal phones Cherry who makes her continuing sexual interest in him clear and agrees to come to the bar. But her mother has been listening in, and when Neal leaves to get his suit, he is arrested on a trumped-up charge. Released after two weeks in jail, he has trouble finding Lizzy's house. When he knocks, no one answers. He waits all day and half the night, but no one comes home.

Neal Cassady was the model for Dean Moriarty in Jack Kerouac's novel *On the Road,* and is routinely credited as the 'true creative genius'—or at the very least, inspiration—behind the Beat literary movement. It's a weighty burden for a dead icon to carry and one that, retrospectively, invites scepticism. Fetishised by Kerouac for his persona and live-fast lifestyle, Cassady published nothing in his lifetime and died youngish in 1968 (aged 42), seemingly of exposure after a hard night's partying, leaving behind a part-written autobiography. This blend of sublime iconic surface and elusive cultural achievement makes him promising movie material and an apt idol for reconsideration in the late 90s, when celebrity has become increasingly virtual, dependent less upon *doing* than upon a PR assisted ability to project *being.*

For audiences intrigued by Cassady's enigma, however, writer-director Stephen Kay's languidly hip, terrifically stylish but rather affectless debut film offers plenty of pleasures but little enlightenment. But then again, it doesn't pretend to, an appropriate stance given the existential philosophy of its subject. Based on one of Cassady's letters to Kerouac, *The Last Time I Committed Suicide* documents an episode in Cassady's life before his *On the Road* period, in which various semi-arbitrary twists of fate diverted him from committing to his depressive girlfriend Joan and settling down into what he termed his "happily ever after".

The Last Time achieves an impressive jump-cut verbal and visual style which correlates well with this inconclusive, inconsequentialist philosophy as well as with the rhythms of Beat writing. Although Cassady's non-marriage to Joan reads on paper like a significant life moment, in the film and—in the context of his multiple real life marriages—it appears as merely one transient incident among many: a momentary distraction from the homosocial bond of mutual admiration between Cassady and his drinking partner Harry. During one pool table exchange, Cassady explains to Harry the human urge to find settled love as more a metaphoric than a literal desire. When, later, he bolts from Joan to go walkabout among his male acquaintances, Harry, assuages his guilt by reassuring him that "sometimes a little distraction's a good thing".

The tone of these male exchanges is philosophical rather than vicious: but the underlying misogyny and possible repressed homoeroticism is clear enough. But though Kay fully acknowledges these dynamics (he's described the Beats as "a boy's club ... who got their love fix from each other") his film replicates these problems without really analysing them. Ironically, the film's narcissistic good looks—half black-and-white photography, half faded colour home movie footage and the camera's love affair with the excellent Thomas Jane as Cassady are largely to blame. Kay portrays the male-female and male-male relations as seductive, thus glamorising and neutralising the tensions at stake. So successfully iconic is Jane's persona that any urge to question his behaviour feels misplaced. As the older Harry, Keanu Reeves invites more ambivalent albeit muted feelings (his age makes his taste for teenage girls seem creepier than Cassady's).

If *The Last Time* is about anything, it is more about its own idolising process of constructing Cassady as icon than the questions of men and women, choice and fate. While its spectacle is seductive, its disengagement from the many questions it raises makes it ultimately hollow viewing, a double irritation since its gorgeous surface wants to be perceived as something more profound.

VILLAGE VOICE, 6/24/97, p. 82, Amy Taubin

Just as style conscious, but more hollow, [The reference is to *Dream With the Fishes*.] Stephen Kay's *The Last Time I Committed Suicide* imagines the final days of Neal Cassady's life as a private citizen—before he left Denver and was reinvented by Jack Kerouac as Dean Moriarty. Hovering on the verge of beatitude, Cassady is torn between the need to prove himself a man by settling down with a fuckable wife and the desire to find his authentic self by cutting loose of ties and responsibilities.

As Cassady, Thomas Jane looks vaguely like James Dean and has about as much complexity as a Calvin model. Jane's blandness might have worked for the film if Kay had been interested in deflating the Cassady myth, but his intention seems to be quite the opposite. *The Last Time I Committed Suicide* is a done-to-death romanticization of the beats, albeit from a Gen X perspective.

Excepting Jane, the actors are quite good, particularly Adrien Brody as an Allen Ginsberg type and Claire Forlani and Gretchen Mol as two of the women Cassady beds and abandons. Keanu Reeves is his enigmatic self as Cassady's pool-shark buddy. I've never been sure whether Reeves is such a riveting screen presence because of, or in spite of, the woodenness of his acting.

Bobby Bukowski's cinematography is as hip as Dorian Harris's editing. Like *Dream With the Fishes*, *The Last Time I Committed Suicide* is pleasingly retro without being at all innovative. Both films suggest that their directors are men of taste and feelings but without much smarts.

Also reviewed in:
NEW YORK TIMES, 6/20/97, p. C16, Stephen Holden
VARIETY, 1/27-2/2/97, p. 77, Dennis Harvey

LATE BLOOMERS

A Strand Releasing release of a One Mind Productions Feature. *Executive Producer:* Jim Jerge and Martha Little. *Producer:* Gretchen Dyer, Stephen Dyer, and Julia Dyer. *Director:* Julia Dyer. *Screenplay:* Gretchen Dyer. *Director of Photography:* Bill Schwarz. *Editor:* Julia Dyer and Gretchen Dyer. *Music:* Ted Pine. *Sound:* Byron Wilson. *Casting:* Nancy Fine. *Production Designer:* Mike McGarty. *Costumes:* Happy Yancey and Mattie O'Neal. *Running time:* 104 minutes. *MPAA Rating:* Not Rated.

CAST: Connie Nelson (Dinah Groshardt); Dee Hennigan (Carly Lumpkin); Gary Carter (Rom Lumpkin); Lisa Peterson (Val Lumpkin); Esteban Powell (Jamie Hooper); Joe Nemmers (Rick Musso); T.A. Taylor (Bill Boardway).

LOS ANGELES TIMES, 7/18/97, Calendar/p. 18, John Anderson

[The following review by John Anderson appeared in a slightly different form in
NEWSDAY, 7/18/97, Part II/p. B12.]

Lesbian chic gives way to applique sweaters and Aquanet in "Late Bloomers," a weirdly mundane morality tale about sapphic love in the South.

Not, mind you, that there is any real sense of place in this movie, produced by siblings Julia, Gretchen and Stephen Dyer, written by Gretchen, directed by Julia. It's set in a suburb, the type insular enough that any extramarital affair—much less one between a math teacher-basketball coach like Dinah Groshardt (Connie Nelson) and a school secretary-faculty wife like Carly Lumpkin (Dee Hennigan)—would tear a Tyson-sized chunk out of the local fabric of life. The gay aspects of the story are almost, if not quite, irrelevant. But, of course, if it didn't have a gay aspect, a movie this pedestrian wouldn't get a second look.

When they're not laughing up their sleeves outright, the sisters Dyer do plenty of nudging and winking, beginning with their opening shot—a bunch of pansies—and moving on to the characters' surnames, the metaphoric turtles that Dinah keeps in her spartan apartment, the dialogue ("There's something fishy going on in this school") and the scene of the crime, Eleanor Roosevelt High School (we all know about Eleanor, don't we?). It's the kind of place where the obtuse principal posts a daily platitude ("You miss 100% of the shots you never take") in order to inspire his student body, who are as uninspiring a group as were ever uninspired by the American educational system.

Much of "Late Bloomers" suggests a visual version of the principal's sloganeering—call it the dark side of Hallmark—and the film possesses a condescending attitude toward its own subject matter. The severe-looking Dinah and the pretty, plump Carly—whose husband, Rom (Gary Carter), has long cooled to her charms—are the two most unhappy folk in town, suggesting that their love is as much about desperation as passion.

The townsfolk are aghast—during a basketball game coached by Dinah, the rumor of their affair literally spreads from ear to ear—but they're also grotesque stereotypes of small-town parents, willing to voice the most Neanderthal opinions without ever suggesting that perhaps adultery, rather than homosexuality, is the more important issue regarding their children.

When Dinah and Carly are fired, ostracized and then decide to get married, the fact that Rom is in attendance, listening to the women's pronouncements of mutual love—he's still Carly's legal husband, after all—is either cruel or stupid, probably the latter. If it's so important that the two women wed, shouldn't Carly get divorced first? I don't know, call me old-fashioned. Call the Dyers smug.

The cast performs well in spite of the material. Both Carter and Lisa Peterson, who plays Carly's daughter Val, are quite good. As are Nelson and Hennigan, even if the most memorable scene will always remain their naked basketball game. They're playing "one on one." Get it? I wish I hadn't.

NEW YORK POST, 7/18/97, p. 46, Larry Worth

Early on in "Late Bloomers," an overweight school secretary tells her colleagues: "I'm either going on a diet or jumping off a bridge." Sadly, she diets.

What results may be cinema's most ludicrous look at latent lesbianism—unfolding at Eleanor B. Roosevelt High School, no less, deep in America's heartland.

The unhappy worker has no sooner lamented her husband's ongoing neglect and children's indifference when she gets turned on by her daughter's butchy gym teacher.

Faster than you can say score, they fall head over sneakers on the basketball court. Playing footsie in the cafeteria quickly segues to yet another shot of the twosome shooting hoops, this time, in the nude.

Things get no prettier when they move in together, much to the horror of the PTA board. The unintentionally hilarious standoff—featuring a movie first: the use of Oreo cookies as a dangerous weapon—nearly justifies sitting through this claptrap.

Actually, the more solemn the tone, the more farcical it seems. Using endless montages and the most inappropriate score imaginable, Julia Dyer stands out as a director of unerringly misguided tastes.

Not surprisingly, the only thing worse than Dyer's inept direction is the absurd script, courtesy of her sister, Gretchen. If stringing one cliche to the next—from precocious children to too-cool teens to dorky adults—was an art form, she'd get a Pulitzer.

And one can only speculate as to which sibling brainstormed the film's most obvious bit of symbolism: shots of two aquarium-bound turtles trying in vain to come out of their shells. It's the equivalent of being hit with a sledgehammer.

And that's not even mentioning the sad-sack, no-talent cast, headed by Connie Nelson and Dee Hennigan as the Bible Belt's answer to Ellen and Anne. Playing the frillier of the pair, Hennigan is an annoying mix of giggles and girth. Meanwhile, Nelson fails to bring new meaning to farmer overalls and bowl haircuts.

As a running joke, director Dyer keeps showing a message board outside the school, bearing slogans like "When the going gets tough, the tough get going." If that holds true for viewers, they'll take off before the opening credits.

VILLAGE VOICE, 7/22/97, p. 72, Elisabeth Vincentelli

Concocted in Dallas by siblings Julia (director) and Gretchen (writer) Dyer, *Late Bloomers* charts the romance between two middle-aged women, both employed at, ahem, Eleanor B. Roosevelt High School. When geometry teacher-girls' basketball coach Dinah (Connie Nelson) and school secretary Carly (Dee Hennigan) unexpectedly fall in love, all hell breaks loose. Dinah finds obscene drawings on her blackboard, Carly's husband Rom laughs nervously, and her daughter Val (the fascinatingly edgy Lisa Peterson) deliberately screws up a pass during a basketball game. After a tense PTA meeting, both women are fired. Figuring that an offense is the best defense, they send wedding invitations to family and colleagues—all of whom show up ready to party, each having undergone a miraculous change of heart in less than two minutes of screen time.

As competent, if banal, as it is, *Late Bloomers* may soon join *Claire of the Moon* in the annals of lesbian infamy, thanks to a rather unfortunate scene—while naked basketball may be an intriguing fantasy, actually seeing it onscreen is quite the cold shower, thank you very much.

Both *Kiss Me, Guido* and *Late Bloomers* testify to the mainstreaming of gay and lesbian subjects in film: these movies may not have been made in Hollywood, but they are permeated by Hollywood-style sentimentality. Obviously neither Vitale nor Dyer has realized that good intentions hardly ever make good art. Worse, they may have realized it but not cared.

Also reviewed in:
NEW YORK TIMES, 7/18/97, p. C12, Stephen Holden
VARIETY, 1/29-2/4/96, p. 65, Godfrey Cheshire

LATIN BOYS GO TO HELL

A Strand Releasing release of a Jürgen Brüning Filmproduktion/Fernando Colomo P.C. proudction in association with Strand Releasing/Stance/GM Films/Pro Fun. *Executive Producer:* Stephen Gallaguer. *Producer:* Jürgen Brüning. *Director:* Ela Troyano. *Screenplay:* Andre Salas and Ela Troyano. *Based on the novel by:* Andre Salas. *Director of Photography:* James Carman. *Editor:* Brian A. Kates. *Music:* Ari Gold. *Sound:* Kristian Petersen. *Sound Editor:* Margaret Crimmins. *Production Designer:* Uzi Parnes. *Costumes:* Uzi Parnes. *Make-up:* Edgar Langer. *Running time:* 86 minutes. *MPAA Rating:* Not Rated.

CAST: Irwin Ossa (Justin Vega); John Bryant Davila (Angel, Justin's Cousin); Alexis Artiles (Braulio); Mike Ruiz (Carlos); Jenifer Lee Simard (Andrea); Guinevere Turner (Sombra); Annie Iobst (Monica); Dashia (Jackie); Norma Maldonado (Mrs. Vega); Jehad Nga (Sylvano); Rebecca Sumner Burgos (Luz); Umberto Gonzales (Rodrigo); Yvonne Washington (Gladys); Reynier Molenaar (Eduardo); Iris Prado Salas (Braulio's Mom); J.R. Valdes and William Gonzalez (Bartenders); Adrian Sanchez (Italian Guy); Fil Fernandez (Cashier); Ari Gold (Trash Popstar); Pepper Burns and Veronica Fox (Gender Illusionists); Jose Muñoz (Mr. Bully); Carmelita Tropicana (Mrs. Bully).

LOS ANGELES TIMES, 9/5/97, Calendar/p. 10, Kevin Thomas

"Latin Boys Go to Hell"—and so does this rambling, diffuse picture set in Brooklyn. In the foreground is a potentially tender tale of a shy young man (Irwin Ossa), heretofore into denial in regard to his sexual orientation, who finds himself attracted to his straight cousin (John Bryant Davila), a likable, easy-going young man visiting from Chicago.

Ossa's Justin is deep into *telenovelas* (soap operas), as is his friend Braulio (Alexis Artiles), who's having an affair with the handsome, unfaithful Carlos (Mike Ruiz). First-time director Ela Troyano clearly means to be saying something about the blurring of melodramatic *telenovela* fantasy with everyday, reality, but it's beyond her present ability to make her point in a coherent fashion.

Troyano would have been better off sticking with working out a credible story set in a macho Latino culture between Justin and his cousin, since Ossa and especially Davila are promising actors. It should be noted that this technically mediocre movie, clocking in at 70 minutes, apparently once had an 86-minute running time.

At the recent outfest, "Latin Boys Go to Hell" caused quite a stir on account of one-sheets and stills featuring the smoldering, nearly naked Ruiz, who looks as if he just stepped out of a Calvin Klein ad. Buyer beware: Don't judge the picture by the poster.

NEW YORK POST, 9/13/97, p. 24, Larry Worth

Judging from "Latin Boys Go to Hell," writer-director Ela Troyano comes off as Almodovar's biggest fan. Also judging from "Latin Boys," the sentiment will never be returned.

It's practically, home-movie time as Troyano trains her camera on a bunch of shirtless gay hunks who experience unrequited amour—in-between viewings of their favorite soap opera, "Dos Vidas."

In a style to do "All My Children" clones proud, a night of lovemaking ends with an exploding pinata. That's about as sharp as the alleged satire gets.

As campy catfights turn murderous, amateurish acting and dopey dialogue overwhelm the boy's ardor. Accordingly, viewers experience "Hell" in a manner that no one truly deserves.

SIGHT AND SOUND, 12/97, p. 45, Paul Julian Smith

New York City, the present. Teenage Justin, undecided about his sexuality, lives with his mother in Brooklyn and works as a photographer's assistant in Manhattan's East Village. He and his friends are avid fans of Spanish-language television soaps. At first, Justin is none too pleased when he hears he will have to share a room with Angel, his cousin from Chicago, but gradually he succumbs to Angel's charms. When the two cousins go clubbing there is a confrontation with the jealous Braulio, whose faithless lover Carlos has unsuccessfully tried to pick up Justin. Braulio's best friend Andrea warns him of Carlos' infidelities, but Braulio chooses not to believe her.

Later at the club, Angel is attracted to Andrea. Carlos approaches Justin again. Seeing Angel with Andrea, the jealous Justin has sex with Carlos. Justin is disillusioned by Carlos' cynicism and selfishness in lovemaking. Meanwhile, Angel poses nude for Monica, the photographer for whom Justin works as an assistant. Discovering Carlos' infidelities, Braulio goes to his apartment and murders him. Now clearly deranged, Braulio confesses to Andrea that he has murdered Carlos and plans to kill Justin. As they struggle with a gun, Braulio accidentally kills Andrea and then leaves for a party at Monica's. On the roof of Monica's building, Justin tells Angel of his love for him. Angel gently rejects his advances. Braulio bursts on to the roof with a gun, but Angel takes the bullet meant for Justin. As Braulio jumps to his death from the roof, Justin cradles the wounded Angel in his arms.

The rough cut of *Latin Boys Go to Hell* shown at the 1997 London Lesbian and Gay Film Festival was cut to music borrowed from Almodóvar movies. And the fond reminiscence of the Madrid master is clear in this, the first feature from Ela Troyano, a Cuban exile resident in New York. And so we find in this an Almodovarian labyrinth of unrequited passions, a scatter-shot plot full of red herrings and loose ends and, most importantly, sudden shifts of genre: from romantic comedy, to melodrama, to murder mystery. But in spite of the Spanish influence (co-producer Fernando Colomo is also famed as the director of Madrid comedies), *Latin Boys* trails a heady whiff of Manhattan.   Troyano makes good use of the glamorously seedy locations (including the famous club La Nueva Escuelita) and the cute actors apparently chosen for their diversity of body types: from skinny, street urchin Angel to gym-toned model Carlos by way of curvaceous ephebe Justin.

In its erotic treatment of such bodies, *Latin Boys* plays unselfconsciously with stereotype. In the opening sequence, Troyano cuts from the virginal Justin nursing his gold crucifix to the naked Braulio holding a skull in front of his genitals as a photographer asks him for "some of that Latin-boy love".   Other unlikely *cache-sexes* in the photo sessions include sombreros and corn cobs. In similiar imagistic fashion, Justin's melancholy is represented by a weeping Madonna, Braulio's madness by cutaways to an ominously full moon.   Sometimes the allusions are heavy-handed, as when the shower scene preceding Carlos' murder cites *Psycho*.   More often overemphasis is defused by offbeat burnout: the prurient straight neighbour, anxious for a glimpse of Carlos' bedroom, finds him slumped on the floor with his severed penis in his mouth.   Or again, Braulio's madness is revealed by his uncharacteristically unkempt appearance: a friend remarks that he must be crazy to go a party with his hair in such a mess.   It is typical of the comic dimension that even sex, the source of all the characters' pleasures and problems, is not taken as seriously as soap opera: in an early sequence Braulio brushes off the amorous Carlos to catch up on his favourite *telenovela*.

If the bilingual dialogue has its moments (some of them in Spanish with the longsuffering mothers), then the photography also has its pleasures with atmospheric night shots of glistening streets and incandescent subway stations. And the editing also transcends the norm. One striking sequence recreates Justin's first sexual experience through quick crosscutting between different locations (Carlos' flat, the nightclub, Justin's fantasies about Angel) before culminating in an explosion of glitter across the screen.

But, in spite of the frankness with which the film addresses a gay audience's demand for beautiful bodies, the world of *Latin Boys* is not based on a binary divide between gay and straight.   Rather it assumes a sexual continuum sometimes thought to be typically Latino. The young men live with their mothers, but there are no anguished scenes of coming out and no visible conflict between the boys' loyalties to their families and to their lovers. Angel, in his own words, "can't go in that [gay] direction", but he is happy to sleep in the same bed with his love-struck cousin. Gays and straights mingle in the same nightclubs and the closest relationships may be between gay men and straight women. One of the tenderest scenes involves gay Braulio being made up for a party by his best-female-friend Andrea. Sharing mascara may be the closest these boys and girls get to true love.

This sexual continuum runs parallel to a fluid fusion of national influences. That rare thing, a US-German-Spanish-Japanese co-production, *Latin Boys* boasts walk-ons by the likes of perfor-mance artist Carmelita Tropicana and lesbian icon Guinevere Turner as a Latin soap diva. With Hispanics set to make up the majority of US public-school students in the next decade, the real significance of *Latin Boys* may be in the evidence it provides for a new source of creative energy for US queer independents. Troyano's feature may be uneven, but it is a significant and very pleasurable pointer to the rich potential of cultural crossover between queer and Latin communities.

VILLAGE VOICE, 9/16/97, p. 89, Vince Aletti

When it comes to mining the heavily trafficked intersection of film and soap opera, Buñuel and Almodóvar are the established masters—going over the top without ever losing control.   If director Ela Troyano seems barely in control of her first feature, the *telenovela*-inspired *Latin Boys Go to Hell*, she still knows how to make bad acting, cheap sentimentality, gross stereotypes, and overheated homoeroticism work for her.   When her story splinters and drifts, Troyano gets by on sheer nerve—the sort of seat-of-the-pants looniness that leads long-running soaps into surrealism.

Latin Boys is a tangle of jealousy, madness, and revenge played out among a group of young New York Latinos.   It's tragedy as trash, full of sex and fights and petty misunderstandings. In other words, it's a comedy where nearly everyone dies, but it's rarely a camp. At its center is Justin (Irwin Ossa), a confused, baby-faced Brooklyn boy who escapes to an East Village dance club whenever he can. In the club's bathroom one night, he's accosted by rapacious superhunk Carlos (Mike Ruiz), who's used to taking what he wants. Rebuffed, Carlos tells his boyfriend, Braulio (Alexis Artiles), that Justin tried to feel him up, setting in motion a clash of good and evil as classic as it is queer.

Justin's inevitable seduction (its climax accompanied by the festive bursting of a piñata) and abandonment provide *Latin Boys* with an appropriately melodramatic centerpiece. And the complex web of associations that radiates from this coupling keeps the plot boiling over. Troyano's formula—think Kenneth Anger meets Latino Fan Club: the softcore version—is hilariously volatile. When it explodes, you can't say you weren't well prepared.

Also reviewed in:
CHICAGO TRIBUNE, 1/2/98, Friday/p. A, Achy Obejas
NEW YORK TIMES, 9/12/97, p. C14, Stephen Holden
VARIETY, 6/30-7/13/97, p. 67, Dennis Harvey

LAY OF THE LAND, THE

A Northern Arts Entertainment release of a JKG Production presentation of a Jonathan D. Krane production. *Executive Producer:* Edward Oleschak and Ralph R. Clemente. *Producer:* Jonathan D. Krane and Sally Kellerman. *Director:* Larry Arrick. *Screenplay (adapted from his play):* Mel Shapiro. *Director of Photography:* Frederic Goodich. *Editor:* Richard Brummer. *Music:* Jeff Lass. *Sound:* Scott Graham and Derrick Bell. *Production Designer:* Clare Brown. *Costumes:* Judy B. Schwartz and Beverly Safire. *Running time:* 94 minutes. *MPAA Rating:* R.

CAST: Sally Kellerman (M.J. Dankworth); Ed Begley, Jr. (Harvey Dankworth); Sandra Taylor (Muriel Johanson); Stuart Margolin (Carmine Ficcone); Tyne Daly (Dr. Guttmacher); Rance Howard (Dr. Brown); Avery Schreiber (Dean Bill Whittier); April Shawhan (Erma Whittier); Tom Nowicki (Bob Chambers); Elisabeth Redford (Blanche Cafferty).

LOS ANGELES TIMES, 9/26/97, Calendar/p. 12, Gene Seymour

[The following review by Gene Seymour appeared in a slightly different form in
[NEWSDAY, 9/26/97, Part II/p. 813.]

Knowing at the outset that adultery with a voluptuous college coed is a major plot element in "The Lay of the Land" makes its title the first of a series of embarrassments for its makers. Aiming for sophistication and wit, the movie achieves only a diverting frenzy of mood swings and—academic setting notwithstanding—the jokes don't get any more subtle.

Still, Sally Kellerman, also a co-producer, and Ed Begley Jr. try hard to make the best of a bad story. As M.J. and Harvey Dankworth, married college professors edging their way toward emotional free fall, they manage to make us care what happens to their characters even though you probably wouldn't want either one of these basket cases at your next party.

M.J., a lapsed documentarian teaching film, has a psychosomatic hand rash and suspects her husband is cheating on her. She tells this to her psychiatrist (Tyne Daly) well before Harvey, a Russian lit professor, decides to act on his lust for a flirtatious graduate student (Sandra Taylor).

There's a whole lot of contrivances scattered around this oft-told tale of a troubled marriage. Some are straight out of Sitcom City, others from Soapy Gulch and still others (like some fantasy sequences involving Daly and Kellerman in pointlessly exaggerated analysis) are Strictly From Nowhere.

Is this a comedy or melodrama? Hard to tell, and any script that decides to waste Stuart Margolin's talents as an Italian P.I. isn't smart enough to be both at the same time. To be sure, it isn't smart enough to know quite what to do after Harvey fesses up and is kicked out by M.J., who then runs off to Brazil to make the movie of her dreams. Don't ask what happens afterward. Just know that it's squishier than anything that came before.

Director Larry Arrick helped fashion this mess with Mel Shapiro from the latter's two-character play. Maybe that's why characters created for this movie, such as Margolin's, Daly's and even Taylor's, seem jerry-built from third-hand diagrams. Also, we see the Dankworths' two sons in the beginning of the movie and only hear about them afterward—and not very much at that. It seems, at the very least, peculiar that these kids' parents are breaking up and falling apart, and we don't get to see how they feel about it.

NEW YORK POST, 9/26/97, p. 48, Larry Worth

About an hour into "The Lay of the Land," Sally Kellerman wanders into the woods and screams at the top of her lungs. Those who've wasted $8.50, never mind their precious to join her.

And though it's nice to see Kellerman back in the spotlight, she can't work miracles on the pathetic script.

It certainly doesn't miss any cliches, beginning with college professor Harvey Dankworth (Ed Begley Jr.) desiring more than an apple from his new student, an all-bust-and-no-brains coed (Sandra Taylor).

Meanwhile, discouraged spouse M.J. (Kellerman) grows increasingly aware that something's missing from their sex life, namely sex. A psychiatrist (Tyne Daly) and private detective (Stuart Margolin) help her understand why—and set the stage for the stupidest showdown since Godzilla squared off with the Smog Monster.

For starters, director Larry Arrick tries to segue from silly sex antics to "Who's Afraid of Virgina Woolf?," broken up by fantasies featuring M.J.'s female shrink as Sherlock Holmes in drag. Here, nothing's elementary.

But Mel Shapiro's script is equally misguided, expanded from a two-character play that had two characters too many.

Speaking of which, the real question is whether Kellerman or Begley overacts to worse effect, bringing sound and fury, but no Faulkner-like inspiration, to their fights. They're embarrassing to watch, but hearing Kellerman's husky crooning—a mistake she first committed in Ross Hunter's disastrous "Lost Horizon" remake—is the final nail in the coffin. As for the title, its a salacious nickname attributed to Begley's mistress. Sadly, the rest of the film makes that seem subtle.

VILLAGE VOICE, 9/30/97, p. 84, Hillary Rosner

Roughly 10 minutes into *The Lay of the Land*, a soft-focus kind of girl enters the office of Professor Harvey Dankworth (Ed Begley Jr.) and announces that she is his new comp lit grad student. She's one of those straight-from-the-Kansas-farm-to-the-*Playboy*-centerfold types and you know, without a doubt, that this married father will become obsessed with her, jeopardize his marriage, and ruin his chances for tenure. And you have a pretty good idea, only a short time later, that M.J., his filmmaker-professor wife (Sally Kellerman), will grow suspicious, hire a private detective, and escape to the arms of another man. The only thing you can't predict is just how bad it will be. Not only is the story hackneyed, the script contrived, and the acting (with the exception of Kellerman) forced, but there is a sense that everyone involved knows this, and is trying to compensate. There are attempts at creativity, like the cryptic dream sequences involving M.J. and her shrink (Tyne Daly), but these are so out a of place that they leave you longing to get back to the main story. Until you get there.

Also reviewed in:
NEW YORK TIMES, 9/26/97, p. E18, Lawrence Van Gelder
VARIETY, 9/29-10/5/97, p. 67, Howard Feinstein

LEAVE IT TO BEAVER

A Universal Pictures release. *Executive Producer:* Ben Myron, David Helpern, and Lynn Arost. *Producer:* Robert Simonds. *Director:* Andy Cadiff. *Screenplay:* Brian Levant and Lon Diamond.

Based on the TV series created by: Bob Mosher and Joe Connelly. *Director of Photography:* Thomas Del Ruth. *Editor:* Alan Heim. *Music:* Randy Edelman. *Music Editor:* David Bondelevitch. *Choreographer:* Duane M. Foster. *Sound:* Thomas Brandau and (music) Elton Ahi. *Sound Editor:* Scott Hecker and Dennis Drummond. *Casting:* Joanna Colbert. *Production Designer:* Perry Andelin Blake. *Art Director:* Peg McClellan. *Set Decorator:* Lisa Robyn Deutsch. *Set Designer:* Easton Michael Smith. *Set Dresser:* Scott Getzinger, Thomas Scott Craig, Kevin Chambers, Larry J. White, II, Taylor Black, and Edson Moreno. *Special Effects:* Joshua Hakian. *Costumes:* Jean Pierre Dorleac. *Make-up:* Cheri Montesanto-Medcalf. *Stunt Coordinator:* Brian K. Burrows and Chris Howell. *Running time:* 88 minutes. *MPAA Rating:* PG.

CAST: Christopher McDonald (Ward Cleaver); Janine Turner (June Cleaver); Cameron Finley (Beaver Cleaver); Erik von Detten (Wally Cleaver); Adam Zolotin (Eddie Haskell); Barbara Billingsley (Aunt Martha); Ken Osmond (Eddie Sr.); Frank Bank (Frank); Erika Christensen (Karen); Alan Rachins (Fred Rutherford); E.J. De La Peña (Larry Mondello); Justin Restivo (Lumpy); Geoff Pierson (Coach Gordon); Louis Martin Braga, III (Gilbert Bates); Glenn Harris, Jr. (Punk); Grace Phillips (Miss Landers); Sam Gifaldi (Richard Rickover); Brighton Hertford (Judy Hensler); Shirley Prestia (Claire Hensler); Brenda Song (Susan); Fran Bennett (Dr. Beaumont); Wendy Walsh (Female Reporter); Lindsay Boyd (Lusty Girl); Heather Lauren Olson (Tamara); Matthew Thomas Carey (Kyle); George Fisher (Bert the Pie Man); Kate C. Sklar (Cute Girl); Darryl Smith (Referee).

LOS ANGELES TIMES, 8/22/97, Calendar/p. 2, Kevin Thomas

"Leave It to Beaver," the latest vintage TV series to get the big-screen treatment, is probably going to please a lot of people with its affectionate depiction of idealized small-city family life. Its makers have rounded up a good cast, headed by Cameron Finley as the adorable 8-year-old Beaver who's forever trying to do the right thing but tends to get derailed momentarily by older kids and adults. Warmth and humor abound.

The trouble is that the picture is hopelessly synthetic. Writers Brian Levant and Lon Diamond try to straddle the '50s and the '90s only to get lost in a limbo of make-believe. They've come up with a timeless story about Beaver coping with a father whose expectations of his son's football prowess at the age of 8 put undue pressure upon the boy, who also has to deal with the theft of his expensive new bike.

But the film's producers and its director Andy Cadiff, who is fresh off the sitcom "Home Improvement," don't seem to have thought through the kind of world in which "Leave It to Beaver" could come alive. Bad matchups between Universal's overly familiar standing sets and Santa Paula locales just don't work.

The filmmakers needed to go for an overall stylized look, to create some kind of background against which emotion could seem real on some level, by way of contrast. (The picture would have worked much better as a period piece.) The film is entirely too literal, its sentimental view of traditional family life unleavened by wit or style.

"Leave It to Beaver" instead is crass visually and its production design mediocre at best—the interiors of Beaver's home are surprisingly fussy and cluttered. For some reason, the stalwart Christopher McDonald as Beaver's unctuous but loving father Ward Cleaver looks more heavily made up and dyed than Janine Turner as his perfect '50s wife June, who wears pearls even when she vacuums. McDonald is an actor and comedian of admirable versatility and range, but the way he's made to appear distracts attention from an amusing and effective performance.

The youngsters fare better, though their characters are Hollywood precocious. Finley is pretty lovable, and Erik von Detten as his older brother Wally and Adam Zolotin as their obnoxious friend Eddie are capable. The original June Cleaver, Barbara Billingsley, cameos as the boys' great-aunt.

But unless you are a die-hard fan of the original series or are looking for a picture suitable for youngsters, you're better off leaving "Leave It to Beaver" alone.

NEW YORK POST, 8/22/97, p. 41, Thelma Adams

Why can't a TV show just be a TV show?

As much as I liked "Leave It to Beaver" as a kid, I gave it up with Lucky Charms and training wheels. There's nothing new about Andy Cadiff's desperate revival from a script by the pair that exhumed "The Flintstones," Brian Levant and Lon Diamond.

The return of the Cleavers is about as welcome as the evil spirits in "Poltergeist." More frozen than Dorian Gray, the Beaver, a.k.a. Theodore Cleaver (cutie Cameron Finley) is still adorably dopey and oppressed by fate.

Beaver's older brother, Wally (Erik von Detten), remains blessedly normal. Eddie Haskell (Adam Zolotin) is still brownnosing and Lumpy (Justin Restivo) stuffs his face. Ward and June Cleaver are the acid flashbacks of sitcom perfect parents.

As June, the housewife who has the audacity to vacuum in pearls and the peculiarity of baking challah bread in WASPville, Janine Turner seems to be suffering the "Northern Exposure" curse. Like Rob Morrow, a film career evades the talented actress.

Christopher McDonald is so cartoony as Ward that the filmmakers might as well have asked Disney to animate him. The return of TV cast members Barbara Billingsley and Ken Osmond has no impact on the plot; they are waxy time travelers and no more.

As for the plot, it, too, is frozen in time. Will Beaver get a bike for his birthday? Will he get his bike back once it's stolen? Will Wally get the girl? Will Ward blow his stack?

Even Eddie gets into the act. He doesn't just moon over Karen (Erika Christensen). He stalks her. Watching his dream girl drinking a soda, Eddie says, "Man, I wish I were that straw."

There's something to be said for adults sharing childhood memories with a new generation—but I thought that was why God invented Nick at Nite. The main trouble with Cadiff's inflated small-screen comedy is that there's no remote control to change channels. I'd rather flip to "Leave it to Beavis."

NEWSDAY, 8/22/97, Part II/p. B5, John Anderson

"From Beav to Beavis" could be, and probably is, the title of university classes in the study of Image and Adolescence in Multi-Media America: How TV Has Defined Childhood and Family From Eisenhower to Clinton and What It All Means to the Unsuspecting Viewer. An unavoidable part of such a course should be the back seat that movies have taken to television in assuming a pre-emptive role in molding youth—or at least our perceptions thereof.

By every indication, the near-mythic "Leave It to Beaver" practically defined America's view of itself, its kids and the way it was supposed to conduct its family life throughout the late '50s and early '60s. Dad, although subject to the occasional episode of bemusement, was sage and even-tempered; Mom stayed home, baked and never broke a sweat in her chiffon and pearls. Wally and Beaver were kids, of course, but by the end of each evening's moral crisis, they had learned something about life and the inherent evil of Eddie Haskell.

What we have in the new "Leave It to Beaver"—in which Ward Cleaver (Chris McDonald), June Cleaver (Janine Turner) and Wally and Beaver Cleaver (Erik von Detten and Cameron Finley) wrestle the psychic trauma of new bikes, pee-wee football and adolescent love—is the latest in Hollywood's compulsion to remake "classic" television shows.

This compulsion has resulted in, just to name a few, "The Brady Bunch," "The Beverly Hillbillies," "McHale's Navy" and "The Flintstones." These shows have often been remade for no particular reason at all. Well, not no reason, of course "George of the Jungle," for instance, has been one of the summer's top moneymakers. But the connection between the old show and the new movie is usually just a ripoff of the title and ultimately a desecration of the show's memory (if, in fact, the show was even worth one).

But "Beaver" is good-natured and goofy, with a la "Brady Bunch"—a nod to the passage of time and the changes therein. June still vacuums in pearls—and it turns Ward on. Eddie Haskell (Adam Zolotin) is still a smarmy wiseguy—but he's threatened with a restraining order for stalking the lovely Karen (Erika Christensen). Beaver tries to get out of playing football and disappointing his dad by doing badly enough in class to require extra help—but then the whole family has to appear before the school psychologist.

There are a couple of totally incongruous references to vulgarity (without the actual vulgarity) and one sex joke delivered, naturally, by Eddie. But overall, pretty mild, and pretty harmless.

Barbara Billinglsey, the original June, makes an appearance as the boys' Aunt Martha and Ken Osmond, the original Eddie, appears as Eddie Haskell Sr. As Beaver, 9-year-old Cameron Finley will never be Jerry Mathers, but he's not supposed to be. And "Leave It To Beaver," the movie, makes a narrow escape from ignominy by not *really* trying to be the original.

Also reviewed in:
CHICAGO TRIBUNE, 8/22/97, Friday/p. C, Michael Wilmington
NEW YORK TIMES, 8/22/97, p. C8, Lawrence Van Gelder
VARIETY, 8/18-24/97, p. 33, Joe Leydon
WASHINGTON POST, 8/22/97, Weekend/p. 37, Stephen Hunter

LEO TOLSTOY'S "ANNA KARENINA"

A Warner Bros. release of an Icon Production film. *Executive Producer:* Stephen McEveety. *Producer:* Bruce Davey. *Director:* Bernard Rose. *Screenplay:* Bernard Rose. *Based on the novel by:* Leo Tolstoy. *Director of Photography:* Daryn Okada. *Editor:* Victor Dubois. *Music:* John Stronach. *Music Editor:* Dean Beville. *Choreographer:* Maria Sudorenko. *Sound:* Peter Glossop. *Sound Editor:* Todd Toon. *Casting:* Marion Dougherty. *Production Designer:* John Myhre. *Art Director:* Sergei Shemyakin. *Set Decorator:* Marthe Pineau. *Special Effects:* Andy Williams. *Costumes:* Maurizio Millenotti. *Make-up:* Paul Le Blanc. *Stunt Coordinator:* Graeme Crowther. *Running time:* 120 minutes. *MPAA Rating:* PG-13.

CAST: Sophie Marceau (Anna Karenina); Sean Bean (Count Vronsky); Alfred Molina (Constantine Dmitrich Levin); Mia Kirshner (Princess Ekaterina "Kitty" Scherbatsky); James Fox (Alexei Alexandrovich Karenin); Fiona Shaw (Lydia Ivanova); Danny Huston (Prince "Stiva" Oblonsky); Phyllida Law (Countess Vronskaya); David Schofield (Nikolai); Saskia Wickham (Dolly); Jennifer Hall (Betsy); Anna Calder-Marshall (Princess Shcherbatsky); Valerie Braddell (Ambassador's Wife); Niall Buggy (Doctor); Anthony Calf (Serpuhovskoy); Vernon Dobtcheff (Pestov); Hamish Falconer (Seriozha); Stefan Gyff (Korunsky); Barbara Horne (Miss Edwards); Larissa Kousnetsova (Agatha); Jeremy Sheffield (Boris); Justine Waddell (Countess Nordston); Mikail Hmelev (Mahotin); Ksenia Rappoport (Maria); Peter Sholohov (Kapitonich); Julia Krasnova (Annushka); Ludmila Kurepova (Princess Sorokin); German Maximov (Priest); Tatiana Zaharova (Midwife); Sergei Scherbina (Korney); Gelena Ivleva (Lizaveta); Vadim Sadovnikov (Inn Priest); Sergei Parshin (Doctor's Doorman); Valery Kukhareshen (Specialist Doctor); Nora Griakalova (Myagkaya); Oleg Kosminsky (Titus); Victor Gurianov and Leonty Varenstov (Peasants); Igor Efimov (Servant); Konstantin Lukashov (Moscow Railway Worker); Alexandra Lavrova (Young Anna).

LOS ANGELES TIMES, 4/4/97, Calendar/p. 14, Kevin Thomas

"Leo Tolstoy's Anna Karenina" is not Tolstoy's classic novel of timeless passion but rather a traditional British period film at its most solemn and conventional. Not only does Bernard Rose's handsome, meticulous production lack that passion, but it also suffers from a miscast Anna, the married Russian aristocrat who risks everything for love in 1880 St. Petersburg. Alas, the film is almost as stodgy as Rose's take on Beethoven, "Immortal Beloved." Only die-hard romantics are likely not to come away disappointed.

French star Sophie Marceau can be a lovely and capable actress in the right circumstances, but she hasn't the radiant, transcendent beauty and doesn't project the noble soul necessary to bring to life one of literature's great heroines. But then Scarlett O'Hara herself, Vivien Leigh, in a 1948 version of "Anna," did not enjoy the acclaim Greta Garbo did, first in the 1927 silent "Love" (which was released in both sad and happy endings) and in the 1935 talkie remake, "Anna Karenina." The irony is that the 70-year-old "Love" seems a less dated take on Tolstoy than this sumptuous 1997 release.

Although the incredibly ornate, authentic period settings are most effective in conveying the oppressiveness of the lives of Russia's upper classes, we don't get much of a sense of the oppressiveness experienced by the *lower* classes that were exploited to support such luxury—a perspective that one might expect from a movie released in 1997.

This "Anna Karenina" is certainly beautiful to behold, and it does have its pluses in its other performances. Sean Bean is a dashing Count Vronsky who sweeps the unhappy Anna off her feet. James Fox is a splendid Karenin, a stern and proper but loving husband whose capacity for forgiveness is nipped in the bud by the lethally puritanical Lydia Ivanova, played by the always-riveting Fiona Shaw, who brings to the film a spark it otherwise too much lacks.

In counterpoint to the story's miserable triangle, Alfred Molina and Mia Kirshner represent a happy couple; Molina's Levin also serves as Tolstoy's alter ego, an aristocrat who learns to question the values and mores of his class.

Not all the classical music that "Leo Tolstoy's Anna Karenina" draws upon had actually been composed by the film's time period, 1880-1883, but its use of selections from Tchaikovsky, Rachmaninoff and Prokofiev is most effective.

NEW YORK POST, 4/4/97, p. 44, Michael Medved

The title character of Leo Tolstoy's immortal 1876 novel is a force of nature—a powerful, passionate woman whose irresistible vitality overwhelms those around her. To play Anna in the past, Hollywood has used Greta Garbo (twice), Vivian Leigh (less successfully) and Jacqueline Bisset (in a 1985 made-for-TV version).

Whatever their dramatic shortcomings, each of these stars presented a formidable screen presence, but the same cannot be said for pouty, petulant Sophie Marceau in the latest, most lavish "Anna Karenina" of them all.

With her wan, wounded-sparrow appearance and her nearly impenetrable French accent, Miss Marceau (who played the Princess of Wales in "Braveheart") grows into her role only when showing Anna's sad disintegration, leaving altogether unanswered the pressing question of why important men would ever have felt drawn to her in the first place.

Unfortunately, Marceau's disastrous presence in the central role spoils an otherwise noble, sumptuous and grandly ambitious adaptation of Tolstoy's sprawling text. Writer-director Bernard Rose (who previously shaped the similarly handsome—and misguided—Beethoven bio "Immortal Beloved") enjoyed unprecedented access to authentic locations in St. Petersburg and elsewhere in Russia, and the result is the most stunning recreation to date of the elegant world of the Czarist aristocracy.

Rose also audaciously attempts to capture Tolstoy's original dramatic structure, balancing Anna's famous story of doomed infidelity with the contrasting, little-known tale of spiritual seeker and devoted husband Koslya Levin who, in key elements, resembles Tolstoy himself. Thanks to Alfred Molina's heartfelt, engagingly vulnerable performance in that role, this difficult plot line merges with unexpected force.

Sean Bean ("Patriot Games") also does a solid job as Count Vronsky, the dashing but shallow officer who captures Anna's amorous attentions but ultimately feels trapped by his own "grand passion." James Fox is less convincing as her stodgy, aging husband who here seems unable to project the genuine adoration of Anna and their son that is such an important factor in the novel.

Filmmaker Rose appropriately but promiscuously pirated Beethoven's music for "Immortal Beloved" and here inserts distracting chunks of Tchaikovsky, Rachmaninoff and Prokofiev. The soundtrack most conspicuously features Tchaikovsky's "Pathetique" symphony, which may be particularly suitable for a film that presents its celebrated literary heroine as merely pathetic rather than as tragic or grand.

NEWSDAY, 4/4/97, Part II/p. B13, John Anderson

If you've always wished that Tolstoy had written nude love scenes, you can rest easy. "Anna Karenina," which possesses all the pomp and few of the circumstances of the original, has arrived, doing for Russian literature what Russia did for Chechnya.

Bernard Rose, the less-than-distinguished director of "Candyman" and "Immortal Beloved" (which basically did for Beethoven what Demi Moore did for Hawthorne), has created what is essentially an illustrated version of the novel, without the novel. The cinematography is breathtaking and the set design is ornate and fabulous, but when you start noticing set design there's something wrong with the picture.

"Anna Karenina" is one of the great, tragic love stories, but what the motivation was for the filmmakers is a mystery. Tolstoy was about spirituality, culture, the Russian soul. Here, however, there are characters without moorings, too many pretty scenes without purpose, too many profundities without context, and a love story that, lacking any connection with the kind of religious complexities found in the book, lies there like a damp dog.

The movie is officially titled "Leo Tolstoy's Anna Karenina," but let's give Count Leo a break. He needs one. Anna, one of the three great adulteresses of 19th-Century literature (the others being Hester Prynne and Emma Bovary) is played by France's Sophie Marceau, who follows Greta Garbo, Vivien Leigh and Jacqueline Bissett in the role, and continues the downward, trajectory. Marceau is beautiful—she recalls Isabelle Adjani in "The Story of Adele H."—but when she opens her mouth, literature trembles. Marcel Marceau would have been a better choice.

It's not just her fault, of course. Anna is supposed to be a woman of profound emotional complexity, whose ill-fated affair with Count Vronsky (the ill-used Sean Bean) is partly about her obsession with living and her inability to cope with life—this, and the suffocating restraints of 19th-Century Russian society. Accompanying her tragic symphony is the story of Levin (Alfred Molina), one of the great characters in literature (and Tolstoy's stand-in), whose parallel search for spiritual fulfillment provides a counterpart to Anna's downfall.

Rose includes both stories, but their connection is incomprehensible, and the love story itself—involving, as it does, such shallow characters—elicits little but a shrug when it all goes badly. Edward Fox delivers the warmest performance, as Anna's dispassionate husband, Karenin, who's never been a bad guy. But neither should he be the repository of all our sympathies.

Rose does take some liberties. I haven't read the novel for some time, but was Anna Karenina addicted to opium? I think he's gotten her confused with Emma Bovary and arsenic. But it may be appropriate: Given the option of seeing this film again, I'd take the arsenic.

SIGHT AND SOUND, 6/97, p. 45, Liese Spencer

Moscow, the 1880s. Returning to the city from his farm, the writer Levin meets Kitty, the sister of his old friend Stiva. Levin proposes to Kitty at a house party that evening, but she refuses. Levin argues with Kitty's preferred suitor Count Vronsky about spiritualism and then leaves in disgust. The following day Stiva goes to the station to pick up his married sister Anna who has arrived from St Petersburg. There he meets Vronsky, who's come to collect his mother. Vronsky is mesmerised by Anna. She is horrified when an engineer is crushed under the wheels of the train. At a ball that evening, Vronsky and Anna dance, enraptured, to Kitty's distress. The following evening, Anna takes a train back to St Petersburg. Vronsky follows her and declares his love. They begin an affair.

At his farm, Levin recovers from a broken heart by throwing himself into his work. Anna falls pregnant. She cannot disguise her feelings for Vronsky and some days later, she and Karenin have an angry confrontation; Anna admits to the affair. Levin proposes to Kitty again and they marry. Anna suffers a miscarriage. Vronsky tries to kill himself but cannot do it. Eventually, Vronsky and Anna leave for Italy, but they feel rootless there. Anna keenly misses her son, Seriozha, and they return to Moscow, but Karenin refuses Anna access to Seriozha. Kitty gives birth to a son. While Anna and Vronsky wait for Karenin to grant her a divorce, Anna is unable to go out in society. Trapped in the house while Vronsky socialises, she begins to take opium and suspects him of having an affair. In despair, Anna throws herself under a train and is killed. Some time later, Levin meets a devastated Vronsky on a train bound for the Slovenian war. Levin offers him words of spiritual support.

A man runs panting through moonlit snow, pursued by wolves. The camera cuts between his stumbling panic and the galloping carnivores. He falls, and finds himself hanging half way down a well as the animals prowl above. This picturesque nightmare which opens Bernard Rose's adaptation of *Anna Karenina* plunges us confidently into the picture. It's an exemplary start, echoing Tolstoy's own determination to grab his readers by the scruff of the neck with that arresting first sentence: "All happy families are alike but an unhappy family is unhappy after its own fashion".

The stuff of Grimm fairy tales, the scene is also redolent of the mythic Russia last seen in *Doctor Zhivago*, a resemblance borne out by the grandiose landscapes with which Rose, like Lean, chooses to frame his tragedy. Where the two diverge is in the obviousness of Rose's subsequent direction, which focuses on the psychology of the novel. No opportunity is missed to capitalise on the romance of Tolstoy's story: Anna's capitulation to Vronsky is communicated with a shot of ice thawing on the river; when she dies, a huge candle fills the screen and is snuffed out. Even the lacy signature intertitles look cheap. It's as if Tolstoy has been remade as Georgette Heyer.

Which isn't to say that there aren't many things to enjoy here. As the screenwriter, Rose's devotion to the text means Levin and Kitty's relationship is given the weight it needs to counterbalance that of Anna and Vronsky's doomed adultery. More important perhaps, Anna is no hostage to sentimental victimhood. Instead, sympathy is spread equally between Anna, Vronsky and Karenin to convey the ineluctable fate worked out in Tolstoy's omniscient narrative.

Many other scenes and exchanges have been translated directly from page to screen so that despite a bracing overall pace, allusions can still be made to the wider social issues that inform Tolstoy's portrait of Russian society. The book's interests in mysticism, hypocrisy and the importance of faith are all touched upon, as is its pragmatic take on marriage. Some of Rose's details may be hackneyed, but the casting and performances are generally good. With his stocky frame and soulful eyes Alfred Molina seems entirely right as Levin. Sophie Marceau is properly proud and sensual as Anna, while Sean Bean has the cruel good looks for Vronsky. James Fox embodies Karenin's progress from arid repression to stunted compassion perfectly.

In terms of production, the film's as rich as a box of Belgian chocolates. The beautiful costumes, well-photographed location shots, lavish red, black and gold interiors of the Russian palaces are all enchanting. There are also some fine set pieces, such as the ball scene which opens with an excited Kitty half running, half walking onto the dance floor to find Vronsky and ends with a breathless Anna reversing the path, escaping Vronsky through a series of gilded doorways which seem to stretch off to a dark vanishing point.

All that's missing, in fact, is psychological and emotional depth, a directorial interpretation that goes beyond the level of analysis in GCSE pass notes. But perhaps the subtlety of Tolstoy's writing will always arrive on screen as melodrama. *Anna Karenina* has been filmed at least four times in English already, including Selznick's Garbo vehicle and an unusual dud from the king of historical epics, Alexander Korda. Now Bernard Rose has added his banal version to the list. *Immortal Beloved*—Rose's bombastic stab at classicism which focused on Beethoven—should have told us what to expect.

VILLAGE VOICE, 4/15/97, p. 72, Leslie Camhi

Spurred perhaps by a lack of imagination and a thirst for authenticity, filmmakers these days are mining great 19th-century novels and the true grit of history for compelling stories. *Leo Tolstoy's Anna Karenina* belongs entirely to Bernard Rose, who condenses the 900-page epic into 110 highly digestible minutes by leaving out most of the novel's passion and philosophical complexity. Bruce Beresford's *Paradise Road*, based on the accounts of women who survived Japanese internment during World War II, is certainly inspirational, but its undeveloped plot and sketchy characters get lost along the way.

In *Anna Karenina*, the major scenes of Tolstoy's novel fly by faster than Cliff's Notes. The beautiful Anna Karenina, wife, mother, and Imperial Russian aristocrat, falls from social grace when she returns the unchecked adulterous ardor of a handsome and equally high-born cavalry officer, Count Vronsky. Meanwhile, the energetic Constantine Levin, who professes a deep disdain for urban society, overcomes several obstacles to marry the jilted Princess Kitty Shcherbatsky; together they find a measure of happiness in the country.

Rose's screen version is saved from inanity by the radiant Sophie Marceau, whose fervent yet selfish tenderness makes hers a compelling performance in a cast full of false notes. (Fiona Shaw, as Countess Lydia Ivanovna, is another exception.) As Vronsky Sean Bean looks appropriately virile in uniform; his initial declarations of devotion are wooden but his performance grows as love turns to regret. With his thick London accent, the likable Alfred Molina seems to have stepped directly from *Masterpiece Theatre* into a role beyond his means as the embodiment of Tolstoy's complex psychology.

Filmed almost entirely in the palaces of St. Petersberg and surrounding country villas, *Anna Karenina*'s sets are sublime, and its period score is equally stunning. A pity, then, that it lacks the novel's subtlety and passion, and its sense of the transformative power of time and emotion.

Also reviewed in:
NEW REPUBLIC, 5/5/97, p. 25, Stanley Kauffmann
NEW YORK TIMES, 4/4/97, p. C18, Stephen Holden
VARIETY, 4/7-13/97, p. 44, Todd McCarthy

LIAR LIAR

A Universal Pictures and Imagine Entertainment release. *Executive Producer:* James D. Brubaker and Michael Bostick. *Producer:* Brian Grazer. *Director:* Tom Shadyac. *Screenplay:* Paul Guay and Stephen Mazur. *Director of Photography:* Russell Boyd. *Editor:* Don Zimmerman. *Music:* John Debney. *Music Editor:* J.J. George. *Sound:* Jose Antonio Garcia and (music) Shawn Murphy. *Sound Editor:* Michael Hilkene. *Casting:* Junie Lowry-Johnson and Ron Surma. *Production Designer:* Linda DeScenna. *Art Director:* Richard A. Toyon. *Set Designer:* Thomas Betts and Colin de Rouin. *Set Decorator:* Ric McElvin. *Set Dresser:* Alan Easley. *Special Effects:* Burt Dalton. *Visual Effects:* Jon Farhat. *Costumes:* Judy L. Ruskin. *Make-up:* Nena Smarz. *Stunt Coordinator:* Mickey Gilbert. *Running time:* 86 minutes. *MPAA Rating:* PG-13.

CAST: Jim Carrey (Fletcher Reede); Maura Tierney (Audrey Reede); Justin Cooper (Max Reede); Cary Elwes (Jerry); Anne Haney (Greta); Jennifer Tilly (Samantha Cole); Amanda Donohoe (Miranda); Jason Bernard (Judge Marshall Stevens); Swoosie Kurtz (Dana Appleton); Mitchell Ryan (Mr. Allan); Chip Mayer (Kenneth Falk); Eric Pierpoint (Richard Cole); Randall "Tex" Cobb (Skull); Cheri Oteri (Jane); S. W. Fisher (Pete); Ben Lemon (Randy); Jarrad Paul (Zit Boy); Marianne Muellerleile (Ms. Berry); Krista Allen (Lady in Elevator); Stephen James Carver (Police Officer); Don Keefer (Beggar at Courthouse); Paul Roache (Beggar at Office); Randy Oglesby (Detective Bryson); Charlie Dell (Restroom Man); Jim Jansen (Pilot); Terry Rhoads (Co-Pilot); Michael Leopard (Tow Yard Employee); Charles Walker (Skycap); Ed Trotta (Mechanic); Ernest Perry, Jr. (Bailiff); Skip O'Brien (Court Guard); Tony Carreiro (Cop); Amanda Carlin (Publicist); Matthew Michael Goodall and Samantha Heyman (Cole Children); Anthony Lee (Fred); Eric Sharp (Sharpo the Clown); Christine Avila (Lupe); Hope Allen (Playground Teacher); Carrie Armstrong (Stenographer); Craig Barnett (Deputy); Brandi Burkett (Flight Attendant); Charles Emmett (Macho Attorney); Steven M. Gagnon, Moon Jones, and Rick Hill (Jail Guards); Mike Grief (Driver); Matthew Arkin (Colleague); Kelly Anne Conroy and Richard Jones (Passengers on Plane); Dennis Napolitano (Piano Player).

CHRISTIAN SCIENCE MONITOR, 4/15/97, p. 13, David Sterritt

[*Liar Liar* was reviewed jointly with *Paradise Road*; see Sterrit's review of that film.]

LOS ANGELES TIMES, 3/21/97, Calendar/p. 1, Kenneth Turan

Maybe Jim Carrey will never make a great film. Maybe he's fated to start in substandard vehicles that couldn't get to public access cable without his help. Maybe a lot of things, but the truth is, so what?

For as "Liar Liar" proves one more time, there is probably no more consistently funny performer working in film today. How much does it matter that this picture is an awkward mixture of Carrey's brilliant physical comedy and a sappy plot about, hold on to your seats, the importance of being a good dad? Not a lot, because Carrey could turn Dr. Spock's "Baby and Child Care" into a comic tornado.

Under the direction of Tom Shadyac, who's become adept at rehabbing comics by reminding they're supposed to be funny (Eddie Murphy's "The Nutty Professor" was his last outing).

Carrey seems fully recovered from the abyss of "The Cable Guy," willing and able to make people laugh.

His L.A. lawyer Fletcher Reede is a lot like Jerry Maguire before he saw the light, eager to say whatever it takes to get the job done and win cases. Intent on a partnership and with the slave-driving Miranda (Amanda Donohoe) as his boss, Fletcher never met a falsehood he wouldn't embrace.

Of course this kind of mendacity doesn't make for family happiness. Fletcher's long-suffering wife, Audrey (Maura Tierney), is now his ex-wife, happily involved with a milquetoast hospital administrator (Cary Elwes). And when son Max (Justin Cooper) is asked at school what his dad does for a living, the boy's sad response is: "He's a liar."

Though this may sound like the setup for a black comedy, that is one thing "Liar Liar" is not. Intent for some reason on giving the film heart, writers Paul Guay & Stephen Mazur have made sure to paint Fletcher as a great guy who really loves his son. He's just too self-absorbed to get his priorities straight, especially with a big new case coming up involving a sexy adulteress (Jennifer Tilly) and the wealthy husband she wants to soak.

Then one night, after Fletcher has told yet another fib to his woebegone boy, Max turns the tables. He makes a birthday wish that for just one day his dad couldn't tell a lie. And, because this is a movie after all, that wish comes immediately true and the real fun begins.

For Fletcher discovers soon enough what's happened to him and ends up in a series of boggling battles with his own body as he tries to force himself to tell his usual lies. A scene with a blue pen he'd very much like to label as red is especially funny but the truth is when Carrey gets rolling everything he touches both verbally and physically leads to laughter.

The king of body twists and rubbery contortions, with as much energy as James Brown in his "hardest working man in show business" phase, Carrey is equally adroit at turning his hand into a mock-monster called the Claw or disguising himself, improbable as it sounds, as a piece of luggage.

An impetuous imp capable of anything at all, Carrey also makes faces like no one alive and is in many ways the comic counterpart of horror legend Lon Chaney, the man who had a thousand of them. In one of "Liar Liar's" defter moments, when son Max worries if he'll suffer any ill effects from the boyish faces he likes to make, Fletcher reassures him with a calm, "In fact, some people make a good living that way."

For Carrey's co-stars, straight persons one and all, the hardest part of the job must be keeping from laughing. To emphasize that point, "Liar Liar" ends with a credit sequence punctuated by bloopers and outtakes from the production that are completely amusing.

For audiences, the hardest part of watching "Liar Liar" is marking time through the duller moments of exposition, wishing the film were as sharp overall as Carrey is himself. Still, as Bette Davis said to Paul Henreid at the close of the very different "Now, Vovager," "Don't ask for the moon. We have the stars."

NEW YORK, 4/7/97, p. 58, David Denby

What would happen to a lawyer who was unable to lie? In *Liar Liar*, Jim Carrey, whose body is a supple as Johnnie Cochran's mind, shows us exactly what would happen: Standing in court, with clients and judge in attendance, Carrey goes through the terrors of the damned. His lips tremble and flap like a roof in a tornado, he seems to be swallowing a sheep, his face collapses, he stutters out a few fragments and then claws the air like a cartoon figure trying to stuff the words back into his mouth. Everyone is looking for good lawyer jokes, and Paul Guay and Stephen Mazur, who wrote *Liar Liar,* seem to have found one: A lawyer physically incapable of lying would not be able to say a word. He would have to swallow his tongue, lacerate his brain.

Liar Liar, directed by Tom Shadyac (responsible for the *Ace Ventura* series and Eddie Murphy's *The Nutty Professor*), shoves this brilliant conceit into the middle of a sentimental family comedy. Carrey, a Los Angeles legal hotshot, manipulative and dishonest, has broken up with his wife (Maura Tierney). His little boy (Justin Cooper), lonely for Dad, and often betrayed, makes a wish on his 5th birthday—that Dad be unable to tell a lie for 24 hours. The movie works toward reconciliation: Dad will honestly admit he loves his little boy. Unfortunately, Jim Carrey as a loving dad is more frightening than Jim Carrey as an absent father. He's so demonically demonstrative with young Cooper, he nearly eats the kid alive, and Maura Tierney, as his wife, has to hold on for dear life just to establish herself on the screen. Someone has to get Jim Carrey to take it down a level or two. In virtually every scene, he loses his balance and hits the deck, waving his arms so violently that he's like a windmill trying to fly.

If the realistic frame of the movie had been quieter, then the wild central section would have been set off more, and *Liar Liar* might have been a classic fable. The lawyer, truth-bound, tells off everyone in his office and comments on bad breath and weird hairdos. Every time he speaks some excoriating truth, he's excruciatingly guilty, yet the mad impulse to blurt it out makes him crazily happy too. In its frantic way, the movie acknowledges that our ordinary social world is held together by little more than genteel evasions. If we were forced to tell the truth, civilization would come tumbling down.

NEW YORK POST, 3/21/97, p. 41, Michael Medved

Jim Carrey as a passionate advocate of family values? Don't laugh—or, rather do, since "Liar, Liar" is not only surprisingly touching but also outrageously funny.

If its hyperactive star occasionally lurches over the top with his rubber-faced, sadistic slapstick excesses, the movie still represents his most coherent and human performance to date.

Carrey plays a slick L.A. trial lawyer whose successful career depends on utter disregard for the truth. His lies prove particularly frustrating to his long-suffering ex-wife (the intensely likable Maura Tierney of TVs "News Radio") and their adorable 5-year-old son (newcomer Justin Cooper).

The boy still adores his preternaturally playful Papa, despite innumerable broken promises, but then Carrey misses the child's birthday party because he's engaged in steamy sex with a ruthless, predatory partner in his firm (Amanda Donohoe).

As he tearfully blows out the candles on his birthday cake, the stricken child makes a solemn wish that his father should be compelled to tell nothing but the truth for an entire 24 hours.

That wish comes true immediately—forcing Carrey, back at his office, into a destructively candid (and hilarious) comment about the quality of the coupling he's just completed with Donohoe.

The movie sets up elaborate shtick as Carrey tries to force his own mouth to return to his comfortable, customary lies, but true words come out against his will, leading to one embarrassing confrontation after another.

The script (by Paul Guay and Stephen Mazur, who previously wrote the disappointing recent remake of "Little Rascals") offers witty insights about daily equivocations and distortions we can all recognize.

The material is broader and less amusing when Carrey enters a courtroom, attempting to represent a selfish, faithless bimbo (Jennifer Tilly) in a vicious divorce case.

Director Tom Shadyac previously worked with Carrey on "Ace Ventura: Pet Detective" and with Eddie Murphy in "The Nutty Professor." In both cases, he turned his stars loose in formless, wildly uneven, one-man comic showcases. This time, however, Shadyac shapes a film with direction, structure and a first-rate supporting cast (including Anne Haney as Carrey's shrewd secretary).

The underlying message ("just spend more time with your precious kids") may be reassuringly simplistic, but the star does develop charming, convincing chemistry with the winning kid who plays his son, and their interaction features the movie's single best laugh.

To test whether his Dad must really tell the truth, the boy makes the kind of ridiculously distorted face that parents routinely discourage.

"Is that really gonna hurt me later on?" he asks.

"No!" Carrey promptly and honestly declares. "Some people make a good living that way."

NEWSDAY, 3/21/97, Part II/p. B2, Jack Mathews

"Do you know how to tell when a lawyer is lying? His lips move."

Thus goes one of the simpler and more cutting entries on the miles-long list of lawyer jokes. It is also the uncredited premise of the new Jim Carrey film, "Liar Liar," one of the funniest assaults ever launched on the subject.

Let's call this a low high-concept picture, with the hyper-animated Carrey playing a slick, fast-rising and spectacularly untruthful attorney who, because of his heartsick son's wish for his fifth birthday, cannot push a lie past his lips for 24 hours. One day, he's shucking everyone from his secretary to his clients to a jury, and failing to keep promises to his son (Justin Cooper). The next day, lies get stuck in his throat like fish hooks and blunt truths leap out like salmon.

"Was it good for you?," asks Fletcher's predatory boss (Amanda Donohoe), as they lie in bed at the very moment his son's across-town wish goes into effect.

"I've had better," he blurts out.

In the morning, he's trying to run away from his own mouth, leaving behind a trail of cruel truths about his colleagues' looks, complexions and weight. When one of his regular mob clients calls for legal advice, he screams into the phone, "Stop breaking the law!" His loyal secretary (Anne Haney) packs and leaves after she asks—and he truthfully answers—why she didn't get that promised raise. And in court, where he's representing a promiscuous wife (Jennifer Tilly) in a high-stakes divorce case, he leaves his client defenseless.

"Liar Liar" is a star vehicle in the best sense of the phrase. There is scarcely more than an idea in Paul Guay and Stephen Mazur's script, yet Carrey—vamping madly in one scene after another—takes it all the way. The comic seizures he puts himself through, trying to force lies out of Fletcher and hold back truths, aren't just outrageously funny, they seem to expand the bounds of human movement.

As in all of his movies, Carrey often goes too far, or sticks with a physical joke too long. There's an entire sequence with Fletcher beating himself up in a bathroom that isn't worth the enormous physical energy he expends on it. But there are few lulls or miscues in what, overall, may be Carrey's best performance.

Fletcher Reede is a cartoon character with real heart. He loves his son and his ex-wife, and is merely caught up in ambition and in a career that seems to value deception and dissembling. Imagine how quickly the Simpson case would have ended if a truth wish had descended over the Dream Team.

Carrey, through all his flamboyant gestures and craziness, makes us believe in Fletcher's rediscovery of himself, and the sentimentality in his later scenes with his son Max and ex-wife Audrey (Maura Tierney) are more emotionally involving than you'd ever expect from this kind of silliness.

Tom Shadyac, the former stand-up comedian who directed Carrey's first "Ace Ventura" movie and the Eddie Murphy hit "The Nutty Professor," has a real gift for exploiting the strengths of his stars. All three of Shadyac's films play off comic set-ups—strings of sketches that put different spins on the same theme while relying on the actors' inventiveness to make each one unique.

Carrey is the current master of this brand of comedy, and in "Liar Liar," he's at the top of his game.

NEWSWEEK, 3/24/97, p. 82, Jeff Giles

For better and worse, Tom Shadyac's *Liar Liar* is the most conventional movie Jim Carrey has ever made: "The Cable Guy" weirded people right out of theaters, so now he's making nice. Sort of. Carrey plays a dirt-bag lawyer named Fletcher Reede. Reede's young son (Justin Cooper) is so sick of being fibbed to that he makes a birthday wish that magically comes true: Dad can't lie for an entire day. Fletcher's trying to win a bogus case and sleep his way up the corporate ladder. What's a lawyer to do?

"Liar" has a clunky first act, and two actresses get handed the same stereotype: Amanda Donohoe plays Boss Slut, and Jennifer Tilly plays Client Slut. (Fletcher's ex, not a slut, is played warmly by Maura Tierney.) But once Fletcher starts telling the truth against his will, the movie delivers some perfect laughs. Fletcher maniacally abuses his firm's partners and literally beats himself up in a john. For 30 minutes, this is the best volcano movie of the year.

But Carrey, a true subversive, shouldn't be wasting his time rattling the bars of ordinary, Michael Keaton-y scripts like this one. When Fletcher inevitably becomes caring and chants "I love my son," you cringe. Would Ace Ventura deliver lines like these? Sure—from his famous talking backside.

SIGHT AND SOUND, 5/97, p. 47, Leslie Felperin

Successful, smooth-talking, Los Angeles-based defence attorney Fletcher Reede perpetually lets down his five-year-old son Max by failing to show up for visits and lying about it. Fletcher's ex-wife Audrey is disgusted, and is considering moving back east with her dull but nice boyfriend Jerry. On the phone, Fletcher lies to Max about his reason for not making Max's birthday party (he's actually having sex with his boss, Miranda). As he blows out the candles on his birthday cake, Max makes a wish that Fletcher won't be able to lie for exactly one day.

The wish is granted. Fletcher cannot lie to Miranda when she asks how was the sex for him (he says he's had better); he can't make up reasons not to take calls he's been avoiding, and he can only tell colleagues the truth about what he thinks of them. Finding out how his situation came about from Max, Fletcher goes on with his day. In court, he has to defend an unfaithful wife, Samantha Cole, who is suing for half her husband's estate. Fletcher wins the case by finding a legal loophole. Realising that his victory means nothing without his family, he rushes to the airport to stop Audrey and Max from leaving with Jerry. While endeavouring to catch the pilot's attention, Max breaks both his legs. In the hospital, Audrey and Max have stayed behind, and Audrey seems ready to make another go of their marriage.

After its schmaltzy moment of closure in which a nice nuclear family is finally reconciled, the credits for the amiable film *Liar Liar* roll against a background of out-takes from the film we've just seen. This time, we see Jim Carrey fluffing his lines and ad-libbing wackily to peals of jollity from the technicians offscreen. Co-stars 'corpse' or crack-up with mirth. Swoosie Kurtz, who has just been playing a humourless Marcia Clark-like prosecutor substitutes the word 'over-acting' for another word in the speech she said earlier and Carrey explodes with laughter at the wit of her gentle jibe. It's a common device now, but by including these out-takes a minor rule of representational etiquette is breached. It's hardly Godardian, but it is a faintly disturbing kind of primal scene, to see an actor stop playing a role and become himself in midstride. Here, it's bogus because obviously the actors and Carrey in particular are still performing in a way. And there is something terribly ineffective in this case precisely because there's been so little difference established between Fletcher and Carrey himself, despite the public relations hype that this film is meant to be a further stretch of Carrey's acting abilities. At least when *Being There* (1979) made the credit out-take sequence its own, the pleasure lay in recognising the feat of mimicry and seeing the palpable difference between Peter Sellers playing idiot savant Chance the gardener and being his real jaded, old self.

It's ironic because *Liar Liar* is centrally concerned with dissembling. The neat conceit at its heart is that Carrey's glib prevaricating lawyer is forced to tell the truth for one whole day because his son wished earnestly for it while blowing out his birthday candles. Like *Groundhog Day* and *Multiplicity, Liar Liar* could be filed under 'magical surrealism', a micro-genre in which supernatural, absurdist (but ultimately humanising conditions) are visited upon ordinary, typically arrogant men. The idea is funny enough and chimes sufficiently with modern (and especially American) contempt for lawyers to carry the film through its sloppy patches. When the son Max realises he's got his dad over a barrel, his quizzes him about all the lies grownups feed kids, such as whether he really will go blind from watching too much television and whether if he crosses his eyes they'll get stuck that way for ever (Fletcher has to confess to this last query that no, they won't, and even if they did some people make a good living out of it).

Still, the film falls a little flat overall for the good, old-fashioned reason that you don't buy Carrey's lawyer act in the first place. His jerky, extraordinarily physical style of comedy is too hyperbolic, throwing any sense of realism off kilter from the start. Seeing him in a typical stance such as that featured on the film poster, with his arms outstretched in a menacing offer of embrace and his teeth bared like a Halloween skeleton, you instinctively know you wouldn't buy a used car from this man, let alone permit him to represent you in a court of law. He's too desperate and excessive in his energy, both before and after being visited by catastrophe. Carrey is clearly trying to prove himself as an actor, which is understandable after the relative poor showing of his first 'serious' film *The Cable Guy* (which now has many quiet defenders), but he can't seem to stop being maniacally insincere and director Tom Shadyac (who launched Carrey in *Ace Ventura Pet Detective)* can't seem to keep him under control either. Fans of Carrey are left wishing he'd find a way to make his *schtick* fresh.

TIME, 3/24/97, p. 88, Richard Schickel

Fletcher Reede is a divorced dad, hardworking and ambitious, trying to make partner at a law firm. His adorable son Max (Justin Cooper) is constantly disappointed by his father's failures to keep their dates for ball games and birthday parties, and weary of his lame excuses for going AWOL. Puffing out the candles on his fifth-birthday cake, Fletcher's telephonic explanations for blowing off the event still ringing in his ears, the kid wishes that his father could be forced to tell the truth for 24 hours.

Magically, Max's dream comes true. The premise of *Liar Liar* is that all the false promises and compliments that ease our paths through the day, all the little evasions that oil the wheels of social and professional, as well as sexual, intercourse are suddenly unavailable to Fletcher. And remember, he's a lawyer.

Carrey is, of course, less an actor than a nuclear reactor. His answer to even innocent questions is a lightning fugue of hugely exaggerated facial ticks, bodily contortions and subverbal bleatings. His genius is for orchestrating these infantile responses in ways that are unduplicative, unduplicatable and explosively subversive. Since the curse Max lays on Fletcher makes him his own worst enemy, Carrey is led into long, hilarious wrestling matches with himself.

As directed by Tom Shadyac, there's enough surrealism in *Liar Liar* to content all but the most exigent Carrey fans. But there's something worrisome about the film's attempts to socialize and sentimentalize the '90s' designated anarchist. It's wrong to push characters like Carrey's toward mainstream lovability. Danger, with just the slightest touch of lonely-guy geekiness, is his business. Maybe *The Cable Guy* was miscalculated, but one would rather see Carrey heading for those dark woods than toward sun-splashed suburbia and the cheerfully romantic ending of this film.

VILLAGE VOICE, 4/1/97, p. 63, J. Hoberman

Jim Carrey's vehicle *The Cable Guy* may have been among the most ambitious and interesting commercial movies of the past few years, but it only grossed $60 million (while offending the sensibilities of *The New York Times*'s chief critic). Now, Carrey is doing penance.

"I had parents come up to me and say that their lad was crying when they left [*The Cable Guy*]," the star told *Premiere*. Carrey goes on to criticize that response, as well as the "Stepford mentality that life has to be completely happy all the time" (see, for example, *Volga Volga*), but *Liar Liar* is clearly designed to be parent-friendly. The story of a workaholic attorney too sleazy for *L.A. Law* who learns to make time for his five-year-old son (a whey-faced lump of curdled adorability) is replete with Stepford tendencies—heart-warming music, anxious reaction shots to flag the jokes, and creepily excessive romantic protestations of undying paternal love. Indeed, the spectacle of Carrey as fun-guy dad is as unsettling in its way as that of Arnold Schwarzenegger doing day care in his similarly calculated *Kindergarten Cop*.

Although *Liar Liar* is rated PG-13, the premise is predicated on a five-year-old's birthday wish. Jilted once more, a little boy wishes that his father be compelled to tell the truth—if only for a single day. Carrey's compulsive honesty is thus a form of Tourette's syndrome, a condition that the actor experiences as maximally visceral. *Liar Liar*'s middle 40 minutes offers some of the most adroit physical comedy since Steve Martin merged with his feminine side in *All of Me*. Most of Carrey's contortions defy description. To avoid blurting out any more unpleasant truths, he plants his fingers in his ears and prances screaming through the office. There's also a reverse Tourette's: because this shyster can no longer lie, he's reduced to speaking in tongues (with faces to match) when asked to articulate his strategy in a tawdry divorce case.

With lawyer Carrey objecting to his own courtroom questions, the trial scene is a minor classic. In desperation, the star mugs himself in the bathroom. (This scene, as my daughter immediately noted, is a self-reflexive riff on the most distasteful bit in *The Cable Guy*—complete with attempted toilet-seat concussion.) An actor who can transform a shit-eating grin into a three-minute exercise in three-dimensional Picasso-ism, Carrey is nothing if not self-aware. In the midst of the sequence, he pauses to assure a bemused spectator that "I'm just kicking my ass." A few more times, Jim, and you'll be ready for your Oscar.

Also reviewed in:
NEW REPUBLIC, 4/28/97, p. 30, Stanley Kauffmann
NEW YORK TIMES, 3/21/97, p. C3, Janet Maslin
NEW YORKER, 3/31/97, p. 107, Anthony Lane
WASHINGTON POST, 3/21/97, p. B1, Rita Kempley
WASHINGTON POST, 3/21/97, Weekend/p. 48, Desson Howe

LICENSED TO KILL

A Deep Focus Productions release.   *Producer:* Arthur Dong.   *Director:* Arthur Dong.
Screenplay: Arthur Dong.   *Director of Photography:* Robert Shepard.   *Editor:* Arthur Dong.
Music: Miriam Cutler.   *Running time:* 80 minutes.   *MPAA Rating:* Not Rated.

LOS ANGELES TIMES, 4/18/97, Calendar/p. 8, Kenneth Turan

What is most surprising—and most provocative—about "Licensed to Kill," Arthur Dong's strong and disturbing documentary on men who kill homosexuals, is the way it overturns our expectations. Nothing you've heard about the plague of violence against gay men will lessen the shock value of this chilling look at the real face of evil.

Winner of the Filmmaker's Trophy at Sundance, "Licensed to Kill" is written, directed, produced and edited by Dong ("Coming Out Under Fire"), a gay man who counts personal experience as the impetus behind this work.

In 1977, Dong explains in a brief voice-over prologue, he was attacked by four gay-bashing teenagers in San Francisco and escaped only by throwing himself on the hood of a passing car. Still attempting years later to understand the roots of this violent behavior, he decided to do "the most difficult thing" and confront men "whose contempt for homosexuals led them to kill people like me."

"Confront" may not be the right word because one of "Licensed to Kill's" strength is the coolness of its technique, the almost clinical matter-of-factness of its presentation. Dong never appears on camera and wisely allows the half dozen convicted murderers he interviews to tell their own stories unimpeded by any kind of hectoring or editorializing.

That does not mean that "Licensed to Kill" is no more than a collection of talking heads. Intercut with Dong's six prison interviews are various kinds of relevant material, including TV news reports and unsettling police evidence tapes and photos of the murders his interviewees committed.

Equally disturbing are the selections from homophobic statements by prominent fundamentalist leaders, psychotic phone messages of the "Save America/Kill a Fag" variety, a home video of a gay man being viciously beaten up by a neighbor and a police interrogation tape in which a young man calmly describes how he came to stab a gay man 27 times.

But though this material is all relevant and to the point, "Licensed to Kill" is that rare documentary that would fascinate and horrify even if it were nothing but talking heads. Because while Hollywood's movies have acclimated us to clichéd bigots, cardboard monsters like James Woods in "Ghosts of Mississippi" or the white racists in "Rosewood," it's a shock to see how various, how unexpectedly well-spoken, how deeply troubled and haphazard the evil that walks our streets can be.

Who would expect to encounter someone like Jay Johnson, an articulate, initially closeted gay man who was raised in a religious, violently anti-homosexual household? Feeling loathing toward all things gay, even "to the extent that I was doing it, I was disgusted with myself," Johnson was more horrified to discover that his mixed race was a handicap to cruising that made him "unsuccessful at something I already hated." A series of slayings attempting to frighten gay men off the streets of Minneapolis is what followed.

For some of the prisoners, the murders they committed were almost an afterthought or a whim, the casual byproduct of robberies of gay men who were the classic easy targets. Faced with the choice of a 7-Eleven and its video camera or victims who "because of the fact that they're a homosexual and they don't want people to know it, they're not gonna go report it to the police," says Donald Aldrich, "who you gonna go rob?"

The most disconnected story belongs to Kenneth Jr. French, a career Army man who killed four people at random in a North Carolina restaurant to protest President Clinton's relaxing of the ban on gays in the military. And one of the sadder histories is that of William Cross. Raped by a friend of the family when he was 7, he "never felt the same afterward, never felt like I was even a man anymore." The irrational but deadly result was anti-homosexual rage.

What many of these men have in common, Dong's film suggests, is the way society's attitudes in general, and the hostility of fundamentalist religion in particular, gave them an almost literal license to kill, a feeling that slaying gay men meant, as Jeffrey Swinford puts it, "just one less problem the world had to mess with." "Religion," muses Jay Johnson, "is a vicious thing."

To look these people in the face, to hear their horrific but always recognizably human stories, is much more affecting and unsettling than printed summations can indicate. To hear an unrepentant Aldrich coolly comment on the new Texas hate crimes statutes his murder resulted in by saying, "maybe something good will come of this after all," is to be confronted with the human condition in all its awful complexity.

NEW YORK POST, 4/2/97, p. 38, Larry Worth

Delving into a murderer's mindset isn't exactly a new concept for moviemakers. But rarely has it been examined with the bone-chilling effects of "Licensed to Kill."

Writer/director Arthur Dong, who lensed 1994's Oscar-nominated documentary "Coming Out Under Fire," gets up close and personal with seven killers, each of whom took at least one life in the name of gay-bashing.

Dong's camera travels into the prisoners' jail cells, lettting them justify—or not—their "license to kill" homosexuals. Some have regrets, more don't.

Predictably, the reasons for the savage acts vary—ranging from one Bible-thumper who quotes "that men who lie with men should be put to death" to a confused victim of child molestation to a "patriot" upset by President Clinton's efforts to allow gays to serve in the military.

Without exception, their words speak volumes about the nature of hate crimes. But Dong makes each tale more vivid by integrating high school yearbook shots of the future killers as well as graphic photos of victim.

Manipulative? Maybe, but it's hard to dismiss the likes of "K-I-L-L" written in one victim's blood over his corpse.

VILLAGE VOICE, 4/8/97, p. 85, Elliott Stein

We've seen a slew of documentaries and features on homophobia and gay-bashing made from the victim's point of view. Arthur Dong's chillingly informative Licensed To Kill switches the focus, profiling seven convicted killers of gays. Obsessed with the subject of homophobic violence ever since he was attacked by a gang of teenagers in San Francisco, the filmmaker felt he needed to understand these acts and decided to meet the men whose contempt for gays led them to kill people like him.

His investigation intercuts the murderers' tales with courtroom testimonies and graphic clips of forensic evidence from police files. The release of this harrowing doc could not be more timely—a just-published report by the New York City Gay and Lesbian Anti-Violence Project informs that while there has been an overall drop in crime, last year saw a 6 per cent increase in incidents of violence against lesbians and gays.

Dong's interviews took place in prisons all over the country and involved a wide range of people: an army sergeant, stationed in North Carolina, enraged over the issue of gays in the military; a Chicagoan, alleged victim of child abuse, whose defense had been "homosexual panic"; a man from Arkansas who had read in an encyclopedia that the Bible urged the execution of gays; a gay man in Minneapolis who had been raised in a strict religious household and who seems to have killed because of his own troubled sexual orientation.

It's clear that Dong somehow gained the complete confidence of his gallery of murderers. Their hair-raising confessions and self-justifying rhetoric come pouring out as rambling but often wrenching soliloquies. Corey Burley, a Texan, who killed an immigrant from Vietnam, declares, "It was a going thing to beat up homosexuals. We had it embedded in our heads that they're weak and wouldn't put up a fight. It wasn't me, it was the bullet I fired that killed him." He can't even recall the name of his victim.

Sergeant Kenneth French feels that our military, is going down the drain. The proof? Why, you can't even hang a Confederate flag up in the barracks anymore. "I just needed to voice my opinion about Clinton letting gays in the army." He voiced it by creating four corpses in a restaurant.

William Cross, the killer from Chicago, is soft-spoken, hunk handsome with a cute cleft chin—matinee-idol material. Anyone, gay, or straight, might unwarily let him in the door. You might bolt it at the sight of shifty-eyed Jeffrey Swinford, the encyclopedia reader. "Life's just one big opinion. My opinion of homosexuals is that they should all be taken care of," he explains.

Dong's own opinions are unvoiced. He doesn't editorialize. But you don't have to spend years cooped up with Freud to come to the conclusion that most of these guys are, on some level, closet cases. On the whole, they're unrepentant and remarkably affectless. The most devastating remark comes from Swinford, who notes that if he hadn't been arrested for the murder he committed he probably would have forgotten all about it.

Also reviewed in:
NATION, 4/28/97, p. 35, Stuart Klawans
NEW YORK TIMES, 4/3/97, p. C16, Janet Maslin
VARIETY, 2/10-16/97, p. 67, Emanuel Levy

LIFE APART, A: HASIDISM IN AMERICA

A First Run Features release of an Oren Rudavsky production. *Executive Producer:* Arnold Labaton. *Producer:* Menachem Daum. *Director:* Oren Rudavsky. *Screenplay:* Menachem Daum and Robert Seidman. *Director of Photography:* Oren Rudavsky. *Editor:* Ruth Schell. *Music:* Yale Storm. *Sound:* Gautam Ghoudbury, William Sarokin, and Matthew Sigal. *Running time:* 96 minutes. *MPAA Rating:* Not Rated.

NARRATORS: Leonard Nimoy; Sarah Jessica Parker

NEW YORK POST, 7/25/97, p. 51, Michael Medved

Have you ever wondered about some bearded, black-suited, otherwordly figure encountered on the street or the subway?

In a series of beautifully shot, startlingly intimate interviews, the stunning documentary "A Life Apart: Hasidism in America" presents a series of Hasidic families and individuals, definitely demystifying a segment of Orthodox Judaism that previously appeared impenetrable to outsiders.

With insightful narration read by Leonard Nimoy and Sarah Jessica Parker, the film goes back to the origins of Hasidism as an emotional, 18th-century protest against the scholarly rationalism of the reigning Jewish establishment. It focuses special attention on the handful of charismatic leaders who, after the devastation of the Holocaust, achieved the near-miraculous reconstitution of Eastern European Hasidic dynasties in New York.

Even the most skeptical viewers will be moved by visions of joyously improbable mass gatherings of Hasidim, including the lighting (in a snowstorm!) of a huge menorah at the onetime center of anti-Semitic atheism in Moscow's Red Square, or the aged, ecstatic Bobover Rebbe dancing at the Brooklyn wedding of his great-granddaughter.

"A Life Apart" is however, more than a sentimental celebration of Hasidic survival, since it includes many comments from critics of this strain in Judaism.

As might be expected from a 96-minute treatment of a vast subject, the movie also features some glaring omissions, with little hint of the mesianic claims of many followers of the late Lubavitcher Rebbe, and no mention that the Lithuanian *misnagdim* (Orthodox opponents of Hasidism) similarly rebuilt their own flourishing communities and rabbinic seminaries in America.

After viewing this important documentary, secular Americans might well ask if their own sacrifices (for the sake, of money, adventure, unpredictability, or fun) could be similarly justified.

VILLAGE VOICE, 7/29/97, p. 78, J. Hoberman

Whether or not, as *New York* magazine predicts, the Hasidim turn out to be the last unassimilated Jews in America, they are the last Jews whose children grow up speaking Yiddish. Thus, this highly sympathetic, quasi-inside documentary (a hit at the last New York Jewish Film Festival), feels pleasingly old-timey despite the fact that much secular Yiddish culture was either a rebellion against or an aestheticizing of Hasidic ways.

A poor person's religion, antirational and steeped in the notion that (almost) everything is holy, Hasidism is relatively recent—a product of an 18th-century split between heart and head in East European Judaism. The Hasidim enjoy a devout relationship with their charismatic rebbes but a complicated one with other Jews—not to mention, as *A Life Apart* hints, other others. Although the filmmakers suggest there's a sense in which Hasidim don't truly live in America, they're still American enough to understand their traditions as a "lifestyle" decision. Ultimately, that's the level in which *A Life Apart* presents them. No Satmar bad boys here, the portrait of community is sufficiently idealized to inspire a *bisl* envy.

Also reviewed in:
CHICAGO TRIBUNE, 1/17/98, Friday/p. M, John Petrakis
NEW YORK TIMES, 7/25/97, p. C3, Janet Maslin
VARIETY, 8/4-10/97, p. 36, Dennis Harvey

LIFE LESS ORDINARY, A

A Twentieth Century Fox release of a Figment film. *Producer:* Andrew MacDonald. *Director:* Danny Boyle. *Screenplay:* John Hodge. *Director of Photography:* Brian Tufano. *Editor:* Masahiro Hirakubo. *Music:* Randall Poster. *Choreographer:* Adam Shankman. *Sound:* Douglas Cameron. *Sound Editor:* Andy Kennedy. *Casting:* Donna Isaacson. *Production Designer:* Kave Quinn. *Art Director:* Tracey Lang Gallacher. *Set Designer:* Linden Snyder. *Set Decorator:* Marcia Calosio. *Set Dresser:* Kevin Milburn and John Reneau. *Special Effects:* Bob Shelley. *Costumes:* Rachel Fleming. *Make-up:* Katherine James. *Make-up (Special Effects):* Douglas White Effects. *Animation Director:* Mike Mort. *Stunt Coordinator:* Jeff Jensen. *Running time:* 103 minutes. *MPAA Rating:* R.

CAST: Holly Hunter (O'Reilly); Delroy Lindo (Jackson); Dan Hedaya (Gabriel); Cameron Diaz (Celine); Ian McNeice (Mayhew); Ewan McGregor (Robert); Frank Kanig (Ted); Mel Winkler (Frank); Anne Cullimore Decker (Ms. Gesteten); Stanley Tucci (Elliot); K.K. Dodds (Lily); Tony Shalhoub (Al); Ian Holm (Naville); Christopher Gorham (Walt); Maury Chaykin (Tod); Timothy Olyphant (Hiker); Robert Kellogg (Karaoke Cowboy); David Stifel (Felix); Duane Stephens (Attendant); Jayceen Craven (Cashier); Crystal Martinez (Bank Teller); Jan Hanks (Customer); Mary-Cristina Schaub (Bank Daughter); Kitty Brunson (Bank Teller); Chuck Gowdy (Client); Judith Ivey (Celine's Mom); Toni Lynn Byrd (Secretary).

LOS ANGELES TIMES, 10/24/97, Calendar/p. 1, Kenneth Turan

Be careful what you wish for, you might get it. And it might turn out to be "A Life Less Ordinary."

The latest effort from the crew that made "Trainspotting" so exciting—writer John Hodge, director Danny Boyle, producer Andrew MacDonald and star Ewan McGregor—"A Life Less Ordinary" sounds like everything audiences weary of business-as-usual major studio romances would be happy to embrace.

After all, this film has charismatic stars and a non-cookie-cutter script whose fondness for the unexpected means it didn't go anywhere near development hell. But the result is no more than a forced fable, a self-consciously smarty-pants concoction that is too clever by half—and too pleased with itself in the bargain.

That's even more of a shame because the chemistry between McGregor and co-star Cameron Diaz is especially powerful and periodically threatens to rescue the movie all by itself. It can't, but even so, Diaz's gift for romantic comedy, coming after her success in "My Best Friend's Wedding," should place her in the "next Julia Roberts-new Sandra Bullock" slot Hollywood is always eager to fill.

Producer MacDonald is the grandson of Emeric Pressburger, the longtime partner of British director Michael Powell, and, like that pair's David Niven-starring "A Stairway to Heaven"/"A Matter of Life and Death," "A Life Less Ordinary" revolves around heaven's influence on earthly romance.

The film opens in a bleached-out, whiter-than-white hereafter where Gabriel (Dan Hedaya) functions as a chief of police. He tells two of his veteran detective-angels, O'Reilly (Holly Hunter) and Jackson (Delroy Lindo), that the deity is peeved at how dysfunctional modern relationships have proved to be, how few couples manage to stay "bonded in eternal harmony." Their assignment is to bring two people together and, as an extra incentive, if they don't succeed they won't be allowed back through the gates of eternity.

It's an especially tough assignment that O'Reilly and Jackson are given. The man and woman they have to manipulate into failing in love are so disparate in every way (except, as the casting ensures, in star quality) that in the ordinary course of events they would never even meet.

Celine (Diaz) is the classic bored little rich girl with a life that's like an upscale perfume ad. She takes time off from swimming in a pool big enough to float the Titanic only to shoot apples off the head of the trusty butler employed by her tycoon father, Naville (Ian Holm).

Robert (McGregor), on the other hand, is one of Naville's lowliest employees, a janitor *manqué* so inconsequential he can be replaced by a robot. As an unambitious, naive, would-be trash novelist, he is also dropped in favor of an aerobics instructor by a girlfriend who insists, "I want a man, not a dreamer."

Determined to have his say about his lost job, Robert bursts into Naville's office while the great man is chatting with Celine, and ends up, more by accident than on purpose, kidnapping the tycoon's daughter and spiriting her away to a remote cabin he somehow stumbles upon.

Decisive action is not Robert's strength, but the avaricious Celine, who's been kidnapped before, soon swings into action, masterminding a demand for ransom and in general giving the hapless Robert fits. Not very promising material for an eternal romance, but with expulsion from heaven as the alternative, O'Reilly and Jackson are not easily deterred.

Reduced to a bare outline, "A Life Less Ordinary" sounds promising, and in fact the film sporadically amuses with lines like Robert's complaint to Celine, "That's all I am to you, the latest kidnapper, a lifestyle accessory."

But though it wears its arbitrariness proudly, there is simply too much over-elaborate silliness masquerading as wit here, not to mention a grating self congratulatory tone. The supporting actors are similarly all over the place, especially the angels, with the usually unflappable Lindo looking lost and Hunter trying on a succession of accents as if they were outfits by Prada. "A Life Less Ordinary" is so intent on being a film out of the ordinary that it doesn't notice how unsatisfying it's become.

Still, there are Diaz and McGregor to enjoy, and that is no small thing. She is a former model without an extensive acting background before her debut in "The Mask," but she excels within her range, and she is every bit the sparkling equal of the trained, experienced McGregor, who is virtuoso enough to have appeared in the very different "Trainspotting," "Emma" and "The Pillow Book," all in the same year. Unlikely as it sounds, these two make a swell match on screen. At least heaven got that much right.

NEW YORK POST, 10/24/97, p. 47, Michael Medved

"A Life Less Ordinary" features numerous scenes of various characters taking gunshots in the leg, which is only appropriate for a project that's indefensibly lame.

It's an audacious but unlikable attempt to fashion a hip "screwball" comedy that gives new meaning to the phrase painfully unfunny"—since the film's biggest intended laugh-getters are scenes of spurting blood, graphic wounds, hurtling bullets, car crashes and mutilations.

The movie's most matchable moments come in the cleverly animated end-credits and one opening sequence displaying the undeniably gorgeous Cameron Diaz in a bathing suit.

She plays a bored, spoiled heiress whose father (Ian Holm) is a ruthless Utah tycoon. One of his lowliest employees, a pathetically ineffectual janitor played by Ewan NcGregor, forces a confrontation when he loses his job, and then stumbles into kidnapping the pampered princess.

This suits the purposes of two angels (Holly Hunter and Delroy Lindo) sent from a bustling celestial police station with orders to jump-start a romance between the hapless kidnapper and his jaded victim.

As this relationship develops, the movie stresses sexual role reversal—with the heroine tough, nasty, mean, cynical, competent and a crack shot, while the romantic lead is helpless, hypersensitive, emotional and shy about sex.

Diaz handles her part of the equation with self-confident aplomb and megawatt star power, but McGregor's nervous, dim-bulb. gelatinous loser is merely annoying, never endearing. The "Trainspotting" trio behind the film (director Danny Boyle, producer Andrew MacDonald, writer John Hodge) show brief flashes of inventiveness and flair, like a wacky cowboy bar karaoke scene in which the lovebirds perform "Beyond The Sea."

But most of their patently padded story feels either slack or sadistic. Knowing nods to better work by Capra, Tarantino, Michael Powell and others only dilute the focus even further.

The only sexual encounter between the characters occurs after Diaz challenges McGregor to a tequila-drinking contest and, typically he's too drunk (and the audience too confused) to know if anything actually happened between them, despite the heroine's swaggering boasts.

Another sequence shows Stanley Tucci as one of her jilted suitors, a dentist recovering from a bullet wound in the head who tortures the hero by removing yet another bullet from his rival's thigh. This interlude unfolds in a dentist's chair, as if to signify that the entire project provides nearly as much fun as root canal surgery.

SIGHT AND SOUND, 11/97, p. 47, Liese Spencer

In Heaven, Gabriel orders angels Jackson and O'Reilly to make rich Celine Naville and poor Robert, a janitor in her father's company, fall in love. If they don't get results, they'll have to stay on Earth. Robert is sacked, and when he returns to harangue Naville, Celine forces him to kidnap her. At a mountain hideout, Celine and Robert decide to split the ransom.

Hoping to make Celine and Robert fall in love by putting them in jeopardy, the angels have themselves hired as bounty hunters by Naville. At a local karaoke bar, Robert and Celine sing and dance together. Later at a rendezvous, Jackson threatens to kill Robert but Celine rescues him. During their getaway, they rob a bank and Robert is shot. Celine takes him to Elliot, a dentist and former suitor of hers, who removes the bullet. When Robert finds Celine and Elliot flirting, he knocks Elliot unconscious. Celine and Robert argue and part.

Resigned to staying on Earth now, the angels kidnap Celine to make some money. Robert chases them to their hideout where he declares his love for Celine. Naville's henchman Mayhew appears and shoots the angels. Naville demands his ransom back. Celine is tied up and put in the boot of the car. Robert pretends the ransom is stashed at the cabin, so they drive there. Gabriel asks God to intervene. Neighbour Tod hears Celine's cries from the boot and lets her out. Armed with a pistol, she orders Mayhew to release Robert; Mayhew uses Robert as a shield. Celine's bullet passes through Robert's heart, leaving him unscathed and Mayhew dead. Robert and Celine get married. The angels ascend to Heaven.

There are times in *A Life Less Ordinary* when it is possible to see the sexy, surreal comedy that director Danny Boyle, writer John Hodge and producer Andrew MacDonald were aiming to make. But, poorly paced, incoherent and uneven, in the end this ambitious film is fascinating only for the comprehensiveness of its failure. A departure from the macabre delights of the team's first two films, *Shallow Grave* and *Trainspotting*, this is an attempt to apply their stylised, pop-culture subversiveness to a new genre: the screwball romance as comic book. Pitched somewhere between *A Matter of Life and Death* (1946) and *It Happened One Night* (1934), the plot maps the well-trod territory of an oddball couple on the run. Divided by class and temperament, Ewan McGregor's janitor and Cameron Diaz's rich girl are a throwback to Gable and Colbert, but while Capra's duo fizzed with wit and the greedy momentum of delayed passion, McGregor and Diaz are a pair of damp squibs .

McGregor and Diaz might have seemed like the perfect box-office pairing, but they are entirely lacking in sexual chemistry. With their blamelessly bland faces neither is capable of suggesting the ingenuity or passion his or her role demands. Hodge's attempt to dandy-up convention with a spot of role-reversal simply exacerbates this flaw. Playing the cool cynic, Diaz is nasty without being vulnerable, while McGregor lacks the roguish charm necessary to make him attractive rather than just plain dim.

More fundamentally, the problem lies in the poor script. While 30s screwball sublimated sex into sparkling banter, Hodge's dialogue lumbers around, labouring dull gags about characters being left by their partners for aerobics instructors. Towards the end of the film, things are a little enlivened unintentionally with purple passages. McGregor delivers such lines as, "You saved my life when you pierced my I heart with an arrow of your love" with all the stilted embarrassment of his first school play. Such language accompanies the film's strenuous stabs at a hip kind of magical realism, but these hackneyed phrases weaken what should be revealing and hallucinatory moments of escapist fantasy. Another scene shows Robert and Celine breaking into a choreographed dance routine. Reaching towards the spectacular transcendence of the musical, it merely looks like a belated rip-off of a Dennis Potter musical moment.

Also echoing such heavenly comedies as *It's a Wonderful Life* (1947) and *Here Comes Mr. Jordan* (1941), the couple's love is meant to be engineered by two angels, there to make Robert and Celine fall in love by "putting them in jeopardy". But it's hard to worry too much about Robert and Celine when you know the 'psychopathic' bounty hunters hounding them are their own guardian angels. What surprises do remain in the story are so clumsily integrated as to appear out-takes from another film (Robert and Celine's bank robbery, Stanley Tucci's mad dentist, to name but two).

Unlike the set-bound *Shallow Grave* and *Trainspotting, A Life Less Ordinary* was shot mostly on location. Paradoxically, it often feels more stagey than either of the earlier films. Making little use of the dramatic Utah landscape, Boyle offers a composite of clichés about the US, creating little sense of place or atmosphere. If his previous films revealed persuasive portraits of British subcultures, Boyle's view of the US is more Americana than American. When Celine briefly stays with her mother in a sleazy mobile home, it's presumably to feed the British appetite for trailer-trash kitsch.

Occasionally, elements of Boyle's previous films filter through. When Robert is dumped by his girlfriend at the start of the film, McGregor's face, peering into a fisheye lens, recalls memories of that other, more charismatic loser, Renton. Later, Robert is attacked through the floorboards with an axe in a scene reminiscent of *Shallow Grave*. What *A Life Less Ordinary* lacks is a look or tone of its own. Its wild gestures at fantasy achieve moments of stylishness, but leached of emotion or narrative conviction, they remain meaningless. About half way through the film, at their mountain cabin hideout, Celine describes a romantic novel she is reading: "This girl, she meets this guy, they fall in love. It's bullshit." This is devastatingly ironic self-referentiality, but maybe not quite the kind the filmmakers intended.

TIME, 11/3/97, p. 117, Richard Schickel

The great thing about *A Life Less Ordinary* is its reckless lack of cultural calculation. In an age ruled by the demographic imperative, it is bound to confuse, if not actually offend, its natural constituencies—nostalgic oldsters, transgressive youngsters—who are antithetical in the first place. Nor in its weirdness does it offer anything but befuddlement for the general movie audience out for a good, conventionally generic time.

Its very title is mystifying. It seems to belong on a memoir by a minor, faintly boring old poet. It perches rather uneasily atop a story in which Robert, a sweet, dim maintenance man (a woolly Ewan McGregor), replaced by a robot, decides to revenge himself on his rich, cruel boss (Ian Holm) by kidnapping the boss's daughter Celine (a sleek Cameron Diaz). She, naturally, turns out to be spoiled, smart, willful and eager to collaborate in ripping off Daddy.

O.K., you say, at heart it's a romantic comedy, *It Happened One Night* with an edge. Not so fast. You haven't taken the angels into account. They're ferociously played by diminutive Holly Hunter and massive Delroy Lindo, and Gabriel (Dan Hedaya) has sent them back to Earth to bring these crazy kids together. If these dysfunctionals can be made to function in harmony, there is hope, he thinks, for a world riven by romantic discord. Well, why not? A little dollop of

Here Comes Mr. Jordan or *Stairway to Heaven* never hurt anyone—except that these seraphs have a mean streak unknown to their more beamish movie predecessors.

For they are, after all, creations of the filmmaking team-director Danny Boyle, writer John Hodge and producer Andrew Macdonald—who gave us *Trainspotting* and *Shallow Grave* and who have yet to make a movie that is less than extraordinary, stylistically speaking. Boyle is a director who has never encountered a radical angle he doesn't like, a dislocating cut between two of them that doesn't capture his fancy, an eccentric minor character he won't encourage to subvert a cliché.

He and Hodge also have nice taste in dream sequences. There's nothing here that quite equals McGregor's dive down the toilet in *Trainspotting*, but there's a dance number, to the antique strains of *Beyond the Sea,* that begins in a karaoke bar and ends in a romantic delirium that's just wonderful. And not at all the sort of thing you'd expect to arise out of the sere Utah landscape where the fugitives have taken refuge from Celine's implacably pursuing pop.

But that's the thing about this movie. It never leaves well enough, or good enough, alone. It keeps looking—sometimes a little too hard—for ways to transform the ordinary into the discomfiting. Somehow, though, one wishes *A Life Less Ordinary* well as it bops chipperly along a road less traveled.

VILLAGE VOICE, 10/28/97, p. 79, Amy Taubin

More pushy than Satan, *A Life Less Ordinary*'s pair of angels (Holly Hunter and Delroy Lindo) have the unenviable task of convincing a bratty heiress (Cameron Diaz) and an unemployed Scottish immigrant (Ewan McGregor) that they were made for each other.

The first Hollywood film by director Danny Boyle, writer John Hodge, and producer Andrew Macdonald (the team responsible for the smart-alecky *Shallow Grave* and the flashy *Trainspotting*) is a cynically contrived affair that hashes together every movie hook that we stupid Americans have been known to fall for: shootouts, car chases, angels, predestination in matters of the heart, wacky road-houses, awesome Utah landscapes, and aggressive babes with perfect bodies who have the hots for sweetly bumbling guys.

Diaz swings her perfect hips, but can't act a jot. McGregor's haircut is pure *Partridge Family* and he behaves as if he's auditioning for *The Fresh Scot of Bel Air*. There's zip chemistry between them. At the preview screening, Hunter scored the film's biggest laugh when, thrice run-over and bleeding from a dozen bullet wounds, she heaves herself onto the hood of her car, ready to start over. Like Wile E. Coyote, angels never die. Still, one joke doesn't make a movie. *A Life Less Ordinary* is the disaster these self-important filmmakers deserve.

Also reviewed in:
CHICAGO TRIBUNE, 10/24/97, Friday/p. F, Michael Wilmington
NATION, 11/24/97, p. 36, Stuart Klawans
NEW YORK TIMES, 10/24/97, p. E12, Janet Maslin
NEW YORKER, 11/3/97, p. 114, Anthony Lane
VARIETY, 10/13-19/97, p. 77, Derek Elley
WASHINGTON POST, 10/24/97, Weekend/p. 54, Desson Howe

LIKE A BRIDE

Director: Guita Schyfter. *Running time:* 115 minutes. *MPAA Rating:* Not Rated.

CAST: Claudette Maille (Oshinica Mataraso); Maya Mishalska (Rifke Groman); Eresto Laguardia (Saavedra).

NEW YORK POST, 10/3/97, p. 52, Larry Worth

The generation gap has been done to death on film, as "Rebel Without a Cause" and its umpteen successors illustrate. Ditto for a Jewish father's insistence on tradition, with "Fiddler on the Roof" being only one of many.

But in "Like a Bride," director Guita Schyfter puts a fresh face on both themes. Her focus? Two Sephardic Jewish girls who come of age in Mexico City during the politically charged 1960s.

By turns humorous, dramatic and poignant, the film is a bit slow to get going. But once the pacing kicks in, the rewards come quickly, not the least of which is understated acting from Claudette Maille and Angelica Aragon as the duly confused heroines.

The ambitious script also conveys an outsider's hurt, the divisiveness of religious factions, the pain of forbidden love and history's role in the present. More remarkable still: Schyfter presents each in a manner that neither James Dean or Tevye would ever recognize.

VILLAGE VOICE, 10/7/97, p. 80, Gary Dauphin

Early in *Like a Bride's* finely nuanced tale of two Mexican-Jewish girlhoods, Oshinica (Claudette Maille) remembers loving her grandmother and her "very Jewish" way of explaining everything with a story. Her friend Rifke (Maya Mishalska) laughs in recognition but mostly remembers growing up sad and different, wishing for Christmases that never come for her. Oshinica is solely ensconced in her clan while most of Rifke's relatives were killed by the Germans.

Bride is an odd kind of coming-of-age film, its background full of sometimes somber historical notes—from the Holocaust to the creation of modern Israel to '60s-era student revolts—while the foreground just about trills with Rifke and Oshinica's response to their families' demands that they marry, and marry Jewish. It's a soapy tale (Rifke falls for a campus rebel, while Oshinica outrages her mother's canasta-playing set by wanting to become a painter), but director Guita Schyfter whips up great suds, choosing details that often have gemlike clarity.

Also reviewed in:
NEW YORK TIMES, 10/3/97, p. E22, Lawrence Van Gelder

LILIES

An Alliance Communications/Triptych Media/Galafilm coproduction with the financial participation of Telefilm Canada/Ontario Film Development Corporation/SODEC/Gouvernement du Quebec/National Arts Centre of Canada/Ontario-Quebec Commission for Cooperation/ Canadian Film and Video Production Tax Credit/Rogers Telefund developed with the assistance of the Fund for Pay Television. *Producer:* Anna Stratton, Robin Cass, and Arnie Gelbart. *Director:* John Greyson. *Screenplay (based on his play "Les Feluettes ou La Répétition d'un drame romantique"):* Michel Marc Bouchard. *Director of Photography:* Daniel Jobin. *Editor:* André Corriveau. *Music:* Mychael Danna. *Choreographer:* Alain Gaumond. *Sound:* Don Cohen and (music) Daniel Pellerin. *Sound Editor:* Jane Tattersall. *Casting:* Dorothy Garder. *Production Designer:* Sandra Kyabartas. *Art Director:* Marie-Carole de Beaumont. *Set Decorator:* Sonia Venne. *Special Effects:* Intrigue Pierre Rivard. *Costumes:* Linda Muir. *Make-up:* Stephen Lynch. *Stunt Coordinator:* Stéphane Lefebvre. *Running time:* 95 minutes. *MPAA Rating:* Not Rated.

CAST: Brent Carver (Countess Marie Laure de Tilly); Marcel Sabourin (Bishop Jean Bilodeau); Matthew Ferguson (Young Jean Bilodeau); Danny Gilmore (Count Vallier de Tilly); Alexander Chapman (Lydie-Anne de Rozier); Gary Farmer (Timothée Doucet); Robert Lalonde (Baron Geoffroy de Hue); Rémy Girard (Baroness Sylvia de Hue); Aubert Pallascio (Older Simon Doucet); Jason Cadieux (Young Simon Doucet); Ian D. Clark (Chaplain/Father Saint Michel); John Dunn-Hill (Warden); Paul-Patrice Charbonneau (Chauffeur); Michel Marc Bouchard (Photographer); Hilliard Ensemble, The (Choir); Jerome Godbout (Harmonica).

LOS ANGELES TIMES, 10/17/97, Calendar/p. 12, Jack Mathews

[The following review by Jack Mathews appeared in a slightly different form in
NEWSDAY, 10/10/97, Part II/p. B7.]

In 1952 Quebec, Catholic Bishop Bilodeau is summoned to a maximum security prison to hear the confession of Simon Doucet, a dying man convicted of murder. But no sooner is he seated in the confessional than the bishop learns he's there to rehash his own sins and to make his own confession.

Canadian director John Greyson's gay romantic tragedy "Lilies," adapted from a 1987 play by Michel Marc Bouchard, is so richly conceived and fluidly executed it's a shame that he chose to give it the distracting artifice of drag theater. Every role in the story is played by a man, and the actors playing women make no effort to conceal that fact.

The female characters appear in flashbacks that transport the bishop, and the audience, from the prison to northern Quebec province 40 years earlier.

It's there, on the estate of the swank Hotel Roberval, that three 18-year-old men—Simon (Jason Cadieux), his lover Vallier (Danny Gilmore) and his ex-lover Bilodeau (Matthew Ferguson)—spend a critical summer struggling with their identities, their consciences and the expectations of their elders.

Simon is in love with Vallier, but, with the affection shown him by the exotic Parisian Lydie-Anne (Alexander Chapman, doing a sort of earthy RuPaul), he's determined to put his homosexual affairs behind him and get interested in girls.

That decision is devastating to Vallier, who declares his love for Simon before shocked guests at a dinner party, and to Bilodeau, who offers to give up plans for seminary school if Simon will go off with him.

Simon's rejection of Bilodeau has tragic consequences, whose lingering mysteries can only be revealed—40 years later—by the bishop.

Greyson stages all this on three levels. The prison chapel, encircled by barbed wire, is converted into a theater where Simon's fellow inmates do a slide show and perform scenes from a play that re-creates the mood at Roberval in 1912, and recalls the sexual tension among Simon, Vallier and Bilodeau.

With amazing smoothness, the gray prison stage dissolves to the actual setting at Roberval, in all its colorful beauty, where the story picks up in period costume, and with the same prison inmates in all the various roles.

From there on, Greyson intercuts scenes from Roberval with confrontations between the older Simon (Aubert Pallascio) and Bilodeau (Marcel Sabourin), whom we see in both the prison setting and as observers in scenes from the countryside.

Greyson's technical virtuosity, however, is ultimately the story's emotional undoing. There are simply too many things being attempted simultaneously for the human drama to take hold. Bouchard writes in a neo-Shakespearean style, which makes the period story theatrical enough, but with principal characters—Lydie-Anne and Vallier's wounded mother, the Countess Marie (Brent Carver)—portrayed by husky-voiced men, the illusion is lost completely.

NEW YORK POST, 10/10/97, p. 49, Larry Worth

Last year, "Lilies" won Canada's Academy Award for best picture. It's safe to say Oscar won't follow suit.

The film is built around an interesting concept. But the script begs for a major overhaul—and a better director than John "Zero Patience" Greyson.

The story opens in 1952 as an aged bishop visits a prison to comfort a "dying" convict named Simon. He's quickly barricaded inside the confessional and forced down memory lane as Simon and fellow inmates perform a 40-year-old tale of love and murder for his benefit.

The scene dissolves to 1912 and a remote Northern Quebec village. There, the bishop grew up as a priggish youth battling jealousy over young Simon's intimacy with another boy, the dashing Vallier. The arrival of a beautiful countess, who's also attracted to Simon, precipitates amorous encounters and betrayals that lead to tragedy.

It all boils down to a condemnation of religious hypocrisy. But how many closeted skeletons can one bishop possibly have? Here, there's enough to fill a boneyard.

That's in addition to the preposterousness of Simon setting up such an elaborate ruse, never mind fellow prisoners going along with it. Things get even worse with director Greyson's insistence on constantly jumping between 1912 and 1952.

There's more. The prisoners who dress up and play roles for the bishop's gaze enact the same parts after the action fades to 1912. That means the men also fill out the ladies' roles.

The only actor to truly rise above such silliness is Brent Carver. The Tony winner from "Kiss of the Spider Woman" is surprisingly effective as Vallier's liberal mother. Wearing a dress but no makeup, Carver renders sexuality moot, which is no mean feat.

In addition, the teen-age Simon, played by Peter Gallagher lookalike Jason Cadieux, ignites convincing sparks with Danny Gilmore as Vallier. The rest of the troupe, however, ranges from adequate to awful.

But the real villain is Greyson. His failure to convey an admittedly unique vision makes "Lilies" wilt before viewers' eyes.

SIGHT AND SOUND, 1/98, p. 49, Rob White

Quebec, 1952. Bishop Bilodeau arrives at a prison to hear a convict's confession. In the prison chapel, he is locked in the confessional by other prisoners while they stage scenes from his adolescence. 1912: after rehearsing the story of St Sebastian together, schoolboys Simon Doucet and Vallier kiss. The young Bilodeau espies this and denounces them, but is tied up and kissed by Simon. Vallier's mother, the Countess de Tilly, sees this and applauds the "play". Later, she describes what she has seen to other parents. The play is cancelled.

Several years later, Simon is engaged to a young woman named Lydie-Anne. At a dinner to celebrate Simon's imminent wedding, the Countess persuades Simon and Vallier to perform the St Sebastian play. A distraught Lydie-Anne tells the Countess that she knew the Countess' husband was a bigamist. That night, urged on by the Countess, Vallier and Simon have sex. Afterwards, watched by Bilodeau, Vallier carries out the Countess' wish to be strangled. Bilodeau finds Vallier and Simon in the school attic. He tries to persuade them to run away with him, explaining that the police know Vallier has been starting fires. Bilodeau smashes a lamp which sets fire to the attic and locks the door. In the present, the Bishop confesses to setting the fire and relates how he went back to rescue Simon, left Vallier, and framed Simon. The prisoner-actors leave the chapel. Alone with Simon, the Bishop confesses that he was in love with him and begs his forgiveness. Simon kisses him, drawing blood. The Bishop begs Simon to kill him, but Simon refuses.

Lilies' director John Greyson, a video artist and activist, is best known outside Canada for his polemical musical, *Zero Patience,* a formally inventive film about Aids and the medical industry. *Lilies* also has a gay subject matter, exploring the bitter aftermath of a schoolboy love affair in the oppressive climate of 1916 Quebec. However, unlike *Zero Patience,* this story is not well served by its experimental style or its over-earnest concern with identity politics.

The film has the makings of a powerful drama, with its central doomed relationship between two boys at an exclusive school in Quebec, around which are spun parental beatings, a matricide, arson and a fiery death for one of the leads. Plus, one of the main female characters is played in drag by a black actor—indeed, all the female roles in *Lilies* are played by men. This is dramatically licensed by the play-within-the-play conceit which has convicts re-enacting the story's events 40 years on in a prison chapel. Norms of performance and categories of gender are meant to be subverted and repressive society critiqued by this effect. But this ambitious strategy has little emotional or psychological bearing on the simpler core-story of two young men kept apart by homophobia. The actors in drag play their roles 'straight', with minimal recourse to camp mannerisms—without, that is, any self-referentiality, and so come across as naively adhering to realist conventions. Even though some of these naturalistic performances are very good, the overall effect is unproductively disorienting in such an intellectually self-aware film.

The same can be said of *Lilies'* structuring devices. The film slips between penal stagecraft and the tragic events of the past, filmed on location in full period costume with such spectacular accessories as a hot-air balloon and a bear. In addition, there are moments when characters from the present physically visit the past, while water and leaves intrude uncannily into the chapel. Again there are rewards in this kind of formal sophistication: we move, or are caught, between history and memory, the everyday world and fantasy. But for each experimental flourish, something is detracted from the authenticity of the human crises underpinning the film. *Lilies* is aesthetically and conceptually very impressive, but it is less than the sum of its parts, its intelligence not sufficiently balanced and buttressed by the careful observation of character.

VILLAGE VOICE, 10/21/97, p. 85, J. Hoberman

The oxymoron "serious fun" might have been coined to describe the earnestly playful, correctly queer cinema of Canadian filmmaker John Greyson, best known for his 1993 AIDS musical, *Zero Patience*.

Draping himself, none too snugly, in the mantle of the late Derek Jarman, Greyson delivers a professional adaptation of Michel Marc Bouchard's modernist prison drama—a baroque play within a play contrived by a convicted murderer to prick the conscience of his boyhood chum, the Catholic bishop who—lured into the pen to hear the dying convict's last confession—becomes its captive audience.

Bouchard's plan is replete with echoes of Jean Genet and *Marat/Sade*, but *Lilies*, which was included in last year's New York Film Festival, is way too solid for the script's ethereal reality-hopping literary conceits. Still, what the movie lacks in spontaneity, it makes up for in its grim phantasmagoria of a Quebec resort town in the waning days of summer 1912. *("Lilies* recruits fantasy to subjugate bigotry" is the filmmaker's martial formulation.) Awash in liturgical music, the production has a solemn gravity that ultimately suits the repression that is its subject.

The prosaic delirium is enhanced by the allegedly dangerous cons who play a variety of middle-aged women. (The all-male cast has the effect of normalizing the adolescent homosexual passions that provide the dramatic motor.) The least heavy-handed performance belongs to Brent Carver, who won a Tony for *Kiss of the Spider Woman* and here gives a memorable, witty turn as the delusional mother of a schoolboy martyr.

Also reviewed in:
CHICAGO TRIBUNE, 2/6/98, Friday/p. K, Patrick Z. McGavin
NEW YORK TIMES, 10/10/97, p. E14, Stephen Holden
VARIETY, 9/9-15/96, p. 121, Derek Elley

LISBON STORY

A Fox Lorber release of a Road Movies Filmproduktion production in association with Madragoa Filmes, Lisboa 94, WDR Cologne.   *Executive Producer:* Joao Canijo.   *Producer:* Ulrich Felsberg and Paolo Branco.   *Director:* Wim Wenders.   *Screenplay (English, German and Portuguese dialogue):* Wim Wenders.   *Director of Photography:* Lisa Rinzler.   *Editor:* Peter Przygodda and Anne Schnee.   *Music:* Madredeus and Jurgen Knieper.   *Sound:* Vasco Pimentel.   *Art Director:* Ze Branco.   *Running time:* 100 minutes.   *MPAA Rating:* Not Rated.

CAST: Rüdiger Vogler (Phillip Winter); Patrick Bauchau (Friedrich Monroe); Teresa Salgueiro (Teresa); Manoel de Oliveira; Madredeus.

NEW YORK POST, 8/1/97, p. 41, Thelma Adams

When the committee at Lisboa '94 commissioned a feature-length film about their fair city, they showed their commitment to European unity by hiring Wim Wenders. It was one of those imperfect decisions by committee that would be comparable to having Dolly Parton write and perform an anthem to Manhattan: She could do it, but why?

You can see the results at the Anthology Film Archives, which is giving Wenders' 1995 "Lisbon Story" a delayed New York theatrical release. While the movie played Cannes, fueled by the "Paris, Texas" director's name, it's not so much an overlooked masterpiece as an artifact in this German director's adventurous, if uneven, career.

"Lisbon Story," is part meditation on cinema's lost innocence, part travelogue. Like the stereotypical white man trying to dance, Wenders has trouble capturing the rhythms of the hilly Portuguese capital on the Tagus River.

Wenders approaches his subject like an art-school project, jury-rigging pre-existing concerns with assigned materials. He concocts a thin, whimsical—or Wimsical—plot around a lame sound engineer named Phillip Winter (Wenders regular, Rudiger Vogler).

Winter comes to Lisbon at the request of self-obsessed director Friedrich Monroe (Patrick Bauchau). When Winter arrives, Fritzy has disappeared; the comical director is in a film funk, on a doomed search for cinema unchained from 100 years of history.

Monroe tries to recapture the innocence of the silents (more than frustrating for sound man Winter). He ends up recycling Buster Keaton. "Lisbon Story" is full of flat-footed pratfalls and heavy-handed Germanic humor. Winter, played with anti-charisma by the dog-faced Vogler, reminds Monroe that cinema is moving pictures; at their heart, movies must move.

Almost incidentally, we view Lisbon's stunning light and toffee-roofed, terraced grace. Wenders introduces us to the seductive rhythms of Madredeus, Portugal's foremost pop artists, although we must endure a tepid romantic subplot involving Winter and lead singer Teresa Salgueiro. The don of Portuguese cinema, Manoel de Olveira, faces Wenders' camera and lectures us on the meaning of cinema.

Wenders' travelogue reaffirms the old saw: You can travel the world but you can't escape your self. This is what is both charming and irritating about "Lisbon Story."

NEWSDAY, 8/1/97, Part II/p. B11, John Anderson

A man without a clue, on a continent without moorings, in a city that's an enigma. It's got to be a movie about cinema.

And it is, although "Lisbon Story," the latest by the celebrated and occasionally worrisome Wim Wenders, is about so much more it may, in fact, be about everything.

Wenders, who has wrestled with elusive spirituality and fractured hope in such films as "Paris, Texas" and "Wings of Desire," ties cinema to art to God and vice versa in this new hybrid comedy, which the director feels is his most entertaining film. He's probably right. With music by the New Age-traditionalist Portuguese group Madredeus (whose members play themselves in the film), a soliloquy on divinity from the venerated Portuguese director Manoel de Oliveira and a Keaton-esque performance by Rudiger Vogler, Wenders makes some heavy meditations very palatable.

But even as his film percolates happily along, Wenders' purpose is sober, even sobering. Phillip Winter (Vogler), a film sound recordist, has been summoned to Lisbon by his old director, Friedrich Monroe (Patrick Bauchau), whose postcard says he needs help with a new documentary. His foot in a cast, Phillip arrives—after a comic nightmare, in which his car gets a flat, loses its muffler, overheats and some Japsnese tourists donate Coca-Cola for his radiator—to find that Friedrich has disappeared. So he moves into Friedrich's house, expecting his friend to return soon, and begins work with the footage he finds.

Phillip befriends the musicians he meets, including the singer Teresa (Madredeus vocalist Teresa Salgueiro), with whom he falls in quite obvious love. A group of children—including the charmers Joel Ferreira and Sofia Benard Da Costa—surrounds Phillip, and their rapport is immediate and real. When Phillip, standing in an adjacent room, amuses them with his soundman's bag of tricks (recreating roaring lions and frying eggs), the result is a distillation of theater, a near-dismissal of image-driven art.

The whole sequence is very warm, because Phillip, with his pliant, pudding face, is a child himself. But as the film progresses and Friedrich's absence continues, Phillip loses his innocence. "Vidiots!" he screams at the kids when they videotape him during work, and then he smiles at his own verbal ingenuity. It's an unfamiliar moment, this creativity, and Phillip revels in it.

What he's doing, of course, is finding his way free of Friedrich's influence, making his own decisions and becoming a metaphor in the process. Phillip is a country left to its own devices; he's a consumer culture cutting up its charge cards. When Friedrich is finally found, Phillip learns that Friedrich has abandoned the film he's been working on, because the director can no longer cope with the burden of a hundred years of cinema—it's too much history, too many images. It's up to Phillip to change his mind.

All of the footage we see—and what Friedrich would like to recapture—is the kind of cinema the Lumiere brothers created on their *cinematographe* back in the 1890s. Wenders was part of the "Lumiere & Company" project of 1995, and made 50-second films on the original Lumiere camera: it must have prompted soul-searching, and a yearning for artistic simplicity, because in "Lisbon Story" what Wenders is after, and occasionally produces, is a nugget of alchemized truth.

VILLAGE VOICE, 8/5/97, p. 74, Amy Taubin

Too slight to be obnoxious (unlike the ponderously romantic *Faraway, So Close!*), Wim Wenders's *Lisbon Story* is attractively photographed by Liza Rinzler and suggests that the director still has a talent for summoning existential dread. A soundman (Wenders regular Rüdiger Vogler) searches sun-bleached Lisbon for a director who's vanished, leaving an uncompleted film on his editing table. If this is to be read as a metaphoric search for self, then I hope it's the director who made the great *The American Friend* that Wenders is looking for. Twenty years is a long time to go missing.

Also reviewed in:
CHICAGO TRIBUNE, 11/28/97, Friday/p. L, Michael Wilmington
NEW YORK TIMES, 8/1/97, p. C3, Janet Maslin
VARIETY, 3/13-19/95, p. 50, David Rooney
WASHINGTON POST, 1/21/98, p. D1, Stephen Hunter

LOCUSTS, THE

An Orion Pictures release of a Brad Krevoy & Steve Stabler production. *Executive Producer:* Adam Duritz, Beth Holden, Charles B. Wessler, and Cynthia Guidry. *Producer:* Brad Krevoy, Steve Stabler, and Bradley Thomas. *Director:* John Patrick Kelley. *Screenplay:* John Patrick Kelley. *Director of Photography:* Phedon Papamichael. *Editor:* Kathryn Himoff and Erica Flaum. *Music:* Carter Burwell and Happy Walters. *Music Editor:* Adam Smalley. *Sound:* Pud Cusack. *Sound Editor:* Barney Cabral. *Production Designer:* Sherman Williams. *Art Director:* Roy Metcalf. *Set Decorator:* Sally Nicolaou. *Set Designer:* Adele Plauché. *Set Dresser:* Debra Sugerman. *Special Effects:* Lars Sloan. *Costumes:* Gail McMullen. *Make-up:* Melanie Hughes. *Make-up (Ashley Judd):* Ben Nye, Jr. *Stunt Coordinator:* Chris Howell. *Running time:* 124 minutes. *MPAA Rating:* R.

CAST: Kate Capshaw (Mrs. Delilah Potts); Jeremy Davies (Flyboy); Vince Vaughn (Clay Hewitt); Ashley Judd (Kitty); Paul Rudd (Earl); Daniel Meyer (Joel); Jessica Capshaw (Patsy); Jessie Robertson (Ellen); Jimmy Pickens (Cameron); Jerry Haynes (Harlan); Jason Davis (Wrangler).

LOS ANGELES TIMES, 10/3/97, Calendar/p. 14, Jack Mathews

[*The following review by Jack Mathews appeared in a slightly different form in* NEWSDAY, 10/3/97, Part II/p. B11.]

Move over, Harry's Bar and the Bad Hemingway Contest. We think we have the winner of the first Terrible Tennessee Williams competition. Not that we're aware of such an event, but how else to explain John Patrick Kelley's brazenly ripe screenplay for "The Locusts"?

Conceived as a play when Kelley was a college student in Kansas, and further developed during his film studies at New York University, "The Locusts" is now a tortured movie melodrama, a tale combining sexual bullying and ambivalence, gulped bourbon, dark pasts, a sultry *femme fatale*, a rural nymph, a virile stranger, a repressed child and enough cigarettes to launch a brand.

This is a film that cries out for obvious symbols, and Kelley provides two doozies, one by way of the title insects, the other by way of bull scrotum. When was the last time you got turned on by farm analogies?

"The Locusts" parts from Williams' favored Southern locale, setting up in Kelley's native Kansas. But there's no skimping here on the sexual depravity and moral decadence that fueled many a Williams play, and "The Locusts" main female character, a boozy, sexually insatiable cattle rancher's widow (Kate Capshaw), is a prairie blend of Blanche Dubois, Alexandra Del Lago and Maggie the Cat.

Capshaw's Delilah Potts (judges, remember to score the names, too) inherited her modest ranch from a husband who hanged himself after catching her in bed with a lover, and eight years later, she's still warming the sheets with whomever she cuts from her herd of ranch hands. Meanwhile, her frail and-largely mute 21-year-old son Flyboy (Jeremy Davies), recently home from a mental hospital, is doing her housekeeping and trying to ignore the traffic to his mother's bedroom.

Into this happy domestic 1960s scene comes Clay Hewitt (Vince Vaughn), a quietly confident drifter, harboring secrets of his own. In short order, Hewitt straightens out the local tough guy (Daniel Meyer), takes over his frisky girlfriend Kitty (Ashley Judd) and becomes a ranch hand in residence at the Potts farm. Before the sweaty stranger can change T-shirts, Delilah's bourbon-soaked tongue is on the floor and the stage is set for some serious sexual tension.

The main relationship in the story, however, is that of Clay and Flyboy, whose liberation from Delilah becomes the intruder's obsession. The kid is severely emotionally disturbed, haunted by the circumstances of his father's death, petrified of his callously controlling mother and incapable of expressing himself to anyone other than Jim, his father's prize bull and the movie's symbol of endangered masculinity.

Why Clay adopts Flyboy as a mission seems to draw from murkier Williams territory, suggesting Clay's own sexual ambivalence. This is a big brother seduction that, combined with Clay's ability to withhold sex from such eager beauties as Kitty and Delilah, makes you wonder. It sure does.

Vaughn, who caught Hollywood's attention in the sneak hit "Swingers," and Davies, the self-abusing hero of "Spanking the Monkey," bring a sincerity to each of their roles that gives "The Locusts" its one compelling dramatic thread. Davies, playing the film's most tragic figure, does such a brilliant physical mime of a frightened boy in a slumping adult body that it's almost impossible to spot the acting that went into it.

Capshaw has an even tougher task, making human a character of such off-putting self-pity and hostility, and through all the smoldering poses in her performance, for all the anguished revelations she delivers about Delilah's past, she doesn't overcome the psychological emptiness of the part.

The talented Judd has one of the most thankless roles of her fresh career. As Kitty, she isn't asked to do much more than appear sexy and flash Kodak smiles. She does both with ease, but there's too much going on behind this actress' eyes to waste in throwaway roles.

Note to filmmakers who cannot shoot a scene without a cigarette in it: Have someone cough once in a while, just so we know the smokes are real.

NEW YORK POST, 10/3/97, p. 49, Larry Worth

Sometimes, superb acting can compensate for the most flawed scripts. "The Locusts" is a textbook example.

In particular, Jeremy Davies, known to art-house fans as the hero of "Spanking the Monkey," delivers Oscar-caliber work as an emotionally crippled man-child, caught in a tragic tug-of-war between his emasculating mother and a well-meaning mentor.

The action takes place in Kansas in the '60s as a handsome drifter finds work on a cattle run by a booze-swilling, lust-driven widow. Problems begin when the hunk pays less attention to the widow than to her seemingly mute son (Davies), who's treated like a servant.

There's nothing sexual between the men, merely one person helping another for a cause that doesn't become apparent until later. But the dragon lady isn't about to lose control for any reason, setting the stage for a tale of Gothic drama, dark secrets and lost love that might as well be dedicated to Tennessee Williams.

That's not to say that first-time writer/director John Patrick Kelley has fashioned his own "Sweet Bird of Youth." Far from it. For starters, the script is weighed down by creaky symbolism about the short-but-sweet life, of locusts, never mind an all-too-literal took at farm-animal castration.

Kelley fares better behind the camera, having nicely evoked a time and place through use of light and shadows. Such touches contribute to a succession of incredibly moving scenarios, even if they're greater than the sum of their parts.

Clearly, star power drives this vehicle, reaching a zenith whenever Davies is on screen. It may be the year's most heartbreaking performance. His every trick, stutter and stunted movement, is natural and unmannered, like watching a new-born, defenseless colt trying to stand on its own.

And as the well-meaning interloper, Vince Vaughn is a perfect complement. Looking like a young Marlon Brando in his stained T-shirt, he exudes a tenderness and charisma that's almost palpable. His scenes with Davies are honed by a delicacy and warmth that define excellence.

The ever-reliable Ashley Judd and Paul Rudd complete a standout cast, with Kate Capshaw being the only shaky link. As the matriarchal shrew, she's properly malevolent but in need of a bit more shading.

The film's downbeat tone and refusal to buy into a happy ending may not please some moviegoers. But if Davies gets the attention he deserves, it's a happy ending regardless.

VILLAGE VOICE, 10/14/97, p. 90, Dennis Lim

Unfolding over one long summer in early '60s Kansas, *The Locusts* is a torpid melodrama in which everyone sweats and has secrets to hide. Despite repeated insinuations to the contrary, the plot contains no surprises. Clay Hewitt (Vince Vaughn), a drifter fleeing a requisite dark past, finds work on a cattle ranch owned by man-eating widow Delilah Ashford Ports (Kate Capshaw), and feels compelled to emancipate the vamp's emotionally stunted son, Flyboy (Jeremy Davies).

First-time writer-director John Patrick Kelley works through some relatively meaty themes (psychosexual pathology, the legacy of abuse), but he does so with numbing predictability. Trapped for the most part in single dimensions, the actors flounder. Clay is the only character with a trace of complexity, but Vaughn appears too limited a performer to exploit it; Capshaw, weighed down by the clunkiest lines, hits one wrong note after another. Skittish and chronically shy, Flyboy is like a severely damaged relation of Davies's character in the recent *Going All the Way*. Still, rote performances aren't exactly out of place in a film that's so methodically Southern Gothic it seems less overheated than reheated.

Also reviewed in:
CHICAGO TRIBUNE, 10/3/97, Friday/p. H, Michael Wilmington
NEW YORK TIMES, 10/3/97, p. E22, Stephen Holden
VARIETY, 9/8-14/97, p. 79, David Rooney
WASHINGTON POST, 10/3/97, p. B4, Stephen Hunter

LONG WAY HOME, THE

A Seventh Art Releasing presentation of a Moriah Films production. *Producer:* Marvin Hier and Richard Trank. *Director:* Mark Jonathan Harris. *Screenplay:* Mark Jonathan Harris. *Director of Photography:* Don Lenzer. *Editor:* Kate Amend. *Music:* Lee Holdridge. *Running time:* 119 minutes. *MPAA Rating:* Not Rated.

NARRATOR: Morgan Freeman
VOICES: Edward Asner; Ruth Gruber; Martin Landau; Miriam Margolyes; Sean Astin; David Paymer; Nina Siemaszko; Helen Slater; Michael York.

LOS ANGELES TIMES, 9/17/97, Calendar/p. 3, Kevin Thomas

[*The following review by Kevin Thomas appeared in a slightly different form in* NEWSDAY, 9/19/97, Part II/p. B11.]

Mark Jonathan Harris' superb documentary, "The Long Way Home," covers much familiar territory concerning the Holocaust and its aftermath. Yet in focusing on the three turbulent wars between the end of World War II and the formation of the state of Israel, it offers epic dimension and admirable clarity and calmness to a complex and wrenching chain of events.

The result is an eloquent saga of historical importance that is as timely and significant as today's headlines reporting the tragic flight of refugees in Africa, Bosnia and Central America.

In only a two-hour running time, Harris has in effect synthesized events dealt with by filmmakers who preceded him, linking these events without diminishing their individual importance. By doing so, he gives scope to the entire terrible ordeal experienced by European Jews from the advent of Hitler through the further hardships of the postwar years.

Harris has not only come up with astutely assembled and remarkably wide range of archival footage, but he has presented it in the very best restored condition possible, helping give his film a heightened, often harrowing, immediacy. Shrewdly, he has limited his interviewees to only those who witnessed or participated in crucial experiences, which allows their presence on camera to serve as punctuation rather than interruptions in his assemblage of period clips.

On the soundtrack, however, we hear the words of countless others, spoken by Edward Asner, Sean Astin, Martin Landau, Miriam Margolyes, David Paymer, Nina Siemaszko, Helen Slater and Michael York. Morgan Freeman serves splendidly as the film's narrator. Composer Lee Holdridge has created a score as dignified as it is stirring.

Harris spends the first 10 minutes presenting footage of the concentration camps as they were liberated by Allied forces at the end of the war. Many of us have seen these images of hell on earth countless times. Surely, such images should have signaled the immediate end of a suffering so hideous as to be beyond the comprehension of anyone who did not endure it personally. That was not to be the case, and that's why it was essential for Harris to include the atrocity footage yet again. There might be an end to starvation and other Nazi atrocities, but many Jews who tried to return to their homes found their houses destroyed or confiscated by others. Many also learned that most or all of their relatives were dead or missing. And they were greeted with blatant anti-Semitism; in a village near Vilna, Lithuania, five returning concentration camp survivors were found murdered. In their pockets was the message, "This will be the fate of all surviving Jews."

Most survived, however, only to be placed behind more barbed wire in displaced-persons camps, noted for overcrowding and substandard living conditions. No wonder the desire of emigrating to Palestine to establish a Jewish homeland blossomed in such circumstances.

Harris does a masterful job in outlining the formidable, disgraceful obstacles to realizing this dream in a world that was so caught up with postwar recovery and growing anti-communist paranoia that it was by and large indifferent to the continuing suffering of Europe's Jews.

Harris makes it very clear that Britain, given a League of Nations post-World War I mandate to administer Palestine, placed paramount importance in the immediate post-World War II period in ensuring access to Arab oil. Clearly, Britain didn't want to irk the Arab world with the idea of Jews emigrating there to form a Jewish state.

Because of this, some 200,000 European and Eastern European Jewish Holocaust survivors were restricted to emigrating to Palestine at a mere 1,500 a month. Despite this restriction, however, as Harris succinctly demonstrates, the refugees were determined to reach Palestine—an incredible, dangerous and illegal mission that culminated in the founding of Israel.

"The Long Way Home" is a major accomplishment on the part of Moriah Films, the Simon Wiesenthal Center's film division, with the center's dean and founder Rabbi Marvin Hier serving as the film's coproducer along with Richard Trank, Moriah Films' executive producer.

NEW YORK POST, 9/19/97, p. 55, Larry Worth

It's commonly assumed that the suffering of Holocaust survivors ended with their liberation from concentration camps. "The Long Way Home" shows otherwise.

The relentlessly harrowing documentary, written and directed by Mark Jonathan Harris, throws fresh light on a four-year nightmare endured by prisoners making their way from Auschwitz to Israel.

Told with a mix of haunting archival footage and first-person recollections, the detailed narrative relates the battle against all-too-convenient emigration quotas, midnight runs across the Alps, being smuggled aboard ship into hostile ports (only to be surrounded by yet more soldiers with guns) and on and on.

Movingly narrated by Morgan Freeman (with assists from Edward Asner, Martin Landau, Helen Slater and Michael York), the production is a fascinating, heartbreaking, unforgettable look at a world where—as "The Long Way Home" reminds viewers indifference and anti-Semitism still thrive.

VILLAGE VOICE, 9/30/97, p. 84, Lisa Katzman

As Netanyahu plays a bully's shell game with the peace process, Zionism's global credibility grows tarnished. Mark Jonathan Harris's *The Long Way Home* makes clear how the massive postwar *aliyah* of Holocaust survivors led to Israel's statehood. Harris's documentary begins by revealing appalling treatment of Holocaust survivors in Displaced Person Camps—many of which were concentration camps a few months earlier. While a GI liberator confesses revulsion toward the desiccated survivors of Dachau, General Patton, inspecting a D.P. camp, describes Jews as *subhuman*. The camps' liberation no more effectively vanquished anti-Semitism than emancipation did racism.

Through newsreel footage, the film documents international callousness toward Jewish resettlement, especially the murderous reprisals against Jews returning to Eastern Europe and Britain's rebuke of refugees to Palestine. The film explains the Jewish resistance movements, the heroic smuggling of refugees, and even the terrorist campaigns against the British. But Harris's comprehensive approach makes his elision of the Arab-Zionist conflict all the more troubling: the blindsiding of Palestinian claims provokes wonder over Israel's lifespan as a Jewish homeland.

Also reviewed in:
NEW YORK TIMES, 9/19/97, p. E14, Janet Maslin
VARIETY, 2/3-9/97, p. 44, Emanuel Levy

LOST HIGHWAY

An October Films release of a CiBy 2000/Asymmetrical production. *Producer:* Deepak Nayar, Tom Sternberg, and Mary Sweeney. *Director:* David Lynch. *Screenplay:* David Lynch and Barry Gifford. *Director of Photography:* Peter Deming. *Editor:* Mary Sweeney. *Music:* Angelo Badalamenti. *Music Editor:* Marc Vanocur. *Sound:* Susumu Tokunow and (music) Jiri Zobac. *Sound Editor:* Frank Gaeta. *Casting:* Johanna Ray and Elaine J. Huzzar. *Production Designer:* Patricia Norris. *Set Decorator:* Leslie Morales. *Costumes:* Patricia Norris. *Make-up:* Debbie Zoller. *Stunt Coordinator:* Chris Howell. *Running time:* 135 minutes. *MPAA Rating:* R.

CAST: Bill Pullman (Fred Madison); Patricia Arquette (Renee Madison/Alice Wakefield); John Roselius (Al); Lou Eppolito (Ed); Jenna Maetlind (Party Girl); Michael Massee (Andy); Robert Blake (Mystery Man); Henry Rollins (Guard Henry); Michael Shamus Wiles (Guard Mike); Mink Stole (Forewoman); Leonard Termo (Judge); Ivory Ocean (Guard Ivor); Jack Kehler (Guard Johnny Mack); David Byrd (Doctor Smordin); Gene Ross (Warden Clements); Balthazar Getty (Pete Dayton); F. William Parker (Captain Luneau); Guy Siner (Prison Official #1); Alexander Folk (Prison Official #2); Gary Busey (Bill Dayton); Lucy Butler (Candace Dayton); Carl Sundstrom (Hank); John Solari (Lou); Al Garrett (Carl); Heather Stephens (Lanie); Giovanni Ribisi (Steve 'V'); Scott Coffey (Teddy); Natasha Gregson Wagner (Sheila); Amanda Anka (Girl #1); Jennifer Syme (Junkie Girl); Richard Pryor (Arnie); Robert Loggia (Mr. Eddy/Dick Laurent); Matt Sigloch (Assistant #1); Gil Combs (Assistant #2); Greg Travis (Tail Gate Driver); Jack Nance (Phil); Lisa Boyle (Marian); Leslie Bega (Raquel); Marilyn Manson (Porno Star #1); Twiggy Ramirez (Porno Star #2).

FILM QUARTERLY, Spring 1998, p. 57, Eric Bryant Rhodes

The ever quotable pop artist and underground filmmaker Andy Warhol reportedly stated that films are "better talked about than seen." With his latest film adventure, *Lost Highway*, David Lynch has given audiences a complex and perplexing story to ponder and some astonishingly brilliant images to enjoy. Yet the majority of critical responses to Lynch's new horror noir have denounced the film's narrative as being interesting but impenetrably chaotic at best, and some have even gone as far as to call the film unwatchable. Even the cinephiles who have recognized the significant aesthetic achievements of Lynch's film have announced that he is unconcerned with narrative logic in *Lost Highway*. Perhaps part of this critical response is due to a reluctance to embrace the robust eroticism and taste for violence displayed in Lynch's works. Lynch has ventured beyond linear film narratives and left incredulous critics and puzzled onlookers muttering that either his picture is obscure by accident or that he is engaged in some frivolous form of cinematic gamesmanship. Some reviewers have expressed their opinions in a tone of righteous indignation and used the supposed "mess" of this film to exact some type of petty revenge upon those who acclaimed Lynch upon the triumph of *Blue Velvet*.

Lost Highway may be destined to baffle devotees of traditional narrative forms in cinema, but should filmgoers be discharged from recognizing the structure and formal mastery of Lynch's film? Although many have suggested that Lynch has gone too far in yielding free reign to his eccentric set of visual obsessions, the film is contained within a formally rigorous and well-defined thematic structure. The difficulties with *Lost Highway* lie with the movie's unremitting dream-like images and Lynch's uncompromising determination to sustain an eternal sense of mystery and wonder throughout the film. He has designed a film with an open architecture in which equally plausible interpretations of the film can be constructed, and which enables the audience to use its imagination to fill in the blanks. The strategy of posing open questions is reminiscent of Antonioni in films like *L'Avventura*. A large part of what has confounded spectators in Lynch's enterprise is how to distinguish between scenes that reflect the characters' fantasies, and those that belong to the narrative "reality." *Lost Highway* is a film that would appear to have a complete disregard for differences in ontological levels. Only a recognition that its visual language communicates a descent deeper and deeper into madness can reveal *Lost Highway*'s intricate conceptual meaning. Lynch has given notice that his film takes its structure from the circular form of the Möbius strip, and herein lies the constraint against which he weaves his thematic concerns.

Fred Madison (Bill Pullman) is living a nightmare: his mind is racked by suspicion, paranoia, and anxieties about the fidelity of his sensuous but emotionally cold wife, Renee (Patricia Arquette), a dark-haired sex kitten decked out in Betty Page-styled fetish attire. Although Fred, a darkly handsome, thirtyish alto saxman in a neo-Bop jazz band, would appear on the surface to be evenly matched with his mysterious and sexually powerful wife, he is incapable of arousing in her any enthusiastic sexual response. Events quickly take a sinister bend when the Madisons begin receiving unmarked videotapes on the front steps of their ominously underdecorated modernist house. When the tapes reveal that an intruder has invaded the Madisons' home and taped them while they were asleep, the terrorized couple call for police help, which arrives in the form of a comical detective duo who find no evidence of forced entry. Unsettled by the violation of their private space, Fred falls into a twitchy, zombie-like state. A third videotape arrives and he sits down to view it. He screams out in horror when the picture reveals Fred looking into the camera's eye beside Renee's savagely bloodied corpse. Although we see nothing of the crime on screen, Fred is summarily sentenced to execution for his wife's murder, and swiftly ensconced in a cell on death row. Isolated in a primitive 19th-century-styled prison cage, Fred has no memory of what happened to Renee on the fatal night, and his mind is shattered by excruciating headaches, unrelenting insomnia, and strange hallucinations (all marvelously captured in the film's mesmerizing visual effects).

Suddenly, in *Lost Highway*'s Kafkaesque center sequence, a prison guard discovers a bewildered and bruised stranger in Fred Madison's cell. A brief investigation by prison authorities determines the identity of the stranger: Pete Dayton (Balthazar Getty), who lives in Van Nuys with his parents, and has absolutely no recollection of how he mysteriously materialized to replace Fred Madison in prison. Pete is enthusiastically welcomed back to normal life and his job at Arnie's auto garage. Delighted with Pete's return, Mr. Eddy (Robert Loggia), a notorious gangster prone to comically capricious outbursts of violence, provides Pete with work on his vintage luxury motor cars. When Mr. Eddy brings in his 50s model Cadillac for a routine tune-up, Pete fatally falls for Alice Wakefield (also Patricia Arquette), Mr. Eddy's seductively carnivorous platinum blonde bombshell, and they embark on a furtive and—for Pete at least—obsessive affair. When the menacing Mr. Eddy's suspicions are aroused, Alice's risky and hastily devised plan of escape takes full advantage of Pete's obsession. She manipulates him into a classic film noir plot—reminiscent of *Double Indemnity* and *Body Heat* to rob one of Mr. Eddy's associates in the pornographic underworld. As the plot unfolds and inevitably spirals down into disaster, Pete is horrified when he discovers that the object of his desire is an unscrupulously mercenary and debauched queen of porn.

As the film progresses, Pete descends deeper into darkness and confusion. At an isolated desert cabin the lovers await the arrival of one of Alice's acquaintances who is to help them escape. But at this point the two tracks of the narrative intersect. Fred Madison reemerges from Pete, and the Mystery Man (Robert Blake)—a kind of dark angel of vengeance—urges him to kill Mr. Eddy. Flames engulf the cabin—or do they?

It should be acknowledged straightaway that *Lost Highway* is, by design, extremely resistant to reduction into a definitive narrative account; by the film's end, it is evident that Lynch has intentionally withheld the answers to questions inevitably provoked by the narrative's elusive and elliptical plot. It is virtually impossible to reconstruct a definitive and rational account of what happens in *Lost Highway*.

According to the majority of its detractors, what happens in the film's prison sequence is that Fred is transformed (think "Metamorphosis") into Pete Dayton via some type of supernatural intervention. Throughout the second half of the film, Pete's parents and girlfriend, Sheila (Natasha Gregson Wagner), allude cryptically to the mysterious and ominous circumstances of the fateful night that something strange happened to Pete. Although Pete has no recollection of that night, we repeatedly see Pete's parents and Sheila in front of the Dayton's house under a threatening evening sky, crying out to avert some impending catastrophic event. *Lost Highway* features several visual images that give some weight to a metamorphosis thesis. After all, for the most part, the film proceeds as if the central narrative has shifted from Fred's "story" to Pete's "story." While Fred agonizes in his prison cell, images of lightning flashes and horrific distortion fill the screen with overtones of extraworldly visitation. Nevertheless, the idea that Fred is literally morphed into a man with a new identity obscures more than it clarifies the subject of *Lost Highway*.

Lynch has publicly called his film a "psychogenic fugue," a term that in this context refers to a mental state in which a person is delusional although seemingly fully aware, a state from which he emerges with no memory of his actions. It also involves losing oneself and taking on an entirely new identity. Most of what occurs during the second movement of *Lost Highway* can be best understood as an elaborate journey into the hallucinations of such a state. The early sequences of the film demonstrate that Fred's consciousness is disturbed by suspicion, paranoia, and nightmares. He also has a pronounced tendency to daydream. This is made most evident when he tells the police detectives, "I like to remember things my own way ... How I remembered them. Not necessarily the way they happened." Fred's tenuous grip on reality is undermined by his voluntary flights into fantasy.

Lynch provides few signals that equal degrees of reality should not be attributed to all the actions of the film. By contrast, in Buñuel's *Belle de jour* the viewer is given cues, like the jingling of bells on the sound track, to distinguish fantasy from reality. The most persuasive evidence for an interpretation of *Lost Highway* as a subjective film understood primarily as Fred's hallucination occurs during the prison sequences. During his time in jail, Fred is plagued by unrelenting insomnia. Hints of his delusional state of mind can be gleaned from the sound of seagulls on the sound track as he slumps in the prison exercise yard overwhelmed by a combination of excruciating headaches and exhaustion. Hallucinations also occur in his prison cell: Fred sees the flames of an exploding desert cabin run backwards—an image that occurs again at the end of the film when Fred "returns" to replace Pete. However the key image that provides evidence for the hallucination thesis is a distorted close up of Fred's face shaking violently back and forth before he screams out in horror. This image occurs twice: in prison before we are introduced to Pete, and just prior to the film's conclusion. The flashes of lightning and out-of-focus visuals are all evidence that Fred's mind is spinning wildly out of control. Between the parentheses, Fred creates a parallel universe in his mind that takes on a will of its own.

The two parallel stories of *Lost Highway* are two manifestations of one essential story: a man obsessed with possessing the *wrong* woman. Although Fred and Pete are played by different actors and have distinct identities, they can be understood as representing the same self. Lynch's casting of the same actress in the roles of both Renee Madison and Alice Wakefield adds further credence to the notion that *Lost Highway* contains two mythic representations of the same couple. In Fred's tormented mind, Alice embodies his obsession with the now dead (and maybe murdered by him) Renee. (The use of one actress in twin roles recalls Buñuel's playful use of two actresses for the role of the tormenting Conchita in *That Obscure Object of Desire*, or, perhaps, Hitchcock's use of Kim Novak as one woman impersonating another in *Vertigo*.) Fred's hallucination is partly all escape into fantasy and partly a terrifying ride into a nightmare beyond his will.   By envisioning Pete's story, Fred creates a new incarnation of the object of his obsession, but in the end his hallucinated encounter with a seductive and compliant temptress is no less catastrophic than his earlier attempts to control the remote and withheld body and soul of his wife.

The structure of *Lost Highway* is modeled on the form of the Möbius strip: a strip twisted 180 degrees and then looped by connecting the opposing ends. In the first image of *Lost Highway* we are speeding down the center of a desolate two-lane flattop along the dashed canary-yellow center line; we hear the industrial beat and the haunting baritone of David Bowie's "I'm Deranged" flowing over the credits on the sound track. This image opens and closes the film. It forms a frame, provides symmetry, and evokes both the closing of a circle and a sense of the infinite (as if this dream or nightmare could go on forever). The circular structure also enables Lynch to construct a world where conventional notions of time are obliterated. In the film's first scene, a disheveled-looking Fred is at home and roused into action when he hears a voice giving an enigmatic and unnerving message over the intercom: "Dick Laurent is dead." When he goes to the window, the speaker has vanished. In the closing scene of the film it is Fred outside his own house who delivers the same message: "Dick Laurent is dead." In the end, we find out who Dick Laurent is and the two parallel stories are linked together, but many of the film's mysteries remain.

Despite the accusation that the film is chaos, or that Lynch is unconcerned with narrative logic, *Lost Highway*, is contained within what Sontag terms (in *Bergman's "Persona": Styles of Radical Will* [New York: Anchor Books, 1991] p. 135) a theme-and-variation narrative. Instead of a conventional story, chronology or plot line, a theme-and-variation form of narration is nonlinear and uses the subject material as a thematic resource to develop variations on the central theme of the film: here, mirroring. The theme, which implies both duplication and opposition, manifests itself on many levels.   The primary example of mirroring is captured in Arquette's characterization of two sides of the same woman: Renee (who appears passive and elusive) and Alice (who determines the action). On the superficial level of appearances, Arquette's Renee has dark hair and favors long dark silhouettes, while Arquette's Alice is a bleached blonde with a taste for revealing necklines and short skirts. However, they are the same in that each evokes a luxurious sense of carnal potency—one withheld, the other flaunted—and each wears fetishist-friendly platform high heels.   The theme-and-variation narrative form enables Lynch to use devices of duplication, opposition, repetition, deviation, and inversion. Arquette's characters have opposing temperaments: Renee is quiet, removed. and cool; Alice is white-hot. The notion of duplication is explored when both Renee and Alice appear in the same photograph; of repetition when Alice and Renee repeat the same dialogue, and when the film's Mystery Man repeats dialogue in the two separate parallel stories of the movie.

Variations on the mirroring theme are worked throughout the film.   Early on we see Fred fervently playing his saxophone, and later Pete listens to the same piece of music over the radio as he works on a car at Arnie's garage. However, Pete's reaction constitutes the emotional inverse of Fred's sensibility: in a fit of annoyance, as if he was subconsciously disturbed by the music's manic intensity, he shuts the radio off. Lynch also employs doubling when characters are introduced in pairs at various points of the film: the odd pair of police detectives, the two prison guards, and the two surveillance cops who follow Pete after his release from prison. Several of *Lost Highway*'s key images—like the two-lane highway, shots of long corridors, the exploding cabin shown in reverse, the frantic scene in front of the Dayton home are also repeated, emphasizing the film's self-referential character and clear intention to pursue a theme-and-variation form of narration. Together, the complex combination of the circular structure and elliptical story line invites repeated journeys along the twisted strip of the film's narrative in search of its closely guarded secrets.

Lost Highway's greatest success is that it deftly subsumes its experiments in structure and form under the aesthetics of hallucination and the iconography of horror. The primary attraction of a Lynch film lies in his virtuosity as a visualist and his ability to conjure up moods with disturbingly visceral impact. Although *Lost Highway* starts out looking like the "real" world, it quickly becomes a "constructed" world: an extravagant phantasmagoria with twilight-zone metaphysics. The structure, form, and visuals all conspire to construct a self-contained allegorical nightmare where the sense of time is eviscerated.

The first clear indication that we are within some kind of alternate universe is the appearance of the Mystery Man. When a mysterious stranger with a mask-like face and pancake-white makeup approaches Fred during a festive party, all the background sounds magically recede away. The Mystery Man claims that he is presently at the Madisons' house and challenges Fred to call him there right now. Confused by the absurdity of the claim, Fred reluctantly dials his own number ... to find the Mystery Man's voice answering at the other end of the line. Frightened, bewildered, and angry over yet another invasion of his private space, Fred asks for an explanation, but the Mystery Man only lets out a Vincent Price-style cackle and walks away.

The establishment of a constructed world permits Lynch and cinematographer Peter Deming to develop the film's aesthetics of hallucination. One of the film's most visually effective scenes occurs when slow-motion photography captures the electricity and longing in the initial gaze between Pete and Alice Wakefield. The mythic mood of the image derives part of its considerable emotional power from the perfect congruence between sight and sound. The slow burn of Arquette's sultry blonde bombshell is heightened by the languid sound of roaring electric guitars. Perhaps the aesthetic highpoint of *Lost Highway* is the love scene in the desert. When Pete and Alice begin their impromptu sexual encounter in the middle of the windswept desert night, their incandescent naked bodies are brightly illuminated by automobile headlights, creating a mood of intoxicating ecstasy and reverie. In the desert, the windblown golden sand and Arquette's radiant hair and torso explain Pete's total surrender to her overpowering sexual energy. The emotional mood shifts from dream to nightmare with disorienting suddenness when the headlights dissolve into darkness and the music's floating lyricism creeps into a brooding drone of synthesizers. Throughout the film, Lynch keeps the emotional tone of the movie within a dream-like register, and he changes keys between images that appear idyllic and icons of the horror genre.

Lost Highway, is a decidedly dark work. In the majority of the film's interior scenes, Lynch favors murky shading and low lighting to elicit the fear of the unknown: long, dark corridors used in a variety of ways to evoke feelings of disorientation: a hallway where Fred is completely swallowed by darkness. Later in the film, Pete's walk along a corridor is accompanied by flashes of lightning and special effects that are the standard fair of the horror genre; his walk down a hallway to find the bathroom is a frightening hallucination: lightning flashes illuminate numbered doors, one of which Pete opens to find a woman, apparently Alice, taunting him. Pulsating music and red filters add to the disorienting effect. The images fittingly project Pete's turmoil in the moments just after discovering the profoundly sordid elements of Alice's life.

Lost Highway's labyrinthine construction enables Lynch to subordinate traditional cinematic concerns with dialogue and plot to a visual language that communicates moods and emotions. Although the dialogue in the film is spare, the drama of a man driven mad by his obsession with the woman he loves has an extraordinary emotional vividness. *Lost Highway* is a mystery, a fable, an allegorical nightmare. Although it can in some moments resemble our notion of reality, Lynch has basically jettisoned the tyranny of logic to take the viewer on an enigmatic journey beyond the limits of reason and reality—down some lost highway. Despite denunciations of the movie as irredeemably chaotic, it actually—with its haunting circularity and endless narrative loop—adheres to a disciplined aesthetic formality. Like *Eraserhead*, the film evokes the interior world of one man's bad dream, the mystery and confusion of a consciousness afflicted by obsession, suspicion, and passion.

LOS ANGELES TIMES, 2/21/97, Calendar/p. 10, Kenneth Turan

No one has ever needed to tell David Lynch to stop making sense. From "Eraserhead" through "Twin Peaks: Fire Walk With Me," his films have focused on the creepy illogic of nightmare, on mocking reason and celebrating the dream state. With this director, what you get is what you see.

"Lost Highway," troublesome but also the director's most accomplished work since "Blue Velvet" a decade ago, takes this tendency even further. Beautifully made but emotionally empty, it exists only for the sensation of its provocative moments. Garnished with sex and violence, it alternates scenes that exquisitely marry sound and image with moments that seem to come from a metaphysical stag film.

Working with co-screenwriter Barry Gifford (who wrote the novel Lynch's "Wild at Heart" was based on), the director has taken traditional film noir elements—gangsters, youthful hunks, jazz musicians, unattainable women and implacable fate—and tossed them into a conceptual Mixmaster. The result is one weirded-out movie that plays as if it were coming and going at the same time.

Though "Lost Highway" presents enough traditional mysteries to mimic the shape of something that might make sense, it has no intention of offering anything like solutions. This film answers no questions, solves no riddles and treats questions of traditional logic as if they came from a different universe.

In fact, "Lost Highway" is set up around the theme of parallel worlds, around the notion of people switching places and shapes and doubling back on themselves through alternate universes in a way that can be neither argued with nor explained.

Introduced first are Hollywood Hills residents Fred Madison (Bill Pullman) and his wife, Renee (Patricia Arquette). He's a tenor sax player who hangs at the Luna Lounge; she's a dark-haired stunner who seems to have no occupation except to look sexually provocative.

The Madisons don't seem to have the happiest of marriages, and they're not made any cheerier by the arrival on their doorstep of a series of increasingly explicit videos of unknown origin that have been mysteriously taken inside their house. The police don't know what it means, and neither will you.

Making things worse for Fred is a chance meeting at a party thrown by one of Renee's kinky friends with someone known simply as Mystery Man. Disconcertingly played by Robert Blake as a living death's head with a laugh like the Shadow, Mystery Man has no trouble living up to his name. Able to be in several places at the same time, he's unnerving, intriguing and completely opaque.

If all this weren't strange enough, midway through "Lost Highway" Fred gets these killer headaches and abruptly turns into another person. That would be Pete Dayton (Balthazar Getty), a handsome young garage mechanic from the Valley with Gary Busey for a father, Natasha Gregson Wagner for a girlfriend and Richard Pryor for a boss.

Pete's best client is the wealthy Mr. Eddy (Robert Loggia), an aging gangster who, in the film's wackiest scene, displays a startling passion for road courtesy when he acts on his credo that "tailgating is one thing I cannot tolerate."

Mr. Eddy's best girl is Alice Wakefield, who is not only as blond as Renee Madison was dark, she is also played by Arquette. When, in a sizzling melding of vocals and picture, Alice gives Pete the come-hitherest of looks as Lou Reed's version of "This Magic Moment" hits the soundtrack, it's clear that Pete will have the same kind of trouble with her that doppelganger Fred had with Renee.

More in its imagery than in its baroque plotting, "Lost Highway" is best at creating a sense of unease. Working with cinematographer Peter Deming and longtime composing, collaborator Angelo Badalamenti, Lynch has put together some thoroughly spooky situations. In the hands of this crew, even something as straightforward as a ringing phone in an empty room can create the feeling that the most awful thing is about to happen.

Less successful, though sometimes effective, is the film's stylized use of dialogue. Lynch favors a flat, uninflected acting style and likes having throwaway lines like "Who the hell owns that dog?" read as if they were pregnant with meaning. It takes a strong performer to make an impression under those conditions and, aside from Blake, only Arquette's uncompromisingly sensual presence has the force to do so.

But though it can seem intriguing at any given moment, those moments have a tendency to get ultra-violent and sexually exploitative. Plus, it's difficult to sustain Lynch's kind of showy nihilism for 2 hours and 15 minutes, no matter how much skill is involved. "I like to remember things my own way, how I remember them, not how they actually happened," says Fred Madison, speaking for a director not shy about amusing himself with on-screen games and not really worried if an audience wants to come along for the ride or not.

NEW YORK, 3/3/97, p. 53, David Denby

If an animal—a wolf, say—eats its own tail and then continues eating until it consumes itself, hoof and whisker, and if it then turns into an antelope that uses its horns to make watercolor drawings of a wolf, we may think that it has pulled off quite a trick. We may also think it's a pretty screwed-up beast. David Lynch's new movie, *Lost Highway* performs comparable contortions and transformations and undergoes comparable rebirths. The picture is a virtuoso exercise in spooky unintelligibility. It seems to be grinning at itself in facing mirrors.

Formally, *Lost Highway* hangs together: There are recurring images and various "rhyming" devices in the plot and a sustained atmosphere of erotic anguish. But none of it makes any particular sense. A man (Bill Pullman) who is sent to prison for murdering his wife (but did he really murder her?) is transformed, somehow, into a younger man (Balthazar Getty) who falls in love with what appears to be the same woman, who ... Here also is a ghost, or at least a ghostly personage (played by Robert Blake), who makes home videos; a good deal of mock pornography; and much doomed driving-about at night, headlights penetrating into the unfathomable darkness, which receives the oncoming beams into its womb of annihilation—or something like that.

David Lynch may be a failure as an artist, but he's not a phony. In this two-hour narrative movie, he has sustained the obsessional weirdness of his most extreme works. He's consistently sick, and consistently indifferent about pleasing us. Which is a shame, because the beginning of *Lost Highway* suggests some interesting possibilities. Patricia Arquette and Bill Pullman play a married couple living together in tense silence and distrust. Pullman is all awareness, and Arquette seems completely drugged, so they make a provocative and unstable combination. Erotic tension gathers in the blank spaces between their words. The couple begins receiving videotapes, first of the exterior of their house, then of the interior and the two of them in bed. Some sort of intruder is plaguing them, and we gather he has a mysterious connection to Arquette's past.

This mix of voyeurism and violation could easily power a great erotic thriller—but then Lynch lets everything go but the eroticism. He escapes into visual fantasia, just as he did after the opening episodes of *Twin Peaks,* when it became clear (to our disappointment) that he wasn't going to provide any great payoff to the fantastic mysteries he had created earlier (he seemed to care who murdered Laura Palmer less than we did). We get the usual menacing Lynchian soundtrack, with its moaning wind-tunnel relentlessness. There are hallucinated corridors illuminated by lightning, and much gangsterish violence. Women solemnly pull off their clothes and offer themselves for male inspection; a pornographic image of Patricia Arquette plays on a screen in an endless monotony of ecstasy.

Arquette, who seems thick and dulled, as if she's had too much sex but isn't really interested in anything else, appears first with long black hair, then with long blonde hair. Whether she's two women or one is impossible to say, but she's certainly the ultimate *noir* girl, Veronica Lake and Jane Greer combined and naked at last, an entirely available and inexhaustible sexual possibility. The movie seems to be about the annihilation of consciousness—people wiped out by sex or death or metamorphosis. *Lost Highway,* if it doesn't wipe out the audience as well, might be interesting to talk about in bed.

But that's the only place, apart from a few film journals, where it will cause much discussion.

NEW YORK POST, 2/21/97, p. 47, Thelma Adams

"Lost Highway" won't win new fans for David ("Eraserhead") Lynch but the aging hipster's cult will make the trip.

"I like to remember things my own way," says saxophonist Fred Madison (Bill Pullman). If we ever had any doubts, Lynch reminds us that his reality isn't ours. The die is cast. Audiences—and critics—be damned.

Before "Lost Highway" turns on its tail, ending at its beginning (a vogue that includes "Pulp Fiction" and "Before the Rain"), the blandly handsome Pullman proves that he makes a fine president (see "Independence Day") but really excels at being a patsy (see "Malice" and "The Last Seduction").

Pullman's musician lives a good sax, bad sex life. His Mulholland Morticia, the auburn-haired Renee (Patricia Arquette), might be having a thing on the side. When the two begin receiving mysterious videos at their haunted condo, poor Fred gets pulled into a Lynchian knot of murder, mayhem, doppelgangers, devils, betrayal and heavy set decoration.

Arquette is a better actress than the material requires. Sure, she can expose her "Twin Peaks" as well as Sherilyn Fenn can; but she's not shallow enough to gloss over the fact that even though she plays two parts, there's less than one character on the screen. Whether Arquette's a dangerous blonde seducing a naive mechanic (Balthazar Getty) or a dipsomaniac brunette, the dual role, recycled from Cain and Chandler, is like a document that has been photocopied too many times.

As a midlife Nosferatu shadowing Fred, Robert Blake is menacing and satirical, beguiling but opaque. The character is a gimmick, a Lynchian dwarf with height. The "In Cold Blood" star doesn't have any more of a fix on why he's there than we do. His downbeat demon with a cell phone echoes Joel Grey in "Cabaret."

Even if there's no *there* there on the "Lost Highway," Lynch is too suave a filmmaker not to inject some new juice into the old pulp fiction. Just as the plot becomes predictable, one character switches place with another following the disturbing dream logic that morphs your high school English teacher, say, with Adolf Hitler, or your sainted mother with Hillary Rodham Clinton. Suddenly, the story takes off, crab-like, in an unforeseen direction.

Such tricks yank the audience back to attention; we're momentarily riveted, riding shotgun on Lynch's psychedelic highway of desire and broken dreams. We're aroused, tickled, amused, disgusted and, ultimately, adrift in a cryptic world that's warped for warped sake.

Lynch might not mind that we're all dressed up in "Blue Velvet" with nowhere to go. He might even be so delusional as to think that's the point. But we've already made the *hajj* to "Twin Peaks." Lynch has our attention. Now tell us something new. Shock us with a deeper, richer vision of the world. We love you, Dave, but pull off this "Lost Highway."

NEWSDAY, 2/21/97, Part II/p. B13, Jack Mathews

Setting aside his major studio pictures, "Elephant Man" and "Dune," David Lynch's films—and his cult TV series, "Twin Peaks"—have all centered on the conflict between the ego and the id of American life. He's fascinated with the massive gulf between the world governed and shaped by society at large, and the one percolating beneath the surface, inscrutable and potentially lethal.

At the opening of his masterful 1986 "Blue Velvet," Lynch announces the film's theme with deliberate obviousness, giving us a glimpse of life in a bucolic small town before his camera digs below the surface, into the wet sod where insects are scurrying about. The rest of "Blue Velvet" is a collision of these adjacent worlds, the surface and the subterranean, and unprepared audiences were left reeling.

Since then, Lynch has gotten more and more obscure in his symbolism, taking "Twin Peaks" from high camp mystery into metaphysical bunk and in the process lost all but his most faithful fans.

With "Lost Highway," Lynch returns to near "Blue Velvet" form and ought to reclaim some of his stray fans. The movie, of course, is patently weird, and only liars will walk out claiming to have unraveled all of its mysteries. But it is a fascinating, dreamlike psychological mind game, with Lynch finding beetles not beneath the surface of polite society but inside the individual human psyche.

"Lost Highway" is constructed as two doomed love stories told back-to-back, the first about a jazz musician (Bill Pullman) being driven mad by doubts of his wife's fidelity, the second about a young auto mechanic (Balthazar Getty) who begins a dangerous affair with a mobster's mistress. But here's your ticket to Lynchville: The two men may be the same person, though they are played by different actors, and their lovers, both played by Patricia Arquette, are almost certainly the same woman. The four characters are two sets of alter egos. Maybe.

With a pace and style that is almost hypnotic, Lynch begins his first story, slowly introducing us to Fred and Renee Madison (Pullman and Arquette), who live in a modern, sparsely decorated home in what appears to be the Hollywood Hills. They speak to each other in sleepy monotones and make love like total strangers. There doesn't appear to be any emotional connection between them, yet when Fred blows his sax at the jazz club every night, it's with a passion fueled by murderous jealousy.

In the second story, the young mechanic, Pete (Getty), who seems to spring full blown from the mind of Fred Madison, falls in love with Alice Wakefield (Arquette again), a blonde sexpot who comes on to him so strongly that he overlooks her relationship with cold-blooded killer Mr. Eddy (Robert Loggia). Like dozens of B movies from the '40s and '50s, Pete is lured by the femme fatale into committing murder for her, and having to face the consequences.

To say more about the plot would be to fill in too many pieces of the puzzle, but I'll add this. As the second story unfolds, we start to double back on characters and events from the first story, eventually coming full circle. The movie begins and ends with the camera chewing up the yellow line of a desert highway caught in the beams of a car's headlights.

What happens in between doesn't always make sense, and you and your friends will go through a pot of after-screening espresso just reconstructing the stories and itemizing the clues. "Lost Highway," written by Lynch and Barry Gifford, is less a psychological thriller than a psycho-analytic mystery, and even if you know the meaning of dreams, it will keep you guessing.

It's easily Lynch's best work since "Blue Velvet," and we welcome him back.

NEWSWEEK, 2/24/97, p. 68, Jack Kroll

With *Lost Highway*, David Lynch has made a movie that will drive you bananas. His films ("Blue Velvet," "Wild at Heart") and his groundbreaking TV series "Twin Peaks" fused reality with dreams. In "Lost Highway," reality has become a dream. But Lynch has forgotten how boring it is listening to someone else's dream. You know, the ones where you become someone else, your mother becomes your cat and your spouse becomes the microwave. In "Lost Highway" (co-written by Barry Gifford), Fred Madison (Bill Pullman) is a jazz musician who suspects his wife, Renee (Patricia Arquette), is having an affair. When she's gruesomely murdered, he's tried and sentenced to the electric chair. In his cell he suddenly turns into Pete Dayton (Balthazar Getty), an auto mechanic. The flabbergasted cops release Pete, who soon meets Alice (Arquette), the girlfriend of sadistic mob boss Mr. Eddy (Robert Loggia), who's also sadistic mob boss Dick Laurent. Alice is a blond Renee look-alike—or is she Renee? And is Pete Fred? And who in hell (literally) is the Mystery Man (Robert Blake), a corpse-faced galoot who can be in two places at the same time?

These mysteries become not fascinating but maddening, a Rubik's Cube that's metastasized into 256 sides. Yes, yes, "lost highway" is the highway we're all on, careering to nowhere. *Oui, oui,* identity has lost its solidity in the postmod world of image scrimmage. *Da, da,* violence lurks in every human heart. Lynch has become the Heisenberg of cinema, telling us that the uncertainty principle rules our lives. Sex is either frantic (Pete with Alice) or failed (Fred with Renee). Murder is the true orgasmic activity of millennial man. Lynch tells us this with the most dazzling style of any filmmaker. (The soundtrack is a tone poem that fuses '90s nihilism from Nine Inch Nails to Marilyn Manson with the neo-noir dronescapes of Angelo Badalamenti and Barry Adamson.) But "Lost Highway" takes us on a joyride to emptiness. It's a dead end.

SIGHT AND SOUND, 9/97, p. 48, Kim Newman

Los Angeles. Saxophonist Fred Madison discovers on his doorstep a videocassette of his house, shot from the outside. The next day, another videocassette includes footage of a track through his home, showing Fred asleep with his brunette wife Renee. The Madisons call the police, who have no explanation. Renee takes Fred to a party thrown by Andy, a shady character, and Fred is accosted by a mystery man, whose face he has glimpsed in the shadows. The mystery man claims to have met Fred at his house, and that he is there right now. He produces a mobile phone so that Fred can confirm this, by phoning home and talking to him. The next videotape shows Fred with the dismembered corpse of Renee. Convicted of his wife's murder, Fred suffers strange headaches and in prison transforms into another person entirely—a young mechanic named Pete Dayton.

The authorities return Pete to the charge of his parents, and Pete picks up his life, doing work for his gangster patron, Mr Eddy. Mr Eddy's mistress, Alice Wakefield—a blonde incarnation of Renee—begins an affair with Pete. Alice talks him into robbing Andy, an associate of Mr Eddy's who lured her into prostitution and working in pornographic films. During the robbery, Andy is killed and Pete notices a photograph of Andy and Mr Eddy with Alice and Renee. Pete drives into the desert, where Alice has arranged to meet a fence. She disappears into a shack—and, as it turns out, from the photograph at Andy's—and Pete transforms back into Fred. Mr Eddy appears on the scene, and is executed by the mystery man. Fred returns to the city to deliver a message to his own home that Mr Eddy, also known as Dick Laurent, is dead, and drives again into the desert, with the police in hot pursuit.

The legend of Luis Buñuel's collaboration with Salvador Dali is that if either included an image or incident open to rational explanation or interpretation, it would be dropped. Yet *Un chien andalou* and *L'Age d'or* afford many meaningful readings. It may well be that with *Lost Highway*, director David Lynch and co-screenwriter Barry Gifford—author of the novel *Wild at Heart*—have succeeded where Buñuel and Dali failed, creating an almost entirely meaningless, or perhaps senseless, film.

A synopsis can only be tentative, since the film delights in contradictory or unexplained events, fracturing narrative logic at every turn. At a party, the film's first protagonist Fred asks the host who the mystery man is. Fred is told that he is a friend of the recently deceased Dick Laurent. But later it emerges that the gangster Mr Eddy is also called Dick Laurent—and when Eddy dies in the course of the film, Fred drives to deliver the news of his death, apparently to his own house. While in Lynch's *Blue Velvet* and *Twin Peaks* the *noir* plots are surprisingly worked through and explained, *Lost Highway* goes out of its way to be inexplicable. The twinning of Fred's wife Renee and Mr Eddy's moll Alice is impossible to rationalise as a *Vertigo* (1958) imposture, a *High Plains Drifter* (1972) resurrection or a *Mirror Images* twinsister exchange. As a photograph at one point demonstrates, Renee and Alice are sometimes separate and sometimes one. If this bothers you, then there is no way into or out of *Lost Highway* for you.

The opening 'Fred Madison' section of the film, climaxing with Fred's transformation, is so powerful that the 'Pete Dayton' sequence inevitably disappoints. Fred and Renee receive the videocassettes, each showing more as the camera gets closer to them. Then Fred encounters the mystery man—Robert Blake in Bela Lugosi make-up, delivering arguably the most frightening performance in 90s cinema—and by this point Lynch fulfills his declared intention to fashion "a twenty-first-century *noir* horror film". He invests the Madisons' house with shadows that, in Raymond Chandler's phrase, betoken "something more than the night". Lynch has always excelled at sidesteps into pocket-sized universes—behind the radiator in *Eraserhead*, within the Black Lodge in *Twin Peaks*—but here he makes the simple shadowed corner into which Fred fades the most dreadful place his cinema has ever taken us.

Though the film slackens off when Balthazar Getty takes over the lead, Bill Pullman, an older version of the characters previously played by Kyle MacLachlan, represents Lynchian Man at his most susceptible to the forces of darkness, as demonstrated in the astonishing first encounter with the mystery man. More significant, perhaps, is Fred's explanation to the cops that he hates video cameras because "I like to remember things my own way ... how I remember them, not necessarily the way they happened". This whole film is not necessarily the way things happened. The Fred/Pete transformation just about makes emotional sense in terms of the entrapment of the *noir* hero within the narrative and the wiles of an eternally reborn *femme fatale*; while the twinning and melding of Alice and Renee play perfectly, thanks to Patricia Arquette's mastery of the art of holding back. But the 'Pete Dayton' section of *Lost Highway* founders a little on its lack of specificity. Have Fred and Pete exchanged bodies, with Pete coming out of some limbo to usurp Fred's place in the world (as Bob did with Agent Cooper in the last episode of *Twin Peaks*?) Or has Fred transformed only into a *physical* likeness of Pete, retaining his own memories and personality? On the one hand, Pete has his own skills at intuitive engine tuning—"The best goddamn ears in town", Mr Eddy comments, patting the film on the back for its consistently superb soundtrack, designed by Lynch himself—but on the other, he seems disturbed by Alice's resemblance to Renee.

Fred Madison lives in a horror story where an ordinary life can be pulled apart because of a stray thought and none of the trappings of American success can offer more than illusory comfort. But Pete Dayton's world is culled from the *noirs* Gifford extemporises on in his distinctive book of movie reviews, *The Devil Thumbs a Ride and Other Unforgettable Films*. Robert Loggia's Mr Eddy, like Frank of *Blue Velvet* and Bobby Peru of *Wild at Heart*, is a parody crime boss, brutally pistol-whipping an obnoxious motorist who has tailgated him, forcing him to promise to learn his highway code, and repeatedly emphasising the punishment he would inflict on anyone who slept with his mistress.

The Pete scenes trot out *noir* motifs—fleeing lovers, double crosses, a fall-guy protagonist—as landmarks rather than events, but the potency of the Fred scenes is never entirely dissipated.

Among the most disturbing moments in the film are a terrifying phonecall from Mr Eddy and the mystery man (lying together in suggestive darkness) to Pete, and later Alice's reminiscence of being forced at gunpoint to strip for Mr Eddy (with Marilyn Manson proving against the odds that it is possible to outdo Screamin' Jay Hawkins with a more demented rendition of 'I Put a Spell on You'). Fred returns at a desert site where time has run backwards, so that the mystery man's shack is first seen in flames and then de-explodes to wholeness. The last section of the film, which jumbles elements from all that has gone before, is all momentum where most movies would be all explanation, fading out with the lost highway of the title (a stray phrase from Gifford's novel *Night People*, not a reference to Hank Williams) and a high-speed car chase into a desert darkness.

As always with Lynch, it is hard to distinguish between a fictional universe created to force a reassessment of your relationship with the real one, and a personal world that suggests an unsympathetic interpretation of its creator's feelings. The abused and murdered women of *Blue Velvet* and *Twin Peaks* are again featured, though there is more eroticising here of living bodies than of dead ones. However, when it comes to genuine film fear—as opposed to Wes Craven's rollercoaster scariness with pop-culture footnotes—Lynch's is the only game in town. This is post-genre horror: playing down explicit shock (even Andy's head-impaling on the corner of a glass table is not given set-piece treatment), it works on the evocation of unease through subtle sounds and blaring doom metal, offering blurred moments that resolve briefly into dreadful clarity. After 100 years of cinema, it is still possible to make a truly terrifying picture.

TIME, 3/3/97, p. 83, Richard Corliss

One reviewer emerged from an early screening of *Lost Highway* with the cry of "Garbage!" Well, David Lynch must be doing something right. The creator of *Twin Peaks* describes his first film in four years as a "21st century noir horror film." It has a battered suitcase of references to old Hollywood film noir, the requisite gore for a scare show and, in the spooky presence of Robert Blake—with his pancake white face, shaved eyebrows and sickly smile—an eldritch harbinger of death like the dwarf in *Twin Peaks*. So whatever that critic may think, *Lost Highway* isn't refuse. But it ain't revelation either. What's missing is the shock of the new.

The plot, which cunningly loops itself like a Möbius strip with sprocket holes, starts with a couple, Fred (Bill Pullman) and Renee (Patricia Arquette), troubled about intrusions into their home and their private lives. Renee vanishes, and the film changes lanes. It follows Pete (Balthazar Getty), a grease monkey who dumps his girlfriend (Natasha Gregson Wagner) and takes up with a gangster (Robert Loggia) and his moll. Damned if this new femme fatale doesn't look exactly like Renee, but with platinum blond hair.

Several motels and murders later, and in between cameos by such veteran outragers as Richard Pryor, Henry Rollins and Mink Stole, we notice the signposts, This is a milder *Wild at Heart,* the 1990 road movie that, like this one, Lynch wrote with novelist Barry Gifford.

If *Lost Highway* had preceded *Wild at Heart* (or *Eraserhead* or *Blue Velvet*), it might give off a sense of otherworldly menace. But we've visited this planet before, become familiar with its obsessions and grotesqueries until they hold as little terror as garden gnomes. And while it's always a tonic in this timid film age to see directors try something different, *Lost Highway* is the same different. Someone should tell Lynch that noir is a genre, but weird isn't.

VILLAGE VOICE, 2/25/97, p. 63, J. Hoberman

"This is some spooky shit we got here" a prison guard informs his deadpan colleague at a key moment in David Lynch's *Lost Highway*. Do tell: A convicted wife-killer, it would seem, has inexplicably metamorphosed, while in his jail cell, into an "innocent" teenage boy.

Lost Highway, Lynch's first movie in four years, seems founded upon a similar longing for regression. Neither as empty nor as stylish as it may initially appear, the film is perilously close to self-parody in its earnestly lysergic, tenderly adolescent evocation of rockabilly badness. Like: Down the two-lane blacktop of unspeakable sex urge a man must go, the wide screen lit by an enormous close-up of a glowing cigarette.

So much for the spirit of youthful abandon. *Lost Highway,* which Lynch cowrote with noir specialist Barry Gifford, is actually most successful when communicating the miasma of conjugal paranoia that engulfs a depressed pair of L.A. hipsters (Bill Pullman and Patricia Arquette). Pullman, a cold fish at best, is rendered all the clammier for being made up to resemble a degenerate version of Lynch's earlier alter ego, Kyle McLachlan. Arquette, meanwhile, seems permanently prepped for Halloween as Morticia Addams—swaddled in black satin, with lipstick to match, her entire performance weighed down by a mass of dark tresses.

Steeped in '40s noir, *Highway's* first half hour has a sinister, antiquarian feel. (The unhappy couple might live on the same Hollywood Hills street where Maya Deren shot *Meshes of the Afternoon.*) The early scenes are weirdly underplayed, but they lodge in the mind like shards—a strobe-lit jazz club, an aggressively artless videotape of Pullman and Arquette asleep in their bedroom produced by an unknown intruder, a pool party where Pullman is approached by the androgynous Mystery Man who's been haunting his dreams (Robert Blake made up to resemble Al Lewis's Bela Lugosi as Dracula in *The Munsters*).

Borderline terrible but compelling nonetheless, *Lost Highway* is characterized by a strenuous striving for absolute creepiness. If the dialogue is not up to the ideas, the leads are even less adequate to their roles. Dull normals Pullman and Arquette never seem to know where they are in the funny-scary-wiggy proceedings, which presently escalate to bloody murder. Perhaps that's the point. This is the first Lynch movie set in Southern California, and the landscape is sveltely depopulated. *Lost Highway's* compositions feel oppressively unfixed and disconcertingly vacant—there's too much air around the figures, themselves too often just standing around.

Around a third of the way through, Lynch pulls a dramatic switch that may or may not involve the transmigration of souls. Instead of Pullman, the hero is now the scarcely more charismatic Balthazar Getty, a grease monkey who still lives with his folks at home. (Hilariously, his sympathetic parents, played by Gary Busey and Lucy Butler, suggest Ozzie and Harriet as a pair of retired bikers.) The closest thing to a jolt of performative energy is provided by Robert Loggia as an ogreish gangster who patronizes the garage where Getty works. To establish his outsize rage, Lynch gives him an entertaining faux-Dennis Hopper scene, running a hapless tailgater off the road.

Things take a decidedly oedipal turn when Loggia shows up with a blond babe also played, by Patricia Arquette. In the neatest privileged moment, Lynch accompanies a slow-motion exchange of meaningful glances with Lou Reed doing his affectedly affectless version of "This Magic Moment." Arquette is even witchier here than she was as the Black Dahlia—an ethereal devil-woman whose peachy complexion sets off her pointy teeth. Events from here on move with the speed of fantasy. Still, the doomed passions remain as remote as the movie's convoluted time-space continuum seems abstract.

Whatever *Lost Highway* lacks in emotional resonance it makes up in ambition. Aspiring to be a pulp masterpiece, the movie draws on the history of L.A. noir, from *Double Indemnity* to *Kiss Me Deadly*, while carrying strong intimations of *Vertigo*. Unfortunately, once the blood begins to flow, *Lost Highway* more often suggests a classy, enervated Wes Craven film. Some of the effects are astoundingly corny: The movie is full of unmotivated thunder and lightning, both inside and out. Every house has its corridor of disco spookiness.

Given Lynch's tabloid sense of morality and horrified fascination with murder-porn, one wonders what he would have done with the original Quentin Tarantino script for *Natural Born Killers*. As boldly phantasmagoric as it is, *Lost Highway* only becomes a bore once the filmmaker starts searching for some ultimate depravity—Marilyn Manson singing "I Put a Spell on You." It takes a while for the sense of sordid scuzz to kick in. Once it does, *Lost Highway* is a sad, sad story—a ghost movie about the ghost of Lynch movies past.

Also reviewed in:
NATION, 3/17/97, p. 44, Stuart Klawans
NEW YORK TIMES, 2/21/97, p. C1, Janet Maslin
NEW YORKER, 3/10/97, p. 98, Terrence Rafferty
VARIETY, 1/20-26/97, p. 44, Todd McCarthy
WASHINGTON POST, 2/28/97, Weekend/p. 43, Desson Howe

LOST WORLD, THE: JURASSIC PARK

A Universal Pictures release of an Amblin Entertainment production. *Executive Producer:* Kathleen Kennedy. *Producer:* Gerald R. Molen and Colin Wilson. *Director:* Steven Spielberg. *Screenplay:* David Koepp. *Based on the novel "The Lost World" by:* Michael Crichton. *Director of Photography:* Janusz Kaminski. *Editor:* Michael Kahn. *Music:* John Williams. *Music Editor:* Kenneth Wannberg. *Sound:* Gary Rydstrom and (music) Shawn Murphy. *Sound Editor:* Richard Hymns. *Casting:* Janet Hirshenson and Jane Jenkins. *Production Designer:* Rick Carter. *Art Director:* Jim Teegarden. *Set Designer:* Pamela Klamer and Linda King. *Set Decorator:* Gary Fettis. *Special Effects:* Don Elliott. *Full Motion Dinosaurs:* Dennis Muren. *Live Action Dinosaurs:* Stan Winston. *Special Dinosaur Effects:* Michael Lantieri. *Dinosaur Motion Supervisor:* Randal M. Dutra. *Costumes:* Sue Moore. *Make-up:* Christina Smith. *Stunt Coordinator:* M. James Arnett and Gary Hymes. *Running time:* 134 minutes. *MPAA Rating:* PG-13.

CAST: Jeff Goldblum (Ian Malcolm); Julianne Moore (Sarah Harding); Pete Postlethwaite (Roland Tembo); Arliss Howard (Peter Ludlow); Richard Attenborough (John Hammond); Vince Vaughn (Nick Van Owen); Vanessa Lee Chester (Kelly Curtis); Peter Stormare (Dieter Stark); Harvey Jason (Ajay Sidhu); Richard Schiff (Eddie Carr); Thomas F. Duffy (Dr. Robert Burke); Joseph Mazzello (Tim); Ariana Richards (Lex); Thomas Rosales (Carter); Camilla Belle (Cathy Bowman); Cyd Strittmatter (Mrs. Bowman); Robin Sachs (Mr. Bowman); Elliott Goldwag (Senior Board Member); J. Patrick McCormack (Board Member); Ross Partridge (Curious Man); Ian Abercrombie (Butler); David Sawyer (Workman); Geno Silva (Barge Captain); Alex Miranda (Barge Captain's Son); Robert "Bobby Z" Zajonc (InGen Helicopter Pilot); Jim Harley (Harbor Master); Colton James (Benjamin); Carey Eidel (Benjamin's Dad); Katy Boyer (Benjamin's Mom); David Koepp (Unlucky Bastard); Eugene Bass, Jr. (Attorney); Bari Buckner (Screaming Woman); Ransom Walrod (Ship Driver); David Gene Gibbs (Police Helicopter Pilot); Vincent Dee Miles (Screaming Hunter); Bernard Shaw (CNN Reporter/Himself).

LOS ANGELES TIMES, 5/23/97, Calendar/p. 1, Kevin Thomas

"Jurassic Park," the biggest worldwide box-office hit of all time, proves to be impossible to top or equal. Its sequel, "The Lost World: Jurassic Park," has stupendous production values and special effects and works best as a family entertainment, but the thrills and chills are not up to the original.

It's not just that we've been there before but also that Steven Spielberg and his associates simply haven't been able to imagine as many flat-out scary moments this time around. But the dinosaurs are once again utterly convincing and irresistible, and that, along with other pluses, will most likely be more than enough to ensure the film's popularity.

From Frame 1 Spielberg et al are clearly aware of the challenge facing them in attempting a sequel, yet are surely correct in assuming moviegoers the world over would be only too happy to see such totally believable and endearing dinosaurs again.

To that end Spielberg and writer David Koepp, also returning from "Jurassic Park," go for lots of disarming humor in incorporating Michael Crichton's sequel to his original novel into the screenplay. It seemed such a mistake in "Jurassic Park" to sideline early on its most interesting character, the brilliant, free-thinking and outspoken chaos theorist Ian Malcolm (Jeff Goldblum) with a broken leg, but in its most inspired stroke, "The Lost World" brings back Malcolm and places him front and center.

Some of its best moments are its earliest. Spielberg and Koepp know they're going to have to do some fast talking to get a sequel off the ground. As zillions of people will recall, Jurassic Park was to be the ultimate theme park, the brain child of British entrepreneur John Hammond (Richard Attenborough), who filled a Costa Rican island with genetically engineered dinosaurs only to have his dream turn into a nightmare, resulting in the destruction of all the animals. Jurassic Park and its fate have remained secret.

Well, maybe not *all* the dinosaurs were destroyed, after all. Aha! The irrepressible Hammond summons Malcolm to his mansion to inform him that dinosaurs are running freely on a *second* island, having been genetically engineered at a facility there. Hammond believes that inevitably this island will be discovered and wants Malcolm to lead a team to photograph the dinosaurs as proof of their existence and lead to their protection. "From capitalist to humanist in four years!" snorts Malcolm, whom Hammond cleverly maneuvers into the assignment he absolutely does not wish to accept.

It's a pleasure to watch such wily pros as Goldblum and Attenborough spar with each other with wit and assurance. Unfortunately, the kind of rich characterization they display while deploying a great deal of necessary expository information is, apart from Goldblum's character, not sustained throughout the rest of the picture.

Besides Malcolm and his rather colorless team, the adventure on Isla Sorna also involves Malcolm's girlfriend Sarah (Julianne Moore), a paleontologist so eager to prove that dinosaurs are great at nurturing their young that it seems never to occur to her that the animals might not welcome a nosy human. Vanessa Lee Chester, as Malcolm's neglected young daughter, is a stowaway on the expedition.

Not surprisingly, Hammond has been removed as head of his company, InGen BioEngineering, in the wake of the Jurassic Park debacle, but his greedy but dimwitted nephew Peter (Arliss Howard) has a plan to replenish company coffers and sends off to Isla Sorna his own team, headed by great white hunter Roland Tembo (Pete Postlethwaite). Along with Goldblum and Attenborough, only Postlethwaite gets a chance to register a vivid, engaging presence.

The stage is set for lots of action-adventure, cliffhanging episodes and disaster sequences, which Spielberg stages with dispatch. There are elements familiar from everything from "King Kong" to "Planet of the Apes," and if "The Lost World" is not particularly fresh, it's not unduly violent. As Malcolm leads the struggle to leave the dinosaurs free from the interference of humans, it poses the inevitable timeless question: Who's the truly monstrous, man or beast?

"Jurassic Park" represented a breakthrough in the use of computer-generated imagery, and the Oscar-winning team that created the dinosaur effects for the 1993 film—Dennis Muren, Stan Winston and Michael Lantieri—is back. They fill the screen with examples of *Tyrannosaurus rex* in all sizes, from adorable hopping babies to a giant mother *T-rex* who wants her infant back—right now. (There are on view other kinds of dinosaurs briefly, but it's a *T-rex* show.)

Also back are ace production designer Rick Carter and composer John Williams, whose score contributes strongly toward creating an aura of excitement. The only key member of Spielberg's creative team who is not a "Jurassic Park" alum is Spielberg's "Schindler's List" cinematographer Janusz Kaminksi, who gives "The Lost World" a darker look than it needs.

Many people will find much to divert them in "The Lost World," and not worry whether or not it falls short of "Jurassic Park." Given the kind of spectacular and harmless enterprise that it is, you wouldn't want to begrudge any viewer any pleasure he or she, children most of all, might derive from it.

NEW STATESMAN, 7/18/97, p. 43, Jonathan Coe

The Lost World Jurassic Park—to give it its full, even more elegant title, *The Lost World Jurassic Park (TM)*—is apparently the highest grossing film of all time; or at least, it was for about a week, until the next highest grossing-film-of-all-time came along. (Funny how these records keep getting broken. I suspect it has more to do with population increases and rising ticket prices than with Hollywood's ability to make bigger and better films.) Producers are always talking about a film's "gross", and the word certainly popped into my mind often enough during *The Lost World Jurassic Park:* in fact it must be among the grossest, not to mention goriest and most sadistic films ever to have been awarded a PG certificate in this country. There's so much violence and bloody mayhem that it makes *Crash* look like a mid-1970s edition of *Blue Peter*. What can James Ferman and friends have been thinking of?

But then the gross-out factor, the audience's shrieks of delighted revulsion, the exquisite calculation of just how much violence the kids can take—these are all part of Spielberg's peculiar genius. He's up there with Disney and Hitchcock in the pantheon of cinema's most shameless and brilliant torturers. The same goes for his way with pathos. There are some shots here of a baby T Rex being used as a huntsman's bait, tethered to the ground and whimpering plangently, which brought tears to my jaded old critic's eyes. Afterward, of course, I realised that I had been weeping over a piece of computer-controlled plastic, and hated myself for it. But that's part of Spielberg's genius, too.

The utter realism of the dinosaurs is something we simply take for granted, after the first film. There's none of the build up to their first appearance, no gasps of wonder at our first glimpse; in fact the entire exposition is garbled and perfunctory, something that has to be rushed through for form's sake. A quick dialogue scene between Jeff Goldblum and Richard Attenborough (establishes that the original island was just a sideshow, and the real dinosaur action is taking place on something called "Site B". Goldblum decides he has to go there, for some reason (who cares?), and on arrival finds that his girlfriend—or maybe his wife (who cares?)—Julianne Moore has preceded him, and is busy doing some sort of research (into dinosaur mating habits? Who cares?) Also installed are Pete Postlethwaite, as the last of the Great White Hunters, determined to have a T Rex to fit into his trophy case, and a bunch of baddies led by Arliss Howard, who want to turn the island into a theme park. (At least I think that's what they want—but then who, for God's sake, cares?)

What follows is an unrelenting barrage of action sequences, many of which are admittedly stunning. *The Lost World Jurassic Park* stands in much the same relation to its predecessor as *Aliens* to the original *Alien*. Knowing that the mere sight of the occasional monster is no longer going to fill us with terror, the filmmakers now bombard us with the things. Dinosaurs fly at the luckless protagonists from all angles, crushing them to death, bashing them to the ground with their tails, snapping their heads off, chomping greedily, and so on. One particularly horrific scene has a man covered from head to foot in dozens of tiny, screeching lizards, one of which gnaws half of his upper lip away in loving closeup.

As the film races from one such extraordinary scene to another—most of them taking place at night, many in the rain, and accompanied by a bone-rattling soundtrack of special effects and symphony orchestra—you start to realise with a certain awe that you're watching some kind of apotheosis of the action movie. The analogy with roller-coaster rides is hackneyed but accurate. Spielberg has made a theme park, not a movie (although on one level the film seems to regard itself, laughably, as a critique of theme park culture), and the real genetic monstrosity here is not the velociraptor or the pterodactyl, but the mutation of what was once intended as an art-form into a mere machine for quickening the pulse. And by far the most scary thing about the film is what it tells us about Spielberg: that although he does seem to have a grasp of concepts such as human interest and imaginative sympathy—as the genuinely affecting *Schindler's List* testifies—he seems to bring just as much energy and commitment to bear on projects that don't even give them the most perfunctory look-in.

That title still exercises me, by the way. Is this, I wonder, the start of a new fashion for simply tacking the name of a successful film onto the name of its sequel? Suppose they now make a sequel to *TLWJP* called *Monster Island*—will it be billed as *Monster Island The Lost World Jurassic Park (TM)?* And supposing *that* is a huge success: will there be a follow-up called *Four Dinosaurs and a Funeral Monster Island The Lost World of Jurassic Park (TM)?*

What was wrong with plain old *Jurassic Park 2,* in the first place?

NEW YORK, 6/2/97, p. 51, David Denby

The Lost World—Steven Spielberg's sequel to *Jurassic Park*—is rather dispiriting. The adventure sequences certainly have spectacular energy and panache; no other director could match them. But the heart has gone out of the material—the awe, the giddy sense of curiosity and fear, the overwhelming violence and startling power. This movie is exciting but impersonal. I didn't much care about anyone in it, and I was indifferent to how it came out. At the beginning, Dr. Ian Malcolm (Jeff Goldblum), the chaos theorist who so correctly predicted the disasters in *Jurassic Park,* journeys to a second, hitherto secret island, also near Costa Rica, where the dinosaurs for the original park were bred. A hurricane has destroyed the facilities at the secret island, but some of the animals have survived in the wild. The visionary but irresponsible entrepreneur John Hammond (Richard Attenborough), now elderly and ill, sends Malcolm to the island with a team to record the wonders for posterity, and Malcolm, who knows how terrifying the dinosaurs are, agrees to go for one reason only—his paleontologist girlfriend, the headstrong

Dr. Sarah Harding (Julianne Moore), is already there, on the loose. What Hammond doesn't know is that his snooty nephew (Arliss Howard), who has taken over Hammond's company, has sent another, larger team to capture some of the fangy beasts and take them back to a stadium in San Diego.

Now, it seems thoroughly unbelievable that any of these people would go near the creatures that hunted men and women so devastatingly in *Jurassic Park*. In particular, Sarah Harding seems infuriatingly dense, and though Julianne Moore may be a great actress, she is bizarrely miscast here and comes off goggle-eyed, disconnected, and entirely humorless. Sarah and an animal-rights-activist-photographer (Vince Vaughn) carry a wounded baby *T. Rex* back to the team's trailer—perhaps the stupidest act in the history of the movies—provoking Mommy-and Daddy-saurus to come looking. The sequence that follows, with the animals pushing the trailer over a cliff as the humans hang on inside, is one of Spielberg's most physically inventive, but it's just spectacle and nothing else. The high-minded attempt to save these particular animals seems almost dotty. If it were treated as dotty, that would be fine, but the movie lays on a glaze of sanctimoniousness in between the horrifying sequences. Spielberg and screenwriter David Koepp seem both timid and exploitative, afraid to offend the animal-rights movement even while using animals to rip humans to shreds.

The action of *Jurassic Park* was an example of what Jeff Goldblum called chaos, or the tendency of large systems to go haywire. That movie had a strong, simple idea—the madness of using technology to control nature. But *The Lost World* has no idea at all. The two teams on the island, one sent to preserve the animals, the other to exploit them, join forces and flee from the aroused dinosaurs; the movie becomes a simple chase and hunt, with characters we don't care about moving through the night and getting lost and then picked off in jungles or fields. There are pesky new creatures, the squeaking little *Compsognathi*, which hunt in packs and nip people to death. And the velociraptors turn up and maim with their usual malicious skill, though they are less entertaining out in the open than in the enclosed space of *Jurassic Park*'s kitchen, where they slid along polished counters and batted the pots and pans.

In an homage to *King Kong,* a giant *T Rex,* shipped back to San Diego, breaks loose and terrorizes the swimming pools and shopping districts of America's most placid city. The San Diego scenes are almost witty, but by this time, *The Lost World* has become decadent—an example of extravagant spectacle for its own sake. Again and again, characters who seem important fade away with no explanation. *The Lost World* hasn't quite been pulled together. It's a visually exhilarating movie, but in all the other ways that matter, it's inert.

NEW YORK POST, 5/23/97, p. 45, Michael Medved

"The Lost World: Jurassic Park" isn't just a dinosaur movie—it's a dinosaur of a movie: prehistoric, lumbering, ungainly, thick-skinned and cold-blooded. This eagerly awaited sequel has been cautiously and self-consciously cloned from the cinematic DNA of its predecessor, but the result is a pale, fuzzy, unfocused copy that is altogether lacking in vitality. In fact, no other film in Steven Spielberg's astonishing career—no, not even "1941"—has seemed so emotionless, formulaic and calculating.

The story begins when "chaos theorist" Dr. Ian Malcolm (Jeff Goldblum), one of the scarred-for-life survivors of the first film, meets with the ailing John Hammond (Sir Richard Attenborough), visionary instigator of the disastrous attempt to create a theme park on a Costa Rican island displaying genetically engineered dinosaurs.

It turns out that the great beasts have continued to thrive without human interference on a nearby island (code named "Site B"), and Hammond persuades the reluctant Malcolm to join his paleontologist girlfriend (Julianne Moore) in reporting on the dinosaurs.

They're joined by Malcolm's precocious daughter (Vanessa Lee Chester) from a previous relationship, who stows away on the voyage, and by a nature photographer/environmental activist (Vince Vaughn).

Their respectful, responsible mission to photograph and research the dinosaurs collides, however, with a more exploitative expedition led by big game hunter Pete Postlethwaite and dispatched by Hammond's greedy nephew (Arliss Howard) to capture the beasts for stateside display.

This silly, convoluted plot takes forever to crank itself up and to begin delivering on the movie's simple-minded promise: lots of thrilling scenes of various human victims chased and devoured by special-effects dinosaurs.

Those creatures (brought to life by a combination of robotic animation and computer graphics) are impressively detailed and frightening, and Spielberg does choreograph one ingeniously and outrageously extended sequence where the lead characters dangle by ropes off the edge of a cliff.

Unfortunately, the grainy, shadowy, incongruously "artistic" cinematography (by Janusz Kaminski of "Schindler's List") serves such scenes less effectively than the crisp, lurid visions of its predecessor.

The locations are also a problem: Spielberg finds this "Lost World" in sound-stage sets that resemble cheesy theme-parks, or in redwood forests of Northern California, and in both cases the settings bear little resemblance to the tropical paradise (filmed in Hawaii) of the first film.

In the end—in desperation—Spielberg resorts to over-the-top, insider comedy: turning his tyrannosaurus loose on the unsuspecting city of San Diego in a smirking, tongue-in-cheek evocation of all those fondly remembered Godzilla movies.

This jokey, hokey tone conflicts with the gory, graphic details of this film, which offers far more specific and sadistic images of munching, mutilation and disemberment than "Jurassic Park."

This shift in emphasis may be viewed as a forlorn attempt to give some teeth to a disappointing sequel that is altogether lacking in bite.

NEWSDAY, 5/23/97, Part II/p. B15, Jack Mathews

Here's a movie I wouldn't mind seeing: Scientists in some future century are digging through the rubble where Hollywood once stood and happen onto a cache of amber, inside which are suspended the intact DNA of screenwriters Ben Hecht, Dalton Trumbo, John Huston and Joseph L. Mankiewicz. The DNA is extracted and cloned, and the genetically coded embryos grow up to re-introduce humanity to "the plot!" The plots interbreed, multiply and beget subplots. In this hothouse atmosphere, character is born, nuance begins to develop, and before long, complete stories are being told. With beginnings, middles and ends. Conflict, tension, resolution. And the cosmos is suddenly dizzy with ... notions!

In the meantime, we'll have to settle for the likes of Steven Spielberg's "The Lost World," which is both more and less a clone of "Jurassic Park." More, in the sheer number of dinosaurs, their movement and their human encounters. Less, in the dramatic rationale conjured up for their existence.

"Jurassic Park," adapted from Michael Crichton's captivating novel, told of a corporate scheme to engineer dinosaurs from the DNA of fossilized amber and make them the main attraction of a theme park on a Costa Rican island. But the dinosaurs didn't become extinct for nothing, and after turning on their resurrectors, the dumb beasts are fireballed back to the ice age.

In "The Lost World," we—and Jeff Goldblum's disgraced scientist, Ian Malcolm—learn that only the mature "Jurassic Park" dinosaurs were killed. Turns out, there's another island, 80 miles south, where the animals were actually bred, and it's still heavily populated with T-Rexes, velociraptors, triceratops and the compsognathus, a prehistoric jackal that looks like a naked bird and feeds in packs, like piranha.

What brings man back in contact with these ungrateful creatures is a scheme, by the biochemical company financing the experiment, to export some of the animals to San Diego, whose exposure to Sea World, the San Diego Zoo and the NFL Chargers (I kid you not, this is in the script) has softened it for a Jurassic Park landing. Also, Richard Attenborough's John Hammond, the man who dreamed up the dinosaur farm, is now a reformed capitalist anxious to turn the breeding island into a protective animal preserve.

Almost before you've settled into your seat, Goldblum's Ian is back among' em, leading a small expedition force comprised of his daredevil girlfriend Sarah Harding (Julianne Moore), photojournalist Nick (Vince Vaughn), techno-handyman Eddie (Richard Schiff), and Ian's daughter, Kelly (Vanessa Lee Chester). Opposing them is a safari led by coldhearted CEO Peter Ludlow (Arliss Howard) and big-game hunter Roland Tembo (Pete Postlethwaite).

"The Lost World," of course, is a reference to Arthur Conan Doyle's classic about a scientific expedition that encounters prehistoric monsters. It was the inspiration for "King Kong," and though the T-Rex loosed on San Diego here looks and behaves more like Godzilla, that's Spielberg's inspiration as well.

More money was spent on "The Lost World" than on "Jurassic Park," the highest-grossing picture in history, and it all seems to have gone into effects. These dinosaurs are more than visual spectacles, they're flesh and blood. You don't see them merely galloping over the countryside in computerized herds, or making scary leaps from dark corners. In "The Lost World," the camera moves among them, touches them, smells their breath, and feels their pulse. They are outrageously realistic.

The problem is, the dinosaurs are more realistic than the characters. Goldblum has a lot of fun mocking the proceedings. "That's the way it always starts," Ian says, when his expedition gets excited over their first look at grazing dinosaurs. "Then later, there's the running and screaming ..."

Running, screaming, hanging from cliffs. Spielberg doesn't miss a trick on this outing, and there are a couple of moments where the audience is screaming as loudly as Julianne Moore. And she screams almost as loudly as Fay Wray did upon seeing King Kong.

"The Lost World" is beautifully choreographed by Spielberg and shot by Janusz Kaminski ("Schindler's List"), and if you keep reminding yourself "it's only a movie," the ride is at least as thrilling as the first. Parents be warned: One of the nicest characters becomes a T-Rex snack, and a dog is eaten, off camera.

SIGHT AND SOUND, 7/97, p. 44, Jonathan Romney

Isla Sorna, near Isla Nubar, the site of the prehistoric theme resort Jurassic Park. A young girl is attacked by a group of tiny dinosaurs, compsognathi. In New York, chaos theorist Ian Malcolm is summoned by Jurassic Park's founder John Hammond, head of the InGen corporation. Following the Jurassic Park disaster, InGen has been taken over by its board, headed by Hammond's nephew Peter Ludlow. Hammond explains that the company's Site B on Isla Sorna, where the dinosaurs were bred, has become a self-supporting ecosystem with a thriving dinosaur colony. He asks Malcolm to join a new team documenting the island's population. Malcolm reluctantly agrees when he learns that his girlfriend, palaeontologist Sarah Harding, is already there.

Malcolm arrives on Isla Sorna accompanied by video-maker Nick Van Owen and equipment specialist Eddie Carr. They meet Sarah, and find that Malcolm's daughter Kelly has also sneaked along. A team from InGen arrives on the island, headed by Ludlow and hunter Roland Tembo, and begins catching dinosaurs for transportation back to a new Park in San Diego. Secret eco-warrior Van Owen frees the dinosaurs, which stampede and destroy the InGen camp. He and Sarah bring a wounded baby tyrannosaurus to their trailer for treatment, but its parents follow them and push the trailer off a cliff; trying to rescue his companions, Eddie is killed.

The team is joined by Ludlow's party—they must all now trek to the original InGen encampment to find a radio. En route, Tembo's sidekick Dieter is killed by compsognathi and the party is attacked first by tyrannosauri, then by velociraptors. Van Owen reaches the encampment, followed by Malcolm, Sarah and Kelly, who ward off a velociraptor attack. They are airlifted out.

In San Diego, Ludlow and assembled press await the ship carrying the captive adult tyrannosaurus, but the dinosaur escapes and rampages through town. Malcolm and Sarah lure it back to the ship using its baby as bait, but Ludlow is killed. The dinosaurs are shipped back to Isla Sorna, and Hammond announces that the island will remain an isolated sanctuary.

The brand logo for the sequel to *Jurassic Park* is almost identical to that of the original—the same dinosaur skeleton, but this time looking calcified and distressed. it could be read as an admission that the new film is destined to be an atrophied repeat of the original. *The Lost World Jurassic Park* gamely wears its bad faith on its sleeve. As the film's new cast, arriving on the island, marvel at the lofty appearance of a stegosaurus herd, Goldblum's Malcolm reminds us that we've been here before and should know what to expect: "That's how it always starts, the 'oos', the 'ahs'—but later there's running and screaming."

The Lost World is a post-miracle film. Where *Jurassic Park* was predicated on the sense of the unique, the never-before-seen, its sequel must inevitably be about the *déjà vu*, about the domestication of the marvellous. Not only are the dinosaurs themselves familiar, but so is the technology: since *Jurassic Park*, we have seen saurian CGI repeatedly used and abused in films that implicitly or explicitly echo that film, from *DragonHeart* to the grotesque parody of the live-action *Flintstones*.

Jurassic Park promised a cinematic and public phenomenon so momentous that its genre derivation was occulted in the process. So *The Lost World* attempts to save itself from the trap of mere repetition by capitalising on genre repetition (the film's explicit theme is, after all, reproduction), presenting itself as a patchwork of allusions. If nothing else, this at least allows Spielberg to have some fun as a filmmaker and film buff, often at his own expense. So the film refers us not only to *Jurassic Park* but also to its models. Michael Crichton's title signals an obvious debt to the Conan Doyle original, filmed twice as *The Lost World* in 1924 and 1960. There are echoes of *Hatari!* in the dinosaur hunt with jeeps, of *Bambi* in the poignant sequences of the bellowing baby T-rex, of the *Road Runner* cartoon in the stampede of freed dinos. The San Diego sequences, a cursory closing play on *King Kong*, take us back to earlier Spielberg territory in a jokey reprise of the uncannily invaded suburbia of *E.T.* and *Poltergeist*.

Most significantly, the film carries its own critique of *Jurassic Park*'s reliance on pure revelation by returning to the emphasis on suspense and the unseen—the jaws effect. In the film's most powerful sequences, we don't look at dinosaurs, but inter them from their ghastly approach: treetops seen from above begin to rustle as the T-rexes move in; and in an extraordinary shot, unseen velociraptors make diagonal tracks towards their prey through a field of long grass. The film's most chilling moment, it reveals *The Lost World* for what it really is—the closest Spielberg has yet come to making his own Vietnam film. This is a story about over-confident US militia moving heavy firepower into a world that's unfamiliar to them, and being outflanked by a far cannier indigenous force: the velociraptors and the disarmingly small, mobile compsognathi are the Vietcong, operating by stealth in their host terrain. Finally, InGen's militaristic initiative defeated, John Hammond makes a presidential-style address to the nation, declaring a new policy of non-intervention.

This doesn't remotely make *The Lost World* a political film, however. It is purely a co-opting of Vietnam iconography in the service of Spielberg's familiar theme of benevolent responsibility. *Jurassic Park*'s theme of parenthood is pushed even further to the fore, stressing the parental duty both to let go and to be protective when appropriate. Where Hammond has learned to release his creations, InGen's new board are exploitative disciplinarians: "We patented it, we own it," says Ludlow of the T-rex. Malcolm is given a lecture on good parenting by his daughter—who, for unexplained reasons, is black—and who upbraids him for not being tougher, especially since her mother is absent. Since we know next to nothing about the mother or about Kelly's own back-story, her sudden appearance seems a contrived look for younger viewers, and as much an arbitrary creation *ex nihilo* as the dinosaurs themselves. The sentimental parenting theme does at least take on a macabre twist at the end: as the baby dinosaur finally crunches on the hapless Ludlow, we seem to see in its parent's artificial eye a glint of benign approval.

The film's ending is, if anything, more cloying than the first, which gave us a hero discovering his paternal instincts and a shot of pelicans (read: childbirth-signifying storks) gliding over water. Here Hammond beseeches us, "Trust in nature: life will find a way," as we see saurians romping in blissful coexistence on their island utopia—an image that suggests a kitsch airbrush painting on the cover of a Christian Science manual. The very last shot is an imposingly luminous image of a pterodactyl coming in to land, silhouetted in a gorgeous sunbeam. But what exactly does it mean? That these creatures, previously unseen, have naturally, spontaneously evolved on the island? Is it a pure formal rhyme with the pelicans? Or a suggestion that the colony now features one species that won't be so easily contained on the island: that we can expect another sequel organically, naturally, to evolve—flying lizards over Vegas, perhaps?

TIME, 6/30/97, p. 65, Richard Corliss

Hollywood rules. Moviegoers in almost every foreign country prefer American films to their own. They love our action pictures, with their size and tempo and assurance, and all those pretty people realizing outrageous dreams. Our directors know how to fulfill Alfred Hitchcock's aim: to make the Japanese audience scream at the same time as the American audience. Perhaps they know it too well. Amanic roteness now envelops action films; the need to thrill has become a drab addiction. Isn't there more to moviemaking than having your finger on the pulse of the world public? Can't the megalo-melodrama be infused with passion and ingenuity? The answer so far, and with just one exception, is no—not this season. For this is the Summer of Dumb.

Maybe this is not new. Some years back, a film critic observed that the problem with summer pictures wasn't that they were bad movies; it was that they were the same bad movie. But more than ever this summer, with the moguls at the sausage factories sending out a new slice of action salami each week—The *Lost World: Jurassic Park*, followed by *Con Air*, *Speed 2: Cruise Control*, *Batman & Robin*, *Face/Off* and *Men in Black*—the big films look like instant remakes, retreads or reductions ad absurdum of last Friday's film, which wasn't all that hot either. Some of the movies have incidental felicities, and, to abort all suspense right now, *Face/Off* is damn fine. But in sum, these films offer evidence that the action-adventure has reached a point of exhaustion. Seen as one 12-hour epic, this multiplex six-pack moves less on cruise control than on automatic pilot. This is zombie entertainment: cinema with motor skills but a dead brain.

At the end of a genre cycle, directors jettison character and story for bustle and special effects—noise and toys. Here are four reasons movies aren't better.

SMALL MINDS THINK ALIKE. It's as if Hollywood had just one huge brainstorming session for all its summer movies. Someone says, "I took a boat ride last week. Let's have a climactic boat chase." *Speed 2* ends with one, and so, for no maritime reason, does *Face/Off.*

Somebody else says, "How about if we have a kid seeing something really scary out a second-story window, but his parents don't believe him, and then the scary thing does its dirty work?" Swell: a dinosaur in The *Lost World,* a runaway cruise ship in *Speed 2.*

A third guy looks up from his PC and says, "Computers!" So half of the pictures either have someone laboriously logging on or, as in *Speed 2,* hand the villain a Mighty Morphin PowerBook as his tool of terror.

A fourth guy says, "All movies are comic books these days. Let's do more movies based on comic books!" Not just *Batman & Robin* and *Men in Black* but also two August releases, *Spawn* and *Steel,* are comic book-inspired. This junk-culture trend must please the kids in the Development departments; no more novels to read, with all those annoying words.

CLUELESSNESS. Melodrama at its best involves a conflict between intelligent good and cunning evil. But it's easier just to have smart people do dumb things. The noble intentions of *The Lost World*'s team of scientists—trying to protect the dinosaurs from a group of rapacious hunters—are undercut by some laughably inane fieldwork. They take close-up photos of the beasts with incredibly noisy cameras that are bound to startle any dino into a frenzy; they kidnap a *T. rex* baby to mend its leg while Big Mama prowls closer. It's knaves vs. fools in the Jurassic jungle.

For all its special-effects frissons, Steven Spielberg sequel lacks the shock of the new; it has the familiarity of a child's second trip to Disneyland. Its formula heroes (American) and villains (European) aren't a hindrance; after all, this is a monster movie. But what about the dinosaurs? Though they ooze attitude, they have no specific character. Viewers were moved by the lovelorn King Kong, and appreciated the creature's maternal rage in *Aliens*; but the *Lost World* beasts are just big, undifferentiated lizards. Memo for the inevitable *Jurassic 3*: try creating a dinosaur with star quality—with a personality, a grudge or a heart.

But Hollywood hardly knows what to do with its human stars. Sandra Bullock became one as the resourceful bus driver of *Speed,* yet in the sequel she can only squeal, hide and get kidnapped, while no-voltage Jason Patric attends to all the heavy heroics. In *Batman & Robin* the guest villains are Uma Thurman as Poison Ivy and Arnold Schwarzenegger as Mr. Freeze. Thurman has sexy fun with her villainous eco-freak, but Arnold is encased in an icy truss of a costume that obscures his rippling charisma. Memo to the Batman team: next time you pay a star $25 million, let us see him.

BRUTALITY. What they lose in personality, they make up in body count. In these sociopathic action films, the hero has a bad case of blood lust. The psychos, like the Steve Buscemi serial killer in *Con Air*, are comic, sympathetic sorts. And anyone who's not a major character is called for icing by Mr. Freeze, or blithely sideswiped by *Speed 2's* Bullock during the most deplorable driving-test scene in film history. Something is wrong with Hollywood if the answer to every story problem is a crash. Even the otherwise canny Disney cartoon *Hercules* has an isn't-it-funny-that-a-whole-Greek-marketplace-falls-down scene.

Male movie stars didn't always have to act like commandos to assert their machismo. How many bad guys did Clark Gable or Cary Grant kill in their careers as Hollywood heroes? Precious few, because life—even a villain's life was held more precious then. Maybe the old movies were naive, but we'll take naiveté over the thoughtless, numberless carnage that makes the modern action film a Bosnia for fun and profit.

FACETIOUSNESS. Jokiness is the current handmaiden of brutality. Violent death provides the punch line for the two-hour string of gags that is the modern action movie. And when the stars aren't killing off the supporting players, they are cracking wise-lamely. All right, nobody goes to hear an action movie, but the verbal humor in *The Lost World* didn't have to be so stilted. In *Con Air* and *Batman & Robin* the lines have the rhythm of wit but not the content; they are their own rim shots.

At least *Men in Black* is a comedy—a fact that may surprise and disappoint the zillions who expect it to be this *Independence Day*'s answer to last year's *Independence Day*. Director Barry Sonnenfeld (*The Addams Family, Get Shorty*) is just the chef to blend comedy and creepiness. as is writer Ed Solomon (It's *Gary Shandling's Show*, the *Bill & Ted* adventures). Early on, they do right by Lowell Cunningham's comic-book premise: that extraterrestrials have landed, that they are a scuzzy lot who deserve to be treated like illegal aliens and that the government has an elite corps of FBI-style agents (notably Will Smith and Tommy Lee Jones) to keep them in line. Ah, this explains everything: Velcro, liposuction, the microwave oven and why the 1964 World's Fair was held in Queens.

This mad, mad world is inventively drawn; Smith and Jones make a finely mismatched pair. But, as in many comedies, all the good stuff is in Act 1. So much energy is spent on the premise that little is left for the payoff. *Men in Black* suffocates from the facetiousness that gave it life, and the movie ends up less like *Independence Day* than like the hectic *Mars Attacks!*

Action movies don't have to fail. The *Fugitive, The Rock, The Long Kiss Goodnight* satisfy the dramatic utilities while kicking beaucoup butt. And sometimes a gifted director can go beyond the conventional pleasures. With *Face/Off*, John Woo, the Hong Kong auteur *(The Killer, Hard Boiled),* has made his smartest, wildest, positively Woo-siest American thriller. Working from a vigorous script by Mike Werb and Michael Colleary, Woo weaves his familiar touches—the slo-mo, the gleaming candles, the long coats flying in the breeze, the doves flying in a chapel as an omen of death—around the central fantasy of male bonding gone berserk.

Sean Archer (John Travolta) is an FBI agent determined to nail Castor Troy (Nicolas Cage), the terrorist who killed Sean's young son. He does so, apparently killing Castor. In order to find a bomb that ... oh, never mind; it's too weird. Just know that Sean has Castor's face sewn on him. And then a revived Castor puts on Sean's face. The men are trapped in the personalities of their worst enemies.

For once, a movie knows how to use its stars. That's important, because, on one level, *Face/Off* is a comedy about acting—Really Big Acting. Cage, who must have been taking Christopher Walken lessons, is spooky-nuts as Castor, then wonderfully poignant as Sean. And Travolta, after shucking his dour FBI persona, shows a gaily dangerous side as Castor. He's a charming, reckless slime.

As the actors go bigger, so does the film; it's the most delirious major-studio melodrama since *Natural Born Killers*. But it's also dead serious—because Woo has restored moral gravity to acts of violence. This isn't just a thrill ride; it's a rocket into the thrilling past, when directors could scare you with how much emotion they packed into a movie.

Studios would be wise to lure more foreign directors like Woo, who knows how to transform summer's dumb-and-dumber product into a gnarly, white-knuckle action film for all seasons.

VILLAGE VOICE, 6/3/97, p. 65, J. Hoberman

Beyond good and evil, as inevitable as its own sequel-friendly happy ending, Steven Spielberg's *The Lost World: Jurassic Park* has arrived to herald summer—and incidentally conquer all universes, known and unknown, with its beyond-state-of-the-art special effects and substandard human ones.

Were it not that *The Lost World* is the follow-up to what was, before Star War's re-release, the highest-grossing movie ever made, its premise would be pleasingly irrational. Seems that the mad Santa played by Sir Richard Attenborough, only mildly deterred by the flaming disaster of his cloned-dinosaur theme park, has decided to protect the re-created species. To the best of my understanding, his plan is to bring back a few specimens from their secret island breeding ground and go *mano a mano* with Flipper by installing them adjacent to the San Diego Zoo. (Attenborough's near-deathbed conversion from, as Goldblum puts it, "capitalist to naturalist" is sure to calm those eco-crazies protesting the intention of Spielberg's Dreamworks to construct its studio on Los Angeles's last remaining wetlands.)

Accordingly, two parties are dispatched to the Caribbean. The first is a team of scientists who, despite the presence of Cassandra-fusspot Jeff Goldblum, want nothing more than to cuddle the baby dinos. (These are the dull good guys: Goldblum's wiseguy cynicism evaporates in the first blast of enraged dino-breath while chief cuddler Julianne Moore gives a performance that consists mainly of running fast, looking flushed, and hyperventilating through clenched teeth.) A second group—sent by Attenborough's evil nephew—is a gang of degenerate-looking thrill seekers, led by Pete Postlethwaite (a great white hunter, referred to optimistically as "Ahab"). They put the dinos in shackles and stun-gun the little critters just for fun.

Sound familiar? Twenty-one summers have passed since *Jaws*—weakly alluded to in *The Lost World*'s opening sequence—pioneered the blockbuster as force of nature. Less story-driven than *Jaws* or even *Jurassic Park, The Lost World* eliminates transitional scenes, recapitulating its predecessor's thrills as if running down a checklist. (The major innovation is a half-hour elaboration on the *North by Northwest* Mount Rushmore scene complicated by rain, recreational vehicles, and a pair of rampaging tyrannosauri.) Despite the mini-dinos who attack en masse and the yucky spectacle of a T. Rex tongue, there's nothing here as memorable as the cuteosaurus splatter attack on the schlub from *Seinfeld*—and, at two hours and 14 minutes, much of it is just unpleasantly nerve-racking.

The dinos are, of course, miraculous at interfacing with the humanoids although, in this viewer, these computer-generated antics inspire a longing to leave the footage deconstructed, the better to study the Stegosaurus strut and to revel in the sequences of sweaty, screaming, panic-stricken actors running away from nothing. Compared to *Jurassic Park*, which at least had the theme-park metaphor to riff on, *The Lost World* is better crafted but less fun—that is until the T. Rex comes ashore in San Diego, allowing Spielberg to express his own deepest impulses by contriving a full-scale suburban apocalypse. This sequence is framed as the ultimate illegal-immigration nightmare although, in bringing the dino home, *The Lost World* apes its unacknowledged namesake—the 1925 Conan Doyle-derived *King Kong*-anticipating spectacular in which a dinosaur enclave is discovered in the Amazon jungle and a brontosaurus tramples London.

Kong died for love but, scarcely an exercise in any sort of *l'amour fou, The Lost World* reeks of family values—although I'm not certain if the presence of Goldblum's African American daughter (Vanessa Lee Chester) is a matter of implied depth or calculated demographics. If *The Lost World* insures that children of all species are repeatedly placed in jeopardy, that's because it's all about parenting. Indeed, Julianne Moore's announced reason for visiting what the natives call the Island of Five Dino-Deaths is to demonstrate that, no matter what you may have heard, the T. Rex was a fundamentally nurturing creature.

Also reviewed in:
NEW YORK TIMES, 5/23/97, p. C1, Stephen Holden
NEW YORKER, 6/2/97, p. 91, Terrence Rafferty
VARIETY, 5/19-25/97, p. 48, Leonard Klady
WASHINGTON POST, 5/23/97, p. B1, Stephen Hunter
WASHINGTON POST, 5/23/97, Weekend/p. 42, Desson Howe

LOVE ALWAYS

A Persistence of Vision Films and Legacy Releasing release of an Isaac Artenstein production. *Executive Producer:* Ken Branson and Coop Cooprider. *Producer:* Isaac Artenstein. *Director:* Jude Pauline Eberhard. *Screenplay:* Jude Pauline Eberhard and Sharlene Baker. *Based on the novel "Finding Signs" by:* Sharlene Baker. *Director of Photography:* Xavier Perez Grobet. *Editor:* Joel Goodman. *Music:* Jaime Valle and Anton Sanko. *Sound:* Kevin Hyde. *Casting:* Doreen Lane. *Production Designer:* Mauricio de Aguinaco. *Art Director:* Eugenio Caballero. *Costumes:* Judi Sarafian. *Running time:* 93 minutes. *MPAA Rating:* R.

CAST: Marisa Ryan (Julia Bradshaw); Moon Zappa (Mary Ellen); Beverly D'Angelo (Miranda); Michael Reilly Burke (Mark Righetti); Doug Hutchinson (James); Beth Grant (Stephanie); Jerry O'Donnell (Mac); Tracy Fraim (David); Aaron Kuhr (AWOL Marine).

LOS ANGELES TIMES, 10/10/97, Calendar/p. 16, Kevin Thomas

"Love Always" is no more than a minor accomplishment, but it does build to an unexpected and rewarding conclusion and serves as an effective showcase for vibrant and attractive Marisa Ryan. Ryan manages to be engaging even as the film wavers under first-time director Jude Pauline Eberhard.

There was probably a better picture to be made from "Finding Signs," a novel written by Sharlene Baker, who adapted it to the screen with Eberhard.

Ryan's Julia is a young Spokane actress caught up in a romance with law student Mark (Michael Reilly Burke) but is not getting anywhere in her career and is not ready to settle down. She lands in San Diego, where, after an interval, she receives a postcard from Mark saying that he's passed the bar and asking her to come back and marry him. Still unsure, she nevertheless decides to see him at least "one more time."

Mark's proposal sets up the film's key gimmick, which is to present Julia as that rarity, a female on the road—especially one as pretty as Julia. No Greyhound for her, Julia hitchhikes in a thirst for experience and, perhaps unconsciously, as a way of putting off a decisive reunion with Mark.

Although it's refreshing to see the filmmakers back away from the instant paranoia induced by the notion of a pretty woman hitchhiking alone, they carry sidestepping the dangers to the extreme. Julia winds up taking an exceedingly roundabout way to get back to Spokane and is caught up in a series of comic adventures with a bunch of largely unbelievable characters drawn with lots of shtick.

Until Spokane at last comes into view, Eberhard displays a shaky sense of geography and an even shakier sense of time and distance.

Like the character of Julia, actress Ryan seems to know how to take care of herself in front of a camera, which here is crucial. For the way Eberhard directs, too much of the time you have the sense of watching actors act instead of becoming the characters they are portraying.

Luckily, the film's climactic sequence is so well-written and conceived that it kicks the film into high gear, but unfortunately this also has the perverse effect of making what has gone before seem all the more mediocre.

NEW YORK POST, 10/10/97, p. 48, Michael Medved

"Love Always" is an amateurish road picture about one free spirit's unstoppable (and interminable) quest to reach the dazzling, fabled, exotic destination of ... Spokane, Washington.

The non-action begins in this bland mid-sized Western town with two enchanted lovers (Marisa Ryan and Michael Reilly Burke) skipping and waltzing across Spokane's various bridges and plazas as if they were in Paris or Bora Bora.

They then make love in artsy, slo-mo style, over-acting transports of ecstasy in order to emphasize the heroine's fierce independence when she inexplicably turns her back on this bliss and her lover's proposal of marriage.

Finding herself in San Diego as an unemployed actress, she gets a postcard from her rejected beau saying he's just passed the bar exam and still wants to marry her.

Without deciding on a response, she hits the road for Spokane, but incompetence, whimsy and bad luck combine to send her instead careening around the country between Boston, Las Vegas and Seattle. Along the way she attends the wedding of her best friend (Moon Zappa), makes love with a bearded nature photographer (Tracy Fraim), meets her favorite all-girl rock band (known as "the Virgin Sluts"), rides with a mumbling hippie burnout (Doug Hutchison), an AWOL Marine (Aaron Kuhr), a middle-aged wife who sculpts ceramic cows (Beth Grant), and other cutesy caricatures.

None of this is the least bit interesting or plausible.

Even the process of the main character hitching her rides seems hopelessly fake. Instead of raising her thumb in the traditional manner, she merely strides down the highway with her bedroll and backpack and various strangers pull up spontaneously asking for a chance to help her.

Unfortunately, Marisa Ryan (a series regular on TV's "Major Dad") projects no trace of the incandescent charisma that's supposed to make her character irresistible. She might someday develop a career as an intelligent character actress in the future, but not as a romantic leading lady.

Debuting writer-director Jude Pauline Eberhard (inspired by a Sharlene Baker novel) scripts all supposedly poetic or insightful lines ("You defy gravity!") that fall to earth like leaden banalities. In the end, moviegoers would be better with a romantic weekend in Spokane.

NEWSDAY, 10/10/97, Part II/p. B6, John Anderson

If there seemed to have been dozens of movies this year with "Love" in their titles ("Love and Other Catastrophes," "love jones," "Love Serenade," etc., et al., ad nauseam), there seemed to be hundreds about post-adolescents adjusting to life, love and oh, I don't know, just the lack of meaning in their lives. Maybe it just seemed like hundreds.

Not that a journey of self-discovery is a bad thing, or even a bad thing to watch. But when most of the miles are being logged by the director in pursuit of a story, the whole thing gets tiresome very quickly.

In "Love Always," the first feature by Jude Pauline Eberhard, there's a lot of fruitless motion, and plenty of angst and yearning. It's a movie set in a universe where, when one character says "I quit my job," another says "Congratulations"—employment being not only irrelevant but an obstacle to happiness. The opening sequence has already established Julia Bradshaw (Marisa Ran) and her boyfriend Mark (Michael Reilly Burke) as passionate urban types, frolicking about San Diego, walking, talking, dancing and having sex in the middle of the day, so they're either chronically unemployed or independently wealthy, in which case they've immediately become even less interesting than they already were.

Mark wants to marry Julia, who's got too much life to live to settle down, so when Mark later writes from Spokane and says he's passed the bar, she bolts for the great Northwest. Who needs self-discovery when you've got a lawyer who needs you?

It takes a profoundly long time to get to Spokane. In the interim Julia meets a collection of roadside attractions James, the apparent speed freak (Doug Hutchinson); Stephanie, the truck driver (Beth Grant); Mae, the bookie (Jerry O'Donnell) and the rock band Virgin Sluts—all of whom have cars and into these cars Julia immediately jumps. This would be totally irresponsible as well as illogical filmmaking, if anything else were believable.

"Love Always" in essence is a budget and a soundtrack (Iris DeMent, Booker T & the MGs, The Supremes, Leonard Cohen) in search of direction and purpose. Take the encounter between Julia and David (Tracy Fraim), the sensitive, woodsy photographer she meets, greets and beds inside of an evening (all this, lest we forget, while she's on her way to her true love, Mark). He snaps a shot of them together, and she says she'd love to have the picture. But no. "I'd like to keep it," he says meaningfully, "if you don't mind"—as if it were the last exposure on the last roll of film in the Western Hemisphere. In "Love Always"—imagine "Mad About You" without the jokes or the irony—making sense never gets in the way of making statements, however smarmy or trite they may be.

VILLAGE VOICE, 10/14/97, p. 96, Dennis Lim

Love begins with a credit sequence that dares you to keep watching: a moist-eyed couple float through various amusement park rides, cycle home on a tandem, dance in their underwear, and have sex in soft-focus close-up. Accompanied by a rancid Kenny G-style saxophone score, it's reminiscent of a deodorant commercial. Hopelessly malformed, Jude Pauline Eberhard's first film features a horribly perky heroine, Julia (Marisa Ryan), a self-described 'militant optimist' who, according to her drippy boyfriend, Mark, is like "a cluster bomb that explodes in a thousand different directions at once." Living up to her billing, Julia sets off on a meandering road trip, in the process bonding with a gallery of character-building eccentrics. The script is horrendous, sometimes to the point of seeming mistranslated (Mark sighs to Julia, "Someday, you're gonna love somebody with all the intensity of the southern hemisphere"), and the syrupy life lessons that constitute the purported payoff make most telemovies appear profound.

Also reviewed in:
CHICAGO TRIBUNE, 10/10/97, Friday/p. I, John Petrakis
NEW YORK TIMES, 10/10/97, p. E20, Lawrence Van Gelder
VARIETY, 11/18-24/96, p. 62, Emanuel Levy

love jones

A New Line Cinema release of an Addis-Wechsler production. *Executive Producer:* Julia Chasman, Jay Stern, Amy Henkels, and Helena Echegoyen. *Producer:* Nick Wechsler and Jeremiah Samuels. *Director:* Theodore Witcher. *Screenplay:* Theodore Witcher. *Director of Photography:* Ernest Holzman. *Editor:* Maysie Hoy. *Music:* Darryl Jones. *Music Editor:* Richard Ford. *"Stepping" Choreographer:* William Perry Casper. *Sound:* Scott D. Smith and (music) Stephen Krause. *Sound Editor:* Larry Blake. *Casting:* Jane Alderman and Robi Reed-Humes. *Production Designer:* Roger Fortune. *Art Director:* Cydney M. Harris. *Set Decorator:* Amelia Hochberg. *Set Dresser:* Troy Borisy. *Special Effects:* Sam Barkan. *Costumes:* Shawn Barton. *Make-up:* Cat'Ania McCoy Howze and Linda Melazzo. *Stunt Coordinator:* Rick LeFevour. *Running time:* 110 minutes. *MPAA Rating:* R.

CAST: Larenz Tate (Darius Lovehall); Nia Long (Nina Mosley); Isaiah Washington (Savon Garrison); Lisa Nicole Carson (Josie Nichols); Bill Bellamy (Hollywood); Leonard Roberts (Eddie Coles); Bernadette L. Clarke (Sheila Downes); Khalil Kain (Marvin Cox); Cerall Duncan (Troy Garrison); David Nisbet (Publisher); Simon James (Roger Lievsey); Oona Hart (Model, Lievsey Studio); Jaqueline Fleming (Lisa Martin); Manao DeMuth (Nina's assistant); Marie-Francoise Theodore (Tracey Powell); Reginald Gibson (Himself); Kahil El Zabar (Percussionist); Darryl "Munch" Jones (Bassist); Teodross Avery (Saxophonist); Everette Dean (Porter); Benjamin LeVert (Savon's Son); John M. Watson, Sr. (Tiki Room Bartender); William Yancey (Sanctuary Bartender); Ernest Perry (Male Model); Helena Echegoyen (Woman on Train); Malik Yosef (Himself); Troy Borisy (Taxi Driver); Michelle Poole and Kevin Bell (Kissing Couple).

LOS ANGELES TIMES, 3/14/97, Calendar/p. 1, Jack Mathews

[*The following review by Jack Mathews appeared in a slightly different form in* NEWSDAY, 3/14/97, Part II/p. B9.]

The unusual thing about Theodore Witcher's otherwise routine "love jones," the audience winner at the recent Sundance Film Festival, is its color. Not its film color, although that's certainly up to snuff. We're talking about the color of its characters, who are all black.

And what's so unusual about them is that there isn't a racial stereotype in the crowd. These are young, middle-class Chicago singles, struggling with the same problems twentysomethings have been struggling with since the sexual revolution—how to combine romance, honesty and intimacy in one relationship. In other words, how to know when they're in love.

It's often easier for friends to spot the real thing before the people involved and, in the case of "love jones," the audience is among the knowing observers. From the moment writer Darius Lovehall (Larenz Tate) and photographer Nina Mosley (Nia Long) meet in an upscale bar that hosts nightly poetry readings, we see in their exchange a deeper connection than a potential fling. But do they?

Darius is an egocentric writer who fancies his reputation as a poet Lothario, while Nina is coming out of a long, abusive relationship with little interest in starting another. In that first night at the bar, Darius dedicates a poem, laced with graphic sexual allusions, to Nina, who later thanks him for the thought but reminds him that love is a richer topic for a poet than sex.

Nevertheless, Darius and Nina are soon sleeping together, convincing themselves—and trying to convince their friends—that they're in a sexual relationship without strings or love. The rest of "love jones" follows the lie from one frustrating breakup to another until the pain of separation makes its case.

This story, of course, has been told in dozens of previous movies and, in ways, "love jones" feels like a copy of another Chicago love story, "About Last Night..." That 1986 film starring Rob Lowe and Demi Moore was adapted from David Mamet's one-act play "Sexual Perversity in Chicago," and the play—if not the movie—captured perfectly the dilemma of modern courtship: It's easier and safer to communicate sexual desire than honest feelings.

It should come as a shock to no one that the dilemma is the same for African Americans. But the plain truth is that nonracial casting is so rare in American movies that "love jones" seems new. Witcher, a recent film school graduate making his debut as both writer and director, includes a few racial references, but, with few changes, the same script could have been used for an all-white production.

New Line deserves credit for taking the chance with a black love story aimed at a traditional mainstream audience, and one hopes the film is successful enough to make "love jones" one of many Hollywood takes on life among middle class minorities. But commercial rooting aside, it's not a particularly engaging movie.

There are some effective group scenes with Darius and Nina and their friends, but Witcher's dialogue and direction more often show the craft than the naturalism he's after. It is also hard to surrender to a romance with only one sympathetic partner; Darius is much too self-absorbed to give us a real stake in the outcome of his courtship—he sees the love of his life every time he looks in the mirror.

Nina, played with warmth and humor by Long, is by far the smartest, most talented and most mature. She deserves more, and it's hard to believe her determination to settle for less.

NEW YORK POST, 3/14/97, p. 51, Bill Hoffmann

Romantic comedies either click or they don't, and "love jones" doesn't.

The all-black cast of characters is bland, the story muddled and the downtown Chicago setting surprisingly lifeless.

That's a shame, because the producers of "love jones" (their idea to lower-case, not ours) are hyping it as a movie that breaks from Hollywood's stereotyping of African Americans as either action heroes or hoods.

Director Theodore Witcher says his production is different from others targeting African Americans because "there's not one lethal weapon in the film, and the only wound is a broken heart."

That's true, but romantic movies should at the very least have emotional pyrotechnics—and there are few in "love jones," which moves so slowly youll be checking your watch halfway through.

Nia Long ("Boyz 'N the Hood") plays Nina Mosley, a struggling twentysomething photographer in heavy crisis: She's been canned from her job, and her longtime boyfriend has bolted.

Enter Darius Lovehall (Larenz Tate), a writer who quits his job to write a novel and falls for Nina at a poetry reading.

This begins a series of contrived plot twists more challenging than any of the emotional issues these two face.

For instance, why does Nina fall straight into bed with Darius after spending the opening scenes swearing off men and sex?

Just what drives these two relationship-wary people to fall for each other so hard and so quickly? That's hard to figure out since both characters are poorly drawn and seem to be acting from the script, not from the heart.

Darius faithfully bangs away at his typewriter, but we know almost nothing about the book he's writing—only that he gets frustrated and sometimes hurls the poor machine off the desk.

And Nina. How does she afford that drop-dead gorgeous loft that only seems available in the movies? And how does she suddenly end up as a top fashion photographer when about the toughest photo assignment we see her on is trying to convince Darius to strip naked for her camera?

We also know so little about her break from her old boyfriend, their attempted reconciliation means little to us.

Will there be a happy ending for Nina and Darius? In this cookie-cutter plot you can bet on it. It's also a good bet that if "love jones" was minus the profanity and brief nudity, it could easily have passed as one of those original "movies" on the USA Network.

SIGHT AND SOUND, 7/97, p. 46, John Wrathall

After splitting up with her fiancé Marvin Cox, photographer Nina Mosley moves home to Chicago and vows never to fall in love again. At a poetry club called The Sanctuary, she meets Darius Lovehall, a writer who goes up on stage and dedicates an explicitly sexual poem to her. In return, Nina promises Darius she will write a poem for him one day, but one about love, not sex.

Nina is looking for an Isley brothers record at the shop run by Darius' friend Sheila when Darius arrives and asks her out. Nina refuses, but Darius gets her address off the back of a cheque and drops round with the Isley Brothers record she wanted. This time she agrees to go out with him. They sleep together on the first date, yet, though obviously smitten, they both tell their friends it's not a "love thing".

Marvin asks Nina to come back to New York with him, and when Darius doesn't object to her leaving, she goes. Unable to find work in New York, she quarrels with Marvin and returns to Chicago. Before she rings Darius she sees him in the street with another woman, Lisa Martin. Nina starts dating Darius' friend Hollywood but, at a party with Hollywood, she sees Darius and leaves alone. Darius follows and helps her get a cab. Reconciled, they start dating again. However, Nina is unable to trust Darius, and they split up. Nina's best friend Josie tells Darius that Nina has got a job in New York and is leaving on the noon train, but Darius arrives too late to see her off.

One year later, Darius' novel is just out when Nina returns to Chicago for a photo shoot. Chancing upon a copy of the novel, she discovers that it's dedicated to her. She goes to The Sanctuary and recites a poem about memories of love. Unable to see Darius in the crowd, she leaves. But he follows her outside and they agree to give it another try.

The actor Larenz Tate comes to *love jones* fresh from two films with the Hughes Brothers, *Menace II Society* and *Dead Presidents*, and the mere fact that he is called upon here to drink wine and recite poetry rather than murder Korean grocers or hold up armoured cars marks this classy romantic comedy as something of a minor revolution in recent black American film-making. When Tate's character Darius tries to impress Nina (Nia Long) into going on a date with him, she jokes that he's "a renaissance black man", and at times 27-year-old writer-director Theodore Witcher's debut feels like a self-conscious attempt at a 'renaissance black film', as it tries to cram in references to as many aspects of African-American culture as possible. jazz, reggae, poetry, photography and 'stepping' (the indigenous Chicago style of ballroom dancing) are all namechecked, while rap and hiphop, the ubiquitous accompaniment to most black American films of the 90s, is only heard on the car stereo of Hollywood, a caricature sexist stud who briefly dates the heroine. *(love jones* also features a fine jazz score by former Miles Davis bassist Darryl Jones, featuring fellow Miles alumnus Wallace Roney on trumpet, though predictably none of it is included on the sound-track album.)

Part and parcel of this anti-gangsta stance is the more positive portrayal of women. Long's Nina has the confidence to walk out on untrustworthy men in order to pursue her career and, in one tantalising scene, to reverse the clichés of sexual roles by ordering Darius to strip while she photographs him. Paradoxically, while Nina's raw, black-and-white photographs are said in the film to be inspired by the work of Gordon Parks, it was the *Life* photographer- turned-director's own 1971 feature *Shaft* which set mainstream black filmmaking on exactly the blaxploitation path from which such films as *love jones* are now turning away.

When Nina shows her work to a smart New York picture editor, he rejects it, telling her it needs to be "slicker, less raw, a bit more polished". While we're supposed to think that he's just a square white guy who doesn't know where it's at anymore, ironically, Theodore Witcher seems to have followed his advice to the letter. (The cinematographer, Ernest Holzman, is a veteran of *thirtysomething*, and his work here could not be more slick and polished.) But again, as Witcher has pointed out, making something that looks this smooth and shiny is a deliberate attempt to go against preconceptions about what kind of films young black directors make. In the time-honoured Hollywood tradition, the twentysomething protagonists of *love jones* have no visible means of support and live in spectacular split-level apartments, even though Nina, it turns out, is merely house-sitting for a rich friend.

Beyond presenting a very positive image of a confident, affluent, young, black middle class, *love jones* doesn't pretend to offer any new twists on the old "will they or won't they?" romantic formula we have seen so many times before. But the cast are sexy and self-assured, the dialogue is consistently sharp—and any film whose hero's seduction technique involves listening to John Coltrane's version of 'In a Sentimental Mood' is all right by me.

VILLAGE VOICE, 3/18/97, p. 69, Gary Dauphin

A slickly easy-on-the-eyes (and brains) first film, *love jones* is a commendable confection of a romance that echos with recent Gen-X Hollywood. It's also a film aimed so directly at a certain segment of the population that, despite knowing better, its members might get sucked into its glossily self-absorbed universe. There have been plenty of films about underemployed hipsters in love, but if you're young, black, straight and live in the Fort Greene environs where parts of it were shot, *love jones* could very well fool you into thinking it's the first film you've ever seen about your black (and at times cheating) heart.

Things get started in the poetry lounge that offers *love jones* its central social scene, the kind of place where folks smoke, drink, and dress, doing the art thing for the good of the race while also taking advantage of the opportunity to meet and greet the opposite sex. It's there that Darius (Larenz Tate), a poet with some kind of vague magazine-related day job, first spots Nina (Nia Long). She blows him off in full view of the circle of other young and pretty black folk that'll become *love jones*'s core group (most notable among them is Bill Bellamy playing a slightly crass would-be player), but the flirty, performative aspects of the exchange insures they'll be running into each other soon. Their relationship takes muted, fitful turns—pursuit, delayed first sex, moving in, a backstabbing involving Bellamy, and so on—all of it directed by Theodore Witcher in a smoothly understated style that pairs the characters' native pretensions with slickly pretty visuals. You're not exactly sure in the end if *love jones* actually knows much about relationships or the ways in which youth, love, and work mix, but it's most definitely no *Booty Call*, which is something.

Also reviewed in:
NEW REPUBLIC, 4/14/97, p. 28, Stanley Kauffmann
NEW YORK TIMES, 3/14/97, p. C14, Janet Maslin
VARIETY, 1/27-2/2/97, p. 75, Todd McCarthy
WASHINGTON POST, 3/14/97, Weekend/p. 44, Esther Iverem

LOVE AND OTHER CATASTROPHIES

A Fox Searchlight Pictures release of a Screwball Five/Beyond Films production in association with The Australian Film Commission. *Producer:* Stavros Andonis Efthymiou. *Director:* Emma-Kate Croghan. *Screenplay:* Yael Bergman, Emma-Kate Croghan, and Helen Bandis. *Based on a story by:* Stavros Andonis Efthymiou. *Director of Photography:* Justin Brickle.

Editor: Ken Sallows. *Music:* Oleh Witer. *Sound:* Martin Kier. *Sound Editor:* Craig Carter. *Art Director:* Lisa Collins. *Make-up:* Jane Frances Kyle. *Running time:* 80 minutes. *MPAA Rating:* R.

CAST: Alice Garner (Alice); Frances O'Connor (Mia); Matthew Dyktynski (Ari); Matt Day (Michael); Radha Mitchell (Danni); Suzi Dougherty (Savita); Kim Gyngell (Professor Leach); Suzanne Dowling (Dr. Russell); Torquil Neilson (Toby); Christine Stephen-Daly (Susan); Dominic McDonald (Zac); Alvin Chong (Alvin); Myles Collins (Myles); Anthony Neate (Tony); Brigid Kelly (Brigid); Emma de Clario (Emma); Shanti Gudgeon (Shanti); Maurie Annese (Computer Geek); Nicholas Crawford Smith (Nick); Adrian Martin (Himself); Leroy Ryan (Nazi); Sanjot Kaur Sekhon (Sanjot); Caroline Lloyd (Carol); Kate Croghan (Office Worker); Joyce Yuen (Lecturer); Paul Harris (Professor Novak).

LOS ANGELES TIMES, 4/4/97, Calendar/p. 1, Kenneth Turan

What is more lively, spirited and unexpected than a youth movie that actually feels youthful? Mostly they show up DOA, compromised by aging, out-of-touch filmmakers and a lack of talent—or both. "Love and Other Catastrophes," however, takes delight in beating the odds.

Made for about $30,000 in 17 days by a gang of fresh, young Australians and directed by 23-year-old Emma-Kate Croghan, "Catastrophes" comes by its wacky charm naturally. A breezy story of university students confused about love or looking for it, it has the exact sense of a culture that comes only from being told from the inside.

More than that, it is pure fun to be around.

"Catastrophes" gets comic mileage out of the self-centered cluelessness of its protagonists. Each is so absorbed in his or her own dramas, so convinced that "my life is a complete disaster," that everyone acts at amusing cross-purposes, missing obvious connections in classic screwball fashion.

It starts with the elfin Mia (Frances O'Conner) and best friend Alice (Alice Garner), film students and roommates in search of a third person to share their funky Melbourne warehouse apartment.

The obvious choice would be Mia's girlfriend Danni (Radha Mitchell), but Mia isn't sure she's ready for that much commitment. And Danni's association with a silent but devoted shadow named Savita (Suzi Dougherty) is nothing if not irritating.

Scattered Mia has another crisis to deal with, or at least she thinks it's a crisis. Her favorite professor, the author of "Feral Cinema," has switched departments and Mia is determined to go with him. But blocking her way on this last day to make the change is nothing less than a comic opera obstacle course, with a $663 library fine serving as only the first act.

Roommate Alice has her own difficulties. Her thesis, "Doris Day as Feminist Warrior," is four years late. And she has to decide whether to chuck her rules for potential boyfriends—must be honest, left-handed and like the same films she does—because she has an eye on Ari (Matthew Dyktynski), a hunky classics major known as the campus Warren Beatty.

And then there is earnest, decent Michael (Matt Day), who shares a class with Ari but is as square as the big guy is cool. He also is trapped in an apartment with non-stop party animals and is desperately seeking a new place to live.

It's the pleasure of "Catastrophe's" script to make all these comings and goings feel spontaneous as well as charming. The action is broken up with literary quotes like Nikki Giovanni's "We love because it's the only true adventure" and Nikos Kazantzakis' "Life is trouble," and though the plotting eventually runs to the thin side, a lively pop soundtrack and surprisingly well-defined characters overcome all obstacles.

"Catastrophes" is also notable for its accepting yet casual attitude toward its characters' sexuality, its refusal to make a big deal about who sleeps with whom or why. Especially after all those Sundance films about morose young people confused about their gender, it's one more thing this captivating film makes look easy.

NEW YORK POST, 3/28/97, p. 53, Thelma Adams

Don't change your name, Matthew Dyktynski. In "Love and Other Catastrophes," Emma-Kate Croghan's hip and breezy first feature, the characters are as quirky and unpolished as Matthew's last name.

Dyktynski plays Ari, the campus Warren Beatty, in a college comedy about a day in the life of room-mates Alice (Alice Garner) and Mia (Frances O'Connor). The chatty pair, one straight and one gay, begin the day looking for a third roommate and end up discovering the meaning of life: Love conquers all.

Shy med student Michael (Matt Day) and Danni (Radha Mitchell), a lipstick lesbian with Jessica Lange looks, step in to put the world in perspective. All five scholars are navigating a world where sex roles are slipping and everything is acceptable—but it's no easier to maintain a monogamous relationship or find the perfect mate than it was in the Doris Day era.

Croghan's gift is her ability to treat her characters comically while taking their emotions seriously. The script, which she co-wrote with Yael Bergman and Helen Bandis, has a wispy, madcap plot and amusing dialogue that's never quite as hilarious as it could be.

Fresh and attractive newcomers Garner and O'Connor flirt with the camera, perfectly capturing what it's like to be young and intelligent and without a clue about one's place in the universe.

"Love and Other Catastrophes" recently played to sold-out houses at "New Directors/New Films" and brings to the screen a sweet and potent vision of what it's like to be a contemporary young woman.

NEWSDAY, 3/28/97, Part II/p. B8, John Anderson

If you're among those who think young American directors engage in obsessive navel-gazing, philosophical thumbsucking and pseudo-intellectual head-scratching, the Australian "Love and Other Catastrophes" will offer some happy news: We are not alone.

From the 24-year-old Emma-Kate Croghan comes this precious little package, a day in the life of five university students whose problems range from overdue library fines to feudal department heads to a lecturer's death-by-doughnuts to ill-starred romance. That the main character, Mia (Frances O'Connor), is a lesbian makes it *au courant,* but no less interminable.

That the film should open home movie-style, with a video of Mia and Alice (Alice Garner) moving into their new apartment, is apt. "Love etc." is an exercise in self-obsessive storytelling, albeit without much of a story. Mia and Alice need a third roommate; Michael (Matt Day), a socially inept medical student, needs a place to live. Alice and Michael need someone to love. Alice, a cinema studies major (naturally), thinks she'll find it with Ari (Matthew Dyktynski), a classics student and part-time prostitute. She's wrong. Even Ray Charles could see that Alice and Michael are going to intersect with the inevitablility of a 5:30 pileup on the LIE.

O'Connor makes Mia matter-of-factly lesbian and her relationship with the ditzy Danni (Radha Mitchell) is as parasitic as any comparable hetero-romance in a state of collapse. Alice is pleasant; Michael is nice. But despite the characters' charms (we won't mention Ari's uber-Beatles haircut) there's not a lot going on here. And what is has gone on before.

It's what you might call a paradoxical situation. Or, a revoltin' development. The rise of independent and faux-independent cinema has been a good thing overall, but it's also led to the misapprehension among aspiring auteurs that by merely creating a milieu and an attitude they've said something profound. And at this, I'm giving Croghan the benefit of the doubt. What she's done, despite all the cinema-savvy quoting that goes on in her film, is follow the lead of countless other fledgling directors who've decided to chronicle the oh-so-agonizing experiences of people on the cusp of adulthood as if no one has gone through it before. There may be something new to say about all this, but Croghan isn't saying it. And what she is saying is irritatingly coy.

On the other hand, there are very commercial reasons for making movies for young adults, and then disguising them as independent works by fresh new talent. Whether these films then deserve the imprimatur of Lincoln Center and the Museum of Modern Art—which have included "Love and Other Catastrophes" in the current New Directors/New Films series—is another, question. The film was one of the few that came to the series with a distribution deal in hand, so let's just say that commercial movies and the co-opting of art-film audience are an insidious and ongoing business.

SIGHT AND SOUND, 5/97, p. 48, Laura Miller

Melbourne, Australia, the present. Two friends, Alice and Mia, both film students, share a flat but need a third roommate. Ari, another student, works as a gigolo. Mike, a medical student, wants to move out of his raucous shared home. As Alice and Mia drive to school, Alice chides Mia for her chronic lateness and fear of commitment. Mia counters that Alice's thesis is overdue and teases her for the lack of romance in her life. On campus, Mia discovers that her attempt to switch departments has been stymied by a large library fine. Mia drops by the cafe where Alice works and, when Ari comes in, Alice reveals to Mia that she has a crush on him. Danni, Mia's girlfriend, and Savita join them, and Mia wheedles Danni out of the money for her fines. Mike eyes Alice in the café, but she is oblivious, and instead approaches Ari.

In the library men's room, Mike meets Ari, who tells him that Alice and Mia need a roommate. Mia pays off her fine, and is told she must now obtain Professor Leach's signature, but he refuses. In a lecture hall, Leach announces to his students that they will be studying Hitchcock on his course. They groan. He imagines groups of students dressed as Quentin Tarantino, Woody Allen and Spike Lee. In another cafe, Mia interviews Mike for the house. Danni storms in and accuses Mia of forgetting their lunch date. They argue and break up.

Mia obtains a crucial signature, and returns to Leach's office but finds he has died suddenly. She encounters Danni, who asks Mia to return the money she borrowed and explains that she's going to the country with Savita. Ari and Alice discuss love and truthfulness over coffee. They meet up with Mia, and the three sneak into Leach's office to obtain his signature stamp for Mia's forms.

Alice and Mia have a party that evening. Alice films the guests, Mia broods jealously about Danni and Savita and Mike drifts around awkwardly. Mia reconciles with Danni. Ari kisses Alice, then they seek out Mia and Danni, and all four get stoned. Each recites his/her three favourite movies, and are then joined by Mike. Asked the same question, Mike responds with a list identical to Alice's, and Alice realises he is her soulmate. The next morning, Alice shows her thesis to Mike, and Mia asks Danni to move in.

Emma-Kate Croghan's ensemble story of a day in the life of several feckless twentysomething friends is the quintessential film student project, so it's no surprise to learn that the director was only 23 when she made it. The casual treatment of gay characters, the satirical portrait of Ari's leather-clad undergraduate alienation, and the callow, theoretical conversations about love and the inevitable party scene are classics of the genre, and *Love and Other Catastrophes* is more successful than many. The film doesn't aim to do much more than charm, and when it fails, it's the result of trying too hard. It has a bemused, rueful, slightly overeducated tone that could be dubbed 'Woody Allen lite'.

Nevertheless, what makes for a fine senior thesis doesn't always set a theatrical audience on fire. Compared to, say, Whit Stillman's witty portrait of a similar crowd in *Metropolitan:*, *Love and Other Catastrophes* feels decidedly thin.

The performances are uneven, although all of the leads have likeable, attractive screen presences. As Alice, Alice Garner is the most relaxed and convincing, and Matt Day, despite his shy, nerdy role as Mike, has the blunt good looks of a young Mel Gibson. As Mia, Frances O'Connor occasionally clicks, but mostly she suffers from the film's overall weakness: visibly straining to appear effortless. In general, the actors aim at conveying personality rather than character, a bad habit encouraged by the laziness of the screenplay, which favours gimmickry. The film professor who cantankerously interferes with Mia's attempt to switch majors, for example, is repeatedly shown gorging on donuts, for no apparent reason other than to stuff 'amusing' quirks onto the screen.

The creators of *Love and Other Catastrophes* (it was jointly written by Croghan and producers Yael Bergman and Helen Bandis) claim two American inspirations: the grubby, independent just-me-and-my-friends ethos of Richard Linklater (*Slacker*) and Kevin Smith (*Clerks*) and the exquisite froth of 30s Hollywood screwball comedy. It's an uneasy mix, resulting in a film that's too airy to settle into mordant realism and too phlegmatic to effervesce. Plot points such as Alice's thesis on "Doris Day as Feminist Warrior" and the notion that similar cinematic tastes equal spiritual compatibility seem to be included as mockeries of various film student pretensions, but the film's so self-congratulatory about its own satire that the jokes are spoiled.

Croghan sprinkles quotes from directors, writers and painters among the cutaway scenes, suggesting the hothouse mentality of student artists whose most powerful experiences come second hand and (as is often said about Tarantino) whose movies are chiefly about other movies. But *Love and Other Catastrophes* never manages to get beyond that myopia, or the film-makers' and performers' conviction that their own are the cutest, hippest, wackiest and most insouciantly unconventional of lives. Some more indulgent audiences will no doubt forgive them that vanity, but for many who remember all too well their own collegiate narcissism, this film may be too embarrassing a reminder to be enjoyed.

VILLAGE VOICE, 4/1/97, p. 72, Justine Elias

What a tough way for Emma-Kate Croghan to begin a career: at 24, the Australian writer-director is going to endure such destructive praise as "cute," "endearing," and "promising." Her first film, a campus comedy about cinema students in love, was picked up for distribution at last year's Cannes Film Festival.

This is not the best thing that could have happened to *Love and Other Catastrophes.* For one thing, the screenplay is clever without being particularly well written. The movie's offbeat inspiration is Doris Day in *Calamity Jane,* a performance revered by Alice (Alice Garner), a shy cinema-studies major who sees Day as an unsung feminist warrior. Alice's bisexual best friend (Frances O'Connor) juggles her latest flames, her debts, and her desire to enroll in a different department. Their male acquaintances include a dorky medical student (Matt Day of *Muriel's Wedding*) and a pseudointellectual (Matthew Dyktynski) who works parttime as a hustler, exclusively servicing women. That this nasal-voiced, helmet-haired John Doe #2 is cast as a stud is one of the many plot points that don't quite ring true.

Wisely, Croghan peppers her film with title-card quotations, including a priceless one from *Calamity Jane,* to give the illusion of speed and unity. Toward the end, she begins to succeed, and she allows her appealing cast some room to shine.

O'Connor, with her mischievous eyes and smoky voice, emotes like a younger Judy Davis, and she's well supported by Garner and Day as the two awkward romantics who are meant to be together. But until its winning final scenes, the movie is consistently undermined by ragged technique.

Croghan has cited Kevin Smith's *Clerks* as an inspiration, but Smith's shaky black-and-white camera work looks like genius next to the jaundiced, grainy footage in Croghan's film. Worse still is the director's tendency to telegraph her jokes: the med student's apartment hunt, a minor character's obsession with adult penile circumcision, and a student rebellion against their Hitchcock-loving lecturer cry out for editing. It may seem cruel to harp on the technical deficiencies of such a young filmmaker, but it's not enough for Croghan and her ilk to get excited about making movies because someone else did it for next to no money. Why doesn't anyone get inspired by the idea of young Ernest Hemingway doing a lot of rewriting before he published his stories, or from the idea that Spike Lee spent more hours on script and post-production than he did on shooting his first film? Despite Croghan's and her cast's obvious talent, it would be hard to imagine this movie getting into theaters if it didn't feature a quirky soundtrack and a few frisky lesbians. Wait for her next film and hope that Croghan's premature debut doesn't ruin her chances at making the accomplished movie she is capable of.

Also reviewed in:
NEW YORK TIMES, 3/26/97, p. C18, Janet Maslin
VARIETY, 5/20-26/96, p. 34, David Stratton

LOVE SERENADE

A Miramax Films release of a Jan Chapman production in association with the Australian Film Finance Corporation. *Producer:* Jan Chapman. *Director:* Shirley Barrett. *Screenplay:* Shirley Barrett. *Director of Photography:* Mandy Walker. *Editor:* Denise Haratzis. *Music:* Christine Woodruff. *Sound:* Gary Wilkins and (music) Peter Smith. *Sound Editor:* Frank Lipson.

Casting: Alison Barrett. *Production Designer:* Steven Jones-Eveans. *Art Director:* Tony Campbell. *Costumes:* Anna Borghesi. *Make-up:* Stephanie Larman. *Make-up (Special Effects):* Nik Dorning, Ann-Maree Hurley and Laura Morris. *Stunt Coordinator:* Johnny Hallyday. *Running time:* 101 minutes. *MPAA Rating:* Not Rated.

CAST: Miranda Otto (Dimity Hurley); Rebecca Frith (Vicki-Ann Hurley); George Shevtsov (Ken Sherry); John Alansu (Albert Lee); Jessica Napier (Deborah); Jill McWilliam (Curler Victim); Ryan Jackson (Boy on Ride); Sabrina Norris (Beautiful Baby).

LOS ANGELES TIMES, 8/1/97, Calendar/p. 4, Kenneth Turan

"Love Serenade" offers as precise and merciless a comic vision as anyone could want. A wickedly funny examination of obsessive romantic behavior, its satiric vision of women in love and men on the make was devastating enough to earn writer-director Shirley Barrett the highly prized Camera d'Or at Cannes, given to the best first film both in and out of competition.

Barrett is Australian, the latest in a slew of filmmakers adept at creating bizarre psychological landscapes where comic delusion is the rule. "Love Serenade's" producer, Jan Chapman, has worked with both Jane Campion and Gillian Armstrong, and though this is Barrett's debut, she gives every evidence of belonging in their company.

A perfectly acted four-character drama, "Love Serenade" is set in the completely parched hamlet of Sunray, where time has not so much stood still as been baked in its tracks. The local radio station, 101.4 on your FM dial, is so bedraggled it's never so much as seen a compact disc, and no one has broadcast from there for months.

Into the studio and the surrounding lunar landscape comes a refugee from the wider world. Ken Sherry (veteran Australian actor George Shevtsov), once the Drivetime King of Brisbane radio, arrives in town, complete with aviator sunglasses, reptilian smile and lounge lizard manner.

An aging hipster who favors shirts open to mid-chest level, Ken Sherry has a seductive voice that drowns its listeners in waves of ennui. He has a taste for rambling personal monologues and the funkadelic sounds of Barry White, and the whole package has a devastating effect on a pair of unwary twentysomething sisters whom fate has placed in the house next door to this self-proclaimed "fool where women are concerned."

Vicki-Ann (Rebecca Frith) is the oldest, a prim beautician who may be the only person in town to have heard of Ken Sherry. She casts covetous eyes on the new arrival from the big city, bombarding him with a baffling string of homemade casseroles and perky smiles.

Vicki-Ann, it develops, sees the world exclusively in glowing romance magazine terms. "Ken Sherry," she earnestly informs her mopey sister Dimity, "has come to Sunray to heal. Slowly, bit by bit, he may learn to love again."

Dimity (Miranda Otto, winner of an Australian Oscar for Armstrong's "The Last Days of Chez Nous") is not so sure about any of this. Awkward, ill-at-ease but more scheming than her dog-bound psyche would indicate, Dimity (who works at the local Chinese restaurant) doesn't see why uneaten casseroles need be the only route to a man's heart.

Never mind that Ken Sherry is a pig in a poke, a dissipated Barry Manilow wannabe addicted to fake intimacy. To Dimity and Vicki-Ann, he is closer to Prince Charming than they ever expected to get and, mutually and madly infatuated, they engage in a peevish rivalry for his wandering affection.

Drawn into this battle from time to time is Albert Lee (John Alansu), Dimity's boss, a man of almost regal formality and comic diction who has always admired Vicki-Ann "from a distance". A stern moralist and spare-time nudist, Albert takes a strong dislike to Ken Sherry when he rashly questions the freshness of the establishment's prawns, and little happens to make him change his mind.

Beautifully consistent in tone from its waspish beginning to a savage, surreal ending, "Love Serenade" is one of those films that shows how essential it can be for writers to direct their own work. No one but Barrett could understand the bizarre nuances of this arch and heavily ironic comedy of obliviousness, with its subtext of men being another species altogether, or guide its actors so expertly toward understanding characters who have no insight themselves.

This is a pitiless kind of comedy, and it works especially well against the backdrop of the sullen romantic ballads of Barry White, including "Never Gonna Give You Up," "I'm Gonna Love You

Just a Little Bit More Baby" and the song that gives the film its name. In this cracked, hot house world, those throaty extravaganzas begin to sound as if they're making sense. "We're all odd," Ken Sherry says, and this film is not about to argue the point.

NEW YORK POST, 8/1/97, p. 42, Thelma Adams

"Be cheerful, strive to be happy," says Ken Sherry.

After his third divorce, the deeply depressed deejay has left the relative hustle and bustle of Brisbane for the fictional backwater of Sunray, Australia.

We have to take his new neighbor Vicki-Ann Hurley's word when she tells her sister that Sherry (George Shevtsov) was big in Brisbane, despite the fact that his sports car is dusty and old, his wardrobe cries disco and his brown face is as wrinkled and stiff as a dime store Indian's.

At first, we swallow the bait. But before long, we discover that, like most things in Shirley Barrett's off-kilter comedy, "Love Serenade," the cheery hairdresser played so well by Rebecca Frith is as falsely bright as the highlights in her hair. Surface details can't be trusted.

The apparently conventional Vicki-Ann has a habit of telling little white lies—and then believing them. A woman who frequently goes fishing, she tells fish tales that grow in the retelling—along with her delusions.

By the time the 26-year-old tells her little sister Dimity (Miranda Otto) to her face that she's odd, we're already skeptical of Vicki-Ann's opinions. As it turns out, she couldn't be more right about Dimity.

At night, Dimity waits tables at the shabby, ironically named Emperor's Palace; by day, the bike-riding 21-year-old circles the ghostly, ghastly, economically depressed Sunray (a "rural paradise on the banks of the Murray River," Vicki-Ann tells Sherry).

Dimity isn't necessarily the oddest fish in Sunray. Her boss (the deliciously deadpan John Alansu) is a pontificating nudist. And what about Sherry? What are those peculiar slits behind his ears that leak fat? Could they be gills?

Fish are the movie's outsized metaphor. Dimity and Vicki-Ann go fishing together. In the case of newcomer Sherry (played with exquisite sleaze by the slim, repulsive Shevtsov), both women go angling for love. Sherry lets both girls "ease his loneliness," and sibling rivalry turns into a bizarrely comic game of fish-eat-fish.

The cast wisely underplays the dark humor. Otto ("The Last Days of Chez Nous") combines gawkiness and a desperate boldness with the scrubbed, freckled appeal of a young Mel Harris; her strip tease for Sherry is fresh and achingly funny. Frith, in her film debut, makes eating a sandwich on white bread interesting.

The winner of the Camera D'Or for best first film at Cannes, "Love Serenade" gets its title from the Barry White hit. The soulful soundtrack is the comedy's safety net; who can resist the stroking sound of white's voice or such ridiculously suggestive rhymes as : "Take off that brassiere, my dear?"

NEWSDAY, 8/1/97, Part II/p. B11, Jack Mathews

If men are heartless ogres in Neil LaBute's "In the Company of Men," they're a different species altogether in Australian writer-director Shirley Barrett's charmingly eccentric comedy "Love Serenade." It appears, from the odd flaps on the neck of "Love's" leading cad that we are ... fish?

It's amazing how two filmmakers can come to the same conclusion—that men are cold-blooded creatures put on Earth to use and abuse women—in such wildly diverse ways. "In the Company of Men" feels like a stoning with sharp rocks, while "Love Serenade" is more of a spanking with kid gloves. The spanking's better.

"Love Serenade," which won Barrett the Camera d'Or for best first feature at the 1996 Cannes Film Festival, is set in a small town so remote that its lone radio station still plays music from vinyl records. That's the depressing news awaiting Ken Sherry (George Shevtsov), an exiled radio personality from Brisbane, when he shows up to take over the one-jock operation.

Sherry, a middle-age narcissist given to gaseous philosophical rants on the air, may be washed up in the big market, but he's hot stuff in desolate Sunray, particularly to the lovelorn sisters living next door. Within days of his arrival, he's deflowered eager 21-year-old Dimity (Miranda Otto), and has his eye on 26-year-old Vicki-Ann (Rebecca Frith).

Vicki-Ann's virginity is uncertain. She talks about having once been engaged, but her boyfriend had a run-in with a chain saw, presumably with that part of the body where men in love do most of their thinking.

These sisters are fabulous characters, simple dreamers with unplumbed depths of naiveté. Vicki-Ann, a self-deluded romantic, has her own hair salon, in a town where the wind does most of the styling. And the aptly named Dimity, when she's not pulling whopping fish out of the river, serves tables in a perpetually empty Chinese restaurant.

Without filling in background details, Barrett portrays the sisters as soulmates who've raised themselves in this tired outpost, seeding their acres of boredom with Dimity's fish tales and Vicki-Ann's romantic fantasies. The exotic appearance of the tall, dark and brooding Sherry creates immediate sibling rivalry, and unleashes years of repressed hostilities, all of which is casually exploited by him.

The three performances are superb. The lanky, silky-voiced Shevtsov makes Sherry a deliciously smarmy creep, just the sort of bad luck you'd expect to enter the lives of the innocent (Dimity) and the desperate (Vicki-Ann). Frith, as required, wears her entire character on her sleeve. The overdressed Vicki-Ann is the product of too much isolation and too many romance novels, and as she courts Sherry with casseroles and idolatry, she leads with her heart.

As plain-looking, tomboyish Dimity, the pivotal character in the triangle, Otto is a revelation. She plays Dimity as a child-woman straddling the line between fantasy and reality, going after Sherry to spite her sister, and with no idea what she's getting into. The scene where she awkwardly strips and offers herself to Sherry is both hilarious and sad.

Afterward, she compares the event to "going to the dentist, only you have to take your clothes off."

There is a touch of magical realism throughout "Love Serenade," most of it coming from Dimity's point of view. Her escape from loneliness is a world of fish, and the gills that she discovers on Sherry's neck may or may not exist. And it's a mystery that Barrett, one of the bright new talents from Down Under, keeps to the film's darkly whimsical ending.

NEWSWEEK, 7/28/97, p. 70, David Ansen

This Australian comedy by writer-director Shirley Barrett won the Camera d'Or for Best First Film at the 1996 Cannes festival. Deservedly: its sense of humor is deliciously different. It concerns the love-starved Hurley sisters, Dimity (Miranda Otto) and Vicki-Ann (Rebecca Frith), denizens of the tiny, forlorn town of Sunray. Their sisterly bond is sorely tested with the arrival next door of the mellifluous-voiced Ken Sherry (George Shevtsov), an over-the-hill deejay from Brisbane setting up shop in this backwater burg, which he floods with the sepulchral tunes of Barry White. Rarely has a less appropriate love object come into movie view. The jaded, fortysomething, thrice-divorced Sherry, with a face as mournful as a basset hound's, a body as spindly as Ichabod Crane's and a reptilian style of seduction, is Mr. Wrong incarnate. Just how fishy this character is cannot be revealed, for it would spoil Barrett's weirdest conceit, which spins the movie into the territory of fable. Suffice it to say that this minimally populated, very funny movie gets odder and darker as it wends its confident way to a very unexpected conclusion.

VILLAGE VOICE, 8/5/97, p. 72, Abby McGanney Nolan

Love Serenade is an Australian comedy that surrounds an awkward young woman of rather grim circumstances with musical hits from the '70s. That the soundtrack features not ABBA but Barry White, Van McCoy, and Billy Paul only begins to explain why Shirley Barrett's directorial debut is several cuts above the goofy, gaudy, but similarly themed *Muriel's Wedding.*

This film has a far more engaging heroine in Miranda Otto's desperately skittish Dimity Hurley and an enthrallingly unlikely seducer in George Shevtsov's Ken Sherry, a thrice-divorced Brisbane DJ who's relocated to the drab, dusty town of Sunray. The only irritating reminder of *Muriel's Wedding* surfaces in Dimity's marriage-obsessed sister Vicki-Ann, played with cheerful mania by Rebecca Frith.

At the film's opening, the two Hurley sisters have established a comfortable routine: they fish regularly on the murky Murray River and lunch together during the work-week on white-bread sandwiches. Twenty-year-old Dimity is the waitress at a usually deserted Chinese restaurant, while her thirtyish sister is an equally in-demand hairdresser.

But when Ken takes over the town's one-man radio station and sets up house next door, all the old customs are abandoned. Vicki-Ann starts to cook meals for Ken instead of her sister (who might have appreciated them more), while Dimity soaks up the soul music Ken broadcasts and imagines finding some slice of heaven in his arms.

It is the eventual odd coupling between Ken and Dimity that makes *Love Serenade* satisfying. Shevtsov, a veteran actor apparently new to American screens, has transformed himself into a creature who seems both oily and dried out; his sun-baked skin gives him a lizardlike appearance and his voice drips with disdain or concern depending on whom he's talking to. His on-air patter, a mixture of everyday uplift and Barry White bass, sometimes gets defensive. "All I've done is love a little too much a little too hard and for that I've been tried and executed many times over." Our young heroine, meanwhile, listens to this chatter with great sympathy, eager to help ease Ken's supposed loneliness. His romantic pronouncements—"Lucky for you, Dimity, virgins are my special-i-ty" couldn't have found a better audience.

Barrett skillfully manages a magic-realist undercurrent for her hyper-realist images and sounds (there are a lot of loud buzzers and squealing teapots in this movie). And the off-kilter naïveté Otto has devised for Dimity is somehow the perfect vehicle for the vengeance she and her sister will try to exact. Put all together, *Love Serenade* has a strange magnetism not unlike those stirring songs of the '70s.

Also reviewed in:
NEW YORK TIMES, 8/1/97, p. C32, Janet Maslin
VARIETY, 5/20-26/96, p. 32, David Stratton
WASHINGTON POST, 8/8/97, p. D1, Rita Kempley
WASHINGTON POST, 8/8/97, Weekend/p. 32, Eve Zibart

LOVE! VALOUR! COMPASSION!

A Fine Line Features release of a Krost/Chapin production. *Executive Producer:* Ruth Vitale, Jonathan Weisgal, and Amy Labowitz. *Producer:* Doug Chapin and Barry Krost. *Director:* Joe Mantello. *Screenplay (based on his play):* Terrence McNally. *Director of Photography:* Alik Sakharov. *Editor:* Colleen Sharp. *Music:* Jackie Krost and Harold Wheeler. *Music Editor:* Steve Livingston. *Sound:* Don Cohen and (music) Gary Lux. *Sound Editor:* Kelly Cabral. *Choreographer:* John Carrafa. *Production Designer:* François Seguin. *Set Decorator:* Anne Galéa. *Costumes:* Jess Goldstein. *Make-up:* Donald Mowat. *Running time:* 115 minutes. *MPAA Rating:* R.

CAST: Jason Alexander (Buss Hauser); Randy Becker (Ramon Fornos); Stephen Bogardus (Gregory Mitchell); John Glover (John & James Jeckyll); John Benjamin Hickey (Arthur Pape); Justin Kirk (Bobby Brahms); Stephen Spinella (Perry Sellars).

LOS ANGELES TIMES, 5/16/97, Calendar/p. 6, John Anderson

[The following review by John Anderson appeared in a slightly different form in
NEWSDAY, 5/16/97, Part II/p. B8.]

When you know going in that Terrence McNally's Tony-winning "Love! Valour! Compassion!" was a hit on the New York stage, one thing becomes stunningly clear: Stage dialogue has a hard time making the trip to a big screen. It's paradoxical, really. In the theater, there's an implicit understanding that distances, both spatial and emotional, must be breached; in the cinema, the intimacy is so immediate that passions must be tempered.

And there's nothing temperate about "Love! Valour! Compassion!," which McNally, who adapted the script, intended as Anton Chekhov cross-pollinated with Oscar Wilde but which arrives at something closer to "The Boys in the Band" meets "The Big Chill."

That this is the first film for director Joe Mantello, who was nominated for a Tony for directing the stage version, may be compounding the problem. But frankly, if someone wanted to do a parody of a gay film like this, it's hard to imagine the sloganeering being much different.

What we have are eight gay "types" rather than full-blooded characters—billboards of earnestness who over several summer weekends meet, grieve, rail and bond at the country home of dancer-choreographer Gregory Mitchell (Stephen Bogardus). Among his guests are longtime lovers Perry and Arthur (Stephen Spinella and John Benjamin Hickey), the icily British pianist John Jeckyll (John Glover), Gregory's lover Bobby (Justin Kirk), who's blind, and John's much younger inamorata, Ramon (Randy Becker), who's hot.

Oh yes, and let's not forget the late-arriving, Broadway-musical quoting Buzz Hauser, played by "Seinfeld's" newly enriched Jason Alexander, who's as brightly over the top as need be (and is the only cast member who was not in the stage play).

McNally is expert at establishing the labyrinth of interrelationships among the men—who loves, loved, loathes and would like to sleep with whom—as well as the men's often impenetrable facades, which may have been erected out of fear but are left standing out of habit. Ramon, lusted after by most of the group, in turns desires Bobby (the sex object responding to the blind man is a bit much, but OK). Bobby's betrayal of Gregory exacerbates the latter's fear of age; Ramon's roaming about makes John more bitter than he already was.

The film works best as a parable of youth and age, and how both are distorted by AIDS. When John's HIV-positive twin brother James (also played by Glover, who's excellent) arrives and begins dying—just as Buzz falls in love with him—it throws much of what is happening in the men's lives into perspective. AIDS, McNally is telling us, is a disease like any other, in the sense that it only hastens the inevitable. The concerns of the stricken—how to best make use of one's time on Earth, how to love as well as one can—aren't exactly limited to the plague-stricken. They're timeless, universal priorities that aren't any different for gays than straights, and that of course is the point. But preaching to the converted is a waste of time, as is saccharine-laced sincerity.

NEW YORK POST, 5/16/97, p. 42, Michael Medved

It's difficult to connect with the eight characters in the new film version of "Love! Valour! Compassion!" not because they all happen to be gay, but because they all come across as so maddeningly shallow and spoiled.

We get to know every feature of their taut, beautifully muscled bodies (Jason Alexander is the only non-hunk in the cast), but we learn next to nothing about their work, their ambitions, their family backgrounds or their passions outside the bedroom.

The eight men gather for three weekends in the country (Memorial Day, July Fourth, Labor Day) at the Victorian lakeside home of a semi-retired choreographer (Stephen Bogardus).

In the course of these stagily structured three acts, they flirt, go skinny-dipping, trade witticisms, trade insults, flirt some more, go skinny-dipping again, show off their lesions, compare AIDS regimens, discuss Broadway's decline, endure short-lived lovers' spats, go skinny-dipping, and flirt some more.

With Terrence McNally's crisp dialogue (he adapted the script from his Tony Award-winning play), such activity might easily carry an intimate stage presentation; but on the big screen, it feels like time-killing fluff. We're trapped in a tedious party of gifted conversationalists who can't think of anything significant or compelling to discuss. The talented cast (nearly intact from the 1994 Broadway production) make a game but doomed attempt to lend some depth to this thin material.

Stephen Spinella and John Benjamin Hickey are endearing as a respectable yuppie couple who are celebrating their 14th year of marriage with their friends.

"We're role models," they declare. "It's very stressful."

John Glover does a silly "evil twin" bit, playing identical British brothers who, were repeatedly informed, represent extremes of cruelty and saintliness. Unfortunately, we never see why the bad twin is supposed to be so rotten, or why the good twin is so noble—except for the fact that he's dying of AIDS.

Meanwhile, the nasty brother brings along his latest lover, a stereotypically hot-blooded but dim-witted Puerto Rican dancer (Randy Becker), whose rugged physique inspires lustful attention from all the others.

Alexander is the only newcomer to the cast, taking over the flamboyant role of the lonely, lacerating "musical comedy queen," played on stage by Nathan Lane. Venturing far from his "Seinfeld" persona, Alexander does a decent job but makes the character far less obnoxious and dominating than Lane thereby depriving the group of its dynamic center.

Stage director Joe Mantello (here making his big-screen debut) makes the most of a stately, 19th-century home (actually near Montreal) that becomes a ninth character in the movie, and also offers lyrical visions of a sylvan lake, but it's too bad that his characters spend all their time splashing around in the shallowest end of the water.

SIGHT AND SOUND, 9/97, p. 49, Paul Julian Smith

At a late nineteenth-century house on a private lake, two hours' drive from New York City during Memorial Day weekend, a choreographer named Gregory in his forties awaits the arrival of his extended family of gay friends: his younger, blind lover, Bobby; HIV-positive Buzz; and easy-going Arthur and uptight Perry, who have been partners for some time. The cynical Englishman John also arrives with his latest young lover, Ramon, a Puerto Rican dancer. As the guests settle in, tensions emerge: John, fearful for his brother in England who is gravely ill with Aids, is disruptive. Ramon's beauty challenges and disturbs the older men. That night Ramon secretly seduces Bobby.

On the Fourth of July weekend, the friends return once more, this time accompanied by John's identical twin James, as good-hearted as his brother is misanthropic. Buzz and James gradually fall in love, while Bobby confesses his infidelity to Gregory, who asks him to leave the house.

On the last holiday of summer, Labour Day weekend, the friends return a final time. Buzz cares tenderly for the gravely ill James, but is terrified by his own approaching death. Gregory confronts Ramon over his affair with Bobby. The friends rehearse a transvestite version of *Swan Lake* for an Aids benefit at Carnegie Hall and go skinny dipping together in the moonlight. During this, a voiceover foretells how each character will die.

Premiere's Libby Gelman-Waxner (the pseudonym of New York gay playwright Paul Rudnick) claims that there should be a new category at the Sundance Film Festival: most original use of a sitcom star on a hiatus. At first glance, *Love! Valour! Compassion!*'s casting of the straight Jason Alexander (*Seinfeld*'s George) as musical-comedy queen Buzz should win hands down. Avoiding the curse of the comedy vehicle (see the disastrous cinematic ventures by *Friends'* cast members), Alexander enters into this low-budget Broadway adaptation with gusto: a spread in *Out* magazine had him delightedly putting his hand down hunky Randy Becker's shorts.

Fans of the sardonic Libby and *Seinfeld* alike, however, will be disheartened by the opening sequence of *Love! Valour! Compassion!* In a smug voiceover, Stephen Bogardus' Gregory sings the praises of the film's sole setting: "I love my house. Every body does. It was built in 1895 and still has most of the roof." As Alik Sakharov's camera lovingly pans over the antiques to Harold Wheeler's saccharine score, a weekend in such a setting threatens to be a season in hell. Fortunately sceptical Britons have a built-in identification character: John Glover's unloved and unloving John, smoking furiously through the exquisite dinner parties. UK audiences may be less willing than Americans, however, to have their hearts warmed by the youthful narcissism of Ramon or the lightly sketched artistic dilemmas of the saintly Gregory. It is no doubt a convention of the country-house genre that people leave their social context back home in the city, but still the contemplation of mortality in such cosseted conditions does not always inspire the desired emotional engagement. Even in the US, access to a private lake is not generally a priority for people with Aids.

Nonetheless, opening up the claustrophobic set and actualising what was merely mimed on stage, first-time director Joe Mantello does manage some moments of purely cinematic pleasure. Becker's unabashed nudity on location will inspire the same delight it did on stage and the editing makes some swift and economical points, as in the packing sequence where jeans and handcuffs go into one friend's case, musical comedy CDs and Aids medication into another's. Best of all is the precise social observation: the fastidious house guests who, disapproving of their host's towels, bring along their own; the conversational minefield of race and disability, even among this group of relatively homogeneous middle-class professionals. (It is interesting here to compare *Love! Valour! Compassion!* with *My Night with Reg* and *Boyfriends,* UK stage-to-camera works whose focus is more on class.) And the dialogue has the sparkle worthy of the play's Tony awards: Buzz's little bedroom is "the Patty Hearst Memorial Closet", his nightmare is a revival of *West Side Story*, starring Cher. The consummate craftsman of the well-made play, scriptwriter Terrence McNally rings the changes on the characters as the plot progresses: long-suffering Gregory takes revenge on philandering Ramon (surely the most original use of a waste disposal in a gay comedy); hardened John reveals a softer side by confessing a teenage S&M encounter; even the "gay imp" Buzz turns bitter, imagining the cast of *The Sound of Music* wiped out by an avalanche.

For all its fuzzy edges, then, *Love! Valour! Compassion!* often succeeds in its aim of revealing those precious moments when the everyday and the eternal coincide. The details of gay domesticity (the trimming of hair in a life-partner's ears) and the tokens of a love which come almost too late (the kissing of a lesion) are tenderly recreated. And the plot guides us towards the sober virtues and modest rewards of fidelity and solidarity. Most surprising of all are the final voiceovers in which we are told the fate of each character: vibrant Ramon will meet his end in a plane crash, loveless John will never change. It is a sobering and most un-American moral: that even survivors must die one day and that some of us will not be redeemed suffering.

VILLAGE VOICE, 5/20/97, p. 78, Elliott Stein

I'd never been any kind of fan of Terrence McNally's work until I saw his play *Love! Valour! Compassion!* in what seemed a definitive production by Joe Mantello. I was greatly affected by this tale of AIDS-era gay life, a far cry from Matt Crowley's preliberation classic, *The Boys in the Band,* with its self-loathing roster of bickering male bitches. *Love! Valour!* recounts the betrayals, seductions, the highs and lows of four male couples with humor and some pathos, but these gents are loving friends, reaching out and trying to get through it all together.

The screen version, adapted by McNally, sticks close to the original: over the course of three holiday weekends, a group of buddied-up urban professionals leaves the city to gather at the upstate New York Victorian summer house belonging to Gregory (Stephen Bogardus), a choreographer struggling with an aging body. Relationships form, sunder, re-form; a couple of illnesses worsen; the characters foretell their own deaths. There's no strong narrative arc, rather a series of touching, lightly Chekhovian variations on the theme of interlacing gay lives.

Mantello, making his directorial debut in films, again shows his fine hand with actors—the performances are all, save one, remarkable—but he's not yet at home behind the camera. As cinema, this is a stodgy affair. And although six of the seven members of the original cast repeat their roles, the part of Buzz, the outrageously flamboyant musical comedy queen, whooped up memorably by Nathan Lane on Broadway, has been given to Jason Alexander, best known as George on *Seinfeld.* He has no flair for camp; the body language rings false. Miscast, he's a serious liability, as is Harold Wheeler's unrelentingly treacly musical score.

Also reviewed in:
NEW REPUBLIC, 6/9/97, p. 30, Stanley Kauffmann
NEW YORK TIMES, 5/16/97, p. C10, Stephen Holden
VARIETY, 2/3-9/97, p. 45, Emanuel Levy
WASHINGTON POST, 5/23/97, Weekend/p. 42, Desson Howe

LOVE'S DEBRIS

An In Pictures release of an MC4 and Imalyre/VTCOM production. *Producer:* Wieland Schultz-Keil, Jean-Pierre Bailly, Anne Cauvin and Christoph Meyer-Wiel. *Director:* Werner Schroeter. *Screenplay (French, English, Italian and German with English subtitles):* Werner

Schroeter. *Director of Photography:* Elfi Mikesch. *Editor:* Juliane Lorenz. *Music:* Elisabeth Cooper. *Costumes:* Alberte Bersaqe. *Running time:* 122 minutes. *MPAA Rating:* Not Rated.

WITH: Anita Cerquetti; Martha Mödl; Rita Gorr; Carole Bouquet; Isabelle Huppert.

NEW YORK POST, 7/23/97, p. 42, Larry Worth

Under the best of circumstances, the world of opera has made a shaky transition to cinema. Even directors like Franco ("Otello") Zeffirelli and Joseph ("Don Giovanni") Losey tanked with stilted, lifeless efforts.

But those stilted, lifeless efforts are bona-fide masterpieces next to "Love's Debris." Werner Schroeter's documentary on three aging divas is not only interminable, it earns negative numbers for lack of cohesion and accessibility.

That's because Schroeter's more concerned with getting his mug on camera than identifying the speakers. And since his lineup is considerably more arcane than Beverly Sills, all but the most devout opera fans will be left in the dark.

The central trio—Anita Cerquetti, Martha Modl and Rita Gorr—comment on aging, their professional triumphs and personal lives, then interact with myriad others to sing or converse. But since no background or reference points are forthcoming, it's a waste of time and celluloid.

Potential viewers should also brush up on their French, Italian and German: Almost no arias are subtitled. Yes, that means audiences don't know who's singing, or what's being sung. And, for that matter, what's with all the lesbian tableaux?

It wouldn't take Einstein to see the problem here: Lyrics with no translation render Schroeter's bizarre imagery meaningless. In a typical scene, one performer appears to be singing about love as a man rides nude on horseback into a domed arena. Huh?

Out of the blue, French actresses Isabelle Huppert and Carole Bouquet then appear in the 13th-century abbey that serves as the documentary's setting. Although Bouquet's presence is never explained, Huppert is gradually revealed as an amateur opera singer. Ironically, watching Huppert stretch her vocal cords turns into one of the film's few highlights.

And, of course, the professionals' voices are undeniably lovely. So, why not catch them on CD rather than suffer through the agony of "Love's Debris"?

VILLAGE VOICE, 7/29/97, p. 76, Amy Taubin

A German filmmaker and stage director with a passion for opera, Werner Schroeter gathered nearly a dozen of Europe's reigning divas in a 13th-century French abbey to explore his theory: "that everything we express with our voice is the product of our quest to come even closer to someone, our need for love, and all manner of attendant emotions." The film that resulted, *Love's Debris*, is an acute and moving depiction of the process by which opera singers balance their immersion in the music, their interpretation of a character, and the unique expression of their own psyche.

Though the conversations between Schroeter and the artists (among them Anita Cerquetti, Martha Modl, and Rita Gorr) are fascinating, the joy of the film is in the singing. Working with only piano accompaniment, the barest suggestions of sets, and a camera that scrutinizes every movement, Schroeter elicits stunningly modern readings of familiar arias from such 19th-century warhorses as *Traviata, Carmen*, and *Bohéme*. Essential viewing for singers, actors, and directors, it might also win new fans for a very old form.

Also reviewed in:
NEW YORK TIMES, 7/23/97, p. C13, Stephen Holden
VARIETY, 11/11-17/96, p. 61, Emanuel Levy

MA VIE EN ROSE (MY LIFE IN PINK)

A Sony Pictures Classics release of an Haut et Court/La Sept Cinema/TF1 Films Production/WFE/RTBF/Freeway Films coproduction with the participation of Belgique European Coproduction Fund and Eurimages/Canal+/Cofimage 8/Avance surrecettes/CNC/Centre du Cinema et de l'Audiovisual de la Communate Francaise. *Producer:* Carole Scotta. *Director:* Alain Berliner. *Screenplay (French with English subtitles):* Chris vander Stappené and Alain Berliner. *Director of Photography:* Yves Cape. *Editor:* Sandrine Deegen. *Music:* Dominique Dalcan and Eric Michon. *Sound:* Ludovic Henault. *Casting:* Brigitte Moidon. *Set Designer:* Veronique Melery. *Costumes:* Karen Muller Serreau. *Make-up:* Kaatje Van Damme. *Running time:* 88 minutes. *MPAA Rating:* Not Rated.

CAST: Georges Du Fresne (Ludovic); Michèle Laroque (Hanna); Jean-Philippe Écoffey (Pierre); Hélène Vincent (Elisabeth); Julien Rivière (Jerôme); Cristina Barget (Zoe); Gregory Diallo (Thom); Erik Cazals de Fabel (Jean); Daniel Hanssens (Albert); Laurence Bibot (Lisette); Jean-Françoise Gallotte (Thierry); Caroline Baehr (Monique); Anne Coësens (Schoolteacher); Raphaelle Santini (Chris); Marie Bunel (Child Psychologist); Morgane Bruna (Sophie); Marine Jolivet (Fabienne); Vincent Grass (School Director); Catherine Hirsch (Secretary); Kevin Martin (Kevin); Marie-Beatrice Paillard (Manon); Peter Bailey (Jeremie); Charly Esposito (Tristan); Jeremy Durieu (Lucien); Michael Cordera (Ben); Erwan Demaure (Jonathan); Simon Poitier (Bertrand); Alexandra Génovès (Pam Girl); Alice Detrouleau (Kissing Girl); Michel Forget (Hand of God); Sabrina Leurquin (Voice of Speaker); Bruno Georis (Voice of Ben); Baptiste Hupin (Voice of Schoolchild); Alexandra Isaye (Voice of Birthday Child).

LOS ANGELES TIMES, 12/26/97, Calendar/p. 1, Kenneth Turan

The family is giving a party, and upstairs someone small is getting ready. The dress, the earrings, the lipstick, everything is selected with care. But when the 7-year-old is introduced, the neighbors gasp, and so do the parents. For this perfectly dressed little girl is actually Ludovic, a little boy.

A serious comedy about gender confusion, "Ma Vie en Rose" (My Life in Pink) is a lively, high-spirited film that is at once light and serious, sentimental and smart. Though it's the debut for its Belgian director, Alain Berliner, "Ma Vie" is so delicate and assured it manages to avoid the traps a venture like this might be thought to fall into.

Though it seems it must, "Ma Vie en Rose" has nothing to do with sexual orientation but says a great deal about childhood, fantasy, acceptance and the gap between adults and younger folks. For it's in no way clear what Ludovic's sexual orientation might or might not be as an adult, and that's the point: For right now, no matter what anyone says, he is a child all the way.

A good deal of the credit for "Ma Vie's" success must go to Georges Du Fresne, without whose exactly calibrated performance as the 7-year-old Ludovic this picture can't even be imagined. With huge saucer eyes in a grave, sphinx-like face that occasionally breaks into a pleased smile, the preternaturally calm Du Fresne gives the most guileless and natural impression of a boy who doesn't understand why his conviction that he is really a girl should be a big deal to anyone.

But a big deal it most certainly turns out to be, though at first his father Pierre (Jean-Philippe Ecoffey) and mother Hanna (Michèle Laroque) try to be amused by their son's desire to dress up and resist any trims to his carefully maintained Prince Valiant hairstyle.

Equally understanding at first is his sports car-driving grandmother Elizabeth (Hélène Vincent), who smiles on Ludovic's identification with the Barbie-like TV character Pam and counsels understanding for someone searching for his identity.

But then Ludovic, who is nothing if not determined, starts insisting that he and Jerome, the son of a neighbor who just happens to be his father's boss, are going to get married in the future "when I'm not a boy." Ludo, as his parents call him, doesn't want to cause trouble, but when what to him is a simple and straightforward desire gets combined with the boy's will of iron, things soon spin out of control.

The problem, not surprisingly, is the adults, starting with the family's neighbors and the parents of the other children at Ludo's school. By turns unnerved, threatened and made insecure by the boy's insistence, the nominal grown-ups show themselves to be more limited in their thinking than the children, eager to place inappropriate and offensive labels on anything that makes them uncomfortable.

Speaking of "Ma Vie" at its Cannes debut, director Berliner said his film "begins like Tim Burton's 'Edward Scissorhands' and ends like Ken Loach" and then added, "in the middle it's Billy Wilder." This unexpected combination of bright fairy-tale fantasy, sharp satire and naturalistic empathy for its characters is what gives Berliner's work (he also co-wrote the screenplay with Chris vander Stappen) more resonance than might be expected.

The other great thing about "Ma Vie en Rose" is its fairness. Though Ludo's mother and father do not behave like a couple out of Parenting magazine, the film resists the temptation to portray them as ogres and is instead careful to cast them in an extremely sympathetic light. If in truth no one is lonelier than the child who is different, the plight of the people who love him, this graceful film insists, can be just as hard.

NEW YORK POST, 12/26/97, p. 41, Thelma Adams

What's a mother to do when her darling boy thinks he looks pretty in pink? In Belgian director Alain Berliner's assured debut, fantasy and fiction converge. "Ma Vie en Rose (My Life in Pink)" is an original social comedy about a 7-year-old by who believes he's a girl.

With a sensitive, understated performance from child actor Georges Du Fresne, the movie explores the impact of Ludovic's cross-dressing and love for the boss' boy on his siblings, parents, grandmother, the neighbors and the community at large.

Good-natured but never treacly, "Ma Vie" resists sitcom possibilities. From its images of cars backing up simultaneously in neighboring driveways to its gentle hero, "Ma Vie" echoes Tim Burton's homegrown fairy tale about difference in suburbia, "Edward Scissorhands."

The movie won the best picture prize at the Karlovy Vary Film Festival in the Czech Republic and was screened at Cannes and the New York Film Festival.

NEWSDAY, 12/26/97, Part II/p. B8, Jack Mathews

Imagine the confusion facing a 7-year-old boy who is absolutely certain he was meant to be a girl. In first-time Belgian director Alain Berliner's simultaneously fanciful and poignant "Ma Vie en Rose (My Life in Pink)," the confusion facing young Ludovic is not his—as we said, he knows who he is—but that of his family, schoolmates, and neighbors.

A hit on the festival circuit since May's Cannes Film Festival, "Ma Vie en Rose" is a fable about gender identification that doesn't preach tolerance as much as inspire it. And it does so without offering audiences a clear, tidy resolution to the question on the mind of every other character in the film: What will Ludovic be when he grows up?

Is he a genetically programmed homosexual? Will his showmanship and yearning to dress as a girl lead him to the stage and future productions of "La Cage aux Folles"? Will he, worst case scenario, save up his money and have his sexual paraphernalia surgically corrected? Or is he, as the people surrounding him devoutly hope, just going through a phase?

In other words: Has nurture lost out to nature, or simply reached a non-lethal crossroad?

Since "Ma Vie en Rose" was written by a lesbian who claims to have gone through a similar early crisis, it's likely that Ludovic was leaning on the page toward a life in pink. But Berliner is as interested in the behavior of those around him, particularly of those in Ludovic's family, who may be said to be temporarily living their lives in red.

The Fabre family has just moved into a manicured, close-knit Brussels suburb, across the street from the man Pierre Fabre (Jean-Philippe Ecoffey) works for, and signs of trouble first appear at a backyard barbecue they're hosting to introduce themselves to the neighbors. This is Pierre's wife, Hanna (Michele Laroque), "the pretty one," their oldest son Tom, "the brainy one," youngest son Jean, "the naughty one," and as another son appears in a princess costume, a pageboy haircut, high heels, and make-up, "Ludovic, the jokey one."

It's a smashing appearance. Ludovic, played to wide-eyed perfection by 11-year-old actor Georges Du Fresne, has an androgynous beauty. And unless someone told you whether the actor is a boy or girl—here goes: Georges is a boy—you wouldn't know.

Ludovic's cross-dressing is no joke to the Fabres, and becomes less so when Ludovic gets his heart set on mating later in life with Pierre's boss' son, whom he is caught kissing in a mock marriage ceremony. Soon, Ludovic's behavior is a community scandal, threatening Pierre's job and Ludovic's schooling, and testing family bonds.

Attempts to dissuade Ludovic of his notions—dad makes him play soccer, mom enlists a child psychologist, his hair—is shortened—do nothing to change his outlook, or to ease adult fears, and the family is suddenly faced with ostracism.

All this over the apparent inclinations of a 7-year-old? The reaction of the adults is played straight, but is intentionally overstated by Berliner to show the effects of pressure placed on a child.

In fact, the movie spends a lot of time in either exaggerated reality or outright fantasy. Charming scenes from Ludovic's recurring dream, about the star of a TV show who doubles as his guardian angel, are intercut with actual events and sometimes merged with them. If the special effects, angel dust, sets and so on, seem a little unsophisticated, remember, it's all produced in a child's mind.

Besides Du Fresne, the film features superb performances from Ecoffey and Laroque as the parents and veteran French actress Helene Vincent as Ludovic's empathetic grandmother.

Sony Pictures Classics did well to save the release of "Ma Vie en Rose" for the holidays. Belgium's official entry in the Academy Award competition for best foreign-language film is a warm and sentimentally restrained portrait of a family wrestling with demons of society's making. If you believe that family values are rooted in love and not conformity, "Ma Vie en Rose" can be this season's "It's a Wonderful Life."

NEWSWEEK, 12/22/97, p. 84, David Ansen

[*Ma Vie en Rose* was reviewed jointly with *Wag the Dog*; see Ansen's review of that film.]

SIGHT AND SOUND, 11/97, p. 48, Michael Temple

A young boy, Ludovic, lives in a suburb with his professional father Pierre, his affectionate mother Hanna, his big sister and two rather dull brothers. He believes deeply that though mistaken for a boy he is profoundly a girl, and will one day grow up to be a woman. At first, his parents and his many friendly neighbours perceive this quirk as harmless. But when he stages his 'wedding' to Jérôme, son of his father's Catholic fundamentalist boss, opinions begin slowly to change, and trouble brews within family and community.

Ludovic is bullied at school; there's pressure for Pierre at work and tension for Hanna within the tight-knit network of mothers. Despite intervention from a psychotherapist and Hanna's understanding grandmother, conflict also develops between husband and wife, father and son, and eventually between the innocent but determined Ludovic and an increasingly exasperated Hanna. A crisis is reached when Pierre loses his job, the family is forced to move, and Ludovic is sent to live with Granny until things cool down.

The family begins to settle again in a new suburban community, and Ludovic, shorn of his girlish locks, appears slowly to be re-entering both family and school, until a final act of misunderstanding forces an emotional confrontation. At a fancy-dress party, a tomboy forces Ludovic to exchange his musketeer outfit for a frock. Hanna explodes into a fit of recriminatory violence, and Ludovic runs away in tears. When Hanna comes to her senses and Ludovic reappears, this excess seems to have effected an uneasy catharsis and a fragile reconciliation.

Before a single shot, French popstar Zazie's Gainsbourgian theme-song sets the tone of pop-sweet perversity which will pervade the following 90 minutes of screen-time: "*Rose/je lis tous les romans/à l'eau de/rose/j'en souligne des passages/au crayon/rose/ le bonheur m'obsède/à la nèv-/rose ...*" ("*Rose/I only read stories/tinted with/rose/I underline extracts/in the colour/rose/happiness haunts me/to the point of/neu-ros-is...*").

From these opening bars onwards, Alain Berliner's debut feature *Ma vie en rose* bears many such generous gifts and surprises, not least the relief that despite its title we are to be spared any samples or even mentions of Edith Piaf. Most precious of these is certainly Georges Du Fresne's extraordinary performance as Ludovic, the most persuasive case yet for making cross-dressing obligatory in primary education. Much as Mathieu Kassovitz's central enchantment successfully held together the questioning and questionable complexity of *A Self-Made Hero*, so the young Du Fresne maintains the charm and uncertainty of *Ma vie en rose* as it unfolds its sexual themes of identity, preference, difference and community. Round the essential glow of this one actor's absorbing appearance (from his delicate features to his sensitive movement and timing), characters such as his parents and siblings radiate uneven conviction and faltering sympathy, expressive of the ambiguity they feel towards him. The performers outside the family relationships also draw great force from Ludovic's central presence, which considerably simplifies their jobs. They only have to look at Ludovic, react to what he does and stick to the stereotypes which the film assigns them. But without Du Fresne at the centre, none of it would work.

The material aspects of *Ma vie en rose* are noteworthy for two contrasting reasons: location and decor. This is the kind of bland suburbia more routinely associated with Britain or the US, one cluttered with garden barbecues, ill-advised wardrobes, bad dancing and spacious mobile homes. Such unexpected textural details will be a pleasant surprise for a non-French audience more accustomed to the chic Parisian settings or Mediterranean glamour of French cinema. Berliner's compositions exploit shapes and colours with relish rather as Tim Burton's did in *Edward Scissorhands*, but at the same time the film has a sobriety reminiscent of made-for-television social dramas. This prosaic aspect amplifies through contrast the film's frequent excursions into richer and kitschier textures, where bright pinks and yellows and special effects overflow. This is the case especially of the scenes where Ludovic escapes into a parallel universe ruled by Barbie-and-Ken-like toys 'Pam and Ben', the romantic children's show he draws inspiration from. But the boundaries between these different spaces, the realistic one and the fantasy one, become blurred at key points in the narrative, such as the wedding-scene between Ludovic and his little chum Jérôme, or at the climactic moment when Ludovic's deranged mother Hanna magically climbs through a billboard advertising 'Pam and Ben' and accidentally slips into her son's fantasy-world.

It should not be forgotten that this is a first film, and so though some will no doubt object that it fails to address the issues properly—or to identify the proper issues at all—allowances should perhaps be made. *Ma vie en rose* is a generous and at times gorgeous instance of cinema's true powers and promise.

TIME, 1/12/98, p. 84, Richard Corliss

The effect is stunning: a seven-year-old in lipstick and a borrowed pink dress. Anyway, the sight stuns the parents of the boy who makes his entrance so gaily bedecked. He is Ludovic (Georges Du Fresne), a sweet child convinced he's a girl. No point in lecturing the lad; Ludo blithely pursues his obsession. Of a school chum, he says, 'We're going to marry when I'm not a boy."

In the genially subversive Franco-Belgian *Ma Vie en Rose,* the town where Ludo and his family live is cheerily color-coordinated (each garage door is painted a different pastel), but the emotions that the boy's cross-dressing provokes are darker. Everyone goes instantly agog. Wives scold; husbands threaten. Schoolboys turn into bullies, ready to take the natural law into their own hands. The film, directed by Alain Berliner from an original script by Chris vander Stappen, has the scheme of a socially fretful TV movie. Yet at heart, *Ma Vie en Rose* is a delightful comedy, both in its buoyant dream sequences and in Ludo's vagrant, clumsy stabs at embryonic machismo. Staring at himself in the mirror, he shoots off an imaginary gun, just like the other kids, and—he's really trying—adjusts his crotch.

This is no tract; all the characters have reasons for their outbursts. But the film is most sympathetic to Ludo's desperate, deadpan certitude that he'd enjoy being a girl. Like last year's magnificent *Ponette, Ma Vie en Rose* is an inside report—neither cloying nor condescending—from the enchanted, irradiated island of childhood.

VILLAGE VOICE, 12/30/97, p. 66, Amy Taubin

Ludovic, the seven-year-old hero of Alain Berliner's cartoonish confection *Ma Vie en Rose*, refuses to accept that anatomy is destiny. Dressed in his sister's pink ruffled dress and his mother's red spike heels, he makes a conversation-stopping entrance into the lawn party his parents are throwing to celebrate their arrival in a bourgie French suburb that seems a relic of the split-level '50s. Although his parents and siblings reassure themselves that "he's just going through a phase," Ludovic is adamant in his desire to become a girl and to marry his schoolmate—who inconveniently happens to be the son of his father's bigoted boss.

Directed with a light and affectionate hand by Alain Berliner, *Ma Vie en Rose* is a comedy of manners about sexual difference and social conformity. Ludovic's parents are baffled by their son's belief that he's a girl. Their admirably supportive impulses falter when the outside world takes revenge against the entire family for Ludovic's supposedly unnatural behavior.

Ma Vie en Rose bears more than a passing resemblance to Todd Haynes's more intelligent and moving 30-minute made-for-TV film *Dottie Gets Spanked*. Like the fragile seven-year-old in *Dottie*, Ludovic idolizes a female TV personality who appears in his dreams as a creature with magical powers. The brightly colored, cardboard-like mise-en-scène of *Ma Vie en Rose* is a reflection of Ludovic's obsession with this Barbie look-alike named Pam.

As Ludovic, Georges Du Fresne is sweet, grave, and vulnerable. The adult actors, on the other hand, rely on an overly broad sitcom style that makes the film too glib for its subject matter. Stylish but slight, *Ma Vie en Rose*, barely probes the surface of Ludovic's dilemma.

Also reviewed in:
NEW REPUBLIC, 1/26/98, p. 24, Stanley Kauffmann
NEW YORK TIMES, 12/26/97, p. E33, Stephen Holden
VARIETY, 5/19-25/97, p. 57, Lisa Nesselson

MAD CITY

A Warner Bros. release of an Arnold Kopelson production in association with Punch Productions. *Executive Producer:* Stephen Brown, Jonathan D. Krane, and Wolfgang Glattes. *Producer:* Arnold Kopelson and Anne Kopelson. *Director:* Costa-Gavras. *Screenplay:* Tom Matthews. *Story:* Tom Matthews and Eric Williams. *Director of Photography:* Patrick Blossier. *Editor:* Francoise Bonnot. *Music:* Thomas Newman. *Music Editor:* Bill Bernstein. *Sound:* Bertrand Lenclos and (music) Dennis Sands and Tom Winslow. *Casting:* Amanda Mackey Johnson and Cathy Sandrich. *Production Designer:* Catherine Hardwicke. *Art Director:* Ben Morahan. *Set Designer:* Mark Worthington, Steve Lauberth, and Charlie Vassar. *Set Decorator:* Jan Pascale. *Special Effects:* David Kelsey. *Costumes:* Deborah Nadoolman. *Make-up:* Allan Appone. *Stunt Coordinator:* Bud Davis. *Running time:* 114 minutes. *MPAA Rating:* PG-13.

CAST: John Travolta (Sam Baily); Dustin Hoffman (Max Brackett); Mia Kirshner (Laurie Callahan); Alan Alda (Kevin Hollander); Robert Prosky (Lou Potts); Blythe Danner (Mrs. Banks); William Atherton (Dohlen); Ted Levine (Alvin Lemke); Tammy Lauren (Miss Rose); William O'Leary (CTN Junior Executive); Raymond J. Barry (Dobbins); Lucinda Jenney (Jenny Baily); Akosua Busia (Diane); Ebbe Roe Smith (Travis Bartholomew); Bingwa (Nat Jackson); Chris Byrne (KXBD Cameraman); Dyllan Christopher (Sam's Son); Kiersten Nally (Cliff's Daughter); Sylvia Short (Mrs. Baily); Scanlon Gail (Bob); Charlie Holliday (Banker); Kevin Cooney (Principal); John Landis (Doctor); Susan Segal (Tabloid Reporter); Jenna Byrne (Reporter KMUR); Jason Cottle (Hollander's Assistant); Randall Batinkoff (CTN Junior Executive); Julian Wall (British Reporter); Laura Davis (Hollander's Producer); Nick Scoggin (Statz); Julio Oscar Mechoso (Air Force Sergeant); Rueben Grundy (Reporter Rueben); David Clennon (Street Preacher); Jay Leno (Himself); Stephen E. Kaufman (Hollander's Lawyer); Richard Portnow (Brackett's Agent); Bill Rafferty (Bill Gottsegen); Kurt Johnson (Macho

Parent); Susan Burig (Stage Manager); D. Seifert (Minister); J.P. Bumstead (Fisherman); Sean O'Kane (Lemke's Assistant); Donald O'Sullivan (Policeman); Lee Ann Manley (Rachel's Mother); Velina Brown (Bonnie's Mother); Michelle Pelletier (Max's Mother); Patricia Smith (Jenny's Mother); Adina Goldman (Lou's Assistant); Roger Shamas (Hollander's Driver); Stephen Brown (Hollander's Associate); Richard Gross (FBI Agent); Adam M. Koppekin (Assistant); Aaron Lucich (Sniper); Caryn Matchinga (Mother); Tom Fridley (Young Man); Christopher Michael Moore (Bowler #1); Dirk Blocker (Bowler #2).

LOS ANGELES TIMES, 11/7/97, Calendar/p. 10, Kenneth Turan

Like the reporters whose exploits it details, a film about journalism has to maintain credibility or it has nothing at all. Director Costa-Gavras and stars Dustin Hoffman and John Travolta give "Mad City" a base of believability but it's not fated to last.

Costa-Gavras directed and co-wrote the electric "Z," but that was back in 1970. Here, working from a script by Tom Matthews, he's made a film that has more in common with Billy Wilder's celebrated 1951 "Ace in the Hole," starring Kirk Douglas as a journalist who wouldn't hesitate to auction off his mother if it helped him get a story.

But what seemed prescient nearly half a century ago now comes off as predictable, simplistic and tame. "Mad City" is an example of how enervated polemical filmmaking can become when its plot loses contact with plausibility. While a case could be made for each of the elements of this worst-case scenario happening, putting them all into the same story is a flagrant case of piling on.

"Mad City" opens with what looks like a carefully planned robbery of a savings institution in fictional Madeline, Calif., but it's only a local news team from KXBD Channel 6 trying to get a hit-and-run interview from a recalcitrant bank official.

Leading that attack is the ever-brash Max Brackett (Hoffman). Once a nationally known network reporter based in Manhattan, Brackett has been exiled to Madeline for offenses not immediately revealed, and he's desperate enough to try anything to get back.

Attempting to control Brackett is weary editor Lou Potts (Robert Prosky). While the reporter wants to move the line that defines acceptable journalistic behavior, the editor worries about what the community will think. And when Brackett gets too pushy, Potts sends him and dewy-eyed intern Laurie (Mia Kirshner) to do a puff piece on budget cuts at the local Museum of Natural History.

Simultaneously headed for the museum is recently laid off $8-an-hour security guard Sam Baily (Travolta). All he wants is the chance to plead with Mrs. Banks (Blythe Danner), the museum's patrician director, for his old job. But when she tries to throw him out Baily takes an automatic weapon from his bag, shoots someone and ends up, much to his chagrin, as a takeover artist with a bunch of schoolchildren as hostages.

A lost soul who couldn't be more hapless as a criminal mastermind, Sam is way out of his depth from minute one of these misadventures. All he wants is the status quo, and when he sees himself castigated on TV for his part in the shooting, he angrily scolds the talking head, "It was an accident, moron."

The reason Sam Baily is on TV at all is that Max Brackett just happened to be occupied in the men's room when the weapon went off. After alerting his station, Brackett proceeds to mentor Baily in the finer points of hostage-taking, advising him whom to talk to, what to say to them, what to ask for and how to get it. As to what the reporter wants, that's clear to us if not to Baily: a story hot enough to get him back to New York.

Under Brackett's expert manipulation, the saga of Sam Baily gets increasingly bigger until it turns into just the kind of bogus human drama that catches the attention of the network boys in New York. Much against his will, it even piques the interest of Brackett's nemesis, anchor Kevin Hollander (Alan Alda), "the man America trusts for news" and the reason Brackett is in exile in the first place.

Though its basic situation is hardly new, "Mad City" does have something going for it. While Travolta looks as uncomfortable in his part as his character does brandishing an automatic weapon, Hoffman, who was originally thought of for the Baily role, does excellent work as the newsman, giving a sharp, focused and intelligent performance that adds a note of complexity to a film that generally does without it.

The problem with "Mad City" is that in its eagerness to make its point about journalistic excess as strong as possible, the film just about buries it. Everyone from the FBI to militant militias shows up and everything that can possibly go wrong with the coverage does, from bogus accusations of prejudice to complete strangers being interviewed as Baily's friends.

Reporters sneak into hospital rooms, trample on flower gardens, and even innocent young intern Laurie gets turned into a conniving careerist in the blink of an eye. Everyone hustles, manipulates and looks for the exploitable angle, which makes them not all that much different from the people responsible for this trying film.

NEW STATESMAN, 7/10/98, Gerald Kaufman

At first it seems that this is to be yet another hostage movie. Blundering into a museum in a small California town comes overweight, middle-aged Sam Baily (John Travolta). It is immediately obvious that he is not very bright. It soon becomes obvious that he is trouble. Producing a gun and a bag of dynamite, he demands that the museum's curator (Blythe Danner) give him back his job as a security guard. She refuses. His gun goes off accidentally, hitting and wounding a black security guard patrolling outside the museum.

Inside the men's room is Max Brackett (Dustin Hoffman), a TV reporter who has come to cover a story about budget cuts at the museum and is in radio contact with his control van nearby. He tells his assistant to notify the studio and the authorities that a hostage situation has arisen. For inside the museum is a party of young schoolchildren.

We are, it seems, in familiar territory. Brackett, displaying heroism and daring, will find a way of saving the children and delivering Baily to justice. But that is not this film's purpose at all. It is Brackett's intention not to end the crisis but to manipulate it. What we are watching is not a replay of *Dog Day Afternoon* but a 1990s replica of Billy Wilder's *Ace in the Hole*.

Wilder's 1951 melodrama dealt with a corrupt journalist's attempt to increase newspaper sales by delaying the rescue of a man trapped in a cave. *Mad City* is a savage satire about the whole panoply of media manipulation at the end of the millennium; and—what might have been impossible to imagine Tom Matthews' screenplay manages to transcend Wilder in cynicism and dark humour.

"You're the best show in town, Sam," Brackett tells Baily. On to the scene swarm hordes of TV crews. From New York arrives network star Kevin ("I'm the man America trusts for news") Hollander (Alan Alda). But Brackett is the man in charge: "Born for the job—a pig in shit," say his envious colleagues. It is he who, from the siege museum, orchestrates the action, who instructs his TV station to win sympathy for Sam by interviewing his family, his neighbours, his clergyman.

It is Brackett who, when Sam decides as a token of goodwill to release one child who happens to be white, tells him to set free a black child as well because the guard he shot was black. The networks take polls and find that "Sam Baily is tapping into something the working class can relate to". "Fifty-nine per cent of the people are showing compassion for an armed felon," snarls Hollander.

The networks begin to haggle with Brackett about the scheduling for freeing all the children: prime time, evening, a Thursday, when ratings are weak. Others get into the action. Baily T-shirts are sold outside the siege museum. Blacks and racists stage separate demonstrations. The police chief, at first unwilling to cooperate with Brackett, is exhorted, "Sam Baily is making you the most famous cop in the United States of America".

Television cameras intrude into the hospital room where the wounded guard is fighting for his life. Against doctors' advice, his wife agrees to an on-air interview. "We need the money," she says and, symbolising low working-class aspirations and network cynicism, is paid a paltry $10,000. The museum curator, wise to Brackett's intentions, warns Sam against him, only to be tempted by Brackett with the prospect of the museum's new fame attracting donations to solve its cash problem.

And Sam, too, yields to temptation. At first troubled by his notoriety—"I'm famous in a bad way"—he is reassured by Brackett: "It doesn't make any difference on television: people know who you are." Soon he is convinced, boasting: "Dave Letterman knows who I am." Before long he is participating in a phone-in on Larry King Live and rebuking Brackett for prompting him with answers.

No technique of TV is left unscathed by Matthews' script. There is a cunning sequence—a warning to anyone participating in sound-bite interviews—when the vox-pop interviews in Sam's favour are re-edited to vilify him.

Costa-Gavras directs this admonitory narrative at breakneck pace, choreographing the scavenging TV crews as in a ballet. The performances are merciless. Alda, as the network star determined to beat Brackett, is the embodiment of crafty amorality. John Travolta, whose sultry self of 20 years ago can be seen in the current re-release of Grease, provides a portrayal unlike anything he has previously done: plump, shambling, worried, sad, remorseful, but given to sudden rages, and so real that we can almost smell his sweat.

Dustin Hoffman as Brackett is the puppet-master, his constantly darting eyes revealing his hyperactive thought processes as he keeps recalculating the odds and the moves. A wonderful episode right at the end shows that he has done his work too well. At the outset, Brackett's demurely black-clad young camera-woman, Laurie (Mia Kirshner), dashes across to help the security guard who has been shot. Brackett later tells Laurie that she should have taken her camera with her. When she protests that her hands would have been too full to help the guard, he explains patiently that the camera comes before the help.

During the siege Laurie is seduced—by fame and money, not sex, for this film is too busy to bother with that—into swapping allegiances and going to work for Hollander. When in the final confrontation Brackett staggers, hurt, out of the museum and makes to brush blood off his forehead, Laurie—now dressed in dramatic scarlet—stops him. Leave it, she tells him, "it's good television".

And that is this film's alarmingly accurate message—not simply about one fictional episode in a movie but about the way, far too often, television turns real-life tragedies into pap to win ratings. As the jaded, disillusioned Brackett explains: "It's about show business."

NEW YORK, 11/17/97, p. 74, David Denby

Dustin Hoffman is at the top of his game in *Mad City*, Costa-Gavras's glum morality tale about the depredations of the media. Hoffman plays Max Brackett, a former bigtime TV reporter who has been busted down to a local California station after running afoul of the network's star anchor (Alan Alda). Max is doing a nothing story at a local natural-history museum when a fired employee—Sam Baily (John Travolta), a guard—barges back into the museum to plead for his job with his ex-boss (Blythe Danner). Hoping to be taken seriously, Sam, who isn't too bright, carries a gun, and when the gun goes off by accident, wounding another guard, and Sam locks the door, shutting in some schoolchildren, Max knows that he's right in the middle of a media gold mine—a hostage situation. Grabbing the spotlight, he works the moment for all it's worth.

Hoffman plays Max the relentless opportunist very quietly, as a man who knows how to charm, a man who even knows how to listen. Some of Hoffman's best moments come when he's just watching John Travolta, who gives a big, sweaty performance as the unhappy guard. Travolta tries very hard, but he's been caught, I think, in a trap not of his own making. Both Costa Gavras and the screenwriter, Tom Matthews (working from a story he created with Eric Williams), are so determined to make Sam a bumbling innocent—a pure American sap, a victim—that they rob him of will and finally of interest. Our curiosity leaves Sam and shifts back to Max, who makes the bitter discovery that television, which he thinks he's master of, has a demonic energy that he can't possibly control. Hoffman, keeping the performance quiet right to the end, very subtly runs through shades of regret, pity, disgust, and self-disgust.

Mad City is an intelligent and heartfelt attempt to shake us up, but we've been over this ground before—in better movies like *Dog Day Afternoon*, in the many media mea culpas following the death of Princess Diana. What we feel when watching *Mad City* is not so much shock or rage as sorrow. The movie says that television appropriates human tragedy for its own benefit. True enough, though the real problem is that few of us have the strength to turn off the set.

NEW YORK POST, 11/7/97, p. 57, Thelma Adams

Director Costa-Gavras' cheap shot at cheaper journalism, "Mad City," recalls a burg descended from "Network." It's a city where all the citizens are mad as hell and aren't going to take it anymore.

Sam Baily (John Travolta) is mad because he lost his job as a security guard at the natural history museum.

Max Brackett (Dustin Hoffman) is mad because he lost his job as a network reporter and has been bounced to the boonies.

Anchorman Kevin Hollander (Alan Alda) is mad because that's what it takes to become America's most trusted newsman.

When Baily attempts to regain his job by waving a shotgun in front of his ex-boss, Mrs. Banks (a whispery Blythe Danner), he ends up taking a passel of schoolkids hostage in the shadow of the dinosaurs.

Meanwhile, in the museum loo, Brackett just happens to be interviewing his male anatomy (I kid you not). Taking time out from that big story, the downtrodden newsman seizes the day. If Baily's misguided crime isn't the story of a lifetime, Brackett will manipulate the news to salvage his career.

Over the course of the movie, Brackett somehow gains a conscience (Tom Matthews' absurd debut script expects a leap of faith here). Brackett's wide-eyed assistant (Mia Kirshner) gets her eyes opened wider by network smoothie Hollander.

And, somehow, Baily slips from being a blue-collar hero forced against the wall by nonprofit arts downsizing to a nincompoop who doesn't have the sense to come in out of the publicity rain of terror.

As stories about journalistic integrity go, this isn't news. Who cares about Brackett's redemption or Baily's crucifixion?

As Baily, Travolta leaps backward, acting with huge sideburns and hunched shoulder, but no real humanity. Hoffman mumbles and shuffles and cons, but he's dead behind the eyes.

In "Mad City," Travolta and Hoffman are, always feverishly acting, acting. I can only suppose that these stars put their trust in the famous Costa-Gavras. The director of "Z" and "State of Siege" lets not only them down but the audience, as well.

NEWSWEEK, 11/17/97, p. 90, Jack Kroll

The Greek-born director Costa-Gavras became a world figure in 1969 with the fiercely exciting "Z," the true story of a political murder that brought down the repressive Greek regime. "Z's" explosive mix of speed, action and dialogue gave ideology an emotional heat absent from the screen since the great Soviet directors. His subsequent films made Costa-Gavras a one-man school of the politically committed movie. But the end of the cold war has dampened his fires. His American films of the '80s, like "Betrayed" and "Music Box," had little impact. *Mad City* strikes a spark, but the flame sputters.

In "Mad City," Costa-Gavras takes aim at that bullet-riddled target the media. Max Brackett (Dustin Hoffman), a former hotshot national TV reporter who had an on-camera fight with his anchor, has been banished to a local California station. Max sees his way out of the hinterland when a schoolkids' outing at the local museum turns into a hostage situation. A laid-off-guard, Sam Baily (John Travolta), turns up with a rifle and dynamite. When he accidentally wounds a guard, the local media swarm to the scene. But the slick Max takes control coaching the dim-witted Baily and wangling exclusive access from the cops. His former anchor, Kevin Hollander (Alan Alda), shows up and pulls rank, offering Max a network job if he moves to the background.

The result is tragic, fueled by media lust for a mini-Waco. TV execs adjust their coverage to the shifting polls on sympathy for Sam, the $8-an-hour guy with a family to support. Camera crews force their way everywhere. Interviews are inane, some edited to falsify context. Larry King does his classic remote like the Wizard of Disaster. Watching "Mad City" is like watching a thousand TV stories. Such familiarity kills impact. The genius of Oliver Stone, however controversial, in movies like "Natural Born Killers," has been to leap beyond reality, taking it to such a pitch of mad surrealism that he touches the profound pathology of a media-driven culture. And long before Stone, Billy Wilder's 1951 "The Big Carnival" (which is the source for Tom Matthews's "Mad City" screenplay) was a Swiftian take on a cynical reporter milking a small-town disaster to further his career.

Hoffman's Max is a corporate dilution of the Kirk Douglas character in "The Big Carnival." Travolta is more interesting. He's done a De Niro, gaining weight so that his potbelly and mutton-chopped jowls seem like the very protoplasm of the loser. Calming his kid hostages with Indian stories and junk food, Travolta's Sam focuses the residue of Costa-Gavras's once raging social concern. But "Mad City" is not mad enough.

SIGHT AND SOUND, 7/98, p. 46, David Tse

Madeline, California. During a routine story on the local museum of natural history, television reporter Brackett surreptitiously reports live a confrontation between fired security guard Sam Baily and his former employer. Baily accidentally shoots a fellow guard. The image of the wounded man stumbling out of the museum is filmed by Brackett's assistant Laurie and broadcast, effectively jump-starting a siege crisis. A group of visiting schoolchildren and Brackett become hostages. Brackett acts as mediator between Baily and the police in order to generate a career-reviving exclusive. Baily's live interview with Brackett is a success, and Baily is hailed "the poster child of the disenfranchised".

Network anchorman, Kevin Hollander arrives to muscle in on the story. The network offers to hire Brackett if he persuades Baily to talk to Hollander, but Brackett refuses when he realises Hollander is out to crucify Baily. Public opinion sways when the wounded guard dies and Brackett's initial manoeuvrings are exposed. Baily lets the hostages go, then blows up the museum with himself in it. Laurie, now working for Hollander, interviews a shell-shocked Brackett.

Given that Costa-Gavras has been frequently grouped with Sidney Lumet as a director of topical melodramas, it is perhaps fitting that he should make *Mad City*, a 90s update of Lumet's *Dog Day Afternoon* (1975). Like Lumet's recent *Night Falls on Manhattan*, *Mad City* is a response partly to the O.J. Simpson media circus, though the filmmakers also cite the 1993 Waco standoff as a departure point. Locating the felon-under-siege plot inside a museum instead of a bank makes *Mad City* a less claustrophobic film than *Dog Day*, but this also lightens the dramatic momentum. Nonetheless, Tom Matthews' screenplay delights in effective reversals (the felon is a disgruntled ex-security guard of the museum), and demonstrates an insider's knowledge of newsroom politics. Borrowing from Billy Wilder's journalism satire *Ace in the Hole*, the hostaged reporter Max Brackett's attempts to manipulate the situation to his advantage are darkly humorous.

The movie presents a damning picture of journalism as a game of Chinese Whispers. Most of the burnout and tension derive from the fact that Baily (John Travolta, wonderfully scuzzy and confused) is too dumb to play the media game, and has to be constantly prompted by Brackett. "You've got to have realistic, concrete demands, or you make them very nervous," he advises. "Remember, that's your jury pool out there." The movie deftly parallels Brackett's coaching of Baily inside the museum with Brackett's rivals interviewing the guard's family and friends: the interviewees reflexively follow the reporters' cues, or are later edited to suit the commentators' purposes. Brackett's nemesis Hollander is also regularly prompted by his assistants, and has sheepishly to 'lead in' with Brackett's reports.

Though it makes a rousing yarn, the polarisation of Hollander's network sensationalism with small, honest news stations is reductive. Costa-Gavras is not subtle. You have to accept the heavy-handed melodramatic style to enjoy this film: when Brackett corners a corrupt banker, a down-and-out tap dancer performs in the background; a rainstorm breaks out when the plot thickens; and the film closes with a top shot of microphones converging like vultures on a distraught Brackett. The function of Mia Kirshner's Laurie is to be seduced by Hollander's shiny corporate world and reject Brackett's investigative spirit, thus setting a negative example for us all.

What is unusual about *Mad City* in the context of Costa-Gavras' oeuvre is that, in contrast to his previous martyred investigative journalists (as in *Missing)*, the journalist is now the anti-hero. As a wartime correspondent, Brackett's ingenuity and initiative would be esteemed, here, in a civilian setting, he's a self-aggrandising trickster. There is real pathos in the second act as Brackett finds himself increasingly sympathetic to the guard, and discovers his efforts to save this hapless man have been torpedoed by his earlier opportunism.

The movie spreads itself too thinly by going for too many hot buttons: there are perfunctory nods towards the problems of museum funding, Native American rights, and fundamentalism. Indeed one can argue the movie is guilty of the same sensationalism that it indicts. But despite its easy social conscience, the movie is often hilarious and zeroes in on an essential, heartless truth about journalism. In a crucial scene, on learning that Laurie has dropped the camera while attending to a wounded man, Brackett chastises her. He tells her there is no way one can participate in a situation and also report it. He means he prefers the latter, of course, but that's exactly the line he himself has crossed. For better or for worse, compassion and impartial reportage are mutually exclusive.

VILLAGE VOICE, 11/18/97, p. 85, Amy Taubin

In Costa-Gavras's *Mad City*, John Travolta plays a decent husband and father who goes berserk when he's laid off from his job as a museum guard. Armed and desperate, he goes to the museum, accidentally shoots a colleague, and winds up with the museum director, some two dozen children, and Dustin Hoffman (playing a former star TV reporter, now demoted to the sticks) as hostages.

Wildly uneven in tone, *Mad City* lurches between *Network* and *Dog Day Afternoon,* with overtones of King Kong (Travolta's working-class stiff has a brute-beast innocence that's meant to be both touching and frightening—and occasionally is).

The TV reporter realizes that the hostage taker is his ticket back to the big time. He's egocentric enough to believe that he can manipulate the story to make himself and the hostage taker come out with public opinion wildly on their side. Some people never learn. The same powermad forces that went after him in the past are after him again, and they don't care how many innocents get slaughtered in the process. Violence is better for the ratings, and so forth.

Mad City doesn't become gripping until the last third. That's when you might start to suspect that Costa-Gavras's over-ingratiating tone in the beginning of the film was a ploy to implicate the audience in the nasty stuff to come. It doesn't quite work, but it does make *Mad City* slightly more interesting than what passes for a political thriller these days.

In any case, Sam Fuller, newshound that he was, would not have approved. R.I.P., Sam. *Pickup on South Street* was the first movie I fell in love with. We will not see your like again.

Also reviewed in:
CHICAGO TRIBUNE, 11/7/97, Friday/p. A, Michael Wilmington
NEW REPUBLIC, 12/15/97, p. 28, Stanley Kauffmann
NEW YORK TIMES, 11/7/97, p. E14, Janet Maslin
NEW YORKER, 11/17/97, p. 114, Anthony Lane
VARIETY, 10/27-11/2/97, p. 42, Emanuel Levy
WASHINGTON POST, 11/7/97, p. G7, Stephen Hunter
WASHINGTON POST, 11/7/97, Weekend/p. 49, Desson Howe

MAN WHO KNEW TOO LITTLE, THE

A Warner Bros. release of a Regency Enterprises presentation of an Arnon Milchan/Polar production. *Executive Producer:* Elisabeth Robinson and Joe Caracciolo, Jr. *Producer:* Arnon Milchan, Michael Nathanson, and Mark Tarlov. *Director:* Jon Amiel. *Screenplay:* Robert Farrar and Howard Franklin. *Based on the novel "Watch That Man" by:* Robert Farrar. *Director of Photography:* Robert Stevens. *Editor:* Pamela Power. *Music:* Chris Young. *Music Editor:* Andy Glen. *Choreographer:* Aletta Collins. *Sound:* Simon Kaye and (music) Dick Lewzy. *Sound Editor:* Bob Risk. *Casting:* Michelle Guish. *Production Designer:* Jim Clay. *Art Director:* Chris Seagers. *Set Decorator:* Maggie Gray. *Special Effects:* George Gibbs. *Costumes:* Janty Yates. *Make-up:* Frances Hannon. *Stunt Coordinator:* Wayne Michaels. *Running time:* 92 minutes. *MPAA Rating:* PG.

CAST: Bill Murray (Wallace Ritchie); Peter Gallagher (James Ritchie); Joanne Whalley (Lori); Alfred Molina (Boris); Richard Wilson (Daggenhurst); John Standing (Gilbert Embleton); Simon Chandler (Hawkins); Geraldine James (Dr. Ludmilla Kropotkin); Anna Chancellor (Barbara Ritchie); Nicholas Woodeson (Sergei); Cliff Parisi (Uri); John Thomson (Dimitri);

Janet Henfrey (Ms. Goldstein); Terry O'Neill (Spenser); Isabel Hernandez (Consuela); Donald Pickering (Sir Duncan); Venetia Barrett (Sir Duncan's Wife, Felicity); Terence Harvey (Herr Schuster); Cate Fowler (Frau Schuster); Richard Dixon (Rupert); Sarah Crowden (Sylvia/Fiona); Barnaby Kay (Swat Team Leader/PC in James'); David Hounslow (Wilkie); Addam Fogerty (Newman); Jacqueline Phillips (Annabel); Inday Ba (Des); Dexter Fletcher (Otto); Josephine Gradwell (WPC, Wendy); Linda Broughton (Middle-Aged Woman); David Boyce (Middle-Aged Man); Jo Dow (Hotel Manager); Bob Holmes (Husband in Hotel Room); Paul Shearer (TV Reporter); Yoshinori Yamamoto (Japanese Man); Toshie Ogura (Japanese Woman); Charles Simon (Aged Desk/Night Clerk); Roger Morlidge (PC Cohrane); Ashley Gunstock (Second Policeman in Car); Judith Dawson (TV Newscaster); David Michaels (M15 Agent); Damian Myerscough (Stage Manager); Jason Round (Policeman); Andrew Woodall (Det. Sgt. Malloy); Malcolm Storry (Chief Inspector Cockburn); Eddie Marsan (Mugger #1); Tat Whalley (Mugger #2); Fred Whitman (Toastmaster); Daryll Kay and Linzi Lazlor-Carr (Liveried Children); Richard Cubison (Immigration Officer); Sarah Greene and Mike Smith (TV Presenters); J.E. Freeman (CIA Man); Maxwell Caulfield (British Agent); Mike Justus (Waiter).

LOS ANGELES TIMES, 11/14/97, Calendar/p. 23, Kevin Thomas

[*The following review by Kevin Thomas appeared in a slightly different form in* NEWSDAY, 11/14/97, Part II/p. B12.]

"The Man Who Knew Too Little" is too little, too late. At a time when the James Bond franchise struggles to keep *au courant*, a sendup of those Cold War spy capers of the '60s and '70s requires considerable imagination. Unfortunately, Bill Murray, Joanne Whalley, Peter Gallagher and Alfred Molina can't make a dent in this stale and hopelessly contrived comedy.

A naive Blockbuster clerk from Des Moines whose knowledge of life would seem to come entirely from the movies, Murray's Wallace Ritchie pops up unannounced at the posh London residence of his rich brother James (Gallagher), just as James and his wife are preparing for a formal dinner for a representative of a German investment firm involving a deal that could yield James millions.

What to do with the nerdy Wally, the kind of guy who'll say anything that crosses his mind? Wallace ends up packed off with a ticket to London's newest interactive experience, the Theater of Life, which simulates all manner of adventures for its participants. One phone call is all it takes for the participant to get instructions for what he or she is to do next.

You may have already guessed where director Jon Amiel and his writers are taking us: The trouble Wally is about to got into is not a performance but for real, involving some old spy types eager to heat up the Cold War, but Wally nonchalantly takes every danger as a put-on.

Their shenanigans are resolutely mechanical, uninspired and unfunny. To be sure, Wally will be rewarded for his impregnable stupidity. Murray and others are game, but you really don't need to know more about this dud. "The Man Who Knew Too Little" isn't likely to give "Austin Powers" a run for its money.

NEW YORK POST, 11/14/97, p. 50, Michael Medved

"The Man Who Knew too Little" is a tired, wheezing, one-joke movie in which even that single gag turns out to be a dud.

Bill Murray plays a goofy video clerk from Iowa who shows up unexpectedly at the London home of his banker brother (Peter Gallagher) on the night the brother is hosting an important business dinner.

In order to get his embarrassing relative out of the way, Gallagher arranges an evening of interactive drama with the "Theater of Life," in which professional actors will lead Murray through elaborately staged adventures.

Of course, Murray accidentally stumbles into a real-life conspiracy involving secret agents and contract killers, but remains convinced that he is merely part of the show, thereby startling everyone with his apparent fearlessness.

This especially impresses Joanne Whalley, a call girl trying to blackmail the minister of defense, while British spymaster Richard Wilson wants to eliminate her along with her mysterious new American protector.

For this purpose, he calls upon a former Soviet hit man (Alfred Molina, in the film's only genuinely funny performance) as part of the effort to disrupt a gala British-Russian "friendship" banquet and to reignite the Cold War.

Under the slack direction of Jon Amiel ("Copycat," "Sommersby"), Bill Murray's humbling innocent keeps declaring how much fun he's having, but the movie remains so grim and dreary that it's impossible to believe him.   Only in the climactic banquet scene, when he improvises a few moves as part of a colorfully costumed Russian folk-dance troupe, does the famous funnyman finally earn a few laughs.

By then it's too late, especially in view of the appallingly misleading "PG" rating. With tacky scenes of leather-clad sadomasochism, and graphic references to prostitution and oral sex, those who would consider taking kids to what's misleadingly sold as a Bill Murray romp can only be pitied as "Parents Who Know Too Little."

SIGHT AND SOUND, 6/98, p. 50, Peter Matthews

Wallace Ritchie arrives in London to celebrate his birthday with his brother James who gives him a ticket to the Theatre of Life, an interactive dramatic experience. A mix up over a phone call sends Wallace to bump off a call girl and steal some incriminating letters while a hitman named Spenser takes Wallace's call and ends up killing a member of the theatre company.

Wallace meets Lori the call girl. The blackmailed minister Gilbert Embleton breaks into her flat to retrieve the letters, but Wallace frightens him away. Then Lori is attacked by Spenser, who's obtained the correct address; Wallace fights him off, still thinking it's part of the game. It transpires that Gilbert is embroiled in a plot to sabotage the signing that night of the English-Russian peace accord. Gilbert contacts his commander in chief Sir Roger Daggen burst to warn him of the dangerous American, whom he takes to be Spenser. Sir Roger alerts his confederate Sergei, who calls out hitman Boris to deal with Wallace, Wallace later discovers the corpse of Spenser, recently murdered by Boris.

Sir Roger offers to exchange the letters for money with Wallace and meets him at the Grand Plaza Hotel. Boris abducts Wallace and Lori. Having figured out by now that Wallace isn't Spenser, the conspirators threaten to bring on the world-renowned torturer Dr Ludmilla Kropotkin. Wallace and Lori escape. Tipped off by Wallace, James rushes to the Grand Plaza, where he falls into the hands of Dr Ludmilla. At the peace accord reception, Wallace accidentally disables a bomb. A mix up with briefcases results in Sir Roger and Sergei stealing the bomb which later blows them up. In the Caribbean with Lori, Wallace is approached by two hitmen who beg him to join their team. He accepts still believing that they refer to his fantastic acting ability.

If one were to take a solemnly auteurist approach to *The Man Who Knew Too Little,* one could say that it extends in a bold new direction the fascination with role playing and illusion reality, games first shown by director Jon Amiel in his work on Dennis Potter's BBC mini series *The Singing Detective* and subsequently developed in such theatrical features as the serial killer mystery *Copycat* and the romantic melodrama *Sommersby*. One might add that the story parodies Alfred Hitchcock's 1956 version of the political intrigues in *The Man Who Knew Too Much*, while also incorporating the wrong man in jeopardy situation from *North by Northwest*. Moreover, the primary conceit of a simpleton being mistaken for a superman carries overtones of Chance Gardener in *Being There*. But that would be giving too much pedigree to a film maker who has become a hard-working journeyman by now—and to a comedy whose likable quality rests on its being of no importance whatsoever.

Stylistically, the movie reaches its peak in the animated title sequence (directed by Graham McCallum), where technicians' names sprout legs or eyes and go skittering across the screen in imitation of those graphic gizmos that designers like Fritz Freleng *(The Pink Panther)* used to dream up for the openings of silly 60s spy spoofs. Thereafter, the visuals settle down into a sort of compromise between pop boldness and outright tackiness which suitably expresses the peculiar creative synergy of cinematographer Robert Stevens (from the *Naked Gun* series) and production designer Jim Clay *(The Crying Game)*. Amiel employs a token hand-held technique in a few scenes with the evident idea of sending up the hero Wallace's belief that he is extemporising his way through an elaborately contrived theatrical happening. However, the director's most vital contribution would appear to be the fostering of a laid-back atmosphere where the actors can horse around and embroider freely on the rather asinine script.

Always at his best playing insincere creeps, Bill Murray is disappointingly cast as a well-intentioned doofus; but the triumph of Wallace's nerdy enthusiasm over the combined forces of European reaction is satisfying just the same—and it's hard not to break up at Murray's fatuous delivery of throwaway lines like "Don't ever show your face on this *mews* again!" Nearly all the supporting actors down to the bit players communicate a sense of easygoing fun with the usually dour Alfred Molina having an obvious ball as Boris the Butcher and Richard Wilson lending his familiar waspish tones to vulgarisms like "Doesn't that just bite it?" in the role of Sir Roger.

While the humour can be politely described as basic ("flush" and "floater" figuring prominently among the double entendres), the movie is at least an efficient machine that keeps its numerous farcical components whirring and clicking without losing track of any of them. If the result is something less than a comic seizure, it's because the filmmakers don't fully lay hold of their lowbrow opportunities. For instance, one looks forward to the appearance of world ranking torture expert Dr Ludmilla Kropotkin and her inevitable collision with Wallace's straight-laced brother James; but the most Amiel can think to do is have the good doctor pull a few ugly faces, while James emerges unscathed with only a slightly mussed hairdo. The fact is that one laughs anyway, just as one can't help laughing at the impromptu Russian folk dance by which Wallace ultimately saves the day, though it falls short in slapstick inventiveness.

The amiable lack of pretension makes it possible to forgive everything even a disconcertingly wholesome tone that never lets you forget the movie has been certificated for pre-pubescents (who should indeed eat it up). Sometimes a quick and painless 94 minutes or so is all one wants, and that's what *The Man Who Knew Too Little* cheerfully and quite enjoyably supplies.

VILLAGE VOICE, 11/25/97, p. 100, Gary Dauphin

I imagine that sliding into middle age and smaller budgets is a real bitch if you're a onetime star like Bill Murray, which is probably why *The Man Who Knew Too Little* is such a poignant (kind of) surprise. *Man*'s slapsticky tale posits Murray as a Des Moines Blockbuster video employee mistaken for a secret agent while on vacation in the United Kingdom. (Given tickets to a night of "interactive theater," he thinks the guys shooting at him are actors.) Various predictable hijinks ensue as Murray smirkily saves the day, but this rube succeeds not because he's too stupid to be afraid but because stupidity frees him to be, well, a real actor. It's a nice turn, Murray strolling though shtick cobbled together from various espionage sendups (from *Austin Powers* to Roger Moore-era Bond) with a kind of Zen-like peace until he literally gets to look into the camera and declaim, "I can't act." He can't, of course, but whereas usually that particular joke is usually on the audience, here it's on him.

Also reviewed in:
CHICAGO TRIBUNE, 11/14/97, Friday/p. H, Michael Wilmington
NEW YORK TIMES, 11/14/97, p. E22, Lawrence Van Gelder
VARIETY, 11/10-16/97, p. 40, Todd McCarthy

MANDELA: SON OF AFRICA, FATHER OF A NATION

An Island Pictures release of a Clinica Estetico production. *Executive Producer:* Chris Blackwell and Dan Genetti. *Producer:* Jonathan Demme, Edward Saxon, and Jo Menell. *Director:* Jo Menell and Angus Gibson. *Director of Photography:* Dewald Aukema and Peter Tischhauser. *Editor:* Andy Keir and Mona Davis. *Music:* Cedric Gradus Samson and Hugh Masekela. *Sound:* Tony Bensusan. *Sound Editor:* Magdaline Volaitis. *Running time:* 120 minutes. *MPAA Rating:* Not Rated.

NARRATOR: Patrick Shai.

LOS ANGELES TIMES, 3/21/97, Calendar/p. 8, Kevin Thomas

[*The following review by Kevin Thomas appeared in a slightly different form in* **NEWSDAY, 3/21/97, Part II/p. B13.**]

When long-exiled South African filmmaker Jo Menell, producers Jonathan Demme and Chris Blackwell and co-director Angus Gibson joined forces to make the stirring Oscar-nominated documentary "Mandela," they decided to abide by a statement the South African president had made in regard to what was most difficult about life after 27 years in prison: "Getting people to see me as a human being, not as a messiah or a demigod."

They certainly succeed in presenting Mandela as a human being, a man of considerable humor and unpretentiousness; in conversation or at the podium, Mandela is one of the most well-spoken men of his times. But he's such an extraordinary man that the more they delve into his life, the harder it becomes not to think of him as a messiah. His sister Mabel says she long ago realized that "he belongs to the nation... We can see that this is the job God gave him ..."

As an "official" film biography, "Mandela" had its charismatic subject's full cooperation, yet it has a quality of considerable candor, perhaps because Mandela may be one world leader who actually may have little or nothing to hide. The film neither dwells on nor skirts the controversy surrounding Winnie Mandela, and it lets stand without further comment Mandela's public declaration of his enduring love for her when he announced that they were divorcing.

Mandela, however, does not counter his first wife Evelyn's remark that with him politics came first, family second—a sentiment echoed by Winnie. There's not much of Mandela's private life in the film. We're left with the feeling that Mandela, even apart from his long imprisonment, has had little time for that.

The film reinforces the indelible impression that Mandela has made around the world as a man of awesome dignity, courage, faith and determination. Perhaps that Mandela was born into the royalty of the Xhosa tribe has something to do with his bearing and self-discipline.

In covering familiar territory—after all, Mandela is one of the most famous men in the world—the filmmakers nevertheless succeed in conveying how astonishing is the distance he has covered in his nearly 80 years. We learn how he turned his back on an ancient tribal way of life to escape an arranged marriage, fled to Johannesburg in 1941, became a boxer and subsequently a partner in South Africa's first black law firm. He became increasingly involved in the struggle against apartheid, which resulted in 27 years imprisonment, 13 at hard labor in a lime quarry. "It keeps you in shape," says Mandela, who today is lean and elegant and in his youth was well-built and handsome.

The succinct, briskly paced "Mandela" was culled from 200 hours of footage plus 100 more of archival materials. Skillfully assembled and enlivened by an intoxicating array of African music on the soundtrack, it conveys forcefully not merely the well-known evils of apartheid but also the astonishing strength and wisdom of Mandela. Here is a man whose dream—for a South Africa with a one-man, one-vote rule—and whose ideal—of a "democratic and free society in which all peoples live together in harmony with equal opportunities"—now actually has a chance of coming true.

NEW YORK POST, 3/21/97, p. 52, Larry Worth

Few would argue that Nelson Mandela's triumph over South Africa's antiquated apartheid system is one of the decade's most inspirational stories. So why isn't the documentary charting that saga equally inspiring?

"Mandela: Son of Africa, Father of a Nation" isn't a bad film, but it unfolds with the excitement of a history book in need of dusting off. Adopting a straightforward approach to Mandela's journey from spear-carrying youngster to South Africa's first black president, the production balances interesting minutiae against lackluster presentation.

Yes, it's intriguing to hear how Mandela received his first name from a frustrated school teacher, or his tale of being circumcised at age 16 via un-sterilized spear. But such moments are balanced against standard newsreel footage and endless talking-head shots.

In addition, co-directors Jo Menell and Angus Gibson approach the material in a somewhat reverential manner. They mention Mandela's divorce from first wife Evelyn almost in passing, then ignore little chestnuts like F.W. DeKlerk's contribution to the peace process.

That's not to say the production doesn't have its assets: terrific archival photos of Mandela as a Johannesburg lawyer, beautiful shots of the South African countryside and a rousing, eclectic soundtrack.

The filmmakers also deserve points for rounding up some interesting speakers, including Mandela's most famous spouse—the ever-feisty, increasingly controversial Winnie—and some of Mandela's equally outspoken ANC colleagues.

Then again, no matter how interesting the story, Menell and Gibson let them run on too long. And is there any real reason to show Mandela shaving, cleaning his razor and turning down his bed? Some healthy editing would have done wonders for the film's languid pacing.

Regardless, it earned entry in last year's New York Film Festival, then garnered a best-documentary nomination in Monday's Oscar derby. But "Mandela" would stand a better chance of grabbing the gold had it proved half as compelling as its title character.

SIGHT AND SOUND, 4/97, p. 45, Kevin Macdonald

A film biography of Nelson Mandela, ANC leader and first democratic president of South Africa, the film opens with atmospheric shots of Robben Island prison, where Mandela was kept incarcerated for more than 20 years by successive apartheid governments. The story then flashes back to his childhood, and outlines his life chronologically. An interview with Mandela provides a voice-over to many of the images. Interwoven with this is archive footage—some it previously unseen—and numerous interviews with colleagues, friends and family, including his sister Mabel, his first wife Evelyn, the writer Anthony Sampson, ANC mentor Walter Sisulu, Archbishop Desmond Tutu and Winnie Mandela.

Born into a Royal household in the Transkei region of South Africa in 1918, Mandela experienced a traditional tribal childhood, before becoming the first member of his family to receive a western-style education. He arrived in Johannesburg in 1941, running away from an arranged marriage, and soon joined the ANC. In 1952, Mandela opened the first black law firm in South Africa, together with future ANC president Oliver Tambo. Throughout the 50s Mandela was involved in non-violent anti-apartheid protests and in 1956 he and 156 other leading activists were arrested and charged with high treason. This notorious case lasted for four years but ended in victory for the ANC. Soon afterwards Mandela and the ANC decided that armed struggle was the only solution. In 1962, Mandela was arrested again and sentenced to life imprisonment on Robben Island, where he became a focus for worldwide anti-apartheid feelings. In 1990 Mandela was released and started immediate negotiations with President F. W. de Klerk for South Africa's first multi-racial elections. In May 1994, he was elected President. Interspersed throughout are sequences where Mandela revisits locations which hold special significance for him: the village where he grew up, his old school, the prison on Robben Island and, finally, his ancestral burial ground, where he himself will be buried.

Most of us are disabused of the notion that the American Academy Awards are a true measure of cinematic excellence at about the same age as we stop believing in Santa Claus. Nevertheless, no two awards are as debased as those for best short and best feature-length documentary. This sorry state of affairs was highlighted two years ago when *Hoop Dreams*, widely regarded as one of the most entertaining and influential documentaries of recent years—and certainly the most popular—failed to even gain a nomination. The subsequent furore was justified. But the Academy members hardly seem to have learnt their lesson, and last year gave the award to a thoroughly pedestrian film on Anne Frank. The Academians clearly have difficulty telling the difference between an important, worthy subject and a good documentary.

It is no surprise then that this very disappointing documentary Mandela should find itself among this years nominees. Stylistically the film lingers somewhere between the undistinguished and the crass. The video to film transfer has not helped, particularly in the numerous musical montage sequences where the directors seem to have varied the speed of numerous shots, resulting in an unattractive jumpiness of the image. The combination of interviews and archive footage is never surprising; rarely, if ever, does it bring one up cold with a sense of understanding of Mandela or the anti-apartheid struggle. Worst of all are the soft-focus 'poetic reconstructions'—Mandela the boy playing the traditional warlike game of *thinti*, or standing elegiacally in his cell on Robben Island. These would have felt clichéd even in the context of a regional current affairs programme.

The directors, Jo Menell and Angus Gibson, are both South Africans and must have experienced at first hand the horrific injustices and petty humiliations of apartheid, but they resolutely fail to humanise Mandela's struggle—what apartheid felt like for ordinary black individuals is never brought home to us.

Only infrequently does the documentary come alive during rare moments of observation (why are these so rare when the crew apparently spent seven months filming with Mandela?). There is a lovely scene in which we simply watch Mandela shave—using an old fashioned bristle brush to lather up his face—that subtly expresses much about his character: the meticulousness, the dignity and the calm. Elsewhere we hear Mandela's assistant gently chastise him—like a daughter to a much-beloved father—for wearing the same shirt for too many days in a row. Perhaps the most telling sequence also concerns clothes: a discussion about what Mandela should wear to his official inauguration ceremony. Mandela, typically, does not wish to appear too elegantly or expensively dressed—it would seem improper when so many of those who voted for him are so poor.

Mandela is very much the authorised biography. The President must have aided the film-makers in their efforts to gain access to his close family and colleagues. This is not to say that the film is a whitewash. It does, for instance, go into the failure of Mandela's first marriage to Evelyn (he admits that politics was more important to him than his family) and doesn't shy away from the unpleasant accusations which have been levelled at Winnie. But however much many of us may think that Mandela is as close to a modern day saint as there is, the film-makers should still have tried harder to humanise him and the great struggle he led by opening up the complexities rather than closing down into pat clichés. Too often while watching *Mandela* I was left with the unpleasant sense that this was a corporate video for ANC PLC.

VILLAGE VOICE, 3/25/97, p. 86, Ed Morales

There has always been something a little otherworldly about Nelson Mandela. He first came into general consciousness as the unglimpsed, incarcerated leader of the Soweto uprisings of the '70s, an absent hero who existed as a handsome visage on antiapartheid buttons and posters. His was the consummate political prisoner legend—when he was finally released in 1989, it was as if a demigod banished from the world had returned to live as an ordinary mortal once again.

It's this kind of premature deification that the makers of *Mandela: Son of Africa, Father of a Nation* work to dispel. While everyone knows how Mandela brought apartheid to its knees and became the first black president of South Africa, few of us know much about his life before prison. Beginning with his origins in the southern veld, *Mandela* revels in the ethereal, mist-shrouded landscape of the East Cape, cleverly switching gears with grainy black-and-white footage of South Africa's history.

One of *Mandela*'s strengths is its riveting testimonials, from his sister Mabel's gruff insistence that he was a leader from childhood to Mandela's candid storytelling, as when he reveals that a schoolteacher gave him his Christian name. (His tribal name is Rolihlahla Dalibunga Madiba Mandela.) Old films of children fighting with sticks fade to Mandela exposing his calf to show a mark that remains from his youthful jousting. Mandela, also seen in boxing trunks and other sporty poses, is portrayed as the physical type, later to be compared with his more intellectual ANC comrade Oliver Tambo. The scene where Mandela describes his teenage circumcision, with its burning huts and flickering footage of tribesmen in jaguar paint, is one of the eeriest you'll ever see in a documentary about a Nobel Prize winner.

The well-assembled soundtrack gives the film an exuberant momentum while underscoring the contrast between Mandela's rural beginnings and his urban manhood—African jazz and rhythm-and-blues acts mix with roots Capetown music. Full of exotic swing, songs like "Ylyole" by the Havana Swingsters and "Vuka Vuka" by the Manhattan Brothers (one of Mandela's favorite bands) instill '40s and '50s South Africa with a hip feel.

As the narrative switches to wartime Johannesburg, Mandela is taken under the wing of pioneering black businessman Walter Sisulu, and becomes involved with the ANC. He lives a vital, politically involved urban lifestyle, making crucial contacts and alliances as well as polemical points. The movie makes clear that the apartheid government had to lock Mandela up not only because of his political savvy but his remarkable charisma; he comes off like a cross between Malcolm X and Muhammad Ali.

Unfortunately, *Mandela* begins to lose intensity with his incarceration. After the Sharpeville massacre of 1960, static videotape footage takes over and Mandela becomes less interesting in his role of absent deity, then exonerated saint. The film takes on first a hackneyed music-video quality, then starts to look like the kind of in-house film you'd see at one of our national conventions. Complex political struggles between the ANC and the Zulus are oversimplified; the arrest of Winnie Mandela for murder and kidnapping is also treated hastily. But perhaps the fluffy treatment by directors Jo Menell and Angus Gibson was the price of their intimate access to their subject. *Mandela*'s up-close-and-personal style ultimately redeems it. When a staff member suggests he wear a different shirt that day, Mandela, looking like he never notices the camera, shoots back, "Everybody just looks at my face." *Mandela* manages to avoid being dwarfed by its larger-than-life subject.

Also reviewed in:
NEW REPUBLIC, 4/7/97, p. 26, Stanley Kauffmann
NEW YORK TIMES, 3/21/97, p. C12, Stephen Holden
VARIETY, 10/21-27/96, p. 83, Godfrey Cheshire

MARGARET'S MUSEUM

A Cabin Fever Entertainment and CFP Distribution release of a Malofilm Communications presentation of a Ranfilm/Imagex/Tele Action/Skyline production. *Executive Producer:* Marilyn A. Belec. *Producer:* Mort Ransen, Christopher Zimmer, Claudio Luca, and Steve Clark-Hall. *Director:* Mort Ransen. *Screenplay:* Gerald Wexler and Mort Ransen. *Based on "The Glace Bay Miner's Museum" by:* Sheldon Currie. *Director of Photography:* Vic Sarin. *Editor:* Rita Roy. *Music:* Milan Kymlicka. *Music Editor:* Steve Wener. *Sound:* Yvon Benoît. *Sound Editor:* Raymond Vermette. *Casting:* Stuart Aikins, Anne Tait, Lulu Keating, and Mary Vingoe. *Production Designer:* William Flemming and David McHenry. *Art Director:* Emanuel Jannasch. *Set Decorator:* Ian Greig. *Special Effects:* Augustus White. *Costumes:* Nicoletta Massone. *Make-up:* Donald Mowat. *Stunt Coordinator:* John Walsh. *Running time:* 118 minutes. *MPAA Rating:* R.

CAST: Helena Bonham Carter (Margaret MacNeil); Clive Russell (Neil Currie); Craig Olejnik (Jimmy MacNeil); Kate Nelligan (Catherine MacNeil); Kenneth Welsh (Angus MacNeil); Andrea Morris (Marilyn Campbell); Peter Boretski (Grandfather); Barry Dunn (Mr. Campbell); Norma Dell'Agnese (Mrs. Campbell); Glenn Wadman (Willy); Elizabeth Richardson (Sister); Ida Donovan (Sarah); Gordon Joe (Hum Sing); Wayne Reynolds (Fraser); Murdoch MacDonald (Clerk); Yow Wah Chee (Chinese Cook); Terry O'Keefe (Miner); Liam Hussey (Peter); Mary Alvena Poole (Woman); Carol Kennedy (Tourist Woman); Bruce MacCleod (Mountie); Emma Fahey (Alma McLaren); Sam White (Young Man); Amy Jo Lamb (Young Margaret MacNeil); Ian Mugford and Billy Fraser (Little Boys); David B. Lamb (Roddie MacKenzie); Kyle MacNeil and Stewart MacNeil (Band); Jenipher Roland (Fiddler); Aaron Schneider (Tourist Man); Paul Young, Sean Hewitt, and Matt Zimmerman (Doctors); Peter Marinker (Hiring Man).

LOS ANGELES TIMES, 3/14/97, Calendar/p. 14, Kevin Thomas

"Margaret's Museum" is one of those gratifying, intimate films in which all elements seem to mesh perfectly. A love story set against a deepening drama of social protest, it has a distinctive psychological twist to which won't be relieved here.

A lyrical, romantic period piece of intense passion, it stars Helena Bonham Carter in a strikingly successful departure from her usual upper-crust roles.

Set in the late '40s or early '50s in the picturesque town of Glace Bay on Cape Breton, Nova Scotia, it opens in a Chinese restaurant where Margaret, who's also a hospital charwoman, works as a waitress. In walks Clive Russell's Neil Currie, who's very tall, shaggy-haired, bearded—and somewhat drunk, his reaction to haveing been fired from the nearby coal mine for speaking Gaelic on the job. Margaret's boss throws him out when he starts playing his bagpipes.

Margaret is a natural beauty with a fiery temperament and Neil is a man of imposing, looming physical presence. You might think, consdering time and place, that youv'e stumbled on a Canadian "Picnic," but that's not the case at all: Neil may be a free spirit with a poetic soul, but he's a serious man, a stayer, not a drifter, who respects Margaret's desire to marry as a virgin.

Because mine disasters claimed her father and older brother and because her grandfather is dying of black lung disease, Margaret is understandably obsessive in her determination that neither Neil nor her younger brother Jimmy (Craig Olejnik), end up in the mines. But what are the alternatives for Neil and Jimmy in a small, remote one-industry town?

What a paradox the film's setting presents: a seaside region of idyllic natural beauty whose way of life is also a way of death.

Adapted by director Mort Ransen and Gerald Wexler from stories by Sheldon Currie, "Margaret's Museum" recalls the fatalism of Irish drama, John Millington Synge's "Riders to the Sea" in particular. (It also inevitably recalls "Germinal," the powerful French film from the Emile Zola novel protesting coal mining conditions and starring Gerard Depardieu.)

It has a somewhat literary quality—Margaret, Neil and others are notably well-spoken—and Neil, of whom we know little, could be Lady Chatterley's lover himself, the earthy natural man. (Come to think of it, Bonham Carter and Russell could be terrific in a new version of the D.H. Lawrence novel.)

With the singular exceptions of David Cronenberg and Atom Egoyan, English-speaking Canadian filmmakers tend to be traditionalists (French-Canadians are a different matter). In style, Ransen is typically conservative, but the familiar Canadian virtues of restraint and clarity are just what's needed to offset the tempestuousness of Margaret's nature and the film's ever-growing criticism of coal mining conditions.

To say that "Margaret's Museum," although contemporary in its sexual candor, has the feel of a film actually made in the period it depicts is meant as a compliment. It is a film of supporting performances as splendid as those of its stars and of telling details and nuances.

Kate Nelligan as Margaret's mother, a good, caring woman beneath an understandably thick layer of bitterness and cynicism, has a barrage of tart lines.

The film has a firm grasp of the idiosyncrasies of human nature. For example, Margaret, in her realism, demands that Neil use condoms because she doesn't want to bring into the world a child she cannot afford to feed. Yet when he, with equal realism, suggests they leave town to find better prospects elsewhere, she says she cannot leave until Jimmy is on his way, dreaming incredibly that somehow this nice, ordinary kid is going to become a doctor.

In another example, a miner, recovering from broken legs suffered in an accident, admits that he can't wait to get back to work, with camaraderie outweighing dire conditions.

A very brief and deliberately oblique prologue sets up succinctly the film's totally logical—if you think about it—and stunning climax. As tender as it is angry, "Margaret's Museum" is wholly memorable, a triumph for all concerned, especially Bonham Carter.

NEW YORK POST, 2/7/97, p. 48, Thelma Adams

It's the pits being a coal miner's daughter. If you're Loretta Lynn, you sing to drown out the sound of your pain. If you're the title character of "Margaret's Museum," you open a gallery to rival Vincent Price's "House of Wax".

Canadian director Mort Ransen's grim, gilded social drama about the horrors of the mining life is a labor of love that loves labor in an old-fashioned, PBS sort of way that's more quaint than stirring.

Inspired by Sheldon Currie's short stories, Ransen and cowriter Gerald Wexler dig into the past—the '40s—and travel to Nova Scotia's remote Cape Breton Island. The hamlet of Glace Bay is a breathtaking setting where, man and nature collide. The birds live in splendor, the men in squalor.

Culture is the miner's saving grace. A Scotch-Irish stew, they have the balm of bagpipes (a mixed blessing) and Celtic airs to soothe rough lives of dusty desperation. For Currie, et. al, preserving the Gaelic traditions and, specifically the language, becomes a holy and political mission. If these people lose their tongue, they lose their souls.

Margaret, as played by Merchant-Ivory poster girl Helena Bonham Carter ("A Room With a View"), is a knockabout outcast who resists the miner's life even while she can't escape it. Her father and brother died in the pits. Meg refuses to marry a miner—until she meets pipe-playing, drunken roustabout Neil Currie (Clive Russell).

The charismatic Carter swears and sits with knees spread, but she's one of those fine-boned, creamy-complected stars who has the ability to make a flour sack shift, black socks and clunky shoes like my Aunt wore during World War II look ready for the runway. She bares her breasts and she still seems like she's in costume. I love Carter, and she's watchable curating this "Museum," but her Margaret is as believable as Sharon Stone's death row inmate in "Last Dance."

As Neil, Russell is more surprising. A Gaelic Kevin Kline with a touch of Paul Bunyan, this 6-foot-6 actor takes a break from playing villains to create a memorable romantic figure. In earthy love scenes that appear like hiccups in the grim social realism, Russell approaches Carter with an abiding gentleness. Their embraces seem like a lion making love to an antelope.

Kate Nelligan plays Margaret's mum, Catherine, an angry widow with a clairvoyant streak and none of Neil's gentleness. Nelligan begins at such a high pitch she has no where to go. Catherine not only alienates Meg but deflects the audience from her pain. She's as upbeat as she gets when she gives the following blessing to her newlywed daughter: "You'll be happy or miserable as the case may be."

With "Margaret's Museum," it's clear from the beginning that there's only one option. That's why it's much less affecting than it could be. It's as if we examine our horror, passion, pain and disappointment through thick glass: We're impressed but unmoved.

NEWSDAY, 2/7/97, Part II/p. B9, Jack Mathews

On a grassy bluff overlooking the sea from Cape Breton, Nova Scotia, is a small shack, made of scrap wood and windows, with a glass-enclosed loft. From the brief conversation of a couple we see driving toward the shack, we assume it is a museum, and, since the movie we're watching is titled "Margaret's Museum," we assume we know the name of the woman greeting them.

We're right about both of these things, but it's not wise to assume anything more. Mort Ransen's "Margaret's Museum," adapted from Sheldon Currie's short stories about life in a coal town in post-World War II Nova Scotia, follows a deceptively complex emotional trail, starting and ending at that shack, and passing hope, horror, and despair on the way and in about that order.

I don't recommend this movie as a cure for depression. It's about the hard lives led by an immigrant population—mostly Scots and Irish who came to Nova Scotia with high hopes and got on a treadmill to hell instead. The men worked in the mines, dying young in cave-ins, or in middle-age of black lung disease, leaving jaded widows and sisters behind.

"Margaret's Museum" focuses on one family, or what remains of it. There's Catherine MacNeil (Kate Nelligan), an embittered woman who's lost her husband and son to cave-ins, tends a father dying of black lung and has a son coming of age in a place where there is only one career. She also has a grown daughter, Margaret (Helena Bonham Carter), who's determined not to marry a miner.

So she marries a dishwasher instead, the flaky Irishman Neil Currie (Clive Russell), a gentle giant who staggers into her life one day, full of liquor and hot air, and with an armful of bagpipes to let off the steam. It's Neil who builds that shack on the bluff, and the glass enclosure where the couple tangle up in nightly lovemaking.

Margaret and Neil share as much of an idyllic life as you can imagine in so desolate a place. But when Neil is forced to take a job in the mines, the fragile natures of their relationship and of Margaret's relationship with her mother, are exposed, and emotionally, it takes us all down in the mines.

Ultimately, "Margaret's Museum" is a primal cry against abuse by the mine owners, whose disregard for their workers' health destroyed generations of lives. The performances of Carter and

Nelligan are primal cries in themselves, and, by the time you return to Margaret's museum, you may be too drained or numb to cry yourself.

SIGHT AND SOUND, 5/97, p. 49, Peter Matthews

Cape Breton Island, Nova Scotia, the late 40s. Margaret MacNeil is a rebellious young woman who lives with her cantankerous mother Catherine, her 16-year-old brother Jimmy and an asthmatic grandfather in the village of Glace Bay. Resentment runs high against the powerful mining company that oversees nearly every aspect of daily life in the community. Recognising its monopolistic advantage, the company keeps wages low and ignores basic safety provisions; a siren often signals yet another mining disaster. Years ago, one such accident claimed the lives of Margaret's father and elder brother, and she will have no more to do with the men of the mines. However, Margaret's resolve melts when she meets Neil Currie, an ex-miner who washes dishes at the Pink Blossom Café, although Catherine foretells calamity for the lovers. Margaret, smitten by Neil's charm and bagpipe-playing, agrees to marry him, but insists he stays out of the mines.

Meanwhile, Jimmy begins a sexual relationship with his dancing partner, Marilyn. He also lands a job in the mines, despite the family's connivance to keep him barred. Neil loses his job at the café, and the couple becomes perilously short of money. One day, Margaret informs Neil that she has no wish to bring babies into this miserable world. When Neil finally concedes defeat and joins Jimmy at the pit, Margaret leaves him. The pair are soon reconciled, but Catherine predicts tragedy. The next time the siren sounds, it turns out to be a death knell for both Neil and Jimmy. Margaret carts the bodies over to her mother's for washing—only to discover that Grandpa, left unattended, has choked to death. Insane with grief, Margaret performs one last defiant act: she carves up her loved ones, removing grandpa's coal-blackened lungs, Neil's lungs and fingers and Jimmy's penis. After two years, Margaret is released from the asylum and opens a very unusual exhibit, which she calls the Miner's Museum.

Margaret's Museum has, at least, the virtue of a genuine shock ending—which is the only thing genuine about it. You sit there innocently hibernating through the roguish burnout and lilting dialogue that comprise the movie's idea of daily life in a Nova Scotian mining community 50 years ago. But then the pace begins to pick up alarmingly, the melodramatic disasters proliferate, and before you know it, poor, unhinged Margaret has dismembered and pickled three of her relatives. It's as if John Ford had decided to enliven *The Quiet Man* (1952) with a last-minute bloodbath; and there's always the hope that the director Mort Ransen and his co-writer Gerald Wexler are a couple of spry Dadaists, instead of the humbling fellows they appear to be.

But alas, the tone is too earnest to leave much room for doubt. Even in the catastrophe, Ransen (who has directed numerous limited-release Canadian films) settles for a single, decorous spurt of blood on our plucky heroine's face; and the camera glides so euphemistically over her pickle jars that it seems to be aiming at a Gothic atrocity movie the whole family can enjoy. Admittedly, a certain amount of heavy-handed foreshadowing appears to be going on down in Glace Bay. You can't help feeling that the continually sullen, overcast sky bodes no good; and if that isn't enough, the movie includes one character—Margaret's acidulous mother Catherine—whose entire dramatic function consists in issuing dire warnings. But you really do need clairvoyance to predict that a folksy charmer like Margaret's husband Neil, who murmurs such endearments as "I'll buy you moonshine," between bouts of lyrical bagpipe-playing will end up sliced and diced. The Southern American writer Flannery O'Connor also visited Gothic violence on plain folk; but her Bible Belt characters were like gnarled outcroppings of the landscape. The assorted mock-primitives here are about as rooted in collective memory as the knickknacks at a tourist shop—so that maybe Margaret, with her pickle jars, has the right idea after all.

Ransen and Wexler run into a more purely structural problem in that their script condenses two or three short stories from Sheldon Currie's collection *The Glace Bay Miner's Museum*. This means that the viewer is lulled to sleep in the initial, interminable build-up of local colour; but then the several climaxes erupt all at once—the mines collapse, Grandpa keels over and Margaret has her heroic inspiration. It all suggests a Thomas Hardy novel gone haywire, but one can see glimmerings of thematic intent planted along the way. Where the other yokels take their cue from gloomy Catherine in casting themselves as pawns of fate, Margaret learns that her bitter lot is man-made and specifically the result of corporate callousness and greed. When she gets busy with her knives, it's supposed to be an angry political gesture.

All of which possibly explains the movie's enormous critical success in Canada where it seems to have been taken as a courageous airing of historical guilt. And while the real-life victims of the 40s mining disasters aren't necessarily best-served by this embalming in homogenised hokum, no doubt for many viewers Ransen's bloodless, academic style represents craftsmanship. The actors can't do much with their hand-me-down roles, but Kate Nelligan's crusty Catherine provides the one entertaining note in the whole show. Helena Bonham Carter clearly relishes the chance to play a slattern after all those pale English roses. As Margaret, she sports flour sacks and a mop of greasy hair; and you can see her tensely concentrating to get the slurred Cape Breton vowels just right. But her diligent performance is self-defeating, for it never once strikes that keynote of romantic abandon which might make the heroine's actions remotely plausible.

VILLAGE VOICE, 2/11/97, p. 74, Michael Atkinson

The John Entwhistle of national cinemas, Canadian films have never been renowned for their unique voice and character; Canuck "identity" has been as easy to nail down as a blob of mercury. But, worthwhile or not, Canadian movies are almost always pervaded by a telling sense of lostness, emptiness, provincial desolation; they're like movies made by exiles from culture, and that includes the rogue personas like David Cronenberg and Guy Maddin. Think of how that hopeless borderland sensibility has resonated through Cronenberg's films, including *Crash*.

This hard-bitten Canadian-ness can creep you out, bore you, or add to a film's impact, and in *Margaret's Museum* it does all three. An off-kilter Nova Scotia melodrama bleary with remote idiosyncrasy and working-class rancor, Mort Ransen's tiny grungefest centers on Helena Bonham Carter as Margaret, a quirky, antisocial misfit whose nose never stops running, living with her mother and young brother in a remote coal-mining corner of Cape Breton. Margaret quickly meets up with, and falls for, Neil (Clive Russell), a brawny but sensitive Irishman who has similar problems with authority and orthodoxy. Neil is pie-eyed and blowing bagpipes when we meet him, but he's never defined exclusively as a drunk—an hour into the film, all you're sure he is is Irish. Likewise, for the whole first half, you're not sure what the film's about, and then you find out: the hapless mortality and calamity of communities built around coal mines, where much of Margaret's family has died already and more will die before the film is through.

Margaret's Museum has the fatal, unrealistic scent of fiction-workshop literariness about it, where characters are defined by eccentric behavior and neatly contrived histories, but after a while—perhaps by sheer dint of having them linger longer than you'd like they become convincing. (Margaret's embittered mother, played with dead-eyed zest by Kate Nelligan, talks like she walked right out of a Mamet play.) The film more or less rests with Carter, who's sadly miscast: she's a cherub, Margaret is a hardened, hands-on-hips crankcase, and the two just don't jell. If you can wait out its tiresome offbeatness and affect, *Margaret's Museum* does pay off. But what resonates is that haunting Canadian emptiness; this movie happens on the edge of civilization in more ways than one.

Also reviewed in:
NEW REPUBLIC, 2/24/97, p. 25, Stanley Kauffmann
NEW YORK TIMES, 2/7/97, p. C18, Janet Maslin
VARIETY, 6/12-18/95, p. 60, Brendan Kelly

MASTERMINDS

A Columbia Pictures release of a Byars/Dudelson/Pacific Motion Pictures production. *Executive Producer:* Matthew O'Connor and David Saunders. *Producer:* Robert Dudelson and Floyd Byars. *Director:* Roger Christian. *Screenplay:* Floyd Byars. *Story:* Floyd Byars, Alex Siskin, and Chris Black. *Director of Photography:* Nic Morris. *Editor:* Robin Russell. *Music:* Anthony Marinelli. *Music Editor:* Terry Wilson and Pat Caird. *Sound:* Michael McGee and (music) Mark Curry. *Sound Editor:* John Nutt and Bill Sheppard. *Casting:* Andrea Stone. *Production Designer:*

Douglas Higgins. *Art Director:* Doug Byggdin. *Set Decorator:* Mark Lane. *Special Effects:* Randy Shymkiw. *Costumes:* Monique Sanchez and Derek J. Baskerville. *Make-up:* Connie Parker. *Stunt Coordinator:* Jacob Rupp. *Running time:* 106 minutes. *MPAA Rating:* PG-13.

CAST: Patrick Stewart (Raf Bentley); Vincent Kartheiser (Ozzie); Brenda Fricker (Principal Maloney); Brad Whitford (Miles Lawrence); Matt Craven (Jake); Annabelle Gurwitch (Helen); Jon Abrahams (K-Dog); Katie Stuart (Melissa); Michael Macrae (Deroy); Callum Keith Rennie (Ollie); Earl Pastko (Captain Jankel); Jason Schombing (Marvin); Michael David Simms (Colonel Duke); David Paul Grove (Ferret); Akiko Morison (Janet); Teryl Rothery (Ms. Saunders); Vanessa Morley (Gabby); Bruce Pinard (Happy Boy Guard); April Telek (Sexy Girl); Steve Makaj (Captain Majors); Jay Brazeau (Eliot); Douglas Newell (Science Teacher); Frank Cassini (Cop); Kimberly Unger (Flight Attendant); Pamela Martin (Female TV Reporter); Andrew Wheeler (Bank Officer); Merret Green (Male TV Reporter); Michael Benyaer (Taxi Driver).

LOS ANGELES TIMES, 8/22/97, Calendar/p. 18, Gene Seymour

[The following review by Gene Seymour appeared in a slightly different form in **NEWSDAY, 8/22/97, Part II/p. B15.]**

"Masterminds" has "teen product" stamped all over its shiny surface. It boasts a 16-year-old hero who looks as if he just came from a Seattle mosh pit. He's also way cooler and a whole lot smarter than the grown-ups, all of whom, of course, don't understand him. Power-amped guitar-fills are used to patch the spaces between action sequences. And, as seems to be the case with every movie released this summer, it loves to squeeze your insides with high-concept—and highly implausible—action.

Still, compared with all the other action thrillers made for the 17-year-old in all of us, "Masterminds" delivers its' routine suspense with relative restraint and even a little ingenuity. It doesn't brutalize its characters or its audience with gratuitous, excessive violence.

And even if it is "high concept," give its makers some credit for being even a little novel. If you were making the pitch, you'd probably call it "'Hardy Boys' Meets 'Die Hard.'" That is, if Joe or Frank Hardy had some of Bart Simpson's antisocial tendencies.

Of course, Ozzie Paxton, as played by moody, handsome Vincent Kartheiser (from last year's late-summer family flick "Alaska"), looks nothing like Bart and doesn't quite have the Simpson kid's way with a wisecrack. Nonetheless, he is, like Bart, defiantly underachieving, a cyber whiz who finds little reason at home or school to put his considerable mental prowess to productive use.

Ozzie is in so much trouble at the movie's start that he's even willing to deliver his bratty stepsister (Katie Stuart) to the tony private school he used to attend before getting tossed out for terminal attitude. The tough-talking principal (Brenda Fricker) had been so undone by Ozzie's pranks the previous year that she had hired a suave security specialist (Patrick Stewart) to build an air-tight, high-tech system.

But just when Ozzie's about to administer a *coup de grace* to the school, there's a turn of events that puts Ozzie in an unexpected role. Ozzie finds himself inside the school, having the time of his life with the kind of freewheeling subterranean mischief that would make both Bugs Bunny and Bruce Willis proud.

This is unapologetic wish-fulfillment for teenage outcasts everywhere. Like most fantasies, it stretches credulity like pizza dough. (Mostly, you wonder how it's possible that, despite the surplus of explosions, electrocutions and other mayhem, no one loses his or her life.)

Still, after watching so many recent movies that persist in showing children in perpetual helplessness, it comes as something of a relief to see a movie where a kid actually takes charge of a situation. There are worse things for movies to do than give kids a sense of autonomy.

And it's a pleasure to watch "Star Trek's" Stewart having so much fun being bad. He doesn't eat the scenery so much as dine on it, and he carries his villainy in a charming, smarmy manner that almost makes you root for him. Or, at least, for he and Ozzie to pool their malcontent imaginations together so they can annoy the slugs who cramp their styles.

NEW YORK POST, 8/22/97, p. 48, Thelma Adams

"Masterminds" wasn't produced by brain surgeons. It's a slick, low-budget "Die Hard" meets "Home Alone" clone that knows exactly who its audience is: teen-age boys.

Directed by Roger Christian, scripted by Floyd Byars, "Masterminds" pits teen cyberbrat Ozzie (Vincent Kartheiser) against military-trained security guru Rafe Bentley (Patrick Stewart).

Ozzie has been suspended from the ritzy Shady Glen day school for blowing up the science lab: Bentley has been ejected from a high-tech conglomerate for embezzling. Now they share something else: Bentley kidnaps Shady Glen's richest kids and outcast Ozzie is the only one who can foil the evil scheme.

Aside from the usual Hollywood dysfunctional family guilt trip—Ozzie must rescue his stepsister, make peace with his stepmom, recapture the attention of his workaholic dad and get over the loss of a birth mom who walked—"Masterminds" is a primer for being true to your school by blasting it to bits.

In Ozzie's efforts to put the brakes on Bentley, the techno-geek Ozzie blows the Shady Glen boiler, blasts the swimming pool and demonstrates how to evade pursuers by heating a doorknob with a Bunsen Burner and pouring nitric acid on the lab floor.

Kartheiser ("Alaska") has prettier lips than stepmom Annabelle Gurwitch—which must add to the competitive tension. But when it comes to action, he's the son of Bruce Willis and Steven Seagal, unfazed by opponents who are older, more experienced and have the ability to grow beards.

Stewart is the movie's secret weapon. He adds the drumroll of "Richard III" to such throwaway orders as "send in the ferret."

VILLAGE VOICE, 9/2/97, p. 78, Gary Dauphin

If you can imagine a low-body-count *Die Hard* set an exclusive private school and starring one of those longhairs from Hanson, you pretty much get the gist of *Masterminds*. A harmless bit of early adolescent cool, the movie tells the tale of how hacker-troublemaker Ozzie Paxton (Vincent Kartheiser) foils the mass-kidnap plans of ex-British Secret agent Ralph Bently (Patrick Stewart), not only saving the well-heeled students of his old school (he's been expelled over a prank) but redeeming himself in the eyes of his workaholic parents.

Soon after the movie opens, Ozzie finds himself trapped on the grounds of the Shady Glen School, which gentleman terrorist Bently has taken over. Ozzie immediately slips into Man Inside mode, taking to the air vents and subbasements while the more legit, uniformed rescuers bumble around outside. Knowing more about computers, telephone switch boxes, and security systems than your average SWAT team member, Ozzie becomes a roachlike annoyance to the kidnappers, which turns out to be just fine with the Bald One, as now he's got a 'worthy opponent.' Except for Stewart's game-but-controlled hamming, *Masterminds* has the look and feel of an over-caffeinated Nickelodeon movie, making it just about perfect for kids on the verge of that difficult transition from kid TV to MTV.

Also reviewed in:
CHICAGO TRIBUNE, 8/22/97, Friday/p. F, John Petrakis
NEW YORK TIMES, 8/22/97, p. C5, Stephen Holden
VARIETY, 8/25-31/97, p. 74, Leonard Klady
WASHINGTON POST, 8/22/97, p. D6, Stephen Hunter

MATCHMAKER, THE

A Gramercy Pictures release of a PolyGram Filmed Entertainment presentation of a Working Title production. *Executive Producer:* Lyn Goleby. *Producer:* Tim Bevan, Eric Fellner, and Luc Roeg. *Director:* Mark Joffe. *Screenplay:* Karen Janszen, Louis Nowra, and Graham Linehan. *Based on a screenplay by:* Greg Dinner. *Director of Photography:* Ellery Ryan. *Editor:* Martin Smith. *Music:* John Altman. *Music Editor:* Mike Higham. *Sound:* Brendan Deasy and (music)

Geoff Foster. *Sound Editor:* Nigel Heath and Julian Slater. *Casting:* Ros Hubbard, John Hubbard, Amanda Mackey Johnson, and Cathy Sandrich. *Production Designer:* Mark Geraghty. *Art Director:* Terry Pritchard. *Set Dresser:* Fiona Daly. *Special Effects:* Maurice Foley. *Costumes:* Howard Burden. *Make-up:* Maire O'Sullivan. *Stunt Coordinator:* Patrick Condren. *Running time:* 100 minutes. *MPAA Rating:* R.

CAST: Janeane Garofalo (Marcy); Jay O. Sanders (McGlory); Denis Leary (Nick); Olivia Caffrey (Annie); Joan Sheehy (Bus Passenger); Anne Gildea (Airport Assistant); Paul Hickey (Declan); Claude Clancy (Michael); James Ryland (Sergeant Riley); David King (Local Lad No. 1); Niall McDonnell (Local Lad No. 2); Milo O'Shea (Dermot); Maria Doyle Kennedy (Sarah); Sinead Murphy (Bettina); David McDonagh (Little Joe); David O'Hara (Sean); Peter Dix (Tony); Tommy Tiernan (Vince); David Kelly (O'Connor); Rosaleen Linehan (Millie); Akemi O'Tani (Japanese Bride); Kieran Aherne (MC); Frankie McCafferty (Jimmy); John Joe Murray (Irish Dancer); Stuart Dunne (Head Bang Man); Gerry O'Brien (Fisherman); Donncha O'Faolain (2nd Aran Singer); Jimmy Keogh (O'Hara); Conor McDermottroe (Paul); Linda Lee (Campaign Assistant); Joe Dillon (Aran Local); Ned Dennehy (1st Aran Singer); Vincent Walsh (Philip); Ellery Ryan (Philip's Friend); Saffron Burrows (Moira); Owen O'Neill (Garda); Seamus Corcoran (Local Cynic); Robert Mandan (McGlory Senior); Nancy O'Neil (Journalist); David Ian ("McGlory" MC); FAKE McGLORYS: Siobhan Vaughan (Brigid); James Hickey (Paddy Jr.); Robert Hickey (Michael).

LOS ANGELES TIMES, 10/3/97, Calendar/p. 22, John Anderson

The following review by John Anderson appeared in a slightly different form in:
NEWSDAY, 10/3/7, Part II/p. B11.]

When the Irish finally take over the world, it'll be the likes of "The Matchmaker" that people look back on and say, "Ahhhh, that's how they caught us with our pants down ..."

You know the movie drill: singing, praying, quaint traditions, barely comprehensible accents and someone doing the John Wayne-quiet man routine. Or in the case of Janeane Garofalo—star of "The Matchmaker"—the decidedly unquiet woman.

Taking a large, large cue from Bill Forsyth's "Local Hero," Mark Joffe's comedy finds Garofalo's jaded politico Marcy Tizard in a land long ago and far away: Ireland, circa 1997, where she's looking for the roots of her boss, the very un-Kennedy-esque John McGlory (Jay O. Sanders).

McGlory is an uninspiring and possibly stupid Massachusetts senator, and a guy who'd like to keep his job. Abetted by his scrofulous campaign manager Nick Ward (Denis Leary), the senator has dispatched Marcy to Ireland to find and /or create a link for him with the Ould Sod.

Marcy winds up in the tiny town of Ballinagra, which has little in the way of McGlorys, but is in the middle of a matchmaking festival. With the unwanted assistance of local marriage consultant Dermot (the elfin Milo O'Shea), her life gets turned around and upside down.

Garofalo, likable if prickly, has perfected a persona based on a very '90s sense of ennui and purposeful impatience and cynicism. In "The Matchmaker" these qualities serve her well, although she has an entire nation to provide the counterpoint. It's a charming place, and Marcy—as she becomes more disenchanted with Boston politics and more enamored of her Irish hosts—becomes more charming, too.

Her chief antagonist/fascination is Sean—played by David O'Hara, the lone Irish warrior of "Braveheart," who shows a real talent for low-key comedy and understated seduction. Sean is assigned as Marcy's unofficial guide, and when they get stuck on an island during a genealogical excursion, things warm up. When they get back to the mainland and Sean's beautiful wife (Saffron Burrows) makes an appearance, the temperature plunges.

It's becoming a cliche to say this, of course, but if you can't see where this romance is going, you're blind. In "The Matchmaker," director Joffe does a lot of what he did in his 1992 comedy "Spotswood"—in which Anthony Hopkins' uptight efficiency expert was won over by his blue-collar factory workers.

But while Joffe does swing a big shillelagh's worth of Irish cliché, he also manages to get around the stereotypes frequently enough, at least, to provide some human comedy among the pseudo-leprechauns.

NEW YORK POST, 10/3/979 p. 48, Larry Worth

Consistently proving superior to her scripts, Janeane Garofalo has worked more magic with lame material than David Copperfield has. But Houdini himself couldn't escape from "The Matchmaker" unscathed.

It's a romantic comedy that's neither romantic nor comedic. Set in Ireland, the gorgeous scenery can't begin to compete with the nonstop stupidity.

Under Mark Joffe's brainless direction, it's kind of like "Local Hero," minus the charm, delightful characters and whimsical spirit of the Bill Forsyth classic.

Garofalo plays Marcy, a cynical political aide who's dispatched to the Emerald Isle to find her smarmy boss' relatives. For reasons unknown the pol's declining popularity will be aided by a photo op with a bunch of lads and lassies.

Naturally, Marcy runs into a wee bit of trouble when a matchmaking festival over-takes the town she's staked out. The big question is whether she'll abandon her fruitless mission and find her own true love before the end credits.

Those unsure of the answer are the only ones who'll appreciate this claptrap, composed of one silly sequence after another.

It's made all the worse as Joffe—who recently tried to show the funny side of a mental ward in the despicable "Cosi"—injects slapstick into the proceedings. By the time a dog urinates on the heroine's luggage, all hope is gone.

At least Joffe is consistent. He makes every development completely predictable and telegraphs each supposed twist long before it arrives. In addition, the script tries so hard to play up the crazy locals that it could pass for—God forbid—"Cosi II."

That's not to say Garofalo doesn't fight the good fight. She's as appealing as a presence as ever, infusing an energy and dry wit into a production that never merits her efforts.

Veteran Irish actor Milo O'Shea is also an engaging presence. But in the title role, a sort of Celtic version of Dolly Levi, he's practically asked to wink at the camera. He deserves better.

So does Denis Leary as a sleazy spinmeister, Jay O. Sanders as the corrupt campaigner and newcomer David O'Hara as the Irishman with whom Marcy is meant to fight—and subsequently fall for head over heels.

The bottom line: Even diehard Garofalo fans will find no love lost for "The Matchmaker."

VILLAGE VOICE, 10/14/97, p. 94, Laurie Stone

Janeane Garofalo has a frantic look on her face, a mood inspired less, one suspects, by playing Marcy, a politician's aide sent to scare up Irish roots for her boss, than by realizing she's in a turkey. How many times must director Mark Joffe (perpetrator of the equally gobble-worthy *Cosi*) have called out, "Smile, smile bigger, smile with condescending compassion'? The movie is a one-sentence concept inflated with reaction shots: Big-city working girl meets Sean (David O'Hara), a shaggy-haired Irish dreamer, and discovers, well, nothing. She arrives at a seaside town smack in the middle of a matchmaking festival, so all the rooms are taken, except for an attic hole with a spine-crunching bed. And whom should she find in her bathtub in the obligatory meet-cute scene but twinkly Sean. Python-esque weirdness momentarily erupts when a fake family the pol intends to videotape declares that its shit bucket has room for more turds. Otherwise, for nearly two hours, Garofalo's wit is drained along with O'Hara's charm as they witness punishing scenes of step dancing and pub singing. Garofalo would destroy this treacle in stand-up.

Also reviewed in:
CHICAGO TRIBUNE, 10/3/97, Friday/p. B, Mark Caro
NEW YORK TIMES, 10/3/97, p. E16, Stephen Holden
VARIETY, 9/29-10/5/97, p. 66, Todd McCarthy
WASHINGTON POST, 10/3/97, p. B7, Rita Kempley
WASHINGTON POST, 10/3/97, Weekend/p. 46, Desson Howe

McHALE'S NAVY

A Universal Pictures and The Bubble Factory release of a Sheinberg production. *Executive Producer:* Lance Hool and Perry Katz. *Producer:* Sid Sheinberg, Bill Sheinberg, and Jon Sheinberg. *Director:* Bryan Spicer. *Screenplay:* Peter Crabbe. *Story:* Peter Crabbe and Andy Rose. *Director of Photography:* Buzz Feitshans, IV. *Editor:* Russell Denove. *Music:* Dennis McCarthy. *Music Editor:* Rich Harrison. *Sound:* Fernando Cámara and (music) John Richards. *Sound Editor:* Richard Legrand, Jr. *Casting:* Lisa London and Catherine Stroud. *Production Designer:* Gene Rudolf. *Art Director:* Kim Hix. *Set Decorator:* Patrice Laure. *Set Dresser:* Macedonio Ramos. *Special Effects:* Jesus "Chucho" Duran. *Costumes:* Michael T. Boyd. *Make-up:* Gina Homan. *Make-up (Tom Arnold):* Bob Mills and Carla Palmer. *Stunt Coordinator:* Gary Jensen. *Running time:* 109 minutes. *MPAA Rating:* PG.

CAST: Tom Arnold (McHale); Dean Stockwell (Binghampton); Debra Messing (Carpenter); David Alan Grier (Parker); Tim Curry (Vladakov); Ernest Borgnine (Cobra); Bruce Campbell (Virgil); French Stewart (Happy); Danton Stone (Gruber); Brian Haley (Christy); Henry Cho (Willie); Anthony Jesse Cruz (Roberto); Honorato Magaloni (Castro); Guillermo Rios (Jose); Eduardo Lopez Rojas (Gonzalez); Tom Ayers (Henchman Carl); Scott Cleverdon (Henchman David); Robert Schuch (Boat Henchman); Tommy Chong (Armando/Ernesto); Paco Mauri (Doctor); Juan Rebolledo (Juan); Diego Vazquez (Rey); Lucy Moreno (Hermina); Mineko Mori (Mystic Woman); Luis Lemus (Sergeant); Alejandro Reyes (Manuel); Alex Cole (Guard); Joe Keyes (Officer); Tomas Leal (Monkey Owner); Luisa Huertas (Nurse); Joe Minjares (Pharmacist/Barber); Fima Noveck (Russian Leader); Eric Champnella (Stan); John Pyper Ferguson (Interrupting Henchman); Anthony Azizi (Bad News Henchman); Bryan Spicer (Unlucky Henchman).

LOS ANGELES TIMES, 4/19/97, Calendar/p. 6, John Anderson

[The following review by John Anderson appeared in a slightly different form in **NEWSDAY, 4/19/97, Part II/p. B5.]**

Although it comes under the increasingly crowded category of Why Did They Bother, "McHale's Navy" does offer an example of a movie that tries to be all things to all people. As long as they're 13 and male.

It has, and I mean it, everything: Adolescent comedy. Numerous massive explosions. A terrorist subplot. White male patriarchy. Loud Hawaiian shirts. And let's not forget name recognition, even if the TV series ran only from 1962-66 and was largely forgettable. Inspired by "Sgt. Bilko" and the precursor of "F Troop" (1965-67), it starred Ernest Borgnine as a Navy commander chasing both Japanese ships and whatever illicit profits he and his cohorts could make in the Pacific Theater of World War II.

A lot has changed in McHale's Navy. For one thing, McHale's not in the Navy. Played by the occasionally amusing Tom Arnold as a guy lost somewhere between "Animal House" and "Donovan's Reef", McHale makes his money selling beer, ice cream and girlie calendars (no nudes, because this is a family film, which is why there are so many explosions) to the real Navy personnel (real, of course, being relative) and living the life of ease on his own private island.

All of which comes to a screeching halt when Capt. Binghampton (Dean Stockwell) arrives to shake things up a la Capt. Queeg, and terrorist Tim Curry makes things hot for McHale's personal village-full of locals. Stockwell, with his voice jacked up an octave, does a passable homage to Joe Flynn, the original Binghampton. Curry, playing one more goateed villain, is the Russian Vladakov, although his accent wanders everywhere from Finland to Greece.

Other changes? Ensign Parker, originally Tim Conway, is now black and played by David Alan Grier. The toadying Lt. Carpenter is now a woman (Debra Messing). The esteemed Borgnine plays Cobra, a military bigwig with a secret identity (take a shot, you can't miss). No one calls Binghampton "Leadbottom," although if one more sailor yelled, "Hey, Skip!" at McHale, I was going to throw myself overboard.

The cast is generally as nondescript as the original, although Bruce Campbell (star of Sam Raimi's classic "Army of Darkness"), who plays Virgil, is the focal point of the movie's funniest scene, a bar fight in Havana, in a Cuba that looks like Club Med with an attitude.

One question: McHale's crew lives on San Ysidro, and the only San Ysidro I know was the site of the 1984 massacre of 21 people at a McDonald's in California. Is this a stupid joke? Or just a mistake? Either way, coming from "McHale's Navy," it isn't all that surprising.

NEW YORK POST, 4/18/97, p. 45, Larry Worth

TV's service sitcom "McHale's Navy" remained an American staple for four glorious years. The current big-screen update won't keep Americans' interest for four days.

Yes, end credits confirm that the production is based on the '60s classic. But fans will be hard-pressed to find connections.

Rather than sending up its small-screen predecessor (a la "The Brady Bunch Movie") or building on its humor (a la "Wayne's World"), this retooled '90s version opts for a new slant. It puts supposedly exciting action-adventure sequences and heart-tugging tableaus alongside their alleged yuks. Predictably, It's a lethal combo.

Of course, the first tip-off for disaster comes with Tom Arnold stepping into Ernest Borgnine's waterlogged wingtips as the smart-talking leader of a company of goofballs. So when McHale's PT73 is blown up after 35 minutes, his apparent death seems a mercy kill.

No such luck. Arnold resurfaces to confirm that—in the wake of "The Stupids," "Carpool" and "Big Bully"—his "True Lies" success was a fluke. Here, his girth again outweighs his talent.

But blame should be shared with director Bryan Spicer and an unintelligible screenplay. For instance, the introduction of an East German terrorist (eyeballpopping Tim Curry) in the Caribbean setting makes less sense than the subplot about a boys' baseball team.

Aside from embarrassing French Stewart, David Alan Grier, Bruce Campbell, Debra Messing and Dean Stockwell (aping Joe Flynn's blustery Captain Binghampton), the saddest moments belong to Borgnine as a high-ranking officer. Having had the good sense to skip 1965's "McHale's Navy Joins the Air Force," why jump aboard this sinking ship?

No one would deny that the series left viewers doubled over. This version may do the same, but the cause is now no laughing matter.

Also reviewed in:
NEW YORK TIMES, 4/19/97, p. 14, Stephen Holden
VARIETY, 4/21-27/97, p. 60, Leonard Klady

MEET WALLY SPARKS

A Trimark Pictures release in association with Largo Entertainment. *Producer:* Leslie Grief, Elliot Rosenblatt, and Harry Basil. *Director:* Peter Baldwin. *Screenplay:* Rodney Dangerfield and Harry Basil. *Story:* Harry Basil. *Director of Photography:* Richard H. Kline. *Editor:* Raul Davalos. *Music:* Michel Colombier. *Choreographer:* Charles Picerni. *Sound:* Stephen Halbert. *Casting:* Fern Champion and Mark Paladini. *Production Designer:* Bryan Jones. *Art Director:* Steve Karman. *Costumes:* Alexandra Welker. *Stunt Coordinator:* Charles Picerni. *Running time:* 105 minutes. *MPAA Rating:* R.

CAST: Rodney Dangerfield (Wally Sparks); Debi Mazar (Sandy Gallo); Cindy Williams (Emily Preston); Burt Reynolds (Lenny Spencer); David Ogden Stiers (Gov. Floyd Preston); Alan Rachins (Judge Randall Williams).

LOS ANGELES TIMES, 2/3/97, Calendar/p. 6, John Anderson

[The following review by John Anderson appeared in a slightly different form in NEWSDAY, 2/3/97, Part II/p. B7.]

Roseanne. Geraldo. Rolanda. Sally Jessy.
Bob Saget. Jerry Springer. Richard Bey. Tony Danza.
Burt Reynolds. Stuttering John. Morton Downey Jr.
Donner. Cupid. Michael Bolton.

But ya know ... Rodney Dangerfield never gets any respect. And considering the people he's hanging out with in this movie, it's no surprise.

But then again, there may be a method to his madness. If you're going to star in a movie as bad as "Meet Wally Sparks"—the most inept collection of hoary gags, stale slapstick routines and baggy-pants comedy since the last "Police Academy" debacle—then why not drag every other tasteless hack on stage and screen down with you?

Dangerfield, goggle-eyed and ready to tip over, is Wally Sparks, prototypal trash-talk TV star and stunted adolescent. He incurs the wrath of advertisers (which seems unlikely) for hosting programs about lesbian alien Elvis impersonators and "Sex After 10 Years of Marriage—Should the Wife Know About It?" He also becomes the target of a Southern governor (David Ogden Stiers), whose reelection bid becomes tied to Sparks and his show. The fate of a nation lies in the balance.

What ensues, of course, is a creaky plot about cross-cultural collision and the eventual armistice between fundamentalist rigidity and media licentiousness. Also, one long Dangerfield stand-up routine virtually unencumbered by narrative.

Make no mistake: Like Wally Sparks himself, there is no redeeming social value inherent in this debut feature by Peter Baldwin, who is apparently—and successfully—shedding whatever wholesomeness has attached itself to him by virtue of his work on "The Wonder Years," "Newhart" and "Family Ties." What we get here is comedy of the frenetic phallic or flatulent variety.

Dangerfield is Dangerfield, an acquired taste; "Wally Sparks" is nowhere near his career-defining work in, let's say, "Caddyshack," but he's a known commodity. What's surprising is how many others should be caught up and demolished by this sweeping wave of excremental nonsense. Stiers, Cindy Williams, Debi Mazar, Lesley Anne Down, all supporting actors of some note. But then, so is Dangerfield. What "Wally Sparks" really needed was a star. And while I never thought I'd ever say this, what Wally really could have used was a Chevy Chase.

NEW YORK POST, 2/1/97, p. 21, Bill Hoffmann

Rodney Dangerfield is an absolute scream as a sex-crazed tabloid talk-show host in the low-brow, shaggy-dog comedy "Meet Wally Sparks."

Forget the plot, which is about as lame as they come. The whole show is Rodney—and when he's on, which is most of the time, he's hot as a pistol.

This is Dangerfield doing his classic stand-up—with the emphasis on sex, sex and more sex.

With eyes bugged out and pants often at ankles, the 75-year-old comic takes no prisoners as he cheerfully rattles off irresistible one-liners, such as:

"I saved a girl from being attacked last night—I changed my mind!" and "My dog's named Egypt because every room he visits he leaves a pyramid!"

It doesn't matter if a joke falls flat—he's got a million more of 'em.

Dangerfield is Wally Sparks, a leering but lovable TV chatmeister whose gross gabfest goes far beyond Sally Jessy Raphael, Geraldo Rivera or Jerry Springer (who appear in cameos ripping Sparks' cheesy act).

The network boss (Burt Reynolds) wants Wally off but gives him a week's reprieve to clean up his act. This leads him to a party thrown by a stuck-up Southern governor (David Ogden Stiers), where all hell breaks loose.

It's classic slapstick and staccato-speed schtick. Is it a good movie? No. But neither were most of those churned out by Abbott and Costello. And who cares? It's great to have Rodney back doing what he does best—keeping us in stitches.

Also reviewed in:
NEW YORK TIMES, 2/1/97, p. 15, Stephen Holden
VARIETY, 2/3-9/97, p. 43, Leonard Klady

MEN IN BLACK

A Columbia Pictures release of an Amblin Entertainment production in association with MacDonald/Parkes productions. *Executive Producer:* Steven Spielberg. *Producer:* Walter F. Parkes and Laurie MacDonald. *Director:* Barry Sonnenfeld. *Screenplay:* Ed Solomon. *Story:* Ed Solomon. *Based on the Malibu Comic by:* Lowell Cunningham. *Director of Photography:* Don Peterman. *Editor:* Jim Miller. *Music:* Danny Elfman. *Music Editor:* Ellen Segal. *Sound:* Peter F. Kurland and (music) Shawn Murphy. *Sound Editor:* Skip Lievsay. *Casting:* David Rubin and Debra Zane. *Production Designer:* Bo Welch. *Art Director:* Thomas Duffield. *Set Decorator:* Cheryl Carasik. *Set Designer:* Sean Haworth, Lawrence A. Hubbs, Marco Rubeo, and Patrick M. Sullivan, Jr. *Special Effects:* Peter M. Chesney. *Visual Effects:* Eric Brevig. *Animation Supervisor:* Rob Coleman. *Costumes:* Mary E. Vogt. *Make-up:* Kathrine James. *Special Make-up Effects:* David Le Roy Anderson. *Make-up (Alien Effects):* Rick Baker. *Make-up (Will Smith):* Laini Thompson. *Stunt Coordinator:* Brian Smrz. *Running time:* 113 minutes. *MPAA Rating:* PG-13.

CAST: Tommy Lee Jones (K); Will Smith (J); Linda Fiorentino (Laurel); Vincent D'Onofrio (Edgar); Rip Torn (Zed); Tony Shalhoub (Jeebs); Siobhan Fallon (Beatrice); Mike Nussbaum (Gentle Rosenberg); Jon Gries (Van Driver); Sergio Calderon (Jose); Carel Struycken (Arquillian); Frederic Lane (INS Agent Janus); Richard Hamilton (D); Kent Faulcon (1st Lt. Jake Jensen); John Alexander (Mikey); Keith Campbell (Perp); Ken Thorley (Orkin Man); Patrick Breen (Mr. Redgick); Becky Ann Baker (Mrs. Redgick); Sean Whalen (Passport Officer); Harsh Nayyar (News Vendor); Michael Willis (Cop in Morgue); Willie C. Carpenter (Police Inspector); Peter Linari (Tow Truck Driver); David Cross (Morgue Attendant); Charles C. Stevenson, Jr. (MIB Agent Bee); Boris Leskin (Cook); Steve Rankin and Andy Prosky (INS Agents); Michael Goldfinger (NYPD Sergeant); Alpheus Merchant (Security Guard); Norma Jean Groh (Mrs. Edelson); Bernard Gilkey (Baseball Player); Sean Plummer and Michael Kaliski (First Contact Aliens); Richard Arthur (2nd First Contact Alien); Debbie Lee Carrington (Alien Father); Verne Troyer (Alien Son); Mykal Wayne Williams (Scared Guy).

CHRISTIAN SCIENCE MONITOR, 7/11/97, p. 12, David Sterritt

[*Men in Black* was reviewed jointly with *Contact*; see Sterritt's review of that film.]

LOS ANGELES TIMES, 7/1/97, Calendar/p. 1, Kenneth Turan

Go ahead, admit what you've always suspected. A certain percentage of people met in daily life are so strange, so out-and-out weird, they have to be aliens from another universe. Now, at last, comes a major motion picture that dares to tell you it's all true.

Wised-up and offhandedly funny, "Men in Black" introduces us to the super-secret government agency, known as MiB for short, that makes those aliens toe the line. Starring the inspired pairing of Tommy Lee Jones and Will Smith, "Men in Black" is a genially twisted riff on the familiar alien invaders story, a lively summer entertainment that marries a deadpan sense of humor to the strangest creatures around.

Based on obscure comic-book material, "Men in Black" has maintained the energy and sass of the form while taking on, in Ed Solomon's screenplay, a hipster attitude that extends to the protagonists' ever-present black suits and the Ray-Ban sunglasses they always wear.

Barry Sonnenfeld is an excellent director for this point of view, and "Men in Black" is a blend of the strengths of his previous films, the knowing humor of "Get Shorty" and the visual razzmatazz of "The Addams Family." And Sonnenfeld also oversaw the smooth blending of the different comic styles of the picture's two leads.

Jones, as his dead-on reading of the most memorable line in "The Fugitive" revealed, has a definite flair for gruff, acerbic humor. His Agent K is a no-nonsense government operative who suddenly shows up at a routine Border Patrol investigation of a suspicious truck near the Texas-Mexico line. One of its passengers, it turns out, has come from a lot farther than Cuernevaca.

In the meantime, James Edwards (Smith), a New York City cop with a glib, engaging cockiness, is doing his best to chase down a suspicious person with the unnerving, practically extraterrestrial, ability to just about leap tall buildings in a single bound.

Though MiB boss Zed (Rip Torn) is worried about Edwards' insouciance, K admires his perseverance and is soon recruiting the cop to sever all human contact and join "the best of the best of the best" as Agent J. But not before a whole lot of explaining is taken care of.

Unbeknownst to most people, the planet Earth has volunteered its services as a safe zone where political refugees from other galaxies can live in peace, "kind of like Casablanca without Nazis," in K's helpful phrase. Mostly they're law-abiding citizens, but MiB is around to hold the line when they turn rogue, which means using outlandish weaponry on some pretty weird individuals.

A good deal of the fun of "Men in A Black" is joining Agent J as he gets acquainted with the variety of wacky aliens masquerading as humans that form K's beat. Created by four-time special-effects Oscar winner Rick Baker, with an assist from Industrial Light & Magic, these include beings that sprout new heads like weeds, intergalactic emperors tiny enough to live in hollowed-out skulls and much larger and more formidable beings.

Though its charm is in its attitude and premise (and Danny Elfman's rousing score), "Men in Black" does have a serviceable plot that kicks in when a rusty flying saucer crash-lands in a rural area.

Out comes an unseen-for-now creature who promptly rips off (literally) the ill-fitting skin of a local resident named Edgar (Vincent D'Onofrio) and lurches around Manhattan looking for the Arquillian galaxy, one of the treasures of the universe. That search involves considerable mayhem, which is where the boys make contact with the city's deputy medical examiner, mistress of sangfroid Dr. Laurel Weaver (Linda Fiorentino).

"Men in Black" is set in New York at the suggestion of its director, a native son, and that sets up inventive use of such landmarks as the Guggenheim Museum, the old World's Fair grounds in Queens and the Battery Park vent room for the Holland Tunnel, plus the expected jokes about what percentage of cabbies are not of this Earth.

Hard to ignore because it's partly unexpected is the film's slime factor. "Men in Black" has periodic moments of gross-out humor that will not be to everyone's taste, and when Edgar the invader finally reveals himself, he turns out to be more disturbing and off-putting than the film's genial tone would have you expect.

But mostly what you get with "Men in Black" is the opportunity to spend some quality time with the Kings of Cool in a world where inconvenient memories get erased and supermarket tabloids offer the most reliable alien tips. It's not the traditional world where only the bad guys wore black, but you already knew that, didn't you?

NEW YORK, 7/7/97, p. 53, David Denby

In *Men in Black*, Tommy Lee Jones says outrageous things in his rapid, matter-of-fact manner, his tone implying that he alone is in touch with reality. Yet the reality that Jones is in touch with is so strange that he seems to us like the greatest hipster who ever lived. Barry Sonnenfeld, the former cinematographer who directed the *Addams Family* movies and *Get Shorty,* has gone big-budget without losing his wits. In this inventive and sometimes hilarious summer-season spectacle, Jones, dressed in funereal black, plays a government agent devoted to monitoring aliens in the United States. Aliens? The Mexicans who cross the Rio Grande? No, people like *that* Jones lets into the country with a few welcoming words of Spanish. The aliens he monitors are exraterrestrials who have been landing here since the sixties and who have often taken slightly strange-looking human forms—fitting right into New York, say. That guy down the street with the big jaw and the funny gait—he's one of them. Many of the aliens pad around the Village harmlessly.

They're here, all right, but unlike the killers in *Independence Day* and the pods in *Invasion of the Body Snatchers,* they aren't taking over. In truth, they're a manageable problem most of the time. Some of them are famous political figures or movie stars (it's a good laugh when we see their faces put up on a board); some, still in space-creature form, even work in Jones's home office in New York—those little crawly guys hanging out at the coffee machine and gossiping like crazy. The humor of *Men in Black* comes right out of Tommy Lee Jones's everything-is-normal personality: The extraordinary is treated as routine business. (When Jones hears an extraterrestrial has announced that the world is coming to an end, he asks, without skipping a beat, "Did he say when?" A civil-service worker, after all, needs precise information.) Jones rides herd on the aliens, shakes some of them down for information, visits the morgue—all the clichés of cop and G-man movies get put to use as far-out comedy. Jones recruits Will Smith from the NYPD as a new agent and leaves him to handle the human wife of an alien, who is giving birth in the back of a car somewhere in Jersey. Sonnenfeld poses Tommy Lee in the foreground of the shot and lets him rattle on, while deep in the background, maybe 30 feet away, Will Smith, wrapped in giant tentacles, gets flipped around like a toy by the creature that has just emerged front the womb.

There's usually plenty of fantasy in the summer season, but very little play; Sonnenfeld, working with Ed Solomon, who adapted the Lowell Cunningham comic book, likes to put on a magic show. Everything in *Men in Black* is a bit off, and most of the surprises have a charge of strangeness. Perhaps Jones and Smith get slimed by exploding creatures once too often, but the rest of the jokes are goofy and fresh. As we learned in *The Addams Family,* Sonnenfeld also likes to mix the human and the creaturely together; he turns the macabre into farce. Rick Baker, the great makeup-effects designer, works here with his usual ferocious skill but with a new spirit of gothic wit that he may have picked up from Sonnenfeld. Vincent D'Onofrio, playing a back-country primitive—not an alien but one of God's creatures—gets swallowed by a visitor (a giant cockroach, I believe), which then takes over D'Onofrio's skin; the trouble is, the alien doesn't quite fit inside. Playing this new hybrid thing, D'Onofrio staggers around like Frankenstein's monster, his limbs jerking suddenly, his mouth and jaw askew, his bulk shifting uneasily underneath his clothes. The character suggests Kafka in reverse: A cockroach awoke from uneasy sleep one day and found himself a man.

The roach in human form is determined to destroy the world for some reason I never quite understood, and only the men in black can stop him. By the middle of the picture, Will Smith, doing his street-smart thing, has pulled even with Jones. Arching his elegant eyebrows (they play off the Dumbo ears: Smith's face is a visual joke in itself), Smith gets to engage in sex badinage with Linda Fiorentino's mortician, who has a thing for dead bodies with strangely alien insides. *Men in Black* is a successful absurdist fiction. When Jones wants to find out what's really going on in the world, he reads the supermarket tabloids. All those UFO spottings, those freakish occurrences, the two-headed babies, the mysterious disappearances and miraculous returns ... Right, you guessed it: The tabs have been telling the truth all along. *Men in Black* is as clever and knowing a large-scale entertainment as we are likely to get this season.

NEW YORK POST, 7/1/97, p. 33, Michael Medved

"Men in Black" features nifty special effects, a funny script, a tangy Danny Elfman score, formidable star power and a sensational trailer. Why then, is it so difficult to feel excited about its release?

Partly because nearly everything worth watching in this movie has already been displayed in that action-packed trailer, and partly because convincing characterization—that elusive element of humanity—is so sorely lacking.

No one expects a midsummer thrill-ride movie (from Spielberg's thrill factory at Amblin Entertainment, no less) to approximate Chekhov in its meditations on the human condition, but is it really too much to ask that people in the film should seem as real and compelling as, say, the personalities in "Independence Day"?

In last summer's blockbuster, Will Smith played a jet jockey who came across as swaggering, heroic, witty and captivating, but here his part is a smug cipher with no visible motivation, and whose juvenile jokes seem much less amusing than his smirking would suggest.

Smith's anemic performance leaves crucial empty space at the center of "Men in Black" that is never entirely filled by the movie's formidable assets—including Tommy Lee Jones in precisely the sort of role as a stictly business, dedicated professional that won him his Oscar in "The Fugitive."

Here he plays a veteran agent for a super-secret, quasi-governmental operation charged with monitoring and regulating the few thousand aliens who have come to Earth, taken on superficial human form and live in our midst—with Newt Gingrich, Sylvester Stallone and Dennis Rodman, the film suggests, counted among them.

Jones and his fellow Men in Black (including the chief of operations, Rip Torn) face their biggest challenge when a deadly intergalactic bug crashes his saucer in upstate New York, takes over the dead body of a boorish farmer (the scene-stealing Vincent D'Onofiio, in a brilliant performance aided by stunningly effective makeup), and then refuses to play by the established rules, threatening all life on Earth.

As the MiB do their best to overcome this dire threat, Jones tries to train a cocky New York City cop (Smith) as his new partner, and they repeatedly cross paths with an increasingly suspicious (and seriously sexy) city pathologist (Linda Fiorentino).

Director Barry Sonnenfeld ("Get Shorty" and both "Addams Family" movies) possesses an energetic gift for dark comedy, and "Men in Black" offers its share of laughs.

There's also a wonderfully original chase scene through the Queens-Midtown Tunnel and a clever, spectacular climax which, in contrast to this summer's other blockbusters, constitutes a genuine highlight rather than letdown.

The aliens come in a dazzling array of shapes and sizes, but it's not necessarily a good sign when a movie's cunningly constructed, briefly glimpsed interstellar insects and reptiles come across as so much more intriguing and substantive than its human personalities.

NEWSDAY, 7/1/1979 Part II/p. B2, Jack Mathews

Let me ask you skeptics a question: What if the headlines you see in the supermarket tabloids—you know, "Man Eaten by Bench in Central Park!" "Farmer Finds Live Baby in Watermelon!" "Cheating Hubbie Frank Gifford Says 'Aliens Made Me Do It!'"—were true?

It's a nifty premise for a science-fiction comedy and Barry Sonnenfeld's "Men in Black," adapted from a little-known comic strip, could provoke the most outrageous headline of the summer: "Imaginative Movie Released by Hollywood!"

With special effects from George Lucas' Industrial Light and Magic, and fabulous character and creature designs by Oscar-winning makeup whiz Rick Baker, "Men in Black" offers an inventively loopy, surprise-filled alternative to the other $100-million pictures exploding on screens.

The film stars Tommy Lee Jones as Agent K, a well-traveled veteran of a super-secret government agency whose mandate is to find the illegal aliens in our midst. Not border jumpers, but aliens who arrive on spaceships, snatch bodies and cause the kind of subversive mayhem that, unchecked, can bring about the end of the world—just as the tabloids predict.

Jones teams up with Will Smith, a feisty young cop he recruits to train as Agent J, his eventual replacement. Together, they set out to uphold the agency's motto, "To Protect the Earth From the Scum of the Universe." After encounters with "Beetlejuice"-like aliens, J and K focus their attention on the virulent Edgar Bug (Vincent D'Onofrio), an ambitious alien who inhabits the rapidly decaying body of the farmer who happened onto his wreck. The world is at stake as Edgar lumbers into Manhattan, in search of the diamond crucial to his plan, and only J and K, dressed like the Blues Brothers, can stop him.

Sonnenfeld, an award-winning cinematographer before directing "The Addams Family" and "Get Shorty," has the perfect dead-pan touch for "Men in Black." His characters seem to be both dedicated to their tasks and in on the joke. When K walks into an agency coffee room, and carries on a conversation with a clutch of gremlin-size friendly aliens, Jones' offhand manner gives the whole surreal scene an added layer of whimsy.

K and J make a familiar cop team, the wily veteran and the rambunctious rookie, and Jones and Smith play well off each other. D'Onofrio is very funny behind his "Dawn of the Dead" makeup, and Rip Torn has some fun as Zed, the no-nonsense agency chief. There's also good work from Linda Fiorentino as Laurel, the sharp medical examiner who keeps discovering alien innards in the corpses sent to her, only to have her memory of them erased before she can sound the alarm.

There's a lot of fancy hardware on display, but the trickiest gadget of all is a chrome-plated, cordless phone-size object that erases someone's short-term memory. You see, MiB agents are always among us, ferreting out and destroying aliens, but to stave off general panic, they erase the memories of eyewitnesses. Inevitably, a few eyewitnesses escape the aim of the memory erasers, thus those occasional scoops in the supermarket tabs.

"Men in Black" is very original, completely silly and loads of fun. Unlike the vacuous "Batman & Robin," Sonnenfeld's film is exactly what a comic-book movie should be. Tell your friends at the supermarket.

SIGHT AND SOUND, 8/97, p. 47, Mark Kermode

One night, while busting a truckload of illegal Mexican immigrants, US state troopers are overruled in their arrest by two mysterious government agents who swiftly identify a disguised extraterrestrial named "Mikey' among the foreign party. Startled, Mikey attacks and is shot dead by agent K, whose ageing partner D realises that he has finally grown too slow for his job. Using a high-tech memory eraser, K blanks the troopers' memories of the encounter, and then erases his former partner's memory of his entire career.

In Upstate New York a flying saucer deposits an alien who removes and dons the skin of wife-baiting hick named Edgar. In New York, athletic cop James Edwards pursues an agile fugitive whose space-age weapon dematerialises. Racing to the top of a tall building, the fugitive (an alien) predicts the end of the world before throwing himself to the ground below. At Police headquarters, Edwards' report provokes derision from all except morgue technician Laurel, but K's unexpected arrival wipes all their memories except Edwards'. K enlists Edwards' help to identify the alleged weapon from a barrage of toys being sold by local extraterrestrial store owner Jeebs and then wipes Edwards' memory. Impressed by the new recruit, K has Edwards recruited by the MiB, a top-secret agency policing alien activity on earth. Edwards becomes K's new partner, and is given the name J. When two friendly aliens attempt to leave New York in a hurry, K's fears are aroused.

Following a story in a tabloid newspaper, K and J interview Edgar's wife, erase her memory, and begin to track the alien in Edgar's skin back to Manhattan, where he has committed a murder in a restaurant. During Laurel's post-mortem examination of Edgar's prey, K and J discover a tiny alien, whom K recognises as a high-ranking extraterrestrial. The tiny alien tells them to search for a galaxy on "Orion's belt" before expiring. Meanwhile, an interstellar force threatens to destroy the earth if the aforementioned galaxy is not returned safely. Understanding that scale is relative, K and J trace the galaxy (which Edgar is also after) to a pendant hanging from the collar of the tiny extraterrestrial's pet cat, Orion.

As their various paths converge, K, J and Laurel race against the clock to retrieve the galaxy and prevent the earth's destruction. A lengthy chase climaxes in a bout of close physical combat with Edgar's now bug-like form. In the course of the battle, K allows himself to be swallowed whole by the bug-alien to retrieve his gun, an experience which convinces him that he, too, has grown tired of working for the MiB. Having destroyed the bug and retrieved the galaxy, K asks J to wipe his entire career memory. Some time later, J and newly recruited MiB agent Laurel spy a tabloid paper headline telling of K's emergence from a lengthy coma, and subsequent reunion with his childhood sweetheart.

Far and away the most consistently impressive of this year's summer blockbusters, *Men in Black* is a hugely enjoyable romp which demonstrates that spectacular special effects and whiz-bang visuals need not preclude witty, intelligent screenwriting or engaging characterisation. Having served as a director of photography on such visually arresting projects as the Coen Brothers' *Blood Simple* and *Raising Arizona* before directing the two effects-heavy *Addams Family* features, Barry Sonnenfeld is clearly relaxed and confident enough to be able to orchestrate the on-screen pyrotechnics efficiently, without letting them dominate or overshadow the drama. It's a tribute to his even-handed direction that the *Bill and Ted* films' screenwriter Ed Solomon's script retains such prominence, lashing together elements of sci-fi comic-book satire and 60s spy-television chic with enthusiasm and ease. Incorporating the same brand of hip, dry humour that made *Get Shorty* such a jazzy treat, *Men in Black* nods its head towards such disposable cultural landmarks as *The Man from U.N.C.L.E.* in a manner which is both mockingly modern and winningly cool.

To this end, the picture benefits too from tapping into an unlikely chemistry between Will Smith and Tommy Lee Jones, both of whom riff merrily on Solomon's abrasively affectionate odd-couple dialogue with cocky charm. Smith in particular continues to impress as a rising star whose experience in the areas of television and music video have expanded, rather than diluted, his ample screen talents. While *Independence Day* established him as a quirky ensemble player who could hold his own amidst lavish special effects, *Men in Black* sees him blossoming into a fully fledged leading man, blessed with genuine star quality, oodles of charm, and a smart sense of comic timing which perfectly complements his obvious physical assets.

Jones, meanwhile, has one of the few faces whose granite-like features can allow him to deliver lines like "Put up your hands, and all of your flippers" without cracking so much as a smirk, but which still retains enough mobile sensitivity to suggest genuine pathos when remembering his lost childhood love. He can also downshift into red-neck parody when the moment demands, as in one wonderful scene in which he ploughs his turbo-charged jet-car through a tunnel-bound traffic jam with Elvis' chugalug version of Chuck Berry's 'Promised Land' blaring from the car stereo. "Elvis didn't die," he later assures his new partner, "he just went home." In anybody else's mouth, it would be a cheap and corny Kit Kat-advertisement gag, but delivered in Tommy Lee's seen-it-all drawl, the claim takes on such a bizarre sincerity that it achieves a seriousness which is profoundly comic.

Only the imposing Linda Fiorentino gets somewhat lost in the heady mix—we could well have tolerated more of her spikily incisive and spike-heeled mortician, and indeed *Men in Black*'s final coda suggests that the probable sequels may pursue this avenue. In a market-place increasingly dominated by empty spectacle, the promise of such a continuing franchise spicing up next summer's slate of blockbusters is enticing indeed.

TIME, 6/30/97, p. 65, Richard Corliss

[*Men in Black* was reviewed jointly with *The Lost World: Jurassic Park;* see Corliss' review of that film.]

VILLAGE VOICE, 7/8/97, p. 69, J. Hoberman

Who says we don't live in the Land of the Free? The choice this July 4th weekend is between two mega-million buddy-buddy action-packed fever dreams, both celebrating precisely the sort of clandestine guv'mint shenanigans we're all supposed to fear and loathe in waking life.

What's more, neither of the movies is half bad. So, okay, patriots: you can elect to watch men-in-black Tommy Lee Jones and Will Smith battle state-of-the-art interstellar dung beetles or, alternatively, opt to see manic doppelgängers John Travolta and Nicholas Cage switch identities mid movie and face off against each other, undercover FBI guy versus master terrorist. The former spectacle, directed by Barry Sonnenfeld, is suavely understated; the latter, by John Woo, is relentlessly over-the-top.

Timed, like the upcoming *Contact,* to coincide with the golden anniversary of the Roswell Incident, Sonnenfeld's *Men in Black* takes its premise from an obscure comic book to parody the Roswell-popularizing *X Files*. Ridiculously cool Tommy Lee Jones is a top field operative in an extraterrestrial immigration agency that's based in the air shaft of the Brooklyn Battery Tunnel (and financed by the patents for such alien technologies as the microwave and liposuction). His job is to protect our borders by unmasking the slime creatures hiding inside Mexican illegals as well as to monitor the sizable population of resident E.T.s who, unbeknownst to all but a few, already walk among us.

Sound metaphoric? Something more than a hack and less than an auteur, Barry Sonnenfeld has a knack for the civilized evisceration of promising genre junk. Devil-worshiping premise aside, his Addams Family flicks contained nothing more subversive than the title *Addams Family Values,* while the undeniably genial *Get Shorty* was a prime example of Tarantino fire. Given its humongous budget and baroque special-effect violence, *Men in Black is* beyond proficient and, at times, even engagingly offhanded in its throwaway sight gags. But, like all of Sonnenfeld's films, it's a bit thin, somewhat slow, and ultimately overfamiliar—a delayed echo of *Ghostbusters* (which was similarly predicated on the fun of expulsive, mucousy textures).

Like Sonnenfeld's earlier films, *Men in Black* is helped by its coherent production design—which, linked to the Jetson era, includes a prolonged riff on the 1964 World's Fair—and eccentric casting. For the first half, Rick Baker's assortment of aliens are a wildly varied bunch of geeks. Moreover, it's a relief that Jones is finally underplaying a role—his stoicism serves to ground sidekick Smith's smart-mouth yapping. Linda Fiorentino is briskly businesslike as the world's sexiest morgue attendant ("I hate the living," she remarks), while Vincent D'Onofrio gives a highly choreographed stunt perf as a corpulent yahoo taken over by a belligerent alien and all but falling out of his grungy, decomposing skin.

Sonnenfeld told *The New York Times* that his model for *Men in Black* was *Dr Strangelove* but, as usual, he's oblivious to social satire. Manhattan is the preferred dwelling place for the aliens, who are also supposed to include such out-of-town celebs as Newt Gingrich and Sylvester Stallone. The identification between E.T. and *Entertainment Tonight*—clinched by the running gag that the supermarket tabs (or "hot sheets" as Jones calls them) offer Earth's best investigative reporting—suggests a missed opportunity for the sort of critical parody that enlivened John Carpenter's anti-Reagan *They Live*. Instead, it's another round at the *Star Wars* cantina.

Also reviewed in:
NEW YORK TIMES, 7/1/97, p. C9, Janet Maslin
NEW YORKER, 7/7/97, p. 76, Antony Lane
VARIETY, 6/23-29/97, p. 93, Todd McCarthy
WASHINGTON POST, 7/2/97, p. C1, Rita Kempley
WASHINGTON POST, 7/4/97, Weekend/p. 42, Desson Howe

METRO

A Touchstone Pictures release in association with Caravan Pictures. *Executive Producer:* Mark Lipsky and Riley Kathryn Ellis. *Producer:* Roger Birnbaum. *Director:* Thomas Carter. *Screenplay:* Randy Feldman. *Director of Photography:* Fred Murphy. *Editor:* Peter E. Berger. *Music:* Steve Porcaro. *Music Editor:* Brent Brooks. *Sound:* Willie Burton and (music) Shawn Murphy. *Sound Editor:* George Watters, II *Casting:* Ellen Chenoweth. *Production Designer:* William Elliott. *Art Director:* Greg Papalia. *Set Designer:* James Claytor, Dawn Swiderski, and William R. Beck. *Set Decorator:* Jerie Kelter. *Set Dresser:* Emilio Armendia. *Special Effects:* Larry Cavanaugh. *Costumes:* Ha Nguyen. *Make-up:* Wynona Y. Price. *Make-up (Eddie Murphy):* Toy Russell Van-Lierop. *Prosthetic Make-up:* Matthew W. Mungle and John E. Jackson. *Stunt Coordinator:* Mickey Gilbert. *Running time:* 117 minutes. *MPAA Rating:* R.

CAST: Eddie Murphy (Scott Roper); Kim Miyori (Detective Kimura); Art Evans (Lieutenant Sam Baffert); James Carpenter (Officer Forbes); Michael Rapaport (Kevin McCall); Donal Logue (Earl); Jeni Chua (Debbie); Dick Bright (Bank Manager); David Michael Silverman (SWAT Officer Jennings); Denis Arndt (Captain Frank Solis); Frank Somerville (Reporter 1); Malou Nubla (Reporter 2); Carmen Ejogo (Ronnie Tate); Nino Degennaro (Repoman); Michael Wincott (Michael Korda); Val Diamond (Screaming Lady); Charleston Pierce (Ronnie's Boyfriend Greg); Paul Ben-Victor (Clarence Teal); Will Marchetti (Detective Glass); Trevor Denman (Racetrack Announcer); Joe Vincent (SWAT Captain); Corie Henninger (Jewelry Salesgirl 1); Nellie Cravens (Jewelry Customer Dotson); Danny Teal (Jewelry Manager); Karen Kahn (Jewelry Salesgirl 2); Jeff Mosley (Cable Car Brakeman); Ralph Peduto (Bail Bondsman Hawkins); James Cunningham (Postrio Waiter); C.W. Morgan (Jail Laundry Room Guard); Nick Scoggin (Property Room Sergeant Frank); Marie Villatuya (Tahitian Waitress).

LOS ANGELES TIMES, 1/17/97, Calendar/p. 1, Kevin Thomas

[The following review by Kevin Thomas appeared in a slightly different form in NEWSDAY, 1/17/97, Part II/p. B13.]

Since "Metro" stars Eddie Murphy and since it opens in a quiet week, this stale action thriller may well attract audiences who can't get enough of Murphy, or mindless, bone-crunching violence, no matter how totally uninspired and credibility-defying the circumstances.

Cast as a San Francisco police department hostage negotiator, Murphy, is his usual witty, charismatic self, which serves only to underline how inferior this film really is. There's just got to be better action scripts out there for Murphy, and in the wake of the acclaim he's accrued for, "The Nutty Professor," he ought to hold out for them.

By-the-numbers doesn't begin to describe how cliché-ridden Randy Feldman's script is. Once past a not-bad opening sequence set in a bank, in which Murphy's Scott Roper demonstrates how fearless and skilled a negotiator he is, "Metro" pretty much runs out of gas. What story there is set in motion when Roper's pal, a veteran lieutenant (Art Evans, ever-reliable), is slain. Sure enough, the enraged and grief-stricken Roper is forbidden to work on the case. But wouldn't you know, there are more twists and turns involving a vicious and elusive crook (Michael Wincott) who manages a $10,000 heist in jewelry from the venerable Shreve & Co.

There needs to be a moratorium on star policemen like Roper bursting into squad rooms like a tornado every time they enter and police captains who tell such stars they can't work on their friends' murders when we already know they will anyway.

Equally predictable is that Roper will be estranged from the woman in his life; very few movie policemen over the last 25 years have had stand-up wives or girlfriends. Since Roper's girlfriend Ronnie (Carmen Ejogo) is a San Francisco newspaper photographer, you would think that she would understand how central Roper's work is in his life. You would also think that, if she had trouble dealing with this, she'd back off at the first hint that her own life could be in danger, instead of drawing closer to him. Ejogo deserves a lot of credit for making Ronnie as plausible as she does. Not much is made of Roper's new partner, a deceptively nerdy type played affably by Michael Rapaport.

Then there's the inevitable set-piece chase scene, which in this case involves a runaway cable car—hey, it's San Francisco—and is a stunt work tour de force, but which is way out of proportion for this movie's meager material. The streets of San Francisco are strewn with so many wrecked cars over such a wide area that this catastrophe has got to be the city's worst disaster since the Loma Prieta earthquake of 1989 or maybe even the 1906 quake and fire. Yet no one ever refers to this major occurrence once it is over.

No effort has been stinted in polishing this painfully derivative picture as if it were a diamond instead of strictly paste. Director Thomas Carter keeps things moving, Fred Murphy's camera work gleams, but at three minutes short of two hours, "Metro" seems drawn-out and wearying. Well, here's something, at least: It *does* leave you mildly curious as to why the bad guy is called Michael Korda—the very name of a noted author and editor in his own right.

NEW YORK POST, 1/17/97, p. 41, Michael Medved

The newspaper ads for "Metro" (with their intriguing tag line, "Life Is a Negotiation") seem to promise a different sort of heroic cop—focusing on an expert hostage negotiator who relies on psychology, charm and the gift of gab rather than brawn or bullets.

Unfortunately, those ads are totally misleading, since Eddie Murphy's character does precious little negotiating after the movie's opening five minutes.

Instead, he busies himself with the standard pursuits of all motion picture police officers—gun fights, knife fights, fistfights, avenging dead partners, bucking superiors, conducting reckless high-speed chases, crashing countless cars, and consigning bad guys to huge, fiery explosions.

It's all terribly familiar and totally predictable—and a horrible waste of talent. The movie simply forgets (or throws away) the idea that its main character's main weapon is his mouth—just as it forgets that Eddie Murphy's chief asset is his comic genius and charisma, and not his muscle-flexing action skills as a Stallone wannabe.

The undernourished plot centers on a psychotic, brilliant and ferociously violent jewel thief (played with memorable menace and flair by Michael Wincott) who develops a personal (and improbable) vendetta with Murphy's character, hostage negotiator for the San Francisco Police Department.

The script (by Randy Feldman, who previously wrote Sylvester Stallone's "Tango & Cash") tries to give this hero some depth by making him a compulsive gambler who's flat broke and has recently been rejected by his gorgeous Afro-British girlfriend (Carmen Ejogo)—but then never explains where he gets the dough to buy that girlfriend a first-class vacation to Tahiti.

There's also the inevitable new partner (Michael Rapaport), who's initially resented and resisted by Murphy, but then becomes his indispensable best friend.

Some of the action scenes (especially a wild chase down the hilly streets of San Francisco involving a runaway cable car and more than a dozen automobiles flying through the air) are spectacularly and elaborately staged—though utterly lacking in plausibility. Director Thomas Carter (an acclaimed TV veteran whose one previous feature was the dreary melodrama "Swing Kids") is reasonably skillful at setting up this splashy nonsense but why does he need Eddie Murphy for such feats of derring-do?

The best part of the "Beverly Hills Cop" movies was their mixture of subversive wit and intense action, but "Metro" (the odd title is never explained) offers precious few laughs, keeping its star occupied by twice jumping onto speeding, out-of-control vehicles.

Traditionalists may also thrill to a ludicrous updating of the old maiden-tied-to-the-railroad-tracks scenario straight out of silent films. There's even a big, devoted, galumphing dog thrown in for good measure, but not even his adorable drooling face can add lovability to this fast-paced, slick, hyper-violent and ultimately empty and charmless film.

SIGHT AND SOUND, 5/97, p. 50, Toby Manning

San Francisco, the present. Police hostage negotiator Scott Roper is summoned to a bank heist. Events get out of hand and he ends up shooting the gunman. Afterwards, Roper's colleague, Sam Baffert, makes a routine visit to jewellery dealer, Michael Korda, but Korda murders him. Later, when Roper starts to investigate his friend's death, he is taken off the case by his boss. Calling on Ronnie, an old flame, Roper is further dispirited when Greg, her current boyfriend, shows up. Meanwhile Korda berates his slow-witted cousin Clarence for leading Baffert to him and thereby putting a major diamond smuggling operation in jeopardy. Roper is assigned a new partner, McCall, and they are called to a jewellery store hold-up engineered by Korda who tricks Roper into shooting a hostage, and then escapes. After a chase involving cable cars and automobiles, Roper and McCall finally overwhelm Korda in a parking lot.

Roper and Ronnie are re-united. Meanwhile the imprisoned Korda persuades Clarence to murder Ronnie. Roper arrives at the apartment in time to hear Ronnie's screams. He rescues her and kills Clarence. Roper visits Korda in prison to warn him off, but Korda is unrepentant, and promises he will have his revenge. Korda escapes and kidnaps Ronnie as she and Roper are packing for a holiday in Tahiti. Korda demands the stolen diamonds in exchange for the girl. Roper illicitly gets hold of the diamonds, and arrives at a dockside warehouse with McCall covering him. Ronnie is strapped to a metal cutter. Roper gives Korda the diamonds, and struggles to free Ronnie from the cutter when Korda refuses to set her free. As Korda drives away, McCall shoots him. Roper and Ronnie go to Tahiti.

The cop thriller is hardly alien territory for Eddie Murphy. He made his film debut with *48 Hrs.* in 1982, which was soon followed by *Beverly Hills Cop*, a film originally earmarked for Sylvester Stallone. Murphy is one of the few black actors who get cast as an action lead and his comic persona usually counts as much in these action films as in his comedies. *Metro*, for which Murphy is executive-producer, furthers the cause of gags and guns but aims not just for more action (it's the most physical role of Murphy's career) but also dramatic depth. This time, the familiar Murphy wiseass persona is not merely chastened by experience, he's in crisis. From the opening scene in which Roper, a virtuoso negotiator, is forced to fall back on firepower during a bank robbery hostage situation, Murphy reveals a character whose verbal facility won't do the business any more—a predicament one could ascribe to Murphy himself.

Roper's crisis finds its apotheosis in the moments when he is tricked into shooting a hostage and when his girlfriend is taken hostage. Metro conveys this sense of looming disaster in effective, if formulaic ways, with cars cracking up in the San Francisco hills and cable cars cutting loose. Murphy proves that he can carry tense scenes (his face-to-face confrontations with Korda, for instance, are fine), but the film's queasy lurches back to comedy are fainthearted and undermining to the film's psychological drama. Murphy's comic persona has, after all, never offered much in the way of complexity.

Television director Thomas Carter (*Equal Justice*) seems to have been chosen as a safe pair of hands: efficient but never exceptional, his use of locations—cavernous banks, eerily deserted dockyards—is never anything but predictable. The other performers are given little room to manoeuvre, and although Michael Wincott makes good use of his subordinate role, the fine Michael Rapaport (*True Romance; Mighty Aphrodite*) is sadly underused as McCall. The part of

Ronnie (Carmen Ejogo, who played Blinda in Dennis Potter's *Cold Lazarus*) is another fudge: initially granted a part that promises more than the usual stock love interest, she is soon reduced to a trusty victim in a low-cut dress.

TIME, 1/27/97, p. 68, Richard Corliss

The movie audience's relationship with a favorite star is like a long-term, off-and-on affair. The star seduces us, he disappoints us; after years of the same-old, we take him for granted; then he does something wonderful to win back our love. Eddie Murphy, from his explosion on *Saturday Night Live* in 1981 to his current turn in the cop drama *Metro*, has been a beguiling, exasperating beau. With his horse laugh and his wizardry at impressions, he rose to eminence as the little guy who can take charge. But he became addicted to adulation and lost the common touch. His appeal waned; the comeback attempts proved futile. Until, that is, last summer's *The Nutty Professor*.

That hit comedy—which won Murphy the year's Best Actor award from the National Society of Film Critics and, in a just world, would snag him an Oscar nomination—was like a great date with an old lover fresh from rehab. Eddie was once again cute, dazzling, working overtime to please. Relocating his strength as a mimic, he played seven characters, all brilliantly. The one unattractive figure, Buddy Love, was a wicked stretch of the Eddie Murphy personality that moviegoers had tired of: sleek, preening, abrasive, an overdog in love with itself. The other characters were marvels not just of makeup but also of comic sympathy; Sherman Klump and his pudgy, putrefactive family had humor and heart. The $130 million box-office take showed how much affection filmgoers still had for Murphy. They hoped it heralded a new Golden Age for the Golden Child.

On the evidence of *Metro*, maybe *The Nutty Professor* was less a trend than a fluke. This cop thriller bears a surface similarity to the early Eddie hits *48 HRS.* and *Beverly Hills Cop*, but it's lame and lazy, inefficient even as the sort of action machine Hollywood can tool up in its sleep. The mandatory car chase is woefully generic; it disregards the laws of physics without raising more than vagrant musings in the viewer. Why, for example, would a cable-carful of passengers be too timid to apprehend the lone bad guy while he's busy wrestling with the hero?

Murphy is Scott Roper, a San Francisco cop making up his own rules in edgy face-offs with the criminal class of the Bay Area. Roper is no Dirty Eddie; he's a negotiator who has to ingratiate himself with the malefactors before he can blow their heads off. This offers plenty of chances for Murphy-style comedy, none of which writer Randy Feldman or director Thomas Carter bothered to exploit. Except for a decent scene in which Roper mimics a white bandit as a test for his galoot partner (Michael Rapaport), there's no room for Eddie to be Eddie. It's as if Carter thought the project was a smooth vehicle that Murphy could simply ride in, when it's really a hunk-a-junk the star needed to transform.

Roper is issued a regulation villain (Michael Wincott, whose menacing baritone was used to better effect in the recent Jim Jarmusch corpse opera *Dead Man)* and a girlfriend in peril (British stunner Carmen Ejogo). A shame the star wasn't given a character to play, witty dialogue to speak or clever plot twists to unravel. But though Roper is often at gunpoint, Murphy wasn't when he agreed to make *Metro*. In his bumpy tryst with filmgoers, how long will he make us wait for another *Nutty Professor?* How long until we can love Eddie again?

VILLAGE VOICE, 1/28/97, p. 70, Laurie Stone

If only we could have gotten to know the bad guy. His name is Michael Korda—an homage to/vendetta against the writer-publisher? Played by Michael Wincott, he's cute in a dangerous, intellectual way, speaking with a Tom Waits growl and exuding a millenial-fevered disaffection à la David Duchovny. Your basic jazz-hip (Ellington is playing in his tasty boho pad) grad school dropout, could-be-a-sociopath/could-be-a-sexual-compulsive type. Alas, he's given no personal history, no reason for being homicidal. He's just an incarnation of menace that has to endure until his car blows up, a threat that could as easily have been green slime, a cyborg, or a killer virus.

Even without a raison d'être, Korda has more personality than anything else in this movie. *Metro* (to what does the title refer?), written by Randy Feldman, is like a ransom note devised out of cut-and-pasted bits from *Dog Day Afternoon, Bullitt,* and every Schwarzenegger film. There is not an original moment onscreen. Eddie Murphy plays Scott Roper, a hostage negotiator, and, as luck would have it, in the span of a week there are two big crises in San Francisco, the movie's location. Following them is an endless car-and-trolley chase up and down the city's hills, and then more senseless automobile slaughter after Korda escapes and continues to wreak havoc.

Roper is the only character we're allowed to know anything about, but he, like the movie, is a hodgepodge of plastic parts. He's wrestling with a gambling habit, trying to romance a former girlfriend, and breaking in a rookie partner, but these elements are worn like accessories. Having won back fans with *The Nutty Professor,* in which he lampooned the strutting rooster he'd become, Murphy now seems desperate to cement approval and prove he can be ol' Eddie, endearingly street and fast with the quips. He's not ol'Eddie. That guy was a kid, who really was straight from the margins—not a homeboy but authentically inside the caustic wit of black male outsideness.

In *Metro,* he looks lost and desperate. The stand-up patter that erupts from his mouth comes off like a Tourette's tic, strained, from left field. His flirting style of hammering at a woman until she gives in has curdled. Flop sweat and fear rise off this movie with a metallic tang. Having been cocksure, then chastened, Murphy doesn't know how to make comedy or something tender out of his experience. But nothing will throw an artist off his true scent more than truckling.

Also reviewed in:
CHICAGO TRIBUNE, 1/17/98, Friday/p. A, Michael Wilmington
NEW YORK TIMES, 1/17/97, p. C3, Stephen Holden
VARIETY, 1/13-19/97, p. 151, Howard Feinstein
WASHINGTON POST, 1/17/97, p. D1, Jacqueline Trescott
WASHINGTON POST, 1/17/97, Weekend/p. 38, Kevin McManus

MIDNIGHT IN THE GARDEN OF GOOD AND EVIL

A Warner Bros. release of a Malpaso production in association with Silver Pictures. *Executive Producer:* Anita Zuckerman. *Producer:* Clint Eastwood and Arnold Stiefel. *Director:* Clint Eastwood. *Screenplay:* John Lee Hancock. *Based upon the book by:* John Berendt. *Director of Photography:* Jack N. Green. *Editor:* Joel Cox. *Music:* Lennie Niehaus. *Music Editor:* Don Harris. *Choreographer:* Doris Wood. *Sound:* Willie Burton. *Sound Editor:* Alan Robert Murray and Bub Asman. *Casting:* Phyliss Huffman. *Production Designer:* Henry Bumstead. *Art Director:* Jack G. Taylor, Jr. and James J. Murakami. *Set Designer:* Jann Engel, Peter Kelly, Joseph G. Pacelli, Jr., and Cate Bangs. *Set Decorator:* Richard Goddard and John Anderson. *Special Effects:* Joe Pancake and Steve Riley. *Costumes:* Deborah Hopper. *Make-up:* Tania McComas. *Running time:* 155 minutes. *MPAA Rating:* R.

CAST: Kevin Spacey (Jim Williams); John Cusack (John Kelso); Jack Thompson (Sonny Seiler); Irma P. Hall (Minerva); Jude Law (Billy Hanson); Alison Eastwood (Mandy Nichols); Paul Hipp (Joe Odom); Lady Chablis (Chablis Deveau); Dorothy Loudon (Serena Dawes); Anne Haney (Margaret Williams); Kim Hunter (Betty Harty); Geoffrey Lewis (Luther Driggers); Richard Herd (Henry Skerridge); Leon Rippy (Detective Boone); Bob Gunton (Finley Largent); Michael O'Hagan (Geza von Habsburg); Gary Anthony Williams (Bus Driver); Tim Black (Jeff Braswell); Muriel Moore (Mrs. Baxter); Sonny Seiler (Judge White); Terry Rhoads (Assistant D.A.); Victor Brandt (Bailiff); Patricia Herd (Juror 1); Nick Gillie (Juror 20); Patrika Darbo (Sara Warren); J. Patrick McCormack (Doctor); Emma Kelly (Herself); Tyrone Lee Weaver (Ellis); Gregory Goossen (Prison Cell Lunatic); Shannon Eubanks (Mrs. Hamilton); Virginia Duncan, Rhoda Griffis, and Judith Robinson (Card Club Women); JoAnn Pflug (Cynthia Vaughn); James Moody (Mr. Glover); John Duncan (Gentleman in Park); Bess S. Thompson (Pretty Girl); Jin Hi Soucy (Receptionist); Michael Rosenbaum (George Tucker); Dan Biggers (Harry Cram); Georgia Allen (Lucille Wright); Collin Wilcox Paxton (Woman at Party); Charles Black (Alpha); Aleta Mitchell (Alphabette); Michael "Kevin" Harry (Phillip); Dorothy Kingery (Jim Williams' Sister); Amanda Kingery (Amanda, Jim Williams' Niece); Susan Kingery (Susan, Jim Williams' Niece); Ted Manson

(Passer-by); Margaret R. Davis (Ruth); Danny Nelson (Senator); Bree Luck (Woman at Club);
Ann Cusack (Delivery Woman); Jerry Spence (Hair Dresser).

CHRISTIAN SCIENCE MONITOR, 11/21/97, p. 15, David Sterritt

[*Midnight in the Garden of Good and Evil* was reviewed jointly with *The Rainmaker*; see
Sterritt's review of that film.

LOS ANGELES TIMES, 11/21/97, Calendar/p. 1, Kenneth Turan

"Midnight in the Garden of Good and Evil" boasts 2 million hardback copies in print after
spending three years on national bestseller lists, but unless you already knew those facts you'd
never guess them from the uninvolving film that Clint Eastwood has cobbled together from bits
and pieces of the original story.

It's not necessary to have read John Berendt's nonfiction book about a murder trial set amid the
brandy-soaked decadence of Savannah, Ga., to feel let down by what Eastwood and screenwriter
John Lee Hancock have created. Listless, disjointed and disconnected, this meandering two-hour,
32-minute exercise in futility will fascinate no one who doesn't have a blood relation among the
cast or crew.

But looking at the book does provide a road map that shows just how this particular accident
happened. It starts, not surprisingly, with garden-variety Hollywood hubris, because if ever a
bestseller was an unlikely candidate for a satisfying motion picture, this was it.

At its core, "Midnight in the Garden" is a Southern Gothic Arabian Nights, a charming
compilation of eccentric, unexpected and often pointless stories and characters to which the
nominal murder-mystery plot is almost incidental. What the movie has done is flip-flop the
original's components, paring down the stories and emphasizing and even adding to the book's
Perry Mason elements, which is the equivalent of clear-cutting a lush forest and asking everyone
to admire the few stumps that remain.

Though Eastwood can do wonders as a director, his minimalist tendencies are better suited to
containing overripe material like "The Bridges of Madison County." Adding his deliberate touch
to a script that has already shredded gossamer-thin material makes what should be lively and energetic flat and uninvolving.

While author Berendt lived off and on in Savannah for eight years, his film surrogate, New
York journalist John Kelso (John Cusack), is flown down on assignment for Town & Country
magazine to cover a celebrated Christmas party given by the mysterious Jim Williams (Kevin
Spacey).

A preservationist and restorer of antebellum mansions, the self-proclaimed nouveaux riche Williams is a key figure in Savannah society. A collector of "the trappings of aristocracy," he
smokes King Edward cigarillos, owns enough Faberge eggs to make a czar jealous and calls Kelso
"sport" whenever possible.

On his first night in town the journalist also meets Mandy Nichols (Alison Eastwood, the director's daughter) and Joe Odom (Paul Hipp), a pair of—dare one say it—free spirits who party
with enough intensity to convince Kelso that Savannah is "like 'Gone With the Wind' on
mescaline."

At the big Christmas bash, Kelso witnesses an altercation between Williams and Billy Hanson
("Gattaca's" Jude Law), "a walking streak of sex" (or so the book calls him). Very much the
profane and trashy street hustler, and nominally the host's part-time employee, Hanson's position
as Williams' lover becomes clearer when Williams later shoots him, he claims in self-defense,
and is charged with murder. Sensing a good story, Kelso decides to stick around and write a
book on the situation.

Unlike Berendt's position in the original as a detached observer, Kelso here is in the thick of
the story, serving as a key witness and a detective, investigating leads, finding critical evidence
and sharing information with Williams' lawyer Sonny Seiler (Jack Thompson) and his voodoo
advisor (don't ask) Minerva (Irma P. Hall). While this sounds interesting compressed into a
single sentence, dragging it out at the film's glacial pace is another story.

As what was serendipitous in "Midnight" now is plodding, so characters who were fully drawn in the book, like disgruntled inventor Luther Driggers (Geoffrey Lewis), are now reduced to shallow and eccentric cameos, brief stops on a tour bus' itinerary.

The Lady Chablis, the drag queen who plays herself in the film, presents a different kind of problem. While she is one of the book's most memorable personalities, she had no relation to the trial or anyone in it. But she's been, pardon the pun, dragged into everything here, and her weary "Birdcage" antics are given so much time she's allowed to hijack, the movie without knowing quite what to do with it.

While some of "Midnight's" difficulties, like condensing the book's four trials into one, are more or less unavoidable, others are of its own making, like contriving an unnecessary romance between Kelso and Mandy that is formidably unconvincing.

Unlike Berendt, who penetrated the normally closed inner circles of Savannah, director Eastwood (who wisely chose to turn the film's soundtrack into a tribute to native son Johnny Mercer) has not been able to find a way into this material. If the book made readers feel as if they were lifelong local residents, the movie version of "Midnight in the Garden of Good and Evil" treats us like tourists, on the outside looking in.

NEW YORK, 12/1/97, p. 120, David Denby

Playing a homosexual in *Midnight in the Garden of Good and Evil*, Kevin Spacey gives what is perhaps the straightest performance of his career—that is, the least mischievous, menacing, and ambiguous. In such films as *The Usual Suspects,* Spacey has become something of a legend—an actor's actor with uncanny skills of sinister self-effacement that somehow make him more dominating than the most flamboyant of performers. Spacey can achieve miracles by draining the obvious emotion out of lines, modulating into dry-ice sarcasm with no more than subtle inflections of his beautiful baritone. At times, he seems to be amusing himself, riffing on our credulity. The man is definitely a tease; his reserved manner can suggest depths without limit. We don't know him; we *can't* know him—that's Spacey's pride. In *Midnight,* by contrast, Spacey is a civilized, refined fellow who is very eager to appear solid through and through. He plays Jim Williams, the real-life Savannah plutocrat and antiques dealer who empties a gun into his nasty young lover (Jude Law) and goes on trial for murder. The movie, adapted from John Berendt's best-seller by screenwriter John Lee Hancock and directed by Clint Eastwood, preserves Berendt's portrait of Savannah as an odd but vibrant moss-hung backwater of the old South, a place devoted to social rituals of traditional formality and gentility—but a place that is also bursting with eccentric life beneath the surface. The eccentricity is able to flourish precisely because of the exquisite dedication to manners and propriety. Jim Williams wants to play the game by the rules and survive. His defense, in part, depends on his social standing, his friends, his reputation. Refinement is part of his armor; irony is not.

Even in this plain style, Spacey is very good, but the performance doesn't expand—his Jim Williams is always trying to convince people that he *has* no secrets, that the surface is his true nature. The movie doesn't expand, either, and perhaps it's in the nature of the material that it can't. John Berendt (who was editor-in-chief of this magazine from 1977 to 1979 and hired, among other people, me) presents himself in the book as an unencumbered New Yorker who just wanders into Savannah. Through a series of random meetings, he gets drawn into the life of the town and suddenly finds himself in the middle of a murder trial. What has made the book so popular, I think—apart from the author's skill, his great ear, his feeling for anecdote—is Berendt's spirit of relaxed tolerance, his plain, friendly affection for a rather fantastic bunch of characters. He writes like Truman Capote without the mean streak.

Midnight in the Garden of Good and Evil is a leisurely, atmospheric, and digressive movie made from a leisurely, atmospheric, and digressive book. Clint Eastwood's taste is now unimpeachable. There's nothing vulgar or forced or too explicit in the movie, and he shares and even amplifies Berendt's live-and-let-live manner (something of a change, in middle age, for a man who once used to beat up creeps and homosexuals in his movies). *Midnight,* however, suffers from a rare fault: It's a little underpowered and almost too pleased with its own easy affability. We want more concentration, a quickening of the tempo, and more insight.

Berendt's autobiographical writer figure has been given a name, John Kelso (John Cusack, charming as always), given a love interest (Alison Eastwood, Clint's appealing daughter), and made more active than the author's modest, recording "I." Kelso arrives with a specific magazine assignment—to write about Jim Williams's famous parties—and once the trial begins, he makes it clear that he's staying to write a book; he even enters into an ethically dubious arrangement with Williams and his lawyer (Jack Thompson) to share his information about the case and even help the defense, in return for access. At first, as Kelso wanders about, the movie seems a kind of sunshiny, high-style travelogue. People keep taking him by the arm and walking him past beautiful restored houses and through stunning squares with splashing fountains as they teach him local history and acquaint him with the oddities of the street people. But what was charming and ruminative in the book feels rather arbitrary and disconnected here. In part, the time scale of the two media are different: A movie always demands greater economy, a stricter, even ruthless, sense of relevance.

Berendt gives quite a bit of space to the witty black transvestite Lady Chablis, who has only a marginal connection to Jim Williams and his lover, and Eastwood uses her heavily, too—uses the real Lady Chablis (né Frank Deveau), who has a dynamite figure, arms like blades, and a richly insinuating manner sharp enough to ... well, to peel a grape. Lady Chablis grabs at her moment of cinematic glory with upraised talons: Eastwood may have been too amused (or intimidated) by her to shut her off. And, like Berendt, he indulges the black voodoo lady Minerva (Irma P. Hall), who mutters imprecations in the cemetery at night and may or may not affect the outcome of the trial with her charms and spells. I have to admit that in both versions of the material, I found Minerva a bit much.

The movie compresses four trials stretching over eight years into a single trial (dominated by Jack Thompson, the superb Australian actor doing an expert imitation of a good old boy). In the end, *Midnight* is a meditation on the unknowability of the truth. A strict accounting of justice (in the legal sense) is not possible. Spacey's Jim Williams, talking to Kelso, defends his love affair with young Billy Hanson—a stud, a tornado, a pain in the neck—with eloquent simplicity. He tried to teach the young man to make something of himself and got some comfort in return, but the boy was destructive and unmanageable. We get the sense that Williams was indeed guilty of murder but that Billy would have killed him sooner or later. Is it murder, then, or a kind of preemptive self-defense? Perhaps the mumbling Minerva speaks the truth after all. "There are no answers," she tells Kelso, in her most intelligible moment.

NEW YORK POST, 11/21/97, p. 53, Thelma Adams

Regrettably, the most authentic thing about Clint Eastwood's "Midnight in the Garden of Good and Evil" is the drag queen, The Lady Chablis.

Like the naive protagonist John Kelso (John Cusack), who arrives in Savannah and hops a red tour bus into town for a few pungent factoids about America's most romantic city, we feel like we are being taken on a guided tour of the highlights of John Berendt's best seller by a not-so-bright guide.

Screenwriter John Lee Hancock ("A Perfect World"), of necessity, must speed up Berendt's nonfiction. The book had the leisure to chat about Johnny Mercer (Savannah's famous musical son), eccentrics like the man who has horseflies leashed to his coat, or the insatiable host whose nightly house parties are thrown in the stately town homes he "appropriates."

Like the flies on the eccentric, Berendt floated above and through his narrative, appearing to surprise himself when he buzzed into the sensational murder trial of Savannah's most powerful arriviste: antiques dealer Jim Williams (Kevin Spacey).

Hancock in many ways is too faithful to the book, failing to reinvent it with a satisfying cinematic structure. The drama digresses with tableaux that give the gracious, partying locals the look of figures in Disneyland's Pirates of the Caribbean, then hastens to the central dramatic event.

Did Williams shoot his assistant/lover, hustler Billy Hanson (Jude Law) in cold blood? Journalist Kelso, on hand to cover Williams' legendary Christmas party for Town and Country magazine, suddenly shifts into investigative reporter gear.

Kelso taps drag performer Chablis (played by the transvestite him/herself, a character in the book and a shrewd self-promoter) to sound the depths of forbidden Savannah. The Yankee reporter also romances Mandy Nichols (Eastwood's daughter Alison) and accompanies Williams on a visit to voodoo priestess Minerva (Irma P. Hall). The film takes its title from these nocturnal rituals at the cemetery.

Throughout "Midnight," Eastwood's pacing is awkward, the scenes static, the characters more opaque than mysterious. The courtroom sequences that dominate the second half are poor-man Perry Mason. Because the trial drama is incoherent, Chablis' key testimony seems superfluous. She becomes another fly on a string, making a lot of noise buzzing around the story.

Eastwood, a strong director elsewhere, is well-intentioned but out of his element. He can't establish and maintain the wide cast of characters in a story that cries out for a Robert Altman or Alan Rudolph. The action sequences are rudimentary and the supernatural scenes never strike the right tone.

A tense-jawed Cusack is less charming than vacant. He delivers his backstory sorrows without conviction, he romances Mandy without heart (Alison Eastwood's Blanche Dubois accent makes us long for the subtleties of Sondra Locke).

Spacey, after an Oscar and a long run of great acting, seems lost. He doesn't wear his mustache and hairpiece; they wear him.

Eastwood's "Midnight in the Garden of Good and Evil" captures much of the plot, but little of the spell that kept Berendt's book on the best-seller list the past 3½ years.

NEWSWEEK, 12/1/97, p. 87, David Ansen

Sent to Savannah, Ga., to cover an elegant, black-tie Christmas party for Town and Country, New York writer John Kelso (John Cusack) finds himself knee deep in Southern eccentrics and embroiled in a murder case. To the horror of Savannah society, the party's "bachelor" host, Jim Williams (Kevin Spacey), is arrested for shooting his hustler lover (Jude Law). On the phone to a friend back home, the discombobulated journalist describes his Savannah experience: "It's like 'Gone With the Wind' on mescaline."

If only one could say that about Clint Eastwood's *Midnight in the Garden of Good and Evil*. The fans who have kept John Berendt's nonfiction tale on the best-seller list for more than three years may come away feeling they've seen "Perry Mason" on Valium. Eastwood and screenwriter John Lee Hancock faced a knotty problem of adaptation: what's beguiling about the book isn't the unsatisfying murder-mystery plot but the supremely odd cast of characters, the drenched-in-decadence atmosphere, the evocation of a community blissfully insulated from the mundane. Perhaps this could have been captured in a leisurely mini-series (the PBS "Tales of the City" offers a model). Eastwood's strangely lackluster 2-hour, 35-minute version feels both too long for a tensionless courtroom drama and too short to do justice to its characters.

Much of the casting, however, is dead on. Kevin Spacey's creepy, dead-eyed gentility fits the nouveau riche antiques dealer Williams like a velvet glove; Jack Thompson seems born to play the heartily charming attorney Sonny Seiler, and Cusack has the right mix of irony and intelligence to play the authorial stand-in (who has been given a lame, unnecessary romantic involvement with Alison Eastwood's colorless Mandy). One of the true treats is getting to see The Lady Chablis play her transvestite self: her salty drag-queen energy is an always-welcome distraction. Chablis gets to shine in the movie's one surefire scene, when she jeeringly misbehaves at a black debutante ball. Irma T. Hall's voodoo priestess Minerva fares less well: Eastwood's depictions of her occult cemetery rituals are hopelessly stagy.

The one crucial miscasting is Eastwood as director. He approaches the story like a tourist. He seems to think that by using real locations and casting Savannah socialites as extras that he's captured the soul of the book. What he's missed is that Berendt's "nonfiction" reads like fantasy and requires a more baroque visual style—that touch of mescaline—to transport us into this alternate reality. Anyone who hasn't read Berendt's book first may be hard pressed to understand its long-lived allure.

SIGHT AND SOUND, 3/98, p. 52, Jonathan Romney

Savannah, Georgia. Writer John Kelso arrives in town to write an article about the lavish Christmas party held by wealthy antique dealer Jim Williams. He meets assorted local characters, including fly-by-night Joe Odom and his sometime girlfriend Mandy. Shortly after the party,

Williams shoots and kills his gay lover Billy Hanson. Kelso decides to write a book about the case, and makes a deal with Williams and his attorney Sonny Seiler for co-operation. Williams takes Kelso on a graveyard excursion with voodoo practitioner Minerva.

Williams is jailed on a murder charge. Drag queen The Lady Chablis testifies in court about Billy's violent nature. She and Mandy assist Kelso on a trip to the morgue to look for clues relating to the key question of whether Williams fired at Billy in self-defence. Kelso finds key evidence, but Williams confides to him that Billy never fired at him at all. However, Seiler has found a flaw in the police's procedures and Williams' version remains a secret. Williams is acquitted, but after his release he dies of a heart attack—Billy has apparently avenged himself from beyond the grave. Kelso stays on in Savannah with Mandy.

One of the stranger aspects of John Berendt's true-crime bestseller *Midnight in the Garden of Good and Evil* is that his characters—the real citizens of Savannah, Georgia—keep asking who will play them when his book is filmed. What ought to make this adaptation fascinating is that, in some cases, the answer is: themselves. Two key figures in the book appear as themselves: the briefly glimpsed pianist Emma Kelly, and the limelight-hungry drag queen The Lady Chablis, already a media star with her own book and numerous chat-show appearances under her belt. The real lead defence attorney Sonny Seiler himself also plays the judge presiding over the Williams trial. In addition, the film was shot on Savannah locations, including Jim Williams' house and the very room in which the shooting took place.

All this raises two questions. One is: what kind of deals did Clint Eastwood have to do with Savannah and the people involved to get his film made? This is pertinent because in the book, everything seems a little too easy: John Berendt always seems to be in the right place to meet the right people and gain their confidence. His screen surrogate John Kelso, however, has to broker several compromising deals to get his story, and Lennie Niehaus' ominous chords are always there to accompany John Cusack's bemused scowl whenever he's in too deep. The second question is a more resonant one about the film's relation to truth. What does it mean, for example, that Chablis a real person whose entire *raison d'être* is to be constantly performing—plays a fictionalised version of herself, repeating lines she speaks in the book and is supposed to have said in reality? Indeed, she becomes here part of an even flashier narrative than Berendt's: previously just a star local eccentric, she is now an integral figure in the trial and Kelso's conspirator in a farcical morgue raid.

It must be said that Chablis' performance is one of the film's few compelling attractions—a non-stop appeal to the gallery, at once presumptuous and self-mocking, that marks her out as a 'natural', however inappropriate that word is. Of course, she also totally unbalances the film, which in effect is strong between three Chablis routines—her stage show, her outrageous disruption of the black debutantes' sedate cotillion, and her court appearance. It's just as well that everyone else in this world is a performer too—Berendt is at pains to point out that all Savannahians really are 'full-blown literary characters'. In a book, of course, this peculiarity of place comes across as a compelling paradox, but in a screen drama, we expect the characters to be characters, so that the extremity of the situation only really comes across when Chablis commandeers it.

Unfortunately the ontological ramifications of this extraordinary compaction of real and false layers are lost on a director as sober-sided as Eastwood—you can only imagine what the Altman of *Pret-A-Porter* might have done with this grotesque tragi-farce.

The paradoxes never emerge because the film is too concerned to arrange a compellingly messy story into a neat courtroom drama, playing fast and loose in the process: Kelso is turned from involved chronicler into implicated detective and given a listless romance with another of Berendt's bystanders, Mandy. Eastwood and screenwriter John Lee Hancock excise what makes the book breathe—more time spent with Savannah's minor players, and the political chicanery behind the case. Nor is Eastwood that interested in the minutiae of evidence procedure, which might at least have given us a touch of *Murder One*. Instead, the courtroom scenes are on the sluggish level of *Perry Mason* to which Seiler is unwisely made to allude.

The most serious casualty is the inscrutably complex accused Jim Williams, who represents all that is most unflappably play-actorish about Savannah life but who may also be psychopathic. Everything rides on the impersonation of him. Kevin Spacey puts in yet another effortlessly suave turn, suggesting deep turbulence under a glacial surface. Spacey gets the act down pat: a *nouveau riche* playing the Old Southern grandee, this Williams is a man successfully creating a cartoon of himself, tying it all up in his quizzical little tic, 'Mmm hmmm. But we are so used to Spacey playing monsters (he's in danger of becoming his generation's Anthony Perkins) that the film is content to let these connotations do all the work. The character's subtleties collapse entirely in the risible denouement, as Billy's phantom materialises sneering on the carpet. All the film's credibility vanishes in this last-minute metamorphosis into a Tale of the Unexpected.

As for the town that seems to have turned into its own theme park long before Berendt got there —well, its famous squares look lovely, but in a curiously literal, unevocative way. Berendt may have made Savannah the most exotic locale of American true fiction since Hunter S. Thompson's Las Vegas, but for all that Eastwood can do with it, you wouldn't want to live there, and it's not such a thrilling place to visit either.

TIME, 12/1/97, p. 84, Richard Corliss

John Berendt's nonfiction best seller has yet to appear between soft covers. So the film, directed by Clint Eastwood, serves as the audiovisual paperback version. It is likely to disappoint the book's acolytes and tax the patience of newcomers.

Jim Williams (Kevin Spacey) deals in antiques and other old secrets, with a suavity that beguiles the gentry. When he kills a young punk who was his lover, Williams loses a few friends but attracts the attention of a Yankee journalist (John Cusack) who becomes his fond, skeptical biographer.

Screenwriter John Lee Hancock fuses Williams' four murder trials into one but is faithful to the local fauna: the gun-waving doyen, the man who walks an invisible dog, the voodoo priestess, the man haloed by horseflies. Eastwood has cast Williams' attorney as the trial judge and, as him(her)self, the Lady Chablis, a drag queen of note—one note—in a turn that will make no one forget Jaye Davidson.

Like the way-too-wide-eyed Cusack, Eastwood lingers over these mild deviates from the norm as if they were the critter in *Alien Autopsy*. This film might have trusted more in Spacey's sly glamour, and in Williams as a wily game player to the death. Possibly his own.

VILLAGE VOICE, 12/2/97, p. 84, Amy Taubin

If you're anything of an auteurist, you'll appreciate the films of Clint Eastwood—those he's directed and those he's starred in. Eastwood has probably never made a truly great film—not even the seductive and much praised *Unforgiven*. Like John Sayles, he's overly restrained in matters of cinematic expressiveness. But taken together, his films form a serious critique of masculinity and its contradictions.

It's as part of that critique that *Midnight in the Garden of Good and Evil* is engaging for most of its 155 minutes. Of the many films of 1997 that are too long for their own good, Eastwood's adaptation of John Berendt's bestseller has the reasonable excuse. The leading character in the book is the city of Savannah, where the pace of life is slow and the punctuation of gunshots therefore more dramatic.

A novelistically plotted nonfiction, Berendt's book revolves around a shooting death. Famed Savannah antiques dealer Jim Williams was tried four times for the murder of his employee-lover Danny Hansford (Billy Hanson in the film). Williams claimed self-defense. Soon after the last trial, he died of a heart attack. (I'm not giving away anything that at least 2 million readers don't already know.) In any event, neither the book nor the film is a conventional whodunit. Rather, their fascination depends on their depictions of characters who are a lot more complicated than they might appear, in part because their sexuality is not exactly straight-arrow.

Although Berendt's book is a logical choice for Eastwood after the success of *The Bridges of Madison County* (there's safety in bestsellers), the issues involved are closer to *White Hunter, Black Heart,* Eastwood's biopic of John Huston. Like *White Hunter, Midnight in the Garden* takes a real-life situation as a jumping-off point for an exploration of the fiction of identity. As an actor and star, Eastwood has a working knowledge of how identity is constructed—how much is will, how much escapes conscious control. Eastwood's Man With No Name was as much a drag act in that sense as is the Lady Chablis.

Two of three principal characters in the film of *Midnight in the Garden* present themselves in ways that are not altogether in accord with certain facts of their existence. The Lady Chablis (played by the real Lady Chablis) lives out her fantasy of femininity, and not just when she's onstage. Though a shade too PG-13, she gives the film a jolt of energy whenever she appears.

Then there's Williams, the murder suspect (played by Kevin Spacey), who by virtue of his exquisite taste has worked his way into the upper reaches of Savannah society. Williams prides himself on passing as "old money" when in reality he was born lower middle class. He's also in the closet. No one is more surprised than he that influential Savannahians don't rally around him after he's accused. He's lived for so long as an insider, he half believes he is one.

Compared with these two, the film's leading man, as it were, is mere cardboard. Eastwood and screenwriter John Lee Hancock have transformed the relatively transparent first-person narrator of the book into an active character, a young New York journalist named John Kelso (John Cusack) who comes to Atlanta to cover Williams's party for a national magazine, happens on a juicy killing, gets involved with the locals, and even falls in love. In the novel, Berendt's evasiveness about his own sexuality was irritating enough. In its desperation to provide him with solid heterosexual credentials, the film is downright ridiculous.

Despite Jack Green's dreamy, hyperrealist cinematography, the film fails to evoke the Southern Gothic atmosphere that was so essential to the book's success. The scenes in the cemetery involving the voodoo witch Minerva (and there are a bunch of them) seem whimsical rather than spooky.

Midnight in the Garden of Good and Evil is most absorbing when Spacey is on the screen. He manages to convey—without any of his usual mugging—that Williams's seemingly effortless grace masks an extraordinary need for control and an inner chaos that the man himself cannot totally comprehend. It's this sense that subjectivity is inaccessible, not only to others but to the self, that Eastwood captures in two brief, heart-stopping sequences.

The second of them occurs during the last of three replays of the crime. To describe it would give too much away, so I'll just say that it's a moment that's as shocking as it's inevitable, and it's well worth waiting two and a half hours for. The first of them is a three-shot sequence that happens quite early in the film. We see Hanson's bloody body lying on the carpet in Williams's study. Then there's a cutaway to police activity outside the house. And then we see Williams alone, sitting stock-still on a sofa, holding a cat in his arms. It's the way Eastwood separates the shot of the dead boy from the shot of the man who killed him that lets us know that no matter what follows, we can never know what passed between these two people, that there are limits to what can be represented in words and images, and that art exists to make those limits known.

Also reviewed in:
CHICAGO TRIBUNE, 11/21/97, Friday/p. A, Michael Wilmington
NEW REPUBLIC, 12/29/97, p. 28, Stanley Kauffmann
NEW YORK TIMES, 11/21/97, p. E1, Janet Maslin
NEW YORKER, 12/8/97, p. 121, Daphne Merkin
VARIETY, 11/24-30/97, p. 63, Todd McCarthy
WASHINGTON POST, 11/21/97, p. C1, Rita Kempley
WASHINGTON POST, 11/21/97, Weekend/p. 52, Desson Howe

MIMIC

A Dimension Films release. *Executive Producer:* Michael Phillips. *Producer:* Bob Weinstein, B.J. Rack, and Ole Bornedal. *Director:* Guillermo Del Toro. *Screenplay:* Matthew Robbins. *Story:* Matthews Robbins. *Based on the short story by:* Donald A. Wolheim. *Director of Photography:* Dan Laustsen. *Editor:* Patrick Lussier. *Music:* Marco Beltrami. *Music Editor:* Stuart Goetz and Chris McGeary. *Sound:* Glen Gauthier and (music) John Kurlander. *Sound Editor:* Robert Shoup and Phil Benson. *Casting:* Billy Hopkins, Suzanne Smith, and Kerry Barden. *Production Designer:* Carol Spier. *Art Director:* Tamara Deverell. *Set Decorator:* Elinor Rose Galbraith. *Set Dresser:* Brenton Brown. *Special Effects:* Ted Ross. *Visual Effects:*

Brian M. Jennings. *Creature Design:* Rob Bottin and Tyruben Ellingson. *Creatures Created by:* Rick Lazzarini. *Costumes:* Marie-Sylvie Deveau. *Make-up:* Donald J. Mowat. *Make-up (Mira Sorvino):* Collier Strong. *Stunt Coordinator:* Branko Racki. *Running time:* 105 minutes. *MPAA Rating:* R.

CAST: Mira Sorvino (Susan Tyler); Jeremy Northam (Peter Mann); Alexander Goodwin (Chuy); Giancarlo Giannini (Manny); Charles S. Dutton (Leonard); Josh Brolin (Josh); Alix Koromzay (Remy); F. Murray Abraham (Dr. Gates); James Costa (Ricky); Javon Barnwell (Davis); Norman Reedus (Jeremy); Pak-Kwong Ho (Preacher); Glen Bang (Yang); Margaret Ma (Chinese Woman); Warna Fisher (Bag Lady); Alan Argue (Skeletal Bum); Charles Hayter (Homeless Man); Julian Richings (Workman); James Kidnie (Subway Repairman); Eve English (Homeless Woman); Bill Lasovich, Doug Jones, and Roger Clown (Long John).

LOS ANGELES TIMES, 8/22/97, Calendar/p. 20, Kenneth Turan

Imitation, "Mimic" tells us, is nature's most protective form of flattery. Flies can evolve to look like spiders, caterpillars can take on the markings of snakes. Given how hostile humans are to the insect kingdom, it's not hard to guess what bugs would imitate, if only they had the chance.

Based on a short story by Donald A. Wolheim and run through four screenwriters, "Mimic" is basically genre all the way, and much of its plotting and characterization is standard issue. But "Mimic" also has Guillermo Del Toro, a director with a gift for horror, and that makes a considerable difference.

As those familiar with Del Toro's previous work, the haunting Mexican vampire film "Cronos," already know, that gift is a disturbing thing to observe. Del Toro is an expert at the ominous, using a striking visual sense to drench his films with an atmosphere suffocatingly thick with undefined menace.

Though Del Toro must know that what is left unseen is more terrifying than what the camera reveals, the mass-market nature of "Mimic" demands a much higher gross-out quotient than the more artistic "Cronos," which won the International Critics Prize at Cannes. Still, even within the box office's insistence on off-putting sequences dedicated to making the audience squirm, Del Toro understands how to bring a sense of style to the genre's oldest tricks.

Both the film's creepy credits: sequence (done by Imaginary Forces, the outfit that did the similar work for "Seven") and its opening sequence tell the same back story: A tragic epidemic called Strickland's disease has raged across Manhattan for two years, threatening to kill an entire - generation of children.

To stop it, the Center for Disease Control's Dr. Peter Mann ("Emma's" Jeremy Northam) has asked Dr. Susan Tyler (Mira Sorvino), the usual brilliant scientist who heads the department of entomology at the American Museum of Natural History, to find a way to attack the disease's carrier, the common cockroach.

Not one to disappoint, Dr. Tyler uses genetic engineering to create a new species of superbug called the Judas breed, which takes out more roaches than the Orkin man. The epidemic is stopped and now, three years later, doctors Tyler and Mann are happily married working professionals.

Things are not so swell, however, in the dark caverns beneath the city. Strange predators have been killing people and dragging them underground, observed only by a withdrawn little boy (Alexander Goodwin of "Nobody's Fool") who works for his shoe-shining grandfather (Giancarlo Giannini). Gifted at imitating sounds and a wizard at identifying footwear, the boy is stumped by what he sees. "Mr. Funny Shoes" is the best ID he can come up with.

Meanwhile, Dr. Tyler, dubbed "the bug lady" by the media, is handed a suspicious-looking box of cornflakes by two kids out to make a buck. Inside she discovers a baby Judas bug, something that was not supposed to happen, since the breed tested 100% sterile in the lab. "They were designed to die," she tells her old prof and bug guru (F. Murray Abraham), "and they are breeding."

Determined to investigate, the two doctors enlist a young assistant (Josh Brolin) and an understandably reluctant subway cop (an emphatic and empathetic Charles S. Dutton). Everyone eventually ends up in the nasty tunnels of a dark and awful subterranean world, sucked deeper and faster than they imagined possible into an ever-unfolding nightmare.

It's evidence of Del Toro's skill at creating the ambience of dread that even during the film's horror film time lag, when the audience knows what's going on but the characters don't, he manages enough visual brio to keep us from feeling impatient.

Collaborating with Danish cinematographer Dan Laustsen, production designer Carol Spier (who works frequently with David Cronenberg) and editor Patrick Lussier, Del Toro has created a true landscape of unease for "Mimic." Even nominally neutral sights, like a hospital room filled with gauze tents, statues of saints draped in plaster and a deserted snow-covered children's playground, play as spooky in this gifted crew's hands.

In fact, the argument could be made that "Mimic" is considerably more effective before the dread creatures—enormous human-looking insects created by Rick Lazzarini, who also did the more playful Bud Frogs for the beer commercials—make their appearance.

Though he can handle it, Del Toro's heart doesn't seem to be in the out and out repulsion the bug attacks require. His gift is for the whiff of nightmare, not its more obvious components, and those with stomachs strong enough to withstand the shocks will be gratified to discover in "Mimic" an impressive horror film that has the ways and means to scare and scare again.

NEW YORK, 9/1/97, p. 72, David Denby

I suppose almost anything is fair in a horror movie, but really, how low do filmmakers have to sink in order to put children in jeopardy from giant cockroaches? In *Mimic*, directed by Guillermo del Toro, two little boys like to sell the strange insects that they find in New York to the "bug lady"—an entomologist (Mira Sorvino) who once genetically engineered a special cockroach in order to fight some other disease-carrying roaches. The boys wander around subways looking for some really big ones, and that's when they run into trouble. *Mimic* is set in New York, mainly underground—a vast, dark, wet network of tunnels, crawlways, and abandoned rooms. It is a netherworld, all muck and yuck, with huge pullulating nests yielding Sorvino's creatures, which have now evolved, very rapidly, into predators.

The bugs themselves are rather grand. At full height, they stand in caped and courtly black, their claws brought together in what appears to be the two halves of a face—a human face. They are, you see, mimicking their most serious predators—us. Hence the movie's title. There are the usual stern, philosophical remarks from authorities about the hubris of man, the arrogance of science, and so on, but for all the solemn talk, this movie partakes of the eternal stupidity of horror films, in which characters back away in the dark from one menace only to be attacked by another. Del Toro, who is Mexican, does not hesitate to use Catholic symbolism for creepy effect (for some reason, the creatures hole up in an abandoned church).

I'm not sure what such attractive and talented young actors as Mira Sorvino and Jeremy Northam are doing in this junk. *Mimic* gets the job done, I suppose, yet despite the A-level cast and technical crew (Rob Bottin did the crawlers), there isn't a touch of poetry, and as far as this bug-hater is concerned, a horror film without beauty is like a horse race without Thoroughbreds.

NEW YORK POST, 8/22/97, p. 43, Michael Medved

Now that the politicians have totally cured New York's crime problem, the city must confront a formidable new menace: giant, genetically engineered insects that arise from beneath the streets to devour unsuspecting residents.

What makes these creepy critters more frightening than your normal man-eating movie monsters is that they quickly evolve to "mimic" their natural enemies—human beings—by developing an eerie resemblance to tall, shadowy, black-cloaked stalkers.

And what makes "Mimic" far more chilling than your run-of-the-maul, creature-in-the-basement picture is the way it disarms its natural enemies—film critics—by taking on the protective coloration of more substantive, challenging fare—complete with cold, clammy, expressionistic visuals (think "Seven" meets "Batman"), smart writing and world-class acting.

Mira Sorvino stars as a brilliant scientist who recombines DNA of various species to create a short-lived new life form ("the Judas breed") that succeeds in eradicating an epidemic that threatened the lives of the city's children.

Three years later, she and her health-official husband (Jeremy Northam of "The Net" and "Emma"), discover that the artificially designed species has not only survived (imagine that!), but quickly evolved in horrifying and profoundly dangerous directions. With the grudging aid of a cynical, world-weary transit authority cop (the excellent Charles S. Dutton) and advice from a world-famous scientist (F. Murray Abraham), the intrepid couple finds its way down long-abandoned, antique subway tunnels, where the evil beasts seem to be germinating.

Director-writer Guillermo del Toro (who previously created the classy, acclaimed 1993 Mexican vampire movie "Cronos") makes these winged multi-legged monstrosities utterly and indescribably disgusting—which is, of course, the entire point of the movie.

The pacing is expert and seductive, with enough sudden shocks to jolt you several times out of your chair. Sympathetic performances, complete with uncanny romantic chemistry between the surprisingly athletic Sorvino and the smart, smoldering Northam, provide an unexpected bonus.

Unfortunately, a few self-consciously "artsy" details mar the otherwise absorbing proceedings—including too much preachiness about the dangers of "man's tampering with nature" and an especially bizarre subplot featuring the elegant Giancarlo Giannirxi as a shoeshine man (of all things), whose weirdly babbling, autistic 8-year-old grandson (Alexander Goodwin) develops some odd spiritual connection with the creatures.

New Yorkers may resent the movie's excesses in using steam and filth and shadows and rotting garbage and endlessly dripping surfaces to evoke an incomparably ugly and nightmarish vision of the city—especially since this grim Gotham happened to be shot in Toronto.

Nevertheless, those unforgettable insects can rip apart and swallow up all such objections, and if you can settle into the properly perverse mood they may seriously bug you.

NEWSDAY, 8/22/97, Part II/p. B3, John Anderson

Crunch. Squirt. Add gothic-Catholic iconography. Stir. Simmer.

What you get is "Mimic," the new Guillermo Del Toro conscience-and-horror epic with side orders of mortality, divinity, entomology and the kind of graphic exterminations that call to mind Alejandro Jodorowsky (probably Del Toro's greatest influence). That is, when it's not evoking Sam Raimi and David Cronenberg, or cutting its own niche in the horror genre.

As in "Cronos," his vampires-and-gilded-cockroach epic of several years back, Del Toro's feature attraction here is bug life, although not of the Mexican archeological variety. More of the Frankenstein variety. Mira Sorvino who else?—begins by saving New York's children from an insidious disease and ends by saving the entire city from the cure. The man-plays-God and God-gets-mad theme is given added edge by the fact that everyone's intentions were good; they just don't pay quite enough attention to the wonders of genetic mutation.

To make the perfect horror movie, given the evolution of the genre, it's not enough for the stomach to react. The mind has to follow suit. If you lose both, so much the better. "Mimic" has more than its share of bloodshed and sick jokes—Charles S. Dutton, as the transit cop who helps in the search for the terror below, is consistently funny as a civil servant acting above and beyond the call. The sounds of squashing are often as stimulating as the sight of a 6-foot mosquito spiriting Sorvino down a subway tunnel.

The film also spends most of its time under ground, in a subway system full of grottos and ruins and mutant killer insects, which provides a ripe metaphor for modern guilt: Hidden from view, inhabited by the dregs of society, the underground is everything society has abandoned, ignored and betrayed. And it's coming back to get us.

Less garish than Jodorowsky ("El Topo," "Santa Sangre"), and far more humorous than Cronenberg's more bizarre work, "Mimic" borrows, but makes its own place in fright cinema. The creepiness begins immediately, as the credits roll against a backdrop of pinned butterflies, muffled nightmare voices and pictures of children—the kind you see in the files of city agencies. The creepiness is maintained throughout our travels through Del Toro's vision of urine-marinated New York subway system, the disappearance of the idiot-savant-for-shoes Chuy (Alexander Goodwin of "Nobody's Fool") and the search by his shoemaker father, played by Giancarlo Giannini (by the way, no parent with a missing child would be told by the police to call back in 48 hours).

It continues via the gradual releasing of insect factoids and the denouement, which isn't as science-based as the rest of the film, and succumbs to drippy sentimentality. But maybe I shouldn't have used the word drippy, because "Mimic" certainly sticks to the roof of your brain.

NEWSWEEK, 8/25/97, p. 72, Ray Sawhill

Mimic is undoubtedly the best mutant-cockroach horror thriller ever made. Even granting that there hasn't been much competition, this is intended as a high compliment. Director Guillermo ("Cronos") Del Toro's giddy, elegant scare picture is also a mutant among current movies: it never sacrifices its story or characters to its special effects, and its thrills aren't extensions of theme parks or videogames. It works on your emotions rather than your nerves.

The script, from a short story by Donald Wolheim, tells a classic nature-takes-revenge-on-us-for-messing-with-her story. Mira Sorvino and Jeremy Northam are scientists who have stopped a cockroach-borne epidemic in New York City by releasing genetically engineered roaches programmed to breed and then die. A few years later signs of a different problem appear: some of the designer bugs may have outwitted their DNA, mutating into scary new forms. The two scientists set out to solve the problem they have created.

A virtuoso at tension and atmosphere, Del Toro orchestrates sounds, shadows and textures with expressionist malice, and sets the action amid damp, vaulted spaces and in tunnels full of forgotten industrial debris—the city as a roach nest. Sorvino, with her air of Yuppie expertise and her face puffy with guilt and fear, is touching as the top bug-fighter. Playing her mentor, F. Murray Abraham hits eerie bass notes. Charles S. Dutton, warm and humorous, is the cop who leads the team underground.

As a yuck!-and-eek! extravaganza, the film is an effective successor to "Scream"—audiences at New York previews have been shrieking, giggling and talking back to the screen.

Yet "Mimic" is also a feast for film buffs, recalling such cult favorites as 1985's "Re-Animator" and the Italian vampire movies of the '60s. In one long sequence, the investigators take shelter in an abandoned subway car deep under the city. All around are scaffolding and crud; above, far out of reach, beckons an enormous, befogged skylight. The image has the flamboyant poetry that silent movies are still treasured for. Then the giant cockroaches attack. "Mimic" is just an exploitation movie with artistic touches, but it gives us the creeps about all the creatures we share our cities with.

SIGHT AND SOUND, 7/98, p. 47, Philip Strick

An epidemic threatens New York City's children. Dr Susan Tyler and her husband Dr Peter Mann identify cockroaches as the plague-carriers and develop a new species to kill them: the Judas breed secretes a poison fatal to the roaches and the children are saved. Three years later, Susan realises that the Judas breed has been evolving and anxiously tries to monitor its progress. Nearby, autistic 8-year-old Chuy investigates the shrouded visitors to a derelict chapel. They carry him deep into the city's subway tunnels. His grandfather Manny searches for him.

With Peter and their assistant Josh, Susan hunts the subways for Judas breed specimens, recruiting security cop Leonard as a reluctant guide. Susan is stalked by a giant insect that mimics human appearance. Seizing her, it vanishes into the tunnel network. Josh stumbles across a giant cache of eggs and is killed. Peter and Leonard encounter Manny, who helps them find Susan. Reunited, they take refuge in an old subway carriage as the mimic bugs attack. Leonard sacrifices himself so that the others can escape. They find Chuy, but the mimics kill Manny After putting Susan and Chuy into a service lift to return them to the surface, Peter finds the centre of the bug colony and sets off a huge gas explosion that destroys it. A male mimic escapes and confronts Susan but is crushed by a subway train. Peter rejoins Susan and Chuy amid the debris in the street above.

First planned as a short episode in a film anthology, *Mimic* was inspired by a two-page story by veteran editor-publisher Donald A. Wolheim. Although the scenario was worked on by a surprising range of contributors including John Sayles and Matthew Robbins *(*batteries not included)*, the finished product shows scant sign of their influence. Instead, it has become what its director Guillermo del Toro terms an 'atmospheric fable', with enhancements that could only have originated with the director himself as an extension of the tangled ambiguities of his vampire film *Cronos*.

With *Cronos,* del Toro unleashed a scuttling heap of roaches from the eye of an angel, their origin related to the immortal occupant of a golden scarab. This rich muddle of icons continues in *Mimic* with bigger and more numerous bugs, some loathed plague-carriers and others seemingly members of a privileged brotherhood with a "Jesus Saves" neon sign and its own Masonic codes. "Maybe," suggested the Buñuelian recluse of *Cronos*, "insects are God's favourite creatures." It's a concept that del Toro is clearly tempted to take seriously.

If Wolheim's story was another variant on science fiction's persistent fear of body snatching, del Toro's vision of a nonhuman species living unnoticed among us provides a diverting original parallel. His film's first half tells two stories: the *Outbreak*-style account of disease containment and its consequences, and *The Shining*-style relationship between a child with unusual skills and his brooding environment. Frustratingly, their complexities suggest more than is ultimately delivered. In what seems like a direct reference to *Cronos*, for example, the researcher's hand is pierced by a bug's claw, but immortality is no longer an issue and the incident passes without further comment.

At first, the story of the boy, with his exceptional recognition of the sounds made by footwear and his aptitude for insect communication, more than compensates for these uncertainties. But the empathy between Chuy and his grandfather, another apparent update from *Cronos*, carries implications which never quite surface, despite the pathos of the grandfather's death in the grip of Chuy's 'disciples'. The monkish sect of unidentified humanoids in the derelict chapel may be God's favourites but they reveal a Satanic malevolence. It also seems strangely inconsistent of them to carry both child and entomologist undamaged into the underworld while ripping everyone else apart.

Although a wondrous territory of soaring buttresses and unlikely skylights, the subway system provides a sobering familiarity, with expendable cast members scrabbling through tunnels to meet their doom. Its second half an anticlimactic reminder of *Them*, *Aliens* and *Starship Troopers*, complete with transfixing claws, del Toro's fable runs out of atmosphere until, returning to form with a bang, it blasts the city streets. Del Toro can handle this kind of spectacle as well as anybody. What makes him more interesting is his delight in detail, his affection for visual symmetry, and his savouring of the unexpected—as when a falling body produces a splash of white paint instead of blood; or when, in a single tracking shot, a silent figure sprouts terrifyingly into an unimaginable predator. Teasingly, the film's final image of the 'saved' features a crucifix: true to form, del Toro leaves us to make what we like of that.

TIME, 8/25/97, p. 70, Richard Corliss

Dr. Susan Tyler (Mira Sorvino) paces edgily on a deserted New York City subway platform. A brilliant scientist who has recently used genetic engineering to eradicate an epidemic, Susan is not smart enough to realize she's in a horror movie and ought to be wary of approaching a tall, hooded stranger to ask the time. The stranger turns and reveals its hideous face—*ewwww*, a killer cockroach! It enfolds Susan in its great wings and flies off into the subway's dank underworld.

A great horror moment, like this one in Guillermo Del Toro's *Mimic*, works as both pulp and poetry. It gets scare shivers tickling the lay audience while connoisseurs nod sagely at the canonical resonance; think of the creature as Dracula spreading its capelike wings and Sorvino as both a Frankenstein whose experiment went bad and a Fay Wray to the insect world's King Kong. The roach and its sibs are Susan's mutant creations; they have the gift of mimicking other species. If Susan's commando crew doesn't Off the bugs quick, New York could become a slightly less fabulous place to live.

"Maybe insects are God's favorite creatures," says an old man to a doting grandchild in Del Toro's fine 1992 *Cronos*. The same themes and similar characters show up here; the director is apparently buggy for bugs and for strange, trusting children. For its first hour-up to and including that airborne kidnapping of our heroine—*Mimic* is a suavely creepy essay in entomophobia. Then the film gets a severe case of the stupes. The creatures keep Susan alive (inexplicable unless she is meant to be mated with the king bug), and they stop evolving into humans (so we never, alas, see the final stage of a really uggy bugman). Horror-film heroines are typically doomed to lose their wits halfway through the picture. This time it happened to the director.

VILLAGE VOICE, 8/26/97, p. 73, Amy Taubin

An arty bug movie with enough yech factor to appeal to 13-year-olds, Guillermo Del Toro's *Mimic* stars Mira Sorvino as the Dr. Frankenstein of recombinant DNA technology. She overreaches and fucks up royally (think of *Mimic* as the anti-*G.I. Jane*), but since she acts in the interest of saving children's lives, we're supposed to love her despite her stupidity.

When a mysterious roach-borne virus threatens an entire generation of young New Yorkers, the lady scientist engineers a mutant bug that's supposed to wipe out the roaches and self-destruct in the process. She makes an error, however, in designing the reproductive DNA. Instead of dying off, the new bugs hole up beneath the Delancey Street subway station and rapidly evolve into six-foot flying mantises that have the ability to mimic the physiognomy of their primary enemy —humans. Standing upright on a subway platform, they look like Darkman until, throwing back their cloaklike outer shells, they swoop down on their prey, consuming them on the spot or carrying them, like groceries, back to their lair.

Mimic will probably hold your attention—and might even elicit a scream or two—but it won't haunt your dreams. After the preview, most of the audience plunged into the subway without a murmur, a nervous giggle, or, I suspect, a second thought.

Also reviewed in:
CHICAGO TRIBUNE, 8/22/97, Friday/p. A, Michael Wilmington
NEW YORK TIMES, 8/22/97, p. C3, Janet Maslin
VARIETY, 8/18-24/97, p. 30, Todd McCarthy

MISSION TO MIR

An Imax Corporation and Lockheed Corporation release in association with the Smithsonian Institution's National Air and Space Museum. *Producer:* Toni Myers and Graeme Ferguson. *Director:* Ivan Galin. *Director of Photography:* James Neihouse. *Editor:* Jane Morrison. *Music:* Micky Erbe and Maribeth Solomon. *Running time:* 40 minutes. *MPAA Rating:* Not Rated.

WITH: Mission Crew Members of Mir.

NEW YORK POST, 10/17/97, p. 49, Larry Worth

In Russia, mir is the word for peace. In America, Mir represents malfunctioning solar panels, ripped cable cords and every other debacle that's put the 11-year-old Russian space station in the headlines.

But before all that, Mir was known as the man-made satellite where American astronauts like Shannon Lucid and Norm Thagard spent months with their Slavic counterparts.

"Mission to Mir" takes viewers to that more peaceful period of the orbiting orb's history, via the glory of IMAX giant-screen photography.

The results prove pretty entertaining, starting with a generous number of newsreels encapsulating the space race from the '60s through Mir's launch in February of '86.

After a fascinating sequence of the training period at Moscow's Star City, the bulk of the material takes place aboard ship, starting with an extensive tour of Mir's six interlocking modules and their unique accessories.

The story is humanized chiefly by Lucid's comments about her time in orbit, as when telling how her daughter sent a sci-fi novel to Mir that was missing its conclusion. Only then did Lucid truly feel the isolation of outer space.

Filmed over 2½ years, most of the footage was shot by the astronauts, several of whom were trained to operate the 85- and 176-pound IMAX cameras. That's a feat in itself.

But whether showing a Mir's-eye view of Tibet, the docking procedure with the American shuttle Atlantis or the buddy-buddy U.S. Russian astronauts singing a chorus of "Moscow Nights," the interest level is consistently maintained.

Now if they could just make the space station work as well as "Mission to Mir," there'd be happy endings all around.

Also reviewed in:
NEW YORK TIMES, 10/17/97, p. E14, Stephen Holden

MR. MAGOO

A Walt Disney Pictures release of a Ben Myron production. *Executive Producer:* Henry G. Saperstein, Andre Morgan, and Robert L. Rosen. *Producer:* Ben Myron. *Director:* Stanley Tong. *Screenplay:* Pat Proft and Tom Sherohman. *Director of Photography:* Jingle Ma. *Editor:* Stuart Pappé, David Rawlins, and Michael R. Miller. *Music:* Michael Tavera. *Music Editor:* Michael T. Ryan. *Sound:* Rob Young and (music) Robert Fernandez. *Sound Editor:* Tim Chau and Donald J. Malouf. *Casting:* Marcia Ross and Donna Morong. *Production Designer:* John Willett. *Art Director:* Doug Byggdin. *Set Decorator:* Elizabeth Wilcox. *Costumes:* Tom Bronson. *Make-up:* Sandy Cooper. *Make-up (Leslie Nielsen):* Judy Lovell. *Stunt Coordinator:* Ailen Chun Wai Sit. *Running time:* 85 minutes. *MPAA Rating:* PG.

CAST: Leslie Nielsen (Mr. Magoo); Kelly Lynch (Luanne Leseur); Matt Keeslar (Waldo); Nick Chinlund (Bob Morgan); Stephen Tobolowsky (Agent Chuck Stupak); Ernie Hudson (Agent Gus Anders); Jennifer Garner (Stacey Sampanahoditra); Malcolm McDowell (Austin Cloquet); Miguel Ferrer (Ortega Peru); L. Harvey Gold (Schmitt); Art Irizawa (Gosha); John Tierney (Hebzinski); Terence Kelly (McManus); Rick Burgess (Molinaro); Jerry Wasserman (Javier); Bill Dow (Museum Curator); Frank C. Turner (Ralston, Stage Manager); Monique Rusu (Rosita); Robert Metcalfe (Desk Clerk); Danny Steele (Tenor); Dolores Drake (Female Tourist); Claire Riley (Newswoman); Pat Waldron (Soprano); Michael Puttonen (Security Guard); Pamela Diaz (Tour Guide); Chancz Perry (Train Station Porter); Marke Driesschen (Radio Announcer); Brenda MacDonald (Opera Patron); Joseph Davies (TV Trainer); Shaun MacDonald (Cook Show Host); David Neale (Fix It Guy); Carrie Cain Sparks (Rosita's Dresser).

LOS ANGELES TIMES, 12/24/97, Calendar/p. 13, John Anderson

[The following review by John Anderson appeared in a slightly different form in
NEWSDAY, 12/24/97, Part II/p. B11.]

Among those who attend early movie screenings with some regularity, there is a man who is known as the Laugher. Always in the front of the house, always ahead of the crowd, the Laugher's laugh is loud and lusty. And you would hear him anyway. Because when the Laugher laughs, the Laugher laughs alone.

It was a virtual aria the Laugher performed at last week's screening of "Mr. Magoo," which stars the usually hilarious Leslie Nielsen as the myopic millionaire and '60s cartoon character Quincy Magoo. When Magoo mistook his toothpaste for Ban de Soleil, the Laugher was in stitches. When Magoo and his faithful dog Angus played fetch with a priceless stolen ruby, the Laugher was in hysterics. And when Magoo tried to cook a chicken while watching an exercise show ("Lift those legs!!"), people were ready to call the paramedics. Yes, there's a certain infectious quality to the Laugher's laugh. But unless Disney can clone him, it's unlikely that your experience will be as mirthful as ours, which was kind of like being locked in a room with the Laugher.

"Mr. Magoo," Disney's live-action version of what was never really classic animation, may be crashingly unimaginative, but its real offense is making such poor use of Nielsen. When he gets to be really goofy, the film is close to funny. But his director, Stanley Tong, accustomed to working with the likes of Jackie Chan, seems intent on moving his film along at such a rate of speed—and with such little sense of comic continuity—that anything but purely physical comedy simply can't survive.

In fact, the whole blundering-Magoo concept—which earlier this year stirred the wrath of the National Federation of the Blind, compelling Disney to include a blathersome disclaimer about the sightless being able to live satisfying lives, etc., etc.—goes by the wayside in favor of a hackneyed jewel-heist-action-chase plot line. This is, of course, territory far more familiar to Tong—and us, unfortunately—than the kind of stuff one wants from Nielsen.

They should have given more screen time to the dog, who exerts a lot of energy keeping Quincy from killing himself or losing the ruby. Ernie Hudson and Stephen Tobolowsky play the bumbling FBI and CIA agents and it doesn't matter which is which. Kelly Lynch is the villainess Luanne, inspiring wonder (as in, "I wonder how someone goes from 'Drugstore Cowboy' to 'Mr. Magoo' in only one career?"). You also have to ask yourself why Disney is remaking a cartoon with such a little recognition factor among those whom it's apparently aimed at (the under-7 demographic) or why, with all the resources at its disposal, the company couldn't come up with anything less feeble than "Mr. Magoo." Of course, it's the holidays. People are busy. And besides, they made the Laugher very, very happy.

NEW YORK POST, 12/24/97, p. 34, Michael Medved

One of the great things about adapting cheesy source material like the old "Mr. Magoo" cartoons is that no one can accuse you of violating the lofty artistic standards of the original.

Since the nearsighted nitwit first stumbled into animated existence in 1949, Magoo has been a bad joke: an eccentric, good-natured old man who won't acknowledge his impaired vision but somehow survives one disastrous mistake after another.

The movie infects that tired formula with the new energy of (you will pardon the expression) eye-popping stunts and a silly, convoluted plot with a sneakily sexy villainess.

That naughty girl is an international jewel thief, seductress and martial arts expert played by the hugely entertaining Kelly Lynch, demonstrating astonishing athleticism and an utterly unexpected, surprisingly subtle flair for comedy.

As she steals a priceless ruby from philanthropist Magoo's newly dedicated museum, she also steals the movie. Leslie Nielsen plays the bumbling Magoo, replacing the cartoon character's bald pate with his own trademark thatch of snow-white hair.

In fact, this Magoo bears less resemblance to any cartoon character than to all those other lovable idiots Nielsen has played so well in the past. Aided by his clean-cut nephew Waldo (Matt Keeslar) and his protective, resourceful bulldog Angus (played by four well-trained pooches), Magoo takes on a vicious crime boss (Malcolm McDowell) and an international summit of gangsters in his efforts to recover the lost gem.

Ernie Hudson and Stephen Tobolowsky provide so-so comic relief as dueling representatives of the CIA and FBI, but the film's saving grace, aside from the lovely Lynch, is exhilarating direction by Stanley Tong. This veteran of Jackie Chan action films cunningly choreographs madcap mayhem on a ski slope, busy city streets (of Vancouver), in an opera house, a crowded harbor and, most spectacularly, at an awe-inspiring South American waterfall.

The superior slapstick and adrenalin-pumping thrills will captivate kids (especially small boys), while parents will laugh in spite of themselves—especially at the hilariously PC disclaimer appended to the conclusion of the adventure: "The preceding film is not intended as an accurate portrayal of blindness or poor eyesight."

SIGHT AND SOUND, 7/98, p. 49, Nick Thomas

Quincy Magoo, a near-sighted millionaire, hosts a benefit at the local museum whose prize exhibit is the star of Kuristan, a priceless ruby. In the crowd are two thieves, Leseur and Morgan, who later return and steal the gem. They escape on a ferry, but as they fight over the jewel, it falls into Magoo's adjacent fishing boat, his trusty bulldog Angus realises its value, though Magoo is oblivious to its presence. Later, while Magoo sings in an opera (to which his nephew Waldo invites the Kuristan government's representative, Stacey), he unwittingly sees off the pursuing pair of villains. By now, however, the theft has alerted both the CIA and FBI.

Disguising herself as a journalist, Leseur seduces Magoo, who invites her to his house. Morgan drives off with the gem in Magoo's ancient Studebaker, pursued in vain by Magoo, now aware of the jewel, in a giant eggplant-shaped car. Magoo, disguised as crime baron Ortega Peru, heads for the hideout of evil mastermind Austin Cloquet, where the jewel is being auctioned off to the highest bidder, but Leseur runs off with the ruby, with Magoo in pursuit.

In Brazil, the real Peru plans to pay Leseur $15m for the ruby as a gift for his bride-to-be. Magoo dons the bride's dress, and as the police close in, jumps on the fleeing Peru's helicopter, along with Leseur. After a struggle, Magoo and Leseur end up at the edge of a waterfall. Leseur is winched to safety and arrested, while Magoo parascends with the jewel, which is restored to the museum.

John Hubley's famously myopic cartoon character, made for UPA in the 50s and voiced so distinctively by Jim Backus, is hardly an obvious candidate for a 90s Disney live-action treatment. Largely absent from UK television schedules in recent years, Mr. Magoo as a character has virtually no currency with its intended audience.

Meanwhile, with reference to other audiences, the disclaimer offered in the end credits that the film "is not intended as an accurate portrayal of blindness or poor eyesight" is presumably to appease those who feel that the hero's disability is not an appropriate subject for humour. Blindness has not, it must be admitted, proved a great source of screen comedy—only Marilyn Monroe in *Gentlemen Prefer Blondes* and Mr Muckle, W C. Fields' dyspeptic nemesis in *It's a Gift* spring to mind—and this version of Mr Magoo adds little to the genre.

At least Disney had the wit to hire Hong Kong action director Stanley Tong, most notable for such Jackie Chan vehicles as *Rumble in the Bronx, Supercop* and *First Strike*. With those, Tong excelled in a genre common in Hong Kong but rare in contemporary Hollywood—the action comedy. While American martial artists' humour tends to be of the unintentional variety, Chan's films seamlessly combine high kicks with low comedy.

It might have worked here, if it wasn't for the fact that Mr. Magoo and the art of kung-fu are not natural companions. "This hep cat has a black belt in mayhem," cries Magoo when faced with his pursuers. Unfortunately, as a qualification, it's not enough. The most impressive physical feats come from Kelly Lynch as the chameleon-like Leseur, but the venerable Magoo, the focal point of the film, is no action hero, and because of this, the crucial emulsion of action and comedy fails.

The action itself is sometimes impressive: in their opening up of the physical space of the film, most notably in the scenes at the museum and over the waterfall, Tong and cinematographer Jingle Ma (another Chan alumnus) use swooping cameras and vertiginous crane shots to create the sense of panorama which the film's central character crucially lacks. They take their cue from the original cartoons, neatly homaged in the impressive animated opening and closing sequences. These also set up the permanent sense of physical danger surrounding Magoo, which Tong tries to bring to the live action here.

The comedy, though, fails to ignite. Leslie Nielsen's reputation as a comic performer dates from his earlier collaborations with writer Pat Proft on brilliant television series *Police Squad!* and his turn in *Airplane!* Much of the humour played on Nielsen's previous incarnation as a wooden and deadly serious second lead. His straightness was the perfect foil for the absurd comic scenarios of his writers. Now, after a series of increasingly desperate spoofs which have relied on his comic mugging rather than the original incongruity, Nielsen's comic stock has fallen and there is little here to raise it.

VILLAGE VOICE, 1/6/98, p. 68, Gary Dauphin

A possible holiday diversion for under-10s who've either already seen *Anastasia* thrice or who might be creeped out by all the crawling and scurrying in *Mouse Hunt*, Disney's live-action update of the marginally beloved, UPA animated series *Mr. Magoo* stars Leslie Nielson as the eponymous, nearsighted millionaire. The movie's basic shtick is that Mr. Magoo won't wear his glasses, and optical ignorance being broad, politically incorrect comedy bliss, this reluctance allows him to walk blithely up to the paddlewheels of riverboats (Ah! An escalator, harrumph, chim-chim!") or slide down a slick mountain on an ironing board ("Ah! A snowboard, harrumph, chim, chim!"). Most important to the film's stitched-together excuse for a story, Magoo mistakes a huge, stolen ruby for a toy belonging to his quick-witted dog Angus. Although the animated bits that bookend the movie reveal that Nielsen in no way actually resembles the original Mr.

Magoo, the actor does do a good job of incessantly muttering and jabbering to himself à la Jim Backus.

Hong Kong action veteran Stanley Tong *(Supercop, Rumble in the Bronx)* obviously learned a few things staging physical comedy for Jackie Chan, and he throws in a stunt finale involving Magoo, a helicopter, an inflatable raft, and a really big waterfall that's so out of nowhere you have to admire the director's determination to put shoulder to Hollywood grindstone and make the best of what's essentially an English language résumé-builder. No adult in their right mind should actually want to sit through Mr. Magoo—unless, as in my case, there's money involved—but it's unlikely that anyone will go postal while on an obligatory family outing. What more can you ask for this Christmas?

Also reviewed in:
NEW YORK TIMES, 12/24/97, p. E8, Lawrence Van Gelder
VARIETY, 12/22/97-1/4/98, p. 60, Joe Leydon
WASHINGTON POST, 12/25/97, p. C11, Rita Kempley
WASHINGTON POST, 12/26/97, Weekend/p. 36, Rita Kempley

MOLOM: A LEGEND OF MONGOLIA

A Norkat Company release of a Lung-Ta proudction. *Executive Producer:* Fabien Quaki. *Producer:* Marie Jaoul de Poncheville. *Director:* Marie Jaoul de Poncheville. *Screenplay (Mongolian with English subtitles):* Marie Jaoul de Poncheville. *Director of Photography:* Jacques Besse. *Editor:* Danielle Anezin. *Music:* John McLaughlin and Trilok Gurtu. *Production Designer:* Abderrahmane Sissako. *Costumes:* Kh. Amarjagal and N. Batbayer. *Running time:* 93 minutes. *MPAA Rating:* Not Rated.

CAST: Tseded (Molom); Yondejunai (Yonden).

LOS ANGELES TIMES, 3/27/98, Calendar/p. 18, Kevin Thomas

Marie Jaoul de Poncheville's "Molom—A Legend of Mongolia" is a lyrical epic that takes us into a vast, unspoiled landscape in which an old man, Molom (Tseded), encounters a boy, Yonden (Yondejunai), cared for by wolves after being abandoned by his drunken father.

In the telling of Poncheville's enchanting tale, you're asked to view Molom as a kindly grandfatherly type with some remarkable psychic gifts and healing powers. He takes the boy, who's not a true "wild child"—he's able to speak—and guides him on the path of Buddhist wisdom.

You're also invited to consider that Molom is half-shaman, half-priest, a mediator between the gods and men whose purpose is to protect and enlighten all he meets. That you can take "Molom" on two levels gives it clarity and suggestiveness; anchored to reality, it soars in the imagination.

As Molom and Yonden travel the countryside, the man entertains the boy with wonderful tales of the glories of Mongolia's past. They experience various adventures and meet many people, but all the while Molom is guiding Yonden in the ways of Buddhism, teaching him of the quest for Shambala, the Buddhist paradise.

As Poncheville shifts effortlessly from the everyday to the exquisitely fantastic, Molom steers Yonden toward his greatest lesson: understanding that the elusive "sacred pearl" he glimpses in the palm of an old woman—or is she a witch?—is in fact his soul and that he can find it only within himself.

"Molom" could be taken as part of a glorious trilogy that includes Nikita Mikhalkov's Oscar-nominated "Close to Eden" and Xie Fei's "A Mongolian Tale." All three evoke a timeless way of life only to jolt us with the unexpected intrusion of a raw, bustling present. Mikhalkov saw an Eden endangered, and Xie commented on the corrupting powers of urban values. Poncheville clearly perceives these dangers, yet her film is an expression of faith that the spiritual values embodied in Buddhism will endure.

The beauty and simplicity of this film, which makes exceptionally effective use of soundtrack narration, is absolutely exhilarating, and though Tsededorj is a celebrated acting veteran, 12-year-old Yondejunal is one of those miraculously natural actors, completely undaunted by the presence of a camera.

"Molom—A Legend of Mongolia" marks the feature debut of Poncheville, a documentarian and journalist best known for "Lung Ta: The Forgotten Tibet." That 1990 documentary, made with Franz-Christophe Glercke, offers a convincing vision of a Shangri-La turned into a nightmare by Chinese forces and policies.

NEW YORK POST, 8/8/97, p. 52, Larry Worth

Depicting a spiritual journey is always an iffy proposition, maybe since the search for life's meaning rarely translates to the big screen. It's even tougher when the subject matter becomes redundant, as in "Molom."

The chief pleasure here is the stunning scenery and expansive vistas of Mongolia, as evidenced earlier, this year in the heartbreaking "A Mongolian Tale" and Nikita Mikhalkov's 1992 gem, "Close to Eden."

Like its predecessors, "Molom" has an ageless quality in its look at a culture that hasn't changed over the centuries, what with residents still residing in tent-like yurts, dressing in animal skins and making a living as farmers on the steppes.

But unlike "Eden" and "Tale," the simplistic story generates limited a sort of myth, the plot revolves around a Mongolian shaman, the titular Molom, who travels to High Asia in search of a protege.

He's no sooner touched down than he sets eyes on an urchin raised by wolves, your basic Romulus sans Remus. Together, man and boy trek from one adventure to the next, all of which test the youth's physical and mental strength as he comes to appreciate Buddha.

It's soon a case of seen-one-epiphany, seen-'em-all. In between hiking, bathing, skipping stones and digesting homegrown philosophy with Molom, the kid encounters magic pearls, sacred stones, ghostly birds and fortune-telling bones. Sadly, none of them provide the secret to compelling cinema.

On the other hand, screen newcomer Yondejunai is a perfectly cute youngster whose expressive face conveys more than is required. And as Molom, the elderly Tseded delivers warmth and surprising authenticity to the mumbo-jumbo which passes for sage counsel.

Then there's director Marie Jaoul de Poncheville, who ably captures the landscape's eerie beauty. But she's far too heavyhanded with flights of fancy and temptation-to-redemption scenarios. In addition, interest appreciably lags when the protagonists move into a 20th-century setting.

That's why 'Molom' is the proverbial mixed bag, taking one steppe forward for every two back.

VILLAGE VOICE, 8/12/97, p. 74, Gary Dauphin

There's a struggle between good and evil in *Molom,* but it's more child-sized than what one gets in *Spawn* [See Dauphin's review of that film]. Adapted from local Mongolian folklore surrounding wandering shamans (the "molom" of the title), the film opens with one of the wise men finding a young boy named Yonden living with wolves. Yonden's been abandoned by a drunk, wolf-hunting father, and Molom is the first human he's seen in years. The two take to traveling together.

Not much happens beyond that, the pair moving in a straight line from the steppes to Ulan Bator, where Yonden can be educated by Buddhist monks. Molom offers Yonden succinct pearls of wisdom, their interaction the gentle kind you might find between a grandfather and grandchild. Director Marie Jaoul de Poncheville illuminates a nomadic lifestyle in tiny strokes that can border on the imperceptible. The steppes are a vast blankness, the rolling depressions and random piles of rock evoking the receding glaciers, while the wide-eyed camera plays hide-and-seek with a world of detail. (Billowing flowerbeds are revealed during close-ups only to disappear into the bruise-colored background during long shots.) For anyone interested in a ground-level look at a storied but little-seen place, it's the only show in town.

Also reviewed in:
NEW YORK TIMES, 8/8/97, p. C12, Stephen Holden
VARIETY, 8/1-7/94, p. 46, Lisa Nesselson

MON HOMME

An Artificial Eye Film Company release of a Les Films Alain Sarde/Plateau A with Studio Images 2 and the participation of Canal +. *Producer:* Alain Sarde. *Director:* Bertrand Blier. *Screenplay (French with English subtitles):* Bertrand Blier. *Director of Photography:* Pierre Lhomme. *Editor:* Claudine Merlin. *Sound:* Paul Bertault. *Sound Editor:* Pierre Gamet. *Casting:* Gérard Moulévrier. *Production Designer:* Willy Holt and Georges Glon. *Set Decorator:* Jacques-Albert Leguillon. *Costumes:* Christian Gasc. *Make-up:* Thi-Loan N'guyen. *Running time:* 98 minutes. *MPAA Rating:* Not Rated.

CAST: Anouk Grinberg (Marie Abarth); Gérard Lanvin (Jeannot); Valéria Bruni-Tedeschi (Sanguine); Olivier Martinez (Jean-François); Dominique Valadié (Gilberte); Jacques François (2nd Client); Michel Galabru (3rd Client); Robert Hirsch (M. Hervé); Bernard Fresson (Personnel Director); Jacques Gamblin (4th Client); Jean-Pierre Darroussin (Gilbert's Client); Bernard Le Coq (Inspector Marvier); Ginette Garcin (Woman in Shawl); Dominique Lollia (Mélissa); Aurore Clément (Woman of the World); Jean-Pierre Léaud (M. Claude); Roger Carel (Passerby in Hat); Sabine Azéma (Bérangère); Mathieu Kassovitz (1st Client).

LOS ANGELES TIMES, 9/12/97, Calendar/p. 13, Kevin Thomas

That formidable fabulist, French writer-director Bertrand Blier, returns with "Mon Homme," one of his finest films, even arguably his best.

For nearly 25 years, starting with "Going Places," Blier has been fascinated with the twists and turns of human behavior. With the mercurial relationships between men and women and with what happens to individuals who have the courage to act on their impulses and follow their hearts.

"I like money. I like men. I like selling dreams," says Anouk Grinbigrg's beautiful, petite Marie, the happiest of hookers. "A man is never ugly if you look at him right."

Arriving home late one night, she comes across a whiskered man in ragged clothing huddled at the bottom of the staircase leading to her small but charming garret apartment. He asks for spare change. She has none but offers him food, shelter and finally herself.

Beneath the layers of clothes and the bushy board we can see that no one could consider him ugly. But Marie, in her risky act of compassion—and in her unabashed passion for men, sex and love—has been rewarded beyond her own wildest dreams. The homeless man, whose name is Jeannot (Gérard Lanvin), proves to be a virile, well-built man whose sexual prowess carries the highly experienced Marie to new heights of ecstasy. Think of a Gallic Robert Mitchum.

Their love scene is one of searing intensity, and Blier presents it with the utmost seriousness. To suggest that their lovemaking is a profoundly rapturous experience for Marie and Jeannot, Blier selected for musical accompaniment excerpts from the elegiac music of Henryk Mikolaji Gorecki, explaining that "eroticism is always linked to liturgy." That his other, music of choice is a selection of Barry White songs suggests the wide range of shifting tones that Blier manages with his usual dexterity. (When "Mon Homme" goes into second runs, some enterprising exhibitor surely will book it with "Love Serenade," which also features White songs and an unorthodox take on men and women.)

Marie suggests that Jeannot become her pimp, but he can't resist also turning out his pretty manicurist, whom he calls Tangerine (Valéria Bruni-Tedeschi) as well. But Blier goes way beyond the familiar squaring away of the eternal triangle to create a modern odyssey of Marie and Jeannot pursuing their respective destinies.

Security is an illusion, suggests Blier, so you might as well take your chances in life as in love. There is the sense in this superb picture that life rewards, though not necessarily in material riches, those who disregard convention. It's not too much to say that Marie is a contemporary Candide.

Blier inspires his actors to carry off dizzying changes of moods, attitudes and emotions, often within a single scene. His stars, including Olivier Martinez as another key man in Marie's life, dazzle, and Mathieu Kassowitz, Michel Galabru and Jean-Pierre Leaud are among the well-known actors who make deft cameo appearances as Marie's clients. There's a delightful special appearance by Sabine Azéma.

"Mon Homme" finds a master storyteller and modern moralist at the top of his form.

NEW YORK POST, 8/15/97, p. 42, Thelma Adams

After "Mon Homme," director Bertrand Blier deserves a good dressing down—but the kinky Frenchman might enjoy it.

Welcome to Blier's erotic fantasy: A happy hooker trips over a homeless bum. She drags him upstairs to her atelier, feeds him stew, pours him wine and gives him a corner to curl up in.

As an afterthought, the fresh-faced, slim-hipped Marie (Anouk Grinberg) offers Rasputin's double a freebie. When Jeannot (Gerard Lanvin) climbs on—his fingernails filthy, his knuckles black with soot he gives her the rough ride of her very busy life.

Gag me. It's not enough that Marie loves her work as much as Bill Gates loves his ("Joy, pure joy"), but one night of grinding with Jeannot turns to mutual love. Cue the Barry White tunes. I can't get enough of your grime, baby.

In a post-coital flush, Marie—no great thinker—makes Jeannot her pimp. He cleans up well in a swell suit, suave coif and, thankfully, a manicure. But Jeannot didn't fall to the gutter on his looks; he's a rotter with a sex drive that Roto-Rooter would envy.

Jeannot takes his pimping seriously. He immediately starts recruiting new women like Sanguine (Valeria Bruni-Tedeschi), a shy manicurist. Fortunately, she did not see Jeannot in his natural state.

Back at work making men "hear great music,' Marie bumps away. But her heart and purse belong to papa pimp—until she learns that he's fondling other fishnet stockings in the sea of love.

Meanwhile, famed French actor Jean-Pierre Leaud and rising star Mathieu Kassovitz blow by, while the beautiful Olivier Martinez briefly makes Marie an honest woman.

Blier's high-cast, self-assured booty comedy follows a career rooted in the '70s flaunting of middle-class mores ("Going Places," "Get Out Your Handkerchiefs"). It's just more boorish than provocative when, 20 years later, the director has become wealthy and middle-aged himself.

In the end, the beaten pimp, who has followed his Johnson to jail and back, apologizes to Marie and, facing the camera, to women in general.

Sorry, Monsieur Blier. That isn't good enough.

NEWSDAY, 8/15/97, Part II/p. B9, John Anderson

She's an awfully happy hooker. Marie (Anouk Grinberg), the kind-hearted gamine of Bertrand Blier's "Mon Homme," works overtime with problematic clients, refuses money if the pleasure is mutual and exhibits such an infectious enthusiasm for her work she can convert a patrician Parisian to streetwalking in about four minutes. She loves selling erstaz love, but when it comes for real—in the person of a homeless brute she saves from becoming rat food—her life turns into Zola-esque nightmare.

It's a disconcerting, disorienting tale Blier tells. Combining elements of "Nana," "La Bohéme," "Last Tango" and "Down and Out in Beverly Hills," he seems to vascillate between making an apology on behalf of the entire male sex and spinning a pan-human parable about the perversity of human nature and its incapacity for satisfaction. Either way, it's never boring. And it's certainly her never static.

Take Jeannot (Gerard Lanvin), whom Marie finds sleeping in a doorway—dirty, bloodied, probably drunk. Her good nature demands that she wake him up and move him out, but then she's compelled to offer him a place on her floor, and then we watch all this in Grinberg's gorgeous face—the idea of offering herself to him dawns on her, initially horrifies her, eventually becomes irresistible. Is he grateful? For anything? No, he's brutal. But he's good: By the time they're done, she's in love and asks Jeannot to be her pimp.

From here, the film takes off in several directions, not all of them well-marked or particularly navigable. But we stay with it, because Blier is a twisted assassin of expectations and bourgeoise sensibilities. Take Marie's occupation—is she being exploited? By whom? She is pure joy, an original who defies us to pigeonhole her, to make her into a type. Conversely (and much less pleasantly), there's Jeannot, who may not be grateful but *is* a metaphor. Having been pledged Marie's body, money and undying loyalty, he immediately goes on the prowl, finding and seducing the manicurist Sarah (Valeria Bruni-Tedeschi), whom he dubs Tangerine and coerces into turning tricks. She gets busted. They're all arrested. Marie is devastated (she doesn't even know about Jeannot's third girlfriend) and when Jeannot is jailed she tries to make a new life for herself with Jean-Francois (Olivier Martinez, of "Horseman on the Roof").

It doesn't quite work out, of course. It never did in 19th-Century Russian novels or French plays, so why should it here? What "Mon Homme" has in common with old literature is that while Blier is forcing his audience to accept uncompromised characters, the characters themselves are compromised in a snare of fiction and resignation: Marie has been made a whore, so she revels in it; Jeannot has been made a pimp, so he pimps like a champ. Blier, likewise, is a smasher of complacency. And "Mon Homme" is a wrecking ball.

SIGHT AND SOUND, 6/97, p. 59, Ginette Vincendeau

Marie is a prostitute happy in her profession; she initiates a bourgeois woman into the joys of prostitution and comforts old and young male clients. She rescues a homeless man named Jeannot who sleeps in her doorway and after sex invites him to be her pimp. Although Marie and Jeannot are happy together, he meets a manicurist, Sanguine, and tries to turn her into a prostitute. He is unsuccessful but they become lovers. He also has sex with other women he meets in the street or next door to his flat.

Eventually, Jeannot is arrested as a pimp and it is revealed to Marie that he was seeing Sanguine and might have been a pimp in the past. After Jeannot's arrest, Marie and Sanguine go to a nightclub and, instead of seeing a lawyer as planned in order to help Jeannot, they decide to abandon him and become housewives. In a café, Marie selects a young man, Jean-François, to be the father of her children. After he comes out of jail, Jeannot is taken up by a housewife named Bérangère. Marie and Jean-François live in poverty in Lyons with their two children. Jeannot unsuccessfully attempts to find work and Marie, equally unsuccessfully, tries prostitution again. Jeannot returns to Marie's flat, while Sanguine appears, pregnant with Jean-François' child. Despite Jean-François' protests that he is scared of childbirth, he and Sanguine are bundled off to the hospital by Marie. Jeannot sits down and faces the camera. His last words are: "Sorry Marie, sorry women".

Ever since *Les Valseuses* in 1973, Bertrand Blier's films have provoked strong reactions and disagreements. The trenchant vulgarity of his humour repels and attracts in equal measure. His depiction of gender relations has been perceived as misogynist but some have championed Blier's own line that his films are about male anxieties about women's power, while others see his women as pleasurably strong characters. *Mon homme* is Blier's latest contribution to this debate.

Even though *Mon homme* features Barry White rather than Mistinguett on the soundtrack, French viewers immediately make the connection between the film's title and Mistinguett's 20s song 'Mon Homme' about the joys of being cheated on and beaten by one's man. Like Mistinguett, Marie is a plucky and funny woman who turns abuse and exploitation into a show of strength. Better to be like her, the film says, than a dreary housewife, such as the one she initiates into prostitution or pathetic, mousy-haired Sabine Azéma. Indeed Anouk Grinberg infuses Marie with a nervously energetic performance, especially in the first half of the film. The early scenes in which she takes her customers up to her room are very funny, and illustrate Blier's strategy of staying one step ahead of feminist critique. Marie is a 'sex worker' empowered by a job which gives her independence and good money, as well as her sexual pleasure. When she discovers Jeannot's betrayal, she does not hate her rival, but teams up with her. She then chooses to be a wife and mother and picks a man for his looks, thus, turning him into a sex object. Moreover, in this film men are inadequate liars and cheats, emasculated by old age or unemployment, or wimps scared of childbirth.

Why is it then that this film affords little pleasure, especially from a feminist perspective? First of all, the choice of prostitute and pimp represents a stark reduction of the complexities of male-female sexual relations. The 'Mon Homme' song, and others in the same tradition, were sung by powerful and talented women (Mistinguett, Fréhel, Piaf) but written by men; their underlying celebration of female victimhood finds an echo in Grinberg's Marie. This is relayed cinematically in the sanctification of the star as prostitute. As Blier tellingly says in the press-book, "Why a prostitute? Think of Louise Brooks, Arletty, Irma la Douce, La Dérobade. Like guns and gangsters, it is part of the cinema!" At a basic level, the tale of the prostitute narratively justifies plenty of sex scenes. But despite Marie's assertion that she is "happy in her sex" as well as her head, she amounts to little more than a server of male desire whose talent is to "make the sap spurt". Under the pretence of modernising an old myth, the film celebrates and perpetuates it. The same is true of her treatment of men. This is partly obscured by Blier's nods towards modernity. Despite the contemporary details (Grinberg's punkish looks, references to unemployment, and to Aids), the film refuses naturalism, distancing us through the flash-forwards of Jeannot's arrest and, among other devices, characters speaking directly to camera.

Mon homme is at its best in the first half when Blier displays his talent for directing comedy. Most of his successful films—Les Valseuses, Get Out Your Handkerchiefs (1977), My Best Friend's Girl (1983), Tenue de soirée/Menage (1986)—used the cream of French stars (Gérard Depardieu, Patrick Dewaere, Michel Blanc, Miou-Miou, Coluche and Isabelle Huppert) to great comic effect. Grinberg and Lanvin, as well as Bruni-Tedeschi as the tiresome Sanguine, are excellent actors, but not quite in the same league. They lack the charisma as well as the weight of their predecessors, possibly one reason why the film was not a success in France. Another may be the maudlin sentimentality of the second half, with its theatrically epic scenes such as Jean-François' search for work, Marie walking through the crowd. Blier's early films belonged to the libertarian café-théâtre in their grotesque excess; they were incisive and exuberant in their misogyny but they captured the sensibility of the May '68 generation. In Mon homme, to use a metaphor in tune with the film, that energy is spent. Rather than male anxiety we are left with male self-pity and rather than empowered women, a nostalgic celebration of female sexual availability.

VILLAGE VOICE, 8/19/97, p. 81, Leslie Camhi

A woman who's happy, independent, and successful seeks fullfillment through a man who will use and abuse her. This punishing and all-too-familiar scenario provokes the plot of Mon Homme, Bertrand Blier's latest feature. Anouk Grinberg plays Marie, an adorable waif and self-employed prostitute. She's got a gift to "make a sap flow" and she uses it liberally, with young and the old, the fit and the fat, who enjoy her services.

Alas, one evening she has a moment of pity for a filthy homeless man she finds sleeping by her garbage. She offers him a warm corner, a hot meal, and some torrid sex, Jeannot (Gérard Lonvin) may have forgotten his name, but he remembers a few essentials. Marie, love-struck, makes him a proposition: he can be her pimp, with total control over her money. With a bath, a haircut, a splash of cologne, and a snappy new suit, Jeannot soon looks like one of the manlier hunks in contemporary French cinema. But dressed like a pimp, he quickly begins to act the part. He falls in lust with Sanguine (Valéria Bruni-Tedeschi), a sweet blond manicurist who becomes his mistress.

The perversity of desire is Blier's great theme, and his gift is to make the most offensive men appear more than a bit appealing. There are funny moments here, as when Jeannot sings the praises of domesticity: mending a bra while his girl turns a trick and his chicken simmers in the oven. There's a sharp dialogue and a sexy soundtrack. But when Jeannot starts to slap Marie around, Blier takes his exploration of perversion too far for me. What begins as a charming Gallic celebration of unrestrained sexuality ends up feeling like a bit of an apology for pimps, cheats, and wife beaters.

Also reviewed in:
CHICAGO TRIBUNE, 4/3/98, Tempo/p. 4, Michael Wilmington
NEW YORK TIMES, 8/15/97, p. C8, Janet Maslin

MONDO

A Shadow Distribution release in association with Upstate Films of a film by KG Productions with the participation of Canal Plus and the Centre de Cinematographie. *Producer:* Michèle Ray-Gavras. *Director:* Tony Gatlif. *Screenplay (French with English subtitles):* Tony Gatlif. *Based on a story on:* J.M.G. Le Clézio. *Director of Photography:* Eric Guichard. *Editor:* Nicole D.V. Berckmans. *Music:* Alain Weber. *Set Designer:* Denis Mercier. *Running time:* 80 minutes. *MPAA Rating:* Not Rated.

CAST: Ovidiu Balan (Mondo); Philippe Petit (The Magician); Pierette Fesch (Thi-Chin); Schahla Aalam (The Magician's Companion); Jerry Smith (Dadi); Maurice Maurin (Giordan); Catherine Brun (Church Soloist).

LOS ANGELES TIMES, 6/27/97, Calendar/p. 10, Kevin Thomas

Tony Gatlif's "Mondo" is even more magical than "Latcho Drom," his mesmerizing celebration of Gypsy music and culture retracing the migration of the Rom people from India to Europe 1,000 years ago. Instead of finding rapturous beauty in the often vast, gorgeous nomadic locales of "Latcho Drom," Gatlif, an Algerian-born French national of Gypsy origin, discovers similar glories of nature in an unexpected, more challenging locale: the chic, prosperous South of France resort of Nice and its environs.

He sets its busy boulevards against wide overhead shots that show the majesty of the seaport's setting. He explores the lush foliage of the hillside villas, pausing to contemplate a dewdrop on a petal. He allows us to appreciate the beauty of the shamefully disintegrating estate in nearby Menton of once-famous writer Vicente Blasco Ibáñez, whose World War I novel, "The Four Horsemen of the Apocalypse," became the film that launched the legend of Rudolph Valentino. Above all, Gatlif takes us into the company of free spirits, individuals who live apart from the rush of daily life.

In adapting a 1978 novel by the esteemed Nice-born author Jean-Marie Le Clézio, Gatlif acquaints us with these people through their contact with a boy named Mondo (Ovidiu Balan, an 11-year-old Romanian Gypsy). Le Clézio began his story stating that "no one knew where Mondo came from," and Gatlif takes it from there. Mondo doesn't seem either to know or want to say how he happened to pop up in Nice one day, but he's a handsome kid with a radiant smile unafraid to go, up to a stranger and ask, "Would you like to adopt me?"

Although no one does in the formal sense, Mondo, who is likable, resilient and resourceful, has no trouble making friends and surviving. He'll unload produce, collect coins for a street magician/tightrope walker (none other than Philippe Petit, who famously crossed the two towers of the World Trade Center on a wire), learn how to read from an elderly sailor-fisherman (Maurice Maurin) and hang out with a homeless Scotsman (Jerry Smith), who becomes a key father figure. Most important, he is offered permanent refuge by the kindly Thi Chin (Pierette Fesch), an older woman who tells him she is a Vietnamese Jew and who lives in a fine old villa above the city.

(Fesch is in fact the widow of Jacques Fesch, who was guillotined in 1957 at age 27 for having shot to death a policeman in the course of a botched bank robbery, but has been submitted for beatification by the cardinal-archbishop of Paris for the intensity of his religious conversion in prison. You would not know this from the film, any more than you would probably be able to figure out that the oranges covered with writing that Mondo collects at the beach bear pleas for help from Algerian women.)

What Gatlif has done with such consummate artistry is to catch us up in a parallel universe, one that is at one with nature, that exists unobtrusively alongside the workaday world of Nice. What Gatlif—and Le Clézio—are saying is that society threatens this world at the danger of losing its soul.

The climax of "Mondo" is an absolute stunner, requiring the greatest finesse to pull off on the screen. At that point, we realize there has been some exceedingly deft foreshadowing, but this is one allegory that doesn't reveal itself to be one until its astonishing finish.

NEW YORK POST, 5/30/97, p. 53, Michael Medved

"Mondo" is an improbably poetic French import that asks its questions in such lush and lyrical ways that you hardly notice that it offers no answers.

The title character (played by 11-year-old Ovidiu Balan) is a handsome, sensitive Gypsy boy who lives on the streets of the affluent, gleaming Riviera resort city of Nice.

No one knows when or how he arrived in town, or what might have happened to his parents, as he hides from police and occasionally smiles at strangers with the question, "Would you like to adopt me?"

His many friends include: a homeless old man who travels with white doves in his valise (played by a real-life homeless fisherman named Jerry Smith); a magician who wins coins from tourists with his mystical feats (played by world-famous tight-rope walker Philippe Petit); a fisherman (Maurice Maurin) who teaches the homeless boy the alphabet with letters scratched on smooth stones; and an elderly Jewish woman (Pierette Fesch) who lived for years in Vietnam and seems to have imbibed the wisdom and tranquility of the East.

No one in the cast is a professional actor, but all these inexperienced players give remarkably natural and nuanced performances.

Despite his uncertain life and his constant search for food and shelter, Mondo revels in the beauty of his world, celebrating the splendor of sea and sun and even the occasional tropical rain. Every detail—of lizards and scented gardens and ripe pomegranates and dew drops glistening on broad green leaves—is luminously captured in the glorious cinematography of Eric Guichard.

Director Tony Gatlif, best known for 1993's film festival favorite "Latcho Drom," is an Algerian-born Gypsy of French nationality who fills his soundtrack with seductive, exotic, Kurdish, Gypsy and other music with an insinuating Middle Eastern flavor.

His adaptation of the 1978 story by the revered French author J.M.G. Clezio may have timely political resonance at home, where the French electorate just showed unprecedented support for the anti-immigrant agitation of an ultra-nationalist political party.

Even without knowledge of this context, however, and without comprehension (or acceptance) of the gentle, fragile blessing a homeless boy is supposed to confer on an entire town, it is possible to appreciate this captivating challenge on its own visceral and sensual terms.

NEWSDAY, 5/30/97, Part II/p. B11, John Anderson

In his rightfully acclaimed and virtually wordless Gypsy documentary "Latcho Drom," writer-director Tony Gatlif chronicled the music and life of a lost people. In "Mondo," he tells the story of a lost boy. He's clearly a Samaritan, a poetical saver of souls.

His subject here, adapted from the story by the celebrated French author J.M.G. Le Clezio, is Mondo (Ovidiu Balan), a homeless boy who wanders the streets of Nice striking up friendships with bakers and fishermen, but never the police, who want to lock him up. Sleeping in doorways or trees, eating the occasional pomegranate, he is a wild child, a con artist, an open soul.

He asks strangers if they'd like to adopt him, with a smile that's simply devastating; he follows attractive families around the supermarket, eating pilfered Lu cookies while trying to insinuate himself. He knows enough to flee when a weirdo offers him popcorn.

Where Mondo came from is unclear; where he's going becomes a subject of increasing concern.

"Mondo" is a fable, of course, and like many fables it welcomes a variety of interpretations. Seeing the boy simply for what he is—homeless and alone—is fine; seeing him as a metaphor for a society that accepts disposable humanity is fine, too. Taking it much further would probably be a mistake.

But "Mondo" is an absorbing film, as much for Balan's smile as for Gatlif's very personal direction. His focus on detail—insects as well as minutiae—and his passion for the story are embracing. The story, of course, is innately tragic, and each of Mondo's little victories—learning the alphabet, being taken in by the charitable Thi-Chin (Pierette Fresch)—is bittersweet.

"Mondo" is an unusual film, because it tries so little to make you embrace it, and succeeds so easily in making you do just that.

VILLAGE VOICE, 6/3/97, p. 65, J. Hoberman

The perfect feature to pair with last week's *Ponette,* Tony Gatlif's *Mondo* is similarly a movie less sentimental than it sounds that's spun around a notable child performance. This tot epic is set in the south—rather than the north—of France and is not so much a Cartesian exercise in prekindergarten logic as it is a fable trafficking in urchin supernaturalism.

"No one knew where Mondo came from," a voice informs us of the engaging 10-year-old ragamuffin who materializes one day in the Nice marketplace. Homeless and without family, Mondo sleeps in the street (to wake every morning with a perfectly pouffed coiffure and a well-scrubbed face) and spends his days visiting various adult friends—a fisherman, an old clochard, an elderly lady with a comfy villa, and a magician (daredevil aerialist Philippe Petit). Mondo is a sweet little scamp of goodness to be sure, but Ovidiu Balan, the Romanian Gypsy boy who plays the role, doesn't mug the camera. Gatlif, best known for directing the estimable Gypsy-music film *Latcho Drom,* goes for a relaxed form of magic realism, with a world music backbeat and a Bonnard palette. The Mediterranean light and French largesse equal a ban vivant's heaven on earth.

Deceptively tasteful and slight, *Mondo* is at least half a kids'movie—albeit one in the tasteful poetic tradition of *The Red Balloon.* This is the sort of production where statues whisper their secret thoughts and the blue sea is suddenly filled with bobbing Moroccan oranges. Scarcely overwrought, however, the movie suffers from an absence of tension until the final reel, when it becomes the sort of bittersweet fairy tale perfected by Hans Christian Andersen. Who was that strange lad—stray dog or visiting angel?

Also reviewed in:
CHICAGO TRIBUNE, 9/12/97, Friday/p. C, Michael Wilmington
NEW YORK TIMES, 5/30/97, p. C18, Stephen Holden
VARIETY, 3/24-30/97, p. 34, Ken Eisner

MONDO PLYMPTON

A Bill Plympton production. *Producer:* Bill Plympton. *Director:* Bill Plympton. *Screenplay:* Bill Plympton, Peter Vey, and Maureen McElheron. *Director of Photography:* Andrew Willson, John Schnall, John Donnelly, and Bob Lyons. *Editor:* June Althschuler, Stephen Barr, Merrill Sterns, Nico Sheers, and Holly Fadson. *Music:* Timothy Clark, Maureen McElheron, and Damian Boucher. *Sound Editor:* David Rovin. *Production Designer:* Bill Plymton. *Running time:* 80 minutes. *MPAA Rating:* Not Rated.

VILLAGE VOICE, 9/30/97, p. 86, Gary Susman

Apparently released as a stopgap until Bill Plympton completes his next feature of new material (*I Married a Strange Person, Mondo Plympton* recapitulates the 51-year-old cartoonist's entire oeuvre of very funny but oft recycled shorts with all the charm of a grant proposal. Amid this hastily edited anthology, a cynically crude caricature of Plympton patiently answers a trite set of frequently asked questions about his work (e.g., "Where do you get your ideas from?"). Plympton's inventively sadistic pencil draws the human body as endlessly malleable, to an extent that might horrify even David Cronenberg. One new short, "Nosehair," turns a man's battle against unwanted sproutings into a struggle of cosmic significance that is also 12-year-old-boy-pleasingly gross. Excerpts from his little-seen live-action work and *Strange Person* indicate that, while his style is becoming refined and even more surreal, his taste is as gleefully offensive as ever. Still, a little Plympton goes a long way, and most of the material here has been around and around the block.

Aso reviewed in:
NEW YORK TIMES, 9/24/97, p. E5, Lawrence Van Gelder
VARIETY, 8/25-31/97, p. 75, Dennis Harvey

MONEY TALKS

A New Line Cinema release. *Executive Producer:* Chris Tucker. *Producer:* Walter Coblenz and Tracy Kramer. *Director:* Brett Ratner. *Screenplay:* Joel Cohen and Alec Sokolow. *Director of Photography:* Russell Carpenter and Robert Primes. *Editor:* Mark Helfrich. *Music:* Lalo Schifrin. *Music Editor:* Steve McCroskey. *Sound:* Kim Ornitz and (music) Tim Boyle. *Sound Editor:* Tim Chau and Don Malouf. *Casting:* Valerie McCaffrey. *Production Designer:* Robb Wilson King. *Art Director:* John Marshall. *Set Designer:* Alicia MacCarone and Jeff Ozimek. *Set Decorator:* Lance Lombardo. *Set Dresser:* Ron Patterson, Dean Katz, Ara Darakjian, Frankie "Bean" Lombardo VII, John Maxwell, and Vartan "V.T." Tashjian. *Special Effects:* Dennis Dion. *Costumes:* Sharen Davis. *Make-up:* Rea Ann Silva. *Make-up (Charlie Sheen):* Gabriel Solano. *Make-up (Heather Locklear):* Lisa Christy. *Special Effects Make-up:* Myke Williams. *Stunt Coordinator:* Buddy Joe Hooker. *Running time:* 92 minutes. *MPAA Rating:* R.

CAST: Chris Tucker (Franklin Maurice Hatchett); Charlie Sheen (James Russell); Heather Locklear (Grace Cipriani); Gerard Ismael (Raymond Villard); Damian Chapa (Carmine); Elise Neal (Paula Hatchett); Michael Wright (Aaron); Veronica Cartwright (Connie Cipriani); David Warner (Barclay); Paul Gleason (Detective Bobby Pickett); Daniel Roebuck (Detective Williams); Larry Hankin (Roland); Frank Bruynbroeck (Debray); Paul Sorvino (Guy Cipriani); Robertson Dean (Mercedes Owner); Victor Ferreira (Hector); Marty Levy, Mark Benninghofen, and David Lee McLain (Ticket Customers); Victor Ferreira and Gary Briggs (Car Wash Employees); Nathan Anderson (Tom, News Cameraman); Richard Noyce (Detective at Carwash); Faizon Love (Cellmate); Ralph Odum (Prison Bus Guard); Doug Llewelyn (News Anchor); Paul Guyot (Newsroom Colleague); Jeff Brockton and Gary Price (Cops at Diner); Tycho Thal (Patron); Vahe Berberian (Cabby at Pier); Jake (Himself); Jon Chardiet (Red Camel Doorman); Tom Huff (Store Owner); Rosey Brown (Aaron's Bodyguard); Kevin Lowe (Detective at Precinct); Tawny Little (News Reporter); Viveca Paulin (Auctioneer); Mojoe Nicosia (Carmine's Driver); Dexter Tucker and Norris Tucker (Aaron's Boys); Buddy Joe Hooker (Pierre); Matt Brandstein (Cameraman); Rance Howard (Reverend).

LOS ANGELES TIMES, 8/22/97, Calendar/p. 6, Kevin Thomas

"Money Talks"—but nobody talks faster than comedian Chris Tucker. In "The Fifth Element," he was the most hyper, outrageous drag queen imaginable, and now he's the most frenetic con artist you'll ever see.

His Franklin Hatchett is working as a ticket scalper when Charlie Sheen's James Russell, a TV news man desperate for a story, zeros in on him at a carwash. Franklin's subsequent arrest catches both him and James in a comedy-action adventure that actually *is* funny and diverting (so many that are meant to be these days *aren't).*

As his own executive producer, Tucker, whose talent and persona ranges hilariously between Eddie Murphy and Little Richard, clearly knows how to showcase himself and make others, Sheen in particular, look good. too.

This handsome New Line Cinema release is a straightforward genre film, but writers Joel Cohen and Alec Sokolow and director Brett Ratner have fun with a formula plot and bring lots of imagination and humor to the twists and turns of its unfolding.

They further have the good fortune to be working with a production designer, Robb Wilson King, and a pair of cinematographers, Russell Carpenter and Robert Primes, who really know how to make the most of striking Los Angeles locates. Franklin and his no-nonsense girlfriend (Elise Neal) live at the once-grand old Rosslyn—now Frontier—Hotel at 5th and Main streets, and an auction of ultra-high-end cars is held amid the Art Deco splendor of the Pantages Theater. The film's lighting gives a noirish shading to this color picture that stylishly sets off all the slam-bam action and knockabout humor. Adding to the film's flair is Lalo Schifrin's energetic score.

The action kicks in at yet another cherished locale, the beautiful Beaux Arts 1st Street Bridge that spans the Los Angeles River. Right in the middle of it, a bus carrying prisoners is suddenly commandeered by armed gunmen, and Franklin reluctantly escapes, handcuffed to the nasty

Villard (Gerard Ismael), who turns out to be a diamond smuggler (with a current cache worth $15 million).

A couple of swift plot developments land Franklin in the care of James, who wants to hold on to him through the weekend so that his exclusive story will hit a sweeps week. (James' smart, ruthless boss is played sharply by David Warner, a nice casting touch, since the Brits seem to lead the world these days in sensational journalism.)

As it happens, James is about to be married. He is facing pre-wedding festivities at the wonderfully vulgar Second Empire estate—supposedly in Beverly Hills but most likely Pacific Palisades—of his future in-laws, the jovial Guy Cipriani (Paul Sorvino) and his sour-puss wife (Veronica Cartwright), parents of his beautiful fiancée Grace (Heather Locklear), whose trust and loyalty are about to be severely tested.

Tagging along is Franklin, who introduces himself as none other than Vic Damone Jr., son of the famous singer and his former wife Diahann Carroll. (Never mind that Franklin is too old to have been their son, for Guy embraces "Vic Jr." as a paisano).

Amid all of Franklin's constant conning, there emerges, through bracing humor, a sense of how an enterprising yet poor and uneducated young black man has to be fearlessly on his toes to try to get ahead in this world.

Unfortunately, the realities of the marketplace dictate that an action picture aimed at urban male audiences include plenty of violence and mayhem. To be sure, "Money Talks," which culminates in a showdown in the Coliseum that looks like the start of World War III, is no exception. Yet its makers bring a saving humor even to its fiery climax.

NEW YORK POST, 8/22/97, p. 42, Thelma Adams

"Money Talks." Logic walks.

Brett Ratner's improbable buddy comedy is shamelessly familiar. Franklin Hatchett (Chris Tucker) is black. James Russell (Charlie Sheen) is white. One's motor-mouthed and fresh, the other's as stiff as the wind off Nantucket.

The pair would never share the front seat of a car until now: Franklin's ticket scalper is the fall guy in an elaborate jailbreak/jewel heist; Russell's failing tab TV reporter sees Frank as his ticket to "60 Minutes."

The snappy script's premise? If Russell can keep Franklin quiet for 48 hours, he can wed his Beverly Hills princess (Heather Locklear) on Sunday, make sweeps week on Monday and clear Franklin's name.

Ratner, working from a foul-mouthed scenario from "Toy Story" tellers Joel Cohen and Alec Sokolow, uses "48 Hours" as his bible, while leafing through "The Front Page" and skimming "Six Degrees of Separation."

In the Eddie Murphy role, Tucker shoots his lines like a speed freak with spiders in his drawers. So good in "The Fifth Element," the rising star can be sweet and edgy, even tragic, while never losing the comic beat. But the script substitutes obscenities for quips.

As Tucker is straight man, Sheen puts his father Martin's "Apocalypse Now" voice on auto-pilot. He tries hard to pretend he's someone who's actually held down a job.

As the romantic lead, Sheen's soft where Nick Nolte was hard. Locklear has little more to do than look cute and brush her teeth at the same time (for her fans—and you know who you are—that will be enough).

"Money Talks" crests at the L.A. Coliseum with a bigger-is-better climax that unites the bad boys with a rogue cop, French smugglers and Mafia money-lenders. Before the final fireball—as inevitable as July 4th fireworks—Raymond Villard's scene-stealing ghetto gun runner levels the villains with a rocket launcher.

Weapons of mass destruction can be a thing of beauty and vaporize loose plot points.

NEWSDAY, 8/22/97, Part II/p. B11, John Anderson

It's one thing asking audiences to root for a street-smart, wisecracking, ticket-scalping, corner-cutting, edge-of-the-law-skirting L.A. hustler with a rapid-fire mouth and enough body English to suggest there's an earthquake going on. But it's another to ask us to root for someone with no sense of self-preservation.

Franklin Hatchett (Chris Tucker) loses the sympathy vote afforded most oppressed but shady characters, because whenever trouble comes, he has asked for it. He can't shut up, he isn't that funny, and he's ... well, he's a jerk, basically. He flouts both laws the police and the street's—and when he gets in hot water somebody else has to get him out. And as we all know, movie rogues are to be preferred when they're self-sufficient.

So what we have here—after Franklin gets arrested, survives a bloodbath/jailbreak by virtue of being handcuffed to the baddest guy on the jail bus, and calls Charlie Sheen's nerdy TV reporter/groom-to-be "white boy" for 90 minutes—is a comical sidekick playing the lead role. Tucker was moderately amusing in "The Fifth Element" playing the futuristically flamboyant E!-type reporter, but unlike anything else in that film, he came in regulated doses. Here, his relentlessly verbal shtick suffers from a both a slack script and overexposure.

Director Brett Ratner seems to get bored, too, because the movie makes a turn from straight urban comedy to action thriller complete with bloodbath and shock troops. The carnage of the jail-bus inferno was bad enough, but the climactic shootout in the football stadium—Ratner must have had a big pile of nonrefundable film stock—is ludicrously long and pointless.

Lovers of highly developed acting technique will, however, get the chance to see Sheen and Heather Locklear making like Lunt and Fontanne (and in a drawing room yet!). On second thought, open fire.

SIGHT AND SOUND, 4/98, p. 44, Xan Brooks

Los Angeles, the present. Streetwise ticket scalper Franklin Hatchett is jailed thanks to a campaign by reporter James Russell. In prison, Hatchett is handcuffed to international diamond smuggler Raymond Villard, so when Villard's gang engineers a breakout, Franklin is dragged along too. He escapes from Villard but finds himself hunted by the LA police, who believe him to be behind the break-out and blame him for a cop's death.

Franklin hooks up with Russell, who agrees to shield him in return for his exclusive story. Russell introduces Franklin to his fiancée Grace and prospective father-in-law Guy, but Franklin's freewheeling personality plays havoc with the newsman's lifestyle. Franklin steals Villard's diamonds from the vintage Jaguar they're stashed in, and Villard retaliates by holding Russell hostage. Franklin organises a rendezvous at the LA Coliseum, which culminates in an explosive shoot-out: Villard's gang, supported by dirty cop Pickett, battles with Russell, Franklin and Franklin's gangster friend Aaron. The cops arrive to save the day and Villard is killed attempting to escape in his helicopter. Franklin keeps a few of the diamonds for himself and inserts one into Grace's wedding ring.

Afro-American actor Chris Tucker wears his influences on his sleeve. "Eddie Murphy is my idol," he has said. "He took action-comedy to another level and that's what I want to do for my generation."

Accordingly, *Money Talks* (which Tucker stars in and co-executive produced) comes straight out of the Murphy cookie-cutter. It's an ebony-and-ivory buddy-pic: bickering black guy and white guy in uneasy alliance. One might dub it *Another 48HRS.* had Murphy himself not already used that title. Indeed, in the last decade no one has been recycling the Eddie Murphy myth quite so cynically as Murphy himself. That said, Tucker comes close. His Franklin Hatchett is a karaoke reprise of *48HRS.'* Reggie Hammond, or *Trading Places'* Billy Ray Valentine. He's shrill and speedy; irrepressibly anarchic with a twist of camp. Co-star Charlie Sheen (as stuffed shirt newsman James Russell) is reduced to a testy stooge, standing stiffly to one side as Tucker does his *schtick*.

To be fair, 24-year-old Tucker is capable of more than a low-rent Murphy impersonation, as his edgy performance in the Hughes Brothers' *Dead Presidents* has already demonstrated. However, here debut director Brett Ratner's indulgent handling affords Tucker more than enough rope to hang himself. The film itself clings like a limpet to its odd-couple-in-trouble format, and its rash of subplots ultimately adds up to very little. What fuels it are frequent inconsequential bursts of action (car chases, shoot-outs) and low comedy. It is casually racist ("How those 7-11s going?" quips Hatchett to an Asian millionaire) and mildly homophobic (in jail, Franklin fights off the advances of a bullish gay man). But there is no dynamism, no internal engine to drive the action and anchor the wit. As a substitute, Ratner trusts his soundtrack to do the work. Ominous military drums crop up during the prison scenes; a funky wah-wah guitar gets us through a car chase. Later, when Hatchett and Russell visit a shady black night spot, the audience is treated to a blast of Curtis Mayfield's 'Pusher Man', just to underline the point.

A few crisp lines and genial performances glitter amid the gloom. Hatchett's spiralling fascination with Italian crooner Vic Damone makes for some decent, quirky humour, while Paul Sorvino radiates good-natured bonhomie as Russell's prospective father-in-law. Yet on the whole, there's not a great deal to take away from *Money Talks*. It leaves a jumbled, chaotic impression: a lot of windows being shot out by numerous cops, an extended who's-shooting-whom finale and frequent, fantastical talk of buttocks. The "ass", you see, looms large as a reference point throughout *Money Talks*. Characters invite their rivals to "bite my ass" and "kiss my ass". They request each other to "move your ass". They "want your ass dead", and make several solemn promises to "beat your ass". In the end, it all becomes a bit much. To paraphrase a certain hotelier in the "Waldorf Salad" episode of *Fawlty Towers,* everything's bottoms with these people.

VILLAGE VOICE, 8/26/97, p. 78, Gary Dauphin

If you pare Chris Tucker's comic appeal down to fundamentals, you end up with a helium-inflated, vaguely phlegmy sound. With only *Dead Presidents, Friday,* and *The Fifth Element* to its credit, Tucker's voice is already an identifiable trademark (think Eddie Murphy's laugh or Martin Lawrence's ears), and it's been used to good effect in supporting roles so far, the young comedian spitting out words in a barely controlled tumble that jitters up and down his personal scale of conning lows and just plain screaming highs.

Money Talks is Tucker's first starring role, and forced to carry a roundly mediocre picture, he sounds mostly like a loose bolt rattling in a used car, something small and hard and about to give. Directed by Brett Ratner with none of the saturated and glossy visual style that made his videos MTV staples, *Money* opens with ticket scalper and fence Franklin Hatchett (Tucker) going to L.A. county lockup after snubbing TV reporter James Russell (Charlie Sheen). Franklin is accidentally busted out of jail by a French diamond thief and his *copains,* quickly becoming the improbable object of a shoot-first police manhunt. He ends up back with the soon-to-be-married Russell, crashing his rehearsal dinner and posing as Vic Damone and Diahann Carroll's love child when he's not dodging gun-toting Gauls.

Money Talks is predictable black-guy-white-guy action shtick, but although it shouldn't sink Tucker (I mean, look at Charlie Sheen—he's still working), quite a few audience members may decide he's just talking that same old shit.

Also reviewed in:
NEW YORK TIMES, 8/22/97, p. C5, Stephen Holden
VARIETY, 8/18-24/97, p. 33, Leonard Klady

MONGOLIAN TALE, A

A New Yorker Films release of a Beijing Youth Film Studio/Media Asian Films coproduction. *Producer:* Ma Fung-kwok and Wellington Fung. *Director:* Xie Fei. *Screenplay (Mandarin and Mongolian with English subtitles) based on his novel "Black Steed":* Zhang Chengzhi. *Director of Photography:* Fu Jing-sheng. *Editor:* Xie Fei and Zhao Xiuqin. *Running time:* 104 minutes. *MPAA Rating:* Not Rated.

CAST: Tengger (Beiyinpalica); Naranhua (Someyer); Dalarsurong (Nai Nai).

LOS ANGELES TIMES, 5/16/97, Calendar/p. 14, Kevin Thomas

Xie Fei's beautiful "A Mongolian Tale" is a deceptively simple tale of love and loss, redemption and forgiveness. As a story set in Mongolia and dealing with the inevitability of change, it will surely be compared with Nikita Mikhalkov's somewhat similar and equally splendid 1992 "Close to Eden." The difference between Mikhalkov's Oscar-nominated film and this exquisite film, based on Zhang Chengzhi's popular 1982 novel "Black Steed," is primarily one of perspective, in that it is told by an insider rather than an outsider.

When a city man becomes widowed, he turns over his small son to be raised by his own foster mother, who follows an ancient way of life as a nomadic shepherd. The boy, Beiyinpalica, grows up in an idyllic existence with his beloved Grandma (majestic veteran actress Dalarsurong) and her daughter Someyer, who is roughly the same age as he is. In its first hour the film, set in magnificent grasslands and snowy winter camps, celebrates the life these three lead, close to nature and full of love for one another. However, just as we're thoroughly immersed in a long-ago world, Beiyinpalica, stretched out in a field, watches a jet streaking across the sky overhead. Very shortly, his father will be summoning him back to the city for veterinary studies; somehow a planned eight-month sojourn stretches out to three years. Even so, the now-adult Bayinbulag (Tengger, a major pop singer-composer) forsakes college to return to the steppes to marry his true love Someyer (Naranhuar, the star of Xie's celebrated "Girl From Hunan").

An incident, however, has occurred during Beiyinpalica's absence that will so wound his immature male pride that he turns around and leaves, not to return again for another 12 years. This is the heart of the matter, for the film suggests with a subtle power that true morality derives from nature—that city life can inspire judgments at once abstract and cruel.

However, it takes Beiyinpalica so long to grow up that the consequences of his angry departure are unalterable, both for him and for Someyer. Yet "A Mongolian Tale" holds out for the possibility that in spirit individuals can transcend circumstances—that the values of the past, therefore, have crucial meaning in the present.

There's a poetic quality, combined with a novel's depth of characterization, that makes "A Mongolian Tale" a memorable experience, superbly acted, gorgeously photographed and plaintively scored by Tengger himself.

NEW YORK POST, 4/2/97, p. 38, Bill Hoffmann

Theaters are crammed with movies about lost love, broken hearts and unsettled souls—but few have been set in Mongolia.

That's the secret power behind "A Mongolian Tale," which takes the age-old story of youthful defiance and doomed romance and sets it in the harshly beautiful terrain of a land far, far away.

It's a moving tale of the strength—and stubbornness—of the human spirit.

Nai-Nai (Dalasurong) is a feisty, never-say-die grandma whose life revolves around raising foster kids in the wilds of Inner Mongolia.

Into her brood come a sweet Chinese boy, Beiyinpalica (Tengger) and a delicate Mongolian girl, Someyer (Naranhua), who she decides will one day marry.

Everybody agrees, but first, our young man must go off to the big city to study for eight months. Someyer vows to wait—but when those months turn into three years, our now-worldly teen returns to find a new wrinkle.

His betrothed has been seduced by the local rogue who has gotten her pregnant and doesn't mind boasting about his conquest.

This braggadocio drives our hero up a wall, and he can't accept that his bride-to-be has been compromised. Off he goes, traveling the land as a troubadour, singing painful songs about his screwed-up love.

Someyer, meantime, weds somebody else and begins popping out kids. When Beiyinpalica returns years later, emotional sparks fly.

Director Xie Fei keeps us engrossed until the bitter end, thanks to his expert handling of a fine cast, soul-stirring Mongolian scenery and timeless Eastern philosophies.

Mongolia is the end of the world, to most folks. But it's one dynamite locale for a movie, and "A Mongolian Tale" takes full advantage of that fact for all of its 104 minutes.

VILLAGE VOICE, 4/8/97, p. 79, J. Hoberman

The landscape is the star of Chinese director Xie Fei's *A Mongolian Tale*. As anyone who has seen Nikita Mikhalkov's *Close to Eden* or Tian Zhuangzhuang's *Horse Thief* knows, few vistas are more sensationally photogenic than the Mongolian grasslands. Grooving on cosmic emptiness, however, you may realize that looks aren't everything.

A Mongolian Tale's sappy plot and stilted characterizations would've seemed old to D. W Griffith. A Chinese boy and a Mongolian girl are raised together by their kindly adoptive granny in a little yurt on the steppes. The foster sibs plan to marry but, while the boy is away studying music in the big city, the girl (Naranhuar, last seen here as the sexual victim in Xie's 1986 *Girl From Hunan)* succumbs to the local seducer and the boy—well, if you've seen *Chasing Amy,* you know how guys are. Years later and filled with regret, he returns to the steppe to find his lost love married to a drunk, presiding over a house filled with squalling brats.

Like *Girl From Hunan, A Mongolian Tale,* has the flat, posterish quality characteristic of pre-Fifth Generation Chinese movies. Although it is neither sufficiently well acted nor even scenic enough to command much attention, the maudlin situation has a cumulatively wistful effect, and I can almost guarantee that you'll learn more than you knew before about life in a yurt.

Also reviewed in:
NEW REPUBLIC, 3/31/97, p. 26, Stanley Kauffmann
NEW YORK TIMES, 4/3/97, p. C16, Janet Maslin
VARIETY, 9/4-10/95, p. 78, David Stratton

MORTAL KOMBAT ANNIHILATION

A New Line Cinema release of a Lawrence Kasanoff/Threshold Entertainment production. *Executive Producer:* Alison Savitch, Carla Fry, and Brian Witten. *Producer:* Lawrence Kasanoff. *Director:* John R. Leonetti. *Screenplay:* Brent V. Friedman and Bryce Zabel. *Story:* Lawrence Kasanoff, Joshua Wexler, and John Tobias. *Based on the videogame created by:* Ed Boon and John Tobias. *Director of Photography:* Matthew F. Leonetti. *Editor:* Peck Prior. *Music:* George S. Clinton. *Music Editor:* Mike Flicker. *Sound:* John Midgley and (music) John Whynot. *Sound Editor:* Miguel Rivera. *Casting:* Fern Champion and Mark Paladini. *Production Designer:* Charles Wood. *Art Director:* Nathan Schroeder. *Set Designer:* Martin Roy Mervel and Jamie Carr. *Set Decorator:* Simon R.S. Wakefield. *Special Effects:* Ron Trost. *Visual Effects:* Jessica Huebner. *Prosthetic Make-up Designer:* Gary Pollard. *Animatronic Model Designer:* Chris Barton. *Costumes:* Jennifer L. Parsons. *Make-up:* Melissa Lackersteen. *Stunt Coordinator:* Pat Johnson and Eddie Stacey. *Running time:* 93 minutes. *MPAA Rating:* PG-13.

CAST: Robin Shou (Liu Kang); Talisa Soto (Kitana); James Remar (Rayden); Sandra Hess (Sonya Blade); Lynn Red Williams (Jax); Brian Thompson (Shao-Kahn); Reiner Schoene (Shinnok); Musetta Vander (Sindel); Irina Pantaeva (Jade); Deron McBee (Motaro); Marjean Holden (Sheeva); Litefoot (Nightwolf); Chris Conrad (Johnny Cage); John Medlen (Ermac); J.J. Perry (Cyrax/Scorpion); Tyrone Wiggins (Rain); Dennis Keiffer (Baraka); Ridley Tsui Po Wah (Smoke); Keith Cooke Hirabayashi (Sub-Zero); Lance LeGault (Elder God #1); Carolyn Seymour (Elder God #2); Dana Hee (Mileena); Ray Park (Rayden Double).

LOS ANGELES TIMES, 11/10/97, Calendar/p. 10, Bob Heisler

Rule No. 1 of fantasy movies: Box office rules.
The mortal world was saved for a generation in 1995, when Liu Kang (Robin Shou) defeated the champion of the Outworld in "Mortal Kombat," the movie.
Case closed. Now, everyone, back to the video game to train for the next battle in, say, 20 years. The portal between the Realm of Earth and the Outworld was closed with the solemn promise that things would remain hunky-dory for Liu and his friends.
Not so fast, pathetic humans.
The Elder Gods didn't count on "Mortal Kombat" making more than $100 million, including rentals. And that's not counting foreign sales.
So rip open the portal and prepare Earth to meet its doom.
With holdovers playing Liu and his romantic interest Kitana (Talisa Soto), a new director, (John R. Leonetti) and a new flock of martial artists leaping, kicking and twirling, "Mortal Kombat Annihilation" arrived Friday. The sequel is quite serious, charmless and critic-proof (in fact, it

wasn't screened for the media), and it may attract the teenagers who have made the game so popular.

Then again, it may not.

Unlike with the video game, the outcome here is as certain as an episode of "Mighty Morphin Power Rangers." There will be a martial arts fight to the finish between good and evil. In this corner, the folks who play by the rules, the puny mortals. In the other corner, the folks who don't, the Outers, who really mess up things—at least geographically—before they're through.

Unlike with the video game, there is no apparent violence. Mortal and monster alike tumble from tall buildings, fall against crumbling walls, bounce off a variety of surfaces with no bruises or blood. Oh, a couple of bad guys dissolve, females get to fight in the mud and Jax (Lynn Red Williams) has to tear off his cybernetic, arm-length gloves before he can do his thing, but people only die when thrown into a pit of fire or when their necks are snapped with a loud soundtrack crack. Oddly, amazingly, the neck is the only bone broken anywhere.

There are lessons, of course. Underestimating the power of the human spirit gets you into trouble every time. Earth does not bend to the will of tyrants. Cheaters never win. What closes can also open again. And vice versa.

Characters from the first movie appear in this one, at least briefly, and because they are played by new faces, they must be introduced by name. So you'll see Johnny Cage and Sub-Zero, but don't blink.

The martial arts sequences themselves are carefully choreographed dance routines but provide neither spiritual enlightenment nor enthralling action. The video game elements—multilevel sets, the tendency for a bad guy to suddenly morph or throw out a dragon-headed coil from his midsection—are simply curves in the same thrill ride.

More than a few hands will reach for a joystick to get more involved, but alas, this is not a game. It's only a movie.

NEW YORK POST, 11/22/97, p. 23, Larry Worth

The ad proclaims: "Destroy all expectations."

But why would those who saw the dismal "Mortal Kombat" have any expectations for "Mortal Kombat Annihilation"?

The first was no work of art, but it had more to offer than this makes-no-sense knockoff, a virtual blur of flying fists and legs, pyrotechnics galore, snthesizer-heavy music and cheesy special effects.

Once again two muscle-bound hunks, two babe-a-licious fighting machines and the God of Lightning(!) try to save Earth from evil, this time taking shape as a bald behemoth and his army of freaks.

Perhaps because of embarrassment, only two of the original cast members (Robin Shou and Talisa Soto) have resurrected their characters. Doesn't matter—no one would know the difference anyway.

There's a new director this time, too. Under John R. Leonetti's guidance, the men's costumes tend more toward RoboCop while the ladies look like S&M parlor escapees. At one point, two scantily clad beauties even have a knockdown, drag-out sludge fight, after which the lead guy slobbers, "Ummm-ummm-ummm, you do look good in mud."

Teen-age boys, the film's presumed audience, will probably howl in delight. They'll be equally forgiving of unimaginative computer-generated monsters, endless mumbo jumbo about "opened portals from Outworld" and non-stop choke holds between sad-sack ninjas and overgrown Power Rangers.

All other viewers will get the message loud and clear when one of the villains looks into the camera and yells: "Suckers."

SIGHT AND SOUND, 4/98, p. 45, Andy Richards

Having defeated the evil sorcerer Shang Tsung in the tournament of Mortal Kombat, martial artists Liu Kang, Sonya Blade, Johnny Cage and Princess Kitana are attacked by Shao-Kahn, Emperor of Outworld. Cage is killed. Nice deity Lord Rayden explains to Liu and the others that

Kahn has decided to eschew Mortal Kombat's rules and create a "hell on earth" by allowing Outworld to merge with the human world.

Sonya teams up with Commander "Jax" Briggs and they defeat the evil robot Sektor, while Liu and Kitana defeat the robot Cyrax. Kitana is then captured by Scorpion. Liu meets Nightwolf, who helps him understand his own "animality". Sonya fights and defeats the knife-wielding Mileena. Rayden visits the shrine of the Elder Gods, to complain about Kahn's rule violation. Meanwhile, Kahn appoints Queen Sindel his general. Liu rescues Kitana, and they reunite with Sonya and Jax. Rayden tells them that Kahn is his brother, and that their father—a renegade Elder God—is behind the plot to destroy the earth. They enter Outworld. Kahn kills Rayden. Liu and Kahn battle, transforming themselves into a dragon and a hyena respectively. The remaining Elder Gods appear, and imprison Kahn's father. Liu defeats Kahn, and the surviving combatants return to earth, where a reformed Sindel is reunited with her daughter Kitana, and Rayden is resurrected as a new Elder God.

The manifold failings of *Mortal Kombat 2 Annihilation* highlight the obvious problems of creating coherent and sustained narrative drive from material that is inherently repetitive and overpopulated. As with its game-derived predecessors *Street Fighter and Super Mario Bros.*, this film only succeeds in provoking a desire for the more involving pleasures of the game itself. In fact, both *Mortal Kombat* films function more as extended advertisements than as satisfying experiences in their own right.

The premise of Paul Anderson's original *Mortal Kombat* derived directly from Robert Clouse's *Enter the Dragon* in which a motley group of fighters convene on an island for a supreme tournament. The sequel attempts to extend the series' mythical pretensions through the contrivance of a family feud involving Lord Rayden, his brother Kahn and their corrupt Elder God father. Unfortunately, the plotting is so haphazard, it quickly becomes irrelevant, merely serving to set up the next bone-crushing one-on-one between adversaries. The sequel's action sequences are superior to those of its predecessor, but the violence on display in both films is restrained when set against the graphic bloodshed of the games themselves. It is hard not to assume that the film's core game-playing audience will find the whole translation—with not a decapitation or evisceration in sight—somewhat tame.

While the film's optical effects and action sequences may qualify as acceptable on their own terms (its first-time director John R. Leonetti was the cinematographer of *The Mask),* with this rampantly illogical screenplay it becomes increasingly hard to care about the outcome of events. Characters inexplicably appear and disappear from the story. The reuniting of Kitana with her mother Sindel, which Rayden assures us will be the key to final victory, is a bathetic aftermath to the climactic showdown. At one point, Kahn's father states his desire for an heir "strong enough to kill his own brother"; later, however, Rayden is invited to rejoin his father and brother to rule over the earth. Most incoherently, Liu Kang's efforts to comprehend his own 'animality' are ultimately rendered useless since he doesn't use the skills when he finally kills his enemy Kahn. Such wanton disregard for consistency quickly becomes infuriating, dissipating any vestiges of tension and leaving only a predictable cavalcade of face-offs.

Also reviewed in:
CHICAGO TRIBUNE, 11/27/97, Tempo/p. 9, John Petrakis
NEW YORK TIMES, 11/22/97, p. B10, Lawrence Van Gelder
VARIETY, 11/24-30/97, p. 64, Daniel M. Kimmel

MOST WANTED

A New Line Cinema release of an Ivory Way production. *Executive Producer:* Keen Ivory Wayans and Tony Mark. *Producer:* Eric L. Gold. *Director:* David Glenn Hogan. *Screenplay:* Keenen Ivory Wayans. *Director of Photography:* Marc Reshovsky. *Editor:* Michael J. Duthie and Mark Helfrich. *Music:* Paul Buckmaster. *Music Editor:* Tom Kramer. *Sound:* Michael Hogan and (music) Keith Grant. *Sound Editor:* Andrew DeCristofaro. *Casting:* Valerie McCaffrey. *Production Designer:* Jean-Philippe Carp. *Art Director:* Arlan Jay Vetter. *Set Decorator:* Alex Carle. *Set Dresser:* Rich Baum and Lisa A. Corbin. *Special Effects:* Joe D.

Ramsey. *Costumes:* Ileane Meltzer. *Make-up:* Ken Diaz. *Stunt Coordinator:* Charles Picerni, Jr. *Running time:* 90 minutes. *MPAA Rating:* R.

CAST: Keenen Ivory Wayans (James Dunn); Robert Kotecki (Marine Lieutenant); Rick Cramer (Bus Guard 1); Kenn Whitaker (Bus Guard 2); Wolfgang Bodison (Capt. Steve Braddock); Jon Voight (Casey/Woodward); Eddie Velez (Sgt. Peyton); Michael Marich (Omega 3); Simon Baker Denny (Stephen Barnes); Jill Hennessy (Victoria Constantini); Donna Cherry (First Lady); Robert Culp (Donald Bickhart); Eric Roberts (Spencer); Paul Sorvino (Ken Rackmill); John Diehl (Police Captain); Michael Milhoan (SWAT Leader); Tucker Smallwood (Police Chief William Watson); Amanda Kravat (Charlie); Mario Vitale (Bartender); Ping Wu (Patrolman); Andy Hogan (Video Tech); Casey Lee (Randy); Richard Noyce (Policeman in Hospital 1); Jerry Rector (Policeman in Hospital 2); Chris Geier (Laundry Orderly); Lee Debroux (Commander Goldstein); Sasha Foo (Newscaster); Dave Oliver (Lt. Scruggs); Karen Folkes (Checkpoint Officer); Thomas G. Waites (Sargeant); Martin Grimes (Hot Dog Vendor); David Groh (TV Station Manager); Benny Moore (Man on street); Kaye Wade (Grocery Woman); L.V. Sanders (Gangbanger #1); Tito Larriva (Gangbanger #2); Michael D. Roberts (Homeless Man); Vernon P. Thompson (Homeless Camp Police Officer); David Basulto (Library Security Guard); Melanie Van Betten (VA Hospital Clerk); Mitchell Marchand (Card Player 1); Antonio T. Arnold, Jr. (Card Player 2); Ernie Lee Banks (Card Player 3); Brian Macon (C.I.A. Agent); Christine Devine (Hearing's Reporter).

LOS ANGELES TIMES, 10/10/97, Calendar/p. 8, Jack Mathews

[The following review by Jack Mathews appeared in a slightly different form in NEWSDAY, 10/10/97, Part II/p. B7.]

Keenen Ivory Wayans, writer, producer and star of the chase film "Most Wanted," is said to have done some of the research for his story on the Internet, which is just one more reason to fear the influence of this technological monster.

"Most Wanted" is nonsense on what looks to be a $30-million, maybe $40-million budget. Great-looking sets, intricately staged stunts, elegantly moody photography, spectacular fireball explosions, big crowd scenes and not a nanosecond of plausibility—even by the low standards of the contemporary Hollywood action-thriller.

Stop me if you hear something that rings true here. Wayans plays Sgt. James Dunn, a wrongly imprisoned Marine sniper who is freed by a covert military team and given the choice of returning to the gallows or being the triggerman in an assassination. He chooses the latter, but before he can get a shot off at his intended target, an industrialist with close ties to the White House, a bullet rips through the chest of the first lady, who is standing next to the man.

Suddenly, Dunn is being chased all over Los Angeles by the LAPD, the FBI, the CIA, members of his own covert team, and possibly, the Cookie Monster. It's often too dark to tell. Wayans is better known to most of us as one of the creative talents behind TV's "In Living Color," but this is no joke. "Most Wanted," and most particularly, Dunn, are dead serious, and director David Glenn Hogan stages every ludicrous scene as if he were dramatizing historical events.

Instead, he's dramatizing material that makes you wonder which Web site Wayans was on. The story has the first lady's campaign for veterans' rights running her afoul of a billionaire biotechnology mogul (Robert Culp) and the sadistic rogue general (Jon Voight) he's paying to cover up a lethal biochemical test done with unsuspecting soldiers. Where's the Toxic Avenger when you need him? Wayans has fashioned for himself the role of a silent superhero, a brooding tough guy with an arsenal of techno-guerrilla skills.

He can break into guarded mansions and secured computer systems with equal ease. He can outrun mobs and fusillades of bullets. He's a martial arts expert and can leap tall buildings—or at least leap between them—in a single bound. What he can't do is hold the screen.

Wayans has great looks and size, but he has no interior presence. There is no weight to his character, and even his voice. Even when he's threatening someone, he sounds like a student who's been asked to raise his voice in class.

The performances are all best described as deadpan. As the deputy CIA director, Paul Sorvino looks as if he'd rather be singing opera, and Voight, affecting a terrible southern accent, has the rigid manner of someone who's just had back surgery.

Finally, as the obligatory ally, an eyewitness who can prove Dunn's innocence, Jill Hennessy has little to do other than pester him about what to do next. But she looks great asking.

NEW YORK POST, 10/10/97, p. 49, Larry Worth

Ten years ago, Keenen Ivory Wayans proved himself a first-rate comedian. More recently, he has shown himself to be a second-rate talk show host. And in "Most Wanted," he's a third-rate action hero.

Can fourth-rate dramatist be far behind? Sadly, that has arrived, too: Wayans penned the all-too-familiar, hopelessly illogical script for "Most Wanted."

Here's the setup: Wayans stars as James Dunn, a Gulf War veteran whos about to be executed for killing a superior officer (in self-defense, of course). En route to his hanging party, James is waylaid by the leader of the "Black Sheep," an ultra-secret government-sanctioned assassination squad.

To win his freedom, James must join Operation Wrath, the goal of which is offing a black-market industrialist who's squiring the First Lady around Los Angeles. Faster than you can say Lee Harvey Oswald, the right-wing group has murdered the president's wife and is pointing the finger at you-know-who.

Not to worry. As luck—and hackneyed screenplays—would have it, a gorgeous doctor videotaped the real sharpshooter on a nearby balcony. Naturally, the Black Sheep goons want her dead, too, so James must snatch up the damsel in distress.

All that's left is for the dynamic duo to put Black Sheep members out to pasture, expose a mole in the CIA hierarchy and save the Western Hemisphere from a power-hungry madman.

OK did Wayans miss any cliches? If he did, it was an oversight.

Thankfully, his on-screen presence, even when trying to wax dramatic, clearly outshines his conspiracy scenarios. Looking cool in a spaghetti-western-style duster coat, Wayans' appeal —evidenced on TVs "In Living Color"—is muted but not altogether lacking.

Also serving as producer, he at least had the smarts to surround himself with a great supporting cast.

First and foremost, Southern accented Jon Voight chews scenery with delicious panache as the Black Sheep's manic leader. In contrast, Paul Sorvino is refreshingly laid-back as a head honcho at the CIA.

Likewise, Eric Roberts provides a fun change-of-pace as Sorvino's scholarly, suspender-wearing aide. Then there's Jill Hennessy, who holds her own as Wayans' reluctant sidekick, and Robert Culp's amusing turn as the First Lady's smarmy escort.

Director David Glenn Hogan is more of an unknown, and will remain so if he continues in this mode. Hogan gives viewers scene after silly scene of what's been done before, and appreciably better. Only a multiple car crash late in the proceedings is vaguely memorable.

The bottom line is that Wayans should think long and hard about his future. No one questions his talent, only his wasting it on the likes of "Most Wanted."

SIGHT AND SOUND, 6/98, p. 51, Andy Richards

Sgt James Dunn was imprisoned during the Gulf War for killing a superior officer after he refused to shoot a young Iraqi soldier. Dunn is transferred to Death Row. En route, he is rescued by a covert operations unit called "The Black Sheep", headed by Lt Col Grant Casey. Dunn reluctantly agrees to take the 'kill shot' in an assassination operation on Bickhart, a prominent industrialist, who will be presiding over an opening ceremony with the First Lady. When the First Lady is assassinated before Dunn can kill Bickhart, he realises that he has been set up by Casey.

Dunn flees, pursued by the LAPD and Casey's military squad. He tracks down Victoria Constantini, whose home videotape of the ceremony proves his innocence. Together they discover that the First Lady was on the verge of exposing illegal vaccine research carried out by Bickhart's bio-weapons division. Bickhart offers a $10m public reward for Dunn's capture. Dunn sends the videotape to a news station, but it is intercepted and doctored by Casey's team.

Dunn contacts a man named Rackmill at the CIA who wants to flush out Casey. Dunn infiltrates Casey's HQ, and locates the key to his incriminating computer files. He escapes, and is 'brought in' by Rackmill. Rackmill meets with Casey, and agrees to exchange the files for $5m of the reward money. Casey, having implicated himself, is then executed by Dunn.

Like other recent paranoid action films (*Shadow Conspiracy, Conspiracy Theory,* even Stone's *JFK), Most Wanted* (directed by David Glenn Hogan, director of *Barb Wire)* is content to borrow scenarios and tropes from the classic paranoia cycle of the 70s *(The Parallax View, The Conversation, Three Days of the Condor)* while also offering the kind of triumphant closure that was anathema to the far more cynical, defeatist tone of those Watergate-era films. These new films assume that the cancer of corruption is something that can be cut out cleanly, whereas the older films disturbingly suggested that the rot is everywhere and hard to pinpoint.   The assassinations and framings are all present and correct, but this new cycle conceives of its heroes in wholly uncomplicated terms. Here, Wayans' James Dunn's only crime is his failure to obey an order to shoot an Iraqi boy-soldier in cold blood which led to his killing a superior in self defence.   Voigt is quickly established as the ruthless villain of the piece (reprising his role as intelligence mole from De Palma's *Mission Impossible,* only this time with a faintly ludicrous Southern drawl). It's easy to anticipate the final outcome of this particular plot; Dunn's ability to restore order and justice is never in doubt.

If one accepts the film's limitations, it is still possible to enjoy the efficiency of its construction. The plot information unfolds thick and fast, with Wayans hurtling around LA from one location to the next, plausibly failing to find the time to entangle himself romantically with Jill Hennessy's Victoria Constantini. Wayans, through his production company Ivory Way, is clearly seeking to broaden his range from comedy into action.   Surprisingly, given Keenen Wayans' grounding in comedy material, it is in the film's (mercifully few) humorous interludes that the blandness of his character and the overall slightness of *Most Wanted* becomes most apparent.   Conspiracy films, it would seem, work better with a straight face.

Also reviewed in:
NEW YORK TIMES, 10/10/97, p. E20, Janet Maslin
WASHINGTON POST, 10/10/97, p. D6, Rita Kempley

MOUSE, THE

A Strand Releasing release of an Early Morning Films production. *Executive Producer:* Richard Segedin, Charlie Irish, and Jimmy Walter. *Producer:* Hank Blumental, Harris Tulchin, and John Savage. *Director:* Daniel Adams. *Screenplay:* Daniel Adams. *Director of Photography:* Denise Brassard. *Editor:* Victoria Street. *Music:* Johnathan Edwards. *Sound:* Dave Pastecchi and Alex Wolfe. *Casting:* Shelia Jaffe and Georgianne Walken. *Production Designer:* Gay Studebaker. *Art Director:* Richard Devine.   *Set Dresser:* Chris Rego-Marquiis and Anthony Caruso. *Costumes:* Deborah Newhall. *Make-up:* Heide Kulow. *Stunt Coordinator:* Don Hewitt. *Running time:* 98 minutes. *MPAA Rating:* Not Rated.

CAST: John Savage (Bruce "The Mouse" Strauss); Angelica Torn (Mary Lou Strauss); Rip Torn (Trucker, God); Charles Bailey-Gates (Joe); Irina Cashen (Jamie Strauss); Tim Williams (Frank "Gator" Lux); Edward Lynch (Ron "Butcher" Stander); Rhasaan Orange (Shamster 1); Gary Galone (Shamster 2); Danny Venezia (Shamster 3); Burt Young (Himself); Ray "Boom Boom" Mancini (Larry); Richard Segedin (Sammy); Randall "Tex" Cobb (Himself); Vinny Pazienza (Himself); Sean O'Grady (Himself); Vito Antuofermo (Trainer); Tommy Makem (Commissioner Adams); Domic Chianese (Al the Trainer); Keena Keel (Ann); Gerald Orange (Pete); Verdell Smith (Marty McCormick); Jack Celli (Flashback Promoter); Mario Cianfione (Lopez); John Nacco (Bernie); Ed Begine (Don the Promoter); Steve Brito (Dead Boxer); Frank Gio (Commissioner Brennan); Charlie Irish (Drunk); Michael A. Biase (Ear Doctor); George Van Voorhis (Dead Boxer Trainer); Frank "The Gator" Lux (Lopez Newscaster); Ron "the Butcher" Stander (Bar Patron); Bruce "The Mouse" Strauss (Angelo); Rebecca Rae Adams

(Ginny); Danny Campbell (Himself); Mitch Fennel (Ryan Trainer); Daniel Welch (Flashback); Susan Youngs (McCormick Heckler 1); Michael Cambell (McCormick Heckler 2); Edward Biggine (McCormick Heckler 3); Randy Gordon (Fan); Jim Tunney (Himself); Kip Diggs (Himself); Dick Ryan (Himself); Guy Strauss (Finger Referee); Richard Pitts-Wiley (McCormick Referee); Nick Hasomeris (Flashback Referee); Bill Galvin (Lopez Reporter 1); Tim Miller (Lopez Reporter 2); James Paul Ludwig (Lopez Reporter 3); Wendy Adams (Round Card Girl 1); Tonya Jeria (Round Card Girl 2); Tom Kemp (Commissioner Collins); Lance Norris (Bear Bartender); Burke Carroll (Bear); William J. Devany (McCormick Trainer); Bernie Barry (Lopez Referee).

LOS ANGELES TIMES, 11/14/97, Calendar/p. 24, Kevin Thomas

[The following review by Kevin Thomas appeared in a slightly different form in **NEWSDAY, 11/14/97, Part II/p. B13.]**

Dan Adams' "The Mouse" is a warm, affectionate boxing movie about an actual prizefighter, Bruce "The Mouse" Strauss, whose claim to fame is that he's been knocked out more than any other boxer in history. Indeed, when we meet him, his fondest dream is to be knocked out in every continent in the world. Mouse is played beautifully by John Savage, who physically resembles the real-life Strauss.

Savage's Omaha-based Strauss comes across as a dese, dem and dose guy whose speech belies a cagey philosopher and an old pro with an original take on the rules. Early on, Mouse—who had been a bouncer in a topless bar—discovers he just loves to box and that that was the point rather than winning. The other point is that in carefully calculating losing vs. occasionally winning he discovered a way to secure longevity doing what he loved and in the process earning a decent living for his family.

There are two catches, however. First, by being on the road so much of the time, Mouse puts an increasing strain on his marriage to his loving but fed-up schoolteacher wife (Angelica Torn, the talented daughter of Rip Torn and the late Geraldine Page) and neglects his daughter (Irina Cashen). (He's proud of her skill as a gymnast but loathes the fiercely competitive aspect of her sport.)

While a marital crisis is at the heart of "The Mouse," the film dodges the darker implications of Strauss' career. It treats in jokey fashion the fact that Strauss shamelessly resorts to any ruse to avoid the requisite three-month layoff between being knocked out.

"The Mouse" is intent on being a sweet, modest little comedy, but it's just impossible to sit through it without being forced to think about the brutal aspects of Strauss' way of life and how dangerous all those knockouts are to his brain and to his very existence. Furthermore, Savage has made Mouse such a likably distinctive guy we can't help but become concerned about him. "The Mouse" would have been a stronger movie had it found a way to deal with such realities of the ring.

At the same time "The Mouse," whose fine cast includes Charles Bailey-Gates and Rip Torn (as a trucker convinced he's God) is very good at depicting an individual so consumed by doing what he loves best and the toll that can exact on the lives of those he loves best. You don't have to be a boxer to identify with the Mouse.

NEW YORK POST, 11/14/97, p. 51, Thelma Adams

Who's a bigger loser than Mike Tyson?

In the sleeper comedy "The Mouse," writer/director Dan Adams introduces movie audiences to a fabulous footnote in boxing history: the sorry saga of Bruce ("The Mouse") Strauss, a pugilist who was born to lose. He sacrificed most of his 300 fights—an astonishing record considering most pros top out at 50 bouts.

"Call me Mouse," says John Savage ("The Deer Hunter"), giving yet another joyously idiosyncratic performance as a little man who would rather fight and fall than do an honest day's work. Strauss, who's alive and well and living in Omaha, perfected the shamster: a professional opponent who pocketed a small purse by going a few good rounds before kissing the canvas.

World champs Ray ("Boom Boom") Mancini, Vinny Pazienza and Sean O'Grady weigh in for local color. Angela Torn does an appealing, Susan St. James-turn as Strauss' long-suffering wife.

And Torn's father, Rip, plays God as a trucker. Even with God in his corner, "The Mouse" gets trounced.

With Savage's winning performance, Adams creates an ironic American hero: an athlete who refuses to train, a professional loser who wins at his own game, a family man who neglects his kin and has the decency to take a fall when his wife's new boyfriend throws him a roundhouse punch. This low-budget labor of love is really "The Mouse" that roared.

VILLAGE VOICE, 11/11/97, p. 86, Steven Boone

The Mouse is another low-budget indie doing Hollywood's supposed job for it—that is, providing us with light, broad entertainment. This joky boxing tale is based on the real Bruce "the Mouse" Strauss, a professional tomato can who actually liked eating canvas. Mouse (Hollywood dropout John Savage) is proud of his unique world records, such as the one for having been knocked out in every continent but Australia. He has learned to make a living from taking dives. Mouse believes there's triumph in anything done with skill and grace, even losing a fight. Call him a reverse Rocky.

Writer-director Dan Adams provides *The Mouse* with a quirky atmosphere reminiscent of Ron Shelton's sports comedies for what looks like one-tenth the price. Like Shelton, Adams loads up on fast-flying sports lingo and lovable, eccentric fools. The impressive lineup includes Rip Torn as a truck driver who claims to be God and Tim Williams as Mouse's dim, bear-wrestling protégé. *The Mouse* is the kind of harmless escape the studios continually fail at making; like an overzealous prize fighter, they're too busy chasing the cash.

Also reviewed in:
NEW YORK TIMES, 11/14/97, p. E28, Stephen Holden
VARIETY, 11/18-24/96, p. 64, Dennis Harvey

MOUSE HUNT

A DreamWorks Pictures release of an Alan Riche/Tony Ludwig production. *Producer:* Alan Riche, Tony Ludwig, and Bruce Cohen. *Director:* Gore Verbinski. *Screenplay:* Adam Rifkin. *Director of Photography:* Phedon Papamichael. *Editor:* Graig Wood. *Music:* Alan Silvestri. *Music Editor:* Jacqueline Tager and Dan DiPrima. *Sound:* Keith A. Wester and (music) Dennis Sands. *Sound Editor:* Scott Martin Gershin and Larry Kemp. *Casting:* Densise Chamian. *Production Designer:* Linda DeScenna. *Art Director:* James Nedza. *Set Decorator:* Ric McElvin. *Set Designer:* Lauren Cory, Mary Finn, Al Hobbs, and Stan Tropp. *Set Dresser:* John Ceniceros. *Special Effects:* Michael Lantieri. *Visual Effects:* Jenny Fulle. *Costumes:* Jill Ohanneson. *Make-up:* Julie Hewett. *Mouse and Cat trained by:* Boone's Animals for Hollywood. *Stunt Coordinator:* James Arnett. *Running time:* 97 minutes. *MPAA Rating:* PG.

CAST: Nathan Lane (Ernie Smuntz); Lee Evans (Lars Smuntz); Vicki Lewis (April Smuntz); Maury Chaykin (Alexander Falko); Eric Christmas (The Lawyer); Michael Jeter (Quincy Thorpe); Debra Christofferson (Ingrid); Camilla Soeberg (Hilde); Ian Abercrombie (Auctioneer); Annabelle Gurwitch (Roxanne Atkins); Eric Poppick (The Banker); Ernie Sabella (Maury); William Hickey (Rudolf Schmuntz); Christopher Walken (Caesar); Cliff Emmich (Mayor McKrinkle); Melanie MacQueen (Mayor's Wife); Brianna Shebby (Becky); Danielle Shebby (Betty); Leslie Upson (Leslie Reinhart); Mario Cantone (Zeppco Suit #1); Peter Anthony Rocca (Zeppco Suit #2); Steve Bean (Lester Dinkus); Suzanne Krull (Waitress #1); William Frankfather (Mr. Texas); Pat Thomas (Construction Worker #1); Peter Gregory (Doctor); E.J. Callahan (Historical Clerk); Susan Blommaert (Ms. Park Avenue); Valorie Armstrong (Franklin's Wife); Michael Rae Sommers (Paramedic); Michael Ross (Cop); Jose Rey (Cuban Postal Worker); Carmen Filpi (Pallbearer #4); Harper Roisman (Factory Worker #1); David Fresco (Factory Worker #2); Scott Smith (City Paramedic); Sarah Dampf (Crying Child); Orville Stoeber (Expert #1); David Weisenberg (Expert #2); Fred Pierce (Large-Nosed

Man);   Clement E. Blake (Homeless Man);   Saverio Carubia (Photographer);   Pep Torres (Bus Boy).

LOS ANGELES TIMES, 12/19/97, Calendar/p. 8, Jack Mathews

[The following review by Jack Mathews appeared in a slightly different form in
NEWSDAY, 12/19/97, Part II/p. B8.]

"Home Alone," with a mouse.

When you can pitch a movie idea in five words, you're talking major studio release, and sure enough, here comes DreamWorks' "Mouse Hunt."

With a three-inch field mouse in the Macaulay Culkin role, and Nathan Lane and Lee Evans doing the honors as his bumbling pursuers, "Mouse Hunt" is a virtual replay of the original "Home Alone." It's darker, meaner, sillier, more scatological, and, in rare moments, funnier. But its comedy notion—two oafs being put through the wringer by a wily little opponent—is identical.

The oafs are the Smuntz brothers, Ernie (Lane) and Lars (Evans), who move into the run-down but architecturally priceless Victorian mansion they've inherited from their father (the late William Hickey), only to learn that it's already occupied by a singularly wise and unaccommodating rodent. The brothers' plan is to clean the place up and sell it to the highest bidder. But before the house, the mouse!

In the ensuing hunt, Ernie and Lars are blown up, burned, dunked in a frozen pond and nearly drowned in sewage. The weird exterminator (Christopher Walken) they hire fares even worse; he's tortured and driven mad (which is the least he deserves, after eating mouse droppings).

Screenwriter Adam Rifkin and first-time director Gore Verbinski, whose work on those Budweiser bullfrog commercials is said to have prepared him for the task, are equal-opportunity pack rats. Besides "Home Alone," they've also borrowed heavily from the Road Runner cartoons, Tom and Jerry, Laurel and Hardy, the Coen brothers, and the French team of Jean-Pierre Jeunet and Marc Caro, whose stylishly macabre "Delicatessen" seems to have contributed a few of the darker ideas.

The reliably outrageous Lane, and Evans a gifted British stand-up introduced to film audiences in the 1995 "Funny Bones," are doing pretty much straight-on impressions of Laurel and Hardy. Lane even does a signature Oliver Hardy gesture, fluttering his tie at a pair of pretty ladies. But someone should have reminded them to lower the decibels for their frequent screaming fits. Laurel and Hardy were in muted mono. With digital stereo sound, their screeching pierces the brain like darts.

According to the production notes, 60 field mice were trained at various tasks to perform in the movie, and with an occasional assist from animatronic and computer-generated models, not to mention some very clever camerawork, the mouse is a charmer. But it doesn't take long for cute mouse tricks to get old; most of these tricks were old to begin with.

NEW YORK POST, 4/98, 12/19/97, p. 55, Thelma Adams

Dreamworks SKG is having a tough freshman year. "The Peacemaker" made too much peace and too little cash.

"Amistad" is no "Schindler's List." And now, along comes "Mouse Hunt," a black comedy about a mouse that could be a wry metaphor for that other, big-eared studio—but isn't.

It's not that "Hunt" is bad; it's just not the hit the fledgling studio so desperately needs, and one that megabucks and megatalent could, you would think, toss off in a Monday morning pitch meeting. In fact, "Mouse Hunt" works best as a pitch.

It's "Home Alone" with a three-inch, furry field mouse in the Macaulay Culkin role. Think of this: No pesky father-managers to deal with; no puberty to cut short the franchise.

Add the fabulous Nathan Lane as Ernie Smuntz. This son of a string king inherits an unraveling factory and a tumbledown mansion that could be worth a fortune with a little polishing.

And as a Laurel to Lane's Hardy, cast Lee Evans as Ernie's soft-hearted sibling, Lars. The British star of "Funny Bones" (a drop-everything, must-rent comedy) is a knockabout physical comedian with a gentle spirit that complements Lane's edge.

"Ernie, do you remember how close we were as kids?" Lars asks. "No," Lane responds in a perfect deadpan.

What stands between the battling Smuntz brothers (hilariously played by Lane and Evans) and a mountain of moolah? One tiny mouse. And director Gore Verbinski ought to be able to wrangle big laughs out of one rodent with adorable pink ears and more intelligence than his tiny brain cavity suggests.

Who is this genius Verbinski? Why, he's the guy who brought you the croaking frogs in the Budweiser television commercials. Certainly those constitute sufficient credentials to carry off a comedy running 97 minutes.

Well, maybe not. Verbinski does get the right dark texture, a kind of Coen brothers-meet-Tim Burton hysterical edge. But, working from an uneven script by Adam Rifkin, Verbinski seems trapped in an endless joke loop, with the same gags repeating like backdrops in a Tom & Jerry cartoon.

The supporting players distract from these failings. Christopher Walken is a hoot as an extreme exterminator with some unconventional methods for tracking his prey. The late William Hickey anticipates his own impending deathbed speech as the senior Mr. Smuntz.

And so, with "Mouse Hunt" chasing its own tail despite many great elements, DreamWorks ends its first year as a Hollywood player. It hasn't been a nightmare, but the folks over at Disney are no longer losing sleep over their new competitors.

SIGHT AND SOUND, 4/98, p. 47, Leslie Felperin

When their father dies, Ernie and Lars Smuntz inherit the family string factory and a large dilapidated house. Although the string-making business is failing, Lars wants to carry on with it, but Ernie is tempted to sell up. They move into the house, intending to sell that instead. But the house has another inhabitant: a mouse. Following its scratchings, they discover architectural plans which reveal that the house was designed by the esteemed architect Charles La Rue; the house could be worth millions if they sell it at auction.

Ernie and Lars throw themselves into repairs and set their minds on exterminating the mouse (Ernie has loathed vermin ever since a cockroach ruined his reputation as a chef). However, the mouse continually outwits them: he sets off their traps unharmed, and despatches both a psychopathic cat and a professional exterminator. Finally, during the auction, the brothers' attempt to flush him out of the wall cavities with a hose-pipe results in the destruction of the house itself. The mouse follows them to the string factory which they will now have to sell. But the mouse rigs the factory's machinery to make string out of gourmet cheese. A new delicacy is born, and the brothers become rich making cheese-string. The mouse is placed in charge of quality control.

Mouse Hunt opens with a quotation, attributed to one Rudolf Smuntz, which reads: "A world without string is chaos." Because of the semiotic coding for epigraphs, the sound of the name, and the solemnity with which the quote is introduced, you assume that Rudolf Smuntz must be some little known, Central-European writer, perhaps a contemporary of Franz Kafka or Bruno Schultz, the author of *The Street of Crocodiles*. In fact, Smuntz is a character only from the film's own world, whose funeral is the first scene we see. But the gnomic absurdist bathos of his words is perfectly apropos here, as fitting and as profound within these terms of reference as a line of Kafka's.

Mouse Hunt may appear from its marketing to be a harmless bit of slapstick for the kiddies, *Home Alone* with a rodent, as two brothers are bedevilled by a mouse while the they try fix up their inherited home. But its meanings resonate imperceptibly on a supersonic level as only the best slapstick or children's fiction can. True to Smuntz's words, here is a world constantly threatened by chaos: things fall apart, literally, as the brothers face financial ruin unless they keep their homestead from falling to bits, an entropy provoked by their own efforts to kill the mouse, who may or may not be the reincarnation of the building's mad architect or of their father Rudolf Smuntz himself. It is indeed string that ties it all up in the end: both real string, made from their factory and which serves as a motif in the film, and the string of coincidences that knits together the plot.

Director Gore Verbinski made commercials before this, and that training shows not just in the proficiency of the special effects, and the eye-grabbing quality of the film's overall design (recollecting Heath Robinson's machines; Terry Gilliam's dystopian landscapes of obsolescence), but in the economy which makes this short, slight film seem bursting with energy and ideas. *Mouse Hunt* has the compactedness of classic Warner Bros or MGM cartoons, self-consciously invoked often, especially when the cat they buy to chase the mouse ("We need a ferocious feline, preferably with a history of mental illness") plummets down the dumbwaiter with Wile E. Coyote wail and Foley-artist's thud.

There is a lot of *Tom and Jerry,* as you would expect given the story, but there's also a lot of the cruelty of vaudeville slapstick, buttressed brilliantly by the spot-on timing of stars Nathan Lane and Lee Evans who, fat and thin, simmering and sweet respectively, evoke Laurel and Hardy, right down to Lane's coy Hardy-esque wave of his tie to two Belgian hair models with whom he's flirting. Meanwhile, Adam Rifkin's easily overlooked script also flirts deliciously with vaudevillian language rhythms and Abbott and Costello-style backchat—an expert on the house's architect points to his footwear,. "See these shoes?" "La Rue's?" asks Lane. "No, but he would have liked them," is the reply. Take that staccato dialogue, the cruelty, and the sense of the sublime chaos just about to engulf and remember that Beckett's Vladimir and Estragon also had a thing about string—and Rudolf Smuntz doesn't seem so remote from Kafka and his peers.

VILLAGE VOICE, 12/30/97, p. 61, Dennis Lim

A broadly stylized and imaginatively vicious live-action cartoon, *Mouse Hunt* generates just about enough laughs to neutralize its potentially deadly *Home Alone*-with-a-rodent plot. Showing up the softheaded likes of *Flubber,* DreamWorks's third release and first kids' comedy fulfills its brief to a greater degree than either *The Peacemaker* or *Amistad.*

The film's Laurel and Hardy are the mismatched Smuntz brothers, Ernie (Nathan Lane) and Lars (Lee Evans), who inherit from their father (the late, Lugosi-like William Hickey) the family string business and a derelict mansion. When it transpires that the latter is of considerable architectural value, the siblings set about exterminating the property's unusually territorial mouse (a composite of animatronics, computer generation, and the real thing).

First-time director Gore Verbinski and screenwriter Adam Rifkin keep up the trend of mean-spirited family fare, but in their case it's as much a throwback to old cartoons as it is a concession to populist sadism. The filmmakers find inspiration not only in pain but in absurdity; even the upbeat postcript is ridiculous enough not to be cloying.

Both stars are cast according to type: jug-eared, high-pitched Brit comic Evans as the befuddled buffoon, Lane as the theatrical clown. Christopher Walken shows up briefly as a pest-control expert, wise in matters of rodent psychology. Walken is wheeled on all too often by lazy directors for an easy giggle, but here, his whispery loon is irresistible. At a stretch, *Mouse Hunt* could pass for throwaway Coen or lightweight Tim Burton—which isn't such a bad thing in this season of the distended epic.

Also reviewed in:
NEW YORK TIMES, 12/19/97, p. E20, Janet Maslin
VARIETY, 12/22/97-1/4/98, p. 59, Joe Leydon
WASHINGTON POST, 12/19/97, Weekend/p.52, John F. Kelly

MOUTH TO MOUTH

A Miramax Films release of a Sogetel, S.A./Bocaboca Producciones/Star Line Productions film in collaboration with Sogepaq. *Executive Producer:* César Benítez and Fernando Garcillán. *Producer:* César Benítez, Joaquín Oristrell, and Manuel Gómez Pereira. *Director:* Manuel Gómez Pereira. *Screenplay (Spanish with English subtitles):* Joaquín Oristrell, Juan Luis Iborra, Naomi Wise, and Manuel Gómez Pereira. *Director of Photography:* Juan Amorós. *Editor:* Guillermo Represa. *Music:* Bernardo Bonezzi. *Sound:* Carlos Faruolo. *Sound Editor:* James Muñoz. *Art Director:* Luis Velle. *Costumes:* Nereida Bonmatí. *Make-up:* Karmele Soler. *Running time: 97 minutes. MPAA Rating: R.*

CAST: Javier Bardem (Victor Ventura); Josep María Flotats (Ricardo); Aitana Sánchez-Gijón (Amanda); Mariá Barranco (Angela); Myriam Mézières (Shiela); Jordi Bosch (Thug); Sam Mackenzie (Oswaldo); Fernando Guillen-Cuervo (Raul); Ampara Baró (Margot); Candela Peña (Tanya).

LOS ANGELES TIMES, 9/5/97, Calendar/p. 6, Kevin Thomas

"Mouth to Mouth" is a gloriously giddy Spanish farce of consistent humor and invention that embraces romantic comedy, the thriller, a sharp satire of Hollywood pomposity and even a nudge to gays to get out of the closet. It might also establish Javier Bardem, best known in the U.S. as the amiable stud of Bigas Lunas' "Jamon, Jamon," as an international star.

Bardem plays Victor Ventura, a struggling actor from Cartagena who's having such a struggle surviving in Madrid that he's driven to go to work for a phone sex agency. Since Ventura really has talent and imagination, plus compassion, he's an instant hit, especially with a gay caller who uses the name Bill (Josep Maria Flotats). Victor then gets a call from a woman he connects with so strongly that, in violation of the rules, they end up in a scorching rendezvous. She turns out to be none other than Bill's wife, Amanda (Aitana Sanchez-Gijon), who is in need of Victor's help in ensuring that she gets custody of her two small sons.

Just as Victor, who's fallen in love at first encounter, is about to leave himself wide open to big trouble, his tenacious agent (Maria Barranco) has landed him an interview and possible test for a major Hollywood production to be shot in Madrid. From here on the plot thickens with delightful, inspired dizziness.

"Mouth to Mouth"—the name of the disco that figures in the story is a sensational showcase for Bardem. One moment he's a passionate lover, the next he's doing a disastrous audition, which requires him to do Gene Kelly's famous "Be a Clown" number, and then come on to the Hollywood casting agent (Myrian Mezieres) as the smoldering Latin lover stereotype that she expects—and he despises. Bardem is in fact indubitably sexy, but he can play against his image and also beyond it. His Victor has no small amount of courage and sensitivity, not to mention intelligence and humor.

Director Manuel Gomez Pereira, a whiz at juggling plot and players, and his co-writers have surrounded Bardem with lots of equally fine actors. Flotats is wonderful as the middle-aged, intensely closeted Bill, an eminent plastic surgeon, who in the course of the movie's mayhem, is forced to face up to being gay only to discover that hardly anybody cares.

Sanchez-Gijon's Amanda is herself formidably sexy, gorgeous yet vulnerable, and Barranco's agent is a real heroine, an elegant woman, whose loyalty to her client is put to the test—and then some. Sam Mackenzie is amusing as a Hollywood director who's the Ugly American incarnate. If you enjoyed the German comedy "Maybe ... Maybe Not," you'll probably like ... "Mouth to Mouth" as well.

NEW YORK POST, 9/5/97, p. 58, Thelma Adams

Spanish director Manuel Gomez Pereira's phone sex comedy "Mouth to Mouth" doesn't have the bite of a Pedro Almodovar sextravaganza.

Hunky Javier Bardem, who appeared in Almodovar's "High Heels," stars as an unemployed actor. Victor is about to return to the provinces after trying to make it big in Madrid.

In the collision of coincidences that criss-cross this farce, written by Pereira and Joaquin Oristrell, Victor is delivering pizzas to a phone sex "hot line" just as he hears from his agent, Angela (Maria Barranco), that he's up for the part of a red-hot Latin lover in a Hollywood movie.

Victor takes a job as a phone sexologist so that he can hang on to his acting dream in Madrid for one more month.

"I am an actor," he says. Portraying the sexual fantasies of women—and men—is just another role.

As it turns out, the "hot line" gig is the role of a lifetime for the sexy Titan ill-concealed by goofy Cary Grant glasses. The repressed Victor was born to talk dirty. Not only does he make money, but he releases his inner actor and demonstrates star power.

Victor also unleashes the pent-up desires of a deeply closeted husband, Ricardo (Josep Maria Flotats). Ricardo's jealous wife Amanda (Aitana Sanchez-Gijon) tries to entrap them both, only to fall for Victor. Spitfire Sanchez-Gijon is familiar to American audiences; she took Keanu Reeves for "A Walk in the Clouds."

While the acting crackles, the long-delayed comedy, with its wink-wink, nudge-nudge gay jokes, feels as old as a 1994 telephone book. Phone sex reached its peak in "The Truth About Cats and Dogs," but in general it's better heard not seen.

Pereira tries hard to get the audience hot under the receiver, but it's just that effort that makes the movie a wrong number.

NEWSDAY, 9/5/97, Part II/p. B8, Jack Mathews

How do you say screwball comedy in Spanish? How about *"Boca a Boca"*? Literally, that translates to "Mouth to Mouth," the adopted title for the American release of Manuel Gómez Pereira's story of a Madrid actor/phone sex operator. But screwball comedy it is.

At its best reminiscent of Blake Edwards, and at its worst reminiscent of John Hughes, "Mouth to Mouth" follows the adventures of Victor Ventura (Javier Bardem), a struggling young actor with a heart bigger than his ambitions.

Having lost his job as a pizza delivery man, and facing eviction from his apartment, Victor takes a job at a phone-sex salon. His agent (Maria Barranco) has him lined up for an audition for a major role in an American movie about to be shot in Spain, and he figures he can pay his rent in the meantime by sweet-talking his predominantly homosexual callers until he gets the job.

Life gets quickly complicated when Victor's lone female client lures him into a face-to-face, mouth-to-mouth, etc.-to-etc. meeting. This woman Amanda (Aitana Sanchez-Gijon) is stunningly beautiful (imagine Ingrid Bergman's Ilsa in a Victoria's Secret catalog), but before Victor can say, "I hope it was as good for you as it was for me," she's announcing that she's really the wife, of one of Victor's clients, and she had set up their encounter out of spite.

But now, of course, Victor and Amanda are in love, and the only way they can be together, she explains to him, is for Victor to lure her husband, Ricardo (Josep Maria Flotats), into bed for a compromising photo op. She could then blackmail him into giving her a divorce and custody of their two kids. There is one question: Is Amanda *really* really Ricardo's wife, or is she involved in this secondary plot to have him killed?

Furthermore, can Victor solve this mystery in time to make his audition, or even better, make the resolution part of the audition?

The script, which has more authors than the Inquisition, is true Hollywood mulch—at the end, Pereira essentially thanks Hollywood for the inspiration, and the cynic in me wonders if Miramax didn't pick this movie up with an American remake in mind. It has it all—passion, intimations of violence, romance, modern sexual confusion, bicultural barbs.

At the same time, its sense of humor goes below the belt in ways that are uniquely Spanish. When was the last time you saw an entire comic sequence set up by a man getting caught in his zipper?

The problems in "Mouth to Mouth" are mainly in the performances. Bardem is not very convincing as an actor of raw talent; he seems more an honest schlemiel with a case of self-delusion. And Flotats makes Ricardo's coming out seem slightly pathetic; he's homosexual as victim, a man expressing his liberation in spasms of limp-wristed femininity. It's a great role for Robin Williams.

VILLAGE VOICE, 9/9/97, p. 86, Gary Dauphin

Before the words "phone-sex comedy" get your eyes-a-rolling, be advised that *Mouth to Mouth* (or *Boca a Boca* in the original Spanish) is a nifty little movie. Alternately zany and heated, *Mouth* is light enough on its feet to avoid bogging down in any of its many tangents; it says a few smart things about sex without slouching on the entertainment.

The main mouth belongs to an out-of-work actor named Victor Ventura (Javier Bardem, from *High Heels* and *Jamón Jamón*). In order to survive until his big break, the broke Victor takes a job at the Hot Line, a phone-sex joint catering mostly to male callers. Meanwhile, his actor's audition reel has ended up in the hands of some stereotype-seeking American producers hoping to cast one of Spain's "biggest actors" as a tall, dark, animalistic stud.

At the Hot Line, Victor's a natural at turning on the callers, a situation the script attributes simply to his skills as an actor. Soon after one client ("Bill") becomes a regular, Victor gets a call from "Amanda" (*A Walk in the Clouds's* Aitana Sánchez-Gijón), whom he falls for rather mechanically and immediately. Amanda and Victor meet in person, and *Mouth* promptly careens off into screwball comedyland, where Amanda is really Bill's wife and various revenge scenarios ensue. Usually a film like this falls apart when the hit man appears, but director Manuel Gómez Pereira holds things together like an old-style Hollywood pro.

To its credit, *Mouth* is too good-natured to treat poor Bill as badly as it seems it will at first. He becomes an ally in even screwier shenanigans involving Amanda but he never lets Victor forget the intensity of their initial connection. There's similar playfulness during the audition subplot. The Americans are mostly an oozing bunch of slimes projecting their equally slimy images of Latin heterosexuality onto the goodlooking yet nerdy Victor. He obliges as any struggling actor would, but not without exaggerating his transformation, donning tacky clothes and slicking his hair back with olive oil, his eye set in a near crossed leer. (Bardem has a nice set of chops, believable whether he's playing to Bill, Amanda, or the Americans.) There is a closing boy-girl clinch for Victor, but its so like the one that will close his cheesy Hollywood debut you have to laugh. *Mouth to Mouth* seems to be saying (with a wink, course) that no matter how ambiguous his offscreen life, the real Victor is whoever the biggest audience will pay to see.

Also reviewed in:
NEW YORK TIMES, 9/5/97, p. C8, Janet Maslin
VARIETY, 1/8-14/96, p. 73, Jonathan Holland

MRS. BROWN

A Miramax Films release of an Ecosse Films production for BBC Scotland and WGBH/Mobil Masterpiece Theatre in association with Irish Screen. *Executive Producer:* Douglas Rae, Andrea Calderwood, Rebecca Eaton, and Nigel Warren-Green. *Producer:* Sarah Curtis. *Director:* John Madden. *Screenplay:* Jeremy Brock. *Based on an idea by:* George Rosie. *Director of Photography:* Richard Greatrex. *Editor:* Robin Sales. *Music:* Stephen Warbeck. *Sound:* Alistair Crocker. *Sound Editor:* John Downer. *Casting:* Michelle Guish. *Production Designer:* Martin Childs. *Art Director:* Charlotte Watts. *Costumes:* Deirdre Clancy. *Make-up:* Lisa Westcott. *Stunt Coordinator:* Andy Bradford. *Running time:* 90 minutes. *MPAA Rating:* PG.

CAST: Judi Dench (Queen Victoria); Billy Connolly (John Brown); Geoffrey Palmer (Henry Ponsonby); Antony Sher (Benjamin Disraeli); Gerard Butler (Archie Brown); Richard Pasco (Doctor Jenner); David Westhead (Bertie, Prince of Wales); Bridget McConnel (Lady Ely); Georgie Glen (Lady Churchill); Catherine O'Donnell (Lady in Waiting); Sara Stewart (Princess Alexandra); Finty Williams (Princess Helena); Clair Nicolson (Princess Louise); Hattie Ladburty (Princess Alice); Oliver Kent (Prince Alfred); Alex Menzies (Prince Arthur); Simon McKerrell (Prince Leopold); Rupert Farley (Bertie's Valet); Elaine Collins (Mrs. Grant); Jimmy Chisholm (Mr. Grant); Jason Morell (Lord Stanley); Rebecca Charles (Assistant Dresser); Cherith Mellor (Mary Ann Disraeli); George Hall (Speaker of the House); Robin Marchal (Commons Counter); Oliver Ford Davies (Dean of Windsor); Patrick Hannaway and John Ramsay (Journalists); Delia Lindsay (Society Lady); James Vaughan (Sir Charles Dilke); Brendan O'Hea (Barney); Theo Steele (Footman).

LOS ANGELES TIMES, 7/18/97, Calendar/ p. 12, Kenneth Turan

If "Mrs. Brown" is to be believed, and there's no reason it shouldn't, Queen Victoria was quite a handful. A tyrannical termagant, she insisted on initiating all conversations and spoke of herself in the regal third person. And, like many a Hollywood star, she was surrounded by people who didn't dare tell her when she was acting like a brat.

There was, however, an exception to this rule. John Brown.

A Scottish servant known for good reason as "a Highlander of independent mind," Brown was as difficult as Victoria, every bit her equal in stubbornness and pugnacity. And though the turbulent yet affectionate relationship between these two depicted in "Mrs. Brown" sounds like yet another made-for-the-movies pairing, it turns out to be largely true.

Partly financed by WGBH/Mobil Masterpiece Theatre, "Mrs. Brown" is, not surprisingly, a decorous, always involving costume drama about a love too genteel to speak its name. What puts it ahead of the curve are the impressive, commanding performances by Judi Dench as the mighty monarch and Billy Connolly as the sterling Scot.

A favorite of Albert, the Queen's husband, Brown had first met Victoria while the Prince Consort was still alive. But in 1864, when he is called back to her service, Albert has died and the Queen is in deepest mourning. "She is in a state of unfettered morbidity," wrote Sir Henry Ponsonby (Geoffrey Palmer) to his wife. "We are all prisoners of the Queen's grief."

Brown is called up in the hopes of breaking through Victoria's gloom, but at first he merely irritates her by his tendency to "speak how I find." As Stanley Weintraub wrote in his authoritative "Victoria: An Intimate Biography," Brown was "rough but shrewd [and] addicted to homely, outspoken observations that ignored rank and status."

Surrounded by flummery and flatterers, many of whom were her own children, Victoria increasingly warmed to Brown's plain speaking and complete devotion to both the truth and her royal person. The type who would just blurt out, "Lift your foot, woman," when he was helping the Queen onto her horse, Brown brought a smile to Victoria's face more readily than anyone else.

Naturally their relationship, plus Brown's contempt for protocol, made nothing but enemies among the snobbish and insecure at the stuffy royal court, which took in just about everybody. When he gets the Queen to dance a Highland jig and threatens to turn her into a party animal, no one but Her Majesty is very much amused.

Typical were the remarks of one high-ranking lord, quoted by Weintraub: "Long solitary rides, in secluded parts of the park; constant attendance upon her in her room; ... everything shows that she has selected this man for a kind of friendship which is absurd and unbecoming her position. The Princesses—perhaps wisely—make a joke of the matter, and talk of him as 'Mama's lover.'"

Though historians are convinced physical intimacy between this unlikely couple was out of the question, that didn't stop contemporary gossips, who dubbed Victoria "Mrs. Brown," called Mr. B "the Queen's stallion" and even speculated in print that she had given birth to his child. What the Globe would have done with the situation is thankfully beyond speculation.

Under the careful direction of journeyman John Madden ("Ethan Frome," "Golden Gate"), Jeremy Brock's script satisfyingly illuminates this unexpected but real bonding. There was, however, apparently no dramatic crisis in this relationship, and no evidence that, as the ads grandly claim, "their extraordinary friendship transformed an empire." So "Mrs. Brown" cheerfully invents a drama and drags in Prime Minister Benjamin Disraeli, deliciously played by Antony Sher, as a prime mover. A little less huffing about sacrifice and duty might have been nice, but maybe that's why the sun has yet to set on Hollywood's empire.

Though she is one of the reigning monarchs of British acting, Dench has never had the lead in a theatrical feature before. She is a thorough treat here in one of those tour de force performances, able to scrunch her face up like a regal prune whenever she feels her authority threatened.

Connolly, who has built a career out of being an unconventional stand-up comedian, was a smart choice to play opposite Dench. Their personality types match up splendidly with the characters they play as well as each other, and "Mrs. Brown's" greatest pleasure is seeing and hearing them spar. Even with the gloves on, this is a battle well worth observing.

NEW YORK, 7/28/97, p. 43, David Denby

The legendary British actress Judi Dench does a wicked imitation of royal grief in the early passages of *Mrs. Brown*, a surprisingly satisfying movie about Queen Victoria after the death of her beloved Prince Albert. The picture begins in 1864, when Albert has been gone for three years, and the queen, 45 years old, remains in deep mourning, apparently so depressed she can hardly speak. Presiding over ghastly dinners, Dench presents a closed and masklike mien. Yet there's always a suggestion of conscious power and royal prerogative—even mischief—in her bearing. This woman, we realize, has made a deliberate withdrawal from life. She is able to perpetuate her silence because she can get away with it. At dinner, as everyone waits for Her

Majesty to say something, the queen eats purposefully, rapidly, silently, and then abruptly stops, which causes everyone else to stop, whether sated or not. Finally she speaks, only to censor one of the younger ladies of the court for not eating *enough*. Anguish and perversity join together in her tyrannical silence.

However dim the current royals, the old kings and queens apparently remain a source of wonder to British playwrights, directors, and actors. *Mrs. Brown* is not as powerful as *The Madness of King George,* but it's fascinating and bleakly funny. The theater and TV director John Madden (who also adapted *Ethan Frome* for the movies) successfully captures the immense weight of the imperial state as it awkwardly follows in the wake of Victoria's sorrow. At each of the royal residences, a quartet of black-gowned ladies-in-waiting must halt and recover their position behind the queen whenever she stops to gaze out of a window. The graceful but hurried movement of these four—a kind of wafted scurrying—is close to ballet. The ladies sustain their composure, but the court still comes close to despair. How can you show extreme deference to someone who will not live? You can never outdo the queen for discretion and cleanliness, never appease her desire for order and silence. She practices her one-upmanship with excruciating force.

At his wit's end, the queen's secretary. Sir Henry Ponsonby (the baleful Geoffrey Palmer). hits on the idea of calling back into royal service Prince Albert's groom, John Brown (Billy Connolly), a highlands Scot that the prince had been fond of. Brown shows up and tells the queen, to the court's shocked dismay, that she looks awful. He treats her as a friend who can be brought out of her funk with affectionate raillery, summoning her to life by treating her as an ordinary person. At the same time, of course, he is a servant: he can't go past a certain point of familiarity. Amused—and perhaps secretly relieved—to be treated as a woman, the queen suffers Brown's impertinence, and they become friends, at which point the London scandal sheets begin referring to her as "Mrs. Brown."

Billy Connolly, a TV actor and comic, has fiery eyes burning beneath downward-arching brows, a great black beard. and a roaring voice. Without ever saying so, the queen obviously admires this imposing Scottish masculinity of kilts and exposed knees and vigorous, direct speech. Connolly might be a working-class lover out of D. H. Lawrence—hearty and happily dominating—yet this lover possesses no erotic drive that we can see, or, rather, his drive all flows into an ecstasy of service. Brown imagines himself the only one at court truly concerned with the queen's welfare. He lords it over the other servants; insults the aristocratic Ponsonby; even insults the queen's son, the Prince of Wales (and future Edward VII). In his way, he becomes the craziest of courtiers: He believes he possesses the queen.

Mrs. Brown has its tremulous, precious side—they will touch, but will they kiss?—and the movie could easily have become insufferable. But Madden and the screenwriter, Jeremy Brock, stick to the psychological realities of the situation and don't embarrass us. *Mrs. Brown,* with its misty highlands and severely luxurious royal rooms, is very handsome, but the dim light of rectitude rules the court, and I was highly grateful for the enlivening presence of the actor and author Antony Sher, who plays Prime Minister Benjamin Disraeli. Short, with a tuft of beard that he points like a lance, Sher's Disraeli is a dandy delight—calculating, good-humored, a devastating flatterer. For Disraeli lives in a world in which cleverness is as much prized as seriousness is at the court, and Sher, whose every word is dipped in irony, really seems the most intelligent man in England. Disraeli is the only one shrewd enough to know that Brown, Victoria's half-mad imaginary lover, is the man to bring Victoria back into the public's eye, which is finally the only place she belongs.

NEW YORK POST, 7/18/97, p. 46, Thelma Adams

"Mrs. Brown" highlights the love that dare not speak its name in contemporary Hollywood: a powerful bond between two articulate, intelligent, middle-aged, white heterosexuals.

She's the mighty Queen of England. He's a plain-spoken, whiskey-drinking groom from Balmoral. But you won't see pics of him sucking her toes in the pages of the Star.

Working from Jeremy Brock's sharp script, John Madden's bracing historical romance pairs the grieving widow Queen Victoria (Judi Dench) with her servant, John Brown (Billy Connolly).

Following Prince Albert's death from typhus in 1861, the queen, then in her 40s, retreats behind castle walls, shunning her obligations as head of state.

Her retainers recruit Brown, a favorite of the late prince consort to get her up off her duff, onto her pony and out of her funk. They succeed too well. As Brown says, "All Highlanders are good for the health." Before long, the queen is riding regularly. She moves further from the seat of power, shifting the court from Windsor to distant Scotland. At Balmoral (still a favorite haunt of Prince Charles), the irreverent Scot rises to become the queen's confidant.

At the height of their passion, the two kiss each other's hands. The closest they come to dirty dancing during their Highland fling is a flush-inducing Scottish country dance.

Their alliance does more than put heather in the queen's cheeks. It threatens the Prince of Wales, her eldest son, and plays into the hands of the Republican movement, putting the monarchy at risk.

The contemporary tabs have a field day, nicknaming Victoria "Mrs. Brown." Enter Tory Prime Minister Disraeli (overplayed with pinched cheeks by Antony Sher, the recent star of Broadway's "Stanley'). To preserve his party's power—and his own—Disraeli enlists Brown's aid to return the queen to public life.

In '90s jargon, the relationship between Victoria and Brown had "rebound" written all over it. Director Madden ("Ethan Frome") delivers all the sweet sadness of a doomed upstairs-downstairs romance that was no less intimate for all the layers of cloth, the kilts and the crinolines between the man and woman.

Dench ("Hamlet") makes a commanding queen with human frailty. Her hands order and her mouth dictates, but her mournful eyes are trapped behind the castle walls of her royal face. Connolly draws Dench out with the confidence of a hunter flushing quail.

The British comic has Sean Connery's defiant charm—a coincidence, considering Connery was cast several decades ago to play Brown opposite Elizabeth Taylor's Victoria in one of the greatest movies never made.

NEWSDAY, 7/18/97, Part II/p. B7, Jack Mathews

Let's cut to the chase. Did Queen Victoria and John Brown, her Scottish stable master, sleep together, or was their affair strictly a matter of public speculation?

At a luncheon after the premiere of John Madden's "Mrs. Brown" at the recent Cannes Film Festival, Scottish actor and stand-up comedian Billy Connolly, who plays the robust stable man, said he had no doubt that John Brown and the queen mussed the royal sheets. Dame Judi Dench, the brilliant British stage actress who plays Victoria, said she doubted it.

That the actors aren't sure how intimate their characters were speaks well of Jeremy Brock's screenplay and Madden's delicate direction. "Mrs. Brown," the nickname given Victoria—Queen of the United Kingdom from 1837 to 1901—by her critics, has weighter social and psychological issues on its mind, and the relationship is so authentically characterized that we are left convinced that whatever the attraction between them, it was strong stuff. So were the ramifications.

The story takes place in the years following the death of Prince Albert, with whom Victoria had nine chidren. In a debilitating depression, the queen has isolated herself at the Scottish castle of Balmoral, and has virtually abandoned her ceremonial and political responsibilities, all of which is fueling a campaign in London to end the monarchy.

Into this bleak situation comes John Brown, summoned by the queen's attendants to attempt to lure her out of her doldrums and into the invigorating air of the countryside. It takes some doing, but the single-minded Brown works the miracle, and, after winning the queen's trust, takes over the household and assumes personal power that is a threat all the way to Parliament.

Connolly, looking like the Grizzly Adams of the Highlands, is perfectly cast as this larger-than-life figure, a man capable of boisterous, alcoholic bullying of the royal staff while being a devoted, sentimental confidant to the queen. The ultimate test of Brown's loyalty comes in a visit to the castle by a sharply manipulative Prime Minister Benjamin Disraeli (Antony Sher), who attempts to convince him that only by releasing his grip on the queen can she and the monarchy be saved.

Connolly, who's done character roles in several British films, has a great presence on screen, and we can expect to see him in more leading roles after this. Dench, meanwhile, gives us the most fully developed Victoria yet. She plays the queen at the least popular moment in her 64 years of rule, and as her relationship with Brown evolves, we see the full range of her character, from the darkness of self-pity to the flashes of the generous spirit and royal manner that would, at least until the age of Prince Charles and Diana, keep the monarchy safe from efforts to abolish it.

NEWSWEEK, 7/28/97, p. 69, David Ansen

Mrs. Brown. That's the malicious nickname given Queen Victoria (Judi Dench) by the gossips who were scandalized by her close relationship with a brusque Scottish servant named John Brown (Billy Connolly). In 1864, Brown was summoned to the palace in hopes of drawing the queen out of her deep three-year depression after the death of her beloved Prince Albert. Her withdrawal from the public eye had left her nation edgy and the monarchy imperiled. Oblivious to protocol, the whisky-drinking highlander cuts through her grief with his rude (and shrewd) attentions, and the two forge an unlikely friendship so close it outrages the court. As the fiercely protective Brown's power over the queen grows and rumors of an affair whip from Windsor to Westminster, their relationship threatens the stability of the government, prompting the Machiavellian intervention of Prime Minister Disraeli (Antony Sher). This true story, deftly embellished by writer Jeremy Brock and directed at a bracing English trot by John Madden, is a splendid showcase for its three superb leads. Dench, Connolly and Sher, each with a distinct charisma, offer a fascinating study of the varieties of political and personal power. "Mrs. Brown" doesn't soar, but it certainly seduces.

SIGHT AND SOUND, 9/97, p. 50, Colin McArthur

A grieving widow in 1861, Queen Victoria is joined on the Isle of Wight by her Highland pony and its handler, John Brown. He quickly antagonises her family and courtiers by his abrupt manner and plain speaking, but begins to coax the Queen out of her cocoon of widowhood. Increasingly imperious with the other servants and contemptuous of those around the Queen, Brown becomes her closest personal servant, obsessively concerned about her health and security.

Back in the Highlands, he prises her further out of the court circle and thwarts an attempt by journalists to spy on her. However, persuaded by Prime Minister Benjamin Disraeli that the monarchy is threatened by the Queen's continuing withdrawal from public life and by the rumours casting her as "Mrs Brown", Brown influences her to return to public life. Perceiving this as a betrayal of their close friendship, the Queen re-establishes a chilly, formal relationship with him.

His obsession with her security continues and he foils a would-be assassin, but his frenzied dash into the cold Balmoral night to confront an imagined interloper brings on a fatal bout of pneumonia. He and the Queen are reconciled on his deathbed.

In the rendering of the assured *Mrs. Brown*—the story of Queen Victoria's relationship with John Brown, one of her grooms—experienced television director John Madden (*Inspector Morse*) delivers an acute portrait of the petrified court at Osborne House: vast arrays of servants are frozen into immobility yet ready to jump to the sovereign's merest whim; great swathes of black fabric rustle as the Queen and her attentive entourage sweep through the corridors; and elegantly languid compositions and camera movements provide appropriate formal correlatives of the social milieu depicted. It is into this funereal, Byzantine world that John Brown blows like a great northern gale. Indeed, it is the clash between Brown's values and those of the court that is the centre of dramatic tension in the film. The narrative shift is delivered via Brown's gradual 'rescue' of the Queen from the suffocating artificiality of the court.

Although British film (and television) historical drama is often ideologically pernicious, its virtues are considerable. British set and costume design surpass those of most other countries and the quality of British acting training particularly favours historical subjects. *Mrs. Brown* is further proof of this, with the supporting performances by Geoffrey Palmer as the Queen's private secretary Henry Ponsonby, and Anthony Sher's shamelessly camp depiction of Benjamin Disraeli, testifying to the depth of talent and tradition in British historical drama. However, their roles also function as embodiments of the effete English establishment against which the Queen and Brown must struggle. Precisely because their roles involve struggle, Judi Dench and Billy Connolly are permitted depths and nuances not available to the other characters.

The narrative requirement of popular cinema that heterosexual love be at the centre of every story is handled with considerable subtlety in the writing, directing and playing here. When the

Queen and Brown arrive back at Balmoral from a jolly sojourn at a ghillie's cottage, the royal physician puts down the flush in her cheeks to drink. Ponsonby demurs but forbids the physician to speculate further about the reason for Victoria's flushed cheeks.

One scene in particular, however, testifies to the film's subtlety. Brown indicates to the Queen that in order to preserve her reputation he should resign and withdraw from her circle. In the course of their verbal exchanges, she utters the words "I cannot live without you." In a modern context, such words would carry a heavy erotic charge. Without wholly losing this charge, the film shifts the meaning much more towards the sense that Brown is her indispensable support in the performance of her regal role. Although such nuances spring primarily from Dench, because it is her assignment to make the dramatic transition from atrophied widow to reawakened woman, the film also hints at darkly paranoid depths in Brown's character, indications strengthened by our familiarity with the usually manic quality of Connolly's performances.

So accomplished are *Mrs. Brown*'s writing, directing, acting and technical features that they tend to mask the extent to which it is operating an ideological con trick. Brown is constructed to represent a breath of earthy air entering the musty court of St James. What is obscured, however, is that his apparent irreverence (for example, he habitually addresses the Queen as "Woman") conceals a deeper servitude which leaves the institution of monarchy unquestioned. Brown is the direct analogue, in those US-made films about the antebellum south, of the 'house nigger', whose licensed insolence masks the cruel injustice of slavery. And there is much talk in *Mrs. Brown* of the threat of republicanism but no hint that it might be rather a good idea. There is another sense in which *Mrs. Brown* is ideologically suspect. Although it is an infinitely superior film to *Braveheart*, it shares with that and the other so-called 'kilt movies' a traditional, indeed hegemonic, conception about Scotland in which the English are portrayed as élitist, repressed and effete while the Scots are depicted as demotic, 'natural' and warm-hearted. Apparently complimentary to the Scots, this is in fact a discourse which confirms their subjection. As is so often the case with British films, Mrs. Brown's excellence as a film diverts attention from its questionable subtexts.

TIME, 7/21/97, p. 70, Richard Corliss

The richest woman around has been in mourning for her late husband so long that her sorrow has become a career. Her family can't console her; the managers of the conglomerate she heads are afraid to challenge her. Then her death-in-life is changed by a humble—actually, a quite arrogant horseman named John Brown. He speaks boldly to her and rudely to her children. He takes her on long walks, gives her counsel; most important, he makes her laugh. She is, again, a woman in love. Gossips derisively call her "Mrs. Brown."

This might be a *Gaslight*-style melodrama. *Mrs. Brown*, though, is a true story, about Queen Victoria (Judi Dench) and her long grief after Prince Albert's death. When her intimacy with Brown (Billy Connolly) becomes known, demands to abolish the monarchy ring through Parliament, forcing Prime Minister Disraeli (Antony Sher) to call on Brown. Her Majesty must be coaxed out of hibernation and back to her people.

As written by Jeremy Brock and directed by John Madden, this British film has the regal, clubby aura of Masterpiece Theatre (which co-produced *Mrs. Brown*). Nicely, it lets viewers decide whether Brown is a devoted servant or a devious bully and whether the Queen's long bereavement is partly stubbornness masquerading as principle. It also provides a field day for some wonderful actors too little seen on this side of the Atlantic. Sher is a wily, puckish delight; and Dame Judi, her face clamped in anguish, radiates the stern ecstasy of grief. This queen of English understatement embodies Victoria's belief: that mourning is the only way survivors can consummate their love for the dead.

VILLAGE VOICE, 7/22/97, p. 65, Leslie Camhi

The name of Queen Victoria is synonymous with repression. An immense, iron-willed, and absolute monarch, clothed for 40 years in mourning, she seems hardly the type to have been swept away. But the Victorians were a complex lot—tight lacing has its pleasures—and apparently the Queen herself was capable of monumental, sentimental indiscretion. *Mrs. Brown* explores her intimate attachment, after the death of Prince Albert, to a headstrong Scottish servant.

The longest-running romance in cinema is the camera's adoration for the trappings of royal omnipotence. When John Brown (Billy Connolly) brings the Queen's white pony from Balmoral, her Highland holiday home, to Windsor, he finds that Victoria (Judi Dench) brooks no dissent from an elaborate regime of mourning. Meals are silent; rooms are cold; servants stand frozen as mannequins.

Connolly's Brown is alternately ribald and reverent as he strides around in his kilt and horsehair ornaments, addressing the Queen as "woman" and shaking up court society. Dench's Victoria begins a forbidding figure, but soon becomes a tender devotee of Scottish culture: moving with Brown back to Balmoral, filling the castle with bagpipe music, dressing in tartans, and publishing her Highland journals. Meanwhile, the scene shifts to London, where the beleaguered Tories groan and the journalists lampoon her. So parliamentarian Benjamin Disraeli (Antony Sher)—arch, affable, and oily—is dispatched to coax her back to royal duty.

With care and a scrupulous regard for history, director John Madden has skillfully rescripted the gendered conventions of romance and power. But, once the characters have had their Highland fling, there's hardly anywhere the plot can go. Lives of reticence and seclusion don't usually lend themselves to drama.

Also reviewed in:
NEW REPUBLIC, 8/4/97, p. 26, Stanley Kauffmann
NEW YORK TIMES, 7/18/97, p. C5, Janet Maslin
NEW YORKER, 8/4/97, p. 77, Anthony Lane
VARIETY, 5/19-25/97, p. 58, Emanuel Levy
WASHINGTON POST, 7/25/97, p. D6, Rita Kempley
WASHINGTON POST, 7/25/97, Weekend/p. 48, Desson Howe

MURDER AT 1600

A Warner Bros. release in association with Regency Enterprises of an Arnold Kopelson production. *Executive Producer:* Anne Kopelson, Michael Nathanson, and Stephen Brown. *Producer:* Arnold Kopelson and Arnon Milchan. *Director:* Dwight Little. *Screenplay:* Wayne Beach and David Hodgin. *Director of Photography:* Steven Bernstein. *Editor:* Billy Weber and Leslie Jones. *Music:* Christopher Young. *Music Editor:* Thomas Milano and Will Kaplan. *Sound:* Bruce Carwardine and (music) Bobby Fernandez. *Sound Editor:* J. Paul Huntsman and Victor Iorillo. *Casting:* Amanda Mackey Johnson and Cathy Sandrich. *Production Designer:* Nelson Coates. *Art Director:* Dan Yarhi. *Set Designer:* Elis Lam, Michael Shocrylas, and Gordon White. *Set Decorator:* Tedd Kuchera. *Special Effects:* Neil Trifunovich. *Costumes:* Denise Cronenberg. *Make-up:* Marilyn Terry. *Stunt Coordinator:* Shane Cardwell. *Running time:* 110 minutes. *MPAA Rating:* R.

CAST: Wesley Snipes (Detective Harlan Regis); Diane Lane (Nina Chance); Alan Alda (Alvin Jordan); Daniel Benzali (Nick Spikings); Ronny Cox (President Jack Neil); Dennis Miller (Detective Stengel); Diane Baker (Kitty Neil); Tate Donovan (Kyle Neil); Harris Yulin (General Clark Tully); Tom Wright (Cooper); Nicholas Pryor (Paul Moran); Charles Rocket (Jeffrey); Nigel Bennett (Burton Cash); Tamara Gorski (Young Woman in Bar); Douglas O'Keefe (John Kerry, Assassin); Tony Nappo (Luchessi); Mary Moore (Carla Town); George R. Robertson (Mack Falls); Ho Chow (Tepper); James Millington (Lt. Marty Dill); John Bourgeois (Captain Farr); Peter James Haworth (Treasury Guard); David Gardner (Speaker of the House); Cliff Mcmullen (Carl, Sniper); Keith Williams (Randy Queeg, Lawyer); Grace Armas (Screaming Cleaning Woman); David Fraser (Brack Electronics); George Sperdakos (Reporter, Last Press); Sandra Caldwell (Mrs. Wallace); Frank Moore (Captain Ford Gibbs); Richard Blackburn (Coroner Jimmy Foley); James Gallanders (Law Student); Victor Ertmanis (Cop Bartender); Richard Fitzpatrick (Law Professor); Michael Ricupero (Landlord); Chris Gillett (V.P. Gordon

Dylan);   J. Craig Sandy (1st FBI Agent);   Robert Bidamen (V.P. Aide);   Carol Anderson (Captain's Farr's Assistant);   Christopher Kennedy (Techy);   Mike Kinney (Reporter, Jail); Michael Hambrick (CNN Reporter);   Jackie Bensen, Maureen Bunyan, and Kathryn Klvana (TV Reporters);   Dan Duran (1st CNN Reporter);   Sheldon Turcott and Sandi Stahlbrand (CNN Newscasters);   Tom Urich (CNN News Anchor);   Tino Monte (Local Newscaster);   Raven Dauda (Waitress);   Michael Dyson (Treasury Drone);   Aron Tager (2nd Treasury Guard);   Doris E. McMillon and Lewis Grenville (Network Reporters); Moe Kelso (Gorgeous Woman);   Junior Williams (Medic);   Donald Jones (Reporter C).

CHRISTIAN SCIENCE MONITOR, 4/18/97, p. 15, David Sterritt

Many of today's headlines deal with actual or potential government scandals. Yet polls suggest that many Americans are only mildly troubled by such stuff, as long as the country keeps running on a reasonably steady course.

Hollywood hasn't gotten this message. According to the studios, American attitudes toward government range from surly to hostile, and there's nothing an audience likes better than seeing Washington trashed. Any doubt about this was dispelled when "Independence Day" parlayed a wildly anti-Washington plot—complete with space invaders blowing up a White House presided over by a dithering president—into the biggest box-office numbers of 1996.

But it's risky to rely on Hollywood for up-to-the-minute news about public opinion, since feature films take a long time to work their way to the multiplex. The popularity of "Independence Day" failed to reignite this year in "Absolute Power," a quickly forgotten melodrama pitting Clint Eastwood against Gene Hackman as a president who is downright evil. "Mars Attacks!" also crash-landed with its satirical view of a Washington.

"Murder at 1600," directed by Dwight Little, probably won't do much better. Taking a cautious route, it fills the White House with a veritable army of shifty-looking suspects while ultimately assuring us that the highest brass wouldn't do any harm. Some moviegoers may find a certain naughty attraction in a story that mixes sex and violence with military strategy and presidential politics. But most will find the plot so hokey and the action so predictable that a dollop of trendy government-bashing isn't nearly enough to justify the price of a ticket.

The ever-cool Wesley Snipes plays Harlan Regis, a Washington homicide detective assigned to find out who killed a 25-year-old woman in the White House after a sexual rendezvous. Suspicion falls on everyone from a cleaning attendant to the chief executive himself, with particular attention settling on his randy young son.

Regis has a hard job facing him, and it gets harder when White House insiders start blocking his path. Further complicating the hunt is a national-security crisis: American soldiers are being held hostage by North Korea's government. Americans are curious about how their president will get these boys home, when he can't even defend his own house from mayhem and disorder.

"Murder at 1600" tries for psychological depth. Lest we wonder whether the president is manly enough to lead, for instance, he gets to sock a bad guy during the climax. But most of the movie's slender interest lies in Snipes's likable acting, which is subtle enough to balance Alan Alda as a White House operative and Diane Lane as a Secret Service agent.

Since the US film industry remains a largely white domain, it's always refreshing to see a fine African-American talent like Snipes land a major role, even if the movie is less than impressive. Still, it's worth noting that most big-studio films starring black men break Hollywood's pattern of letting hero and heroine pair off.

"Murder at 1600" joins other recent movies like "Courage Under Fire" and "The Pelican Brief" in keeping the black male protagonist and his white female counterpart at a conspicuously safe distance from each other. Even in the supposedly unbiased '90s, it appears, the combination of race and romance is still too hot for Hollywood to handle.

LOS ANGELES TIMES, 4/18/97, Calendar/p. 10, Kenneth Turan

What with the recent fuss over pricey sleepovers in the Lincoln bedroom and coffee at costs Starbucks would envy, Bill Clinton may think he has White House problems. But those are as dust in the wind compared to what President Jack Neil has to contend with in "Murder at 1600."

It's not just a domestic policy initiative that's dead in the water, there's an actual corpse bleeding all over a White House bathroom floor from multiple stab wounds. That kind of thing can cast a hell of a shadow over an administration already dealing with a hostage crisis in North Korea. Especially when unflappable, unstoppable D.C. homicide Det. Harlan Regis starts digging around.

Starring Wesley Snipes as the suave Regis, "Murder at 1600" is the modern equivalent of the routine B-picture, diverting in a small potatoes kind of way, though its budget and stars are big league. Eager to provide its hero with convenient back doors to get out of and its heroine with tight sweaters to wear when the going gets tough, "Murder at 1600" plays out like an airport paperback, serviceable at passing the time if nothing else is available.

That corpse turns out to be Carla Town, one of the more lithesome employees of the Office of Protocol. She's glimpsed very much alive under the opening credits, having sex with an unknown man somewhere in the White House as portraits of George Washington and Thomas Jefferson look on unperturbed.

Equally blasé is Det. Regis, the kind of smooth operator capable of disarming a potential suicide on his coffee break. He and his partner (Dennis Miller) are called in to investigate because the White House is in Washington, after all, but, except for fatherly National Security Advisor Alvin Jordan (Alan Alda), no one is particularly happy to see them.

Most unhappy is Nick Spikings (Daniel Benzali of TV's "Murder One"), head of, the White House security forces. Haughty, bullet-headed, with the stare of a malevolent Buddha, Spikings, feels personally aggrieved that a murder should have taken place on his turf, and Regis' presence steps on his last nerve.

Still, Spikings does assign Secret Service agent Nina Chance (Diane Lane) to be Regis' liaison. Neither is initially happy with the matchup, but that just makes their becoming buddies inevitable. Soon he's showing her his scale models of Civil War battlefields (surely the oddest movie cop hobby in memory), and she's telling him about the gold medal she won as an Olympic sharpshooter. If you don't think that skill comes in handy down the road, this movie is not for you.

Even with his friendship with agent Chance, Regis has trouble getting arrested, so to speak, in the evidence gathering department. The Secret Service impounds everything that's not tied down and calls it classified, and at various times Regis is followed, spied on, beaten up, misled and lied to. Does this seriously impede his investigation? Did Tiger Woods have trouble at the Masters?

Director Dwight Little, with straight-ahead action movies like "Marked for Death" and "Rapid Fire" to his credit (as well as "Free Willy 2"), does not embarrass himself here, but without Snipes, his charisma and his gift for making the absurd believable, "Murder at 1600" would be in a lot worse shape.

Almost dripping with charisma, Snipes is making a career out of being the best thing in indifferent movies, and a Wayne Beach & David Hodgin script, with more inexplicable gaps than the White House Watergate tapes, doesn't make his job any easier.

Though both Lane and Benzali are excellent foils for Snipes this time around, "Murder at 1600" mostly makes you hope that the actor could find more time on his schedule for films like "The Waterdance" or "White Men Can't Jump." Saving the presidency and saving this picture along with it may seem like quite an accomplishment, but Snipes is one actor who is capable of more.

NEW YORK POST, 4/18/97, p. 37, Thelma Adams

Erect nipples and pearl earrings. That's pretty much all we know about the White House murder victim who's discovered minutes after having steamy sex on the Presidential Seal with an unidentified white male.

After "Absolute Power" and more than four years of Bill Clinton, we'll pretty much believe any nutty theory thrown our way in Dwight Little's flat-footed thriller "Murder at 1600."

More muscular and vital than the script (by Wayne Beach and David Hodgin) is Wesley Snipes, action star. He plays sexy D.C. homicide cop Harlan Regis with an Eddie Murphy sheen and a naivete about the way the District works that will elicit giggles inside the Beltway.

Regis' white sidekick is not Kathie Lee, but Dennis Miller. The wisecracking cop enters the scene with "target" written all over him, but not enough room in the script to really let fly. This is a shame, because a Snipes and Miller comic mystery would be a kick.

Rounding out "The Mod Squad" for the '90s is Diane Lane. The once-promising actress twitches from the get-go as Secret Service agent Nina Chance, a former Olympic gold-medalist sharpshooter. The only dramatic range her character knows is the rifle range.

Before Chance takes the trio into the line of fire, we discover that the president (Ronny Cox) is a dove named Jack who shares mistresses with his son, a girlfriend-beating sex addict whose goal is to fornicate in every room in the White House.

A hawkish Alan Alda, as national security adviser Alvin Jordan, and the person most likely to play Nosferatu in any remake, Daniel Benzali (late of TVs "Murder One"), as the White House security chief, run rings around the weakling leader of the Free World.

The portrait of White House political infighting is so elementary that a meeting to decide whether the United States should to war over a Korean hostage crisis plays like a weekly faculty klatch at a small upstate college. Even Hollywood honchos' compensation negotiations are more subtle and complicated.

"I think Washington is drowning in a sea full of bulls---," Regis tells Alda's D.C. insider after jogging *a deux*. And Hollywood is paddling frantically alongside.

NEWSDAY, 4/18/97, Part II/p. B2, John Anderson

There's probably something profoundly Freudian in the fact that "Murder at 1600" opens with an obligatory gun scene before it gets to the obligatory sex scene. But in terms of dramatic development—something very important here—the gun scene sets up only Wesley Snipes' character. The sex scene sets up the entire impulse behind the movie.

There they are—and who *they* are will have to wait—making the beast with two backs in what appears to be the Oval Office. Portraits of Washington and Jefferson overlook the sweaty scene. Are they disapproving? Or amused? They should be laughing their bewigged heads off. After all; neither of *them* was a monk. But it's poor Bill Clinton who takes the implied rap anytime sex and the presidency are mentioned in the same breath.

But murder is the real crime here, and conspiracy theories the point. When the woman engaged in the previous scene winds up ventilated in a White House bathroom, the president's security force closes ranks, its chief, Nick Spikings (Daniel Benzali) starts making surveillance tapes disappear, and the national security adviser brace yourself, it's Alan Alda—brings in D.C. detective Harlan Regis (Snipes) to get to the bottom of things. Why? That's a good question, although the ace detective never asks it.

We've met Harlan minutes earlier, when he punched out a potential suicide (Charles Rocket) who was waving a pistol around a congested Washington intersection. "Shoot him," suggests his partner, Stengel (the ever-compassionate Dennis Miller), "he's ----- up traffic." Harlan's ability to end the stalemate with a right cross proves him not only a man of action but a sensitive guy as well.

Oddly, Snipes doesn't seem to be on screen as much as he might be. Sure, he's the star, and a good star he is. But a lot of time is devoted to Secret Service agent Nina Chance (Diane Lane), who is assigned to keep Harlan in line, yet eventually she has to betray her agent's code or see an innocent man framed for the murder. Lane is OK, it's nice to see her in a major movie; but Nina is something of a innocent, given that she's protecting the president.

While the investigation goes on—with Harlan being shadowed, his house bugged and his Civil War-buff's battle scenes disturbed—there's a hostage situation in North Korea involving 13 soldiers (as in original colonies, I guess) that's distracting President Neil (Ronny Cox). He may or may not be involved in the murder, but he's certainly under pressure to bomb North Korea to kingdom come.

That's enough background. Basically, "Murder at 1600" is all about secret governments, White House plots and the corruption that, in so many recent Hollywood movies, is eventually pinned on one character at the same time it's being presented as systemic. In constructing this full-frontal assault on the integrity of the U.S. government, director Dwight Little (of the Steven Seagal epic "Marked for Death" and the equally bloated "Free Willy 2") isn't afraid to drag out a whole Lincoln bedroom full of clichés, including some that are merely annoyances:

If there has to be a chase scene in the White House, does it have to go through the kitchen so the guys with the trays get knocked over? When Harlan and Stengel are watching news reports about the murder at a D.C. bar, does the bartender have to turn the TV off as soon as the pertinent news is over? (This would never happen in real life. And sports would be on anyway.) When Nina tells Harlan she was an Olympic sharpshooter (setting up her later display of crack marksmanship) does she have to say, "I brought home the gold"? Do real people speak like this? Or just NBC announcers?

"Murder at 1600" is exciting in its way. It's also exciting to see if the cast can get through the script, and if you can keep from laughing when Alda's character delivers his "you never served in the military" tirade to President Neil. Maybe you'll have better luck than I did.

SIGHT AND SOUND, 7/97, p. 49, Robin Dougherty

Homicide cop Harlan Regis is summoned to the White House when the corpse of a 25-year-old woman is found in one of the private bathrooms. Evidence points to a janitor, but Regis has his suspicions, particularly when the autopsy indicates the woman had consensual sex shortly before she was killed.

In the course of his investigation, Regis is stymied by White House security officer, Nick Spikings, who may have lied about the number of people present at the executive mansion at the time of the murder. Regis teams up with Nina Chance, the Secret Service agent assigned to help him. However, her reticence to talk about the case makes him even more suspicious. By the time the janitor is arrested, Regis believes he's stumbled onto a cover-up that implicates President Jack Neil and the President's son, Kyle Neil.

At the same time, the President is caught in a foreign policy crisis. North Korea is holding American servicemen hostage, but—against the advice of his military advisers—the President refuses to take action. Meanwhile, a surveillance tape surfaces that reveals who actually had access to the victim on the night of the murder. Regis realises that the President is being blackmailed by a cabinet member who resents his pacifist approach. Regis and Chance, along with Detective Stengel, enter the White House via underground tunnels just minutes before the President is about to resign. The mastermind behind the murder and the blackmail turns out to be the President's National Security Advisor, who is shot and killed in the final struggle.

By unofficial count, the Clinton presidency has inspired more movies about besieged presidents (*Nixon, Independence Day*), corrupt administrations (*Absolute Power, Dave*) and botched personal lives (*The American President*) than any other. The problem, of course, is that no mere movie can match the real-life headlines about any of the recent administrations. This is aptly illustrated by *Murder at 1600*, which steals plot elements and themes from such political embarrassments as the Iran-Contra scandal and the William Kennedy Smith rape case, yet still fails as a statement about the nature of power and corruption.

Anyone who missed the incident a few years ago when the body of Clinton's advisor Vincent Foster was found lying in a public park with a bullet in his head is invited to be horrified for the first time at the notion of a conspiracy and cover-up at 1600 Pennsylvania Avenue. That's the address given to homicide detective Harlan Regis (Wesley Snipes) when the corpse of a 25-year-old woman is discovered in one of the executive bathrooms. While Regis and Secret Service agent Chance chase down details that indicate a high-level cover-up, the President is embroiled in a foreign affairs debacle involving North Korea that threatens his popularity at home. His military advisors are urging action, but the President is hesitant to send in more fire power. Each plotline inches forward to a predictable conspiratorial conclusion.

Director Dwight Little (*Rapid Fire, Free Willy 2*) puts his actors through chase sequences that are remarkably lacking in suspense. The film's one atmospheric turn—its evocation of Washington in the grip of summer haze during the day and blinding rain storms at night—is not enough to keep us interested. As treacherous as any cover-up is, there's nothing shocking about it anymore, and thus both Regis and Chance come off as mind-bogglingly naive while the plot thickens and it becomes obvious that someone is trying to frame the President for the murder.

The lack of complexity here is a missed opportunity since Regis and Chance make a good team—even if Regis is the only black man ever born who collects little statuettes of defender-of-slavery Stonewall Jackson. As Chance, Lane is no woman in peril. She's the rare movie heroine who actually gets to be more competent than the goons who are on her trail. By contrast, late-night television comedian Dennis Miller (cast as Regis' friend Stengel) is gratuitously used as an expository device, called in when Regis needs to explain something to the audience. Still, by the time these three manoeuvre themselves through the White House's tunnels and into the executive mansion just minutes before the President is about to resign, there's very little the audience hasn't already figured out, much less still cares about.

VILLAGE VOICE, 4/29/97, p. 82, Justine Elias

The District was laid out before him like a wanton goddess without any clothes on, and detective Wesley snipes "was getting wicked pissed-off about crime," the pulp filmmakers wrote. "Someone at the top—a political insider—has killed a beautiful woman inside the most sacred building in the world. Snipes' only ally: a tough, tight-fitting Treasury agent (Diane Lane). But can he trust her? Sometimes a D.C. cop's got to take a secret tunnel to the Oval Office, bitch-slap a few thugs, and throw the nasty pols a look that seems to say, 'I could give you such a pinch!'"

In this shrewd, preposterous thriller, the mystery really develops as in a cheap novelette, with Snipes cast as both the hardheaded cop and the exquisite, tempestuous babe in trouble. Snipes, a multitalented actor who can share the screen with any type of firearm, has no trouble locating the murderer, who is obvious as soon as he makes his entrance, pursing his lipless mouth and pretending to be nice. *Murder at 1600* proves quite capably that there's no place in our government for sneaky, ugly people.

Also reviewed in:
NEW YORK TIMES, 4/18/97, p. C23, Janet Maslin
VARIETY, 4/14-20/97, p. 91, Emanuel Levy
WASHINGTON POST, 4/18/97, Weekend/p. 44, Desson Howe

MY BEST FRIEND'S WEDDING

A TriStar Pictures release of a Jerry Zucker/Predawn production. *Executive Producer:* Gil Netter and Patricia Whitcher. *Producer:* Jerry Zucker and Ronald Bass. *Director:* P.J. Hogan. *Screenplay:* Ronald Bass. *Director of Photography:* Laszlo Kovacs. *Editor:* Garth Craven and Lisa Fruchtman. *Music:* James Newton Howard. *Music Editor:* Andrew Silver. *Sound:* Ed Novick and (music) Dennis Sands. *Sound Editor:* John Morris. *Choreographer:* Toni Basil. *Casting:* David Rubin. *Production Designer:* Richard Sylbert. *Art Director:* Karen Fletcher Trujillo. *Set Designer:* Kurt Sharp. *Set Decorator:* William Kemper Wright. *Special Effects:* Thomas Ryba. *Costumes:* Jeffrey Kurland. *Make-up:* Noriko Watanabe. *Make-up (Julia Roberts):* Richard Dean. *Stunt Coordinator:* Rick LeFevour. *Running time:* 112 minutes. *MPAA Rating:* PG-13.

CAST: Julia Roberts (Julianne Potter); Dermot Mulroney (Michael O'Neal); Cameron Diaz (Kimmy Wallace); Rupert Everett (George Downes); Philip Bosco (Walter Wallace); M. Emmet Walsh (Joe O'Neal); Rachel Griffiths (Samantha Newhouse); Carrie Preston (Amanda Newhouse); Susan Sullivan (Isabelle Wallace); Chris Masterson (Scott O'Neal); Cassie Creasy (Flower Girl); Lucina Paquet (Kimmy's Grandma); Aida Baggio (2nd Old Woman); Shirley Kelly (Oldest Lady); George Bozonelos and Loretta Paoletti (Party Guests); Joseph Sikora and Shale Marks (Stoner Guys); Phillip Ingram (Wedding Singer); Rose Abdoo (Seamstress); JoBe Cerny (Tailor); Paul Giamatti (Richard, Bellman); Charlie Trotter (Himself, Chef); Guillermo Tellez (Chef); Ned Schmidtke (Captain); Mark Swenson (Karaoke Singer); Mara Casey (Karaoke Girl); Tonray Ho (Karaoke Waitress); Michelle Hutchinson (Drunken Trashy Girl); Robert Sutter (Crabhouse Pianist); Nydia Rodriguez Terracina (Walter's Secretary); Mike Bacarella (Office Janitor); Larry Santori (Conductor); Gene Janson and Kevin Michael Doyle (Sports Magazine Guys); Scott Kuhagen (Werner); Harry Shearer (Johnathan P.E. Rice); Jennifer McComb (Excited Woman); Mary-Pat Green (Angry Woman); Davenia McFadden (Angrier Woman); Jo Farkas (Loony Woman).

LOS ANGELES TIMES, 6/20/97, Calendar/p. 1, Kenneth Turan

The Smile is back.

After a run of roles dour enough to do credit to Calvin Coolidge, Julia Roberts in "My Best Friend's Wedding" returns to the kind of smart romantic comedy she's especially good at, playing a young woman who decides she's in love with a great pal only when he announces he's marrying someone else.

Fortunately for all parties, the director here is Australian P.J. Hogan, whose lightly mocking but sympathetic tone made "Muriel's Wedding" a major success. Based on a script by Ron Bass, who's been known to let bathos get the best of him, this "Wedding" benefits from Hogan's subversive temperament, his skill at leeching out excess sentiment. The director's ability to approach formula material with a fresh eye keeps this film bright and lively even when it verges on wearing thin.

Hogan's tartness is on display as early as the gleeful opening credit sequence, when a bride and bridesmaids in full wedding regalia, picture-book pretty but with the devil in their eyes, drolly lip-sync their way through Ani DiFranco's version of the old standard "Wishin' and Hopin.'" Business as usual this is not.

The same can be said for a winning Roberts, whose relaxed and confident performance is, along with superb supporting work from Rupert Everett, the film's triumphant cornerstone. But she is not a conventional romantic heroine, and her smiles come noticeably on her own terms. As New York restaurant critic Julianne Potter, Jules to her friends, Roberts manages to play not only the film's older female character, but a sometimes bad girl as well, someone who uses her smile as a weapon calculated to distract and disarm opposition.

The opposition in this case includes the people she should be rooting hardest for, starting with sportswriter and ex-boyfriend turned best friend Michael O'Neal (Dermot Mulroney at his most handsome). For nine years these two have joked that if they didn't marry by age 28, they'd wed each other. But when Michael phones on a Wednesday night to announce that he's marrying someone else in Chicago on Sunday, Jules flies in, determined to use those four days to get him to change his mind and marry her.

Naturally, her main target is Michael's endearing intended, the well-scrubbed, barely-out-of-her-teens Kimmy Wallace, bright-eyed and beautiful and unspoiled by her wealthy family. It's an ultimate ingenue role, the kind Roberts herself might have taken in a previous incarnation, and Cameron Diaz, who seems to improve with every role, plays it perfectly.

Since time is short, Jules gets right to work, trying to sow dissension and undermine the relationship any way she can, especially as regards to whether Michael will stay in his "low-paying, zero respect" sportswriting job. Her confidant in this, and the film's sole voice of reason, is her gay editor, George Downes, superbly played by Everett (the impatient Prince of Wales in "The Madness of King George"), who has all the film's best lines. "I don't send you men anymore," he tells Jules. "You don't have the faintest idea what to do with them."

Helped by Hogan's sharp directing and expert acting all around, these shenanigans are amusing, but "Wedding" really gets into gear when George appears in Chicago to lend moral support. A desperate Jules introduces him to everyone as her fiance, and the comic madness that results, culminating in a wild group sing-along of "I Say a Little Prayer" at an unsuspecting seafood restaurant, enables Everett to well and truly steal the picture from everyone concerned.

As if echoing the script's description of Jules' machinations as "a series of underhanded, despicable, not terribly imaginative things," "My Best Friend's Wedding" feels repetitive at times, but its star power and willingness to undercut convention come through at the end. With so many good things on its plate, it's no wonder this picture has what it takes to make Roberts finally smile.

NEW YORK, 7/21/97, p. 48, David Denby

My Best Friend's Wedding is a handsome-looking romantic comedy, with a vibrant star performance by Julia Roberts and lots of eccentric life breaking out in the corners and background. Yet the movie doesn't work in certain fundamental ways, and it leaves one dissatisfied and cranky. I've heard many people complaining about it, and each complaint is different. When this kind of general dissatisfaction sets in, it usually means that the movie's basic fantasy hasn't taken hold—with the result that everyone's irritable preoccupations come to the surface (the movie is demeaning to women ... to gays ... to heterosexuals). Well, maybe, but the real problem is that it's a bad movie. Screenwriter Ronald Bass, who worked on *Rain Man* and other commercially successful pictures, can't spring loose from the bear trap that he's created for himself, and the Australian director P.J. Hogan (*Muriel's Wedding*) is caught there, too, though he manages to wiggle a lot.

Julia Roberts plays a New York restaurant critic, Julianne—or Jules as everyone calls her—who is stunned when her old lover, Michael (Dermot Mulroney), a sports journalist in Chicago, tells her that in a few days he is going to marry a rich young woman. In Jules's head, Michael has always belonged to *her*. She has, however, never realized how much she loves him until she's threatened with losing him forever. Determined to break up the wedding, she rushes to Chicago (which looks dazzling here), and for four days, she plays one low, stupid trick after another.

In the movies she made after her big hit, *Pretty Woman*, Julia Roberts has seemed rather demure, even wan; she was all too willing, I thought, to recede into a scene, to renounce the egotistical prerogatives of stardom. She was so quiet, in fact, that one no longer looked forward to seeing her: She seemed to be running away from what her own talent and the endless media attention had made her. But she's too big a girl and too idiosyncratically beautiful—with a spectacular figure and that wide mouth set in a long face—to hide in a movie, and in *My Best Friend's Wedding,* she seems very large indeed, physically liberated and temperamentally alive, with energy to burn and a horselaugh that breaks out violently.

The audience is with her from the beginning, and that is why the picture's strategy is so perverse. For when Jules gets to Chicago she discovers that her rival, young Kimmy (Cameron Diaz), a junior at the University of Chicago, is a very nice girl and quite selflessly in love with Michael—so selflessly that she is willing (despite misgivings) to give up her prospective career for him. It's hard to tell what the filmmakers want us to think of Kimmy. Cameron Diaz is nervous and giggly, and wails piteously whenever things go wrong with Michael. But how can we root for Jules to send Kimmy packing? We can't.

It's hard as well to know what Bass and Hogan expect us to make of Michael. Here's a young sports reporter who gets all huffy about his integrity, yet he's marrying the daughter of the owner of the Chicago White Sox. Is he merely deluded? Stupid? What causes two beautiful women to knock themselves out for him? Dermot Mulroney is a handsome young man, but he's been made quite inarticulate (if this guy's a writer, I'm a tennis pro), and his temperament is sludgy. He seems self-centered and dim, and he hardly notices a thing (that Jules loves him deeply, for instance).

The movie has the structure of a romantic comedy, but its characters don't fit into that structure. Julia Roberts keeps struggling and striving and expending endless energy and emotion, yet she's working for something—marriage to Dermot Mulroney—that doesn't make sense for her. The movie has nowhere to go; all it can do is spin around, though some of the spinning is highly entertaining. Rupert Everett, who has played highborn louts in his English movies, makes a triumphant appearance as Jules's gay editor, George, who understands her better than she understands herself. George makes wise and witty remarks, like someone's perceptive aunt. At a certain point, the filmmakers throw up their hands and let Rupert Everett take over the movie. We're not entirely ungrateful. Everett, at least, knows what he's doing.

NEW YORK POST, 6/20/97, p. 45, Thelma Adams

Not since Katharine Hepburn brought up Baby in 1938 has a spoiled heiress been as appealing as Kimmy Wallace in "My Best Friend's Wedding.

Kimmy's pretty in pink. She drives Daddy's BMW as if there were two sets of laws: one for her and one for everyone else.

She sings karaoke—horrendously—and receives wild applause.

Kimmy's thoughts go straight from her heart to her mouth without editing. Since meeting sportswriter Michael O'Neal, she confesses she's become "just a sentimental [schmo] like all those nitwits I'd always pitied."

There's only one problem. This is Julia Roberts' summer comeback comedy and Cameron Diaz plays Kimmy.

In "Feeling Minnesota," Diaz slummed in the Courtney Love role. She was a girl behaving badly in "She's the One." Neither part prepared us for this fresh-faced zing, this star power in a bottle blonde.

Roberts isn't the switch-hitter Diaz is, playing good girls and bad girls with ease. Caught by her limits as an actress, Roberts has dropped the Irish brogues of her recent efforts ("Michael Collins," "Mary Reilly"). In P.J. Hogan's black comedy, she returns to familiar territory, but she has to work harder to hold onto her star.

With leonine curls that command their own acting coach and her patented appeal—crying spaniel eyes and spotlight grin—Roberts is amiable even when her character isn't. Julianne Potter is a food critic who hasn't had a taste for commitment until her best friend, O'Neal (Dermot Mulroney), invites her to his wedding.

O'Neal and Potter had "one hot month' while studying at Brown (a stretch, judging by Roberts and Mulroney). When things cooled, they vowed to wed each other if they were both single at 28. Flash forward. On the eve of his 28th birthday, Michael gets engaged—to Kimmy. Julianne sets out to bust up Michaels match and win the set.

Mulroney strains in a role that cries for Cary Grant. But Rupert Everett, as George, Julianne's gay boss and confidante, is magnificently cast. The star of "The Madness of King George" hotwires every scene he's in. He has more sparks with Roberts than Mulroney, even when he's crisply deflating her: "It's amazing the clarity that comes with psychotic jealousy."

Aussie Hogan, best known for "Muriel's Wedding," stages a pitched battle between fizz and fizzle. Working Ronald ("Rain Man") Bass' original script, Hogan struggles to maintain the central tension between Michael and Julianne while making his own distinct comic voice heard.

The center doesn't hold, but the supporting actors contribute enough helium to keep the comedy aloft. The best scene comes at the rehearsal dinner when George, impersonating Julianne's fiancé, describes their relationship as "some glittering Doris Day-Rock Hudson extravaganza."

Everett leads the table in a rousing rendition of the Burt Bachrach classic "I Say a Little Prayer," while lobster-mitted waiters sway in the background. For one, effusive, irreverent moment, I wished Muriel was getting married, not Julianne's best friend.

NEWSDAY, 6/20/97, Part II/p. B9, Jack Mathews

Australian director P.J. Hogan, who made his feature debut with the magically inventive comedy "Muriel's Wedding," ties the knot Hollywood style with "My Best Friend's Wedding," and the magic's gone.

It's not Hogan's fault, necessarily. You can't blame him for cashing in on the international success of "Muriel's Wedding," which he also wrote, and which he made for the price of a studio couch. But he might have held out for a script that had in more in common with his first film than the title ritual.

"Muriel's Wedding" was about a good-hearted ugly duckling's eventful search for true romance; "My Best Friend's Wedding" is about a mean-spirited beauty named Julianne who's trying to sabotage her former lover's engagement and reclaim him for herself.

For the first "Wedding," Hogan adopted a jaunty musical, near fanciful tone to help audiences relate to Muriel and cheer her on. He occasionally attempts it in the second, too, with one sensational success in a restaurant sequence. But even with Julia Roberts back in "Pretty Woman" form, flashing the keyboard smile and erupting in that Looney Tunes laugh, Julianne is nobody's idea of a heroine.

Written by Oscar winner Ron Bass ("Rain Man"), who hadn't attempted anything approaching screwball comedy before. "My Best Friend's Wedding" is set mostly in Chicago, where Julianne a feared New York restaurant critic, has just four days to separate sportswriter/best friend/former lover Michael (Dermot Mulroney) from baseball heiress Kimmy (Cameron Diaz). And she'll do anything to pull it off, except tell him she loves him (the word sticks in her throat like over-cooked brisket).

The midsection of the movie is devoted to Julianne's schemes to diminish her younger rival in Michael's eyes, and it's a mission that turns Julianne from narcissistic snob to a word that rhymes with witch to delusional obsessive to lawbreaker. Being all these things and sympathetic, too, is a challenge that perhaps only Roberts, or perhaps Sandra Bullock, could meet. Put Demi Moore or Rebecca De Mornay in this role and audiences would stone the screen. Whether Roberts succeeds is the issue that, will separate people who love the movie from those who find it excruciating.

For those of us in the second group, the one genuine grace note in the film is Cameron Diaz, who is an even better comedy actress than Roberts and whose character is about as perfect—honest, devoted, sensitive. and unspoiled—as she seems. She's a wonderful ingenue, whom Bass may have fashioned after Elizabeth Taylor's turn in "Father of the Bride."

As soon as we get to know the two women, Michael's choice is a no-brainer, but his relationship with Julianne has gone on so long and been so close, that we can't be sure where his loyalty lies. Mulroney plays the wanted man with a convincing innocence.

The movie's scene stealer, however, is Rupert Everett, as Julianne's gay editor and co-conspirator, George. It's an over-the-top performance in a film that can't quite decide whether it wants to be sentimental or madcap, and Everett is terrific in a scene where he leads an entire restaurant in a rendition of the Dionne Warwick hit, "Say a Little Prayer."

That scene, and an opening credit number, are the only true Hogan moments in an otherwise full-blooded star vehicle. Welcome to Hollywood.

NEWSWEEK, 6/23/97, p. 76, David Ansen

Julianne (Julia Roberts), a food critic, and Michael (Dermot Mulroney), a sports-writer, are former lovers, current best friends and about to turn 28. Once they made a vow that if neither had fallen in love by 28, they would marry each other. Now Michael has lost his heart to someone else—and when he tells Julianne the news, just four days before the wedding, she is suddenly convinced she's been in love with Michael all along. Obsessed with derailing the nuptials, Julianne speeds to Chicago, determined to change roles from bridesmaid to bride.

If the delightful and surprising romantic comedy *My Best Friend's Wedding* played by the usual rules, the woman our heroine is trying sabotage—the rich and beautiful Kimmy (Cameron Diaz)—would be played as either a prig or a goody-two-shoes. But as written by P.J. Hogan ("Muriel's Wedding") Kimmy is more than a creditable competitor, and Julianne's motives are riddled with neurotic and ambiguous undertones. Because Julianne is Julia, back in glorious comic form, we are inclined to root for her, but "Wedding" is daring enough to employ the Uncertainty Principle. Should we be rooting for her? The movie keeps you wondering. As her other best friend (Rupert Everett) asks her: do you really love him—or is it just about winning?

A romantic comedy for an era of diminished expectations, "Wedding" is at its funniest when Everett arrives on the scene and the duplicitous Julianne pretends that her gay friend is her fiancé successfully arousing Michael's jealousy. Indeed, the chemistry between Roberts and Everett—who's never been so charming or hilarious—far surpasses any charge between her and Mulroney, whose function is more decorative than substantial. Here, it is the friendship between a straight woman and a gay man that has the nuances and depths of a good marriage. At a time when the Hollywood romantic comedy feels like an endangered species (try sitting through "'Til There Was You") the buoyant. bitter-sweet "Wedding" puts new fizz in an old form.

SIGHT AND SOUND, 9/97, p. 50, Darren Arnold

Julianne Potter is astounded to learn that her best friend and former lover Michael O'Neal is about to marry heiress Kimmy Wallace in four days' time. Nervous about the event, Michael asks Julianne to fly to Chicago to be with him. Realising she still loves Michael, Julianne goes intending to break the couple up, but is momentarily disarmed by Kimmy's likeableness. Julianne tries gently to persuade Michael that Kimmy isn't his type. After several attempts to cause friction between them, Julianne convinces Kimmy to ask her father Walter to offer Michael a job, knowing Michael would hate the idea. The suggestion causes an argument between the couple, but they make up.

Needing support, Julianne calls her gay friend George, who arrives in Chicago. Julianne pretends George is her fiancé, but this ruse fails to make Michael sufficiently jealous. Julianne uses Walter's e-mail account to write a letter to Michael's boss in order to make it look as if Walter wants Michael sacked. She backs out of actually sending it, but the e-mail is later sent by mistake. Michael's boss writes to let him know what kind of family he's marrying into. Disgusted, Michael breaks up with Kimmy, but neither he nor Kimmy actually tells anyone or cancels the wedding.

On the big day, Julianne finally confesses to causing all the trouble and how she really feels to Michael. They kiss, but Kimmy sees them and runs away. Realising that Michael loves Kimmy more than herself, Julianne finds Kimmy and convinces her to come back and marry him. At the reception, Julianne dances happily with George.

P.J. Hogan's *My Best Friend's Wedding* opens amusingly with a saucy blonde bride and her pink-frocked maids singing "Wishin' and Hopin'" straight to camera. Colourful and slightly surreal, they look as if they could have stepped straight out of the same director's *Muriel's Wedding*. It's also an oddly protracted sequence, and because the women look squarely at the viewer it almost seems like a hellish advertisement for marital bliss. It's something of a disappointment that the film that follows is so much more generic than Hogan's last, bittersweet feature. Still, while *My Best Friend's Wedding* lacks the raw edge of *Muriel*, it's nonetheless an exemplary take on an overworked genre.

A film where two attractive women vie for the attention of the same man is by no means original, but it's the delicate shading applied to this simple premise that sets the film apart. Arguably its most interesting aspect is how the two main female characters are presented: Hogan wisely eschews the good girl/bad girl dichotomy that has become synonymous with the modern romantic comedy (David Burton Morris' *Jersey Girl* being a prime example). Instead, the personalities are carefully balanced so that ultimately viewer sympathies will probably be determined by a prior preference for either Cameron Diaz or Julia Roberts. Both are extremely engaging, with Roberts showing restraint and range in the more unflattering role of Julianne the scheming heroine, and Diaz bringing a certain steeliness to the squealing Kimmy. The film's biggest mystery is how either could be so besotted with Dermot Mulroney's wooden Michael.

In fact, the film seems far more interested in the friendship between Julianne and George, her gay friend, than in any of the other relationships in the film. The Michael scenario almost seems a mere foil to allow this tender, more subtle story to shine through *(Muriel's Wedding* also had characters ultimately preferring friendships over romances, which makes this theme, along with weddings, a kind of directorial watermark). Rupert Everett beautifully plays the role of George to the extent that he even survives the script's intentions to reduce him to an effete, camp clown.

The screenplay by Ronald Bass is what occasionally shackles the film, by paying more attention to plot development than characterisation. Thankfully, Hogan always ensures that we care about the characters and throws little stylistic curve balls to freshen things up. There is one scene in particular that stands out as queasily surreal. Michael's younger brother and two friends give a helium-assisted recitation of John Denver's 'Annie's Song', which overlaps disconcertingly with a grave and crucial exchange between Michael and Julianne. It's the film's most unsettling and simultaneously funny moment and, like the opening credits, appears to belong to another work altogether.

TIME, 6/23/97, p. 78, Richard Schickel

She's cool. A restaurant critic who nibbles at life as if it were a dubious meal, Julianne Potter (Julia Roberts) has, shall we say, neglected her emotional growth.

He's dim. A good-natured sportswriter who actually likes the bad pay and long road trips, Michael O'Neal (Dermot Mulroney) is one of those guys who believe the unexamined life is the only one worth living.

Sometime lovers who have decided to be best friends instead, they once made one of those silly promises no one expects to be held to: to marry if nothing better turns up before they reach the age of desperation, which, in their youthful innocence, they imagine to be 28. Now that the year is upon them, he suddenly announces he is getting married—to an heiress, no less—and she decides to put a stop to that nonsense.

Well, all right. Busting up society weddings has always been good comedic sport. We like to see spoiled, if redeemable, brats be embarrassed in front of their rich friends. In the classics of this sub-genre (it *Happened One Night, The Philadelphia Story*), it was the man (Clark Gable, Cary Grant) who caused the ruckus. But different tropes for different folks. And different times. It is theoreticary O.K. to place a woman in the terminator role. And Roberts, that realest of nice girls, much of the time makes us believe that her insanity is temporary.

But there are too many moments in *My Best Friend's Wedding* when her ferocity reads as near motiveless malignity, especially as it is largely directed at Cameron Diaz's Kimmy, the bride-to-be. She's pert and pretty, smart and spunky—not at all someone we wish ill. When our sympathies shift to her, the movie sours. It is no help either that Ronald Bass neglected to write (or Mulroney was unable to find) a character in Michael. Why all this fuss over this lox, we keep wondering. Director P.J. Hogan (*Muriel's Wedding*) stages a couple of marvelously giddy musical numbers, and Rupert Everett is terrific as the voice of sweet homosexual reason in the midst of this heterosexual hubbub. He—and the songs—probably belong in a different, better movie. But they give this one what edge and clarity it has.

VILLAGE VOICE, 7/8/97, p. 74, Justine Elias

The funniest things about weddings are the hideous gowns that have been forced on the bridesmaids, and the best running gag In this amiable, meandering romantic comedy is the sight of Julia Roberts in a too tight, too girly, colored frock, trying not to hate herself. The look of animal terror in her eye, as she catches sight of herself in a bridal-shop mirror, is the most eloquent expression of emotion that Roberts has offered on film in a long while.

Much of the movie, directed by P. J. Hogan (*Muriel's Wedding),* casts Roberts as a scheming homewrecker, determined to steal her old boyfriend (Dermot Mulroney) away from his devoted fiancée (Cameron Diaz). Trouble is, Roberts never seems to be desperate to win Mulroney, whose generic guy's guy sportswriter becomes more boring the longer he's onscreen, and Diaz—who at first glance seems to be a simpering air-head—is on second, third, and fourth meeting as charming, effusive, and natural as, well, as a character Julia Roberts might have played circa 1990. It's left to the congenitally debonair Rupert to play the Oscar Wilde ex machina. He's the wise, romantically satisfied homosexual authority figure who stops the movie just as the situation becomes completely cloying.

Also reviewed in:
NEW REPUBLIC, 7/28/97, p. 26, Stanley Kauffmann
NEW YORK TIMES, 6/20/97, p. C3, Janet Maslin
NEW YORKER, 6/16/97, p. 107, Terrence Rafferty
VARIETY, 6/16-22/97, p. 35, Leonard Klady
WASHINGTON POST, 6/20/97, p. C7, Stephen Hunter
WASHINGTON POST, 6/20/97, Weekend/p. 37, Rita Kempley

MY MOTHER'S COURAGE

A National Center for Jewish Film release of a Sentana Film/Little Bear/Wega Filmproduktion coproduction. *Executive Producer:* James Mitchell. *Producer:* Michael Verhoeven. *Director:* Michael Verhoeven. *Screenplay (German with English subtitles):* Michael Verhoeven. *Based on the novel by:* George Tabori. *Director of Photography:* Michael Epp and Theo Bierkens. *Editor:* David Freeman. *Music:* Julian Nott and Michael Verhoeven. *Sound:* Johannes Rommel and (music) Richard Lewzey. *Sound Editor:* Les Wiggins. *Casting:* Michelle Guish. *Production Designer:* Wolfgang Hundhammer. *Set Decorator:* Claude Garnier and Sarah Beckmann. *Special Effects:* Otto Franke and Rosta Debef. *Costumes:* Rosemarie Hettman. *Make-up:* Gerlinde Kunz and Paul Schmidt. *Stunt Coordinator:* Jaroslav Tomsa. *Running time:* 88 minutes. *MPAA Rating:* Not Rated.

CAST: Pauline Collins (Elsa Tabori); Ulrich Tukur (SS Officer); Heribert Sasse (Kelemen); Natalie Morse (Maria); Robert Giggenbach (Cornelius Tabori); Günther Bothur ("Moustache"); Simon Verhoeven (Young SS Man); Jens Harzer (Young Man in Pajamas); Buddy Ellas (Rabbi); Peter Radtke (German Teacher "Wireless"); Otto Grünmandl (Julius); Hana Frejkova (Martha); George Tabori (Himself); Tatjana Vilhelmova (Olga); Istvan Iglódi (Usicky); Eddi Arent (Klapka); Wolfgang Gasser (Iglodi); Johanna Mertinz (Tram Conductor); Jindrich Bonaventura (Greenshirt with Chalk); Jirl Knot (German Bookkepper); Stanislav Triska (Doctor 'monocle');

Vladimir Volek (Doctor 'pince nez'); Jitka Smutná (Sister Liebgart); Horst Hiemer (German Professor); Peter Mohrdiek (Bald German, Saloon Car); Axel Scholtz (Butcher); Alexandra Millard (Little Elsa); Jiri Ornest (Elsa's Father); Petra Berndt (Young German Nurse); Josef Vajnar (Stranger, Cattle Car); Eva Holubová (Twins' Mother); Radka Mayerova (Young Whore, Saloon Car); Miroslav Táborsky (Barber); Jaroslav Tesitel (Mr. Buchbinder); Ondrej Skoch (George Tabori, Aged 16); Jaroslava Kretschmerova (Young Emma); Petr Billy (Shoe-shine Boy); Lilian Malkina (Woman at Shoe-Shine); Petr Janis (Man with Pass); Mikulas Roth (Praying Man); Darlene Charles (Wardrobe Girl); Ladislav Koci (Man Missing Luggage); Valerie Kaplanova (Blind Woman); Rudolph Starz (Sarcastic Man, Cattle Car); Stanislav Hajek (Man with Books); Arnost Goldflam and Marcela Kralova (Jewish Couple); Jiri Raisky-Kastner (Policeman).

NEW YORK POST, 9/10/97, p. 40, Larry Worth

If a Holocaust-based comedy sounds like an impossibility, chalk up writer-director Michael Verhoeven as a modern-day miracle worker.

That's not to say that "My Mother's Courage," the based-on-truth story about Verhoeven's mother being sent to Auschwitz, recalls "Springtime for Hitler." Rather, it's filled with moment upon moment of gentle whimsy, O. Henry-like ironies and unbelievable absurdity.

Set in the Budapest of 1944, the film opens as the eternally optimistic Elsa Tabori (Pauline Collins) is arrested by Hungarian police. But that doesn't seem a big deal to someone who sports her yellow star like a corsage.

Even when being herded into a cattle car, Elsa assumes she's headed to a Swedish resort. Therein lies the film's ever-growing poignancy, particularly as Elsa relives her past glories to maintain an upbeat demeanor.

Within the last half hour, Verhoeven changes tone yet again, setting the pace for a finale with as much heart-stopping suspense, as "Schindler's List." Better still, it's played out with Nazi officers who avoid the goose-stepping stereotype.

Maybe that's why one forgives Verhoeven's flaws. As with his earlier "The Nasty Girl," the film is slow to build and seems initially unfocused. Its movie-within-a-movie format also distracts.

But Pauline Collins, best known for her remarkable work as "Shirley Valentine," exhibits enough charm, selflessness and strength as the cheery heroine to dispel all draw backs. Along with Ulrich Tukur's enigmatic SS officer and Natalie Morse as a traumatized victim, the cast is virtually flawless.

But chiefly due to Verhoeven, "My Mother's Courage" amuses, moves and horrifies in a virtually unprecedented manner, making it one of the year's most unconventional entertainments.

NEWSDAY, 9/10/97, Part II/p. B5, Jack Mathews

One summer morning in 1944 Budapest, an amiable Jewish housewife named Elsa Tabori was stopped on her way to her sister's home, and handcuffed. She was to be deported, she was told, and was then herded along with hundreds of other Hungarian Jews, all wearing the mandated Star of David on their chests, into crowded cattle cars supposedly bound for Sweden.

Elsa was one of an estimated 760,000 Jews living in Hungary before the German occupation in 1944, and one of only 260,000 still alive a year later. How she survived that train ride, and what she saw and learned on the way, is the subject of a novel and play by her son George Tabori, and now the subject of German director Michael Verhoeven's film adaptation, "My Mother's Courage."

George Tabori, who left Hungary before the war and enjoyed a career as a Hollywood screenwriter ("Crisis," "I Confess"), created his story from his mother's reminiscences, and appears at the beginning and end of the movie, as its sardonic host. As he did with his Oscar-nominated "The Nasty Girl," Verhoeven occasionally breaks through the "fourth wall" here, giving us a glimpse of the contemporary studio surroundings as the film opens, and even having Tabori interrupt a flashback scene of his father's arrest, to point out that his captors are Hungarian Nazis, not Germans.

I'm not sure why Verhoeven chose to do this with "My Mother's Courage." Reminding us that no dramatic recreation can convey the actual horror merely subverts the illusion of reality, and forces us out of the story.

Thankfully, Verhoeven abandons the device fairly quickly, and we are allowed to identify with Pauline Collins' Elsa as a trusting, warmhearted optimist totally unprepared for the grotesque lessons she's about to learn. As the train hurtles through the countryside, headed not for Sweden but Auschwitz, she gets to know the teenager Maria (Natalie Morse), whose day began with her rape by Nazis and with her sister being drowned by them.

While standing along the tracks, waiting to board a second train, a young man bends over to pluck a wildflower for a girl, and is shot to death by a guard. Earlier, twin girls are yanked out of their mother's arms and sent off with a nurse, destined no doubt for Dr. Mengele's medical experiments. A man claiming to have a Red Cross pass is escorted into an office and murdered.

Elsa's fate, and that of Maria's, rest with an SS officer (Ulrich Tukur) with gentle blue eyes and a perversely corrupted conscience. He's a vegetarian because he can't understand "how a person can chop up another living being and eat it." Yet, he has no problem transporting thousands of people to their deaths.

The officer is a fascinatingly conflicted character, and Tukur plays both sides of his personality in ways that leave us as confused about his humanity as Elsa apparently was throughout the rest of her life.

"My Mother's Courage," like many European coproductions, was intended as an English-language film, which explains the casting of Collins. It was later decided to release the film in subtitled form, with Collins' voice dubbed into Hungarian. The dubbing is apparent, but not a major distraction. Collins' performance is mostly internal, with Elsa's range of emotions read through her eyes, and her body language.

It's a smart and involving performance, and whether Verhoeven likes it or not, I believed it.

SIGHT AND SOUND, 1/98, p 49, Nick Kimberly

The author George Tabori, addressing the camera, explains that he is celebrating his eightieth birthday on the set of a movie about his mother Elsa. He meets the actor who plays his mother. Tabori then 'goes' to Budapest in 1994, his birthplace, to introduce his parents. Elsa (played by the actor from the studio), wearing the gold star used to identify Jews, is taken into custody. Her captors manage to lose her, but rather than escape, she joins a crowd of Jews being herded to the railway station. Another Jew explains they are going to Auschwitz, "the Jewish bakery". They're herded into cattle cars and taken from the city. We glimpse Nazi soldiers on the train and their commander, an SS officer. Eventually, they reach their first destination. The Jews are marched to a huge grain store. Elsa risks death to explain to the SS officer that she shouldn't be there because she has a Red Cross pass.

To her surprise, the SS officer allows her to return to Budapest with him. When their train stops, the SS officer advises her to make her escape. This she does, emerging in contemporary Berlin. Elsa ends up back at her sister's in Budapest, where she resumes the cardgame she should have started before the transportation. Over the closing credits, television footage shows the SS officer explaining that he played no part in the deportations and that, in any case, it was too long ago to remember.

Theodor Adorno suggested that, after Auschwitz, there could be no poetry. He was right only if we see poetry as no more than a balm to soothe away pain, and with it, all memory of pain. And, of course, there's more to poetry than that. Auschwitz demanded, and continues to demand, poetry and every other kind of art. Michael Verhoeven's film is brave in not only responding to that demand, but doing so with humour. The moments when it stands outside the story it's telling only serve to invite us further into that story.

Nor does it find it necessary to shout, or to draw easy morals from the tale of author George Tabori's mother Elsa and her extraordinary escape. It's extraordinary because it is so simple: she asks to be allowed to go home, and her request is granted. That doesn't, needless to say, amount to an exoneration of the SS officer who grants her request. He is a vegetarian, but his feeling for his fellow creatures only goes so far. Verhoeven risks making a caricature of him, not least in a scene where the soundtrack exaggerates every slurp and swallow he makes while eating a plum, yet Ulrich Tukur's performance is so precisely chilling that he never comes across as a caricature.

Why he should grant Tabori's mother freedom is a mystery the film deliberately never solves. In a curious way, by rejecting a solution, this renders more painful the thought of the fate of all those who didn't ask for their freedom (not that the Nazis would have granted it, of course). In its quietly quizzical way, *My Mother's Courage* isn't about Auschwitz at all, but about the memory of what Auschwitz meant, about the experience of *not* dying there. If that seems an evasion, it isn't. In one phantasmagoric image, more forceful than any blunt realism, Verhoeven encapsulates the enormity of the Holocaust: in the cattle truck, the camera picks out the gold star on Tabori's mother's breast, then draws back to show her face (Pauline Collins in defiant mode), then draws back further until the screen fills with dozens of gold stars, glowing in the truck's darkness.

It's an image of appalling beauty, asking us to look at history again: a process of re-examination that history itself forces on us. *My Mother's Courage* achieves its aims with something of a twinkle in its eye. For that, it's rather remarkable, in its understated way.

VILLAGE VOICE, 9/16/97, p. 98, J. Hoberman

For an East European Jew to survive the Holocaust was, in the deepest sense, an absurdity—or what a religious person would term a miracle. Such is the premise of Michael Verhoeven's gently absurdist *My Mother's Courage,* adapted from George Tabori's play and detailing the circumstances by which Tabori's mother Elsa, a sixtyish Hungarian Jew, managed to escape deportation to Auschwitz.

Spanning a single day during the summer of 1944, *My Mother's Courage* is as would-be Brechtian as its title suggests. The movie opens with documentary footage of a former Nazi officer denying the very Budapest deportations that Verhoeven will stage, then shows the 80-year-old Tabori meeting Pauline Collins, the Irish actress who plays his mother. The mood is deceptively light, at times almost slapstick. Because Hungary was, for most of the war, a passive Axis ally, the deportation of the nation's Jews (who were far more integrated than the Jews of Poland or Romania) did not begin until after the Germans occupied the country in March 1944. Hence the bewilderment of those caught up, along with Mrs. Tabori, in the movie's "test" roundup.

Verhoeven a calm and principled filmmaker whose previous features include such exemplars of German antifascism as *The White Rose* and *The Nasty Girl*—takes his cues from anti-Hitler Hollywood comedies like *The Great Dictator* and *To Be or Not To Be*, as well as the Czech movies of the 1960s. (Budapest stands in here for Prague.) As played by Collins, Mrs. Tabori is a wide-eyed innocent—trusting, cheerful, and, above all, proper.

That she so resembles her most famous creation, Shirley Valentine, gives the movie a further unsettling dimension—she truly is anybody's middle-aged mother packed up and bound for the gas chamber.

My Mother's Courage was received so stormily at the 1995 Toronto Film Festival that Verhoeven felt compelled to drop the most controversial scene—one victim makes sexual advances to another in a packed cattle car—and further amplify the "happy" ending. But the movie's antic tone hardly diminishes its detailed account of the mechanics of deportation. Nor does the grotesque whimsicality of one SS commandant mitigate the horror of the German death machine. On the contrary. *My Mother's Courage* shows that blue skies and sunshine can be as devastating as night and fog.

Also reviewed in:
NEW REPUBLIC, 9/29/97, p. 26, Stanley Kauffmann
NEW YORK TIMES, 9/10/97, p. C16, Stephen Holden
VARIETY, 4/8-14/96, p. 63, Derek Elley

MY SEX LIFE...OR HOW I GOT INTO AN ARGUMENT

A Why Not Productions/La Sept Cinéma/France 2 Cinema coproduction with the participation of Canal Plus and the Centre National de la Cinématographie. *Producer:* Pascal Caucheteux and Grégoire Sorlet. *Director:* Arnaud Desplechin. *Screenplay (French with English subtitles):* Arnaud Desplechin and Emmanuel Bourdieu. *Director of Photography:* Eric Gautier. *Editor:* François Gedigier and Laurence Briaud. *Music:* Krishna Lévy. *Sound:* Laurent Poirier and (music) Didier Lizé. *Sound Editor:* Mathilde Muyard. *Casting:* Claude Martin, Stephane Batut, and Jeanne Biras. *Production Designer:* Antoine Platteau. *Costumes:* Claire Gérard-Hirne and Delphine Hayat. *Make-up:* Bernard Floch, Isabelle Legay, Jeanne Milon, and Nurith Barkan. *Running time:* 178 minutes. *MPAA Rating:* Not Rated.

CAST: Mathieu Amalric (Paul); Emmanuelle Devos (Esther); Emmanuel Salinger (Nathan); Marianne Denicourt (Sylvia); Thibault de Montalembert (Bob); Chiara Mastroianni (Patricia); Denis Podalydès (Jean-Jacques); Jeanne Balibar (Valérie); Fabrice Desplechin (Ivan); Hélène Lapiower (Le Mérou); Michel Vuillermoz (Frédéric Rabier); Roland Amstutz (Chernov); Marion Corillard (Ivan, the Student); Solenn Jarniou (Pascale); Philippe Duclos (Spiritual Accompanist); Elisabeth Maby (Tatie); Paule Annen (Mrs. Chernov); Anne-Katerine Normant (Esther's Friend); Vincent Nemeth (Friend); David Gabison (Diocese Delegate).

NEW YORK POST, 9/17/97, p. 61, Thelma Adams

Arnaud Desplechin's, elliptical, witty, gorgeously acted ensemble comedy about grad students groping for the meaning of life and love while dealing with jealousy, academic and otherwise, has no right to be as good as it is.

"My Sex Life ... or How I Got Into an Argument," a hidden treasure of last year's New York Film Festival, combines the sublime and the ridiculous with astonishing assurance from the young French director of "La Sentinelle."

For nearly three hours we are immersed in the romances, friendships and ambitions of a close-knit group of friends. Provocative, funny, emotionally wrenching, it makes us come to know a little more, and question a little more, about ourselves through the interplay of Bob, Paul, Nathan, Esther, Valerie, Sylvia and their dialectics of sex.

Paul (Mathieu Amalric) is Bob's cousin, Nathan's biggest fan, Esther's reluctant boyfriend. He covets Nathan's girl, the sultry Sylvia, but learns the steps of the masochistic tango from Valerie, a hyper-intelligent nutcase.

Amalric earned a Cesar (the French Oscar) for best newcomer in 1996 for his Paul. This small, eager, charming skirt-chaser is stuck in a rut: His dissertation is incomplete; his archrival (Michel Vuillermoz) has stepped over him to assume a full professorship in epistemology; and his 10-year relationship with Esther (Emmanuelle Devos) is in a state of perpetual breakup.

Paul, almost 30, has become an almost habitual drifter, his adolescence delayed. He sacrifices Esther in a misguided attempt to grow up, moons over Sylvia (Marianne Denicourt), spars with Valerie (Jeanne Balibar).

As Paul seems to shrink before us, branding himself with a scarlet "L" for loser, psychologically frozen, the women caught in his gaze grow in size and majesty. They come into focus in astonishing depth: Esther's tragic and true love for Paul despite his faults, Sylvia's insecurity behind her cool sensual stare, Valerie's predatory rage.

By the end, we feel a little older, a little wiser and enormously satisfied. Even when the dollar is up and air fares are down, "My Sex Life ... " is the best way, short of enrolling in the Sorbonne, of immersing oneself in an insider's Paris.

SIGHT AND SOUND, 8/97, p. 46, Michael Temple

Paul is a young philosophy lecturer at Nanterre University in Paris. Unlike his male contemporaries, be they friends or rivals, he has yet to complete his doctoral thesis. His romantic life has reached a similar impasse: infidelity and mutual contempt have eaten into the soul of his longstanding relationship with his girlfriend Esther. Most powerfully, the lingering traces of an idealised affair with Sylvia, the beautiful fiancée of his best friend Nathan, still haunt his mind and prevent him from fully committing to Esther.

As distraction from this double paralysis, he enters into a desperate relationship with the intensely disturbed Valérie, girlfriend of Paul's friend Jean-Jacques. All around him, Paul observes his friends in variegated but analogous states of post-adolescent uncertainty. Sooner or later, he must face up to his sexual and intellectual responsibilities. He finally breaks with Esther, abandoning her to a clinical depression, while on the intellectual front, his surprise resignation from the university paradoxically enables him to finish his thesis and open up a different professional future. A kind of double resolution is reached when Nathan proposes that Sylvia should help Paul prepare his thesis for publication. This brings the ex-lovers together again, which may allow them to conclude their relationship one way or another at last.

For the first half hour of *Ma Vie sexuelle* (*How I Got Into an Argument*) or *My Sex Life* (why keep the title in French?), you could imagine yourself watching a kind of Eric Rohmer derivative. What we seemingly have here is the familiar ensemble cast of semi-bourgeois twentysomethings living out their entertaining but trivial existential problems in the highly photogenic scenery of contemporary Paris and its suburban environs. Less than eloquent but more than prolix, the characters spend much time analysing their so far brief and simple lives within a philosophically and psychologically literate framework.

These dialogues are shot and assembled with a sharp, low-budget intelligence, which brings the cinematic form as close as it will ever get to the cynical but sentimental elegance of the late nineteenth-century prose fiction of a Guy de Maupassant. The frequent interventions of an anonymous but all-knowing narrator and the overarching *Bildungsroman* structure take Arnaud Desplechin's second full-length feature (following *La Sentinelle* of 1992) even closer to literariness than Rohmer's longstanding filmic "comédies et proverbes" project.

However, as *Ma vie sexuelle* slowly unfolds its full three-hour dramatic complexity, we begin to realise that Desplechin's work needs to be distinguished from Rohmer's in a number of ways. The most important is that the young director's ambition is serious and weighty, whereas the older man's ultimate purpose seems to be the attainment of a cosily ironic detachment. What at first seem like reflections of Rohmer's famously light touch (the self-conscious inanity, the monotonous and supposedly oxymoronic gag of a pretty girl quoting Hegel) are gradually transformed into something much darker and deeper in scope. These characters really are suffering! These professional and emotional mutations really hurt!

Desplechin achieves this transformation first and foremost by the sheer scale of the piece, its psychological force and violence increasing in intensity and conviction as the film stretches out into its final third hour. The central narrative strand of the protagonist Paul's relationships with three women is given perspective as well as comic relief by the interpolation of secondary plotlines, such as his friend Ivan's bizarrely erotic conversion to Catholicism (or, at least, his decision to become a priest, which in this case is not quite the same thing), and the mysterious, ancient rivalry between Paul and his former close-friend-turned-philosophy star Frédéric Rabier. (This episode comes to a climax when Paul salvages Rabier's dead pet monkey from behind a radiator.)

Depth of character-analysis likewise stems from the gradual accumulation of detail and nuance we witness. For example, the portrayal of Esther's slow depressive descent into melancholy after Paul's decision to put their extenuated bond out of its misery is subtly nuanced, as is Valérie's abusive and counter-abusive relationship with the wimpish Jean-Jacques.

Ultimately, the film will either stand or fall according to the quality and conviction of its acting, and on this count Desplechin has succeeded in obtaining excellent performances all round, both from the major and minor characters, thus assuring the ensemble has the necessary pace and balance to sustain its length and range. This is no doubt partly explained by the fact that many of the young cast have played together before, either for Desplechin himself (Emmanuelle Devos, Emmanuel Salinger, Marianne Denicourt all appeared in *La Sentinelle*) or for other directors (Mathieu Amalric, Denis Podalydès and Chiara Mastroianni performed in Danièle Dubroux's 1995 *journal du séducteur*). Indeed, the whole cast of *Ma vie sexuelle* figured prominently in a recent issue of the earnest film-journal *Positif* devoted to the new generation of screen and stage actors currently injecting (according to *Positif)* some youth and dynamism into the French film-scene.

The very idea of an actor-led rather than auteur-inspired wave of energy running through French film perhaps suggests an exceptional phenomenon, sufficiently curious at least to warrant our sustained further attention. In the meantime, Desplechin's *Ma vie sexuelle* may fascinate or infuriate its no doubt modest British audience, but if you give it some time and patience you can be sure you won't see another film like it all year.

VILLAGE VOICE, 9/23/97, p. 90, Amy Taubin

A tour de force of cross-purposes and mixed emotions, rapt looks and furtive glances, compulsive chatter and inspired one-liners, Arnaud Desplechin's *My Sex Life ... or How I Got Into an Argument* is also a brilliant meshing of form and content. To describe *My Sex Life ...* simply as novelistic (which it is) obscures the inventiveness and purity of Desplechin's filmmaking. It's hard to think of another contemporary film in which camera movement and editing are as subtly synced to a character's perceptions of and responses to his world.

The character is Paul Dedalas (Mathieu Amalric), a 29-year-old Parisian graduate student in philosophy whose nervous energy, quixotic humor, and guilty but irrepressible eroticism belie his complete paralysis vis-a-vis some important areas of his life. Paul is as incapable of definitively breaking up with Esther (Emmanuelle Devos), his girlfriend of 10 years, as he is of finishing his dissertation. Burdensome though they are, girlfriend and dissertation connect him to his adolescence and defend him from the terrors of beginning "his life as a man."

In any case, Paul doesn't want to be an academic, he wants to be a writer, and we can think of *My Sex Life ... or How I Got Into an Argument* as the bildungsroman he will write after he's broken through his blockages.

The mechanism for this breakthrough appears in the form of a man in a white designer suit with a monkey on a leash. He is Frederic Rabier (Michel Vuillermoz), Paul's former classmate who has become the chairman of his department. While Paul's relatively busy sex life encompasses the dependent Esther, the enigmatic Sylvia (Marianne Denicourt), who inconveniently happens to be involved with his best friend Nathan (Emmanuel Salinger), and the flamboyantly defiant Valerie (Jeanne Balibar), his "argument" is with Rabier, the poseur, whose meteoric rise is based on his vaporous dissertation for which Paul has complete contempt. Painful as it is, Paul's encounter with Rabier has the cathartic effect of forcing his repressed anger and competitiveness into the open, thus loosening the hold of the past.

If this sounds either pat or grim, it's not. *My Sex Life ...* is an extraordinarily generous, psychologically astute, sharply erotic romantic comedy. As mercurially paced as a great screwball, it feels less than half as long as its three-hour running time. After three viewings, I'm still not sure where the flashbacks begin and end, but let me assure you, it's nothing to get hung up about. The libido knows not the niceties of linear time.

Fine as the supporting actors are (particularly Devos, who in her last scenes suggests an alternate film routed through her subjectivity rather than Paul's), *My Sex Life ...* would be inconceivable without Amalric's performance. Almaric seems to wear his nervous system outside his skin, and his remarkable eyes can look simultaneously evasive, mischievous, defensive, seductive, and besotted.

Desplechin's fluid, richly textured misc-en-scène takes its queue from those eyes. Aided by Eric Gautier's right-handed cinematography, Desplechin radicalizes the Hollywood ideal of invisible camera and editing (the camera follows the actors, the cuts are camouflaged by activity in the frame), transforming it into a precise and delicate mapping of attention and desire. "I'm no Don Juan, but the one pleasure I can count on is when I stick my hand for the first time in the panties of a girl I don't know," says Paul. A catchy line, it's more than matched by the three-second shot in which the camera mimes Paul's glance as it travels down from the face to the thighs of his object of desire—as she herself slides her dangling legs into a standing position—and back up to her face again. Everything you need to know about the push and pull of sexual attraction is in that shot—which, in the context of the film, is not at all unique. In *My Sex Life ...*, the simplest movements are as dizzying as revelations.

Also reviewed in:
CHICAGO TRIBUNE, 8/15/97, Friday/p. J, Michael Wilmington
NEW YORK TIMES, 9/17/97, p. E5, Janet Maslin
VARIETY, 5/20-26/96, p. 31, Stephen O'Shea
WASHINGTON POST, 10/10/97, Weekend/p. 48, Stephen Hunter

MYTH OF FINGERPRINTS, THE

A Sony Pictures Classics release of a Good Machine production in association with Eureka Pictures. *Executive Producer:* James Schamus and Ted Hope. *Producer:* Mary Jane Skalski, Tim Perell, and Bart Freundlich. *Director:* Bart Freundlich. *Screenplay:* Bart Freundlich. *Director of Photography:* Stephen Kazmierski. *Editor:* Kate Williams and Ken J. Sackheim. *Music:* David Bridie and John Phillips. *Music Editor:* Steve Hamilton. *Sound:* Peter Schneider, Jesse Feigelman, and (music) Simon Polinski. *Sound Editor:* Steve Hamilton. *Casting:* Douglas Aibel. *Production Designer:* Susan Bolles. *Art Director:* John McFarlane. *Set Decorator:* Catherine Pierson. *Set Dresser:* Brian Buteau. *Costumes:* Lucy W. Corrigan. *Make-up:* Tracy Warbin. *Stunt Coordinator:* Christopher Lee. *Running time:* 90 minutes. *MPAA Rating:* R.

CAST: Randee Allen (Waitress); Arija Bareikis (Daphne); Justin Barreto (Young Jake); Chris Bauer (Jerry); Nicholas Bourgeois (Young Warren); Tom Cumler (Man at Train Station); Blythe Danner (Lena); Hope Davis (Margaret); Christopher Duva (Tom); Kelsey Gunn (Young Leigh); Laurel Holloman (Leigh); Brian Kerwin (Elliot); James LeGros (Cezanne); Julianne Moore (Mia); Polly Pelletier (Young Mia); Pamela Polhemus (Bookstore Woman); Michael Rupert (Warren's Psychiatrist); Roy Scheider (Hal); Michael Vartan (Jake); Noah Wyle (Warren).

LOS ANGELES TIMES, 9/26/97, Calendar/p. 22, Kenneth Turan

Home, poet Robert Frost wrote, is "the place where, when you have to go there, they have to take you in." But don't assume they're happy to do so or that you'll be any happier once you're inside. Few things in life are as frustrating as family.

Bart Freundlich's "The Myth of Fingerprints" deals with the paradoxes of family, the wariness that we sometimes have with the people we're nominally closest to, the way blood relations can get under the skin like no one else. It's a decorous film, conventionally well-made, but don't be fooled. Its emotional impact is considerable.

Writer-director Freundlich is only 27, and like any self respecting young person he debuted "Fingerprints" at Sundance, but, not surprisingly, a prize was not in the offing. For this is not the kind of fashionable, on-the-edge filmmaking that captivates tastemakers. It is rather a picture that brings youthful passion and involvement to old-fashioned themes and concerns, that has the ability to deal with traditional relationship problems as if they hadn't been touched on before.

"Fingerprints" is not without its problems; not all of its elements work, and it can seem precious and self-conscious at moments. But these are only moments, and mostly we are thankful for Freundlich's gift for creating character, his ear for the awkwardness, bickering;, and free-floating anxiety that coexist uneasily with love when families dare to gather.

The setting this time is Maine, the time Thanksgiving, the participants four adult children coming together at their parents' home for the first time in three years. Two of them are arriving with new partners, but everyone's romantic lives are in for a shock before the weekend is over.

Presiding over the family is Hal, the sour, misanthropic father who'd much rather everyone .0 stayed away. As expertly drawn by Roy Scheider in one of his best performances, Hal is forever exasperated and out of sorts, and not even the ministrations of nurturing wife Lena (Blythe Danner) can shield the family from the effects of his baleful disposition.

It's the always-angry Mia (Julianne Moore) who is the most like him, a hostile terror who has a bad word for everyone and every situation. She arrives with boyfriend Elliot (Brian Kerwin), a therapist, but he is no better at dealing with her moods than anyone else.

Oldest son Jake (Michael Vartan) has been influenced by his family in another way: He can't admit to love or commit to his girlfriend Margaret (Hope Davis), whose bubbly personality appeals to the family's perky youngest child, the practical joking Leigh (Laurel Holloman).

The most openly vulnerable-and in many ways the most appealing-sibling is Warren (Noah Wyle, Dr. John Carter on TV's "ER"). Taunted by Mia for being his "usual normal, insecure, depressed self," Warren is still trying to get over his breakup with Daphne (Arija Bareikis), the woman he feels he will never replace.

When Warren finds out that Daphne is also back in town for the holidays and asking about him, a rapprochement seems inevitable. But these two have never fully confronted the reasons they split, and that process leads to the film's most moving revelations.

Also unpredictable but considerably less convincing is Mia's rediscovery of her old kindergarten beau, Leonard Morrison, who now improbably calls himself Cezanne (James LeGros). Though Moore and LeGros are among the most reliable of current performers (and worked especially well together in Todd Haynes' "Safe"), their relationship is not well-grounded m reality and is the film's weakest aspect.

Along with a script that has an affecting feeling for how people react to one another, Freundlich's ability to get the actors to flesh out his words is a further reason for the film's success. Each member of the "Fingerprints" ensemble is someone we recognize, and the group always seems like a family on screen.

Grappling with the sense of being trapped in the personalities of people they'd rather not be, wondering if it's necessary to come from a healthy family to have a successful relationship, the characters never lose their individuality. Is it more difficult to be a child or a parent under these circumstances? Sensible to the end, "The Myth of Fingerprints" says it's too close to call.

NEW YORK POST, 9/17/97, p. 61, Thelma Adams

Glossy and affecting, "The Myth of Fingerprints" captures the mixed emotions of a family Thanksgiving: the rush to arrive and the desperation to leave; the elation, the laughs, the frustration; the unfinished business and the business that can never be finished; the sibling tension and the sexual tension as significant others join the fray.

In Bart Freundlich's debut feature, a Sundance Film Festival fave, the writer-director has brought everything to the screen but the turkey and stuffing.

After a three-year absence, Warren (Noah Wyle, of TVs "ER") returns home. It's a rambling Maine Victorian, cheerily decorated by his mom (Blythe Danner) with spindle beds and mismatched chenille pillows, and coldly inhabited by his dad (Roy Scheider).

As Warren tells his therapist at the outset, "It's been long enough that I can't remember that I shouldn't go.

But go, he must. This wounded modern Yankee, movingly portrayed by Wyle, reunites with his siblings Jake (Michael Vartan), Mia (Julianne Moore) and Leigh (Larel Holloman). And then there's Daphne (Arija Bareikis): the gal who broke his heart three years before.

Warren's father overshadows him. As the patriarch, the sour-faced Scheider is rigid, inert, bottled up; his Hal never learned how to love big grown children as he did when they were young. The kids have become rivals for the unconditional love of sweet, and sweetly rationalizing, Danner.

Of the remaining siblings, Jake can't express his love for girlfriend Margaret (the adorable Hope Davis); Leigh observes over the pages of her journal, unattached but untouched by the surrounding dysfunction; and Moore's Mia rivals Wyle's Warren for the story's broken heart.

Moore's pained porcelain princess type who rarely gets screen time: beautiful, self-assured, independent, this woman is angry and she doesn't know why. Even her sexuality is an act of aggression. When Jake confronts her bitchiness to the family, she replies: "Aren't they the first people you're supposed to be hostile to?"

With a bit of therapy and the passage of time, Warren confronts the pain of a family that on the surface has everything but is locked in a battle for dominance, a struggle for each separate voice to be heard or silenced, a battle between action and inaction.

The anguish is felt most strongly in glancing pin pricks, the confrontations that are not confrontations, the stolen ecstatic moments of release and relief.

Like the family reunion the film dramatizes, the pretentiously titled "Myth" has big moments and dry spells—but the universally excellent cast never lets the family down. The bombshell revelation about Hal, Warren and Daphne seems slight, but the downbeat, low-key ending, with half the conflicts left unraveled, is deeply satisfying.

Sufficient questions are left unanswered for another Maine reunion, in the big house where the wind batters the shutters and memories rattle the present.

NEWSDAY, 9/17/97, Part 11/p. B11, Jack Mathews

As the holidays approach, so, inevitably, do the movies about reunions of dysfunctional families. First up, freshman writer-director Bart Freundlich's "The Myth of Fingerprints," and if it's a harbinger of what's to come, it's going to be a long, sloppy season.

The angst-ridden reunion is a staple of domestic drama because most of us endure our own variations of it, and can identify with the specifics. People change between get-togethers, throwing off the family rhythms and forcing adjustments. Grown children bring along new mates or lovers, adding strangers to the mix. Family skeletons rattle behind conversations, threatening to surface and cause open hostility.

Usually, we ride the goodwill of the occasion to a successful day, and sign off with plans for the next gathering. Whether we end up feeling that way about a movie family depends on how well we get to know its members, and how much we like them. And after enduring Thanksgiving weekend with the last-name-unknowns in "The Myth of Fingerprints," I hope I never see any of them again.

The WASP New England clan is a former unit of six. The father, Hal (Roy Scheider), the mother, Lena (Blythe Danner), brothers Warren (Noah Wyle) and Jake (Michael Vartan), and sisters Mia (Julianne Moore) and Leigh (Laurel Holloman). The strangers in their midst are Jake's sexually frisky, plain-talking girlfriend, Margaret (Hope Davis), and Mia's milquetoast boyfriend, Elliot (Brian Kerwin).

The key dynamics are these: Hal is a dour, emotionally insulated creep who harbors but cannot express deep affection for his children; Lena is a gentle, nurturing mother who suffers her husband's acrid behavior in silence; Warren is a fragile, psychologically damaged loner; Jake is an insecure skirt-chaser fighting the reality that he's in love; Mia is a self-absorbed crank; and Leigh, the youngest, is an impetuous late teen with naive faith in the family bonds.

Freundlich, an NYU film school graduate, has a fluid directing style and a fair command of dialogue, but rarely will you see a storyteller devote as much time to characters without making them familiar.

Most of "The Myth of Fingerprints" is consumed by sarcastic or loaded exchanges between the three oldest siblings. Their father is such a strange, aloof figure, you'd think they'd be united by shared experiences of surviving him. Instead, they each adopt their own weekend agenda. Warren gets back together with his high school sweetheart (Arija Bareikis). Mia takes up with an old sweetheart (James LeGros). Jake is kept busy keeping Margaret sexually satisfied. And Leigh has her eyes on Mia's abandoned boyfriend, Elliot.

The story eventually settles on Warren, and his scarred relationship with his father. There's a moment of revelation about Hal and Warren late in "Myth" that is meant to be a stunner, but which seems little more than an embarrassment. In any event, it's not a strong enough dramatic device to engross us for the long, cold weekend, or to be thankful for it.

SIGHT AND SOUND, 12/97, p. 48, Peter Matthews

Hal and Lena are a middle-aged couple living in Maine. Their four adult children are coming home for the Thanksgiving weekend. Lena looks forward to the reunion, but Hal resents the intrusion. Younger son Warren turns up a day early. College student Leigh returns and meets her big sister Mia and Mia's boyfriend Elliot at the train station. Finally, elder son Jake shows up with his girlfriend Margaret.

That night, Jake and Margaret make love, as do Mia and Elliot, and Lena and Hal. The next morning, Warren goes to meet his ex-girlfriend Daphne. Hal 'kills' a turkey by pumping a store-bought one full of lead. Mia begins reading a book called *The Scream of the Rabbits*. Daphne explains to Warren why she broke off with him four years ago: Hal made a pass at her one drunken evening and she hated Warren for being unable to stand up to his father. Mia is vexed that her book is incomplete because Hal tore out some pages for kindling. Desperate to learn the end, she visits a bookshop in town and meets Cezanne, a childhood playmate who has read the book.

The next day, Lena explains to Leigh how she loves Hal despite everything. Mia meets Cezanne, who finishes the story for her. After Thanksgiving dinner, Hal dances with Daphne, but won't let Warren cut in. Angry, Warren hurls his father to the ground. Hal retreats to the basement to view old home movies. Early in the morning, Elliot leaves a note for Mia and departs alone. Warren also creeps away without a word, though surreptitiously watched by his father from a bedroom window. Hal calls out Warren's name, but no one hears.

Why does Lena, the matriarch of the troubled clan in writer-director Bart Freundlich's debut feature *The Myth of Fingerprints,* keep baking soda in the refrigerator? If you are halfway acquainted with the anguished-family genre, you already know the answer: "It takes away all the rotten smells." In another metaphorically loaded moment, shrewish daughter Mia reads a novel that climaxes with the accidental smothering of some baby rabbits and hysterically rages 'why doesn't he do something?' The putative 'he' is the novel's gardener hero, who loves the furry creatures but won't properly care for them. The real negligent gardener, needless to say, is Mia's stern, uncommunicative father Hal—the kind of freeze-dried parent who invariably turns up in the these family sagas of stifled emotions and autumnal regrets.

Hal's chilliness is meant to explain why Mia is such a bitch, and also evidently accounts for the permanent look of fear in the eyes of baby brother Warren—though Freundlich's script is subtle enough to imply that Warren (as in rabbit warren) is actually Hal's favourite child. There are, on the other hand, a couple of subsidiary siblings, ebullient Leigh and straight-arrow Jake, who don't appear to have been scarred much at all. That's presumably the point of the title: children may share the same gene pool and basic formative experiences, but still grow up in radically unpredictable ways.

Freundlich presents the family (or at least this family) as a puzzle without a definite solution. The relative absence of determinism is what mainly distinguishes this movie from some earlier, patter portrayals of upper-middle-class anguish. The Warren figure in Robert Redford's *Ordinary People* is played by Timothy Hutton as a blobby mass of insecurities on account of his soul-destroying mother. Fortunately, a life-affirming psychiatrist is around to sort things. In Mark Rydell's *On Golden Pond,* Jane Fonda's tense, embittered daughter somehow irons out her difficulties with her crusty father by successfully performing the backflip dive she was afraid to attempt as a child.

Fingerprints has its own version of that therapeutic backflip: Warren finally acquires the balls to stand up to Hal, who once made a drunken pass at girlfriend Daphne and now obligingly re-enacts the scene. However, the father-son showdown is over with so quickly there's little sense of a catharsis. Indeed, none of the delicate, muted epiphanies that each of the dozen or so characters experiences during the long holiday weekend seems especially decisive and this is what makes the film rather interesting. Structurally, it doesn't plot a linear progression towards a big truth; it splinters into countless local truths which bump it against one another in molecular fashion—all relative, all conditional, all subject to revision. In terms of *mise en scène,* Freundlich composes his actors in clusters amid the nooks and crannies of the rambling family homestead, and this vast yet cosily accommodating abode is well suited to express the idea of a decentred space.

It's symptomatic that the therapist figure here—Mia's lover Elliot—has no privileged voice in the narrative, but is just a houseguest. In Freundlich's view, there's no point diagnosing the family since there isn't any cure for it: all one can do is simply muddle through. The advantage of this resignation is that it takes some of the heat off the usual suspects. Hal isn't the great castrating Father so much as a dad whose fallibility is accorded a good deal of sympathy (his belated calling of Warren's name provides the movie's emotional climax). Freundlich conscientiously avoids schematics and abstraction, seeming to endorse Tolstoy's famous proposition that "each unhappy family is unhappy in its own way".

However, Tolstoy would have gone on to link individual destinies with larger historical forces. The chief drawback of Freundlich's refusal to interpret his subject matter is that it keeps the movie on a level of microscopic perceptions. You have to settle instead for tiny shocks of recognition which self-consciously don't add up. Freundlich works almost by a principle of subtraction—he offers teasing fragments of behaviour and motive, and then invites the viewer to fill in the dots. You need to project a lot onto this spare, elliptical movie in order to enjoy it. If it were a novel, there would be plenty of white on the pages.

VILLAGE VOICE, 9/23/97, p. 96, Laurie Stone

Warren (Noah Wyle) tells his shrink he can go home after a three-year absence: "It's been long enough that I can't remember why I shouldn't go." Like hell. He knows he saw his father (Roy Scheider) make a pass at his girlfriend, and he neither confronted his father nor explained his passivity to her. First-time writer-director Bart Freundlich misses the chance to turn his predictable family anatomy into a messy, intriguing tale. He presents sibling rivalry and dinner-table tension as if their ordinariness were noteworthy. Meanwhile, the disturbing father—Scheider doing Pinter in an episode of *Relativity*—is treated as a boilerplate depressive. In a home movie, he sadistically cracks eggs over young Warren's head, yet his children don't discuss him or weigh the cost of their mother's (Blythe Danner) obliviousness. The actors default to "business" amid the bland dialogue, with the exception of James LeGros, who plays the oddball childhood sweetheart of the what's-her-problem angry sister Mia (Julianne Moore) with charm.

Also reviewed in:
CHICAGO TRIBUNE, 10/3/97, Friday/p. M, John Petrakis
NEW REPUBLIC, 10/6/97, p. 28, Stanley Kauffmann
NEW YORK TIMES, 9/17/97, p. E5, Stephen Holden
VARIETY, 2/3-9/97, p. 48, Todd McCarthy

NAPOLEON

A Goldwyn Entertainment Company release of a Herald Ace Inc. and Furry Feature Films production in association with Nippon Herald Films, Fuji Television, Pony Canyon. *Executive Producer:* Masato Hara and Ron Saunders. *Producer:* Michael Bourchier and Mario Andreacchio. *Director:* Mario Andreacchio. *Screenplay:* Mario Andreacchio, Michael Bourchier, and Mark Saltzman. *Director of Photography:* Roger Dowling. *Editor:* Edward McQueen-Mason. *Music:* Bill Conti. *Sound:* James Currie and Craig Carter. *Casting:* Christine King. *Production Designer:* Vicki Niehus. *Running time:* 81 minutes. *MPAA Rating:* G.

VOICES: Jamie Croft (Napoleon); Philip Quast (Birdo); Carole Skinner (Cat); Dame Edna Everage (Kangaroo); Frank Whittle (Koala); Anne Lambert (Earless Wallaby/Spider); David Argue (Frill-Necked Lizard); Joan Rivers (Mother Penguin); Steven Vidler (Turtle/Snake); Brandan Little (Owl/Wombat); Susan Lyons (Napoleon's Mother).

LOS ANGELES TIMES, 10/14/97, Calendar/p. 3, Gene Seymour

[*The following review by Gene Seymour appeared in a slightly different form in* NEWSDAY, 10/13/97, Part II/p. B2.]

"Napoleon" labors under what its plucky little hero characterizes as the curse of cuteness. Think of "The Incredible Journey" with an Australian accent, and there isn't that much more to think about except how you can keep yourself from sighing "awwwwww ..." every time an animal does something adorable on screen.

The story begins where most trouble begins: at a children's birthday where Muffin (voiced by Adam Wylie), a golden retriever pup living a cozy fenced-in existence with his mum, dreams of being among the wild dogs of the Outback, where he is known as Napoleon. Somehow he finds himself in a basket with enough balloons to lift him out of his backyard and out to sea.

A galah (sort of a pinkish parrot) named Birdo (Bronson Pinchot), who's somehow strayed from his flock, helps Muffin/Napoleon come to a safe landing on a south Australian beach. The pup thinks he's finally found the frontier he's been searching for.

Except he's still afraid of water. (I thought all dogs were natural swimmers. Let's move on.) Nevertheless, no pond, stream or waterfall can keep Napoleon from finding the source of the howling he hears in the distance. Not even a psychotic house cat who's been stranded in the wild for so long he thinks the puppy's a big yellow mouse.

Think I'm making this up as I go along? I'm not, but it often seems as if the people who made this movie did. The pokey storytelling has some charm, and the animal encounters are well-edited enough to make you wonder how they managed to get birds, beasts, lizards and koalas to coexist so well on screen. The encounter between the puppy and a slumbering iguana is as startling as anything recalled from one of those Disney true-life adventures of the 1950s.

A few famous voices pop up here and there on screen. Dame Edith Everage sings a very silly hippety-hop tune as—what else?—a kangaroo. Joan Rivers is heard briefly as mother to a vacationing family of penguins. The use of light and landscape is adroit, and the dingo pups are almost as beguiling as Napoleon. Bill Conti's music, though not his best, serves the story well without getting in its way.

Because the real-life animals talk like humans, comparisons will be made to "Babe," especially since both films share an Aussie pedigree. But not only don't the creatures here have computer-generated moving mouths, they don't have nearly as many interesting things to say. A few dumb jokes slip in here and there, but they don't add up to enough to make "Napoleon" anything more than the sweet-natured trifle it is.

If I were between 5 and 9 years old, I'd love "Napoleon." Beyond that, I doubt I'd push it too hard.

NEW YORK POST, 10/11/97, p. 19, Larry Worth

It's a winning formula: family film, cute talking animal, Australian setting. Well, at least it worked for "Babe."

"Napoleon" changes a few components. Substituting an adorable golden retriever for an adorable piglet is OK. But substituting ennui for charm isn't.

The sap starts flowing as mischievous little Muffin—who calls himself Napoleon—flies away in a balloon basket from his doghouse in Sydney. Minutes later, he's lost in the wilderness, where he's fending off dragon-like lizards, sibilant snakes and most fearsome of all, a mad house-cat.

As if that weren't silly enough, each member of the animal kingdom sings some of the worst lyrics on record. For example, parakeet-like friend Birdo Lucci (get it?) induces Napoleon to turn rabbits into dinner by belting out: "At last you're off your leash; turn them into bunny quiche."

Here, "Napoleon's" Waterloo comes in the form of director Mario Andreacchio, who didn't even bother coordinating the animals mouths with their words. Instead, he opts for Disney's "Homeward Bound: The Incredible Journey" approach of lackluster voiceovers.

Then there's the typical avalanche of bad puns. So when Napoleon horrifyingly tumbles down a cliff in his wicker airship, Birdo cracks: "I knew he was a basket case."

The actors supplying the voices are equally cringe-inducing, with Jamie Croft's Aussie-flavored intonations making Napoleon too precious for words, while Philip Quast's Birdo sounds like a drag queen on the prowl. Cameos from Joan Rivers, Stuart Pankin, Casey Siemaszko and Dame Edna Everage (a.k.a. Barry Humphries) don't register one way or the other.

Accordingly, kids will be twiddling thumbs long before the pup trades his call-of-the-wild mindset for "there's no place like home." So why not cut to the chase and simply rent "The Wizard of Oz"? Toto never looked better.

Also reviewed in:
CHICAGO TRIBUNE, 7/22/98, John Petrakis
NEW YORK TIMES, 10/11/97, p. B11, Anita Gates
VARIETY, 1/13-19/97, p. 152, David Stratton

NENETTE AND BONI

A Strand Releasing release. *Executive Producer:* Françoise Guglielmi. *Producer:* Georges Benayoun. *Director:* Claire Denis. *Screenplay (French with English subtitles):* Jean-Pol Fargeau and Claire Denis. *Director of Photography:* Agnes Godard. *Editor:* Yann Dedet. *Music:* Tindersticks. *Sound:* Jean-Louis Ughetto and (music) Vincent Arnardi and Thierry Lebon. *Set Designer:* Arnaud de Moleron. *Costumes:* Elisabeth Tavernier. *Running time:* 103 minutes. *MPAA Rating:* Not Rated.

CAST: Grégoire Colin (Boni); Alice Houri (Nenette); Valeria Bruni-Tedeschi (The Baker Woman); Vincent Gallo (The Baker); Jacques Nolot (Mr. Luminaire); Gerard Meylan (The Uncle); Alex Descas (The Gynecologist); Jamila Farah (The Wise Woman).

LOS ANGELES TIMES, 10/24/97, Calendar/p. 14, Kevin Thomas

"Nenette and Boni" is another understated triumph for gifted French writer-director Claire Denis. It is an exquisitely evoked expression of an aching longing for love and family set in working-class Marseilles.

Denis has immense, steadfast respect for seemingly ordinary people and their lives. Her films have a quality of gravity—yet are often hilarious. They also have an intimacy and flow that seem spontaneous and at the same time precisely right.

Grégoire Colin's Boni is a tall, sturdy 19-year-old pizza worker given to pouring out his sexual fantasies (involving the neighborhood baker's wife, Valeria Bruni-Tedeschi) in his journal. She is a ravishing earth mother incarnate, radiating health and happiness, as voluptuous as the pastries her devoted, hard-working American husband (Vincent Gallo) makes. In contrast to Boni and his sister Nenette (Alice Houri), the bakery couple, who have several children, live in rare contentment.

Except for his loneliness, Boni seems otherwise satisfied with his routine existence. He has a rabbit for a pet and lives in an apartment that's awfully small but has a great view of the harbor from its rooftop. He has some pals, a flexible work schedule, and it's hard to understand why he doesn't have—or try to have—a girlfriend. Maybe it's because his mother, who apparently adored him, has only recently died.

That Nenette, who is off at boarding school, never came to visit while their mother was dying sets off Boni's rage when she turns up. She has run away from school because she's finally faced the fact that she's pregnant. The heart of "Nenette and Boni" is how—with much wariness—brother and sister thrash through an attempt at some kind of harmonious relationship.

At one point the father (Jacques Nolot), who abandoned his family some time in the past, turns up with a lavish offering of food—pathetically craving a reconciliation. Their mother, he tries to explain, "was never a 'real woman' with me."

"Nenette and Boni," which has a gentle Tindersticks score, is a tender, impassioned celebration of life—about making pizza, about giving birth and about how the two are connected. Colin, Houri and Nolot never let us catch them acting.

NEW YORK POST, 10/3/97, p. 48, Larry Worth

Clair Denis has built an impressive resume over the last decade, starting with her 1988 gem "Chocolat". But she's managed to outdo herself with "Nenette and Boni."

This slice-of-life look at a troubled 19-year-old, Boni, and his pregnant younger sister, Nenette, is an emotional roller coaster about family love, particularly the ties one wouldn't expect to bind.

With a succession of gray, Marseilles-based days befitting the story's moodiness, the errant siblings debate their respective fates, as well as the future of Nenette's swelling belly. The results are never predictable, thanks largely to a script (co-written by Denis) that's filled with fantasy sequences, understated action, droll humor and electrically charged, surprisingly intimate dialogue.

The first-rate cast is equally amazing, headed by Gregoire Colin and Alice Houri in the title roles, Valeria Bruni-Tedeschi as the married object of Boni's affections and Vincent Gallo's hilarious cameo as a love-struck baker.

Viewers should be warned that "Nenette and Boni," never ties into a neat little package. But after tapping into Dennis' uniquely lyrical visions, one wouldn't want it to.

VILLAGE VOICE, 10/7/97, p. 80, Leslie Camhi

Brothers and sisters are bound to each other in that are cryptic and irrevocable. Claire Denis's *Nenette et Boni* is a love story, set among siblings who can barely stand each other. Grégoire Colin plays Boni, a 19-year-old who earns a meager living driving a pizza van around Marseilles. Cut off from the world, with no high school diploma, he spends his days kneading dough, baking pies, and serving slices, while indulging in furious erotic fantasies about a shapely, married baker (Valeria Bruni-Tedeschi).

One morning his 15-year-old sister shows up at the house he shares with assorted unemployed companions. Nenette (Alice Houri) has bolted from boarding school, pregnant by someone she won't identify. The bonds between brother and sister are wary and tinged with aggression; their mother is dead and they're estranged from their father, a sometime gangster, who sells chandeliers when he's not in trouble. For Nenette, her pregnancy is a source of torment and savage resentment, but it slowly awakens Boni from his sexual torpor with the promise of new life.

Denis's camera stays close to the bodies of her two beautiful, bewildered principals, adrift on a sea of listless social services and internal confusion. Boni's adolescent male fiefdom of rage and sexual craving is tendered astonishingly vivid and replete with irony: his lust for the baker and for his new coffeemaker, her fuzzy pink slippers, and his pet white rabbit mingle in feverishly panting wet-dream sequence. Denis evokes the smell of hamburger buns, unwashed sheets, and old sweaters and the feel of pizza dough, whipped cream, and brioche to create the air of hectic sensuality informing this story of the act made flesh. For at the center of all this anger and disorder is the small, unseen body taking shape within Nenette's belly.

Denis manages yet again to draw stellar performances from her leading actors, in particular Grégoire Colin, whose Boni is a model of raw teenage fury, tempered by frustration and the first stirrings of empathy. Valeria Bruni-Tedeschi is endearingly comic as the unsuspecting object of his s/m daydreams, and the very young Alice Houri makes a fine Nenette. Jacques Nolot plays their vain and ineffectual father, adding a thick dose of local color with his rich provincial accent, and Vincent Gallo (as the baker's American husband) provides a dollop of tender surrealism.

Marseilles's teeming immigrant community forms a vibrant backdrop to this story of shattered and displaced family ties. A vignette about fake telephone cards sold to unsuspecting immigrants is woven into Denis's greater theme, the need to remain connected, by wires however thin, in a world of mass migration and seething indifference.

Also reviewed in:
CHICAGO TRIBUNE, 11/28/97, Friday/p. B, Michael Wilmington
NEW YORK TIMES, 10/3/97, p. E18, Stephen Holden
VARIETY, 8/26-9/1/96, p. 62, Derek Elley

NICK AND JANE

An Avalanche Releasing release of a Prophecy Pictures Ltd. presentation of an Emerald Productions Inc. *Producer:* Bill McCutchen, III. *Director:* Richard Mauro. *Screenplay:* Richard Mauro, Neil W. Alumkal, and Peter Quigley. *Story:* Richard Mauro. *Director of Photography:* Chris Norr. *Editor:* Wendey Stanzler and Richard Mauro. *Music:* Mark Suozzo. *Casting:* Eve Battaglia. *Production Designer:* Mark Helmuth. *Art Director:* Stacy Tanner. *Costumes:* Liz McCaffrey. *Running time:* 96 minutes. *MPAA Rating:* R.

CAST: Dana Wheeler-Nicholson (Jane); James McCaffrey (Nick); John Dossett (John); Lisa Gay Hamilton (Vickie); David Johansen (Carter); Gedde Watanabe (Enzo); Clinton Leupp (Miss Coco); Saundra Santiago (Stephanie); George Coe (Mr. Morgan).

LOS ANGELES TIMES, 10/14/97, Calendar/p. 20, Kevin Thomas

[The following review by Kevin Thomas appeared in a slightly different form in **NEWSDAY, 10/14/97, Part II/p. B13.]**

Richard Mauro's "Nick and Jane" is a well-made Manhattan romantic comedy that could have been better if it didn't surround its engaging principals with so many caricatures.

Every time we're beginning to take seriously a romance between a workaholic financial analyst (Dana Wheeler-Nicholson) and an establishment dropout cabby-artist James McCaffrey), Mauro cuts to their sidekicks. Lisa Gay Hamilton bubbles away with much charm as the analyst's pushy but genuinely concerned best pal, so why does her character have to turn out to be the office dominatrix? And why does the cabby's roommate (Gedde Watanabe), a no-talent, layabout rap artist, have to be a determined foot fetishist?

Comic relief is traditionally supplied by second leads in the telling of a love story, but these sexual hang-ups play lots more contrived than amusing. The effect is to inject the entire film with an unnecessary sense of the artificial. Faring better are the film's two gay characters, the bitchy, elegant Carter (David Johansen), yet another of Jane's office colleagues, and Miss Coco (Clinton Leupp), the cabby's neighbor, a wise drag queen. They're occasionally amusing stereotypes, but presented with clear respect and affection.

It's apparently because Watanabe's Enzo is such a deadbeat, unable to come up with his share of the rent, that McCaffrey's Nick is facing eviction from his apartment in a Lower East Side tenement. If it weren't for that prospect he wouldn't have accepted an offer of $1,500 from Wheeler-Nicholson's Jane to pose as a financial whiz kid at a crucial office party. Nick and Jane, who caught her boyfriend and coworker (John Dossett) in the sack with another colleague (Saundra Santiago), have met cute a couple of times already.

Since Mauro and his co-writers have taken considerable pains to establish credibility for their two-people-from-different-worlds romance, it's too bad that they sabotaged it with too much sidebar shtick. In any event, Wheeler-Nicholson and McCaffrey are attractive and effective, with McCaffrey, last seen in "The Truth About Cats and Dogs," possessing that something extra in looks, presence and personality that could just take him on to bigger and better pictures.

NEW YORK POST, 11/14/97, p. 50, Larry Worth

Once upon a time, Dick and Jane were elementary school icons. "Nick and Jane," on the other hand, is simply elementary.

He's a blue-collar cabbie. She's an upper-crust executive. He's from the Lower East Side. She's the Upper West. He's laid-back. She's a go-getter. Can head-over-heels love be far behind?

First—at least in writer-director Rich Mauro's book there has to be a labored setup. So after dumping her two-timing beau-cum-colleague, Jane can't get ahead at work, at least unless she pretends Nick is her fiance.

The setup will sound particularly familiar to those who saw "Picture Perfect" this summer. It's virtually the same scenario, but with little-knowns Dana Wheeler-Nicholson, James McCaffrey and John Dossett trying—and failing—to generate Jennifer Aniston, Jay Mohr and Kevin Bacon's star power.

Will "Nick and Jane" have a happy ending regardless? That's a no-brainer, much like the film itself.

VILLAGE VOICE, 11/25/97, p. 102, Hillary Rosner

It's almost worth the admission price just to watch *GQ*-bound James McCaffrey deliver an endearing performance in a terribly bland role. But even McCaffrey, as a down-and-out cabdriver who builds scrap-metal art, can't rescue this unfunny and mildly offensive romantic comedy. It's the tale of corporate analyst Jane (Dana Wheeler-Nicholson), who conspires to drive her ex-boyfriend crazy by hiring Nick (McCaffrey, scrubbed, shaved, and costumed in a Wall Street suit) to masquerade as the new power-man in her life. If this sounds like the '80s, it might well be: the film features Gedde Watanabe (*Sixteen Candles*'s Long Duck Dong) and makes a little too much of Nick's drag queen neighbor. But the film's biggest disappointment is its message that any starving artist would and should be thrilled to be paraded around at all the right parties. It is only after Nick saves Jane's ass on the corporate line that she is able to look behind his cabdriver exterior to the whirring business mind within, and finally falls in love with the guy who just might be able to rise to her level.

Also reviewed in:
CHICAGO TRIBUNE, 11/14/97, Friday/p. K, John Petrakis
NEW YORK TIMES, 11/14/97, p. E33, Janet Maslin
VARIETY, 11/17-23/97, p. 64, Lael Loewenstein

NIGHT FALLS ON MANHATTAN

A Paramount Pictures release of a Spelling Films presentation of a Mount/Kramer production. *Producer:* Thom Mount and Josh Kramer. *Director:* Sidney Lumet. *Screenplay:* Sidney Lumet. *Based on the novel "Tainted Evidence" by:* Robert Daley. *Director of Photography:* David Watkin. *Editor:* Sam O'Steen. *Music:* Mark Isham. *Music Editor:* Annette Kudrak. *Sound:* Les Lazarowitz and (music) Stephen Krause. *Sound Editor:* Ron Bochar. *Casting:* Hopkins, Smith & Barden. *Production Designer:* Philip Rosenberg. *Art Director:* Robert Guerra. *Special Effects:* Conrad Brink. *Costumes:* Joseph G. Aulisi. *Make-up:* David Craig Forrest. *Stunt Coordinator:* Jack Gill. *Running time:* 115 minutes. *MPAA Rating:* R.

CAST: Andy Garcia (Sean Casey); Richard Dreyfuss (Sam Vigoda); Lena Olin (Peggy Lindstrom); Ian Holm (Liam Casey); James Gandolfini (Joey Allegretto); Colm Feore (Elihu Harrison); Ron Leibman (DA Morgenstern); Shiek Mahmud-Bey (Jordan Washington); Dominic Chianese (Judge Impelliteri); Paul Guilfoyle (McGovern); Bonnie Rose (Instructor); Norman Matlock (Detective); Sidney Armus (Judge); Jim Murtaugh (Man in Asylum); Melba Martinez (Legal Aid Attorney); Santo Fazio (Eduardo); Anthony Alessandro (Shmuel); David Wolos-Fonteno and John Seitz (Captains); Stephen Beach (2nd Cop); Nafisah Sayyed (Half-naked Girl); Vincent Pastore (3rd Cop); Robert Sean Miller (3rd Captain); Marcia J. Kurtz (Eileen); Jude Ciccolella (Lieutenant Wilson); John Randolph Jones (Captain Lawrence); Chuck Pfeiffer (Captain Gentile); Clark D. Williams, Bill Boggs, and Tamara Phillips (News); Louis Guss (Court Clerk); Richard Bright (64th Precinct Lieutenant); Ronald von Claussen (64th Precinct Sergeant); John Dibenedetto (2nd Patrolman); Kevin Ramsey (Sean's Assistant); Kermit Frazier (Jury Foreman); Veronica Hall (Pier Cop); Vic Noto (Diver); Jim Moody (Mayor Williams); Socorro Santiago (Lab Assistant); Fran Anthony (Moderator); Donna Hanover, Jack Cafferty, and Kaity Tong (TV Newspersons); Allen Collodow and Dennis Paladino (Cops); Mike Cammallere (1st Sergeant); Jim Mauro (1st Lieutenant); Salvatore Paul Piro (4th Cop); Frank Vincent (Captain); Mike Sheehan (2nd Sergeant); Joe Mosso (2nd Lieutenant); Teddy Coluca, Roslyn Cohn, and Elliot Cuker (Reporters); Yvette Mercedes (Meter Maid); Kristina Lear (Girl in Restaurant); Joe Drago (D.A. Driver); Catherine Schreiber (Sean's 2nd Assistant); Bobby Cannavale (Vigoda's 1st Assistant).

LOS ANGELES TIMES, 5/16/97, Calendar/p. 8, Kevin Thomas

Director Sidney Lumet marks his 40th year in films with his 40th movie, "Night Falls on Manhattan," and it is gratifying to report that it's one of his best. Significantly, he's made nearly three-quarters of his films in Manhattan, where he became the quintessential New York director well before Woody Allen came along. As it is happens, "Night Falls" is also quintessential Lumet.

To Lumet, people count for more than fancy camera angles and special effects. He is perennially concerned that, in a corrupt world, the choices that individuals of character and principles make do in fact matter and have real-life consequences for themselves and others and even society at large.

The great thing about Lumet is that he is not cynical but instead finds an amusing irony in exploring the art of the possible, in discovering that point at which decent people in positions of power and responsibility can be capable of working together privately, of looking the other way if necessary, for the greater good of all concerned.

This is the lesson that Andy Garcia's Sean Casey needs badly to learn. (Garcia as a character named Sean Casey? We eventually learn Sean's late mother's maiden name was Nuñez.) He is the son of veteran cop Liam Casey (Ian Holm) and was a policeman himself before becoming an assistant district attorney.

A chain of events rapidly propel the younger Casey into becoming the district attorney, fiercely idealistic and seriously inexperienced. In the aftermath of the sensational case that made his career a mere eight months after becoming an assistant D.A., Casey now finds as his first order of business the related discovery of the corpse of an ex-cop turned go-between for drug kingpins and cops on the take.

To experience the pleasure of surprise after surprise in watching this picture, it's clearly better not to have read Robert Daley's "Tainted Evidence," which Lumet adapted to the screen, or to know much about the plot. The film is a classic example of Aristotle's belief in the dramatic power of the improbable—of how much more potent the improbable can lie than the easily plausible if you can make it credible. A string of unlikely events and coincidences set off "Night Falls," and Lumet makes them believable the old-fashioned way: through interaction with a screen full of strongly drawn, fully dimensioned, psychologically valid characters.

Along with excellence in all aspects—Mark Isham's spare, elegiac score; David Watkin's brooding, shadowy images; production designer Philip Rosenberg's evocative, wide-ranging settings; Sam O'Steen's sharp yet subtle editing—there are many richly shaded portrayals, a Lumet hallmark.

Had "Night Falls" been made 20 years ago, the role of Sean Casey most surely would have gone to Al Pacino. Yet it is hard to imagine anyone doing a finer job than Garcia in making Sean come alive in all his passion and torment. British actor Holm, who added so much pleasure to "The Fifth Element" as a priest with cosmic secrets, in "Night Falls" has one of his great screen roles as a decent, dedicated cop and loving father called upon to defend his entire career.

Alan Dershowitz himself couldn't do a better spin on events than does Richard Dreyfuss, as a savvy liberal attorney in defending a drug kingpin/cop killer (played with unsettling, barely controlled rage by Shiek Mahmud-Bey) in what seems to be a baldly open-and-shut case.

Ron Leibman is Sean's bombastic mentor; Colm Feore is Leibman's WASPY, Harvard-educated antagonist; and James Gandolfini is Holm's partner on the force of many years. Lena Olin plays a key member on Dreyfuss' team, a worldly woman who makes her attraction to Garcia clear yet in her sophistication rightly worries that she just might not be good enough for so rigorous a man.

All of these actors and many others are memorable. Somehow the people in Lumet movies look more real than they do in most other director's films, perhaps because they're not all young or attractive. Typical of his attention to supporting players is Marcia J. Kurtz as the kind of dedicated, dependable secretary you would expect a Manhattan D.A. to have.

Anyone who has seen Lumet's terrific 1990 "Q & A," in which Timothy Hutton played a similarly idealistic novice assistant district attorney happening upon corruption in high places, is likely to see "Night Falls on Manhattan" as a companion film. They both take us into darkly paneled settings of power as well as dangerous streets and *gemütlich* old Manhattan bars.

In both instances, Lumet creates—with warmth, wisdom and humor—a vibrant world in which good and evil are in constant combat and in which possibilities in relationships between people are fluid and infinite.

The jolting opening of "Night Falls" shows how adept Lumet is at creating edge-of-your-seat suspenseful action with economy and dispatch. But the heart of the matter for Lumet is daring to take the time to let people actually talk and even listen to each other.

It's surprising that Paramount did not release "Night Falls" when it was ready last autumn, since it is the kind of expertly crafted prestige item often held for year-end release for the Oscar race. However, as an intelligent and mature major American film, "Night Falls on Manhattan," while hardly what one would call a summer movie, opens virtually without competition.

NEW YORK, 6/2/97, p. 53, David Denby

In *Night Falls on Manhattan*, which is Sidney Lumet's twenty-ninth movie set in New York, the Manhattan D.A. (Ron Leibman) stands on a desk and harangues his staff with lurid profanities. The sequence is entertaining, but one's pleasure in it just barely survives the realizations that (a) Leibman's "shocking" language is an awfully easy way of getting laughs, and (b) almost everyone talks this way in Lumet films. The D.A. is a caricature of urban Jewish overbearingness, brimming with knowing ethnic insults, intrusive presumptions about everyone and everything, an enjoyment of bluster for its own sake.

The movie also sets up its moral conflicts in ways that are familiar. A veteran Queens cop (Ian Holm) gets shot three times when attempting to arrest a notorious Harlem drug dealer. The dealer, who has been paying off cops for years, surrenders himself to a William Kunstler-type liberal lawyer (Richard Dreyfuss), and the case goes to trial. The D.A. wants to improve his own chances for re-election, so he seizes on the wounded cop's son (Andy Garcia), a young prosecutor, to try the case. The trial and its aftermath sorely test the idealism of the young prosecutor, whose own father may be involved in corruption.

Is moral behavior in public office possible, or even desirable? Does compromise necessarily destroy the compromiser? The movie wrestles with these familiar Lumet themes, but what it's really about is Lumet's fantasy of New York—a city endlessly loud and confrontational. The noise level! Characters suddenly begin shouting in close-up. Running up and down a long table, collapsing on a couch, Leibman uses the D.A.'s office space as if it were a stage set that had to be brought to life. Lumet works for intense emotion, and that's why he may not notice or care that except for Richard Dreyfuss, everyone in the movie is miscast—that neither Andy Garcia nor the excellent British actor Ian Holm seem like Queens Irish, and that Lena Olin, suppressing her accent as a lawyer who falls in love with Andy Garcia, doesn't seem like much of anyone. *Night Falls on Manhattan* is never dull, and there are some touching moments, but I wish it had been done with more precision, more quiet observation, and more taste. You would think that no one lived in this city but screamers and the morally anguished.

NEW YORK POST, 5/16/97, p. 37, Michael Medved

The acting in "Night Falls on Manhattan" is so satisfying and superb that its easy to overlook the film's many other brilliant elements—such as masterfully crisp editing, revealing and eloquent production design, a subtly affecting film score (by Mark Isham) and, above all, a probing, complex and unabashedly intelligent screenplay.

Director Sidney Lumet wrote the script himself (adapting Robert Daley's melodramatic novel "Tainted Evidence") and here returns to the top of his filmmaking form after several recent creative or box-office disappointments.

As in so much of his previous work ("Serpico" "Prince of the City" "Q & A"), Lumet's subject is police corruption in New York, but this time the moral ambiguities confronting his characters are presented more movingly than ever before.

Andy Garcia stars as a former street cop who attends law school at night, then gets a frustrating, low-level job in the Manhattan district attorneys office.

The impassioned, ambitious and savvy DA (Ron Leibman, in an adrenaline-pumping, career-topping turn) puts Garcia in charge of a high-profile case for public-relations reasons, and Garcia's career as a prosecutor (and politician) quickly takes off.

His progress greatly pleases his proud papa (the splendid Ian Holm, with a flawless New York accent), a 37-year-veteran of the police department, and bemuses Richard Dreyfuss (in a riveting, Oscar-worthy performance) as a cunning, idealistic, radical lawyer who comes up against Garcia in court.

All of these people are tainted good guys, trying their best to combat drugs and crime but willing to bend rules and the truth to pursue their aims.

Equally complicated are Lumet's (surprisingly sympathetic) bad guys: the troubled but unfailing likable James Gandolfini as Ian Holm's long-time police partner, and Shiek Mahmud-Bey, a scene-stealing young actor with a truly imposing physical presence, as an African-American drug dealer and cop-killer prosecuted by Garcia.

The only weak link in the splendid cast is Lena Olin, whose slight Swedish accent is a needless distraction in her puzzling role as the pampered rich girl (and opposing lawyer) who becomes Garcia's love interest.

At times, Garcia himself also seems a bit dull, dim and confused when compared to the spellbinding performers around him, but by the end of the film the character gradually wises up, demonstrating that his understated, ordinary-guy limitations represented an essential element in Lumet's dramatic structure.

Many other films have tried to present a gritty, insider's view of the messy collusion between idealism and corruption in New York politics, but unlike tacky confections such as Al Pacino's recent "City Hall," Lumet's latest triumph gets all the details right, and feels piercingly authentic in describing even the smallest elements in its characters' lives.

Lumet (who has shot 28 previous films entirely on location in New York City) has never won an Oscar in the course of his remarkable career, but "Night Falls on Manhattan" gives him his best chance since "Dog Day Afternoon" (or maybe even since "Network") to remedy that situation.

NEWSDAY, 5/16/97, Part II/p. B3, John Anderson

What is that? There's something happening at the beginning of Sidney Lumet's new crime drama "Night Falls on Manhattan" that sounds like an orchestra tuning up. Is that what it is? Or is it just the low roar of The City itself, engines lubed and impatient, gearing up to bring one more good man down?

It could be either: There's something symphonic about "Night Falls on Manhattan," even if it's an old score being played. Pitching the principled individual against the system, after all, has been Sidney Lumet's stock in trade since the '50s. He's the Zola of cinematic New York, whose better films ("12 Angry Men," "Serpico," "Dog Day Afternoon," "The Verdict") have shown a perverse affinity with Frank Capra in that they acknowledge corruption as the norm, and the triumph of goodness even if it's only in the eye of the beholder—as all but miraculous.

But having established the beachhead, Lumet has been joined by a lot of support troops—some of whom are producing television shows like "NYPD Blue" and "Homicide"—and when it comes to the only quasi-fictionalization of the nightmare that is our cities, the stakes have risen precipitously.

Lumet, meanwhile ... well, to say he's spinning his wheels would be wrong because his anger is still fresh, his outrage untempered. "Night Falls" isn't 5 minutes old before you're despairing. Partners Liam Casey (Ian Holm) and Joey Allegretto (James Gandolfini) are staking out a vicious killer and drug dealer named Jordan Washington (Shiek Mahmud-Bey), and when they try to take him, Liam is mowed down with Uzi fire. Should they have waited? It's a toss-up. When the rest of the force does arrive, the chaos and incompetence are so unbridled that cops are executed by Washington, one dies by friendly fire and the suspect gets away in a stolen police car.

Liam, however, survives, and when Washington is brought in, the shoot-from-the-hip district attorney, Morgenstern (Ron Liebman) has only one candidate in mind to prosecute the case. Liam's son, Sean Casey (Andy Garcia), a former cop and new assistant DA, who has never tried a major case.

You can buy Morgenstern's move, because he's a shameless politician. You can buy the defense attorney, Sam Vigoda—played by a sensational Richard Dreyfuss and modeled on the late William Kunstler—because he's a shameless politician. You can buy Jordan Washington—played with sullen fury by Mahmud-Bey and modeled on Larry Davis (charged in a 1986 shootout with cops and acquitted after Kunstler convinced a jury he acted in self-defense)—even if he isn't "born again" while in police custody. But Sean? That's a bit of a tough one to swallow.

He wins the case and, after Morgenstern has a heart attack, is elected district attorney. But during Washington's case, Vigoda has raised questions about drug dealers' payoffs to police and a network of dirty cops. Is Liam involved? Can Sean do the right thing? Is his affair with Vigoda's assistant Peggy Lindstrom (Lena Olin) going to lead to an additional scandal? What to do, what to do ...

Lumet gets some really fine work out of his actors, notably Holm and Garcia, who are particularly good together. But the drama is a bit monotonal. And as a platform for moralizing, "Night Falls" has the same structural weaknesses as the recent "City Hall." When push comes to shove, there seems little question what these characters will or should do—even if what they do doesn't adhere to any moral absolutist's point of view. We know too much about the way these types of administrations, bureaucracies and even individuals operate—thanks in large part to Sidney Lumet, who in "Night Falls on Manhattan," is mining gritty urban realism and finding something like nostalgia.

SIGHT AND SOUND, 9/97, p. 51, David Tse

Manhattan, the present. A group of Assistant District Attorneys attend their initiation lecture. Among them is Sean Casey, whose father is the veteran cop Liam Casey. Liam and his partner Joey Allegretto try to arrest top Harlem drug dealer Jordan Washington. Washington wounds Liam and kills several cops in his escape. A media scandal erupts. Attracted by the publicity value and as a slight to his ambitious Prosecution Counsellor Elihu Harrison, DA Morgenstern appoints Sean as prosecutor to the case.

Radical defence attorney Sam Vigoda arranges for Washington's public surrender and trial. Vigoda evokes sympathy for Washington by alerting the jury to the protection racketeering and assaults by the local police. Washington is convicted. Sean begins an affair with Vigoda's aide Peggy Lindstrom. When Morgenstern suffers a stroke, Sean is pushed to run for DA's office against Harrison. Sean wins the election, and Vigoda persuades him to seriously investigate police corruption.

The corrupt Allegretto pressures Sean to influence Internal Affairs, but Sean refuses. Liam admits to Sean his arrest warrant for Washington was forged. Allegretto commits suicide. Liam confesses to a reputable judge. Lindstrom accidentally discovers the warrant and confronts Sean, accusing him of withholding evidence. The judge condones the offence by privately validating the warrant. Sean considers resignation, but Vigoda counsels him to accept an imperfect system and continue in office. Sean addresses a new group of Assistant DAs.

Nothing has done so much to undermine Sidney Lumet's reputation as a key figure in New York cinema as Pauline Kael's essay on the making of *The Group*. Reprinted in *Kiss Kiss Bang Bang*, this implied that Lumet, for all his gifts, retained the mind-set of a director for live television (which is where he had started), and was popular with the industry primarily for his ability to wrap in time and come in under budget. Certainly in a 40 films in 40-year career (a frequency matched only by that other high-minded Jewish New Yorker, Woody Allen) surely suggests a certain mechanical cast to his creative mind, and perhaps a director who treats topical issues with at best workaday efficiency. But in *Night Falls on Manhattan*, these vices are never damaging enough to stop it from being a compelling police procedural drama. Lumet's perennial preoccupation is the fallibility of the criminal justice system; this movie is a response to—and aims to restore faith in—the judicial system in a post-O.J. Simpson media landscape. Andy Garcia's Sean Casey isn't a crusading movie DA; he's a potential political posterboy thrust into the job, trying to survive without forfeiting justice.

Lumet has his roots in off-Broadway and television literary adaptations. His theatrical mind-set is evident in the ambitious three-act structure: the first part concerns the botched arrest of a top Harlem drug dealer and subsequent power struggle within the DA's office; the middle act conforms to the rules of Lumet's favourite genre, courtroom drama. The third act retreads Lumet's own 1981 *Prince of the City* (which like this movie was adapted from a Robert Daley novel), as the focus narrows from the public to the personal with corrupt cops cracking up under internal investigations. The movie is described by Lumet in the press notes as "a moral melodrama about personal choice". This sounds fine, until you recall how in his astute-but-folksy book *Making Movies* Lumet defines 'drama' as a genre where characters determine the plot, and 'melodrama' as the reverse, which makes the above quote, in his terms, something of a putdown. What the film boils down to is three sets of relationships, each in a crisis of conflicting professional and emotional loyalties: Casey and Lindstrom, the defence aide who is also his lover; Casey and Allegretto, his cop father's corrupt partner; and the final father-and-son showdown. If one of the principal motors of drama is the divided self, then poor Casey's three-way split is really overdoing things.

Lumet's didacticism can appear dogmatic. Defence attorney Vigoda (Richard Dreyfuss, groomed to resemble Alan Dershowitz) is an ex-60s radical, but it eventually transpires his real intent is exposing police corruption. In Lumet's films, centres of moral fortitude are invariably represented by grouchy old men. With his father under suspicion, Casey finds two alternative (Jewish) mentors in Vigoda and ex-DA Morganstern. So, on the one hand, we have a highly schematic narrative (three acts, three relationships, three father figures), and the legal situations are rigged to illustrate didactic points; on the other hand, the film is richly dramatic. Lumet's clipped docudrama style has an urgency and clarity that wins you over. And because the opening scenes set up the world of New York judicial *realpolitik* so believably, we buy the melodrama in the later acts. The real-life parallels with the Simpson and Rodney King trials are handled intelligently, not sensationally, while the contending viewpoints in the trial are arranged constantly to readjust our perceptions of the case.

Lumet is one of the few film-makers still working with an imaginary proscenium arch. His camera here remains always at an objective distance, allowing us to judge the morality of the Byzantine legal dealings for ourselves. *Night Falls* is shot almost entirely with a medium lens and in natural light; the no-frills, quasi-documentary visual style is constantly in service to the out-standing cast. Special praise must go to Ron Leibman's Morgenstern, the tough older District Attorney: Leibman brings to this role a no-nonsense *chutzpah*.

Night Falls amounts to a credible overview of the ills and sheer difficulty of modern-day law enforcement. Moreover, it gives us an ending that casts a vote for those who administer the law (even if it tips the scale by using a *deus ex machina* of a beneficent judge). The movie argues that despite the in-fighting, the crippling technicalities and habitual briberies, there's still hope the system can deliver justice. And yes, as Kael might observe, Casey's monologue that bookends the film is a preachy theatrical device, but it's a measure of the film's ability to absorb that you take in every word of it. Judicial procedures have their fascinations, but the drama is finally about Casey's navigation of moral grey areas through pragmatic ethical persistence: he has learned to function in a flawed bureaucracy without compromising his youthful ideals. Sidney Lumet is 73, and in today's sea of junky legal thrillers, it is a pleasure to watch a filmmaker who treats law and ethics with the seriousness and intelligence that they deserve.

VILLAGE VOICE, 5/20/97, p. 76, Amy Taubin

If Frears errs on the side of clarity and control, at least his wheels never creak. [The reference is to *The Van*; see Taubin's review.] Not so Sidney Lumet, who even in such admirable films as *Running on Empty* can't resist overloading the obvious. And that's hardly the worst of *Night Falls on Manhattan*. Lumet, who wrote and directed, uses a twisted version of the Larry Davis case as a jumping-off point for yet another oedipally inflected, hackneyed tale of police corruption. (It's *so* twisted it makes Oliver Stone seem like a stickler for historical accuracy—no, Lumet doesn't use real names, but does that matter?)

For those with short memories, Davis was a big-time dealer who wounded several cops during a drug bust. Having eluded arrest, he hired William Kunstler as a lawyer, turned himself in, and pleaded self-defense. His story was that the cops who'd been using him since he was 15 to sell drugs for them wanted not to arrest him but to kill him on the spot. The jury believed Davis and acquitted him of attempted murder, though it found him guilty of weapons possessions and other lesser charges. It was one of the first big cases in which the jury's mistrust of the police determined the verdict.

In Lumet's version, the Kunstler clone (Richard Dreyfuss) loses the case to an idealistic assistant district attorney (Andy Garcia). Does the Kunstler clone appeal? No. It turns out that he believes the drug dealer is the scum of the earth and that he took the case not to win his acquittal, but in the hope of bringing police corruption to light. If the idealistic assistant D.A.—who's become so famous overnight that he's elected D.A., defeating his smarmy, Giuliani look-alike opponent by a landslide—makes the pursuit of police corruption his priority *no matter where it leads,* the Kunstler clone will back him all the way. Since the newly elected D.A. has a father (Ian Holm, the only actor in the film to resist chewing the scenery) who's not just a cop but a cop shot while attempting to bust the Larry Davis-like drug dealer, is there anyone who doesn't know where this is leading?

Wouldn't it be great if someone made a movie about the real Larry Davis? But please, not Sidney Lumet.

Also reviewed in:
NEW REPUBLIC, 6/16/97, p. 28, Stanley Kauffmann
NEW YORK TIMES, 5/16/97, p. C3, Janet Maslin
VARIETY, 5/12-18/97, p. 63, Leonard Klady
WASHINGTON POST, 5/16/97, p. B1, Stephen Hunter
WASHINGTON POST, 5/16/97, Weekend/p. 45, Eric Brace

NOTHING TO LOSE

A Touchstone Pictures release of a Bregman production. *Executive Producer:* Louis A. Stroller. *Producer:* Martin Bregman, Dan Jinks, and Michael Bregman. *Director:* Steve Oedekerk. *Screenplay:* Steve Oedekerk. *Director of Photography:* Donald E. Thorin. *Editor:* Malcolm Campbell. *Music:* Robert Folk. *Music Editor:* J.J. George. *Sound:* Maury Harris and (music) Thomas Vicari and Frank Wolf. *Sound Editor:* Michael Hilkene. *Casting:* Gretchen Rennell Court. *Production Designer:* Maria Caso. *Art Director:* James J. Murakami and Kevin Constant. *Set Designer:* Sig Tinglof. *Set Decorator:* Cloudia. *Set Dresser:* Jennine Rimer. *Special Effects:* Josh Hakian. *Costumes:* Elsa Zamparelli. *Make-up:* Larry Wayne Abbott. *Make-up (Martin Lawrence):* Kim D. Davis. *Make-up (Tim Robbins):* Cristina Bartolucci. *Stunt Coordinator:* Manny Perry. *Running time:* 97 minutes. *MPAA Rating:* R.

CAST: Martin Lawrence (T. Paul); Tim Robbins (Nick Beam); John C. McGinley (Davis "Rig" Lanlow); Giancarlo Esposito (Charley Dunt); Kelly Preston (Ann); Michael McKean (Phillip Barrow); Rebecca Gayheart (Danielle); Susan Barnes (Delores); Irma P. Hall (Bertha); Samaria Graham (Lisa); Marcus Paulk (Joey); Penny Bae Bridges (Tonya); Steve Oedekerk (Security Guard Baxter); Mary Jo Keenen (Grace); Lisa Mende (Emma); Clark Reiner (Alan); Ned Gill (Zach); Patrick Cranshaw (Henry); Randy Oglesby (Sheriff); Steven M. Porter (Sheriff Officer #1); Robert Louis Kempf (Hillbilly Attendant); Dave Lea (English Driver); Dan Martin (LAPD Sergeant); Lance August (LAPD Officer); Joe Minjares (Security Guard); Carl Sundstrom (Overweight Security Guard); Hank Garrett (Manny); Selma Stern (Old Woman in Elevator); Caroline Keenan (Ann's Sister); Jim Meskimen (Business Suit Man); J.J. Boone (Ginger); Kid Kim (Mary Ann); Jodi Jinks (Girl at Checkout); Willy Parsons (Truck Driver); Victoria Restall (Woman in Bar).

LOS ANGELES TIMES, 7/18/97, Calendar/p. 1, Kenneth Turan

"Nothing to Lose" is Exhibit A in what's right and what's wrong with current Hollywood comedy. There's no lack of wickedly funny people to place in films, but once they're cast, no one seems to know exactly what to do with them.

Written and directed by Steve Oedekerk, who's written for both Jim Carrey and Eddie Murphy, "Nothing to Lose" stars Martin Lawrence and Tim Robbins as a pair of opposites-attract guys thrown together by the whim of capricious fate. It's a clever pairing, and the comic skill and presence of the actors are enough to make the film sporadically quite funny.

The problem is that "Nothing to Lose's" exploration of what happens when a tall white advertising executive turns the tables on a short black carjacker is less a plot than a concept, a hook to hang various bits of business on.

Given the strength of the performers, a fair number of these random sequences are seriously funny, but too much of the film does no more than take up space. For not the first time, comedy stars function as the equivalent of special effects, elements whose presence ensures audience turnout and allows the filmmakers to more or less ignore problem areas.

Though he's moved on to directing serious films like "Dead Man Walking," comedy has always been one of Robbins' strong areas as an actor, and "Nothing to Lose" makes good use of his expertise as an irritable straight man, irked and exasperated at the lunatic events that take place around him.

When the film starts, however, Robbins' Nick Beam, secure in the love of his wife (Kelly Preston) and the respect of his boss (Michael McKean), could be the most contented guy in all of L.A. But circumstances conspire to change his point of view, and Nick is so devastated by events he drives around some of the more dangerous parts of town in a seething fog.

Into his GMC Yukon jumps the gun-toting T. Paul (Lawrence), determined to take possession of the vehicle. "You picked the wrong guy on the wrong day," is Nick's furious response as he takes off on a maniacal ride that has T. Paul pleading, "not the sidewalks, people got to walk there."

As the hyperkinetic would-be carjacker, Lawrence ("Bad Boys," "You So Crazy," TV's "Martin") demonstrates once again why he's the livest wire on screen. With the devil in his eyes and cleverness on his tongue, Lawrence is an unstoppable comic imp, equally at home with disbelieving double takes and profane verbal riffs. He has the gift of making every word he says sound funny, a gift the film would be lost without.

The Arizona desert is where this odd couple ends up when Nick finally stops driving, and where circumstances conspire to turn them into a cockeyed criminal team. Somehow they get on the bad side of a pair of real goons (John C. McGinley and Giancarlo Esposito), which leads to nominal complications that drag things out even more.

As a former stand-up and Carrey's collaborator on the scripts for both Ace Venture movies (he directed the sequel), Oedekerk understands the need to get out of the way of talented performers and allow them to simply be funny on screen. But "Nothing to Lose" over-relies on car crashes and plodding physical humor, and never manages to get any consistent comic momentum going.

The film does contain some priceless bits, like an aged hardware store clerk (Patrick Cranshaw) forced to decide whether Nick or T. Paul has the more menacing robbery style. Perhaps the film's funniest sequence, a demented dance routine by a too-cool flashlight-toting security guard, turns out to be performed by the director himself. Nice going, Steve.

Yet aside from these successes, "Nothing to Lose" has nowhere compelling to go, not even when it reveals that T. Paul is a bright solid citizen who has turned to thievery (he calls it "dabbling in future used goods") after an extended job search that failed because he was not the corporate color.

While it is a small surprise to have even a hint of social consciousness here, that, like too much of the rest of "Nothing to Lose," is too obvious to be effective. It turns out to be easier to put together a racially integrated comedy team than to have a film that feels integral and whole.

NEW YORK POST, 7/18/97, p. 39, Michael Medved

The traditional highwayman's threat "Your money or your life!" works only if the intended victim actually wants to go on living.

First-time carjacker Lawrence makes this inconvenient discovery when he pulls a gun on LA advertising executive Tim Robbins as the well-groomed yuppie stops his shiny new sports utility vehicle at a traffic light in a dangerous and decrepit neighborhood.

Unbeknownst to the nervous crook, Robbins has just minutes before glimpsed his adored and adoring wife (Kelly Preston) engaged in some late afternoon intimacy with his slimy boss (Michael McKean).

Driving around aimlessly, feeling suicidal and self-pitying with his see perfect life suddenly shattered, Robbins urges Lawrence to go ahead and pull the trigger ... and then speeds off on a wild ride out to the desert, taking the would-be thief along as a startled hostage.

After this cleverly contrived set-up, most moviegoers will sink back in their seats with dreary expectation of yet another interracial, bickering buddies formula picture (in the 40-year-old tradition of "The Defiant Ones") about two guys who start off as bitter enemies but eventually learn (group hugs, everyone!) that they need and love one another.

"Nothing to Lose," however, packs some potent surprises, conquering predictability with its ingenious plotting, consistently witty writing and shockingly rich characterizations.

Robbins, an actor whose most serious work ("The Shawshank Redemption," "The Player") often seems blank, bland and enigmatic plays his juiciest, most emotionally varied and altogether appealing role since "Bull Durham."

Martin Lawrence also shows unexpected depth, starting out as a hyperkinetic, smart-mouthed cartoon, but eventually etching an indelible portrait of a bright but wounded unemployed father who'll do anything to keep the respect of his glowingly portrayed (and somewhat idealized) family.

Giancarlo Esposito and especially John C. McGinley (complete with nose ring) are also excellent in colorful supporting roles as a pair of vicious, filthy armed robbers, driving through the desert while listening to the composer Pachelbel in their jalopy.

The biggest scene-stealer, however, is Steve Oedekerk as an office building security guard who performs a laugh-out-loud hilarious disco routine with a flashlight when he thinks no one is watching.

Oedekerk deserves this moment of glory since he's the one who wrote and directed this smart, funny and touching film.

His skillful, supremely self-assured handling of both funny and emotional moments creates a bond with the audience that's finally as warm and surprising as the connection between the story's two stars.

NEWSDAY, 7/18/97, Part II/p. B3, Jack Mathews

Los Angeles ad executive Nick Beam (Tim Robbins) is having a bad day. A very bad day. First, he comes home from work early to find his wife in bed with his boss. Then, while driving around in a depressed daze, some street thug named T. Paul (Martin Lawrence) leaps into his car, holds a gun to his head and starts demanding money.

Suddenly, something snaps in Nick's head. Figuring that life is no longer worth living anyway, he hits the door lock button, stomps on the accelerator and speeds off toward the desert with his stunned hostage pinned to the back of his seat. T. Paul's not having his best day, either.

The opening to Steve Oedekerk's "Nothing to Lose" holds terrific promise for a freewheeling summer comedy, and for the most part, it delivers. Oedekerk, who wrote last year's hit "The Nutty Professor" and wrote and directed the second "Ace Ventura" movie, doesn't know when a joke has run its course, but in a summer where laughs are as rare in theaters as good ushers, we'll take our rations and go quietly.

Like all buddy movies, and there have only been a few thousand this year, "Nothing to Lose" relies heavily on the chemistry of its stars. And it does well by Robbins, whose gawky amiability comes into good use, and Lawrence, the fast-talking stand-up who seems to give the film a burst of energy every time it starts to sag.

Given the conventions of the genre, there are few surprises in the evolving relationship between Nick and T. Paul. Through the first half of the film, they're the odd couple on the road, the yuppie and the hood, bickering with each other while managing to get themselves into trouble with both the law and the pair of highway outlaws (John C. McGinley and Giancarlo Esposito) who will follow them all the way back to L.A.

Eventually, they become unlikely allies in a scheme to break into Nick's company and steal his boss' personal fortune. It's revenge for Nick, and a way out of the ghetto for T. Paul and his hard-pressed family.

So much of this works that we can only wonder why Oedekerk stretched the scenes beyond their usefulness. He seems to feel that the lanky, rubbery-faced Robbins is kindred comic spirit to Jim Carrey, and encourages the same kind of outlandish behavior. But Robbins' appeal comes from a much quieter place; he's a more introspective actor than Carrey, and every time he lurches into over-the-top physical comedy, both Robbins and Nick are out of character.

Oedekerk is more successful at giving his story a measure of social weight, in the subplot about T. Paul's personal crises. He's not a street thief by choice. Despite earning correspondence school degrees, he can't get a job, and he has a loving wife (Samaria Graham), an endearingly brassy mom (Irma P. Hall), and two adorable kids to feed. This could get real icky, but in this instance, at least, Oedekerk does know when to pull back.

SIGHT AND SOUND, 11/97, p. 48, Andy Richards

Nick Beam is a happily married LA advertising executive. Returning home one day after an appointment is cancelled, he sees what he thinks is his wife Ann having sex with his boss, Phillip. Without confronting them, he leaves his house in a daze and drives downtown, where sometime criminal T. Paul attempts to carjack him. Ignoring the gun pointed at his head, Nick speeds out into the Arizona desert, effectively kidnapping T. Paul.

After much bickering, Nick agrees to return T. Paul to LA. En route, T. Paul robs a gas station, and the pair are chased by a police car, which collides with a pickup. Nick hits on the idea of robbing Phillip's personal safe. Nick himself then holds up a gas station when the owner tries to pull a gun on him. Nick and T. Paul are then held at gunpoint by another pair of robbers, Charlie and Davis, but manage to escape after a tense four-way stand-off.

Nick returns T. Paul to is home, where he rejoins his wife and children. Nick notices T. Paul's engineering certificate, along with a pile of job rejections. The pair break into Phillip's office and steal his store of cash. Still embittered, Nick reveals his identity to the security camera, and smashes the phallus on Phillip's prize primitivist statue. They hide out in a hotel, where a despondent Nick is almost seduced by an acquaintance but he backs down from having sex with her. Meanwhile, Charlie and Davis, who have traced Nick through a dropped business card, steal the money from T. Paul. Nick calls Ann, who explains to him that it was her sister and her fiancé that he saw. Elated, Nick pursues Charlie and Davis with T. Paul, and retrieves the money from them at gunpoint. Nick tells T. Paul that he now wants to return the money. T. Paul is unwilling, but finally relents. Nick returns to Ann. T. Paul removes the incriminating footage of Nick from the security tapes, and Nick offers T. Paul a job with the company.

With his impressive achievements in recent years as an actor (*The Player, Short Cuts, The Shawshank Redemption*) and director (*Bob Roberts, Dead Man Walking*), it comes as something of a disappointment to find Tim Robbins contributing his talents to this light-headed caper-comedy. Its depiction of two superficially dissimilar men reaching across the American racial and class divides is stunningly uncomplicated, plotted to subsume all the tensions it generates into a reassuring sense of closure.

That the film throws up sporadic flashes of wit, and puts an occasional humorous spin on a worn cliché, is attributable to the skill of its lead performers and the sporadic merits of director Steve Oedekerk's script. But it lacks any sustained ingenuity, or meaningful treatment of its themes. Given Oedekerk's background as a stand-up comic and writer-director on *Ace Ventura When Nature Calls*, and considering that Robbins and Lawrence have both directed their own material (the latter with *A Thin Line Between Love and Hate*), it is hard not to see this film as an unsatisfactory fusion of disparate comic styles and sensibilities. Some of the slapstick—Nick and T. Paul outside a diner, brawling in the dirt for possession of a stolen credit card, then hit by the diner's owner with a frying pan—severely tries the patience. Much of the banter between the pair is lazily contrived, with Lawrence redeploying the repertoire of grimaces and doubletakes that sustained his breakthrough performance in Michael Bay's *Bad Boys*.

The film's opening scene is more impressive: a hilarious two-hander between Robbins and Preston, played with a restrained confidence and excellent comic timing almost entirely absent from the remainder of the film, which is breezy to the point of complacency. What are we to make of Nick's 'mistake' over his wife's infidelity, which the film makes absolutely nothing of? Preston's Ann is so underwritten that she isn't even afforded an opportunity to chide her husband for his mistrust. It hardly helps, of course, that this fundamental plot contrivance and its eventual outcome are so obviously signposted for the audience.

If sexual politics are given short shrift, racial politics are also handled in a patronising manner. It is implied that within T. Paul's black man ("not exactly the corporate colour", he notes ruefully) there is a white man struggling to get out, with his eventual 'reward' being the dignity of a support systems job in a white-dominated company. Nick, on the other hand, is supposedly a man going off the rails because of a perceived betrayal, but he never loses his grip as Michael Douglas' D-Fens so intriguingly does in Schumacher's *Falling Down*. Nick's petty robberies are committed with a white-collar sense of propriety, and his theft is performed purely through a fatalistic desire for revenge. Thus, Nick and T. Paul remain distinct identities with distinct agendas.

Here, then, is a film that strains to assert that there are good and bad white and black people, that the metaphorical Grand Canyon of race can be bridged with a little goodwill and vision from both sides, and that things are never as bad as they seem.

VILLAGE VOICE, 7/22/97, p. 70, Laurie Stone

Tim Robbins's pudding features make his taut intelligence a continual surprise, and this pleasing tension lofts Steve Oedekerk's largely boilerplate buddy pic to occasional winning flights. A la *48 Hours* and *Men in Black*, Oedekerk serves a white guy/black guy pairing, with Martin Lawrence playing T., a novice carjacker who picks on the wrong whitey. Believing he's caught his wife in flagrante with his boss, Robbins's Nick, an LA. ad exec, is pumped with so much pain it makes him fearless, and he winds up taking T. hostage and driving to Arizona.

Usually in such movies the men start as opposites and gradually thaw into camaraderie, but almost from the get-go Nick and T. show a similar sappy decency mixed with a yearning to be bad. The flicks rivalry isn't between Nick and T. but between this couple and a black/white combo of legit desperadoes, Charlie and Rig, played with cartoon malice by Giancarlo Esposito and John C. McCinley. Believing they've caught Nick and T. robbing a service station, Charlie and Rig ram Nick and T.'s yuppie van with a scarred, outlaw sedan worthy of Cronenberg's *Crash*. Reveling in their pierced-flesh, lollipop-sucking self-regard, they cry, "We're the only professional criminals on this strip!"

The movie goes dead whenever women enter the scene: Nick's wife (Kelly Preston); a bar trick Nick turns down; and T.'s wife (Samaria Graham), a treacly perfect black mom. Oedekerk isn't interested in what happens between men and women but rather in exploiting the libidinous energy between men. The partners flirt with each other, Lawrence flashing his toothy grin and seductively tagging the much taller Robbins "lanky." The bad guys flirt too, and dub Nick and T. with women's names. There's nothing new about boys wallowing in grunge as a time-out from domesticity, but pleasure here ripples from the recognition that no one is ever hard enough. Without women around, the males are free to get soft, flap around in the dirt, and weep at Pachelbel's Canon. Homoerotic doesn't come off as patently psycho or sissy, nor is it sanitized with overhearty camping. In the age of *Ellen, Nothing To Lose* is a posthomophobic farce.

Also reviewed in:
NEW YORK TIMES, 7/18/97, p. C12, Janet Maslin
VARIETY, 7/14-20/97, p. 44, Emanuel Levy
WASHINGTON POST, 7/18/97, p. B1, Stephen Hunter
WASHINGTON POST, 7/18/97, Weekend/p. 41, Desson Howe

NOTHING PERSONAL

A Trimark Pictures release of a Channel Four Films presentation with the participation of the Irish Film Board, British Screen and Little Bird Productions. *Executive Producer:* James Mitchell. *Producer:* Jonathan Cavendish and Tracy Seaward. *Director:* Thaddeus O'Sullivan. *Screenplay (based on his novel "All Our Fault"):* Daniel Mornin. *Director of Photography:* Dick Pope. *Editor:* Michael Parker. *Music:* Philip Appleby. *Sound:* Peter Lindsay. *Sound Editor:* Nick Adams. *Casting:* Ros Hubbard and John Hubbard. *Production Designer:* Mark Geraghty. *Art Director:* Fiona Daly. *Costumes:* Consolata Boyle. *Make-up:* Maire O'Sullivan. *Running time:* 86 minutes. *MPAA Rating:* Not Rated.

CAST: Ian Hart (Ginger); John Lynch (Liam); James Frain (Kenny); Michael Gambon (Leonard); Gary Lydon (Eddie); Ruaidhri Conroy (Tommy); Maria Doyle Kennedy (Ann); Jeni Courtney (Kathleen); Gerard McSorley (Cecil); Gareth O'Hare (Michael); Ciaran Fitzgerald (Young Liam); Antony Brophy (Malachy); B.J. Hogg (Jake); Jim Duran (Billy); Cathy White (Lizzie); Lynne James (Gloria); Joe Rea (Joe); Amanda Maguire (Susan); Robbie Doolin (Drunk Fella); Oliver Maguire (Marty); Frankie McCafferty (Lizzie's Husband); Stephen Kennedy (Danny); Andrew Roddy (Nationalist); Frank McCusker (Man); Seamus Ball (Jimmy); George Shane (Sammy); Danny McElhinney (Pub Bomber); Janet Moran (Waitress); Lydia Courtney (Penelope); Noah Ehli Davis (Scruffy Young Man); Alan Burke (Ginger's Brother); Colm O'Brien (Young Kenny).

LOS ANGELES TIMES, 4/30/97, Calendar/p. 1, Kenneth Turan

The chaos of riot and revenge in Northern Ireland, characterized with deceptive mildness as "the troubles," goes on and so does the passion to make films about it. In 1984, a young actor named John Lynch made his feature debut as an IRA lad in the affecting "Cal," went on to 1993's "In the Name of the Father," and now is back on the streets of Belfast yet again in "Nothing Personal," a work that stands strongly on its own.

Given all that similar cinema, it's inevitable that "Nothing Personal" feels familiar at first. When it opens in a busy Belfast pub in 1975 with ominous Irish drumbeats, everyone except the pint drinkers knows a bomb is about to go off.

But as directed by Thaddeus O'Sullivan, whose fine but very different "December Bride" won a pan-European Felix Award, "Nothing Personal" soon goes its own way, both in focus and tone. It's one of those films that tears you to pieces emotionally, but it displays a love for language and character along the way.

Adapted by Daniel Mornin from his novel "All Our Fault," "Nothing Personal" departs from the norm by focusing most of its attention on the Protestant battle lines. Not that that makes much difference, for in clannishness and loyalty to a tit-for-tat ethic of retaliation, both sides are more each other's mirror image than they want to acknowledge.

As "December Bride" (as well as his delightful debut short, "The Woman Who Married Clark Gable") showed, O'Sullivan has a gift for character and the ability not to cross the line into emotional overkill. Determined not to be maudlin, he's dedicated this film to Gilo Pontecorvo's classic "Battle of Algiers" because it managed to "represent conflict in an emotional way that's not sentimental."

Helpful here is the way director of photography Dick Pope, a veteran of several films with Mike Leigh, can catch reality on the fly, as well as screenwriter Mornin's graceful dialogue. It's a cliché to comment on the Irish gift for self-expression, but it's hard to hear lines like "If I can't pity myself once in a while, who can I pity?" and "If you had a brain in your head it'd feel lonely" without saying a silent thank you.

"Nothing Personal" is set during a 24-hour period when exhausted Protestant and Catholic leaders, feeling "it's time we got the nutters off the streets," declare a shaky cease-fire. The film's larger question is not whether the truce will last but whether it can last, whether a culture based on random violence can be modulated or brought to a halt.

As a noncombatant, Catholic Liam Kelly (Lynch) cares only about the cease-fire because he wants the streets around his house safe for his two children (Jeni Courtney, Ciaran Fitzgerald) to play in. Out of work and separated from his wife, he finds himself somewhere on the Protestant side of the barricades on that cease-fire night and being in the wrong place at the wrong time sets up a fateful chain of events.

The Protestants we meet are committed to military action. While leader Leonard (the protean Michael Gambon) is starting to feel worn down, his younger subordinates are drugged on violence and power, capable of kneecapping a young man as casually as lighting a cigarette.

Loyalist squad leader Kenny (a nicely ambivalent James Frain) has sacrificed his family to what he believes is service to his country. Kenny's pal Ginger (Ian Hart, winner of the best supporting actor award in Venice), has only surface interest in political reasons. He's an unthinking, smug hothead who increasingly loves the killing for its own sake.

"Nothing Personal" is especially good at showing how these cycles of violence in Belfast spiral out of control, at revealing the poison of hatred and revenge spreading without check to a younger and still impressionable generation like a new kind of gang warfare.

Because O'Sullivan doesn't believe in stinting on horrors, "Nothing Personal," with some graphic scenes of torture and death, can be hard to take. In its decisions about who shall live and who shall die, the film is also open to the charge of being unnecessarily schematic. But even if your mind has problems with plot points, your emotions are always affected.

The most painful thing about "Nothing Personal" is the realization that today, 20-plus years further on, a solution is not necessarily any closer. The words of Yeats that open the film are as applicable now as they ever were: "The blood-dimmed tide is loosed, and everywhere the ceremony of innocence is drowned. The best lack all conviction, while the worst are full of passionate intensity."

NEW YORK POST, 4/25/97, p. 48, Bill Hoffmann

Movies about the conflict in Northern Ireland can easily be maudlin and depressing affairs because the issue can overwhelm the plot and there is never a happy ending.

"Nothing Personal" escapes that fate, but not because it concludes with roses and sunshine—it sure doesn't.

Instead, Thaddeus O'Sullivan's drama places a sharp focus on how "the troubles" affect a small community in Belfast, presenting us with a small, unforgettable cast, of characters who live atop a ticking time bomb.

At its heart "Nothing Personal" reveals that, tragically, the many similarities Protestants and Catholics have are repeatedly side-swiped thanks to deep-rooted political madness that's impossible to untangle.

It's 1975, and Protestant loyalist Kenny (Frain) is a squad leader the cause, so much so that he's basically blown off his wife and family.

A firm believer in avenging the violent deaths of innocent people, he's infuriated by a negotiated ceasefire between his boss (Michael Gambon) and the Nationalists.

But what really drives Kenny to question his devotion to the cause are his secret marching orders to kill off one of his group's most bloodthirsty men as kind of a peace-offering to the other side.

Will Kenny actually turn on his own man, all for the sake of a shaky ceasefire? It's a question that shakes the foundation of his very soul as he weighs the allegiance he has pledged to his mates and to a cause that seems to become more fragmented by the second.

O'Sullivan does a bang-up job of mounting tension from the very first minute—and keeping it high throughout.

The film opens in a crowded Belfast pub as customers down pints of Guinness, play darts and sing. But it is almost immediately evident that all is not right.

What happens in this pub is a jolter—and its sets the scene for a consistently insightful look at a conflict that everybody is sick to death of, but seems impossible to solve.

NEWSDAY, 4/25/97, Part II/p. B13, Jack Mathews

An adolescent girl is walking through the nighttime streets of Belfast, looking for her father. She walks into a pub, recoils from patrons' questions about where she lives, then asks the teenage doorman if she can leave.

"Go anywhere you like," the boy says, feeling rejected. "It's a free country."

Oh, but it's not. Not for the boy, who's Protestant, or for the girl, who's Catholic, or for anyone of either faith in the war-ravaged neighborhood. In different circumstances, the girl might return the boy's interest, but here, where Catholics and Protestants would rather hate than date, there is no point.

The title of Thaddeus O'Sullivan's "Nothing Personal" is both ironic and accurate. It's nothing personal when someone heaves a rock or a Molotov cocktail into a crowd on the other side of the barrier, yet how can it not be personal when someone wants to kill you for who you are?

Adapted from his own novel by Belfast writer Daniel Mornin, "Nothing Personal" burrows into the "Irish problem" by following two families for a day after the bombing of a Protestant bar. One is the fractured family of Protestant paramilitary leader Kenny (James Frain), whose murderous hatred of Catholics has disconnected him from his wife and kids. The other belongs to the Catholic Liam (John Lynch), Kenny's boyhood friend and now a single father trying to keep himself and his children out of harm's way.

Over the next 24 hours, Kenny and Liam will meet again, and Kenny will be challenged to see if there is enough humanity left, in him to save Liam from his gang—particularly the sociopathic Ginger (Ian Hart)—who are determined to give Liam "the message," Belfastese for executing members of the other faith.

"Nothing Personal" is brutally hard to sit through. O'Sullivan, a native of tranquil Dublin, is guiding us into a hell of human making, introducing us to people who are instantly believable in both their convictions and fears. It's a strangely eerie world where normal folks try to live normal lives on the front lines of an ongoing street war.

In the midst of this gloomy scene is Liam's daughter Kathleen (Jeni Courtney), the girl wandering the streets in search of her father. She's a tragic heroine, full of hope and dread, her life hanging in the balance of a feud she doesn't remotely understand.

Like the recent "Some Mother's Son," and any serious movie on the subject, the point of "Nothing Personal" is that violence begets violence, and that there are no winners where there are innocent victims. It is, as Brad Pitt says in "The Devil's Own," an "Irish story, not an American story," and it may never end.

SIGHT AND SOUND, 2/96, p. 50, Trevor Johnston

Belfast, 1975. At the height of The Troubles, a bomb explodes in a Protestant pub, reducing it to a pile of rubble, and leaving passers-by (among them Liam, a Catholic) to rescue the survivors. In another part of the city, high-ranking Republican and Loyalist paramilitaries Cecil and Leonard meet in seclusion to negotiate a ceasefire, after which Leonard warns Loyalist squad commander Kenny to keep his men under firmer control. Although Kenny himself has his reservations that the peace deal is a sell-out, Leonard's admonition grows stronger when Kenny's psychotic right-hand man Ginger viciously burns a Catholic youth to death with a petrol bomb during a flare-up between the two communities along the Peace Line. At the point when the ceasefire has been signed, Leonard orders Kenny "to put to sleep that nauseating wee shite".

Single father Liam however, has been caught up in the disturbance and finds himself taking shelter in a Protestant household, where, coincidentally, Kenny's ex-wife Ann looks after his wounds. Liam's own children, Kathleen and Young Liam, are beginning to get worried by their dad's absence, with Kathleen and her older friend Michael resolving to look for him—even if it means crossing into the other community. Kenny, Ginger and regular partner Eddie meanwhile, draw teenager Tommy into their circle by making him doorman at the local paramilitary-run drinking den, and then taking him along on a regular nocturnal patrol, during which they spot the returning Liam on the street and bundle him away for questioning.

While tension escalates between virulently anti-Catholic Ginger and dedicated Loyalist soldier Kenny during the violent interrogation, Kenny recognises Liam as a childhood friend, accepts his innocence and lets him go. Yet as the release takes place on one of the streets separating the two sides, Michael appears with a pistol, sees the gunmen with Liam and prepares to fire, fatally wounding Kathleen by accident as she tries to stop him.

As the Loyalists take flight in their car, Ginger's gloating over the little girl's death incites Kenny to shoot him, in so doing purposefully attracting fire from a British army patrol, who riddle the vehicle with bullets. Later, when Kathleen and Kenny are buried on opposite sides of the same cemetery, Liam and Ann offer each other their condolences while the respective paramilitary representatives look on.

In Northern Ireland they don't count angels on the top of pinheads, they just ask them what school they went to, which football team they support and listen whether they pronounce H-Block with an 'aitch' or a 'haitch'. It's no surprise that this tiny nation (if it is one) produced a Nobel Prize-winning poet in Seamus Heaney, for the decoding of language and cultural information for any lurking indications of bias or covert intent is an ongoing pastime. It's an environment where unilateral political attitudinising has long since stood in for progressive and meaningful dialogue, the Peace Process notwithstanding.

Although Thaddeus O'Sullivan's new drama, an Anglo-Irish production, has been adapted by Belfast-born writer Daniel Mornin from his novel All Our Fault, you can't help but feel the filmmakers are running into a celluloid minefield. The piece has some perceptive things to say about the Ulster Protestant psyche and a fair degree of credibility in the home truths it breaches, yet the problem, as ever, in dealing with Northern Ireland is that by telling one story, you invite castigation for not telling all the others. In a place of diametrically-opposed traditions, both sides will trawl though any work of art looking for crumbs of self-justification as well as sins of omission: the demands of political one-upmanship are such that everyone wants to be right, and if a film doesn't endorse your particular opinion, then you have to make a point of dismissing it. Simply responding to it 'as a film' isn't in it, when cultural trophy-taking is an integral element of one's ideological self-definition.

To approach Nothing Personal with something like even-handedness then, some perception of the spectrum of opinion on both sides might be a start, but that can be a fraught process in itself.

This particular reviewer, for instance, has to declare his own 'Moderate' Unionist background in a quiet suburb of East Belfast, and let the reader make of that what they will. The opening sequence is calculated to raise the emotional ante when an IRA bomb blast in a Protestant pub leaves a mass of casualties under rubble. The reality of Republican violence is thus swiftly established—or it would be if budgetary restrictions hadn't made the explosion's aftermath look all-too-obviously phoney (certainly when compared with contemporary television news footage of such atrocities). What's crucial about the fudging of this particular sequence is that without the shadow it ought to have cast throughout the rest of the film, the concentration elsewhere on Protestant violence tips the balance in a way that the producers may not have fully intended, thus laying the piece open to the accusations of Republican bias which emerged in the British press when it was premiered at Venice.

Since John Lynch takes another beating as the sympathetic Liam and the needless death of his daughter Kathleen provides the film's key moment of Rossellinian moral outrage, it's easy to read the film's over-riding sensibility as green-tinted. Yet what shouldn't be overlooked is the honesty and equanimity with which Mornin and O'Sullivan focus on the Loyalist paramilitary cause. Michael Gambon's Leonard is a leader who insists that 'things are bad enough without men behaving like beasts," positing a common decency within the conflict that's very much the way Ulster Protestants (many of them churchgoers) like to see themselves.

In the film's most commanding performance by a young actor of enormous promise, James Frain's Kenny also conducts what is for him in essence a military campaign with as much integrity as the circumstances allow, even at the cost of his own marriage. His ability to distinguish between defined strategic objectives and indiscriminate hatred against the Catholic community is underlined by his willing release of his childhood pal Liam when he's satisfied he knows nothing of importance.

In contrast, Ian Hart's trigger-happy Ginger is psychotic bigotry made manifest, a character who demonstrates that the political struggle has provided a window of opportunity for sadists and psychotics to indulge their darker impulses. If Hart's portrayal seems to have a bit too much of Robert De Niro's Johnny Boy from *Mean Streets* in him, and his accent is as approximate as Gambon's, the film's command of the distinctive local patter adds to its significance in giving the Loyalists the most serious consideration they've received on the big screen thus far (although O'Sullivan's previous feature *December Bride* was another trenchant look at a turn-of-the-century rural Protestant community).

For this viewer though, the film's nod to Gilo Pontecorvo's *Battle of Algiers* in the end-credits is rather compromised by its curious lack of a sense of place—it was shot entirely in Dublin, without so much as a couple of second-unit inserts to add in some genuine images of Belfast—and by the obvious contrivances in a narrative that crams its action into a 24-hour time-frame and a mere handful of locations. Unfortunately, it's only in the section where Kathleen goes looking for her Catholic dad in the Protestant drinking club that the paranoia endemic in such surroundings and the awful, inevitable feeling of divisions being handed down through generations, is really most effective. O'Sullivan's bustling, small-scale film is so busy cramming its plot into 85 minutes it never quite brings home the emotional impact it ought to have done. Finally, whether you see it as another step in the demonisation of the Ulster Prod or as a sincere attempt to examine some of the strengths and stresses of the Loyalist agenda, it's still a film to laud for the courage and sincerity of its aspirations rather than its modest, perhaps muffled achievement.

VILLAGE VOICE, 4/22/97, p. 77, Amy Taubin

As ebullient and trustworthy as Hart is in *Hollow Reed,* that's how twisted and feral he is in *Nothing Personal.* (The performance won him the best supporting actor award at the Venice film festival.)

Set in Belfast in 1975, *Nothing Personal* is about a small group of "loyalist" extremists at war with the IRA. A brief against terrorism, the film shows its effects on three men. Kenny (James Frain), the terrorist leader, sees himself as the defender of an embattled community, but in fact, he's become addicted to revenge and killing. Ginger (Hart), his right-hand man, is a psychopath who needed no excuse to become a killer; what the circumstances give him is the opportunity to do unlimited damage. Ginger is so trigger-happy that even Kenny thinks about "putting him to sleep." Caught in the violence is Liam (John Lynch), a divorced father with two children. Although Liam is a Catholic, he and Kenny were childhood friends. But the crucial difference between them now is that Liam wants peace and Kenny wants war.

Taut, brutal, and stomach-churningly predictable (it's clear from the start that bad things are going to happen to good people), *Nothing Personal* is basically a gang-war genre film with a smattering of politics and nicely nuanced performances. Hart, whose jaw seems to have receded several inches from its position in *Hollow Reed,* gives Ginger a face that makes you think of the cork on a Molotov cocktail. Unlike Hart, Lynch has a visage that's always with him. He can't help seeming haunted and anguished; it's a matter of bones and muscles. But whatever he lacks in flexibility, he makes up for with intensity. His Liam is as tender as Hart's Ginger is vicious. Too bad that *Nothing Personal* is less than the sum of their parts.

Also reviewed in:
NEW REPUBLIC, 4/14/97, p. 28, Stanley Kauffmann
NEW YORK TIMES, 4/25/97, p. C4, Janet Maslin
VARIETY, 9/11-17/95, p. 107, David Stratton

NOWHERE

A Fine Line Features release of a Why Not production. *Executive Producer:* Nicole Arbib, Pascal Caucheteux, Gregoire Sorlat, and Ilene Staple. *Producer:* Gregg Araki and Andrea Sperling. *Director:* Gregg Araki. *Screenplay:* Gregg Araki. *Director of Photography:* Arturo Smith. *Editor:* Gregg Araki. *Music:* Peter M. Coquillard. *Sound:* Christopher Taylor. *Casting:* Rick Montgomery, Dan Parada, Mary Margiotta, and Karen Margiotta. *Production Designer:* Patti Podesta. *Art Director:* Dan Knapp and Pae White. *Set Decorator:* Jennifer M. Gentile. *Special Effects:* L. Matt Hill. *Costumes:* Sara Slotnick. *Make-up:* Jason Rail. *Running time:* 85 minutes. *MPAA Rating:* R.

CAST: James Duval (Dark); Rachel True (Mel); Nathan Bexton (Montgomery); Chiara Mastroianni (Kriss); Debi Mazar (Kozy); Kathleen Robertson (Lucifer); Joshua Gibran Mayweather (Zero); Jordan Ladd (Alyssa); Christina Applegate (Dingbat); Sarah Lassez (Egg); Guillermo Diaz (Cowboy); Jeremy Jordan (Bart); Alan Boyce (Handjob); Jaason Simmons (The Teen Idol); Ryan Phillippe (Shad); Heather Graham (Lilith); Scott Caan (Ducky); Thyme Lewis (Elvis); Mena Suvari (Zoe); Beverly D'Angelo (Dark's Mom); Charlotte Rae (Fortune Teller); Denise Richards (Jana); Teresa Hill (Shannon); Kevin Light (Noah); Traci Lords (Val Chick 1); Shannen Doherty (Val Chick 2); Rose McGowan (Val Chick 3); John Ritter (Moses Helper); Christopher Knight (Mr. Sigvatssohn); Eve Plumb (Mrs. Sigvatssohn); Lauren Tewes (Julie the Newscaster); David Leisure (Egg & Ducky's Dad); John Enos III, Nicolette Gato, and Brian Buzzini (The Scary Drag Queens); Aaron Smith, Tres Trash Temperilli, and Sara Jane (The Atari Gang); Devon Odessa (What); Stacy Keanan (Ever); Gibby Haynes (Jujyfruit); Keith Brewer (Surf); Derek Brewer (Ski); Roscoe (The Alien).

LOS ANGELES TIMES, 5/9/97, Calendar/p. 14, Kevin Thomas

[The following review by Kevin Thomas appeared in a slightly different form in NEWSDAY, 5/9/97, Part II/p. B11.]

As the credits unroll for the high-energy "Nowhere," Gregg Araki's most ambitious movie to date, we bear the voice of Dark (James Duval) observe, "L.A. is like nowhere. Everybody who lives here is lost." This most sweeping—and familiar—of generalizations certainly applies with bleakly comic force to 18-year-old Dark and his pals.

Yet Dark, for all the apocalyptic feelings he experiences—and he's not alone in this—is a sweet, dreamy, sometimes klutzy youth who is simply looking for love and, in doing so, affirms its possibility.

What a risky picture "Nowhere" is. Araki plays compassion for his young people against a sendup of virtually every teen movie classic you can think of since "Rebel Without a Cause"—not to mention "Melrose Place" and "Beverly Hills, 90210"—and even borrows from those beloved monster movies of the '50s.

The world may be coming to an end, dreadful things befall some of his kids, but Araki resolutely feels that that's no excuse for losing your sense of humor. "Nowhere," which has a a scorching mix of songs from contemporary rock acts, is stylized to the max with production designer Patti Podesta's bold yet simple key settings establishing the film's fantasy tone. Take this picture literally and you're in trouble; better to view it as an allegory on youthful despair in which Araki deftly scores serious points without taking himself too seriously.

Even though Dark, who's working on a video for a class project, is clearly the film's hero—and perhaps Araki's alter ego—there seems to be almost as many people in "Nowhere" as there are in your usual Robert Altman movie. Dark is "totally" in love with his lifelong girlfriend Mel (Rachel True). While she thinks he's just "precious," she's a conscientious, upfront hedonist and switch-hitter with a girlfriend, Lucifer (Kathleen Robertston), who engages in nonstop insults with Dark. Mel is the kind of girl who postpones talking about a relationship she actually regards as nonexistent to go off with a pair of blond surfer twins (Keith and Derek Brewer).

"Nowhere" takes place within a 24-hour period in which Dark and some of his friends meet at breakfast and look forward to an evening of Kick the Can, involving dropping pills washed down with beer, to be followed by a really big party given by an ultra-decadent guy named Jujyfruit (Butthole Surfers singer Gibby Haynes).

Among the many—many—people we meet are a lovely girl nicknamed Egg (Sarah Lessez) picked up by a TV series hunk (actual "Baywatch" hunk Jaason Simmons, here truly terrifying), who goes on fatuously about the miseries of celebrity only to prove to be a real Jekyll and Hyde, and Cowboy (Guillermo Diaz), whose boyfriend and bandmate Bart (Jeremy Jordan) is plunging deeply into drugs and kinky sex.

The most innocent couple, despite their adult sexual sophistication, are Mel's likable younger brother Zero (Joshua Gibran Mayweather) and his devoted girlfriend Zoe (Mena Suvari), who want only to manage to get into Jujyfruit's party. There is a slew of familiar actors in cameos, including Beverly D'Angelo as Dark's mom.

Whether "Nowhere's" Alien (Roscoe) is real or a figment of an hallucinogenic—or, in fact, Satan himself—doesn't matter. He's funny yet represents the sense of fear and danger that so many of these young people experience, whether they admit it or not.

Araki is a marvel at controlling shifting tones, and "Nowhere," a confident, intricate work, has a great Pop Art look, yet its emotions are real. The most chilling moments occur when, reaching the rock-bottom moments of their young lives, Egg and Bart, in the isolation of their respective bedrooms, have only a slick and dangerous TV evangelist (John Ritter) to turn to.

If there is a sense of finality to "Nowhere," it is entirely appropriate, for Araki considers it the conclusion of a trilogy on disaffected youth that includes "Totally F***ed Up," a serious and engaging attack on suicide among gay teens, and "The Doom Generation," a tale of sexually ambiguous crooks on the run.

Artistically and emotionally, Araki, one of the most distinctive American filmmakers to emerge in the past decade, has expressed just about all that he can about young people feeling adrift in a spiritual void. It will be fascinating to see where he takes us next.

NEW YORK POST, 5/9/97, p. 51, Larry Worth

Pushing the cinematic envelope has been a long-standing tradition for Gregg Araki, the writer-director who could pen the book on nihilistic youths. But at some point, even the most cutting-edge auteurs get redundant.

Welcome to "Nowhere."

Advertised as Araki's sequel to "Totally F --- ed Up" and "The Doom Generation," his latest look at teens in turmoil gets its message out within 10 minutes, then spends the next 75 repeating itself.

As ever, the principals are largely bisexual, thrive on punk rock, sport multi-hued hairdos, obsess on a coming apocalypse, and sport more tattoos than Popeye and enough pierced body parts to qualify as pin cushions. Naturally, their language of choice is a variation on Valley-speak, and counterculturalism is a way of life.

That's all well and fine, particularly when, as in "Doom Generation," Araki focuses on two or three individuals. This time around, though, he widens the canvas to include 20-odd characters, many of whom seem totally interchangeable.

As the film opens, hunky hero Dark fantasizes in the shower about his pretty girlfriend (who's attracted to a lusty lesbian named Lucifer), then segues to the angelic-looking man of his dreams. Startled from the reveries by his smoke-belching mom, it's off to a day of sex, drugs and rock 'n' roll with his friends and trying to defeat a gun-toting mini-Godzilla from another planet.

It's all in a day's work for an Araki boy-toy, but the sharp humor that generally complements the goings-on is in perilously short supply. Here, the emphasis is on ugliness, as when one character's nipple rings are torn off with a pair of pliers. Not pretty.

Nor are tiresome diatribes against organized religion, traditional dating rituals and parents who just won't listen. And while Araki's arresting editing proves diverting, his subject matter—as when cross-cutting among multiple bondage scenes—is a feeble attempt at shock treatment.

Saving graces come by way of striking visuals and inventive lighting, along with amusing cameos from a host of former TV stars, ranging from John Ritter's New Age messiah to, quirky bits from Lauren "Love Boat" Tewes and "Brady Bunch" kids Christopher Knight and Eve Plumb.

For the most part, they prove considerably more engaging than James Duval's ever-confused Dark or colorful playmates Rachel True, Chiara Mastroianni, Debi Mazar, Kathleen Robertson, Christina Applegate and Nathan Bexton.

Like the rest of the production, they seem all dressed up with "Nowhere" to go.

SIGHT AND SOUND, 6/98, p. 52, Liese Spencer

Los Angeles, 1997. High school student Dark Smith meets up with his girlfriend Mel and her lesbian lover Lucifer and the three of them drive to a coffeeshop called The Hole. On the way, they pick up Montgomery. At The Hole, Dark sees Cowboy, who is looking for his lover Bart; their rock band has a rehearsal that day. The friends agree to meet later for a game of 'kick the can' before their friend Jujyfruit's party that evening.

Also at The Hole are female friends Dingbat, Alyssa and Egg. When the bulimic Egg goes to the toilet, a famous soap opera star and teen idol walks in. They leave together on a date.

Alyssa is picked up by her biker lover Elvis. Mel and Lucifer go rollerblading on Venice Beach. Wandering along the road, Dark sees an alien exterminate three Valley girls. Cowboy looks for Bart at the house of his heroin dealer, and eventually finds him on Venice Beach. He tells him their relationship is over unless he stops taking drugs.

Mel appears at Dark's house and they make love. Elsewhere, Alyssa spanks Elvis. In a hotel room, the teen idol rapes Egg. In a sado-masochism parlour, Bart is tortured by a dominatrix. Back at Dark's house. Dark asks Mel to marry him. Mel tells him that she cannot commit to any one person or gender.

At a deserted sports centre, Dark, Mel, Alyssa, Lucifer, Montgomery, Dingbat and Egg's brother Ducky meet up to play kick the can. After taking Ecstacy, they run and hide. While looking for the others, Dark sees Montgomery being abducted by an alien.

At Jujyfruit's party Cowboy gets a phone call from Bart's parents. Bart has committed suicide. Dark and Lucifer are unhappy because Mel disappears with male twins Surf and Ski. Ducky discovers Egg has committed suicide, and throws himself in the swimming pool. Elvis attacks and kills a drug dealer called Handjob. At home Dark tells his video diary he's had a bad day Montgomery appears at his window. The boys get into bed together and profess their love for each other. Suddenly Montgomery turns into a giant cockroach.

There's a scene in Gregg Araki's latest film *Nowhere* where a man called Elvis bludgeons someone called Handjob to death with a tin of Campbell's soup. Elvis, onlookers and victim are splattered with blood, but it might as well be Warhol's Own Brand Ketchup. The third film in Araki's 'teen apocalypse trilogy' (following *Totally F***ed Up* and *The Doom Generation),* *Nowhere* revels in such cartoon camp; its storm of sex and violence celebrates American pop culture with punning, postmortem artifice. Andy would have liked it.

Like *Totally F***ed Up*, *Nowhere* concerns the "lifestyles of the bored and disenfranchised". But its glossy look and hip, indie soundtrack place it closer stylistically to Araki's big budget sequel to *Totally F***ed Up*, *The Doom Generation*. Swapping his old, experimental video *vérité* aesthetic for day-glo hyper-realism, Araki produces an eye-scorching trip through the millennial madness of contemporary Los Angeles. With giant billboards screaming "God Help Me" and television evangelists preaching empty redemption, Araki's city is a high fashion hinterland of lost souls. Wallowing in the angst of its teenage inhabitants, Araki directs like Fassbinder on fast forward, abandoning the crude political messages of such earlier movies as *The Living End* for something more oblique and superficially apolitical, all hormonally heightened emotion and omnivorous sexuality.

While *Totally F***ed Up* opened earnestly with statistics on suicides among gay teens, *Nowhere*'s credits drift straight into the fantasies of its bisexual hero, Dark Smith (James Duval). just as his mental montage reaches its onanistic climax, however, there's a bang on the door and a grotesque close up of the mouth of his mother (Beverly D'Angelo) fills the screen. All shouting red mouth and acid green face mask, she brings Dark back down to earth, or at least to Araki's surreal version of it, like a soap-opera directed by John Waters.

If *The Living End* with its HIV-positive protagonists on a crime spree was Araki's queer take on the road movie, *Nowhere* is his subversion of the all-American high-school movie. Focusing on an 'ordinary' day in the life of a group of LA teens, the film hurtles between romance, tragedy and magical realism as it builds towards its inevitable climax: the house party. Using rapid cuts, Araki makes a slick daisy chain of a large ensemble cast which mixes Araki regulars such as Duval with ironically cast imports from television. *Baywatch* hunk Jaason Simmons, for example, appears as 'the teen idol' who, after winning one girl's sympathy with lines about the loneliness of celebrity, brutally rapes her. The assault is not just on innocence, one suspects, but on the white-washed morality of *Baywatch* itself and shows like it. Meanwhile, *Beverly Hills 90201* star Kathleen Robertson is cast as a lesbian called Lucifer and gets to spit lines like "lick my box".

Eschewing causal links for a more anarchic expressionism, Araki records the narcissism and naivety of his school kids with a mixture of infatuation and sardonic amusement. In one scene, the camera gazes down on a circle of bulimic girls as they dive into a huge slice of cake; in another it stares up through a glass table on which the girls are sniffing fat lines of coke. Whichever way you cut it, Araki seems to be saying, his teens are in trouble.

Nonetheless, styled to the hilt in blue wigs, biker gear and other hip accessories, Araki's gorgeous bulimics, drug addicts, dominatrices and rape victims are not so much real characters as 'drag' teens parodying the highly sexed solipsism of adolescence. "We all know deep down in our souls that our generation is going to witness the end of everything," cries Dark in his video diary, "I'm only 18 years-old and already I'm totally doomed."

Between the MTV visuals and cool Californian surf speak lie trivial rites-of-passage rituals that are played disconcertingly straight, such as the scene where Dingbat (Christina Applegate) lunges to kiss a boy during a game of 'kick the can' and chips his tooth with her brace. For the most part, however, *Nowhere* plays like *The Breakfast Club* on acid. Taking the heterosexual mating games of the high-school movie, Araki twists them into a transgressive cartoon of polymorphous perversity. Skipping Thermonuclear Catastrophes class, Araki's teens float around in a liberated, libidinous soup. In one scene Mel (Rachel True) abandons both her boyfriend and her lesbian lover for the blonde twins Surf and Ski (Keith and Derek Brewer). In another a heterosexual couple yell "Daddy" and "Mummy" as they reach their frantic climax.

Like the sex, Araki's violence is explicit yet comic. Whether it's the legs of the dead Egg (Sarah Lassez) sticking up from behind her bed, or the torso of Bart (Jeremy Jordan) protruding from his parents' oven, Araki's carefully composed frames allude not to reality but to comic book horror. Elsewhere, a B movie alien crashes in from a 50s sci-fi film to reduce a trio of big haired Valley girls (including Waters' star Traci Lords) to pastel puddles. When Nathan Bexton's dreamy Montgomery is turned into a more literal space cadet by the same green monster, Araki's script reaches new levels of tongue-in-cheek banality. Eventually, returning to earth, Montgomery tells Dark that he was abducted by aliens. "No way," drawls Dark; "Way," Montgomery gravely replies.

Lacking the avant-garde invention of earlier gay film-makers such as Derek Jarman *(The Last of England)* or the intellectual rigour of Queer directors such as Tom Kalin *(Swoon)* or Todd Haynes *(Safe)*, Araki seems content with such wilful superficiality. Art-directed to within an inch of its life, *Nowhere* could just as easily be retitled 'Nothing', its failure to engage with any real emotion not so much a comment on air-headed youth as a symptom of it. Indeed, one often feels Araki is less interested in subversion than in mere inversion. One wouldn't want hectoring, but there's a slightly troubling lack of analysis or depth here that similarly mars his earlier films.

Araki described *The Doom Generation* as a heterosexual movie for homosexuals, in the way that films such as *Philadelphia* were homosexual movies for heterosexuals. With *Nowhere*, his integration of Queer New Wave with Hollywood commercialism goes one step further. Araki's most technically accomplished movie to date, it is also his most formally conservative—the guerrilla distanciation of *Totally F***ed Up* is replaced by consumer friendliness.

As it draws to a close with a blissful image of two boys in bed, it almost looks as though *Nowhere* may even succumb to a feel-good ending. Happily, Araki chooses instead to have Montgomery undergo a Kafkaesque metamorphosis. As a giant roach explodes through Montgomery's stomach wall and beetles out of the picture, Dark is left alone. Dazed and confused and splattered with blood, he looks something like the way Araki's audience might feel after watching this self-reflexive assault on mainstream cinema.

VILLAGE VOICE, 5/13/97, p. 79, J. Hoberman

Fast, lurid, less arousing than enjoyably numbing, Gregg Araki's new sex-and-splatter youth flick is the ultimate drive-in miasma. Everybody knows this is *Nowhere*. The L.A.-based indie filmmaker has made much of taking his inspiration from *Melrose Place* and *Beverly Hills 90210* and, indeed, his sixth and most lavish production suggests nothing so much as the Aaron Spelling version of *Naked Lunch* (the movie, of course), complete with tacky horror-movie visitations.

Narcotic without being narcoleptic, *Nowhere* juggles a half-dozen or so plots while picking up more or less where the 1995 *Doom Generation* (Araki's self-proclaimed "heterosexual" feature) left off. It's casually apocalyptic sci-fi—set on a teenage planet of model-pretty, spandex-swathed, purple-haired twinkies (many of them on wheels) and mapping a dimension of pure libido cum universal confusion. If the viewer can't keep the various relationships (or even orientations) straight, neither can the principals—among them Araki axiom James Duval, *Craft*ress Rachel True, *90210*'s Kathleen Robertson, and *Married With Children* soubrette Christina Applegate, plus a matched set of dominatrices played by ubiquitoids Debi Mazar and Chiara Mastroianni.

Nominally enrolled in the University of Beverly Hills (where they seem to major in doomsday ecology), the Arakians spend most of their time coupling, cruising, and hanging out at a campus coffee bar called the Hole—there to gorge on Fruit Loops and up-chuck in the unisex toilet. It's in that very john that one vulnerable lass is picked up by a hunky TV star from *Baywatch* (Jaason Simmons). "Are we still in reality?" she wonders as he feeds her the line, "You have no idea how sucky it is to be a celebrity." The interpenetration of glitz fame and wannabe yearning gives *Nowhere* its particular local color: For the non-celebs, the basic choice is between hedonism and Jesus (promoted on the tube by the likes of evangelist John Ritter).

Some drop by the wayside but few convert. *Nowhere*'s erotic mode is polymorphously perverse—although, for all the enthusiastic face-chewing and a scene where someone takes pliers to someone else's nipple ring, it isn't particularly explicit. Like Burroughs, Araki has a taste for baroque, conceptional entanglements and seems turned on less by sex than by violence—the yuckier and more regressive the better. The climax of the film's last-reel bachanalia has a biker named Elvis bludgeon to death a hapless bystander with a 32-ounce can of tomato sauce.

Although no longer "Los Angeles's lowest-budget filmmaker," as *Variety* once dubbed him, Araki still favors a billboard mise-en-scène. Bathed in hot pink and orange lighting, every room is a brash designer concept, e.g., the polka-dot fever spawned perhaps by the plates of moldy food littering the floor of these teenage boudoirs. The soundtrack mixes wall-to-wall power punk with prose-poems in exaggerated Valspeak. (Is this the first movie to feature the contraction "whatev'"? There's a throwaway bit in which space aliens strafe a bus stop, vaporizing a gabby trio of aging Val Chicks—Shannen Doherty, Traci Lords, and Rose McGowan—down to their bite plates, but *Nowhere* makes something like *Earth Girls Are Easy* seem as quaintly innocent as MTV 101.

Everything considered, *Nowhere* really should be funnier than it is; the movies best running gag is Araki's tender regard for the lovesick Dark (Duval), a dim Keanu Reeves type longing for a real teen romance with a cheerfully wanton girlfriend (True). In blatant contradiction, the movie opens inside Dark's febrile brain as he takes his morning shower—a steamy reverie of hetero-, homo-, maso-whatev, interrupted by the reality principle in the form of his greenfaced mother (Beverly D'Angelo).

By dawn most of Dark's fantasies have come true—after a fashion. "It's been a gnarly day," he tells the video-camera suspended over his bed. Could *Nowhere* simply be the extended masturbation scenario of a lonely adolescent? Stay tuned—before the 37-year-old enfant terrible exceeds the militant youth-film statute of limitations and lapses into the middle-aged morass of stealing beauty.

Also reviewed in:
NEW YORK TIMES, 5/9/97, p. C17, p. Stephen Holden
VARIETY, 2/10-16/97, p. 66, Emanuel Levy

O AMOR NATURAL

A First Run Features and First Run/Icarus Films release of a Pieter van Huystee Film & TV/NPSTV production. *Producer:* Pieter van Huystee. *Director:* Heddy Honigmann. *Screenplay (Portuguese with English subtitles):* Heddy Honigmann. *Director of Photography:* José Guerra. *Editor:* Marc Nolens. *Sound:* Noshka van der Lely. *Running time:* 76 minutes. *MPAA Rating:* Not Rated.

NEW YORK POST, 12/31/97, p. 32, Larry Worth

Hearing elders talk dirty has long been a cheap yuk in American comedies, as when some tough-as-nails granny uses the F-word on an unsuspecting passerby. Ha-ha-ha.

So, if nothing else, director Heddy Honigmann deserves applause for letting seniors chat about their randy pasts while treating them with the utmost respect.

Then again, that's a slim frame to build a quasi-documentary around, as those who check out "O Amor Natural," will quickly discover.

Dutch filmmaker Honigmann takes her camera to sun-splashed beaches, crowded barbershops and sundry other hot-spots in Rio de Janeiro. The purpose? To get golden-agers' feedback on a posthumously released book of erotic verse from Brazilian poet Carlos Drummond de Andrade.

The M.O. is to have the utterly unembarrassed elders read a sexually graphic poem of their choosing, then comment. And almost without exception, that leads to their own reveries of passionate clinches and heavy breathing.

But while never exploitational, things start getting tired after the first six or seven septuagenarians have their say. No matter how poignant, ribald, amusing or liberating their anecdote, they soon sound redundant.

Ditto for the actual poetry. In fact, de Andrade's descriptions of sensual delights come across like an awestruck adolescent's carnal yearnings. At its best, the book—also titled "O Amor Natural"—is completely unremarkable.

So is Honigmann's direction, as she showed in her 1992 documentary on Peruvian cab drivers, "Metal and Melancholy." Competent, yes. Inspired, no.

On the other hand, travelogue-like scenes of Rio seem wonderfully inviting, and the sound of the poet's voice—heard only once on a scratchy recording—generates considerable interest.

That's why the production is a mixed blessing. At its best, "O Amor Natural" is a heartfelt celebration of seniors' vitality. At its worst, the routine feels older than the participants.

NEWSDAY, 12/31/97, Part II/p. B27, John Anderson

It's apropos of something: After a movie season in which cinema was virtually propped up on words—adaptations of novels having crowded the 10-best lists and beyond—we get a movie that pays tribute to literature.

And not only literature, but sex, memory and the sensual frankness of aging Brazilians. "O Amor Natural," by Peruvian-born Dutch director Heddy Honigmann, is not a documentary about

Brazilian poet Carlos Drummond de Andrade, or even the poetry for which he was so highly celebrated during his life.   Instead, Honigmann uses the erotic poetry Drummond never published—in a volume titled "O Amor Natural," which appeared after his death in 1987—and makes of it a small, sensual journey through the erotic life of his native land.

It's a heady trip. After a strange introduction that seems inadvertently to peg Drummond as a poet of the bourgeoisie—laborers and merchants don't know him, but middle-class matrons do?—Honigmann goes on to trace, through the often graphic but always love-struck poems of Drummond, a chord in the people she interviews. Most of them are in their 80s—and more apt to be acquainted with the poet and their reticent but gradually enthusiastic readings of his love poems open up floodgates of sexual memories, as well as an awareness among them and us of how powerful the right words can be.

There are few good films about writers, fewer still about poets and what they do—"The Postman" ("Il Postino") was a welcome aberration—and virtually none that treats sex with such tender nobility. This is to Honigmann's credit, but also to that of her "cast"—one older man, whose own daughter draws out of him tales of infidelity, his view of love, his late wife's indulgences; two proper women, one of whom is prompted by a Drummond poem to recall a ferocious tryst with a fisherman; an 81-year-old former Olympian swimmer who reads a heated work about love in the shower, which mirrors her own relationship to water; the denizens of a barbershop, who between clips and trims comment on the merits of Drummond's appetites.

It's an unusual film, one that goes in a seemingly impossible direction to mine an elusive quantity with an improbable tool. But by avoiding the documentary conventions, the talking heads, the droning analyses, and focusing on the ready sensuality of Rio de Janeiro and the minds of its people, Honigmann creates a worthy work of literary criticism as well as an entertaining film.

VILLAGE VOICE, 1/6/98, p. 62, Elliott Stein

It's doubleheader time in New York for Heddy Honigmann. The Dutch documentarian's first feature, *Au Revoir* (1995), was the highlight of last week's series of films from Holland. Her new doc, *O Amor Natural* (1996), an intriguing window onto the fervid landscape of Brazilian sexuality, is now warming up a screen at Film Forum. This largely irresistible movie comes in the shape of an idiosyncratic homage to Brazil's most beloved poet, Carlos Drummond de Andrade (1902-1987). Although Drummond never intended his erotic poems to be made public, they were published posthumously. Honigmann takes a copy through the streets of Rio and asks an array of seniors—the men and women interviewed are all well over 60—to recite portions of *O Amor Natural,* and to respond to the book's graphic imagery by answering candid questions about their memories and fantasies of sexual love. Brazil is among the least puritanical countries on earth: nearly all of the interviewees turn out to be deliciously salty-mouthed.

It's a lovely film. My sole reservation is that while a doc that breaks the taboo about talking with old people about sex is refreshing, it seems arbitrary for Honigmann to have limited the discourse to one age group. In the liveliest scene, the director calls on bandleader Delegado and widowed singer Neuma, both from the celebrated Mangueira samba school. In cracked voices, the pair manage to get through a charming samba about Drummond and Charlie Chaplin. Then, a brief passage from the poems is all it takes to set Neuma off into a Molly Bloomish, graphic reverie about *l'amour.* Finally, she turns to the camera, and as if confessing to the poet himself, declares: "You know, I killed my husband with all my fucking, I think."

Also reviewed in:
NEW YORK TIMES, 12/31/97, p. E8, Stephen Holden
VARIETY, 4/28-5/4/97, p. 101, David Rooney

OFFICE KILLER

A Strand Releasing release in association with Good Machine and Kardana/Swinsky Films. *Executive Producer:* Tom Carouso, John Hart, Ted Hope, and James Schamus. *Producer:*

Christine Vachon and Pamela Koffler. *Director:* Cindy Sherman. *Screenplay:* Elise MacAdam and Tom Kalin. *Story:* Cindy Sherman and Elise MacAdam. *Director of Photography:* Russell Fine. *Editor:* Merrill Stern. *Music:* Evan Lurie and Randall Poster. *Sound:* Neil Danziger. *Sound Editor:* Eliza Paley and Paul P. Soucek. *Casting:* Billy Hopkins, Suzanne Smith, and Kerry Barden. *Production Designer:* Kevin Thompson. *Art Director:* Ford Wheeler. *Set Decorator:* Amy Silver. *Set Dresser:* Thi-Linh Le. *Special Effects:* Drew Jiritano. *Costumes:* Todd Thomas. *Make-up:* Evelyn A. Ortmann. *Make-up (Special Effects):* Rob Benevides. *Running time:* 81 minutes. *MPAA Rating:* Not Rated.

CAST: Florina Rodov (Receptionist); Jason Brill (Delivery Man); Eddie Malavarca (Brian the Mailboy); Carol Kane (Dorine Douglas); Molly Ringwald (Kim Pool); Barbara Sukowa (Virginia Wingate); Jeanne Tripplehorn (Norah Reed); Mike Hodge (Mr. Landau); Doug Baron (Ted); Linda Powell (Naomi); Albert Macklin (Brad); Michelle Hurst (Kate); Paula Cale (Paula); Harley Kaplan (Steve); Michael Imperioli (Daniel Birch); David Thornton (Gary Michaels); Alice Drummond (Carlotta Douglas); Marla Sucharetza (Mrs. Gary Michaels); Rachel Aviva (Young Dorine); Marceline Hugot (Young Carlotta); Wayne Maxwell (Jimmy the Homeless Man); Julia McIlvaine (Linda the Girl Scout); Cleopatra St. John (Girl Scout #2); Danny Morgenstern (Ted's Secretary); Timothy D. Stikney (Paramedic #1); Christopher Tracy (Paramedic #2).

LOS ANGELES TIMES, 12/5/97, Calendar/p. 4, John Anderson

[The following review by John Anderson appeared in a slightly different form in **NEWSDAY, 12/5/97, Part II/p. B11.]**

Cindy Sherman's Hollywood-puncturing "Untitled Film Stills"—photos recently sold to the Museum of Modern Art for Hollywood-style money—feature their maker in a variety of counterfeit movie poses intended to evoke the irony of the familiar, the seductive glamour of the superficial. As a work of art, they're a one joke routine. But they're also funny, at least in the fleeting light of first impression.

With "Office Killer"—an ostensible sendup of the exploitation-horror genre that never rises above anemic homage—Sherman joins the ranks of those she would parody. It's almost, ironically, ironic: Her post-Modernist photography is about pop-cultural packaging and presumptions; "Office Killer" is about selling the people and the product and making the work nearly incidental.

It's the first in an announced series of arty horror films from the people of Good Machine (the New York company behind Ang Lee, Hal Hartley and Edward Burns, among others), and its producer is the maverick Christine Vachon ("I Shot Andy Warhol," "Kids," "Stonewall"). The co-writer is director and Vachon associate Tom Kalin ("Swoon"). Todd Haynes ("Safe," "Poison") contributed dialogue. Elise MacAdam, a Columbia University student of Good Machine's James Schamus, wrote the original script.

Thus armed and loaded, "Office Killer" bears an acknowledged debt to Dario Argento ("Suspiria") and unacknowledged ones to George Romero ("Carrie", "Dilbert").

Dorine (Carol Kane), a gray, besweatered functionary at the struggling Constant Consumer magazine, lives for her job and is one of those dinosaurs through whom many publications avoid embarrassment: the one who knows how to spell, how to write, where goes the semicolon.

As overlooked as she is valuable, Dorine is put on part time as part of the downsizing campaign of the ferociously ambitious editor's assistant, Norah Reed (Jeanne Tripplehorn) and, after accidentally electrocuting the office creep, Gary (David Thornton), goes a tiny bit haywire. Systematically killing off co-workers and hiding their rotting corpses in the house she shares with her nagging invalid mother (Alice Drummond), Dorine gets in touch with her muse, which is Death.

The actors—who also include Michael Imperioli as what passes as the hero, and Fassbinder favorite Barbara Sukowa as the magazine's chain-smoking, Eurotrash editor—are barely directed. And MacAdam's script paves no new ground: The characters are types, whom one expects to be perverted for purposes of such arch comedy but who are caught up in a salad spinner of confounding sensibilities and purposes.

"Office Killer" would at least have been fun had Sherman gone for pure camp, rather than letting the film morph into a quasi-topical morality tale. As it is, there's more to chew on in one Sherman still than in 81 minutes of her not-so-moving picture.

VILLAGE VOICE, 12/9/97, p. 69, Amy Taubin

A fairy tale of a different order, [the reference is to *Good Will Hunting*] Cindy Sherman's *Office Killer* opens promisingly in the anxiety-drenched headquarters of a magazine that's about to be downsized. The mise-en-scène has a flat, soft-colored look, like a '50s comic recyled as a 90s girl zine. With Evan Lurie's score tinkling sinisterly in the background, the actors move like robots one step from the scrap heap. The scene is stylish and all of a piece, but it lasts only 10 minutes. After that, the film turns into an aimless satire on teen-kill horror that's both gory and soporific. If Sherman, a brilliant sensual artist has any filmmaking talent, it's not in evidence here. A couple of punchy static images do not make a movie. Given the context, they don't even make an impression.

Also reviewed in:
CHICAGO TRIBUNE, 2/27/98, Friday/p. P, John Petrakis
NEW YORK TIMES, 12/3/97, p. E5, Stephen Holden
VARIETY, 8/25-31/97, p. 76, Derek Elley

100 PROOF

A George Maranville production. *Executive Producer:* Jay Faires. *Producer:* George Maranville. *Director:* Jeremy Horton. *Screenplay:* Jeremy Horton. *Director of Photography:* Harold Jarboe. *Editor:* George Maranville. *Music:* Michael Mosier and George Nicholas. *Sound:* Jordan Chassan. *Production Designer:* Patrick McNeese. *Costumes:* Peggy Watts. *Running time:* 94 minutes. *MPAA Rating:* Not Rated.

CAST: Pamela Stewart (Rae); Tara Bellando (Carla); Jack Stubblefield Johnson (Arco); Minnie Bates Yancy (Sissy); Larry Brown (Eddie); Jim Varney (Rae's Father); Kevin Hardesty (Roger); Loren Crawford (Trudy); Joe Ventura (Ted).

NEW YORK POST, 9/24/97, p. 44, Bill Hoffmann

"100 Proof" will shock your socks off.

It's an ultra low-budget Southern Gothic horror picture that'll have you clutching your seat, wincing in discomfort and gasping for air.

That said, anybody who wants to see the remarkable and dazzling debut of a young filmmaker—in this case, 27-year-old Jeremy Horton—should rush on down to Film Forum.

Horton follows the appalling existence of two coked-up losers, Rae and Carla, who lie, cheat, steal and hook their way through a dying Kentucky town.

As brilliantly played by Pamela Stewart and newcomer Tara Bellando, these two prime examples of American trailer-trash live only for the second. There is no such thing as the future in their grimy, misfitted lives.

The film opens with Rae bathing a senile, half-dead old man named Arco (Jack Stubblefield Johnson), who spits out a terrifying monologue of bile and hatred, culminating in his explicit detailing of how to kill a cat.

Rae, desperate to get her hands on Arco's welfare check, shoves his hand up her shirt for a complimentary grope, then rips him off.

This triggers a chain of events that lead Rae and Carla to commit a stomach-churning series of murders. Without a doubt, the final 20 minutes deliver one of the most harrowing and jolting movie sequences in years.

Compounding the shock is the fact that it's all based on the true exploits of two soulless female outlaws who stormed Kentucky 11 years ago.

There's also a great turn by Jim Varney (of infamous "Ernest" fame) as Rae's nasty, abusive dad.

Don't enter the Film Forum looking to be uplifted. But for some stunning cinema, "100 Proof" is 100 percent explosive.

VILLAGE VOICE, 9/30/97, p. 86, Dennis Lim

The oppressively grim *100 Proof* would have lived up to a title like *Kicked in the Head*, or *Poked in the Eye*, or anything else suggesting momentary but intense pain. With this writing-directing debut, Jeremy Horton joins a group of (mostly male) filmmakers who seem to think that if they carry female bonding to its logical extreme, the result will be a bloodbath.

Case in point: Rae (Pamela Stewart) and Carla (Tara Bellando), certified sociopath and passive tagalong respectively, on the loose in Lexington, Kentucky, snorting coke, swigging whiskey, and ultimately, slaughtering innocents. Loosely based—like *Fun, Heavenly Creatures,* and *Sister, My Sister*—on a true story, *100 Proof* slips in one foiled kiss between its two protagonists, and so qualifies as the latest entry in the increasingly exploitative lesbian-killer subgenre. Stewart's performance is just a marginally more nuanced version of Amanda Plummer's strident, tic-laden hysteric in Michael Winterbottom's execrable *Butterfly Kiss,* the worst of the bunch so far.

On purely technical terms, Horton is resourceful and competent enough, but as a dramatist, he lacks sophistication. Inspired by a 1986 crime spree, he's simply thrown in undergraduate-level psychology and a hint of artiness, and left the results to stew in a thick soup of indie-nihilist dread.

Also reviewed in:
CHICAGO TRIBUNE, 2/20/98, Friday/p. J, John Petrakis
NEW YORK TIMES, 9/24/97, p. E5, Stephen Holden
VARIETY, 2/24-3/2/97, p. 90, Joe Leydon

187

A Warner Bros. release of an Icon production. *Producer:* Bruce Davey and Stephen McEveety. *Director:* Kevin Reynolds. *Screenplay:* Scott Yagemann. *Director of Photography:* Ericson Core. *Editor:* Stephen Semel. *Music:* Chris Douridas. *Music Editor:* Lisé Richardson. *Choreographer:* JoAnn Jansen. *Sound:* Geoffrey Patterson. *Sound Editor:* Jay Wilkinson. *Casting:* Marion Dougherty. *Production Designer:* Stephen Storer. *Art Director:* Mark Zuelzke and Harry Darrow. *Set Designer:* Gary Sawaya. *Set Decorator:* Marcia Calosio. *Special Effects:* Andre Ellingson. *Costumes:* Darryle Johnson. *Make-up:* Marietta Carter-Narcisse. *Stunt Coordinator:* Eddie Watkins. *Running time:* 120 minutes. *MPAA Rating:* R.

CAST: Samuel L. Jackson (Trevor Garfield); John Heard (Dave Childress); Kelly Rowan (Ellen Henry); Clifton Gonzalez Gonzalez (Cesar); Tony Plana (Garcia); Karina Arroyave (Rita); Lobo Sebastian (Benny); Jack Kehler (Hyland); Jonah Rooney (Stevie); Demetrius Navarro (Paco); Ebony Monique Solomon (Lakesia); Yannis Bogris (Barsek); Dominic Hoffman (Victor); Martha Velez (Mrs. Chacon); Method Man (Dennis Broadway); Sage Allen (Teacher); Kathryn Leigh Scott (Anglo Woman); Donal Gibson (Animal Regulation Officer); Lisa Del Mundo (Asian Girl); Vic Polizos (Assistant Coroner); Leonard L. Thomas (New York Assistant Principal); Antwon Tanner (Augie); Gannon Brown (Tywan); Larry Costales (Hispanic Man); David Reyes (Investigator); Joanna Sanchez (Iris); Richard Riehle (Walter); Harri James (Librarian); Esther Scott (Mrs Ford); Esther "Tita" Mercado (Mrs. Santana); Chase A. Garland (Straggling Student); Guy Torry (Voice in Crowd); Anthony Aguilar (Chicago Tagger).

CHRISTIAN SCIENCE MONITOR, 8/1/97, p. 12, David Sterritt

High school science teacher Trevor Garfield has a problem at the beginning of "One Eight Seven," the new movie about inner-city education.

His classroom talents have earned respect from his peers and his better-motivated pupils. But the corridors of his Brooklyn school don't exactly ring with civilized values, and failing a hostile student can be as dangerous as dissing a stranger in a dark alley. Trevor learns this the hard way, suffering a near-fatal attack from a "gang-banger" with a chip on his shoulder and a tenpenny nail in his fist.

Trevor recovers from his wounds, moves his life and work to the other side of the country, and dips back into teaching as a substitute in the Los Angeles schools. But adversity recurs. Surly students take a dislike to him on Day 1, and a dispute over a stolen watch makes the toughest troublemaker into his mortal enemy. His only friends are a computer teacher as threatened as he is, and a history teacher whose moral sense was burned out years ago.

Trevor remembers when he was idealistic, optimistic, and ethical to a fault. Can he recapture those days amid the chaos and confusion that a major American city has the audacity to call an educational system? Or does a job in the jungle require an adjustment in one's personal and professional morality?

Those are the big questions raised in "One Eight Seven"—the police code for homicide, written "187" in the movie ads—by director Kevin Reynolds and screenwriter Scott Yagemann, who taught in L.A.'s public schools for seven years before penning this script. They pull no punches in depicting the darkest sides of today's urban and educational environments, and their sympathy with embattled teachers will please many education-minded people.

The picture would be more persuasive if it didn't use over-the-top melodrama to illustrate its points, however. Some scenes pour on so much terror and destructiveness that one suspects the filmmakers are less interested in outlining a social problem than in stirring up our vengeful instincts, so we'll be primed to cheer when the mayhem-filled climax finally arrives.

Worse, the film strongly suggests that vigilante violence cloaked as "taking personal responsibility" instead of "being a victim"—may have a part to play in returning law and order to the schoolroom. The movie hedges its bets by taking an ambivalent, sometimes murky stance toward the plot's take-charge hero. Still, this aspect of the story will repel viewers who feel the most likely effect of violence is to beget more of the same, simply prolonging a (literally) vicious circle.

Samuel L. Jackson gives a powerful performance as Trevor, lending three-dimensional life to a character who might have seemed schematic and even self-contradictory in less able hands. As a bonus, the nuanced acting of this gifted African-American star helps soften the movie's discomfiting racial undertones, which arise from its harsh portrayal of intolerably decayed ghettos swarming with dysfunctional members of racial and ethnic minorities.

John Heard and Kelly Rowan are also fine as the history and computer teachers. Reynolds keeps the action moving at an energetic pace, although his visual style often sweats and strains surprisingly hard for such a relatively straightforward story; the editing is punchy and the camera is forever turning, craning, revolving, and otherwise knocking itself out.

Ericson Core did the colorful cinematography, and music supervisor Chris Douridas assembled the eclectic soundtrack songs, which range from hip-hop to strains of an Indian sitar that seems to have wandered in from some other movie.

LOS ANGELES TIMES, 7/30/97, Calendar/p. 1, Kenneth Turan

The most disheartening line in "187" is its last, written in bold type across the screen just before the credits roll: "A teacher wrote this movie." It's enough to make you weep, and not just because it's painful to think that this muddled and manipulative film was penned by someone in a position to mold impressionable minds.

No, that line is disturbing because it shows that screenwriter Scott Yagemann, director Kevin Reynolds and producers Bruce Davey and Stephen McEveety are suffering from the group delusion that they've made a serious movie about Something Important, that, to quote Davey, everyone involved "shared the vision that this story needs to be told."

What they've actually made is an unconvincing piece of trash about crime in the schools and one teacher's reaction that has no discernible purpose outside of feeding our paranoia. Making things worse, it's a film that wants to have it both ways. It condemns school violence while providing heroically lit portraits of the perpetrators, and it angles for a "Death Wish"-type vigilante reaction from its audience while being too self-important to actually deliver. What a mess.

Director Reynolds, who included in the press kit a list of "startling statistics" about school violence and a boast that his film "is going to challenge and unsettle some people," must have slept through a great deal of recent cinema if he thinks no film has previously dared to so much as hint that schools are the most dangerous places on Earth.

Starting as far back as "Rebel Without a Cause" through "Lean on Me," "Stand and Deliver," "Dangerous Minds" and other films too repetitive to remember, Hollywood has so consistently delivered the message that public schools are sulfurous pits of hell that today's parents may be forgiven if they want to strap on an Uzi before venturing out to Open House Night.

Trevor Garfield (Samuel L. Jackson) starts the film as a dedicated teacher in one of those snake pits, Roosevelt Whitney High School in Brooklyn's Bedford-Stuyvesant section. He's unsettled one day to find his name and the numbers "187," apparently gang slang for murder, written on every page of a textbook. He expects an attack, and it almost immediately happens.

Fifteen months later, Garfield has moved to Los Angeles and is working as a substitute teacher. He is still dedicated, still someone who prays every morning "for strength and serenity," but it's more than a stiffness in the way he walks that marks a change in the man since that incident in Brooklyn. Garfield is more guarded less spontaneous and more, shall we say, open to the idea that hooligans must be dealt with on their own terms.

His new assignment certainly does not lack for bad boys, the worst of whom, Cesar (Clifton Gonzalez Gonzalez) and Benny (Lobo Sebastian), practically drool with evil as card-carrying members of a group that calls itself K.O.S., "Kapping Off Suckers."

Yet though we're supposed to regard these guys as scum of the Earth, "187" cinematographer Ericson Core, whose background, not surprisingly, is in music videos, can't help but visually glorify them, using lighting and camera angles that portray the K.O.S. members as fierce if misguided warriors. Witness its brief use of unnecessary nudity; "187" can't, quite swear off the use of exploitative techniques even while insisting that its aims are pure.

Not much help to Garfield (or the film) are the two clichéd teachers he ends up spending the most time with. Dave Childress (John Heard) is a crude slob who's seen too much, and Ellen Henry (Kelly Rowan) is a blond beginner who is overmatched by the system.

Worse still are the representatives of that system, the principals and other administrators whom the film, in its most interesting and possibly true-to-life touch, presents as careerist bureaucrats who spend more time worrying about lawsuits from coddled students than the safety of the faculty.

Despite this noticeable lack of support, Garfield still tries to do the right thing, encouraging Rita (Karina Arroyave), the inevitably talented you person trapped in poverty, and trying to convince the gangbangers that macho pride isn't worth dying for. Yet even Garfield, like Charles Bronson in "Death Wish," ultimately finds it hard to resist doing something a little more tangible than offer encouragement.

Unfortunately, blustery director Reynolds ("Robin Hood: Prince of Thieves," "Waterworld," "Rapa Nui"), aside from being someone who thinks "subtlety" is a word best left in the dictionary, is also too conflicted about what kind of film he's worked on to make Garfield's problem and its farfetched resolution creditable or involving. To say that not even Jackson, one of the most convincing of actors, can turn Trevor Garfield into a person worthy of concern is to only hint at how lacking "187" turns out to be.

NEW YORK POST, 7/30/97, p. 36, Michael Medved

For most of its running time, "187" plays like a standard-issue heroic-teacher-versus-gang-invested-high-school melodrama in the honorable (if formulaic) tradition of "Stand and Deliver" and "Dangerous Minds".

About two thirds of the way toward its conclusion, however, director Kevin Reynolds ("Water World," "Robin Hood: Prince of Thieves") springs a shocking surprise which instantly transforms his movie into something different—and much worse.

With a sudden plot twist about a psycho killer on the loose, Reynolds and his collaborators sacrifice all credibility and all compassion for the characters, utterly wasting the intense, affecting performances by a uniformly talented cast.

Chief among the victims of this abrupt crack-up is Samuel L. Jackson, as an uncompromising science teacher who refuses to give up on his profession, He's assigned to the fictional "John Quincy Adams High School," a hellish, graffiti-scarred institution where violent, drug-addicted Chicano gangsters dominate his class.

Clifton Gonzalez Gonzalez and Lobo Sebastian are thoroughly convincing (and utterly hateful) as the two most dangerous thugs, while the sultry Karina Arroyave is similarly forceful as a bright but troubled girl inspired by the new teacher—and trying to seduce him.

Unlike most other movies about inner city schools, "187" never reassures the audience by investing its teacher protagonist with superhuman powers to "reach" his afflicted students.

Director Reynolds, whose best work ("Rapa Nui," "The Beast") involved similarly offbeat, politically incorrect and risky shockers, uses cutting-edge music (by the British band Massive Attack and others) along with first-rate cinematography and editing to portray the yellow-tinged, smoggy, poisonous world of an L.A. smothered in moral haze.

But then comes that startling plot reversal, demeaning all the film's worthwhile moments.

The title "187" refers to the section of the California penal code indicating homicide, and seems appropriate to a film that murders its own good intentions.

NEWSDAY, 7/30/97, Part II/p. B2, Jack Mathews

Do you know someone who's heading off to college this fall, with plans to become a high school teacher? Ask them if they can answer this simple multiple choice question before they begin:

Your students are totally out of control. They won't listen to you, they taunt you, they spit in your hand, and yell in your face. One or two are even threatening to kill you.

The proper disciplinary approach is.

a. Cane them.

b. Shoot them with morphine darts, and cut their fingers off while they're unconscious.

c. Murder them.

d. Challenge them to a game of Russian roulette.

e. Take them to see Kevin Reynolds' "187" and tell them to behave or they may get all of the above.

From "Blackboard Jungle" to "Dangerous Minds," with dozens of pictures in between, Hollywood has turned out a dizzying number of horror movies about decent teachers thrust into anarchic classrooms, and having to get by without any support from the administration. But none has offered as despairing a view of education and life in school as "187."

Reynolds, working from a script by former teacher Scott Yagemann, paints a picture of the inner-city high school environment so hopelessly grim that it's hard to imagine anyone other than the kids showing up. And they wouldn't miss it. On a typical day, the guys get to spray-paint graffiti on the walls and gang-rape whomever they choose, while the rest of the girls egg them on like cheerleaders from hell.

In the midst of these scenes is Samuel L. Jackson's Trevor Garfield, a science teacher who has dedicated his life to the profession only to discover that his life may be the cost of doing business. "187" follows Trevor on assignments on both coasts, first at a school in the Bed-Stuy section of Brooklyn, then, months after recuperating from a vicious stabbing there, at a barrio school in Los Angeles.

What these high schools have in common is their savage student bodies. They don't need teachers at these places, they need lion tamers. You get the impression that the class valedictorian will be determined by number of kills.

I'd like to assume that Reynolds and Yagemann intend "187" as a dark fable of a post-apocalyptic world, a glimpse at the end of the road we're on. But fables bear morals, and the only message here is that some students are beyond the range of a kind teacher's influence and probably deserve to be caned, mutilated or killed, all of which are suggested.

The title—"one-eight-seven"—refers to the police code for homicide, and is used the students to warn teachers of their impending deaths. Trevor finds "187s" all over the book of the Bed-Stuy student who will soon attack him with a 10-penny nail. And he finds them all over his house in Los Angeles, before the incorrigible Cesar (Clifton Gonzales Gonzales) and his gang come after him.

All this because he wants to teach them!

Jackson, as always, brings tremendous intensity to his role, but Trevor is really being used by the filmmakers to lead the audience into a revenge mode. We're meant to share his growing sense of hopelessness, and urge his violent impulses. But Reynolds' gimmicky direction is such a distraction that the film doesn't even work as exploitation.

We're too busy wondering why Reynolds is blurring faces with focus distortion, or has his camera swooping in and around scenes, to go through the tension/release cycle that is the pulse of vigilante movies. For the run of "187," we're stuck with a man going through a slow spiritual death.

John Heard, playing a cynical, drunken teacher who has a war chest of handguns at home, offers some comic relief, but nothing comes of his character, either.

The one relationship that might give the story sympathetic underpinnings, between Trevor and a white teacher (Kelly Rowan), is abruptly cut off. If they were afraid of injecting interracial romance, they should have cast the role with a black actress. The audience needs some emotion other than despair to get through this.

SIGHT AND SOUND, 9/97, p. 52, Robin Dougherty

New York City. High-school science teacher Trevor Garfield finds the figure 187 scrawled throughout his textbook. He realises that the number—a penal code for homicide—is a threat on his life. Later, he's stabbed repeatedly in the school hallway by a student.

Fifteen months later, Garfield has relocated and finds a job as a teacher in an inner-city school in LA. He inspires a student, Rita, who asks him to tutor her. At his house, she mistakenly thinks he wants sex in return for lessons. Benny, a gang member who's also Garfield's student, finds another kid painting over his territorial graffiti markings along a LA River culvert. Benny shoots the offender dead, leaves the scene and never returns to school. Garfield befriends Ellen, the computer-science teacher who is being stalked by Benny, and invites her to dinner. Later at school, he gives a lesson on drugs, using his own prescription morphine and his watch to drug a lab rat and time its sedation. When the watch disappears, he accuses a student named Cesar, also a gang member. Garfield confronts Cesar at the boy's home in the projects. Soon, Benny's body is found near the culvert. Ellen's dog is found dead and the figure 187 is sprayed all over Garfield's house.

After a drug-induced hallucination, Cesar discovers his index finger has been cut off. The police don't believe Garfield is responsible, but Ellen becomes suspicious of Garfield when she finds Benny's rosary at his house. Cesar appears at Garfield's house with two buddies. They find Garfield waiting for them. He admits to killing Benny and mutilating Cesar. They force him to play Russian roulette with a loaded gun. Garfield pulls the trigger three times—all blanks. Then he insists that Cesar play, too. After Garfield shoots himself in the head, Cesar pulls the trigger once more, killing himself.

Scott Yagemann, himself a former substitute schoolteacher, wrote the screenplay for 187, apparently intending to elicit sympathy for the public servants who battle daily against ignorance, poverty, and other social conditions that make maintaining American public education a Sisyphean task. Ironically, the movie virtually rebukes anyone who would defend teachers by citing horrifying conditions, the inhumanity of the students, and the infrequent victories which can't stem the tide of failures. Since the hero ultimately turns on those he thinks he's trying to save, the message thoroughly undercuts its proteaching stance.

At the centre of 187—the title refers to the California state penal code for murder—is Samuel Jackson, who gives the most enigmatic performance of his career. His Trevor Garfield is at first a dedicated teacher who in the film's gorgeous opening scenes rides his bike over the Brooklyn Bridge and into Bedford-Stuyvesant in order to give his students a lesson in centripetal force once he arrives. Apparently, he's the last person who deserves to be violently stabbed by a student, presumably the one who has scrawled "187" all over Garfield's book.

For much of the story, however, Garfield is impenetrable. His colleagues think he's nuts for caring so much about teaching. But we don't learn much about him while he's in New York, so when he resurfaces, 15 months after the stabbing attack, as a substitute in South Central Los Angeles, we can't crack him. Is he meek and restrained because of the attack or was he always like that? Is he all-but-defeated or is he making an honest attempt to reconnect with the job?

Most of all, is his jumpiness when, for example, a student hits him with a paper wad, the result of post-traumatic stress disorder or was he always deranged? These issues become important once Garfield begins to encounter violence again.

The film is an intriguing mess, partially thanks to director Kevin Reynolds (*Waterworld*). Reynolds is hardly a subtle craftsman, and here he can't decide whether he's helming a social essay or a thriller. At times, *187* seems to be a stalker film about a gang member harassing a teacher; at other times, it's a condemnation of a system that cares more about the superficial virtues of students' rights than about teaching them responsibility. When the turning point arrives that establishes Garfield as the person responsible for the violence, it comes as an off-putting surprise. Reynolds' skill in editing for narration is practically non-existent. But as a piece of filmmaking, *187* isn't at all dull. Cinematographer Ericson Core has a great eye and makes a scene following a gang murder uncannily beautiful by shooting the sunlight bouncing off the river trickling through a culvert. He captures the odd beauty of concentric circles of headlights on the LA freeway at night—the inner circle red, the outer circle white. He even manages to make the often-photographed Brooklyn Bridge look like it holds new mystery. That's more than can be said for the movie as a whole.

VILLAGE VOICE, 8/12/97, p. 72, Ed Morales

On paper, Kevin Reynolds's *187* seems like a decent attempt to keep his career from going under after *Waterworld*. You'd think Samuel L. Jackson as a brainy, passionate high school science teacher who quotes Thomas Wolfe and listens to Miles Davis would make for a warm and fuzzy setup. Watch him charm, cajole, educate, and talk some sense into those wild gangsta kids!

Who else will they listen to? But this latest update on the old *Blackboard Jungle* riff is nothing less than a macabre cross between *Stand and Deliver* and *Death Wish*. Written by Scott Yagemann, an ex-teacher who served a seven-year sentence in L.A. schools, *187* tries to call attention to the plight of thousands of teachers and students who are physically attacked every year in public, but only serves to distort the issue.

The Reynolds-Yagemann team immediately establishes a climate of fear and loathing. In the opening minutes, Jackson's character, Trevor Garfield, is brutally stabbed by a student in his Brooklyn high school because he gave him a failing grade. He relocates to the L.A. sprawl, and on his first day at Adams High, he's looked over by gang boys like a new inmate in prison-fresh meat. Shifting demo-graphics, *187* becomes a spixsploitation movie—with one gringo exception, all of Garfield's tormentors are cartoon Chicano thugs, members of the KOS (Kap Off Suckers) crew. While *187* is supposed to be a reference to the California penal code number for murder, it seems to have more to do with Proposition 187. There's plenty of fuming done by the teachers about having to speak Spanish; the principal, Mr. Garcia, is a spineless minority bureaucrat defending gang kids; and even the good girl, Rita (an early-Rosie Perez facsimile), feels she has to get naked on Garfield's couch in exchange for tutoring.

Though Garfield is motivated by the idealism of educating the masses and a desire to put trauma behind him, he develops a vengeful streak through a platonic interracial romance with a wispy fellow teacher, Ellen Henry (Kelly Rowan). The moody trip-hop and cool jazz soundtrack enhances Jackson's sensitive, nuanced performance, but he's sabotaged by *187*'s ridiculous and cynical plot twists. The film resorts to the Russian roulette sequence in *The Deer Hunter* to frame the final confrontation between Garfield and gang leader Cesar (Clifton Gonzalez Gonzalez) with wildly bloody results. A weak murder mystery disguised as an issues film, *187* is ultimately defined by its helicopter-tracking panoramas of L.A., so detached from its subject that its vision becomes a total blur.

Also reviewed in:
NEW YORK TIMES, 7/30/97, p. C15, Janet Maslin
VARIETY, 7/28-8/3/97, p. 57, Todd McCarthy
WASHINGTON POST, 7/30/97, p. C2, Stephen Hunter
WASHINGTON POST, 8/1/97, Weekend/p. 30, Desson Howe

ONE NIGHT STAND

A New Line Cinema release of a Red Mullet production. *Executive Producer:* Robert Engleman. *Producer:* Mike Figgis, Annie Stewart, and Ben Myron. *Director:* Mike Figgis. *Screenplay:* Mike Figgis. *Director of Photography:* Declan Quinn. *Editor:* John Smith. *Music:* Mike Figgis. *Music Editor:* Nigel Heath. *Sound:* Pawel Wdowczak and (music) Steven Price. *Sound Editor:* Nigel Heath. *Casting:* Nancy Foy. *Production Designer:* Waldemar Kalinowski. *Art Director:* Barry Kingston. *Set Designer:* Theodore Sharps. *Set Decorator:* Florence Fellman and Carolyn Cartwright. *Special Effects:* Gary Bentley. *Costumes:* Laura Goldsmith and Enid Harris. *Make-up:* Kathryn Bihr. *Stunt Coordinator:* Jeff Imada and Jeff Ward. *Running time:* 103 minutes. *MPAA Rating:* R.

CAST: Wesley Snipes (Max Carlyle); Nastassja Kinski (Karen); Kyle MacLachlan (Vernon); Ming-Na Wen (Mimi Carlyle); Robert Downey, Jr. (Charlie); Marcus Paulk (Young Charlie); Natalie Trott (Saffron); John Calley (Charlie's Father); Glenn Plummer (George); Amanda Donohoe (Margaux); Zoë Nathenson (Mickey); Thomas Haden Church (Don); Vincent Ward (Nathan); John Ratzenberger (Phil); Thomas Kopache (Merv); Annabelle Gurwitch (Marie); Susan Barnes (Malinda); Michelle Jonas (Malissa); Margaret Makinen (Receptionist); Mike Figgis (Hotel Clerk); Johanna Torell (Doctor Olsson); Julian Sands (Nurse Chris); Donovan Leitch (Kevin); Ione Skye, Xander Berkeley, and Greta Gaines (Charlie's Friends); Crystal Pite (Title Dance Sequence/Featured Dancer); Christopher Bauer (Bartender); Anne Lambtron and Nick Sandow (Muggers); Michela Zanchi and Tiffany Hecht (Armani Women); Bill Raymond (Gridlock Taxi Driver); Tracy Thorne (Helicopter Traffic Woman); Oscar Colon and Ahmed Ben Larby (Delegate in Lines); Saffron Burrows (Supermodel); Robie Yamamoto (Featured Male Model); Chris Edwards, Richard Caselnova, and Jeffrey Howard Kaufman (Policemen); Joseph John Scott (Flower Vendor); Trula Marcus (Party Guest); Tava Smiley (Hotel Receptionist); David Acosta (Caterer); Aixa Maldonado (Caterer's Assistant); Nadira Hall (Middle Eastern Musician); Daniel Hawk Hicks and Lee Wells (Doormen); Xavier Urquieta (Pakastani Diplomat); Rachel Escalera (Nanny).

LOS ANGELES TIMES, 11/14/97, Calendar/p. 2, Kenneth Turan

In creating "One Night Stand," writer-director Mike Figgis has, like the celebrated Dr. Frankenstein, come up with something of a monstrosity: a pompous, pretentious sex farce. If that sounds unnerving, you have no idea.

With an overload of contrivance and a weakness for fake intimacy, "One Night" has unmistakable farce components. But Figgis, humorless enough to think he's being profound, is so determined to bring this to the level of "Tristan and Isolde" that you don't know whether to laugh at the wrong places or cry out in frustration.

"One Night Stand" is being conspicuously marketed as the newest work "from the director of 'Leaving Las Vegas,'" a designation that doesn't help the new film and makes the old one look worse by comparison. Seeing the same visual and aural techniques used on unintentionally preposterous material might embarrass those who thought the earlier film was in any way profound.

Though they tend to look like smoke and mirrors here, Figgis' stylistic touches are all present. Cinematographer Declan Quinn is back from "Las Vegas" to add his jittery, eye-catching camerawork. And Figgis himself has once again come up with a moody jazz score that is undeniably the picture's strongest element. "Without the music," the director has said, "I would have no interest in filmmaking."

People who think like that may make wonderful music, but they really shouldn't be writing their own scripts. What results here is bathetic lines, like "Everything in me that was hollow and false seemed so clear suddenly," that sound like parody but are meant to be taken with dreadful seriousness.

Almost from its opening moments, when L.A. commercial director Max Carlyle (Wesley Snipes) faces the camera on a Manhattan street and reveals he's a happily married 35-year-old husband and father with quite the successful career, "One Night Stand" starts on the wrong foot.

There is an air of false and unearned closeness about that mock-documentary technique that creates distance despite trying hard for connection.

Things soon get worse when Max uses his trip to New York to reconnect with Charlie (Robert Downey Jr.), a gay performance artist who used to be his best friend. Not only is Charlie such a defensive pain in the neck it's difficult to imagine him as anyone's best friend, but making him HIV-positive feels manipulative in the worst way.

It's in a hotel restaurant that Max and the beautiful Karen (Nastassja Kinski) first notice each other. But he's happily married, remember, and as it turns out so is she. End of story, right? Of course not.

Instead what happens is an ever-widening series of coincidences, from ink on a shirt to a shared love of the Juilliard String Quartet to massive Manhattan gridlock to a mugging that would never happen now that crime fighter Rudolph Giuliani is still New York's mayor. Figgis' script becomes so insistent in offering excuses and mitigating circumstances out of fear that we'll dislike this couple for cheating that audiences will be tempted to shout, "Enough already, do whatever you want, just get on with it."

The act itself, it we're to judge by the elaborate way it's been staged and accompanied by a trumpet solo played by Figgis himself, was apparently a prime Kodak moment for the concupiscent couple. Karen heads off to parts unknown and Max returns to L.A. to pick fights with his gorgeous wife, Mimi (Ming-Na Wen), and get secretly grumpy because the purity of that one night reveals the rest of the world for the dross it is.

All this time Max's pal Charlie is getting sicker and sicker, and soon a return trip to New York is unavoidable. That's the point where "One Night Stand's" coincidences and improbabilities go into mind-numbing overdrive and, as the coup de grace, Charlie gets so ill that, in true movie fashion, he becomes an all-knowing sage able to offer Max the wisdom he's sorely in need of.

Unaware that they're being betrayed by their own movie, both Snipes and Kinski (who does bite her lip a bit too often) work hard and with acceptable effectiveness, but "One Night Stand" is beyond salvation. "Life is short," says Charlie in one of his bursts of Talmudic insight, "the tree-huggers are right." Too short to waste on foolishness like this.

NEW YORK, 12/8/97, p. 63, David Denby

Mike Figgis's great 1995 movie *Leaving Las Vegas*, starring Nicolas Cage and Elisabeth Shue, chronicled the wrenching final days of a lowlife Tristan and Isolde. His new romantic drama, *One Night Stand*, is smoother, sleeker, and, though hardly without skill, not nearly as interesting. The picture reminded me of something intelligent but essentially novelettish and chic from Europe 30 years ago—something like Claude Sautet's *Les Choses de la Vie*, in which the French bourgeoisie smoked too much, played at adultery, and smashed up their cars. A successful Los Angeles advertising director, Max (Wesley Snipes), visits an old friend in New York who has AIDS (Robert Downey Jr.), misses his plane home, and spends a night with a lovely woman he meets in the city (Nastassja Kinski). Max goes back to Los Angeles, but now he's dissatisfied with his high-powered job and his snappish, sexually demanding wife (Ming-Na Wen), who orders him around and bores and exhausts him in bed. Poor Max! When he returns to New York a year later to see his friend, now dying, he runs into his one-night stand, and the flame, as they say, is relit.

The situations are so obvious that the audience giggles, but *One Night Stand,* like everything else Figgis has done (including *Stormy Monday* and *Internal Affairs),* has style and more than a little flavor. Figgis, a musician as well as a writer-director, likes to work off-center, concentrating more on the embellishments and variations than on the main tune. The episodes illustrating Max, a commercial director, at work are very glitzy and MTV-ish indeed, but the scenes of friendship, sex, and marital discord play in expressive fits and starts, with inadvertent moments, stolen glances, repressed laughs, and unfinished thoughts dominating the meager spoken dialogue. Figgis gets a lot out of Wesley Snipes, who has been known to bluster his way through movies. This time, Snipes conveys a real sense of privacy—his face is always alive, and we can see a man registering both dissatisfactions and pleasures that he's not eager to share. Nastassja Kinski smiles and has very little to say, but she's charming, and Robert Downey Jr. gives an intense and bitter performance as the dying young man. At his insistence, his friends give a big party on the day of his funeral, and everyone gets laid. Figgis has a show-business sense of things encompassing an idiosyncratic moral view. The meaning of the movie seems to be that adultery is a celebration of life. Well, maybe.

NEW YORK POST, 11/14/97, p. 50, Thelma Adams

After "Leaving Las Vegas," director Mike Figgis goes bicoastal for "One Night Stand." He exchanges contemplative drunks and hookers for contemplative yuppies: beautiful successful people with issues of the heart and soul.

Max (Wesley Snipes) is cruising. At 35, he's a high-powered Hollywood commercial director. He's like a Talkin Heads song: He has a beautiful wife, beautiful kids, a beautiful life. He doesn't know it yet, but it's stopped making sense.

And then, on a business trip to New York, Max meets Karen (Nastassia Kinski). She's not just any married rocket scientist. She's a beautiful blonde with a mysterious accent, a mysterious vulnerability, a mysterious mysteriousness. They click.

For one night, Max and Karen make love like a cool jazz song, long and soulful. Max returns to his bright, sunny life, his wife, his kids, his dog, his job. But he can't get Karen out of his head.

Figgis, who wrote the script, gives the creaky plot an immediacy, a contemporary rhythm and flavor. We feel this is the New York-L.A. axis as it's really lived by the privileged, sushi-eating, expense-account class.

As Max, Snipes seduces. He introduces himself directly to the camera, confessing that he used to be "the most promising director on the Lower East Side" before he headed for the coast and commercials.

After the affair, Max begins to recede inside himself, behind slogans he doesn't half-believe. Snipes won a best actor award at the Venice Film Festival for this intimate performance.

His Max is a man standing at the uneasy intersection between art and commerce, love and infidelity.

Figgis supports Snipes with an ensemble of well-cast characters who seem fully capable of spinning the movie on its axis and carrying it in another direction, to tell other stories of fast-lane life.

Chief among these characters is Charlie (Robert Downey). He's an HIV-positive Manhattan artist and Max's best pal from his young and restless downtown days. Downey seizes the screen with vigor, charm and real pain, addiction-wracked body a perfect stand-in for the rigors of AIDS.

As Max's wife, Ming-Na Wen ("The Joy Luck Club") is a revelation. Her sexy mom knows what she wants and how to get it. She's a funny straight talker who appears so natural on screen it's as if she could walk off the celluloid corner with her shopping bags and meet you in front of the theater.

In "One Night Stand," the pain and passion feel real, but the details are often high gloss. Max's kids are accessories, his character lacks specificity and Kinski's Karen is a composite dream woman, a scientist in the perfect little black dress.

"One Night Stand" plays like an elegant, arty "thirtysomething." That's not an insult: It's crisp, current, entertaining, intelligent, funny and moving. But it doesn't withstand deeper scrutiny.

NEWSDAY, 11/14/97, Part II/p. B15, Jack Mathews

In movies, expectation is often the forerunner of disappointment, and so it follows with Mike Figgis' "One Night Stand," the director's first film since "Leaving Las Vegas." Again, Figgis' attention is on a man following his self-destructive impulses, only this time he is on a far less lethal path. In fact, Wesley Snipes' Max Carlyle may be on the path of enlightenment.

"Leaving Las Vegas" is the story of an alcoholic on a planned suicidal bender, and the lonely prostitute who attempts to see him through it. "One Night Stand" is about a married man who has lost his way, and only begins to, realize it when he bumps into a married woman with whom he'd had a brief encounter a year before, and finds himself in love with her.

Theirs was no ordinary one night stand, if there is such a thing. Take the wedding rings away from Max and Karen (Nastassja Kinski) and their one night stand has the arc of a typical New York romance, a courtship of weeks or months condensed into a layover.

They meet, they go to a concert, they get mugged, they go to bed. Figgis takes care and devotes a lot of time, making clear that their relationship bears no resemblance to that of the groping lovers in "Fatal Attraction." Max, a successful director of TV commercials, is surrounded by beautiful women every day, and has no trouble resisting temptation. Karen is a business woman from upstate New York, equally faithful to her husband.

But when they meet, by chance in a Manhattan hotel lobby, their attraction is genuine, and by the time they end up in each other's arms, they've developed such a strong romantic bond that the sex is a greater expression of feeling than passion.

That feeling is missing from Max's marriage, and having attained it with Karen, its absence begins to push him away from both his wife, Mimi (Ming-Na Wen), and his unfulfilling job. A year later, when Max returns to New York to spend time with a friend (Robert Downey Jr.) dying from AIDS, he discovers—to his surprise, apprehension and eventual delight—that Karen's husband is his friend's brother (Kyle MacLachlan), and that the feelings they shared are still alive.

Figgis takes some wrong turns from that point, and the film begins to feel like a modern Hollywood screwball comedy. In fact, there is a lot of humor throughout "One Night Stand," including an hilarious bit when Max returns home from his first tryst, bearing a tell-tale scent that only the family dog detects. But where the story ultimately takes us is contrived, emotionally false and too cute by a mile.

It's too bad because the early and middle going are tremendously compelling. Snipes and Kinski have great chemistry, and create a plausibly deep and satisfying romantic relationship in that one night stand.

The performances are all good. Downey has one of the longest death bed scenes on film, and playing a man fighting his fear of death and racing time to resolve issues with friends and family, he makes our hearts ache. And MacLachlan is wonderfully smarmy, so homophobic, he wears gloves when he visits his dying brother in the hospital.

Figgis' films are always heavily stylized, and on this one, he broaches self-indulgence. The film percolates with in-and-out fades, to the rhythms of a score (written by Figgis) that often overwhelms the dramatic action and even makes it hard at times to hear dialogue spoken in an otherwise quiet setting. Ultimately, the style takes more away from the experience of "One Night Stand" than it adds, making the film promise more in its detail than it delivers in emotional impact.

SIGHT AND SOUND, 12/97, p. 49, John Wrathall

In New York on business, commercials director Max visits his friend Charlie, a gay choreographer, who has just found out he is HIV positive. Back at his hotel, Max notices another guest, Karen. The next day, his pen leaks in his shirt pocket. Karen points out the stain and, since Max has already checked out of his room, invites him back to hers to change. Accidentally missing his plane, Max goes to the string quartet concert Karen said she would be attending that night, and meets her there. In the street afterwards, they are mugged. Max goes back to the hotel with Karen to comfort her, and she offers him the spare bed in her room. During the night, they make love. The next morning, Max returns to Los Angeles, but his life now seems empty. He quarrels with colleagues at work and with his wife Mimi.

One year later, Max returns to New York to visit Charlie, who is dying. At the hospital, he meets Charlie's brother Vernon, who turns out to be married to Karen, When Mimi arrives from LA, the two couples go out for dinner together. Vernon and Mimi talk animatedly, while Max and Karen scarcely speak. Visiting Charlie one day, Max finds Karen there. Charlie wakes up to see them kissing. When Karen has left, Max confesses to Charlie about his one night stand. Charlie tells him he has to work things out for himself.

Charlie dies. At the wake, Max and Karen sneak off to the summer house to make love and catch Vernon and Mimi in flagrante. Exactly one year later, the four of them meet up again. When they part, it transpires that Vernon is now with Mimi, and Max with Karen.

Mike Figgis has written in *Sight and Sound* of his enthusiasm for François Truffaut's *The Woman Next Door*, and it was perhaps an echo of that film (the story of former lovers whose marriages are disrupted when they meet again through an unlikely coincidence) which attracted him to Joe Eszterhas' original script for *One Night Stand*. So thoroughly has Figgis reworked the material that Eszterhas' name has now gone from the credits altogether. What was once described as an "erotically charged thriller" has now emerged as something much more tender and, despite its thoroughly American settings, much more European.

For a product of the US mainstream, *One Night Stand* is a very hard film to classify. It's at once comic and tragic, naturalistic and stylised, simple and sophisticated, shallow and deep. The plot is drawn in broad strokes, almost playfully neat in its construction. But within this framework, Figgis homes in on the tiniest of gestures and emotions. At the same time, he seems to take utterly for granted the hot potatoes of inter-racial adultery and gay-straight male friendship, out of which most American films, if they dared allude to them at all, would surely make a meal.

After the triumph of *Leaving Las Vegas,* Figgis has apparently been allowed to make a film completely on his own terms, as he most certainly was not on *The Browning Version* and *Mr Jones.* And, free from studio interference and budget restrictions, he shows himself to be a filmmaker in complete control of his medium. He is now credited as sole writer, but it's not so much as writer-director but as composer-director that he really comes into his own. Figgis often allows the music to drown out the dialogue, so we concentrate not so much on how characters speak to each other as on how they simply are together. At the Juilliard Quartet concert they attend together, Max and Karen whisper to each other, but we don't hear a word, we just see the growing intimacy between them, and Beethoven does the rest, Figgis often changes music abruptly mid-scene, almost in the style of Godard, except that here he is using his own music, as well as other people's. For example, the scene in which Max quarrels with his wife Mimi in their bedroom is intangibly enhanced by the way Figgis accompanies it, starting with a funky, repetitive bass riff, cutting momentarily to silence as Mimi hits Max, then bringing in the Beethoven quartet Max heard earlier with Karen.

With his editor John Smith, Figgis gives the film a wonderfully light, evanescent rhythm. Slow and fast motion are employed, but the dominant stylistic trope is the fade, which he uses to extraordinary effect. In the early scenes, when Max notices Karen in the hotel foyer, the handheld camera captures the way people look at each other with a breathtaking tracery of glances and subtle shifts of focus, the momentary fade-outs almost like the blinking of an eyelid. Later, when Max and Karen unexpectedly meet again by Charlie's hospital bed, Figgis fades again as they catch each other's eye—a visual punctuation which makes the moment all the more charged by seeming to undercut it.

Max and Karen's relationship is mapped out in looks, not words. The intimacy we sense between them comes less from conversations in which they get to know each other than from the way Figgis frames them together. The first time the two couples eat out together at a sushi restaurant, Vernon and Mimi talk incessantly, while Max and Karen exchange complicit glances, wincing at their spouses' brashness. When Karen reveals that she is a rocket scientist, Max does a wonderful doubletake: it's as much of a surprise to him as it is to us.

Though the film opens with Max talking straight to camera, elsewhere Figgis seems to be eavesdropping on his characters, almost like a documentarist. He elicits correspondingly detailed and truthful performances from his cast: Wesley Snipes deservedly won the Best Actor award at Venice, while Robert Downey Jr has the showy role as the dying Aids-victim Charlie (in scenes which make *Philadelphia* seem overblown and fake by comparison). But perhaps the most impressive and surprising work here is from Kyle MacLachlan as Charlie's brother Vernon. We first meet him outside Charlie's hospital room, where he chats away to Max, inappropriately bright and casual. When Max excuses himself, Figgis captures the tiniest darkening of MacLachlan's features, and we know that Vernon is just putting a brave face on his own grief.

Where Figgis really confounds expectations, however, is in his treatment of the "one night stand" itself. As scripted by Eszterhas and directed by Adrian Lyne, who was once attached to the project, this would no doubt have been a thrashing sexual *tour de force.* Once Max and Karen have returned to her hotel room, Figgis takes his time building up to the big moment, with more fade-outs tantalisingly drawing out their sleepless night in separate beds. When they finally come together, it's for the briefest, tenderest of embraces, before Figgis cuts to the tiny speck of Max's plane high in the sky as he flies back to Los Angeles the following morning (perhaps an allusion to a sperm, and to a similar shot Godard used to show the moment of conception in *Je vous salue, Marie*). Max returns to his wife Mimi, with whom he has the athletic, vocal, vigorous—and empty—sex which almost every other filmmaker would pass off as the real thing.

In fact, the whole film seems to take on the quality of a one night stand. At once light and heavy, it's rich in possibilities. It could mean nothing, or it could change your life.

VILLAGE VOICE, 11/25/97, p. 91, Michael Atkinson

An elliptical, jazzy study in sensual obsession that for all its interracial humpery and HIV empathy comes off lacquered in various shades of vanilla, Mike Figgis's *One Night Stand* doesn't explore its topic so much as flirt with it. Figgis shoots as if in a dozy, postcoital stupor (fading to black and back again in midscene), while the often beguilingly informal contours of his script inevitably edge it toward haphazardness. In the end what you get is a character study that never becomes intimate with its subject.

Figgis also scores his films, and the way *One Night Stand's* lazy-man's-jazz soundtrack runs roughshod over the dialogue makes you wonder where his loyalties lie. When you can hear him, Wesley Snipes broods at the film's center as a smug commercial director enjoying a career acme, a sexy Asian American wife (Ming-Na Wen), and an *Architectural Digest*-bound Beverly Hills home. After visiting his old partner Robert Downey Jr. (a snippy gay performance artist looking down an HIV gun barrel) in New York, Snipes meets cute with Nastassja Kinski. They share a Beethoven string quartet, a mugging, and softcore sex.

Back home, Snipes's primary concern is dodging the suspicion of infidelity, which even the family dog harbors. (His distraught reaction shots are the funniest thing in the film.) Meanwhile, Snipes gets vaguely dyspeptic with his wife and coworkers, until everyone is summoned back to Downey's deathbed for an extended elegy and subsequent Irish-style bash. Rather than plumb the characters or the issues, Figgis goes for the O. Henry windup and wallows in upmarket hepness—all cigarettes, sax solos, and long looks across the room.

VILLAGE VOICE, 12/2/97, p. 84, Dennis Lim

The star turn in Mike Figgis's *One Night Stand* belongs not to Wesley Snipes or Nastassja Kinski (whose moody, pouty characters share the title encounter) but to Ming-Na Wen, who makes the most of a love triangle's least advantageous comer. A spark plug of life in a film that's often barely awake, Wen sidesteps the many pitfalls of a role that, as scripted, must have been one-dimensionally vacuous. (She's obviously used to rising above her material, having comfortably survived two seasons an NBCs routinely insipid *The Single Guy*.)

Playing Snipes's extrovert wife, Mimi (a character who in the original Joe Eszterhas script was, physically at least, "a Cindy Crawford type"), Wen's main concern was to instill a degree of complexity. "I wanted to make sure she wasn't a woman that Wesley's character could easily leave. In doing so, he faces a difficult, adult choice." Wen defends the film's casually multiracial cast as more than tokenistic contrivance. "The fact that race isn't an issue is interesting. The film is subtle—its about not being judgmental. Mimi's a woman, who happens to be Asian, happens to be a wife and mother, happens to love sex, loves dominating during sex."

In a hilarious sex scene with Snipes, Wen takes charge, spitting out instructions of near military precision. "I remember Mike wanted me to keep getting louder," she laughs. "It was very improvised. You really can't calculate those scenes. I had no idea how it would turn out. When I first saw it, I was squirming in my seat, but it made me feel better that people found it funny."

Next year, Wen will be seen in *Parallels*, an ABC sci-fi movie of the week, and on Broadway in *Golden Child*, a play by David Henry Hwang. She also provides the lead voice in next summer's Disney animation, *Mulan*, which she describes as "an epic coming-of-age story set in China. I play a young woman warrior who dresses up as a boy and joins the army to save her father."

Wen, who's perhaps still best known for her role in *The Joy Luck Club*, has landed a number of roles (among them, Mimi) originally intended for white actresses. Asian American women in Hollywood are, she says, still expected to be "the exotic beauty or the war victim." But, she notes, "men have it even worse—gang member, the geeky waiter, the kung-fu master, the corrupt anything. Some of these roles can be legitimate if the script is good, but often that's not how it is."

Also reviewed in:
CHICAGO TRIBUNE, 11/14/97, Friday/p. F, Mark Caro
NEW YORK TIMES, 11/14/97, p. E19, Janet Maslin
VARIETY, 9/8-14/97, p. 77, David Rooney
WASHINGTON POST, 11/14/97, p. D7, Stephen Hunter
WASHINGTON POST, 11/14/97, Weekend/p. 50, Desson Howe

OPERATION CONDOR

A Dimension Films release in association with Media Asia Distribution. *Executive Producer:* Raymond Chow. *Producer:* Leonard Ho. *Director:* Jackie Chan. *Screenplay:* Jackie Chan and Edward Tang. *Editorial Consultant:* Rod Dean. *Director of Photography:* Wong Ngok Tai. *Editor:* Cheung Yiu Chung. *Music:* Stephen Endelman. *Sound:* Glenn T. Morgan. *Art Director:* Oliver Wong. *Art Director:* Eddie Ma and Lo Ka Yiu. *Costumes:* Thomas Chong and Carroll Gordon. *Running time:* 92 minutes. *MPAA Rating:* PG-13.

CAST: Jackie Chan (Jackie); Carol Cheng (Ada); Eva Cobo de Garcia (Elsa); Shoko Ikeda (Momoko); Alfred Brel Sanchez (Adolph); Ken Goodman (Adolf's Guard #1); Gregory Tartaglia (Adolf's Guard #2); Lyn Percival (Adolf's Guard #3); Bruce Fontaine (Adolf's Guard #4); Archer Wayne (Adolf's Guard #5); Brandon Charles (Adolf's Guard #6); Low Houi Kang (Adolf's Guard #7); Peter Klimenko (Adolf's Guard #8); Christian Perrochaud (Adolf's Guard #9); Jonathan Isgar (Tasza); Daniel Mintz (Amon); Bozidar Smiljanic (Duke Scapio); Mark King (Duke's Guard #1); Bryan Baker (Duke's Guard #2); Charles Yoemans (Man with Stolen Clothes).

LOS ANGELES TIMES, 7/18/97, Calendar/p. 14, Kevin Thomas

Jackie Chan's terrific 1990 "Armour of God II," a martial arts variation on "Raiders of the Lost Ark" with Jackie in search of Nazi gold in the heart of the Sahara Desert, has been painstakingly reworked into an English-language version and retitled "Operation Condor." Trimmed by 13 minutes and fitted out with a dynamic new score and sound design, the film becomes far more accessible to Chan's mainstream fans.

Until Chan's recent U.S. breakthrough, his countless films, many of them delightful, inspired entertainments, could be seen outside Chinatown only in art theaters and only occasionally—and always in Cantonese with English subtitles. ("Armour of God" refers to an ancient suit of armor, a sacred relic, which Jackie tracked down in the first film.)

The first of Chan's films directed-and co-written-by himself to get wide distribution in America, "Operation Condor" is simplicity itself. Dimension Films' production notes tell us that Jackie is playing "the world's greatest secret agent," code name Condor, and who would argue with that?

He's been summoned to the U.S. Embassy in Madrid, where a U.N. representative hands him an ultra-urgent assignment: locate 240 tons of Nazi gold buried somewhere in the Sahara before a terrorist group does.

In taking on the assignment he winds up accompanied by three beautiful women: Carol Cheng as his nominal boss, Eva Cobo de Garcia as the blond granddaughter of the German officer in charge of hiding the gold—she says she wants "to clear his name"—and Shoko Ikeda, who just turns up. They're on hand mainly for pulchritude purposes and some mildly risque banter, much like the glamour girls in an old Bob Hope movie or TV show.

Transforming "Armour of God II" into "Operation Condor" has rendered its story line extremely vague, almost to the point of nonexistence; some soundtrack narration could have helped. But you go to a Jackie Chan movie not for the plot but for his fabulous, pyrotechnic acrobatic and martial arts skills, his sunny personality and flawless grace as a world-class screen comedian.

In any event, Jackie is swiftly off to Morocco, with lots of high jinks and derring-do in a picturesque old caravansary-style hotel and then on to the desert, where the gold turns up hidden in a vast subterranean fortress.

Spacious, dramatic settings are the inevitable locales for the all-important climactic sequences in action-adventure thrillers, and this fortress fits the bill for "Operation Condor," especially since it's equipped with an enormously powerful wind machine that allows for some amazing stunt work.

Chan does his own stunts, and he has said that as a result, "My films show what is humanly possible." And that's why even adventure fantasies as slight and preposterous as "Operation Condor" are fun.

NEW YORK POST, 7/18/97, p. 47, Michael Medved

Like other Jackie Chan movies, "Operation Condor" is so cheerfully unpretentious, so straightforward in its silliness and shabbiness, that normal cinematic standards apply.

Sure, the script is inane, the dubbing dreadful, the acting (especially by the various villains) is embarrassingly awful, and the special effects are pathetic.

The movie still provides its superstar's indestructible athleticism and likability, some very funny, self-deprecating gags daring stunts (performed, as usual, by Jackie himself) and enough furiously frenetic, elaborately choreographed fight scenes to satisfy the legion of Chan fans.

This time the picture also delivers some authentic-looking locations—a far cry from "Rumble in the Bronx," which portrayed rough neighborhoods of New York with the snowcapped peaks of Vancouver visible in the background.

"Condor"—a re-dubbed version of a 1991 Chan movie called "Armour of God II: Operation Condor" opens with a thoroughly entertaining prologue on a jungle mountaintop in the Philippines where our hero emulates Indiana Jones by stealing a glowing gem from an idol in a cave; he barely escapes with his life, descending the treacherous slopes inside a handy-dandy inflatable device that gives new meaning to the phrase "follow the bouncing ball."

The movie itself then follows an odd bounce to Madrid, where Chan gets an assignment from some U.N. officials conveniently assembled in the American embassy. He's a secret agent (for someone or other) who's code-named "Condor" but consistently addressed as Jackie.

Teamed with a pretty expert in desert survival (Carol Cheng), he's sent to the Sahara to recover 240 tons of gold buried there by Nazis. Along the way, they're joined by the blonde, leggy granddaughter (Eva Cobo de Garcia) of the German officer who buried the treasure, and a ditzy spiritual seeker (Shoko Ikeda) with a pet scorpion named "Ding Ding."

To reach their destination beneath the burning sands of Morocco, Jackie and his three babes must of course fight off various terrorists, paramilitary thugs, and even an aging Nazi in a wheelchair (Alfred Brel Sanchez) imaginatively named "Adolf."

Even by the low standards of the genre, the repeated stereotypes of violent, stupid, devious and greedy Arabs (all played by non-Arabs) are grotesquely—and gratuitously insulting.

In contrast to his previous U.S. box-office triumphs, Chan directs this one himself and significantly alters the way his character functions. Rather than an invincible superhero, smoothly dispatching scores of opponents, this struggling protagonist sometimes even loses one-on-one encounters.

In fact, there's an almost masochistic edge to all the painful chops and hops and falls Chan stages for himself. These hurts hardly matter, however, since the last third of the movie (shot on a sound stage representing a Nazi underground lair and abandoned wind tunnel) is so shadowy that the interminable action is often incoherent, and the elaborate expenditure of hot air represents a blown opportunity.

NEWSDAY, 7/18/97, Part II/p. B7, John Anderson

Like a smiling rubber ball in a particularly hostile pinball machine, action god Jackie Chan -is all recoil and reflexes, his movies an exercise in voyeuristic sado-masochism: knowing he does all the physics-defying stunts himself gives them even more of an edge, a virtual titillation. Watching the outtakes that standardly run with his closing credits which are as agony-oriented as "America's Funniest Home Videos," except they're funny—makes you realize how much he goes through for his art.

We share a bit too much of his pain, however, in "Operation Condor," an older Chan feature, released in 1991, that's been dubbed and recut by Chan and the Miramax offspring, Dimension

Films. They probably should have left it alone. The mouths and the dialogue are like trains leaving different stations at different times, in different directions. The substitute voices of the women characters—particularly Ada (Carol Cheng) and Elsa (Eva Cobo de Garcia), who accompany Jackie on his search for hidden Nazi gold—are whiny enough that any indignation you feel about them being slapped will evaporate like the movie's plot line.

The abusive types include the film's comedy Arabs, who are about the most cartoonish ethnic stereotypes you're likely to see in a major motion picture. If you laugh at them, forgive yourself. It's not that they're funny, it's just that they're so unlikely. Pro-Arab pickets were outside this week's premiere at Manhattan's Ziegfeld Theater, putting a cramp in everyone's good time. Their complaints turned out to be understated.

The line on Chan is that his earlier films "Drunken Master," for instance, or his earliest directing efforts, "Fearless Hyena" and "The Young Master"—far surpass his later efforts, marrying comedy and action with unsurpassed style. "Condor" comes out of a middle period, after some of Chan's celebrated major injuries and before his more Hollywood-oriented efforts (including the most recent "First Strike" and "Rumble in the Bronx"; last year's "Supercop" was another reissue). But even the "Police Story" series contains more sophistication than "Condor," which borrows all but the theology from "Raiders of the Lost Ark" and is punctuated by Cheng and Cobo de Garcia screaming like girls, getting in Jackie's way and beating up mercenaries with helmets while performing a kick-line.

Chan, however, always delivers the action and there are several sequences that might make your hair fall out. Always a gifted comedian (he's the Hong Kong Buster Keaton) and his own best director, Chan is a walking, talking and occasionally limping human special effect. Whether "Condor" has wings remains another story.

VILLAGE VOICE, 7/29/97, p. 71, J. Hoberman

Another sort of '80s nostalgia is induced by the belated commercial opening of Jackie Chan's *Armour of God II: Operation Condor*. [The reference is to *Air Force One*; see Hoberman's review of that film.] Released in Chinatown six years ago, this most expensive of Chan productions has been rescored and dubbed (or, in the case of some actors, redubbed) into English, courtesy of Miramax's Dimension division—who may be thanked (or not) for eliminating a particularly egregious instance of karaoke accompaniment.

Operation Condor, as the title has been shortened, is basically Jackie in the Temple of Doom. Accompanied by a gaggle of action babes, the affable star searches for Nazi gold in the depths of the Sahara. (Next time: Switzerland.) Given the doggedly neocolonialist cast of credulous, comic natives and stupid, villainous Arabs, *Operation* might have been improved had the dubbing been scripted by the Firesign Theater. As it is, the movie is mondo cheese, albeit bracketed by two inventive set pieces—a motorcycle chase through old Madrid and a comic slugfest in a wind tunnel.

Playing the klutz until he goes into action, Chan is the most inventively kinetic movie star since Fred Astaire—his martial arts/acrobatic/ stunt riding virtuosity is matched only by a comic ability to convert anything into a weapon. Part of the Chan mystique is his refusal to use a stunt double; too bad that he developed an American crossover audience after his capacity for physical punishment had considerably diminished. His new fans would have been far better served by the rerelease of his mid-'80s classics: *Project A, Police Story*, and the original *Armor of God*.

Also reviewed in:
NEW YORK TIMES, 7/18/97, p. C14, Anita Gates
VARIETY, 7/21-27/97, p. 39, Derek Elley
WASHINGTON POST, 7/18/97, p. B6, Rita Kempley

OSCAR AND LUCINDA

A Fox Searchlight Pictures release in association with the Australian Film Finance Corporation and the New South Wales Film and Television Office of a Dalton Films production. *Producer:*

Robin Dalton and Timothy White. *Director:* Gillian Armstrong. *Screenplay:* Laura Jones. *Based on the novel by:* Peter Carey. *Director of Photography:* Geoffrey Simpson. *Editor:* Nicholas Beauman. *Music:* Thomas Newman. *Music Editor:* Bill Bernstein. *Sound:* Ben Osmo and (music) Shawn Murphy and Tom Winslow. *Sound Editor:* Andrew Plain. *Casting:* Alison Barrett and Kathleen Mackie. *Production Designer:* Luciana Arrighi. *Art Director:* Tom Nursey, John Wingrove, John Ralph, and Paul Ghiradani. *Set Decorator:* Sally Campbell. *Special Effects:* Steve Courtley. *Costumes:* Janet Patterson. *Make-up:* Kirsten Veysey. *Stunt Coordinator:* Rocky McDonald and Graeme Crowther. *Running time:* 131 minutes. *MPAA Rating:* R.

CAST: Ralph Fiennes (Oscar Hopkins/Oscar's Great Grandson); Cate Blanchett (Lucinda Leplastrier); Ciaran Hinds (Reverend Dennis Hasset); Tom Wilkinson (Hugh Stratton); Richard Roxburgh (Mr. Jeffris); Clive Russell (Theophilus); Bille Brown (Percy Smith); Josephine Byrnes (Miriam Chadwick); Barnaby Kay (Wardley-Fish); Barry Otto (Jimmy D'Abbs); Linda Bassett (Betty Stratton); Polly Cheshire (Young Lucinda); Gillian Jones (Elizabeth Leplastrier); Robert Menzies (Abel Leplastrier); Adam Hayes (Young Oscar); James Tingby (13-Year-Old Oscar); Matyelok Gibbs (Mrs. Williams); Sonia Ritter (Fanny Drabble); Peter Whitford (Mr. Ahearn); Lynette Curran (Mrs. Ahearn); Ron Blanchard (Steamer Captain); Colin Taylor (Frazer); Michelle Doake (Hotel Maid); Karen Vickery and Elspeth MacTavish (Society Gossips); Andrea Moor (Miss Shaddock); Leverne McDonnell (Miss Malcolm); Geoff Morrell (Charley Fig); Christian Manon (Mr. Tomasetti); Douglas Hedge (Dog Pit Caller); Lucy Knight (Belgian Girl); Tobias Saunders (Belgian Boy); Marianne Borgo (Belgian Grandmother); Vanessa Seydoux (Belgian Mother); Catherine Harvey (Melody); Ray MaCallan (Purser's Assistant); Mark Denny and Andrew Davis (Leviathan Stewards); Paul Rogers and Matt Potter (Gambling Stewards); Billie Pluffer and Louella Pluffer (Rabbit Girls); David Page (Aboriginal Busker); Norman Kaye (Bishop Dancer); Michael Duggan (The Dean); Basil Clarke (Elderly Parishioner); Babs McMillan (Mrs. Judd); Mary Kavanagh (Trevis Girl); Treffyn Koreshoff (Trevis Boy); Patrick Blackwell (The Verger); Lucy Bell (Mrs. Mary Hasset); Wing Hall (Fan Tan Croupier); Cassy Huang and Meng Soh (Fan Tan Players); Chris Haywood (Mr. Judd); Judi Farr (Mrs. Smith); Stuart Campbell (Glass Worker); Leslie Daymon (Glassworks Foreman); Andre Lillis (Waiter); Janet Foye and Dacre King (Diners); Andrew S. Gilbert, Sandy Winton, and Damian Monk (Expeditioners); Greg Segal (Young Carpenter); Paul Shillingsworth and Walangari Karntawara (Narcoo Guides); Roy Gordon, Kevin Walker, and Brett Laurie (Kumbaingiri Men); Steve Rodgers (Man in Tavern); Kim Hillas (Publican's Wife); Elma Kris (Aboriginal Woman); Fiona Press (Mrs. Trevis); Elaine Hughes (Kumbaingiri Woman); Philip Dodd (Government Inspector); Patrick Andrews (Oscar's Son); Taleah Melenhorst (Oscar's Great-Great-Granddaughter); Geoffrey Rush (Narrator).

LOS ANGELES TIMES, 12/31/97, Calendar/p. 8, Kevin Thomas

Gillian Armstrong's highly assured "Oscar and Lucinda," based on the Peter Carey novel Armstrong has long cherished, is such an audacious and unusual tale of love and destiny that you want to be bowled over by it. It has wit and style to burn, and creates an impeccable re-creation of Victorian society undergoing an industrialization that ultimately would have profound impact on the status of women. It has dash, both scope and intimacy and a poignant surprise finish—not to mention considerable complexity and substance.

Yet whether you ultimately will be bowled over by it will depend on how you react to Ralph Fiennes. As in the overrated "The English Patient," Fiennes here so swiftly projects a quality of such intense apartness and capacity for suffering that he taps a streak of showy martyrdom. For some of us that's a turnoff, for others it's yet further proof of what good training performing Shakespeare can be for British actors. In any event, Fiennes gives off a disproportionate aura of exquisite vulnerability.

Armstrong, working from Laura Jones' adroit adaptation, succinctly introduces us to Fiennes' Oscar and the beguiling Cate Blanchett's Lucinda, who meet on a ship bound from London to Sydney in the mid-19th century. Oscar, a would-be missionary, has endured a harsh, rural religious upbringing from his father only to discover a passion for gambling; eventually, he will come to view a belief in God as a bet.

Like Oscar, Lucinda has also had a single-parent rural childhood, but her mother was not only a rebel but rich. Lucinda's adult life has been a gamble, turning her back on the quiet married country life society would expect of her, to invest successfully in a Sydney glass factory with a rugged minister (Ciaran Hinds), who shares her passion for beautiful glass.

Oscar and Lucinda, clearly mutually attracted, seem made for each other with their risk-taking temperament and imagination, but the one thing that the clenched Oscar can't do is to declare his love for her in a direct manner, especially in the light of Lucinda's partnership with the imposing man of the cloth.

The means he ultimately hits upon to express it are so dramatic, involving such obsessive folly, that the film will inevitably bring to mind Werner Herzog's "Fitzcarraldo," inspired by a true story in which an Irishman hauled a ship over a mountain in an Amazonian jungle as part of a plan to finance the construction of an opera house in Manaus, Brazil.

Flawless contributions by Armstrong's crew make "Oscar and Lucinda" a vibrant period piece, buoyant yet incisive, and easily sustaining interest, if not generating deep involvement, throughout a just-under two-hour running time. Blanchett's naturalness throws Fiennes' theatricality in bold relief, and Armstrong's detachment allows for a coolness when her film could use more warmth.

Despite reservations about Fiennes' off-putting portrayal, "Oscar and Lucinda" is the most venturesome movie yet made by one of the best filmmakers of her time. Any picture made by the director of "My Brilliant Career," "Starstruck," "Mrs. Soffel," "The Last Days of Chez Nous," "Little Women" and especially "High Tide" is worth a gamble.

NEW STATESMAN, 3/27/98, p. 44, Gaby Wood

There was a moment about a third of the way through a screening of *Oscar and Lucinda,* when the Australian director Gillian Armstrong realised her preview audience had been "slightly misled". The people recruited in the Santa Monica mall thought they were coming to see, as Armstrong puts it with a faux-flouncy manner, "a *lovely* period drama from that *lovely* woman that did *Little Women,* starring *lovely* Ralph Fiennes."

Her laughter at the misconception is significant, since many might describe the film in exactly this way, even those who feel well disposed towards it. She attributes the preview audience's shock to the darkness and violence of Peter Carey's Booker prize-winning novel on which the film is based. But she does herself little justice.

There are other reasons why Armstrong's work is unlovely in the best of ways. Her subtle, well-crafted direction is consistently undercut by a devotion to oddness and difference. The pioneering heroines she has portrayed since *My Brilliant Career* in 1979 are not just strong, they are triumphantly awkward.

On the face of it, Armstrong herself couldn't be more accommodating. When I met her at the Dorchester she struck me as serene and full of good humour, pulled together and laissez-faire. Her face is a pleasure to watch and she speaks with such modesty one would assume it false were she not so simple and direct in everything she says.

My Brilliant Career, an adaptation of Miles Franklin's novel about a young woman with literary ambitions growing up in the outback and resisting the convention of marriage, is remembered fondly by tough women the world over. But its effect on the Australian film industry was far more dramatic. Armstrong was the first Australian woman to make a feature film in 50 years and she set the pace for her female compatriots, what she calls the "exciting mix" of Jane Campion, Jocelyn Moorhouse, Shirley Bassett and others, all of whom acknowledge their huge debt to her. When questioned on this subject, though, Armstrong is self-effacing: "Well," she says of that film, "I think it was very helpful—it certainly was being watched and judged, so luckily for us, it did well."

It is one of the happy peculiarities of recent Australian history that film and feminism grew up as sisters. Cinema had thrived there early in the century (Australia was one of the first four countries to be "wired for sound"). Women got the vote in Australia in 1902, 16 years before Britain. But by the time Armstrong became a student in the sixties, there was no longer any Australian film industry to speak of. Typing skills were her only ticket to a job—and Armstrong wasn't much of a typist.

She came to study film at Swinburne Art School through "one of those flukes in life". After waitressing, making tea for film crews and working on commercials, Armstrong joined the first year of the Australian Film and Television School—a "pilot" director's course. This was in the early 1970s. The Australian Film Commission wasn't set up until 1975, and the Australian Film Finance Corporation not until 1988. She became the only woman director in the group now known as the Australian New Wave: Peter Weir, Fred Schepisi, Bruce Beresford, George Miller, Philip Noyce. Armstrong helped to change those times, and when the industry was born again, newly liberated women were its leading figures.

She is quick to remark on the strength and charisma of her latest leading lady. Cate Blanchett as Lucinda changes from shot to shot; when she's off-screen you want her to come back so you can see what she'll look like next. Both of the main actors "had to be odd, off-centre," Armstrong says. "But you couldn't say what that oddness was going to be."

Blanchett and Fiennes play fidgety soul-mates who come together on a ship from England to Australia. They are both gamblers, in circumstances where that is not only improper but profoundly damaging. Their habit fuels the plot and it embodies the pull between them: they don't quite know how to love each other, but they are nonetheless addicted. Adrenaline and misunderstanding lead to the enactment of an impossible dream, an unwinnable bet; a church made of glass is carried down a river.

The story's route to the screen has been long and circuitous but seemingly inevitable. Carey and Armstrong have been friends for years, and he gave her the manuscript of *Oscar and Lucinda* more than ten years ago. Her account of their working relationship is rather touching. When she and the screenwriter Laura Jones changed the ending, they "nervously put the idea past Peter, and he said, 'I wish I'd thought of it.'"

When he first saw the film, he cried and was then "deeply embarrassed".

Initially Armstrong thought it would be impossible to film in Australia. She passed on it at first, and returned to the project only when John Schlesinger, for whom the rights had been bought, backed out. "The thing was," Armstrong says, "six years ago, this was the reaction: people won't go and see a film where the actors speak in English accents, people won't go and see a period film, no one will sit through a film two hours long. It's too tragic, can't you rewrite it? And you have to find a star to play Oscar."

Accents are something she is very funny about. Returning to the subject of her education in film, she tells me that she saw her first Australian feature in her last year at college. It was Tim Burstall's *2,000 Weeks*, "and I have to say I was ashamed to hear Australian accents in the cinema, they sounded so weird and thin. Because we were so used to hearing American or even English accents: I mean, don't forget in the sixties the British film industry was burgeoning. I went and saw *Georgie Girl*, and *A Hard Day's Night* ten times."

What's piquant about hearing this recent history from her is that her position is both central and idiosyncratic. She describes the turning point for the industry as the moment when "Peter Weir made *Picnic at Hanging Rock*, which I think was the first time people said: 'My God, there's an Australian film and we're not embarrassed.'"

Armstrong, unlike Carey, still lives and works in Australia. Even when her films are produced by a Hollywood studio, she has earned the right to do postproduction at home. There is an Armstrong community: she and Jane Campion often work with the same first assistant director, the same producer, the same scriptwriter. "The only problem is that we all worry about Jane and I shooting at the same time ... We'll be fighting over our First AD, tearing him apart!"

The light and the heavy heat of Australia are inescapable in Armstrong's *Oscar and Lucinda*. She herself grew up in the suburbs, "where they shoot, uh, *Neighbours*. They were all orchards and now they're housing estates."

But there are also parts of Australia many have never seen. "We tried to capture that feeling of Sydney being on the water. I had to say to the studio, about the journey with the church up north, this is not the outback, it's really tropical rain forests."

Armstrong was worried because the sun was always behind the clouds as they were filming. She thought the film would come out "grey and depressing". But when she saw the rushes she was pleased. I think of the country she has never left, of the eeriness most famously seen in *Picnic*, as she says proudly of her own film, "you actually feel the heat and feet the strangeness. There is some quality of fear there. Australia is a strange land."

NEW YORK POST, 12/31/97, p. 31, Thelma Adams

What a difference a year makes. In 1996, Ralph Fiennes was "The English Patient." While he didn't win an Academy Award himself, despite a nomination, his devastatingly romantic performance in the title role led the movie to an Oscar sweep.

Now, in Gillian Armstrong's addled Victorian romance, the closest Fiennes will get to an Academy Award is his character's name. He is the Oscar of "Oscar and Lucinda," Laura Jones' misguided adaptation of Peter Carey's Booker Prize-winning novel about romantic misfits mucking up their lives in the Australian outback.

While other characters repeatedly refer to Oscar as a scarecrow, he resembles the Mad Hatter at a literary tea. With red hair, a weak face and body parts stitched together at random, Fiennes plays a young English cleric with an eccentric problem: He loves to gamble as much as he hates the sea.

In a whimsical turn, Oscar goes missionary. Despite his phobia, he embarks on the good ship Leviathan. He heads for Australia in the misguided step cure. The turn of events seems all the more whimsical because Jones (she scripted "A Thousand Acres," another literary misfire) cannot attach Carey's characters to a satisfying dramatic arc.

On the ship, Oscar meets a dashing young Aussie heiress—a glass manufacturess—whose gambling jones is as big as his own. Dear Lucinda (played with pluck by Cate Blanchett, last seen hobbling down "Paradise Road") is one of those fabulous female individualists, a square peg in holes, that Armstrong has brought to the screen throughout her brilliant career. (She also directed "Little Women.")

It's not quite love at first bet for "Oscar and Lucinda." First we must travel to labored metaphor country, a territory even a trek to the outback cannot escape.

The priest and the heiress build a testament to their star-crossed and unconventional passion, a glass church. The striking image of the crystal cathedral floating down river on its barge in the Australian wilderness opens and closes the movie.

The floating church becomes Armstrong's "Fitzcarraldo," her cry in the wilderness for art, faith, love and divine impracticality. But the literary adaptation that surrounds this memorable image is so herky-jerky, Geoffrey Rush's voiceover narration is so heavy-handed, that the metaphor, like the church, drowns under its own weight.

NEWSDAY, 12/31/97, Part II/p. B14, John Anderson

"Sumptuous" would be one way to describe director Gillian Armstrong's adaptation of Peter Carey's "Oscar and Lucinda," a film composed of some of the most riveting pictures ever put on screen. Another way would be "dim": For all the interesting faces inhabiting this big old period drama, there's not a lot going on behind them.

Had it worked, it might have been a minor miracle, anyway. Carey's Booker Prize-winning work is one of those all-absorbing reads, a 20th-Century novel with 19th-Century aspirations, a book full of fantastical people and unlikely occurrences. They seem less unlikely, of course, when they are part of a sprawling tale full of evolving characters. But even with a generous length of two hours and 12 minutes, Armstrong must skip along the book's various plot points as if they were stones in a rather treacherous stream, and for all her obvious good intentions she ends up all wet.

Ralph Fiennes, reminding one all too readily of the late Stan Laurel, is Oscar Hopkins, whose Proustian moment with a forbidden Christmas pudding sets his soul on the road to pain, and maybe perdition. The son of a forbidding and so-humorless-he's-humorous minister, Oscar's life is built on religion and superstition, and while Carey knew what he was up to it's not certain Armstrong's quite up to speed on all this.

Oscar is a repository for the misguidance of others, and for most of the movie, Fiennes' face is a blank slate. A far more interesting set of expressions belongs to the up-and-coming Cate Blanchett, the only interesting thing about the ill-begotten war movie "Paradise Road" and a captivating presence despite the errant arc of the story.

Armstrong's interest and those of screenwriter Laura Jones ("Angel at My Table," "Portrait of a Lady") were no doubt piqued by Blanchett's character, Lucinda Leplastier, a proto-feminist entrepreneur who harbors a fascination with glass, a tidy inheritance, and an addiction to dice and cards. Lucinda buys a destitute glass factory, has an uncoordinated romantic flirtation with the too-proper Rev. Dennis Hasset (Ciaran Hinds), and has the bad luck to hook up with fellow gambler and dusty cleric Oscar. In frustration and defiance, she agrees with his plan to transport a glass church through the Australian bush country to Hasset's remote congregation. And by the time this all happens, one doesn't know whether to laugh or go blind.

"Oscar and Lucinda" is, however, one of the most beautiful films to look at. The production design of Luciana Arrighi and the cinematography of Geoffrey Simpson combine for a look that is starkly beautiful and shamelessly baroque, and make me want to see the film again—all things considered, a ringing endorsement.

NEWSWEEK, 1/12/98, p. 61, David Ansen

When a movie comes along as handsome, literate and ambitious as Gillian Armstrong's *Oscar and Lucinda*, it should be a cause for rejoicing. This picaresque tale of Victorian Australia and England, adapted by Laura Jones from Peter Carey's Booker Prize-winning novel, is made with passion, skill and a commendable disdain for the predictable. It has a lovely score by Thomas Newman, stunning production design, striking costumes and gorgeous cinematography. Unfortunately, it just doesn't jell.

"Oscar and Lucinda" is a classic example of a highly literary novel whose virtues stubbornly resist translation to the screen. It's the tale of two singular misfits whose fates collide because of a shared passion for gambling. Oscar (Ralph Fiennes) is a naive, guilt-stricken man who breaks with his fundamentalist father and goes to Oxford to become an Anglican priest. There he discovers the giddy glories of racetrack gambling. Realizing that his addiction stands in the way of his vocation, he decides (with the flip of a coin) to sail to Australia to become a missionary. On the voyage he meets the obsessive gambler Lucinda (Cate Blanchett), a wealthy, independent Australian heiress who's bought a glass factory in Sydney. These two may seem meant for each other, but the unworldly and self-punishing Oscar is convinced she loves another man. To win her, he engages her in a wager: that he can build and transport a glass church to a remote town in New South Wales where the minister he thinks she loves resides.

By the time "Oscar and Lucinda" arrives at its highly symbolic conclusion, the movie has become tangled in its own intricate cosmology, caught in a narrative gridlock of eccentric details. Oscar and Lucinda's rarefied compulsions seem willed by literary fiat, not flesh and blood. Having no entree to their inner lives, we have to be constantly told by the narrator (Oscar's great-grandson) what they are feeling. Fiennes, made up to resemble an ascetic Harpo Marx, gives an arch, theatrical performance so stylized it's hard to understand Lucinda's attraction to him. It's easier to see Lucinda's allure—Blanchett is a fiery delight. Since there's no emotional glue holding Carey's flights of fancy together, what should seem magically unpredictable too often feels merely whimsical. A noble failure, "Oscar and Lucinda" wins your respect, but not your heart.

SIGHT AND SOUND, 4/98, p. 48, John Wrathall

As a boy in nineteenth-century England, Oscar Hopkins runs away from his father, an austere preacher, and studies to become an Anglican minister. But at Oxford he discovers a new passion: gambling. To escape temptation, he decides to go to New South Wales as a missionary. Meanwhile, in Australia, heiress Lucinda Leplastrier buys a glass works in Sydney, where she makes friends with fellow glass enthusiast the Reverend Hassett, and discovers the joys of the card table. Returning to Australia after a trip to England, Lucinda finds herself on the same boat as Oscar, and asks him to hear her confession. Visiting her cabin, he discovers their mutual passion for gambling. But after gleefully playing cards with her, he collapses in a fit of remorse. Embarrassed, Lucinda avoids him after that.

In Sydney, Oscar meets Hassett before the latter, his reputation tarnished by his friendship with Lucinda, is exiled by his superiors to the remote, chapel-less village of Bellingen. Oscar and Lucinda meet again in a gambling den. When his anti-gambling landlady throws Oscar out, Lucinda takes him in. The two of them make a pact never to gamble again. But, to prove himself to Lucinda, Oscar makes one last bet: that he can take the glass chapel she has designed cross-country to Bellingen. The expedition sets off, with the bullying Jeffris as second-in-command. When Jeffris and his guards massacre a group of aboriginals, Oscar kills Jeffris in

self-defence. Oscar eventually reaches Bellingen by floating the chapel down a river on a raft.
Exhausted, he collapses and is seduced by a local widow, Miriam Chadwick. Oscar is asleep in
the chapel at its moorings in the river when it sinks. He is drowned. Lucinda has the chapel
salvaged from the river bed. When Miriam gives birth to Oscar's son, he is baptised inside the
chapel, now erected in Bellingen.

As she demonstrated in her first feature, *My Brilliant Career* (1979), and in two of her
subsequent US-based films, *Little Women* and the underrated *Mrs. Soffel,* Gillian Armstrong has
a flair for probing beneath the frills of costume drama to uncover her characters' psychological
quirks. She is reunited on *Oscar and Lucinda* with Laura Jones, who wrote her 1987 film *High
Tide* and has since proved herself with two skilful literary adaptations for Jane Campion, *An
Angel at My Table* and *The Portrait of a Lady*.

But this dream team has bitten off more than it can chew with Peter Carey's 1988 Booker Prizewinner *Oscar and Lucinda*. It's not that Armstrong and Jones fail to capture Carey's peculiar tone
or to bring to life his more inspired visions—the glass chapel floating up the river at the end of
the film is indeed a wonder to behold. But the sheer breadth of Carey's extraordinary imagination
poses structural problems for film-makers (Wim Wenders, for one, came unstuck filming the
Carey-scripted *Until the End of the World*).

Even racing through highly compressed accounts of Oscar and Lucinda's parallel childhoods,
with the help of Geoffrey Rush's beautifully spoken narration, Armstrong cannot bring her
protagonists together until an hour into the film. Once Ralph Fiennes and Cate Blanchett are
allowed to play off each other, the film comes alive in the exuberant scene where Oscar arrives
in Lucinda's cabin to hear her confession, but cannot contain his excitement when he discovers
her interest in card games. He goes on to deliver a marvelous speech in which, inspired by
Pascal's theory that God requires us to gamble on the fact of his existence, he argues that
gambling is divinely sanctioned. Nervous and obsessed, but enormously sympathetic, Oscar may
be Fiennes' most likable film role to date, and he is perfectly matched by Blanchett. Headstrong
and gauche in equal measure, her Lucinda is an engaging eccentric who can't help defying social
strictures, in the tradition of Judy Davis' Sybylla in *My Brilliant Career* and Kerry Fox's Janet
Frame in *An Angel at My Table*.

Unfortunately, having contrived to unite these strange kindred spirits, the plot abruptly separates
them again. A great passion which is never consummated, nor even admitted to, can't help but
prove a flimsy and ultimately frustrating basis for an episodic, 132-minute film. The final act,
when Oscar sets off on his *Fitzcarraldo*-style mission across the outback, provides a gripping
dramatic climax that's both whimsical and shocking, but it leaves Lucinda entirely out in the cold.

Always a sensitive director, Armstrong does justice both to the novel's strange, poetic detail and
to its emotional range, from almost slapstick comedy (here, largely at the expense of Sydney's
bourgeoisie) to the full-blown tragedy of Oscar's death. But something eludes her. In the end,
despite the best intentions, Carey's novel resembles Lucinda's glass church: a beautiful,
mysterious creation which, when you try to transport it, shatters and sinks.

TIME, 12/22/97, p. 81, Richard Schickel

It's a sight to behold and image to cherish—a little country church, improbably fashioned out
of glass and wrought iron, bobbing down an untamed river deep in the 19th century Australian
wilderness. How in the world did it and the man delivering it—a nice, pious (if defrocked)
clergyman named Oscar Hopkins (Ralph Fiennes)—end up in these unlikely precincts?

Logically enough, if your definition of the logical encompasses the inherent illogic of human
passion. For gangly Oscar, nervous yet nervy in Fiennes' gloriously addled performance, is a
gambling man. Gambling is an activity that as he sees it, permits him leaps and tests of faith,
with all his winnings going to churchly charities. He has bet that he can deliver this fragile
edifice by a certain date despite the roughness of both the country and the crew that's helping
with the tugging and hauling.

His wager is with Lucinda Leplastrier (the luminous and spunky Cate Blanchett), also a
gambling addict. For her, gambling is a way of asserting herself against gentility and separating
herself from some of the money she has inherited but doesn't really want. Equally unlikely for
a woman of her time, she is an industrialist. That church is a product of her glass factory, and

it is intended as reparation to another clergyman who has been exiled for being seen in her raffish company.

O.K., you say, you know where *Oscar and Lucinda* is heading—toward the kind of happy, reconciling ending that usually crowns romantic period adventures. Don't get too comfortable with that thought. For this story, adapted from Peter Carey's Booker Prize-winning novel by Laura Jones and directed by Gillian Armstrong, is as wayward as its main characters—comic, fierce, digressive. Its business is to turn sure-thing expectations into a game of chance, and provide us with that rarity—a genuinely eccentric yet deeply insinuating film.

VILLAGE VOICE, 1/6/98, p. 68, Amy Taubin

Adapted from Peter Carey's dense Booker Prize-winning novel, Gillian Armstrong's *Oscar and Lucinda* is both a story of impossible love and a parodic social history of mid-19th-century Australia—a country where Victorianism was an even more uneasy fit than it was in England or America. The novel is darker and more ironic than the film; treacherous undercurrents ripple under its crystalline surface.

In Armstrong and screenwriter Laura Jones's adaptation (faithful throughout in action and dialogue), Oscar (Ralph Fiennes) is an Anglican minister, a free spirit by temperament knotted up by religious guilt. The impetuous, secular, protofeminist Lucinda (Cate Blanchett) is an heiress who invests her fortune and her fantasy in a glass-manufacturing factory. Oscar and Lucinda are drawn together by their shared obsession with gambling, which Oscar regards as a vice that may well damn him to hell. Diametrical opposites, Oscar and Lucinda are as made for each other as Grant and Hepburn in *Bringing Up Baby,* but the very differences that inspire their mutual attraction also make them act at cross-purposes.

Armstrong's most inspired choice was to cast Ralph Fiennes as Oscar and to allow the character to be as much the "oddbod" onscreen as he is on the page. Stammering and flailing about, Fiennes is like a combo of Jean-Louis Barrault as the lovesick mime in *Les Enfants du Paradis*; Jonathan Miller on a particularly stressful day; and a silent-movie virgin, shielding herself from the villain with that palms-out gesture that signals "touch me not." "Oddbod," of course, desires—as much as he fears—to touch and be touched. He is both the shyest of nerds and the most ardent of romantics, his paralyzing phobias his only defense against the oceanic drives of his unconscious.

Risking his matinee idol status, Fiennes not only goes through the entire movie in a near hysterical state, he's also extremely feminine without being at all campy. And I daresay it's the gender-bending aspect of the performance, rather than the ticks and twitches, that male members of the audience find so off-putting.

Nothing else in the film is as fully realized as Fiennes's Oscar. Blanchett is a skillful and appealing actress, but a bit too soft for Lucinda (a young Judy Davis was needed). Armstrong brings out the best in the actors, but her direction gets bogged down in picturesque detail. Though a bit plodding, *Oscar and Lucinda* is still a more rewarding costume drama than such crowd pleasers as Jane Campion's woolly-headed *The Piano* (her worst film) or Iain Softley's insipid, prurient *Wings of the Dove.*

Also reviewed in:
CHICAGO TRIBUNE, 1/23/98, Friday/p. A, Michael Wilmington
NEW YORK TIMES, 12/31/97, p. E5, Janet Maslin
NEW YORKER, 1/12/98, p. 84, Anthony Lane
VARIETY, 12/8-14/97, p. 110, Emmanuel Levy
WASHINGTON POST, 1/30/98, p. D6, Rita Kempley

OTHER VOICES, OTHER ROOMS

An Artistic License Films release of a Golden Eye Films presentation. *Executive Producer:* Robert C. Stigwood and Lili Mahtani. *Producer:* Peter Wentworth and David Rocksavage.

Director: David Rocksavage. *Screenplay:* Sara Flanigan and David Rocksavage. *Based on the novel by:* Truman Capote. *Director of Photography:* Paul Ryan. *Editor:* Cynthia Scheider. *Music:* Chris Hajian. *Music Editor:* George Craig. *Sound:* Jeffree Bloomer and (music) Gary Chester. *Sound Editor:* Budge Tremlett. *Casting:* Billy Hopkins, Suzanne Smith, and Kerry Barden. *Production Designer:* Amy McGary. *Art Director:* Glen Rivers. *Set Decorator:* Sally Peterson. *Costumes:* Jane Greenwood. *Make-up:* Herta Jones. *Running time:* 98 minutes. *MPAA Rating:* Not Rated.

CAST: Lothaire Bluteau (Randolph Skully); Anna Thompson (Amy Skully); David Speck (Joel Sansom); April Turner (Missouri Fever, 'Zoo'); Frank Taylor (Edward 'Ed' R. Sanson); Leonard Watkins (Jesus Fever); Audrey Dollar (Idabell Thompkins); Elizabeth Byler (Florabell Thompkins); Moses Gibson (Little Sunshine); Terri Dollar (Ellen Kendall); Jayne Morgan (Cafe Woman); Brian Moeller (Roger); Lonnie Hamilton (Old Man on Bus); Yami Hidalgo (Dolores); Wayne Capabas (Pepe); Bob Kingdom (Narrator); Todd Langenfeld and Mark Stender (Attackers); Kyle Steven Walden (Joel at Age 4); Charles Barber (Young Ed Sansom); Emilly Petta (Mrs. Sansom); Guy Mercer II (Good Samaritan).

LOS ANGELES TIMES, 12/19/97, Calendar/p. 16, Kevin Thomas

David Rocksavage's film of Truman Capote's first published novel, "Other Voices, Other Rooms," comes to the screen as a beguiling mood piece—dripping in Southern decadence that verges on parody, but so chilling that it's no wonder that the story has been described as Southern Gothic.

We hear on the soundtrack what sounds like Capote's famous slurred baby voice—it belongs to Ben Kingdom, veteran of Capote one-man shows—lending occasional narration, which proves to be an inspired device.

It's the Deep South, 1938, and 12-year-old Joel, whose mother is dead, hears his aunt and her husband, who regards the child as a mama's boy, discussing how Joel's long-absent father now wants his son to come to live with him.

A bus and finally a horse-driven cart take Joel to a remote plantation dominated by a superb but dilapidated manor house, complete with columns. In its way, Skully's Landing is surely as awe-inspiring to Joel (David Speck) as was Manderley to Rebecca. He is greeted by a pretty woman, Amy Skully (Anna Thomson, memorable as the disfigured prostitute in "Unforgiven"). In time he meets her cousin Randolph (Lothaire Bluteau, co-star of "Bent") and both are full of delays as to when Joel is actually going to get to be reunited with his father.

The mansion is filled with fine antiques and curios, just the sort of place that an imaginative boy like Joel would find fascinating. However, he's been thrust into a dark and psychologically complex household just as he's verging on coming of age. Randolph is a thin, handsome aesthete, full of effete charm and booze, and beneath a veneer of Southern graciousness, Amy is a desperately unhappy woman, devoted to her self-destructive cousin. "Everything's going to be all right," Randolph says soothingly. "When is everything going to be all right?" asks Amy in desperation. Amy and Randolph could be close relatives to Blanche DuBois.

Amy and Randolph are bound by a dark secret, which involves the reason why Joel has been summoned. (No, they are not his real parents.) Anyone who as a child was in the care of someone who combined living in the past with aristocratic pretensions will know .how potent and permanent an effect an individual like Randolph has upon you. This beautifully acted, carefully wrought film leaves you feeling that in Randolph you're seeing the man that Truman Capote became.

NEW YORK POST, 12/5/97, p. 56, Michael Medved

How can a filmmaker convey a languid, smothering, plantation-Gothic atmosphere without boring an audience beyond endurance?

It's a problem never quite solved by "Other Voices, Other Rooms," based on Truman Capote's first published novel.

1032 FILM REVIEW ANNUAL

The vaguely autobiographical tale shows a solemn 13-year-old "mama's boy" (superbly played by David Speck) summoned, after his mother's death, to join the father who abandoned them nine years before.

Arriving at a remote, crumbling, seemingly haunted mansion, the child meets the haughty, dotty spinster (Anna Thomson) who presides over the rotting house and her flamboyant, melodramatic cousin (Lothaire Bluteau of "Jesus of Montreal" and the current "Bent").

Neither of these aristocratic eccentrics will allow the boy to even see his father until he's "settled in," but one bright spot involves the good-hearted, ill-fated black servant girl who becomes the boy's primary protector (played with easygoing earthiness by April Turner).

In contrast, the central performance by strikingly handsome Lothaire Bluteau is a collection of self-conscious mannerisms, taking his chain-smoking, hard-drinking, oil-painting role beyond the rearm of bizarre characterization and into the territory of hammy caricature—with his cause further undermined by a distracting, utterly inappropriate French accent.

First-time director David Rocksavage (a veteran documentarian for British TV) rearranges Capote's novel to withhold a major shock until the movie's end, but by that point most members of the weary audience will be past caring.

Painstaking production design, lyrical camera work and lush music are all first rate, providing artful, even gaudy wrapping for what seems in the end an empty package.

NEWSDAY, 12/5/97, Part II/p. B8, John Anderson

It may have swaddled some of this century's more precocious prose, but it was the dust jacket on "Other Voices, Other Rooms"—Truman Capote's first novel, published in 1948 that produced the first demi-scandal of the fledgling "celebutante's" writing life: Pictured in a rather blatant sprawl, Capote and his languorous posture left little to doubt about him or his style.

The book jacket was a gesture of and about its time and place, but gestures always played a large part in the life of Capote, creator of "Breakfast at Tiffany's," "In Cold Blood" and, of course, the social suicide known as "Answered Prayers." Gesture also has much to do with the film version of "Other Voices," which has been brought to the screen with much of the languor but a lot less of the poetry than is contained in the author's writing.

In telling the story of Capote manqué Joel Sansom—who, a la Capote, is sent to live among his southern relatives at an impressionable age—director and co-screenwriter David Rocksavage exhibits a flair for the Blanche DuBois-isms of life but not much feel for making a period piece. And so he has delivered a two-headed creature that wants to sup of the political correctness of the '90s at the same time it sips mint juleps in the quasi-feudal '30s.

He does get a first-rate performance out of Lothaire Bluteau, the striking Canadian actor who was so good in "Jesus of Montreal" and "Black Robe" and who makes Joel's debauched uncle, Randolph Skully, a benevolent nightmare. Joel, expecting to find his father waiting when he arrives at the ruined old Skully house, finds instead Randolph, his sister Amy (Anna Thomson) and an atmosphere of entrenched corruption—much of which is portrayed quite well by Rocksavage. Joel doesn't find his father, not at first, and the elder's whereabouts become the object of much mystery and strange disclosures.

Capote, who was farmed out to his relations from about the age of 2, had a jaundiced eye about southern gentility, which was infused with as much decay as grandeur. But in portraying his own outlook, he always seemed to stand outside his younger self, recognizing the vulnerability of a young boy wounded by abandonment and looking for something to cling to. Young David Speck, who was in "The Client," is far too defiant and modern to be anyone's Capote, or Joel Sansom, and his performance as much as anything is Rocksavage's downfall. Anna Thomson, on the other hand, plays Amy Skully like every southern belle plus Florence Henderson, and that's too weird not to be interesting.

SIGHT AND SOUND, 7/99, p. 51, Rob White

Thirteen-year-old Joel rides a bus to Noon City in the deep south of the US. He remembers how a letter had arrived at his aunt Ellen's house in New Orleans from his long-absent father summoning him to live in his mansion at Skully's Landing. When he finally reaches the house he meets his aunt Amy and cousin Randolph, but there's no sign of his father. He befriends Jesus

Fever, the elderly servant, and Jesus' daughter Zoo, as well as Idabell, the fiery daughter of the neighbour. He discovers his paralysed and autistic father in an attic bedroom. It was Randolph who wrote the letter.

Amy steals the letters he tries to send to New Orleans while Randolph slowly captivates him with stories of Cuba and his futile love for Pepe (whom Randolph writes to, care of all the world's capital cities). Jesus dies. Zoo runs away but returns after she has been raped and beaten in the road. Joel and Idabell run away but return when Joel is bitten by a snake. Aunt Ellen visits, bringing Joel's things which Amy hides. Joel finds them and confronts a drunken Randolph who confesses to shooting and paralysing Joel's father. Joel leaves Skully's Landing.

Other Voices, Other Rooms was Truman Capote's first novel, published to enormous acclaim in 1948 (when the author was only 24). Told from the point of view of Joel Sansom, a 13-year-old boy uprooted on false pretences in order to stay with relatives in the deep south, it's a claustrophobic chamber piece, part gothic saga of family secrets, part coming-of-age memoir. It was always going to be a difficult novel to adapt to the screen. Lacking the film-friendly premises of *In Cold Blood* (1967) or *Breakfast at Tiffany's* (1961), it's more purely a writer's book, full of subtly subjective narration and ornate descriptions of the fecund swamplands where the dilapidated Skully house sits, and the wasted, tormented people who occupy it. So it was a risky choice of source material for a first feature for documentarian David Rocksavage, and this isn't a particularly distinguished debut.

There are too many curious experiments and evasions. The character of neighbour Idabell, prominent in the novel, is underdeveloped here, making her presence inexplicable. Instead of accentuating how the southern setting would appear to an adolescent and adopting the visual style of, for example, *The Night of the Hunter* (where everything is primal, enlarged, threatening to the senses), the film-makers give us swamps which are a little too muddy, a mansion just a little too peeling and battered. And while a framing voiceover delivered by a Capote soundalike is forgivable, the fantasy flashbacks where bibulous cousin Randolph remembers lost-love Pepe and imagines Joel with them are simply bizarre in their staginess. They look like out-takes from Fassbinder's *Querelle* and—the very muted homoeroticism of Capote's book notwithstanding—seem entirely inappropriate. On the other hand there are two very powerful moments involving the servants Zoo and Jesus: an improvised prayer service in which father and daughter sing an exquisite spiritual, and a brief slow-motion sequence in which she's chased on an empty road before (we later discover) being raped.

What remains are the lead performances. David Speck as Joel could have been better coached and his diction is often awkward, but he has a wonderfully still, thoughtful face. Anna Thomson as the dipsomaniac Amy moves through the film like a ghost—pallid, crushed, tears always at the edge of her eyes. Lothaire Bluteau luxuriates in the decadence and the guilty, inward looking maudlinity of Randolph. Both these adult players are compelling but finally too wan, too overcome by ennui, too eviscerated to lift the film beyond the ordinary.

VILLAGE VOICE, 12/9/97, p. 79, Elizabeth Weitzman

Truman Capote's tale of a boy (David Speck) who travels to a faded plantation to find his father, only to be snared by a wild-eyed spinster (Anna Thomson) and her alcoholic cousin, Randolph (Lothaire Bluteau), surely seemed fresher when he published it half a century ago. But Rocksavage and his crew have imaginatively re-created the rotten beauty of Capote's autobiographical novel with a quiet, effective moodiness. The mansion that becomes 13-year-old Joel's prison, stripped of its glories outside and smotheringly debauched within, is as much a masterwork of period detail as are the meticulously chosen 1930s costumes. Thomson and April Turner (as the servant Zoo) turn characters straight off the Southern Gothic assembly line into touching portraits, but there's no question the film belongs to the delicate, complicated Randolph. In fact, though Capote always claimed young Joel as his alter ego, one would have to wonder what he'd make of Bluteau's sharpwitted, bitterly lonely aesthete.

Also reviewed in:
CHICAGO TRIBUNE, 2/14/98, p. 32, Michael Wilmington
NEW YORK TIMES, 12/5/97, p. E10, Stephen Holden
VARIETY, 10/30-11/5/95, p. 74, Emanuel Levy

OUT TO SEA

A Twentieth Century Fox release of a Davis Entertainment Company production. *Executive Producer:* Dylan Sellers and Barry Berg. *Producer:* John Davis and David T. Friendly. *Director:* Martha Coolidge. *Screenplay:* Robert Nelson Jacobs. *Director of Photography:* Lajos Koltai. *Editor:* Anne V. Coates. *Music:* David Newman. *Music Editor:* Alex Gibson and Tom Villano. *Choreographer:* Kim Blank. *Sound:* Jim Webb and (music) Bruce Botnick. *Sound Editor:* John A. Larsen. *Casting:* Jackie Burch. *Production Designer:* James Spencer. *Art Director:* William F. Matthews. *Set Decorator:* Anne D. McCulley. *Set Designer:* Glenn Williams and Lauren Cory. *Set Dresser:* Rich Cline, Michael Rutgard, Scott Kennedy, and Gregory Griffith. *Special Effects:* Ed Felix. *Costumes:* Jane Robinson. *Make-up:* Steve LaPorte. *Make-up (Walter Matthau):* Linda V. Melazzo. *Make-up (Jack Lemmon):* Steve LaPorte. *Stunt Coordinator:* Roydon E. Clark and Chris Howell. *Running time:* 106 minutes. *MPAA Rating:* PG-13.

CAST: Jack Lemmon (Herb); Walter Matthau (Charlie); Dyan Cannon (Liz); Gloria De Haven (Vivian); Brent Spiner (Godwyn); Elaine Stritch (Mavis); Hal Linden (Mac); Donald O'Connor (Jonathan); Edward Mulhare (Carswell); Rue McClanahan (Mrs. Carruthers); Alexandra Powers (Shelly); Sean O'Bryan (Allan); Esther Scott (Maria); Allan Rich (Sebastian); Estelle Harris (Bridget); Leon Singer (Willie); Concetta Tomei (Madge); Goh Misawa (Tanaka); Kim Blank (Dance Instructor); Louisa Abernathy (Edie); Michael Laskin (Purser); Hector Mercado (Parrot); Carol Barbee (Flight Attendant); Dale Raoul (Sylvia); Lomax Study (Shapiro); Beverly Polcyn (Pearl); Shaun Toub (Bettor in Front); Bert Rosario (Cab Driver); Paul Kievit (Ship Captain); Henk Ijdens (Ship Officer); Frank Patton (Dealer); Natalia Momtchilova (Shopgirl); Rod Phillips (Julian); P.D. Mani (Floor Person); Trevor Denman (Track Announcer); Bubba Dean Rambo and Allen Walls (Dance Hosts).

LOS ANGELES TIMES, 7/2/97, Calendar/p. 12, Kevin Thomas

The "Grumpy Old Men" movies reunited Jack Lemmon and Walter Matthau with box-office success, but "Out to Sea" is more like it. Much more. Here's a movie mainly about people who are considerably over 21 without a single old codger joke and without anyone apologizing for his or her maturity. "Out to Sea" generates both considerable laughter and emotion.

Robert Nelson Jacobs' script, his first to be produced, is a wonder, a classic shipboard farce that gives full play to Lemmon's and Matthau's formidable comic gifts that are deftly played against genuine sentiment.

What's more, Jacobs has come up with a raft of roles for a wide array of esteemed veterans who glow under the direction of Martha Coolidge, who can always be counted upon to bring out all the gleaming facets of both script and cast. Coolidge has brought to films as diverse as "Rambling Rose," "Three Wishes" and now this comedy a sense of unity and pace while never losing focus on the human heart and its often mysterious workings. Coolidge has always been interested in people rather than special effects, and this kind of concern is a terrific anchor for the freewheeling mayhem of "Out to Sea."

Lemmon plays Herb, a retired department store salesman and grieving recent widower, whose brother-in-law Charlie (Matthau), a fearless, lifelong gambler and con man, maneuvers him onto a Caribbean cruise where they wind up as "dance hosts" aboard a luxury liner. Under the impression that Charlie has won them a free trip, Herb is appalled to discover too late that if he in fact resists working as an unpaid taxi dancer he'll have to cough up for the expensive trip.

Charlie's motives are unapologetically base. Having never married, he figures it's time to snag a rich wife, and what better hunting grounds could there be than a cruise ship loaded with wealthy divorcees and widows of a certain age? In regard to Herb, however, there's some actual altruism in contriving to bring him along. He feels Herb ought to start living again. What Charlie, who's been caught up in conniving his entire life, doesn't count on is falling in love—for the first time—himself.

But how could he possibly resist Dyan Cannon's Liz, a gorgeous, sexy divorcée with a wicked sense of humor who seems to respond to Charlie's basset-hound charm, even though he's older than her salty mother (Elaine Stritch, in typically astringent form)? Meanwhile, Herb meets a lovely recent widow, Vivian (Gloria De Haven, in a most welcome return to the screen). Despite his mourning, he has to admit he's attracted to her.

Such are the sturdy emotional underpinnings of a wacky farce with Charlie pulling every scam in the book and complicating Herb's life and burgeoning romance in every conceivable way. Charlie and Herb's nemesis is the liner's deliciously prissy cruise director (Brent Spiner), a self-important, ambitious martinet who imposes military discipline upon his dance hosts while also serving as the ship's absurdly terrible singing star. Spiner is so hilarious he comes close to stealing the show.

What a delightful cast "Out to Sea" has. Hal Linden and none other than Donald O'Connor also play dance hosts. The late Edward Mulhare, who memorably took over for Rex Harrison as Henry Higgins in the original company of "My Fair Lady," is Charlie's handsome rival for Liz, and Rue McClanahan, the ship's bejeweled owner, winds up as Charlie's sole dance partner in a classic scene of awesome, undaunted clumsiness on his part.

Cinematographer Lajos Koltai brings a burnished look to the film, and designer Jane Robinson must be cited for her splendid costumes. All the actresses have beautiful wardrobes, keyed to the characters they are portraying yet elegant in their considerable variety—glamour for Cannon, understated good taste for De Haven, lush extravagance for McClanahan and a smart, witty look for Stritch. In a key scene Cannon wears a clinging, shimmering evening gown that is surely one of the most dazzling creations she has ever worn on the screen.

"Out to Sea" uses lots of sets and fakery, sometimes amusingly so, when it leaves the ship, but production designer James Spencer manages to make this strategy give the film a vintage feel that reminds us fondly of the kind of studio movies O'Connor and De Haven used to make in Hollywood's Golden Era. But this is only a nod to nostalgia, as appealing as it is, for "Out to Sea" is fast and funny, tart and clear-eyed about love and mortality.

NEW YORK POST, 7/2/97, p. 37, Thelma Adams.

Vulgar, cranky, sex-starved, unemployed, two-dimensional? The butt of every joke in a three-mile radius? No, the stars of "Out to Sea" aren't Beavis and Butt-head. They're those canny cash cows of the senior set, the odds-buster's of the Screen Actors Guild: Jack Lemmon and Walter Matthau.

There's life after 70—but the jokes aren't getting any younger. Tighten up your borscht belt and surrender to another geriatric Grumpy and Grumpier. As the live wire, Matthau prods stick-in-the-mud Lemmon, "You're still alive. Hasn't anyone told you?"

As the plot creaks, gambler Matthau drags his widowed brother-in-law (Lemmon) on a luxury cruise. He fails to mention that they're going steerage. The pair must pay their way as dance hosts for lonely widows and aggressive gold diggers.

Enter Gloria DeHaven. She debuted in "Modern Times," but learned everything she needed for her part as Lemmon's shipboard squeeze from turns on "The Love Boat" and "Fantasy Island."

Dyan Cannon rips a lesson from the Dorian Gray handbook: Surround yourself with geezers and you'll look forever young. Plastic surgery, peekaboo dresses and a disdain for undies don't hurt.

Anyone who ever questioned Cannon's acting ability will have new appreciation for the actress. A post-coital glow after bedding Matthau? That's acting! Was that the earth moving, or your, artificial leg uncoupling?

Martha Coolidge's direction is seaworthy; she serves ham with a *joie de vivre* that Julia Child would appreciate. Robert Nelson Jacobs' script rocks with sight gags and one-liners without racing ahead of the stars. This isn't "Speed 2."

Coolidge plays her best cards in the casting. Brent Spiner—TV's favorite android, Data—sports a wavy hairdo and a pencil mustache as the smarmy cruise director. He sings a drop-dead version of' "Oye Como Va," all Latin rhythms and Anglo pelvis, his diction as clipped as a prize poodle.

Also on board, a grouchy Elaine Stritch shows off gams that never grow old and spouts the movie's best, if typical, vulgarity.

There's more to "Out to Sea" than gutter-mouthed seniors. On the dance floor, Stritch goes toe-to-toe with Donald O'Connor. The legendary song-and-dance man gets two chances to tap a stairway to heaven. When he hoofs a solo to the Latin hustle, O'Connor shuffles a classic scene into a disposable, if harmless, comedy.

Also reviewed in:
NEW YORK TIMES, 7/2/97, p. C11, Janet Maslin
VARIETY, 6/30-7/13/97, p. 65, Joe Leydon
WASHINGTON POST, 7/2/97, p. C10, Stephen Hunter
WASHINGTON POST, 7/4/97, Weekend/p. 42, Rita Kempley

PAPERBACK ROMANCE

An MGM release of a Goldwyn Entertainment Company presentation in association with Generation Films, Lewin Films and Pandora Cinema. *Producer:* Bob Weis. *Director:* Ben Lewin. *Screenplay:* Ben Lewin. *Director of Photography:* Vince Monton. *Editor:* Peter Carrodus. *Music:* Paul Grabowsky. *Choreographer:* Teresa Blake. *Sound:* John Phillips. *Casting:* Liz Mulinar. *Production Designer:* Peta Lawson. *Art Director:* Victoria Hobday. *Set Dresser:* Daryl Mills and Denise Goudy. *Special Effects:* Peter Stubbs and Jeff Little. *Costumes:* Anna Borghesi. *Make-up:* Kirsten Veysey. *Stunt Coordinator:* Chris Peters. *Running time:* 93 minutes. *MPAA Rating:* R.

CAST: Gia Carides (Sophie); Anthony LaPaglia (Eddie); Rebecca Gibney (Gloria); Jacek Koman (Yuri); Sioban Tuke (Kate); Lewis Fiander (Bruce Wrightman); Robyn Nevin (Anne-Marie Lepine); Marshall Napier (George LePine); Mary-Anne Fahey (Myra); Michael Edward-Stevens (Benny); Steady Eddy (Nicholas); Michael Vietch (Det. Sgt. Scott); Russell Fletcher (Det. Tyrone); Nicholas Bell (Sophie's Doctor); Kurt Ludescher (Ernst); Max Bruch (Diamond Cutter); Lynda Gibson (Library Clerk); David Watson (Professor-Type at Party); Kirk Alexander (Celebrant); Paul Karo (Defense Lawyer); Terry Norris (Judge); Alvin Chong (Chinese Doctor); Ernie Grey (Doctor at Wedding); Agnieszka Perepeczko (Woman at Wedding); Carolyn Bock (Hotel Hospitality Lady); Maggie Stevens (Mrs. Wrightman); Cliff Ellen (Airline Porter); Alexandra Lewin (Music Student); Paul Wishart (Courier); Mandy Bowden (Marjorie); Alan Levy (Wrong Man at Party); Geoff Lipton (Taxi Driver); Suzanne Chamberlain (Woman in Hotel Lobby); Petru Gheorghiu (Party Host); Phillipa Lee (Woman at Party); Teresa Blake (Woman on Greek Island); Pandora Finch (Madelaine); Eli Yanay (Man on Greek Island); Kareb Davitt (Arist); Tasilimn Emiabata (Artist's Model); Teresa Blake (Female Catburglar); Daniel Witton and Michael Collins (Male Catburglars); Mitch Bartlett (Man in Ski Chalet); Zan McMillan (Woman in Ski Chalet).

LOS ANGELES TIMES, 8/15/97, Calendar/p.8, John Anderson

[The following review by John Anderson appeared in a slightly different form in
NEWSDAY, 8/15/97, Part II/p. B9.]

Sophie (Gia Carides) writes fabulously erotic novellas about women on holiday and godlike Greeks and white-washed huts and wind-blown sex, but has this habit of reading her work out loud. In public. And one night, in the library, Eddie (Anthony LaPaglia), a jewel dealer, over-hears her. He gets very interested. He asks her out. She says no, of course, and we soon see why: Having waited for him to leave, she hobbles to her feet, the kaa-clang of her leg brace echoing through the unlit stacks.

This is the stuff of a romance novel itself, or something starring Valerie Bertinelli, or maybe a viscious spoof on"'The Jenny McCarthy Show." But "Paperback Romance," which stars the real-life couple Carides and LaPaglia as a couple of charmers with secrets, voids any maudlin sentiment. And because it does, its sad subtext becomes merely a foundation for Australian outrageousness.

Imagine the same film made in Hollywood and you'll see what I mean. Julia Roberts would be Sophie, all earnestness and winsomeess. Mel Gibson would play Eddie as slightly psychotic; he'd go to medical school between jewel heists and would have Sophie running wind sprints by the end of the picture.

In "Paperback Romance," the inspiration comes from Sophie's willingness to throw caution to the wind and find love outside her fertile imagination. And from the penchant of writer-director Ben Lewin ("The Favor, the Watch And the Very Big Fish") for understating almost all the gags, or even creating some of them in the first place.

Things happen here that are strictly out of Australia, which has exported such unorthodox and dark-hued recent comedies as "Strictly Ballroom," "Muriel's Wedding" and "Priscilla, Queen of the Desert." Sophie's accident, for instance, is a mad bit of the unexpected: Shadowing Eddie in the mall where he's been met by his humorless (but very funny) fiancée Gloria (Rebecca Gibney), she's desperate not to let him see her limp. One thing leads to another, and she ends up in a shopping cart hurtling from the second floor to the first. It may be due to the Pavarotti impersonator she lands on, but the whole thing is very funny and—given the relatively low-key tone the film has had so far—pretty hilarious.

The accident gives Sophie the break she needs, and with her leg in a cast she can pursue Eddie into what she figures will be a short-lived but high-perspiration relationship. "Paperback Romance" isn't much more than predictable in plot line—Eddie's shady jewelry operation comes into it, as does his pursuit by a former cellist/KGB agent named Yuri (Jacek Koman). But the script and the performances more than compensate, as does Carides, who plays Sophie as half-naif and half-Machiavelli, and a character who wouldn't stoop to being a symbol of anything noble.

NEW YORK POST, 8/15/97, p. 43, Thelma Adams

What is the Trojan Horse position? We never learn the answer in "Paperback Romance," a silly Australian erotic comedy about a romance novelist and a jewelry dealer overcoming personal handicaps to find true love and great sex.

Married actors Gia Carides and Anthony La Paglia—antagonists in "Brilliant Lies"—are Sophie and Eddie. These opposites meet cute in a library.

Sophie's writing about a menage a trois on a Greek-island she's never visited. For plot's sake, she recites as she goes. Eddie overhears the overheated prose while checking out the provenance of a diamond necklace. They're attracted to each other like moths to a desk lamp.

As if stock characters in a bodice ripper, Sophie and Eddie both harbor dramatic secrets. Their relationship must also survive external meddling. His domineering fiancee, Gloria (Rebecca Gibney), ferrets out Sophie's secret. Meanwhile, Yuri (the tragically comic Jacek Koman), an undercover cop on Eddie's trail, trips for the romance novelist.

As directed by Ben Lewin ("The Favor, The Watch and The Very Big Fish"), Carides and La Paglia are playful and appealing. We believe that this self-sufficient yet delicate damsel with lust in her pen can redeem the lovable scamp who has lust everywhere else—almost.

Romance fiction is among the most formulaic in literature. What tickles about Lewin's script is that it's no cookie-cutter comedy. It floats in its own fantasy, spinning out erotica between plot points, both adoring and mocking such overblown images as a flame-haired female artist lovingly creating a plaster cast of a naked male while plaster of Paris drips sensuously down his buttocks.

VILLAGE VOICE , 8/26/97, p. 84, Rebecca Louie

Ashamed of her polio-damaged leg and afraid of intimacy with men, Sophie (Gia Carides) feeds her starved sexual appetite by writing yarns of erotica. Eddie (Anthony LaPaglia), a corrupt jeweler, overhears her whispering a tale from her notebook and becomes smitten. Desperate for love and affection, she tries to deceive him into thinking she has two "normal" legs.

The moral of Ben Lewin's *Paperback Romance* is disability happens. In addition to Sophie, each of the film's principal characters taste the physically challenged life: Eddie severs his tongue, his fiancée Gloria breaks her arm, and police officer Yuri, who lovingly compares Sophie to the tragic women of Russian literature, wears unexplained bandages over his nose. Lewin presents deforming accidents as part of the slapstick humor of everyday life.

While the film's self-conscious portrayal of Sophie's fantasies are ludicrously fun, the predictable and often banal circumstances of *Paperback Romance* are the fluff that supermarket Harlequins are made of.

Also reviewed in:
CHICAGO TRIBUNE, 8/29/97, Friday/p. G, Mark Caro
NEW YORK TIMES, 8/15/97, p. C8, Stephen Holden

PARADISE ROAD

A Fox Searchlight Pictures release of a Village Roadshow Pictures/YTC Pictures production in association with Planet Pictures. *Executive Producer:* Andrew Yap and Graham Burke. *Producer:* Sue Milliken and Greg Coote. *Director:* Bruce Beresford. *Screenplay:* Bruce Beresford. *Based on a story by:* David Giles and Martin Meader. *Based in part on the diaries of Betty Jeffrey in "White Coolies":* Betty Jeffrey. *Director of Photography:* Peter James. *Editor:* Tim Wellburn. *Music:* Christine Woodruff. *Music Editor:* Christo Curtis. *Choreographer:* Russell Page and Kate Dunn. *Sound:* Gary Wilkens and (music) Michael Gissing. *Sound Editor:* Gary O'Grady. *Casting:* Alison Barrett, Joseph Middleton, and Patsy Pollock. *Production Designer:* Herbert Pinter. *Art Director:* Ian Gracie. *Set Decorator:* Brian Edmonds. *Special Effects:* Brian Cox. *Costumes:* Terry Ryan. *Make-up:* Nikki Gooley. *Stunt Coordinator:* Glenn Boswell. *Running time:* 110 minutes. *MPAA Rating:* R.

CAST: Glenn Close (Adrienne Pargiter); Frances McDormand (Doctor Verstak); Pauline Collins (Margaret Drummond); Cate Blanchett (Susan Macarthy); Jennifer Ehle (Rosemary Leighton-Jones); Julianna Margulies (Topsy Merritt); Wendy Hughes (Mrs. Dickson); Johanna Ter Steege (Sister Wilhelmina); Elizabeth Spriggs (Mrs. Roberts); Pamela Rabe (Mrs. Tippler); Clyde Kusatsu (The Snake); Stan Egi (Captain Tanaka); David Chung (The Interpreter); Sab Shimono (Colonel Hirota); Penne Hackforth-Jones (Mrs. Pike); Pauline Chan (Wing); Lisa Hensley (Edna); Susie Porter (Oggi); Anita Hegh (Belt); Tessa Humphries (Celia Roberts); Lia Scallon (Mrs. O'Riordan); Marta Dusseldorp (Helen van Praagh); Marijke Mann (Mrs. Conje); Aden Young (Bill Seary); Paul Bishop (Dennis Leighton-Jones); Stephen O'Rourke (William Pargiter); Vincent Ball (Mr. Dickson); Nicholas Hammond (Marty Merritt); Noel Ferrier (Robbie Roberts); Steven Grives (Westmacott); Robert Grubb (Colonel Downes); Arthur Dignam (Mr. Pike); Tanya Bird (Siobhan O'Riordan); Alwine Seinen (Millie); Kitty Clignett (Sister Anna); Shira Van Essen (Antoinette van Praagh); Yoshi Adachi (Mr. Moto); Mitsu Sato (Rags); Taka Nagano (Boris); Koji Sasaki (Lofty); Julie Anthony (Female Vocalist); Geoffrey Ogden-Brown (Band Leader); Cafe Society Orchestra (Band); Jason Arden (Edgar); Kristine McAlister (Matron Heffernan); Jesse Rosenfeld (Danny Tippler); Phillip Stork (Michael Tippler); John Elcock (Seaman Francis); Hamish Urquhart (Aran O'Riordan); Jemal Blattner (Older Aran O'Riordan); John Proper (Captain Murchison); Shigenori Ito (Doctor Mizushima); Geoff O'Halloran (Sailor); Chi Yuen Lee and Ping Pan (Chinese Men).

CHRISTIAN SCIENCE MONITOR, 4/15/97, p. 13, David Sterritt

"Paradise Road," the new movie starring Glenn Close and recent Oscar-winner Frances McDormand, tells a true story that many moviegoers will find compelling.

At the height of World War II, a large group of women were captured by Japanese forces as they fled Australia on a ship gunned down at sea. Transported to the island of Sumatra, they were kept for years in a prison camp where British and Dutch refugees were also held.

Conditions were brutally bad, and morale was often perilously low. But many of the women gained spiritual strength by singing in a "vocal orchestra," immersing themselves in great music whose beauty helped them cope with their ordeal.

This extraordinary tale has several fine qualities. It reveals a little-known historical episode that ended in triumph for those who survived it. It celebrates the power of music to inspire and uplift people's lives.

It centers on strong, creative women whose courage and ingenuity help them meet challenges that would overcome many of the male heroes who fill today's movie screens.

But if this sounds like a picture you might enjoy, think twice before rushing to the box office.

In addition to its scenes of musical beauty, wartime bravery, and friendship under adversity, "Paradise Road" contains explicit views of women being threatened, assaulted, and beaten; prison authorities treating inmates as if they were animals instead of human beings; one character being tortured for hours of unrelenting pain; and even a helpless woman being burned alive before the horrified eyes of her comrades.

The story had to include these ingredients, of course, as part of its real-life tale. But it didn't have to spill them across the screen in such harrowing detail.

In the end, "Paradise Road" presents a box-office paradox. On one hand, people who want to see an unflinching portrayal of prison-camp brutality won't be much interested in long scenes of emotional bonding and ethereal singing. On the other, people seeking an uplifting tale about friendship and artistic exaltation will be appalled at the picture's outbursts of ultraviolence, however true these may be to the historical record.

If this contradiction hurts ticket sales for "Paradise Road," studio executives may wonder what crimped the picture's success.

A key answer may be that Hollywood movies are often designed by groups—including everyone from scriptwriters to marketing experts—whose members are motivated by different, sometimes conflicting interests. One faction may suggest emphasizing lovely classical music to attract refined viewers with a taste for culture. Another may insist on plenty of violence to draw younger audiences.

Sometimes, such compromises work. Other times, competing goals cancel each other out and kill a movie's chances before opening day.

"Paradise Road" is not the only current film to suffer from the made-by-committee blues. "Inventing the Abbotts," about class tensions and romantic longings in a Midwestern town during the 1950s, has a nostalgic atmosphere and sensitive performances that mature audiences might find very appealing—urless they object to the four-letter language, sex, and nudity that earn the picture an R rating.

Even the animated "Cats Don't Dance," which sports a refreshing G rating, seems driven by conflicting goals. Kids will love the cartoonish action that ensues when a starry-eyed young cat pulls up his small-town stakes and heads for Hollywood to become a musical-comedy star. But how many youngsters will understand the old-movie references that pepper nearly all the dialogue—apparently hoping to please grown-ups who accompany their children to the theater?

Nothing in Hollywood is simple, of course, and there are cases where seemingly mixed motives have surprising box-office potency. "Liar Liar" couples a largely child-centered plot—about a little boy who wishes his fast-talking dad won't be able to lie for 24 hours—with a steady barrage of vulgar words and sex-related humor.

This could have been a recipe for disaster, A la Jim Carrey's recent bomb, "The Cable Guy," which turned off almost everyone by gluing slapstick comedy onto a stalker-movie plot. Audiences have been flocking to "Liar Liar," though, revitalizing Carrey's career and giving Hollywood a financial lift as it awaits the potentially profitable warm-weather season.

It remains to be seen whether "Paradise Road" will soar as effortlessly as its music or sink under the weight of its harrowing violence. If the latter possibility comes true, studio chiefs should ask themselves afresh whether they really know what audiences they want to attract—or whether they're wedded to a scattershot approach that tries to please everybody and ends up making nobody happy.

LOS ANGELES TIMES, 4/11/97, Calendar/p. 12, Kenneth Turan

Trivia collectors take note: "Shine" is no longer the only Australian film to use classical music as the key to a sentimental drama about the unbreakable resilience of the human spirit. "Paradise Road" takes the same path, but another "Shine" it's not.

Set during World War II and dealing with the state of war that existed between Japanese captors and their charges in an all-women prisoner of war camp, "Paradise Road" is also at war with itself. A warmhearted horror show that puts clichéd movie people into a realistic situation, the signals it sends out are nothing but mixed.

Written and directed by Bruce Beresford, whose better-known works include "Driving Miss Daisy," "Tender Mercies" and "Breaker Morant," this film is intended as a tribute to a group of women who found a unique source of strength that enabled them to survive years of nightmarish imprisonment.

But try as it might, "Paradise Road" can't help being too purposefully uplifting for its own good, filled with non-surprising surprises and emotional epiphanies that are unenviable on the nose. Watching it serves to underscore how skillful "Shine" was in sidestepping some of those same obstacles and cannily simulating emotional reality.

Based on a true story, "Paradise Road" begins in Singapore on a February night in 1942. The colony's British residents are taking their ease at a fancy dress ball at the legendary Raffles Hotel, feeling smug and making derogatory comments about the capabilities of the Japanese armed forces.

An exploding bomb just outside the door changes everyone's tone. Almost immediately comes the announcement that the city will fall in a few days and a hurried plan to evacuate women and children by sea is put into effect. "It's a nice night," one woman says dryly, "for the collapse of an empire."

These opening sections, energized by a sense of urgency, are strong and promising. But once a series of mishaps leads these women, the most visible of whom is tea planter's wife Adrienne Pargiter (Glenn Close), to a Japanese prison camp on the island of Sumatra, the emotional texture gets dicier.

In the 40-odd years since the classic "The Bridge on the River Kwai" was set in a P.O.W. camp for men, standards for allowable on-screen brutality have considerably loosened, and "Paradise Road" takes full advantage of the change.

Under the direction of the vengeful Capt. Tanaka (Stan Egi), eager to act on his belief that "the time for rules has ended," the camp's guards unleash a barrage of savage beatings and graphic brutality on their prisoners, a scenario not likely to do much for Japan's current image abroad.

But if "Paradise Road" is realistic on a physical level, showing these women shoveling out latrines and coping with malaria as well as torture and foul food, its delineation of them as characters is considerably more pro forma. With nothing for these people to do that isn't familiar or expected, the characters tend to lose individual identity and blend together more than they ought to.

Some performers do stand out, though not always for the best reasons. Pauline Collins, the erstwhile star of "Shirley Valentine," smoothly handles the role of Miss Drummond, a saintly, unflappable missionary. Less successful is Frances McDormand, unusually at sea as the German Jewish Dr. Verstak, who calls everyone "darling" in a castoff Marlene Dietrich accent.

Equally visible is Close as Mrs. Pargiter, she of the short-cropped hair and stiff upper lip. Together with Miss Drummond, Pargiter, a music student before she married, comes up with the scheme of forming their fellow inmates into a vocal orchestra, in effect having the women delicately hum their way through some of the great pieces of the classical music repertoire. It's an endeavor that ends up touching even the stony hearts of their captors.

That story can't help but be a bit heartening in its way, but it's also a little too obvious at every turn. The same goes for the film's digs at a prewar society where women were forced to be wives or even nuns when what they really wanted to do was make music or repair trucks. It's not that that point isn't well worth making, it's rather too bad that the film doesn't trust us to discover its truths more on our own.

NEW YORK POST, 4/11/97, p. 45, Thelma Adams

"Nice night for the collapse of an empire," says American wife Topsy Merritt (Julianna Margulies) at the swinging start of Bruce Beresford's old-fashioned but feminist concentration camp drama, "Paradise Road."

It's Singapore, 1942. Before long all the white women in their evening dresses will be eating bugs and snakes, and bowing to the Japanese flag in Sumatra.

These include society wife Adrienne Pargiter (the imperial Glenn Close), English rose Rosemary Leighton-Jones (Jennifer Ehle), shy Ausie nurse Susan Macarthy (Cate Blanchett) and poodle - toting grand dame Mrs. Roberts (Elizabeth Spriggs).

The most affecting—and shocking—scenes arrive early. As Singapore falls, husbands and soldiers pack the Western women onto ships. Just as our gang—the sharp-tongued, the alkie, the silent, the soigne, the impossible—approaches international waters and safety, a flock of planes etches the horizon.

The Japanese bomb the ship into twigs and screws. As the women jump overboard, they leave one life behind and enter another. No more cricket club. No more gin fizzes. Just one scared, wet dog and the spirits they were born with.

"It could be worse, I suppose," says nurse Blanchett.

"Do you think so?" asks Close, in conversational tea talk as they dog paddle in the debris.

Beresford ("Driving Miss Daisy") smoothly controls the expository scenes in his fact-based story. They're sharp, intelligently written (by the director), and the characters pop out, pulling our emotions along with them without any resistance.

After some rough going, the survivors land in Sumatra. Japanese Soldiers round them up with a barbarism that mirrors the civility they left behind. They are beaten with sticks; decapitated heads grimace from poles in village squares.

Once the club women and nurses arrive at a Sumatran concentration camp, the film struggles between strong characters and stronger cliches. The cast expands to include a German Jewish doctor (played with a cynical swagger by Oscar-winner Frances McDormand), a singing missionary (Pauline Collins), a sympathetic Asian (Pauline Chan) and a whiskey-drinking nun (Johanna Ter Steege).

While the women don't tunnel out of the camp as men would do (the prime plot mover in movies from "Stalag 17" to "The Great Escape"), they find a spiritual escape in music. What Beresford gains in Dvorak, he loses in suspense.

Close, looking more stringy and masculine as time wears on, her eyes piercing blue in a saintly, skeletal face, revives her early interest in music (Mrs. Pargiter trained at the Royal Academy but abandoned all to be a society wife). She forms a vocal orchestra and the campers' performance of the New World Symphony give them strength and gain their jailed respect.

There's something very pat—and troubling—about Beresford's idea of concentration camp as spiritual Club Med where women become empowered through deprivation.

If they were really empowered, they wouldn't have been as obedient to their Japanese captors as they were previously to their fathers and husbands. They would have gotten the hell out—or somehow turned the tables on their captors rather than setting them for tea.

What makes "Paradise Road" a path worth taking is a blissful international cast that transcends its limitations and carries the drama almost to paradise.

NEWSDAY, 4/11/97, Part II/p. B2, John Anderson

Can a movie be based on fact and still make "Hogan's Heroes" seem like a documentary? To paraphrase Oscar Wilde, would it require someone with a heart of stone not to laugh at Glenn Close directing POWs singing "Bolero"?

The answers to these questions are strictly subjective, but they might occur to you while watching "Paradise Road," a film so noble it collapses under the weight of its own sincerity. Based on the experiences of female prisoners of the Japanese during World War II (Claudette Colbert served a similar sentence in 1950's "Three Came Home"), it concerns a multinational group on Sumatra that, in the face of relentless abuse, humiliation and its own internecine warfare, forms a "vocal orchestra."

For all its glorious Ravel and Dvorak, however—sung in a jungle that sounds like Alice Tully Hall—the film exalts its women beyond the bounds of believability, demonizes the Japanese beyond the limits of good taste and chronicles cruelty without establishing a point.

Director Bruce Beresford, who once made such films as "Breaker Morant" and "Black Robe"—and has more recently cranked out such softheaded, pseudo-sociology as "Last Dance"—is so constrained by formula that he loses track of what he's about. The initial setting is Singapore, 1942, where the self-satisfied colonials dance as if it's the end of the world, while maintaining a willful ignorance of the approaching Japanese. This lack of preparedness is presumably the fault of the men, since the women are mere accessories. But when the society wives voice the most virulently racist opinions about the enemy, dramatic tradition demands that their subsequent suffering be viewed as something they've brought on themselves. So which is it? Retribution or sexism?

It doesn't really matter, because the real purpose of the film is to subject its female characters to incessant peril. Even here, however, Beresford misfires. He attaches the same sense of indignation to the women being rudely awakened—the guards bang on their beds with batons—as he does to their physical beating. The abuse is constant, painful to watch and borders on the inane. At one point, a Chinese woman, Wing (Pauline Chan), is set on fire for dealing in contraband quinine (malaria is rampant and untreated). The actions of the Japanese may be historically accurate, but why did anyone feel compelled to recreate them? A movie like "Paradise Road" needs to teach a lesson, and it's hard to find one here, except as ethnic propaganda.

The movie's ostensible inspiration—the group organized by Adrienne (Close) and the missionary Margaret (Pauline Collins, of "Shirley Valentine") to sing wordless orchestral music—is also based on fact, but rings as falsely as anything else, including recent Oscar winner Frances McDormand's performance as a German-Jewish doctor who seems like a refugee from a Kurt Weill road show. The constant wisecracking is merely off-putting, but the ripest moment occurs when the Japanese guards, sent to break up the singers' premiere performance, are stopped in their tracks by the beauty of the music. Literally. The vicious, sadistic tormenters, rendered helpless by the "New World Symphony." If Adm. Halsey had only known ...

The importance of music to despairing captives was done, and to infinitely better effect, in "Playing for Time." And for all the courageousness of "Paradise Road," there are a few peculiar historical omissions. There are no rapes, for one thing—which, given the Japanese military's record concerning "comfort women," would have seemed an inevitability. The women are, however, herded to a nearby officers club and given the option of trading sex for three hots and an occupied cot. "Are Japanese officers any worse than most of the creeps we've known?" asks Topsy (Julianna Margulies). She's talked out of it, but not all the women are. "I just lost four sopranos," Adrienne mourns.

Close is unmercifully earnest, but Cate Blanchett is convincing as the insecure prisoner Susan, and Johanna Ter Steege, as the Dutch nun Wilhelmina, supplies some welcome comic relief. It's odd, but in the film's press notes, no mention is made—either in the plot synopsis or among the cast biographies—of any of the film's Asian male actors. This just reinforces the sense that "Paradise Road" is a kind of vanity production, a nest of raging egos co-opting the stories of brave, real-life women for their own shallow posturing.

SIGHT AND SOUND, 12/97, p. 50, Nick Kimberley

In 1941, bombs interrupt a society dance in Singapore. Women and children are shepherded into boats, one of which, carrying Australian and Dutch as well as British women, is sunk off the coast of Sumatra. Adrienne Pargiter, Rosemary Leighton-Jones and Susan Macarthy swim ashore where they encounter Captain Tanaka. He takes them to the nearest town where they are brutally rounded up by Japanese soldiers and reunited with other survivors from their boat including a German Jew, Dr Verstak, and Wing, a Chinese who reveals that Tanaka belongs to the Japanese secret police.

The Japanese bully the women nickname "The Snake" marches them to a prison camp. Tension between the women repeatedly interrupts their routines. Verstak observes with wry detachment while treating the sick. When posh Mrs Roberts falls ill, Wing risks her life to get quinine for her. Someone betrays her to Tanaka. Before the whole camp, he douses her with petrol and lights it. Later, Pargiter and missionary Margaret Drummond hatch the idea of forming a "vocal orchestra".

The best-looking prisoners are offered the chance to work as unpaid prostitutes for better conditions and some accept. Pargiter is caged for hitting a soldier, but freed thanks to Drummond's intervention with Colonel Hirota. Tanaka tortures Macarthy for a perceived slight, but she survives. Hirota finally allows Pargiter's orchestra to perform Ravel's *Boléro*. The Japanese are entranced.

When the camp is moved, the women learn that the Japanese are losing the war, but many women die including Drummond. At her funeral, Tanaka taunts Pargiter, who responds by banging out *Boléro* with some stones. All the prisoners join in. Eventually, Hirota announces that the war is over and the women embrace.

It's both an advantage and a drawback of prison-camp movies that they make it all too easy to distinguish between the good guys (gals in this case) and the bad guys. Bruce Beresford knows that if he lets his narrative framework become too schematic our sympathies might evaporate; but he also knows that you can't make heroes out of torturers and prison-camp commandants. Besides, there's a large element of fact in the story he's telling. There really was a women's vocal orchestra put together in a Japanese prisoner-of-war camp on Sumatra, and while *Paradise Road* no doubt makes free with the historical details, it honours the spirit of the women's bravery.

In the process, of course, Beresford is obliged to make the Japanese gruesome and it has to be said that his actors co-operate. Clyde Kusatsu's performance as The Snake achieves a bestial intensity, its brutality made the more physical by the fact that Beresford provides no subtitles for the sections of Japanese dialogue, so that we, like the women, have to guess at what is being said. Here, the Japanese communicate by means of facial contortion, vocal volume and sheer terror and that terror has an almost physical effect on the movie's audience.

Yet there are dramatic problems the film never quite resolves. It's a myth (which is not to say it's untrue) quite deeply embedded in the modern psyche that certain torturers, whether in Nazi Germany or in Ariel Dorfman's play *Death and the Maiden,* have a predilection for classical music. But the sadism of the women's tormentors can't be made to disappear in a beatific smile and a puff of tobacco smoke simply by a rendition of *Boléro* in multipart vocalisation. At least the movie makes it clear that the music's beneficial effects on the prison camp staff last no longer than the performance itself.

In the end, what matters to Beresford, and hence to us, is the spirit that allows these women to cope with the abysmal conditions in the camps, even though many of them are hopelessly ill-equipped to deal with anything but a life of cosseted luxury. Although Glenn Close's Pargiter and Pauline Collins' Drummond are a little too good to be true, the network of relationships between the women is convincingly multi-faceted. There are gripers and shirkers as well as paragons and saints, and the racial superiority voiced time and again by the Japanese finds an echo, albeit faint, in the petty prejudices of the English women, only too eager to believe the Dutch women have stolen their soap in the showers. And in a neatly underplayed moment, we see the Jewish Dr Verstak extracting gold teeth from corpses, exactly as the Nazis were doing to Jewish corpses in Europe at the very same time. Verstak's motive is honourable, if still distasteful: she sells the teeth to the Japanese in exchange for medical supplies.

Paradise Road, to its credit, never wholly abandons the generic tropes of the women's prison movie. We may get no lesbian love, but we do get the shower scene, the torn-hair fight, and in a scene where a Dutch nun repairs a truck that the Japanese mechanic can't manage, we get the sweet innocent who proves sparkier than any man. We also get a powerful ensemble performance that knows exactly how to jerk our tears. It's a manipulative movie, certainly, in which emotions have priority over everything, but there's no dishonour in that. Just don't expect sophisticated political analysis.

TIME, 4/14/97, p. 96, Richard Schickel

Singapore: Raffles Hotel, early 1942. The colonial swells are having a party—black ties, a ricky-ticky dance band lulling them with torpid tunes. As they swill their bubbly, they mutter contempt for the advancing Japanese army in smug racist terms.

Don't these folks know they're fox-trotting on the edge of a volcano? No, of course not. They never do. But we do. We've been partying with their heedless ilk on the eve of disaster since we started going to the movies. We know that when the pretty girl and the handsome lad start moonily planning their future, the *crump-crump-crump* of an artillery barrage is but a moment away.

We also know that we are in for a very long day's journey on writer-director Bruce Beresford's endlessly predictable *Paradise Road.* Do we know that the ship carrying the women and children to safety as Singapore surrenders will be sunk, Red Cross markings or not? Can we predict that the well-spoken Japanese officer some of the survivors meet when they stumble ashore on Sumatra will turn out to be a sadist? When the commandant of the camp where they're interned appears, are we not instantly certain he studied penology with Colonel Saito over on the River Kwai?

And we're just getting started. We have much familiar hardship and vile torment to go. Not to mention the inevitable triumph of the human spirit. One day Adrienne Pargiter (Glenn Close) and Margaret Drummond (Pauline Collins) get to humming the theme from a symphony. The former once studied music seriously; the latter is a missionary who knows how inspiring a good tune can be when you're in the dumps. Or trying to survive in one. Soon enough the prisoners form a symphonic chorus, which sings wordless versions of great orchestral works. Even the more selfish and cynical prisoners—among them recent Academy Award winner Frances McDormand, rather miscast as a Viennese Jewish doctor—register awe and wonder at this feat.

We are assured that this all really happened. Survivors have imparted their memories to Beresford. The vocal arrangements they made still exist and are used in the movie. But in shaping their tale for the screen, shouldn't he have honored their courage—and, yes, inventiveness—with something other than clichés?

VILLAGE VOICE, 4/15/97, p. 72, Leslie Camhi

Another tale of women under duress [the reference is to *Leo Tolstoy's Anna Karenina*], *Paradise Road* follows a group of mostly British and Australian expatriates who were evacuated from Singapore in 1942 on the eve of Japanese occupation. When their boat is bombed, they jump ship, and several women manage to swim to shore in Sumatra. There their troubles begin in earnest; they're captured and interned with local Dutch women in a Japanese prison camp, where they're starved, tortured, and nearly worked to death. In an act of spiritual resistance, the women form an orchestra of voices, rehearsing complex modernist works in secret and performing to a stunned audience of inmates and jailers.

Bruce Beresford has assembled an impressive ensemble of luminaries and newcomers. Glenn Close stars as a British society woman who conceives of the orchestra with her friend, a mild-mannered missionary played by the excellent Pauline Collins. Julianna Margulies is winning as a tough, pretty American, and Cate Blanchett portrays a young Australian nurse with an upper lip that is alternately stiff and trembling. Frances McDormand lends her considerable talents to the role of an aloof, German-Jewish refugee; unfortunately, her harsh accent makes her sound like Colonel Klink, and her satiric performance seems spliced in from another movie.

In fact, these characters must endure not only their jailers' brutality but also all the cinematic conventions of the prison and concentration-camp genres. Yes, there's a perennial nay sayer in this group, and, needless to say, she's a smoker. There's a beautiful girl who pines away for love, and several traitors who sleep with the enemy. *Paradise Road* does have some uncommonly moving moments, but when the women start to die in droves, the film itself begins to fade. History alone can't keep a film alive.

Also reviewed in:
NEW YORK TIMES, 4/11/97, p. C12, Stephen Holden
NEW YORKER, 4/14/97, p. 89, Anthony Lane
VARIETY, 4/7-13/97, p. 42, Emanuel Levy
WASHINGTON POST, 4/18/97, p. C1, Rita Kempley
WASHINGTON POST, 4/18/97, Weekend/p. 44, Desson Howe

PEACEMAKER, THE

A DreamWorks Pictures release. *Executive Producer:* Michael Grillo and Laurie MacDonald. *Producer:* Walter Parkes and Branko Lustig. *Director:* Mimi Leder. *Screenplay:* Michael Schiffer. *Based on an article by:* Leslie Cockburn and Andrew Cockburn. *Director of Photography:* Dietrich Lohmann. *Editor:* David Rosenbloom. *Music:* Hans Zimmer. *Music Editor:* Adam Milo Smalley. *Sound:* Tom Nelson and (music) Alan Meyerson. *Sound Editor:* J. Paul Huntsman and Victor Iorillo. *Casting:* Risa Bramon-Garcia and Randi Hiller. *Production Designer:* Leslie Dilley. *Art Director:* Dennis Bradford, Keith Gonzales, William Ladd Skinner, Ivo Husnjak, and Neno Pecur. *Set Designer:* Joshua Lusby. *Set Decorator:* Rosemary

Brandenburg and Alan Hicks. *Special Effects:* Martin Gutteridge. *Visual Effects:* Michael Backes. *Costumes:* Shelley Komarov. *Make-up:* Rolf John Keppler. *Stunt Coordinator:* G.A. Aguilar. *Running time:* 122 minutes. *MPAA Rating:* R.

CAST: George Clooney (Colonel Thomas Devoe); Nicole Kidman (Dr. Julia Kelly); Armin Mueller-Stahl (Dimitri Vertikoff); Marcel Iures (Dusan Gavrich); Alexander Baluev (Alexsander Kodoroff); Rene Medvesek (Vlado Mirich); Gary Werntz (Hamilton); Randall Batinkoff (Ken); Jim Haynie (General Garnett); Alexander Strobele (Shummaker); Holt McCallany (Appleton); Michael Boatman (CPN Beach); Joan Copeland (Senator Bevens); Carlos Gomez (Santiago); Slavko Juraga (Stevo); Alexander Reskov (Vassily); Dejan Acimovic (Driver); Harsh Nayyar (Doctor Taraki); Matt Adler (Alan); Tamara Tunie (Jody); Alexander Yatsko (Russian Corporal); Bruce MacVittie (DOE Helo Tech); Luboir Paulovic (Pockman); Charles Dumas (Branigan); Ramsey Faragallah (Cabbie); Murphy Guyer (INS Agent); Leslie Dilley (New York Priest); David Lomax (FBI agent 2); Adina Porter (New York Female Cop); Hubert Kramar (Kordech Guard); Alma Cuervo (UN Representative); Sébasatian Roche (German Backpacker); Blaise Corrigan (FBI agent 1); Gordon Catlin (Gunner); John Ottavio (FBI Agent 3); Goran Visnijic (Bazta Sergeant); Jay Acovone (Cop); Hannah Werntz (Piano Student); James Colby (Limo Driver); Jean Rogers (Sarajevo CNN Representative); Matt Winston (UN Official); Terry Serpico (Sniper 1); Thom Mathews (Major Rich Numbers); Jerry Dixon (Sniper 2); David Lagle (Pilot 3); Lou Moustillo (Costello); Bozidar Smiljanic (Serb Minister); Michael Potts and Richard Poe (DOE Haz-mat Techs); Slobodan Dimitrijevic (Serb Official); Martin Nikodym (Polish IFOR Soldier); Charles Cavalier (Angry Motorist); Jerome Hardeman (Pilot 1); David Hamilton Simonds (Philly Agent); Irmelin Mai Hoffer (Vienna Cafe Singer); Chuck Cooper (NYPD cop); Jono Kouzouyon (Bazta Merchant); Jared Chandler (Marine); Evert Sooster (Praporshik); Branko Lustig (Man with Poodle); Mathew Sussman (National Guard Captain); Bill Christ (DOE Agent); William Hill (Agent); Bernie McInerney (Carey); Andrea Doven (Kelly Girl); James Dumont (Young Sniper); Mark Johnson (CIA Agent); Alexander Kuznetsov (Russian Controller); Ed Semenov (Radio Officer); Bruce Gray (CNN Newscaster); Endre Hules (Older Major).

CHRISTIAN SCIENCE MONITOR, 10/3/97, p. 12, David Sterritt

Gone are the days when Hollywood studios were truly "dream factories," cranking out illusions with assembly-line regularity. Today's studios are less like factories than finance companies, doling out money to artists and technicians who do the hands-on work of filmmaking.

Yet the dream-factory image lives on, and in what may prove to be the most important show-business development of the 1990s: DreamWorks, the first major studio since the '30s to be created from the ground up. Its products range from movies and TV series to CDs and computer games.

If the names of its founders are any indication, it could have a huge impact on American enter-tainment. Movie mogul Steven Spielberg, media executive Jeffrey Katzenberg, and music mag-nate David Geffen are three of the savviest—and most successful—figures in their field.

If the quality of its first movie is any indication, though, excitement could fizzle out fast. "The Peacemaker" is a warmed-over story told with little conviction and less imagination. It may pull in box-office dollars from die-hard action fans, but anyone hoping for fresh approaches is in for a disappointment.

"The Peacemaker" begins with a gang of greedy terrorists hijacking a trainload of nuclear weapons in the Russian countryside, setting off a blast to cover their tracks. Alerted to this crisis, two American experts—a brainy atomic scientist and a brawny intelligence officer—scoot from Washington to Eastern Europe and finally New York, tracking first the nuclear thieves and then a lone psychopath with a bomb in his backpack.

These ingredients are hardly original—ruthless villains, odd-couple heroes, ticktocking count-downs, colorful explosions—but they can still be effective if cleverly used. Sad to say, they seem more trite than true in the hands of director Mimi Leder, making her big-screen debut after years of "ER" and other TV shows.

While she keeps the action hopping from one flash point to the next and cooks up a couple of exciting sequences in the last 30 minutes, she doesn't develop the narrative momentum needed to sustain a two-hour story.

Nor does she instill much inspiration in her stars. George Clooney was more expressive wearing his "Batman & Robin" mask than toting his military medals here. And whose idea was it to make Nicole Kidman a multi-lingual nuclear specialist? The same show-biz agent who pitched her as a brain surgeon in "Days of Thunder"? The oddest thing about "The Peacemaker" is that DreamWorks appears to have cut corners on the production—a peculiar decision, given the importance of a rip-roaring success to inaugurate the studio. The budget has been reported at $50 million. That's about average for today's Hollywood, but a tad stingy for a picture relying on high-speed adventure and high-tech effects (always popular in the non-English-speaking market overseas).

DreamWorks may become more impressive when its next movies appear. Spielberg's historical drama "Amistad" promises to be another serious-minded venture in the "Schindler's List" vein, and the comedy "Mouse Hunt," starring Nathan Lane and Christopher Walken, sounds like fun.

But the fact that things may improve doesn't mean "The Peacemaker" is worth the price of a ticket. Older studios have barraged us with more than enough eye-popping chase scenes, strung-out villains, and movie stars outrunning fireballs. DreamWorks is overstuffed with money, talent, and clout. It should be aiming much higher than its dreary debut suggests.

LOS ANGELES TIMES, 9/26/97, Calendar/p. 1, Kenneth Turan

"The Peacemaker" is one of those "what was that all about?" movies, where events rush by so fast you're convinced you must have seen something but you're not sure exactly what.

Quick assassinations, cold-blooded double-crosses, train wrecks, car chases through crowded streets of European capitals, the fate of civilization as we know it—they've all been shoe-horned into the much-anticipated first film from DreamWorks, Hollywood's newest studio.

Whether viewed as a bellwether for what to expect from the new guys or simply on its own merits, "The Peacemaker" comes across as a strictly genre project done with more than the usual amount of polish and skill. So while it's nice to see a high craft level on an action thriller, it's hard to get excited about something that's so business-as-usual at its core.

The crispness with which events move along can be credited to first-time feature director Mimi Leder and her team, including cinematographer Dietrich Lohmann, editor David Rosenbloom ("Primal Fear") and composer Hans Zimmer, whose score pounds away at a fierce clip.

Leder, who's won Emmys for her work on "ER," the show of the moment on network TV, does not linger on any shot or any situation. Though she has a tendency to feature as many close-ups of worried faces as the Oscar telecast, Leder has a zest for action and does it well.

What "The Peacemaker" doesn't do well, though it tries, is bring much in the way of emotion or character development to the table. While Michael Schiffer's script, based on research done by Andrew Cockburn and Leslie Cockburn on nuclear weapons smuggling out of the former Soviet bloc, is strong on event, its moments of personal agony and regret are uniformly unconvincing.

Mostly, however, what we get in the way of dialogue are people screaming, "It doesn't make sense," and demanding to talk on a secure phone. If you think that means a telephone that's firmly attached to a nearby wall, you've got a lot to learn about the world of international espionage and intrigue.

Here to fill you in are Dr. Julia Kelly (Nicole Kidman), a top scientist and acting head of the White House Nuclear Smuggling Group, and Lt. Col. Thomas Devoe (George Clooney), an intelligence officer with Army Special Forces. Unlikely allies, it takes something as powerful as a 75-kiloton nuclear explosion to blow them together.

That bomb blast in the Urals deep in the former USSR signals that a nefarious scheme is under-way to steal nuclear warheads and sell them ($200 million apiece seems to be the going rate) to whatever enemies of truth, justice and the American way can afford to pay the tariff.

Teamed up by the urgency of the situation, Kelly and Devoe tackle the problem via brains (hers) and brawn (his). While the good doctor tries to figure out who would be in the market for a warhead, the lieutenant colonel, a take-charge type who doesn't hesitate to break noses when the mood is on him, gets physical and justifies it by saying: "This is how things work in the real world."

Both Kidman and Clooney give dependable, movie-star performances in these James Bond-ish roles. While Kidman's Dr. Kelly is too much the cliched frazzled female at times, the script balances that with scenes of strength and competence. And though Clooney is the same dark-eyed smiling rogue he's played in just about all his feature roles, it's a characterization that is effective.

Also worth noting is Romanian actor Marcel lures as Dusan Gavrich, a Serbian piano teacher with a soulful face and a date with destiny. But though "The Peacemaker's" plot is international enough to have technicians credited in 10 countries, the film manages to treat Sarajevo and Pale, the capital of the Bosnian Serb republic, as if they were the same place, which is like confusing Benjamin Netanyahu and Yassir Arafat. With all that hustle and bustle going on, maybe they figured no one would notice.

NEW YORK, 9/29/97, p. 51, David Denby

Perhaps the most interesting thing about *The Peacemaker*—the ballyhooed first film released by the ballyhooed new studio DreamWorks—is that the director is a woman. Mimi Leder's experience is limited to series TV, but she plunges into large-scale action here with all the hard expertise and relentless momentum of Wolfgang Petersen or Andrew Davis. People jump from one moving train to another, cars play smash palace in Vienna's narrow streets, and George Clooney dangles from a helicopter. Leder appears to have an instinctive feeling for how a big thriller should go. She lays on the weight, noise, and power right at the beginning with a mysterious sequence of trains moving out of a station (crunch, crunch, CRUNCH!) somewhere in Russia late at night. The dark-toned, heavy-metal opening is portentous but appropriate: Some disaffected Russian military types are in the process of stealing an SS-18 nuclear missile with multiple warheads. *The Peacemaker is* taut, powerful, consistently exciting. It's also, I'm afraid, a great deal too much like many other thrillers made recently.

Playing a brilliant lady scientist (you can't make these movies anymore without one), Nicole Kidman, her body covered in pants and long-sleeved white shirts, may not be very convincing when she speaks techno jargon, but she's extremely charming. Taking a deep breath before speaking, she really acts the part of someone unused to exercising authority; she allows herself to seem a woman repelled by brutality. George Clooney, whose clipped, self-sufficient manner is the latest style in smart-ass one-upmanship, is the special-ops colonel who thinks he can teach the scientist the nasty facts of life.

Here's the deal: A rogue Russian general has stolen the nukes from a train; the general then wrecks the train and detonates one of the warheads in order to cover his tracks. Clooney thinks that nothing but money is at stake—a quick sale to Iran, perhaps. Kidman says no; she fears a fanatic with a single warhead more than a greedy cynic with eight warheads. They are both right: The Russian wants money, and a Bosnian Serb, who gets one of the warheads, wants revenge for the death of his family in the civil war.

The movie turns into an elaborate chase, with Kidman and Clooney tracking the thieves by means of electronic surveillance, then helicopter, and at last, rather breathlessly, on foot through the crowded streets of Manhattan. For all its professed horror of a nuclear catastrophe, *The Peacemaker* is rather casual about the bomb that does go off in the Urals. But Ms. Leder can certainly move the metal with the best of them.

NEW YORK POST, 9/26/97, p. 41, Michael Medved

If the first big release from Steven Spielberg's much-heralded new partnership, DreamWorks SKG, is any indication, then this company won't distinguish itself with novel projects; it will just do them much better than anyone else. "The Peacemaker" is, quite simply, the most exciting—and plausible—terrorist thriller yet filmed.

The format is familiar: one courageous superhero (George Clooney) saving the world from deadly schemes by a charismatic wacko. What makes this effort best of its breed is the shockingly sophisticated and topical script (from Michael Schiffer, of "Crimson Tide") and the taut, expertly edited effort by director Mimi Leder (an Emmy Award-winning TV veteran in her knockout big-screen debut).

The movie begins, quite literally, with a bang as a nuclear explosion in Russia grabs the attention of the White House and Pentagon brass. Nicole Kidman plays a Princeton-educated, national-security rookie who is assigned by the president to follow up reports that nine similar bombs disappeared after the blast and may be headed for terrorists or arms merchants.

She's teamed with a cocksure Army lieutenant colonel and intelligence expert (Clooney). Together they fly to Europe in a desperate effort to find the missing nukes.

In Vienna, they connect with a worldly-wise former KGB honcho (and Clooney's old friend), Armin Mueller-Stahl, searching for a corrupt Russian general (Alexander Baluev) who may lead the conspiracy to steal the bombs.

Absorbing techno-thriller details, such as pinpoint satellite surveillance monitoring the progress of a single truck, come across more convincingly and less distractingly than in the Tom Clancy film adaptations; a splendidly choreographed car chase provides an unforgettably chilling experience precisely because neither our hero and heroine nor their borrowed (and ultimately battered) vehicle comes across as invulnerable or implacable.

Clooney is an ideal leading man for this material, with a diffident charm that makes his derring-do endearing rather than intimidating.

Kidman is the perfect counterpart, facing personal danger for the first time with impressive athleticism and unmistakable smarts.

Best of all is Marcel Iures as the intellectual, sad-eyed Bosnian terrorist whose comprehensible motivation makes his actions all the more chilling.

NEWSDAY, 9/26/97, Part II/p. B3, Jack Mathews

Mimi Leder's "The Peacemaker" marks the first day of issue for the film division of spanking new DreamWorks SKG, the studio formed by Steven Spielberg, David Geffen and Jeffrey Katzenberg, and today's date will be writ neither in infamy nor triumph. This action-thriller is as routine Hollywood fare as the summer weather that should have greeted it.

Starring George Clooney and Nicole Kidman as competitive allies chasing nuclear terrorists from Bosnia to Russia to New York, "The Peacemaker" is undiluted high-tech adventure, filled with heavy-breathing exposition, calamitous chases, impossible feats of derring-do, a jackhammer musical score and rare seconds of plausibility.

It's not the hijacking of nuclear weapons, so superbly choreographed in the opening sequence, that strains credulity. Given the almost instant collapse of the Iron Curtain, it's no stretch to believe a few nukes would be copped by resourceful Russian thieves and sold to anti-West terrorists. What sucks the air out of your lungs is that the fate of so many millions of people, not to mention real estate values in targeted Manhattan, are entrusted to so unlikely a set of superheroes.

There are references to the Pentagon and to the president, but when 10 plutonium bombs are taken from a train in Russia, the task of finding and disarming them falls to nuclear scientist Julia Kelly (Kidman), acting head of the White House Nuclear Smuggling Group, and her military liaison, Lt. Col. Thomas Devoe (Clooney). For Kelly, it's a big job, a big opportunity and a big crock. There is actually a scene in the movie where the president's national security adviser asks her if she's willing to risk World War III to follow her instincts and violate Russian air space.

"Yes, I am," she says, firmly.

Well, all righty then, go to it. Give us a call, let us know how it turns out.

Mimi Leder, a multiple-Emmy winner for episodes of "China Beach" and "ER," directs her first feature without prejudice. She takes the overheated script and her unlikely cast, and fashions something resembling frenzied docudrama. It's as if she were directing "The Guns of Navarone" under the lash of Oliver Stone.

Using quick cuts, close-ups, shifting camera angles and Hans Zimmer's re-duh-duh-duh-duh-dundant score, Leder creates such a quick-paced illusion of actuality that audiences may be swallowing events before they feel the hooks. She has an obvious gift for action (or did boss Spielberg lend a hand?), which is best demonstrated in a terrific sequence where she turns a car chase into a metaphor for a toughest-man contest.

But inevitably, the film hangs on the veracity of its two main characters, and they have none. Clooney's Devoe is like some sweaty incarnation from an Ollie North fever dream. He's handsome, headstrong, quick-witted, athletic, patriotic and—where there's a task at hand—immune from the laws of society. It's a role tailored to the strengths of a major action star, which Clooney, to date, is not.

Kidman is almost comically miscast. A centerfold scientist to the rescue. Not that the White House Nuclear Smugging Group, if such a thing existed, wouldn't be led by a beautiful woman, but that she'd also be put in charge of the globe-hopping mission to recover the weapons, to engage in hand-to-hand combat, and to race a ticking clock to disarm a plutonium warhead is the kind of scenario you get out of a bong.

Lost in the smoke is a provocatively unconventional villain. Dusan, convincingly played by the Romanian actor Marcel Iures, is a man whose wife and daughter were killed by snipers in Sarajevo, and who is now driven by depression and bitterness to nuke the UN "peacemakers" he blames for his grief.

There's solid human drama in that, to be sure, but it's a subject to explore in a serious context, not in a summer movie. Even one that comes out in the fall.

NEWSWEEK, 9/29/97, p. 71, David Ansen

Nuclear scientist Nicole Kidman and army intelligence officer George Clooney put aside their temperamental differences to save the world from a terrorist with a nuke. That, in a nutshell, describes the globe-hopping action-thriller *The Peacemaker*, the first release film the much-ballyhooed DreamWorks. No one will accuse it of breaking the mold with this one, a competent summer movie that happens to arrive in the fall. Director Mimi Leder, a veteran of "ER," starts things with a bang, strikingly staging a train hijacking in which 10 nuclear warheads are stolen by a renegade Russian general and an 11th explodes. In its set pieces—a car-crushing shoot-out in Vienna, a wild bomb hunt in New York"—"Peacemaker" fills the mindless-action-movie quota quite stylishly.

The trouble is, "The Peacemaker" thinks it has a mind. (As proof of its seriousness, it dispenses with a star romance.) It's the first studio movie to touch upon the war in Bosnia, but it does this so meretriciously that you wish it had stuck to fantasy. Most egregious is its piano-playing Serb villain, to whom the movie attempts to give tragic depths by showing us his daughter's death by snipers. (In Sarajevo, it wasn't Serbs who were killed by sniper fire.) Nothing about this man—his motives, his odd politics—makes any sense. Leder tries to bring a sense of grief to a body-count-happy genre, but you can't have it both ways. Every time Kidman and Clooney take a break from their movie-star bantering to mourn a death, it rings hollow. You don't cast Nicole Kidman as a nuclear scientist and then expect the audience to furrow its brow over world events. Where's mindlessness when we really need it?

SIGHT AND SOUND, 11/97, p. 49, Andy Medhurst

In Russia's Ural Mountains, two trains collide, producing a nuclear explosion. Amid the confusion this causes, a number of nuclear warheads are smuggled out of Russia by a small group of profiteers led by rogue soldier Alexsander Kodoroff. The American response to the crisis is headed by nuclear scientist Julia Kelly and military agent Col. Thomas Devoe, who has doubts concerning both Kelly's gender and inexperience. Kelly and Devoe fly to Vienna to meet Dimitri Vertikoff, a Russian friend of Devoe's, who gives them vital information but is killed by Kodoroff's associates. Kodoroff's gang is tracked down to a small road near the Iranian border where Devoe leads a mission to ambush and capture them.

In the battle that follows, Kodoroff and most of his gang are killed, but one escapes with a single warhead. He delivers this to Dusan Gavrich, a Bosnian politician about to attend a summit conference in New York. Once a believer in democratic processes, Gavrich has been pushed towards violent revenge by the death of his wife and child in Sarajevo and what he sees as western complicity in the bloodshed in Bosnia. By the time Kelly and Devoe have identified him and traced his movements, both Gavrich and the bomb he now carries have eluded them. He plans to detonate the bomb at the UN, thereby focusing world attention on the situation in Bosnia. After a desperate chase though the streets of New York, Kelly and Devoe corner the wounded Gavrich in a church. Before dying, he primes the bomb to explode, but Kelly saves the day and earns Devoe's respect by defusing it.

This is an impossible, and therefore fascinating, film. What it wants to be is a politically subtle action thriller, but its chosen genre simply has no room for the moral complexity to which it aspires, resulting in a deeply fractured text. An audience that allows itself to enjoy action thrillers, to relish their spectacle, tension and expense, always has to leave its ideological sensitivities at home unless, of course, it's an audience so reactionary as to positively relish the naked racism of, say, *True Lies*. Certain films of the genre invite that amnesia either by being spectacularly naive (my favourite example of this tendency is *Rambo III*'s version of Afghanistan) or so complex and fanciful it's impossible to grasp what the politics on offer actually are *(Mission Impossible)*.

The Peacemaker refuses to take either option, striving instead to blend the thick-ear pleasures of explosions and chases with a sincere attempt to address the recent and current tragedies of Eastern Europe. The ambiguities of that project are nicely captured in its title: who or what precisely is "the peacemaker"? The United States? The United Nations? Clooney's all-American hero? The despairing Bosnian Gavrich? The nuclear device which he intends to use for his desperate purpose? Juggling all these possibilities while still pushing the required generic buttons puts an insupportable strain on the film, but even if it can't hope to succeed, its noble failure demands a certain degree of respect.

The real strengths of the film lie outside its top-line stars, though both are on reasonable form. Clooney is even more scrumptious in army gear than he was in Batman drag, and looks increasingly set to be a key male star of mainstream Hollywood's next decade, while Kidman does what she can with the now clichéd role of the gorgeous-yet-brainy female lead. Their sparring has an occasional zinginess that suggests they'd make an outstanding team in a romantic comedy. Here, though, both are outclassed by the little-known Marcel Iures, in the pivotal role of Dusan Gavrich. His character is saddled with a degree of stereotyping—he has soulfully suffering eyes and is given to playing moodily classical piano—but in general he delivers an affecting performance that gives the film real weight. It's rare indeed for Hollywood film to concede that a 'terrorist' determined to blow the heart out of a US city might in fact be someone with complex motivations well beyond the simplistic model of 'evil' usually wheeled on in films of this type. Yet this raises a generic problem, for if the usual villain figure is for once treated with dignity and even sympathy, who is the gung-ho hero going to kick around the screen?

The part of Clooney's punchbag and all-round slimebag is occupied by Kodoroff, suggesting that though the intractable messiness of the Bosnian situation precludes demonising Dusan, there will always be a reliably diabolical Russian to hunt down and destroy. Even here, though, *The Peacemaker* distances itself from a purely moronic Cold War mentality by counterposing Kodoroff with the avuncular, likeable Vertikoff, whose brutal killing is intended to legitimate much of the US-instigated mayhem that follows.

Mimi Leder, in charge of her first film after impressing Steven Spielberg with her work directing *ER*, shows no sign of nerves on being entrusted with such a blockbuster. Indeed, the film's supple visual dynamism should lay to rest forever those tired industry truisms about women's inability to handle action pictures, with the vertiginous fight over a gorge at the Iranian border and the panic-inducing editing of the climactic New York pursuit constituting two especially impressive sequences.

The tensions between visceral pleasure and political responsibility make this a schizophrenic film—Kidman's attempts to map out the convolutions of Balkan politics are more than once rudely disrupted by another car chase or military alert, while the way the script scatters names like Chechnya and Azerbaijan may alienate some insular US audiences, leaving them impatient for imperialist fisticuffs. Nonetheless, *The Peacemaker* is at least trying to widen the remit of action cinema, to inject a little complication into a traditionally reductive genre, and as such stands as one of the most intriguing Hollywood films of the year.

TIME, 9/29/97, p. 95, Richard Corliss

Three years in the making! At a cost of $2.7 billion! From three of the most powerful men in show biz! Ladies and gents, DreamWorks SKG proudly presents: *The Peacemaker*!

Actually, the film cost a thrifty $50 million; the $2.7 billion is for the startup of the multimedia company that Steven Spielberg, Jeffrey Katzenberg and David Geffen created in 1994. But since

DreamWorks has been on the pokey side delivering boffo product from its TV and music divisions, the release of *The Peacemaker* has sparked anxious anticipation. Shouldn't the studio's first film, like the opening bars of a symphony, make a statement about the outfit's ambitions?

Not this one. The picture is an urgent if conventional thriller about the theft of a nuclear bomb by a Serbian terrorist. Every nation wants to defuse the bomb since the terrorist says he will use it to blow up the United Nations. But in Michael Schiffer's script the task is pretty much left to a cowboy and a lady: U.S. Army Colonel Tom Devoe (George Clooney) and nuclear scientist Julia Kelly (Nicole Kidman). They race around the globe (the film was shot in 10 countries), kill villains, crash cars and tap on computers.

Standard action-film stuff, including the big-vehicle-dangling-off-a-precipice scene from Spielberg's *Lost World.* It works well for a while, thanks to Mimi Leder's bustling direction and to Clooney, who has a gift for eroticizing impatience. ("Women!" his stare says. "Can't live with 'em; they can't live without me.") Then the film finds sympathy for its villain and goes softly nuts with him. In the final chase everyone's IQ drops about 20 points.

The rest of *The Peacemaker* moves with familiar efficiency. It ain't DreamWorst. It's just an odd little film for the big guys to say hello with.

VILLAGE VOICE, 9/30/97, p. 84, Gary Dauphin

If the first film to be released by DreamWorks SKG (that's Messrs. Spielberg, Katzenberg, and Geffen to you and me) is any omen of the studio's fortunes, expect things to start slow, pick up steam, and then plateau at a level where money and high technology tend to mask a general lack of ideas. *The Peacemaker* is a semirealistic Bond flick without the Bond, an expensive globe-trot wherein an untested NSC nuclear scientist (Nicole Kidman, frosty even when she's nice) and a loose-cannon army intel officer (George Clooney, looking at times like a younger, thinner Al Gore) chase a stolen Russian nuclear warhead from the Iranian border to Bosnia to East 44th Street.

The film is front-loaded with 45 minutes of ponderous warhead-stealing and bickering between Kidman and Clooney, but once our heroes leave the monitor-strewn situation rooms of Washington, *Peacemaker* gets going quite nicely. First-time feature director Mimi Leder seems at ease with the large-scale deployments of men and material that are part of any action flick starring the U.S. government, and the second half of *The Peacemaker* would have made a pretty good summer multiplex entry. The last reel, where New York City falls under federal emergency management, is a real gem, especially when the NYPD starts cuffing and grabbing every man, woman, and child in Manhattan wearing a backpack even though the bomber's face has been on the wires for hours. Apparently even in the high-tech world of global counter-terrorism, some things are still best done by hand.

Also reviewed in:
CHICAGO TRIBUNE, 9/26/97, Friday/p. A, Michael Wilmington
NATION, 10/27/97, p. 34, Stuart Klawans
NEW REPUBLIC, 11/3/97, p. 28, Stanley Kauffmann
NEW YORK TIMES, 9/26/97, p. E10, Janet Maslin
NEW YORKER, 10/6/97, p. 125, Anthony Lane
VARIETY, 9/22-28/97, P. 37, Todd McCarthy
WASHINGTON POST, 9/26/97, p. C1, Stephen Hunter
WASHINGTON POST, 9/26/97, Weekend/p. 49, Desson Howe

PEST, THE

A TriStar Pictures and The Bubble Factory release of a Sheinberg production. *Executive Producer:* Robert A. Papazian. *Producer:* Sid Sheinberg, Jon Sheinberg, and Bill Sheinberg. *Director:* Paul Miller. *Screenplay:* David Bar Katz. *Story:* David Bar Katz and John Leguizamo. *Director of Photography:* Roy H. Wagner. *Editor:* Ross Albert and David Rawlins. *Music:*

Kevin Kiner. *Music Editor:* Adam Kaye. *Choreographer:* Fatima Robinson. *Sound:* Mark Ulano and (music) Chris Papastephanou. *Sound Editor:* Cindy Marty. *Casting:* Wendy Kurtzman. *Production Designer:* Rodger E. Maus. *Art Director:* Suzette Ervin. *Set Designer:* Carole Lee Cole. *Set Decorator:* Jim Duffy. *Set Dresser:* Margot Manfredi and Charley Brady. *Special Effects:* Paul Lombardi. *Costumes:* Tom McKinley. *Make-up:* Lon Bentley. *Stunt Coordinator:* Norman Howell. *Running time:* 82 minutes. *MPAA Rating:* PG-13.

CAST: John Leguizamo (Pestario Vargas, The Pest); Jeffrey Jones (Gustav Shank); Edoardo Ballerini (Himmel Shank); Freddy Rodriguez (Ninja); Tammy Townsend (Xantha Kent); Aries Spears (Chubby); Joe Morton (Mr. Kent); Charles Hallahan (Angus); Tom McCleister (Leo); Ivonne Coll (Gladyz); Pat Skipper (Glen Livitt); Jorge Luis Abrell (Piercer); Judy Ann Elder (Mrs. Kent); Jennifer Broughton (Bank Employee); Yau Gene Chan (Cook); Paul Harris (Karaoke Singer); Joe Jokubeit (Laphroig); David Bar Katz and Will Potter (White Guys); Les Lannom (Bagpipe Player); Jim Lau (Mr. Cheung); Barrie Mizerski (Host); Hugh Murphy (Emcee); Kristin Norton (Trixy); Yelba Osorio (Malaria); Tony Perez (Felix); Cantor Aviva Rosenbloom (Cantor); Julian Scott Urena (Sergio).

LOS ANGELES TIMES, 2/10/97, Calendar/p. 4, Kevin Thomas

"The Pest" is the worst. Talented and versatile actor-comedian John Leguizamo indulges himself so totally with incessant mugging, mimicking and all-around showing off that he begins to wear out his welcome before the opening credit sequence is over.

Leguizamo collaborated with screenwriter/co-producer David Bar Katz on this joyless would-be laugh riot in which he plays a frenetic Miami con man who becomes quite literally the target of a crazed German hunter (Jeffrey Jones, with a wavering accent) who wants Leguizamo's head for his trophy wall. Meanwhile, Leguizamo is on the run from the *Scottish* Mafia.

You can only wish that one or the other of them had caught up with him long before the picture's 82 minutes were up.

NEW YORK POST, 2/8/97, p. 21, Bill Hoffmann

John Leguizamo is all the Marx Brothers rolled into one in "The Pest," a rollicking, rude and politically incorrect comedy that's a non-stop laugh riot.

Leguizamo always has been one of America's most underrated comic treasures, with brilliant one-man shows such as "Mambo Mouth" and "Spic-o-Rama." But they were just a little too hot to get him accepted by Middle America.

In "The Pest," Leguizamo aims for the mainstream and hits the bull'seye, tempering his arsenic-laced agenda just enough and mixing it perfectly with 82 minutes of beautifully timed slapstick.

Leguizamo plays goofy Miami con man Pestario Vargas, known as "The Pest" for his amazing ability to wing his way through life without spending a dime—a "career" that is driving his proud Latino dad up the wall.

The Pest scams a bag lunch from a fat schoolkid, cons a Peking duck dinner from a nervous Chinese restaurant boss, jostles tourists for cash as a blind three-card-monte dealer, and so on. Life is one big wacky rip-off after another—until he gets in debt to Scottish mobsters for $50,000. Luckily for The Pest, a crazed German named Gustav (Jeffrey Jones), with a penchant for hunting humans and mounting their heads, decides The Pest has just the right kind of spunk to be his next challenge.

If The Pest can stay alive for just 24 hours, he'll be rewarded with ta-da!—$50,000, all of which leads to a fast and furious chase through south Florida.

The erratic script by David Bar Katz, based on a story by Katz and Leguizamo, ricochets all over the place, hitting the mark more than not.

But even when it sputters, Leguizamo rides to the rescue with a smashing sight gag or zippy one-liner. He takes no prisoners, skewering ethnic groups, gays, Eurotrash, wildlife, TV, fashion and anything else that crosses his path.

Jim Carrey, Robin Williams and Howard Stern have rightfully ruled American comedy for years. Now it's time for them to make room for another comic genius: John Leguizamo.

NEWSDAY, 2/10/97, Part II/p. B2, John Anderson

At the rate at which we rediscover and venerate the "lost masterpieces" of our high-velocity culture, John Leguizamo's "The Pest" should be reaching the status of unappreciated classic in, oh ... about two weeks. But until the culture catches up to it, "The Pest" will have to languish in the limbo of critical misunderstanding.

Which is really a shame, because among the current class (and I use that word guardedly) of young male comedians minoring in irritation—Chris Farley, Pauly Shore, Adam Sandler—it's John Leguizamo who's the most naturally talented, the quickest and probably still the one most likely to succeed, even after "The Pest."

But Leguizamo is also an improvisational virus in need of an antibiotic. Drawing his major inspiration from Harpo Marx, all three Stooges, pre-abstinence Robin Williams and Daffy Duck, Leguizamo is a 45-rpm performer in a 33 1/3 world, much of whose work is lost in a blur of pancultural references and high-impact comedy. "What'd he say?" you'll ask, and no one will have a clue.

As Pest—which seems to be short for any number of Hispanic handles he tosses off in the course of his curriculum vitae—Leguizamo's a guy you wouldn't mind seeing stopped in his tracks. Which is the plan when a rich German named Gustav (Jeffrey Jones) lures Pest to his remote island compound, where Pest is to be on one end of a gun, and the hunter Gustav on the other.

This is a lift from Richard Connell's famous short story "The Most Dangerous Game," which has been the basis for action movies such as "Hard Target," but never before a comedy. It's as good a premise as any, though, since Leguizamo's rapid-fire delivery is the real attraction, along with his penchant for the disgusting (there are prolonged scenes involving defecation, vomiting and bird droppings) and the politically incorrect: Jokes are directed at the nationality of the Scot mobsters to whom Pest owes money ("It's Sean Connery's birthday!") and the German villains ("So what if you started a few wars? Actually, you started every war. But who's counting!"). Jews gets ribbed; gays get gaffed. PBS will not be airing "The Pest" anytime soon, but if you head down to a theater, you can catch it after 20 minutes of commercials.

Pest and his pal Chubby (Aries Spears) do a Beavis and Butt-head impersonation at one point and it's a bit more than apt: Leguizamo is an animated cartoon character, and his film aspires to the cerebral depth of a cartoon. This would be original. If only it were.

Also reviewed in:
NEW YORK TIMES, 2/8/97, p. 14, Stephen Holden
VARIETY, 2/10-16/97, p. 64, Joe Leydon

PICTURE PERFECT

A Twentieth Century Fox release of a 3 Arts production. *Executive Producer:* William Teitler and Molly Madden. *Producer:* Erwin Stoff. *Director:* Glenn Gordon Caron. *Screenplay:* Arleen Sorkin, Paul Slansky, and Glenn Gordon Caron. *Story:* Arleen Sorkin, Paul Slansky, and May Quigley. *Director of Photography:* Paul Sarossy. *Editor:* Robert Reitano. *Music:* Carter Burwell. *Music Editor:* Thomas Drescher. *Choreographer:* Allison Diftler. *Sound:* Les Lazarowitz and (music) Michael Farrow. *Sound Editor:* Dan Sable. *Casting:* Mary Colquhoun. *Production Designer:* Larry Fulton. *Art Director:* John Wright Stevens. *Set Decorator:* Debra Schutt. *Set Dresser:* Peter J. Von Bartheld, Jeff Naparstek, Mark Simon, William J. Kolpin, and Mark Selemon. *Costumes:* Jane Robinson. *Make-up:* Fern Buchner. *Stunt Coordinator:* Douglas Crosby. *Running time:* 100 minutes. *MPAA Rating:* PG-13.

CAST: Jennifer Aniston (Kate Mosley); Jay Mohr (Nick); Kevin Bacon (Sam Mayfair); Olympia Dukakis (Rita); Illeana Douglas (Darcy O'Neal); Kevin Dunn (Mr. Mercer); Anne Twomey (Sela); Faith Prince (Mrs. Mercer); John Rothman (Jim Davenport); Margaret Gibson (Mrs. Davenport); Paul Cassell (Brad); Ivar Brogger (1st Ad Executive); Peter McRobbie (2nd Ad Executive); Bray Poor (3rd Ad Executive); Daryl Edwards (4th Ad Executive); Jenna Stern

(5th Ad Executive); Bellina Logan (Ad Agency Receptionist); Sean Patrick Thomas (Ad Agency Researcher); Andrea Bendewald (Pregnant Friend); Marcia DeBonis (Rosie); Matthew Sussman (Darcy's Husband); Jim Ryan (Anchor Person); Doug Easley (Maitre D'); Ali Marsh (Snack Lady); Richard Spore (Watch Seller); Amelia Campbell (Susan); Vimesh Thakar (The Maharishi); Faran Tahir (Sajit); David Cromwell (Minister); Jessica Cushman (Bride); Barry Del Sherman (Groom); Kaley Cuoco (Little Girl).

LOS ANGELES TIMES, 8/1/97, Calendar/p. 18, John Anderson

[The following review by John Anderson appeared in a slightly different form in NEWSDAY, 8/1/97, Part II/p. B3.]

There's a joke to be made here about friends in low places, but let's first examine the evidence: a film comedy about a woman in her 20s who just can't find the right man (one demerit, triteness). A woman with a strong sense of her own individuality and integrity who goes into the advertising business (two demerits, illogic). A woman who is supposed to be smart, savvy, sassy, but can't find a dress that fits over her already obvious abundantness (three demerits, acreage).

But "Picture Perfect" has its moments, even if they have to fight to get our attention. The centerpiece is Jennifer Aniston, the "Friends" star and fledgling film actress who brings unconventional sexiness and no particularly comedic gifts to the role of Kate Mosley. She is, however, surrounded by talented supporting players, including Kevin Dunn, Faith Prince and Illeana Douglas, a Joan Blondell for the '90s, whose Darcy O'Neal gets Kate in trouble to begin with.

Actually, she's in trouble already. Her career at Mercer Advertising is on the slow track, thanks to her lack of personal commitments (mortgage, kids, etc.; the boss, played by Dunn, doesn't want his people to be too mobile). And because she dresses like the Artist Formerly Known as Princess. Even though she's come up with the winning slogan for a multimillion-dollar mustard account—a well-known brown substance spread so thickly over this film it doesn't need to be mentioned here—she is cut out of the actual campaign, until Darcy invents a fiancé; wedding photographer Nick, played by "Jerry Maguire" villain Jay Mohr. Kate suddenly has the proper Mercer profile.

She also, suddenly, becomes very attractive to the office hunk-heel, Sam Mayfair (Kevin Bacon, the movie's biggest stretch), who's only interested because she's unavailable; that Kate never quite gets this is one of the movie's bigger potholes. They go to bed (a safe-sex sequence at the beginning of the movie apparently covers all subsequent bed-hopping), and she's smitten. So is he. So is Nick. It gets complicated. Or tiresome. It all depends on whether you've ever seen a romantic comedy before.

Without charting the actual troop movements within "Picture Perfect," Kate gets herself in hot water, and is in general an unsympathetic character. As such, she joins Julia Roberts ("My Best Friend's Wedding") and Meg Ryan ("Addicted to Love") in this summer's most peculiar development, the rise of the morally bankrupt screen heroine. They do things that are despicable, but we cheer for them anyway, because they're pretty and we've been trained so well. Just give us a tin cup and an organ grinder. We'll be set for life.

Director-co-writer Glenn Gordon Caron—onetime writer of the Bruce Willis-Cybill Shepherd series "Moonlighting" and the director of the infamously nutty "Wilder Napalm"—takes a few chances, such as having his characters make fun of the movie's own jokes. This is grace under pressure. Olympia Dukakis, playing Kate's oppressive matchmaking mother, makes periodic appearances complaining about the men Kate's not marrying ("He's gay, Ma!" "So?").

The product placement is astounding, and Carter Burwell, composer, shouldn't have scored the movie's emotional climax with James Newton Howard's music from "Dave." It only serves to remind one of better movies, at a time when one needs no reminders.

NEW YORK, 8/18/97, p. 51, David Denby

In *Picture Perfect*, Jennifer Aniston, as an advertising-world striver looking for a guy, jumps in and out of clothes, pouts, suffers, and shakes her hot little body with amusing impatience. When Aniston looks at a man, you can believe she wants something from him. In this contemporary screwball comedy, directed by Glenn Gordon Caron, Aniston hits the right notes of sexual candor and straightforward ambition. She's intensely likable, and the movie succeeds as romantic comedy, which is not something one can say about a certain recent monster hit that ended with the heroine in the arms of a homosexual. Aniston, bucking for promotion at her appearance-conscious firm, pretends to be engaged to a stranger played by blond Jay Mohr (from *Jerry Maguire*), a state of unavailability that immediately attracts the irresistible office cad, Kevin Bacon. The nice thing about Bacon's character is that you find him increasingly more intelligent and sympathetic as the movie goes along, without your thinking for a moment that he's the right guy for Jennifer Aniston. As our girl's eventually authentic lover, Jay Mohr is a little indecisive (Mohr always looks like he's about to say something other than what he does say). But he'll do.

NEW YORK POST, 8/1/97, p. 37, Michael Medved

In her first starring motion picture role, Jennifer Aniston provides the humor and sexiness her "Friends" fans expect, and wears an eye-popping (and implausible) assortment of revealing outfits. But her warm-hearted performance emphasizes vulnerability, seducing the audience with an endearing, everywoman quality as the saucy, slightly klutzy, girl next door.

Thanks to Aniston's effortless earthiness and charm, and a nicely nuanced little-girl-lost aspect to her role, even the most hormone-addled males in the audience will identify with the character at the same time they feel attracted to her, transforming the convoluted and contrived silliness of "Picture Perfect" into a mildly entertaining romantic comedy.

Aniston plays a 28-year-old New Yorker with an exciting job in advertising but a disastrous social life. Much to her chagrin, her generally sympathetic, suspender-wearing boss (Kevin Dunn) passes her over for a key promotion because he feels that her lack of a husband or boyfriend makes her an unstable, unpredictable quantity.

In real life, of course, this decision would no doubt provoke some nasty discrimination lawsuit, but here it leads Aniston—and her best friend (Illeana Douglas) to fabricate a fiancé to facilitate her advancement.

They produce a photograph of Aniston posed with a handsome man (Jay Mohr) she briefly met at a friend's wedding. Later they pay him to travel from his home in Boston to continue the charade.

A fringe benefit of Aniston's suddenly attached status is that it provokes instant interest from her sultry, fashionable co-worker Kevin Bacon, who limits his romantic focus to women who are unavailable.

All of this confuses the heroine's nagging, overprotective, hairdresser mother, played by the always effective Olympia Dukakis.

Since both Aniston and Dukakis are, in real life, Greek-Americans, their fuzzy, indeterminate, all-purpose ethnicity in the movie seems something of a wasted opportunity.

Jay Mohr made a strong impression as the ruthless sports-agent rival to Tom Cruise in "Jerry Maguire," but he's even better here, playing the phony fiancé as a tender, undemanding, sensitive, salt of the earth saint who, in the hands of a lesser actor, would have seemed much too good to be true.

Director Glen Gordon Caron is best known as the creator of TV's fondly remembered "Moonlighting," but his previous movie work ("Clean and Sober," "Wilder Napalm," Warren Beatty's "Love Affair") suffered from a strained seriousness and grandiosity.

Here he returns to his breezy, TV comedy roots, using his long-ago experience at an advertising agency to inspire a refreshing portrayal of a top Madison Avenue firm as an exciting, demanding place to work rather than as an outright madhouse.

The outcome of the painfully improbable urban fairy-tale plot is unmistakably obvious a full half hour before the end of the picture, so the resolution feels sluggish and padded. Still, watching with this much charisma and chemistry is never an altogether unpleasant chore.

SIGHT AND SOUND, 12/97, p. 51, Philip Kemp

Kate Mosley, who works for Mercer Advertising, feels her life is in a rut. Her career is stalled, her love-life limited to unsuitable dates foisted on her by her mother Rita. She is attracted to her colleague Sam, but he only goes for women who are already attached. Choosing a team to pitch for the Gulden's Mustard account, Kate's boss Alan Mercer makes clear that only employees with commitments—and therefore with something to lose—can expect to get on in the firm.

At an out-of-town wedding Kate meets wedding-videomaker Nick. To help her, her friend and colleague Darcy puts it about that Kate and Nick are engaged. Kate is indignant. But when she's chosen to head the Gulden's team and Sam makes a move on her, she goes along with the deception. However, Nick becomes famous when he saves a child in an accident, and Mercer invites Kate and her supposed fiancé to dinner at a smart restaurant. Kate seeks out Nick and offers him money to act the role and stage a bust-up at the dinner table.

Bemused at first, Nick agrees to cooperate, but finds himself increasingly attracted to Kate and tries to evade the public row. Kate forces it on him, accusing him of having a mistress. Out of sympathy, Mercer promotes Kate to creative head, but she realises that Nick really loves her, and that she loves him. She tells everyone the truth, ditches Sam and seeks out Nick at a wedding he's filming. They embrace, warmly applauded by the whole congregation.

So far, apart from Courteney Cox's likeably self-mocking turn as the predatory television reporter in *Scream*, attempts by the *Friends* team to make it on the big screen haven't met with much success. *Picture Perfect*, Jennifer Aniston's latest starring vehicle, looks unlikely to change the pattern. An inconsequential piece of comedic fluff, it makes occasional hopeful lunges towards smartness and sophistication, but finally bogs down in a soft-centred romantic formula. Still, what else could be expected from a film whose climax is that irritating romantic-comedy cliché, the principal couple falling into each other's arms while a roomful of total strangers beamingly applaud?

This mix—conventional humour overlaid with mildly audacious street-smart—is familiar enough: it's the archetypal stuff of mid-evening US television sitcom, which is where most of those involved with the film, along with its star, come from. The director, Glenn Gordon Caron, made his name on the series *Moonlighting*, in which Bruce Willis leapt to fame. That series rode on the simmeringly antagonistic chemistry (off-screen as well as on, by all accounts) between its two leads, Willis and Cybill Shepherd. And it's just that kind of edgy relationship that's missing here.

Aniston, as yet, lacks the presence to carry a whole feature. The way she ceaselessly fiddles with her hair suggests an uneasy awareness that she's being upstaged by her own coiffure. As her eventual partner Nick, Jay Mohr is amiably bland. But both are decisively outclassed by the second leads, Illeana Douglas (the star of *Grace of My Heart*) as Kate's manipulative friend Darcy, and the engagingly amoral Kevin Bacon. You can't help feeling that these two would have made a sexier—and wittier—teaming.

All the same, the film has its diverting moments, and gets in a few shrewd jabs at the slick, superficial world it depicts. When Kate protests at the fake-boyfriend fabrication foisted on her, Darcy retorts, "We're in advertising, Kate. I didn't lie—I sold." But Kate's final come-clean confession at a client meeting, when she denounces herself for letting professional ambition rule her life, rings gratingly false, a throwback to all those debilitating 40s comedies when a career woman admits that what she really wants is frilly domesticity. *Picture Perfect,* setting out to satirise emotional dishonesty, ends up skewered on the same charge.

TIME, 8/11/97, p. 75, Richard Schickel

The boss likes his staff settled down and therefore a little desperate: you know, mortgage, car and tuition payments, maybe a few bills from the orthodontist. When obligations exceed income, the folks at his ad agency work harder and more loyally. That's his theory, anyway, and Kate (Jennifer Aniston) doesn't fit it. She's single and living within an income that does not match her talent. A friend suggests she invent a fiancé to get a raise based on this spurious evidence of stability. A wedding videographer named Nick (Jay Mohr) agrees to go along with the gag, hoping to turn their fake affair into the real thing.

What say, fans of romantic comedy? Can you accept the slightly silly place *Picture Perfect* is coming from? Can you predict the blissful place it's heading? Of course you can. What may surprise you—given the desperate energies being applied to this genre these days—is the film's confident, unforced air. Some of that derives from Aniston's performance, a nicely judged blend of intelligence and inexperience, briskness and softness. She is, as she proves every week on

Friends, an actress who serenely lets the comedy come to her instead of frantically searching for it. Director and co-writer Glenn Gordon Caron, late of *Moonlighting*, operates in the same smart, patient manner. You might wish he and his colleagues had toasted Nick, their studmuffin, a little more crisply—enough of these puff-pastry leading men—but the rest of the roles are crunchy, and *Picture*, if not quite perfect, makes a nice light snack for a hot summer's day.

VILLAGE VOICE, 8/12/97, p. 74, Jennifer Vandever

It's no accident Jennifer Aniston's on this month's *Cosmopolitan* cover, since her new film is like a feature piece entitled, "How To Judge a Guy by His Hair." Aniston plays Kate, an ambitious advertising exec who's so eager to please her boss that she invents a fictive fiancé to give the appearance of a "perfect" life. Once the boss thinks she's hitched, Kate becomes immensely popular and everyone loves her innovative marketing ideas for mustard (supermodels). It's a creaky premise at best and not helped by the fact that this is basically a $30 million promo for Gulden's mustard. The moral dilemma hinges on Jennifer's choice between her "fiancé" (a charming turn by Jay Mohr) who has unextraordinary J. Crew nice-guy hair, and a terribly miscast Kevin Bacon, who has longish hipster hair. Kevin's coif denotes that he's sexy and dangerous but actually points up his one not so hidden character flaw—he's a sleaze. Will Jennifer figure it out in time? As every Cosmo girl knows, the answers to the quiz are pretty obvious.

Also reviewed in:
NEW YORK TIMES, 8/1/97, p. C10, Janet Maslin
VARIETY, 7/28-8/3/97, p. 58, Todd McCarthy
WASHINGTON POST, 8/1/97, p. B1, Rita Kempley

PILLOW BOOK, THE

A Cinepix Film Properties release of a Kasander & Wigman Productions/Alpha Films/Woodline Films production in association with Channel Four Films/Studio Canal Plus/De Lux Productions. *Executive Producer:* Jean-Louis Piel, Denis Wigman, and Terry Glinwood. *Producer:* Kees Kasander. *Director:* Peter Greenaway. *Screenplay (English, Japanese, Mandarin and Cantonese with English subtitles):* Peter Greenaway. *Director of Photography:* Sacha Vierny. *Editor:* Chris Wyatt. *Sound:* Garth Marshall. *Sound Editor:* Nigel Heath. *Production Designer:* Wilbert van Dorp. *Costumes:* Dien van Straalen, Koji Tatsumo, Margaret Margiela, and Paul Smith. *Make-up:* Sara Meerman. *Running time:* 126 minutes. *MPAA Rating:* Not Rated.

CAST: Vivian Wu (Nagiko); Yoshi Oida (The Publisher); Ken Ogata (The Father); Hideko Yoshida (The Aunt/The Maid); Ewan McGregor (Jerome); Judy Ongg (The Mother); Ken Mitsuishi (The Husband); Yutaka Honda (Hoki); Barbara Lott (Jerome's Mother); Wichert Dromkert (The Book of the Innocent); Martin Tukker (The Book of the Idiot); Wu Wei (The Book of Old Age); Tom Kane (The Book of the Exhibitionist); Kheim Lam (The Book of the Seducer); Daishi Hori (The Book of Youth); Kinya Tsuruyama (The Book of Secrets); Eiichi Tanaka (The Book of the Betrayer); Rick Waney (The Book of Silence); Masaru Matsuda (The Book of Birth & Beginnings); Wataru Murofushi (The Book of the Dead); Ronald Guttman (Lecturer); Ryuko Azuma (Grandmother); Seitaro Koyama and Tatsuya Kimura (Nephews); Yoshihiko Nagata and Atsushi Miura (Husband's Friends); Kazushi Ishimaru (Baby Nagiko); Hikari Abe (Nagiko's Baby); Junko Matsumori (Pregnant Nagiko Double); Kazuko Abe (Breast Feeding Nagiko Double); Arnita Swanson (Edele); Jim Adhi Limas (Man in Lift); Miho Tanaka, Fabienne de Marco, and Tania de Jaeger (Model Friends in Café Typo); Lu Jinhua (Wife of Calligrapher); Kumi Komino (Elderly Secretary); Yuki Hayashi (Young Female Secretary); Maskai Taketani (Young Male Secretary); Mr. & Mrs. Lo (Old Servant and Wife); See Yan Leung (Bookshop Manager); François van den Bergen (Book of Seducer).

LOS ANGELES TIMES, 6/6/97, Calendar/p. 11, Kenneth Turan

Despite its arresting visual style, its wave after wave of creative and hypnotic images, "The Pillow Book," as its name hints, slowly but inexorably leads to sleep.

Written and directed by Peter Greenaway, "The Pillow Book" is more coherent and plotted than his last film, the understandably little seen "The Baby of Macon." But it shares with that and earlier works like "The Cook, the Thief, His Wife and Her Lover" and "Prospero's Books" both an air of smug pretension and a cold and gleeful delight in the poetry of excess.

There can be no doubt that Greenaway, working as usual with veteran cinematographer Sacha Vierny (who shot both "Hiroshima Mon Amour" and "Last Year at Marienbad" for Alain Resnais), is an exceptional visual stylist with an aesthetic that prides itself on being self-consciously artistic.

But "Pillow Book" demonstrates, as do the others the limits of style as a filmmaking be-all and end-all. A director who communicates sparingly with his actors if at all, Greenaway doesn't notice or care about the dramatic weakness of his films. If they look spectacular, as they inevitably do, that is enough for him.

In this, Greenaway can be seen as the art-house equivalent of blockbuster-oriented French director Luc Besson, whose "The Fifth Element," the most expensive film ever made in Europe, is similarly contemptuous of all but the flimsiest forms of emotional connection. For these directors and the audience they appeal to, surface sensation is all that matters.

Told in both Japanese and English, "The Pillow Book" explores the life of Nagiko, introduced as a child in Kyoto whose master calligrapher father (Ken Ogata) paints a greeting on her face every year on her birthday.

On the same day, her aunt reads to her from one of the classics of Japanese literature, "The Pillow Book," a 10th century journal and collection of lists written by Sei Shonagon. One of the pleasures of this "Pillow Book' is the beautiful way Greenaway and Vierny illustrate the book's "List of Splendid Things," displaying a large garden covered in snow or indigo-colored flowers.

As she grows into a beautiful young woman, Nagiko (Vivian Wu of "The Last Emperor" and "The Joy Luck Club") becomes increasingly obsessed with having herself written on, even taking calligraphic prowess into account when considering potential lovers.

Nagiko also feels haunted by a sense of unfinished business with her father's publisher (Yoshi Oida), a predatory homosexual who has had a murky relationship with her parent that has always discomfited her.

Moving to Hong Kong, Nagiko meets a dilettantish English translator named Jerome ("Trainspotting's" Ewan McGregor) who, to compensate for his poor calligraphy, offers his body for her to write on. This reversal doesn't end well, but Nagiko embraces the general idea, and before the movie is finished, she carefully inscribes 11 different books on the skins of a series of full frontally nude young men.

All this is illustrated in the most lavish style possible, with images overlapping and blending into one another. The screen is split any number of times and any number of ways, including a black strip left along the bottom to accommodate elegantly written subtitles. Stately and hypnotic, "The Pillow Book" is best appreciated as a series of visuals slowly washing over the mind.

But minds tend to be pesky things, demanding more than visual pleasures, and "The Pillow Book," with mechanical, undirected line readings adding to its problems, is much too icy to play half as interesting as it may sound. For all his skill, Greenaway wants to be no more than a puppet master, and puppets, though beautiful, have limitations of their own.

NEW YORK POST, 6/6/97, p. 45, Thelma Adams

In Peter Greenaway's "The Pillow Book," not everything is as clear as the nether regions of Ewan McGregor—or the family jewels of Tom Kane, Martin Tukker, Kheim Lam and a host of other men.

Matter of fact, male frontal nudity is nothing new for the painterly director of "The Cook, the Thief, His Wife & Her Lover" and the unreleased "The Baby of Macon," which features Ralph Fiennes and Julia Ormond rolling around together in the altogether.

As his use of male and female nudity suggests, Greenaway rarely blinks—but sometimes he can stare at a subject too long to please American audiences. "The Pillow Book" is a challenging mixture of carnality and sensuality, storytelling and intellectual posturing.

Greenaway's film refuses to be taken at face value. Viewers must let the images and text wash over them with eyes—and subconsciouses—wide open.

The story begins like a fairy tale, only to become a fever dream. (As usual, Greenaway, working from his own script, has greater control over the imagery than the drama—although he embarks with self-possession here.)

Every year on Nagiko's birthday, the little girl receives a gift from her father, a Kyoto calligrapher. He paints her eyes, nose and mouth and signs his work on the nape of her neck. Each year, her aunt reads to her from "The Pillow Book," a courtesan's diary that will turn 1,000 on Nagiko's 28th birthday.

Flashback: The 10th-century diarist lists life's pleasures. Sei Shonagon equates the beauty of paper with a lover's skin. She celebrates the apparently simple, though infinitely complex ability to communicate through writing, as well as the sensual pleasure of putting pen to paper.

Flash forward: Nagiko (Vivian Wu) has become a wealthy Hong Kong model. Troubled by a failed marriage and, to simplify, her father's prostitution by his male publisher, she has an odd fetish. She beds calligraphers and they write on her flesh; she exchanges sex for text.

When Nagiko meets an English translator (McGregor, of "Emma"), he urges her to take pen in hand and write on his body. She begins her own pillow book, written in artful calligraphy on the bodies of naked men. Nagiko becomes subject, not object.

In the sensual union of writer and translator, East meets West and art is made flesh. On the screen, text and image coexist, black and white bleed to color, the screen splits and opens up Greenaway's world. Until the final, overheated half hour—after Greenaway has indulged his own fetish for desecrating corpses on screen—there has rarely been a film that so inspired viewers to engage in art, not just watch it.

NEWSDAY, 6/6/97, Part II/p. B8, Jack Mathews

Controversial British filmmaker Peter Greenaway, whose credits include the grotesquely sensual "The Cook, The Thief, His Wife & Her Lover" and the kaleidoscopic "Prospero's Books," says his audiences fall into three groups: (1) those who walk out after five minutes, hurling insults on their way; (2) those who wait 40 minutes, then hit the aisle, and (3) those who stick around, and return over and over again.

I claim a fourth category: critics who watch Groups 1 and 2 with envy, but feel duty-bound to go the distance, once!

In interviews promoting his ninth film, "The Pillow Book," Greenaway has cast himself as the messiah of an exalted video-film esthetic that will, after a century of wasted opportunity, mark the moving picture at last as a true art form. Claiming that, himself aside, there is no major talent in cinema, Greenaway sees a future where there will also be no theaters, no plots, and no emotional connection between movies and their audiences.

In their stead will be three-dimensional audio-visual experiences, more sensual and tactile than intellectual, with no boring beginnings, middles and ends.

Can you stand the wait?

If all this proves true, "The Pillow Book" is going to be a great embarrassment to Greenaway. Despite its arcanely erotic subject, and enough experimental flourishes to mark it as distinctly his, the film has an almost conventional storyline, its lead character is fully accessible, and for an artist so resolutely misanthropic, there beats here the faint pulse of a romantic.

"The Pillow Book" is the story of Nagiko (Hong Kong actress Vivian Wu), a Japanese woman with an Electra complex and a fetish for body painting. Every birthday from her earliest childhood, her father, an expert calligrapher, paints a sensuous message on her face, while her aunt reads to her from "The, Pillow Book," Sei Shonagon's 10th-Century book of amorous reminiscence.

When she turns 18, Nagiko's father stops the ritual, and she is left a woman with sexual desires that can only be satisfied by men with the talent and patience to paint exquisite text all over her body. Still, Nagiko doesn't find true fulfillment until she falls in love with the bisexual Jerome

(Ewan McGregor), an Englishman who suggests that they switch roles, that he become the tablet and she the brush.

She agrees, and her work is so spectacular, Nagiko takes Jerome to her father's homosexual publisher to show it off. The results of this encounter, combined with Nagiko's lingering resentment over the publisher's earlier humiliation of her father, leads to tragic—and, at the same time, sensually graphic—results.

Ordinary folks with modern sensibilities might see "The Pillow Book" as a cautionary tale about child abuse. Nagiko's dad surely didn't mean to send his daughter on a fruitless quest for strong writing and weird sex, but the most casual reader of Ann Landers could see that's where her sensuous childhood has her headed.

Greenaway, of course, has no interest in such mundane human issues. His own obsession, exercised in various forms throughout his films, is the esthetic of sensation—whether of taste (of fine food, feces and human flesh in "The Cook, The Thief... "), pain (from pancreatic cancer in "The Belly of an Architect") or decay ("A Zed & Two Noughts"). Sex and death are the only primary colors on Greenaway's palette, and for him, "The Pillow Book" only exists at the point of contact, where the brush meets the skin.

No mistaking, "The Pillow Book" offers an exotic menu. Full frontal nudity, of both Wu and Nagiko's men, are frequent, and the body calligraphy with all the dissolves, split screens and multiple images in Greenaway's editing arsenal—is indeed a moving exhibit of Japanese art.

Members of Group 3, the Greenaway faithful, don't need any encouragement, but if you're only going to give the self-proclaimed pioneer of cinematic art one chance, let "The Pillow Book" be it.

SIGHT AND SOUND, 11/96, p. 57, Claire Tovey

On each birthday during her childhood in Kyoto, Nagiko Kiohara has a creation greeting painted onto her face by her calligrapher father. Her aunt reads to her nightly from The *Pillow Book of Sei Shonagon* and encourages her to keep her own diary. On Nakigo's fifth birthday, she witnesses an arrangement her father has with his homosexual publisher: sex in return for money and publication.

At 18, Nagiko is married off to the publisher's nephew, a boorish archery enthusiast. He refuses to paint her face and they quarrel often. One day, he burns her diaries, setting fire to their house. Nagiko flees to Hong Kong. While working in a restaurant kitchen, she learns English and typing. A job with a dressmaker leads to a successful modelling career. Now wealthy, she seeks out calligraphers as lovers, offering sex in exchange for their writing over her body. Hoki, a Japanese photographer, becomes obsessed with her.

At the Cafe Typo, Nagiko meets an English translator, Jerome, who suggests she should switch to writing on her lovers' bodies. She refuses at first, but later experiments on herself and a sleeping man, allowing Hoki to photograph the results. Hoki convinces her to transcribe the writing so he can take it to a publisher he works for. However, the manuscript is rejected. Furious, Nagiko sets out to seduce the publisher. At the publisher's shop, Nagika is struck by its resemblance to her father's publisher's place. The publisher turns out to be the same man, and Jerome is his lover. Her only hope is to seduce Jerome. She makes a rendezvous with him at the Cafe Typo, they fall in love and she confesses that she wants to be a writer.

Jerome proposes that Nagiko write on his body so that he can present himself to the publisher. Jerome strips for the publisher, revealing a beautiful advertisement for 13 books of erotic poetry. Enthralled, the publisher has it transcribed, but Jerome forgets his bargain with Nagiko. Furious, Nagiko starts sending other men with further erotic books written on them. The publisher becomes obsessed with the men, ignoring Jerome, who is remorseful and seeks a reconciliation with Nagiko. Hoki, out of jealousy, persuades Jerome to fake a suicide in her apartment, which then proves fatal. Nagiko buries his body, beautifully decorated with love poetry, burns all her possessions and returns to Kyoto.

Hoki tells the publisher that Jerome is dead. The publisher has the body disinterred and flayed. The skin is turned into a pillow book. When Nagiko, now pregnant, hears of this outrage, she starts sending the publisher the remainder of the thirteen books, one by one, on young men's bodies. The publisher's shop is burnt down by environmentalist protestors, and he shuts down his business. On the eve of the millennium he receives the thirteenth book, inscribed on a Sumo wrestler.   After the publisher has handed over the skin book, the wrestler cuts his throat. Nagiko's 28th birthday, and her child's first, is celebrated by Nagiko painting the greeting on the child's face, and by the burial of the Jerome book under a Bonsai tree.   Nagiko can now begin her own pillow book.

As Japanese hieroglyphs run golden down the screen, we look through them at scenes from the family life of a young Japanese girl, Nagiko, shot in black and white (from a low angle that seems an Ozu-homage).   A birthday creation greeting is written in paint onto her face by her father; later she watches him making a sexual bargain with his publisher.   Sometimes excerpts from the tenth-century text, *The Pillow Book of Sei Shonagon*, fill the screen with characters, or appear dramatised in a separate frame.   When the film moves into Nagiko's adult life, into colour and Hong Kong (shot from a higher, more distanced perspective), we frequently see her naked, surrounded by gorgeous textual and interior decoration, and being written on with more hieroglyphs. Later still she becomes a writer/illustrator, despatching young men beautifully covered with erotic poetry to a publisher.   We see her coupling with her decorated lover, Jerome, through diaphanous erotic Japanese art images.

The Pillow Book, it is clear, gathers up the two concerns that have driven so many of Peter Greenaway's films: the question of sex and power and the question of cinematic representation, of developing a kind of 'denser' film than the linear narrative of mainstream Hollywood cinema allows.

That these are his twin obsessions may be what marks him out as an inheritor of the 60s European art movie—for it was the concern with formal experimentation, and with a sexuality that couldn't be found in mainstream cinema, which gave 60s European art cinema its signature. Yet what is interesting about Greenaway is that he tends, when talking about his own work, to foreground the representation rather than the sex.

Perhaps this is because sex is always a dangerous bargain in his films.   *The Draughtsman's Contract* ties together sexual favours with social power—a similar situation to the one in which Nagiko's father is embroiled in *The Pillow Book*.   Sex leads to multiple (offscreen) rape in *The Baby of Macon* and to cannibalism in *The Cook the Thief His Wife & Her Lover*, not to mention the death of Jerome in the present film.

But what is remarkable about *The Pillow Book*, in relation to his recent films, is that sex seems at times not only a liberating compact but a sensuous one.   For instance, the effect of the elegant calligraphy on the bodies of the two main actors, Vivien Wu and Ewan McGregor, is often breathtaking (if troubling) and sometimes erotic.

But the importance of the sensuousness is greater than this implies—for one way of seeing the film is to see it as a riposte, whether consciously or not, to other recent art films about hetero-sexual sex and representation, such as Jacques Rivette's *La Belle Noiseuse*.   Where in that film the scratching of Michel Piccoli's pen on paper seems an analogue to a penetrative assault on Emmanuelle Béart's body, in *The Pillow Book* the direct painting on the bodies seems rather to offer aesthetic enhancement and pleasure.   But most importantly what really separates Greenaway's from Rivette's is that in *The Pillow Book* the heroine stops being the canvas on which the man writes and becomes the writer herself, taking control of her destiny, ready to begin a new life.

So it's clear that if Greenaway is indebted to the 60s, he is not slavishly so.   What marks *The Pillow Book* out is not merely its partial setting at the millennium, but its millenial or utopian longings.   Greenaway seems here to have found a form through which he can imagine past, present, and future on the screen simultaneously (via overlay); he can bring east and west together (through Vivian Wu and Ewan McGregor); and through the Japanese hieroglyph can bring together word and image—since the word is an image, *The Pillow Book* may have the characteristic 'violence' motifs of a Greenaway film: it also has a curious—and curiously mov-ing—utopian quality.

TIME, 7/7/97, p. 106 Richard Corliss

At the end of the last millennium, the Japanese courtesan Sei Shonagon wrote *The Pillow Book* which survives as a masterpiece of erotic and political intrigue.   A thousand years later, the English filmmaker Peter Greenaway (*Drowning by Numbers, The Cook The Thief His Wife & Her*

Lover) has created a severe, rhapsodic fable about body painting—about a woman's desire to make of herself a living work of erotic art.

As a birthday present each year, little Nagiko's father would write a sensuous sentiment, in elegant Japanese calligraphy, on the child's face. Twenty years later, Nagiko (Vivian Wu) tries to duplicate, erotically, the touch of her father's brush. She challenges her lovers to write their lust all over her body. Then she finds a handsome Englishman (Ewan McGregor) who convinces her that she should do the writing, on his body. Finally, she will be not the paper but the pen—an artist writing love notes in the medium of flesh.

Any Greenaway film is a complex word-and-picture game—of stories within stories, images within images, like a Chinese puzzle box. The director also insists that his actors throw themselves, soul and especially body, into his complex revenge scenarios. Wu is a fine, supple tabula rasa; McGregor (*Trainspotting*) shows again that he is one of the boldest, most charming young actors.

It's lovely that, in an age when pop culture dances with the dunces, someone has the mandarin urge to arouse and test his audience. Lovelier still when, as in *The Pillow Book,* text and texture meet so exquisitely. Sex is a visual art, Greenaway says, and writing is a matter of life and death.

VILLAGE VOICE, 6/10/97, p. 69, J. Hoberman

The attractive, frequently unclothed heroine of Peter Greenaway's new film is in the habit of making lists—elegant things, splendid things, things that irritate, things that make the heart quicken. She may be one of the latter, but *The Pillow Book,* I fear, is not.

Greenaway is out to reinvent the whole notion of cinema. As he wrote in *Sight and Sound,* "The visual language experiments of *Prospero's Books* are continued in *The Pillow Book.* Neither has a guilty conscience about putting the word 'book' in their titles, if only because this demonstrates the equivocations of a film tradition that always starts with text before it moves on to image. ... "The riskiest thing about this soporific experiment is placing the word "pillow" in the title—might give the viewer ideas. In contrast to the abrasively hysterical *Prospero's Books,* an exercise in logorrhea whose main attraction was John Gielgud's withered tush, this cold, contemptuous, and interminable Oedipal saga is just a big, static snooze.

Little Nagiko grew up in Kyoto having daddy (Ken Ogata) paint a sensuous birthday message on her face. Once matured into lissome Vivian Wu, she still likes to be inscribed. Ditching her noncompliant husband, she moves from Tokyo to cramped noisy crazy Hong Kong to search for the ideal lover-calligrapher, becomes one herself, and, having fallen in love with Ewan McCregor, starts inscribing her books on the bodies of men. Humorlessly satirizing Barthes's notion of textual erotics, Greenaway withholds his trademark nastiness far too long. *The Pillow Book*'s pretensions are boundless but, for all its desperate fashion and layered imagery, It's a staggering bore—vacantly petulant as Kate Moss's stare.

Also reviewed in:
NEW YORK TIMES, 6/6/97, p. C10, Janet Maslin
VARIETY, 5/20-26/96, p. 32, David Stratton
WASHINGTON POST, 6/20/97, Weekend/p. 38, Desson Howe

PIPPI LONGSTOCKING

A Legacy Releasing release of a Nelvana Ltd./TFC Trickompany GmbH/AB Svensk Filmindustri/Iduna Film Productiongesellschaft production with the participation of Telefilm Canada. *Executive Producer:* Michael Hirsh, Patrick Loubert, and Clive Smith. *Producer:* Hasmi Giakoumis and Merle-Ann Ridley. *Director:* Clive Smith. *Animation Director:* Robin Budd and Bill Giggie. *Story:* Susan Snooks. *Based on the books by:* Astrid Lindgren. *Editor:* Noda Tsamardos. *Music:* Anders Berglund. *Sound:* Glenn Barna. *Art Director:* Clive Powsey. *Production Designer:* Paul Riley. *Running time:* 75 minutes. *MPAA Rating:* G.

VOICES: Melissa Altro (Pippi Longstocking); Catherine O'Hara (Mrs. Prysselius); Carole Pope (Teacher); Dave Thomas (Thunder-Karlsson); Gordon Pinsent (Capt. Longstocking).

LOS ANGELES TIMES, 8/22/97, Calendar/p. 14, Gene Seymour

[*The following review by Gene Seymour appeared in a slightly different form in* **NEWSDAY, 8/22/97, Part II/p. B12.**]

Paul Bunyan, Batman and the White Power Ranger have their place. But to 8- or 9-year-olds, Pippi Longstocking is the first superhero they can truly embrace as one of their own.

For one thing, she's their age, give or take. For another, she can probably wrestle each of the aforementioned powers to the ground without once forsaking her broad, imperturbable grin.

And, most important to a child's fondest wish-fulfillment, she does whatever she wishes to do and can take care of herself without being mean to anyone. Even to those who deserve otherwise.

Astrid Lindgren's epic heroine in scarlet pigtails deserved an epic live feature movie, which this animated version of her 1945 debut novel is not. Still, this feature-length cartoon works well enough within its self-imposed boundaries to be a competent, no-frills rendering of Lindgren's whimsical universe of dull-witted authority figures and supremely intelligent pets, of circus strong men, silly thieves and kids walking backwards for the fun of it.

In case you've forgotten the story, Pippi (voice by Melissa Altro) is the globe-trotting daughter of a ship's captain, the latter of whom is swept overboard during a storm. She is thus forced to return to the town of Villa Villekula to take care of herself, her monkey named Mr. Nilsson, her horse named Horse and a large chest filled with gold coins.

Mrs. Prysselius (voice by Catherine O'Hara), the town busybody, thinks Pippi should be placed in a children's home. Two career criminals (one of whom is voiced by O'Hara's fellow "SCTV" alum Dave Thomas) think her treasure should be placed in their hands. The kids next door think everyone should let her be. Two daffy policemen think they should go fishing. Pippi thinks life would be complete if she could only learn a few newfangled dance steps.

Enough of the "Pippi" spirit is contained in this "Pippi" movie to excuse its gratuitous, eminently forgettable songs and standard-issue animation. Compared with the bombast of most summer movies, it entertains with modest efficiency. You may want to wait for the home-video version. One doubts whether your children will.

NEW YORK POST, 8/22/97, p. 48, Michael Medved

The new "Pippi Longstocking" is a well-intentioned Canadian-Swedish-German coproduction that isn't going to offend anyone, but it won't thrill anyone either.

Based on the durable children's book character created in 1944 by Swedish writer Astrid Lindgren, this new film is personally approved by the 90-year-old author, and features pleasant, pastel-hued animation, four relentlessly perky songs, and a capable cast of voices that includes a pair of moderately famous names (Catherine O'Hara and Dave Thomas) in supporting roles.

The red-haired, pigtailed 9-year-old heroine "sails the seven seas" with her ship-captain father until he falls overboard in a storm, and she returns to his picturesque country house with her swaybacked horse and her mischievous pet monkey.

While Pippi's quirky, independent ways win friendship from two neighbor kids, the local busybody Mrs. Prysselius (O'Hara) wants to place the unsupervised imp in a children's home.

Meanwhile two comical burglars (who bear a family resemblance to the bungling bad guys of "Home Alone") escape from jail to steal the chest of gold coins in Pippi's Victorian home.

The multinational filmmakers faced a series of challenges which frankly defeated producers of several previous (and consistently wretched) live-action, "Pippi" pictures: in adapting an eccentric, 50-year-old tale set in a Swedish village to appeal to jaded contemporary tastes, they've opted here for a bland visual world that looks like anywhere and nowhere.

Obvious questions (such as the origins of Pippi's superhuman strength at lifting horses and bulky burglars) are, never even asked, while the child's penchant for gaily disregarding all adult authority (and even family relationships) hardly makes her an ideal role model.

While boasting a $10 million budget, the flat, flaccid animation bears less resemblance to big studio cartoon blockbusters than it does to the world of Saturday morning kiddie shows—and its 75 minutes pass by just about as painlessly and pointlessly.

Also reviewed in:
CHICAGO TRIBUNE, 8/22/97, Friday/p. Q, Monica Eng
NEW YORK TIMES, 9/22/97, p. C22, Lawrence Van Gelder
VARIETY, 8/25-31/97, p. 75, Howard Feinstein

PLAYING GOD

A Touchstone Pictures release in association with Beacon Pictures. *Executive Producer:* Armyan Bernstein and Thomas A. Bliss. *Producer:* Marc Abraham and Laura Bickford. *Director:* Andy Wilson. *Screenplay:* Mark Haskell Smith. *Director of Photography:* Anthony B. Richmond. *Editor:* Louise Rubacky. *Music:* Richard Hartley. *Music Editor:* Tass Filipos. *Sound:* Mark Weingarten and (music) Phil Chapman. *Sound Editor:* Darren Paskal. *Casting:* Johanna Ray and Elaine J. Huzzar. *Production Designer:* Naomi Shohan. *Art Director:* Troy Sizemore. *Set Decorator:* Evette Frances Knight. *Costumes:* Mary Zophres. *Make-up:* Naomi Donne. *Make-up (Special Effects):* Gabe Bartalos. *Stunt Coordinator:* B.J. Davis. *Running time:* 93 minutes. *MPAA Rating:* R.

CAST: David Duchovny (Eugene Sands); Timothy Hutton (Raymond Blossom); Angelina Jolie (Claire); Michael Massee (Gage); Peter Stormare (Vladimir); Andrew Tiernan (Cyril); Gary Dourdon (Yates); John Hawkes (Flick); Will Foster Stewart (Perry); Philip Moon (Casey); Pavel D. Lynchnikoff (Andrei); Tracey Walter (Jim); Sandra Kinder (Sue); Bill Rosier (Jerry); Keone Young (Mr. Hsi); Eric DaRe (Digiacomo); Gareth Williams (Phelps); Teo (Adonis); Stacey Travis (Nurse); Max Lazar (Dimitri); Frank Ensign (Len); Bob A. Jennings (Dr. Clifford); Ross Kettle (Resident Surgeon); Nikki Lee (Anaesthesiologist); John Roselius (Surgeon #1); Damon White (Winston); Dan Hildebrand, J.P. Jones, and Jerry Sloan (Russian Thugs); Alphonse V. Walter (Isaac); Melvin Jones (Rasta Doorman); Mara Duronslet (Jessica); Ernest Garcia (Burt); Alex Désert (Bartender); Sarah Stavrou (Woman); Jesse Perez (Crack Dealer); Daniel Rey Silvas (Basketball Player); Michael Chong (Chinese Security Guard #2); Alexander Folk (South African Businessman); Stella Garcia (South American Businesswoman); Guy Siner (Dutch Businessman); Al Ahlf (FBI Agent).

LOS ANGELES TIMES, 10/17/97, Calendar/p. 14, Jack Mathews

[*The following review by Jack Mathews appeared in a slightly different form in* NEWSDAY, 10/17/97, Part II/p. B9.]

Normally, when the star of a hit TV series is tested with the lead role in a major studio movie, film critics raise their noses and wonder, "Can he make the leap?" In the case of "X-Files" double-Emmy nominee David Duchovny, tapped for the Disney/Touchstone star vehicle "Playing God," it's more a question of whether he can survive the crash.

It's not his fault, necessarily. "Playing God," a self-conscious neo-noir thriller, was destined for no better than mediocrity by Mark Haskell Smith's lamely derivative script. It was also saddled with weak casting in supporting roles, and it was finished off by the clumsy direction of British feature film rookie Andy Wilson. Neither the studio nor Duchovny's agent did the actor any favors.

"Playing God" stars Duchovny as a defrocked surgeon who, in order to pay for the drug habit that cost him his license, becomes the house doctor for a Los Angeles mob that's at war with the local branch of the Russian syndicate. Bullet wounds are his specialty. The pay is good—$10,000 per patch-up—but the boss (a blond Timothy Hutton) is bug nuts, and his girlfriend (Angelina Jolie) is a quietly cool siren who will soon get him into a lot of trouble.

Stirring things up on the sidelines are brooding Russians with names like Vladimir and Dimitri, a pair of white-trash lackeys who seem to be doing scenes from "Dumb & Dumber" and an over-zealous—and overacted—FBI field agent (Michael Massee) trying to link Hutton to a Chinese smuggling operation. Guns are blazing from all directions, blood is spilling like oil from the

Exxon Valdez and Duchovny's Dr. Sands is busier than a White House apologist on the Sunday morning news circuit.

The major failing is that all of these characters, from the inept FBI man to the mob boss to the most psychopathic thugs, are meant to be quasi-lovable and darkly amusing, like the John Travolta and Samuel L. Jackson hit men in "Pulp Fiction." But the roles are not well defined, and the actors—aimlessly directed as they are—can't pull that off on their own.

To be fair to Wilson, his background in theater and television drama leaves him ill-prepared for a routine Hollywood genre film that is about equal parts posturing, precious dialogue and overblown action. In other words, "Playing God" needed an experienced hack, someone who could at least make a cross-town car chase in L.A. look as if it was hard to do.

Mainly, what's missing in "Playing God" is any sense of urgency or passion. Duchovny, who is from the Jason Patric school of low-key action hero, seems bewildered by his surroundings and unconvinced—as he should be—of the notion that his character is a self-destructive overachiever seeking redemption. Nothing about the doctor's drug addiction rings true.

Duchovny does deliver a few good deadpan lines, and Hutton brings occasional humor to his standard psycho-mobster. Angelina Jolie, Jon Voight's stunning 22-year-old daughter, gives her *femme fatale* Claire a world-weariness beyond her years, plus a hint of intelligence that contradicts her circumstances.

But "Playing God" is Duchovny's film to rise or fall on, and the elevator is definitely not going up.

NEW YORK POST, 10/17/97, p. 49, Michael Medved

"Playing God" centers on a seriously suffering surgeon (smoldering David Duchovny of TVs "The X-Files") who goes one night to a seedy, after-hours club to score some drugs.

Suddenly, murderous thugs come up to the bar and pump several rounds into the dreadlocked stranger who was drinking at the bar alongside the depressed doc.

As he collapses in a puddle of blood, no one is willing to call 911 because of the victim's obvious criminal connections, so Duchovny, after initial hesitation, makes a fateful decision to improvise emergency treatment.

This compassionate act brings dire consequences, since the troubled, drug-addicted physician had lost his license to practice medicine some months before, and he's now swept up in a thrilling new career as "a gunshot doctor," quietly treating wounded crooks who can't risk visits to a hospital.

This juicy premise provides a showy role for Duchovny, who does a solid (if somewhat understated) job portraying a profoundly flawed but powerfully sympathetic antihero.

But it's the villain who steals the show, thanks to a rip-roaring, riveting performance by Timothy Hutton (of all people) as a psychotic crime boss with spiky, bleached-blond hair and pseudo-existentialist flourishes.

Hutton tears into the role with such captivating glee that he may launch an entirely new career for himself playing quirky bad guys.

And speaking of launched careers, 21-year-old Angelina Jolie (daughter of screen legend Jon Voight) makes a knockout impression as Hutton's languid, leggy mistress; with her lavishly luxuriant lips, shiny, brittle (and broken) surface, she's nearly perfect as a wounded neo-noir heroine.

Michael Massee is also strong as an amoral, manipulative FBI agent.

In fact, even the smallest roles seem fresh, imaginatively conceived and expertly acted—so why should "Playing God" feel so disappointing when it ends?

The problem is a plot that is significantly less compelling than the people who propel it—complete with ho-hum, only adequate confrontations and car chases, together with a climax that feels simultaneously far-fetched and familiar.

Portentous, pretentious voice-over narration by Duchovny ("If you're in the business of saving lives, you better start with your own") adds an especially leaden and ludicrous touch.

In the end, this intriguing doctor's dilemma deserved more audacious and effective long-term treatment.

SIGHT AND SOUND, 1/99, p. 53, Liese Spencer

Struck off the register for operating while high on amphetamines, drug-addicted Los Angeles surgeon Eugene Sands spends his time trying to score synthetic heroin. At a bar one night someone gets shot. Sands saves their life. Later Sands is kidnapped by gangster Raymond Blossom, who gives him $10,000 for saving his employee and offers him a job treating wounded criminals who cannot be taken to hospital.

Sands joins Blossom's gang which is battling for territory with the Russian mafia. Sands grows close to Blossom's girlfriend Claire. The Russians raid Blossom's warehouse and steal his fake designer goods. Blossom captures an injured Russian called Vladimir. Sands saves his life, but discovers Blossom has only kept him alive long enough for questioning.

An FBI agent tells Sands that to avoid arrest he must inform on Blossom. Sands is wired up to record Blossom's meeting with a Chinese gangster, eager to import Blossom's counterfeit goods into China. During an FBI raid Claire is shot. Sands and Claire escape to a car, driven by Blossom's henchman Cyril; Sands sees an FBI microphone on Claire's chest. Cyril tries to kill Sands, but Claire stabs Cyril.

After operating on her in a bar, Sands takes Claire to his parents' house in the country and comes off heroin. The FBI insist Claire return to LA to entrap Blossom. Back in LA, Blossom sends two surfers to kill Sands, but he escapes. Blossom shoots the Chinese businessman. He and Claire are pursued by the FBI and Sands. During the car chase, Sands rescues Claire and runs down Blossom.

A wretched Tarantino rip-off, this trashy thriller aspires to flip black comedy but manages only moments of unintentional hilarity. As a Hollywood calling card from Andy Wilson (one of the British directors of the television series *Cracker)* it's a derivative disaster. As a vehicle for David Duchovny (this was his first feature before the *X Files* movie) it's a tragedy which could have buried the star's spin-off career before it even began.

The film opens with a portentous voice-over musing on the significance of day-to-day decisions, causality, or what "the Greeks call character". The voice belongs to Eugene Sands, a famous Los Angeles surgeon who has had his licence revoked for operating while high on amphetamines and now spends his days trawling seedy bars in search of heroin to feed his addiction.

In one such bar he saves a gun-shot victim's life with a coat hanger and soon finds himself in the employ of Timothy Hutton's gangster, who hands him fat envelopes of cash to perform emergency operations on various low-lifes.

If we are to believe Duchovny's hypnotically monotonous voice-over, this arrangement is some kind of Faustian pact, with Sands selling his soul to the Mob in return for a chance to practise his profession. "Hell doesn't always look like hell," he drones, "on a good day it can look a lot like Los Angeles."

Since Wilson handles his story with all the wit and sophistication of a bad episode of *Charlie's Angels,* it's hard to give *Playing God* much credit as a morality tale of any profundity. What's left is an impression of relentless, poorly staged but graphic violence, whose genuine B-movie texture is supposed automatically to qualify as 'ironic', as if unbelievable characters, crude performances, plastic sets, second-hand dialogue and other clichés (sinister FBI agents, car chases, slow-motion shoot-outs) were somehow innately witty.

Eager to impress on viewers his technical virtuosity, Wilson gratuitously shoots each scene from a different, ever more ludicrous angle. His frenetic framing is complemented by some enthusiastic over-acting from a peroxide-cropped Hutton. Risibly camp and flamboyant, Hutton's performance provides a pleasing foil for Duchovny, who doesn't so much sleepwalk his way through the film as remain in a coma, barely bothering to open his mouth to mumble a line (go back to the amphetamines, Eugene).

What is it that Claire sees in him, you wonder, to lure her away from Hutton? Is it the blank eyes or the sheen of sweat? But that would probably be investing too much motive, too much of what the Greeks call character into Claire—her main purpose is to pout, which Angelina Jolie does admirably. During their brief sojourn in a comfortable country cabin ('My parents' summer house,' he tells her, failing to explain why he spends the rest of his time in a squalid flat), Sands decides to come off heroin. The cold-turkey scenes in which a well-fed Duchovny affects withdrawal symptoms take the film to a new low.

VILLAGE VOICE, 10/28/97, p. 84, Dennis Lim

Barely adequate by straight-to-video standards, *Playing God* stars David Duchovny as Eugene Sands, a junkie surgeon who, in the fashion of junkie surgeons, loses his medical license. After an impromptu lifesaving operation in a nightclub, Eugene finds himself working first for Timothy Hutton's bottle-blond Zen-master psychopath (a villain that would appear overpitched in a Bond movie), and later for some FBI goons. Containing only the vaguest semblance of a plot, this is an oddly ragged picture, cobbled together from mismatched clichés traditional Russian and Chinese bad guys coexist with inept and jokey hoods from the Tarantino collection.

Most effective when ironically inscrutable, Duchovny is ill served by Mark Haskell Smith's script, which burdens him with an exhaustingly overwritten narration and a surplus of stillborn lines. Director Andy Williamson makes a brief, curious foray into expressionism (to illustrate Junkie Hell), but otherwise plays it safe and anonymous.

Also reviewed in:
CHICAGO TRIBUNE, 10/17/97, Friday/p. D, Mark Caro
NEW YORK TIMES, 10/17/97, p. E18, Stephen Holden
VARIETY, 10/20-26/97, p. 71, Leonard Klady
WASHINGTON POST, 10/17/97, p. D6, Stephen Hunter

PONETTE

An Arrow Releasing presentation of a Les Films Alain Sarde and Rhône-Alpes Cinéma coproduction with the participation of la Région Rhône-Alpes/Centre National de la Cinématographie and Canal+. *Executive Director:* Christine Gozlan. *Producer:* Alain Sarde. *Director:* Jacques Doillon. *Screenplay (French with English subtitles):* Jacques Doillon. *Director of Photography:* Caroline Champetier. *Editor:* Jacqueline Lecompte. *Music:* Philippe Sarde. *Sound:* Dominique Hennequin and (music) John Timperley. *Sound Editor:* Jean-Claude Laureux. *Casting:* Antoinette Boulat, Christine Baras, Sophie Blanvillain, Brune Compagnon, Lola Doillon, Eve Guillou, Marick Hermet, Magali Montoya, and Sandrine Revet. *Art Director:* Henri Berthon. *Costumes:* Astrid Traisssac. *Make-up:* Laurence Azouvy-Jarnau. *Running time:* 92 minutes. *MPAA Rating:* Not Rated.

CAST: Victoire Thivisol (Ponette); Matiaz Bureau Caton (Matiaz); Delphine Schiltz (Delphine); Léopoldine Serre (Ada); Luckie Royer (Luce); Carla Ibled (Carla); Antoine Du Merle (Antoine); Marie Trintignant (Ponette's Mother); Claire Nebout (Aunt Claire); Aurélie Vérillon (Aurelie, a Boarder); Xavier Beauvois (Ponette's Father); Henri Berthon (Primary School Teacher); Marianne Favre (Marianne).

LOS ANGELES TIMES, 6/20/97, Calendar/p. 10, Kevin Thomas

To watch Jacques Doillon's "Ponette"—one of the most sensitive, luminous films about the very young ever made—is to be reminded that the French cinema has traditionally paid more attention to children than that of any other country. Even in the many French films not primarily concerned with youngsters, they are a vivid presence and are taken seriously. In dealing with the impact of death on a 4-year-old, "Ponette" will inevitably recall Rene Clement's similarly themed "Forbidden Games" (1952), a classic among French films.

A young woman has been killed in a car accident, leaving her widower (Xavier Beauvois) to cope with their daughter, Ponette (Victoire Thivisol, age 4), who refuses to accept that she will never see her mother again. Her father leaves Ponette in the care of their child's aunt (Claire Nebout), who lives in the country with her own two children, Matiaz (Matiaz Bureau), about Ponette's age, and Delphine (Delphine Schiltz), who looks to be 6 or 7.

Ponette has landed in a loving, idyllic atmosphere, but like so many people of all ages, she discovers that she is essentially alone in coping with such a loss. Her father is a flat-out atheist, and her well-meaning aunt tells Ponette of Christ's Resurrection to comfort her only to inadvertently give her the hope that her mother will experience a Second Coming herself. (Alas, it clearly never occurs to these adults to get their stories straight for the child's benefit.)

As Ponette interacts with her sweet-natured cousins (the angelic Matiaz especially) and with other children at school, we get a good idea of how hard it is for small children to make sense of so much contradictory and incomplete information of the various ways in which people deal with life and loss. The effect of all this input is simply to reinforce Ponette's firm belief that if she prays hard enough to God her mother surely will appear to her.

In tackling such a story, Doillon has pulled off something of a miracle as he takes us into the world of the very young, letting us experience with them their sense of constant fresh discovery and gradual comprehension. How ever did he get these toddlers to respond to the camera without a trace of self-consciousness? How did he get such performances from them?

And performances, no matter if they're essentially playing themselves, is what they are. How did he create such spontaneity, such a quality of authenticity? (The information that Doillon and his assistants set up workshops with the children does not begin to explain the magnitude and quality of his own inspiration.) All the children in the film emerge as distinct individuals and personalities, not just Ponette.

You well understand how the judges at the Venice Film Festival last year named Victoire Thivisol best actress. As the grief-stricken yet doughty Ponette, she takes us steadfastly through all of Ponette's moods—her pain, her fleeting joys, her resolution. So acute and constant an observer is Doillon, a 20-year film veteran whose work almost never reaches America, that he carries off moments that a lesser filmmaker could never hope to attempt.

Intimate, tender yet resolutely clear-eyed, "Ponette" is in all its aspects a remarkable achievement.

NEW STATESMAN, 6/26/98, p. 51, Gerald Kaufman

[*Ponette* was reviewed jointly with *The Object of My Affection*; see Kaufman's review of that film in Film Review Annual, 1999.]

NEW YORK, 6/9/97, p. 79, David Denby

Exquisitely molded faces, softened by natural light; Rubenesque lips, ripe and full; an enormous seriousness and responsibility before the world's sorrows—the children in *Ponette* are very beautiful, and perhaps beauty at this level of intensity is all we need. The 4-year-old girl Ponette (Victoire Thivisol) has lost her mother in a car crash, and writer-director Jacques Doillon tells the story of her grief entirely from her point of view. Ponette's father, young and tense, conscious of his responsibility yet also terrified, tries to console his daughter but then leaves, dumping the girl into the arms of her aunt, who lives in the country somewhere in the French Alps. The aunt does all she can, and so do Ponette's cousins, especially little curly-haired Mathias (Matiaz Bureau), who offers his protection with romantic tenderness and the readiness of a cavalier. But Ponette still has to bear up by herself. She does so by not letting go of her sorrow, holding to her grief as closely as she does to her little rag doll.

Jacques Doillon keeps the camera low to the ground and respectfully records lengthy conversations among the children, their metaphysical speculations and their ideas about marriage and love and singleness. Shot in the country, much of the movie is physically beautiful, and one has to say that these are exceptional, even idealized, children. Except for one moment, they don't chant, and I heard no poopy-doopy jokes, no Barney chatter. Neither pop culture nor vulgarity has touched them. Despite its concentration on grief, the movie is something of an idyll: the children are seen as profoundly serious. Doillon doesn't offer any "mature" view of death because, of course, there isn't any. Ponette manages her unbearable loss as well as anyone ever does. Flinching from nothing, she's a true heroine.

NEW YORK POST, 5/23/97, p. 50, Bill Hoffmann

"Ponette" is one of those rare movies about children that works.

And it introduces a 4-year-old actress who gives a truly remarkable performance—one that is so moving I'll even compare it to that of Jean-Pierre Leaud in "The 400 Blows."

The story is simple: A little girl named Ponette is told of her mother's death in a car crash, and begins the long and difficult task of trying to cope with it.

But before you dismiss the plot as too depressing, take it from me: Little Victoire Thivisol, who plays the newly motherless child, grabs your heart from the first frame and never lets it go.

So instead of being one big downer, "Ponette" is a life-affirming movie that provides new insights into the way we learn to perceive the concepts of life and death.

Soon after Ponette is given the tragic news by her bitter father, who blames his wife's careless driving on the tragedy, the girl is shipped off to her aunt's home in the French countryside to "heal."

But Ponette's grief manifests itself in questions about the existence of God and whether He has the power to bring people back from the dead.

She has sad "conversations" with her mom and bears the often cruel barbs of her cousins, who try to tell her like it really is.

Thivisol is one terrific little actress, totally natural and affecting at every turn.

Part of the strength of director Jacques Doillon's film is that he focuses his complete attention on Ponette. And yet, the same focus also provides the movie's one weakness.

"Ponette" yearns for a bit of conversation between adults. If only we could have seen the girl's father talking about her agony with other adult family members. It would have added an extra dimension to our understanding of Ponette's psyche and her mental gremlins.

Still, the complete immersion into Ponette's world is a daring step for a filmmaker. Doillon has taken that step with great success.

NEWSDAY, 5/23/97, Part II/p. B8, John Anderson

"Joyful as a child" is a description that doesn't sit particularly well with little Ponette (Victoire Thivisol), a child in transition. "I'm not joyful being a child," she says quite frankly, and no, she's not. Her mother is dead, she can't come to grips with it and she's growing up far faster than she should.

But death's intrusion on—and interruption of—childhood is just one of the themes of Jacques Doillon's elegantly wounding "Ponette," which may assume a 4-year-old's perspective on mortality but transcends age. What goes on around Ponette as she fights the acceptance of her mother's passing—all the confused and confusing theories of death and heaven and Jesus and zombies—is a babble of superstition and optimism. The point: No one knows, wants to know, or will admit they don't know but will always say what they feel to a child who can't possibly fathom the weight of death. Ponette feels it all quite profoundly, thanks, including a certain resentment at a world so lacking in satisfactory answers.

Doillon accomplishes several quite wonderful things in "Ponette"—the most spectacular being the performance he gets out of little Victoire Thivisol, who was voted best actress at last year's Venice Film Festival. She's heartbreaking, naturally—a motherless child can hardly be otherwise—but the way Ponette seesaws between mortifying grief and frank wisdom is disturbingly real. And with her crushed rosebud mouth and hurt eyes, young Victoire is also lovely to watch.

But Doillon manages to hit on a basic truth about childhood—that children are accepting of what they don't see and have total faith in what they do, and that these are qualities that aren't always lost to age. He also captures, or perhaps creates, a very convincing world of unsullied affection and intimacy. Among the different children in his film—such as Ponette's cousins (Matiaz Bureau, Delphine Schiltz), with whom she goes to stay—there are expressions of such innocent affection that it takes one's breath away, perhaps out of guilt, perhaps out of admiration for the director.

What happens to Ponette within the confines of the film is the quite inevitable confrontation with her mother's mortality (Mom being played by the enormously talented Marie Trintignant). That we care so much about what happens to Ponette once the credits roll and her story ends is a testament to the director, who has tapped into something quite basic and maybe transforming.

SIGHT AND SOUND, 7/98, p. 51, Michael Temple

A woman and her four-year-old daughter Ponette are involved in a car crash. The mother dies, while Ponette escapes with a broken arm. Ponette's father tells her simply that her mother is dead. Ponette's loss and confusion are then exacerbated by her father's departure on a business trip. He leaves her with her aunt and two cousins in a small mountain village.

Despite the care and understanding of those around her, Ponette enters into an extended period of mourning, refusing to believe that her mother will not soon return. Her aunt, her cousins, and her school friends all relate religious, legendary, and fantastic stories to Ponette which they hope will console her. But the stories gainsay and contradict each other, so Ponette picks out the narrative fragments she needs in order to build structures of belief. Finally, miraculously, her mother appears in the flesh and instructs Ponette to "learn to be happy".

This film marks an extreme development in Jacques Doillon's long-running investigation of children, their behaviour, their language, their psychology, and their potential as screen actors and objects of cinematic scrutiny. With *La Fille de quinze ans*, Doillon explored the topic of adolescent sexuality, and with *Le Jeune Werther* he focused on a young boy's suicide. Both of these films play to some extent on the spontaneity and inarticulacy of youth, but with *Ponette* Doillon takes his project into previously uncharted territory. Its leading actress, Victoire Thivisol, was only four years old when the film was made, while its story engages with what might be hazardous material for a cast of performers one would normally expect to be gurgling or gooing on the fringes of a family-based comedy or melodrama.

The sudden loss of a beloved parent, the complex process of grief—how can a child so young begin to understand events like these, let alone tread the fine line between detachment and commitment required by such a part? Is it the actress Victoire Thivisol's confusion or Ponette's pain that we see as the bereaved child struggles to make sense of the words, reasons, and stories provided by the people around her? It would be wrong, however, to start accusing Doillon of exploitation of children or trivialisation of grief, for this is a highly serious and sincere piece of film-making. What will make many viewers uncomfortable is the brutality of Doillon's premise, along with the film's powerful and unsettling distortion of cinematic identification.

On a personal level, identification with Ponette-Victoire is made extraordinarily easy by the engaging simplicity of the direction and by Doillon's refusal to prioritise viewpoints. The father's coarse atheism and the aunt's pious Catholicism are indistinguishable in presentation and impact from the muddled mythologies of death rehearsed by the children. Deprived of clear ideological or perceptual reference points, all we can do is watch Ponette struggling to come to terms with the absoluteness of death. And the simple impossibility of her philosophical task renders her failure strangely accessible.

Equally, Doillon offers us identification by one of cinema's shortest routes: the close-up, constantly bringing us nearer to Ponette's seemingly enormous eyes, her tired and reddened complexion, her disproportionately large and almost distorted face. So rare is it to see little children photographed in this degree of detail that once again the viewer's sense of who is who and what is what begins to stretch and blur. This distortion is eventually carried over to all the children, their bodies appearing at times to fill up the whole screen. Contrasting with this intense photographic intimacy is the clear and open landscape of green grass, big trees, stunning mountains, and infinite skies. This sudden, vertiginous shifting between the infinite and the tiny suggests some kind of metaphysical manipulation on Doillon's part, although he has strongly denied any such intention, claiming that the 'resurrection' at the end of the film was not of his confection, but came from the thousands of nursery-school children he interviewed while researching the film.

In France there was a good deal of debate around *Ponette*, with most opinions willing to grant Doillon artistic licence rather than condemn him to ethical censure. The generally positive reaction was in part facilitated by the media deployment of Marie-Hélène Encrevé, a psychoanalyst whom Doillon had asked to keep an eye on the children, notably Victoire Thivisol. The agreement between director and analyst was that the shooting of the film would cease as soon as Encrevé saw any signs of distress. According to the analyst, the children were reportedly quite happy to "play amongst themselves" between takes, and then switch over to playing *Ponette* for the camera. Encrevé's account is intriguing, not least because of the elements she foregrounds and those she elides. She informs us that Victoire seemed to have perfectly grasped Diderot's "paradox of the actor", but does not elaborate on Victoire's 'technique' for producing tears, which apparently involved 'asking' Doillon to tell her off very sternly. Whatever conclusion one comes to regarding *Ponette,* whether it be expressed in ethical or personal terms, it is clear that

Doillon is committed to pushing to the limit his particular conception of cinema, and that in so doing he has already taken his films into areas he didn't know they could explore.

TIME, 6/16/97, p. 76, Richard Corliss

[*Ponette* was reviewed jointly with *Gabbeh*; see Corliss' review of that film.]

VILLAGE VOICE, 5/27/97, Film Supplement/p. 22, J. Hoberman

An authentic tour de force, Jacques Doillon's chastely enchanting *Ponette* challenges description. How do you discuss this movie in which a young child refuses to accept the reality of her mother's death—without making it appear far more sentimental and precious than it actually is?

Four-year-old Ponette (Victoire Thivisol) is introduced, sucking her thumb through a hole in an arm cast, hospitalized in the aftermath of the car crash that critically injured her mother. She is informed that her mother might die and then, soon afterward, that her mother is dead, as she and her agonized, angry father (director Xavier Beauvois) drive through the countryside. They park, Ponette pouts, and, while scrambling around on the hood of the car, offhandedly remarks that her mother must be "flying with her magic mirror."This will not be the last theory that she offers (or receives) on the afterlife.

Sent to stay with cousins approximately her own age, Ponette regales them with stories that her mother visits her by night. These dreams are scarcely dispelled by her aunt's earnest attempts to impose an adult theology. Ponette is told that her mother is with Jesus in heaven and further reminded of Jesus's resurrection. While the cousins are content to play "resurrection," logical Ponette reasons that if Jesus could return from the dead, so could her mother. Gathering an assortment of offerings, the child spends several days stubbornly waiting for her. (In effect she starts her own religion.) Too drily directed to even seem pathetic, the scene is given a mordant postscript when Ponette's father explains that he doesn't believe in Christ's resurrection: "That's not for us." The girl is furious with her aunt: "Daddy said that's not true. It's not nice to lie to me."

An unsmiling charmer in Osh Kosh overalls, Victoire Thivisol won the best-actress award at the last Venice Film Festival (just before she entered kindergarten). Watching her, it is as easy to imagine that her pudgy features have assumed the permanent veil of sadness one associates with those who lose a parent in childhood, as it is impossible not to speculate on the technical aspects of her performance. While a few of the more emotional scenes benefit from editing-room sleight of hand (Ponette is more apt to begin a scene in tears than begin crying on cue) "Thivisol's line readings have the offbeat spontaneity of a pint-sized Kim Stanley.

The film's script was evidently developed out of a half year's worth of workshops with four- and five-year-old children. Indeed, once Ponette is placed in some sort of boarding school, Doillon is responsible for directing an entire, chattering three-feet-tall ensemble. Setting his camera down in the midst of their play, Doillon keeps close to the kids, making a quasi-ethnographic observation as the vulnerable Ponette comes under the influence of a nascent cult leader, perhaps a year older than she, who bosses her through a series of initiatory ordeals. The movie is scarcely *Lord of the Flies* but neither is childhood sentimentalized. In fighting with another kid over a toy gun, Ponette is informed that she deserved to have her mother die.

The amazing thing, given its heartbreaking premise, is that *Ponette* is scarcely a weepie. The purity of the child's concentration and will—even when, in the movie's riskiest scene, she digs for her mother in the graveyard—is almost matched by the clarity of the filmmaker's structure and analysis. Ultimately, *Ponette* is not so much a movie about bereavement and loss (and magical thinking and denial) as it is about the ways in which all of these inform religious thinking—including, of course, the religion of mass entertainment, for which one need only imagine the Hollywood remake with Robin Williams, Meg Ryan, and the hideous little bugger from the last Jim Carrey flick.

Doillon's scenario has its miraculous aspects to be sure—and he would have required the genius of Carl Dreyer to pull off the final scene. But, because even its innocent, ineffably single-minded protagonist cannot truly bring her mother back to life, *Ponette* precisely concerns the failure of the spell so spuriously cast in nearly every happy-ending movie around, from *Liar, Liar* to *The Fifth Element*.

Also reviewed in:
NEW REPUBLIC, 6/2/97, p. 28, Stanley Kauffmann
NEW YORK TIMES, 5/23/97, p. C14, Stephen Holden
VARIETY, 9/9-15/96, p. 116, David Stratton
WASHINGTON POST, 6/27/97, Weekend/p. 44, Rita Kempley

PORTLAND

A Zentropa Entertainment release in association with DR TV and the Danish Film Institute. *Producer:* Peter Aalbaek Jensen. *Director:* Niels Arden Oplev. *Screenplay (Danish with English subtitles):* Niels Arden Oplev. *Director of Photography:* Henrik Jongdahl. *Editor:* Henrik Fleischer. *Music:* Sons of Cain and Morten Olsen. *Sound:* Kristian Eidness Andersen and Torsten Bolvig Hansen. *Production Designer:* Lars Kofoed-Hansen. *Costumes:* Ingrid Soe. *Running time:* 103 minutes. *MPAA Rating:* Not Rated.

CAST: Anders Wodskou Berthelsen (Janus); Michael Muller (Jakob); Ulrich Thomsen (Lasse); Iben Hjejle (Eva); Birthe Neumann (Mother); Baard Owe (Kaj); Edith Thrane (Mrs. Eriksen); Helle Charlotte Dolleris (Irene); Susanne Birkemose Konsgaard (Minna).

NEW YORK POST, 5/28/97, p. 49, Thelma Adams

Great Danes they're not! In "Portland," Niels Arden Oplev's Danish "Trainspotting," an ex-con teaches his younger brother Drug Dealing 101: arm-busting, granny-snuffing and profit-sniffing.

Copenhagen burns in Oplev's harsh, acidly funny shocker about Danish bottom-feeders. Shot in brilliant black and orange by cinematographer Henrik Jongdahl, "Portland" is probably the only movie in history to be named after a brand of cement.

Welcome to post-industrial Denmark. It's no "Babette's Feast."

"Anyone happy in this town is on something," says Janus (Anders Wodskou Berthelsen). The feral heavy metaller returns from a trip "up country" unrepentant.

Janus' first civilian act is to boost a car, get high and slalom across three lanes in a drug-crazed rave with his younger brother, Jakob (Michael Muller), riding shotgun.

There's a pain driving the 23-year-old toward disaster, but it's as hidden as his pie face behind black, stringy hair.

"From now on, we'll stick together," Janus tells his 17-year-old brother. We always hurt the ones we love.

Jakob is a soulful-eyed blond with a bowl cut and the noble look of a Viking hero on his first foray to Greenland.

There's a poetry in the youth's full lips; it's clear from the first grinding of the gears that those lips will be drinking poison before the movie ends.

What we take away from "Portland" is not Jakob's final, mirthless laughter, the hardened set of his mouth. We carry the echo of an earlier moment: the lanky teen dancing the Texas two-step with two blondes dressed as cowgirls, swooning into schoolboy kisses with one lovely just before dawn.

There's nothing throwaway about the scene, a fleeting vision of the sweet man Jakob could have been. Hope dies, but newcomer Oplev rises from the ashes with the help of Lars von Trier's Zentropa Studios.

"Portland"'s visceral, drug-fueled mood swings—at times screaming, speeding, at times whispering, slo-mo—recalls the blazing mood and energy of Wong Kar-Wei's "Chungking Express."

The aptly named Sons of Cain provide a menacing score that's all the more disturbing for its gasps of whispery romanticism.

NEWSDAY, 5/28/97, Part II/p. B9, John Anderson

There aren't any babies in strollers in the Danish "Portland," the debut feature by the talented Niels Arden Oplev. But there's one in a crib. And the scene surrounding him is enough to upset the comforting supposition that there are better worlds than this.

What happens is less important than what we think might happen, because by the time the wee Dane arrives on the scene Oplev has already stripped away our protective layer of Planet Hollywood-issue apathy and made mayhem something new. And unifying: In "Portland," Oplev is his own World Court, issuing a global indictment of spiritual laxity, moral complacency and collaboration with the corporate/entertainment enemy.

That the film is often bleakly, blackly funny makes its Cain-and-Abel-esque story entertaining as well as unsettling. Janus (Anders Wodskou Berthelsen) is just out of jail on a drug-dealing charge, where he's met the same kind of problem as his customers: He's heavily in debt to his dealer, Lasse (Ulrich Thomsen), for the pills that got him through his prison stay. Met at the jail door by his babe-in-the-woods brother, Jakob (Michael Muller), Janus proceeds to get high, sharpen a screwdriver and pop the lock on a car, which he then steals and heads for the city at something more than a reckless pace.

Which is how "Portland" itself proceeds, as it pushes Janus toward a somewhat twisted love with Lasse's half-sister Eva (Iben Hjejle), Jakob toward a life like Janus' and both of them on a collision course with Lasse. His characters are far more important to Oplev than plot, but so is the depiction of a world in which hope is a luxury and moral strength is not just unaffordable but undefinable: Is Jakob weak because he finds the casual ruthlessness of his brother's world a shock? Or is Janus weak because he can't find it within himself to resist the easy money, easy drugs and easy violence that eases his roiling psyche? For all the appalling brutality of "Portland," Oplev is a moralist, because he makes the brutality appalling.

After all, violence in movies is so ubiquitous it's almost anesthetic. What would we do if such-and-such didn't eviscerate so-and-so? Storm the projection booth? Or just question our worldview?

Oplev—whose debut feature was made within "Breaking the Waves" director Lars von Trier's Zentropa Films—simply wants to redefine our worldview. And he accomplishes a curious marriage of cliche and insight: When Janus blames their negligent mother for his and Jakob's plight, we know too much about him to think he believes entirely in what he says. When he tells Jakob, "It's us against the world," it sounds like a line he heard in a movie. That it was a movie he probably saw in jail separates Janus, perhaps not too dramatically, from the rest of the world. But his desperate state and Oplev's uncompromising vision separate "Portland" from the rest of the class.

VILLAGE VOICE, 6/3/97, p. 74, Gary Dauphin

The grittily random future-primitive underworld of *Portland* is a far cry from the well-ordered, forward-looking place that usually comes to mind when thinking of Denmark. The Portland of the title refers to a brand of cement, and Jakob and Janus, the two Danish siblings in Niels Arden Oplev's curiously fatigued first feature, live the low life in the shadows of rectilinear concrete high-rises and gently sloping highways. Alternately clinging to each other and clawing each other like black-clad chicks falling from the same nest, the brothers are not only victims of Europe's depersonalized cities but test cases in how old metaphors about boys running wild at the fringes of society stand up to the approaching millennium. *Portland* maybe intoxicated with new-tech trends in audio (industrial-music dissonance) and video (nameless cities glow in amber, the pixelation suggesting a landscape under constant watch by surveillance cameras and night sights), but it's basically asking an old question: do things that don't kill young men still make them stronger?

The film begins with Jakob (Michael Muller, whose eyes will become as hard by movie's end as they're soft and pained at its opening) waiting for older brother Janus (an oily Anders Wodskou Berthelsen) to be released from prison. They don't hug so much as exchange mild blows, the proof of their mutual love Janus's willingness to share a smoke. Janus is a thin-hipped pill-popping freak and after teaching Jakob his basic street ethos ("You have to be cold to survive"), he introduces him to an odd kind of reverse drug dealing: divesting poor retirees of prescription meds for street-level resale.

Portland doesn't give the pair much to do besides procure, so they move with a wry aimlessness through a violently repetitive series of incidents where Jakob's weakness plays against Janus's lack of affect. There are strange moments of levity (Jakob goes to a line dance, while the dealer they report to cries about the violent demands of his business), but Jakob predictably hardens up while Janus softens enough to tell his girlfriend, 'I love you' (only after beating the crap out of her, of course). *Portland* is more keen on grungy atmosphere than substance or character, but in the end the quality of hoplessness that shapes Janus and Jakob's world is made pretty clear: the horror isn't that things get worse in life, but that nothing changes except attitude.

Also reviewed in:
NEW YORK TIMES, 5/28/97, p. C14, Stephen Holden
VARIETY, 3/4-10/96, p. 76, David Stratton

POSTMAN, THE

A Warner Bros. release of a TIG production of a Kevin Costner film. *Producer:* Jim Wilson, Steve Tisch, and Kevin Costner. *Director:* Kevin Costner. *Screenplay:* Eric Roth and Brian Helgeland. *Based on the novel by:* David Brin. *Director of Photography:* Stephen Windon. *Editor:* Peter Boyle. *Music:* James Newton Howard. *Music Editor:* Jim Weidman. *Choreographer:* Ellen Bromberg. *Sound:* Kirk Francis and (music) Shawn Murphy. *Sound Editor:* Bruce Stambler. *Casting:* Mindy Marin. *Production Designer:* Ida Random. *Art Director:* Scott Ritenour. *Set Decorator:* Ron Reiss. *Set Designer:* Thomas Betts, Susan Lomino, James Murakami, Bill Taliaferro, and Darrell Wight. *Set Dresser:* Christian Kastner. *Special Effects:* Terry Frazee, Don Frazee, Donald E. Myers, Jr., William Greg Curtis, Ralph Allen Winiger, and Eugene Crum. *Costumes:* John Bloomfield. *Make-up:* F.X. Perez. *Stunt Coordinator:* Norman Howell. *Running time:* 170 minutes. *MPAA Rating:* R.

CAST: Kevin Costner (The Postman); Will Patton (Bethlehem); Larenz Tate (Ford); Olivia Williams (Abby); James Russo (Idaho); Daniel Von Bargen (Sheriff Briscoe); Tom Petty (Bridge City Mayor); Scott Bairstow (Luke); Giovanni Ribisi (Bandit #20); Roberta Maxwell (Irene March); Joe Santos (Getty); Ron McLarty (Old George); Peggy Lipton (Ellen March); Brian Anthony Wilson (Woody); Todd Allen (Gibbs); Rex Linn (Mercer); Shawn Hatosy (Billy); Ryan Hurst (Eddie); Charles Esten (Michael); Anne Costner (Ponytail); Ty O'Neal (Drew); Kirk Fox (Gangly Recruit); Ken Linhart (Disappointed Conscript); Korey Scott Pollard (Thin Recruit); Kayla Lambert (Shakespeare Girl); Austin Howard Early (Shakespeare Boy); Ellen Geer (Mrs. Thompson); Randle Mell (Village Mayor); Cooper Taylor (Tony); Dylan Haggerty (Slow Recruit); Michael Milgrom (Holnist Projectionist); Keith C. Howell (Holnist Scout); H.P. Evetts (Holnist Soldier); Jeff Johnson and Jeff McGrail (Rope Bridge Soldiers); Lily Costner (Lily March); Gregory Avellone (Pineview Man); Andy Garrison (Pineview Sentry); Rusty Hendrickson (Pineview Minister); Marvin Winton (Pineview Old Man); Tom Novak and Richard Joel (Benning Gatekeepers); George Wyner (Benning Mayor); Brooke Becker and Eva Gayle Six (Benning Women); Todd Lewis (Benning Man); Joe Costner (Letter Boy); Kathi Sheehan (Mother of Letter Boy); Amy Weinstein and Betty Moyer (Elvis Women); Joseph McKenna (Holnist Captain); Neal Preston Coon (Bridge City Boy); Rick Wadkins (Bridge City Man); Shiree Porter (Bridge City Woman); Anthony Guidera (Bridge City Guard); Jade Herrera (Carrier); Greg Serano (California Carrier); Derk Cheetwood (Carrier Twelve); Mark Thomason (Adult Letter Boy).

LOS ANGELES TIMES, 12/24/97, Calendar/p. 14, Kenneth Turan

The year is 2013. America's consumer society lies in ruins, a hodgepodge of faded Coppertone billboards and tilted Union 76 globes. Heartless bandit hordes rape and pillage at will. Who dares stand in their way? Can anyone rise to the challenge of speaking out for what's good and decent? To the strains of "deliver the letter, the sooner the better," a hero does arise. Believe it or not, it's "The Postman."

The first film to be directed by and star Kevin Costner since "Dances With Wolves" won seven Oscars, "The Postman" sounds like it's going to be "Dirtworld," a land-locked version of Costner's most notorious film, the much-derided but finally adequate "Waterworld."

But "The Postman" turns out to be something much sillier than that. Goofy and gee-whiz when it isn't being post-apocalyptic glum, it is such an earnest hodgepodge that only by imagining "Mad Max" directed by Frank Capra can you get even an inkling of what it's like.

Working with cinematographer Stephen Windon and production designer Ida Random, Costner does display the sense of epic storytelling that characterized his work in "Wolves" and "Waterworld," as well as the belief that any film that doesn't approach three hours isn't worthy of his attention.

But the actor-director doesn't seem to realize or care how unintentionally funny the Eric Roth and Brian Helgeland scenario (adapted from the novel by David Brin) plays on that wide screen. While some of the film's choicer lines were apparently cut after wiser heads intervened, others have remained. "You're a godsend, you're a savior," breathless folk say to Costner's nameless drifter, to which he replies, with the humility and solemnity of a medieval saint, "No, I'm just the postman." True enough.

Costner tries to combat the unlikeliness of a postman as a mythic figure, able to inspire devoted legions and the key to the revival of the Restored United States of America, by playing his character as a reluctant hero, an aw-shucks kind of guy who stumbles onto greatness all unawares.

Introduced by an awe-filled voice-over that announces, "In those days he walked alone, a solitary witness to the chaos that reigned," Costner's drifter is an itinerant actor who wanders the West with his trusty mule Bill, reciting snippets of Shakespeare in the hopes of getting a free meal.

It is the drifter's bad luck to run across the path of Gen. Bethlehem (Will Patton), a former copy machine salesman who now commands a ragtag army that spreads terror wherever it can. Conscripted into the general's militia, he suffers through multiple screenings of "The Sound of Music" (no kidding) before escape becomes possible.

On the run, the drifter stumbles on a letter carrier's uniform. Seeing the impersonation as a way of scamming free meals, he puts it on and tells people in the nearby hamlet of Pine View that the government is starting up again and mail delivery will resume.

"Stuff is getting better" is the essence of his message, and it certainly starts getting better for the Postman. The uniform attracts the attention of the fetching Abby (British stage actress Olivia Williams), a married woman with a sterile husband who's in search of just the right drifter to serve as the "body father" for her future child.

Things are so hopeless in Pine View that against his will the Postman attracts followers desperate for something to believe in. Prime among them is the grandly named Ford Lincoln Mercury (an ill-at-ease Larenz Tate), who soon enough starts shouting deranged things like "I'm a postman, I'm not running from anything."

The film's all-time gee-whiz line, however, goes to Abby, who has to look our hero in the eye and tell him straight on, "You give out hope like it was candy in your pocket. You have a gift, Postman." There's only one word for this, and those who remember what Costner himself told Madonna about her show in the "Truth or Dare" documentary will know what it is: neat.

With its logic-defying mixture of tones and acting styles (rock star Tom Petty is especially problematical), "The Postman" shows what can go wrong when you trust movie stars to direct themselves. What Costner and company have ended up with is a 2-hour-and-50-minute vanity project, an elaborate and expensive frame that exists to display the kind of role he likes to play. Whether anyone beyond the actor's most loyal fans will think that's neat is another story.

NEW YORK POST, 12/24/97, p. 34, Michael Medved

The best fun associated with "The Postman" involves thinking up appropriately insulting headlines playing off its title. How about "This 'Postman' Doesn't Even Ring Once." Or, "'Postman' Is a Dead Letter"? Or, "Kevin Costner Goes Postal"? Or, "The 'Postman' Is Fourth Class Male"? Or, simply, "Return to Sender,"?

Kevin Costner's first directorial effort since "Dances With Wolves" is an idiotic, overlong, insanely indulgent movie that is so lavish, so flamboyant in its awfulness that it becomes perversely entertaining.

For one thing, the film is seldom less than visually stunning, with breathtaking locations (mostly in Oregon and New Mexico), elaborate, intriguing sets and hundreds of carefully crafted costumes. Unfortunately, these images add up to a story even less coherent or structured (and more soggy) than Costner's previous post-apocalyptic adventure, "Waterworld."

Once again, our hero is a lonely wanderer in a ruined world, traveling the West in 2013 after a war destroyed the United States. Finding a mail-carrier's uniform in a rusted old jeep, Costner puts it on and takes the stack of mail, telling suspicious town-people that long-suspended postal service has returned and that he is an official representative of the "restored government of the United States."

Inspired by his lies, a group of young idealists (led by Larenz Tate) rallies to actually deliver mail and to defy the oppressive rule of psychotic warlord Will Patton, dressed and made up to resemble Robert E. Lee.

Among many other atrocities, Patton kidnaps Costner's main squeeze (played by incandescent British newcomer Olivia Williams), whom the Postman has inherited after her husband asked him to impregnate her. Don't ask.

None of this makes sense, as survivors use electricity but no phones or telegraphs, and possess all sorts of guns and artillery but no cars. These arbitrary absences justify innumerable horseback scenes, including massed cavalry charges, which Costner shoots with genuinely lyrical intensity.

The script strains for similar lyricism, featuring lines like, "You have a gift, Postman. You give out hope like it was candy in your pocket."

There's also pseudo-biblical narration, declaring, "In those days, he walked alone, a silent witness to the insanity." You may become witness to the insanity of this film, but there is no reason to remain silent.

NEWSDAY, 12/24/97, Part II/p. B7, Jack Mathews

Wherever Kevin Costner is living these days I bet you'd find a large Remington-style sculpture of a man crouched on the back of a charging horse, reaching for a piece of mail held up by a small boy. A filmmaker of Costner's stature takes home whatever memento from a production he wants, and the sculpture of the legendary hero of "The Postman" embodies both the spirit of the movie and the outsized ego of its creator.

"The Postman," the first film Costner has officially directed since "Dances With Wolves," is patriotic hokum on a massive scale, and its overt similarities to "Waterworld," the pre"Titanic" record-holder for cost overruns, leaves you wondering what Costner and the powers at Warner Bros. must have been thinking.

Some steps were obviously taken to avoid a "Waterworld." For one thing, the movie was made4 in a publicity vacuum, and arrives in the midst of the high season with less advance buzz than "Mouse Hunt." Apparently, it's better to have no word-of-mouth than even the chance of negative word-of-mouth.

More importantly, Costner has avoided the cold, silent-but-deadly action hero archetype he played in "Waterworld" and fallen back on the shy charms that made him a major star in the first place. His character here, a post-apocalypse drifter who dons a mail carrier's uniform and inadvertently becomes the great white hope of a reclaimed civilization, has humor, vulnerability, an easy smile, and a manner as comfortable as an old shoe.

But those wise moves don't begin to compensate for the bad ideas and the interminable time devoted to "The Postman." The movie is nearly three hours long, and its central story doesn't begin until the end of the first hour. If you're going, you'd better like Kevin Costner a lot!

Costner took a leisurely approach to "Dances With Wolves," another story about a solitary man finding purpose on the frontier after a devastating war. But "The Postman," adapted from David Brin's sci-fi novel, is a futuristic fable, taking place after an imaginary war, on an imaginary frontier in the Pacific Northwest, where isolated pockets of survivors take orders from a villain out of a bad B-western.

That villain is Bethlehem (Will Patton), a sadistic looter who has formed an army of marauders who run roughshod over the scattered townships, drafting their men, raping their women and pillaging their possessions and provisions. Costner plays a Bethlehem draftee who escapes into the mountains, and returns, wearing a mail carrier's uniform taken from a skeleton for warmth, to carry on a ruse for food.

Costner calls himself the Postman, and delivers some 13-year-old mail, found with the uniform, to the residents of Pineville, whose sense of restored contact with the outside world makes him a hero. There's food, a bath, a shave, and a party. A beautiful woman named Abby (Olivia Williams), whose husband is infertile, asks him to impregnate her. Neither rain nor snow nor gloom of night can keep him from completing this task.

The drifter makes up stories to burnish his image. He's not only a federal employee, but a personal emissary of the current president, who has sent him to assure Americans that the nation is being rebuilt.

From such bold myth a legend is born, and carried on the wind. Soon, there is a postal youth movement. Its carriers, mostly teenagers recruited by Postman acolyte Ford Lincoln Mercury (Larenz Tate), deliver the mail with religious fervor, and the Postman is their god.

Naturally, Bethlehem doesn't take the news well, and another war begins. This time, it's an outmanned United States—i.e., the deluded mail carriers—against the armed marauders. Only a genuine hero can lead the righteous underdogs to victory.

The story, adapted by the talented Eric Roth ("Forrest Gump") and Brian Helgeland ("L.A. Confidential"), is such bunk it's hard to watch without giggling. Nothing makes sense if you give it a moment's thought, and though the film's humor often distracts you from those thoughts, the ending is such complete sentimental nonsense, it makes the three hours taken to get there feel like penance for being suckered in.

SIGHT AND SOUND, 4/98, p. 49, Philip Strick

In 2013, the US consists of isolated communities struggling to recover from World War Three. A loner wanders between villages, performing scenes from Shakespeare. He is conscripted into the marauding army of General Bethlehem. Intrigued by his captive's intransigence, Bethlehem determines to break him, but the man escapes. Finding a mail van and a postman's uniform, he demands entry to the town of Pineview with a bag of letters, claiming to be an official representative of the restored government. He is welcomed as the Postman.

Soon, he recruits postal workers and builds up a network for deliveries. A local girl, Abby, asks him to help her and her husband by impregnating her. The new mood of confidence enrages Bethlehem, who launches an attack on the town of Benning when, inspired by the Postman, its townsfolk refuse him entry. Wounded, the Postman escapes with the help of Abby, now widowed, and she nurses him through a hard winter.

Recovered, he finds the new postal service is flourishing, and he is acclaimed as a folk-hero. But Bethlehem's murderous attacks intensify until, horrified by the carnage, the Postman acknowledges defeat and retreats to a remote town, Bridge City. Forced to return by Bethlehem's capture of Ford, his most loyal supporter, the Postman arranges a final confrontation in which he and Bethlehem fight hand-to-hand for the leadership. Bethlehem's death heralds a new era, celebrated years later by the unveiling of a commemorative statue of the Postman by his daughter.

After its interestingly metaphorical opening in which a drifter finds his vocation (originally published separately), David Brin's novel of reformation, on which *The Postman* is based, quickly gets entangled in a jumble of less charming post-apocalyptic notions, including a malfunctioning computer, a militant feminist movement, and a contest between muscle-enhanced super villains called "Augments". Wisely discarding these attractions, the screenplay for *The Postman* by the high pedigree team of Eric Roth *(Forrest Gump)* and Brian Helgeland *(L.A. Confidential,* concentrates on more homely matters. It is only too tempting to detect in this Gump-like hints of absurd idealism and Ellroy-influenced examples of fakery and deceit. Still lurking rather confusingly in the background is British neo-Nazi arch-fiend Nathan Holn, the late founder of the survivalist Holnist movement. Very much in the foreground, by contrast, is star and director Kevin Costner, poised as ever between two worlds.

Once again taking the role of untouchable, Costner plays his mailman as part pony express rider and part Robin Hood. "I'm just a performer," he murmurs, "Shakespeare and stuff like that." But grand dramatic gestures are hardly his style and on stage he's a shambling disaster. Instead, emerging fully stubbled from the Utah salt flats like a fusion of Eastwood and Everyman, no ties, no past, he is an animal-loving nonentity whose rather laboured sense of humour and brow-wrinkling indignation at injustice just about redeem him. Belatedly, we learn that the Postman was also once a Holnist, a revelation that at least provides some vague background. His main opponent, too bloodthirsty to form an obvious alter ego, sums him up to mutual satisfaction after one glance at his binoculars: "You like to keep your distance, don't you?"

Detachment, leading to recruitment—the formula inevitably evokes Costner's *Dances with Wolves* in which the exiled soldier mediates in the wasteland between the Army and the Indians. As if firmly staked to safe territory, Costner repeats a number of themes and predicaments from the earlier film: the partnership between man and mount (here, a mule called Bill who also plays Macduff); the edgy relationship with a woman in mourning; the solo ride between two armies drawn up for battle; the beatings which, filmed subjectively, make us share the victim's blackouts. Among many striking resemblances, the staging of the vicious Pawnee being trapped and killed beside a river in *Dances with Wolves* is repeated in the execution of a Holnist in *The Postman*, distanced with the same sense of necessity and regret. Above all, *The Postman* is an extended elaboration on the delicate scene in *Dances with Wolves* in which the Lieutenant and the Indian can at last speak to each other through an interpreter and are soon firm friends. "Communication makes us strong," says the Postman's daughter, emphatically named Hope, summarising his message some 30 years later.

Unfortunately, the truism derives no fresh vitality from the Costner treatment. Where *Dances with Wolves* enjoyed a remarkable certainty of pace and place, *The Postman* with its nervous editing and fidgeting camera, clearly lacks confidence in the sillier twists of its narrative, a would-be Western somewhere between *Jeremiah Johnson* and *She Wore a Yellow Ribbon* (which it has the brass nerve to copy directly at one point). However, the plot gets lost among a welter of odd costumes and pointless atrocities. Magnificent landscapes and huge vistas of horsemen make pleasant viewing but, like the ludicrous intervention by a lion, their validity soon becomes questionable. Stuck with playing a dystopian destroyer knowingly after Dennis Hopper in *Waterworld*, Will Patton mainly convinces us that copying machine salesmen are not to be trusted, while Olivia Williams, in an appealing debut, looks both vulnerable and intelligent enough to pray, along with the rest of us, that the Postman won't ring twice.

VILLAGE VOICE, 12/30/97, p. 76, Dennis Lim

Not quite as funny as its trailers indicate, *The Postman* is a disappointingly unspectacular disaster, a nearly three-hour rumble of low-level idiocy that would have been more entertaining had it erupted more frequently into full-blown lunacy. The year is 2013; the stereotypically dilapidated landscape is the result of a world war, horrible plagues, and various ecological disasters; and that messianic, Mad Max-ish figure emerging from the horizon on his mule, well, that's Kevin Costner.

The Postman's high concept (drifter delivers mail, saves America) is the stuff of high farce, but Costner—directing his delayed follow-up to *Dances With Wolves* (though he patched together *Waterworld* after Kevin Reynolds bailed)—pretends not to notice. Straight-faced and simpleminded, the film takes refuge in blind patriotism—it's a paean to the restorative power of communal ties.

Costner's character—nameless, but known variously as Shakespeare, The Postman, and Only the Greatest Man Who Ever Lived—is, to begin with, some kind of renegade performance artist in the arid postapocalypse. The film's half-hour preamble includes a spirited run-through of Shakespeare's greatest hits, starting Kevin and his mule. (Under the circumstances, *Macbeth's* "a tale told by an idiot, full of sound and fury, signifying nothing" leaps out at you.)

Being of "suitable ethnic foundation," Costner is soon conscripted by the Holnists, a tyrannical army led by one General Bethlehem (Will Patton, putting on an unattractive sideshow of herniated villainy). Escaping into the wilderness, Kevin stumbles upon a dead postman and a sackful of 15-year-old mail; presenting himself as a uniformed representative of the "Restored United States," he delivers the letters to their addressees in a nearby community. It's not long before the pose takes on a life of its own; in what turns, out to be a faith-healing exercise, youngsters across the American Northwest (including a poorly used Larenz Tate) relaunch the pony express.

As it happens, our accidental hero has good semen, too. Having been spared "the bad mumps," he's able to fertilize the happily married Abby (Olivia Williams), who, once impregnated with the child of Costner, is conveniently widowed. "You give out hope like it was candy in your pocket," an appreciative Abby later tells The Postman.

Costner is too limited a performer to be his own director as well; apart from Matthew McConaughey (and perhaps Leonardo DiCaprio), no contemporary actor utters his lines with such unmodulated disregard for context. His bland direction slides into sluggish bombast, eventually resorting to the slo-mo self-mythologization that made Mel Gibson's *Bravehear*t unbearable. But unlike Gibson, Costner (who's most appealing as a rumpled loser) doesn't have the makings of a megalomaniac; *The Postman* is pure hubristic hokum, yet it's notable mainly for its sheer ordinariness.

Also reviewed in:
NEW YORK TIMES, 12/24/97, p. E1, Stephen Holden
VARIETY, 12/22/97-1/4/98, p. 57, Todd McCarthy
WASHINGTON POST, 12/25/97, p. C10, Rita Kempley

PREFONTAINE

A Hollywood Pictures release of an Irby Smith/Jon Lutz/Mark Doonan production. *Producer:* Irby Smith, Jon Lutz, Mark Doonan, and Peter Gilbert. *Director:* Steve James. *Screenplay:* Steve James and Eugene Corr. *Director of Photography:* Peter Gilbert. *Editor:* Peter Frank. *Music:* Mason Daring. *Music Editor:* Stuart Goetz. *Sound:* Robert Marts and (music) Michael Golub. *Sound Editor:* Clancy Troutman and James Troutman. *Casting:* Pam Dixon Mickelson. *Production Designer:* Carol Winstead Wood. *Art Director:* Gregory A. Weimerskirch. *Set Decorator:* Nina Bradford. *Set Dresser:* Michael DeSilva. *Special Effects:* Tom Knott. *Costumes:* Tom Bronson. *Make-up:* Bill Corso. *Stunt Coordinator:* Stan Barrett, Sr. and Chris Howell. *Running time:* 106 minutes. *MPAA Rating:* PG-13.

CAST: Jared Leto (Steve Prefontaine); R. Lee Ermey (Bill Bowerman); Ed O'Neill (Bill Dellinger); Breckin Meyer (Pat Tyson); Lindsay Crouse (Elfriede Prefontaine); Amy Locane (Nancy Alleman); Laurel Holloman (Elaine Finley); Brian McGovern (Mac Wilkins); Kurtwood Smith (Curtis Cunningham); Adrian Amadeus (Finnish Teammate); Laurence Ballard (O'Hara); Ryan Brewer (12 Year Old Black); Robert Karl Burke (Young Pre); Kevin Calabro (3rd Airport Reporter); George Catalano (Patron #1); Wade Clegg (German Security); Wally Dalton (Dick Burke); Adam Fitzhugh (Thomas Becker); Jim Freeman (Patron #2); Tom Glasgow and David Grosby (NCAA Press); Geoff Haley (German Soldier); Dag Hinrichs (Jeff Galloway); Tracy Hollister (Lasse Viren); Peter Anthony Jacobs (Ray Prefontaine); Eric Johnson (Olympic Trials Reporter); Eric Keenleyside (James Buck); Steve Kelley (U of O Reporter); Stephen J. Lang (Bar Back); Shannon Leto (Bar Patron); Eric Liddell (Gary Powers); Jochen Liesche (German Newscaster); Henry Lubatti (Frank Shorter); Jeff McAtee (Reporter at Village Gate); Michael Patten (Munich Stadium Official); John Charles Pavlich (Husband); Wendy Ray (Himself); Gaard Swanson (1st Reporter at Airport); Brad Tuinstra (Finnish Runner); Brad Upton (Neighborhood Man); Bruce Walker (Olympic Village Reporter); Hugh P. Wallace (Man on Winding Road); Mac Wilkins (Track Official); Phaedra Wilson (German Security Girl); Paul Yarnold (Reporter at Trailer Park).

LOS ANGELES TIMES, 1/24/97, Calendar/p. 1, Kenneth Turan

Steve Prefontaine was, to crib a line from Bruce Springsteen, born to run. And to win. The ultimate competitive animal, he finished first in more than 75% of his races and remains the only person ever to hold the U.S. records in every distance from 2,000 to 10,000 meters.

But there is another side to this charismatic runner, who knew he was good and wasn't fearful about sharing the knowledge. Prefontaine became an early spokesman for athletes' rights and helped put Nike on the map by accepting its sponsorship, when it was just a wee Oregon company. More poignantly, Steve Prefontaine died in an automobile accident when he was 24 years old, leading to his apotheosis as the James Dean of track and field.

It's taken more than 20 years, but Hollywood has finally caught up to Prefontaine's appeal, and for a while two projects were, yes, racing to reach theaters. A Robert Towne-directed version called "Pre" starring Billy Crudup is scheduled for fall release, well behind the current "Prefontaine."

Directed and co-written by Steve James, the director of "Hoop Dreams," and co-produced and photographed in Super 16-millimeter by his "Hoop" partner Peter Gilbert, "Prefontaine," not surprisingly, takes a documentary approach to its story.

This means that it not only starts off with newsreel footage and shoots as much as possible in a loose, hand-held style, but also frames the narrative around talking head shots of actors often in unconvincing aging makeup-playing key participants in Prefontaine's life who comment on the man they knew.

While documentaries like "Hoop Dreams" come with the grittiness of reality automatically included, dramatic films have to manufacture their own, and "Prefontaine" can't. Though it is always pleasant and agreeable, this film has the bland and undemanding texture that characterizes movies made for network TV. Worshipful without really trying to be, it's more an illustrated scrapbook than an involving motion picture.

The man who "turned distance running into a blood sport" grew up in Coos Bay, Ore., not sure where to channel his fearful determination to succeed. The discovery of running answered that question, though Prefontaine (played by look-alike Jared Leto) does find time to have a sweet relationship with down-home girlfriend Elaine Finley (Laurel Holloman).

The two go to the University Of Oregon where Pre, as, everyone calls him, switches romantic allegiances to the more upscale Nancy Alleman (Amy Locane) and comes under the tutelage of irascible coach Bill Bowerman (R. Lee Ermey), a crusty autocrat who, believe it or not, has a caring heart under that gruff exterior.

It's Bowerman who moves Pre from the mile to the less publicized longer distances, correctly, assuring him that, with his personality, he'll make everyone care about these races. In a kind of sporadic inside joke, Bowerman, who went on to co-found Nike, is seen continually experimenting, not always successfully, with different kinds of homemade running shoes.

The turning point in Pre's young life is his participation in the 1972 Munich Olympics, both his memorable 5,000-meter race against Finland's Lasse Viren and his emotional response to the massacre of Israeli athletes. One result was his determination to fight the Amateur Athletic Union (here presented as a mythical organization called the ATU) to gain conditions comparable to those of cosseted European athletes.

Though "Prefontaine" takes a certain amount of power from its protagonist's personality and the events he lived through, Steve James' script (co-written by Eugene Corr) is filled with overly familiar situations and lines like "He ran his heart out" and "Nobody can coach desire." Equally self-evident is that nobody can ensure that a memorable story will get the kind of nuanced treatment it deserves.

NEW YORK POST, 1/24/97, p. 48, Larry Worth

If there's anything harder than achieving a breakthrough success, it's following up a breakthrough success. Just ask Quentin Tarantino.

That's why director Steve James earns extra credit. After hitting a bull's-eye with the documentary "Hoop Dreams," he's now exploring another side to his talent in "Prefontaine."

This time, he turns the tables by fashioning a faux documentary, complete with "home movies," celeb interviews and reflections on legendary distance runner Steve Prefontaine. The results are anything but conventional.

First and foremost, the film succeeds because James, who co-wrote the script with Eugene Corr, makes Steve a flawed, complex individual.

A golden boy narrative would have been the easiest course. Instead, Steve comes off as a Jekyll and Hyde: appealing and affectionate one minute, cocky, defensive and arrogant the next.

As made manifest by his behavior at the Munich Olympics, he's driven to run, partly because of childhood insecurities, more from obsessive competitiveness. Even when amusing some youngsters, Steve can't let a 6-year-old appear to beat him.

But Steve's off-putting ways never go over the top. That's because of a portrait imaginatively painted in shades of gray, an all-but-endangered species in Hollywood.

And while James deserves applause, it's to be shared with Jared Leto. The handsome actor, best known from TV's "My So-Called Life," is an unexpected knockout.

Beyond the demanding scenes of Steve's physical prowess, Leto convincingly evolves from soft-spoken youth to a man haunted by multiple demons. It's all conveyed in the subtlest of gestures and soulful glances.

Nice backup comes from Ed O'Neill and R. Lee Ermey as Steve's coaches, Lindsay Crouse as his German-accented mom and Amy Locane as his ever-loyal girl-friend.

Some subplots fare less well. For instance, the politics of amateur vs. pro deals may leave non-sports fans confused. Further, James relies too heavily on period tunes to convey the feel of the late '60s and early '70s.

But even before a tragic conclusion, the escalating drama proves undeniably moving. It's yet another indication of James' and Leto's complementary skills.

A second version of the same story—"Pre"—is due this fall. Clearly, star Billy Crudup and director Robert Towne have their work cut out for them.

NEWSDAY, 1/24/97, Part II/p. B2, Jack Mathews

Did you know that Jesus Christ was a distance runner at the University of Oregon?

Neither did I before seeing "Prefontaine," Which is purported to be the true story of '70s track star Steve Prefontaine but whose tone resembles nothing so much as "King of Kings." This is the story of a man of divine talent and determination who suffered for the faithful and died a young martyr.

Making films about sports stars is always dicey business. People iconize athletes with the most despicable natures; Dennis Rodman leaps to mind quicker than a head butt and a kick to the groin. But popular athletes cut down in the prime of life are the stuff of a screenwriter's dream.

This year, more than two decades after his death, the Prefontaine story is being told twice. Later in the year, we see "Pre," by writer-director Robert Towne, whose 1982 "Personal Best" is among the finest and least sentimental films on track and field. But first, there's "Prefontaine," which marks the feature debut by "Hoop Dreams" director Steve James, and it ranks near the bottom of the canon.

What dooms the picture to banality is James and co-writer Eugene Corr's eagerness to burnish the legend of Prefontaine, the free-spirited track star with flowing blond hair whose brashness translated into charisma and whose death, in a car accident in 1974, had sports writers memorializing him as the James Dean of track and field.

The movie deals with Prefontaine's tangible achievements—he held the American records at every distance between 2,000 and 10,000 meters, and led a revolt against the autocratic Amateur Athletic Union—but barely hints at his role as a symbol of the campus rebellion sweeping the country. His brashness, his looks, his Joe Namath-style gift for self-promotion, and his defiance of the AAU are the things that made him stand out.

Structuring the film as a documentary, with figures from the runner's past talking to the camera and leading us into flashbacks, James treats Prefontaine as a latter-day Jim Thorpe, the outsider as front-runner. With Prefontaine's family, friends and coaches all pitching in (and, off-camera, acting as consultants), we follow a kid who's too small for team sports compensating by putting his back to the wind and running to solo glory.

The film's coup is the casting of newcomer Jared Leto, who bears an uncanny resemblance to Prefontaine. Leto's likeness allowed James, shooting with Super 16-mm. film and blowing it up to 35mm., to blend new track footage with newsreel clips of the real Prefontaine in action and effect an amazing verisimilitude. However, as soon the races are over, the story descends immediately into clichés.

"Prefontaine" plays like a sports movie from the '40s, where adorably gruff coaches speak dialogue suitable for epitaphs ("They don't know how great a runner they're watching," says R. Lee Ermey's Bill Bowerman), where relatives tremble in the stands, rivals are compelled to shake their heads in awe, and old roommates choke back tears remembering where it all began.

The truth of his life is that Prefontaine died before achieving his dream of winning an Olympic gold medal. He had his chance, at the 1972 Munich Games, but ran fourth, a fact that the film audaciously blames on the distraction caused when Arab terrorists took Israeli wrestlers hostage, and the Olympics shut down while the world watched the tension build to slaughter.

The movie leaves the impression that Prefontaine is peeved by the delay. He was ready to go. How could they do this to him? That may confirm James' point that Prefontaine was blessed with singleminded determination, but it also points up the foolish importance we place on competition.

VILLAGE VOICE, 2/4/97, p. 76, Brian Parks

As worn and musty as a pair of old track shoes, *Prefontaine* is the flat-footed biopic of 70s Olympian Steve Prefontaine. Aiming to "turn distance running into a blood sport," Pre—as he's called—bursts out of his starting block in rural Oregon on a race to change the face of American athletics.

Prefontaine's story is basically a morality tale of how an asshole can learn a bit of humility before dying tragically. Vain and cocky, Pre joins the University of Oregon track team, his eyes already on the Olympics. Arrogant but talented, he quickly becomes a national sensation. (The film flashes newspaper headlines to prove this, but they don't spin as fast as they do in old movies.) Success follows success, and Pre gets to dump his soulful high school girlfriend for a bland blond babe he meets while jogging.

Prefontaine is directed by Steve James, who also made *Hoop Dreams*. James borrows from his previous outing, offering *Prefontaine* as a fake documentary: aging versions of the characters—done up in clumsy "old" makeup—regularly interject memories of the ill-fated runner. James also intersplices grainy footage (it was a grainier decade) of the '72 Olympics, a tactic that offers plenty of opportunity to compare how much the original Pre looks like the guy playing him (Jared Leto). The attack on the Israelis at Munich is the movies greatest drama, but it's only used here as a way to force Pre to think about somebody other than himself.

An accidental parody of the athlete-dying-young movie ("Watch Pre defeat the evil bureaucrats of amateur track!"), the film is most enjoyable for its parade of bad mustaches. And in the oddest scene, Pre's wise old coach—who moonlights as a cobbler of running shoes—gives the track star a pair of his newest creations, decorated with a primordial Nike swoosh. We might as well be witnessing the birth of the baby Jesus.

Also reviewed in:
CHICAGO TRIBUNE, 1/24/97, Friday/p. L, John Petrakis
NEW YORK TIMES, 1/24/97, p. C12, Janet Maslin
VARIETY, 1/27-2/2/97, p. 75, Todd McCarthy

PRETTY VILLAGE, PRETTY FLAME

A Cobra Film Department release of an RTV Serbia/Ministry of Culture of the Republic of Serbia. *Executive Producer:* Goran Bjelogrlic and Milko Josifov. *Producer:* Goran Bjelogrlic, Dragan Bjelogrlic, Nikola Kojo, and Milko Josifov. *Director:* Srdan Dragojevic. *Screenplay (Serbo-Croatian with English subtitles):* Vanja Bulic, Srdan Dragojevic, and Nikola Pejakovic. *Inspired by the war report as published in "Duga" by:* Vanja Bulic. *Director of Photography:* Dusan Joksimovic. *Editor:* Petar Markovic. *Music:* Aleksandar Sasa Habic. *Sound:* Martin Jankov Tomica and (music) Laza Ristovski. *Sound Editor:* Svetolik Mica Zajc. *Production Designer:* Milenko Jeremic. *Set Decorator:* Zivan Todorovic. *Costumes:* Tatjana Strugar Dragojevic. *Make-up:* Radmila Todorovic. *Special Make-up Effects:* Martina Subic Dodocic. *Running time:* 128 minutes. *MPAA Rating:* Not Rated.

CAST: Dragan Bjelogrlic (Milan); Nikola Kojo (Velja Kozic); Dragan Maksimovic (Petar, "Professor"); Velmir Bata Zivojinovic (Gvozden Maksimovic); Zoran Cvijanovic ("Speedy"); Milorad Mandic ("Fork"); Dragan Petrovic (Laza); Lisa Moncure (Liza Linel); Nikola Pejakovic (Halil); Petar Bozovic (Sloba); Marko Kovijanic (Marko); Dragan Zaric (Nazim);

Admir Sehovic (Little Milan); Milos Duricic (Little Halil); Vera Dedovic (Schoolmistress); Branka Katic and Milena Pavlovic (Nurses); Branko Vidakovic, Dubravko Jovanovic, and Uros Duric (Profiteers); Radoslav Milenkovic (Doctor); Feda Stojanovic (Dzemo); Boris Milivojevic (Young Muslim); Bojan Zirovic (Soldier); Mira Banjac (Velja's Mother); Reneta Ulmanski (Milan's Mother); Melita Bihali (Halil's Mother); Milica Ostojic (Aunt Fanny); Svaba and Musa (Junkies); Nebojsa Ilic (Milos Kozic, Velja's Brother); Drakula (Evil Attendant); Darko Tomovic (Camerman); Natalja Lucanin and Sandra Ilic (Nurses); Nenad Milenkovic Sanela (Waitress); Suzana Zlatanovic (Little Girl's Mother); Irena Sladic (Little Girl); Tanja Bukusic (Pioneer); Olivera Viktrovic (Nazim's Wife); Jelena Ivanisevic (Nurse); Rodoljub Dokovic Zuca (Buba's Father); Savo Radunovic (Functioneer); Milko Josifov (Turk).

LOS ANGELES TIMES, 1/16/98, Calendar/p. 16, Kevin Thomas

Srdjan Dragojevic's "Pretty Village, Pretty Flame" makes a stunning companion film to Emir Kusturica's "Underground" as a brutal, bravura allegory on the terrible disintegration of Yugoslavia. It has much the same passion, pain, anger and sooty humor of the Kusturica film and similarly boasts an array of vital, earthy characterizations.

Both filmmakers are too sophisticated to send conventional anti-war messages but instead create epic panoramas of human folly and suffering fueled by unbridled racism.

Dragojevic moves back and forth in time with supreme confidence, but his key shifts occur between 1980, the day Tito dies, and 1992, when war breaks out in Bosnia between Serbs and Muslims. The setting is an idyllic mountain community, where nine years before Tito, seen in newsreels, is dedicating—with appropriate pomp and ceremony—the Brotherhood-Unity train tunnel connecting Zagreb and Belgrade.

By 1980, the tunnel is seen full of scaffolding, and two little boys are afraid to enter it, believing it is inhabited by an ogre. Although one is a Serb and the other a Muslim, the boys are best friends, and they still are as adults, in the spring of 1992. "Will there be a war?" wonders Halil (Nikola Pejakovic). "What war?" replies Milan (Dragan Bjelogrlic), as they sit in a sunny roadside cafe on the top of a mountain.

Events, however, overtake them like a forest fire raging out of control, and they find themselves suddenly enemies. Halil believes Milan burned down his garage; Milan hears that two men in Halil's patrol killed his mother.

By now, Dragojevic is widening his perspective as the war progresses, moving beyond the two former friends to depict Serbian soldiers on a savage rampage throughout the area, burning, slaughtering and looting with a rock'n'roll glee and abandon. Eventually, however, a small group of Serbs find themselves trapped in that tunnel, among them Milan. Among their Muslim captors is, inevitably, Halil.

The film, in effect, unfolds as a flashback, in the memory of Milan as in 1994 he lay in a Belgrade hospital bed, recuperating from serious war injuries. Nearby is a fellow survivor of the 10-day tunnel siege, the Professor (Dragan Maksimovic).

Milan's memories of the siege constitute the bulk of the film, where Milan and other Serb soldiers, plus an American journalist (Lisa Moncure) with a camcorder, are holed up, contemplating their fate, dipping into their own memories and dreams. Having characterized the Serbs as savages, Dragojevic now uncovers their humanity.

The sequences set in the increasingly symbolic tunnel present Dragojevic with another kind of challenge: sustaining interest and momentum throughout the long siege. However, whereas "Pretty Village," which could be shorter, is for sure grueling, Dragojevic has succeeded in creating a film that is largely compelling over the long haul, building to climactic sequences that can only be described as devastating, as over-used as that word may be.

Dragojevic is a formidable director of actors, and it's good to see Moncure, as the sole American in the picture, making such a strong impression amid native actors of such presence.

"Pretty Village, Pretty Flame" is strong on irony, nuance and telling detail. After one of the Serbs goes on about how Serbia is the oldest state in the world and how Serbs were eating with forks while the Germans and English were still eating with their hands, Dragojevic later shows how swiftly a fork can be turned into a weapon.

NEW YORK POST, 10/10/97, p. 49, Larry Worth

Many may think of "All Quiet on the Western Front" as the definitive anti-war film. It probably still is. But "Pretty Village, Pretty Flame" isn't far behind.

Much like Emir Kusturica's dazzling "Underground," it's set in the former Yugoslavia. But while the Serbo-Croatian war was only one chapter of the epic "Underground," carnage-strewn battlefields are the basis for "Village."

Specifically, most of the action takes place in a long-abandoned mountain tunnel built decades ago by Marshal Tito's army. The film opens with newsreel footage of a ribbon-cutting ceremony at which scissors accidentally slice into one man's thumb. It's a messy precursor for the blood to flow on that soil.

Told from the hospital bed of a half-mad Serb, he recalls the cave as a shelter for himself, a handful of fellow recruits and a pretty American journalist. The group is trying to outlast a troop of Muslims that taunt and terrorize them from outside the cavern.

But since the Muslims can't get in and the Serbs can't get out, it's a no-win situation, much like the conflict itself.

Within that context, director Srdjan Dragojevic fashions a deeply disturbing treatise on the futility of war, despite an unmistakably pro-Serb sentiment. Thankfully, that's diluted by themes about the arbitrariness of political alliances and solid characterizations of each factions' followers.

Told in a non-linear style, the film demands attention and patience, partially since Dragojevic takes viewers' knowledge of Yugoslavia's fate for granted. But once you get past the sometimes confusing narrative, payoffs multiply.

Without exception, the actors prove outstanding, with Dragan Bjelogrlic brilliantly leading the pack as the central Serb survivor.

The end result is hauntingly effective and properly jarring. And while there's nothing pretty about "Pretty Village, Pretty Flame," it remains a work of exceptional beauty.

SIGHT AND SOUND, 1/98, p. 51, John Wrathall

Bosnia, 1980. Two boys, Milan and Halil, don't dare go into the abandoned tunnel in the hills outside their village because they believe that an ogre is sleeping there. If they wake him up, he will burn their village. Bosnia, 1992. Milan and Halil, who now work together in a garage, discuss the prospect of civil war. Two years later, after the outbreak of war, Milan, now fighting with a Serbian unit, shoots his comrades when they set fire to Halil's garage. Later, he returns home to find his mother murdered. Sloba, the local cafe owner, tells him the Muslims are responsible.

Outside the village, Milan's unit comes under attack by Muslim forces. Milan and five colleagues—leader Gvozden, Velja, Petar aka 'Professor', 'Fork' and Laza—take refuge in the tunnel. They are joined by an ambulance, carrying Red Cross worker 'Speedy' and an American television reporter, Liza. As the Muslims lay siege to the tunnel, they taunt the Serbs through loudspeakers. Milan recognises Halil's voice. The Serbs are picked off one by one. As each one dies, he flashes back over how he came to join up. Milan gets the ambulance running again. The survivors try to break out and are shot to pieces. Milan makes it to the end of the tunnel unscathed and finds Halil waiting. When they ask each other why they have done such terrible things, Halil says the ogre is responsible. He is killed when the tunnel explodes.

1994. Milan, Professor and the comatose Speedy lie in a Belgrade hospital ward. The next room houses a wounded Muslim. When Speedy dies, Milan vows to kill the Muslim, and crawls towards him, despite his injuries. Professor tries to stop him and they collapse in a pool of blood. 1980. The boys find the entire population of the village, including their older selves, dead in the tunnel.

The opening dedication, "to the film industry of a country that no longer exists", strikes a similar note of bitter nostalgia as the title "Once upon a time there was a country" at the start of *Underground*. Like Kusturica's film, *Pretty Village Pretty Flame* takes a despairing, ironic and largely apolitical look at the chaos which engulfed Yugoslavia in the 90s, and has been criticised for its overtly Serbian point of view. Though the film focuses on the friendship of the Serb Milan and the Muslim Halil, and its destruction by the war, it is seen entirely through Milan's eyes.

Halil, a sympathetic figure in the flashbacks, is just a mocking, disembodied voice outside the tunnel in the war sequences.

But to see the film as Serbian propaganda is to miss the point. Like Kusturica, director and co-writer Srdan Dragojevic focuses on the Serbs not to excuse them but to examine how they were duped into going to war. Though an unconvincing figure in her own right, the American journalist serves as a surrogate for the Western viewer, arriving with preconceptions which are by no means unjustified ("I'm fully aware of the Serbian concern for women in this war," Liza scoffs), before uncovering the huge diversity of attitudes motivating the cross-section of Serbs trapped in the tunnel. The captain, Gvozden, is a Yugoslav People's Army veteran, still devoted to the memory of Tito, and still proud of his heroic achievement walking 350 kilometres to the great man's funeral; the simple-minded brothers-in-law, Laza and Fork, are steeped in mystical mumbo jumbo about ancient Serbian civilisation; Velja is just a black marketeer who joined up to save his brother from the draft; and the intellectual Petar has the four Cs painted on his helmet, an acronym meaning "Only Unity Can Save the Serbs", and one of the key slogans of Serb nationalism with its pseudo-historical justifications for expansion. Milan, meanwhile, may seem the most level-headed of the Serbs, but he ends up the most crazed in the hospital scenes, desperate to murder the wounded Muslim in the next ward even if he dies in the attempt. It's as if, once "the ogre" is released, even the most reasonable cannot help succumbing to bloodlust in the end.

Blaming the war on the ogre—the atavistic force of madness and violence lurking in the tunnel that Tito built—might seem like an attempt to shirk Serbian responsibility. But at the same time Sloba, the local war profiteer who whips up hatred and loots the houses of his former friends but stays safe and prosperous in his cafe, is presented as an unmistakable caricature of the Serbian leader Slobodan Milosevic.

Moving deftly back and forth across several time-scales—from the opening spoof newsreel set in 1971, through the boys' childhood and the confinement in the tunnel, to the gruelling scenes in the hospital—Dragojevic builds up a devastating, kaleidoscopic picture of lives shattered by war. The tone is bitterly cynical, from the shots of Serbs looting and burning cut to an inane rock song, the lyrics of which go "the whole of Yugoslavia's dancing rock and roll", to the scene where the Serbs in the tunnel are reduced to taking swigs from a bottle of urine, prompting Speedy to sing a Coca-Cola jingle. But Dragojevic's nihilism has a romantic grandeur reminiscent of Peckinpah, who is evoked explicitly in Fork's bloody demise and in the famous lines from *The Wild Bunch* (1969) "Let's go." "Why not?"—spoken by Liza and Speedy before they run down the tunnel to certain death. As Peckinpah showed in *Cross of Iron* (1977), and countless Vietnam movies have demonstrated since, soldiers don't have to be fighting for a just cause to deserve our compassion.

VILLAGE VOICE, 10/14/97, p. 94, Gary Dauphin

Splattering even the quiet scenes with saturated Technicolor hues, *Pretty Village, Pretty Flame* is an aggressively lurid film from the former Yugoslavia, believable even when you know color this vivid only exists in the movies. A brutally violent outing set on the front lines of the Bosnian civil war, *Village* is an odd antiwar film. Jazzed on testosterone-fueled combat sequences and made by Serbs but critical of Serbian nationalism, this is a movie where deep inside every looter and village burner beats the heart of a (semi-)lovable grunt straight out of *The Longest Day*. As a storytelling strategy that works in the short run, overpowering and seducing, but the long-term verdict will have to wait until the wound *Village* depicts becomes less raw.

The film opens with a Tito-era newsreel about the opening of a "Peace Tunnel" in Bosnia-Herzegovina, a perfectly staged reenactment of Communist ritual that lurches into director Srdjan Dragojevic's preferred nutty territory when the Party ribbon cutter nearly lops off his own thumb. Flash-forward to the early '90s where wounded Serbian fighter Milan (Dragan Bjelogic) lies in a Belgrade hospital, trapped between garishly lit fever dreams about the war and a waking desire to literally fork the Muslim POW in the next room to death. Milan grew up near the quickly abandoned Peace Tunnel, and as a boy he and his best bud and future enemy Halil (Nikola Pejakovic, playing a Bosnian Muslim, of course) dreamt of exploring the spooky ruin when they were bigger and "better armed"

Milan's hospital nightmares center on the day he and his group of Serbian irregulars were chased into the tunnel by Halil's Muslim fighters. While they try to wait out the Muslims, the film drops in and out of the prewar lives of these losers and misfits. Even though the Serbs commit most of the onscreen atrocities, each is given a mitigating internal life by good performances and finely crafted, emblematic details. In contrast, Halil's Muslims are invisible ciphers, voices shouting and shooting into the tunnel. Milan and Halil do get a final face-to-face, but what's most disturbing about it is that like any family squabble, this one's terms and outcome were decided years ago.

Also reviewed in:
NEW YORK TIMES, 10/10/97, p. E14, Lawrence Van Gelder
VARIETY, 9/9-15/96, p. 120, Emanuel Levy
WASHINGTON POST, 11/21/97, Weekend/p. 54, Desson Howe

PRISONER OF THE MOUNTAINS

An Orion Classics release of a Karavan Joint Stock Company/BG Productions/Cinema Committee of the Russian Federation production. *Producer:* Boris Giller and Sergei Bodrov. *Director:* Sergei Bodrov. *Screenplay (Russian with English subtitles):* Arif Aliev, Sergei Bodrov, and Boris Giller. *Based on an idea by:* Boris Giller. *Director of Photography:* Pavel Lebeshev. *Editor:* Olga Grinshpun, Vera Kruglova, and Alan Baril. *Music:* Leonid Desyatnikov. *Music Editor:* Minna Blank. *Sound:* Ekaterina Popova-Evans. *Art Director:* Valery Kostrin. *Running time:* 98 minutes. *MPAA Rating:* R.

CAST: Oleg Menshikov (Sacha Kostylin); Sergei Bodrov, Jr. (Vania Zhilin); Susanna Mekhralleva (Dina); Dzhemal Sikharulidze (Abdul-Murat); Aleksandr Bureev (Hasan); Valentina Fedotova (Zhilin's Mother); Aleksei Zharkov (Maslov, the Russian Commander).

CINEASTE, Vol. XXIII No. 1, p. 47, Louis Menashe

Prisoner of the Mountains belongs in a way to that venerable genre, the Russian war film. Only things have been turned inside out. Russia's enemies here are not the ferocious counter-revolutionary White Armies of the Civil War (as in, say, *Chapayev*), or the savage German invaders of World War II (*The Rainbow, Fate of a Man*, and numerous memorable others). In Sergei Bodrov's film, Russians are the invaders, their Chechen opponents are tough, but noble, and war itself is the cruel enemy.

Bodrov (b. 1948), formerly, a journalist and scriptwriter, came to prominence as a director during the liberating, *glasnost* wave of the Gorbachev years, when once forbidden subjects and styles filled Soviet screens. To cite two of his best known films: *The Non-Professionals* (1987) follows a troupe of young amateur musicians through rural Kazakhstan in a detached, semidocumentary way, while *Freedom is Paradise* (1989) is an unadorned look at Soviet society through the eyes of a lad who escapes from his reform school to seek out his father in a distant prison camp. Bodrov is clearly animated by humanist concerns, and by something I've heard more than one Russian in the film world describe as essential for the health of post-Soviet society —compassion. The director has said that he wanted to make a film set in a contemporary battleground—Bosnia, for example, or the former Soviet republic of Tadjikistan—not in order to engage political issues or take political sides, but to claim eternal human values amid war's ravages. When the smoldering situation in the Northern Caucasus flared into a full-scale war of Chechen independence from Moscow, Bodrov had an ideal dramatic vehicle for expressing his compassion that war plus a Tolstoy short story about an analogous war a century and a half earlier.

It took a certain amount of courage for a Russian director to craft a pacifist film about the Chechen war, and one, moreover, in which the Chechens are presented more positively than the Russians. (Many Russians have objected to the film on these grounds.) Passions run very high in both camps. The Chechens, a Muslim people numbering about a million and a half today, have been battling Russian control since the early nineteenth century. In 1944 Stalin ordered wholesale deportations of the Chechen population to Central Asia for collaborating with the Germans. After the U.S.S.R. broke up in 1991, they started their drive to independence.

From the Russian side, the popular view of the Chechens is of a sullen minority involved in illegal activity (like other ethnic groups from the Caucasus, they are known derisively in Russian as "Blacks") and blamed for much of the organized criminal violence around such areas as drug trafficking and gun-running that have plagued major cities in post-Soviet Russia. From the official point of view, the Chechen quest for independence threatens, if successful, the unity of the fragile Russian Federation, made up of dozens of non-Russian minorities.

None of these issues appear in Bodrov's film, nor, consequently, is the exceptional ferocity of the two-year war explained. The Russians have resorted to massive aerial bombardment and artillery barrages, while the Chechen guerrilla campaign has seen mass hostage talking. The site of the film's action is not even identified as Chechnya. (It was shot in neighboring Dagestan.) It is a given that we are in Chechnya, and that the Russian army is there. Why it is there, and why the Chechens give battle, is left to the audience to intuit. I see in these omissions not only, Bodrov's above-the-fray pacificism (both sides are victimized by the war, whatever the issues), but the severe post-Communist 'reaction-formation' of so much of the Russian intelligentsia, filmmakers included, against all 'politics' and political ideologies. What counts for them are the 'normal' human currencies of love, decency, loyalty, friendship, kindness—or Bodrov's compassion.

Which brings us back to Tolstoy, and another peculiar (minor) omission. The film credits the story to "an idea of Boris Giller," one of its producers and screenwriters, but any educated Russian knows it is derived from a spare and touching Tolstoy short story written for young people in 1872, based on the author's experiences as a Russian officer in the Caucasus a generation earlier. In *A Prisoner of the Caucasus* (subtitled, *A True Story*), two Russian officers are captured and held in shackles for ransom by a Chechen villager. One of them escapes with the assistance of the Chechen's young daughter, a girl of thirteen, who is moved by pity and compassion (and perhaps something else) for the Russian.

Flash forward a century and a half for Bodrov's film, based on the outline of the Tolstoy story, embellished and transferred artfully to contemporary Chechnya. The Russians are still there, and the Chechens are still fighting them and taking them hostage. In other works, Tolstoy's descriptions of the hatred the Chechens felt for the Russians even read like the dispatches of journalists there in our own day.

Bodrov's *Prisoner* is a handsome and melancholy war drama set in the spectacular Caucasus, with Pavel Lebeshev's camera roaming beautifully in panoramic long shots across the flat-topped roofs of mountain villages. (Lebeshev is the talented cinematographer whose work may be seen in many of Nikita Mikhalkov's films, including *Slave of Love* and *Oblomov*). Bodrov's two captured Russians are a hard-drinking cynical veteran NCO played with effective swagger by Oleg Menshikov, the dark messenger of death in Mikhalkov's *Burnt by the Sun,* sporting a moustache here and looking like a carefree Russian Errol Flynn; and a young and innocent recruit—Sergei Bodrov, Jr., the director's son, not a professional actor but turning in a superb performance as a reluctant soldier who learns some life—and death—lessons in the Chechen killing fields. The two are brought closely together in captivity after a nicely shot opening ambush scene.

The film unfolds in a series of episodes that are paced briskly by Russian standards, rather glacially by Western norms, especially for an adventure film. But taking time with the story works to its advantage; we get the full flavor of several different relationships as they develop. There is the buddy aspect in the older soldier/young recruit pairing. They see the world differently and get on each other's nerves, but they recognize they are in this thing together and must bear it with patience and humor—the very Russian characteristics of endurance, and indifference to danger. In one scene they dance rollickingly to Louis Armstrong's "Let My People Go." In another, the crusty Sasha (Oleg Menshikov) lapses into nostalgia and despair, and reaches to touch the young Vanya's hand as the soundtrack soars with the patriotic hymn "The Slavyanka": a very moving moment. (Leonid Desyatnikov's haunting score alternates Caucasian motifs of reeds and woodwinds with Russian tunes, especially "The Blue Scarf," a sentimental ballad popular during World War II.)

The second important relationship involves the two Russians and their captor Abdul (the Georgian actor Djemal Sikharuklidze), an imposing figure who wants to exchange them for his son, held by the Russian army, and resists the demand of some elders to kill the two. His dramatic act of kindness in the film's denouement matches the tenderness shown by his young daughter. Her relationship with the young recruit Vanya is both central to the film's narrative and its emotional core. Played brilliantly by another nonprofessional (Susanna Mekhralieva, discovered by Bodrov in a Dagestan schoolroom), the dark-eyed Nina is captivated by Vanya, by his plight of course, but perhaps by budding romantic feelings for him as well. She talks to him, dances for him, dresses for him, and ultimately frees him in a courageous act of defiance against all the force of patriarchy and customs (Unlikely? Well, Tolstoy wrote that it was a true story, and anyway it serves Bodrov's purpose well.)

Vanya, fearing the trouble her act will cause her, refuses to escape. The powerful climax follows: a long, long walk past a cemetery (a nice touch) as Abdul leads Vanya to his execution ('dead man walking,' Chechen style). Abdul is bound now to avenge the killing of his son by the Russians during an escape attempt, but in a heart stopping moment as we wait with Vanya for the fatal bullet, Abdul fires into the air and walks away somberly, back to the camera. Enough of killing, that walk seems to say.

I should note that some have interpreted that last scene differently. Since we never see Abdul fire into the air, and since the traditional code of vengeance would strongly suggest otherwise—Abdul would shoot him, period—the alternate explanation has a now dead Vanya magically trying to wave off the Russian helicopter gunships overhead as they target the village. And in a ghostly voice-over afterword, Vanya tells of trying to dream of the villagers "he came to love." This interpretation is fueled by two episodes in which the executed Sasha-Sasha's ghost—appears to Vanya. (Sasha had killed two Chechens cold-bloodedly in an attempted escape; his throat is cut in retaliation.) So why not have Vanya's ghost turn up as well? I think Bodrov's two brief excursions into magic realism are ill-conceived and clumsily brought off, but in that last scene, either way, the 'real' Vanya or the 'magic' Vanya conveys the same message: the merciful Chechens, people he developed an affection for, are repaid with brutality.

There is one other clumsy scene in an otherwise consistently moving and well-made film that amply earned its Academy Award nomination in the foreign-language category. Bodrov stages a folkloristic tableau of Chechen warriors dancing, drinking, wrestling, and roasting some meat at a campfire. It comes off as kitschy and patronizing. The film has plenty of authentic local color without it in numerous village scenes. The contrast between premodern village life shown in the film and the very modern instruments of war (on both sides, though the Russians have the overwhelming fire power), is striking.

As of this writing, the guns are silent in Chechnya. A peculiar peace has materialized: the Chechens claim independence and act that way, while the Russians deny their independence but agree to let them act that way. There were rumors in Moscow last year that President Boris Yeltsin asked for a private screening of *Prisoner of the Mountains,* and was so affected by the film that it impelled him to redouble efforts for peace. Wonderful, if true. Now that would be real good magic realism.

LOS ANGELES TIMES, 2/7/97, Calendar/p. 2, Kenneth Turan

One hundred and fifty years ago, Russian writer Leo Tolstoy wrote a short story set in the Caucasus at a time when his country was locked in a miserable war with intractable rebels. How little some things change.

Simple, powerful, convincing, "Prisoner of the Mountains" is the Tolstoy plot updated to the recent conflict with Chechnya, but its story needs no specific time or place to be effective. A spare, poetic tale of the traps of conflict and fate, of how much and how little humanity counts for in a state of war, it could be told about any location where killing is casual and options for survival few.

Directed by veteran Russian filmmaker Sergei Bodrov (who had a hand in the script and cast his son Sergei Bodrov Jr. as one of the leads), "Prisoner" won the International Critics Prize at Cannes and is Russia's entry for best foreign language film in the 1996 Academy Awards.

Despite its, official status, Bodrov's work is remarkable for not taking sides in the conflict. The film's measured, unsentimental sympathies are rather for those whose lives are fractured by war's pointless savageries, no matter what their political allegiance.

Bodrov Jr. plays a young crewcut recruit named Vania, first glimpsed being inducted assembly-line style into the Russian army. Boyishly eager to serve, he asks where he's headed. "Wherever your country sends you," is the gruff reply.

That turns out to be the Caucasus mountains, where the large but lackadaisical Russian force engages in massive drinking and random weapon firing, all of which arouses the contempt of the devoutly Muslim local people who have bitterness, feuds and long memories of their own to contend with.

Out on patrol in the hinterlands, Vania gets shot in an ambush, and only he and Sacha, another badly wounded soldier, survive the attack. Chained together, they're taken to a remote mountain village where they find themselves the personal prisoners of an unbending local patriarch named Abdoul Mourat (Jemal Sikharulidze).

Played by the quicksilver Oleg Menshikov, who was Nikita Mikhalkov's nemesis in "Burnt by the Sun," the mustachioed Sacha is not the kind of person you want to be shackled to. A cocky, selfish veteran who loves nothing but his AK-47, Sacha is at home in the cynical ambience of combat. Contemptuous of his chain-mate's reluctance to kill the enemy, he insists. "You have to, Vania. It's war."

Not surprisingly, Sacha and Vania do not remain at each other's throats but form a wary camaraderie. Also to be expected is the relationship of sorts that forms with their guards, especially Abdoul's young and suspicious daughter Dina (Susanna Mekhralieva). But these familiar elements are handled with clarity and integrity and don't play out in completely expected ways.

The core of "Prisoner of the Mountains" is why these men have been taken captive in the first place. Abdoul's own son has been imprisoned by the Russians and he hopes, with a parent's defiant logic, that he will be able to exchange his first-born for these two foreign invaders.

But in the corrosive atmosphere of war, with not a thimbleful of trust on either side, what ought to be a simple trade becomes anything but. The villagers want the soldiers killed out of hand, the Russians don't believe the hostages even exist and the intractability of the situation narrows the possibilities for those who believe that there is value in even a single human breath. But, because they do believe, they can't help but persevere.

Beautifully shot by Pavel Lebeshev, cinematographer on a number of Mikhalkov films, "Prisoner" is strengthened by its scenes showing village customs and traditions that have endured for generations. And the acting, both by veteran Menshikov and newcomer Bodrov, stresses the characters' individuality.

But "Prisoner of the Mountains" is successful mostly because of its determination to trust the pared-down ruthlessness of the situation. By doing so, the filmmakers underline one of the truisms of Eastern European cinema: The best of films often come from the worst of times.

NEW YORK, 3/3/97, p. 54, David Denby

In *Prisoner of the Mountains*, a company of armed Russians fighting in the war with Chechnya is ambushed by the rebels; two Russian soldiers survive and are held as prisoners in a Muslim village in the Caucasus Mountains. The older one, Sacha (Oleg Menshnikov), a professional soldier with a devil-may-care attitude, is disgusted by Vania (Sergei Bodrov Jr.), the raw recruit he's stuck with. Sacha is violent, witty, experienced, Vania a lamb caught in a life-and-death situation. Shackled together, the two men are kept in a stinking dark hut. In time, they grow to like each other and to admire some of the villagers who guard them. The village elder, an enormous, fierce-looking man (Jemal Sikharulidze), wants to keep them alive so he can trade them for his son, who is held prisoner by the Russians nearby. For a while, a deal seems possible—maybe. This Russian-made movie, based on a Tolstoy novella, is about the decent human emotions that get squashed by the iron logic of war.

Prisoner of the Mountains has great purity of intention and sweetness of feeling, and I wish I admired it more. The director, Sergei Bodrov, stages complex actions in a choppy and fragmentary style that isn't always convincing. And he does more to suggest an emotion than to create it. He does well, however, with the faces of the mountain people (most of them nonactors), which are hooded and closed off. And Bodrov suggests something of the odd, anomalous atmosphere of a sputtering neocolonial war, in which the participants intermingle, talk—then suddenly shoot each other. Betrayal has become a way of life.

There is a good attempted-escape sequence, a mad dash up streams, through ravines, the two men lost in the wasteland of rugged mountains. Bodrov, in his slightly haphazard way, captures the rawness, the unpredictability, the stop-and-go violence of war. The entire movie has a spontaneous and rather casual feeling to it. On the other hand, we don't always know what's going on: some sequences feel halfhearted and arbitrary, dropped in out of nowhere. Bodrov needs to tighten his grip on basic technique: his casualness is cutting off meaning. The humanist message—that what holds people together is more important than the political and religious differences that divide them—seems a little wan and perfunctory when your technique is better at conveying chaos than at evoking the ties that bind.

NEW YORK POST, 1/31/97, p.42, Michael Medved

"Prisoner of the Mountains" is both timeless and topical, ingeniously adapting a Leo Tolstoy short story from 150 years ago ("Prisoner of the Caucasus) to the cruel realities of today's war in Chechnya.

Director/co-writer Sergei Bodrov never identifies the precise location of his story or specifically refers to the Chechen fighting, adding to the movie's ageless, universal atmosphere. Except for the brief appearance of helicopters and other modern equipment, the story might have unfolded any time in the last three centuries of Russian warfare against the fierce Muslim fighters of the Caucasus.

Vania (played by the director's son, Sergei Bodrov Jr.) is a wide-eyed teenage draftee from Moscow whose mountain patrol is ambushed by local rebels. The entire detachment is slaughtered, except for Vania and his tough sergeant, Sacha (Oleg Menshikov), a macho veteran who revels in the thrill of combat.

These two survivors are loaded onto donkeys and taken to a remote mountain village, where the gaunt, scowling patriarch, Abdul (magnificently well-played by the riveting Dzhemal Sikharulidze) plans to exchange them for his own son, who's been captured by the Russians. If they won't trade, he fully intends to kill his prisoners.

Meanwhile, Abdul's shy, lovely daughter (12-year-old Susanna Mekhralieva) brings bread and water to the captives and begins to feel sympathy for their plight. The movie beautifully recreates the world of this ancient village, precariously perched on the edge of barren mountains that suggest a lunar landscape in their lonely grandeur (it was actually filmed in the Republic of Dagestan, about 200 miles from the Chechen front).

"The wind frightens the heart of any strangers here" declares a plaintive local song, and you can readily believe it. The middle section of the film depicts the edgy relationship between the two Russian captives, chained together with leg irons and in rather formulaic fashion representing the struggle between innocence and cynicism.

Menshikov, a popular Russian star ("Burnt by the Sun"), who here bears an unmistakable resemblance to Kevin Kline, makes the sergeant an irresistibly dashing rogue, while young Bodrov conveys the fumbling, gullible simplicity of the frightened young soldier without succumbing to excesses of sweetness that would have ruined the movie's balance.

If some of the plot elements seem painfully predictable, that is, perhaps, the price you pay for working with eternal themes. And beyond the story line, the senior Bodrov offers images of such exotic, forlorn splendor, and such gorgeously subtle coloration, that the visual poetry alone should satisfy most moviegoers.

NEWSDAY, 1/31/97, Part II/p. B15, John Anderson

Like many an old western, "Prisoner of the Mountains" uses conflict between warring, culturally dissimilar forces—Russian cowboys vs. Muslim Indians, in this case—without taking much of a political stand. Filmed only a few hundred miles from Chechnya, Sergei Bodrov's humanistic film seems to beg for a judgment call on present-day Russian imperialism, but opts instead for using the motherland's oppression for allegorical purposes.

As such, it works pretty well, even if one feels hung out to dry among the breathtaking Caucasus Mountains and barbarous Muslim warriors who take Sacha (Oleg Menshikov) and Vania (Sergei Bodrov Jr.) hostage.

Their tank ambushed by a troop led by the fearsome Abdul (Dzhemal Sikharulidze), they are to be his means to a trade for his own captive son, who is in Russian hands. In the meantime, Sacha and Vania, shackled together, get to know each other all too well, and plot ways to escape.

The two soldiers, caught up in a Third World nightmare, comprise their own metaphor for First World conflict. Sacha (who looks like a Russian Kevin Kline) is a ruthless veteran who never forgets that what he's in is a war, never questions his duty to kill and escape; his failure to shed this scaly demeanor is Bodrov's most political statement.

Vania, on the other hand—younger, less cynical, more easily bruised—succumbs to the hard-scrabble charms of the Muslim village, the good-heartedness of Abdul's young daughter, Dina (Susanna Mekhralieva), and the doubt that plagues all thinking people. He is the type to create art, perhaps, but never empires.

The Muslims too are a hardened lot; Abdul has lost two sons to violence and is determined not to lose a third. His naivete, however, is rather touching: He has both Sacha and Vania write to their mothers to facilitate a trade for his sons.

Sacha, of course, has no mother. Vania's, just as predictably, comes immediately to Abdul to win her boy's release.

But things go wrong, as they usually do in a film whose moral instruction is about not letting one stupid act lead to another. Bodrov, in addition to creating some precisely composed pictures and some equally precise characterizations, imbues his film with a staunchly Russian sense of ironic resignation, a stoic recognition of the cosmic joke at play.

At no time do Sacha or Vania experience fear. It's more like chagrin at being caught, at becoming the victims of fate they've probably laughed about a thousand times.

Abdul never laughs, of course. But his fate is no joke, and his plight is no game, political or otherwise.

SIGHT AND SOUND, 3/98, p. 34, Julian Graffy

Ivan (Vania) Zhilin, a newly conscripted Russian soldier, is thrown straight into a Caucasian conflict zone. In an ambush, only he and his sergeant Sasha survive. They are held in captivity in a mountain village by a man called Abdul-Murat, who aims to trade them for his son, who was captured by the Russians. They are looked after by his young daughter, Dina, and guarded by a dumb man, Hasan. An attempt is made to effect the exchange, but both sides withdraw, distrusting each other The two men are made to write letters to their mothers to get them to intercede. While Abdul is in the local Russian-occupied town, another Caucasian tries to shoot them.

The Russian commander, Maslov, refuses to meet Abdul. He tells Vania's schoolteacher mother that the locals will only trick her, so she makes her own arrangements to contact Abdul. At night, Vania and Sasha are abducted by a local Caucasian commander and made to clear a minefield. For their courage, they are taken to a feast for local fighters. Vania and Sasha escape. Hasan tries to recapture them and Sasha kills him. They run off. Sasha kills a shepherd and steals his rifle but they are recaptured. Sasha has his throat cut, but Vania is taken back to Abdul. Sasha's ghost appears to Vania and summons him to happy death.

In the town, the old man who had tried to kill them shoots his own son, Mamed, who was working in the Russian police. In the confusion, Abdul's son escapes, but he too is shot down. Because of this, Dina tells Vania that he will be killed the next day. She releases him but, to protect her, he refuses to run away. Abdul takes him into the mountains to shoot him, but instead lets him go. As Vania wanders through the mountains, four Soviet helicopters appear overhead, on their way to a revenge bombing of the village.

The plot of *Prisoner of the Mountains* is fashioned from a string of conventional motifs. Two very different captives (Russian soldiers Vania and Sasha) are drawn through adversity into bond of trust. They gradually develop an affection for their Caucasian captors which, in the case of the younger prisoner and the girl guarding him, borders on love. Their observation of the customs of their 'enemies' provokes interest and growing respect, while their alien skills are found useful (only Vania can mend Caucasian Abdul's broken watch). But their escape attempt brings tragic, unwished-for consequences. Recapture is followed by reprisal, and a reassertion of the harsh imperatives of war and killing. These elements are familiar from stories and films about wars the world over, but director Sergei Bodrov revisits them with a winning combination of professionalism and humanity.

The Caucasus region has long fascinated Russians as the nearest manifestation of the unfathomable Orient, and nineteenth-century Russian literature abounds with encounters between young Russians (often army officers) and this Muslim part of their empire. The Russian title of Bodrov's film *Prisoner of the Caucasus,* was used in poems by Pushkin and Lermontov and in a story by Tolstoy which also provides the names of Bodrov's characters here.

The real-life Russian encounter with the Muslim world over the last 20 years of has often been characterised by violence rather than attempts at understanding, with the Afghan war of the early 80s, the recent Chechen war and a number of smaller engagements along the former Soviet border. These wars have is found their way into Russian cinema. One notable example is Vladimir Khotinenko's 1995 film *The Muslim* in which a young Russian soldier returns to his village after a period of captivity, having embraced the Muslim faith, and is met with incomprehension and violence.

But however well intended this and other films on the subject may have been, Bodrov makes a distinctive contribution by setting his film entirely among the Muslim rebels. He shows a startling even-handedness in his depiction of the victims on *both* sides. This film was begun before the Russian invasion of Chechnya in December 1994 and it contains no direct reference to that conflict. But it opened in Moscow in the summer of 1996, when the war was still raging, and its insights were not lost on Russian audiences. *Prisoner of the Mountains* plunges both its heroes, and the viewer, with disorienting suddenness into a Dagestani *aul,* the mountain village of the Russians' captivity. This is a place of flinty unmade roads, where wheat is still threshed by mules, where people step out on to their roofs to be awed by the stark beauty of the surrounding mountains (stunningly photographed by Pavel Lebeshev). It is a place of immemorial codes—about dress, about marriage, about deference to elders and, above all, about vengeance for wrongs suffered. But it is, repeatedly, a place of small and large kindnesses offered to the prisoners.

For all this, Bodrov's central concern is with the experience of the two Russian captives: the innocent, unworldly private Vania, his life under threat before it has even begun, and the sophisticated, bantering sergeant Sasha, who begins by teasing the lad and ends up fiercely protective of him. Neither actor is absent from the screen for any length of time. Oleg Menshikov, who plays Sasha, is one of the biggest stars of Russian cinema, familiar to British audiences from Nikita Mikhalkov's *Burnt by the Sun.* He brings a brilliant doomed raillery to the part of Sasha, his wit masking an awareness of death's long shadow. He is superbly complemented by Bodrov's son and namesake as Vania. His is an affecting performance of great naturalness, reminiscent of the hero of Grigori Chukhrai's *The Ballad of a Soldier* (1959), another young Russian thrown in the maelstrom before he has had time to live. Bodrov Jr has since become one of the favourite actors of young Russian audiences for his mesmerising performance in Aleksei Balabanov's 1997 hit *Brother,* in which he played a young Chechen war veteran who turns into a Petersburg killer (a chilling gloss on the possible fate of his character here).

Both Russians and Caucasians are portrayed by Bodrov with sympathetic attention, since none of them is responsible for the tragedy that engulfs them. This evocative balance extends to the film's score—the plaintive song of the *aul* ("We are the children of the mountains/The mountains will protect us") is counterpointed by the melancholic strains of well-loved songs from past Russian campaigns, the pre-revolutionary 'On the Hills of Manchuria' and the World War Two 'The Blue Kerchief', another register of valour betrayed. Even the two opposed commanders are shown as driven to acts of savagery by circumstance and ignorance. The real orchestrators of this tragedy are, eloquently, absent. It is this rare combination of unrelenting tension and almost leisurely observation that makes *Prisoner of the Mountains so* effective, and illustrates Bodrov's assertion that "I like telling good stories".

Sergei Bodrov was born in 1948 and is the director of seven feature films. In several (including *Non-Professionals,* 1986; *Freedom Is Paradise,* 1989; *I Wanted to See Angels,* 1992.) he displayed a striking ability to coax natural, unforced performances from young actors. More than 20 films have been made from his screenplays. He has recently worked largely out of LA, but he began his career in Kazakh cinema and *Prisoner of the Mountains* was made as a Russian-Kazakh co-production since that gave him greater freedom to tell the tale as he wanted. The film struck a powerful chord with Russian audiences—it was one of the very few recent Russian films to recoup its cost—and was equally popular with critics. In 1996, at the Sochi Kinotavr, now the leading Russian film festival, it won the Grand Prix, and Menshikov and Bodrov Jr. shared the male acting prize. It then swept the board at the 1997 Nikes (the Russian Oscars), where it took five of the main prizes, again including Best Film. It was pipped for the 1997 Oscar for Best Foreign Language Film by Jan Svera's *Kolya* (another tale of the encounter between two initially incompatible people, a man and a little boy). It thus comes to London garlanded with prizes. It is regretful that it was not released here when the events it alludes to were fresher in the public mind, but one hopes it will find the audience it deserves.

VILLAGE VOICE, 2/4/97, p. 69, J. Hoberman

A more discreet form of magic realism casts its spell over Sergei Bodrov's *Prisoner of the Mountains*. [The reference is to *Saint Clara*; see Hoberman's review of that film.] Skillfully updating a story by Leo Tolstoy in which a Chechen village elder captures two Russian soldiers to trade for his own POW son, Bodrov has produced a movie that's highly topical and timeless as a western.

However well regarded, Bodrov's earlier, Soviet-era films scarcely found an American audience, even on the festival circuit. Here, he brings his wonderfully understated and precise style to blatantly picturesque material. Their tank ambushed its first time out in the field, two soldiers—a rakish sergeant (played, for maximum charm, by Russian star Oleg Menshikov) and a dazed young recruit (the director's own 20-year-old son) are taken prisoner, chained together, and held hostage, somewhere above the cloud-line, in a town seemingly carved from a mountain cliff.

The Prisoner script modifies the boys' adventure aspect of the Tolstoy original (which billed itself as a true story), but—filled with indigenous music and local customs, populated by young girls in flowered babushkas and dourly mustachioed men in conical lambswool hats—the movie is still a chastely glamorous ethnographic pageant. The mountain town is surrounded by a stone garden of stalagmite tombs and set in a landscape suggesting in equal measure Colorado and Mars. At one point, Bodrov pans from a seeming desert to the shores of a tropical sea. Such creative geography underscores the movie's casually fantastic interpolations—the mysterious radio transmission (Louis Armstrong singing "Go Down Moses") that inspires the prisoners to escape or the subsequent appearance of a cheerful ghost. And, no less than *Saint Clara*, *Prisoner of the Mountains* features a miracle-working 13-year-old girl.

Despite a guerrilla-camp roisterfest that's a veritable John Milius wet dream of vodka swilling, lamb roasting, music, dancing, and celebratory wrestling, the war here is a dirty one. While one Russian soldier barters his revolver for a few bottles of vodka, his craven commander scarfs down the local caviar with a soup spoon, chasing it with a juicy hunk of melon in each hand. *Prisoner of the Mountain* occasionally turns sentimental, but it's scarcely *The Deer Hunter*. Indeed, one need only imaginatively transpose its location from the Caucasus to Indochina to appreciate the exotic quality of its humanist zing.

Also reviewed in:
NATION, 2/17/97, p. 36, Stuart Klawans
NEW REPUBLIC, 2/24/97, p. 24, Stanley Kauffmann
NEW YORK TIMES, 1/31/97, p. C3, Janet Maslin
VARIETY, 5/20-26/96, p. 38, Leonard Klady
WASHINGTON POST, 2/7/97, Weekend/p. 42, Desson Howe

PRIVATE PARTS

A Paramount Pictures and Rysher Entertainment release of a Northern Lights Entertainment production. *Executive Producer:* Daniel Goldberg, Joe Medjuck, and Keith Samples. *Producer:* Ivan Reitman. *Director:* Betty Thomas. *Screenplay:* Len Blum and Michael Kalesniko. *Based on the book by:* Howard Stern. *Director of Photography:* Walt Lloyd. *Editor:* Peter Teschner.

Music: Van Dyke Parks. *Music Editor:* Dick Bernstein. *Sound:* Tod A. Maitland. *Sound Editor:* John Dunn. *Casting:* Phyllis Huffman and Olivia Harris. *Production Designer:* Charles Rosen. *Art Director:* Rick Butler. *Set Decorator:* Beth Kushnick. *Special Effects:* Conrad F. Brink. *Costumes:* Joseph G. Aulisi. *Make-up:* Sharon Ilson. *Stunt Coordinator:* Doug Coleman and Daniel W. Barringer. *Running time:* 90 minutes. *MPAA Rating:* R.

CAST: Howard Stern (Himself); Robin Quivers (Herself); Mary McCormack (Alison Stern); Fred Harris (Himself); Paul Giamatti (Kenny); Gary Dell'Abate (Himself); Jackie Martling (Herself); Carol Alt (Gloria); Richard Portnow (Ben Stern); Kelly Bishop (Ray Stern); Henry Goodman (Moti); Jonathan Hadary (Griff); Paul Hecht (Ross Buckingham); Allison Janney (Dee Dee); Michael Murphy (Roger Erlick); James Murtaugh (Payton); Reni Santoni (Vallesecca); Lee Wilkof (Marvin Mamoulian); Melanie Good (Brittany); Theresa Lynn (Orgasm Woman); Amber Smith (Julie); Althea Cassidy (The Kielbasa Queen); Jenna Jameson (Mandy); Bobby Borriello (Howard, age 7); Michael Maccarone (Howard, age 12); Matthew Friedman (Howard, age 16); John Michael Bolger (Music Awards Technician); Steven Gilborn (Howard's Agent); Curtis McClarin (Airline Representative); Richard B. Shull (Symphony Sid); Evan Roberts (Elliot); Gabriel De Silva (Herbie); Jennifer Gareis and Mandy Steckelberg (Co-eds); Ali Marsh (Blind Co-ed); Scott Cohen and James Villenaire (Friends); Wendy Hoopes (Elyse); Richard Russell Ramos (Film Professor); Gordon Joseph Weiss (Unshaven Deejay); Allison Forman (Barb); Julie Gawkowski (Patricia Fonfara); Davenia McFadden (Nurse); Michael Gwynne (Duke of Rock); Irene DeCook (The Leather Weather Lady); Jordan Derwin (Rubberbound Man); Stuart Rudin (Trembling Patient); Richard Ziman (Salesman); Adam Lefevre (Sales Manager); Janine Lindemulder (Camp Director's Wife); Scott Lawrence (News Guy); Christine Tucci (Doctor); Kim Chan (Waiter); Nick Wyman (Douglas Kiker); Stephen Pearlman and Catherine Wolf (Couple Looking for Apartment); Tom Tammi (Corporate Executive); Luke Reilly (Imus); Rick Levi and Peter Jacobson (Lawyers); Leslie Bibb (NBC Tour Guide); Joanne Camp (Reenie); Peter Maloney (Researcher); Sarah Zinsser (Kenny's Secretary); Barry Papick (Engineer); Christine Toy and Alison Stern (NBC Switchboard Operators); Susan Pratt (Stewardess); Sasha Martin and Sarah Jane Hyland (Howard's Daughters); Larry Grey (Doctor Larry); John "Stuttering" Melendez, George "Cracked Bob" Harvey, and Nicole Bass (Themselves); Camille Donatacci (Bikini Girl in Westchester); Danna Bradley and Seth Silver (Transvestites); Carrie Flaska (Wife in Car); Steve Ballot (Husband); Brian Costantini and Barnett Milton Lloyd (DC Cops); Aimee Luzier (Betty Jean Rushton); David Letterman (Himself); Mia Farrow (Herself).

CHRISTIAN SCIENCE MONITOR, 3/7/97, p. 15, David Sterritt

Radio has become an all-time winner in the mass-media sweepstakes by allowing listeners to develop strong bonds with the personalities who talk to them over the airwaves.

These bonds are based on fantasy as much as reality, since the personalities are heard but rarely seen. Successful radio stars cultivate the illusion that they're speaking directly, even intimately to each of us as we listen in our homes, cars, and offices.

So when a particular disc jockey or talk-radio host becomes not just a star but a superstar, it's certain he (or occasionally she) is saying something lots of people want to hear—whether to agree or disagree, cheer or boo, swoon with affection, or boil with anger.

That's why the huge popularity of a Howard Stern shouldn't be shrugged off by anyone interested in the state of contemporary mass culture even if studying it means putting up with a walloping dose of vulgarity, offensiveness, and childishness that would have been literally unheard-of in broadcasting just a few decades ago.

"Private Parts," the movie based on Stern's life and career, begins with a woman who gazes into the camera and tells us from the get-go how "offensive, obnoxious, disgusting" he is. The next scene brings all those adjectives to life—with a comedy routine so gross that Stern himself claims to be embarrassed by it—and makes you wonder what grotesqueries the picture will trot out for an encore.

From here on, the movie is designed to please Stern's hard-core fans while enticing new followers into his vast radio audience. In this way, it's a full-fledged member of the Hollywood marketing club initiated by "Star Wars" and its ilk, in which every media-related commodity exists largely to promote *other* media-related commodities.

So the next few scenes try to win over anti-Stern skeptics by portraying him as a likable youngster who dreams of celebrity while staging goofy puppet shows and bumbling his way through college-radio programs.

His only enemies are stuffiness, prudery, and hypocrisy. Stuffiness, prudery, and hypocrisy are obviously bad things. So what fun-loving person wouldn't be on his side?

The picture eventually settles down to business, spending long stretches in Stern's crowded studio while he sizzles the microphone with sexual skits and scatological gags, spiced with sexist, racist, and homophobic humor calculated to make fans feel bold and adventurous for daring to laugh at it. Equally calculated is the large amount of time allotted to his long-suffering but devoted wife and his energetic African-American radio partner. He couldn't really be a bigoted male-chauvinist pig if those nice women adore him!

Maybe he couldn't, maybe he could. All that's certain from "Private Parts" is that Stern is a consummate capitalist who'll say anything to raise his ratings and profits. He drives his network managers crazy, but in the end he wins every battle by pointing out how many dollars he's raking in for them.

Staking out a similar stance, "Private Parts" steers clear of cultural arguments over censorship, freedom of the airwaves, and other complex public issues. "The People vs. Larry Flynt," a movie that treats these matters with some seriousness, hasn't fared very well at the box office. Stern and his handlers aren't going to make the same mistakes. If idiocy sells, idiocy is what they'll peddle. And if old fogies object, Stern will make rude noises at them on the radio.

Surely there's a lesson in this worth pondering.

"Private Parts" was directed by Betty Thomas from a screenplay by Len Blum and Michael Kalesniko, based on Stern's book. Stern and his co-host, Robin Quivers, portray themselves.

LOS ANGELES TIMES, 3/7/97, Calendar/p. 1, Jack Mathews

[The following review by Jack Mathews appeared in a slightly different form in **NEWSDAY, 3/7/97, Part II/p. B2]**

The opening chapter of radio deejay Howard Stern's best-selling autobiographical riff "Private Parts" recalls the supposedly true story of a Long Island businessman who became so aroused by an on-air interview between Stern and a lesbian that he had to pull over to the side of the expressway during rush hour and relieve himself.

That chapter is titled "My Philosophy," and it's no joke. While some suspended adolescent males dream of hitting the winning home run in Game 7 of the World Series, or becoming a famous rock star, or dating a contortionist, Stern seems to fantasize a crowning moment when the world will pull off the road to listen, moan and swear allegiance to the King of All Media.

In the meantime, Stern himself is moving to the middle of the road. In Betty Thomas' tamed yet very funny film version of "Private Parts," the 6-foot-5, long-haired shock-jock plays himself as an over-compensating Alvy Singer, Woody Allen on growth drugs. He's a once-timid Jewish boy from Long Island who was driven into a shell of fantasies by a father who called him a moron and never allowed him to speak.

Once Stern broke out of that shell, sometime in the early days of his radio career, according to "Private Parts," a testosterone-charged id came storming out, guided only by wit and ambition, and the warning went forth: Women and children, get away from the radio!

That Howard Stern, the one who first caught the Federal Communication Commission's attention by having an on-air guest play the piano with his penis (no, his selection was not the Rach 3), is hardly present in the movie. The radio Stern—part-scripted, part-improvised—vacillates wildly between comic brilliance and sophomoric glibness, between locker room taunting and outright cruelty. In contrast, the movie's Stern is an earnest cuddle bear, a bit outrageous, perhaps, but at worst a class clown, and at best ... well, a loyal friend, devoted husband and the most honest personality in America.

In the film, which might have been called "The People vs. Howard Stern," the radio star assumes the voice of reason and becomes a champion of free speech, standing his ground against the FCC and hypocritical station bosses who love his ratings but hate how he's getting them.

After being warned against using obscene words by his New York program manager (played with eyeball-bulging gusto by Paul Giamatti), Stern orchestrates a game show bit where co-hosts Robin Quivers, Fred Norris and Jackie Martling (all playing themselves) are asked to fill in the missing parts of the words "(blank)willow" and "(blank)-a-doodle-doo." When Stern's show is cut off in the middle of a massage being administered to him by a naked lady, he charges into the manager's office and succeeds in confronting him on the air.

Stern's acting is often awkward, particularly in the sentimental moments with his spectacularly tolerant wife, Alison (Mary McCormack). In fact, he appears so ill at ease kissing his co-star, you can believe his frequent claim of 22 years of marital fidelity.

But there's no denying Stern's natural presence or his gift for self-deprecating charm. Of all the celebrities we've seen playing themselves in adoring biographies, he may be the one most up to the task—and certainly the one most anxious. "Private Parts" is the promo-op of a lifetime.

Thomas, with a script by Len Blum ("Stripes," "Meatballs") and Michael Kalesniko, has turned Stern's life into a sequence of "best of" anecdotes. Some of them are plenty raunchy, but there is little of the mean-spiritedness that often creeps into the radio show. And the raunch itself is within the range of mainstream sexual comedy.

Wisely, Thomas chose not to depict Stern's male listeners in the throe of side-of-the-road ecstasy—that would have been as revolting as the freak show extreme on the radio show. Instead, we watch a spectacular blond, in the privacy of her living room, following Stern's instructions to straddle the woofer on her stereo speaker, crank up the bass and turn up the volume.

Nor does the film go into the seamy particulars of the FCC fines leveled against the deejay's stations. He's just a humorist showing his listeners a good time, while the regulators are cynical, mirthless spoil-sports.

His polished persona will be hard for Stern's detractors to swallow, in the event any show up. And it may even be too sanitized for some of his most ardent followers. But setting expectations aside, "Private Parts" is a supremely crafty, smartly written and—given the number of "himselfs" and "herselfs" on the cast list—surprisingly well-acted piece of pop kitsch.

NEW YORK, 3/24/97, p. 90, David Denby

What to make of Howard Stern? It was obviously a stroke of Jewish genius to turn a small member into a major asset. Howard Stern has killed off some genuine taboos and eliminated certain chagrins in the only way possible in the media—by turning them into boasts.

As a source of comic shtick, he's gotten more mileage out of his ding-a-ling than Jack Benny did out of stinginess. So Howard Stern can't simply be shrugged off. But he shouldn't be lionized either. With his shoulder-length hair and pointed chin, Stern looks like a naked *philosophe,* a sort of crumbum Voltaire. In the movie *Private Parts*, made from his 1993 mock autobiography (same title), Stern chronicles his Horatio Howard ascent from suburban Nowheresville. The movie has countless scenes of Stern demonstrating to us how much he loves his wife and parents and how good he is to his employees while he's rotten to everyone in authority. All of which may be true, but it's embarrassing to see such flagrant self-testimonials on the screen. Before Stern's megalomania takes over, the movie has a likably slapdash quality. But when it goes bad, it goes really bad.

With the help of the writers Len Blum and Michael Kalesniko and director Betty Thomas, Stern has created an effective screen character for himself as a boy and young man—Howard the oversized, underdeveloped Long Island nerdo thinking dirty thoughts. He wants only to please people and fit in, but outrageous impulses always break free. The filmmakers steal whatever they can from *Annie Hall,* but they steal well and gracefully. Stern narrates his life, and the scenes of his childhood are fast, light, and funny in Woody Allen's vignette style. Sitting on a locker-room bench, the teenage Howard stares in misery as a variety of naked black boys go past him, heading for the showers. In the movie (but not always on the air), Stern gets away with masochistic jokes by not dwelling on them—one quick moment and then on to the next riff. There are also mild little Allen-type alienating devices: Stern, apologizing to the audience, plays himself as a college student at Boston University, an absurdly tall gawky geek in a mustache and black mop of hair. Standing in for himself at 20, Stern has a surprisingly young and tender face, as if memory of old failures had softened his features.

His early career in radio is done swiftly as a series of professional disasters and moral victories. At some awful Westchester station, he tries to play it straight, using a mellifluous, hello-you-nice-people voice on a morning show, but he can't go through with it. At a Midwestern station, doing the news, he cuts for a "remote" to some trouble spot and imitates a female black agitator: "Kill, kill de white man." Howard Stern, at his best, is a casual satirist of hypocrisy and identity politics; he's a throwback to the heroic age of radio, when a few spontaneous madcaps broke up the long patches of mediocrity and pleasant boredom. Though he presents his upward surge from obscurity to celebrity as a titanic struggle, he didn't actually struggle for very long; He was a big star by the time he was 30 or 31. His achievement was to turn urban nihilism, white hetero division, into commercial sport. Howard Stern isn't just successful in the marketplace; he *is* the marketplace. Derision and crass race- and woman-baiting are now the essence of salesmanship. And salesmanship that works has become irresistible for almost everyone. As if commercial success made Stern hip, the *Times* and *The New Yorker* have eagerly jumped on the bandwagon while casually dumping everything they believe in. It's a measure of Stern's power that he can get people to misrepresent themselves so obviously.

Private Parts becomes painful once Stern makes it big. We are treated as if we were all worshiping fans, fascinated by the assembling of Howard's immortal team (Robin Quivers, Fred Norris, Jackie Martling), and we're supposed to cheer for the team's humiliating anyone who tries to stop them or restrict them in any way. The persecution of a disapproving NBC executive, played by the diminutive Paul Giamatti, amounts to outright sadism—even after Stern has triumphed, the guy is pulled back for another kick in the rear. And how funny is the team? Sometimes very funny. But don't make the mistake of listening to the show too often. Howard Stern has a fifties idea of sexual humor: Get a big blonde to take off her clothes. His jeering at ethnics and women has the dull ritual gamesmanship of a guy at a bar going for easy laughs.

It's fine with me if celebrities who put on airs get cut up. Howard Stern destroys the phonier kinds of high-mindedness, but he also destroys any kind of high-mindedness. And the movie, in imitation of Stern, plays the same stupid trick on the audience that *The People vs. Larry Flynt* tried to play: It implies that anyone disapproving of its hero is either a religious fundamentalist or a stuffed shirt. The trick is pulled off by dumping so many turds on the enemy that he's reduced to angry spluttering or pained dignity.

How can you argue with a man who puts himself down so openly? You can't. But Howard Stern's member is a double-edged sword. With every swing, he destroys taboos—and says that dignity is an illusion. Whatever Milos Forman may think, the real Larry Flynt liberated not some healthy carnality in the working man but white-guy resentment and rage. Men who feel out of it identify with the losers who become big media winners and get to tell off women and immigrants. In a shameless society, no one has any way of knowing when he's been patronized.

The trouble with small-dick boasting, as opposed to the usual kind of boasting, is that it's unappeasable. The glare of Howard Stern's self-promotion is blinding. In the second half of the movie, as Stern becomes a celeb, he tells us again and again that he can have any woman in town but that he will remain faithful to his wife (Mary McCormack). He makes himself into a martyr of denial. Power, apparently, is what really turns him on. At some level, he fancies himself a leader. But of what? The movie shows crowds gathering together to celebrate his ratings triumph over Don Imus. Whoopee. He raises his arms as the masses salute. Then it's back to spanking lesbians. Howard Stern, despite his victories, is a jerk's idea of a free man.

NEW YORK POST, 3/7/97, p. 39, Thelma Adams

Shock jock Howard Stern's "Private Parts" will irritate his enemies. Why? Because it's obscene? Racist? Sexist? UnAmerican? No. Because it's irresistibly funny.

Howard tells it like it might have been in a coming-of-age romp based on his best seller. Directed by Betty Thomas from an entertaining script by Len Blum and Michael Kalesniko, "Private Parts" profiles an ugly duckling who doesn't become a swan—but unites his fellow mallards into a powerful populist lobby willing to shed millions for the good of the Stern.

Stern's humor succeeds because he never spares himself. Surveying his personal history, everyone gets a chance to diss the dork: his father ("Shut up, you moron!"); a blind college coed (she feels his face and rejects him); his former boss ("offensive, obnoxious, disgusting").

The multi-millionaire deejay and self-styled King of All Media describes high school locker-room hell: "[I was] hung like a 3-year-old."

"Private Parts" follows Stern's rise from an obscure Westchester station, where he was pulled off the air for having a lousy voice, to becoming the voice to be reckoned with, the highest-paid disk jockey on radio.

Stern (who plays himself with ease) found his voice by letting it all hang out. He created a push-pull by trying to be as candid as he could possibly be while forcing others to say and do the things they might only feel comfortable with in the privacy of their own bathrooms.

The deejay surrounded himself with a merry band of men and women (Sternmates Robin Quivers and Fred Norris successfully play themselves). The gang faced its greatest challenge when Stern made the big time—NBC radio in New York City—and the mighty peacock tried to crush his spirit.

The scenes in which Stern & Co. bait Kenny (Paul Giamatti), the overeager NBC exec who attempts to tame Stern, are priceless. In a classic example of what the FCC called "barnyard radio," Stern, Quivers and Norris find a creative way to evade Kenny's bans on certain anatomical words. The hilarious bits are a liberating display of creative anarchy.

It wouldn't be the Howard Stern show without bare breasts and suggestive sausage swallowing. This is the man who proved his motto "lesbians equal ratings." But the comedy is surprisingly tender. Stern's winning and wooing of Alison (Mary McCormack), a pretty social worker and the once and future Mrs. Stern, reveals the private, unspeakable side of Stern: the conservative family man.

Like Stern, Director Thomas ("The Brady Bunch Movie") packages outrageous subject matter in a mainstream vehicle. I wonder how John ("Hairspray") Waters, an inflammatory humanist like Stern, would transform a life of Howard. Will we ever know how Stern's superhero, "Fartman," would appear in Odorama?

Until then, expose yourself to "Private Parts."

SIGHT AND SOUND, 7/97, p. 49, Ben Thompson

Media personality Howard Stern is on the plane home. His bid to make a flashy entrance at an awards show has backfired. As he laments his inability to secure the respect he deserves, a beautiful woman sits down next to him and, recognising him, pulls a disgusted face. He vows to win her round by telling her his life story.

Stern grows up in Roosevelt, Long Island, the only geeky Jewish kid in a tough, black area. Raised by his strict radio-engineer father and an overprotective mother, Howard seeks validation in performing from an early age. From putting on obscene puppet shows as a youth, he progresses to studying radio engineering at college in Boston. There he first encounters his beautiful wife-to-be Alison, whom he woos by persuading her to star in his experimental film. As his career as a radio disc jockey takes off, Stern leads two separate lives. At home he is a loving family man: on air, a taboo-busting 'shock jock'. From college radio to stations in Westchester County, Detroit, Washington and eventually NBC in New York, he hones his salacious persona. By his own definition of marital fidelity—which encompasses cavorting with porn stars before an audience of millions and making jokes about his wife's miscarriage on air—he remains faithful.

However, his painstakingly assembled "radio family"—including side-kicks Robin Quivers and Fred Norris, and later Gary Dell'Abate and Jackie Martling—is threatened with dissolution in the course of a power struggle between Stern and his new bosses at NBC. Howard seems to let them down when he refuses to resign in support of newsreader Quivers after the corporation fires her. However, via a campaign of reckless insubordination and popular protest, he gets her reinstated. The show is syndicated nationwide and Stern becomes an idol to millions and a hate-figure to almost as many.

Back in the present, the woman on the plane is totally at his mercy by the end of his story. Arriving at the airport, Howard introduces her to his wife and daughters who have come to meet him, and bids her a wistful goodbye.

Whatever else *Private Parts* has or hasn't achieved, there's no doubt that it represents a landmark in the history of the biopic. With a heroic egotism that will come as no surprise to anyone who has heard his radio show, seen him on US television or read the best-selling autobiography on which this film is based, Howard Stern makes his acting debut playing himself. From now on, all prospective cinematic biographies will have to consider the option (traceable back to Al Jolson's example) of putting their subject in the leading role. But is *Private Parts* the long overdue next step forward from *Wayne's World* in the long march toward metatextual nirvana? Well, yes and no.

The film starts out promisingly with Stern, unapologetic low-culture supremacist that he is, succeeding in grossing out an MTV awards show audience by descending from on high in character as "Fart Man". And yet, while it goes against everything Stern stands for to say it, *Private Parts* the movie is a rather less satisfying manifestation of his compellingly problematic personality than the original book of the same title. It's not that director Betty Thomas (*The Brady Bunch Movie*) or screenwriter Len Blum (*Meatballs*) have done in explicitly bad job. It's just that where *Private Parts* the airport blockbuster laid bare the inner Stern so effectively that even those who might have supposed themselves his sworn enemies could not help but be bowled over by it, the film is ultimately a disappointingly conventional rags-to-riches story.

"I just sat down and emoted" is how Howard Stern sums up his cinematic debut, and if there is a problem with his acting, it's that it is too good. For British audiences spared until now the fearsome ubiquity the self-styled "King of All Media" has attained in his homeland—it is all too easy to believe that this is not the real Howard Stern but just a competent actor who bears a vague resemblance to the original (a casting strategy pursued in Thomas' tele-film *The Late Shift*, wherein two jobbing thespians strive manfully to impersonate US talk-show hosts Jay Leno and David Letterman). There is one moment early on where Stern's voiceover prefaces a flashback with the caveat that "I look a little old to be in college. but for this movie you've got to suspend disbelief". Alas, if only Howard had dared to play himself at the ages of 7, 12 and 16 as well as 21, this film might have captured the larger-than-life renegade aura that is the stuff of his enduring appeal.

As it is, what we're left with is *Talk Radio* as if scripted by Kelvin Mackenzie, *The Chris Evans Story* as played by Joey Ramone. Even in its attempts to be offensive *Private Parts* falls somewhat between two stools. The relentless sexism for which Stern is justly notorious is acknowledged but not wallowed in. The only authentic nod to the bad taste which is his bread and butter comes when he repeatedly throws a frisbee into the face of a mentally disordered man while accompanying his wife's social work charges on a picnic, but even this is done in a bid to entertain.

It's not that this film is a whitewash, either personally or professionally. The audience is left in no doubt as to just how long-suffering Stern's wife Alison is (she is the only one of Howard's inner circle not playing themselves here, and Mary McCormack brings an aggrieved nobility to a rather thankless part). And Stern's radio routines are here in all their barrel-bottom-skimming glory. Some of them, especially the ones where he hauls his would-be censors in the NBC boardroom over hot coals of wilful obscenity, are extremely funny. But the problem is the same one that attends all of radio's forays into cinema, which is that the whole point of the first medium is that you don't have to look at the person who's talking, and the whole point of the second is that you do.

TIME, 3/10/97, p. 95, Richard Corliss

This has to be considered a love story: Howard Stern says, "I love you, Alison" even more often than "penis." The mostly genial *Private Parts*, written by Len Blum and Michael Kalesniko and directed, with more style and verve than absolutely necessary, by Betty Thomas, is like Stern's radio show: self-obsessed, paranoiac, very funny and way too long.

It is best in its first half, when Stern, looking like a taller Weird Al Yankovic with his geeky posture, vulture profile and Afro hairdo, plays the familiar failure—a disappointment to his parents and bosses. Only his wife Alison (Mary McCormack from TV's *Murder One*) sees that this guy has star potential if he'd just be his horny self on the air. Howard gets to rant, vomit, expose his cellulite buttocks, flaunt the cinema's all-time-funniest erection and defame Don Imus and the WNBC brass. It's get-even time for the guy they called Howeird.

Now he also wants to be How Nice. Stern hopes to be "understood"—as a caring husband, a faithful friend, a mensch for all seasons. Don Rickles did this for decades, of course, insulting his listeners before sucking up to them (*I hate you! Love me!*). Stern just does it on radio.

Maybe he really cares for his audience as much as he does for his wife. In the movie he expresses that love by making radio jokes about her miscarriage and telling a woman who's about to strip in his studio that Alison died of cancer. Yeah, Howard. Love you too.

VILLAGE VOICE, 3/11/97, p. 78, Colson Whitehead

Private Parts does such a good job of redeeming Howard Stern that it's hard to figure out who the movie is for. His mob—the folks you see on the news teeming at his book signings, or slouched at midnight waiting to sell out Madison Square Garden for an advance screening of the flick—will relish this further proof that he's a misbegotten loser like them, but then they've already cleared their dance cards. His tight-lipped legions of detractors will stay home, safely smug in their visions of American decline. Cleverly structured, the movie would win over a fair portion of this latter group if they were ever to see it.

Director Betty Thomas (*The Brady Bunch Movie, The Late Shift)* makes a big effort of placing Stern in "context" opening this heehawing hagiography as he departs the MTV Video Awards stage in his infamous Fartman costume. He knows he's made an idiot of himself, and as he passes Flavor Flav, Hammer, Ted Nugent, and Ozzy Osborne backstage, all of whom stare at him incredulously, Stern is immediately the hapless, misunderstood jackass we are meant to follow for the rest of the movie. Not Stern the racist, sexist, homophobic loudmouth, but Stern the high school geek with an ostrich face. On his defeated ride back to New York, he sits next to one of the unconverted and recapitulates his life—his childhood in Long Island, a succession of lame DJ jobs before he finds his signature style, his rise to the number one radio spot in New York City—in an attempt to win her over.

Engineered thusly as a plea for understanding, the movie describes his on-air rage not as the bile of a misanthrope, but the kidding around of a quirky dude who's all id.

After a half hour of guilty giggles, I felt nostalgic for the juvenile goofs of my childhood, and was not surprised to learn that *Private Parts* was cowritten by Len Blum, author of low-comedy classics *Meatballs* and *Stripes*. Of Stern's material, they've chosen the more broadly juvenile over the patently insulting and utilize it well. What could have been set pieces instead illustrate key points in Stern's career, most effectively in the final third of the film, which details Stern's battles with NBC suits—it's very nerds vs. preppies, as in most of those '80s teen comedies. Stern looks deeply sad and pathetic for a lot of the movie and comes off as extremely likable, particularly in the scenes with his wife Allison (played by *Murder One*'s Mary McCormack), who stands by her man with remarkable forbearance. Who knew he could be such a sweetheart?

Also reviewed in:
NATION, 4/28/97, p. 36, Stuart Klawans
NEW REPUBLIC, 4/7/97, p. 26, Stanley Kauffmann
NEW YORK TIMES, 3/7/97, p. C3, Janet Maslin
VARIETY, 3/3-9/97, p. 67, Todd McCarthy
WASHINGTON POST, 3/7/97, p. B1, Rita Kempley
WASHINGTON POST, 3/7/97, Weekend/p. 32, Desson Howe

QUIET ROOM, THE

A Fine Line Features release in association with Domenico Procacci of a Vertigo/Fandango production. *Producer:* Domenico Procacci and Rolf de Heer. *Director:* Rolf de Heer. *Screenplay:* Rolf de Heer. *Director of Photography:* Tony Clark. *Editor:* Tania Nehme. *Music:* Graham Tardif. *Sound:* Peter D. Smith. *Production Designer:* Fiona Paterson. *Art Director:* Beverley Freeman. *Running time:* 91 minutes. *MPAA Rating:* PG.

CAST: Celine O'Leary (Mother); Paul Blackwell (Father); Chloe Ferguson (Girl, Age 7); Phoebe Ferguson (Girl, Age 3).

NEWSDAY, 3/21/97, Part II/p. B13, John Anderson

A different kind of suspense film, "The Quiet Room" takes place largely in the mind of a 7-year-old girl (Chloe Ferguson) who for reasons only gradually explained has stopped talking. And she's good at it. "You can't trick me," we hear her think, as Mother (Celine O'Leary) or Father (Paul Blackwell) pose questions that literally beg for answers. She resists their pleading, their anger, their wrath. She's driving them a little mad.

But "The Quiet Room," a deft bit of psychological business from Australia's Rolf de Heer, is about a world gone mad. It's the girl's world, granted, but since we're inside her head, it's all we have. And that's apt: As her parents go through the quiet pains of eventual marital breakup, they're oblivious to the fact that what they're dismantling is their child's entire universe.

This isn't a moralizing film, per se, but it certainly puts a new slant on a subject taken for granted. The Girl (she has no name as such) flashes back to herself at age 3 (played by Ferguson's sister, Phoebe), wanting to be loved the way she was when she was little. Her rationale carries the self-absorbed logic of childhood: Her parents may have stopped loving each other, but by doing so they've unavoidably changed their love for their daughter.

"The Quiet Room" is one quiet movie—you adopt the Girl's silence, and it keeps you on the edge of your seat. If there's a fault here, it's that the Girl—given a very affecting reading by Chloe Ferguson—swings a bit broadly from innocence to irony (not that kids aren't capable of it, but this is a movie). And when she thinks a line like "You're hurting my heart," it may indeed be true, but doesn't sound like it.

"The Quiet Room" is an odd film, a taut tale of modern woe that will leave you moved. "Are you and Dad making progress?" she asks her mother, having at last broken her code of silence, adopting the euphemistic language of adults and slipping away from us even as we watch.

VILLAGE VOICE, 3/25/97, p. 84, Leslie Camhi

A silent child is a sad reproach to the adults around her. In *The Quiet Room,* silence is a seven year-old's weapon of choice in an ongoing war between the members of her family. The unnamed girl (played well by Chloe Ferguson) lives in a suburban Australian apartment with her mother and father, who don't get along. As they fight over everything from carpet cleaning to child rearing, she retreats into a world of isolation and to say no more.

Her mother brushes the girl's long hair and remarks that at least the child no longer complains that it hurts. Her father tries to trick her into speaking with little-girl games that simply don't work. Though her parents go to therapy, they remain painfully blind to the obvious: their child refuses to speak because she is disgusted with the nonsense spoken by adults.

The Quiet Room is intentionally ambiguous about what exactly ails the girl; is it autism or simple alienation? At times she comes perilously close to madness: she regresses and makes unintelligible sounds and rocking motions. Nevertheless, her aphasia seems to be a remarkably coherent strategy. "You'll speak to each other before I'll speak again," she silently tells her parents.

The mute child's interior monologue runs through the film in a continuous voice-over. Her barbed commentary on her parents' half-truths and her world's absurdity is both amusing and touching, though after a while the convention begins to seem as stifling as the girl's illness. And though the film is well-shot, sensitive, and affecting, its cause and effect logic ultimately undermines the complexity of the child's inner life. Compared with the tangled reality of autism, it's as simple and innocent as a fairy tale.

Also reviewed in:
NEW YORK TIMES, 3/21/97, p. C12, Stephen Holden
VARIETY, 5/6-12/96, p. 81, David Stratton

RATS IN THE RANKS

A Film Australia and Arundel Films production in association with Channel 4, La-Septe-Arte, Australian Broadcasting. *Executive Producer:* Chris Oliver. *Producer:* Bob Connelly and Robin Anderson. *Director:* Bob Connolly and Robin Anderson. *Director of Photography:* Bob Connelly. *Editor:* Ray Thomas and Bob Connelly. *Sound:* Robin Anderson and Robert Sullivan. *Running time:* 98 minutes. *MPAA Rating:* Not Rated.

NEW YORK POST, 2/26/97, p. 44, Larry Worth

Lies, back-stabbing and dealing. Yes, it's just another day on the campaign trail Down Under.

Mayoral candidates in the Sydney suburb of Leichhardt, Australia, will do anything—short of murder, presumably—to rule over the council chamber, as cleverly documented by Bob Connolly and Robin Anderson in "Rats in the Ranks."

Connolly and Anderson prove once and for all that small-town elections are as nasty as, if not nastier than, big-time politicking. For the most part, the point is proven by incumbent Larry Hand, who's desperately hoping for a fourth one-year term.

Despite his sleaziness and false bravado, Larry actually seems the best of a repulsive lot, with strong competition coming from his Lady Macbeth-like deputy mayor and her equally treacherous arch-rival.

Take-no-prisoners attitudes, ever-changing alignments and the art of slinging the bull are mere warmup exercises in this modern-day jousting contest.

Filmed over nine months and concluding with down-to-the-wire election eve results, the end product is both eye-opening and amusing, due largely to the participants' ease at letting it all hang out in front of the camera.

The pols' bickering and blatantly illegal actions seem even more alarming since the bucolic little town—population 60,000—could pass for the Aussie version of Mayberry, right down to its sweet-looking town hall.

Admittedly, the film will be of interest chiefly to those intrigued by the political process. All others could justifiably equate it with a cable-access filming of the local selectmen's meeting.

Also Connolly and Anderson should have fine-tuned the editing. But that's a common quibble with documentaries in general.

For the most part, "Rats in the Ranks" is a sad commentary on the road to attaining office, and an even sadder affirmation of politics' universal ugliness.

VILLAGE VOICE, 3/4/97, p. 72, Elliot Stein

Codirectors Robin Anderson and Bob Connolly are best known for their remarkable documentaries on the legacy of colonialism in New Guinea: *First Contact* (1983), *Joe Leahy's Neighbors* (1989), and *Black Harvest* (1992). After this "Highlands Trilogy," one of the great achievements of Australian cinema, the pair returned home to make *Rats in the Ranks,* a vérité investigation of another kind of tribal culture—local politics Down Under.

Rats was shot over a nine-month period in a suburb of Sydney, the municipality of Leichhardt, a polyglot community of old working-class stiffs, multicultured immigrants, and middle-class professionals. The directors turn their unblinking gaze on the town's 1994 mayoral campaign, a nasty power clash between incumbent Mayor Larry Hand and the councillors who covet his job. A master wheeler-dealer and baby kisser, "His Worship" is popular with the citizenry, but the mayor is elected by the council members. It comes as a shock to discover that in this doc on politics, there's hardly a mention of political issues—politics is simply about "getting the numbers."

Hand, a former Labor Party member, has become an Independent. On the eve of the election, when the Laborites on the council are unable to agree on a candidate, desperate double crosses are topped by perfidious triple crosses. All the while, the tireless Hand, whether in black leather jacket and jeans or in the more formal ermine of his office, is busy manipulating this opposition and confiding his strategies directly to the camera in a series of shamelessly self-congratulatory soliloquies. Sleazeball he may be, but this amiably blatant ham has star quality. The Aussie accents are occasionally mumbly and impenetrable, but attention will be rewarded—this engrossing doc is bright, suspenseful, and blackly droll.

Also reviewed in:
CHICAGO TRIBUNE, 9/5/97, Friday/p. F, John Petrakis
NEW YORK TIMES, 2/26/97, p. C16, Janet Maslin
VARIETY, 7/22-28/96, p. 53, David Stratton

RED CORNER

A Metro-Goldwyn-Mayer Pictures release of an Avnet/Kerner production. *Executive Producer:* Wolfgang Petersen and Gail Katz. *Producer:* Jon Avnet, Charles B. Mulvehill, and Rosalie Swedlin. *Director:* Jon Avnet. *Screenplay:* Robert King. *Director of Photography:* Karl Walter Lindenlaub. *Editor:* Peter E. Berger. *Music:* Thomas Newman. *Music Editor:* Bill Bernstein. *Choreographer:* Jamal Graves and Edgar Dizan. *Sound:* Jeffrey Wexler, (music) Dennis Sands and Tom Winslow. *Sound Editor:* George Watters, II. *Casting:* David Rubin. *Production Designer:* Richard Sylbert. *Art Director:* Virgina Randolph-Weaver. *Set Designer:* Peter J. Kelly, Patricia Klawonn, George R. Lee, Hugo Santiago, Barbara Ann Spencer, and James F. Truesdale. *Set Decorator:* William Kemper Wright. *Set Dresser:* Frank Calvert, Kurt Hulett, Nick Rymond, and Russ Anderson. *Special Effects:* Jan Aaris. *Costumes:* Albert Wolsky. *Make-up:* Fern Buchner. *Make-up (Richard Gere):* Felicity "Fizz" Bowring. *Stunt Coordinator:* Buddy Joe Hooker. *Running time:* 119 minutes. *MPAA Rating:* R.

CAST: Richard Gere (Jack Moore); Bai Ling (Shen Yuelin); Bradley Whitford (Bob Ghery); Byron Mann (Lin Dan); Peter Donat (David McAndrews); Robert Stanton (Ed Pratt); Tsai Chin (Chairman Xu); James Hong (Lin Shou); Tzi Ma (Li Cheng); Ulrich Matschoss (Gerhardt Hoffman); Richard Venture (Ambassador Reed); Jessey Meng (Hong Ling); Roger Yuan (Huan Minglu); Li Chi Yu (General Hong); Henry O. (Procurator General Yang); Li Jia Yao (Director Liu); Lu Yukun (Director Liu's Associate); Robert Lin (Director Liu's Interpreter); Steve Beebe (Disco DJ); Wei De Zhong and Grace Zhan (Beijing Opera Performers); Yvonne Wang (Disco Waitress); Gao Qiang (PSB Captain); Gao Xiao-Hua and Yao Wang (PSB Arresting Officers); Gu Xiao Yang and Hans Hanbo Cui (Prison Guards); Zong Ping (Captain Feng); Lei Yin (Feng's Assistant); Paul Chen (Visitor's Room Assistant); Jeffrey Dong (Prison Doctor); Jian Rui Chao (Yuelin's Aide); Zhang Daxing (Procurator Ma); Ding Yi Wang (Procurator Ma's Assistant); Lily L. Lin (People's Housewife Assessor); Mike Wu (People's Accountant Assessor); Bing Yang (Male Court Interpreter); Hua Wahrman (Female Court Interpreter); Ming Lo (Medical Examiner); Ken Leung (Peng); Liu Baifang (Chinese TV Reporter); Danny Wang (PSB Escort); Kenny Ki (Guard at Hotel Door); Jack C. Huang (Guard at Phone Center); Mei-Juin Chen (Phone Clerk); Jin Zheng Hui (Phone Center Supervisor); Kent Faulcon (Marine Guard).

LOS ANGELES TIMES, 10/31/97, Calendar/p. 1, Kenneth Turan

Its population is estimated at 1.2 billion, but China only sounds like a large and powerful country. In fact this would-be colossus is no match at all for Richard Gere when he gets his dander up. Or so "Red Corner" would have you believe.

Directed by Jon Avnet, no friend of subtlety, "Red Corner" is a sluggish and uninteresting melodrama that is further hampered by the delusion that it is saying Something Significant. But its one-man-against-the system story is hackneyed and the points it thinks it's making about the state of justice in China are hampered by an attitude that verges on the xenophobic.

Gere plays Jack Moore, a top attorney and negotiator for an American firm eager to get the rights to beam trash TV into China via satellite. He wears glasses to show he's smart and knows just the right quote from Chairman Mao to throw into conversation when things get sticky.

What Moore apparently doesn't do is watch his own product, or else he'd know that he's being set up when a sultry Beijing fashion model starts eyeing him seductively. But, like too many men, he assumes he's irresistible and spirits the woman off to his hotel room for a night of genteel debauchery.

That doesn't seem like such a good idea the next morning, when a hung-over Moore awakens to discover that the woman has been murdered and his bloody fingerprints are on everything but the remote control. Making things worse, she turns out to be the daughter of a powerful Chinese general. And is he ever in a bad mood.

In fact the Chinese that "Accused Moore," as everyone takes to calling him, comes into contact with are among the most sinister and unsmiling group of Asians to emerge from Hollywood since the "Beasts From the East" movies of World War II. And the justice system and prisons they work for make traditional Hollywood penitentiaries seem like spa vacations by comparison.

Instead of being read his rights, Moore is informed he has no rights and that the easy-to-remember motto of the country's judicial system is "Leniency for those who confess, severity for those who resist." Moral education of criminals is the aim in China, and judges tend to get mightily offended if the accused is not properly repentant.

Moore's typically Western response is to get arrogant and pushy, which just steps on their last nerve as far as the Chinese are concerned. They beat him unmercifully, wash his dinner plate in the nearest latrine and break his glasses, which he doesn't seem to miss and looks better without anyway.

While no one is suggesting that Chinese justice would pass muster before an international tribunal at The Hague, presenting the situation in such a heavy-handed and obvious manner does not create dramatic interest. And as the aggrieved Moore, who spends much of his time losing his patience and screaming things like "Do you have any idea what I've been through?," Gere contributes no more than a rigid and graceless performance.

Naturally, Moore's only line of defense is a woman just as attractive as the one who was murdered in his hotel room but much more resistant to his charms. Shen Yuelin (Bai Ling) quizzes Accused Moore closely about his one-night stand with the general's daughter ("Is this the typical duration of your relationships?") and tells him that, big as China is, she's yet to run across "a man not threatened by a woman's intelligence."

Still, as Shen Yuelin gradually comes to believe in Moore's innocence, the two of them end up making a heck of a team. She maneuvers behind the scenes and he simultaneously hijacks China's legal system and outwits the entire Beijing police department. All that remains are a spate of final courtroom surprises that fans of the exploits of Perry Mason will find familiar.

For the script by Robert King, whose previous credits include the best-forgotten "Speechless," never strays from the generic. Inspired by an incident King witnessed in Italy that first got changed to Russia before ending up in China, the peripatetic "Red Corner" takes a sledgehammer approach to what may well be a serious problem. You just wouldn't know it from this film.

NEW YORK POST, 10/31/97, p. 43, Michael Medved

If Chinese President Jiang Zemin felt a sudden spasm of homesickness during his visit to our shores, he could always dodge into a matinee showing "Red Corner" to enjoy some sights and sounds of good old Beijing.

Actually, the movie's re-creation of the mainland capital might not fool a native, but it still seems remarkably convincing for a project filmed—except for some brief footage shot in China without authorization—entirely on artfully assembled sets in California.

Unfortunately, the preposterous plot feels far more phony than these ambitious sound stages, but charisma and chemistry among the key performers and a few cleverly staged surprises still make for an above-average thriller.

Richard Gere (whose offscreen activism for Tibetan independence already ruined his popularity among Chinese ruling circles) stars as an entertainment lawyer trying to negotiate a major TV deal in Beijing.

At a lavish fashion show, a willowy model (Jessey Meng) catches his eye and they retire to a posh hotel for a lushly lyrical erotic interlude.

The next morning, the police awaken the badly hung-over Gere at the same time they haul away the bloody body of his concupiscent companion.

Charged with her murder, he faces a nightmarish legal system with a 99 percent conviction rate, total disregard for civil liberties, and swift, certain punishment.

His court-appointed attorney (played by luminous Chinese actress Bai Ling) represents his only hope. At first she urges a guilty plea (in line with the systems slogan, "Leniency for those who confess, severity for those who resist")—but she becomes increasingly convinced of his innocence and fearlessly tracks a complex conspiracy to the very pinnacle of Party power.

Most of the well researched courtroom details feel authentic, until the story line collapses in its last half-hour in an orgy of Perry Mason pyrotechnics and missing evidence suddenly (and implausibly) recovered.

There's also a silly back story about Gere's tragically (and conveniently) departed wife and daughter: a detail intended to humanize the edgy antihero but hardly needed since Gere does a such a strong, smart job with his complicated part.

Even better is Bai Ling—projecting brains, courage and ethereal beauty in such a captivating combination that anyone with a pulse will fall for her character.

NEWSDAY, 10/31/97, Part II/p. B3, Jack Mathews

As Chinese President Jiang Zemin wraps up his eight-day visit to the United States, we hope he'll find some time to visit one of our fine multiplexes, indulge himself with a large Coke, a tub of popcorn and some Milk Duds, and take in a good old-fashioned American movie. We recommend Jon Avnet's "Red Corner."

The film is fairly conventional political melodrama, mixing elements of the Cold War thriller with the courtroom histrionics of Perry Mason, but it will do two things for Jiang. It will give him a nostalgic glimpse of images from home—Tiananmen Square during the '89 massacre, archival footage of mass executions, and so on. And it will illustrate for him, even more rudely than Bill Clinton has, what Americans really think of his government's human rights policies.

Even though Jiang will only understand the Chinese dialogue, generously laced throughout the film, he'll get the drift of the story, about an American lawyer framed by corrupt Chinese profiteers for the murder of a Beijing model, and its Tiananmen Square message—No Longer Silent!   The president may also recognize the film's star, Richard Gere, the pain-in-the-neck actor who called for Tibetan independence during the Academy Awards show a few years back.

In "Red Corner," Gere plays Jack Moore, a slick, skillfully condescending international lawyer who has come to Beijing to close a multi-billion-dollar satellite communications deal. He has learned enough Chinese to appear sincere, and enough party politics to provide its officials with a moral rationalization. So what if the satellite brings in images of bouncing babes from "Baywatch" and other temptations of free-world decadence; didn't Mao say something about discouraging western values by mocking them?

Though Jiang may find the gullibility of the Chinese officials a bit of a stretch, it works for the movie, and Moore is so certain of success that he decides to celebrate with a night of champagne and sex with the vivacious model he meets in a Beijing bar. But one moment he's teaching her English words—like "lips," "tongue," "breast"—and the next, he's being rousted out of a drug stupor by the Red Guard and being charged with killing his playmate, who turns out to be the daughter of a powerful general.

The arrest not only negates his satellite deal, but puts him at odds with both the Chinese system, which won't even allow him his own lawyer, and officials of the U.S. embassy, who don't want to risk the fragile Sino-American relationship by contesting what appears to be an open-and-shut case. Ultimately, Moore's only hope is Shen Yuelin (Bai Ling), his Chinese public defender, who will have to risk her own career and life in attempting to prove his innocence.

The soul of Kafka lurks in this premise of a man being tried for a capital crime he did not commit, in a country whose language he doesn't speak, by a judicial system that boasts "Leniency for those who confess, severity for those who resist." And the scenes where Moore—growingly confused, frustrated and desperate—attempts to apply the principles of American justice in a Chinese courtroom are powerful.

Great care was taken by Avnet ("Fried Green Tomatoes") and the brilliant production designer Richard Sylbert ("Chinatown") to create a plausible Beijing environment. Jiang may even be surprised to learn that the "hotung," a commercial/residential neighborhood of low buildings and narrow passageways where Avnet stages one of the year's most elaborately gratuitous chase scenes, was built on a seven-acre plot near Los Angeles International Airport.

Screenwriter Robert King ("Speechless") has essentially dramatized America's appeal for democracy in China. "Red Corner" gives the country a thorough scolding by showing how the suppression of speech works against it. Only through an open search for truth can the victim's bereaved father see justice, and the public defender's courage in challenging her country's implacable code of silence is the film's overt political message.

Some simplistic speech-making is justifiable in this kind of cross-cultural thriller, but not the lame cliché of courtroom drama that fill a last act so rife with revelations of guilt, it would make Perry Mason blush. After making a mockery of China's criminal justice system, "Red Corner" makes a mockery of ours. Call it Hollywood diplomacy.

NEWSWEEK, 11/10/97, p. 78, Yahli Chang

Bai Ling's friends in China tell her that the Chinese government hates her new movie, *Red Corner*. In it Richard Gere plays an American lawyer framed for murder in Beijing, and Bai Ling—a Chinese movie star tackling her first major Hollywood role—is the attorney who guides him through China's corrupt and sinister judicial system. Gere has already been banned from entering China for his pro-Tibet activities. Bai Ling, who now divides her time between China, New York and Los Angeles, could be banned, too. Or the government could let her back in and prevent her from leaving, forbid her from acting—and throw her in jail. Her friends warn her not to talk to the press. But when she sits down with a reporter, she talks, nonstop, for 2½ hours. "Should I say, 'Oh, I'm just an actress; I'm an idiot?' " she says. "I cannot. This is not an anti-China movie. We're criticizing the judicial system because we want to make things better. Whatever happens, I'll live with it."

Her problems have already begun. She says a Chinese director who had planned to cast her in a movie has decided against it, telling her, "I don't want to get into trouble." Under pressure from his friends, a Chinese journalist has killed a story he was going to write about her. A visiting friend called the Chinese Embassy here to get her number and was warned not to contact her. Bai Ling defends her decisions but sometimes wavers. She hasn't told her family about "Red Corner"—most of them still live in China—because she doesn't want them to worry. "I hope that nothing happens to them," she says. "I don't want to think about that ... I don't know what to do."

Bai Ling, 27, was brought up by her grandparents in Sichuan province. Her parents, both university professors, chose opposing sides in the Cultural Revolution and separated. When she was 14, Bai Ling joined the People's Liberation Army in Tibet as an entertainer. She was mostly ignorant of politics and was told only that the Tibetans carried knives and were very dangerous. One day an army leader confiscated her diary, saying, "Bai Ling, you're young, and we want to promote you. But if you don't let us see what you're thinking, how can we help you?" Bai Ling left the army after three years and began acting. She soon became one of China's biggest movie stars.

In 1989 Bai Ling joined the Tiananmen Square protests. "I saw a lot of people die, she says. "You know, we did not believe they were going to shoot. When the army came, we lay on the ground. When the gunshots stopped, we got up—but a lot of people next to me could not. Afterwards, it rained for a whole month. The sky was mourning." In 1992 she left stardom in China for waitressing in New York. She learned English by osmosis and eventually landed a role as a Chinese mafia moll in "The Crow." Now she's fielding offers from Hollywood and sending money back to her family.

Bai Ling usually spends half the year in China and hopes to continue visiting. While shooting "Red Corner" in L.A., she would linger on the sets after hours because they reminded her of home. "Here I'm more free, but isolated and lonely," she says. "But there's a lot of anger in China. People hide themselves; they hold back the truth and become twisted. China needs to open up and not be afraid."

SIGHT AND SOUND, 6/98, p. 53, Philip Horne

In Beijing, Jack Moore negotiates with media minister Lin Shen to establish the first Chinese American joint satellite venture for the McAndrews corporation. Celebrating in a nightclub with Lin Dan, the minister's son, he takes model Hong Ling back to his hotel for sex. In the morning, woken by police, Moore finds himself blood stained and Hong Ling murdered. Moore is jailed and urged to confess. A Chinese lawyer must defend him, while Hong Ling's father General Hong seeks revenge. In court, Moore is enraged when his female defender, Shen Yuelin, pleads guilty to win leniency. Later, discovering Moore was truthful about a missing locket, she suspects a frame up. Moore is released into her custody to prepare his defence. They revisit the crime scene. On television, Moore sees a rival media mogul triumphing with Lin Dan; Moore's disgrace has scotched the agreement.

An assassin attempts to shoot Moore in the street: he flees to the US embassy but, realising his escape jeopardises Shen Yuelin, resurrenders himself. In court, she rebels and is removed, but appeals to General Hong and is supported by the Procurator General. The locket arrives, containing a picture of Lin Dan with Hong Ling—he had his mistress murdered to frame Moore. General Hong shoots Lin Dan. Freed, Moore parts tearfully with Shen Yuelin at the airport.

Red Corner is possibly, producer turned director Jon Avnenet's best film, if only because, in the words of the journalist heroine of his last, *Up Close & Personal,* "we are only as good as the story we tell." Not that *Red Corner* altogether eschews the standard tricks of clichéd dialogue, posturing and unjustifiable fantasy plotting that disfigure *Close.*   Although the Avnet team has spent a year researching Chinese legal procedures, and there's covertly made footage of Beijing, these features don't help to achieve an air of reality. But the high-budget concern with 'accuracy' does add some interesting twists. The use of so many Chinese actors speaking Mandarin, and the often dramatically vivid presentation of falsely accused American Jack Moore's language problems, do create a world we do not see often in a mainstream movie.

Furthermore, the film's liberalism, albeit soft centred, prevents it from wholeheartedly endorsing the unrestricted flow of western entertainment into China. The real Chinese villains are not isolationists opposing contact with the West, but corrupt, westernised yuppies, prepared to sacrifice lives for personal gain, who love the softcore 'Beachside' show (clearly *Baywatch)* being sold by the McAndrews corporation. Exchanges between Moore and his brief Shen Yuelin balance Chinese authoritarianism against statistics of American poverty and crime. Moore's trajectory involves a recognition of the moral insufficiency of his McAndrews work and even of the craven US diplomats in the Beijing embassy, whom he finally tells to "go to hell".

So while the film does not promote contemporary America as a corporate and political package, the values Moore discovers through Yuelin and she through him are recognisably western: the courageous defence of truth and justice against formalities and regulations. They discover a spiritual kinship which transcends the boundaries of culture and ideology (in defending him she atones for her childhood acquiescence in the Cultural Revolution). In their *Casablanca*-esque farewell, Yuelin assures the bereaved Jack, who has lost his wife and daughter years before, that despite their separation, "You will always have a family." It is a measure of the excellence of the luminous Bai Ling, making her western film debut, that she manages to lend conviction to such lines as: "You're a part of my life now, Jack Moore."

Red Corner is much less anti-Chinese than it may at first appear. For justice to be finally done, a good half dozen Chinese individuals are required to depart from the Party line, question authority, and take risks. This certainly damages the believability of the plot, but evokes a more differentiated and flexible Chinese society than the ethnophobic aspect of the story might lead one to expect. The film can even seem to be idealistically trying to wish into existence a mutual moral reformation, based as much on individual contact and friendship between peoples as on economics.

And as a courtroom thriller with a twist, if one accepts its sometimes extortionate demands on one's credulity, *Red Corner* just about satisfies. It benefits from a sincere, contained performance from Richard Gere, and where the expert hero is cloyingly congratulated ("I like your style, Jack") his polish and glibness are at least shown up later as evil or venal, while his expertise is later seen as inauthentic. And while one gasps at the script's cheeky corniness when Moore spots the embassy's fluttering Stars and Stripes during his rooftop escape bid, his later rejection of official US help is a welcome irony.

VILLAGE VOICE, 11/4/97, p. 84, Dennis Lim

Like its less enlightened predecessor, *Midnight Express, Red Corner* crudely exploits the primal Western fear of alien judicial systems. In Beijing to negotiate a landmark telecommunications merger, silver-cropped, silver-tongued lawyer Jack Moore (Richard Gere) wakes from a one-night stand to find himself accused of murder. Facing the hard-line version of *The People's Court,* he's made to watch videos of executions and repeatedly reminded, "Leniency for those who confess, severity for those who resist." But Jack has his own, pithier mantra. "I'm an American citizen" he mutters a couple of times, shell-shocked.

Directed by polymorphous hack Jon Avnet (who's maneuvered with alarming ease from *Fried Green Tomatoes* to *The War* to *Up Close and Personal) Red Corner* is far too ludicrous to be in any way offensive. In fact, it works best when it's overtly ludicrous. A showy chase sequence—through Beijing's (well, the elaborate soundstage's) narrow back alleys all the way to the American embassy—finally jump-starts the film about an hour in.

Robert King's screenplay does little more than superimpose a brain-dead murder-mystery plot onto an exotically resonant, but strictly-one-dimension backdrop. Though masquerading as con-troversial political critique, the film doesn't deliver on the hints of sinister government conspiracies or, to its credit, pander much to xenophobic impulses. It's too busy ogling its protagonist's towering nobility.

Jack's court-appointed advocate, Shen Yuelin (Bai Ling), puts her good name on the line to get him out on bail. When Jack realizes this, he relinquishes the safety of the embassy, marching out to a swelling symphonic score, staring a throng of Party guards and a likely death sentence in the face. The spiral of martyrdom continues, Jack and Yuelin outdoing each other with increasingly self-sacrificial behavior. Gere, for his part, is perfectly watchable as long as he doesn't try to act too aggrieved.

Despite being lumped in with *Kundun* and *Seven Years in Tibet* as Hollywood's China irritants du jour, *Red Corner* should cause less annoyance than the pro-Tibet epics. The courts are cartoon Kafka, but the authorities seem curiously tolerant of lawyerly histrionics. *Red Corner* lapses often into legal-thriller crud, complete with heckled objections, free-form grandstanding, and a no-nonsense woman judge. "I will not tolerate this line of questioning," thunders the conveniently bilingual Presiding Chairman (Tsai Chin, not at all scary, maybe because she was also one of the mothers in *The Joy Luck Club).*

The film is, of course, utterly patronizing. At the end, teary-eyed Yuelin, a child of the Cultural Revolution, thanks Jack for liberating her ("I will never be the same"), even though his chief contribution throughout has been a Richard Gere-like opaqueness. Still, you have to admire the nerve of a movie that presents Richard Gere as a counterrevolutionary force.

Also reviewed in:
CHICAGO TRIBUNE, 10/31/97, Friday/p. A, Michael Wilmington
NEW REPUBLIC, 11/24/97, p. 30, Stanley Kauffmann
NEW YORK TIMES, 10/31/97, p. E20, Janet Maslin
VARIETY, 11/3-9/97, p. 98, Todd McCarthy
WASHINGTON POST, 10/31/97, p. B1, Stephen Hunter
WASHINGTON POST, 10/31/97, Weekend/p. 53, Desson Howe

RELIC, THE

A Paramount Pictures release in association with Cloud Nine Entertainment of a Pacific Western production. *Executive Producer:* Gary Levinsohn and Mark Gordon. *Producer:* Gale Anne Hurd and Sam Mercer. *Director:* Peter Hyams. *Screenplay:* Amy Holden Jones, John Raffo, Rick Jaffa, and Amanda Silver. *Based on the novel by:* Douglas Preston and Lincoln Child. *Director of Photography:* Peter Hyams. *Editor:* Steven Kemper. *Music:* John Debney. *Music Editor:* Tom Carlson. *Choreographer:* John Alexander and Adam Shankman. *Sound:* Gene S. Cantamessa and (music) John Richards. *Sound Editor:* Wylie Stateman and Glenn T. Morgan. *Casting:* Penny Perry. *Production Designer:* Philip Harrison. *Art Director:* Eric Orbon and James Murakami. *Set Designer:* Lina King, Louis Montejano, and Christopher S. Nushawg. *Set Decorator:* John Anderson and Patricia Malone. *Special Effects:* Gary Elmendorf. *Costumes:*

Dan Lester. *Make-up:* Stephen Abrums. *Stunt Coordinator:* Brian Smrz. *Running time:* 110 minutes. *MPAA Rating:* R.

CAST: Penelope Ann Miller (Dr. Margo Green); Tom Sizemore (Lt. Vincent D'Agosta); Linda Hunt (Dr. Ann Cuthbert); James Whitmore (Dr. Albert Frock); Clayton Rohmer (Detective Hollingsworth); Chi Muoi Lo (Greg Lee); Thomas Ryan (Parkinson); Robert Lesser (Mayor Owen); Diane Robin (Mayor's Wife); Lewis Van Bergen (John Whitney); Constance Towers (Mrs. Blaisedale); Francis X. McCarthy (Mr. Blaisedale); Audra Lindley (Dr. Zweizig); John Kapelos (McNally); Tico Wells (Bailey); Mike Bacarella (Bradley); Gene Davis (Martini); John Di Santi (Wooton); David Proval (Johnson); David Graubart (Eugene); Ronald Joshua Scott (Josh); Jophery C. Brown (Frederick Ford); Thomas Joseph Carroll (Evans); Montrose Hagins (Chanting Woman); Santos Morales (Captain Borne); Ralph Seymour (Sergeant); La Donna Tittle (Teacher); Edward Jemison (Museum Worker); David Hollander (Charlie); Amanda Ingher (Donna); Don Harvey (Spota); Ken Magee (Coroner's Assistant); Aaron Lustig (Dr. Brown); Kent George (Student); Lynn A. Henderson (Perri Masai); Ron Cummins (Dr. Gross); Matthew Daniel Mosoes (Crazy Man); Elwood Forbes (Furlin Graduate Student); Dina Bair (Reporter); Mark Lake (SWAT Team Guy); Ned Schmidtke (Captain Martin); Vincent Hammond and Brjilan Steele (Kothoga); Gary Hecker (Kothoga Vocalization); Craig Hosking and Dirk Vahle (Helicopter pilots).

LOS ANGELES TIMES, 1/10/97, Calendar/p. 6, John Anderson

[The following review by John Anderson appeared in a slightly different form in
NEWSDAY, 1/10/97, Part II/p. B2.]

If you can buy Penelope Ann Miller as a doctor of evolutionary biology, you can buy just about anything, and that certainly includes the fusion of genetics and voodoo behind "The Relic." But Peter Hyams' film isn't about fact, or even narrative fiction. It's about sound and light, and for much of the time its reliance on purely visceral terror keeps one plastered to one's seat—and, except for the occasional involuntary outburst, very, very quiet.

It's a thrill ride, of course, one with an overly generous helping of gross-out shots and alarming cuts. Miller, as the pert and principled Dr. Margo Green, may be rather hard to accept as one who spends her life among bone-scouring beetles and fund-lusting lab wonks. But the all too rarely seen Tom Sizemore as Lt. Vincent D'Agosta—who's investigating the gruesome murders at Green's Chicago museum—is believably beleaguered. Hyams' own cinematography (he does double duty here) is for much of the time a masterwork of half-light and the sound—"The Relic" should be seen only in theaters equipped for it—may be the real star of the picture.

Hyams the director ("Sudden Death," "Timecop," "The Star Chamber") operates at too much of a fevered pitch for things not to eventually get out of hand—accelerating violence and horror eventually hit maximum velocity and warp into nonsense, no matter how erudite the script. But for much of the movie, apprehension prevails. And that's because "The Relic"—imagine "Predator" crossed with "Phantom of the Opera"—operates on the most basic, and soundest, of dramatic principles: What we can't see is always the most terrifying thing of all—far scarier than anything cooked up in the makeup department of a Hollywood studio, or on its computers, either. Not knowing what's behind the string of stunning eviscerations/decapitations—the creature haunting the institution (exteriors were shot at Chicago's Field Museum) is after the hypothalamus of its victims, which requires some cranial intrusions—is key. Once we see it, it loses much of its attraction. But, hey, there's a lot in life that works exactly the same way.

"The Relic" suffers from some of the stock inanities of the science-horror genre: Two scientists, for instance—in this case Green and her mentor Dr. Albert Frock (James Whitmore)—talking to each other but really talking to us, because they already *know* the stuff they're explaining to each other. And while "The Relic" isn't as guilty as some films on this point, do people whose lives are in peril tell this many jokes? And will someone please explain why characters in movies who are caught up in the police investigation of a murder—the murders of co-workers, at that—act as if they're being subjected to the world's biggest inconvenience? In Green's case, it makes her look like the most self-absorbed creature alive (except for the monster, perhaps) and that's obviously not Hyams' intention.

Easier to swallow are the objections from museum director Ann Cuthbert (Linda Hunt) that the investigation is going to delay the museum's gala opening of its show on myth and superstition—which will provide major funding, as well as the kind of crowd scenes necessary for a truly climactic blood bath. The gala also allows Miller the opportunity to spend the second half of the movie in a little black something that shows off her legs. The symbolic surrender of her high heels just prior to the ultimate confrontation is a bit much, but the point is made: Don't mess with a woman in need of grant money, no matter how skimpily she's dressed.

NEW YORK POST, 1/10/97, p. 48, Michael Medved

Is it a giant insect? A killer reptile? A man-eating plant? A savage god from the Brazilian rain forest? Or a human being horribly transformed by a jungle virus altering his DNA?

By the time "The Relic" finally gives you a glimpse of its mutant monster, you don't much care, because the movie has already worn out its welcome with silly scenes in which its characters stagger endlessly down dimly lit passageways with flashlights.

The maddeningly fuzzy camera work (in which even major characters are hard to recognize) may be an attempt to cover up the short-comings of the ambitious special-effects creature—or it may be simple sloppiness.

Either way, director Peter Hyams has no one to blame but himself since, as usual, he also served as cinematographer. It's a sad comedown from his straight-ahead, handsome work on "Sudden Death" (the best, vehicle yet for Jean-Claude Van Damme) and reflects the deadly impact of a few pretensions of atmospheric "artistry" on this sort of pulpy fare.

Just as the killer creature gives evidence of clumsy assemblage by committee, so, too, the screenplay (based on the work of six credited writers) plays like an awkward hybrid.

A brilliant evolutionary biologist (Penelope Ann Miller) in the Chicago Natural History Museum investigates a few crates shipped to her basement lab by an anthropologist who is missing in the rain forest. At the same time, a cynical police lieutenant (Tom Sizemore) investigates a hold full of bodies in a mysterious ship that has just arrived at a Lake Michigan port from the same part of South America.

Before long, a hideous force is running wild in the museum, ripping the heads off each victim to devour the brain's hypothalamus—the same body part that's mysteriously missing from the victims on that boat.

Tough cop Sizemore wants to shut down the museum till he solves the crimes, but he can't stop the gala, black-tie opening for a new exhibition on "Superstition" that the mayor himself is atttending.

Miller is a lightweight screen presence who registers terror effectively, but can't plausibly portray brilliance or determination. Sizemore makes a good character actor, but with his moody mumbling, he is miscast as a leading man.

Filmmaker Hyams is on to something in depicting the eeriness of a great museum after closing time, but he kills this whole approach by filling that museum with big crowds of partying, prominent people and turning his creature-in-the-basement movie into a bloated disaster trick—like a landlocked "Poseidon Adventure."

When the lavish special effects finally kick in during the last 20 minutes, they do provide a few effective chills, but it's a terrible sign when the museum exhibits intended as background seem more intriguing than the story line.

This movie is missing more than its hypothalamus.

SIGHT AND SOUND, 6/97, p. 61, Rob White

An anthropologist, John Whitney, observes a native ritual in Brazil and drinks a drugged potion. Later, he tries unsuccessfully to stop some crates being shipped to the Chicago Museum of Natural History. He climbs into the hold unnoticed. Six weeks later in Chicago, a cop, Lt Vincent D'Agosta, discovers decapitated crew-members in the hold.

At the museum, biologist Margo Green is told by the director, Ann Cuthbert, to press her case for a grant at an upcoming exhibition gala. She also tells Green that another researcher, Greg Lee, has applied for the grant. In the basement, Whitney's crates from Brazil are found to contain only some fungus-covered leaves which Green examines. A security guard is killed by an unidentified creature. D'Agosta arrives to examine the corpse and question staff. The pathologist points out that the guard's brain is missing its hypothalamus, as were the bodies found on the ship. D'Agosta tries unsuccessfully to stop the gala. Green squashes a huge bug which had earlier been seen eating some of the fungus.

As the gala opens, Green and the museum curator are locked in the basement by Lee. The fungus-creature kills some cops. At the gala, a headless body falls from the ceiling: there is a panic in which people arc crushed to death. D'Agosta finds Green and the curator. Green, running a computer analysis of the fungus, explains how it mutates whatever eats it. The curator explains his theory of aberrant evolution and relates this to a story about a South American tribe who created a homicidal, brain-eating monster—the Kothoga—to slay its enemies. The creature kills off many people, including the curator. A computer analysis reveals that the two-thirds reptilian creature is 33 per cent John Whitney. Green encounters the creature in the basement laboratory. She starts a chemical fire which consumes the creature as she hides in a maceration tank.

The Relic, in spite of its *Raiders of the Lost Ark*-style archaeological caper title, is a monster-on-the-rampage movie, produced by Gale Anne Hurd (producer of *Aliens,* the *Terminator* films, and *The Ghost and the Darkness* and Sam Mercer (*Congo*), directed by Peter Hyams (*Capricorn One, Outland, 2010, Time Cop*), and with a creature designed by the veteran Stan Winston (*Aliens, Jurassic Park*).   This is quite a team, who have made a film which is solid and enjoyable but desperately unoriginal genre fare.

Though set in the (fictional) Chicago Natural History Museum, the film-makers make virtually nothing of this promising setting. Instead much of the action takes place either in dank underground tunnels (which could just as easily be on another planet or in a derelict medieval castle), or in a basement laboratory which houses the computer equipment needed to drive the plot. The lab is a functional space—like the kitchen in *Jurassic Park* or the loading-bay in *Aliens*—which the monster invades only to meet its end because of a protagonist's ingenious use of equipment and effects that are ready to hand. (The most notable item of which in *The Relic* is a maceration tank—a container in which animal carcasses are boiled down then stripped of their flesh by beetles prior to being exhibited in museums.) The major plot point—the monster really gets to work when the museum is full of visiting dignitaries—leaves room for a whole array of stock characters. Much like the authorities in many disaster movies from *Jaws* to *Dante's Peak,* the sycophantic mayor (Robert Lesser) ignores the warnings of Detective Lt Vincent D'Agosta (played by Tom Sizemore, who was wonderful in *Heat* and deserves better parts than this) that the gala to which dignitaries are invited should be cancelled.   For museum curator (James Whitmore), the monster's existence is confirmation of a long-cherished theory about evolutionary 'aberrations' (needless to say, you don't need to be Stephen Jay Gould to know that this is ridiculously bogus science). He stares at the creature before being killed with just that look of rapt admiration which Bob Peck directed at the velociraptor in *Jurassic Park.* The reptilian mutant creature itself is almost laughably like an identikit monster.   It has the arachnoid composite mouth-parts of an adult Alien; the sabre-fangs of a Predator; the reptile-cum-big cat body of a velociraptor; and the tripartite feet of a Tyrannosaurus Rex.

The lack of invention on display is nicely summed up by a scene quite early in the film, in which heroine Margo Green (Penelope Ann Miller) is attacked by a bug which has mutated after eating the Brazilian fungus which can create the monster. The bug is *huge,* like a giant turtle. But neither Green nor her mentor, the curator, comment on its outlandish size or the spectacle of the animal, so immersed are they in dissecting it and trying to confirm its species. The two screen scientists resemble the makers of *The Relic,* who are adept at their craft, instinctively aware of how each generic bit fits with every other, so deft at anatomising and replicating sci-fi and action movie elements that they don't notice the grotesque, improbable surface and shape of their creation.

Also reviewed in:
CHICAGO TRIBUNE, 1/10/97, Friday/p. C, John Petrakis
NEW YORK TIMES, 1/10/97, p. C1, Stephen Holden
VARIETY, 1/13-19/97, p. 151, Emanuel Levy

RHYME & REASON

A Miramax Films release of a City Block and Aslan Pictures production. *Executive Producer:* Helena Echegoyen. *Producer:* Charles X Block, Peter Spirer, and Daniel Sollinger. *Director:* Peter Spirer. *Director of Photography:* Peter Spirer, Daniel Sollinger, George Mitas, Sean Adair, Brennan McClean, Alex Rappaport, and Antonio Ponti. *Editor:* Andy Robertson and David Wilson. *Music:* Benedikt Brydern, Happy Walters, and Andrew Shack. *Sound:* Antonio Arroyo, Scott Evans, Craig Keil, Whit Norris, Fred Aubry, Steve Willer, Jordan Chassan, Jim Manson, and (music) Casey Stone. *Running time:* 90 minutes. *MPAA Rating:* R.

WITH: Busta Rhymes; A Tribe Called Quest; Method Man of Wu-Tang Clan; Pharcyde; Wyclef of the Fugees; Catastrophe of The Alkoholiks; The Alkoholiks; Raekwon/Wu-Tang Clan; The Notorious B.I.G.; Kurtis Blow and Crew; Heavy D; Grand Master Caz; Salt-N-Pepa; Speech; Biz Markie; DJ Lord Jazz of the Lords of the Underground; DJ Scratch of DAS EFX; DJ Rip-One of Air Force Crew; Mr. Animation of Air Force Crew; Crew Chico of Air Force Crew; Lil' Caesar; Wise Intelligent; Andre Charles; Chuck D; Erick Sermon; Lords of the Underground; Craig Mack; LBC Crew; Suave (Pharcyde Manager); Redman; Diezzle Don; Mack 10; KRS-ONE; DJ Muggs of Cypress Hill; MC Eiht; Chaz Hays (E-40 Manager); Whodini; Guru; Spearhead; Lauryn Hill of the Fugees; Praz of the Fugees; Ras Kass and Crew; Parrish Smith; Kris Kross; Xzibit; NAS; "Puffy" Combs; Paul Stewart; Sen Dog; Security at JTR; Kid of Kid N' Play; The Luniz; Adario Strange; Keith Murray; Girls (It's Your Birthday - JTR); Kool Herc; Red Alert; LL Cool J; Da Brat; Tupac; Cypress Hill; Spice 1; Spice 1 - Mom; LV; Master P; Lost Boyz; Suga T; E-40; Too-Short; Melly Mel; Scorpio; Young MC; The Rza; Dogg Pound; Jermaine Dupri; Jay-Z; Homicide; DAS EFX; Dr. Dre.

LOS ANGELES TIMES, 3/5/97, Calendar/p. 4, Kenneth Turan

Rap music and the hip-hop culture that spawned it are a $3 billion a year industry, but to most Americans, who hear only complaints about the violence and misogyny of selected lyrics, it's a world so unfamiliar it might as well be on the far side of the moon.

Ideally, a documentary on this self-contained universe would serve as a guide to the perplexed, introducing a specific sensibility, as "Hype!" did with grunge rock, to a wider audience. "Rhyme & Reason" is a welcome step in the right direction but not as large a one as necessary.

Directed by Peter Spirer, "Rhyme & Reason" offers tantalizing glimpses of the film it might have been, poignant sequences and pithy quotes, that illuminate why hip-hop and rap mean so much to so many people. But finally its approach is too haphazard, its chosen technique too rough and ragged. More than just preaching to the converted, "Rhyme & Reason" seems intent on informing the already educated.

Part of the film's scattershot quality comes from the number of artists participating—more than 80 according to the press material, far too many for a 90-minute film. Though fans will likely recognize each and every personality, for the non-pro it's a confusing welter of names and faces. Even when people are identified, it's only once, and no attempt is made to provide any clue about reputation or status. If you don't know what separates Heavy D from the Notorious B.I.G., don't look to this film for an answer.

Maybe because their faces are the most familiar, or maybe because the increasing years made them more thoughtful, the most articulate artists in "Rhyme & Reason" turn out to be the veterans of the business, people like the late Tupac Shakur, Ice-T, Salt-N-Pepa and Dr. Dre.

The strongest and most powerful points "Rhyme & Reason" makes are about rap's value as a crucial means of self-expression for those who wouldn't ordinarily be heard. "At its best," one performer says, "hip-hop music can grab the nation by the neck and make people realize what's going on. It's a voice for oppressed people who in many ways don't have any other voice."

Equally provocative are discussions centering around the considerable sums rappers make, the different ways they're handling their wealth and whether the responsibility many of them feel to "stay real" affects their decision to move out of the old neighborhood once they can afford to.

Ice-T, for instance, explains the difference between how police treat him now and in the past and talks about what it means to his friends to see "a brother like myself" succeed "without giving in to the man." And his point that "there's no black community, it's a poor community" is echoed by Shakur, almost radiant in a few brief clips, who says that "the same crime element that white people are scared of black people are scared of."

But for every strong section in "Rhyme & Reason," like the segment about the performers' devotion to their mothers, other parts, like the attempt to give a brief history of the roots of rap and hip-hop, are too sketchy and insubstantial. It sometimes feels that the filmmakers used whoever was handy to make their points rather than searching out the best and most articulate spokespeople.

That is especially true for the soft-soap sections on violence and the abuse heaped on women in rap lyrics. Though one performer's point about no one objecting when Arnold Schwarzenegger wipes out battalions of people is a good one, the half-hearted responses female rappers have to unfriendly lyrics feel makeshift and unconvincing.

"Rhyme & Reason's" anarchic approach to its subject may be intentional, an off-shoot of covering a world that doesn't necessarily value tidy summations. And the film does offer a snapshot, however hurried, of the sense of the moment in the hip-hop scene. But documentary opportunities to examine the subject may not be all that frequent, and it's too bad that this chance was not utilized to the fullest.

NEW YORK POST, 3/5/97, p. 37, Larry Worth

There's no in-between with rap music: You either love it or hate it.

Ironically, those who utterly despise it may get the most out of "Rhyme & Reason," a fascinating documentary on the unique blend of lyrics and beat that, according to one speaker, "represents an oppressed culture ... It's what we see daily and what we feel daily."

The film proves downright informative for those who aren't in the know. For starters, it defines the difference between rap and hip-hop, the origins of break-dancing, the art of graffiti, and how they all tie together.

The info is conveyed through a colorful selection of rappers, ranging from the entertaining Salt-N-Pepa, bigger-than-life Ice-T, controversial Chuck D and no-nonsense Da Brat to the late and ever-incisive Tupac Skakur. (In footage of his memorial service which concludes the film, he's hailed by colleagues as "a prophet.")

Director Peter Spirer keeps the pacing brisk, mixing some sharp black-and-white footage of the flood with a soundtrack that nicely illustrates the speakers' points.

The production also earns kudos for refusing to sanitize the likes of gangsta rap, addressing the horrors of East Coast vs. West Coast turf wars, exposing the danger of guns as "an everyday accessory" and being candid about anger at the white community.

Yet, there's also a surprising amount of humor, as when one rapper tells how cops he once intimidated now send him Christmas cards. Equally amusing is when teen-ager Kris Kross can't recall the first time he heard himself on radio because it was "too long ago."

Such bits turn "Rhyme & Reason" into an all-round crowd-pleaser. While rap fans revel in the music, those who resist rap's allure will—at the very least come closer to understanding it.

VILLAGE VOICE, 3/11/97, p. 74, Gary Dauphin

If you wanted to give someone a succinct introduction to the history of hip hop, you could do worse than *Rhyme & Reason*. Director Peter Spirer tackles his subject with the kind of savvy professionalism that was so sorely lacking from last year's *The Show*, trading the occasionally meandering slice-of-life approach for the more fruitful tack of traveling around the Hip Hop Nation doing interviews and location shoots. The result can seem earnestly traditional at times, but *Rhyme* at least respects its subjects enough to ask them serious questions.

Rhyme opens in the Bronx, while voice-overed luminaries from KRS-One to Dr. Dre to the RZA identify the street corners and playgrounds as the birthplace of hip hop. Spirer sketches a unified field theory of the Bronx Old School, with sequences on the genealogy of break beats and scratching, the lost art of break dancing, and the artistic merits of graffiti. It was a golden age that ended at about the time the music industry discovered hip hop's profitability.

Rhyme is close to encyclopedic, featuring artists from just about every generation and region. Spirer gets consistently good quotes, his subjects speaking on a range of topics with the verbal fat pretrimmed. Chuck D remembers how the crack plague changed hip hop, Ice-T meditates on how he was probably better at stealing than rapping, and Nas figures that making music was his only way to get by and survive. On the visual side, Spirer displays a keen, occasionally ironic eye, putting the right people in the right locations: Notorious B.I.G. sits resplendently large on his sofa unwrapping platinum and gold albums, Q-Tip sits atop a sunny park jungle gym chatting with kids, while Craig Mack good-naturedly washes some dishes in his kitchen, speaking on the cheating ways of managers and labels.

There is internal criticism of sexism in rap lyrics and violence in gangsta rap, but its contained in discrete blocks of interview that don't open up onto each other. Even though Salt and Pepa and Lauren of the Fugees speak eloquently on women and matters of respect, its not long before male rappers are eagerly checking out bikini-clad behind in *Rhyme*'s segment on the Jack the Rapper Convention. A little more cross-talk might have added something more to the mix, but even without it *Rhyme & Reason* more than lives up to its name.

Also reviewed in:
NEW YORK TIMES, 3/6/97, p. C18, Stephen Holden
VARIETY, 3/10-16/97, p. 80, Leonard Klady
WASHINGTON POST, 3/7/97, Weekend/p. 33, Esther Iverem

RIDING THE RAILS

An Artistic License Films release of an Uys-Lovell production. *Producer:* Michael Uys and Lexy Lovell. *Director:* Michael Uys and Lexy Lovell. *Screenplay:* Michael Uys and Lexy Lovell. *Director of Photography:* Samuel Henriques. *Editor:* Howard Sharp. *Music:* Jimmie Rodgers, Doc Watson, Woody Guthrie, Brownie McGhee, Sonny Terry, Elizabeth Cotton, Jay Sherman-Godfrey, and Jimmy Weinstein. *Sound:* Neil Riha. *Running time:* 72 minutes. *MPAA Rating:* Not Rated.

WITH: Jim Mitchell, Clarence Lee, René Champion, Peggy De Hart, John Fawcett, and Bob (Guitar Whitey) Symmonds.

LOS ANGELES TIMES, 9/5/97, Calendar/p. 2, Kevin Thomas

During the Great Depression, an estimated 4 million Americans left home and boarded boxcars in a desperate search for work. Of that number, about 250,000 were teenagers, and filmmakers Michael Uys and Lexy Lovell had the inspired idea to solicit letters from them.

From among their 3,000 or so respondents, Uys and Lovell selected 10 vital, engaging individuals to tell their stories in their irresistible documentary, "Riding the Rails," as the first in a series of four documentaries, each of which will play one week.

Although their subject seems sure-fire, Uys and Lovell have made an exemplary documentary, the kind of which has been raising the standards of the form in recent years. This means that the film-makers and their colleagues have done the astonishingly comprehensive research that has become expected in the field.

Even those of us born during the Depression and familiar with hard times images of the era all our lives will be amazed at how Uys and Lovell have mined archival sources to create a broad canvas of an America in dire straits from coast to coast. Images of bread lines, beggars, Hoovervilles and hobo jungles mingle with footage of young people actually riding the rails, sometimes in the process of either fleeing much-despised railroad detectives or being arrested by them.

In short, they've brought alive the past in a way that places their 10 participants in as rich a context as possible. The filmmakers' assemblage of their people and materials has the charm and artistry of a fine old crazy quilt.

A couple of lines from some of those 3,000 letters, an old photo there, a visit to a rusty railroad train track, plus folk songs of the era on the soundtrack—these are the kinds of lovely bits and pieces that frame the interviews and the vintage footage. "Riding the Rails" is the splendid mosaic that represents documentary filmmaking at its most engaging.

Not everyone left home and headed for the nearest railroad track for the same reasons and in the same circumstances, although they almost all are from small towns or rural areas. Peggy De Hart, the one woman in the film, ran away from home at age 15 in 1938 with her best friend (whom she did not know was pregnant) after an argument with her father. John Fawcett, whose father was a prosperous ophthalmologist and who had a happy family life, took off in 1936 at age 16 for pure adventure.

For the others, the lure of adventure may have been there, but it was blended with a heavy dose of sheer necessity. And whereas Charley Bull, who took off in 1930 at age 19, says he wouldn't consider riding the rails now for $200 a day—"$500, you might talk to me"—Bob "Guitar Whitey" Symmonds incredibly is still riding the rails, during the summer months purely for the fun of it.

Clarence Lee, the one African American among the 10, recollects painfully that when he was 16 in 1929, his father felt forced to order him to leave home. "He told me, 'Go fend for yourself. I cannot afford to have you around any longer."'

Lee points out what one would assume: that young blacks had a harder time on the road than their white counterparts. He observes that where a white teen on occasion might actually be invited to sit at a farmhouse dining room table and even allowed to sleep inside the house, a black teen automatically would be fed on the porch and might be permitted to sleep on a haystack in the barn.

Where Uys and Lovell really prove their mettle as first-rate documentarians is in the ever-so-gradually darkening tone of their film. As the Depression wore on and on and times got tougher and tougher—culminating in the cruel and arduous Dust Bowl emigration—the stories of the 10 witnesses get grimmer accordingly.

Yet these people have such an enduringly indomitable spirit that "Riding the Rails" never gets depressing. Instead, it is infinitely moving as we realize these individuals, now in their 70s and 80s, have been profoundly affected by what they experienced and survived.

What "Riding the Rails" leaves us with is a much better idea of what the Great Depression meant for our parents, grandparents and great-grandparents—even if they didn't head for the boxcars themselves and even if they managed to avoid outright hunger. The next time an older relative strikes you as being unnecessarily frugal, you'll understand why.

NEW YORK POST, 9/12/97, p. 47, Thelma Adams

What kid hasn't fantasized about running away from home with a bandanna sack tied to a stick? Few travel farther than around the block.

During the Great Depression, running away from home became an epidemic—250,000 boys and girls hit the road, Jack. In Michael Uys and Lexy Lovell's exhilarating, heart-wrenching, historically accurate "Riding the Rails," a handful of golden-agers reflect on the experience that changed their lives.

Men and women, black and white, these individuals took to the roads and jumped freight cars in the 1930s. Pushed by poverty, inspired by adventure, escaping brutality, searching for romance or pregnant, these teens grew up fast—and hungry—in speeding boxcars, hobo jungles and along dusty rural roads.

Howard Sharp, assisted by Roger Schulte, dynamically edited stock footage, stills, crisp interviews and contemporary landscapes. The images roll to the folk ballads of Jimmie Rodgers, Doc Watson and Woody Guthrie. "Riding the Rails" is a moving commentary on youthful adventure, mature wisdom and the historical forces that ripen a child into an adult, ready or not.

NEWSDAY, 9/12/97, Part II/p. B13, Jack Mathews

"We thought it was the magic carpet ... romance, the click of the rails." With that idealized memory, spoken by a man looking back more than 60 years to his adventures as a teenage freight-hopper during the Great Depression, the quietly poignant documentary "Riding the Rails" begins.

It's a beautiful beginning, evoking the romantic lure of the railroad, which from its earliest days had symbolized opportunity, escape, adventure and new beginnings. For millions of people thrown into jobless despair after the crash of the stock market in 1929, the train was all of those things, and for some, the only hope.

Plenty of books and movies have attempted to chronicle the transient life along America's railroads in the 1930s, but Michael Uys and Lexy Lovell's "Riding the Rails" is one of the few to narrow its focus to the children on the rails. William Wellman directed a cautionary film "Wild Boys on the Road" in 1933, intending to scare kids away from the tramp life. But by the middle of the decade, an estimated 250,000, adolescents were out there, living in hobo "jungles," picking fruit, begging food, and running from police' and club-wielding railroad guards.

Uys and Lovell decided to document that story on film and announced their intentions in magazines catering to senior citizens. Within weeks, they received 3,000 letters. Ten of those respondents, now ranging in ages from 72 to 85, appear in the film, all with incredible stories of hardship, inevitably leavened with the romance of adventure.

Some were asked to leave home by parents who could no longer care for them, some set out planning to find work and send money home, some left because there wasn't anything else to do. For many, their schools had closed, there were no jobs at home, and their friends had left. One of them never got the thrill of the ride out of his system, and at 74 is still hopping freight trains as a leisurely pastime.

The interviews are the heart and soul of "Riding the Rails," but Uys and Lovell make great use of archival footage, film clips, and their own material to illustrate the individual stories and give their documentary visual energy and pace. They have, in fact, opted to chronicle this tragic chapter in American life through the filtered memories of their witnesses.

There's a romantic gauze over the most harrowing tales. Peggy De Hart, on the road at 15, laughs her way through a story of how she escaped from a man who'd given her a ride with ulterior motives. There was special danger for girls, many of whom ended up working as prostitutes, selling themselves at 50 cents a man.

Their experiences on the rails obviously shaped each of the subject's lives in critical ways, and though there is the natural tendency to hyperbolize youthful adventures, all of them know it was no magic carpet ride. While explaining his loneliness on the road, after being asked by his sharecropper father to leave home at 16, Clarence Lee could barely get the words out before collapsing in sobs.

"It hurts even now," he says.

Also reviewed in:
NEW REPUBLIC, 10/13/97, p. 31, Stanley Kauffmann
NEW YORK TIMES, 9/12/97, p. C10, Janet Maslin
VARIETY, 2/3-9/97, p. 48, Dennis Harvey

RIPE

A Trimark Pictures release of a C & P production. *Executive Producer:* Patrick Panzarella and Michael Chambers. *Producer:* Suzy Landa and Tom Razzano. *Director:* Mo Ogrodnik. *Screenplay:* Mo Ogrodnik. *Director of Photography:* Wolfgang Held. *Editor:* Sarah Durham. *Music:* Anton Sanko. *Sound:* Jonathan S. Gaynor. *Casting:* Eve Battaglia. *Production Designer:* Sally Petersen. *Art Director:* Hannah Moseley. *Costumes:* Katherine Jane Bryant. *Running time:* 93 minutes. *MPAA Rating:* Not Rated.

CAST: Monica Keena (Violet); Daisy Eagan (Rosie); Gordon Currie (Pete); Ron Brice (Ken); Vincent Laresca (Jimmy); Karen Lynn Gorney (Janet Wyman).

LOS ANGELES TIMES, 5/30/97, Calendar p. 4, Kevin Thomas

The thought of a venturesome set of runaway 14-year-old fraternal twin sisters taking refuge on a military base, of all places, sounds potentially, lurid.

Remarkably, feature-debuting filmmaker Mo Ogrodnik has taken this highly charged circumstance and turned it into "Ripe," a compelling fable of all-American sex and violence, death and desire.

When the father of twins Violet (Monica Keena) and Rosie (Daisy Eagan) strikes a deer while driving down a forest road, he loses control of his car, which hits a tree and bursts into flames. The twins escape, but their parents die.

We're left to assume that their mother was totally ineffectual because they do not grieve her loss. Their father, on the other hand, was a monster not above pointing a rifle at his terrified daughters. Rosie sells Violet on a dream of their running off to some vague paradise in Kentucky.

Along the way, hungry and tired, they wind up at a derelict military base somewhere in the South, given shelter by the base's newly hired groundskeeper, Pete (Gordon Currie).

Ogrodnik manages to come up with a reason for Pete to let them stay with him in his shack, and he even passes them off to the base's commanding officer as his nieces. Even so Pete, though likable, is not exactly strong on good judgment; he in fact has already let himself be seduced by the commander's bored wife (Karen Lynn Gorney, John Travolta's leading lady in "Saturday Night Fever").

Complicating matters greatly is that Rosie is in love with her beautiful sister, who is experiencing mutual attraction with Pete, a sexy, long-haired vegetarian who offers a contrast to the soldiers.

Ogrodnik pulls us deeply into this most volatile of situations to convey just how powerful the onslaught of sex and emotion can be on girls of such troubled background. She makes this point with considerable daring and imagination and with formidable portrayals from her two young stars.

NEW YORK POST, 5/2/97, p. 54, Bill Hoffmann

"Ripe" purports to be a poignant, coming-of-age story about 14-year-old twin sisters and how each loses her virginity.

In reality, it's a hackneyed mishmash of genres that can't decide whether it wants to be a teen flick, a sex movie, an expose on Army life or a Gothic horror picture.

So, it throws in a little of each and hopes for the best. Sorry, Charlie—none of it works.

Violet (Monica Keena) and Rosie (Daisy Eagan) are twins as different as night and day. While sexy Violet flirts with any guy who walks past, tomboy Rosie is busy killing insects and rats she catches copulating.

In a mind-numbing plot device, their parents are conveniently wiped out in a car crash, allowing the twins to wander off to an Army training base.

They move in with Pete (Gordon Currie), a hippie handyman who lives in a ramshackle home on the base, where nobody seems interested in why two curvy teens have suddenly materialized.

Violet trots around braless in a shirt that all but spells "jailbait," teasing every gal-starved soldier she bumps and grinds by. One good-guy soldier teaches the sisters to shoot—a deed that raises not one eyebrow among the brass.

The movie delivers the goods at the end: Both girls get tanked up at a dance, and Violet hits the mattress with Pete and Rosie abandons her innocence with a drunken soldier against a wall.

If things had ended there, "Ripe" might have escaped its bottom-of-the-barrel, one-star rating.

Instead, it goes for broke, suddenly turning into a cheesy horror flick as Rosie, furious that Pete has soiled her sister, blows him away in a closet.

Then, feeling guilty about it, she plays a long, torturous game of Russian roulette with the barrel of a gun in her mouth. Too bad she didn't turn the weapon on the film crew.

NEWSDAY, 5/2/97, Part II/p. B12, John Anderson

When young soldiers whistle and howl, Violet (Monica Keeria) can't help but smile—appreciatively—unlike her sister, Rosie (Daisy Eagan), who can't help but give them the finger. These two are sisters, all right, but in the great tradition of fictional twins they're too close, too much like opposite sides of the same coin, too poised on the edge of disaster for us not to want them to jump already and put us out of our misery.

And "Ripe," in which first-time director Mo Ogrodnik gives terrifying new connotations to the words "first-time director," is too much like some self-analytic, pseudo-Freudian exercise in autoerotic thumbsucking to make its point, which is hardly a ,point at all. Children turn sexual, the transition is often painful, decisions made in youth are frequently misguided. Ogrodnik contributes nothing to illuminate these truths, but she does put the nubile Monica Keena in some salacious situations, and for many audiences that's more than enough.

What we see in flashback is how the girls' father would playfully chase them around the house at gunpoint. Despite all this quality time, Rosie leaves both parents in the burning wreckage of the family car while dragging Violet to safety and then convincing her to run away. They end up on an Army base, where a newspaper with an apparently widespread circulation plasters their pictures on the front page, but no one notices. One gets the feeling not everyone is being all they could be.

The trajectory of "Ripe" is taking Violet to her inevitable deflowering, Rosie to possible full-fledged Ellen-hood and both of them to a calamity of uncertain description. Toward these ends they meet Pete (Gordon Currie), the handsome base gofer, about whom swirl some serious hygiene questions but who lets them stay in his house. And Ken (Ron Brice), an MP who takes Rosie under his wing and teaches her to shoot a pistol. Considering the way the rest of "Ripe" is progressing, the appearance of a gun in such unstable hands is only going to mean one thing.

Ogrodnik creates a convincing milieu: The base itself is squalid, the people rank and there's a distinctly homoerotic flavor to the relationships among the GIs, who wrestle naked and keep gay magazines hidden about the place. The two young actresses are also quite good: Eagan, theatergoers may recall, was the youngest actress ever given a Tony, for her role in "The Secret Garden," and she made a touching acceptance speech back in 1991. But that was then, and "Ripe" is now, and one walks away from Ogrodnik's film, like so many others recently, wondering why anyone felt it should be made.

VILLAGE VOICE, 5/6/97, p. 86, Amy Taubin

Mo Ogrodnik's debut feature, *Ripe*, is about orphaned 14-year-old fraternal-twin-girl runaways who grow up too fast when they take refuge on an army base. Though nothing in the film comes close to its fragmented opening sequence—as nightmarish and elemental as a fairy tale by the brothers Grimm—*Ripe* suggests that Ogrodnik is not only talented but also willing to take big risks. Which, given the preponderance of safety-first indies, shouldn't be underestimated.

When the twins' mom and their gun-toting ogre of a dad are killed in a car crash, Rosie (Daisy Eagan) pulls Violet (Monica Keena) from the wreckage and they hit the road. They wind up on a rundown army base where Pete (Gordon Currie), a flaky handyman, lets them pass themselves off as his orphaned nieces. Rosie views the base as just a temporary refuge, but Violet, who looks 14-going-on-25, revels in the newfound male attention. Inevitably, it's a man who comes between the two girls—with disastrous results.

In attempting to walk a tightrope between realism and fantasy, *Ripe* gets tripped up by kinks in its narrative logic. It works best when it seems to be taking place within the imagination of Rosie, the tomboy twin who has a penchant for bashing creepy-crawly things (bugs and frogs) to death while they're fucking. Rosie is desperately attached to Violet, who inspires her rescue fantasy and her fear of abandonment.

While the narrative scuttles awkwardly in and out of Rosie's subjectivity (when Ogrodnik loses control of the point of view, the results are downright prurient), the look of the film is scarily expressive. Ogrodnik and cinematographer Wolfgang Held set their bleached-out peach and green pallete against a glaringly overcast sky. There are no dark shadows to hide in. Everything the girls do is overexposed. And if Ogrodnik, like too many young directors, relies on a gun to hype up the action, she is nevertheless a real filmmaker—someone who connects emotions and ideas to images that are both ghostly, and vivid, and occasionally unique.

Also reviewed in:
NEW YORK TIMES, 5/2/97, p. C16, Stephen Holden
VARIETY, 4/22-28/96, p. 92, Todd McCarthy

RIPOUX CONTRE RIPOUX (MY NEW PARTNER AT THE RACES)

An Interama release and of a Films 7/Orly Films/Sedif/TF1 Films production. *Director:* Claude Zidi. *Producer:* Pierre Gauchet. *Screenplay (French with English subtitles):* Simon Michael and Claude Zidi. *Director of Photography:* Jean-Jacques Tarbes. *Editor:* Nicole Saunier. *Music:* Francis Lai. *Sound:* Jean-Louis Ughetto. *Sound Editor:* Amina Mazani. *Art Director:* Françoise Deleu. *Set Decorator:* Odile Hubert and Frédérique Menichetti. *Special Effects:* Philippe Silvain and Jean-François Cousson. *Costumes:* Olga Pelletier. *Make-up:* Eric Pierre. *Stunt Coordinator:* Jean-Claude Laguiez. *Running time:* 107 minutes. *MPAA Rating:* Not Rated.

CAST: Philippe Noiret (René); Thierry Lhermitte (François); Guy Marchand (Inspector Felix Brisson); Line Renaud (Simone); Grace De Capitani (Natacha); Michel Aumont (Commissioner Bloret); Jean-Pierre Castaldi (Inspector Guy Portal); Jean-Claude Brialy (Banker); Jean Benguigui (Cesarini); Christian Bouillette (Jeweler); Roger Jendly (Albert Le Fourgue); Georges Montillier (Clothing Shop Assistant); Ren Morard (Fernand); Alain Mottet (Superintendent); Bernard Freyd (Guichard); Patricia Karim (Boutique Shop Assistant); Jacques Richard (Jean-Marie Laroche); Antoine Valette and Daniel Breton (Guichard's Assistants); Tansou (Police Sergeant); Daniel Milgram (Cop in Natacha's Bar); Martial Bretter (Cop in Boutique); Christian Pernot (Commissioner Le Guyaver); Gérard Beaume (Natacha's Boss); Valérie Leboutte (Gypsy Prostitute); Roland Waden (Handsome Man "Present"); Louba Guertchikoff (Inspector Brisson's Mother); Lauertine Milebo (Cook in Foyer); Billy Kong Lobo (Natacha's Black Client); Bertrand de la Fontaine (Bistro Owner); Simon Michael and Denis Brandon (Thugs); Salah Cheurfi (Miloud); Denis Seurat (Record Shop Assistant); Raymonde Mauffroy (Bank Employee); Marie Manten (PMU Employee).

NEW YORK POST, 9/24/97, p. 44, Larry Worth

French superstar Philippe Noiret is always worth watching. Indeed, he's the only reason to watch "Ripoux Contre Ripoux."

The film is actually a sequel to 1984's silly Gallic farce "My New Partner." In that, Noiret played a corrupt cop who led goody-two-shoes colleague Thierry Lhermitte down the primrose path.

With director Claude Zidi again at the helm, the characters' further adventures pick up years later as bad boy Lhermitte is overcome by a troubled conscience. But he quickly discovers—to Noiret's delight that honesty isn't the best policy.

A predictable, drawn-out scenario follows, with Noiret's amusing asides and laid-back style providing welcome relief. Released in France in 1989, viewers might wonder—at least initially—why "Ripoux," at Anthology Film Archives, took so long to cross the Atlantic. All too soon, they'll have the answer.

SIGHT AND SOUND, 7/91, p. 54, Kim Newman

Montmartre. François, an idealistic young policeman who has been initiated into the ways of corruption by his partner René, decides to go straight. René insists that no one on their patch is honest, proving his point by hauling in at random a passerby, a bank manager, and scaring from him a confession of some past wrongdoing. When the pair retrieve money stolen from a shopkeeper, René keeps half but François returns the rest to the woman, an old girlfriend of René's, who accuses the pair of stealing all the money, forcing Bloret, their superior, to institute corruption proceedings against them.

These are upheld by the crooks and businessmen of Montmartre, and the pair are suspended while Felix and Guy, two straight-arrow cops, are brought in to replace them. René and François retreat to the country, where René tries to make money fixing a horse race. The witnesses who testified against them then turn up, explaining that Felix and Guy have proved even more brutally corrupt and extortionist than they, and begging them to return. When they arrive at the Paris station, René and François are harassed by Felix and Guy, to whom they have evidently been sold out by one of the underworld figures. François apparently agrees to go into partnership with the other two, while René is left to retire.

But Felix and Guy learn that François is only trying to amass evidence against them, and René and François realise that all the Montmartre hoods have sold them out. However, discovering that Felix and Guy are keeping their loot in the bank run by the man they earlier pulled in, René and François set their rivals up, stealing their money and then framing them for the bank robbery. Felix and Guy are arrested and the police commissioner commends René and François for their honesty, promoting them to the Internal Affairs department. François tries to hand over the money Felix and Guy made, but René has already stolen it.

Le Cop 2 finds itself in the frequent sequel bind of having to come up with a new story to build on the original, in which the central dramatic crisis—the attempts of charmingly corrupt cop Philippe Noiret to turn his unreasonably honest junior Thierry Lhermitte into a younger version of himself—was satisfactorily resolved. As with *Another 48 HRS.*, an arbitrary plot wedge has to be driven between two characters who were reconciled in the original. Here François' doomed and dramatically unconvincing attempts to go straight after having succumbed to René's blandishments are compounded by the pointless plot byway which has François deserting René for his even more crooked successors, as part (presumably) of a scheme to bring them to justice.

The business of the cheerful amorality of the central pair is rather heavy-handedly expanded by the central suggestion that absolutely nobody in Montmartre is honest or well-intentioned. The five caricature crooks all rat on the heroes at every turn, and smooth banker Jean-Claude Brialy, in a pointless cameo, turns out to be guilty of some unspecified malfeasance. The idea of charmingly corrupt cops wore pretty thin in Claude Zidi's original and is stretched well beyond breaking point here. Sentimental accordion music and nostalgic views of Paris and the French countryside spuriously try to make a distinction between the caring, twinkling, amusing rottenness of the heroes and the humourless, brutal, mean-spirited criminality of their successors.

VILLAGE VOICE, 9/30/97, p. 88, Elliott Stein

Claude Zidi hit the box-office jackpot in 1984 with *Les Ripoux* a cynical farce about an odd couple of corrupt Parisian policemen. *Ripoux contre Ripoux* (1990), its mechanical sequel, rounds up most of the original cast, headed by Philippe Noiret as a slobbish old-fashioned cop and Thierry Lhermitte as his handsome partner. Both pad their salaries with bribes and racketeering. When they're suspended for corruption, their replacements are an even sleazier pair of gendarmes. The bulk of this overlong and underfunny saga involves the two jokers' attempts to regain their jobs.

Zidi's Paris has been photographed with some artistry by cinematographer Jean-Jacques Tarbes. It's a city populated, however, by dull caricatures. The women are all hookers with hearts of gold; there's one gay character, a swishy cabaret owner, enamored of his poodle. In an alarming scene, a suspect is struck hard on the head with a telephone book. This is meant to be hugely comic, but somehow, abusive and thieving policemen don't seem all that droll.

Also reviewed in:
NEW YORK TIMES, 9/24/97, p. E5, Lawrence Van Gelder
VARIETY, 3/21/90, p. 21, Leonard Klady

ROCKETMAN

A Walt Disney Pictures release in association with Caravan Pictures of a Roger Birnbaum/Gold/Miller production. *Executive Producer:* Jon Turteltaub, Oren Aviv, and Jonathan

Glickman. *Producer:* Roger Birnbaum. *Director:* Stuart Gillard. *Screenplay:* Craig Mazin and Greg Erb. *Story:* Oren Aviv, Craig Mazin, and Greg Erb. *Director of Photography:* Steven Poster. *Editor:* William D. Gordean. *Music:* Michael Tavera. *Music Editor:* Michael Ryan. *Choreographer:* Tony Savino. *Sound:* Pud Cusack and (music) Robert Fernandez. *Sound Editor:* Larry Kemp. *Casting:* Rick Montgomery and Dan Parada. *Production Designer:* Roy Forge Smith. *Art Director:* Michael Rizzo and Joseph Hodges. *Set Decorator:* Brenda Meyers-Ballard. *Set Designer:* Gary Sawaya and Tom Dornbusch. *Special Effects:* Jeff Jarvis. *Visual Effects:* Barry Watkins. *Costumes:* Daniel Orlandi. *Make-up:* John M. Elliott, Jr. *Make-up (Special Effects):* Thomas Burman. *Stunt Coordinator:* Danny Virtue and Russell Towery. *Running time:* 93 minutes. *MPAA Rating:* PG.

CAST: Harland Williams (Fred Z. Randall); Jessica Lundy (Julie Ford); William Sadler ("Wild Bill" Overbeck); Jeffrey DeMunn (Paul Wick); James Pickens, Jr. (Ben Stevens); Beau Bridges (Bud Nesbitt); Peter Onorati (Gary Hackman); Don Lake (Flight Surgeon); William Arthur Jenkins and Ken Farmer (Mission Controllers); Blake Boyd (Gordon A. Peacock); Brandon Kaplan (Young Fred); Paxton Whitehead (British Reporter); Don Armstrong (Anchorman); Pamela West and Marjorie Carroll (Nuns); Claire Birnbaum (School Kid #1); Sean Tweedley (NASA Lab Tech); Cindy Hogan and Felcia Griffin (Reporters); Lidia Porto (Gary's Nurse); Richard Dillard (The President); Gil Glasgow (Bartender).

LOS ANGELES TIMES, 10/10/97, Calendar/p. 14, Kevin Thomas

"Rocketman" is one of Disney's decidedly lesser efforts, a space adventure so stale, mechanical and predictable that even the small children at the press preview were mainly unresponsive. Not even the special effects are very special.

Harland Williams stars as Fred Z. Randall, an ultra-nerdy, ultra-klutzy genius who has designed the operating system for the spaceship Pathfinder. All it takes is a couple of flukes to land Randall on the first manned space mission to Mars aboard Pathfinder. Less than thrilled at the prospect of having Randall along on the journey are Pathfinder's seasoned commander "Wild Bill" Overbeck (William Sadler) and mission specialist Julie Ford (Jessica Lundy). The other passenger is a chimpanzee.

As written by Craig Mazin and Greg Erb and directed by Stuart Gillard, "RocketMan" plays like a live-action cartoon that should have been a work of animation in the first place. The infinite plasticity of the form might well have gone a long way toward unshackling "RocketMan" from its triteness.

More frenetic than funny, Williams does lots of impressions—and they all just happen to be characters from vintage Disney films. Unfortunately, his Randall is not at all distinctive and seems but a carbon copy of countless nerds before him. On the whole the cast is dull, with only Beau Bridges making a dent as a conscientious veteran astronaut back at NASA headquarters in Houston.

NEW YORK POST, 10/10/97, p. 41, Michael Medved

The same studio that gave the world all those cheap but profitable comedies starring Jim Varney and Pauly Shore now believes that our civilization needs yet another goofball comic. The result is "RocketMan," which introduces Harland Williams, the latest comedic discovery of the shameless (but shrewd) Walt Disney Co.

While this rubber-faced Canadian (who played a small part in "Dumb and Dumber") lacks the explosive energy of Jim Carrey, or even the eccentric, easily imitated personalities of a Varney or a Shore, he does project a sheepish, indestructible, bumpkin likability, along with the deadpan timing to win a few laughs.

Williams plays Fred Z. Randall, a klutzy, sideburned computer nerd who's been fascinated from boyhood by the space program. He's programmed the operating systems for the first manned mission to Mars, and when the astronaut assigned to operate the navigational computer is injured in training, Randall takes his place at the last minute.

He's accompanied on his interplanetary adventure by a gung-ho, all-American commander (Bill Sadler), a no-nonsense but comely Mission Specialist (Jessica Lundy) and a mischievous chimpanzee (played by a remarkably charismatic, scene-stealing 3-year-old beast named Raven). Beau Bridges and Jeffrey DeMunn play key members of Mission Control with their usual authority and professionalism.

Many of the in-flight gags are painfully predictable (Fred whining "I have to go tinkle" or breaking wind and inflating his space suit), but others are more elaborate and inventive (involving a "hyper-sleep" chamber that's supposed to place the crew members in suspended animation for eight months of their voyage).

Made with considerable cooperation from NASA, the technical details feel surprisingly authentic and the sets and special effects, while hardly world-class, are far better than you'd expect from a film of such distinctly limited ambition.

The potty humor (complete with accidental ingestion of laxatives) of will appeal to naughty little boys of all ages, while slightly more sophisticated viewers may enjoy knowing retro references—with Williams crooning "If I Were King of the Forest" "When You Wish Upon a Star."

No one could accuse this picture of many demands on the intelligence or attention span of its audience, but it does manage to return its hard-working crew to Earth with a smooth, soft landing.

NEWSDAY, 10/10/97, Part II/p. B6, Jack Mathews

If you think Jim Carrey's a clown, meet his clone, Harland Williams. From the woods of Canada, where as a lonely forest ranger he presumably did stand-up for the local fauna, Williams emerges in a full head-banging, face-making, animal-impersonating, gas-passing, pun-dropping gallop as the star of Disney's "RocketMan."

Williams is cut from the same agitated bundle of neurons as Carrey; he's a blur of screwy physical shtick and cartoon mannerisms. But as Fred Z. Randall, a computer specialist pressed into service on the first manned mission to Mars, he's kept on a short PG leash, compelled to stay within the bounds of infantile propriety. That means he can O.D. on laxatives, get his head stuck in a toilet and pass gas through another astronaut's air hose. But that's it.

Kids will love this guy. He speaks their language. "Are we there yet?" "Can I drive?" "I'm hungry." He does terrible impersonations of TV characters, plays with his food, even though it's just astronaut paste, and draws pictures on the walls of the space shuttle.

But deep down, everybody loves a child, and when Fred appears on the first Mars broadcast and begins singing "I've Got the Whole World in My Hands," he's got the whole world in his.

I will see "RocketMan" again, when I'm captured by terrorists and forced at gunpoint. It's like being stuck in a room with Bill Nye the Science Guy. But the film does have an infectious spirit, Williams is a clear upgrade from past Disney discovery Pauly Shore, and best of all, the movie is only 90 minutes long!

Director Stuart Gillard ("Teenage Mutant Ninja Turtles III") and his clutch of writers throw in enough advanced humor to get you past some of the bowel jokes. But in the end, no pun intended, "RocketMan" flies or falls on the antics of its child-man star, and a little of this guy goes a long way.

Also reviewed in:
CHICAGO TRIBUNE, 10/10/97, Friday/p. H, Rick Kogan
NEW YORK TIMES, 10/10/97, p. E 14, Lawrence Van Gelder
VARIETY, 10/13-19/97, p. 78, Joe Leydon

ROMY AND MICHELE'S HIGH SCHOOL REUNION

A Touchstone Pictures release of a Laurence Mark production in association with Bungalow 78 Productions. *Executive Producer:* Barry Kemp and Robin Schiff. *Producer:* Laurence Mark. *Director:* David Mirkin. *Screenplay:* Robin Schiff. *Director of Photography:* Reynaldo Villalobos. *Editor:* David Finfer. *Music:* Steve Bartek. *Music Editor:* Angie Rubin. *Choreographer:* Smith Wordes. *Sound:* David Ronne and (music) Robert Fernandez and Alan

Meyerson. *Sound Editor:* David Eichhorn. *Casting:* Marcia Ross. *Production Designer:* Mayne Berke. *Art Director:* Jan O'Connell. *Set Decorator:* Jackie Carr. *Special Effects:* Larz Anderson. *Costumes:* Mona May. *Make-up:* Kevin Haney. *Make-up (Mira Sorvino and Lisa Kudrow):* Collier Strong. *Stunt Coordinator:* Cliff McLaughlin and Randy Fife. *Running time:* 91 minutes. *MPAA Rating:* R.

CAST: Mira Sorvino (Romy); Lisa Kudrow (Michele); Janeane Garofalo (Heather); Alan Cumming (Sandy Frink); Julia Campbell (Christie); Mia Cottet (Cheryl); Kristin Bauer (Kelly); Elaine Hendrix (Lisa); Vincent Ventresca (Billy); Camryn Manheim (Toby); Justin Theroux (Cowboy); Jacob Vargas (Ramon); Tami-Adrian George (Receptionist at "Singled Out"); Neil Dickson (Boutique Manager); E.J. Callahan (Mr. Lish); Kathy Long (Kick Boxing Instructor); Betsy Folsom (Spinning Instructor); Zack Phifer (Head of Personnel); Ricky Paull Goldin (Guy at Rehab Meeting); Robb Skyler (Creepy Manager); Deezer D and Kivi Rogers (Service Guys); Brian McGregor (Brat); Pat Crawford Brown (Truck Stop Waitress); Victor Wilson (Bartender Vic); Paul Keeley (Suit Salesman); Elizabeth Norment (Irate Customer); Rick Pasqualone (Mark); Tate Taylor (Casey); Linda Clements (Beverly Hills Lady); Alan Purwin (Helicopter Pilot).

LOS ANGELES TIMES, 4/25/97, Calendar/p. 4, Jack Mathews

[The following review by Jack Mathews appeared in a slightly different form in
NEWSDAY, 4/25/97, Part II/p. B2.]

There are two versions of the title event in director David Mirkin's "Romy and Michelle's High School Reunion." One occurs as a dream, the other as an actual event, and it is a pleasure to report that the second is as goofy and fantastic as the first.

The urge to compare "Romy and Michele" to other movies and characters is irresistible. It's a bit of "Clueless" mixed-in with the outrageous humor of "Strictly Ballroom," its theme combines "Revenge of the Nerds" with "Thelma & Louise," and its two main characters are Beavis and Butt-head with breasts. Heh-heh. Cool.

Adapted by Robin Schiff from her play "Ladies Room," "Romy and Michelle" is the story of two suspended-adolescent women, lifelong friends, and former high school geeks-in-arms, who decide to attend their reunion at Tucson's Sagebrush High, hoping to dazzle their former tormentors with their trumped-up success as the inventors of Post-its.

In fact, Romy (Mira Sorvino) is a clerk at a Los Angeles Jaguar dealership and Michelle (Lisa Kudrow) is an unemployed clothing designer. They're roommates, soul mates and co-dependents who still talk and think like Valley girls, and while their lights upstairs are dim, the girls are bright enough to know their classmates will still find them dull.

The dead-pan performances of Sorvino and Kudrow, who played Michelle in the original play, are perfect. Romy and Michelle are cartoon characters, but the actresses make them both real and enormously sympathetic. Kudrow plays Michelle as the picture of honest, blissful ignorance, while Sorvino adds to those qualities the melancholy of a woman carrying a teenager's torch.

For Michelle, the whole point of going to the reunion is to have a good time, maybe sleep with someone. For Romy, there's the hope of finally catching the eye of the jock who never gave her a look.

Mirkin introduces the main characters at the reunion through a series of anecdotal flashbacks that Romy and Michelle share while thumbing through the Sagebrush annual. There's Billy (Vincent Ventresca), Romy's airhead dreamboat; his snooty prom queen girlfriend Christie (Julia Campbell); super-geek Sandy Frink (Alan Cumming), who has a debilitating crush on Michelle; and Heather (Janeane Garofalo), a disheveled loner who seems to have majored in anger.

All these characters reappear in delightfully surprising ways in both Michelle's dreamed-up re-union and the real one. Garofalo's manner finally begins to grate—she isn't given much to do other than scowl and swear—but the movie skips along too quickly for the sour notes or its many flat moments to spoil the party.

Mirkin, a first-time director whose TV comedy writing credits include "The Tracey Ullman Show" and "The Simpsons," knew exactly what he had here and composed it like frames in a comic strip, ordering cheerful snow-cone colors for everything from the girls' childlike outfits to the decor of a Laundromat. In fact, there's a jaunty spirit to every element in the film, from

Reynaldo Villalobos' photography to Mayne Berke's production design to Mona May's funky costumes to Steve Bartek's score.

But beneath the endless silliness of the movie beats a real heart, and its theme of loyal friendship keeps propping it up every time the thin walls of the story seem about to collapse. Though "Romy and Michele" doing Tucson doesn't take us much further than Beavis and Butthead doing America, the ride, and the company, are a lot more fun.

NEW YORK POST, 4/25/97, p. 49, Thelma Adams

You can go home again—but why? It's the high school reunion dilemma.

The daffy, disarming comedy "Romy and Michele's High School Reunion" pairs Lisa ("Friends") Kudrow and Oscar-winner Mira Sorvino. They're Beavis and Butt-head with hairspray.

Ten years out of Tucson's Sagebrush High, Romy (Sorvino) is a cashier and Michele (Kudrow) is unemployed. They live in Venice Beach. They're short on boys and high on binge eating. They share common interests.

"I hate throwing up in public," says Michele. "Me, too." agrees Romy.

Their little lives of quiet denial and loud clothing are thrown into a tailspin. Successful Sagebrush alum Heather (Janeane Garofalo) bumps into Romy while buying a Jag and tells her about their 10-year reunion.

Flash to the past. Romy tells Michele at the senior prom that they'll move to L.A. and "everything is going to happen for us there and well never look back." What a deludinoid!

The simple setup, punchily directed by David Mirkin from a familiar, funny script by Robin Schiff, leads to flashbacks in which yearbook photos are cleverly reanimated, a trip to Tucson and a Fellini-lite nightmare.

"Romy and Michele" culminates in a fantasy dance number that works in the awkwardly loopy way Woody Allen aspired to in "Everyone Says I Love You."

Kudrow and Sorvino score with Judy Holliday surface playfulness and lethal timing. Romy and Michele may be ditzy, but they know that girls just wanta have fun—and there's heartbreak along the way. They must confront existential questions: Who is the Mary and who is the Rhoda of the duo?

It's these kind of issues that can end a friendship that started in the sandbox.

And who can slice an ego with her tongue? Cow-eyed Garofalo delivers another tragicomic performance that leaves us wanting more. Heather is a link in the high school food chain—hurt and hurting, wounded and wounding.

In high school, Heather watched her one true love and science partner, the ridiculous Sandy Frink (Alan ["Emma"] Cumming), moon over Michele.

Now, a rich inventor, Heather returns to Tucson to claim her man. Meanwhile, the "Frinkizoid" has his own surprises.

The plot takes some jolting turns into left field and occasionally unravels, but the leads' good-natured performances knit the story back into place. The message is sure and simple: staying friends and looking fabulous is the best revenge of the nerds.

Were we that pathetic in high school? As Michele so sagely puts it: "Duh."

SIGHT AND SOUND, 9/97, p. 54, Liese Spencer

Venice Beach, California. Romy and Michele are flatmates in their twenties. Romy works as cashier at a car company, where she meets Heather, a misfit classmate from high school. Now rich and successful, Heather tells Romy about a high-school reunion planned for a few weeks' time, but says she's not going.

Back at the flat, Romy and the unemployed Michele remember their school-days. In flashback, we see the 'A,' 'B' and 'C' groups of the class: the glamorous 'A' group of girls think Romy and Michele are 'freaks', Abrasive loner Heather smokes between classes and pines after nerdish Sandy Frink, himself in love with the uninterested Michele. The girls remember how Romy was spurned by class jock Billy at their prom night.

Deciding to go to the reunion, Romy and Michele resolve to diet, and to find boyfriends and a job for Michele before the event. After failing in all areas, they decide to lie about their lives.

Romy borrows a car from work, they dress as businesswomen and on the way decide to say they invented Post-It notes.   After an argument between them, Michele falls asleep and has a nightmare. Later, at the party, Heather turns up and blows their cover, humiliating them in front of the 'A' group. They make up and decide just to have a good time. A former classmate who is now an editor for Vogue compliments them on their outfits and the 'A' group are toppled. Romy gets her revenge on Billy before Sandy, now a millionaire, arrives and whisks them away in his helicopter. From the air, they see Heather in a clinch with another boy who ignored her at school. Some time later, Romy and Michele are working in their own Frink-funded fashion boutique.

The camera speeds over the sea, over Venice Beach and through the window of a beach-side apartment, moving seamlessly into a close-up of a television screen showing *Pretty Woman*. As the camera revolves to reveal Romy and Michele watching the movie for the umpteenth time, Michele captures the double-edged and definitively girly pleasures of ridiculing and revelling in *Pretty Woman*'s pulp escapism, drawling "poor thing—they won't let her shop".

It's a cute piece of bubblegum self-reflexivity, since *Romy and Michele's High School Reunion* offers the same winning combination for audiences, both celebrating and satirising its heroines' shopping, fashion and boyfriend-oriented lifestyle. A cross between *Clueless* and *Muriel's Wedding* in its colourfully kitsch design and fairytale plot, this is marked from the start as an ironic chick flick, knowingly exploiting all those teenage fantasies of love, success and revenge that linger in the still-teenage hearts of sensible grown-up women. It's a buddy movie that archly plays on the reactionary romantic sensibilities of its female audience, but is finally less interested in marriage than in female friendship.

Executive producer and screenwriter Robin Schiff developed the script from her stage play *The Ladies Room,* and the movie demonstrates a fine ear for the rhythms and idiom of West Coast girl-speak, delivering a sharp gag about once a minute. It helps of course to have Lisa Kudrow, Mira Sorvino and Janeane Garofalo voicing her lines, actors effectively if predictably cast in roles which play heavily on their established screen personae. Thus Kudrow reprises the ditz but earnest inarticulacy of her television character from *Friends*, Sorvino offers a Californian take on her *Mighty Aphrodite* part and Garofalo rerehearses her usual tough-talking-but-vulnerable *shtick* (as in *The Truth About Cats & Dogs*). Resplendent in matching big blonde hair and trashy Versace-style outfits courtesy of *Clueless* costumier Mona May, Kudrow and Sorvino brilliantly deadpan Schiff's dumb banter while retaining sympathy for their airhead heroines. So successful is the droll superficiality of Schiff's dialogue that one of the funniest moments of the movie comes when Romy jokes that she has secured a sportscar for them to arrive in at the reunion by spending the day giving her male co-workers handjobs, only to be aghast when an appreciative Michele accepts this news without turning a well-sprayed hair.

Using the familiar formula of the high-school reunion, the movie slyly parodies such reunion films as *The Big Chill* and *Peggy Sue Got Married*, with their sentimental combination of lost youth, adult self-knowledge and nostalgic soundtracks. Here, Romy and Michele's self-realisation is limited to deciding that friendship is important and life is about having fun. Meanwhile a soundtrack composed of dire pop hits from the 80s induces a wincing flood of recognition as it works its way through a kind of anticlassic back catalogue, including "Footloose" by Kenny Loggins and 'Our Lips Are Sealed' by the Go-Gos.

The film is the directorial debut of David Mirkin, who brings a suitably breathless pace and cartoonish camerawork to the girls' adventures. He squeezes in some nice gags, such as the pair setting off in their sportscar, 'Footloose' on the radio, shouting "Watch out Tucson, here we come!"—only to have it stall, repeatedly, forcing them to reprise their battlecry with every false start. *Romy and Michele's High School Reunion* could easily have been an infantile farce, but the detailing provides many incidental pleasures, such as the way the class snobs reappear at the reunion as smugly righteous 'homemakers', all simultaneously pregnant in *Stepford Wives* fashion.

That said, the movie is more successful in the nominally realist first half, as it intercuts the girls' everyday lives with scenes of bad-haired humiliation at high school. Later, climactic fantasy sequences are betrayed by facile mugging and poor make-up, with Michele's prolonged dream sequence particularly misjudged. The 70-year time-jump to Romy and Michele as feuding, prosthetically aged hags smacks of the dead-weight satire of *Death Becomes Her*.   It's an imaginative and potentially funny scene that would have worked as animation, but Mirkin, once a producer of *The Simpsons*, here fails to translate it into live action. These cavils apart, this is a delicious slice of feel-good wish fulfilment that should strip the thin layer of adult cynicism from its audience and have them quoting lines and reliving scenes with all the relish of, say, *Pretty Woman* fans.

VILLAGE VOICE, 5/6/97, p. 79, Justine Elias

How beautiful, thin, and rich does a woman have to become before her old high school tormentors will decide she's cool enough for them? For Romy White, a former teenage outsider who has transformed herself into a stunning. fashion-mad club girl, the first reaction from the almighty in crowd will always be: "Oh, you were the chubby one, weren't you?" That's even after Romy (Mira Sorvino) and her best pal Michele (Lisa Kudrow) concoct an absurd success story, whip up some homemade haute couture, and show up at their 10th reunion looking as invincibly minx-like as Marilyn Monroe and Jane Russell did in *Gentlemen Prefer Blondes*.

Romy and Michele covers familiar territory, but this generally good-natured comedy has the advantages of snappy direction by *Simpsons* veteran David Mirkin, a sharp and funny script by Robin Schiff, and likable performances all around, especially by Irish actor Alan Cumming as a geek who once dared to love a girl above his station (the younger Michele, cheerful despite her huge back brace). Even when the pace slackens towards the end, and the jokes on the mean prom king and queen turn a bit ugly, there's the pleasure of watching Kudrow's Michele, who has nervously hung on her best friend's every word, startle herself by expressing an independent thought.

And when its three high school losers stun their classmates by performing a ridiculously long dance number, *Romy and Michele* becomes something other than a typical teenage fantasy. It ends as happily as *Gentlemen Prefer Blondes* might have, if those two dangerously talented showgirls had decided to postpone their hasty marriages and open up a dancing school for misfits instead.

Also reviewed in:
NEW YORK TIMES, 4/25/97, p. C5, Janet Maslin
VARIETY, 4/28-5/4/97, p. 100, Todd McCarthy
WASHINGTON POST, 4/25/97, p. G6, Rita Kempley
WASHINGTON POST, 4/25/97, Weekend/p. 49, Desson Howe

ROSEWOOD

A Warner Bros. release of a Peters Entertainment production in association with New Deal Productions. *Executive Producer:* Tracy Barone. *Producer:* Jon Peters. *Director:* John Singleton. *Screenplay:* Gregory Poirier. *Director of Photography:* Johnny E. Jensen. *Editor:* Bruce Cannon. *Music:* John Williams. *Sound:* Veda Campbell. *Casting:* Marion Dougherty. *Production Designer:* Paul Sylbert. *Art Director:* Chris Gorak. *Set Designer:* Mark Garner. *Set Decorator:* Dan May. *Costumes:* Ruth E. Carter. *Stunt Coordinator:* Glenn Randall, Jr. *Running time:* 122 minutes. *MPAA Rating:* R.

CAST: Jon Voight (John Wright); Ving Rhames (Mann); Don Cheadle (Sylvester Carrier); Bruce McGill (Duke); Loren Dean (James Taylor); Esther Rolle (Sarah Carrier); Elise Neal (Scrappie); Catherine Kellner (Fannie Taylor); Michael Rooker (Sheriff Walker); Catherine Kellner (Fanny Taylor); Akosua Busia (Jewel); Paul Benjamin (James Carrier); Kevin Jackson (Sam Carter); Mark, Jr. Boone (Poly); Muse Watson (Henry Andrews); Badja Djola (John Bradley); Kathryn Meisle (Mary Wright); Jaimz Woolvett (Deputy Earl);

CHRISTIAN SCIENCE MONITOR, 2/25/97, p. 14, David Sterritt

Filmmakers still love fantastic yarns like "Dante's Peak" and "Scream." But stories based on reality are also in fashion, from the coming Mafia thriller "Donnie Brasco" to celebrity-centered films like "Shine" and "The People vs. Larry Flynt."

Reality takes second place to dramatization in such movies, of course, and savvy audiences don't expect them to provide full-fledged historical truth. But in the more responsible examples, enough real-life material glimmers through the Hollywood touches to give us a glimpse of actual events.

This certainly happens in "Rosewood," which takes its title from the name of a Florida town destroyed in a race war about 75 years ago. Directed by John Singleton, the picture contains a number of melodramatic flourishes that cut into its credibility and ironically weaken its impact. Yet it retains more than enough believable details and credible characterizations to give it the ring of tragic truth.

Judging from the movie's evidence, the most important single fact about Rosewood appears to have been the economic and cultural success achieved by its poor but honorable African-American citizens. They built their town into a thriving community—complete with proud homeowners, a well-attended church, even a music teacher for the local kids—that's more impressive than anything the white folks in the nearby village of Sumner can boast of.

It's risky for black people to outshine their white neighbors in the Deep South of 1923, and some of Sumner's rednecks take petty revenge by exploiting and abusing African-Americans, who are prevented by law and custom from defending themselves. Things reach a boiling point when a promiscuous white woman gets horribly beaten by a sadistic white lover, and she tries to cover the facts by claiming she was assaulted by a black man on the run from a chain gang.

The good ol' boys of Sumner grab their dogs, load their rifles, and crank up their hatreds for a furious manhunt in the nearby woods and swamps, which quickly escalates to an all-out attack on the black community. Their shotgun shells fly as wildly as their emotions, taking a toll in human lives that grows more horrifying by the hour. Aside from the outcries of the besieged blacks, the only voices of reason are a handful of whites—a sheriff trying to enforce the law, a shopkeeper with many black customers, his deeply religious wife whose commitment to the black victims can't be trusted to extend very far.

It's astonishing to think that such an event could happen. But happen it did, just a few decades ago, and the film's final credits tell of survivors still remembering the disaster. The actuality and urgency of the story call into question the filmmakers' strategy of using melodramatic formulas to heighten its visceral appeal.

It is possible, for example, that during the real incident a new Rosewood resident named Mann stayed off attacks on his life and aided his fellow blacks by leading women and children to safety through the wilderness. But it is unlikely that he fended off a berserk mob with two blazing pistols, made a strenuous escape after literally being lynched, and received help in his exploits from a horse that seems smarter than many of the human characters.

This aside, "Rosewood" marks an impressive comeback for director Singleton, who followed his electrifying debut in "Boyz N the Hood" with letdowns in the pretentious "Poetic Justice" and the uneven "Higher Learning."

Ving Rhames, an actor so gifted that even the wretched "Striptease" gained greatly from his presence, gives the heroic Mann as much humanity and believability as the screenplay allows. Jon Voight, one of Hollywood's more thoughtful and creative denizens, is excellent as the white merchant with divided loyalties.

Standouts in the supporting cast include Esther Rolle as a dignified Rosewood matron, Elise Neal as a schoolteacher caught in the cross-fire, and Michael Rooker as the hard-pressed sheriff.

Bruce McGill is also particularly real (and frightening) as a white man who sees the chaotic episode as a chance to teach his little boy what "manhood" means, and this character brings out an unstated but important subtext in the movie. Every one of the rampaging killers in "Rosewood" is a male—a reminder that gender attitudes as well as racial bigotry have played strong roles in causing such American tragedies, and that more attention to enlightened conceptions of manhood could have a healing influence on today's society.

CINEASTE, Vol XXIII No. 1, p. 45, Ed Guerrero

John Singleton's *Rosewood* grapples with a powerful, daunting contradiction. Put simply, how does one make a slick, Hollywood action-adventure-entertainment flick, with big box-office expectations, about one of history's ultimate nightmares: genocidal racism? Singleton is not alone in attempting to negotiate this contradiction, since other mainstream filmmakers have attempted to do so before. Posed as question, this contradiction reverberates with a number of issues, raised most recently by the work of Steven Spielberg in *Schindler's List* (1993), Mario and Melvin Van Peebles in *Panther* (1995), Costa-Gavras in *Betrayed* (1988), and even Kevin Costner in *Dances with Wolves* (1990).

Singleton answers the challenge of his material by casting this true and horrific tale in the mold of the Hollywood revisionist Western, with its lone, gunslinging hero "aimin' to settle down" in a prosperous little town in need of his talents and abilities. This Western is revisionist because the hero is black; the cultural focus is on African America; the scene is the South in the 1920s; and the issue is lynching and mass murder.

Rosewood is based on the terrible, historically-repressed events that took place in the small, thriving black town of that name, located on the edge of the Florida cypress swamps. Fueled by economic competition and jealousy, and finally ignited by an adulterous white woman's charge of abuse against a black man—the mythical and historically indispensable black *other*—a legally-sanctioned lynch mob from the nearby white town of Sumner descended on Rosewood and burned it to the ground. In the process, the mob managed to kill 'several people' (the body count was probably much higher than officially reported) and managed to drive several hundred of the town's residents into hiding in the surrounding swamps.

Yet the repressed does return, and the story was featured in 1983 on CBS-TV's *60 Minutes*, indebted to the long memories of twenty Rosewood survivors and descendants, including Arnett Doctor, and the investigative reporting of Gary Moore of the *St. Petersburg Times*. After another eleven years of political haggling and hearings, the Florida State Legislature, in a first-of-its-kind gesture, voted monetary reparations for Rosewood's victims.

Of course, it's a long way from historical actuality to the big Hollywood screen, with its ultimate imperative that *everybody's* story be measured by its box-office potential—that is, be reduced to its commodity status. Thus, the nagging contradiction between commercial form and historical content pops up almost immediately in a self-conscious moment in *Rosewoods* opening scene when World War I vet Mann (Ving Rhames), flush with his discharge money and packing a couple of .45 automatics, rides into town. In the age of the automobile, a young boy asks the obvious question: Why is he riding a horse?

But the tension between content and form is present in other more significant and obvious ways. Hollywood always depicts the collective sufferings and struggles of oppressed peoples through the tale of the hyperbolic, heroic individual. Certainly, Spielberg's viewing the Holocaust this way in *Schindler's List*, or Spike Lee's masking his celebrity persona as Shorty, konked and Zoot Suiting his way through *Malcolm X*, or the Van Peebles trying to understand the political rise of the Black Panther Party through nostalgic eyes in *Panther*, are but the most recent variations on this gambit.

Singleton's prime attribute and contribution to black filmmaking has much to do with his ability to survive in the 'movie business' as a mainstream director moving from project to project. In this regard, one hopes that, by example and networking, he will help hold that space open for other emerging black directors of the same persuasion. From Singleton, then, one has come to expect industry convention rather than experimentation and subversion of form, no matter how socially insurgent the content of his films.

Thus, in dutiful big-screen manner, the story unfolds with Mann looking at a piece of property he wishes to buy, connecting closely with Rosewood's leading family, the Carriers—Sylvester (Don Cheadle) and Aunt Sarah (Esther Rolle)—and taking a liking to their comely, schoolteacher daughter, Scrappie (Elise Neal). Added to this stock mix of plot and characters are a number of ambivalent whites, including the sexploitative storekeeper, John Wright (Jon Voight), who becomes reluctantly instrumental in saving many of the citizens of Rosewood, and Sheriff Walker (Michael Rooker), who tries to control the drunken lynch mob from Sumner he has deputized. Of course, this Hollywood adaptation would not be complete without the displacement-by-class of all evil onto the poorest of Southern whites. These folks are most notably represented by a bo' hog-hunting, whisky-drinking, murderous, racist lunatic named Duke (Bruce McGill) and a 'trashy' young white woman named Fannie Taylor (Catherine Kellner), who initially yells "nigger" and sets things off.

What makes *Rosewood* an interesting and even powerful film, however, resides not in its form or formula, but in the way its visual spectacle and argument manage to break through the smothering, controlling embrace of Hollywood liberalism. In spite of itself, *Rosewood* manages to shake up the expectations of even the most jaded mall-multiplex *cinéaste*.   Singleton's rendering of the Twenties town of Rosewood and its culture evokes notions of a stable, homogenous, unified, and self-sufficient black community between the world wars, while simultaneously depicting the climate of racism and black/white power relations that made such a black world necessary and, ironically, possible.

With all the fine detail of a mainstream-cinema period piece, in the film's most seductive scenes the protagonist Mann breaks bread with the Carrier family and the next night attends a community New Years' Eve dance. In these fleeting moments—in the social world of black hospitality, dance, and celebration—*Rosewood* transcends formula. The costumes, the moves on the dance floor, even the brothers discreetly sipping from a jug and ruminating on the fringe of the gathering, nostalgically call up a world receded from our generational memory. But Singleton has a thing for parties, and one can contrast this Twenties community and social gathering with the other communities and parties across the great political divide of the civil rights movement— the Nineties 'hood 'Bar-B-Q' in *Boyz N the Hood* or the picnic in *Poetic Justice*. The paradigm has shifted and the problems have grown, but the beat goes on.

Rosewood's real power, however, dwells in the way the film, with its quite graphic scenes of racist, genocidal violence, "dialectically shocks " us, as Frederic Jameson would say, into new realizations about ourselves and our communal relations. As a national audience, both cinematic and televisual, we have become quite addicted and inured to the graphic verisimilitude of action-adventure violence as entertainment. What gives us that extra jolt of unease in *Rosewood,* however, is the subtle current of repressed history running through the film, no matter how commercially masked, that resonates with the Holocaust, the evils of ethnic cleansing in the former Yugoslavia, or the genocide/countergenocide of the Hutu/Tutsi disaster in Rwanda. That is to say, the film forces us to recognize all of that seething fear and hatred reserved for the *other* in the planetary political unconscious, waiting to explode in our collective faces at the next economic downturn, the next instance of racial scapegoating, or the next spell of 'war fever' and communal suicide.

At the height of the film's action, the disturbing sight of black men and women hanging from trees and telephone poles, highlighted by the flames of their burning community, seamlessly merges with those old *Life, Jet*, and archival photographs of real lynchings in America's historical gallery of horrors. (consequently, *Rosewood*'s spectacle of violence is decidedly *not* escapist entertainment in that mainstream-cinema sense. Violence, here, demands a regurgitation of barely hidden collective nightmares and guilty complicities, as well as a painful examination of the national conscience. These are all things we as a national audience don't like to face, even in the darkness and anonymity of our cinemas. These concerns are symbolized in one of the film's closing scenes, when the rabid Duke, proud of his crimes, forces his young son to look at a pile of black bodies awaiting disposal. Here, all of humanity's body counts are evoked, from Auschwitz, to Wounded Knee, to My Lai. Singleton's obvious point—as the child rejects his father's wretched path and runs away from home—is that hope resides in the next generation.

To be certain, Singleton's film is full of messages of the more obvious, liberal, movie-industry variety, including those about some whites being rational, good, and perhaps heroic in evil times, to historic black arguments about self-defense and active struggle against racism. Even though trapped in a Hollywood black/white buddy configuration, Jon Voight and Ving Rhames do a reasonable job of lifting the film's messages above editorial didacticism. Voight's performance as a circumstantial hero—an ambivalent, exploitative white storekeeper in the black community, who finds his conscience in the heat of the massacre—shows his subtle and consummate skill as an actor. Rhames is equally outstanding as the quintessentially laconic, Hollywood tough guy who, in this instance, stakes a clear claim for black manhood and resistance in the face of oppression.

Rhames's Mann makes this point in a scene best described as 'popcorn' violence. While riding on his 'hoss' out of town, Mann is wildly fired upon by several whites who chase him deep into the woods. Finally, Mann turns, stands his ground, and opens up with both his .45s. Cut to the whites hauling ass out of the woods, with the punch line coming when they exclaim that they were ambushed by a gang of "ten to fifteen niggers." The audience explodes with laughter. Singleton's timing and editorial touch, with this classic scene from the archives of the cinematic West, proves just right.

Some of *Rosewood*'s messages, however, are not so entertaining or edifying. These moments find their origins in the film industry's habit of reflexively devaluing those powerless groups not at the center of its discourse or at the top of its representational caste system. Hollywood films, no matter who makes them, continue to be plagued by some very obvious color and gender problems. In the case of *Rosewood,* one must ask why it is that the darkest black woman in the cast (Akosua Busia as Jewel) literally opens the film with her legs spread wide and squealing in the pain/pleasure of miscegenation, and then, in the film's closure, is symbolically punished by having her murdered corpse gruesomely displayed —face up, eyes open—in a close-up. The existence of a devaluing, color-caste hierarchy in this instance focused on those whom Alice Walker has referred to as "*black* black" women—continues to be a disturbing reality in commercial cinema.

Disturbing, as well, is how the liberal 'problem-picture' mechanism of displacement works when ultimately assigning blame and punishment for the genocidal operations of a systematic and collectively racist society. Unquestionably, the adulterous white woman, Fannie Taylor, is initially responsible for the horrific sequence of events that transpires in *Rosewood.* For certain, she bears the historical burden of articulating the repeatedly deployed, false accusation against black men as rapists and/or criminals. As is well known from the Susan Smith case and more recent spectacles in our televisual media circus, the electronic evocation of the black bogeyman is still big business. Moreover, Singleton does a reasonable job of looking into Fannie's motivations with some psychological subtlety. We see her abject misery and how she garners sympathy from the town's upstanding white women with her false charges.

In *Rosewood*'s final scene, however, we're dealing with Hollywood's 'trickle-down' theory of punishment, with the most powerless individual in the hierarchy taking the rap for the collective. As *Rosewood* ends, the camera looks down in a long shot on a shack, and we hear the screams and blows of Fannie, as she is brutally beaten by her husband, mixed with the lush, poignant music signifying ideological and narrative resolution. In Singleton's defense, one could argue that a society that could burn and murder an entire black town on impulse would have no trouble thrashing one defenseless, lower-class, white woman (although perhaps this is too subtle an insight for an action-adventure flick, even one with epic, historical pretensions). Hollywood films always argue for what they show in their action, and not necessarily for a director's intentions. So the film's narrative concludes with an act of symbolic punishment, one displacing all blame for the genocide of a racial minority onto yet another out group—women.

Ultimately, however, in spite (or perhaps because) of the tangle of contradictions that characterize *Rosewood,* John Singleton has made a film that prods the collective, national psyche. Although *Rosewood* wasn't commercially successful at the box office, the issues it explores will continue to resonate for some time to come, since the film is sure to have a long run in the video store, in the classroom, and within the critical discourse about Black Cinema.

LOS ANGELES TIMES, 2/21/97, Calendar/p. 1, Kenneth Turan

The need to bear witness against atrocity, to testify that something wicked this way came, is the powerful drive that animates "Rosewood," the story of an American tragedy so horrific no one talked about it for more than half a century.

Hidden for all that time was what took place in a small Florida town during the first week of 1923, when a prosperous African American community of several hundred people was obliterated in an orgy of racism and violence. At least six blacks and two whites were killed, many more wounded, with the survivors of that burnt-out place fleeing into pine wood swamps, too traumatized to ever return home.

Directed by "Boyz N the Hood's" John Singleton, "Rosewood" is an impressive film that is significant both for bringing its story to a wide audience and also because, as Singleton has acknowledged, "no black man has had the opportunity before to direct a film like this in this context, and on so wide a canvas."

Yet despite its real virtues, the nagging feeling remains that "Rosewood" illustrates more than it illuminates. As written by Gregory Poirier and produced by Jon Peters, whose credits are mostly of the blockbuster variety, the film is broader and more simplistic than it needs to be, settling more than it should for obvious emotions and situations.

Anger, obviously, leaves little room for subtlety, and it was perhaps not possible for Singleton and company to be dispassionate in the face of their overpowering need to show and tell. And because its awful story is difficult to erase from the mind, "Rosewood" is finally stronger than the awkwardness and the flaws in its telling. It's just unfortunate there isn't less of that to overcome.

A quiet hamlet in western Florida, Rosewood is a place where large, close-knit African American families own their own land and businesses. But even though music teacher Sylvester Carrier (Don Cheadle of "Devil in a Blue Dress") is modern enough to risk standing up to white people in nearby Sumner, his mother Sarah (Esther Rolle) warns him that no matter what he might think, "times ain't never changed for crackers."

As determined as Sylvester to believe that things can be different is Mann (Ving Rhames), a Shane-like stranger who rides into town, catches the eye of winsome schoolteacher Scrappie (Elise Neal) and thinks about spending some of the money he earned as a soldier in World War I to bid on a piece of land and settle down. An actor of imposing presence, Rhames can be hard when he needs to be but also softens enough to make his courtship scenes with Scrappie warm and affecting.

Mann's rival in the land auction in Rosewood's only white resident, merchant John Wright (Jon Voight), pithily described as "half-way decent for a white person, if there was such a thing." The concern he has for his black customers doesn't stop Wright from exploiting them, and though Voight tries to bring life to this conflicted, ambivalent character, the well-meaning storekeeper estranged from a Bible-reading wife is too much of a stock character for his efforts to succeed.

Similarly, the part of Fannie Taylor (Catherine Kellner), though historically accurate, is overly familiar. The slutish wife of a sawmill worker, her patently false claim of being raped by a black man is the spark that starts the fire that alcohol, mob hysteria and racism turn into a monstrous conflagration.

If Fanny's character has a soap opera quality to it, the same is true for the town's unbridled racists, particularly the vicious, bearded Duke (Bruce McGill). Though these people undoubtedly existed, there is an obviousness and a lack of subtlety about the way they're depicted on screen that diminishes "Rosewood's" dramatic impact.

What has undeniable force are the sequences of torture and violence that make up the heart of the film. Singleton's direction, Johnny E. Jensen's cinematography and Bruce Cannon's editing convincingly capture the feeling of a nightmare time when as a survivor interviewed on a Discovery Channel documentary called "The Rosewood Massacre" starkly put it—"they killed everything that was black."

Even here, however "Rosewood" can't avoid overreaching, with shots of a drunken white mob intercut with a blacks child's birthday party. And the closer the film gets to the end, the more Hollywood it becomes, unable to resist a few show-b-biz plot twists that are closer to the spirit of Peters' "Money Train" than to the aspirations of the rest of the picture.

Still, incompletely realized though it is, "Rosewood's" story is as difficult to ignore as it is to completely embrace. Its message continues to be relevant, and its true-to-history emphasis on African Americans standing up for themselves, as well as its portrayal of interracial cooperation, are laudable. But understanding that this is a story that needs telling doesn't cancel the wish that it was a bit better told.

NEW YORK POST, 2/21/97, p. 46, Thelma Adams

On the surface, "Rosewood" is exactly the kind of serious movie that John Singleton should be directing. The first African-American director ever to be nominated for an Oscar ("Boyz N the Hood"), Singleton dramatizes a historical incident of rampant racism.

In 1923, a white mob razed the black town of Rosewood on Florida's Gulf Coast. What fueled them? A white woman's false claim that a black man beat her.

"Rosewood" is an honorable endeavor—it just isn't a good film. Working from a script by Gregory Poirier, which plays fast and loose with the facts, Singleton creates a world in which "The Waltons," played by African-Americans, meets "Deliverance."

"Rosewood" starts slowly with that patented golden glow that's supposed to reflect the past.

(Steven Spielberg used a silver glowy black and white in "Schindler's List," a movie that reportedly influenced Singleton. "Schindler" composer John Williams scored "Rosewood.")

As a trained historian, I hate to tell these guys: It didn't glow any more then than it does now—unless, of course, it's Chernobyl.

Singleton's Rosewood is the kind of town in which kids play ring-a-round-the-rosie, the town idiot balances himself innocently on the railroad tracks, and a horrible tragedy of epic proportions lurks right around the bend just behind the jolly steam engine.

Singleton introduces the white grocer (played as an aging buck caught in the headlights by Jon Voight) having sex with his black clerk in the store room. The town matriarch and midwife Sarah (the unflappable Esther Rolle) describes the grocer as "a halfway decent white man if there ever was that sort of thing."

In nearby white Sumner, evil white-trash daddy Duke (Bruce McGill) teaches his son life's basics: fishing, hunting and noose-making. When the town slut, the aptly named Fannie (Catherine Kellner), gets beaten senseless by her lover (a scene so graphic that we are treated to purple boot marks on her lily white back), she claims a black stranger battered her.

The townsfolk put together a lynching party as if it were the annual barbecue.

Meanwhile, Mr. Mann (Ving Rhames) rides into Rosewood on his trusty charger. The WWI vet romances the local maiden, Scrappie (Elise Neal), befriends her piano-playing cousin (Don Cheadle) and prepares to settle down.

But those damn "crackers" won't let him. As the prime suspect in Fannie's beating, Mann's gonna have to save the whole town before he gets his girl.

Hackneyed and ham-fisted, "Rosewood" wastes Rhames, Voight, Cheadle (Oscar-worthy in "Devil in a Blue Dress") and Rolle. Stymied by stock situations, the saintly blacks and the demon whites never exist in three dimensions.

Does the director expect a guilty white audience to take their punishment and like it? "Rosewood" is not a prestige film that escapes the cliches of the hood, but the work of an unimaginative filmmaker who learned everything he knows about humanity from watching other people's movies.

NEWSDAY, 2/21/97, Part II/p. B2, Jack Mathews

While everyone is taking notice of the dominance of independent films in this year's Academy Awards race, John Singleton's new picture, "Rosewood," helps explain why Hollywood is being left out of the biggest party of the year. This is a major studio movie made for $28 million that would have been better at half the price with half the ambition.

"Rosewood" is based on a true story, the razing of a small black community in rural 1923 Florida by a white mob incited by a white woman's claim that she'd been beaten by a black man. The number of blacks killed is unclear. Survivors of the Rosewood massacre have testified that they saw mass graves. But the record accounts for just eight deaths—of six blacks and two whites.

That's four more people than were killed in the gunfight at the O.K. Corral, and if Singleton had stuck just to the known facts, he'd have had a powerful drama on his hands. But the director of "Boyz N the Hood" wanted something far more epic in scale, something the size of a John Ford Western, and though he certainly got the big look he wanted, its exaggerated action and clichéd fictional heroism almost overwhelm the history.

You can see the Western influence in Mr. Mann (Ving Rhames), a survivor of both World War I and, from the scars on his neck, a lynching or two. He rides into Rosewood on a black horse, dressed in black, packing a gun, a big smile, and a hoarse whisper of a voice. He's John Wayne, or Clint Eastwood.

Mr. Mann sticks around long enough to fall in love with the young schoolmarm (Elise Neal), befriend her relatives, and to bid on five acres across from a store owned by John Wright, the town's only white man (Jon Voight). But when a married slut in nearby Sumner decides to blame the beating by her white boyfriend on an anonymous black man, Mr. Mann figures he's the obvious target and leaves.

Soon there is a mob of drunken white men marching toward Rosewood in a hang-'em-first, ask-questions-later rage, and the once-peaceful black community is turned into a smoldering holocaust. Blacks are hanged and shot, women and children are chased into the adjacent marshes, and their one defiant hero, the music teacher Sylvester Carrier (Donald Cheadle), is left to take on the mob by himself.

Eventually, Mr. Mann returns, on a trick horse that must have studied under Trigger, and joins the conscience-stricken John Wright to rescue the survivors. Rhames has a powerful presence, but Mr. Mann is such a tangle of movie-hero clichés that he's a distraction from the real-life horror of the story. Cheadle is much more effective as Carrier, whose rejection of the authority of his white trash neighbors represents the emerging self-reliance of southern blacks. Strong in other key roles are Esther Rolle, as Carrier's mother, and Michael Rooker, as the weak sheriff who can't control the mob.

Oddly, the best-written role went to Voight. His shopkeeper is a mixed-up widower who has remarried but can't keep his hands off the black teenager who works for him. He patronizes his black customers, exploiting them while taking credit for helping them, and when the storm comes, his first concern is for his store. But he has a basic decency that ultimately rises against the mob, and he follows the right instincts.

Much of "Rosewood" is very good and very powerful. But the further Singleton pushes the action—there are chases on horseback, in cars, and in trains—the further he gets from the story's human dimension. The film almost stops at the beginning of the riot, and transforms into a Western shoot-em-up, with so many people—white and black—being killed that they have no identities.

For a movie about the sanctity of life, that's a pretty big mistake.

TIME, 3/3/97, p. 83, Richard Schickel

More than 70 years ago, two tiny hamlets stood virtually side by side at the edge of the central Florida swamps. One of them, Sumner, was populated completely by whites. The other, Rosewood, more prosperous and civilized, was almost entirely black. During the first week of 1923, the citizens of the former community rose up against the latter, razing most of it, killing many of its residents and driving off the rest of them. In a matter of days, a ghost town was created.

Even in an era when lynchings were commonplace in the South, this genocidal frenzy was astonishing in its barbarism. Equally remarkable is the fact that it was banished from history for more than a half-century, until a newspaper reporter stumbled on the story in 1982. Since then there have been television and magazine accounts of this outrage, and now director John Singleton has made a film that is bound to arouse controversy over its approach to this tragedy.

For in shaping *Rosewood,* he and screenwriter Gregory Poirier have commingled the relatively few known facts of this matter with a lot of very obvious, very movieish fictions. Some of this was doubtless inevitable. Like the terrible end of the story, its ludicrous beginnings—a trampy white woman falsely accuses an anonymous black man of brutally assaulting her, thereby whipping up a mob spirit in Sumner—is known and powerfully shown. What is not available in the historical records is anything very specific about the people, victims and victimizers alike, who lived this story. Nor, apparently, does it offer a suitably heroic figure on whom to center audience attention or a suspenseful and emotionally releasing climax.

The moviemakers therefore create a character named Mann (Ving Rhames), who drifts into town on horseback just as the tragedy is beginning to unfold. In essence, he's the mysterious stranger of a thousand westerns, eager to avoid conflict but miraculously adept at the killing arts when he is finally obliged to employ them. Ultimately he and John Wright (Jon Voight), the white storekeeper in the town and a reality-based character, make common, inspiring cause to rescue Rosewood's surviving women and children from the swamp where they have taken refuge from the blood-crazed posse searching for them. There is some historical truth to this passage, but not to the well-staged, high-impact action sequence that brings the film to an end. In fact, the psychologically devastated survivors of the massacre embraced silence and anonymity until the few still remaining began talking to investigators in the early 80s.

Ordinarily such trespasses against truth would be enough to condemn such a movie, but Rhames' gravity and grace, Voight's pinched anguish as he wills himself to do right, the moving work of actors like Don Cheadle and Esther Rolle do much to redeem this film for human if not historical reality. *Rosewood* finds, in a shameful bygone moment, sources of pride for contemporary audiences. There are worse things to do with the past.

VILLAGE VOICE, 3/4/97, p. 76, Gary Dauphin

If John Singleton's latest movie looks unblinkingly (and remarkably fairly) at a long-hidden racial atrocity, it's not so much because of the film's politics as its choice of genre. *Rosewood* is the young black director's best work to date, an effective and often courageous example of what movies can do with the black past, but it's also pure Hollywood—a broadly earnest period piece cut from the familiar dusty bedrock of the western.

Since the story was rediscovered by the Florida media a few years ago, the facts behind the film have been fairly well documented: In 1923, a married white woman is beaten by her white lover, and accuses an unknown black male of the deed to hide her infidelity. By week's end the entire town of Rosewood, Florida, had been burned to the ground, with over 150 black men, women, and children murdered and buried in unmarked graves. *Rosewood* sticks to the facts quite closely, but draws on the testimony of a core group of survivors to turn the depressingly familiar tale of Southern lynch mobs into a big-screen ode to black (and white) heroism. The immediate spark that sets mobs of swamp crackers rampaging through Rosewood's streets is a shooting, an act of self-defense wherein a music teacher named Sylvester Carrier (played with typical little-man intensity by Don Cheadle) opens fire on a mob intent on lynching him. (One of the good old boys drawls, by way of explanation, "That nigra's got a piano up in there.")

While Carrier stands in front of the homestead, understandably defending kith and kin, it falls to Mann (Ving Rhames) to explain to audiences why those outside the circle of black family should care about what happened. A fictional avatar of those who came to Rosewood in search of a better life, Mann arrives just before the purported assault, a WWI vet and drifter who in the wise words of Sylvester's mother "might find Rosewood a place to settle." Things are indeed relatively good for black folk. A town of prosperity, home ownership, and family feeling, it's an idyll offered to Mann (right down to a young, pretty future wife) and then wrenched quickly away. No surprise, then, that he'd take up a gun to save what's left of it after the initial assault. It's telling that the fictional black male stand-in kills the most whites and also suffers the most contemporary loss, namely his belief in the possibility of black communities that are more than depressed, violent hells.

Singleton and *Rosewood* will be praised (and deservedly so) for the way they handle the white people in this story. Whites in Rosewood are either unmitigated racists or men who, after some mighty wrestling with their own best interests, offer succor to their black neighbors. Of the latter there are but a handful: Johnny Wright (a nervous Jon Voight), who owns the local store and likes to screw his black salesgirl; the town sheriff (a hoarse Michael Rooker), who loses control of the situation before it begins; and the kindly conductor of the local freight train, who figures prominently in the film's climax. (With momentary exception, the white women are mostly neurotics, simpletons, and saintly Bible-thumpers.) Despite their hemming and hawing over the obvious, the white male characters exhibit courage and complexity that allow even the most racially uncomfortable white folks a safe entrée into this film, no small matter if *Rosewood* is to survive at the box office. Part of me thinks it's unfortunate that so much attention has to be paid to the roles of "good" whites in order to make a story like *Rosewood,* but that's Hollywood.

Also reviewed in:
NEW YORK TIMES, 2/21/97, p. C18, Janet Maslin
VARIETY, 2/17-23/97, p. 68, Todd McCarthy
WASHINGTON POST, 2/21/97, p. B1, David Nicholson
WASHINGTON POST, 2/21/97, Weekend/p. 43, Desson Howe

ROUGH MAGIC

A Rysher Entertainment and Goldwyn Entertainment Company release of an UGC Images and Recorded Picture Company presentation in association with Martin Scorsese. *Executive Producer:* Yves Attal, Jonathan Taplin, and Andrew Karsch. *Producer:* Laurie Parker and Declan Baldwin. *Director:* Clare Peploe. *Screenplay:* Robert Mundy, William Brookfield, and Clare Peploe. *Based on the novel "Miss Shumway Waves A Wand" by:* James Hadley Chase. *Director of*

Photography: John J. Campbell. *Editor:* Suzanne Fenn. *Music:* Richard Hartley. *Sound:* Mark Ulano and Salvador De La Fuente. *Sound Editor:* Eddie Joseph. *Casting:* Elisabeth Leustig. *Production Designer:* Waldemar Kalinowski. *Art Director:* Barry M. Kingston and Brigitte Broch. *Set Decorator:* Florence Fellman and Andre Krassoievitch. *Set Dresser:* Grant Sawyer, Michael Broaddus, Kevin Coyle, Stephen O. Pfauter, Aaron Stearnlicht, and Antonio Munohierro. *Special Effects:* Andre Ellingson and Laurencio Cordero. *Costumes:* Richard Hornung. *Make-up:* Kate Shorter. *Stunt Coordinator:* Phil Neilson. *Running time:* 104 minutes. *MPAA Rating:* PG-13.

CAST: Bridget Fonda (Myra Shumway); Russell Crowe (Alex Ross); Jim Broadbent (Doc Ansell); D.W. Moffett (Cliff Wyatt); Kenneth Mars (Magician); Paul Rodriguez (Diego); Andy Romano (Clayton); Richard Schiff (Wiggins); Euva Anderson (Diego's wife/Tojola); Michael Ensign (Powerbroker); Gabriel Pingarron (Telegraph Man); Santos Morales and Rene Pereyra (Policemen); Gregory Avellone (Burly Usher); Mark Del Castillo (Clayton's Assistant); Chris Otto (Mechanic); Jose Escandon (Waiter); Ana Cristina Vasquez (Maid).

LOS ANGELES TIMES, 5/30/97, Calendar/p. 4, John Anderson

[The following review by John Anderson appeared in a slightly different form in NEWSDAY, 5/30/97, Part II/p. B9.]

Like a car constructed out of scavenged parts, "Rough Magic" sputters, coughs, wheezes, lurches, spins out of control and runs smack into the springtime of our discontent. Of course, it's a miracle it moves at all.

Starring the inscrutable Bridget Fonda and the very talented but consistently misused Russell Crowe, "Rough Magic" has a '50s setting (we see Nixon deliver the Checkers speech), a '40s wardrobe (Fonda tries to out-Bacall Bacall), a '60s sense of the absurd and, of course, a strictly '90s sense of narrative poverty.

While the cast is likable—it includes Kenneth Mars and Jim Broadbent, who occupy a similar status on their respective sides of the Atlantic—the story is an irritatingly obtuse attempt to make bedfellows of magic, Mexican spiritualism, film noir and the Atomic Energy Commission. It's hard to say whether director Clare Peploe actually intended to make "Rough Magic" such an unnatural act, but what she has delivered is a *ménage á trois* of Don Siegel, Carlos Castañeda and Captain Kangaroo.

But let's get to the meat of this ham sandwich: Myra Shumway (Fonda) is the gifted understudy to a mysterious magician (Mars), who doesn't want her to marry the oily, mustachioed, uranium-wealthy Senate candidate Cliff Wyatt (D.W. Moffett). During a decidedly arch interlude in their dressing room, Cliff shoots the magician from the confines of a guillotine while Myra takes a photo and then splits for Mexico while Cliff puts the seedy ex-reporter Alex Ross (Crowe) on her trail.

Together, Myra and Alex head south, where Doc Ansell (Broadbent) is trying to get the recipe for a secret elixir out of a Mayan shaman (Euva Anderson) who would like to turn him into a toad. They all hook up, Myra and Alex bond, a nasty guy named Diego (the unforgivable Paul Rodriguez) gives them a dose of pre-NAFTA diplomacy, Myra communes with the white witches of the Mexican outback and Cliff turns out to be a homosexual.

"Magic, my dear, comes from the heart, not the head," says the worldly old magician—and while death, resurrection and cohabiting rabbits finish up "Rough Magic," you'll be holding your head, wondering just when hip became hell and overripe became over-the-top and why, if Peploe really had been thinking, she didn't toss in a few dinosaurs.

NEW YORK POST, 5/30/97, p. 52, Michael Medved

"Rough Magic" displays plenty of rough spots but very little magic in a wildly uneven (but undeniably energetic) attempt to blend *film noir,* romantic comedy and Latin America magic realism.

Bridget Fonda plays a plucky magician's assistant (in 1952 Los Angeles) who has been chosen as a suitable bride by a politically ambitious uranium millionaire (D.W. Moffett).

After the final performance of her nightclub act, a backstage mishap involving her shabby but mystical mentor, (Kenneth Mars) threatens to destroy the electoral ambitions of her all-powerful intended.

She runs off to Mexico with incriminating film of the incident, while her fiance hires a cynical American reporter (Russell Crowe) to track her down. He falls hard for Fonda without telling her he's been paid to keep her under surveillance.

Meanwhile, a rubber-faced English quack (Jim Broadbent) hawking "miracle elixir" to Mexican peasants helps guide Fonda to a Mayan pyramid to connect with the legendary shaman (Euva Anderson) she's been taught to revere.

After her initiation into ancient mysteries, Fonda displays odd, unpredictable magic powers that go far beyond her old mastery of sleight of hand.

These funky forces even help her with vicious, vengeful Paul Rodriguez, a gas station proprietor and bandito in the "I-don't-need-no-stinkin-badges" "Sierra Madre" tradition.

Rodriguez won't win any "image awards" from Chicano organizations for his outrageously stereotypical performance, but he does make the part simultaneously hilarious and terrifying.

The other performers are similarly impressive, including Russell Crowe in his engaging Robert Mitchum turn.

Fonda also handles the ridiculous demands of her role with uncanny aplomb, mixing vulnerability with Golden Girl glamour.

The problem is that all the actors are ultimately undone by the uncertain tone and peculiar pacing of director/co-writer Clare Peploe, whose previous features include the little-seen "High Season" and "Sauce for Goose."

Though the first half of the film emphasizes haunting Mexican (and Guatemalan) locations handled with occasionally overwrought mysticism and solemnity, the movie concludes with rude, crude comedy.

It's easy to admire the disconnected elements of this mix, but the nearly incoherent handling leaves the whole bewildering business several enchiladas short of a combination plate.

VILLAGE VOICE, 6/3/97, p. 74, Amy Taubin

Set in post-World War II California and Mexico, Clare Peploe's *Rough Magic* combines film noir with magic realism. The result is as tedious as it is incoherent. As a magician's assistant who discovers that she has real powers of transformation (enough to turn a person into a sausage), Bridget Fonda maintains her poise. Shelved for a year after its completion, *Rough Magic* should have just disappeared.

Also reviewed in:
NEW YORK TIMES, 5/30/97, p. C12, Stephen Holden
NEW YORKER, 6/2/97, p. 92, Terrence Rafferty
VARIETY, 9/11-17/95, p. 108, David Stratton

RUDYARD KIPLING'S THE SECOND JUNGLE BOOK MOWGLI AND BALOO

A TriStar Pictures release of an MDP Worldwide and Sharad Patel presentation of a Kiplinbook/Rajel Patel production. *Executive Producer:* Sharad Patel and Mark Damon. *Producer:* Raju Patel. *Director:* Duncan McLachlan. *Screenplay:* Bayard Johnson and Matthew Horton. *Based on the classic tale by:* Rudyard Kipling. *Director of Photography:* Adolfo Bartoli. *Editor:* Marcus Manton. *Music:* John Scott. *Casting:* Don Pemrick and Dean Fronk. *Production Designer:* Errol Kelly. *Art Director:* Paul Takis and Sunil Wijeratne. *Costumes:* Ann Hollowood. *Make-up:* Mustaque Ashrafi. *Mechanical Effects:* Robert E. McCarthy. *Stunt Coordinator:* Solly Marx. *Running time:* 88 minutes. *MPAA Rating:* PG.

CAST: Jamie Williams (Mowgli); Bill Campbell (Harrison); Roddy McDowall (King Murphy); David Paul Francis (Chuchundra); Gulshan Grover (Buldeo); Cornelia Hayes O'Herlihy (Emily Reece); B.J. Hogg (Col. Reece); Amy Robbins (Molly Ward); Hal Fowler (Capt. Ward); Albert Moses (Conductor); Wijeratne Warakagoda (Engineer); Simon Barker (Train Official); E.A. Piyasena (Porter); Raja Sumanapala (Buldeo's Servant); Sunil Hettiarachchi (Rickshaw Man).

LOS ANGELES TIMES, 5/16/97, Calendar/p. 8, John Anderson

[The following review by John Anderson appeared in a slightly different form in **NEWSDAY, 5/16/97, Part II/p. B9.**]

Disney's live-action "Jungle Book" of 1994 had lofty production values, a taut script, a fine supporting cast and, most of all, Jason Scott Lee, who was as cunningly convincing a loincloth-clad hero as anyone was likely to cast.

Now we get the non-Disney "Rudyard Kipling's The Second Jungle Book: Mowgli and Baloo"—Mowgli being the jungle boy, Baloo being the bear—which is a mouthful, and more words are about all it adds to this particular *oeuvre.* The film does boast a charismatic lead actor—11-year-old Jamie Williams, who is wonderfully expressive as the young Mowgli. But the film looks undernourished—as do many of the animals—and you're a bit distracted from the story worrying whether everyone is getting enough to eat.

Set in 1890s India, it's full of primeval landscapes and jungle beasts—Baloo, Mowgli's good friend; Grey Wolf, leader of the pack that has raised the boy from infanthood; and Bagheera, the black panther—although a lot of it looks as if it were shot through an old Viewmaster.

Director Duncan McLachlan gives us twitty Raj-era Brits and daffy Indians, and one American—Harrison (Bill Campbell), a talent scout for P.T. Barnum, who wants to capture the boy and bring him back to New York. Harrison will, of course, come to his moral senses, especially after Mowgli is put in peril by his Uncle Buldeo (Gulshan Grover), who has inherited Mowgli's late father's estate and doesn't want any 11-year-olds asserting their rights to the property.

A reasonable amount of "The Second Jungle Book" is energetic and occasionally fun; Roddy McDowall makes an appearance as a mad old soldier and lifts the film out of its doldrums. The chimpanzees are antic, but the less controllable animals—the wolves, the panther—are shot in ways that clearly called for as little control and as little film as possible. That these failings are so noticeable doesn't do much for the old suspension of disbelief, and combined with the insipid narration and predictable slo-mo animals sequences, it makes the script seem even more lame.

"I'll be a monkey's uncle," Harrison says during a particularly momentous scene, "the animals are cooperating with each other..." Well, if he were, they'd have to be. But the fact that I'm searching so strenuously for jokes is an indication of how tough things can be in the jungle.

NEW YORK POST, 5/16/97, p. 43, Larry Worth

In Walt Disney's classic animated version of "The Jungle Book," Mowgli the man-cub and Baloo the bear sang about "The Bare Necessities."

But those necessities apparently didn't get a second thought from the producers of "The Second Jungle Book: Mowgli and Baloo," TriStar's prequel to Disney's dismal '94 live-action retelling.

The script supposedly is based on Rudyard Kipling's literary children's favorite, but the only discernible similarities involve the characters' names. Yes, Mowgli's back (this time at age 10, rather than a teen approaching manhood), along with fleeting appearances from Baloo, Bagheera the panther, Kaa the python and Shere Khan the tiger.

It's the quartet of new characters—an Indiana Jones-like talent scout for P.T. Barnum, Mowgli's murderous uncle, a local thief and a tracker who looks more serpentine than his pet snake—that proves problematic. Each is searching for Mowgli within India's dense undergrowth—and up to no good.

Ditto for director Duncan McLachlan. The neophyte storyteller has no feel for comedy or adventure, making for some painfully unfunny attempts at humor, and some hilariously bad drama.

The latter erupts early on, as the narrator states that Mowgli is being chased by two giant monkeys. But it's hard to feel any suspense when the relentless pursuers are no bigger than Tarzan's Cheetah.

For the most part, the plot boils down to a three-part formula: boy captured, boy escapes, cut to stupid animal trick (monkey smokes, monkey bicycles, monkey overacts). And repeat.

The dialogue is equally painful, evidenced by gems like, "In the jungle, the hunter can become the hunted." Or, "The animals want to save him from those mysterious apes called man." Or, best of all, "I'll be a monkey's uncle."

Faint praise goes to those who can repeat such drivel with a straight face: Jamie Williams' wild child, Bill Campbell's tired-looking adventurer and Roddy McDowall as a mad "Man Who Would Be King" leftover.

And while the scenery of Sri Lanka is undeniably lovely, matte backdrops of a legendary monkey city (where the last "Jungle Book" also concluded) look pretty hokey in this age of sophisticated special effects.

Collectively, "The Second Jungle Book" is enough to send Baloo—never mind moviegoers—into permanent hibernation.

Also reviewed in:
NEW YORK TIMES, 5/16/97, p. C12, Lawrence Van Gelder
VARIETY, 5/12-18/97, p. 64, Leonard Klady

SAINT, THE

A Paramount Pictures release in association with Rysher Entertainment of a David Brown and Robert Evans production. *Executive Producer:* Paul Hitchcock and Robert S. Baker. *Producer:* David Brown, Robert Evans, William J. MacDonald, and Mace Neufeld. *Director:* Phillip Noyce. *Screenplay:* Jonathan Hensleigh and Wesley Strick. *Story:* Jonathan Hensleigh. *Based on the character created by:* Leslie Charteris. *Director of Photography:* Phil Meheux. *Editor:* Terry Rawlings and Tim Grover. *Music:* Graeme Revell. *Music Editor:* Joe E. Rand. *Sound:* Ivan Sharrock and (music) Chris Dibble. *Sound Editor:* Jim Shields. *Casting:* Patsy Pollock and Elisabeth Leustig. *Production Designer:* Joseph Nemec, III. *Art Director:* Alan Cassie, Leslie W. Tomkins, Lucy Richardson, and Nick Palmer. *Set Decorator:* Peter Young. *Special Effects:* George Gibbs. *Visual Effects:* Robert Grasmere. *Costumes:* Marlene Stewart. *Make-up:* Paul Engelen. *Stunt Coordinator:* R.A. Rondell. *Running time:* 115 minutes. *MPAA Rating:* PG-13.

CAST: Val Kilmer (Simon Templar); Elisabeth Shue (Dr. Emma Russell); Rade Serbedzija (Ivan Tretiak); Valery Nikolaev (Ilya Tretiak); Henry Goodman (Dr. Lev Botvin); Alun Armstrong (Chief Inspector Teal); Michael Byrne (Tretiak's Aide, Vereshagin); Evengy Lazarev (President Karpov); Irina Apeximova (Frankie); Lev Prigunov (General Sklarov); Charlotte Cornwell (Inspector Rabineau); Emily Mortimer (Woman on Plane); Lucija Serbedzija (Russian Prostitute); Velibor Topic (Skinhead); Tommy Flanagan (Scarface); Yegor Pozenko (Scratchface); Adam Smith (Young Simon Templar); Pat Laffan (Catholic Priest); Verity Dearsley (Agnes); Michael Marquez (Boy in Orphanage); Lorelei King (TV Reporter); Alla A. Kazanskaya (Old Russian Lady); Ronnie Letham (Old Russian Man); Tusse Silberg (Prostitute's Mother); Peter Guinness (Frankie's Curator); Stefan Gryff (President's Aide); Malcolm Tierney (Russian Doctor); Stephen Tiller (Russian Policeman); Christopher Rozycki (Russian Chief of Police); Etela Pardo (President Karpov's Wife); Nikolai Veselov (Red Square Tramp); David Schneider (Rat Club Comedian); Oxana Popkova (Ilya's Girlfriend); Agnieszka Liggett (Rat Club Party Girl); Lydia Zovkic (Rat Club Beauty); Alexander Tutin (Russian Colonel); Vadim Stepashkin (Russian Soldier); Ravil Isyanov (Tretiak Guard); Alexander Kadanyov (Tretiak's Security Guard); Petar Vidovic (Tretiak's Builder); Susan Porrett (Orphanage Nun); Cliff Parisi (Pub Waiter); Richard Cubison and Tony Armatrading (Customs Officers); Benjamin Whitrow (Chairman at Oxford); Julian Rhind-Tutt (Young Student); Kate

Isitt (Second Student); Barbara Jefford (Academic Woman); Sean O'Kane (Running Student); Lucy Akhurst (Policewoman); Nigel Clauzel (Marine Guard); Eric Loren (Embassy Official); William Hope (State Department Official); Michael Cochrane (Cold Fusion Broker); Ginny Holder (Jamaican Video Girlfriend); Akiko (Japanese Video Girlfriend); Melissa Knatchbull (English Video Girlfriend); Caroline Lee Johnson (Private Hotel Receptionist); Roger Moore (Voice on Car Radio).

LOS ANGELES TIMES, 4/4/97, Calendar/p. 1, Kenneth

What's the Saint doing in "The Saint"?

Directed by Phillip Noyce, best known for "Patriot Games" and, "Clear and Present Danger," both Tom Clancy adaptations, "The Saint" is meant to be that kind of James Bond/Batman franchise picture, a large-scale action adventure with running and chasing and things blowing up all over town.

But as played by Val Kilmer, the Saint is one weirded-out dude, such a cold and manipulative game player that by the time he says, "My life is very strange, I don't do anything normal," it comes off as too modest a statement.

It's an odd characterization, which Kilmer takes to almost too readily. And the Saint's tortured, duplicitous soul, his eagerness to disguise his real self, belongs to quite a different film than the boy's adventure Noyce and screenwriters Jonathan Hensleigh and Wesley Strick have put up on screen.

Simon Templar, a.k.a. the Saint, a reformed professional thief with a taste for the high life and a weakness for doing good deeds, was created by Leslie Charteris in 1928 and subsequently featured in more than 50 novels and the very different Roger Moore-starring TV series. But the circumstances of his change of heart are nowhere noted, and that's the lingering question "The Saint" has been constructed to answer.

It all started, a brief prelude announces, in "the Far East yesterday," at an orphanage where a young Simon Templar demonstrates a facility for sleight of hand and a stubborn refusal to acknowledge his identity.

An accident at the orphanage further darkens his character, and by the time Kilmer takes over the role, Templar has become a calculated and cynical rogue who hires himself out to the highest bidder in the hopes of amassing the $50 million in fees he feels he needs to retire.

And does this guy ever love disguises. Though audiences may be forgiven for losing count, Kilmer is officially credited with playing more than a dozen characters, including a stern Russian bodyguard, a gawky, bucktoothed journalist and a longhaired, leather pants-wearing poet.

Those who remember how tenaciously the actor embraced a Southern accent as Doc Holliday in "Tombstone" won't be surprised at the relish with which he approaches this aspect of his character. Gradually, however, this fetish for false chins and elaborate wigs becomes as unnerving as it is entertaining, a kind of indulgent, actorish game-playing that is always threatening to throw the rest of the proceedings off balance.

A film like this is incomplete without a villain, and for "The Saint" the evil-doer is Ivan Tretiak ("Before the Rain's" Rade Serbedzija), a billionaire oil. magnate and Slavic nationalist by day and the decadent head of the Russian mafia in whatever time he has left over from plotting world domination.

Templar comes to the attention of Tretiak and his equally noxious son Ilya (Valery Nikolaev) when he successfully burglarizes their headquarters. Respecting professionalism wherever he finds it, Tretiak Sr. promptly hires Templar to go to England and steal the secret to a successful experiment with cold fusion from the scientist who made the breakthrough.

That would be the winsome Dr. Emma Russell (Elisabeth Shue), a particularly girlish and vulnerable genius who Templar decides is susceptible to a poetic seduction. Soon enough an elaborate trap is set and the inevitably bizarre disguise is created to go with it.

But if Templar gets more disoriented than he planned when he tangles with the naive and spirited doctor, audiences will share his confusion. For the future, the Saint is such an unpleasant and predatory manipulator, it's difficult to root for romance. And when Kilmer's mightily convincing Ice King begins to melt, it's so out of character with what's gone before that its believability is touch and go.

Aside from the Saint's character, the rest of "The Saint" is pretty much as it should be for a film like this, with director Noyce and company investing the usual bravura set pieces with a showy sense of pace and the two screenwriters contributing some clever moments. But whereas something like "Clear and Present Danger" was briskly all of a piece, "The Saint" has difficulty making us believe that its diverse elements belong in the same motion picture.

It's also interesting to note that, as reported by the trade press, pressure was exerted on the filmmakers to change the original ending to a more upbeat one than planned. Seeing how uneasily Kilmer's malevolent characterization fits the current film, it's difficult not to wonder about the quality of the presumably darker "Saint" that got left behind.

NEW YORK, 4/21/97, p. 52, David Denby

The Saint is what big-studio Hollywood desperately wants to make and what it entirely deserves to fail with. Director Phillip Noyce, who should know better, has given himself over to an obvious attempt to revisit the 007 genre, with Val Kilmer in the would-be franchise role of a charming but "cold" orphan who has become an inscrutable master thief and seducer (George Sanders in movies and Roger Moore on TV did the role in the past). Produced on a monstrous scale, *The Saint* is mainly an endless chase with some striking use of Moscow backgrounds and some nastily energetic Russian and Eastern European actors. Elisabeth Shue is wasted in an unplayable role as a "brilliant" but humanly inept scientist, and there isn't a ghost of a point anywhere. The movie is ostensibly about cold fusion and the future of Russia, but it's all weightless nonsense, made with speed but no discernible style. In the past, Noyce, the director of *Clear and Present Danger,* had seemed a master of the Hollywood machine, but this time he gets steamrolled by it.

NEW YORK POST, 4/4/97, p. 39, Thelma Adams

There's such a thing as karma. Badboy Val Kilmer finds the ideal role in "The Saint"—and the movie crumbles around him.

Kilmer shrewdly hung up his Batman cape; the character has become the black hole at the center of the franchise. Hollywood's Caped Crusader is a study in comic-book co-dependency: He must play straight man for every wacky villain while shouldering angst.

Kilmer's Simon Templar is an action hero tailor-made to the star's mercurial talents. A tortured Catholic with a love for magic and miracles and enough guilt to last two lifetimes, Templar has grown into an international thief.

Templar's physical agility is matched by his swift wit and mastery of disguises. Kilmer's Saint is seductive not because he has James Bond's unshakable confidence but because there's a lost little schoolboy trapped beneath all that chest hair.

Kilmer distances himself from the smoothie played on TV's "The Saint" by Bond alum Roger Moore; the 90s Templar is a hero both shaken and stirred.

"The Saint" starts strong, directed with a sure hand and a high sense of adventure by A-list actioner Phillip Noyce. The helmer of "A Clear and Present Danger" is so nimble and Kilmer so diverting that an hour passes before Wesley Strick and Jonathan Hensleigh's sludgy script slows down the whole effort.

Templar, going for the inevitable last score (also known as the screenwriters' last gasp), gets involved in stealing a scientific formula for a Russian oil magnate (Rade Serbedzija). Templar's mark is American-born, Oxford-based genius Dr. Emma Russell (Elisabeth Shue in a feat of miscasting reminiscent of Melanie Griffith in "Shining Through").

Shue, the hapless hooker in "Leaving Las Vegas," is just no nuclear physicist, no mother of cold fusion. Costumer Marlene Stewart's idea of dressing the blonde with the dentist's daughter's smile in dirty lab coats and black knee-top stockings doesn't make Shue look any more like Einstein.

Noyce is bolder at action than romance (his Tom Clancy movie adaptations spring to life when the wife is out of the picture). He ineptly shoots Shue in nursery white lingerie and saggy anklets while shyly ignoring his main man. Kilmer makes a sinfully sexy "Saint' but, because the movie doesn't keep pace with his inventive performance, the actor may not come marching in for a well-deserved sequel.

NEWSDAY, 4/4/97, Part II/p. B2, Gene Seymour

More than any actor before him (yes, including even Roger Moore), Val Kilmer was born to play "The Saint." It's difficult to imagine anyone else among his generation of actors who's better equipped to convey Simon Templar's ambiguous heroism and ramrod cunning.

As the globe-trotting Robin Hood, Kilmer gets to wear different costumes and funny wigs, talk in exotic accents and indulge in the kind of flamboyant shtick that's made him a cult figure and an almost-big star. He has just enough fun with the role to make you think there's some life left in Leslie Charteris' venerable franchise.

But the movie lets both Kilmer and Charteris' creation down with a thud.

Set a couple of years into the future (meaning the very brink of That Scary Millennium), director Phillip Noyce's update of "The Saint" imagines a Russia that is itself on the brink of an apocalyptic retreat from democracy.

A ruthless billionaire (Rade Serbedzija) is a referendum away from being annointed czar of a new Russian empire, and he believes that possessing the secret to cold fusion could allow him to—dare we say it?—*rule the world!*

The problem is that this valuable secret rests solely in the demure, reclusive head of Emma Russell (Elisabeth Shue), an American physicist based at Oxford.

Enter Templar, a master thief recruited by the aspiring czar to obtain the formula by hook or crook. Naturally, he does it both ways, peeking into Russell's private notebooks and using such intimate knowledge to accidentally-on-purpose approach her disguised as her ideal date.

He gets the goods, but he feels like a heel. She, in turn, tracks him down to Russia and unwittingly walks into the hands of her pursuers. An elaborate chase ensues through the sewers, basements and cramped high-rise housing projects of contemporary Moscow, with Templar and Russell struggling to evade the billionaire's leather-clad goons.

At some point, you may be struggling to evade a migraine from all the claustrophobic shuffling around.

Noyce has a well-deserved reputation as an ace screen adapter of such Tom Clancy spy novels as "Patriot Games" and "Clear and Present Danger."

But though he was able to cut through the suffocating narrative density of those books, Noyce seems intent on making this version of "The Saint" seem as ponderous as, well, a Clancy novel.

The patchwork plotting is made even worse by excessive handwringing over whether Templar is basically "sinner" or "saint."

As if!

With Moore's TV "Saint," one just took it for granted that Templar was a little bit of both, and he wore his duplicity as effortlessly as he wore one of his expensive suits. And though the old TV series (to which the filmmakers make a couple of gratuitous references) may have run into some sticky melodramatic patches here and there" I remember there being more charm, more *fun* in those stories than can be found here.

Kilmer, as noted, gamely holds onto his own charm through the film's drearier stretches. (Shue fares less well in a thankless role.)

As for fun, that doesn't really happen until the very end, when Kilmer's Templar deftly eludes Scotland Yard en route, presumably, to another adventure.

If so, let's hope for his sake that he'll get a chance to lighten up a little.

SIGHT AND SOUND, 5/97, p. 52, José Arroyo

A Catholic orphanage in late 70s Britain. A small boy refuses to utter the name he's been given, even after a caning. All the girls are sent away and the boys deprived of food. The boy picks the lock of the caged-in food and goes to free his girlfriend, announcing that his name is now Simon Templar. While helping the girl to climb over fencing, the boy rouses the presiding monk, who sets his guard dog loose. The dog pushes the girl over the balcony to her death.

The present. Simon is the Saint, a gentleman thief and master of disguises. Close to his retirement target of $50 million profit, he accepts a contract to steal a microchip in Moscow. While oil magnate and would-be dictator Ivan Tretiak is making a speech, the Saint infiltrates his building and cracks the safe. Discovered by Ivan's coke-addict son, Ilya, he escapes after a fight and gets his contraband through customs. An impressed Tretiak then hires him to steal a formula for a new energy process called cold fusion, newly developed by scientist Emma Russell, an American working at Oxford.

The Saint breaks into Emma's apartment to discover all he needs to seduce her. Posing as an eccentric poet, Thomas More, he steals the formula, but he also falls in love with Emma. He nonetheless turns over the formula to Tretiak because Emma's life will be endangered if he doesn't. Emma goes to the police, discovers that the thief's aliases always involve saints' names and tracks him down to Moscow. She turns him over to the Russian police only to be arrested as well. They escape but realise Tretiak has a plot to take over the government. In order to prevent this, Emma has to complete the cold fusion formula so that it works. She does so, the Saint brings it to a Russian scientist and they thus foil Tretiak's plot to embarrass the incumbent president. Simon and Emma are eventually reunited in England.

As a film, *The Saint* can at least count on our fondness for the old television series. Unbelievable and rather tacky, the show is nevertheless likeable. The moment at the beginning of each episode when Roger Moore looks above his head at his halo and then raises an eyebrow at the audience is a promise of charming naughtiness and small-screen glamour. A more extensive version of the show—with designer clothes and cars, glitzy locations and a light touch—would have been enough to turn the material into a valuable film franchise. Instead, the film-makers condescendingly try to upgrade the material by adding 'depth' to it. Director Phillip Noyce *(Sliver, Clear and Present Danger)* has said that he wanted to tell the story of how a sinner becomes a saint, [of] one man's struggle for redemption." Then why make a film about glamorous thieves, sexy scientists, and cartoon villains? What has been enjoyed by generations obviously wasn't good enough for the film-makers, and this forfeits the immense audience goodwill.

The Saint is a series of errors in judgement from the start. The film shows us how a young 'bastard' orphan became The Saint, an element of Simon Templar's psychological history previously, and perhaps wisely, ignored by Leslie Charteris, author of the novels, the television series and the various early film adaptations. In the first few minutes of the film, chiaroscuro lighting, skewed angles and distorting lenses are used to show an upmarket précis of *Oliver Twist*, with orphans being denied food, physically abused and being chased by guard dogs until one of them falls to a brutal death. Unfortunately, it takes more skill than Phillip Noyce has at his disposal to begin a sophisticated caper comedy like a Gothic melodrama.

The film could have recovered if Val Kilmer's performance wasn't so misguided. George Sanders and Roger Moore each made a success of the part because they could be suave, throwing away lines with utter nonchalance and appearing unruffled after every fist-fight. In that charmingly implausible tradition, Elisabeth Shue (last seen in *Leaving Las Vegas)* plays her scientist as if she were attending a chemistry class in *Clueless*. She wears knee-stockings and mini-skirts and recites her scientific jargon as if hyping the latest make-up range from Revlon. And she comes off best. Kilmer, however, has decided to Act with a capital A. The film seems designed to show us how well he can do nerdy scientist, gay German, butch Russian Commissar and sensitive poet (the last turn laughably bad). He throws himself with vigorous intensity into each impersonation as if it were a Method exercise, and for the most part he succeeds. But none of his turns evoke the wit and elegance formerly associated with *The Saint*.

It is ironic that this version tries so hard to improve, supposedly, its source material only to come across as a cut-rate *Mission Impossible*. Like the latter, the hero here uses fancy gadgets and physical prowess to steal from seemingly impenetrable places, his quest taking him to various exotic locations where he comes into contact with glamorous women. *Mission Impossible,* however, delivers the requisite action and suspense. *The Saint* tries so hard to be something better that it ends up being something much worse. It's like throwing béarnaise sauce on Rice Krispies: no meat: no snap, crackle or pop—and entirely indigestible.

VILLAGE VOICE, 4/8/97, p. 88, Gary Dauphin

· It's hard to imagine exactly what possessed Val Kilmer to abandon a sure gig like Batman for the big-screen version of *The Saint*. Kilmer his a rep for being a little on the difficult side, but after sitting through *The Saint*'s barely warm reheat of current spy-tech clichés—from missing cold-fusion secrets to apocalyptic Russian ultranationalists—he seems a little crazy too, pinning franchise hopes on a dim rerun memory like series hero Simon Templar. Not exactly the work of an actor fully in command of his wits. Some will say he was pushed.

The Saint opens in a strange place for all attempted techno-espionage coolfest—the childhood trauma school of action heroism. Much the way Batman obsesses over his dead parents, Simon Templar has a thing about his name. An on orphan initially named by some priests after Saint John, he takes "Simon Templar" after reading up on gnostic magician Simon Magus and the Knights Templar; it's the very stuff of Catholic schoolboy fantasy, if the movie's to be believed. Fast-forward from there to Moscow, where an all-grown Templar is in the process of robbing the aforementioned Russian ultra-nationalist of a computer chip (it disappears into *The Saint's* murky plot soon after making a hotly contested appearance). The Russians are taken with Simon's ballsy approach to international crime and hire him to steal the cold-fusion theory of babe physicist Emma Russell (Elisabeth Shue, who is quite fetching but not very believable). Emma and Simon fall for each other, and it isn't long before the pair are dodging the Russian army and various law enforcement agencies, trying to save the world and Russian democracy between moony looks.

The original Roger Moore series was a low-key breath of '60s international cool, nestled between the mod extravagances of *The Avengers* and the arcane technophilia of *Mission: Impossible* (my mother remembers it as "quiet, like *Columbo* with spies"). This *Saint* gets part of that formula right. Kilmer never draws a gun, for instance, and favors quick wits and disguises over hacking and fisticuffs. Unfortunately, though, director Phillip Noyce has created more of a rip-off than an ode, a patchwork quilt of bits from recent movies that are themselves rip-offs. This Simon Templar is a man of a thousand faces, all right, and, believe me, you've seen all of them.

Also reviewed in:
NEW YORK TIMES, 4/4/97, p. C24, Janet Maslin
NEW YORKER, 4/14/97, p. 88, Anthony Lane
VARIETY, 3/31-4/6/97, p. 103, Todd McCarthy
WASHINGTON POST, 4/4/97, p. B1, Rita Kempley
WASHINGTON POST, 4/4/97, Weekend/p. 43, Desson Howe

SAINT CLARA

A Kino International release of a Transfix production. *Producer:* Marek Rozenbaum and Uri Sabag. *Director:* Ari Folman and Ori Sivan. *Screenplay (Hebrew and Russian with English subtitles):* Ari Folman and Ori Sivan. *Based on the novel by:* Pavel Kohout. *Story:* Yelena Machinova. *Director of Photography:* Valentin Belanogov. *Editor:* Dov Steuer. *Music:* Barry Saharov. *Sound:* Gil Toren. *Casting:* Orit Azoulay. *Production Designer:* Ariel Glaser. *Set Dresser:* Simcha Speizer. *Costumes:* Tzipi Anglischer. *Make-up:* Orit Yitzhak. *Running time:* 85 minutes. *MPAA Rating:* Not Rated.

CAST: Lucy Dubinchik (Clara Chanov); Halil Elohev (Eddie Tikel); Johnny Peterson (Rosy Rosenthal); Maya Mayron (Libby); Israel Damidov (Elvis Chanov); Yigal Naor (Headmaster Tissona); Maya De Fries (Eleanor Galash); Tal Feignboim (Galit Biron); Tal Ben Bina (Tikel's Mother); Menashe Noy (Tikel's Father); Jenia Doudina (Clara's Mother); Ronald Hairlovsky (Clara's Father); Joseph El Dror (Teacher Mounitz); Orly Zilberschatz-Banai (TV Reporter); Ronny Bachar (Vered Rosenthal); Tomer Patlock (Asthma); Divan Sivan (Baby Chanov); Helena Zoubtov (Seismographic Engineer).

NEW YORK POST, 1/29/97, p. 39, Larry Worth

Despite the title, it's safe to assume "Saint Clara" will never be confused with "The Song of Bernadette."

In reality, the film is closer to "Carrie"—as lensed by Israel's answer to Tim Hutton and penned by the Czech equivalent of Jim Jarmusch.

Specifically, neophyte writer-directors Ari Folman and Ori Sivan inventively blend the surreal, the magical and the off-beat into a New Age "Twilight Zone."

Set in Israel's Golda Meir Junior High of 1999, the tale opens as exasperated administrators scream at a classroom of punks; each pupil has aced a particularly tough exam. Coincidence? Not likely.

Clara, a stunning, purple-eyed Russian transfer student, admits to anticipating the test questions and sharing her clairvoyant insights. But that's just the beginning of her otherworldly abilities.

That's not to say Folman and Sivan end up treading on Stephen King turf. Instead, they center on a fractured teen-age love triangle, complemented by sendups of parents and Israeli politics.

It's an arresting mix, all filtered through a quirky sense of humor and vaguely dreamlike quality. Folman and Sivan's penchant for the loopy is best exemplified in a scene of two confused youngsters discussing their future on a couch—in the middle of a swamp.

For that matter, the filmmakers' study of pill-popping, androgynous adolescents is admirably unconventional. Much credit for that goes to Lucy Dubinchik, who's ethereal, vulnerable and sexy as the titular heroine. And as the boys vying for her affection, Halil Elohev and Johnny Peterson prove unexpectedly engaging.

Collectively, they give adventurous film fans ample reason to believe in the power of "Saint Clara."

VILLAGE VOICE, 2/4/97, p. 69, J. Hoberman

Russians may have never set foot on the moon, but to judge from *Saint Clara* and *Prisoner of the Mountains* [See Hoberman's review of *Prisoner of the Mountains*.], two exceptionally fine "small" movies opening in New York this week—their mere presence is sufficient to imbue the barren landscape of central Israel or the rugged heights of the Caucasus with a hallucinatory lunar quality.

Saint Clara, set on the eve of the millennium and at the edge of the Negev, in a Bauhaus *povera* model town overshadowed by an industrial-strength seismographic institute, is an insouciant punk vision. This tale of teenage clairvoyance (from the land of Uri Geller) is like a benign *Carrie* or a cross between *Welcome to the Dollhouse* and *Village of the Damned*—tracking a crisis in pedagogic authority that begins when an entire class of seventh-graders at the Golda Meir School manages to score identically perfect marks on a math test.

The class ringleaders—longhaired Eddie and his more ideologically hardcore pill-popping cohort, the skinhead Rosy—are hauled in to the principal for questioning. "This is an act of revolt he warns, searing the screen with his iridescent red suit. Soon, however, the principal is dreaming of revolution himself—the miraculous occurrence has been traced to the psychic intervention of the enigmatic Clara, as gravely beautiful as a medieval icon, a recent émigré from deepest Russia who lives in a trailer at the edge of town with her suitably goofball family (themselves a mélange of uncanny weirdos drawn mainly from the Russian-Israeli Gesher theater).

Clara is adolescent power incarnate, although her telepathic powers are rationally explained by her childhood in a radioactive dump. "The questions just jumped into my head," she explains. From whose head did *Saint Clara* jump? Israeli cinema has never been distinguished for its sardonic comedies although *Saint Clara* is actually the second such to appear in New York this year. (One hopes some enterprising distributor managed to catch Igal Bursztyn's cerebral slapstick *Everlasting Joy,* which teleported Baruch Spinoza from 17th-century Amsterdam to contemporary Tel Aviv, when it was shown at the New York Jewish Film Festival.) Written and directed by the team of Ari Folman and Ori Sivan (both in their early thirties), adapted from a novel by the Czech writer Pavel Kohout, and shot by Russian-born cinematographer Valentin Belanogov, *Saint Clara* is an Israeli film with attitude—much of it East European.

Saint Clara's sci-fi ambience, strident colors, eccentric performances, exaggerated wardrobes (each character has a trademark garish accessory), deftly low-budget special effects, and undercurrent of psychedelic rock seem closer in spirit to the Russian-American indie smash *Liquid Sky* than to any Israeli models. Even more East European is the films pervasive sense of entropy. "Everything's falling apart" the anarchist Rosy exults. "The system is paralyzed." That system is, in fact, charactered not only by the universal regime of junior high school but by an ossified socialism and a decrepit cult of personality. Golda Meir's photograph is ubiquitous, and, while

Saint Clara may bug some for being an Israeli feature that makes no mention of the Palestinian question, it will surely shock others by including an image of a life-size Meir sculpture hung by the neck from a schoolroom ceiling and set aflame.

Clara is not responsible for trashing the school, but, like the baby witch in the old ABC sitcom, she is nonetheless an idol of youthful anarchy. Given an impossible equation to solve at the blackboard, she retaliates by conjuring a fiery mass vision that climaxes with a bird crashing through the schoolroom window. Nor are her miracles restricted to class. She correctly predicts the winning lottery combination for Eddie's father—as well as for 300 other people, thus precipitating a near-riot of blasphemous crowds chanting, "God Almighty is a joke, all our dreams up in smoke!" In the end, however, this is a film about first love. (Folman and Sivan have assembled an excellent cast of kids, including teen rocker Halil Elohev, who plays Eddie, and the gravely self-possessed Lucy Dubinchik, herself a 14-year-old Russian immigrant, as Clara.) As the friends Rosy and Eddie battle for Clara's favors, the "Saint" herself forecasts an earthquake—most likely so that she can attend the movies with Eddie. As the town empties out, the rock drone turns unexpectedly mellow, and the remaining couples pair off. (Even the hardcore punkette Libby doffs her pilot's helmet and lets down her hair.) Alone in the theater, Eddie and Clara have the movie to themselves. The building crumbles, the screen gently explodes as these shy teenagers exchange their first kiss.

Disaster is a weird source of solace. This anarcho-punk teen romance is not only extremely comic but unexpectedly sweet. A movie that would surely be the hit of Sundance, *Saint Clara* is at once an enchanting vision of Israel "normalcy" a slap in the face of public taste, and a poem about the unbridgeable gap between adults and children.

Also reviewed in:
NEW YORK TIMES, 1/30/97, p. C18, Stephen Holden
VARIETY, 12/11-17/95, p. 88, Deborah Young

SALUT COUSIN!

A Seventh Arts Releasing release of a JBA Productions film.   *Producer:* Jacques Bidou. *Director:* Merzak Allouache. *Screenplay (French and Arabic with English subtitles):* Merzak Allouache and Caroline Thivel. *Director of Photography:* Pierre Aim. *Editor:* Pierre Abela. *Music:* Safy Boutella. *Production Designer:* Oliver Raoux. *Running time:* 102 minutes. *MPAA Rating:* Not Rated.

CAST: Gad Elmaleh (Alilo); Mess Hattou (Mok); Magaly Berdy (Fatoumata); Ann Gisel (Laurence).

LOS ANGELES TIMES, 6/13/97, Calendar/p. 2, Kevin Thomas

"Salut Cousin!" is the timeless story of the naive stranger coming to the big city, and Franco-Algerian filmmaker Merzak Allouache brings to it a freshness, vitality and beguiling rueful humor.

The film is too long by 10 minutes at least, but it is such a warm and endearing picture that you're likely to forgive Allouache for milking his finale for all its worth.

No small part of the picture's impact is in the Paris it shows us: the City of Light as experienced by the poor foreigner who has to reside in a shabby tenement neighborhood in the 18th *arrondissement*.

Alilo (Gad Elmaleh) is a gangly young man with curly hair and expressive eyes who arrives in Paris from Algiers on what is supposed to be a quick round-trip to pick up a large suitcase crammed with copies of designer gowns to be sold at great profit back in Algeria. Wouldn't you know that Alilo has lost the name and phone number of his Paris contact—and that his boss back home has taken off for Morocco for five days? It's a clever excuse for Allouache and his co-writer, Caroline Thivel, to keep Alilo in Paris for the kind of experiences sure to transform his life.

He stays with his cousin Mok (Mess Hattou) in a tiny, ancient apartment. The Paris-born Mok, with his sideburns and goatee, is desperate to make it as a rapper; he lifts from La Fontaine's fables, of all sources. Mok is up to his ears in the latest—Parisian slang and trendy punk attire and lives by his distinctly limited wits. There's a likability, even sweetness, about Mok, with his beloved goldfish and flamboyant wardrobe, but he's wildly unreliable and dangerously foolish.

The adventures that Alilo embarks on with his cousin are funny, but as the film progresses, its serious undertones begin to surface. "Salut Cousin!" is very much about the pain of surviving in an often nakedly racist and unjust society and the pain of contemplating an Algeria beset with strife and oppression. Alilo meets a number of fellow countrymen who long to return to Algeria but feel that it will never be possible to do so.

In telling his story, Aflouache shows us a Paris that never seemed more like Los Angeles in its rich yet volatile multicultural diversity, its graffiti-scarred shabbiness and its garish sex industry establishments. Elmaleh, Hattou and others are totally winning, as is the seductive, exuberant Arabic music of Safy Boutella's score.

"Salut Cousin!" leaves us longing, to see Allouache's 1994 "Bab El Oued City," his indictment of Islamic extremist violence in his homeland that turned him into an exile himself.

NEW YORK POST, 2/21/97, p. 42, Thelma Adams

If there's anything new to say about odd couples, culture clashes, loan sharks and the search for true love, "Salut Cousin!" doesn't find them.

That's not to say the film fails. It's a mixed bag, with the comedy-drama getting off to a slow start but hitting full stride about halfway through.

Director and co-writer Merzak Allouache taps into similar themes from his earlier "Bab el-Oued City." Specifically, he explores an Arab neighborhood, but this time in Paris rather than his native Algiers.

The story is bookended by an arrival and departure from Gay Paree, with a naive black market-eer fresh from Algeria lodging with his "worldly" cousin-cum-rapper. What quickly becomes obvious is that the "city boy" is far less savvy than his Old World relative.

Thankfully, Allouache quickly moves beyond the black-and-white characterizations, developing the principals into three-dimensional anti-heroes. That's what gives viewers a reason to stick around for long-delayed plot twists and an O. Henry-inspired finale.

Allouache also scores on ambience, showing a dirty side of Paris' back alleys that definitely isn't on the tourist maps. In addition, he poignantly address Arabs' mixed feelings on their roots.

Then there's the down side: a litany of subplots that diffuse the main storyline, inclusion of an inappropriate fantasy sequence and a lack of skill in the editing room.

The acting falls somewhere in-between. As the would-be man around town, Mess Hattou is convincingly sad and propriately annoying while Gad Elmaleh's ingenue is less focused, maybe because his role isn't as well defined. As their respective love interests, Ann Gisel Glass and Magaly Berdy fail to impress one way or another.

So do the production's merits outweigh the flaws? Ultimately, yes. But in "Salut Cousin!" everything's relative.

VILLAGE VOICE, 2/25/97, p. 70, Leslie Camhi

Alilo from Algiers shows up at his cousin Mok's in Paris. He's there on "bizness" for his smuggler boss, picking up a suitcase full of haute couture *shmattas* to sell in the war-torn streets of home. "Like a donkey," he loses his contact's address and must spend a few days in town.

Mok lives in the 18th arrondissement, in the crumbling and colorful Moscova district, home to an assortment of immigrants and bohemians. His neighbors include West Africans in the "import-export" business and an out-of-work Shakespearean actor. Mok's a would-be singer who sets La Fontaine's poetry to rap-fusion music; he's got a goldfish named Nobody, a tall blond girlfriend whose thug boyfriend is after him, and a load of debts. Still, he tries to show Alilo around.

In the Barbès quarter, Allio runs into an ex-police officer from Algiers, now running a fake-Rolodex operation. In the projects, he spots an imam with a shady Algerian past. In Moscova, he meets a beautiful West African woman.

Salut Cousin! has the naive charm, good looks, and tender heart of its hero. With a light touch, French Algerian director Merzak Allouache conveys the picturesque appeal of Paris's piebald districts, though he leaves out their seamy and sordid side. Beyond the hood, his street scenes cannily capture the mutual paranoia that currently informs French-Algerian relations. But the real heart of this film, like that of its exiled director, is, one senses, elsewhere: in the ravaged country that his hero has momentarily left behind. When Mr. Maurice, an Algerian Jew in the Paris rag business who'll never go back, talks lovingly about the streets of the medina, we're moved, but Allouache doesn't linger long on such melancholy moments. This film is his distraction from the thought of home.

Also reviewed in:
NEW YORK TIMES, 2/21/97, p. C12, Stephen Holden

SCHIZOPOLIS

A Northern Arts Entertainment release of a Point 406 Ltd. production. *Producer:* John Hardy. *Director:* Steven Soderbergh. *Screenplay:* Steven Soderbergh. *Director of Photography:* Steven Soderbergh. *Editor:* Sarah Flack. *Music:* Cliff Martinez, Joseph Wilkins, Mark Mangini, and Harry Garfield. *Running time:* 96 minutes. *MPAA Rating:* Not Rated.

CAST: Steven Soderbergh (Fletcher Munson); Betsy Brantley (Mrs. Munson/Attractive Woman No. 2); David Jensen (Elmo Oxygen); Eddie Jemison (Nameless Number Headman); Scott Allen (Right-hand Man); Mike Malone (T. Azimuth Schwitters); Katherine LaNasa (Attractive Woman No. 1).

LOS ANGELES TIMES, 5/23/97, Calendar/p. 18, Kevin Thomas

"Schizopolis" represents a minor act of self-indulgence on the part of the sometimes eccentric Steven Soderbergh but results in major tedium for the viewer. The gifted filmmaker, who made a splashy debut with "sex, lies, and videotape," this time is relentlessly zany without being funny. It's as if Soderbergh, who also stars in dual roles, were out to put a surreal spin on the earlier film but without sufficient inspiration to make it work.

The first third of the film is especially insufferable as his Fletcher Munson, an extravagantly neurotic employee of a famous self-help guru, struggles with the assignment of writing a speech for his boss. In the meantime, Soderbergh, who in appearance could pass as Woody Harrelson's brother, piles on all the nonsense vignettes and subplots he can come up with to little positive effect.

The film gets better when Munson discovers a carbon copy of himself, a dentist, who in turn is having an affair with his—Munson's—wife (Betsy Brantley). To top it off, a woman who is *her* double turns up at the dentist's office as a new patient.

Actually, Soderbergh is on to something that kicks in but too late to matter much. When Munson passes himself as the dentist to his wife, he gains a unique opportunity to see himself as she does—a hopelessly preoccupied individual. This doubling allows Soderbergh to suggest how couples need literally to get outside themselves to recharge a marriage gone stale.

In his own playing and that of the lovely, poised Brantley, Soderbergh succeeds quite well in this. But you suspect that he's afraid this concern may play as too obvious and banal. He may therefore feel he must distract us with all manner of dreary slapstick and asides. This is too bad because, as he has proved in his criminally neglected 1993 second feature, "King of the Hill," about an abandoned boy coping in the Depression, he can bring terrific poignancy and immediacy to the straightforward narrative.

To be sure, Soderbergh suggests that we're living in a universe of mind-boggling absurdity while so craving recognition and self-respect that we not only spawn phony prophets but also individuals hungering for the attention that attempting to assassinate them would bring. Soderbergh has lots to say but this time seems to lack the confidence to express himself seriously.

NEW YORK POST, 4/9/97, p. 39, Larry Worth

Steven Soderbergh his yet to repeat himself on the big screen, having veered from the indie classic "sex, lies and videotape" to Spalding Gray's most compelling filmed monologue, "Gray's Anatomy."

So there's good reason to believe "Schizopolis" can be written off as the director's sole attempt at experimental, pretentious, incoherent moviemaking—a beginning-to-end waste of celluloid for one and all.

The utterly incomprehensible, purposely confusing plot has Soderbergh playing a speechwriter who's experiencing problems on the work front and home front. Aside from enduring the boss from hell, his wife is having an affair with her dentist, who happens to be a mirror image of hubby.

Still following? It gets worse: The wife also has an identical twin—known as Attractive Woman No. 2 who's being romantically pursued by the lookalike dentist.

And that's not even mentioning the various subplots, one of which concerns a movie within the movie as a sex-crazed bug exterminator turns guerrilla fighter. Huh?

Believe it or not, Soderbergh's writing is even worse than his direction. Much of the dialogue consists of exchanges like "Generic greeting" and "Generic greeting returned," while other bits are delivered entirely in code.

In addition, Soderbergh inserts pointless title cards, employs fast-motion, dubbing that isn't meant to match actors' mouth movements, irreverent newscasts and black-and-white dream sequences. It's like a casebook example of how not to make a movie.

And that may be part of Soderbergh's big joke, along with his unique takes on society's identity crises, ho-hum existences, communication problems and sexual hangups. But should filmgoers be expected to pay perfectly good money for such an indulgence?

Midway through the production one scene stands out: a hand-held shot of a sign taped on a tree that says "idea missing." When it comes to "Schizopolis," no more need be said.

NEWSDAY, 4/9/97, Part II/p. B9, John Anderson

Bearing more than a hint of Heaven's Gate and something less than a pie in the face for Scientology, Steven Soderbergh's "Schizopolis" is a vaudevillian's search for identity, and may even be the director's send-up of himself.

Does it work? Not usually, although its intentions seem serious. As far as Heaven's Gate goes, the movie's connection with it seems just a matter of good, or at least curious, timing. But the character T. Azimuth Schwitters (Mike Malone), his philosophy-in-book-form "Eventualities" and his Dilbertesque corporate religion, are all pretty pointed. And occasionally funny. More often, however, we're like Admiral Stockdale, wondering who we are and why we're here.

Introducing the movie himself, Soderbergh—who also stars as several intersecting characters and personalities who isn't/aren't as confused as he/they might be by all the goings-on—tells us that any questions we have about the film are our fault. That we'll have to see the movie many, many times (spending many, many dollars) in order to clear. things up. This will not be happening.

There are Monty Pythonesque bits of recurring goofiness—a naked escapee from an institution who's pursued for most of the film—and a daisy chain of adulteries, in which Munson (Soderbergh), who's been given the assignment of writing an important speech for Schwitters, discovers that his dentist/doppelganger, Dr. Korchek (Soderbergh again), is having an affair with his wife (Betsy Brantley). Or is it Korchek's wife? He promptly forgets her when he falls in love with—the same woman!

If you see where all this is going, your engagement with this review may be coming to a screeching halt any time now.

Soderbergh's career, and his engagement with it, have been on something of a roller coaster since he burst on the scene with "sex, lies and videotape." "Kafka"—which this film calls to mind in more ways than one—wasn't very well received; "King of the Hill," a minor masterpiece, was largely ignored, and "The Underneath" was treated similarly. His most recent film, "Gray's Anatomy," was basically a Spalding Gray vehicle, although infinitely enhanced by Soderbergh's direction.

But Soderbergh's own sense of destination seems vague. He equates Hollywood with mind control—Elmo (David Jensen), a bug exterminator, is turned into an egomaniacal action star by a couple of Hollywood casting directors who may as easily be cult recruiters.

And the language used by his characters—"Generic greeting!" "Generic greeting returned!"—implies a society looted of its culture.

Ostensibly a comedy, "Schizopolis" makes more than its share of sad observations about the state of the world. And the movies.

VILLAGE VOICE, 4/15/97, p. 74, Gary Dauphin

There are all kinds of curiosity-piquing gags in *Schizopolis,* first and foremost the opening bit where writer, director, and star Steven Soderbergh informs the audience that they'd better see this "very important film" as many times as is necessary to understand it. The director of *sex, lies and videotape* et al. is only partly right. *Schizopolis* is mostly reminiscent of absurdist sketch comedy à la Monty Python, but besides being significantly less funny than Python, but also more pretentious (in a bad way), showing flashes of ambition that are tantalizing but continually unrealized.

Schizopolis is divided into three loosely connected sections, most of them dealing with speechwriter Fletcher Munson (Soderbergh) and his work for an L. Ron Hubbard-like guru. (The religion-cum-publishing empire is called "Eventualism.") Munson has three days to write an important address, but he's bedeviled by a lack of inspiration, a zipless marriage, a chronic masturbation habit, and a tendency to daydream in high-speed video clips. If his problems seem semi-straightforward, its all in the retelling. Writer-director Soderbergh is in full pseudo-Python mode in the first section, breaking up the slight plot with random sight gags, dream sequences, and subplots that only come together in the film's last minutes.

The main repeating interjection involves an exterminator who beds down housewives like some stud Orkin man. While no great shakes as comedy, all the dialogue in those scenes is curiously cut and pasted into nonsense exchanges like: "Jigsaw halibut erosion?" "Candied yarn jigsaw." In the second section the transpositions become more literal, Munson stumbling upon a doppel-gänger whose identity he adopts. *Schizopolis* settles down considerably at that point, becoming a fitful satire about yuppie angst. It briefly comes to life when it turns out Munson's wife (played by Betsy Brantley, Soderbergh's real-life ex-wife) is having an affair with his doppelgänger. The third (and best) section replays earlier sequences from the wife's perspective, and *Schizopolis* becomes the movie Soderbergh must have seen in his head—an understated dance of morphing characters locked into one-sided relationships. It's a passing epiphany though, as in the end Soderbergh settles for the gags that overpopulated the early parts of the film. *Schizopolis* takes a complicated road to nowhere, and although it might say something about suburban thirtysome-things or provide Soderbergh with some working therapy, that doesn't mean you want to sit through it.

Also reviewed in:
CHICAGO TRIBUNE, 11/21/97, Friday/p. L, John Petrakis
NEW YORK TIMES, 4/9/97, p. C13, Janet Maslin
VARIETY, 5/27-6/2/96, p. 66, Todd McCarthy

SCREAM 2

A Dimension Films release of a Konrad Pictures production in association with Craven/Maddalena Films. *Executive Producer:* Bob Weinstein, Harvey Weinstein, and Kevin Williamson. *Producer:* Cathy Konrad and Marianne Maddalena. *Director:* Wes Craven. *Screenplay:* Kevin Williamson. *Director of Photography:* Peter Deming. *Editor:* Patrick Lussier. *Music:* Marco Beltrami. *Music Editor:* Bill Abbott. *Choreographer:* Adam Shankman. *Sound:* Jim Stuebe and (music) John Kurlander. *Sound Editor:* F. Scott Taylor. *Casting:* Lisa Beach. *Production Designer:* Bob Ziembicki. *Art Director:* Ted Berner. *Set Designer:* Martin Roy Mervel. *Set Decorator:* Bob Kensinger. *Set Dresser:* Josh Elliot, Eric Fishman, and Bryan Shupper.

Costumes: Kathleen Detoro. *Make-up:* Carol Schwartz. *Make-up (Courteney Cox):* Beth Katz. *Make-up (Jada Pinkett):* Judy Murdock. *Make-up (Special Effects):* Howard Berger. *Stunt Coordinator:* Tony Cecere. *Running time:* 122 minutes. *MPAA Rating:* R.

CAST: Jada Pinkett (Maureen); Omar Epps (Phil); Paulette Patterson (Usher Giving Out Costumes); Rasila Schroeder (Screaming Girl Up Aisle); Heather Graham ('Stab' Casey); Roger L. Jackson ("The Voice"); Peter Deming (Popcorn Boy); Molly Gross (Theater #1); Rebecca McFarland (Theater #2); Neve Campbell (Sidney Prescott); Elise Neal (Hallie); Liev Schreiber (Cotton Weary); Kevin Williamson (Cotton's Interviewer); Sandy Heddings-Katulka (Girl in Dorm Hallway); Joe Washington (Reporter #1); Angie Dillard (Reporter #2); John Patrick (Reporter #3); Craig Shoemaker (Artsy Teacher); Sarah Michelle Gellar (Cici); Josh Jackson (Film Class Guy #1); Walter Franks (Film Class Guy #2); Timothy Olyphant (Mickey); Nina Pertronzio (Film Class Mopey Girl); Jamie Kennedy (Randy Meeks); Jerry O'Connell (Derek); Courteney Cox (Gale Weathers); Duane Martin (Joel); Laurie Metcalf (Debbie Salt); Stephanie Belt (Reporter #4); Richard Doughty (Reporter #5); Lewis Arquette (Chief Hartley); Rebecca Gayheart (Sorority Sister Lois); Portia De Rossi (Sorority Sister Murphy); David Arquette (Dewey Riley); Marisol Nichols (Dawnie); Cornelia Kiss (Coroner at Cici's House); Lucy In (ER Doctor); Philip Pavel (Officer Andrews); Timothy T. Hillman (Captain Down); Nancy O'Dell (Tori's Interviewer); Tori Spelling (Herself); Luke Wilson ('Stab' Billy); David Warner (Drama Teacher Gus Gold); Greg Meiss (Zeus); Adam Shankman (Ghost Dancer); Jack Baun (Tackled Cell Phoner); Corey Parker (Library Guy); Chris Doyle (Officer Richards); Mark Oliver (Reporter #6); Jason Horgan (Fraternity Brother #1); D.K. Arredondo (Fraternity Brother #2); John Embry (Fraternity Brother #3); Jennifer Weston (Reporter #7); Shelly Benedict (Reporter #8).

LOS ANGELES TIMES, 12/12/97, Calendar/p. 1, Kevin Thomas

You can't blame the makers year's terrific sleeper horror picture "Scream" for trying to cash in on its runaway success. Yet in striving mightily not merely to duplicate its impact but improve upon it, director Wes Craven and writer Kevin Williamson have raised the ante to the degree that contrivance and a horrendous body count combine to yield a morbid effect for discriminating filmgoers, despite a comic tone. Still, there's enough ingenuity and scariness to please plenty of fans of the first film.

Once past an elaborate and gory pre-credit sequence involving the premiere of a horror movie called "Stab," we learn that it was adapted from a best-selling book by that indomitable newscaster Gale Weathers (Courteney Cox) on the killings that occurred in "Scream."

Weathers is back on the scene, at an inviting old Midwestern college where a seeming copycat killer—hidden behind a black cloak and an Edvard Munch "Scream" mask—is terrorizing the campus. In jeopardy are other "Scream" survivors Neve Campbell (a drama student), David Arquette (a local cop), Jamie Kennedy (a film buff and now also a college student) and Liev Schreiber (wrongly accused by Campbell of murdering her mother).

As before, the movie is loaded with film references, and Williamson not only raises the old question of the relationship of screen violence and real-life violence but also jokes about the question of whether sequels can ever be as successful as the originals. As clever, witty and adroit as the filmmakers are in covering their bases they cannot dispel the feeling that their sequel is not as good as their original, even though it abounds in confident stylistic and technical flourishes that are the result of Craven's long experience as a horrormeister.

The cast is large and consistently capable. Campbell is a lovely, skilled actress of much poise and Cox and Arquette excel in the film's most fully dimensional roles. David Warner turns up most effectively as Campbell's drama professor, and Jada Pinkett and Omar Epps score as a couple who have the misfortune to choose going to that "Stab" premiere over the latest Sandra Bullock movie. (In one of the movie's many amusing moments Tori Spelling plays Campbell in "Stab.")

For a film with so many smarts, "Scream 2" has a curious lapse that undermines its credibility needlessly. Why doesn't the college close down or why isn't the state police or National Guard called in when the corpses pile up to the point you lose count?

NEW YORK POST, 12/12/97, p. 49, Thelma Adams

Horror movies don't kill. People who watch horror movies kill.

With "Scream 2," Wes Craven—the horrormeister who dreamt up "Nightmare on Elm Street"—continues to tease celluloid thrill-seekers while posing that question.

This time around, the answer is less pressing, the questions less pointed, but the gore is as good as ever. With the one-two punch of "Wes Craven's New Nightmare" in 1995 and the box-office bonanza "Scream" in 1996, Craven single-handedly revived the flagging teen genre.

How did Craven do it? By combining "Beverly Hills 90210" slickness with a video geek's running commentary and the ability, to deliver the shocks that sent audiences leaping from their seats, crying: "Don't open that door! Don't answer that phone!"

With "Scream 2," Craven returns to the scene of the crime with "Scream" screenwriter Kevin Williamson. The original's chief victim, Sidney (Neve Campbell), has graduated from Woodsboro High and attends Windsor College.

"Scream" survivor Sidney is trying to put that yucky Woodsboro murder spree behind her. But the past is creeping up on the perky "Party of Five" star.

"Stab," a movie-within-the-movie based on the Woodsboro slaughter and starring Tori Spelling (a running gag in the original), has opened at a campus theater.

Based on a best seller by smarmy ambush journalist Gale Weathers (Courteney Cox), "Stab" has become inspiration for a local psycho. The copycat killer is making sure life imitates art—and Sidney's freshman year is murder.

With David Arquette, Jamie Kennedy and Liev Schreiber returning, and the addition of hunk Jerry O'Connell, wise-cracking Timothy Olyphant and movie-goers Omar Epps and Jada Pinkett, Craven sets the scene for a bigger body count, more carnage and a more twisted path to the hand that holds the knife.

Along the way the characters wink at the audience. They chat about the rules of sequels and what generally makes them "s———" with the exceptions of "The Godfather, Part II" and "Aliens." And then, whether they're silly sorority sisters in fuzzy pink sweaters or handsome frat boys with cleft chests, the knowing victims still open that door, answer that phone, go back to that damn room.

Craven's latest sequel doesn't break—or bloody—new ground, but it's not second-class. Audiences will want to scream and scream again!

NEWSDAY, 12/12/97, Part II/p. B8, John Anderson

Fright master and lapsed academician Wes Craven has been redefining the horror genre since "Nightmare on Elm Street," which treated dreams the way "Jaws" treated the beach. But as he's moved along the gore-spattered path of his movie-making career, Craven has been less and less concerned with what scares us than why. And how.

With "Scream 2"—which, needless to say, is the sequel to last year's blockbuster "Scream"—Craven has taken his genre-busting, movie-within-a-movie strategy to a point of no return: The movie opens in a theater showing a movie called "Stab," which is based on the "real-life" case told in "Scream," on a night when those Munch-inspired masks and fake knives are being handed out—all the better to disguise the killer who quickly butchers two members of said audience.

The only way Craven can take this any further will be to have real killers stalking the audiences of "Scream 2"—and given that "Scream 3" is a virtual fait accompli, he may be filming now. So be very careful.

Craven really started deconstructing the horror movie with "Wes Craven's New Nightmare," in which the film's script prophesied the mayhem to come. In "Scream," the characters made fun of horror-film conventions, which of course then all came true.

In "Scream 2," what we have is a sequel-critiquing sequel—"Sequels suck" says one film student and victim-to-be—which is always aware of itself as a movie, makes dry, topical jokes about portable phones, reckless celebrity, O.J. Simpson and the Internet, all the while managing to scare us through the most mundane tactics imaginable. It's as if Craven wants to show us how easy it is, while appealing to multiple audiences at once. And he succeeds. The wonder is how he reins himself in and keeps his pictures looking like cheesy exploitation films while at the same time the ideas are so ambitious and contradictory.

All the major "Scream" players are back, even if they haven't quite recovered from the last movie. David Arquette's ex-cop Dewey Riley is the most visibly wounded, his hand crippled from a "Scream" attack. Neve Campbell is the beleagured Sidney Prescott, who keeps her head while all those around her are losing theirs, and Courteney Cox, whose Turtle-Waxed looks have seldom served a character better, is the hard-shelled TV reporter Gale Weathers.

We will abide by Dimension Films' request not to disclose exactly what happens, but it isn't giving anything away to say that Craven is among the smartest of filmmakers, whose use of the horror genre is no happy accident. He knows what pushes our buttons; he knows how easily they're pushed.

What he's done in "Scream 2" is create that oft-advertised but seldom realized creation, a movie for everybody. Well, maybe not for the faint of heart or stomach, but for everyone else it's a movie that makes you laugh, makes you squirm and makes you say "Oh yeah."

SIGHT AND SOUND, 5/98, p. 55, Kim Newman

Windsor, Ohio. At a preview of *Stab,* a film about the Woodsboro murders (the story of the film *Scream),* a copycat masked murderer kills students Phil and Maureen. Sidney Prescott and Randy Meeks, survivors of the rampage of Sidney's mad boyfriend Billy Loomis, are at nearby Woodsboro College. Sidney's new boyfriend is Derek; her friends include film students Cici and Mickey and roommate Hallie. Drawn to town by the new murders are reporter Gale Weathers, whose account of the Woodsboro murders formed the basis of *Stab,* Dewey Riley, an ex-deputy, who is offended by Gale's mercenary exploitation of the events; and Cotton Weary, once unjustly imprisoned for one of Billy's murders.

Randy reasons the new murderer is mounting a "sequel" to the original crimes and, after Cici is killed, the police give Sidney constant protection. The killer murders Randy and stabs Dewey. After slaughtering Sidney's guards and Hallie, the killer pursues Sidney to the campus theatre. There, he reveals himself to be Mickey and murders the helpless Derek, explaining that he intends to use his trial to test out a defence that he was compelled to kill because of his addiction to violent movies. Mickey is acting in concert with local reporter Debbie Salt, who is actually Billy Loomis' equally mad mother, out for revenge. Sidney and Gale, assisted by Cotton, overcome and execute the killers, and it turns out that Dewey has survived. Sidney allows Cotton, who has wished to exploit his tangential part in the original murders to become famous, to be acclaimed as a hero.

Wes Craven has already delivered the ultimate post-modem sequel in *Wes Craven's New Nightmare,* which withdraws from the frame of the *Elm Street* series to ask questions about what the whole thing means. So he is in something of a quandary with *Scream 2,* which is hipper and slicker than *New Nightmare,* but zooms in rather than pulls back. Though characters express sentiments like "sequels suck!" and Randy the Movie Nerd is on hand to explain the rules of sequels as he once explained the rules of slasher movies, this pointedly never evokes *New Nightmare* or the underrated *Psycho II.* Instead, it plays riffs not only on disappointing sequels (don't forget Craven's *The Hills Have Eyes, Part II)* and the 80s run of campus-set slasher movies (such as *The House on Sorority Row)* which co-existed with the high school-set slasher movies referenced by *Scream.*

There is on the surface quite a lot going on here. *Scream's* screenwriter Kevin Williamson reunites with Craven to intersperse the scares with jokes that call into question the whole issue of performance. Derek tries to win back Sidney by imitating Tom Cruise's serenade from *Top Gun.* Drama professor David Warner directs theatre major Sidney in an amazingly pretentious student production which has her pursued by a killer chorus in Greek masks. Extracts from *Stab* recreate scenes from *Scream* with worse acting (Tori Spelling plays Sidney) and more obvious horror effects, itself quite an achievement. And one murderer's rant that he intends to use the 'effects' controversy as the basis of his defence is one-upped by his partner's admission that she's killing people for good old-fashioned revenge.

By explicitly setting out the rules by which the story operates within the narrative itself, Williamson borrows a trick from the writer John Dickson Carr, who was wont to drop essays on locked-room murders into his fictions. A less happy debt is to Agatha Christie, who realised that without exactly cheating you could have two apparently unrelated murderers act in concert and thus get away with it by giving them both alibis. As with the out-of-nowhere motivations and heavily misleading set-ups that seem to put all the characters into the frame, this means the finale isn't quite satisfying. As in *Clue*, the film based on the board game, *Scream 2* could have been shot with any number of endings, revealing any of the characters as guilty, so each possible resolution has equal weight.

Though a superbly crafted scare-and-smirk machine, *Scream 2* is ultimately affectless. The early deaths of Jada Pinkett and Sarah Michelle Gellar, staged with flair in the unusual setting of a crowded cinema and the almost insultingly archetypal one of a deserted sorority house, are shocking and saddening, but only because the actresses are so appealing. The film is obliged to spend most of its time with Sidney, who through no fault of Neve Campbell—is the least realised character in sight. When the ostensible hero is murdered near the end, the show's almost over so there's no point getting worked up about him.

Nevertheless, *Scream 2* deserves points for including so many infallible indices of guilt among its suspect list—Dewey's nerve-damaged handicap (how many crippled villains have risen from their wheelchairs for the finish?); David Warner and Laurie Metcalf's familiar faces in apparently minor roles (Roy Thinnes and Farley Granger had similar turns in horror films and were guilty); Jamie Kennedy's resentment at being a supporting character (an equivalent geek in *The Dorm that Dripped Blood* is the killer). The glee in all this knowingness is infectious, but in cleverness and self-awareness the film becomes all surface. Viewed as a follow-up to Craven's best work—from *The Last House on the Left* and *The Hills Have Eyes* through *A Nightmare on Elm Street* to *New Nightmare*—*Scream 2:* is rootless, a picture whose immediately engaging factors are eerily bereft of anything like a subtext.

VILLAGE VOICE, 12/23/97, p. 84, Amy Taubin

A copycat movie about a copycat killer, *Scream 2* tries to make derivativeness a virtue, but the film-buff reflexivity that was so winning without being exactly fresh in the original is seriously tired the second time around. Everyone who was left alive at the end of *Scream*—including Randy (the irresistibly sardonic Jamie Kennedy) and Deputy Dewey (the secretly glamorous David Arquette)—congregates on the campus of Windsor College, where Sidney Prescott (Neve Campbell), the resourceful heroine of *Scream*, is trying to get on with her life. Unfortunately for Sidney, ambitious TV reporter Gale Weathers (Courtney Cox) has written a book about the Woodsboro murders, which has been turned into a movie titled *Stab*. When *Stab* opens at Windsor College's local movie theater, it inspires a whole new round of murders and mayhem. The killer's first victims are a squabbling couple played by Jada Pinkett and Omar Epps. Since they're the wittiest actors onscreen, it's downhill after that.

Kevin Williamson's dialogue should appeal to everyone who's taken Film Studies 101, but Wes Craven's direction is heavy-handed and strictly by the numbers. If you don't guess the murderer within the first 20 minutes, you must be a virgin to the genre.

Also reviewed in:
NEW YORK TIMES, 12/12/97, p. E16, Janet Maslin
VARIETY, 12/8-14/97, p. 111, Leonard Klady
WASHINGTON POST, 12/12/97, p. C1, Stephen Hunter
WASHINGTON POST, 12/12/97, Weekend/p. 56, Richard Harrington

SCREWED: AL GOLDSTEIN'S KINGDOM OF PORN

A Cinema Village Features release of a St. Dympna production. *Producer:* Andrew Gurland and Todd Phillips. *Director:* Alexander Crawford. *Director of Photography:* Alexander Crawford. *Editor:* Alexander Crawford. *Running time:* 85 minutes. *MPAA Rating:* Not Rated.

WITH: Al Goldstein, Dave Clark, and Curtis Sliwa.

LOS ANGELES TIMES, 1/9/97, Calendar/p. 15, Kevin Thomas

Before there was Larry Flynt, there was Al Goldstein, publisher of Screw Magazine and host of the cable-access show "Midnight Blue," two legendary mainstays of Manhattan's X-rated scene. Goldstein apparently became the first man ever to beat a federal obscenity charge—before Flynt even started publishing Hustler. Arrested 19 times by his own count, Goldstein is proud that he's never cut a deal with a prosecutor.

As with Flynt, Goldstein is important in the cause of 1st Amendment rights. But his story, told in Alexander Crawford's documentary "Screwed," makes "The People vs. Larry Flynt" look like "Pollyanna."

Clearly a shrewd, reflective man of superior intelligence, Goldstein can use four-letter words with the effect of a blowtorch. He's famously a no-holds-barred kind of guy, and filmmaker Crawford has wisely understood that nothing less than a no-holds-barred documentary will do. Crawford follows Goldstein everywhere, including the sets of the X-rated movies he makes. "Screwed" is as blunt as its subject.

Crawford also puts Goldstein in the context of his audience. He spends time with a heavyset young man searching for a hooker, with an older man interested in sadomasochistic sex and with a one-legged man who collects pornography, who says, "A world without pornography is a world without imagination."

Brooklyn-born Goldstein, who held down a variety of jobs before launching Screw in 1958 with $150, calls his magazine "a compendium of everything sexual" and he calls "Midnight Blue" more "revenge than entertainment" By this Goldstein means that the program's concern with sex gives him a chance to blast anyone who angers him, especially hypocrites. "I don't defend porn as much as I defend porn's right to exist," he says.

Goldstein has been honing his bombastic public persona for so long you sense that he probably means to be in total control of how he comes across on film. It is possible that he may not like that you come away from "Screwed" with a sense of just how much alike he is to many of his readers and viewers: middle-aged, seriously overweight and not very successful with women. Indeed, as the film unfolds he's experiencing the breakup of his fourth marriage. Yet he also seems to want us to take seriously his own longing for love. At one point, he says, "I am the audience Screw targeted."

He is an angry man, and much of that anger is directed at women as well as hypocrites on the issue of sex. A man who has known him a long time remarks, "He's a terrible enemy and a wonderful friend."

Crawford waits until nearly end of his film to ask Goldstein what the price of being Al Goldstein has been. Goldstein, who tells him that it is his best question, replies, "No one takes you seriously ... They're amazed you ever read a book ... You're regarded as a cartoon character with no depth ... You make yourself into a joke so that no one can hurt you."

NEW YORK POST, 1/10/97, p. 49, Bill Hoffmann

Like rats and cockroaches, Al Goldstein is one of those infamous New York institutions that help give our great city a notorious distinction.

We could certainly do without him, but geez, the Big Apple would lose a good chunk of its unique character if he wasn't here.

That's the message behind "Screwed"—an affectiomate look at the 60-year-old porn king who created Screw magazine, makes adult movies and hosts the kitschy cable show "Midnight Blue." Years before Larry Flynt and Howard Stern battled obscenity laws, the cigar-chomping Goldstein took on the feds, Time Warner and others on free-speech issues.

But while Flynt and Stern gained national prominence, Goldstein, a self-described "300-pound Brooklyn-born, Jewish pornographer," largely remained a New York phenomenon.

Director Alex Crawford shows Goldstein at his outrageous best—or obnoxious worst—as he spouts unprintable venom about his four ex-wives and boasts about his sexual prowess.

To demonstrate that prowess, a gleeful Goldstein has a fledgling porn star strip and performs a hardcore sex act on her as she squeals in delight.

Well, why not? After all, Goldstein publishes what he calls "the world's most honest magazine."

The movie reveals that honest or not, "Screw" caters to the maladjusted lonely men who need hookers and porn flicks for gratification and come off like raincoat-wearing patrons from a 42nd Street grindhouse out of the '60s.

Goldstein may be more maladjusted than any of them.   In his world, women are faceless pleasure machines, not to be trusted.

But the movie never quite cracks the enigma of Goldstein, who despite his credulity is an intellectual with a vast knowledge of history, art and politics.   Too often, he runs rampant with Goldstein schtick a la his Channel 35 show.

The only one to rip the smut king here is Curtis Sliwa, whose amusing anti-porn monologue makes him sound like a paid spokesman for Disneyfication.

Still, "Screw" is a fascinating portrait of a patented New York City odd-ball.

NEWSDAY, 1/10/97, Part II/p. B13, John Anderson

Compared Al Goldstein, Larry Flynt is Alfred Knopf.   So it's no surprise that "Screwed: Al Goldstein's Kingdom of Porn" makes "The People vs. Larry Flynt" seem like something that should have been narrated by Alistair Cooke.

But such lack of refinement is the redeeming quality—for lack of a better word—of Alexander Crawford's low-budget, high-intensity exploration of Goldstein's fetid world.   Crawford takes great delight, it seems, in showing us the gamiest aspects of Goldstein's warped counter-culture of hardcore publications, fetishists and street hustlers.   But as long as sex publishers are enjoying such currency, we may as well see one in his native element.

Goldstein, born and raised in Williamsburg, Brooklyn—a self-described "shy, introverted, Jewish guy"—started Screw magazine in 1968 and became the whipping boy (no judgments intended) of crusading moralists everywhere.   Long before Larry Flynt had his highly publicized First Amendment victories, Goldstein was fighting in the trenches.   "I had four subscribers in Kansas," he says, describing events leading up to his federal obscenity indictment, which was filed in Wichita.   "And three were postal inspectors."

So Goldstein has a sense of humor, which separates him from his detractors.   Also, a sense of desperation and rage.   He describes his ability to bestow sexual "awakenings" on women as the equivalent of "bringing sight to Helen Keller." He heaps scathing abuse on his ex-wives from the pulpit of his "Midnight Blue" late-night TV show (on leased public-access cable) and practices his own brand of a self-delusion.   And, although few of his critics would find justification in it, Goldstein seems to have been grievously disappointed by the women in his life—beginning with his mother—which explains at least a little bit why he's so intent on degrading them.

Where Crawford goes right is in making Goldstein anything but heroic, and in displaying the people who subscribe to Goldstein's paper (and his ideas) as rather pathetic and seamy.   But he also paints pornography's opponents as a rather blinkered group.   Guardian Angel and radio personality Curtis Sliwa is given a large amount of screen time to display his cultivated inarticulateness, as he decries the "transsexuals, transformers and herkama-jerks" that populate the rapidly disappearing porn palaces of Times Square.   But other than voicing knee-jerk indignation, he contributes little besides serving as a shining example of middle-American repugnance of what ranges from an obsession to a sickness.

Of course, even one of Goldstein's editors, questioned about the First Amendment-protected porn of Screw, finds it "hard to say how it really serves the public." It's left to a female dominatrix to explain porn's one defensible purpose: that it accommodates people whose sex drives can't otherwise be fulfilled.   So it's about charity ... although there's very little of that in "Screwed."

VILLAGE VOICE, 1/14/97, p. 63, Patricia Thomson

To see the truth, you have to look a girl right in the asshole.   So says "Big Bob," proud owner of 8000 porn videos and an avid reader of *Screw,* one of America's raunchiest sex rags.

Big Bob's insights are about as deep as they get in *Screwed,* a documentary about Al Goldstein, publisher of *Screw.*

No doubt the makers of *Screwed*—director Alexander Crawford and producers Todd Phillips and Andrew Gurland (who also run the New York Underground Film Festival)—are hoping to ride the coattails of *The People vs. Larry Flynt* and make the most of the fact that Goldstein got there first—his magazines been around longer (29 years) and he was first to be vindicated after a Federal obscenity bust (in 1977).

But *Screwed* is no *Larry Flynt*. Though Goldstein is a colorful character and the film offers a few peeks at people doin the nasty, *Screwed* remains surprisingly flat. Part of the problem is that the film treads lightly wherever it goes. Whether interviewing *Screw* readers like Big Bob, street hookers, editors, or Goldstein himself, the filmmaker lobs only softball questions.

"What do you think about when you do porn?" he asks a towel-clad actress.

"Fucking," she says. "I'm sorry, that's what it's about."

"That's cool."

Not what you'd call a probing follow-up. Ditto after Goldstein trashes his four ex-wives, and spews venom at women and his industry. Unchallenged, Goldstein remains master of this tour. There's not an unguarded moment.

Asked what price he's paid for being Al Goldstein, the porn king replies, "You become a cartoon character," acknowledging, "You make yourself into a joke so no one can hurt you." Unfortunately, *Screwed* lets Goldstein get away with his self-caricature intact.

Also reviewed in:
NEW YORK TIMES, 1/10/97, p. C22, Stephen Holden
VARIETY, 1/13-19/97, p. 152, Todd McCarthy

SELENA

A Warner Bros. release of a Q Productions, Inc.-Esparza/Katz production. *Executive Producer:* Abraham Quintanilla. *Producer:* Moctesuma Esparza and Robert Katz. *Director:* Gregory Nava. *Screenplay:* Gregory Nava. *Director of Photography:* Edward Lachman. *Editor:* Nancy Richardson. *Music:* Dave Grusin and Sidney James. *Choreographer:* Miranda Garrison. *Sound:* Bayard Carey. *Casting:* Roger Mussenden. *Production Designer:* Cary White. *Art Director:* Ed Vega. *Set Designer:* Adele Plauche. *Set Decorator:* Jeanette Scott. *Costumes:* Elisabeth Beraldo. *Running time:* 127 minutes. *MPAA Rating:* PG.

CAST: Jennifer Lopez (Selena Quintanilla Perez); Edward James Olmos (Abraham Quintanilla, Jr.); Jon Seda (Chris Perez); Constance Marie (Marcela Quintanilla); Jacob Vargas (Abie Quintanilla); Lupe Ontiveros (Yolanda Saldivar); Jackie Guerra (Suzette Quintanilla); Richard Coca (Bobby - Dinos 1961); Panchito Gomez (Young Abraham, Dinos 1961); Sal Lopez (Juan Luis); Victoria Elena Flores (Young Suzette); Rafael Tamayo (Young Abie); Leon Singer (Concert Promoter); Rebecca Lee Meza (Young Selena).

LOS ANGELES TIMES, 3/21/97, Calendar/p. 1, Kenneth Turan

Americans love success stories, particularly those with humble beginnings and unhappy endings. So when the phenomenally popular Selena Quintanilia Perez, the Grammy-winning Queen of Tejano Music, was shot to death in March 1995, scant weeks before her 24th birthday, "Selena" the movie was only a matter of time.

In the tradition of "Lady Sings the Blues," "The Rose," "What's Love Got to Do With It" and other sudsy tales of singers and their woes, "Selena" is in part a completely predictable Latino soap opera that should satisfy those who complain they aren't making movies like they like used to.

"Selena" is also reminiscent of "La Bamba's" story of Ritchie Valens, and not just because its subject is Mexican American. Selena's father, Abraham Quintanilla, the film's executive producer, had complete script approval, and the price of family cooperation, not to mention the use of Selena's music, was the inevitable sanitizing and sentimentalization that are also Hollywood's stock in trade.

Yet, despite all this, there are chunks of "Selena" that only a stone could resist. This movie turns out to be a celebration not only of the singer but also (as "What's Love" was for Angela Bassett) of the actress who plays her, Jennifer Lopez.

Even in forgettable films like "Money Train" and "Jack," Lopez's presence and ability made her seem just one role away from stardom, and with "Selena" she's seized the opportunity and turned in an incandescent presentation that is especially strong during the film's numerous musical numbers.

Though Lopez lip-syncs to Selena's voice, she makes use of her background as a dancer (she was a Fly Girl on "In Living Color") to project an irresistible joy in performance that both does justice to Selena's appeal and helps burn away the film's saccharine haze.

Written and directed by Gregory Nava ("Mi Familia," "El Norte"), "Selena" makes full use of Lopez's charisma in its opening scene, a re-creation of the singer's triumphant appearance before the biggest Astrodome crowd ever just a few weeks before her death. From the chaos backstage through Selena's solo walk through a curtain to the rapture of her adoring fans, it's just the first of the film's string of pure Hollywood moments.

That adrenaline jolt is needed to hold attention for the next half hour, when an extensive sequence of flashbacks goes into Selena's family history, starting with her father's attempt to start a doo-wop group called Los Dinos in Corpus Christi, Texas, in 1961.

Defeated by a combination of racism and the resistance of Mexican Americans to anything you can't dance to, Abraham Quintanilla (Edward James Olmos) puts music out of his mind until he discovers that his youngest daughter Selena (played by 10-year-old Becky Lee Meza) has a voice like the mature Ethel Merman.

Much to the discomfort of wife Marcela (Constance Marie), Quintanilla insists that Selena and her two siblings (once grown, played by Jacob Vargas and Jackie Guerra) form a group. He even quits his job to open a restaurant so they'll have a showcase. Quintanilla even teaches his daughter to sing in Spanish though she doesn't know the language because "you've got to be who you are, you can't change it, and you're Mexican deep inside."

Speeches like that, and a later one about the difficulties of being a Mexican American ("You've got to be twice as perfect ... It's exhausting") indicate that even without Quintanilla's supervision, Nava would likely have made this kind of a soft film. While the writer-director's fearlessness in the face of emotion has its charms, Nava's willingness to state everything in the most obvious terms and the film's lack of dramatic texture do get bothersome.

Most of "Selena" is taken up with the singer's gradual but inexorable rise to the top. Despite resistance of Mexican Americans to a female tejano star and the skepticism of Mexicans about a woman whose command of Spanish was less than perfect, Selena easily wins everyone over and her willingness to accept herself as she is turns her into a key role model for Latinas.

Unlike, say, Tina Turner in "What's Love Got to Do With It," however, the young adult Selena is presented without any life-threatening problems. Her main conflict, hardly shattering, was a budding romance with handsome, heavy metalish lead guitarist Chris Perez (Jon Seda) that father Abraham is determined to quash.

Overall, Selena's most persistent difficulty turns out to be dealing with her father, a man with a fierce temper and a will of iron who threw one of many fits when she first tried out her trademark bustier on stage. It's a measure of how stern a taskmaster the senior Quintanilla must have been that despite this film's tendency to whitewash, as played by Olmos he comes off as a single-minded tyrant who loved his daughter but was determined to run her life.

"Selena" closes with documentary footage of the real singer, and it's a shock to realize that Lopez so much resembles her that for a instant you can't tell one from the other. And it's in fact a melding of the two, of the real story and the actress' ability to convey it, that creates emotional connections destined to outlive the doses of biopic boilerplate that surround it.

NEW YORK POST, 3/21/97, p. 49, Michael Medved

In crafting a movie biography of the late Tejano singing sensation Selena Quintanilla Perez, writer-director Gregory Nava faced a nearly impossible balancing act: keeping faith with millions of devoted fans while simultaneously engaging other moviegoers who know nothing about her other than the brutal fact of her murder two years ago at age 23.

Facing the conflicting pressures of this assignment, Nava achieves an honorable compromise—a sweet if simple-minded fan letter which, like his previous films "El Norte" And "My Family/Mi Familia," amounts to a warmhearted celebration of the indestructible bonds of family.

The Quintanillas come across here as a fun-loving musical clan of irresistible wholesomeness—a spicy Latino answer to Ozzie and Harriet.

Edward James Olmos (who reportedly gained 50 pounds for the role) plays the patriarch, who leaves his job at a Texas oil company and risks his family's suburban home to start a Mexican restaurant that can highlight the musical talents of his three kids.

This venture fails with an utterly gratuitous political dig ("It's that Ronald Reagan. Reaganomics. A lot of small businesses have gone broke.") and the family hits the road to perform at fairs and carnivals.

As Selena grows up, the lead role passes from spunky 10-year-old Becky Lee Meza to glamorous Jennifer Lopez, who soon defies her domineering father with her love for the sulky lead guitarist (Jon Seda) in the family's band.

Lopez may bear only a passing resemblance to the real Selena, but she is captivating in her own right, showing depth and range far beyond her previous, mostly decorative performances in movies like "Money Train" and "Blood and Wine."

Constance Marie is marvelous as her wise, doting mother, while the reliable Olmos brings unforgettable dignity to a role that could have been a nasty caricature.

Some of the dialogue feels hackneyed and clunky ("She is special! And she's gonna make it!" or "Being a Mexican-American is tough. You've got to be twice as perfect as anybody else."), but it can't defeat this gifted, passionate ensemble cast.

More troubling are the long stretches of lip-syncing and heavily edited film meant to recreate Selena's live performances. I'm not qualified to judge their authenticity, but even those with a hearty appetite for bouncy Tejano tunes will begin to feel bored.

A more serious flaw involves the movie's puzzling, anticlimactic treatment of Selena's murder—by far the most dramatic element in her short life. The incident is summarized in brief news reports but never dramatized—perhaps to avoid bloody scenes that might have threatened the movie's PG rating and its strong family appeal.

Like the rest of the film, this decision demonstrates admirable sensitivity, but produces little substance or satisfaction.

NEWSDAY, 3/21/97, Part II/p. B9, Jack Mathews

Writer-Director Gregory Nava's screenplay for "Selena," a film biography of the slain *tejano* singer Selena Quintanilla Perez, goes easy on a father who, by most other accounts, managed her life and career as a tyrant, and whose approval Nava needed for every detail from casting to dialogue. And for reasons we can only guess (legal? Dad again?), the movie doesn't even bother to dramatize the most dramatic event—her murder by a distressed employee.

Still, in capturing the essential appeal of Selena to the millions of Latinos who adored her, Nava has come up with one of the most joyous and effective celebrations of an entertainer's life in memory.

The "Selena" sound track, using recordings released before and after her death, is likely to recruit millions more fans to the reggae-polka-*conjunto*-blended music long popular along the American-Mexican border. And the movie is going to make a star of Jennifer Lopez.

The 25-year-old Lopez, who played one of the central characters in Nava's "La Familia," gives an astonishingly confident performance as Selena, both in creating a psychologically complete character, and in miming the star's boundless performance energy. Lopez not only bears an eerie physical resemblance to Selena, she has her dance steps and stage manner down perfectly.

"Selena" tips its hand to the father's influence early, opening with Abraham Quintanilla (Edward James Olmos) sending Selena—out to the stage of a sold-out Houston Astrodome, for a concert held shortly before her death. The film then cuts back a quarter-century, to when Abraham was a member of a Mexican-American trio whose ethnicity kept them out of white clubs and whose pop-rock ballads got them run out of clubs in the Latino community.

The frustration of his short-lived music career is meant to explain Abraham's compulsion to raise his own children as an act. Selena sings, older sister Suzie is on drums and brother Abie plays guitar—mostly against their wishes. Even their mother (Constance Marie) considers Abraham's guidance a form of child abuse, but the impression intended—and left by Olmos' often comically engaging performance—is of a man selflessly looking after his family's interests.

Watching the story unfold, knowing that the family had total control over its content, I had the feeling that Nava had put the untouchable elements out of his mind and simply concentrated on what he could do, which was tap into the childlike joy that Selena got from her music and from performing. In fact, if you accept Abraham as approved by Abraham, the moments with the family resemble a Mexican-American "Father Knows Best."

Taking the story as told, "Selena's" strength is its exaltation of ordinary people undergoing extraordinary success. Her brief life is spectacular but uncomplicated. She was raised in Texas, and had to learn her Spanish phonetically when she first sang in public at her parents' Mexican restaurant. She was touring and recording at 15, eloped with a band member (warmly played by Jon Seda) at 20, and had gold and platinum albums by 23.

She also had her own clothing line and owned several boutiques, and was recording her first English-language album when she went to a Corpus Christi motel room to meet with Yolanda Saldivar, who had embezzled thousands of dollars while running Selena's fan club and cooking the books for her other businesses. In real life, Selena ran out of that motel room with a bullet wound, and bled to death. Saldivar claimed she fired her gun accidentally, but she was convicted of murder and is serving a life sentence.

The movie doesn't even go to the motel, let alone inside the room. Instead, Nava intercuts newsreel footage of the scene outside with scenes of Selena's grieving family and fans. There are also shots in the final montage of the real Selena in performance, underscoring the brilliance of Lopez' performance.

Given the extended postscript he made of Selena's tragic end, Nava would have had a better movie, certainly more streamlined, if he'd simply skipped it altogether.

TIME, 3/24/97, p. 86, Richard Corliss

Elvis has Graceland. Jim Morrison's plot at Père-Lachaise in Paris has been the subject of such devotion and commotion that the cemetery's keepers have threatened to expel the coffin. But on a recent Friday afternoon at the Seaside Memorial Park in Corpus Christi, Texas, no poignant notes or fresh flowers bedeck the black gravestone of Selena Quintanilla Perez. The place is deserted—until two young people approach to pay their respects. Roddy Gómez, 27, and his fiancé Lisa Castro, 18, moved from Arizona two months ago, simply to live in the city of their idol. "It looks so plain, it's hard to believe she's buried here," says Gómez. Castro thinks the site is pretty. "But somehow I thought it would be bigger."

No matter. The fans of Selena, Queen of Tejano, are about to get a $23 million memorial, and they needn't make a pilgrimage to this Gulf-port city either. Two years after the Mex-Tex singer was killed by the president of her fan club, a reverent Hollywood biopic is opening around the country. *Selena*, from writer-director Gregory Nava *(El Norte, Mi Familia)*, stars Jennifer Lopez in a Spanish-accented version of the old star-is-born tale. Urged on by her father (Edward James Olmos), a gifted girl rises to the top of her niche market. She falls in love and elopes with her band's guitarist (Jon Seda)—a defiant gesture that tests but doesn't defile her dad's love. She's ready to ride the pop mainstream when Yolanda Saldivar, a trusted friend, cuts Selena down at 23. End of a life, beginning of a legend.

"I didn't do the movie to exploit my daughter," insists Abraham Quintanilla Jr., 57, who formed the group Selena y Los Dinos when the girl was just nine and served as its manager and goading spirit. "I did it because there's an insatiable desire from the public to know more about her." Nonetheless, *Selena* is the latest, largest artifact in the kind of postmortem career maintenance that not only honors but also profits from a slain celebrity. Selena still has three albums on *Billboard*'s Latin Top 50 chart. Music awards continue to come her way. The family has kept promoting Selena hair salons, Selena fashions and a new Selena doll ($22 plus tax).

Scavengers are also circling. E! the Entertainment Channel aired a re-enactment of Saldivar's trial and plans to rebroadcast it soon. And in *Selena's Secret,* the newest of at least half a dozen unsanctioned bio books about the star, author and Univision hostess María Celeste Arrarás coyly hints that Selena kept a secret diary and was planning to torpedo her career for a tryst with the Mexican plastic surgeon who administered her liposuction treatments. The family denies these scandals.

The *Selena* film studiously avoids the sensational. It dares to be a slow, stolid film about goodness, to build its story on the rock of family love. The main conflict is over Selena's love for long-haired Chris, the metal guitarist who plays pappy pop when he joins the band—he's a rebel without a chord. Chris is also the excuse for a later tearful reconciliation between Selena and Dad. Though then, are often at loggerheads, they are never at loggerhearts. Selena's too devoted for that. She's a modern-day saint in spandex.

To give it a tang in the common consciousness, any new form of pop music needs an emblematic satyr or a martyr. Rock had Elvis; reggae, Bob Marley. Selena was no wild woman, though onstage she zestily displayed her full figure in spangled bustiers. She succeeded in Tejano (a blend of Mexican *ranchera*, polka, country and pop, Colombian *cumbia*, even reggae) by projecting an aerobic perkiness—Gloria Estefan tinged with Janet Jackson.

Her songs, usually written and arranged by her brother Abraham III, are perky too, cheerful rather than soulful. The early ones, with their tinny, Tijuana Brass charts and keyboards that evoke calliopes, are ideal for the fairground or merry-go-round. Later efforts had broader pop inflections; they complement Selena's expert mimicry of everything from Edith Piaf's melodramatic contralto to the coloratura riffs of Mariah Carey. But the sound is still lightly Hispanic; the tunes are infectious fluff. Los Dinos was a band for a fiesta or wedding, where the bride has a sweet last dance with her father.

Selena's father, known as Abraham to distinguish him from his composer son ("A.B."), was protective and demanding of the budding star. In the film he is portrayed as a short-tempered klutz who would do anything to see his kids make the musical mark that he didn't achieve on his own. Some onlookers believe that Abraham, who served as the film's executive producer, wielded control over it as he did over Selena's life. "The guy has been so adamant about controlling the spin on this," says Joe Nick Patoski, a *Texas Monthly* writer and author of the acclaimed *Selena: Como la Flor*. "He's as manipulative as Joe Jackson ever was."

Quintanilla may wish his kids had had the success of the Jackson 5. But, he says, "I'm not a mean person. I'm just a father who was protecting his children in the music business, which is a vicious business." Moctesuma Esparza, who produced the film with Robert Katz, says Abraham was dogged but malleable. "He didn't want any mention of Yolanda, but we convinced him that the full arc of the story wasn't there without what happened at the end." Says director Nava: "One reason for doing the film was that the fans need catharsis, and if you don't show her death, you can't get that."

The whole family was involved, providing insights and details. Lopez, who gives a feisty, buoyant performance that could set her on a star path similar to the singer's, moved in with Selena's sister Suzette and got scolded by the singer's mother for bad eating habits. "She told me I was just like Selena"—a reproach that to Lopez was high praise. When Nava finished the script, he read it to the family. "They stopped us many times," Esparza says, "because they were crying so hard."

The elder Quintanilla confesses that some days I can cope with it. Other times I have a knot in my throat all day long." He occasionally has dreams of Selena. In one, he sees her sleeping in her bedroom and then she suddenly wakes. "In the dream, I told her, "We better let the media know you're not dead, because they'll think we played a hoax for the publicity."'

Quintanilla is often shaken into silence by the ghost and the guilt. "Sometimes I feel like I'm to blame," he says. "Me and my wife were in bed talking about this the other night—that had we not chosen this path for our kids, Selena would still be alive." He also chose Saldivar to run the Selena fan club, after the woman had left more than a dozen insistent messages on his answering machine. "I actually feel sorry for her sometimes," says Abraham, who adds he believes Saldivar was demonically possessed at the time of the murder. "But Yolanda is not really in my mind. Selena is in my mind."

Selena is also in music stores; expect a surge in the sales of her eight albums, and of the soundtrack CD. And this week, with the release of this earnest little weepie, Selena may finally get to fulfill her crossover dream into the mainstream, that River Jordan for Latino musicians. Surely she and her family deserve some sort of Hollywood happy ending.

VILLAGE VOICE, 4/1/97, p. 70, Daisann McLane

It's no surprise that *Selena*, Gregory Nava's film about the murdered Tejano singer, is more hagio than biography. In the two years since Quintanilla was shot by her assistant in a Days Inn, she's become a role model akin to a saint (She may be the only chart-topper whose fans carry votive candies.) Yet even as hagiographies go, *Selena* misses the inspirational beat.

The film's opening scene is meant to record a triumph and set us up for the tragic finale. It's Selena's last, sellout show at the Houston Astrodome and Nava pulls out all the cinematic stops, cutting from a radiant and sequined Selena (astonishingly twinned by Jennifer Lopez) to the cheering audience, then to shots of a white rose (innocence!) and a big Texas moon (dreams and fate!). But then the band strikes up the intro to Selena's final performance, the proof of her imminent cross-over to mainstream stardom. And her last song? A medley of Donna Summer's disco classics.

Unintentionally funny like this may be the result of too many agendas. Selena's fiercely protective father and manager had final approval over Nava's script, and so the story of Selena's climb from the rickety stages of Texas state fairs to the Grammys and stardom has all the showbiz grit of a *Partridge Family* episode: a talented girl is pushed by her demanding but lovable dad (Edward James Olmos) to become a singer. Director Nava tries to squeeze more juice from the formula—his specialty is sweeping, heroic sagas of Mexican American struggle and heartbreak like *El Norte* and *Mi Familia*—but the showbiz, middle-class Quintanilla family doesn't quite fit into Nava's mold. Meanwhile, there's the marketing bottom line—guess what the first single is.

Nava sidelines the figure of Yolanda Saldivar, Selena's killer, so much so that viewers unfamiliar with Selena's true story may be confused about the circumstances of her murder. There's only one subplot that enlivens this otherwise tedious memento mori: the forbidden romance between Selena and her guitarist, Chris Perez (played by the hunky Jon Seda). Fresh from eloping with Perez in a flashy red convertible, Selena lifts her arms to the sky as the hot Texas breeze flies through her hair. The film takes off for that moment and you get a sense of what a fascinating character this impulsive, determined young woman must have been. Maybe someday someone will make a movie about *her*.

Also reviewed in:
NEW YORK TIMES, 3/21/97, p. C16, Stephen Holden
VARIETY, 3/24-30/97, p. 33, Todd McCarthy
WASHINGTON POST, 3/21/97, p. B1, Richard Harrington
WASHINGTON POST, 3/21/97, Weekend/p. 48, Eric Brace

SELF-MADE HERO, A

A Strand Releasing release of a Aliceléo, Lumière/France 3 Cinéma/M6 Films/Initial Groupe production in association with Cofimage 7 and Studio Images 2 with the participation of Canal Plus, the Centre National de la Cinématographie, and the support of the PROCIREP. *Executive Producer:* Françoise Galfré. *Producer:* Patrick Godeau. *Director:* Jacques Audiard. *Screenplay (French with English subtitles):* Alain Le Henry and Jacques Audiard. *Based on the novel by:* Jean-François Deniau. *Director of Photography:* Jean-Marc Fabre. *Editor:* Juliette Welfling. *Music:* Alexandre Desplat. *Sound:* Jean-Pierre Duret and (music) Didier Lizé. *Sound Editor:* Nicolas Naegelen. *Casting:* Serge Boutleroff and Florence Botel. *Production Designer:* Michel Vandestien. *Art Director:* Dominique Douret. *Set Decorator:* Emmanuel Maintigneux. *Special Effects:* Georges Demetrau, Grégoire Delage, and Olivier Zeninski. *Costumes:* Caroline de Vivaise. *Make-up:* Mayté Alonso. *Special Make-up Effects:* Dominique Colladant. *Running time:* 105 minutes. *MPAA Rating:* Not Rated.

CAST: Mathieu Kassovitz (Young Albert Dehousse); Anouk Grinberg (Servane); Sandrine Kiberlain (Yvette); Jean-Louis Trintignant (Old Albert Dehousse); Albert Dupontel (Captain Dionnet); Nadia Barentin (The General's Wife); Bernard Bloch (Ernst); François Chattot (Louvier); Phillippe Duclos (Caron); Danièle Lebrun (Mme Dehousse); Armand de Baudry d'Asson (Englishman); Wilfred Benaiche (Nervoix); François Berléand (Monsieur Jo); Philippe Berodot (Leguen); Gilles Del Frate (The Partisan); Stéfan Elbaum ("Little Versailles" Man 1); Marc Ernotte (De Vaincourt); Jérôme Floch (Etienne); Isabelle Gruault (Lutétia, Young Woman); Donatien Guillot (Knickerbocker); Philippe Harel (Information Officer); Christophe

Kourotchkine ("Little Versailles" Man 2);   Philippe Lehembre (Maitre Becquard);   François Levantal (Delavelle);   Patrick Ligardes (Malbert);   Clotilde Mollet (Odette);   Phillippe Nahon (The General);   Yann Pradal (FFI 1);   Bruno Putzulu (Meyer);   Georges Siatidis (Beauchamps); Laurent Vacher (Maldoror Man);   Yves Verhoeven (Boutin);   David Fernandes (Albert, Child); Xavier Arcache (Jean Caron, Child);   Eléonore Godeau (Little Girl at Kiosk);   Thomas Vindevogel (Lout);   Anne Villette and Dominique LeMonier (Violin Players, Orchestra); Geneviève Strosser (Alto, Orchestra);   Vincent Segal (Cello, Orchestra);   Marc Marder (Double-bass, Orchestra);   Emmanuel Strosser (Piano, Orchestra).

LOS ANGELES TIMES, 12/3/97, Calendar/p. 10, Kenneth Turan

Duplicity is always intriguing, but impostors, people who painstakingly create false identities from the ground up, fascinate most of all.   "The best lives are invented, someone said that," remarks Albert Dehousse, the protagonist of Jacques Audiard's smart and provocative "A Self-Made Hero," before blandly adding, "I think it was me."

Directed and co-written (with Alain Le Henry) by Audiard, an experienced French screenwriter who now directs as well, "A Self-Made Hero" is an acute psychological study of a man who made himself up as he went along, a delicious piece of work that succeeds in making the audience a willing accomplice in the deception.   Winner of the best screenplay prize at Cannes, it is as precisely written as it is thought out, and beautifully acted in the bargain.

For most of the film Dehousse is played by Mathieu Kassovitz (best known as the director of "La Haine"), but when we first meet the character it's as a much older man played by Jean-Louis Trintignant, the subject of a documentary looking into the unique circumstances of his life. (Using these two actors is also something of an inside joke, for they were the stars of Audiard's first film as a director, 1994's excellent but still unreleased "Regarde Les Hommes Tomber.")

It's the nature of Dehousse's deception that makes him worthy of this documentary.   More or less unaffected by World War II, he was able, in the chaotic peacetime months of 1945, to pass himself off as a valued and heroic member of the French Resistance.   This concern with the malleability of morality in wartime and after, with how easily the French nation as a whole was able to slough off its history of collaboration, was what attracted Audiard to the Jean-François Deniau novel the film is based on.

Audiard is especially fortunate in the way actor Kassovitz brings the correct combination of earnestness, timidity and bravado to the role of the simultaneously guileless and ruthless Dehousse.   Though we may think we'll be put off by the man's dishonesty, there is something ingratiating and amusing about how desperately Dehousse wants to become an insider.   A callow youth with surprising reserves of cleverness, able to hide pure calculation under the mask of boyishness, Dehousse is an entertaining master magician who turns his own life into the greatest act of all.

One of the unstated themes of "A Self-Made Hero" is that though he wasn't aware while it was happening, Dehousse's entire life as a preparation for his supreme deception.   He in effect grew into his vocation, picking up tips and techniques from a variety of unrelated sources.

As a child, growing up in genteel poverty in rural France, young Albert got his first lesson in deception when he realized his own mother has misled him about his late father's past.   Already a lover of words and make-believe, he acts out the novels of youthful adventure he reads, and when he meets future wife Yvette (Sandrine Kiberlain), he tells her he's a writer and proves it by copying out passages from the latest book he's read and passing them off as his own.

However, Dehousse will not invent on the page, but rather with life itself.   After a wartime spent as a salesman learning about self-presentation, he runs off to Paris on Liberation Day out of embarrassment at how little he did during the conflict.   There he comes under the influence of the Captain (Albert Dupontel), a real Resistance hero who "loved deceit in every form."   He tells his young protégé that he's at a rare moment in history when anything goes, and advises him, should he try to be false, "to make it all up, to invent everything from A to Z."

Which is what Dehousse sets out to do.   Beginning with easy things, like bluffing his way into Resistance reunions, he soon turns to deception's heavy lifting.   "A Self-Made Hero" is especially good at showing the painstaking hard work that goes into making yourself over: the reading, the memorization, the socializing, the willingness to practice lines as conscientiously as any actor.

The more he does it, the more Dehousse discovers he has a gift for this business, an ability for outfoxing the suspicious, for knowing how to say, "Need I say more?" when saying more would be fatal. He eventually meets a woman (Anouk Grinberg) who is very nearly a match for him, and he finds himself almost turning, like the protagonist of Roberto Rossellini's classic "General Della Rovere," into something like the person he's pretended to be.

Writer-director Audiard has not only put together a script that works like an intricate clock, he's also collaborated with cinematographer Jean-Marc Fabre ("Moi Ivan, Toi Abraham") to give the film a sense of cinematic style. Among the playful touches he includes are shots of a chamber ensemble playing the film's Alexandre Desplat score. No matter how real I've made it seem, he's saying, never forget that we're making it up here just like that rascal Albert Dehousse.

NEW YORK POST, 9/12/97, p. 47, Larry Worth

If stories of the Resistance remain a sensitive subject for Gauls, Jacques Audiard just became a man without a country.

In "A Self-Made Hero," the up-and-coming French director has fashioned a fast-paced, wildly irreverent comedy of World War II posturing, alongside a scathing commentary on the essence of reality.

Mathieu Kassovitz, the director of last year's brilliant "Hate," steps in front of the lens as Albert Dehousse, a born liar whose engaging tales of derring-do propel him to the heights of postwar politics.

It starts with the simple parroting of colleagues' anecdotes, words which soon become his own. Albert ultimately connives, seduces and reinvents his way from conscription-dodging teen to revered military honcho, setting a new standard for amoral carpetbaggers in the process.

More remarkably, audiences can't help but cheer him on, largely due to an appealing lead performance. Kassovitz—who resembles a young Matt Lauer—invokes Peter Sellers' classic Chauncey Gardiner role in "Being There," by way of Woody Allen's human chameleon in "Zelig." It's a stunning tour de force, proving him as good an actor as director.

Sandrine Kiberlain and Anouk Grinberg—whose resemblance to Juliette Binoche is almost uncanny—are heartbreakingly incisive as the women in Albert's life. And equally entrancing are Jean-Louis Trintignant's droll asides as Albert's latter-day self.

But the real star remains Audiard. He recognizes the all-too-human tendency to reinvent one's life, then boldly spins that concept to the max.

Using the Resistance movement as a means to explore the nature of truth, Audiard incorporates faux documentary interviews, period World War II footage, eclectic camerawork and most audaciously—shots of an orchestra playing the movie's background music, underscoring the illusory quality of filmmaking itself.

With a mood that changes from whimsical to tragic in a heartbeat, the results deliver on various levels. As entertainment, innovation and thought-provoking cinema, "A Self-Made Hero" triumphs.

NEWSDAY, 9/12/97, Part II/p. B11, John Anderson

During the reunification of Germany a few years ago, this joke made the rounds: Question: Did you hear that the two Germanys have decided on a new capital? Answer: Yes, Paris.

In a way, Jacques Audiard's "A Self-Made Hero" is the long version of the joke, a prolonged puncturing of France's image as a nation that resisted fascism throughout World War II, a lengthy muttering of nasty words, like "collaborationist." Its "hero," Albert Dehousse (Mathieu Kassovitz), a stand-in for France, recreates his own history, attains respect and position. He is eventually found out, but—in his audacity, at least—he's an object of begrudged admiration.

Based on the novel by Jean-Francois Deniau, "A Self-Made Hero" is both revisionist history and a caustic reflection of current-day celebrity. Think of Albert as a child of television" of C-span: He's been reared on lies and therefore cultivates them. Contrary to what his mother's told him, his father wasn't a World War I hero; he was a drunk who dropped dead outside the local café. When he meets Yvette (Sandrine Kiberlain), he claims to be a novelist and then spends hours copying the work of others to give to her. They marry, but Albert is perceived as so untrustworthy that only at the end of the war does he discover that his father-in-law ran the local

Resistance unit—and that his wife was part of it. He's gifted, though, and what he's gifted at is lying.

He leaves town, heads for Paris and parlays his talent into invitations to Resistance reunions, a job interrogating actual collaborationists, and eventually gets a military commission and access to the bed of the lovely officer, Servane (Anouk Grinberg).

You want to say he's despicable, but as played in unassuming fashion by Mathieu Kassovitz, a director in his own right ("Cafe au Lait," "Hate"), Albert is more of a cipher. But he's so good at what he does that you tend to root for him. Director Audiard and co-writer Alain Le Henry structure "A Self-Made Hero" partly as mock-umentary—JeanLouis Trintingnant plays Albert as an old man, reflecting on his past. The film makes occasional forays into the surreal, with characters speaking of their own imminent death.

Albert's strange appeal actually lends a certain smugness to the film. The few people who suspect his deceit are cast as villains, and the overriding implication is that Albert could have been a great man had he not been trying so hard to pretend he was a great man. If France is to be castigated for convenient memory, shouldn't Albert be condemned, too? Ah well, you know what Rick said: We'll always have Paris.

SIGHT AND SOUND, 4/97, p. 47, Michael Temple

Provincial France, the 30s. A fatherless boy, Albert Dehousse, is brought up by his widowed mother. He fills the social void with various games and fantasies. A friend reveals to him that his father was not a war-hero, as his mother maintains, but the town drunk, dead from cirrhosis. During the German Occupation of 1940-44, Albert is unfit for active service. He meets Yvette and wins her heart by passing for a budding novelist. They marry and his father-in-law initiates him into the persuasive arts of the travelling salesman, thereby helping Albert avoid 'voluntary' labour in Germany. At the Liberation of France, Dehousse discovers that his wife and father-in-law were involved in the Resistance, while his mother's collaboration is publicly punished. Albert disappears to Paris.

There, he spectacularly reinvents himself as a Resistance hero. He soon learns that people will believe what they want to hear regarding a period they would rather forget. Two key encounters trigger off his reassimilation: he meets Monsieur Jo, a profiteer of foreign origin, who gets caught out when he reconverts to patriotism and Captain Dionnet, a genuine if cynical Resistance hero and double agent, who abruptly disappears with a handsome GI. So convincing is Albert's infiltration of the *anciens réistants* that soon he is identified as a reliable, apolitical judge of others, and appointed firstly to weed out traitors in France, and then (as Lieutenant Colonel Dehousse) to run psychological and propaganda operations in occupied Germany.

Despite winning over his initially hostile fellow soldiers, Dehousse starts to crack: contradictions arise in his past history and present life; between the sheets of intimacy, he confesses all to his lover, Servane, herself an intelligence agent. Albert is called upon to round up a group of French Wehrmacht volunteers, now on the run. Faced with the choice between public trial and discreet execution, Albert opts for the fatal solution, having first promised the traitors that, for the record, they will have died in action. Albert then signs and submits his own confession. Political expediency, however, demands that scandal should not be added to ridicule, and so he is convicted on a minor charge of bigamy (for his relationships with Yvette and Servane). We are given to understand that ex-Lieutenant Colonel Dehousse went on to enjoy a post-war political career appropriately tinged with suspicion, myth, and double-dealing.

As the elaborate twists and turns of the synopsis above will suggest, Jacques Audiard has produced a complex and suggestive tale of private fantasy and public myth, touching upon some extremely problematic areas of contemporary French history in the process. 50 years after the events, it is still difficult, in aesthetic terms, to find an appropriate form which can explore the complicities and connivances of World War Two resistance and collaboration. It is still politically sensitive to expose the monumental self-deception beneath the post-war Gaullist mythology of heroism, patriotic fidelity, and triumphant rebirth into a morally pure modernity. The bizarre and controversial reception afforded Pierre Péan's 1994 biography of the young François Mitterand (*Une jeunesse française*) told us as much about the French public's current anxieties, taboos, and perversities, as it did about this sombre period and the awkward questions it continues to pose. One might indeed speculate whether Audiard could have drawn equal inspiration from that affair as he did from Jean-François Deniau's 1989 novel Un *héros très discret* (literally, "a very discreet hero", although "a self-made hero" is an excellent translation in context).

It is important to make some remarks concerning the way in which Audiard treats the basic narrative material, not least because he has himself declared in interview that he wanted the themes of fakery and fabrication fully integrated into the *mise en scène*.   He is clearly less interested in pointing the finger at identifiable baddies than he is in making everyone feel the narcissistic little baddy inside. In order to achieve this effect, he doubly frames the story of Albert Dehousse. Firstly, he uses the ageing and iconic Jean-Louis Trintignant, so famous he must first and foremost be 'Trintignant' rather than 'Dehousse', in order to portray the character of Albert in the present day, directly addressing the camera and audience and commenting on the tale. These sequences are cut into the narrative as a distanciation effect: they spoil the possibility of certain narrative resolutions, and they remind us of our present position as spectator, disrupting our identification and undermining our judgement.

Secondly, Audiard sets up his film as a fake documentary: the work jumps back and forth in time from past to present, editing in mock-interviews with Albert's supposed contemporaries and 'specialists' of the period, as well as newsreel material taken indifferently from Pétain's Vichy, and De Gaulle's Liberation. This confusion of false historical documents with genuine historical fictions gives a provocative political edge to the elaborate psychological exploration of lying and self-delusion. There are two further alienation techniques employed by Audiard: the insertion of deliberately improbable scenes shot against a darkened backdrop, in which we see the young Albert flying, fighting, and variously fancying himself; lastly, the periodical sequences showing us the musicians playing the soundtrack.

If the aim of such (Godardian) methods is largely to disrupt our relationship with the filmic illusion, we need also to examine the ways in which *A Self-Made Hero* ceaselessly draws us in to its many identificatory traps. These psychological moves are unsurprisingly focused on the central figure of Albert, and therefore on the remarkable presence of Mathieu Kassovitz (director, as we know, of *Métisse* and *La Haine*). As spectators, we are invited to play our part in his passive-aggressive, narcissistic-voyeuristic world. We watch him perform: rehearse, repeat, fluff and perfect a whole series of parts and lines. And we watch him watch: most strikingly in three parallel sequences, where first Albert as a child watches some neighbours playing a game of tennis, then some German soldiers playing on the same court during the Occupation, and finally in Germany where Lieutenant Dehousse is caught watching his comrades playing and is forced into making a humiliating spectacle of himself as a totally incompetent player.   At this psychological level, then, our own passage from viewer to player to viewer again is far from comfortable and less than comforting.

On the question of discomfort, there are two final matters which also concern alienation and identification which Audiard seems either unhappy to address or unwilling to foreclose: sexuality and otherness. Firstly, there is a double strand of doubt running through and around Albert's sexuality. He is unconvincing, we hear repeatedly, in his role as male heterosexual lover; he is not quite there, as if a void were revealed when the mask slips in bed. This doubt is developed in his encounter with the Captain, who by contrast is frankly out, and happily promiscuous. Their intimacy is short-circuited, however, by the disappearance of the Captain: the fleeting glance they later exchange in Germany is left as a question mark (as is the exact nature of Albert's relationship with his German manservant and 'father', and Yvette's relationship with the bisexual Servane).

In a similar vein, Audiard wilfully leaves in suspense the status of the racial 'other' in this historical tale of two countries' complementary destinies. France and Germany form a conflictual but collaborative couple, from the Great War to mutual occupation and collaboration, Adenauer and De Gaulle, Mitterrand and Kohl. In a third, less certain position, however, we find the foreigner in the form of 'Monsieur Jo', hoist by his own petard, and Dehousse-Kassovitz who, at a critical moment of his reinventions 'passes' for a Jew called Rozinsky, whom he knows to have been deported to the camps during the Occupation. This gives us a 'French' director directing a 'Jewish' actor-director playing a 'French' faker passing as a disappeared 'Jew'... It would be interesting to know what the two protagonists think about these issues, and how consciously they are woven into the shifting and absorbing structures of *A Self-Made Hero*.

TIME, 10/20/97, p. 105, Richard Corliss

Noir! The very word sounds like a French lion's growl. In its undiluted form, film noir (named after *Série Noir,* a French publisher's line of crime novels) is tart and murky, like cheap Parisian coffee, and as mean as any Marseilles street a gangster could skulk down. These dank moral tales are about the evil that taints everyone—especially the hero, who must end up dead or disgraced. This disqualifies Hollywood neo-noir like *L.A. Confidential,* where at the fade-out two guys and a gal grin as if they'd just seen *Singin' in the Rain.* In true noir there is no reprieve.

Maybe we should leave noir to the French and other outsiders; they are less likely to go simple with sentiment. Two handsome films, Jacques Audiard's *A Self-Made Hero* and Arturo Ripstein's *Deep Crimson,* take a smart, stony-eyed look at chicanery in the '40s. Some cunning insects are on display, and not a tear needs to be shed for them or their victims.

A man lying to himself: that is delusion. A nation lying to itself: that is policy. Thus the death of half a million American Indians is euphemized as manifest destiny. The French, after their craven accommodation to the occupying Nazis, had their own little lie. Collaborators? *Mais non*—we were all in the Resistance!

A Self-Made Hero could be called *The Secret Life of Walter Vichy.* Albert Dehousse (Mathieu Kassovitz) is a slow-witted fellow with a gift for mimicry. He was not called for war service, so when a true Resistance hero relates his adventures, Albert uses these particulars to dress up his life. He soon finds he needn't tell many lies about himself, others will sketch the rest of his imagined exploits out of their urgent need for heroes.

The film—a deadpan comedy cloaked in noir atmosphere (fog, dark alleys, secret meetings)—does not merely point a gnarled finger at French gullibility; it gets at the universal impulse to create alternative truths. Lying is a way to stay alive. "When Death comes," says Albert, "we'll lie to it. We'll say, 'You've got the wrong guy.'" This anti-*Hero* leaves an indelible taste, somehow both bitter and savory.

Evil can be passive, like Albert's, or gross, like Coral's in the Mexican *Deep Crimson.* Coral (Regina Orozco), a nurse, is fat, lazy, a bust at everything but loving Nico (Daniel Gimenez Cacho). Movie-mad Coral wants a man like Charles Boyer. Well, Nico does wear a toupee. And like Boyer in *Gaslight,* he is a thief of women's affections and inheritances. Coral, at first a mark, proves his accomplice and inspiration. Dumping her two kids in an orphanage and posing as Nico's sister, she prods him to romance, rob and kill his ladies; then the swindlers make sweaty lust in the shed. And why do they do it? "To be together," the lovers say. "United in blood and death."

Based, like the 1970 *The Honeymoon Killers,* on the case of lonely-hearts murderers Raymond Fernandez and Martha Beck, this poisonous, beautifully acted tragicomedy exerts a cold fascination. Virtually every scene is a single shot (no intercutting to cue emotion); the camera prowls like a smooth, stealthy voyeur. Yet the film is true to the ferocity of mad love. There is a deep crimson in the couple's passion that, in the end, can only fade to noir.

VILLAGE VOICE, 9/16/97, p. 98, Leslie Camhi

World War I gave France military heroes whose names adorn every town and city; World War II produced a humiliating defeat, four years of collaboration, and scars that still haven't healed. De Gaulle propagated the myth of widespread Resistance to promote national unity; alas, the truth was much more murky.

Jacques Audiard's *A Self-Made Hero?,* based on Jean-François Deniau's novel, was inspired by this continuing scandal. Mathieu Kassovitz (director of *La Haine)* plays Albert Dehousse, a provincial French wimp growing up in the '20s and '30s. Albert's mother gives him his first lessons in lying; she says his father died bravely in battle, though he succumbed to cirrhosis. Albert resolves to become a hero, but in World War II he avoids conscription, marrying Yvette (Sandrine Kiberlain), the beautiful daughter of a close-knit Communist family. At the war's end, he learns that Yvette's family was part of the Resistance.

Shamed by his own blindness, Albert sets off for Paris, where he meets the Captain (Albert Dupontel), a true Resistance fighter. The Captain is captivated by the scams of the postwar period, where people change identities more quickly than shirts: "losers posing as winners, cowards posing as heroes, devils as saints." Taking a lesson, Albert decides to fabricate a history with himself as a paradigm of Resistance. Furiously, he memorizes maps of London, and the names and politics of Resistance circles; soon he's passing himself off as a member and he's appointed to an important post in Germany. There he meets Servane (Anouk Grinberg), a stunning sergeant who fought with the Free French in Algeria.

In Kassovitz, Audiard has found a consummate actor for this story about the pleasure, rewards, and fascination of pretending. (The great Jean-Louis Trintignant plays an elderly Dehousse with a sly panache.) The narrative is cunningly cut with pseudo-interviews of historical witnesses, in a parody of the genre initiated by *The Sorrow and the Pity*. This false documentary framework raises the very questions of truth, invention, and duplicity that plague both Dehousse's story and French cultural memory. *A Self-Made Hero* is an amusing and finely crafted exercise in the betrayal of history.

Also reviewed in:
CHICAGO TRIBUNE, 1/2/98, Friday/p. C, Michael Wilmington
NATION, 9/22/97, p. 42, Stuart Klawans
NEW REPUBLIC, 9/22/97, p. 30, Stanley Kauffman
NEW YORK TIMES, 9/12/97, p. C8, Janet Maslin
VARIETY, 5/20-26/96, p. 32, Lisa Nesselson

SEVEN YEARS IN TIBET

A TriStar Pictures release of a Mandalay Entertainment presentation of a Reperage and Vanguard Films/Applecross production. *Executive Producer:* Richard Goodwin, Michael Besman, and David Nichols. *Producer:* Jean-Jacques Annaud, John H. Williams, and Iain Smith. *Director:* Jean-Jacques Annaud. *Screenplay:* Becky Johnston. *Based on the book by:* Heinrich Harrer. *Director of Photography:* Robert Fraisse. *Editor:* Noëlle Boisson. *Music:* John Williams and Yo-yo Ma. *Music Editor:* Ken Wannberg. *Sound:* Ken Weston and (music) Shawn Murphy. *Sound Editor:* Peter Pennell. *Casting:* Priscilla John and Francine Maisler. *Production Designer:* At Hoang. *Art Director:* Pierre Queffelean. *Set Decorator:* Jim Erickson. *Special Effects:* Dean Lockwood. *Costumes:* Enrico Sabbatini. *Make-up:* Paul Engelen. *Make-up (Brad Pitt):* Jean Black. *Make-up (David Thewlis):* Christine Blundell. *Stunt Coordinator:* Nick Gillard. *Running time:* 134 minutes. *MPAA Rating:* PG-13.

CAST: Brad Pitt (Heinrich Harrer); David Thewlis (Peter Aufschnaiter); B.D. Wong (Ngawang Jigme); Mako (Kungo Tsarong); Danny Denzongpa (Regent); Victor Wong (Chinese "Amban"); Ingeborga Dapkunaite (Ingrid Harrer); Jamyang Jamtsho Wangchuk (Dalai Lama, 14 Years); Lhakpa Tsamchoe (Pema Lhaki); Jetsun Pema (Great Mother); Ama Ashe Dongtse (Tashi); Sonam Wangchuk (Dalai Lama, 8 Years); Dorjee Tsering (Dalai Lama, 4 Years); Ric Young (General Chang Jing Wu); Ngawang Chojor (Lord Chamberlain); Duncan Fraser (British Officer); Benedick Blythe (Nazi Official); Tom Raudaschl (Lutz Chicken); Wolfgang Tonninger (Hans Lobenhoffer); Samdup Dhargyal (The Garpon); Chemchok (Garpon's Agent); Tenzin Jangchub (Declaration Monk Official); Angphurba Sherpa (Tibetan General); Tsering Wangdue and Yama Nugdup Cheshatsang (Burly Guides); Kalsang Dhundop Lungtok (Vendor Ice-Skates); Sonam Bidhartsang (Jacket Vendor); Lama Champa Tsondu (Watch Vendor); Geshe Lobsang Nyma (Ling Rinpoche); Geshe Yeshi Tsultrim (Trijang Rinpoche); Lama Champa Chandu (Dalai Lama's Room Attendant); Pemba Norbu Sherpa (Young Sherpa); Karma Apo-Tsang (Messenger to Great Mother); Ngawang Tenzin Gyatso (Jokhang Monk Official); Choeden Tsering and Lama Jampa Lekshe (Military Instructors); Lama Thupten Nugdup (Head of Security's Aide); Daniel Tedeschi (Marchese); Gerardo Ebert (Horst Immendorf); Sebastian Zevalia (Rolf Harrer, Younger); Philipp Kriechbaum (Rolf Harrer, Older).

CHRISTIAN SCIENCE MONITOR, 10/10/97, p. 15, David Sterritt

Religion, history, and politics play important parts in "Seven Years in Tibet," now opening in theaters after a well-received premiere at the international filmfest here.

But the most important factor in getting it "green-lighted" by Hollywood was probably the participation of superstar Brad Pitt, whose handsome face is filmed so glowingly that it almost outshines the magnificent Himalayan mountains that surround him throughout much of the story.

The movie is a star vehicle at heart, aimed more at marketing Pitt's popularity than probing complexities of empire-building and cultural clash that trouble the Tibetan region to this day. Still, the story takes clear stands on moral and ethical issues—such as China's outrageous occupation of its peace-loving neighbor—and may foster new understanding of this ongoing situation.

Pitt plays Heinrich Harrer, a real-life Austrian adventurer famed in the 1930s for his mountain-climbing exploits. (He wrote about his adventures in the 1953 book "Seven Years in Tibet.") Portrayed as a talented but self-involved man, he flees from mounting responsibilities at home and heads for Nanga Parbat, one of the highest Himalayan peaks.

War has erupted in Europe, though, and Harrer is confronted by British soldiers who haul him from the mountainside and whisk him into an internment camp. He escapes with help from fellow prisoners, whom he promptly abandons, preferring to trek toward safety on his own.

A two-year journey brings him to the isolated Tibetan city of Lhasa, center of the country's Buddhist faith. It is also the home of Tibet's spiritual leader, the Dalai Lama—still a boy, tantalized by a little knowledge of Western culture and eager for a teacher who'll expand his horizons.

Harrer becomes his tutor, developing a mutually enlightening friendship with him. The movie culminates with China's invasion, Harrer's return to Europe, and his pupil's escape to India.

This is fascinating material to work with, and director Jean-Jacques Annaud decks out Becky Johnston's screenplay with the sort of outdoorsy vitality he cultivated in "The Bear" and "Quest for Fire." Pitt is commendably earnest as Harrer, ably supported by David Thewlis as his fellow traveler and several gifted Asian performers, including Jamyang Wangchuk as the Dalai Lama, in the Tibetan roles.

Its merits notwithstanding, the impending release of "Seven Years in Tibet" was clouded by news reports that Harrer had been an active Nazi during the '30s, not a politically apathetic figure as the film originally implied. In response, the producers have dubbed in a small amount of extra dialogue that admits his Nazi connection and indicates his subsequent regret about this.

The movie could have benefited from further improvements, such as reducing the story's Eurocentric bias—the Dalai Lama seems infatuated as much with Western cars and movies as with the ancient traditions of his own land—and delving more deeply into spiritual questions. The story acknowledges how wrenching it was for pacifist Buddhists to take up arms against the Chinese, for instance, but fails to tell us why Tibetans didn't confront the invasion through alternative means, such as a Gandhian commitment to nonviolent resistance.

Such shortcomings aside, "Seven Years in Tibet" is one of the season's more substantial large-scale entertainments, using colorful storytelling and Pitt's appealing presence to spotlight an imperialistic event that continues to cry for correction.

LOS ANGELES TIMES, 10/8/97, Calendar/p. 1, Kenneth Turan

"Seven Years in Tibet" opens not with a spectacular mountain vista, not with a shot of Lhasa's fabled golden-roofed Potala but with a single word, impressive in the size of its capital letters: BRAD. It's only a quirk of the credit design that the name appears that way, but it really tells you all you need to know about the two hours and 11 minutes that follow.

Despite all the media buzz about "Tibet's" unflattering portrait of the Communist Chinese and the newly revealed Nazi past of the film's real-life protagonist, mountaineer Heinrich Harrer, what we have here is an old-fashioned star vehicle that has more in common with "Lost Horizon" than with anything remotely political.

It may be cold up on the roof of the world, but that doesn't mean star Brad Pitt isn't given the opportunity to go bare-chested to appease his determined fans.

Though Pitt is as attractive as ever, "Seven Years" offers other things to look at and in fact functions better as a travelogue than as a drama. Set partly in Tibet just after World War II, when fate cast Harrer in the role of unofficial tutor to the young Dalai Lama, its Robert Fraisse cinematography is strong on the country's vivid pageantry and colorful costumes.

Logistics and political problems led director Jean-Jacques Annaud to shoot in the foothills of the Andes, on the Argentina-Chile border, but his passion for authenticity led him to import both yaks from Montana and nearly 100 Tibetan monks from a monastery in India. When publicists say no expense was spared, this is what they mean.

Annaud ("The Lover") has always been a director partial to wide-screen exotica, but his best films, "Quest for Fire" and "The Bear," do without conventional dialogue. The script here is by Becky Johnston, whose last feature was another star vehicle, "Prince of Tides." It is burdened with lines like "Buttered tea was never my cup of tea" and has a tendency to simplify everything, from Harrer's domestic situation to the reason China was able to take over Tibet.

That's OK in theory, this being a movie after all, but "Tibet" is also hampered by an overall sluggishness. Harrer not only spends seven years in Tibet, it takes him almost that much time to get there, and the journey seems to take forever. And waiting for the film's obvious and not very dramatic theme to kick in is also not worth the wait.

None of this is particularly Pitt's fault. He does what he can with what he has, smiling his one-of-a-kind smile and giving a respectable star's performance. One thing he can be faulted for is his newly minted Austrian accent, painful at moments but mostly just an unnecessary hindrance that pulls you out of the picture. Some actors would be well-advised not to bother with foreign accents, and Pitt is one of them.

"Seven Years in Tibet" introduces us to Pitt's Heinrich Harrer in 1939, handsome as an Aryan god and about to coldly leave his pregnant wife for a chance to join a German-sponsored expedition led by Peter Aufschnaiter (David Thewlis) that will attempt to climb Nanga Parbat, one of the highest of the Himalayas.

This icy farewell turns out to be characteristic of Harrer, depicted for most of the script as an arrogant egotist, self-centered and aloof, someone who never apologizes and never feels remorse. When Aufschnaiter says to him, "No wonder you're always alone, no one can stand your miserable company," it's a judgment even the man himself accepts as accurate.

Harrer's character doesn't even change during years spent in a British prisoner of war camp in India, where his mountain-climbing team ends up when World War II breaks out. While he's secretly pining away for the son he fears he'll never see (sniff, sniff), on the surface he's the same rotter he's always been.

Intercut with Harrer's difficulties are scenes of the boy Dalai Lama, the spiritual and secular leader of Tibet, growing up lonely in Lhasa's Potala palace. What he yearns for, aside from more companionship than his mother (played by the real Dalai Lama's sister, Jetsun Pema), is knowledge of the West. Clearly these two have a date with destiny. Harrer and Aufschnaiter manage to escape from the British and bicker their way across the rigors of the Himalayas, sneaking into Tibet despite an anti-foreigner policy strict enough to satisfy Gov. Pete Wilson. Once inside Lhasa, they compete for the affections of Pema Lhaki (Lhakpa Tsamchoe), the only English-speaking Western-style female tailor in the entire city. And she's attractive, too.

Harrer gets a bit involved in Tibetan politics and the machinations of rivals played by B.D. Wong and Mako. But mostly he ends up as unofficial tutor/best buddy to the 14-year-old Dalai Lama (Jamyang Jamtsho Wangchuk), who tells him he wants to know everything from "Where is Paris?" to "Who was Jack the Ripper?"

Perhaps suspecting that his audience is falling asleep, Annaud ends "Tibet" with violent but pointless scenes of the 1950 Chinese invasion.

The film's theme, that working with the Dalai Lama redeems the bratty Harrer, takes so long developing that it has dissipated its welcome before it arrives. And we don't actually see the transformation; Harrer just wakes up one day and mends his ways. Maybe it's just too hard to be selfish in that thin mountain air.

NEW YORK, 10/13/97, p. 94, David Denby

Seven Years in Tibet, appears to be an epic made for the people of Southern California. A selfish bastard and glory freak from Austria named Heinrich Harrer (Brad Pitt) climbs enormous

Himalayan peaks in 1939, gets thrown into a British prison camp at the start of the war, escapes, links up with another escapee, fellow Austrian climber Peter Aufschnaiter (David Thewlis), and penetrates the mysterious holy city of Lhasa, Tibet, where he attains humility and peace and even selflessness, largely through friendship with the teenage Dalai Lama. When the Communist Chinese attack Tibet in 1950, Harrer—a real person, still alive today—does what he can to help the defense, but the jig is up, and he returns to Europe, where he resumes his career as a climber and national hero.

Harrer's book (same title), which I have not read, has a good reputation, but the movie made by Jean-Jacques Annaud is a kind of mountain-air morality play, made without fervor or intelligence. Annaud opens up huge physical spaces, and the mountains, high valleys, and famous walled city are good to see (even if the Andes sometimes sub for the Himalayas), but with someone as bland as Brad Pitt at the center of the movie, the peaks are less a visual metaphor of striving and spiritual ambition than an inert picture-postcard background. Pitt is lithe and very blond, but there's nothing going on in his face and nothing at stake in the movie. In the beginning, he doesn't look arrogant; he looks merely puppyish and snarly, and when he reforms, he just seems becalmed, even bored.

A few of Harrer's adventures with Aufschnaiter are mildly amusing, but the movie is devoid of drama. Whether Heinrich Harrer loses his arrogance and becomes a nice man is hardly a question any grown-up can find interesting. (Brad Pitt may be an actor for teenage girls and no one else.) The cynical will say: "Harrer was stuck in Tibet during the war years; what else could he do but become 'unselfish'? The Dalai Lama was the only game in town." Remarks like these would be inadmissible if the movie were not so feeble. The theatrics of Buddhism in the temples of Lhasa—the basso chanting and the severe piety of the monks—are very pleasing, but the young Dalai Lama is just a nice kid with bright eyes and a charming smile, a nice kid who wants a friend, and the scenes between him and Harrer lack any kind of tension or illumination. Harrer becomes an older brother who is docile yet reverent. But why is he reverent? Where are the spiritual qualities in the boy that would transform a grown man into a different personality? We don't see them.

The Dalai Lama has a following even today among movie-colony seekers (like Richard Gere), and it's something of a sick joke that when an enormous film at last gets made embodying this obsession it should end in disgrace. For Heinrich Harrer, it turns out, was no innocent Austrian mountain climber but a Nazi and an active member of the S.S. The German magazine *Stern* outed him about five months ago, when the movie was almost done. (A few hastily written voice-over lines spoken by Pitt allude to the party membership.) Perhaps it's characteristic of the empty-headed piety behind movies like this that the people involved in it did years of preparation and managed not to discover the single most important fact about their hero.

NEW YORK POST, 10/8/97, p. 47, Thelma Adams

Like its star, Brad Pitt, "Seven Years in Tibet" is gorgeous on the surface. Based on the journal of legendary mountaineer Heinrich Harrer, Becky Johnston's screenplay plots the athlete's spiritual trek from arrogant Austrian to acolyte of the Dalai Lama.

With Jean-Jacques Annaud ("Quest for Fire") at the helm, we view the twin peaks of earthly beauty: Nanga Parbat, the world's ninth-highest crest, and Pitt's honey-gold coif.

Four and a half years in a British prison camp and Harrer's hair still has swing.

Annaud kicks things off as Harrer is caught behind enemy lines in India in 1939. He and fellow climber Peter Aufschnaiter (David Thewlis) finally make their escape: a magnificent 1,500-mile trek across Tibet.

Once in Lhasa, the climbers wait out the war. Harrer becomes the personal tutor to the youthful Dalai Lama. He teaches him about cars and builds a cinema. (Will they play "Hello, Dalai?")

Meanwhile, Aufschnaiter shacks up with a local tailor. With his sneering lips and stringy body, Thewlis ("Naked") is a visual foil for Pitt. Both actors struggle with accents, which Thewlis later abandons like a climb beset by an avalanche.

On the political front, while the Nazis are losing the war, the Chinese threaten Tibetan autonomy. Like Martin Scorsese's forthcoming "Kundun," the movie adopts Tibet as Hollywood's favorite pet cause.

The Dalai Lama stands firm against the Chinese, but a Tibetan courtier (B.D. Wong) betrays his people and hands the small but spiritual nation over to the enemy.

While Annaud and company are busy condescending, however, they overlook a crucial historical parallel.

Harrer was more than an s.o.b. He was also a Nazi and an early one. According to reports published in Men's Journal and Germany's Stern magazine after Annaud shot the movie, the climber joined the Nazi storm troopers in 1933 and the S.S. by 1939.

That the storm troopers assisted in the overthrow of the Austrian government makes the film's indictment of Tibetan traitor Wong hollow. In his journal, Harrer failed to mention that the Nazis had a Tibetan agenda and that he might very likely have been part of it.

Whether Harrer was, in historian Michael H. Kater's words, "a heavy Nazi," is only part of the story. In post-production, Annaud added a scene in which Pitt's Harrer accepts a swastika as he rushes through a train station. Later, in voice-over, he says: "The will to overcome weaker people fills me with shame."

The shame is that there is a better story here—and Pitt is capable of playing it. We don't need the trite, great-white-father-helps-the-little-Lama theme, or the Freudian subplot that has Harrer pining for the son he's never met.

Few doubt that, whatever Harrer's youthful sympathies, Tibet transformed him. He has spent a lifetime scaling mountains others could hardly reach and treating the indigenous people with a respect that was ahead of his time.

From storm trooper, to spiritual seeker—now there's a story! Truth is stranger—and surely better—than fiction.

NEWSDAY, 10/8/97, Part II/p. B2, John Anderson

Brad Pitt wears some really fabulous Zen-wear in "Seven Years in Tibet," especially those black sashed pajamas. They look chic. Durable. And really comfortable.

And being comfortable is what it's all about. Thanks to explorer Heinrich Harrer's memoir of his years in Tibet and his relationship with the young Dalai Lama, what we have is the foundation for one of the older formulas in Hollywood adventure film: the Adonysian westerner, cast among the off-white tribes, where he both gains and imparts knowledge (while also engaging in some manner of action, flirting with love and developing into a changed but better man).

It's the kind of romance we'd almost lost, thanks to all those nettlesome multicultural types and the development of a less than totally egocentric worldview among First Worlders. But thanks to one of the century's great adventurers—and a guy who was a bit more than a Nazi sympathizer—we have the classic form restored to its proper place, because this is a fact-based film and fact forgives everything.

And it's certainly something Hollywood can slip into like a set of silk pajamas, especially with Brad Pitt in the leading role and rivaling the breathtaking landscape for our attention. This is a star-powered, mountain-climbing, spirit-enlightening vehicle for Pitt and he's such a charmer you almost forgive him the accent. Of course, if cinema tradition were really a concern, Pitt wouldn't have had to assume that uneven Austrian accent at all; movie stars played foreign roles without risking their dignity with attempts at authentic inflection. It is, however, the year 1997, or 20 A.S. (After Streep), so Pitt is almost required to take a shot at it.

And as Harrer, who in his youth must have been a real louse, Pitt sneers and snarls and makes the other members of his 1939 Himalayan climbing team miserable—including the team leader, Peter Aufschnaiter (David Thewlis), who will accompany Harrer both to a British POW camp after the war breaks out and to Tibet once they escape the camp (and where Aufschnaiter, not Harrer, wins the lovely Tibetan tailor played by Lhakpa Tsamchoe).

Aufschnaiter may be German, but he's still a mensch, and we sympathize with him as Harrer makes a colossal ass of himself all the way across south-central Asia. They encounter bandits, hellacious weather and unfriendly Tibetans who refuse them entrance to the forbidden city of Lhasa, but Harrer (and this is to Pitt's credit) still seems like the biggest obstacle to anyone's happiness. Only after disguising themselves do the two get inside of Lhasa, where life is sweet but in very great danger.

It's Harrer's bond with the young Dalai Lama (played by various actors at various ages) that gives his story its historic resonance and it's a very engaging friendship. Although Harrer must be circumspect, the young boy is interested in things like movies and Harrer regales him with tales of the outside world. And Harrer, of course, grows too, as the Lama's Buddhist serenity casts its power over him.

It doesn't work on the Chinese, however, and their march into Lhasa and the subsequent destruction of Tibetan culture and self-governance is depicted with enough cruelty to spark popcorn throwing in theaters all over these United States. Whether "Seven Years in Tibet" will have the kind of power to overturn Favored Nation agreements is one thing. That it tries at all to make its audience angry is something very much in its favor.

SIGHT AND SOUND, 12/97, p. 53, Mark Kermode

Germany, 1939. Austrian adventurer Heinrich Harrer leaves his pregnant wife Ingrid to climb the Himalayan peak Nanga Parbat with mountaineer Peter Aufschnaiter and others. After an avalanche, the expedition is abandoned, and the explorers are arrested by the British and sent to Dehra POW camp because World War Two has started. While languishing in Dehra, Heinrich receives divorce papers from his wife, repeatedly attempts to escape, and frequently writes letters to his son Rolf. Finally, in September 1942, he breaks out with Peter and several other POWs and flees to Northern India. A two-year trek with Peter through the Himalayas into Tibet brings the couple to the forbidden city of Lhasa, which they enter in disguise.

Housed by a generous city dweller, and discreetly sponsored by local diplomat Ngawang, Heinrich and Peter are befriended by a beautiful tailor, Pema, whom Peter woos and weds. In 1945, after news of the Allied victory, Heinrich receives word from Rolf asking him not to contact him ever again.

Dismayed, Heinrich falls into a depression from which he is saved by a summons to meet the young Dalai Lama, "Kundun". Eager to learn the ways of the Western world, "Kundun" asks Heinrich for tutelage and commissions him to build a cinema.

Meanwhile, Chinese forces mobilise to reclaim Tibet, routing the Tibetan army at a key location. Although ordered to offer no surrender, the Tibetan resistance collapses when the traitorous Ngawang destroys their own munitions rather than fight the far-larger army. Heinrich insists that "Kundun" flee, but he refuses, instead telling Heinrich that he must return home to be a father to his own child. Having witnessed "Kundun"s initiation as Tibetan spiritual leader, Heinrich travels to Austria and, in 1951, finally meets his son to whom he gives a musical box beloved of "Kundun". Later, reconciled, Heinrich teaches his son to climb.

The most obvious problem with Jean-Jacques Annaud's lavish Tibetan tipple is that it shares a similar relationship to Martin Scorsese's forthcoming *Kundun* that Patrick Bergin's woe-begotten *Robin Hood* bore to Kevin Costner's celebrated *Robin Hood Prince of Thieves:* it's the film that has been released just before the more famous one comes out. Since expectations of Scorsese's long-awaited movie are so high, Annaud's only real claim to fame is that he got there first, and is thus now presumably able to play golf with Richard Gere, safe in the knowledge that he has "done Tibet" in a big way. But the anticipation of *Kundun* constantly undercuts what would otherwise have been merely a glossy, good-natured travelogue with modest philosophical pretensions.

In particular, Scorsese's star-free cast list will make Annaud's use of a beach-blonde Brad Pitt, cosmetically rugged throughout, seem at best dodgy, and at worst plain stupid. From his opening line, when he announces in a cod Austrian accent that he's leaving at once for "Da Himalayas! Da Himalayas!" to the closing moments in which he manfully mouths "Vell done, son, vell done!", Pitt's head is placed beautifully on the critical chopping block, inviting enthusiastic axing.

Ironically, though, despite so much potential for failure, *Seven Years in Tibet* is nowhere near as grim as it could have been. The design is eye-pleasing, the vistas spectacular, the political allegiances present and politically correct. There are also moments of wry intimate wit: when Pitt is first summoned to meet "Kundun", the Dalai Lama, the boyish bafflement and abashed charm Pitt exhibits reminds us just how good an actor he can be when not behaving like a film-star. All this is admirable, as is Robert Fraisse's cinematography, and indeed Annaud and Noëlle Boisson's editing which manages to cram an awful lot of (admittedly episodic) action into a relatively compressed period of time. (Annaud seems to like films with Eastern settings, having also directed the film based on Marguerite Duras' novel *L'Amant*, while his taste for panoramic vistas must have been sharpened during the making of his *Wings of Courage*, the first, and maybe the only, feature Imax 3-D film ever made.)

The movie's true shortcomings are ultimately far less cosmetic, and centre on the philosophical problem of making any allegedly anti-imperial movie which rests upon the presence of a Hollywood star. While Becky Johnston's screenplay rails boldly against the oppression of the expansive Chinese empire, the movie itself paints a bizarrely skewed, odd picture of a Disneyfied Tibetan culture.

This interpretation is as suspiciously imposed from on high as the impending Communist rule is on the Tibetans themselves. From the beautiful tailor who doles out philosophical platitudes about the indigenous religion, to the curiously enthusiastic Dalai Lama who seems to accept Heinrich as his spiritual equal, the occupants of Lhasa behave more like loveably exotic foreigners thrilled by this multiplex tourist trade than as a people proudly isolated within their own culture. "What's a molotov cocktail?" "Kundun" demands with wide-eyed wonder when first introduced to a noticeably unhumbled Heinrich. "What's an elevator? Who's Jack The Ripper? And can you build me a movie house!"

This, of course, is the key. Throughout the film, we are left with the impression that the person "Kundun" is addressing is not an Austrian explorer, but a Hollywood icon, a glamorous American actor spreading benevolent goodwill through the miracle of cinema, rather than a former Nazi with an irrepressibly arrogant wanderlust. In the film's most heavy-handedly self-congratulatory moment, the holy child actually asks Pitt, "Do you think some day people will look at Tibet on the movie screen and wonder what happened to us?"

Maybe so. The question, though, is whether they'll see the real Tibet, or just some sanitised movie theme park with quasi-philosophical concession stands. A film with a political message is a fine and noble thing, but only if that message can be heard over the sound of the film-makers enthusiastically slapping their own and each other's backs.

VILLAGE VOICE, 10/14/97, p. 96, Michael Atkinson

The lead credit for Jean-Jacques Annaud's ubermensch fairy-tale *Seven Years in Tibet* begins with a routinely glorious Brad and climaxes with the dissolve-in of a mountainous, looming Pitt, letting us know exactly where we, and the Tibetans, stand. Make no mistake, this is Spielbergian pop history for the mall minions, complete with a movie-star Nazi saving the innocent tribes from oppression. (And what would a visit to Lhasa be without a few Lhasa apsos?) As mountaineer—Aryan rebel god Heinrich Harrer, Pitt even gets to teach the Tibetans how to ice-skate, which must be something like teaching Polynesians how to tan.

No Tibetan gets quite as upset about the Chinese invasion as Brad does, either—he even gets to rough up a Lhasa dignitary for having betrayed the homeland. The film's sense of obviousness to irony and shame is overpowering. (That Harrer has recently been outed as an SS member warrants only an extra line of narration, not the donning of hair shirts as you'd reasonably expect.) Based on Harrer's memoir about his self-imposed exile in Tibet during World War II, during which time he apparently taught the Dalai Lama everything he knows, Annaud's film would be merely a pious bore if it weren't for the Buddhism For Dummies bromides (somewhat less enlightened than Bill Murray's *The Razor's Edge*), the *Indiana Jones*-ish treatment of Asian locals, and the god-awful blondness of its hero.

Come to think of it, it's a pious bore anyhow. Annaud specializes in international epics that take up space like half-inflated parade balloons; the narrative rhythm of *Seven Years* can only be described as icebound. But that Brad—is there no limit to his majesty? Other gone-native white guys in the *Dances With Wolves* paradigm can only go green (although the only gorgeous, English-speaking chick in Lhasa unaccountably falls for coadventurer David Thewlis). Look at the bright side: Brad's redemption among the bumpkins should alert for some time the impulse to remake *Lost Horizon* again.

Also reviewed in:
CHICAGO TRIBUNE, 10/10/97, Friday/p. A, Michael Wilmington
NEW YORK TIMES, 10/8/97, p. E1, Janet Maslin
VARIETY, 9/22-28/97, p. 37, Derek Elley

WASHINGTON POST, 10/8/97, p. D1, Rita Kempley
WASHINGTON POST, 10/10/97, Weekend/p. 48, Desson Howe

SHADOW CONSPIRACY

A Hollywod Pictures release of an Andrew G. Vajna presentation of a Cinergi production. *Executive Producer:* Andrew G. Vajna and Buzz Feitshans. *Producer:* Terry Collis. *Director:* George P. Cosmatos. *Screenplay:* Adi Hasak and Ric Gibbs. *Director of Photography:* Buzz Feitshans, IV. *Editor:* Robert A. Ferretti. *Music:* Bruce Broughton. *Music Editor:* Patricia Carlin and Robin Katz. *Sound:* Keith A. Wester and (music) Paul Holme. *Sound Editor:* Hamilton Sterling and Jerry Ross. *Casting:* Karen Rae. *Production Designer:* Joe Alves. *Art Director:* Bill Hiney. *Set Designer:* Thomas Minton and Johnathan J. Short. *Set Decorator:* Anne D. McCulley. *Set Dresser:* Melissa Berent, Jamie Bishop, R. Mark Hughs, and Stephen G. Shifflette. *Special Effects:* Thomas L. Fisher. *Costumes:* April Ferry. *Make-up:* David Atherton. *Make-up (Charlie Sheen):* Carol Rippy. *Stunt Coordinator:* Vic Armstrong. *Running time:* 103 minutes. *MPAA Rating:* R.

CAST: Charlie Sheen (Bobby Bishop); Linda Hamilton (Amanda Givens); Donald Sutherland (Chief of Staff Jake Conrad); Stephen Lang (The Agent); Sam Waterston (President); Ben Gazzara (Vice President Saxon); Henry Strozier (Treasury Secretary Murphy); Charles Cioffi (General Blackburn); Stanley Anderson (Attorney General Toyanbee); Nicholas Turturro (Grasso); Theodore Bikel (Professor Pochenko); Dey Young (Janet); Reginald Davis (Basketball Player #1); Johnny Newman (Basketball Player #2); Antonio Todd (Basketball Player #3); Bobby Zajonc (Helicopter Pilot); Casey Biggs (Stokes); Richard Bauer (Grolier); Penny Fuller (Dr. Olson); Gore Vidal (Congressman Page); Tom Quinn (Reporter #1); Jonas Elmblad (Jergon); James A. Chory (Man); Paul Gleason (Blythe); Terry O'Quinn (Frank Ridell); Vicki Ross-Norris and Bob Child (News Reporters); Beverly Brigham (Cafe Waitress); Harold Surratt (Marine Colonel); Helen Carey (Tamara Yarshov); Walt MacPherson (Hickman); Scott Wesley Morgan (Agent Wyndham); F.T. Rea (Security Man #1); James L. Byrd (Security Man #2); Thomas Shelton (Street Vendor); Jeffrey Thompson (Taxi Driver); Karen Bralove (First Lady); Katrina Tabori (Situation Room Assistant); Brian Smyj (Rawlings); Ralph Cosham (Driver); Ramon Estevez (Mr. Jones); Nicholas A. Puccio (Cabinet Member #1); Karyn V. Cody (Cabinet Member #2); Charles Bowen (Cabinet Member #3); Michael Cunningham (White House Desk Clerk); Oscar Pitts, Jr. (Restaurant Patron #1); Reginald C. Colbert (Restaurant Patron #2); Dominick De Marco (Restaurant Patron #3); J. Williams Midkiff, Jr. (Restaurant Patron #4); Richard A. Mention, III (Tech); Nick Olcott (Secret Service #1); Roy Bordon (Secret Service #2); Andreas Brandt (Secret Service #3); John Leisenring (Man in Accident #1); Lawrence Leonard (Man in Accident #2); Richard Turner (Senator).

LOS ANGELES TIMES, 1/31/97, Calendar/p. 10, John Anderson

[The following review by John Anderson appeared in a slightly different form in **NEWSDAY, 1/31/97, Part II/p. B10.]**

In a cozy, covert U.S. government research facility, bearded refuseniks drink tea and contemplate their screen-savers. Suddenly a gunman enters and systematically slaughters the staff—all except one, who throws the assassin a curve by hiding his tea setting in a sideboard.

"Three Days of the Condor"? No, and it's not quite Robert Redford either. The one with the highly coveted info is Theodore Bikel, playing another Eastern Bloc intellectual, who draws Corvette-driving, basketball-playing presidential advisor/frat boy Bobby Bishop (Charlie Sheen) into a nasty nest of clandestine government and anti-American subterfuge.

"Shadow Conspiracy" is one of those movies that would make you ask, "Where do they *get* this stuff?," except you probably know the answer already. "Condor." "The Parallax View." Any of Hitchcock's "wrong man" movies. In one scene, a marquee advertising "Touch of Evil" tries to implicate Orson Welles in this mess, and the relentless killer played by Stephen Lang seems straight out of "Terminator II."

Speaking of which: The recently resuscitated Linda Hamilton is in the cast, as a member of the White House press corps with bad taste in hats and even worse taste in men—she and Bishop have a history (of course), which intrudes itself on an already crowded narrative. Desperately, the two try to outrun the traitors at the high end of the governmental food chain who want to usurp the president (Sam Waterston) by any means necessary and install a government that best resembles their idea of civilization.

Did we mention "Seven Days in May"? How about the Ollie North trials? It hardly matters. The overriding problem with "Shadow Conspiracy," which was never meant to be taken seriously anyway, is that there isn't an appealing person in it. Donald Sutherland, as the White House chief of staff, looks as if he's prepping for "The Jack Kevorkian Story." Ben Gazzara, as the vice president, reminded me a lot of Dick Morris. Hamilton and Sheen deserve each other and Gore Vidal, in a cameo as the crooked Congressman Page, seems to be mortified, probably because he's found himself in this movie.

Watching the direction of George P. Cosmatos—who's been responsible for "Rambo II," "Cobra" and "The Cassandra Crossing," as well as the far more palatable "Tombstone"—one begins to admire Lang's efficiency as a trained killer. You might even root for him.

Cosmatos' chase scenes are perfunctory exercises that generate little or no suspense. The first chase comes too soon (because you know it's too early for the hero to die), and others come too late (because the nation must survive and Bobby's the only one who can save it). There's even a pursuit inside the White House and its network of subterranean tunnels that is not just prolonged but in defiance of several laws of physics.

And as each member of the cast tries, none too successfully, to convince us there are vital matters at risk here, the howlers multiply, as do the lines for the exits.

NEW YORK POST, 1/31/97, p. 42, Larry Worth

Long before Oliver Stone came along, government conspiracy movies were already a genre in and of themselves.

When done well, they became classics, a la "The Parallax View," "Seven Days in May" and "The Manchurian Candidate." But even the flops never approached the blatant stupidity of "Shadow Conspiracy."

Typical of most inadvertently laugh-out-loud productions, its big problem is a ridiculously awful script, as penned by Adi Hasak and Ric Gibbs. Based on their hilarious handiwork, Hasak and Gibbs could put new life into TV's "Saturday Night Live." As for drama ...

Try this on the absurd-o-meter: A trusted adviser to the president of the United States runs smack into a panicked researcher who's screaming about a deadly political cover-up. Seconds later, the bookworm gets a bullet in the forehead.

The adviser (Charlie Sheen) is subsequently chased all over D.C.—along with his ex-girlfriend (Linda Hamilton), a crusading journalist—by a one-man killing machine in a white duster. Naturally, the assassin's aim is dead-on, except when Sheen and Hamilton enter his rifle's cross hairs.

It gets worse, culminating in a finale that seems out of a Monty Python sketch. That's in addition to a script with less credibility than O.J.

More puzzling than any aspect of the plot is why people as gifted as Donald Sutherland, Ben Gazzara, Nicholas Turturro, Sam Waterston, Theodore Bikel, Stephen Lang and Gore Vidal would be party to such nonsense.

For that matter, why did Charlie Sheen sign on as the lead? Sheen, who demonstrated his abilities in "Platoon" and "Wall Street," made a comeback last year with "The Arrival." Here, he takes a giant step back to the likes of "Terminal Velocity."

Linda Hamilton fares no better as the feisty reporter. She's a joke from the moment her character shows up at a news conference in a picture hat. And despite her experience fighting off "Terminator"-like killers, Hamilton's damsel in distress is as lame as they come.

Then there's director George P. Cosmatos, who last embarrassed himself via the dismal "Tombstone." Now he delivers a thriller without thrills, despite using everything from lightning-and-thunder storms to carving knives in an effort to generate suspense.

But the only anticipation attached to "Shadow-Conspiracy" is whether viewers laughter will drown out the cornball dialogue.

SIGHT AND SOUND, 7/97, p. 53, Philip Kemp

Washington, DC. A hitman known as the Agent enters the Center for Civic Responsibility, a civil-liberties watchdog body, and wipes out its staff. Only Professor Yuri Pochenko escapes. He tries unsuccessfully to contact his former pupil Bobby Bishop, a special advisor to the President. The President is about to announce drastic defence cuts and a freeze on government contracts. This alarms several cabinet members, especially Vice President Saxon and Pentagon chief, General Blackburn. Bobby, at the suggestion of his mentor Jake Conrad, the Chief of Staff, persuades the President to hold off for a few days. He succeeds, and deflects rumours at a subsequent press conference despite the questioning from journalist Amanda Givens, Bobby's former lover.

Pochenko warns Bobby of a government traitor, but the professor is gunned down by the Agent. Pursued by the hitman, Bobby calls Conrad for help: Conrad sends security guards to bring him in, but the Agent kills several of them, and Bobby, realising there must be a leak inside the White House, goes on the run again. He phones Amanda, and also her editor, Frank Ridell. Amanda meets Bobby at the newspaper office, where they find Ridell dead. Bobby enters the apartment of Pochenko's girlfriend, Tamara Yarshov, and finds a list of suspect members of the White House staff. The Agent shows up and kills the returning Tamara, but with Amanda's help Bobby gets away.

The pair penetrate Conrad's computer files at the White House and discover that he ordered Pochenko's death. They escape the building, follow Conrad to a rendezvous with Saxon and Blackburn and overhear a plot to assassinate the President at a meeting at Adams Hall. Bobby gets into the hall, where the Agent has smuggled in a lethal toy helicopter. The remote-controlled device kills several people, including Saxon and Blackburn, but Bobby contrives to destroy it and shoot the Agent. Conrad kills himself later. Bobby, now the head of the President's new jobs programme, keeps a date with Amanda.

Shadow Conspiracy isn't so much a film as an anthology. There's scarcely a scene, theme or visual device on offer that hasn't been lifted front elsewhere, and not only from other thrillers: among the movies plundered are such political-intrigue stories as *North by Northwest* (1959), *The Anderson Tapes* (1971), *Three Days of the Condor* (1975), *All the President's Men* (1976) and *No Way Out* (1986), but also Barry Levinson's *Toys* (the lethal toy helicopter) and *Once Upon a Time in the West* (1968) (the hitman's ankle-length white duster coat). One subway chase sequence manages to tip its hat simultaneously to *Diva* and Fritz Lang's *Man Hunt* (1941). It's a tribute of sorts to director George Pan Cosmatos *(Rambo: First Blood, Part II)* and his fellow filmmakers that they've succeeded in stitching this ragbag of off-cuts into a reasonably coherent and even at times passably exciting thriller.

Two elements, though, are notably absent from the mix: surprise and suspense. These days, no film that introduces Donald Sutherland acting grizzled and avuncular in the first reel is going to any great pains to conceal its chief baddie. And once the action gets started, it soon becomes evident that roughly every seven minutes Charlie Sheen and (after they've teamed up) Linda Hamilton will be plunged into yet another perilous strait from which they'll narrowly extricate themselves unscathed except for a few cosmetic grazes. However, just to prove they really were in danger, various minor characters are killed around them without anyone evincing much regret, let alone grief. (Among the actors thus wasted—in both senses—are Ben Gazzara and Theodore Rikel.) Nor does the film shrink from hackneyed contrivances to advance the plot: at one point the lead conspirator even sets up one of those helpful "OK guys, let's run through the plan one more time" meetings in a place where the hero can comfortably eavesdrop on them.

Maybe in the hope of disguising its secondhand components, *Shadow Conspiracy* makes great play with technology. Computer screens feature copiously, and state-of-the-art satellite surveillance dominates much of the action. "I've got your ass!" exults Nicholas Turturro's geeky boffin, as his screen zeroes in from outer space on a single car number plate in a Washington backstreet. In the film's final shot, the camera describes a reverse of this trajectory, zooming vertiginously out from a view of a couple in a park to take in the entire continent, while a babel of international voices floods the soundtrack. There might be a message there, but it's more likely that the film-makers, kleptomaniac to the last, simply saw the same shot elsewhere and pounced on it for a neat ending.

VILLAGE VOICE, 2/11/97, p. 74, J. Hoberman

Getting a jump on the season's other White House crime-scene scenarios (including next week's *Absolute Power*), *Shadow Conspiracy* is an action cartoon with a four-word pitch: Stephanopoulos versus the Terminator. Charlie Sheen plays the youthful adviser to an out-of-control president ("Since he won reelection, he's not listening to anybody!"), who inexplicably splits for Camp David so an implacable one-man hit team can implicate his staff in an orgy of murder decimating half of Georgetown. Briskly glazed, Sheen battles the Conspiracy, abetted by Linda Hamilton (a low-rent Sandra Bullock). Neither has as much fun as Nicholas Turturro, the government computer nerd who shuts down spy satellites over Cuba to track Sheen through Foggy Bottom. *Shadow Conspiracy* is irrational without being interesting, but, as directed by George P. Cosmatos *(Rambo, Cobra)*, almost buoyant in the absence of Sylvester Stallone.

Also reviewed in:
NEW YORK TIMES, 1/31/97, p. C6, Stephen Holden
VARIETY, 2/3-9/97, p. 43, Daniel Kimmel

SHALL WE DANCE?

A Miramax Films release of a Daiei, NTV, and Nippon presentation of an Altamira Pictures production. *Executive Producer:* Hiroyuki Kato, Seiji Urushido, Shigeru Ohno, Kazuhiro Igarashi. *Producer:* Shoji Masui, Yuji Ogata, and Yasuyoshi Tokuma. *Director:* Masayuki Suo. *Screenplay (Japanese with English subtitles):* Masayuki Suo. *Director of Photography:* Naoki Kayano. *Editor:* Jun'ichi Kikuchi. *Music:* Yoshikazu Suo and Taeko Ohnuki. *Sound:* Kiyoshi Yoneyama. *Sound Editor:* Kiyoshi Yoneyama. *Production Designer:* Kyoko Heya. *Running time:* 110 minutes. *MPAA Rating:* PG.

CAST: Koji Yakusho (Shohei Sugiyama); Tamiyo Kusakari (Mai Kishikawa); Naoto Takenaka (Tomio Aoki); Eriko Watanabe (Toyoko Takahashi); Akira Emoto (Toru Miwa); Yu Tokui (Tokichi Hattori); Hiromasa Taguchi (Masahiro Tanaka); Reiko Kusamura (Tamako Tamura); Hideko Hara (Masako Sugiyama); Syuichiro Moriyama (Ryo Kishikawa); Masahiro Motoki (Hiromasa Kimoto); Misa Shimizu (Natsuko); Hiroshi Miyasaka (Maccho); Kunihiko Ida (Teiji Kaneko); Amie Tojo (Hisako Honda); Ayano Nakamura (Chikage, Sugiyama's Daughter); Katsunari Mineno (Shinichi Hirayama); Tomiko Ishii (Haruko); Maki Kawamura (Eiko); Takako Matsuzaka (Fusako Hattori); Koichi Ueda (Torakichi); Mari Nishino (Wakako, Toyoko's Daughter); Yuri Kawachi (Marika); Emiko Hara (Akiko Hattori); Rie Misawa (Suzune); Mizue Kihara (Nami Suzuki); Taro Ikemura (Yutaka Kawai); Kenji Nakagawa (Visitor at Dance Hall); Katsuhisa Shirota (Chu); Kaoru Shinoda (Shinji); Yoko Noma (Fumiko); Kie Sugata (Mai, as a Child); Hanako Onuki (Student); Akiko Hatakeyama (Aya Komatsu); Shuichiro Moriyama (Ryo Kishikawa); Kyoko Kagawa (Keiko Kishikawa); Takashi Takemura (Announcer at Dance Competition); Mika Takanishi (Pro Dancer at Dance Hall); Kazunari Hashimoto (Tetsu Mambo); Masaaki Takarai (Student); Robert Hoffman, Naena Hoffman, and Angelique Roehm (Blackpool Dancers); Paradise Yamamoto (Band Leader); Hidekazu Tanaka (Tokihiko Okada); Yoko Tanaka (Naoko); Goro Kataoka (Jo Blues); Ren Osugi (Sugiura); Yudai Ishyama (Hama Jitterbug); Hirotaro Honda (MC at Mai's Farewell Party).

LOS ANGELES TIMES, 7/11/97, Calendar/p. 13, Kevin Thomas

Every once in a while a foreign film comes along that seems to be able to connect to that larger audience that normally doesn't care to sit still for subtitles.

"Cinema Paradiso," with its love of movies, and "Like Water for Chocolate," with its love of food (and romance), were two such films. "Shall We Dance?" just might be another. Most everybody, after all, loves to dance or watch dancing.

Even more than Australia's "Strictly Ballroom," Masayuki Suo's "Shall We Dance?," which won all 13 of Japan's equivalent of the Oscars, is much more than a lot of dazzling rug-cutting. World-class charmer that it is, it is also a wry comment on the way a tradition of impassive formality can inhibit ordinary Japanese people in their daily lives even as the 20th century draws to an end.

Tokyo office manager Shohei Sugiyama (Koji Yakusho) while riding a commuter train, glimpses a beautiful young woman peering somberly out the window of a fourth-floor ballroom dancing school. It's an image that recalls an Edward Hopper painting and has such an impact on him that he eventually will feel compelled, despite overwhelming feelings of shyness and self-consciousness, to seek her out.

At 42, Shohei is a settled man, with a wife (Hideko Hara) and daughter (Misa Shimizu) and a recently acquired house in the suburbs that he worked very hard to afford and will take a long time to pay off. He doesn't enjoy the after-hours drinking typical of many Japanese office workers, and he's hit a vaguely bored and dissatisfied passage in his life.

The strangely sad young woman, Mai (Tamiyo Kusakari, a top ballerina in Japan and the director's wife), proves to be very cold and later on even brutal to him. But Shohei goes ahead and signs up for a Wednesday evening group class, a decision that will transform both their lives in ways neither they nor we could predict.

Painfully awkward, Shohei struggles manfully to master the traditional ballroom dances under the kindly instructions of a pretty smiling middle-aged woman, Tamako (Reiko Kusamura). (He can't afford Mai's individual lessons.) Gradually, Shohei starts to relax, to move gracefully, to improve his posture and to emerge as the tall, slim and handsome man that he actually is. On the dance floor and off, Yakusho is a marvelously self-effacing actor, heading an outstanding cast.

At first, Shohei's wife, Masako, is so reflexively traditional in her thinking that, sensing her husband's malaise, she worries that he's *not* staying out late and having fun. But when it's soon clear that there's a new happiness and contentment in him, she automatically suspects he's having an affair.

Not quite so old school as to resign herself to that possibility, she nevertheless finds it easier to hire a private detective than to ask him what's going on, and Shohei in turn is much too embarrassed to admit to her that he's doing something so radical as taking ballroom dancing lessons. Why, that would be tantamount to asking your own wife to dance!

Shohei and Masako, in short, are caught up unconsciously in a Japanese concept of marriage so old-fashioned that it wouldn't occur to them to be full-fledged partners in their relationship, sharing experiences, any more than it would be to be partners merely on a dance floor.

Suo sandwiches these serious observations in lots of humor and swirling waltzes. As did classic Hollywood comedies of the 30s, "Shall We Dance?" has a pair of second leads as a source of much humor and some poignancy.

Naoto Takenaka plays one of Shohei's employees, unexpectedly a classmate, equally secretive but determinedly flamboyant—the tango is his specialty—on the dance floor. Often the most vibrant presence on screen, Eriko Watanabe is Toyoko, a plump, outspoken middle-aged woman who supports herself and her daughter with several menial jobs and dreams of becoming a ballroom dancing champion.

Suo shrewdly bides his time in allowing ice princess Mai to melt and confront the reasons for her own unhappiness.

"Shall We Dance?" is a great-looking, great-sounding film, and Yoshikazu Suo's lilting, sometimes wistful score is a major component in the picture's success. You don't want to sit this one out.

NEW YORK, 7/28/97, p. 44, David Denby

Hollywood's virtual abandonment of dancing has been one of the industry's greatest follies of the past twenty years. To our chagrin, it is now up to other countries to put dance into the movies. The Japanese, perhaps, are not ready to make a full-scale dance musical, but in the gravely charming *Shall We Dance?* they have made a shy and tender pass at one. Ballroom dancing, we learn, is a secret passion in Japan. The hero, Shohei Sugiyama (Koji Yakusho), a fortyish accountant, with a wife and daughter tucked away in a suburban house, sneaks off to a dancing school as if indulging a hidden vice. There he meets the other guilty men, all of whom, overcoming hideous shyness, stumble through beginner's agonies in the waltz, tango, and rumba. The teachers, accomplished woman dancers, do what they can with this recalcitrant material, and Shohei falls in love with one of them, Mai (Tamiyo Kusakari), a tall, lovely girl who has her own guilty secret. At times, the movie (written and directed by Masayuki Suo) comes close to embarrassment: For us. all this exquisite Japanese tact seems so nuttily beside the point. Yet it's hard not to be touched when the men speak of their pleasure in movement, and when Shohei. though not a natural, dons a beautiful tux and achieves a proud competency in a ballroom competition. Obsessed, Shohei practices in the rain with an imaginary partner—just enough of a reminder of Gene Kelly to make an American sigh with bitter regret.

NEW YORK POST, 7/11/97, p. 41, Michael Medved

If you've ever visited Tokyo, you've seen them on the commuter trains: impeccably neat, poker-faced suburbanites who exhaust themselves at their mind-numbing office jobs to maintain their respectable middle-class lifestyles.

In the enchanting import "Shall We Dance?" Koji Yakusho plays one such forty-something survivor, whose tidy, drab little wife (Hideko Hara) are suddenly not enough for him. Each night on the way home from work, his train stops at a station where he sees the face of an incandescently beautiful woman (Tamiyo Kusakari) gazing out the window of the fourth floor of a shabby building into the gathering twilight.

Haunted by her look of loneliness and yearning, he gets off the train one night and stumbles into the ballroom dancing school where she works. He signs up for a group class for clumsy, middle-aged beginners taught by a much older woman, just so he can be close to his willowy beauty.

Much to his surprise, the tired businessman begins to enjoy the lessons but keeps his new hobby a secret from his increasingly suspicious wife. She hires a private detective to determine why he's coming home so late and so exhausted, but he becomes even more involved with dancing, preparing to risk humiliation by entering a low-level ballroom competition.

Yakusho makes a supremely sympathetic everyman, as the kinetic magic of the dance gradually brings new warmth to his frozen life.

The lovely Tamiyo Kusakari, one of Japan's most distinguished ballerinas makes an overwhelmingly effective movie debut, investing every step, every turn of her superbly controlled body with eloquence and elegance. There is also a scene-stealing and heartbreaking supporting role by Naoto Takenaka, as a balding, bespectacled accountant who dons a wavy, shoulder-length wig to lead a secret life as a master of the tango and a ballroom "Latin lover."

These characters (and a half-dozen others) are so captivating and convincing, that it's easy to forgive writer-director Masayuki Suo for the fact that his slight story and lengthy amateur dance sequences begin to drag at several points, and that his principals suffer from a distressing habit of declaring their innermost thoughts in long, implausible confessionals.

Nevertheless, it's obvious why "Shall We Dance?" swept all 13 Japanese Academy Awards. With this superbly accomplished cast, and this lyrical and affectionate director, "Shall We Dance?" is an invitation that is impossible to resist.

NEWSDAY, 7/11/97, Part II/p. B8, Jack Mathews

When director Masayuki Suo began writing "Shall We Dance?," its subject, ballroom dancing, was a hobby generally indulged in the privacy of clubs and dance classes in Japan, and its practitioners rarely spoke of it in public. Today, after the movie collected $30 million in ticket sales and 11 Japanese Oscars, ballroom dancing in Japan is said to be a craze, and those who do it well are envied.

What is the strange power of this movie to transform a stubborn culture's attitude? Well, though "Shall We Dance?" may not be quite as magical as Baz Luhrmann's deliriously comic "Strictly Ballroom," or as joyous a celebration of dance's liberating energies as "Flashdance" and "Footloose," it has enough spirit to put a spring in everyone's step. Even of the reserved Japanese. "Shall We Dance?" is not so much about dance as it is about self-discovery.

It's the story of a Japanese worker in midlife crisis, trying to find some meaning, to his existence beyond putting in a good day's work and being a good husband and father. (Suo says he set out to make a movie to lift the spirits of Japan's so-called "salarymen,"joyless fellows who conduct their lives under a cloud of depression.)

Each night, on his subway ride home, Shohei (Koji Yakusho) glances up at a dance studio, occasionally spotting a beautiful woman in leotards staring out the window, lost in thought. Imagining who she is and what she's thinking about becomes such an obsession with Shohei that he gets off the train one evening and drops into the studio. The mystery woman, Mai (Tamiyo Kusakari), is a teacher there, he learns, and he promptly signs up for classes.

So far, it sounds like the opening of "Swing Time," where Fred Astaire pops into a dance studio, asks to have Ginger Rogers as his teacher, then pretends—to the music of "Pick Yourself Up"—to be a stumbling amateur. But there's nothing coy about Shohei. He *is* a stumbling amateur, a genuine double-left-footed klutz and easily the worst in his very bad beginners group.

But there's worse news. Mai only works with advanced dancers, leaving Shohei quietly stuck with an older teacher, who holds no mystery for him at all. If he ever hopes to get close to Mai—and all he wants, in case you're getting ahead of the story, is to know her and dance with her—he has to get good.

"Shall We Dance?" is awash in culturally rich issues, some of which are foreign to Westerners in more ways than one. Shohei's behavior seems maddeningly shy until we realize what a wild thing he is merely to show up in the dance class, and to keep his quasi-scandalous adventure from his family and friends.

Although the film has tremendous humor, most of it is provided by the early dance lessons and by a bewigged rhumba king (Naoto Takenaka) who turns out to be Shohei's disguised boss, director Suo is dead serious about the consequences of his character's actions. Shohei's wife puts a detective on his trail, never thinking of secret dance lessons as a possible alternative to an affair, and the fear of being found out at work all but paralyzes him.

It's not spilling anything to say this is all headed toward a climactic dance competition where Shohei's partner may or may not be Mai (OK, it is). This is the kind of story that demands a big payoff, and Suo provides it. But there's nothing cheap or facile about it. Shohei, played with tremendous depth of feeling by Yakusho, is transformed by his experience, not only left a better dancer for it, but a better man.

"Shall We Dance?" You bet.

SIGHT AND SOUND, 5/98, p. 56, Philip Kemp

Shohei Sugiyama commutes between his good but dull office job and his happy but unexciting marriage. One evening on the train he spots a mysterious beauty, Mai, gazing from the window of a ballroom-dancing school. On impulse he signs up for lessons and is assigned to the beginners' class along with two other men, Tanaka and Hattori. Among the other pupils he discovers an office colleague, Aoki, disguised and dancing a flashy rumba. Under the tuition of the school's director Tamako, Shohei gains aptitude, but can't bring himself to tell his wife Masako and daughter Chikage what he's doing.

Shohei invites Mai to dinner. She refuses, rebuking him for using dance to pursue her. Stung, he applies himself assiduously and finds joy in dance for its own sake. Noticing the change in him, Masako suspects an affair and hires a private detective, Mr Miwa. Shohei makes such progress that another regular at the school, Toyoko, suggests he should partner her at a major forthcoming competition. Mai, impressed by his dedication, tells him how she blighted her dancing career while competing in the World Championship at Blackpool.

Having discovered Shohei's secret, Miwa invites Masako and Chikage to attend the competition. Aoki and Tanaka also enter and do well, but Shohei and Toyoko score a triumph until Chikage shouts out encouragement. Shocked at his family's presence, Shohei trips, tearing off Toyoko's dress. Crestfallen, he promises Masako he will give up dancing, and avoids the farewell party for Mai who, her confidence restored, is off to compete again at Blackpool. But at the last moment he reconsiders, and he and Mai share an ecstatic waltz together.

References to *Shall We Dance?* as a Japanese *Strictly Ballroom* are misleading—all the two films really have in common is their fascination with the arcane conventions of ballroom dancing. Where Baz Luhrmann's *tour de force* was all Cuban heels, embroidered bolero jackets and brash

Aussie extroversion, Masayuki Sou's comedy—which has become the highest-grossing Japanese film ever in the US—is sober suits and acute social embarrassment. As the introductory voice-over (in English) explains, in a country "where married couples don't go out arm in arm, much less say 'I love you' in public", ballroom dancing has taken on the allure of a secret vice. What to most British—or indeed Australians—seems absurdly old-fashioned in its formality looks daring in a society where public physical contact is taboo.

In some ways *Shall We Dance?* has more in common with Fredrik Thor Fridrikssoifs *Cold Fever,* where a bemused Japanese visitor encounters alien mores in Iceland. As with *Cold Fever,* much of the humour in Suo's film derives from the anomalies of culture clash, the attempt by members of one highly coded society to lock on to patterns laid down by another, one no less coded but by quite different assumptions. "It's a British sport, after all," muses the watching detective when a stylish but inconsiderate pair of contestants are marked down for "ungentlemanly attitude." Part of the perilous attraction of culture clash is the chance it offers to switch under cover of the alien culture: not so much a fish out of water as a much more colourful fish in different water. The film is all but stolen by Naoto Takenaka's bravura performance as Aoki, transmuting himself from shy, despised office drudge into Danny Aoki the Latin-American dance demon, launching into a ferocious rumba with flashing teeth and black shag-pile wig.

Aoki's extravagant double act serves as a burlesque variant of the transformation experienced by Shohei—drawn out of himself, learning to let go, but only fully liberated once he's renounced his hopeless passion for the graceful Mai and begun to love dance for its own sake. Though even then he's too embarrassed to tell his wife what he's doing, let alone invite her to join him at the classes, while she in turn is too embarrassed to ask questions, and assumes he's having an affair. (As indeed he is, but with dance.) For all the genuine affection between them, they spend most of the film hopelessly out of step. It takes their daughter, more forthright and less inhibited than her parents, to persuade them to make the obvious move and dance together. The responsiveness to one's partner Shohei has learnt on the dance floor can at last be applied to his marriage.

As well as two previous features, Suo has directed documentaries on Juzo Itami (director of *Death Japanese Style* and *Tampopo).* The affinity is evident: Suo shares Itami's fascination with the Japanese concern for social ritual, the fear of becoming conspicuous by failing to do the right thing. He also shares Itami's generosity towards his characters. There are no villains in *Shall We Dance?* and its sense of the ridiculous never precludes sympathy. This is a warm, immensely likable film. And besides, how can you resist a movie where the ultimate in exoticism and sophistication is represented by Blackpool?

TIME, 6/16/97, p. 76, Richard Corliss

[*Shall We Dance?* was reviewed jointly with *Gabbeh*; see Corliss' review of that film.]

VILLAGE VOICE, 7/15/97, p. 68, Amy Taubin

Although he hasn't admitted it to himself, Shohei, a Japanese salaryman, is bored silly with his job, his suburban domesticity, and the daily two-hour railroad commute between them. Leaving work one evening, he sees a tall, slender, sad-eyed young woman looking out the neon-framed window of a ballroom dancing school. In Japan, where it's considered unseemly—even for married couples—to touch in public, social dancing is beyond the pale. For Shohei, the dancing school is not very different from a pre-Disney Times Square massage parlor. The shock of seeing a vulnerable and virginal beauty in such sordid surroundings is enough to make him fall instantly in love.

In the course of Masayuki Suo's irresistible *Shall We Dance?,* Shohei (Koji Yakusho) learns how to love not the dancer but the dance, thereby solving his midlife crisis while keeping his marriage intact. Combining conservative sexual politics with a liberating vision of self-expression through the mastery of a form, *Shall We Dance?* is an art-house *Saturday Night Fever.*

When Shohei works up the courage to enter the dancing school, he finds a kind of secret society of middle-class men and women just like himself—although not nearly so handsome. Each student has to find his or her own way to overcome inhibitions or delusions of grandeur so that their dancing can be, as Martha Graham used to say, the landscape of their souls.

Though Suo's filmmaking style is undistinguished, he gets wonderfully subtle, understated performances from Yakusho and Tamiyo Kusakari as the sad-eyed lady who's in the midst of a life crisis herself. *Shall We Dance?* is charming enough to overcome American resistance to subtitles. Dance, after all, has a language of its own.

Also reviewed in:
NEW YORK TIMES, 7/11/97, p. C18, Janet Maslin
VARIETY, 6/10-16/96, p. 42, Leonard Klady
WASHINGTON POST, 7/18/97, Weekend/p. 41, Stephen Hunter

SHE'S SO LOVELY

A Miramax Films release of a Hachette Premiere & Cie production in association with Clyde Is Hungry Films. *Executive Producer:* Bernard Bouix, John Travolta, and Gérard Depardieu, and Sean Penn. *Producer:* Rene Cleitman. *Director:* Nick Cassavetes. *Screenplay:* John Cassavetes. *Director of Photography:* Thierry Arbogast. *Editor:* Petra Von Oelffen. *Music:* Joseph Vitarelli and Amanda Scheer Demme. *Music Editor:* Allan K. Rosen and Patty Von Arx. *Sound:* Jim Stuebe and (music) Daniel Wallin and Nicholas Viterelli. *Sound Editor:* Mike Le-Mare. *Casting:* Matthew Barry. *Production Designer:* David Wasco. *Art Director:* Daniel Bradford. *Set Designer:* Amy K. Skjonsby-Winslow. *Set Decorator:* Sandy Reynolds-Wasco. *Set Dresser:* R.A. Tony Poland. *Special Effects:* Grergory C. Landerer. *Costumes:* Beatrix Aruna Pasztor. *Make-up:* Deborah Larsen. *Make-up (John Travolta):* Frank H. Griffin, Jr. *Running time:* 100 minutes. *MPAA Rating:* R.

CAST: Sean Penn (Eddie); Robin Wright Penn (Maureen); John Travolta (Joey); Harry Dean Stanton (Shorty); Debi Mazar (Georgie); Gena Rowlands (Miss Green); James Gandolfini (Kiefer); David Thornton (Saul); Kelsy Mulrooney (Jeanie); Susan Traylor (Lucinda); Bobby Cooper (Cooper); John Marshall Jones (Leonard); Chloe Webb (Nancy Swearingen); James Soravilla (Avi); James Bozian (Intern #1); Paul Johansson (Intern #2); Justina Machado (Lady Ticket Taker); Tito Larriva (Lead Singer); Tony Marsico (Band Member); Ilya Brodsky (Taxi Driver); Burt Young (Lorenzo); Neill Barry (Mario); Clayton Landey (Attendant #1); Jason O'Malley (Attendant #2); Dennis Fanning (Cop #1); John Cundari (Cop #2); Noon Orsatti (Cop #3); Nina Barry (Helen Caldwell); Chris Kinkade (Security Guard); Kristina Malota (Rosie); Nicollette Little (Dolly); Lester Matthews (Black Dude).

CHRISTIAN SCIENCE MONITOR, 8/29/97, p. 15, David Sterritt

"She's So Lovely" has enough powerful star names—John Travolta, Sean Penn, Robin Wright Penn to make it a must-see item in the opening days of the World Film Festival here, and to brighten its marquee value as it now arrives in American theaters.

But for many moviegoers, the name to consider is farther down in the credits: Cassavetes, identifying both the director (Nick) and the writer (John) of the tale.

The father of this father-son team, the late John Cassavetes, was best known as a Hollywood actor with hits like "Rosemary's Baby" and "The Dirty Dozen" on his résumé.

Using his earnings from this, he forged an even more important career as writer, director, and frequent star of his own movies—shaggy, boisterous, unbelievably energetic human dramas that capture the flavor of real experience in ways Hollywood rarely approaches.

Pictures like "Faces" and "A Woman Under the Influence" reflected his conviction that a meaningful film should not be "entertainment" but "exploring" and "asking questions of people," to quote him from critic Raymond Carney's excellent book "The Films of John Cassavetes."

Cassavetes's films often deal with families, and he saw filmmaking as a family affair, often featuring his wife—Gena Rowlands, a major star in her own right—in leading roles.

Now their son, Nick Cassavetes, has picked up where John left off. The younger Cassavetes directed his mother in last year's "Unhook the Stars," about a woman reaffirming her sense of adventure through her relationship with a troubled young neighbor. This year he returns with

"She's So Lovely," based on a script his father wrote some 20 years ago but never brought to the screen.

Mr. Penn and Ms. Penn play Eddie and Maureen, a working-class couple who lives an undisciplined but basically satisfying life. Eddie has a troubling weakness for violence, and an attack on Maureen by an eccentric neighbor sends him over the edge, landing him in prison for a long stretch.

Returning to society, he finds Maureen now married to a more conventional fellow who obviously loves her very much. How should the men react to each other, and where do Maureen's loyalties ultimately lie? Nobody knows for certain, producing an emotional puzzle that galvanizes the movie's last portion.

At its best, "She's So Lovely" has the anything-goes turbulence and on-the-edge audacity that made John Cassavetes a cinematic legend whose reputation keeps rising steadily to this day. At its weakest, it courts roughness and rawness for their own sakes. Speaking to journalists at this spring's Cannes filmfest, the younger Cassavetes said he didn't change the script much except to remove some things he didn't understand.

In all, "She's So Lovely" is second-best Cassavetes but still one of late summer's more adventurous releases, helped by strong performances from its talented stars and from the great Rowlands in a minor role.

In an admirable move, Miramax Films is launching the movie with "Love on the Edge," a mini-retrospective of six John Cassavetes films: the rarely shown "Love Streams" and "Minnie and Moskowitz" and the classic "Shadows," "Faces," "Husbands," and "A Woman Under the Influence." The series continues through Sept. 4 in New York and Boston and just finished a Los Angeles run. In their first New York weekend, according to Miramax, the films had the city's highest per-screen average earnings, out-drawing every new movie in town.

LOS ANGELES TIMES, 8/29/97, Calendar/p. 10, Jack Mathews

[The following review by Jack Mathews appeared in a slightly different form in **NEWSDAY, 8/27/97, Part II/p. B9.]**

The script for Nick Cassavetes' "She's So Lovely," a strange and uneven comedy of mad love starring Sean Penn, Robin Wright Penn and John Travolta, is an inheritance from his father, the writer, director and chronicler of floundering romantic souls, John Cassavetes.

The senior Cassavetes wrote the original screenplay in the late '70s, intending to cast himself and his wife Gena Rowlands as married pub-crawlers Eddie and Maureen. And one of his pals—Ben Gazzara or maybe Peter Falk—would doubtless have played Joey, whom Maureen marries after Eddie is put in a mental hospital.

The script languished for a decade before Sean Penn got interested in playing Eddie and John Cassavetes rewrote it for him. But Cassavetes died before anything could come of that alliance. Later, Penn optioned the script, planning to both star and direct. Nothing came of that, either.

Finally, while directing his first picture, "Unhook the Stars," Nick Cassavetes showed his father's unproduced screenplay to one of that film's producers, and "She's So Lovely's" 20-year journey from script to screen ended at this May's Cannes Film Festival, where Penn's performance earned him the jury's best actor award.

That's the good news. Penn's instincts were correct. Eddie is a terrific John Cassavetes character, a man under the influence, and for the first half of the movie, as Eddie and Maureen blindly answer to both their passions and their demons, Penn does some of the best acting of his career. So does Wright Penn, and Travolta shows up at the half-way mark to do an irresistible turn in a rare supporting role.

But there are two distinct halves to "She's So Lovely," and they are so wildly different you might wonder whether 15 or 20 pages of crucial transition hadn't fallen out of the script somewhere along the line.

The first half is chip-off-the-old-block Cassavetes, with the characters and Thierry Arbogast's cameras prowling the streets, bars and tenements, creating that same quirky, nervously honest, often darkly funny mood that made John Cassavetes one of the defining filmmakers of the turbulent '70s. The second half, picking up 10 years after Eddie was institutionalized, is pure screwball comedy. It's as if Cassavetes had written the first half for himself to direct, and the second for Carl Reiner.

When we rejoin them, Eddie is leaving the hospital, appearing more sedated than cured, to visit Maureen, who's now living in an upscale suburban neighborhood with the devoted, good-hearted and possibly mob-connected Joey. They have three children, including the daughter Maureen was carrying when Eddie short-circuited and shot a paramedic.

Eddie and Maureen are different people now. Not just sobered-up different, *different*. But they both know, without speaking or seeing each other for a decade, that they're still madly in love. The only question for Maureen is, what to do about Joey? She's been honest with him about his runner-up position in her heart, but with the dreaded reunion at hand, Joey's not sure whether to throw her out or beg her to stay, whether to kill his rival or befriend him.

Travolta is at a great advantage appearing in only one of the two halves of the picture. He doesn't have to come out of the dark, dingy, urine- and blood-stained shadows of the first half and into the bright, sitcom suburbia of the second half. People bleed in the first; they bounce in the second. And the ever-charming Travolta bounces very well these days.

It's hard to judge the second-half work of Penn and Wright Penn, or of Harry Dean Stanton and Debi Mazar, who play depressing barflies in the first half, and Fred and Ethyl Mertz in the second. Continuity was an issue for no one.

The abrupt shift in style and tone may be intended to show that love, like bacteria, can survive the extremes. But the principle doesn't apply to movies.

NEW YORK POST, 8/27/97, p. 43, Thelma Adams

Tough guys don't cry—except in Cassavetes movies.

In "She's So Lovely," opening today, director Nick Cassavetes, working from a leftover script by his late, great director dad John, finds himself swept away by those same old "Love Streams."

The younger Cassavetes casts Sean Penn and John Travolta as Eddie and Joey, macho men both. The are thinkers (but not intellectuals), lovers and losers. They spar over the same woman, Maureen (Robin Wright Penn, Sean's, real-life wife).

Cassavetes puts Penn, not disco king Travolta, in the dancing role. In a defining scene, Eddie and "Mo," barflies both, visit a decrepit dance hall. More than simulated celluloid sex, the tender, rhythmic, hungry dance between Eddie and Mo reveals everything about their intimacy, their wordless core of drunken interaction, their passion and grace.

To paraphrase Eddie, dance puts the light in your eyes. The pair have the kind of love that lights up their eyes, but they're as doomed together as Bonnie and Clyde, and not nearly so swift.

In a script that leaves the motivations to the performers, Eddie goes nuts after Maureen gets beaten and bopped by a fellow drunk. Ten years later, the big-hearted bum emerges from the sanitorium, older and shakier. Not only has Mo never visited Eddie in the asylum, she's divorced him and married Joey, a trigger-tempered contractor. Now, she's living the suburban dream with three lovely daughters, one of them Eddie's. The lights are out in Maureen's eyes, but at least she's got a home.

Mrs. Penn doesn't take her cues from Gena Rowlands, who appears here in a cameo. The elder Cassavetes' muse and widow, the younger's mother and lead in his debut "Unhook the Stars," lends even the slimmest part a glamour and sympathy, a solidity that defies the role as written.

The younger actress plays Mo with a Mia Farrow whine, a Jennifer Jason Leigh beat-me vulnerability, a bone china fragility. "I hate being alone," Maureen says early in the film. L'amour fou, crazy love, is the movie's theme, its drunken truth. But acting is what makes "She's So Lovely."

Penn rips himself open and sews himself up; he's fearless, funny and just insane enough to make crazy Eddie a romantic hero. Travolta doesn't dance, but as a loving husband who tries to set events straight in a crooked world, he can lose the girl and still emerge the winner.

TIME, 8/25/97, p. 70, Richard Corliss

In the 1984 documentary "I'm Almost Not Crazy ..." John Cassavetes defines filmmaking as "waiting around ... for your dynamic turn." That surely applies to his own improvisatory works: *Shadows, Faces, Husbands, Minnie and Moskowitz*. They are anguished home movies of actors searching for the precise pitch of rage or love. The films mean to grapple with painful truth, but it can seem ages between epiphanies. A Cassavetes movie often plays like two hours in the waiting-waiting-waiting room of the Actors Studio.

The weird thing about *She's So Lovely* is that a script by the impresario of improv, directed by his son, should become a tight, slight, goofy romance. As the lovestruck Eddie, Sean Penn denounces his wife's perfume as "a good smell to cover up bad smell." John Travolta, as the second husband of Eddie's beloved Maureen (Robin Wright Penn), snaps at his young stepdaughter, "You haven't lived long enough for me to argue with you. You're just a glorified piece of blue sky." The film has the soul of a sailor after a few drinks, and the mouth of a randier Damon Runyon.

The guilty secret of John Cassavetes' films was that they relied on Hollywood star quality. His lupine smile sent out laser beams of frantic menace, and Gena Rowlands had (still has) a face the camera can't stop watching. When she shows up in *She's So Lovely* to hear Penn murmur, "You're a very beautiful woman, and I haven't been around the kindness of women in some time," it's a sweet tribute from this generation of Method mesmerizers to the one who taught them how.

Director Nick Cassavetes is less a full-fledged auteur here than a cheerleader and referee, keeping the stars fighting without biting. Wright, like Maureen, is game for any outsize challenge, but her bantam desperation sounds shrill; at times she is overrun by the wild gestures that seize Maureen. Travolta, though, balances nicely on a seesaw of caring and exasperation; and Penn has every garish shade of Eddie in his palette. He gets the pain, charm and drive, the stumbling humor of a guy whose only religion is the woman who betrayed him. He turns a jerk into a heroic figure: St. Doofus.

VILLAGE VOICE, 9/2/97, p. 73, Amy Taubin

Among the loose ends John Cassavetes left behind when he died in 1989 at age 59 was a film script titled *She's DeLovely*. Written shortly after he made his masterworks, *A Woman Under the Influence, The Killing of a Chinese Bookie*, and *Opening Night*, it's yet another angle on the messy conundrums that inspired all his films: love and marriage, madness and marriage, mad love. Had Cassavetes brought *She's DeLovely* to the screen, it might have been a great film. At the least, it would have spared his son, Nick Cassavetes, the embarrassment of following so inadequately in his father's footsteps.

Sean Penn and Robin Wright Penn play Eddie and Maureen, married alcoholics with poor impulse-control clinging to a can't-live-with-you-can't-live-without-you seesaw. They're crazy in love, connected by something more ineffable than sexual heat. When Eddie returns from a bender to discover that Maureen's been raped, he goes berserk, shoots a cop, and gets sent to the looney bin. Believing that Eddie will never recover, Maureen, who's pregnant and destitute, opts for suburban security with Joey (John Travolta). Ten years later, Eddie is released and comes for Maureen, expecting to pick up where they left off. Maureen has to choose between the stability of family life and the chaos of *l'amour fou*.

In the roles that Gena Rowlands and Peter Falk would have ben slightly too old to play in the late '70s (and perhaps that's one of the reasons the film wasn't made then), Penn and Wright are simply dreadful. Pouty and posy, Penn's performance lacks even a semblance of a center. Wright's naive Rowlands imitation is totally undermined when the real Rowlands turns up in a tiny part midway through the film and shows us what we've been missing. (She plays the psychiatric social worker who certifies Eddie's release.)

Travolta, however, proves himself the equal of any actor in the elder Cassavetes' stock company. Travolta makes his first appearance midway through the film (after the title "10 years later") and we know in an instant what hell his character has been going through. Joey has been forced to play the reality principle in this triangle, and his frustration with the role, not to mention the problem of his wife being in love with another man, has made him as crazy as Eddie and Maureen. He's been haunted for so long by a fantasy of Eddie that by the time the flesh-and-blood version shows up on his doorstep, he's a passive-aggressive basket case.

None of this is ever spelled out in the script, but we can read it from the confusion in Travolta's eyes, his simultaneously clenched and flaccid facial muscles, and his misplaced bursts of hostility. John Cassavetes stripped his films of everything that could come between the actors and the audience. That's what made them so discomfiting and so revelatory. Nick Cassavetes, whose main objective as a director is to prove he's not his father (why else would he open a film about blindered people with a helicopter shot, for Chrissake?), gussies up *She's So Lovely* with atmospheric lighting and flashy camera moves. Travolta effortlessly punches through the slick surface to the film that might have been.

Also reviewed in:
CHICAGO TRIBUNE, 8/29/97, Friday/p. A, Mark Caro
NEW YORK TIMES, 8/27/97, p. C9, Janet Maslin
NEW YORKER, 9/8/97, p. 91, Anthony Lane
VARIETY, 5/26-6/1/97, p. 64, Emanuel Levy
WASHINGTON POST, 8/29/97, p. B1, Rita Kempley
WASHINGTON POST, 8/29/97, Weekend/p. 47, Desson Howe

SHILOH

A Legacy Releasing release of a Utopia Pictures/Carl Borack production in association with Zeta Entertainment. *Executive Producer:* Carl Borack and Mark Yellen. *Producer:* Zane W. Levitt and Dale Rosenbloom. *Director:* Dale Rosenbloom. *Screenplay:* Dale Rosenbloom. *Based on the novel by:* Phyllis Reynolds Naylor. *Director of Photography:* Frank Byers. *Editor:* Mark Westmore. *Music:* Joel Goldsmith. *Production Designer:* Amy Ancona. *Costumes:* Charmain Schreiner. *Running time:* 93 minutes. *MPAA Rating:* PG.

CAST: Michael Moriarty (Ray Preston); Blake Heron (Marty Preston); J. Madison Wright (Samantha); Scott Wilson (Judd Travers); Ann Dowd (Louise Preston); Rod Steiger (Doc Wallace); Bonnie Bartlett (Mrs. Wallace).

CHRISTIAN SCIENCE MONITOR, 4/28/97, p. 13, David Sterritt

A boy and his dog. It's one of the oldest stories in the world, but it still makes a good movie from time to time.

The latest specimen of the breed is "Shiloh," named after a shy little pooch—a beagle, actually, like Snoopy but somewhat less articulate—whose adventures begin when he's bought for $35 by Judd Travers, a West Virginia hunter. Judd had a difficult childhood, we eventually learn, and he takes out his lingering frustrations on the animal kingdom—rabbits and raccoons he tracks down and sells, and hunting dogs he mistreats if they don't behave the way he wants.

Shiloh doesn't like this new owner and runs away the first chance he gets. He's rescued by Marty Preston, an 11-year-old boy who lives with his family not far from Judd's ramshackle home. Marty wants to buy Shiloh from Judd and give him a better life, but Judd won't hear a word of it—either because he likes Shiloh as a hunting dog, or because he's so ornery he just doesn't like to see anyone happy.

Marty returns Shiloh to Judd, but when the beagle escapes a second time, Marty hides him away and claims to have no idea of his whereabouts. Judd is suspicious, and so is Marty's father, who sympathizes with his son but won't come between a dog and its legal owner. He also hates lying. The climax pits Marty and his dad against Judd and all the mean habits he's accumulated in his sadly disgruntled life.

"Shiloh" is refreshing partly because it's a well-made family picture that tells a good, clean story without relying too much on cute animal tricks or sentimental plot twists. For a movie aimed at family audiences, it also takes a surprisingly sophisticated view of the moral issues involved.

Marty has trouble "doing the right thing" because he's caught between two right things to do: telling the truth and returning Shiloh to his legal owner, or saving the dog from a life of obvious misery. The solution he eventually finds—agreeing to keep quiet about Judd's illegal trapping if Judd sells him the dog—is far from ideal. But it teaches Marty, and us, that the world is too complicated for a few simple rules to resolve every problem.

"Shiloh" is extremely well acted by a human cast including young Blake Heron as the hero, Michael Moriarty and Ann Dowd as his parents, and the great Rod Steiger as the local veterinarian who treats Shiloh's wounds after a bad scrape. Best of all is Scott Wilson as Judd, whose meanness is unforgivable but at the same time understandable, considering that he grew up with hardships as bad as the ones he's giving Shiloh now.

Dale Rosenbloom directed the movie from his own screenplay, based on a novel by Phyllis Reynolds Naylor that has won a large number of prizes including the prestigious Newbery Medal for children's literature. Frank Byers did the cinematography, vividly capturing the backwoods settings where much of the story unfolds.

"Shiloh" is easily the best family film so far this year, and a healthy reminder that movies suitable for young viewers don't have to be bland or boring for the grown-ups who take them to the theater.

LOS ANGELES TIMES, 4/25/97, Calendar/p. 8, Kevin Thomas

"Shiloh" is an uncommonly intelligent and thoughtful family film—although too intense for children under 8 or so—that captures that moment when a child, raised in normal circumstances, begins to realize how painful and contradictory life can really be.

Marty Preston (Blake Heron), already a fine actor of considerable reserves and range) is an 11-year-old boy living with his parents, Ray (Michael Moriarty) and Louise (Ann Dowd), and two younger sisters (Tori Wright, Shira Roth) in a rural West Virginia community where Ray works as a mail carrier.

Living in the vicinity is Judd Travers (Scott Wilson), a lifelong friend of Ray's, whose home is a tar-paper shack and who hunts for a living. He is training a year-old beagle one day when the animal barks at just the wrong moment. Judd strikes it on its head with a stick, causing the dog to run off, winding up in Marty's arms.

Of course, it's love at first sight between the boy and the dog. But Marty's love for the creature he names Shiloh, after a nearby bridge, will be tested immediately—and with increasing severity.

First of all, the reason why he doesn't already have a dog is that his grandmother has died recently and so expensively that Ray was forced to take out a second mortgage on the modest Preston family home. A stern, patriarchal moralist whose view of right and wrong is clear-cut, Ray declares the family can't afford a dog until it pays off its debts. In any case, in Ray's view the dogs are Judd's property, and that's that.

But Marty has good reason to believe that Judd will at the very least beat the animal severely again—he does in fact threaten, to break all its legs—or simply destroy him as worthless. Even though Marty realizes his father's sense of right and wrong clashes with his own, he feels he must do everything he can to protect Shiloh.

What Marty above all learns is that it can take an awful lot of time and effort to get adults to listen to you and to take you seriously. Only when an opportunity presents itself for Marty to sit down with the local doctor (Rod Steiger) does the boy get support in deciding to fight to keep Shiloh.

What's so good about this film, adapted from the Phyllis Reynolds Naylor novel by its skilled director Dale Rosenbloom, is that it takes its time in letting us get to know its people—yet it lasts only a modest 93 minutes.

At the outset you have no idea how crucial a role Steiger's doctor will play, and that both Ray and even Judd will acquire such dimension. In a strong yet appropriately understated directorial debut, Rosenbloom turns his cast, which includes Bonnie Bartlett as the doctor's kindly wife and J. Madison Wright as his little granddaughter Samantha, into an effective ensemble. And Shiloh, played by a beagle named Frannie, is a winner, too.

You can actually believe these people live where they do and behave as they do. It was Steiger who suggested Wilson for Judd Travers, and Wilson helps us understand a man who is almost too easy to hate. Since this handsome film, shot on location, has so much going for it, it's a shame it's stuck with such a trite, smarmy score that goes for the very sentimentality that "Shiloh" takes such pains to transcend.

NEW YORK POST, 4/25/97, p. 48, Michael Medved

"Shiloh" is a moving film about dogs and kids that avoids all the most prominent pitfalls of such projects, never condescending to either its characters or its audience.

Debuting writer-director Dale Rosenbloom mobilizes a strong, committed cast of Hollywood old hands to craft a view of childhood that is honest and intense, but not harsh, and in the process frames significant moral issues with exceptional impact and clarity.

Scott Wilson (who has played character roles in films from "In Cold Blood" to "Dead Man Walking") is superbly nuanced and unexpectedly complex as a bearded hunter in West Virginia who lives alone with his guns and his dogs.

One night, as he takes aim at a raccoon, a newly acquired beagle lets out a yelp that spoils the shot, leading the infuriated mountain man to slam the butt of his rifle into the animal's head.

Injured and terrified, the beagle runs away and takes refuge in the forest until he meets an 11-year-old (Blake Heron) crossing a creek in the woods. The boy befriends the wounded dog, names him "Shiloh" after the bridge where he has found him, and wants to adopt him permanently.

Unfortunately, his father (Michael Moriarty) is a rural mail carrier who can barely feed his family and insists that they return the beagle (who's adorable but not supernaturally smart or sensitive) to the abusive owner who's determined to keep and train the valuable dog.

When Shiloh runs away once more, the boy faces a painful dilemma and decides to defy and deceive his parents. He builds a makeshift shelter for the dog, secretly steals table scraps to feed him, and desperately tries to devise some plan to keep him permanently.

Young Blake Heron, veteran of numerous TV movies, portrays the main character as intelligent and unfailingly decent, yet with a rugged quality that makes him one of the more believable, engaging child actors in recent films. Moriarty, as his father, also balances toughness and tenderness, skillfully combining with Ann Dowd as the mother to create a functional screen family that is both loving and plausibly imperfect.

Even Rod Steiger, as the retired village doctor and grandfather of the boy's best friend, is uncharacteristically restrained and deeply affecting. Based on an award-winning young readers novel by Phyllis Reynolds Naylor, the story line provides twists and revelations that are, refreshingly enough, impossible to predict.

The film's biggest shortcoming is the bland, blank nature of its locations, suggesting some autumnal anywhere rather than a specific small town, reflecting apparent restrictions of the budget. Nevertheless, passionate performances and loving direction transcend these limitations, and transform simple material into an altogether memorable and commendable family film.

NEWSDAY, 4/25/97, Part II/p. B7, John Anderson

Even if it were well directed and had an original story and weren't so ham-handed in its sense of righteous indignation, "Shiloh" would have a kind of carpetbagger quality about it: the feeling that everyone involved has just landed and will be out as soon as the checks clear.

Not that there are going to be checks, or that the film has anything but apparently noble intentions. Nothing blows up; nobody dies. But this tale of a boy and the abused dog he adopts (well, steals, actually) is set in rural West Virginia. And for all the aerial shots of fields and farms and the funky ambience, there's more verisimilitude in "Deep Space Nine." By imposing a suburbanite's view of the world on its backwoods universe, "Shiloh" exhibits a grievous lack of understanding, or willingness to understand. Which is something of a misstep when you're making a movie about understanding.

Marty Preston (Blake Heron), the all-too-indignant, preteen hero of the film, finds a dog with a bleeding head wound and immediately decides to keep him. Never mind that his father, postman Ray Preston (Michael Moriarty), is in debt because of Marty's ailing grandmother, or that the dog rightfully belongs to the unsavory Judd Travers (Scott Wilson), a trapper and hunter who makes his money with his dogs and can't afford to be sentimental about them.

No, Marty acts as if he's never heard of animals being worked, or killed, and as if he didn't grow up in the place where he lives. His sense of outrage is not just overly theatrical; it's foreign. And the dog? He seems to be a graduate of the PETA School for Pack Hounds: A well-timed yelp ruins Judd's shot at a raccoon, and Judd gun-butts the pooch. Why he wants the dog back is anybody's guess.

Yes, Judd is a brute, and the messages of "Shiloh"—being kind to animals, working hard for the things you want, etc.—are noble, and kids should be exposed to them. Parents, however, will be turning feral by the end of the first act. Director Dale Rosenbloom never entertains the idea that there are other ways of life in this country, that some people might actually survive by hunting or trapping, and never makes it possible to transfer the lessons of the film to another place and time—a slaughterhouse supplying meat to Long Island, for instance, or someone running dog fights in an inner city.

The cast is good, overall. Moriarty exudes patriarchy—and honor, when he insists that Marty take the dog back. Wilson is nicely seedy as Judd, and Rod Steiger—when you can get past the fact that he's in this film—is fine as the kindly grocer-physician, Doc Wallace. J. Madison Wright is quite engaging as Marty's girlfriend (sort of) Samantha, too. But young Blake Heron is too much, especially when Marty's telling Judd, "You better not hurt that dog or else," and Judd isn't breaking Marty over his knee. "Shiloh" is yet another movie about children made by people who don't seem to know any. And I'm not sure about dogs either.

VILLAGE VOICE, 4/29/97, p. 78, Francine Russo,

How old do you have to be before you feel condescended to by a film that footnotes every dramatic moment with a platitude? I figure by 10, you're pushing it.

Shiloh, based on the Newberry Award-winning novel, is a story of boy gets dog, boy loses dog, boy ... Well, why spoil the ending? Young Marty, a West Virginia country kid, wants to keep the injured puppy he's found. But he belongs to Judd, the mean mountain man, who abuses his animals just like his own pa abused him. Marty determines to save that dog, even if he has to fight Judd with his bare prepubescent hands.

Dale Rosenbloom writes and directs with the same heavy hand. You can hear his computer keys clicking while the kid's mouth spills righteous words.

Sentimentalized death is the ticket here, and love and pluck. But between bouts of scoffing, I found my eyes getting moist. And I wasn't the only critic so afflicted. So, who knows? Maybe they can got *Shiloh* past the 10-year-olds.

Also reviewed in:
NEW YORK TIMES, 4/25/97, p. C8, Anita Gates
VARIETY, 10/28-11/3/96, p. 71, Dennis Harvey

SHOOTING PORN

A John Tilley and Caryn Horwitz release. *Producer:* Caryn Horwitz and Doug Lindeman. *Director:* Ronnie Larsen. *Screenplay:* Ronnie Larsen. *Director of Photography:* Bruce McCarthy. *Editor:* James Lyons. *Sound:* Juan Martinez. *Running time:* 75 minutes. *MPAA Rating:* Not Rated.

WITH: Gino Colbert; Chi Chi LaRue; Blue Blake; Bryan Kidd; Adam Rom; Hunter Scott; Rip Stone; Adam Wilde; Mickey Skee; David Widmer.

LOS ANGELES TIMES, 10/3/97, Calendar/p. 8, Kevin Thomas

Strictly for adults, Ronnie Larsen's "Shooting Porn" is a forthright, funny, occasionally graphic and ultimately serious and comprehensive took at the world of gay porn video-making. Having written the popular satirical play "Making Porn," Larsen now takes us onto the sets of two top porn video-makers, Gino Colbert and Chi Chi La Rue, and interviews their stars and many others involved in the industry.

Colbert and La Rue, are both veteran professionals. On the set, they are supportive but no-nonsense; La Rue says he is amazed that anyone would believe he'd wear drag to work. (At parties and personal appearances, La Rue always appears in drag, resembling a younger, better-looking Divine. Without drag, he says, "I'd be just a fat boy standing in the corner.") Key among the actors are Blue Blake and Hunter Thompson, both popular stars and possessed of a formidable sense of humor, especially about themselves.

"Shooting Porn" is often outrageous and sometimes hilarious. There are moments when some audiences might wish Larsen had not been quite so candid about all the clinical aspects of preparing for a sex scene, but he presents porn actors as human beings, not merely the objects of carefully calculated' sex fantasies.

Most of the actors admit to a certain uneasiness at the outset of their careers but clearly lose their inhibitions swiftly. Not surprisingly, they are all good-looking and in shape, but they also seem to have acquired a certain detachment about themselves and what they're doing, something essential to success and survival in most endeavors but absolutely crucial in the transitory world of porn.

Larsen makes clear why resilience is so important in pointing out the realities that porn actors have to deal with—like having to decide whether or not to tell your parents what you're doing for a living, for starters. (The consensus: Tell them before they find out.)

Then there's the issue of sexual orientation, since a number of the most famous stars in gay porn claim to be straight. These so-called "gay for pay" actors are sometimes derided by openly gay actors. (The consensus: It's not possible for any totally straight actor to function in porn). Self-proclaimed straight men, however, are attracted to gay porn because they are treated with more respect and earn more money than in straight porn. (The only thing the men of porn apparently are coy about is their earnings, and how they report it on their income tax returns.)

"Shooting Porn" goes for a humorous, light touch, but Larsen is too smart not to overlook the dark side of porn—the way in which some young men self-destruct on the fast track. The classic example is Joey Stefano, a handsome young man who died of a drug overdose in a seedy Hollywood motel room at the age of 26. Stefano was also HIV-positive, which raises the specter of AIDS in porn.

While Stefano is described by many as a troubled, vulnerable individual, La Rue's remark that in regard to Stefano's death "the industry had nothing to do with it" seems a bit disingenuous. Although safe—or rather safer—sex is nowadays the rule in gay porn, Larsen does not make mention of the huge toll AIDS has exacted on porn actors of previous decades.

In his apt concluding remarks to "Shooting Porn," critic David Widmer, citing the outpouring of grief over Stefano's death, wonders whether porn actors realize how much they mean to legions of lonely gay men, especially those who are isolated in small, remote towns.

NEW YORK POST, 7/11/97, p. 41, Larry Worth

Those who snoozed through biology class can get all their questions answered—at least about the male anatomy—in "Shooting Porn." The bad news: It's more than you ever wanted to know.

Ronnie Larsen's documentary on gay pornography—specifically, the lensing of hard-core flicks—goes out of its way to be graphic. Accordingly, Larsen's intents seem far less educational than exploitive.

For most part, the film segues between directors Chi Chi LaRue (who appears both in and out of drag) and Gino Colbert. Both are seen working on their latest gay projects, allowing for convenient demonstrations of whatever points they're making.

More often than not, that involves the showcasing of body parts and sexual doings which needed no visualization. It seems as if Larsen inserted them strictly to satisfy his presumably gay following.

That's unfortunate, since the topic of porn certainly raises issues of much broader interest. Here, one of those issues is glimpsed when addressing the drug-induced death of a 26-year-old gay porn icon.

In addition, there's a relatively provocative debate about "gay for pay actors"—avowed hetrosexuals who cavort with men when the camera's rolling. Since three gay porn headliners fall into that category, the ensuing comments prove duly intriguing.

But all too soon, Larsen is back indulging sexual fantasies or veering into completely foreign turf. How he segues to video clerks complaining about cassettes' soiled jackets defies all logic.

As ever, Larsen's presentation sacrifices focus for alleged titillation. So, whether showing tricks of the trade, actors' endless prepping or just unrelated minutiae, the results neither engage or amuse.

Actually, there is one big laugh, though unintentional: when LaRue comments that gay hardcore is in danger of becoming "too mainstream." That's as delusional as "Shooting Porn" pretending to be more than a skin flick.

VILLAGE VOICE, 7/15/97, p. 74, Elliott Stein

Ronnie Larsen decided to do a film scrutinizing the gay video industry while researching background for his play *Making Porn,* a broad comedy that has proved a huge Off-Broadway hit. The resultant *Shooting Porn* was, in turn, one of the hits of this year's recent New York Lesbian & Gay Film Festival. A diverting doc, with a few steamily explicit scenes, it offers such a rosy view of the business, however, that it almost seems as much a fiction as the directors feel-good stage piece.

The film is loosely structured around visits to the sets of two prolific gay directors, Chi Chi La Rue and Gino Colbert. The flamboyant and garrulous La Rue is often seen in drag; his films seem to feature mostly boy-next-door performers. Colbert, who makes both straight and gay sex flicks, uses beefier, slightly older hunks. Larsen's pic tells us nothing of the stylistic differences of these auteurs of arousal; it's frustrating not to see any clips from their finished work.

Much of the movie is devoted to in-between-takes interviews with the two directors and their retinue of stars and technicians. A good deal of this stuff is drolly piquant—an actor preparing for a bathroom sex sequence squats on a toilet seat, gross wiener peering out of his Jockey shorts, as he orders a full menu of Italian takeout; La Rue, directing a performer, urges: "Wink your butt hole at me, Josh, wink it in and out." Aficionados of enemas will get their fill—several are performed on camera. An interesting polemic erupts briefly about "gay-for-pay" performers—apparently some of the biggest queer porn stars are heterosexual. But just how het can they be? Colbert remarks dryly: "The straight guys do the best cock sucking."

At 75 minutes, this is a relatively short feature; James Lyons' brisk editing never permits the pace to lag. Still, I could have done with one less enema and a bit more information. How many gay porn features are made annually? How has AIDS affected the industry? What happens to older gay porn stars? These and other pertinent questions are not asked; others, involving drugs and prostitution, are simply skimped.

Also reviewed in:
NEW YORK TIMES, 7/11/97, p. C10, Stephen Holden
VARIETY, 6/23-29/97, p. 96, Dennis Harvey

SICK: THE LIFE AND DEATH OF BOB FLANAGAN, SUPERMASOCHIST

A Cinepix Film Properties release of a Kirby Dick production. *Producer:* Kirby Dick. *Director:* Kirby Dick. *Director of Photography:* Jonathan Dayton, Kirby Dick, and Geza Sinkovics. *Editor:* Kirby Dick and Dody Dorn. *Music:* Blake Leyh. *Sound:* Alan Barker and Kip Gynn. *Running time:* 90 minutes. *MPAA Rating:* Not Rated.

WITH: Bob Flanagan; Sheree Rose; Cathy Flanagan; Bob Flanagan, Sr.; Tim Flanagan; Sarah Doucette.

LOS ANGELES TIMES, 11/7/97, Calendar/p. 19, Kevin Thomas

"Sick: The Life and Death of Bob Flanagan, Supermasochist:"is a title sure to turn off lots of people, and indeed Kirby Dick's astute documentary is not for the faint of heart. It's one of those pictures, however, worth knowing about even if you never see it.

That's because of the way in which Flanagan and his wife, Sheree Rose, integrate extreme behavior within everyday existence. They come across as decent, decidedly courageous individuals with an extraordinary degree of self-knowledge. They command respect even if you are repelled by their specific activities.

Cystic fibrosis combined with a Catholic upbringing lead Flanagan to conclude that he could alleviate the pain of his disease through masochistic behavior. ("Jesus," he declares, "is the most famous masochist.") Rose is right when she says her husband was lucky to meet her, for she is a sadist. Beyond these dovetailing predilections, Flanagan and Rose prove to be an exceptionally creative and intelligent couple who were able to turn, their obsessions into art, albeit of a highly specialized kind and involving at times an overwhelmingly brutal exhibitionism. Flanagan became a writer, visual artist and performance artist while Rose, along with assisting in his performance art, became a photographer and video artist, and in those roles she in fact contributed significantly to this film.

Still, "Sick" is hard to take. If elaborate public and private displays of sadomasochism are not your thing—even if meant to represent a triumph of the spirit and will over the pain of disease—it becomes a serious turnoff. (Not everyone, after all, enjoys watching a man drive a nail through his penis.) On top of this, the film is a record of Flanagan's death from cystic fibrosis in January 1996 at the age of 43.

He comes across as a gallant, darkly humorous man determined not to go gently into the night. Yet as his always-shaky health deteriorates, so does his relationship with Rose, who has difficulty accepting that he has finally reached the stage where he's no longer up to submitting to her stinging ministrations—not even 42 "little spanks by the hand" to celebrate his birthday. Love proves stronger than a passion for S&M, however, and Rose remains loyal and caring to the end and beyond.

While the film focuses foremost on Flanagan and to a lesser extent Rose, it offers insights to others as well. We meet a beautiful teenager, also stricken with cystic fibrosis, who via the Make-a-Wish Foundation gets to meet Flanagan, whose way of coping with their disease has captured her imagination, and most significantly, Flanagans' parents, who knew nothing about the bizarre aspects of their son's behavior until late in his life.

His mother, who lost two of her three daughters to cystic fibrosis, sees irony in her son's deliberately endangering the life she and her husband strived to protect. His father has come to see his son as he saw himself, his life an act of defiance against God for the curse of cystic fibrosis. Flanagan was once the poster boy for cystic fibrosis, and in his unique way, remained so.

NEW YORK POST, 11/7/97, p. 57, Larry Worth

Ever wonder what makes a sadomasochist tick?

"Sick: The Life and Death of Bob Flanagan, Supermasochist" supplies the answer. But the price is an hour and a half of seat-squirming for even the hardiest viewers.

Director Kirby Dick puts the camera on Bob Flanagan, who battled against his cystic fibrosis by mutilating the body he hated so much.

Shot on video over the two years leading up to Bob's demise at age 43, the film follows Bob to his randy poetry readings and graphic performance-art exhibits, then talks with his understandably confused parents and brother.

But, make no mistake: Most of the time is spent as Bob and his companion—an odious dominatrix named Sheree—explore their unique relationship.

The camera is spared virtually nothing, whether Bob is spitting phlegm into a cup or screaming his way through various cuttings and piercings. But the most controversial scene is near the finale, when Bob drives a nail (in unbelievable closeup) through his most sensitive body part, then pulls it out as blood spurts into the camera lens.

It's excruciating to watch. More than that, it distracts from the humanity that is the essence of Bob's story. He was also a man of great humor, but that's lost in the shuffle too.

Director Dick certainly deserves credit for bringing attention to a man who dealt with a death sentence in the only way that made sense to him. And while the results certainly aren't entertaining, they're undeniably enlightening. And shocking. And repulsive. And deeply disturbing.

Accordingly, viewers may exit "Sick" questioning if the end justifies the means.

NEWSWEEK, 3/24/97, p. 79, Jack Kroll

[*Sick* was reviewed jointly with *Crash*; see Kroll's review of that film.]

SIGHT AND SOUND, 2/98, p. 48, Mark Cousins

A documentary about Bob Flanagan, which establishes the facts about his life through his own performance pieces, and through captions and interviews with his parents and brother. Born in 1952 and brought up in California, Flanagan was diagnosed with cystic fibrosis and given six-to-seven years to live. Two of his siblings also died from the disease. He, too, "should be dead by now".

At an early age, he hung himself from his parents' doors and put pins in his belt. A comic video letter from 1983 tells of his new relationship with Sheree Rose. Sheree says her domination skills are 'motherly'. In 'Autopsy 1992', she pierces Bob's penis and inserts a steel ball in his anus. In 1994, Bob's seven-screen crucifixion piece, 'The Scaffold', is unveiled, with other installations. At the opening, he and Sheree mingle with crowds and he's interviewed. Afterwards, he's depressed. She tells him he's the hit of New York. Sarah, a young woman interested in S&M, writes to Bob asking if they can meet. They do, and later Bob and Sheree discuss whether Sheree is jealous.

Bob appears in the Nine Inch Nails video 'Happiness in Slavery' and plays at cystic-fibrosis summer camp. In a close shot, he nails his own penis to a block of wood, then removes the nail. Bob's health deteriorates. He goes to hospital and Sheree visits but he eventually dies. Her photographs show his full body and closeups of his genitals, crowned by thorns. One month after Bob's burial, Sheree unwraps a jar full of liquid from his lungs. As his 1995 poem "Why" is read, images from his childhood are shown.

It is a very good thing that Kirby Dick's likeable, award-winning film *Sick The Life & Death of Bob Flanagan, Supermasochist* will have a theatrical release in the UK. Its immensely private scenes benefit from being shown in public. Men in particular might find it hard to watch close-ups of Bob Flanagan's innocent looking little penis trussed up and nailed down, but libertarians will cheer. To experience *Sick* is to feel cinema, and cinema-going, mature in some way. This is not to say that the film is a great creative contribution to the history of documentary. Despite the awards and the unflinching compassion, especially at the end, *Sick* is a weaker film than it should be. Individual scenes are disturbing and complex, but the overall organisation of the material is flawed.

The problem stems from what kind of non-fiction film *Sick* thinks it is. Its subtitle clearly leads us to expect a portrait of a life which will explore layers of personality. And indeed most of the scenes in the film are either of Flanagan talking about himself, performing his autobiographical poetry or making his installations. We hear from his family and see him with his wife Sheree. Most of the time, however, director Dick takes Flanagan, his friend, at his own estimation. The impression is always of someone face-on, consciously aware that he's accounting for himself. This results in a portrait of disappointing one dimensionality. The film's point-of-view doesn't move, but rather takes a seat in the front row of the stalls. The best documentary portrayals of people for example, such films as *Marlene* by Maximilian Schell or the Maysles-Hovde Meyer film *Grey Gardens*—construct troubling, non-linear, oblique relationships between film-maker and subject. *Sick* doesn't do this.

What is interesting is that, despite the film's title and concerns, Kirby Dick says it isn't a portrait film at all. He prefers to think of it as an essay about how Flanagan's cystic fibrosis has in some way helped to create his intense body awareness and how Flanagan found an aesthetic response to it through his art. But if this is an essay and not a portrait, then the frontality of his portrayal of Flanagan is not appropriate. If the film is an essay, like the films of Chris Marker or Marcel Ophuls, you'd then expect it to follow the contours and themes and ideas raised by Flanagan's art rather than his life. You'd think it would put Flanagan in other contexts, or consider how other illnesses inspired artists, such as Dennis Potter or Marcel Proust. And it would surely evaluate Flanagan's work itself.

Sick begins in this way, but its first 15 minutes signal a discursive range which is not followed through. It sets up the connections between the illness, art and pain with ease and wit, and Flanagan himself is most engaging in these early sequences, but it fails to advance from here. Flanagan's art itself is inadequately explored, leaving the suspicion that in objects such as a teddy bear done up in bondage gear, there isn't much there. Only the final poem 'Why', which Dick illustrates with what looks like 8mm footage from his subject's childhood, seems to get close to the heart of what Flanagan really has to say.

There is a scene towards the end of this film, when Flanagan and Sheree are at home, after the opening in Manhattan of his latest exhibition. He is depressed, and she's irritated with him and filming their conversation on low-grade videotape. She wonders why he's depressed since everyone is talking about him. This tense exchange is one of the film's most revealing moments. It shows something of her interest in publicity. It reveals the Warholian nature of some of their ambitions. More of this scepticism and candour throughout would have improved the film.

Despite these weaknesses, *Sick* is an important film. Its director has said that the penis nailing and anal insertion scenes are not really crucial to what it's trying to say. This is surely wrong because it's the very boldness of the raw material, the tenderness (in both sense of the word) of the nailing scene in particular, which gives the film its power. Kirby Dick's instinctive editing decision to show us it all, the full monty, is a fine tribute to his friend Bob Flanagan.

TIME, 11/3/97, p. 114, Richard Corliss

He could have emerged from Jesse Helms' darkest nightmare of an NEA-performance psyche: a guy who nails his penis to a board and calls it art. Yet Bob Flanagan, masochist with a cause, might win the sympathy of any stony conservative, for he was one of the longest-lived survivors of cystic fibrosis, a lung disease that takes most of its victims in childhood. His daft wit even turned his affliction into a *Mary Poppins*-style ditty: "Supermasochistic Bob has cystic fibrosis/ He should've died when he was young, but he was too precocious / A lifetime of infection and his lungs all filled with phlegm/ The CS would have killed him if it weren't for S&M/ Hum-diddle-iddle-iddle I'm gonna die ..."

Since Kirby Dick's *Sick: The Life & Death of Bob Flanagan, Supermasochist* displays all of its subject's creative carpentry skills, it is not for the faint of stomach. (When the song *The Hammer of Love* starts playing, go out for popcorn.) But like the 1994 *Crumb*, this deadpan documentary transcends its sensational topic. Flanagan's artful self-mutilation, and especially his corrosively comic descriptions of it, amounted to a heroic decision to take the punishment that God or nature meted out to him into his own hands.

His long relationship with the dominatrix Sheree Rose is a ferocious metaphor for any intense, complex liaison. Whatever welts she inflicted, whatever pain he endured and enjoyed, they surely deserved and loved each other. Flanagan's most poignant work of art—the culmination of a life in agony—is his death at age 43. It is recorded here with a grace that nearly matches the blithe heroism of a man most viewers might, at the beginning of this funny, disturbing, stirring film, have too quickly labeled sick.

VILLAGE VOICE, 11/11/97, p. 86, Dennis Lim

It's a remarkable film that can offer a garishly blood-splattered close-up of an impaled penis and still appear wholly non-sensationalist. *Sick*, Kirby Dick's portrait of Bob Flanagan, the poet, per-formance artist, and 'Supermasochist" who died in January 1996, is a manifesto of defiant survival and improbable self-empowerment. While it clearly owes its pathos and potency to Flana-gan, Dick's documentary is as honest and complicated as it needs to be.

Far more than most artists, Flanagan suffered for his art. Or, more to the point, he translated acute, lifelong suffering into radical, life-preserving art. Diagnosed with cystic fibrosis as a child, Flanagan learned to eroticize pain; he explored, indulged, and drew sustenance from his masochism, and became one of the longest-living survivors of the incurable lung disease. "The CF would have killed me if it weren't for S&M," he sings in one of his incongruously cheery ditties.

In collaboration with his dominatrix lover, photographer Sheree Rose, Flanagan subjected his emaciated body to ritual, sometimes public, abasement. Virtually a stand-up comic who, while stripped, scarred, sutured, or strung up, remained Mr. Congeniality, Flanagan was a serious artist with a keen sense of the absurd.

Interspersed with videos of his performances and installations (and, no less memorably, with his wheezy coughing jags), *Sick* is a poignant account of one man confronting a death sentence conferred at birth. For Flanagan, wresting control of his mortality meant laughing in its face (the audience's inevitable nervous mirth is a comparable impulse). The movie opens with him announcing his own death to the camera; as the end credits roll, he sings about how it's "fun to be dead." For all the insistent gallows humor (or perhaps because of it), the images of Flanagan on his deathbed, disoriented and scared, followed by Rose's snapshots of his newly dead corpse, are ineffably sad.

Without attempting overt analysis, *Sick* provides lucid insights into the psychological dynamic of an s/m relationship. Crucially, it also debunks the myth of masochist as victim. Flanagan is probably best known for being tortured and disemboweled in Nine Inch Nails' "Happiness Is Slavery" video, but that persona is aberrational. In interviews here, he speaks of the control implicit in masochism, pointing out, "I'm more the mad scientist than the guinea pig." Dick brings intense scrutiny to bear on Flanagan and Rose's relationship, as if daring the viewer to pass judgment. For the most part, their union seems a blissfully fortuitous one, but there are signs, too, of stress eroding its foundations. With Flanagan close to death, barely able to breathe, Rose throws a tantrum: "If you loved me, you'd submit to me."

Sick leaves conventional notions of complicity in tangles, its voyeuristic, freak-show aspect balanced (but hardly neutralized) by its emphatically collaborative nature. The need for an underlying explanation is addressed most forcefully by Flanagan himself, in his torrential poem, "Why," (used here in a devastating concluding voiceover). Equally instructive, however, are the thoughts of his parents. "I see a young man who hates his body," says Flanagan's mother. I concur with her husband, a sensible man who prefers to see his son's supermasochism as a way of telling God, "Go fuck yourself."

Also reviewed in:
NEW YORK TIMES, 11/7/97, p. E24, Stephen Holden
VARIETY, 2/3-9/97, p. 44, Emanuel Levy

SIMPLE WISH, A

A Universal Pictures and The Bubble Factory release of a Sheinberg production. *Producer:* Sid Sheinberg, Bill Sheinberg, and Jon Sheinberg. *Director:* Michael Ritchie. *Screenplay:* Jeff Rothberg. *Director of Photography:* Ralf Bode. *Editor:* William Scharf. *Music:* Bruce Broughton. *Music Editor:* Richard Harrison and Nick Meyers. *Sound:* Doug Ganton and (muisc) Armin Steiner. *Sound Editor:* Richard Legrand, Jr. *Casting:* Rick Pagano. *Production Designer:* Stephen Hendrickson. *Art Director:* Peter Grundy. *Set Decorator:* Jaro Dick. *Set Dresser:* Jacques-Alexander Veilleux. *Special Effects:* Martin Malivoire. *Visual Effects:* Tim Healey. *Costumes:* Luke Reichle. *Make-up:* Patricia Green. *Stunt Coordinator:* Alison Reid and Danny Aiello, III. *Running time:* 95 minutes. *MPAA Rating:* PG.

CAST: Martin Short (Murray); Kathleen Turner (Claudia); Mara Wilson (Anabel Greening); Robert Pastorelli (Oliver); Amanda Plummer (Boots); Francis Capra (Charlie); Ruby Dee (Hortense); Teri Garr (Rena); Alan Campbell (Tony Sable); Jonathan Hadary (Lord Richard); Deborah Odell (Jeri); Lanny Flaherty (Duane); Clare Coulter (Ms. Bramble); Neil Foster (Manny); Jaime Tirelli (Joe); Jack McGee (Officer O'York); Lillian Ritchie and Miriam Ritchie (Schoolgirls); David Crean (Tony's Agent); Kwok-Wing Leung (Grocer); Adam David (Sable's Chauffeur); Rick Fox (Pianist); Derek Carkner (Shaw's Assistant); Henry Gomez (Investor); Frank Cee (Vendor); John Douglas Williams (Paperboy).

LOS ANGELES TIMES, 7/11/97, Calendar/p. 18, Kenneth Turan

[*The following review by Kenneth Turan appeared in a slightly different form in*
NEWSDAY, 7/11/97, Part II/p. B9.]

If you put a gleeful performance inside an indifferent movie, does the film get better or does it remain an indifferent piece of work with an asterisk next to it? This is no abstract question, it's what audiences will be deciding should they see "A Simple Wish."

The engaging acting comes courtesy of Martin Short, a comic actor who's been memorable in short bursts (the obsequious Franck in "Father of the Bride" and the impossible agent in "The Big Picture") but has rarely had the run of an entire picture.

In "A Simple Wish" he plays Murray, the world's only male fairy godmother, a bow-tied dervish recently certified as a wish-fulfiller but uncertain at best about his powers. Antic, manic, easily perturbed and prone to petulant, sarcastic remarks ("That's Mr. Fairy to you," he says to a nonbeliever), Short's Murray is quite a piece of business and guaranteed to be as funny a performance as the year will see.

The rest of "A Simple Wish," written by Jeff Rothberg and directed by the veteran Michael Ritchie, is more miss than hit, with more haphazard moments than clever ones. And though it clocks in at only 89 minutes, a surprising amount of that is no more than marking time.

Conceptualized (like much of recent Disney animation) as a kid film spiced up with references to things like collagen and old Bette Davis movies to keep the adults occupied, "A Simple Wish" is also loaded with computer-generated special effects, and that turns out to be unfortunate.

Though they no doubt cost the Earth, the effects here, illustrating the tricks fairy godfolk can do with their wands, are only marginally involving. And the film has a tendency to go to them too quickly, simply because it can, in what feels like an effort to disguise how flimsy much of the script is.

The heart of the film is a 7-year-old with a lot of problems. Motherless Anabel Greening (kid veteran Mara Wilson) has a brother who torments her (Francis Capra) and a singing father (Robert Pastorelli) who drives a hansom cab in Central Park but might relocate the whole family to Nebraska if he doesn't get the lead in an upcoming Broadway musical.

That show, "Two Cities," is one of the film's more amusing sidelights. Based on the Dickens novel and scheduled to be the 23rd consecutive hit for Lord Richard (an amusing Andrew Lloyd Webber parody by Jonathan Hadary), "Two Cities" comes complete with an onstage guillotine and dead-on songs like "It's a Far Better Thing I Do" that director Ritchie wrote to music by Lucy Simon.

Hoping to get her dad the leading role of Sidney Carton, young Anabel puts out a call for a fairy godmother and ends up with the unnervingly nontraditional Murray instead, someone who looks and acts like an absent-minded symphonic conductor. So new at the wish game he keeps referring to written instructions, Murray has the annoying habit of having his spells go "ever so slightly awry," which leads to big-time complications for Anabel and her family.

More than that, Murray is soon forced to tangle with the dread Claudia (Kathleen Turner), a former godmother who was kicked out of NAFGA (North American Fairy Godmothers Assn., "a not-for-profit organization") for giving in to the dark side. Bored with kids and "their insipid wishes," Claudia is bucking to be the queen of mean, and has some dirty tricks in store for NAFGA's members. Only Murray, it turns out, has even a prayer of stopping her.

Turner is very much in the spirit of things as Claudia, as is Terri Garr as NAFGA member Rena. But not enough of "A Simple Wish" measures up to Short's inspired lunacy, to riffs like his wicked imitation of Turner's vocal patterns. That clever a film would probably be too much to hope for but, after all, what are fairy godmothers for?

NEW YORK POST, 7/11/97, p. 41, Thelma Adams

Do you believe in magic?

Anabel Greening does.

Played with metropolitan savvy by Mara Wilson, this winning little New Yorker knows that sometimes, to accomplish something really big, you have to delegate. She has "A Simple Wish" to transform her unemployed actor dad (Robert Pastorelli) into a Broadway star.

If Anabel fails, her family has to move to Nebraska. To a wee Manhattanite, this is a fate worse than family court. In times of crisis, it pays to recruit a fairy godmother.

Enter Martin Short in prickly nerd mode with a red wig, rabbit teeth and a waistcoat. His Murray is an inexperienced wish-granter trying to break the gender barrier of the North American Fairy Godmothers Association (NAFGA).

Anabel thinks her worries are over until Murray starts waving his wand. Instead of conjuring up a rabbit, he creates an 80-foot *rabbi* with the short fuse of a man who just entered the 23rd hour of his Yom Kippur fast. As if that weren't bad enough, Murray turns Anabel's dad to bronze.

Meanwhile, a political schism within NAFGA threatens his ability to reverse the spell. He must overpower Claudia (Kathleen Turner), a fallen fairy godmother. Stripped of her magic wand by the clan, the witch plots to topple NAFGA by stealing their wands.

Turner pairs Glinda the Good Witch looks and Witch of the West wickedness in a deliciously silly turn. She revels in overblown costumes that recall the darkly sexy apple-giver of Disney's "Snow White and the Seven Dwarf." Amanda Plummer collars her intensity to comic ends as Claudia's sidekick, a dog-turned-club-kid.

Michael Ritchie's delightful family film doesn't quite match the seamless cruel comedy of the best Roald Dahl stories brought to film, as in Nicolas Roeg's "The Witches." The director who began with "Downhill Racer," made us "Smile" and then delivered "The Bad News Bears," achieves a milder magic working from Jeff Rothberg's uneven script.

Ritchie and Rothberg grant a parent's simple wish for family fare that doesn't involve cranky mommies, overcompensating divorced daddies, rampaging dinosaurs with a taste for little girls, bats clad in S & M gear and boats of mass destruction.

And, more than that, it puts special effects back where they belong: in the wands of fairy godmothers who only have to say "Shasha-sha boom!" to transform the world into a happier place.

SIGHT AND SOUND, 11/97, p. 51, Charlotte O'Sullivan

Motherless, seven-year-old Anabel doesn't want to leave NYC for Nebraska, but this will happen if her father fails to get the lead in a Broadway musical. He's been called back for a second audition, but the show's backers would prefer a big name. Anabel's prayer for a fairy godmother is answered with Murray, the very first male fairy godmother.

Meanwhile, the other fairy godmothers are holding their annual get-together. Two unwanted guests appear: the megalomaniacal Claudia, who went over to the dark side and was stripped of her wand, and her awestruck sidekick Boots. Claudia casts some heavy spells and steals the wands of the assembled godmothers: she now controls every wand but her own—which is in Murray's hands.

Murray accidentally magics himself and Anabel to Nebraska, then turns Dad into a statue in Central Park. With Dad's second audition imminent, Murray stalls for time by causing the big-name rival to vomit toads. With Anabel's brother Charlie, Murray and Anabel visit fairy-godmother HQ and release the chief fairy godmother from Claudia's spell. She tells them they must restore Dad before midnight.

At Claudia's castle a battle of wits ensues, resolved when Murray turns Boots against Claudia. Claudia is magically imprisoned in fragments of a mirror and the rest rush back to Central Park. Missing the midnight deadline, they join forces and break the spell anyway. Dad gets the job and Murray skips off into the sunset with Boots.

It's strange that while kids seem to prefer movies *sans* children (such as *Batman & Robin* and *Men in Black*) the industry insists on churning out films like this—bland odes to the magic of pre-adolescence. Even so, need this film have been so disappointing? Actress Mara Wilson (the star of *Matilda*) is not to blame—as Anabel, a little girl who still believes in fairy godmothers, she smiles gravely, her dark eyes and vulnerable stillness reminiscent of the children in *The Spirit of the Beehive* or *The White Balloon*. You can well believe she has lost her mother.

Moreover, the idea behind the story is good. For a wish to come true, Anabel must imagine what she wants. So when she asks to go to Central Park and is shaboomed with Murray to Nebraska, his question is understandable: "Were you thinking about Nebraska?" "Maybe," replies Anabel, trembly-lipped. As the top fairy godmother explains, "There is no simple wish." Freud got here first, but screenwriter Jeff Rothberg seems a willing disciple, tackling the problem "What do children want?" with sly gusto. Dad is clearly having an affair with Jeri, his female agent, so if the family stays in NYC—as Anabel seems to want—she'll be getting a new mommy. This not only makes sense of Nebraska but also the 'wish' that paralyses Dad—it's her attempt to restrain his sexuality. And evil godmother Claudia, all rage against men and 'masochistic' girls, could be a displaced mom come uncontrollably back to life.

Unfortunately, the film deserts such pleasantly murky territory. This is Martin Short's show: it's lovable Murray that's meant to matter, not an angst-ridden kid. Everything that goes wrong is down to his incompetence. Torn between crude Ken Dodd-style arm waving and sub-Tim Burton strangeness, Short repels the attention he demands. He is too obviously from this world, a stand-up comic hogging the stage.

The audience want Anabel and Claudia to meet, but they're kept apart almost until the end, when we discover Claudia has no designs on the child. Unlike such twisted sisters as Snow White's stepmother or Oz's Wicked Witches, she never gets personal, or scars our psyches. In a tantalising scene in her castle, she and Anabel play together, curiously compatible. But this game is quickly ended by Murray, as he and Claudia engage in old-fashioned sex-war banter. "Never send a man to do a woman's job," she purrs (Kathleen Turner apparently having fun), but it's campy pantomime stuff.

Compounding everything is the film's sheer stylistic ineptitude. We gasp the first time Claudia flattens someone in cartoon style; the second time we yawn. Director Michael Ritchie (*The Candidate*, 1972) may not be to blame—*A Simple Wish* looks like the work of many panicked hands. 'Magic' and 'childhood' have never seemed more estranged.

Also reviewed in:
NEW YORK TIMES, 7/11/97, p. C18, Lawrence Van Gelder
VARIETY, 7/14-20/97, p. 44, Todd McCarthy
WASHINGTON POST, 7/11/97, p. B7, Stephen Hunter
WASHINGTON POST, 7/11/97, Weekend/p. 38, Jane Horwitz

SIXTH MAN, THE

A Touchstone Pictures release of a Mandeville Films production. *Executive Producer:* Jody Savin. *Producer:* David Hoberman. *Director:* Randall Miller. *Screenplay:* Christopher Reed and Cynthia Carle. *Director of Photography:* Michael Ozier. *Editor:* Eric Sears. *Music:* Marcus Miller. *Music Editor:* Gedney Webb. *Sound:* Rick Patton. *Sound Editor:* Dave McMoyler. *Casting:* Dan Parada. *Production Designer:* Michael Bolton. *Art Director:* Eric Fraser. *Set Decorator:* Lin MacDonald. *Set Dresser:* Chuck Robinson and Gordon A. Clapp. *Special Effects:* Stewart Bradley. *Visual Effects:* John T. Van Vliet. *Costumes:* Grania Preston. *Make-up:* Jan Newman. *Stunt Coordinator:* Jacob Rupp. *Running time:* 107 minutes. *MPAA Rating:* PG-13.

CAST: Marlon Wayans (Kenny Tyler); Kadeem Hardison (Antoine Tyler); David Paymer (Coach Pederson); Michael Michele (R.C. St. John); Kevin Dunn (Mikulski); Gary Jones (Gertz); Lorenzo Orr (Malik Major); Vladimir Cuk (Zigi Hrbacek); Travis Ford (Danny O'Grady); Jack Karuletwa (Luther LaSalle); Chris Spencer (Jimmy Stubbs); Kirk Baily (Coach Nichols); Saundra McClain (Camille Tyler); Harold Sylvester (James Tyler); Octavia L. Spencer (Nativity Watson); Danielle Saklofsky (Cheryl); Christopher Turner (Jordy); Scott LaRose (Ernie); Paul Ben-Victor (Bernie); Emil Pinnock (Young Antoine); Allan Lindo (Young Kenny); Tyronne L'Hirondelle (Doctor); Tony Marr (Paramedic); Rod Crawford (Man in Bathroom); Jody Savin (Reporter #1); Dave Young (Reporter #2); Randall Miller (Booster); Lauro Chartrand (Husky Mascot); William Sasso (Guy in Bar); Flex (Jerrod Smith); Brent Kerray (Wilson); Greg Collins (Ref #1); Keith Gibbs (O'Neil); Kevin Benton (Ref #2); Howard Storey (Ref #3).

LOS ANGELES TIMES, 3/28/97, Calendar/p. 14, Jack Mathews

[The following review by Jack Mathews appeared in a slightly different form in
NEWSDAY, 3/28/97, Part II/p. 8.]

If there's such a thing in Hollywood as being too smart for your own good, Disney's marketing gurus may qualify for releasing a movie on a weekend when it will have to compete with its own subject.

Disney-Touchstone's "The Sixth Man" is a ghost comedy about a college basketball team reaching the Final Four, and on Saturday, while its fictional heroes are trying to scratch out a win in that event on the big screen, every basketball fan worth his Air Jordans will be home watching the real thing on television.

On Sunday, the movie's target audience figures to be out playing the game. And on Monday, they'll be back in front of their TVs for the NCAA Championship itself.

Tuesday, however, looks good.

For those who haven't had enough March Madness by then, "The Sixth Man" is recommended. This is old-fashioned cornball fun, an "Angels in the Back Court" fantasy about a college superstar who returns from the dead to help his younger brother lead their Washington Huskies team to the Final Four.

Kadeem Hardison is Antoine Tyler, a national phenom who suffers a fatal heart attack after slam-dunking an alley-oop pass from younger brother Kenny (Marlon Wayans) The team goes into a deep mid-season slump after Antoine's death, but a prayer from Kenny is answered, and Antoine is soon back on the court, unseen but still an all-star.

The team suddenly can't lose. Antoine sits on the Huskies' basket, casually flicking away opponents' shots. He enters the bodies of his teammates to put a heavenly spring in their step, and enters the bodies of their rivals to throw up some bricks. He even starts riots on the other team's bench.

This is like stealing—*exactly* like stealing—and as the Huskies head for the Final Four, the mortal players become conscience-stricken and plead with Kenny to kick the ghost off the team.

Randall Miller, who directed "Houseguest" and "Class Act" for Disney, has given "The Sixth Man" the pace of a run-and-gun offense, and the games have authentic settings. Big arenas, big crowds, good players, blathering sportscasters and a parade of big-name opponents with famous coaches—UCLA and its past-master Jim Herrick among them.

All this gives "The Sixth Man" enough verisimilitude to hook young basketball fans, and Eric Sears' quick-cut editing covers most of the seams of the film's under-budgeted special effects.

The script by husband-wife team Christopher Reed and Cynthia Carle lays the brotherly love sentiment on a little too thick at times and includes a romantic subplot about Kenny's relationship with a suspicious female sportswriter (Michael Michele) that goes nowhere. But "The Sixth Man" has an irresistible team spirit, and stars Hardison and Wayans seem to be having too much fun to be acting.

While the filmmakers embrace the clichés of the sport, they admirably avoid the racial stereotypes. It's refreshing to see black youths portrayed positively and without the street language that many screenwriters seem to think is genetic. Frankly, it's hard to understand "The Sixth Man's" cautionary PG-13 rating; the referees missed the call.

NEW YORK POST, 3/28/97, p. 45, Thelma Adams

"The Sixth Man" has all the elements of a great Disney family comedy: appealing stars Kadeem Hardison and Marlon Wayans, great special effects and a funny script with a strong black family at its core.

Antoine and Kenny Tyler (Hardison and Wayans) are basketball playing brothers. The two Washington Huskies are just a breath away from their dream—becoming NCAA champs—when tragedy strikes. Older bro' and ball-hog Antoine dunks himself to death. His heart fails during the important Huskies vs. UCLA Bruins match.

Kenny, always the follower, watches the Dawgs lose their bite without his brother. Before the season is over, a ghostly Antoine returns to unleash the beasts. The team's sixth player leads the Huskies all the way to the championship. The setup makes for a series of funny, "Son of Flubber" special effects that are less strained and strenuous than the "Space Jam" histrionics.

The effects start with a hilarious haunted locker room. Later, we see Antoine rough-housing with Kenny, and then watch the team react as they see the solo survivor contort himself. Before long, Antoine's ghost becomes less friendly than Casper.

The older brother interferes in Kenny's romance with a female sports reporter (Michael Michele) and slams an opponent into the backboard. For Kenny, letting go is hard to do, but he realizes that if he's ever going to be a champ, he has to do it on his own.

Wayans and Hardison are well-matched. They're both strong physical comedians with excellent timing—and Wayans brings a particular sweetness to his role as the younger brother.

Director Randall Miller ("Houseguest") sets the situation up so that you feel how tight these brothers are and understand how that connection might go beyond the grave. Miller also deftly handles Antoine's death so that the moment is emotionally powerful but is quickly deflected back into a comic mode.

But "The Sixth Man" deserves a penalty for unnecessary lewdness. The script, by husband-and-wife. team Christopher Reed and Cynthia Carle, includes throwaway gutter talk that adds nothing to the story and lessens its value as a family movie.

Wayans and Hardison might lift "the game to a higher level," as the comedy's tag line goes, but the Disney scriptwriters pander to the lowest common denominator.

Also reviewed in:
NEW YORK TIMES, 3/28/97, p. C21, Lawrence Van Gelder
VARIETY, 3/31-4/6/97, p. 86, Joe Leydon

SLAVES TO THE UNDERGROUND

A First Look Pictures release of a Neo Motion Pictures production. *Executive Producer:* Joel Soisson, Jeffrey Thal, and Judy Friend. *Producer:* Kristine Peterson, Bill Cody, and Raquel Caballes Maxwell. *Director:* Kristine Peterson. *Screenplay:* Bill Cody. *Director of Photography:* Zoran Hochstatter. *Editor:* Eric Vizents. *Music:* Mike Martt. *Production Designer:* Michael Moran. *Costumes:* Maggie Brown. *Running time:* 94 minutes. *MPAA Rating:* Not Rated.

CAST: Molly Gross (Shelly); Marisa Ryan (Suzy); Jason Bortz (Jimmy); Bob Neuwirth (Big Pal; Natacha La Ferriere (Zoe); Claudia Rossi (Brenda); James Garver (Brian); Peter Szumlas (Dale).

NEWSDAY, 11/14/97, Part II/p. B15, Gene Seymour

Suzy (Marisa Ryan) loves Shelly (Molly Gross), who thinks she loves Jimmy (Jason Bortz), who *also* loves Shelley. The story's as old as France in the 1870s and as up-to-date as Seattle in the 1990s. Which happens to be where "Slaves to the Underground," an amiable, bittersweet romantic comedy takes place. In fact, this movie is so up-to-date that the "grunge rock" that helped deliver the Emerald City of the Pacific Northwest to cultural prominence is now ancient history. The subculture depicted by writer Bill Cody and director Kristine Peterson has sharper edges and tougher politics than the soulful anomie associated with grunge.

The guerrilla-feminist rock band led by Suzy and Shelley is a symbol for this restlessness. In between their roughneck gigs at a local club, the band plays quick-hit pranks on sexist talk-radio jocks and porn shops. The rage thrills Shelley as does sex with the volatile Suzy. But she also looks wistfully at the more placid satisfactions offered by her nice-guy-ex Jimmy, who, like a lot of young writers in town, would rather put out his own "zine" than work for anyone else.

The interpersonal dynamics between this trio and their assortment of proto-punk and proto-slacker buddies can be both fun and unsettling to watch. Ryan, who used to be "Major Dad's" oldest stepdaughter, makes a startling first impression when she jumps off the stage to break a suspected rapist's nose. Her Suzy dares you to flinch in her presence and give her a warm hug at the same time. She, like the rest of the cast, wins you over through energy and nerve.

A few words should also be said for Shelley's ongoing exegesis of "The Graduate," her "mom's favorite movie" and one that "defined her mother's generation." She's not wild about the film or about its two lovelorn protagonists (Dustin Hoffman's Ben is described as a "selfish, irresponsible proto-slacker"), and her disdain shows one form of romanticism peering down witheringly at another. If you're a 1960s partisan, you might resent this. But if you've been wondering where the spark for a new 1960s insurgency is coming from, you might be mildly encouraged.

VILLAGE VOICE, 11/18/97, p. 85, Abby McGanney Nolan

Trying hard to be current, *Slaves to the Underground* immerses itself in Seattle's post-grunge subculture and winds up feeling more than a little dated; It may be scruffier than *Singles* but it doesn't have any more of an edge. Focusing an Shelly (Molly Gross), a rock musician in her early twenties, director Kristine Peterson and screenwriter Bill Cody delve into questions of loyalty and sexuality—Shelly is torn between the outspoken lead singer in her band (Marisa Ryan) and her old boyfriend (Jason Bortz)—but never build dramatic momentum. The targets of the film's social commentary are absurdly overdrawn (like the talk-radio host who rails against Medicaid, "if you can't afford to get sick, don't get sick") and the solutions (zines and rock'n'roll) way too pat. And since when does someone have to move to D.C. to be an activist?

Also reviewed in:
NEW YORK TIMES, 11/14/97, p. E33, Stephen Holden
VARIETY, 1/27-2/2/97, p. 79, Godfrey Cheshire

SLEEPOVER

An Artistic License Films release. *Producer:* Jim McNally. *Director:* John Sullivan. *Screenplay:* John Sullivan. *Director of Photography:* Joaquin Baca-Asay. *Editor:* Jim McNally. *Music:* Elliott Goldkind. *Sound:* James Good. *Production Designer:* Roshelle Berliner. *Running time:* 82 minutes. *MPAA Rating:* Not Rated.

CAST: Michael Albanese (Mark); Karl Giant (Sean); Shannon Barry (Anne); Heather Casey (Brooke); Ken Miles (Ken); Megan Shand (Megan).

LOS ANGELES TIMES, 10/25/96, Calendar/p. 28, Kevin Thomas

The Grande 4-Plex continues its American Independent Film Series with John Sullivan's "Sleepover," a remarkably detached and mature evocation of coming of age set against a harrowing incident inspired by an event Sullivan actually experienced.

Sullivan shows us nothing we haven't seen before, but that thought never occurs to you as you're watching his exceptionally adroit, unfussy film set in an attractive Connecticut town at the end of summer.

"Sleepover" is as American as apple pie, but it has the unpretentious, throwaway sophistication of a French film. Its half-rural waterside setting is one of those places in which young people are experiencing the transition to adulthood with too much time on their hands, which is the perfect atmosphere in which a bully may flourish—until those he dominates start outgrowing him.

Saddled with totally obtuse and uninterested parents, Michael Albanese's Mark is a good-looking auburn-haired youth who knows how to turn on the charm but most of the time is throwing punches and pushing people around as he expresses the rage that has him in its constant grip. He's a truly deplorable, brutal control freak, but he has enough charisma to make it comprehensible that Karl Giant's Sean, a likable, perfectly normal kid, would let Mark dominate him—just as it's understandable why Heather Casey's poised, patrician Brooke would be turned on by him, even when she knows better.

A meandering, restless summer culminates when Sean; Brooke; her 14-year-old younger sister Anne (Shannon Berry); her pretty, sensitive friend Megan (Megan Shand), to whom Sean is attracted; and Sean's friend Ken (Ken Miles)—the one African American in the neighborhood—are persuaded to pile into a car with Mark. A supposedly innocent outing turns into a nightmare as Mark is forced to realize he's losing his grip on his pals.

"Sleepover" is a first film for most everyone involved, but cast and crew alike impress, especially Albanese, who shows us the pitiable kid beneath Mark's macho posturing. "Sleepover" is a most accomplished debut film for NYU film school graduate Sullivan.

NEW YORK POST, 3/7/97, p. 50, Larry Worth

Why, one might ask, is the title for "sleepover" all lowercase in the movie's credits and advertisements?

Whatever the reasoning, it accurately reflects a production where high points are nowhere to be found.

Made on a shoestring by NYU grad John Sullivan, it's yet another coming-of-age-in-suburbia story. But unlike superior predecessors (particularly "American Graffiti" and "Summer of '42"), there's no reason for audiences to care about the fate of its characters.

Worse, Sullivan falls into pretensions of artiness as he incorporates hazy flashbacks, time-lapse photography, a too-cool soundtrack and slo-mo sequences.

The action, or lack thereof, takes place over a two-day period in a middle-class Connecticut community as three schoolboys—a bully, his sensitive pal and a lonely African-American—seek to score with the opposite sex. When meeting up with a pretty cheerleader type, her bookish chum and a tag-along younger sister, their players seem answered.

What follows is a long night in which the sextet explore drinking, driving, drugs, racism, intercourse, friendship, MTV, peer pressure, guns, tragedy and you-name-it. Clearly, the themes merit discussion, but addressing them in such a superficial manner accomplishes virtually nothing.

But in any slice-of-life story, the one essential ingredient is credibility. Here, the stilted dialogue and paint-by-number developments make viewers think they're eavesdropping on a high school play's first rehearsal.

The cast of unknowns are likely to remain such, at least if they don't head directly to an acting workshop. In particular, Michael Albanese's turn as the truculent anti-hero feels embarrassingly hollow and consistently artificial.

Accordingly, Sullivan's good intentions in "sleepover" are all for naught. As a film about alienation, it succeeds only at alienating its audience.

VILLAGE VOICE, 3/11/97, p. 78, Amy Taubin

Clumsier but more affecting than *The Daytrippers,* John Sullivan's *sleepover* follows three uneasily bonded adolescent boys as they attempt to score some sex on a summer weekend. One is shy, one seems to be the only African American in a middle-class small town, and one is a badly wounded narcissist, a glamour-boy bully in a rage at a world that offers him minimal attention or opportunities. Writer-director Sullivan and actor Michael Albanese have created a memorable character—seductive, manipulative, and bound for self-destruction. He's the reason that *sleepover* is not merely an afterschool special.

Also reviewed in:
NEW YORK TIMES, 3/7/97, p. C4, Stephen Holden

SMILE LIKE YOURS, A

A Paramount Pictures and Rysher Entertainment release of a David Kirkpatrick production. *Executive Producer:* Robert Harling. *Producer:* David Kirkpatrick and Tony Amatullo. *Director:* Keith Samples. *Screenplay:* Kevin Meyer and Keith Samples. *Director of Photography:* Richard Bowen. *Editor:* Wayne Wahrman. *Music:* William Ross. *Sound:* Doug Axtell. *Production Designer:* Garreth Stover. *Art Director:* Chris Cornwell. *Set Designer:* Larry Dias. *Costumes:* Jill Ohanneson. *Running time:* 97 minutes. *MPAA Rating:* R.

CAST: Greg Kinnear (Danny Robertson); Lauren Holly (Jennifer Robertson); Joan Cusack (Nancy Tellen); Jay Thomas (Steve Harris); Jill Hennessy (Lindsay Hamilton); Christopher McDonald (Richard Halstrom); Donald Moffat (Dr. Felber); France Nuyen (Dr. Chin); Marianne Muellerleile (Nurse Wheeler); Shirley MacLaine (Martha).

LOS ANGELES TIMES, 8/22/97, Calendar/p. 10, Kevin Thomas

[The following review by Kevin Thomas appeared in a slightly different form in
NEWSDAY, 8/22/97, Part II/p. B8.]

In the funny, well-done "A Smile Like Yours," Lauren Holly and Greg Kinnear's Jennifer and Danny Robertson seem to have it all. They are deeply in love, uncommonly attractive and successful. She runs a San Francisco perfume boutique with her best friend Nancy (Joan Cusack), and he's a sought-after elevator contractor. They have a gracious suburban home.

All that's missing is a baby. Danny takes a whenever-it-happens-it-happens attitude, but Jennifer is becoming increasingly desperate to conceive. She even goes so far as to attempt to concoct an aphrodisiacal perfume, even though we're told they make passionate love every night.

Infertility scarcely seems a cause for humor. But it is the measure of debuting director Keith Samples and his co-writer Kevin Meyer that this movie is all the more rewarding for tackling such a ticklish issue with wit as well as compassion.

Indeed, the Robertsons' difficulty in conceiving a child deftly becomes a metaphor for all the pressures that bear upon—and undermine—contemporary marriage. For several generations, the media have held up fearsome standards for perfect connubial bliss. Couples must be great-looking and be great lovers; they must have great jobs, live in great homes and, of course, have great kids.

With affectionate humor, the filmmakers bring the Robertsons to that inevitable moment of truth that dictates they seek out a fertility clinic, and at this point the film takes on a nifty satirical edge. They're immediately made to feel intimidated by the intense, implacable authority of the clinic's doctor (France Nuyen, subtly amusing) and its gloriously insensitive head nurse (scene-stealing Marianne Muellerleile), of whom Danny observes that he now knows what happened to that nurse in "One Flew Over the Cuckoo's Nest."

Having raised such a delicate subject so boldly, the filmmakers unfortunately smudge their fade-out in the film's climax. But "A Smile Like Yours" is nonetheless an uncommonly thoughtful and intelligent mainstream entertainment, painstaking and stylish in every aspect.

Always a good sign, the entire cast shines, not just the stars. Key are Jay Thomas as Danny's wise best pal and co-worker; Jill Hennessey, a standout as a vampy architect; Christopher McDonald as a smooth cosmetics tycoon; and Donald Moffat as a pompous physician.

There's also a sparkling unbilled cameo by a legendary star whose identity won't be revealed here.

NEW YORK POST, 8/22/97, p. 42, Michael Medved

"A Smile Like Yours" manages a seemingly impossible cinematic transformation making innumerable sex scenes involving the lovely Lauren Holly look silly, mechanical and altogether resistible.

She plays a ditzy San Francisco wife who's gone off the pill without telling her husband and now approaches him day and night in a variety of provocative get-ups, hoping this amiable every-man (Greg Kinnear) will help conceive the child she desperately wants.

Though lines of dialogue repeatedly describe their sex as "great," the film never portrays these couplings as intense or erotic or satisfying; Holly's interest in her husband seems merely calculating rather than carnal.

This is a crucial flaw in the film because we're supposed to care enough about this couple and this heroine to cheer them through a series of entirely arbitrary threats to their wedded bliss.

Holly eventually drags her man to a fertility clinic, where he withstands a barrage of utterly predictable gags about masturbatoriums and turkey basters and a fat, fascistic nurse (Marianne Muellerleile).

Then there's the pending big-bucks sale of a devastating perfume Holly has developed with her partner (Joan Cusack) in an aroma shop; for idiotic reasons she keeps the transaction a secret from her spouse.

Meanwhile, Kinnear works as a subcontractor at a construction site, where he's ruthlessly plagued by a leggy architect (Jill Hennessy) who comes across as an outrageously implausible figure of male fantasy.

No explanation is ever offered as to why this stunningly sexy, successful professional would invest untold money, effort and embarrassment in a single-minded effort to seduce a painfully ordinary married man.

So many American couples face problems of infertility that the dilemma might yet provide a serviceable subject for bittersweet comedy, but "A Smile Like Yours" handles the situation even more awkwardly than the misbegotten 1990 Gene Wilder project "Funny About Love."

Here, first-time director (and long-time production executive) Keith Samples clumsily unleashes blaring musical cues ("I Feel Good," "The Pink Panther") to try to comment on the action and connect his woozy montages.

The few moments of tenderness—like Kinnear's declaration to his wife that he wants their baby to have "a smile like yours"—quickly sink beneath the turgid tide.

The movie's single best scene shows the troubled couple tearily watching a video of the classic "I Love Lucy" episode in which Lucy lets the unsuspecting Ricky know she's pregnant.

This antique reference is no accident, since Lauren Holly's lame idea of how to play romantic comedy ineptly apes Lucille Ball's girlish, goo-goo-eyed mugging.

It's unclear who turned a graceful and glamorous star into this cloying cutie-pie, but whoever it was, as Ricky Ricardo would say, has got a whole lot of 'splainin' to do.

VILLAGE VOICE, 9/2/97, p. 82, Jennifer Vandever

Hollywood's ongoing love affair with the redemptive power of babies continues here with Greg Kinnear and Lauren Holly starring as a yuppie couple trying desperately to get pregnant. Their efforts rapidly escalate from afternoon quickies to a fertility clinic featuring scary gynecological equipment and frequent trips to the "masturbatorium."

Unfortunately the script appears to have taken a few trips to the masturbatorium as well in this self-indulgent hodgepodge of sitcom setups and unfunny anal-probe humor. The film revels in the obvious and the corny: Kinnear is menaced by a Vaseline-fingered, commandant-style nurse as Holly gazes tearfully at double strollers.

Veering wildly from broad slapstick to hokey melodrama, Kinnear braves the rapids more successfully than Holly, whose characterization is so inconsistent it verges on incoherence. Supporting players Joan Cusack and Jay Thomas turn in smarter and more interesting performances than the film's leads. A final note: there are extended portions of this film during which one is forced to consider the nature of Greg Kinnear's sperm, as well as a bizarre, unbilled cameo by Shirley MacLaine, who shows up to thrust a banana into a coke. Take that!

Also reviewed in:
CHICAGO TRIBUNE, 8/22/97, Friday/p. L, Mark Caro
NEW YORK TIMES, 8/22/97, p. C5, Janet Maslin
VARIETY, 8/25-31/97, p. 74, Joe Leydon

SMILLA'S SENSE OF SNOW

A Fox Searchlight Pictures release of a Constantin Film Produktion GmbH in co-operation with Smilla Film A/S/Greenland Film Production AB/Bavaria Film GmbH. This film was supported by Eurimages/FFA, Filmfernsehfonds Bayern/Danish Film Institute/Hans Hansen/Nordic Film & TV Fund. *Producer:* Bernd Eichinger and Martin Moszkowicz. *Director:* Bille August. *Screenplay:* Ann Biderman. *Based on the novel "Froken Smillas fornemmelse for sne" by:* Peter Hoeg. *Director of Photography:* Jörgen Persson. *Editor:* Janus Billeskov-Jansen and Pernille Bech-Christensen. *Music:* Hans Zimmer and Harry Gregson-Williams. *Music Editor:* Adam

Smalley. *Sound:* Friedrich M. Dosch and (music) Paul Hulme. *Sound Editor:* Chris Munro. *Casting:* Leonora Davis. *Production Designer:* Anna Asp. *Art Director:* Jörgen Strasser. *Set Decorator:* Ivar Baungaard. *Special Effects:* Peter Hutchinson. *Costumes:* Barbara Baum. *Make-up:* Gerlinde Kunz and Horst Stadinger. *Stunt Coordinator:* Paul Weston. *Running time:* 115 minutes. *MPAA Rating:* R.

CAST: Julia Ormond (Smilla Jasperson); Gabriel Byrne (Mechanic); Richard Harris (Tork); Robert Loggia (Moritz Johnson); Jim Broadbent (Lagermann); Mario Adorf (Captain Sigmund Lukas); Bob Peck (Ravn); Tom Wilkinson (Professor Loyen); Emma Croft (Benja); Peter Capaldi (Birgo Lander); Jürgen Vogel (Nils Jakkelsen); Vanessa Redgrave (Elsa Lübing); Ono Fleischer (Inuit Hunter); Agga Olen (Juliane); Patrick Field (Policeman); Matthew Marsh (Detective); Charlotte Bradley (Mrs. Lagermann); Charles Lewson (Pastor); Ann Queensberry (Mrs. Schou); David Hayman (Telling); Ida Julie Anderson (Smilla as a Child); Maliinannguaq Markussen-Molgard (Smilla's Mother); Alvin Ing (Licht); Erik Holmey (Hansen); Peter Gantzler (Maurice); Lars Brygmann (Verlaine); Clipper Miano (Isaiah).

LOS ANGELES TIMES, 2/28/97, Calendar/p. 1, Kenneth Turan

When Peter Hoeg's "Smilla's Sense of Snow" was published in Denmark in 1992, no one anticipated the kind of international sales and celebrity this singular book would have. Yet, in an irony its author might appreciate, that level of success ensured that the inevitable film version wouldn't be just as memorable.

Because once Hoeg's literate, philosophical thriller started selling all those copies in dozens of languages, it was only a matter of time until it became, if not an actual Hollywood feature, then one of those bland and stodgy international co-productions that homogenizes and standardizes everything it encounters.

So though "Smilla's" Danish director is Bille August, this stolid film has more in common with his multicultural version of Isabelle Allende's "House of the Spirits" (which was produced, as is "Smilla's," by German Bernd Eichinger) than his Oscar—and Palme d'Or-winning Danish-language "Pelle the Conqueror."

Actually, a comparison with the deadly "Spirits" is unfair, because "Smilla's" has some things going for it, including the original book's involving plot and a respectable performance by Julia Ormond as the accidental detective who gives the book its title.

But though it's a handsomely mounted, professional piece of work, "Smilla's" has too many components, from its use of English to its cross-cultural cast, that are useful for international sales but make this film more routine than it ought to be. And Ormond, who works hard and has to carry the entire picture, has what even director August acknowledges as an almost impossible task.

"The structure of the novel is exceptionally sophisticated," he admits in a making-of-the-movie-book published by the Noonday Press. "Converting that into something as concrete as film is extremely difficult. ... Smilla is highly intelligent and very philosophical and has a most intriguing outlook on life, but there is no way that this can be transferred directly onto film."

Just so.

Smilla Qaavigaaq Jaspersen, a half-Inuit scientist who lives in Copenhagen, is introduced walking home on a snowy December evening. An ambulance with its siren on passes her, and she is taken by a premonition that turns out to be true: Someone she knows has died.

It turns out to be Isaiah, a 6-year-old boy who lies motionless in the snow in front of her apartment building. The police tell her Isaiah was playing on the roof and accidentally fell to his death, but, for several interconnected reasons, Smilla is suspicious.

One is that she knows the boy, knows that his fear of heights made fun and games up there unlikely. Another is that, as the daughter of a Greenland woman who was a celebrated hunter, Smilla inherited a sixth sense about snow, and what she sees of Isaiah's footprints on the roof indicate that he was not frolicking but fleeing in terror.

The final reason is Smilla's own temperament. Brought to Copenhagen at age 6 by her American father (Robert Loggia), Smilla's feeling of displacement has turned her into the angriest woman on film, abrupt, abrasive and in a constant mistrustful rage against the world. Smilla's so sullen, we see in flashbacks, it took an act of will for Isaiah, a fellow Greenlander, to get close to her. Not the kind of person, in short, likely to accept the official explanation of anything.

Though Ormond comes off more petulant than the "rough all over" woman she's supposed to be, she does look appropriately gaunt and severe and, fortunately, she is good at being determined. Because, helped by a neighbor known as the Mechanic (Gabriel Byrne), what Smilla does is follow one clue after another about Isaiah's fate all across Copenhagen and beyond. Without the book's involving language, this becomes fairly routine, though enlivened by supporting performances by Richard Harris as a mining tycoon and Vanessa Redgrave as one of his former employees who now considers herself a bride of Jesus.

Though it is written by American Ann Biderman ("Copycat," "Primal Fear"), there is an awkwardness to the use of language here that makes scenes sound like the product of a multinational commission. Entire segments of the film, like Smilla's bitter relationship with her father's new girlfriend Benja (Emma Croft), come off as completely flat. With interiors shot on studio stages, "Smilla's" isn't particularly Scandinavian in its look, with one exception: The credits sequence, filmed on the glaciers and ice fields of Greenland, creates a sense of mystery and majesty the rest of the film lacks. Though enlivened by occasional touches, "Smilla's" is like the food at Taco Bell: exotic only to someone who hasn't experienced the real thing.

NEW YORK POST, 2/28/97, p. 45, Thelma Adams

The worst title so far this year is "Smilla's Sense of Snow". Amazingly it improves on the original title of Peter Hoeg's international best-seller: "Miss Smilla's Feeling for Snow." For American audiences, "Melissa's Sense of Snow" might be slightly better. "Snowsense" is nonsense.

What about "Tiny Footprints in the Snow"? Too Agatha Christie. "The Case of the Inuit Boy"? Too Sherlock and the Danish author's fans would be left out in the cold, unaware that Bille August's thriller adapts the novel Time magazine named book of the year in 1992.

What do you do about a character named Smilla? If you're August ("Pelle the Conqueror") you cast Julia Ormond. After her charmless "Sabrina," the unwatchable "Captives" and the drippy "Legends of the Fall," in which Ormond's beauty paled in comparison to Brad Pitt's, I was pleasantly surprised at how strong the British actress is playing the half-Inuit, half-American loner whose insular world is shattered when a neighbor's son falls from a Copenhagen roof.

What's sadder than a child's casket'? The sense that the death was needless.

Smilla doesn't believe the police report that her 6-year-old Inuit buddy, also a refugee from Greenland, fell by playing in the snow. By reading his footprints in the ice, the moody mathematician with a crush on slush detects foul play. Before you can say rogue meteors and prehistoric worms, Smilla is on the trail of a corporate conspiracy that leads back to her native Greenland.

Joining her on her quest to expose the boy's killers is the mysterious mechanic (Gabriel Byrne).

Smilla is a rare—and welcome—screen female. Attractive, smart, aggressive, contradictory, athletic, angry, she commands center stage, Byrne (who could use a sexual magnetism check) is her sidekick and love object.

The only relationship Smilla seems capable of sustaining is the one with the boy but as we see in flashbacks, even that had a rough start. "You, smell bad," she tells the big-eyed boy when they meet. Byrne asks: "Why does such a nice person have such a rough mouth?" Because Smilla's jagged on the inside.

Screenwriter Ann Biderman effectively captures the tensions between Danes and Inuits internalized in Smilla's psychological turmoil. Biderman, who also penned "Copycat" and "Primal Fear," is gaining a reputation for scripting uncommonly intelligent adult thrillers.

The characters here are lively, the dialogue is pointed and the situations—initially, at least—are unexpected. But Biderman and August lose hold on the crime thriller in the third act, awkwardly condensing events and characters from the book, slashing and burning scenes, as the mystery overheats on the way to its anticlimax.

"Smilla's," said to be the first feature to be shot on Greenland, opens with a staggering, beautifully shot special effect more mysterious than "Twister." A lone ice fisherman tries to outrun an Arctic tidal wave. It eventually overtakes and eliminates him. This is also what happens to

"Smilla's." It stumbles just short of becoming a satisfying intellectual thriller: Michael Crichton with Scandinavian soul.

NEWSDAY, 2/28/979 Part II/p. B2, Jack Mathews

On the blue-white crust of the frozen sea off 1859 Greenland, an Inuit stands over a hole he'd carved in the ice, his harpoon raised over his head as he waits patiently for a seal to surface. His dogs are sleeping a few feet away, as if experience has taught them this might take all day.

Suddenly, the dogs are roused, and in the sky behind the hunter, a yellow streak of light races toward the earth, slamming into it like an atomic bomb and creating a tidal wave of ice and water that surges violently toward the Inuit, his dogs ... and us.

This powerful opening scene in "Smilla's Sense of Snow" is not in the Peter Hoeg best-seller from which the film is adapted, but it's a good addition. Followed by the scene that does begin the novel, of a woman (Julia Ormond) returning to her modern-day Copenhagen apartment building to learn of the death of an Inuit boy she'd befriended, it immediately establishes the framework of a mystery that otherwise takes a few miles of Hoeg's teasing prose to accomplish.

Sadly, it's about the only good thing to be said for the adaptation, directed by Denmark's Bille August ("Pelle the Conqueror") from a script by the American Ann Biderman ("Primal Fear"). The rest of the film is an awkward mix of plodding suspense and over-the-top action, building toward a climax back in Greenland that plays like James Bond on a budget.

Biderman's story is relatively faithful to the book, but without the subtleties and narrative voice it flattens out. Instead of building the momentum that the ominous score assures us we ought to be feeling, it merely advances an inch at a time, like the winter freeze.

"Smilla's Sense of Snow" is a dense tale of scientific intrigue, corporate greed and murder, all emanating from that spectacular space-to-Greenland collision in 1859. The story getting us back there takes the form of an old-fashioned murder mystery. Smilla Jasperson (Ormond) is a half-Inuit, half-Scandinavian woman with a brilliant mathematical mind and a long history of rebellion. She's a contentious loner who only befriends 5-year-old Isaiah (Clipper Miano) because of their shared ethnic and Greenland roots.

When police tell her the boy fell while playing on the roof of the apartment building, she knows it's not true. First, Isaiah had a phobia about heights, and second, she can tell from his footprints in the snow that he was being chased when he fell. As she begins her own investigation, she runs into a cover-up that seems to include the Copenhagen police, coroner, district attorney, perhaps the fellow tenant (Gabriel Byrne) so anxious to help her and the huge Greenland Mining Co., where the trail leads.

Ormond, last seen in the title role of "Sabrina," has a dominating presence, but we simply learn too little about her to understand the complex nature of her hostility toward Denmark, which until 1979 administered Greenland; toward her rich father, Moritz (Robert Loggia), and toward herself.

Loggia shows a gentle side we don't often see in him, but everyone else Byrne, as Smilla's neighbor and eventual lover; Richard Harris, as the profiteering scientist Tork, and Emma Croft as Moritz' airhead mistress are playing genre stereotypes.

More than anything, what's lost in the transition from page to screen are the cultural and psychological conflicts between the Greenlanders and the Danes. Hoeg's novel contains as much of this detail as a textbook, but, coming out of Smilla's self-examination, it's fascinating stuff.

August's best movies—"Pelle the Conqueror," "Best Intentions" and the upcoming "Jerusalem"—are deep character studies. As he demonstrated with his first English-language film, the star-studded disaster "The House of the Spirits," he has no intuitive gift for classic Hollywood storytelling, and with "Smilla's Sense of Snow," he shows little improvement.

SIGHT AND SOUND, 11/97, p. 52, Geoffrey Macnab

Greenland, 1859. A huge meteor crashes into the snow. Copenhagen, the present day. Smilla Jasperson, a half-Greenlander, returns home to her apartment to find that Isaiah, the six-year-old son of Smilla's alcoholic Greenlandic neighbour, has fallen to his death, allegedly after playing on the roof. Smilla is immediately suspicious. She had befriended Isaiah, knew he was terrified of heights, and suspects he may have been murdered.

Smilla's investigations into Isaiah's death are hampered by the police, but she discovers that Isaiah's mother is being paid a pension by a sinister corporation, Greenland Mining. Isaiah's father died suspiciously during an expedition to Greenland on which his son accompanied him. Smilla's neighbour, a man she knows as Mechanic, helps her and the two soon become lovers. But she is perplexed when she sees him talking with Tork, a Greenland Mining scientist.

Smilla manages to board the *Kronos*, a huge tanker bound for Greenland. She discovers that scientists from Greenland Mining are aboard. So is Mechanic, who tells her he is an undercover agent for the government. She learns that Tork has found the meteorite and plans to transport it back to use as a source of energy. But the meteorite has brought back to life deadly microbes which were responsible for the death of Isaiah's father. The little boy himself was infected, which was why he was kept under observation by scientists. There's a shoot-out in the remote cave enclosing the meteorite. Tork is wounded, but manages to escape. Smilla pursues him as he tries to clamber across the ice floe back to the ship. She talks him through the events leading to Isaiah's death. He loses his footing and drowns beneath the ice as Mechanic blows up the cave.

Smilla Jasperson, the half-Greenlandic protagonist of Peter Hoeg's novel *Miss Smilla's Feeling for Snow*, is a distinctive creation. She speaks in the first person, and everything that happens in the book is seen from her perspective. As she meditates about her diet ("I eat mostly fatty meat"), talks about mathematics and folklore, and then investigates the death of her six-year-old neighbour, her tone is intimate and confessional.

Transforming such an introspective heroine into a film character was always going to be difficult. Director Bille August and his scriptwriter Ann Biderman dispense with the first-person narration. This is a thriller, after all, and to have Smilla telling the story in flashback would strip the film of any suspense. But the downside is that they deprive Smilla of her unique voice. To compensate, they distil some of her poetic musings into the dialogue, with often extremely stilted results. "Mathematics is a vast, open landscape," she observes to her lover, Mechanic, in what passes for small talk.

August has assembled a bankable international cast, but in the process risks stifling any sense of local identity. Characters speak English in a variety of different accents. Julia Ormond gives Smilla a hint of a Greenlandic intonation while Robert Loggia as her father is American, Gabriel Byrne and Richard Harris both have an Irish burr to their voices, and Mario Adorf as the ship skipper sounds German. The effect is reminiscent of such Cold War thrillers as *Gorky Park* in which American and British actors used to adopt ridiculous Russian accents. Presumably, August would not have been able to raise finance without the stars, but given that he himself argues that *Miss Smilla* is "about roots and identity", the casting seems perverse. The film takes both its mood and tempo from Ormond's Smilla, in virtually every scene. To her credit, the actress does not attempt to make the character sympathetic. Smilla is dogged, spiky and bad-tempered, and Ormond conveys both the loneliness and hostility of a woman living in a city she hates. "Beat it, you little shit," is how she greets the doe-eyed Greenlandic boy Isaiah when he first turns up at her door.

The Danes have a guilty conscience about their treatment of Greenland, a country which they colonised. Smilla, Isaiah and Isaiah's alcoholic mother are all portrayed as outsiders, marginalised within Danish society. In spectacular flashback sequences, we're presented with Nanook-like images of Inuit hunters and of Smilla as a child in the Arctic wilderness. August hints at a lost Edenic lifestyle and tries to remind us of some of the old wrongs.

Unfortunately, the lyricism is often muted as the film switches into thriller mode. The surly, intelligent Smilla of the early scenes gradually gives way to an athletic action heroine. At least the normal gender stereotyping is knocked on the head—she's courageous and self-reliant while the men around her are dithering and cowardly—but that doesn't make the film-making any less formulaic. The deadly meteorite is the kind of McGuffin you'd expect to find in a James Bond film. (Some of the sets even look like backdrops of the sort used on the 007 sound stages at Pinewood.) By the time Smilla actually reaches Greenland, August is so busy cranking up the tension that he shows precious little feeling for the landscapes. (Miss Smilla may have a sense of snow but he palpably doesn't.) Rather than attempt to capture the awesome beauty of the ice floes and vast, empty plains, he treats them merely as somewhere to stage the explosive finale.

Miss Smilla is August's second international, English-language co-production after *House of the Spirits,* and he has already almost finished a third—a new version of *Les Misérables.* Such films look spectacular, feature high-profile stars, and sometimes rake in returns at the box office (*The*

House of the Spirits is one of the most successful films ever in South America) but they're always likely to lack the conviction that filmmakers can bring to more modest projects, made in their own language and rooted in their own culture.

TIME, 3/10/97, p. 90, Richard Schickel

Smilla's Sense of Snow is more than a climatological instinct. It is the projection of a wintry soul over which a long, cold Arctic night settled long ago.

When we meet her in director Bille August's intricate and compelling realization of Peter Hoeg's bestselling novel, Smilla Jaspersen has given her professional life over to the frozen music of mathematics, her private life over to bone-chilling isolation. The set of Smilla's face, the carriage of her body, as Julia Ormond plays her, says, "Don't ask, don't touch." She relents—angry at the show of weakness—for just one person. That is a lonely little boy named Isaiah, who lives in her apartment building.

Her identification with the child is more than that of one solitary with another. He was born in Greenland, as she was. Both of his parents are Inuits, natives of the region, as her mother was. Both have lost parents at an early age. And now, like Smilla before him, the boy finds himself trying to make a new life in Copenhagen, which to them is hardly the Danny Kaye song's "friendly old girl of a town." August makes us see it as dark and claustrophobic, stressing its contrast to the bright and limitless horizons of the land, essentially untouched by modern civilization, where they were born.

One day Smilla comes home from work and finds Isaiah dead, the victim of a fall from their building's rooftop. An accident, the police insist. A murder, her intuition tells her. This suspicion is confirmed by the increasingly hostile behavior of the authorities as she begins to investigate the case. It will come as no surprise to devotees of the paranoid thriller—is there any other kind nowadays?—that the victim is accidentally privy to information that threatens the secret plans of a powerful mining corporation to exploit and sully Greenland's purity. It will come as no surprise to them either that as the conspiracy surrounding Smilla begins to take form, the movie loses some of its superbly shadowed sense of menace.

What will surprise everyone is the dry iciness, the burning coldness of Ormond's Smilla. Up to now she has trafficked largely in vulnerability—melting in *Legends of the Fall,* perhaps a shade too winsome in *Sabrina.* Here, she is all contained fury, except for the flashes of anger and contempt that burst without warning from the darkness within. It's not exactly diva acting such as we used to get from the great ladies of the movies' classic era. She achieves her effects with less obvious calculation. But like a Barbara Stanwyck or a Bette Davis, she takes us into that country where strength shades into neurosis, and we fear that she can never be reclaimed for the more orderly pleasures of ordinary life.

It is Gabriel Byrne's duty as an enigmatically watchful neighbor-lover-ally patiently to offer her that option, and he does it with his customary brooding grace. It's the duty of a lot of good character actors to keep driving her in the opposite direction, toward the end of her very taut tether. It is the very great pleasure of this movie (well written by Ann Biderman) that its truly haunting suspense derives not from Smilla's conflict with her external enemies but from her own demons.

VILLAGE VOICE, 3/4/97, p. 72, Amy Taubin

Smilla Jasperson, the heroine of Peter Hoeg's classy 1993 bestseller, is the daughter of a Greenland Inuit mother and Danish father. When her mother is drowned hunting walrus, Smilla is sent to Copenhagen to live with her father, an anesthesiologist who's made a fortune relieving Europe's elite of their pain.

A mixed-race outsider, Smilla takes refuge in a passion for higher mathematics and a specialized knowledge of the qualities of snow. She also is obsessed with finding out the truth about the death of a young boy, a Greenland exile like herself. Smilla believes the boy has been murdered and that powerful people in the government and the scientific community are involved in a cover-up.

A first-person suspense novel with sci-fi elements its *(Alien* must have been an influence) set in an exotic though hilly landscape, *Smilla* has obvious widescreen potential. It's also filled with pitfalls. The action-packed narrative slows to a crawl in the second half (when the location changes from picturesque Copenhagen to the dank confines of a freighter bound for Greenland) only to climax a bit too precipitously amid arctic ice floes. And while Smilla herself is among the most seductive female characters in contemporary fiction, her uniqueness is less a matter of what she does than of how she perceives the world from her alienated position.

August's most dire mistake was to cast Julia Ormond as Smilla. A delicate but bland beauty who wears clothes with great flair, Ormond has none of Smilla's intensity or toughness of mind, body, and spirit. Trekking across the awesome arctic expanses, she looks more like a well-brought-up English schoolgirl on her way to hockey practice than a woman who takes comfort in the most inhospitable landscape imaginable.

Ormond doesn't get much help from screenwriter Ann Biderman, who seems to think that a one-line quote from Euclid's *Elements* sufficiently demonstrates the workings of a mind shaped by mathematical abstractions. Nor from August, who relies on an awkward five-second shot of a child sucking at her mother's breast to express the enormity of maternal loss.

August also seems possessed of the delusion that tight close-ups reveal inner thoughts. Thus, the film alternates between wide shots of handsomely furnished interiors or atmospherically lit exteriors and close-ups of actors smirking knowingly or suspiciously—to no end whatsoever. The heaviest smirker is Gabriel Bryne, playing a mysterious character known only as "the mechanic," but Richard Harris, as an evil businessman, Robert Loggia as Smilla's guilt-ridden father, and Vanessa Redgrave as a personnel director turned religious fanatic are no slouches in the lifted-eyebrow department.

Hoeg's novel is about a woman who, excluded from a powerful old-boy network because of her sex and race, nevertheless gains access to its secrets. It's Smilla's desire to penetrate the male inner sanctum—where science and big business determine the future of the planet—that makes the book a compelling read. But August, though an experienced director, lacks the most basic sense of how to use the camera to reveal the dynamic relationships between insiders and outsiders.

Smilla's Sense of Snow is an utterly flat film—narratively, psychologically, visually. Though covering a vast terrain, it winds up going nowhere.

Also reviewed in:
NEW YORK TIMES, 2/28/97, p. C3, Janet Maslin
NEW YORKER, 3/10/97, p. 99, Terrence Rafferty
VARIETY, 2/17-23/97, p. 68, David Stratton
WASHINGTON POST, 3/14/97, p. G6, Rita Kempley
WASHINGTON POST, 3/14/97, Weekend/p. 44, Desson Howe

SOUL FOOD

A Fox 2000 Pictures release of an Edmonds Entertainment production. *Executive Producer:* Kenneth "Babyface" Edmonds. *Producer:* Tracey E. Edmonds and Robert Teitel. *Director:* George Tillman, Jr. *Screenplay:* George Tillman, Jr. *Director of Photography:* Paul Elliott. *Editor:* John Carter. *Music:* Wendy Melvoin and Lisa Coleman. *Music Editor:* Dan Garde. *Choreographer:* Vanessa Truvillion. *Sound:* David Obermeyer. *Sound Editor:* Lawrence H. Mann. *Casting:* Robi Reed-Humes. *Production Designer:* Maxine Shepard. *Art Director:* Cydney M. Harris. *Set Decorator:* Joe Bristol. *Set Dresser:* Aaron C. Holden, Jr. *Special Effects:* Tom Ryba. *Costumes:* Salvador Perez. *Make-up:* Cat'Ania McCoy-Howze. *Make-up (Vanessa L. Williams):* Kate Best. *Special Effects Make-up:* Jeffrey Lyle Segal. *Running time:* 120 minutes. *MPAA Rating:* R.

CAST: Vanessa L. Williams (Teri); Vivica A. Fox (Maxine); Nia Long (Bird); Michael Beach (Miles); Mekhi Phifer (Lem); Brandon Hammond (Ahmad); Jeffrey D. Sams (Kenny); Gina Ravera (Faith); Irma P. Hall (Mother Joe); Carl Wright (Reverend Williams); Mel Jackson (Simuel); Morgan Méchelle Smith (Kelly); John M. Watson, Sr. (Uncle Pete); M.T. Alexander (Jada); Lawrence Petty (Harome); Marcia Wright (Nicole); Bernard Mixon (Dr. Benson); Hamp Clemons (Hamp); Theron Touché Lykes (Blimp); Martell Hill Edmond (Ahmad, Age 4); Ras Majah Couzan (Dread Man); James W. Boinski (Foreman); Mike Bacarella (Printing Company Owner); Joan Collaso (Choir Member #1); Donn C. Harper (Funeral Minister);

George Brashear (Blimp's Henchman #1); Larry C. Tankson (Blimp's Henchman #2); Austin Curtis (Family Member); Sylvester Phifer (Bartender); Malik Yoba (Studio Engineer); Kenneth "Babyface" Edmonds (Band Member #1); Kevon Edmonds (Band Member #2); Melvin Edmonds (Band Member #3); Jo Jo Hailey (Band Member #4); K-Ci Hailey (Band Member #5); Simon Horrocks (Band Member #6); Randy Walker (Band Member #7); Tamara Braun (Teri's Secretary).

LOS ANGELES TIMES, 9/26/97, Calendar/p. 20, Kevin Thomas

[The following review by Kevin Thomas appeared in a slightly different form in NEWSDAY, 9/26/97, Part II/p. B7.]

"Soul food cooking is cooking that comes from the heart," says Mother Joe, matriarch of an African American family. So does "Soul Food," a warm and embracing family drama, written and directed by George Tillman Jr.

Tillman drew inspiration from his own Milwaukee family, his beloved grandmother in particular. Humor, sentiment and melodrama strike a balance as he brings to life nine major characters and a host of others as well.

For 40 years, the now-widowed Mother Joe (the majestic Irma P. Hall) has served a sumptuous Southern-style Sunday dinner in her fine old Chicago home and in doing so has held together her family of three daughters and their families. But Mother Joe is hit with a life-threatening illness, and soon her daughters are battling right over her hospital bed as she slips into unconsciousness.

Her eldest daughter Teri (Vanessa L. Williams) is a successful lawyer and her relatives' financial mainstay—a fact she is reminding them of constantly. Her relationship with her sister Maxine (Vivica A. Fox) has been strained since Maxine stole her boyfriend and married him happily.

Teri doesn't get along much better with her youngest sister, Bird (Nia Long) . Bird has made a success of her beauty salon, but Teri won't let her forget that it was she who lent her the money to get it started.

On top of all this, Teri's marriage is troubled. She looks upon her husband's desire to give up law to pursue a career as a musician as foolhardy. The demands of her career and her lack of support for her husband Miles (Michael Beach) leave him vulnerable to the attentions of her visiting cousin, Faith (Gina Ravera), a onetime stripper determined to make it as a Broadway dancer. Maxine's marriage is rock solid, but Bird's is undermined when her new husband Lem (Mekhi Phifer) is thrown out of work because he lied on his job application about felony convictions.

Soon there are enough conflicts and crises to launch a soap opera, but "Soul Food" works because Tillman really cares about these people. He sees them in three dimensions and judges none of them.

On the surface, Teri is unsympathetic, but Tillman—plus Williams' fierce intelligence and honesty—allow us to see the isolation she feels because she possesses greater drive and intellect than her relatives. (Teri, who disapproves of Faith even before she becomes involved with Miles, would be surprised that her cousin has developed a similar craving for success.)

For much of the film, Lem becomes its focal point; he is representative of countless black men with a criminal record who find it all but impossible to find work once they have served their time.

"Soul Food" will find particular resonance with those of us who happened to be the favored grandchild, and as children were the center of attention of a large extended family forever coming and going in a big old house. Brandon Hammond's bright young Ahmad—-son of Maxine and her husband—is Tillman's alter ego in "Soul Food" and its narrator.

"Soul Food" reaches a deftly motivated send-'em-home happy ending, but not before Tillman convinces you he knows what life's inevitable changes and losses are all about and how in your heart of hearts you never really get over them. He couldn't have made this movie otherwise.

NEW YORK POST, 9/26/97, p. 49, Thelma Adams

If music is the "Soul Food" of love, play Babyface.

Kenneth ("Babyface") Edmonds, the music impresario and Grammy-winning writer of "Exhale (Shoop Shoop)," joins wife Tracy E. to produce their first movie, "Soul Food."

And it cooks, simmers and smokes.

Writer-director George Tillman Jr. lovingly recalls the Sunday feasts of his childhood following a recipe as old-fashioned as sweet potato pie, as satisfying as home-fried chicken.

Tillman showers affection on his fictional Mid-western African-American clan. Big Mama (Irma P. Hall) has been dishing out dinners and wisdom for 40 years.

With Big Mama's diet, it's no surprise that the diabetic matriarch falls ill. While she's comatose, her three daughters battle for the soul—and control—of the family's future.

Bitchy lawyer Teri (Vanessa L. Williams) reminds everyone she's footing the bill. She resents the domestic bliss of Maxine (Vivica A. Fox), Big Mama's heir apparent. Maxine's happily married to Kenny (Jeffrey D. Sams), Teri's old flame.

Meanwhile, hairdresser Bird (Nia Long) bounces between her bickering sibs. She can't cook, but she's got a bun in the oven.

Maxine's canny son Ahmad (Brandon Hammond) plays narrator. From the opening sequence, the wedding of Bird and Lem (Mekhi Phifer), Big Mama's favorite grandson, has plenty to tell. Stripper cousin Faith (Gina Ravera) seduces Teri's hubby Miles (Michael Beach), Lem loses his job and returns to jail, and Teri flips out during Maxine and Kenny's anniversary party.

With a strong cast led by diva Williams and Fox, "Soul Food" is honest, humorous and heartfelt. Like "Waiting to Exhale," it invites audience participation. When Miles dropped his pants for Faith, the woman seated in front of me yelled: "Don't do it."

But "Soul Food" isn't all gloss. When Lem lashes out at Bird, gets tanked and brandishes a gun he shouldn't possess, writing his own ticket back to prison, the situation is complex and unexpectedly affecting. Tillman doesn't need to lean on Babyface's tunes to strike an emotional cord.

Occasionally, "Soul Food" digs itself into heavy cornbread or settles too easily on the sitcom couch. But, as Big Mama tells Ahmad: "If you let bad things stop you, you won't be here for the good things."

SIGHT AND SOUND, 7/98, p. 53, Liese Spencer

Every Sunday in Chicago, Mother Joe's family gathers for dinner, prepared by her and her daughters Teri, Maxine and Bird. Other diners include Teri's husband Miles, Maxine's husband Kenny, Bird's new husband Lem, Cousin Faith and Maxine's son Ahmad. One Sunday, Maxine gives birth to a daughter. During a leg amputation for diabetes, Mother goes into a coma.

In her absence, the family splinters. Lem loses his job, while Maxine argues with Miles over his giving up law for music. When Bird gets a new job, they argue violently and Lem pushes her. Teri sends a gang of heavies to rough up Lem; he pulls a gun and is arrested. Miles and Faith are seen having sex by Teri. At Maxine and Kenny's wedding anniversary, Teri threatens to sell mother's house, then tries to attack Faith. Later, Mother dies. Maxine and Bird meet Teri and tell her they will not let her sell the house. Bird is pregnant. Teri gets Lem released from jail. Pretending to know where Mother kept her fortune, Ahmad tricks the family into meeting for Sunday lunch where they talk over their problems and find the stash of money.

From the opening soft-focus montage of family photographs to the treacly voice-over that draws it to a close, Soul Food is a resolutely bland potboiler that offers little in the way of sustenance, but plenty of life lessons. Like many movies before it, this second feature from writer/director George Tillman Jr (his first was Scenes for the Soul uses the staple device of the family gathering (weddings, anniversaries, funerals—you name it, they're all in here) to serve up familiar conflicts for a spread of stereotypical characters, including a money-grabbing sister, a good-natured housewife and an adulterous exotic dancer. All are observed through the eyes of cute child narrator Ahmad.

At least the performances are workmanlike. The rivalries and jealousies between the three sisters are vigorously portrayed by Nia Long, Vivica A. Fox and Vanessa L Williams. Fox in particular injects much-needed vivacity into her goody-two-shoes wife and mother. Unfortunately, such supporting characters as Bird's gay hairdressing friends or Carl Wright's lecherous family minister verge on pantomime. occasionally Tillman's sexy script spices things up, but for the most part he's content to have his characters say such lines as, "Seems like everything I love, I lose." The film's soft-soap polemics are equally basic: a hasty speech from Ahmad at the film's close explains how slavery led black folks "to express their love for each other through food".

The sleeper success in the US of *Soul Food* with its all-black cast and soundtrack from bands including BLACKstreet and Boyz II Men, proves how hungry audiences are for African-American stories. Let's hope scared studios give audiences something a bit more substantial to chew on soon.

VILLAGE VOICE, 9/30/97, p. 80, Steven Boone

First-time director George Tillman Jr. guides this sweet, shamelessly manipulative ode to the Black Family with often dazzling efficiency. *Soul Food* feels likes one big, gauzy Kodak moment interrupted by what my mother would call "ugliness." The trouble starts when Big Mama (Irma P. Hall), the elderly head of a middle-class African American family, slips into a coma after a diabetes-induced amputation. Without Big Mama's cooking, peacekeeping, and wisdom spouting, her twenty-and thirtysomething offspring plummet into tragedy and conflict. The ensuing twists and turns are contrived but it doesn't matter; Tillman has assembled a flawless cast so charismatic, our belief in them smothers all cynicism about the plot.

Vivica A. Fox and Vanessa Williams cut up as long-feuding siblings who take the gloves off when Big Mama is gone. Nia Long plays baby sister, whose attempts to help her new, ex-convict husband (Mekhi Phifer) blow up in her face. As Fox's thoughtful son, young Brandon Hammond narrates and instigates the action. His doe-eyed, completely virtuous character doesn't grate, except for the endless narration Tillman gives him. Most of it is obvious and unnecessary ("Big Mama went into the hospital"—cut to Big Hama in the hospital). Mekhi Phifer *(Clockers),* a fierce screen presence, hijacks the movie whenever he appears.

Soul Food is a crowd pleaser because it knows its crowd intimately. At an advance screening, a mostly African American audience gave the film the loudest, most enthusiastic reception I've observed since Robert Townsend's *The Five Heartbeats.* Tillman is as shameless an entertainer as Townsend, with the same uncool yet disarming faith in family values. And in the manner of *Like Water for Chocolate* and other art-house feast-flicks, *Soul Food* stars plates of yams, steaming pots of collard greens, and glazed, garnished hams.

Also reviewed in:
CHICAGO TRIBUNE, 9/26/97, Friday/p. C, Mark Caro
NEW YORK TIMES, 9/28/97, p. E10, Janet Maslin
VARIETY, 9/22-28/97, p. 38, Godfrey Cheshire
WASHINGTON POST, 9/26/97, Weekend/p. 50, Lonnae O'Neal Parker

SOUL IN THE HOLE

A Northern Arts Entertainment release of an Asphalt Films production. *Executive Producer:* Cis wilson and Mel Lawrence. *Producer:* Lilibet Foster. *Director:* Danielle Gardner. *Screenplay:* Danielle Gardner and Lilibet Foster. *Director of Photography:* Paul Gibson. *Editor:* Melissa Neidich. *Sound:* Steven Robinson. *Running time:* 100 minutes. *MPAA Rating:* Not Rated.

WITH: Kenny Jones; Ronnet Jones; Ed (Booger) Smith; Kenyetta Jones.

LOS ANGELES TIMES, 2/20/98, Calendar/p. 16, Kenneth Turan

First "Hoop Dreams," now "Soul in the Hole." What is it about basketball that makes it the source of excellent documentary films?

Partially it's the game itself, fluid, swirling, quintessentially visual. To watch the spectacular no-look passes and the all-but-indescribable moves to the hoop featured in "Soul" is to understand why it has so many passionate followers.

While "Hoop Dreams" concentrated on two players trying to make their mark in organized high school and college ball, "Soul" focuses on the more harum-scarum world of New York City street basketball, where the game tends to be flashier, the players more individualistic as well as occasionally more personally troubled.

Set during a recent summer so hot, as a radio DJ puts it, "I saw the devil on a bed with a fan," "Soul" follows one particular team, Kenny's Kings of the Bedford-Stuyvesant section of Brooklyn, as it competes in the self-contained universe of the summer game, playing in intense tournaments like "It's a Fila Thing," "The Mecca" and the one that gives the film its name.

The on-court star of Kenny's Kings is Ed Smith, universally known as Booger, an uncommonly talented guard with skills so dazzling that Sports Illustrated featured him on its cover last year as "King of the Streets," describing a wizard who "controls the ball as if it were secretly hooked to his hand and couldn't possibly get away."

But it's more than the flash of the game that makes street basketball so intoxicating and this film so involving. It's the knowledge of the poverty and emotional destitution these players often come from and are always in danger of returning to. It's the understanding of how street ball becomes a reason to believe because it gives players and spectators the chance to be taken out of themselves, to soar literally and metaphorically. Since the downside is so abrupt and chilling for those who aren't able to use basketball to change their lives, this game is more life and death than sports usually are.

Trying to help his players survive in their world is the coach and namesake of Kenny's Kings, Kenny Jones. Though his own livelihood as a liquor store clerk is problematical, Jones and his wife Ronnet work to create a surrogate family for the young players he coaches. Hot-tempered and insistently profane, Jones is hardly a classic role model, but he cares about these kids, and one of the things "Soul" demonstrates is how much can be accomplished by one man who simply cares.

The drama of "Hole in the Soul" is two-fold: Will Kenny's Kings get through the summer undefeated and will Kenny Jones be able to keep his star player on an even keel and away from the myriad dangers of life on the streets that has a fatal attraction for Booger Smith?

Men with two more different styles would be hard to imagine. Jones is a bulldog, forceful and confrontational, always speaking his mind. Booger, though confident and charismatic, is quieter, someone who glides through his life like he glides on the court while nurturing his own particular dreams. "If I don't make it to the NBA, I'm gonna be a drug dealer," he says at the start of the film. "Somehow I've gotta get me a Lexus. Whatever it takes."

Making their relationship more complex than the average player-coach dynamic is that 18-year-old Booger, estranged from his mother and with no contact with his father, has lived with the Jones family for the past three years, making Kenny Jones the closest thing to a parent he's ever had.

Jones has few delusions about Booger: "Ninety-nine percent of the time he's lying," he says of his charge. "The other 1% he's asleep. "Yet despite—or maybe because of no one else caring about this kid—Jones became determined to "civilize him as much as possible," a goal that leads to "Soul in the Hole's" most affecting moments.

Director Danielle Gardner and producer Lilibet Foster hung out in New York's playgrounds and neighborhoods for years working on this film, and that time paid off. Because its documentary style is completely nonjudgmental, "Soul in the Hole" creates a strong sense of street verisimilitude. It doesn't judge or psychoanalyze. It focuses on the ambience of the street game as much as on the players. "Soul" places us firmly in this unforgiving world, and it's one we won't forget.

NEW YORK POST, 8/8/97, p. 53, Larry Worth

The comparisons to "Hoop Dreams" are inevitable. After all, basketball documentaries that chart inner-city kids' struggles are rarer than a mid-court swish.

As such, "Soul in the Hole" holds it own, and then some. It's not only considerably pithier than the overlong "Dreams" but comes up with protagonists that are every bit as fascinating.

The real-life drama unfolds in the summer of '93 on the asphalt courts of Bed-Stuy's neighborhood playgrounds, during which liquor store owner Kenny Jones coaches "Kenny's

Kings" through one colorfully named tournament ("Soul in the Hole." "The Malcolm X Invitational," "It's a Fila Thang") after another.

But the heart of the goings-on rests in Kenny's paternal relationship to 18-year-old star point guard Ed Smith, referred to strictly by his nickname, Booger. Having lived with Kenny and his wife since being kicked out of his own home, Booger is supremely talented, undeniably charismatic and a frighteningly loose cannon.

The dynamic between the two men is as touching as it is funny, and as volatile as it is heartbreaking. Scenes of Kenny breaking down, as when his players pull a no-show at a crucial game, or Booger's reception at an Arizona junior college, prove indelible images.

But what's equally remarkable is the manner in which neophyte filmmaker Danielle Gardner captures Kenny and Booger's complex dealings. She then goes one better by tapping into the energy and excitement of street basketball in general and the spirit of Bed-Stuy in particular.

For once drugs and guns aren't Bed-Stuy's main characters, though their temptation to Booger is clear. Rather, the focus is on Kenny turning Booger and his peers into virtual magicians, along with the sideline wagering, women fans ogling players' heaving chests and high-voltage disputes between foul-mouthed referees.

Gardner drops the ball chiefly in her cursory looks at some of Booger's colleagues, later expecting viewers to respond to their fates. In addition, some of the photography is unnecessarily grainy.

But those are minor quibbles in a uniformly impressive production. Thanks to Gardner, the soul displayed in "Hole", makes it a winner for sports fans and devotees of the human comedy.

NEWSDAY, 8/8/97, Part II/p. B9, John Anderson

The comparisons with "Hoop Dreams" will be inevitable and relentless, so let's make like a healthy Muggsy Bogues and get it over with: Yes, "Soul in the Hole" is a movie about inner-city black kids playing basketball, kids for whom the basket is both the gold ring and the life preserver, who shoot as if everything depends on it because it probably does.

But where "Hoop Dreams" found its drama in the upwardly mobile aspirations of two young men with their eye on the NBA, Danielle Gardner's smaller, fluid, electric and poetic documentary about Brooklyn playground ball isn't really about winning.

It's about pure survival and character and whether one gifted player, who's been flagrantly fouled by life, can keep off the slippery slope of easy money and the night-town of the projects. And it's the kind of movie that makes you wait in acute apprehension for the postscript you know is going to appear at the end of the picture.

"If I don't make the NBA I'm gonna be a drug dealer," says Ed (Booger) Smith, who smiles when he says it, but not in a way that's completely convincing. Either way, he adds, he's going to buy a Lexus. And within this agonizingly limited view of life's possibilities, Booger's future squirms and writhes.

He's a local legend, the star of Kenny's Kings, the glamor team among the many competing in the 1993 version of Brooklyn's marathon of summer tourneys—Soul in the Hole itself being the ultimate shootout for Bed-Stuy bragging rights. They play on asphalt courts that are virtually melting, where the tempers are hairtrigger and the threat of violence is always in the air. The team is coached by Kenny Jones, a volatile fireplug of a man, who can give as good as he takes ("Oh _____, did we win *again*?" he crows), and who, with his wife, Ronnet, took Booger in when his mother threw him out.

The games are great to watch, the players sparkle; Charles Jones, who starred at Long Island University this year and was the nation's top scorer, is among them. But it's Booger and Kenny who are the heart of the story.

Gardner uses no narration, swings between film and video, shoots under daunting conditions and manages to achieve a level of intimacy and immediacy that's as thrilling as any last-second three-point shot.

Brooklyn often comes off as a perpetual street party, a garden of unearthly delights, and Booger, a prodigy on the court but a child-man off it, teeters on the brink of what might be wild success or total destruction. College becomes a possibility; so does some long-term trouble with the law. Kenny, who carries himself like the baddest mutha in town but cries when he ought to, watches Booger's progress as if every step was his first.

"Soul in the Hole" is a basketball movie, sure, but you won't find many more urgent or convincing portraits of, uh, male bonding, or what these guys would probably be embarrassed to call love.

VILLAGE VOICE, 8/12/97, p. 67, Amy Taubin

Listen up: the great summer picture has arrived. Of the people, for the people, and directed by the fanatically dedicated Danielle Gardner, *Soul in the Hole* is proof that the movies as populist entertainment have not perished from the earth.

Set in Brooklyn during one steamy summer, *Soul in the Hole* follows Kenny's Kings, a Bed-Stuy street basketball dream team, as it goes from tournament to tournament on what could be an unstoppable winning streak. But it's also the story of the love of Kenny Jones, the teams irrepressible coach, for Ed "Booger" Smith, the inspired point guard who becomes his surrogate son.

The best film ever made about basketball—and about growing up black, male, and street—*Soul in the Hole* is, dare I admit it, a documentary. Not a middle-class-über-alles PBS-style documentary (no way PBS could air a film that opens with the invocation "Why doncha play some fuckin' defense, you buncha sorry-assed fucks" and continues in the same vernacular for 90 minutes), but a passionate, nonjudgmental depiction of a street culture that almost never appears uncensored on the screen—not even in the collected works of Spike Lee. That director Danielle Gardner is a 32-year-old white woman who loves playground hall and who spent a year hanging with Kenny's Kings before she brought in professional moviemaking equipment only adds a layer or two of complexity to what's onscreen. Are those guys riffing about "borrowing" clothes from stores more guarded because it's a white female behind the camera? Maybe, or maybe not, or maybe guarded in a different way than they would have been if the film were more clearly an inside job. This film calls into question easy assumptions about insiders and outsiders—especially when a camera's involved.

But putting aside sticky matters of gender, race, and power, *Soul in the Hole* is a joy to watch. It moves, as jock and film historian Paul Arthur wrote of it, "with the drive and rhythm of a continuous fast break." It has, in Kenny and Booger, two extremely compelling, complicated characters. Kenny treats his team (among them Charles Jones, who became a Division I leading scorer in 1997 at L.I.U., and Javone Moore, who graduated an Academic All-American from Canisius College) like an extended family, but Booger is his favorite child and it's Booger's future that's most in doubt. Keeping Booger out of the projects where he grew up and still feels most at home and getting him on a plane to college in Arizona where a full scholarship awaits matters more to Kenny than winning tournaments. The problem is that the charisma, daring, and unpredictability that make Booger a genius on the court turn self-destructive on the street. Tender but unsentimental, *Soul in the Hole* shows how dire is the predicament of this heartbreak kid.

Also reviewed in:
NEW YORK TIMES, 8/8/97, p. C8, Stephen Holden
VARIETY, 2/19-25/96, p. 51, David Rooney
WASHINGTON POST, 9/12/97, Weekend/p. 41, Desson Howe

SPAWN

A New Line Cinema release in association with Todd McFarlane Entertainment of a Dippé/Goldman/Williams production. *Executive Producer:* Todd McFarlane and Alan C. Blomquist. *Producer:* Clint Goldman. *Director:* Mark A.Z. Dippé. *Screenplay:* Alan McElroy. *Story:* Alan McElroy and Mark A.Z. Dippe. *Based on the comic book by:* Todd McFarlane. *Director of Photography:* Guillermo Navarro. *Editor:* Michael N. Knue. *Music:* Graeme Revell. *Music Editor:* Joshua Winget. *Sound:* Jim Thornton and (music) Mitch Zelezny. *Casting:* Mary Jo Slater and Bruce H. Newberg. *Production Designer:* Philip Harrison. *Art Director:* Eric W. Orbom. *Set Designer:* Sharon Alshams, Fanee Aaron, Dorn Merrill Kennison, and Barry

Lehrman. *Set Decorator:* Dena Roth. *Costumes:* Dan Lester. *Special Effects:* Garry Elmendorf. *Visual Effects:* Steve "Spaz" Williams. *Make-up:* Cindy Jane Williams. *Special Make-up:* Robert Kurtzman, Gregory Nicotero, and Howard Herger. *Animation:* Dennis Turner. *Stunt Coordinator:* Charles Croughwell. *Running time:* 97 minutes. *MPAA Rating:* PG-13.

CAST: John Leguizamo (Clown); Michael Jai White (Al Simmons/Spawn); Martin Sheen (Jason Wynn); Theresa Randle (Wanda); Melinda Clarke (Jessica Priest); Miko Hughes (Zack); Sydni Beaudoin (Cyan); Nicol Williamson (Cogliostro); D.B. Sweeney (Terry Fitzgerald); Michael Papajohn (Zack's Dad); Frank Welker (Voice of The Devil Malebolgia); Robia Lamorte (XNN Reporter); Caroline Gibson (News Anchor); John Cothran, Jr. and Tony Haney (African Liaiso); Marc Robinson, Chris Coppola, and Jay Caputo (Punks); Darryl Warren (Security Guard); Mike Akrawi and Romeo Akrawi (Foreign Dignitaries); Jack Coleman (Doctor); Laura Stepp (Angela); Garrison Singer (Anesthesiologist); Todd McFarlane (Alley Bum).

LOS ANGELES TIMES, 8/1/97, Calendar/p. 20, John Anderson

[The following review by John Anderson appeared in a slightly different form in **NEWSDAY, 8/1/97, Part II/p. B9.**]

If you're in the mood for Julie Harris in "The Belle of Amherst," there's probably no need to read any further. If, however, what you want is an anguished superhero from hell whose face looks like the inside of an all-weather radial, "Spawn" might just be the movie for you.

Based on Todd McFarlane's nightmare comic book, "Spawn" stars Michael Jai White (HBO's "Tyson") as Al Simmons, a rogue member of a rogue agency who is sent to hell by his superior, Jason Wynn (Martin Sheen), when he's virtually incinerated during a germ-warfare "experiment" in North Korea. Why Simmons didn't go in the other direction is not explained, and I don't want to ask, but once down there he makes a pact with Satan: By agreeing to lead the forces of hell against heaven at Armageddon, he is allowed to return to Earth and see his beloved wife, Wanda (Theresa Randle).

Inspired by the Tim Burton school of gothic urban decay, and with a few episodes of the old "Beauty and the Beast" series under his belt, director Mark A.Z. Dippé does a considerable job recreating the feel of McFarlane's books; the scenes in hell are particularly ghoulish and other-worldly; the fire-scarred Simmons, who has metamorphosed into Spawn, takes the disquiet and self-loathing of the modern comic hero to new heights—or depths—especially when you consider that he's already dead. The special effects are effective and aggressive, although one might occasionally confuse a divine vortex with a flushed toilet.

Any questions will be answered in the sequel, which seems inevitable given that the final words of "Spawn" tell us in no uncertain terms that the story hasn't ended. But then, "Spawn" is mostly about establishing its hero and seeking revenge: Spawn, cape aswirl and eyes aglow, wants Wynn and is relentless in his pursuit.

Spawn doesn't actually return to Earth until five years have passed; finding Wanda married to his best friend Terry (D.B. Sweeney) doesn't help his disposition. Neither does the fact that he's caught on the horns of an infernal dilemma. The evil Clown, played by an antic but very funny John Leguizamo (he gets all the good lines), is intent on filling Satan's army with lost souls; to that end, he devises a scheme whereby Spawn's killing of Wynn will unleash an unstoppable viral plague. Nicol Williamson, posturing like hell's *boulevardier*, is Cogliostro, another hellian who urges Spawn to reject Satan and preserve life. Spawn, already in need of some serious dermatology, now has this end-of-the-world thing to worry about.

There's lots of action and lots of dubious theology, and the religious right will be tying itself in knots trying to figure out whom to boycott (New Line is owned by Time Warner, if that's any help). "Spawn," meanwhile, does what it's supposed to do, which is make a comic come to life. Or is it death?

NEW YORK POST, 8/1/97, p. 43, Thelma Adams

And the award for the most fireballs goes to ... "Spawn."

The gates to hell are a fiery wormhole. The crimson cape of the title warrior—a Marine who reneges on a Faustian deal with the devil—swirls with flame. A control tower turns into a burning torch and a Korean chemical weapons factory becomes a sprawling inferno.

Fireplaces don't just crackle and swirl, they shoot flame gushers into otherwise tasteful living rooms. Between scenes, agitated first-time director Mark A.Z. Dippe sweeps the screen with cleansing fire.

Working from a script by Alan McElroy, the pyromaniacal Dippe (the production notes insist that it's not pronounced "DIP-ee") has concocted a swirling, spinning action-adventure based on the top-selling comic book also named Spawn.

Spawn, the soldier formerly known as Al Simmons (buff, stoic Michael Jai White), gets double-crossed by his mentor, Jason Wynn (played by Martin Sheen, who must be taking career advice from his son Charlie). The devil resurrects the deep-fried hero to lead his minions to the "gates of heaven."

Simmons accepts the invitation to do Lucifer's bidding in order to revisit his wife, Wanda (Theresa Randle). So what if the Earth's fate weighs in the balance?

After five years in limbo, Simmons returns to Earth with a scarred, rubbery mug, a super-powered exoskeleton and matching magic cape. He's not pretty.

He scares little children—but not as much as his blue-faced clown sidekick, played with worm-eating, gaseous gusto by John Leguizamo. The wise-cracking goon from below the Borscht Belt is Spawn's guardian devil.

On the side of good are an ancient Crusader (Nicol Williamson, a touch of class overwhelmed by crass) and Simmon's best-friend-turned-romantic-rival Terry Fitzgerald (the limp D.B. Sweeney). Of course, the bad guys have more fun and Clown gets the best lines, such as they are.

With dazzling, nonstop special effects from Industrial Light and Magic and gross-out humor, "Spawn" is perfectly pitched for teen-age boys. For the rest of us, the live-action comic book burns out quickly. It's half-baked.

Scarred in face and spirit, White's character bears an uncanny resemblance to the crispy Ralph Fiennes of "The English Patient." The patient is not everybody's model for a hero—and certainly someone we don't want to stare at for any length of time.

SIGHT AND SOUND, 10/97, p. 57, Kim Newman

Colonel Al Simmons, an assassin working under Jason Wynn of the US government's covert A-6 agency, is double-crossed while destroying a bioweapons facility in North Korea; Simmons is killed by Wynn and his sidekick Jessica Priest.

Five years later, hideously burned, Simmons appears in a New York slum, and is teased separately by two mystery figures, a squat figure named Clown and the 500-year-old Cogliostro. They reveal to him that he has been granted a body of mutable necroplasm and returned to Earth by a demonic entity known as Malebolgia on the condition that he leads the armies of Hell.

The Clown, who is really an insectile demon called the Violator, encourages Wynn in his plan to control the world with a bioweapon stolen from the Koreans. Meanwhile, the Violator sets up Simmons, now known as Spawn, to kill Wynn in revenge, thus damning his own soul.

Spawn, who can convert his body into versatile armour, makes an attempt to assassinate Wynn but, after killing Priest, is forced to retreat. He discovers his wife Wanda has married his best friend, Terry Fitzgerald, and that they are raising his daughter, Cyan, with whom he makes contact. His conscience awakened by his feelings for his family and by the teachings of Cogliostro, Spawn rebels against the Violator and, mastering his powers, defeats the Violator and the hordes of Malebolgia.

By refusing to kill Wynn, Spawn saves his soul and turns down the command of Hell's armies. Wynn is arrested and exposed, and Cogliostro, tired of the struggle, hands over the job of battling the forces of Malebolgia on Earth to Spawn.

Artist-writer Todd McFarlane, noted among comics connoisseurs for introducing "funky webbing" to the long-running comic *Spider-Man*, created *Spawn* in 1992. It would form the cornerstone of an empire/universe Image Comics were founding as an alternative to the shaky Marvel-DC duopoly that had dominated the superhero-comic industry since the 60s. Whereas DC's *Superman* and *Batman*, both from the late 30s, and Marvel's early 60s *Spider-Man* and *X-*

Men all began as comic strips and evolved gradually into properties, *Spawn* was conceived from the first as not merely a comic-strip character but a spin-off source for action figures, animated television shows (a *Spawn* series has already been made), crossovers with other companies' heroes (*Spawn* has met *Batman*, twice in comics) and, inevitably, a movie blockbuster.

Given the canniness McFarlane has shown in controlling and quality-controlling *Spawn* and related merchandise (his company is co-producer of the film), it is astonishing that he should have allowed his baby into these hands. Alan McElroy is a screenwriter responsible for the dire and derivative *Halloween 4: The Return of Michael Myers*, and Mark A. Z. Dippé is a director with a special-effects background but no apparent storytelling ability. While the 'origin' story of *Spawn* was told in mosaic form over the first dozen issues of the comic as the dead and confused Simmons remembers more and more of his backstory, the film trots it out in dollops. The first major flashback—Clown takes Spawn back to Hell, where he made a deal with Malebolgia to lead his armies on the condition he be allowed to return to see his wife—is positioned just after the offer itself, so that one wonders why it wasn't just told straight.

Arriving after such indie superheroes as the Mask and the Crow have shot their bolts, the real problem is that *Spawn* is so indebted to earlier comic-to-movie transformations that it never establishes an identity of its own. Like the Crow, Spawn is literally a zombie (he has a Freddie Krueger burn-face); like the Mask, he can do all manner of smart CGI trucks with his cloak and chains (which are a tad reminiscent of *Hellraiser*'s Cenobites); and like Batman in the Tim Burton films, he is shut out of normal family life by a deep-rooted trauma (in this case, his own death). There is even some unsuccessful jokiness at the expense of this lack of originality: Spawn refers to his mentor Cogliostro (a bewildered Nicol Williamson doing his Merlin act) as "Yoda". However, merely using heroic archetypes doesn't automatically mean that they will carry the right resonance. The old sense of the term "comic book" as a jibe denoting shoddy plotting and too-easy sentiment has rarely been more applicable than it is here. It suits the dreadful happy family scenes, complete with dog, intended to show us what Spawn is missing, and the ropey circularity of the conspiracy-bioweapon storyline in which the whole thing is stuck.

Top-billed John Leguizamo, encased in a make-up bubble as the midget clown or replaced by CGI as the towering Violator, is intended to steal the film, poaching a lot of Burtonisms from Michael Keaton's *Beetlejuice*. However, the sound mix has been biased so heavily towards great noise effects and a trendy soundtrack that almost all his tossed-off jokes and routines are inaudible ("every time someone farts, a demon gets his wings").

Michael Jai White is bland as Simmons, the family-man covert assassin, and swamped by effects as Spawn, a hero constantly upstaged by his own magical costume. (McFarlane draws the best capes in comics, and Spawn's red whirlwind is faithfully recreated.) The rest of the cast are forced to mouth speech balloons. There are the expected compensations of spectacular (if repetitive) infernal visions, monstrous transformations and hero-villain slugfests, but this is a tiresome adventure, shackled by its '12' certificate whenever it tries to deal with real evil.

In the end, one is forced to wonder why, if Hell can only pick a general for its armies every 400 years, Malebolgia bothered with the deep-down, nice-guy, liberal-wimp Al Simmons. He could have recruited Melinda Clarke's Jessica Priest, a conscience-free psychopath in a black leather catsuit who not only has the required ruthlessness but also proves that she's a better killer than Simmons by murdering him.

Of course, the reason Simmons is the hero is because the plot of *Spawn* has been contrived to create a continuing hero. After the first few issues of Spawn, McFarlane was criticised for delivering great art and ordinary scripting. He then went out of his way to bring in top-rank comics writers (Alan Moore, Neil Gaiman, Dave Sim, Grant Morrison) to shape things up. If there are going to be more movies, he would do well to remember the lesson and get hold of some proper writers and directors.

VILLAGE VOICE, 8/12/97, p. 74, Gary Dauphin

Already hardwired into the midbrains of millions of kids on either side of the PG-13 speed bump, *Spawn* makes its loud and digitally rendered way into theaters virtually presold. *Spawn* the movie isn't as good as Todd McFarlane's comic book or HBO's late-night animated series, but it is coolly effective, low-fuss summer moviemaking.

As directed by first-timer Mark Dippé, *Spawn* tells the tale of a reluctant soldier in the war between heaven and hell. Al Simmons (Michael Jai White) is a government black-ops specialist whose psych profile labels him a "borderline psychotic." Murdered by his own boss (a scenery-chewing Martin Sheen), Simmons goes straight to hell without passing Go, but instead of frying he's asked to lead the hosts of Hell in the coming Armageddon. Simmons takes the job providing he can see his comely wife again and take revenge on both Sheen and a rather zanily bloated and foul-mouthed minor demon played by John Leguizamo. Although there's plenty of gunplay, Simmons's main weapons are of the T1000 hard-soft variety, his skin/suit sprouting blades, chains, and hooks, his swirling red cape as likely to carry him aloft as it is to solidify into a bulletproof barrier.

Although he's a certifiable bad-ass, Simmons has the standard comic-book sensitivities/liabilities: he's a killer with a deep love for his wife, a loyal soldier working for disreputable villains. Simmons is also black in the offhand but profound way of most black superheroes—you never forget his race, but his skin is hidden under layers of scars and prostheses. *Spawn* relies heavily on action moves and a headlong soundtrack (the demographic buckshot hits everyone from Marilyn Manson to DJ Spooky), but in the end it's the black and brooding heart Todd McFarlane first sketched out in the early '90s that carries the movie. Spawn is a superhero, but he's also the most fundamentally screwed superhero in recent memory. He tries to do the right thing, but all he can manage is an uneasy détente with the powers that be. If merchandise sales are any indication, kids love that kind of thing these days.

Also reviewed in:
NEW YORK TIMES, 8/1/97, p. C10, Stephen Holden
VARIETY, 8/4-10/97, p. 34, Todd McCarthy
WASHINGTON POST, 8/1/97, Weekend/p. 30, Rita Kempley

SPEED 2: CRUISE CONTROL

A Twentieth Century Fox release of a Blue Tulip production. *Executive Producer:* Mark Gordon. *Producer:* Steve Perry, Jan De Bont, and Michael Peyser. *Director:* Jan De Bont. *Screenplay:* Randall McCormick and Jeff Nathanson. *Story:* Jan De Bont and Randall McCormick. *Based on characters created by:* Graham Yost. *Director of Photography:* Jack N. Green. *Editor:* Alan Cody. *Music:* Mark Mancina. *Music Editor:* Zigmond M. Gron. *Sound:* Robert Janiger and (music) Steve Kempster. *Sound Editor:*Gregg Baxter. *Casting:* Risa Bramon Garcia and Randi Hiller. *Production Designer:* Joseph Nemec, III and Bill Kenney. *Art Director:* Bill Skinner. *Set Designer:* Jeff B. Adams, Jr., Douglas D. Berkeley, Daniel Bradford, Mark Garner, Stephanie Seaman Girard, J. Mark Harrington, Duncan Kennedy, Carlos Menendez, Martin Roy Mervel, Derrick W. Smith, and Darrell L. Wright. *Set Decorator:* Cindy Carr, Chris Grantz, Michael Calabrese, George Capetanos, Richard L. Manalia, Frederick Valentine, Cary Whitaker, Larry A. Cornick, Lisa K. Sessions, and Kristen Jones. *Set Dresser:* Jane Johnson and Tyler Patterson. *Special Effects:* Al DiSarro. *Costumes:* Louise Frogley. *Make-up:* G. Dennis Liddiard, Jr. *Make-up (Sandra Bullock):* Pamela Westmore. *Stunt Coordinator:* Dick Ziker. *Marine Stunt Coordinator:* T. Bahr. *Running time:* 110 minutes. *MPAA Rating:* PG-13.

CAST: Sandra Bullock (Annie Porter); Jason Patric (Alex Shaw); Willem Dafoe (John Geiger); Temuera Morrison (Juliano); Brian McCardie (Merced); Christine Firkins (Drew); Michael G. Hagerty (Harvey); Colleen Camp (Debbie); Lois Chiles (Celeste); Francis Guinan (Rupert); Tamia (Sheri); Jeremy Hotz (Ashton); Enrique Murciano, Jr. (Alejandro); Jessica Diaz (Isabel); Connie Ray (Fran); Patrick Darbo (Ruby); Kimmy Robertson (Liza, Cruise Director); Charles Parks (Frank); Susan Barnes (Constance); Bo Svenson (Captain Pollard); Royale Watkins (Dantes); Alex Montesino (Control Room Chief Engineer); Mark Adair-Rios (Engine Room Crew Member #1); Xavier Coronel (Engine Room Crew Member #2); Tyler Patton (Engine Room Crew Member #3); Craig A. Pinckes (Engine Room Crew Member #4); Glenn Plummer (Maurice); Allison Dean (Marifa); Michael Robinson (Muster Deck Officer #1); Joe d'Angerio

(Muster Deck Officer #2); Joe Foster (Pool Officer); Richard Speight, Jr. ("C" Deck Officer); Michael O'Hagan (Supertanker Captain); Christopher Wynne (Supertanker Officer #1); Robert Herrick (Supertanker Officer #2); Ivory Broome (Supertanker Crew Member #1); Tim Conway (Mr. Kenter); Thomas J. Huff (Diaper Van Driver); Jay Lacopo (Real Estate Salesman); Alexander De Bont (Little Boy at Condo); Kathryn Rossetter (Mother at Condo); Mark Beltzman (Convertible Owner); Mark Kriski (News Reporter); Ben Meyerson (Bridge Officer #1); Ben Siegler (Policeman); Gustavo Laborie (Bridge Officer #2); Jennifer S. Badger (Passenger #1); Cheryl Bermeo (Passenger #2); Jeff Brockton (Passenger #3); Don Pulford (Passenger #4); Cliff McLaughlin (Passenger #5); Matthew Taylor (Passenger #6); PJ Wagner (Passenger #7); May R. Boss (Passenger #8); Nancy Collet (Passenger #9); Wilma Edward (Woman on Phone).

LOS ANGELES TIMES, 6/13/97, Calendar/p. 1, Kenneth Turan

The Seabourn Legend has everything a movie cruise ship needs, including five passenger decks, swimming pool, health club, beauty salon, plus a mad terrorist to call its very own.

It's completely appropriate that "Speed 2: Cruise Control" centers on the hijacking of the Legend, because this movie is a form of creative abduction. Director Jan De Bont has lifted both the title and star Sandra Bullock from the original "Speed" and placed them in a movie that otherwise has little connection to the earlier hit.

A film that wouldn't have been considered, let alone made, if De Bont hadn't been so successful the first time around, "Speed 2" suffers from its derivative origins. Though it displays enough perils to put a dent in future cruise ship sales, the film has a makeshift, slapdash quality that is the opposite of its predecessor.

That film, De Bont's directing debut, took the quirky idea of a booby-trapped Santa Monica bus that would explode if it slowed below a certain speed and turned it into an expert piece of commercial filmmaking, one of the most deserved action hits of 1994.

Though co-star Keanu Reeves considered this new trip unnecessary, the "Speed 2" crew has packed in lots of references from the original. These include cameos for returning actors, a stunt in an elevator and the repeated use of the film's "relationships based on extreme circumstances never work out" tagline.

As noted, Bullock's Annie Porter is back, with a new boyfriend she thinks has a low-stress job as a beach cop in Venice. But, as Annie finds out in the film's opening sequence, Alex Shaw (Jason Patric) is another daredevil SWAT team operative who practically needs leg irons to keep him from risking his life.

That sequence, with Shaw on a motorcycle chasing a truck and dodging large cartons on a winding mountain road, is in many ways the film's best. De Bont's fine kinetic sense, his expertise at pacing action, is on more display in is warmup than in the film's more expensive and cumbersome climactic stunts.

To make up for misleading Annie about his job, Alex asks her to join him on a Caribbean cruise. A week of quality relaxation time together, he says, and we'll really get to know each other better. As if.

Since anyone who cares knows that the cruise's tranquillity isn't fated to last, one of the film's flaws is that it's too slow getting into the bulk of the action. Though tyro screenwriters Randall McCormick and Jeff Nathanson have no gift for character or chitchat, "Speed 2" spends so much time with its forgettable characters that it begins to resemble a wide-screen episode of "The Love Boat."

The film does have that terrorist, passenger John Geiger (Willem Dafoe), ill enough to show up with his own jar of leeches, and he finally shows his cards. A disgruntled former employee of the cruise line who now thirsts for revenge, Geiger is intent on widening his eyes, laughing maniacally and destroying the Seabourn Legend, not necessarily in that order.

Only one man has the expertise and the nerve to stop him, and it's not the overweight representative of Fatbusters. As the confident and capable Shaw, Patric, one of the most interesting of today's young actors, gives the film's best performance. Tense and intense, unwilling to raise his voice above a whisper, he has charisma as well as the physicality to make his action sequences convincing.

Regrettably, the jeopardy situations "Speed 2" dreams up are overly familiar and not compelling. While "Speed" had a kind of originality, the sequel is the kind of "ship at risk" epic that has been done often before, perhaps most memorably in Richard Lester's little-seen "Juggernaut" from 1974. Even the film's big-ticket closing stunts are more impressive for their size than for any excitement they generate.

"Speed 2" is inescapably a movie where most people, including a largely unchallenged Bullock, are doing no more than going through the paces. When her stressed-out character says, "I swear I'm never leaving the house again," it's to be hoped that future "Speed" sequels are what she's ruling out.

NEW YORK, 7/7/97, p. 54, David Denby

In *Men in Black*, Tommy Lee Jones deals with anyone who knows too much about the aliens by holding up a skinny little instrument and blanking out his memory. That is what I imagine the studios would like to do to the film audience—wash out our memories of recent summer block-busters. so they could start all over. In *Speed 2,* you can feel the desperation of Jan De Bont as he tries to top things he did in the original *Speed.* This one's set aboard a cruise ship, and Sandra Bullock is back but with a new daredevil partner, Jason Patric, who replaces Keanu Reeves. There's also a new villain, Willem Dafoe, who apparently has more teeth than William F. Buckley. Dafoe plays a disappointed maritime-software designer who got fired and now wants to destroy the ship whose computer systems he devised. Of course he can't simply blow a hole in the ship's hull below the water line—if he did, there would be no summer-season movie. Grinning and popping his eyes, Dafoe booby-traps the liner, causing engines to overheat, fire doors to lock, the ship's course to change—he does everything but place carpenter ants in the bingo lounge.

The first *Speed* worked an enormous number of changes on the simple theme of a bus that had to keep going fast or blow up: the movie was exciting and even elegant because the restricted situation forced the filmmakers to invent. But this movie is just silly—an endless chase through studio-set corridors. There's a fairly exciting sequence in which Patric, underwater, tries to wrap a cable around the propeller to stop the ship from plowing into a tanker, but most of the action is whipped-up nonsense made dynamic by rapid cutting. In the grand finale. the ship plows into a little town on St. Martin, coming right down the street long after a real ship would have run aground.

The big summer movies have created the means of their own extinction. They have become more and more ludicrous, and now some of us feel like pashas who have seen too many naked bodies: we didn't ask to become jaded, but still we are stupefied by the sight of immense resources wasted on idiotic stories. We can refresh ourselves by seeing small movies—or by quitting altogether.

NEW YORK POST, 6/13/97, p. 49, Thelma Adams

Sink the Love Boat! Welcome to "Speed 2: Cruise Control."

Three summers ago, director Jan De Bont leapt to the Hollywood A List on the back of an L.A. bus in "Speed." Last summer, he tore up screens with "Twister."

This summer, De Bont deserves a vacation. What he gets is Willem Dafoe's leech-loving computer psycho hijacking a cruise ship in the Caribbean. All we get is a cumbersome actioner that works very, very hard to top its predecessor.

The first "Speed" was a fluke hit, a lean and mean action machine mounted on the unlikely chassis of a Los Angeles bus. It also had the combustible pairing of Keanu Reeves, making his first run at action stardom, and Sandra Bullock, not yet a marquee name.

"Speed 2" is more predictable, another movie of mass destruction.

It begins with a wink to the original: Annie (Bullock) fails a driving test while speedily explaining away Keanu's Jack.

"Relationships based on extreme circumstances never work out," she tells the terrified driving examiner (Tim Conway, in a welcome comic cameo).

Jack's gone, long live Alex (Jason Patric). Annie's new beau is another daredevil cop, which simplifies things for formula-following writers Randall McCormick and Jeff Nathanson.

Annie and Alex look great together, and they tingle when they touch, but they have commitment issues.

What better way to solve them than by cruising the Caribbean? This leads to the movie's romantic thread—a case of proposal interruptus—and puts the square-jawed duo right in Dafoe's path.

Geiger (Dafoe) has a bee in his bonnet—or a leech on his body—because years of designing computer navigational systems have poisoned his physique with copper.

Once he became terminally ill, the cruise company that "leeched" Geiger's expertise tossed him overboard. Now the cyber-nut wants payback—and he doesn't mean shuffleboard and midnight buffets.

How Geiger can control an entire cruise ship from a computer wristband when I can't even get my fax modem to work is another question for the writers, but let's take it on faith. He plots a course for disaster; Alex and Annie must save the day.

Having set up a high-tech, high-seas hijacking, De Bont overloads the adventure. Explosions, collisions, close encounters with propellers, looming cliffs and oil tankers—the series of events that build to the ramming of St. Martin drag on the suspense. Call it the slow boat to China syndrome.

After St. Martin's fall, a final, breathless, humor-spiked speed-boat chase pulls "Speed 2" out of disaster-movie disaster. The reason we still care by the end is that Patric makes a straight-ahead, muscular, morally grounded action hero—and the sparks between the "Sleepers" star and Bullock can't be doused, even if they play half their scenes soaking wet.

NEWSDAY, 6/13/97, Part II/p. B3, Jack Mathews

I'm rushing across the street to hail a cab after a screening of Jan De Bont's "Speed 2: Cruise Control" when an elderly woman going the other way catches my attention.

"Excuse me," she says. "'Swan Lake.' One intermission, or two?"

Somehow, it's the perfect ending to a surreally bad night. First, I'm dumbfounded sitting through an action movie that showcases not one single exhilarating scene or enticing idea, then stumped by a question hurled at me from the twilight zone. "I don't know," I answer, apologetically.

The next day, as I tap these words into my computer, my mind keeps returning to the conundrum of "Swan Lake." Why did the lady want to know? Why did she ask me? Would that I could beat these odds in the lottery.

There are no lingering questions over "Speed 2." Like Steven Spielberg's "Jurassic Park" sequel last month, this is merely a return to the gold mine. The first film, a brilliantly shot thriller about a bus on the run, exploded onto screens in the summer of '94, making stars of director De Bont, LAPD daredevil Keanu Reeves and cute-as-a-button bus driver Sandra Bullock, and making a sequel mandatory.

But a bus doesn't have the follow-up potential of an island chockablock with dinosaurs, so "Speed 2" had to literally find another vehicle. And the best De Bont and his screenwriters Randall McCormick and Jeff Nathanson could come up with was a Love Boat.

The ship is the Seabourn Legend, Caribbean-bound with a passenger list that includes Bullock's blathering Annie; her new boyfriend, Alex (Jason Patric), a modest SWAT team hero, and Geiger (Willem Dafoe), a disgruntled former cruise line employee who pops pills and bathes with leeches while plotting a takeover of the ship. Seems that in designing, the Seabourn's sophisticated computer system, Geiger was exposed to metal toxins that left him terminally ill, which, in turn, cost him his job, which, in turn, makes him scarier than a postal employee carrying a brown bag.

If you've seen the trailer, you know the rest of the story. The ship gets locked in on a course headed full steam for, first, an oil tanker, and, second, a picturesque island resort harbor. Can Alex and Annie outwit Geiger and save this ship of fools? Will Alex get up the nerve to propose to Annie by the final reel? Will the deaf child and the frisky dog be rescued?

"Speed 2," like most banal sequels, makes the mistake of overplaying the presumed strengths of the original. In this case, that's Bullock's innate cuteness, her ability to smile away her characters' gabby airheadedness. A recent poll had Bullock ranked 62nd on a list of America's most "fun personalities." Surrounded as she is by death and terror in "Speed 2," she's going for No. 1.

De Bont, who sandwiched "Twister" between his two "Speeds," has attributed the success of the first film to the audiences' concern for the characters. A pretty weird delusion. It succeeded because of its nifty premise—a bus is rigged to explode when its speed dips below 50—and because of its super-executed, nonstop action pace. There's plenty of action in "Speed 2," as well, but at no time does it equal the suspense, tension or originality of the first film.

I've never been more aware of an action film's score, and it's because the music is doing all the work for scenes that have no emotional impact of their own. Composer Mark Mancina has to cover for the stars, too. There's no chemistry whatsoever between Patric and Bullock.

To his credit, Dafoe seems to be having more genuine fun than anyone else. Geiger is a pure psychopath, and not since Scott Glenn swallowed a worm in "Urban Cowboy" has an actor had a more disgusting scene than the one where Dafoe plucks live leeches from a container and sets them, sucker-side down, on his bare chest.

But that's as good as it gets in this tedious wretch of a movie. One intermission, or two? I wish.

SIGHT AND SOUND, 8/97, p. 53, Richard Falcon

Three years after her adventure with a runaway bus, Annie Porter is now dating Alex Shaw, an LA cop who has told her he works a safe bicycle patrol on Venice Beach. During a driving test, she blunders into a high-speed motorcycle pursuit, to discover Alex is a SWAT daredevil. He mollifies her with a Caribbean cruise aboard the luxury liner *Seabourn Legend*, on which he intends to propose.

On the ship, a fellow passenger, John Geiger—a designer of computer systems for luxury cruisers—embittered after being sacked for being terminally ill, plants timers and explosives around the ship and hacks into the ship's computer system. Forcing the crew to evacuate the ship after throwing the captain overboard, Geiger steals a guest's diamond collection and puts the ship on auto pilot to collide with a supertanker in the harbour off the island of St Martin.

Alex and Annie save passengers trapped in a hanging lifeboat and—after flooding the hold in a vain attempt to slow the ship down—Alex rescues 14-year-old Drew, a hearing-impaired girl trapped in a lift. Alex fails to block the ship's propellers with the anchor line, and Geiger escapes, taking Annie hostage. Alex and ship's photographer Dantes use the submerged bow thrusters and the anchors to avert the collision, but the liner then crashes into the harbour and the centre of town. After a high-speed chase, Alex rescues Annie from Geiger's seaplane and Geiger crashes into the tanker, dying in the inferno. Annie now accepts Alex's proposal.

"You'll never drive in this town again," says Annie's driving instructor after *Speed 2 Cruise Control*'s promisingly kinetic opening chase sequence. But with the shift from the freeways of LA to the open sea comes a cargo of insuperable problems, which bedevil the breathless adrenaline rush a *Speed* sequel demands. The camera swoops desperately around the 459-foot liner in an attempt to simulate the excitement of velocity, but while this may evoke the director Jan De Bont's cinematography on *The Hunt for Red October*, it makes the instructor's *bon mot* seem an admission of defeat.

With former *Speed* star Keanu Reeves spending more time with his rock band, Jason Patric's task as Alex is to be the genre's most inconspicuous action hero, allowing Sandra Bullock as Annie to further define her star persona as the girl-next-door who rises to extreme circumstances. But with hero and heroine a team from the outset, the narrative has serious difficulty finding a use for her. Too much time is devoted to her quest to find out whether he is the kind of man she can "look after", and the static opening reel is unsuccessful screwball comedy, from driving lesson to lovers' bickering on the liner.

The passengers—including hearing-impaired Drew, two weight-watchers and a woman kicking cigarettes—veer perilously close to characters from a Zucker Brothers disaster spoof. However, Drew is also to some extent Annie's rival—a character clearly in need of an action hero to look after her. After the botched proposal, we see Annie watching Kubrick's *Lolita* on television and identifying herself with Sue Lyons (later Annie paints her toenails *Lolita*-style)—but the mixed messages here, about Annie's desires, show up the lack of any romantic spark between the leads which could have kept the opening reels afloat, besides opening up a fairly queasy subtext. Rescuing Drew from the flooded hold, Alex deals with Drew's sign-language declaration of love by using the line Annie had used to deflect his proposal, "relationships based on extreme circumstances never work out". Again the romantic dilemma is rendered paradoxical: with wafer-thin plotting like this, responses to extreme circumstances are all that can define both character and romance. Annie needs to be rescued and needs an action hero. The resulting comic-movie heroine can defuse a grenade without realising she is still holding it, can chainsaw open a locked door but forget to turn the chainsaw off and can race the villain on jet skis but needs her boyfriend's underwater kiss to save her from drowning.

Replacing Dennis Hopper's evocative madman, Dafoe has be a stereotyped villain motivated by revenge against what he describes as lack of "understanding from senior management" as he tips the ship's captain overboard. Despite a novel scene—Geiger takes a bath with a bottle of leeches—the emaciated actor contents himself with a by-the-numbers selection of strange giggles, teeth-baring and eye-rolling.

Which would all be beside the point if *Speed 2* delivered the popcorn. Despite the apparent rigours of shooting—with reports of the crew contending with three separate hurricanes—and the spectacular destruction of an island resort (a mixture of digital effects and a full-size replica of the ship's prow colliding into the set), *Speed 2* fails to excite in the set pieces. All urban audiences take lifts, buses and subways, but being trapped on the world's most luxurious liner requires a different kind of suspended disbelief. This shouldn't matter, but it is a mark of the film's lack of mastery over its own genre machinery that we become aware how little of it relates to a recognisable everyday environment—to what Richard Dyer defined, apropos *Speed,* as the "indispensable human coordinates of the real world". When these co-ordinates become blips on the ship's maritime radar, their absence leaves *Speed 2*, and us, all at sea.

TIME, 6/23/97, p. 79, Richard Schickel

The human propensity to tamper with a good thing is probably ineluctable. In the movie game it is known as the Curse of the Sequel Monster. Or, more properly, the Monster Sequel.

The latest, but surely not the last, case in point is *Speed 2: Cruise Control,* unworthy successor to the last action movie that ran as much on wit as it did on special effects. That film was in touch, however goofily, with some of our everyday anxieties—a runaway bus on a screwed-up freeway is not entirely beyond our ken. At the very least we can imagine being caught in the resulting traffic jam.

But a Caribbean cruise ship, its controls fritzed by a mad computer genius (there's no other kind in the movies these days) and set on a collision course first with a loaded oil tanker, then with a resort island? No, this is not a scenario that haunts our sleepless nights.

What's worse, that ship is packed with standard-issue fools, whose function is to react badly to all the movie's fires, floods and explosions. In this melee it's hard to develop characters we can get behind. Sandra Bullock, of course, is back as Annie, but the combination of pluck and vulnerability that made her so winsome in the Ur-*Speed* is missing here. This time she exists mainly to get tied up and abducted by Willem Dafoe, an actor who can never quite transcend (or enjoy) his inherent weirdness the way Dennis Hopper does. Jason Patric and his rippling pecs fill in for willowy Keanu Reeves as Annie's protector (and, in this case, lover). He's stalwart and athletic, but fundamentally uninteresting.

This is not entirely his fault. The screenwriters, Randall McCormick and Jeff Nathanson, and the director, Jan De Bont, have no interest in providing their actors with stuff to act. Their job is to keep the whammos coming. Our job is to sit there, absorb the blows and pretend to like their cold expertise. With De Bont's quick wit and tense minimalism on the first *Speed* still fresh in mind, that's hard work.

TIME, 6/30/97, p. 65, Richard Corliss

[*Speed: Cruise Control* was reviewed jointly with *The Lost World: Jurassic Park*; see Corliss' review of that film.]

VILLAGE VOICE, 6/24/97, p. 75, Justine Elias

Jan De Bont makes short work of action-movie clichés: It takes a mere 10 minutes for our intrepid-yet-helpless heroine to tell her new boyfriend (who's just thrown himself into the path of a speeding diaper truck, revealed that he's actually a member of LA.'s S.W.A.T. team, *and* hinted that he'd like to settle down), "I don't even know who you are anymore!" As entertainment, *Speed 2: Cruise Control* is so frantic, cluttered, and migraine-inducing that even the most avid explosion junkies may find it difficult to enjoy. De Bont, renowned cinematographer, made a famously assured directorial debut with *Speed,* a streamlined thrill ride, that never violated its own mad logic. But his sequel is a product of and for disordered minds, a seemingly endless frenzy of vehicular destruction that always seems to be five minutes away from a finale that never arrives. Sandra Bullock seems to be in a major funk for much of the movie: though she's ostensibly the main character, she's made to whine that her holiday is ruined, even as the ship's going down and people are getting killed. Her savior this time around is Jason Patric, an incurably intense actor who can say more words, more authoritatively, than Keanu Reeves can. The villain is a disgruntled electronics genius (Willem Dafoe), who fumes and grimaces like one of the nasty apple trees in *The Wizard of Oz.* Whether he's dry-swallowing a handful of pills, attaching leeches to his body, or clubbing an over-friendly ship's porter in the head, Dafoe seems to be having a screamingly good time in an imaginary theme park called Summer Movie Land. Too bad he's the only one who knows how to get in.

Also reviewed in:
NEW YORK TIMES, 6/13/97, p. C12, Janet Maslin
NEW YORKER, 7/7/97, p. 77, Anthony Lane
VARIETY, 6/16-22/97, p. 34, Emanuel Levy
WASHINGTON POST, 6/13/97, p. B1, Stephen Hunter
WASHINGTON POST, 6/13/97, Weekend/p. 41, Desson Howe

SPIKE AND MIKE'S 1997 FESTIVAL OF ANIMATION

A Mellow Manor Productions release of an international collection of animated shorts. *Running time:* 89 minutes. *MPAA Rating:* Not Rated.

LOS ANGELES TIMES, 4/4/97, Calendar/p. 12, Kristine McKenna

If you head for "Spike & Mike's 1997 Festival of Animation" with visions of Betty Boop dancing in your head, be warned: They don't make cartoons like they used to.

Opening today at the Nuart, this year's animation survey comprises 14 shorts, only five of which use pen and ink. Whereas mainstream animation has come to be dominated by the brightly bland Disney style, underground animation is in the grip of clay animation, a technique combining clay figures and stop-action photography.

Anyone familiar with work by giants of animation such as Max and Dave Fleischer, Tex Avery or Chuck Jones must be forgiven for dismissing clay animation as strictly for amateurs. During the '30s, one recalls, the Fleischer brothers took animation to unprecedented heights with the creation of Betty Boop and Popeye the sailor, characters who resided in a hallucinatory universe that was truly amazing. The astonishing thing about Fleischer cartoons was the detail and depth of field; you could look far into their picture plane and discover all manner of things happening simultaneously, because every inch of the image was alive.

Only one short at the Nuart, British artist Karen Kelly's "Stressed," aspires to that degree of visual complexity—and she pulls it off, too. A cautionary tale about the pace of modern life, "Stressed" is a stunning montage of fluid, washy drawings that flicker by at an accelerating pace.

Three more shorts get high marks, but they succeed on wit rather than technical virtuosity. "Political Correction," a drawn short created at Cal Arts by Steve Fonti, is a hilarious sendup of the effects of political correctness on language: Refer to your dog as a "canine American," Fonti advises, lest he bite you on the leg.

Russian artist Louriy Tcherenkov's "The Great Migration," the story of a bird who loses his flock while flying south for the winter, derives its charm from the humor in Tcherenkov's drawings. His birds are ungainly creatures who are just as confused as the humans on the ground below them, and they flap their wings frantically in order to stay aloft.

Acing the clay animation division is British animator Nick Parks' Oscar-winning "A Close Shave." One in a series of adventures starring crackpot inventor Wallace and his dog Gromit, "A Close Shave" is infused with a loopy brilliance that puts one in mind of Jay Ward, the great American who gave us "Rocky and Bullwinkle." Park gets the clenched-jaw elocution peculiar to the British just right, and the idea of a detective story about sheep rustling in the heart of London—and a heroic lamb who trots around in a handknit sweater trimmed in pink—is so deliriously ridiculous you're willing to overlook the fact that clay animation moves with the jerky artificiality of a video game.

Also notable for its humor is Anthony Hodgson's "Hilary," a clay animation short that would work just as well as a spoken word radio drama; it's the voice-over monologue rather than the images that pull you into this story. Notable for their creepiness are clay animation shorts "Trainspotter" (about a blind man), "Barflies" (about drunk flies) and "Stiffy" (about a dead dog). The chance of a cartoon about a dead dog being amusing isn't good, and Canadian filmmaker Brian McPhail falls far short of the task.

VILLAGE VOICE, 6/24/97, p. 88, Dennis Lim

The original 'toonfest returns with a haphazard, passably entertaining mix of new work and established favorites (no Wallace or Gromit, but Bill Plympton's *Nosehair,* for one, has been on the program before). This year's two obvious duds are Steven Fonti's *Political Correction,* a facile spoof of p.c. lingo, unamusingly attired as a *Schoolhouse Rock* number, and Mike Johnson's *The Devil Went Down to Georgia,* a mediocre music video (with Primus's Les Claypool on vocals to boot). Most of the other lows can be ascribed to a regrettably widespread weakness for gross-out humor (the very kind cultivated by Spike & Mike's companion, the Sick & Twisted Festival).

Amid the blur of claymation and stop-motion, computer images and pencil sketches, the visual standout is *Stressed* Karen Kelly's flickering montage of expressionist watercolor squiggles. Top honors, however, must go to Anthony Hodgson, for *Hilary,* a droll bedtime story that starts off deadpan creepy, but nimbly sneaks in a tender coda.

Also reviewed in:
CHICAGO TRIBUNE, 6/5/98, Friday/p. G, John Petrakis
NEW YORK TIMES, 6/20/97, p. C12, Stephen Holden

SPRUNG

A Trimark Pictures release of a Darin Scott production. *Executive Producer:* Mark Amin. *Producer:* Darin Scott. *Director:* Rusty Cundieff. *Screenplay:* Rusty Cundieff. *Director of Photography:* Joao Fernandes. *Editor:* Lisa Bromwell. *Music:* Stanley Clarke. *Sound:* Oliver L. Moss. *Production Designer:* Terrence Foster. *Art Director:* Jim Moores. *Set Decorator:* Melanie Paizis. *Costumes:* Tracey White. *Running time:* 105 minutes. *MPAA Rating:* R.

CAST: Tisha Campbell (Brandy); Rusty Cundieff (Montel); Paula Jai Parker (Adina); Joe Torry (Clyde); John Witherspoon (Detective); Jennifer Lee (Veronica); Clarence Williams, III (Grand Daddy).

LOS ANGELES TIMES, 5/14/97, Calendar/p. 8, John Anderson

[*The following review by John Anderson appeared in a slightly different form in*
NEWSDAY, 5/14/97, Part II/p. B13.]

By burlesquing rap culture almost to the point of absurdity, the talented young writer-director-actor Rusty Cundieff made the mockumentary "Fear of a Black Hat" into one of the funnier movies of recent years.

Cundieff again proves himself adept with the new romantic comedy "Sprung," which is genre-busting without being a pretentious pain. While it can be viewed on one level as a straight, bawdy reading on the current condition of love, the new film sends up both the extremes of much African American comedy and the self-conscious, cloying qualities of over-earnest film romance in general. Imagine "Four Weddings and a Funeral" meets "Booty Call."

Like "Four Weddings," Cundieff's "Sprung"—a term referring to the condition whereby one's perfectly normal self-absorption has been undone by love—opens with Montel (Cundieff) arriving late for a wedding. We assume it's his, but it doesn't matter. From this point, we flash back to the auguries of tortured romance between Montel and Brandy (Tisha Campbell), an affair destined to be blighted by all the usual afflictions of '90s love—money, sexism, perilous assumptions—but mostly by the misguided attempts at matchmaking/breaking by their friends Clyde (Joe Torry) and Adini (Paula Jai Parker).

Clyde is an iron-pumping, gold-lamé-wearing, burger-joint-managing man on the prowl, whose tools of courtship include a borrowed Porsche and a purloined ATM receipt. At a sorority party, he and Montel meet Brandy and Adina. Adina is the queen of the gold diggers, whose assessment of available men begins at their wallets: Through her mind's eye we see the kind of instantaneous computer readouts used in films like "The Hunt for Red October" but that for Adina provide appraisals of phony Rolexes and cheap suits. The fantasy visuals work both ways. When Montel and Clyde first arrive, they visualize Brandy in a baby-doll nightie and Adina decked out as a dominatrix.

Clyde's counterfeit wealth fools Adina; they go to bed and engage in what might be called Extreme Sex. When she finds out she's been played, her revenge is ugly—and funny. Montel and Brandy, meanwhile, develop a more meaningful relationship, which upsets Clyde and Adina—because it means they'll have to see more of each other.

En route to real love and hot sex, there's a lot of playful, stylized mischief executed by Cundieff—Adina looks in the mirror and sees a lollipop labeled "sucker"; when she belts Clyde, little birds circle his head. Cundieff is casting his characters as cartoonish, if not outright cartoons, but his willingness to be this goofy is refreshing.

Montel's love talk can be cloying—Cundieff himself is not quite as convincing as his co-stars—and the structure of "Sprung" is a bit stilted: This kind of four-handed game of hot pursuit has been done to death. But it's a genuinely romantic and genuinely funny film. Cundieff's story is dedicated to the proposition that real love exists—and is available, if you're honest enough. The movie is honest, too, about the silly things people often do for love.

NEW YORK POST, 5/14/97, p. 39, Bill Hoffmann

Remember the frat boy in "Animal House" who has a dead drunk nymphet in his room and is wrestling with his conscience about what to do?

On one side of his brain, the devil is taunting him to ravage her without mercy. "Don't do it!" begs an angel on the other side.

If you recall those opposite ends, you've got a good idea of what to expect in "Sprung," Rusty Cundieff's energetic, if one-note comedy about a pair of pals hunting for babes.

Clyde (Joe Torry) is a jive, sex-mad ladies man whose non-stop goal is to end up in the sack, while Montel (Rusty Cundieff) wants romance and commitment before anything else.

They meet their matches in Adina (Paula Jai Parker), a gold-digger who wants her men wealthy, and Brandy (Tisha Campbell), a good-hearted girl leery of the male species, period.

After Clyde tricks Adina into thinking he's loaded, the duo have acrobatic sex as funny as it is heated.

Meanwhile, Brandy and Montel fall for each other, sending their sexed-up friends into a desperate mission to bust them up.

This leads to a fast-paced succession of deceptions, emotional eruptions and a predictable happy ending.

The material grows tiresome after a while. You can only listen to endless chatter about sex for so long after all.

"Sprung" has some hilarious moments, but its one-note characters and plodding script boil down to just another case of "been there, done that."

VILLAGE VOICE, 5/20/97, p. 80, Gary Dauphin

This fitfully funny tale of romance hatched, foiled, and then regained starts out with light-skinned nice guy Montel (director Rusty Cundieff) being tutored in black-mack style by his darker bud Clyde (the ever reliable Joe Torry). The gotta-be-hard nostrums sound like audition tips for *Booty Call 2*, but since this movie is mostly about *acting* black, the fellas hook up with freak Adina (Paula Jai Parker doing a gold-digger routine that's so single-minded it's almost impressive) and nice girl Brandy (Tisha Campbell). Clyde trades rutting-dog/Mandingo love-scene notes with Adina, while Montel and Brandy just get "sprung," their niceness combining into a spun-sugar thing they call love. Clyde and Adina join forces to first break their friends up and then bring them back together, their combined energies keeping the film modestly forward propelled.

Director Cundieff *(Fear of a Black Hat, Tales From the Hood)* has always struck me as a smart guy, but he struggles mightily trying to put dog-movie yuks in the service of his better and wryly ironic instincts. To make a smart dog movie you have to be kind of crazy, I think, diving into the mire of sexual stereotypes that surround black people and swimming until you either drown or come out the other side covered in shit yet transformed. For better or worse, *Sprung* and Cundieff are just a little too nice for that.

Also reviewed in:
NEW YORK TIMES, 5/14/97, p. C16, Lawrence Van Gelder
VARIETY, 5/19-25/97, p. 49, Andrew Hindes
WASHINGTON POST, 5/16/97, Weekend/p. 45, Stephen Hunter

SQUEEZE

A Miramax Films and Robbins Entertainment release of a ca.thar.tic filmWorks and Danan/Moreno Films production in association with Dorchester Youth Association Collaborative Extreme Close-Up. *Executive Producer:* Mitchell B. Robbins. *Producer:* Ari Newman, Garen Topalian, Stephanie Danan, and Patricia Moreno. *Director:* Robert Patton-Spruill. *Screenplay:* Robert Patton-Spruill. *Director of Photography:* Richard Moos. *Editor:* Richard Moos. *Music:* Bruce Flowers. *Sound:* Lenny Manzo. *Production Designer:* Maximillian Cutler. *Art Director:* Ben Dulong. *Set Dresser:* William Sutherland. *Costumes:* Sheila Gentile. *Make-up:* Robert Fitz. *Special Effects:* Brian Ricci. *Stunt Coordinator:* Norman Mclean. *Running time:* 89 minutes. *MPAA Rating:* R.

CAST: Tyrone Burton (Tyson); Eddie Cutanda (Hector); Phuong Duong (Bao); Geoffrey Rhue (JJ); Russell G. Jones (Tommy); Leigh Williams (Marcus); Robert Agredo (Uzi); Beresford Bennett (Derick); Jennifer Maxcy (Lisa); Harlem Logan (Fiend); Diane Beckett (Aunt C.); Ingrid Askew (Pearl); James Spruill (Psychiatrist); William Butler (Jason); Daryl Bugg (Mason); Maleah Liggins (Tisha); Pinky Lugo (Pinky); Milagros Jones (Angela); James Spruill (Homeless Man); Catherine Oberg (Cat Fighter); Patrick Ruth (Male Catfighter); Sean Henderson (Bad Kid #1); Johnny Henderson (Bad Kid #2); Lynda Patton and Georgette Leslie (Women in Car); Bruce Serefin (Police Officer); Gerry Nuzollo (Gas Station Attendant); Jessica Edwards (Marrisa); Victor Nunez (Julio); Alfred Rivera (Doorman); John Bonaparte (Man with Burning Book); Juanita Rodriguez (Youth Center Receptionist); Monique Douglas (Female Yuth Worker); Sparkle Henderson, Nicole Kelly, and Melissa Khomblassen (Girls with Rakes); Aaron Stewart and Roy J. Lynch (Barbers); Max Cutler (Hospital Patient).

LOS ANGELES TIMES, 6/13/97, Calendar/p. 8, Kevin Thomas

[The following review by Kevin Thomas appeared in a slightly different form in **NEWSDAY, 6/13/97, Part II/p. B8.]**

"Squeeze" is the perfect title for Robert Patton-Spruill's sensitive and comprehensive depiction of the world of three teenage boys from some of Boston's meaner streets, where the pressures on them to enter a life of crime become increasingly intense. "Squeeze" grew out of Patton-Spruill's experiences in conducting acting workshops at the Dorchester Youth Collaborative, an anti-violence media arts organization in the old suburban Boston neighborhood in which virtually the entire film was shot.

While making the point that creative youth centers can be life-savers, Patton-Spruill resists preachiness. If anything, we don't get enough of the idea of what the programs at the center in his film really are—the kids seem perpetually raking leaves around the neighborhood.

No matter; the center's leader JJ, as played with admirable persuasiveness by Geoffrey Rhue, suggests vividly what a challenge is to rescue kids teetering on the edge of an urban abyss. In this instance, the boys who concern JJ are Tyson (Tyrone Burton), a bright 14-year-old African American, and his best pal Hector (Eddie Cutanda), who is Puerto Rican. Occasionally they hang out with Bao (Phuong Duong), a Vietnamese refugee every bit as much a homeboy as Ty and Hector. They are such likable, good-humored guys you quickly want nothing bad to happen to them.

Danger, however, not surprisingly looms swiftly and seriously. The boys are earning a little money filling gas and cleaning windshields at a neighborhood station when a local gang drives them off, claiming the boys invaded its turf.

In anger, Hector leads an attack on one of the gang members but doesn't stop there; he steals the guy's money despite Ty's feeling that this theft is a huge mistake. He feels his and Hector's lives are suddenly in such danger he must seek protection from the local drug lord, who offers it—in exchange for the boys peddling his drugs on the street.

Working from stories written by Dorchester Youth Collaborate cofounder Emmett Folgert, Patton-Spruill suggests how such a chain of events can occur with a rapidity that is downright dizzying, making us feel powerfully the sheer precariousness of these boys' existence and the huge effort it takes by concerned individuals like JJ even to attempt a rescue that, should it succeed, might well prove tentative at best. At the same time Patton-Spruill suggests with equal force that Ty and Hector have at some point got to take a step back and decide what paths they're going to try to take with their lives.

For all of its passionate concerns—and surely because of them—Patton-Spruill has created a whirlwind of a movie, fast-moving and exciting. These concerns are vividly expressed through Richard Moos' constantly moving camera and Bruce Flowers vital score, incorporating lots of rap music that contributes both energy and commentary. But what makes "Squeeze" really work, of course, are the completely natural portrayals of its three charismatic young stars—Burton, Cutanda and Duong.

NEW YORK POST, 6/14/97, p. 27, Bill Hoffmann

A tiny picture called "Squeeze" squeezes into theatres this weekend in the shadows of such blockbusters as "Con Air" and "The Lost World."

That takes guts. But "Squeeze" has plenty.

This little movie—made on a bus-fare budget—has as many visceral thrills and wrenching dramas as most of the power-charged, Dolby-enhanced box-office monsters you'll catch this summer.

Director Robert Patton-Spruill takes us through the dark and grimy backstreets of the Dorchester section of Boston as three 13-year-old street kids are jettisoned into a hair-raising fight for their lives.

As played by Tyrone Burton, Eddie Cutanda and Phuong Duong, these lads are streetwise but straight, swaggering but sweet.

But trouble erupts when they beat up a nasty crack dealer and grab his wad of cash.

That's like signing their own death warrant, and the chase is on as the kids hit the pavement in a desperate effort to stay alive.

What gives this film much of its power is the natural, unaffected acting or the young trio, whom director Patton-Spruill plucked from a theater group of troubled kids called Extreme Close Up, in Dorchester.

There are some missteps: The use of freeze frames at the end of key scenes seems stagy; some heavy-handed symbolism doesn't work—particularly a gruesome and unnecessary scene of a hamster being crushed by a snake; and the last 15 minutes have one too many climaxes.

Still, "Squeeze" works. It's also nice to see Miramax releasing the kind of independent film it was famous for before being bought by Disney.

VILLAGE VOICE, 6/17/97, p. 66, Amy Taubin

An affecting after-school special, *Squeeze* centers around a director-actor collaboration. Robert Patton-Spruill developed his first feature while working with young performers in Extreme Close Up, an acting troupe nurtured by the Dorchester Youth Collaborative, a Boston-area center for at-risk teenagers.

The film focuses on three 13-year-olds (Tyrone Burton, Eddie Cutanda, and Phuong Duong), who beat up a vicious crack dealer for disrespecting them and then make a bad mistake by impulsively stealing his money. In desperate need of protection, they take refuge in a youth center by day and deal crack for their nemesis's rival at night.

Patton-Spruill has an eye for off-kilter compositions and kinetic camera movements that are expressive of his young protagonists' terrors and desires. Visually arresting, the film is never slick or hyped-up. The ensemble acting is exceptionally honest and Tyrone Burton—who carries the heaviest narrative load— has an emotional intensity and fluidity that's rare in adolescent performers. Miramax, which, for the most part, has been cold-shouldering films this small, knows it's never too early to cozy up to talent.

Also reviewed in:
NEW YORK TIMES, 6/13/97, p. C8, Anita Gates
VARIETY, 4/29-5/5/96, p. 135, Daniel M. Kimmel

STAR MAPS

A Fox Searchlight Pictures release of a Flan De Coco Films production in association with King Pictures. *Executive Producer:* Esther Shapiro, Chris Iovenko, Scott King, Mitchell Kelly, and Beth Colt. *Producer:* Matthew Greenfield. *Director:* Miguel Arteta. *Screenplay:* Miguel Arteta. *Story:* Miguel Arteta and Matthew Greenfield. *Director of Photography:* Chuy Chavez. *Editor:* Jeff Betancourt, Tom McArdle, and Tony Selzer. *Music:* Lysa Flores. *Music Editor:* Thomas Morse. *Sound:* Yehuda Maayan. *Sound Editor:* Donald Sylvester. *Production Designer:* Carol Strober. *Casting:* Belinda Gardea. *Set Decorator:* Natalie Cohen. *Set Dresser:* David L. Bush. *Costumes:* Melanie Stavinski. *Make-up:* Melanie Stavinski. *Stunt Coordinator:* B.J. Davis. *Running time:* 95 minutes. *MPAA Rating:* R.

CAST: Douglas Spain (Carlos); Efrain Figueroa (Pepe); Kandeyce Jorden (Jennifer); Martha Velez (Teresa); Lysa Flores (Maria); Annette Murphy (Letti); Robin Thomas (Martin); Vincent Chandler (Juancito); Al Vicente (Fred); Herbert Siguenza (Cantinflas' Ghost); Jeff Sanna (Frank Rivers); Jeff Michalski (Bartender); Beth Colt (Carmel County Stage Manager); Zak Penn and Michael White (Carmel County Writers); Alisa Steen (Carmel County Casting Director); Anna Padgett (Nanny); Danny De La Paz (Hotel Guard); Mark Beltzman (Angry Customer); Hana Delaney (Bel Air Woman); Bill Gordon (Bel Air Man); Andrew Garcia (Young Carlos); T.J. Forster (Jennifer's Son); Kate Movius (Carmel County Actress); Joshua Fardon (Carmel County Actor); Adam Parker (Man Mistaken for Customer); Joe Mayesh (Guard at Gate); Michael Caldwell (Tourist); Rachel Winfree (Tourist Woman); Doug Kieffer (Waiter).

LOS ANGELES TIMES, 7/23/97, Calendar/p. 1, Kenneth Turan

The selling of maps to movie stars' homes is one of those only-in-L.A. institutions, right up there with Forest Lawn, Angelyne and the Doo-Dah Parade. A different kind of local landmark are the young people who dream of stardom, who want to become bigger than life themselves. "Star Maps" joins both of these L.A. preoccupations in an unusual kind of film package.

A word-of-mouth success at this year's Sundance Film Festival, "Star Maps" is balanced between contrivance and reality. Heavy on melodramatic elements, it nevertheless exerts a powerful emotional pull. That's because a truth exists underneath the quasi-clichéd situations, a truth that is unlikely but undeniable.

Part of what makes "Star Maps" different is its potentially exploitative subject matter, its fictional thesis that some of those cute young people out there selling maps on our streets are in reality male prostitutes on call to potential customers of both sexes. Writer-director Miguel Arteta has given this story both sweetness and edge, as well as an explosive father-son relationship that is a considerable strength.

Though he's coming into town on a bus from Mexico, 18-year-old Carlos (Douglas Spain) grew up in L.A. and has only been gone for two years. In that time, however, the dream of becoming an actor and a star has so taken him over that the fantasy follows him everywhere.

The reality Carlos has to deal with would drive anyone to dreaming. His mother Teresa (Martha Velez) has had a nervous breakdown and enjoys imaginary conversations with the ghost of the great Mexican actor Cantinflas. His brother Juancito (Vincent Chandler) has become a damaged couch potato. And his sister Maria (singer Lysa Flores, who also put together the film's driving soundtrack) is chafing at her role as the sane caregiver who holds everything together.

There is a father in this family, and he is the film's most frightening and most involving character. Pepe (Efrain Figueroa) is a pimp who was turned out onto the street by his own father and is intent on doing the same thing with his son. Abusive, with a pimp's terrifying charm, Pepe scoffs at his son's ambitions. "I had dreams, but my father taught me to be a man," he says, convinced that he knows what is best for Carlos.

As for Carlos, though unwilling to give up on his dream, he's willing to work for his father for a chance to connect with some of the Hollywood types Pepe says he knows. "I'm not going to let it get to me," he confidently tells his sister, but, as with most 18-year-olds, the shy and earnest Carlos turns out to be not nearly as tough and street-wise as he imagines.

Given some rudimentary training by Letti (Annette Murphy), Pepe's hooker girlfriend who also isn't as wised up as she thinks she is, Carlos is placed on L.A. street corners with a sign and maps and told "stand here and look pretty."

It's in what happens to Carlos on that corner that "Star Maps" gets more difficult to credit. Jennifer (Kandeyce Jorden), the gorgeous lead in a popular TV show, turns out to be a star maps client, addicted to extramarital sex with impoverished Latinos. She connects with Carlos and offers to help him with his career, but this is not to Pepe's liking, and how that complicated equation works out is where the drama of "Star Maps" lies.

Though Carlos and his dreams are pleasant to experience, it's the son's interaction with a father devoid of family feeling that is the emotional core. While parts of "Star Maps" are awkward, predictable and not quite believable, the film's confidence when dealing with this particular relationship never falters. It gives the film a bedrock veracity it wouldn't otherwise have, and allows the story to make more of an impact than some of those flaws would have you believe.

NEW YORK POST, 7/23/97, p. 42, Thelma Adams

Meet Hollywood's invisibles: the gardener with the leaf blower; the washer-woman waiting for the Wilshire bus dwarfed by shopping bags; the boy selling "Star Maps" to stars' homes.

These are Hollywood's living extras, the brown-faced workers without speaking roles. They are the L.A. kin of the Mexican deaf-mutes of today's headlines. They have risen a few steps up the immigrant ladder from the slave laborers who dole out baseball keychains, whose faces we ignore as we bury our noses in the newspaper on the subway.

With "Star Maps," Miguel Arteta makes the invisible visible. His honest, if awkward, debut gained the writer-director visibility at this year's Sundance Film Fest with an inspired Hollywood hook: What if those Chicano youths were only selling maps as a cover for a male prostitution ring? It's "El Norte" meets "Johns."

Arteta takes audiences on a guided Greyhound Bus tour of Hollywood's invisibles with Carlos (newcomer Douglas Spain) riding shotgun. With a face that glows like the moon (according to his mother, well-played by Martha Velez), bedroom eyes and a teasing mole that rivals Cindy Crawford's, Carlos doesn't plan to stay invisible for long.

Carlos "sells maps" for his father, Pepe (Efrain Figueroa, a tightly coiled, square-headed smoothy in the Harvey Keitel vein). But the boy has Sunset Boulevard dreams: he wants to become the next Antonio Banderas. He envisions his face on the cover of Spin with the headline: "Carlos! Carlos! Carlos!"

The young man's dreams approach reality when Pepe pairs Carlos with Jennifer (Kandeyce Jorden), a breezy Jacqueline Bisset type who stars in a night-time soap. Carlos fantasizes about being Jennifer's co-star; she "just wants a poor Mexican boy to ..." mow her lawn, so to speak.

The plot is no more contrived than any other Hollywood fantasy; it's an Hispanic "Pretty Woman." Yet Arteta brings to certain moments a piercing union of beauty and pain, truth and impossibility, fantasy and reality.

In one kinky scene, Carlos and Pepe's mistress Letti (Annette Murphy) perform in front of an old, hairy mogul and his twentysomething wife. The paired couplings are grotesque, but oddly tender. Letti soothes the savage Carlos with embraces that border on making love—and yet he is still having sex with his father's girlfriend in front of strangers.

The set piece plays like a sex video choreographed by Frida Kahlo. With the Mexican artist's passion, if not her polish, Arteta has added to the vibrant, synthetic, contradictory Border Art movement while striving for a Hollywood dream of his own.

NEWSWEEK, 7/28/97, p. 69, David Ansen

It's the oldest story in the books—the innocent kid who hits Hollywood with dreams of stardom in his eyes and discovers the tarnish beneath the tinsel. But it doesn't feel old the way first time writer-director Miguel Arteta tells it here, with healthy swabs of melodrama, frank sexuality, a sprinkle of magic realism, a dark sense of humor and a rock *en español* beat. Carlos (Douglas Spain), a second-generation immigrant, returns from Mexico to his massively dysfunctional family in L.A. with fantasies of becoming the next Antonio Banderas. His father, Pepe (Efrain Figueroa), puts him on the street selling maps to stars' homes—Dad's clever cover for his prostitution ring. The sweet, ambitious Carlos doesn't care if his clients are men or women, as long as he gets to make Hollywood contacts, and he thinks he's hit pay dirt when he services Jennifer (Kandeyce Jorden), the star of a TV soap, who promises him a bit part. Complications ensue, what with a raging bull of a father, a crazy mom who talks to the spirit of Cantinflas. a hulking, retarded brother, a saintly sister trying to escape the family madness, and the demands of his hustling career—which obligate him to sleep with his father's mistress for the delectation of an appreciative gringo couple. It may sound sordid, but Arteta manages to bounce from brutality to comedy with only a few missteps—and without the sweaty moralism that usually attends melodrama. The low-budget "Star Maps" may not be fully realized, but it's fully alive.

VILLAGE VOICE, 7/29/97, p. 76, Amy Taubin

Looking at L.A. with outsider eyes, Miguel Arteta, like Godard and Brecht before him (to cite only the classiest progenitors), sees prostitution as a grand metaphor for economic and social relations as well as a literal fact of life.

Carlos (Douglas Spain), the sweet-faced, 18-year-old Chicano protagonist of Arteta's *Star Maps*, becomes a hustler (1) to please his Dad and (2) as a way of launching his movie career. Carlos' psycho father Pepe (Efrain Figueroa) is a pimp who was prostituted by *his* father and now wants his son to follow in his footsteps. When a satisfied customer offers Carlos a part on her TV show, Pepe twists arms to prevent his heir apparent from escaping his clutches.

Conceived under the influence of the Menendez case, *Star Maps* is a nasty comedy about dysfunctional Latino patriarchy. While the films most exploitable scene is an unappetizing bedroom four-way involving Carlos, Pepe's girlfriend, and the Anglo couple who have hired them to perform, Arteta is most inspired when he's orchestrating the family dinner-table scene from hell. However sluggishly it turns, *Star Maps*'s motor is fueled by oedipal rage more than racial or class conflicts.

No cookie-cutter indie, *Star Maps* is packed with ideas, most of them transgressive. With the positive-minority-images crowd already gunning for the film, I'd like to be more on its side than I am. Unfortunately, Arteta's filmmaking skills are not yet equal to his intelligence or ambition. The script meanders, the actors (with the exception of Spain, who has the catatonic appeal of the young Martin Sheen) are wooden, and the mise-en-scène is inexpressive. (Low-budget $2.5 million for worldwide rights after *Star Maps*'s not particularly auspicious Sundance debut? Could it be that the promise of young, kinky Latino sex (which, in fact, peters out after breasts are bared and hands fumble at waist bands) guarantees an audience? If so, constraints are no excuse for the endless succession of two-shots.) And, rather than carrying the film, the lively rock-en-español score only points up the tepidness of the imagery. (If this seems harsh, imagine what Buñuel or Arturo Ripstein would have made of this material.)

Also reviewed in:
NEW YORK TIMES, 7/23/97, p. C11, Janet Maslin
NEW YORKER, 7/28/97, p. 78, Terrence Rafferty
VARIETY, 2/3-9/97, p. 49, Dennis Harvey
WASHINGTON POST, 8/22/97, Weekend/p. 36, Eve Zibart

STARSHIP TROOPERS

A TriStar Pictures and Touchstone Pictures release of a Jon Davison production. *Producer:* Jon Davison and Alan Marshall. *Director:* Paul Verhoeven. *Screenplay:* Ed Neumeier. *Based on the book by:* Robert A. Heinlein. *Editor:* Mark Goldblatt and Caroline Ross. *Music:* Basil Poledouris. *Music Editor:* Curtis Roush. *Sound:* Joseph Geisinger and (music) Tim Boyle. *Sound Editor:* Stephen Hunter Flick. *Casting:* Johanna Ray and Elaine J. Huzzar. *Production Designer:* Allen Cameron. *Art Director:* Steve Wolff and Bruce Robert Hill. *Set Decorator:* Bob Gould. *Set Dresser:* Mara Massey. *Special Effects:* John McLeod. *Creature Visual Effects:* Phil Tippett. *Spaceship Visual Effects:* Scott E. Anderson. *Costumes:* Ellen Mirojnick. *Make-up:* John Blake. *Stunt Coordinator:* Vic Armstrong. *Running time:* 129 minutes. *MPAA Rating:* R.

CAST: Casper Van Dien (Johnny Rico); Dina Meyer (Dizzy Flores); Denise Richards (Carmen Ibanez); Jake Busey (Ace Levy); Neil Patrick Harris (Carl Jenkins); Clancy Brown (Sgt. Zim); Seth Gilliam (Sugar Watkins); Patrick Muldoon (Zander Barcalow); Michael Ironside (Jean Rasczak); Rue McClanahan (Biology Teacher); Marshall Bell (General Owen); Eric Bruskotter (Breckinridge); Matt Levin (Kitten Smith); Blake Lindsley (Katrina); Anthony Ruivivar (Shujimi); Brenda Strong (Captain Deladier); Dean Norris (Commanding Officer); Christopher Curry (Mr. Rico); Lenore Kasdorf (Mrs. Rico); Tami-Adrian George (Djana'D); Teo (Corporal Bronski); Steven Ford (Lt. Willy); Ungela Brockman (Corporal Birdie); Curnal Aulisio (Sgt. Gillespie); Greg Travis (Net Correspondent); Bruce Gray (Sky Marshall Dienes); Denise Dowse (Sky Marshall Meru); John Cunningham (Fed Net Announcer); Julianna McCarthy and Timothy McNeil (Experts); Robert David Hall (Recruiting Sergeant); Brad Kane (Lanny); Amy Smart (Pilot Cadet); Timothy Omundson (Psychic); Patrick Bishop (Engineering Officer); Hunter Bodine (Young Cap Trooper); Travis Lowen (Little Boy Trooper); Patrick Wolff (Late Cadet); Mara Duronslet (Communications Officer); Dale A. Dye (General); Michael Stokey (Officer with Morita); Tyrone Tann (Student); Matt Entriken (Marco); Eric Dare (Medic); Ronald L. Botchan (Jumpball Referee); Walter Adrian (Judge); Stephanie Erb (Young Mother); Mylin Brooks (Female Trooper); Armand Darrius and Kai Lennox (Male Troopers).

LOS ANGELES TIMES, 11/7/97, Calendar/p. 1, Kenneth Turan

Forget the Terminator, it's the Exterminator you'll be looking for after experiencing "Starship Troopers." A film whose self-proclaimed motto is "Kill anything that has more than two legs," this picture has what it takes to premiere at a Roach Motel and be reviewed by the makers of Raid.

Based on Robert A. Heinlein's classic 1959 science-fiction novel, "Starship Troopers" presents the evildoers almost no one can abide, the one kind of villain not likely to hold press conferences protesting small-minded stereotyping. It's us vs. the bugs, big time, and as one character resolutely puts it, "we're in this for the species, boys and girls."

Put together by Paul Verhoeven ("RoboCop," "Basic Instinct," "Showgirls"), a director for whom excess is never enough, "Troopers" does not fit any reasonable definition of a quality motion picture. But it certainly is a jaw-dropping experience, so rigorously one-dimensional and free from even the pretense of intelligence it's hard not to be astonished and even mesmerized by what is on the screen.

Part of the reason is those darn bugs. Besides the hordes of gigantic Warriors, who attack in unstoppable waves like the Japanese in xenophobic World War II movies, there are flying bugs, crawling bugs, gargantuan fire-breathing Tanker bugs and even, Lord protect us, a deep-thinking Brain bug that knows lots more than we'd like it to.

Constructed out of a complex combination of model and miniature work and computer-generated imagery, "Starship Troopers'" impressive futuristic world of bugs, spaceships and total war makes you wonder about the sanity of the technicians who spent lonely hours making innumerable insects look good on camera. There must be less taxing ways to make a living.

But where "Starship Troopers" has it all over similar effects-laden efforts likes "Independence Day" and "Twister" is its complete lack of pretense. There's no mock emotion here, none of the nauseating pseudo-sensitivity that, for instance, marked Judd Hirsch's character in "Independence Day."

What Ed Neumeier's script provides instead is a cheerfully lobotomized, always watchable experience that has the simple-mindedness of a live-action comic book, with no words spoken that wouldn't be right at home in a funny paper dialogue balloon. Not just one comic book either, but an improbable and delirious combination of "Weird Science," "Betty and Veronica" and "Sgt. Rock and His Howling Commandos."

Also thrown into this high-energy mix, in case anyone was thinking of getting bored, is the fascist utopianism of the original Heinlein novel. Introduced via infomercials and news broadcasts playing on a computer screen, "Troopers" takes us to a militaristic future where video bulletins encourage young people to "Join the Mobile Infantry and save the world" and schools teach that "violence is the supreme authority" and nothing solves problems with the efficacy of "naked force."

"Troopers" opens with its own teaser trailer, a TV broadcast of Earth's attack on bug stronghold Klendathu, in the heart of the Arachnid Quarantine Zone, the dread AQZ. "This is an ugly planet, a bug planet," an on-screen reporter huffily reports before getting eviscerated on the spot by an understandably outraged local resident.

Now that it's got our attention, "Trooper" flashes back a year and goes into its Betty and Veronica mode, introducing its key characters as students at a high school located for unknown reasons in Buenos Aires. These youthful performers are by and large not familiar faces but they all have the shiny photogenic glow of a shampoo commercial, not to mention a sleek superficiality that makes Luke Skywalker seem like Hamlet by comparison.

Square-jawed hero Johnny Rico (Casper Van Dien) is captain of the football team and in love with the beautiful Carmen Ibanez (Denise Richards). But while Carmen is flirting with handsome Zander Barcalow (Patrick Muldoon), Johnny is oblivious to the fact that vixenish Dizzy Flores (Dina Meyer), his attractive quarterback (the game has changed some over the years), is carrying a major torch for him. And brainy Carl Jenkins (Neil Patrick Harris, TV's Doogie Howser) is too busy perfecting his mind-reading techniques to even have a girlfriend.

All this romantic plotting comes to a boil at graduation. Both Carmen and Zander head off to Fleet Academy to become hotshot pilots, and Johnny, under the influence of hard-nosed teacher Jean Rasczak (Michael Ironside), dismays his parents by joining the rugged Mobile Infantry in the hopes of impressing Carmen. And who should turn up in the same platoon but old pal Diz. Talk about complications.

Of course, everyone's personal life takes a back seat when those pesky bugs, who have been trouble before, launch a devastating sneak attack on Earth. Fearless, egoless and hard to kill, the bugs are a heck of an opponent and they seem to know that after years of skirmishing this will be a battle to the death.

A very messy death it turns out to be, for "Starship Troopers" offers no shortage of all manner of carnage. The bugs are both nuked and blown away by what's been reported as the most ammunition ever used in a major motion picture, while the hapless humans are repulsively chomped up, dismembered, impaled, beheaded and completely slimed on by the enemy. "Bugs don't take prisoners," our troops are warned and, for better and worse, neither does "Starship Troopers."

NEW YORK, 11/17/97, p. 72, David Denby

At the repulsive climax of *Starship Troopers*, which is about endless war between earthlings and giant outerplanetary spiders, a human captive is dragged forward and made to face an enormous "brain bug." At last! We're about to get an answer to the question tormenting us. Throughout the war, it's been understood that the bugs have been too stupid to win. But recently, arachnid intelligence has been improving. After all, they have managed to wipe out Buenos Aires (or is it all of South America? Anyway, they kill a lot of people). Where does the new intellectual prowess come from? Finally, we find out: The brain bug plunges a tubelike tentacle into the captive's head and sucks out his gray matter. So that's how they do it. But we wonder: Is there also a hidden metaphor here? Director Paul Verhoeven, who began his career back in the Netherlands with such elegant entertainments as *Soldier of Orange* and *The Fourth Man*, seems to have undergone, in Hollywood, a draining operation of his own. Since arriving here, Verhoeven has made not elegant entertainment but such violent near-trash as *RoboCop, Basic Instinct, Total Recall*, and *Showgirls*. Of course, Verhoeven is not likely to see the matter as I do. He's made *Starship Troopers* in the "ironic" style of current pop movies: The picture seems to be making fun of the very idiocy that it's so desperately packaging and selling to us. A director may relinquish his intelligence, but he still tries to save his self-respect. Pulling the rug out from under his own work, he may even convince himself that he's doing something witty.

In form, this depressing super-production is less science fiction than World War II platoon movie. just as in a picture like *Sands of Iwo Jima*, a group of guys gather together in basic training, go to war, and suffer triumph or death according to a strict plan of virtue rewarded and weakness punished. Verhoeven and screenwriter Ed Neumeier, adapting a Robert Heinlein novel, have moved the old generic war plot into the future, but with a feminist slant. The boys and girls now train together, stripping off their uniforms for communal showers, fighting and dying side by side. Physically, the men and women are just bodies—the men with square jaws, the women with full figures and tawny hair. The actors, obviously chosen for their muscular anonymity (Casper Van Dien? Dina Meyer?), deliver such lines as "A citizen has the courage to make the safety of the human race a personal responsibility" with the dim enthusiasm of teens in a beach-blanket movie. The simplicity, the gung ho, let's-kill-bugs spirit is no doubt meant satirically, but it will also function well in the international market. No one in Bangkok is likely to have the slightest trouble understanding *Starship Troopers*. Well-built, naked Americans and dead bugs are popular everywhere.

Verhoeven throws in a variety of government recruiting videos in which the bug-fighters are made to look like uniformed Fascist hordes. The videos are meant as satire, too. But of course it's these very Fascist hordes that the rest of the movie is celebrating—indeed, we are told that the world will be annihilated without them.

So what's the point of the joke? Verhoeven may be cheering himself up with these sportive flourishes, but he's not doing a thing for the rest of us. The spirit *of Starship Troopers* is grim and sanguinary. We spend most of our time watching men and women pump bullets into disgusting creatures that seem to be all sexual organs—waving green tentacles and devouring vulvas. Even though the special effects are spectacular (the creatures fly in, hop over rocks by the hundreds, erupt from underground), *Starship Troopers* is fatally lacking in lightness, play, invention. Human bodies are gutted and eviscerated, the limbs pulled off, the heads drilled. Are children supposed to enjoy this literal-minded, grisly bloodbath? As you watch the endless carnage, you become sure that Hollywood has gone completely, utterly mad. But how can you fight the success of "ironic" stupidity? Verhoeven may have had his brains removed, but it's the audience that winds up with a hole in the head.

NEW YORK POST, 11/7/97, p. 49, Michael Medved

"Starship Troopers" is such an blood-pumping, hyper-macho exercise the mere act of watching it may make moviegoers feel more muscular.

Loosely based on Robert Heinlein's classic novel, the streamlined story follows four high school friends who eagerly enlist in the military in order to earn citizenship in a New World Order of the future.

Played by an earnest but unknown cast of spectacularly attractive young people, these principals include a brilliant, buxom golden girl (Denise Richards), who trains as an elite starship pilot while her utterly infatuated boyfriend (chiseled-featured super-hunk Casper Van Dien) enrolls in the mobile infantry.

He's joined in that branch by dazzling, tousle-haired Dina Meyer, who's been trying to get his attention for years, while mutual pal Neil Patrick ("Doogie Howser) Harris uses mysterious psychic powers to advance rapidly in military intelligence.

All four friends soon find themselves caught up in all-out intergalactic war against a mysterious breed of giant extraterrestrial insects that menace life on Earth.

Early stages of the struggle show human forces grievously underestimating their hard-shelled foes and suffering appropriately grisly consequences.

Director Paul Verhoeven ("RoboCop," "The Fourth Man") ingeniously frames the action with amusing, ironic blasts of jingoistic propaganda that offer the 'official' version of events on the computer net of Earth's fascistic federation.

Entertaining details of training and discipline suggest timeless aspects of military organization: despite high-tech gadgetry available to these futuristic forces, they are still an assemblage of expendable adolescents with everything in common with "grunts" who've slogged through all previous human battles.

To stress the "war is hell" theme, Verhoeven displays an ugly obsession with maiming and mutilation of the most horrifying sort, but his uniformly great-looking, hard-bodied, male and female soldiers still seem to be having a grand time especially in a steamy, coed group shower scene.

The intrepid, rock-jawed hero Van Dien survives this encounter, and many amazing feats of derring-do, without once mussing a single strand of his perfectly coifed hair.

Ultimately, it's the battling bugs who save "Starship Troopers" from an uncomfortable resemblance to "Melrose Place in Outer Space."

These largely computer-generated beasts have been conceived and deployed with altogether admirable imagination and skill making some of huge combat scenes irresistibly absorbing.

Like "Independence Day," this breathlessly paced adventure recycles old rah-rah war movie cliches with a winning combination of reverence and subversive wit, and should please (and draw) crowds on a similar scale.

NEWSWEEK, 11/10/97, p. 78, Jeff Giles

Fourteen-year-old boys have their ways of sneaking into R-rated movies, and this weekend they'll all converge on *Starship Troopers*. Let your son go if you must, but don't go with him. Paul Verhoeven's sci-fi epic is an empty videogame of a movie about interplanetary pest control. The plot? Alien insects from Klendathu decimate Buenos Aires, and Earth retaliates by sending an army of Aaron Spelling actors into space.

Years ago the Dutch-born Verhoeven made a splashy Hollywood entrance with two thrilling, inventive sci-fi pictures, "RoboCop" and "Total Recall." Then he formed an unholy alliance with Joe Eszterhas and unleashed "Basic Instinct" and "Showgirls." "Troopers" is a welcome U-turn, but though Verhoeven rehashes "RoboCop" gimmicks—parodying newscasts, splashing cybertext across the screen—there's no soul in this machine. The dewy cast of unknowns has nothing to do but wait to get their brains sucked out by bugs.

The battles and the bugs, to be fair, are magnificent. Special-effects designer Phil Tippett has the time of his life here: his sprawling army of giant spiders, beetles and wasps outdoes even his famed Velociraptors from "Jurassic Park." Ultimately, though, it's depressing to see a director as good as Verhoeven give audiences nothing but special effects and gore. If "Starship Troopers" becomes a smash—and it may, though it's not as rousing as "Independence Day" nor as funny as "Men in Black"—it will confirm the director's basest instincts. And it will be a wonder if he ever makes another good movie.

SIGHT AND SOUND, 1/98, p. 53, Andrew O'Hehir

At some point in the distant future, democracy on earth has been replaced by military rule. The planet prepares for war against the Bugs, an alien arachnid race. In Buenos Aires, four high school friends prepare to do their part: outstanding student Carmen hopes to become a starship captain; Johnny, her boyfriend, enlists in the infantry; computer whiz Carl is assigned to military intelligence; and Dizzy, a girl Johnny has spurned, follows him into the infantry. Johnny nearly quits boot camp when his blunder causes a death.

The Bugs launch a surprise attack on Earth, destroying Buenos Aires, and Johnny rejoins the infantry for the assault on Klendathu, the Bugs' home planet. Carmen has become a rising starship officer, breaking off her relationship with Johnny along the way and teaming up with Zander, a fellow officer, instead. She saves her ship from destruction during the disastrous invasion of Klendathu, which results in heavy casualties and full-scale retreat. Faced with evidence that the Bug race is intelligent, Earth generals—including Carl, who has become a leading strategist—resolve to attack the outer reaches of the Bug empire first.

In an extended series of battles, human forces begin to turn the tide. Johnny proves himself in combat and rises to the rank of lieutenant. Dizzy finally gets Johnny into bed, but is killed soon thereafter. In a daring mission, Zander and Carmen rescue Johnny and the dying Dizzy. A climactic battle ensues in which Zander is killed, but he, Carmen, Johnny, and Carl are all instrumental in capturing a Brain Bug, an arachnid mastermind. The war goes on, but humanity has seized a dramatic advantage as the three friends are reunited.

Featuring astonishing special effects and some of the most harrowing battle scenes in movie history, *Starship Troopers* is the crowning achievement of Paul Verhoeven's film-making career to date. It also offers an opportunity to rethink his peculiar genius. For all his love of virile spectacle and evident desire to engage a mass audience, Verhoeven retains an inscrutable ironic streak that constantly threatens to undermine his quest for commercial success. Despite the artery-constricting pace and remarkably fluid photography, *Starship Troopers* may strike many viewers as a chilly, off-putting work, lacking the reassuring moral certitude and myth-informed sentimentality of a Lucas or Spielberg epic. It also offers a curious mixture of genres, half World War Two guts-and-glory, half *Melrose Place*. While the fearsome Bugs (special effects artist Phil Tippett far outdoes his *Jurassic Park* work here) will please the crowds, rather more unnerving is *Starship Troopers'* presentation of the fascist flavoured utopia, based on Robert A. Heinlein's original novel.

In *Starship*'s future, the twentieth century is remembered as an age when "social scientists brought our world to the brink of chaos", and the generals seized the reins, as Michael Ironside's history teacher-cum-infantry lieutenant informs his charges. Inspired by the philosophy of Ayn Rand and others, Heinlen's "utopia" may have been a deadly earnest prescription, but for Verhoeven it becomes an aesthetic and ideological field of play. As in *RoboCop* (and, less effectively, *Total Recall)*, he constructs a half ironic future landscape, a densely textured mix of historical imagery, Swiftian satire, and, most importantly, movie allusions.

This is a world where male and female soldiers fight, shower, and bunk together with comradely nonchalance; where battlefield nuclear weapons and psychic powers have become nearly commonplace; where a murderer convicted in the morning will be executed that night on live television. Nonconformity, along with racial and ethnic divisions, has been swept away by a hegemonic Anglo-American monoculture. As usual, Verhoeven wants to play both ironist and devil's advocate. He maintains a plausible sardonic distance, while doing little to discourage viewers who may find the film's orderly universe appealing.

It's also a universe crowded with free-floating fragments of earlier fictions. In a broadcast called *Why We Fight* (the title of a World War Two US produced propaganda series), citizens proclaim, "I'm doing my part!" and "The only good bug is a dead bug!" A tough as nails infantry officer defending an impossible position rallies his troops by hollering: "Come on, you apes! You want to live forever?" *Starship Troopers* clearly follows the pattern of numerous war pictures: a group of civilians is moulded into a warrior band and tested in the crucible of combat where some are killed and others hardened. Furthermore, the film echoes assorted World War Two events: from the Bugs' sneak attack (Pearl Harbor), via the disastrous invasion and pell-mell retreat from Klendathu (Dunkirk) and the series of strategic peripheral attacks (island-hopping in the Pacific), to the decisive turning point (D-Day).

But if classic war films offer unambiguous good guys and bad guys, Verhoeven here pulls an almost invisible moral bait-and-switch. Of course, we'll root for the human race against a teeming hive of insects. But the humans in this film look and act more like the Nazis than the

Allies. As Carl, the intelligence officer, Neil Patrick Harris boasts the wardrobe and insouciant smirk of a youthful *Ubersturmführer*. Moreover, we are told at first that the Bugs have no personalities and no civilisation, but the discovery of the caste of Brain Bugs scotches all such theories. For all the movie's humans know, there are arachnid poets greater than Milton.

Furthermore, if you understand the movie as an elaborate confidence game to illustrate the untrustworthy yet irresistible nature of narrative, its implausibly superficial characters (and no star cast, drawn largely from US prime time soaps) begin to make sense. With his Aryan cast for whom we're meant to root, Verhoeven seems to be commenting on the power of popular dramatic forms to mask noxious ideologies. As the relentlessly gung-ho Johnny, Casper Van Dien is less a handsome hunk than a 50s comic book illustration of one, with his squarish, dimpled jaw and Popeye biceps. Boasting supermodel eyebrows, startling electric-blue eyes, and an infinitesimally upturned nose, Denise Richards, as the faithless Carmen, can muster only two expressions: happy and sad. Verhoeven seems to be simultaneously ridiculing this style of vapid, televisual melodrama and celebrating its power.

Add the parodic snippets of interactive television interspersed throughout the film—in which adorable tots play with live ammunition or stomp insects on suburban streets ("Know Your Foe!") and the whole enterprise feels closer to Buñuel than to George Lucas. Like Fritz Lang and Ernst Lubitsch before him, Verhoeven is a European director who has learned to translate his artistic concerns into the Hollywood idiom. Verhoeven also lived under Nazi occupation as a small child in Amsterdam, and it's tempting to read *Starship Troopers* as a fable in which that occupation never ended. But it's not entirely clear what that child brought from that experience, in growing into the most duplicitous and diabolical mainstream film-maker since another tormented expatriate, Alfred Hitchcock. Verhoeven seems both hypnotised and horrified by the mass audience, imprisoned by his own need to attract a crowd and then feel superior to it. The results are fascinating, but when will the crowd, and the conjurer, tired of the game?

TIME, 11/10/97, p. 102, Richard Schickel

Welcome to the retrofuture. It's a time when they're fighting a high-tech intergalactic war but talking about it in the kind of lowbrow rhetoric—hysterical jingoism—we haven't heard issuing from movie screens since World War II.

Besides the weaponry and the enemy—monstrous, profoundly malevolent bugs—a few other things have changed. There's a world government now, and the combat troops are fully gender integrated—to the point where they take showers together. This implies, of course, that more saltpeter than ever is being dumped into their rations.

Essentially, however, it's business as usual in *Starship Troopers*. Basic training is still brutal. The platoon we follow from the first day of enlistment to battlefield apotheosis contains many familiar types—supermacho drill sergeant, dopey yokel and, at its center, Johnny (Casper Van Dien, a newcomer with a useful, uncanny resemblance to the old B-picture star John Agar), who is the traditional spoiled and aimless kid. He has—need one say?—joined up for the wrong, selfish reasons, but when his hometown is destroyed, Pearl Harbor-style, he embraces the right, vengeful-idealistic rationales for merciless slaughter and achieves heroism.

Johnny has a high school girlfriend, Carmen (Denise Richards), who becomes the hottest pilot in the star fleet. This gives director Paul Verhoeven, always a coldly calculating craftsman, and writer Ed Neumeier, adapting a Robert A. Heinlein novel, a chance to satirize old-fashioned aerial-combat movies too. Johnny also has a frustrated high school admirer, Dizzy (Dina Meyer), who lands in his platoon, finally gets his attention and then heroically dies. This gives the filmmakers a chance to strike that note of romantic self-sacrifice—death transfigured—that is integral to movies of this kind.

There is not, indeed, a base they fail to touch. The enemy is never particularized, so we never have a sympathetic thought for them. And scattered through the movie are online equivalents of those old-fashioned, pseudo-documentary short subjects designed to keep the home front heated up—cheerfully massed soldiers stretching as far as the lens can see, overheated descriptions of atrocious enemy behavior, that sort of thing.

Pretty funny. But not always very funny. For *Starship Troopers* contains an unexplored premise. There are two classes in this futureworld: civilians, who have sacrificed voting privileges for material ease, and warriors, who earn the right to rule by their willingness to die for the state. In short, we're looking at a happily fascist world. Maybe that's the movie's final, deadpan joke. Maybe it's saying that war inevitably makes fascists of us all. Or—best guess—maybe the filmmakers are so lost in their slambang visual effects that they don't give a hoot about the movie's scariest implications.

VILLAGE VOICE, 11/11/97, p. 77, J. Hoberman

Call it the new secular humanism. Instinctual insect fear mixes with goofy macho in *Starship Troopers*, Paul Verhoeven's long-awaited, megamillion-dollar adaptation of Robert A. Heinlein's once controversial, sternly ideological ray-gun blaster.

Not for the arachnophobic, this intergalactic Raid campaign is surely on Verhoeven's wavelength. After *RoboCop* and *Total Recall, Basic Instinct* and *Showgirls,* the transplanted Dutchman has become something like our Fritz Lang—Hollywood's comic-book artist deluxe, the suavely brutal purveyor of hardcore pulp. Verhoeven may lack Lang's visionary conviction and cultural pessimism, but he has a boldly cartoonish graphic sensibility and a corresponding gusto for caricatured postmodern shibboleths. Somewhere beyond irony, *Starship Troopers*'s clever opener dares the viewer to position the movie as kissing cousin to a Hitler Youth recruitment ad.

More than one observer has called Heinlein's novel borderline fascist. *Starship Troopers* was written during the period of Sputnik anxiety to protest a proposed suspension of nuclear testing and, rejected by Heinlein's longtime publisher as too militaristic for kids, was brought out in 1959 by another house as an adult novel. Baldly synopsized, it sounds like a straight-arrow precursor of William S. Burroughs's *Nova Express.* Heinlein's philosophical treatise transposes the World War II-platoon scenario to outer space, anticipating the New Frontier mystique of the Green Berets as rich kid Johnny Rico achieves his battlefield destiny amid the Terra Federation's struggle for control of the galaxy, against the arachnoid collectivists known as the Bugs.

Verhoeven ups the Darwinian ante by casting his movie with (mainly unknown) prime young human specimens—the square-jawed Casper Van Dien and dishy Denise Richards are not only the most physically perfect but also the most enthusiastic of warriors, surviving a basic-training regimen that includes routine bone breaking and public floggings. The movie has no difficulty conceptualizing the human race as fundamentally American. (Buenos Aires, where Van Dien and Richards are introduced graduating high school, is here less Latin than *Beverly Hills 90210.*)

Cynical enough to stage an attack with 10 million casualties, then riff on audience outrage at the death of a single dog, Verhoeven doesn't dwell unduly on the Heinlein worldview. A class on "the failure of democracy" briefly alludes to the process by which veterans took over and made citizenship contingent on military service. The atmosphere of steroid-pumped survivalism seems extrapolated from Desert Storm U.S.A. In this postliterate world, personal letters can wind up publicly broadcast, the Internet advertises televised executions, and football has mutated into an even more violent indoor sport. Perhaps because the film was bankrolled by Warner Bros., CNN is not on hand to cover the apocalypse—or is it that the script called for the battlefield reporter ("This is a bug planet, an ugly planet") to be dismembered mid-telecast?

An altogether more stylish, sardonic, and efficient entertainment machine than *Independence Day, Starship Troopers* substitutes gender equality for ethnic balance. Showgirls go to war. The army is coed. Male and female soldiers get to shower and, on at least one occasion, bunk down together ... in the name of species solidarity? The most intense sci-fi combat film since James Cameron's *Aliens, Starship Troopers* subsumes a plot-driven class struggle between infantry and air force in the visceral excitement of all-out, hand-to-tendril interspecics warfare—most spectacularly in the sensationally animated, artfully corpse-splattered, nerve-wracking attacks of the scuffling, screaming crustacean-spider hordes.

That the movie has no more depth than the early-'80s video games that were based on Heinlein's novel is Verhoeven's ultimate joke. Every planet not only resembles the Dakota badlands but has an earthling-compatible atmosphere. Oxygen is everywhere. Considering that the spider-monsters are apparently capable of targeting earth cities with meteors launched from deep space, it takes the Terra Federation a remarkably long time to realize that the Bugs might actually be intelligent.

Also reviewed in:
CHICAGO TRIBUNE, 11/7/97, Friday/p. A, Michael Wilmington
NEW YORK TIMES, 11/7/97, p. E14, Janet Maslin
VARIETY, 11/3-9/97, p. 98, Todd McCarthy
WASHINGTON POST, 11/7/97, p. G1, Rita Kempley
WASHINGTON POST, 11/7/97, Weekend/p. 48, Desson Howe

STEEL

A Warner Bros. release of a Quincy Jones-David Salzman Entertainment production. *Executive Producer:* Shaquille O'Neal, Leonard Armato, and Bruce Binkow. *Producer:* Quincy Jones, David Salzman, and Joel Simon. *Director:* Kenneth Johnson. *Screenplay:* Kenneth Johnson. *Based upon characters from DC comics created by:* Louise Simonson and Jon Bogdanove. *Director of Photography:* Mark Irwin. *Editor:* John F. Link. *Music:* Mervyn Warren. *Sound:* Susumu Tokunow. *Casting:* Shana Landsburg and Laura Adler. *Production Designer:* Gary Wissner. *Art Director:* Gershon Ginsburg. *Steel's Suit Design:* Greg Cannom. *Costumes:* Catherine Adair. *Special Effects:* Mark Franco. *Stunt Coordinator:* M. James Arnett. *Running time:* 93 minutes. *MPAA Rating:* PG-13.

CAST: Shaquille O'Neal (John Henry Irons); Annabeth Gish (Susan Sparks); Judd Nelson (Nathaniel Burke); Richard Roundtree (Uncle Joe); Irma P. Hall (Grandma Odessa); Ray J. (Martin); Charles Napier (Col. David); Kerrie Keane (Senator Nolan); Thom Barry (Sgt. Marcus); Hill Harper (Slats); George Lemore (Cutter).

LOS ANGELES TIMES, 8/18/97, Calendar/p. 4, Bob Heisler

[*The following review by Bob Heisler appeared in a slightly different form in*
NEWSDAY, 8/18/97, Part II/p. B7.]

Would it surprise you to learn that a recurring motif in "Steel" involves Shaquille O'Neal trying—and initially failing—to throw things into baskets? Would it surprise you to learn that "Steel" has a recurring motif at all?

There's a funny, entertaining, good vs. evil movie built around O'Neal—lots of plot and strong support from "Suddenly Susan" boss Judd Nelson, Richard Roundtree, Annabeth Gish and the city of Los Angeles, home of Shaq's day job with the Lakers.

Based very loosely on the DC Comic metal-covered character, "Steel" leads quickly and seamlessly through its story to the final confrontation between the very good John Henry Irons (O'Neal) backed by his computer whiz Army buddy Sparks (Gish) and the very bad Nathaniel Burke (Nelson), who is drummed out of the Army after a stunt that puts Sparks in a wheelchair and who now wants to sell to the highest bidders the Sonic Eliminator weapon they all developed. The test marketeers are a street gang-rats as the exceedingly nasty Burke calls them.

Before you can say "Holy Batplot," Irons has abducted Sparks from a St. Louis VA hospital, the good guys have set up a massive computer and counter-weapons operation buried in the work pile of junkyard artiste Uncle Joe (Roundtree) and our hero has fashioned a funky metal suit that turns him into a 7-foot-2 robocop with a winning smile and ready to fight crime.

Gangs are props in "Steel"; a subplot involving Irons' little brother Martin (Ray J) flashes a glossary full of street language but little meat. Los Angeles, mostly by night, plays the role of beleaguered city—a chopper-filled skyline, a free-fire zone in Pershing Square and a mostly befuddled LAPD.

Writer-director Kenneth Johnson could have dropped a couple of unnecessary scenes and backed down on the soundtrack attack, but there's a confident hand at the helm when Roundtree can make a "Shaft" joke and O'Neal can use Arnold Schwarzenegger's voice in a phone call.

And give Shaq a little slack. The tall fellow doesn't hide behind the suit, the computer gadgetry or a very impressive hammer-shaped weapon (John Henry was a steel-driving man, after all). While his range of emotions goes from real cute to real mad without stopping often enough in between—wisely, the camera avoids close-ups and cuts off his head in some shots—he knows the difference between a movie and a public appearance.

In the end, he gets the girl, even if he doesn't quite kiss her.

NEW YORK POST, 8/16/97, p. 26, Larry Worth

Shaquille O'Neal's sport is basketball, not baseball. But with his third cinematic strike, he's hopefully out of the movie biz.

After going from collegiate hoop recruit in "Blue Chips" to sassy genie in "Kazaam," it seemed he'd hit rock bottom. But who could have foreseen "Steel"?

It's the latest in a seemingly endless series of comic book characters transferred to the screen, this time depicting a former defense weapons expert who dons a suit of armor to battle evil in L.A.

Just for starters, how does a 7-foot-1, 300-pound behemoth think his dual identity won't be detected by those around him?

"What the hell *is* that?" an antagonist asks when first seeing Shaq in superhero gear. Good question.

Steel looks like a scrap-metal version of RoboCop, but with Catwoman-like helmet. Go figure Typically, he's assisted by junkyard-owning uncle (Richard Roundtree), a brainy, beautiful and handicapped computer whiz (Annabeth Gish) and a savvy street kid (Ray J).

As written and directed by Kenneth Johnson, it all comes off like a sub-par variation on the Incredible Hulk (which Johnson not coincidentally directed in TV-movie form). The mix of silly plot twists, ho-hum special effects and painfully weak humor seem all too familiar.

As if that's not bad enough, it's 45 minutes before Steel even dons his metallic duds. Then, it's accompanied by cornball lines like "You gotta fight fire with fire."

In fairness, "Steel" is no worse than this month's earlier comic outing, "Spawn". In fact, it's less offensive. On the other hand, Judd Nelson's by-the-numbers villain can't hold a candle to the deliciously campy Uma Thurman in "Batman and Robin."

And then there's Shaq, whose atonal histrionics are clunkier than his 75-pound suit. Even when parodying his prowess on the court (Steel can't hit a basket to save his life), he's like a run-on joke with no punchline.

Only Annabeth Gish, who showed such promise in "Desert Bloom" and "Mystic Pizza," comes off with dignity intact. Clearly she deserves better than "Steel." So do moviegoers.

Also reviewed in:
NEW YORK TIMES, 8/16/97, p. 16, Lawrence Van Gelder
VARIETY, 8/18-24/97, p. 33, Leonard Klady

SUBURBIA

A Sony Pictures Classics release of a Castle Rock Entertainment/A Detour Filmproduction film. *Executive Producer:* John Sloss. *Producer:* Anne Walker-McBay. *Director:* Richard Linklater. *Screenplay (based on his play):* Eric Bogosian. *Director of Photography:* Lee Daniel. *Editor:* Sandra Adair. *Music:* Randall Poster. *Sound:* Jennifer Murphy. *Sound Editor:* Tom Hammond. *Casting:* Judy Henderson and Alycia Aumuller. *Production Designer:* Catherine Hardwicke. *Art Director:* Seth Reed. *Set Director:* Keith Fletcher. *Set Dresser:* Joe Herlocker and Bart Brown. *Costumes:* Melanie Armstrong. *Make-up:* Candi Duke. *Stunt Coordinator:* Walter Strait. *Running time:* 118 minutes. *MPAA Rating:* R.

CAST: Giovanni Ribisi (Jeff); Steve Zahn (Buff); Amie Carey (Sooze); Kitt Brophy (Sooze's Mom); Jonn Cherico (Shopping Channel Host); Samia Shoaib (Pakeesa); Ajay Naidu (Nazeer); Ketih Preusse (Officer Chip); Eric Park (Officer Gary); Nicky Katt (Tim); Dina Spybey (Bee-Bee); William Martin Hayes (Scuff); Jayce Bartok (Pony); Bill Wise (Limo Driver); Parker Posey (Erica); M.J. Lin (Restaurant Hostess).

LOS ANGELES TIMES, 2/7/97, Calendar/p. 4, Jack Mathews

[The following review by Jack Mathews appeared in a slightly different form in
NEWSDAY, 2/7/97, Part II/p. B9.]

Richard Linklater is making a career out of stalking Gen Xers. His first film, the $16,000 "Slacker," follows various losers and dropouts around Austin, Texas. His follow-up, "Dazed and Confused," spends a day with some aimless high schoolers in the same town. And his last film, "Before Sunrise," gets off a train with a young couple who'd just met and follows them as they wander the streets of Vienna.

Linklater, almost alone, is fascinated with that awkward stage in life between adolescence and adulthood where individuality is defined more by attitude than character, and where knowledge is just beginning to gain a foothold. With each succeeding picture, Linklater seemed to grow as a filmmaker, just as his characters became more defined and developed.

But with his fourth picture, "subUrbia," he takes two giant steps backward. Back to the 'burbs, back to the dazed and confused, back to material he has done before and much better.

"subUrbia," with a script adapted by Eric Bogosian from his off-Broadway play, is a darker and nastier bit of business than Linklater ever conjured for himself, and it is totally absent the empathy of his earlier films. If you dig deep enough into your psyche, you may be able to identify with the phony self-importance of some of its young characters, a clutch of post-high school friends who hang out in the parking lot of a convenience store. But nothing that happens in "subUrbia" will necessarily make it worthwhile.

The group is composed of types. There's Jeff (Giovanni Ribisi), the budding intellectual on the elusive trail of the meaning of life; Buff (Steve Zahn), a manic geek who acts freshly graduated from "Porky's"; and Tim (Nicky Katt), the obligatory brooding loner.

Apparently, the three buddies collect at the same place every night in fictional Burnfield to drink beer, argue among themselves and harass the industrious Pakistani couple who run the store. On this particular night, they're expecting a visit from Pony (Jayce Bartok), who's gone on to an actual career as a rock singer, and are joined in their wait by Jeff's perky girlfriend Sooze (Amie Carey), a would-be performance artist, and her depressed friend Bee-Bee (Dina Spybey), fresh out of rehab. When Pony shows up in his limo, with his sexually available assistant Erica (Parker Posey), the scene is set for a blizzard of regrets, accusations, rivalries, jealousies and confrontations, not to mention enough sloppy intellectual thumb-sucking to wrinkle the screen.

The main issue dividing the group is inertia. With the exception of Pony and Sooze, who naturally gravitate toward each other, these people are on a slacker's sabbatical, taking time off from time to time, as if being 20 is a condition, like barrel fermentation, that can take five or 10 years. No question, Linklater and Bogosian are dealing with truths about that age, but they have nothing new or particularly interesting to offer, and they've created such an unpleasant group, it certainly isn't inviting.

NEW YORK, 2/10/97, p. 49, David Denby

The 20-year-olds in suburbia don't even have a place to go. College dropouts, dreamers, and premature failures—a couple of the men are sliding into alcoholism and racist bitterness—they hang out every night in a convenience-store parking lot somewhere in suburban Texas. As a group, they have gathered at this gruesome cement corner since high school. Most Americans would see them as posing losers, and in many ways they are. But playwright-screenwriter Eric Bogosian and director Richard Linklater treat them tenderly; the kids are losers of a special kind —embittered idealists trapped in the nowheresville of American pop commercialism. What if you see through society, and you think that everything is crap? What do you do then? You're stuck with your perception. All you can do is refine it.

Bogosian exercises his famous talent for self-serving rant; Linklater specializes in moods of youthful sloth, drunken euphoria, and futility. The two men join strengths and weaknesses. *SubUrbia* is intensely written and played, and though it whirls around and goes nowhere, passages of it are affecting. Everyone knows kids like this, at least in fantasy—they're what we fear our own children may become.

NEW YORK POST, 2/7/97, p. 47, Michael Medved

The movie "subUrbia," as the pretentiously contrived lettering of the title suggests, tries too hard to make a significant sociological statement—thereby detracting from its own moments of real power and a collection of truly superb performances.

Director Richard Linklater ("Slacker," "Dazed and Confused") again demonstrates enormous skill in working with an ensemble cast comprised largely of unknowns. The characters are a few years out of high school, still living at home and feeling trapped and desperate in the bland, charmless suburb of "Burnfield," which could be located in any corner of America.

Jeff (Giovanni Ribisi) lives in a pup tent in his parents' garage, working as a box boy while perfecting his pose of alienation ("It's my duty as a human being to be p--- ed off").

His girlfriend, Sooze (Amie Carey) is a would-be feminist performance artist with spiky hair, a ring through her eyebrow, and a dazzling smile. Jeff's best friend is Tim (Nicky Katt), a brooding Air Force dropout with tattoos, a violent streak and a serious drinking problem, while his other pal Buff (Steve Zahn) is a hyperactive doofus who works at a pizza joint and energetically embellishes tall tales about his own alleged sexual exploits.

A visit from an old high school pal produces an all-night crisis that disrupts their dreary lives, because Pony (Jayce Bartok) has become a successful rock musician who drives into town in a stretch limousine, accompanied by his "publicist" (Parker Posey), a sexy sophisticate from L.A.

The most sympathetic character in the film is an older outsider who hates and judges these aimless kids: Ajay Naidu plays a Pakistani immigrant who owns an all-night convenience store and tries to keep the reckless punks from hanging out on his property.

Based on Eric Bogosian's searing play (performed at Lincoln Center in 1994), the script offers several surprising twists and throws the characters together in unexpected and revealing combinations. The fine young cast proves uncannily successful in showing these people as simultaneously horrifying and sympathetic, though the film never gets far in attempting to explain their rage or despair.

Linklater's montages of bleak suburban suburban sprawl (one of them accompanied by the old Gene Pitney song "Town Without Pity"), never seem quite as appalling as he seems to intend, and the movie works best when treating its characters with humor and pity, rather than blowing up their dilemma in melodramatic, tragic or even emblematic terms.

NEWSWEEK, 2/17/97, p. 66, Jack Kroll

Seven paid-up members of Generation X hang out in the parking lot of a convenience store, grimly determined to do nothing. Except talk. And swill beer. Well, one of them Rollerblades. Their talk is the lingua franca of the grunge mind as it oozes into the millennium. America, says one, is a "caldron of spiritual oatmeal." But wait, this is Eric Bogosian's *subUrbia*, which was so effective as a play. Why has it thinned out as a movie? Richard Linklater, whose "Slacker" gave a shrewd charm to the chaotic ramblings of Gen-Xers in Austin, Texas, has filmed "subUrbia," but he hasn't movie-ed it. Onstage, trapped in the mini-wasteland of the parking lot, the creeped-out kids crackled like lightning in a bottle. Linklater's meager attempts to open up the movie drain its energy: it's as if Bosch threw in a few homey vignettes to mitigate the horrors of his pictures of hell.

Onstage, Bogosian had created a hellish vision. Jeff the college dropout, Tim the racist air force vet, Buff the idiot Rollerblader, Sooze the would-be performance artist, Bee-Bee the desperate druggie, Pony the rock semi-star who limos back to revisit his burned-out buddies, Erica his sleekly slutty publicist, all embody what hell is—scorching futility. On screen, the youthful cast does its damnedest, but Bogosian's punk eloquence is strangely flattened out. All you think is, "Oh, shut up, I've got my own problems."

SIGHT AND SOUND, 10/97, p. 59, Claire Monk

Jeff, Tim, Buff, Jeff's girlfriend Sooze and Sooze's friend Bee Bee, all in their early twenties, live in Burnfield, a US suburb. College dropout Jeff, racist cynic Tim and clownish Buff spend most nights drinking outside the convenience store, causing friction with the shop's owners Nazeer and Pakeesa. One evening, news that Pony, a high-school friend turned rock star, may drop by prompts contrasting reactions, from Buff's eagerness to taste the rock lifestyle to Jeff's rejection of its hollow materialism. Pony arrives in a limo with his publicist, Erica, and tensions intensify, particularly between Jeff and Sooze, who are already in conflict over Sooze's plans to study performance art in New York and Jeff's refusal to go with her. The distressed Bee Bee—a recovering alcoholic—vanishes unnoticed.

Intrigued by Tim's thumbnail analysis of herself, Erica stays behind driving with him while the others go a ride in Pony's limo. Pony's rekindling of an old attraction to Sooze causes Jeff to leave the car, and he returns to store where Bee Bee is drinking bourbon alone and swallowing pills. Absorbed in his own crisis, Jeff resolves to go to New York with Sooze after all, but when the limo returns it seems he has lost her to Pony. Meanwhile Eric has vanished, and Sooze, Pony and Buff go to look for her. Nazeer has the increasingly aggressive, abusive Tim arrested, whereupon Tim 'confesses' to Jeff that he has beaten Erica to death. Debating whether to report the murder, Jeff is interrupted by Buff, boasts of spending a torrid night with Erica—who then turns up unharmed.

Released, Tim returns intending shoot Nazeer. Prevented by Jeff, he climbs onto the store roof, where finds Bee Bee's unconscious, probably dead, body. As an ambulance is called, Tim triumphantly threatens to implicate Nazeer in the tragedy.

After the retro-trip of *Dazed and Confused* and *Before Sunrise*'s 24-hour romantic tour of Vienna, the latest feature from America's most consistently intelligent chronicler of unfocused youth returns to the present and to home territory. Literally so: the location for *SubUrbia*'s fictional US suburb is actually Linklater's adopted home town of Austin, Texas—famously the setting for his 1991 debut, the zeitgeist-defining *Slackers*. But while *SubUrbia*'s cast of perpetual students and workless cynics shares some cross-over territory with *Slackers*' creative loafers and conspiracy theorists, is a darker, more pessimistic film than its predecessors. Where Linklater's earlier films celebrated the art of doing very little, *SubUrbia*'s twenty-somethings inhabit various states of stagnation. With a visit from an old friend as catalyst, this stasis is primed to spill over into conflict, violence (in the case of the semi-psychopathic Tim) and tragedy (for the fragile alcoholic Bee Bee).

Adapted by Eric Bogosian (of *Talk Radio* fame) from his own off-Broadway play, *SubUrbia* is Linklater's first work to originate with another writer—with mixed consequences. Bogosian and Linklater share many concerns: *SubUrbia*'s ironic take on the suburban ideal, focus on alienated young adulthood, half-parodic debates about idealism and compromise, and 24-hour timespan make it a seamless addition to the Linklater canon. But the film remains bound by the limits of its theatrical origins: for too much of the time, the nine main characters remain fixed on the stage of their underpopulated store carpark hang-out, though the exclusion of the viewer from other locations in which the story unfolds is only occasionally a plot necessity. (For example, we—and Jeff, the gang's 'serious' thinker—are tricked into believing that rock star Pony's rich-girl publicist Erica has been beaten to death by Tim, when in fact she has spent the night partying with pizza cook Buff.)

But if this sense of spatial constriction is disappointing after the free-wheeling wandering of *Slackers* and *Before Sunrise*, it is compensated for by astonishingly rich characterisation which leaves few of our first impressions unchallenged. The feminist, punk would-be performance artist Sooze (Amie Carey gives the stand-out performance in an excellent cast) seems the most strong-willed and likely to succeed, yet her hilariously unlikely enthusiasm for Pony's half-witted acoustic ballads makes us question the substance behind her surface, while her professed anti-racism too proves hollow in the face of Tim and Buff's baiting of the long-suffering Asian store-owners Nazeer and Pakeesa. Conversely Buff, who seemed pre-ordained never to gain a piece of the action, ends up winning the rock-video-directing contract, the trip to LA and the girl.

The shift which most tellingly signals the maturing of Linklater's own perspective, however, occurs in the depiction of the film's central figure Jeff. Though he initially functions as Linklater and Bogosian's mouthpiece, as events progress his justification of his inertia as existential resistance ("I don't need a limousine to know who I am") acquires an increasingly ironic tinge—and the tragic denouement (in which his navel-gazing stops him from taking steps to save Bee Bee's life) shows his 'principled' inaction to be as damaging as any other kind. There's a reason after all why *SubUrbia*'s white slackers rarely stray from the parking lot: they are literally going nowhere. And as the film draws to an unresolved close, it's significant that the final comment comes from Nazeer—little older than the gang, yet light years away in his aspirations (he plans to finish his engineering degree, sell the store, and move on to better things). "You people!" he cries, "You throw it all away!"

VILLAGE VOICE, 2/11/97, p. 70, J. Hoberman

A quintet of suburban post-teens—the depressed would-be writer Jeff, the manic MTV-hound Buff, the aspiring performance artist Sooze, the dope-addled Bee-Bee, and the high school quarterback turned cynical lush Tim—hang out on the strip waiting for the return of their erstwhile classmate Pony—a dork with a guitar who has somehow become a minor rock star. The five friends are dreaming their own escapes but (ironically) Pony turns out to be weirdly nostalgic for the good old days, while Erica, the hard-edged LA. publicist who manages his life, finds Burnfield, Texas, almost exotic.

Best seen as a kind of Beavis and Butt-head Do Chekhov, Eric Bogosian's *subUrbia* made for entertaining theater—despite, or perhaps because of, its less-than-convincing cluck-cluck-cluck over the self-destructive antics of the latest generation of crazy mixed-up kids. Bogosian's performer-driven rantfest, staged at Lincoln Center in the spring of 1994, had the advantage not only of his own Marty-meets-the Ramones repartee but of a crackerjack ensemble and the hyper-real elegance of Derek McLane's faux-7-Eleven set.

The choice of Richard Linklater to film Bogosian's show would seem over-determined, given Linklater's résumé, not to mention the references to dazed and confused slackers sprinkled throughout the play's reviews. *subUrbia* shares the same voyage-to-the-end-of-night structure as Linklater's more sweetly romantic *Before Sunrise,* but, despite the promising use of Gene Pitney's "Town Without Pity" under the opening credits, the director doesn't do much more than repackage Bogosian's material for mass consumption. The camera placement is determinedly unobtrusive, the action cautiously opened up to add a few new scenes in various mall locations.

Steve Zahn recreates his role as the hyperactive Buff—a fount of subsurfer slang and inane bits of business. The only other original cast member is Samia Shoaib, one of the Pakistani shop-keepers who reproach the brats of America with the bitter wisdom of the Third World: "You threw it all away." Still, eloquently blank Sundance icon Parker Posey is shrewdly cast as the Bel Air princess, and Linklater gets solid performances from Giovanni Ribisi, Nicky Katt, and Jayce Bartok. The weak link is Amie Carey's overheated turn as Sooze, the community-college feminist bound for SVA so ferociously, embodied onstage by Martha Plimpton. (In the movie, not only the character is needy: so is the actress.) Still, Carey's inept enthusiasm accentuates her character's performance-work-in-progress as the movie's sarcastic high point.

Fact is, *subUrbia* pretends to be about the young and the marginal of the American heartland but is really concerned with the more self-absorbed issue of how one's peers handle one's success. Dropping the term "postmodern," referring to their own "alienation" referencing Sarajevo and Charles Bukowski, dreaming of video and performance art, Bogosian's characters are less East Texas than East Village. *subUrbia* may invert the bogus claptrap of *Rent* but it's a far better evocation of Avenue B.

Also reviewed in:
NATION, 3/3/97, p. 35, Stuart Klawans
NEW YORK TIMES, 5/27/97, p. C5, Janet Maslin
NEW YORKER, 2/10/97, p. 85, Terrence Rafferty
VARIETY, 10/14-20/96, p. 58, Godfrey Cheshire
WASHINGTON POST, 3/7/97, Weekend/p. 32, Rita Kempley

SUDDEN MANHATTAN

A Phaedra Cinema release of a Marcia Kirkley production. *Executive Producer:* Paul D'Addario, Jeff Sine, and Larry Lavine. *Producer:* Marcia Kirkley. *Director:* Adrienne Shelly. *Screenplay:* Adrienne Shelly. *Director of Photography:* Jim Deanult. *Editor:* Jack Haigas. *Music:* Pat Irwin. *Sound:* Bill Kozy. *Casting:* Ellen Parks. *Production Designer:* Teresa Mastropierro. *Art*

Director: Tina Khayat. *Set Decorator:* Christina Manca. *Costumes:* Cherish Cullison. *Running time:* 85 minutes. *MPAA Rating:* R.

CAST: Adrienne Shelly (Donna); Tim Guinee (Adam); Roger Rees (Murphy); Louise Lasser (Dominga); Hynden Walch (Georgie); Chuck Montgomery (Bearded Man); Paul Cassell (Ian); Jon Sklaroff (Alex).

NEW YORK POST, 3/7/97, p. 47, Thelma Adams

There's nothing sudden about "Sudden Manhattan," Adrienne Shelly's laid-back, mildly depressed, black comedy. When a character doodles "I have nothing to do" in her journal at the movie's beginning, it's cause for concern. When that character is the star, writer and director, it's time to worry.

Shelly, who recalls a whimsical Rosanna Arquette, is best known for starring in two of Hal Hartley's strongest films, "Trust" and "The Unbelievable Truth." In her feature debut as a director, she plays Donna, an unemployed twentysomething who must fend off adoring suitors while she tries to eke out the meaning of life between cheese omelettes and black-and-white milkshakes.

Before Donna has time to check her cholesterol, she stumbles across a shooting in Greenwich Village. Like Hartley, guns present an exaggerated (and, possibly, unnecessary) feeling of danger in a life that is otherwise running along directionless but without external threats.

Did Donna witness a murder or is she nuts? Whichever it is, Shelly is refreshingly polite about the hazards of city living when your hair is a perfect strawberry-blonde poof. "You went to all the trouble of stalking me," Donna tells a stranger at her door. "I guess it would be rude of me to send you away."

An appealing actress who injects charm into moments that would be dead on the page, Shelly has gathered a loopy gang of crackpots played by spirited actors: an unemployed actor and health inspector (Tim Guinee), a lovesick Irish landlord (Roger Rees), a bearded brute with multiple personalities (Chuck Montgomery) and a man-obsessed pill-popper (Hynden Walch).

Shelly's biggest find is Louise Lasser, Woody Allen's comic muse in his blessed "Bananas" phase. Lasser's kooky New Age fortune teller delivers just the magical whimsy that could be Shelly's hallmark. In one scene, the now-puffy Lasser raises her arms—and hem—to deliver a spell. When she reveals her fluffy, full thighs, a wicked bit of realism creeps in: So that's why Allen has hooked up with Soon-Yi.

NEWSDAY, 3/7/97, Part II/p. B15, John Anderson

Somehow, you just can't imagine a movie that tries to mix Woody Allen, Jean Anouilh and the old "Abbott & Costello Show" being called "Sudden Lindenhurst." No, as a movie backdrop, New York City presumably forgives all, and apparently provides an alibi for anything.

Which brings us to the sweet-faced Adrienne Shelly, best known for her daffy naivete in two Hal Hartley movies, who has made a feature titled "Sudden Manhattan." And while this in itself is no reason for alarm, apprehension wouldn't be unreasonable. Neither would a certain awe: In the first few moments, Shelly's character, Donna, rises from her bed and recites, mantra-like, "I have no reason to get up. No reason to brush my teeth. No reason to wash my face." And you've already begun asking yourself the type of question that a first-time director ordinarily requires at least 30 minutes to provoke.

As Donna ambles through her day, and life, she sees a murder re-enacted regularly on a Greenwich Village street; eggs in a diner rumble like Los Angeles; her writing teacher/landlord, Murphy (Roger Rees), woos her pathetically; a theater director/health inspector named Adam (Tim Guinee) stalks her, spooks her, fails her in bed. A gypsy fortune teller named Dominga (Louise Lasser) predicts torture and death. It's an unhappy group in an unhappy scenario, being barely buoyed along by Shelly's guileless charm but eventually scuttled by a lack of substance. Or point.

Incongruity doesn't equal profundity; absurdity doesn't equal art. These are concepts elusive to "Sudden Manhattan," which isn't evil, but might drive you to commit some.

VILLAGE VOICE, 3/11/97, p. 74, Justine Elias

We all know someone like Donna, a bright woman caught up in a stream of continual apologies; as her best friend says, "You ask her for something and she gets it for you, like some kind of Zen waitress." Writer and director Adrienne Shelly, best known as the heroine of Hal Hartleys movies, has created an ideal role for herself in her first feature film. Wearied by her own obsessive thoughts and aural hallucinations, Donna embarks on a journey into screwball fantasy, a world populated by unemployed artists, playwrights-to-be, and guys who like to quote Dostoyevsky in bed. Though the movie's eccentric touches eventually wear out their welcome, Shelly wisely allows her costars—including Tim Guinee, Louise Lasser, Hynden Walch, and half the Cucaracho Theater company as many funny lines as she saves for herself. Unlike Woody Allen and other solipsistic filmmakers she obviously admires, Shelly is as fascinated by other people's peculiarities as she is by the little earthquakes in her head.

Also reviewed in:
NEW YORK TIMES, 3/7/97, p. C12, Stephen Holden
VARIETY, 4/29-5/5/96, p. 135, Andrew Hindes

SUNDAY

A Cinepix Film Properties release of a Goatworks Films production in association with Sunday Productions and Double A Films. *Producer:* Jonathan Nossiter and Alix Madigan. *Director:* Jonathan Nossiter. *Screenplay:* James Lasdun and Jonathan Nossiter. *Director of Photography:* Michael Barrow, John Foster, and Daniel Lerner. *Editor:* Madeleine Gavin. *Sound:* Neil Riha. *Production Designer:* Deana Sidney. *Art Director:* Stephen Beatrice. *Set Decorator:* Anne Park. *Costumes:* Kathryn Nixon. *Running time:* 93 minutes. *MPAA Rating:* Not Rated.

CAST: David Suchet (Oliver/Matthew); Lisa Harrow (Madeleine Vesey); Larry Pine (Ben Vesey); Jared Harris (Ray); Joe Grifasi (Scotti Elster); Arnold Barkus (Andy); Bahman Soltani (Abram); Willis Burks (Selwyn); Joe Sirola (Subalowsky); Henry Hayward (Sam); Kevin Thigpen (David).

LOS ANGELES TIMES, 8/22/97, Calendar/p. 16, John Anderson

[The following review by John Anderson appeared in a slightly different form in NEWSDAY, 8/22/97, Part II/p. B11.]

When you're a kid, September is the cruelest month. And Sunday, naturally, is the cruelest day of the week. It marks the end of freedom, the resumption of work, the cusp of hope and horror. It's time you spend the way you spend your last dollar, with all the unbridled joy of the condemned.

This sentiment fades, of course, but does it ever really go away? (Think right now about last Sunday night or the melancholic, fast-approaching September.) And what is it that makes a Sunday a Sunday? That a person has somewhere to go—and something to do—on Monday. When they don't, then Sunday is likely no day at all. And every day.

In Jonathan Nossiter's complex, unsettling, disquieting "Sunday," We have two people with nowhere to go: Oliver (David Suchet), a downsized IBM accountant living in a Queens men's shelter, and Madeleine (Lisa Harrow), a middle-aged English actress with an estranged husband, an adopted daughter and no work.

They meet in a swirl of fiction. "You're Matthew Delacorta," she says to Oliver on the street one early Sunday morning, "the film director." Oliver agrees that he is. They eat, mate, bond and wrap their manufactured mystery around themselves like a psychic lifeline.

Nossiter, whose previous feature was the Quentin Crisp film "Resident Alien," is trying—and largely succeeding—to give us an autopsy on fiction itself. When Madeleine asks him to tell her a story, Oliver obliges with his own, complete with the very fabrication they're experiencing at that moment. She replies with a story of her own, which is her own story, albeit with a horror-movie ending—real life being not too boring but simply too brutal.

Cutting occasionally away from Madeleine and Oliver, and checking in with the other wandering residents of the genteel/squalid men's home (played by, among others, Jared Harris, Joe Sirola and Willis Burks), Nossiter creates atmosphere. But he also is suggesting the existence of multiple realities, multiple identities, multiple stages of ego disintegration, the varied interpretations of Oliver's life. The cinematography (by Michael Barrow, John Foster and Daniel Lerner) is clean and bright and crisp; the effect is a cool beauty and bracing disinterest.

But the real disturbance in "Sunday"—which won the feature and screenplay prizes at this year's Sundance Film Festival—lies in the truths the characters tell each other. Even as they dismiss them.

Or use them for protection. Or wield them as weapons—against Madeleine's unpleasant husband, Ben (Larry Pine), for instance—and the way the line of demarcation always blurs. What is real and what is fiction, after all, is never a case of truth: When Oliver explains the plot of his "new movie"—about a middle-class everyman who's lost everything—Madeleine tells him what a marvelous story it would be. Even as she's in it. Even as we watch.

Suchet, who plays Hercule Poirot on the PBS "Mystery!" series and is quite unrecognizable here, gives a virtuoso turn as Oliver. a man who's as physically uncomfortable with the world as the world is with him; he is, after all, the unpleasant detail of a thriving economy, the homeless man who doesn't fit the derelict profile.

Harrow, always so powerful and quietly moving, here is a Londoner cast adrift in Queens (itself cast as a land of the lost) and gives a tremendous performance.

Oliver and Madeleine dwell in different hells together, very personal states from which they cannot escape save perhaps through each other—and then Nossiter burdens them with too much insight for such a neat trick.

It might have been depressing, of course, all this frustrated humanity, but "Sunday" has such a sense of its own self-possession—and the all-embracing reach of its own fiction—that its downbeat rhythms are something close to exhilarating.

NEW YORK POST, 8/22/97, p. 43, Thelma Adams

Jonathan Nossiter's affecting film "Sunday." unfolds like a Borges short story.

Two strangers meet on a Sunday under the elevated train tracks in Queens. She is hidden behind the potted plant she carries. He hides behind enormous eyeglasses.

Madeleine (Lisa Harrow) is English. She is a Shakespearean actress trapped in a failed marriage, in what she perceives as a failed borough, in a body that is past its prime.

Oliver (David Suchet) is a downsized upstate IBM accountant who has spiraled into a church-run homeless shelter in Queens.

When Madeleine mistakes Oliver for a famed director named Matthew Delacorta, she begins her audition right there on the street, continues it in her cozy parlor, and consummates it on her untidy landing.

As the two tell each other stories and reinvent their identities, the movie, like Borges' fiction, begins to turn on itself, to shift back and forth in time and perspective, tacking to chart its true course. The unusual drama won awards at the Sundance Film Festival for both best film and best screenplay.

Nossiter, working from a script he co-wrote with James Lasdun from a Lasdun short story, tries to approximate both the way we live and the fantasies that shape our lives.

For Madeleine and Oliver, their lives have taken radical twists, and their senses of self are at odds with the homes and homeless shelters they return to each night. They are alienated from the people who surround them and alienated from themselves.

Aided by strong support from Jared Harris, as a shelter pervert, and Larry Pine, as Madeleine's strange and estranged husband, Suchet (PBS' Poirot) and Harrow ("The Last Days of Chez Nous") give darkly dazzling performances.

Even when Madeleine and Oliver are stripped bare physically, they reveal the delicate folds of human consciousness and ego. As "Sunday" darkens into dusk, the pair peel away layer upon layer, but they cannot strip bare emotionally in front of each other.

Romantic, raw, streaked with humor, beautifully shot, textured in its sound, "Sunday" remains mysterious. We are never clear what facts the duo recognize as true, how extensive is their mutual and self-deception. We know only that Monday will inevitably follow Sunday, a day in which there's only a brief rest for weary romantics.

VILLAGE VOICE, 8/26/97, p. 84, Laurie Stone

With Piaf warbling about Paris on the soundtrack and an anxious camera shooting through gauzy curtains, *Sunday,* a first feature by Jonathan Nossiter, begins with promising mystery and unease. We can't find our bearings, as a gaggle of men of various races and ages stumble through bathroom ablutions and launch bits of conversation over a noisy TV. Eventually we unravel that we're in a men's shelter in Queens, amid inhabitants who have mostly lost hope, and we see that the confused, dread-soaked atmosphere is seeping from Oliver (David Suchet), a downsized IBM technician, who has spiraled out of safety and marriage. Overweight, bald, and clinging to dignity with his folded towel draped on the grimy communal sink, he is George Costanza stranded in his worst nightmare.

And just like George, who should he encounter a few steps into his depression-hobbling Sunday walk but an intense, needy woman. She is Madeleine (Lisa Harrow), an out-of-work British actress, carrying a wilted palm, who declares he is the director Matthew Delacorta. Oliver doesn't correct her, and screenwriters Nossiter and James Lasdun suggest that Oliver might *be* Matthew, scouting locations for a project. This and other affectations sabotage the characters, whom we can't really penetrate since they might be lying. The filmmakers substitute murk for a throughline about flirted-with themes: dislocation and cultural cacophony. The shelter's denizens become window dressing.

It's a shame, because, as opposed to the characters they play, Suchet and Harrow do a disinhibited dance, exposing their middle-aged flesh in sex scenes and listening attentively as each unfolds a tale of drift in Queens. Spilling the story of Oliver's decline, Suchet is a marvel of sweaty despair and irrepressible hunger, clutching this opportunity to feel rather than stay numb. Strapped for funds, Madeleine has landed in a ramshackle house with an estranged husband who plays a tug-of-war over their adopted Asian American daughter. With her clipped Royal Shakespeare diction, Harrow's Madeleine casts out hysteria like a lure, then reels it in to steady herself. Too often, though, she's portrayed as the embodiment of chaos, a moody, sharp-tongued succubus, wielding garden clippers and exulting in her penchant (unexplored) for half-dead plants and tottering males. Is she a fatal woman? Is Matthew a director? Instead of harnessing the loneliness and wariness that rise off his actors, Nossiter thins his movie with trivial pursuits.

Also reviewed in:
CHICAGO TRIBUNE, 9/26/97, Friday/p. K, Michael Wilmington
NATION, 9/8-15/97, p. 36, Stuart Klawans
NEW YORK TIMES, 8/22/97, p. C8, Stephen Holden
NEW YORKER, 9/15/97, p. 74, Daphne Merkin
VARIETY, 2/3-9/97, p. 42, Joe Leydon
WASHINGTON POST, 9/12/97, Weekend/p. 41, Desson Howe

SUZANNE FARRELL: ELUSIVE MUSE

A Seahorse Films, Inc. production. *Producer:* Anne Belle and Catherine Tambini. *Director:* Anne Bell and Deborah Dickson. *Director of Photography:* Don Lenzer, Tom Hurwitz, and Wolfgang Held. *Editor:* Deborah Dickson. *Running time:* 115 minutes. *MPAA Rating:* Not Rated.

WITH: Suzanne Farrell; Jacques d'Amboise; Maria Calegari; Arthur Mitchell; Helene Alexopoulos; Paul Mejia; Maurice Béjart; Isabelle Guerin; Susan Jaffe; Peter Boal; Marie-Christine Mouis.

NEW YORK POST, 3/28/97, p. 55, Larry Worth

Though nominated, "Suzanne Farrell: Elusive Muse" didn't win as best feature-length documentary at Monday's Oscar ceremony. But that doesn't diminish its triumphs.

As directed by Anne Belle and Deborah Dickson, it may be the year's most entertaining mix of drama, dance and unadulterated soap opera.

Specifically, New York City Ballet superstar Suzanne Farrell reflects on being part of a bizarre lovers' triangle in the '60s with choreographer George Balanchine and the man she subsequently wed—another member of Balanchine's troupe.

Farrell was forced to choose between love and career, and the surprising results cast everyone in a pretty unflattering light. Long before the fascinating finale, each comes off as a serious candidate for Doctor Freud's couch.

Since premiering at last fall's New York Film Fest, the production has been trimmed by about 10 minutes. And while the pacing is undeniably quicker, the directors would have been wiser to plug up some narrative holes particularly regarding Farrell's suitable-for-sainthood hubby, Paul Mejia.

But any flaws are more than outweighed by remarkable dance footage, music that ranges from Igor Stravinsky to Richard Rodgers and comments by a host of luminaries. Even ardent ballet haters will come away with a new appreciation for its artistry.

Then again, the production isn't geared to ballet fans. Rather, "Suzanne Farrell" will appeal to anyone intrigued by the mysteries of the human heart.

VILLAGE VOICE, 4/1/97, p. 72, Richard B. Woodward

It is hard to watch *Suzanne Farrell: Elusive Muse,* especially anywhere within Lincoln Center, and not hear the dancer's heartbroken recital of her love affair with Balanchine as a bid to insinuate herself as his rightful heir. No word is ever said in the film about the New York City Ballet's tattered reputation since his death, and no mention made of the venomous attacks on Peter Martins and the cheerleading for Farrell to replace him from some dance critics, notably Arlene Croce. But what isn't spoken—and who isn't on camera adds a swirl of subtext to Farrell's already kinky life story. This may be the first straight documentary of an American ballerina that also qualifies as a slanted political manifesto.

To hear Farrell and her students tell it, she is the "channel" to Mr. B. A parade of her male partners—Jacques d'Amboise, Arthur Mitchell, and her husband, Paul Mejia—testify that she was the last muse of the genius. Balanchine's discovery of the willful, innocent 18-year-old from Cincinnati when he was 60, and his rage when she decided to marry, is a juicy episode in many books, and forms the core of Farrell's autobiography, *Holding on to the Air.* Their love affair in class and on-stage—more passionate, we are led to believe, because unconsummated—made her the Balanchine dancer of the '60s. (She replaced Diana Adams, who erred in becoming pregnant.)

But to see how this hopeless union translated into choreography is to appreciate anew Balanchine's cruel gifts, his manipulation of worshipful young dancers and his blind, Lear-like self-pity. At a benefit performance of *Don Quixote* in 1965, seen here in priceless footage, he cast himself as the dottering Don pursuing an incandescent Dulcinea. Farrell recalls their staying up all night after the event to talk about their shared excitement in collaboration. It was the night, she says, that she first tasted champagne.

When the film taps Farrell's ardent memories of Balanchine, it is easy to believe how strongly he burns as her guiding light. In an anecdote that indicates an awesome faith in her own strength of mind, she recalls looking down Columbus Avenue after his death and thinking that she could will him back to life. A lovely throwaway moment at their lakeside home shows Farrell and Mejia tying up their boat to the dock. They perform the task like courtiers, their bodies obeying orders from an unseen ballet master. Balanchine still governs both their lives.

As a portrait of a human being, however, *Elusive Muse* is missing too many pieces. Farrell's stage mom, who abandoned her husband in Ohio and slaved 20-hour days as a nurse in New York so her daughters could dance, makes a strange cameo, but dad and sister are never heard from or even discussed. And none of Farrell's female contemporaries step forward to offer commentary. Did Allegra Kent, Patricia McBride, Merrill Ashley not wish to speak or did the film's star ask that they not be interviewed? It feels as if the Farrell-Balanchine plot line, so reminiscent of *The Red Shoes,* determined what parts of this life were fit to be filmed. The filmmakers, Anne Belle and Deborah Dickson, might have sensed that if these shoes fit too comfortably in a documentary format, don't wear them. The lasting impression left by Farrell is of someone with a lot of murky, unresolved issues. She may be a brilliant teacher, but I'm not sure that anyone should trust a ballet company in her hands.

Also reviewed in:
NEW YORK TIMES, 3/28/97, p. C16, Jennifer Dunning
VARIETY, 10/14-20/96, p. 59, Godfrey Cheshire

SWAN PRINCESS, THE: ESCAPE FROM CASTLE MOUNTAIN

A Legacy Releasing release of a Nest Entertainment/Seldon O. Young/Jared F. Brown/K. Douglas Martin presentation of a Rich Animation Studios production. *Producer:* Richard Rich and Jared F. Brown. *Director:* Richard Rich. *Screenplay:* Brian Nissen. *Story:* Richard Rich and Brian Nissen. *Editor:* James D. Koford. *Music:* Lex de Azevedo and Clive Romney. *Music Editor:* Douglas Lackey. *Sound:* Tim Grace and (music) Robert Abeyta. *Casting:* Bernard Van De Yacht. *Animation:* Richard Rich. *Running time:* 75 minutes. *MPAA Rating:* G.

VOICES: Michelle Nicastro (Odette); Douglas Sills (Derek); Jake Williamson (Clavius); Christy Landers (Uberta); Joey Camen (Knuckles); Steve Vinovich (Puffin); Doug Stone (Speed); Donald Sage MacKay (Jean-Bob); Joseph Medrano (Lord Rogers); James Arrington (Chamberlain); Owen Miller (Bromley); Rosie Mann (Bridget).

LOS ANGELES TIMES, 7/21/97, Calendar/p. 4, Kevin Thomas

[The following review by Kevin Thomas appeared in a slightly different form in
NEWSDAY, 7/21/97, Part II/p. B9.]

"The Swan Princess," the German fairy tale that is the basis for the beloved "Swan Lake" ballet, emerged in, 1994 as a pleasant animated musical fantasy aimed at children, especially little girls. Its sequel, "The Swan Princess; Escape from Castle Mountain," opened Friday without benefit of press preview. While it's true that the original film's villain—and its key asset —Rothbart (voiced with zesty relish by Jack Palance) got killed off, the sequel otherwise is much like the original, although not as inspired.

Prince Derek (Douglas Sills) and Princess Odette (Michelle Nicastro) have settled down to domestic life at their Swan Lake castle along with their pals, Speed the Turtle, Jean-Bob the Frog and Puffin the Bird. A conscientious ruler, Derek has trouble delegating authority, leaving Odette feeling neglected and longing, in song, for the days when her husband slew dragons on her behalf.

She gets her wish speedily, for the departed Rothbart's partner in evil, Clavius (Jake Williamson), residing nearby in a mountain lair, is determined to get his hands on the Magic Orb stored in the bowels of Swan Lake castle. As Clavius relates in vigorous song, he who gets his hands on the glowing transparent ball becomes charged with a laser-like power to "create, change, rearrange and destroy" with just a little zap here, there and everywhere. Today, Swan Lake castle and its rulers, tomorrow the world—that's Clavius' agenda.

In the ensuing adventures, Odette, with the help of an old witch, must turn into a swan to try to save her husband but how to turn back into a woman?

As before, director Richard Rich, a noted Disney alumnus, makes good use of his actors' voices, and his sequel, like the original, is traditional in style, featuring the usual painterly storybook back-drops, with the equally typical simply drawn humans and anthropomorphized animals. Two songs have been reprised from the first film, and Lex de Azevedo has contributed three new numbers, all of them effective in the context of the story.

Small children are likely to be delighted with "The Swan Princess: Escape From Castle Mountain," but just as with the original, adults may find it old-fashioned, mainly in style.

SIGHT AND SOUND, 11/97, p. 54, Leslie Felperin

A few years ago, Princess Odette had been turned into a swan by the sorcerer Rothbart, but was released from the spell by the love of Prince Derek. Now, the two are married but Derek is constantly called away from his bride on business. Among his distractions are the fires and traps set by Niles, the henchman of Clavius who was once Rothbart's partner in sorcery. Clavius is determined to retrieve the Black Arts, powers encased in a magic orb hidden by Rothbart somewhere in Derek's castle. Niles' fires are lures to ensnare Derek so that Clavius can extort the Black Arts from him. Clavius kidnaps Derek's imperious mother Uberta on her birthday and sends a ransom note to Derek. When Derek goes to meet him, Clavius sneaks into the castle and tries to abduct Odette. But she, aided by her friends Jean-Bob (a frog), Speed (a turtle) and Puffin (a puffin), manages to break away. Her maid Bridget uses the newly found Black Arts to turn Odette into a swan so that she can fly away and warn Derek.

Clavius acquires the magic orb and returns to his mountain lair; the animals stowaway on his getaway balloon. Bedevilled by Niles but helped by Odette, Derek arrives at the lair and vanquishes Clavius, but the Black Arts orb is destroyed in the battle and Jean-Bob killed. It is feared that Odette may never return to human form. At the lake which she once frequented and where she was returned to human form years ago, the magic of the moonbeams works again; Odette is humanised and Jean-Bob brought back to life. Derek resolves to spend more time with her, despite his pressing duties of state.

One of the few virtues of *The Swan Princess The Secret of the Castle* is that it feels little need to waste much time explaining its backstory, told in *The Swan Princess*. The film's airy attitude to exposition might be read as an oversight that the earlier film was so dull an experience, it was easy to forget. Actually, it's more likely this reflects the film-makers' assumption that only ardent fans of the original would bother with this continuation of its characters' adventures.

The logic of the first *The Swan Princess'* narrative, concerned as it was with establishing the true love of its protagonists, left the film-makers hardly anywhere else to go in the sequel, given the generic restrictions. After all, it's a strange decision to pick up where "... and they lived happily ever after" leaves off, the tag having such a ring of finality to it. Yet *The Secret of the Castle* concerns keeping that happiness fresh, despite the distractions of blazing fields and visiting kings. But where a romantic comedy for adults would find impediments in the characters themselves to be overcome, here it is that creaky plot devices—the evil partner/spouse of the earlier film's baddie—seeking that which they feel is rightfully his or hers. As with the first film, director Richard Rich (a veteran of such Disney films as *The Black Cauldron*) is less interested in fashioning an original story than in reworking familiar motifs for a child audience.

Clavius is a more entertaining villain than the last film's, playing an air-guitar of pink electrical magic as he rhapsodises over his magic powers. There are some inventive moments like this, including the quasi-Tex Avery reactions of Jean-Bob. There's also a reasonably exciting catch-the-magic-orb chase scene around the castle, although it's marred by a ludicrous chant of 'No Fear!' on the soundtrack, as if by an invisible chorus. But the central characters remain wooden, unengagingly drawn contrivances, given to singing absurd ballads with synthesiser accompaniments which could plausibly pass for best-forgotten Eurovision Song Contest entries. Indeed, the film's look mostly recalls supermarket children's books translated from obscure languages. Very Eurovision.

Also reviewed in:
NEW YORK TIMES, 7/19/97, p. 16, Lawrence Van Gelder

SWEET HEREAFTER, THE

A Fine Line Features release of an Alliance Communications presentation of an Ego Film Arts production. *Executive Producer:* Robert Lantos and Andras Hamori. *Producer:* Camelia

Frieberg and Atom Egoyan. *Director:* Atom Egoyan. *Screenplay:* Atom Agoyan. *Based on the novel by:* Russell Banks. *Director of Photography:* Paul Sarossy. *Editor:* Susan Shipton. *Music:* Mychael Danna. *Sound:* Ross Redfern. *Sound Editor:* Sue Conley. *Production Designer:* Philip Barker. *Art Director:* Kathleen Climie. *Set Designer:* Patricia Cuccia. *Costumes:* Beth Pasternak. *Make-up:* Sylvain Cournoyer. *Stunt Coordinator:* Peter Szkoda. *Running time:* 110 minutes. *MPAA Rating:* R.

CAST: Ian Holm (Mitchell Stephens); Sarah Polley (Nicole Burnell); Bruce Greenwood (Billy Ansell); Tom McCamus (Sam Burnell); Gabrielle Rose (Dolores Driscoll); Arsinée Khanjian (Wanda Otto); Alberta Watson (Risa Walker); Maury Chaykin (Wendell Walker); Brooke Johnson (Mary Burnell); Earl Pastko (Hartley Otto); David Hemblen (Abbott Driscoll); Stephanie Morgenstern (Alison); Caerthan Banks (Zoe Stephens); Peter Donaldson (Schwartz); David Hemblen (Abbott); Kirsten Kieferle (Stewardess); Simon Baker (Bear); Sarah Rosen Fruitman (Jessica); Marc Donato (Mason); Devon Finn (Sean); Fides Krucker (Klara); Magdelena Sokoloski (Young Zoe); James D. Watts (Young Mitchell); Allegra Denton (Jenny); Russell Banks (Dr. Robeson).

LOS ANGELES TIMES, 11/21/97, Calendar/p. 10, Kenneth Turan

The exquisite and overwhelming emotional tapestry that is "The Sweet Hereafter" plays its credits over the simplest and most primal of scenes. An infant and its parents, unclothed and drowsy under white sheets, share the same quiet bed. It's a pristine moment, an idyllic fantasy of togetherness that almost seems to mock us as a much darker vision of the scenarios that can devastate families gradually unfolds.

While it's usual to call films haunting, "The Sweet Hereafter" is more accurately described as haunted, both by children who've died and those who are alive yet distant and estranged. Directed by Atom Egoyan from Russell Banks' celebrated novel of a small town's response to a cataclysmic school bus accident, "The Sweet Hereafter" is a delicate and assured exploration of what different kinds of tragedies do to the parents and children who experience them.

Though his six previous features (including "Exotica" and "The Adjustor") have made him one of Canada's most respected writer-directors, matching Egoyan's highly personal sensibility with this lucid, unadorned book was not an obvious choice. But speaking at Cannes, where "Hereafter" won three major awards, Egoyan said that after years of telling nothing but his own interior stories, he was eager for the challenge of a straightforward adaptation.

Fortunately, Egoyan is incapable of being completely straightforward. Instead "Hereafter" joins the list of exceptional films, ranging from Jean-Luc Godard's "Contempt" to David Lynch's "The Elephant Man," that result when directors with strong personal visions take on conventional material and make it very much their own.

Starting with an unnerving opening shot taken from the point of view of a man trapped inside a car wash, Egoyan and cinematographer Paul Sarossy know how to keep audiences consistently off-balance. Using unexpected juxtapositions and unsettling angles, "Hereafter" has the subtle ability to never provide quite what we're expecting.

While Banks' novel fragments his story by telling it through four characters, Egoyan's screenplay opts for one point of view and instead breaks up its narrative through the use of multiple time frames. "The Sweet Hereafter" moves intricately back and forth between the accident itself, the time before it and the time afterward, and it's only gradually that we're able to fit the pieces together and understand what happened when.

The character at the center of "The Sweet Hereafter" is Mitchell Stephens (Ian Holm), a successful negligence attorney who comes to Sam Dent, British Columbia, (moved from the novel's New York state) intent on filing a class-action suit on behalf of the 14 children who died when the town's school bus left the highway and plunged into a frozen lake.

It is a younger version of Stephens, probably, that we see in bed under the opening credits, and before we observe him in action in British Columbia we are shown his current relationship with that child, his daughter Zoe (played by the novelist's daughter Caerthan Banks).

Angry, suspicious, quite possibly still addicted to drugs despite being in and out of numerous clinics, Zoe is a cause of tremendous rage and frustration for a father who now relates to her only as a shrill voice on his mobile phone. So the controlled outrage Stephens brings to his work in Sam Dent is fueled as much as anything by his own terrible anger at having a child irretrievably lost without the solace of having anyone to blame, anyone to sue.

As he moves through the desolate grandeur of Sam Dent in winter, Stephens, played with fluid precision by the masterful Holm, is almost preternatural in his effectiveness. He knows what to say to the grieving parents, knows the time to tell them, "I will represent you only in your anger, not your grief," the time to insist "there is no such thing as an accident, the word means nothing to me." When he pleads, "Let me direct your rage," it is of course a well-thumbed line, but that doesn't change the fact that he's sincere in his desire, and his need, to do just that.

The people of Sam Dent whom Stephens talks to are glimpsed on both sides of the accident, trying to peer through the numbness of their grief to decide if a lawsuit would help anesthetize the pain. We meet the college-educated Ottos (Arsinee Khanjian and Earl Pastko), the morose Walkers (Maury Chaykin and Alberta Watson) who run the Bide-a-Wile motel, and the three key townspeople who were co-narrators with Stephens in the novel.

Dolores Driscoll (Gabrielle Rose) is the chatty school bus driver, walrus-mustached Billy Ansell (Bruce Greenwood) is a single parent who lost both his children, and, most poignantly, there is 14-year-old Nicole Burnell (Sarah Polley), once the light of the town, now paralyzed and forced to restart her life as a self-described "wheelchair girl."

Though this is Egoyan's first adaptation, "The Sweet Hereafter" could serve as a model for how to do it right. He is in sync with the essence of the novel, the overwhelming nature of the tragedy as well as the unmistakable glimmers of healing and reconciliation, while adding vital elements of his own. It was Egoyan's idea, for instance, to have Nicole read the Robert Browning/Kate Greenaway version of "The Pied Piper of Hamlin" to Billy Ansell's children in the days before the accident, a touch that adds a beautiful layer of emphasis to the narrative.

Aside from Holm, many of the actors in "The Sweet Hereafter" are Egoyan regulars, and he directs them expertly, getting an especially subtle performance out of young Polley, well-known in Canada for her television work, whose role becomes more and more central as the story progresses.

What Egoyan has done best is suffuse this story with a almost stately restraint. Unafraid of necessary silences, willing to let scenes play out, Egoyan understands how potent a deliberate pace can be, how effective it is in making already powerful material strong enough to tear at your heart.

NEW STATESMAN, 9/26/97, p. 56, John Diamond

There's an old joke about Wagner, told by Wagnerians, that "he isn't as boring as he sounds". You want to say the same thing about the Canadian director Atom Egoyan. His films (and *The Sweet Hereafter,* although markedly different in crucial respects, is no exception) all creak along, frame by studied frame, scene by significance-heavy scene. But still, and this is the point, you want to make the journey.

It's no less true, though, that the slow chug-chug-chug can also make you itch to pull the emergency stop at times. Egoyan's work has a kind of baffling, irksome seductiveness about it. The flaws are evident and the *longueurs* long, but while the film is on you can forget how unentertaining it all is.

This lack of entertainment is pertinent. It's obvious. And it is more obvious here than in, say, *Speaking Parts* or *Exotica.*   This film of Russell Banks' novel could have been made in Hollywood, and the same could not be said of Egoyan's earlier movies.

The Sweet Hereafter tells the story of a small Canadian community in the shocked aftermath of a school bus crash. Mitchell Stevens, an ambulance-chasing lawyer played by Ian Holm, has come, in his words, to represent the people in their anger. Their reactions to him, as well as his to them, make up a large part of the film's narrative.

In Hollywood hands this would have been a film about how "tragedy unites the residents of a small town" and, interestingly enough, this is exactly how the producers bill the movie. But that is not at all how the movie is played. If anything, this is how tragedy disunites a community.

True, the ending (and this is hardly giving much away) seems to indicate that the meddling lawyer can be got rid of and the town rekindle its identity and integrity, but that is the least satisfying part of the film. According to Egoyan and Banks, what is meant to be an act of courage and solidarity—and I don't want to give away too much plot here—comes across as something very different: aggressive, accusatory, even.

But plot and the old who-what-why is pointedly not what Egoyan's film is about. Stevens, who claims he has come to help the townspeople find out who is to blame for the accident, by his own actions bears false witness. In trying to assuage people's grief by making them believe there could be a reason for their suffering, he obscures the real message: that there is no answer, no cause, no truth to unturn.

Made by a Hollywood studio, this would have been a very different film: for one thing, Ian Holm would be reunited with his junkie daughter, or find romance with her sympathetic old school pal next to whom he finds himself seated on a plane. Not that either the almost-absent, always-phoning daughter or the attractive old school friend are exactly underplayed here. It's hard to imagine that the suggestive relationship between Nicole (Sarah Polley, a regular Egoyan troupe member) and Papa would be played quite as it is—if at all—in a Hollywood version, but these days who knows?

Egoyan is often talked about as a cerebral film-maker, but his messages are too overstated to be complex. The idea of lost children—the lawyer-father who has lost his child to drugs, the townspeople who have lost theirs to death, the sonorous recounting of *The Pied Piper*—is rammed home a little too unsubtly; you can make the connections without having all the dots joined up for you. But Egoyan's real gift is as a sensualist. This is a beautiful-looking film. The light drips, glows, reflects in pools throughout, imbuing the film with a muted radiance you can't take your eyes away from.

All his films are beautiful constructs but this one is different: the images are less harsh, more kindly. Earlier films seemed all about disembodied sex and alienated souls: here there is a hopefulness that lies not just in the light. The opening scene, of a woman, a man, a small child curled together, is tender, full of domestic sweetness; even if, midway through the film, we learn that the opening image is a picture before the fall, the knowledge of that fall takes none of the earlier intimacy away. This may be a trite observation, but this is surely a film made by a new father.

NEW YORK, 11/24/97, p. 68, David Denby

The Sweet Hereafter is a rarity—a glum, rather painful movie that is so beautifully made, so complexly imagined, that one accepts its sadness, at first grudgingly and then willingly, as an artist's necessary voice. The artist in question is the Canadian filmmaker Atom Egoyan *(Exotica)*, who has adapted Russell Banks's 1991 novel devoted to the aftermath of a devastating school-bus accident. In form, *The Sweet Hereafter* appears to be a kind of detective story. A big-city lawyer, Mitchell Stephens (Ian Holm), enters a snowy, forlorn town in British Columbia after fourteen children have died, and travels about interviewing the parents and survivors. Stephens is an adroit and intelligent man; he is also a fanatic, desperate to enlist everyone, including the teenage survivor, Nicole (Sarah Polley), in a grievance suit. "There's no such thing as an accident," he says, insisting that culpability lies somewhere—perhaps not in the female bus driver, an utterly responsible person, but in the company that made the bus or the company that built the guard rail running along the icy road where the bus skidded, broke through, and sank in a half-frozen lake. *Someone* must be responsible. As Stephens investigates, we see what led up to the accident—the family life of the town, with its fissures and its secrets, including adultery and a suggestion of incest—and eventually we see the accident itself. The film cuts backward and forward in time, and we expect that Stephens will uncover some amazing circumstance that will explain everything.

But *The Sweet Hereafter* is far less conventional than that. The detective story yields to a moral inquiry about the value of community and the nature of bonds, both corrupt and pure, between parents and children, with Stephens less the hero of the inquiry than its fool. He is, to be sure, a most remarkable fool, a figure of almost Dostoevskian torment. From the first, Egoyan shows us what's driving him. Stephens's own daughter, Zoe, is a drug addict, a lost, lying girl, always in trouble, and she telephones him constantly, drawing on Stephens's love for her even as she betrays that love. Stephens is trapped—caught between adoration and contempt, and left with an unappeasable desire to avenge the destruction of children everywhere. But he wants to avenge what cannot be avenged, what can only be healed.

This is Ian Holm's greatest role in the movies. His Stephens, fully able to take control of shattered people, is himself in a state of barely controlled despair, and Egoyan keeps the camera very tight on Holm, who registers the tiniest shifts in consciousness with movements of his eyes and lips. Holm's performance is economical but dazzlingly expressive—a masterly demonstration of the art of film acting. He has often played hard, bitter men, but here, playing an intelligent man who doesn't know himself, he attains the stature of a tragic villain. Without meaning to, Stephens breaks the grieving town wide open, exposing wounds that are trying to close.

Atom Egoyan has a rapt, mysterious style, a beautiful solemnity, precise and intelligent, that depends for its haunting effect on something withheld—a word unspoken, an emotion deflected or turned inside out. His previous movie, the erotic drama *Exotica,* was finally, for all its skill, too much a puzzle. But *The Sweet Hereafter* works toward a greater and greater radiance. The transitions from one location to another and one time frame to another are managed effortlessly, with trancelike calm and beauty. Egoyan uses the cold winter landscapes for their tranquil menace, but he knows when to play for a larger, more sinister effect. The camera flies over the hills, trailing that school bus as it rides toward disaster. There's no suspense: We know roughly what's going to happen, but we need to see it for ourselves. We need to feel, and understand, the parents' intimacy with horror, and we experience the accident through the eyes of Billy (Bruce Greenwood), who is driving behind the bus and is the father of two of the children. Billy *sees;* he's the hero of the movie, an unillusioned man, rejecting avenging lawyers and bad-luck omens in favor of the most bitter reality. Bruce Greenwood, one of several actors in the film with whom Egoyan has worked before, has a gap-toothed smile, a slow, deliberate way of speaking, and a sullen wit. He's an assured male presence who pulls off one of the hardest tasks for an actor—he plays an ordinary man who is also, in his way, a great man. His adulterous scenes with Alberta Watson (the mother in David O. Russell's *Spanking the Monkey*) have an acrid intimacy.

The actors are all excellent in a plain style that avoids irony, pose, perversity. This blunt Canadian virtue is not all that we want from acting, but in this case, a slight blandness is part of the point. The deliberate tone is a product of the cold, the open spaces, the lonely life; it's natural to the small northern town, whereas the edgy fervor of the intrusive lawyer is not. These people, so measured and restrained, know how to pull themselves together. Nicole, the survivor, reads, in flashback, Robert Browning's version of "The Pied Piper of Hamelin" to two of the children who later die. The Pied Piper, of course, kills the rats, and when he receives no pay, he takes revenge by leading the town's children away. The poem becomes a kind of narration, a haunting refrain that teasingly promises both annihilation and safety. We wonder: Who in the movie is the piper? Is it the bus driver? The lawyer who wants vengeance? Or is it Nicole, who tells a lie and leads the town to safety? This is a movie about redemption that doesn't feel forced or phony. Even poor Stephens gets his small share of grace. Two years after the inquiry, he's still trying to save his daughter, the daughter he saved from death as an infant many years earlier. By the end of the movie, everything comes together—the answer to the detective inquiry is all that is most difficult to face in life. If there were many movies as reality-bound as this one, I think I would go mad. That this one exists, however, is almost a blessing.

NEW YORK POST, 11/21/97, p. 53, Thelma Adams

Canadian Atom Egoyan has always been a challenging, cerebral, visually inventive filmmaker on the intellectual fringe. With his latest drama, the "Exotica" director makes a great leap forward. "The Sweet Hereafter" is his most mature, emotionally charged and accessible work, a masterpiece of contemporary filmmaking.

Artfully adapted by Egoyan from the superb Russell Banks novel, "The Sweet Hereafter" won the Grand Prize at the Cannes Film Festival. Having screened in the prestigious centerpiece slot at this fall's New York Film Festival, it was the festival's most passionate film, its beating heart, and the movie that sent me from the theater weeping.

"The Sweet Hereafter" is the wrenching, morally complex story of an ambulance-chasing lawyer and the rural town he changes forever, a story of class conflict and common humanity. Brilliantly played by Ian Holm, attorney Mitchell Stephens travels from the city to remote Sam Dent, British Columbia, to exploit a devastating schoolbus accident.

The bus, driven by local matron Dolores Driscoll (Gabrielle Rose), swerved off an icy road one wintry morning. Nearly two-dozen children died. Driscoll survived to bear witness, along with Nicole Burnell (the luminous Sarah Polley), a popular teen crippled by the crash.

While stirring up the grief-stricken rural community in the name of righteous anger and a big settlement, Stephens exposes the society's frayed edges. "It's up to me to ensure moral responsibility in this society," he tells a bereft parent.

Stephens' voyage to the town that has lost its children also changes the lawyer. He gradually confronts his personal loss, breaking through the hard ice of his denial. He confronts his feelings for his demanding, drug-addicted daughter Zoe (heartbreakingly acted by the author's daughter, Caerthan Banks). She is as lost to him as the children of Sam Dent.

Beautifully shot by Paul Sarossy, the panoramic drama, with its majestic mountainscapes and big skies, never loses its intimate grasp of the feelings and motivations of its characters. Initially crushed, Nicole uses her changed circumstances to liberate herself from the cycle of incest perpetuated by her father. She gains the courage to stand up for a truth larger than the facts and rescue the town from litigation hell.

Egoyan remains true to the novel's moral and emotional core. Grief changes us, but it also contains the power to heal, to connect us with what is valuable in life: our children, our families, our communities, a morality that must be an individual choice, not the product of a class action lawsuit.

Through the aftermath of a tragic schoolbus accident, Egoyan and Banks describe a world that has lost its children—through drugs, mass media, neglect, incest, violence. But Nicole's courage gives the movie its redemptive final note. She says in voiceover. "All of us, Dolores, me, the children who survived ... we're all citizens of a different town now, a town of people living in the sweet hereafter.

If a movie this powerful comes once a year, then it's a good year at the movies. Will the Academy be brave enough to follow the lead of the Cannes jury?

NEWSWEEK, 11/24/97, p. 73, David Ansen

On a snowbound, wintry day outside the small town of Sam Dent, in British Columbia, the local school bus plunges off the side of a hill and sinks into a frozen lake. Fourteen of the town's children die. Among the few survivors are the bus driver, Dolores Driscoll, and the beautiful teenager, Nicole Burnell, who will be wheelchair-bound for the rest of her life. In the face of such a calamity, how does a community survive? How do the parents cope? Who do they turn to for solace—and where do they look for scapegoats? These are among the big questions raised by Canadian filmmaker Atom Egoyan's strong, harrowing *The Sweet Hereafter*, taken from Russell Banks's novel.

In the book, the tale was told by a handful of narrators. There was the well-liked Dolores (Gabrielle Rose). There was Nicole (Sarah Polley), who hid a dark family secret, and the Vietnam vet Billy Ansell (Bruce Greenwood), a widower who lost his twin children in the accident. The fourth narrator, the big-city lawyer Mitchell Stephens, has become the focal point of Egoyan's remarkable adaptation, which recently won the Grand Prize at Cannes. Stephens (Ian Holm) arrives in the aftermath of the tragedy, promising financial recompense to the parents of the victims. "Let me represent your anger," pleads the lawyer, a man who's convinced there's no such thing as an accident. Someone must pay.

Is this man a vulture, preying on the weak? It's not quite that simple. Stephens is driven by more than greed: he's haunted by the daughter he's lost to heroin, a loss he can deal with only through the surrogacy of this lawsuit. As Holm plays him, with buttoned-down rage, we see what a superb actor this lawyer must be, adapting his performance to suit the emotional needs of his clients in the class-action lawsuit. It's the only stage he's at home on: confronted with his own daughter, he turns to ice.

Obviously, a story so infused with grief could easily become mawkish, but Egoyan is no sentimentalist. As in his earlier, even more stylized films ("The Adjuster," "Exotica"), Egoyan transforms the most extreme experiences into something almost ritualistic. There's a mesmerizing clarity to "The Sweet Hereafter": you're moved by it, but you never feel the filmmaker is milking your emotions. It's rare that a literary adaptation can at once be so faithful to its source and yet have a voice and tone so entirely its own.

Led by the superb Holm, the subtle Polley and the charismatic Greenwood, the largely Canadian ensemble here reveals to us the sins, wounds and secret strengths of a community rocked by a vicious fate. Amid the sorrow, there is the harsh beauty of survival.

SIGHT AND SOUND, 10/97, p. 60, Tony Rayns

Lawyer Mitchell Stephens arrives in Sam Dent, a small town in British Columbia, where the community is paralysed by a recent accident: the school bus, driven by Dolores Driscoll and carrying 22 children, went off an icy road and plunged into a lake, causing 14 deaths. Stephens hopes to mobilise the bereaved parents into a class-action lawsuit against the bus company; he will act without a fee, against one-third of any settlement reached. (Stephens himself has deep emotional problems; divorced from his wife Klara, he keeps his drug-addicted, drop-out daughter Zoe at arm's length.)

He turns to the local motel owners Wendell and Risa Walker for advice on which grieving parents to approach. He also meets Dolores (and her husband Abbott, victim of a stroke) and hears her account of the day of the accident. The first to sign up for his class action are the Ottos, Hartley and Wanda, who lost their adopted son Bear. Risa is the next, followed by Sam and Mary Burnell, whose daughter Nicole survived the accident but is now wheelchair-bound. (Stephens provides a computer for Nicole, to sweeten the deal.) But garage-owner Billy Ansell, a widower who lost both his children, threatens Stephens with violence and advises others in the community to have nothing to do with him.

Called to give her legal deposition about her experience of the accident, Nicole (who has previously insisted that she will not tell lies) destroys the law-suit by testifying that Dolores was driving too fast. Stephens is left smarting, but the community regains a sense of solidarity and learns to come to terms with its grief.

This narrative is intercut with flashbacks to the periods before, during and immediately after the accident, centred on the day-to-day lives of the main characters. Billy regularly hires Nicole to babysit his children while he pursues a secret affair with Risa. Nicole is trying to make it as a rock singer, and has an incestuous relationship with her father Sam. Stephens himself recalls an episode from Zoe's infancy, when he and Klara raced against time to get her to a hospital in a medical emergency. There are also glimpses of the future: some time later, Stephens is on an internal flight and finds himself sitting next to Allison, a childhood friend of Zoe's. The encounter forces him to go over the gradual breakdown of his relationship with his daughter and to describe his deeply unresolved feelings for her. On arrival at his destination, he sees Dolores driving a hotel shuttle-bus. In Sam Dent, Nicole feels that the community has entered a new and happier phase which she dubs "the sweet hereafter". But her own thoughts still centre on the days when she used to babysit Billy's children—and dreamed of marrying Billy herself.

Atom Egoyan has been notably frank about his reasons for adapting Russell Banks' novel and making—for the first time—a film not based on an original screenplay of his own. "I felt I had made a number of films inspired by stories that came from the universe that was in my own head, but it was becoming all too familiar for me. I wanted to find something that would challenge me and still provide a framework on which I could impose my own structural concepts, and this was the perfect story for that." He is also eager to cement a direct link between this film and its predecessor: "*Exotica* ends with a shot of Christina walking towards the house. What happens there has had a great deal of influence on her life. She is not protected in the house. And *The Sweet Hereafter* takes us inside the house." (Both quotes are from the Alliance Communications pressbook.)

This is a not uncommon syndrome among writer-directors who base their work on deeply personal preoccupations and use it to confront issues they want to resolve for themselves or to exorcise personal demons: they tend to reach a point (sometimes temporary, sometimes permanent) when the well runs dry. Fassbinder dealt with it by co-opting favourite books (*Effi Briest, Berlin Alexanderplatz*) or by giving a revered classic a good kicking (*Nora Helmer*). Paul Schrader dealt with it by remaking *Cat People*. Egoyan has taken what seems at first sight the Cronenberg route of filming an 'unfilmable' novel. His adaptation of *The Sweet Hereafter* certainly looks like an Atom Egoyan film; simply as an exercise in superimposing one sensibility on to another, the film is so ingenious, so skilful and so nuanced that it's easy to forget that it has literary roots at all.   All of which makes it hard to explain why the film is ultimately so disappointing.

The core problem seems to be that Egoyan has miscast himself as the adapter of a novel in which a sense of community is paramount.   Few directors have *less* sense of community than Egoyan: his work has always centred on obsessives and eccentrics trapped in solipsistic worlds, most of whom have cause to regret their forays into social and sexual intercourse, and the surly bonds that interest him most are those within families.   Here he does not even present a plausible topography of the town, which never feels like anything but a patched-together collection of locations, let alone provide any inkling of the ways its citizens interact socially.   For the purposes of the film, Sam Dent is a group of five unhappy households, a garage and a civic courthouse.   And the only elements which knit the households together prior to the accident are an adulterous affair and the feelings of a young woman trapped in an incestuous affair with her father who dreams of marrying the town's most eligible widower and becoming a 'mother' (rather than just a babysitter) to his kids.   In short, Egoyan's Sam Dent is not a million miles from *Peyton Place*.

Banks' novel is divided into four sections, each with its own narrator: the structure helps the author to build a real sense of the community which has been struck by the tragedy.   In line with his earlier films, Egoyan appears to replace the idea of plural voices with an omniscient directorial point-of-view.   *The Sweet Hereafter* has a fantastically complicated time structure: it has hardly begun before it plunges into free-range cross-cutting between the pasts, presents and futures of its characters, and it feels free throughout to make connections across all bounds of time and space.   Egoyan's method of constructing and narrating his films has always had an element of tease: he likes to drop hints, make insinuations, leave room for the viewer to speculate... and to surprise with sudden revelations.   *The Sweet Hereafter* does all these things, only more so.   It's as if what Egoyan responds to most strongly in the novel is simply the range of characters and time-frames it provides as grist to the mill of his structural machinations.

The most surprising (and daring) of the film's countless linkages is that between the bus accident itself and the day when Stephens' then-infant daughter Zoe almost died from the side-effects of an insect bite.   Egoyan effects the link simply by presenting one event after the other.   The implications are anything but clear-cut: the juxtaposition could be suggesting that Stephens' quest to mount the Sam Dent class-action suit is an oblique expression of his unresolved rage at the breakdown of his own marriage and the loss of his own daughter—not to an insect bite and an insufficiently concerned doctor but later, to narcotics.   The one thing which is clear (and Egoyan underlines it heavily by using the image of the Stephens family asleep moments before the calamity strikes Zoe as the background to his main title at the front of the film) is the directorial sleight-of-hand which equates a community tragedy with a family crisis.

It's revealing that the 'glue' which Egoyan uses to weld the many disparate fragments together is 'The Pied Piper of Hamelin'.   The poem is first heard as Nicole's bedtime reading to Billy's children: it subsequently blankets the film, appearing on the soundtrack even when, at some unspecified point in the future, Stephens discusses Zoe's fate with one of her old friends on a plane. (Browning's poem is not in the novel, although Banks now says he wishes it had been.) The prominent use of the poem 'rhymes' Sam Dent with Hamelin and implies that the children who died in the bus-crash were somehow 'culled' as a punishment for the sins of their parents. (It also, of course, identifies Nicole with the "lame child" left behind by the piper.) This is a smart and snazzily post-modern way of connoting 'community', but Egoyan cannot make it stick when nothing in the rest of the film supports it.   Five pained/guilty families do not a community make.

Banks and Egoyan do, however, reach simultaneous climaxes with the crucial scene of Nicole's testimony about the crash, the only genuinely moving moment in the film.   For Egoyan, Nicole's rationally inexplicable decision to scuttle the law-suit by lying represents both an act of tremendous courage and a decisive break with "what happens to her inside the house"—her incestuous idylls with her father, which take place in a barn dangerously festooned with candles. His respect for the novel obliges him to show Nicole's action having a community-wide effect, something he attempts in a rather bizarre way with a shot of a ferris wheel over which Nicole's voice enthuses about everything being "strange and new".   But he follows this by showing Nicole's retreat into her memories of the days when she was Billy's babysitter, closing the film as he began it: with an image of domestic bliss which we know will very soon be shattered.   On the face of it, a classic Egoyan moment. But it doesn't kick either emotionally or intellectually, because the ingenuity of the adaptation has obstructed the real thrust of the film.

TIME, 12/1/97, p. 84, Richard Schickel

No one knows why the school bus swerved off the road and into the lake. All that is known by the inhabitants of the profoundly isolated small town in British Columbia, already buried in snow and melancholy, is that 14 of their children are dead and many more are injured. After such tragedy, what redemption?

None, of course. Unless you can find cold comfort in cold cash. Which is why a sardonic God invented negligence lawyers. Russell Banks, author of the novel from which Atom Egoyan derived *The Sweet Hereafter*, has, however, improved on His handiwork, creating in Mitchell Stephens (Ian Holm) a man who chases settlements with a chills-and-fever passion that can be explained not by greed but by the suppurating wounds life has inflicted on him. The man, whom Holm plays with superbly controlled fanaticism, wants compensation from an unfair universe but finds momentary relief in squeezing more readily available targets.

It is necessary for the townsfolk, who are stupid and sinful in more ordinary ways, to avoid being drawn into his vengeful scheming, to find a sweet hereafter in which they can at least partly heal. It is a young woman (Sarah Polley)—surely the daughter Stephens wishes he might have had—who opens them to that state of grace in this solemn, subtly structured, beautifully acted and ultimately hypnotic movie.

VILLAGE VOICE, 11/25/97, p. 91, J. Hoberman

Somewhere in rural Canada, in the middle of *The Sweet Hereafter*, a kid-filled school bus skids off the road into an icy lake. It's filmed in long shot; long anticipated and long withheld, it shatters the winter world's clear, cold crystal. Adapted by Atom Egoyan from Russell Banks' 1991 novel, the movie—which won a jury prize at Cannes and had its local premiere at the last New York Film Festival—is as restrained in its effects as it is devastating.

The big-budget disaster flick may be in the midst of a new Hollywood cycle, but heart-wrencher of heartwrenchers, *The Sweet Hereafter* charts the ways in which disaster resonates through the communal psyche. The spectacular backdrop, the images of isolation and loneliness give the movie a chilling, ethereal quality. Grief is only partially cauterized. The material is so overwhelming that it takes a second viewing to get some critical perspective.

As the title suggests, the worst has already happened when *The Sweet Hereafter* opens. The town has been transported into the phantom zone. But where the novel's overlapping action is divided among four narrators, the movie travels effortlessly back and forth in time, creating a brilliantly edited vortex of suspense and dread as it circles around the catastrophe. Repeatedly, Egoyan puts his camera in a helicopter, follows the doomed bus, and then abruptly swoops away into the sky—suspending, for a few minutes longer, the fatal accident.

This ballad structure is reinforced by Egoyan's use of Robert Browning's "The Pied Piper of Hamlin"—read to two sleepy children on the last night of their lives by their teenage baby-sitter Nicole (Sarah Polley, expanding on a similar role in Egoyan's *Exotica*). It's a tremendously suggestive juxtaposition that only makes metaphoric sense once the movie is over. Save for the school-bus driver, Nicole is the accident's sole survivor. And no less than the lame boy of Browning's poem—left bereft as the only child in Hamlin—she was maimed, albeit invisibly, even before the bus plunged into the lake.

The Sweet Hereafter is a disaster movie with neither heroes nor villains. An ambulance-chasing lawyer up from the city encourages the town's bereaved parents to sue—the government, the bus manufacturer, whomever. "There is no such thing as an accident," he tells them with righteous fury. As in Banks's novel, religion per se does not exist. The spellbinding lawyer offers the closest thing to faith. (The director might have had more faith in Ian Holm's grimly fastidious performance—illustrating one particularly sensational flashback that the actor could easily have put over on narrative alone.)

The lawyer is himself a distraught parent—father of an HIV-infected junkie—and consumed by helpless rage each time his investigation is interrupted by a phone call from his own lost daughter. In one deftly Egoyan touch, he receives a transmission while locked in a car wash. In another, Egoyan allows the lawyer to tell his story to the model daughter (a childhood friend of his own) whom he happens to meet on an airplane—another detached, hermetic environment, somewhere in the clouds.

The Sweet Hereafter is Egoyan's first adaptation after a half-dozen highly personal, even idiosyncratic, features, but he nevertheless manages to find all of his recent themes—family ties, media simulation, unspeakable loss, and professional exploitation. As the lawyer has a more than passing resemblance to the grandiose title character of *The Adjuster,* so the tangled relations between parents and children—specifically fathers and daughters—in the context of terrible loss hark back to *Exotica.*

The presence of absence is a longstanding Egoyan obsession. When the bus finally goes down, an eerie videotape of its wrecked interior signals that the film has become, finally, a ghost story. With the accident at the movie's dead center, the last half focuses on Nicole—lost object of her father's fantasies. What court can put a price on that? Even lawyers weep when the truth is a lie.

Also reviewed in:
NATION, 12/8/97, p. 35, Stuart Klawans
NEW REPUBLIC, 12/8/97, p. 30, Stanley Kauffmann
NEW YORK TIMES, 11/21/97, p. E18, Janet Maslin
NEW YORKER, 11/24/97, p. 138, Daphne Merkin
VARIETY, 5/19-25/97, p. 54, Brendan Kelly
WASHINGTON POST, 12/26/97, p. C1, Stephen Hunter
WASHINGTON POST, 12/26/97, Weekend/p. 35, Stephen Hunter

SWITCHBACK

A Paramount Pictures and Rysher Entertainment release of a Pacific Western production. *Executive Producer:* Keith Samples, Mel Efros, and Jeb Stuart. *Producer:* Gale Anne Hurd. *Director:* Jeb Stuart. *Screenplay:* Jeb Stuart. *Director of Photography:* Oliver Wood. *Editor:* Conrad Buff. *Music:* Basil Poledouris. *Sound:* David Kelson. *Casting:* Pamela Dixon Mickelson. *Production Designer:* Jeff Howard. *Art Director:* Carl Sfensel. *Costumes:* Betsy Heiman. *Running time:* 129 minutes. *MPAA Rating:* R.

CAST: Dennis Quaid (Frank LaCrosse); Danny Glover (Bob Goodall); Jared Leto (Lane Dixon); R. Lee Ermey (Sheriff Buck Olmstead); Ted Levine (Deputy Nate Booker); William Fichtner (Chief Jack McGinnis); Leo Burmester (Shorty); Merle Kennedy (Betty); Julio Oscar Mechoso (Jorge Martinez); Orville Stoeber (Saldez).

LOS ANGELES TIMES, 10/31/97, Calendar/p. 12, Jack Mathews

[The following review by Jack Mathews appeared in a slightly different form in NEWSDAY, 10/31/97, Part II/p. B6.]

Before he exploded onto the scene of commercial screenwriting with his back-to-back scripts for "Die Hard" and "The Fugitive," young Jeb Stuart wrote a screenplay in a college workshop program that showed enough promise to earn him a Hollywood agent. Now, that early script has been dusted off and made into a major motion picture, with Stuart himself directing, and it is a spectacular mess.

"SwitchBack" looks fabulous, with Oliver Wood's cinematography providing breathtaking panoramas of the snow-clad Rockies, and the film's action sequences and literal cliffhangers are first-rate in their design, stunt work and special effects. But beneath its high production gloss, and its casting of action pros Danny Glover and Dennis Quaid, is a story of jaw-dropping banality.

"SwitchBack" is a serial killer thriller, about an obsessed FBI agent following the bloody trail of a psychopath into the wintry wilderness of the Southwest. Quaid's Frank LaCrosse is on a solo manhunt. The killer, Bob Goodall (Glover), has tricked the FBI into pinning his 18 murders on another man, but Frank, who's been after him for 18 months, knows better. Goodall kidnapped

Frank's 7-year-old son, just to get him taken off the case, and then sent him a riddle telling him how to get the boy back.

It seems that Goodall wants to die, but he wants to do it as part of a game of hide-and-seek, and before Frank can get to the part where he might be able to sing "Olly-olly-oxen-free!," he has to overcome local police resistance, a stupid subplot about a sheriff's election, clumsy attempts by his own agency to stop him, and the whims of mother nature.

You can feel the student's hand all over this story. Stuart creates conflict and motivation out of thin air. The killer's MO is to sever the femoral arteries of his random victims, but no explanation for that peculiar fetish is ever given. Nor do we learn why Goodall wants to die, or why he's suddenly killing all of his old friends.

In fact, the only plausible person in the film is R. Lee Ermey's Buck Olmstead, a wise old Texas sheriff who becomes Frank's ally.

Frank is a one-note character played in a trance-like, monotone funk by Quaid. In contrast, Glover hams it up with relish as the villain. In the early going, when he and his hitchhiker (Jared Leto), a medical student dropout used first as a red herring, then a foil, and finally a messenger, are driving into the Rockies, Glover's gregarious manner is good fun.

But when his dark side is revealed, it's almost laughably incongruous. He goes from charmer to maniac in a nanosecond, and right back again. Strobe Man. This is definitely a pathology worth exploring, but hey, Stuart is a screenwriter not a psychologist. If you want human dimension, if you want professionalism, rent Hitchcock.

NEW YORK POST, 10/31/97, p. 51, Thelma Adams

What do you call a train obsession? Amtrakmania?

Jeb Stuart has trains on the brain. The most memorable sequence in Stuart's script for "The Fugitive" is the runaway train that nearly catapults off the screen, setting the hero free to run for his plot.

When Stuart chose to make his directing debut with the thriller "SwitchBack," an early screenplay he wrote at Stanford, his hero all but goes choo choo.

The movie's expository set piece—a Halloween-ready screamer with a baby sitter in mortal danger—cuts to a little boy upstairs. What's he doing? He's obliviously playing with his Brio train set.

From that moment until the film's caboose, the energetic fight-to-the-death aboard a rickety train in the Rocky Mountains, Stuart works his story like an engineer, pushing it faster and faster until it threatens to leap the rails but never does.

There's a certain grimness to Stuart's determination that parallels his hero, FBI agent Frank LaCrosse (Dennis Quaid). Quaid buries his "Big Easy" smile and turns to the Harrison Ford school of jaw-grinding, physically fit family men on a tear against evil.

Agent LaCrosse is in-hot pursuit of a serial killer—and, yes, this time it's personal. (We know his sorrow, but we still want to say, "Lighten up.")

Stuart tosses around the suspects: Could the slasher be the buck-toothed mystery man in the opening scene. The blue-eyed hitcher, Lane Dixon (Jared Leto), who's carrying a burden as big as his backpack? The jovial ex-railroad man, Bob Goodall (Danny Glover), who picks Dixon up on the road to Salt Lake City?

Will the pursuit of justice interfere with the heated sheriff's election between Buck Olmstead (R. Lee Ermey) and rival Jack McGinnis (William Fichtner) in Amarillo? There's a lot happening in "SwitchBack," all of it precise and well-oiled, none of it new.

In "SwitchBack," every hick bar is a brawl waiting to happen. Every diner has a patron choking, poised for resurrection. Every cheap motel room has corpses in the tub.

Why does the killer kill and kill again? Because it makes for a good cat-and-mouse plot, a good thriller engine. Is that reason enough? After the movie ended, the improbability of the killer's actions stayed with me like the echo of a train whistle after the train has passed.

Stuart's direction is sturdy, his script entertaining, but he doesn't live up to his best line. Sheriff Olmstead says about LaCrosse: "He told the truth. And once you've heard the truth, everything else is just cheap whiskey."

VILLAGE VOICE, 11/4/97, p. 84, Michael Atkinson

Reviewers have been implored not to reveal the surprising plot twists and ending of *SwitchBack*, the publicity notes alluding so royally to the film's special structure that I thought perhaps writer-director Jeb Stuart decided to remake Melville's *Le Doulos*. No one needed to worry. Stuart's screenplay—his first, written in college—is a veritable Western Union of telegraphed thriller ka-thunks, taking a page out of the Joe Eszterhas of-course-he's-the-killer-there's-nobody-else-around school of plot finesse; it all hangs on the elaborate designs of yet another genius serial killer.

Somebody should pull the stats, but surely a Harper's Index item on the annual ratio of serial killer movies to actual living serial killers would push 10 to 1. And you can cough up cultural studies theses all you want about how this reflects our cultural dreads and weaknesses, but if you asked Stuart, author of *Die Hard, The Fugitive*, and *Just Cause*, I bet he'd say all you need is cash.

A work of meaningless, ineffectual professionalism, *SwitchBack* follows two parallel stories which, surprise, intersect in the end. Number one: Dennis Quaid is an embittered fed hunting down the serial killer who kidnapped his son. His investigation brings him to rural Colorado, right smack in the middle of a testy election for sheriff between crusty incumbent R. Lee Ermey and ratlike hopeful William Fichtner. Number two: angelic hitcher Jared Leto gets picked up by the overbearing Danny Glover, whose Lincoln interior is covered with lacquered centerfolds. Their trip westward is punctuated with a crazy roadhouse bar fight, lots of hazardous mountain driving, jovial encounters with Glover's pals, and so many heavy-handed visual and music portents indicating that Glover is in fact the serial psycho from story number one you wonder what other conclusion you're supposed to reach.

As in *Sleepless in Seattle,* the two stars meet only at the very end, amid a hailstorm of flummery about train schedules and clearing the Rio Grande. Produced within an inch of its life, *SwitchBack* has a rip-roaring way with cliff-hanging stunt scenes, but the actors are just there to pay bills—Quaid seems only occasionally on the verge of an emotion, and Glover works every word of dialogue like week-old taffy. Ermey, whose drill-sergeant cadence makes every line delivery snap, crackle, and pop, steals the show. Which doesn't seem quite worth his time. As usual, the serial killer is merely an abominable macguffin with no history or motive, just an m.o. so pointlessly obtuse it could've been conceived only in film school.

Also reviewed in:
CHICAGO TRIBUNE, 10/31/97, Friday/p. J, Mark Caro
NEW YORK TIMES, 10/31/97, p. E20, Stephen Holden
VARIETY, 10/27-11/2/97, p. 42, Leonard Klady
WASHINGTON POST, 10/31/97, p. B1, Rita Kempley
WASHINGTON POST, 10/31/97, Weekend/p. 53, Desson Howe

TANGO LESSON, THE

A Sony Pictures Classics release of an Adventure Pictures presentation of an OKCK Films/PIE/NDF/Imagica/Pandora Film/Cinema Projects/Sigma Pictures coproduction. *Producer:* Christopher Sheppard. *Director:* Sally Potter. *Screenplay:* Sally Potter. *Director of Photography:* Robby Müller. *Editor:* Herve Schneid. *Music:* Sally Potter. *Choreographer:* Pablo Vernon. *Sound:* Jean-Paul Mugel, Gerard Hardy, and (music) Franck Lebon. *Casting:* Irene Lamb. *Production Designer:* Carlos Conti. *Art Director:* Graciela Oderigo. *Set Dresser:* Marianna Sourrouille. *Special Effects:* Tom Cundom and Christian Talenton. *Costumes:* Paul Minter. *Make-up:* Thi-Loan Nguyen. *Stunt Coordinator:* Patrick Cauderlier. *Running time:* 101 minutes. *MPAA Rating:* PG.

CAST: Sally Potter (Sally); Morgane Maugran (Red Model); Geraldine Maillet (Yellow Model); Katerina Mechera (Blue Model); David Toole (Fashion Designer); George Yiasoumi (Photographer); Michele Parent, Claudine Mavros, and Monique Couturier (Seamstresses);

Matthew Hawkins and Simon Worgan (Bodyguards); Pablo Veron (Pablo); Carolina Iotti (Pablo's Partner); Howard Lee (Man at Tea Dance); Heathcoat Williams (Builder); Juan Jose Czalkin (Waiter); Gustavo Naveira (Gustavo); Fabian Salas (Fabian); Horacio Marassi (Shoe Man); David Derman, Oscar Dante Lorenzo, and Omar Vega (Salon Dancers); Carlos Copello (Carlos); Olga Besio (Olga); Cantilo Pena (Hotel Porter); Maria Noel, Fabian Stratas, and Gregory Dayton (Movie Executives); Peter Eyre (English Tango Fan); Emmanuelle Tertipis (Woman in Dressing Room); Ruben Orlando Di Napoli (Master of Ceremonies); Tito Haas (Taxi Driver); Alicia Monti (Carlos' Partner); Maria Fernanda Lorences (Woman Opening Door); Luis Sturla and Amanda Beita (Couple Opening Door); Marcos Woinski (Man Opening Door); Eduardo Rojo (Janitor); Oscar Arribas (Man at Synagogue).

LOS ANGELES TIMES, 12/24/97, Calendar/p. 12, Jack Mathews

[The following review by Jack Mathews appeared in a slightly different form in **NEWSDAY, 11/14/97, Part II/p. B12.]**

Given the amount of ego essential to sustaining the careers of filmmakers, it's surprising that more movies aren't made as self-portraits. At least, it's surprising until you suffer through something like Sally Potter's "The Tango Lesson."

Potter, a British director ("Orlando"), performance artist and former dancer, has trained the script and camera on herself with such a steady, self-admiring gaze, it almost forces you to look away. What she sees—a woman of intellectual depth and sensitivity, professional integrity, sensuality, grace, courage, determination and talent—is not particularly what we see, which is a woman smothering herself with her own affection.

"The Tango Lesson" is done as a reflective docudrama, chronicling Potter's obsession with learning the tango. She has worked up a story of sorts, about herself and her relationship with Pablo Veron (as himself), the tango dancer she engages for lessons. Soon, they are getting not only their feet tangled up, but their emotions. Through most of the film, Sally and Pablo confine their passions to the dance floor, alternately fighting and making love.

Potter can tango, and with the flowing black-and-white cinematography of Robby Muller, the graceful editing of Herve Schneid, and a wonderful tango soundtrack, the dance sequences are pleasurable enough to watch. But in the end, tango is the movie's only strength, and for those of us compelled to watch even vanity productions, we can be thankful that Potter didn't decide to learn the polka.

NEW YORK POST, 11/15/97, p. 28, Thelma Adams

It's no longer polite to use the word "spinsters."

There was a time, though, when actresses like Katharine Hepburn and Maggie Smith arrived at that difficult age when they were no longer young but not yet ready to abandon their sexuality and play madwomen in the attic. So they played spinsters, women of independent means and minds, women who experienced their last burst of sexuality in a foreign country in the arms of a younger man.

Sally Potter, the inventive, if self-conscious, director of "Orlando," now leads us through "The Tango Lesson," a post-modern version of the spinster romance "Summertime" or "Love and Pain (and the Whole Damn Thing)."

In this last tango in Paris, London and Buenos Aires, a filmmaker named Sally, played by Potter herself, travels to France. Sally takes up the tango—and Argentine tango star Pablo Veron.

Shot largely in gravitas-giving black and white by noted cinematographer Robby Muller ("Breaking the Waves"), the drama has the improvisational feel of a dance being created as we watch within a defined rhythm and structure.

The pale, bird-like Potter, with tense thin lips and fair locks yanked into prim buns, is well-cast. We look into her, intelligent face and see the child that she must have been, the old woman that she will become, and her ardent, midlife desire to rekindle a fire in her life and art.

As her muse, "Tango Argentina" star Veron makes a strong movie debut.

Veron leads the audience through a number of well-shot tango numbers, although he is hampered in duets with Potter, who has the steps but not the moves. Director Potter uses the conceit to explore leading and following, dominance and submission, the push-pull of relationships between men and women.

In the end, though, "The Tango Lesson" is a case study in smart women, stupid choices. By the time Potter lets her hair down and dons tight T-shirts the movie has become a vanity production.

SIGHT AND SOUND, 12/97, p. 54, Claire Monk

Sally Potter, a London-based film director, is working on a new script. During a research trip to Paris, she wanders into a theatre and is mesmerised by the Argentinian tango being danced on-stage by a couple. Afterwards, she approaches the male dancer, Pablo Veron, and arranges for him to give her tango lessons.

After one lesson, Sally returns to London to work on her script but becomes restless. When her study's floor needs extensive work, she escapes to Buenos Aires and immerses herself in learning the tango from two dancers, Gustavo and Fabian. A fax from some interested US producers sends her back to London to finish her script. Afterwards, she returns to Pablo in Paris. He is startled by her progress and they start dancing together, fall in love and strike a bargain: if he will make her a tango dancer, she will make him a film star.

In Hollywood, studio executives praise Sally's script but want to change most of its distinctive qualities. Disillusioned, she abandons the film. A new idea for a film about the tango takes root. Meanwhile, Pablo asks her to perform in a show with him. But on New Year's Eve, he breaks a date they have made. Later, he proposes they sublimate their attraction to each other their work. Their dancing ceases to be harmonious: Pablo attacks Sally's every movement. After their public performance, he criticises her furiously. After a row, they split up.

Rethinking, Sally offers Pablo reconciliation, but on one condition: if she is to put him in a film, he must learn to follow *her*. They return to Buenos Aires and start work on the film with Gustavo and Fabian. The hard search for locations causes the men to rebel, until Sally takes charge. Now it is Pablo who feels vulnerable, and he starts to ask questions about himself and their relationship. Reunited, the pair embrace, and Sally expresses her love in a song.

The director and star of *The Tango Lesson* Sally Potter has described her film as one which "exists, perilously, on the knife edge between reality and fiction". Potter's previous feature *Orlando* (based on a Virginia Woolf novel which was part fictionalised biography, part historical time-travel and part love letter) also balanced on this knife edge, but the fact that it was a literary adaptation made the combination safer. By contrast, *The Tango Lesson,* based on real experiences from Potter's life, is a significant personal risk, one intensified by Potter's decision to play herself on screen.

Shot mostly in exquisite black and white by veteran cinematographer Robby Müller, it dramatises/documents Potter's fascination with the Argentinian tango. The film shows her single-minded desire to learn the dance and her fluctuating emotional relationship with her teacher/partner Pablo Veron (a real-life tango star, also playing himself, who comes across as macho, predictably over-accustomed to adulation, and prone to giving ego-bruising criticism of the older, female Potter.

Given Potter's near-constant presence on screen in an allegedly autobiographical film, *The Tango Lesson* will inevitably be rejected by some viewers and critics as self-indulgent. But for a film-maker like Potter who has never marketed herself as a media or screen personality, the experience must have been closer to self-exposure. Miraculously, she transforms this highly personal material and uses her ambiguous screen presence (is it Potter we are watching, or a construction named "Sally Potter"?) well to make a film which is mostly intriguing and affecting rather than embarrassing. This has the same light touch, the same playfulness about gender relations and the magical aura which made *Orlando* a pleasure. The film's weaknesses (of which the chummy casting of poet Heathcote Williams as an unlikely builder is one) are generally minor, although the 'happy ending', in which Potter serenades Pablo by the Buenos Aires docks, is not just cheesy but unsatisfying.

To criticise *The Tango Lesson* in such terms, though, misses the point. Its real richness lies in the multilayered themes which Potter's immersion in the dance allows her to explore. She has written that the film is about: "the attraction of opposites: between Anglo-Saxon and Latin-American cultures; between male and female; between the watcher and watched ... [and] about power". Obviously, *The Tango Lesson* is also about the imbalance of power between man and woman—a theme for which the tango itself stands as a potent metaphor.

To be a satisfactory tango partner, a woman must learn to "do nothing", to follow. When Sally, used to taking charge as a film director, fails to achieve this passivity, Pablo rages that she has "destroyed [his] freedom to move". But, more interestingly, *The Tango Lesson* is also an exploration of the relationships between pleasure and work, life and art. Rather than dramatising the distance between rehearsal and performance, inspiration and artefact, *The Tango Lesson* constantly continuity-edits them together. Crucially, Pablo's insistence that personal and professional relationships should be kept distinct results in the disintegration of his relationship with Sally.

Thus our uncertainty about whether Potter's presence on screen is personal or professional, and the related 'problem' the film seems to pose—why, some might ask, has Potter pursued this personal project rather than a more mainstream movie?—are exactly the subjects *The Tango Lesson* seeks to explore. Potter's dramatisation in the film of her dissatisfaction with *Rage*, the film project she abandoned in real life, and with her abortive encounter with Hollywood executives, provocatively suggests that her powerlessness as a woman and tango amateur are not so different from her position in an industry in which films and directors are fundamentally commodities. With ironic aptness, *The Tango Lesson*'s only colour sequences (highly reminiscent of *Orlando*'s lavish spectacle) are imagined glimpses from this parallel film which wasn't made. For those who wonder why Potter has followed *Orlando* with a film which seems to retreat from the mainstream—while recalling the more stringent political critiques of her earlier work—*The Tango Lesson* offers its own answer.

VILLAGE VOICE, 11/18/97, p. 82, J. Hoberman

Sally Potter's *The Tango Lesson,* is hardly cinema verité, but it does operate in the gap between narrative fiction and documentary truth while questioning the nature of stardom . Call it a structuralist-minimalist-feminist dance-musical psychodrama or a post-*Evita* analogue to Yvonne Rainer's more strenuously avant *The Lives of Performers*.

Potter—best known for her 1992 adaptation of Virginia Woolf's *Orlando*—plays herself, a primly humorless British filmmaker writing an outlandish Hollywood script called *Rage* (visualized as a woman in red, chased by a legless dwarf). Fortunately, she allows herself to be seduced from this task by an obsession with tango, striking a bargain with the young and hunky Paris-based dancer Pablo Veron (also playing himself). If he teaches her to tango, she'll put him in the movies. In the short run, the alliance is quite successful. The self-possessed Potter, whose perfect carriage suggests professional training more than holds her own.

Although the dance scenes can be wonderfully kinetic—Vernon choreographs a terrific number around the people mover at the Buenos Aires airport—*The Tango Lesson* aspires to more, foundering on a series of unconvincing developments. The partners discover that they are both Jews, fall in love, discuss the movie they are making, quarrel over Potter's need to lead. What's disarming (or not, depending on your perspective) is that in this age of unlimited self-improvement, her narcissism is taken for granted.

Also reviewed in:
NATION, 12/22/97, p. 36, Yvonne Marceau
NEW YORK TIMES, 11/14/97, p. E19, Janet Maslin
VARIETY, 9/8-14/97, p. 78, David Rooney
WASHINGTON POST, 12/25/97, p. C14, Desson Howe
WASHINGTON POST, 12/25/97, Weekend/p. 34, Desson Howe

TAR

A Mongrel Movies release. *Producer:* Abigail Hunt. *Director:* Goetz Grossmann. *Screenplay:* Goetz Grossmann, James A. Pearson, and Gilbert Giles. *Director of Photography:* Lloyd Handwerker. *Editor:* Sabine Krayenbuhl. *Music:* John Hill. *Running time:* 90 minutes. *MPAA Rating:* Not Rated.

CAST: Kevin Thigpen (Curtis); Nicole Prescott (Tracy); Seth Gilliam (Tyrone); Ron Brice (Jamal).

NEW YORK POST, 11/26/97, p. 46, Larry Worth

Fans of blaxploitation films have reason to cheer. But they'll be the only ones celebrating "Tar."

Stereotypes flourish as gun-toting African-American radicals kidnap and murder rich white businessmen to battle the system's inequities. A slew of racist Caucasian cops rounds out the usual suspects.

Trying not to leave a cliche unturned, director-and-cowriter Goetz Grossmann also tells a story of star lovers, with a pretty black cop having a crisis of conscience after falling for a childhood pal-turned-criminal.

Kevin Thigpen and Nicole Prescott are completely charismatic as the dynamic duo, while Seth ("Starship Troopers") Gilliam's turn as a man of divided loyalties deserves its own showcase. Sadly, "Tar" is too focused on fanning the flames of black-and-white dissension to even notice.

Also reviewed in:
NEW YORK TIMES, 11/26/97, p. E5, Lawrence Van Gelder

TELLING LIES IN AMERICA

A Banner Pictures release of a Joe Eszterhas presentation of a Banner Entertainment production in association with Kuzui Enterprises and Ben Myron productions. *Executive Producer:* Brian Swardstrom, Mickey Liddell, and Naomi Eszterhas. *Producer:* Ben Myron and Fran Rubel Kuzui. *Director:* Guy Ferland. *Screenplay:* Joe Eszterhas. *Director of Photography:* Reynaldo Villalobos. *Editor:* Jill Savitt. *Music:* Nicholas Pike. *Music Editor:* Mark Green and Michael Jay. *Choreographer:* Thomas Clark and Elizabeth Knowle. *Sound:* Jonathan Andrews and (music) Julie Last. *Sound Editor:* Tim Chau. *Casting:* Emily Schweber and Susan Brown. *Production Designer:* James Gelarden. *Set Designer:* Thomas Paul. *Set Decorator:* Sarah Young. *Costumes:* Laura Cunningham. *Make-up:* Jeanee Josefczyk. *Running time:* 101 minutes. *MPAA Rating:* PG-13.

CAST: Kevin Bacon (Duane, "Billy Magic"); Brad Renfro (Karchy Jonas); Maximilian Schell (Dr. Istvan Jonas); Calista Flockhart (Diney Majeski); Paul Dooley (Father Norton); Jonathan Rhys Meyers (Kevin Boyle); Luke Wilson (Henry); Damen Fletcher (Amos); Jerry Swindall (Andy "Croak" Stas); K.K. Dodds (Justine); James Kisicki (Cecil Simms); J.J. Horna (The Blind Kid); Ben Saypol (Timmy Morelli); Tony Devon (Danny Hogan); Rohn Thomas (Sergeant Disapri); Joe Baka (Detective Carpenter); Tuesday Knight (WHK Receptionist); Dave Buckel (WHK Newscaster); Matt Miller (Assistant DA); Jack Skelley (Immigration Judge); Jane Jean Miller and Wendy Waltz (Groupies); Angelique Osborne (Giggly Girl); Abdullah Bey (Old Man); Kevin Willigham (Driver); Patrick White (School Kid); Molly McDougal (Good Looking Girl at Diner).

LOS ANGELES TIMES, 10/24/97, Calendar/p. 12, Kenneth Turan

It's always a pleasant surprise to find something real and touching in a film. Even in one written by Joe Eszterhas. Especially in one written by Joe Eszterhas.

Recent credits like "Basic Instinct," "Showgirls," "Sliver" and "Jade" and their emphasis on eroticized violence have made Eszterhas perhaps the highest-paid screenwriter in today's Hollywood. But while it might be thought easier for a camel to go through the eye of a needle than for Eszterhas to write a largely heartfelt film like "Telling Lies in America," he has done so with an unexpected degree of success.

Drawing on elements from his own youth growing up as a Hungarian refugee in Cleveland, Eszterhas and director Guy Ferland have come up with a poignant immigrant's tale set in that city in the early 1960s. Though it's hampered by numerous plot contrivances that are overly conventional and predictable, "Telling Lies" has an affecting emotional texture at its core that makes up for a lot.

The film is also strengthened by a pair of adroit lead performances by Brad Renfro and Kevin Bacon, actors who completely understand their characters and know how to make the most of them on screen.

Still only 15, Renfro is a remarkably instinctive performer who brought a natural intensity to films like "The Client" and "Sleepers." His Karchy Jonas is a 17-year-old senior on scholarship at Cleveland Latin High School. It's a Catholic school with upper-middle-class students who make life difficult for someone whose ever so slightly European demeanor and inflection mark him as an outsider.

More than anything, Karchy wants to be with it, to be cool. He loves the sound of rock 'n' roll music and has a crush on Diney Majeski (Calista Flockhart), the slightly older girl he works with at an after-school job. But whatever he wants, even the ability to pronounce "th" like a native-born American, seems fated to be always frustratingly beyond his reach.

The epitome of everything that Karchy thinks is worth having is rock jock Billy Magic (Bacon), the Joe Cool mainstay of WHK Radio. While the film lets us know that Billy is something of a con artist with a propensity for getting fired, Karchy sees things differently. To him, Billy's red Cadillac, hipster slang and callous manipulation of women represent all the promise of America, the new land.

Given how familiar a character this is, it says a lot for Bacon's energized, completely realized performance that he makes the hustling Billy as compelling a person as he does, equally believable as a role model for Karchy and in some of his less savory aspects.

It also turns out that Billy is on the lookout for a high school kid with some of Karchy's qualities. He calls the boy Chuckie and Slick, helps him with his wardrobe and in making that "all-important love connection" and even hires him as a gofer and assistant for $100 a week.

What Billy sees in Karchy, and it is the film's most telling element, is a facility for lying that's born out of a combination of embarrassment and shame. Karchy tells people he's going to Princeton when he's barely getting out of high school and answers, "Sure, lots of times," when asked if he's done anything he in fact hasn't. When Diney asks him why he has to show off so much, he replies with the melancholy truth, "I ain't got that much to show."

Going nowhere academically and with no more than vague ambitions of being a writer, Karchy thinks he's figured out how this country works. When his serious father (a small but indispensable performance by Maximilian Schell) asks why Billy pays him so much, Karchy tells him, "This is America, Pop." But one of the reasons "Telling Lies in America" is such an evocative title is that Karchy comes to see that he doesn't understand as much about either lying or America as he thinks he does.

Though director Ferland has a gentle, pleasant touch, there's not much he can do with "Telling Lies'" more hackneyed elements, like Karchy's fumbling encounters with sex, his nightmare date from hell with Diney and his friendship with a black classmate. Like Karchy, we just have to survive these disappointments in hopes of getting to the good stuff underneath.

One of the most pleasing elements of "Telling Lies in America" is its classic soundtrack of early '60s rock, nearly 20 songs on a par with "Lonely Teardrops," "Sleepwalk" and "Shimmy Shimmy Ko-Ko Bop." They help make Eszterhas' trip back in time one that the rest of us can take pleasure in as well.

NEW YORK POST, 10/17/97, p. 48, Thelma Adams

For years, critics have been urging multi-million-dollar screenwriter Joe Eszterhas to reject his "Basic Instinct" and use his talent for good, not evil ("Showgirls").

Apparently, he listened. The result is "Telling Lies in America," which had its U.S. premiere last week at the New York Film Festival.

Directed by Guy Ferland ("The Babysitter"), this heartfelt, if overly familiar, coming-of-age story is about Karchy Jonas (Brad Renfro). The Hungarian teen gets an unsentimental education from shady dee jay Billy Magic (Kevin Bacon).

"America" is set during the slacks-and-ties era in Cleveland, Ezsterhas' youthful stomping ground. It opens with a "Happy Days," all-the-retro-money-can-buy feel.

"Did you hear that new Pat Boone song? It's neat," says one of Karchy's fellow outcasts in the high school cafeteria. Karchy's white-collar refugee father (Maximilian Schell) strains at a blue-collar job to send his son to the exclusive Catholic prep school the boy hates.

Karchy, like all great artists-in-waiting, just doesn't fit in. His greatest talent, creative storytelling (a.k.a. fibbing), is matched by his love for the infant rock 'n' roll. Both loves come to bear when he rigs an election to be selected by a real radio station as an outstanding high school senior.

At the radio station, Karchy meets Billy Magic. Bacon ("Picture Perfect") adds Magic to his list of seductive cads. His deejay is a fascinating study in gray and white. He honestly loves black music, but isn't above cheating an up-and-coming African-American band out of its royalties. He appreciates Karchy in a way that no one else does, but he's not above using him in a dirty payola scam.

Karchy, disarmingly played by Renfro ("The Client"), is one of those put-upon, precocious fictional teens who slips a copy of "Huckleberry Finn" to the older woman he adores.

"I think I'm gonna be a writer," he tells Diney (Calista Flockhart), "I haven't written anything yet."

In part, Eszterhas seems to be answering critics with a reminder that he, too, was a sensitive boy once. He wasn't always a big-bucks schlockmeister. The son of Hungarian refugees, he attended that Cleveland Catholic school of hard knocks alongside Karchy.

Like his adorably dishonest young hero, Eszterhas learned the eminently self-serving lesson that lying paid off in the new land. A naturalization judge agrees with Karchy: No one really believes that George Washington chopped down the cherry tree and came clean to his father.

Soundtrack-driven to the point of annoyance (we're deep in "Shimmy Shimmy Ko-Ko Bop" territory), "America" is saved from this defensive, I-suffered-too, semi-autobiographical posturing by the excellent performances of Renfro, Bacon and the monumental Schell.

NEWSWEEK, 10/20/97, p. 70, David Ansen

Here's a surprise. Joe Eszterhas, the writer who inflicted "Showgirls" and "Basic Instinct" upon the world, redeems himself with this autobiographical tale of Hungarian-born teenager Karchy Jonas (Brad Renfro) struggling to decode the American way of life in early '60s Cleveland. His mentor in mendacity is a slick, corrupt deejay named Billy Magic, a cynical hipster played to sleazy perfection by Kevin Bacon. While the elements in this coming-of-age saga may seem familiar—losing one's virginity to a doo-wop beat, payola in the music biz—Eszterhas brings a fresh, immigrant's-eye perspective to his tale. Sensitively directed by Guy Ferland, it features fine turns by Calista Flockhart as the grave, working-class girl Karchy desires and Maximillian Schell as Karchy's father. "Telling Lies" tells bittersweet truths about the moral cost of success in America.

SIGHT AND SOUND, 4/98, p. 54, Mark Sinker

Cleveland, 1960. Recently fired for payola, a rock and roll DJ takes the name Billy Magic and starts a popularity contest, with high-school students voting for a new on-air winner every week. Harassed and poor at a rich school, Karchy Jonas has persuaded co-worker Diney to date him if he wins. He does, by sending in hundreds of nominations himself. Amused by Karchy's lying denials of cheating, Magic hires him as a gofer, collecting the DJ's bribes.

Karchy too wants to be a DJ, but thinks his slight Hungarian accent rules this out. On the date, Karchy sneaks Diney an aphrodisiac: she gets sick and dumps him. Elated after one of Magic's girls seduces him, he picks up Diney in the DJ's Cadillac. They become friends again. Magic hears Karchy's friend Amos sing, and gets him a record deal. Later, Amos angrily tells Karchy the contract is a ripoff. The cops quiz Karchy about payola: he must shop Magic, or it will affect his and his father's naturalisation.

Karchy begs Diney for help, and they sleep together, but she tells him she's engaged. Magic has used him, the police insist. He confronts the DJ, demanding he tear up Amos' contract. Magic laughs, but Amos reveals he now has an honest deal. Asked in court about envelopes stuffed with cash, Karchy denies all—and realises his accent has vanished. The judge ignores police pleas, and Karchy and his father become US citizens. The judge sees Karchy alone: he knows he lied, but doesn't mind.

Arriving from Hungary in Cleveland as a child, quick to grasp that a slackness with the strict facts is one of his adoptive nation's strengths, screenwriter Joe Eszterhas is still rare in being so explicitly prepared to defend the higher value of the fib. *Telling Lies in America*'s crooked DJ Billy Magic's magic is tarnished but not dispelled by this semi-autobiographical picture's conclusion. Meanwhile, hero Karchy's *Billy Liar*-style fabrications are considered no more a moral failing than his inability to pronounce the 'th' sound.

The film's root context is also fashioned from a moral conundrum. White youth's mesmerised 50s love of rock and roll was a product of the money-hungry abuse of media power: key Cleveland DJ Alan Freed was famously scapegoated by the industry for payola in the early 60s, and was, in rock's founding myth, a martyr to anti-racism. Alluding to this, the first time we see Billy Magic, he's drinking, whoring and giving himself a job by claiming he lost the last one because the discs he spun were too black.

Director Guy Ferland (*The Babysitter*) sets all this in the vanished pre-60s, pre-Beatles America that Barry Levinson celebrated and lamented in *Diner* and *Tin Men:* a Cleveland leafily unwoken in its look, less suburban-claustrophobic than stranded in cultural quarantine. Yet this rites-of-passage film dares to omit all the Hollywood archetypes we've come to dread. Maximilian Schell's widowed immigrant dad treats his son with gentle, trusting equality; Paul Dooley's teacher-priest is wrongheaded, but not a stock figure. Even the ritual counter-humiliation of a bullying jock at school has a pyrrhic countertwist. Refusing formula, this is by far the most dialectically un-American pro-America project Eszterhas has undertaken.

It's a cliché that his plots obsess on the good and the bad of mutual exploitation. As such exploiters, Karchy and Magic are both flagrant. Each well grasps the deal—that's why the threatened recriminations never materialise. But no agenda-free relationships exist here, though one is sentimentalised: perhaps inevitably in a script written by a former *Rolling Stone* journalist, black singer Amos, pressuring Karchy to help him find pop success, is somehow given a PC purity of motive. Implausible when he lurches into politicised rage, he's really little more than a pretext for a required moral twist. What's more, Amos' potential hit ('Medium Rare', written by Kevin Bacon himself) is closer as pastiche to those worthily unvulgar 50s R&B cuts prized by cultists for *not* charting than to music that sold in 1960-6. And if the DJ's louche sexiness is so liberating, must the black character really act out *no* naughty hungers of his own?

As it is, he's an uninterestingly noble patsy-cum-plot-device—yet Calista Flockhart's amused, unhappy, intelligent Diney is all the truer for her diminishment into cowardice. Compare *Billy Liar* again. Diney's is the betrayal that forces Karchy to realise that even good people can't always do good things, even though it's Magic's that leads Karchy to his first responsible lie. Magic may skip town, Julie Christie-style, but it's Diney's decision to desert and hurt that forces us to review John Schlesinger's 1963 sleepytown Brit classic, and its contempt for Tom Courtenay's dreamy escapism. For where the Christie character's similar decision is fetishised as flyaway heroic-sexy, Diney's is humanised.

You can be whoever you want to be: this founding American lie has left many stellar careers strewn with casualties, the no-longer-needed tossed aside like yesterday's couture. A star himself today, Eszterhas' claim that you have to have idolised and been let down before you can grow up is unlikely to be motive-free. But when Karchy-Eszterhas realises he no longer needs an idol's approval to affirm his own worth, he's hinting that a different myth might be a truer, trickier American creed: *you can discover who you are, and be that.* Which is unexpected and heartening—in a sleight-of-hand sort of a way.   The title of the film, a pet project since Eszterhas' first Hollywood success in the mid-80s, should have been *Telling Lies IS America*.

VILLAGE VOICE, 10/21/97, p. 94, Dennis Lim

Though relatively unsalacious, *Telling Lies in America* is still recognizable as a Joe Eszterhas effort—it's a specious, ham-fisted film with cardboard characters, stock scenarios, and a reference to teeth marks and fellatio in the first half hour. Set in the early '60s Cleveland of the screen-writer's boyhood, this is a schematically nostalgic rite-of-passage movie, filtered through the immigrant experience of Hungarian-born schoolboy Karchy Jonas (an earnest Brad Renfro), who believes that lying well and being able to pronounce "th" are essential to making it in America. Handpicked to work as lackey for an unctuous lady-killer disc jockey called Billy Magic (Kevin Bacon, making the most of a caricature), Karchy wises up, gets laid, and finds himself implicated in the payola scandal. Guy Ferland *(The Babysitter)* directs with close attention to surface detail, but he never gets to the heart of the story—quite possibly because there isn't one to begin with.

Also reviewed in:
CHICAGO TRIBUNE, 10/24/97, Friday/p. C, Michael Wilmington
NATION, 11/24/97, p. 35, Stuart Klawans
NEW YORK TIMES, 10/9/97, p. E5, Stephen Holden
VARIETY, 9/15-21/97, p. 78, Todd McCarthy
WASHINGTON POST, 10/24/97, Weekend/p. 54, Desson Howe

TEMPTRESS MOON

A Miramax Films release of a Tomson (Hong Kong) Films Co. Ltd. production. *Executive Producer:* Sunday Sun.   *Producer:* Tong Cunlin and Hsu Feng.   *Director:*   Chen Kaige. *Screenplay (Mandarin with English subtitles):* Shu Kei and Wang Anyi. *Story:* Chen Kaige. *Director of Photography:* Christopher Doyle. *Editor:* Pei Xiaonan. *Music:* Zhao Jiping. *Sound:* Lai Qizhen and (music) Zhang Zhengdi. *Art Director:* Huang Qiagui. *Set Designer:* Zhang Xianzhi. *Costumes:* William Chang and Chen Changmin. *Make-up:* Xu Guangrui. *Running time:* 113 minutes. *MPAA Rating:* Not Rated.

CAST: Leslie Cheung (Yu Zhongliang, aka Xiao Xie);   Gong Li (Pang Ruyi);   Kevin Lin (Pang Duanwu); He Saifei (Yu Xiuyi, Zhongliang's Sister); Zhang Shi (Li Niangjiu); Lin Lianqun (Pang An); Ge Xiangting (Elder Qi); Xie Tian (Boss); David Wu (Jingyun); Zhou Jie ("The Woman of Heavenly Lane"); Zhou Yemang (Pang Zhengda); Ren Lei (Yu Zhongliang, Child); Wang Ying (Pang Ruyi, Child); Ge Lin (Pang Duanwu, Child).

LOS ANGELES TIMES, 6/13/97, Calendar/p. 1, Kevin Thomas

Chen Kaige's exquisite yet harrowing "Temptress Moon" takes us into chaotic China in its transitional 1920s to spin a heady tale of love and revenge as the worlds of the Shanghai underworld collide with that of a decaying ancient noble family, sealed off in its vast country estate.

Thirteen-year-old Zhongliang, orphaned in the revolution as it swept over Shanghai, arrives at the ancient palatial estate of the Pangs in the countryside outside Shanghai, at the invitation of his sister (Zhang Shi), the wife of the Young Master Pang (Zhou Yemang).

Eager to participate in the new society that will be emerging after 2,000 years of imperial rule, Zhongliang has dreams of going to Beijing and becoming a scholar. Although he sometimes has the chance to play with Ruyi, the Young Master's younger sister, and her cousin Duanwu, he has been forced to become a servant, a slave even, to his sister and brother-in-law, a dedicated smoker of opium. When his brother-in-law eventually expects the boy to participate in erotic fun and games, something happens behind closed doors that propels Zhongliang back to Shanghai, where we catch up with him 10 years later.

We are left to imagine how Zhongliang (Leslie Cheung) has survived during this period. But when we meet him again, the '20s are roaring through glamorous, corrupt Shanghai's gaudy, neon-lit avenues, and he has become the sleekest most debonair of gigolos, an expert at blackmailing women for his, deeply paternal boss (Xie Tien), a loving but diabolical underworld kingpin whose favorite he has become. "Temptress Moon" really gets underway when the boss orders Zhongliang to lure Ruyi (Gong Li), now head of the Pang family, to Shanghai as part of some undisclosed plan to grab what's left—which seems considerable—of the Pang fortune.

At this point, the world of "Shanghai Triad" collides with that of "Raise the Red Lantern"— films directed by China's other leading director, Zhang Yimou—as the cynical young gangster zeros in on the innocent, though headstrong, heiress, who has never been anywhere and never expects to go anywhere. Zhongliang remains consumed with rage over his treatment by the Pangs, and, given his acquired expertise in seduction, has no trouble bewitching Ruyi.

What Zhongliang doesn't count upon is the impact of this ravishingly beautiful innocent upon him, setting in motion a tug-of-war between two proud, willful individuals—think of Jennifer Jones and Gregory Peck in "Duel in the Sun."

What's crucial here is that Chen, who previously teamed Cheung and Gong in his epic "Farewell My Concubine," has been able to transform the emotional extravagance of melodrama into an eloquent romantic tragedy in which we can perceive an entire society undergoing wrenching change. If Ruyi and Zhongliang are on the one hand the pawns of fate, they nonetheless are able to exercise their freedom to make drastic choices.

Clearly, Chen wants us to see in "Temptress Moon" a timeless parable of circumstance and choice that applies to modern China as well as its own traumatic transitional era. At the same time, the film works very well as a singularly tempestuous period tale, churning with danger, adventure and steamy passion.

This is an absolutely gorgeous-looking film, beautifully photographed (by Australia's Christopher Doyle) amid fabulous settings and accompanied by a grand romantic score. Gong deftly creates Ruyi as a stunning enigma, while the protean Cheung once again summons that full range of emotions that also charged "Farewell My Concubine."

A final note: As has been the fate of so many films made by major Chinese directors, "Temptress Moon" remains banned in China.

NEW STATESMAN, 10/10/97, p. 38, Jonathan Meades

Buried in Chen Kaige's film is a tragedy as compressed, emotionally harrowing, brutal and hermetic as that which his leading lady, Gong Li, played out in the wonderful *Judou*, a work whose elemental potency and structural limpidity recalled Racine. But Chen ignores the truism that classicism augmented is drama mitigated and opens out the tight core as though he is expanding a stage piece for the screen. What should have been a chamber work is deformed with a load of context, with great dollops of reverence, with right-on moralising, with impasto period colour—with, indeed, a broad gamut of centrifugal distractions. It's not so much that he's failed to adhere to the dictum of nothing outside the story; rather you get the feeling he didn't quite know what the story was till he had told it, and that even then he was incapable of dispensing with the dross.

It all begins promisingly enough, with a shot that recalls one of Lewis Carroll's tawdry exercises in kiddy-porn: a half-dressed little girl gazes dreamily into the camera while smoke describes sinuous scrolls around her and her unseen father speaks a paean to opium, "the source of inspiration". The camera hangs around till she smiles the beatific smile of opiate intoxication. This is a scene of great economy; it is also perverse, shocking and familiar enough to indicate the sort of milieu Chen intends to lead us into. But this is a director who doesn't trust his audience's cognitive faculties. So he follows it with a parchment shot—you know, several metres of antique distressed Naugahyde on which is inscribed a GCSE history lesson: 1911, the overthrow of the Qing dynasty, the foundation of the republic. And since the audience is liable to be composed of illiterates, there is a word-for-word voiceover. Next up is a longer—much longer—sequence of scene setting, a series of setups infuriatingly punctuated by subtitles proclaiming "six months later", "four years later" and so on. We are introduced to the Pang family, representatives of the old regime, their hundreds of retainers, their labyrinthine palace and their labyrinthine familial rivalries. This is a story of O, and father, son and daughter Ruyi are all in thrall to the drug; that is, they're victims of the British Empire.

They spy on each other, break crockery and steal up behind each other to put their hands over unwitting eyes—motifs that persist throughout the film. When the father dies the elders (this is a family which makes the Corleone mob look nuclear) decree that Ruyi is its new head. This is because the son is now a living vegetable, rendered thus by his brother-in-law, whom he treated like a houseboy and who has had his revenge by lacing an opium pipe with arsenic. At this stage the brother-in-law wisely scarpers to Shanghai to pursue a career in the seduction and blackmailing of married women. He also gains the favour of his gang boss, a wizened oldster played by a walnut crossed with Noel Coward.

Chen's version of Shanghai seems to have been entirely learnt from other movies, notably from von Sternberg: it's all dancehalls, Anna May Wong bobs, co-respondent shoes, minatory glances, art direction, spray-on "decadence".

When Ruyi arrives in this neon city she is stripped of all the wiles she displayed at home and is turned, improbably, into a bucolic bumbler. Across a courtyard she is made to spy on the gigolo at work with a woman he actually loves—one of the rare scenes which achieves a proper tension. And in one of many self-referential internal symmetries Ruyi places a white cloth over the woman's face after she has leapt to her death. She also apes the dead woman's Occidental marcel wave in an attempt to win the gigolo who, several twists later, gets to work with his special recipe pipes again.

It all ends horribly—not that anyone is likely to care, for the countless incidental felicities add up only to a scrappy patchwork. The clumsy structure, which includes characters giving narrative summations and, in an otherwise sequential piece, the use very late on of flashback, work against the subject and give the unities no chance at all. There is too much causal "psychology" for tragedy, not enough for an episodic saga of familial dysfunction. And while there are many striking tableaux—banished concubines being punted across a lake full of gunnera-like plants, tablecloths laden with mah-jong pieces being pulled by the mischievous, stoned Ruyi—the elliptical, soft-edged style of the cinematography (by the Australian Christopher Doyle) is invariable in scene after scene. It's an imposed *look*.

NEW YORK POST, 6/13/97, p. 49, Thelma Adams

"Temptress Moon" has been orbiting since the New York Film Festival, while Miramax Films dickered with an element that is beyond micromanaging: The plot is as complicated as a Chinese puzzle box and the text is in Mandarin.

I adore "Temptress Moon." It's as beautiful as anything you will see on screen this year, particularly if you missed "Cyclo" at the Film Forum. The tragic period romance is sweeping and old-fashioned, a kinky, Asian "Gone With the Wind," a Chinese potboiler that occasionally winks at the audience because it is so overripe and over-the-top.

But Miramax has cause for concern. The plot is arcane. Artistic decisions Kaige ("Farewell My Concubine") made to lend mystery to the already-twisted plot can simply be mystifying to anyone who hasn't paid close attention to the opening narration or who had the misfortune to be in the slow popcorn line.

Where to begin? It's the 1920s. The Chinese Emperor has abdicated. A new world order has begun, but not before a few old stories are played out.

Leslie Cheung ("Farewell My Concubine") is a gigolo; Gong Li ("Shanghai Triad") is the beautiful head of the Pangs, an old, powerful family of opium addicts. Corruption, true love, incest and a past that has a nasty way of catching up with the present entangle the two lovers.

The pair's decadence (and the house of cards built and blown away in Shu Kei's screenplay) leads to their fall and the rise of Li's subservient cousin (Kevin Lin). It is this twist—the dullard's supple ascension to the seat of power as the convoluted romantic melodrama distracts the audience—that has been read as a jab at President Zhang Zeming.

You don't need a degree in China studies to bask in the glow of "Temptress Moon." It's a sensual film that's as intoxicating and inexplicable as expensive perfume. Fluid camera movements from hot-shot cinematographer Christopher Doyle, delicious period costumes, and exuberant performances from the leads and supporting players make this as much a rich and guilty pleasure as it is a political parable.

NEWSDAY, 6/13/97, Part II/p. B9, John Anderson

Chen Kaige is not just one of the world's more prominent provocateur-directors, he's one of its more resolute. Although he occupies what seems to be a peculiar but very special place in the hierarchy of the Chinese arts, he continues to make what can be seen as allegorical critiques of the state of his country; Beijing, which gives him grudging respect, probably because of the reflected glory, continues to ban his movies. In its bureaucratic perfection, the situation is a work of art in itself.

But life goes on. And with "Temptress Moon"—wherein Chen works for the first time with the Australian hipster-cinematographer Christopher Doyle—he moves in new directions, at least visually. Even Chen's more devoted followers will be taken aback by the hallucinogenic quality of his imagery and the film's occasionally frantic disposition (his pre-"Farewell My Concubine" films, after all, included the cooler-than-cool "King of the Children" and "Life on a String"). But what he's after is the psychological quality of an opium high. And he apparently just about gets it, too.

The film opens in 1911, with the fall of the Qing dynasty and the birth of the Chinese republic. Its story is set within the corrupt embrace of an enormously influential Shanghai clan, which itself is in the warm embrace of opium. Caught up in this maelstrom of political, social and domestic upheaval are three children, who will form a sexual and emotional triad that is the stuff of profound character study and considering recent developments in Chinese politics, subtle satire as well.

Since the film played at Cannes last year and subsequently at the New York Film Festival, Miramax Films and Chen have added a preamble that explains its historical context as well as the framework of its narrative. It helps immensely.

Ruyi (played as an adult by the fabled Gong Li) has been brought up on opium smoke by her father, the patriarch of one of China's wealthiest and most powerful families. Zhongliang (Leslie Cheung), the orphaned brother of Ruyi's brother's wife (see, already it's getting complicated), has been brought into the household not, as he thinks, to better his situation, but to be a servant. He does something—what it is we're not quite sure—but after he prepares his brother-in-law's opium pipe, said brother-in-law is left brain dead.

Zhongliang disappears but, like Heathcliff, will return with money and a new occupation: Seducing and blackmailing wealthy married women. Ruyi, meanwhile, has assumed head-of-the-household status (her brother being a virtual vegetable) but only because the elders could assign the poor relation Duanwu (Kevin Lin) to assist her. Ruyi's sister-in-law (and Zhongliang's sister) Xiuyi lurks ominously in the background. The sexual tension bubbles and boils.

Last week, someone said that movie reviews contain too much plot synopsis, so we're going to take the hint. Chen does a far better job of laying out this Byzantine tale than we can here, and has created a lush, dizzyingly mobile film about overheated emotions, overheated glands and overheated brains. Although obscured by a haze of opium smoke, "Temptress Moon" is as provocative as Chen himself.

SIGHT AND SOUND, 10/97, p. 61, Tony Rayns

1911. The young Yu Zhongliang comes to the Pang family estate in the countryside near Suzhou to join his sister Xiuyi, who is married to the family's eldest son Pang Zhengda. His hopes of studying in Beijing recede as he finds himself treated as a servant; his chief job is to prepare Zhengda's opium pipes. Zhengda perceives that the bond between Zhongliang and his sister is overly close. Six months after the birth of Republican China, on the day that Zhengda succumbs to opium poisoning and loses his mind, Zhongliang flees the house, intending to travel to Beijing.

1921. Zhongliang has become the most popular gigolo in Shanghai, carrying out 'stings' on married women on behalf of his boss, an aged roué. He works under the name Xiao Xie. The 'stings' are masterminded by his boss' right-hand man Li Niangjiu. Meanwhile Old Master Pang dies, and Zhengda's mental incapacity rules him out as new head of the household. The clan elders decide to appoint Zhengda's younger sister Ruyi to the role, with male cousin Duanwu as her ward. Ruyi, also an opium smoker, has always been headstrong; her first action is to send home her late father's concubines. News of these developments reaches Shanghai, and Zhongliang's boss decides to send him back to the Pang estate to seduce Ruyi and steal the family fortune. Zhongliang very reluctantly agrees to go. His reunion with his sister is stormy (he rejects her near-incestuous overtures), but he soon falls in love with Ruyi. The feeling is mutual, and Ruyi takes the adoring Duanwu to bed (oblivious to his feelings) to practise sex before offering herself to Zhongliang. Zhongliang promises to help Ruyi and Duanwu escape to Beijing, but he abandons them and runs away to Shanghai.

Zhongliang's boss is heartbroken to realise that he has 'lost' his favourite to Ruyi: he sends Li Niangjiu to the estate to fetch Ruyi and contrives a plan to show her that Zhongliang is actually a heartless gigolo. Li brings Ruyi to a room in Heavenly Lane, opposite the house where Zhongliang is to 'sting' Mrs Shen, the one 'client' he felt for sincerely. Ruyi duly witnesses the 'sting'... and Mrs Shen's subsequent suicide. She returns to the estate sadder and wiser, to find that her former fiancé Jing is eager to rekindle their relationship. She resolves to give up opium before marrying him. Zhongliang chases Ruyi to the estate and begs her to run away with him. She tells him that she no longer loves him. Zhongliang prepares one last opium for her, and adds arsenic to it—as he did ten years earlier when he deliberately poisoned Zhengda. He leaves the household, only to be shot down at the quay by the clan elders. Smoking the pipes leaves Ruyi brain-dead. Duanwu is appointed the new head of the Pang family.

In so far as Chen Kaige and Zhang Yimou are the creative and professional rivals they're usually seen as these days, then *Temptress Moon* has to be seen as the film in which Chen finally ventures into sexual themes and issues. Zhang centred his films on sexually aware and active characters from the very start (*Red Sorghum* and *Ju Dou*); Chen's films from *Yellow Earth* to *Life on a String*, by contrast, bend over so far backwards to avoid a sexual dimension that they suggest at least a deliberate avoidance of the issue and at worst a major blockage. Even *Farewell My Concubine*, notionally centred on the rivalry between a prostitute and a stage transvestite for the loyalty of a 'real man', nervously shied away from the story's sexual implications. In this light, *Temptress Moon* seems like a drastic overcompensation, a film so steeped in torrid emotions and florid sexual gestures that it hovers on the brink of absurdity.

It is at its most cogent when it wonders how much of adult sexual identity and attitude are embedded in childhood experiences: the striking image of Ruyi, Zhongliang and Duanwu facing the camera as children which climaxes the introductory scenes recurs at the very end to pose the question in purely visual terms: were the respective fates of these characters already somehow sealed when they played together as kids? Between the two appearances of this challenging image, Chen and his cinematographer Chris Doyle do their utmost to lyricise the melodramatics of the plot and eroticise the characters, turning the film into the kind of opium-pipe-dream which makes heightened emotions and extreme situations credible. Their strategy is a qualified success: the film does have a rhapsodic sweep (especially in its spectacular visualisation of Shanghai in the 20s) which finesses much of the rhetorical excess. But whenever the script calls for scenes of sexual action, the film seems almost as naive as Ruyi herself. Scenes like Xiuyi's attempt to seduce her brother into a kiss or Duanwu's excitement at having to fend off prostitutes on the streets of Shanghai (he reacts by trying to rape Ruyi) are embarrassingly naked in their determination to breach self-imposed taboos.

The film has had an awkward passage into distribution. It carries an entirely fictitious screenplay credit (to a real Hong Kong writer-director), simply to get past Taiwanese restrictions on the release of films by Mainland China film-makers; it was actually written by the woman novelist Wang Anyi and Chen himself. Then, when it failed to replicate the success of *Farewell My Concubine* in Cannes, its US distributor Miramax demanded a recut: Chen removed some 15 minutes, mostly from the childhood scenes, in an attempt to make the characters' identities and relationships clearer; the original version has been released only in Hong Kong and Taiwan. Miramax itself went on to resubtitle the film in anachronistic slang (in the process removing such apparently incomprehensible subtleties as Zhongliang's use of a pseudonym for his seductions in Shanghai) and to add both a written preamble on the historical background and a stream of captions to identify characters, places and dates, all of which work against the film's oneiric flow by turning it into a history lesson.

As a result, the *Temptress Moon* which finally reaches British screens is a rather muddied reflection of the film Chen intended. The recut has minimised the sense of the action as a series of recurring dreams and imposed a generally unhelpful new 'drive' on the narrative. Most of the more adventurous Steadicam shots have gone, taking with them the implication that the characters were trapped in mental labyrinths of their own making. Substantial pleasures remain, most of them visual, but the present cut reduces the impact of the performances and obscures whatever parallels Chen wanted to draw between the 20s and the present.

TIME, 6/16/97, p. 76, Richard Corliss

[*Temptress Moon* was reviewed jointly with *Gabbeh*; see Corliss' review of that film.]

VILLAGE VOICE, 6/17/97, p. 61, J. Hoberman

If star chemistry could be bottled, they'd call it *Temptress Moon*. Chen Kaige's new feature reunites the two beauties of his 1993 *Farewell My Concubine*—the imperiously girlish Gong Li and the quicksilver matinee idol Leslie Cheung. Wafting, intoxicated, across the screen, the poisonous love of her innocently opium-addled heiress for his tragic gigolo is one sultry gust of cinema.

Chen directs this tale with a conductor's august deliberation, but the movie's third star is cinematographer Chris Doyle—best known for his hyper-calligraphic camera work with Wong Kar-wai and here no less eager to go for baroque. Sinuous and fluttery, set in a designer-decadent 1920s Shanghai, *Temptress Moon* is blatantly mannered; it unfurls amid rattling wind chimes to a continuous backbeat of distant thunder.

The feudal world is crumbling around the aristocratic Pangs—a family of junkies, mired in the obsolete traditions of their fabulous estate, miles outside and light years apart from booming, revolutionary, modernizing Shanghai. The character played by Cheung, a poor relation of the Pangs, had run away to the big city for a life of romancing and blackmailing its richest women. Now the callous Shanghai stud is sent back to the Pangs by the doting old queen who appears to be the town's boss of bosses; his assignment is to seduce the unworldly daughter (Gong) who has been installed as head of the family.

A sense of druggy, lacquered doom compensates for the absence of spontaneity. *Temptress Moon* is a darker, more gestural film than *Farewell My Concubine,* Chen's overrated 1993 career-maker—up until now the most glamorous expression of the New Chinese Cinema. The camera placement here is more judicious (as well as wackier) and the editing (some of it imposed, one suspects, by the American distributor) far snappier. At least 10 minutes shorter than when it was shown at the 1996 Cannes Film Festival, *Temptress Moon* is pleasingly fragmented—a round of tumultuous jolts, bravura star entrances, and staccato displays of cinematographic power.

Where the half-century-spanning *Farewell My Concubine* suffered from a bad case of the Bertoluccis, *Temptress Moon* feels as heedless as its heroine. Chen has the David Lean stuff down and, for all the theatrical lighting and weighty mise-en-scéne, he tosses it away. The teeming overheads, the emotional farewells at railroad platforms, the narrow streets filled with parading soldiers, come and go without benefit of establishing shots. No crowd scene has more weight than any of Doyle's trademark in-and-out-of focus arabesques.

Temptress Moon has its flaws. The big-city decadence is borderline campy, the narrative hits a speed bump 90 minutes into the film, and the final wrap-up is more than a bit glib. (This may be a factor of cuts made in the opening section.) Still, there's no denying the movie's urgency, nor its bold reliance on style and fantasy. Outside, Shanghai is drenched by an unending monsoon; inside, an outrageously decorative woman drops a single crystal tear.

Also reviewed in:
NEW YORK TIMES, 6/13/97, p. C8, Stephen Holden
VARIETY, 5/20-26/96, p. 36, Derek Elley
WASHINGTON POST, 6/20/97, p. C1, Stephen Hunter

TETSUO II: BODY HAMMER

A Manga Entertainment release of a Toshiba EMI presentation. *Producer:* Fuminori Shishido, Fumio Kurokawa, Nobuo Takeuchi, and Hiromi Aihara. *Director:* Shinya Tsukamoto. *Screenplay (Japanese with English subtitles):* Shinya Tsukamoto. *Director of Photography:* Shinya Tsukamoto. *Editor:* Shinya Tsukamoto. *Music:* Chu Ishikawa. *Running time:* 83 minutes. *MPAA Rating:* Not Rated.

CAST: Tomoroh Taguchi (Taniguchi); Nobu Kanaoka (Kana); Shinya Tsukamoto (The Guy).

LOS ANGELES TIMES, 8/15/97, Calendar/p. 8, Kevin Thomas

With "Tetsuo II: Body Hammer," Japan's prodigious visionary Shinya Tsukamoto takes his first film, "Tetsuo: The Iron Man," a logical step further. In the earlier picture, man becomes metal; now he's mutated into a killing machine.

Tsukamoto is an amazing, idiosyncratic filmmaker, able to conjure up a universe and put it on the screen with maximum impact and conviction. In essence, he envisions man transformed into a lethal weapon every time he becomes angry.

The film takes us into a modern metropolis in which everything looks brand-new and shiny (and soulless) and picks out an ordinary-looking young Japanese businessman, Tomoo Taniguchi (Tomoroh Taguchi, who had a similar role in the first film). Taniguchi lives with his wife Kana (Nobu Kanaoka) and small son in a tasteful apartment in a vast highrise.

Taniguchi has no memories of his life before the age of 8, when he was adopted by foster parents. However, he's beginning to have dreams of an open field in a beautiful rural setting. Eventually he envisions a couple with two small sons in that field, peering into the horizon. It's an image that could have come straight out of a classic Ozu film.

In a giant shopping mall, the Taniguchis are accosted by a pair of skinheads and barely escape with their lives. Attacked again, Taniguchi develops superhuman strength in a state of rage, saving his own life.

Zapped by some sort of ray gun, Taniguchi winds up in an immense factory inhabited by a legion of zombie-like mutant skinheads undergoing severe physical training. He's strapped down and his head clamped in some diabolical-looking machinery, which results in speeding his mutation into a walking arsenal, sprouting cyberguns in all directions.

Of course, links emerge between Taniguchi's bizarre fate and his repressed childhood memories. As before, Tsukamoto casts himself as the key adversary, here called "The Guy."

What Tsukamoto does so dazzlingly well is to blur the line between man and killing machine to create a powerful metaphor for the modern world, which he clearly sees in need of destruction so that humans can again live in harmony with nature.

Tsukamoto brings to life his apocalyptic vision with wit, outrageous humor and with images that achieve their own kind of blurring-between comic-book stylization and movie-camera reality. The intensely graphic look of "Tetsuo II" is at once beautiful and eerily surreal, and Tsukamoto creates the familiar equation of masculinity and weaponry with exceptional critical force.

Sometimes "Tetsuo II" is hard to follow, despite subtitles, but there's no mistaking what Tsukamoto expresses—with such dizzying impact—about the clash between nature and society.

NEW STATESMAN & SOCIETY, 11/20/92, p. 34, Jonathan Romney

[*Tetsuo II: Body Hammer* was reviewed jointly with *Twin Peaks*; see Romney's review of that film in Film Review Annual, 1993.]

NEW YORK POST, 6/27/97, p. 42, Larry Worth

There's something about the fusion of man and machine that strikes horror in the heart of moviegoers. The proof? One need only recall the Borg from "Star Trek: First Contact," or, better yet, "The Terminator."

Not so for 1988's "Tetsuo: The Iron Man." But he's baaack anyway in "Tetsuo II: Body Hammer."

The original—relating one's inexplicable transformation into a steel-veined killing machine—at least had a visceral power. But there's no solace to be found in the mind-numbingly stupid sequel.

The simplistic good-vs.-evil plot shows the hero battling an evil scientist's plan to clone cyber soldiers in a smelting factory. Faster than you can say ferric oxide, the protagonists tommy-gun guts pop a la "Alien" from his solar plexus. The rest is a series of gore-drenched splats as the characters square off.

Though director Shinya Tsukamoto's dizzying camerawork and special effects sometimes divert, "Tetsuo II" never coalesces. Rather, it corrodes before viewers' eyes.

VILLAGE VOICE, 7/1/97, p. 96, Michael Atkinson

Calling Shinya Tsukamoto's *Tetsuo II* a sequel to the holocaustic first film is a bit like calling your second pint of mescal a sequel to your first. As ramshackle and batty, if not as relentlessly propulsive, as its predecessor, *Tetsuo II* also tests the torsion resistance of narrative comprehensibility a little less severely—there's actually a plot, and significantly fewer flesh tremors. (Tsukamoto learns the hard way you can't buy inspiration with a larger budget—this film actually seems cheaper.) Tomoroh 'Tomorrow" Taguchi is back as a prototypical Tokyo salaryman, this time beleagured by a mysterious band of thugs who eventually kill his son and transform him into a human Gatling gun. (The cannon barrels only emerge from his chest and hands when he gets angry, like the Hulk.) Taguchi eventually goes up against the entire evil horde of cyborgian punks (who spend time working out seminaked with industrial scrap metal—call David Fincher!) and their insidious leader (Tsukamoto, who also serves as cinematographer, editor, art director, and gaffer). The post-Cronenbergian transformations are no longer sexual, merely homicidal and power mad, and as a result *Tetsuo II* has little subtextual weight. Like its post-atomic cousin *Akira,* the first *Tetsuo* belonged to its moment as a cultural nervous breakdown; its sequel can only mop up afterward.

Also reviewed in:
NEW YORK TIMES, 6/27/97, p. 12, Stephen Holden
VARIETY, 9/28/92, p. 81, Derek Elley
WASHINGTON POST, 7/11/97, Weekend/p. 37, Richard Harrington

TEXAS CHAIN SAW MASSACRE: THE NEXT GENERATION

A Cinepix Film Properties release of an Ultra Micros and River City Films production. *Producer:* Robert Kuhn. *Director:* Kim Henkel. *Screenplay:* Kim Henkel. *Director of Photography:* Levie Isaacks. *Editor:* Sandra Adair. *Music:* Wayne Bell. *Sound:* Scott Szabo. *Production Designer:* Debbie Pastor. *Art Director:* Ann Yzuel. *Set Dresser:* Julia Kirt. *Costumes:* Kari Perkins. *Running time:* 86 minutes. *MPAA Rating:* R.

CAST: Renee Zellweger (Jenny); Matthew McConaughey (Vilmer); Robert Jacks (Leatherface); Tonie Perenski (Darla); Joe Stevens (W.E.); Lisa Newmeyer (Heather); John Harrison (Sean); Tyler Cone (Barry); Vince Brock (Eric); Susan Loughran (Amanda); David Laurence (Jack); James Gale (Rothman).

LOS ANGELES TIMES, 8/29/97, Calendar/p. 16, John Anderson

[The following review by John Anderson appeared in a slightly different form in NEWSDAY, 8/29/97, Part II/p. B9.]

It's prom night, naturally, and the kids have taken a wrong turn down a malevolent-looking country road, and someone has roared out of the darkness and plowed into Barry's father's car. "I'm dead," says Barry (Tyler Cone). "Somebody please kill me."

No problem.

Barry, you see, has already been caught cheating by his whiny, conniving girlfriend Heather (Lisa Newmeyer), and he's told the movie's shrinking-violet heroine Jenny (yes, that's Renee Zellweger of "Jerry Maguire") that she's too ugly to ever get a date. And he's besmirched the integrity of the local road department. So he may as well have a little electronic news zipper scrolling around his forehead reading "Marked for Death."

But that's the way it goes through most of "Texas Chainsaw Massacre: The Next Generation," which is just the kind of film that Wes Craven's "Scream" has now rendered virtually defunct. In recent hit, Mr. Nightmare on Elm Street exploded all the teen-horror conventions, produced a thoroughly entertaining and often very scary movie and made the watching of by-the-numbers chop-'em-ups like "TCM," if not impossible, then at least an exercise in futility.

Inspired by the landmark 1974 film about a family of chainsaw-wielding Lone Star lunatics, the new "TCM" is neither innovative enough nor scary enough nor funny enough to sustain itself. It predates "Scream," of course, regardless of the bogus "May 22, 1996" that opens the film. If it didn't, "TCM," which seems to have been made for about 14 bucks not including the gas for the chainsaws, could never have afforded either Zellweger or Matthew McConaughey—both Texans, by the way, and in McConaughey's case on the road to big-time movies by May of '96.

McConaughey ("A Time to Kill," "Contact"), who provides the only substantial terror and unpredictability, is the head of the world's most dysfunctional family, wearing a remote-controlled mechanical leg (which itself provides a few choice moments) and dictating to the Emerson-quoting W.E. (Joe Stevens), his exhibitionist girlfriend Darla (a weirdly funny Tonie Perenski) and, of course, the raving maniac Leatherface (Robert Jacks).

Leatherface, whose chainsaw ballet should have been a highlight of the movie, is now a sensitive cross-dresser who turns homicidal only when Heather won't stop screaming. We know how he feels.

Zellweger is actually quite all right as the spunky Jenny; she certainly never loses her dignity, even when she's cruelly abused. And she knows, as so few teenagers do in these films, to run off the road and into the woods when there's a crazy person in a pickup trying to run you down. Ah, these kids, they never learn. Not even in sequels.

"TCM" was written and directed by Kim Henkel, who wrote the screenplay for the 1974 Tobe Hooper film (and yes, despite the cutlery reference, Henkel seems to be his real name). He was apparently dissatisfied with sequels II and III, which depended too much on gore than did the largely non-bloody but frenetic original.

He avoids unnecessary bloodshed here, even flirting with some pertinent socio-sexual issues. Heather, for instance, admits that she acts the way she does because she's too shallow to get what she wants any other way. She admires Jenny, whose wallflower act turns out to be a reaction to a family situation. Barry, while he's still around, exhibits all the feminist sympathies of Cro-Magnon man.

But you can get all this stuff, quite frankly, on any afternoon soap. What we want from "Texas Chainsaw Massacre: The Next Generation" is a giddy mix of gruesome horror and campy humor. What we get is less massacre than mess.

NEW YORK POST, 8/29/97, p. 56, Thelma Adams

Back in 1994, before Matthew McConaughey became the next big thing, he had time to kill. In "Texas Chainsaw Massacre: The Next Generation," McConaughey's wicked, one-legged Vilmer had the time, opportunity and motive to slaughter fellow Texan Renee Zellweger.

Now that McConaughey ("Contact") and Zellweger ("Jerry Maguire") have become coveted cover art, Kim Henkel's direct-to-drive-in horror flick about mass murder on prom night has been shipped to movie theaters.

That "The Next Generation" is DOA won't stop some fans from seeing the predictable splatter-fest, a paler shade of red from Tobe Hooper's 1974 cracked comedy about a Texas family who got a charge out of chainsaws.

Henkel wrote the original, but a lot of blood has passed under the bridge in the past 20 years including two chainsaw spinoffs. In his sloppy sequel, Henkel covers no new ground with new gore; he careens between cartoon cut-up, camp and conspiracy theories.

Robert Jacks, in his debut in the role of Leatherface, a chainsaw wielding freak with a mask of borrowed human skin, crosses Divine with Hannibal Lecter to no great effect. Zellweger's Jenny has a face to remember—and he wants to wear it.

Jenny obviously hadn't seen "Scream"—it wasn't made, yet. Otherwise, she'd know that if you're the one girl in your high school who hasn't had a drink or dropped your dress, you'll probably survive prom night. There's no place for sacrificial virgins in contemporary teen horror.

For his part, McConaughey switches into his crazy Woody Harrelson swagger. He's an unapologetic natural-born killer who doesn't give a chainsaw what people think of him.

Zellweger, with her hair mussed and her body covered in frumpy white satin, doesn't seem to be having nearly so much fun as her "Dazed and Confused" co-star. It's far more satisfying to play the victim to Tom Cruise's ego.

NEWSWEEK, 9/8/97, p. 75, Jeff Giles

Recently, there has been a minor controversy over the fact that *Texas Chainsaw Massacre: The Next Generation* is opening on all of 15 screens. Once you've seen it, you can understand why: is 15 too many? Matthew McConaughey and Renee Zellweger, buddies from Austin, Texas, made the bewildering flick in 1994. There's been speculation that when they became stars they tried to block its release. But Zellweger once told NEWSWEEK making the movie was "a blast." McConaughey said it was "a hoot, man."

Not to watch. You'd like "Chainsaw" to be campy fun, but after a funny prom-night opener, you're rooting for almost everyone to die. Zellweger's a wallflower terrorized by the family from hell: Leatherface (Robert Jacks) dances with his chain saw while his demented brother Vilmer (McConaughey) stomps around on his mechanical leg. Then there's more plot stuff that maybe the director can explain. McConaughey's awful but clearly having a ball—frankly, you feel worse for him in "Contact,"—and Zellweger is endearing when she finally tries to save her life. No force on earth however, could have saved the movie.

VILLAGE VOICE, 9/2/97, p. 78, Michael Atkinson

A comparatively unnecessary but jubilant return to the grand days of keep-repeating-it's-only-a-movie—specifically the pioneering 1974 screaming meemies of Tobe Hooper's *The Texas Chainsaw Massacre*—original scripter Kim Henkel's 1994 *Texas Chainsaw Massacre: The Next Generation* would have never seen the weary glare of a projector bulb if it hadn't starred native Texans Renee Zellweger and Matthew McConaughey before they became magazine covers. (Indeed, it opens at a high school prom, suggesting the malformed offspring of *Dazed and Confused*. A refreshingly berserk run through the woods that is bound for a cult, or at least a Joe Bob Briggs pull-quote, Henkel's hypercaffeinated hog-wash begins with the usual lumbering exposition and ponderous setup before exploding into Living Theater absurdity.

Leatherface may look like Weird Al Yankovic, but hey, America, meet McConaughey the howling, nose-biting, script-chewing psychopath. As the bullgoose loony with a homemade hydraulic leg, MM makes Rutger Hauer look like Steven Wright. *Contact*, schmontact, I can never look at him straight again. An utterly charming, uproarious mutant that out-spoofs *Scream, The Next Generation* seethes with that forgotten grindhouse vibe. You can almost smell the mildew.

Also reviewed in:
CHICAGO TRIBUNE, 8/29/97, Friday/p. N, John Petrakis
NEW YORK TIMES, 8/29/97, p. C12, Janet Maslin
VARIETY, 9/1-7/97, p. 75, Joe Leydon

THAT DARN CAT

A Walt Disney Pictures release. *Executive Producer:* Andrew Gottlieb. *Producer:* Robert Simonds. *Director:* Bob Spiers. *Screenplay:* S.M. Alexander and L.A. Karaszewski. *Based on the novel "Undercover Cat" by:* Mildred Gordon and Gordon Gorden. *And the original screenplay by:* Mildred Gordon, Gordon Gordon, and Bill Walsh. *Director of Photography:* Jerzy Zielinski. *Editor:* Roger Barton. *Music:* Richard Kendall Gibbs. *Music Editor:* Allan K. Rosen and Patty Von Arx. *Sound:* Walter Anderson and (music) Robert Fernandez. *Sound Editor:* Michael Hilkene. *Casting:* Gary Zuckerbrod. *Production Designer:* Jonathan Carlson. *Art Director:* Jeremy A. Cassells. *Set Designer:* Gerald Sullivan and Jonathan Short. *Set Decorator:* Susan Lee Degus. *Special Effects:* Ray Bivins. *Costumes:* Marie France. *Make-up:* June Brickman. *Running time:* 89 minutes. *MPAA Rating:* PG.

CAST: Christina Ricci (Patti); Doug E. Doug (Zeke); Dean Jones (Mr. Flint); George Dzundza (Boetticher); Peter Boyle (Pa); Michael McKean (Peter Randall); Bess Armstrong (Judy Randall); Dyan Cannon (Mrs. Flint); John Ratzenberger (Dusty); Megan Cavanagh (Lu); Estelle Parsons (Old Lady McCracken); Rebecca Schull (Ma); Tom Wilson (Melvin); Brian Haley (Marvin); Mark Christopher Lawrence (Rollo); Rebecca Koon (Lizzy); Ned Bellamy (Agent #1); Brad Sherwood (Agent #2); Rob Cleveland (Agent #3); Jeffrey King (Agent #4); Tom Turbiville (Field Agent #1); Libby Whittemore (Another Agent); Cassandra Lawton (Newscaster); Margo Moorer (Teacher); Hillary Tolle (Kid #1); Paula Jones (Kid #2); Kinsey McLean (Kid #3); Jon Kohler (Hollywood Cat Choreographer); Wilbur T. Fitzgerald (Scientist #1); Terrence Gibney (Scientist #2); Harvey Reaves (Cop #1); Michael Genevie (Cop #2); Bill Coates (Old Ticket Man); Alex Van (Trash Man); Michelle B. Cooper (Female Nurse); Stephen Michael Ayers (Disbelieving Cop #1); Douglas Myers (Judge); Frank Smith (Announcer); Larue Stanley (Widow); David Wayne Evans and Margaret Ellis (Agents); Mike Banks (Helicopter Pilot).

LOS ANGELES TIMES, 2/14/97, Calendar/p. 16, Kevin Thomas

[The following review by Kevin Thomas appeared in a slightly different form in NEWSDAY, 2/14/97, Part II/p. B13]

Disney's reworking of its beloved 1965 "That Darn Cat" is too contrived and drawn out to have much appeal for audiences beyond small children, who may be diverted by the antics of a clever feline but who may also start to squirm before the crime comedy at last wraps it all up.

This new version finds bright 16-year-old Patti (Christina Ricci) bored out her mind living in an idyllic Massachusetts town with her genial bookseller father (Michael McKean) and her prissy, obtuse mother (Bess Armstrong), who would drive most teenagers crazy. Patti's key consolation is her alley cat, D.C., who brings excitement into her life when he comes home with a wristwatch around his neck, which becomes a clue in a kidnapping. Action of sorts kicks in when Patti takes off for Boston and convinces a rookie FBI agent (Doug E. Doug)—she will soon describe him accurately as "painfully inept"—to investigate.

Amazingly, this bit of fluff was originally written by the same writing team—Scott Alexander & Larry Karaszewski, this time using the initials "S.M." and "L.A." in the credits instead of their first names—who wrote the hard-edged "The People vs. Larry Flynt." (They have said in interviews that most of the original "Darn Cat" dialogue they wrote long ago was subsequently changed.)

Although most of what ensues in "Darn Cat" is inane, there are a couple of pluses. Although Doug's FBI agent is made to seem idiotic, Patti is well-written and well-played by Ricci under Bob Spiers' direction. Armstrong is especially amusing as the tiresome mother. Dean Jones, who was in the original film, and Dyan Cannon are the classy couple whose housekeeper is the kidnap victim.

Other familiar players include George Dzundza as Doug's huffy boss; Peter Boyle, the local soda fountain proprietor; and Estelle Parsons as the town's crazy old lady. None of these sterling actors has much of a chance to shine in this film, which was first announced for release last year.

But Elvis, cast as D.C., is one smart, scrappy feline. And Edgeville, S.C., which stands in for the fictional Edgefield, Mass., is quaint. But that's about all you can say for this "Darn Cat."

NEW YORK POST, 2/14/97, p. 51, Thelma Adams

It's a good thing the English have a special appreciation for failure, because Bob Spiers, the director of the addictive British black comedies "Absolutely Fabulous" and "Fawlty Towers" just made his Hollywood debut helming "That Darn Cat." Meow!

It's not that Disney's recycling of the 1965 pet detective comedy is bad, it's just not "The Love Bug." Even the Hayley Mills original wasn't the best of breed.

"Cat" starts out upbeat, pumping to a rap song with a "That Darn Cat" refrain. The adorable Christina Ricci ("The Addams Family") keeps pace as Patti. The black-wearing teen outcast hates her twee, Technicolor town. Nothing ever happens in the edgeless Edgefield—but that's about to change.

One morning, Patti's pet, Darn Cat (Elvis, a big-headed, fluffy-ruffed, broom-tailed tomcat), wanders home sporting a Timex. It's trouble time. The watch is a kidnapping clue. Patti contacts the FBI. As a joke, G-man George Dzundza assigns bumbling agent Doug E. Doug (of TVs "Cosby") to follow the bouncing furball.

Spiers assembles a jolly supporting cast: Disney staple Dean Jones, Dyan Cannon, Peter Boyle, Rebecca Schull, Estelle Parsons and John Ratzenberger. Michael McKean and Bess Armstrong make a playful pair as Patti's indulgent dad and prissy perfect mom.

The problem is that the fleabitten script has only three lives and one good act. Having drawn a dozen characters and a town that is folksy by day and freaky by night, scribes S.M. Alexander and L.A. Karaszewski lead the audience on a less-than-merry chase. A cat is only as good as his material .

Also reviewed in:
NEW YORK TIMES, 2/14/97, p. C12, Stephen Holden
VARIETY, 2/17-23/97, p. 69, Joe Leydon
WASHINGTON POST, 2/14/97, Weekend/p. 69, Jane Horwitz

THAT OLD FEELING

A Universal Pictures and The Bubble Factory release of a Sheinberg production in association with Boy of the Year and All Girl Productions. *Executive Producer:* Tom Joyner. *Producer:* Leslie Dixon and Bonnie Bruckheimer. *Director:* Carl Reiner. *Screenplay:* Leslie Dixon. *Director of Photography:* Steve Mason. *Editor:* Richard Halsey. *Music:* Patrick Williams. *Music Editor:* George A. Martin. *Choreographer:* Anne Wootten. *Sound:* Bruce Carwardine and (music) Charles Pollard. *Sound Editor:* Robert L. Sephton. *Casting:* Nancy Nayor. *Production Designer:* Sandy Veneziano. *Art Director:* Alicia Keywan. *Set Decorator:* Steve Shewchuk. *Set Dresser:* Dan Conley. *Costumes:* Robert De Mora. *Make-up:* Patricia Green. *Make-up (Bette Midler):* Angela Levin. *Stunt Coordinator:* Ted Hanlan. *Running time:* 103 minutes. *MPAA Rating:* PG-13.

CAST: Bette Midler (Lilly); Dennis Farina (Dan); Paula Marshall (Molly); Gail O'Grady (Rowena); David Rasche (Alan); Jamie Denton (Keith); Danny Nucci (Joey); Blu Mankuma (Bar Pianist); Jayne Eastwood (Aunt Iris); Michael J. Reynolds (Senator Marks); Joan Luchak (Senator Marks' Wife); Mike Wilmot (Man at Wedding); Lula Franklin (Granny Tapper); George Hevenor (Bandleader); Arlene Meadows (Inn Proprietress); Don Allison (Desk Clerk); Ian Clark (Rufus); David Huband and Tony Craig (Cops); Kim Bourne and Cara Chisholm (Waitresses); Pedro Salvin (Waiter); Doug Murray (Best Man); John Nightingale (Sanford, Usher); Scott Gibson (Gordon, Usher); Mary Jo Eustace (Girl at Tabloid); Simon Barry (Bushboy); Ian Downie (Minister); Marjorie Lowe, Michelle Carberry, and Justina Taglialatela (Bridesmaids); Tabitha Lupien, Brittney Kuczynski, and Alexandra Longo (Flower Girls); Gerry Mendicino (Maitre d'); Jerry Schaeffer (Male Fan); Madeline Lee (Woman at Sidewalk Cafe).

LOS ANGELES TIMES, 4/4/97, Calendar/p. 10, John Anderson

[The following review by John Anderson appeared in a slightly different form in **NEWSDAY, 4/4/97, Part II/p. B2.]**

She may not be your cup of vinaigrette, but Bette Midler knows who she is, and what it is she should do: Walk loudly and carry a big shtick.

She's done it for a long time, and she does it well. And she's seldom been more Bette than as the brassy, sassy and lethally theatrical Lilly of "That Old Feeling," a shticky situational comedy that pays tribute to director Carl Reiner's roots in television while giving some well-deserved exposure to a lot of talented people.

These include Dennis Farina, who plays Lilly's ex-husband, Dan, from whom she's been divorced for 14 years—and for whom she harbors a lethal reservoir of venom. Dan returns the affection. The two can't be in the same room without an EMS unit on call.

How two such profoundly ethnic characters had such a homogenized daughter as Molly (Paula Marshall) is a credit to the miracle of movie casting, but when Molly gets married, Lilly and Dan go on the honeymoon. Beginning with some Porsche-rocking congress in the parking lot at Molly's reception, their mutual hatred turns to lust and they leave their respective spouses behind for a whirlwind tour of a luxury Manhattan hotel suite.

As well as things are going for them, they don't start well for us. Reiner actually has the nerve to open with a scene of Molly choking on her engagement ring, which was placed in her chocolate mousse by order of her unctuous fiancée, Keith (Jamie Denton). It's the kind of thing that, had you seen it walking into the theater, might prompt you to turn around and walk out. The movie gets better.

Actually, "That Old Feeling" is a very traditional comedy in a surreal sort of way. Both Dan and Lilly are married to people with whom they cheated while married to each other. And both of the new people are losers. Lilly's husband, Alan (a very funny David Rasche), is a self-help author and therapist whose own psyche is a bit unhinged. Dan's wife, Rowena (Gail O'Grady, formerly of "NYPD Blue"), is a closet harpy. The moral lesson is that the first marriage should never have been put asunder—which, given the hair-trigger tempers on both parties, is a little hard to swallow.

As is Molly's virginity, which isn't actually mentioned but exists as a kind of sexual Godot. The Dan-Lilly disappearance puts Molly's honeymoon on hold. So when she recruits Joey the *paparazzo* (Danny Nucci) to help find Mom, and things heat up between them, her deflowering becomes a subject of high suspense. It's quaint and, considering the animal coupling going on everywhere else in the movie, a little weird.

But "That Old Feeling" is generally fun, thanks to old pros Midler and Farina, and Nucci, who plays Joey as a combination Joe Pesci-Jerry Lewis and provides an antidote to the rigidity of Molly and Keith. In fact, forget what I said about "traditional" values: Dan and Lilly are having too much fun to be role models for anyone.

NEW YORK POST, 4/4/97, p. 44, Thelma Adams

"That Old Feeling" pretty much describes Carl Reiner's adultery comedy. With Bette Midler and Dennis Farina as "toxic parents" who reunite at their daughter's wedding, much to their current spouses' chagrin, the movie is never as fresh as the first half-hour promises.

Midler is energetic but not brilliant as a self-obsessed Hollywood star. Her Lilly loves to hate her paparazzi. She feels virtually undressed if Joey the Cockroach (Danny Nucci) isn't stalking her with his Nikon.

The diva with a touch of Streisand is best when the material in Leslie Dixon's uneven script rises to her anger: "I'm not neurotic," Lilly tells daughter Molly (Paula Marshall). "I'm a bitch."

Farina, best known for playing cops or robbers ("Get Shorty"), makes sparks fly with Midler. As Dan, a mystery writer who has a tendency to kill off actresses in his books, Farina shows that he can trade barbs, kiss hard and samba.

Listening to Midler aim a love song in his direction proves to be beyond Farina's range. He doesn't seem to know what to do with his mouth in the sappy scene.

"That Old Feeling" clicks in sharp exchanges. Lilly and Dan take off together after Molly's wedding. Spotted on the street, an old woman tells them, "It's so nice to see a mature, loving relationship." Lilly shoots back: "It's adulterous, but thanks."

Screenwriter Dixon ("Mrs. Doubtfire") stumbles when she tries to weave a farcical plot with the many loose ends she creates. Dan's wife Rowena (Gail O'Grady) falls into bed with (Jamie Denton)—and then offers a withering postgame wrap-up. Molly gives cheesy photog Joey a one-minute makeover and a romance blossoms. Lilly's husband, Alan (David Rasche), a couples counselor, comes undone, unable to heal himself.

Alan tells a patient over the phone: "Anger is such a cheap emotion." Unfortunately, it's the only honest feeling fueling the plot. As the story progresses, the one-liners go soft, the sex broadens, the characters become caricatures, and Reiner ("Wheres Poppa?") loses control over the whole menagerie.

Out of all things familiar, an actress emerges who is fresh and appealing. Marshall's Molly has the zing of a young Mary Tyler Moore. Her reactions are natural, her timing assured and she can turn from a laugh to a cry in the time it used to take Moore to toss a hat up in the air.

SIGHT AND SOUND, 9/97, p. 56, Karl Philips

Keith Marks, a prospective congressman running on a family values ticket, proposes marriage to his girlfriend Molly. Molly is worried that her divorced parents, Lilly Leonard and Dan De Mora, will cause trouble. During a shopping trip, Lilly, a famous actress, is hassled by Joey Donna, a paparazzo photographer.

Lilly comes to the wedding with her new husband Alan, and Dan with his young wife Rowena. To everyone's surprise, the divorced couple behave themselves. But afterwards, having rediscovered their attraction for one another, they have sex in a car. This reunion continues in secret at the hotel that night, but they create such a disturbance the distracted newlyweds can't consummate their own marriage. Lilly and Dan leave when their spouses discover the infidelity. Keith, concerned about his career, insists that Molly stop the affair. With Joey's help, Molly finds Lilly and Dan at the Majestic hotel. Lilly leaves Molly and Joey locked in a hotel room together, and unable to escape their predicament they bond. That same night Keith and Rowena have sex together.

Joey spurns the opportunity to photograph Lilly and Dan kissing and gatecrashes a wedding reception at the hotel with Molly. She styles Joey to make him more attractive and he dances with Lilly, while Dan's opinion causes Molly to question her own marriage. Joey reveals his feelings for Molly and they kiss but agree that it could never work out. Lilly and Dan argue and in the commotion Joey drops a concealed camera. Molly, not realising that Joey has already proved himself by not taking any photographs, loses faith in him and they have a row. Keith, Rowena and Alan arrive at the hotel and everybody returns home.

As everyone is gathered at the airport to see off the newlyweds, Molly discovers a hair belonging to Rowena on Keith's jacket. Molly gives her airline tickets to Lilly and Dan. Joey gets his picture at last, but destroys the film and walks off hand in hand with Molly.

At a time when Hollywood would see everyone in neatly arranged nuclear families, *That Old Feeling* suggests that perhaps even the warring Lilly and Dan did get it right first time around and that a couple divorced for 12 years can be reunited. However, while there are swoony wedding-day trappings and second honeymoons aplenty, *Feeling* only delivers on half of its claim to be a 'romantic comedy'.

Carl Reiner proved that he can direct comedy with flair with *The Jerk* and *All of Me*. Here he takes the most direct route possible and rarely hits the right comic mark or develops the themes or characters satisfactorily. For example, you want to know why is Molly so repulsed by the idea of her parents' reunion; beyond concerns for her husband's career there appears to be little reason. If her step-parents Alan and Rowena are as one-dimensional as they are depicted then surely she would welcome her folks getting back together.

Dennis Farina as her father Dan, holidaying from his usual tough-guy roles (see *Get Shorty*), makes his romantic debut, but although his character attempts to give as good as he gets, he seems resigned to playing second fiddle. With Midler centre-stage, the supporting characters are mere set-dressing. David Rasche's Alan, a self-help guru, spouts nothing but psychobabble; Danny Nucci's Joey, a *paparazzo*, is the token shifty kid from across the tracks who comes good; and Gail O'Grady's nipped and tucked Rowena is simply there as a foil for Midler.

Rowena is to *Feeling* what the despised trophy partners were to *The First Wives Club*: younger models to be envied and then humiliated by the wiser, older and more experienced women. As if to prove this, Midler reveals flesh at every opportunity. The film itself is relentlessly about appearances. Midler's Lilly detests Joey because he once published an unflattering picture of her and she will only be photographed on her good side, Rowena is despised for her looks, and even Joey requires a makeover to get served in the up-market hotel.

The film, stemming from Midler's production company, is transparently no more than a vehicle for the brassy, gregarious Bette, and not content with the odd line reminiscent of her standup spiel—"I'm not neurotic, I'm just a bitch!"—she also gets to sing, in a clumsily manufactured scene with the musicians in the bar, and later to show off her dancing skills. The film is supposedly viewed from the daughter's point of view, but Paula Marshall's conventional Molly is a duller version of the repressed Saffron from *Absolutely Fabulous*, who hates her extrovert ex-hippie mother Edina, who (as with Lilly here) always gets the loudest lines and the brightest clothes. This attention to dress is reflected in the other characters' outfits, which are considerably more sombre by comparison. The same detail is noticeable in the two wedding scenes. Molly's and Keith's attire is marked by pastel shades, particularly in its use of flowers, suggesting a pure but ultimately boring partnership. By contrast the gate-crashed wedding reception, virtually a second wedding for Lilly and Dan, features a lively Latino band and bright, loud colours, reflecting the fiery time that the second honeymooners are having.

As a battle of the sexes, *That Old Feeling* also lacks ammunition, something that the black comedy *The War of Roses* had in excess. In that film Michael Douglas and Kathleen Turner demonstrated a sense of cruelty that verged on the maniacal. Here, Midler and Farina's characters just pussyfoot around. *That Old Feeling*, an apt title for a predictable film short on originality, achieves little apart from reminding the viewer that people in their fifties still enjoy sex. If the film has a happy ending it is only because it fails to address the question of whether any of the protagonists will be any happier this time next year, next month, or even next week.

Also reviewed in:
NEW YORK TIMES, 4/4/97, p. C22, Lawrence Van Gelder
VARIETY, 4/7-13/97, p. 43, Leonard Klady
WASHINGTON POST, 4/4/97, p. B6, Rita Kempley

THIS WORLD, THEN THE FIREWORKS

An Orion Classics and Largo Entertainment release of a Muse, Balzac's Shirt and Wyman production. *Executive Producer:* Barr Potter. *Producer:* Chris Hanley, Brad Wyman, and Larry Gross. *Director:* Michael Oblowitz. *Screenplay:* Larry Gross. *Based on a story by:* Jim Thompson. *Director of Photography:* Tom Priestley, Jr. *Editor:* Emma E. Hickox. *Music:* Pete Rugolo. *Music Editor:* Lisle Leete. *Sound:* Coll Anderson and (music) Leslie Ann Jones. *Sound Editor:* Skip Lievsay. *Casting:* Mary Vernieu. *Production Designer:* Maia Javan. *Art Director:* Alison Sadler. *Set Decorator:* Chester A. Spier. *Special Effects:* Michael Schorr and Ronnie Yeskel. *Costumes:* Dan Moore. *Make-up:* Brad Boles. *Stunt Coordinator:* Dean Mumford and Michael Walter. *Running time:* 100 minutes. *MPAA Rating:* R.

CAST: Billy Zane (Marty Lakewood); Gina Gershon (Carol Lakewood); Sheryl Lee (Lois Archer); Rue McClanahan (Mrs. Lakewood); Seymour Cassel (Detective Harris); William Hootkins (Jake Krutz, Private Investigator); Will Patton (Lieutenant Morgan); Val DeVargas (Mexican Doctor); Richard Edson (Joe); Roberta Hanley (Younger Mom Lakewood); Philip Loch (Marty Lakewood's Father); Elisabeth Imboden (Neighbor's Wife); Christian Durango (Little Marty Lakewood); Sloan Cobb (Little Carol Lakewood); Robert Pentz (Lou); Marianna Alacchi (Glenda); Orson Oblowitz (Eugene); Willie Cobbs (Blues Musician); Max Maxwell and Matt O'Toole (Thugs in Bar); Mert Hatfield (Bus Driver); Megan Leigh Brown (Young Carol Lakewood); Tom Keeley (Cousin Lyle); Christopher Jones (Young Marty Lakewood); Thad Mace (Tim); Jonathan Taylor Luthren (Ben); Stephanie Fisher (Claire); Mark Jeffrey Miller (Lloyd); Vincent Schilling and David Curtis (Patrons); Lou Criscuolo (McCloud); Jeffrey Pillars (Galloway); Paul Allan Sincoff (Assistant); John Bennes (Griffith); Barry Bell (Barnett Gibons); David Lenthall (Doctor); Brian Gamble (Undertaker); Terry Neihuis (Minister); Dean Mumford (Captain Miles Archer, Marine); Nick Warner (Real Estate Guy).

LOS ANGELES TIMES, 7/11/97, Calendar/p. 14, Kevin Thomas

[The following review by Kevin Thomas appeared in a slightly different form in
NEWSDAY, 7/11/97, Part II/p. B8.]

Director Michael Oblowitz and writer-producer Larry Gross have a tough time getting a grip on "This World, Then the Fireworks," a lurid, low-down adaptation of a story by legendary hard-boiled writer Jim Thompson. As a result, "This World" lumbers and strains too often when it should snap and crackle.

It's the late '20s and the lives of two small children, brother and sister, are blasted when their father, in your classic fit of jealous rage, takes a shotgun to his lover and her husband, a cop. He's executed for his crime; his wife, who was in the range of fire, is left with a face scarred by pellets. His son and daughter are so traumatized they form a bond so tight that it inevitably blossoms into incestuous passion and a reckless, lawless existence.

Some of the most entertaining and provocative films have resulted from inspired directors taking vintage potboiler material and managing to play it both ways, having fun with its outrageousness yet simultaneously taking it seriously. A prime example is François Truffaut's adaptation of Cornell Woolrich's "The Bride Wore Black," and such diverse directors as André Techiné, R.W. Fassbinder and Brian De Palma have also gotten away with such outré ventures. But "This World" stifles in self-consciousness and ponderousness, leaving us with a screen full of improbable, nasty and uninvolving characters.

After their lives have literally been smashed to smithereens, the mother, who grows into a religious hysteric, starts drifting around the country with her two small children. As the story flashes ahead to 1956, the mother (Rue McClanahan), too weary to keep on moving, has wound up in a farmhouse adjacent to a small West Coast city. Her daughter Carol (Gina Gershon), having seen her marriage break up, has become a hooker working out of a local bar.

The son Marty (Billy Zane) has gone off to Chicago to become a hotshot crime reporter, digging up so much dirt about organized crime and its connection to political corruption that he's got to blow town. (Perhaps as some kind of punishment for his feelings for his sister, Marty has married a homely woman suffering from elephantiasis and they have an equally unattractive son.) In any event, he turns up at the home of his mother, and Marty and Carol's reunion has predictably dangerous results.

What we need at this point is the feeling we got so strongly in Leonard Kastle's classic 1970 "Honeymoon Killers": that its overweight, unhappy nurse and its small-time con man most likely would have continued to lead relatively harmless lives until they met, unleashing within each other a deadly mix of passion and evil. Marty and Carol, reunited, have this kind of impact upon each other, but "This World" doesn't really develop their relationship. The point is that if you're dealing with increasingly outrageous material and want to get away with it, you've got to be working from the firm foundation of a solid script.

Zane's Marty is convincingly brilliant and amoral, Gershon goes for an Ava Gardner look and McClanahan, always a game, accomplished actress, plays boldly against her glamorous image. Sheryl Lee, as a repressed small-town cop, is effective as one of those perfect blond '50s goddesses until she's seduced by the heartless Marty. However, except for McClanahan and Seymour Cassel as a shrewd cop, the others seem to be striking poses and assuming attitudes more than actually acting.

The picture has a fairly authentic period look and feel and a great jazzy, saxophone-heavy Pete Rugolo score too good for it. But the callow "This World" winds up a reminder of how tough it really is to pull off an authentically fatalistic neo-noir—one like Stephen Frears' marvelous Jim Thompson adaptation, "The Grifters."

If it's small-town crime and Ava Gardner you're in the mood for, you might want to pick up the "Whistle Stop" (1946) video currently on sale in many drugstore racks for a couple of bucks. It's not great, but it's the genuine article.

NEW YORK POST, 7/11/97, p. 40, Thelma Adams

"If I sleep with one more sailor, I'll start saluting," says Carol, the twisted sister who shoots off sparks in "This World, Then the Fireworks," Michael Oblowitz's explosive if scattershot noir film.

Adapted by Larry Gross from Jim Thompson's banned 1955 short story, "This World" is so hard-boiled that if it were an egg it would implode.

Gina Gershon's voluptuous Carol is an alley cat on a hot tin roof. It's not for nothing that she's an amoral grifter. In the sharp, shocking exposition—shot from below, like family photos taken by observant kids—Carol and her 4-year-old twin brother, Marty, witness a domestic apocalypse on Independence Day.

Close enough to taste the splattered blood like raindrops, the two children cleave to each other. They also take cleavers—or whatever's handy—to whomever bothers them. This includes their righteous mama, Rue McClanahan (ill-served by Brad Boles' "House of Wax" makeup).

Marty (Billy Zane, in a juicy performance that tops the movie) narrates the story. True to Thompson's body of work (most notably "The Killer Inside Me"), the narrator is an amoral man of above-average intelligence. Capable of reeling in the audience with his charm, he then appalls with monstrous behavior.

Grown up and married to a woman who hardly registers, Marty finds that his heart still belongs to Carol (Gershon, of "Face/Off," beguiles again). When dirty cops run him out of Chicago, he flees to his sister's waiting bed and their mother's rebukes in a small, coastal California town. There, he gets into the girdle of pent-up policewoman Lois (Sheryl "Bliss" Lee).

The siblings scheme to bilk Lois out of her beach house. But the twist has a twist of its own. Before you can say Tijuana abortionist (another plot point that would have shocked contemporary readers), Marty finds himself outmaneuvered.

Thompson delivers a comeuppance that confronts Marty with the emotional and moral complexities that he has been running from ever since that fateful July Fourth when his father's shotgun blasts eclipsed the Roman candles.

The author of "The Grifters" earned his perversions and atrocities with a prose style that was simplicity itself: conversational, direct and modest. Thompson didn't surprise us with hip turns of phrase; he left the surprises to his plot turns.

In contrast, director Oblowitz is too cool to stay as cool as the movie's opening sequence. His camera movements become over-heated, his dramatic fireworks explode too soon.

Despite its sultry cast, "This World, Then the Fireworks" sizzles, then fizzles.

SIGHT AND SOUND, 12/97, p. 55, Linda Ruth Williams

Pursued by the police, Marty Lakewood leaves his wife and son in Chicago to join his mother and twin sister Carol in California. He re-establishes the sexual relationship he has with Carol, a hooker, which was formed in response to the crucial trauma of the twins' lives: their father murdered his lover's husband on the children's fourth birthday, an event witnessed by Marty, Carol and their mother. The father went to the electric chair, and the mother went mad.

After briefly working as a journalist, Marty meets and seduces policewoman Lois Archer. He tries to persuade her to sell the beach house which she owns with her brother, an absent soldier whose photograph is displayed in the house. Though Lois thinks this will allow them to elope, Marty plans to live off the proceeds with Carol. Marty kills a private detective who is tailing his sister, then Carol kills one of her clients by biting his neck. Their mother has sunk further into insanity, so Carol feeds her a fatal dose of sleeping pills.

Carol leaves for Mexico, and the police question Marty about his sister's involvement in the murders. Carol dies at a backstreet abortionist's, and Marty is left with Lois, who has agreed to arrange for the house to be sold. The soldier in the photograph arrives and intrudes on their lovemaking, so Marty kills him. It is then revealed that this man is Lois' husband. Lois takes the blame for the shooting, and her employers, the police department, cover up the scandal, allowing Lois and Marty to pocket the proceeds from the sale of the house.

In the original Jim Thompson story upon which *This World, Then the Fireworks* is based, Marty tells a tale to his traumatised twin sister Carol, with whom he is having an incestuous relationship. "Once upon a time," he says, "there was a little boy and a little girl, and the little boy was her father and the little girl was his mother." Director Michael Oblowitz's rich neo-*noir* adaptation beautifully envisions and unravels Thompson's tale of twisted family romances. When brother and sister get to play mummies and daddies for real, the oedipal desire implicit in post-war *noir* becomes explicit. The secret-feeding hothouse flowers of, say, *The Big Sleep* (1946), are now open Venus fly-traps, consuming whatever comes their way in unnaturally broad daylight. *This*

World is not, however, neo-*noir* by numbers. The *femmes fatales*, bent cops and grifters are there, urged by perverse desires into alienated acts of violence. But crime thrills have been subordinated to sexual subterfuge, and *This World* does not play like pulp fiction. It is a Jacobean tragedy for the 50s fetishist.

Indeed, the *mise en scène* is so meticulously detailed the film's world looks like a surreal 50s theme park. This drama is played out in jewel-primaries (alternating with bleached monotones in the flashbacks). Its score dips and dives across classic vocals, lounge-bar conga-sleaze and breathy tenor sax. Oblowitz (the maker of several low-budget shorts and the feature *King Blank*) and cinematographer Tom Priestley ensure that the film has a consistently glamorous look. However resistant you are to the overwrought content or the underwrought story (there are plot-holes you could drive Sheryl Lee's Pontiac through), it is hard to withstand the sheer brio of a camera move which starts by holding in pristine focus for a second that same Pontiac's chrome front fender, before sliding around its wing to pick out passing people reflected therein. For another shot, the camera lurks behind glass shelves laden with stilettos, which become the frame through which we watch Marty and Carol saunter down the pavement.

This World also takes its *noir*-influences more seriously than other homages. Accompanied by a frenetic burst of Latin percussion, the killing of a detective by Marty clearly echoes Orson Welles' monstrous Quinlan in *Touch of Evil* (1958). Also echoing Welles' *The Lady from Shanghai* (1948), there are mirrors everywhere in *This World*, but Oblowitz's do something quite different from Welles'. Here, characters are doubled in perfectly posed arrangements of face and mirror-image: in one scene, the twins' mother is framed in her daughter's bedroom mirror as she confronts her children's embrace. The positioning of the figures underlines the complexity with which this film reverses the 'normal' flow of family desire. Power and craziness are exchanged between parent and twins, as are the fundamental roles of father-mother-child: here the mother becomes the child intruding on the primal scene (the vision of one's parents having sex). After this knowingly twisted primal scene comes a fatal one when Carol gives her mother a fatal overdose. The sequence of events is pure Thompson; the mirror-framing underscoring it is Oblowitz's.

As the children, Zane and Gershon give convincingly adolescent performances—petulant, rebellious, united against their griping mother. Zane plays Marty like an underground Hamlet, messianic seductiveness alternating with repellent nastiness. Doing his best to live up to one character's prediction that in a film of his life Marty would be played by Marlon Brando, Zane moves easily between crazed theological-psychobabble and flat, inexpressive voiceover exposition. The statuesque Gershon, whose Ava Gardner looks ensure that she was *made* for those dresses, has the chance to be subtler here than in previous performances, despite the lurid subject matter. Anyone who saw her in *Showgirls* or *Bound* might have expected her Carol to be a vengeful *femme fatale* seductress, but Gershon also presents her as vacant, knotted-up, doomed. Set against her is Sheryl Lee's frigid blond ("One's a glass of milk and one's a highball," says Marty). If Gershon is Gardner, Lee is Deborah Kerr, especially when she and Zane roll in the surf in knowing homage to *From Here to Eternity*. Lee, who has turned out some brilliantly complex—and unjustly overlooked—performances, is not particularly stretched here (unlike her Frederick's of Hollywood underwear). Instead, she's simply being asked to switch from uptight repression to wild wantoness to show that the milk wasn't so innocent after all.

A bigger problem lies in *This World*'s status as a crime film. It slides around between genres, even flirting with the vampire film when Carol kills her trick by chewing his throat. There are murders, cons, duplicity, but causes and explanations are refused. In fact, the film's central crime is really incest. Beyond the customary "they fuck you up, your mum and dad" justification (insisted on by the flashback sequences), in this world people do things just *because they do*. Dealing in extremes, the film offers both too much and too little—and this is not a criticism, given its double obsession with emptiness and superfluity. If you want answers, coherence and closure, look elsewhere. *This World* offers instead excessive passions and thin morals, reasons which do not justify unreasonableness. Catching its characters on the brink of dissolution, it finally gives up on explaining the arbitrary violence and psychotic rants which leak out of the cracks fast developing in everyone, everywhere. *This World* is not a subtle work—which makes it hard to respond mildly to it—and it will not be to everyone's taste. But for those who relish films wrought from explosive emotions rather than exploding objects this is a smorgasbord of cinematic spectacle.

VILLAGE VOICE, 7/15/97, p. 65, J. Hoberman

The small-town sheriff as serial killer—a mixture of Bull Connor and Dynamite Bob—is precisely the sort of all-American psycho prized by the alcoholic, ex-Communist pulp writer Jim Thompson.

Only marginally appreciated during his lifetime, Thompson's oeuvre has become a holy grail for neo-noir filmmakers. Written in 1957, rejected by *Playboy,* posthumously published, and now lovingly adapted for the screen by Michael Oblowitz and Larry Gross, the novella *This World, Then the Fireworks* is feverishly perverse even by Thompson's standards. This graphic account of multiple murder and sexual blackmail (as well as incest, matricide, and backstreet abortion) opens on the Fourth of July with a gruesome killing witnessed by four-year-old twins: "We burst into laughter simultaneously... It was funnier even than Charlie Chaplin in the movies, or Krazy Kat in the funny papers. The man on the floor didn't have any head."

Yow! The traumatized tots, a boy and a girl, grow up into a complementary set of amoral hustlers. The movie's major triumph is casting a wondrously matched pair of ripe feline beauties, Billy Zane and Gina Gershon (who deserves to displace Sharon Stone as the movies' reigning bad girl). Sleek panthers preying on the bourgeois sheep of sleepy, mid-'50s L.A., the sibs run their scams pretty much in tandem until Zane's character gets overly involved with the repressed police gal (Sheryl Lee) whom he's idly transformed into a masochistic sex slave.

Set in the sultry armpit of a world where women wear black slips and men sleeveless undershirts and the afternoon sun streams through the venetian blinds to cast a perfect grid of diagonal tiger stripes on the rumpled bedsheets, *This World* has clearly been made by a pair of aesthetes—which may account for the movie's highly theoretical mise-en-scène, at once studied and overwrought. The filmmakers scarcely shy away from Thompson's cartoonish excesses—a sleazy private dick resembling Jabba the Hutt gets his eyeball impaled on his desk paper spike. But if *This World* feels overlong and increasingly airless, it may be because Thompson's flophouse prose poem is treated with the reverence other filmmakers might accord Jane Austen.

Too constricted to give full vent to the story's lunacy (but too enamored to ignore it), *This World* is ultimately smothered by the film-makers' fond fastidiousness—a turgid irony compounded by the final Chet Baker ballad, "You Don't Know What Love Is."

Also reviewed in:
NEW YORK TIMES, 7/11/97, p. C5, Stephen Holden
VARIETY, 1/27-2/2/97, p. 76, Emmanuel Levy

THOUSAND ACRES, A

A Touchstone Pictures release in association with Beacon Pictures and Propaganda Films of a Via Rosa/Prairie Films production. *Executive Producer:* Armyan Bernstein and Thomas A. Bliss. *Producer:* Marc Abraham, Lynn Arost, Steve Golin, Kate Guinzburg, and Sigurjon Sighvatsson. *Director:* Jocelyn Moorhouse. *Screenplay:* Laura Jones. *Based on the novel by:* Jane Smiley. *Director of Photography:* Tak Fujimoto. *Editor:* Maryann Brandon. *Music:* Richard Hartley. *Music Editor:* John Finklea. *Sound:* Richard Lightstone and (music) Armin Steiner. *Sound Editor:* Robert Grieve and Greg King. *Casting:* Nancy Klopper. *Production Designer:* Dan Davis. *Art Director:* James F. Truesdale. *Set Decorator:* Andrea Fenton. *Set Designer:* George R. Lee and Andrew Menzies. *Special Effects:* Martin Becker. *Costumes:* Ruth Myers. *Make-up:* Lizbeth Williamson. *Make-up (Michelle Pfeiffer):* Ronnie Specter. *Make-up (Jessica Lange):* Dorothy Pearl. *Stunt Coordinator:* Rick Le Fevour and Jim Fierro. *Running time:* 101 minutes. *MPAA Rating:* R.

CAST: Michelle Pfeiffer (Rose Cook Lewis); Jessica Lange (Ginny Cook Smith); Jason Robards (Larry Cook); Jennifer Jason Leigh (Caroline Cook); Colin Firth (Jess Clark); Keith Carradine (Ty Smith); Kevin Anderson (Peter Lewis); Pat Hingle (Harold Clark); John Carroll Lynch (Ken LaSalle); Anne Pitoniak (Mary Livingstone); Vyto Ruginis (Charles Carter); Michelle

Williams (Pammy);   Elizabeth Moss (Linda);   Ray Toler (Marv Carson);   Kenneth Tigar (Doctor);   Steve Key (Loren Clark);   Dan Conway (Henry Dodge);   Stan Cahill (Frank);   Ray Baker (Wallace Crockett);   Beth Grant (Roberta);   Andrea Nittoli (Waitress).

LOS ANGELES TIMES, 9/19/97, Calendar/p. 1, Kenneth Turan

Sisterhood is powerful in "A Thousand Acres," and you'd think that would be enough. Certainly it seems to be in those moments when Michelle Pfeiffer and Jessica Lange triumphantly share the screen as embattled siblings in this adaptation of Jane Smiley's Pulitzer Prize-winning novel about the bonds and burdens of kinship and a gift that shatters a family.

Playing sisters has been a longtime aim of these actresses, and they handle the opportunity beautifully. Both strong and vulnerable, they're thoroughly alive individually as well as forming the interlocking halves of a believable, cohesive whole, smoothly complementing each other's work like they've been doing this for years.

But as powerful as sisterhood is, and as memorable as these performances are, it turns out that it's not enough. As directed by Australian Jocelyn Moorhouse ("Proof," "How to Make an American Quilt") from an adaptation by fellow countrywoman Laura Jones, "Acres" has trouble with a group that has rather a history of bedeviling women, namely men. The film doesn't lack for key male characters (there are at least five), and their actions aren't more objectionable than they should be. The problem is how insubstantial the men come off on screen, how hollow and ephemeral they appear. That's not only as opposed to the brio of Pfeiffer and Lange, which is to be expected, but even as opposed to how they're presented in the novel, where considerably more effort is expended delineating their characters.

This lack doesn't take anything away from those lead performances, but what it does do is deprive them of a more substantial and nuanced showcase in which to be seen. And it keeps the film from accomplishing its aims, accentuating a tendency to be cut and dried, to come off as more earnest and predictable than it perhaps intended to.

"A Thousand Acres" opens with a montage of bucolic farm images, pristine enough for a greeting card. But this is almost purposefully deceptive, for the people of the small town of Pike, Iowa, especially the extended family of Larry Cook (Jason Robards), have darker more turbulent lives and more troubled pasts than the surface sunshine would indicate.

The film's narrator is Larry Cook's oldest daughter, Ginny (Lange), married to easygoing Ty Smith (Keith Carradine) but still enough of her widowed father's daughter to walk to his house and cook his breakfast every morning. Childless and turning dowdy before her time, Ginny is the family conciliator, the force for stability who has taught herself to believe that things will surely get better.

Rose (Pfeiffer), a breast cancer survivor with an edgy relationship with husband Peter (Kevin Anderson), is a woman who prides herself on her plain speaking, a quality that often lapses into harshness and hostility. Like Ginny and baby sister Caroline (Jennifer Jason Leigh), a lawyer who lives in Des Moines and is only sporadically present, Rose has created her personality as a form of defense against her overbearing father.

Larry Cook, crusty and land-proud, is the most respected farmer in Zebulon County and sole owner of the unencumbered 1,000-acre establishment that has been in his family for generations. At a family gathering, he shocks everyone by declaring his intention of making a gift of the place to his three daughters as soon as the contracts can be drawn up.

This act of heedless generosity causes problems from the start. When lawyer Caroline cautiously hesitates about accepting, Larry immediately snaps, "If you don't want it, my girl, you're out," and suddenly a family division has risen up out of nowhere.

If this sounds familiar, it's because author Smiley took the bare bones of her story from Shakespeare's "King Lear" and its tale of a monarch who gives his kingdom to daughters Goneril, Regan and Cordelia. But "A Thousand Acres" has concerns outside of Shakespeare's as well as a modern twist on what that act of generosity leads to.

It's a gift that ends up causing chaos because it triggers actions and memories that in turn expose rifts and crimes, secrets and lies, that have been papered over and half-forgotten. As Larry Cook, perhaps regretful over his actions, becomes even more of a sour tyrant than he was before, his daughters begin to realize just how much they've chafed under his authoritarian rule. And they also increasingly notice the presence of the town's newly returned prodigal son, Jess

Clark (Colin Firth, Darcy in the BBC's "Pride and Prejudice"), who seems immediately attracted to Ginny.

Though, according to press reports, director Moorhouse was dissatisfied enough with this cut of "A Thousand Acres" to consider removing her name from the picture, the film succeeds, as the book did, in effectively telling the Lear story from the daughters' point of view, revealing these women as too powerless to protect themselves from being victimized by patriarchal excesses.

Given how important the men are to the film's dynamic, their not having the same texture and reality as the women is "Acre's" major weakness. It removes believability from the crisis-heavy plot, making key events seem artificial and insubstantial and leaving the film limp when its stars do not have each other to work off of.

Combating these drawbacks are the great strengths of those lead performances. If Pfeiffer's resentful Rose supplies much of the film's energy, it is Lange's older sister who changes most over the course of the film. At first Ginny doesn't seem sophisticated enough to be the author of the voice-over she reads. However, her character has the grace to grow into her words, and by the time "A Thousand Acres" ends we know exactly what the price of that personal evolution was.

NEW STATESMAN, 6/12/98, p. 43, Nick Coleman

This way madness lies.

Presumably Americans don't have much of a taste for Manifest Destiny these days, knowing what they know. So when Jocelyn (*How to Make an American Quilt*). Moorhouse shows us, in her new film *A Thousand Acres*, the wide horizon of the agrarian mid-west, and gilds it with a sunset to illuminate the relieving perpendiculars of grain elevator and wind pump and, for good measure, trickles over it some English-style pastoral music as if the very spirit of Delius stalked the cornfields, then you know that something in the barn is worm-eaten.

This is Zebulon County, Iowa, where Daddy Cook presides over the thousand acres that stand for the enterprise and sheer graft of several generations of Cooks, who drained it, nurtured it, then ruled over it with, one suspects, a thick mixture of iron paranoia and Masonic zeal. Daddy has three daughters: Ginny, Rose and Caroline. Ginny is complaisant, Rose bitter and Caroline a lawyer. Daddy decides to divide the farm equally between the three sisters and then gets the hump when Caroline lawyerishly expresses some doubt as to the wisdom of such a gesture. Daddy promptly disinherits her and suddenly the penny drops. We are no longer in American Eden but in King Lear.

Jane Smiley's Pulitzer Prize-winning novel is one of the great American things of the past 20 years or so. It's a story of gradual realisation, of a peeling back of layers, of the slow exposure of the worm in the bud. Smiley forces us to endure the same agonies of discovery as her central character by the simple device of making the reader identify with the methodically ingenuous narration of Ginny/Goneril, the obliging daughter, the one who wants everyone to just get on with it, no matter the cost to truth, honesty and good mental health. It's some trick.

In the film, though, it's obvious from the start that Ginny doesn't have a prayer. She wears ·lothes your mum stopped wearing in the seventies; she walks across muddy fields to tell Daddy his breakfast's ready. Goaded by the uncontained raging of cancer-ridden Rose/Regan ("The more pissed off I am, the better I feel"), she passively participates in the consignment of Daddy to madness and, in so doing, begins to unpick the seams of her neatly stitched life. She discovers the pleasures of forbidden sex, watches her own childless marriage disintegrate and recovers the suppressed memory of Daddy's idea of a good time. It's a bumpy ride straight to the slurry pit.

It's also a ride which, in celluloid form, might have degenerated into a TV-movie-style moral tract, in which self-knowledge is the engine rather than the consequence of redemption. But Moorhouse's film isn't that naff. It's an honest attempt to do the book. It is also a bit of a mess, which might explain why it's taken so long to come out.

A Thousand Acres bears the scars of a thousand hours in the editing suite. It has no rhythm and sustains little atmosphere. It lurches precipitously from epiphany to revelation, from oceanic cornfield to church social, its symbolism overcooked, its secondary characters half-done. Ultimately, Moorhouse's desperate willingness to do justice to the width of the original material leaves her film cramped and gasping for the oxygen of a moment's inconsequentiality. How life-giving it would be, for instance, to have the opportunity to think with Ginny rather than merely to react with her, or even to see what she does with a mess of onions. But no. As narratives go, this one's a parcel of snakes. And an hour and three-quarters of linear plot development does not permit us the luxury of a minute's downtime with the snake-handling equipment.

In the end, the film sells itself to the viewer as an arty melodrama within a Hollywood role-playing game. This is Jessica Lange's umpteenth pop at rendering an archetype of life-bitten agricultural womanliness, and by no means the most convincing. Her Ginny is simply too dim to make her disintegration seem anything other than an inevitability. Indeed, she has it coming from the moment she goes all girly over the kitchen range for the benefit of smouldering Colin Firth, the prodigal prig of Zebulon County, who gets about six lines with which to justify his existence in the film and fails, not surprisingly.

Dowdy-beautiful Michelle Pfeiffer comes off better as rancorous Rose; as do Jason Robards as the granite-faced old loon and Jennifer Jason Leigh as the clay-faced young lawyer. But they all buckle in the end under the weight of a literary big sky, pregnant with heavy weather, before being swallowed up by the corn.

NEW YORK POST, 9/19/97, p. 52, Michael Medved

"A Thousand Acres" might be appropriately retitled "A Thousand Aches"—focusing on incest, adultery, alcoholism, breast cancer, family-busting, lawsuits, sudden-death, lingering death, desertion, miscarriages, brawls at church suppers, child abuse and other horrors as part of a uniquely Hollywood take on "traditional" Midwestern family values.

Clumsily adapted from Jane Smiley's Pulitzer Prize-winning novel, the movie aspires to the status of epic tragedy (complete with heavy-handed, distracting echoes of "King Lear") but comes across like the shoddiest of soap operas.

Wealthy Iowa farmer Jason Robards begins the troubles when he decides, Lear-like, to divide his ancestral 1,000-acre farm among his grown daughters.

Jessica Lange plays the oldest, a sweet, dull, dutiful wife locked in a childless marriage to Keith Carradine. Michelle Pfeiffer is the edgy, angry middle child, married to a crude, occasionally abusive lout (Kevin Anderson) and recovering from a mastectomy.

Jennifer Jason Leigh is the sourpuss youngest, willfully separating herself from the rest of the family and pursuing a legal career in a nearby city.

In response to their father's increasingly demented and possibly senile behavior, the older girls throw him off his own property—providing delayed revenge for the forced sex Pfeiffer says her monstrous old man imposed on her throughout adolescence.

Meanwhile, both Lange and Pfeiffer find themselves romantically drawn toward a curly-headed hippie prodigal (Colin Firth) who has returned after many years' absence to a neighbor's farm.

The stellar cast provides sturdy performances (and Lange's yearning tenderness and palpable sense of loss amount to more than that), but not even the most artful acting can create much connection with these insufferably shallow and self-destructive characters with no one of stature or durable appeal to carry you through the plot's bathetic cascade of melodramatic ordeals.

Australian director Jocelyn Moorhouse provides the same unfocused assemblage of overwrought episodes that marred her previous film, "How to Make an American Quilt," with the same tone-deaf approach to the distinctively American flavor of picturesque rural locations.

This "Thousand Acres" receives plenty of fertilizer, but provides only a stunted harvest of bitter corn.

NEWSDAY, 9/19/97, Part II/p. B10, Jack Mathews

Widower Larry Cook is the lord of all he surveys: 1,000 acres of fertile Iowa farmland. His grandfather carved it out of a flood plain, digging the drains and turning the topsoil himself, and like his father before him, Larry has prospered there. But he's an old man now, and he has no sons to carry it on, only the three daughters that he impetuously, ruinously, decides to give it to.

That's the triggering dramatic device of Jane Smiley's Pulitzer Prize-winning 1991 novel "A Thousand Acres," and of Jocelyn Moorehouse's filmed adaptation. It's an updated, and reversed version of "King Lear," told from the perspective of the two oldest daughters. But it plays less as a Shakespearean tragedy than as an emotional disaster movie.

Structured as a narrative memoir, told by oldest daughter Ginny (Jessica Lange), "A Thousand Acres" tracks a couple of years in the lives of the Cook family, a period of such sustained catastrophe, bitterness, deaths, grief, recriminations and marrow-deep pain that people are advised to indulge it only on days when they're seeing their therapists.

Publicity for the movie focuses on the determination of its two major stars, Lange and Michelle Pfeiffer, who plays middle sister Rose, to work together, and on the efforts of their agents to make that happen with Smiley's novel. Their interest in the material is understandable. Each is offered a distinct character who goes through an enormous arc of change, and their strongest scenes are the ones they share.

They also seem to have got from themselves, and from each other, exactly what they wanted. Ginny, the oldest, and seemingly steadiest sister, and straight-talking Rose, the agitator, are two of the year's best female roles, and Lange and Pfeiffer have tremendous screen rapport.

But for all their pain, heartache and tears (enough to flood a thousand acres), Ginny and Rose are interesting only as victims of an outlandish tyrant. If "King Lear" is about a man suffering the consequences of his generosity, "A Thousand Acres" is about three women suffering the consequences of his very existence.

Larry Cook is a patriarchal monster, abusive, overbearing, duplicitous, and—by the time we meet him—half-mad. He's just decided to retire, split the farm among his three daughters, and turn its management over to Ginny's and Rose's husbands (Keith Carradine and Kevin Anderson). When the youngest daughter, Caroline (Jennifer Jason Leigh), hesitates about accepting the gift, he cuts her out of the deal and turns his back on her, just as Lear did to Cordelia.

But soon, Larry Cook is regretting everything, insisting that Ginny and Rose cheated him out of his property, and reconciling with Caroline—the daughter who left the farm to become a lawyer—whom he enlists in a legal, destructive effort to reclaim the farm.

In the novel, Smiley may have been able to spread Ginny's litany of disasters through filters of time, allowing readers to absorb her characters' more heroic qualities between crises. But there is little sense of passage of time in Moorehouse's film. Someone's cancer seems to come out of remission the day after another family member drowns, which comes a few minutes after learning that dad is crazy, on the morning after one sister learns of the other's affair with the secret love of her life.

That isn't the half of it. At the moment you're wondering what else can go wrong, Rose reveals a family secret that makes everything else look like a Christmas letter from the Bradys.

A subplot lifted from "King Lear" involves Jesse (Colin Firth), the wandering son of a neighboring farmer, a man of passion—at least, in regard to the married Cook sisters—and a calculating eye on his father's land. But his real purpose in "A Thousand Acres" is to serve as the catalyst prompting Ginny and Rose into deeper and deeper revelations.

"A Thousand Acres" is largely a two-character play, with occasional appearances by the father, the younger sister, and the various men in Ginny's and Rose's lives. But Moorehouse, working with a script by Laura Jones ("The Portrait of a Lady"), is having to pack too many traumas into the film to allow audiences time to absorb them, feel them and prepare for the next.

NEWSWEEK, 9/22/97, p. 82, David Ansen

There are many ways in which A Thousand Acres, Jocelyn Moorhouse's film of the Jane Smiley novel, doesn't do justice to the Pulitzer Prize-winning book. But anyone in search of a powerful emotional experience, and anyone who wants to see two of the juiciest performances of the year, shouldn't miss it. Michelle Pfeiffer and Jessica Lange—both of whom, remember, were written off at the start of their careers as disposable Hollywood blondes—have done as much to light up American movies in the past two decades as any other actors I can think of. Paired as the Cook sisters, Rose (Pfeiffer) and Ginny (Lange), in this loose transposition of "King Lear" to the Iowa farmlands, they make an incandescent team.

Rose and Ginny are two of three daughters of a powerful and revered Iowa farmer named Larry Cook (Jason Robards). The third daughter, Caroline (Jennifer Jason Leigh), has become a lawyer in the city. The tragic events in Smiley's novel, as in "Lear," are set off when the patriarch quixotically announces his plans to divide his land among his three offspring. But Smiley turns Shakespeare on its head—for the heroines here are those arch-villainesses Goneril and Regan, and the Lear figure is a malevolent patriarch who has inflicted ghastly psychological damage on his children. From under the family's Grant Wood surface, poisonous fumes rise.

Rose, the mother of two, recovering from a mastectomy, is a woman fueled by rage ("The more pissed off I feel, the better I am"), while the childless Ginny, passive and repressed, tries to smooth over the buried antagonisms that are wrenching this deeply dysfunctional family apart. These complex, fully realized women are Smiley's triumph, and Lange and Pfeiffer, playing an eloquent emotional duet, bring them vividly to life.

Moorhouse and her fellow Australian screenwriter Laura Jones succeed where it counts, capturing the close, sometimes bitterly fraught relationship between the sisters. The men in the tale—Rose's unstable husband (Kevin Anderson), Ginny's virtuous but obtuse mate (Keith Carradine) and the neighbor's seductive son Jess (Colin Firth)—are merely sketched in. The storytelling, full of dark secrets and impassioned outbursts, can seem melodramatic and clunky at times, and Moorhouse doesn't have much feel for the Iowa landscape or for the community that demonizes the two sisters. But if the movie isn't all it could have been, when Pfeiffer and Lange are on screen, you don't want to be anywhere else.

By coincidence, the two stars had neighboring offices at Orison Pictures back in 1992, when both received early galleys of Smiley's novel. They immediately turned to each other and smiled: this was the project they had been waiting for. "In the beginning we didn't really decide who was going to play what character," says Pfeiffer, who admits she always wanted to play Rose. "I loved her struggle, I loved her fight. She had this uncontrollable urge to speak the truth. This movie scared me a lot. This was one that I knew I could fail on in a big way."

Lange was scared, too, at the prospect of playing Ginny. "Ginny's passive. I've never had to play a character like that before. At the beginning of the film I used to walk around the set and say, 'God, I haven't got a clue what I'm doing here.' But I always had the novel as my guideline. I kept it with me every second of the day."

Though it was a five-year struggle to get the movie made, the shoot itself, according to the stars, was mainly harmonious. "Jessica and I didn't know each other very well before this movie. I didn't even really talk to her until we were literally walking to the set to do our first scene together. But the work was effortless." Lange agrees: "There was not one moment in that suspended reality that I didn't believe that she was Rose and that she was my sister."

The problems came after the shooting ended, when Moorhouse ("How to Make an American Quilt") turned in her cut. Everyone was disappointed. The story meandered; the emotion got lost. The producers hired an outside editor to come in and work alongside Moorhouse's editor. The director stormed off, threatening to take her name off the movie.

With the input of the stars and the producers a new version emerged. "My feeling was the storytelling was not clear," says Lange of that first cut. "I had no problem shooting with Jocelyn," says Pfeiffer. "Post-production was the hard thing. It may have been that she was too close to it. We were all too close to it. It took bringing in a new editor who was objective and brutal. It's still Jocelyn's movie."

In this age of the auteur, interfering with a director's "vision" is a great heresy. But in the real world, not all directors are created equal, and not all directors are always right. Movies are a collaborative art. Whatever Moorhouse's side of the story is (she declined to be interviewed), she has kept her name on the picture, and she deserves credit for creating the conditions that allowed Pfeiffer and Lange's magic to blossom. It may have taken fights to get there, but the movie still feels like a labor of love.

SIGHT AND SOUND, 7/98, p. 55, Peter Matthews

Iowa farmer Larry Cook announces his retirement and divides the farm equally among his three daughters. Afraid to cross their autocratic father, the elder siblings Ginny and Rose accept, but the youngest Caroline expresses misgivings; Larry instantly disowns her. Though married, Ginny begins an affair with Jess, a neighbour's son. Relations sour between Larry and his two eldest daughters as he becomes increasingly irrational, culminating in them locking him out during a thunderstorm. Later, Rose confesses to Ginny that Larry sexually abused her throughout her adolescence. At first, Ginny cannot remember ever suffering the same abuse, but the memory is triggered at a later date. Larry and Caroline sue the sisters for the return of the farm, charging mismanagement.

After her husband Peter is killed in a car accident, Rose confesses to Ginny that she has also been conducting an affair with Jess. At the court hearing, the judge rules in favour of the two sisters after Larry begins babbling on the witness stand. Ginny abandons the farm and moves to another city. Ginny's husband Ty signs her share of the property over to Rose and leaves for Texas. Some months later, Ginny is called home by the news that Rose is fatally ill with cancer. Before dying, Rose pleads with Ginny to adopt her two daughters. Larry succumbs to a heart attack and the family's 1,000 acres are taken over by a big corporation.

Proof, a cold, crafty psychodrama with some of the nasty charge of *The Servant* (1963), brought Australian Jocelyn Moorhouse to wider notice as a tough-minded young talent. But Hollywood still tends to offer women film-makers messagey scripts (Kathryn Bigelow being the most conspicuous exception). Saddled with the feminist uplift of *How to Make an American Quilt* for her US debut, Moorhouse did what she could to redeem the coy material. Based on Jane Smiley's Pulitzer Prize-winning novel, *A Thousand Acres* is even more high-toned. But whether Moorhouse felt cowed by the enterprise's cultural prestige or merely exhausted at the thought of another sorority drama, it seems to have broken her spirit at last. The movie practically defines mediocre respectability, and contains not one single memorable shot.

This is surprising given that the story (loosely based on *King Lear)* concerns three sisters who come to grief over an enormous tract of Iowa farmland. While Moorhouse and cinematographer Tak Fujimoto offer numerous boundless vistas, the prosaic framing doesn't encourage one's heart to soar; though filmed on a studio backlot, *Gone with the Wind* had a stronger romantic feeling for the soil. A few strategically placed low-angle shots would have been enough to establish landowner Larry Cook as an object of fear and fascination for his daughters rather than the obstreperous hick he seems here. At least Moorhouse gives some scope for the kind of tentative, exploratory emotions one never gets in the more cartoonish forays into sisterly bonding (see *Steel Magnolias* or *Waiting to Exhale*) directed by men.

Unfortunately, the moments of womanly soul-searching don't sit well beside the baroque excesses of the plot. Smiley weaves the melodrama seamlessly into a naturalistic 400-page fiction. It might conceivably have worked as a miniseries on television. But the film piles up madness, adultery and child abuse in an awful traffic jam, while Ginny's garrulous narration papers over the cracks in the continuity. Probably to maintain a lofty atmosphere, screenwriter Laura Jones has weeded out a few of the more egregious episodes (such as the blinding of the Gloucester-surrogate Harold). The consequence is that the film falls between two stools: it manages to be implausible without ever quite toppling over into campy fun. Fans of the novel will certainly miss Ginny's vindictive attempt to snuff out Rose with poisoned sausages at one point. This disappointing omission has the effect of making the sibling rivalry a toothless side issue in a fairly uncomplicated celebration of female solidarity. While there's something too pat about Smiley's revisionist resolve to speak up for the neglected claims of Goneril and Regan against the bullying Lear and that prissy Cordelia, she distributes blame and sympathy more or less impartially. The simplified moral bookkeeping of Jones and Moorhouse ranges strong, supportive women against men—each one brutal, weak or untrustworthy—so that the movie begins to suggest *The Color Purple* with white people.

Neither Jessica Lange nor Michelle Pfeiffer are especially convincing as weather-beaten farm wives. They are, however, more than up to the task of animating an old-fashioned star vehicle with the force of big colourful personalities, and on this level *A Thousand Acres* is reasonably entertaining. The performers succeed in putting over the salient contrasts between the women, but they must do so in the absence of a larger context—since Smiley's symbolic equation of the rape of the daughters with that of the land has been unceremoniously dropped. Perhaps the one singularity in this undistinguished movie is the appearance of the credit "Mastectomy Effect" (by Rick Baker). This refers to the scene where Pfeiffer's character Rose displays her post-operative scar at the cancer clinic—a smooth bit of effects magic that deserves to rank with Gary Sinise's missing legs in *Forrest Gump*. But it's precisely the kind of detail that film-makers fuss over these days at the expense of the skills that really count.

TIME, 9/22/97, p. 93, Richard Schickel

Poor Shakespeare—obliged to motivate his tragedies with nothing more than seven terrible, familiar sins and a smattering of Aristotle. How much richer his works might have been had the blessings of postmodernism been his. He might, for example, have been free to draw openly on incest as a theme instead of dropping little hints of it here and there for the scholars to ferret out 400 years later. And what about recovered memory? That's a dramatic device he never dreamed of.

You have to grant a certain credit to novelist Jane Smiley for the unapologetic boldness with which she appropriated the story of King Lear for her Pulitzer prize-winning novel, *A Thousand Acres,* resettling his mythical Britannic majesty and his fractious daughters on a modern Iowa farm. You also have to admire the nerve with which she attached pop-psych subtexts to her rearrangement, the daring with which she turned the whole works into a feminist tract.

It was the sober realism of her style that redeemed the novel, its weight and conviction that prevented readers from noticing (or caring) that by replacing noble enigmas with banal behaviorism, Smiley had downsized tragedy to melodrama. The movie version—bereft of diverting literary stratagems, relentlessly focused on what-next narrative—takes it another step down—to soap opera.

It's not just that the Lear figure, played by Jason Robards, has been renamed Larry and dressed in coveralls, or that he decides to divide his realm among his daughters for tax purposes, although these devices have a certain flattening effect on the tale. The problem is that it is no longer his tragedy but his children's—Goneril, who is here renamed Ginny, and played by Jessica Lange; and Regan, who's called Rose and impersonated by Michelle Pfeiffer; and Cordelia, known now as Caroline and acted by Jennifer Jason Leigh.

The first two, we eventually learn, were incestuously abused by their father when they were children. Rose, who has breast cancer, has never forgotten his long-ago depredations, but they have been buried deep in Ginny's unconscious, from which her sister is determined to dig them out. All this is terribly up to date, "relevant" according to the vulgar standards set for us by the endlessly instructing voices of media shrinks.

But sordid particulars and easy explanations are ever the enemy of tragedy. In this case they transform it—despite a lot of earnest acting of the kind that always seems to have its eye on a year-end prize—into nothing more than a revenge plot. They also rob it of grandeur and universality and deprive us of the pleasure of deriving our own meanings from its characters and events. We know what we think of child molesters, and we are aware of the dread consequences of their acts. On this matter we require no instruction. But a cracked old man, misjudging his powers and the nature of his children? Why yes, we can be moved to vivid identification with him, to pity and terror by his plight. Him we might someday become.

VILLAGE VOICE, 9/30/97, p. 84, Abby McGanney Nolan

With *A Thousand Acres,* her Pulitzer prize-winning novel, Jane Smiley took the side of King Lear's much reviled daughters, Goneril and Regan, putting Shakespearean power plays out under the sun of the big Iowa skies. Lear was transformed into Larry Cook, a major-league farmer who molested his motherless daughters, and Cordelia became Caroline, the little sister who had been shielded from her father's depredations and thus had no clue about his real self. Unfortunately Jocelyn Moorhouse's film adaptation—faithful to the plot but lacking the book's headlong narrative rush—is nearly as flat as the surrounding cornfields.

Jessica Lange and Michel Pfeiffer have shed much of their glamorous exteriors to become Iowa farmwives. Lange is oldest sister Ginny, still in denial about Dad (Jason Robards); Pfeiffer's Rose is her foil, a two-dimensionally angry woman who unaccountably lives across the road from the man who abused her throughout her teens. As with other crucial moments, the scene in which Cook divides his kingdom among his three daughters carries no particular weight, deadened by slack pacing and inappropriate music. From here on, tragedy is planned for tearjerkery.

The novel doesn't lack for activity, on top of Shakespeare's storms and madness (which here reads as Alzheimer's), there are infidelities, car accidents, and cancer. But compressed into a two-hour film, the succession of misfortune is numbing. Lange and Pfeiffer, earnest as they are, seem to be playing to Oscar voters, while the rest of cast—Jennifer Jason Leigh as Caroline,

Kevin Anderson and Keith Carradine as Cook's sons-in-law, Colin Firth as a flirtatious neighbor —seem lost in unfamiliar territory. Director Moorhouse, who made such a sharp debut with *Proof,* apparently clashed with the studio over the final edit and may find more fertile ground back home in Australia.

Also reviewed in:
CHICAGO TRIBUNE, 9/19/97, Friday/p. C, Michael Wilmington
NEW YORK TIMES, 9/19/97, p. E12, Janet Maslin
NEW YORKER, 9/29/97, p. 87, Daphne Markin
VARIETY, 9/15-21/97, p. 69, Godfrey Cheshire
WASHINGTON POST, 9/19/97, p. C7, Rita Kempley
WASHINGTON POST, 9/19/97, Weekend/p. 50, Desson Howe

THRILL RIDE: THE SCIENCE OF FUN

A Sony Pictures Classics release of a New Wave International production. *Executive Producer:* Ben Stassen. *Producer:* Charlotte Huggins. *Director:* Ben Stassen. *Screenplay:* Kurt Frey. *Director of Photography:* Sean Phillips. *Music:* Michael Stearns. *Production Designer:* Ray Spencer. *Running time:* 40 minutes. *MPAA Rating:* Not Rated.

CAST: Harry Shearer (Narrator); Paul Harper (The Coal Miner); Elvira (Mistress of the Dark).

LOS ANGELES TIMES, 7/11/97, Calendar/p. 16, Jan Herman

"Thrill Ride: The Science of Fun" isn't quite the white knuckle adventure its promoters claim. Yet it's exciting even without being in 3-D as you might expect from an Imax movie of this kind.

The large-format picture recounts the history of roller coasters, beginning in 18th century Russia with sleds and wood-framed ice slides, and traces their technological evolution up through the latest versions. At the same time, it blends information with experience.

"Thrill Ride" doesn't just document the twists and turns with archival illustrations and rare film footage of the earliest rides or explain the gravitational dynamics of roller coasters with table-top demonstrations—all of which is fascinating. It takes you on the rides and, what is more intriguing, into the computer-generated hyper-reality of simulated rides signed for pilot and astronaut training, as well as for the entertainment industry.

Naturally a movie about thrill rides that asks, "What is a roller coaster but the promise of pure sensation?" demands to be made in 3-D—especially when its motto is "fear is fun" and its tongue-in-cheek safety warnings remind you to keep your hands and feet inside the theater.

But once you've accepted the disappointment that "Thrill Ride" won't be taking you over the top to into 3-D free fall, you may find yourself feeling grateful. The tamer 2-D format minimizes the chance you might do what astronauts have been known to do in the NASA motion simulator (or as it's been dubbed, the LRV, for Lunch Review Vehicle). (The real reason the picture wasn't made in 3-D, director Ben Stassen says, is that he combined new footage with recent footage of thrill rides already shot in 2-D. "Jumping back and forth from 2-D to 3-D would have been too disturbing," he explains.)

"Thrill Ride" incorporates excerpts from 13 previous "ride" films, including "Superstition" (featuring Elvira), "Secrets of the Lost Temple," "Asteroid Adventure," "Back to the Future: The Ride," "This Is Cinerama" and extensive portions of Stassen's own "The Devil's Mine Ride" (featuring Paul Harper), a live-action film brilliantly enhanced by computer graphics imagery.

Perhaps the most revealing sequences in "Thrill Ride" show how computer designs make use of gravity and kinetic forces to create seemingly impossible rides of uncanny precision dressed out in elaborate, even supernatural environments.

For all their fascination, however, the most entertaining footage has nothing to do with the law of gravity or any of the live-action views shot from various amusement park thrill rides.

It's a storytelling scene made possible by computer technology, in which the old coal miner from "The Devil's Mine Ride" appears backstage and doubles as his look-alike brother, to demonstrate the clever ventriloquism that Hollywood sound designs can create.

Although "Thrill Ride" does not match the visual impact or the natural beauty of "Into the Deep," which, for example, takes an astonishing 3-D dive to the bottom of the sea, it nonetheless ranks among the best Imax documentaries this viewer has seen.

NEW YORK POST, 7/11/97, p. 40, Larry Worth

There's nothing like the mix of exhilaration and terror experienced on a roller coaster. And that couldn't be more obvious after sitting through "Thrill Ride: The Science of Fun."

The new IMAX presentation would seem a perfect vehicle for conveying the stomach-losing drops and hair-raising turns of riding the tracks. But the huge-screen format isn't used to its best advantage here.

For starters, director Ben Stassen filmed the production in ho-hum 2-D rather than the you-are-there 3-D process. Accordingly, the initial roller coaster footage from "This Is Cinerama" is only as effective as it was 40 years ago.

Ironically, that's also the chief highlight in "Thrill Ride," complemented by some wonderful but all-too-fleeting archival looks at the history of roller coasters. Heck, moviegoers don't even get to ride one in its entirety, which wouldn't seem to be asking a lot.

The focus then switches to '80s and '90s technology—specifically, the introduction of simulation rides *a la* Universal Studios' "Back to the Future" attraction. Even then, the effort gets bogged down in explanations and camerawork that barely suggest the unique mix of overpowering images and physical jostling.

By the time Stassen moves on to computer-generated thrill rides, which constitute the bulk of the screen time here, interest has pretty much ebbed.

Lackluster narration from Harry Shearer and Paul Harper's dopey bits as a brain-warped prospector-cum-guide don't help. Though meant to fill viewers with anticipation about what's ahead, Harper's cornpone antics make spending time with him seem a scarier concept.

On the plus side, there's an amusing cameo from Elvira, Mistress of the Dark; a clever explanatory segment on acoustics, and a few interesting factoids thrown in as distractions. But they can't distract from the overall sensation of disappointment.

So, why settle for "Thrill Ride"? True adventure seekers should head for Coney Island's Cyclone and check out the real thing instead.

NEWSDAY, 7/11/97, Part II/p. B9, Jack Mathews

The films shown in Imax theaters have less in common with movies than theme-park attractions, and "Thrill Ride: The Science of Fun," produced by Sony Pictures Classics, cuts to the gut of the theme-park experience. It's an attempt to put audiences in the seats of America's scariest rides and toss us around in front of a screen as big as all outdoors while hoping we don't toss our lunch on the people in the row in front of us.

At its best, "Thrill Ride" is topsy-turvy excitement. More than half its 40-minute running time is devoted to various rides, either in the camera operator's seat aboard Magic Mountain's Viper, Busch Garden's Kumba and Montu, Las Vegas' The Big Shot, and Universal Studio's "Back to the Future" attraction, or in make-believe coasters careening wildly through some fabulous computer-generated tunnels and haunted houses.

Seven times, the eight story-high screen does a complete 300-degree loop, usually followed by a hairpin turn, or a plunge down a bottomless pit of rails.

As a kid, I was pounded into the back of my state in another filmed roller coaster ride, that one in "This is Cinerama," a wide-screen travelogue adventure shot and shown with a three-camera, three-projector process. Clips from that are used in "Thrill Ride."

Since then, I've been on many roller coaster rides, including a couple in the IMAX film, and there is no comparison. Not on a flat screen, no matter how big.

It's interesting to imagine how "Thrill Ride" would have played had it been shot in 3-D. Maybe Sony didn't want to pony up the extra expense, not so much in the costs of filming, but in theater cleanup and law suits.

In any event, the rides here are likely to have the same effect on the current generation of kids as "This is Cinerama" had on its. What it also will do, between rides, is bore them silly.

More ride time would strain the audience's comfort, and in padding the film to justify a full-price ticket, Stassen subjects us to the antics of a colossally cornball old prospector (Paul Harper), to lessons on roller coaster history (it started in a mine) and physics (it works on gravity), and to a teasing glimpse at the technology of "simulated rides."

For the latter, we see people belted into stationary, hydraulic-controlled seats, being jerked around in sync with images on a screen we do not see. It appears that these people are being tortured for government secrets, yet their faces say they're having the time of their lives.

And maybe they are. Simulated rides are the current rage at theme parks, but nothing we see in "Third Ride" explains why.

VILLAGE VOICE, 7/22/97, p. 65, J. Hoberman

As suggested by its title, *Thrill Ride: The Science of Fun*, the summer's IMAX extravaganza means to demonstrate that movies are more meta than ever. Roller coasters and more are *Thrill Ride*'s subject, although disappointingly two-dimensional, it only intermittently fulfills its promise of Pure Sensation.

Interpolating ancient footage from *This Is Cinerama* and demonstrating the plunging-skyscraper elevator that is the Las Vegas 'Big Shot' (a falling experience seemingly calculated to summon the rising gorge), *Thrill Ride* showcases a new permutation of Total Cinema—namely the marriage of the NASA-designed "flight simulator" and the technology of wraparound movie projection known as the ride film. Jodie Foster takes one fairly disorienting thrill ride in *Contact*. But it is Zemeckis's first blockbuster *Back to the Future* which has produced the most epic example—and this IMAX movie is basically a giant trailer for it. (Heartening, I suppose, to see Sony so strenuously promoting its rival Universal's attraction.)

Thrill Ride pretends to be futuristic, but experiences like the *Back to the Future* ride transport us back past the origins of movies to 19th-century panoramas and the Hale's Tours that briefly rivaled the nickelodeon. What goes around, comes around. Perhaps this is why we get swastikas from Vega and why the tour guide retrieved for *Thrill Ride* from the Museum of Virtual History insists on impersonating a creature from TV's Stone Age, the garrulous old cowhand Gabby Hayes.

Also reviewed in:
NEW YORK TIMES, 7/11/97, p. C10, Lawrence Van Gelder
VARIETY, 7/21-27/97, p. 39, Howard Feinstein

TICKLE IN THE HEART, A

A Kino International release of a Zero Film in coproduction with Neapel Film. *Producer:* Thomas Kufus, Martin Hagemann, and Edward Rosenstein. *Director:* Stefan Schwietert. *Screenplay (English and Yiddish with English subtitles):* Stefan Schwietert. *Based on an idea by:* Joel Rubin and Rita Ottens. *Director of Photography:* Robert Richman. *Editor:* Arpad Bondy. *Music:* Joel Rubin and the Epstein Brothers. *Sound:* Marc O. Hiker. *Running time:* 84 minutes. *MPAA Rating:* Not Rated.

CAST: Max Epstein; Willie Epstein; Julie Epstein; Peter Solokow; Harriet Goldstein Darr; Pat Merola; Harry Kolestein; Joel Rubin.

LOS ANGELES TIMES, 6/6/97, Calendar/p. 12, Kenneth Turan

"A Tickle in the Heart" is a completely charming documentary about old men and young music, or at least music that sounds young. For though the melodies of klezmer are considerably older than even the three Epstein brothers, in their hands it takes on the kind of vivid, electric life that might raise the dead if the need arose.

The traditional celebratory music of Eastern European Jews, clarinet-based klezmer has roared back to prominence in this country and Europe after having, as one of the Epsteins puts it, "dropped dead for 20 or 25 years."

The Epsteins, proud of "playing this cockamamie music for all our lives," were energized by ears of experience apiece, they even remember back to when "klezmer was an insulting word" - because of its connection with itinerant, penniless musicians. "When you heard that term, you wanted to punch someone in the nose."

It's a tribute to how popular klezmer has come internationally that "Tickle in the Heart" (the title refers to the music's emotional pull) is funded largely through German government arts money and directed by Swiss German filmmaker Stefan Schwietert.

Schwietert and American director of photography Robert Richman have given "Tickle" a crisp, sparkling black-and-white look that, along with the film's restrained and deliberate tone, contrasts nicely with the music's extravagant spirit.

Dispensing with voice-over narration, "Tickle" allows us to find our own way into the world of the Epsteins, who live within hailing distance of one another in the retirement world of South Florida.

Patriarch Max, the 85-year-old wizard of the clarinet, is first glimpsed meticulously washing his car, while drummer Julie demonstrates his recipe for potato latkes. Brother Willie is the keeper of the schedule and "the busiest retired trumpet player in Florida."

Bluff, gruff, on-and-off cantankerous, the Epsteins are not often silent, and their chatter is one the film's pleasures as they genially argue with one another about questions of tempo and range and anything else that's handy.

After glimpsing them at home, much of "Tickle" follows the Epsteins on some of their interna-tional musical journeys. They return to New York in the late 1960s, where a kind word from a powerful, Hasidic rabbi leads to wedding gigs without end. And they pay a poignant visit to Pinsk, their father's much-changed Eastern European hometown.

Especially interesting is their concert in Berlin, a play date Willie Epstein admitted "sounded very strange to us. We thought it would be a tough place for this kind of music to sell." But klezmer turned out to be huge in Berlin, even though the audience is only 5% Jewish, and the brothers' concert was a major success.

Though "Tickle" is expert at photographing the Epsteins setting up on stage and traveling on the road, the film, not surprisingly, is, most alive when these slow-moving men begin to make the liveliest music imaginable. Once they get going, the years truly do fade away.

NEW YORK POST, 1/29/97, p. 39, Michael Medved

When the German government and a Brooklyn yeshiva join forces in funding a documentary film, you can rightly expect something significant and extraordinary—and that is exactly what you get with a "A Tickle in the Heart."

This thoroughly captivating film feels as spicy, filling and homey as one of your grandmother's lovingly prepared old-country meals—serving up irresistible music together with irresistibly earthy personalities.

The three Epstein Brothers represent a living link to the golden age of klezmer music—the alternately festive and mournful tones that enlivened the vanished universe of Eastern European Jews, and that now wail again through a host of hip, young, American klezmer bands.

Though born (beginning in 1912) on Eldridge Street on the Lower East Side, the Epsteins cherished and nourished Old World traditions, even after their joint migration to a retirement community in Florida, where they've continued playing to appreciative audiences at senior centers and synagogues.

The movie portrays this busy life, but focuses more significantly on the recent rediscovery of the Epsteins' music and their sudden arrival on the international concert scene.

"A Tickle in the Heart" is photographed in richly detailed, dramatically lit black and white, then edited with consummate skill by filmmaker Stefan Shwietert—a 35-year-old German-born Swiss Gentile.

Only once does his Teutonic perspective seem to interfere with his loving portraiture: When the Epsteins journey to Pinsk, Belarus, to search for the home their father left in 1906, there is no mention of the Holocaust that wiped out the pre-war Jewish majority in that city.

Nevertheless, the film achieves an eloquently elegiac tone with hints and shadows, even as it largely avoids explicit reference to tragedy.

NEWSDAY, 1/22/97, part II/p. B11, Letta Tayler

If proof ever were needed that reality can be as bizarre as fantasy, the scene from "A Tickle in the Heart" in which three Jewish octogenarians perform klezmer for an adoring Gentile crowd in Berlin would suffice.

"I love a Yiddish song, a heartfelt, beautiful little Hasidic song," the young Berliners blithely sing along in Yiddish, as the wrinkled *klezmorim* strike up a raucous um-pah, um-pah, um-pah.

There are many similarly surreal moments in "A Tickle in the Heart," a documentary about three klezmer-playing brothers from the Lower East Side who retire to Florida, only to find a growing demand for their Eastern European Jewish music in the Sunshine State and, ultimately, in Europe.

Unfortunately, the film barely explores these potent contrasts. We discover little about Max, Willie and Julie Epstein except that they are purists who cook their potato pancakes as fastidiously as they preserve the Old World nuances in their music. We don't end up knowing a whole lot more about klezmer, either.

Though the film lacks profundity, it's awash in atmosphere. The scenes of fragile seniors—most of them Jewish New York retirees—dancing to the Epsteins' music in Florida senior centers are joyous tributes to a people and its culture.

Providing poignant contrast is the Epsteins' visit to their father's hometown in Poland. The Epstein house is long gone, but the brothers do find a lone, gnarled resident who can hum a few bars of a klezmer tune.

Shot in black and white, the film beautifully captures the ticky-tacky kitsch of the Epstein's retirement community in Tamarac, Fla., with its identical bungalows and plastic lawn ornaments. And the Epsteins are a hoot.

"Playing music is fun. Avocation, vocation, the same apple," philosophizes drummer Julie Epstein. "What other thing can you say is that way? Can a doctor go out and say, 'Let's go out on a golf course and you'll cut out your appendix and you'll cut out my left ear?' Can't do that! But in the music business, you can!"

VILLAGE VOICE, 1/28/97, p. 68, Leslie Camhi

Klezmer music, an elderly clarinetist explains to a young disciple, "has nothing to do with ability. It's about tickling the cockles of my heart." *A Tickle in the Heart* emerged from three months that director Stefan Schwietert spent living in a retirement community in Florida that is home to the Epstein brothers—Max, Willie, and Julie—once and future kings of the klezmer circuit. This charming and oblique documentary, shot in ravishing black-and-white, captures the Epsteins' peculiar melding of Eastern European music, Brooklyn roots, and southern Florida lifestyle. Reindeer ornaments grace the handkerchief lawns of split-level houses in subdevelopments where you have to be over 55 to live: "It's God's waiting room," Willie Epstein says.

At a leisurely pace, we follow the brothers as they don tuxedos, pack the car with instruments, and head off for one of their many engagements among the senior community. In the 1960s, they were the band most in demand at Hasidic weddings from Pitkin Avenue to Allen Street. Lately, their career has gotten a second wind from the klezmer revival in Germany. We watch as Max, the charismatic clarinetist and eightysomething leader of this musical family, starts a Yiddish sing-along at a sold-out concert in Berlin. We see them travel by train to the Polish village where their father was born, and where they play a little klezmer for the local population of war amputees and suspicious children. Above all, it's the spirit of klezmer that survives even in its now suburban setting; a music of small losses and pleasures, lilting and plaintive, its emotional wallop is nevertheless intense.

Also reviewed in:
NEW YORK TIMES, 1/23/97, p. C19, Lawrence Van Gelder
VARIETY, 8/12-18/96, p. 34, Dennis Harvey

'TIL THERE WAS YOU

A Lakeshore Entertainment and Paramount Pictures release of a Penney Finkelman Cox production. *Producer:* Penney Finkelman Cox, Tom Rosenberg, and Alan Poul. *Director:* Scott Winant. *Screenplay:* Winnie Holzman. *Director of Photography:* Bobby Bukowski. *Editor:* Richard Marks and Joanna Cappuccilli. *Music:* Miles Goodman and Terence Blanchard. *Production Designer:* Craig Sterns. *Running time:* 120 minutes. *MPAA Rating:* PG-13.

CAST: Jeanne Tripplehorn (Gwen); Dylan McDermott (Nick); Sarah Jessica Parker (Francesca); Jennifer Aniston (Debbie); Karen Allen (Betty); Michael Tucker (Saul); Alice Drummond (Harriet); Ken Olin (Gregory); Nina Foch (Sophia Monroe).

LOS ANGELES TIMES, 5/30/97, Calendar/p. 6, Jack Mathews

[The following review by Jack Mathews appeared in a slightly different form in **NEWSDAY, 5/30/97, Part II/p. B3.]**

"Everything in my entire life has led up to this moment," say the fated lovers of Scott Winant's "'Til There Was You," and the same can be said, without the enthusiasm, for anyone who attempts to endure this trite, sentimental romantic comedy.

"'Til There Was You" is the first feature for both Winant, one of the creators of TV's "thirtysomething," and screenwriter Winnie Holzman, a staff writer for that show, and neither one will be in contention for rookie of the year honors. Their "Sleepless in Seattle" wannabe works so hard to make you root for that first meeting between Jeanne Tripplehorn's Gwen Moss and Dylan McDermott's Nick Dawkan that you can barely stand them when they finally do.

The idea of a romance that doesn't begin until the movie ends is a difficult thing to pull off, and Nora Ephron only managed it on the charismatic appeal of her two stars, Tom Hanks and Meg Ryan. Tripplehorn and McDermott are likable enough in their roles, but Holzman's precious, overwritten script gives them few genuinely honest moments, and no lines to match the wit in "Sleepless."

"'Til There Was You" takes its "my life as pretext" theme almost literally. We meet Gwen and Nick as small children, and learn why she'll grow up to be a hopeless romantic, clinging to the notion of one great love, and he'll grow up emotionally "unavailable." In these early scenes, Gwen's mother fills her head with a poetically idealized account of her meeting with Gwen's father. Nick, meanwhile, is living in a Tennessee Williams story, listening to his melancholy mom berate his alcoholic father every night.

You need a scorecard to keep the players straight through the first half hour of the film, and you will be quizzed later. Virtually everyone you meet in Gwen's and Nick's childhood and college years return, in a series of coincidences that affect their lives, and put them on their intersecting course.

Actually, Gwen and Nick meet once in grade school, when he bumps into her on the stairway, and they share a measured glance. And in college, he accidentally drops a model of a building out a second-story window and sees it land next to Gwen on a bench below.

But most of the time, they're in the margins of each other's world. Nick has a romance with the former child star Francesca Lanfield (Sarah Jessica Parker) whose autobiography is being ghost-written by Gwen. And Gwen is dating a neurotic book editor who insists on taking her to the Awful Truth, a ghastly industrial deco restaurant designed by Nick.

As we follow their near encounters, the only question is precisely what will bring them together. Gwen's letters to the Los Angeles Times, condemning plans by Nick's architecture firm to tear down the historic apartment complex that she lives in, and that Francesca owns? Or could it be something as simple as their shared nicotine addictions? Nothing in Holzman's overly tidy script goes without some later comment, and there's enough second-hand smoke in the picture to pollute the theater.

NEW YORK POST, 5/30/97, p. 53, Michael Medved

The movie "'Til There Was You" offers a fresh, fascinating perspective on the old story of love at first sight—focusing on the 30 years that precede a fateful meeting rather than describing the joys and challenges that follow it.

Like "Sleepless in Seattle," the movie shows the fates working overtime to bring a couple together and overcoming obstacles even more difficult and disturbing: These characters must significantly change themselves, not just their circumstances, in order to prepare for their inevitable connection.

The compelling and convincing manner in which those changes unfold on screen demonstrates the talent of first-time director Scott Winant and screenwriter Winnie Holzman, both veterans of the late, lamented TV series "thirtysomething."

The movie begins with its two principal characters growing up in radically different homes in the 1960s; her mother and father are warm, loving exemplars of the upper-middle-class ideal, while his parents are feuding, dysfunctional, impoverished and quickly estranged.

The two kids briefly attend the same elementary school, and keep crossing paths on many occasions thereafter, but never manage to learn each other's name.

As an adult, Gwen (Jeanne Tripplehorn) is an incurably dreamy romantic—sentimental, silly and appallingly vulnerable. Nick (Dylan McDermott), however, is a selfish, slick-talking charmer who chronically lies about himself and his background.

He's a rising architect with a trendy L.A. firm, while she struggles to make a living as a ghostwriter of celebrity autobiographies.

Her latest client (Sarah Jessica Parker) is the former child star of a '70s TV series, resembling "The Brady Bunch," who has managed to survive drug addiction and other Hollywood horrors. Simultaneously, Parker is involved with McDermott, who's supposed to be designing the sleek replacement for a funky old apartment building she owns. But you'll never guess who happens to rent a place in that beloved historic structure and finds the courage to lead the fight against McDermott's plans and the wrecker's ball.

Throughout the film, Tripplehorn displays unexpected and formidable gifts as a comic.

Minor parts (Jennifer Aniston as Tripplehorn's married best friend; Alice Drummond as her dotty, endearing neighbor) are expertly handled, even if their interweaving into the story seems at times a bit too cute and conniving.

It's also disappointing that the two leads, played by gifted supporting players clearly ready for top billing, spend so much of their screen time smoking cigarettes and making the habit look attractive. Potential influence on the audience is bad enough, but there are also worries about the impact on two flawed but admirably fleshed-out fictional characters who most viewers will come to cherish.

Also reviewed in:
NEW YORK TIMES, 5/30/97, p. C10, Janet Maslin
VARIETY, 4/21-27/97, p. 60, Leonard Klady

TIMOTHY LEARY'S DEAD

A Strand Releasing presentation of a Davids and Mills Prods. production. *Producer:* Paul Davids. *Director:* Paul Davids and Todd Easton Mills. *Screenplay:* Paul Davids and Todd Easton Mills. *Director of Photography:* Paul Helling. *Editor:* David Wilson and Mark Deimel. *Music:* Moody Blues. *Sound:* Ted Gordon. *Running time:* 80 minutes. *MPAA Rating:* Not Rated.

LOS ANGELES TIMES, 6/6/97, Calendar/p. 8, Kristine McKenna

Timothy Leary's year of prostate cancer are more known than such details usually are. Leary considered death the last of what he called the three big taboos (the preceding two being sex and drugs), so he made a point of flaunting the conventions that normally attend it. An unconventional man whose compulsive defiance of authority may have been his greatest gift to society, Leary is such a rich biographical subject that one senses the shortcomings of "Timothy Leary's Dead" all the more.

The directorial debut of Paul Davids who conducted extensive interviews with Leary in the final months of his life, the film purports to be a biography but fails miserably in that regard. We get no sense whatsoever, for instance, of the forces that shaped Leary into the man he became. Why did his four marriages and his relationships with his children fail? The film refers to the myriad books Leary wrote, but what precisely were the books about? What, in Leary's opinion, was the final legacy of the social revolution he helped launch in the '60s? Was anything of lasting value achieved, or was it merely a blip of freedom on the radar screen of societal control? You won't find answers to these questions in Davids' confusing film, which scrambles the chronology of events in Leary's life and lacks a clear narrative arc.

Davids is, of course, to be commended for having the foresight to capture Leary at length on film as his life wound to a close. Leary, seen as a 75-year-old man who was clearly gravely ill, remained remarkably articulate to the end—all that LSD didn't seem to have hurt him. Davids also did a terrific job of tracking down archival footage and still photos and conducted sharp interviews with Leary's colleagues from his days at Harvard—Richard Alpert (a.k.a. Ram Dass) and Ralph Metzner—both of whom have insightful things to say about Leary.

However, the film completely unravels in its final half hour, which includes an interview with a police officer expounding on the dangers of drug use, a blip from a cartoon, interviews with members of a Bay Area nudist organization, shots of Leary's mailbox, a mosh pit at L.A. club Jabberjaw, an acquaintance of Leary's taking a hit off a bong and musicians on the Venice boardwalk performing a song co-written by Davids. None of this adds to our understanding of Leary, nor is it of interest on any other score.

The film takes its final misstep in its handling of the crygogenics question that hovered over Leary's death. Several years ago Leary arranged to have his brain cryonically frozen for future thawing and use, but three weeks prior to his death he announced he was canceling the procedure. Davids' film concludes with a scene that suggests Leary is undergoing some sort of surgical procedure and then cuts to a shot of what may or may not be Leary's head packed in ice.

Davids won't divulge whether the scene was faked, but the closing credits roll over footage of Leary having a plaster cast made of his head. Whatever the truth of the matter, this is a tacky way to bring the curtain down on Leary's life. Love him or hate him, Leary was a repository for many American dreams and nightmares of the last 50 years, and the "cryonics mystery" trivializes all he represents.

NEW YORK POST, 6/6/97, p. 44, Michael Medved

"Timothy Leary's Dead" is the ultimate bad trip—a dismal, incoherent, painfully amateurish documentary that combines pretentious stretches of talking-head tedium with a climax of such tacky and appalling ghoulishness that the movie emerges as one of the decade's most monumentally unpleasant cinematic experiences.

Part of the problem is the heavy reliance by first-time filmmaker Paul Davids on 1995 interview footage from the last months of Timothy Leary's life.

Suffering from inoperable prostate cancer, the 75-year-old psychedelic guru looks wasted and cadaverous, opaque and glassy-eyed, pathetically arrayed in grizzled goatee and paisley Nehru jacket.

His comments display none of his fabled charisma, providing neither insight nor humor concerning his long and complicated life.

There's also no attempt to explore some of the more incongruous aspects of his existence—such as his West Point education, war time service in the Army, or his profitable 10 years on the college lecture circuit (starting in 1982), debating fellow media media icon (and ex-con) G. Gordon Liddy.

Surely, some footage of those debates might have been more compelling than the endless interview with '60s burnouts mumbling reverentially about their LSD mentor's philosophic profundity. The only attempt at providing "equal time" to a skeptical perspective on the psychedelic revolution comes from one angry L.A. cop, posed in front of his police car.

The one indelible image of Leary arises, however, from the painstakingly-planned moment of his death—dutifully captured by these documentarians.

As if this weren't tasteless enough, they also record the attending specialists sawing off Leary's head and placing it into a refrigerated cabinet for cryogenic preservation—in case the body of some brain-dead fellow in the future wants a slightly used (and acid-addled) replacement brain.

This unspeakably grotesque sequence inevitably recalls the 1963 sci-fi stinker "They Saved Hitler's Brain," though it's not nearly as funny. Concerning "Timothy Leary's Dead," the best possible advice remains: "Turn Off. Tune Out. Don't Go."

NEWSDAY, 6/6/97, Part II/p. B9, John Anderson

Long before Timothy Leary turned on, tuned in and dropped out permanently—he died of inoperable prostate cancer last year—the one-time Harvard professor, pioneering acid head and prison escapee had been relegated to the dustbin of '60s countercultural history. But, cliché or not, he'd made a lot of people very nervous. And he always seemed to believe in what he said, which is more than you can say about a lot of the people he was making so nervous. What's clear in "Timothy Leary's Dead" (in which, yes, we do hear the Moody Blues' "Legend of the Mind," whence the title sprang) is that Leary and the rest of his mind-expanding '60s crowd were stoned elitists, even in their small-d democracy.

As serious as they were about the potential of LSD as a means of expanding consciousness—"they" including Leary's Harvard colleague Dr. Richard Alpert, or Ram Dass, who appears at length in the film—they should have realized that most of America was far more concerned with recreation than exploration. And the few people called upon here to declare Leary complicit in the nation's drift into drug abuse are dismissed unfairly.

"Timothy Leary's Dead," directed by the debuting Paul Davids and written by Davids and Todd Easton Mills (son of John), makes a mistake that's not just off-putting but often fatal to a documentary with an agenda (and what other kind is there?): It presumes that the filmmakers' enthusiasm for its subject is shared by the audience. Rather than convince us of why Leary was important—socially, spiritually or pharmacologically—the movie begins at hero worship and comes to rest somewhere on the outskirts of adoration. Anyone offering an opposing point of view is put in a derisive position, no matter how much sense he makes.

There are "revelations"—Leary's claim that John F. Kennedy took LSD; that G. Gordon Liddy (with whom Leary teamed on lecture tours in the '90s) led the drug raid on Leary & Co.'s Millbrook, N.Y., commune in the mid-'60s; and that Leary's first wife killed herself on his 35th birthday—of which nothing is said after Leary mentions it once.

Leary occasionally sounds like a Heaven's Gate recruiter—his body is spoken of as a "vehicle," death as the last trip—although all the discussion of having Leary's head cryogenically frozen does lead neatly to the final scenes, in which ... well, it would be unfair to tell it straight. Suffice to say that Leary's brain and body go in different directions, although the end credits should reassure the squeamish and the skeptical alike.

VILLAGE VOICE, 6/10/97, p. 78, Michael Atkinson

As shagodelic and uncritical as its subject, *Timothy Leary's Dead* is a fairly conventional 100-meter dash through the life of the 20th century's most notorious pharmaceutical pimpernel. If the film rarely seems aware of the irony inherent in Leary's self-made celebrity, it at least has the courage of Leary's convictions, all the way down to the man's last hurrah.

Employing a standard but unavoidably lysergic combo of talking heads and archival news stock, the movie tracks Leary from his initial fame as Harvard psych prof gone trippy to his heyday as a pop outlaw to the lecturing mandarin and Internet ghost of the last decade or so. A happy camera hog, Leary appears neither brilliant nor very serious, and his legacy ends up a catalog of 1001 ways to describe the industrial-strength head trip.

Still, here's a man who practiced what he preached, all the way down to his cancerous "ultimate voyage" and scheduled cryonic beheading—all on film. As postmortems on the '60s go, this one has a distinct millennial chill.

Also reviewed in:
NEW YORK TIMES, 6/6/97, p. C4, Janet Maslin
VARIETY, 11/11-17/96, p. 60, Ken Eisner

TITANIC

A Paramount Pictures and Twentieth Century Fox release of a Lightstorm Entertainment production. *Executive Producer:* Rae Sanchini. *Producer:* James Cameron and Jon Landau. *Director:* James Cameron. *Screenplay:* James Cameron. *Director of Photography:* Russell Carpenter. *Editor:* Conrad Buff, James Cameron, and Richard A. Harris. *Music:* James Horner. *Music Editor:* Jim Henrikson. *Choreographer:* Lynne Hockney. *Sound:* Christopher Boyes, Mark Ulano, Doug Canton, and (music) Shawn Murphy. *Sound Editor:* Tom Belfort. *Casting:* Mali Finn. *Production Designer:* Peter Lamont. *Art Director:* Charles Lee. *Set Designer:* Marco Niro, Dominic Masters, and Peter Francis. *Set Decorator:* Michael Ford, Ali Rubenstein, Claude Roussel, and Jason Shurko. *Special Effects:* Thomas L. Fisher. *Costumes:* Deborah L. Scott. *Make-up:* Tina Earnshaw and Laura Borzelli. *Make-up (Old Rose):* Greg Cannom. *Stunt Coordinator:* Simon Crane. *Running time:* 197 minutes. *MPAA Rating:* PG-13.

CAST: Leonardo DiCaprio (Jack Dawson); Kate Winslet (Young Rose DeWitt Bukater); Billy Zane (Cal Hockley); Kathy Bates (Molly Brown); Frances Fisher (Ruby DeWitt Bukater); Bernard Hill (Captain Smith); Jonathan Hyde (Bruce Ismay); Danny Nucci (Fabrizio); David Warner (Spicer Lovejoy); Bill Paxton (Brock Lovett); Gloria Stuart (Rose Dawson Calvert); Victor Garber (Thomas Andrews); Suzy Amis (Lizzy Calvert); Lewis Abernathy (Lewis Bodine); Nicholas Cascone (Bobby Buell); Anatoly M. Sagalevitch (Anatoly Milkailavich); Jason Barry (Tommy Ryan); Ewan Stewart (First Officer Murdoch); Ioan Gruffudd (Fifth Officer Lowe); Jonny Phillips (Second Officer Lightoller); Mark Lindsay Chapman (Chief Officer Wilde); Richard Graham (Quartermaster Rowe); Paul Brightwell (Quartermaster Hichens); Ron Donachie (Master at Arms); Eric Braeden (John Jacob Astor); Charlotte Chatton (Madeleine Astor); Bernard Fox (Colonel Archibald Gracie); Michael Ensign (Benjamin Guggenheim); Fannie Brett (Madame Aubert); Jenette Goldstein (Irish Mommy); Camilla Overbye Roos (Helga Dahl); Linda Kerns (3rd Class Woman); Amy Gaipa (Trudy Bolt); Martin Jarvis (Sir Duff Gordon); Rosalind Ayres (Lady Duff Gordon); Rochelle Rose (Countess of Rothes); Jonathan Evans-Jones (Wallace Hartley); Brian Walsh (Irish Man); Rocky Taylor (Bert Cartmell); Alexandre Owens (Cora Cartnell); Simon Crane (Fourth Officer Boxhall); Edward Fletcher (Sixth Officer Moody); Scott G. Anderson (Frederick Fleet); Martin East (Lookout Lee); Craig Kelly (Harold Bride); Gregory Cooke (Jack Phillips); Liam Tuohy (Chief Baker Joughin); James Lancaster (Father Byles); Elsa Raven (Ida Straus); Lew Palter (Isidor Straus); Reece P. Thompson, III (Irish Little Boy); Laramie Landis (Irish Little Girl); Amber Waldell and Alison Waddell (Cal's Crying Girl); Mark Rafael Truitt (Yaley); John Walcutt (First Class Husband); Terry Forrestal (Chief Engineer Bell); Derek Lea (Leading Stoker Barrett); Richard Ashton (Carpenter John Hutchinson); Sean M. Nepita (Elevator Operator); Brendan Connolly (Scotland Road Steward); David Cronnelly (Crewman); Garth Wilton (First Class Waiter); Martin Laing (Promenade Deck Steward); Marc Cass and Paul Herbert (Hold Stewards); Emmett James (First Class Steward); Christopher Byrne (Stairwell Steward); Oliver Page (Steward Barnes); James Garrett (Titanic Porter); Erik Holland (Olaf Dahl); Jari Kinnunen (Bjorn Gunderson); Anders Falk (Olaus Gunderson); Martin Hub (Slovakian Father); Seth Adkins (Slovakian 3 Year Old Boy); Barry Dennen (Praying Man); Vern Urich (Man in Water); Rebecca Jane Klinger (Mother at Stern); Tricia O'Neil (Woman); Kathleen Dunn (Woman in Water); Romeo Francis (Syrian Man); Mandana Marino (Syrian Woman); Van Ling (Chinese Man); Bjorn (Olaf); Dan Petterson (Sven); Shay Duffin (Pubkeeper); Greg Ellis (Carpathia Steward); Diana Morgan (News Reporter); I Salonisti (Titanic Orchestra); Gaelic Storm (Steerage Band).

CHRISTIAN SCIENCE MONITOR, 12/19/97, p. 12, David Sterritt

With a reputed cost of more than $200 million, "Titanic" is probably the most expensive movie ever made. The reasons for its mammoth price tag aren't hard to calculate.

First, special effects cost money and filmmaker James Cameron has filled "Titanic" with the sort of high-tech wizardry he mastered in earlier epics like the "Terminator" pictures.

Second, special effects involving water are even more expensive than the dry-land variety, since it's hard to match shots together when the background is rolling and rippling. Remember "Waterworld," the previous most-expensive-movie-ever-made?

Third, "Titanic" clocks in at a whopping three hours and 17 minutes. This accounts for a significant chunk of the budget in itself and may play a role in determining the picture's profitability. Exhibitors will be able to screen it only half as often as a normal-length feature, and some moviegoers might head elsewhere when they realize it's such a long sit. One critic has already dubbed it an interactive film: Since there's no intermission, you make your own whenever you want!

Do all these big-budget dollars and on-screen hours pay worthwhile dividends? The bottom-line answer is yes. "Titanic" is no masterpiece, but it's an absorbing entertainment with enough different moves, moods, and ideas to keep everyone happy at least part of the time.

The story begins not in 1912, when the great ship went down, but in the present. A crew of money-minded adventurers has mounted an undersea expedition to the wreck, hoping to salvage a fabulous diamond from a shipboard safe.

Hauling the strongbox to the surface, they find it contains a mere drawing of the jewel adorning the neck of a beautiful teenager. News of their discovery travels fast, and soon they receive an unexpected visitor: a 100-year-old woman who identifies herself as Rose DeWitt Bukater, the long-ago youngster in the sketch. Her memories reawakened, she describes the Titanic's voyage in vivid detail.

This episode makes a haunting framework for the main body of the film, setting up "Titanic" as a tale of time and memory as well as drama, danger, and disaster.

The next portion is less imaginative: a leisurely account of how love blooms between Rose, engaged to marry a pompous gentleman named Cal, and Jack Dawson, a young artist with a third-class ticket and a rascally streak as wide as the ocean they're crossing. Cameron is a resourceful director but a pedestrian screenwriter, and while these scenes benefit from likable acting by Kate Winslet and Leonardo DiCaprio, they suffer from trite dialogue and predictable romance-movie events.

All of which heightens our anticipation of the tragedy about to strike—and strike it does, with wrenching views of the Titanic's awful encounter with an iceberg too close for the fast-traveling hull to avoid. Here the movie picks up all the steam it lost during the droopy love triangle, nimbly coordinating action-adventure situations (panicky passengers, inadequate lifeboats, Jack chained to a pipe in a rapidly flooding room) with images as crisply realistic as Hollywood's advanced technology can make them.

Cameron's screenplay also takes on flashes of intelligence, as when Cal and his oily assistant both reveal how they "make their own luck," one with money and the other with a gun. This moment suggests that nothing more admirable than naked wealth and brute force supports the social power they wield—and that there may not be much difference between these forms of strength. It's a trenchant commentary on the inequalities that give upper-deck passengers a higher chance of survival than their disadvantaged shipmates.

Production information on "Titanic" is loaded with striking statistics. The original ship was 880 feet long, weighed some 60,000 tons, and carried about 2,223 people. Facilities for the movie included a 775-foot exterior set, a 17-million-gallon pool to sink it in, and 5 million gallons of water to flood it with.

And so on, from the number of wigs worn by the cast (450) to the size of the camera crane (80 feet) used for the most sweeping shots. Moviegoers who admired Cameron's technical savvy in pictures like "Aliens" and "True Lies" will flock to "Titanic" for the thrills these elements provide and that makes sense, since the effects won't translate well to small-size TV screens.

But what's most impressive about "Titanic" is the evidence it shows of new maturity in Cameron's filmmaking priorities. While this is hardly the $200 million art film some moviegoers had hoped for, it cares as much about its characters as about its visual effects and seems genuinely mournful about the human loss caused by the disaster.

Like the musical "Titanic" that has attracted Broadway theatergoers this year, ifs an epic with a heart.

And when a techie like Cameron starts cultivating human values, it bodes well for Hollywood's future.

LOS ANGELES TIMES, 12/19/97, Calendar/p. 12, Kenneth Turan

To the question of the day—what does $200 million buy? the 3-hour-and-14-minute "Titanic" unhesitatingly answers: not enough.

Note that despite the hopes of skeptics, aghast at the largest film budget of modern times, money enough to run a full-dress presidential campaign or put a serious dent in illiteracy, the answer is not nothing. When you are willing to build a 775-foot, 90% scale model of the doomed ship and sink it in a 17-million-gallon tank specially constructed for the purpose, you are going to get a heck of a lot of production value for your money. Especially if your name is James Cameron.

More than that, at "Titanic's" two-hour mark, when most films have sense enough to be winding down, this behemoth does stir to a kind of life. With writer-director Cameron, a virtuoso at large-scale action-adventure extravaganzas serving as ringmaster, the detailing of the ship's agonies (compressed here from a real-life two hours and 40 minutes to a bit more than an hour) compels our interest absolutely.

But Cameron, there can be no doubt, is after more than oohs and aahs. He's already made "The Terminator" and "Terminator 2"; with "Titanic" he has his eye on "Doctor Zhivago" / "Lawrence of Arabia" territory. But while his intentions are clear, Cameron lacks the skills necessary to pull off his coup. Just as the hubris of headstrong shipbuilders who insisted that the Titanic was unsinkable led to an unparalleled maritime disaster, so Cameron's overweening pride has come unnecessarily close to capsizing this project.

For seeing "Titanic" almost makes you weep in frustration. Not because of the excessive budget, not even because it recalls the unnecessary loss of life in the real 1912 catastrophe, which saw more than 1,500 of the 2,200-plus passengers dying when an iceberg sliced the ship open like a can opener. What really brings on the tears is Cameron's insistence that writing this kind of movie is within his abilities. Not only isn't it, it isn't even close.

Cameron has regularly come up with his own scripts in the past, but in a better world someone would have had the nerve to tell him or he would have realized himself that creating a moving and creditable love story is a different order of business from coming up with wisecracks for Arnold Schwarzenegger.

Instead, what audiences end up with word-wise is a hackneyed, completely derivative copy of old Hollywood romances, a movie that reeks of phoniness and lacks even minimal originality. Worse than that, many of the characters, especially the feckless tycoon Cal Hockley (played by Billy Zane) and Kathy Bates' impersonation of the Unsinkable Molly Brown, are clichés of such purity they ought to be exhibited in film schools as examples of how not to write for the screen.

It is easy to forget, as you wait for the iceberg to arrive and shake things up, how excellent an idea it was to revisit for modern audiences the sinking of what was the largest moving object ever built. Numerous films have been made on the subject, with even the Third Reich taking a shot with a version that concluded, not surprisingly, that the sinking was "an eternal accusation against England's greed." As Steven Biel wrote in "Down With the Old Canoe," a fascinating cultural history of public reaction to the event, "The Titanic disaster begs for resolution—and always resists it."

One reason this version is so long is a modern framing story involving nautical treasure hunter Brock Lovett (Cameron veteran Bill Paxton), who is scouring the Titanic's wreck (it was located in 1985) for a fabulously expensive blue diamond called "The Heart of the Ocean" that was lost on board.

What Lovett turns up instead is a drawing of a nude young woman wearing the jewel. News of that find prompts a phone call from 101-year-old Rose Dawson Calvert (Gloria Stuart), who says it's her in the drawing. Lovett flies Rose (whom Cameron modeled on artist Beatrice Wood) out to join his expedition. The bulk of "Titanic" is her recollection of what happened before, during and after that great ship went down.

Young Rose (now played by Kate Winslet) boarded the Titanic as a 17-year-old wearing a very large hat and metaphorical shackles. "To me it was a slave ship," she recalls, "taking me to America in chains." In plainer English she was being forced by her snooty mother Ruth DeWitt Bukater into a (gasp!) loveless marriage with Cal Hockley, an arrogant and wealthy snob for whom the phrase "perpetual sneer" was probably invented.

Rose may be a 17-year-old, but she knows a thing or two. She makes offhanded references to Freud, a wise gentleman no one else on board has heard of, and during an impromptu shopping spree she managed to buy works by Picasso, Degas and Monet despite Hockley's dismissive belief that they "won't amount to a thing." Clearly, this prodigy of taste and discernment deserves better than Mr. Perpetual Sneer, no matter how rich he is.

Enter Jack Dawson (Leonardo DiCaprio), a madcap artist and cherubic scamp who wins his steerage ticket in a dockside card game. Jack is staggered by a glimpse of Rose, and though a conveniently placed Irish lad advises him "you'd as like have angels flying out of your arse as get next to the likes of her," he's not the kind of young man to give up easily.

Sure enough, despite the presence of 2,200 other passengers and crew, it's only Jack who's around to save the day when a distraught Rose considers suicide in a flattering evening gown. Despite the best efforts of mother Ruth (Frances Fisher) and Hockley's snarling valet Spicer Lovejoy (David Warner), Jack and Rose are irresistibly drawn to each other. She improves his manners (not hard to do), he teaches her how to spit like a man, and they spend quality time in photogenic locations like the ship's towering prow.

Both Winslet and DiCaprio are capable actors (though his brash brat routine is wearing thin) but they are victimized, as is everyone else, by dialogue that has the self-parodying ring of Young Romance comics. "You could just call me a tumbleweed blowing in the wind," Jack says, adding later, "sooner or later the fire I love about you is going to burn out." Most weighted down by this kind of blather are the fatuous Hockley, who has to say things like "you filth" and Bates' Molly Brown, a character so relentlessly folksy she'd be at home on "The Beverly Hillbillies."

Finally, after so much time has passed you fear the iceberg has slept through its wake-up call, disaster strikes the ship at 11:50 on the night of April 14. Cameron is truly in his element here, and "Titanic's" closing hour is jammed with the most stirring and impressive sights, from towering walls of water flooding a grand dining room to the enormous ship itself defying belief and going vertical in the water.

These kinds of complex and demanding sequences are handled with so much aplomb it's understandable that the director, who probably considers the script to be the easiest part of his job, not only wants to do it all but also thinks he can. Yet as Cameron sails his lonely craft toward greatness, he should realize he needs to bring a passenger with him. Preferably someone who can write.

NEW YORK, 12/22-29/97, p. 130, David Denby

Perhaps the most powerful emotion inspired by *Titanic* is not awe or excitement but simple relief. For it was by no means clear that the bastards could do it—that *anyone* in Hollywood could put together, in this age of cynicism and ineptitude, a hearty big entertainment in the manner of such broadly pleasing, Oscar-winning movies as, say, *Ben-Hur*. But writer-director James Cameron has pulled it off: The creator of the *Terminator* movies is now the king of the squares. This fabulously expensive watery epic is actually a very good movie—though one must add that there's nothing daring about it, no new themes that might disturb the Republic in its tumultuous sleep of shopping. The generic elements are securely in place: The wine glass trembles, the dishes rattle and fall, the string quartet plays Offenbach on the tilting deck; at the end, the ship turns on its end, stem straight up, and beautifully sinks. *Titanic* is not "important"—except in commercial terms. The only startling thing about it is the centrality of its love story. Instead of making a disaster movie with a thread of romance, Cameron has made a romantic movie in which a fictional love affair is heightened by disaster. The picture is about the big ship memory and desire. It's about the things that died on the morning of April 15, 1912—an earlier form of technological hubris, the class system of pre-World War I England and America. It's also about what was born—not just love but a new spirit in women.

Titanic begins with a contemporary pirate, a treasure hunter, Brock Lovett (Bill Paxton), who is obsessed with the sunken hulk. Lovett's submersible robot enters one of the deluxe staterooms and with mechanical arms retrieves a locked safe. There's a suggestion of violation in the probe, a new form of hubris, and Lovett takes a fall: He finds not the famous diamond he was looking for but only a drawing of a naked young woman wearing the stone. It turns out that the woman, Rose, is still alive; she's a remarkably (perhaps unbelievably) articulate 100-year-old beauty (Gloria Stuart) who joins Lovett at his ship and then holds him and his crew of techno-ruffians in thrall with her story of what happened more than 80 years earlier. The knowing and sarcastic contemporary age gives way to the stiff Edwardian grandeur of the floating palace. Rose's memory controls the flow of events, a framing device that is borderline banal; Rose's statements are rather too beautiful and placid. Yet there's a shrewdly crowd-pleasing emotional logic behind Cameron's idea. We realize that we are seeing the disaster through the lens of hope.

Back in 1912, the 17-year-old Rose DeWitt Bukater (Kate Winslet), dressed in lace and chiffon, with an enormous plumed hat and parasol, boards the ship in utter misery. Rose is accompanied by her awful fiancé, Cal Hockley (Billy Zane), a young but already domineering steel baron from Pittsburgh. Zane, an Australian, plays Cal with a supercilious manner that recalls, at times, Louis Hayward prancing and posing as Louis XIV. Rose is stuck with this sneering horror; her snobbish mother (Frances Fisher), possessed of a good name but nothing else, desperately needs cash. So! A lovely girl about to be sacrificed to a monster—the situation reeks of crude Victorian melodrama, but it works because Kate Winslet (the younger sister in *Sense and Sensibility)* is no ordinary young actress. There's strength of will and more than a little singularity in the large hazel-blue eyes, the thick red hair and downward-turning lips. Winslet is breathtakingly vivid in her emotional transparency. She easily masters the American accent as well as a young upper-class girl's petulant pride.

Onboard, Rose meets her soulmate, Jack Dawson (Leonardo DiCaprio), who is probably meant to evoke Jack London. He's a free-spirited. rootless American—a penniless artist—who cheerfully makes his way around the world. DiCaprio, 23, doesn't have the size or muscled body of most movie heroes; he's very young, slender, even rather delicate, with long straight blond hair and a triangular face that is almost pretty. Yet DiCaprio's lack of muscular weight makes his various audacities seem even more of a risk. Jack may be an idealized figure, but Cameron has chosen the right actor for idealization: Leonardo DiCaprio's cockiness is completely engaging (there's a fundament of gallantry and decency in it), and we accept the movie as a celebration of youthful reckless gaiety. A gambler, Jack has the wit to see that Rose's unhappiness hides a bold, deeply romantic and sexual nature; he leads her up to the bow of the ship, where she spreads her arms as if to fly over the water like the *Winged Victory of Samothrace*. It's a corny but stirring rhetorical moment, with the camera on a crane swooping across the bow.

Cameron does a lot of that high swooping over the ship, and also much rushing up and down grand staircases and through corridors. There's no great distinction in his moving-camera style—the shots never quite escape rousing cliché—but Cameron does convey the enormous scale and variety of the place. There are the stokers in their reddish inferno below; the Babel of Swedish, Italian, and Russian immigrants in steerage; the gowned and tuxedoed swells displaying themselves in the mahogany public rooms. What we see, of course, is meant to be an evilly class-ridden society. Except for the crude, good-hearted Denver millionairess Molly Brown (Kathy Bates)—the "unsinkable Molly Brown" of musical fame—the wealthy are unspeakably rude or just frightened and starchy. (Well, it's not rich people who make movies like this a hit.)

Jack, the interloper, takes Rose down to steerage, where the real people, sweat flowing freely, are having themselves a fine time drinking beer and dancing up a storm. This sort of cheesy stuff is redeemed only by the romantic charge between Winslet and DiCaprio. Indeed, what's most endearing about this enormous movie is the two kids running around the ship looking for a place to make love. Highly preoccupied, they don't know that they're in an epic—that an awesome tragedy is about to enfold them and everyone else. Their frivolous unconsciousness is charming. When Winslet takes off her clothes so that DiCaprio may sketch her naked, the scene is tenderly erotic and naughty in a way that we've never seen before in a big-spectacle movie.

All the observation of individuals and social types pays off, of course, in the way people behave once the ship strikes the iceberg. The scandal of the *Titanic* disaster lay not only in the ship's faulty construction but in the White Star Line's clear intent to save the rich and drown the poor should catastrophe occur. As a piece of movie staging and directing, the sinking is lovely—detailed, agonizingly slow at first and then rushed and panicky and grandly gruesome at the end, a whirl of bodies hurling themselves at restricted lifeboats. Cameron dramatizes the way the third-class passengers were locked below as the first-class passengers were saved, but he makes his point without rubbing our faces in it. The sheer amazement produced by the big ship going down is greater than any Marxist analysis one could make of the event.

Special effect or not, the sight of the stern, with its huge propellers unsheathed, rising straight up out of the water, is enduringly strange. As Jack and Rose hang giddily at the railing, people lose their grip and go crashing down the deck or fall from the heights into the water. After the ship goes under, Cameron has his finest, cruelest moment—the survivors left in the vast expanse of freezing water wailing in confusion. As for Rose, she is delivered into an active and brilliant life. The movie comes full circle, back to Lovett's outfit, and there's a neat surprise ending. The ship may be ponderous, but Cameron's conception stays light in the water.

NEW YORK POST, 12/19/97, p. 47, Michael Medved

Defying the odds and against all logic, "Titanic" turns out to be worth the money.

This insanely ambitious screen epic not only justifies its reported $200 million production budget but, far more important, handsomely repays whatever hard-earned dollars moviegoers will invest to see it.

For 197 utterly spellbinding minutes, writer-director James Cameron delivers awesome spectacle, rich and captivating characters, a great love story, rousing adventure, and a seemingly endless succession of images so grandly cinematic, so poetic and breathtaking, that they unequivocally earn the overused adjective "unforgettable."

Cameron presents his tale with an ingenious framing device, beginning the film with a present-day salvage expert (Bill Paxton) exploring the wreck of the great ship on the ocean floor in search of a priceless diamond once owned by one of its passengers.

As part of his search, he meets a 101-year-old Titanic survivor (the luminous Gloria Stuart) who tells her melodramatic story.

As a 17-year-old (played by the magnificent Kate Winslet) she boarded the huge liner ("the largest moving object ever made from the hand of man") with her mother (Frances Fisher) and her haughty, domineering, wealthy fiance (Billy Zane).

Feeling trapped by the stuffy, socialite's life awaiting her, she was dangerously drawn to a third-class passenger she meets during the voyage: a penniless artist (Leonardo DiCaprio) who won his tickets onto the Titanic in a dockside poker game.

Director Cameron presents his working-class characters as universally earthy, vital and decent while his elegant swells all seem hollow and cruel. But the risky between-decks affair still comes across as authentic, passionate and involving enough to make the audience forget for a time that we're headed for an iceberg.

Amazingly enough, the movie makes the exhilaration, elegance and sheer fun of sharing Titanic's maiden voyage ("when you could smell fresh paint and sleep on sheets never used before") as riveting as the disaster that followed.

Those scenes of suffering, heroism and folly achieve a visceral, gut-churning impact approached by no other film since "Schindler's List."

Imagine the stricken craft, an incongruous island of light and panic, swallowed up by a vast black ocean under an even vaster starry, moonless sky.

Or a lifeboat searching with a lantern for signs of life among hundreds of frozen bodies bobbing in eerie silence in their life-preservers.

The cast is consistently superb, with standout performances even in minor parts, like that of doomed Captain E.J. Smith (Bernard Hill) and proud, gentlemanly shipbuilder Thomas Andrews (Victor Garber).

Winslet is perfectly cast as a headstrong beauty of 1912, with no taints of present-day trendiness to shatter the film's painstakingly precise period atmosphere.

The characters may or may not find a missing diamond among the famous wreckage, but with any justice they should come up with Oscar gold.

NEWSDAY, 12/19/97, Part II/p. B3, Jack Mathews

The sinking of the Titanic has been explored many times, many ways; in books and film, fiction and nonfiction, with and without the accompaniment of "Nearer My God to Thee." We've heard or read scores of survivors' accounts, we've toured the great ship through pre-launch photos and newsreel footage, we've even been to its grave to roam its carcass in documentaries made for the smallest (TV) and largest (IMAX) screens.

The only thing that has eluded our imagination is the sense of actually going down with the ship. Nobody aboard the Titanic that fateful night in 1912 lived to tell *that* story, and no filmmaker has had the resources or the gall to speculate ... until now.

Welcome writer-director James Cameron's "Titanic," a staggering reenactment that cost about 25 times more to make than the original ship cost to build (about $7.5 million to $10 million), takes 25 minutes longer to watch than the Titanic took to sink, and arrives—some five months later than expected—as one of the most perversely thrilling adventures ever put on film.

"Titanic" is not the masterpiece it might have been. Cameron, whose previous films include the "Terminator" movies and "The Abyss," is a magician with special effects, model-work, and action choreography, but his writing leans toward matinee-movie cliché, and the love story at the heart of "Titanic" is too transparently contrived for the kind of epic drama he intends. But as a maker of spectacle, Cameron will end the century on a list that began with D.W. Griffith.

To his credit, Cameron rejected the disaster movie formula that "Titanic" begs to accommodate. He doesn't develop a handful of mini-dramas that come to a boil as the iceberg approaches. Instead, he focuses on two people, the drifter-artist Jack Dawson (Leonardo DiCaprio), who wins his steerage-class ticket in a last-minute poker game, and Rose DeWitt Bukater (Kate Winslet), a 17-year-old American returning home with her domineering mother (Frances Fisher) and the wealthy English snob, Cal Hockley (Billy Zane), with whom she's miserably engaged.

The first-class/steerage romance is a tired but inescapable cliché of Titanic lore. Few times have the lines between social classes been so clearly drawn, or the stakes as carefully measured, as they were with the Titanic. Not only were the passengers segregated by class, but when the ship began to sink, the steerage compartment was sealed off and blocked with armed guards in an attempt to save those holding the higher-priced tickets first.

A romance between a have and have-not, which is also the dramatic linchpin of the current Broadway musical "Titanic," is the most convenient way to bridge the class issue. And Cameron milks it for all it's worth, and then some.

Rose is a caged spirit, buckling under the weight of her mother's greed, her fiancé's ego and the manners of her class, while Jack Dawson, free as the wind, holds the key to her liberation. After a chance meeting—she's about to jump overboard, he happens by to rescue her—and some skittish class foreplay, Jack and Rose begin a lightning, sexually charged romance that will become the scandal of the upper decks.

"Titanic" is framed within a contemporary story about the finding of a sketch of a nude woman in the hull of the sunken ship, and with the reminiscences of the 102-year-old woman (Gloria Stuart) who claims to be the girl in the drawing. That girl is Rose, of course, and with marine scavenger Bill Paxton and others looking on in misty-eyed wonder, she takes us back to that day in April, 1912, when the first of the Titanic's 2,207 passengers begin boarding in Southampton, England.

If the numbers describing the Titanic's size are incomprehensible—three football fields long, 18 stories high—so is Cameron's nine-tenths scale replica. When the elderly Rose begins her story, we see the image of the gray, decayed sunken hull of the Titanic dissolve into its maiden glory, sitting dockside in Southampton, a mountain-size symbol of man's technological genius.

The image on screen is also a symbol of man's technological genius, albeit of another age. There may be telltale moments in "Titanic," particularly those aerial shots of the ship at sea, where the seams of the graphic overlays are faintly visible, or where the water seems to take on a metallic shimmer. But the scale of the ship's exterior is so overwhelming, and its interiors so finely and authentically detailed, that you very quickly surrender to the illusion, and allow the Titanic's inherent drama—the approach of doom—to sweep you along.

"Titanic" takes its time getting there. The iceberg isn't spotted, by lookouts in the crow's nest, until 1 hour and 35 minutes into the movie, after Jack and Rose are madly in love, and being pursued by her furious fiancé and his gun-toting companion (David Warner).

The scenes with Zane's spurned lover and Warner's brooding thug provide the worst moments in the movie. Zane and Warner are playing villains out of a "Perils of Pauline" plot, and the melodrama they create just as the ship begins to sink is truly wretched excess.

But the chase nonsense gives Cameron the opportunity to take us where no moviegoers have gone before, into the imploding bowels of the Titanic, from its flooded boiler room, where the crew is trying to follow rats to safety, to the steerage compartment, where panic is fueling riot, to the forecastle, where Captain Smith (Bernard Hill) stares in catatonic shame, to the decks, where stewards are trying to maintain order while loading the lifeboats, "women and children first."

Cameron devotes minimal time to the actual historical drama played out aboard the Titanic, that being the reckless insistence by a White Star Lines executive (Jonathan Hyde) that the ship travel full-speed through the treacherous ice fields to get to New York a day early. It's there, as subtext, as are such noted Titanic figures as the ship's builder Thomas Andrews (Victor Garber), Molly Brown (Kathy Bates), and super-wealthy passengers John Jacob Astor (Eric Braeden) and Benjamin Guggenheim (Michael Ensign).

But Cameron's aim was to set the most intimate love story possible against one of the century's biggest tragedies, and he very nearly pulls it off. DiCaprio has a captivating presence in a role that might have been written for a young Clark Gable, and Winslet, an Oscar nominee for "Sense and Sensibility," imbues Rose with enough passion to fuel a shelf of romance novels.

In the end, this "Titanic's" weakness seems a small one, Cameron's penchant for overstatement. Maybe that's because he started out making a summer movie, not the heavyweight holiday release/Academy Award front-runner it has become. And it's certainly not enough to sink the ship.

SIGHT AND SOUND, 2/98, p. 50, Laura Miller

The Atlantic Ocean, the present day. Brock Lovett explores the *Titanic* wreck, secretly looking for a famous diamond, the Heart of the Ocean, fabled to have sunk with the ship. In a safe, he finds a sketch of a young woman. After the discovery is reported, an elderly woman named Rose contacts him, explaining that she is the woman depicted and that she knows he's looking for the diamond. She is airlifted to the ship, where she relates her experience of the disaster.

1912. The *Titanic* is boarded by the young Rose, her mother and her wealthy fiancé, Cal. Jack, an artist, wins his steerage passage in a poker game. That evening, Rose almost throws herself over the rail but Jack talks her out of it. Cal promises to give Rose the Heart of the Ocean diamond. Ismay, the Chairman of the White Star Line, demands the ship go faster. The next day, Rose confesses her unhappiness to Jack. He dines with the first-class passengers, then invites Rose to a party in steerage. She asks him to draw her in the nude and leaves the sketch in Cal's safe. The two lovers flee, pursued by Cal's valet, Lovejoy. They make love in a car in storage. The lookouts sight an iceberg, but attempts to evade it fail and it collides with the ship.

Rose and Jack are captured, and Lovejoy plants the diamond on Jack, who is arrested and handcuffed to a pipe. Andrews, the ship's designer, tells the Captain that the ship will sink. The crew distributes lifejackets and begins loading the inadequate number of lifeboats with women and children. Panic ensues. Rose rescues Jack. Cal bribes and lies his way onto a lifeboat. The ship breaks in half, and sinks entirely. Jack and Rose find some driftwood that will only support Rose. She is rescued after he dies from the cold, and once ashore she hides from Cal, changing her name.

Back in the present, the elderly Rose sneaks up to the deck and tosses the Heart of the Ocean diamond overboard. She dies and joins Jack and the other deceased crew and passengers of the *Titanic*.

James Cameron (*Terminator*) heads for old fashioned Hollywood epic territory with *Titanic*, reputedly the most expensive film ever made. Using computer-generated imagery, he succeeds at capturing the visceral terror and awe of the legendary maritime disaster. The minutes when the ship splits in half, its stem tilts upward, exposing its enormous propellers, and the desperate passengers cling to the suddenly perpendicular deck or plummet from its heights into the icy water are particularly effective.

Likewise, Cameron is in his element during the crisp action sequences of the film's second half, in which the characters race through rapidly flooding passages and make several narrow escapes from drowning. *Titanic* is ostentatious in its fidelity to the material aspects of its subject, presenting in detail the handsome staterooms, decks and swankily appointed first-class atrium with its famous staircase. Many of the establishing shots have an air of the guided tour about them, carefully displaying a production design so meticulously created that it has won the approval of minutia obsessed *Titanic* buffs—no small feat. Cameron even commissioned his own underwater footage of the wreck.

Nevertheless, *Titanic* rarely feels like anything more than the most impressive movie money can buy. What grandeur and pathos the film possesses belong to the mythic story of the shipwreck itself, a fantastic confluence of history and the stuff that ballads are made from (as well as several films already, including *A Night to Remember* of 1958). Cameron adds precisely nothing to the sum if you calculate his many gaffes against his commitment to a strict, methodical standard of authenticity.

And even that standard disintegrates when it comes to Cameron's own screenplay, a vulgar, cliché-ridden, anachronistic effort that entirely fails to capture the rigidly stratified manners of the era, despite Cameron's apparent interest in class relations. In fact, what Jack, Rose and Cal most resemble are the teens in John Hughes' high school dramas of the 80s in which noble, if brash, poor boys win the prettiest girls in class away from arrogant, bullying football stars. Having Rose drop vapid references to Picasso and Freud, and Jack reel off a list of stock bohemian adventures (drawing nude prostitutes in Paris, working a shrimp boat in Monterey) only compound the aura of phoniness.

Cameron's appealing young leads do struggle to bring vigour to their thin, cartoonish characters. Winslet often looks stiff and lost, as if affronted by her lines. While DiCaprio mostly just coasts on his insouciant movie-star charm, he's still a bit too unripe to make a convincing leading man. It's only in the minor characters—Victor Garber as the ship's architect Thomas Andrews, the musicians who go on playing as the ship sinks beneath them and Bernard Hill as the *Titanic*'s doomed captain—that the film offers us individuals as interesting as their fate. Not surprisingly, they are substantially based on actual people, and not the products of Cameron's limited powers of dramatic invention. While the film's first half, focused as it is on Rose and Jack's budding romance and the nastiness of Cal (who lacks only a handlebar moustache to twirl), seems overlong, *Titanic* is more crude than inept. The movie works as a simple minded entertainment that provides a setting for spectacular visual effects, and many audiences will find it adequately enjoyable.

That everything about *Titanic*—from its stereotyped characters to its bright, even lighting—feels ersatz and obvious may only trouble the kind of people who dislike the immaculate, synthetic recreations of real places in Disney theme parks. Not everyone who sees *Titanic* will yearn for the movie it might have been had it been made by a film-maker with imagination, and intelligence, rather than just raw ambition, but those who do will find it littered with missed opportunities as well as demonstrations of conspicuous spending. There were many complex and fascinating grown-ups aboard the *Titanic,* and several dozen true stories more compelling than Jack and Rose's teenage love. And there are deep veins of tragedy and mystery in the tale of the star-crossed ship that James Cameron hasn't the sensitivity to tap.

TIME, 12/8/97, p. 91, Richard Corliss

In 85 years, the *Titanic* tragedy has spawned a dozen or so film and TV adaptations. A silent one-reeler, *Saved from the Titanic*, was released just one month after the event and starred an actress who had been onboard. There was a Teutonic Titanic, a Nazi-financed epic featuring an imaginary German hero. The 1958 British A *Night to Remember* is still revered for its balance of newsreel realism and humanist pluck. But diving into crowded waters is James Cameron's M.O. Except for *The Terminator* and *The Abyss*, all his films have been sequels or remakes, each grander and pricier than the movies that preceded it. What gargantuan retread can be next—*History of the World Part 2*?

Bigness was, of course, an attraction of the actual ship. In the film, the ship company's boss says, "I wanted to convey sheer size." Cameron could be his spiritual heir. The man who made *The Terminator* for $6 million has become the high priest of Hollywood bloat. He is also the movies' mad toymaster: he keeps falling in love with an imposing machine (a cyborg, an alien, a submarine, a Harrier jet, an ocean liner) that he then spends great amounts of time and energy destroying.

Fine, Jim—build the damned ship, sink the damned ship. But in the 90 or so minutes before the iceberg slices open the starboard side, some compelling romantic fiction is in order. Here the film fails utterly. It imagines an affair between free-spirited artist Jack Dawson (Leonardo DiCaprio) in steerage and Philadelphia blueblood Rose Bukater (Kate Winslet), unhappily engaged to wealthy Cal Hockley (Billy Zane). DiCaprio has a smooth, winsome beauty, and Winslet, who at first seems bulky beside him, comes to look ravishingly ravaged by the climax. Everyone else is a caricature of class, designed only to illustrate a predictable prejudice: that the first-class passengers are third-class people, and vice versa.

Once the ship starts sinking, people do die becomingly, and the R.M.S. *Titanic* takes on the personality of a magnificent beast— King Kong or Moby Dick in extremis. The brilliantly realized visual effects are invisible and persuasive. The digitized water looks like real water; the computer blobs look like human beings tumbling down to their deaths from the severed ship's nearly vertical stem. But the narrative events that should add emotional heft are substandard action tropes: kids in jeopardy, bad guys menacing pretty women, Jack manacled to a water pipe. "I'll just wait here," he says gamely, and idiotically, as Rose runs for help.

The film doesn't play to Cameron's strength as a ringmaster of burly metaphorical fantasy. His story of Jack, Rose and Cal isn't half as poignant as the true ones known from books and films of the event. On this vast canvas, the problems of these three little people really don't amount to a hill of beans.

Tales of this film's agonizing gestation and tardy birth, though already the stuff of legend, will mean little to moviegoers, who will pay the same $7 or $8 to see Titanic that they spend on films made for a thousandth its cost. Ultimately, *Titanic* will sail or sink not on its budget but on its merits as drama and spectacle. The regretful verdict here: Dead in the water.

VILLAGE VOICE, 12/23/97, p. 79, J. Hoberman

Chugging into theaters half a year late, James Cameron's $200 million mixture of hokiness and hokum is not the disaster it might have been. As the year's preeminent display of cinematic muscle flexing, *Titanic* is the sort of enterprise that would only be truly successful if it sank a studio or two.

The movie, whose running time is given by waggish publicists as two hours and 75 minutes, hits its own equivalent of the fatal iceberg almost immediately. To call the framing story "tacky" does an injustice to its torpor. Still, it's not precisely true that if you've seen *Titanic*'s trailer, you've seen the whole shebang—arrive at your leisure; there is an exciting 40-minute action flick struggling to escape from steerage.

Titanic opens by exhuming what could be the authentic remains of the actual ship two miles below the Atlantic surface. Cameron treats this disturbingly spooky sequence with bizarre irreverence. "Oops, somebody left the water running" one of the crew cracks as their submersible penetrates a Titanic state room. It's a key revelation, desecrating a taboo to express the film's hatred of the real. With defensive crassness, the trauma of the supposedly unsinkable ship is reduced to a treasure hunt for a fabulous jewel that never was. The paper money in the safe has long since been reduced to sludge, yet such is the power of fantasy, a sketch of a naked teenager—dated April 12, 1912—is miraculously preserved. Adding a bit of sci-fi to the mix, a 101-year-old lady ('30s star Gloria Stuart) recognizes her 17-year-old self when the portrait is shown on TV "Wasn't I a dish?" she cackles.

The ensuing flashback is a tiresome cliché parade, sweeping upstairs and down, from Titanic's fabulous Grand Salon to the boozy reel of a raucous third-class party. Smug billionaires cock a snoot at boisterous parvenus and bright-eyed immigrants, while, having won his passage in a dockside poker game, footloose American sketch artist Jack (earnestly callow Leonardo DiCaprio) boards in time to save the unhappy rich girl Rose (hearty, anxious Kate Winslet) from hurling herself overboard, despondent over her engagement to a smarmy tycoon named Cal (Billy Zane).

The tedium of *Titanic*'s first 90-plus minutes is relieved mainly by the gaffes programmed into Rose's character. This daring child smokes in public, cites the still-untranslated Sigmund Freud (naughtily linking Titanic itself to the "male preoccupation with size"), and has superb taste in modern art. (That her luggage includes Picasso's *Demoiselles d'Avignon,* a Degas, and a Monet is actually less unlikely than her enthusiasm for Jack's sketches of picturesque Montmartre.) Strolling on deck, Rose deploys her eagle eye and lightning calculation to announce the ship's insufficient lifeboats, an error for which engineer Thomas Andrews (Victor Garber) regularly offers her an apology.

In moments like these, *Titanic* suggests the movie Cecil B. DeMille might have made in 1928 were he not contemplating a more modern disaster flick about a giant dirigible. Not only is the dialogue as floridly stilted as the least literate silent-movie intertitles, but the correlation between the characters' personal lives and impending doom is absolute. Jack is preparing to sketch Rose in the nude. One iceberg approaches another—or something like that. (Cut to old Rose regaling the enrapt scavenger crew: "It was the most erotic moment of my life.") The earth really did move ...

Actually, the lovers are just kissing when the boat ruptures—although the reason it does is because the sailors on the bridge took their eyes off the ocean to watch the couple smooch! Astonishingly, the current Broadway musical is more coherent in explaining and wringing pathos from, What Went Wrong. (It's even witty in opening the second act with the clueless swells singing how strange it feels to be wearing pajamas in the Grand Salon.) But no show could equal the insane chase Cameron orchestrates through the furnaces and cargo hold of the stricken ship. "This is bad," Jack sagely observes. No, Jack, this is good—at last. Who wants to root against the ship going down?

As riots break out and passages flood neck-high, wicked Cal twirls his nonexistent mustache, Jack suffers the equivalent of being tied to the railroad tracks, and Rose rises to the occasion. The three principals leapfrog through the catastrophe—jumping on and off lifeboats, pausing to save a stray baby, bribe an officer, or accept another apology from Mr. Andrews. A sublime moment of mad love and gunfire in the near-submerged ballroom and the doomsday confusion of the finale are, of course, irresistible. The bridge floods, windows smash, people scream, a courageous priest drones on, and the lovers remember how they met. As the world turns upside down, old Rose offers a final *pensée*: "A woman's heart is a deep ocean of secrets."

Two thousand passengers and not one recognizable human being! With *Titanic* steaming along toward the mythopoeic moment when (as our Freudian Rose might note) the ship goes majestically perpendicular, you might amuse yourself wondering if the miracle of special effects will ever make it possible to replace the three leads with digital images of Diana, Charles, and Dodi. (The giddy *New Yorker* review that preceded the movie's release by nine days reported the Prince of Wales attending a London screening.)

That the sinking of the rigorously class-based society that was Titanic provided a ready-made metaphor for the World War wreck of the 19th-century European order was recognized by all subsequent movie versions, including the 1930 Anglo-German *Atlantic*, 1953 Hollywood *Titanic*, and 1958 British *A Night To Remember.* (The 1943 Nazi *Titanic,* notorious for the director's mid-production arrest and "suicide," was more narrowly conceived as spectacular, anti-British propaganda.)

So what is there for us to worry about? If the Asian markets crash, if we go to war with Iraq, if the Windsors abdicate, if Rupert Murdoch breaks his nose, this *Titanic* may take a similarly retroactive glow of prophetic vision. Otherwise, it's not even *The Poseidon Adventure* of 1997.

Also reviewed in:
NEW REPUBLIC, 1/5 & 12/98, p. 24, Stanley Kauffmann
NEW YORK TIMES, 12/19/97, p. E1, Janet Maslin
NEW YORKER, 12/15/97, p. 156, Anthony Lane
VARIETY, 11/3-9/97, p. 7, Todd McCarthy
WASHINGTON POST, 12/19/97, p. D1, Stephen Hunter
WASHINGTON POST, 12/19/97, Weekend/p. 50, Desson Howe

TO HAVE (OR NOT)

A Cinema Parallel release of a CLP and Dacia Films production. *Producer:* François Cuel and Georges Benayoun. *Director:* Laetitia Masson. *Screenplay (French with English subtitles):* Laetitia Masson. *Director of Photography:* Caroline Champetier. *Editor:* Yann Dedet. *Production Designer:* Arnaud de Moleron. *Costumes:* Caroline de Viviane. *Running time:* 100 minutes. *MPAA Rating:* Not Rated.

CAST: Sandrine Kiberlain (Alice); Arnaud Giovaninetti (Bruno); Roschdy Zem (Joseph); Laetitia Palermo (Hélène); Natalie Villeneuve (Christelle); Didier Flamand (Personnel Officer); Claire Denis (Alice's Mother).

LOS ANGELES TIMES, 6/6/97, Calendar/p. 10, Kevin Thomas

Young people in French films always seem so much more serious and reflective than their American counterparts, and that can be quite beguiling, as in the case of Laetitia Masson's low-key, pitch-perfect first feature, "To Have (or Not)," the second offering in the Grande 4-Plexes "Le Cinema Francais" series.

It's a small, intimate film, and Masson, who has been a camera assistant to Jacques Rivette on "La Belle Noiseuse," displays an easy, assured style and a flawless sense of proportion. She's gotten everything just right; you feel she has a sense of humor, although her film is not a comedy. "To Have (or Not) " also has a subtle glow that should come as no surprise, for her cinematographer Caroline Champetier also shot Jean-Luc Godard's beautiful "Helás pour Moi."

The centerpiece of her film is Alice, played by a striking new actress named Sandrine Kiberlain, who is tall, long-necked and has a strong profile. At one point, Alice, feeling weary, remarks that she looks "like a tired giraffe." Yet Kiberlain is as attractive as she is distinctive looking and has a vibrant presence, radiating strength but also vulnerability.

To top it off, she is an actress of depth and concentration. (In 1995, when this film was released in France, Kiberlain won a Cesar as the most promising young actress.)

When we meet Alice, she is just getting laid off from her fish-cannery job in a northern French town. Facing difficulty finding new work and bored with the bleak locale, she breaks off with her boyfriend and decides to try her luck in Lyon with the idea of figuring out how to pursue her dream of becoming a singer. Meanwhile, we also meet Bruno (Arnaud Giovaninetti, also a gifted actor), a darkly handsome, sensitive construction worker deeply hurt in a broken romance.

Inevitably but not immediately, Alice and Bruno cross paths at a small hotel managed by Bruno's pal Joseph (Roschdy Zem) where they are both staying temporarily. Masson shrewdly has allowed us to get to know them before they get to know each other. They are both most likable and intelligent young people aware of their limited opportunities, yet Alice has developed an ambitiousness that Bruno lacks. He, in fact, represents a blue-collar existence from which he has become determined to try to flee.

Alice's and Bruno's destinies unfold amid a big-city's workaday world, which Masson views with much warmth and compassion. "To Have (or Not)" is inviting and graceful, has a bracing dash of reality and leaves us eager to see what Masson and her actors do next.

NEW YORK POST, 4/19/97, p. 21, Larry Worth

Think "When Harry Met Sally"—minus Billy Crystal's cute mugging, Nora Ephron's perfect pickup lines, Rob Reiner's breezy direction and, of course, Meg Ryan's faked orgasm. The no-frills result would boil down to the likes of "To Have (Or Not)."

Neophyte director-writer Laetitia Masson provides a gritty, slice-of-life take on two down-and-outs in France who may or may not end up together.

Actually, the film's first third centers only on Alice, a delicate young woman who gets fired from a fish-packing factory in Boulogne-sur-Mer. When her romance falls apart thereafter, she packs her bags and moves to Lyon.

Lyon is also home to Bruno, a moody soccer player whose experience with amour is an ongoing disaster. He lives in a rundown hotel where, as luck would have it, Alice ultimately seeks shelter.

It's safe to say Alice and Bruno don't find love at first sight. But the journey they embark on proves consistently intriguing, and refreshingly realistic.

Part of that's because Masson feels no obligation to play by the rules. Her storytelling technique puts less emphasis on arty shots than blistering closeups. Meanwhile, the dialogue has a ring of spontaneity that makes one think she's done her homework on the mating dance.

The down side comes by way of a few too many narrative holes, some continuity troubles and overbearing musical selections.

Thankfully, the two leads are duly distracting. Physical appeal aside, Sandrine Kiberlain's range is impressive; she seems both sweet and on-the-edge without ever going over the top. And as Bruno, Arnaud Giovaninetti delivers an appropriately dark mix of confusion and pain.

Collectively, Masson and her stars make "To Have (Or Not)" the year's most engaging romance to date.

VILLAGE VOICE, 4/22/97, p. 82, Elisabeth Vincentelli

When Alice (the luminous Sandrine Kiberlain) is laid off from a fish-processing factory in the drab port town of Boulogne-sur-Mer, she decides to make a clean break and, leaving both her boyfriend and her apartment, moves to Lyons. A classic tale of restless youth, you might think, but *To Have (or Not)* is more subtle than that, and its quiet charm is worth enduring Anthology's rock-hard seats.

Director Laetitia Masson, making her feature debut, is not afraid to be unabashedly romantic in her portrayal of a prickly young woman. When Alice arrives in Lyons, the camera follows her very closely as she walks amid the lights of the city. She ends up at the Ideal Hotel and the first thing she sees is the sleeping Bruno (Arnaud Giovaninetti); it's Princess Charming discovering Sleeping Beauty. But in this case, Princess Charming is hoping to find a low-paying job and, maybe, a new life as well—she needs to be awakened just as much as the construction worker lying on the couch.

The strength of the movie is that though Masson never loses sight of the forces that shape the characters—Alice and Bruno are both working-class with no immediate means of escape—she never belittles them. Rather, *To Have (or Not)* is a snapshot full of humanity: Masson has affection for all of her characters and by dropping Alice at the Ideal Hotel, she places herself squarely in the poetic-realist tradition of 30s and '40s French films set in a hotel amid employees and guests. Bruno crashes at the hotel because he can't bear going home, while Alice had briefly considered moving to Paris but "got scared that there'd be no room for me." Laetitia Masson is romantic enough, generous enough, to offer both of them shelter in her film.

Also reviewed in:
NEW YORK TIMES, 4/18/97, p. C10, Stephen Holden
VARIETY, 10/9-15/95, p. 63, David Stratton

TOILERS AND THE WAYFARERS, THE

A Outsider Enterprises release of a Keith Froelich production. *Executive Producer:* Marc Huestis. *Producer:* Karen Manion, Ralf Schirg, and Keith Froelich. *Director:* Keith Froelich. *Screenplay (German and English with English subtitles):* Keith Froelich. *Director of Photography:* Jim Tittle. *Editor:* Rob Harriss and Keith Froelich. *Music:* Chan Poling. *Sound:* Matt Ehling. *Casting:* Jessica Nelson. *Set Decorator:* Merrill Stringer. *Costumes:* Sally Englehardt and Jeannie Millett. *Running time:* 75 minutes. *MPAA Rating:* Not Rated.

CAST: Matt Klemp (Dieter); Ralf Schirg (Udo); Andrew Woodhouse (Phillip); Jerome Samuelson (Dieter's Father); Joan Wheeler (Udo's Aunt); Michael Glen; Ralph Jacobus; Douglas Blackstone.

LOS ANGELES TIMES, 8/29/97, Calendar/p. 14, Kevin Thomas

Keith Froelich's "The Toilers and the Wayfarers" is an example of regional filmmaking at its most venturesome and rewarding. It takes us into the Minnesota German American town of New Ulm, an orderly community of much charming vintage architecture—but not exactly the most congenial place for a gay youth to come of age.

Froelich's key figure is Dieter (Matt Klemp), a handsome 16-year-old high school student with a strict father (Jerome Samuelson) who, like most people in the town, speaks German most of the time. Not ready to face up to his sexual orientation, Dieter is repulsed when his best friend, Phillip (Andrew Woodhouse), makes a pass at him. As Phillip regards Dieter as only reason for staying in New Ulm's ultraconservative atmosphere, he runs off to Minneapolis in reaction to Dieter's rejection.

Meanwhile, an ailing lonely woman (Joan Wheeler) in New Ulm has invited her nephew Udo (Ralf Schirg) to come live with her, a decision she regrets almost instantly. Udo, who looks to be somewhere in his early 20s, is a troubled, unreliable yet free spirit, a guy who'll drink a beer at 8 a.m. and shocks his aunt's starchy friends and neighbors with his uninhibited behavior.

With Phillip gone, Dieter quickly becomes friends with Udo, whose influence grows as Dieter's father's becomes increasingly disapproving of their friendship. Udo is apparently straight, or perhaps asexual, and he and Dieter seemingly remain no more than friends. If, however, they are lovers, this is no small issue because Dieter is a minor. Froelich seemingly is trying for a quality of uncertainty or ambiguity in this relationship that is beyond his reach as a first-time feature writer-director.

Dieter is a classic example of the obedient, dutiful youth who, when he rebels, does so in direct proportion to the oppression he has long endured. When his father's censure becomes unbearable, he takes off with Udo to Minneapolis, and they meet up with Phillip. But these young men have almost no means of survival. Udo is prepared to scrub floors, quite literally, before prostituting himself, but both Phillip and Dieter are swiftly caught up in the dangerous business of hustling on the street. That they are gay simply heightens their vulnerability.

The larger point Froelich makes quite well, even though it has been made before, is that teenagers fleeing miserable homes have so few viable alternatives to prostitution when they take off for the big city. Udo's presence adds further dimension in that he also represents the immigrant whose dream of America doesn't match up with the realities.

The narrative line and detailing tend to get fuzzy in "The Toilers," but Froelich holds attention because his people are easy to care about and because he's brought their distinctive world to life with considerable grace and passion. He gets a hefty assist from composer Chan Poling's stirring score and cinematographer Jim Tittle's splendid black-and-white images.

About half the film's dialogue is in German (translated via good English subtitles), and Froelich manages to elicit winning performances from his trio of stars, who move easily back and forth between English and German. "The Toilers" is romantic, even lyrical, in spirit, but it doesn't flinch before blunt realities. Not for a second.

NEW YORK POST, 9/19/97, p. 55, Bill Hoffmann

The "Toilers and the Wayfarers" is one of the most visually striking movies of the year. Jim Tittle's crisp black-and-white cinematography oozes with atmosphere, evoking wistful memories of Minnesota small-town life.

The striking visuals set the stage for an intriguing tale of two teens growing up gay and the turbulence it causes in their quiet German-American village.

The cast of unknowns is good, and Keith Froelich wields a steady directorial hand. While the film's appeal is limited mainly to gay audiences, cinematically, there's a lot for everybody to enjoy.

VILLAGE VOICE, 9/23/97, p. 90, Elliott Stein

Most of the dialogue in Keith Froelich's stale first film is in German. It's an American flick and that's about the extent of its originality. Froelich's gay coming-of-age movie is set largely in a conservative German American Midwestern community where two closeted teens, Dieter

(Matt Klemp) and Phillip (Andrew Woodhouse), lead stifled lives. Phil takes the plunge and runs off to Minneapolis, the small-town virgin becomes a city hustler. After getting spanked once too often by his petty führer father, Dieter leaves home to join his pal, comes out himself, and is soon plying the same shifty trade in order to survive. The inseparable friends, now lovers, are arbitrarily separated again—by the authorities, fuzz, unfeeling adults, you name it—but above all by an undercooked script.

Jim Tittle's excellent black-and-white cinematography is crisply nuanced, but Froelich's direction is strictly from film school. The few tepid skin scenes add no spark to this listless exercise in déjà vu.

Also reviewed in:
NEW YORK TIMES, 9/19/97, p. E20, Stephen Holden
VARIETY, 3/11-17/96, p. 48, Dennis Harvey

TOMORROW NEVER DIES

A United Artists release of Albert R. Broccoli's Eon Productions film. *Producer:* Michael G. Wilson and Barbara Broccoli. *Director:* Roger Spottiswoode. *Screenplay:* Bruce Feirstein. *Based on characters created by:* Ian Fleming. *Director of Photography:* Robert Elswit. *Editor:* Dominique Fortin and Michel Arcand. *Music:* David Arnold. *Music Editor:* Dina Eaton. *Sound:* Chris Munro and (music) Geoff Foster. *Sound Editor:* Martin Evans. *Casting:* Debbie McWilliams. *Production Designer:* Allen Cameron. *Art Director:* Stephen Scott, Giles Masters, Tony Reading, Jonathan Lee, and Ken Court. *Set Decorator:* Peter Young. *Special Effects:* Chris Corbould. *Costumes:* Lindy Hemming. *Make-up:* Norma Webb. *Stunt Coordinator:* Vic Armstrong. *Running time:* 119 minutes. *MPAA Rating:* PG-13.

CAST: Pierce Brosnan (James Bond); Jonathan Pryce (Elliot Carver); Michelle Yeoh (Wai Lin); Teri Hatcher (Paris Carver); Ricky Jay (Henry Gupta); Götz Otto (Stamper); Joe Don Baker (Wade); Vincent Schiavelli (Dr. Kaufman); Judi Dench (M); Desmond Llewelyn (Q); Samantha Bond (Moneypenny); Colin Salmon (Robinson); Geoffrey Palmer (Admiral Roebuck); Julian Fellowes (Minister of Defence); Terence Rigby (General Bukharin); Cecile Thomsen (Professor Inga Bergstrom); Nina Young (Tamara Steel); Daphne Deckers (PR Lady); Colin Stinton (Dr. Dave Greenwalt); Al Matthews (Master Sergeant 3); Mark Spalding (Stealth Boat Captain); Bruce Alexander (HMS Chester Captain); Anthony Green (HMS Chester Firing Officer); Christopher Bowen (HMS Devonshire Commander Richard Day); Andrew Hawkins (HMS Devonshire Lieutenant Commander Peter Hume); Dominic Shaun (HMS Devonshire Lieutenant Commander); Julian Rhind-Tutt (Yeoman); Gerard Butler (HMS Bedford Leading Seaman); Adam Barker (Sonar); Michael Byrne (HMS Bedford Admiral Kelly); Pip Torrens (HMS Bedford Captain); Hugh Bonneville (HMS Devonshire Air Warfare Officer); Jason Watkins (HMS Bedford Principal Warfare Officer); Eoin McCarthy (HMS Devonshire Yeoman); Brendan Coyle (HMS Bedford Leading Seaman); David Ashton (First Sea Lord); William Scott-Masson (Staff Officer 1); Laura Brattan (Staff Officer 2); Nadia Cameron (Beth Davidson); Liza Ross (Mary Golson); Hugo Napier (Jeff Hobbs); Rolf Saxon (Philip Jones); Vincent Wang (Mig Pilot); Philip Kwok (General Chang).

CHRISTIAN SCIENCE MONITOR, 12/22/97, p. 11, David Sterritt

He's everywhere! James Bond's handsome face and dashing image are being used to market everything from wristwatches to credit cards this season. The only question is whether they'll be able to sell the most expensive commodity of all: "Tomorrow Never Dies," his new wide-screen adventure.

It's unlikely the answer will turn out to be no. This is the 18th installment in the Bond saga to date, and while studio publicity should always be viewed with a mountain of skepticism, there's no reason to dispute United Artists' claim that his exploits constitute "the longest-running and most successful film franchise in cinema history."

The new picture is overflowing with the same high-energy heroics that have marked the whole series, so its success seems a foregone conclusion.

Pierce Brosnan makes his second appearance as the secret agent with a license to kill, squaring off against a timely new villain: media mogul Elliot Carver, an exaggerated cross between Rupert Murdoch and Ted Turner, with a hint of Big Brother during his most megalomaniacal moments.

Carver's immediate goal is to influence everyone on Earth through the power of his communications empire. Next on his list of ambitions is that old favorite, world domination, which he plans to achieve by goading Britain and China into a conflict awful enough to usher in a New World Order under his personal control.

As in many of the better Bond pictures, the bad guy is far more interesting and surprising than our all-too-familiar hero. Bond has enough tricks up his sleeve, though—a remote-control car, a cellular phone loaded with gizmos—to give the illusion that the series still has some novelty going for it.

Lending the freshest touch is his new henchperson, a Chinese woman as resourceful as 007 himself.

None of this means "Tomorrow Never Dies" is a particularly admirable accomplishment. Anybody on the lookout for uplifting values, or even civilized ones, will be put off by the very first scene—glorifying violence and military hardware with explosive glee—not to mention the opening credit sequence, adorned with the display of slinky women that has become one of the series' most predictable and exploitative features.

A few of the later scenes generate psychological or narrative thrust for a few minutes at a stretch, but most of the picture has all the warmth and humanity of Bond's robotic car. The filmmakers just push the right buttons and jump out of the way.

Brosnan makes a credible Bond, if not an exciting one, and Hong Kong action star Michelle Yeoh makes an impressive Hollywood debut as his sidekick. Best of all is Jonathan Pryce, who brings a chilling brand of charm to the power-crazed mogul. Joe Don Baker, stage magician Ricky Jay, and the entertainingly weird Vincent Schiavelli make the most of undistinguished parts.

Returning to their alphabetical roles are the inimitable Judi Dench as M and the unstoppable Desmond Llewelyn as Q, marking his 16th appearance in the ongoing 007 saga. Roger Spottiswoode directed.

LOS ANGELES TIMES, 12/19/97, Calendar/p. 2, Kenneth Turan

There's no advertising tag line on "Tomorrow Never Dies," the new James Bond film, but an accurate one might be "Never wake a sleepwalker. Especially one that's turning a nice profit."

As the latest film in a series that dates back to "Dr. No" in 1962, a run of 18 pictures that has earned an estimated $2.5 billion in admissions, "Tomorrow Never Dies" is very aware of its position as the latest incarnation of one of the most lucrative franchises in movie history.

This self-consciousness means more than licensing so many products—notice, please, the BMW car, the Dunhill cigarette lighter, the Omega watch and the Ericsson phone, to name a few—that you half expect Bond to appear covered with a sea of corporate logos like a successful stock car driver. It also mandates that considerable time and effort go toward keeping things the same as they've always been.

So even though the Bond song is now sung by Sheryl Crow instead of Shirley Bassey or Nancy Sinatra, change is not apparent or even allowed in most areas of "Tomorrow Never Dies." The film's producers have calculated, no doubt correctly, that in this chaotic world the Bond audience wants things unchanged as much as possible. Who would have thought that what started out as the racy exploits of a suave secret agent would turn into the movies' version of comfort food?

From its derivative title through the Bond-in-an-eyeball logo and the way-familiar Monty Norman theme, a lot of "Tomorrow Never, Dies" has a stodgy, been-there feeling. Agent 007 still prefers martinis shaken not stirred, still makes increasingly tired double-entendre remarks, still drives a car that's a weapons arsenal on wheels. And gadgetmeister Q (Desmond Llewelyn), though looking like he could have served Queen Victoria, is still handing out gizmos to our favorite undercover operative.

Speaking of undercover, "Tomorrow Never Dies" is so old-fashioned in the romantic area it just about wheezes. Bond's tryst with a Scandinavian professor of linguistics is shot in such a determinedly modest way it comes off as quaint more than sexy. And even the concept of blond Scandinavians as the epitome of sexuality has a comforting, retrograde feeling about it.

Veteran director Roger Spottiswoode has tried to pep the old warhorse up, but the combined inertia of all those pictures over 35 years proves hard to budge. The only place where an updating has been successful is in the addition of the lively Michelle Yeoh, one of Hong Kong's top female action stars, as a sidekick for Mr. B.

Though we've never met him before, even the power-mad villain, intent on nothing less than world domination, feels familiar. As written by Bruce Feirstein and played by Jonathan Pryce, Elliot Carver does have a different occupation than the evil types of the past: He's a media mogul, an exaggerated version of Robert Maxwell or Rupert Murdoch, who believes "words are the new weapons" in a battle to control the hearts and minds of every human being on Earth.

Completely devoted to his credo that "there's no news like bad news," Carver is willing to manufacture events to sell papers and TV time. He and henchman Gupta (Ricky Jay) use computer technology (the all-purpose boogeyman of the moment) to provoke a major diplomatic incident between Britain and China that Carver hopes he can massage into all-out war.

He reckons without the cool intelligence of M (Judi Dench) and the sang-froid of 007 (Pierce Brosnan, once again), who gets assigned to figure out what's up. Fortunately for our side, Carver's wife Paris (Teri Hatcher) is an old, uh, acquaintance of Bond, and its just a matter of time before he finds out enough to battle for the fate of civilization as we know it.

As noted, Yeoh as Wai Lin, a Chinese operative reluctant at first to join forces with "a decadent agent of a corrupt Western power," is a major asset, as are the elaborate stunts that are one of the series' reasons for being. Also breaking the iron-clad bonds of over-familiarity is the terribly amusing Vincent Schiavelii as Dr. Kaufman, who learns that the pride he takes in being the assassin's assassin comes before a fall.

"I am not interested in your stupid escapades," a fed-up superior says to Bond at one point, but the people who bankroll these films feel otherwise. When it says "James Bond Will Return" at the close of the credits, it's a promise you can take to the bank. Literally.

NEW YORK, 1/12/98, p. 48, David Denby

The first hour or so of *Tommorow Never Dies*, the new Bond, is laced with the usual satisfying sexual innuendo and insolent humor. Pierce Brosnan, of course, will never possess Sean Connery's aura of menace—Brosnan is Bond lite ("Bond ... *Jim* Bond")—but Jonathan Pryce is self-amused and amusing as a Rupert Murdoch-like media entrepreneur who foments a war between Britain and China. There is a fine BMW 750IL that can be driven by remote control (i.e., from the backseat), but much of the action—explosions, more explosions, men firing at one another with machine guns—is just as boring as the action in ten other big movies of the past year. You won't miss a thing should you leave well before the end. If more can't be found in Bond than this, I wouldn't object, in principle, to that tuxedo's being hung up in the closet for good.

NEW YORK POST, 12/19/97, p. 55, Michael Medved

Evaluating any 007 film requires separate consideration of each of the four B's Bond, Baddies, Booms and Babes.

When it comes to its Bond, "Tomorrow Never Dies" delivers the goods.

As he proved two years ago in "GoldenEye," Pierce Brosnan is a natural as 007: lithe, athletic, suave and hugely likable.

While lacking Connery's darker, more cynical edge, or Moore's self-mocking smugness, Brosnan projects just enough vulnerability to make his Bond seem more genuinely heroic than his largely superhuman predecessors.

As far as Baddies are concerned, this picture unequivocally excels, since Jonathan Pryce qualifies as one of the best Bond villains of them all.

He brings surprising subtlety and snaky charm to his role as a visionary, malevolent, meshugena media mogul.

A clever script (by humorist Bruce Feirstein) enormously assists this characterization, as Pryce attempts to provoke a war between Britain and China on which his global satellite network could scoop the world—or what's left of it.

In terms of Booms, those special effects and chase scenes that Bond boosters demand, the latest installment is solid if not spectacular.

The slam-bang opening sequence (at a terrorist arms bazaar somewhere in Russia) is exhilarating, but long chase scenes involving a cunningly customized BMW in Hamburg and a motorcycle (pursued by a helicopter) in Saigon (filmed in Bangkok) seem like Bondage as usual.

The climactic confrontation, aboard Pryce's high-tech "stealth" ship, goes on much too long with pointless, head-splitting excesses of automatic weapons and exploding fireballs.

It's in the Babes department that "Tomorrow" truly goes bust ... or rather, falls flat ... or whatever.

Michelle Yeoh plays a brilliant Red Chinese spy who works together with Bond—yet another sign of improving relations. She's a major Asian action star, and while her stunts seem impressively athletic, she generates no electricity at all with Brosnan.

Teri Hatcher is even worse, as the villain's pampered wife and (secretly) Bond's former lover. She looks conspicuously uncomfortable in her ill-chosen costumes, and performs with such dreary, mechanical lifelessness that there's no discernible difference in her acting when she's supposed to be dead.

Nevertheless, the old formula still works when all elements are shaken (not stirred) together, even though you end up almost feeling sorry for 007 for his disappointing love life in this film.

NEWSDAY, 12/12/97, Part II/p. B2, John Anderson

As soon as I knock back this Romanov martini and check the time on my Acropolis wristwatch, I'm going to use my Norse Explorer cell phone to call Birdbath Rent-a-Car and reserve a Bavalium motor car with retractable machine-gun turrets and hustle down to the mall. Because while tomorrow never dies, today is too short for all the shopping one must do.

Think retail. Leaving most product-placing Hollywood producers in their gold-flecked dust, the makers of the latest James Bond extravaganza—"Tomorrow Never Dies" with Pierce Brosnan as our randy secret agent—have accomplished the inevitable: filled their film with enough blatant endorsements to make the film itself incidental.

Forget the vague illogic of the Germanic villains, the mad media mogul (Jonathan Pryce) inciting global incineration or the belated wisdom in casting a beautiful Hong Kong action star (Michelle Yeoh) as a Bond girl. Watching "Tomorrow Never Dies" is like playing "Where's Waldo" with the brand-name merchandise. And if you think the movie's pre-Christmas release is a coincidence, well, you may believe that Teri Hatcher is a man.

Not, of course, that the film's audience is going to expect anything less, or, for that matter, anything more, than what director Roger Spottiswoode has delivered, which could be a spoof of "Austin Powers." Although Spottiswoode shoots Brosnan quite tightly—eliminating the need for the gracefully aging hunk to actually get on a moving vehicle—his Bond remains the invincible stud deluxe, trading innuendo with Miss Moneypenny (Samantha Bond), putting a twinkle in the eye of M (Judi Dench) and driving Q (Desmond Llewelyn) to distraction with his motor skills.

Bond's sense of humor is comprised of atrocious puns and carries a musky Rat Packiness about it (a brief interlude with the mournful-looking Vincent Schiavelli is hilarious, but could have been from another movie). His no-soil suits are a testament to modern dry cleaning, and if ever he's stuck in a high-rise building, Bond is surer to go up than down.

Creating international villainy in the post-Soviet world has presented Hollywood with something of a dilemma; responses have ranged from the creative to the laughable ("Air Force One," for instance) with the current favorites being secret-government functionaries, anyone with an accent and the press.

In "Tomorrow Never Dies," we begin at a "terrorist arms bazaar on the Russian border," where Bond has to elude a missile fired by his own hair-trigger Adm. Roebuck (Geoffrey Palmer, of the old "Butterflies" series) but it's a quick trip to the high-gloss world of Elliot Carver (Pryce), global communications czar and doomsday technician.

Carver's plan is to pit Britain against China and then become the hero by quelling hostilities himself. "Tomorrow" may be campy but its world view is right up to date: Carver's goal is the China market which is dictating our own foreign policy right now. Tarring the media is certainly popular, but Carver could just as easily be a knockoff of Michael Eisner as Rupert Murdoch.

Carver's wife is Paris, an old Bond flame played by Hatcher, who departs the picture early enough to make way for the near-legendary Michelle Yeoh, Hong Kong's premier female action star. Although Bond saves her bacon on several occasions—how else could it be?—Yeoh's Chinese agent Wai Lin may be the most capable and convincing Bond Girl ever.

Which shows at least some progress, as both Brosnan and Bond go wheezing across the millennia. Who'll be the next 007? Leonardo DiCaprio? David Schwimmer? Pauly Shore? The possibilities are endless, although the song remains overwhelmingly the same.

SIGHT AND SOUND, 2/98, p. 52, José Arroyo

The British Secret Service discover that an US-made nuclear encoder is up for sale at a terrorist arms bazaar on the Russian border. They decide to prevent the sale by bombing the site, but realise too late that the bombing will detonate nuclear missiles attached to a Russian aircraft. James Bond steals the plane with the missiles and averts nuclear disaster. The decoder, however, falls into the hands of Elliot Carver, a media mogul who can already topple governments but who will settle for nothing less than world domination.

In order to sell more newspapers and increase ratings, Carver has sunk a British ship and used the decoder to make it look like the work of the Chinese air force. He hopes to create an international incident between China and Britain which will eventually secure him exclusive broadcast rights to China. Bond has 48 hours to avert World War Three. He's sent to Hamburg, where Carver is launching a new service. Bond steals the decoder, meets Wai Lin, a female Chinese secret agent, and rekindles a romance with an old flame, Paris, who is now married to Carver. Carver orders the torture and murder of Bond and his own wife. Bond escapes and bumps into Wai Lin in Saigon where they are caught trying to infiltrate Carver's headquarters. Handcuffed together, they escape, pursued by Carver's evil henchman Stamper. Bond and Wai Lin track down Carver's 'stealth boat', avert his planned missile strike on China, and destroy the boat.

All Bond films have to confront the daunting challenge of simultaneously following the formula set down by previous Bond films, updating the conflicts, and making the production bigger and better than their predecessors. *Tomorrow Never Dies* is responsibly formulaic: there is the spectacular pre-credit sequence (actually disappointing here); the guns, girls and gadgets; the action set-pieces in exotic locations; and the explosive ending which resolves an international conflict. We see the last from several angles, while the explosive orgasm between Bond and the heroine is left to our imaginations. *Tomorrow* also benefits from the updating of Bond and his employer M's characters which took place in *GoldenEye*, and throws in Samantha Bond's shiny new Moneypenny. However, a smell of mothballs emanates from the rest of the characters and the plot.

There are elements of *Tomorrow* which remain stuck in yesteryear, specifically Bond's heyday, the 50s. In this anachronistic world, Britain is still a world power, Russia and China unknowable but deadly threats to the 'Free World'. In the newest Bond, the villains are still somehow associated with a totalitarian Germany: Doctor Kaufman, a torturer, seems to have been trained in some concentration camp. His disciple Stamper, the unfeeling Aryan executioner, evokes both Nazism and Stalinism and is obviously a clone of Robert Shaw's memorable villain in *From Russia with Love* (1963).

Even Carver, who is British (in keeping with the current Hollywood fashion for supervillains) is introduced to us in Hamburg. Indeed, Carver is a good illustration of the limited success *Tomorrow* has in representing the present. Carver is meant to evoke such powerful media moguls as Rupert Murdoch and Robert Maxwell, but his lines evoke various Bond-film baddies of the past, such as Blofeld or Goldfinger. The technology at his disposal is contemporary but his dreams and desires remain definitely Cold War. Strangest of all, he's plotting a nuclear war for ratings, seemingly unaware that this would probably eliminate most of his potential viewers.

The film-makers' attempts at making this Bond film bigger and better seem to have taken the form of merely cannibalising the series' history. As early as the credit sequence, the lack of imagination is evident: a model covered in gold refers to *Goldfinger* (1964), and a diamond-necklaced one references *Diamonds Are Forever* (1971) and so on. Carver's stealth boat is hidden in a Far Eastern archipelago very similar to the one where Scaramanga is hiding in *The Man with the Golden Gun* (1974). Even the set-pieces, although generally satisfactory, attempt to outdo those of the other Bonds by evoking as many of their elements as possible. So, while a fistfight in a moving train was the highlight of *From Russia with Love*, in *Tomorrow* Bond has to dodge bullets in the air, on land and under water and steer, or steer clear of, most types of fast-moving vehicle. But quantity is not enough. Though the film moves too fast for the audience to care much, it often fails to provide adequate motivation for action. (How did that Russian appear at the back of Bond's plane at the beginning? Why doesn't the windshield on Bond's BMW shatter earlier?) It is ironic that in a film which equates bigger with better, the most exhilarating moment is the relatively low-tech one where a fabulous Michelle Yeoh as spy Wai Lin shows off her martial-arts expertise.

Tomorrow is like a photocopy of a collage of previous Bonds: there's more, but it looks second-generation. This extends to the film's visuals. Part of the pleasure of the previous Bonds was that they revelled in design, the high production values providing images of dense texture and glossiness. But even that depth of surface is missing in *Tomorrow*. Each shot is full of things, busy, but this doesn't contribute to the film's overall look. The one memorable image is of Carver in front of an expanse of video monitors. It's a narratively interesting shot because it allows the film to show action in different places simultaneously, and visually interesting since it breaks up the frame into different spheres of action. But, as the filming of video monitors tends to do, even this contributes to the film feeling visually thin.

Tomorrow Never Dies has non-stop action, a dash of glamour, and some witty dialogue, adroitly performed by a very good cast bent on wringing out every nuance of every *double entendre*. The Bond formula is now so fixed that watching the films has become somewhat ritualistic. Unfortunately, in this case, this ritual evokes memories of a higher order of pleasure than the film is able to provide. However, the pleasures on offer in *Tomorrow,* if instantly forgettable, are also considerable. The film is better than the general run of action/spectacle movies, an indication of how little we have come to expect from the genre. But it is far from the premium Bond.

VILLAGE VOICE, 12/30/97, p. 72, Gary Dauphin

The 20th installment in the adventures of Agent 007 of Her Majesty's Secret Service, *Tomorrow Never Dies* is much what you'd expect of a 90s James Bond flick. Like the last Bond movie, *Goldeneye, Tomorrow* ditches a good deal of the series's loungey glamour for technofetishism. Several cuts above the inbred but campy nadir of the Roger Moore years and, of course, patently incapable of reproducing the pleasures of ur-Bond Sean Connery, *Tomorrow* is sure to become one of those fill-in Bond flicks that's just kind of there, one of the many impostors poor Miss Moneypenny has endured since Sean first swept her off her feet.

In case you've recently been released from a block of Arctic ice, James Bond (played by a game but wan Pierce Brosnan) saves the world, this time from a crazed media mogul (Jonathan Pryce) who at various times scans like Rupert Murdoch and at others like the late Robert Maxwell. This particular captain of nefarious industry plans to give his new cable news network a spectacular launch by precipitating a military confrontation between China and Great Britain (right, like the British are going to endanger their Asian trade relations). His only obstacle is a globe-trotting James armed with the usual mix of hard gadgets from M and moist women from around the globe.

The main object of *Tomorrow*'s technophilic attentions is a remote-controlled BMW (a canny touch which makes the inevitable *Tomorrow Never Dies* video game an integral part of the movie), while Hong Kong Queen of Action Michelle Yeoh plays this year's Bond girl. If anything in this film accurately reflects global realities it's probably the casting of Yeoh, but alas, despite her star power and fast feet, she's under-utilized, kept at arm's length from James in what seems a misplayed gesture of trans-Pacific film-industry amity. Yeoh's powerful elusiveness doesn't bring on a new era of gender equality in Bond flicks, but it does rekindle the old feeling that what our hero most needs is a woman who can kick his ass, and royally. That'd make for an interesting Bond flick, but like Miss Moneypenny you could wait a lifetime for Hollywood to provide it.

Also reviewed in:
NEW YORK TIMES, 12/19/97, p. E18, Janet Maslin

VARIETY, 12/15-21/97, p. 57, Todd McCarthy
WASHINGTON POST, 12/19/97, p. D1, Rita Kempley
WASHINGTON POST, 12/19/97, Weekend/p. 50, Desson Howe

TOUCH

A United Artists release of a Lumiere International presentation of a Lila Cazes production. *Producer:* Lila Cazès and Fida Attieh. *Director:* Paul Schrader. *Screenplay:* Paul Schrader. *Based on the novel by:* Elmore Leonard. *Director of Photography:* Ed Lachman. *Editor:* Cara Silverman. *Music:* David Grohl. *Music Editor:* Shari Jo Schwartz. *Sound:* Pawel Wdowczak and (music) Barrett Jones. *Sound Editor:* Steve Borne. *Casting:* Ronnie Yeskel and Mary Vernieu. *Production Designer:* David Wasco. *Art Director:* Daniel Bradford. *Set Decorator:* Sandy Reynolds Wasco. *Set Dresser:* McPherson O'Reilly Downs. *Costumes:* Julie Weiss. *Make-up:* David Atherton. *Make-up (Special Effects):* Todd Masters. *Stunt Coordinator:* Eric Bryson. *Running time:* 100 minutes. *MPAA Rating:* R.

CAST: LL Cool J (Himself); Gina Gershon (Debra Lusanne); Conchata Ferrell (Virginia Worrel); John Doe (Elwin Worrel); Christopher Walken (Bill Hill); Skeet Ulrich (Juvenal); Maria Celedonio (Alisha); Chris Hogan (Scruffy Staff Worker); Anthony Zerbe (Father Donahue); Bridget Fonda (Lynn Faulkner); William Newman (Court Clerk); Tom Arnold (August Murray); Breckin Meyer (Greg Czarnicki); Matt O'Toole (Bailiff); Richard Fancy (Judge); Tamlyn Tomita (Prosecutor); Don Novello (Father Navaroli); Mason Adams (Father Nestor); Richard Schiff (Jerry); O-Lan Jones (Bib Overalls); Brent Hinkley (Arnold); Paul Mazursky (Artie); Janeane Garofalo (Kathy Worthington); Diana Georger (Song Leader); Theo Greenly (Richie Baker); Lolita Davidovich (Antoinette Baker); Richard Coe (Roman Governor); Julie Condra (Shelly); John Gay (Palsied Man); Missy Hargraves (Waitress); Casey Gray (Stripper); Kate Williamson (Edith); Dennis Burkley (Hillbilly).

LOS ANGELES TIMES, 2/14/97, Calendar/p. 2, Kenneth Turan

"Being serious," a character in "Touch" gently suggests, "doesn't mean you have to be solemn," which also sums up the sensibility of this latest film based on a novel by Elmore Leonard, the master of the wised-up fable with a touch all his own.

With a protagonist named after the Roman master of satire, "Touch" is an easygoing sendup of both organized religion and our fascination with tabloid TV. And it comes from a most unlikely source, a filmmaker whose work as a writer ("Raging Bull," "The Last Temptation of Christ") and writer-director ("American Gigolo," "The Comfort of Strangers") has been noticeably more solemn.

But Paul Schrader is a self confessed Leonard fan, and he has been smart enough to stay out of the way of the kind of alive and lively dialogue and character-driven situations that made "Get Shorty," the last Leonard film, so successful. The result is a cynical, lightly amusing movie, one pleased smile from start to finish.

While "Touch" features Leonard's usual crew of genial grifters and infectious eccentrics, there is a difference here. At the center of things is the genuine article, a true saint named Juvenal whose touch can heal and whose presence in contemporary L.A. starts a frenzy among the less spiritually inclined.

First to get the easy money fever is Bill Hill (Christopher Walken), a nominally ordained minister who used to make a good living back in Georgia running services in front of the world's tallest illuminated cross. Temporarily relocated into the motor home and siding business, Bill is still looking for the main chance.

He thinks he's found it when he sees the mysterious Juvenal (Skeet Ulrich) restore the sight of a woman who has been blind from birth. But Juvenal proves hard to pin down, so Bill recruits Lynn Faulkner (an engaging Bridget Fonda), who once twirled a baton during his services, to infiltrate the Sacred Heart Rehabilitation Center and get on the young man's good side.

Also interested in Juvenal is August Murray, the founder of OUTRAGE (Organization Unifying Traditional Rites as God Expects) a conservative paramilitary religious organization (with uniforms modeled on the Ohio State Marching Band) that considers itself "the gray army of the Holy Ghost."

Deliciously played by Tom Arnold in the film's strongest performance, Murray has been following Juvenal's exploits since he was "the Miracle Worker of the Amazon." Likely to say things like, "Do they make a condom that protects the soul?," Murray is determined to use the young man to foster a nationwide religious revival.

The young man, who also bleeds from the wounds of the stigmata, of course, has ideas of his own, including wondering if Lynn has a boyfriend at the moment. Ulrich, who made his debut opposite Winona Ryder in last year's "Boys," is what's needed as a guileless, otherworldly presence who functions as the calm center of a growing comic hubbub.

And "Touch" takes care to surround Juvenal with all manner of sharpies, all nicely played by a smooth ensemble cast. There's Janeane Garofalo as a skeptical reporter, Gina Gershon as a TV talk-show host who claims "controversy is my oxygen," Lolita Davidovich as a topless dancer and even Paul Mazursky as a music producer who knows the Pope sold 2.5 million units only because "he toured."

Writer-director Schrader has thoughtfully parceled out the film's irresistible language to all concerned and kept the tone of the proceedings modulated rather than frenetic. "Touch" is not one of those movies that hurtles toward a slam-bang climax. A bemused gloss on the varieties of religious experience, it knows enough to take its time, making sure we enjoy ourselves along the way.

NEW YORK POST, 2/14/97, p. 50, Michael Medved

In "Touch," the riveting young actor Skeet Ulrich is asked to play a mysterious monk who simultaneously resembles Francis of Assisi and the late Kurt Cobain; a grunge-generation stigmatic (and suspected saint) who emerges from the Amazon rain forest with an inexplicable power to heal.

It's a ridiculous role that might have humiliated a lesser talent, but not even charisma and conviction from Ulrich (who made strong impressions previously with supporting parts in "Boys," "Scream" and "Albino Alligator") can save this disjointed, disappointing movie.

In fact, the otherworldly, yearning quality he displays on screen might actually reflect the actor's sincere, understandable longing to be anywhere else but trapped in this annoying situation. Based on Elmore Leonard's weird, witty 1987 novel, "Touch" centers on Juvenal, an emaciated idealist who returns from assignment in the jungles of Brazil to work with alcoholic patients at a Catholic rehab center in Los Angeles.

Eventually, his periodically punctured palms, as well as his stunning, hands-on cures for blindness and cancer, inspire a fierce struggle between competing eccentrics.

Tom Arnold plays the uniformed head of a paramilitary Catholic fringe group that wants to force the Church back to traditional ways, while the badly miscast Christopher Walken is a fallen evangelist who hopes to use Juvenal as his ticket back to big money and the religious big time.

Bridget Fonda is Walken's protege—and former baton twirler in his church—who is now a Hollywood record promoter asked to get close to Juvenal and probe his secrets. Janeane Garofalo is an initially skeptical reporter (and later an adoring ghostwriter) assigned to the wonder-working Wunderkind, while Gina Gershon is a nasty TV talk host who wants to expose him with her audience.

All of the actors seem to try hard (Arnold, in particular, tries much too hard), but each seems to be operating in a totally different movie. Intimate scenes work best, showing the growing romantic chemistry between Ulrich and Fonda, while the film is at its worst in frantically unfunny efforts at comedy and social commentary aimed at easy targets—like TV talk shows.

Writer/director Paul Schrader, previously noted for brooding, moody, muddled movie meditations, shapes an ungainly, unfocused effort that produces no more laughs than his somber previous efforts such as "Mishima," "The Comfort of Strangers," "Light of Day" or "Light Sleeper."

The satire remains so soggy and inept that you begin to understand why most of the characters mispronounce the protagonist's name as "Juvenile."

NEWSDAY, 2/14/97, Part II/p. B11, John Anderson

Team up two sublimely cynical romantics like Elmore Leonard and Paul Schrader and the result is a sardonic morality play like "Touch," a movie not quite as clever as it thinks it is, but perhaps more on target than it wants to be.

Schrader, still best known for having written the screenplay for "Taxi Driver," is somewhat obsessive about the spirituality of social detritus. And working off Leonard's novel of the same name, "Touch" puts a considerable collection of quasi-human wreckage (or perhaps human quasi-wreckage) at his disposal.

They include Bill Hill (Christopher Walken), a bankrupt minister of the "Uni-Faith" Church currently working in recreational vehicles and vinyl siding; August Murray (Tom Arnold), leader of the reactionary Catholic group Outrage, whose members are pro-Latin and anti-guitar mass; Lynn Faulkner (Bridget Fonda), onetime ecclesiastical baton twirler and pop record promoter; her scabrous boss, Artie (Paul Mazursky), and a self-promoting reporter named Kathy Worthington (Janeane Garofalo).

Oh yes, and Juvenal (Skeet Ulrich), presumably named for the onetime bishop of Jerusalem but more likely for the Roman satirist, whose gift of healing is viewed by the cast of characters above not as an avenue to God, but to big bucks.

The rejection of the blessed has been a plot convention for everyone from St. John to Robert Heinlein, but the rabble at least *accepted* the concept of divinity before they turned ugly. In "Touch" they start ugly and stay ugly (ugly and funny, that is) while both Leonard and Schrader create an ultra-cynical scenario in which religious miracles are still interesting, but only for their profit potential.

The defining scene takes place in a church, as Juvenal, who has spent several years in the Brazilian jungles, places his hands upon the bald head of a boy with cancer. As blood streams from the stigmata wounds on Juvenal's hands, August exhorts his followers to hand out pamphlets; a news photographer shoots away. When the boy is diagnosed cancer-free, Bill uses the incident to get coverage from Kathy (who gets a lucrative book deal), and pitch a Juvenal interview to a TV station (whose producer bites when she finds out the kid's mother, played by Lolita Davidovitch, is also a topless dancer). The interviewer, a venomous harpie played by Gina Gershon, is just one more leech in a long line of bloodsuckers.

"Touch" percolates with pop music and pastel sets, but the film would have been a lot more dynamic with a less anemic twosome than Ulrich and Fonda playing the lovestruck twosome. But Walken is particularly good in a rare comic role, Davidovitch is her usually solid self and Schrader's direction is controlled and insightful. The movie is less than a miracle, but it made a believer out of me.

SIGHT AND SOUND, 6/98, p. 58, Philip Kemp

Bill Hill, former evangelist turned mobile home salesman, sees a young ex-Franciscan monk called Juvenal seemingly restore a blind woman's sight. Eager to find out more, he persuades his friend Lynn Faulkner (once a cheerleader in his church, but now a music promoter) to feign alcoholism and check into the rehab centre where Juvenal works. Sceptical at first, Lynn is convinced by Juvenal's simplicity and sincerity. After he heals an acute alcoholic, she sees bleeding stigmata on his body.

Bill hopes to cash in on Juvenal's gift. But Juvenal is also coveted by August Murray, leader of a splinter group of ultra-conservative Catholics, who sees the 'miracle worker' as a potential source of publicity for his movement. At the dedication of a new church for August's sect, Juvenal heals a young cancer sufferer, Richie Baker, brought along by August for miracle purposes. The healing is widely reported. Lynn, feeling protective of Juvenal, keeps him away from reporters, and the two become lovers. This gets into the papers as well, infuriating August.

Presenting himself as Juvenal's manager, Bill does a lucrative deal with predatory chat-show hostess Debra Lusanne. When Juvenal tries to heal a palsy sufferer nothing happens, and he believes the gift has left him. August breaks into Lynn's flat with a gun planning to kill her, but Juvenal pushes him off the balcony. On her show, Debra accuses Juvenal of hypocrisy and venality prompting Lynn's furious intervention. Debra has August wheeled on encased in plaster. Juvenal, trying to ask August's forgiveness, heals him and he rises from his wheelchair, causing a public sensation. Juvenal and Lynn drive off together towards the mid-west.

Touch is perhaps Elmore Leonard's most deeply felt novel, and certainly his least expected. Centred around a man who may be a miracle worker and is probably a saint, it has little of the flip humour and gleefully convoluted plotting of *Get Shorty* the source of the best Leonard screen adaptation to date, *Jackie Brown* notwithstanding. But while Leonard treats his miraculous healer Juvenal wholly seriously, *Touch* is still very much a comedy. And whatever Paul Schrader's qualities as screenwriter and director, few would describe him as a master of comedy.

Schrader's sole attempt at a comedy till now was the little seen *Witch Hunt,* a poorly mixed blend of fantasy, whodunit and political satire. *Touch* is nowhere near as broken backed, but it still suffers from a crucial uncertainty of tone that leaves several of his actors, Christopher Walken in particular, floundering uneasily where Barry Sonnenfeld and his cast in *Get Shorty,* hit the right note from the off and never looked back, *Touch* sputters and stalls as it tries to get up to speed. Often it seems that the story hasn't been fully rethought in cinematic terms, or that Schrader's admiration for Leonard has made him stay too faithful to the original. The loose-limbed structure that a novel can get away with looks diffuse and unfocused on screen.

Part of the problem may be geographic. Leonard's novel is very specifically located in his hometown of Detroit, not the most lovable of cities but one with a flavour all its own. Schrader's film deracinates the action, relocating it for no good reason to LA, famously skewered by another fine American novelist, Alison Lurie, as "the Nowhere City".

Where the film works best—as might be expected from a director known for his tormented ambivalence about religion—is in dealing with the two characters positioned at the polar opposites of faith: the open minded, all accepting Juvenal and the ferociously, bigoted August. Skeet Ulrich does remarkably well with one of the toughest acting assignments going—playing someone genuinely good without a hint of sickliness. Meanwhile, Tom Arnold brings out all the desperate pathos in August, strutting about in a richly inane uniform that crosses Francoist militia with Boy Scout. They play beautifully off each other: Juvenal, innocent but not naive, recognises just what a clown August is but doesn't reject or condemn him for it. August, used to encountering either fellow-bigotry or scornful hostility finds Juvenal's attitude utterly incomprehensible, squinting at him with baffled suspicion.

The hot-gospelling style offers a barn door target for mockery, and the film can't resist a few easy shots, like Bill Hill's wistful memories of owning "the world's largest illuminated cross, with 'Jesus Saves' in blue neon". But the best of the burnout mines a more subtle vein of absurdity, as when Bridget Fonda's Lynn, T-shirt in hand by the washing machine, pauses to ask worriedly "Do you think it's all right stigmata blood going in the wash?" Here and elsewhere, *Touch* has its pleasures. Gina Gershon's barracuda of a chat-show hostess is spot on, though Janeane Garofalo as the dirt-digging reporter is largely wasted. But the overall impression is that Schrader, for all his admiration of Leonard, can't quite get on his wavelength. His forthcoming adaptation of *Affliction* by Russell Banks (author of *The Sweet Hereafter*) should find him on surer ground.

TIME, 2/24/97, p. 67, Richard Schickel

The cliché used to be that if Christ came back to earth in modern times, he would be either actively scorned or passively ignored by a population lost to materialism. That, of course, was before the talk shows and tabloids began directing the spiritual lives of simple, yearning souls. Nowadays, in his innocence, a Christ figure would be ripe for cheezoid exploitation.

Unless he has adapted to the new era, as has the one who calls himself Juvenal in writer-director Paul Schrader's sly and nicely understated adaptation of novelist Elmore Leonard's *Touch.* Played by Skeet Ulrich, he has done time in the wilderness, suffers the stigmata and can cure the incurable by the laying on of hands. Otherwise, though, he's a cool dude. He likes girls, shows no particular interest in spreading any sort of gospel and turns a politely bemused face toward the hustlers and lowlifes who swarm around when word of his preternatural healing gifts starts to drift out of the rehab center where he has taken refuge.

Among his would-be exploiters are a sometime revivalist (Christopher Walken), now reduced to selling used RVs and aluminum siding; a Catholic fundamentalist (Tom Arnold), prepared to enforce a return to the Latin Mass, at gunpoint if necessary; a dubious record promoter (Paul Mazursky), worried that Juvenal won't tour as the Pope does; a star biographer Janeane

Garofalo), looking for the inside gossip; and, of course, a TV host (Gina Gershon), half smarm, half snarl.

They're all good characters, well cast and well played, and the fun of the movie is watching the scuzzballs unravel when they are confronted by serene, possibly divine, innocence. In Juvenal's case this quality is gently armored by Bridget Fonda's sweetly sexy representation of common American sense and decency. She is supposed to seduce Juvenal on behalf of the siding salesman, but she knows a good man when she sees one, in part because they so rarely traverse the moral flatlands she has been obliged to inhabit. She also knows she had better treasure and protect this one without dithering too long over the matter. Goodness is ever an endangered species—and evil is ever a dangerous one.

Striving for drollness, Schrader sometimes achieves a distancing effect instead. Neither the comedy nor the melodrama is quite as compelling as it might be. But *Touch* was never meant to be *Get Shorty*. It is rather a wintry meditation on the difficulties of sustaining authentic faith in the age of telemortality. For that work, its cynicism, wry but not weary, is very effective.

VILLAGE VOICE, 2/25/97, p. 70, Amy Taubin

If Christ were resurrected in the '90s, he'd work in a rehab center, heal a stripper's leukemic kid, fall in love with a rock promo-girl and narrowly escape being crucified on a TV talk show. He also might have the velvety-brown eyes, sleek facial hair, and unflappable demeanor of Skeet Ulrich.

Faithfully adapted from Elmore Leonard's deadpan comic novel, Paul Schrader's *Touch* is a small, smart, quite likable movie graced by vivid performances, witty dialogue, and a low-key r&b score by Dave Grohl that gives a little bounce to the casually funky pastel mise-en-scène. An antidote to *The People vs. Larry Flynt, Touch* zeros in on the vulgarity of white Christian middle America without either pumping it up or glossing it over. Understated and uneventful, it will no doubt fare better at the video stores than the multiplexes. (And why fault a movie for knowing its place?)

Touch revolves around the relatively passive Juvenal (Ulrich), a former monk who has the power of healing through his embrace. On these occasions, blood oozes from five wounds on his body that correspond to Christ's wounds on the cross. Juvie doesn't bother analyzing his power. "If my mind's doing it, it's psychosomatic; if it's God, it's supernatural," the stigmatist explains with a shrug.

His powers prove more exciting to various con artists and religious fanatics, among them Bill Hill (Christopher Walken), a former fundamentalist turned RV salesman. Bill thinks Juvie's just what's needed to give his bankrupt Uni-Faith ministry a new lease on life. He sends Lynn (Bridget Fonda), a former Uni-Faith baton twirler, to find out whether Juvie is the real thing. Lynn and Juvie fall in love at first sight, getting so wrapped up in each other that they're barely aware of all the hustlers closing in.

As Juvie, Ulrich is amusingly down-to-earth and nice to look at (despite an orange-toned make-up job that foils any possibility of his looking lit up from within), but lacks the necessary charisma. (He's not quite a movie star, no less a God.) Nor does Leonard's dialogue fall trippingly from his tongue; too often, he sounds more like an actor than a person.

Faring considerably better are Fonda and Walken and, in smaller parts, Janeane Garofalo, Paul Mazursky, and Lolita Davidovich. Garbed in an immaculate, off-white acetate suit accessorized with a king-size "Thank you Jesus" tie bar, Walken looks more animated than he has in years, relishing the opportunity to display his Broadway hoofer's physical-comedy skills and an agile vocal delivery that turns falsetto at the least provocation. Where Walken makes light of his flamboyance, Fonda gives panache to her ordinary domestic activities. "Do you think it's all right, " she inquires, holding up Juvie's red-stained shirt, "stigmatic blood going in the wash?"

Also reviewed in:
NATION, 3/17/97, p. 44, Stuart Klawans
NEW YORK TIMES, 2/14/97, p. C5, Janet Maslin
VARIETY, 2/10-16/97, p. 63, Todd McCarthy
WASHINGTON POST, 2/14/97, Weekend/p. 68, Desson Howe

TRAVELLER

An October Films release of a Banner Entertainment production. *Executive Producer:* Robert Mickelson and Rick King. *Producer:* Bill Paxton, Brian Swardstrom, Mickey Liddell, and David Blocker. *Director:* Jack Green. *Screenplay:* Jim McGlynn. *Director of Photography:* Jack Green (uncredited). *Editor:* Michael Ruscio. *Music:* Andy Paley. *Music Editor:* Jonathan Karp. *Choreographer:* Adam Shankman. *Sound:* Carl Rudisill and (music) Mark Linett. Sound Editor: Christopher Sheldon. *Casting:* Joseph Middleton. *Production Designer:* Michael Helmy. *Art Director:* Skye Bailey. *Set Decorator:* Steve Davis. *Costumes:* Douglas Hall. *Make-up:* Rudolph R. Eavey III. *Special Effects Make-up:* Vincent Guastini. *Stunt Coordinator:* Jim Vickers. *Running time:* 100 minutes. *MPAA Rating:* R.

CAST: Bill Paxton (Bokky); Mark Wahlberg (Pat O'Hara); Julianna Margulies (Jean); James Gammon (Double D); Luke Askew (Boss Jack); Nikki Deloach (Kate); Danielle Wiener (Shane); Michael Shaner (Lip); Vincent Chase (Bimbo); Andrew Porter (Pincher); Jean Howard (Bokky's Grandmother); Rance Howard (Farmer); Robert Peters (Farmer's Son); Jo Ann Pflug (Boss Jack's Wife); Scott Schultz (Snipe); John Bennes (Hearse Driver); Barbara Rowan (Pregnant Wife); Trenton McDevitt (Pregnant Wife's Husband); Moses Gibson (Porter); Bonnie Cook (Cashier); John Paxton (Financial Planner); Jim Flowers (Bar Regular #1); Frederick E. Dann (Bar Regular #2); Walter Cobb (Priest); Joanne Pankow (Elderly Woman); Chuck Kinlaw (Elderly Woman's Son); Blaque Flower (Gas Station Owner); Ted Manson (First Trailer Buyer); Kerry Maher (Bartender); John Esterbrook (Trailer Salesman); Mary K. Heneghan (Traveller Camp Dancer).

LOS ANGELES TIMES, 4/25/97, Calendar/p. 11, John Anderson

[The following review by John Anderson appeared in a slightly different form in **NEWSDAY, 4/18/97, Part II/p. B11.]**

It's not a problem, precisely, but in order to get the full drift of "Traveller"—the directorial debut of cinematographer Jack Green ("Twister," "Unforgiven")—you need a little background.

The title refers to the "gypsies" of the British Isles (in Ireland they're commonly called Tinkers) who make their living running con games, selling dubious goods and generally holding to the proposition that life is a matter of them vs. us (not that that last quality makes them particularly unique). And there apparently are, like the better-known Romany Gypsies, Celtic "tribes" in the United States, living an outlaw existence reliant on guile and a casual regard for mainstream morality.

Their ethnic and ethical insularity is both the intriguing aspect of "Traveller" and the flaw in its story. Having brought his dead father back to the tribe for burial, Pat O'Hara (Mark Wahlberg) expects to stay: To be a Traveller, his father told him, was his birthright. Because Dad left the tribe to marry an outsider, however, he was considered a pariah. And that, it is immediately clear to Pat, is his real inheritance.

But Bokky (Bill Paxton), a purveyor of counterfeit driveway sealant and the fair-haired boy of tribal chief Boss Jack (Luke Askew), takes Pat under his wing, introduces him to the scams of the Traveller (the phony sealer scam, the confuse-the-cashier-at-the-diner con) and tries to bring him up to speed.

Paxton, when not chasing or being chased by tornadoes, is really quite a winning performer, and as Bokky he keeps the film on the ground. James Gammon, a terrific character actor, is a gnarled and comic Double D, the non-Traveller scam artist who gets Bokky and Pat into a really big sting. And it's nice to see "ER's" Julianna Margulies out of hospital fatigues and in the role of single mother/bartender Jean, who lures Bokky toward the fate of Pat's father—love at the expense of outcast status.

But with Pat, Wahlberg has the least gratifying role and one that's somewhat problematic. He's on thin ice, yet he chases Boss Jack's daughter Kate (Nikki DeLoach) almost immediately. (For her part, Kate talks about Traveller-hood as if Pat were trying to become an Eagle Scout). Bokky's not all that crazy about Pat either, but rather than make an extra effort to be bad, Pat keeps showing what little talent he has for small-time crime. (Does that make him good?). And he questions the status quo (i.e., the fact that Jack gets a cut of all ill-gotten gains), displaying a flair for the impolitic that will never get him on the tribal fast track.

So it's a mixed bag. The cast is really fine, but the script requires a lot of hard swallowing. The story moves along briskly and colorfully, but gets further and further from the intimate atmosphere that makes it so initially appealing.

The romance of the Travellers provides an intriguing background, although the group's ethos is violated at every turn. And the sound track—featuring Jimmie Dale Gilmore, Lou Ann Barton, Al Green, and Little Charlie and the Nightcats—is terrific, even if it has very little to do with the Irish or Gypsies. So it's settled: I had a good time. I'm just asking myself why.

NEW YORK POST, 4/18/97, p. 44, Thelma Adams

The bagpipes, the granny-spouting homespun wisdom, the country dances performed with more enthusiasm than skill, the quaint little corner of Americana overlooked by Hollywood: this used to be the bread and butter of American independent films like "Belizaire the Cajun" and "Heartland."

Jack Green, Clint Eastwood's cinematographer, steps out from under Dirty Harry's shadow to direct a drama that opens with the rough, loose-limbed, easy feeling of those low-budget movies. Randy Travis sings "King of the Road" while Bokky (Bill Paxton) drives along in his truck, scamming people for 20 bucks here, 8,000 there.

Bokky's a "Traveller," an Irish-American grifter who wanders the North Carolina roadways, ripping off home-owners and living out of banged-up trailers and cheap motels. He's part of a Traveller's collective. The community has its own leaders, music, dances, music, patois, arranged marriages and a history that goes back to itinerant scam artists and horse traders on the Emerald Isle.

After Bokky meets three strangers, he's no longer king of the road. Pat (Mark Wahlberg) returns to Carolina to bury his father, a Traveller who broke ranks to marry an outsider and apprentices himself to Bokky. Grisly Double D (the single-malt-whiskey-voiced James Gammon) leads the pair into a big score against a gang of Turkish con-artists.

Of course, there's no such thing as one last score. Events might not have gotten so hairy if Bokky hadn't lost his heart to outsider Jean (Julianna Margulies), a single mother with a critically ill daughter. Yes, she needs big bucks for an emergency operation.

Screenwriter Jim McGlynn gleefully roasts these old plot chestnuts, tossing them with pungent cultural details that untimely don't mean much. What starts out as a sprightly movie about a little-known community snowballs into a violent, "Straw Dogs" climax for which the workmanlike Green has not prepared us.

Paxton last seen as the squeaky-clean lead of "Twister," underplays nicely here. Not so the edgy Wahlberg, who's one step short of his hunky killer in "Fear" without a clear motivating drive.

The best scenes pair Paxton and "E.R"'s sexy Margulies. Their attraction and mutual distrust peak when Bokky explains how to con during pillow talk: "Look 'em in the eye and lie to yourself." This unsettling exchange is more interesting than the climax where a gun is held to the eye socket of a pretty little deaf girl.

SIGHT AND SOUND, 2/98, p. 53, Charlotte O'Sullivan

Bokky is a con-man, making money for the travellers' community he belongs to (which is based in the backwoods of the Southern US). Young Pat O'Hara wants to join the travellers, but their leader, Boss Jack, doesn't trust him because his traveller father "married out". Bokky takes Pat out on the road and the latter proves a quick learner of Bokky's confidence tricks. One of their victims is Jean, a barmaid. However, when Bokky learns that Jean has lost her job as a result of his scam, he feels both guilt and desire, and returns the money. The attraction proves mutual, but Pat disapproves because she's an "outsider".

Jean tells Bokky that she needs money to pay for an operation for her daughter, Shane. As a result, Bokky agrees to get involved in one of fellow traveller and con-man Double D's "big" scams. The target is a group of Turkish travellers, led by Joe Bimbo, and the scam involves forged money. Bluff is followed by counter-bluff and the three men end up with a suitcase of real money. The 'Turks' take their revenge by killing Double D. They then follow Bokky and Pat to Jean's house where they beat the men and threaten to rape Jean. Just as Bokky's about to be shot, Boss Jack appears and kills the Turks. Pat and Boss lack drive home together; Bokky and his new family take another road.

Traveller is more and less of a film than it seems. Hero Bokky certainly wouldn't look out of place in an old-fashioned Western as the uncivilised but good-hearted loner, indifferent to 'big visions'. He's dishonest, but it's all in a good cause (he's providing money for his community). Meanwhile, his relationships with Pat (who has just lost a father) and patriarch Boss Jack have a familiar ring. Stretching Howard Hawks' 1947 film *Red River's* Oedipal struggles over three generations, *Traveller* positions Bokky as the liberal surrogate son to ruthless Boss Jack, while he's also the surrogate-father to the initially rebellious but increasingly hard-line Pat.

First-time director Jack Green and writer Jim McGlynn add something new to the formula. While maverick cowboys tend to be associated with nature, Boss Jack appears to be the only male living on the land. Bokky boasts to Pat of discovering "virgin territory" and "rich pickings" in his travels. In fact, the Carolina hicks prove wise to his tricks, and Bokky is forced into the towns which aren't shiny, modern spaces. As we keep being reminded, we're in an economic depression. Bokky's world is out of time, with no way forward to civilisation, no way back to nature. The pioneer spirit has nowhere to go.

Such a vision lends a pleasantly dispirited energy to the proceedings and all the fun is in the details. Bokky grins along to an old Clint Eastwood movie *(Every Which Way But Loose)* on the television, an in joke reminder that Jack Green was cinematographer on *Unforgiven* and *The Bridges of Madison County*. Green's debut may be lovingly shot in bleached greys and oppressive greens, but he went there already in the grimy films he made with Clint. Once again, there is no virgin territory.

For a while, Bill Paxton does much to enhance the film's moral complexity. He possesses a blandness of almost religious intensity, but here it works because it makes Bokky's sporadic sexual aggression all the more disturbing. However, as Paxton's role swells to an ever-more-virtuous size (perhaps because he's the producer?) *Traveller* falls apart. Mark Wahlberg is left with little to do and Julianna Margulies (though full of beautiful, rueful smiles) struggles to hold her own. It gets worse. How do we discover Bokky has lost a wife and child? As the Celtic pipes pipe sweetly, we get a shot of the wife's grave and then the camera lurches towards another, emblazoned with the words 'Baby Bridget'. If this film were a song, Dolly Parton would sing it. Sentiment and prejudice often go hand in hand and so it is here. Jean hears about the plan to cheat Turkish traveller Bimbo and tells Bokky she doesn't want him cheating any more people. "This guy ain't people" he growls. This might have been intended as tongue-in cheek machismo, all part of a Mamet-like dissection of the games con-men play, but it doesn't feel like it.

Traveller wants us to believe it's tackling a difficult question of what makes an American: loyalty to private faith or public duty? Pat and Boss represent loyalty to faith—the travellers' insular world in which blood ties are all and big daddy's laws come first. Bokky and lean represent another route, a world in which a man abides by the laws of the wider community but can also choose his own wife. The final tone is quietly triumphant: where else but America could both groups find a home? The "rag-headed Turks" are presumably not considered human, so they don't deserve a home. Far from being iconoclastic, then, *Traveller* ends up preaching the most reactionary and offensive of sermons. *Traveller* probably won't do much business. It's a small film and proclaims itself as such. But in this case, small is ugly.

VILLAGE VOICE, 4/22/97, p. 77, Amy Taubin

Though Bill Paxton gave a memorable performance in *One False Move,* he mostly cruises on charm. That's certainly the case in *Traveller,* where he's meant to be an Irish American gypsy con man who wants out of the stifling Tinker society in which he's been raised. Directed by Jack Green, the movie lacks any sense of subcultural specificity, though it has a superabundant country music score. Tough, sexy, and looking more than ever like a fireplug, Mark Wahlberg has the thankless job of playing sidekick to a star whose attention is inexplicably elsewhere. Wahlberg rises to the non-occasion. He's the best thing in the movie.

Also reviewed in:
NEW REPUBLIC, 5/19/97, p. 26, Stanley Kauffmann
NEW YORK TIMES, 4/18/97, p. C3, Janet Maslin
VARIETY, 3/17-23/97, p. 53, Emanuel Levy
WASHINGTON POST, 5/2/97, Weekend/p. 42, Richard Harrington

TRIAL AND ERROR

A New Line Cinema release of a Larger Than Life production. *Executive Producer:* Mary Parent and Allen Alsobrook. *Producer:* Gary Ross and Jonathan Lynn. *Director:* Jonathan Lynn. *Screenplay:* Sara Bernstein and Gregory Bernstein. *Story:* Sara Bernstein, Gregory Bernstein, and Cliff Gardner. *Director of Photography:* Gabriel Beristain. *Editor:* Tony Lombardo. *Music:* Phil Marshall. *Music Editor:* Tom Carlson. *Sound:* Robert Anderson, Jr. and (music) Steve Krause. *Sound Editor:* Bruce Stambler and Kim Secrist. *Casting:* Terry Liebling. *Production Designer:* Victoria Paul. *Art Director:* Philip J. Messina. *Set Designer:* Ron Yates, Antoinette J. Gordon, Suzanne Feller-Otto, and Kristen Pratt. *Set Decorator:* Kathe Klopp. *Set Dresser:* Deana Albers, Nick Raymond, Greg Moore, Miguel Garcia, Keith McCormick, Dennis Cripps, Fred Paulsen, Mike Higelmire, Tim Caprarelli, Mike Cunningham, and Brian Bilson. *Special Effects:* John E. Gray. *Costumes:* Shay Cunliffe. *Make-up:* Felicity Bowring. *Stunt Coordinator:* Ernie Orsatti. *Running time:* 98 minutes. *MPAA Rating:* PG-13.

CAST: Michael Richards (Richard Rietti); Jeff Daniels (Charles Tuttle); Charlize Theron (Billie Tyler); Jessica Steen (Elizabeth Gardner); Austin Pendleton (Judge Paul Z. Graff); Rip Torn (Benny Gibbs); Alexandra Wentworth (Tiffany); Jennifer Coolidge (Jacqueline); Lawrence Pressman (Whitfield); Dale Dye (Dr. Stone); Max Casella (Dr. Brown); McNally Sagal (Charles' Assistant); Kenneth White (Hank Crabbit); Keith Mills (Buck Norman); Zaid Farid (Bailiff); Rachel Winfree (Mrs. Sussex); Ken Magee (Clerk); Michelle Bonilla (Court Reporter); Mark Davenport (Eric); Kelly Perine (Kurt); Rick La Fond (Phil); Paul Joseph Dworkin (1st Bartender); John Bigham (2nd Bartender); Nancy Linehan Charles (Witness); Jim Cody Williams (Heavy Lowlife); Kurek Ashley (Tattooed Lowlife); Jodi Faith Cahn (Elizabeth's Secretary); Brian Mahoney (Man in Bar); Gerry Spence (Himself); Norman Brennar (Courtroom Janitor).

LOS ANGELES TIMES, 5/30/97, Calendar/p. 12, John Anderson

[The following review by John Anderson appeared in a slightly different form in
NEWSDAY, 5/30/97, Part II/p. B9.]

Most big-budget, dream-cast comedies are a lot like pea soup: A creamy mass, with the occasional lump of ham.

"Trial and Error," starring "Seinfeld's" Michael Richards (in a very Kramer-esque performance), is a pretty soupy mess, but the croutons are fabulous—i.e. the statuesque Charlize Theron ("Two Days in the Valley"), with whom director Jonathan Lynn is either madly in love or knows a good thing when she comes into focus. If someone wanted to make someone else a star, it's hard to imagine a better route than Lynn takes with Theron, who brings the movie to its knees every time she comes on screen.

Which is saying something, given how hard everyone's working to make merry in a pretty silly film. Jeff Daniels is the uptight lawyer Charlie Tuttle, who has to skip the bachelor party arranged by his actor pal Richard Rietti (Richards) because his future father-in-law/boss has sent him out of town to win the unwinnable fraud trial of career liar Benny Gibbs (a terrific Rip Torn). Gibbs is on trial for selling copper engravings of Abraham Lincoln-pennies to be precise—for $17.95 apiece. Richard arrives and takes Charlie on the town, where he gets drunk and has his lights put out by two locals. The justice system is imperiled.

Do you want me to explain how Richard has to handle the court case, while Charlie reassesses his romance with Tiffany (Alexandra Wentworth) and falls in love with waitress Billie (Theron)? I didn't think so.

There's a lot to hate about "Trial and Error," including the title. Are we supposed to assume that the judge (a very funny Austin Pendleton) knows that Richard isn't a lawyer? The way Lynn directs the courtroom scenes you have to assume so, but that sort of upends the entire premise. Of course, very little that goes on in court as Richard does battle with the savvy-but-not-that-savvy prosecutor Elizabeth Gardner (Jessica Steen) doesn't constitute an indictable offense, so a suspension of disbelief—think O.J. jury—is required.

Daniels, who seems to be making a career of playing straight man to physical comics (he starred with Jim Carrey in "Dumb & Dumber", for instance), is as bland as ever. Richards is doing Kramer. Steen is very good as the besieged district attorney and Theron just eats up the screen. As Billie, she knows how to stop a nosebleed, cure an anxiety attack, reads Walt Whitman and shotguns derelict appliances as a form of stress relief. Can she make soup? I don't know, but she knows how to make one palatable.

NEW YORK POST, 5/30/97, p. 47, Thelma Adams

Jonathan Lynn's "Trial and Error" is a trial for the audience and a mild error in judgment for its stars, Michael Richards and Jeff Daniels.

Lynn had a surprise hit with "My Cousin Vinny." The ex-attorney returns to the well with another court comedy about city slickers navigating the hicksville justice system.

Daniels is Tuttle, an uptight corporate clone engaged to the boss' daughter. His best man is Rietti (Richards), a humbling unemployed actor who wouldn't know the truth if it offered him a Screen Actors Guild card. They're Tweedledum and Tweedledummer.

A week before the Beverly Hills wedding, Tuttle's father-in-law dispatches him to settle a suit in the Nevada desert. It's just a matter of gaining a continuance in the trial of the family shyster (Rip Torn).

He's a sleazy con man who sells "engraved copper portraits of the Great Emancipator"—pennies—for $17.99.

A series of improbable stunts leads to an exchange of identities between the leads. Rietti steps up to the bench and Tuttle surrenders his briefs.

The actor has his finest role as a defense attorney who sells his client up the river; the lawyer finds there's life after law school if you only stop and smell the local waitresses.

What's the difference between practicing fraud, practicing corporate law and acting? Not much, moan screenwriting partners Sara and Gregory Bernstein. The lies! The lies! Like Lynn, Mr. B. is also a "recovering" lawyer.

One can only hope he made cases tighter than this script.

"Seinfeld's" Kramer does his Gumby-legged best with Rietti. The movie's high point is a Richards throwaway: an audition piece where the loopy actor solos as a guy confessing to a Mafioso that he loves his girl. Then Richards kicks his own butt all over the stage like a 'toon loon.

Daniels cruises in "dumb" control. He does his neurotic quick burns, his red-faced panic attacks, then rolls over, loosens his tie and woos. Charlize Theron makes his appealing love connection.

Torn rips up the screen in his own defense. His pitch to the jury about being an orphan hero on Halloween—his pathetic little "pumpkin boy" speech—is a comic nugget in an otherwise limp courtroom caper.

"Trial and Error" isn't hard time, but it would be criminal to pay full price to see it. Case closed.

SIGHT AND SOUND, 1/98, p.54, Mark Kermode

Rising lawyer Charlie Tuttle is engaged to his boss' daughter Tiffany. He's despatched to Nevada to demand a continuance in the case against his client, fraudster Benny Gibbs, which means missing his stag party. On arrival, Charlie is met by his best man, actor Ricky Rietti who arranges a surprise party in the hotel bar. Charlie is fed a superstrong cocktail by waitress Billie, gets into a drunken fight and passes out.

Too hungover to work the next morning, Charlie is replaced in court by Ricky, who asks the judge for the continuance only to be refused and forced to face prosecutor Elizabeth Gardner whom he tried to chat up the night before. Charlie and Ricky swap identities, with Charlie prepping Ricky to perform in court. Charlie opts for the infamous "Twinky defence" (which alleges that Gibbs' sugar addiction made him insane). Charlie loses his temper and is eventually expelled from the courthouse.

Charlie starts to fall for grad-school dropout Billie and adopts jeans and leather jacket, while Ricky becomes ever more lawyerly. As the defence collapses, Gibbs demands to take the stand and wins jury support with a sob story. Defeated, Elizabeth offers a lenient plea bargain which Ricky accepts but Gibbs refuses. Besotted, Ricky reveals his deceptions to Elizabeth and declares his love for her. The next day in court, Charlie overhears Ricky's moving, honest summation and promptly breaks up with Tiffany who has arrived unexpectedly. While Charlie and Billie celebrate their relationship, Gibbs is duly convicted, and Ricky woos Elizabeth.

Lacking any of the flair of his previous courtroom drama *My Cousin Vinny*, in which a similarly incompetent lawyer merrily bluffs his way to justice, director Jonathan Lynn's latest is surprisingly inept comic stodge. It's inadequacies clearly lie with Sara Bernstein and Gregory Bemstein's lumpen script, which has none of the economic wit of *My Cousin Vinny*, and which groans with contrivance and predictability.

Of course, true justice prevails in the end. Of course, Charles chooses Billie over Tiffany (and she turns out to be more than just a waitress) and of course uptight prosecutor Elizabeth is revealed as the bike-riding dream girl we all saw in reel one, but only Ricky failed to recognise. That these inevitable ends should come to pass is not the problem. That they should do so with such plodding lifelessness and heavy handed schmaltz is tiresome indeed. Does every character really have to announce the life changes they are going through on this long day's journey into truth? Does Lynn really have to use a soft filter every time a man is enchanted by a beautiful woman, or resort to Timotei-advert techniques (slow-motion with much lustrous hair bobbing) every time someone's thoughts turn to love? And does Phil Marshall's score really have to go all tinkly to tell us that people are feeling dreamy?

On the performance side, Michael Richards raises an early titter with his bad-actor-at-an-audition routine in which he mimes being brutally beaten by thugs. But once the plot kicks in he's left to huff and puff his way through a series of unfunny courtroom showdowns, before revealing his true lovable self in a toe-curling summation. Daniels is far worse, oscillating wildly between repressed hysteria and youthful abandon in a manner which makes you want *not* to mother and love him (as do both Billie and Tiffany), but to strangle him and be done with it. All of which makes Lynn's movie both a trial (for the viewer) and an error (for all those involved). Who ever would have expected such mediocrity from the man behind *Yes, Minister*?

Also reviewed in:
NEW YORK TIMES, 5/30/97, p. C3, Janet Maslin
VARIETY, 5/26-6/1/97, p. 64, Leonard Klady
WASHINGTON POST, 5/30/97, p. B7, Rita Kempley
WASHINGTON POST, 5/30/97, Weekend/p. 41, Desson Howe

TROJAN EDDIE

A Castle Hill Productions release of an Initial Films production with Stratford Production in Ireland for Bord Scannan na hEireann/The Irish Film Board/Irish Screen and Channel 4. *Executive Producer:* Rod Stoneman, Alan J. Wands, Kevin Menton, and Nigel Warren-Green. *Producer:* Emma Burge. *Director:* Gillies MacKinnon. *Screenplay:* Billy Roche. *Director of Photography:* John deBorman. *Editor:* Scott Thomas. *Music:* John Keane. *Sound:* Simon Willis and (music) Steve Price. *Sound Editor:* Pat O'Neill. *Casting:* Hubbard Casting. *Production Designer:* Frank Conway. *Art Director:* John Paul Kelly. *Art Director:* John Paul Kelly. *Costumes:* Consolata Boyle. *Make-up:* Morag Ross. *Stunt Coordinator:* Philippe Zone. *Running time:* 105 minutes. *MPAA Rating:* Not Rated.

CAST: Stephen Rea (Trojan Eddie); Richard Harris (John Power); Stuart Townsend (Dermot); Aislin McGuckin (Kathleen); Brendan Gleeson (Ginger); Sean McGinley (Raymie); Angeline Ball (Shirley); Angela O'Driscoll (Carol); Brid Brennan (Betty); Jason Gilroy (Patsy McDonagh); Maria McDermottroe (Rosy); Sean Lawlor (Gerry); Britta Smith (Lady Cash); Pat Laffan (Matt); Jimmy Keogh (Reg); Gladys Sheehan (Eddie's Mother); Noel Donovan (Arthur); Aoife MacEoin (Landlady); Pecker Dunne (Traveller); Linda Quinn (Travelling Woman); Dolores Keane (Red-Haired Traveller); Orla Charlton (Young Woman); Billy Roche (Man); Des Cave (Priest); Michael Collins (Second Traveller); Aisling O'Flanagan (Daughter #1, Jenny); Roison O'Flanagan (Daughter #2, Rebecca); Eugene O'Brien (Lady's Cash's Son); Charlotte Bradley (Farmer's Wife).

LOS ANGELES TIMES, 9/12/97, Calendar/p. 14, John Anderson

[The following review by John Anderson appeared in a slightly different form in **NEWSDAY, 8/29/97, Part II/p. B9.]**

Irish actor Stephen Rea has spent his career doing the improbable: dominating films while playing the hapless, hopeless or feckless, a bemused husband in "Bad Behavior," a conflicted cop in "Michael Collins," a thoroughly rattled IRA soldier in "The Crying Game."

His characters are satellites, moons, offshore operations, never quite the center of attention. And yet, even though Rea eschews the often theatrical edginess of our more prominent actors and blessedly lacks the tranquilizing effect of our major stars, he's been memorable in everything he's done.

His streak continues in "Trojan Eddie," an ironic Irish drama directed by Gillies MacKinnon of "The Playboys" and last year's well-received Scottish film "Small Faces."

Rea's title character, a low-level hustler who sells goods of dubious origin (transported in a Trojan van, whatever that is), is trying to realize his dream of self-employment, a stable home for his two daughters, some kind of detente with his philandering wife, Shirley (Angeline Ball of "The Commitments"), financial security and peace of mind. But in keeping with Rea's M.O., it's not Eddie around whom its rural Irish community revolves.

That honor goes to John Power (Richard Harris), the leader of the local Travellers (Irish gypsies), who doesn't get around much anymore. He has a big car, a big house and a number of thriving business interests. Power reigns over all he surveys through his own brutality—and few are better than Harris in communicating barely controlled rage—and the help of his thuggish son, Ginger (Brendan Gleeson). Eddie no Traveller himself, is viewed by them with contempt and suspicion, although he's a marvelous salesman. (And the thing he sells best is Eddie.)

In intelligent, understated fashion, MacKinnon transmutes Billy Roche's script into a world of Celtic Corleones, a feudal construct in which law equals strength and people are for sale. When Power becomes infatuated with a beautiful young Traveller girl named Kathleen (Aislin McGuckin), who reminds him of his late wife, he basically buys her. But it's a marriage not just between May and December but between the 19th and late 20th centuries. After a wedding that MacKinnon invests with all the joy of a funeral, the fox-eyed Kathleen absconds with the 11,000-pound marriage purse and Eddie's sidekick, Dermot.

This presents problems for Eddie, of course, and Rea, with his air of profound resignation, is an enigmatic and captivating figure. But so is Harris, who, when his mouth is slightly ajar and he's staring into the abyss of age, can make his shadowed, life-scarred face a thing of terrible beauty. His Power comes to the late realization that he's made an ass of himself; every laugh he hears becomes a laugh at him, any affront a capital offense. He's volatility personified.

Eddie, torn between his quixotic love for Shirley and a stable life with the far more worthy Betty (Brid Brennan), sees in all this romantic mayhem a chance for himself. The resolution is something of a twist, although character rather than plot is the strong suit of "Trojan Eddie." MacKinnon mixes a gritty milieu with the subtleties of deception—and self-deception in a place where the men look at the women with complete befuddlement, and the women see their men as broken promises. You wouldn't want to live in this fractured Camelot, but it's certainly an interesting place to visit.

NEW STATESMAN, 3/21/97, p. 48, Tim Adams

To some of those, including me, who saw Gillies MacKinnon's *Small Faces*, the second-best film to come out of Scotland last year was *Trainspotting*. MacKinnon's semi-autobiographical movie told the story of three brothers growing up in gangland Glasgow in the late sixties. By mixing an acute sense of child's-eye morality with scenes of surreal violence it achieved a tone that fell somewhere between *Just William* and *Reservoir Dogs*, as such it captured perfectly the indiscriminate brutality of boyhood.

MacKinnon had won some critical acclaim for his previous films—most notably for his TV adaptation of John Healy's ragged down-and-out-in-London novel *The Grass Arena*, but *Small Faces* marked a step-change in his career. Not only was the film judged Best Independent Film at the Edinburgh Festival, it received enough attention for MacKinnon to be invited to follow the primrose path of Bill Forsyth and make his next movie in Hollywood in the event, he decided to go only as far as Ireland.

Trojan Eddie, scripted by Billy Roche of *Wexford Trilogy* fame, is a far plainer film than *Small Faces*. MacKinnon sacrifices stylistic bravura to the simple virtues of a traditional narrative. In fact, narratives do not come much more traditional than this: the kernel of Roche's title is contained in an Irish folk song (one of the few things you don't have to buy options in these days). The song's refrain becomes something of a mantra in the film. It goes: "Oh Maids, when you're young don't you wed an old man", and, by way of clarification, continues: "He's got no faloodorum, he's lost his dingdoorum."

The faloodorum and dingdoorum in question in *Trojan Eddie* belong to Richard Harris, who plays, with considerable menace, a kind of gypsy Don Corleone, the psycho-tinker who rules a community of travellers in a particularly damp bit of Ireland.   Harris's character, the imaginatively named John Power, first sees his "young maid" Kathleen (Aislin McGuckin) at his wife's graveside.   After running her boyfriend out of town, conniving with her bare-knuckle champion-boxer father and holding her leather trousers while she plays Susannah to his Elder in the local trout stream, he eventually persuades her to wed him.

It is then, of course, that the trouble begins. At the centre of the trouble is Trojan Eddie himself. Brilliantly played by Stephen Rea, Eddie is Power's hired huckster. Along with his friend Dermot, he sells knock-off goods for knock-down prices in half-demolished warehouses, and gives the proceeds, minus a little cream, to his boss. Troubles have never been too far from Eddie—for one thing his wife has a habit of seducing his friends (and his enemies)—but they begin in earnest when his sidekick Dermot gets inside Kathleen's leathers, and they increase notably when the two elope on the night of the gypsy king's wedding, taking an £11,000 dowry with them.

The motor to MacKinnon's film comes from the charged opposition of the can-do Harris and the can't-do Rea. It begins in their faces: Richard Harris's features have sharpened into an extreme sternness since his Camelot days: bloodless lips and grey eyes are flanked by geometric frown-lines. Rea's face, by contrast, seems to exist in a different gravitational field altogether, full of the bags and sags of the *bona fide* loser. MacKinnon contrives to bring these faces into Smith-and-Jones-like juxtaposition at every opportunity: and there are plenty—usually as Harris considers whether to break Eddie's nose with his forehead. At the heart of their opposition there is also, however, a pressing ethical debate: is it possible to get the girl *and* the money?

Harris and Rea are aided in their quest for the answer to this dilemma by strong performances from Sean McGinley, the only man *below* Eddie in the community's hierarchy, and Brendon Gleeson, who plays Power's deranged son and minder.

The uncredited star of this film, however, is the bog in which long scenes of it are set. Rarely can mud—a particularly peaty black ooze in this case—have played such a part in a film: the men scrap in it; live alongside it; half drown in it; it encroaches on a shop Eddie wants to rent; and it is an uninvited guest at the doomed wedding. Set reports from *Trojan Eddie* attest to the presence of a particularly virulent form of flu, which at various times during production laid most of the cast low; having seen the film the wonder is that they avoided trench foot. MacKinnon has obviously developed a fondness for mud: he is about to begin work on an adaptation of Pat Barker's Somme-based novel *Regeneration*.

NEW YORK POST, 8/29/97, p. 62, Larry Worth

No, "Trojan Eddie" isn't about birth control. Nor does it have any connection to a hollow, wooden horse.

Actually, the subject matter is far more original, principally due to Stephen Rea's most spellbinding performance since "The Crying Game." The Oscar-nominated actor makes the title role into a showpiece for his unique mix of tics, vulnerability and fire.

Nicknamed for the Trojan van in which he travels, Eddie is a sad-sack lackey to a Celtic mobster who rules a group of gypsy-like travellers. Unlucky in love and life, Eddie comes alive only when he's selling his boss' contraband, ranging from the "Rolls-Royce of razors" to far more dangerous wares.

Fate throws Eddie a curve when the aging kingpin opts to take a child bride, with Eddie acting as the hapless go-between. Not surprisingly, the wife-to-be has a few ideas of her own, setting off a chain of betrayal, infidelity and murder.

That subject matter makes a dramatic change of pace for director Gillies Mackinnon, whose work on "The Playboys" and "Small Faces" only hinted at his abilities. He brings a lyrical, poetic sensibility to the admittedly bleak scenario while carefully encapsulating small-town politics.

Unfortunately, Billy Roche's script isn't a perfect complement. It's initially rambling manner makes for unnecessary confusion and a distinct lack of focus. In addition, some of the dialogue borders on trite.

That's when it's Rea to the rescue. His interpretation of a resentful, whey-faced character about to explode is simply amazing. He's a joy to watch, plain and simple.

Ditto for the always reliable Richard Harris. As the power-mad tyrant, he spews rage and venom like no other working actor. His ferocity is as frightening as it is hypnotic.

Rounded out by Angeline Ball and a fine cast of troupers, "Trojan Eddie" is proof positive that a bunch of Irish actors can overcome a paltry plot with the gift of gab.

SIGHT AND SOUND, 4/97, p. 53, Philip Kemp

In a small Irish town, Eddie, a skilled huckster, shifts consumer goods at makeshift auctions. He relies for his stock on John Power, the godfather of the local traveller community. Despised as a 'townie' (non-Romany) by the travellers, Eddie is obliged to hand over most of his profits to Power. Dermot, Power's nephew, acts as Eddie's assistant. Eddie's marriage has collapsed: his wife, Shirley, leaves their two young daughters with him while she runs around with other men, including Power's thuggish son Ginger. Eddie still hankers after her, despite the devotion of his girlfriend Betty.

Power becomes infatuated with a traveller woman named Kathleen and resolves to marry her despite the disparity in their ages. However, Kathleen starts a secret affair with Dermot, much to Eddie's alarm. During the wedding feast, Dermot and Kathleen run off together, taking with them the £11,000 dowry from the guests. Power sends a message to Dermot via Eddie that he will take Kathleen back, but Dermot must return the money. Eddie continues trading, assisted by his seedy friend Raymie. When Dermot contacts him, Eddie devises a plan to split the money with him. On the strength of this plan, he buys lots of stock and takes a lease on premises in Dublin.

Intercepting a call to Eddie, Raymie betrays Dermot's whereabouts to Kathleen's clan, the McDonaghs. Dermot gets away, but the money vanishes. Eddie is reduced to trading from a market stall with Betty and his daughters. Ginger, convinced Eddie knows where the money is, comes after him. Eddie hides, but Raymie taunts Ginger and is murdered by him. At the funeral, Eddie defies Power. Dermot, tired of Kathleen, abandons her and Eddie takes her back to her husband. Realising Raymie took the money, Eddie searches his flat and finds it there. Later, Power and Kathleen, visiting a cinema, are confronted by the triumphant image of Eddie on screen, advertising his spacious new warehouse.

The Irish playwright Billy Roche is best known for his *Wexford Trilogy*, three loosely interlinked plays set in his native city and populated by disillusioned fantasists and starry-eyed no-hopers. *Trojan Eddie*, his screenwriting debut, presents a similar cast of ambiguous characters, at once self-deceiving and wryly self-aware. The director Gillies MacKinnon has always been fascinated with people living on the precarious edge of society: travelling players in *The Playboys*, teenage street gangs in *Small Faces*, the junkie vagrants of *The Grass Arena*. In *Trojan Eddie*, he creates another borderline world, tawdry and poetic, enamoured with its own fragmenting myth.

Here, MacKinnon's view of Romany lore never adopts the woozily indulgent gaze of such films as Mike Newell's *Into the West*. When John Power, godfather of the travellers, meets Kathleen by a woodland stream and embarks on a nostalgic riff about his youth on the road, it could easily have prompted a sentimental approach. Instead, we get it straight: this is an infatuated old man trying to impress a young girl, and her half-puzzled, half-scornful reaction not only foreshadows events to come, but suggests that Power's memories are an index of weakness, not of strength.

Eddie himself first appears even more of a lost cause than the affluent, dominant Power. Stephen Rea's face, soft and rumpled as an unmade bed, radiates failure. His dreams of running his own business seem merely the defensive fictions of a born loser. Used and despised by almost everyone around him, Eddie hasn't even the gumption to ditch his sluttish wife and commit to his patient girlfriend.

However, *Trojan Eddie* follows the pattern of that classic but always serviceable fable, the worm that turns. Eddie reveals hidden reserves of tenacity, and can even command loyalty of a sort: girlfriend Betty sticks by him, and assistant Raymie at the last refuses to betray him to Ginger, dying for it. Power, for all his wealth and attendant muscle, shrinks steadily in stature as his fixation takes hold, snarling helplessly at the mocking laughter he hears always at his back. (The camera lingers dispassionately on Richard Harris' gaunt, ravaged features, as if watching old age and impotence devour him from within.) Meanwhile, Eddie grows, defies Power and kicks ex-wife Shirley out, until in the coda his magnified image, surrounded by gleaming consumer goods, booms gloatingly out at Power from the cinema screen: "Whatever you want—I got."

The despised outsider becomes a mythic figure, beyond the reach of his former patron's dwindling vengeance. For his previous film, *Small Faces* (scripted by himself and his brother Billy), Gillies MacKinnon brought a strikingly fresh perspective to the well worn subject of juvenile delinquency. In *Trojan Eddie*, helped immeasurably by a fine, all-Irish cast and Roche's eloquent script, he presents another unhackneyed take on material that might, in other hands, have verged on banality. It's scarcely surprising that he doesn't capture here quite the same haunting blend of intimacy and strangeness as in the earlier film, given that this time he's not dealing with elements of his own past and that urban Scotland and rural Ireland have such different texture. But *Trojan Eddie* confirms MacKinnon's expanding range and reach as a director, and begins a promising screenwriting career for Roche and this augurs well for the future of films in these islands.

VILLAGE VOICE, 9/2/97, p. 73, Dennis Lim

Audiences should be warned that *Trojan Eddie*'s eponymous hangdog loser, played by the congenitally morose Stephen Rea, turns out to be the film's livliest character. A stubbornly dour melodrama, the Scottish director Gillies MacKinnon's latest feature is set in a particularly damp and boggy outpost of rural Ireland, among a band of travelers whose leader, John Power (Richard Harris), is a gypsy variation on the Godfather, as wretched and crumpled as he is violently psychotic. Rea plays ex-convict Eddie, a huckster in Power's employ, smooth-tongued but resoundingly luckless. (Eddie's wife, the village harlot, sums up his lifelong predicament: "You just keep getting left behind.")

MacKinnon's *Small Faces* a spry Glasgow gang fable, marked him as a supremely surefooted talent. A filmmaker with a distinct painterly touch, he has a way of aestheticizing, without quite romanticizing, the grime to which he's drawn. *Trojan Eddie* wallows in a kind of dilapidated beauty, with saturated colors filling out drab locales and pools of muddy, golden light mysteriously flooding the frame.

Though in many ways inferior to *Small Faces*, *Eddie* shares the earlier film's vivid impressionistic style, its unsentimental outlook, even its capacity for indelible, offhand brutality. The screenplay, by the playwright Billy Roche, is a letdown, though—averse to anything resembling momentum, its self-conscious air of abstraction interrupted by moments of clattering triteness. ("Love makes a fool of you," wails a singer at Power's wedding ceremony, right before the old man's teen bride makes off with his nephew.) MacKinnon probably has a great film in him, but *Trojan Eddie* isn't it. The movie strives for a vaguely mythic resonance, but instead has the viewer itching to point out to its makers the distinction between a myth and a cliché.

Also reviewed in:
NEW YORK TIMES, 8/29/97, p. C3, Stephen Holden
VARIETY, 9/16-22/96, p. 72, Derek Elley

TROMEO & JULIET

A Troma Inc. release. *Executive Producer:* Daniel Laikind, Grant Quasha, and Robert Schiller. *Producer:* Michael Herz and Lloyd Kaufman. *Director:* Lloyd Kaufman. *Screenplay:* James Gunn and Lloyd Kaufman. *Director of Photography:* Brendan Flynt. *Editor:* Frank Reynolds. *Music:* Willie Wisely. *Music Editor:* David Rogers. *Sound:* David Alvarez, Jonathan Slon, and (music) Ezra Gold. *Casting:* Andrew Wiener. *Production Designer:* Roshelle Berliner. *Art Director:* Hannah Mosely. *Set Dresser:* Jennifer Acomb and Alex Ingalls. *Special Effects:* Louie Zakarian. *Costumes:* Kyra Svetlovsky. *Make-up:* Callie French. *Stunt Coordinator:* Marcos Miranda. *Running time:* 107 minutes. *MPAA Rating:* Not Rated.

CAST: Jane Jensen (Juliet Capulet); Will Keenan (Tromeo Que); Valentine Miele (Murray Martini); Maximillian Shaun (Cappy Capulet); Steve Gibbons (London Arbuckle); Sean Gunn (Sammy Capulet); Debbie Rochon (Ness); Lemmy (The Narrator); Stephen Blackehart (Benny Que); Flip Brown (Father Lawrence); Patrick Connor (Tyrone Capulet); Earl McKoy (Monty Que); Gene Terinoni (Detective Ernie Scalus); Wendy Adams (Ingrid Capulet); Tamara Craig Thomas (Georgie Capulet); Antonia Lurie (Brittany); Jacqueline Tavarez (Rosy); Steven Lawrence Loniewski (Harry); John Fiske (Vic); Garon Peterson (Fu Chang); Tiffany Shepis (Peter); Joe Fleishaker (1-900 Hunk); Peter James Kelsch (Bluto Fitzgibbon); Manon Kelley (CD ROM Woman); Joseph Anthony (Flavio, Penis Monster Guy); Caroline Smith (Pauline); Steve Roberts (Fellow with Disgusting Larva); Liz Ip (Fluttery Eyelids Girl in Opium Den); James Gunn (Found a Peanut Father); Kathleen Warner (Found a Peanut Mother); Brian Stefanovic and Marko Stefanovic (Found a Peanut Kids); Lloyd Kaufman (Found His Penis); Mark Manfro (Cop); Craig Adams (Guy Who Says It Will Take Him Only Two Minutes to Have Sex); Charis Michelson (Blind Chick); Merle Allin (Biker Dude); I.M. Smelly (Biker Doody); Neal Ruddy (Nice Man Hit by Car!); Lauren Danielle Gold (Cissy); Karl Unger, Jr. ("Carl"); Ralph Villela (Guy Who Says "You got to work hard to get a head in life"); Lisbeth Kaufman and Charlotte Kaufman (Mutant Kids); Evan Roberts (Boy Dancing in Field with Father Lawrence); Giovanni Giaconi (Giovanni); Brian McCarey (Guy Who Got Pissed Off, Sitting Around Day ....); Wesley Walker (Dog Wearing Visor); Brian Fox (Bill Shakespeare).

NEW YORK POST, 2/28/97, p. 44, Michael Medved

"Tromeo & Juliet" may not be the most brilliant of all recent cinematic adaptations of Shakespeare, but it is easily the most disgusting.

Where else will you find an intense, protracted closeup of the whole process of nipple piercing—or a credit line acknowledging "Sandee Brockwell" for her "stunt nipple"?

What other piece of Shakespearean cinema shows a major character thrown from a car, smashing his head against a fire hydrant, then scooping bloody pieces of his own splattered brains from the sidewalk to try stuffing them back inside his cracked skull?

The cracked skull responsible for this "no holds Bard" approach is Lloyd Kaufman, impresario of Troma Studios, and director of such gaudy ornaments to our civilization as "Toxic Avenger" and "Surf Nazis Must Die."

As always, Kaufman deploys an abundance of adolescent energy in his frantic (largely successful) efforts to gross out his audience, making inventive use of a bare-bones budget and handling his Gen X cast with enough skill to suggest that he's capable of far more than self-mocking exploitation fare.

As if anticipating such questions, the demented director incongruously inserts several scenes in which his leads deliver straight Shakespearean dialogue, as if to prove that these little-known kids (especially the luminous, emotionally transparent Jane Jensen, who plays Juliet) could do the actual play justice if they so desired.

In Kaufman's contemporary Manhattan setting, Montagues and Capulets have become warring gangs aligned with feuding former partners from the porno industry. Juliet's protective nurse is a tattooed and predatory lesbian with pierced lips, nose and eyebrows, who takes repeated advantage of the boss's innocent daughter.

Romeo (or "Tromeo" here, played by Will Keenan) masturbates to explicit computer games, while music from alternative rock bands like Superchunk and Motorhead raves and rants on the soundtrack.

Unfortunately, the movie's occasionally witty excesses are marred by gratuitously dark elements—including a bizarre incest theme involving three different couples and featuring sickening sequences showing Juliet sadistically molested by her lustful, drug-addicted father.

The incest preoccupation also provides a surprise ending that offers an especially grotesque "Tromatic" twist on those ludicrous 18th and 19th century versions of "Romeo" that rewrote the play to enable the lovers to avoid tragic death.

The best part of the movie remains the end credits, however, which include acknowledgement not only of "Best Boy" but also "Worst Boy" and "Wurst Boy"—an appropriate position for a production which, like an irresponsible sausage maker, spices up random leavings from the slaughterhouse floor.

SIGHT AND SOUND, 12/96, p. 54, Kim Newman

Manhattan, the present. Because Cappy Capulet once levered his partner Monty Que out of a profitable exploitation film company and stole Monty's wife, relatives of both partners are involved in a violent feud. Julie Capulet, Cappy's daughter, is pledged in marriage to meat billionaire London Arbuckle, but halfheartedly carries on a lesbian affair with Capulet's servant, Ness.

Tromeo Que, Monty's son, persuades his cousin Benny and friend Murray Martini to go to a fancy dress party at the Capulet house because he knows his sometime girlfriend Rosy will be there. At the party, Tromeo discovers Rosy is faithless, but is struck by love for Julie, who rejects both London and Ness to pursue the affair. Tromeo later breaks into the Capulet house and discovers that Cappy has confined his daughter to a plexiglass jail cell, in which they make love. Tromeo, with Ness' help, smuggles Julie out of the house and the couple are married by a helpful priest.

Meanwhile, the feud erupts into violence as Murray provokes Tyrone Capulet into murdering him, whereupon Tromeo causes Tyrone to be dismembered in a road accident. Juliet, needing to be rid of London, takes a potion which turns her into a mutant cow, prompting her former fiancé to defenestrate himself. Tromeo's love restores her former beauty, but Cappy makes an enraged attempt to murder the lovers which ends with his own death. Cappy's wife tells Tromeo that Cappy was his father, but Tromeo and Juliet decide to remain married even though they are brother and sister, happily raising deformed kids in Tromaville.

Lloyd Kaufman's Troma Pictures (essentially a one-man outfit) works so hard at degeneracy and self-delighted crassness that it's a miracle they have never made a good film. In interviews and such associated items as the company's in-house newspaper *The Troma Times*, Kaufman is an extremely witty man. His scripts, however, maroon genuine laughs among long stretches combining frenetically unfunny routines with a streak of mean-spirited nastiness that squelches any chance of real (as opposed to manufactured) cult appeal. Less than, say, the early films of John Waters, the Troma product lacks the paradoxical sweetness of Waters' *Pink Flamingoes*, though the technique and production values remain on a level with the home movie aesthetic Waters pioneered in the 70s. Too often Troma films seem like an attractive put-down of the expected audience: there is always a sense that Kaufman, with his cheery mix of hype and candour, is giving his viewers not what they want but what they deserve.

There are coups in *Tromeo & Juliet*, but most are compromised. Getting Lemmy of Motorhead to play the chorus is a nice thought, but poor sound recording renders his monologues almost impossible to follow. Most of the gag routines go on far longer than is funny, especially the last-reel rampage that ends with Juliet's father, Cappy Capulet, being electrocuted when the PC monitor that's been rammed over his head is turned on.

Once in a while a funny idea creeps through—the lengthy end-credits, punctuated by despairing screeds from the lonely soul who compiles them, a final anonymous audience comment, "now at least I don't have to read the play". The Shakespeare angle, which stretches to a tiny shot of the Bard supposedly enjoying the joke, means the cast has to cope with iambic pentameter. But the deficiencies of Valentine Miele's Mercutio-equivalent are not covered up by the complete redubbing of his dialogue (by a very recognisable Lloyd Kaufman).

Exploitation aspects are chucked into the comedy without much thought. The sex scenes could come from the motel version of any wretched hardcore schlock, and the violence involves cheesily ropey effects yoked to ideas like Juliet's dream pregnancy disgorging popcorn, rats and maggots, or a stud in an erotic fantasy sprouting an arm-sized penis with a Freddy-style monster head. In fact there are far too many unpleasant asides to catalogue usefully here. As with the unworkable auto-crash/auto-erotic or Aids gags of *The Toxic Avenger* and *Troma's War*, the admirable willingness to transgress is undermined by a fatal uncertainty of tone.

Troma has cultivated a company identity, and most scenes here are weighed down with self-referentiality—guest shots by the Toxic Avenger and Sgt. Kabukiman NYPD, the dressing of every set with posters, videos and promotional items from previous Troma product. Clips from earlier Troma films represent the output of Cappy and Monty's Silky Films. Decrying the way Cappy has taken Silky down-market, Benny Capulet claims Cappy distributes the worst films ever made, with a clip from one of the *Class of Nuke 'Em High* films as an illustration. In theory, the Troma phenomenon is interesting, engaging and amusing; in practice, the films are rarely more than tedious, repulsive and punitively laughless.

Also reviewed in:
NEW YORK TIMES, 2/28/97, p. C7, Stephen Holden
VARIETY, 6/10-16/96, p. 46, Lisa Nesselson

TROUBLESOME CREEK: A MIDWESTERN

An Artistic License/Forensic Films release of a West City Films Inc. production. *Producer:* Jeanne Jordan and Steven Ascher. *Director:* Jeanne Jordan and Steven Ascher. *Screenplay:* Jeanne Jordan and Steven Ascher. *Director of Photography:* Steven Ascher. *Editor:* Jeanne Jordan. *Music:* Sheldon Mirowitz. *Sound:* Jeanne Jordan, Steven Ascher, and George Christ. *Running time:* 88 minutes. *MPAA Rating:* Not Rated.

WITH: The Jordan family (Russel, Mary Jane, Jon, Jim, Pam, Judy, Janet, Jeanne), Tim Wolf, Steven Ascher.

NEW YORK POST, 1/24/97, p. 49, Larry Worth

John Mellencamp's tireless trooping for Farm Aid has sometimes made him seem the Corn Belt's answer to Sally Struthers. But the plight of Russel and Mary Jane Jordan, as documented in "Troublesome Creek: A Midwestern," puts his cause in a whole new light.

That's not to say this real-life account of veteran farmers forced off their Iowa homestead is heavy going. Far from it.

As lensed by Jeanne Jordan and Steven Ascher (Russel and Mary Jane's youngest daughter, and her husband), the sad scenario unfolds with surprising humor and great warmth.

The action begins when a new bank takes over the Jordan's loan and, due to an accumulated $220,000 debt, puts them on the dreaded "troubled account list." The only solution: sell off their machinery, livestock and house furnishings. In short, they're to lose everything but the land, which has been in the family since 1867.

Virtually all of this happens with the cameras rolling, letting viewers watch as dad makes the loan officers squirm, mom hesitates over which curios go in the "sell" and "give away" piles, and the family has a last Thanksgiving dinner on their prized Ethan Allen table.

Along the way, the Jordans not only put a human face on farmers' crises but exemplify how a tough situation can be handled with dignity and grace. Indeed, it's nearly impossible not to care about their fate.

That's in addition to tips on auction etiquette, learning how sons rent a nearby farm while waiting to inherit, and observing the slow death of once-thriving communities. Better still, none of the sidelights deter the production's brisk pacing.

The directors go a step further by framing the proceedings with clips from classic westerns. For instance, a shot of Gary Cooper and Grace Kelly leaving town in "High Noon" precedes the segment when Russel and Mary Jane face their own departure.

So do the good guys win in the end? That would be giving away too much. But suffice to say that "Troublesome Creek" makes viewers the ultimate victors.

NEWSDAY, 1/24/97, Part II/p. B15, John Anderson

Oh good grief, I thought, as the opening moments of "Troublesome Creek" rolled across the screen: a farm film. Waves of grain, fruited plains, dispossessed people, tears of rage. And, ultimately, an unventable anger at bankers, bureaucrats and major corporations. Just what I need.

But it was. "Troublesome Creek" is no arid documentary about the farm crisis, or a political diatribe about unsolvable problems. Amid and around its very basic narrative—in which a family that has farmed its land for 125 years finds itself overextended and underappreciated—swirl the concepts of nationhood, history, the pursuit of happiness and the myths that America has subsisted on for centuries. And which, of course, are casually tossed aside whenever the overriding concept of money enters the picture.

It's also a genuinely honest portrait of a family, without any treacle, but with plenty of heart. Veteran independent filmmakers Jeanne Jordan and Steve Ascher decided to make this film when her father, Russel Jordan, decided to retire from farming. The crapshoot of paying off last year's loans with this year's crop had stopped paying out. Jim Jordan, one of Jeanne's brothers, had been farming leased property with the expectation of buying it, but the land was being sold out from under him. So the plan was for Russel and his wife, Mary Jane, to sell off everything and move to town; for Jim to work the Jordan place with his own equipment, and for one more farm family to reorder itself, and thus survive.

What we're privy to is not just a tragedy that's been repeated for years across the farmlands of America, but an intimate portrait of the Jordans, an intelligent, articulate group who defy every urbanite's stereotype of Midwesterners or farmers (although another brother, Jon, does a dead-on imitation of that very stereotype).

The film, titled after the stream that runs across the Jordans' Iowa land, contains moments of almost overwhelming poignancy, and irony: Russel Jordan's affection for old westerns and their simple code of good and evil is made metaphoric by his own worrisome state of affairs. The auctioning of the Jordans' possessions is wrenching, but so are narrator Jeanne Jordan's reveries about growing up on the farm. Her reminiscence about spending time alone with her father, for instance—which was a rarity in such a large family—is an eloquent statement about parent-child relationships, but also about unsung emotion, something given eloquent voice in "Troublesome Creek."

If there's a flaw in the film, it's in the two filmmakers' reliance on arty shots when the landscape itself proves them unnecessary. But this is a small point. Many of us complain about the lack of substance or "decency" in the cinema, and many of us are right. Those who look to movies and find them wanting in basic human values should go to see "Troublesome Creek," or stop making so much noise.

VILLAGE VOICE, 1/28/97, p. 61, Amy Taubin

Troublesome Creek: A Midwestern won the documentary grand prize at the 1996 Sundance film festival; the morning after, bleary-eyed L.A. and New York sophisticates staggered into a special screening to see what they'd missed. And although Americana comes in all shapes and sizes, it's easier to sell a cosmeticized Hollywood portrait of a scuzzmeister like Larry Flynt than a no-frills documentary about a 70-year-old Iowa farmer and his wife fighting off foreclosure. Even with the Sundance prize and an Academy Award nomination, *Troublesome Creek* had to wait a year for its release.

Informed by Norwest Bank in 1990 that despite four decades of profitable farming, they are now considered a bad risk, Russel and Mary Jane Jordan come up with an ingenious plan whereby they'll sell everything—livestock, machinery, their household goods, including Mary Jane's treasured Ethan Allen dining-room set—everything except their farm itself. The proceeds from the sale will be used to pay off the bank. Russ and Mary Jane will retire to a rented house in a nearby town, while their oldest son Jim, about to have the farm he's renting sold out from under him, takes over the farm that has been in the Jordan family for 120 years and works it with his own equipment.

Named for the twisting stream that crosses the Jordan farm, *Troublesome Creek* is as much about survival as it is about loss. Or as filmmaker Jeanne Jordan, Russ and Mary Jane's youngest daughter, puts it, "What are success and failure in a life, and how do you know which is which?"

A Boston-based documentarian, Jeanne and her husband Steven Ascher decided to record her father and mother's last year on the Jordan homestead. The result is a mix of home movie and social history, about one family's way of coping with an ongoing farm crisis which the government has declared nonexistent. It's about what happens when the local banks that encouraged farmers to modernize and expand in the '70s are taken over by corporate giants like Norwest. It's about how farmers buy up their failed neighbors' possessions knowing that their own farms may be next on the auction block. It's about "good people" who defend themselves against bad circumstances with a well-developed sense of humor. A fan of the western, Russ nicknames the Norwest loan officer—whose too-good-to-be-true real name is Tim Wolf—"the hired gun."

The filmmakers use Russ's beloved westerns as a narrative conceit (in a "Midwestern" Jeanne explains, "it's not sure that the good guys win"). But embedded in *Troublesome Creek* is also a metaphor for its own production. Indeed, independent documentary filmmaking is as tenuous an occupation as family farming. *Troublesome Creek* was financed largely through NEH and PBS grants, a cultural support system that's been downsized to death. When Jordan talks about her parents being on "the losing side of history," she might as well be talking about herself.

Also reviewed in:
NEW REPUBLIC, 2/17/97, p. 26, Stanley Kauffmann
NEW YORK TIMES, 1/24/97, p. C6, Stephen Holden
VARIETY, 2/5-11/96, p. 61, Joe Leydon

TRUTH OR CONSEQUENCES, N.M.

A Triumph Films release of a Higgins/Messick/Wayne production. *Executive Producer:* Phillip M. Goldfarb. *Producer:* J. Paul Higgins, Kevin J. Messick, and Hilary Wayne. *Director:* Kiefer Sutherland. *Screenplay:* Brad Mirman. *Director of Photography:* Ric Waite. *Editor:* Lawrence Jordan. *Music:* Jude Cole and Gary Jones. *Music Editor:* Dan Garde. *Sound:* Walter Anderson. *Sound Editor:* Walter Newman. *Casting:* Janet Hirshenson and Jane Jenkins. *Production Designer:* Anne Stuhler. *Art Director:* Roswell Hamrick. *Set Decorator:* Les Boothe. *Set Dresser:* Josh Persoff. *Special Effects:* Eddie E. Surkin. *Costumes:* Susan Bertram. *Make-up:*Kate Shorter. *Stunt Coordinator:* Chris Howell. *Running time:* 101 minutes. *MPAA Rating:* R.

CAST: Vincent Gallo (Raymond Lembecke); Mykelti Williamson (Marcus Weans); Kieffer Sutherland (Curtis Freley); Kevin Pollak (Gordon Jacobson); Kim Dickens (Addy Monroe); Grace Phillips (Donna Moreland); James McDaniel (Frank Thompson); Rick Rossovich (Robert Boylan); John C. McGinley (Eddie Grillo); Max Perlich (Wayne); Rod Steiger (Tony Vago); Martin Sheen (Sir); Scott Christopher (Frank Pearson); Steve O'Neill (Detective); Marshall Bell (Police Lieutenant); Richard Clark (Don Severt); Mark Lonow (Alan Gryder); Jason Rodriguez (Sir Man #1); Jim Wilkey (Sir Man #2); Craig Cliver (Sheriff); Robert Peters (Market Clerk); Craig Clyde (Patrol Officer); Joan Robinson (Sheriff #1); Colin Patrick Lynch (Sheriff #2);

Peter Iacangelo (Wiseguy);   James Verbois (Man on Hillside);   Tim Parati (Cecil);   Donre
Sampson (Cecil's Man); Bill McIntosh (Warehouse Cop #1); Perry Barndt (Warehouse Cop #2);
John Brimley (Warehouse Cop #3); Bob Jaurgui (Stunt Cop); Maurice Dunster (Dodge Owner);
Dennis Bridwell (Vago Wiseguy #1); Richard Slaughter (Vago Wiseguy #2); Don Shanks (Vago
Wiseguy #3);   Chris Howell (Roadside Bar Fighter);   Craig Hoskings (Helicopter Pilot);   Dan
Rudert (Helicopter Pilot); Manny Rodriguez (Marksman).

LOS ANGELES TIMES, 5/2/97, Calendar/p. 19, Kevin Thomas

The following review by Kevin Thomas appeared in a slightly different form in
NEWSDAY, 5/2/97, Part II/p. B12.]

"Truth or Consequences, N.M." takes us down a familiar killers-on-the-run road only to
swerve in enough unexpected directions to make it a fresh, exciting and thoroughly involving
thriller. It's a strong first directorial outing for Kiefer Sutherland who, in working from Brad
Mirman's smart script, gets the utmost from a fine ensemble cast—including himself.

Vincent Gallo's Raymond leaves prison for the open arms of Kim Dickens' Addy, and these
devoted lovers look forward to a better life. Yet eight months later the drug dealer, Eddie Grillo
(John C. McGinley, at his nastiest), for whom Raymond took a two-year fall, has rewarded him
only with a chump-change warehouse job.

This makes Raymond vulnerable to a plan to hold up Eddie for his stash that will involve
Raymond's prison pal Curtis (Sutherland) and Curtis' associate Marcus (Mykelti Williamson).
While Marcus is the most level-headed member of the gang, Curtis, a two-time loser, is a wild
and crazy guy who starts opening fire at Eddie and an unknown man who happens to be sitting
with him at his desk in the warehouse.

The filmmakers try hard to romanticize Raymond, played by Gallo with the kind of anguish he
might well bring to playing Jesus Christ, and the slightly more intelligent Addy as a latter-day
Bonnie and Clyde. Amazingly, it doesn't matter whether you're able to buy into this hooey or
not, because Mirman's script has some built-in insurance, both in early and climactic surprise
twists and in a couple, Gordon (Kevin Pollak) and Donna (Grace Phillips), held hostage by the
gang when it commandeers their RV.

It's easy to dismiss Raymond and Addy as dangerous, worthless trash for all their caring for
each other, especially after Addy remarks that "Curtis takes the cake for dumb" and you can't
help but think, "Wrong. It's you and Raymond who take the cake for hooking up with a raving
psycho like Curtis in the first place."

But Gordon and Donna, far more interesting than Raymond and Addy, are on hand to take up
our attention. That's because this couple's love for each other becomes increasingly tested as
Gordon starts bonding with the gang, saying at one point to the rightly dismayed Donna that "they
make more money in one week than I make in a year."

With the same kind of aplomb he displays in front of the camera as the wacko Curtis,
Sutherland unerringly steers the film to a boffo finish with style and drive.   Other actors
Sutherland directs to top-notch portrayals include Rod Steiger as a Vegas underworld kingpin who
laments the lack of respect in the modern-day world of crime, Martin Sheen as an amusingly
savage mob enforcer and Max Perlich as Raymond's truly luckless friend. Handsomely photographed in Southwest locales, including the town that gives the film its title, "Truth or Consequences, N.M." delivers the action goods with welcome intelligence.

NEW YORK POST, 5/2/97, p. 46, Bill Hoffmann

Kiefer Sutherland visits over-traveled Tarantino country in "Truth or Consequences,
N.M."—and survives.

As a first-time director, Sutherland has pulled off a neat trick—breathing new life into the now
standard "quirky crime drama" genre that "Pulp Fiction" spawned for better or worse.

For starters, he has cast himself in the role he does better than any other '90s actor—the
trigger-happy psycho whose weird tics and "Twilight Zone" personality are as cheerfully
entertaining as they are absolutely appalling.

And wisely, he doesn't take himself too seriously, nonchalantly moving from belly laughs to blood and gore and back again with the ease of a polished director.

The story is simple. Ex-con Ray Lembecke (Vincent Gallo) has just been released from the pen and wants more than anything to escape to paradise with his cutesy girlfriend, Addy (Kim Dickens).

One last heist will make it all happen, so he gathers his ex-cellmate, Curtis Freley (Sutherland), and an associate, Marcus Weans (Mikelty Williamson).

Unfortunately, Freley doesn't consider any stickup a success until the floor is awash with blood and guts, and that's exactly what happens after the gang finds cocaine, not money, in their victims' possession.

The four dirtbags—along with Addy and a suitcase with millions of dollars worth of the white stuff go on the lam, grabbing two yuppie hostages along the way.

The action is fast and furious and par for the course for this type of movie. But Sutherland is really on the ball, giving his story a big B-12 shot of energy by casting two old pros, Rod Steiger and Martin Sheen, as a couple of blood-thirsty mobsters.

Steiger seems like a pig in a sty and is obviously enjoying himself in the role of Vago, a humorless, foul-mouthed Las Vegas mob kingpin.

And it's neat to see Sheen playing against type as a sadistic enforcer named Sir, who's handy with a set of diabolical surgical tools.

It's true there's really nothing new here—but there's no doubt that Sutherland is off to a flying start on the other side of the camera.

VILLAGE VOICE, 5/6/97, p. 86, Amy Taubin

This years *Feeling Minnesota, Truth or Consequences, N.M.* is a film so pointless and stupid that one has to pity the actors for being involved—all except Kiefer Sutherland who, not content with costuming as a coked-up psycho-killer, also helms. A road map to its director's arrested development, yet another bungling-dope-dealers-on-the-lam flick that despite the stunning absence of narrative logic, imagines making some serious statement about America.

After much driving, interspersed with loopily intimate moments that suggest the actors (Vincent Gallo and Kim Dickens) were taking time out to audition for the Actor's Studio, the film terminates with our antiheroes, the hostages they've acquired on route, and the undercover cop among them caught in a shoot-out between the Vegas Mafia and the DEA.

This film is a consequence of two appalling trends in indie filmmaking: (1) Tarantinoism (yes, we get to see body parts hacked off a living victim) and (2) the belief that a dead-ended acting career qualifies one to direct a movie. Would that they both were over.

Also reviewed in:
NEW YORK TIMES, 5/2/97, p. C33, Stephen Holden
VARIETY, 4/28-5/4/97, p. 100, Godfrey Cheshire

TURBO: A POWER RANGERS MOVIE

A Twentieth century Fox release of a Saban Entertainment/Toei Company production. *Executive Producer:* Haim Saban and Shuki Levy. *Producer:* Jonathan Tzachor. *Director:* David Winning and Shuki Levy. *Screenplay:* Shuki Levy and Shell Danielson. *Director of Photography:* Ilan Rosenberg. *Editor:* Henry Richardson and B.J. Sears. *Music:* Shuki Levy. *Sound:* Neal Spritz. *Production Designer:* Yuda Ako. *Art Director:* Steve Miller and David Lazan. *Set Designer:* Kurt Alex Geisse and Marcos Alvarez. *Set Decorator:* Julie Bolder. *Costumes:* Danielle Baker. *Car Customizer:* George Barris. *Running time:* 99 minutes. *MPAA Rating:* PG.

CAST: Jason David Frank (Tommy, the Red Power Ranger); Steve Cardenas (Rocky, the Blue Power Ranger); Johnny Yong Bosch (Adam, the Green Power Ranger); Catherine Sutherland (Katherine, the Pink Power Ranger); Nakia Burrise (Tanya, the Yellow Power Ranger); Blake Foster (Justin); Paul Schrier (Bulk); Jason Narvy (Skull); Austin St. John (Jason); Amy Jo

Johnson (Kimberly); Hilary Shepard Turner (Divatox); Jon Simanton (Lerigot); Richard Genelle (Ernie).

LOS ANGELES TIMES, 3/28/97, Calendar/p. 2, Kevin Thomas

[*The following review by Kevin Thomas appeared in a slightly different form in* NEWSDAY, 3/28/97, Part II/p. B7.]

"Turbo: A Power Rangers Movie," which once again moves the popular "Power Rangers ZEO" children's TV series to the big screen, has lots of energy and a sensational villainess, Divatox (Hilary Shepard Turner), whose fashion tips come from Ming the Merciless and who has been given all the film's sharpest lines.

Turner delivers lines like "That's right! Bow down to me, you little peons" with the kind of spoofy wit that adults, obliged to take children to a kiddie show like this, will really be grateful for. But then filmmakers Shuki Levy and David Winning have brought much panache and sophistication to the making of this fantasy adventure extolling the good old-fashioned virtues of spirit and courage embodied by the Power Rangers. "Turbo" is a solid follow-up to the entertaining 1995 "Mighty Morphin Power Rangers."

The Rangers are an ethnically diverse group of young people tapped to conquer intergalactic evil with character as well as world-class martial arts skills and a battery of crime-fighting gadgetry that would turn James Bond green with envy. The filmmakers go for that great kitschy vintage comic book/Saturday matinee serial look that's been in vogue since "Raiders of the Lost Ark" and "Conan the Barbarian." They do it very well, and they set it off smartly with top-notch special effects and a hard-driving rock score.

The alien Divatox is determined to free the evil, all-powerful Maligore so that she can marry him and thereby "raid all the riches of the universe." To do this, however, she's got to kidnap the diminutive blue-eyed, golden-bearded alien Lerigot, who holds the special key that keeps Maligore imprisoned in the depths of an active volcano on an island kingdom.

Unfortunately for her, Lerigot has escaped to the planet Earth, where he crosses paths with the Power Rangers (Johnny Yong Bosch, Nakia Burrise, Jason David Frank, Catherine Sutherland and newcomer Blake Foster), a bland though likable and resourceful group of do-gooders. You can pretty much take it from there.

NEW YORK POST, 3/28/97, p. 52, Larry Worth

At least the guillotine was quick. "Turbo: A Power Rangers Movie" is the cinematic equivalent of the rack, stretching the pain of victims—er, viewers—into 99 minutes of sheer torture.

As 1997's answer to Torquemada, directors David Winning and Shuki Levy carry off the impossible: They make one pine for 1995's merely hideous "Mighty Morphin Power Rangers: The Movie."

Sure enough, "Turbo" is the second big-screen production inspired by TV's popular kid show about five teens who assume extraordinary powers to fight all manner of intergalactic villains.

This time around, the color-coded quintet battle everything from an eye-patched lady space pirate who travels in a Capt. Nemo-like sub (minus Jules Verne's inspiration, of course) to a gigantic boa constrictor. A snake's actions have never seemed so heroic.

All the Rangers' derring-do boils down to keeping evil forces away from an all-powerful magician. But it's hard to take the wizard seriously since he looks like a kid in a troll costume that wouldn't pass muster on Halloween.

At least he's consistent with the rest of the sad-sack masks, thrift store costumes and bargain basement special effects. Indeed, the climactic fight between dueling behemoths seems straight out of "Godzilla vs. the Smog Monster."

Then there's the alleged narrative. Those who aren't in the know about Power Rangers history will be left in the dark as references to past adventures and characters fly by with nary an explanation. Newcomers will also need a primer to explain why characters morph into robots, or, better still, how five turbo zords (huh?) coalesce into a super-powerful Megazord (what?).

Clearly, one doesn't expect Oscar-caliber action here. Even so, the principal actors are utterly interchangeable. Barbie and G.I. Joe have more range. If "Turbo" represents the best the Power Rangers can put on the silver screen, it's safe to say the series has run out of steam.

Also reviewed in:
NEW YORK TIMES, 3/29/97, p. 17, Lawrence Van Gelder
VARIETY, 3/31-4/6/97, p. 86, Joe Leydon
WASHINGTON POST, 3/28/97, p. 52, Jane Horwitz

TURBULENCE

A Rysher Entertainment and Metro-Goldwyn-Mayer release of a Martin Ransohoff production. *Executive Producer:* Keith Samples. *Producer:* Martin Ransohoff and David Valdes. *Director:* Robert Butler. *Screenplay:* Jonathan Brett. *Director of Photography:* Lloyd Ahern, II. *Editor:* John Duffy. *Music:* Shirley Walker. *Music Editor:* Thomas Milano. *Sound:* David MacMillan and (music) Michael Farrow. *Sound Editor:* Gregory King and Robert Grieve. *Casting:* Phyllis Huffman. *Production Designer:* Mayling Cheng. *Art Director:* Donald B. Woodruff. *Set Designer:* Daniel Jennings, Peter Kelly, and Henry Alberti. *Set Decorator:* Donald Kraft. *Special Effects:* Al Di Sarro. *Visual Effects:* Mark Vargo. *Costumes:* Robert Turturice. *Make-up:* Gary Liddiard. *Stunt Coordinator:* Billy Burton. *Running time:* 110 minutes. *MPAA Rating:* R.

CAST: Ray Liotta (Ryan Weaver); Lauren Holly (Teri Halloran); Brendan Gleeson (Stubbs); Ben Cross (Captain Sam Bowen); Rachel Ticotin (Rachel Taper); Jeffrey DeMunn (Brooks); John Finn (Sinclair); Catherine Hicks (Maggie); Hector Elizondo (Detective Aldo Hines); J. Kenneth Campbell (Captain Matt Powell); Heidi Kling (Betty); James MacDonald (1st Officer Ted Kary); Gordy Owens (Carl); Alan Bergmann (Mr. Kramer); Danna Hansen (Mrs. Kramer); R.J. Knoll (Kip); Sondra Spriggs (Career Woman); Garrett Brown (LAX Manager); Darryl Theirse (Limato); Michael Harney (Marshall Douglas); Grand L. Bush (Marshall Arquette); Richard Hoyt Miller (Marshall Riordan); Michael F. Kelly (Marshall Green); Fritz Mashimo (Asian Businessman); Tom Todoroff (Mr. Hollywood); Jeffrey Joseph (Detective); Dennis Redfield (Desk Sergeant); Malachy McCourt (Ray, the Doorman); Gary Rodriguez (Rodriguez); Billy Burton (Port Authority Officer); Callie Thorne (Laura); John Elsen (Stone); Bill Cross (William Harris); Tannis Benedict, Don Dowe, and Scott Gurney (Air Traffic Controllers); Cooper Huckabee (Wing Commander); Ken Thatcher, II (SWAT Member); Kevin O'Rourke (Mark Pavone); Scott Lawrence (Felix); Ken Mosley (Tower Air Co-Pilot).

LOS ANGELES TIMES, 1/10/97, Calendar/p. 4, Kenneth Turan

Though it's one of the first films out in 1997, "Turbulence" feels like yesterday's movie. Its plot dynamics, its dialogue, even its special effects, are familiar for having been employed time and time again. And usually to better effect than they are here.

Not for the makers of "Turbulence" is the spending of tens of millions of dollars on computer-generated imagery. Most of the special effects this time around come from simply shaking parts of the set with a venerable device called a gimbal. Hey, it may be old-fashioned, but it works.

What's being shaken but not stirred is a 747 airplane headed from New York to Los Angeles. Because it's Christmas Eve (and because it's cheaper to film that way), the plane is almost empty: just an elderly couple, a rogue skateboarder and a couple of other folks.

Things can't stay quiet for long. Entering the plane en masse are four burly federal marshals escorting a pair of menacing criminals in chains: a bank robber named Stubbs (Brendan Gleeson) and convicted killer Ryan Weaver (Ray Liotta).

Actually, Weaver doesn't seem all that menacing. Though he's earned a reputation as the Lonely Hearts Strangler for having raped and killed five women, he insists he's innocent and seems solicitousness itself as he makes small talk with stewardess Teri Halloran (Lauren Holly).

Herself recently disappointed in love, Halloran insists to co-worker Maggie (Catherine Hicks) that Weaver "doesn't look like a serial killer," a judgment matched in acuity only by whoever told the Titanic's captain he didn't have to worry about icebergs.

Small as the group on the plane is, it's too large for screenwriter Jonathan Brett's purposes, and soon enough everyone else on the flight, from the pilots to the passengers and crew, have been disposed of one way or another, clearing the aisles for a cat-and-mouse game between the only two actors whose names can be found above the title.

As the unstable Weaver, who, it turns out, is so angry at the tough cop who arrested him (Hector Elizondo) that he doesn't care if he lives or dies, Liotta gives a performance that does nothing more than echo the legion of screen madmen who've come before him.

The same could be said for Holly's Teri, not the first woman to look distraught and terrified as a madman chases her around an aircraft and a major storm shakes everything up. Why she ends up having to both hold him off and try to land the plane in her underwear is something a special issue of Ms. Magazine might be devoted to.

Veteran director Robert Butler, whose career (mostly on television) extends all the way back to "The Computer Wore Tennis Shoes," has not managed to lift this predictable drama out of the ordinary. Though it's fortunate for Teri that the plane is on automatic pilot during most of her struggles, it's unfortunate for the audience that the picture is similarly situated all the way to the end.

NEW YORK POST, 1/10/97, p. 43, Michael Medved

Forget about those "Friendly Skies..."

In "Turbulence," two convicts (Ray Liotta and Brendan Gleeson) get loose during an airline trip transporting them from New York to L.A., kill the four federal agents guarding them and make the rest of the flight an exceedingly bumpy ride.

The violent lightning storm over the Midwest that threatens to down the Boeing 747 is merely a showy distraction to the bloody insanity on board the plane, as one plucky flight attendant (Lauren Holly) crawls over the bodies of dead pilots to try to fly the stricken bird to safety.

With this ridiculous premise, you might expect "Turbulence" to soar with all the grace of an ungainly turkey. Instead, the stupid thing is so well shot, so solidly acted and, above all, so slickly edited that it takes wing in spite of itself and remains embarrassingly entertaining.

The script (by feature film first-timer Jonathan Brett) neatly skirts the edge of self-parody until the (literally) slam-bang conclusion where it sails merrily over-the-top. There's even some tacky topical interplay between the two main characters (Liotta and Holly) inspired, perhaps, by all those self-help books in the, "Smart Women/Foolish Choices" tradition.

She's supposed to be a sensitive, romantic vegetarian who's just been jilted by her fiance. On a Christmas Eve flight (with the plane's cabin implausibly decorated with holiday lights and holly) she feels naturally vulnerable to the handsome, handcuffed convict with the piercing blue eyes and the charming, gentle manners. She knows he's a convicted rapist and serial killer, but at first she tends to believe him when he says he's been framed.

Since he first grabbed public attention 10 years ago in "Something Wild," Ray Liotta has shown a special affinity for these charismatic psycho roles, and here he's done it again—alternately fetching, ferocious, frightening and funny. For her part, Holly is lovely to look at (as always), but also displays surprising depth, vulnerability and intelligence, while proving herself a formidably tough action heroine.

The supporting cast is also strong—including the underused Catherine Hicks as Holly's flight attendant best friend, Hector Elizondo as the arresting cop who understands Liotta best, Rachel Ticotin as one of the worried airline supervisors on the ground, and Ben Cross as the stiff-upper-lip British pilot on another plane who helps talk the nervous flight attendant through the controls of the jumbo jet.

Aside from annoyingly intrusive and banal background music (by Shirley Walker), the main problem with "Turbulence" is its gleeful revelry in its own blood-soaked sadism. Director Robert Butler (a 40-year Hollywood veteran best known for his Emmy-winning TV work) skillfully gets us cheering at excessive and expertly rendered violence against a seemingly unstoppable villain, but it's hard to feel good about it after this high-flying foolishness finally comes down to earth.

NEWSDAY, 1/10/97, Part II/p. B9, John Anderson

"I don't think there's ever been a situation quite like this," someone says during the course of "Turbulence." (If you want to add an exclamation point, be my guest.) And he's quite right. An airplane disaster-hostage-serial-killer-sex-assault-murder-Christmas-movie,"Turbulence" is like a three-legged elephant with a trunk, horn and in-dash CD player. The parts are all familiar; the assembly is like nothing you've ever seen.

No cliché is left unturned, as plucky flight attendant Teri Halloran (Lauren Holly), with no pilot training, tries to land a 747 without crashing into Los Angeles while a possible serial killer roams about the all-but-abandoned aircraft.

Seldom have the words "stay calm" carried so much comedic weight.

Is there a gremlin outside, chewing on the wing of the plane? It wouldn't be at all surprising, but no, he's inside, and he's played by Ray Liotta. As Ryan Weaver, a Ted Bundy type who may or may not be the "lonely hearts strangler" sought by Det. Aldo Hines (Hector Elizondo), Liotta is as creepy as he's been since "Something Wild."

But he does get progressively loony, to the point that "Turbulence" begins to look less like an Irwin Allen disaster flick than one by Abrahams, Zucker and Zucker.

Weaver, who has been nabbed by Hines in New York, is loaded aboard a near-empty jumbo jet for the trip to L.A., along with a Cro-Magnon robbery suspect named Stubbs ("Braveheart's" Brendan Gleeson), who's a walking advertisement for mandatory sterilization, complete with obligatory southern accent. Stubbs manages to spark a midair shootout that kills almost everyone, including himself. The pilot is caught in the crossfire; the co-pilot gets his neck broken just sitting in the cockpit.

Weaver keeps his cool while all those around him are losing theirs. The plane, and the plot, accelerate toward catastrophe and illogic. There's a level 6 storm right in front of the plane.

"On a scale of one to ten?" Teri asks ground control.

"On a scale of one to six."

Holly and Liotta are actually good actors, but "Turbulence" and its overload of trite situations are evidence of the creative poverty afflicting Hollywood.

That, and the woeful state of escapist cinema in the era of international marketing.

As a prime example of the kind of movie made for overseas sales, "Turbulence" therefore has not only limited dialogue but inane dialogue. It boasts an overly generous portion of violence. The illogical, unlikely and physically impossible are treated as natural phenomena. And Holly—so courageous, so upstanding, so aeronautical—is eventually reduced to running around in her underwear.

SIGHT AND SOUND, 5/97, p. 55, Kim Newman

New York. Ryan Weaver, an escaped serial killer, is apprehended by the NYPD with the help of advice from Los Angeles detective Aldo Hines, who planted the evidence that originally convicted Weaver. On Christmas Eve, Weaver and a bank robber named Stubbs are to be transported across country via an almost-empty commercial flight. Weaver makes friendly advances to Teri Halloran, a flight attendant who fits his usual victim profile. Stubbs attempts a hijack and kills the federal marshals accompanying the prisoners and the cockpit crew. Weaver kills Stubbs, and convinces Teri that he is an innocent man. However, he conceals from her the fact that both pilots are dead.

With the aeroplane on auto-pilot heading for a storm and the authorities at Los Angeles airport (LAX) alerted, Teri begins to have suspicions about Weaver. He murders Maggie, another stewardess, and pens the surviving passengers and crew in a small cabin. Teri makes contact with LAX, where crisis supervisor Rachel Taper and pilot Sam Bowen talk her through the landing procedure. Weaver menaces Teri and announces that he plans to crash the plane into Los Angeles, whereupon the authorities put a fighter in the air with orders to shoot the plane down. Teri repeatedly fights off Weaver and finally kills him. On the second attempt, Teri lands the plane.

It's taken over 15 years, but the lingering contempt for the disaster movie—brought out into the open by the MAD magazine-style satire of *Airplane!*—has finally worn off. *Twister, Independence Day, Daylight* and *Dante's Peak* have redeemed various sub-genres of disaster. The flight path is finally clear now for the return of that primal problem-with-the-plane movie that dates back before *Airport* (1969) to *The High and the Mighty* (1954) or *Five Came Back* (1939) and which was the template for the Zucker-Adams-Zucker spoof. Coupled with the recent precedent of *Die Hard*-in-the-air *Executive Decision, Turbulence* bids fair to revive the fear-of-flying movie for the 90s.

Recalling the trauma of Karen Black's character in *Airport 1975*, *Turbulence* is constructed around the archetypally naff situation of a ditzy employee who has to land the plane. *Turbulence* literally dispenses with the sub-plots favoured by the classic disaster movies. We get a glimpse of the cocky skateboarding kid, the nervous old couple and the *Variety*-reader travelling first class. But after all the cops and crew on board have been violently wiped out, the villain hustles all this surplus narrative cargo into a locked cabin where they are promptly forgotten about for the remainder of the film. As *Twister* stirred in echoes of *His Girl Friday*, *Turbulence* also reaches out of the disaster genre to yoke in a narrative motors from other formats, such as the unlikable psycho of the *Halloween* or *Friday the 13th* series, overlaid with the viper-in-the-nest, charming murderer that *Turbulence*'s star Ray Liotta exemplified in *Unlawful Entry*.

Given the tangle of contrivances necessary to get its lady and madman plot airborne, *Turbulence* rattles through the set-up quite well, intercutting the cops' capture of villain Weaver with heroine Teri being dumped (on Christmas Eve) by her fiancé. There's a suggestion that Weaver might be an innocent whose quick-thinking in a crisis will be a path to redemption. However, Liotta's character's bonding with Teri—involving a flirtatious discussion of in-flight movie, *It's a Wonderful Life*—is so nauseatingly smarmy that the possibility of his heroism is almost instantly squashed. The bulk of the movie can best be described as efficient tosh, with cutaways to a kindly Ben Cross and a feisty Rachel Ticotin producing hilarity almost of *Airplane!* proportions as they calmly try to gentle Teri through a succession of ordeals. The out of control plane, with its malfunctioning auto pilot, is a lively setting for the familiar business of the psycho chasing the heroine all over the house. This scenario comes equipped with the expected fire extinguishers, automatic doors, axes and dropped bullets that have to be loaded into a dropped gun by a panic-stricken heroine who is being groped by the roller.

Lauren Holly, model-perfect cheekbones fetchingly bloodied, is an old-fashioned, pre-Sigourney Weaver heroine: suitably gutsy at the climax, but still afflicted with periods of plot-extending catatonia. Director Robert Butler (a veteran television director who also helmed the tele-movie *Mayday at 40,000 Ft!* in 1976) keeps the mechanics of chase and attack working. But the film's ultimate inadequacy as a thriller resides in the failure of the two leads to make the necessary cat-and-mouse connection, and indeed the plot locks the two up in different cabins for too much of the film. The nearest *Turbulence* gets to character development is pretty offensive: Weaver tries to play on the gun-holding Teri's liberal distaste for the death penalty by claiming, "you won't kill me, you don't believe in capital punishment," only to be told "I changed my mind," and wind up with a bullet in his brain.

Also reviewed in:
CHICAGO TRIBUNE, 1/10/97, Friday/p. N, Michael Wilmington
NEW YORK TIMES, 1/10/97, p. C3, Stephen Holden
VARIETY, 1/6-12/97, p. 179, Leonard Klady

TWILIGHT OF THE GOLDS, THE

An Avalanche Releasing release of a Showtime presentation of a Regent Entertainment/Below the Belt production. *Executive Producer:* Garry Marshall. *Producer:* Paul Colichman, Mark Harris, and John Davimos. *Director:* Ross Marks. *Screenplay:* Jonathan Tolins and Seth Bass. *Adapted from the play by:* Jonathan Tolins. *Director of Photography:* Tom Richmond. *Editor:* Dana Congdon. *Music:* Lee Holdridge. *Sound:* DJ Ritchie. *Casting:* Valorie Massalas. *Production Designer:* Amy B. Ancona. *Running time:* 92 minutes. *MPAA Rating:* PG-13.

CAST: Jennifer Beals (Suzanne Stein); Jon Tenney (Rob Stein); Faye Dunaway (Phyllis Gold); Brendan Fraser (David Gold); Garry Marshall (Walter Gold); Rosie O'Donnell (Jackie); Sean O'Bryan (Steven); Patrick Bristow (Brandon); John Schlesinger (Adrian Lodge); Jack Klugman (Rob's Father).

NEW YORK POST, 10/24/97, p. 46, Thelma Adams

"The Twilight of the Golds" never lets the audience forget it's in issue film. What, the drama asks, would you do if genetic testing revealed that your unborn child was gay?

Probably, like most of the characters in Ross Marks' movie, our first reaction would be: "The most important thing is that the baby is healthy."

But what next? That dilemma animates the script by Jonathan Tolins and Seth Bass, based on Tolins' Broadway play. Will pregnant Suzanne Stein (Jennifer Beals) abort when she finds that there is a 90 percent probability that her fetus will grow up to march in a gay pride parade?

Suzanne's geneticist hubby, Rob (Jon Tenney), is a member of the research team behind the unusual (and fictional) test. He encourages Suzanne to be tested, but when the results arrive, Rob has trouble facing the personal ramifications of the scientific findings.

Meanwhile, Suzanne's upper-class Jewish parents, Phyliss and Walter Gold (Faye Dunaway and Garry Marshall), get into the act. Does their desire for a grandchild override their misgivings? Do they want to return him like unwanted wedding presents to Saks?

The kicker is that the Gold's adored, opera-loving son David (Brendan Fraser) is gay. The news of the baby's potential orientation forces a family showdown on the impact of David's homosexuality on the Golds.

As David, Fraser makes an appealing departure from his "George of the Jungle" and "Encino Man" loincloth movies. Shiksa goddess Dunaway makes kasha and speaks Yiddish: Who can watch without a snicker? But Dunaway hits her mark in emotional clinches, while funnyman Marshall ("Pretty Woman" director and "Murphy Brown" regular) can deliver a stinger, but flattens when the drama calls for more.

With Rosie O'Donnell thrown in as Suzanne's coworker and director John Schlesinger making an odd appearance as Rob's mentor, the movie brims with vitality as it relentlessly dissects issues from genetic engineering to unconditional love.

"The Twilight of the Golds" has the narrow focus of an Ida Lupino problem movie from the cusp of the '50s, such as "Not Wanted" or "Never Fear." What it needs is director Lupino's sharpness and unsentimentality, her open-endedness.

When the sun sets on the Golds, all debates are tied up with a pretty blue bow, ready for delivery—and we can't believe a minute of it.

VILLAGE VOICE, 11/4/97, p. 84, Dennis Lim

Whatever else it may be—pseudoscientific morality play, glib issue-of-the-week drama—*The Twilight of the Golds* is primarily a sanctimonious bore. Originally aired on Showtime (where it should have remained), the film puts a televisually correct optimistic spin on Jonathan Tolins's critically savaged Broadway production. A one-line synopsis is deceptively provocative: middle-class Jewish couple Suzanne (Jennifer Beals) and Rob (Jon Tenney) discover that their unborn child carries the so-called gay gene, and consider aborting it. To complicate the high-concept scenario, Suzanne's brother, David (Brendan Fraser), is gay, a fact barely recognized by their compulsively suffocating parents (Faye Dunaway and the movie's executive producer, Garry Marshall, both hamming relentlessly). Less an anti-eugenics polemic than a heavy-handed plea for tolerance, the script (by Tolins and Seth Bass) is too callow to even succeed at the level of cheap manipulation. To their credit, Beals and Fraser strive for nuance, albeit with little success. Otherwise, there's atrocious acting across the board, with Dunaway's notion of ethnic color an especially mortifying sideshow.

Also reviewed in:
NEW YORK TIMES, 10/24/97, p. E14, John J. O'Connor
VARIETY, 1/27-2/2/97, p. 78, Dennis Harvey

TWIN TOWN

A Gramercy Pictures release of a Polygram Filmed Entertainment presentation of a Figment Films production in association with Agenda. *Executive Producer:* Andrew MacDonald and Danny Boyle. *Producer:* Peter McAleese. *Director:* Kevin Allen. *Screenplay:* Kevin Allen and Paul Durden. *Director of Photography:* John Mathieson. *Editor:* Oral Norrie Ottey. *Music:* Mark Thomas. `Sound:` Colin Nicolson and (music) Paul Golding. *Sound Editor:* Ross Adams. *Casting:* Nina Gold. *Production Designer:* Pat Campbell. *Art Director:* Jean Kerr. *Special Effects:* David Harris. *Costumes:* Rachel Fleming. *Make-up:* Graham Johnston. *Stunt Coordinator:* Peter Brayham. *Running time:* 99 minutes. *MPAA Rating:* Not Rated.

CAST: Llyr Evans (Julian Lewis); Rhys Ifans (Jeremy Lewis); Dorien Thomas (Greyo); Dougray Scott (Terry); Biddug Williams (Mrs. Mort); Ronnie Williams (Mr. Mort); Huw Ceredig (Fatty Lewis); Rachel Scorgie (Adie Lewis); Di Botcher (Jean); Mary Allen (Olive); Paul Durden (Taxi Driver); David Hayman (Dodgy); Kevin Allen (TV Presenter); Brian Hibbard (Dai Rees); Morgan Hopkins (Chip); Sion Tudor-Owen (Dewi); William Thomas (Bryn Cartwright); Denny Durden (Kazoo Player); Jenny Evans (Bonny Cartwright); Helen Griffith (Lynette); Royston John (Ivor); Julie Davies (Madeline); Gillian Elise (Pat); Steffan Rhodri (Hunky); Nicholas McGaughey (Chunky); Brian Hancock (Drunk in Toilet); Martin Ace (Rocking Sikh); Bhasker Patel (Ranjit); Michael Cunningham (Mr. Waldron); Boyd Clack (Vicar); Keith Allen (Emrya).

LOS ANGELES TIMES, 5/16/97, Calendar/p. 14, Kevin Thomas

Since Welsh films surface on the average of once a decade, you hope that when one pops up it's an occasion to cheer. While "Twin Town" reveals first-time director and co-writer Kevin Allen a go-for-broke talent with a wild and woolly sensibility, his comedy turns so savage that it's difficult to keep on laughing after an engagingly rowdy start. You don't have to be of Welsh descent to be disappointed in "Twin Town," but it makes it worse if you are.

Dylan Thomas once wrote that "Swansea is the graveyard of ambition," to which the old Welsh seaport city fathers replied, "Ambition is critical" spelled out in brass letters embedded in a granite step in the heart of town. It's an admonition spurned exuberantly by the glue-sniffing, car-"borrowing" Lewis twins, Julian (Llyr Evans) and Jeremy (Rhys Ifans), the spindly slacker sons of Fatty Lewis (Huw Ceredig), a bearded, beefy construction worker.

When Fatty complains of cutting corners in a roofing job, he's firmly reminded by his employer Bryn Cartwright (William Thomas), a businessman as successful as he is shady, just who's the boss. When, moments later, Fatty tumbles off a ladder and winds up with a broken leg, he finds himself all of a sudden regarded an independent contractor by Cartwright.

You wouldn't think that Julian and Jeremy would have enough brains between them to know how to go after Cartwright when he flat-out refuses any financial aid whatsoever to their father, but they prove to be a fearless and sometimes imaginative team. It's hilarious when they manage to drop their trousers—and more—on the very disco stage where Cartwright's pretty daughter expects to win the karaoke semifinals to the tune of "I Will Survive"—her father having greased the right palms.

But the skirmishing between the twins and Cartwright and his two key henchman, a pair of corrupt cops, Greyo (Dorien Thomas) and Terry (Dougray Scott), escalates brutally, with the smiles swiftly starting to freeze on your face. Allen's capacity for affection for rambunctious, thumb-your-nose blue-collar guys is equaled by his nonchalant acceptance of how shockingly lethal human nature can be. He goes so far with violence, it's hard for him to be funny; as a comedy, "Twin Town" is way beyond dark.

Before the film turns so grim, there are lots of raunchy laughs generated by a large and uninhibited cast. Amusingly, the twins' sister (Rachel Scorgie) works as a receptionist at a seedy massage parlor her mother insists on calling an "executive health spa." Allen may suggest that anything goes in Swansea, but it certainly looks to be an inviting place.

NEW YORK POST, 5/9/97, p. 50, Michael Medved

The gritty Welsh industrial city of Swansea somehow survived devastating Nazi bombing raids in February, 1941, so it should also manage to survive its characterization in the twisted new comedy "Twin Town"—but just barely.

The most positive aspect of the film and its impact is that it will make audiences feel grateful to live somewhere else—anywhere else. If you want to develop a whole new appreciation for the glittering charms of Secaucus or Bridgeport, then this is the movie for you.

It's not the tacky urban landscape that makes this screen version of Swansea so hateful, but rather the characters who inhabit the place.

Chief among them are the Lewis brothers (played by real-life brothers Llyr Evans and Rhys Ifans), who are universally known as "the twins" even though they are actually several years apart.

These drooling, gurgling sadists and punks steal cars, destroy property and abuse all available drugs while boasting a combined IQ that clearly remains in double digits.

Think of a Welsh-accented version of the two lead characters in "Dumb and Dumber," but with no hint of sweetness or likability.

Their father, Fatty Lewis (Huw Ceredig), suffers a painful accident falling from a ladder during a roofing job, and when the corrupt, conspiratorial contractor (William Thomas) refuses to pay for the mishap, a vicious feud begins. A prized poodle's head is chopped from her body, the builder's pretty daughter (Jenny Evans) is doused with urine during a karaoke contest, and five victims are eventually burned, drowned, strangled or otherwise cruelly dispatched.

None of this is either funny or believable, nor is the subplot about two crooked cops who deal drugs with the criminal contractor.

Writer-director Kevin Allen, best known for documentaries about the fanatic soccer fans of Wales, seems determined to set an all-time movie record for repetitions of the F-word—especially since the Welsh accents make more complex vocabulary difficult to understand.

His idea of cinematic imagination involves suspending one of the characters from a noose connected to his electric garage door, so that when his wife returns and presses the remote control opener she inadvertently hangs him.

There's also a heartwarming touch of nationalism with another principal buried at sea, wrapped in the Welsh flag, while a massed choir at a local pier sings traditional hymns.

The little-known but gifted Welsh cast shows all the varied and impressive professionalism we've come to expect from movie actors in the United Kingdom and they all deserve better projects than this one.

The Welsh poet Dylan Thomas famously described Swansea as a "lovely ugly town," but the movie about the place is better summarized as pretty ugly.

NEWSDAY, 5/9/97, Part II/p. B13, John Anderson

A mixed marriage of the grotesquely funny and the casually cruel, "Twin Town" is set in Swansea, Wales—a place, we're told, that Dylan Thomas once described as "the graveyard of ambition." Responding to this, Swansea's city council has installed a monument stating "Ambition Is Critical." It's not clear whether anyone actually gets the joke, but the joke certainly wasn't intentional.

But nothing feels particularly "intentional" about "Twin Town," the rather rollicking first feature by Welsh documentarian Kevin Allen, who operates fluently in a milieu of natural squalor. While chronicling some appalling acts of revenge within its tiny community, it also portrays that community with disarming honesty and a deep appreciation for the absurd. In what might be the dark side of Bill Forsyth's "Local Hero," or a Preston Sturges farce, "Twin Town" seldom sneers at Swansea, choosing to find humor in the army of eccentrics who inhabit it.

These include the "Lewis twins," who aren't really twins but are inseparable, incorrigible car thieves and pot smokers. Played by brothers Llyr Evans and Rhys Ifans (Ifans being Welsh for Evans), these seemingly lobotomized petty criminals live in a pair of house trailers with their father, Fatty (Huw Ceredig), an itinerant carpenter, Welsh music enthusiast and model-builder; and their sister Adie (Rachel Scorgle), a "receptionist" at a local massage parlor (aka "executive health spa"). They sniff Dad's glue and antagonize Adie and drive the police crazy by stealing every fast car they can get their hands on.

But the twins are only the punctuation for this story, the chickens coming home to roost in a town rife with corruption and class tensions. Local bigwig and roofing contractor Bryn Cartwright (William Thomas) is engaged in a cocaine deal with two detectives—the vaguely psychopathic Terry (Dougray Scott) and the slightly more trustworthy Greyo (Dorien Thomas).

Bryn, whose *nouveau riche* pretensions provide much of the movie's more understated sight gags, treats Swansea as his private fiefdom. But when Fatty falls off a ladder and Bryn refuses to pay compensation, the twins set out on a course of retribution that progresses into triple murder and a collapse of the local social system.

"Twin Town" bears some comparison to the Scottish film "Trainspotting" (whose director, Danny Boyle, and producer, Andrew MacDonald, were executive producers of Allen's movie) because of their British origins, but also for their view of post-Thatcher resignation about life and crime and an unstandardized, loose-limbed approach to comedy. But "Twin Town" is a singular achievement. And it translates beautifully.

SIGHT AND SOUND, 4/97, p. 53, Ben Thompson

Swansea, the present. Jeremy and Julian Lewis, two unruly brothers known as "the twins" even though they aren't, live on a caravan park with their parents and sister Adie, a massage parlour receptionist. In between bouts of solvent and other drug abuses, the brothers terrorise their hometown by joyriding through streets and over rugby pitches. Their anti-social tendencies are well known to local policemen Terry and Greyo—themselves no strangers to criminal behaviour, being currently involved in a major drug deal.

Ignoring the misgivings of the more cautious Greyo, the psychotic Terry is upping the scale of their operation. Meanwhile, the twins' father, Fatty Lewis, is hospitalised when he falls off a roof while working for wealthy local businessman Bryn Cartwright. Cartwright—who turns out to be the brains behind the drug deal—makes a dismissive response to the twins' demands for compensation. They have their revenge at the Barons' nightclub karaoke competition, when the expected triumph of Bryn's daughter Bonny (her father has bribed karaoke king Dai Rees, with whom Bonny, behind her father's back, is also having an affair) turns to humiliation as the brothers urinate on her from behind a curtain. A huge fight ensues and the brothers escape, but Bryn and Terry catch up with them later and administer a sound beating. The twins respond by leaving the severed head of Bryn's wife's poodle in the Cartwright's marital bed.

Commissioned to exact an appropriate vengeance, Terry douses the Lewis' dog's kennel with petrol and sets light to it. In the ensuing conflagration, the dog, Cantona, escapes, but the twins' entire family are killed. The orphaned brothers head for the hills in a stolen hot-dog van. Greyo tries to investigate the triple murder, but Bryn threatens to reveal his involvement in the drug deal. Terry's attempts to fit up Dai bring to light his affair with Bonny. Before Bryn's rage has had a chance to abate, the twins have broken into his house, stolen his car and boat, and trussed him up in a noose connected to his automatic garage door so that his returning wife inadvertently hangs him. Out in the bay, the brothers have kidnapped Terry and tied him to their father's stolen coffin. As massed choirs sing on the dockside in memorial to Fatty, the twins lower the coffin into the sea—drowning Terry in the process and head for Morocco.

Twin Town's director and co-writer Kevin Allen had a bit part in *Trainspotting* (as the hotel manager supervising the climactic drug deal), and his debut feature's eagerness to be to South Wales what *Trainspotting* was to urban Scotland borders on the obsessional. What is surprising is that Danny Boyle and Andrew MacDonald (*Trainspotting*'s director and producer respectively) should have agreed to act as executive producers of a piece of work that is actually a travesty of all their film achieved.

It's not so much that specific instances of direct inspiration—the high octane delinquency opening, the scatological set-piece (this time urine rather than excrement based), even a Celtic-sporting-triumph-as-metaphor-for-national-pride moment (here it's a rugby try as opposed to Archie Gemmill's World Cup goal)—are just too numerous to keep track of. The shocking thing is that for all *Twin Town*'s determination to borrow from *Trainspotting*, it has so signally failed to capture the essence of the earlier film.

Where John Hodge's screenplay gave Renton's nihilism a strangely uplifting, almost spiritual, quality, Allen's script confuses detachment with heartlessness. It seems to take pleasure in its leading characters' lack of any redeeming features, and from the dog's decapitation through the death of the twins' whole family to the concluding clutch of "comic" murders (in themselves enough to drive the most diehard defender of free speech kicking and screaming into the censorship lobby), a streak of sadism as wide as the M4 runs through the entire narrative. To attempt to justify this by claiming that this film somehow concerns "the absurdity of revenge" will just not wash.

Given the freshness of its Swansea locations and an eager cast of talented local actors (many of them refugees from the S4C soap opera *Pobol Y Cwym*), *Twin Town* should at least have been able to take for granted a sense of itself as coming from outside the London-dominated mainstream of UK cultural discourse. But the pervasive pall of cynicism which seems to hang over the whole project is pure Groucho Club. There is no theoretical reason why someone with Allen's Comic Strip background shouldn't make a worthwhile feature film—and his excellent television documentaries *World Cup Hell* and *On the March With Bobby's Army* proved there is more than one string to his bow—but to make that step requires a leap of the imagination that is not evident here.

The most depressing thing about *Twin Town* is that it seems to mark the almost instant decay of a new and exciting cinematic language in British films. One hopes that others will pick up MacDonald, Boyle and Hodge's baton with better faith. For just as all the accusations that were hurled at *Trainspotting*—that it was immoral, irresponsible, gratuitously violent—were proved to be untrue (or, if true, then true *in a good way*) by the life-affirming nature of the film itself, now they can all be dusted down and levelled at *Twin Town*—this time without fear of effective contradiction.

VILLAGE VOICE, 5/13/97, p. 86, Amy Taubin

Thumbing their unidentical noses at the local law enforcement, the Lewis twins, Julian (Llyr Evans) and Jeremy (Rhys Ifans), joyride through the Welsh countryside in luxury vehicles hijacked from their rich, corrupt neighbors. Evans and Ifans, who look like boiled eggs under straw, are the only palatable elements in *Twin Town*, a first feature by Kevin Allen, executive produced by Andrew MacDonald and Danny Boyle—the team that nurtured *Shallow Grave* and *Trainspotting*.

More determinedly offensive than those two upmarket successes, *Twin Town* is part of the burgeoning British regional filmmaking scene, dedicated to homegrown back-stabbing critiques of the most dismal corners of the post-Thatcher U.K. Here it's Swansea, dubbed "shitty little city" (a tiff on Dylan Thomas's more tempered "graveyard of ambition") by *Twin Town*'s coke-dealing plainclothes cop (Dougray Scott).

Twin Town is a nasty comedy of revenge fueled with a variety of illegal substances from airplane glue to magic mushrooms inhaled and ingested by almost all and sundry. When the twins' father Fatty Lewis, an occasional construction worker, falls off a roof while doing a job for Swansea's sleazy tycoon Bryn Cartwright, the twins demand compensation. Bryn, who's in cahoots with the coke-dealing cops, laughs in their twitching faces. Enraged, the twins go backstage during the finals of the Swansea karaoke competition and spray Byrn's daughter with piss just as she launches into "I Will Survive." From that follows all manner of murder and mayhem including a dog decapitation.

Allen keeps things moving at a frantic, unmodulated pace that becomes enervating after the first five minutes. He seems to have been unduly influenced by the Coen brothers. I have no idea what the residents of Swansea will make of Allen's scabrous vision of their hometown. For someone with a more distanced view, *Twin Town* is off the cinematic map.

Also reviewed in:
NEW YORK TIMES, 5/9/97, p. C20, Lawrence Van Gelder
VARIETY, 2/10-16/97, p. 67, Derek Elley
WASHINGTON POST, 5/30/97, Weekend/p. 42, Desson Howe

TWISTED

A Leisure Time Features release of a Don Quixote production in association with Miravista Films. *Executive Producer:* Barry Witz and Mark Wiener. *Producer:* Adrian Agromonte and Bernard Arbit. *Director:* Seth Michael Donsky. *Screenplay:* Seth Michael Donsky. *Director of Photography:* Hernan Toro. *Editor:* Tom McArdle and Seth Michael Donsky. *Music:* Q Lazzarus and Danny Z. *Production Designer:* Scott Bailey. *Costumes:* Rosemary Ponzo. *Running time:* 100 minutes. *MPAA Rating:* Not Rated.

CAST: David Norona (Angel); Keiven McNeil Graves (Lee); William Hickey (Andre); Anthony Crivello (Eddie); Jean Loup (Fine Art); Billy Porter (Shiniqua); Elizabeth Franz (Social Worker); Ray Aranha (Can Man).

LOS ANGELES TIMES, 12/12/97, Calendar/p. 9, Kevin Thomas

Imagine the late William Hickey—maestro of cadaverous. insinuating evil—cast as Andre, a latter-day Fagin, operating a male brothel out of a lavish old Manhattan townhouse rather than running a gang of youthful pickpockets in Victorian London.

Hickey, Oscar-nominated for his ancient Mafia don in "Prizzi's Honor," is every bit as gleefully amusing as you would expect, but the film in which he stars, "Twisted," is not the kind of movie you might expect it to be.

Instead of serving up gay erotica, first-time filmmaker Seth Michael Donsky creates an urban underworld fantasy, a stylized, operatic fable of innocence and corruption in which he's more concerned with souls than bodies. He's primarily concerned with the salvation of Angel (David Norona), a sweet-natured hustler, and Lee (Keiven McNeil Graves), a runaway African American adolescent, who share a passion for music.

Dark and wiry, Angel works as a bartender and writes songs, but he's trapped in a dangerous, coked-up relationship with the abusive Eddie (Anthony Crivello). Eddie's a macho drug dealer who supplies the clientele at Andre's brothel, where Lee has ended up. Eddie also doesn't hesitate to force Angel into prostitution.

Andre is apparently in no hurry to turn Lee into a child prostitute, and Angel starts reaching Lee to play the piano that had belonged to Andre's opera singer-mother. But the more concerned Angel grows for Lee's welfare the more both become vulnerable to the malevolent Eddie and to one of Andre's resident hustlers (Jean Loup) eager to see the kid start paying his way. The strongest force for good in this tale is Shiniqua (Billy Porter), a caring and fearless drag entertainer at the bar where Angel works.

Donsky, who gives his cast the confidence to show considerable emotion, clearly understands that he is working with lurid material, and he plays against it, seemingly as inspired by Dickens as by the silent cinema in which melodrama, in the hands of masters like D.W. Griffith, became a way of expressing the harshness of life. Indeed, Donsky even uses old-fashioned intertitles as a narrative device.

The silent filmmakers often indulged in sentimentality, the obverse side of melodrama, but didn't flinch in depicting cruelty and injustice and the way in which it brutalizes and deforms its victims. Deliberate theatricality, invoking stage and screen techniques of the past allows Donsky and his ace cinematographer Hernan Toro to suggest the eternalness of suffering and the redemptive impulse of self-sacrifice. By the time "Twisted" is over its world and that of Dickens seem one and the same.

NEW YORK POST, 12/5/97, p. 56, Michael Medved

In a defining moment from "Twisted," a vicious drug dealer named Eddie (Anthony Crivello) angrily asks his male lover: "Do you know what it's like to eat out of a garbage can?' ,After watching this miserable movie, I know what it's like—since the film serves up a heaping helping of garbage presented with a rancid seasoning of preening and pretentiousness.

The story supposedly derives from "Oliver Twist," with a wide-eyed black orphan named Lee (Keiven McNeil Graves) serving as updated protagonist.

When his homeless hymn-singing protector (Ray Aranha) gets murdered by thugs, the little Dickens falls in with the Fagin of this story: an effete old fop named Andre (the late William Hickey) who operates an utterly decadent' homosexual brothel.

One member of Andre's stud stable, Fine Art (Jean Loup) wants to sell the tender 10-year-old on the streets, but another associate, Angel (David Norona), is a drug-addled, brutalized, aspiring composer who prefers teaching him piano.

A hefty drag queen (Billy Porter) also desires the best for the boy, defying the sexy and sadistic Eddie/Bill Sykes.

With nothing else to boast about in this appallingly amateurish production, 29-year-old writer-director Seth Michael Donsky proudly points to his budget of less than $80,000 which somehow brought him a lurid array of orange and blue lights, though the wooden acting proves considerably less colorful.

The irrepressible Donsky has already announced his next project: "House of Lear," an adaptation of "King Lear" set in the drag ball circuit of New York. Awaiting its release, I'll be eagerly counting the days.

NEWSDAY, 12/5/97, Part II/p. B8, John Anderson

Young orphan boy, cast among the street scum of a major city, taken in by an underage criminal element and mentored by a seemingly benevolent, ultimately psychotic elderly overseer. It sounds Dickensian. And it is.

"Twisted," first-time director Seth Michael Donsky's variation on "Oliver Twist" gets an A for audacity: the Fagin character, Andre—William Hickey, in one of his last roles before his death this year—controls a stable of young male hustlers, one of whom, Fine Art (Jean Loup) recruits the homeless Lee (Keiven McNeil Graves). Lee, who because of his age is considered a prime commodity, is, naturally, Oliver. Fine Art is the Artful Dodger. Dickens' villain, Bill Sykes, turn up as Eddie (Anthony Crivello), a thuggish drug dealer. As for Angel, Eddie's boyfriend/punching bag (David Norona), everyone knew him as Nancy.

Donsky's movie raises a couple of interesting points. Had Dickens written his novel today, for one, sexual exploitation would probably be presupposed, so his premise is hardly farfetched. At the same time, if audiences weren't given the built-in distraction of tracking the Dickens story as it manifests itself in the Donsky movie, there might not be enough here to keep us entertained.

Think of it: Another story about urban low-lives and how they crush dreams, crush bones and try to seduce a child who's already been betrayed by his family and society. Is this new? No, and with the exception of Hickey's performance, there isn't a lot here that's particularly compelling. Hickey is wonderfully creepy. And he seems to be one of the few who have a sense of the tone of the film—with the exception of Billy Porter, whose in-your-face drag queen Shiniqua is a complete hoot.

A lot of the dialogue is stiff, the editing a bit jumpy, and moments that simply ring false. Loup is nicely nasty as Art, but Norona, whose Angel is the focus of much of the film, plays him like a suburban refugee. But he does have most of the sappier lines, in a film that wants to be flamboyant, but is better when it's being gritty.

VILLAGE VOICE, 12/9/97, p. 69, Dennis Lim

First-time writer-director Seth Michael Donsky has shoved Dickens into a contemporary netherworld that's less squalid (or, indeed, Dickensian) than it is ludicrously tacky. It's a milieu in which you can identity a pusher by his gold chain, a pimp by his smoking jacket, and a drag queen by her heart of gold.

Oliver's character—now Lee (Keivyn McNeil Graves), an African American 10-year-old—hasn't been modified much, but he has been marginalized to make way for the film's flashier alterations. Nancy has become Angel (David Norona)—waiter, sometime rent boy, would-be singer-songwriter, and punching bag of Bill Sykes-like boyfriend (Anthony Crivello). The Artful Dodger is a bottle-blond hustler (Arthur, but people call him Art, as in Fine Art). Most dramatically, Fagin has mutated into a senile pimp (played by the late William Hickey, who oozes deeply creepy Eurotrashiness in his penuitimate role).

There's scads of stilted acting, not to mention some ill-considered flourishes—flashbacksunfold in the present, portentous title cards interrupt the narrative. Still, Donsky, whose background is in theater, does more than wallow in the incongruity of his updated story (which would be the preferred option of most smug young turks). He's also a resourceful visual stylist, and the film's smutty, shadowy look is strangely alluring. For what it's worth, I'd take five enterprising miscalculations like *Twisted* before having to sit through one *Kiss Me, Guido*.

Also reviewed in:
NEW YORK TIMES, 12/5/97, p. E17, Stephen Holden
VARIETY, 7/15-21/96, p. 39, Daniel M. Kimmel

U-TURN

A TriStar Pictures release of a Phoenix Pictures presentation of an Illusion Entertainment Group production in association with Clyde Is Hungry Films. *Executive Producer:* John Ridley. *Producer:* Dan Halsted and Clayton Townsend. *Director:* Oliver Stone. *Screenplay (based on his book "Stray Dogs"):* John Ridley. *Director of Photography:* Robert Richardson. *Editor:* Hank Corwin and Thomas J. Nordberg. *Music:* Ennio Morricone. *Music Editor:* Bill Abbott. *Sound:* Gary Alper. *Sound Editor:* David Kneupper. *Casting:* Mary Vernieu. *Production Designer:* Victor Kempster. *Art Director:* Dan Webster. *Set Decorator:* Merideth Boswell. *Special Effects:* Mark Hendersheid. *Costumes:* Beatrix Aruna Pasztor. *Make-up:* John Blake. *Make-up (Jon Voight):* Ken Diaz. *Stunt Coordinator:* Tierre Turner. *Running time:* 125 minutes. *MPAA Rating:* R.

CAST: Sean Penn (Bobby Cooper); Billy Bob Thornton (Darrell); Abraham Benrubi (Biker #1); Richard Rutowski (Biker #2); Jon Voight (Blind Man); Jennifer Lopez (Grace McKenna); Powers Boothe (Sheriff Potter); Nick Nolte (Jake McKenna); Aida Linares (Jamilla); Sean Stone (Boy in Grocery Store); Ilia Volokh (Sergi); Valery Nikolaev (Mr. Arkady); Brent Briscoe (Boyd); Bo Hopkins (Ed); Julie Haggerty (Flo); Annie Mei-Ling Tien (Short Order Cook); Joaquin Phoenix (Toby N. Tucker); Claire Danes (Jenny); Sheri Foster (Grace's Mother); Laurie Metcalf (Bus Station Clerk); Liv Tyler (Girl in Bus Station).

FILM QUARTERLY, Winter 1998-99, p. 44, Eric Bryant Rhodes

Among A-list Hollywood directors working today, nobody creates deeper fault lines between admirers and detractors more than Oliver Stone. While working within the Hollywood system, Stone has been able to produce a provocative and controversial body of work unrivaled in its ability to aggressively challenge American audiences to critically evaluate their social and political institutions. Although his position within the Hollywood community has been validated by three Academy Awards, he has maintained his status as a maverick by consistently taking risks. Stone's admirers consider him a courageous filmmaker who engages important historical subjects from a personal, and frequently left-wing, perspective. His detractors label him a paranoid and propagandist who uses the powerful medium of film to push a distorted view of recent events in American history. Thus, Stone has become cemented in the collective American consciousness as being primarily an issues oriented and historical filmmaker with a slightly subversive take on the American establishment.

It is a pity that *U-Turn*, Oliver Stone's highest aesthetic achievement to date, appears at a time when the director has become locked in an image as a political radical. *U-Turn*, a purely fictional story adapted from John Ridley's novel *Stray Dogs*, represents a conscious and much welcome strategic retreat from political controversy. Unfortunately, the film stands little chance of being appraised on its own merits. The film has lamentably not received its just recognition for two reasons. The accumulated hostility and pent up bad feeling against Stone among those who find his portrait of the United States to be fundamentally anti-American makes any picture he releases anathema and subject to a whole host of dismissive prejudgments and general indifference, if not ridicule. Among Stone's supporters—who view him as a daring and outspoken filmmaker and enjoy his agitprop approach to cinema—a fictional film that is devoid of political content and not sufficiently engaged is at serious risk of reduced box office receipts by failing to deliver his signature degree of political commitment.

While the name Oliver Stone has become fixed in the public consciousness with a didactic brand of political cinema, the frequent uproars and persistent controversies that greet his work have overshadowed the fact that he has evolved into an exceptional visual artist with an inventive vocabulary of powerful images and cinematic techniques. In many respects *U-Turn* reveals what Stone's career could have been had he taken an alternative route, taking a detour around the political disputes and fierce attacks that have marked his course through the film world.

U-Turn is an adventure in genre fusion. It is Stone's approach to film as an entertainment without political pretensions. It is pure story with no social or political agenda. The film can best be characterized as a Spaghetti Noir taking its inspiration from the tradition of Hollywood Westerns—with a salute to the stylistic innovations and European sense of sophistication Sergio Leone brought to that genre—and *film noir*. The film takes its title from the reversals, ping-pong shifts of advantage, or u-turns that swing the plot and are the picture's primary narrative theme. Stone has characterized the story as "scorpions in a bucket" to describe the double-crossing, dissembling, and debauchery at the center of the moral universe of the main characters. For the characters that inhabit *U-Turn,* Stone draws upon archetypes—like the drifter, the sheriff, and the *femme fatale*—of the Western and *film noir* genres as ingredients in his spaghetti-noir sauce.

U-Turn is the story of Bobby Cooper (Sean Penn), a feckless pill-popping gambler with a bag full of dollars in transit to Las Vegas to pay off outstanding debts to a menacing band of Russian bookmakers. One sweltering hot day he strays into Superior, Arizona, a dusty southwestern town even more corrupt than he is. He rides into town in a Mustang—a red 1964 Ford Mustang—which needs to have a busted radiator hose repaired before he can get back on the road. Bobby, a man who has obviously seen the world, approaches this hick town with all the arrogance and condescension of one of Howard Hawk's heroes, but over the next twenty-four hours Superior humbles this worldly stranger. With steam shooting from beneath the Mustang's hood, Bobby pulls into Harlan's garage, where the bumbling grease monkey mechanic Darrell (Billy Bob Thornton) exploits the stranded motorist's predicament to the hilt. After being given an exorbitant estimate for the routine repair of a radiator hose, Bobby wanders into town to wet his whistle and get a bite to eat. Almost immediately Bobby is bombarded by a bizarre set of people, situations and circumstances that conspire to thwart his effort to return to Vegas to retire his gambling debts. While waiting for his car to be repaired, he becomes infatuated with Grace McKenna (Jennifer Lopez) and gives the coy Apache seductress all his best Bogart lines. Here is where it all goes wrong. Grace fails to mention that she is married to Jake, a much older real estate developer, who walks in on the pair just in time to prevent being cuckolded. Once ensnared in this sordid love circle, Bobby's completely desperate situation gets him reluctantly involved in a few hastily devised subplots of murder for hire. Through all the twists and turns of the plot we are introduced to the quirky inhabitants of Superior, until Bobby embarks on his final chance for escape.

U-Turn is a departure for Stone in several ways. For one, it is definitely the most humorous picture he has made. Although the dark satire of *Natural Born Killers* provided several uproarious moments, the comic scenes of *U-Turn* achieve a wacky and almost slapstick level of hilarity. The series of close calls and near misses, taunts and frustrations, outrages and surprising twists of fate give the film a cartoonish type of lunacy. The extreme set of circumstances and corrupt world of Superior provide the film with several opportunities for twisted visual gags, razor sharp zingers, and gut busting black humor.

Another difference is that Stone is working on a much more manageable scale. In a way, it marks a return to the tight budgets and guerrilla style of filmmaking that first brought Stone to prominence as a director. The monumental scale and sprawling storylines of his historical and biographical pictures made it exceedingly difficult for Stone to cash-out with a satisfactory dramatic effect. The big budgets led to compromises in which Stone had to cast big stars more for their box office bankability than their suitability for the role. *U-Turn*'s smaller scale enables Stone to compress the storyline into a much faster tempo that gives the film an exciting feeling of urgency. In contrast to the indeterminate conclusions of his grand historical films, the viewer receives the extraordinary twists of plot with a sense of confidence that the director is in complete command of the narrative and the story ends on a gratifying note of ironic resolution.

U-Turn, more than any of Stone's others, is told with extraordinary skill in images. In contrast to his epics, Stone has managed to compress a long story into conventional feature length time through the thrifty use of images in a visual shorthand. He makes deft use of time-lapse of photography, reprises beautiful images, and zooms in on key details (like a knowing glance between Grace and Sheriff Potter, her surreptitious lover). Superior's nuances are established quickly in montage shots that give the viewer a sense of the tedium of life in this isolated backwater. Like many of his other pictures, its style is direct and assaultive but Stone has come a long way since the clumsy voice over letter narrative of *Platoon,* and *U-Turn* demonstrates a much greater measure of subtlety. Perhaps being freed from the burden of screen-writing enabled Stone to give full flight to his visual imagination and pour all his energies into set-ups, frame composition, camera angles, symbolism, and detailed attention to the overall atmospherics of the film.

A large part of the credit for the visual splendor of the picture has to be given to the outstanding cinematography of Stone's long-time collaborator Robert Richardson. From the opening aerial shot of Bobby's speeding Mustang leaving a trail of dust along a deserted dirt road until the closing credit panorama shot of the majestic red rocks mountain range, Richardson's camera work takes full advantage of the poetic landscapes of *U-Turn's* locale in the great American Southwest. The picture was shot primarily in color on high contrast Kodak reversal film stock that gives *U-Turn* a wild rough-and-tumble look with overexposed grainy visuals. The high contrast quality and overexposure that are peculiar to reversal film stock captures perfectly the sweltering Arizona heat and absorbs the rich primary colors of Victor Kempster's exquisite production design. The filmmakers' vivid color palette of blazing reds, bright pinks, sandy yellows, and aquamarine facilitates the narrative's rapid shifts in emotional tone from muted naturalism to hallucinogenic dream states. Stone's experiments in style and pioneering juxtaposition of video with different film stocks—particularly in *JFK* and *Natural Born Killers*—did not go unnoticed by acute observers, but in *U-Turn* form serves function better than in any of his previous films.

The camerawork of *U-Turn* illustrates precisely how the aesthetic qualities and technique of the film animate the themes and story of the picture. The opening sequences of the movie are filmed primarily with a handheld 16mm camera that provides *U-Turn* with a Godardian rapid tempo and nervous energy that depicts with near perfection the protagonist's disoriented state of mind upon entering the strange small universe of Superior. What is dazzling about Stone's films since *Natural Born Killers* is how he utilizes camerawork, editing, soundtrack, and contrasting film stocks to build composite images that communicate the interior thoughts, subjective experiences, and differing levels of consciousness of the characters. When Bobby experiences psychic jolts during his constant travails, Stone chooses distorted multiple exposure images, and ruptures between image and sound to convey information about the protagonist's emotional distress. This technique is used most brilliantly when expressing the antagonistic relationship between Bobby and the comically grotesque mechanic Darrell. When Bobby is driven over the edge by Darrell's escalating demands of payment for routine repairs and unauthorized work, an image of Bobby's gun—which he has locked in the trunk of his Mustang—flashes on the screen to depict his murderous intent. When the advantage shifts to Darrell, a character that appears more stupid than he is, we see a frontal portrait shot of the filthy and inept mechanic laughing in Bobby's face. In the film's unhappy ending, as Bobby's last tumble of the dice turns to disaster, Stone's camera shows us the triumphant grin of Darrell in Bobby's final moment of despair. The break in correspondence between auditory and visual sensations is one of Stone's most imaginative innovations. The overall aesthetic sensibility of the film is hallucinogenic as told from the subjective point of view of the drug tripping protagonist. This mood and altered state of perception is illustrated best in the hypnotic scene between Bobby and Grace on the edge of precipice. As Bobby summons up the courage to carry out the murder for hire he has planned with Jake and push Grace over the edge, Stone prolongs our suspense with quick cross cutting and a sweeping aerial shot that flies above the two figures within the sublime beauty of the Arizona canyons. The music, natural sounds, and powerful images all work to intensify Bobby's heightened sense of emotion and delusional state of mind.

Although the betrayals of trust and treacherous subplots of the story are derived from classic *film noir* tropes, the film's visual style is inspired by the aesthetic sensibility of Sergio Leone's

Spaghetti Western. From the visual vocabulary of Leone's pioneering approach to the Western genre, Stone makes frequent use of giant close-ups of the main characters' eyes and lips, and he shoots his hero on a solitary walk against the sky of the desert horizon. Bobby, much like the Clint Eastwood hero of Leone's *Fistful of Dollars* trilogy, acts out of the single motivation of financial gain.

The affinity with the Spaghetti Western is most evident in Ennio Morricone's score and soundtrack for the film. Morricone was, or course, one of Leone's most important collaborators. The soundtrack of country and western popular tunes and Morricone's haunting compositions contributes more to the emotional power and ambiance of the picture than any of the music in Stone's previous films, with the possible exception French *nouveau vague* composer Georges Delerue's work on *Salvador*. The music in *U-Turn* assumes multiple functions with striking results. The C & W songs reinforce place and setting, and the abrupt sonic burst of the music heightens the jarring effect of the stop-and-start internal rhythms of the film. Nothing illustrates this technique better than the robbery scene at the Groceria. When Bobby has the misfortune to be caught up in an armed robbery at the local grocery store, the old lady who owns the place whips out a shotgun and guns down the fleeing criminals. As she blast the robbers, who are attempting to abscond with Bobby's bag of money, her bullets inadvertently shred Bobby's C notes into confetti. At the moment the bills fly into a thousand pieces, Stone uses contrapuntally romantic music and slow motion photography to abruptly shift from the tension of a crime in progress to the surreal turn of the tables. Morricone's score also supports the film's comic tone with the frequent use of quirky sounding instruments and humorous melodic lines. One of the most jarring sound effects that reinforces the genre blending theme is when we hear the whinnying of a horse when the radiator hose of Bobby's Mustang explodes.

The outstanding acting performances of *U-Turn* also make it a much underrated film. Sean Penn's talent as an actor is often simply taken for granted, but as the desperate Bobby Cooper, Penn has to draw upon a deep reservoir of emotions to depict his feelings and expressions in an extreme set of circumstances. At different times, Bobby is angry, frustrated, arrogant, or begging for mercy, and Penn's performance in *U-Turn* is on a par with any of his previous starring roles. He, more than any other actor working in films today, gives himself over completely to the role. Penn is on screen in almost every scene and the role demands that he become at times hysterical and livid, a strongly persuading lover, and a man reduced to sheer desperation through his many ups and downs. In the supporting roles, Stone has assembled a host of talented character actors that collectively constitute a Fellini-esque gallery of monsters. As the female lead, Jennifer Lopez gives a playful performance that is both tender in its vulnerability, yet steaming with eroticism. Her character, Grace, despite her exquisite exterior, is a wounded child, who is primarily motivated by the fear of being alone and the desire to be loved. Nick Nolte, outfitted in a grotesque costume, gives a superb voice performance with much more of a rough edge than audiences have grown accustomed to seeing in him, and Powers Boothe, who plays the hard drinking and corrupt Sheriff Virgil Potter, symbolizes the upside-down moral universe and perversity of this town.

Perhaps the finest of the supporting performances is given by Billy Bob Thornton as Darrell. From the second he appears on screen in his absurd make-up, Thornton is an unrelenting object of farce. Covered in filth, and seemingly unaware of his low IQ and cultural backwardness, Darrell's sheer stupidity constantly causes him to be, underestimated. In a fit of rage Bobby shouts, "You're just an ignorant, inbred, tumbleweed fuck!" but, ultimately, he gets the best of Bobby. Claire Danes also gives a noteworthy performance as Jenny, the town's attention seeking nymphet, who takes an interest in Bobby and drives her ridiculously jealous lover boy into a tizzy. Witnessing Jenny's relentless pursuit of the stranger in town, Toby N. Tucker (Joaquin Phoenix), Jenny's beau, challenges the uninterested Bobby to a fight to defend her honor by saying in a deadpan twang: "You and I got a little man's business to take care of." Jenny and Toby, like the other supporting roles, are drawn as strongly stereotyped caricatures whose outrageous antics and cartoonish behavior frustrate Bobby's attempt to escape the bizarre world of Superior. These constant trials in extreme circumstances test Bobby's character.

In the final movement of the film, the picture's philosophical theme is revealed. *U-Turn*, a picture that at first appears a typical thriller, is ultimately about Bobby's character and his nihilistic view of spiritual matters. This is most evident in Bobby's encounters with the town derelict, a blind man, played by Jon Voight. Voight's blind man, who sees more than the sighted, gives Bobby cryptic clues about his spiritual hollowness and lack of humility. Grace's husband Jake identifies Bobby as a man without scruples and offers to pay Bobby a substantial portion of the insurance money if he kills Grace. Although Bobby protests that he is not a killer, Jake tells him, "You got a killin' in you." Grace also tries to intuit Bobby's true character and manipulate him sexually into doing away with Jake to set her free. When Bobby shrinks back in horror from her wicked plan and tells her, "I'm not a killer Grace," she replies, "It's in you." Despite the fact that he is a soulless rascal and behaves like a scoundrel, Bobby is unwilling to cross a certain moral line. When Grace asks Bobby what he thinks happens to peoples' spirits when they die, he says: "Nothing. They're just dead meat!" The desert peaks, canyons, and valleys are ultimately a metaphor for the desolation and emptiness of Bobby's soul.

The double-crossing, spiritual nihilism, complete lack of trust of the story all come together in the film's surprising climactic sequence. Despite all the turmoil they have been through together, the final confrontation between Bobby and Grace demonstrates the impossibility of happiness between these two notorious characters. As Bobby and Grace fight to the death, he states, "I love you Grace, but I can't trust you." The moment is strikingly captured on celluloid with a comprehensive life-review flashback montage and the brilliant imagery of Native American mysticism.

The fact that *U-Turn* has been overlooked by audiences and critics alike cannot be attributed to stylistic faults, story, or performances. Perhaps the film will be re-evaluated and full consideration will be given to its aesthetic merits when the dark cloud of controversy and visceral reaction that presently accompany the release of any of Stone's pictures recedes from the horizon. *U-Turn* encapsulates all of Stone's stylistic innovations as a filmmaker and works his themes successfully within a fictional narrative. It achieves a much higher level of thematic continuity, dramatic resolution, and fit between subject and scale than his brilliant, but ultimately artistically unsuccessful *Natural Born Killers.*

LOS ANGELES TIMES, 10/3/97, Calendar/p. 1, Kenneth Turan

"U-Turn" is a new turn for director Oliver Stone, but otherwise it's awfully familiar. The latest in an unending series of bleakly comic, nihilistic neo-noirs to reach the screen, "U-Turn's" story of a bad day in an Arizona hell invests a lot of skill and style in a trifling tale. So it manages to sporadically amuse even while it's wasting your time.

Like the often-filmed Jim Thompson novels ("The Grifters," "The Getaway," "After Dark, My Sweet," among others) of which it is a knockoff, "U-Turn's" John Ridley script places a drifting stranger who thinks he's wised up in a situation that runs the gamut from garden-variety criminality to the purest evil.

After a run of thematically ambitious films like "JFK" and "Nixon," Stone probably turned to this smaller-scale project (shot in 42 days for $20 million, which passes for down and dirty in Hollywood) as a change of pace, the way someone might pick up a thriller at an airport newsstand.

But while a film like "L.A. Confidential" feels like its rethought and re-imagined genre material, "U-Turn," despite entertaining diversions like amusing acting and jazzy visuals, merely walks where others have tried before. It's also difficult to shake the curious feeling that Stone, who satirized similar material so effectively in "Natural Born Killers," is now determined to present it straight.

Driving a red 1964 Mustang convertible though the high lonesome deserts of the American Southwest, protagonist Bobby Cooper (a controlled Sean Penn) isn't planning to stop in Superior, Ariz. But then his engine blows up on him and there he is in the worst possible town to stumble onto unawares.

For Superior is wall-to-wall with trailer trash grotesques, devious deviants capable of running a putative tough guy like Cooper around in circles, working their will on him and catching him up in their contagious bad dreams.

Guys like Darrell (Billy Bob Thornton), the shifty, grease-encrusted mechanic who takes a stab at fixing Bobby's car. Or the blind man (an all-but-unrecognizable Jon Voight) who dispenses unfathomable advice while looking after a dog who may or may not be dead. And don't forget the local teen agers, the too-flirty Jenny (Claire Danes) and her pugnacious boyfriend Toby N.

Tucker (Joaquin Phoenix). "People call me TNT," he glowers at Bobby, who can't help but respond: "That's not very imaginative."

Director Stone has obviously gotten a kick out of dealing with this impressive collection of twisted psyches. And the performers themselves, especially the teen lovers, offer periodic dark chuckles as they go about what passes for their daily lives. It's no surprise that Bobby asks at one point: "Is everyone in this town on drugs?"

More central to the plot are "U-Turn's" fun couple, Grace and Jake McKenna. With close-cropped hair and a grizzly beard that bring to mind John Huston's devious power broker in "Winter Kills," Nick Nolte is wickedly effective as real estate developer Jake, believable when he tells Bobby he can literally smell a lack of scruples on a man.

There is also, to borrow another Jim Thompson title, a hell of a woman in town, Jake's wife Grace McKenna. Passionately played by Jennifer Lopez, Grace is the archetypal noir *femme fatale*, sultry, scheming and impossible for men to resist. She's a good part of the reason Bobby stays in town longer than he plans.

Working as usual with virtuoso director of photography Robert Richardson, production designer Victor Kempster and editors Hank Corwin and Thomas J. Nordberg, Stone has given "U-Turn" the jazzy and jumpy took of a cinematic hallucination, which ought to have been protection enough against boredom.

But the film's look and its acting, clever as they are, feel like window dressing on a film whose plotting is overly familiar and as obvious as an early shot of a buzzard and a wolf gnawing at the entrails of a tasty piece of road kill.

Because the exposition is so familiar and pro forma, "U-Turn," despite its notable diversions, is marked by a lack of narrative drive, an inability to involve us in what will happen to its characters. It's so empty emotionally it's difficult to see what the point is, unless it's the celebration of emptiness, an aim that has become so familiar recently it hardly seems worth the trouble everyone has gone to.

NEW YORK, 10/20/97, p. 71, David Denby

Oliver Stone is just horsing around in *U-Turn*. Sean Penn, a small-time bagman, gets stuck in an unspeakable Arizona desert town, where he falls into a preposterous labyrinth of deceit and betrayal. Stone's usual cinematographer, Robert Richardson, has shot the movie with a wonderful feeling for the harshness of southwestern light and color—a reddish glow that almost hurts the eyes to look at. Jennifer Lopez shows up as a femme fatale, and Nick Nolte, reprising John Huston's rasping grandee-rapist bit from *Chinatown* is her double-crossing husband. Sean Penn, who usually freaks other people out, gets freaked out in this movie again and again. It's about time. *U-Turn* goes on too long, but in its malignant way (imagine a barrelful of scorpions in *their* boogie nights), it's often rather funny.

NEW YORK POST, 10/3/97, p. 41, Thelma Adams

Oliver Stone has directed a brilliant, career-making first film with the neo-noir shocker "U-Turn." There's only one problem: He's already made "Platoon," "Salvador" and "Nixon." There's no going back.

Stone's flashy, bloody-but-bloodless, misogynistic black comedy features the best that money can buy or barter, even if the director brags to the press about his quick-'n'-dirty shoot on a modest budget.

With Academy Award-winning lensman Robert Richardson ("JFK") Sergio Leone's house composer, Ennio Morricone ("A Fistful of Dollars"); and John Ridley's script, Stone takes a stellar cast on a kitschy road trip to nowhere. His characters might as well be buzzards, for all the feeling he lavishes on them.

Sean Penn, on a roll of flawless acting that brings a unique scent to even the stinkiest of stock parts, plays a gambler Bobby Cooper, whose car breaks down on the road to Vegas. He finds himself in an Arizona town without pity, playing a deadly game of craps where Jennifer Lopez, in the "She's-my-sister-she's-my-mother" role, is abfab as Grace, a half-Apache seductress who can turn the hanging of drapes into excruciating foreplay. Grace is married to Jake (Nick Nolte, tall and scrawny and wily as a cartoon coyote). Nolte's menacing sugar daddy is so dry, he makes you thirsty.

As a crooked mechanic who holds Bobby's car hostage, Billy Bob Thornton is as appealing as crusty, day-old fried eggs. Joaquin Phoenix and Claire Danes provide more comic relief as dirt-dumb pathological lovers who catch Bobby in their romantic crossfire. Jon Voight fuses a cigar store Indian and Cousin It as the Stone standard: the Native American spiritual advice columnist.

For all its humor, the movie is fundamentally humorless. Incest, revenge, mutilation, greed, claustrophobia: They're all there, in Technicolor. "U-Turn" exists on a plane that is completely referential; there is no reality, only the movies.

Call "U-Turn" neo-noir, call it a pasta western; either way, Stone has hit a genre cul-de-sac. He'd better start listening to those sage native Americans who crop up spouting themes as if they were flashcards. It's time he made an artistic 180. In his violent, parched comedy, only the buzzards appear to fly in from the natural world with a healthy appetite.

SIGHT AND SOUND, 5/98, p. 58, Philip Strick

Bound for Las Vegas to pay off a gambling debt, Bobby Cooper is forced to stop in the town of Superior, Arizona because of a failing engine. Garage-owner Darrell warns him that the repair will take hours. Clutching his case full of cash, Bobby meets the seductive Grace McKenna who takes him off to her villa. Bobby and Grace's tryst is interrupted by her husband Jake who gives Bobby a lift back. He suggests Bobby murder Grace for a share of her insurance money, but Bobby refuses.

However, during a robbery in a grocery store, Bobby's money ends up blasted all over the shop. In a diner, Bobby is befriended by teenager Jenny, until her jealous boyfriend Toby intervenes. Bobby reluctantly goes to Jake's office to discuss Grace's possible death. Jake suggests Bobby push Grace over a cliff during a sightseeing drive. Instead, he rescues her and they become lovers. Grace tells him Jake drove her mother to suicide and molested her as a child for years; she suggests they kill him and take his hoard of money.

Bobby spends his last remaining cash on a bus ticket, but Toby attacks him again and chews the ticket to shreds. Bobby goes out to the McKenna place where he and Grace kill Jake. Using Jake's money, Bobby reclaims his car from Darrell, loads Jake's corpse in the boot and sets out with Grace. When Sheriff Virgil stops them, it emerges that Grace had been planning a similar getaway with him. She shoots Virgil, and later tries to kill Bobby but he kills her instead. He prepares to drive to freedom, but the engine fails.

Embedded in *U Turn* is a vagrant philosopher of no relevance to the story except that he seems to have guessed the outcome already. Played by Jon Voight, this blind Christ figure weirdly updates Oliver Stone's gallery of omniscient commentators (which includes the Indian mystics of *The Doors* and *Natural Born Killers* and Donald Sutherland of *JFK*) to point up both the ironies and the futilities of his latest venture. "Your lies are old," cackles the soothsayer, as much to Stone himself as to the town's latest reckless spirit, "but you tell'em pretty good."

Stone's old lies on this occasion make no claim to be based on fact. Swooping into the small-town no-hoper territory of, say, Charles Williams' *The Hot Spot* or Jim Thompson's *The Kill-Off*, he gleefully indulges here in sun-baked *noir*, prompted by a genre story from a former television scriptwriter, John Ridley. Stone has stated in interviews that he intended to pay homage to the dark post-war output of directors like Robert Siodmak, André De Toth and Jacques Tourneur, but despite the attempt to achieve—by Stone standards—a low-cost quickie (a 42-day schedule on a budget of "only" $20 million), his regular obsessions permeate the entire exercise. The luckless Bobby Cooper's plight echoes those of the idealistic recruit of *Platoon* the bewildered President of *Nixon*, and the drug-taking Morrison of *The Doors,* spectators alike to a seductive anarchy.

Above all, *U Turn*'s character roll call is remarkably like a Westernised *Wall Street* there's the naive outsider, the ruthlessly cash-obsessed community, the corrupt wheeler-dealer the faithless mistress. Nearly circular in its fatalism, Ridley's melodrama also spices up the staple crime-thriller ingredients of desperation and violence with a generous sprinkling of farce. Not generally considered Stone's forte, it's the burnout that makes the difference here. Unexpectedly, he has come up with a raucously joke-filled black comedy, much assisted by Sean Penn's expression of growing perplexity as one absurd encounter after another erodes Bobby's survival prospects.

Stone's anecdotes may be about concealment, but his characters always signal their failings with an exaggerated honesty—and this fondness for exaggeration, sometimes at a pantomime pitch, imperils his more serious arguments. In the hothouse climate of *U Turn* which has no vital message to impart beyond the usual gumshoe-drama precept that things can only go from bad to worse, there's nothing much to lose and the snarling and shrieking seem enjoyably appropriate. More controversially, they are matched with the associative visual cacophony that Stone and his team composed with relish for *Natural Born Killers:* contrary to traditional *noir* restraint, Stone's new wild style converts *U Turn* into a roaring broadside of colliding images.

This delirium, which seems to be taking place inside Cooper's head, suggests a nasty case of sunstroke. It makes for good subjective cinema at times. When Bobby first meets Jennifer Lopez's Grace, her appearance literally shakes the sidewalk. Concentrating so closely on details of skin, lips and eyelashes, the dialogue becomes insubstantial. The flash-shots dominate what would otherwise be transparently banal pieces of the plot and enrich—or obscure—them with deliberate complication. Moments of crisis are accompanied by glimpses of burial mounds, rattlesnakes, scorpions, the moon, stuffed animals, and random flashbacks linked not so much to Bobby's own history (of which we see little) as to a more general undefined subtext about territory haunted by dead Apaches. Responding as if to a Gothic thriller Stone's players enjoy themselves hugely, with Billy Bob Thornton quite superb as the unstable car mechanic and Nick Nolte in full-blooded Lee Marvin mode. Even so, a little less hysteria from their director would probalby have helped.

VILLAGE VOICE, 10/7/97, p. 73, J. Hoberman

"If you analyze it, [life] becomes almost meaningless," Rodney Brooks tells Morris at one point. Such might be the motto for Oliver Stone's self-consciously modest genre effort, *U-Turn*. The movie opens with Sean Penn racing his red Mustang through Monument Valley, top down and radio blasting. He's momentarily invigorating —pure Americana with bells and quotation marks. Then Stone cuts to his first mega-close-up of a slobbering vulture ...

Where *Fast, Cheap & Out of Control* [see Hoberman's review] used a dense montage and a variety of film stocks to make all manner of unexpected connections, *U-Turn* uses the same technique and cinematographer to subtract from the sum of human knowledge. It's clear from the first jazzy, ominous flourishes that the movie is running on empty—it coasts downhill from the credits as Penn gets stuck in an entropic Arizona town populated by the grossest grease monkey in creation (Billy Bob Thornton), an irascible blind Indian sage (Jon Voight) tending a dead dog, and a mighty suspicious sheriff (Powers Boothe), not to mention a dusky little cock tease (Jennifer Lopez) with a saber-toothed husband from hell (Nick Nolte).

Like *Fast, Cheap & Out of Control*, *U-Turn* is also a sort of bestiary. Everyone has their totem animal. Crows caw, bears snarl, vultures vulch—and who planted that dang scorpion on the tap-water spigot?! Can this be the artist that Garry Wills celebrated in *The Atlantic* as America's Dostoyevsky?

Penn plays a natty asshole with enough zip to mask his character's stupidity, accumulating stigmata as he staggers through the movie's big scenery, double-vision dissolves, and subliminal shock cuts. But Stone's empathy for his characters is somewhat less than underwhelming. "You don't know if you want to kill me or fuck me" taunts Lopez—poised, if limited, in a seriously underwritten role. (The rote misogyny is compounded by casting Claire Danes as a piece of dumb-as-dirt jailbait.)

These must be the latter days. (I read in *The New York Times Magazine* of Stone's conversion to Beverly Hills Buddhism.) That, reviewing *U-Turn* from the lofty heights of the Telluride Film Festival, *Variety* could find this fricassee of *NBK* outtakes ranging in tone from the desultory to the dopey to the downright terrible to be "imaginative, daring, and energized," not to mention loaded with "hilariously surreal asides," is a tribute to either the rarefied Rocky Mountain atmosphere or cozy film-klatch self-congratulation or both. Suffice to say that *U-Turn* is an unbelievably clumsy and pretentious attempt to make the sort of mock noir the Coen brothers invented with *Blood Simple* or John Dahl knocked off so sveltely with *Red Rock West*.

"Nothing," the blind Indian tells us, "makes the Great Spirit laugh harder than a man's plans." Almost nothing. Turn that car back to the '60s, man! A few more little U-turns and I fear that, pace Richard Nixon, we won't have Oliver Stone to kick around anymore.

Also reviewed in:
CHICAGO TRIBUNE, 10/3/97, Friday/p. A, Michael Wilmington
NEW REPUBLIC, 10/27/97, p. 27, Stanley Kauffmann
NEW YORK TIMES, 10/3/97, p. E18, Janet Maslin
VARIETY, 9/1-7/97, p. 74, Todd McCarthy
WASHINGTON POST, 10/3/97, p. B1, Stephen Hunter
WASHINGTON POST, 10/3/97, Weekend/p. 46, Desson Howe

ULEE'S GOLD

An Orion Pictures and Jonathan Demme release of a Nunez-Gowan/Clinica Estetico production. *Executive Producer:* Edward Saxon, Valerie Thomas, and John Sloss. *Producer:* Victor Nunez. *Director:* Victor Nunez. *Screenplay:* Victor Nunez. *Director of Photography:* Virgil Marcus Mirano. *Editor:* Victor Nunez. *Music:* Alex Steyermark and Charles Engstrom. *Music Editor:* David Murphy. *Sound:* Pete Winter and (music) Gary Chester. *Sound Editor:* Alberto Garcia. *Casting:* Judy Courtney. *Production Designer:* Robert "Pat" Garner. *Art Director:* Debbie DeVilla. *Set Decorator:* Charles Kulsziski. *Costumes:* Marilyn Wall-Asse. *Make-up:* Marilyn Wall-Asse. *Running time:* 113 minutes. *MPAA Rating:* R.

CAST: Peter Fonda (Ulee Jackson); Patricia Richardson (Connie Hope); Christine Dunford (Helen Jackson); Tom Wood (Jimmy Jackson); Jessica Biel (Casey Jackson); Vanessa Zima (Penny Jackson); Steven Flynn (Eddie Flowers); Dewey Weber (Ferris Dooley); J. Kenneth Campbell (Sheriff Bill Floyd); Traber Burns (Chance Barrow); Ryan Marshall (Charley Myers); Chad Fish (Markie); Will Sexton (Child at Rest Stop); Dale C. Marshall, James T. Whitehurst, and Charles Branner (Beekeeping Assistants).

CHRISTIAN SCIENCE MONITOR, 6/13/97, p. 12, David Sterritt

Independent filmmaking made big strides in popularity with the recent Academy Awards race, even though most of the attention-getting pictures were made by relatively new figures on the "indie" scene.

Some hardy filmmakers have been laboring in that vineyard for a long while, though, including Victor Nunez, who has explored his northern Florida homeland for almost 20 years in human-scaled productions like "A Flash of Green" and "Ruby in Paradise."

Nunez's newest picture, "Ulee's Gold," could be a good bet for next year's Oscars if indies stay in vogue. Again the setting is northern and central Florida; again the story is driven more by characters than plot twists; and again there's a performance—by Peter Fonda this time—so fascinating that everything else seems to cluster around it like bees in a honey-filled hive.

The bee comparison is appropriate, since the title of "Ulee's Gold" refers partly to honey, harvested by the main character from an apiary near his home.

It also refers to his family, which is as much a treasure as any family, but hard for Ulee to appreciate for two reasons. One is that his reclusive nature has led him away from most human contacts since his unhappy days in the Vietnam War. Another is that his particular family seems prone to trouble. His son is in prison, his daughter-in-law has drug problems, and his eldest grandchild has started following her mother's bad example.

The story begins when Ulee learns his daughter-in-law is in the clutches of two unsavory friends who are looking for stolen loot her husband stashed away before going to jail. Spurred by family loyalty, Ulee brings his drug-dazed relative home and sobers her up with help from a compassionate nurse. Then the bad guys from Orlando arrive on his doorstep with demands and threats, and Ulee must fend them off while shielding his household.

This plot sounds melodramatic, and the movie does have outbursts of emotional and physical violence. Nunez's movies are never motivated by sensationalism, though. He pushes the tale through its distasteful moments as briskly as possible, lingering on them just long enough to establish the challenges his characters have to face. This makes their victories over violence and immorality all the more stirring when they finally occur.

One lesson of "Ulee's Gold" is that a contemporary movie can focus on family values and moral issues without seeming preachy or sentimental. Another is that a skilled screenwriter can bring intellectual interests into a story—the name Ulee is short for Ulysses, one of several references to ancient literature in a light-handed way.

One more lesson is that it's never too late for a comeback. Once a '60s icon in antiestablishment classics like "Easy Rider" and "The Trip," the half-forgotten Fonda has been relegated in recent years to second-rate cameos in third-rate pictures.

Yet his portrayal of Ulee—apparently modeled on real-life mannerisms of Henry Fonda, his movie-star father—is as convincing and absorbing as any work of his career.

Patricia Richardson, of TV's popular "Home Improvement" series, heads the supporting cast. Virgil Mirano did the superbly atmospheric camera work.

LOS ANGELES TIMES. 6/13/97, Calendar/p. 1, Kenneth Turan

An unadorned and unexpectedly moving look at personal redemption and the resilience of family, "Ulee's Gold" stands out for its sureness, its quiet emotional force and writer-director Victor Nunez's ability to find and nurture the mystery and power in the events of an ordinary life.

One of the prime movers of the American independent movement, Nunez, who also serves as his own camera operator and editor, has always made well-regarded but little-seen films, from "Gal Young 'Un" in 1979 through 1993's Ashley Judd-starring "Ruby in Paradise." With "Ulee's Gold" he's added a streak of melodrama that if anything heightens the intensity of his work.

Set, like Nunez's other films, in northern Florida (he once joked his camera would break if it crossed the state line), "Ulee's" is built around a compelling performance by Peter Fonda that unmistakably echoes the work of his father Henry while serving as the capstone of the son's long career as well.

Fonda plays Ulee Jackson, a third-generation beekeeper specializing in Tupelo honey, a stubborn and solitary man proud of his self-reliance. A distant, reserved Vietnam veteran who survived the war when his friends did not by being both tricky and lucky, Ulee's intrinsic faith in family has been shaken by the actions of his own kin.

His son Jimmy (Tom Wood) is in jail for robbery and his daughter-in-law Helen (Christine Dunford) has run off and abandoned their daughters, teenage rebel Casey (Jessica Biel) and her soulful younger sister Penny (Vanessa Zima). The girls live with Ulee, who tells Jimmy he keeps them on a short leash because "one round of fools is enough, don't you think?"

Serving as both a counterpoint to this chaos and as a solace to Ulee are his bees, and among the most memorable scenes in "Ulee's Gold" are unhurried examinations of the rhythms and rituals of beekeeping. Serene and simply poetic, these sequences have a profound and mesmerizing quality, benefiting from Nunez's lifetime of craft and his belief in the significance of what he's showing.

A phone call from his imprisoned son puts an end to Ulee's removed life. Jimmy's wife, Helen, has turned up in Orlando, strung out on drugs and staying with the criminal lowlifes who took part in her husband's failed robbery. Though Ulee's initial reaction is a convincing "I could care less and you know it," his core belief that "we don't ask outsiders for help" makes it inevitable that he will become involved.

That involvement takes two forms. One is the strong dynamic—resisted by everyone from Ulee to the initially out of control Helen to even her children—to re-integrate her into her family. Helping here is Connie Hope ("Home Improvement's" Patricia Richardson), a neighbor who works as a nurse and is leery herself of too much personal contact.

More dangerous is the insistence by Eddie Flowers (Steven Flynn) and Ferris Dooley (Dewey Weber), his son's erstwhile criminal partners, that Jimmy knows more than he's saying about the robbery. Either Ulee helps them get at the truth or family lives will be sacrificed.

Nunez and his insightful ensemble cast have taken this familiar material and woven it into an affecting drama of surprising complexity and impact, neither overstating the melodrama nor avoiding how difficult it can be to make lasting human connections. Best of all is Fonda, wearing metal-rimmed glasses that echo his father's, who brings a deliberateness and a weight to Ulee's stillness that say more than pages of dialogue could. His performance holds the film together, and it's one that all generations of Fondas can be proud of.

Not only do these characters have realistic interior lives, but the locale itself, as in all Nunez's films, becomes a palpable presence. As camera operator (working with cinematographer Virgil Mirano) as much as writer-director, Nunez's extensive knowledge of this part of Florida so roots his story in a defined sense of place that it practically grows out of the soil.

Best of all, Nunez has over the years mastered the technique of allowing his narrative to seem to tell itself. "Ulee's Gold," unfolding in its own way and at its own pace, illustrates how much is gained when a filmmaker has the nerve to take his time. There is a quality about this film's use of deliberation that comes at times wonderfully close to magic.

NEW YORK, 6/16/97, p. 51, David Denby

Ulee's Gold is a fine piece of work in an immaculately restrained, upper-middlebrow style that doesn't much interest me. Peter Fonda, pushing 60 but still possessed of that lanky frame and handsome high forehead, plays a Florida beekeeper, Ulee (short for Ulysses, apparently), who is all bottled up inside. Ulee's wife has died; his son is in jail after a bungled robbery; his daughter-in-law has disappeared, only to show up a druggy mess; and Ulee has to hold the family together himself, irritably raising his two granddaughters while carrying on the delicate and exacting work in the marshes of the panhandle that produces an extraordinary honey.

Victor Nunez *(Gal Young 'Un, Ruby in Paradise)* loves this back-country Florida, and he shoots it with a precise, dry color palette. Everything is seen very clearly and plainly, without exaggeration: Ulee's work is repetitive and undramatic; a couple of young Florida hoods are just banal and stupid. Ulee, a hero of day-by-day integrity, has been hurt so much he won't let himself feel anything; he's become joyless and censorious, and the movie, of course, chronicles his slow thawing-out as he tries to pull his family together. The theme is banal, the treatment decent but parched, in the manner of foundation-supported public-TV drama. Peter Fonda has never been an expressive actor, and it's hard to accept him as a man dulled by loss when we can't see the flicker of some earlier light beneath the dimmed-out surface. His performance is too quiet and unvaried.

Ulee's Gold manages to suggest that everything has gone wrong in this family because Ulee's son has not, like his father, and his grandfather before him, taken up beekeeping. Even if one stretches that point into metaphor—with beekeeping standing in for all the specialized crafts that have been abandoned in the modern period—it's a fantasy of an organic social order that makes little sense for this land of the rootless and the self-made. Most of us in America find our own destiny, and doing so doesn't turn us into criminals. When Ulee's son, behind bars but reformed, announces that he plans to devote his life to beekeeping, it's hard to imagine, after watching Fonda's silent, numbing work routine, that the boy is really coming out of prison.

NEW YORK POST, 6/13/97, p. 48, Thelma Adams

It isn't easy keeping bees. Ask Ulee, the oddly named beekeeper at the hub of Victor Nunez's quiet, graceful, gripping American drama.

"Ulee's Gold," which earned star Peter Fonda a well-deserved buzz at Sundance, overflows with a lifetime of hard-won wisdom in a single, gently paced sitting. Like life, sooner or later everybody gets stung. But not everybody recovers.

Ulee is a conservative Florida widower haloed in tragedy. The sole survivor of his Vietnam platoon, coming home rocked his spirit—and his marriage. Now, with his wife six years buried and his only son in jail for armed robbery, Ulee tends his two granddaughters and his many bees with the same philosophy: Show no fear and you won't get hurt.

Once we learn that Ulee stands for Ulysses, it becomes clear that Fonda's slim-hipped grandpa is as American as Ulysses S. Grant, and his search for a home within himself is as classic a quest as that of the Latin Ulysses.

In "Ulee's Gold," the reluctant patriarch has to stop thinking like a drone and open himself up to life in order to make his house a hive. Writer/director Nunez tosses a drug-addicted daughter-in-law, two crazed hooligans, a cooler full of dirty money and a loaded pistol in Ulee's way to shake him out of his torpor.

A regional filmmaker of astonishing heart, the man behind "Ruby in Paradise" and "A Flash of Green" endows his characters and the Florida landscape with subtlety, texture and depth. Under Nunez's direction, Fonda spills open as an actor.

He might look stringy and chiseled like papa Henry; his rangy movements and whispery gentleness recall the senior Clint Eastwood. But the emotional truth is Fonda's alone.

NEWSDAY, 6/13/97, Part II/p. B13, Jack Mathews

Beekeeping, by its nature, is a solitary activity (who's going to go with you?), but for proud workaholic Ulysses Jackson in Victor Nunez' quietly powerful drama "Ulee's Gold," it's also an emotional hideaway, a daily reprieve from the painful grind of human interaction.

Ulee, played with emotional depth heretofore unnoticed in Peter Fonda, is badly damaged goods. He's a Vietnam vet in his sixth year of grieving over the death of his wife—or, more accurately, over the unfinished business of that marriage. He's full of guilt about a son now in prison for bank robbery, and of anger with the daughter-in-law who abandoned her children. And his granddaughters, one in her mid-teens, the other advancing toward puberty, need the kind of attention Ulee is only able to give to his bees in the Tupelo marshes of southern Florida.

When we meet him, the scarred landscape of the marshes, with its trees and stumps scattered through fields of black water and mud banks, matches the landscape of Ulee's state of mind. And things are about to get worse. Two of his son's robbery partners have discovered that before going to prison, he buried some of the bank job's loot at Ulee's bee farm, and they're threatening great bodily harm—to Ulee and the girls—if they don't get the money.

Like Nunez' last film, "Ruby in Paradise," "Ulee's Gold" is a story about personal restoration. Not redemption, not discovery, not survival, but a rehabilitation of the psyche. And this profound transformation is carried out with a dignity and truth that, for thinking moviegoers, serves as a virtual antidote to the numbing simplicity of most mainstream Hollywood films.

Almost every turn in "Ulee's Gold" runs against convention. You watch this film thinking that yes, at 58, Peter Fonda is more than ever his father's son. The looks, the voice, the lanky Midwestern frame. And the reflective nature of his character suggests a role Henry might have played.

However, as the movie wears on, the slow burn of Ulee's personality more closely resembles characters associated with Clint Eastwood. Behind the protective mask is potential danger. Ulee is, after all, a soldier who, alone in his company, survived Vietnam. When his son, Jimmy (Tom Wood), talking about his ex-partners, says to Ulee on a prison visit, "You're the big jungle fighter, kill them!," your Hollywood-trained response is to expect him to do just that.

But expectations are dead ends in "Ulee's Gold." Though he seems fearless in his confrontations with his son's cronies, his actions are never those of an action hero. When the bad guys, Eddie (Steven Flynn) and Ferris (Dewey Weber), carelessly leave a gun unattended, Ulee doesn't risk grabbing it and turning the tables, he takes the more certain route of kicking it into a pond, at least relieving them of the short-term option of shooting him.

Flynn and Weber are welcome relief front the psychopath stereotypes passing for villains elsewhere on the screen this summer. Eddie and Ferris are ignorant, white-trash thieves, run-of-the-mill bottom feeders with barely enough sense to detect an easy score. Their behavior is unpredictable, in the film as it would be in life.

Other good work is done by Christine Dunford, as Helen, Ulee's drug-addicted daughter-in-law; Jessica Biel, as his alienated older granddaughter, Casey; and Vanessa Zima, as the younger Penny.

Nunez' one conventional character is Ulee's new next-door neighbor, Connie Hope ("Home Improvement's" Patricia Richardson), whose last name says it all. She's a nurse, conveniently available to minister to Helen; a divorcee; conveniently available to rekindle Ulee's romantic spirit; and a concerned citizen, conveniently on guard when trouble appears across the street.

But there are no missteps at the story's center. Ulee is one of the most compelling figures to come along in a while, and Fonda, without a moment of histrionics, gives him a breadth of character that marks him an original. Ulee's gold is his Tupelo honey; Nunez' gold is Fonda.

SIGHT AND SOUND, 4/98, p. 56, Philip Kemp

Vietnam vet Ulysses ("Ulee") Jackson, a Tupelo, Florida beekeeper, lives an isolated life with his young granddaughters Casey and Penny. He gets a call from his son Jimmy, jailed for a bank robbery: Jimmy's estranged wife Helen has fallen into the hands of his low-life partners in crime, Eddie Flowers and Ferris Dooley. Reluctantly, Ulee agrees to rescue her. He finds Helen in Orlando, drugged out of her mind. While raving, she revealed that Jimmy secreted $100,000 of robbery loot before being arrested. Eddie and Ferris hand Helen over to Ulee on condition he finds out Jimmy's hiding place. Otherwise, they'll pay his family a visit.

With the help of their new neighbour Connie Hope, Ulee and the girls nurse Helen back to health. Preoccupied with harvesting his honey, Ulee delays visiting Jimmy, but finally learns from him that the cash is hidden in a derelict truck in the swamp. He returns home to find Eddie and Ferris holding Helen and the girls at gunpoint. They tie up the womenfolk and force Ulee to take them to the hiding place. While Eddie and Ferris exult over the cash, Ulee kicks the gun into the swamp, but back in town Eddie spitefully stabs him in revenge. Meanwhile, Connie has released Helen and the girls and alerted the Sheriff. Eddie and Ferris are arrested. Visiting Ulee in hospital, the Sheriff feigns ignorance of Jimmy's connection with the stolen cash. Jimmy is reconciled with Helen and will soon be eligible for parole. Ulee invites Connie over for dinner.

Victor Nunez likes to structure his films around what his characters do—not the amatory or action high peaks of the plot, however, but how they live out their workaday lives. In his last feature, *Ruby in Paradise,* the scenes that said most about his heroine didn't concern her romantic entanglements (which were fairly banal) so much as the prosaic detail of her daily job. *Ulee's Gold* focuses still more strongly on this day-to-day element—as well it might, having such a beguiling, photogenic activity as beekeeping to watch. Virgil Mirano's camera dwells lovingly on the slow, viscous process of honey-gathering, capturing the heaviness of sweet-scented air in dusty swampwood sheds. The whole film seems to derive its texture and pacing from the quality of its eponymous product: this is a movie that gathers itself together and falls in slow, deliberate folds, like fresh-lifted honey off a comb.

As Ulee, Peter Fonda wears his role as assuredly and naturally as if it were an old coat. He's always shared with his father the ability to get inside physical labour, to look like a man doing a job rather than an actor going through the motions (think of Henry Fonda splitting logs in John Ford's *Young Mr. Lincoln,* 1939). He might have been beekeeping all his life. This grounding in quiet solidity in the measured, unhurried pacing, in the performances of Fonda and his fellow-actors, especially Patricia Richardson, likable matter-of-fact as the sympathetic new neighbour—is the film's strength, allowing it to take on board more conventionally dramatic elements than in Nunez's previous films: guns, drugs, crooks, hidden loot. Early on, when Ulee credits his survival in Vietnam to being 'tricky and lucky', it raises fears that at the showdown he may transform into an action hero. But in the event, there's no such jarring of the tone. The violence, and the heroism, stay low key and unforced, and are all the more effective for it.

So it's all the more of a shame that so much attention to lived reality should be lavished on such a predictable storyline. The parable of the misanthropic loner, forced to relate to others and discovering the joys of emotional openness, was hardly new when Dickens used it in *A Christmas Carol* and we've seen it a thousand times since. Nunez doesn't help by ramming home his moral with some self-conscious dialogue. "We don't ask outsiders for help," Ulee announces, and his daughter-in-law improbably tells him: "Your body might have stuck around, but your heart took off years ago."

This narrative overdetermination runs riot in the final reel, where redemption is handed out wholesale. Husband is reconciled to wife, daughters to parents, son to father; Ulee and Connie are neatly paired off, and Jimmy offers to join his father in the beekeeping business. Closure is absolute; nothing can be left tentative and open. Nunez's skill as a filmmaker is undoubted, it would be good to see it applied to far bolder material.

TIME, 7/7/97, p. 108, Richard Schickel

Ulee Jackson (Peter Fonda) keeps bees, which may account for the cautious way he moves through life. He is a widower, which surely explains his pensive silences. His son is in jail, his daughter-in-law is in need of rescue from drugs and low company, and his granddaughters, who live with him, require large helpings of love, patience and understanding. All that, doubtless, justifies the bitter flashes that occasionally illuminate his frozen taciturnity.

What's harder to understand is the critical enthusiasm and good grosses that have so far greeted *Ulee's Gold*. Some of it probably derives from a desire to welcome Fonda back from his long exile on the fringes of moviemaking—B keeping of another kind—and the fact that, in his maturity, he reminds us a little bit of his father. Most of it, though, surely arises from the desire to encourage an alternative cinema of sobriety and humanity in the midst of summer's heavily mechanized silly season. The key moment in writer-director Victor Nunez's film comes when Ulee could pick up a stray gun and blast a pair of bad guys away. He doesn't, and you just know that this austere refusal of the conventionally melodramatic will eventually win *Ulee's Gold* an Independent Spirit Award.

We, meantime, learn more about apiaries than we really need to know. And are left wondering if some dynamics in the direction, some perversity in the development of characters, some surprises in the story-qualities that animated *Lone Star,* which so richly filled this slot last summer—would constitute that much of a sellout. Nunez's film neither floats like a butterfly nor stings like a bee. It just drones on.

VILLAGE VOICE, 6/17/97, p. 66, Amy Taubin

There's something of John Sayles and even more of John Ford in *Ulee's Gold,* which is to say, it's unmistakably a film by Victor Nunez, American indie traditionalist.

In Nunez's latest depiction of Florida, where the light is limpid and warm and the living is slow but not at all easy, tradition goes all the way back to Homer. Having lost his Penelope forever, Ulysses Jackson, a/k/a Ulee, makes an interior odyssey—to find his way back to the family he never left.

Ulee (Peter Fonda) is a bee keeper, a Vietnam survivor with a bum knee, busting his back to eke out a living in a dying cottage industry. Ulee makes extra-tasty honey, but bee-farming has become industrialized, and though the mass-market product is less unique, no one seems to care. (Nunez has been writing, directing, shooting, and editing his own films for 20 years, and if you think *Ulee's Gold* contains a metaphor for its own making, you wouldn't be wrong.)

With his wife dead of cancer, his son Jimmy doing time for bank robbery, and his daughter-in-law Helen run off, Ulee tries to make some sort of stable life for his granddaughters. Nunez takes his time, establishing Ulee's growing sense of loss and the domestic and work routines that barely insulate him from his pain. It's not until we're a quarter of the way through the film that the suspense-genre motor kicks in.

Calling from prison, Jimmy implores Ulee to rescue Helen, who's strung out on Rophynol and hanging around with Jimmy's former partners-in-crime. These two scuzzballs have discovered that before he was arrested, Jimmy stashed away big bucks from the robbery. They tell Ulee to deliver the money or else they'll do bad things to Helen and the kids.

Nunez tried once before, with less success, to combine a genre plot with a realistic, character-driven portrayal of daily life. In *A Flash of Green* (1985), the convoluted criminal investigation overwhelmed the characters. Here, however, Nunez keeps the focus on Ulee, a stand-up guy who's more resourceful coping with the evil in the world than with his own repressed anger and guilt.

Ulee's Gold is essentially a collaboration between director and actor. Longtime underachiever Peter Fonda gives the performance of a lifetime as the emotionally withdrawn Ulee. (One hopes it won't have dimmed in memory when award season rolls around.) Comparisons to Clint Eastwood or to his father Henry, while not unwarranted, miss a crucial point. This Fonda inhabits Ulee's thin skin as an actor rather than a star. Once the shock wears off from seeing that Captain America has become a grandpa with thinning hair and stiffened joints, what one sees on screen is almost all Ulee Jackson.

Nunez's filmmaking style is as understated as Fonda's acting. (The movie was shot in Super 16 because the lighter camera allowed Nunez more mobility, but the new Kodak stocks make the 35mm blowup look like old Technicolor.) The camera is Ulee's mirror but it sees him in ways he can't see himself. It lingers as he pours a cup of tea for a woman he's on the brink of desiring—as if the grace he brings to that quotidian task were the measure of the man. It notes how he tightens his body against the softly ravishing Florida light because to open himself to pleasure means risking being overwhelmed with pain. It observes his tick of fiddling with his glasses—not to see more dearly but to shield himself from other eyes.

Still, one can't completely forget that it's Peter Fonda on the screen. Even stripped of his bad-boy glamour, he embodies a complicated moment in American film history. Not only the privileged and abused son of old Hollywood, Fonda is also the star and one of the creative powers behind the picture that gave the industry a heart attack. *Easy Rider,* a personal film made on the cheap by Hollywood insiders, became a catalyst for the independent film movement. Death trip though it was, it galvanized the creative energy of a generation that had never before recognized itself in the movies.

Nearly 30 years later, *Ulee's Gold* is an elegy for the fragile independence that's been almost entirely co-opted by the industry as well as for a romantic image of a masculine self-sufficiency that no one could live up to. It's a very sad film, though not entirely pessimistic. (If Ulee becomes a better man for learning to mix tenderness with grit, it's because he lives in a house full of women.)

Wanting the best for his characters, Nunez sometimes falls into sentimentality. But just when the film turns unbearably sticky, he gifts us with Van Morrison singing "Tupelo Honey" and comes up with the gold.

Also reviewed in:
NATION, 7/14/97, p. 34, Stuart Klawans
NEW REPUBLIC, 7/7/97, p. 26, Stanley Kauffmann
NEW YORK TIMES, 6/13/97, p. C3, Janet Maslin
NEW YORKER, 6/16/97, p. 108, Terrence Rafferty
VARIETY, 2/3-9/97, p. 42, Todd McCarthy
WASHINGTON POST, 6/20/97, Weekend/p. 37, Desson Howe

ULYSSES' GAZE

A Fox Lorber release of a Theo Angelopoulos Film Productions-Greek Film Center-Mega Channel (Athens)/Paradis Films-La Generale d'Images-La Sept Cinema (Paris)/Basic Cinematografica-Instituto Luce-RAI (Rome) coproduction, in association with Tele Munchen, Concorde films, Channel 4. *Executive Producer:* Costas Lambropoulos and Mark Soustras. *Producer:* Costas Lambropoulos. *Director:* Theo Angelopoulos. *Screenplay (English and Greek with English subtitles):* Theo Angelopoulos, Tonino Guerra, and Petros Markaris. *Director of Photography:* Yorgos Arvanitis. *Editor:* Yannis Tsitsopoulos. *Music:* Eleni Karaindrou. *Sound:* Thanassis Arvanitis. *Production Designer:* Yorgos Patsas and Midrag Mile Nicolic. *Costumes:* Yorgos Ziakas. *Running time:* 180 minutes. *MPAA Rating:* Not Rated.

CAST: Harvey Keitel (A.); Maïa Morgenstern ("Ulysses'" Wives); Erland Josephson (Library Curator); Thanassis Vengos (Taxi Driver); Yorgos Michalokopoulos (Nikos); Dora Volonaki (Old Woman).

LOS ANGELES TIMES, 3/21/97, Calendar/p. 6, Kevin Thomas

The title of Theo Angelopoulos' monumental, magnificent "Ulysses' Gaze" refers to the master Greek filmmaker's longing for the innocent vision of the novice. This longing, in turn, gives way to his larger concern with the tragic history of the Balkans, the ongoing chaos in the former Yugoslavia, in particular.

His near three-hour epic is archetypal Angelopoulos: great, stunning vistas unfolding at a stately pace. Angelopoulos is literally a modern Homer: Virtually all his films are odysseys multilayered in meaning. As such, they are totally demanding and can be enthralling if you're able to—and prepared to—give yourself over to them—totally.

Harvey Keitel plays a Greek-born American filmmaker known only as A. who returns after a 35-year absence to his native country for a presentation of his newest film. We are told that the film is extremely controversial for its religious themes—think of Martin Scorsese's "The Last Temptation of Christ," which is based on Niko Kazantzakis' novel—and this provokes a demonstration in his hometown.

Amid the uproar, A. is actually much more concerned with tracking down three unaccounted-for reels of film taken by the Manakia brothers, real-life figures who, beginning early in the century and for some 60 years, recorded life throughout the Balkans without regard to national borders or ethnic politics and turmoil. We also learn that the brothers operated a theater in Monastir (now Bitolj) until it was destroyed in 1939.

A. becomes increasingly obsessed with the need to track down those reels as a way of revitalizing himself, and his search takes him all over the Balkans, climaxing in strife-torn Sarajevo itself. A.'s odyssey becomes for Angelopoulos, whose principal writer for years has been Italy's distinguished Tonino Guerra, an expression of his love for the cinema and a contemplation of the role of the artist in times of war. It also demonstrates the power of art as an act of defiance in the face of danger and devastation.

A.'s travels take us into such unfamiliar territory you are likely to have trouble following his itinerary (neatly outlined and traced on a map in the press kit) from Korita, Albania, to Skopje, Bucharest, Belgrade and Sarajevo. It is actually not that important to Angelopoulos' themes and concerns that you know at all times precisely where you are—A. doesn't always know that himself. However, a couple of title cards and a little bit of soundtrack narration could make the film more accessible to American audiences. In Sarajevo, he meets the genial, kindly head of the local film archive (Erland Josephson, a favorite from Ingmar Bergman's films).

Along the way, A. has encounters with several women, all of them played by intense, darkly beautiful Maia Morgenstern; in two sequences, Keitel becomes the Manakia brothers and Morgenstern their wives.

Like Fellini, Angelopoulos, working with his formidable cinematographer Yorgos Arvanitis, is a creator of memorable images, and the sight of an immense, dismantled statue of Lenin laid out on a tugboat heading down the Danube is especially striking as well as obviously symbolic.

"Ulysses' Gaze" represents, through Keitel and Angelopoulos, the teaming of two world-class risk-takers. Keitel is more than up to the challenge of playing Angelopoulos' clear alter ego, a sensitive, passionate man given to poetic reflections.

Verging on the surreal, "Ulysses' Gaze" creates its own universe in which loss, suffering and longing are expressed with the utmost dazzling beauty and made more stirring with the accompaniment of Eleni Karaindrou's melancholy score. Angelopoulos has written that "there comes a moment when the filmmaker begins to doubt his own capacity to see things, when he no longer knows if his gaze is right and innocent." Judging from "Ulysses' Gaze," Angelopoulos has nothing to worry about.

NEW STATESMAN & SOCIETY, 2/9/96, p. 34, Lizzie Francke

Theo Angelopoulos is a film-maker for whom the odyssey never ends. His cinema is peopled with those burdened by their strange journeys. Of his more recent films, *A Voyage to Cythera* (1984) follows the film-maker who returns to the Soviet Union after years in exile. In *The Bee Keeper* (1986), Marcello Mastroianni plays a middle-aged man who relinquishes family and work to pursue the pollen trail with his apiary; while *Landscape in the Mist* (1988) is about two children who search in vain for their missing father who may or may not now be living in Germany.

His latest film continues in the tragic trajectory. Its allegorical nature is made quite manifest from the beginning—a film-maker named simply "A" (played by Harvey Keitel) returns to Greece after years of American exile to screen his latest, controversial film, which is projected in an Athens square in spite of the objections of religious extremists. "A" is ushered through a labyrinth of streets while dark-clad shoals of armed police and protesters flood through the city—riot shields and candles their respect totems. But the filmmaker is really back in the old country to commence a "personal journey" in search of three missing and undeveloped films made by the Manakis brothers, turn-of-the-century founders of Balkan cinema. The Manakis, we are told, were trying to record "an era, a new century ... they weren't concerned with politics or racial difference." They were attempting to portray something innocent of the political upheavals around them.

Searching for those lost reels, "A" treks across snow and war-blasted Balkan states, taking taxis and rickety trains from Athens to Sarajevo via Skopje, Bucharest and Belgrade, and finds that his journey is as much about crossing temporal borders as geographical ones as he stumbles over troubled 20th-century history. His odyssey is also marked by futile encounters with various women (all played by Maia Morgenstern, who in one dream sequence also appears as his mother).

Clearly, *Ulysses' Gaze* is about a political history that is locked in an endless replay, but it is also about the history of cinema. The celluloid ghosts cannot be laid to rest; they have a disruptive presence within the film, not only in short bursts of footage from the early era that flicker though *Ulysses' Gaze*, but in "A"s travels. He chances upon derelict cinemas, cold and as uninviting as the shrines of a religion abandoned long ago. He may be looking for that pure, clean moment in film history—that time of innocence—but the suggestion is that this is his delusion. When finally he comes across his holy grail, it is an empty vessel—the film is projected only to reveal a bright blankness. And that is the grand tragedy of this saturnine piece.

One suspects that Angelopoulos is wrestling with his own demons of light and sound as he attempts to tether the world that he projects to the sullied world that he lives in. The unseen movie is the echoing double of the one that we see as beginnings and endings collapse into each other. "A" may stand for Angelopoulos and autobiographical. But it is also for alpha which is entwined with Omega.

The film is an undeniably breathtaking piece, a testament to the power of the moving image as "A" passes from one well-turned symbolic moment to the next. The cinematography by Yorgos Arvanitis is spectacular, and, along with the music, helps envelope one in the muted, dream-like mood of the piece. The vast, gray, wintry landscapes that "A" passes through imply the terrible isolation—while moments smothered in mist and darkness underline just how occluded the vision can be. Indeed, there is something more than haunting about a film that is unafraid to wipe out vision completely that makes darkness visible.

But sometimes those symbolic moments feel too measured. Travelling up the Danube from Bucharest to Belgrade, "A" accompanies a huge statue of Lenin that is being broken up and "spread around for collectors". The relics of communism are exported as a curiosity while, along the river banks, crowds gather to genuflect and cross themselves, perhaps in perverse homage. Later, in the shell of Sarajevo, the inmates of an asylum are left to do an "undead" shuffle through the streets. But the endless pursuit of the eternal feminine as played by Morgenstern jars most of all. It may be part of the mythic trope, but here it feels like a perfunctory gesture empty of emotional resonance. But then *Ulysses' Gaze* is a cold film in every way. "A" may display a range of feelings—but they are not authenticated by the deadened acting style Keitel chooses to adopt here: it is hard truly to emote when you are a cipher. In the final Sarajevo section, "A" befriends "S", the town's film archivist (Erland Josephson), and his daughter (Morgenstern, again). A stroll through the city, though, ends up with "A"'s companions becoming separated from him in the mist, only to be rounded up and shot. The shocking climax is muffled—one can't get inside "A"'s grief. But then surely this is Angelopoulos'intention—for this voyage is not one of personal catharsis but one that throws the audience back from the mythic into the real, bloody world.

NEW YORK POST, 1/17/97, p. 49, Larry Worth

Who says they don't make epics anymore?

True, "Ulysses' Gaze" doesn't have the sweep of David Lean's "Doctor Zhivago." For that matter, it's lacking the narrative power of Homer's "Odyssey," even though the hero's journey equals that of the legendary Ulysses.

But writer/director Theo Angelopoulos has come up with an ambitious, lyrical look at one man's trek from his Greek roots to the midst of battle-scarred Sarajevo. Along the way, the focus veers from the fall of Communism to the horror of ethnic cleansing. And much, much more.

The plot begins in a deceptively straightforward manner: much-celebrated director Mr. A. (Harvey Keitel) embarks on a quest to find three long-lost reels of undeveloped film shot by two Balkan brothers in 1905.

What follows makes the search for the Holy Grail pale by comparison. But as Mr. A. stresses early on, this is a personal journey and a metaphysical one, too. He's soon confronting the ghosts of his mother and grandparents, finding and losing a succession of lovers (all played by the same woman) and blurring fantasy with reality.

Angelopoulos strikes a uniquely poetic tone as the world-weary main character obsesses on finding inner peace.   That comes obvious via a nonstop series of breathtaking, amazingly photographed scenes.

The standout is a 15-minute sequence in which a Colossus-sized Lenin statue is dismantled and placed on a barge for an unforgettable trip, with a Lilliputian Keitel perched on Lenin's Gulliver-like shoulder.

The Sarajevo tableaux are almost as mesmerizing, capped by a juxtaposition of innocence, beauty and unspeakable bloodletting that underscores the central themes of faith and despair.

Complementing the haunting score, Keitel is in top form as the anguished protagonist.   Indeed, his pathos and apt delivery completely overshadow the latest of his now-trademark romps in the buff.   Erland Josephson and Maia Morgenstem also stand out.

But that doesn't mean the production's perfect.   Is its three-hour running time excessive? Yes. Could the dialogue be improved? Sure.   Are the results sometimes pretentious? No question.

At the same time, these abstract pieces of a giant puzzle are always original, ever-intriguing and consistently arresting.   That's why "Ulysses' Gaze" comes off as the most brilliant of jigsaws.

SIGHT AND SOUND, 2/96, p. 55, Nick Kimberley

A, a film director, in exile for 35 years, returns to Greece to show his new film.   The screening is disrupted by religious fanatics.   A says that he is in Greece to locate three fabled reels of film shot in 1905 by the Manakis brothers: the Balkans' first film.   A pursues a beautiful woman, the first of several who accompany his odyssey to recover the old film (most of them played by Maïa Morgenstern).   A takes a taxi to Albania.   At the border, he picks up an old woman visiting her sister for the first time in 47 years.   Up in the mountains, the cabby tells A that Greece is dying after 3000 years in ruins.

A makes his way to Skopje.   The city's film archivist (Morgenstern) learns of his quest for the "film that contains the world".   She joins him on the next stage of his journey, to Bucharest, where A seems to slip into a different time.   He is interrogated about his association with the anarchist Manakis brothers.   Faced with a firing squad, A suddenly rejoins the present.   But the past reemerges as we see his family at a party, spanning consecutive New Year's Eves in the 1940s.

A awakes from his dream and bids farewell to his companion before boarding a barge carrying a huge statue of Lenin to Germany.   He disembarks in Belgrade, where he learns that the Manakis reels went to Sarajevo to be developed.   A sets off with yet another woman (Morgenstern) into the battle zone.   Finally he reaches Sarajevo and finds the film librarian, whose efforts to develop the reels have been curtailed by war.   Spurred into finishing his job, the librarian introduces A to his daughter (Morgenstern), who senses she has known the film-maker for years.

On the streets, fog allows the locals to feel safe from snipers.   Strolling with the librarian and his family, A becomes separated from the others.   Through the fog we hear gunmen kill his new friends.   Distraught, he returns to the newly-developed film.   We see a blank and flickering screen as A wonders what he's been searching for and whether he's found it.

The deafening clash of symbols, the ominous rumble of portents, the distant sound of axes grinding: not all the noises we hear during *Ulysses' Gaze* are there on the soundtrack.   The movie is certainly in some senses autobiographical, yet it also aspires, like much of Theo Angelopoulos' work (in particular his epic trilogy *Days of 36, The Travelling Players* and *The Hunters*) to the status of an epic, one built on a highly schematic and rather fragile structure.

As the film director A takes boat journey after boat journey on his way to Sarajevo, he replays Ulysses' original odyssey, complete with repeated encounters with mysterious women, most of them played by Maia Morgenstem.   Whether the Homeric allusion is useful is open to question. Certainly it would be difficult to find many exact correspondences.   Perhaps in the end it is sufficient that this Ulysses is a figure whose journey can only leave destruction in its path while his goal remains elusive and perhaps illusory.   His quest for the Manakis brothers' silent film might be seen as Angelopoulos' own search for a pristine cinema.   It's a search that necessitates nothing less than a synopsis of our century, which Angelopoulos invites us to read through the simultaneous histories of cinema and of the Balkans, in particular the country that was Yugoslavia.

Almost the first words that we hear from A are "This is a personal journey". On the way we see some awe-inspiring, even terrifying sights. The film's starkest images are almost invariably of something vast and impersonal which threatens to obliterate the merely human: the bleached light high up in the Albanian mountains; the fog that falls on Sarajevo; the two sets of demonstrators, one carrying umbrellas, the other torches, who, facing each other across police lines, silently engulf A and the woman he is pursuing through the streets of Athens. These disturbing moments eerily re-enact the persistent tragedy of the twentieth Century. It is a measure of Angelopoulos' skill that they are mysterious, rather than dogmatic images, none more so than the sight of the shoreline crowds genuflecting as the disassembled statue of Lenin floats by, apparently pointing A towards his destiny.

Yet finally *Ullysses' Gaze* traps itself in its own thick web of allegory. Film director A's name suggests that he is an emblem: Keitel plays him rather too convincingly as a cipher, delivering his lines as if, precisely, reading a script. When his encounters with Morgenstern become sexual, it's more a matter of scrabbling at each other's outer garments than of any truly erotic mingling of bodily fluids. Much of the dialogue is subtitled, but there are long passages in stiff and unyielding English, which Keitel, in particular, delivers as if reading from a phrasebook. Explaining his quest for the Manakis film, he advises us that he is searching for "a lost glance, a lost innocence, an obsession, as if it was my own work, my own first glance, lost long ago," a sequence of clauses clumsily striving for poetic significance, yet defying any attempt to sound natural.

At one point A dismisses one of Morgenstern's multiple incarnations with a sobbed "I'm crying because I can't love you," but not only does he not appear to be crying, the line itself is grotesque, as if quoted in the wrong place. Perhaps Angelopoulos intends us to find A absurd and egocentric, processing misery to his own ends, unable to understand what's going on: having finally made his way to Sarajevo he stands at a crossroads, forlornly repeating, "Is this Sarajevo?" while the citizens hurtle past him not daring to slow down for fear of dying.

The film's closing images are of A muttering solipsistically to a blank screen soon after his new-found friends have been shot: the bitter irony is presumably intentional, a reminder of the sterility of any quest for the "first gaze," for artistic purity. Still the feeling persists that we should see A's quest as truly heroic. The very length of the film suggests as much. In fact, the film's duration works against itself, dulling the impact of the many images which remain with the viewer long after the lights come up. Yet three hours spent in pursuit of A's obsession might lead us to think that this Ulysses set sail in a somewhat leaky vessel.

VILLAGE VOICE, 1/21/97, p. 65, J. Hoberman

What does it take these days to get a reasonably challenging, foreign-language movie to an American audience? Big star? Festival pedigree? Upbeat ending? Two-page *Times* ad? Disney-affiliated distributor? Mad ambition?

Speaking of hubris, *Ulysses' Gaze*, the 1995 cause célèbre by Greek maestro Theo Angelopoulos, has the chutzpah to connote the fin de siècle, the cine-centennial, and the fall of Communism (not to mention the collapse of the Ottoman Empire), while referencing them all to the founding narrative of the Western canon.

After 35 years in America, a Greek-born director named "A" (Harvey Keitel) returns to his native village, ostensibly to screen his latest movie. Once there, however, he embarks on an odyssey that, over the course of a stately three hours, will take him from Greece through Albania, Macedonia, Bulgaria, and Romania, up the Danube and ultimately to Sarajevo, in search of a mythical three undeveloped rolls of film shot in 1905 by a pair of pioneer Balkan filmmakers. *Ulysses' Gaze* is very nearly an allegory of its own tortuous path to New York. (Snubbed by the NYFF, it is opening at Anthology Film Archives.) Indeed, it may be tougher to sell this movie than it is for A to find his three ancient actualities.

For me, Angelopoulos's extended takes and meaning-drenched landscapes have always seemed derivative of '60s art-house gods Michelangelo Antonioni and Miklós Jancsó and, unlike my erstwhile colleague Georgia Brown (who reported on Angelopoulos's "public embarrassment" at Cannes, where his movie lost out to another post-Yugoslavia epic, Emir Kustirica's

Underground), I've not been a partisan of his previous movies. Nor was I predisposed to like *Ulysses' Gaze*. If the premise seemed dubious, the (English) dialogue proved (to put it kindly) banal. The grand metaphors were overly schematic and didn't always jell, and yet ... the images command the screen. The film's rhetoric is triumphantly visual—albeit ably supported by Eleni Karaindrou's rhapsodic, incantatory score.

An epic at once abstract and concrete, *Ulysses' Gaze* does touch greatness—largely because of its formal mastery. No less than Jancsó, Angelopoulos specializes in choreographing fluid shots of groups in motion to present history as an unfolding spectacle—the rain-slicked streets of an otherwise empty town filled with rival demonstrations, one brandishing torches, the other wielding umbrellas. And like that other "A," Antonioni, Angelopoulos sets his figures in unexpectedly eloquent wastelands—a melancholy 10-minute sequence filmed through the windshield of a cab careening through the villages of snowy Albania. Unique is his capacity to choreograph flashbacks in contiguous space—when A arrives in Bucharest, for example, he is met on the platform by his own youthful mother. Later, the first five years of Romanian Communism are telescoped into a seamless series of New Year's eve parties.

Keitel, who is present in virtually every shot, gives a physically heroic performance—all the more so for his having to articulate the ineffable. (It is certainly his riskiest job since *Bad Lieutenant*, and his dedication to the project has extended well beyond the seven months he spent before the camera.) Although the wonderful Romanian actress Maia Morgenstern—last seen here in *The Oak*—is on hand to embody a half dozen manifestations of the eternal *femme*, Keitel plays his most memorable scene opposite the noble brow and gravely unseeing eyes of a dismembered Lenin statue. In a sequence that suggests *Land of the Pharaohs* as much as *Being and Nothingness*, a barge carries the fallen idol past the silently genuflecting masses all the way to Belgrade, where A learns that the lost reels he was seeking have disappeared into the urban rubble of Sarajevo.

It is there, in an abandoned cinemateque in Europe's heart of darkness, that A encounters the last cinephile (Erland Jacobson). The sequence's misc-en-scène of dank postmodern detritus has been anticipated by both Hans-Jürgen Syberberg and Tarkovsky and may best be appreciated as science fiction. Still, to watch this bombed-out cinematheque on the big screen at the not-quite-as-bombed-out Anthology Film Archives, on a derelict stretch of Second Avenue that's light years away from Cannes's blazing noon (or even the West Side hubbub of the New York Film Festival) is moving in itself—you can almost believe that Angelopoulos has created the last European art film.

Also reviewed in:
NEW REPUBLIC, 5/12/97, p. 27, Stanley Kauffmann
NEW YORK TIMES, 1/17/97, p. C6, Janet Maslin
VARIETY, 5/29-6/4/95, p. 53, David Stratton

UNDERGROUND

A New Yorker Films release of a CIBY 2000/Pandora Film/Novo Film co-production. *Executive Producer:* Pierre Spengler. *Director:* Emir Kusturica. *Screenplay (Serbo-Croatian with English subtitles):* Dusan Kovacevic and Emir Kusturica. *Based on the play by:* Dusan Kovacevic. *Director of Photography:* Vilko Filac. *Editor:* Branka Ceperac. *Music:* Goran Bregovic. *Choreographer:* Milena Moravcova. *Sound:* Marko Rodic. *Sound Editor:* Svetouk Zajc. *Production Designer:* Miljen Kljakovic. *Costumes:* Nebojsa Lipanovic. *Running time:* 167 minutes. *MPAA Rating:* Not Rated.

CAST: Miki Manojlovic (Marko); Lazar Ristovski (Petar "Blacky" Popara); Mirjana Jokovic (Natalija); Slavko Stimac (Ivan); Ernst Stotzner (Franz); Srdan Todorovic (Jovan); Mirjana Karanovic (Vera); Milena Pavlovic (Jelena); Bata Stojkovic (Deda); Bora Todorovic (Golub); Davor Dujmovic (Bata); Nele Karajlic (Falling Gypsy); Branislav Lecic (Mustafa); Dragan

Nikolic (Film Director);   Erol Kadic (Janez);   Predrag Zagorac (Tomislav);   Hark Bohm (Dr. Strasse);   Petar Kralj (Dr. Mirkovic);   Emir Kusturica (Dealer);   Pierre Spengler (Russian Driver);   Branko Cvejic (Captain);   Josif Tatic (Police Inspector);   Zdena Hurtecakova (Fat Lady);   Tanja Kecman (Script);   Albena Stavreva (Girl from the Tunnel);   Elizabeta Dorevska (Woman Prompter);   Peter Mountain (Officer);   Mirsad Tuka and Batica Nikolic (Investigators);   Desa Biogradija (Lady in the Theatre Box);   Zoran Mlljkovic and Dusan Nikolic (Partisans)   Radovan Markovic (Commando);   Miodrag Dordevic (Assistant Director);   Ljijana Jovanovic (Prostitute);   Danica Zdravic (Boat Dancer);   Stojan Sotirov (Driver in Tunnel);   Slobodan Salijevic Orchestra (Gypsy Orchestra);   Boban Markovic Orchestra (Gypsy Orchestra in Café);   Soni (Charlie).

FILM QUARTERLY, Winter 1997-98, p. 50, Marianna Yarovskaya

Up until *Underground* (1995), the films of Yugoslavian director Emir Kusturica are all about growing up, about rites of passage, and initiation. This is not to say they are about adolescent infatuation or sexual awakening; instead, they are concerned with initiation as a process, the unfolding of the cosmic mystery and the transformation of boy into man. Such initiations are seen through growing up in Sarajevo *(Do You Remember Dolly Bell,* 1981), childhood under totalitarianism *(When Father Was Away on Business,* 1985), the deadly games of a gypsy boy *(Time of the Gypsies,* 1989), and the impossibility of loving a mother and a daughter equally at the same time—an impossibility from which it's easier to escape to the world of dreams *(Arizona Dreams,* 1993).

But with *Underground,* Kusturica has grown older. As if to illustrate the point, the film opens with a flying fish being served to a burly, black-mustached Balkan. The fish, a memorable icon of freedom in Kusturica's *Arizona Dreams,* suddenly comes to life and jumps off the plate, only to be casually shot dead and eaten, accompanied by a fine wine. It is a shocking visual image, but it merely flashes upon the screen and disappears. For Kusturica, childhood is brutal and finished off quickly. Yet if growing up implies the death of the past, there is one area in which Kusturica refuses to grow up. He refuses to believe that his homeland, the country formerly called Yugoslavia, no longer exists. *Underground* was represented at the 1995 Cannes Film Festival not by Bosnia or Yugoslavia, but by the European Council. This choice (Kusturica's own) signified not a recognition of a new and unified Europe, but a boyish refusal to bury an old and fragmented Europe.

Underground was advertised as a history of a country that had ceased to be—the film's subtitle, incidentally, is *Once There Was a Country.* Recounting the history of a country that doesn't exist, the film spans 50 years, from World War II, postwar reconstruction, and the corruption of Tito's regime up to the current Balkan war. The film concentrates on the destruction of friendship and mutual betrayal between two patriotic Serb-speaking gangsters, Marko and Blacky, who begin as revolutionaries and evolve into guerrilla partisans, directing their black-market operations from an underground cellar before their paths separate and they enter upon a series of betrayals. *Underground* blends the history of the country with the events of its main characters' lives. The two spheres have a surprising amount in common, a situation which Kusturica reinforces through authentic-looking but doctored news footage of Marko appearing with Yugoslav President Tito and other world figures.

Underground won three prizes, including the prestigious Palme d'Or for Best Picture, at the 1995 Cannes Film Festival. Kusturica's work was called "a brilliant and ambitious film filled with the kind of teeming human images that one usually associates with Fellini." (Damian Cannon, *"Underground,"* *Empire,* no. 4, 1996) Another Western critic, Deborah Young, said, "If Fellini had shot a war movie, it might resemble *Underground."* *(Variety,* May 30, 1995) In Russia, *Underground* was called the triumph of the decade.   Nevertheless, the film also sparked a firestorm of controversy.   Some critics at Cannes thought that it exploited notions of vitality and brutality, which had already lost all potential appeal in the light of the bloody and tragic war in Yugoslavia. And *Underground* got a cold reception from Bosnian critics, who described the film as weak and claimed that Kusturica, who is a Bosnian Muslim by birth, won the prize merely because the film was about war.   There were even widespread accusations by Bosnians and enthusiastic French critics that the film was pro-Serb because of the choice of location (Belgrade) and the focus on Serbian characters and their portrayal as revolutionaries or victims of war whose violence only adds to their irresistibility and charm. This was compounded by the fact that the film's world premiere at Cannes was attended by the Serbian secret police chief, flanked by a celebrated war criminal named Arkan (the Rambo of the Balkans). Bosnian critic Stanko Cerovic's newspaper review ("Canned Lies: Yellow Press Heroes," *Bosnia Report,* August, 1995) was scathing:

> Kusturica's reconstruction of history has nothing to do with reality, unless you accept the theories of Serb nationalists; which these days even in Belgrade tend to be confined to the yellow press... His latest film shows real impotence masked by a fireworks display of noise, color and meaningless scenes... In this beautiful and wealthy city, the representatives and favorites of a criminal regime came together with the Western Elite to act out a scenario based on manipulation, stupidity and cowardice. Applauding themselves, their congratulatory phrases were full of humanism, art and love, while in Bosnia—precisely in the name of this false theater—hundreds of innocent people continue to be killed. Western soldiers continue to be humiliated, while Serbia (which Kusturica is defending) is dying in the arms of Slobodan Milosevic and the Serb extremists whom he created and has taught to butcher.

Among the Bosnians of Sarajevo, Kusturica has also been accused of treason for moving to Paris and failing to identify himself with the war-time government of Alia Izetbegovic.

Upset by the failure of the film in his own country, Kusturica re-edited it numerous times and finally claimed he was going to quit filmmaking. (Fortunately, he soon retracted that statement and has now just completed a new film—*Cat Black, Cat White.*) Although most foreign critics treated the film primarily as a political piece, Kusturica associated himself with neither the Muslim nor the Serb tradition in *Underground.* The film reads like the director's own personal repentance and lament for Yugoslavia. However, *Underground* is more than just a political film.

The film can be seen as three separate stories, differing in theme and style: the World War II period, Tito's regime, and the present day (called "The War"). The separations are accurate and useful, if one sees the picture merely as a political allegory or character study. However, *Underground* operates on several levels of interlocking complexity ranging from the political to the psychological. One of the film's most interesting relationships is between its depiction of political ideology and the subconscious aspect of such ideologies/regimes. Kusturica examines the human desire for political power and weaves a complex tapestry in which the film acts as a psychoanalysis of the political regime that grows out of the subconscious sphere. This is not the first time the subconscious has come to the foreground in Kusturica's work. The final scene of *When Father Was Away on Business* delves into the sphere of imagination. In *Time of the Gypsies,* Kusturica goes even deeper into the sphere of dreams and the subconscious. The director is proud of how naturally and organically such a journey/transition was made in *Underground:* "I did what I wanted, I shot every scene on the edge of consciousness, and the transition to the episodes where there are sounds from the other worlds are made smoothly and look like a continuation of reality."

History in Kusturica's films does not reflect objective or factual accounts of historical development; rather, historical movement is represented by the sphere of the collective unconscious, even when it is contained where it should be—under ground. The "heroes" of *Underground*—Blacky and Marko—do not merely use the subconscious; they are symbols of it. Marko Dren is a man from the underground—a word that has multiple meanings in the film. Literally, it is a fictional cellar where these heroes are hiding. It also has a revolutionary meaning, as "resistance," as well as a psychological meaning, where it functions as a synonym for the collective unconscious. (Through Marko, the collective unconscious attempts to politically rule the country and its historical development: Marko becomes an arms dealer and Tito's right-hand man after the war, thereby gaining immense power.)

From the opening sequence, the subconscious is not personified by any one individual; it flows from the images juxtaposed before us. The German bombardment of Belgrade in 1941, signifying the beginning of the war, is devastating the city. At the zoo, where Marko's brother Ivan works, a horde of animals—tigers, chimpanzees, elephants, zebras—liberated from their cages walk among the ruins, symbolizing the free, unfettered impulses of the collective unconscious.

Several years after the bombing, Marko and Blacky, pursued by the Gestapo, hide their families in Marko's grandfather's cellar, where they have put together an underground munitions factory. The hidden community has fashioned its own underground world and Marko is its only link to the outside world while they make weapons for the revolution. Although Blacky is married, he has decided to daringly snatch his object of desire, the actress Natalija, from under the nose of her German admirer, Franz, during a performance at the National Theater. Marko and Blacky make their way to the theater without trouble and Blacky strides onto the stage to shoot Franz in front of the horrified audience. Then, grasping Natalija, he makes his escape.

Blacky and Natalija arrange to be married on a boat moored outside of Belgrade. A great party ensues while everyone waits for the priest. Unfortunately, the cleric never comes, but Franz, who has survived the shooting, does—with a phalanx of soldiers. After a short battle, Natalija runs to her German lover. Blacky is captured and Marko escapes. Hideous torture ensues for Blacky, yet he never cracks. Marko stages a rescue; Blacky is returned to the cellar commune to recover, and Marko and Natalija remain above ground. While Blacky recuperates in the cellar, Marko seduces Natalija. She is a survivor who switches allegiance among the three men according to the degree of power and protection.

As Allied bombers destroy what the Nazis have left of Belgrade, Marko completes his betrayal of Blacky and the resistance, making the refugees in the cellar believe that the war is still going on. Fast forward to 1961: Marko is now an important advisor to Tito and a war hero—and married to Natalija. He unveils a statue of Blacky and says a few words in praise of his "late" friend. A filmed dramatization of Marko's and Blacky's war exploits, primarily as propaganda for Communist Yugoslavia, is under way. Blacky, of course, is still alive in the cellar complex with a group of survivors that has grown in number. A subterranean society has developed over the intervening years, which embraces births, marriages, and deaths as well as weapons production for the war believed to be still raging outside. Marko and Natalija perpetuate this myth so they can sell and profit from the arms produced down below. Matters come to a head when the guilty duo attend the wedding reception for Jovan, Blacky's son, in the cellar. As a drunk Natalija considers revealing all to Blacky, it is revealed that he and Jovan have already planned to leave the hideout on a surprise raid.

As Yugoslavia begins to disintegrate after Tito's death, Marko finds it increasingly difficult to sustain the fiction of a Nazi-occupied Belgrade for Blacky and his friends, who are preparing themselves for a massive assault on the outside. When they finally emerge, Blacky and Jovan stumble across the film set. Convinced that the war is still going on, and enraged by the sight of (the actor playing) Franz, they launch an attack on actors and crew, killing "Franz."

The story continues in the present, when Blacky and the others have escaped the cellar through subterranean tunnels, only to emerge and find their country unrecognizable... and yet unchanged: bombs and bloodshed are everywhere. An aged Natalija and a crippled Marko are still dealing in arms (and drugs) with anyone willing to do business, but they meet a gruesome fate at the hands of a freedom fighter (who happens to be Blacky), dying in flames in a motorized wheelchair circling aimlessly and endlessly in the smoking ruins of war-torn village. Ivan, an innocent figure whose role is to carry the emotional toll of the war, reappears to learn the truth about Marko's treachery and the tragic fate of the country he knew as Yugoslavia.

In the final part of *Underground,* Kusturica focuses on the idea of Yugoslavia inhabiting parallel worlds by creating a network of underground tunnels—inhabited by Yugoslav warriors and refugees, and U.N. peacekeepers—linking Berlin with Bosnia and Croatia. One tunnel exits into a burning village—it is impossible to identify it as Bosnian, Croatian, or Serbian. Everyone has lost, until the film's Felliniesque final scene of a fantasy reconciliation in which all the film's characters, living and dead, celebrate a family-style reunion on a splinter of land that splits off from the mainland and floats gently away.

In Russia, *Underground* garnered a tremendous and favorable critical response. In a poll organized by the Russian magazine *Art of Cinema,* Kusturica and Quentin Tarantino were deemed the leaders in a list of directors of the twenty-first century, and a fantastic synthesis was created: "Quentin Kusturica." Kusturica was compared not only with Fellini but also with Dostoevsky, especially his *Notes from Underground,* and with Tarkovsky. In interviews, Kusturica himself often compares his own works to these of Tarkovsky. Kusturica's films, like Tarkovsky's, are complex, multi-layered, and nonlinear, jumping back and forth in space and time, from objective to subjective visualizations. Though Kusturica and Tarkovsky come from similar cultures and points of view, in *Underground* Kusturica did what Tarkovsky was avoiding—he played the role of psychoanalyst, whose patient is not an individual, but a whole social system.

There is also a comparison to be made between *Underground* and Russian literary sources such as Mikhail Bulgakov's *Master and Margarita,* Maxim Gorky's *The Lower Depths,* and Dostoevsky's *Notes from Underground.* The film's title, in fact, directly references Dostoevsky's work: unrestrained desire triumphs in both. The underground man in Dostoevsky's novella upholds this desire, this *wanting,* as the highest value. He "needs only independent wanting, whatever this independence may cost and wherever it may lead." For the underground man, "one's own free and voluntary wanting, one's own caprice, however wild, one's own fancy, though chafed sometimes to the point of madness—all this is that same ... most profitable profit." Kusturica's heroes realize and achieve this most profitable profit, this independent wanting, giving themselves over to fancy—and that is how they derive happiness. As a result of their actions, blood streams like a river of champagne.

Josef de Maistre, the French philosopher who was ambassador to Russia in the early 18th century, said of the Russians: "Nobody can want as violently as the Russians want... If you lock Russian desire in a prison, the prison will explode." *(Collected Works,* vol. VIII, p. 291) One can easily apply these words to Kusturica's heroes and to his film in general. Desire in Kusturica's film is sadistic by its very nature, but this sadism is not purely malevolent; it is not just a wanton desire to destroy. Rather, it is joyful, and connected with erotic pleasure, with libido. But *Underground* changes after the Regime emerges from the underground. Sadistic desire splits into libidinous and destructive elements, and Marko usurps its libidinous aspect. The embodiment of this usurption is that Natalija, the object of erotic desire (of both enemies and friends), becomes Marko's wife. But Marko betrays his role as the personification of erotic desire. He stands next to Tito; he gives speeches; he dedicates a monument to his "dead" comrade Blacky, and oversees the crew making the propaganda film about Blacky's wartime exploits. Here Marko belongs to the sacred heart of the Communist regime.

Natalija starts to complain about not having a child with Marko. His eros has been wasted on something else—politics. From reproach she turns to action: she tries to seduce him, but finds that he is unable to respond. Having realized his impotence, Marko leaves the political arena. The news of his exit from politics is followed by the ironic remark: "Having learned about it, Tito fell seriously ill, and in 20 years he died." Kusturica therefore dates the fall of the regime not by the moment when its leader passed away, but when the desire that drove the regime, having lost its vitality, faded.

It is Blacky who takes on the destructive aspect of desire—what Freud called mortido or Thanatos (desire for death), and it is juxtaposed with libido or Eros. Paradoxically, de Maistre's metaphor about desire imprisoned gets dramatically embodied in *Underground:* mortido is indeed in some sort of a prison. But the destructive desires of the Regime are never destroyed: mortido is stored in the underground, in the subconscious, and, deprived of the opportunity to realize itself, becomes frustrated. The inhabitants of the underground keep their aggression keyed up by crying out toasts, singing revolutionary songs, producing guns. They even manage to construct a tank. And Blacky constantly tries to come back up to the surface. To him, the war is not over yet, the enemy is still roaming the country and Tito and his regime are still in danger.

De Maistre's metaphor is resolved just as its author had predicted: the tank destroys the underground, Blacky and his son Jovan emerge. The prison blows up and destructive desire is liberated. It happens almost simultaneously with the disappearance of Marko Dren, the personification of the libidinous aspect of desire.

Referring to Tarkovsky, Kusturica often spoke about the importance of the natural elements in his culture. Indeed, water becomes especially significant in the last scenes of *Underground,* when we see Blacky's drowned son, Jovan, reemerge from the water to join the rest of the film's characters (both alive and dead). We see Blacky's wife, Vera, who died while giving birth to Jovan in the beginning of the film, and Jovan's bride, who threw herself into a well. And lastly, on a spit of land that cuts deep into the waters, they begin a big party—the final act of all Russian folk tales. Films usually end with the words, "The End." In Kusturica film there is a title on black: "This story has no end." Indeed, if this story in truth represents the workings of the collective unconscious, then it can have no end.

Underground builds a metaphor for the entire Communist world. The film is set everywhere and nowhere, at no time and always. When I think about what type of film would effectively deal with the chaos in contemporary Russia, I think about *Underground*. But when Russians try to make films about the situation in the mid-90s, they come out with openly absurdist works like *Shirli-mirli (Nonsense)* or *The Hammer and the Sickle* (both 1996), or *Everything Will Be O.K.* (one of the biggest hits of last year, with a huge and very enthusiastic cast, and a score combining a balalaika group with *Porgy and Bess)*, forgetting that even an absurdist plot follows some sort of logical order. Absurdity is the most difficult of styles, the one, ironically, demanding the greatest restraint and discipline. Kusturica often said that his films are closer to the circus or musical theater than they are to serious literature.

French film critic Gerard Lefort wrote in the left-wing Parisian newspaper *Liberation:* "It's a war film ... or, rather, a film in the state of war, a film in occupation: the war is viewed as a rock-and-roll concert. It's the famous speech of Churchill ("I promised you blood and tears") sung to the Sex Pistols." Kusturica voluntarily takes up the comparison: "Have you ever been to the concerts of The Clash or, rather, The Sex Pistols, whom I unfortunately never saw on stage? They never stop, it's a catharsis with no beginning and no end. You know, I play in a rock group and that gives me the best sensations in life."

Underground is indeed a catharsis with no beginning and no end, from the burning zoo to the rift that separates the festive and phantom partygoers from their homeland; from the terrifying decorations of the underground tunnels to Tito's funeral and the famous song "Lili Marleen." The great flights of surreal imagery only serve to intensify the growing horror and sadness. The film is a lament, a song of violence and sadness. In his own way, the filmmaker has rendered a deeply significant service to the cause of reconciliation in a "country that ceased to be."

LOS ANGELES TIMES, 12/26/97, Calendar/p. 2, Kevin Thomas

In 1993 the former Yugoslavia's greatest filmmaker, Emir Kusturica, returned to his homeland after a five-year absence to confront the disintegration of his country with a dazzling epic allegory, "Underground," which took two years to make and which won the Palme d'Or at Cannes in 1995.

Best known for the Oscar-nominated "When Father Was Away on Business" (1985), set in Yugoslavia's harsh Stalinist period, and "Time of the Gypsies" (1989), a chronicle of a youth's induction to petty crime, Kusturica also made the wonderfully offbeat romantic adventure "Arizona Dream" (1993), a revealing funny-sad slice of Americana with an equally wonderfully unexpected cast headed by Johnny Depp, Faye Dunaway, Jerry Lewis and Lili Taylor.

It takes a great deal of passion and sorrow to sustain a 167-minute tragicomic farce, but only occasionally does "Underground" weary. It's a sprawling, rowdy, vital film laced with both outrageous absurdist dark humor and unspeakable pain, suffering and injustice. It spans the years 1941, when Germany bombed and invaded the country—the Allies bombed it, too—until 1992, when warfare was again spreading across the land.

(Ironically, in attempting to take an all-encompassing perspective on the fate of Yugoslavia and in avoiding in taking sides in the current turmoil, Kusturica touched off such a controversy on home ground he announced he was quitting filmmaking. He has since changed his mind and has just signed to direct the late Dennis Potter's adaptation of D.M. Thomas' novel "The White Hotel," a chronicle of a woman's life from 1900 to World War II.)

Wars have always provided lucrative opportunities for unscrupulous profiteers, and the natty, wiry Marko (Miki Manojlovic, star of "When Father Was Away on Business") has enough shrewdness and daring to lure his naive pal Blacky (Lazar Ristovski) into dealing in arms and gold and engaging in guerrilla raids on Nazi convoys, which allows them to emerge as postwar heroes of the burgeoning Communist Party. Indeed, in Marshal Tito's greatest moments of public triumph, Marko—now his close confidant-pops up Zelig-like, standing next to him.

A different fate, however, awaits Blacky, for in one fell swoop Marko steals Natalija (Mirjana Jokovic), the woman the rugged Blacky loves, while he and a host of others, including Blacky's own brother Ivan (Slavko Stimac), continue hiding in the cavernous basement beneath Blacky's elegant country villa outside Belgrade. Periodic recorded bursts of strafing interspersed with snatches of Lale Andersen's famous recording of "Lili Marleen," convince those in hiding that World War II continues long after peace. They go on manufacturing the light weapons—and even a tank—that will turn Blacky into a major arms merchant. Vera (Mirjana Karanovic) may have no talent whatsoever as an actress—this doesn't impede her tremendous popularity, however—but she's no fool. Although passionately in love with Marko, she has an inconvenient conscience about all those people toiling away in her basement that drives her to drink.

Illusion and reality collide spectacularly when a film, an unintentionally Keystone Cops-like treatment of Marko's World War II heroics, commences production. It provides Kusturica with a climax to "Underground," but such is its scope it jumps to an ultimate reckoning between its principals in 1992 and beyond that to an epilogue that is profoundly touching and amusing as well. As all this suggests, Kusturica is nothing if not ambitious, loading his film with potent symbols around its central metaphor as that basement representing a Yugoslavia under a communist system that kept its people in ignorance as it exploited them.

Like Polish master Andrzej Wajda did in his landmark "Man of Marble," Kusturica wickedly skewers the kitschy, ponderous communist bloc taste—ranging from bland realist statuary to displays of power expressed in pompous parades.

Manojlovic's Blacky recalls Giancarlo Giannini's similarly opportunist—though not nearly so smart or lucky—antihero in Lina Wertmüller's "Seven Beauties," set in World War II. Kusturica and his co-writer Dusan Kovacevic, who also wrote the original story, have created roles of a lifetime for his four key actors—Stimac's brother emerges as a figure of gentle betrayed innocence—and they are up to the tremendous range they demand.

"I was born [in 1954] in a country where hope, laughter and the joy of living are stronger than anywhere else," Kusturica has said. "Evil as well. You are perpetrator or the victim."

He has captured all of this and more with wit, compassion and irony in "Underground"—and has even dared to end on a note of hope and reconciliation for the former Yugoslavia.

NEW YORK, 10/20/97, p. 71, David Denby

Underground, Emir Kusturica's astonishing, exhausting epic—a demi-masterpiece, a monstrosity, a conundrum—is finally opening in New York for a regular theatrical run. This quasi-allegorical treatment of recent Balkan history has been brought off in a style of obsessive, riotous burlesque. Two extraordinary scoundrels, Marko (Miki Manojlovic) and his friend Blacky (Lazar Ristovski)—raffishly handsome men, with thick, dark hair and dark eyes gleaming with malice—storm their way through history in a movie that combines a deep love of fraudulence with an equally deep love of theatricalism in all its low-farce varieties. You may not understand all of *Underground,* but you won't be bored.

NEW YORK POST, 6/20/97, p. 45, Larry Worth

There's nothing like the visuals of Federico Fellini or the political satire of Luis Bunuel. But writer-director Emir Kusturica pays homage to both late, great giants of the cinema—as well as to his late, great homeland, Yugoslavia—in the epic masterpiece "Underground."

Covering a 50-year span, it's the story of a particularly unusual lovers' triangle, told in a mood that switches from black comedy to drama to horror to fever dream.

The film opens in 1941 on the eve of Belgrade's destruction by the Germans. But rather than center on humans, the camera stays in the city's zoo, registering animals' reactions as bombs turn their cages into twisted iron shards.

The surreal tone is indelibly set as a goose playfully nips at a tiger—right before the big cat takes the bird's head off—and a woman berates her husband for the previous night's infidelity. This may be the apocalypse, but the meek aren't about to inherit the Earth—at least, not in this scenario.

The principals fit right into this twilight-zone setting, proving as heroic as they are villainous. Marko and Blacky, who profit on the country's newfound misfortune by trafficking in gold, hide from the Nazis in a cellar filled with family and friends.

So it goes until World War II's end, at which point Marko and girlfriend Natalija make the cellar-dwellers—who now include Natalija's former beau, Blacky—believe that the battle is continuing. Their, motive? Making a fortune off the weapons made by their prisoners.

And that's just the launching pad for a tale that continues through the current Serbo-Croatian nightmare, punctuated by endless twists, ever-changing alliances, political shockers, undying passion and lots and lots of revenge.

But Kusturica isn't interested solely in storytelling. As with "When Father Was Away on Business" and "Arizona Dream," he laces his production with subtle metaphors and symbol-laden imagery to compose a cinematic poem—in this case dedicated to Yugoslavia's ongoing tragedy.

Along with amazing photography (complete with separate color schemes for above ground and below it) and Goran Bregovic's mesmerizing score, the brilliant cast includes Miki Manojlovic, Lazar Ristovski and Mirjana Jokovic.

Collectively, they helped Kusturica take home the Palme d'Or at 1995's Cannes Film Festival. And although it has taken another two years, "Underground" is finally seeing the light of day in America. Few would deny that is was worth the wait.

NEWSDAY, 6/20/97, Part II/p. B8, John Anderson

Blaring horns, bleary whores and errant gunshots open Emir Kusturica's "Underground," which alternately ambles and rampages across the screen, but has virtually had to drag itself to these shores. Two years after winning the grand prize at Cannes—and then becoming a cause celebre among sniping French intellectuals—this multiple metaphor for nationalism, communism and the evil of -isms arrives like a bouquet of flowers and a punch in the face.

The Sarajevo-born Kusturica—whose films have ranged from "When Father Was Away on Business" to the Johnny Depp-Faye Dunaway vehicle "Arizona Dream"—has been attacked for his alleged Serb propagandizing; he's also been hailed for what others have seen as a scathing condemnation of totalitarianism. The film is so heavy with metaphor that interpretations are available for everyone—although "Underground" now is a little shorter than it was at Cannes, more coherent and perhaps less antagonizing. But what hasn't really been addressed is the reasonable possibility that Kusturica's film transcends momentary political and military upheavals, and serves as an allegory for the universal, timeless heart of darkness.

It's a movie that's well aware of its status as a piece of transitory entertainment. Opening in 1941, with its ever-present and clearly mad brass band—accompanying the roguish Blacky (Lazar Ristovski) and Marko (Miki Manojlovic) through the slickened streets of Belgrade—"Underground" moves quickly to its most horrific sequence, the bombing of a zoo. Now, the plight of abandoned zoo animals in post-war Europe was a disgrace, and a brilliant metaphor in itself, but Kusturica, with his panic-stricken tigers and crazed apes, is tossing the "war movie" back in his audience's face: Why are we so upset by the gruesome deaths of chimpanzees, when people are being slaughtered too? Because of our humanity?

It's the essence of humanity that's at stake in "Underground." Blacky and Marko have established a heroic-yet-profitable business sabotaging the Nazi war wagon, but when their group of partisans has to take refuge in the cellar beneath Marko's house (a huge, labyrinthian symbol of the Soviet bloc), Marko stays above ground, distributing the arms being manufactured below by the Yugoslav patriots. When the war ends, Marko doesn't tell them—or Blacky—and for 15 years he lets them labor, thinking the Germans are still occupying Belgrade, while he becomes a wealthy cog in Marshal Tito's machine. All Blacky wants to do is get out and fight the fascists. When he finally leaves the cellar, he's primed and loaded.

Life has gone on, both above and below. Natalija (Mirjana Jokovic), playing an actress whom Blacky once kidnaped for love, has becomes Marko's lover-conspirator. Blacky has a son, the simple-minded   Jovan (Srdan Todorovic), Kusturica's emblematic Yugoslav with no pre-communist memory. When father and son break out of the cellar, they kill "Germans" on a movie set; Blacky becomes so engrossed in firing on the set he doesn't notice Jovan drowning. With no one else to kill, Blacky becomes a militiaman, perpetrating crimes against his own countrymen—much the way Marko has been doing all along. Rage, confusion and ammunition are too much in abundance not to be put to use.

Kusturica isn't exonerating anyone; he's indicting everyone. That his film is so rich with his visual poetry, his cross-pollination of Terry Gilliam and Luis Bunuel, his wry incongruities—and a climactic fantasy that's simply heartbreaking—is his way of rejecting the notion that evil is unavoidable, or art irrelevant.

SIGHT AND SOUND, 3/96, p. 53, Tony Rayns

Belgrade. 6 April 1941. Marko raucously celebrates his friend Petar 'Blacky,' Popara's acceptance into the Communist Party.

Part I: The War. The first German bombing raid over Belgrade hits the zoo, where Marko's slow-witted brother Ivan is a keeper. While the region falls to the Nazis, Marko and Blacky begin to thrive as black marketeers. Marko tries to pick up actress Natalija Zolko, but loses her to the dashing Nazi officer Franz. Fearing that a mole is betraying the Communist-led resistance. Marko installs Blacky's cell of resistance fighters in the roomy cellar beneath his grandfather's house. Blacky's wife Vera slips, goes into premature labour, and dies giving birth to a son, Jovan. Ivan enters the cellar with his chimp, Soni, and a parrot.

1943. Natalija now stars in German melodramas at the National Theatre, and Blacky determines to snatch her from the arms of Franz. He stages a daring mid-performance raid and carries Natalija off to a pre-arranged wedding party. But Franz catches up with them the next morning; Natalija surrenders to him and Blacky is arrested and tortured. Marko rescues his old comrade and they retreat back underground, where Blacky's mental and physical injuries are nursed. Marko casts himself as the cell's above-ground liaison man ... and seduce Natalija at the first opportunity.

Easter, 1944. Allied bombers finish off what the Nazis had left of Belgrade. Marko embraces Tito.

Part II: The Cold War. In 1961, Marko attends a tribute to the late war hero Blacky, and announces production of the film *Spring Comes on a White Horse,* based on their wartime exploits in reality, though, Blacky is still hiding in the much-expanded cellar with his resistance fighters, making armaments for the anti-Nazi war which Marko tells them is still raging above ground. Natalija connives in this deception, but guiltily starts hitting the bottle. Drunk one day, she accidentally falls into the cellar, where Blacky finds her and welcomes her to Jovan's wedding. Blacky later finds Marko alone with Natalija (he is urging her to maintain the pretence that the war has never ended) and realises that his best friend has 'stolen' his wife. He gives Marko a gun, with which he shoots himself in the leg. At Jovan's wedding party, Soni triggers an explosion which reveals a network of tunnels leading to all the European capitals.

Blacky and Jovan go to the surface, and find what looks like Franz leading Nazi troops in an attack on the resistance. Unaware that they have stumbled into the filming of *Spring Comes on a White Horse,* Blacky shoots the actor playing Franz and decimates the film crew. Blacky is later arrested by the police while failing to save Jovan from drowning in the Danube. Marko and Natalija meanwhile decide to go out with a bang by dynamiting the cellar. Tito is grief stricken at the disappearance of his comrade Marko, and dies 20 years later. Many heads of state (including Margaret Thatcher) attend his state funeral in 1980.

Part III: The War. In 1991, Ivan flees incarceration in a German mental hospital and tries to return to Yugoslavia via the old network of tunnels. En route, a UN soldier tells him that Yugoslavia no longer exists. Reunited with Soni, Ivan reaches a war-ravaged village where Blacky leads a team of Serbian partisans and Marko trades in black market arms and squires Natalija. Ivan violently attacks his brother and then hangs himself in despair. One of Blacky's guerillas executes Marko and Natalija, burning the bodies. Blacky is drawn into the network of tunnels by Jovan's ghostly voice—and finds himself once more on the banks of the Danube, where Vera is hosting another wedding party for their son. The guests include Marko, Natalija, Ivan and everyone else from the cellar. The party is held on a promontory which breaks free from the bank and floats down river as an island.

Despite winning another Cannes Golden Palm and seeing his film sold for distribution throughout the developed world, Bosnia's most celebrated cinéaste says that *Underground* will be his last film. Emir Kusturica is reportedly distressed at being attacked for his failure to make the film a denunciation of Serbian aggression and war crimes. But his wounded recalcitrance seems as feeble as the attacks which provoked it. The film's real political problem is not that it fails to be 'correctly' partisan but that it rests on nostalgia for a national identity which it simultaneously exposes as a skillfully manipulated illusion. If Kusturica seriously believes (as the film's opening caption has it) that "once upon a time there was a country whose capital was

Belgrade," then he should surely hold to his convictions and stand by their expression in *Underground.*

The script's central contention is that 'Yugoslavia' was a Cold War fiction manufactured by Tito and the Communist ruling class, founded on a siege mentality and sustained by the ideological indoctrination of its population. Life in the film's cellar is in every sense fantastic: workers' playtime in an armaments factory. Blacky, its kingpin, is only a slightly more exaggerated version of the kind of hero of socialism played by Nikita Mikhalkov in *Burnt by the Sun*, a macho meathead whose lusty appetites and comic-strip indestructibility are clearly supposed to make him seem admirable, even loveable, in the community's absurdity. Blacky, in short, is the salt of the earth and his domain is a bunker for peasant joys, sorrows and dreams. That this underground time-capsule turns out to be linked by tunnels to every other capital in Europe presumably reflects old Marxist fantasies of international workers' solidarity.

Marko's above ground world of high-living and realpolitick is more sketchily represented through archive newsreels (some of them digitally doctored, *á la Zelig* or *Forrest Gump*, to incorporate the figure of Marko himself) and the double fiction of the film-within-the-film *Spring Comes on a White Horse* (a parody of Tito's propaganda epics). Even in *Underground's* final section, which attempts to encapsulate the Balkan war in the strafing of a village by guerrillas and the grotesque, Ceaucescu-style executions of Marko and Natalija, Kusturica relies on no more than a few 'shock' images to evoke the reality of five years of bloodshed, internecine strife and ethnic cleansing.

The underlying question here is whether Emir Kusturica's patented visual and dramatic coups can bear the weight of political meaning and heartfelt sentiment he tries to invest them with. Predictably enough, the director of *Time of the Gypsies (Dom Za Vesanje)* frames the film as a circus parade in the manner of late Fellini: the artifice is flamboyant, the music (by a brass brand and a gypsy orchestra, both often on camera) is virtually non-stop, and the spirit is carnivalesque. Some of Kusturica's ideas and images are undeniably potent: the rise of protagonists who sail through the decades essentially unchanged meshes with set pieces like the opening bombing of the zoo and the closing creation of the island to generate a powerful sense of authorial vision.

But too much of the 'poetry' seems closer to Andrew Lloyd Webber than to, say, Jean Vigo or Max Ophuls, both of whom are quoted visually, and the implied claim to political resonances is proportionally weakened. There is also a huge problem of mysogyny, which may well be the element which has prevented the film from pulling substantial audiences in all but the most patriarchal countries. It's amazing that a director as sophisticated as Kusturica thought he could get away with his conception of Natalija, the film's only substantial female character, as a brainless floozy who opportunistically switches her sexual allegiance from scene to scene and sublimates her self-hatred in drink. Who would trust the political or aesthetic nous of a director who still sees women that way?

VILLAGE VOICE, 6/24/97, p. 75, J. Hoberman

The drinking, dancing, scheming anti-heroes of Emir Kusturica's *Underground* are the ultimate wild and crazy Balkin party animals—they're jerked through History's convulsions as if by some hyperactive cosmic puppeteer. This extravagant, controversial movie—sniffed at and passed on by several American distributors—is a bravura succession of bitter japes, not least the use of two heedless, indestructible blockheads to lament the dissolution of a nation.

Underground won the Palme d'Or at the 1995 Cannes Film Festival and (as chronicled in *The New Yorker,* the *Voice,* and elsewhere was immediately thereafter subject to a full-scale Parisian contretemps as, per philosopher Alain Finkielkraut, "a rock, postmodern, over-the-top, hip, Americanized version of the most drivelling and lying Serbian propaganda." Now, thanks to Anthology Film Archives and New Yorker Films, local intellectuals can have their opportunity to denounce Kusturica—or not. Is it cinephilia or political sin? The passions of the early '90s already may be more passé than Yugoslavia itself.

Underground's Serbian title could be translated as *Once Upon a Time There Was a Country*; "catastrophe!" is the recurring exclamation. Kusturica, a nominally Muslim native of Sarajevo and hence the newly established Bosnia's best-known artist, was effectively stateless when he made *Underground*—as well as without effective political cover, being a public supporter of the no-longer-viable Yugoslav federation. Reviled as a traitor in his hometown, the filmmaker invoked the first several years after Tito's death, corresponding to the early phase of his career, as a golden era: "Great movies. Beautiful novels. Great rock-and-roll. We became a superpower in basketball."

This may be the closest Kusturica will come to greatness. Outraged and outrageous, fueled by a host of comic performances and the mournful frenzy of Goran Bregovic's infectious brass score, *Underground* opens with a band charging through the outskirts of Belgrade—the fantastic succession of falling-down drunken antics celebrating the induction of two petty black marketeers into the Communist Party and previewing the grotesque spectacle to come. Part gypsy saber dance, part sped-up Fellini film, *Underground* is a would-be national allegory, aspiring to the class of magic realist novels like *The Tin Drum* and *Midnight's Children*.

World War II is staged as a series of bloody pratfalls. Set free by a German bombing raid, Belgrade's zoo animals wander off through the rubble of collapsed buildings. Throughout the Nazi occupation, the bluff and hearty Blacky (Lazar Ristovski), his hawk-nosed, sad-eyed, duplicitous blood brother Marko (Miki Manojlovic, eponymous star of Kusturica's other Cannes laureate, *When Father Was Away on Business),* and a clueless German officer all vie for the affections of the actress Natalija (Mirjana Jokovic, as supple and rubber-faced as her character is opportunistic). The rondo of romantic betrayals climaxes with Blacky's onstage abduction of the actress and is supplemented by his and Marko's no less madcap commando raids.

Jumping ahead to the early '60s, *Underground*'s middle section is a convoluted allegory suggesting that Tito's Yugoslavia was dependent on preserving the memory of World War II while keeping the population in a condition of mobilized ignorance. The authorities unveil a statue of the partisan martyr Blacky even while he remains alive in the basement (giving the movie its English title), persuaded by Marko that the war wages on, still producing arms to defeat the Germans. In the midst of this, Kusturica stages a subterranean wedding party—the longest, funniest, most apocalyptic thing of its kind since the Russian Orthodox nuptials that kicked off Michael Cimino's similarly reviled (but far less accomplished) *Deer Hunter*.

To further complicate an already exhausting narrative—and, in a way, parallel Kusturica's gumping his characters into wartime newsreels of Tito's victory parade—*Underground*'s first third is reprised, after a fashion, by the ridiculously heroic film that is being shot about Marko and Blacky's wartime exploits. (When Blacky finally leaves his shelter, he inevitably emerges onto the movie set to mistake it for the climactic battle against the fascists.) A final section has the ageless characters enthusiastically playing their gangster roles on opposing sides of the post-Yugoslavia civil wars. The St. Vitus dance continues. To complete the bloody farce, the galvanized corpses have one last celebration even as their little piece of heaven splits off and floats into oblivion.

A nearly sustained marvel of convoluted takes and choreographed energy that never once loses its sardonic brio, *Underground* is truly maniacal. This is the sort of movie in which characters break bottles of slivovitz over their heads. The oompah rhythms could drive even the members of the New York Institute for the Humanities to do the Zorba, critiquing Kusturica while pounding on the closest seat. Perhaps it's this tone that put off the French. Finkielkraut, who launched his first attack on the movie without even having seen it, would complain to *The New Yorker* of "all that terrible Slav sentimentality that I hate—all these weddings and drunken embraces, spilling over into the love of violence." The movie may look like a wedding, but it's more like a wake. Indeed, *Underground*'s vision of Slavs at their most Yugo is a merciless satire of volkish bombast, about as sentimental as a Roadrunner cartoon.

Kusturica responded to the debate over *Underground* by publicly renouncing filmmaking. At last report, however, he is said to be at work on a new movie. Good news to be sure, although I daresay he would have to lose a second homeland to have the rage to ever again let loose so ferocious a howl.

Also reviewed in:
CHICAGO TRIBUNE, 2/6/98, Friday/p. A, Michael Wilmington
NATION, 7/14/97, p. 36, Stuart Klawans
NEW YORK TIMES, 6/20/97, p. C21, Janet Maslin
VARIETY, 5/29/95, p. 55, Deborah Young

UNDERWORLD

A Keystone Pictures release in association with Trimark Pictures of a Robert Vince production. *Executive Producer:* Mark Amin, Michael Strange, and Abra Edelman. *Producer:* Robert Vince and William Vince. *Director:* Roger Christian. *Screenplay:* Larry Bishop. *Director of Photography:* Steven Bernstein. *Editor:* Robin Russell. *Music:* Anthony Marinelli. *Casting:* Abra Edelman and Elisa Goodman. *Production Designer:* John Ebden. *Running time:* 95 minutes. *MPAA Rating:* R.

CAST: Denis Leary (Johnny Crown); Joe Mantegna (Frank Gavilan); Annabel Sciorra (Dr. Leah); Larry Bishop (Ned Lynch);. Abe Vigoda (Will Cassady); Robert Costanzo; James Tolkan; Heidi Schanz; Cristi Conaway; Traci Lords; Jimmie F. Skaggs.

NEW YORK POST, 5/9/97, p. 50, Michael Medved

"Underworld" may set a world's record for powerful lead performances (by Denis Leary and Joe Mantegna) in service of an idiotic and unworthy script. The fact that one of the cast's other superior actors (Larry Bishop) also wrote the altogether inferior screenplay only adds to the irony.

Bishop (son of comedian Joey Bishop and writer-director of the mannered, disappointing "Mad Dog Time") has recycled a Dumpster full of visual and verbal gangland cliches sprinkled with gabby, irrelevant dialogue in the tired Tarantino tradition.

It's supposed to be funny (or surrealistic, or something or other) but, for the most part, the movie is balefully boring and feels vastly longer than its official 95-minute running time.

Leary is undeniably riveting as Johnny Crown, a criminal psycho, specializing in psychobabble, who has just been released from seven years in stir and is determined to even the score for the mob hit that put his papa into a coma.

In the course of one Father's Day, he rubs out a dozen bad guys in a slow-motion massacre full of spurting veins and shattered glass, then kidnaps his old buddy—grim, enigmatic nightclub owner Mantegna. They ride around endlessly in a wet, gleaming Lincoln Continental, playing out the ex-con's elaborate revenge fantasies, speculating on whether or not Mantegna actually participated in the attack on Leary's dad, or whether the brain-dead old man in a hospital bed is really anyone's father.

Or whether veteran, poker-faced mobster Abe Vigoda is Mantegna's father, as Leary asserts. Or whether sexy psychologist Annabella Sciorra, kept in a hotel room like a prostitute-slave, is truly Mantegna's ex-wife.

While another smart-mouthed, clinically depressed mobster (Bishop) pursues his own murderous rampage and occasionally collides with the others, they all search for a missing mystery man named Essex, who never does provide the promised key to comprehending this chaos.

Director Roger Christian (who previously created little-seen oddities such as "Nostradamus" and "The Sender" after winning an Oscar as art director for "Star Wars") offers lots of atmospheric shadows and fog to decorate the lurid, gleaming surfaces of his nightmarish, slick-city world. In the same way, the questions and confusions of the cluttered script serve only to mask the project's appalling emptiness.

NEWSDAY, 5/9/97, Part II/p. B9, John Anderson

If there weren't already a "Fathers' Day" opening today, they might have lifted that title for "Underworld," which takes place on Father's Day and contains contorted messages about patriarchy and progeny. Of course, it might just as easily be called "St. Valentine's Day," since it opens with a particularly hellacious massacre. Or maybe "Luis Bunuel Meets David Mamet," a place where the testosterone turns surreal.

But it's called "Underworld," the name of a club in Chicago where the bad guys—all of whom exist in a vacuum of lawlessness—practice their marksmanship while anticipating the arrival of Johnny Crown (Denis Leary), an ex-con whose father is in a hospital bed and who's orchestrating a bizarre revenge scenario based on psychotherapy and slit throats.

Johnny has just gotten out of prison, where he studied and became the "only working psychopathic psychotherapist in psychopathology." His cat-and-mouse game with Frank Gavilan whom he suspects of being the nefarious Richard Essex, prime suspect in his father's assault—is riddled with Freudian claptrap. In an effort to "make everyone happy," he reunites Frank with his estranged psychiatrist wife, Leah (Annabella Sciorra), and his estranged father (Abe Vigoda). Where this is all going is a mystery, and not one you're aching to have solved.

Director Roger Christian strives for a limpid sensuality, mixing stylized violence with red lampshades, phallic cigars and ephemeral underwear. Waiting for it all to coalesce into something substantial is an exercise in futility, as the dialogue—by Larry Bishop, who also plays arch villain Ned Lynch—is too ponderous and the acting too coy. What works is the film's message about violence—how it spreads like a virus, and is ultimately irresistible.

But Denis Leary is an acquired taste, like gasless dentistry. And "Underworld" doesn't even have the dubious advantage of his sneering wit: Johnny Crown lapses into childishness, or is steered by the script into limp gags and bizarre non sequitur. All of this defuses his wrath and derails the film, which is rife with bloodletting and big guns. Mantegna, as usual, is strong, but largely mute. Is he fighting the dialogue? You couldn't blame him.

VILLAGE VOICE, 5/13/97, p. 79, Justine Elias

[*Underworld* was reviewed jointly with *Breakdown*; see Elias' review of that film.]

Also reviewed in:
NEW YORK TIMES, 5/9/97, p. C14, Anita Gates
VARIETY, 5/20-26/96, p. 39, David Rooney

UNFORGOTTEN: 25 YEARS AFTER WILLOWBROOK

A Castle Hill Productions release of a City Lights presentation in association with HeartShare. *Executive Producer:* Katie Meskell. *Producer:* Danny Fisher. *Director:* Jack Fisher. *Screenplay:* Stuart Warmflash. *Director of Photography:* Eric Lau, Mark Kroll, Alan McPheely, and Richard Mauro. *Editor:* Constantine Limperis, Matthew Mallinsen, and Shelly Toscano. *Music:* Hayes Greenfield. *Running time:* 60 minutes. *MPAA Rating:* Not Rated.

WITH: Danny Aiello (Narrator); Geraldo Rivera (Commentator).

LOS ANGELES TIMES, 10/25/96, Calendar/p. 14, Kevin Thomas

In 1972 Geraldo Rivera received a key from a doctor friend that enabled him to enter Staten Island's Willowbrook State School, a misleadingly named asylum. He left with enough footage to yield an award-winning WABC-TV series so devastating in exposure of horrendous conditions there that it led to the institution's closure.

Producer Danny Fisher and director Jack Fisher commemorate the upcoming 25th anniversary of Rivera's exposé with their moving "Unforgotten: Twenty-Five Years After Willowbrook." They interview several families who had relatives at Willowbrook and how they've coped in the years since. The documentary's two key families' relatives now live in group homes, but as challenging as it is to have a developmentally disabled child or sibling, the Fishers suggest encouragingly that over the last 25 years there have been considerable improvements in resources and attitudes.

The film's most affecting individual is Bernard Carabello, who has managed to create an independent life and career for himself despite having been abandoned by his family at the age of 3 at Willowbrook, where he spent the next 18 years, incorrectly regarded as mentally retarded simply because he is afflicted with cerebral palsy.

Narrated by Danny Aiello, "Unforgotten" presents effective alternatives to Willowbrook but could use more context, informing us as to how well the nation as a whole is handling the care of the developmentally disabled and how such care can be most effectively financed and administered.

NEW YORK POST, 2/14/97, p. 50, Bill Hoffmann

Twenty-five years have flown by since a muckraking reporter named Geraldo Rivera burst into the Willowbrook State School for the profoundly retarded and exposed a house of horrors that sickened and shamed viewers.

Anybody who saw that stomach-churning footage of disabled kids and adults wallowing in their own urine and feces in the Staten Island institution's filthy dorms will never forget it.

As the powerful new documentary "Unforgotten" shows, the story of Willowbrook—and its bittersweet legacy—is as disturbing as the day it was uncovered.

Director Jack Fisher hunted down families who had put their kids there in the '50s and '60s with promises that they would be well cared for.

But the once-model institution went down the toilet after it was hit by massive evidence of mismanagement and was closed soon thereafter.

Also reviewed in:
NEW YORK TIMES, 2/14/97, p. C20, Stephen Holden

VAN, THE

A Fox Searchlight Pictures release in association with BBC Films of a Deadly Films production in association with Beacon Pictures. *Executive Producer:* Mark Shivas. *Producer:* Lynda Myles. *Director:* Stephen Frears. *Screenplay (based on his novel):* Roddy Doyle. *Director of Photography:* Oliver Stapleton. *Editor:* Mick Audsley. *Music:* Eric Clapton and Richard Hartley. *Sound:* Brendan Deasy and (music) Alan Douglas. *Sound Editor:* Peter Joly. *Casting:* Leo Davis. *Production Designer:* Mark Geraghty. *Art Director:* Fiona Daly. *Costumes:* Consolata Boyle. *Make-up:* Morna Ferguson. *Stunt Coordinator:* Patrick Condren. *Running time:* 96 minutes. *MPAA Rating:* R.

CAST: Colm Meaney (Larry); Donal O'Kelly (Bimbo); Ger Ryan (Maggie); Caroline Rothwell (Mary); Neili Conroy (Diane); Ruaidhri Conroy (Kevin); Brendan O'Carroll (Weslie); Stuart Dunne (Sam); Jack Lynch (Cancer); Laurie Morton (Maggie's Mum); Marie Mullen (Vera); Jon Kenny (Gerry McCarthy); Moses Rowen (Glenn); Linda McGovern (Jessica); Eoin Chaney (Wayne); Frank O'Sullivan (Wally); Jill Doyle (Mona); Barbara Bergin (Dawn); Charlotte Bradley (Anne Marie); Ronan Wilmot (Bald Man); Stanley Townsend (Des, Health Inspector); Sheila Fitton (Missis Twix); Alan King (Mechanic); Bernie Downes (Pregnant Woman); Martin Dunne (Garda Sergeant); Tommy O'Neill (Nightclub Barman); Eilish Moore (Bingo Woman); Gavin Keilty (World Peace); Paul Raynor (Pitch & Putt Man); Claude Clancy (Leo the Barman); Eileen Walsh (Crushed Girl); Michelle Gallagher (Girl); Sandra Bagnall (Complaining Woman); Arthur Napper (Nightclub Bouncer); Fionnuala Murphy (Young Woman); Jessie O'Gorman (Kerrie); Michael O'Reilly (Arsenal Supporter); David Kelly (Boy with Choc Ice); Lee Bagnall (Crying Boy); Jamie Bagnall (Other Kid); David Byrne (Barry).

LOS ANGELES TIMES, 5/30/97, Calendar/p. 15, Kevin Thomas

The makers of "The Van" would have been wiser not to point out that it is the concluding installment in writer Roddy Doyle's Barrytown trilogy that began with "The Commitments" (1991), that irresistible tale of young Dubliners forming a '60s-style soul music group, and "The Snapper" (1993), in which the wonderful Colm Meaney plays a working-class father confronted with a pregnant teenage daughter who refuses to name the father of her child.

Compared to that meaty fare, "The Van" is pretty slim pickings—not unlike the grub that two out-of-work guys (Meaney and Donal O'Kelly) serve from their food mobile in their fictional Dublin rowhouse suburb of Barrytown. So thin is this film that it's surprising to discover that the 1990 novel that Doyle adapted to the screen himself was short-listed for the prestigious Booker Prize. What's further surprising is that Doyle and first-rate director Stephen Frears, who also directed "The Snapper," weren't able to make more of the material.

O'Kelly's Bimbo has just been laid off his 25-year bakery job while his best friend Larry (Meaney) hasn't worked in years. When one of their barroom pals directs them to the most-derelict food van you ever saw, Bimbo risks his modest severance check to rehabilitate the van and hire Larry to work with him. They are a success so instant as to needlessly defy credibility, but the grind of work begins to strain Bimbo and Larry's friendship.

"The Van" celebrates male bonding—carried to extremes—without providing much depth or dimension. The first hour or so rambles about with Bimbo and Larry and their pals putting away formidable quantities of ale while their wives (Ger Ryan, Caroline Rothwell) are presented as all-understanding, all-forgiving paragons clearly smarter than their spouses but too self-effacing to let them know it. The effect is to remind us of how many screen hours we've spent with blue-collar British Isles guys in pubs and witnessed their humiliating plight of long-term unemployment.

"The Van" gathers some steam as the free-spirited Larry begins to chafe under the workload and the fact that he's Bimbo's employee and not his partner. However, the changes in Larry seem contrived for the purposes of plot resolution rather than growing out of his character. Like Bimbo, we wonder why Larry isn't profoundly grateful for the chance for gainful employment at a time and place when, it's implied, he's long ago given up any hope of finding a job.

In the absence of strong characterization, the burly, ever-endearing Meaney seems too often to be asked only to show off in displays of antic behavior not all that inspired and therefore not all that funny. In the far more understated role of Bimbo, O'Kelly registers more effectively.

"The Van" overflows with affectionate high spirits, but it doesn't travel nearly as well as "The Commitments" or "The Snapper" did.

NEW YORK POST, 5/16/97, p. 43, Thelma Adams

Get laid off? What next?

Get drunk.

Win the lottery?

Bottoms up.

Bloody your best buddy's lip? "Let's go for a pint," Bimbo (Donal O'Kelly) tells Larry (Colm Meaney), two married pals who brave unemployment in Stephen Frears' "The Van."

The final installment of novelist-turned-screenwriter Roddy Doyle's Barrytown Trilogy ("The Commitments" and "The Snapper") unintentionally serves up a slice of Irish life that makes it clear why there never was an Irish Empire.

Bimbo and Larry prove that friendship is more important than commerce, even if they display all manner of self-destructive behavior in order to reach that epiphany.

Larry, an old hand at being on the dole, teaches Bimbo the ropes after he gets canned. Not content to sit on his duff, Bimbo buys a chip van—a movable feast he calls Bimbo's Burgers. When the burgermeister hires Larry to dip chips, they're no longer unemployed workers united. They've become management and labor.

Set against the 1990 World Cup, Doyle's buddy comedy feels warmed over and structurally unambitious. Despite Eric Clapton's lively original music, "The Van" lacks the soundtrack-driven enthusiasm of "The Commitments."

"The Van" also misses the deep emotional charge of "The Snapper." That sharp family comedy centered on Meaney as a working-class Dublin Da coming to terms with his unmarried daughter's pregnancy—and her stubborn refusal to reveal the father's name.

Still, "The Van" has touching moments, some easy laughs, a general warmth, and a gregarious performance from Meaney, the talented actor best known in the States as Chief O'Brien from "Star Trek: Deep Space 9."

NEWSDAY, 5/16/97, Part II/p. B8, John Anderson

It's money, not music, that soothes the savage breast. And it doesn't take much: A little financial wherewithal, some small sense of fiscal self-respect, and everything else—health, sex, appetite, soccer—improves. Things go better, to paraphrase that old multinational ad slogan, with cash.

In Stephen Frears' delightful, neo-libertarian comedy "The Van"—which is set in Ireland but transcends economic communities and free-trade agreements—the subtle message isn't about money per se. It's about how much it takes to make someone happy. In fact, it may not be about money at all.

The question mark amid all the local color and character is Larry (Irish movie stalwart Colm Meaney) who's habitually unemployed and unmistakably happy when his friend Bimbo (Donal O'Kelly) is let go by the bakery. Larry is all set to show Bimbo "the ropes"—increased golf, increased Guinness and a settling into life on the dole. Bimbo, however, has not yet shaken off the habit of self-sufficiency and decides to parlay his severance into a "chip van"—a vehicle equipped with fryer, grill and countertop—and join the ranks of the self-employed.

Larry becomes his partner, and like a Celtic Kramden and Norton they set about fixing up a wreck of a truck, teaching themselves some rudimentary fast-food business and setting up outside the local pub, where the TV is broadcasting Ireland's bid for the World Cup. Hungry and, for a long time, victorious, the crowds mob Larry and Bimbo's wagon.

A lifetime of sitcom watching will have prepared American audiences for a standardized arc of small victories, huge reversals and an eventual resurrection by Larry and Bimbo, but nothing really works that way. And whether things go wrong or right isn't the point of "The Van." Novelist Roddy Doyle ("Paddy Clarke Ha Ha Ha") has written a script that is rich in character, local color and hilarity. The third in his so-called "Barrytown trilogy" (a name borrowed from an old Steely Dan song), it follows Alan Parker's "The Commitments" and Frears' "The Snapper" and provides Frears with the kind of smaller, humanity-driven story and setting in which he works so well (and did, in "The Grifters, "My Beautiful Laundrette" and "Sammy and Rosie Get Laid"). After the unspeakable "Mary Reilly," doubts were raised about Frears. They may now be dismissed.

So about Larry: Is it the money, or the self-esteem? While his new-found "wealth"—and how much can he and Bimbo make?—doesn't dominate the story, it's a credit to the writing and direction how subtly the world around him changes. Larry's marriage improves, the family gets along better, he starts to lose his tendency toward hair-trigger vulgarity. He becomes a better man just because he has a job. Not revelatory, perhaps, but well-done, and well-aimed. Within the catalog of Thatcher-dominated film and fiction that has been generated by the economically besieged British Isles since the '80s, "The Van" has to stand as one of its more pointed moments.

SIGHT AND SOUND, 12/96, p. 56, Leslie Felperin

Barrytown, Dublin, 1989. Bimbo, a baker, is devastated when made redundant, despite receiving a £3,000 cheque. His unemployed friend Larry comforts him with the thought that they can keep each other company. The two men enjoy golfing and hanging out together, but Bimbo is restless; he decides to buy a dilapidated and engineless 'chipper' van, much to his wife Maggie's horror. Larry helps him push it home, and Bimbo invites Larry to be his business partner. They begin the arduous process of cleaning the van and learning to make battered fish, chips and burgers in time for the World Cup in June.

By the time Ireland's first game comes, the van is ready and Bimbo and Larry, assisted by Larry's daughter Diane, start serving, despite their ineptitude. Business starts to take off and the two men divide the profits. Maggie helps with the planning, though Larry complains to his wife Mary that Maggie is too controlling. By the time Ireland has lost to Italy, they have enough money to buy an engine for the van. Maggie arranges a permit for them to serve at Dollymount beach.

Things begin to sour between the two men: Bimbo feels Larry doesn't take the work seriously enough, while Larry resents Maggie's interference. The two men go for a night out to heal the rift, but it only widens when Bimbo is successful at pulling a woman at a wine bar and Larry isn't. The next morning, Larry wakes with a terrible hangover to learn Mary has earned an 'A' on her leaving certificate and his son Kevin has passed a seven of his exams.

Being the owner of the van, Bimbo decides to pay Larry a wage from now on, so Larry insists on tea breaks and hints at joining a union. One night a health inspector calls. Appalled at the lack of hygiene, he shuts down the business. The two men get drunk together, argue and exchange clumsy blows. Convinced that "killing" the van will be the only way to heal their friendship, Bimbo drives the van into the sea. Larry carries him back to shore and goes home to his wife.

There's a line of slow-acting poignancy spoken at the beginning of *The Van* when long-term "man of leisure" Larry and his newly unemployed friend Bimbo search for a lost golf ball on a pitch-and-putt course. Larry advises Bimbo to "Say 'fuck it' and walk away—then you'll find it." The advice takes on a symbolic resonance, for that's effectively what both men try to do later, after the chip van business they started together collapses. Bimbo abandons the van, the symbol of both their friendship and their strife, in the sea thinking this will help him 'find' his bond with Larry again. Larry, after having felt outgrown by his wife and family and then found and lost a sense of pride in the van's success, ends the film by trudging home to his wife's bosom, to his rediscovered need for her, like a pudgy Leopold Bloom in sandy jeans.

The loveable thing about *The Van* is that resonant, understated touches such as this are deftly done; the annoying thing about it is that they are a bit too deft. There's a literary finickiness about the film's crafted air of naturalness. This is textbook kitchen-sink realism—low on declamatory revelations, but rich with the *mots justes* of Dublin working-class slang. (The dialogue is peppered with such Dublin words as 'yokes' for 'things' and 'battered' for 'drunk'.) *The Van*'s screenwriter, Roddy Doyle, taught English in secondary schools before he won the Booker Prize (for *Paddy Clarke Ha Ha Ha)* and wrote the Rabbitte-family novels on which this film and two others have been based (the others being *The Commitments*, directed by Alan Parker, and *The Snapper*, directed as is *The Van*, by Stephen Frears). As a novelist, Doyle writes with the pared-down simplicity of a teacher who has corrected too many clumsy student essays, with the sparseness of someone who has taught Hemingway or F. Scott Fitzgerald many times (his books are low on description, snippy with dialogue), with the studied casualness of someone who has inspired many a lazy student with a close reading of Salinger's *A Catcher in the Rye.* There's an energy and an immediacy that one can deeply admire, while still feeling that it's a bit retro and tinged with sentimentality.

Doyle's 'chipper'-style—crisp on the outside, a bit mushy on the inside—suffuses the dialogue here, though it's still the best thing about the film. It's particularly flavoursome in the ensemble scenes, when spoken by the film's cast of fine Irish character actors, led by redoubtable Colm Meaney (who starred as the same-but-differently-named character in the previous two films). The scenes in the pubs, in which men nurse slow pints and quiet resentments, are studies in small-talk concealing deeper hostilities, rivalries and alliances. There's a particularly effective dinner scene where Larry and family banter and swear at each other, until the son Kevin gets a little too cheeky. Larry rebukes him with a paternal "Remember who paid for that dinner," to which Kevin, reminding his father of his unemployed status, stingingly replies: "the State". Nothing else in the film better illustrates its central themes of male pride and the way domestic economics subtly shift the balances of power in relationships.

Where *The Commitments* was about the idealism of youth, and *The Snapper* about a girl's transition from teenager to parent, *The Van* is mainly about middle-aged masculinity and its discontents. You would think that Stephen Frears, who's had his fair share of triumphs and later-life disappointments, might have a special feel for the material. But on balance, the best book in Doyle's trilogy is the most lacklustre of the three films. Frears' strategy seems to be to hang back and let the actors do the work. Takes are long and generous, letting the performers work up a comic fire and then letting them douse it with a bit of melodrama. Sometimes that works well, but sometimes it feels as if people are performing in different productions. One protracted take in a wine bar mensroom between Larry (Colm Meaney) and Bimbo (Donal O'Kelly) is typical of Frears' lassitude: Meaney plays broad, drunk and boorish, his gestures over-powering O'Kelly's quiet anxiety. Granted, the characters are meant to be out of synch at this point, but it feels more like Frears can't be bothered to manage them.

The problem may just be one of scale; this sort of delicate drama can disguise its slight flaws easier on a small screen than on a big one, or even turn that smallness into extraordinary intimacy, as happened with Roddy Doyle's teledrama *The Family*. The success of *The Snapper* at film festivals persuaded its producers to give it a theatrical release, and perhaps they thought it would be self-deprecating to give *The Van* anything less. Yet amplified for a theatrical screen, its stage sets look artificial, it quotidianness drab. As television drama, this is fine. As a theatrical release, it is sadly a bit flat.

VILLAGE VOICE, 5/20/97, p. 76, Amy Taubin

In the U.S., workers are downsized; in Britain, they're made redundant. Like the pink slip, downsizing has an emasculating edge that suggests the loss of something more defective than one's paycheck. But it's the literary association in redundancy that gives me the shakes. What could be worse for a writer than being redundant? (Did I need to spell that out?)

The Van is a stubborn, bittersweet comedy about male bonding set against a background of middle-class unemployment. It's the third, and least rambunctious, film adapted by the Irish novelist Roddy Doyle from his Barrytown series. (Barrytown is a fictional suburb of Dublin.) The first two—*The Commitments*, directed by Alan Parker, and *The Snapper*, directed by Stephen Frears—were crowded, noisy, and immediately endearing. *The Van*, also directed by Frears, is sparer and, despite the vivid performances of Donal O'Kelly and Colm Meaney in the leading roles, slightly more labored. Though not lacking in surface humor, it's a film driven by undercurrents. When their tug goes slack, the story stalls.

The Van opens with Bimbo (O'Kelly) fighting back tears. There are few images more startling than an adult male in a suit and tie crying in public. Bimbo has just been made redundant by the bakery where he has worked all his life. He's stopped off in the local pub for a bit of comfort before delivering the bad news to his wife and three kids. Soon his best friend Larry (Meaney), who hasn't worked in years, has him laughing in his beer.

Bimbo and Larry exemplify the attraction of opposites in friendship as well as love. The lanky, still-boyish-looking Bimbo is a resourceful eager beaver with excellent impulse control. His identity is built around being a good provider for his family The beefy Larry plays the id to Bimbo's superego. Larry can be counted on to resist authority and opt for immediate gratification. He feels just guilty enough about being perpetually on the dole to resent anyone who can put a turkey on the table for Christmas dinner. If looks could kill, then the gold-lamé-covered guest at Bimbo's holiday party would have succumbed instantly to Larry's disgruntled stare. (Meaney is a master of hostile, frustrated reactions.) "Larry's been without a job for so long, he's forgotten how to work with anyone else" observes Bimbo worriedly—but by then, it's already too late.

Bimbo has invested his severance pay in a decrepit, filthy, fast-food wagon ("It looks like the inside of a leper") and asks Larry to be his partner. "We'll call it Bimbo's Burgers" says Larry in an uncharacteristically self-effacing burst of enthusiasm. But no sooner does the business score its first success than he wants to change the name to Bimbo and Larry's Burgers. The friendship turns into a power struggle and Bimbo is forced to choose between his relationship with Larry (irrational as it is) and the satisfactions of being a boss.

Rare in that it's focused almost entirely on work, *The Van*. also offers some satisfying glimpses of domesticity. Larry's wife Mary, who's gone back to school and is getting straight A's, knows how to defuse his anger before it takes hold. Larry doesn't give Mary as much back up as she needs, but his admiration for her is boundless and completely convincing. Doyle's characters are rich in constructions and Bimbo and Larry are two of the best.

Frears does terrific work with the actors. O'Kelly and Meaney never make a misstep and the supporting cast is very fine. Still, the film seems a little too controlled and, though Oliver Stapleton is a terrific cinematographer, much too carefully lit. Each scene exists to make a single point; when the point is made, the scene is over. One longs for a little chaos, or at least some overlap. There's a scene late in the film where Bimbo and Larry take a night off to repair their failing friendship. They wind up with two women in a hip Dublin wine bar. When Bimbo discovers that he has the option of scoring, he takes off, in terror, for the loo, pursued by the enraged, humiliated Larry who has struck out. The mix of bafflement, frustration, failed machismo, anger, and guilt is like something out of Cassavetes, and one longs for Frears, who has had his unhinged moments (remember *My Beautiful Laundrette* and *Sammy and Rosie Get Laid?*), to get reckless. He never does.

Also reviewed in:
NEW YORK TIMES, 5/16/97, p. C19, Stephen Holden
NEW YORKER, 5/26/97, p. 89, Anthony Lane
VARIETY, 5/20-26/96, p. 36, David Stratton
WASHINGTON POST, 6/13/97, p. B1, Rita Kempley
WASHINGTON POST, 6/13/97, Weekend/p. 41, Desson Howe

VEGAS VACATION

A Warner Bros. release. *Producer:* Jerry Weintraub. *Director:* Stephen Kessler. *Screenplay:* Elisa Bell. *Based on a story by:* Bob Ducsay. *Director of Photography:* William A. Fraker. *Editor:* Seth Flaume. *Music:* Joel McNeely. *Production Designer:* David L. Snyder. *Costumes:* Carole James. *Running time:* 90 minutes. *MPAA Rating:* PG.

CAST: Chevy Chase (Clark W. Griswold); Beverly D'Angelo (Ellen Griswold); Randy Quaid (Cousin Eddie); Wayne Newton (Himself); Ethan Embry (Rusty Griswold); Wallace Shawn (Dealer); Marisol Nichols (Audrey Griswold); Miriam Flynn (Cousin Catherine); Shae D'Lyn (Cousin Vickie).

LOS ANGELES TIMES, 2/17/97, Calendar/p. 4, Jack Mathews

[*The following review by Jack Mathews appeared in a slightly different form in* **NEWSDAY, 2/17/97, Part II/p. B2.**]

In the first of National Lampoon's "Vacation" movies in 1983, Chevy Chase's Clark Griswold drove his family cross-country with a dead relative on the roof. In the fourth and worst episode, "Vegas Vacation," the Griswolds head from their Chicago suburb to Las Vegas with a dead script on their hands.

This series—conceived by John Hughes, who wrote or co-wrote the first three screenplays—never has been more than a chain of comic sketches, built around the haplessness of a well-meaning family man who can't talk and drive at the same time. The character was tailored to Chase's dead-pan style, and he has delivered a few memorable physical and mental pratfalls.

But there is nothing more memorable about "Vegas Vacation" than the flatness of the writing in Elisa Bell's script and the uninspired direction of first-timer Stephen Kessler. They take a decent comedy premise—how Vegas' potpourri of temptations affects each member of a naive Midwestern family—and lay it out as if the premise itself is all that's necessary.

So we see the luckless Clark repetitiously blowing the family nest egg in the casino, intercut with scenes of his abandoned wife Ellen (Beverly D'Angelo) trying to resist the advances of her idol Wayne Newton, son Rusty (Ethan Embry) getting a fake ID and going on a winning streak that puts him in the good graces of the mob, and daughter Audrey (Marisol Nichols) breaking out of her shell with a job as a go-go dancer.

You can't fault Chase and D'Angelo—or series regular Randy Quaid, who returns as trailer trash cousin Eddie—for anything other than dipping into a dry well. What's tired is not their performances but the series itself, and a script notable for its episodic pointlessness.

There is a long sequence with the family at Hoover Dam that goes nowhere, and another on the road that repeats the scene in the first film where Clark flirts with a passing motorist. It's Christie Brinkley again, in another red convertible, only this time she has a baby in the back seat. That's the whole joke! And, worse news, that's as good as it gets.

This is one "Vacation" you may want to put off until it comes out on video.

NEW YORK POST, 2/15/97, p. 21, Larry Worth

When Clark Griswold (Chevy Chase) tells his family that they're going to Las Vegas, his kids say they're "getting too old for this." They're not the only ones.

Indeed, Chase, Beverly D'Angelo and Randy Quaid sleepwalk through "Vegas Vacation," the latest comedy about the Griswold clan's wacky adventures. It continues the steady downhill slide from "National Lampoon's Vacation" to "European Vacation" to "Christmas Vacation."

Can a trek to Appalachia be far behind?

On second thought, that might prove more fun than this collection of Glitter Gulch clichés, varying only from standard gross-out humor to predictable punch lines.

Most of the action centers on Clark losing the family's bank account at the gaming tables. In between, Wayne Newton (!) puts the moves on Clark's better half (D'Angelo) while weird Cousin Eddie (Quaid) revels in being king of the trailer trash.

First-time director Stephen Kessler could have used any of the above to satirize Sin City's evolution into America's new family hotspot. Instead, he takes the easy route by cruising into one sitcom setup after another.

That's why one can't blame Chase and his cohorts for finding few laughs in enacting the Griswolds' Vegas shenanigans: They came, they gambled, they lost.

What else is new?

But do "Vegas Vacation" viewers have to suffer the same fate?

Also reviewed in:
NEW YORK TIMES, 2/15/97, p. 24, Lawrence Van Gelder
VARIETY, 2/17-23/97, p. 71 Todd McCarthy

VISITING DESIRE

An AB. Productions Inc. release. *Producer:* Beth B. *Director:* Beth B. *Director of Photography:* Beth B. *Editor:* Melody London. *Music:* Jim Filer Coleman. *Sound:* Beth B. *Running time:* 70 minutes. *MPAA Rating:* Not Rated.

WITH: Lydia Lunch; Kembra Pfahler; Shannon O'Kelley; Chloe Dzubilo; Ned Ambler; Cyrus Khambatta; Eric Danville; Annie OK; John Val Jean; Patty Powers; Lysa Cooper; Doug Charles.

NEW YORK POST, 2/7/97, p. 48, Bill Hoffmann

How's this for a plot: A dozen strangers are paired off in a tiny East Village bedroom to act out their wildest fantasies as an inconspicuous video camera captures the action.

A cheesy porn flick? Nope, just the latest cutting-edge exercise from Beth B—a New York original who's ground out some of independent cinema's most intriguing movies over the past 20 years.

"Visiting Desire" opens with five therapists discussing the nature of fantasies—the reasons why we have them, their benefits and their dangers.

This sets the scene for a series of encounters which begin when two people who've never met before are left alone in a bedroom, where a king-sized bed is the main feature, and encouraged to let it all hang out.

To encourage the outrageous, Beth B stacks the deck with a veteran performance artist, a gender-bender, a fetishist, an adult filmmaker and other rock 'n' roll outlaw types who don't mind cursing, kissing and getting naked.

By the end of 70 minutes, we've witnessed wrestling matches, mental breakdowns, crossdressing, masturbation, lesbianism and rampant exhibitionism.

The single set, which seems hopelessly limiting at first, turns into a marvelously claustrophobic space, almost like an undersized cage at a zoo, making it perfect for conflict.

"Visiting Desire," opening today at Cinema Village, does rely a bit too much on the over-the-top antics of Lydia Lunch, a veteran performance artist who's a bit too long in the tooth to still pull off her outrageous schtick.

Lunch seems to he playing to the camera, giving the proceedings a slight whiff of chicanery.

Still, "Visiting Desire" remains edgy and compelling stuff for the most part—an unpredictable mix of comedy, drama and nervous energy.

It easily stands next to "Two Small Bodies," "Salvation," "The Trap Door," "Belladonna" and "Black Box" as another solid Beth B movie.

Perhaps best of all, it's a welcome sign that Beth B—unlike many of her contemporaries like Penelope Spheeris and John Waters—hasn't sold out to Hollywood and watered down her spunky subversive roots.

And for that she deserves a rousing "Bravo."

VILLAGE VOICE, 2/11/97, p. 74, Michael Atkinson

Empty too, though in a far from rewarding way [The reference is to *Margaret's Museum*; see Atkinson's review.] Beth B's new indulgence *Visiting Desire* is, essentially, a series of crudely shot (on video) encounter sessions wherein a gaggle of Beth's narcissistic Downtown friends (Lydia Lunch among them) lounge on a bed and flirt, act out uninteresting sexual fantasies, tease each other, cry, and sometimes fuck. Neither actors nor real people, B's cast rarely manages to suppress embarrassed smirks as they congratulate themselves over and over for their not so unorthodox sexual preferences. (Clitoral stimulation by belt thwacking is a highlight.) And because B managed to muster only a merciful 70 minutes from this unpromising setup, Cinema Village has tacked on a sharp New Zealand short, Andrew Bancroft's *Planet Man,* a hyperbolic, Cannes-selected neonoir that imagines life on earth if all women were suddenly to disappear. (Guess: men turn into alehouse rats.) Sweaty and crude, the film's lickspittle thesis is both trite and mildly homophobic (would a woman ever make a film with the reverse premise?), but formally it's classic NZ cheese, like early von Trier on a pop-stand budget.

Also reviewed in:
NEW YORK TIMES, 2/7/97, p. C10, Stephen Holden
VARIETY, 10/21-27/96, p. 96, Emanuel Levy

VOLCANO

A Fox 2000 Pictures release of a Shuler Donner/Donner and Moritz Original production. *Executive Producer:* Lauren Shuler Donner. *Producer:* Neal H. Moritz and Andrew Z. Davis. *Director:* Mick Jackson. *Screenplay:* Jerome Armstrong and Billy Ray. *Story:* Jerome Armstrong. *Director of Photography:* Theo van de Sande. *Editor:* Michael Tronick and Don Brochu. *Music:* Alan Silvestri. *Music Editor:* Kenneth Karman. *Sound:* Jim Tanenbaum and (music) Dennis Sands. *Sound Editor:* Tom Bellfort and John Larsen. *Production Designer:* Jackson DeGovia. *Art Director:* Scott Rittenour, Tom Reta, William Cruse, and Donald Woodruff. *Set Designer:* Patty Klawonn, Richard Reynolds, Dianne Wager, Les Gobruegge, Beverly Eagen, and Richard Lawrence. *Set Decorator:* K.C. Fox. *Set Dresser:* Loren P. Lyons. *Special Effects:* Dale Ettema. *Special/Mechanical Effects:* Clay Pinney and Marty Bresin. *Costumes:* Kirsten Everberg. *Make-up:* Michael Mills. *Make-up (Tommy Lee Jones):* Michael Germain. *Stunt Coordinator:* Mic Rodgers. *Running time:* 120 minutes. *MPAA Rating:* PG-13.

CAST: Tommy Lee Jones (Mike Roark); Anne Heche (Dr. Amy Barnes); Gaby Hoffmann (Kelly Roark); Don Cheadle (Emmit Reese); Jacqueline Kim (Dr. Jaye Calder); Keith David (Lt. Ed Fox); John Corbett (Norman Calder); Michael Rispoli (Gator Harris); John Carroll Lynch (Stan Olber); Marcello Thedford (Kevin); Laurie Lathem (Rachel); Bert Kramer (Fire Chief); Bo Eason (Bud McVie); James G. MacDonald (Terry Jasper); Dayton Callie (Roger Lapher); Michael Cutt (Armstrong); Kevin Bourland (Bob Davis); Valente Rodriguez (Train Driver); Sheila Howard (Panicked Woman/Nanny); Gerry Black (Train Passenger); Susie Essman (Anita); Lou Myers (Pastor Lake); Gareth Williams (Pete); Juan Gabriel Reynoso (Carlos); Angela Albarez (Lydia Perez); Richard Penn (Middle Aged Man); Jennifer Bill (Nurse Fran); Mickey Cottrell (Councilman Gates); M. Darnell Suttles (Chief Sindelar); Ken Kerman (Museum Guard); Sal Rendino (Chuck); Michael Manuel (Del); Jared Thorne and Taylor Thorne (Tommy); Richard Schiff (Haskins); Brad Parker (Ken Woods); Peter Kasper (Kenny Lopez); Brian Markinson (OEM Staffer #1); Robert Wisdom (OEM Staffer #2); Katie Rich (OEM Staffer #3); Ceal Coleman (OEM Staffer #4); Phil Nee (OEM Staffer #5); Carlos Cervantes (OEM Staffer #6); George Zaver (OEM Staffer #7); Marty Levy (OEM Staffer #8); Wayne Grace (OEM Staffer #9); Mother Love (Traffic Cop); Kayli DeGregorio and Kelsi DeGregorio (5 Year Old Chuckie); Steven Mainz (K-Rail Driver); Josie Dapar (Survivor #1); Joy Baggish (Survivor #2); Ron Perkins (Fire Chief); Todd Sible (Scott); Joshua Fardon (Medic); Catherine Schreiber (Displeased Protestor); David Pressman (Second Protestor); Danny Comden (Ascending Cop); Michael McGrady (Policeman); Michole Briana White (ER

Nurse 1); Steve MacLaughlin (Construction Supervisor); Howard DuVall (Engineer #1); Sam Alejan (Engineer #2); Gary Kent James (Engineer #3); Robert Tittor (Engineer #4); John Perry Edson, Jr. (Engineer #5); David T. Mabowe (Engineer #6); Ken Thomas (Engineer #7); Eddie J. Low (Engineer #8); Georganna Barry (Java Lady); Tom Crabson (Passenger on Train); Rick Rogers (Sgt. Riley).

LOS ANGELES TIMES, 4/25/97, Calendar/p. 1, Kenneth Turan

"Volcano" glows with heat. Lava heat. The coast may be toast, but it's the lava, covering everything like a malevolent tide of melted butter, that makes this a disaster picture that's tastier than usual.

Hollywood's last volcano movie, the misbegotten "Dante's Peak," was particularly stingy in the lava department, barely letting it flow. "Volcano" has no such qualms and though wet blanket scientists may question the likelihood of raging torrents of superheated goo rising from the La Brea tar pits intent on swallowing the Westside, the film's mightily impressive special effects will sway most doubters.

Shot on an 80% scale model of the Wilshire corridor constructed on 17-plus acres of the McDonnell Douglas plant parking lot in Torrance, "Volcano" will be particularly convincing for Los Angeles residents.

Seeing the Los Angeles County Museum of Art, the Art Deco May Co. building and surrounding sites, plus all those elegant Wilshire Boulevard palm trees, consumed by a relentless tide of lava is especially unnerving if you've spent time in the neighborhood.

As written by Jerome Armstrong and Billy Ray, "Volcano" also manages some sly moments that will be appreciated around town. A subway motorman reads "Screenplays That Sell," Metro workers are stigmatized as "the guys who collapsed Hollywood Boulevard" and a huge billboard of local icon Angelyne becomes a victim of the volcano's flames.

It's not surprising that director Mick Jackson highlights these and other funny touches; one of his credits is Steve Martin's "L.A. Story." Jackson also has a background in documentary work, and his ability, working with cameraman Theo van de Sande and editors Michael Tronick and Don Brochu, to move things along and create a sense of continuous urgency is critical to "Volcano's" effectiveness. Because at its core, "Volcano" is another one of those programmatic disaster movies, with dogs in jeopardy and kids wandering off at the worst possible moment. A great deal of its dialogue is of the "I know you're scared, I'm scared too" variety, and there's even room for the everpopular "What is *that?*"

But a great sense of pace is a wonderful thing, and director Jackson and his crew (who made good use of hand-held and Steadicam shots and reportedly averaged an impressive 30 to 40 camera setups a day) move so quickly from shot to shot and location to location that viewers have a limited time to dwell on the film's predictable implausibilities.

"Volcano" also benefits from crisp work from its principals, especially Tommy Lee Jones as Mike Roark, the tireless head of L.A.'s fictional Office of Emergency Management. Few actors can look as indomitable or project the kind of take-no-prisoners fierceness that's a match for any natural disaster.

When strange things start happening below the placid surface of MacArthur Park after a mild earthquake, Roark almost immediately barks, "Find me a scientist who can tell me what the hell is going on." His staff comes up with feisty seismologist Dr. Amy Barnes (Anne Heche) who suspects a volcano. Roark smirks a sexist smirk, but it's not long before his toes are almost literally being held to the fire.

Heche, a strong actress who is rapidly bubbling up from the underground herself, appearing in "Donnie Brasco" and now this, proves to the one of the few performers of either sex capable of standing toe-to-toe with the fierce Jones, and their interaction is one of the film's pluses.

Other supporting players, including Don Cheadle as Emmit Reese, Roark's ambitious second-in-command, and Gaby Hoffmann as Roark's sullen teenage daughter, also manage to do what's necessary without overstaying their welcomes.

As that darn lava threatens to vaporize everything it touches, including Metro passengers who probably wish they'd taken their cars, Roark comes up with a wild and crazy plan to save the city. Hey, he knows it's a longshot, but that's the kind of guy he is.

In everything besides special effects, "Volcano" is allergic to breaking new ground, and viewers have to endure moments of bogus brotherhood and a chauvinist ending that pulls Dr. Barnes out of the line of fire to took for Roark's lost daughter. But it's hard to dislike a film where a character can survey a sea of lava and say, "Better take the freeway. Wilshire looks pretty bad." After the horrendous dramatics of "Twister," "Independence Day" and "Dante's Peak," a disaster movie that's not a complete disaster itself can be reason enough to smile.

NEW YORK, 5/12/97, p. 55, David Denby

I saw *Volcano* in Los Angeles, and so I had the odd experience of watching a movie in which lava flows down the street—Wilshire Boulevard—that I had just taken to get to the screening with my children. Coming out of the theater, we stood at the corner of Westwood and Wilshire and got blown about by the Santa Ana winds. As everyone knows, Los Angeles has lost its old spoiled-rotten complacency, its assurance of limitless pleasure and freedom. Beautiful the city is, but its beauty is precarious, with a sense of dismay right under the lush, golden splendor. A mud slide is coming, the wind is coming, the end of the world is just around the corner. Los Angeles has developed a resilience and humor one doesn't remember from, say, twenty years ago. At the screening, people cheered whenever some hideous local landmark—a big poster, an awful new building—bit the dust, and there were groans when the overfamiliar faces of local news reporters, banal chroniclers of disaster, came on screen. Citizens have survived one calamity after another, and no matter what happens, the palm trees wave in the breeze, pretty people in convertibles cruise the Strip at night, and blacks, Asian-Americans, and Latinos set a lot of the city's tone. The movie, directed by Mick Jackson, a Brit convert to Los Angeles, is a perverse hymn of praise for Los Angeles's creative, multi-ethnic mess. The city is tattered, corrupt, divided, perhaps chaotic, but, for the first time, deeply lovable.

Volcano may not be lovable, but it's certainly likable, which is something one can say of very few disaster movies. It's the least morbid, the most high-spirited and entertaining example of a very rum genre. In this movie, such disaster-film clichés as the Warning Signs of Catastrophe are almost comical: subterranean rumblings, odd emissions of heat and steam from below, and a rather overinsistent gurgling, as of a stew pot gone mad, at the La Brea Tar Pits. The filmmakers seem almost to be teasing us. There is even a small quake that everyone shrugs off with jokes. Banter is the universal style. The guys furiously building the city's controversial subway argue with the head of the Office of Emergency Management, Mike Roark (Tommy Lee Jones); and Roark, in turn, ribs his lieutenant, a swift-talking joker (Don Cheadle) who mans the control center in a turned-around golfer's cap. When a seismologist, Dr. Amy Barnes (Anne Heche), shows up, she and Roark appear to be flirting. Mick Jackson and the screenwriters, Billy Ray and Jerome Armstrong, let us know they are making an entertainment.

When the volcano blows, the sight is almost pretty, like a *son et lumière* show that has gone bizarrely over the top: Enormous columns of red flame shoot up in the night, and lava bombs are flung aloft like flaming cannonballs in an old medieval-siege movie. This is a highly photogenic catastrophe. The lava, like a thick stream of bubbling Italian meat sauce, moves in a stately way down Wilshire, almost as if the boulevard were a sealed corridor. Are there no cross streets? Is there any reason for the lava to move west (menacing the affluent West Side) rather than east or south? The lava has been well-directed. It glows in the dark and burns or melts everything in its path, eating cars, causing buildings to explode, but it always moves slowly, so there's plenty of time for people to stand around looking at it, transfixed, sometimes paralyzed. It takes them a while to realize how dangerous the stuff is.

Tommy Lee Jones is the perfect actor to play take-charge guys who are good at improvising. Jones always seems to be thinking on his feet. He talks in a rapid, almost careless way, as if everything were settled in his mind and communication no more than a necessary follow-through, and he's always racing ahead to the next thing and then the next. Roark is a man too sure of himself, and too unpretentious at heart, to get riled at people not as fast as he is. Jones is very appealing, and so is Anne Heche, who keeps up with him, rattling off her brilliant-seismologist jargon with tremendous facility. These two speedsters, we feel, are the only people who can save the sleepy, quarrelsome city. At times, they seem the only people capable of thought.

In general, disaster movies reduce the audience to sheer spectatorship. We're put in the position of wanting to see the people melt (otherwise, there's no movie); we root for disaster.

At the same time, we're flattered with an appeal to "moral" feelings—all those little incidents of heroism, sacrifice, and nobility. The plot of a disaster movie is a series of conventions assembled to convince a morbidly fascinated audience that it has "heart." Even *Volcano,* fast-paced and shrewd as it is, has a dog that grabs its bone and flees a building about to explode in flames. (The audience cheers derisively.) But the dog, as it turns out, is far more resourceful than the teenage daughter of Mike Roark. This round-faced girl (Gaby Hoffmann) places herself in the path of the lava flow and manages to stand under a building as it is about to fall over, and every time she gets in trouble, her dad has to stop saving the city and rescue her. As a way of anchoring our responses, she's a pathetic and insulting device. Couldn't the filmmakers do better?

Volcano is an odd mixture of contempt and respect. The filmmakers make a pass at promoting multicultural harmony: There's a Korean doctor who selflessly wears herself out attending the injured, and a cocky, pain-in-the-ass AfricanAmerican who antagonizes a white policeman, gets himself arrested, but then, when released, pulls himself together and joins in the effort to save the city. Last summer, at *Independence Day,* I had the sense that the movie was openly yearning for the Martians to arrive: Please, God, let them come! Let them come so we can all fight them together and end the divisions between one ethnic group and another! *Volcano* offers the healing catastrophe: That lava flowing down Wilshire may be the new melting pot.

NEW YORK POST, 4/25/97, p. 43, Thelma Adams

Lava! Valour! Compassion! Mick Jackson's "Volcano" is a hunka, hunka steaming magma with a warm heart at its core.

The disaster pic asks the burning question: What would happen to LaLa Land if it suddenly spouted Krakatoa west of Palmdale? The movie with more magma-per-minute than any feature that has come before dramatizes Rodney Kings famed line, "Why can't we just get along?

The answer: When the La Brea Tar Pits bubble, the MacArthur Park ducks stew in their own lake, and Wilshire Boulevard is a molten river, Angelenos of all stripes stand together—even if it takes the Beverly Center going up in flames to achieve racial unity.

This being Hollywood, it also takes a white guy to rally the troops. Tommy Lee Jones—the actor who specializes in craggy-faced authoritarians we reluctantly adore when has not playing yahoo wackos—steps into flame-retardant shoes as the savior of Mid-Wilshire. When disaster strikes, the buck stops at the desk of emergency czar Mike Roark (Jones).

There wouldn't be enough steaming subplots if Roark's personal life weren't a disaster zone. Roark is divorced, his hostile daughter wants to pierce her nose, and he has no fashion IQ. But when this control freak with the Brillo personality senses that the rumblings beneath MacArthur Park aren't the usual five-point tremors, his life comes into focus. "Find me a scientist!" he shouts.

Enter Anne Heche ("Donnie Brasco"), a perky blonde in the Jean Arthur, Myrna Loy vein. She zestfully pulls off the oxymoron of being a hot-shot seismologist. It's lava at first sight for Dr. Amy when she spots Roark taking charge. They'll have to hang by their fingers 40 feet above a molten river before we know it's the real thing.

Working from a fluid script by Jerome Armstrong and Billy Ray, Jackson ("The Bodyguard") - sketches the human details while moving into one nail-biter set piece after another. "Volcano" gets off the ground quicker than its rival, "Dante's Peak," which now seems as buried as Pompeii.

It's no surprise that when the Earth's crust cracks, Hollywoodies hang tough. But what's cool about "Volcano" is watching familiar landmarks flame out and crumble. We're moved, we're entertained, we're horrified, we're taken so close to the fire we're almost flushed.

With lava bombs bursting in air, flaming palm trees and our prehistoric pal—the plaster wooly mammoth from the La Brea Tar Pits—sinking into phosphorescent orange and yellow goo, "Volcano" is truly spectacular. And it ends on the perfect musical note: Randy Newman singing "I Love L.A."

NEWSDAY, 4/25/97, Part II/p. B3, Jack Mathews

We're told in the production notes for Mick Jackson's "Volcano" that it is conceivable a fissure could occur between the tectonic plates rubbing against each other below southern California, allowing magma and gases to rise, build up pressure and produce a volcanic eruption. And if it were to happen, as it does in the movie, Los Angeles' burbling La Brea Tar Pits seems as likely an exit hole as any.

So, given the kernel of scientific foundation to the story, why is "Volcano" as silly as "The Blob?"

The answer is that the filmmakers, presumably survivors of numerous real-life L.A. disasters, couldn't buy the theory themselves, not enough to imagine how the city might actually respond. It's much easier to follow the prescribed disaster movie formula—introduce a few key characters and throw them all together in the inferno.

In this case, the core group includes single dad Mike Roark (Tommy Lee Jones), the head of L.A.'s emergency response department; his 13-year-old daughter, Kelly (Gaby Hoffmann); his wisecracking assistant, Emmit Reese (Don Cheadle); beautiful geologist Amy Barnes (Anne Heche); samaritan surgeon Jaye Calder (Jacqueline Kim), and the usual assortment of officious baboons who, as the earth rumbles and burps, refuse to react. And, of course, there's a dog.

The clever ad slogan for "Volcano" is "The Coast Is Toast," but nothing of the sort actually happens. Though volcanos are powerful forces, no volcano has ever met the likes of Mike Roark and Amy Barnes. Together, they stop the lava in its tracks at Fairfax and Wilshire, then rush to the Beverly Center, where Barnes has decided it will next emerge.

"We're dealing with very determined stuff here," someone observes of the magma. Well, with Mike and Amy, the volcano doesn't have it so easy either.

For native Angelenos like myself, there's fun in spotting landmarks in the Wilshire District, the location of both the La Brea Tar Pits and the Los Angeles County Museum of Art, and at the Beverly Center, which is adjacent to Cedars Sinai, where the rich and the famous get their organ transplants.

All of these landmarks are key sets, and a 90-percent-scale replica of a block in the district was actually constructed and destroyed during the filming. Those scenes lend an authenticity to the disaster that the numerous computer-generated graphics can't begin to match.

The underlying theme of the story is that ongoing subway development in Los Angeles may be responsible for the fissure giving vent to the earth's gastritis. That creates some tension between Roark and city transportation officials, and gives Jackson an opportunity to take us underground for some terrifying scenes of trapped humans getting the first whiff of the volcano's breath.

The movie is intended as a thrill ride, and after a long, effectively dramatic build-up, it delivers almost nonstop action. There are explosive lava bombs raining from the sky, followed by torrential ash storms. Buildings and cars ignite like dry brush, and Roark leads one hairbreadth escape after another.

Jones, getting a late-life fling as an action star, doesn't have much acting to do, and is generally upstaged by his flashy costar, Heche. But events become so outrageous—at one point, Roark has 20 minutes to blow up a building and 200 yards of highway in which to dam and redirect a river of lava—that character development is no longer an issue.

Jackson, who also directed the parody "L.A. Story," gives the city's stereotypes another workout here. There's a subway conductor working on his screenplay before going on duty, an ongoing confrontation between a feisty black man and the hothead cop he calls "Fuhrman," and a helicopter view of idiots looting in the orange glow of the eruption.

Fires, floods, earthquakes, riots, O.J., and now this. Pardon me as I wipe away a tear, but there is no place like home.

NEWSWEEK, 5/5/97, p. 68, David Ansen

The secret of *Volcano*'s success as a better-than-average disasterama is its nonstop pace. Like the lava that streams down L.A.'s Wilshire Boulevard incinerating everything in its path, the relentless succession of wham-bang images simply rolls over each and every cliché in the script, smothering your objections in the process.

Unlike "Dante's Peak," which postponed the cork-popping for an hour, "Volcano" gets right down to business with a hefty quake, the effect of which is to open the tectonic doors to the volcanic juices lying in wait to destroy Los Angeles. Director Mick Jackson and his screenwriters (Jerome Armstrong and Billy Ray) are smart enough to know we didn't come for "character development." We want to see L.A. trashed. (What other burg can stand in for Sodom and Gomorrah these days?) To document the destruction, Jackson adopts a faux-newsreel style, which makes "Volcano" seem like a continuation of all the other times we've watched L.A. withstand real-life assault from fires, mudslides, tidal waves, quakes, looters, arsonists and, most recently, armed-to-the-teeth bank robbers.

Jackson is the man who directed the affectionately satirical "L.A. Story." This could be seen as its giddily nightmarish sequel. The fun of the movie is in the background details—a giant billboard of Angelyne, L.A.'s self-appointed sex icon, crashing to the streets; a Metro subway driver reading "How to Write Screenplays That Sell" as he heads to his lava-licked fate; the banner at the enflamed County Art Museum announcing its Hieronymus Bosch show. Anyone familiar with the city will be impressed with the movie's recreation of the Miracle Mile district, constructed in a parking lot at a McDonnell Douglas Aircraft plant. The lava heads west toward that burg bunker of consumerism, the Beverly Center, where our hero, Emergency Management Control head Tommy Lee Jones, and our heroine, seismologist Anne Heche, must make one last-ditch effort to save the West Side from deep-frying.

Jones and Heche have to create their characters on the run, and skimpy as these roles are, they give them urgency and a plausible aura of intelligence. Unfortunately, the plot requires Tommy Lee to be concerned about his terrified 13-year-old daughter (Gaby Hoffmann), a tiresome whiner whose survival is hardly a burning issue. A further gaffe is the high-minded subplot about a white racist cop and a black homeboy who learn to work together under the shadow of the volcanic ash, which all too symbolically transforms black and white into the same shade of gray. Oh, well, nobody said "Volcano" was profound. Happily, no bad idea hangs around long enough to become truly noisome. "Volcano," busily and cheerfully hysterical, always has some new fish to fry, new truck to melt, new skyscraper to tumble or new manhole to pop with a radiant gusher of movie magma.

SIGHT AND SOUND, 10/97, p. 62, Tom Tunney

In LA, the Office of Emergency Management's team leader Mike Roark and seismologist Dr Amy Barnes investigate an underground explosion which kills several construction workers. It emerges that the building of a new tunnel has provoked a volcanic disturbance. Barnes goes underground with her colleague Rachel, who loses her life in a second explosion. Barnes makes a narrow escape.

The same explosion traps a subway train and its passengers underground. At the La Brea Tar Pits, manhole covers are blasted hundreds of feet in the air, flaming lava balls hurtle in menacing arcs across the city and a thick stream of molten lava curls through the streets. The media descend on the crisis as panic grips the population. Driving with his teenage daughter Kelly, Roark meets Dr Jaye Calder in the street and helps her deal with the injured crew of a crashed fire engine. One man is trapped in his cab and dies as the lava reaches him. Roark rescues his daughter from the advancing lava. Moving on, Roark meets Dr Barnes and the pair perform another rescue using a fire engine ladder to swing over the molten inferno. Using water from the fire trucks, they manage to cool the lava, thus forming a dam against the hotter material.

A rescue team reaches the trapped subway train and the leader, Stan, sacrifices himself by standing in the lava to hurl the injured train driver to safety. Roark organises a series of concrete barriers to hold back the lava at Cedars-Sinai Hospital, where the lava is about to burst out of the subway tunnel. Meanwhile Dr Barnes searches for Kelly in the evacuating crowd. The demolition of a skyscraper succeeds in diverting the lava into the LA storm drain, from where it proceeds harmlessly into the sea. Roark is reunited with his daughter and Dr Barnes.

Like that of *Earthquake*, made 23 years ago, the dramatic logic of *Volcano* is as simple and functional as its one-word title: an underground volcano erupts in the middle of LA. Every thing leads to and from that premise. Also conforming to the established disaster-movie type, the key characters are given some rudimentary social context before their lives are put in jeopardy: Roark has a daughter; Dr Calder is in a failing relationship; and, most amusingly of all, the subway train driver is reading a book called *Writing Screenplays That Sell*. Commendably, Mick Jackson (who before he directed *The Bodyguard* helmed the made-for-TV British nuclear-disaster drama *Threads*) spends the bare minimum of time setting up the human mechanics of the plot before plunging feet first into the special-effects mayhem.

The sustained violence of the eruption sequences almost suggests an invasion of the city by an alien force. Frighteningly random in their effect, the screaming aerial lava bombs would do justice to *The War of the Worlds* (1952), while the slow but unrelenting progress of the inferno suggests that this is, in part, a straight-faced rip-off of *The Blob* (1958). The violent flowing centrepiece of the film is truly spectacular, but the effect is partially ruined by the film-makers' insistence on guiding the narrative with the babble of reporters, whose upbeat voice-overs constantly intrude on the action.

The reporters are real LA media people and, very depressingly, they all talk with the same blandly modulated fake enthusiasm which is the hallmark of tabloid television. Tim Burton took the inspired decision to kill off the media in *Mars Attacks!* The problem with this film is that none of them ever sounds like they're in danger. The entire disaster is thus reduced to a spectator sport with the cinema audience placed in the same, safely sanitised, position as the television viewer. Such a perspective is perhaps appropriate for a film made by Rupert Murdoch's Twentieth Century Fox, sister company to Sky and News International. However, it would have been a far more exciting film if the lava had fried a couple of camera crews—and Roark's Office of Emergency Management control centre is also strangely insulated from the centre of the action.

The disaster movies of the 70s usually insisted on the flaws of those who were chosen to die, typically an array of ageing and/or second-division stars. Unfortunately, that gleefully sadistic aesthetic no longer seems to apply. Calder's unpleasant husband (who would then probably have been played by Tony Franciosa or Robert Wagner) would have been assured of a spectacularly nasty death. Here, he's merely forgotten about. Instead, almost everyone else gets a chance to be Charlton Heston: there's a soldier who heroically stays with his trapped buddy as the skyscraper blows up (which makes a telling contrast with Marjoe Gortner's demented national guardsman in *Earthquake*) and a cynical black teen and an arrogant white cop who learn to work together while putting up a barrier. At the end, when the survivors are all covered in grey dust, a child announces triumphantly as the video cameras scan them: "Look at their faces, they all look the same!" The symbolism is meant to suggest a kind of news event as *E Pluribus Unum*-message, but the underlying premise is that if it's not on television, it hasn't happened.

TIME, 4/28/97, p. 73, Richard Corliss

Just one more reason not to live in Los Angeles. It seems there's an active volcano under Wilshire Boulevard, and is it steamed! It blows spitballs of lava up through manhole covers. It sends fire chunks into the sky, as if in a malefic Disney World spectacle, and has them land on prime Beverly Hills real estate. It not only exhales scalding air, it also sucks it back in. This monster, writhing undead in its coffin, has a personality. It even growls, basso profundo; imagine Barry White slowly murmuring "Booo!"

We're pretty sure that Nostradamus predicted a premillennial Hollywood plague of natural-disaster movies. Last year *Twister*; this fall *The Flood*. In February, *Dante's Peak* sent small-town folk scurrying from their local Vesuvius; now Mick Jackson's *Volcano* has man tamper in God's domain—by daring to build a subway in L.A. The script, by Jerome Armstrong and Billy Ray, thus exploits two major fears of Angelenos: getting demolished by a horrid subterranean force, and having to take public transportation.

The gookum-like lava is less smothering than the plot clichés: our hero (Tommy Lee Jones) and his perpetually hysterical child (Gaby Hoffmann), ever blundering into catastrophe; the spiky geologist (Anne Heche) who has to exclaim "Oh, God!" 46 times; silliest of all, the ornery whites and blacks who when covered with gray ash learn that, gee, Armageddon is color-blind. And just once in a disaster film, could a dog please die?

All right, nobody cares. You just want to see the volcano that ate L.A. If so, you'll have a hell-lava time.

VILLAGE VOICE, 4/29/97, p. 71, Gary Dauphin

Whether it's alien-produced, as in *Independence Day*, or the work of Mother Mature, à la *Volcano* (this year's Fox Event flick), it seems that a big wave of fire is just the social tonic needed by a moribund America. In no particular order, the lava flow that takes out downtown L.A. brings a parent and child together, reconciles the LAPD with the black community, teaches a wife her husband's an asshole, and allows another asshole to redeem himself via sacrificial self-immolation. Not a bad day's work for a digitally animated river of thousand-degree ooze.

L.A.'s searing road to inner healing begins with a minor tremor that introduces *Volcano*'s cast of quick-sketch characters. Chief among them is the head of the Office of Emergency Management (Tommy Lee Jones), a transplanted flood fighter who is interrupted during some quality time with his sullen, teenage daughter. The county's head geologist (a perky Anne Heche) deduces there might be some lava beneath the city of dreams, which quickly spews up from beneath the La Brea Tar Pits. From there, Jones starts yelling at people to get their asses in gear, the E.R. doc gets to choose between duty and husband, an Angry Black Guy gets to become Helpful Black Guy, and so on, all of them working together to save the city in typical disaster-movie fashion. The lava and volcano effects are properly spectacular, and director Mick Jackson keeps things moving toward the big blowout, the effects and the bit players doing their allotted thing with mechanical precision. *Volcano*'s panoramic views of L.A. partially in flames don't have *ID4*'s apocalyptic grandeur, but they do look enough like the familiar images of riots and hill fires to impress audiences who by now have seen the world end on a regular basis.

Also reviewed in:
NEW YORK TIMES, 4/25/97, p. C1, Janet Maslin
VARIETY, 4/21-27/97, p. 59, Todd McCarthy
WASHINGTON POST, 4/25/97, p. G1, Rita Kempley
WASHINGTON POST, 4/25/97, Weekend/p. 49, Eric Brace

WACO: THE RULES OF ENGAGEMENT

A Somford Entertainment release. *Producer:* William Gazecki and Michael McNulty. *Director:* William Gazecki. *Director of Photography:* William Gazecki and Rick Nyburg. *Editor:* William Gazecki. *Music:* David Hamilton. *Running time:* 135 minutes. *MPAA Rating:* Not Rated.

CINEASTE, Vol. XXIII, No. 3, 1998, p. 45, Peter Bates

Viewed on a purely formal level, *Waco: The Rules of Engagement* appears to have many elements of the classic documentary exposé-tragic events, acrimonious confrontations, government complicity, grainy footage, gut-wrenching photographs, high-tech surveillance, archival material, spunky congressional hearings, doleful music, heroes, villains, victims.

Viewed more deeply, the film quickly engages the viewer. From its opening sequence, it functions as an antidote to the U.S. Government's version of the two 1993 raids on the Branch Davidian religious sect's Mount Carmel Center in Waco, Texas. Against a black background, accompanied by ominous violins and drams, an ATF telephone-negotiation tape plays prior to the Bureau of Alcohol, Tobacco, and Firearms raid on February 28, 1993. A young child asks if they are going to come and kill her. The negotiator, Jim Cavanaugh, reassures her. The film then cuts to its first visual, Mount Carmel in flames from the April 19 FBI raid. An agent's voice claims that the FBI did not introduce fire into the compound. Few documentary opening sequences in recent years have been this powerful.

Who are the Branch Davidians and why did the government go after them? The film explains that they are a sect of religious zealots who splintered from the Seventh Day Adventists in 1935 and that, from the mid-Eighties, their leader was the charismatic David Koresh, aka. Vernon Wayne Howell. Throughout the siege and afterwards, particularly during the Joint Sub-Committee hearings of the U.S. House of Representatives (July-August 1995), the mainstream press portrayed the Davidians as unstable, suicidal, gun-toting cultists. Clearly, they must have antagonized the government and incurred its righteous wrath. Yet many Americans who witnessed the fifty-one-day siege felt that the government may have overreacted. Attorney General Janet Reno was questioned for authorizing the raid (operating from misleading information from the FBI). Aside from a few sound bytes, not many learned Koresh's side of the story and even fewer knew about the extent of government duplicity, aside from a few stories about the introduction of CS tear gas into the center where children were present.

What is the real truth? The film uses a barrage of devices and revelations in an effort to convey it. A snippet from the congressional hearings reveals that the ATF, anticipating favorable publicity, notified the press prior to their raid. Interviews with Branch Davidian survivors belie ATF and FBI assertions that the sect started shooting first or that they ignited their own compound. When the FBI maintains that no pyrotechnic devices were deployed during their assault, director William Gazecki produces photographs of unexploded pyrotechnic devices found in the ashes of Mount Carmel. Negotiator Jim Cavanaugh is also caught lying, as he argues with Koresh about whether ATF helicopters fired on the compound.

When the FBI claims it didn't fire a shot during the assault, Gazecki introduces one of the film's most intriguing segments. He shows a FLIR (Forward Looking Infrared) video taken from a fixed-wing aircraft flying overhead during the April 19 assault (unidentified as an FBI aircraft). Used during the Gulf War, infrared photography shows an areas hot and cold spots. Coupled with an independent expert pinpointing gunfire toward the building, the sequence rivets the viewer, like a *60 Minutes* hidden-camera exposé. The expert, Dr. Edward Allard, a former supervisor of the U.S. Army's Night Vision Laboratory, even opines that the troops might have been firing at people trying to escape. While the footage makes this assertion compelling, the supporting evidence is too sparse. Even the Branch Davidians didn't claim this happened.

Using another documentary device, the film captions each telephone negotiation between the besieged Branch Davidians and the FBI, even though for most of them it is unnecessary, since they are clearly audible. David Hamilton's music provides emotive support for these tense sequences. Jarring, dissonant chords play while the ATF is suiting up for their raid. As helicopters arrive, the music turns percussive, then mournful, when wounded agents stumble into a hospital and Koresh displays his wounds to a home-video camera. As the ATF hands over control of the operation to the FBI, the music becomes martial, quickening volume and tempo, while the FBI rolls in the tanks. Later, a smiling Davidian child waves just before we see a panning shot of the burning compound. The music repeats the elegiac bars, but more slowly, almost funereally. Gazecki's editing is truly impressive. He shows gruesome photographs of charred corpses, as we hear interviews with forensic experts on the effects of CS tear gas on bodies. A survivor's tearful testimony about hearing screams during the fire makes congressman Sonny Bono wince in disgust. Audiences report leaving the film feeling drained, cynical, and angry.

The muckraking style of *Waco,* while hitting its target of government abuse, goes soft on Koresh and his beliefs. In an early interview, James Tabor, a biblical scholar, maintains that the media demonized Koresh. The film then presents a brief history of the Branch Davidians, from their inauspicious beginnings to Koresh's takeover of the leadership through a power struggle. Curiously, the style of this five-minute segment is uncharacteristically banal. Up to this point, the film countered government assertions with powerfully presented facts and the persuasive commentary of opposing experts. Here Koresh's outlook is presented like a Bible-Belt educational film recounting the history of the Republican Party. His power struggle with George Rodin, son of a movement leader, is mentioned briefly as an "armed confrontation," with no details on the shooting and Koresh's subsequent incarceration.

Waco alludes to the Branch Davidian obsession with the Seven Seals symbolism in the Book of the Apocalypse. Yet it skimps on Koresh's personal interpretation, which Dick Reavis (interviewed in the film) explains in his book, *The Ashes of Waco.* The "great sword" carried by the rider of the red horse in the Second Seal is a rifle. As a new leader, Koresh was authorized by this seal to "take peace from the earth," and, by the Fourth Seal, to "kill with the sword." Had Koresh lived and his movement thrived, he probably wouldn't have launched an evangelical raid on neighboring towns. But he might have had more armed spats with rival groups who challenged him, or perhaps even with heretical followers. His creed certainly led him in this direction.

In dealing with the ATF raid, Gazecki brings up the thorny issue of gun ownership. Not only was Mount Carmel heavily armed, but Koresh also legally stockpiled semiautomatic weapons, believing they would accrue value as gun-control legislation became imminent. (A few years later, they did.) He attended gun shows and consorted with dealers. Yet, by his own admission, he did convert some rifles into illegal automatic weapons (perhaps not the forty-eight the FBI claims it uncovered). While the film omits this fact, it does correctly assert that Koresh had a constitutional right to bear arms. Gun ownership is clearly not the central issue in this film about government complicity. But Gazecki did take the time to interview the local sheriff who states that the Branch Davidians were just like every other gun advocate in rural Texas. Had the director questioned such freewheeling gun ownership—constitutional or not—it wouldn't have weakened his case against the FBI attack on Mount Carmel.

The film is also soft on Koresh's supporters. Gazecki must have read Reavis's book, which states that Koresh became a cause célèbre among right-wing groups such as California's Constitution Party (similar to the national Libertarians). The Gun Owners of America circulate Carol Moore's book, *The Massacre of the Branch Davidians*. Even Timothy McVeigh showed up during the fifty-one-day siege to lend his support. Yet the film mentions none of this. Right-wingers (other than government agents) appear only as adversaries, like Ku Klux Klan member Bill Latham, who wanted to help rout Koresh, and some bloodthirsty talk-show callers. It is unlikely that Gazecki omitted mentioning such reactionary adulation of Koresh because he's a right-wing extremist. Perhaps he was just naive. Or perhaps he thought unveiling these facts would diminish the film's argument.

Why did Waco happen? The film waffles on this point. Whether or not the ATF suspected Koresh had illegal weapons, or sought positive publicity because funding decisions were imminent, is inconsequential. According to historian Howard Zinn, the government, obsessed with law and order, often makes preemptive (and illegal) strikes against rural, white extremists. The 1992 Ruby Ridge raid followed the same formula—invent a pretext for going in, take control of the situation, then destroy or cover up as much evidence as possible. Unlike Barbara Trent's documentary, *The Panama Deception* (1992), *Waco* doesn't draw historic parallels to the events it covers. Instead, it provides rationales by quoting experts like Henry Ruth, a Treasury Department report reviewer, who maintains that the Branch Davidians were quashed "to enforce the morals of our society, to enforce the psyche of right thinking."

The film's strategy is to convince us that Koresh was crushed because he was an outsider, a maverick who bucked the system and paid dearly for it. But this outlook misses the point. If he were predictable instead of uncontrollable, the government might have groomed him as a respectable member of the religious right; if his Branch Davidians had chosen to remain on the fringe and disarmed themselves, the IRS might have gone after them for tax evasions like it did with Reverend Moon. It could be argued that Koresh led his cult into a kind of mass suicide, either by believing that public opinion would prevent the FBI from attacking or that God would "translate" them, bodies and souls, into heaven at the instant the bullets started flying. While Koresh's faith clearly clouded his decisions, it does not diminish the resulting atrocity. *Waco's* images are just too appalling: children's charred bodies twisted from effects of CS gas; a body crushed under a tank tread; the compound going up in wind-swept flames. Gazecki's decision to include them in his film when few (if any) other news sources did, attests to his sense of outrage.

Waco is an emotionally powerful indictment of the brutality of the government intervention and certainly deserves the Academy Award nomination it received. By ending the film with commentary lamenting the FBI role as judge, jury, and executioner, Gazecki forces middle America to confront its collective conscience. Two government agencies spun out of control so drastically that their actions alarmed viewers on both the liberal left and the extreme right. *Waco: The Rules of Engagement* forces all Americans to say, "This shouldn't have happened to anyone." Through powerful imagery and often compelling evidence, it also scares us with a truly sinister implication. If the U.S. Government can so ruthlessly eliminate a band of marginal zealots, who else are they willing to go after?

LOS ANGELES TIMES, 8/7/97, Calendar/p. 17, Kevin Thomas

William Gazecki's "Waco: The Rules of Engagement" is a major documentary, a meticulously detailed, step-by-step and terrifyingly persuasive all-out attack on government agencies and officials for their handling of the siege of the Branch Davidian sect outside Waco, Texas, in early 1993, which resulted in more than 80 deaths.

What emerges here is an acute sense of the ongoing struggle in American society between protecting the constitutional freedom of religion and protecting the public from the lunatic fringe.

Gazecki and his colleagues make clear the need for law enforcement agencies—and the public at large—to understand the thinking of religious sects to communicate better with them and, when standoffs occur, to designate highly skilled, highly trained individuals as negotiators.

Drawing from an amazing array of footage from various sources and from many interviews, plus chunks of testimony from the Joint Congressional Committee on Waco held in 1995, Gazecki contends that the Bureau of Alcohol, Tobacco and Firearms raided the Branch Davidian compound in February 1993 as an easy way to garner good publicity—only to have four of its men shot to death and six Davidians killed as well. He then argues that the FBI then moved in and, fueled by feelings of revenge, covered up its actions.

Gazecki challenges the FBI claim that its men never fired a single shot in its 51-day siege by showing footage from an infrared video shot by the FBI itself from a helicopter. Dr. Edward Allard, a former supervisor of the U.S. Army's Night Vision Lab, in examining the footage, concludes that certain flashes could be caused only by FBI gunfire. However, the layman is being asked to take his word for it, because the footage is so blurry.

Gazecki has an easier time in making his case that the FBI, using a strong, highly combustible tear gas combined with a systematic ramming of large holes in the compound walls, through which a prairie wind could flow, caused the complex to catch fire. (Apparently, a large supply of kerosene was also caused to leak because of the attacks.) He does not believe the Branch Davidians set their compound on fire as an act of mass suicide, and he does not flinch in showing just how horrible death was for its victims.

Gazecki maintains a calm, detached tone throughout, which allows us to judge Branch Davidian leader David Koresh for ourselves. Frankly, as a man with a ninth-grade education who not only believed in following a literal interpretation of the Bible, but also an ability to attract followers, he is scary. Even one of his lawyers, an eloquent attacker of the FBI, admits he believes Koresh was guilty of statutory rape. Dick Reavis, who wrote the first book on the standoff, contends that the Branch Davidians' large collection of weaponry, some of it illegal, was an inventory—the sect apparently made money in gun dealing—rather than an arsenal. But this view is scarcely comforting. It is an understatement to say that "Waco: The Rules of Engagement" is provocative in every sense of the word.

NEW YORK POST, 6/13/97, p. 48, Larry Worth

Timothy McVeigh won't be the only one upset by the Branch Davidians' fiery fate in 1993 after the release of "Waco: The Rules of Engagement."

The documentary, which makes a pretty damning case for the FBI's culpability in the tragedy that resulted in the deaths of four federal agents and about 80 men, women and children at the fortified Texas compound, is powerful, unsettling and eye-opening—not to mention a surefire magnet for controversy.

As directed by William Gazecki, the film is unquestionably sympathetic to the Branch Davidians. He begins by tracing their history as an offshoot of Seventh-day Adventists, then charts how David Koresh became their leader.

Lending an unexpected poignancy is the inclusion of tapes made by the Davidians during the 51-day standoff against federal agents at the compound. As each explains what brought him or her into the religion, they come off as reasonable and normal—making a subtitle listing the date of their death almost incomprehensible.

Though well over two hours, the production continues to fascinate, jumping between congressional hearings and news footage of the standoff and subsequent siege. The last half hour's use of infrared footage, to support beliefs that the FBI fired directly on the Davidians, will raise yet more eyebrows.

But whether viewers accept all of Gazecki's theories, taped phone conversations between the FBI and Koresh prove that the government engaged—at the very least—in one lie after another. And political considerations aside, Attorney General Janet Reno doesn't come off as a champion for truth, justice and the American way.

That's not to say that the film is perfect. Gazecki allows too much redundant testimony, and he's unashamedly manipulative.

Still, "Waco" guarantees that audiences will walk away not only disturbed but assured that society's "outsiders"—even those who bear arms and have questionable sexual practices—deserve a better fate.

NEWSDAY, 6/13/97, Part II/p. B8, John Anderson

Although it's been cut by 30 minutes since knocking out Sundance audiences this year, don't think "Waco: The rules of Engagement" has been the victim of government subterfuge. As damning a documentary as one can imagine about the 1993 siege in Waco, Texas, it neither makes a hero of sect leader David Koresh, nor does it suggest that the inferno at the Branch Davidian compound fulfilled his apocalyptic vision of Armageddon—because that would suggest a battle between good and evil. And there's no good here.

A film review isn't the place to draw a conclusion about the guilt, innocence or incompetence of the FBI and Bureau of Alcohol, Tobacco and Firearms—the agencies at one end of the 51-day siege that ended with the deaths of 76 men, women and children. But if I were the prosecution in Denver, I'd be glad it wasn't screened for the McVeigh jurors.

In his painstakingly thorough and even-tempered examination of what went on and what went wrong, director William Gazecki paints a scathing picture of government agencies out of control and intent on avoiding any peaceful end to the standoff—which began with a failed gun raid, led to the deaths of four ATF officers and culminated with the fiery destruction of the compound. Gazecki's film certainly would have been more balanced had he gotten direct rebuttal from federal authorities, who apparently declined to speak because of pending lawsuits. (He uses their public testimony, which he counters at almost every turn.) But the undisputed aspects of the case alone are enough to raise glaring questions:

● Why were three-quarters of the warrants issued for the initial raid concerned with allegations of child abuse, an area completely outside the ATF's jurisdiction?

● Why, supposedly, was no one in command aware that David Koresh had invited authorities to inspect the compound before the raid?

● Although the question of who shot first may never be answered, why would truckloads of ATF agents pull up to the front doors of the compound, in trucks covered only in tarps, if they really thought the Branch Davidians were going to open fire with 50-cal. machine guns? The agency is criticized for being incompetent, not suicidal.

● Why has the videotape of the raid disappeared? Why have those front doors which may be the key to who shot first disappeared as well?

● Why did Sharon Wheeler, an ATF publicist, call the media the night before the raid, thus allowing newspeople to beat the feds to the compound by 30 minutes?

● Why, if there were no plans to incinerate the Davidians—they supposedly started the fire themselves, remember—would an agent ask by phone if there were any fire extinguishers inside, and when told there was only one say, "You oughta get some fire insurance."

● Why was the compound bulldozed after the final attack, in violation of every rule of criminal investigation? Why has there been no independent probe of the fire?

Gazecki also shows us heat-sensitive photography—the type we saw during the Gulf War—to establish convincingly that the feds were lying when they claimed they never fired on the compound during the siege. The all-but-conclusive evidence shows that not only did they shoot at the compound—including the combustible gas and pyrotechnic rounds that probably started the blaze—they shot sect members as they fled the fire.

He also shows us: The 911 tapes. The Koresh home videos. The testimony of a local sheriff as to the good character of his Davidian neighbors. The almost quasi-hysterical conduct of Brooklyn's Charles Schumer and other congressmen, deriding anti-government witnesses during House hearings. The candid and all-too-revealing videos of the government forces amassed and bloodthirsty outside the compound. And the voice of a little girl, asking by phone whether an FBI agent is coming to kill her. "No, no ... nobody's coming," he reassures her. Well, he lied, too.

If people want to reject "Waco," and the idea that their government practices a policy of execution before trial, they can probably do so. But it won't be easy.

VILLAGE VOICE, 6/17/97, p. 61, J. Hoberman

Timothy McVeigh may never take the opportunity to explain himself to a jury of his peers, but William Gazecki's two-hour-plus documentary *Waco: The Rules of Engagement* makes it amply apparent why the siege of the Branch Davidians has become the militia movement's Alamo. Emphasizing the constitutional aspects of the case, while making use of the evidence in the public record (a postmodern mix of home videotapes, recorded 911 calls, infrared surveillance footage, and congressional hearings televised over C-SPAN) this cinematic legal brief is a convincing, indeed devastating, argument against the FBI.

Waco traces the history of the Branch Davidians back to the 1930s, locating them in the local history of Waco, and explaining (too briefly) the violent conflict that resulted in David Koresh's splinter group. The filmmakers seem disinclined to analyze the impact of Koresh's strident preaching—his millennial pronouncements and us-and-them worldview—on his followers. Similarly, *Waco* takes as unremarkable the distinctively Texan form of Christianity that seems rooted in gun-show culture. If *Waco* ultimately documents a small band of armed zealots besieged by an army of better-armed, less responsible, and even stupider zealots, the final attack on the Davidian compound is as horrifying as it is gripping.

Also reviewed in:
CHICAGO TRIBUNE, 9/22/97, Tempo/p. 5, Michael Wilmington
NEW REPUBLIC, 7/14 & 21/97, p. 28, Stanley Kauffmann
NEW YORK TIMES, 6/13/97, p. C13, Stephen Holden
VARIETY, 4/17-23/97, p. 48, Joe Leydon
WASHINGTON POST, 6/20/97, p. C1, Stephen Hunter

WAG THE DOG

A New Line Cinema release of a Tribeca/Baltimore Pictures/Punch production. *Executive Producer:* Michael DeLuca, Claire Rudnick Polstein, and Ezra Swerdlow. *Producers:* Jane Rosenthal, Robert DeNiro, and Barry Levinson. *Director:* Barry Levinson. *Screenplay:* Hilary Henkin and David Mamet. *Based on the book "American Hero":* Larry Beinhart. *Director of Photography:* Robert Richardson. *Editor:* Stu Linder. *Music:* Mark Knopfler. *Music Editor:* Mark Jan Wlodarkiewicz. *Sound:* Steve Cantamessa amd (music) Chuck Ainlay. *Sound Editor:* Tim Holland. *Casting:* Ellen Chenoweth and Debra Zane. *Production Designer:* Wynn Thomas. *Art Director:* Mark Worthington. *Set Designer:* Jeff Markwith. *Set Decorator:* Robert Greenfield. *Special Effects:* Dennis King. *Costumes:* Rita Ryak. *Make-up:* Peter Montagna. *Running time:* 120 minutes. *MPAA Rating:* R.

CAST: Dustin Hoffman (Stanley Motss); Robert De Niro (Conrad Brean); Anne Heche (Winifred Ames); Denis Leary (Fad King); Willie Nelson (Johnny Dean); Andrea Martin (Liz Butsky); Kirsten Dunst (Tracy Lime); William H. Macy (Mr. Young); John Michael Higgins (John Levy); Suzie Plakson (Grace); Woody Harrelson (Sgt. William Schumann); Michael Belson (President); Suzanne Cryer (Amy Cain); Jason Cottle (Assistant Director); David Koechner (Director); Harland Williams (Pet Wrangler); Sean Masterson (Bob Richardson); Bernard Hocke (Technician); Jenny Byrne (Sharon); Maurice Woods (Kid with Shoes); Pops Staples (Himself); Phil Morris (Co-pilot); Chris Ellis (Officer); Edwin T. Morgan (Owner); J. Patrick McCormack (Pilot); Jennifer Manley (Teenage Girl); Edrie Warner (Judge); Richard Lawson (Young Man/CIA); Drena De Niro (Gate Stewardess); Alberto Vasquez (Combine Driver); Brant Cotton (Sharon's Boyfriend); Kenneth Kern (Nashville Engineer); Michelle Levinson (Faye); Ron McCoy (Limo Driver); Derick Morgan (CIA Agent); Garry R. Roleder (USAF Chaplain); Merle Haggard and Jim Belushi (Themselves); George Gaynes (Senator Nole); Rick Scarry (White House Reporter); Cliff B. Howard (Ranger); Furley Lumpkin and Sean Fenton (Raking Dads); Nikki Crawford (Mom); John Franklin and Kevin Furlong (Jockeys); Lu Elrod (Southern Woman); Michael Villani (Male Commentator); Warren Wilson

(Crossfire Interviewer); Terry Anzur (Female Announcer 3); Melissa Gardner (Chris Andrews Reporter); Giselle Fernandez (Female Press Person); Christine Devine and Richard Saxton (Chicago Newscasters); Geffrey Blake and Jerry Levine (Media Guys); Jack Shearer (Sklansky); Emmett Miller (News Break Reporter); Bill Handel (Reporter 7, Andrews AFB); Arlene Afshangol (Albanian Girl); Hope Garber (Albanian Grandmother); Gina Menza (Press Room Reporter); Maggie Mellin (Mrs. Rose); Tom Murray (Aircraft Carrier Reporter); Shirley Prestia (Moderator Named Shirley); Ralph Tabakin (Southern Man); Marguerite Moreau (Teenage Girl in Audience); Jay Leno (Himself).

LOS ANGELES TIMES, 12/24/97, Calendar/p. 4, Kenneth Turan

"Why does a dog wag its tail?" Glad you asked. "Because a dog is smarter than its tail. If the tail were smarter, the tail would wag the dog."

With a title taken from that tart bit of pre-credits philosophy, "Wag the Dog" is set in the topsy-turvy times we live in, where illusion means more than reality and a lie is halfway around the world while truth is still pulling on its boots.

A gloriously cynical black comedy that functions as a wicked smart satire on the interlocking worlds of politics and show business, "Wag the Dog" confirms every awful thought you've ever had about media manipulation and the gullibility of the American public. And it has a great deal of fun doing it.

Directed by Barry Levinson and starring Dustin Hoffman, Robert De Niro and Anne Heche, "Wag" is also that rare major player production that was made on a sane budget of $15 million, not enough money for James Cameron to clear his throat. And it was shot in such an expeditious manner that the producers include a line in the final credits specifically thanking "the cast and crew for completing principal photography in 29 days!"

The reason people accustomed to a more, shall we say, leisurely pace agreed to work so crisply had to be the lure of "Wag's" deft script. Written by Hilary Henkin and David Mamet. from a novel called "American Hero" by Larry Beinhart, "Wag" is a sharp-edged farce where the lines are hard enough to cut glass and the plot's gleeful twists and complications never flag.

Though "Wag the Dog" focuses on a popular president who is scant days shy of reelection, we never see the man. But we are told of his actions, specifically that he badly misbehaved with an underage Firefly girl in the Oval Office. Now the Washington Post has the story and the disloyal opposition, sensing blood, is about to run TV attack ads pegged to the music of "Thank Heaven for Little Girls."

When trouble strikes, or so White House operative Winifred Ames (Heche) reveals, the president has only one motto: Get Conrad Brean. As played by De Niro, Brean may look like a shambling suburban Redskins fan, but beneath that disheveled exterior he's an unflappable political spin doctor, capable of salvaging any situation and keeping the dogs of war at bay.

Brean's mandate is to use any means necessary to distract the American public from the budding scandal. He's a master of planting disinformation, so official spokesmen can honestly deny it and thereby make people believe it's true. His fabrications don't have to prove out, they just have to con the electorate for those few days until the election.

Brean's brainstorm is to concoct a crisis with Albania, insisting that this hapless country is "a staging ground for terrorism." Why Albania? Why not Albania? To make the story stick, Brean and company go out to Hollywood and elicit the support of one of the movie business' top producers, the legendary Stanley Motss (Hoffman). His job, should he accept it, is to manufacture not a real war but a media one, to create the images and campaign that will convince the country that something terribly dangerous is going on in that weak Balkan country.

It's common knowledge in the real Hollywood that the outward appearance of Stanley Motss, his house, his clothing and hairstyle, are inspired by producer Robert Evans, whom Hoffman has been imitating in private since Evans produced the Hoffman-starring "Marathon Man" in 1976.

But Hoffman is able to go way past caricature here. He brings such zest to his characterization that it is Motss' zany passion for producing that ignites Brean's plot and carries the picture. First he pulls together his crack team, including the Fad King (Denis Leary), who can start trends before others even spot them, and resourceful songwriter Johnny Green (Willie Nelson), who complains that Albania is a hard word to rhyme.

Seeing Motss at work is a privilege. Who else could fabricate atrocity footage from war-torn Albania on a local sound stage, simultaneously reassuring a nervous starlet (Kirsten Dunst), telling technicians to "punch up a burning bridge" and arguing with the president ("I hate when they interfere") about what kind of kitten will be optically added to the girl's arms to complete the picture.

No matter the nature of the crises he faces (and this film has an endless number), Motss calls it nothing compared to what he went through in the past, when, for instance, "I was four months into 'Song of Songs' and realized I didn't have the rights."

Motss brazens it out with the CIA, insisting to wavering members of his team that "the war isn't over until I say it's over," and leaves no doubt in anyone's mind that "producing is being a samurai warrior." It's been so long, perhaps since "Tootsie" and "Rain Man," that Hoffman has taken a satisfying comic role that it's good to be reminded of the gift he has for funny business.

It's not only Hoffman but everyone on both sides of the camera who seem to have been energized by the challenge of working fast with quality material. The only sad thing about "Wag the Dog" is that it suggests the kind of films we're missing out on because of an elephantine production system that makes reasonably priced films with major talent as rare as actors seeing any money on studio profit-participation deals.

Underneath the humor, not surprisingly, "Wag" is making serious points about what's wrong with our political system and media culture. Of course we'd like to believe we're not all that gullible, that there is a limit to what we can be manipulated into, but the evidence points elsewhere. When a character says, apropos of everything, "it's a good thing Jimmy Stewart didn't live to see this," "Wag the Dog" leaves you without the power to disagree.

NEW STATESMAN, 3/13/98, p. 47, Jonathan Freedland

Politics is show business for ugly people, say the old Washington hands. They've got a point. Would the likes of David Mellor, Douglas Hogg or Gerald Kaufman get so much facetime in any other sphere? OK, maybe Kaufman could have scratched out an on-screen living, taking a few villainous parts off Donald Pleasance (cream suit, purring kitty on the lap, that sort of thing). But mainly politics is a fast-track to celebrity for those denied the Kate Winslet route.

In America the track has become a two-way street, with showbiz providing easy entrée to government. If you're a star, you can follow the late Sonny Bono or Ronald Reagan and head for Washington yourself—or you can get access to those already there.

In the first weeks of the Clinton administration, the Hollywood stampede to the nation's capital was so heavy, veterans quipped: "On a clear day in Washington, you can see Barbra Streisand forever."

But the best place is the messy little intersection where the two lanes of traffic collide. This they do in *Wag the Dog,* as they have in the US for the last couple of decades. Who knows, something similar might even be happening right here.

Followers of the Zippergate scandal will feel familiar with the film's plot. A president seeking re-election is faced with what the Clintonites used to call a "bimbo eruption": a teenage girl says the boss groped her in the White House. A crisis team is assembled, until spin-surgeon Robert De Niro hits on a strategy: he will distract the nation by sending America to war. Hollywood producer Dustin Hoffman is brought in to fake television pictures of a faraway conflict—thus despatching Bimbogate to the inside pages. Part *Capricorn One*, part *Primary Colours, Wag the Dog* presents the anatomy of a political con.

As an essay in satire, it's hard to fault. Like the best smart bomb, it locks on to its assorted targets and hits dead on. Of course, the film has won plaudits for prescience—foretelling last month's great media switch from Monica Lewinsky to Saddam Hussein with eerie accuracy. The alleged clinch between president and young woman happens in the "small office behind the Oval Office"—just like Bill and Monica. When a television newsreader announces the sex scandal to the nation, there is a shot of the Prez embracing a young woman in a crowd, wearing a dark beret. You will do a double-take: that image is a carbon-copy of the now-infamous video picture of Big Bill hugging young Monica as he works a presidential rope-line. Could director Barry Levinson have pasted in the picture post-Zippergate—for extra effect? As *Wag the Dog* makes clear, they can do that sort of stuff these days.

Even the fading of the Gulf crisis has not depleted the movie's uncanny topicality. De Niro's Dick Morris character decides that the enemy for his cold war will be Albania. "What did the Albanians do to us?" asks Anne Heche, playing a George Stephanopoulos-style White House girl-wonder. "What did the Albanians do *for* us?" says De Niro. When *Wag the Dog* was made, this must have sounded utterly absurd and random. But take a look at your morning paper: chances are, there's a US official talking of the grave and sudden crisis close to ... Albania.

The script, nicely turned by David Mamet and Hilary Henkin, peels back the covers on the US news process, walking us through the familiar cycle: deliberate leak, non-denial, denial, urgent newsflash, bullshit "analysis", late-night jokes on *Jay Leno*, then boredom before the final fickle move to fresher terrain.

Hollywood has done some of this media deconstruction work before, whether in light tales—*Dave* and *The American President*—or in documentaries like *The War Room* (on the 1992 Clinton campaign) or *The Perfect Candidate* (following Oliver North's 1994 quest for a Senate seat). But *Wag the Dog* goes further. It doesn't limit itself to a send-up of the politicians and the press. It satirises the US electorate, too.

The geographic ignorance of the American people is there—where's Albania?—as is the credence lent to television. "We're at war," declares De Niro with satisfaction, "I just saw it on TV." Mamet and Henkin also zero in on Americans' much-overlooked reluctance to go to war. Contrary to the British left's old images of the Yanks as gung-ho warmongers, ordinary Americans are actually scaredy-cats—prepared to let their troops get their kit on only if an unambiguous moral crusade is at stake.

Reagan knew every good war needed an arch-villain—and so he cast the Soviet Union as the Evil Empire. Bill Clinton had to deploy the same language of good and wickedness before Americans would let their boys anywhere near Haiti or Bosnia.

And so Hoffman, as camp LA producer, works to pluck the heartstrings of the heartland. He hires a Hollywood wannabe to dress up as an Albanian villager, shoots her dashing across a sound-stage and—after pressing a few computer-ish buttons—mocks up a burst of "harrowing" war footage. The cynicism is exquisite. "I want sirens, you know, *ooh-aah* Anne Frank sirens," Dustin Hoffman tells the guy conjuring up sound effects. Having sat in the "gallery" during NBC's live broadcast of Princess Diana's funeral—where the director screamed to his camera-man, "Give me TEARS! Is no one fucking *crying* at this funeral?"—I can vouch that *Wag the Dog* is guilty of only the mildest exaggeration.

It's sharp, it's clever and—at 95 minutes—refreshingly lean in the current era of three-hour flabathons. But, like the characters themselves, the film loses the plot somewhere in the last half-hour, lurching dangerously close to unfunny farce. Occasionally the writing is heavy-handed: we're told that "war is show business" and that "the president is a product". But perhaps the greatest flaw is one that has dogged earlier Hollywood attempts at political satire. In the determination to be tart and accurate, the film forgets to be a film. Just like Tim Robbins' *Bob Roberts,* the characters are not so much real people as elements in a single, if elaborate gag.

Still, as political jokes go, watching De Niro and Hoffman guided by Mamet and directed by Levinson makes for a snappy hour and a half. And it's *much* more fun than anything involving Messrs Mellor, Hogg and Kaufman.

NEW YORK, 1/19/98, p. 50, David Denby

Barry Levinson's political and media satire *Wag the Dog* goes as fast as the wind, and that's a relief because the idea behind the movie is thin. Very thin—and at times offensively glib. So if Levinson had directed with a heavy hand, or paused for more than an instant's reflection, he would have killed the nasty fun. It's less than two weeks before an election, and the president, seeking another term, is accused of molesting a teenage girl just outside the Oval Office. That the allegation may be false is not the point: the *Washington Post* is about to run the story. What to do? The president's operative Winifred Ames (Anne Heche) calls in a Dick Morris-like Mr. Fixit, Conrad Brean (Robert De Niro), and Brean, together with a big-deal Hollywood producer, Stanley Motss (Dustin Hoffman), distracts the press and the public. They whip up a nonexistent war with mighty Albania, complete with sinister Albanian terrorists crossing the Canadian border carrying a nuke in a suitcase. Brean is a master of spin; his general method depends on exploiting other people's paranoia and disbelief. He sends out rumors and then denies them—denies, for instance, that the United States has a B-3 bomber, which causes the press to believe that there really is such a plane and that the White House wants it kept secret.

The CIA, refusing to play ball, announces the end of the "war"—which exists, of course, only as media images and rumors put out by the White House—so Brean and Motss, in order to keep things going, create an American hero who was somehow left "behind the lines" in Albania (Woody Harrelson). The entire country goes nuts over the brave soldier who has been "cast off like an old shoe." With a little prodding from a Motss crony known as "the Fad King" (Denis Leary), teenagers all over the country throw old shoes, tied together, up onto telephone poles. Come home, Old Shoe! There are songs, anthems, patriotic events; the scam goes on and on, each snafu provoking a triumphant new lie to keep the press and public happy right up to the election.

Now, satire doesn't have to be responsible, but it does have to be internally coherent, and this idea, however funny, is so extremely opportunistic—and at times so crassly conceived—that it falls into a variety of contradictions of its own making. If the press is as disbelieving as Brean thinks, then it would also not believe in the "war" with Albania, including the easily disproved story of terrorists crossing the border. The disbelieving press would want to know where the instant videos of the war (which producer Motss has manufactured) come from, and so on. The script was written by David Mamet, who claims never to have read the novel—*American Hero*, by Larry Beinhart—that an earlier version of the screenplay (by Hilary Henkin) was based on. The screen credit has been disputed, but Levinson says he shot Mamet's version, and in any case, the dialogue sounds like pure Mamet—brutal, fragmentary, the sound of self-justifying egotists balling their way through existence. How smart is David Mamet's cynicism? The notion that politics is just a series of media images, that everything is manipulated behind the scenes by a few all-powerful insiders, is the kind of hip idea that has been around for decades, and in a way, it smacks of fakery itself and even of vanity. The implication is that no one can fool David Mamet; he can see through absolutely everybody. But this may be the worst illusion a talented writer can fall into.

People more intelligent than Mamet know that intelligence has its limits; a writer of genius like Chekhov approached the human mystery with some degree of humility. Knowingness may be David Mamet's greatest vice—the limitation of his savage voice—but among show-business people, Mamet's wary hostility passes for toughness, even for wisdom. As Jacob Weisberg pointed out in the online magazine *Slate*, people who stage things for a living and spend all their time caught in the secretive, deal-ridden mania of Hollywood film production may very well believe that everything important is arranged behind the scenes for a public composed of imbeciles. Cynicism is *their* way of life; they can't see that politics, for all its manipulativeness and ties, is very different from show business. Ronald Reagan manipulated images, yet Reagan—corny, ignorant, deluded in some ways—was not a phony.

But now, having done my duty as a skeptic of extreme skepticism, I have to say that *Wag the Dog* is accomplished and at times viciously funny. Levinson, shooting very fast and cheaply, creates a likable, low-key world of rogues and scoundrels working together to gull the public; we enjoy their company, we enjoy the pretense that political and media life is like this—fast, wisecracking, devastatingly effective. The picture conveys an irresistible pleasure in fakery for its own sake, and that's its charm.

De Niro gives a light, unemphatic performance as the fixer, a nearly anonymous man who slips into the White House wearing a rumpled tweed hat (he might be a Maryland suburbanite running for a train). De Niro's Brean doesn't have to speak in a loud voice; his intelligence is so obvious that everyone falls silent when he speaks at all. On the other hand, the producer Motss (the t is silent) is a boaster, a raconteur, an endless celebrant of his own triumphs and elegist of his own failure to receive sufficient recognition for those triumphs. He is the voice of purest Hollywood. When we first see Dustin Hoffman, he appears to be lying in a glass coffin. It turns out he's getting a suntan, one of those appalling, perfect Los Angeles tans that looks painted on with brownish gold leaf. His hair fluffed and swept back nobly, Hoffman could be a swank duchess. (A resemblance to the producer Robert Evans has been lovingly noted by a number of observers.) Stan Motss is very vague about details, but he has an unquenchable, let's-put-on-a-show spirit. "This is nothing! Nothing!" he exclaims as some unspeakable disaster befalls the team of scam artists. After all, Stan has produced the *Oscars*. Dustin Hoffman latches on to the producer's vanity and grievances. Increasingly proud of the outrageous con he is working on the country—he considers it a work of art comparable to, oh, *The Ten Commandments*—Stan refuses to remain anonymous. He wants the public glory he doesn't get out of putting a movie together.

Anne Heche is funny, too, in one of Mamet's acidly written parts for women. Her political operative is so boneless morally that she invariably rushes to agree with the most powerful person in the room. Heche has a temperament like pentup electrons; she flows in the direction of whatever circuit opens up to her. Some of the best work in the movie consists of little flashes from Heche and the other actors—things said *sotto voce* in the background of scenes. In many small ways, the movie is inventive and intricately wicked. Willie Nelson, as an alcoholic country-and-western singer, turns up as one of Stan's cronies, a man who can manufacture a croaking, bluesy song at the drop of a hat. What tickles Mamet and Levinson is how cultural "authenticity" is now used to prop up completely ersatz media imagery. In order to support the "war," Willie Nelson writes a Depression-era style folk song and also a patriotic anthem with ecstatic solos for women and blacks. In a recording session devoted to this drivel, the soloists sing so passionately they might be sending George Washington or even Jesus himself to heavenly rest.

NEW YORK POST, 12/26/97, p. 41, Thelma Adams

It's hard to imagine a contemporary political satire that can top recent events: the exhumation of faux war hero Larry Lawrence, the three little bears of DreamWorks sleeping at the White House, the drawn-out puppy naming, the soap opera that is the Paula Jones case.

If Barry Levinson doesn't better the facts in his cynically funny "Wag the Dog," at least he keeps up with the Clintons. The premise, in the hard-edged script from David Mamet and Hilary Henkin, is that the president (code name: Big Bird) has a fire in his fly—or, at least, he's fondled a Firefly Girl while she was touring the White House.

What's his right-hand gal Winifred Ames (Anne Heche) to do, two weeks before Election Day? Get to the bottom of the matter? Comfort the family? Make "Thank Heaven for Little Girls" the national anthem? None of the above. Get the woman a spin doctor!

Enter Conrad Brean (Robert De Niro), a low-key media plumber who gets cash for fixing nasty messes. His first plan of attack is to deny something that didn't happen to get the country's mind off the fearless leader's fly.

Brean's first thought? Start a war. Start a war with Albania. Who cares what's happening within the White House when bombs could potentially be bursting in air on CNN?

Having started spinning, Brean goes into overdrive. He recruits the Hollywood hit squad, led by egomaniacal producer Stanley Motss (Dustin Hoffman). Brean exhorts Motss to produce a war pageant to rival his Oscar telecasts as the two begin to package the presidency.

On hand to dabble with democracy are trends guru Denis Leary, costume designer Andrea Martin and down-home singer Willie Nelson. The country star composes a war song, "The American Dream," with more than a passing resemblance to "We Are the World." All participants are promised back-end profits.

One of the film's funniest moments arrives when the Hollywood gang confess that they haven't voted in any national elections but they all voted for the Oscars.

Hoffman, Heche and De Niro make an excellent Scarecrow, Lion and Tin Man. Having escaped from "Mad City," Hoffman focuses his edgy rage into the figure of a short man whose ego is too big for his skin.

Heche, the sharply dressed professional woman on the verge of a nervous breakdown, reminds us that she's more than Ellen DeGeneres' coming-out party. And De Niro serves the material best by remaining calmly detached.

The parts are greater than the sum of "Wag the Dog." But, given recent events, the dark comedy that fuses Hollywood, electoral politics and image consultants doesn't seem as far-fetched as it might have four years ago.

NEWSDAY, 12/26/97, Part II/p. B3, Jack Mathews

A political consultant, a presidential adviser and a Hollywood movie producer are transporting a violent mental patient in a private jet bound for Washington, D.C. With the antipsychotic drugs almost gone, and the mental patient becoming more paranoid by the second, the adviser is beside herself, and the even super-cool consultant is getting rattled. But not the producer.

"Have you ever shot in Italy?" he asks, calmly. "Try three Italian starlets swacked out on benzedrine and grappa. This is nothing. This is a walk in the park."

Moments later, the plane has crashed, and the survivors are hitching a ride on a wheat thrasher driven by an illegal immigrant. How are they going to explain this to the world, the adviser wants to know. The producer says it's nothing, a piece of cake compared to some of the jams he's been in.

"Try a 10 a.m. pitch meeting, coked to the gills, and you haven't even read the treatment!" he says.

These snapshots come to you from somewhere in the middle of "Wag the Dog," courtesy of director Barry Levinson and screenwriters Hilary Henkin and David Mamet, and trust me, in context they're hilarious.

"Wag the Dog," the story of a White House scheme to create a distraction from an impending presidential sex scandal, is a dizzy inside joke that will play wherever folks with a wicked sense of humor gather. It's a satire that manages to break the skin of both Hollywood and Washington, the axis powers of public manipulation, and though they are minor flesh wounds, it's a riot.

Filmed on the quick, for a relatively paltry $15 million, "Wag the Dog" is little more than a sophisticated, 97-minute skit. But the knowing dialogue, which Levinson credits mostly to Mamet, and the obvious fun being had by the film's illustrious cast keeps it fresh to the very end.

Here's the problem: With less than two weeks to go to the general election, the president's campaign is suddenly threatened by allegations from a Girl Scout that he had assaulted her in the Oval Office after she asked if she could look at his Remington bronze.

Here's the solution: Conrad Brean (Robert De Niro), a crisis management political consultant, comes up with the idea of bringing America to the brink of an imaginary war with ... well, to pull a name out of the hat, Albania.

Here's the method: Brean and the chief of staff go to Hollywood to hire Stanley Motss (Dustin Hoffman), a veteran, big-spending movie producer (the apparent model is "Chinatown" producer Robert Evans) who knows how to get things done fast, get them done right, and damn the costs.

Motss is recruited to produce the fake war, and keep America's attention off the sex scandal until the election's over, and he sees it as his biggest challenge since he remade "Moby Dick," from the whale's point of view. With a slogan specialist (Denis Leary) and a glib songwriter (Willie Nelson), he sets the wheels in motion, and every time the wheels come off, he puts them back on. It's a piece of cake. It's what producers do.

Whether Hoffman was inspired by Evans, whom he worked for on "Marathon Man," or other producers met along the way, he's nailed the stereotype of the narcissistic, big-time Hollywood hustler. Motss dresses well, drinks designer water, tones his skin in a tanning coffin, plays tennis and speaks a language that is made up almost exclusively of movie references. And Hoffman doesn't miss a beat in sending up the whole thing.

De Niro is perfectly laid back as a no-nonsense trickster who's been lurking in the public consciousness since the Nixon days, and Heche is terrific fun as the voice of truth being drowned out by the pragmatism of Brean and the flamboyance of Motss. But some of the film's biggest laughs are provided by Woody Harrelson, in his extended cameo as the mad man recruited from prison to play the folk hero Sgt. Schumann.

"Wag the Dog" isn't ground-breaking stuff as either political or Hollywood satire, but it's more fun than three Italian starlets on grappa, and a lot better than the whale's version of "Moby Dick."

NEWSWEEK, 12/22/97, p. 84, David Ansen

It used to be that at least a couple of Christmas movies were, well, seasonal. You know, "Miracle on 34th Street," "Scrooge," the whole snowflakes-and-good-will-toward-men thing. In 1997, fuggedaboudit. We get ships that sink, ships that carry slaves, a masked man chopping up teenagers, James Bond slaughtering suavely, a president who molests young girls, a violent preacher, a misanthropic neurotic, more Quentin Tarantino gunplay, a cross-dressing child, the Chinese invading Tibet, Kevin Costner saving America in a landlocked "Waterworld" and Woody Allen behaving badly. Does this sound like fun? Well, actually, some of it is. We've made our list, we've checked it twice, a lot of it is more naughty than nice, but hey, that's entertainment. Get used to it.

Case in point: the most wickedly entertaining movie of the season is the one about the president who fondles an underage Firefly girl two weeks before an election. How can he overcome such a scandal? The scathing satire *Wag the Dog* shows you how: by bringing in legendary spin doctor Conrad Brean (Robert De Niro), who instantly surmises that what is required is a massive diversionary tactic. Perhaps a war? Perhaps a war with Albania? A war that will occur not in reality but on prime-time TV. Enter Hollywood producer and legend in his own mind Stanley Motss (Dustin Hoffman) to mastermind the production.

It's a deliciously outrageous premise, and director Barry Levinson and writers David Mamet and Hilary Henkin know just how to spin it, savaging Washington and Hollywood with merciless wit. This knowing political satire takes no prisoners and never goes soft. You can sense the cast's delight getting to play with such razor-edged material: De Niro hasn't been this breezy in ages, Woody Harrelson does a hilariously scary bit as a "war hero" who is inconveniently psychotic and there are sly turns from such co-conspirators as Ann Heche, Denis Leary and Kirsten Dunst as an actress deeply upset that she won't be able to list her performance as an Albanian war victim on her résumé. (She'll be killed if she does.) But the cream of the jest is Hoffman's brilliant impersonation of the egomaniacal, motormouth producer (any resemblance to the overcoiffed Robert Evans is entirely intentional). "Wag the Dog" was made fast (a 29-day shoot), relatively cheaply (a $15 million budget) and with a contagious sense of mischief. It's a hoot.

Woody Allen is back in sharp comic form, too, though it's likely that his abrasive black comedy *Deconstructing Harry* will alienate as many people as it tickles. Let's be frank. Woody has a problem: people always think the characters he plays are him. He's certainly not courting fans by casting himself as novelist Harry Block, the oft-married, selfish, sex-obsessed and generally despicable hero of this smart, nasty and very raunchy comedy. A lot of women fall in love with Harry (you may wonder why), but they all end up furious at him; if he hasn't betrayed them in life, he does so in his novels, where his infidelities are barely disguised as fiction. (Think Philip Roth.)

"Deconstructing Harry" hops brilliantly between Harry's real and fictional lives. (Thus Kirstie Alley, Elisabeth Shue and Judy Davis are "real," while Demi Moore, Julia Louis-Dreyfus and Richard Benjamin play fictitious versions of the real people in Harry's life.) The story-within-the-story called "The Actor," with Robin Williams, is Allen at his most inspired, but I won't spoil it by giving away the joke. In its structure, "Harry" echoes Bergman's "Wild Strawberries"—it's the summing up of a self-absorbed life. It may be the bleakest, most self-punishing comedy Allen has made. Amazingly, it's one of the funniest.

Woody thought of calling his movie "The Meanest Man in the World." This could just as well have been the title of James L. Brooks's new, wildly uneven romantic comedy *As Good as It Gets*. The man in question is Melvin Udall (Jack Nicholson), world-class grinch. An obsessive compulsive who'll use a bar of soap only once, he's also a sneering bigot who insults blacks, Jews and gays and is first seen throwing his gay neighbor's dog down the garbage chute of their New York apartment building. Because it's Nicholson playing Udall—with lip-smacking, eyebrow-raising relish—we know that sooner or later we're going to be asked to fall in love with this guy, who underneath it all is a lonely soul terrified of human connection. The agents of his redemption are: (1) the dog, which he must care for when his artist neighbor is badly beaten in a robbery, (2) the gay artist (Greg Kinnear), a sensitive soul whom Udall will come to befriend and (3) the waitress Carol (Helen Hunt), a no-nonsense saint with a sickly, asthmatic son. She, of course, will teach Udall to love.

The man who made "Terms of Endearment" and "Broadcast News" is too ingenious a writer to serve this sentimental tale straight: he comes at it sideways, mixing the sweet and sour in unexpected—and sometimes hilarious—ways. But the marvelously unpredictable Brooksian moments coexist this time with shameless pandering (the old cute-dog trick), broad sitcom staging and some surprisingly klutzy filmmaking. Brooks seems so worried that Udall will turn us off that he overcompensates with the sort of crowd-pleasing shtik he used to shun. The tough-tender Hunt is terrific, and Nicholson has amazing moments, but does Udall add up to a coherent character? (What does his compulsiveness have to do with his bigotry, anyway? Why his abrupt, unlikely change of heart toward Kinnear?) "As Good as It Gets" works: by the end you'll no doubt be won over by its cranky hero. But for those of us who cherish the quirkily unformulaic Brooks of old, it's a tainted victory.

If it's ravishing filmmaking you want, search no further than *Kundun*, Martin Scorsese's visually exquisite account of the early years of the 14th Dalai Lama, driven into exile from Tibet in 1959 when the Chinese invaded his country. Except for the fact that it unfolds in a world of men, this would seem a total departure for Scorsese. His hero (played by four different Tibetan nonprofessional actors) is the anti-Raging Bull—a man serenely devoted to the principles of nonviolence. This passivity creates a formidable challenge for screenwriter Melissa Mathison, for her protagonist is largely devoid of the internal conflict that is the staple of drama. But "Kundun" doesn't take a novelistic approach. Think of it as an epic poem, in which Scorsese's swirling, headlong baroque camera searches paradoxically for the stillness at the meditative heart of Buddhism. This is not a movie for those who crave plot: at times it gets becalmed in the merely ceremonial. The heartfelt, uncompromising "Kundun" is at its greatest in the magically subjective scenes of childhood and in the stunning and moving final act, when the young Dalai Lama must escape in disguise to the Indian border, and past, present and future become one in Scorsese's impassioned eye.

Robert Duvall plays a very different man of God in his fascinating, fervent *The Apostle*, which he directed, wrote and largely financed himself. "Sonny" Dewey is a devout Pentecostal preacher in Texas with a violent streak and an eye for the ladies. But he's no fraud, and this is no stereotypical Hollywood put-down of redneck religion. Duvall, in as gnarly, passionate and complex a performance as he's ever given, asks us to look at this man in all his troubled, contradictory glory. Sonny flees the law after beating his estranged wife's lover with a baseball bat, and starts a new life in a Louisiana bayou town, where he seeks salvation by starting a new church. Farrah Fawcett, Miranda Richardson, Billy Bob Thornton and John Beasley flourish under Duvall's artful, anthropologically precise gaze. "The Apostle" captures the roof-raising, multiracial evangelical world with fresh, uncondescending eyes.

Another gem, from Belgium, is the not-to-be-missed *Ma Vie en Rose*, the first film of a very talented, funny and tender filmmaker named Alain Berliner. Its extraordinary hero, 7-year-old Ludovic, is a boy quite certain that when he grows up he will be a girl. His unshakable conviction, not to mention his habit of dressing in girls' clothing, throws his suburban bourgeois parents into a tizzy. Their son's difference is a problem for everyone but Ludo himself, the calm center of a storm that shakes the family, and their angry, scandalized community, to its roots. The issue of gender is a delicate one, and Berliner and screenwriter Chris Vander Stappen navigate this tricky terrain with charm, tact and sudden bursts of whimsy as the film takes us inside Ludo's candy-colored, TV-inspired fantasies. Young Georges Du Fresne may be the most enchanting child actor to come along in years. Ludo's story, told with the bold strokes of a fable, will break your heart and make you smile, often at the same time.

The heroine of Quentin Tarantino's *Jackie Brown* is a 44-year-old flight attendant (Pam Grier) busted by the Feds for carrying 50 grand in tainted money and some coke into the country. Jackie gets her revenge on both the ruthless arms dealer Ordell (Samuel L. Jackson), who set her up, and on the cops, when she enlists a tough but decent bail bondsman (Robert Forster) to aid her in an elaborate scam with a half-million-dollar jackpot as the payoff. The tale—faithfully taken from Elmore Leonard's "Rum Punch"—is filled with funny, gritty Tarantino lowlife gab (no director is more enamored of talk) and a respectable body count, but what is most striking is the film's gallantry and sweetness. Above all, it's a loving homage to '70s blaxploitation star Grier's sexy, poignant, middle-aged swagger. Filled with terrific acting—Forster, Jackson and Robert De Niro as a dumb ex-con are especially wonderful—"Jackie Brown" hums down the runway without ever quite taking off. Much too long for its own good, it's an honorable genre movie that falls curiously flat. But Tarantino hits some new and touching notes with Grier and Forster—a sense of what it means to grow old with grace—that make you want to see what he could accomplish without guns and gangsters.

SIGHT AND SOUND, 3/98, p. 57, Robin Dougherty

Washington, DC. Eleven days before the election, presidential aide Winifred Ames and spin doctor Conrad Brean gather with other White House staff to discuss how to handle public reports that the President has molested a teenage girl. Brean suggests that attention could be diverted from this scandal if the White House were to invent an international crisis. Ames and Brean fly to Los Angeles to enlist the help of noted Hollywood producer Stanley Motss.

Motss, taken with the idea of producing a war—or, as Brean puts it, 'the appearance of a war'—gathers together a crew, including country singer Johnny Dean and a character known as 'the Fad King'. Together, with input from the White House and help from digital filmmaking techniques, they produce a video depicting 'war-torn' Albania. News channels pick it up and the Albanian crisis is taken for truth. Then, the CIA intercepts Brean and Ames and announces the end of the Albanian war on television.

As election day approaches, Motss concocts another twist: a soldier named Schumann is invented, and it is reported that he was left behind in Albania. He becomes a legend. To use the soldier's homecoming as a PR ploy, the White House hires a convict to portray him. The plane carrying the convict crashes on its way to Washington, and the convict—in jail for raping a nun—terrorises a woman and is subsequently killed by her father. Motss now stages a public funeral. Motss wants to make a movie about these events. Brean warns him not to talk, and soon Motss turns up dead from an apparent heart attack. The Albanian crisis continues to make news.

As soon as the project was announced, it was clear that the target of *Wag the Dog*'s satire was the Clinton administration. But veteran filmmakers David Mamet (screenplay) and Barry Levinson (direction) could hardly have dreamed that their black comedy would seem to predict actual details surrounding the President's alleged dalliance with a 21-year-old White House intern. Moviegoers will almost certainly gasp when the screen lights up with a photo of the fictional President touching the shoulder of the girl in question because it so resembles a real life video of Clinton and ex-intern Monica Lewinsky together on the White House lawn. And if that doesn't make them uneasy, then the fictional President's campaign advert using the song 'Thank Heaven for Little Girls' surely will.

For these reasons, *Wag the Dog* is destined to be remembered more for its serendipitous timing than for its other merits. That's not entirely a bad thing, since it's basically a one-joke movie that deflates about half way through. Made in a breathtaking 29 days—in the downtime caused by a delay in filming Levinson's upcoming *Sphere*, which also stars Dustin Hoffman—and on a tiny $15 million budget, the final product doesn't feel like something thrown together at all. Using video clips, demonstrations of digital editing, and close-ups of musicians recording in a studio, it amply suggests the sophisticated range of manipulative techniques employed in the marriage between Hollywood and Washington.

Put aside for a moment the fact that President Clinton's ever-growing aggressive stance towards Iraq in January 1998 is just the sort of thing the presidential advisors of *Wag the Dog*—stuck with the burden of inventing a conflict with Albanian terrorists would recommend. No, this film is an extremely well-made trifle, one that, with its cast pulled from disparate parts of the American entertainment universe, has an Altman-like mosaic feel to it. Its allusive cryptogram of a title is the only outward sign that playwright Mamet *(Speed the Plow, Glengarry Glen Ross)* penned the screenplay. Well, the title and the catch phrase "This is NOTHING"—a verbal tic that producer Stanley Motss utters when each phase of the absurd cover-up he's created comes horribly undone.

There's a great deal of nonsense here for film lovers (and political junkies) to chuckle over—Motss and his cronies, one of whom is played by Andrea Martin (from television's SCTV), talk about merchandising profits and back-end deals for the Albanian 'production' they're cooking up. "You've never been at a pitch meeting," Motss replies when Brean thinks their prospects of keeping the Albanian war story are sinking. And, as a special touch, the Hollywood schemers draft in Jim Belushi to speak for Americans of Albanian descent.

All this is fresh but not deep, and that's the shortcoming of *Wag the Dog*. Like many a political satire before it, this film can't keep up with the titillating events of real life. Rather than turn the story into a political intrigue once the CIA is on the tail (and tale) of Brean and Motss, Mamet and Levinson go for farce. The problem is that a movie can veer off in wildly absurd directions and still never be able to compete with the headlines. Presidential aide Winifred Ames, played solidly by Anne Heche, may get us to laugh with her talk about the virtues of being pro-active—as though that were something specific—but all the while, the real drama is being played out far from the darkened theatre.

It's old news, after all, that Hollywood shenanigans have infiltrated politics. The real treat of *Wag the Dog* is the prospect of De Niro and Hoffman working together. (That is, in something more substantial than one scene together in *Sleepers*.) There's not a great deal of chemistry between the two, but that's perhaps because as players in a farce, they don't really have a lot of characterisation to get across. Still, it's a bit disappointing that De Niro makes Brean academic, occasionally sardonic—someone who could have been played by almost any solid actor. In the end, *Wag the Dog* belongs to Hoffman, who plays Motss as the kind of slimeball you almost want to bring home to Mother.

TIME, 12/22/97, p. 83, Richard Schickel

Eleven days before the election, the President is accused of sexual dalliance with a visitor to the Oval Office—an underage visitor, at that. What's needed, the spin doctor (a coolly cynical Robert De Niro) decrees, is a splendid little war to divert the populace. None being handy, one will have to be invented out of rumor and falsified electronic imagery.

That's where Hollywood producer Stanley Motss (Dustin Hoffman) comes in. And *Wag the Dog* takes off. It requires a paranoia that might make Oliver Stone wag his head to believe in the film's overarching proposition; you need too many potentially leaky support personnel to fake a war. But director Barry Levinson and writers Hilary Henkin and David Mamet (no less) have obviously known their share of Stanleys, and we have no trouble believing in him.

Especially as Hoffman, a furiously contradictory blend of hubris and insecurity, venal focus and material distraction, and transparently false charm and roughshod willfulness, plays him. Arranging for the patriotic songs and sentimental images needed to stir our nascent jingoism—a war orphan rescuing her kitten from a bombing, a POW posing for an enemy camera and sending a secret, reassuring message home to Mom—he transcends his origins as a show-biz in-joke. For he is less immoral than pre-moral, childlike in his gleeful wickedness. That somehow completes his perfect embodiment of everything that's awful in American life nowadays and even, curiously, induces a sympathetic pang at his ultimate downfall.

VILLAGE VOICE, 12/30/97, p. 72, J. Hoberman

A low-budget quickie knocked out by high-priced talent (as well as a rare instance of Hollywood political satire), *Wag the Dog* takes as its Frankfurt School premise the midcampaign fabrication of a nonexistent international crisis to divert media attention from an incumbent president's sexual peccadillo.

Sound familiar? The president's emergency spin doctor (Robert De Niro) recruits a credit-hungry Robert Evans-like producer (Dustin Hoffman) to orchestrate the appearance of a war against Albania. De Niro is as low-key and professional here as in *Jackie Brown*, but, as the tanned and coiffed fount of show-biz wisdom, the long-winded Hoffman steals the movie ("try a 10 a.m. pitch meeting when you're coked to the gills and you haven't even read the treatment"), particularly once he senses that, as he puts it, the CIA is trying to shut down his picture.

The state of the art being what it is, *Wag the Dog* rivals *Deconstructing Harry* as the season's best (and best-written) comedy. In addition to the De Niro-Hoffman show, director Barry Levinson has the benefit of an enthusiastic ensemble rattling off David Mamet's dialogue, as well as an unrelentingly cynical succession of Reagan, Clinton, and Gulf War gags: The set piece is the creation of simulated, *Welcome to Sarajevo*-style civil war footage in which the magic of digital imagery transforms a teenage actress clutching a giant bag of corn chips into a pathetic, kitten-cradling refugee in flight from her flaming village.

Suffused in conventional wisdom, yet even more despairing than it may know in acknowledging the absolute authority of TV, *Wag the Dog* is fundamentally about the movie industry—Hollywood's fabrication of titanic pseudoevents, its anxious contempt for the audience, and easy manipulation of the media. Director Barry Levinson may be no one's idea of an auteur, but there are some ways in which *Wag the Dog* (not named for the presidential puppy) is actually the most hearffelt movie of the week.

Also reviewed in:
CHICAGO TRIBUNE, 1/2/98, Friday/p. A, Michael Wilmington
NEW REPUBLIC, 2/2/98, p. 24, Stanley Kauffmann
NEW YORK TIMES, 12/26/97, p. E7, Janet Maslin
NEW YORKER, 1/5/98, p. 68, Anthony Lane

VARIETY, 12/15-21/97, p. 58, Godfrey Cheshire
WASHINGTON POST, 1/2/98, Weekend/p. 29, Desson Howe

WAITING FOR GUFFMAN

A Castle Rock Entertainment release. *Producer:* Karen Murphy. *Director:* Christopher Guest. *Screenplay:* Christopher Guest and Eugene Levy. *Director of Photography:* Roberto Schaefer. *Editor:* Andy Blumenthal. *Music:* Michael McKean, Harry Shearer, and Christopher Guest. *Choreographer:* Andrea Ariel. *Sound:* Dennis Johnson and (music) David Cole. *Sound Editor:* Robert Grieve. *Production Designer:* Joseph T. Garrity. *Art Director:* John Frick. *Set Decorator:* Jenny C. Patrick. *Set Dresser:* Mari Phillips. *Costumes:* Julie Carnahan. *Make-up:* Kate Shorter. *Running time:* 93 minutes. *MPAA Rating:* R.

CAST: Deborah Theaker (Gwen Fabin-Blunt, Councilwoman); Michael Hitchock (Steve Stark, Councilman); Scott Williamson (Tucker Livingston, Councilman); Larry Miller (Glenn Welsch, Mayor); Don Lake (Phil Burgess, Blaine Historian); Christopher Guest (Corky St. Clair); Fred Willard (Ron Albertson); Catherine O'Hara (Sheila Albertson); Parker Posey (Libby Mae Brown); David Cross (UFO Expert); Eugene Levy (Dr. Allen Pearl); Jim McQueen (Singing Auditioner); Turk Pipkin (Ping Pong Ball Juggler); Jerry Turman (Raging Bull Auditioner); Bob Balaban (Lloyd Miller); Paul Dooley (UFO Abductee); Linda Kash (Mrs. Allan Pearl); Lewis Arquette (Clifford Wooley); Matt Keeslar (Johnny Savage); Brian Doyle-Murray (Red Savage); Miriam Flynn (Costume Designer); Jill Parker-Jones (Stage Manager); Margaret Bowman (Costume Dresser); Paul Benedict (Not Guffman).

LOS ANGELES TIMES, 1/31/97, Calendar/p. 1, Kenneth Turan

The municipality of Blaine, Mo., "a little town with a big heart in the heart of the country," is about to celebrate a very special event.

While it seems like only yesterday that an unscrupulous guide abandoned a wagon train after convincing the gullible travelers they'd arrived in California, in fact it's been 150 years since Blaine's glorious founding. And the town is determined to pull off an event that promises to be "the standard by which sesquicentennials will be judged."

For those not fortunate enough to make it to Blaine for the festivities, a documentary crew is on hand to record it all for "Waiting for Guffman," a sly and gleeful comedy showcase that pokes clever fun at the American musical, amateur theatricals and anything else that's not nailed down.

The standard by which all mock-documentaries are judged is, of course, "This Is Spinal Tap," and the moving force behind "Guffman" is Christopher Guest, alive in our memory as Tap's lead guitarist Nigel Tufnel.

Guest directed and co-wrote "Guffman" (with "Second City's" Eugene Levy) and also stars as Corky St. Clair, the creative tornado behind "Red, White and Blaine," the musical pageant that celebrates Blaine in all its misbegotten glory.

For there is more to this town than the legend of its accidental founding. There's the story of how the weary feet of President William McKinley led to Blaine's becoming the Stool Capitol of the World. And then there was the celebrated UFO sighting/potluck dinner of 1946. All of which has to get into "Red, White and Blaine."

Collaborating with Guest on "Guffman's" music and lyrics are his "Tap" cohorts Michael McKean and Harry Shearer. Together they come up with some splendid numbers, including the peppy—"Stool Boom" and the parallel "Nothing Ever Happens in Blaine" and "Nothing Ever Happens on Mars."

But "Waiting for Guffman" offers more than music. We're privileged to be behind the scenes in everything from the choosing of the cast to the inevitable crises of confidence when it looks as if "Red, White and Blaine" might never get to pack the high school gym after all.

Which, given the kind of talent there is in Blaine, would have been a shame. Ron and Sheila Albertson (Fred Willard and Catherine O'Hara), for instance, in private life travel agents who have never ventured out of town, have done enough local theater to be known as "the Lunts of Blaine."

Then there are the newcomers, like Dr. Allan Pearl (Eugene Levy), the tone-deaf dentist who thinks he had a relative who worked in Yiddish theater. Or Libby Mae Brown (Parker Posey at her most irresistible), the soignee Dairy Queen counter girl who wows Corky St. Clair with her spirited version of "Teacher's Pet."

Finally, it does all come down to the charismatic Corky, a veteran of too many years spent as far off Broadway as you can get. Back in Blaine as the high school drama teacher who wanted audiences to "feel the heat" in his legendary staged version of "Backdraft," Corky has the passion and the vision to override skeptics like music teacher Lloyd Miller (Bob Balaban), apparently the only sane individual in town, and get "Red, White and Blaine" up on its feet.

Similarly, there would be no "Waiting for Guffman" without Guest, who came up with the concept, gathered a sprightly group of practiced farceurs around him and even brought the arch Corky St. Clair, with his goatee, bowl haircut and perennially puzzled look, to querulous life.

If Corky has a hidden agenda, it's that "Red, White and Blaine" could become his ticket to Broadway. He confidently expects the arrival of a certain Mr. Guffman, the representative of a powerful New York producing organization, sure that his show has what it takes. That may be an open question, but "Waiting for Guffman" will inspire no such doubts.

NEW YORK POST, 1/31/97, p. 41, Michael Medved

"Waiting for Guffman" contains so many funny bits that you can share the best of them with friends without fear that you'll be spoiling the movie.

For instance, the film's flamboyant, hero, Corky St. Clair (Christopher Guest), proudly displays his collection of priceless Hollywood memorabilia, introducing us to "My Dinner With Andre" action figures and his cherished "Remains of the Day" lunch boxes.

Poor Corky is a grandly ambitious actor/dancer whose New York career amounted to nothing. Now he has carved a niche for himself in tiny Blaine, Mo. After thrilling the locals with his productions of "Barefoot in the Park" and "Backdraft," he's ready for the greatest challenge of his career—a grand musical review called "Red White and Blaine" to celebrate the town's 150th anniversary.

In mounting this historic epic, Corky can count on travel agents Ron and Sheila Albertson (Fred Willard and Catherine O'Hara), who have starred in his previous triumphs, but he also recruits Dairy Queen counter girl Libby Mae Brown (Parker Posey) and Dr. Allen Pearl (Eugene Levy), the local dentist who auditions with an energetic medley of Stephen Foster favorites.

During rehearsals, the effete impressario electrifies his little troupe with the news that he's won a commitment from a top Broadway agent named Guffman to come to opening night with a view to bringing this Middle American extravaganza to New York.

The show itself is hilarious, with ridiculous production numbers and original songs (by Michael McKean, Harry Shearer and Guest) that are downright infectious in their tackiness.

The history of the town (including its 19th century emergence as the Stool Capital of the World, and its UFO encounter/potluck dinner of 1946) is also unusually colorful and engaging.

It, all emerges from a series of talking-head interviews and backstage footage, captured by an unseen camera crew, in the tradition of the dead-pan "rockumentary" filmmakers in "This Is Spinal Tap."

The resemblance is no accident, since Christopher Guest (who directed "Guffman" and co-wrote its script with Eugene Levy) starred as Nigel Tufnel, the lead guitarist of "Spinal Tap."

This time however, no one ever explains why the dutiful documentarians are working on the project in the first place. The characters (who reportedly improvised most of their lines) also make the occasional mistake of going for outrageous laughs at the expense of the crucial feature of believability.

Fred Willard's travel agent, for instance, says that he's never left the town of Blaine, and implausibly boasts about his penis-reduction surgery.

These reservations, however, will be easily overwhelmed by the belly laughs the movie provokes and the affection it inspires for its weird but endearing characters.

NEWSDAY, 1/31/97, Part II/p. B10, Jack Mathews

Blaine, Mo., is what you might describe as a one-horse town ... if it had a horse. It's a hiccup on the east-west highway crossing the "Show Me" state, a burg with an annual budget of $15,000 and a furniture industry that has earned Blaine the title of "Stool Capital of the World."

These are proud folks, the Blaineans. And as the 150th anniversary of the town nears (yes, it's been that long since Col. Blaine told his California-bound party that he could smell the Pacific Ocean and dropped anchor in Missouri), they're getting ready to put on the greatest sesquicentennial show the state has seen.

The centerpiece of the celebration, and of Christopher Guest's small-town put-down, "Waiting for Guffman," is "Red, White and Blaine." It's a historical musical written and directed by Broadway emigré Corky St. Clair (Guest) and starring Corky and such earnest Blaine hams as the dentist Dr. Pearl (Eugene Levy), Dairy Queen counter girl Libby Mae Brown (Parker Posey) and travel agents Ron and Sheila Albertson (Fred Willard, Catherine O'Hara).

"Waiting for Guffman" reunites Guest, lead guitar for Rob Reiner's title rock group in "This Is Spinal Tap," and "Spinal Tap" producer Karen Murphy, and they don't mind if we make the connection. Guest, with writing help from Levy, Michael McKean and Harry Shearer, was clearly out to duplicate the spirit of "Spinal Tap" in fictional Blaine, Mo.

Guest, adopting the faux documentary style, was only partially successful. The story and the performances are as consistently tongue-in-cheek as the earlier film, and there are some hilarious bits laced throughout. But small-town America is too easy a target, and even without Willard's presence to remind us, "Waiting for Guffman" more often feels like "Fernwood 2-Night" than "This Is Spinal Tap."

As in "Spinal Tap," the running joke is that both performers and audience think they're terrific, when they are, in fact, horrible. The show they're putting on would barely pass muster as a grade school production, but their enthusiasm and the joy of the audience are infectious.

Within that broad outline, "Guffman" operates as a series of comic sketches. A dinner scene, to cite the most memorable example, exists solely for a punch line where Willard's obnoxiously gregarious Ron Albertson attempts to show Dr. Pearl—"a medical man"—the results of his penis-reduction surgery.

Levy has some very funny moments as Dr. Pearl, a dentist who believes his own wit is better than a lungful of laughing gas, and Lewis Arquette, as the taxidermist recruited to be the play's narrator, does a nice switch, showing up on opening night to read his lines like a true Broadway veteran. Not that anyone would notice.

Guest saved the best for himself. Corky, whose swishiness and queen-size tantrums raise not the slightest suspicion among Blaine's innocents, is a riot of a Broadway stereotype. Corky lives for the theater, even though the theater can live without him, and neither his bad taste nor his total absence of talent discourages him.

"This Is Spinal Tap" this is not, but "Waiting for Guffman" definitely has its moments.

NEWSWEEK, 2/10/97, p. 66, David Ansen

Hey kids, let's put on a show! The Mickey and Judy spirit is alive, if somewhat talent-challenged, in Blaine, Mo. To celebrate its sesquicentennial, the city council has commissioned a musical show to commemorate Blaine's 150-year history, from its discovery to its heyday as the "stool capital of the world." This show will be written, directed, choreographed and designed by local legend Corky St. Clair (Christopher Guest), the high school's flamboyant drama teacher. Having once resided in the Big Apple, the temperamental Corky is held in something approaching awe by the can-do Blaineans, who hope that the effete impresario will bestow the same magic on "Red, White and Blaine" that he brought to his theatrical production of "Backdraft."

Guest, best remembered as guitarist Nigel Tufnel in "This Is Spinal Tap," has returned to that classic's "mockumentary" form to bring us *Waiting for Guffman*, a *cinéma un-vérité* account of the casting, rehearsal and performance of Corky's show. The movie is, from start to finish, a hoot. Directed by Guest from an outline he developed with costar Eugene Levy—which was then improvised by the terrific cast—"Guffman" is both a savvy satire of small-town boosterism and an affectionate salute to the performing spirit.

Resembling a cross between "Spinal Tap" and the 1975 beauty-pageant satire, "Smile," "Waiting for Guffman" is a comedy for those who appreciated "SCTV" and get off on "The Larry

Sanders Show." Its humor comes not from jokes or plot twists but from the perfect pitch of its straight-faced performers, who never acknowledge that this "documentary" is utterly bonkers.

Guest's Corky is a triumph, a queenly stereotype invested with such enthusiastic conviction it transcends offensiveness. (One of the unstated jokes is that it never occurs to anyone in Blaine that he's gay: he's just "artistic.") The cast that Corky assembles is a classic: for starters, there's travel agents Ron and Sheila Albertson (Fred Willard and Catherine O'Hara), whose audition piece is "Midnight at the Oasis." The Regis and Kathy Lee of Blaine, they seem born to host a morning talk show. Less showbiz-savvy, but just as hungry for the spotlight, is the cross-eyed dentist Dr. Allan Pearl (Eugene Levy). Parker Posey plays Dairy Queen counter girl Libby Mae Brown, Lewis Arquette is the retired taxidermist who will serve as the pageant's "Our Town"-ish narrator and Bob Balaban is Corky's seething rival, the high-school music teacher.

"Spinal Tap" alumni Harry Shearer, Michael McKean and Guest wrote the show's songs, which straddle the thin and hilarious line between competence and catastrophe. In a coda in New York, where Corky has opened his shop of showbiz memorabilia, the irrepressible impresario shows off his unique collection, which includes "action figures" from "My Dinner With Andre." For more in that vein, rush instantly to "Waiting for Guffman."

VILLAGE VOICE, 2/11/97, p. 74, Justine Elias

When the community theater in sleepy Blaine, Missouri, puts together a musical about the town's less than illustrious past, the cast starts dreaming of the big time, they're under the impression that a Broadway producer is coming to check out their show. Christopher Guest (perhaps better known as the guitarist for Spinal Tap) plays the grandiose, multi-untalented director Corky St. Clair, a New York transplant who babbles about "wrasslin" with the muse of theatre." Like *This Is Spinal Tap, Waiting for Guffman* is a pseudodocumentary that captures show business at its most mediocre, but this time, most of the subjects (a dazed Dairy Queen employee, a quietly seething high school music teacher) aren't nearly pretentious enough to poke fun at. Their dreams of escape are so modest that Guest's movie comes off as clever but a bit cruel, rarely rising above the level of a patronizing joke.

Also reviewed in:
NEW YORK TIMES, 1/31/97, p. C6, Janet Maslin
VARIETY, 9/16-22/96, p. 71, Daniel M. Kimmel
WASHINGTON POST, 2/28/97, Weekend/p. 43, Desson Howe

WARRIORS OF VIRTUE

A Metro-Goldwyn-Mayer release of a Law Brothers production. *Executive Producer:* Joseph Law. *Producer:* Dennis Law, Ronald Law, Christopher Law, Jeremy Law, and Patricia Ruben. *Director:* Ronny Yu. *Screenplay:* Michael Vickerman and Hugh Kelley. *Based on characters created by:* Dennis Law, Ronald Law, Christopher Law, and Jeremy Law. *Director of Photography:* Peter Pau. *Editor:* David Wu. *Music:* Don Davis, Eric Harryman, and Torrie Dorrell. *Music Editor:* Lori Eschler Frystak. *Action Choreographer:* Siuming Tsui. *Sound:* Irving Mulch, Kerry Uchida, Guntis Sics, and (music) Armin Steiner. *Sound Editor:* Marc Chiasson. *Casting:* Felicia Fasano. *Production Designer:* Eugenio Zanetti. *Art Director:* Joseph P. Lucky. *Set Decorator:* Fresca Courtois. *Set Dresser:* Gudson "Gus" Olafsson. *Special Effects:* Ya-lin Wang and Jian-ping Xia. *Visual Effects:* John Gajdecki. *Costumes:* Shirley Chan. *Make-up:* Thomas Nellen. *Stunt Coordinator:* Marc Akerstream. *Running time:* 103 minutes. *MPAA Rating:* PG.

CAST: Angus Macfadyen (Komodo); Mario Yedidia (Ryan Jeffers); Marley Shelton (Elysia); Chao-Li Chi (Master Chung); Jack Tate (Yun); Doug Jones (Yee); Don W. Lewis (Lai/Mayor Keena); J. Todd Adams (Chi); Adrienne Corcoran (Tsun); Michael John Anderson (Mudlap); Tom Towles (Grillo); Lee Arenberg (Mantose); Dennis Dun (Ming); Roy Ceballos (Willy

Beest); Jason Hamer (Mosely); Bobby Porter (Ryan's Stunt Double); Rickey D'Shon Collins (Chucky); Michael Dubrow (Brad); Peter Abrahamson (Chila); Stuart Kingston (Dullard); Qu Ying (Barbarotious); Gill Butler and Victoria Schoenke (Villagers); Michael Vickerman (Dragoon Commander); Warren Moon (Coach); Teryl Rothery (Kathryn); Julie Patzwald (Tracey); Kimberly Warnat (Lisa); Adam Mills (Toby); Clay McRae and Hamish Allan-Headley (Football Pals); Lian-Yi Li (Chinese Cook).

LOS ANGELES TIMES, 5/2/97, Calendar/p. 2, John Anderson

[The following review by John Anderson appeared in a slightly different form in **NEWSDAY, 5/2/97, Part II/p. B7.]**

Strategically positioned for a line of its own lunchboxes, "Warriors of Virtue" is an ambitious kung-fu fantasy with a muscular visual style, a fairly consistent level of hysteria and an admirable sense of its own goofiness. At the same time, its manufactured mythology is something less than archetypal, and something close to "Teenage Mutant Ninja Kangaroos."

That's right, kangaroos. The Roo-Warriors of the land of Tao—who might in fact be refugee "humanimals" from the Island of Dr. Moreau—are each associated with a noble virtue and one of the earth's "five elements." Yun (Jack Tate) represents benevolence and water; Yee (Doug Jones), righteousness and metal; Lai (Don W. Lewis), order and wood; Chi (J. Todd Adams), wisdom and fire, and Tsun (Adrienne Corcoran), loyalty and earth. This attempt at distinguishing one magic marsupial from the other is not something that will matter much to audiences, or be remembered by them 10 seconds after it's all been introduced. But it gives an indication of the level of mystical boilerplate in which these warriors are cast.

Their wise leader is Master Chung (Chao-li Chi), who seems modeled after the Ninja Turtles' own Master Splinter and, after one losing battle, the post-physical Obi Wan Kenobi. But recycling, of course, is as important a theme as any other imparted here, which includes the inherent cruelty of teenagers.

Ryan Jeffers (Mario Yedidia), a smart kid with a brace on his leg, provides his high school quarterback with the winning play and as a reward is goaded into an "initiation" in which he falls into an enchanted sewer and pops up in Tao. There, he's befriended by the lovely but troubled Elysia (Marley Shelton) and gets involved in the warfare between the "people" of Tao and the evil Komodo (Angus Macfadyen), who is draining the Lifesprings of Zubrium, because Zubrium offers eternal youth and Komodo is a Zubrium junkie.

Much of the film is fun, but a lot is confusing. Hong Kong director Ronny Yu keeps things fluid in the pre-Tao sequences, and the scenes in which Ryan's wise friend Ming (Dennis Dun) displays his kung-fu cooking style in the kitchen of a neighborhood Chinese restaurant are electric. But the fight scenes in Tao are claustrophobically tight, there's little sense of space and the story bogs down in its own myth and moralizing.

Produced by the four Law brothers—medical doctors born in Hong Kong and working in the United States—the film was made almost entirely in Beijing, and may be a hint from China that the Hong Kong action film will be safe once the city is taken. It's not entirely good news. Half fairy tale, half thriller, "Warriors of Virtue" is having as much of an identity crisis as Hong Kong itself.

NEW YORK POST, 5/2/97, p. 46, Thelma Adams

All-American nerd Ryan Jeffers is the new kid in Tao, an underworld Oz where good faces evil and battling kangaroo-men save the day. In "Warriors of Virtue," director Ronny Yu's first English-language movie, East meets West and if's not exactly love at first sight.

Hong Kong-born and Western-educated, Yu has crossover potential. Working from Michael Vickerman's clunky screenplay, Yu stages the fabulous fantasy kung fu scenes that made his "The Bride With White Hair" a hit in China and on the festival circuit.

The lavish battle scenes, including the climax where the five "Roo" warriors battle the evil Komodo (Angus Macfadyen of "Braveheart"), are fast and furious. Macfadyen's campy villain looks like young Orson Welles on a day when the shoot has gone afoul. While Komodo is a knave we love to hate, the young hero, Ryan, as played by Mario Yedidia ("Jack"), is hardly more likable. This has much to do with scribe Vickerman's overloading the script with lessons in self-esteem.

No endearing Dorothy with the added benefit of a cuddly Toto, Ryan is a charm-impaired teen with a gimpy leg frustrated by his inability to make the football team. Yu makes the athletes as malevolent as flying monkeys so that the handicapped boy's desires seem nothing short of masochistic.

Under the wing of a sage Chinese cook named Ming (Dennis Dun), and via his trip to the Tao netherworld, Jeffers learns "there's no place like me, there's no place like me." It's no ancient Chinese secret, Grasshopper, that "Warriors of Virtue" peaks when the wild fists are flying, and sags when the moral lessons are heavy-handed.

SIGHT AND SOUND, 8/97, p. 57, Robin Dougherty

Ryan is a young loner with a leg brace. Since his mother has to work, he eats a lot of meals at a nearby Chinese restaurant. There he befriends a cook, Ming, who tells him a story about the Warriors of Virtue, who fight with the "powers of fire, metal, wood, water and earth". Ming then gives Ryan an ancient Chinese manuscript.

Ryan is lured into an initiation rite by an older boy, a local bully. The stunt involves walking across a drainpipe suspended over an open water tank. When Ryan attempts it, he falls into the whirlpool below. When he comes to, in a forest surrounded by flickering lights, he finds his lame leg healed and that he is in the Land of Tao. Other residents of Tao include a young princess dressed in white named Elysia, a dwarf, and an evil prince named Komodo who has recovered Ryan's knapsack and the ancient manuscript he thinks will give him eternal life. To Ryan's aid comes Master Chung, who introduces him to four of the Warriors of Virtue—kangaroo-shaped samurais (the fifth Warrior has exiled himself, as a punishment for taking a life). But their powers have weakened and Komodo threatens to take over the world.

With help from Ryan—who realises he must fill in for the missing fifth Warrior—they are able to muster their collective strength and defeat the evil Komodo. Master Chung is killed in battle. Ryan vanishes in a blast of light and reappears back in the sewer atop the pipe. He retreats home, leaving the bullying older boy marooned by a blast of storm drainage.

The marriage of Hong Kong's martial-arts fairytales with children's storytelling plots can be fertile. In such series as *Monkey*, long-tongued storybook beasties and pint-sized samurais do battle, with ancient weapons, all the while tossing themselves into the air with the fascinating abruptness that only cheesy, low-budget editing can provide. That loopy charm is all but absent from *Warriors of Virtue*, a film whose genesis—it's produced by four Hong Kong-born brothers who are now American-schooled doctors—is more compelling than its plot.

Drawing on classic folk tales from a variety of cultures but gleaning nothing unique, this story of a boy warrior in a mythical land is generic, despite its protagonists, the Warriors of the title, being human-sized kangaroos in samurai clothing and their townsfolk being rather charming-looking water buffalo and camels. Even its young hero Ryan, played well enough by Mario Yedidia, isn't much developed as a character. We know we should care for him, but the script give us no reason to.

With its dimestore Zen philosophy and focus on a child who learns to look within himself for strength, the screenplay borrows a great deal of plot structure and Orientalist waffle from *The Karate Kid* series. For example, when young hero Ryan visits his cook friend Ming, Ming shows him an empty cocoon. Ryan asks about the moth it once held, and Ming says, "I interrupted his journey. It's the struggle to free ourselves that gives us the strength to fight." It's only a matter of time before Ryan is given a character-building adventure to help him internalise the lessons of his teacher.

Director Ronny Yu (*The Bride with White Hair*, *The Phantom Lover*) makes use of such Hong Kong conventions as freeze frames, slow-motion chase sequences and phantasmagoric swordplay. The production design, replete with candy-coloured skies and upright-walking mammals, is nearly odd enough to have its own low-budget charm. And there's no denying that Yu uses a kingdom's worth of theatrical dry ice. The leering of two of the characters—the evil prince Komodo and his assistant—suggests a sexual energy that extends beyond the age-group of the film's likely audience. However, despite much colourful and high-energy punctuation of the action, little attention has been given to its rhythm.

Occasionally, Yu allows a little humour to slip in. Unfortunately, the scene with the most energy—in which a breathtaking acrobatic display by chef Ming prevents a many-course dinner from crashing to the ground—comes early on. It leads us to expect more dazzling stunts and imaginative risks, but none is delivered. Nor are any fresh notions about personal growth: the kangaroo Warriors that Ryan meets in the magical Land of Tao are merely preachy vehicles to teach the tenets of co-operation and good form. Despite admirable attempts to provide a new slant on fairytale wisdoms, *Warriors of Virtue* is a story told better many times before.

VILLAGE VOICE, 5/13/97, p. 86, Gary Dauphin

If you need to take a kid in that difficult post-Disney-but-pre-teen demographic to the movies you could do significantly worse than *Warriors of Virtue* which stitches together kid-pic bits and pieces from *The Neverending Story* to *The Karate Kid*, all the while giving it a wire-fu spin. Things start out in the "real world," where martial arts and comix fan Ryan Jeffers (a reasonably spunky Maria Yedidia) is a downtrodden kid with a brace on his leg, his only joy watching the cook at the local Chinese restaurant agilely chop and fry the hell out of the night's special. Ryan falls into a sewer on a dare, but instead of drowning he's transported to the Land of Tao, one of those magical-realm universes where he not only gets to live out his dreams of being a hero but, of course, learns the true meaning of strength, honor, etc. *Warriors* has a tendency to nestle After-School Special homilies about believing in yourself against fortune-cookie adages ("Where there is anxiety, there is error"), but veteran UK director Ronnie Yu *(The Bride With White Hair)* knows his way around a fantasy adventure. *Warriors* is stocked with enough well-paced (albeit bloodless) fights and high-flying derringdo that even a fan of Yu's scarier and significantly harder ghost-story flicks will get the occasional kick.

Also reviewed in:
NEW YORK TIMES, 5/2/97, p. C10, Lawrence Van Gelder
VARIETY, 5/5-11/97, p. 67, Leonard Klady

WASHINGTON SQUARE

A Hollywood Pictures release in association with Caravan Pictures of a Roger Birnbaum production in association with Ann Dubinet. *Executive Producer:* Randy Ostrow. *Producer:* Roger Birnbaum and Julie Bergman Sender. *Director:* Agnieszka Holland. *Screenplay:* Carol Doyle. *Based on the novel by:* Henry James. *Director of Photography:* Jerzy Zielinski. *Editor:* David Siegel. *Music:* Jan A.P. Kaczmarek. *Music Editor:* Christopher Kennedy. *Choreographer:* Elizabeth Aldrich. *Sound:* Michael Barosky and (music) Rafal Paczkowski. *Sound Editor:* Frank Gaeta. *Casting:* Debra Zane. *Production Designer:* Allan Starski. *Art Director:* Alan E. Muraoka. *Set Decorator:* William A. Cimino. *Set Dresser:* Elizabeth A. Weber, F. Dale Davis, Elizabeth H. Bell, John Millard, John Millard, Jeff Stacy, and Kenny Sheehan. *Special Effects:* Douglas Retzler. *Costumes:* Anna Sheppard. *Make-up:* Micheline Trepanier. *Stunt Coordinator:* Jeff Ward and Janet Paparazzo. *Running time:* 115 minutes. *MPAA Rating:* PG.

CAST: Jennifer Jason Leigh (Catherine Sloper); Albert Finney (Dr. Austin Sloper); Maggie Smith (Aunt Lavinia Penniman); Ben Chaplin (Morris Townsend); Judith Ivey (Mrs. Elizabeth Almond); Arthur Laupus (Mr. Almond); Jennifer Garner (Marian Almond); Robert Stanton (Arthur Townsend); Betsy Brantley (Mrs. Montgomery); Nancy Daly (Maureen, Maid); Sara Ruzicka (Catherine Sloper, Age 11); Rachel Layne Sacrey (Sarah Almond, Age 16); Rachel Osborne (Alice Almond, Age 17); Scott Jaeck (John Ludlow); Peter Maloney (Jacob Webber/Notary); Lauren Hulsey (Edith); Sara Constance Marshall (Therese, Maid); Marissa Anna Muro (Paris Singer); Loretto McNally (Midwife); Eva Jean Berg (Sloper's Cook); David Hildebrand (Engagement Party Pianist); James J. Waltz (Engagement Party Singer); Peter Klaus (Engagement Party Guest); Jack Lilley (Carriage Driver).

LOS ANGELES TIMES, 10/10/97, Calendar/p. 1, Kenneth Turan

In 19th century New York, "Washington Square" was as much a state of mind as an address. It represented wealth, status and the power of an autocratic society that was inflexible toward those living under it.

As created by novelist Henry James, the tortured romantic life of Catherine Sloper of Washington Square had a haunting, unsettling quality attractive to filmmakers. Director William Wyler had one of his biggest successes with 1949's "The Heiress," starring Montgomery Clift, Ralph Richardson and Olivia de Havilland, who won an Oscar for portraying the struggling Catherine.

Agnieszka Holland, whose credits range from "The Secret Garden" to "Total Eclipse," is the latest director to be seduced by Catherine's woes. As written by debut screenwriter Carol Doyle, this version of the James novella takes a different tack than the Wyler version, which was based on a successful play. But hampered by widely divergent performances and a troubling tendency toward the obvious, the result is not a success.

This lack of subtlety in "Washington Square" is especially troubling because James was a writer to whom nuance and inference were everything. Even if the brooding, complex "Heiress" hadn't existed as a touchstone, this film's broad-brush sensibility, its insistence, to take one example, on the symbolic value of caged birds, weakens it in terms of dramatic interest.

What this "Washington Square" does have is a determination to open the story up visually. So Jerzy Zielinski's camera promenades through the square itself (shot in Baltimore because New York's has become decidedly bohemian) and visits locales like a large family wedding and a rowdy, distinctly non-Jamesian tavern/bordello.

Time is also taken to illustrate the back story of Catherine and her father, Dr. Austin Sloper (Albert Finney). We see the disaster of her birth, which cost Dr. Sloper his beloved wife and caused him to harden his heart against his infant daughter. And we see the girl as a teenage chubbette, pathetically eager to please the haughty doctor even though it hardly seems possible.

By the time Jennifer Jason Leigh comes on to play the adult Catherine, her personality seems to be set. Plain in looks, awkward in manner, with gauche taste and an inability to be comfortable in her own skin, Catherine is the despair not only of her distant father but also of her flighty aunt Lavinia (Maggie Smith). Her major asset, or so her father thinks, is the sizable inheritance she will come into upon his death.

Then a young man named Morris Townsend (Ben Chaplin) enters Catherine's life. Charming and sensually handsome, he claims to think of her not as awkward but rather as "a woman without guile." Together, he promises, they'll find sanctuary from the world's pain.

Naturally, Catherine flowers under this attention, and the young man is much favored by her romantic aunt. But Dr. Sloper, the autocrat of the breakfast and whatever other tables he occupies, is not so easily moved. To his mind, Townsend's lack of employment makes him a fortune hunter, someone whose purely mercenary nature his daughter is too simpleminded to comprehend.

Because Wyler's "The Heiress" had the advantage of a marvelously ambiguous performance by Montgomery Clift, much of the film's interest was taken up by the question of Townsend's sincerity. "Washington Square," by design, has another, equally valid focus and that is the agony of Catherine's dilemma, forced to choose between a tyrannical father she loves and an equally obdurate suitor who doesn't want to marry without parental permission.

Not for Jennifer Jason Leigh, apparently, are lighthearted characters who have an easy time with, life. Her graceless Catherine, all fidgets and twitches, is squarely within her range and interest, and Jason Leigh provides her with fine moments when she looks truly haunted and on the edge of hysteria.

But even this performance, the film's solid center, could have used some modulation, and when it comes to Finney and Smith, their work is so caricatured and overdone that it throws the entire film out of balance. Even the natural and believable Chaplin, last seen in "The Truth About Cats and Dogs," has a tendency to abruptly change emotional direction like a faucet that runs hot then cold.

"Washington Square's" determination to make its story as simpleminded as possible is its great drawback. Though the argument could be made that Catherine's fate is subtly handled, the film's eagerness to spell everything out in capital letters would probably make James cringe. What he would think about an ending that involves Manhattan's first day-care center and a Marilyn and Alan Bergman song about a piece of string is thankfully beyond imagining.

According to "A Talent for Trouble," Jan Herman's comprehensive Wyler biography, Tom Cruise and director Mike Nichols considered remaking "The Heiress" as recently as 1993. They finally decided against it, concluding "Wyler's version was perfect." More than anything else, "Washington Square" indicates they were right.

NEW YORK, 10/13/97, p. 92, David Denby

In Washington Square, set in upper-class New York in the 1850s, a plain, awkward girl who happens to be an heiress, Catherine Sloper (Jennifer Jason Leigh), meets a handsome young man, Morris Townsend (Ben Chaplin), at an elaborate garden party.   Decorous behavior—the implacable standard of the time—requires control, yet Catherine fidgets, stares, and ducks her head as if suddenly transfixed by a fold in her fringed and gaudy dress; then she stares again. No man of comparable beauty, or any beauty at all, has paid her much attention in her life, which has been led entirely under the gaze of her father, Dr. Sloper (Albert Finney), a widower of sardonic speech and dictatorial temperament. Morris is not only good-looking but also charming, ardent, and, as far as Catherine can tell, entirely taken with her. Is he serious? A mere opportunist? Catherine's father is sure that he is after her fortune.

In this and many other scenes from *Washington Square,* the actors, the director (Agnieszka Holland), and the screenwriter (Carol Doyle) are struggling against the familiarity of the material. Even if you haven't read Henry James's great early (1881) novel, or seen the recent Broadway revival of *The Heiress,* Ruth and Augustus Goetz's theatrical adaptation of the book (first mounted in 1946), or seen the excellent 1949 William Wyler movie based on the Goetzes' work (starring Olivia De Havilland, Montgomery Clift, and Ralph Richardson), you may still find that the material feels generically familiar as a situation: A rich, vulnerable young woman meets a poor but cunning and self-possessed young man with nothing to recommend him but his physical splendor.

What Holland and the others have done is to make the story as dangerous as possible—to take it to an extreme of neurotic energy, passion, and rage without going over the edge into travesty. Holland, the Polish-born director of *Europa, Europa* and *Olivier, Olivier,* gives every emotion its full stop. The characters have developed an elaborate armature of manners, but as far as we can see, they repress or deflect nothing. People run up and down stairs, tremble, and shout. The filmmakers seem determined to expose the elements of melodrama and erotic anguish beneath James's powerfully urbane manner. If the results aren't in line with James's tone—one of suavity yielding to outbursts of candor—the movie often works on its own terms as emotional drama. There are no languid, dead, merely decorative patches here, as there were in Jane Campion's version of *The Portrait of a Lady.*

At first, however, Jennifer Jason Leigh is too rabbity. Her Catherine seems not merely shy and awkward but half insane. She drops things, picks them up, drops them again; and she drops herself too—she can barely remain on her feet. She hardly seems upper-class: Her Catherine has an ineptitude so complete she almost invites cruelty, and I dreaded the return of what I have complained of in the past, Jennifer Jason Leigh's tendency to turn masochism into bravura. Jason Leigh is about half the size of Ben Chaplin, who, though not as handsome as Montgomery Clift, nevertheless has dark liquid eyes, dark hair, full sensual lips, and an enormous eagerness of address. His Morris Townsend nearly devours Catherine, and she's ready to be devoured. Aroused, Jason Leigh arches her back, and in one scene nearly pops out of her dress. Dear God, are they going to fornicate in Dr. Sloper's drawing room? It's one thing to ruffle Henry James, another to torment him. No, they hold back; the movie stays on course.

Albert Finney, however, is something of a brute. He seems to have wandered in from another set, where Dickens was being adapted. Finney's imposing and blustery, a mass of unconscious rages, and his callousness combined with the erotic openness of the younger actors turns the story into that of a grown-up denying young lovers a physical relationship; he becomes a jealous father who acts out of twisted motives (his own wife died giving birth to Catherine). When it turns out that Dr. Sloper is correct about Morris Townsend's motives, it comes as something of a shock. We can't put his acumen together with his obtuseness. James's point is that Dr. Sloper is both right and wrong, both protective and damnably egotistical—that's why the story is so richly ambiguous morally—whereas in Finney's interpretation, Dr. Sloper is virtually a murderer.

But Chaplin and Jason Leigh keep the movie on track. Chaplin's false candor gives way to desperation; the too-sensual face collapses into misery and childishness. Chaplin's fits of self-justification are despicable but touching and recognizably human—we've all had moments like that, moments in which our worst selves have been exposed and our best selves try to break away from the bad behavior and can't. Morris is trapped, and Chaplin's desperation is piteous. And Jason Leigh pulls herself out of masochism and becomes, by degrees, a formidably willful and proud woman. Henry James gave Catherine dignity in withdrawal; Agnieszka Holland, in a series of final radiant close-ups, makes her a force. It's a feminist reading of the text but not a vulgarization of it.

Holland keeps the camera active and the backgrounds fitful. Washington Square itself (Union Square in Baltimore serves as a double) may be an orderly paradise, with children and bicycles and fine ladies and gentlemen, but the rest of 1850s New York is a beehive of nasty activity. The port is buzzing, and men copulate with whores in the back room of a saloon. Filling in what James leaves out is a plausible way to do him in the movies, a plausible way of taking him over while not approaching what he actually is—subtle and brilliant beyond the movies' abilities to capture.

NEW YORK POST, 10/3/97, p. 49, Michael Medved

"Washington Square" amounts to a movie miracle, transforming a century-old tale of a Victorian spinster into perhaps the most passionate motion picture of the year.

Based on the same Henry James story that inspired Olivia de Havilland's Oscar-winning performance in 1949's "The Heiress" and Cherry Jones' Tony Award-winning performance in the 1995-96 Broadway revival of "The Heiress," this new version follows the book more faithfully and provides much better balance among the characters.

Despite the bitter conflicts and betrayals that mark their interactions in the story, each of the four principals emerges as comprehensible, convincing and, in some sense, sympathetic.

Jennifer Jason Leigh (in a performance of overwhelming range, subtlety and power) plays Catherine Sloper, the only child of a prominent New York physician (Albert Finney) whose beloved wife died in childbirth.

Catherine adores her manly, dignified father, but he remains painfully conscious of the fact that his awkward, vulnerable daughter is neither beautiful nor brilliant. She is a perfect target, in fact, for the ardent, silver-tongued Morris Townsend (Ben Chaplin, of "The Truth About Cats and Dogs"), a penniless young man who begins courting her with single-minded, melting-eyed intensity.

Catherine falls wildly in love and wants to marry Morris—even if her protective father is right that he actually cares only for her money.

Meanwhile, babbling, sentimental, widowed Aunt Lavinia (Maggie Smith) does what she can to bring the two young people together, thereby adding to the family's troubles.

Director Agnieszka Holland ("Europa Europa," "The Secret Garden") does such a spectacular job in capturing the complexity of her characters that audiences will continue debating their actions and intentions long after the film.

The dialogue (expertly adapted from James' prose by debuting screenwriter Carol Doyle) rings with intelligence and edge, while the production design (by Allan Starski of "Schindler's List") effortlessly captures the many worlds of 19th century New York without the fussiness, or show-offy splendor, that marred so many other period projects (such as "The Age of Innocence").

The Oscar race begins in earnest with this beautiful and heartbreaking film, which deserves nominations for its director and all four of its stars in their respective categories. It dazzles both eye and imagination with its visions of the past, and ends too soon for an appropriately enthralled audience.

NEWSWEEK, 10/13/97, p. 75, David Ansen

If you've read Henry James's "Washington Square," or seen either William Wyler's 1949 movie "The Heiress" or the play by Ruth and Augustus Goetz, you may think a new version is unnecessary. You may think, as well, that movies of classic 19th-century novels have to be genteel decorative objects more suitable for PBS than your local cineplex. Think again. Polish-born director Agnieszka Holland ("Europa, Europa," "The Secret Garden") shakes the dust off our preconceptions to give us, a *Washington Square* that both respects James's complexities and bitter ironies and adds a visceral kick all its own.

Jennifer Jason Leigh is the wallflower Catherine Sloper—awkward, plain and guileless—who grows up in the shadow of her father's disappointment. Dr. Sloper (Albert Finney), an esteemed physician with a sarcastic wit, can never forgive his daughter for being the agent of his wife's death in childbirth. When a handsome but penniless young man, Morris Townsend (Ben Chaplin), transforms Catherine's expectations with his declarations of love, her father smells a fortune-hunting rat and is determined to prevent a marriage.

The ensuing drama of competing wills is played out in ways at once funny, heartbreaking, savage and subtle. Leigh calibrates Catherine's metamorphosis from timid diffidence to abashed passion to resigned self-knowledge with microscopic precision. Chaplin finds unexpected layers of neediness and self-laceration in the charming, ambiguous Townsend, and Finney brings a slashing sardonic power to Dr. Sloper, a man who is right for all the wrong reasons. Holland and screenwriter Carol Doyle have given James a feminist spin without diminishing the men in the tale: everyone in this painful triangle is granted a near-tragic stature. The broad comic aspects rest in the deft hands of Maggie Smith as the excitable meddler, Aunt Lavinia. No longer a tale of revenge, as "The Heiress" was, Holland's passionate version may be truer to James. He'd be startled by its earthiness, but he'd recognize these bruised, complex hearts as his own.

SIGHT AND SOUND, 6/98, p. 59, Peter Matthews

New York City the 1830s. Dr Austin Sloper's wife dies in childbirth. As the innocent cause of the tragedy his shy and clumsy daughter Catherine is treated by Austin with ill-concealed distaste. One evening, a now mature Catherine accompanies Austin and his sister Lavinia Penniman to a party celebrating the engagement of her cousin Marian. There she meets the groom's cousin Morris, a handsome idler living with his sister. Catherine dances with Morris and is soon smitten. After several visits, Morris declares his love for Catherine. Austin politely inquires about Morris' finances and situation and later bluntly accuses Morris of being a fortune hunter. The doctor informs his daughter that he will disinherit her should she marry without his consent. Austin decides to take her on an extended tour of Europe. Catherine agrees and pleads with Morris to wait for her.

In Europe, Catherine confesses that her feelings for Morris are unchanged. Furious, Austin pours out his contempt for his ungrateful daughter. Catherine returns to New York chastened but now openly defiant of her father. She is reunited with Morris, but he admits when pressed that he doesn't want to marry her without her money. Deeply humiliated, she tells her father that she will not marry Morris during Austin's lifetime. The years pass and Catherine remains unattached despite a number of suitors. Austin dies after trying unsuccessfully to exact a promise from her that she will never marry Morris. Catherine inherits only the house. Sometime later Morris returns and begs for a reconciliation. Catherine orders him to leave.

Nothing else in Agnieszka Holland's film version of Henry James' short novel remotely lives up to the bravura of the opening sequence. From somewhere high above the treetops, we peer down on tiny costumed extras parading through a meticulous recreation of upper class New York circa 1830. The camera dips to street level, selects a house, then passes through an open window. It scoots around the plush interior while a babble of voices swells on the soundtrack culminating in a ghastly shriek. Scrambling up to a bedroom, we run smack into the pale, bloodied corpse of a beautiful young woman whose new-born child is offered tentatively for the inspection of the nauseated father. In one cinematic swoop, Holland discloses the social milieu in both its macro and microcosmic aspects, graphically establishing the primary motive from which the tale's rebounding ironies spring.

The second scene is pretty effective too: the unloved infant has grown into a pudgy adolescent who, commanded to sing at a birthday party, wets herself on the drawing room carpet while a clock ticks away somewhere in the stunned silence. Needless to say, this diuretic episode isn't in the book. From the literal way Holland stages it, she and the screenwriter Carol Doyle might be making a subversive point about those Victorian angels of the hearth having bladders like the rest of us. There's also an oddball shot of the adult Catherine pressing her lips lasciviously against a mirror, and even dotty old Aunt Lavinia is shown surreptitiously fondling and sniffing a tuft of masculine hair.

Such kinky improvements have the intermittent effect of converting the story from a delicate tragicomedy to a slice of Zolaesque naturalism. The film-makers want to exhibit instinctual life heaving beneath the blue-blooded codes of propriety. In a similar vein, the sound mixer has gone wild with multi-tracks and overlapping dialogue in an effort to confer immediacy on the stilted period situations. Few of these visual and aural stunts feel organically connected to the drama since they are basically there as sweeteners, the evident assumption being that no contemporary audience could stomach James' ultra-refined classicism served up neat.

In terms of making technique count for something, Holland expends herself early. After ten minutes or so, the movie becomes psychologically murky and haphazard, less from James' famous ambiguity than from the director's substitution of fussy pictorialism for simple observation. For instance, the tasselled, beribboned blue and yellow hoopskirt that Catherine wears to the Almond engagement party is certainly an eye popper. But it's symptomatic of Holland's loss of grip on the material that you can't tell whether the character is meant to look striking or monstrous in this get up. When Catherine sports a cherry red ball gown in William Wyler's magnificent 1949 adaptation *The Heiress,* there's no mistaking the cruel import of her father's line: "Ah yes, but your mother *dominated* the colour."

Still, the film-makers insist that theirs is the more faithful interpretation, and it's true they have tried to restore the heroine's original emotional trajectory. In the novel, a timid mouse passes through the twin fires of a perfectionist father and a worthless lover, and emerges ruefully enlightened. The theatrically charged Wyler version is more about the worm turning: Catherine becomes the glittering, imperious avenger of her wrongs. (No one who has seen the film will easily forget Olivia de Havilland's basilisk stare as she bolts the door, leaving Montgomery Clift's Morris pounding fecklessly outside.) *The Heiress* is an almost unbearably intense movie, but admittedly, much of its melodramatic power rests on the patriarchal myth that a woman can't be strong unless she is tough as nails and sexually dried up. Holland and Doyle retain James' final sense of hard won independence and inner peace, but they blunt its edge of wry pathos in the interest of an acceptably rosy feminist coda, with Catherine apparently running the Victorian era's first and only day-care centre.

The movie is at least admirably cast. Albert Finney contributes his now imposing bulk to the role of iron-clad paterfamilias Austin Sloper and Maggie Smith is practically inevitable as the whimsical Lavinia. As gold-digging Morris, the uncommonly pretty Ben Chaplin bats his dark liquid eyes in a plausibly coquettish manner. (He's obviously watched *The Heiress* since he echoes much of Montgomery Clift's nervous, courtly phrasing).

True to the stylised form she's known for here, Jennifer Jason Leigh equips Catherine with a full panoply of hysterical giggles and strange, squinty expressions. And where Olivia de Havilland gave you flashes of the wallflower's suppressed intelligence, Leigh plays the character as an unrelieved lump who can't make a move without sideswiping a wall or tumbling headlong into the mud. This Catherine is so comically, abjectly repulsive that you simply don't buy her ultimate ascension to personhood. However, Leigh takes more chances than just about any other contemporary actress, and there's a kind of hubristic grandeur even in so intricately wrong-headed and mannered a performance as this one.

VILLAGE VOICE, 10/7/97, p. 80, Michael Atkinson

Movies are escape, and costume dramas based upon classic novels of quiet romantic struggle are escape cubed—genteel B&B getaways for those of us deeply disgruntled that our lives consist of waiting at traffic lights, reheating food, and doing laundry. However much English-prof meditation a film like *Washington Square* may prompt, we are still there for the time travel. (The mousy housemaids, the dandies in waistcoats, Maggie Smith as a fussy chaperone—will it never end?)

Faultlessly manufactured, Agnieszka Holland's adaptation gets so much right that you tend to wonder if getting things right is all there is. In this genre, it may be so. Holland has managed to imbue most of her films, even *The Secret Garden,* with a mysterious visual energy, but, contracted to do James for Disney, her hands are tied, which is not unlike saying James Ivory has the run of the joint.

The story, thanks to the deathless career of the stage-screen version *The Heiress,* is common coin, but Holland and screenwriter Carol Doyle have endeavored to return the material to its maker. Thus, instead of *The Heiress*'s climactic lockout, we get James's far less cathartic confrontation between insecure waif-turned-embittered spinster Catherine Sloper (Jennifer Jason Leigh) and relentless fortune hunter Morris Townsend (Ben Chaplin), years after he courted her for her father's money. (This last scene contains Doyle's one Campion-esque nod to contemporaneity: Catherine isn't simply toiling on fancywork, but running a full-scale 19th-century day care; "Is your mother working late again?" she asks the last girl to leave.)

Though James junkies may quibble, Holland's film does deliver the book's desperate, ar-rhythmic heart on a silver-plated platter. Of course, the film is performance dependent, and hits one hair-raising balance after another: seemingly frustrated by his own obscenely Irish eyes and lips, Chaplin teeters superbly between earnest ardor and contemptuous gold digging (indeed, the two are not mutually exclusive, one of James's finer points), while Leigh, still the premier submergent actress of her generation, makes every emotional tremor visible to us while still creating Catherine as a terminally bruised wallflower. There's still something coltish and newborn about Leigh that makes this almost typecasting—at 36, she can still produce the embarrassing rictus of a friendless schoolgirl. And as the tyrannical Dr. Sloper, Albert Finney may be no Ralph Richardson, but even he has moments when the eyes glare out of that mountain of a face with something close to dread and understanding.

Also reviewed in:
CHICAGO TRIBUNE, 10/10/97, Friday/p. A, Michael Wilmington
NEW REPUBLIC, 10/20/97, p. 26, Stanley Kauffmann
NEW YORK TIMES, 10/3/97, p. E13, Janet Maslin
VARIETY, 9/15-21/97, p. 76, Todd McCarthy
WASHINGTON POST, 10/10/97, p. D1, Stephen Hunter
WASHINGTON POST, 10/10/97, Weekend/p. 48, Desson Howe

WATERMELON WOMAN, THE

A First Run Features release of a Dancing Girls Productions film. *Executive Producer:* Michael Light. *Producer:* Alexandra Juhasz and Barry Swimar. *Director:* Cheryl Dunye. *Screenplay:* Cheryl Dunye. *Director of Photography:* Michelle Crenshaw. *Editor:* Annie Taylor. *Music:* Paul Shapiro and Bill Coleman. *Sound:* Jack A. Mehlbaum. *Sound Editor:* Jim Ford and Magali Taylor. *Casting:* Gail Lloyd. *Production Designer:* Robert "Ratface" Holtzman. *Set Decorator:* Stacey Byers. *Costumes:* Solomon Wise and Luciana Moreira. *Make-up:* Kathy Robertson. *Running time:* 90 minutes. *MPAA Rating:* Not Rated.

CAST: Cheryl Dunye (Cheryl); Guinevere Turner (Diana); Valarie Walker (Tamara); Lisa Marie Bronson (Fae "The Watermelon Woman" Richards); Irene Dunye (Herself); Brian Freeman (Lee Edwards); Ira Jefferies (Shirley Hamilton); Camille Paglia (Herself); Sarah Schulman (CLIT Archivist); V.S. Brodie (Karaoke Singer); Shelley Olivier (Annie Heath); David Rakoff (Librarian); Toshi Reagon (Street Musician); Christopher Ridenhour (Bob); Kathy Robertson (Yvette); Jocelyn Taylor (Stacey); Bill Wayterra (Photographer); Elaine Freeman (Bride's Mother); Erin Cramer (Bride); Wellington Love (Groom); Toni Nash (Groom's Mother); Zoe Goldberg (Little White Girl); Calder Goldberg (Little White Boy); Shanel Johnson, Olivia Bokelman, Madelyn Bokelman (Little Black Girls); Barry Swimar (Relative in Yarmulka); Sara Vogt ("Plantation Memories" Mistress); Ana Margaret Sanchez ("Souls of Deceit" Mulatto); Eve Oishi (Karaoke White Girl); Joy Malinowski (Emcee); Anthony Christopher (Black Banker on the Street); Suzi Nash (Black School Teacher on the Street); Earl Pittman, Jonathan Ellis, and T. Lamonte McKinnon (Sorry Rosies); S. Elizabeth Evans (Leather Girl on Street); Amadee Braxton and Denise Sneed (Bus Stop Girls); Robert Reid-Pharr (Street

Queen in Library Line); David Hanson (Grungy White Boy); Rita Porter (White Woman at Produce Truck); Brian Balsemore (Produce Man); Gail Lloyd (Diane's Black Date); Tatum Kendall, Tania Galtoni, and Jake Carlo (White Students); Zanobia Webb (Poet); Nana Korantemaa (Drummer); Nana Akousa Agylriwah (Percussionist); Virginia Manning (Annie's Girlfriend); Patricia Ellis (Mrs. Edge-Fletcher); Lillie Hayes (Her Maid); James Charles Roberts (Newsreel Narrator); Robert Sciasci and A. Ron Marigna (Police Officers); Donnita Hamilton (June's Next Door Neighbor).

LOS ANGELES TIMES, 3/28/97, Calendar/p. 18, Kevin Thomas

Philadelphia filmmaker Cheryl Dunye has such a light, easy touch both in front and in back of the camera that you're in danger of not noticing how skillful a craftsman she really is or how deftly she raises serious issues of race and sexual orientation in "The Watermelon Woman."

Her wry and exhilarating comedy, at once romantic and sharply observant and containing within in it a "mockumentary," won the audience award at last year's Outfest, and its opening today at the Nuart provides the occasion for a second look, which serves only to reaffirm the depth and range of Dunye's talent. (To its advantage, the film has lost about five minutes of running time.)

Dunye, who is making her feature debut with "Watermelon," more or less plays herself as a vivacious, beautiful young Philadelphia video store employee whose burning ambition to become a filmmaker leads to her determination to make a documentary on a lovely but obscure black actress who appeared in a number of Hollywood films in the '30s.

Dunye's Fae Richards is a fictional woman but is representative of countless African American actors who appeared in both Hollywood and "race" pictures who virtually disappeared without a trace.

Indeed, in the credits of the film in which Richards first captivates Dunye, Richards is billed simply as "The Watermelon Woman." (Dunye has simulated this movie and other moments in Richards' life to perfection.)

As a lesbian, Dunye becomes obsessed with Richards when she discovers that the actress was rumored to have been the lover of the white female director in whose films she frequently appeared.

Dunye has much to express, and she does it with humor, energy, wit, passion and perception. On a personal level, she reflects on how one's work can undermine both love life and friendships and on her need, as a black lesbian filmmaker, to reclaim whatever heritage she can.

In pursuing the elusive Richards, Dunye calls attention to a wide range of black popular culture that deserves to be rediscovered, reevaluated and enjoyed.

She reveals how racism can work both ways when her best friend and co-worker, the hearty and tart-tongued Tamara (Valarie Walker, a terrific presence), becomes uptight when Cheryl begins a romance with a gorgeous white woman (Guinevere Turner of "Go Fish"). Tamara is even more exasperated when the video store proprietor hires a young, hip and self-possessed white woman (Shelley Olivier). Along the way, Dunye gets Camille Paglia to say something positive about the movies' black mammy stereotypes, and even about the symbol of watermelons in black culture.

Dunye has learned how to start on a comic note and become more serious so gradually that we scarcely realize it's happening. Yet "The Watermelon Woman" never loses its exuberant spirit.

It is ironic that "The Watermelon Woman" last year sparked an ugly National Endowment for the Arts funding debate in Congress over its love scenes, when they are the epitome of discreet eroticism, and they provide more evidence for the old argument that female filmmakers are the supreme sensualists. It is inconceivable that had the actors been of the same race but not the same sex, such a sequence could have caused such a furor.

NEW YORK POST, 3/5/97, p. 37, Bill Hoffmann

Your first reaction to the opening scenes of "The Watermelon Woman" may be: Geez, not another no-budget, shot-on-video vanity project that somehow got distribution.

But hang on. Because you'll soon be hooked by Cheryl Dunye's relaxed, documentary-style feature—an intriguing tale of one woman's exploration of an obscure black actress from the Roaring '20s on.

Dunye—basically playing herself—stars as a fledging lesbian moviemaker who stumbles on an old "race movie"—one of hundreds made during the '30s and '40s with all-black casts for segregated black theaters.

She's bowled over by the beauty of one actress—Fae Richards, known as "The Watermelon Woman"—and discovers Fae was not only gay, but had a fling with the movie's white female director.

Dunye decides to make a movie about the forgotten star—a project that becomes a whimsical journey of self-discovery. She's a natural actress—appealing and good-natured—and by the end, we care about Dunye, her pals and the fictional actress we've seen only in nicely faked '30s film clips.

"The Watermelon Woman" is a warm and vital exploration of the gay feminine psyche—and good filmmaking, too.

SIGHT AND SOUND, 10/97, p. 63, Andrea Stuart

Cheryl is a black, lesbian, video-store checkout clerk who wants to be a documentary film-maker. She and her best friend Tamara are making some money on the side, videoing grad-uations, bar mitzvahs and other events, but Cheryl has bigger ambitions. She is also obsessed with old Hollywood movies, particularly those which used to play the US black-cinema circuit in the 30s and 40s. Through watching these movies, she discovers a handsome young actress, known only as the Watermelon Woman, who crops up again and again as the 'black mammy' in Hollywood spectaculars of that period. Cheryl searches for information and eventually uncovers the Watermelon Woman's real name: Fae Richards. As luck would have it, Fae was also a lesbian.

Meanwhile, back at the video shop, Tamara is determined to fix Cheryl up. Her attempts to match Cheryl to a nice black girl are thwarted, however, by the appearance of Diana, a rich white dyke who coolly and confidently seduces Cheryl. To Tamara's intense disapproval. Cheryl and Diana's interracial relationship evolves. Becoming obsessed with her search for the Watermelon Woman, Cheryl discovers as she prepares a documentary about her that Fae Richards had an exploitative affair with a white female director. Later, she returned to singing and enjoyed a long-term relationship with a black woman. These findings preoccupy Cheryl: both her relationship and her friendship start to fray, but she continues making her film about Fae. After interviewing her own family and friends and visiting a feminist archive collective, she manages to track down the Watermelon Woman herself.

Constructed as a sort of mock documentary or 'mockumentary', *The Watermelon Woman* stars its own director Cheryl Dunye as a wannabe filmmaker who becomes obsessed with a forgotten black female film actor, known only as the Watermelon Woman, whom she fervently hopes is a lesbian. Its *raison d'etre*, rather predictably, is the reclaiming of black lesbian history. Even though it is Dunye's first and only feature, it has attracted a lot of attention on the gay and lesbian festival circuit and won the Teddy Bear for the Best Gay Film at the 1996 Berlin Film Festival. The film's power relies on its audience's desire for the story of the Watermelon Woman, a black lesbian actor from the 30s, to be true, which it isn't. Dunye's justification for her filmmaking strategy, that "we must make our own history", feels like a copout. After all, can downright invention ever be justified by an obliterated past? You can't get past the feeling that Dunye is washing over complexities and contradictions that she could never eliminate so neatly in real life.

You suspect that Dunye aspires here to marry the visual inventiveness of early Spike Lee with that of such lesbian independent films as *Go Fish*. But Dunye's filmic alter ego lacks the fun of Lee's geeky character Mars in *She's Gotta Have It*. Moreover, the rough, shaky cinematography used both in *Go Fish* and *The Watermelon Woman* is hard on the eye and puts even more pressure on a weak plot to carry our interest. The result is that the actual film too often looks like a bad home movie, while Cheryl's footage of weddings and bar mitzvahs looks slick by comparison.

Perhaps the film's problem is that it is too comfortable preaching to the converted. The plot leans heavily on lesbian in-jokes, as in the dating scene. It picks up themes that are mainly of interest to lesbian audiences (such as the politics of interracial dating) but then neglects to develop them or, indeed, to make them relevant to a wider audience. The sense of thematic claustrophobia is only heightened by the film's roll call of lesbian talent, including Guinevere

Turner (from *Go Fish)* and Toshi Reagon (whose mother is part of the right-on *a cappella* group, Sweet Honey in the Rock).

Nonetheless, there are a couple of funny cameos. The lesbian novelist Sarah Schulman portrays a lesbian archive collective member whose earnest, jargon-spouting disorganisation will make anyone who has ever experienced the joy of collective work giggle—or shudder. Motormouth academic Camille Paglia also outdoes herself, babbling on at warp speed about a subject on which she clearly knows nothing. You can't help but wonder whether she realises just how revealing this little portrait is.

This film will no doubt achieve some popularity with lesbian and gay audiences beyond the festival circuit, for whom this series of in-jokes and references will be cosily familiar, but its crossover potential seems rather limited. Indeed it is very unlikely that it will be seen by anyone who wouldn't otherwise go and see an art movie by a black lesbian film-maker. I wish I could say that this is a shame.

VILLAGE VOICE, 3/11/97, p. 74, Gary Dauphin

Who is the Watermelon Woman? That's the question asked by Cheryl Dunye's first full-length feature, a faux documentary wherein "Cheryl," a budding filmmaker and video-store clerk (played by Dunye) investigates the life and times of a forgotten black actress. Cheryl has a habit of special-ordering old mammy-flicks for her personal collection, and when she discovers the actress known only as "The Watermelon Woman," something about the woman's face strikes her. From there starts a journey that takes her from Hollywood to Harlem to a lesbian history archive in New York where the "black files" are kept in a few crates in a corner. It's a wryly funny trip completely in keeping within the neatly modulated presence the writer-director-star has onscreen, but as is the way with the kind of questions Cheryl asks, the answer speaks as much to her own life as her subject's.

First films about making a first film form a distinct genre, but in *The Watermelon Woman*, Dunye has decidedly bigger fish to fry than most. Cheryl's quest—the character's or the director's—is to make a movie about black women and their images, and she uses two lenses, one the recorded fragments of the Watermelon Woman's life, the other Cheryl's day-to-day as a brainy (albeit underemployed) black lesbian literally surrounded by images she hasn't made. The fascination with a minor a (played in perfectly period photographs and clips by Lisa Marie Bronson) is partly a sign of a moviemaker's natural cinephilia (Cheryl would rather stay home and watch some tapes than go out on a date, much to her buddy Tamara's disgust) but it's also DIY history- and family-making.

The Watermelon Woman is definitely a comedy, and a detective story of sorts, but it's also 'a project' in an abstract, academic way. Cheryl interviews people (including Camille Paglia who gets edited at various points midsentence) and there are numerous historical digressions about black-owned film companies and lesbian nightlife in the '40s, Dunye offering some history even as she makes some up. Cheryl gets a new lover, a suspiciously black-identified white girl (Guin Turner), about the time she discovers her subject was involved with the white woman who directed many of her movies, and the film takes on an ominously didactic overtone—at least until Cheryl's black lesbian friends start giving her a hard time.

Dunye rightly reserves her most heartfelt insights for the little details that make up the big picture, so that when she announces that at least she and the Watermelon Woman have "movies and women" in common, she's not talking about categories but the offscreen places where they meet.

Also reviewed in:
CHICAGO TRIBUNE, 11/14/97, Friday/p. J, Achy Obejas
NEW YORK TIMES, 3/5/97, p. C17, Stephen Holden
VARIETY, 6/24-30/96, p. 123, Joe Leydon

WE FREE KINGS (I MAGI RANDAGI)

A Isituto Luce release of a I.P.S. Ideazione Servizi Produzione Servizi in association with Istituto Luce. *Producer:* Francesco Torelli. *Director:* Sergio Citti. *Screenplay (Italian with English subtitles):* Sergio Citti, David Grieco, and Michele Salimbeni. *Director of Photography:* Franco Di Giacomo. *Music:* Ennio Morricone. *Sound:* Bruno Pupparo. *Production Designer:* Danilo Donati. *Running time:* 94 minutes. *MPAA Rating:* Not Rated.

CAST: Silvio Orlando (Melchoir); Patrick Bauchau (Balthazar); Rolf Zacher (Casper); Gastone Moschin (Father Gregorio); Nanni Tamma (God); Laura Betti; Franco Citti; Ninetto Davoli.

NEW YORK POST, 12/5/97, p. 56, Larry Worth

The story of three wise men in search of a messiah is pretty popular this time of year. But "I Magi Randagi"—a.k.a. "We Free Kings" (its American title)—isn't the stuff of church services.

Yes, a trio of gift givers navigates by a star to find the baby Jesus. But that's where the similarities end—and where "Magi" comes closer to Jean-Luc Godard's "Hail Mary."

At one point here, the Virgin Mary appears to be part of a black-market baby ring. But before things get too sacrilegious, it's on to another case of mistaken identity.

Actually, confused characters are the driving force in "Magi," starting with the not-so-wise men. They're actually circus performers corralled into carrying gold, frankincense and myrrh in a small Italian village's nativity pageant.

But a few dreamlike twists and turns later, the costumed actors have embarked on their own search for the Christ child—a series of adventures that produces ribald revelations and social commentary galore.

Taking inspiration from Pasolini's stark locales and Fellini's bizarre visuals, writer-director Sergio Citti devises an alluring hybrid. That includes some intentionally—and hilariously—hokey special effects.

Citti's script is equally memorable, showcasing a world where almost all are motivated by greed. Surreal storytelling seamlessly meshes with a satire on everything from race relations to soap operas. And there's enough irony along the way to have O. Henry green with envy.

That's not to overlook the film's flaws. Aside from some rambling, unfocused passages, Citti gets too heavy-handed for his own good, as when branding mankind as the most ferocious of animals. Is this meant to be a revelation?

Thankfully, the versatile cast always distracts when the need arises. In particular, Silvio Orlando, Rolf Zacher and Patrick Bauchau are hilarious as the bewildered acrobats-cum-wise men.

Granted, "I Magi Randagi" probably won't become a holiday tradition. But it makes this season's moviegoing a bit merrier for cineastes.

Also reviewed in:
NEW YORK TIMES, 12/5/97, p. E12, Lawrence Van Gelder
VARIETY, 12/23/96-1/5/97, p. 42, Deborah Young

WEDDING BELL BLUES

A BMG Independents release of a Curb Entertainment presentation of a Bergman Lustig production. *Producer:* Mike Curb, Carole Curb Nemoy, Ram Bergman, and Dana Lustig. *Director:* Dana Lustig. *Screenplay:* Annette Goliti Gutierrez. *Story:* Dana Lustig and Annette Goliti Gutierrez. *Director of Photography:* Kent Wakeford. *Editor:* Caroline Ross. *Music:* Paul Christian Gordon and Tal Bergman. *Production Designer:* Shay Austin. *Costumes:* Dana Allyson. *Running time:* 111 minutes. *MPAA Rating:* R.

CAST: Illeana Douglas (Jasmine); Paulina Porizkova (Tanya); Julie Warner (Micki); John Corbett (Cary); Jonathan Penner (Matt); Charles Martin Smith (Oliver); Richard Edson (Tom);

Debbie Reynolds (Herself); Joseph Urla; Stephanie Beacham; Carla Gugino; Leo Rossi; John Capodice; Liz Sheridan; Stephen Gilborn; Jeff Seymour; Victoria Jackson.

LOS ANGELES TIMES, 6/13/97, Calendar/p. 6, John Anderson

[The following review by John Anderson appeared in a slightly different form in **NEWSDAY, 6/13/97, Part II/p. B9.]**

Are audiences ready for another movie about the Fate Worse Than Death? That is, being 30 and unmarried? Pretty gruesome, but stick with it, because as trite as "Wedding Bell Blues" seems to be, it gets better. And better.

It may not ever get great, though, because besides suffering from what looks like a bad blowup from 16mm to 35mm, its directing is never quite up to the script. And the script is never quite up to the actresses. But the actresses do some of their best work, as characters who—will wonders never cease?—are more than just variations on the same female theme.

Sure, they all suffer from the husband blues—they don't have any, so they're. blue. Irrational perhaps, but they approach their misery from entirely different directions and ethnic entanglements.

Micki (Julie Warner of "Doc Hollywood") has been jilted just before getting to the altar and has this whole Jewish guilt/no orgasm thing to go through. Tanya (Paulina Porizkova of Sports Illustrated) is the daughter protégée of a beautiful, much-married mother (Stephanie Beacham, "Dynasty") who finds herself pregnant and suddenly boyfriendless. And the prickly Jasmine (Illeana Douglas of "Grace of My Heart") has to deal with the cloying concerns of her Old World family, who are praying for her to get married soon, honeeeeeey, and start reproducing.

Sick and tired of the whole affair—or lack thereof—they decide to go to Las Vegas, marry someone (anyone) quickly, get divorced immediately and get their families off their backs. Illogical? Sure. But consider "Wedding Bell Blues" a metaphor for the burden of procreation or the temporary insanity caused by the relentless attention of relatives.

As silly as it sometimes gets, "Wedding Bell Blues" never loses that thread of truth that keeps it from unraveling entirely. The suffocation of social pressure, the idea of self-worth as defined by men—it all rings true. And the movie also has smart performances: Douglas, whose Jasmine is almost constitutionally incapable of letting down her guard until she meets the earthy Matt (Jonathan Penner); Porizkova as Tanya, who almost turns into her mother and allows the good-hearted Oliver (a warm Charles Martin Smith) to take the paternity rap for her child; and Warner as Micki, who finds the road to paradise with a lusty cowboy named Cary ("Northern Exposure's" disc jockey, John Corbett).

The film also includes some lengthy footage of Debbie Reynolds' nightclub act—cute and she was nice to consent—but whatever other delights "Wedding Bell Blues" contains, it's never so fantastic that it might not happen. The story's a long shot, of course, a punkish fairy tale. But you never get the sense that you're being led down the primrose path. Or any aisle in particular.

NEW YORK POST, 6/13/97, p. 58, Michael Medved

"Wedding Bell Blues" begins with one of those contrived and cutesy high concepts that that suggests a brain-dead disaster in the making, but then the making thing turns around and surprise you—delivering enriched characterizations and some unpredictable plot twists that are seductive.

In the end, the picture becomes a serviceable if tarnished vehicle for the three potently appealing actresses who drive it home.

A shallow, dim-witted fashion plate (Pauline Porizkova), a sexy, fabric designer (Illeana Douglas) with a pierced nose and a leopard-spotted wardrobe, and an offensively stereotypical, uptight, non-orgasmic Jewish princess (Julie Warner) share a house in L.A.

Since they're all going through a moment of crisis (unwanted pregnancy, rejection by a fiancé, and so forth) and worried about the approach of their respective 30th birthdays, they escape together for a road trip to Las Vegas.

They make a pact to each find a guy and get married, then instantly divorced within 24 hours, just so they can say they've been wed before age 30 and reduce the pressure they feel.

So far, so bad—as the movie gets off to a lame cliche-ridden start with this preposterous premise, and you expect similarly hackneyed material when the ladies go off for their wild night of laughter and love in Las Vegas.

Amazingly enough, the men they meet (John Corbett, Charles Martin Smith and particularly Jonathan Penner) turn out to be characters rather than cartoons and the movie is suddenly watchable. Bit players also make solid contributions to the mix, especially Stephanie Beacham as Porizkova's much-married glamour-puss mother, and Debbie Reynolds in an amusing excerpt from her own Vegas show.

The movie never provides particularly profound insights about life or love, and handles an abortion sequence in an especially shallow and thoughtless manner, but there are small and engaging moments—as when Porizkova (the supermodel who's been doing under-appreciated credible work as an actress ever since her debut in 1987's "Anna") laments the common assumption that beautiful people have no real problems.

Douglas is also affecting as the wise-cracking sophisticate who's provided scores of men with "the best sex of their lives" only to discover that they decline to take her home to meet Mom.

Israeli-born Dana Lustig, who's previously co-produced several obscure films like "For Hire," and "Rave Review," makes a reasonably able directorial debut.

By the movies calculated conclusion, Lustig has largely managed the considerable task of making her main characters as appealing to men as they are sympathetic to women.

VILLAGE VOICE, 6/17/97, p. 61, Justine Elias

A tasteful but inexpensive gift is in order for *Wedding Bell Blues*, a subdued comedy from director Dana Lustig and writer Annette Goliti Gutierrez. The movie's formulaic first hour owes something to *The Brothers McMullen* and something more to 1940s women's pictures about three gals with love trouble, but appealing performances make this modest movie worth a look.

Three Los Angeles housemates, never the best of friends, two serious romantic crises: the perky, immature bride-to-be (Julie Warner) is jilted shortly before her wedding; the gorgeous, under-educated shop clerk (Paulina Porizkova) is pregnant and afraid she can't count on her longtime boyfriend; the textile designer (Illeana Douglas) is bored with her roster of artist-musician lovers and weary of her traditional family's prayers that she find herself a nice man. Fortunately, Warner's fiancé leaves his credit card behind to smooth things over, and the women take a consolation trip to Las Vegas, where they plan to find husbands, get married, and file for divorce—all in the course of one weekend. Douglas justifies the cynical agenda this way: "It's much better to be 30 years old and divorced than 30 years old and never married." "Pathetic," they all agree, but somehow "less pathetic." The movie never strains to make this idea into a madcap adventure, nor does it take the easy route of blaming the heroines, their mothers, or men in general for this sorry state of affairs. But a little spark—of anger, of joy—might have helped the movie become much funnier. As it is, *Wedding Bell Blues* is a mild *Big Night* for chicks: good time, good food, and everybody stays friends no matter what.

Also reviewed in:
NEW YORK TIMES, 6/13/97, p. C14, Janet Maslin
VARIETY, 10/28-11/3/96, p. 68, Brendan Kelly

WELCOME TO SARAJEVO

A Miramax Films and Channel Four release of a Dragon Pictures production. *Producer:* Graham Broadbent and Damian Jones. *Director:* Michael Winterbottom. *Screenplay:* Frank Cottrell Boyce. *Based on the book "Natasha's Story" by:* Michael Nicholson. *Director of Photography:* Daf Hobson. *Editor:* Trevor Waite. *Music:* Adrian Johnston. *Sound:* Martin Trevis. *Sound Editor:* Peter Baldock. *Casting:* Simone Ireland and Vanessa Pereira. *Production Designer:* Mark Geraghty. *Special Effects:* Alan Whibley. *Costumes:* Janty Yates. *Running time:* 100 minutes. *MPAA Rating:* R.

CAST: Stephen Dillane (Michael Henderson); Woody Harrelson (Flynn); Marisa Tomei (Nina); Emira Nusevic (Emira); Kerry Fox (Jane Carson); Goran Visnjic (Risto); James Nesbitt (Gregg); Emily Lloyd (Annie McGee); Igor Dzambazov (Jacket); Gordana Gadzic (Mrs. Savic); Juliet Aubrey (Helen Henderson); Drazen Sivak (Zeljko); Vesna Orel (Munira); Davor Janjic (Dragan); Vladimir Jokanovic (Emira's Uncle); Izudina Brutus (Lucky Strike); Labina Mitevska (Sanja); Sanja Buric (Alma); Haris Secic (Altar Boy); Kerry Shale (UN Convoy Official); Majda Tusar (Woman Baker); Miralem Zupcevic (Baker's Husband); Peter Kelly (UN V.I.P.); Dijana Bolanca (Nina Co-Worker); Nino Levi (Zivko); Berina Salijevic (Road Runner); Frank Dillane (Christopher Henderson); Paige Brogan-Smith (Jane Henderson); Petar Arsovski (Joey); Viktorija Peceva (Ajsha); Nikolina Kujaca (Bride); Joana Popovska (Bride's Mother); Natali Rajcinovska (Bride's Sister); Brankica Jankoska (Hairdresser); Dragan Marinkovic (Chetnik Leader); Senad Basic (Black Marketeer Leader); Ines Hadzovic (Hospital Girl); Cesir Adi (Child on Bus); Milan Plistina (Beauty Contest Compere); Ines Fancovic (Woman Shouting at Bread Queue); Haris Sarvan (Black Marketeer #1); Pejdah Dzevad (Black Marketeer 2).

CHRISTIAN SCIENCE MONITOR, 12/12/97, p. 12, David Sterritt

Who would have guessed that Woody Harrelson, who launched his career as a sitcom funnyman in "Cheers," would become a specialist in controversial Hollywood drama?

From the notorious "Natural Born Killers" to last year's "The People Vs. Larry Flynt," his choice of projects has been anything but cautious. His new picture, "Welcome to Sarajevo," pushes fewer hot buttons than those earlier films but still provides plenty to debate.

Harrelson plays an American reporter named Flynn, stationed with several colleagues in Sarajevo at the height of the Bosnian war. Faced with choices between personal safety and professional responsibility—should you risk death or injury to get today's big story?—the journalists handle this pressure in various ways. Flynn takes on the mannerisms of a jaded veteran, using cynical humor as a defense against anxiety. British correspondent Michael Henderson takes a different tack, becoming so concerned over events that his objectivity as a newsman may become the war's next casualty.

This situation boils over when Henderson realizes a local orphanage is under steady bombardment from Bosnian Serb guns. Determined to turn the crisis around, he begins reporting from the orphanage as often as possible, hoping this will spark outrage—and action—in the world community.

Outraged himself when help falls to materialize, he throws away his last shreds of detachment and decides to take individual responsibility for at least one endangered child. Henderson smuggles a little girl to his family in England, where she can live safely until the war ends. He doesn't care what Bosnian law might think of this arrangement—or what skeptics like Flynn might say about lighting one tiny candle in the face of such overwhelming darkness.

"Welcome to Sarajevo" is based on true events, including the decision by Henderson's real-life prototype (TV correspondent Michael Nicholson) to rescue a Bosnian youngster. In keeping with this background, the movie boldly incorporates actual newsreel footage—with authentic images of human suffering, some of them seen in TV reports on the war—into its conventionally scripted and acted story.

Some viewers at the Cannes filmfest and elsewhere have criticized this, calling it disrespectful and even exploitative to mix depictions of real tragedy with Hollywood drama, no matter how well-intended the reasons.

Others disagree, noting that documentary and fiction are both valuable means of exploring situations in need of attention, and that no unbreakable rule forbids mixing these modes in a single movie.

This positive argument carries a lot of weight. In a sense, "Welcome to Sarajevo" is less about its fictionalized scenes than about the actual events behind them: the siege of Sarajevo, the bombardment of the orphanage, a reporter's decision to take personal action. All its dramatized elements, from its scripted dialogue to Harrelson's role as the naysaying cynic, can be seen as devices needed to bring a harrowing but humane story to a popular audience without watering down the very real horrors of a very real war.

The movie was filmed in Sarajevo as well as Croatia and Macedonia by Michael Winterbottom.

LOS ANGELES TIMES, 11/26/97, Calendar/p. 1, Kenneth Turan

"Welcome to Sarajevo" is more than a title, it reflects a fierce and focused determination on the part of its makers to teach the lessons of that city's beleaguered past to a wider world. When a character pleads for the world's attention by saying, "Everyone must know we are dying," she is speaking for the film as well as herself.

Directed by Michael Winterbottom, "Welcome to Sarajevo" blends drama, re-creation and reality in a serious attempt not to be the typical multimillion-dollar film about an embattled region with Woody Harrelson in a leading role. And while it accomplishes this to a considerable extent, complete success is not to be.

What Winterbottom and screenwriter Frank Cottrell Boyce have aimed to do is twofold. On the one hand, they want to tell the tale, based on a book called "Natasha's Story," of how a British journalist became involved in the fate of a 9-year-old Bosnian orphan.

But more than that they want to re-create what Boyce has described as a Dantesque walk through hell. Frustrated with a West that was often indifferent to Sarajevo's horrific plight, a West that chose to change the channel or assume that that city's citizens had little in common with the rest of Europe and America, "Welcome to Sarajevo" is intent on redressing the balance in one compelling cinematic swoop.

Given how difficult it is to awaken a complacent public, that "Sarajevo" manages to make even a dent in the overall lethargy is impressive. Part of the reason is that director Winterbottom, witness his work on last year's "Jude," has a rigorous style that downplays emotional material. So one thing this film is not is awkwardly sentimental.

Also, though "Sarajevo" does have its share of recognizable faces including Harrelson as a larger-than-life American journalist named Flynn and Marisa Tomei as an international aid worker, their roles are carefully circumscribed and kept from taking over the picture.

As played by British stage and television actor Stephen Dillane, Michael Henderson, the ITN network's man in Sarajevo, is presented as the journalistic opposite number of the gregarious, chance-taking Flynn. Humorless, driven, all-business, his self-proclaimed motto is "We're not here to help, we're here to report."

Then happenstance brings Henderson into contact with an orphanage on the city's front lines. Troubled by what he's experienced, and perhaps fed up with his own distance, he does a series of stories on the place and becomes intrigued by a strong-minded girl named Emira (Emira Nusevic). And when Tomei's inexperienced but determined aid worker arrives with a dicey plan to take children out, the journalist is faced with a decision with complex ramifications.

As noted, "Sarajevo" is determined not to be just a single journalist's story, and one way it avoids that is by providing a telling picture of the tenor of life under the siege. Hardly a documentary and not averse to changing details to give its narration more impact and increase its chances of winning hearts and minds, "Sarajevo" nevertheless does an affecting job of re-creating the emotional texture of that city's plight.

But bearing witness can be a complex thing and in its concern to illuminate "Sarajevo" is prone to overkill, to trying too hard to squeeze in every troubling wartime incident. But without an intrinsic reason to be on screen, segments like the discovery of Serb-run concentration camps and Flynn's off-the-cuff comment about why the U.S. didn't support anti-Serb air strikes can feel forced and arbitrary.

Even more jarring is Winterbottom's decision—again made as a reminder of the real horror behind the story—to include approximately 10 minutes of documentary material in the film. This grim footage, which mixes uneasily with the drama and calls attention to its artificiality, is a miscalculation, a gamble that has not paid off. But while "Welcome to Sarajevo" may not be the kind of film you fall in love with, you can't help but respect it the morning after.

NEW STATESMAN, 11/21/97, p. 44, John Dugdale

If you feel like getting your guts kicked, go and see a Michael Winterbottom movie. Anthony Minghella, the other emotional Englishman on Miramax's books, does it with Bach and star-crossed love. But Winterbottom can do it any old way you want it, from cop show *(Cracker)* to domestic tragedy (Roddy Doyle's *Family*), costume classic *(Jude)* to *Thelma and Louise* meets *Brookside (Butterfly Kiss)*.

Based on the experiences of Michael Nicholson, *Welcome To Sarajevo* is his first attempt at faction, a tricky genre which denies a director suspense while compensating him with the extra frisson of fact. A UK audience, at least, knows that Nicholson succeeded in bringing out and adopting a young Bosnian girl, which leaches tension from the central storyline; but being aware that the victims are not just synthetic creations reinforces the wrenching impact of every shooting.

Roland Joffe's *The Killing Fields* and Oliver Stone's *Salvador* also dramatised books by journalists, but Winterbottoms's electric opening sequence affirms a return to an earlier, European model in its homage to the death of the Anna Magnani character in Rossellini's *Rome, Open City,* an overtly partisan film about a devastated capital and its people, not a study of an outsider's moral awakening.

Sensitive, handsome and lacking any hardened hackist traits, Stephen Dillane ("Henderson") is no more ITN veteran Nicholson than Emily Lloyd, as the television reporter who traces Serb detention camps, is Penny Marshall. Winterbottom and screenwriter Frank Cottrell Boyce seem anyway pretty unengaged by the question of journalistic ethics. For them, dispassionate war reporting is a vulture-like activity the humane swiftly grow out of, and when Henderson switches from "news" to "campaigning" by repeatedly filming a bombarded orphanage, the only puzzle is why it took him so long.

Equally straightforward are the film's politics, presupposed rather than argued: the west criminally flew in elderly statesmen to talk to the aggressors, instead of taking (unspecified) decisive action; the Bosnian Serb leadership were monsters, massacring civilians and running concentration camps; and Sarajevo's women and children should have been evacuated when the siege started.

Superficially, this looks like a clearing-out of complexity to get on with the important business of gut-kicking. More precisely, *Welcome To Sarajevo* thrives on a disparity between the crudity of what it has to say and the sophistication of the way in which it says it: the skill in Winterbottom's handling of action sequences (brilliantly, if not unproblematically, layering reconstruction, ITN footage and 1992 pop tracks) and the less showy craftsmanship of Cottrell Boyce's script.

Rather than depicting a monotony of slaughter, the film expertly ensures that each of its many, many deaths is differently nuanced. Achieving "raw emotion", the team's stated objective, is rarely pursued through simple shock tactics. Usually a string of scenes—as with the shooting of Henderson's local fixer carefully but casually acquaint the audience with the future victim.

The hack pack's joshing dialogue has a fluent, *vérité* feel, never giving the oppressive sense of making a tendentious point about a character or issue. The unusually smooth integration of mandatory Hollywood stars (Marisa Tomei and Woody Harrelson) is impressive. Harrelson's reporter is an intriguing jumble of contradictions—brashly Yankee but the only journo to learn Bosnian, a jester but also the co-discoverer of the camps—which to the film's credit are never tidied up.

Like *Jude, Welcome To Sarajevo* promises to be grimly uniform yet turns out to be vividly diverse, made up of many moods, colours and people. If Winterbottom accepts the Hollywood offers that seem certain, will that rich texture characteristic of his British, television-backed work be thinned out, its subtleties and loose ends and caprices obliterated?

Here his first upbeat ending—a cello concert on a hill above the city, as embarrassing as the use of Lennon's "Imagine" to close *The Killing Fields*—is an ominous preview of the consequences of seeking more universal appeal. If *Welcome To Sarajevo* ensures his welcome to LA, it won't (as Minghella found) necessarily be an occasion for rejoicing.

NEW YORK, 12/1/97, p. 121, David Denby

Welcome to Sarajevo, which follows the adventures of some Western journalists during the siege of the city in 1992, is a noble try, but it's a thing of shreds and patches—a mix of documentary footage, acted-out scenes based on true stories, and a general atmosphere of suffering, bravado, and endurance. Written by Frank Cottrell Boyce and directed by Michael Winterbottom (both Brits), *Welcome to Sarajevo* doesn't really work as a movie—there are too many powerful fragments, too many scenes only half developed—but I'm still very glad I saw it. The sardonic title captures the spirit of the American and British workhorses covering the war—gallant ruffians in the service of truth—and although such types have become familiar from earlier, better movies (Roger Spottiswoode's *Under Fire* and Oliver Stone's *Salvador)*, they are still among the most appealing and courageous members of the profession, and there's no reason they shouldn't be celebrated again.   Woody Harrelson is the prime peacock here, a flippant, often drunk, but secretly brave and caring star reporter (loosely based on *Newsday*'s Roy Gutman, who won a Pulitzer Prize for his Bosnia reporting). Woody and his colleagues—female as well as male—find it hard to leave Sarajevo, even after they have awakened the world to the outrages being committed there and elsewhere in Bosnia. Many months go by, and they are still hunkering down at night in the dark hotel, drinking and making mock passes at one another. They have become attached to the city as a cause as well as addicted to their own courage in covering it; they combine daring and egotism in ways that aren't easy to judge.

The documentary scenes of massacre and destruction—the torn corpses in the streets, the gutted buildings and trashed, piled-up cars—are a lot more powerful on the big screen than they ever were on TV, where they fitted all too easily into a disposable entertainment system and could easily be ignored. In the movie, the journalists covering the story appear to know that, particularly the British TV reporter, Michael Henderson, played by Stephen Dillane (based on ITN's Michael Nicholson), a man who wanders through the ravaged city in a bleak, unappeasable rage. Henderson centers his anxieties on some children in an orphanage, covering their story again and again, and when relief help shows up (in the unconvincing presence of Marisa Tomei), he tries to sneak one 9-year-old girl out as his adopted daughter. The girl turns out to have an actual mother in Sarajevo—a woman who long ago abandoned her child—and the movie faces the moral ambivalence of the situation with honorable straightforwardness but no particular power. In general, the shifts back and forth between documentary and acted scenes aren't very successful. Some of us may find it hard to put up with actors striking resolute poses right after scenes of people lying on the street with their legs blown off. Inevitably, the "upbeat" story of a reporter taking a girl out of hell and relocating her to a sunny, idyllic garden in England strikes us as a sentimentalization of what the documentary camera, in the rest of the movie, can't help seeing—the fabric of life ripped, torn, and almost obliterated.

NEW YORK POST, 11/26/97, p. 45, Michael Medved

When faced with news from Bosnia, most Americans feel an irresistible impulse to yawn and change the channel, but moviegoers should resist this instinct for the sake of "Welcome to Sarajevo"—one of the finest, most moving films of 1997.

Based on true stories, this courageous British production concentrates on jaded members of the international press corps covering the brutal siege of Sarajevo in 1992.

Gathering each night in the basement bar of their shell-scarred, generator-lit hotel, these hardened, hard-drinking journalists swap war stories and complain of the indifference of audiences back home.

Though they've risked their own lives to gather shocking footage of a bloody breadline massacre, their scoop gets bumped from broadcasts everywhere by coverage of the separation of Andrew and Fergie, Duke and Duchess of York.

Woody Harrelson plays a loud-mouthed American TV correspondent, famous for his reckless courage and well-nourished ego; Marisa Tomei portrays an initially naive volunteer hoping to rescue children from an orphanage in the besieged city.

The central character, played with edgy intensity by British stage actor Stephen Dillane, becomes obsessed with those same orphans, yearning to tell the world of infants and toddlers who in some cases watched their own parents murdered by snipers.

Developing a relationship with one particular girl with pinched face and haunted eyes (Emira Nusevic), he loses his detachment and gambles everything on a long-shot effort to bring the child home with him to his family in London.

Like "The Killing Fields," "The Year of Living Dangerously" or "Beyond Rangoon," this film focuses on pampered Westerners permanently transformed by exposure to hellish atrocities in exotic locales, but "Welcome to Sarajevo" projects greater immediacy and authenticity than any of its predecessors.

Director Michael Winterbottom (acclaimed veteran of British TV and creator of the moody feature "Jude") expertly blends archival footage with utterly riveting restaged sequences shot in war-ravaged Sarajevo immediately after the 1996 ceasefire.

Mad, ironic details (like the "Miss Besieged Sarajevo" beauty pageant) lend a haunting, surrealistic reality while handsome Croatian actor Goran Visnjic nearly steals the movie as a fearless, compassionate driver employed by the foreign press.

The film's political perspective is one-sidedly pro-Muslim and relentlessly anti-Serb, but it nonetheless succeeds in making the unimaginable agony of ordinary people (more than 200,000 civilians died in the Bosnian war!) urgent and unforgettable.

NEWSDAY, 11/26/97, Part II/p. B11, Jack Mathews

Newsday's Roy Gutman, who won a Pulitzer Prize for his reporting on concentration camp atrocities early in the Bosnian conflict, recently previewed British director Michael Winterbottom's docudrama "Welcome to Saravejo" and, in a Nov. 16 FanFare article, declared the film a journalistically unacceptable pastiche of half-truths, invented characters, contrived events and manipulated chronology.

The movie, largely based on British TV reporter Michael Nicholson's book about his Bosnian tour and his efforts to smuggle a young Muslim girl out of the country, condenses time, herds geographically separated events into its Sarajevo setting, and attributes the work of many journalists to a handful of TV reporters.

Gutman is right about the movie's distortion of detail, and his frustration is understandable. It's annoying to have filmmakers fudge what you know to be the truth, from behind the rationale of artistic license. As Gutman asks, why alter events when reality is powerful enough?

Two answers: Docudramas and journalism are very different things, and "Welcome to Sarajevo's" transgressions are not those of Oliver Stone's "JFK."

Winterbottom isn't re-imagining history and motivation with titillating theories from the fringe. He's taking events the world was scandalously uninterested in, shaping them into a cohesive dramatic structure, and driving home greater truths, leaving viewers stunned, heartbroken and perhaps feeling a bit guilty.

Millions of us were shocked at the stories, emanating from the former Yugoslavia, of "ethnic cleansing," of the relentless sniper and artillery attacks on civilians in Sarajevo, and of the raping of Muslim women. But those were snippets of bad news in otherwise ordinary days, horror stories from a distant place. "Welcome to Sarajevo" brings those stories home.

The movie is roughly a two-part dramatization and summary of the conflict. The first half, often mixing actual newsreel footage with matching re-enactments, gives us an unflinching look at the carnage in Sarajevo during the Serbian siege of 1992. The second half follows the determined efforts of British TV reporter Henderson (Stephen Dillane) to get Emira, a savvy young girl he meets in a besieged orphanage, out of the war zone. The shift in focus is abrupt, but essential. It marks the moment Henderson crosses the line of objectivity, going from observer to participant.

For those who watch people in peril on the news and wonder why the reporters don't drop everything and help, here's one who does. It's not an entirely selfless act. Henderson has covered a lot of wars, seen a lot of death and endured a lot of frustration. As he tells his colleagues in Sarajevo, his report on the "bread-line massacre" was downplayed at home, in favor of an update on a marital rift in the British royal family. Henderson needs to save this girl to save himself.

The melodrama that emerges, as Henderson and the girl (Emira Nusevic) stow away with a busload of orphans being taken out of Bosnia by Jewish aid workers, is potent stuff. A scene where the bus is halted and boarded by gun-toting Serbian paramilitaries is almost unbearably chilling.

There are fine performances throughout. Dillane, well-known in Britain for his television and stage work, makes us feel Henderson's range of often-contradictory emotions. Woody Harrelson is very effective in his supporting role, as a grandstanding American TV reporter who—like Dan Rather donning a caftan in Afghanistan—knows that the best way to assure exposure at home is to make yourself part of the news. Marisa Tomei has her obnoxious gene under control as the American aid worker leading the children's exodus. Croat actor Goran Visnjic has compelling presence as Henderson's driver/translator. And the 10-year-old Nusevic, a Sarajevo native, gives a remarkably believable performance as the girl Henderson saves, and eventually adopts.

What seems a serious oversight is the film's failure to point up the potential consequences of Henderson's action. It's not just his and the girl's lives that he risks, it's also the lives of his journalist colleagues, in this war and every other. The lives of war correspondents are tenuous enough, but when they're viewed as the enemy, they become primary targets.

If it oversimplifies the complications of the Bosnian war, "Welcome to Sarajevo" isolates with laser precision the reasons the West should have been more involved. The movie's most revealing moment is a quiet one, where Henderson is in Sarajevo talking to his wife in England. She asks him the time. He notes that it's one hour later in Sarajevo. All of Europe is no more than one time zone away, and nobody wanted to know what was going on there.

SIGHT AND SOUND, 11/97, p. 56, Xan Brooks

Sarajevo, 1992. International news reporters risk their lives to cover the siege of the city by Bosnian Serbs. Flynn, a US television reporter, causes controversy for his flashy, gung-ho reportage. One of his British counterparts, Henderson, favours a more discreet and objective stance, aided by his producer Jane and Bosnian driver Risto. But Henderson is outraged by the West's apathy towards the crisis. To ensure increased media coverage he adopts a more human-interest angle. He files reports from the stricken Ljubica Ivezic orphanage and lambasts the UN for allowing its sick and starving inhabitants to remain in danger.

With the aid of Nina, an American aid worker, Henderson arranges to evacuate a group of the youngest orphans from Sarajevo. But Henderson has also made a personal promise to rescue Emira, an older orphan for whom no home can be found. She insists on bringing the baby she's been looking after. He decides to adopt the girl, and smuggles her out illegally with the rest of the evacuees. En route in a coach through war-torn Bosnia, they are stopped by Serbian Chetniks, who seize all of the children of Serbian birth, including the baby. Henderson brings Emira to London where she settles comfortably in with his own family. Months later, Henderson learns from Sarajevo that Emira is not, in fact, an orphan: her mother is alive and wants her back. Henderson returns to the city which has now sunk further into chaos. Risto is killed by a sniper's bullet. Henderson locates Emira's mother, who reluctantly agrees to sign the adoption papers and allow Emira to continue living in the UK.

Considering the pro-and-con debate which preceded its release in the UK, some people might have reasonably assumed that Michael Winterbottom's *Welcome to Sarajevo* was the first feature film to examine the war in the former Yugoslavia. Of course, it isn't: Theo Angelopoulos' *Ulysses' Gaze* and Emir Kusturica's *Underground*, to name but two, both trod similar ground with rather less attendant noise. But where these two precedents were personal, idiosyncratic affairs, Winterbottom's film is a broad-brushed, weighty thing, epic in its scope and ambitious in its intentions. And therein lies the problem. At this year's Cannes Film Festival (where it was tipped to win the Palme d'or and then conspicuously failed to do so), critics accused the film of unseemly haste in raking over the coals of the Bosnian conflict; of aestheticising atrocity; and of converting complex contemporary issues into bite-sized human drama.

Whatever its eventual shortcomings, *Welcome to Sarajevo* is a heartfelt movie. From first to last, Winterbottom's handling is fuelled by righteous indignation. Harrowing newsreel footage is juxtaposed with the weasel rhetoric of politicians, while broadcast news is damned for its bias towards fluffy, domestic stories (such as the Fergie-Andrew split). The West's complacency—and subsequent culpability—over the Bosnian tragedy is the constant subtext underpinning *Welcome to Sarajevo*.

Technically, too, it's a *tour de force*. Winterbottom has already shown his skill on the quirky *Butterfly Kiss* and last year's dank and downbeat *Jude*. But neither prepared us for the sheer sweep and scale he exhibits here. The film's *vérité* ambience teeters at times on the verge of documentary-style realism, then shifts off down more overtly stylised avenues (a rash of freeze-frames, a stretch of luminous Super-8 footage). Trevor Waite's editing brings an urgent, kinetic rhythm to the tale, and while the film's forward momentum leaves little room for character development, the ensemble cast work well inside tight parameters. Stephen Dillane's Henderson proves a nicely unglamorous, sour-tempered hero and makes a bracing contrast with Woody Harrelson's larger-than-life Flynn (an allusion, perhaps, to maverick Vietnam War photographer

Sean Flynn), But for much of *Sarajevo* the principal star is the city itself, a Bedlam landscape of grinding hardship and sudden, indiscriminate tragedy. For the news corps through whose eyes Winterbottom views the tale—it's a place of surreal horror and strange fascination. Flynn, for example, could leave and yet opts to stay put. Sarajevo, he says, "is like a virus you can't get rid of".

Then, 40 minutes into this fevered, free-flowing stuff, a central storyline takes shape. Henderson's rescue of orphan girl Emira starts off low down in the mix but soon comes to dominate the film. This personalises the conflict and gives some shape and coherence to the chaos we've been witnessing. However, it brings problems too. Although based on the experience of ITN journalist Michael Richardson, the Henderson-Emira saga sits awkwardly with all that surrounds it. Its arrival sees the film change gear, narrow its focus, turn almost cosy and contrived. Just as Henderson adopts a human-interest angle to focus media attention on the wider issues in Bosnia, one senses Winterbottom has, as a film-maker, chosen the same tack. *Welcome to Sarajevo* never suggests adoption is the sole solution to Bosnia's woes, but the ascendancy of Emira's story does tip the argument in that direction. That story's conclusion is uncharacteristically soft-centred, depressingly feel-good.

Another problem is the soundtrack. At one point, Winterbottom cuts newsreel footage of war casualties to the Rolling Stones' yowling rendition of 'Waiting on a Friend'. Elsewhere, he leans heavily on a brooding indie-rock backdrop (Stone Roses, Stereo MCs). But Sarajevo's songs are not particularly date-specific. They are, rather, your standard trendy youth anthems, fashionable garnish on grim imagery.

Then again *Welcome to Sarajevo* is nothing if not an awkward customer. It's a film that sticks in the memory and nags at the conscience. It cannibalises recent history, takes political pot-shots at those in power, and uses footage of casualties as ballast for its drama. Yet for all that *Sarajevo* remains a sincere, sometimes shattering and often courageous attempt to cram the hell of Bosnia into one 100-minute spell. It's a film that grasps the nettle, and hangs on for dear life.

TIME, 12/1/97, p. 82, Richard Schickel

Henderson (Stephen Dillane) knows the drill: check into the best hotel still standing in some chaotic corner of the world; sally forth each day with your cameraman to gather images of anonymous suffering that will, ironically, make you famous to television viewers around the globe; beat it back to the journalists' bar each night to swap war stories with your colleagues.

It's a life that can be made to look dashing—you know, the trench-coated stand-upper with the rubble of some dreadful, war-torn landscape stretching out behind the minor media star. It's also a life that can begin to seem feckless—you know, the endless trafficking in scenes of human misery that, no matter how widely they are broadcast, do nothing to halt the flow of tragedy

Welcome to Sarajevo is painfully alert to this bitter contradiction. You read it first in Dillane's wary eyes, the weary set of his shoulders, the willed affectlessness of his voice. His Henderson is based on a real British TV journalist named Michael Nicholson, who covered 15 wars in 25 years, and the actor carries the weight of that experience, the need somehow to shift it, most affectingly.

It begins with his determination to make the struggles of an orphanage the center of his coverage. This is not, by the standards of TV, a very sexy story—not compared with carnage in the streets—but he sticks with it. Before he quite realizes what he's doing, Henderson is adopting Emira (played by Emira Nusevic, herself a child of the war), getting her out of the country via a terrifying bus ride through country controlled by Serb guerrillas, then voluntarily, dangerously returning to Sarajevo a year later to complete legal adoption, ensuring that she never has to make this return journey.

This could have turned out to be an exercise in easy sentiment, easy to shrug off. But Frank Cottrell Boyce's script is carefully understated, and director Michael Winterbottom has achieved a remarkably seamless blend of fictional and factual footage. You gain from their work—and from a wonderfully real cast that includes Woody Harrelson—a very powerful impression of a population trying to maintain the small comforts of quotidian routines, common civility, as the only available defense against the surrounding anarchy. And you begin to see the goodness of Henderson's deed not as a carefully considered moral act but as a rather desperate improvisation, an instinctive gesture he needs to make in order to assure his survival as a fully human being. He is surprised, puzzled by his own grace under pressure. The movie, in turn, respects his mystery, and by its refusal of glib inspirationalism earns our emotionally profound regard.

VILLAGE VOICE, 12/2/97, p. 79, J. Hoberman

Welcome to Sarajevo begins in 1992 with the Serb conquest of Vukovar. Then it's on to the Bosnian capital where, in a jazzed-up video frenzy, unseen snipers shoot down a wedding party as it approaches a church. The terror has been well telegraphed but director Michael Winterbottom freezes the image on the international press descending like a contagion on the bloody scene—then inserts documentary footage of actual corpses.

Winterbottom's movie means to be an essay on the inadequacy of images to move an audience to action, but it is more a demonstration of the inadequacy of acting. Who would dispute that the war in Bosnia is a genocidal horror—but what, as the Russians used to say, is to be done? The solution for *Welcome to Sarajevo* is to alternate sluggish sentiment with shock brutality. The movie incorporates atrocious carnage, then asks the viewer to respond to the nominal narrative's parade of cardboard types: noble, suffering Bosnians; sub-human, savage Serbs; adorable war orphans; callous (but good-hearted) Western journalists. Woody Harrelson is the only performer who makes much of an impression—possibly because, cast as he is as the obligatory Ugly American, he doesn't have to wax sanctimonious.

Based on the (published) personal experiences of British war correspondent Michael Nicholson, *Welcome to Sarajevo* argues that it's better to light one candle—or make a movie—than curse the darkness. A depressed British newsman (low-keyed Stephen Dillane) becomes obsessed with the plight of the city's children, in part as a ploy to keep alive home interest in the story. Winterbottom follows his lead. The film's emotional high point is the orphan exodus led by Marisa Tomei, a nerve-wracking caravan past roadside slaughter of civilian families. Less affecting—although also factual—is the hero's rescue of a single child. Her idyllic new life in the English countryside feels all the more an abstract sop each time the narrative collapses into documentary footage of the burning National Library or the starving prisoners in a Serb concentration camp.

Also reviewed in:
CHICAGO TRIBUNE, 1/9/98, Friday/p. A, Michael Wilmington
NEW REPUBLIC, 12/29/97, p. 28, Stanley Kauffmann
NEW YORK TIMES, 11/26/97, p. E5, Janet Maslin
NEW YORKER, 12/1/97, p. 101, Anthony Lane
VARIETY, 5/12-18/97, p. 64, Derek Elley
WASHINGTON POST, 1/9/98, Weekend/p. 41, Desson Howe

WES CRAVEN PRESENTS WISHMASTER

A Live Entertainment release of a Wes Craven presentation of a Pierre David production. *Executive Producer:* Wes Craven. *Producer:* Pierre David, Clark Peterson, and Noel A. Zanitsch. *Director:* Robert Kurtzman. *Screenplay:* Peter Atkins. *Director of Photography:* Jacques Haitkin. *Editor:* Dorian Vernaccio. *Music:* Harry Manfredini. *Sound:* James Hilton. *Casting:* Cathy Hernerson-Martin and Dori Zuckerman. *Production Designer:* Dorian Vernaccio and Deborah Raymond. *Make-up (Special Effects):* Robert Kurtzman. *Running time:* 90 minutes. *MPAA Rating:* R.

CAST: Tammy Lauren (Alexandra Amberson); Andrew Divoff (The Djinn/Nathaniel Demerest); Robert Englund (Anthony Beaumont); Tony Todd (Johnny Valentine); Wendy Benson (Shannon Amberson); Tony Crane (Josh); Chris Lemmon (Nick Merritt); Jenny O'Hara (Wendy Derleth); Kane Hodder (Merritt's Guard).

LOS ANGELES TIMES, 9/22/97, Calendar/p. 6, Gene Seymour

[The following review by Gene Seymour appeared in a slightly different form in
NEWSDAY, 9/22/97, Part II/p. B9.]

The joke goes something like this: Somebody rubs a lamp. A genie appears and says, "What is thy bidding?" or whatever. The lucky lamp-rubber says, "Make me a million dollars!" "Done!" the genie says and turns the guy into a pile of money.

How funny this joke is—and you're giggling yourself hoarse right now, aren't you—depends on what the poor sap wishes for; a cheese sandwich, a door, a contract. (Lenny Bruce once used malted milk in the punch line.) However this joke is played, it wouldn't seem that it could be the basis of a movie.

But hanged if some people haven't gone and done that very silly thing with "Wes Craven Presents Wishmaster," a gross-fest designed to make you never again associate genies with Barbara Eden and Robin Williams.

The genie—sorry, the proper name is "djinn"—lives in a ruby opal that's been stuck for several centuries in a statue of a sacred god. The statue breaks open, the opal is pocketed and soon finds its way into the hands of a gemologist (Linda Hamilton look-alike Tammy Lauren), who unwittingly stirs the djinn (Andrew Divoff) from slumber. (Guess how?)

Once Mister Djinn is out of his glass enclosure, it's party time. He goads everyone he meets into making wishes he grants in the most elaborately brutal manner. For instance, some idiot comes across Mr. D. committing some atrocity. "I wish I didn't have to see this," he wails. You can imagine what the follow through is on this, given that Wes Craven is listed as executive producer.

Some of these transformations are just as predictable and a tad labored. But give "Wishmaster's" makers a little credit for keeping things moving at a brisk pace. It would be nice to think that Craven helped with the rhythm, but my guess is his name is being used mostly as audience bait.

The film is also certifying its schlock-shock pedigree with the presence of "Nightmare on Elm Street's" Robert Englund, who's not bad as a twitty gallery owner, and "Candyman's" Tony Todd, who deserved a better cameo than the bouncer he plays here. Some of the banter is clever, the effects are as gaudy and icky as you'd expect, and it's always nice to see a heroine like Lauren, who wears her pluck without resorting to whimper-whines.

Otherwise, there's not much else to say except—dang! The folks in these movies sure smoke a lot of cigarettes, don't they?

NEW YORK POST, 9/20/97, p. 25, Larry Worth

Wes Craven, the man who gave birth to Freddy Krueger, is at it again. But in "Wishmaster" he attempts to repeat his success via a mean-spirited genie. Therein lies the problem.

Virtually nothing is scary about this centuries-old demon, explained at infinite length as an evil force that personifies "the face of fear." Putting appreciable distance between the Robin Williams- or Barbara Eden-style genie, it's officially called a djinn (pronounced like gin, which viewers may subsequently seek out).

Looking like a cross between "Creature From the Black Lagoon" and "Predator," but with pointier teeth, the evil one plots to open up the gates of Hell. But before that can happen, three wishes must be granted to some unfortunate Earthling.

The movie opens in the Persia of 1127 A.D., when a king's request to "witness wonders" turns into a court full of exploding skulls, flayed bodies and dangling intestines. The ruler wisely avoids wish two.

Flashing to 1997, Djinn sees a troubled blonde beauty as his meal ticket when she accidentally rubs the fire opal where he resides. (Apparently, the Aladdin's lamp home-base idea is a modern-day misconception.) So begins the battle of babe vs. Beelzebub.

Were this ridiculous scenario to take off, it would need Craven in peak form. But as executive producer, he's put newcomer Robert Kurtzman in the directors chair—a decision that's deadlier than anything in Djinn's bag of tricks.

Suspense is kept to a minimum, with most jolts, coming by way of amplified crashing noises. Worse, Kurtzman believes buckets of blood are an acceptable substitute for bona fide horror.

Further detriments include a script devoid of cleverness or originality, a finale that doesn't play by its own rules and endless bad puns ("The guard opened up for me," Djinn says, after walking through a gutted corpse.).

Then there's the cast, which includes wasted cameos from horror vets Robert ("Freddy Krueger") Englund, Tony ("Candyman") Todd, Kane ("Jason Vorhees") Hodder and Angus ("Mortuary") Scrimm. Meanwhile, heroine Tammy Lauren screams far more than anyone in the audience, Chris Lemmon remains a walking kiss of death and Andrew Divoff's Djinn could induce snoring.

Indeed, if Craven thinks his new monster will rival Freddy on the nightmare circuit, he's more of a wishful thinker than Djinn.

Also reviewed in:
CHICAGO TRIBUNE, 9/24/97, Tempo/p. 2, John Petrakis
NEW YORK TIMES, 9/20/97, p. B11, Lawrence Van Gelder
VARIETY, 9/29-10/5/97, p. 67, Joe Leydon

WHEN THE CAT'S AWAY

A Sony Pictures Classics release of a Vertigo Productions/France 2 Cinema co-production with the participation of Canal+. *Producer:* Aissa Djabri, Farid Lahouassa, and Manuel Munz. *Director:* Cédric Klapisch. *Screenplay (French with English subtitles):* Cédric Klapisch. *Director of Photography:* Benoît Delhomme. *Editor:* Francine Sandberg. *Sound:* Olivier Le Vacon and (music) Dominique Dalmasso. *Sound Editor:* Philippe Heissler. *Casting:* Bruno Levy. *Art Director:* François Emmanuelli. *Costumes:* Pierre-Yves Gayraud. *Make-up:* Isabelle Nyssen. *Stunt Coordinator:* Daniel Vérité and Gilles Conseil. *Running time:* 95 minutes. *MPAA Rating:* R.

CAST: Garance Clavel (Chloé); Zinedine Soualem (Djamel); Renée Le Calm (Madame Renée); Olivier Py (Michel); Simon Abkarian (Carlos); Frédéric Aufray (Photographer); Olivier Bamy (Black Workman); Jane Bradbury (Model); Joël Brisse (Benoît 'Bel Canto', the Painter); Olympe Brugeille (Madame Brugeille); Franck Bussi (Aggressive Guy); Marilynne Canto (Policewoman); Aline Chantal (Madame Doubrowsky); Antoine Chappey (Drunk Guy); Pascal Chardin (House Painter); Andrée Damant (Madame Dubois); Hélène de Fougerolles and Marine Delterme (Models); Carlos Donoso (Salsa dancer); Marcelle Dupuy (Concierge); Romain Duris (Jean-Steph, the Drummer); Eriq Ebouaney (Black Workman); Denis Falgoux (Denis); Marthe Fouquet (Madame Vilchenu); Philippe Garcia (Assistant Stylist); Michel Glasko (Michel's Buddy); Danielle Hoisnard (Madame Georgette Verligodin); Mille Japy (Victoire); Jean-Marie and Lila (Patrons at "The Taillandiers"); Jacqueline Jehanneuf (Madame Henriette Clavo); Nicolas Koretzky (Assistant Photographer); Kristelle (Herself); Gisèle Laquit (Gisèle); Estelle Larrivaz (Flo, the Hairdresser); Liane Leroy (Model); Franck Manzoni (Claude, Michel's 2nd Buddy); Madeleine Marie (Madame Sureau, Who Keeps Getting Lost); Felipe Moya (Troudo); Aurélia Petit (Blance, the Barmaid); Suzanne Plasson (Odile); P'tit Louis (EDF, the Moving Man); Paola Ramirez (Salsa Dancer); Francis Renaud (Aggressive Guy); Marie Riva (Publicity Woman); Eric Savin (Militant); Hiam Soualem (Courtyard Woman); Marina Tomé (Stylist); Jean-Marc Truong (Bouncer); Coraly Zahonero (Baker); La Fanfarniente (Band).

LOS ANGELES TIMES, 7/3/97, Calendar/p. 16, Kenneth Turan

"When the Cat's Away" is a bit of close-up magic, graceful enough to make something out of nothing. Small and intimate, it expands from its slight romantic comic premise to deal playfully with loneliness and love, providing a wry mash note to the city of Paris along the way.

Not the tourist Paris we usually see, but the workaday metropolis, specifically the neighborhood in transition that is the Bastille district. "When the Cat's Away" shows a city in flux and an arrondissement where old people are evicted and older buildings demolished as the hip quickly replace the humble.

Writer-director Cedric Klapisch put this film together a little bit on the fly, but you'd hardly know it. A filmmaker whose latest work, "Un Air de Famille," won three Cesars, the French Oscars, Klapisch has an impeccable feeling for people and their foibles. His gentle assurance and ability to push "When the Cat's Away" in gently surprising directions give this film its unmistakable charm.

It all starts with that cat, Gris-Gris, black with a white spot, and Gris-Gris' mistress Chloe (Garance Clavel), a waif-like young woman who works as a makeup stylist on high fashion photography shoots.

Chloe is going off on vacation and is desperate for someone to look after Gris-Gris. Her concierge laughs, her gay roommate Michel (Olivier Py) suggests tossing it out of a car window, so she ends up trusting it to Madame Renee (Renee Le Calm), the neighborhood cat woman.

"Men have often let me down, but cats never," says Madame Renee, a feisty gnome who has five or six of the animals around at any given time. But when Chloe returns from her trip, she finds Madame Renee distraught: Gris-Gris has disappeared, probably out an open apartment window to a life on the rooftops of Paris.

Though her acquaintances don't understand, Gris-Gris' loss is a major one for Chloe. Frightened by men, by life, by everything but her cat, Chloe's only friend is Gris-Gris. She must get it back. Or so she thinks.

For it is, of course, the gentle paradox of "When the Cat's Away" that Chloe's loss forces her to connect more with both her neighborhood and the rest of Paris than she'd ever thought to before.

First she meets the legion of eccentric cat fanciers, dotty elderly parties like the president of Cats Are People, Too, who divide all Paris into militaristic search zones and call to keep her posted on their progress even when there's none to report.

Then, as Chloe puts posters up and becomes something of a local celebrity, she meets other neighbors, like Djamel (Zinedine Soualem), who is slightly deranged; a sad painter named Bel Canto (Joel Brisse); and a handsome young man (Romain Duris) she keeps crossing paths with. The more Chloe mixes in life, the more she craves it, but she's so new to things she hardly knows where to begin.

Shot in semi-documentary style, "When the Cat's Away" mixes professional and nonprofessional actors so adroitly you keep having to remind yourself that what you're watching isn't really happening. The most memorable performance is from one of the non-pros, Le Calm, who is in fact a real-life neighborhood cat lady whose experiences help inspire the film.

Only 35 years old, writer director Klapisch is perhaps the most promising of the current bunch of young French filmmakers, able to charm both critics and audiences. "When the Cat's Away" has played in Paris for over a year. Klapisch has the wonderful gift of appreciating the humor in his characters without robbing them of their humanity. To his film's hope that prosperity doesn't alter Paris beyond recognition should be added the wish that success doesn't do the same to him.

NEW YORK, 8/4/97, p. 56, David Denby

Chloé (Garance Clavel) is a not quite beautiful girl with a long neck and a warming smile that almost never breaks out. Chloé is a little slow to talk. She's not stupid, nor is she depressed, exactly, but she's definitely running in low gear. She has a rather unsatisfying job as a makeup girl for fashion photo-shoots, and she lives in a shabby stretch of the Right Bank, near the Place de la Bastille, with a gay male friend who can't give her much. One of the thousands of stranded young women in the big city, Chloé is attached to her black cat, whom she calls Gris-Gris (Gray-Gray). The fat, yellow-eyed creature sits contentedly on his mistress's chest, but when Chloé goes on vacation, she leaves him with an old woman—an animal-lover with lots of cats—and Gris-Gris apparently escapes through the kitchen window. Returning, Chloé searches the area with the old lady and soon with everyone else in the neighborhood; after a while, a battalion of old-lady cat lovers, quivering with excitement, are phoning one another like air-raid spotters in wartime Britain. Chloé, meanwhile, has acquired a new pet even more faithful than Gris-Gris—a young man of North African descent who fell off a roof as a child and is now a little slow but would do anything for Chloé.

When the Cat's Away, written and directed by young Cédric Klapisch, feels at first like a strung-together collection of gentle anecdotes—an improvisation, always charming and funny, but minor, in which some not terribly important people are observed in their ruffled, natural state. It's only after the movie has been going for a while that we realize what a genius of melancholy Klapisch really is, for what he's done is nothing less than capture the tone and tenor of loneliness in the big city—and also the ways loneliness might end. *When the Cat's Away* is about the state of being lost and the deliverance of being found. Klapisch handles such events as a ghastly night spent looking for companionship, or an encounter with one's roommate's lover, or the raillery of some neighborhood types drinking their way through the evening, with such superlative delicacy that one thinks—one prays—that here at last is a successor to both Renoir and the New Wave, a young Frenchman with an instinct for human solidarity as well as first-rate lyrical skills. *When the Cat's Away* could be an early peak in a great directing career.   Don't miss it.

NEW YORK POST, 6/20/97, p. 44, Thelma Adams

Skip the bat and go for the cat.   Cédric Klapisch's deceptively light Parisian comedy, "When the Cat's Away," proves something "Batman & Robin" director Joel Schumacher hasn't stopped long enough to figure out: The most powerful special effects are detonated in the human heart.

The plot is whisker thin.   Sulky makeup artist Chloe (Garance Clavel) boards her cat with neighbor Madame Renee (Renee Le Calm) for a much-needed vacation.   When the alienated hipster returns, the cat's disappeared and Renee's consumed with guilt.

Renee recruits a network of old ladies and lonely bachelors to find the perversely named Gris-Gris (the cat is black, not gray).

"Why not Blacky?" asks the down-to-earth Renee, who describes Chloe to her cronies as if the lonely young woman were a stray cat herself, "a little pale ... tight jeans and showy sweaters."

Part Shelley Duvall, part Isabelle Adjani, Clavel charms effortlessly.   She grows on us by curling into the role as if it were an old sofa.   Her Chloe doesn't struggle for our affections; even Gris-Gris seems stand-offish with his mistress.

Through the cat search, Chloe connects with her neighbors and sheds her alienation like her chic skinny black cardigan.   In a final, exhilarating epiphany, Chloe realizes that love, like Gris-Gris, was right under her nose.

Under Klapisch's gentle touch, Paris emerges as a union of small villages, on the verge of being sacrificed to gentrification—and remains, triumphantly, the City of Love.

NEWSDAY, 6/20/97, 11/96, Part II/p. B8, Jack Mathews

A lonely, young makeup artist in Paris loses her closest companion, a black cat named Gris-Gris, and sets out to find it.   During her relentless search, she meets neighbors she'd never met before, is pursued by men she'd never noticed, and finds romance where she'd least expected it. And in Cedric Klapisch's "When the Cat's Away," she does all this in what occasionally feels like real time.

"When the Cat's Away" is a sweetly peculiar film that is as much about the decaying, multi-ethnic neighborhood of Bastille where Chloé (Garance Clavel) lives than it is about her loneliness. Writer-director Klapisch once lived here, and local knowledge would undoubtedly enhance the experience.

Reportedly inspired by a friend's similar cat hunt in Bastille, Klapisch's interest is in how a seemingly mundane crisis can become a common cause, drawing the best out of strangers, and creating relationships out of thin air.   Remember, the cat's away.

Klapisch took his crew into the same neighborhood, and even cast non-professional locals in key roles.   Most prominent among the amateurs is Madame Renee (Renee Le Calm), an elderly cat lover whose apartment, in real life as in the film, is filled with strays and boarded pets.   It is from her flat, while Chloé is holidaying at the beach, that Gris-Gris disappears, and it is Madame Renee's guilt that inspires the scope of the cat-hunt.

Madame Renee is a terrific personality, and Klapisch couldn't have gotten the loopy honesty of her performance from the most seasoned pro.   Clavel, too, is a real find, having just one previous role in a TV movie to her credit. She brings Chloé's aching loneliness so much to bear, you'll feel the urge to help her out yourself.

But this film, largely improvised and shot in a near documentary style, is ultimately more tedious than endearing. Events move not at a cat's pace but a snail's, with Klapisch's camera following Chloé, Renee and the others with the kind of repetitive determination that breeds boredom.

The stitching between scripted and improvised scenes often shows, too, in the awkwardness of shots "grabbed" on the streets. And in the playing Chloé's gay roommate, Michel, veteran stage actor Olivier Py is so over the top, you'll wish it was he rather than Gris-Gris who got lost.

SIGHT AND SOUND, 11/96, p. 62, Chris Darke

Chloé is a young Parisian makeup artist sharing a flat in the 11th arrondissement with her gay friend Michel. Chloé needs a minder for her cat Gris Gris so that she can go on holiday and is put in touch with a Madame Renée. When Chloé returns from her holiday, Gris Gris has gone missing. Chloé's concierge introduces her to the local handyman, Djamel, who will help her look for her cat. Mme. Renée recruits a network of friends to help. Chloé meets a painter nicknamed 'Bel Canto'. Djamel, Michel and Chloé poster the neighbourhood. One night, Chloé is woken by the sound of Michel having sex with his new boyfriend. Unable to sleep, Chloé searches for a friend in a bar but cannot find her.

At work, her colleagues tell her that she's letting herself go and that evening, before going out, she tries on various outfits. She sees Djamel searching the alleyways for Gris Gris. In a bar, a hip-looking guy she'd noticed before offers her a light but they are interrupted by a drunk, who chats her up. Chloé flees to the toilets where the drunk's girlfriend—who turns out to be Chloé's colleague from work—angrily berates her. Chloé is harassed by a group of men and Blanche the barwoman offers to accompany her home. Blanche tries to kiss her, but Chloé refuses. That night, out of loneliness, Chloé shares a bed with Michel and has a nightmare. She gets a call from one of Madame Renée's circle telling her that a cat's body has been found on some derelict ground but it is not Gris Gris'.

Arriving back at her apartment she sees Djamel climbing onto the roof in pursuit of a cat. The cat is not Gris Gris and Djamel almost falls off the roof. Chloé meets the hip guy again and they go to his apartment and have sex. Chloé realises that she is more interested in him than he is in her and leaves. Djamel tells Chloé that Mme Renée is ill. They visit her and discover Gris Gris trapped behind the cooker. Bel Canto is moving out to the suburbs so Chloé helps him. In the local cafe, the painter and Chloé bid each other a lingering goodbye and promise to meet soon. Chloé watches Bel Canto's van pull away and runs home elated.

When The Cat's Away epitomises present-day Parisian cinema. Marketed in France as a youth comedy, it has the slimmest of plots—a lonely young woman searching for her feline companion finds love—on which is hung a bittersweet story of urban isolation and companionship. Sitting somewhere between the sophisticated perambulations of an Eric Rohmer film, the feel-good neighbourliness of Wayne Wang and Paul Auster's Smoke and the virtuoso stylistics of Wong Kar Wai's Chungking Express, When the Cat's Away succeeds in making its hair-thin storyline come to life through a documentary-like attention to the life of a particular Parisian quartier: the 11th arrondissement, known as Popincourt.

During the late 1980s, since the development of the Bastille Opera house, the area has undergone a process of gradual gentrification. Cédric Klapisch, who established himself as an acute comedy director with 1994's Le Peril Jeune, roots his film in the observation of this transformation, a central motif of which is the demolition of the beautiful old church, Notre Dame d'Espérance. Gentrification is seen as an ambiguous but unstoppable process. The film returns repeatedly to rubbish-strewn wastelands awaiting development. The ultra-hip Pause Café is unfavourably contrasted with the local café de quartier by Madame Renée, who can't understand why people choose a place where coffee is four times more expensive. Madame Renée is herself treated as something of an icon representing the old area; authentic, aged and soon to be replaced by new money and fashionable young things. Bel Canto's decision to move out is another sign. Gentrification of an area is often foretold by its popularity with artists. Popincourt had a reputation with artists before many were forced out by rent increases. The film's rootedness in the neighbourhood has led to its being identified by *Cahiers du cinéma* as part of a tendency of the young French cinema to combine the street-level shooting style of the *nouvelle vague* with the lightly-handled, social-observation comedy that characterised the French cinema of the 30s and early 40s. In this respect, *Cat* is close to Pierre Salvadori's *Les Apprentis*. Like the odd couple in that film, these characters are of a specific time and place. Benoît Delhomme's cinematography conveys both the cramped apartments in which the older generation lives and the fugitive encounters of young Parisian street life. Chloé's run-in with the hip young guy she keeps noticing on the street—a cooler-than-thou fashion victim whose vocabulary barely extends beyond "ouaii, mortel" ("yeeah, wicked")—is one of many contingent encounters.

There is much here that is acute about the way people live together in the city. The casual cruelty, for example, extended to Djamel, the good hearted *beur*, when Chloé sees him searching the alleyways of a trendy street for Gris Gris. The comedy pitches itself quietly, juxtaposing unlikely types, and through careful pacing and some neat editing. Chloé's holiday is shown as a brief interlude, a sunny beat between entering and leaving the same Metro stop; swimming in the sea, she barely has time to breath between strokes before she's back on the Paris streets. The only filmic misjudgement here is her bad dream, which provides unnecessary access to her interior life—the most nightmarish thing about it is its resemblance to a tacky perfume advertisement.

Despite the slightness of the story, there is a cumulative sense of people's loneliness being held at bay by street-level encounters. The euphoric final image of Chloé running through the street, propelled by the promise of love in bloom, arrives with an unexpected force that indicates that, for all its appearance of off-the-cuff improvisation, this is a carefully structured, charming film that makes the city feel like home.

VILLAGE VOICE, 6/24/97, p. 75, J. Hoberman

Slight but fully realized, disarmingly droll and discreetly free-wheeling, *When the Cat's Away* is one more sign that France still breathes. No postmodern, over-the-top, hip Americanized whatever this. Cédric Klapisch cuts a slice from the gritty quiche of city life, tracking the comic search of a thin, grave, not-quite-chic makeup artist for her lost house pet.

The wanly depressed Chloé, played by newcomer Garance Clavel, returns from two weeks at the seaside to discover that her beloved black cat Gris-Gris has disappeared from the apartment of the eccentric, cat-boarding Madame Renée. Chloé's solitary vacation is rendered with wonderful economy—a single shot of her partially immersed in the ocean. She subsequently scours the newly fashionable quarter around La Bastille escorted by a dim young handyman Djamel, among other local flakes, and assisted by a network of neighborhood crones (most of them playing themselves).

Klapisch, who studied film at NYU in the mid 1980s, uses this anecdotal plot as pretext for an understated documentary. Chloé's serendipitous expedition is played out against a backbeat of eviction, demolition, and gentrification. Although *When the Cat's Away* flirts with urban romance and the heroine's work allows Klapisch to have a bit of fun with vacant models, the tone is bittersweet and nostalgic enough to include a bar full of old-timers singing "Paris, Queen of the World." In a season of brain-dead behemoths, Klapisch's celebration of chance encounters amid the urban flux has a nimble insouciance. With *When the Cat's Away*, the mice really do play.

Also reviewed in:
NEW REPUBLIC, 6/30/97, p. 27, Stanley Kauffmann
NEW YORK TIMES, 6/20/97, p. C21, Janet Maslin
VARIETY, 2/26-3/3/96, p. 73, Emanuel Levy
WASHINGTON POST, 7/11/97, p. B7, Rita Kempley
WASHINGTON POST, 7/11/97, Weekend/p. 37, Desson Howe

WILD AMERICA

A Warner Bros. release of a James G. Robinson presentation of a Morgan Creek production in association with The Steve Tisch Company. *Executive Producer:* Gary Barber, Steve Tisch, and Bill Todman, Jr. *Producer:* James G. Robinson, Irby Smith, and Mark Stouffer. *Director:* William Dear. *Screenplay:* David Michael Wieger. *Director of Photography:* David Burr. *Editor:* O. Nicholas Brown and Stuart Pappe. *Music:* Joel McNeely. *Sound:* Mary H. Ellis. *Casting:* Pam Dixon Mickelson. *Production Designer:* Steven Jordan. *Art Director:* Jack Balance. *Costumes:* Mary McLeod. *Running time:* 110 minutes. *MPAA Rating:* PG.

CAST: Jonathan Taylor Thomas (Marshall Stouffer); Devon Sawa (Mark Stouffer); Scott Bairstow (Marty Stouffer, Jr.); Frances Fisher (Agnes Stouffer); Jamey Sheridan (Marty Stouffer Sr.); Tracey Walter (Leon); Don Stroud (Stango); Zack Ward (D.C.); Claudia Stedelin (Carrie); Anastasia Spivey (Donna Jo); Leighanne Wallace (Tanna); Amy Lee Douglas (Julie Anne).

LOS ANGELES TIMES, 7/2/97, Calendar/p. 11, Kevin Thomas

"Wild America" is a delightfully far-fetched family adventure inspired by the real-life exploits of three teenage Arkansas brothers during the summer of 1967. Credibility is stretched at every turn, but that adds rather than detracts from the fun because, even if everything didn't quite happen in real life as this movie depicts it, it should have.

Buoyed by solid acting, characterization and direction, this Warner Bros. film plays like a fantasy adventure. And writer David Michael Wieger and director William Dear anchor it persuasively in the real contradictions within the character of the boys' father.

Marty Stouffer Sr. (Jamey Sheridan) and his wife, Agnes (Frances Fisher), live on a small Fort Smith, Ark., farm where Stouffer runs a used carburetor business and tinkers with rebuilding a World War II training plane. Their eldest son, Marty Jr. (Scott Bairstow), is a Hemingway admirer who nevertheless decides he'd rather shoot animals with a camera than a gun.

The middle son, Mark (Devon Sawa), is in the process of discovering girls, and the youngest, Marshall (Jonathan Taylor Thomas), the story's narrator, is mainly concerned with surviving his older brothers' bullying. Marshall has an underdog's resourcefulness and seems the shrewdest of the brothers.

Writer Wieger soon manages to maneuver the boys onto their summer odyssey, driving around the country in an old truck carrying an even older 16mm camera, with which Marty hopes to shoot enough exotic wildlife footage to end up with a documentary to sell to television. (All three brothers did end up in TV, with "Marty Stouffer's Wild America" running 11 years on PBS.)

The boys plunge swiftly into more perils than Pauline, but the extreme danger of most of them is deflected with much humor. (This is not the kind of film, however, for kids who might be tempted to emulate some of the Stouffers' riskier derring-do.)

In reality, the boys' parents would have been out of their minds to let their young sons go off on such a quest since they're clearly not remotely responsible, experienced or old enough to undertake it. But this is an escapist movie with a lot of comedy in which the boys are armed with infallible pluck and luck.

The boys' father is a familiar archetype, here sharply defined. He fires his sons with the American dream that says you can achieve any goal you set through dint of hard work and determination, yet he feels angry and slighted when they seem less than enthusiastic about joining him in rebuilding carburetors for the rest of their lives.

There's some substance as well as wonderment in the cliffhanger that is "Wild America."

NEW YORK POST, 7/2/97, p. 39, Michael Medved

In a summer of numbingly predictable blockbusters, "Wild America" is a splendid surprise—and a most welcome reminder of the crucial difference between "kiddie movies" and family films.

The former aim to please very young moviegoers without causing accompanying parents too much boredom or embarrassment.

Family films, on the other hand, simultaneously engage adults and children, connecting with both audiences in very different ways.

"Wild America" definitely falls into the latter category, offering a thrilling cinematic experience for all viewers above age 4 while providing very special resonance for those of us who spent part of our youth in the late '60s.

Inspired by the true story of the three Stouffer brothers (famed producers of nature documentaries), the movie dramatizes the beginning of their career in the summer of 1967.

It's told from the point of view of the youngest of the boys, 12-year-old Marshall (pre-teen heartthrob and "Home Improvement" star Jonathan Taylor Thomas), who stows away with his two teen-age brothers (the especially expressive Scott Bairstow and the charismatic Devon Sawa) on a cross-country road trip.

They've just acquired a used, 16mm camera, with which they intend to capture images of rare or endangered species, hoping their work as wildlife photographers will help them escape the grimy family business of salvaging automobile carburetors in Arkansas.

Jamey Sheridan is excellent as their macho, highly skeptical father, and Frances Fisher is equally convincing as their more comprehending mom.

In fact, the movie projects these bittersweet family ties with vigorous, full-bodied complexity—including the fundamentally affectionate relationships among three battling brothers, and the diabolical (and decidedly dangerous) cruelty the two older boys devise for tormenting the long-suffering youngest cub in the clan.

In the last few years, the strangely unheralded Bill Dear has quietly accumulated credentials as one of the best directors of family films in the business. And "Wild America," like his admirable precious efforts "Harry and the Hendersons" and "Angels in the Outfield," mixes humor and excitement with an abundance of heart and soul.

For moviegoers of any and all ages, that a difficult combination to resist.

Also reviewed in:
NEW YORK TIMES, 7/2/97, p. C22, Stephen Holden
VARIETY, 7/14-20/97, p. 44, Leonard Klady
WASHINGTON POST, 7/2/97, p. C5, Stephen Hunter
WASHINGTON POST, 7/4/97, Weekend/p. 42, Kevin McManus

WILL IT SNOW FOR CHRISTMAS?

A Zeitgeist Films release of an Ognon Pictures production with the participation of Centre National de la Cinématographie and Canal + and the participation of the Caisse Centrale D'Activities Sociales du Personnel des Industries Électrique et Gaziére. *Producer:* Humbert Balsan. *Director:* Sandrine Veysset. *Screenplay (French with English subtitles):* Sandrine Veysset. *Director of Photography:* Hélène Louvart. *Editor:* Nelly Quettier. *Music:* Henri Ancillotti. *Sound:* Didier Saïn. *Sound Editor:* Christophe Winding. *Art Director:* Jack Dubus. *Costumes:* Nathalie Raoul. *Running time:* 90 minutes. *MPAA Rating:* Not Rated.

CAST: Dominique Reymond (Mother); Daniel Duval (Father); Jessica Martinez (Jeanne); Alexandre Roger (Bruno); Xavier Colonna (Pierrot); Fanny Rochetin (Marie); Flavie Chimenes (Blandine); Jeremy Chaix (Paul); Guillaume Mathonnet (Rémi); Éric Huyard (Yvan); Loys Cappatti (Bernard); Marcel Guilloux-Delaunay (Schoolteacher); Bouaza Annah and Bouziane Bouakline (Arab Workers); Julie Peysson and Irène Calitzine (Students); CAVAILLON FAMILY: Andrée Toussaint (Woman); Annette Pradler (Nasty Sister); Babeth Roger (Another Sister); Fabrice Veysset (Son); Stéphane Veysset (Another Son); Jeanne Moto (Ida, the Fat Lady); Andrée Veysset (Woman in Vineyard); Laurent Guibert (Mechanic).

LOS ANGELES TIMES, 12/19/97, Calendar/p. 8, Kenneth Turan

Love and family. Hope, redemption and the resilience of spirit that carries individuals through hard times. All the themes that characterize classic French cinema are given an assured and modern spin in the deeply felt, emotional "Will It Snow for Christmas?" Though it's slotted for only one week at only one theater, don't be misled. This is one of the most affecting, naturally touching films of the year.

Winner of both the Prix Louis Delluc, the most venerable French film award, and the Cesar for best first film, "Christmas's" story of several seasons in the life of a farm family introduces Sandrine Veysset as a writer-director who's a clear descendant of such great humanist directors of the French tradition as Jean Renoir and Marcel Pagnol.

Yet though this story is poignant enough to evoke tears, it would be a mistake to anticipate a sentimental wallow. For Veysset's accomplishment is a clear-eyed determination to create empathy without getting mushy, to tell a moving story without fogging the lens.

This ability to be even-keeled goes together with a willingness to let the story develop instead of dictating it. Rather than being told what happens or what to think, we're allowed the welcome luxury of observing and coming to our own conclusions.

What is presented to us are scenes from rural life in southern France, snapshots of a farm so poor there's no indoor plumbing. Seven children make their home here, playing or working in the fields depending on their age, and all cherished by their protective and loving mother (Dominique Reymond, winner of the best actress prize at the Paris Film Festival).

Their father (Daniel Duval) is not there all the time, but when he is around he's especially hard on the children, bringing them to tears of frustration and rage. The mother defends them, angrily when need be, and though it's clear that the parents care for one another, it doesn't sound implausible when the mother tells him, "One day, I'll stop loving you."

Set over a boiling summer, a cool fall and a frigid winter, "Christmas" allows us what feels like the privilege of living this family's life along with them and experiencing the power of a mother's love. Veysset has a gift for making care what happens, and for getting considerable emotion out of small but potent moments like the mother standing alone in front of a mirror, brushing her hair and dreaming, it seems likely though it's never stated, of what might have been.

Because we're not directly informed, it's not until we've connected to this family that we realize where some of the tension has been coming from. The father has another farm nearby, where he lives with his legal wife and their much older offspring. He is not married to the mother we've become so attached to, and their children are illegitimate.

Though the emotional connection between father and mother is palpable, that situation makes strains in their relationship inevitable. Because of this, plus the poverty and the hard work, we come to feel that every day is a struggle for these people, every situation brings on the threat of a possible disaster to children and a mother whose earnest decency has won us over.

While "Will It Snow for Christmas?" does contain some plot twists that dance on the edge of melodrama, the effect they have is earned. Always at the center is the mother, refusing to let her children be exploited, determined to do whatever it takes to preserve both their humanity and their dignity. Writer-director Veysset dedicated this film to her own mother, and a more heartfelt piece of work is hard to imagine.

NEW YORK POST, 12/17/97, p. 60, Larry Worth

Bing Crosby wasn't the only one dreamed of a winter wonderland. In Sandrine Veysset's debut film, seven kids in the French countryside continually wonder: "Will It Snow for Christmas?"

But that's as close as Veysset gets to the crooners warm and fuzzy holiday sentiments. In fact, she may have come up with the most depressing, least sentimental yuletide movie on record.

Ironically, that's not only its most appealing feature but the biggest drawback: While never taking the easy way out with cute kid shots, neither does Veysset give viewers much stake in their welfare.

The story unfolds on a rural Gallic farm as the kids labor in the field alongside their long-suffering mom. When making his occasional visits, dad treats them as cheap slave labor, saving his affections for his "real" wife and "legitimate" children on a nearby estate.

"Bastards should be kept hidden," declares the woman with his wedding ring, setting the tone for an ensuing maelstrom. But even then, Veysset underplays the emotional sparring to create more of a mood piece.

That nets mixed results. For instance, she purposely overbleaches all exterior shots as if to drain the picture-perfect locale of any beauty and romance. Good idea, except the characters prove equally colorless.

None of the children assumes much identity or exhibits distinct personality traits. The parents—who don't even get names, referred to only as father and mother—are somewhat underwritten, too.

Refusing to accept such limitations, Dominique Reymond's eyes communicate the mix of love, exhaustion and desperation that define the mother's existence. Reymond's efforts have already been recognized in France, where "Snow" earned her a best-actress accolade last year.

By the same token, Daniel Duval refuses to make the father into a cardboard villain. Even while barking out inhuman orders he conveys enough *je ne sai quoi* to justify the love of two women.

Indeed, "Will It Snow for Christmas?" isn't without gifts. But more thought should have gone into their wrapping.

NEWSDAY, 12/17/97, Part II/p. B11, John Anderson

Slavery is Steven Spielberg Official Territory this holiday season, the nobility of the oppressed has been co-opted by the Natalie Portman-powered "Diary of Anne Frank," and women's issues seem to have fallen, inadvertently enough, into Woody Allen's lap. Nothing, however, says more about enslavement, breeding-for-labor or the poetry of the powerless than one small French film by one 30-year-old Frenchwoman.

Had Jean Renoir used Dickens as a screenwriter, he might have conjured something, like "Will It Snow for Christmas?", whose elegant austerity is a holiday gift. Counterbalancing almost everything Americans get to see out of today's young French cinema—largely urban, largely angry—this debut feature by Sandrine Veysset is ultra-natural in its observations, deft in its control, and places the young director in the honorable and endangered Gallic tradition of rendering the archetypal out of the ordinary.

It's a deceptively simple story: On a dusty farm in the south of France, a mother (Dominique Reymond, who might be Juliette Binoche with a work history) lives with her seven illegitimate children. They are visited—all too frequently—by the children's father, who lives with his wife and older children on a nearby farm while using his "bastards" as cheap labor. Their unnamed mother is paid a wage, her needs are provided for begrudgingly; her children are treated like migrant workers and, barring an intrusion by social services, their plight is all but inescapable.

Generating equal parts affection and indignation, "Will It Snow?" is more than precise in its depictions of the main characters' motivations. The father is a miserly farmer, but he's less than evil. The mother, whose children adore her, is in denial about the harm being done her kids, at least until the father makes a pass at the oldest girl (an act we never see, and the details of which remain vague). She has no real recourse and her own feelings are always masked by devoted maternity.

Relating what has clearly been an oft-told tale, she regales the children with the story of a dream: God made her run a race, and when she lost, He sentenced her to have seven children. The kids themselves are delighted by their divine origin; the mother's sentiments are ripe for interpretation.

"Will It Snow for Christmas?" has an ending that's oblique to the point of irritation, but the film is both a parable and that rare movie that prompts us to ask who and what and where we are in relation to the work itself. Where Veysset puts us is in the corner, off to the side, occasionally treated to an intimacy with the characters, but more generally with restricted access to the mother and her happy children, making their bond all the more inviolate. We want to get in and we can't. The privilege bestowed by "Will It Snow for Christmas?" is that we're here at all.

SIGHT AND SOUND, 11/97, p. 57, Jane Clarke

A mother and her seven children live on a farm in rural France with no toilet, bathroom or proper heating. The farm is owned by the children's father who is married to someone else and lives with his other, official family on an estate called Cavaillon. He treats his mistress and the children badly, using them as cheap labour to work alongside his legitimate sons, Yvan and Bernard.

In the summer, the family works hard harvesting vegetables. The children fear their father, but they adore their mother. She struggles bravely to keep the children cheerful and ensures they have a relationship with their father, even when he disgusts her by chasing young women students working on the farm. The father insists the young children come to Cavaillon to plant cabbages. Homesick, they get into trouble by revealing their paternity to a neighbour.

Autumn comes and the children return to school. The mother works in the fields with her baby beside her. The father catches her talking with one of the workmen and flies into a jealous rage, but later makes a pass at his own eldest daughter Jeanne. In despair, the mother wants to leave but feels the children live a better life in the country than they would in a city council flat. For Christmas, she borrows a gas heater from the school, and spends all the money they have earned on presents. They have a candlelit feast, and then she pulls all the children's mattresses into one room with her and when they are asleep, turns the gas on. However, a bad dream wakes her; she sees that it's snowing and flings the window open, shakes all the children awake and makes them go play in the snow.

Will It Snow for Christmas?, Sandrine Veysset's remarkable first feature film about rural poverty and maternal passion, is peculiarly reminiscent of Chantal Akerman's *Jeanne Dielman 23, Quai du Commerce, 1080 Bruxelles* (1975). The similarity has less to do with the content of Veysset's film than with her insistence on showing everyday events as they are lived. just as Akerman made us watch her Belgian housewife going about her daily rituals, so Veysset forces us to look at areas of life rarely evoked in cinema. Repeatedly, we watch this woman, known only as Mother, and her seven children engaged in the back-breaking drudgery of farm work. Yet this is also a love story: she is a mother who is so deeply attached to her children, she contemplates killing them to save them from depending on a cruel father who may harbour incestuous feelings.

The opening pre-title sequence places the story firmly in the children's universe, as the camera follows the younger children crawling excitedly through tunnels made from bales of hay. We hear their shrieks of excitement as they chase each other and the camera twists and turns with them. In an exterior shot of a sunlit farmyard, the children play in the mud, creating their own farmyard and town. But the Edenic quality of these brief opening scenes gives way very quickly as a van draws up and their father calls them into the barn where they will sort onions for the rest of the day.

Against the innocence of the children is set the weary experience of the mother, both burdened and shored up by her love for her children. At one point she tells an anecdote that encapsulates the double-edged nature of these feelings. She tells the children of a dream she once had where she met God in a cave of light. She is forced to run a race with an enormously fat woman in order to be let free, and the other woman beats her. God says to her, "You've lost. Your punishment is that you'll have seven children". As she tells this story, the children huddle around her and climb onto her lap as the camera moves in tight on this family group. The framing suggests that her punishment, the seven children, is also her reward. The fact that she con-templates killing them later illustrates a further paradox, encountered occasionally in news stories: for a distressed parent, killing one's children can sometimes seem like an act of love.

Why does this film carry such a punch? I think its power lies in the way it mixes this heart-wrenching content with an intimate visual style. The extraordinarily natural, almost neo-realist, performances of Dominique Reymond as the mother and her seven children involve the viewer in the texture of these lives. The style favours handheld camera, while natural light and extreme close-ups place us right in the quick of the action and in the swirl of emotion. Events are brought so close, we cannot distance ourselves. Indeed, the film is almost shockingly intimate. All this is achieved without recourse to the usual musical means of manipulation. In fact, after the opening title song there is no music at all in the film until the very end when, at the deeply moving climax, a sorrowful song starts up: "Down comes the snow/And my heart is clad in black".

VILLAGE VOICE, 12/23/97, p. 79, J. Hoberman

Another sort of love story [The reference is to *Titanic;* see Hoberman's review], Sandrine Veysset's *Will It Snow for Christmas?* confines its disaster to a farm in southern France. The movie opens with a gaggle of cute towheads playing with toy animals until an outraged adult male puts them to work. A law unto himself, this studly peasant has fathered a second family of illegitimate children, using them and their fertility-goddess mother for unpaid labor.

Essentially timeless, *Will It Snow for Christmas* maps a pre-feudal social order in which unrestrained patriarchy enslaves the child-subjects of a benign, natural matriarch. What's best about the movie is its unblinking representation of physical work. Veysset's highly touted debut feature is remarkable for its scenes of picking cabbages, washing radishes, and sorting leeks, among other types of backbreaking labor in blazing sunlight. This concrete detail supports some highly abstract characterizations. The leads are only known as the Father, the Mother, and the Children. He's as stingy as she is generous, but they're both shining stars. Working like a mule scarcely impairs her innate chic; he's never less than debonair in demanding a mid-harvest quickie. The film never suggests the Mother might be Catholic; she presumably had all seven children for love. And what a wondrously well-behaved brood they are—making *The Brady Bunch* look like *Lord of the Flies.*

Will It Snow for Christmas? is talented and affecting, but it's as fake in its way as *Titanic.* The fairy tale here is just a bit more knowing. *Titanic* concludes with a tautological vision of the afterlife as first-class passage on the Ship of Dreams; the emotionally more complex *Will It Snow for Christmas?* introduces a gratuitous mysticism to sentimentalize the heaven-on-earth of its own shock ending.

Also reviewed in:
NEW REPUBLIC, 12/15/97, p. 28, Stanley Kauffmann
NEW YORK TIMES, 12/17/97, p. E1, Stephen Holden
VARIETY, 5/27-6/2/96, p. 74, Lisa Nesselson

WIND IN THE WILLOWS, THE

A Columbia Pictures and Allied Filmmakers release of a John Goldstone production. *Producer:* John Goldstone and Jake Eberts. *Director:* Terry Jones. *Screenplay:* Terry Jones. *Based on the novel "The Wind in the Willows" by:* Kenneth Grahame. *Director of Photography:* David Tattersall. *Editor:* Julian Doyle. *Music:* John Du Prez. *Choreographer:* Arlene Phillips. *Sound:* Andre Jacquemin. *Casting:* Irene Lamb. *Production Designer:* James Acheson. *Special Effects:* Peter Hutchinson. *Costumes:* James Acheson. *Make-up:* Jan Sewell. *Running time:* 87 minutes. *MPAA Rating:* PG.

CAST: Steve Coogan (Mole); Eric Idle (Rat); Terry Jones (Toad); Anthony Sher (Chief Weasel); Nicol Williamson (Badger); John Cleese (Mr. Toad's Lawyer); Stephen Fry (Judge); Bernard Hill (Engine Driver); Michael Palin (The Sun); Nigel Planer (Car Salesman); Julia Sawalha (Jailer's Daughter); Victoria Wood (Tea Lady); Robert Bathurst (St. John Weasel); Don Henderson (Sentry); Richard James (Geoffrey Weasel & Mole's Clock); Keith Lee Castle (Clarence Weasel); Roger Ashton-Griffiths (Prosecution Counsel); Bernard Padden (Clerk of the Court); Sarah Crowden (Samantha); Hugo Blick (Justin); William Lawrance (Policeman); Richard Ridings (Guard); Peter Whitfield (Detective 1); John Levitt (Detective 2); John Boswall (Elderly Gentleman); David Hatton (Booking Clerk); Graham McTavish (Drunken Weasel).

LOS ANGELES TIMES, 11/1/97, Calendar/p. 2, Kevin Thomas

Terry Jones' reworking of Kenneth Grahame's 1908 children's classic, "The Wind in the Willows," for the screen looks great but plays dull. Rather than zesty and engaging, it comes across as arch and tedious, too often mechanical and lifeless.

The pervasive, precious quality of the film suggests strongly that it would have been far better suited to the limitless possibilities of fantasy provided by animation than the photographic realism of live action.

One fine day timid Mole (Steve Coogan) finds his comfy, well-appointed subterranean home shaken as if by an earthquake. His pompous, idiotic friend Toad (Jones), heir to a grand English estate, has sold off its meadow, long Mole's home, to Weasel (Anthony Sher) to satisfy his cravings to purchase these newfangled machines, automobiles. Toad not only wrecks them as soon as he drives them but now this indulgence threatens his entire holdings.

It is Weasel's plan to erect a dog food factory on the meadow, which he has swiftly plowed over—thus the earthquake effect—and to tear down Toad's stately home and build a plant to process anything and everything supplied by destroying the riverbank that borders Toad's estate. But it's the riverbank that protects animals from the "wide world" into which Mole's friend Rat (Eric Idle) says neither he nor any of his friends, which includes Badger (Nicol Williamson), dare venture.

What we have here from Jones is an ultra-contemporary ecological message about as subtle as the giant meat grinder that is the centerpiece of Weasel's new factory. Such bald protest doesn't mesh well with the material's gossamer quality because the fable's characters, played by a swath of England's first-rate actors, lack depth and dimension. (A couple of wan musical numbers are of little help.) James Acheson's production and costume design is period perfection itself, full of whimsy and color, but this "Wind in the Willows" fails to work up much of a breeze.

NEW YORK POST, 10/31/97, p. 51, Thelma Adams

"The Wind in the Willows" is as welcome and wonderful as mucking about in a boat followed by a riverside picnic. It's simply the best live-action children's movie of the year—and that's not even employing the hyperbole of that glorious hedonist, Toad.

If you've never visited Toad Hall and the gang—Mole, Rat, Badger and the rest—get thee to a library. Kenneth Grahame's 1908 novel is one of the most beloved volumes of children's literature in the English language.

There have been animated "Willows" in the past, but Monty Python alum Terry Jones, who wrote the script, casts actors as Toad, et al., and sends them on a new adventure.

Jones himself steps into Toad's spry boots (and green pancake makeup), talking nonsense before snatching a fly from the air with a perfectly awful pink tongue. What a grand nincompoop! I's Toad's love for motorcars and his inability to drive them that gets all the animals on the river in trouble with the Weasels (Anthony Sher chief among them). Both the insecure Mole (Steve Coogan) and the gruff Badger (Nicol Williamson) lose their homes as a result, and Rat's (Eric Idle) beloved river turns to mud.

Jones, who directed "Monty Python's the Meaning of Life" and "Life of Brian," captures what it is that children and adults love about the great children's books—"Alice in Wonderland" or "The Wizard of Oz."

We enter a world that's a mirror image of our own. Through the looking glass, magic can happen and animals can talk, but they're really saying all the things we'd like to say and doing all the things we'd like to do, foolish or not.

Because these books rarely preach or judge and ring true to human behavior, they have longevity; they continue to entertain both young and old. Jones' fabulous "Wind in the Willows" fits into this category.

Yes, there are lessons to be learned about community and friendship, self-interest and greed, but we'd all be nincompoops if we stressed that over the pure pleasure of being in the delightful company of Mole, Rat, Badger and old "greenhead" himself, Toad.

The Python influence is as strong as Grahame's characters. John Cleese steals a scene as Toad's defense attorney, a lawyer who finds his client indefensible. Michael Palin shines as the sun. And Toad even does drag, dressing in a tea lady's frock to escape prison and flouncing about the countryside in heels and bonnet. How jolly!

SIGHT AND SOUND, 11/96, p. 63, Geoffrey Macnab

One morning, while spring cleaning in his burrow, Mole is interrupted by a huge trembling. He ventures to the surface to discover a bulldozer above him. In fright, he hurries to the riverbank. Here, he runs across Rat, who is preparing a picnic. Rat invites Mole to join him. They set off in a boat. Eventually Rat and Mole reach Toad Hall. They tell Toad what has happened to Mole's home. Toad admits he sold the field to the untrustworthy weasels, but insists he had no idea they were going to destroy Mole's burrow. The three go on an expedition in Mole's brand new caravan. All are in good spirits until they're almost driven off the road by the very latest invention, a motorcar. Excited, Toad decides to buy a car for himself.

Over the following weeks, Toad crashes dozens of cars. The weasels provide him with new vehicles, but make him sign away most of his property. Rat and Mole ask their wise old friend, Badger, for advice. Despite their efforts, Toad is soon hauled up in court, charged with stealing someone else's car, and sentenced to 100 years in prison. The weasels take over the riverbank and build an enormous dog food factory. The next scheme is to destroy Toad Hall. Rat and Mole resolve to help Toad escape jail so he can save his ancestral home. But Toad has already bought his own freedom by making a deal with the jailer's daughter and the tea lady. Toad, Rat, Mole and Badger escape the authorities by leaping onto a high speed train. They avoid being minced at the dog food factory, and when the Chief Weasel tries to blow up the Hall, his factory goes up instead—Rat has switched the explosives.

Toad vows to give up his wild ways. But one afternoon, while the others are celebrating at a Regatta, he sneaks off. Before they can stop him, he has taken to the air in his brand new glider.

Much of the enduring appeal of Kenneth Grahame's novel, The Wind in the Willows (first published in 1908, though not well known until the 20s) surely lies in its mood of yearning. It's a gentrified, Home Counties version of the Falstaff myth; a lament for a Merrie England of rivers, meadows and rolling country lanes, but also an attempt at summoning up the lost innocence of childhood. Grahame's vision was essentially reactionary: his idealised little world was a buffer against the forces of modernity. The best way to deal with society beyond the woods was to ignore it ("Don't ever refer to it again," Rat tells Mole) and to hope it went away.

Adapting Grahame's story 88 years on inevitably blurs the focus. Now, the nostalgia is not just for a vanished pastoral idyll but for the Edwardian era itself. By one of those odd heritage industry ironies, the early 1900s England, which Grahame professed to hate, becomes part of the Wind in the Willows package. In his preface to his recent stage adaptation of the novel, Alan Bennett suggests that the "Wild Wooders", avaricious weasels, were intended by Grahame as symbols of the "militant proletariat." In the film, by another reversal, they're treated as arch-Thatcherite yuppies. (At times this even seems like an allegory about infighting in the Tory party, with Toad as the old-style 'Shire Tory' and the chief weasel as his modern-day nemesis.)

Characters aren't decked out in full animal costume, but are each given one or two attributes of the creatures they're playing. This Toad has sickly green skin, an enormous embonpoint, and an elastic, long-reaching tongue, Rat is dressed in blazer and boating cap, but has whiskers and a tail, while Mole wears a miner's helmet for barrowing. Most of the cast appear to be doing pantomime turns rather than giving performances. Anthony Sher plays the Chief Weasel as if he's Brecht's Arturo Ui, a little Hitler on the make. As Badger, a saturnine soul whose lair is deep in the bowels of the earth, Nicol Williamson seems at times to be reprising his Merlin from John Boorman's Excalibur while Michael Palin smiles down at the world with his most unctuous grin as the sun.

Toad, Rat warns Mole, is boastful and conceited: he is obsessed with machinery, speed and explosions; enjoys the sound of his own voice and always takes credit for other people's efforts. The same might be said of Terry Jones, who writes, directs, stars (appropriately enough as Toad) and provides some of the music. Just as Toad quickly grows bored of river trips and leisurely caravan journeys, Jones (who has Monty Python and the Holy Grail, Monty Python's Life of Brian, and Monty Python's the Meaning of Life to his credit, and Erik the Viking to his discredit) seems to have become exasperated with the rambling, episodic nature of his source material. By trying to inject danger and conflict he risks destroying the whimsical, evanescent quality of the original. Rat may talk of the pleasures of "messing about on the river," but there's precious little time for picnics here. From the opening in which bulldozers trample over Mole's home, to the high voltage denouement, the pace is frantic. The comedy and the songs have a forced, desperate quality, as if the filmmakers aren't quite sure whether they're pitching at an adult or child audience, and think that making a lot of noise is the best way of grabbing the attention of both.

At times, Jones resorts to the style of bawdy, carnivalesque humour that he helped patent in his *Monty Python* days. The knockabout sketches in which Toad's prison lawyer John Cleese in best Basil Fawlty-mode) gets him sentenced to 100 years in prison, or where a lusty guard is taken in by Toad's tea-lady disguise and tries to kiss him, are funny enough in themselves, but such hyperbolic burnout has precious little to do with Grahame's fey little fantasy world. The grindingly unfunny sequences set in the dog food Factory, which seems to have been copied straight from Chaplin's *Modern Times*, offer laboured visual gags about spanners in the works, and end up stalling the narrative in the process.

The film occasionally quickens into life. It benefits from witty anthropomorphism (rabbits dressed in Edwardian bicycling outfits kissing under hedgerows). It sometimes catches the sense of yearning which runs through the book (for instance, Rat's dewy-eyed description of the perfect winter picnic) and even works up a head of steam during an exhilarating, if pointless, railway chase. At least, this *Wind in the Willows* isn't mawkish: the loud humour and slapstick keep smug, treacly Home Counties sentiment at bay.

There's no attempt to hint at the dark underside of the story, Grahame's own unhappy marriage and the subsequent suicide of the son for whom he wrote the book. Above all, the film seems a testament to the Toad-like egotism of its director. The amphibious hero suffers from a "dementia brought about by motor cars." Movie cameras unhinge Jones in the same way if this recklessly self-indulgent offering is anything to go by.

Also reviewed in:
NEW YORK TIMES, 10/31/97, p. E24, Lawrence Van Gelder
VARIETY, 11/3-9/97, p. 99, Todd McCarthy

WINGS OF THE DOVE, THE

A Miramax Films release of a Renaissance Films production. *Executive Producer:* Bob Weinstein, Harvey Weinstein, and Paul Feldsher. *Producer:* Stephen Evans and David Parfitt. *Director:* Iain Softley. *Screenplay:* Hossein Amini. *Inspired by the novel by:* Henry James. *Director of Photography:* Eduardo Serra. *Editor:* Tariq Anwar. *Music:* Ed Shearmur. *Music Editor:* Tim Handley and Dashiell Rae. *Choreographer:* Stuart Hopps. *Sound:* Peter Lindsay and (music) Steve McLaughlin. *Sound Editor:* Martin Evans, Matt Grime, Nick Lowe, Nigel Mills, and Mike Wood. *Casting:* Michelle Guish. *Production Designer:* John Beard. *Art Director:* Andrew Sanders. *Set Decorator:* Joanne Woollard. *Costumes:* Sandy Powell. *Make-up:* Sallie Jaye. *Running time:* 101 minutes. *MPAA Rating:* R.

CAST: Helena Bonham Carter (Kate Croy); Linus Roache (Merton Densher); Alison Elliott (Millie Theale); Charlotte Rampling (Aunt Maude); Elizabeth McGovern (Susan); Michael Gambon (Kate's Father); Alex Jennings (Lord Mark); Ben Miles (Journalist 1); Philip Wright (Journalist 2); Alexander John (Butler); Shirley Chantrell (Opium Den Lady); Diana Kent (Merton's Party Companion); Georgio Serafini (Eugenio); Rachele Crisafulli (Concierge).

LOS ANGELES TIMES, 11/7/97, Calendar/p. 2, Kenneth Turan

Despite a dense, convoluted writing style that makes no concessions to readers in a hurry, magisterial novelist Henry James has lately become a favorite of movie-makers. This last year has seen Jane Campion's "Portrait of a Lady," Agnieszka Holland's "Washington Square" and now Iain Softley's unlikely success with "The Wings of the Dove," which against some odds turns out to be the most emotionally involving of the group.

As written by Hossein Amini, who also did the adaptation for "Jude," this is inevitably a stripped-down version of James, with the novel's plot pared away and rerouted and everything so plainly stated that James purists are likely to get all huffy if they even bother to see the film at all.

But for everyone else, even simplified James is more complex and absorbing than most of what reaches the screen. The author's great underlying themes and his gift for character are all in play here and help make this melancholy story of love, delusion and misguided sacrifice unexpectedly moving and satisfying.

Like many of James' novels, "The Wings of the Dove" examines lovers and would-be lovers trapped in a limbo between the avaricious, cynical and status-obsessed world of Europe and the more innocent and open society of newly wealthy America, invariably represented by a young and vulnerable heiress. It shows that though the webs convention spins may be gossamer-thin, they bind like steel. And it unmistakably illustrates how both the possession of money and the zeal to acquire it can lead to genteel but crushing tragedy.

In telling this story, director Softley and his crew (including cinematographer Eduardo Serra, production designer John Beard and costume designer Sandy Powell) have in part taken the Merchant Ivory approach. "Wings of the Dove" is richly appointed and beautifully mounted, with lush location shooting in Venice given the place of honor.

But Softley and screenwriter Amini have gone further, adding a decidedly bodice-ripper tone to the proceedings. "Wings" features sexual encounters, nudity and a visit to an opium den, and its embracing of pulp rapture is reminiscent of the director's debut, the Beatles-themed "Backbeat."

"Wings" also takes advantage of subtle acting across the board especially from star Helena Bonham Carter. Physically at home at the turn of the century as few other actresses are, Bonham Carter, who graced both "A Room With a View" and "Howards End," here gives her most mature performance to date. She conveys romantic longing and passion both repressed and expressed, and even convincingly wears the enormous and elaborate hats of the period.

Her character, Kate Croy, is introduced just after she has been acquired as a ward by her aunt, the commanding and aristocratic Maude (Charlotte Rampling). Maude gives Kate clothes, jewels and status and also provides funds for the girl's reprobate father, but there is of course a price to paid. Kate is forbidden to marry for love alone or do anything else that might offend the sensibilities of the status-obsessed ruling class.

This is a problem because Kate is in love with the radical journalist Merton Densher (Linus Roache of "Priest"). He wants to marry her as soon as possible, but Kate, "not good at being impulsive," is also reluctant to jeopardize both her own and her father's security.

Also the year is 1910 (moved up nearly a decade from the book's setting), a time when society's strictures are beginning to come undone. Women are smoking, enjoying erotica and starting to take offense when men say, "There's far too much going on behind those pretty lashes." Why, Kate is thinking, can't both money and love be available to her?

Then American heiress Millie Theale (Alison Elliott), "the world's richest orphan," appears in London. Impulsive, warm-hearted and free-spirited, she becomes fast friends with Kate, but that doesn't mean the women share all their secrets. Millie is not told about Merton, and when Kate finds out the real reason for her friend's trip to Europe, she constructs a nervy plan that is fraught with more peril than she can imagine.

A lot of actresses have played James' susceptible heiresses over the years, from Cybill Shepherd in "Daisy Miller" to Nicole Kidman in "Portrait of a Lady." So it's saying quite a bit to note that almost no one has caught the requisite artlessness and lack of affectation as well as Elliott. As different here from the role she played in "Spitfire Grill" as that was from Steven Soderbergh's "The Underneath," Elliott has that rare chameleon-like ability to become truly different people every time she appears on screen.

Finally, however, the success of this film rests on the work of Bonham Carter. Though the filmmakers have smartly placed her in a more positive light than James did, Kate is still an ambiguous character, a causer of pain but also heartbreaking when she says, "I hurt so much, you can't imagine." As the personification of the unknowability, the unpredictability of the human heart, her performance is outstanding.

NEW YORK, 10/10/97, p. 60, David Denby

Agnieszka Holland's recent adaptation of the early Henry James novel *Washington Square* was an abrupt and fiery affair, with people shouting and throwing themselves about. But the new *The Wings of the Dove*, adapted from one of James's last books, from 1902, is passionate in a different style—quieter, with a fine-textured, sustained directness that builds to a considerable intensity. *The Wings of the Dove* is about money, class, and sexual desire: it's also about the varieties of control and duplicity—people hiding their motives, lying to help others but also to advance their own interests. The movie gives deception an almost voluptuous power and danger: Deception becomes a form of seduction; it is also a snake that coils and then strikes itself. The director, Iain Softley, *(Backbeat)*, a Brit, brings us close to faces whose mysteries we try to penetrate and decipher. The evenness of the movie's tone, and its alert, lambent attention to its complex characters, is satisfying and even exciting in an old-fashioned way.

The movie differs from James's novel in a hundred particulars, but the great point is that it works on its own terms, which is all one can ask. What, after all, are filmmakers to do with a book that begins with the following sentence: "She waited, Kate Croy, for her father to come in, but he kept her unconscionably and there were moments at which she showed herself, in the glass over the mantel, a face positively pale with the irritation that had brought her to the point of going away without sight of him"? The way that extraordinary sentence circles back on itself suggests Kate's confinement and frustration, and I suppose that such a state of mind could be conveyed by slowly turning the camera back to a starting point. But a director proceeding this way moment by moment would never get anywhere. James, in his elaborate and super-subtle later books, did not write filmable scenes; *The Wings of the Dove* consists of dense pages of analysis and bursts of highly elliptical dialogue. But James, it turns out, also has a superb story to tell, and Softley and the screenwriter Hossein Amini deftly pluck it out. Coping with James's inexhaustible sensitivity, they have made everything more brisk, decisive, and direct—and in a few cases crude—but they have not falsified the core of James's great novel.

At the center, there are two young people who love each other but need money. Kate Croy (Helena Bonham Carter), clever, beautiful, and distinguished, lives in London with her wealthy aunt (Charlotte Rampling), who is determined to marry her off to a rich man and who does what she can to break up Kate's relationship with the charming but penurious young journalist Merton Densher (Linus Roache). I regret that I once intimated in these pages that Helena Bonham Carter was too short to play starring roles. Short she is, but her dark eyes and piled dark hair give off an almost witchlike allure. She has become a confident and powerful actress. We are drawn to Bonham Carter's intelligence, even though her Kate is calculating and unromantic—not a brave enough person to live with Densher in poverty. Kate plays for the largest stakes; she wants her handsome young man and she wants to be rich, too. By degrees, and without his quite understanding it, Densher gets pulled into a conspiracy that Kate engineers. For there is another young person in their social circle, the fabulously wealthy American heiress Millie Theale (Alison Elliott), who is sweet, generous, and wasting away from some nameless disease (leukemia, perhaps). Millie needs a lover; she needs to live. Kate, who genuinely likes her, wants Millie to be happy and to know love—with Densher, who would then inherit the money, after Millie's death, that would allow Kate to marry him. Kate's motives are mixed, both selfless and selfish, benevolent and sinister, and she corrupts Densher with her provocative ambivalence.

Linus Roache, the lead in *Priest,* has an open, handsome face and a fine profile, and in this movie he is suave yet incisive, too, and convincingly ardent. His Densher is meant, I think, to be a kind of cultivated masculine ideal. Because he's such a splendid fellow, Densher's puzzlement as Kate pushes him into Millie's arms is painful; his anger and sexual aggression as he realizes how he is being used become the dramatic high point of the movie. The complicating factor—Henry James always has a complicating factor—is that Densher falls for Millie; or rather, he falls for her desire to experience everything she can before dying. Alison Elliott, as Millie, is merely good—soft, smiling, intelligent, a woman who lights up when an attractive man pays her attention.

The filmmakers have aggressively bumped the period ahead from 1902 to 1910; the characters take the subway and dodge automobiles; they smoke cigarettes furiously and attend a gallery exhibit of Klimt's decadent nudes. The women are dressed in the new looser clothes, and at the end of the movie, Bonham Carter slowly removes her corset and is naked. We get the point: Kate Croy and Merton Densher are modern personalities, rebels against the constrictions of their time (they seem to have skipped over the Edwardian period into the twenties). Rebellion is certainly not something that Henry James had in mind, but it's a minor vulgarization.

The movie begins in sumptuous private dwellings in London, and moves to Venice, the mysterious, labyrinthine, sensuously overwhelming Venice where death lurks in the very pursuit of pleasure. Softley shows us the jostling gondolas in the darkened canals at night and the swirling gaiety of a masked ball. In the dark city, perversities of will and desire swiftly unfold, and betrayal gives way to self-betrayal. Despite an immense simplification of the novel, *The Wings of the Dove* is still the most complexly motivated, the most noble, pathetic, and emotionally involving movie around.

NEW YORK POST, 11/7/97, p. 57, Thelma Adams

Dark water shimmers in a Venetian canal. A silver-laden table drips lobsters. A woman's hat is a universe unto itself, an overturned cornucopia. Riding "The Wings of the Dove" is a visual swoon.

We have entered Merchant Ivory territory, but the images are, overripe, as intoxicating as opium, as fetid as day-old caviar. This is "Masterpiece Theater" as if directed by Peter Greenaway looking over Gustav Klimt's shoulder.

In beauty there's death. And in "The Wings of the Dove" there are a few surprises.

The first is that Iain Softley directed this baleful romance. Neither "Backbeat" nor "Hackers," his precocious debut and American sellout, prepared us for this lovers' triangle set in London and Venice in 1910.

Surprise two: Henry James has never been so sexy. His chilly 1902 novel has been adapted by Hossein Amini with a loner's slow hand. Don't expect to skim the pages of "Wings" and find lovers coupling in a Venetian alley or sealing their love's end on a big brass bed in a shabby bed-sitter.

The final surprise is Helena Bonham Carter. Under Softley's direction, the Merchant Ivory poster girl ripens from that exquisite object of desire in a "A Room With a View." Carter descends from her ivory tower to embody penniless, but smoldering, Kate Croy.

Kate is the focus of intense familial manipulaiion. Her father (Michael Gambon) is an opium addict. To sustain his habit, he bartered his daughter to his dead wife's sister.

Wealthy Aunt Maude (Charlotte Rampling) takes Kate under her wing and introduces her to polite society—but at a price. Kate must renounce her father and her beau, a poor journalist named Merton Densher (seductively underplayed by Linus ["Priest"] Roache).

Then Kate meets Millie Theale (a glistening Alison Elliott), a wealthy American orphan with a troubling pallor. By throwing Millie and Merton together, Kate schemes to have it all: impoverished writer and the fortune that will buy her access to society.

One of the themes of "The Wings of the Dove"—a phrase that refers to the soul's ascent to heaven—is that corruption, as one character says, "is a gradual process." Kate's shortcut to happiness, her attempt to manipulate love, becomes a slippery slope to hell.

Softley suavely moves Kate, Merton and Millie to Venice, a city that is as aesthetically pleasing as it is physically rotting. The three cannot survive the test of this deceptively romantic backdrop: Kate's actions darken, Merton's loyalty divides, Millie becomes more angelic as she approaches death.

Softley offers a bold and sensual conclusion to his bold and sensual adaptation, but it's sadly bereft of an emotional payoff, like sex cut off from love, labored and without feeling. At the very end, Softley loses his "Wings," but Carter and Roache are heaven-sent.

SIGHT AND SOUND, 1/98, p. 55, Peter Matthews

London, 1910. After the death of her mother, Kate Croy becomes the ward of her wealthy aunt Maude who hopes to unite Kate to Lord Mark. Although in love with journalist Merton Densher, Kate renounces him. Kate meets American heiress Milly Theale. The two become friends, but Lord Mark is also attracted to Milly. Hoping to meet Kate, Merton crashes another party with an older woman. He follows Kate to the billiard room, where she gives vent to her jealousy. The two kiss passionately. Later, Milly runs into Kate, who introduces her to Merton. Milly is attracted to him. Lord Mark invites Kate and Milly to his country estate. One night, he reveals to Kate that Milly is terminally ill. He proposes to marry Milly for her money; after she dies, he and Kate can live off the inheritance. Kate angrily repulses him. Later, Milly asks Merton to join her and Kate on a holiday excursion to Venice.

In Venice, Kate informs Merton of Milly's illness and of her suspicion that the heiress is in love with him. Kate suggests that he seduce Milly to make her final days happy. Kate returns to London but, having second thoughts, visits Lord Mark who goes to Venice to tell Milly of Merton's ongoing affair with Kate. Merton denies everything, but Milly says it doesn't matter: she loves both her friends. Shortly after, Milly dies. In London, Kate arrives at Merton's flat bearing Milly's last letter which he refuses. Merton tells Kate he plans to abandon any claim to Milly's money. Kate agrees to marry him if he will give his word that he is not in love with Milly's memory. Merton is silent.

One of the most compelling reasons to see this film of Henry James' novel *The Wings of the Dove* is that the frocks are magnificent. Costume designer Sandy Powell has outfitted the two female leads in a series of plush, semi-stylised creations which are a pleasure to gawk at, but which also underscore the story's basic meanings and contrasts. Dazzling but darkly passionate and devious, Kate Croy is arrayed in dramatic blues and blacks, varied at one crucial juncture by flaming scarlet. Her victim, ardent, naive and mortally sick Milly Theale, appears in verdant floral patterns which grow progressively paler and culminate in pure, angelic whites. Since James is a celebrated master of the oblique, it's cunning of Powell and director Iain Softley to have largely relegated expression of character motivation to the *mise en scéne*. James himself was usually too caught up in the convolutions of consciousness to bother with much external description, but the film-makers have found a way to flesh out his cerebral universe without sacrificing its core of ambiguity.

Softley and screenwriter Hossein Amini should perhaps be awarded a medal of valour for undertaking this movie at all. It's easy to understand why film-makers have generally opted for the works of James' middle period before his narrative form dissolved into sheer nuance and equivocation. First published in 1902, *The Wings of the Dove* is a prime example of late James, so one could get light-headed from pondering all its imponderables.

Does Milly Theale find a friend or an implacable enemy in Kate Croy? Is Kate scheming to prop up the illusions of a dying girl or is she acting from self interest? And is Milly herself entirely the ethereal dove of the title or is she also playing a game with people's hearts?

James' mature fiction exasperates some people because it's hard to grasp at anything substantial. The stealthily dropped hints and circumlocutions become the whole subject. There was probably no way to preserve the book's tortuously rarefied tone without antagonising half the audience. However, Softley and Amini have done a smooth job of desublimating the text to the acceptable dimensions of a costume drama. It's a slightly dull one, because it leaves out James' fine-spun critical intelligence and all that remains is an attenuated upper-class atmosphere where nothing much happens. Softley may have recognised the problem, since he tries to bestir the viewer with visual tricks—overhead shots, complicated dissolves, endless tracking—producing a statelier version of his MTV style in two earlier pictures, *Backbeat* and *Hackers*.

There's also the now-customary attempt (pioneered by Jane Campion in *The Portrait of a Lady*) to sex up the notoriously celibate James. Kate and her illicit lover Merton Densher do it like rutting animals down a squalid alleyway. Then, they do it again with more melancholy when their well-laid plans have gone awry. Everyone (including poor Milly) must be brought down to the universal itch. The film-makers have updated the story to 1910, presumably to take advantage of the lifting of Victorian repression. The sumptuous production design (by John Beard) explicitly invokes the sensuality of Pre-Raphaelite and Decadent art. But there's an additional, more strictly cinematic reference point to *film noir*: shrouded in shadows, Kate becomes a sort of Ur-*femme fatale*, making Merton her libidinal confederate and Milly the chump.

Sadly, Amini's script goes and spoils it all by making the protagonists sympathetic. James certainly takes account of the harsh economic realities determining Kate's ruinous course, but he remains too much the nineteenth century patrician to view her as other than a pushy modern materialist, while the finer grained Milly is idealised as "the heir of the ages". One can appreciate why Milly's more difficult attributes have been junked and her character humanised. What's more objectionable is the movie's softening of Kate, who is turned into a rebel against stuffy bourgeois convention. Though you can't exactly blame the film-makers for modulating James' snobbish moralism, the shift in emphasis effectively eliminates the story's sense of nameless evil: it becomes a tale of some nice, misguided people, and that's about it. Softley and Amini haven't licked the perennial problem of how to modernise a classic writer whose greatness depends on attitudes completely foreign to us. This skilful, graceful movie is a good deal more *likeable* than the book, but therein lies the whole difficulty.

VILLAGE VOICE, 11/11/97, p. 88, Leslie Camhi

The enigma of personality was something Henry James explored in prose as oblique and inward-turning as thought. *The Wings of the Dove*, his 1902 novel, focuses intently on the uncertain motivations of a few confused people. Director Iain Softley's artful adaptation relies heavily on physiognomy and fin de siècle trappings, but manages to preserve a good deal of the story's ambiguity.

Kate Croy (Helena Bonham Carter)—beautiful, minxlike, and willful—has become the ward of her fabulously wealthy Aunt Maude (Charlotte Rampling) after her mother's death and father's precipitous social decline. Maude intends to provide for Kate as long as she marries a suitable, aristocratic suitor. But Kate loves Merton Densher (Linus Roache), a principled but penniless journalist with the sensitive face of a wounded puppy.

Softley has moved the story forward to 1910, setting it more emphatically in this century and linking the couple's passionate trysts—in elevators and the brand-new Tube—with the sleeping currents of modernity. Soon a red-haired young American imbued with democratic values arrives to shake up London high society. Millie Theale (Alison Elliott), perfectly pleasant and "the world's richest orphan," soon captivates all the cash-poor aristocrats whose castles need repairing. Millie's secret (known to some) is that she's dying, of an unnamed illness with few apparent symptoms. The young women with their sad mysteries are drawn to each other but keep separate counsels, and Millie soon falls for Kate's "friend," Merton. On an impromptu trip to Venice, Kate—filled with cryptic ambition—devises a plan to soothe all their suffering, and the three become locked in a triangle whose sides are continually shifting.

Softley's prewar London is faintly reminiscent of the '60s in its love affair with the accoutrements of exoticism (Egyptianate fashions, neo-Moorish architecture, Gustav Klimt paintings), though not in its stuffy, hidebound conventions. With a permanent whiff of scandal about her, Charlotte Rampling's Aunt Maude seems less a model of Victorian propriety, than a wily, wealthy bohemian. The women look wonderful in their sealskin coats, black-and-yellow striped skirts, green mink-lined embroidered cloaks, and serpentine, plumed turbans, as well as, later on, in Venice, where they're clothed in Fortuny.

The director's Venice is carnal and carnivalesque, its cathedrals and fish markets equally overpowering; but the city's ethereal magic at night is something he grasps for and misses. Similarly, he's better at rendering the cunning and sensual Kate and her beautiful, indecisive beau than he is at drawing the lines of Millie's more transendent character. Finally, his film errs where the medium usually does on the side of the literal and the fleshly, when its subject is memory and the spirit.

VILLAGE VOICE, 11/25/97, p. 100, David Yaffe

With paragraphs that sprawl for pages, verbs that are as inactive as nouns, and that have to be absorbed like individual lines of a lyric poem, Henry James's *The Wings of the Dove* hardly screams box office boffo. In order to convert the novel into marketable product, director Iain Softley replaced semi-colons with sex, risking the alienation of Jamesian literalists in favor of mainstream success. One of those Jamesians, biographer Fred Kaplan, was approached by Miramax to help them market the film. Kaplan agreed to watch the movie and demanded no money up front (a decision he says he later regretted). Once he made his views known, Miramax looked elsewhere.

Though finding it "visually beautiful and interesting," Kaplan says now that he feels certain no one but Hossein Amini had actually read James's daunting book, and that even Amini seemed deaf to the subtleties of James's tone. Much of the novel is about absence: we never learn the particulars about Millie's illness, Lionel Croy's "unmentionable deed," or the physicality of Merton and Kate's lovemaking; the film literalizes all these mysteries. Kaplan also quarrels with the film's change of setting from 1902 to 1910—in no way neccessary for the film's representation of trains, phones, or clothes. "If it were my film," says Kaplan, "I would have said, 'Fuck that.' In 1902, the underground was already in place, the phones were already in place, probably even the lift in the subway station was in place. Don't stir up people who know the novel."

But Kaplan considered the film's time shift unimportant compared with its depiction of Kate Croy (Helena Bonham Carter). "The movie turns her into a manipulative schemer, an insecure Romantic who loses her nerve at the last minute. In the novel, she never loses her nerve." And Kaplan says the last few minutes would have horrified the prudish James." The final scene was anti-James in every way. Kate Croy is naked. She has been depicted throughout the film as materially ruthless and now is using sex to get what she wants. The scene in the film is the act of two characters very different from the characters in the novel. The sex scenes are well done, but have nothing to do with the novel. But they have a lot to do with how a modern writer and audience might rewrite *Wings* to reflect not James and his times, but us and now."

Also reviewed in:
CHICAGO TRIBUNE, 11/14/97, Friday/p. A, Michael Wilmington
NEW REPUBLIC, 12/1/97, p. 32, Stanley Kauffmann
NEW YORK TIMES, 11/7/97, P. E16, Stephen Holden
NEW YORKER, 11/10/97, p. 121, Daphne Merkin
VARIETY, 9/8-14/97, p. 76, David Stratton
WASHINGTON POST, 11/14/97, p. D7, Rita Kempley

WINNER, THE

A Live Entertainment release of a Mark Damon Productions presentation in association with Village Roadshow-Cupsal Film Partnership of a Ken Schwenkar production. *Executive Producer:* Mark Damon and Rebecca DeMornay. *Producer:* Kenneth Schwenker. *Director:* Alex Cox. *Screenplay (based on her play "A Darker Purpose"):* Wendy Riss. *Director of Photography:* Denis Maloney. *Editor:* Carlos Puente. *Music:* Daniel Licht. *Music Editor:* Mark Killian, David J. Bondelevitch, and Carlos Puente. *Sound:* Mark Ulano and (music) Larry Mah. *Sound Editor:* Christopher Sheldon and Perry Robertson. *Casting:* Jeanne McCarthy. *Production Designer:* Cecilia Montiel. *Art Director:* Felipe Fernandez. *Set Designer:* Paul Meraz. *Special Effects:* J.D. Streett. *Costumes:* Nancy Steiner. *Make-up:* Desne Holland. *Stunt Coordinator:* Dan Bradley. *Running time:* 90 minutes. *MPAA Rating:* R.

CAST: Rebecca DeMornay (Louise); Vincent D'Onofrio (Philip); Richard Edson (Frankie); Saverio Guerra (Paulie); Delroy Lindo (Frank Kingman); Michael Madsen (Johnny, 'Wolf'); Billy Bob Thornton (Jack); Frank Whaley (Joey); Luis Contreras (Guy in Couple); Ed Pansullo (Man with Broken Arm); Sy Richardson (Bartender); Craig Vincent (Man); Biff Yeager (Philip's Father); Del Zamora (Cellmate); Roger Jennings (Croupier); Alex Cox (Gaston).

LOS ANGELES TIMES, 7/25/97, Calendar/p. 20, John Anderson

[The following review by John Anderson appeared in a slightly different form in NEWSDAY, 7/25/97, Part II/p. B8.]

Three low-rent operators named Frankie, Paulie and Joey (Richard Edson, Saverio Guerra and Frank Whaley) are sittin' around a decrepit desert bus station, contemplating the most recent phenomenon in nearby Las Vegas: a roulette-playing idiot savant who only bets on Sundays and hasn't lost in weeks. How, they ask, can they avail themselves of his good luck?

If only his name weren't Philip, Joey says. If only it were something significant—like, maybe, Jesus. "I need a sign!" he says. And one promptly falls off the bus station wall.

Careening between baggy-pants comedy and film noir parody and shored up by really terrific performances by Rebecca DeMornay and Whaley, Alex Cox's "The Winner" seems to have everything you need—or that Hollywood thinks it needs—for success. There is DeMornay's Louise, the sexy singer-hooker with the heart of gold; a Christ figure/angel *manque* in the spaced-out Philip (Vincent D'Onofrio); a psychopath, in Philip's brother Johnny (Michael Madsen);

broad comedy, from the three aforementioned stooges; a scary man with power (Delroy Lindo's unhappy casino owner); and Billy Bob Thornton in a really bad rug.

Set in Las Vegas, which has become the Monument Valley of postmodern movie America and where the dream of something for nothing can be tarted up like a middle-class tax cut, "The Winner" is a goof. A very stylish goof, but a goof just the same. Its story mines numerous noir clichés, in a way that's almost disarmingly blunt: Louise owes money to the mob. Philip falls in love with her and promises her salvation at the roulette table. Johnny, who arrives in town with their dead father over his shoulders, has a history with Louise (so does everyone else). Kingman (Lindo) and his henchman Jack (Thornton) are plotting. The manic Joey perpetrates a blood bath. The plot line spins off into a vaporous nexus of met expectations, where the only mooring is incongruity.

Where Cox takes his hard left, of course, is in the character of Philip, as unlikely an American as possible: Until he meets Louise, he doesn't care if he wins or loses. Some people might be tempted to say the same about the English-born Cox, who since "Repo Man" and "Sid and Nancy" has been flying well below the radar (the mostly Spanish-language "Highway Patrolman" was quite good, and different, but got limited exposure).

"The Winner" is not an uninteresting film—the Wendy Riss script is smart, Denis Maloney's cinematography is fluid and Cox is a gifted filmmaker. But it *is* a joke. And to really enjoy it, I'm afraid, you have to want to *get* the joke.

NEW YORK POST, 7/25/97, p. 48, Thelma Adams

Alex Cox's stylish, brassy black comedy follows a gaggle of Las Vegas losers as they try to fleece "The Winner."

Vincent D'Onofrio ("Men in Black") is Philip, a loser on a mystical winning streak, a lonely bear with a thorn in his paw. As his brother, Michael Madsen is still paddling around in "Reservoir Dogs" territory. His howling Wolf with a wiggle in his hips is a felon capable of untold violence and obscene sexual magnetism.

Lounge singer Louise (Rebecca DeMornay, who also served as executive producer) has had both men, but she wants to go out on a winner. DeMornay tingles with tackiness, unafraid to be funny and freaky simultaneously. Squeezed into bras beyond wonder, she slings her breasts around like a rodeo rider casting a lariat.

Billy Bob Thornton tickles under a toupee; Delroy Lindo waxes mysterious; Frank Whaley whacks out again, the crazy little creep under the Bob's Big Boy 'do. Richard Edson, a fixture on the independent scene, offers his ugly mug as a foil for those actors in on the action.

Originally shown on cable TV, "The Winner" was wrongfully resurrected as a tease for lovers of renegade director Cox's "Sid and Nancy," 'Repo Man" and the profoundly mysterious, rarely seen, Spanish-language "Highway Patrolman"—"The Winner" turns out to be a freeway off ramp to nowhere. Despite Cox's visual inventiveness, it's a dead-end ensemble comedy. Working from Wendy Riss' hip but hapless script, Cox gets his wild characters stirred up and speeding along; then he shoots all his guns, turns off the lights and disappears.

SIGHT AND SOUND, 2/98, p. 55, Jonathan Romney

Las Vegas. Gangsters Joey, Frankie and Paulie plan to cash in on the success of Philip, a gambler who has been on a winning streak at the Pairadice Casino. He plays every Sunday and never loses. Also conspiring to fleece Philip are Jack, a hitman for casino owner Kingman, and Louise, a singer in serious debt to Kingman. Louise seduces Philip, who is ready to marry her; she tells Jack to wreck her apartment to make Philip think she is in danger from the Mob. Jack obliges, leaving behind a severed hand belonging to his last victim—Philip's father. Philip is approached by Joey, posing as a journalist, and Philip tells him how gambling saved him from suicide.

Philip's brother Wolf arrives carrying their dead father, and they bury him in the desert. Wolf investigates his murder; but Louise tells Jack she is convinced Wolf is the killer. Philip gets into a bar-room fight; he realises his luck is out, and tells Louise he could lose next Sunday. Wolf is arrested, but escapes. Philip borrows a large sum to cover Louise's debt in case he loses. On Sunday, he gives Louise the money; she starts to leave town with it, but drives back and returns it to him. Joey stabs Wolf and mounts an armed attack on the casino, just as an angry Jack enters with a gun. The ensuing shoot-out becomes a massacre, and Louise dies in Philip's arms. He cashes in all the money for a single chip, and plays it on the big wheel. Kingman hits a switch, killing all the lights in the casino, in Las Vegas, and the stars in the sky.

The Winner should, perhaps, properly be seen less as the new Alex Cox film than as the missing piece in the Alan Smithee canon. It has a chequered history, to say the least: as Cox points out in his letter to January's *S&S*, he regards it as his only "work for hire" to date; and the version now released was re-cut by the producers. They also replaced the original Pray For Rain score with what Cox describes as "muzak"—if not quite that, it's certainly distracting, that glib cocktail jazz pastiche that has become genre shorthand for comedy-thriller flipness. Cox regards the present cut, with only slight exaggeration, as "incomprehensible", and attempted to get his name removed from the credits. So it seems almost inappropriate to review the film at all, at least as a film "by" its director. As for attempting to piece together imaginatively a vision of what the film might have been, suffice to say this is no *Magnificent Ambersons*.

Indeed, Cox-watchers might justifiably feel that much of what is wrong with *The Winner* has a familiar stamp of Cox about it: a taste for sometimes grating incongruity, a tendency to let the movie-making seams show through the drama, and an over-indulgence for trash Americana. if it really was a "gun for hire" project, it nevertheless seems to have been peculiarly tailored to Cox's tastes (and at the very least, he's left his signature in it with a cameo as a French choreographer).

What we can't really speculate on is the film's peculiar syntax, which may or may not have originated in the director's own urge to experiment, but is certainly its most rebarbative aspect. A characteristic trick is the use of long tracking shots, with a weaving camera following actors who appear to be improvising around their parts.

Elsewhere, the long takes are hacked up with spasmodic volleys of jump cuts. The result of both effects, and of the avoidance of close-ups, is to leave us stuck at some distance from the characters. What may have been designed as a tone of ironic coolness actually leaves the film looking all the more threadbare, as though the technique had been adopted to save time on expensive set-ups.

The film's main selling point is its catalogue of name character players, but their various routines never coalesce into genuine ensemble work, largely because the script is structured as a series of duets. This, presumably a legacy of screenwriter Wendy Riss' original stage play, creates an often claustrophobic stasis. Rebecca DeMornay, archly sexy as a piece of upmarket trailer trash, dominates the film with nervy style, but then, as executive producer, she may have been in a position to ensure that the editing worked to her advantage. Billy Bob Thornton and Delroy Lindo are largely sidelined; Michael Madsen drifts in and out in his usual hard-ass guise. And Frank Whaley's gibbering psycho in a pompadour might have cut muster as a bit part in *Lost Highway* but is cut far too much slack here. The worst liability is Vincent D'Onofrio, a vacant centre to the film, whose moments of anguished confusion look as though he's running through a series of Actors' Studio warm-up exercises.

The style of *The Winner* might have been less annoying applied to a simple comic-strip gangland lark, but the film's moral and metaphysical pretentions jar horribly. Its observations about American voracity and about gambling as grand metaphor are banal and this is only highlighted by the extremely cheap feel of the whole project everything, from the decor of the Pairadice Casino to the Casio-style backing track to Louise's stage act, is strictly bargain basement. *The Winner* seems all the more pointless a venture since Paul Thomas Anderson's neglected debut *Hard Eight* proved that cheapness and claustrophobia could be used to enormous metaphoric effect in a gambling context.

VILLAGE VOICE, 8/5/97, p. 67, J. Hoberman

There's another form of integrity on view in *The Winner*. [The reference is to *In the Company of Men*; see Hoberman's review.] Hardcore maverick Alex Cox flies beneath the radar once again with a film whose title is so saturated with irony you might as well take it at face value. Self-destruction is Cox's theme *(Sid and Nancy, Walker, Highway Patrolman)* as well as his game (ditto). He repossesses his obsession in this visually astute *film maudit*—a deftly directed, highly disposable, low-rent entertainment, resurrected by a small theatrical distributor after having been thrown away on cable TV.

One more negative career move, *The Winner* is derived from a play by Wendy Riss which might originally have had something to do with the idea of Jesus in Vegas: An enigmatic naif (Vincent D'Onofrio) who only plays roulette on Sundays is in the midst of a five-week winning streak. Because this big, dumb country boy invariably gives his money away, he's being staked out as a mark by a trio of geeky stooges as well as his dissolute older brother (Michael Madsen) and most importantly, an aging lounge singer (Rebecca DeMornay, also credited as an executive producer). All schemes unfold under the watchful eye of the Pair-A-Dice casino's psychobabbling boss (Delroy Lindo).

The Winner could have been tiresome. Everyone, the lunar settlement of Las Vegas included, is revisiting old roles—the only exception is Billy Bob Thornton as DeMornay's depressed patsy. Still, Cox manages to charge this hackneyed material with a combination of morbid humor and scuzzball poetry The result is wackier and less preening than the average overacted guyfest—a rancid Hollywood fable in which Divine Providence functions as a sort of cosmic weatherman and a love scene between DeMornay and D'Onofrio is tendered all the more peculiar for being staged in the Liberace Museum. Advancing the action with adroitly managed jump cuts, the director never loses formal control—no matter how his performers froth and even when the hitherto comically economical violence escalates into a strobe-styled, bloody shoot-out of down-faced carnage.

Cox gives himself a bizarre cameo but the scene closest to his heart might be D'Onofrio's attempt to keep his winning streak alive by playing the nickel slots in a Mexican cantina. *The Winner* is all about trying to conjure up something out of nothing—and that's what it is as well.

Also reviewed in:
NEW YORK TIMES, 7/25/97, p. C10, Stephen Holden
VARIETY, 9/23-29/96, p. 71, Emanuel Levy

WINTER GUEST, THE

A Fine Line Features release in association wih Capitol Films, Channel Four Films, and The Scottish Arts Council Lottery Fund of an Edward Pressman/Ken Lipper production. *Producer:* Ken Lipper and Edward R. Pressman. *Director:* Alan Rickman. *Screenplay:* Sharman Macdonald and Alan Rickman. *Adapted from the play by:* Sharman Macdonald. *Director of Photography:* Seamus McGarvey. *Editor:* Scott Thomas. *Music:* Michael Kamen. *Sound:* Colin Nicholson and (music) Stephen McLaughlin. *Sound Editor:* Kevin Brazier and Stephen Griffiths. *Casting:* Joyce Nettles. *Production Designer:* Robin Cameron Don. *Art Director:* Elli Griff and Ben Scott. *Special Effects:* Howard Minkow. *Costumes:* Joan Bergin. *Make-up:* Morag Ross. *Running time:* 110 minutes. *MPAA Rating:* R.

CAST: Phyllida Law (Elspeth); Emma Thompson (Frances); Sheila Reid (Lily); Sandra Voe (Chloe); Arlene Cockburn (Nita); Gary Hollywood (Alex); Sean Biggerstaff (Tom); Douglas Murphy (Sam); Tom Watson (Minister); Jan Shand (Café Proprietor); Sandy Neilson (Passer-by); Bily McElhaney (Bus Driver); Helen Devon (Woman in Tea Shop); Harry Welsh (Boy in Teashop); Christian Zanone (Young Man in Church); Ross Lewis (Jamie).

LOS ANGELES TIMES, 12/24/97, Calendar/p. 10, Kevin Thomas

"The Winter Guest" is a beautiful, deeply moving film that teams Emma Thompson with her mother, veteran actress Phyllida Law, and marks an auspicious film directorial debut for actor Alan Rickman. It is not quite the picture you might expect when a celebrated star and her mother, also a much-respected player, are playing a mother and daughter. You are prepared for high drama, but "The Winter Guest" goes against all manner of theatrics—and as it turns out, this is all for the good.

It doesn't seem that way, however, at first. That's because just when Law and Thompson are working up some steam, Rickman cuts away to one of several other stories. But when all their strands start pulling together you appreciate just how effective the strategies of "The Winter Guest" really are.

The setting is a Scottish coastal town so cold that Law's Elspeth can remember only one other time in her life the sea has actually frozen over. When we meet her, she's trudging through the snow from some distance to visit her daughter Frances, who lives in a lovely old townhouse with her teenage son Alex (Gary Hollywood). Clearly, Frances has gone through some wrenching experience, and we soon realize her husband, beloved by his wife and son alike, has recently died.

Around the time Elspeth is finally arriving at her daughter's home, Rickman is already starting up parallel stories. A pretty girl, Nita (Arlene Cockburn), waiting for a bus across the street from Frances' house, is coming on to Alex; two elderly ladies, Lily (Sheila Reid) and Chloe (Sandra Voe), are also waiting for the bus. Later on, we'll meet two boys, Sam (Douglas Murphy) and Tom (Sean Biggerstaff), who look to be about 13, who are poking around the rocks by the sea.

Frances is not thrilled with the prospect of a visit by her mother. Elspeth is garrulous, opinionated, outspoken and, in a word, tiresome. She's also gutsy, canny and vital, with a passionate love of nature. She's too judgmental to be any real comfort to her daughter, but as the day progresses we realize just how physically frail Elspeth is; not surprisingly, she's in total denial in regard to it.

While proclaiming her independence and self-reliance, she is actually hoping for a chance to be closer to her daughter, who she fears may move to Australia. In any event, both Elspeth and Nita try to persuade mother and son to start letting go of the dead husband and father. Meanwhile, Lily and Chloe, who have nothing better to do than attend funerals, talk of death as the two boys, most engaging and authentic, talk of life.

In a highly affecting, wholly implicit way, "The Winter Guest," which Rickman and Sharman Macdonald adapted from her play, reminds us that no matter how much of a cliché it may be, people really do need people, whether they admit it or not. People also need people who do not necessarily need them in return, however, and in this instance Frances must come to a decision about her mother.

"The Winter Guest" is inevitably about love, friendship and responsibility. The frozen sea is of course a symbol of the state of the mother-daughter relationship, but at the end it acquires a different meaning: Life itself is like walking on ice with all its adventures and perils.

You can sense that "The Winter Guest" started out as a play, but its transposition to screen has been accomplished with an elegant ease, and its setting has much visual splendor. It's a virtual given that an actor as accomplished as Rickman will get the luminous portrayals from his cast that he does, but beyond this he displays an acute sense of pacing, of knowing when to pause and how long to hold a scene to let meaning and emotion seep in.

Law and Thompson are glorious together in this admirably understated movie. "You have great bone structure" Elspeth says to Frances. "You get it from me"and indeed Law and Thompson are strikingly similar-looking beauties. We now also know where Thompson got at least some of her formidable acting ability, too.

NEW YORK POST, 12/24/97, p. 35, Michael Medved

How's this for a Hollywood high concept: Two embittered widows, mother and daughter, spend a full day bickering at one another in a remote Scottish fishing village in the dead of winter.

"The Winter Guest" may be thin on plot and altogether devoid of thrills, but it does offer an audacious, oddball antidote to the slam-bang, star-studded extravaganzas that seem to dominate most theaters this holiday season.

Marking the directing debut of character actor Alan Rickman, this British import ultimately overcomes its forbidding premise with, superlative acting and unmistakable affection for its quirky characters.

Emma Thompson plays a gifted photographer who is still recovering from the illness and death of the husband she adored. Her mother (played with crusty conviction by Thompson's real-life mother, Phyllida Law) shows up one morning, uninvited and unexpected, to nag her daughter out of her lethargy and self-pity.

While they walk and talk through the frozen streets of a deserted seaside town, director Rickman simultaneously focuses on three other couples who similarly need and resent one another.

Thompson's teen-aged son (played by Gary Hollywood) spends the day alternately attracted and repelled by a seductive, dangerous, incongruously innocent village girl, played by an utterly bewitching newcomer named Arlene Cockburn.

Two lonely old ladies (Sheila Reid and Sandra Voe) take the bus out of town to indulge their favorite pastime, attending a stranger's funeral.

Meanwhile, two pre-teens (Douglas Murphy and Sean Biggerstaff) play hooky from school, building a fire by the frozen ocean, adopting a lost kitten and worrying over the unpromising size of their private parts.

Director Rickman (who co-wrote the script, based on an acclaimed play he developed and directed on the London stage) shows each of these ill-assorted pairs drawing closer as protection against the piercing cold and overwhelming emptiness of the world.

His frosty visions of the Scottish coast unfold with haunting splendor. The mother and daughter at the drama's center, with their eerie resemblance to one another, are both such formidable performers and presences that it feels like a privilege to overhear even their occasionally nattering and empty conversations.

NEWSDAY, 12/24/97, Part II/p. B10, John Anderson

The advantage (to us) of the ubiquitous actor-turned-director is his or her natural sympathy for the performance itself. Resisting industry standards—i.e., having everything move along just as rapidly as the eye can follow—the best of the converts allow their actors to stretch out, breathe, expand, grow, develop. With any luck, they're also working with structures that can stand all the stress.

Alan Rickman has played some terrific American villains ("Die Hard") and English romantics ("Truly, Madly, Deeply") but it's harder to imagine a more misguided project than "The Winter Guest" with which to make one's movie-directing debut. The play on which it's based, by Sharman Macdonald (with whom Rickman wrote the script) is an ungainly construct at best: Set on the "coldest day in memory" in a Scottish coastal town (the audience will please disregard the absence of frozen breath, or that puddle on the ground) it involves four sets of characters with few discernible connections besides their eventual date with death—the title character—and who recite dialogue that is arch beyond redemption. Making it worse, the actors are indulged to the point of anarchy.

The performances are strong enough, but as a character drama, "The Winter Guest" raises an inordinate number of questions about motivations off-screen. What, for instance, would intrigue an American company to release this film? Easy: Having the prestigious / bankable Emma Thompson and her mother, stage actress Phyllida Law, cast as its main characters. What would intrigue Thompson and Law about Macdonald's play? Perhaps the chance to act together on screen, portraying characters who can survive purely on the strength of performance.

And what got Rickman so worked up? The seriousness of the play, perhaps, or the chance to make his debut directing Thompson and Law—yes, there's a roundness to it all, more so, anyway, than in the film itself.

In a shot that seems to have been lifted from "Thirty-Two Short Films About Glenn Gould," Law's gloveless and hatless and less-than-surefooted Elspeth comes gallumphing out of a stark white landscape en route to Frances (Thompson), like terror on two legs. Frances, clearly depresssed, hides in the bathroom as soon as Mom arrives, and we don't blame her. The house is unheated, son Alex (Gary Hollywood) has gone to school and she's more or less a sitting duck.

It takes an enormously long time to have one's suspicions confirmed about what's ailing Frances (her dead husband), that she's considering going back to Australia with her son and that Elspeth is a profound pain. Which is probably wise, because once we do know all this we have even less reason to hang out with them.

But we don't have to, because we make intermittent visits to the drama's several other twosomes: Lily and Chloe (Sheila Reid and Sandra Voe), two elderly bus-riding, funeral-watching ladies who have a moment with mortality; Sam and Tom (Douglas Murphy and Sean Biggerstaff), school-skipping lads who wax elegiac about life, death and penis size; and Alex and the comely

Nita (Arlene Cockburn), who do a bit of a dance around each other while edging steadily toward a tryst in Alex' unheated house.

Soggy with theatricality, "The Winter Guest" has a few inadvertently funny moments. When Frances has a crying jag at one point, throwing stones at something off screen, you almost hope Elspeth's not in the way.

When Elspeth, rejecting one of Frances' various acts of solicitation, says "I eat when I'm hungry, I drink when I'm dry" it's not only unjustifiably edgy in terms of the drama, it's unnatural language as well. When young Tom delivers his seaside soliloquy about death, the words and cadence sound like something out of an early sea play by Eugene O'Neill—which would be fine, if he weren't 10 years old.

Although his appreciation for sea-freezing temperatures seems a bit awry, Rickman shows an admirable camaraderie with his actors and an appreciation for the importance of performance. Not enough, however, to make this "Guest" any more welcome.

SIGHT AND SOUND, 1/98, p. 56, Demetrios Matheou

A Scottish seaside village in winter. Frances, a recently widowed photographer, languishes in bed, griefstricken, while her 15-year-old son Alex attempts to look after them both. Frances' mother, Elspeth, makes the arduous journey across frozen countryside to visit her, hoping to restore their relationship which suffered during Frances' married life. She persuades Frances to go for a walk around the village. On his way to school, Alex meets Nita who is new to the area and clearly attracted to him. The two spend the day together, eventually going to his now empty house. Meanwhile, two elderly friends, Chloe and Lily, are making one of their many journeys to local funerals chosen from the obituary columns. Two boys, Tom and Sam, skip school to investigate the coastline.

Frances and Elspeth come across the boys, who are playing on the beach. While Elspeth talks to Sam, Frances takes photographs and the tension between the two women eases. On returning from the funeral, Chloe suddenly feels panic-stricken, but is helped by her friend. Alex and Nita start to make love, but Alex holds back, put off by countless photographs of his father. Nita starts to knock them down, but cuts herself on the broken glass and leaves. Frances and Elspeth return to the house, where Frances—who has been talking of emigrating to Australia suggests that she may stay after all. The two boys wander onto the frozen sea and disappear into the fog.

From the opening shots—of an elderly woman in a fur coat struggling across snow covered fields and icy crags; a tiny village nestling against an ice-covered sea; a younger woman tossing and turning amid brilliant white sheets—it's apparent that landscape is to play a key physical and symbolic role in *The Winter Guest* For his debut behind the camera, the actor Alan Rickman has found the perfect wintry hinterland in which to locate the isolated characters of Sharman Macdonald's original play. He uses his Fife locations with a vigour that prevents the film from being throttled by its theatrical roots.

Rickman and Macdonald skillfully weave their plot around four sets of couples—two boys, two teenage lovers, a pair of pensioners and a mother and daughter. Through the prism of these different generations, the film explores how people cope with loss and loneliness, fear of death, and, in particular, families. These couples may only cross paths occasionally, but their concerns and experiences constantly echo each other. Frances' dead, remembered husband is a thread throughout the film, his absence the catalyst for Elspeth's attempted reconciliation with her daughter. Elspeth experiences the loneliness of a parent who, having devoted her life to her child, is no longer wanted. Bemoaning her daughter's refusal to be comforted, Elspeth cries: 'You taught me to care. How do you stop all that caring?'

Meanwhile, Alex, neglected by parents obsessed with each other, is traumatised by a lack of attention. Offered a potential relationship of his own with Nita, he cannot act. At the youngest end of the spectrum, the thoughtful Sam, tired of the rules imposed by his parents, sighs with melancholy, "I did not ask to be born." Between them, these characters offer a compelling dialectic on the potential, and the potential damage of family life.

As well as loneliness and fear, another force that connects these couples is the lurking presence of death. It's there in the nagging signs of illness that bedevil Elspeth; in the risky ventures onto the ice of both Alex and Nita, and Sam and Tom; and, not least, in Chloe and Lily's gleeful pursuit of funerals—though this hobby barely conceals their mindfulness of their own advancing years.

All this would be far too gloomy if not for the humour that pervades the film. Frances hides in her bathroom while Elspeth potters about the house, singing songs and misremembering the past, which Frances pulls her up on. Outside, trying to escape, Alex tells Nita: "My gran's in there. My mother's had a haircut. It's a bloody battlefield." Chloe and Lily are a blackly comic double act, bemoaning the fact that you'll catch your death before you catch a bus, arguing over the relative merits of burial and cremation, treating themselves to post-funeral cream cakes. Throughout the film, people pine for or argue about such unappetising snacks as a "Menzies pie", a 'Skinners meringue', even a Mars bar. It's never made clear what killed Frances' husband, but a poor diet could be a possibility.

Much has been made of the pairing of real-life mother and daughter Phyllida Law and Emma Thompson. There's certainly chemistry between the two, but one should credit their acting for that. If anything, such novelty casting is a distraction. What is most striking about Rickman's debut is his control of mood, delicately teasing out the metaphorical possibilities of freezing and ice.

Rickman and his talented cinematographer Seamus McGarvey create a series of ravishing, resonant images, many of them crisply framed close-ups that allude both to Frances' stills photography and to her and others' emotional isolation. While the identity of the 'winter guest' is left ambiguous (as is the boys' fate), it is tempting to assume that the guest is the winter itself—an icy stage for these delicate personal dramas, and a clean slate on which new relationships can be built.

VILLAGE VOICE, 12/30/97, p. 66, Amy Taubin

Based on a play by Sharman Macdonald, *The Winter Guest* is about the conflict between autonomy and dependency that bedevils all relationships. The script is full of interesting ideas, but the rigid construction of the scenes and the poetic dialogue are more suited to stage than screen.

The Winter Guest is set in a remote village on the Scottish coast, where the harsh weather defines the character of the inhabitants. That the frozen North Sea, on whose shore much of the action takes place, has been digitally enhanced adds to the hybridity, but also to the awkwardness, of the film. Alan Rickman, who directed the original play, makes his debut here as a filmmaker; despite his potent movie acting career, his directorial impulses are more theatrical than cinematic.

A bit of a dog and pony show, *The Winter Guest* stars real-life daughter and mother Emma Thompson and Phyllida Law. Thompson plays a recently widowed woman who's toying with the idea of leaving her painful past behind and moving to Australia. Law plays her elderly mother, whose defiance of the elements (she walks the icy beach without a cane) belies her terror of being abandoned by the daughter on whom she's increasingly reliant. The daughter is endlessly irritated that her mother still treats her like a child; the mother realizes that the daughter is irritated, but she can't break the habit. "I don't need you to care for me," says the daughter. "You taught me to care for you," the mother replies. "I can't stop just because you've grown."

This is familiar stuff, but from time to time, Thompson and Law find the precise formulation of emotional ambivalence that makes the words sound fresh. And although they inhabit the screen like grand dames, they are only one among a quartet of couples discovering how to negotiate the relationships that are necessary for survival. *The Winter Guest* gives almost equal time to a teenage boy and girl finding first love; a pair of elderly women whose pleasure is attending funerals; and two 11-year-old boys who play hooky from school, worry about the painfully slow development of their genitalia, and rescue a pair of kittens who've been abandoned on the beach. The boys (nicely played by Sean Biggerstaff and Douglas Murphy) run away with the picture.

The unconvincingly digitalized sea notwithstanding, *The Winter Guest* is a striking-looking film. The cold blue grays and grayish whites of the landscape evoke the ominous but seductive presence of the Winter Guest (guess who?) as do the pale, translucent faces of the actors. More metaphoric than human, these personages are so bloodless, their cheeks never redden in the cold.

Also reviewed in:
CHICAGO TRIBUNE, 1/16/98, Friday/p. C, John Petrakis

NEW REPUBLIC, 1/5 & 12/98, p. 24, Stanley Kauffmann
NEW YORK TIMES, 12/23/97, p. E5, Stephen Holden
NEW YORKER, 1/5/98, p. 77, Daphne Merkin
VARIETY, 9/8-14/97, p. 78, Deborah Young
WASHINGTON POST, 1/16/98, Weekend/p. 33, Desson Howe

WONDERLAND

A Fox Lorber release of a Rhinestone production in association with Good Machine. *Executive Producer:* Ted Hope, David Linde, and James Schamus. *Producer:* John O'Hagan. *Director:* John O'Hagan. *Director of Photography:* John O'Hagan. *Editor:* John O'Hagan. *Music:* Tracy McKnight. *Running time:* 80 minutes. *MPAA Rating:* Not Rated.

WITH: Eddie Money; Keelin Curnuck; Roy Curnuck; Bill Griffith.

LOS ANGELES TIMES, 10/24/97, Calendar/p. 8, John Anderson

[The following review by John Anderson appeared in a slightly different form in NEWSDAY, 10/24/97, Part II/p. B11.]

The fact that the greater Western world is now wired for celebrity, sound bites and media savvy hasn't made us wary. On the contrary. Most people now walk around with a news segment's worth of well-rehearsed hot copy on their lips, waiting for a rolling camera and live mike. We have something to say, we say, and we're going to say it; Warhol's fabled 15 minutes of fame is no longer a phenomenon, it's a right. We are significant, although to prove it, it takes a global village.

In "Wonderland," John O'Hagan's sardonic look at that less-than-global but internationally renowned village of Levittown, Long Island, we see people who are more often than not living in time capsules—in some cases, the decor hasn't changed since William Levitt started building this cookie-cutter community back in 1947. At the same time, they're creature of their times. They embrace the camera, they perform, they open their souls and, like a million people they've seen on television, they tell us things we never wanted to know.

Chronic candor isn't their fault, merely a symptom of our freakish times, and O'Hagan is as much a part of this process as anyone. He doesn't start out to ridicule Levittown or its people, and I'm not sure he ever really does; there's an undercurrent of real affection for the subjects he includes, partly for their honesty and candor, partly because of the simple things that make their lives complete.

But after a fairly conventional opening-stock footage, a "March of Time" interview with Levitt himself, a discussion of the postwar housing crunch that prompted the building of this first mass-produced community with its cloned streets and GI-friendly prices—things start to get weird.

One woman discusses in great length the ghost in her house; another, in therapy, castigates, Levittown itself for every problem. A woman reads a passage from a pornographic novel. "Isn't that lovely?" she asks. Another, discussing the early years, states matter-of-factly that "one of the principal amusements was wife swapping." (There's some difference of opinion, but apparently Levittown was never Cleaverville.)

There is no such thing as an objective documentary. A director's imprint is evident in everything from the camera angles through the editing process. Although O'Hagan never actually intrudes on the scene and allows his Levittowners to speak for themselves, one senses a violation of the pact, as Janet Malcolm has put it, between the chronicler and his subjects: These people had no idea how their words and images were going to be used, how they would be juxtaposed with others and possibly made to look ridiculous.

On the other hand, they're adult enough to know how these things work, and their verbal enthusiasm belies any fear of broken contracts.

Basically, the movie is funny and sad. Dreams are modest: One man wants to bowl a perfect game; another wants a mink coat for his wife. War veterans perform a ceremonial flag burning with earnestness and awkward dignity; here, O'Hagan almost dares you to laugh, and shame yourself.

The well-known Levittowners he interviews—cartoonist Bill Griffith of "Zippy the Pinhead" fame and aging rocker Eddie Money—got out when they got famous. Miss New York 1996, Keelin Curnuck, pumps iron poolside. A bartender and his wobbly patrons try to remember the words to "The Star-Spangled Banner." And we try to remember when a place like Levittown was a phenomenon, people were assigned houses in alphabetical order, and anonymity was the norm, not an embarrassment.

VILLAGE VOICE, 10/28/97, p. 84, Michael Atkinson

Just as *Crumb* and *Martha & Ethel* proved that there could very well be an amazing film hidden somewhere inside every family, John O'Hagan's *Wonderland,* a sneaky and charming doc about the rise and ridiculous equilibrium of Levittown, Long Island, proves that there could be a film hidden in every town. Levittown, after all, isn't very unique; as O'Hagan makes clear with idiosyncratic resident interviews and news footage of "the first planned suburban city," Levittown's most famous for being utterly ordinary. Taking a page out of the Errol Morris hornbook, O'Hagan shoots straight and gives each everyday schmo enough rope to hang him- or herself. That includes, it seems, anybody who's everybody in L-town: nondescript blue-collar homeowners, second-generation neurotics, hapless realtors, Eddie Money, Zippy creator Bill Griffith, eccentric collectors, and a woman sharing her house with a destructive ghost. Tales of wife swapping, visions of an elderly woman modeling her vast collection of "native dress," sessions in the office of a psychologist specializing in Levittown identity disorder—idealizing and roasting suburbia in one smirking swipe, O'Hagan has succeeded in making it downright seductive.

Also reviewed in:
CHICAGO TRIBUNE, 5/22/98, Friday/p. F, John Petrakis
NEW YORK TIMES, 10/24/97, p. E22, Stephen Holden
VARIETY, 2/3-9/97, p. 50, Dennis Harvey

YEAR OF THE HORSE

An October Films release. *Executive Producer:* Bernard Shakey and Elliot Rabinowitz. *Producer:* L.A. Johnson. *Director:* Jim Jarmusch. *Director of Photography:* L.A. Johnson and Jim Jarmusch. *Editor:* Jay Rabinowitz. *Music:* Neil Young and Crazy Horse. *Sound:* Tim Mulligan. *Running time:* 106 minutes. *MPAA Rating:* Not Rated.

WITH: Ralph Molina; Frank (Poncho) Sampedro; Billy Talbot; Neil Young.

LOS ANGELES TIMES, 10/17/97, Calendar/p. 20, John Anderson

[*The following review by John Anderson appeared in a slightly different form in*
NEWSDAY, 10/17/97, Part II/p. B13.]

The fine-tuned avalanche that is the music of Neil Young and Crazy Horse is treated with wary respect by Jim Jarmusch in his new "Year of the Horse," a concert film-group portrait that captures as well as any other music movie the natural, untethered essence of live rock. As he would with any uncontrollable force of nature, Jarmusch knows enough to get out of the way and let the good times roll.

Welding performances from the band's 1996 European and U.S. tours to footage shot in both '86 and '76 ("Like a Hurricane," played 20 years apart, is a trip), Jarmusch portrays a band that is, its members are quick to admit, far better than its parts. They bring to one another an energy that individually eludes them; on stage, the union manifests itself in occasionally angelic harmonies, nuclear guitar playing and the overall elevation provided by Young's songwriting.

Where Young ends and Crazy Horse begins has always been a question—not a burning one, granted, but for inquisitive fans the relationship is enigmatic. Young, between other projects (even his long-ago sojourn with Crosby, Stills & Nash), has played with the ramshackle Horse for almost 30 years and refers to the group simply as Crazy Horse. The others—drummer Ralph Molina, bassist Billy Talbot and guitarist Frank "Poncho" Sampedro, all of whom sing—always refer to their band as Neil Young and Crazy Horse. Such rock 'n' roll diplomacy probably says a lot about why they've stuck together.

So does the music, of course, which requires a certain indulgence on the part of the listener, just as it thrives on the self-indulgences of the band. Jarmusch, trying to emulate the aesthetic of Crazy Horse on film, lets them have their head, as it were, using complete performances of songs, with their overheated jams and elaborate endings that are pure bombast and final chords that seem like 140-decibel exclamation points.

While Jarmusch may occasionally accent a performance with roughhewn landscapes and other visual ephemera (a hand-drawn choo-choo, for instance, which is a reference to Young's model train obsession), he never gets in the way, never edits a song. It's their film, and by getting out of the way as much as he does, Jarmusch makes "Year of the Horse" as much a statement about creative freedom as it is about music itself.

The Jarmusch-Young collaboration began when Young did the soundtrack to Jarmusch's underappreciated "Dead Man," continued with Jarmusch's direction of a Young video, and has progressed to "Year of the Horse," which, besides being a concert film, tries to tell the band's story. It's a group with a high mortality rate—original guitarist Danny Whitten (Sampedro's predecessor) died of a heroin overdose in the early '70s, and producers David Briggs and roadie Bruce Berry also have died.

They all get tributes, while Jarmusch gets heckled; you think you can capture the essence of a group that's been together 30-odd years just by bringing around your camera and making a movie so people think you're cool? Sampedro's macho routine is good-natured, but frankly, if they had any sense, the guys in Crazy Horse would thank Jarmusch for creating such a complimentary and kinetic portrait of their tie-dyed, T-shirted and occasionally transcendent band.

VILLAGE VOICE, 10/14/97, p. 96, Michael Atkinson

If you're left craving perspective and modesty, there's always Jim Jarmusch's *Year of the Horse,* in which Neil Young cements his paunchy, shorts-and-black-socks rep as the Robert Duvall of rock. A wistful concert film-cum-autumnal portrait of the aging Crazy Horse, Jarmusch's grainy record (shot mostly on Super 8 and, as the credits say, proud of it) nobly focuses on the band as a democratic unit: Young, bassist Billy Talbot, guitarist Poncho Sampedro, and drummer Ralph Molina. We know Young as much more, but just as the band's perfs are a series of never ending monk-huddle thunderstorms, Jarmusch's visuals keep everything so down to earth you get the impression Neil and the boys just aren't getting enough sleep. No one can say Crazy Horse, or Jarmusch, hunger for glory, but they sure could use a nice salad.

Also reviewed in:
NEW YORK TIMES, 10/6/97, p. B3, Janet Maslin
VARIETY, 6/2-8/97, p. 54, Dennis Harvey

YO SOY DEL SON A LA SALSA

An RMM Film Works release. *Executive Producer:* Ralph Mercado. *Producer:* Rigoberto López. *Director:* Rigoberto López. *Screenplay (Spanish and English with English subtitles):* Rigoberto López and Leonardo Padura. *Director of Photography:* Luis Garcia and José M. Riera. *Editor:* Miriam Talavera. *Running time:* 100 minutes. *MPAA Rating:* Not Rated.

LOS ANGELES TIMES, 10/3/97, Calendar/p. 18, Kevin Thomas

Rigoberto Lopez Pego's "Yo Soy del Son a la Salsa" ("I Am, From *Son* to Salsa") documents the evolution of salsa music from its roots in Cuba to its development there and later on in Puerto Rico and New York.

The music, of course, is well-nigh irresistible, and its makers form an uncommonly ingratiating group of individuals, each quick to give credit to mentors and influences. There's a special poignancy here in that salsa has had to transcend political borders, given the United States long-standing embargo of Cuba.

Lopez Pego simultaneously aims at the salsa specialist and the layman. He has laid out this music's history meticulously throughout this century, charting its variations and presenting its premier artists in chronological order. (Musicians of the '20s—such as the late members of the pivotal Trio Matamoros, formed in 1925—are represented in archival film and television footage.)

With many veteran performers still alive and active, such as Israel "Cachao" Lopez, "Yo Soy" gives us the feeling that we're being given a pretty comprehensive picture, even though we're cautioned that by no means have all performers been included.

Not to worry if you're not a salsa specialist and find yourself a bit bowled over by the amount of information the picture provides. All you have to do is simply sit back and listen to the music.

The most famous musician in the film is probably the late Perez Prado, and the first person to acknowledge that Prado was the King of Mambo is none other than Cachao himself—even though it was he and his late brother Orestes who came up with mambo 60 years ago.

Singer Celia Cruz is represented in performance in vintage clips and in a vivacious interview, and we see Tito Puente in performances both past and present and in a substantial interview. Singer Isaac Delgado is "Yo Soy's" gracious and knowledgeable host.

The film ends appropriately with a long session with today's top Cuban group, the mesmerizing and distinctive Los Van Van.

NEW YORK POST, 9/13/97, p. 24, Larry Worth

As movie documentaries of music movements go, "Yo Soy, Del Son a la Salsa" is as out of step as they come.

Writer-director Rigoberto Lopez crams so much information into this history of salsa that virtually none of it registers. Fans of the phenomenon—a mix of Afro-Cuban rhythms and R&B—will already know the particulars, and newcomers won't retain the names and jargon that speakers throw out at lightning speed.

Speaking of which, all but Evelyn Wood graduates may have trouble keeping up with double-deck subtitles that remain onscreen for about two seconds. Equally fleeting are songs and comments from the likes of Tito Puente and Celia Cruz, who play second fiddle to "host" Issac Delgado. Audiences will get his number as soon as he looks into the camera and says "Nice to meet you.

"Yo Soy, Del Son a la Salsa" could have done with a little less folksiness, and a lot more focus.

Also reviewed in:
NEW YORK TIMES, 9/13/97, p. 14, Stephen Holden

ZEUS AND ROXANNE

An MGM/UA release of a Rysher Entertainment presentation of a Frank Price production. *Executive Producer:* Laura Friedman and Hilton Green. *Producer:* Frank Price, Gene Rosow, and Ludi Boeken. *Director:* George Miller. *Screenplay:* Tom Benedek. *Director of Photography:* David Connell. *Editor:* Harry Hitner. *Music:* Bruce Rowland. *Music Editor:* Richard Bernstein and Shirley Libby. *Sound Editor:* Eric Lindemann. *Production Designer:* Bernt Capra. *Art Director:* Alfred Kemper. *Set Decorator:* Beth Kushnick. *Set Dresser:* Jim Branigan. *Special Effects:* Eric Roberts. *Costumes:* Marion Boyce. *Make-up:* Amanda Rowbottom. *Stunt Coordinator:* Mike Nomad. *Running time:* 98 minutes. *MPAA Rating:* PG.

CAST: Steve Guttenberg (Terry);   Kathleen Quinlan (Mary Beth);   Arnold Vosloo (Claude Carver); Dawn McMillan (Becky); Miko Hughes (Jordan); Majandra Delfino (Judith); Jessica Howell (Nora); Duchess Tomasello (Mrs. Rice); Shanon K. Foley (Linda); Jim R. Coleman (Phil); Alvin Farmer (Floyd); Harri James (Airline Attendant); Justin Humphrey (Craig); James Stone (Security Guard); Maury Covington (Reverend); Michael A. Xynidis (Messenger).

LOS ANGELES TIMES, 1/27/97, Calendar/p. 4, Kevin Thomas

That PG rating for "Zeus and Roxanne" should be taken seriously: No adult should see this picture unaccompanied by a child, preferably no older than 10. Way too contrived and gooey for most grown-ups, it might well delight youngsters, especially its dramatic underwater sequences.

Zeus is a sandy-haired dog belonging to a musician, Terry (Steve Guttenberg), and his small son (Miko Hughes), who have come to the Bahamas for a short stay. Next door is another single parent, Mary Beth (Kathleen Quinlan), a marine biologist with two daughters (Majandra Delfino and Jessica Howell).

Roxanne is a captive dolphin Mary Beth is determined to help return to the wild. When Zeus and Roxanne become soul mates, Mary Beth believes she's witnessing interspecies communication, which could be a breakthrough in her work—and that could save her from the alternative of working as an aquarium tour guide in Minnesota. Meanwhile, she has a villainous colleague (Arnold Vosloo) just waiting to co-opt her research. It's one of those movies in which the animals are smarter than the humans, and the children smarter than the adults.

Any grown-up, however, can see where director George Miller (the "Man From Snowy River" George Miller, not the "Mad Max" George Miller) and writer Tom Benedek are heading: The kids will play matchmaker for their parents, there will be a glitch in their romance, the villain will strike, etc, Your attention may wander.

As children's entertainment, "Zeus and Roxanne" nevertheless works. Guttenberg and Quinlan are attractive, capable players able to bring some degree of reality to their single parents. Their kids are precocious (natch), and youngsters in the audiences will be delighted with Zeus and Roxanne and their friendship. The film has a nice bright and shiny look and gorgeous photogenic locales, but Bruce Rowland's relentless, violin-heavy score doesn't make sitting through "Zeus and Roxanne" any easier.

NEW YORK POST, 1/25/97, p. 21, Larry Worth

George Miller may not be talented, but at least he's consistent.

Miller not only misdirected "The Man From Snowy River" but went on to botch "The Aviator," "Gross Misconduct," "The Neverending Story II" and, most recently, the seal saga "Andre." Why should "Zeus and Roxanne" have been any different?

Actually, Miller—who usually limits himself to traditional family fare—has strayed a bit. Any film that concerns scruffy canine Zeus (officially a Portuguese Podengo) falling for dolphin queen Roxanne is venturing into uncharted waters.

Unfortunately, the rest of the plot, which takes place in the scenic Florida Keys, is all too charted. A goofy musician (Steve Guttenberg), his son and their frisky pooch become neighbors to a prim biologist (Kathleen Quinlan), her two daughters and their cat.

Natch, it's hate at first sight. But faster than you can sing the opening words of "The Brady Bunch" theme song, the love bug has bitten. Worse, the pooch is stowing away on the ravishing researcher's boat and making eyes at the dolphin she's tracking to get a grant.

When the dog slips into the drink, his aquatic beloved saves him from being shark bait. The rest is history. Or, it is at least until a rival researcher plans to steal Zeus, which sets off another nonsensical chain of events.

The rest of the production ranges from the requisite montage of mom and dad prepping for their big date to labored scenes of the heavy's huffing and puffing. That's as original as Miller gets.

What's really sad is seeing actors as appealing as Steve Guttenberg and Kathleen Quinlan reduced to such silliness.

It's particularly embarrassing for Quinlan, straight off her Oscar-nominated turn in "Apollo 13." But Guttenberg's also seen to disadvantage, trying so hard to act cool with his shades, earring and motorcycle that there's no room for emoting.

Predictably, the animals acquit themselves best. The dog is cute, even though his main talent is tipping his head from side to side. The dolphin, meanwhile, swims and cackles with proper panache.

Those who have secretly hoped to see Lassie and Flipper head into the sunset together should be thrilled with the results. All others would be better off at the local aquarium—or pound.

Also reviewed in:
NEW YORK TIMES, 1/25/97, p. 18, Lawrence Van Gelder
VARIETY, 1/27-2/2/97, p. 82, Timothy M. Gray

ADDENDUM

The following review arrived too late to be included in this or previous issues of FILM REVIEW ANNUAL. The issue of FILM REVIEW ANNUAL in which the credits and film reviews appear are given in parenthesis after the name of the film.

ZERO KELVIN *(Film Review Annual, 1997)*

LOS ANGELES TIMES, 3/7/97, Calendar/p. 14, Kevin Thomas

What a grand force of nature is Stellan Skarsgard, who came to international acclaim as the husband in "Breaking the Waves." A big, husky man, Skarsgard, in the Lars von Trier film, expressed a lusty, uninhibited sweetness soured by tragedy. Now in Norwegian filmmaker Hans Petter Moland's compelling "Zero Kelvin," Skarsgard is again earthy and robust, but from the outset his Randbaek is a brutal, caustic man suffering from some terrible secret torment.

A Greenland fur-trapper of much experience, Randbaek is less than thrilled to meet his new partner, Larsen (Gard Eidsvold), a young Oslo poet with a contract to write a book about his experiences during the yearlong expedition. The third man with whom the trappers will be living in a hut in a snowy wasteland is Holm (Bjorn Sundquist), a bald, burly scientist of few but forceful words.

At heart, "Zero Kelvin," adapted by Moland and Lars Bill Lundholm from a novel by Peter Tutein, is a classic clash of temperament and personality between two very different men. What the film accomplishes so admirably is to make these men so individual and their conflict so fresh that we're kept involved from start to finish by a seamless blend of crisp, brisk writing, direction and acting.

From the outset, the film avoids clichés. Larsen is no namby-pamby pushover, but a remarkably self possessed young man who doesn't hesitate to stand up to Randbaek—and who has no trouble at all in fur-trapping. Randbaek, by same token, is no mindless brute but the possessor of a savage intelligence. The key to their conflict is that Larsen has a girlfriend (Camilla Martens) whom he loves, an emotion Randbaek thunderingly insists does not exist; he speaks of sex in the crudest of terms. Randbaek is in fact starving for love and affection and friendship but is so full of rage he understandably puts off the others. The flash point is that Randbaek takes out that anger on the men's sled dogs, insisting that Larsen is undermining their capacity to obey by treating them like pets.

In the intensifying hostility between Randbaek and Larsen, the poet is not entirely innocent. In his awkward, abashed way Randbaek tries to make amends to Larsen after an especially nasty brawl between them by preparing a festive Christmas celebration, only to have his efforts coolly dismissed by Larsen. But then this incident gives way to "Zero Kelvin's" larger concern with the loss of innocence as a virtually inevitable part of the rites of passage. Again, it is amazing how effective "Zero Kelvin," which is set in 1925, catches us up in what so easily could be an overly familiar struggle. There's no question that it gains considerable impact from the icy grandeur of its setting, heightened by Terje Rypdal's spare score. "Zero Kelvin" is as much a journey into an anguished soul as it is to a remote land.

Also reviewed in:
CHICAGO TRIBUNE, 1/17/97, Friday/p. F, Michael Wilmington

AWARDS

ACADEMY OF MOTION PICTURE ARTS AND SCIENCES
70th Annual Academy Awards — March 23, 1998

BEST PICTURE — *Titanic*
Other Nominees: *As Good As It Gets; The Full Monty; Good Will Hunting; L.A. Confidential*

BEST ACTOR — Jack Nicholson in *As Good As It Gets*
Other Nominees: Matt Damon in *Good Will Hunting*; Robert Duvall in *The Apostle*; Peter Fonda in *Ulee's Gold*; Dustin Hoffman in *Wag the Dog*

BEST ACTRESS — Helen Hunt in *As Good As It Gets*
Other Nominees: Helena Bonham Carter in *The Wings of the Dove*; Julie Christie in *Afterglow*; Judi Dench in *Mrs. Brown*; Kate Winslet in *Titanic*

BEST SUPPORTING ACTOR — Robin Williams in *Good Will Hunting*
Other Nominees: Robert Forster in *Jackie Brown*; Anthony Hopkins in *Amistad*; Gregg Kinnear in *As Good As It Gets*; Burt Reynolds in *Boogie Nights*

BEST SUPPORTING ACTRESS — Kim Basinger in *L.A. Confidential*
Other nominees: Joan Cusack in *In & Out*; Minnie Driver in *Good Will Hunting*; Julianne Moore in *Boogie Nights*; Gloria Stuart in *Titanic*

BEST DIRECTOR — James Cameron for *Titanic*
Other Nominees: Peter Cattaneo for *The Full Monty*; Gus Van Sant for *Good Will Hunting;* Curtis Hanson for *L.A. Confidential*; Atom Egoyan for *The Sweet Hereafter*

BEST FOREIGN-LANGUAGE FILM — *Character* (The Netherlands)
Other Nominees: *Beyond Silence* (Germany); *Four Days in September* (Brazil); *Secrets of the Heart (Spain); The Thief* (France/Russia)

BEST ORIGINAL SCREENPLAY — Ben Affleck and Matt Damon for *Good Will Hunting*
Other Nominees: Mark Andrus and James L. Brooks for *As Good As It Gets*; Paul Thomas Anderson for *Boogie Nights*; Woody Allen for *Deconstructing Harry*; Simon Beaufoy for *The Full Monty*

BEST ADAPTED SCREENPLAY — Brian Helgeland and Curtis Hanson for *L.A. Confidential*
Other Nominees: Paul Attanasio for *Donnie Brasco*; Atom Egoyan for *The Sweet Hereafter*; Hilary Henkin and David Mamet for *Wag the Dog;* Hossein Amini for *The Wings of the Dove*

BEST CINEMATOGRAPHY — Russell Carpenter for *Titanic*
Other Nominees: Janusz Kaminski for *Amistad*; Roger Deakins for *Kundun;* Dante Spinotti for *L.A. Confidential*; Eduardo Serra *The Wings of the Dove*

BEST FILM EDITING — Conrad Buff, James Cameron, and Richard A. Harris for *Titanic*
Other Nominees: Richard Francis-Bruce for *Air Force One*; Richard Marks for *As Good As It Gets*; Pietro Scalia for *Good Will Hunting*; Peter Honess for *L.A. Confidential*

BEST ART DIRECTION — Peter Lamont with set decoration by Michael Ford for *Titanic*
Other Nominees: Jan Roelfs with set decoration by Nancy Nye for *Gattaca*; Dante Ferretti with set decoration by Francesca Lo Schiavo for *Kundun;* Jeannine Oppewall with set decoration by Jay P. Hart for *L.A. Confidential*; Bo Welch with set decoration by Cheryl Carasik for *Men in Black*

BEST COSTUME DESIGN — Deborah L. Scott for *Titanic*
Other Nominees: Ruth E. Carter for *Amistad;* Dante Ferretti for *Kundun*; Janet Patterson for *Oscar and Lucinda*; Sandy Powell for *The Wings of the Dove*

BEST MAKE-UP — Rick Baker and David LeRoy Anderson for *Men in Black*
Other Nominees: Lisa Westcott, Veronica Brebner, and Beverly Binda for *Mrs. Brown*; Tim Earnshaw, Greg Cannom, and Simon Thompson for *Titanic*

BEST ORIGINAL MUSICAL OR COMEDY SCORE — Anne Dudley for *The Full Monty*
Other Nominees: Stephen Flaherty (music), Lynn Ahrens (lyrics), and David Newman (orchestral score) for *Anastasia*; Hans Zimmer for *As Good As It Gets*; Danny Elfman for *Men in Black*; James Newton Howard for *My Best Friend's Wedding*

BEST ORIGINAL DRAMATIC SCORE — James Horner for *Titanic*
Other Nominees: John Williams for *Amistad*; Danny Elfman for *Good Will Hunting*; Philip Glass for *Kundun*; Jerry Goldsmith for *L.A. Confidential*

BEST ORIGINAL SONG — "My Heart Will Go On" from *Titanic*, music by James Horner and lyric by Will Jennings
Other Nominees: "Go the Distance" from *Hercules*, music by Alan Menken and lyric by David Zippel; "How Do I Live" from *Con Air*, music and lyric by Diane Warren; "Journey to the Past" from *Anastasia*, music by Stephen Flaherty and lyric by Lynn Ahrens; "Miss Misery" from *Good Will Hunting*, music and lyric by Elliott Smith

BEST SOUND — Gary Rydstrom, Tom Johnson, Gary Summers, and Mark Ulano for *Titanic*
Other Nominees: Paul Massey, Rick Kline, D.M. Hemphill, and Keith A. Wester for *Air Force One*; Kevin O'Connell, Greg P. Russell, and Arthur Rochester for *Con Air*; Andy Nelson, Anna Behlmer, and Kirk Francis for *L.A. Confidential*

BEST SOUND EFFECTS EDITING — Tom Belfort and Christopher Boyes for *Titanic*
Other Nominees: Mark P. Stoeckinger and Per Hallberg for *Face/Off*; Mark Mangini for *The Fifth Element*

BEST VISUAL EFFECTS — Robert Legato, Mark Lasoff, Thomas L. Fisher, and Michael Kanfer for *Titanic*
Other Nominees: Dennis Muren, Stan Winston, Randal M. Dutra, and Michael Lantieri for *The Lost World: Jurassic Park*; Phil Tippett, Scott F. Anderson, Alec Gillis, and John Richardson for *Starship Troopers*

BEST DOCUMENTARY FEATURE — *The Long Way Home*
Other Nominees: *Ayn Rand: A Sense of Life; Colors; Straight Up; 4 Little Girls; Waco: The Rules of Engagement*

BEST DOCUMENTARY SHORT — *A Story of Healing*
Other Nominees: *Alaska: Spirit of the Wild; Amazon; Daughter of the Bride; Still Kicking: The Fabulous Palm Springs Follies*

BEST ANIMATED SHORT — *Geri's Game*
Other Nominees: *Famous Fred; La Veille Dame et Les Pigeons (The Old Lady and the Pigeons); The Mermaid; Redux Riding Hood*

BEST LIVE ACTION SHORT — *Visas and Virtue*
Other Nominees: *Dance Lexie Dance; It's Good to Talk; Sweethearts?; Wolfgang*

HONORARY AWARD

Stanley Donen

GORDON E. SAWYER AWARD

Don Iwerks, co-founder of Iwerks Entertainment "for accomplishments in the field of motion picture science and technology."

SCIENTIFIC AND TECHNICAL AWARD (Oscar Statuette)

Gunnar P. Michelson for "the development of an advanced electronic precision light valve for machines that strike movie prints; this light valve is capable of making changes in printing beam intensity faster and more accurately than devices previously available."

SCIENTIFIC AND TECHNICAL AWARDS (Plaques)

Eben Ostby, Bill Reeves, Sam Leffler and Tom Duff, for "creation of the Marionette Three-Dimensional Computer Animation Systems."

Richard Shoup, Alvy Ray Smith and Thomas Porter, for "development of digital paint systems."

Kirk Handley, Ray Meluch, Scott Robinson, Wilson Allen and John Neary, for "the Dolby CP500 Digital Cinema Processor."

Craig Reynolds, for "contributions to 3-D computer animation."

John Gibson, Rob Krieger, Milan Novacek, Glen Ozymok and Dave Springer, for "development of the geometric modeling component of the Alias Power Animator system."

Dominique Boisvert, Rejean Gagne, Daniel Langlois and Richard Laperriere, for "creation of the "Actor" animation component of the Softimage computer animation system."

Bill Kovacs and Roy Hall, for "engineering efforts leading to Wavefront Visualizer computer graphics system."

Joel Johnson, for "design improvement in fluid-head camera counter-balancing techniques in O'Connor Laboratories "Model 2575."

Al Jensen, Chuck Headley, Jean Messner and Hazem Nabulsi for "production of a self-contained, flicker-free Color Video-Assist camera."

SCIENTIFIC AND TECHNICAL AWARDS (Certificates)

Clark F. Crites, for "development of the ELF 1-C Endless Loop Film Transport and storage system."

Dan Leimeter and Bob Weitz, for "the development of a portable adjustment tool for T-style slit lens assemblies."

Greg Hermanovic, Kim Davidson, Mark Elendt and Paul Breslin, for "their procedural modeling and animation components of the Prisms 3-D software package."

Jim Keating, Michael Wahrman and Richard Hollander, for "work leading to development of the Wavefront Advanced Visualizer computer graphics system."

James M. Reilly, Douglas W. Nishimura and Monique C. Fisher, for "creation of A-D Strips, a diagnostic tool for detecting vinegar syndrome in processed acetate-based movie film."

Philip C. Cory, for "the design of the Special Effects Spark Generator."

Jim Frazier, for "the concept,and Iain Neil and Rick Gelbard for "the development of the Panavision/Frazier Lens System for motion picture photography."

James F. Foley, Charles Converse and F. Edward Gardner; and to Bob Stoker and Matt Sweeney for "the development of Liquid Synthetic Air System, for fog effects in motion pictures."

Richard Chuang, Glenn Entis and Carl Rosendahl, for "the Pacific Data Images Animation System."

James A. Cashin, Roger Hibbard and Larry Jacobson for creation of a projection system analyzer."

NATIONAL SOCIETY OF FILM CRITICS
January 4, 1998

BEST PICTURE — *L.A. Confidential*

BEST ACTOR — Robert Duvall in *The Apostle*

BEST ACTRESS — Julie Christie in *Afterglow*

BEST SUPPORTING ACTOR — Burt Reynolds in *Boogie Nights*

BEST SUPPORTING ACTRESS — Julianne Moore in *Boogie Nights*

BEST DIRECTOR — Curtis Hanson for *L.A. Confidential*

BEST SCREENPLAY — Brian Helgeland and Curtis Hanson for *L.A. Confidential*

BEST FOREIGN-LANGUAGE FILM — *La Promesse* (Belgium)

BEST DOCUMENTARY — *Fast, Cheap & Out of Control*

BEST CINEMATOGRAPHY — Roger Deakins for *Kundun*

SPECIAL CITATION — *Nightjohn*, a film about slavery, whose "exceptional quality and origin challenge strictures of the movie marketplace."

NEW YORK FILM CRITICS
January 4, 1998

BEST PICTURE — *L.A. Confidential*

BEST ACTOR — Peter Fonda in *Ulee's Gold*

BEST ACTRESS — Julie Christie in *Afterglow*

BEST SUPPORTING ACTOR — Burt Reynolds in *Boogie Nights*

BEST SUPPORTING ACTRESS — Joan Cusack in *In & Out*

BEST DIRECTOR — Curtis Hanson for *L.A. Confidential*

BEST SCREENPLAY — Curtis Hanson and Brian Helgeland for *L.A. Confidential*

BEST CINEMATOGRAPHER — Roger Deakins for *Kundun*

BEST FOREIGN-LANGUAGE FILM — *Ponette* (France)

BEST DOCUMENTARY — *Fast, Cheap & Out of Control*

BEST FIRST FEATURE — Neil LaBute for *In the Company of Men*

SPECIAL CITATION — Daniel Talbot "whose New Yorker Films and Lincoln Plaza Cinemas have been so invaluable to serious film audiences."

GOLDEN GLOBE
55th Annual Awards — January 18, 1998

BEST PICTURE (drama) — *Titanic*

BEST PICTURE (musical or comedy) — *As Good As It Gets*

BEST ACTOR (drama) — Peter Fonda in *Ulee's Gold*

BEST ACTOR (musical or comedy) — Jack Nicholson in *As Good As It Gets*

BEST ACTRESS (drama) — Judi Dench in *Mrs. Brown*

BEST ACTRESS (musical or comedy) — Helen Hunt in *As Good As It Gets*

BEST SUPPORTING ACTOR — Burt Reynolds in *Boogie Nights*

BEST SUPPORTING ACTRESS — Kim Basinger in *L.A. Confidential*

BEST DIRECTOR — James Cameron for *Titanic*

BEST SCREENPLAY — Matt Damon and Ben Affleck for *Good Will Hunting*

BEST ORIGINAL SCORE — James Horner for *Titanic*

BEST ORIGINAL SONG — "My Heart Will Go On" from *Titanic*, music by James Horner and lyric by Will Jennings

BEST FOREIGN-LANGUAGE FILM — *Ma Vie en Rose (My Life in Pink)* (Belgium)

CECIL B. DeMILLE AWARD FOR LIFETIME ACHIEVEMENT — Shirley MacLaine

LOS ANGELES FILM CRITICS ASSOCIATION
December 13, 1997

BEST PICTURE — *L.A. Confidential*

BEST ANIMATED FILM — (tie) *Hercules* and *Spirit of Christmas*

BEST ACTOR — Robert Duvall in *The Apostle*

BEST ACTRESS — Helena Bonham Carter in *The Wings of the Dove*

BEST SUPPORTING ACTOR — Burt Reynolds in *Boogie Nights*

BEST SUPPORTING ACTRESS — Julianne Moore in *Boogie Nights*

BEST DIRECTOR — Curtis Hanson for *L.A. Confidential*

BEST SCREENPLAY — Curtis Hanson and Brian Helgeland for *L.A. Confidential*

BEST CINEMATOGRAPHY — Dante Spinotti for *L.A. Confidential*

BEST SCORE — Philip Glass for *Kundun*

BEST PRODUCTION DESIGN — Peter Lamont for *Titanic*

BEST FOREIGN-LANGUAGE FILM — *La Promesse* (Belgium)

BEST DOCUMENTARY FILM — *Riding the Rails*

INDEPENDENT/EXPERIMENTAL FILM/VIDEO — *Finished*

CAREER ACHIEVEMENT AWARD — Peter Bogdanovich

NEW GENERATION AWARD — Paul Thomas Anderson

NATIONAL BOARD OF REVIEW
1997 NBR Awards — February 9, 1998

BEST PICTURE — *L.A. Confidential*

BEST ACTOR — Jack Nicholson in *As Good As It Gets*

BEST ACTRESS — Helena Bonham Carter in *The Wings of the Dove*

BEST SUPPORTING ACTOR — Greg Kinnear in *As Good As It Gets*

BEST SUPPORTING ACTRESS — Anne Heche in *Donnie Brasco* and *Wag the Dog*

BEST DIRECTOR — Curtis Hanson for *L.A. Confidential*

BEST FOREIGN-LANGUAGE FILM — *Shall We Dance?* (Japan)

CAREER ACHIEVEMENT AWARD — Robert Duvall

ENSEMBLE ACTING AWARD — the cast of *The Sweet Hereafter*

BREAKTHROUGH PERFORMER — Bai Ling in *Red Corner*

CANNES FILM FESTIVAL
50th Annual Awards — May 18, 1997

BEST PICTURE (Golden Palm Award) —(tie) *The Eel* (Japan) and *The Taste of Cherries* (Iran)

BEST DIRECTOR — Wong Kar-wei for *Happy Together*

BEST ACTOR — Sean Penn in *She's so Lovely*

BEST ACTRESS — Kathy Burke in *Nil By Mouth*

GRAND PRIX — *The Sweet Hereafter* (Canada)

JURY PRIZE — *Western* (France)

BEST SCREENPLAY — James Schamus for *The Ice Storm*

TECHNICAL PRIZE — (tie) Thierry Arbogast for *She's So Lovely* and Luc Besson for *The Fifth Element*

CAMERA D'OR (Best First Film) — *Suzaku* (Japan)

PALME D'OR (Short Film) — *Is It the Design on the Wrapper?* (U.K.)

JURY PRIZE (Short Film) — (tie) *Leonie* (Belgium) and *Les Vacances* (France)

FIPRESCI INTERNATIONAL CRITICS AWARD — *The Sweet Hereafter* (Canada)

50TH ANNIVERSARY PRIZE — Youssef Chahine for the totality of his work

INDEX

CAST

PRODUCERS

DIRECTORS

SCREENWRITERS

Padura, Leonardo, 1480
Palin, Michael, 462
Palud, Hervé, 733
Parkinson, Eric, 586
Patrick, Vincent, 348
Patterson, James, 746
Patton-Spruill, Robert, 1229
Pearson, James A., 1268
Pejakovic, Nikola, 1082
Peploe, Clare, 1134
Pereira, Gilvan, 721
Pereira, Manuel Gómez, 949
Perry, Nickolas, 171
Pettengill, Theresa, 210
Pfarrer, Chuck, 704
Phelan, Anna Hamilton, 672
Pink, Steve, 587
Pistone, Joseph D., 364
Platnick, Jonathan, 405
Plympton, Bill, 933
Pogue, Charles Edward, 762
Poirier, Gregory, 1126
Potter, Sally, 1264
Preston, Douglas, 1108
Proft, Pat, 922

Quigley, May, 1053
Quigley, Peter, 983

Rafelson, Bob, 138
Raffo, John, 1108
Ramos, Juan Antonio, 362
Ranga, Dana, 384
Ransen, Mort, 886
Ray, Billy, 1400
Reback, Katherine, 485
Reed, Christopher, 1198
Reichle, Franz, 760
Renouslio, Jacqueline Galia, 1
Rich, Richard, 1252

Rickman, Alan, 1473
Ridley, John, 233, 1361
Rifkin, Adam, 946
Riss, Wendy, 1470
Robbins, Matthew, 915
Robinson, Steven, 1213
Roche, Billy, 1337
Rocksavage, David, 1031
Roodt, Darrell, 306
Rosa, Andy, 895
Rose, Bernard, 802
Rosenberg, Craig, 635
Rosenberg, Scott, 236
Rosenbloom, Dale, 1186
Rosenfeld, Seth Zvi, 184
Rosie, George, 952
Ross, Kenneth, 705
Roth, Eric, 1074
Rothberg, Jeff, 1195
Rubin, Joel, 1300
Ruby, Cliff, 210
Rudnick, Paul, 677
Rudolph, Alan, 17
Rymer, Michael, 76

Sachs, Ira, 337
Sagan, Carl, 253
Salas, Andre, 795
Salimbeni, Michele, 1439
Salles, Walter, 498
Saltzman, Mark, 980
Samples, Keith, 1202
Saura, Carlos, 477
Schaeffer, Eric, 438
Schamus, James, 650
Schiff, Robin, 1122
Schiffer, Michael, 1044
Schneider, Dan, 561
Schrader, Paul, 1327
Schroeter, Werner, 867
Schulman, Tom, 396
Schultz, John, 104
Schwartz, Steven S., 297
Schwietert, Stefan, 1300

Scott, Allan, 672
Seidman, Robert, 814
Seifert, Heath, 561
Seitzman, Michael, 442
Shabtai, Sabi H., 96
Shafransky, Renée, 577
Shapiro, Mel, 798
Shaw, Bob, 619
Shawn, Wallace, 340
Shelly, Adrienne, 1246
Sheridan, Jim, 162
Sherman, Cindy, 1007
Sherman, Martin, 46, 130
Sherohman, Tom, 922
Shu Kei, 1272
Shusett, Ronald, 39
Sichel, Sylvia, 49
Sigal, Clancy, 672
Silver, Amanda, 1108
Silver, Scott, 729
Simonson, Louise, 1241
Singer, Isaac Bashevis, 1
Siskin, Alex, 890
Sivan, Ori, 1143
Slansky, Paul, 1053
Smiley, Jane, 1290
Smith, Kevin, 211
Smith, Mark Haskell, 1064
Snooks, Susan, 1062
Soderbergh, Steven, 1147
Sokolow, Alec, 934
Solarz, Ken, 228
Solomon, Ed, 898
Sorkin, Arleen, 1053
Stabile, Savatore, 573
Stagg, Bima, 686
Stern, Howard, 1093
Stern, Tom, 52
Stopkewich, Lynne, 756
Streitfeld, Susan, 456
Strick, Wesley, 1138
Stuart, Jeb, 476, 1262
Suleiman, Elia, 226
Sullivan, John, 1201
Suo, Masayuki, 1177
Svankmajer, Jan, 249

Tabassum, Wanda, 736
Tabio, Juan Carlos, 595
Tabori, George, 969
Tamasy, Paul, 22
Tang, Edward, 1021
Taplitz, Daniel, 234
Tarantino, Quentin, 710
Tavernier, Bertrand, 198
Taylor, Finn, 378
Taylor, Joan, 485
Taylor, Samuel W., 481
Thivel, Caroline, 1145
Thomas, Daniela, 498
Thomas, Theodore, 505
Thompson, Caroline, 189
Thompson, Jim, 1286
Tillman, George, Jr., 1210
Tobias, John, 939
Tolins, Jonathan, 1353
Tolstoy, Leo, 802
Tong, Elliot, 717
Tong, Stanley, 717
Tramontane, Nick, 717
Troyano, Ela, 795
Tsukamoto, Shinya, 1278
Turteltaub, Saul, 496
Twohy, David, 515
Tzudiker, Bob, 72

Uys, Michael, 1114

Vander Stappen, Chris, 869
Van Dormael, Jaco, 401
Veber, Francis, 451
Vercel, Roger, 198
Verhoeven, Michael, 969
Vey, Peter, 933
Veyssat, Sandrine, 1457
Vickerman, Michael, 1426
Villard, Dimitri, 672

Villard, Henry S., 672
Villiers, Nick, 138
Villis, Ray, 683
Vitale, Tony, 753

Wakefield, Dan, 557
Walker, Keith A., 507
Waller, Anthony, 52
Walsh, Bill, 481, 1282
Wang Anyi, 1272
Ward, Jay, 553
Warmflash, Stuart, 1392
Waters, Mark, 639
Wayans, Keenen Ivory, 941
Wells, Audrey, 553
Wondore, Wim, 407, 823
Werb, Mike, 426
Wexler, Gerald, 886
Wexler, Joshua, 939
Whedon, Joss, 39
White, Noni, 72
White, Peter, 586
Wiburd, Margot, 504
Wieger, David Michael, 1456
Williams, Eric, 873
Williamson, David, 180
Williamson, Kevin, 645, 1149
Wise, Naomi, 949
Witcher, Theodore, 853
Wolheim, Donald A., 915
Wong Kar-Wai, 610
Woodley, Richard, 363

Yagemann, Scott, 1009
Yellen, Linda, 405
Yew, Katy, 193
Yonfan, 193
Yost, Graham, 1220
Young, Lance, 136

Zabel, Bryce, 939
Zidi, Claude, 1119
Zurinaga, Marcos, 362

CINEMATOGRAPHERS

Ackerman, Thomas, 553
Adair, Sean, 1112
Adcock, Steve, 171
Adefarasin, Remi, 625
Ahern II, Lloyd, 1350
Ahlberg, Mac, 561
Aim, Pierre, 1145
Albert, Arthur, 134
Alberti, Maryse, 648
Almond, Alan, 187
Amorós, Juan, 949
Anchia, Juan Ruiz, 362
Anderson, Jamie, 587
Arbogast, Thierry, 466, 1182

Archambault, Noel, 659
Arvanitis, Yorgos, 130, 1375
Ascher, Steven, 1344
Aukema, Dewald, 882

B., Beth, 1399
Baca-Asay, Joaquin, 1201
Bailey, John, 90
Ballhaus, Michael, 24
Barrow, Michael, 1248
Bartkowiak, Andrzej, 309, 343
Bartoli, Adolfo, 1136
Batigne, Marc Andre, 226

Belanogov, Valentin, 1143
Beridze, Guiorgui, 218
Beristain, Gabriel, 1335
Bernstein, Steven, 958, 391
Berryman, Ross, 331
Besse, Jacques, 925
Biddle, Adrian, 412, 462
Bierkens, Theo, 969
Blossier, Patrick, 873
Bode, Ralf, 1195
Bollinger, Alun, 499
Bowen, Richard, 616, 1202
Boyd, Russell, 806
Braham, Henry, 496

Brandon, Maryann, 1290
Brassard, Denise, 944
Brickle, Justin, 856
Bridges, David, 405
Budd, Robin, 1062
Bukowski, Bobby, 557, 790, 1303
Burgess, Don, 253
Burmann, Hans, 595
Burr, David, 1456
Burstyn, Thomas, 228
Burton, Geoff, 180
Burum, Stephen H., 451
Butler, Bill, 67
Byers, Frank, 1186

Campbell, John J., 1135
Cape, Yves, 869
Carman, James, 795
Carpenter, Russell, 934, 1307
Carvalho, Walter, 498
Champetier, Caroline, 1067, 1318
Charters, Rodney, 762
Chavez, Chuy, 1231
Choquart, Alain, 198
Clark, Tony, 1100
Collins, Andy, 171
Collister, Peter Lyons, 128
Connell, David, 1481
Connelly, Bob, 1102

EDITORS

MUSIC

PRODUCTION CREW